# JOB SEEKERS GUIDE TO EXECUTIVE RECRUITERS

CHRISTOPHER W. HUNT

SCOTT A. SCANLON

John Wiley & Sons, Inc.
New York · Chichester · Weinheim · Brisbane · Singapore · Toronto

This text is printed on acid-free paper.

Chapters One, Two, and Three consist of material adapted from
the following books by Richard H. Beatty: *The Resume Kit,*
*The Perfect Cover Letter, The Five-Minute Interview.*

*Library of Congress Cataloging-in-Publication Data:*

Hunt, Christopher W.
    Job seekers guide to executive recruiters / by Christopher W.
Hunt, Scott A. Scanlon.
        p.    cm.
    Includes index.
    ISBN 0-471-17932-9 (pbk. : alk. paper)
    1. Executives—Recruiting.    2. Job hunting.    I. Scanlon, Scott A.
II. Title.
HD38.2.H86    1997
650.14—dc21                                                    96-53178
                                                                 CIP

Printed in the United States of America

10 9 8 7 6 5 4 3 2 1

# Contents

# *Introduction*

CHRISTOPHER W. HUNT AND SCOTT A. SCANLON
Editors in Chief, *Executive Search Review, Executive Recruiters of North America,* and *Workplace America*

Whether you have been the victim of a layoff as a result of corporate America's downsizing movement or are currently employed and in the midst of a career transition, searching for a job today can be a difficult and daunting task. To achieve the best results, your job hunt will require energy, creativity, aggressiveness, and a lot of patience—a tall order. Realizing that you are the only one in control of your future can be frightening; however, career transitions, while difficult, are pivotal times of tremendous opportunity: The possibilities are infinite. You have the chance to take the skills and lessons you've gleaned from your past experience and use them to build the future of your dreams.

Even in the most turbulent economic times, one fact remains constant: Companies need innovative and dedicated people in order to survive and grow, and the right people are not always easy to find. This is where executive recruiters can be of assistance: giving you insights into your career and potential that you may not have considered, and matching you with opportunities that you may have been unaware of. Companies know that the hundreds of resumes they receive in response to a classified ad can reveal little or nothing about a candidate's drive to succeed or how he or she will respond to daily work situations. Executive recruiters help companies by examining their employment needs, and then prescreening and narrowing the field of potential candidates to present only those who seem to be a good fit. This works to your advantage: A search consultant can brief you on prospective companies and what sort of employees they are looking for, give you frank advice about your interview style, and prepare you for the sort of questions to expect. You can also be reassured that because the company has gone to the expense of contacting a recruiter, they have a genuine interest in filling the position promptly. Executive recruiters can also be helpful if you *don't* get a certain job: They can tell you why another candidate was chosen, and can coach you on how to improve for your next interview. Always remember: When an executive recruiter tries to contact you, take his or her call. It might be a new beginning for you.

## THERE ARE TWO TYPES OF EXECUTIVE RECRUITERS

Although there are a number of ways to effectively market yourself, this book deals exclusively with executive recruiters, also known as headhunters of executive search consultants. What is an executive recruiter and what role can he or she play in your success? There are two basic types: retained and contingency. Both are paid by the companies that hire them, not by job seekers, but they differ on the methods, and sometimes the salary level, on which they operate.

Retained executive recruiters are headhunters who work on a contract with a client company. They are hired by companies to find a particular executive for a specific position and are subsequently paid a retainer fee (one-third at inception, one-third at the halfway point, and one-third when the candidate is chosen and hired). These recruiters often handle the absolute crème de la crème. IBM chairman Lou Gerstner, Kodak's chairman and CEO, George Fisher, and NFL Commissioner Paul Tagliabue, for example, were all placed by headhunters in this category. The average placement, however, is most often a rung or two lower. Though retained recruiters may be hired to fill a position with compensation in the millions or as low as $50,000, the average assignment generally runs between $75,000 and $125,000.

Contingency recruiters fill the gap between entry-level placements (generally handled by employment agency professionals) and those handled by the retained recruiter. The compensation level starts at about $30,000 and peaks at about $50,000. There are, however, exceptions, as a handful of contingency recruiters will place professionals with compensation levels exceeding $100,000. Recruiters in this category handle the bulk of lower to middle management and general management assignments. They are referred to as contingency recruiters because their fee is paid at the conclusion of the assignment or "contingent upon" the successful placement.

## GETTING THEIR ATTENTION

Job seekers who wish to become part of recruiters' "preferred lists" (meaning that they deem you a strong candidate whom they will consider for any appropriate position) should employ certain steps in order to stand out from the rest of the crowd: Firms such as Korn/Ferry International, Spencer Stuart, Heidrick & Struggles, Russell Reynolds Associates, Management Recruiters, and others collectively receive in excess of one million resumes annually.

First, prior to sending your resume to any executive recruiter, make certain that you contact the search firm first to see if it is the proper firm to handle someone with your background. While many large search firms are labeled as generalist firms because they place executives in most functional disciplines and industries, they are often comprised of several specialty practice areas, such as financial services, automotive, health care, manufacturing, and so on. Large firms may also divide their practices functionally as well, into areas such as general management, human resources, sales and marketing, finance, and so forth. Making sure that your resume is being sent to the appropriate recruiters is time well spent.

Also, don't discount numerous smaller firms, or specialty boutiques, which may prove to be an even better fit for someone with your background and experience. For example, you may locate a firm which specializes in placing senior administrators into educational or nonprofit positions or legal professionals into law firms or corporations. For every position that exists in the corporate world, there seems to be a firm or recruiter that specializes in that area. Check the industry and function specialization categories in this book, and don't hesitate to call firms and ask them about their specialties if you have any questions. Again, a little digging on your part may pay off, saving you countless hours of following up with recruiters who are not able to help you, and saving on postage and paper as well!

## NOW WHAT?

After you target recruiters or firms that specialize in your industry or function, make certain that you are specific as to what you've done and what you are seeking. Don't generalize your credentials—the main question client companies have when reviewing resumes is, "What can this person do for us?" Answer that question on your resume by giving concrete examples of your accomplishments, and how your past companies have benefited from your contributions. Rather than simply saying you were a systems engineer responsible for implementing new technologies, talk about the time and money you saved your company, and how you did it. It's impossible that you made no difference to your past company. Even if you feel your contribution was small, mention it. Think of your resume and cover letter as an outline for what you'll talk about when you meet a recruiter face-to-face.

Also use your resume, cover letter, and interview as a chance to focus on what you expect to accomplish in the future. For example, if you are a compensation and benefits professional but want to expand your skills, make sure that that is clear in your cover letter and on your resume. Also, if there are certain jobs that you are qualified for but are adamant about not doing, say so, and save your recruiter and yourself from arranging interviews for jobs that you wouldn't accept anyway. The mistake that often plagues many job seekers is trying to be every-thing to everyone. Another advantage to being specific about what you want is that if a client company calls with an opening that meets your criteria, the headhunter will be more likely to think of you. Being realistic about your qualifications is also helpful to both your headhunter and yourself. If you have 15 years of experience as a middle management investment banking professional, it is not prudent to think that you will land a position as a book editor because your college minor was journalism. Instead, think through your capabilities and what sort of job might be a good bridge between your past experience and future expectations. By not "sticking with your knitting" you may find yourself in a perpetual gray area.

## USE EVERY CONTACT AS AN OPPORTUNITY

One potential pitfall in the preparation of your credentials is the urge to stretch the truth. There is nothing wrong with highlighting or emphasizing various responsibilities or accom-plishments. But in the desperation of trying to land a job, the temptation is strong to make cer-tain "adjustments" to your credentials. A five-year stint at your last company may turn into seven years because the company you want to work for requires it. Or in describing your posi-tion as director of sales and marketing you may be inclined to state you increased sales by $500,000 when the reality is that they only grew by $250,000. Although you may think you're getting an edge by what you may perceive as inconsequential padding, the truth is that recruiters can smell these embellishments a mile away—it's what they do for a living. Keep in mind that if you're caught lying, the recruiter will not deal with you again (if they do, perhaps be suspicious of *their* integrity). Also, executive search is in many ways a close-knit communi-ty—there's a good chance that other recruiters may learn what you're up to. And, if you by some chance land the job anyway, you may find yourself in a position you are not qualified for, which could, in an extreme case, mean lawsuits for you and possibly your headhunter.

Though it may seem obvious, *always* return your recruiters' calls promptly and politely. Use every contact as an opportunity to give them more confidence in you both as a candidate and as someone they'd like to help. And don't overlook the possibility that you can be helpful to them, too. If a recruiter mentions an opening that's inappropriate for you but might interest someone else you know, say so. Your honesty will be appreciated and remembered. Providing a valuable contact to a recruiter is not only a nice thing for you to do for someone but it may also be rewarding to you somewhere down the line.

For those of you who are currently employed but are always keeping your eye open for other career opportunities, the above suggestions certainly apply to you, but we would offer a few additional tips. You may at some point in your professional life receive a call from a recruiter. It may come during a time that you are completely content with your career and the company you work for and you may not be interested in even taking the call. We would recom-mend that you not ignore a call from a recruiter for three reasons. First, given the unpredictable nature of corporate downsizings and restructurings today, any corporate employee is at risk to be cut loose. Second, although you are a happy camper, a recruiter might be considering you for an even better position. In fact, the only way you might be able to enhance your career is to change locations. And third, the job the recruiter is considering you for may in fact not suit you. But it might be ideal for a colleague or friend who is unemployed or unhappy in his or her job.

Many employed executives are also concerned about confidentiality if they decide to speak with a recruiter. Don't hesitate to mention this if it is a potential problem—recruiters are used to these situations and know more secrets than Mata Hari. If your situation is highly sensi-tive, instruct your headhunter to leave messages on your home answering machine—just be sure to check your messages frequently during the day. If you reach the interview stage with a recruiter, the majority of meetings will naturally be held off-site, generally at the office of the recruiter or even perhaps at your residence. Again, professional recruiters are very sensitive to confidentiality and therefore all meetings are kept very discreet.

There is no doubt that finding a new job can be a challenging experience. Although executive search professionals should represent only a portion of your job search efforts, know-ing how to utilize this valuable asset is essential. I hope that we have been able to provide you with a sense of the marketplace today, which recruiters are best for you, and how you can effectively work with them. Best of luck!

Chapter 1

# Introduction to Resumes

The employment resume—its style, organization, and content—has long been a topic of considerable discussion and debate. Like religion and politics, this is a subject fraught with controversy. It is one of those topics where there are many "experts" who will provide you with considerable "professional" advice and counsel as long as you are willing to listen.

Should you wish to put this statement to the test, let me suggest that the next time you are at lunch or dinner with a group of friends or business colleagues, introduce the subject of "resume preparation" and ask a few of the following questions:

1. How long should a resume be?
2. What is the best resume format? How should it be organized?
3. Should there be a statement of job objective? If so, how should it be worded?
4. Should the resume contain personal data—age, height, weight, marital status, number of children?
5. Should hobbies and extracurricular activities be included?
6. How important is salary history? Should it be shown at all?
7. Where should education be described—near the end or the beginning of the resume?
8. What writing style is the most effective?
9. What is the best format for computer scanning and resume database search?

These, and similar questions, are guaranteed to spark a lively discussion punctuated with considerable difference of opinion. There will be those who claim that "Everyone knows that a resume should never be longer than a single page." Others will assert that "Two pages are quite acceptable." Still others will be adamant that "Two pages can never begin to do justice to 10 years of professional experience and accomplishment." All may use logical and persuasive arguments, with each sounding more convincing than the last. Who is right? Which argument should you believe? What works best?

As a consultant and executive with considerable employment experience, I can tell you that there are good answers to these questions. There is a right and a wrong way to prepare an employment resume. There are items that should definitely be included in the resume, and there are those that are best left out. There are resume formats that have consistently proven more effective than others, and there are those that should be avoided.

There are appropriate answers to these and many other questions associated with the subject of effective resume preparation. But you cannot expect to get expert advice on resume preparation over casual dinner conversation with a few friends whose expertise consists mainly of preparation of their first resume and a few articles read somewhere in a trade journal. This is hardly the type of advice that you need to prepare a resume that will be successful in launching you on a new and prosperous career track.

What I am about to share with you are the observations and advice of a human resources consultant and former personnel executive who has had considerable experience in the corporate employment function of a major Fortune 200 company. This is knowledge gleaned from years of employment experience—knowledge gained from the reading of thousands of employment resumes and the hiring of hundreds of employees at the professional, managerial, and executive level. This advice is based on firsthand observation of those resumes that resulted in job interviews and those that did not. This is advice based on "inside" knowledge of what makes professional employment managers tick—what motivates them to respond favorably to one resume and "turns them off" on the next. It will guide you in preparing a resume that will best display your qualifications and maximize your potential for landing interviews.

This chapter will provide you with an understanding of what happens in a typical company employment department. Where does your resume go? Who reads it? What is the basis for determining interest or lack of interest? What does the employment manager look for in a resume? How is the resume read? Who makes the final decision on your resume? Answers to these and similar questions should provide you with valuable insight that will enable you to design your resume to successfully compete for an employment interview. They will also serve as the basis for better understanding the recommendations made later in this chapter on such topics as resume format, content, style, appearance, and so on.

## COMPETITION

In larger companies, it is not uncommon for the corporate employment department to receive as many as 40,000 to 50,000 resumes during the course of an average business year. Some receive considerably more. The annual employment volume of such firms typically runs in the range of 200 to 300 hires per year. Assuming an average of two to three interviews per hire, these firms will interview 400 to 900 employment candidates in meeting their employment requirements. This means that only 400 to 900 of the total 40,000 to 50,000 resumes received will result in an employment interview. In other words, only one or two out of every 100 resumes will result in an employment interview. Those are not very encouraging odds!

You are thus beginning your employment search at a decided statistical disadvantage. For every 100 resumes mailed to prospective employers, on the average you can expect only one or two interviews to result. These statistics alone should persuade you of the importance of a well-prepared and effective resume.

It is estimated that the average employment manager of a major corporation will read more than 20,000 resumes a year. Assuming no vacation time and 260 workdays in a year, this is equivalent to a weeknight workload of more than 75 resumes. Since employment managers must frequently travel, however, and most do take time off for holidays and vacations, it is estimated that this number is actually closer to 100. Since each resume averages 1½ pages in length, the employment manager has an average of 150 pages of reading to do each evening— a sizable chore!

Since the employment manager frequently spends the entire workday interviewing employment candidates, most resumes are normally read during the evening hours. Additionally, since evenings are often used by the manager to plan employment strategies, write recruitment advertising, and do other planning work necessary to the employment process, the amount of evening time left to read resumes may be only an hour or two.

In many cases, the employment manager is unable to read resumes until later in the evening. The early evening hours must often be used by the manager to make telephone calls to make job offers, follow up with candidates on outstanding offers, prescreen prospective candidates, and so on. These calls can usually be made only during the early part of the evening, leaving resume reading until later.

As you can well imagine, by 10 or 11 P.M. (following a full day of interviewing and several early evening phone calls) the typical employment manager is probably tired. He or she must now read an estimated 150 pages of resumes before retiring for the evening. You can well imagine how thoroughly these resumes will be read.

The technique used by most employment managers in reviewing resumes is not an in-depth, step-by-step reading process. Instead, it is a process of rapidly skimming the resume in a systematic way to determine whether or not the individual has qualifications and career interests consistent with the company's current employment requirements.

Considering all of these factors, resumes that are poorly prepared, sloppy, or in any other way difficult to read will receive very little consideration. Resumes are thought to be indicative of the overall personal style of the writer. Thus the inference that is frequently drawn from such poorly written resumes is that the applicant is likewise a sloppy, uncaring, of disorganized individual. Why then should the employment manager risk bringing this individual in for interviews? In such cases, the resume will more likely than not be stamped "no interest," and the employment manager will quickly move on to the next resume.

By now I hope that you are convinced that the general appearance of the resume is critical to its impact and effectiveness. It should be obvious that readability is likewise a major criterion for resume success. Resume organization and format are therefore extremely important factors to consider if your resume is to be successful in this difficult and competitive arena.

We now move on to a general discussion of the organization and operation of the typical company employment department. We carefully trace the steps through which your resume will likely pass, from the point of receipt by the department to final determination of application status.

## RESUME PROCESSING

In the case of a company with a large employment department, the department is normally subdivided into functional specialties with each employment manager having accountability for a given area. For example, there may be an Administrative Employment Manager who has accountability for all administrative hiring: Accounting, Finance, Law, Data Processing, Human Resources, and so on. A Technical Employment Manager may also exist with accountability for all technical hiring: Research and Development, Central Engineering, Technical Services, Quality Control, and so on. Likewise, there may be an Operations Employment Manager with responsibility for all hiring related to manufacturing or plant operations. Marketing and Sales may also be represented by a separate employment manager.

As resumes are received by the employment department, there is usually one person who is designated to open and sort the mail into the appropriate categories for distribution to the individual employment managers. Once received by the employment manager's administrative assistant, the screening process will begin with the assistant "screening out" those resumes that are clearly not of interest to the employment manager. Thus if the employer is a steel company, the resumes of botanists, foresters, artists, and so forth are likely to be "screen out" at this point. Likewise, the administrative assistant may eliminate illegible, sloppy, or otherwise undesirable resumes.

The next step is for the employment manager to read the resume to determine whether there is an opening that is an appropriate match for the applicant's credentials. If not, the resume is usually marked "no interest," coded, and sent to Word Processing where an appropriate "no interest letter" is prepared and sent to the applicant. A copy of this letter along with the original resume is then returned to the employment department for filing and future reference.

At this point, "no interest" resumes are normally divided into two categories: (1) those in which the employer will probably have no future interest and (2) those having a high likelihood of interest at some future time ("future possibles"). Those in which the company is likely to have future interest are normally placed in an active file for future reference and review. In some cases, these "future interest" resumes are electronically scanned and stored on a computer resume data base. The remaining resumes are placed in a dead file with no possibility of future review.

When the employment manager determines that there is a reasonable match between the candidate's qualifications and the employment needs of a given department, the next step is a review of the resume by the hiring manager (the manager having the employment opening). Having reviewed the resume and determined that there is a probable match between the candidate's qualifications and interests and the requirements of the position, the hiring manager then notifies the employment manager of this interest and requests that the employment manager schedule the candidate for an interview. If, on the other hand, there is no interest, the hiring manager indicates this to the employment manager, and the resume is processed as described above.

In the case of the more sophisticated employers, there is usually one additional step in the process prior to extending an invitation for an interview. This step is referred to as the "telephone screen." This means that either the hiring manager or the employment manager will phone the candidate for the purpose of conducting a mini-interview. This telephone interview is intended to determine whether the candidate has sufficient qualifications and interest to warrant the time and expense of an on-site interview. Additionally, employers frequently use this preliminary interview to determine the validity of the information provided on the resume—a good reason to be factual in describing your qualifications and accomplishments!

There are three critical points in the resume-processing procedure at which your resume may be screened out and marked "no interest":

1. Administrative Assistant—screened for obvious incompatibility, incompleteness, sloppiness, or illegibility.
2. Employment Manager—screened for incompatibility with current openings and required candidate specifications.
3. Hiring Manager—screened for insufficient or inappropriate qualifications when compared with job requirements.

The highly competitive nature of the employment market, coupled with the thorough screening provided by the prospective employer, makes the preparation of a professional and effective resume an absolute must if one expects to be successful in the employment or job-hunting process! The resume cannot be left to chance. It must be carefully and deliberately designed if it is to successfully survive the rigors of the company's screening process.

Let's now take a closer look at the process used by the employment manager to screen resumes. How does he or she read a resume? What is the employment manager looking for? What will determine which resumes are screened out?

## CANDIDATE SPECIFICATION

The very first step in the typical employment process is the preparation of an "employment requisition" by the hiring manager. This document is normally signed by the hiring manager's function head and human resources manager and is then forwarded to the appropriate employment manager. The purpose of the employment requisition is normally threefold:

1. Provides management authorization to hire.
2. Communicates basic data about the opening—title, level, salary range, reporting relationship, maximum starting salary, key job responsibilities, and so on.
3. Communicates basic or fundamental candidate specifications—type and level of education required, type and level of experience sought, technical and administrative skills required, and so forth.

Any good professional employment manager knows that the employment requisition seldom provides sufficient information to do a professional job of identifying and recruiting a well-qualified candidate. Considerably more information will usually be needed, and the employment manager is quick to arrange a meeting with the hiring manager to develop a more thorough and comprehensive candidate specification. The following are examples of typical "candidate specs."

Both of these candidate specs are highly detailed and very particular about the kind of qualifications that will satisfy the employment requirement. Very little has been left to chance. There is a clear understanding of both the educational and experience requirements for candidates who would receive serious consideration for employment.

Job Title:      Chief Project Engineer
Job Level:      600 Points
Department:     Central Engineering
Group:          Mechanical
Education:
  Preferred:    M.S. Mechanical Engineering
  Acceptable:   B.S. Mechanical Engineering
Experience:
  Eight plus years experience in the design, development, installation, start-up, and debugging of Herrington Winders and auxiliary equipment. Demonstrated project leadership of projects in the eight to ten million range. Must have managed groups of five or more professionals.
Maximum Starting Salary:   $85,000

Now let's look at another example.

Job Title:        Director—Human Resources
Job Level:        1,200 Points
Department:    Human Resources
Reporting Relationship:   Sr. Vice President—Administration
Maximum Starting Salary:   $100,000
Estimated Bonus:   20% to 30%
Education:    Masters in Human Resources Management
Experience:
Requires a minimum 15 years experience in Human Resources in a corporation of 20,000 plus employees. Experience must include a broad range of Human Resources experience to include: Employment, Compensation & Benefits, Training & Development, and Employee Relations. Must be up-to-date with modern concepts in such areas as Human Resources Planning, Organization Effectiveness, and Executive Assessment. Experience must include demonstrated management leadership in the direction and guidance of decentralized, autonomous division Personnel functions in a multidivision and highly diversified company. Must have played key role in the development and execution of corporate-wide labor relations strategy in a multiunion setting. Must have managed a staff of at least 20 mid-management and professional level Human Resource professionals.

## HOW RESUMES ARE READ

The candidate specification, as shown in the examples, is the basic tool of the employment manager when it comes to reading an employment resume. Actually the term "reading" is misleading when describing the process by which most employment managers review employment resumes. More precisely, the experienced employment manager rapidly scans for basic qualification highlights. The question that is constantly being asked by the employment manager is "Does this individual meet all of the critical qualifications of the candidate spec?"

The typical employment manager does not bother to read a resume in any degree of detail unless the preliminary scan indicates that the applicant has some of the essential skills and experience sought. In such cases, as key phrases and headings begin to match the candidate spec, the manager slows down and begins to read with a more critical eye. If several key criteria appear to be met, the employment professional will usually return to the beginning of the resume and begin a more thorough, detailed reading. To the contrary, if quick scanning of the resume indicates that few, if any, of the candidate's qualifications appear to match the current requirements, no time is lost in moving on to the next resume.

## QUICK "KNOCKOUT" FACTORS

In scanning the employment resume, the employment manager is looking for key "knockout" factors—factors that clearly spell no interest and signal the employment manager to stop reading and move on to the next resume. Some of these quick knockout factors are:

1. Job objective incompatible with current openings
2. Inappropriate or insufficient educational credentials
3. Incompatible salary requirements
4. Geographic restrictions incompatible with current openings
5. Lack of U.S. citizenship or permanent resident status
6. Resume poorly organized, sloppy, or hard to read
7. Too many employers in too short a period of time
8. Too many pages—a book instead of a resume

Any of these factors quickly signals the employment manager that it would be a waste of time to read any further. These are generally sure knockout factors and warrant use of the no interest stamp. These same factors should be consciously avoided when preparing your employment resume.

## CRITICAL READING

Having successfully passed the quick knockout factors test and avoided the no interest stamp, your resume must now undergo a more thorough and critical scanning. Concentration is now centered on the Work Experience section of the resume as the following questions are considered:

1. Are there sufficient years and level of experience?
2. Is experience in the appropriate areas?
3. Is the candidate missing any critical experience?
4. Does the candidate have sufficient breadth and depth of technical knowledge?
5. Does the applicant have sufficient management or leadership skills?
6. Are any technical or managerial skills missing?
7. Is there a solid record of accomplishment?
8. How does this candidate compare with others currently under consideration?
9. Based on overall qualifications, what are the probabilities that an offer would be made—50%, 75%, 90% (as measured against past candidates with similar credentials)?

There is little advice that can be given to the resume writer in this area. You are what you are, and the facts cannot be changed. You either have the qualifications and experience sought, or you don't. At best, you can hope that through diligent application of professional resume preparation techniques, you have done an excellent job of clearly presenting your overall skills, knowledge, accomplishments, and other pertinent professional qualifications.

There is nothing mysterious or mystical about the resume-reading process. It is essentially logical and straightforward. It is a process whereby the employment manager or hiring manager simply compares the candidate's qualifications and interests with the candidate's hiring spec in an effort to determine the candidate's degree of qualifications and the desirability of moving to the interview (or phone screen) step. Neatness, clarity, organization, style, and format are the key ingredients; they are critical to the impact and effectiveness of the employment resume.

*Chapter 2*

# *Introduction to Cover Letters*

The cover letter that accompanies your employment resume is perhaps one of the most important letters you will ever write. Other than your resume, it is the single key document that will introduce you to a prospective employer and, if well-written, pave the way to that all-important job interview. It is an integral part of your overall job hunting campaign, and it can make or break you, depending upon how well it is written. Construction of this document should therefore be given very careful attention. The care that you give to writing this letter will certainly be a major factor in getting your job search off to an excellent start. Conversely, a poorly written letter will surely scuttle your campaign before it even begins.

## THE PURPOSE OF THE COVER LETTER

Before you can expect to write an effective cover letter, you must understand its purpose. Without a clear understanding of what this letter is intended to accomplish, chances are it will be poorly designed, vague, and totally ineffective. On the other hand, understanding the purpose of this letter is truly paramount to maximizing its impact and effectiveness.

What is the purpose of the cover letter? What is it intended to do?

Well, first and foremost, it is a business letter used to transmit your resume to a prospective employer. So, it is a business transmittal letter. Second, it is a letter of introduction. It is used not only to transmit your resume but also to introduce you and your background to the employer. Third, and importantly, it is a sales letter, intended to convince the prospective employer that you have something valuable to contribute and that it will be worth the employer's time to grant you an interview.

To summarize, then, the purpose of a cover letter is:

1. To serve as a business transmittal letter for your resume.
2. To introduce you and your employment credentials to the employer.
3. To generate employer interest in interviewing you.

Certainly, knowing that these are the three main objectives of a well-written cover letter will provide you with some basic starting points. For now, it is important to simply keep these objectives in mind as we further explore the topic of effective cover letters.

## FROM THE EMPLOYER'S PERSPECTIVE

When contemplating good cover letter design and construction, it is important to keep one very important fact in mind: The cover letter must be written from the employer's perspective.

Stated differently, good cover letter writing must take into consideration that the end result you seek is employer action. More specifically, you want the employer to grant you an interview, so it is important to understand those factors that will motivate an employer to do so.

To understand this important phenomenon, it is necessary to realistically address the following questions:

1. How does the employer read the cover letter?
2. What are the key factors the employer is looking for (and expects to find) in the cover letter?
3. What are the motivational factors that will pique the employer's curiosity and create a desire to interview you?

I think you will agree that these are some very important questions to ask if you are to be successful in designing cover letters that will be truly helpful to your job hunting program. You must pay close attention to the needs of the prospective employer, rather than just your own, if you expect to write cover letters that will motivate him or her to take action. Cover letters must, therefore, be "employer focused" rather than "job searcher focused" if you want to really maximize their overall effectiveness.

Top sales producers have always known that the most important principle in sales success, whether selling goods or services, is selling to the needs of the buyer. What is the customer really buying? Where are the priorities? What specific needs does he or she need to satisfy? Without knowing the answers to these questions, it is easy for the salesperson to emphasize product characteristics and attributes that have absolutely no relationship to the customer's real needs, and deemphasize characteristics and attributes that are truly important. The result—no sale!

In the ideal sense, therefore, it is important to research your target companies very well to determine what it is that they are buying (i.e., looking for in a successful employment candidate). If you are conducting a general broadcast campaign covering several hundred companies, such individual company research may simply not be feasible. If, on the other hand, you are targeting a dozen or so employers for whom you would really like to work, such research is not only feasible but should be considered an "absolute must." Careful advance research, in this case, will pay huge dividends, returning your initial investment of time and effort manyfold.

Even in the case of the general broadcast campaign, where you have targeted several hundred companies, there are clearly some things that you can do to focus your cover letters on the real needs of these employers. Here are some guidelines for conducting meaningful employer needs research:

1. Divide your target list of employers into industry groupings.
2. Using industry trade publications and key newspapers (available in most libraries), thoroughly research each industry grouping for answers to the following questions:
   a. What is the general state of this industry?
   b. What are the major problems faced by companies in this industry?
   c. What are the barriers or roadblocks that stand in the way of solving these problems
   d. What knowledge, skills, and capabilities are needed to address these problems and roadblocks?
   e. What major trends and changes are being driven by companies in this industry?
   f. What new knowledge, skills, and capabilities are needed to successfully drive these changes and trends?

Having conducted this research, you are now in a position to better focus your cover letter on key needs areas of interest to the majority of companies in each of your targeted industry groupings. This provides you with the opportunity to showcase your overall knowledge, skills, and capabilities in relation to those important needs areas. Such focusing substantially increases your chances for hitting the employer's bull's-eye, which will result in job interviews.

Where you can narrow your list to a dozen or so key companies, individual company research can have even greater payoff. Here, you have the opportunity to really zero in on the specific needs of the employer, and you can bring into play a number of research techniques for doing so. The research you do here can, in fact, be tailored to each individual firm; so you can substantially increase your probability of success and up by quite a bit the number of potential interview opportunities.

In many ways, the methodology used in conducting single-firm research is similar to that already described for industry-wide research. You will note some of these similarities as you review the following guidelines for researching the single firm.

1. Determine the firms you would like to target for individual research (firms for which you would really like to work).
2. Using industry trade publications and key newspapers (available at your local library) as well as annual reports, 10K forms, and product literature (available from the target firm's public affairs and marketing departments), thoroughly research for answers to the following questions:
   a. What is the general state of the company?
   b. How does it stack up against competition?
   c. What are the key problems and issues with which it is currently wrestling?
   d. What are the key barriers that must be removed in order to resolve these problems/issues?
   e. What knowledge, skills, and capabilities are needed to remove these key barriers?
   f. What are the company's strategic goals?
   g. What are the key changes that will need to come about for realization of these goals?
   h. What new knowledge, skills, and capabilities will be needed to bring about these critical changes?

Here, as with research of industry groupings, individual company research enables you to use the cover letter to highlight your knowledge, skills, and capabilities in areas that are of importance to the firm. In the case of individual firm research, however, there is the added advantage of being able to tailor the cover letter to target your qualifications to very specific, known needs of the employer. This can provide you with a substantial competitive advantage!

Another technique that you should employ when doing individual firm research is networking. If you don't already belong, you might consider joining specific industry or professional associations to which employees of your individual target firms belong. Using your common membership in these organizations as the basis, you can call these employees for certain inside information. Here are some questions you might consider asking:

1. Is the firm hiring people in your functional specialty?
2. Are there openings in this group now?
3. Who within the company is the key line manager (i.e., outside human resources) responsible for hiring for this group?
4. What are the key things this manager tends to look for in a successful candidate (e.g., technical knowledge, skills, style)?
5. What key problems/issues is the group currently wrestling with?
6. What kinds of skills and capabilities are they looking for to address these issues?
7. What are the major strategic changes this group is attempting to bring about?
8. What qualifications and attributes is the group seeking to help them orchestrate these strategic changes?

Answers to these questions can give you a tremendous competitive advantage when designing an effective cover letter and employment resume. You will have substantial ammunition for targeting and highlighting those qualifications of greatest interest to the employer. Here, you can make the most of your opportunity for successful self-marketing by focusing on the critical needs not only of the organization but of the functional hiring group as well. Clearly, this is a technique you should employ if you want to maximize your chances of getting hired!

The underlying principle behind this needs research methodology, whether industry grouping or individual company research, is that organizations are always looking for individuals who will be "value adding"—that is, individuals who can help them solve key problems and realize their strategic goals. These are the candidates who are seen as the value-adding change agents—the leaders who will help move the company ahead rather than cause it to stand still. Employer needs research will allow you to design effective cover letters that can truly set you apart from the competition and substantially improve your chances for landing interviews.

# Chapter 3

# Introduction to Interviewing

## INTERVIEW THEORY

By definition, the employment interview is a two-way discussion between a job applicant and a prospective employer with the objective of exploring the probable compatibility between the applicant's qualifications and the needs of the employer, for the purpose of making an employment decision. It is the intent of both parties during this discussion to gain as much relevant information as possible on which to base this decision. Further, it is their intent to use the information obtained during the interview process to predict, with some level of accuracy, the probability for a successful match.

Modern interview theory subscribes to a single, universal theory around which almost all employment selection processes are designed. This theory is as follows:

Past performance and behavior are the most reliable factors known in predicting future performance and behavior.

With this theory in mind, it is important for the interviewee to know that the employer's basic interview strategy will be to use the interview discussion to uncover past performance and behavioral evidence in those areas that the employer considers important to successful job performance. These important areas are commonly known as selection criteria. It is against these criteria that the employer will be comparing the qualifications of prospective candidates, and eventually arriving at a final employment decision.

It should be evident that, as the candidate, it will be necessary for you to get some definition of these selection criteria if you expect to be successful in developing an effective counterstrategy. The key to accomplishing this is to force yourself to think as the employer does. Specifically, the question to ask is, "How does the employer go about developing candidate selection criteria?"

## DEVELOPING THE CANDIDATE SPECIFICATION

The first step used by the employer in structuring an interview strategy is usually development of what is commonly known in professional employment circles as the candidate specification. This document typically describes the candidate sought by the employer in terms of such qualifications as knowledge, skills, experience, and other dimensions thought to be necessary to successful job performance. The candidate specification is normally prepared by the hiring manager, with occasional assistance provided by other department managers and/or the human resources department.

When well-prepared and carefully thought out, this specification can be a very valuable document. It frequently serves as the focal point for the employer's entire interview strategy. Advance knowledge of the contents of the document could prove equally as valuable to the interviewee, since it could be used as the basis for formulating an effective counterstrategy. Since this is not a practical consideration, the candidate must go through the same process as the employer in attempting to construct this specification.

When preparing the candidate specification, most hiring managers will review such things as the position description, current year's objectives, business plans, and so on. In essence, the manager is reviewing the general responsibilities of the position in an effort to determine the kind of person needed to meet these requirements. Such review typically results in a candidate specification that includes the following general categories: (1) education, (2) knowledge, (3) experience, (4) skills, and (5) personal attributes.

A typical candidate specification would probably read as follows:

*Education.*    BS degree in mechanical engineering preferred; degree in chemical engineering acceptable.

*Knowledge.*    Paper machine project engineering; wet end sheet formation.

*Experience.*    Two plus years in design, installation, and start-up of tissue and/or towel machines; twin wire-forming machine experience helpful.

*Skills.*    Solid engineering skills in mechanical design; project leadership of contractor personnel.

*Personal Attributes.*    Intelligent, articulate; able to work effectively in fast-paced construction/start-up environment; willing to work long hours, including frequent evenings and weekends; willing to travel at least 40 percent of the time, including weekend travel.

Although admittedly a fairly abbreviated description, this candidate specification is very similar to those used by most organizations.

The employer's strategy now becomes one of interviewing to determine how well the prospective candidate meets this specification. In my example, some of the candidate's qualifications for the position will be evident from a quick review of the applicant's resume. However, such areas as "level of engineering knowledge" and "level of intelligence" cannot be measured by using the applicant's resume. These can only be ascertained through the interview process.

## INTERVIEWEE STRATEGY

Considering the employer's interview strategy, as defined earlier in this chapter, how can the interviewee formulate a meaningful counterstrategy? What steps can the interviewee take to maximize the potential for a favorable interview outcome?

In my judgment, there are a number of things you can do to duplicate fairly accurately the employer's thinking process, thereby allowing yourself to plan an effective counterstrategy that will allow you to "stack the deck" in your favor. Here are some of them:

### Advance Information

You will want to obtain as much information as possible about the position, prior to the actual interview. Although much of this information is readily available just for the asking, it has always amazed me how few employment candidates ever bother to request it.

Don't be shy about requesting this information since many employers are willing to provide it to you if it is available. The strategic advantage of acquiring this information in advance of the interview far outweighs the risks of an employer politely declining your request.

Where available without too much difficulty, you should request the following in advance of your visit:

1. Position job description
2. Job objectives—current year
3. Department objectives—current year
4. Departmental or functional business plan
5. Annual report

### Candidate Specification

During your initial telephone conversation with the employer, you should make it a point to ask for a verbal description of the kind of person they are seeking. Ask the employer to tell you not only what qualifications they are seeking, but also which of these qualifications they consider to be the most important. If time allows, and you can avoid sounding pushy, ask why these factors are considered to be important.

If the employer begins to balk, suggest that you need this information to determine whether or not you are interested in the position and whether you feel you have sufficient qualifications to warrant investing your time in further discussions. This should seem a reasonable request at this stage of the relationship and you will usually get what you want.

It is best to request answers to these questions at the beginning of your discussions, since you will lose considerable leverage once the employer has ascertained that you are interested in the position and are prepared to go to the next step.

## Position Analysis

As with the employer, one of your first steps in formulating your interview strategy is to conduct an analysis of the position for which you will be interviewing. This procedure is similar to the employers' when they form the candidate specification. You will need to review the key responsibilities of the position in an effort to translate these into probable candidate selection criteria. The advance documents that you have collected from the employer should prove very helpful at this point.

The following set of questions should help you to walk through this process in a logical and thorough fashion. Space is provided for you to fill in your answers as you go along.

1. What are the *key ongoing responsibilities* of this position? (Job description should prove helpful here.) _____

    _____

    _____

    _____

2. What are the *key technical problems* to be solved, and *challenges* to be met, in satisfying these ongoing responsibilities? _____

    _____

    _____

    _____

3. What *technical* and/or *professional knowledge* does this suggest that a person must have in order to successfully solve these problems and meet these challenges? _____

    _____

    _____

    _____

4. What are the *specific objectives* for this position for the *current year*? _____

    _____

    _____

    _____

5. What are the *key technical challenges* that must be met and *problems* that must be solved if these objectives are to be successfully achieved? _____

    _____

    _____

    _____

6. What *technical* and/or *professional knowledge* does this suggest that a person must have in order to successfully solve these problems and accomplish these objectives? _____

    _____

## Combined Candidate Specification

You now have two sources from which to construct a candidate specification. The first is the initial telephone conversation with the prospective employer, and the second is the position analysis that you have just completed.

Chances are, if you have done a particularly thorough job with your position analysis, you may well have given more thought to the qualifications necessary to successful job performance than has the employer with whom you will be interviewing. This could serve to place you at a decided strategic advantage during the interview, allowing you to highlight important aspects of your background that are critical to achievement of desired organizational results.

Be careful not to get carried away with your newfound power, however, since this could serve to alienate the interviewer and cause you to be labeled as a show-off or "know-it-all."

Now, pause for a moment to review the overall candidate requirements as defined by both you and the employer. With these requirements in mind, use the following set of questions to help you to translate these overall requirements into a combined candidate specification.

1. *Formal Education:*  Considering the technical challenges of this position and the knowledge required, what formal education/training should the ideal candidate have (degree level and major)? Why? _____

_____

_____

2. *Training:*  What informal education (training courses, seminars, etc.) would likely provide the required knowledge? _____

_____

_____

3. *Experience:*  What level (number of years) and kind of experience would likely yield the depth and breadth of knowledge necessary for successful performance in this position? _____

_____

_____

4. *Related Experience:*  What related or similar kinds of experience might yield the same kind of knowledge, and would therefore be an acceptable alternative?

_____

_____

_____

5. *Skills:*  What specific skills ar required by the position, and how might these be acquired? _____

_____

_____

6. *Personal Attributes:*  What personal attributes and characteristics are probably important for successful performance of this position? _____

_____

_____

# Job Seekers Guide to Executive Recruiters

**Abbatiello, Christine Murphy** — *Information Technology Recruiter*
Winter, Wyman & Company
1100 Circle 75 Parkway, Suite 800
Atlanta, GA 30339
Telephone: (770) 933-1525
**Recruiter Classification:** Contingency; **Lowest/Average Salary:** $30,000/$60,000; **Industry Concentration:** Generalist with a primary focus in Consumer Products, Financial Services, Healthcare/Hospitals, High Technology, Information Technology, Insurance, Manufacturing, Pharmaceutical/Medical, Publishing/Media, Real Estate; **Function Concentration:** Generalist

**Abbott, Dale** — *Principal*
Mixtec Group
31255 Cedar Valley Drive
Suite 300-327
Westlake Village, CA 91362
Telephone: (818) 889-8819
**Recruiter Classification:** Contingency; **Lowest/Average Salary:** $60,000/$90,000; **Function Concentration:** Generalist with a primary focus in General Management, Marketing, Research and Development, Sales

**Abbott, Peter** — *Partner*
The Abbott Group, Inc.
530 College Parkway, Suite N
Annapolis, MD 21401
Telephone: (410) 757-4100
**Recruiter Classification:** Retained; **Lowest/Average Salary:** $90,000/$90,000; **Industry Concentration:** Generalist with a primary focus in Aerospace/Defense, Automotive, Chemical Products, Electronics, Environmental, High Technology, Information Technology, Manufacturing, Non-Profit, Packaging, Publishing/Media, Transportation, Venture Capital; **Function Concentration:** Generalist with a primary focus in Engineering, Finance/Accounting, General Management, Human Resources, Marketing, Research and Development, Sales, Women/Minorities

**Abby, Daniel** — *Account Executive*
Bill Hahn Group, Inc.
2052 Highway 35
Suites 203, 204
Wall, NJ 07719
Telephone: (908) 449-9302
**Recruiter Classification:** Contingency; **Lowest/Average Salary:** $50,000/$60,000; **Industry Concentration:** Biotechnology, Consumer Products, Manufacturing, Pharmaceutical/Medical; **Function Concentration:** Engineering

**Abe, Sherman** — *Vice President*
Korn/Ferry International
The Transamerica Pyramid
600 Montgomery Street
San Francisco, CA 94111
Telephone: (415) 956-1834
**Recruiter Classification:** Retained; **Lowest/Average Salary:** $90,000/$90,000; **Industry Concentration:** Generalist; **Function Concentration:** Generalist

**Abell, Vincent W.** — *Executive Recruiter*
MSI International
8521 Leesburg Pike, Suite 435
Vienna, VA 22182
Telephone: (703) 893-5669
**Recruiter Classification:** Contingency; **Lowest/Average Salary:** $30,000/$75,000; **Industry Concentration:** Generalist with a primary focus in Financial Services, Healthcare/Hospitals, High Technology, Information Technology, Manufacturing; **Function Concentration:** Generalist with a primary focus in Administration, Engineering, Finance/Accounting, General Management, Marketing, Sales

**Abernathy, Donald E.** — *Consultant*
Don Richard Associates of Charlotte
2650 One First Union Center
301 South College Street
Charlotte, NC 28202-6000
Telephone: (704) 377-6447
**Recruiter Classification:** Contingency, Executive Temporary; **Lowest/Average Salary:** $30,000/$40,000; **Industry Concentration:** Generalist; **Function Concentration:** Finance/Accounting

**Abramson, Roye** — *Associate*
Source Services Corporation
379 Thornall Street
Edison, NJ 08837
Telephone: (908) 494-2800
**Recruiter Classification:** Contingency; **Lowest/Average Salary:** $30,000/$50,000; **Industry Concentration:** Financial Services, Information Technology; **Function Concentration:** Engineering, Finance/Accounting

**Abruzzo, James** — *Vice President/Managing Director*
A.T. Kearney, Inc.
153 East 53rd Street
New York, NY 10022
Telephone: (212) 751-7040
**Recruiter Classification:** Retained; **Lowest/Average Salary:** $90,000/$90,000; **Industry Concentration:** Generalist with a primary focus in Education/Libraries, Entertainment, Non-Profit; **Function Concentration:** Generalist with a primary focus in Administration, Human Resources

**Ackerman, Larry R.** — *Vice President*
Spectrum Search Associates, Inc.
1888 Century Park East, Suite 320
Los Angeles, CA 90067
Telephone: (310) 286-6921
**Recruiter Classification:** Contingency; **Lowest/Average Salary:** $30,000/$50,000; **Industry Concentration:** Financial Services; **Function Concentration:** Finance/Accounting

**Acquaviva, Jay** — *Software Engineering Recruiter*
Winter, Wyman & Company
950 Winter Street, Suite 3100
Waltham, MA 02154-1294
Telephone: (617) 890-7000
**Recruiter Classification:** Contingency; **Lowest/Average Salary:** $40,000/$75,000; **Industry Concentration:** High Technology, Information Technology, Publishing/Media; **Function Concentration:** Engineering

**Adams, Amy** — *Executive Recruiter*
Richard, Wayne and Roberts
24 Greenway Plaza, Suite 1304
Houston, TX 77046-2493
Telephone: (713) 629-6681
**Recruiter Classification:** Retained; **Lowest/Average Salary:** $50,000/$90,000; **Industry Concentration:** Generalist with a primary focus in Financial Services; **Function Concentration:** Generalist with a primary focus in Finance/Accounting

**Adams, Gary** — *Manager Midwest Region*
Management Recruiters International, Inc.
7171 West Mercy Road, Suite 252
Omaha, NE 68106-2696
Telephone: (402) 397-8320
**Recruiter Classification:** Contingency; **Lowest/Average Salary:** $30,000/$75,000; **Industry Concentration:** Generalist; **Function Concentration:** Generalist

**Adams, Jeffrey C.** — *Managing Principal*
Telford, Adams & Alexander/Jeffrey C. Adams & Co., Inc.
455 Market Street, Suite 1910
San Francisco, CA 94105
Telephone: (415) 546-4150
**Recruiter Classification:** Retained; **Lowest/Average Salary:** $50,000/$90,000; **Industry Concentration:** Generalist with a primary focus in Consumer Products, Financial Services, Healthcare/Hospitals, High Technology, Information Technology, Insurance, Manufacturing, Non-Profit, Pharmaceutical/Medical, Public Administration, Real Estate, Transportation; **Function Concentration:** Generalist

**Adams, Len** — *Executive Vice President*
The KPA Group
150 Broadway, Suite 1802
New York, NY 10038
Telephone: (212) 964-3640
**Recruiter Classification:** Contingency, Executive Temporary; **Lowest/Average Salary:** $20,000/$40,000; **Industry Concentration:** Financial Services, Information Technology; **Function Concentration:** Finance/Accounting, Human Resources

**Adams, Michael** — *Senior Associate*
CG & Associates
P.O. Box 11160
Pittsburgh, PA 15237
Telephone: (412) 935-1288
**Recruiter Classification:** Contingency; **Lowest/Average Salary:** $30,000/$60,000; **Industry Concentration:** Real Estate; **Function Concentration:** Generalist with a primary focus in Administration, Engineering, Finance/Accounting, General Management

**Adams, Ralda F.** — *President*
Hospitality International
181 Port Watson Street
Cortland, NY 13045
Telephone: (607) 756-8550
**Recruiter Classification:** Contingency; **Lowest/Average Salary:** $40,000/$60,000; **Industry Concentration:** Entertainment, Healthcare/Hospitals, Hospitality/Leisure; **Function Concentration:** Finance/Accounting, General Management, Human Resources, Marketing, Sales, Women/Minorities

**Adelson, Duane** — *Director*
Stanton Chase International
5050 Quorum Drive, Suite 330
Dallas, TX 75240
Telephone: (214) 404-8411
**Recruiter Classification:** Retained; **Lowest/Average Salary:** $75,000/$90,000; **Industry Concentration:** Generalist; **Function Concentration:** Generalist

**Adkisson, Billy D.** — *President*
James Russell, Inc.
2817 Reed Road, P.O. Box 427
Bloomington, IL 61702-0427
Telephone: (309) 663-9467
**Recruiter Classification:** Retained; **Lowest/Average Salary:** $60,000/$90,000; **Industry Concentration:** Healthcare/Hospitals; **Function Concentration:** Administration, General Management

**Afforde, Sharon Gould** — *Executive Recruiter*
Jacobson Associates
150 North Wacker Drive
Suite 1120
Chicago, IL 60606
Telephone: (312) 726-1578
**Recruiter Classification:** Contingency; **Lowest/Average Salary:** $20,000/$50,000; **Industry Concentration:** Insurance; **Function Concentration:** Generalist

**Agins, Ted** — *Account Executive*
National Restaurant Search, Inc.
910 West Lake Street, Suite 108
Roselle, IL 60172
Telephone: (708) 924-1800
**Recruiter Classification:** Retained; **Lowest/Average Salary:** $50,000/$50,000; **Industry Concentration:** Hospitality/Leisure; **Function Concentration:** Generalist with a primary focus in General Management

**Ahearn, Jennifer** — *Consultant*
Logix, Inc.
1601 Trapelo Road
Waltham, MA 02154
Telephone: (617) 890-0500
**Recruiter Classification:** Retained; **Lowest/Average Salary:** $60,000/$75,000; **Industry Concentration:** High Technology; **Function Concentration:** Engineering

**Aheran, Jennifer** — *Consultant*
Logix Partners
1601 Trapelo Road
Waltham, MA 02154
Telephone: (617) 890-0500
**Recruiter Classification:** Retained; **Lowest/Average Salary:** $60,000/$75,000; **Industry Concentration:** High Technology; **Function Concentration:** Engineering

**Aiken, David** — *Partner*
Commonwealth Consultants
4840 Roswell Road
Atlanta, GA 30342
Telephone: (404) 256-0000
**Recruiter Classification:** Contingency; **Lowest/Average Salary:** $30,000/$90,000; **Industry Concentration:** High Technology; **Function Concentration:** Sales

**Ainsworth, Lawrence** — *Account Executive*
Search West, Inc.
1888 Century Park East
Suite 2050
Los Angeles, CA 90067-1736
Telephone: (310) 284-8888
**Recruiter Classification:** Contingency; **Lowest/Average Salary:** $40,000/$60,000; **Industry Concentration:** Aerospace/Defense, Chemical Products, Electronics, Pharmaceutical/Medical; **Function Concentration:** Marketing, Sales

**Aki, Alvin W.** — *Executive Recruiter*
MSI International
2170 West State Road 434
Suite 454
Longwood, FL 32779
Telephone: (407) 788-7700
**Recruiter Classification:** Contingency; **Lowest/Average Salary:** $30,000/$75,000; **Industry Concentration:** Generalist with a primary focus in Manufacturing; **Function Concentration:** Generalist with a primary focus in Engineering

**Akin, Gary K.** — *Manager Southwest Region*
Management Recruiters International, Inc.
3934 FM 1960 West, Suite 105
Houston, TX 77068-3518
Telephone: (713) 580-6020
**Recruiter Classification:** Contingency; **Lowest/Average Salary:** $30,000/$75,000; **Industry Concentration:** Generalist; **Function Concentration:** Generalist

**Akin, J.R.** — *President*
J.R. Akin & Company Inc.
7181 College Parkway, Suite 30
Fort Myers, FL 33907
Telephone: (941) 395-1575
**Recruiter Classification:** Retained; **Lowest/Average Salary:** $75,000/$90,000; **Industry Concentration:** Generalist with a primary focus in Aerospace/Defense, Electronics, Healthcare/Hospitals, High Technology, Information Technology, Insurance, Manufacturing; **Function Concentration:** Generalist with a primary focus in Administration, Engineering, Finance/Accounting, General Management, Human Resources, Marketing, Sales, Women/Minorities

**Albanese, Matt J.** — *Manager Pacific Region*
Management Recruiters International, Inc.
211 South Glendora Avenue, Suite C, P.O. Box 1998
Glendora, CA 91741-1998
Telephone: (818) 963-4503
**Recruiter Classification:** Contingency; **Lowest/Average Salary:** $30,000/$75,000; **Industry Concentration:** Generalist; **Function Concentration:** Generalist

**Albers, Joan** — *Manager Operations*
Carver Search Consultants
9303 East Bullard, Suite 1
Clovis, CA 93611-8211
Telephone: (209) 298-7791
**Recruiter Classification:** Contingency; **Lowest/Average Salary:** $50,000/$75,000; **Industry Concentration:** Biotechnology, Healthcare/Hospitals, Pharmaceutical/Medical; **Function Concentration:** Administration, General Management

**Albert, Richard** — *Associate*
Source Services Corporation
One CityPlace, Suite 170
St. Louis, MO 63141
Telephone: (314) 432-4500
**Recruiter Classification:** Contingency; **Lowest/Average Salary:** $30,000/$50,000; **Industry Concentration:** Financial Services, Information Technology; **Function Concentration:** Engineering, Finance/Accounting

**Albores, Sergio** — *Manager*
Management Recruiters International, Inc.
Av. Domingo Diez 1589, Suite 121
Cuernavaca, Moreios, MEXICO 62250
Telephone: (527) 311-4045
**Recruiter Classification:** Contingency; **Lowest/Average Salary:** $30,000/$75,000; **Industry Concentration:** Generalist; **Function Concentration:** Generalist

**Albrecht, Franke M.** — *Manager Southwest Region*
Management Recruiters International, Inc.
10700 Richmond, Suite 217
Houston, TX 77042-4900
Telephone: (713) 784-7444
**Recruiter Classification:** Contingency; **Lowest/Average Salary:** $30,000/$75,000; **Industry Concentration:** Generalist; **Function Concentration:** Generalist

**Albright, Cindy** — *Executive Recruiter*
Summerfield Associates, Inc.
6555 Quince Road, Suite 311
Memphis, TN 38119
Telephone: (901) 753-7068
**Recruiter Classification:** Contingency; **Lowest/Average Salary:** $20,000/$30,000; **Industry Concentration:** Generalist with a primary focus in Information Technology; **Function Concentration:** Generalist

**Alden, Brian R.** — *Executive Recruiter*
MSI International
8521 Leesburg Pike, Suite 435
Vienna, VA 22182
Telephone: (703) 893-5669
**Recruiter Classification:** Contingency; **Lowest/Average Salary:** $30,000/$75,000; **Industry Concentration:** Generalist with a primary focus in Fashion (Retail/Apparel); **Function Concentration:** Generalist with a primary focus in Administration, Engineering, Finance/Accounting, General Management, Marketing, Sales

**Alderman, Douglas** — *Manager Eastern Region*
Management Recruiters International, Inc.
167 Avenue at the Common, Suite 7
Shrewsbury, NJ 07702
Telephone: (908) 542-9332
**Recruiter Classification:** Contingency; **Lowest/Average Salary:**
$30,000/$75,000; **Industry Concentration:** Generalist; **Function
Concentration:** Generalist

**Alekel, Karren** — *Associate*
ALW Research International
60 Canterbury Road
Chatham, NJ 07928
Telephone: (201) 701-9700
**Recruiter Classification:** Retained; **Lowest/Average Salary:** $60,000/$75,000;
**Industry Concentration:** Generalist with a primary focus in
Aerospace/Defense, Automotive, Biotechnology, Board Services, Chemical
Products, Consumer Products, Electronics, Energy, Environmental,
Healthcare/Hospitals, High Technology, Manufacturing, Non-Profit, Oil/Gas,
Pharmaceutical/Medical, Publishing/Media; **Function Concentration:**
Generalist with a primary focus in Engineering, General Management, Human
Resources, Marketing, Research and Development, Sales, Women/Minorities

**Alexander, Craig R.** — *Manager Pacific Region*
Management Recruiters International, Inc.
Park Center, Suite 220
290 Bobwhite Court
Boise, ID 83706-3966
Telephone: (208) 336-6770
**Recruiter Classification:** Contingency; **Lowest/Average Salary:**
$30,000/$75,000; **Industry Concentration:** Generalist; **Function
Concentration:** Generalist

**Alexander, John T.** — *Managing Principal*
Telford, Adams & Alexander/Human Resource Services
402 West Broadway, Suite 900
San Diego, CA 92101-3542
Telephone: (619) 238-5686
**Recruiter Classification:** Retained; **Lowest/Average Salary:** $50,000/$75,000;
**Industry Concentration:** Generalist with a primary focus in Automotive,
Education/Libraries, Financial Services, Real Estate; **Function Concentration:**
Generalist with a primary focus in Administration, Finance/Accounting,
General Management, Human Resources, Sales

**Alexander, Raymond** — *Vice President Healthcare Search
Division*
Howard Fischer Associates, Inc.
1800 John F. Kennedy Boulevard, 7th Floor
Philadelphia, PA 19103
Telephone: (215) 568-8363
**Recruiter Classification:** Retained; **Lowest/Average Salary:** $90,000/$90,000;
**Industry Concentration:** Healthcare/Hospitals; **Function Concentration:**
Generalist

**Alfano, Anthony J.** — *Managing Director*
Russell Reynolds Associates, Inc.
200 Park Avenue
New York, NY 10166-0002
Telephone: (212) 351-2000
**Recruiter Classification:** Retained; **Lowest/Average Salary:** $90,000/$90,000;
**Industry Concentration:** Generalist with a primary focus in Financial Services;
**Function Concentration:** Generalist

**Alford, Holly** — *Associate*
Source Services Corporation
5429 LBJ Freeway, Suite 275
Dallas, TX 75240
Telephone: (214) 387-1600
**Recruiter Classification:** Contingency; **Lowest/Average Salary:**
$30,000/$50,000; **Industry Concentration:** Financial Services, Information
Technology; **Function Concentration:** Engineering, Finance/Accounting

**Allard, Susan** — *Partner*
Allard Associates
39811 Sharon Avenue
Davis, CA 95616
Telephone: (916) 757-1649
**Recruiter Classification:** Retained; **Lowest/Average Salary:** $60,000/$75,000;
**Industry Concentration:** Financial Services; **Function Concentration:**
Generalist with a primary focus in Administration, General Management,
Marketing, Sales, Women/Minorities

**Allen, Cynthia** — *Recruiter*
Roberson and Company
10752 North 89th Place, Suite 202
Scottsdale, AZ 85260
Telephone: (602) 391-3200
**Recruiter Classification:** Contingency; **Lowest/Average Salary:**
$50,000/$60,000; **Industry Concentration:** Healthcare/Hospitals,
Pharmaceutical/Medical; **Function Concentration:** Generalist

**Allen, David A.** — *Assistant Vice President*
Intech Summit Group, Inc.
5075 Shoreham Place, Suite 280
San Diego, CA 92122
Telephone: (619) 452-2100
**Recruiter Classification:** Retained; **Lowest/Average Salary:** $75,000/$90,000;
**Industry Concentration:** Healthcare/Hospitals; **Function Concentration:**
Administration, Engineering, Finance/Accounting, General Management,
Human Resources, Research and Development, Sales

**Allen, Donald** — *President*
D.S. Allen Associates, Inc.
823 South Springfield Avenue
Springfield, NJ 07081
Telephone: (201) 376-4800
**Recruiter Classification:** Contingency; **Lowest/Average Salary:** $/$90,000;
**Industry Concentration:** Generalist with a primary focus in Entertainment, High
Technology, Information Technology; **Function Concentration:** Generalist with
a primary focus in Engineering, General Management, Marketing

**Allen, Douglas** — *Vice President*
Sullivan & Associates
344 North Woodward, Suite 304
Birmingham, MI 48009
Telephone: (810) 258-0616
**Recruiter Classification:** Retained; **Lowest/Average Salary:** $90,000/$90,000:
**Industry Concentration:** Generalist; **Function Concentration:** Generalist

**Allen, John L.** — *Partner*
Heidrick & Struggles, Inc.
One Post Office Square
Boston, MA 02109-0199
Telephone: (617) 423-1140
**Recruiter Classification:** Retained; **Lowest/Average Salary:** $75,000/$90,000;
**Industry Concentration:** Generalist with a primary focus in Financial Services;
**Function Concentration:** Generalist

**Allen, Rita B.** — *Vice President*
R.D. Gatti & Associates, Incorporated
266 Main Street, Suite 21
Medfield, MA 02052
Telephone: (508) 359-4153
**Recruiter Classification:** Contingency; **Lowest/Average Salary:**
$40,000/$75,000; **Industry Concentration:** Generalist; **Function
Concentration:** Human Resources

**Allen, Scott** — *Executive Recruiter*
Chrisman & Company, Incorporated
350 South Figueroa Street, Suite 550
Los Angeles, CA 90071
Telephone: (213) 620-1192
**Recruiter Classification:** Retained; **Lowest/Average Salary:** $75,000/$90,000;
**Industry Concentration:** Financial Services, Information Technology,
Insurance, Real Estate, Venture Capital; **Function Concentration:** Generalist

**Allerton, Donald T.** — *Partner*
Allerton Heneghan & O'Neill
70 West Madison Street, Suite 2015
Chicago, IL 60602
Telephone: (312) 263-1075
**Recruiter Classification:** Retained; **Lowest/Average Salary:** $90,000/$90,000;
**Industry Concentration:** Generalist with a primary focus in Biotechnology,
Electronics, High Technology, Pharmaceutical/Medical; **Function
Concentration:** Generalist with a primary focus in Engineering, General
Management, Human Resources, Research and Development,
Women/Minorities

**Alley, Glenwood** — *Manager Midwest Region*
Management Recruiters International, Inc.
Meramec Valley Center
200 Fabricator Drive
Fenton, MO 63026
Telephone: (314) 349-4455
**Recruiter Classification:** Contingency; **Lowest/Average Salary:**
$30,000/$75,000; **Industry Concentration:** Generalist; **Function
Concentration:** Generalist

**Allgire, Mary L.** — *Vice President*
Kenzer Corp.
625 North Michigan Avenue, Suite 1244
Chicago, IL 60611
Telephone: (312) 266-0976
**Recruiter Classification:** Retained; **Lowest/Average Salary:** $50,000/$90,000;
**Industry Concentration:** Consumer Products, Entertainment, Financial
Services, Packaging, Venture Capital; **Function Concentration:** Generalist with
a primary focus in Administration, Finance/Accounting, General Management,
Human Resources, Marketing, Research and Development, Sales

**Allred, J. Michael** — *Director*
Spencer Stuart
One Atlantic Center, Suite 3230
1201 West Peachtree Street
Atlanta, GA 30309
Telephone: (404) 892-2800
**Recruiter Classification:** Retained; **Lowest/Average Salary:** $90,000/$90,000;
**Industry Concentration:** Aerospace/Defense, Electronics, Financial Services,
High Technology, Information Technology, Venture Capital; **Function
Concentration:** Generalist with a primary focus in General Management,
Marketing, Sales

**Alpeyrie, Jean-Louis** — *Partner*
Heidrick & Struggles, Inc.
245 Park Avenue, Suite 4300
New York, NY 10167-0152
Telephone: (212) 867-9876
**Recruiter Classification:** Retained; **Lowest/Average Salary:** $75,000/$90,000;
**Industry Concentration:** Generalist with a primary focus in High Technology;
**Function Concentration:** Generalist

**Alphonse-Charles, Maureen** — *Associate*
Pendleton James and Associates, Inc.
One International Place
Boston, MA 02110
Telephone: (617) 261-9696
**Recruiter Classification:** Retained; **Lowest/Average Salary:** $90,000/$90,000;
**Industry Concentration:** Generalist; **Function Concentration:** Generalist

**Alringer, Marc** — *Associate*
Source Services Corporation
4510 Executive Drive, Suite 200
San Diego, CA 92121
Telephone: (619) 552-0300
**Recruiter Classification:** Contingency; **Lowest/Average Salary:**
$30,000/$50,000; **Industry Concentration:** Financial Services, Information
Technology; **Function Concentration:** Engineering, Finance/Accounting

**Altieri, Robert J.** — *Vice President*
Longshore & Simmons, Inc.
Plymouth Corporate Center
625 Ridge Pike, Suite 410
Conshohocken, PA 19428-3216
Telephone: (610) 941-3400
**Recruiter Classification:** Retained; **Lowest/Average Salary:** $50,000/$90,000;
**Industry Concentration:** Healthcare/Hospitals; **Function Concentration:**
Generalist

**Altreuter, Ken** — *Senior Consultant*
ALTCO Temporary Services
100 Menlo Park
Edison, NJ 08837
Telephone: (908) 549-6100
**Recruiter Classification:** Executive Temporary; **Lowest/Average Salary:**
$30,000/$60,000; **Industry Concentration:** Consumer Products, Packaging,
Pharmaceutical/Medical; **Function Concentration:** Engineering, Human
Resources, Research and Development, Women/Minorities

**Altreuter, Kenneth** — *Senior Search Consultant*
The ALTCO Group
100 Menlo Park
Edison, NJ 08837
Telephone: (908) 549-6100
**Recruiter Classification:** Contingency; **Lowest/Average Salary:**
$50,000/$60,000; **Industry Concentration:** Consumer Products, Packaging,
Pharmaceutical/Medical; **Function Concentration:** Engineering, Human
Resources, Research and Development

**Altreuter, Rose** — *President Interim Professionals*
ALTCO Temporary Services
100 Menlo Park
Edison, NJ 08837
Telephone: (908) 549-6100
**Recruiter Classification:** Executive Temporary; **Lowest/Average Salary:**
$20,000/$30,000; **Industry Concentration:** Consumer Products, Electronics,
Financial Services, Manufacturing, Packaging, Pharmaceutical/Medical;
**Function Concentration:** Finance/Accounting, Human Resources, Marketing,
Women/Minorities

**Altreuter, Rose** — *Manager Interim Professionals*
The ALTCO Group
100 Menlo Park
Edison, NJ 08837
Telephone: (908) 549-6100
**Recruiter Classification:** Contingency; **Lowest/Average Salary:**
$20,000/$30,000; **Industry Concentration:** Generalist with a primary focus in
Aerospace/Defense, Automotive, Biotechnology, Chemical Products,
Consumer Products, Electronics, Financial Services, High Technology,
Information Technology, Insurance, Manufacturing, Non-Profit, Packaging,
Pharmaceutical/Medical; **Function Concentration:** Administration,
Finance/Accounting, Human Resources, Women/Minorities

**Alvey, Frank C.** — *Vice President*
Robert Sage Recruiting
127 East Windsor
Elkhart, IN 46514
Telephone: (219) 264-1126
**Recruiter Classification:** Contingency; **Lowest/Average Salary:**
$30,000/$75,000; **Industry Concentration:** Automotive; **Function
Concentration:** Generalist

**Amato, Joseph** — *President*
Amato & Associates, Inc.
388 Market Street, Suite 500
San Francisco, CA 94111
Telephone: (415) 781-7664
**Recruiter Classification:** Contingency; **Lowest/Average Salary:**
$50,000/$75,000; **Industry Concentration:** Insurance; **Function
Concentration:** General Management, Marketing, Sales

**Ambert, Amadol** — *Recruiter*
Bryant Research
466 Old Hook Road, Suite 32
Emerson, NJ 07630
Telephone: (201) 599-0590
**Recruiter Classification:** Contingency; **Lowest/Average Salary:**
$50,000/$90,000; **Industry Concentration:** Biotechnology,
Pharmaceutical/Medical; **Function Concentration:** Research and Development

**Ambler, Peter W.** — *President*
Peter W. Ambler Company
14651 Dallas Parkway, Suite 402
Dallas, TX 75240
Telephone: (214) 404-8712
**Recruiter Classification:** Retained; **Lowest/Average Salary:** $50,000/$90,000;
**Industry Concentration:** Generalist with a primary focus in Board Services,
Chemical Products, Consumer Products, Financial Services, Energy, Fashion
(Retail/Apparel), Financial Services, Healthcare/Hospitals, High Technology,
Information Technology, Manufacturing, Non-Profit, Oil/Gas, Packaging;
**Function Concentration:** Generalist with a primary focus in Administration,
Engineering, Finance/Accounting, General Management, Human Resources,
Marketing, Research and Development, Sales

**Ameen, Edward N.** — *General Manager*
Management Recruiters International, Inc.
3527 Ridgelake Drive, P.O. Box 6605
Metairie, LA 70009
Telephone: (504) 831-7333
**Recruiter Classification:** Contingency; **Lowest/Average Salary:**
$30,000/$75,000; **Industry Concentration:** Generalist; **Function
Concentration:** Generalist

**Ames, George C.** — *President*
Ames O'Neill Associates
330 Motor Parkway
Hauppauge, NY 11788
Telephone: (516) 582-4800
**Recruiter Classification:** Contingency; **Lowest/Average Salary:**
$40,000/$60,000; **Industry Concentration:** Generalist with a primary focus in
Aerospace/Defense, Biotechnology, Electronics, High Technology, Information
Technology, Manufacturing; **Function Concentration:** Generalist with a
primary focus in Engineering, Human Resources, Marketing, Research and
Development, Sales

**Amico, Robert** — *Associate*
Source Services Corporation
71 Spit Brook Road, Suite 305
Nashua, NH 03060
Telephone: (603) 888-7650
**Recruiter Classification:** Contingency; **Lowest/Average Salary:**
$30,000/$50,000; **Industry Concentration:** Financial Services, Information
Technology; **Function Concentration:** Engineering, Finance/Accounting

**Amsterdam, Gail E.** — *Managing Director Retail Practice*
D.E. Foster Partners Inc.
570 Lexington Avenue, 14th Floor
New York, NY 10022
Telephone: (212) 872-6232
**Recruiter Classification:** Retained; **Lowest/Average Salary:** $90,000/$90,000;
**Industry Concentration:** Consumer Products, Fashion (Retail/Apparel);
**Function Concentration:** Generalist with a primary focus in
Finance/Accounting, General Management, Human Resources

**Ancona, Donald J.** — *Manager Midwest Region*
Management Recruiters International, Inc.
Chanhassen Office Complex
80 West 78th Street, Suite 230
Chanhassen, MN 55317-9705
Telephone: (612) 937-9693
**Recruiter Classification:** Contingency; **Lowest/Average Salary:**
$30,000/$75,000; **Industry Concentration:** Generalist; **Function
Concentration:** Generalist

**Anderson, David C.** — *Managing Partner*
Heidrick & Struggles, Inc.
2200 Ross Avenue, Suite 4700E
Dallas, TX 75201-2787
Telephone: (214) 220-2130
**Recruiter Classification:** Retained; **Lowest/Average Salary:** $75,000/$90,000;
**Industry Concentration:** Generalist with a primary focus in High Technology;
**Function Concentration:** Generalist

**Anderson, Dean C.** — *Partner*
Corporate Resources Professional Placement
4205 Lancaster Lane, Suite 107
Plymouth, MN 55441
Telephone: (612) 550-9222
**Recruiter Classification:** Contingency; **Lowest/Average Salary:**
$40,000/$60,000; **Industry Concentration:** Electronics, High Technology,
Manufacturing; **Function Concentration:** Engineering, Research and
Development

**Anderson, Dennis** — *Chief Executive Officer*
Andcor Human Resources
539 East Lake Street
Wayzata, MN 55391
Telephone: (612) 821-1000
**Recruiter Classification:** Retained; **Lowest/Average Salary:** $40,000/$75,000;
**Industry Concentration:** Generalist; **Function Concentration:** Generalist

**Anderson, Glenn G.** — *Principal*
Lamalie Amrop International
Key Tower, 127 Public Square
Cleveland, OH 44114-1216
Telephone: (216) 694-3000
**Recruiter Classification:** Retained; **Lowest/Average Salary:** $90,000/$90,000;
**Industry Concentration:** Generalist; **Function Concentration:** Generalist with a
primary focus in General Management

**Anderson, Janet** — *Consultant*
Professional Alternatives, Inc.
601 Lakeshore Parkway, Suite 1050
Minneapolis, MN 55305-5219
Telephone: (612) 449-5180
**Recruiter Classification:** Executive Temporary; **Lowest/Average Salary:**
$30,000/$40,000; **Industry Concentration:** Generalist; **Function
Concentration:** Generalist with a primary focus in Finance/Accounting, Human
Resources, Marketing

**Anderson, Jim L.** — *Manager Pacific Region*
Management Recruiters International, Inc.
3100 Mowry Avenue, Suite 206
Fremont, CA 94538-1509
Telephone: (510) 505-5125
**Recruiter Classification:** Contingency; **Lowest/Average Salary:**
$30,000/$75,000; **Industry Concentration:** Generalist; **Function
Concentration:** Generalist

**Anderson, Mary** — *Managing Director*
Source Services Corporation
425 California Street, Suite 1200
San Francisco, CA 94104
Telephone: (415) 434-2410
**Recruiter Classification:** Contingency; **Lowest/Average Salary:**
$30,000/$50,000; **Industry Concentration:** Financial Services, Information
Technology; **Function Concentration:** Engineering, Finance/Accounting

**Anderson, Matthew** — *Associate*
Source Services Corporation
161 Ottawa NW, Suite 409D
Grand Rapids, MI 49503
Telephone: (616) 451-2400
**Recruiter Classification:** Contingency; **Lowest/Average Salary:**
$30,000/$50,000; **Industry Concentration:** Financial Services, Information
Technology; **Function Concentration:** Engineering, Finance/Accounting

**Anderson, Richard** — *Vice President*
Grant Cooper and Associates
795 Office Parkway, Suite 117
St. Louis, MO 63141
Telephone: (314) 567-4690
**Recruiter Classification:** Retained; **Lowest/Average Salary:** $60,000/$90,000;
**Industry Concentration:** Generalist with a primary focus in Board Services,
Consumer Products, Electronics, Fashion (Retail/Apparel), Financial Services,
Healthcare/Hospitals, Manufacturing, Non-Profit, Pharmaceutical/Medical;
**Function Concentration:** Generalist with a primary focus in Administration,
Engineering, Finance/Accounting, General Management, Human Resources,
Marketing, Sales

**Anderson, Roger J.** — *Principal*
BioQuest, Inc.
100 Spear Street, Suite 1125
San Francisco, CA 94105
Telephone: (415) 777-2422
**Recruiter Classification:** Retained; **Lowest/Average Salary:** $75,000/$90,000;
**Industry Concentration:** Biotechnology, Pharmaceutical/Medical; **Function
Concentration:** Engineering, Finance/Accounting, General Management,
Marketing, Research and Development, Sales

**Anderson, Shawn** — *Manager*
Temporary Accounting Personnel, Inc.
955 East Henrietta Road
Rochester, NY 14623
Telephone: (716) 427-9930
**Recruiter Classification:** Executive Temporary; **Lowest/Average Salary:**
$20,000/$30,000; **Industry Concentration:** Generalist with a primary focus in
Financial Services; **Function Concentration:** Finance/Accounting, Human
Resources

**Anderson, Thomas** — *Consultant*
Paul J. Biestek Associates, Inc.
9501 West Devon Avenue, Suite 300
Rosemont, IL 60018
Telephone: (708) 825-5131
**Recruiter Classification:** Retained; **Lowest/Average Salary:** $60,000/$90,000;
**Industry Concentration:** Generalist with a primary focus in Automotive,
Biotechnology, Chemical Products, Consumer Products, Electronics,
Environmental, High Technology, Pharmaceutical/Medical; **Function
Concentration:** Generalist with a primary focus in Engineering, General
Management, Human Resources, Marketing, Research and Development, Sales

**Andre, Jacques P.** — *Partner*
Paul Ray Berndtson
101 Park Avenue, 41st Floor
New York, NY 10178
Telephone: (212) 370-1316
**Recruiter Classification:** Retained; **Lowest/Average Salary:** $90,000/$90,000;
**Industry Concentration:** Financial Services; **Function Concentration:**
Generalist

**Andre, Richard** — *President*
The Andre Group, Inc.
2655 North Ocean Drive, Suite 300
Singer Island, FL 33404
Telephone: (407) 844-4070
**Recruiter Classification:** Retained; **Lowest/Average Salary:** $75,000/$90,000;
**Industry Concentration:** Generalist; **Function Concentration:** Generalist with a
primary focus in Human Resources

**Andrews, J. Douglas** — *Partner*
Clarey & Andrews, Inc.
1200 Shermer Road, Suite 108
Northbrook, IL 60062
Telephone: (847) 498-2870
**Recruiter Classification:** Retained; **Lowest/Average Salary:** $90,000/$90,000;
**Industry Concentration:** Generalist with a primary focus in Automotive,
Consumer Products, Electronics, Healthcare/Hospitals, High Technology,
Manufacturing, Pharmaceutical/Medical; **Function Concentration:** Generalist
with a primary focus in Administration, Finance/Accounting, General
Management, Human Resources

**Andrews, Laura L.** — *Associate*
Stricker & Zagor
342 Madison Avenue, Suite 926
New York, NY 10173
Telephone: (212) 983-0388
**Recruiter Classification:** Retained; **Lowest/Average Salary:** $90,000/$90,000;
**Industry Concentration:** Generalist with a primary focus in Consumer
Products, Fashion (Retail/Apparel), Financial Services, Hospitality/Leisure,
Packaging; **Function Concentration:** Generalist with a primary focus in
Administration, Finance/Accounting, General Management, Human Resources,
Marketing, Research and Development, Sales

**Andrick, Patty** — *Executive Recruiter*
CPS Inc.
One Westbrook Corporate Centre, Suite 600
Westchester, IL 60154
Telephone: (708) 531-8370
**Recruiter Classification:** Contingency; **Lowest/Average Salary:**
$30,000/$50,000; **Industry Concentration:** Generalist with a primary focus in
Automotive, Biotechnology, Chemical Products, Consumer Products, High
Technology, Insurance, Manufacturing, Oil/Gas, Packaging,
Pharmaceutical/Medical; **Function Concentration:** Engineering, Research and
Development, Sales, Women/Minorities

**Andujo, Michele M.** — *Executive Recruiter*
Chrisman & Company, Incorporated
350 South Figueroa Street, Suite 550
Los Angeles, CA 90071
Telephone: (213) 620-1192
**Recruiter Classification:** Retained; **Lowest/Average Salary:** $75,000/$90,000;
**Industry Concentration:** Generalist; **Function Concentration:** Generalist with a
primary focus in Finance/Accounting, General Management, Human
Resources

**Angel, Steven R.** — *Manager Central Region*
Management Recruiters International, Inc.
Watterson Towers
1930 Bishop Lane, Suite 426
Louisville, KY 40218-1966
Telephone: (502) 456-4330
**Recruiter Classification:** Contingency; **Lowest/Average Salary:**
$30,000/$75,000; **Industry Concentration:** Generalist; **Function
Concentration:** Generalist

**Angell, Tryg R.** — *Principal*
Tryg R. Angell Ltd.
4021 Main Street
Stratford, CT 06497
Telephone: (203) 377-4541
**Recruiter Classification:** Contingency; **Lowest/Average Salary:**
$30,000/$75,000; **Industry Concentration:** Chemical Products, Energy,
Manufacturing, Oil/Gas, Packaging; **Function Concentration:** Generalist with a
primary focus in Engineering, Finance/Accounting, Human Resources,
Marketing, Research and Development, Sales

**Anglade, Jennifer** — *Senior Associate*
Korn/Ferry International
237 Park Avenue
New York, NY 10017
Telephone: (212) 687-1834
**Recruiter Classification:** Retained; **Lowest/Average Salary:** $90,000/$90,000;
**Industry Concentration:** Generalist; **Function Concentration:** Generalist

**Angott, Mark R.** — *Manager Central Region*
Management Recruiters International, Inc.
2530 South Rochester Road
Rochester Hills, MI 48307-4441
Telephone: (810) 299-1900
**Recruiter Classification:** Contingency; **Lowest/Average Salary:**
$30,000/$75,000; **Industry Concentration:** Generalist; **Function
Concentration:** Generalist

**Ankeney, Dan R.** — *Manager Midwest Region*
Management Recruiters International, Inc.
109 South 2nd Street
Norfolk, NE 68701-5327
Telephone: (402) 379-8212
**Recruiter Classification:** Contingency; **Lowest/Average Salary:**
$30,000/$75,000; **Industry Concentration:** Generalist; **Function
Concentration:** Generalist

**Ankus, Joseph E.** — *Search Consultant*
H. Hertner Associates, Inc.
6600 Cowpen Road, Suite 220
Miami Lakes, FL 33014
Telephone: (305) 556-8882
**Recruiter Classification:** Contingency; **Lowest/Average Salary:**
$50,000/$90,000

**Annesi, Jerry** — *Manager Eastern Region*
Management Recruiters International, Inc.
Powers Building, Suite 225
16 Main Street West
Rochester, NY 14614-1601
Telephone: (716) 454-2440
**Recruiter Classification:** Contingency; **Lowest/Average Salary:**
$30,000/$75,000; **Industry Concentration:** Generalist; **Function
Concentration:** Generalist

**Anterasian, Kathy** — *Consultant*
Egon Zehnder International Inc.
California Plaza, Suite 2625
300 South Grand Avenue
Los Angeles, CA 90071
Telephone: (213) 621-8900
**Recruiter Classification:** Retained; **Lowest/Average Salary:** $90,000/$90,000;
**Industry Concentration:** Generalist; **Function Concentration:** Generalist

**Antil, Pamela W.** — *Vice President*
Norman Roberts & Associates, Inc.
1800 Century Park East, Suite 430
Los Angeles, CA 90067
Telephone: (310) 552-1112
**Recruiter Classification:** Retained; **Lowest/Average Salary:** $60,000/$90,000;
**Industry Concentration:** Education/Libraries, Information Technology, Public
Administration, Real Estate; **Function Concentration:** Generalist with a primary
focus in Administration, Finance/Accounting, General Management,
Women/Minorities

**Anwar, Tarin** — *Managing Director*
Jay Gaines & Company, Inc.
450 Park Avenue
New York, NY 10022
Telephone: (212) 308-9222
**Recruiter Classification:** Retained; **Lowest/Average Salary:** $90,000/$90,000;
**Industry Concentration:** Financial Services, Information Technology; **Function
Concentration:** Finance/Accounting, General Management, Marketing, Sales

**Apostle, George** — *President*
Search Dynamics, Inc.
9420 West Foster Avenue, Suite 200
Chicago, IL 60656-1006
Telephone: (312) 992-3900
**Recruiter Classification:** Contingency; **Lowest/Average Salary:**
$40,000/$90,000; **Industry Concentration:** Aerospace/Defense, Automotive,
Chemical Products, Consumer Products, Electronics, Energy, Environmental,
Healthcare/Hospitals, High Technology, Information Technology,
Manufacturing, Oil/Gas, Pharmaceutical/Medical, Utilities/Nuclear; **Function
Concentration:** Administration, Engineering, General Management, Research
and Development

**Appleton, Diane** — *Co-Manager*
Management Recruiters International, Inc.
Executive Center, Suite 200
555 Republic Drive
Plano, TX 75074
Telephone: (214) 516-4227
**Recruiter Classification:** Contingency; **Lowest/Average Salary:**
$30,000/$75,000; **Industry Concentration:** Generalist; **Function
Concentration:** Generalist

**Aquavella, Charles P.** — *President*
CPA & Associates
5925 Longo Drive
The Colony, TX 75056
Telephone: (214) 370-1111
**Recruiter Classification:** Contingency; **Lowest/Average Salary:**
$20,000/$50,000; **Industry Concentration:** Consumer Products,
Hospitality/Leisure, Manufacturing; **Function Concentration:** Administration,
Finance/Accounting, General Management, Human Resources, Sales

**Archer, John W.** — *Executive Director*
Russell Reynolds Associates, Inc.
200 Park Avenue
New York, NY 10166-0002
Telephone: (212) 351-2000
**Recruiter Classification:** Retained; **Lowest/Average Salary:** $90,000/$90,000;
**Industry Concentration:** Generalist with a primary focus in
Healthcare/Hospitals; **Function Concentration:** Generalist

**Archer, Sandra F.** — *Director*
Ryan, Miller & Associates Inc.
4601 Wilshire Boulevard, Suite 225
Los Angeles, CA 90010
Telephone: (213) 938-4768
**Recruiter Classification:** Contingency; **Lowest/Average Salary:**
$50,000/$60,000; **Industry Concentration:** Generalist with a primary focus in
Financial Services, High Technology; **Function Concentration:** Generalist with
a primary focus in Finance/Accounting

**Ardi, Dana B.** — *Partner*
Paul Ray Berndtson
2029 Century Park East
Suite 1000
Los Angeles, CA 90067
Telephone: (310) 557-2828
**Recruiter Classification:** Retained; **Lowest/Average Salary:** $90,000/$90,000;
**Industry Concentration:** Generalist; **Function Concentration:** Generalist

**Argenio, Michelangelo** — *Director*
Spencer Stuart
277 Park Avenue, 29th Floor
New York, NY 10172
Telephone: (212) 336-0200
**Recruiter Classification:** Retained; **Lowest/Average Salary:** $90,000/$90,000;
**Industry Concentration:** Fashion (Retail/Apparel), Financial Services,
Manufacturing; **Function Concentration:** Generalist with a primary focus in
Finance/Accounting, General Management

**Argentin, Jo** — *Consultant*
Executive Placement Consultants, Inc.
2700 River Road, Suite 107
Des Plaines, IL 60018
Telephone: (847) 298-6445
**Recruiter Classification:** Contingency; **Lowest/Average Salary:**
$40,000/$75,000; **Industry Concentration:** Generalist with a primary focus in
Consumer Products, Financial Services, Healthcare/Hospitals, Information
Technology, Manufacturing, Packaging, Pharmaceutical/Medical,
Transportation; **Function Concentration:** Finance/Accounting, Human
Resources, Women/Minorities

**Ariail, C. Bowling** — *Principal*
Ariail & Associates
210 West Friendly Avenue
Greensboro, NC 27401
Telephone: (910) 275-2906
**Recruiter Classification:** Retained; **Lowest/Average Salary:** $90,000/$90,000;
**Industry Concentration:** Manufacturing; **Function Concentration:** Engineering,
General Management, Marketing, Research and Development, Sales

**Ariail, Randolph C.** — *Principal*
Ariail & Associates
210 West Friendly Avenue
Greensboro, NC 27401
Telephone: (910) 275-2906
**Recruiter Classification:** Retained; **Lowest/Average Salary:** $90,000/$90,000;
**Industry Concentration:** Manufacturing; **Function Concentration:** Engineering,
General Management, Marketing, Research and Development, Sales

**Arms, Douglas** — *Legal Consultant*
TOPAZ Legal Solutions
383 Northfield Avenue
West Orange, NJ 07052
Telephone: (201) 669-7300
**Recruiter Classification:** Executive Temporary; **Lowest/Average Salary:**
$40,000/$75,000; **Industry Concentration:** Chemical Products, Consumer
Products, Electronics, Entertainment, Environmental, Financial Services, High
Technology, Manufacturing; **Function Concentration:** Generalist with a
primary focus in Women/Minorities

**Arms, Douglas** — *Legal Consultant*
TOPAZ International, Inc.
383 Northfield Avenue
West Orange, NJ 07052
Telephone: (201) 669-7300
**Recruiter Classification:** Contingency; **Lowest/Average Salary:**
$40,000/$75,000; **Industry Concentration:** Chemical Products, Consumer
Products, Electronics, Entertainment, Financial Services, High Technology,
Manufacturing, Pharmaceutical/Medical; **Function Concentration:** Generalist
with a primary focus in Women/Minorities

**Arnold, David** — *Senior Vice President*
Christian & Timbers
One Corporate Exchange
25825 Science Park Drive, Suite 400
Cleveland, OH 44122
Telephone: (216) 464-8710
**Recruiter Classification:** Retained; **Lowest/Average Salary:** $90,000/$90,000;
**Industry Concentration:** Generalist with a primary focus in Consumer
Products, High Technology, Information Technology; **Function Concentration:**
Generalist with a primary focus in General Management, Marketing, Research
and Development, Sales, Women/Minorities

**Arnold, David J.** — *Partner*
Heidrick & Struggles, Inc.
Greenwich Office Park #3
Greenwich, CT 06831
Telephone: (203) 629-3200
**Recruiter Classification:** Retained; **Lowest/Average Salary:** $75,000/$90,000;
**Industry Concentration:** Generalist with a primary focus in Consumer
Products; **Function Concentration:** Generalist

**Arnold, Janet N.** — *Manager Southwest Region*
Management Recruiters International, Inc.
1401 Walnut, Suite 302, P.O. Box 2279
Boulder, CO 80306
Telephone: (303) 447-9940
**Recruiter Classification:** Contingency; **Lowest/Average Salary:**
$30,000/$75,000; **Industry Concentration:** Generalist; **Function
Concentration:** Generalist

**Arnold, Jerry** — *Executive Vice President*
Houtz-Strawn Associates, Inc.
11402 Bee Caves Road, West
Austin, TX 78733
Telephone: (512) 263-1131
**Recruiter Classification:** Retained; **Lowest/Average Salary:** $90,000/$90,000;
**Industry Concentration:** Biotechnology, Pharmaceutical/Medical; **Function
Concentration:** Finance/Accounting, General Management, Marketing,
Research and Development

**Arnold, Sheridan J.** — *Vice President*
William B. Arnold Associates
600 South Cherry Street, Suite 1105
Denver, CO 80222
Telephone: (303) 393-6662
**Recruiter Classification:** Retained; **Lowest/Average Salary:** $60,000/$90,000;
**Industry Concentration:** Generalist; **Function Concentration:** Generalist

**Arnold, William B.** — *President*
William B. Arnold Associates
600 South Cherry Street, Suite 1105
Denver, CO 80222
Telephone: (303) 393-6662
**Recruiter Classification:** Retained; **Lowest/Average Salary:** $60,000/$90,000;
**Industry Concentration:** Generalist; **Function Concentration:** Generalist

**Arnson, Craig** — *Regional Manager*
Hernand & Partners
333 West Wacker Drive, Suite 700
Chicago, IL 60606
Telephone: (312) 346-5420
**Recruiter Classification:** Executive Temporary; **Industry Concentration:**
High Technology, Information Technology; **Function Concentration:**
Engineering

**Aronin, Michael** — *Senior Consultant*
Fisher-Todd Associates
535 Fifth Avenue, Suite 710
New York, NY 10017
Telephone: (212) 986-9052
**Recruiter Classification:** Contingency; **Lowest/Average Salary:**
$50,000/$75,000; **Industry Concentration:** Generalist with a primary focus in
Biotechnology, Consumer Products, Entertainment, Fashion (Retail/Apparel),
Financial Services, Healthcare/Hospitals, Hospitality/Leisure, Information
Technology, Pharmaceutical/Medical, Publishing/Media, Transportation;
**Function Concentration:** Generalist with a primary focus in Administration,
General Management, Marketing, Research and Development, Sales,
Women/Minorities

**Aronow, Lawrence E.** — *President*
Aronow Associates, Inc.
One Pennsylvania Plaza, Suite 2131
New York, NY 10119
Telephone: (212) 947-3777
**Recruiter Classification:** Contingency; **Lowest/Average Salary:**
$50,000/$75,000; **Industry Concentration:** Financial Services; **Function
Concentration:** Finance/Accounting, General Management, Marketing, Sales

**Arons, Richard** — *Managing Director*
Korn/Ferry International
One Palmer Square
Princeton, NJ 08542
Telephone: (609) 921-8811
**Recruiter Classification:** Retained; **Lowest/Average Salary:** $90,000/$90,000;
**Industry Concentration:** Generalist; **Function Concentration:** Generalist

**Arozarena, Elaine** — *Executive Director*
Russell Reynolds Associates, Inc.
200 Park Avenue
New York, NY 10166-0002
Telephone: (212) 351-2000
**Recruiter Classification:** Retained; **Lowest/Average Salary:** $90,000/$90,000;
**Industry Concentration:** Generalist; **Function Concentration:** Generalist

**Arrington, Renee** — *Consultant*
Paul Ray Berndtson
301 Commerce Street, Suite 2300
Fort Worth, TX 76102
Telephone: (817) 334-0500
**Recruiter Classification:** Retained; **Lowest/Average Salary:** $90,000/$90,000;
**Industry Concentration:** Generalist; **Function Concentration:** Generalist

**Arseneault, Daniel S.** — *Executive Recruiter*
MSI International
200 Galleria Parkway
Suite 1610
Atlanta, GA 30339
Telephone: (404) 951-1208
**Recruiter Classification:** Contingency; **Lowest/Average Salary:**
$30,000/$75,000; **Industry Concentration:** Generalist with a primary focus in
Electronics, High Technology; **Function Concentration:** Generalist with a
primary focus in Administration, Engineering, Finance/Accounting, General
Management, Marketing, Sales

**Artimovich, Lee J.** — *Vice President*
Korn/Ferry International
4816 IDS Center
Minneapolis, MN 55402
Telephone: (612) 333-1834
**Recruiter Classification:** Retained; **Lowest/Average Salary:** $90,000/$90,000;
**Industry Concentration:** Generalist; **Function Concentration:** Generalist

**Ascher, Susan P.** — *President*
The Ascher Group
25 Pompton Avenue, Suite 310
Verona, NJ 07044
Telephone: (201) 239-6116
**Recruiter Classification:** Executive Temporary; **Lowest/Average Salary:**
$50,000/$90,000; **Industry Concentration:** Generalist with a primary focus in
Consumer Products, Fashion (Retail/Apparel), Financial Services, Information
Technology, Insurance, Manufacturing, Pharmaceutical/Medical,
Publishing/Media; **Function Concentration:** Generalist with a primary focus in
Administration, Finance/Accounting, General Management, Human Resources,
Marketing, Women/Minorities

**Ashton, Barbara L.** — *President*
Ashton Computer Professionals Inc.
#1498 - 1090 West Georgia Street
Vancouver, British Columbia, CANADA V6E 3V7
Telephone: (604) 688-1134
**Recruiter Classification:** Contingency; **Lowest/Average Salary:**
$30,000/$60,000; **Industry Concentration:** Electronics, High Technology,
Information Technology; **Function Concentration:** Engineering, General
Management, Marketing, Research and Development, Sales

**Ashton, Edward J.** — *President*
E.J. Ashton & Associates, Ltd.
P.O. Box 1048
Lake Zurich, IL 60047-1048
Telephone: (847) 540-9922
**Recruiter Classification:** Contingency; **Lowest/Average Salary:**
$30,000/$60,000; **Industry Concentration:** Insurance; **Function
Concentration:** Generalist with a primary focus in Administration,
Finance/Accounting, General Management, Marketing, Sales

**Aslaksen, James G.** — *Partner*
Lamalie Amrop International
225 West Wacker Drive
Chicago, IL 60606-1229
Telephone: (312) 782-3113
**Recruiter Classification:** Retained; **Lowest/Average Salary:** $90,000/$90,000;
**Industry Concentration:** Generalist with a primary focus in Chemical Products;
**Function Concentration:** Generalist with a primary focus in Marketing, Sales

**Asquith, Peter S.** — *Vice President*
Ames Personnel Consultants, Inc.
P.O. Box 651
Brunswick, ME 04011
Telephone: (207) 729-5158
**Recruiter Classification:** Executive Temporary; **Lowest/Average Salary:**
$30,000/$60,000; **Industry Concentration:** Generalist with a primary focus in
Chemical Products, Environmental, High Technology, Manufacturing,
Packaging, Utilities/Nuclear; **Function Concentration:** Generalist with a
primary focus in Engineering, Finance/Accounting, General Management,
Human Resources, Marketing, Research and Development, Sales

**Ast, Steven T.** — *Partner*
Ast/Bryant
One Atlantic Street
Stamford, CT 06901
Telephone: (203) 975-7188
**Recruiter Classification:** Retained; **Lowest/Average Salary:** $75,000/$90,000;
**Industry Concentration:** Education/Libraries, Environmental, Non-Profit;
**Function Concentration:** Women/Minorities

**Aston, Kathy** — *Director*
Marra Peters & Partners
Millburn Esplanade
Millburn, NJ 07041
Telephone: (201) 376-8999
**Recruiter Classification:** Retained; **Lowest/Average Salary:** $/$90,000; **Industry
Concentration:** Generalist with a primary focus in Biotechnology, Consumer
Products, Entertainment, Financial Services, Information Technology,
Manufacturing, Pharmaceutical/Medical; **Function Concentration:** Generalist
with a primary focus in Administration, Engineering, Finance/Accounting,
General Management, Human Resources, Marketing, Research and
Development, Sales

**Atkeson, George G.** — *Managing Director*
Ward Howell International, Inc.
One Landmark Square
Suite 1810
Stamford, CT 06901
Telephone: (203) 964-1481
**Recruiter Classification:** Retained; **Lowest/Average Salary:** $75,000/$90,000;
**Industry Concentration:** Consumer Products; **Function Concentration:**
Generalist

**Atkins, Laurie** — *Senior Associate*
Battalia Winston International
300 Park Avenue
New York, NY 10022
Telephone: (212) 308-8080
**Recruiter Classification:** Retained; **Lowest/Average Salary:** $90,000/$90,000;
**Industry Concentration:** Generalist with a primary focus in Consumer
Products, Electronics, Healthcare/Hospitals, High Technology, Manufacturing;
**Function Concentration:** Generalist with a primary focus in General
Management, Human Resources

**Atkinson, S. Graham** — *Principal*
Raymond Karsan Associates
522 East Genesee Street
Fayetteville, NY 13066
Telephone: (315) 637-4600
**Recruiter Classification:** Contingency; **Lowest/Average Salary:**
$30,000/$90,000; **Industry Concentration:** Generalist with a primary focus in
Biotechnology, Chemical Products, Environmental, Healthcare/Hospitals,
Information Technology, Insurance, Manufacturing, Pharmaceutical/Medical;
**Function Concentration:** Generalist

**Attell, Harold** — *Vice President*
A.E. Feldman Associates
445 Northern Boulevard
Great Neck, NY 11021
Telephone: (516) 466-4708
**Recruiter Classification:** Contingency; **Lowest/Average Salary:**
$50,000/$75,000; **Industry Concentration:** Fashion (Retail/Apparel); **Function
Concentration:** Generalist with a primary focus in Administration, Engineering,
Finance/Accounting, General Management, Human Resources, Marketing,
Research and Development, Sales, Women/Minorities

**Aubin, Richard E.** — *Chairman*
Aubin International
Somerset Court, 281 Winter Street
Waltham, MA 02154
Telephone: (617) 890-1722
**Recruiter Classification:** Retained; **Lowest/Average Salary:** $90,000/$90,000;
**Industry Concentration:** Generalist with a primary focus in Board Services,
Electronics, High Technology, Information Technology, Manufacturing, Venture
Capital; **Function Concentration:** Generalist

**Austin, Jessica L.** — *Recruiter*
D.S.A. - Dixie Search Associates
501 Village Trace, Building 9
Marietta, GA 30067
Telephone: (770) 850-0250
**Recruiter Classification:** Contingency; **Lowest/Average Salary:**
$30,000/$50,000; **Industry Concentration:** Biotechnology, Consumer
Products, Hospitality/Leisure, Manufacturing, Packaging, Transportation;
**Function Concentration:** Generalist with a primary focus in Engineering,
Finance/Accounting, General Management, Human Resources, Marketing,
Research and Development, Sales

**Aydelotte, G. Thomas** — *Partner*
Ingram & Aydelotte Inc.
430 Park Avenue, Suite 700
New York, NY 10022
Telephone: (212) 319-7777
**Recruiter Classification:** Retained; **Lowest/Average Salary:** $90,000/$90,000;
**Industry Concentration:** Generalist with a primary focus in Board Services,
Consumer Products, Education/Libraries, Financial Services,
Healthcare/Hospitals, Insurance, Pharmaceutical/Medical, Publishing/Media;
**Function Concentration:** Generalist with a primary focus in
Finance/Accounting, General Management, Human Resources, Marketing

**Azzani, Eunice** — *Vice President*
Korn/Ferry International
The Transamerica Pyramid
600 Montgomery Street
San Francisco, CA 94111
Telephone: (415) 956-1834
**Recruiter Classification:** Retained; **Lowest/Average Salary:** $90,000/$90,000;
**Industry Concentration:** Generalist; **Function Concentration:** Generalist

**Bacher, Philip J.** — *Vice President*
Handy HRM Corp.
250 Park Avenue
New York, NY 10177-0074
Telephone: (212) 557-0400
**Recruiter Classification:** Retained; **Lowest/Average Salary:** $90,000/$90,000;
**Industry Concentration:** Generalist; **Function Concentration:** Generalist with a
primary focus in General Management, Human Resources

**Bachmeier, Kevin** — *Agribusiness Recruiter/Manager*
Agra Placements International Ltd.
Valley Office Park, Suite 214
10800 Lyndale Avenue South
Minneapolis, MN 55420
Telephone: (612) 881-3692
**Recruiter Classification:** Contingency; **Lowest/Average Salary:**
$20,000/$30,000; **Industry Concentration:** Generalist with a primary focus in
Biotechnology, Chemical Products, Energy, Financial Services, Manufacturing;
**Function Concentration:** Administration, Engineering, Finance/Accounting,
General Management, Human Resources, Marketing, Research and
Development, Sales

**Bacigalupo, Terry** — *Manager Midwest Region*
Management Recruiters International, Inc.
1101 Edgewater Pointe Boulevard
Lake St. Louis, MO 63367-2906
Telephone: (314) 625-1780
**Recruiter Classification:** Contingency; **Lowest/Average Salary:**
$30,000/$75,000; **Industry Concentration:** Generalist; **Function
Concentration:** Generalist

**Bacon, Michael** — *Manager Eastern Region*
Management Recruiters International, Inc.
Cold Stream Office Park
116-C South River Road
Bedford, NH 03110-2131
Telephone: (603) 669-9800
**Recruiter Classification:** Contingency; **Lowest/Average Salary:**
$30,000/$75,000; **Industry Concentration:** Generalist; **Function
Concentration:** Generalist

**Bacorn, Debra** — *Branch Supervisor*
Accountants on Call
One Lincoln Centre, Suite 1050
Oakbrook Terrace, IL 60181
Telephone: (708) 261-1300
**Recruiter Classification:** Contingency; **Lowest/Average Salary:**
$20,000/$30,000; **Industry Concentration:** Generalist; **Function
Concentration:** Finance/Accounting

**Bader, Sam** — *President*
Bader Research Corporation
6 East 45th Street
New York, NY 10017
Telephone: (212) 682-4750
**Recruiter Classification:** Contingency; **Lowest/Average Salary:**
$75,000/$90,000; **Industry Concentration:** Financial Services, Real Estate

**Badger, Fred H.** — *Chief Executive Officer*
The Badger Group
4125 Blackhawk Plaza Circle, Suite 270
Danville, CA 94506
Telephone: (510) 736-5553
**Recruiter Classification:** Retained; **Lowest/Average Salary:** $90,000/$90,000;
**Industry Concentration:** Generalist with a primary focus in Consumer
Products, Electronics, Financial Services, Healthcare/Hospitals, High
Technology, Information Technology, Manufacturing; **Function
Concentration:** Generalist with a primary focus in Engineering,
Finance/Accounting, General Management, Marketing, Research and
Development, Sales

**Baer, Kenneth** — *Associate*
Source Services Corporation
701 West Cypress Creek Road, Suite 202
Ft. Lauderdale, FL 33309
Telephone: (954) 771-0777
**Recruiter Classification:** Contingency; **Lowest/Average Salary:**
$30,000/$50,000; **Industry Concentration:** Financial Services, Information
Technology; **Function Concentration:** Engineering, Finance/Accounting

**Bagg, Keith** — *President/Consultant*
Keith Bagg & Associates Inc.
36 Toronto Street, Suite 520
Toronto, Ontario, CANADA M5C 2C5
Telephone: (416) 863-1800
**Recruiter Classification:** Contingency, Executive Temporary; **Lowest/Average
Salary:** $40,000/$60,000; **Industry Concentration:** Chemical Products,
Electronics, Manufacturing, Pharmaceutical/Medical; **Function Concentration:**
Engineering, General Management, Marketing, Research and Development, Sales

**Bagg, Mary** — *Vice President/Consultant*
Keith Bagg & Associates Inc.
36 Toronto Street, Suite 520
Toronto, Ontario, CANADA M5C 2C5
Telephone: (416) 863-1800
**Recruiter Classification:** Contingency, Executive Temporary; **Lowest/Average
Salary:** $40,000/$60,000; **Industry Concentration:** Financial Services,
Insurance, Non-Profit; **Function Concentration:** Administration,
Finance/Accounting, Human Resources, Marketing

**Bagley, James W.** — *Managing Director*
Russell Reynolds Associates, Inc.
200 Park Avenue
New York, NY 10166-0002
Telephone: (212) 351-2000
**Recruiter Classification:** Retained; **Lowest/Average Salary:** $90,000/$90,000;
**Industry Concentration:** Generalist; **Function Concentration:** Generalist

**Baglio, Robert** — *Associate*
Source Services Corporation
8614 Westwood Center, Suite 750
Vienna, VA 22182
Telephone: (703) 790-5610
**Recruiter Classification:** Contingency; **Lowest/Average Salary:**
$30,000/$50,000; **Industry Concentration:** Financial Services, Information
Technology; **Function Concentration:** Engineering, Finance/Accounting

**Bagwell, Bruce** — *Senior Partner*
Intersource, Ltd.
72 Sloan Street
Roswell, GA 30075
Telephone: (770) 645-0015
**Recruiter Classification:** Retained; **Lowest/Average Salary:**
$50,000/$60,000; **Industry Concentration:** Generalist with a primary focus
in Consumer Products, Electronics, Financial Services, Healthcare/Hospitals,
High Technology, Hospitality/Leisure, Information Technology,
Manufacturing; **Function Concentration:** Finance/Accounting, Human
Resources, Sales

**Baier, Rebecca** — *Associate*
Source Services Corporation
5429 LBJ Freeway, Suite 275
Dallas, TX 75240
Telephone: (214) 387-1600
**Recruiter Classification:** Contingency; **Lowest/Average Salary:**
$30,000/$50,000; **Industry Concentration:** Financial Services, Information
Technology; **Function Concentration:** Engineering, Finance/Accounting

**Bailey, David O.** — *Consultant*
Paul Ray Berndtson
101 Park Avenue, 41st Floor
New York, NY 10178
Telephone: (212) 370-1316
**Recruiter Classification:** Retained; **Lowest/Average Salary:** $90,000/$90,000;
**Industry Concentration:** Chemical Products, Consumer Products, Information
Technology; **Function Concentration:** Generalist

**Bailey, Joseph W.** — *Executive Director*
Russell Reynolds Associates, Inc.
200 Park Avenue
New York, NY 10166-0002
Telephone: (212) 351-2000
**Recruiter Classification:** Retained; **Lowest/Average Salary:** $90,000/$90,000;
**Industry Concentration:** Generalist; **Function Concentration:** Generalist

**Bailey, Linda S.** — *Associate*
Kenzer Corp.
1600 Parkwood Circle NW, Suite 310
Atlanta, GA 30339
Telephone: (770) 955-7210
**Recruiter Classification:** Retained; **Lowest/Average Salary:** $50,000/$90,000;
**Industry Concentration:** Generalist; **Function Concentration:** Generalist

**Bailey, Lisa** — *Associate*
Nordeman Grimm, Inc.
717 Fifth Avenue, 26th Floor
New York, NY 10022
Telephone: (212) 935-1000
**Recruiter Classification:** Retained; **Lowest/Average Salary:** $90,000/$90,000;
**Industry Concentration:** Generalist; **Function Concentration:** Generalist

**Bailey, William A.** — *Vice President*
TNS Partners, Inc.
12655 North Central Expressway
Suite 900
Dallas, TX 75243
Telephone: (214) 991-3555
**Recruiter Classification:** Retained; **Lowest/Average Salary:** $75,000/$90,000;
**Industry Concentration:** Generalist with a primary focus in
Aerospace/Defense, Biotechnology, Electronics, Fashion (Retail/Apparel),
Financial Services, Healthcare/Hospitals, High Technology, Hospitality/Leisure,
Information Technology, Manufacturing, Oil/Gas, Packaging,
Pharmaceutical/Medical, Public Administration, Venture Capital; **Function
Concentration:** Generalist with a primary focus in Administration, Engineering,
Finance/Accounting, General Management, Human Resources, Marketing

**Baillou, Astrid** — *Associate*
Richard Kinser & Associates
919 Third Avenue, 10th Floor
New York, NY 10022
Telephone: (212) 593-5429
**Recruiter Classification:** Retained; **Lowest/Average Salary:** $90,000/$90,000;
**Industry Concentration:** Generalist with a primary focus in Board Services,
Entertainment, High Technology, Publishing/Media; **Function Concentration:**
Generalist with a primary focus in General Management, Marketing

**Baird, Blaine T.** — *Associate*
Physicians Search, Inc.
1224 Katella Avenue, Suite 202
Orange, CA 92667-5045
Telephone: (714) 288-8350
**Recruiter Classification:** Contingency; **Lowest/Average Salary:**
$75,000/$90,000; **Industry Concentration:** Biotechnology,
Healthcare/Hospitals, Pharmaceutical/Medical; **Function Concentration:**
Generalist

**Baird, David W.** — *Principal*
D.W. Baird & Associates
10751 Falls Road, Suite 250
Lutherville, MD 21093
Telephone: (410) 339-7670
**Recruiter Classification:** Contingency; **Lowest/Average Salary:**
$40,000/$60,000; **Industry Concentration:** Chemical Products, Manufacturing;
**Function Concentration:** Engineering, General Management, Marketing,
Research and Development, Sales

**Baird, John** — *Contract Recruiter*
Professional Search Consultants
3050 Post Oak Boulevard, Suite 1615
Houston, TX 77056
Telephone: (713) 960-9215
**Recruiter Classification:** Executive Temporary; **Lowest/Average Salary:**
$50,000/$90,000; **Industry Concentration:** Generalist with a primary focus in
Aerospace/Defense, Chemical Products, Energy, Environmental,
Healthcare/Hospitals, Information Technology, Manufacturing, Oil/Gas;
**Function Concentration:** Engineering, Sales

**Baitler, Simon C.** — *Vice President*
The Stevenson Group of Delaware Inc.
9744 Wilshire Boulevard, Suite 307
Beverly Hills, CA 90212
Telephone: (310) 285-0003
**Recruiter Classification:** Retained; **Lowest/Average Salary:** $75,000/$90,000;
**Industry Concentration:** Chemical Products, Consumer Products, Electronics,
Financial Services, Insurance, Pharmaceutical/Medical; **Function
Concentration:** Generalist

**Baker, Charles E.** — *Associate*
Kenzer Corp.
Fifth Street Tower, Suite 1330
150 South Fifth Street
Minneapolis, MN 55402
Telephone: (612) 332-7700
**Recruiter Classification:** Retained; **Lowest/Average Salary:** $50,000/$90,000;
**Industry Concentration:** Generalist; **Function Concentration:** Generalist

**Baker, Gary M.** — *Vice President*
Cochran, Cochran & Yale, Inc.
955 East Henrietta Road
Rochester, NY 14623
Telephone: (716) 424-6060
**Recruiter Classification:** Contingency; **Lowest/Average Salary:**
$40,000/$60,000; **Industry Concentration:** Generalist with a primary focus in
Biotechnology, Consumer Products, Electronics, Financial Services, High
Technology, Manufacturing, Packaging, Pharmaceutical/Medical; **Function
Concentration:** Administration, Finance/Accounting, Women/Minorities

**Baker, Gary M.** — *President*
Temporary Accounting Personnel, Inc.
955 East Henrietta Road
Rochester, NY 14623
Telephone: (716) 427-9930
**Recruiter Classification:** Executive Temporary; **Lowest/Average Salary:**
$20,000/$30,000; **Industry Concentration:** Generalist with a primary focus in
Financial Services; **Function Concentration:** Finance/Accounting, Human
Resources

**Baker, Gerry** — *Partner*
Baker, Harris & Partners Limited
130 Adelaide Street West, Suite 2710
Toronto, Ontario, CANADA M5H 3P5
Telephone: (416) 947-1990
**Recruiter Classification:** Retained; **Lowest/Average Salary:** $60,000/$90,000;
**Industry Concentration:** Generalist with a primary focus in Electronics, High
Technology, Information Technology, Manufacturing; **Function Concentration:**
Generalist with a primary focus in Engineering, General Management,
Marketing, Research and Development, Sales

**Baker, Jerry H.** — *Partner*
Schuyler, Frye & Baker, Inc.
1100 Abernathy Road N.E., Suite 1825
Atlanta, GA 30328
Telephone: (770) 804-1996
**Recruiter Classification:** Retained; **Lowest/Average Salary:** $90,000/$90,000;
**Industry Concentration:** Generalist; **Function Concentration:** Generalist

**Baker, Jim** — *Sales Recruiter*
Southwestern Professional Services
2451 Atrium Way
Nashville, TN 37214
Telephone: (615) 391-2722
**Recruiter Classification:** Contingency; **Lowest/Average Salary:**
$20,000/$30,000; **Industry Concentration:** Generalist with a primary focus in
Non-Profit; **Function Concentration:** Generalist with a primary focus in Sales

**Baker, Judith** — *Vice President*
Search Consultants International, Inc.
4545 Post Oak Place, Suite 208
Houston, TX 77027
Telephone: (713) 622-9188
**Recruiter Classification:** Contingency, Executive Temporary; **Lowest/Average
Salary:** $60,000/$75,000; **Industry Concentration:** Chemical Products, Energy,
Environmental, Manufacturing, Oil/Gas; **Function Concentration:** Generalist
with a primary focus in Engineering, General Management, Marketing

**Baker, Kerry** — *Manager North Atlantic Region*
Management Recruiters International, Inc.
Pickens Office Complex
509 Lake Road, Suite One
Dyersburg, TN 38024-3814
Telephone: (901) 287-8386
**Recruiter Classification:** Contingency; **Lowest/Average Salary:**
$30,000/$75,000; **Industry Concentration:** Generalist; **Function
Concentration:** Generalist

**Baker, S. Joseph** — *President and CEO*
Search Consultants International, Inc.
4545 Post Oak Place, Suite 208
Houston, TX 77027
Telephone: (713) 622-9188
**Recruiter Classification:** Contingency, Executive Temporary; **Lowest/Average
Salary:** $60,000/$75,000; **Industry Concentration:** Chemical Products, Energy,
Environmental, Manufacturing, Oil/Gas; **Function Concentration:** Engineering,
General Management, Marketing

**Baker, Walter U.** — *Partner*
Lamalie Amrop International
Northdale Plaza, 3903 Northdale Boulevard
Tampa, FL 33624-1864
Telephone: (813) 961-7494
**Recruiter Classification:** Retained; **Lowest/Average Salary:** $90,000/$90,000;
**Industry Concentration:** Generalist; **Function Concentration:** Generalist with a
primary focus in General Management, Marketing, Sales

**Baker-Greene, Edward** — *Senior Recruiter*
Isaacson, Miller
334 Boylston Street, Suite 500
Boston, MA 02111
Telephone: (617) 262-6500
**Recruiter Classification:** Retained; **Lowest/Average Salary:** $75,000/$90,000;
**Industry Concentration:** Generalist with a primary focus in Education/Libraries,
Environmental, Healthcare/Hospitals, Non-Profit, Public Administration,
Transportation; **Function Concentration:** Generalist with a primary focus in
Administration, Finance/Accounting, General Management, Human Resources,
Women/Minorities

**Bakken, Mark** — *Associate*
Source Services Corporation
5429 LBJ Freeway, Suite 275
Dallas, TX 75240
Telephone: (214) 387-1600
**Recruiter Classification:** Contingency; **Lowest/Average Salary:**
$30,000/$50,000; **Industry Concentration:** Financial Services, Information
Technology; **Function Concentration:** Engineering, Finance/Accounting

**Bakker, Robert E.** — *Manager Central Region*
Management Recruiters International, Inc.
Building 200, Suite 6
400 North 136th Avenue
Holland, MI 49424-1830
Telephone: (616) 396-2620
**Recruiter Classification:** Contingency; **Lowest/Average Salary:**
$30,000/$75,000; **Industry Concentration:** Generalist; **Function
Concentration:** Generalist

**Balch, Randy** — *Executive Recruiter*
CPS Inc.
One Westbrook Corporate Centre, Suite 600
Westchester, IL 60154
Telephone: (708) 531-8370
**Recruiter Classification:** Contingency; **Lowest/Average Salary:**
$30,000/$50,000; **Industry Concentration:** Generalist with a primary focus in
Automotive, Biotechnology, Chemical Products, Consumer Products, High
Technology, Insurance, Manufacturing, Oil/Gas, Packaging,
Pharmaceutical/Medical; **Function Concentration:** Engineering, Research and
Development, Sales, Women/Minorities

**Balchumas, Charles** — *Managing Director*
Source Services Corporation
5343 North 16th Street, Suite 270
Phoenix, AZ 85016
Telephone: (602) 230-0220
**Recruiter Classification:** Contingency; **Lowest/Average Salary:**
$30,000/$50,000; **Industry Concentration:** Financial Services, Information
Technology; **Function Concentration:** Engineering, Finance/Accounting

**Baldi, Virgil** — *Vice President*
Korn/Ferry International
One Landmark Square
Stamford, CT 06901
Telephone: (203) 359-3350
**Recruiter Classification:** Retained; **Lowest/Average Salary:** $90,000/$90,000;
**Industry Concentration:** Generalist; **Function Concentration:** Generalist

**Baldock, Robert G.** — *Partner*
Lovas Stanley/Paul Ray Berndtson Inc.
Royal Bank Plaza, South Tower, Suite 3150
200 Bay Street, P.O. Box 125
Toronto, Ontario, CANADA M5J 2J3
Telephone: (416) 366-1990
**Recruiter Classification:** Retained; **Lowest/Average Salary:** $90,000/$90,000;
**Industry Concentration:** Generalist with a primary focus in Financial Services;
**Function Concentration:** Finance/Accounting, General Management

**Baldwin, Keith R.** — *President*
The Baldwin Group
550 West Campus Drive
Arlington Heights, IL 60004
Telephone: (847) 394-4303
**Recruiter Classification:** Retained; **Lowest/Average Salary:** $75,000/$90,000;
**Industry Concentration:** Generalist with a primary focus in
Aerospace/Defense, Chemical Products, Electronics, Financial Services, High
Technology, Manufacturing, Non-Profit, Pharmaceutical/Medical; **Function
Concentration:** Generalist

**Balkin, Linda E.** — *Consultant*
Witt/Kieffer, Ford, Hadelman & Lloyd
2015 Spring Road, Suite 510
Oak Brook, IL 60521
Telephone: (708) 990-1370
**Recruiter Classification:** Retained; **Lowest/Average Salary:** $75,000/$90,000;
**Industry Concentration:** Healthcare/Hospitals; **Function Concentration:**
Generalist with a primary focus in General Management

**Ballantine, Caroline B.** — *Partner*
Heidrick & Struggles, Inc.
125 South Wacker Drive
Suite 2800
Chicago, IL 60606-4590
Telephone: (312) 372-8811
**Recruiter Classification:** Retained; **Lowest/Average Salary:** $75,000/$90,000;
**Industry Concentration:** Generalist with a primary focus in Financial Services;
**Function Concentration:** Generalist

**Ballein, Kathleen M.** — *Shareholder*
Witt/Kieffer, Ford, Hadelman & Lloyd
2015 Spring Road, Suite 510
Oak Brook, IL 60521
Telephone: (708) 990-1370
**Recruiter Classification:** Retained; **Lowest/Average Salary:** $75,000/$90,000;
**Industry Concentration:** Healthcare/Hospitals; **Function Concentration:**
Generalist with a primary focus in General Management

**Ballenger, Michael** — *Partner*
Heidrick & Struggles, Inc.
Four Embarcadero Center, Suite 3570
San Francisco, CA 94111
Telephone: (415) 981-2854
**Recruiter Classification:** Retained; **Lowest/Average Salary:** $75,000/$90,000;
**Industry Concentration:** Generalist with a primary focus in
Healthcare/Hospitals; **Function Concentration:** Generalist

**Balter, Sidney** — *Associate*
Source Services Corporation
120 East Baltimore Street, Suite 1950
Baltimore, MD 21202
Telephone: (410) 727-4050
**Recruiter Classification:** Contingency; **Lowest/Average Salary:**
$30,000/$50,000; **Industry Concentration:** Financial Services, Information
Technology; **Function Concentration:** Engineering, Finance/Accounting

**Baltin, Carrie** — *Account Executive*
Search West, Inc.
340 North Westlake Boulevard
Suite 200
Westlake Village, CA 91362-3761
Telephone: (805) 496-6811
**Recruiter Classification:** Contingency; **Lowest/Average Salary:**
$40,000/$60,000; **Industry Concentration:** Consumer Products, Electronics,
High Technology, Manufacturing; **Function Concentration:** Engineering,
Marketing, Research and Development, Sales

**Ban, Jean T.** — *Executive Vice President*
The Paladin Companies, Inc.
875 North Michigan Avenue, Suite 3218
Chicago, IL 60611
Telephone: (312) 654-2600
**Recruiter Classification:** Executive Temporary; **Lowest/Average Salary:**
$50,000/$90,000; **Industry Concentration:** Generalist; **Function
Concentration:** Marketing

**Ban, Michael P.** — *Chairman and CEO*
The Paladin Companies, Inc.
875 North Michigan Avenue, Suite 3218
Chicago, IL 60611
Telephone: (312) 654-2600
**Recruiter Classification:** Executive Temporary; **Lowest/Average Salary:**
$50,000/$90,000; **Industry Concentration:** Generalist; **Function
Concentration:** Marketing

**Banker, Judith G.** — *Executive Vice President Search Services*
R.D. Gatti & Associates, Incorporated
266 Main Street, Suite 21
Medfield, MA 02052
Telephone: (508) 359-4153
**Recruiter Classification:** Contingency; **Lowest/Average Salary:**
$40,000/$75,000; **Industry Concentration:** Generalist; **Function
Concentration:** Human Resources

**Banko, Scott** — *Associate*
Source Services Corporation
3 Summit Park Drive, Suite 550
Independence, OH 44131
Telephone: (216) 328-5900
**Recruiter Classification:** Contingency; **Lowest/Average Salary:**
$30,000/$50,000; **Industry Concentration:** Financial Services, Information
Technology; **Function Concentration:** Engineering, Finance/Accounting

**Banks, Renate** — *Manager South Atlantic Region*
Management Recruiters International, Inc.
AmSouth Center
200 Clinton Avenue West, Suite 802
Huntsville, AL 35801-4933
Telephone: (205) 536-7572
**Recruiter Classification:** Contingency; **Lowest/Average Salary:**
$30,000/$75,000; **Industry Concentration:** Generalist; **Function
Concentration:** Generalist

**Barack, Brianne** — *President*
The Barack Group, Inc.
885 Third Avenue
New York, NY 10022
Telephone: (212) 230-3280
**Recruiter Classification:** Retained; **Lowest/Average Salary:** $75,000/$90,000;
**Industry Concentration:** Consumer Products, Entertainment; **Function**
**Concentration:** General Management, Marketing

**Baran, Helena** — *Associate*
Michael J. Cavanagh and Associates
30 St. Clair West
Toronto, Ontario, CANADA M4V 3A1
Telephone: (416) 324-9661
**Recruiter Classification:** Retained; **Lowest/Average Salary:** $75,000/$90,000;
**Industry Concentration:** Generalist with a primary focus in
Aerospace/Defense, Automotive, Board Services, Consumer Products,
Electronics, Healthcare/Hospitals, Information Technology, Manufacturing,
Non-Profit, Packaging, Pharmaceutical/Medical, Real Estate, Transportation,
Venture Capital; **Function Concentration:** Generalist with a primary focus in
Administration, Engineering, Finance/Accounting, General Management,
Human Resources, Marketing

**Baranowski, Peter** — *Associate*
Source Services Corporation
71 Spit Brook Road, Suite 305
Nashua, NH 03060
Telephone: (603) 888-7650
**Recruiter Classification:** Contingency; **Lowest/Average Salary:**
$30,000/$50,000; **Industry Concentration:** Financial Services, Information
Technology; **Function Concentration:** Engineering, Finance/Accounting

**Baranski, David J.** — *Co-Manager*
Management Recruiters International, Inc.
2 North Riverside Plaza, Suite 1815
Chicago, IL 60606-2701
Telephone: (312) 648-1800
**Recruiter Classification:** Contingency; **Lowest/Average Salary:**
$30,000/$75,000; **Industry Concentration:** Generalist; **Function**
**Concentration:** Generalist

**Baranski, Glenda A.** — *Co-Manager Midwest Region*
Management Recruiters International, Inc.
2 North Riverside Plaza, Suite 1815
Chicago, IL 60606-2701
Telephone: (312) 648-1800
**Recruiter Classification:** Contingency; **Lowest/Average Salary:**
$30,000/$75,000; **Industry Concentration:** Generalist; **Function**
**Concentration:** Generalist

**Barao, Thomas** — *Principal*
Korn/Ferry International
One International Place
Boston, MA 02110-1800
Telephone: (617) 345-0200
**Recruiter Classification:** Retained; **Lowest/Average Salary:** $90,000/$90,000;
**Industry Concentration:** Generalist; **Function Concentration:** Generalist

**Barber, Toni L.** — *Executive Recruiter*
MSI International
200 Galleria Parkway
Suite 1610
Atlanta, GA 30339
Telephone: (404) 951-1208
**Recruiter Classification:** Contingency; **Lowest/Average Salary:**
$30,000/$75,000; **Industry Concentration:** Generalist; **Function**
**Concentration:** Generalist with a primary focus in Administration, Engineering,
Finance/Accounting, General Management, Marketing, Sales

**Barbosa, Franklin J.** — *Senior Vice President*
Boyden
55 Madison Avenue
Suite 400
Morristown, NJ 07960
Telephone: (201) 267-0980
**Recruiter Classification:** Retained; **Lowest/Average Salary:** $75,000/$90,000;
**Industry Concentration:** High Technology; **Function Concentration:** Generalist
with a primary focus in Engineering, Finance/Accounting, General
Management, Human Resources, Marketing, Research and Development,
Sales, Women/Minorities

**Barger, H. Carter** — *President*
Barger & Sargeant, Inc.
22 Windermere Road, Suite 500
P.O. Box 1420
Center Harbor, NH 03226-1420
Telephone: (603) 253-4700
**Recruiter Classification:** Retained; **Lowest/Average Salary:** $90,000/$90,000;
**Industry Concentration:** Generalist with a primary focus in Consumer
Products, Fashion (Retail/Apparel), Financial Services, Healthcare/Hospitals,
High Technology, Insurance, Manufacturing; **Function Concentration:**
Generalist with a primary focus in Finance/Accounting, General Management

**Bargholz, Harry** — *Manager North Atlantic Region*
Management Recruiters International, Inc.
4006 Oleander Drive, Suite 4-B
Wilmington, NC 28403
Telephone: (910) 791-2999
**Recruiter Classification:** Contingency; **Lowest/Average Salary:**
$30,000/$75,000; **Industry Concentration:** Generalist; **Function**
**Concentration:** Generalist

**Barick, Bradford L.** — *Co-Owner/Manager*
Management Recruiters International, Inc.
Dubay Professional Centre
1117W County Road DB
Mosinee, WI 54455
Telephone: (715) 341-4900
**Recruiter Classification:** Contingency; **Lowest/Average Salary:**
$30,000/$75,000; **Industry Concentration:** Generalist; **Function**
**Concentration:** Generalist

**Barick, Linda R.** — *Co-Owner/Manager Midwest Region*
Management Recruiters International, Inc.
Dubay Professional Centre
1117W County Road DB
Mosinee, WI 54455
Telephone: (715) 341-4900
**Recruiter Classification:** Contingency; **Lowest/Average Salary:**
$30,000/$75,000; **Industry Concentration:** Generalist; **Function**
**Concentration:** Generalist

**Barilone, John** — *Account Executive*
Search West, Inc.
750 The City Drive South
Suite 100
Orange, CA 92668-4940
Telephone: (714) 748-0400
**Recruiter Classification:** Contingency; **Lowest/Average Salary:**
$40,000/$60,000; **Industry Concentration:** Generalist; **Function**
**Concentration:** Marketing, Sales

**Barker, Mary J.** — *Manager Central Region*
Management Recruiters International, Inc.
124 North Division, Suite D-2
Traverse City, MI 49684
Telephone: (616) 947-8000
**Recruiter Classification:** Contingency; **Lowest/Average Salary:**
$30,000/$75,000; **Industry Concentration:** Generalist; **Function**
**Concentration:** Generalist

**Barker, Mary J.** — *General Manager*
Management Recruiters International, Inc.
500 Country Pine Lane, Suite 1
Battle Creek, MI 49015-4282
Telephone: (616) 979-3939
**Recruiter Classification:** Contingency; **Lowest/Average Salary:**
$30,000/$75,000; **Industry Concentration:** Generalist; **Function**
**Concentration:** Generalist

**Barlow, Ken H.** — *Associate*
The Cherbonnier Group, Inc.
805 South Wheatley Street, Suite 160
Ridgeland, MS 39157
Telephone: (601) 952-0020
**Recruiter Classification:** Retained; **Lowest/Average Salary:** $75,000/$90,000;
**Industry Concentration:** Generalist with a primary focus in Chemical Products,
Electronics, Energy, Environmental, Financial Services, Healthcare/Hospitals,
High Technology, Information Technology, Manufacturing, Oil/Gas,
Utilities/Nuclear, Venture Capital; **Function Concentration:** Generalist with a
primary focus in Administration, Engineering, Finance/Accounting, General
Management, Marketing, Research and Development, Sales

**Barnaby, Richard** — *Associate*
Source Services Corporation
3 Summit Park Drive, Suite 550
Independence, OH 44131
Telephone: (216) 328-5900
**Recruiter Classification:** Contingency; **Lowest/Average Salary:**
$30,000/$50,000; **Industry Concentration:** Financial Services, Information
Technology; **Function Concentration:** Engineering, Finance/Accounting

**Barnes, Richard E.** — *President*
Barnes Development Group, LLC
1017 West Glen Oaks Lane, Suite 108
Mequon, WI 53092
Telephone: (414) 241-8468
Recruiter Classification: Retained; Lowest/Average Salary: $50,000/$75,000;
Industry Concentration: Generalist with a primary focus in Automotive, Board
Services, Chemical Products, Electronics, Healthcare/Hospitals, Information
Technology, Insurance, Manufacturing, Non-Profit, Transportation; Function
Concentration: Generalist with a primary focus in Administration, Engineering,
Finance/Accounting, General Management, Human Resources, Marketing,
Research and Development, Sales

**Barnes, Roanne L.** — *Executive Vice President*
Barnes Development Group, LLC
1017 West Glen Oaks Lane, Suite 108
Mequon, WI 53092
Telephone: (414) 241-8468
Recruiter Classification: Retained; Lowest/Average Salary: $50,000/$75,000;
Industry Concentration: Generalist with a primary focus in Automotive, Board
Services, Chemical Products, Electronics, Financial Services,
Healthcare/Hospitals, Insurance, Manufacturing, Non-Profit, Packaging,
Pharmaceutical/Medical, Transportation; Function Concentration: Generalist
with a primary focus in Administration, Engineering, Finance/Accounting,
General Management, Human Resources, Marketing, Research and
Development, Sales

**Barnett, Barney O.** — *Manager Central Region*
Management Recruiters International, Inc.
1203 Mt. Eden Road, Suite 1
Shelbyville, KY 40065-8822
Telephone: (502) 633-6100
Recruiter Classification: Contingency; Lowest/Average Salary:
$30,000/$75,000; Industry Concentration: Generalist; Function
Concentration: Generalist

**Barnett, Kim M.** — *Manager Central Region*
Management Recruiters International, Inc.
6200 Som Center Road, Suite B-20
P.O. Box 39361
Solon, OH 44139-2911
Telephone: (216) 248-7300
Recruiter Classification: Contingency; Lowest/Average Salary:
$30,000/$75,000; Industry Concentration: Generalist; Function
Concentration: Generalist

**Barnett-Flint, Juliet** — *Consultant*
Heidrick & Struggles, Inc.
2740 Sand Hill Road
Menlo Park, CA 94025
Telephone: (415) 854-9300
Recruiter Classification: Retained; Lowest/Average Salary: $75,000/$90,000;
Industry Concentration: Generalist with a primary focus in High Technology;
Function Concentration: Generalist

**Barnette, Dennis A.** — *Partner*
Heidrick & Struggles, Inc.
125 South Wacker Drive
Suite 2800
Chicago, IL 60606-4590
Telephone: (312) 372-8811
Recruiter Classification: Retained; Lowest/Average Salary: $75,000/$90,000;
Industry Concentration: Generalist with a primary focus in Financial Services;
Function Concentration: Generalist

**Barnum, Toni M.** — *Partner*
Stone Murphy & Olson
5500 Wayzata Boulevard
Suite 1020
Minneapolis, MN 55416
Telephone: (612) 591-2300
Recruiter Classification: Retained; Lowest/Average Salary: $60,000/$75,000;
Industry Concentration: Generalist with a primary focus in Electronics, Energy,
Financial Services, High Technology, Insurance, Manufacturing,
Publishing/Media; Function Concentration: Generalist with a primary focus in
Engineering, Finance/Accounting, General Management, Human Resources,
Marketing, Women/Minorities

**Baron, Harvey J.** — *Manager Pacific Region*
Management Recruiters International, Inc.
9455 Ridgehaven Court, Suite 205
San Diego, CA 92123-1632
Telephone: (619) 565-6600
Recruiter Classification: Contingency; Lowest/Average Salary:
$30,000/$75,000; Industry Concentration: Generalist; Function
Concentration: Generalist

**Baron, Jon C.** — *Physician Recruiter*
MSI International
201 St. Charles Avenue
Suite 2205
New Orleans, LA 70170
Telephone: (504) 522-6700
Recruiter Classification: Contingency; Lowest/Average Salary:
$30,000/$75,000; Industry Concentration: Generalist with a primary focus in
Healthcare/Hospitals, Pharmaceutical/Medical; Function Concentration:
Generalist with a primary focus in Administration, Engineering,
Finance/Accounting, General Management, Marketing, Sales

**Baron, Len** — *President*
Industrial Recruiters Associates, Inc.
20 Hurlbut Street, 1st Floor
West Hartford, CT 06110
Telephone: (860) 953-3643
Recruiter Classification: Contingency; Lowest/Average Salary:
$30,000/$50,000; Industry Concentration: Generalist with a primary focus in
Aerospace/Defense, Automotive, Biotechnology, Chemical Products,
Electronics, Environmental, High Technology, Manufacturing, Packaging,
Transportation; Function Concentration: Generalist with a primary focus in
Engineering, Finance/Accounting, General Management, Marketing, Research
and Development, Sales, Women/Minorities

**Barone, Marialice** — *President*
Barone-O'Hara Associates
29 Emmons Drive
Princeton, NJ 08540
Telephone: (609) 452-1980
Recruiter Classification: Retained; Lowest/Average Salary: $60,000/$90,000;
Industry Concentration: Pharmaceutical/Medical; Function Concentration:
Generalist with a primary focus in Engineering, General Management,
Marketing, Research and Development, Sales

**Barowsky, Diane M.** — *Partner*
Lamalie Amrop International
225 West Wacker Drive
Chicago, IL 60606-1229
Telephone: (312) 782-3113
Recruiter Classification: Retained; Lowest/Average Salary: $90,000/$90,000;
Industry Concentration: Generalist with a primary focus in
Healthcare/Hospitals; Function Concentration: Generalist with a primary focus
in Administration, Finance/Accounting

**Barr, Ronald** — *Account Executive*
Search West, Inc.
3401 Centrelake Drive
Suite 690
Ontario, CA 91761-1207
Telephone: (909) 986-1966
Recruiter Classification: Contingency; Lowest/Average Salary:
$40,000/$60,000; Industry Concentration: Publishing/Media; Function
Concentration: Administration, Engineering, Finance/Accounting, General
Management, Marketing, Research and Development, Sales

**Barrett, Betsy** — *Associate*
Russell Reynolds Associates, Inc.
333 South Grand Avenue
Suite 3500
Los Angeles, CA 90071
Telephone: (213) 253-4400
Recruiter Classification: Retained; Lowest/Average Salary: $90,000/$90,000;
Industry Concentration: Generalist; Function Concentration: Generalist

**Barrett, Dan E.** — *Manager North Atlantic Region*
Management Recruiters International, Inc.
600 Peachtree Parkway, Suite 108
Cumming, GA 30131-6822
Telephone: (404) 889-5250
Recruiter Classification: Contingency; Lowest/Average Salary:
$30,000/$75,000; Industry Concentration: Generalist; Function
Concentration: Generalist

**Barrett, J. David** — *Partner*
Heidrick & Struggles, Inc.
245 Park Avenue, Suite 4300
New York, NY 10167-0152
Telephone: (212) 867-9876
Recruiter Classification: Retained; Lowest/Average Salary: $75,000/$90,000;
Industry Concentration: Generalist with a primary focus in Financial Services;
Function Concentration: Generalist with a primary focus in
Finance/Accounting

**Barrucci, Jim** — *Temp-to-Perm Accounting Recruiter*
Winter, Wyman & Company
950 Winter Street, Suite 3100
Waltham, MA 02154-1294
Telephone: (617) 890-7000
Recruiter Classification: Contingency; Lowest/Average Salary:
$20,000/$50,000; Industry Concentration: Generalist; Function
Concentration: Finance/Accounting

**Bartels, Fredrick** — *Associate*
Source Services Corporation
4510 Executive Drive, Suite 200
San Diego, CA 92121
Telephone: (619) 552-0300
Recruiter Classification: Contingency; Lowest/Average Salary:
$30,000/$50,000; Industry Concentration: Financial Services, Information
Technology; Function Concentration: Engineering, Finance/Accounting

**Bartesch, Heinz** — *Director*
The Search Firm, Inc.
595 Market Street, Suite 1400
San Francisco, CA 94105
Telephone: (415) 777-3900
Recruiter Classification: Contingency; Lowest/Average Salary:
$40,000/$75,000; Industry Concentration: Electronics, High Technology,
Information Technology

**Bartfield, Philip** — *Associate*
Source Services Corporation
5 Independence Way
Princeton, NJ 08540
Telephone: (609) 452-7277
Recruiter Classification: Contingency; Lowest/Average Salary:
$30,000/$50,000; Industry Concentration: Financial Services, Information
Technology; Function Concentration: Engineering, Finance/Accounting

**Barth, Cynthia P.** — *Principal*
Longshore & Simmons, Inc.
Plymouth Corporate Center
625 Ridge Pike, Suite 410
Conshohocken, PA 19428-3216
Telephone: (610) 941-3400
Recruiter Classification: Retained; Lowest/Average Salary: $50,000/$90,000;
Industry Concentration: Healthcare/Hospitals; Function Concentration:
Generalist

**Barthold, James A.** — *Associate*
McNichol Associates
620 Chestnut Street, Suite 1031
Philadelphia, PA 19106
Telephone: (215) 922-4142
Recruiter Classification: Retained; Lowest/Average Salary: $75,000/$90,000;
Industry Concentration: Environmental, Healthcare/Hospitals, High
Technology, Pharmaceutical/Medical, Transportation; Function Concentration:
Generalist with a primary focus in Administration, Engineering,
Finance/Accounting, General Management, Human Resources, Marketing,
Research and Development, Sales, Women/Minorities

**Bartholdi, Ted** — *Consultant*
Bartholdi & Company, Inc.
14 Douglass Way
Exeter, NH 03833
Telephone: (603) 772-4228
Recruiter Classification: Retained; Lowest/Average Salary: $60,000/$90,000;
Industry Concentration: High Technology, Information Technology, Venture
Capital; Function Concentration: Generalist with a primary focus in
Engineering, Finance/Accounting, General Management, Marketing, Research
and Development, Sales

**Bartholdi, Theodore G.** — *President*
Bartholdi & Company, Inc.
8260 East Raintree Drive, Suite 211
Scottsdale, AZ 85260
Telephone: (602) 596-1117
Recruiter Classification: Retained; Lowest/Average Salary: $60,000/$90,000;
Industry Concentration: High Technology, Information Technology, Venture
Capital; Function Concentration: Generalist with a primary focus in
Engineering, Finance/Accounting, General Management, Marketing, Research
and Development, Sales

**Barton, Gary R.** — *Partner*
Barton Raben, Inc.
One Riverway, Suite 2500
Houston, TX 77056
Telephone: (713) 961-9111
Recruiter Classification: Retained; Lowest/Average Salary: $75,000/$90,000;
Industry Concentration: Generalist with a primary focus in Board Services,
Consumer Products, Electronics, Energy, Financial Services, High Technology,
Information Technology, Manufacturing, Packaging, Publishing/Media, Real
Estate, Transportation, Venture Capital; Function Concentration: Generalist
with a primary focus in Administration, Finance/Accounting, General
Management, Human Resources, Marketing, Sales

**Barton, James** — *Associate*
Source Services Corporation
1 Gatehall Drive, Suite 250
Parsippany, NJ 07054
Telephone: (201) 267-3222
Recruiter Classification: Contingency; Lowest/Average Salary:
$30,000/$50,000; Industry Concentration: Financial Services, Information
Technology; Function Concentration: Engineering, Finance/Accounting

**Bartone, Robert J.** — *Managing Director*
MRG Search & Placement Inc.
2693 Whitney Avenue
Hamden, CT 06518
Telephone: (203) 230-1088
Recruiter Classification: Contingency; Lowest/Average Salary:
$40,000/$90,000

**Bascom, Roger C.** — *Co-Manager Central Region*
Management Recruiters International, Inc.
P.O. Box 2970
North Canton, OH 44720-0970
Telephone: (330) 497-0122
Recruiter Classification: Contingency; Lowest/Average Salary:
$30,000/$75,000; Industry Concentration: Generalist; Function
Concentration: Generalist

**Bascom, Shirley R.** — *Co-Manager*
Management Recruiters International, Inc.
P.O. Box 2970
North Canton, OH 44720-0970
Telephone: (330) 497-0122
Recruiter Classification: Contingency; Lowest/Average Salary:
$30,000/$75,000; Industry Concentration: Generalist; Function
Concentration: Generalist

**Bason, Maurice L.** — *President*
Bason Associates Inc.
11311 Cornell Park Drive
Cincinnati, OH 45242
Telephone: (513) 469-9881
Recruiter Classification: Retained; Lowest/Average Salary: $60,000/$90,000;
Industry Concentration: Generalist with a primary focus in Automotive,
Biotechnology, Board Services, Chemical Products, Consumer Products,
Environmental, Fashion (Retail/Apparel), Financial Services, Healthcare/Hospitals,
High Technology, Insurance, Manufacturing, Packaging, Pharmaceutical/Medical,
Public Administration; Function Concentration: Generalist with a primary focus in
Administration, Engineering, Finance/Accounting, General Management, Human
Resources, Marketing, Research and Development, Sales

**Bass, Nate** — *Managing Director*
Jacobson Associates
Five Neshaminy Interplex
Suite 113
Trevose, PA 19053
Telephone: (215) 639-5860
Recruiter Classification: Contingency; Lowest/Average Salary:
$60,000/$75,000; Industry Concentration: Financial Services, Insurance;
Function Concentration: Generalist with a primary focus in Administration,
Finance/Accounting, General Management, Marketing, Research and
Development, Sales

**Bassler, John P.** — *Managing Director*
Korn/Ferry International
2 Logan Square, Suite 2530
Philadelphia, PA 19103
Telephone: (215) 496-6666
Recruiter Classification: Retained; Lowest/Average Salary: $90,000/$90,000;
Industry Concentration: Generalist with a primary focus in Consumer
Products; Function Concentration: Generalist

**Bassman, Bob W.** — *Co-Manager*
Management Recruiters International, Inc.
18333 Preston Road, Suite 500
Dallas, TX 75252
Telephone: (214) 931-5242
Recruiter Classification: Contingency; Lowest/Average Salary:
$30,000/$75,000; Industry Concentration: Generalist; Function
Concentration: Generalist

**Bassman, Robert** — *Chairman and CEO*
Kaye-Bassman International Corp.
18333 Preston Road, Suite 500
Dallas, TX 75252
Telephone: (214) 931-5242
Recruiter Classification: Executive Temporary; Lowest/Average Salary:
$40,000/$60,000; Industry Concentration: Biotechnology, Chemical Products,
Financial Services, Healthcare/Hospitals, High Technology, Information
Technology, Pharmaceutical/Medical, Transportation; Function Concentration:
Generalist

**Bassman, Sandy** — *Executive Vice President*
Kaye-Bassman International Corp.
18333 Preston Road, Suite 500
Dallas, TX 75252
Telephone: (214) 931-5242
Recruiter Classification: Executive Temporary; Lowest/Average Salary:
$40,000/$60,000; Industry Concentration: Biotechnology, Chemical Products,
Financial Services, Healthcare/Hospitals, High Technology, Information
Technology, Pharmaceutical/Medical, Transportation; Function Concentration:
Generalist

**Bassman, Sandy M.** — *Co-Manager Southwest Region*
Management Recruiters International, Inc.
18333 Preston Road, Suite 500
Dallas, TX 75252
Telephone: (214) 931-5242
**Recruiter Classification:** Contingency; **Lowest/Average Salary:**
$30,000/$75,000; **Industry Concentration:** Generalist; **Function
Concentration:** Generalist

**Bastoky, Bruce M.** — *President*
January Management Group, Inc.
5503-E Briardale Lane
Dublin, OH 43016
Telephone: (614) 717-4555
**Recruiter Classification:** Retained; **Lowest/Average Salary:** $75,000/$90,000;
**Industry Concentration:** Generalist; **Function Concentration:** Generalist

**Bates, Nina** — *Senior Associate*
Allard Associates
39811 Sharon Avenue
Davis, CA 95616
Telephone: (916) 757-1649
**Recruiter Classification:** Retained; **Lowest/Average Salary:** $60,000/$90,000;
**Industry Concentration:** Generalist with a primary focus in Financial Services;
**Function Concentration:** Generalist with a primary focus in Administration,
General Management, Marketing, Research and Development, Sales

**Bates, Scott W.** — *Vice President*
Kittleman & Associates
300 South Wacker Drive, Suite 1710
Chicago, IL 60606
Telephone: (312) 986-1166
**Recruiter Classification:** Retained; **Lowest/Average Salary:** $50,000/$75,000;
**Industry Concentration:** Healthcare/Hospitals, Non-Profit; **Function
Concentration:** Finance/Accounting, General Management, Marketing,
Women/Minorities

**Battalia, O. William** — *Chairman*
Battalia Winston International
300 Park Avenue
New York, NY 10022
Telephone: (212) 308-8080
**Recruiter Classification:** Retained; **Lowest/Average Salary:** $90,000/$90,000;
**Industry Concentration:** Generalist with a primary focus in Chemical Products,
Consumer Products, Electronics, Information Technology,
Pharmaceutical/Medical; **Function Concentration:** Generalist with a primary
focus in Finance/Accounting, General Management, Human Resources,
Marketing, Sales

**Batte, Carol** — *Associate*
Source Services Corporation
520 Post Oak Boulevard, Suite 700
Houston, TX 77027
Telephone: (713) 439-1077
**Recruiter Classification:** Contingency; **Lowest/Average Salary:**
$30,000/$50,000; **Industry Concentration:** Financial Services, Information
Technology; **Function Concentration:** Engineering, Finance/Accounting

**Battistoni, Bea** — *Area Vice President*
Accountants on Call
911 Main Street, Suite 620
Commerce Tower
Kansas City, MO 64105
Telephone: (816) 421-7774
**Recruiter Classification:** Contingency; **Lowest/Average Salary:**
$20,000/$30,000; **Industry Concentration:** Generalist; **Function
Concentration:** Finance/Accounting

**Battistoni, Bea** — *Area Vice President*
Accountants on Call
1990 Post Oak Boulevard, Suite 720
Houston, TX 77056
Telephone: (713) 961-5603
**Recruiter Classification:** Contingency; **Lowest/Average Salary:**
$20,000/$30,000; **Industry Concentration:** Generalist; **Function
Concentration:** Finance/Accounting

**Bauer, Bob** — *Manager Midwest Region*
Management Recruiters International, Inc.
19350 South Harlem Avenue, Suite 203
Frankfort, IL 60423
Telephone: (815) 464-5992
**Recruiter Classification:** Contingency; **Lowest/Average Salary:**
$30,000/$75,000; **Industry Concentration:** Generalist; **Function
Concentration:** Generalist

**Baugh, Amy** — *Executive Recruiter*
Richard, Wayne and Roberts
24 Greenway Plaza, Suite 1304
Houston, TX 77046-2493
Telephone: (713) 629-6681
**Recruiter Classification:** Retained; **Lowest/Average Salary:** $40,000/$60,000;
**Industry Concentration:** Generalist; **Function Concentration:** Generalist

**Bauman, Martin H.** — *President*
Martin H. Bauman Associates, Inc.
375 Park Avenue, Suite 2002
New York, NY 10152
Telephone: (212) 752-6580
**Recruiter Classification:** Retained; **Lowest/Average Salary:** $90,000/$90,000;
**Industry Concentration:** Generalist with a primary focus in Board Services,
Chemical Products, Consumer Products, Financial Services, Manufacturing,
Transportation, Venture Capital; **Function Concentration:** Generalist with a
primary focus in Administration, Engineering, Finance/Accounting, General
Management, Human Resources, Marketing, Research and Development,
Sales, Women/Minorities

**Bawulski, Fred B.** — *Manager Central Region*
Management Recruiters International, Inc.
Bingham Office Park, Suite 285
30300 Telegraph Road
Bingham Farms, MI 48025-4509
Telephone: (810) 647-2828
**Recruiter Classification:** Contingency; **Lowest/Average Salary:**
$30,000/$75,000; **Industry Concentration:** Generalist; **Function
Concentration:** Generalist

**Baxter, Robert** — *Vice President*
Korn/Ferry International
303 Peachtree Street N.E.
Suite 1600
Atlanta, GA 30308
Telephone: (404) 577-7542
**Recruiter Classification:** Retained; **Lowest/Average Salary:** $90,000/$90,000;
**Industry Concentration:** Generalist; **Function Concentration:** Generalist

**Beal, Richard D.** — *Vice President*
A.T. Kearney, Inc.
Lincoln Plaza, Suite 4170
500 North Akard Street
Dallas, TX 75201
Telephone: (214) 969-0010
**Recruiter Classification:** Retained; **Lowest/Average Salary:** $90,000/$90,000;
**Industry Concentration:** Generalist with a primary focus in Environmental,
High Technology, Manufacturing; **Function Concentration:** Generalist with a
primary focus in Engineering, Research and Development

**Beall, Charles P.** — *President/Managing Director*
Beall & Company, Inc.
535 Colonial Park Drive
Roswell, GA 30075
Telephone: (404) 992-0900
**Recruiter Classification:** Retained; **Lowest/Average Salary:** $90,000/$90,000;
**Industry Concentration:** Generalist with a primary focus in
Aerospace/Defense, Consumer Products, High Technology, Manufacturing,
Venture Capital; **Function Concentration:** Generalist

**Beals, Calvin H.** — *Manager South Atlantic Region*
Management Recruiters International, Inc.
4100 Center Pointe Drive, Suite 105
Fort Myers, FL 33916-9450
Telephone: (941) 939-2223
**Recruiter Classification:** Contingency; **Lowest/Average Salary:**
$30,000/$75,000; **Industry Concentration:** Generalist; **Function
Concentration:** Generalist

**Bean, Bill** — *Contract Recruiter*
Professional Search Consultants
3050 Post Oak Boulevard, Suite 1615
Houston, TX 77056
Telephone: (713) 960-9215
**Recruiter Classification:** Executive Temporary; **Lowest/Average Salary:**
$60,000/$75,000; **Industry Concentration:** Energy, Manufacturing; **Function
Concentration:** General Management, Sales

**Bean, Bob** — *Manager North Atlantic Region*
Management Recruiters International, Inc.
4 Carriage Lane, Suite 301
Charleston, SC 29407
Telephone: (803) 556-6461
**Recruiter Classification:** Contingency; **Lowest/Average Salary:**
$30,000/$75,000; **Industry Concentration:** Generalist; **Function
Concentration:** Generalist

**Bearman, Linda** — *Vice President*
Grant Cooper and Associates
795 Office Parkway, Suite 117
St. Louis, MO 63141
Telephone: (314) 567-4690
**Recruiter Classification:** Retained; **Lowest/Average Salary:** $60,000/$90,000;
**Industry Concentration:** Generalist with a primary focus in Board Services,
Consumer Products, Electronics, Financial Services, Healthcare/Hospitals,
Manufacturing, Non-Profit, Pharmaceutical/Medical; **Function Concentration:**
Generalist with a primary focus in Administration, Engineering,
Finance/Accounting, General Management, Human Resources, Marketing, Sales

**Beatty, Jane** — *Consultant*
Paul Ray Berndtson
10 South Riverside Plaza
Suite 720
Chicago, IL 60606
Telephone: (312) 876-0730
**Recruiter Classification:** Retained; **Lowest/Average Salary:** $90,000/$90,000;
**Industry Concentration:** Generalist; **Function Concentration:** Generalist

**Beaudin, Elizabeth C.** — *Partner*
Callan Associates, Ltd.
1550 Spring Road
Oak Brook, IL 60521
Telephone: (708) 832-7080
**Recruiter Classification:** Retained; **Lowest/Average Salary:** $90,000/$90,000;
**Industry Concentration:** Generalist with a primary focus in
Aerospace/Defense, Automotive, Biotechnology, Chemical Products,
Consumer Products, Electronics, Energy, Environmental, Fashion
(Retail/Apparel), Financial Services, High Technology, Information Technology,
Manufacturing, Oil/Gas; **Function Concentration:** Generalist with a primary
focus in Administration, Engineering, Finance/Accounting, General
Management, Human Resources, Marketing, Research and Development,
Sales, Women/Minorities

**Beaudine, Frank R.** — *Chairman and CEO*
Eastman & Beaudine
13355 Noel Road, Suite 1370
Dallas, TX 75240
Telephone: (214) 661-5520
**Recruiter Classification:** Retained; **Lowest/Average Salary:** $75,000/$90,000;
**Industry Concentration:** Generalist; **Function Concentration:** Generalist

**Beaudine, Frank R.** — *Senior Vice President*
Eastman & Beaudine
One Ravinia Drive, Suite 1110
Atlanta, GA 30346
Telephone: (770) 390-2720
**Recruiter Classification:** Retained; **Lowest/Average Salary:** $75,000/$90,000;
**Industry Concentration:** Generalist; **Function Concentration:** Generalist

**Beaudine, Robert E.** — *President and COO*
Eastman & Beaudine
13355 Noel Road, Suite 1370
Dallas, TX 75240
Telephone: (214) 661-5520
**Recruiter Classification:** Retained; **Lowest/Average Salary:** $75,000/$90,000;
**Industry Concentration:** Generalist; **Function Concentration:** Generalist

**Beaulieu, Genie A.** — *Director Communications*
Romac & Associates
183 Middle Street, 3rd Floor
P.O. Box 7040
Portland, ME 04112
Telephone: (207) 773-4749
**Recruiter Classification:** Executive Temporary; **Lowest/Average Salary:**
$/$60,000; **Industry Concentration:** Financial Services, Healthcare/Hospitals,
High Technology, Hospitality/Leisure, Information Technology, Insurance;
**Function Concentration:** Finance/Accounting

**Beaupre, Joseph** — *Director*
Price Waterhouse
1250 Rene-Levesque Blvd. Ouest
Suite 3500
Montreal, Quebec, CANADA H3B 2J4
Telephone: (514) 938-5600
**Recruiter Classification:** Retained; **Lowest/Average Salary:** $60,000/$90,000;
**Industry Concentration:** Generalist; **Function Concentration:** Generalist

**Beaver, Bentley H.** — *Managing Director*
The Onstott Group, Inc.
60 William Street
Wellesley, MA 02181
Telephone: (617) 235-3050
**Recruiter Classification:** Retained; **Lowest/Average Salary:** $90,000/$90,000;
**Industry Concentration:** Generalist with a primary focus in Chemical Products,
Consumer Products, Electronics, Financial Services, High Technology,
Information Technology, Manufacturing; **Function Concentration:** Generalist
with a primary focus in Engineering, Finance/Accounting, General
Management, Human Resources, Marketing, Research and Development, Sales

**Beaver, Robert** — *Associate*
Source Services Corporation
1290 Oakmead Parkway, Suite 318
Sunnyvale, CA 94086
Telephone: (408) 738-8440
**Recruiter Classification:** Contingency; **Lowest/Average Salary:**
$30,000/$50,000; **Industry Concentration:** Financial Services, Information
Technology; **Function Concentration:** Engineering, Finance/Accounting

**Beaver, Robert W.** — *Vice President*
Executive Manning Corporation
3000 N.E. 30th Place, Suite 405/402/411
Fort Lauderdale, FL 33306
Telephone: (954) 561-5100
**Recruiter Classification:** Retained; **Lowest/Average Salary:** $75,000/$90,000;
**Industry Concentration:** Generalist with a primary focus in
Aerospace/Defense, Automotive, Chemical Products, Consumer Products,
Electronics, High Technology, Manufacturing, Pharmaceutical/Medical;
**Function Concentration:** Generalist

**Beck, Barbara S.** — *Principal*
Rhodes Associates
555 Fifth Avenue
New York, NY 10017
Telephone: (212) 983-2000
**Recruiter Classification:** Retained; **Lowest/Average Salary:** $90,000/$90,000;
**Industry Concentration:** Financial Services, Insurance, Real Estate, Venture
Capital; **Function Concentration:** Generalist

**Beck, Charlotte** — *Consultant*
Witt/Kieffer, Ford, Hadelman & Lloyd
2015 Spring Road, Suite 510
Oak Brook, IL 60521
Telephone: (708) 990-1370
**Recruiter Classification:** Retained; **Lowest/Average Salary:** $75,000/$90,000;
**Industry Concentration:** Healthcare/Hospitals; **Function Concentration:**
General Management

**Beck, Jerry** — *Senior Associate*
Financial Search Corporation
2720 Des Plaines Avenue, Suite 106
Des Plaines, IL 60018
Telephone: (708) 297-4900
**Recruiter Classification:** Contingency; **Lowest/Average Salary:**
$30,000/$50,000; **Industry Concentration:** Generalist; **Function
Concentration:** Finance/Accounting

**Beck, Michael** — *Consultant*
Don Richard Associates of Richmond, Inc.
7275 Glen Forest Drive, Suite 200
Richmond, VA 23226
Telephone: (804) 282-6300
**Recruiter Classification:** Contingency; **Lowest/Average Salary:**
$30,000/$50,000; **Industry Concentration:** Information Technology

**Beckvold, John B.** — *Principal*
Atlantic Search Group, Inc.
One Liberty Square
Boston, MA 02109
Telephone: (617) 426-9700
**Recruiter Classification:** Contingency; **Lowest/Average Salary:**
$20,000/$60,000; **Industry Concentration:** Generalist with a primary focus in
Biotechnology, Consumer Products, Electronics, Financial Services, High
Technology, Information Technology, Manufacturing, Real Estate; **Function
Concentration:** Finance/Accounting

**Bedford, Jennifer** — *Senior Associate*
Korn/Ferry International
1800 Century Park East, Suite 900
Los Angeles, CA 90067
Telephone: (310) 552-1834
**Recruiter Classification:** Retained; **Lowest/Average Salary:** $90,000/$90,000;
**Industry Concentration:** Generalist; **Function Concentration:** Generalist

**Beebe, Colin** — *Associate Recruiter*
Klein, Landau, Romm & North
1725 K Street NW, Suite 602
Washington, DC 20006
Telephone: (202) 728-0100
**Recruiter Classification:** Contingency; **Lowest/Average Salary:**
$50,000/$90,000

**Beer, John** — *Vice President*
People Management Northeast Incorporated
One Darling Drive, Avon Park South
Avon, CT 06001
Telephone: (860) 678-8900
**Recruiter Classification:** Retained; **Lowest/Average Salary:** $75,000/$90,000;
**Industry Concentration:** Generalist with a primary focus in Financial Services,
Insurance; **Function Concentration:** Generalist

**Beerman, Joan** — *Associate*
Kenzer Corp.
777 Third Avenue, 26th Floor
New York, NY 10017
Telephone: (212) 308-4300
**Recruiter Classification:** Retained; **Lowest/Average Salary:** $50,000/$90,000;
**Industry Concentration:** Generalist; **Function Concentration:** Generalist

**Beeson, William B.** — *Vice President*
Lawrence-Leiter and Company
4400 Shawnee-Mission Parkway, Suite 204
Shawnee-Mission, KS 66205
Telephone: (913) 677-5500
**Recruiter Classification:** Retained; **Lowest/Average Salary:** $75,000/$90,000;
**Industry Concentration:** Generalist with a primary focus in Consumer
Products, Electronics, Fashion (Retail/Apparel), Financial Services, Insurance,
Manufacturing, Non-Profit; **Function Concentration:** Generalist

**Behringer, Neail** — *President*
Neail Behringer Consultants
24 East 38th Street
New York, NY 10016
Telephone: (212) 689-7555
**Recruiter Classification:** Retained; **Lowest/Average Salary:** $50,000/$90,000;
**Industry Concentration:** Fashion (Retail/Apparel); **Function Concentration:**
Generalist with a primary focus in Administration, General Management,
Marketing

**Beir, Ellen Haupt** — *Vice President*
Korn/Ferry International
237 Park Avenue
New York, NY 10017
Telephone: (212) 687-1834
**Recruiter Classification:** Retained; **Lowest/Average Salary:** $90,000/$90,000;
**Industry Concentration:** Generalist; **Function Concentration:** Generalist

**Belden, Charles P.** — *Consultant*
Raymond Karsan Associates
2500 Mosside Boulevard, Suite 218
Monroeville, PA 15146
Telephone: (412) 373-5433
**Recruiter Classification:** Contingency; **Lowest/Average Salary:**
$30,000/$90,000; **Industry Concentration:** Generalist with a primary focus in
Insurance; **Function Concentration:** Generalist

**Belden, Jeannette** — *Associate*
Source Services Corporation
10220 SW Greenburg Road, Suite 625
Portland, OR 97223
Telephone: (503) 768-4546
**Recruiter Classification:** Contingency; **Lowest/Average Salary:**
$30,000/$50,000; **Industry Concentration:** Financial Services, Information
Technology; **Function Concentration:** Engineering, Finance/Accounting

**Belford, Paul** — *Principal*
JDG Associates, Ltd.
1700 Research Boulevard
Rockville, MD 20850
Telephone: (301) 340-2210
**Recruiter Classification:** Contingency; **Lowest/Average Salary:**
$50,000/$90,000; **Industry Concentration:** Biotechnology, Education/Libraries,
Energy, Environmental, Non-Profit, Pharmaceutical/Medical, Public
Administration; **Function Concentration:** Administration, General
Management, Human Resources, Marketing

**Belfrey, Edward** — *Vice President*
Dunhill Professional Search of Irvine, Inc.
9 Executive Circle, Suite 240
Irvine, CA 92714
Telephone: (714) 474-6666
**Recruiter Classification:** Contingency; **Lowest/Average Salary:**
$60,000/$75,000; **Industry Concentration:** Aerospace/Defense, Electronics;
**Function Concentration:** Generalist with a primary focus in General
Management, Marketing

**Bell, Cathy** — *Co-Manager Eastern Region*
Management Recruiters International, Inc.
Dorsey Hall Professional Park
5044 Dorsey Hall Drive, Suite 204
Ellicott City, MD 21043-7739
Telephone: (410) 884-1363
**Recruiter Classification:** Contingency; **Lowest/Average Salary:**
$30,000/$75,000; **Industry Concentration:** Generalist; **Function
Concentration:** Generalist

**Bell, Danny** — *Co-Manager*
Management Recruiters International, Inc.
Dorsey Hall Professional Park
5044 Dorsey Hall Drive, Suite 204
Ellicott City, MD 21043-7739
Telephone: (410) 884-1363
**Recruiter Classification:** Contingency; **Lowest/Average Salary:**
$30,000/$75,000; **Industry Concentration:** Generalist; **Function
Concentration:** Generalist

**Bell, Jeffrey G.** — *Managing Director*
Norman Broadbent International, Inc.
200 Park Avenue, 20th Floor
New York, NY 10166
Telephone: (212) 953-6990
**Recruiter Classification:** Retained; **Lowest/Average Salary:** $90,000/$90,000;
**Industry Concentration:** Generalist with a primary focus in Financial Services;
**Function Concentration:** Generalist with a primary focus in
Finance/Accounting, General Management

**Bell, Lindy** — *Executive Recruiter*
F-O-R-T-U-N-E Personnel Consultants of Huntsville, Inc.
3311 Bob Wallace Avenue, Suite 204
Huntsville, AL 35805
Telephone: (205) 534-7282
**Recruiter Classification:** Contingency, Executive Temporary; **Lowest/Average
Salary:** $30,000/$50,000; **Industry Concentration:** Generalist with a primary
focus in Automotive, Consumer Products, High Technology, Manufacturing;
**Function Concentration:** Generalist

**Bell, Lisa** — *Information Technology Recruiter*
Winter, Wyman & Company
950 Winter Street, Suite 3100
Waltham, MA 02154-1294
Telephone: (617) 890-7000
**Recruiter Classification:** Contingency; **Lowest/Average Salary:**
$30,000/$60,000; **Industry Concentration:** Generalist with a primary focus in
Information Technology; **Function Concentration:** Generalist

**Bell, Michael** — *Director*
Spencer Stuart
One University Avenue
Suite 801
Toronto, Ontario, CANADA M5J 2P1
Telephone: (416) 361-0311
**Recruiter Classification:** Retained; **Lowest/Average Salary:** $90,000/$90,000;
**Industry Concentration:** Generalist with a primary focus in Financial Services,
Insurance, Non-Profit; **Function Concentration:** Generalist with a primary
focus in Human Resources

**Bell, Peter P.** — *Director*
Cantor Concern Staffing Options, Inc.
330 West 58th Street
Suite 216
New York, NY 10019
Telephone: (212) 333-3000
**Recruiter Classification:** Executive Temporary; **Lowest/Average Salary:**
$40,000/$50,000

**Bellano, Robert W.** — *Director*
Stanton Chase International
10866 Wilshire Boulevard
Suite 870
Los Angeles, CA 90024
Telephone: (310) 474-1029
**Recruiter Classification:** Retained; **Lowest/Average Salary:** $75,000/$90,000;
**Industry Concentration:** Generalist with a primary focus in Board Services,
Consumer Products, Energy, Healthcare/Hospitals, Hospitality/Leisure,
Insurance, Oil/Gas, Pharmaceutical/Medical, Publishing/Media, Venture
Capital; **Function Concentration:** Generalist with a primary focus in
Finance/Accounting, General Management, Human Resources, Marketing,
Sales

**Belle Isle, Charles** — *Partner*
Belle Isle, Djandji Inc.
1200 McGill College Avenue
Suite 2250
Montreal, Quebec, CANADA H3B 4G7
Telephone: (514) 878-1991
**Recruiter Classification:** Retained; **Lowest/Average Salary:** $75,000/$90,000;
**Industry Concentration:** Generalist; **Function Concentration:** Generalist

**Bellshaw, David** — *Senior Recruiter*
Isaacson, Miller
334 Boylston Street, Suite 500
Boston, MA 02111
Telephone: (617) 262-6500
**Recruiter Classification:** Retained; **Lowest/Average Salary:** $75,000/$90,000;
**Industry Concentration:** Generalist; **Function Concentration:** Administration,
General Management, Women/Minorities

**Bellview, Louis P.** — *General Manager*
Management Recruiters International, Inc.
317 South Friendswood Drive
Friendswood, TX 77546
Telephone: (713) 996-0008
**Recruiter Classification:** Contingency; **Lowest/Average Salary:**
$30,000/$75,000; **Industry Concentration:** Generalist; **Function Concentration:** Generalist

**Bellview, Sibyl M.** — *Manager Southwest Region*
Management Recruiters International, Inc.
317 South Friendswood Drive
Friendswood, TX 77546
Telephone: (713) 996-0008
**Recruiter Classification:** Contingency; **Lowest/Average Salary:**
$30,000/$75,000; **Industry Concentration:** Generalist; **Function Concentration:** Generalist

**Benabou, Donna** — *Associate*
Kenzer Corp.
777 Third Avenue, 26th Floor
New York, NY 10017
Telephone: (212) 308-4300
**Recruiter Classification:** Retained; **Lowest/Average Salary:** $50,000/$90,000;
**Industry Concentration:** Generalist; **Function Concentration:** Generalist

**Benjamin, Maurita** — *Associate*
Source Services Corporation
8614 Westwood Center, Suite 750
Vienna, VA 22182
Telephone: (703) 790-5610
**Recruiter Classification:** Contingency; **Lowest/Average Salary:**
$30,000/$50,000; **Industry Concentration:** Financial Services, Information
Technology; **Function Concentration:** Engineering, Finance/Accounting

**Bennett, Delora** — *President*
Genesis Personnel Service, Inc.
10921 Reed Hartman Highway
Suite 226
Cincinnati, OH 45242
Telephone: (513) 891-4433
**Recruiter Classification:** Contingency; **Lowest/Average Salary:**
$20,000/$50,000; **Industry Concentration:** Consumer Products,
Healthcare/Hospitals, Pharmaceutical/Medical; **Function Concentration:**
Administration, Engineering, Finance/Accounting, Marketing, Sales,
Women/Minorities

**Bennett, Jo** — *Vice President*
Battalia Winston International
300 Park Avenue
New York, NY 10022
Telephone: (212) 308-8080
**Recruiter Classification:** Retained; **Lowest/Average Salary:** $90,000/$90,000;
**Industry Concentration:** Generalist with a primary focus in Board Services,
Chemical Products, Consumer Products, Electronics, Healthcare/Hospitals,
High Technology, Insurance, Manufacturing, Non-Profit, Venture Capital;
**Function Concentration:** Generalist with a primary focus in Engineering,
Finance/Accounting, General Management, Human Resources, Marketing,
Sales, Women/Minorities

**Bennett, Joan** — *Director Research/Recruiter*
Adams & Associates International
978 Hampton Park
Barrington, IL 60010
Telephone: (847) 304-5300
**Recruiter Classification:** Retained; **Lowest/Average Salary:** $75,000/$75,000;
**Industry Concentration:** Generalist with a primary focus in Electronics,
Packaging; **Function Concentration:** Generalist with a primary focus in
Engineering, General Management, Marketing

**Bennett, Ness** — *Recruiter*
Technical Connections Inc.
11400 Olympic Boulevard, Suite 770
Los Angeles, CA 90064
Telephone: (310) 479-8830
**Recruiter Classification:** Contingency; **Lowest/Average Salary:**
$40,000/$75,000; **Industry Concentration:** High Technology, Information
Technology; **Function Concentration:** Generalist

**Bennett, Richard T.** — *Senior Recruiter*
Isaacson, Miller
334 Boylston Street, Suite 500
Boston, MA 02111
Telephone: (617) 262-6500
**Recruiter Classification:** Retained; **Lowest/Average Salary:** $75,000/$90,000;
**Industry Concentration:** Generalist with a primary focus in Public
Administration; **Function Concentration:** Administration, General
Management, Women/Minorities

**Benson, Edward** — *Associate*
Source Services Corporation
1601 East Flamingo Road, Suite 18
Las Vegas, NV 89119
Telephone: (702) 796-9676
**Recruiter Classification:** Contingency; **Lowest/Average Salary:**
$30,000/$50,000; **Industry Concentration:** Financial Services, Information
Technology; **Function Concentration:** Engineering, Finance/Accounting

**Benson, Kate** — *Associate*
Rene Plessner Associates, Inc.
375 Park Avenue
New York, NY 10152
Telephone: (212) 421-3490
**Recruiter Classification:** Retained; **Lowest/Average Salary:** $75,000/$90,000;
**Industry Concentration:** Generalist with a primary focus in
Aerospace/Defense, Consumer Products, Fashion (Retail/Apparel), Insurance,
Pharmaceutical/Medical; **Function Concentration:** Generalist with a primary
focus in Administration, Finance/Accounting, General Management, Human
Resources, Marketing, Research and Development, Sales

**Bentley, David W.** — *Partner*
Nordeman Grimm, Inc.
717 Fifth Avenue, 26th Floor
New York, NY 10022
Telephone: (212) 935-1000
**Recruiter Classification:** Retained; **Lowest/Average Salary:** $90,000/$90,000;
**Industry Concentration:** Generalist; **Function Concentration:** Generalist

**Berarducci, Arthur** — *Partner*
Heidrick & Struggles, Inc.
One Post Office Square
Boston, MA 02109-0199
Telephone: (617) 423-1140
**Recruiter Classification:** Retained; **Lowest/Average Salary:** $75,000/$90,000;
**Industry Concentration:** Generalist; **Function Concentration:** Generalist

**Berenblum, Marvin B.** — *Partner*
Heidrick & Struggles, Inc.
Greenwich Office Park #3
Greenwich, CT 06831
Telephone: (203) 629-3200
**Recruiter Classification:** Retained; **Lowest/Average Salary:** $75,000/$90,000;
**Industry Concentration:** Generalist with a primary focus in Consumer
Products, Publishing/Media; **Function Concentration:** Generalist

**Bergen, Anthony M.** — *Vice President*
CFO Associates, Inc.
1055 Parsippany Boulevard
Suite 501
Parsippany, NJ 07054
Telephone: (201) 402-2005
**Recruiter Classification:** Executive Temporary; **Lowest/Average Salary:**
$90,000/$90,000; **Industry Concentration:** Generalist with a primary focus in
Consumer Products, Manufacturing; **Function Concentration:** Administration,
Finance/Accounting, General Management, Marketing, Sales

**Berger, Emanuel** — *Senior Recruiter*
Isaacson, Miller
334 Boylston Street, Suite 500
Boston, MA 02111
Telephone: (617) 262-6500
**Recruiter Classification:** Retained; **Lowest/Average Salary:** $75,000/$90,000;
**Industry Concentration:** Generalist with a primary focus in Education/Libraries,
Environmental, Healthcare/Hospitals, Non-Profit, Public Administration,
Transportation; **Function Concentration:** Generalist with a primary focus in
Administration, Finance/Accounting, General Management, Human Resources,
Women/Minorities

**Berger, Jay V.** — *Partner*
Morris & Berger
201 South Lake Avenue, Suite 700
Pasadena, CA 91101
Telephone: (818) 795-0522
**Recruiter Classification:** Retained; **Lowest/Average Salary:** $60,000/$90,000;
**Industry Concentration:** Generalist with a primary focus in Biotechnology,
Board Services, Chemical Products, Education/Libraries, Electronics,
Environmental, Financial Services, Healthcare/Hospitals, High Technology,
Information Technology, Manufacturing, Non-Profit, Packaging,
Pharmaceutical/Medical, Public Administration, Real Estate; **Function
Concentration:** Generalist

**Berger, Jeffrey** — *Associate*
Source Services Corporation
10300 West 103rd Street, Suite 101
Overland Park, KS 66214
Telephone: (913) 888-8885
**Recruiter Classification:** Contingency; **Lowest/Average Salary:**
$30,000/$50,000; **Industry Concentration:** Financial Services, Information
Technology; **Function Concentration:** Engineering, Finance/Accounting

**Berger, Joel** — *President*
Meridian Legal Search
25 West 43rd Street, Suite 700
New York, NY 10036
Telephone: (212) 354-9300
**Recruiter Classification:** Contingency; **Lowest/Average Salary:**
$60,000/$90,000

**Berger, Judith E.** — *President*
MDR Associates, Inc.
9360 Sunset Drive, Suite 250
Miami, FL 33173
Telephone: (305) 271-9213
**Recruiter Classification:** Retained; **Lowest/Average Salary:** $90,000/$90,000;
**Industry Concentration:** Healthcare/Hospitals; **Function Concentration:**
Generalist

**Berk-Levine, Margo** — *Executive Vice President*
MB Inc. Interim Executive Division
505 Fifth Avenue
New York, NY 10017
Telephone: (212) 661-4937
**Recruiter Classification:** Executive Temporary; **Lowest/Average Salary:**
$60,000/$75,000; **Industry Concentration:** Generalist with a primary focus in
Consumer Products, Entertainment, Fashion (Retail/Apparel), Financial
Services, Publishing/Media; **Function Concentration:** Generalist with a primary
focus in General Management, Human Resources

**Berke, Carl E.** — *Vice President*
The Cassie Group
Professional Office Center
800 W. State St., Ste. 103
Doylestown, PA 18901
Telephone: (215) 348-1222
**Recruiter Classification:** Retained; **Lowest/Average Salary:** $75,000/$90,000;
**Industry Concentration:** Pharmaceutical/Medical; **Function Concentration:**
Marketing, Research and Development, Sales, Women/Minorities

**Berkowitz, Carol** — *Account Executive*
Career Management International
197 Route 18
East Brunswick, NJ 08816
Telephone: (908) 937-4800
**Recruiter Classification:** Retained; **Lowest/Average Salary:** $20,000/$30,000;
**Industry Concentration:** Fashion (Retail/Apparel); **Function Concentration:**
Generalist with a primary focus in Sales

**Berlet, William** — *Principal*
KPMG Executive Search
P.O. Box 31, Stn. Commerce Court
Toronto, Ontario, CANADA M5L 1B2
Telephone: (416) 777-8500
**Recruiter Classification:** Retained; **Lowest/Average Salary:** $75,000/$90,000;
**Industry Concentration:** Generalist; **Function Concentration:** Generalist

**Berlin, Marc** — *Branch Manager*
Accountants on Call
970 West 190th Street, Suite 420
Torrance, CA 90502
Telephone: (310) 527-2777
**Recruiter Classification:** Contingency; **Lowest/Average Salary:**
$20,000/$30,000; **Industry Concentration:** Generalist; **Function
Concentration:** Finance/Accounting

**Berman, Kenneth D.** — *Physician Recruiter*
MSI International
6345 Balboa Boulevard
Suite 335
Encino, CA 91316
Telephone: (818) 342-0222
**Recruiter Classification:** Contingency; **Lowest/Average Salary:**
$30,000/$60,000; **Industry Concentration:** Generalist with a primary focus in
Healthcare/Hospitals; **Function Concentration:** Generalist with a primary focus
in Administration, Engineering, Finance/Accounting, General Management,
Marketing, Sales

**Berman, Wendy** — *Senior Recruiter*
Klein, Landau, Romm & North
1725 K Street NW, Suite 602
Washington, DC 20006
Telephone: (202) 728-0100
**Recruiter Classification:** Contingency; **Lowest/Average Salary:**
$50,000/$90,000

**Bermea, Jose** — *Executive Recruiter*
Gaffney Management Consultants
35 North Brandon Drive
Glendale Heights, IL 60139-2087
Telephone: (708) 307-3380
**Recruiter Classification:** Retained; **Lowest/Average Salary:** $60,000/$90,000;
**Industry Concentration:** Generalist with a primary focus in
Aerospace/Defense, Automotive, Chemical Products, Electronics, High
Technology, Manufacturing, Transportation, Venture Capital; **Function
Concentration:** Generalist with a primary focus in Engineering, General
Management, Research and Development, Women/Minorities

**Bernard, Bryan** — *Associate*
Source Services Corporation
520 Post Oak Boulevard, Suite 700
Houston, TX 77027
Telephone: (713) 439-1077
**Recruiter Classification:** Contingency; **Lowest/Average Salary:**
$30,000/$50,000; **Industry Concentration:** Financial Services, Information
Technology; **Function Concentration:** Engineering, Finance/Accounting

**Bernas, Sharon** — *Associate*
Source Services Corporation
3 Summit Park Drive, Suite 550
Independence, OH 44131
Telephone: (216) 328-5900
**Recruiter Classification:** Contingency; **Lowest/Average Salary:**
$30,000/$50,000; **Industry Concentration:** Financial Services, Information
Technology; **Function Concentration:** Engineering, Finance/Accounting

**Berne, Marlene** — *Vice President*
The Whitney Group
850 Third Avenue, 11th Floor
New York, NY 10022
Telephone: (212) 508-3500
**Recruiter Classification:** Retained; **Lowest/Average Salary:** $75,000/$90,000;
**Industry Concentration:** Generalist with a primary focus in Financial Services,
Real Estate, Venture Capital; **Function Concentration:** Generalist with a
primary focus in Sales

**Bernstein, Charles Page** — *Consultant*
Paul Ray Berndtson
191 Peachtree Tower, Suite 3800
191 Peachtree Street, NE
Atlanta, GA 30303-1757
Telephone: (404) 215-4600
**Recruiter Classification:** Retained; **Lowest/Average Salary:** $90,000/$90,000;
**Industry Concentration:** Generalist; **Function Concentration:** Generalist

**Berrong, Barbie H.** — *Co-Manager*
Management Recruiters International, Inc.
Homestead Professional Building
4333 State Road 261
Newburgh, IN 47630-2668
Telephone: (812) 853-2511
**Recruiter Classification:** Contingency; **Lowest/Average Salary:**
$30,000/$75,000; **Industry Concentration:** Generalist; **Function
Concentration:** Generalist

**Berrong, Ray** — *Co-Manager Central Region*
Management Recruiters International, Inc.
Homestead Professional Building
4333 State Road 261
Newburgh, IN 47630-2668
Telephone: (812) 853-2511
**Recruiter Classification:** Contingency; **Lowest/Average Salary:**
$30,000/$75,000; **Industry Concentration:** Generalist; **Function
Concentration:** Generalist

**Berry, Chuck** — *Manager Southwest Region*
Management Recruiters International, Inc.
165 South Guadalupe, Suite 150
San Marcos, TX 78666-5531
Telephone: (512) 392-3838
**Recruiter Classification:** Contingency; **Lowest/Average Salary:**
$30,000/$75,000; **Industry Concentration:** Generalist; **Function
Concentration:** Generalist

**Berry, Harold B.** — *Vice President*
The Hindman Company
Browenton Place, Suite 110
2000 Warrington Way
Louisville, KY 40222
Telephone: (502) 426-4040
**Recruiter Classification:** Retained; **Lowest/Average Salary:** $50,000/$90,000;
**Industry Concentration:** Generalist with a primary focus in
Aerospace/Defense, Automotive, Chemical Products, Consumer Products,
Electronics, Financial Services, High Technology, Manufacturing, Oil/Gas,
Pharmaceutical/Medical, Transportation; **Function Concentration:** Generalist

**Berry, John R.** — *Partner*
Heidrick & Struggles, Inc.
125 South Wacker Drive
Suite 2800
Chicago, IL 60606-4590
Telephone: (312) 372-8811
**Recruiter Classification:** Retained; **Lowest/Average Salary:** $75,000/$90,000;
**Industry Concentration:** Generalist with a primary focus in Hospitality/Leisure;
**Function Concentration:** Generalist with a primary focus in General
Management

**Bertok, Ken** — *Vice President Recruiting Services*
The Wentworth Company, Inc.
The Arcade Building
479 West Sixth Street
San Pedro, CA 90731
Telephone: (800) 995-9678
**Recruiter Classification:** Retained; **Lowest/Average Salary:** $/$90,000; **Industry Concentration:** Generalist; **Function Concentration:** Generalist

**Bertoux, Michael P.** — *Vice President*
Wilcox, Bertoux & Miller
100 Howe Avenue, Suite 155N
Sacramento, CA 95825
Telephone: (916) 977-3700
**Recruiter Classification:** Contingency; **Lowest/Average Salary:**
$40,000/$75,000; **Industry Concentration:** Financial Services; **Function
Concentration:** Administration, General Management

**Bertsch, Phil L.** — *Manager Midwest Region*
Management Recruiters International, Inc.
11701 Borman Drive, Suite 250
St. Louis, MO 63146
Telephone: (314) 991-4355
**Recruiter Classification:** Contingency; **Lowest/Average Salary:**
$30,000/$75,000; **Industry Concentration:** Generalist; **Function
Concentration:** Generalist

**Bertsch, Phil L.** — *Manager Midwest Region*
Management Recruiters International, Inc.
3301 Rider Trail South, Suite 100
St. Louis, MO 63045-1309
Telephone: (314) 344-0900
**Recruiter Classification:** Contingency; **Lowest/Average Salary:**
$30,000/$75,000; **Industry Concentration:** Generalist; **Function
Concentration:** Generalist

**Besen, Douglas** — *President and CEO*
Besen Associates Inc.
115 Route 46 West
Building C-21
Mountain Lakes, NJ 07046
Telephone: (201) 334-5533
**Recruiter Classification:** Contingency; **Lowest/Average Salary:**
$50,000/$90,000; **Industry Concentration:** Generalist with a primary focus in
Biotechnology, Chemical Products, Consumer Products, High Technology,
Manufacturing, Pharmaceutical/Medical; **Function Concentration:** Generalist
with a primary focus in Administration, Engineering, General Management,
Human Resources, Marketing, Research and Development, Sales,
Women/Minorities

**Bethmann, James M.** — *Executive Director*
Russell Reynolds Associates, Inc.
1900 Trammell Crow Center
2001 Ross Avenue
Dallas, TX 75201
Telephone: (214) 220-2033
**Recruiter Classification:** Retained; **Lowest/Average Salary:** $90,000/$90,000;
**Industry Concentration:** Generalist; **Function Concentration:** Generalist

**Bettick, Michael J.** — *Recruiter*
A.J. Burton Group, Inc.
120 East Baltimore Street, Suite 2220
Baltimore, MD 21202
Telephone: (410) 752-5244
**Recruiter Classification:** Contingency; **Lowest/Average Salary:**
$40,000/$75,000; **Industry Concentration:** Consumer Products, Energy,
Financial Services, Healthcare/Hospitals, Manufacturing; **Function
Concentration:** Finance/Accounting

**Betts, Suzette** — *Associate*
Source Services Corporation
520 Post Oak Boulevard, Suite 700
Houston, TX 77027
Telephone: (713) 439-1077
**Recruiter Classification:** Contingency; **Lowest/Average Salary:**
$30,000/$50,000; **Industry Concentration:** Financial Services, Information
Technology; **Function Concentration:** Engineering, Finance/Accounting

**Bhimpure, Anita** — *Account Executive*
Career Management International
197 Route 18
East Brunswick, NJ 08816
Telephone: (908) 937-4800
**Recruiter Classification:** Retained; **Lowest/Average Salary:** $30,000/$40,000;
**Industry Concentration:** Fashion (Retail/Apparel); **Function Concentration:**
Generalist

**Bickett, Nicole** — *Associate*
Source Services Corporation
111 Monument Circle, Suite 3930
Indianapolis, IN 46204
Telephone: (317) 631-2900
**Recruiter Classification:** Contingency; **Lowest/Average Salary:**
$30,000/$50,000; **Industry Concentration:** Financial Services, Information
Technology; **Function Concentration:** Engineering, Finance/Accounting

**Bicknese, Elizabeth** — *Partner*
Heidrick & Struggles, Inc.
One Peachtree Center
303 Peachtree Street, NE, Suite 3100
Atlanta, GA 30308
Telephone: (404) 577-2410
**Recruiter Classification:** Retained; **Lowest/Average Salary:** $75,000/$90,000;
**Industry Concentration:** Generalist; **Function Concentration:** Generalist

**Biddix, Maryanne** — *Consultant*
Tyler & Company
1000 Abernathy Road N.E.
Suite 1400
Atlanta, GA 30328-5655
Telephone: (770) 396-3939
**Recruiter Classification:** Retained; **Lowest/Average Salary:** $60,000/$90,000;
**Industry Concentration:** Healthcare/Hospitals, Insurance; **Function
Concentration:** Generalist

**Bidelman, Richard** — *Managing Director*
Source Services Corporation
1601 East Flamingo Road, Suite 18
Las Vegas, NV 89119
Telephone: (702) 796-9676
**Recruiter Classification:** Contingency; **Lowest/Average Salary:**
$30,000/$50,000; **Industry Concentration:** Financial Services, Information
Technology; **Function Concentration:** Engineering, Finance/Accounting

**Biegel, Sandy** — *Vice President - L.A. Wholesale*
Evie Kreisler & Associates, Inc.
865 South Figueroa, Suite 950
Los Angeles, CA 90017
Telephone: (213) 622-8994
**Recruiter Classification:** Contingency; **Lowest/Average Salary:**
$30,000/$75,000; **Industry Concentration:** Fashion (Retail/Apparel); **Function
Concentration:** Generalist

**Biestek, Paul J.** — *President*
Paul J. Biestek Associates, Inc.
9501 West Devon Avenue, Suite 300
Rosemont, IL 60018
Telephone: (708) 825-5131
**Recruiter Classification:** Retained; **Lowest/Average Salary:** $60,000/$90,000;
**Industry Concentration:** Generalist with a primary focus in Automotive,
Biotechnology, Chemical Products, Consumer Products, Electronics,
Environmental, High Technology, Pharmaceutical/Medical; **Function
Concentration:** Generalist with a primary focus in Engineering, General
Management, Human Resources, Marketing, Research and Development, Sales

**Biggins, J. Veronica** — *Consultant*
Heidrick & Struggles, Inc.
One Peachtree Center
303 Peachtree Street, NE, Suite 3100
Atlanta, GA 30308
Telephone: (404) 577-2410
**Recruiter Classification:** Retained; **Lowest/Average Salary:** $75,000/$90,000;
**Industry Concentration:** Generalist with a primary focus in Financial Services,
Non-Profit; **Function Concentration:** Generalist

**Biggins, Joseph** — *Information Technology Recruiter*
Winter, Wyman & Company
950 Winter Street, Suite 3100
Waltham, MA 02154-1294
Telephone: (617) 890-7000
**Recruiter Classification:** Contingency; **Lowest/Average Salary:**
$30,000/$60,000; **Industry Concentration:** Generalist with a primary focus in
Information Technology; **Function Concentration:** Generalist

**Billingsly, Dorothy M.** — *Executive Vice President/ Managing Director*
DHR International, Inc.
Seville-on-the-Plaza
500 Nichols Road, Suite 430
Kansas City, MO 64112
Telephone: (816) 756-2965
**Recruiter Classification:** Retained; **Lowest/Average Salary:** $60,000/$90,000;
**Industry Concentration:** Generalist; **Function Concentration:** Generalist

**Billington, Brian** — *President*
Billington & Associates
3250 Wilshire Boulevard, Suite 914
Los Angeles, CA 90010-1502
Telephone: (213) 386-7511
**Recruiter Classification:** Retained; **Lowest/Average Salary:** $50,000/$60,000;
**Industry Concentration:** Generalist with a primary focus in Consumer
Products, Entertainment, Healthcare/Hospitals, Hospitality/Leisure,
Manufacturing, Non-Profit, Pharmaceutical/Medical, Transportation; **Function
Concentration:** Administration, Finance/Accounting, General Management,
Human Resources

**Billington, William H.** — *Partner*
Spriggs & Company, Inc.
1701 East Lake Avenue
Suite 265
Glenview, IL 60025
Telephone: (708) 657-7181
**Recruiter Classification:** Retained; **Lowest/Average Salary:** $60,000/$90,000;
**Industry Concentration:** Generalist with a primary focus in Board Services,
Consumer Products, Electronics, Financial Services, Manufacturing,
Pharmaceutical/Medical, Utilities/Nuclear; **Function Concentration:** Generalist
with a primary focus in General Management, Human Resources, Marketing,
Sales

**Billotti, Lisa** — *Director Research*
Bryant Research
466 Old Hook Road, Suite 32
Emerson, NJ 07630
Telephone: (201) 599-0590
**Recruiter Classification:** Contingency; **Lowest/Average Salary:**
$50,000/$90,000; **Industry Concentration:** Biotechnology,
Pharmaceutical/Medical; **Function Concentration:** Research and Development

**Bilz, Deirdre** — *Partner*
Johnson Smith & Knisely Accord
101 Federal Street, Suite 1900
Boston, MA 02110
Telephone: (617) 342-7441
**Recruiter Classification:** Retained; **Lowest/Average Salary:** $90,000/$90,000;
**Industry Concentration:** Generalist; **Function Concentration:** Generalist

**Biolsi, Joseph** — *Associate*
Source Services Corporation
15260 Ventura Boulevard, Suite 380
Sherman Oaks, CA 91403
Telephone: (818) 905-1500
**Recruiter Classification:** Contingency; **Lowest/Average Salary:**
$30,000/$50,000; **Industry Concentration:** Financial Services, Information
Technology; **Function Concentration:** Engineering, Finance/Accounting

**Bird, Len L.** — *Manager Southwest Region*
Management Recruiters International, Inc.
2200 Space Park Drive, Suite 420
Houston, TX 77058-3663
Telephone: (713) 335-0363
**Recruiter Classification:** Contingency; **Lowest/Average Salary:**
$30,000/$75,000; **Industry Concentration:** Generalist; **Function
Concentration:** Generalist

**Birns, Douglas** — *Associate*
Source Services Corporation
155 Federal Street, Suite 410
Boston, MA 02110
Telephone: (617) 482-8211
**Recruiter Classification:** Contingency; **Lowest/Average Salary:**
$30,000/$50,000; **Industry Concentration:** Financial Services, Information
Technology; **Function Concentration:** Engineering, Finance/Accounting

**Bishop, B. Susan** — *Vice President/Managing Director*
DHR International, Inc.
325 East Eisenhower Parkway, Suite 106
Ann Arbor, MI 48108
Telephone: (313) 662-8284
**Recruiter Classification:** Retained; **Lowest/Average Salary:** $60,000/$90,000;
**Industry Concentration:** Generalist; **Function Concentration:** Generalist

**Bishop, Barbara** — *Vice President*
The Executive Source
55 Fifth Avenue, 19th Floor
New York, NY 10003
Telephone: (212) 691-5505
**Recruiter Classification:** Executive Temporary; **Lowest/Average Salary:**
$75,000/$90,000; **Industry Concentration:** Generalist with a primary focus in
Financial Services, Insurance, Venture Capital; **Function Concentration:**
Human Resources

**Bishop, James F.** — *President*
Burke, O'Brien & Bishop Associates, Inc.
1000 Herrontown Road
Princeton, NJ 08540
Telephone: (609) 921-3510
**Recruiter Classification:** Retained; **Lowest/Average Salary:** $90,000/$90,000;
**Industry Concentration:** Generalist; **Function Concentration:** Generalist

**Bishop, Sandy** — *Manager Eastern Region*
Management Recruiters International, Inc.
7 St. Albans Circle
Newtown Square, PA 19073
Telephone: (610) 356-8360
**Recruiter Classification:** Contingency; **Lowest/Average Salary:** $30,000/$75,000;
**Industry Concentration:** Generalist; **Function Concentration:** Generalist

**Bishop, Susan** — *President*
Bishop Partners
708 Third Avenue
New York, NY 10017
Telephone: (212) 986-3419
**Recruiter Classification:** Retained; **Lowest/Average Salary:** $90,000/$90,000;
**Industry Concentration:** Entertainment, Information Technology,
Publishing/Media; **Function Concentration:** Generalist with a primary focus in
General Management, Marketing, Sales, Women/Minorities

**Biskin, Donald** — *Partner*
Heidrick & Struggles, Inc.
1301 K Street N.W., Suite 500 East
Washington, DC 20005
Telephone: (202) 289-4450
**Recruiter Classification:** Retained; **Lowest/Average Salary:** $75,000/$90,000;
**Industry Concentration:** Generalist with a primary focus in
Healthcare/Hospitals; **Function Concentration:** Generalist

**Bitar, Edward** — *Senior Vice President*
The Interface Group, Ltd./Boyden
2828 Pennsylvania Avenue, N.W., Suite 305
Washington, DC 20007
Telephone: (202) 342-7200
**Recruiter Classification:** Retained; **Lowest/Average Salary:** $75,000/$90,000;
**Industry Concentration:** Generalist with a primary focus in Consumer
Products, Energy, Environmental, Financial Services, High Technology,
Information Technology, Manufacturing, Non-Profit, Transportation; **Function
Concentration:** Generalist with a primary focus in Engineering,
Finance/Accounting, General Management, Women/Minorities

**Bittman, Beth M.** — *Senior Associate*
Norman Roberts & Associates, Inc.
1800 Century Park East, Suite 430
Los Angeles, CA 90067
Telephone: (310) 552-1112
**Recruiter Classification:** Retained; **Lowest/Average Salary:** $60,000/$90,000;
**Industry Concentration:** Energy, Environmental, Public Administration, Real
Estate, Transportation; **Function Concentration:** Generalist with a primary focus
in Administration, Engineering, General Management, Human Resources,
Women/Minorities

**Bizick, Ron** — *Manager Central Region*
Management Recruiters International, Inc.
1201 Broughton Road, Suite 1
Pittsburgh, PA 15236-3469
Telephone: (412) 650-9610
**Recruiter Classification:** Contingency; **Lowest/Average Salary:** $30,000/$75,000;
**Industry Concentration:** Generalist; **Function Concentration:** Generalist

**Black, Douglas E.** — *Executive Recruiter*
MSI International
200 Galleria Parkway
Suite 1610
Atlanta, GA 30339
Telephone: (404) 951-1208
**Recruiter Classification:** Contingency; **Lowest/Average Salary:**
$30,000/$75,000; **Industry Concentration:** Generalist with a primary focus in
Manufacturing; **Function Concentration:** Generalist with a primary focus in
Administration, Engineering, Finance/Accounting, General Management,
Marketing, Sales

**Black, Frank S.** — *General Manager*
Management Recruiters International, Inc.
1100 Wayne Avenue, Suite 710
Silver Spring, MD 20910
Telephone: (301) 589-5400
**Recruiter Classification:** Contingency; **Lowest/Average Salary:**
$30,000/$75,000; **Industry Concentration:** Generalist; **Function Concentration:** Generalist

**Black, James L.** — *Executive Vice President/Managing Director*
DHR International, Inc.
22525 S.E. 64th Place, Suite 201
Issaquah, WA 98027
Telephone: (206) 557-3681
**Recruiter Classification:** Retained; **Lowest/Average Salary:** $60,000/$90,000; **Industry Concentration:** Generalist; **Function Concentration:** Generalist

**Black, Nancy C.** — *President*
Assisting Professionals, Inc.
2000 North Woodward, Suite 250
Bloomfield Hills, MI 48304-2255
Telephone: (810) 647-9800
**Recruiter Classification:** Executive Temporary; **Lowest/Average Salary:** $50,000/$75,000; **Industry Concentration:** Generalist; **Function Concentration:** Generalist

**Blackmon, Sharon** — *Vice President*
The Abbott Group, Inc.
530 College Parkway, Suite N
Annapolis, MD 21401
Telephone: (410) 757-4100
**Recruiter Classification:** Retained; **Lowest/Average Salary:** $90,000/$90,000; **Industry Concentration:** Generalist with a primary focus in Aerospace/Defense, Electronics, Energy, High Technology, Information Technology, Non-Profit; **Function Concentration:** Generalist with a primary focus in Engineering, General Management, Human Resources, Marketing, Women/Minorities

**Blackshaw, Brian M.** — *Partner*
Blackshaw, Olmstead & Lynch
1010 Monarch Plaza
3414 Peachtree Road N.E.
Atlanta, GA 30326
Telephone: (404) 261-7770
**Recruiter Classification:** Retained; **Lowest/Average Salary:** $75,000/$90,000; **Industry Concentration:** Generalist; **Function Concentration:** Generalist

**Bladon, Andrew** — *Vice President/Executive Director*
Don Richard Associates of Tampa, Inc.
100 North Tampa Street, Suite 1925
Tampa, FL 33602
Telephone: (813) 221-7930
**Recruiter Classification:** Contingency, Executive Temporary; **Lowest/Average Salary:** $20,000/$50,000; **Industry Concentration:** Generalist with a primary focus in Automotive, Financial Services, High Technology, Information Technology, Real Estate; **Function Concentration:** Generalist with a primary focus in Administration, Finance/Accounting, Research and Development

**Blair, Kelly A.** — *Partner*
The Caldwell Partners Amrop International
Sixty-Four Prince Arthur Avenue
Toronto, Ontario, CANADA M5R 1B4
Telephone: (416) 920-7702
**Recruiter Classification:** Retained; **Lowest/Average Salary:** $/$90,000; **Industry Concentration:** Generalist with a primary focus in Consumer Products, Hospitality/Leisure, Non-Profit, Pharmaceutical/Medical, Public Administration; **Function Concentration:** Generalist

**Blair, Susan** — *Director Recruitment*
Simpson Associates
Trump Parc
106 Central Park South
New York, NY 10019
Telephone: (212) 767-0006
**Recruiter Classification:** Contingency; **Lowest/Average Salary:** $60,000/$90,000; **Industry Concentration:** Fashion (Retail/Apparel); **Function Concentration:** Finance/Accounting, Human Resources, Marketing, Sales

**Blake, Eileen** — *Consultant*
Howard Fischer Associates, Inc.
1800 John F. Kennedy Boulevard, 7th Floor
Philadelphia, PA 19103
Telephone: (215) 568-8363
**Recruiter Classification:** Retained; **Lowest/Average Salary:** $90,000/$90,000; **Industry Concentration:** Healthcare/Hospitals; **Function Concentration:** Generalist

**Blakslee, Jan H.** — *President*
J: Blakslee International, Ltd.
49 Hillside Avenue
Mill Valley, CA 94941
Telephone: (415) 389-7300
**Recruiter Classification:** Retained; **Lowest/Average Salary:** $90,000/$90,000; **Industry Concentration:** Biotechnology, Board Services, Pharmaceutical/Medical, Venture Capital; **Function Concentration:** Generalist with a primary focus in Engineering, Finance/Accounting, General Management, Human Resources, Marketing, Research and Development, Women/Minorities

**Bland, Walter** — *Associate*
Source Services Corporation
925 Westchester Avenue, Suite 309
White Plains, NY 10604
Telephone: (914) 428-9100
**Recruiter Classification:** Contingency; **Lowest/Average Salary:** $30,000/$50,000; **Industry Concentration:** Financial Services, Information Technology; **Function Concentration:** Engineering, Finance/Accounting

**Blanton, Thomas** — *Partner*
Blanton and Company
P.O. Box 94041
Birmingham, AL 35220-4041
Telephone: (205) 836-3063
**Recruiter Classification:** Contingency; **Lowest/Average Salary:** $75,000/$75,000; **Industry Concentration:** Generalist with a primary focus in Biotechnology, Chemical Products, Electronics, Healthcare/Hospitals, Information Technology, Manufacturing, Packaging, Pharmaceutical/Medical; **Function Concentration:** Generalist with a primary focus in Engineering, General Management, Human Resources, Marketing, Research and Development, Sales

**Blassaras, Peggy** — *Associate*
Source Services Corporation
111 Monument Circle, Suite 3930
Indianapolis, IN 46204
Telephone: (317) 631-2900
**Recruiter Classification:** Contingency; **Lowest/Average Salary:** $30,000/$50,000; **Industry Concentration:** Financial Services, Information Technology; **Function Concentration:** Engineering, Finance/Accounting

**Blecker, Jay** — *Executive Recruiter*
TSS Consulting, Ltd.
2425 East Camelback Road
Suite 375
Phoenix, AZ 85016
Telephone: (602) 955-7000
**Recruiter Classification:** Contingency; **Lowest/Average Salary:** $60,000/$75,000; **Industry Concentration:** Aerospace/Defense, Electronics, High Technology; **Function Concentration:** Engineering, General Management, Marketing

**Blecksmith, Edward** — *Vice President*
Korn/Ferry International
601 South Figueroa
Suite 1900
Los Angeles, CA 90017
Telephone: (213) 624-6600
**Recruiter Classification:** Retained; **Lowest/Average Salary:** $90,000/$90,000; **Industry Concentration:** Generalist; **Function Concentration:** Generalist

**Blessing, Marc L.** — *Vice President Corporate Development*
Management Recruiters International, Inc.
200 Public Square, 31st Floor
Cleveland, OH 44114-2301
Telephone: (216) 696-1122
**Recruiter Classification:** Contingency; **Lowest/Average Salary:** $30,000/$75,000; **Industry Concentration:** Generalist; **Function Concentration:** Generalist

**Blickle, Michael** — *Associate*
Source Services Corporation
One South Main Street, Suite 1440
Dayton, OH 45402
Telephone: (513) 461-4660
**Recruiter Classification:** Contingency; **Lowest/Average Salary:** $30,000/$50,000; **Industry Concentration:** Financial Services, Information Technology; **Function Concentration:** Engineering, Finance/Accounting

**Bliley, Jerry** — *Senior Director*
Spencer Stuart
One University Avenue
Suite 801
Toronto, Ontario, CANADA M5J 2P1
Telephone: (416) 361-0311
**Recruiter Classification:** Retained; **Lowest/Average Salary:** $90,000/$90,000; **Industry Concentration:** Generalist with a primary focus in Automotive, Board Services, Electronics, Financial Services, High Technology, Information Technology, Manufacturing, Packaging, Transportation; **Function Concentration:** Generalist with a primary focus in Finance/Accounting, General Management, Human Resources, Marketing, Sales

**Blim, Barbara** — *Principal*
JDG Associates, Ltd.
1700 Research Boulevard
Rockville, MD 20850
Telephone: (301) 340-2210
**Recruiter Classification:** Contingency; **Lowest/Average Salary:**
$50,000/$90,000; **Industry Concentration:** Aerospace/Defense, Electronics,
Financial Services, High Technology, Information Technology; **Function
Concentration:** Engineering, Research and Development, Sales

**Bloch, Suzanne** — *Associate*
Source Services Corporation
701 West Cypress Creek Road, Suite 202
Ft. Lauderdale, FL 33309
Telephone: (954) 771-0777
**Recruiter Classification:** Contingency; **Lowest/Average Salary:**
$30,000/$50,000; **Industry Concentration:** Financial Services, Information
Technology; **Function Concentration:** Engineering, Finance/Accounting

**Blocher, John** — *Managing Director*
Source Services Corporation
10300 West 103rd Street, Suite 101
Overland Park, KS 66214
Telephone: (913) 888-8885
**Recruiter Classification:** Contingency; **Lowest/Average Salary:**
$30,000/$50,000; **Industry Concentration:** Financial Services, Information
Technology; **Function Concentration:** Engineering, Finance/Accounting

**Block, Laurie** — *Executive Recruiter*
Richard, Wayne and Roberts
24 Greenway Plaza, Suite 1304
Houston, TX 77046-2493
Telephone: (713) 629-6681
**Recruiter Classification:** Retained; **Lowest/Average Salary:** $50,000/$90,000

**Block, Randy** — *President*
Block & Associates
20 Sunnyside Avenue, Suite A332
Mill Valley, CA 94941
Telephone: (415) 389-9710
**Recruiter Classification:** Retained; **Lowest/Average Salary:** $90,000/$90,000;
**Industry Concentration:** Electronics; **Function Concentration:** Generalist

**Bloom, Howard C.** — *Principal*
Hernand & Partners
5000 Quorum Drive, Suite 160
Dallas, TX 75240
Telephone: (214) 661-1485
**Recruiter Classification:** Executive Temporary; **Industry Concentration:**
High Technology, Information Technology; **Function Concentration:**
Engineering

**Bloom, Howard C.** — *Co-Owner*
The Howard C. Bloom Co.
5000 Quorum Drive, Suite 770
Dallas, TX 75240
Telephone: (214) 385-6455
**Recruiter Classification:** Retained; **Lowest/Average Salary:** $50,000/$90,000;
**Industry Concentration:** Generalist; **Function Concentration:** Generalist

**Bloom, Joyce** — *Co-Owner*
The Howard C. Bloom Co.
5000 Quorum Drive, Suite 770
Dallas, TX 75240
Telephone: (214) 385-6455
**Recruiter Classification:** Retained; **Lowest/Average Salary:** $50,000/$90,000;
**Industry Concentration:** Generalist; **Function Concentration:** Generalist

**Bloom, Joyce** — *Principal*
Hernand & Partners
5000 Quorum Drive, Suite 160
Dallas, TX 75240
Telephone: (214) 661-1485
**Recruiter Classification:** Executive Temporary; **Industry Concentration:**
High Technology, Information Technology; **Function Concentration:**
Engineering

**Bloomer, James E.** — *Vice President*
L.W. Foote Company
110-110th Avenue N.E.
Suite 680
Bellevue, WA 98004-5840
Telephone: (206) 451-1660
**Recruiter Classification:** Retained; **Lowest/Average Salary:** $75,000/$75,000;
**Industry Concentration:** Generalist with a primary focus in Biotechnology,
Electronics, Entertainment, High Technology, Manufacturing,
Pharmaceutical/Medical; **Function Concentration:** Generalist with a primary
focus in Engineering, General Management, Marketing, Research and
Development, Sales

**Bloomfield, Mary** — *Senior Associate*
R.D. Gatti & Associates, Incorporated
266 Main Street, Suite 21
Medfield, MA 02052
Telephone: (508) 359-4153
**Recruiter Classification:** Contingency; **Lowest/Average Salary:**
$40,000/$75,000; **Industry Concentration:** Generalist; **Function
Concentration:** Human Resources

**Blue, C. David** — *Manager North Atlantic Region*
Management Recruiters International, Inc.
Memorial Professional Building, Suite 302
2511 Memorial Avenue
Lynchburg, VA 24501
Telephone: (804) 528-1611
**Recruiter Classification:** Contingency; **Lowest/Average Salary:**
$30,000/$75,000; **Industry Concentration:** Generalist; **Function
Concentration:** Generalist

**Bluhm, Claudia** — *Associate Executive Search Consultant*
Schweichler Associates, Inc.
200 Tamal Vista, Building 200, Suite 100
Corte Madera, CA 94925
Telephone: (415) 924-7200
**Recruiter Classification:** Retained; **Lowest/Average Salary:** $90,000/$90,000;
**Industry Concentration:** Electronics, High Technology, Information
Technology; **Function Concentration:** Administration, Engineering,
Finance/Accounting, General Management, Human Resources, Marketing,
Research and Development, Sales

**Blumenthal, Deborah** — *Consultant*
Paul Ray Berndtson
101 Park Avenue, 41st Floor
New York, NY 10178
Telephone: (212) 370-1316
**Recruiter Classification:** Retained; **Lowest/Average Salary:** $90,000/$90,000;
**Industry Concentration:** Generalist; **Function Concentration:** Generalist

**Blumenthal, Paula** — *Partner*
J.P. Canon Associates
225 Broadway, Suite 3602
New York, NY 10007
Telephone: (212) 233-3131
**Recruiter Classification:** Contingency; **Lowest/Average Salary:**
$30,000/$60,000; **Industry Concentration:** Generalist; **Function
Concentration:** Generalist

**Blunt, Peter** — *Account Executive*
Hernand & Partners
770 Tamalpais Drive, Suite 204
Corte Madera, CA 94925
Telephone: (415) 927-7000
**Recruiter Classification:** Executive Temporary; **Industry Concentration:**
High Technology, Information Technology; **Function Concentration:**
Engineering

**Boag, John** — *Senior Consultant*
Norm Sanders Associates
2 Village Court
Hazlet, NJ 07730
Telephone: (908) 264-3700
**Recruiter Classification:** Retained; **Lowest/Average Salary:** $90,000/$90,000;
**Industry Concentration:** Information Technology; **Function Concentration:**
Generalist

**Boal, Robert A.** — *Manager Central Region*
Management Recruiters International, Inc.
3511 Center Road, Suite E-A
P.O. Box 178
Brunswick, OH 44212-0178
Telephone: (216) 273-4300
**Recruiter Classification:** Contingency; **Lowest/Average Salary:** $30,000/$75,000;
**Industry Concentration:** Generalist; **Function Concentration:** Generalist

**Boccella, Ralph** — *Senior Recruiter*
Susan C. Goldberg Associates
65 LaSalle Road
West Hartford, CT 06107
Telephone: (860) 236-4597
**Recruiter Classification:** Contingency; **Lowest/Average Salary:**
$40,000/$75,000; **Industry Concentration:** Aerospace/Defense, High
Technology, Manufacturing; **Function Concentration:** Finance/Accounting

**Boccuzi, Joseph H.** — *Senior Director*
Spencer Stuart
277 Park Avenue, 29th Floor
New York, NY 10172
Telephone: (212) 336-0200
**Recruiter Classification:** Retained; **Lowest/Average Salary:** $90,000/$90,000;
**Industry Concentration:** Biotechnology, Pharmaceutical/Medical; **Function
Concentration:** Generalist

**Boczany, William J.** — *Director*
The Guild Corporation
8260 Greensboro Drive, Suite 460
McLean, VA 22102
Telephone: (703) 761-4023
**Recruiter Classification:** Contingency; **Lowest/Average Salary:**
$40,000/$50,000; **Industry Concentration:** Aerospace/Defense, Electronics,
High Technology, Information Technology; **Function Concentration:**
Engineering, Finance/Accounting, General Management, Research and
Development

**Bodnar, Beverly** — *Co-Manager Eastern Region*
Management Recruiters International, Inc.
1230 Parkway Avenue, Suite 102
West Trenton, NJ 08628
Telephone: (609) 882-8388
**Recruiter Classification:** Contingency; **Lowest/Average Salary:**
$30,000/$75,000; **Industry Concentration:** Generalist; **Function
Concentration:** Generalist

**Bodnar, Robert J.** — *Co-Manager*
Management Recruiters International, Inc.
1230 Parkway Avenue, Suite 102
West Trenton, NJ 08628
Telephone: (609) 882-8388
**Recruiter Classification:** Contingency; **Lowest/Average Salary:**
$30,000/$75,000; **Industry Concentration:** Generalist; **Function
Concentration:** Generalist

**Bodner, Marilyn** — *President*
Bodner, Inc.
372 Fifth Avenue, Suite 9K
New York, NY 10018
Telephone: (212) 714-0371
**Recruiter Classification:** Contingency; **Lowest/Average Salary:**
$30,000/$75,000; **Industry Concentration:** Generalist; **Function
Concentration:** Finance/Accounting

**Boehmer, Jack** — *Senior Consultant*
KPMG Executive Search
Marsland Center
20 Erb Street West
Waterloo, Ontario, CANADA N2L 1T2
Telephone: (519) 747-8800
**Recruiter Classification:** Retained; **Lowest/Average Salary:** $75,000/$90,000;
**Industry Concentration:** Generalist; **Function Concentration:** Generalist

**Boerkoel, Timothy B.** — *Executive Director*
Russell Reynolds Associates, Inc.
200 Park Avenue
New York, NY 10166-0002
Telephone: (212) 351-2000
**Recruiter Classification:** Retained; **Lowest/Average Salary:** $90,000/$90,000;
**Industry Concentration:** Generalist with a primary focus in Consumer
Products; **Function Concentration:** Generalist

**Boesel, James** — *Consultant*
Logix Partners
1601 Trapelo Road
Waltham, MA 02154
Telephone: (617) 890-0500
**Recruiter Classification:** Retained; **Lowest/Average Salary:** $60,000/$75,000;
**Industry Concentration:** High Technology; **Function Concentration:**
Engineering

**Boesel, Jim** — *Consultant*
Logix, Inc.
1601 Trapelo Road
Waltham, MA 02154
Telephone: (617) 890-0500
**Recruiter Classification:** Retained; **Lowest/Average Salary:** $60,000/$75,000;
**Industry Concentration:** High Technology; **Function Concentration:**
Engineering

**Bogard, Nicholas C.** — *Vice President and Principal*
The Onstott Group, Inc.
60 William Street
Wellesley, MA 02181
Telephone: (617) 235-3050
**Recruiter Classification:** Retained; **Lowest/Average Salary:** $90,000/$90,000;
**Industry Concentration:** Financial Services, Insurance, Real Estate, Venture
Capital; **Function Concentration:** Generalist with a primary focus in
Administration, Finance/Accounting, General Management, Human Resources,
Marketing, Sales

**Bohle, John B.** — *Partner*
Paul Ray Berndtson
2029 Century Park East
Suite 1000
Los Angeles, CA 90067
Telephone: (310) 557-2828
**Recruiter Classification:** Retained; **Lowest/Average Salary:** $90,000/$90,000;
**Industry Concentration:** High Technology; **Function Concentration:** Generalist

**Bohn, Steve J.** — *General Manager*
MSI International
2170 West State Road 434
Suite 454
Longwood, FL 32779
Telephone: (407) 788-7700
**Recruiter Classification:** Contingency; **Lowest/Average Salary:**
$30,000/$60,000; **Industry Concentration:** Generalist with a primary focus in
Financial Services, Healthcare/Hospitals, High Technology, Information
Technology, Manufacturing; **Function Concentration:** Generalist with a
primary focus in Administration, Engineering, Finance/Accounting, General
Management, Marketing, Sales

**Bole, J. Jeffrey** — *President*
William J. Christopher Associates, Inc.
307 North Walnut Street
West Chester, PA 19380-2623
Telephone: (610) 696-4397
**Recruiter Classification:** Contingency; **Lowest/Average Salary:**
$30,000/$90,000; **Industry Concentration:** Generalist with a primary focus in
Packaging; **Function Concentration:** General Management, Marketing, Sales

**Bolger, Thomas** — *Vice President*
Korn/Ferry International
3950 Lincoln Plaza
500 North Akard Street
Dallas, TX 75201
Telephone: (214) 954-1834
**Recruiter Classification:** Retained; **Lowest/Average Salary:** $90,000/$90,000;
**Industry Concentration:** Generalist; **Function Concentration:** Generalist

**Bolls, Rich** — *Manager Southwest Region*
Management Recruiters International, Inc.
Cigna Tower, Suite 2110
1360 Post Oak Boulevard
Houston, TX 77056
Telephone: (713) 850-9850
**Recruiter Classification:** Contingency; **Lowest/Average Salary:**
$30,000/$75,000; **Industry Concentration:** Generalist; **Function
Concentration:** Generalist

**Bommarito, Bob C.** — *Manager Central Region*
Management Recruiters International, Inc.
302 South Water Street
Marine City, MI 48039-1689
Telephone: (810) 765-3480
**Recruiter Classification:** Contingency; **Lowest/Average Salary:**
$30,000/$75,000; **Industry Concentration:** Generalist; **Function
Concentration:** Generalist

**Bond, Allan** — *Senior Consultant/Director*
Walden Associates
1601 Trapelo Road
Waltham, MA 02154
Telephone: (617) 890-8885
**Recruiter Classification:** Retained; **Lowest/Average Salary:** $90,000/$90,000;
**Industry Concentration:** High Technology, Information Technology; **Function
Concentration:** General Management

**Bond, James L.** — *Vice President*
People Management Northeast Incorporated
One Darling Drive, Avon Park South
Avon, CT 06001
Telephone: (860) 678-8900
**Recruiter Classification:** Retained; **Lowest/Average Salary:** $75,000/$90,000;
**Industry Concentration:** Generalist with a primary focus in Information
Technology; **Function Concentration:** Generalist

**Bond, Robert J.** — *Managing Partner*
Romac & Associates
125 Summer Street, Suite 1450
Boston, MA 02110
Telephone: (617) 439-4300
**Recruiter Classification:** Executive Temporary; **Lowest/Average Salary:**
$/$60,000; **Industry Concentration:** Financial Services, Healthcare/Hospitals,
High Technology, Hospitality/Leisure, Information Technology, Insurance;
**Function Concentration:** Finance/Accounting

**Bonifield, Len** — *Consultant*
Bonifield Associates
3003E Lincoln Drive West
Marlton, NJ 08053
Telephone: (609) 596-3300
**Recruiter Classification:** Contingency; **Lowest/Average Salary:**
$40,000/$60,000; **Industry Concentration:** Financial Services, Insurance;
**Function Concentration:** Generalist with a primary focus in Administration,
Finance/Accounting, General Management, Human Resources, Marketing,
Research and Development, Sales

**Bonnell, William R.** — *President*
Bonnell Associates Ltd.
One Morningside Drive North
Westport, CT 06880
Telephone: (203) 226-2624
**Recruiter Classification:** Retained; **Lowest/Average Salary:** $75,000/$90,000;
**Industry Concentration:** Generalist with a primary focus in Financial Services,
Healthcare/Hospitals, Insurance; **Function Concentration:** Generalist with a
primary focus in Finance/Accounting, General Management, Human
Resources, Marketing, Sales

**Bonner, Barbara** — *Principal*
Mixtec Group
31255 Cedar Valley Drive
Suite 300-327
Westlake Village, CA 91362
Telephone: (818) 889-8819
**Recruiter Classification:** Contingency; **Lowest/Average Salary:**
$60,000/$90,000; **Function Concentration:** Generalist with a primary focus in
Marketing, Research and Development, Sales

**Bonner, Rodney D.** — *Manager Southwest Region*
Management Recruiters International, Inc.
12600 West Colfax Avenue, Suite C-440
Lakewood, CO 80215-3736
Telephone: (303) 233-8600
**Recruiter Classification:** Contingency; **Lowest/Average Salary:**
$30,000/$75,000; **Industry Concentration:** Generalist; **Function
Concentration:** Generalist

**Book, Cheryl** — *Medical Recruiter*
Aureus Group
8744 Frederick Street
Omaha, NE 68124-3068
Telephone: (402) 397-2980
**Recruiter Classification:** Contingency; **Lowest/Average Salary:**
$30,000/$40,000; **Industry Concentration:** Healthcare/Hospitals; **Function
Concentration:** Administration, General Management

**Boone, James E.** — *Managing Director*
Korn/Ferry International
303 Peachtree Street N.E.
Suite 1600
Atlanta, GA 30308
Telephone: (404) 577-7542
**Recruiter Classification:** Retained; **Lowest/Average Salary:** $90,000/$90,000;
**Industry Concentration:** Generalist; **Function Concentration:** Generalist

**Booth, Otis** — *Vice President*
A.T. Kearney, Inc.
Biltmore Tower
500 South Grand Avenue
Los Angeles, CA 90071
Telephone: (213) 689-6800
**Recruiter Classification:** Retained; **Lowest/Average Salary:** $90,000/$90,000;
**Industry Concentration:** Generalist with a primary focus in
Aerospace/Defense, Board Services, Environmental, Manufacturing, Non-Profit,
Oil/Gas; **Function Concentration:** Generalist with a primary focus in General
Management

**Booth, Ronald** — *Associate*
Source Services Corporation
5343 North 16th Street, Suite 270
Phoenix, AZ 85016
Telephone: (602) 230-0220
**Recruiter Classification:** Contingency; **Lowest/Average Salary:**
$30,000/$50,000; **Industry Concentration:** Financial Services, Information
Technology; **Function Concentration:** Engineering, Finance/Accounting

**Bopray, Pat** — *Executive Recruiter*
Personnel Unlimited/Executive Search
25 West Nora
Spokane, WA 99205
Telephone: (509) 326-8880
**Recruiter Classification:** Contingency; **Lowest/Average Salary:**
$30,000/$60,000; **Industry Concentration:** Generalist; **Function
Concentration:** Generalist

**Borden, Stuart** — *Vice President*
M.A. Churchill & Associates, Inc.
Morelyn Plaza
1111 Street Road
Southampton, PA 18966
Telephone: (215) 953-0300
**Recruiter Classification:** Contingency; **Lowest/Average Salary:**
$50,000/$75,000; **Industry Concentration:** Financial Services, Insurance;
**Function Concentration:** Marketing, Research and Development, Sales

**Borel, David P.** — *Co-Manager*
Management Recruiters International, Inc.
2814 New Spring Road, Suite 217
Atlanta, GA 30339
Telephone: (404) 436-3464
**Recruiter Classification:** Contingency; **Lowest/Average Salary:**
$30,000/$75,000; **Industry Concentration:** Generalist; **Function
Concentration:** Generalist

**Borenstine, Alvin** — *President*
Synergistics Associates Ltd.
400 North State Street, Suite 400
Chicago, IL 60610
Telephone: (312) 467-5450
**Recruiter Classification:** Retained; **Lowest/Average Salary:** $75,000/$90,000;
**Industry Concentration:** Generalist with a primary focus in Information
Technology; **Function Concentration:** Generalist

**Borland, James** — *Senior Vice President*
Goodrich & Sherwood Associates, Inc.
521 Fifth Avenue
New York, NY 10175
Telephone: (212) 697-4131
**Recruiter Classification:** Retained; **Lowest/Average Salary:** $60,000/$90,000;
**Industry Concentration:** Generalist with a primary focus in Board Services,
Chemical Products, Consumer Products, Financial Services,
Healthcare/Hospitals, Information Technology, Insurance, Manufacturing,
Oil/Gas, Publishing/Media, Venture Capital; **Function Concentration:**
Generalist with a primary focus in Administration, Finance/Accounting,
General Management, Human Resources, Marketing, Sales

**Borman, Theodore H.** — *Senior Partner*
Lamalie Amrop International
200 Park Avenue
New York, NY 10166-0136
Telephone: (212) 953-7900
**Recruiter Classification:** Retained; **Lowest/Average Salary:** $90,000/$90,000;
**Industry Concentration:** Generalist with a primary focus in Biotechnology,
Chemical Products, Healthcare/Hospitals, Pharmaceutical/Medical; **Function
Concentration:** Generalist with a primary focus in General Management,
Research and Development

**Bormann, Cindy Ann** — *Manager*
MSI International
5215 North O'Connor Boulevard
Suite 1875
Irving, TX 75039
Telephone: (214) 869-3939
**Recruiter Classification:** Contingency; **Lowest/Average Salary:**
$30,000/$60,000; **Industry Concentration:** Generalist with a primary focus in
Financial Services, Healthcare/Hospitals, High Technology, Information
Technology, Manufacturing; **Function Concentration:** Generalist with a
primary focus in Administration, Engineering, Finance/Accounting, General
Management, Marketing, Sales

**Bos, Marijo** — *Executive Director*
Russell Reynolds Associates, Inc.
333 South Grand Avenue
Suite 3500
Los Angeles, CA 90071
Telephone: (213) 253-4400
**Recruiter Classification:** Retained; **Lowest/Average Salary:** $90,000/$90,000;
**Industry Concentration:** Generalist with a primary focus in Consumer
Products; **Function Concentration:** Generalist

**Bostic, James E.** — *Vice President Operations*
Phillips Resource Group
330 Pelham Road, Building A
Greenville, SC 29615
Telephone: (864) 271-6350
**Recruiter Classification:** Contingency; **Lowest/Average Salary:**
$40,000/$50,000; **Industry Concentration:** Generalist with a primary focus in
Chemical Products, Electronics, Environmental, High Technology, Information
Technology, Manufacturing, Packaging, Utilities/Nuclear; **Function
Concentration:** Generalist with a primary focus in Administration, Engineering,
General Management, Human Resources, Marketing, Research and
Development, Sales, Women/Minorities

**Bostick, Tim** — *Consultant*
Paul Ray Berndtson
301 Commerce Street, Suite 2300
Fort Worth, TX 76102
Telephone: (817) 334-0500
**Recruiter Classification:** Retained; **Lowest/Average Salary:** $90,000/$90,000;
**Industry Concentration:** Generalist; **Function Concentration:** Generalist

**Bosward, Allan** — *Associate*
Source Services Corporation
1290 Oakmead Parkway, Suite 318
Sunnyvale, CA 94086
Telephone: (408) 738-8440
**Recruiter Classification:** Contingency; **Lowest/Average Salary:**
$30,000/$50,000; **Industry Concentration:** Financial Services, Information
Technology; **Function Concentration:** Engineering, Finance/Accounting

**Bothereau, Elizabeth A.** — *Vice President*
Kenzer Corp.
Fifth Street Tower, Suite 1330
150 South Fifth Street
Minneapolis, MN 55402
Telephone: (612) 332-7700
**Recruiter Classification:** Retained; **Lowest/Average Salary:** $50,000/$90,000;
**Industry Concentration:** Generalist; **Function Concentration:** Generalist

**Boucher, Greg** — *Recruiting Manager*
Southwestern Professional Services
2451 Atrium Way
Nashville, TN 37214
Telephone: (615) 391-2722
**Recruiter Classification:** Contingency; **Lowest/Average Salary:**
$20,000/$20,000; **Industry Concentration:** Generalist; **Function
Concentration:** Generalist with a primary focus in Sales

**Bouer, Judy** — *Principal*
Baker Scott & Company
1259 Route 46
Parsippany, NJ 07054
Telephone: (201) 263-3355
**Recruiter Classification:** Contingency; **Lowest/Average Salary:** $50,000/$75,000;
**Industry Concentration:** Generalist; **Function Concentration:** Generalist

**Bourbeau, Paul J.** — *Managing Director*
Boyden
1250, boul. Rene-Levesque ouest
Bureau 4110
Montreal, Quebec, CANADA H3B 4W8
Telephone: (514) 935-4560
**Recruiter Classification:** Retained; **Lowest/Average Salary:** $75,000/$90,000;
**Industry Concentration:** Generalist; **Function Concentration:** Generalist with a
primary focus in Engineering, Finance/Accounting, General Management, Human
Resources, Marketing, Research and Development, Sales, Women/Minorities

**Bourbonnais, Jean-Pierre** — *Managing Partner*
Ward Howell International, Inc.
420 McGill Street, Room 400
Montreal, Quebec, CANADA H2Y 2G1
Telephone: (514) 397-9655
**Recruiter Classification:** Retained; **Lowest/Average Salary:** $75,000/$90,000;
**Industry Concentration:** Generalist; **Function Concentration:** Generalist

**Bourque, Jack J.** — *Manager Eastern Region*
Management Recruiters International, Inc.
140 Willow Street, Suite 6, P.O. Box 1017
Winsted, CT 06098-1017
Telephone: (860) 738-5035
**Recruiter Classification:** Contingency; **Lowest/Average Salary:** $30,000/$75,000;
**Industry Concentration:** Generalist; **Function Concentration:** Generalist

**Bourrie, Sharon D.** — *Director*
Chartwell Partners International, Inc.
275 Battery Street, Suite 2180
San Francisco, CA 94111
Telephone: (415) 296-0600
**Recruiter Classification:** Retained; **Lowest/Average Salary:** $90,000/$90,000;
**Industry Concentration:** Generalist with a primary focus in Board Services,
Consumer Products, Financial Services, High Technology, Information
Technology, Insurance, Real Estate, Transportation, Venture Capital; **Function
Concentration:** Generalist with a primary focus in Finance/Accounting,
General Management, Human Resources, Marketing, Women/Minorities

**Bovee, Camille** — *Account Executive*
Search West, Inc.
340 North Westlake Boulevard
Suite 200
Westlake Village, CA 91362-3761
Telephone: (805) 496-6811
**Recruiter Classification:** Contingency; **Lowest/Average Salary:**
$40,000/$60,000; **Industry Concentration:** Fashion (Retail/Apparel); **Function
Concentration:** Administration, Marketing

**Bovich, Maryann C.** — *Principal*
Higdon Prince Inc.
230 Park Avenue, Suite 1455
New York, NY 10169
Telephone: (212) 986-4662
**Recruiter Classification:** Retained; **Lowest/Average Salary:** $90,000/$90,000;
**Industry Concentration:** Generalist with a primary focus in Biotechnology,
Board Services, Consumer Products, Energy, Financial Services,
Healthcare/Hospitals, Information Technology, Manufacturing, Oil/Gas,
Packaging, Venture Capital; **Function Concentration:** Generalist with a primary
focus in Finance/Accounting, General Management, Marketing, Sales,
Women/Minorities

**Bowen, Tad** — *Vice President*
Executive Search International
60 Walnut Street
Wellesley, MA 02181
Telephone: (617) 239-0303
**Recruiter Classification:** Retained; **Lowest/Average Salary:** $75,000/$90,000;
**Industry Concentration:** Generalist with a primary focus in Financial Services,
Healthcare/Hospitals, High Technology, Transportation; **Function
Concentration:** Generalist with a primary focus in General Management

**Bowen, William J.** — *Vice Chairman*
Heidrick & Struggles, Inc.
125 South Wacker Drive
Suite 2800
Chicago, IL 60606-4590
Telephone: (312) 372-8811
**Recruiter Classification:** Retained; **Lowest/Average Salary:** $75,000/$90,000;
**Industry Concentration:** Generalist with a primary focus in Education/Libraries,
Healthcare/Hospitals, Non-Profit; **Function Concentration:** Generalist

**Boxberger, Michael D.** — *President*
Korn/Ferry International
120 South Riverside Plaza
Suite 918
Chicago, IL 60606
Telephone: (312) 726-1841
**Recruiter Classification:** Retained; **Lowest/Average Salary:** $90,000/$90,000;
**Industry Concentration:** Generalist with a primary focus in Board Services,
Energy; **Function Concentration:** Generalist

**Boyd, Michael** — *Branch Manager*
Accountants on Call
2099 Gateway Place, Suite 440
San Jose, CA 95110
Telephone: (408) 437-9779
**Recruiter Classification:** Contingency; **Lowest/Average Salary:**
$20,000/$30,000; **Industry Concentration:** Generalist; **Function
Concentration:** Finance/Accounting

**Boyd, Sara** — *Area Director*
Accountants on Call
7677 Oakport Street, Suite 180
Oakland, CA 94621
Telephone: (510) 633-1665
**Recruiter Classification:** Contingency; **Lowest/Average Salary:**
$20,000/$30,000; **Industry Concentration:** Generalist; **Function
Concentration:** Finance/Accounting

**Boyd, Sara** — *Area Director*
Accountants on Call
44 Montgomery Street, Suite 1250
San Francisco, CA 94104
Telephone: (415) 398-3366
**Recruiter Classification:** Contingency; **Lowest/Average Salary:**
$20,000/$30,000; **Industry Concentration:** Generalist; **Function
Concentration:** Finance/Accounting

**Boyer, Dennis M.** — *Partner*
Heidrick & Struggles, Inc.
300 South Grand Avenue, Suite 2400
Los Angeles, CA 90071
Telephone: (213) 625-8811
**Recruiter Classification:** Retained; **Lowest/Average Salary:** $75,000/$90,000;
**Industry Concentration:** Generalist with a primary focus in Consumer
Products, Hospitality/Leisure; **Function Concentration:** Generalist

**Boyer, Heath C.** — *Senior Director*
Spencer Stuart
2005 Market Street, Suite 2350
Philadelphia, PA 19103
Telephone: (215) 851-6200
**Recruiter Classification:** Retained; **Lowest/Average Salary:** $90,000/$90,000;
**Industry Concentration:** Generalist with a primary focus in Chemical Products,
Consumer Products, Healthcare/Hospitals, Manufacturing, Packaging,
Pharmaceutical/Medical, Utilities/Nuclear, Venture Capital; **Function
Concentration:** Generalist with a primary focus in Finance/Accounting,
General Management, Human Resources, Marketing

**Boyle, Russell E.** — *Consultant*
Egon Zehnder International Inc.
55 East 59th Street, 14th Floor
New York, NY 10022
Telephone: (212) 838-9199
**Recruiter Classification:** Retained; **Lowest/Average Salary:** $90,000/$90,000;
**Industry Concentration:** Generalist with a primary focus in Biotechnology,
Financial Services, High Technology, Manufacturing, Pharmaceutical/Medical;
**Function Concentration:** Generalist

**Braak, Diana** — *Managing Associate*
Kincannon & Reed
2106-C Gallows Road
Vienna, VA 22182
Telephone: (703) 761-4046
**Recruiter Classification:** Retained; **Lowest/Average Salary:** $90,000/$90,000;
**Industry Concentration:** Biotechnology; **Function Concentration:** Generalist

**Brackenbury, Robert** — *Financial Recruiter*
Bowman & Marshall, Inc.
P.O. Box 25503
Overland Park, KS 66225
Telephone: (913) 648-3332
**Recruiter Classification:** Contingency; **Lowest/Average Salary:**
$30,000/$50,000; **Industry Concentration:** Automotive, Chemical Products,
Consumer Products, Fashion (Retail/Apparel), Financial Services, Insurance,
Manufacturing, Packaging, Pharmaceutical/Medical, Publishing/Media;
**Function Concentration:** Finance/Accounting

**Brackin, James B.** — *Partner*
Brackin & Sayers Associates
1000 McKnight Park Drive, Suite 1001
Pittsburgh, PA 15237
Telephone: (412) 367-4644
**Recruiter Classification:** Contingency; **Lowest/Average Salary:**
$30,000/$60,000; **Industry Concentration:** Generalist with a primary focus in
Chemical Products, Consumer Products, Electronics, Energy, Financial
Services, Healthcare/Hospitals, High Technology, Information Technology,
Manufacturing, Packaging, Pharmaceutical/Medical, Publishing/Media,
Transportation; **Function Concentration:** Generalist with a primary focus in
Administration, Finance/Accounting, General Management, Human Resources,
Marketing, Sales

**Bradshaw, John W.** — *Vice President*
A.T. Kearney, Inc.
3050 Post Oak Boulevard, Suite 570
Houston, TX 77056
Telephone: (713) 621-9967
**Recruiter Classification:** Retained; **Lowest/Average Salary:** $90,000/$90,000;
**Industry Concentration:** Generalist with a primary focus in Energy; **Function
Concentration:** Generalist with a primary focus in Engineering, Marketing,
Research and Development, Sales

**Bradshaw, Monte** — *Vice President*
Christian & Timbers
One Corporate Exchange
25825 Science Park Drive, Suite 400
Cleveland, OH 44122
Telephone: (216) 464-8710
**Recruiter Classification:** Retained; **Lowest/Average Salary:** $90,000/$90,000;
**Industry Concentration:** Generalist; **Function Concentration:** Generalist

**Brady, Colin S.** — *Managing Director*
Ward Howell International, Inc.
3350 Peachtree Road N.E.
Suite 1600
Atlanta, GA 30326
Telephone: (404) 261-6532
**Recruiter Classification:** Retained; **Lowest/Average Salary:** $75,000/$90,000;
**Industry Concentration:** Automotive, Chemical Products, Manufacturing,
Transportation; **Function Concentration:** Generalist with a primary focus in
General Management

**Brady, Robert** — *Executive Recruiter*
CPS Inc.
One Westbrook Corporate Centre, Suite 600
Westchester, IL 60154
Telephone: (708) 531-8370
**Recruiter Classification:** Contingency; **Lowest/Average Salary:**
$30,000/$50,000; **Industry Concentration:** Generalist with a primary focus in
Automotive, Biotechnology, Chemical Products, Consumer Products, High
Technology, Insurance, Manufacturing, Oil/Gas, Packaging,
Pharmaceutical/Medical; **Function Concentration:** Engineering, Research and
Development, Sales, Women/Minorities

**Bragg, Garry** — *Vice President*
The McCormick Group, Inc.
9401 Way Point Place
Jacksonville, FL 32257
Telephone: (904) 739-0760
**Recruiter Classification:** Retained, Contingency; **Lowest/Average Salary:**
$50,000/$60,000; **Industry Concentration:** High Technology, Information
Technology; **Function Concentration:** Engineering, Marketing, Sales

**Brand, John E.** — *Co-Manager*
Management Recruiters International, Inc.
5652-B Highway 90
Milton, FL 32583
Telephone: (904) 626-3303
**Recruiter Classification:** Contingency; **Lowest/Average Salary:**
$30,000/$75,000; **Industry Concentration:** Generalist; **Function
Concentration:** Generalist

**Brand, Karen M.** — *Co-Manager South Atlantic Region*
Management Recruiters International, Inc.
5652-B Highway 90
Milton, FL 32583
Telephone: (904) 626-3303
**Recruiter Classification:** Contingency; **Lowest/Average Salary:**
$30,000/$75,000; **Industry Concentration:** Generalist; **Function
Concentration:** Generalist

**Brandeis, Richard** — *Executive Recruiter*
CPS Inc.
One Westbrook Corporate Centre, Suite 600
Westchester, IL 60154
Telephone: (708) 531-8370
**Recruiter Classification:** Contingency; **Lowest/Average Salary:**
$30,000/$50,000; **Industry Concentration:** Generalist with a primary focus in
Automotive, Biotechnology, Chemical Products, Consumer Products, High
Technology, Insurance, Manufacturing, Oil/Gas, Packaging,
Pharmaceutical/Medical; **Function Concentration:** Engineering, Research and
Development, Sales, Women/Minorities

**Brandjes, Michael J.** — *Principal*
Brandjes Associates
16 South Calvert Street
Suite 500
Baltimore, MD 21202
Telephone: (410) 547-6886
**Recruiter Classification:** Contingency; **Lowest/Average Salary:**
$50,000/$75,000; **Industry Concentration:** Financial Services; **Function
Concentration:** Generalist with a primary focus in Administration,
Finance/Accounting, General Management, Human Resources, Marketing,
Research and Development

**Brandon, Irwin** — *President*
Hadley Lockwood, Inc.
17 State Street, 38th Floor
New York, NY 10004
Telephone: (212) 785-4405
**Recruiter Classification:** Retained; **Lowest/Average Salary:** $90,000/$90,000;
**Industry Concentration:** Financial Services; **Function Concentration:**
Generalist

**Brandt, Brian S.** — *Director Business Development*
The Paladin Companies, Inc.
875 North Michigan Avenue, Suite 3218
Chicago, IL 60611
Telephone: (312) 654-2600
**Recruiter Classification:** Executive Temporary; **Lowest/Average Salary:**
$50,000/$90,000; **Industry Concentration:** Generalist; **Function
Concentration:** Marketing

**Brassard, Gary** — *Associate*
Source Services Corporation
111 Monument Circle, Suite 3930
Indianapolis, IN 46204
Telephone: (317) 631-2900
**Recruiter Classification:** Contingency; **Lowest/Average Salary:**
$30,000/$50,000; **Industry Concentration:** Financial Services, Information
Technology; **Function Concentration:** Engineering, Finance/Accounting

**Brassard, Phillipe** — *Associate*
KPMG Executive Search
1155 Rene-Levesque Boulevard
Montreal, Quebec, CANADA H3B 2J9
Telephone: (514) 875-9123
**Recruiter Classification:** Retained; **Lowest/Average Salary:** $75,000/$90,000;
**Industry Concentration:** Generalist; **Function Concentration:** Generalist

**Bratches, Howard** — *Senior Partner*
Thorndike Deland Associates
275 Madison Avenue, Suite 1300
New York, NY 10016
Telephone: (212) 661-6200
**Recruiter Classification:** Retained; **Lowest/Average Salary:** $75,000/$90,000;
**Industry Concentration:** Generalist with a primary focus in Board Services,
Consumer Products, Entertainment, Fashion (Retail/Apparel), Financial
Services, Healthcare/Hospitals, Hospitality/Leisure, Information Technology,
Insurance, Manufacturing, Pharmaceutical/Medical, Publishing/Media, Venture
Capital; **Function Concentration:** Generalist with a primary focus in
Finance/Accounting, General Management, Human Resources, Marketing,
Sales

**Braun, Jerold** — *Principal*
Jerold Braun & Associates
P.O. Box 67C13
Los Angeles, CA 90067
Telephone: (310) 203-0515
**Recruiter Classification:** Contingency; **Lowest/Average Salary:**
$50,000/$75,000; **Industry Concentration:** Fashion (Retail/Apparel); **Function
Concentration:** Generalist

**Brazil, Kathy** — *Research Associate*
Bryant Research
466 Old Hook Road, Suite 32
Emerson, NJ 07630
Telephone: (201) 599-0590
**Recruiter Classification:** Contingency; **Lowest/Average Salary:**
$50,000/$90,000; **Industry Concentration:** Biotechnology,
Pharmaceutical/Medical; **Function Concentration:** Research and Development

**Breault, Larry J.** — *Manager South Atlantic Region*
Management Recruiters International, Inc.
756 SE Port St. Lucie Boulevard
Port St. Lucie, FL 34984
Telephone: (561) 871-1100
**Recruiter Classification:** Contingency; **Lowest/Average Salary:**
$30,000/$75,000; **Industry Concentration:** Generalist; **Function
Concentration:** Generalist

**Bremer, Brian** — *Associate*
Source Services Corporation
5 Independence Way
Princeton, NJ 08540
Telephone: (609) 452-7277
**Recruiter Classification:** Contingency; **Lowest/Average Salary:**
$30,000/$50,000; **Industry Concentration:** Financial Services, Information
Technology; **Function Concentration:** Engineering, Finance/Accounting

**Brennan, Jerry** — *President*
Brennan Associates
P.O. Box 29026
Dallas, TX 75229
Telephone: (214) 351-6005
**Recruiter Classification:** Contingency; **Lowest/Average Salary:**
$50,000/$60,000; **Industry Concentration:** Automotive, Manufacturing;
**Function Concentration:** General Management, Marketing, Sales

**Brennan, Patrick J.** — *Managing Director and COO*
Handy HRM Corp.
250 Park Avenue
New York, NY 10177-0074
Telephone: (212) 557-0400
**Recruiter Classification:** Retained; **Lowest/Average Salary:** $90,000/$90,000;
**Industry Concentration:** Generalist with a primary focus in Financial Services;
**Function Concentration:** Generalist with a primary focus in General
Management, Marketing

**Brennan, Timothy** — *Vice President*
Brennan Associates
P.O. Box 29026
Dallas, TX 75229
Telephone: (214) 351-6005
**Recruiter Classification:** Contingency; **Lowest/Average Salary:**
$50,000/$60,000; **Industry Concentration:** Automotive, Manufacturing;
**Function Concentration:** Research and Development, Sales

**Brennan, Vincent F.** — *Vice President*
Korn/Ferry International
237 Park Avenue
New York, NY 10017
Telephone: (212) 687-1834
**Recruiter Classification:** Retained; **Lowest/Average Salary:** $90,000/$90,000;
**Industry Concentration:** Generalist; **Function Concentration:** Generalist

**Brennecke, Richard C.** — *Manager North Atlantic Region*
Management Recruiters International, Inc.
330 Pelham Road, Suite 109B
Greenville, SC 29615
Telephone: (864) 370-1341
**Recruiter Classification:** Contingency; **Lowest/Average Salary:**
$30,000/$75,000; **Industry Concentration:** Generalist; **Function
Concentration:** Generalist

**Brennen, Richard J.** — *Senior Director*
Spencer Stuart
401 North Michigan Avenue, Suite 3400
Chicago, IL 60611-4204
Telephone: (312) 822-0080
**Recruiter Classification:** Retained; **Lowest/Average Salary:** $90,000/$90,000;
**Industry Concentration:** Generalist with a primary focus in High Technology,
Information Technology; **Function Concentration:** General Management,
Research and Development, Sales

**Brenner, Mary** — *Recruiter*
Prestige Inc.
P.O. Box 421
Reedsburg, WI 53959
Telephone: (608) 524-4032
**Recruiter Classification:** Contingency; **Lowest/Average Salary:**
$50,000/$90,000; **Industry Concentration:** Automotive, Consumer Products,
Financial Services, Healthcare/Hospitals, Insurance, Manufacturing; **Function
Concentration:** Generalist

**Brenner, Michael** — *Partner*
Lamalie Amrop International
200 Park Avenue
New York, NY 10166-0136
Telephone: (212) 953-7900
**Recruiter Classification:** Retained; **Lowest/Average Salary:** $90,000/$90,000;
**Industry Concentration:** Generalist; **Function Concentration:** Generalist with a
primary focus in General Management, Marketing, Sales

**Brent, Art** — *Vice President*
Goodrich & Sherwood Associates, Inc.
250 Mill Street
Rochester, NY 14614
Telephone: (716) 777-4060
**Recruiter Classification:** Retained; **Lowest/Average Salary:** $60,000/$90,000;
**Industry Concentration:** Generalist; **Function Concentration:** Generalist

**Brentari, Michael** — *Senior Consultant*
Search Consultants International, Inc.
4545 Post Oak Place, Suite 208
Houston, TX 77027
Telephone: (713) 622-9188
**Recruiter Classification:** Contingency, Executive Temporary; **Lowest/Average
Salary:** $60,000/$75,000; **Industry Concentration:** Chemical Products, Energy,
Environmental, Manufacturing, Oil/Gas; **Function Concentration:** Engineering,
General Management, Marketing, Research and Development

**Brenzel, John A.** — *Partner*
TASA International
Hurstbourne Place
9300 Shelbyville Road
Louisville, KY 40222
Telephone: (502) 426-3500
**Recruiter Classification:** Retained; **Lowest/Average Salary:** $90,000/$90,000;
**Industry Concentration:** Generalist; **Function Concentration:** Generalist

**Brewster, Edward** — *Associate*
Source Services Corporation
9020 Capital of Texas Highway
Building I, Suite 337
Austin, TX 78759
Telephone: (512) 345-7473
**Recruiter Classification:** Contingency; **Lowest/Average Salary:**
$30,000/$50,000; **Industry Concentration:** Financial Services, Information
Technology; **Function Concentration:** Engineering, Finance/Accounting

**Brieger, Steve** — *Principal*
Thorne, Brieger Associates Inc.
11 East 44th Street
New York, NY 10017
Telephone: (212) 682-5424
**Recruiter Classification:** Retained; **Lowest/Average Salary:** $90,000/$90,000;
**Industry Concentration:** Generalist with a primary focus in Biotechnology,
Chemical Products, Consumer Products, Electronics, Financial Services,
Healthcare/Hospitals, High Technology, Manufacturing, Packaging;
**Function Concentration:** Generalist with a primary focus in Administration,
Engineering, Finance/Accounting, General Management, Human Resources,
Marketing, Research and Development, Sales

**Briggs, Adam** — *Vice President*
Horton International
10 Tower Lane
Avon, CT 06001
Telephone: (860) 674-8701
**Recruiter Classification:** Retained; **Lowest/Average Salary:** $90,000/$90,000;
**Industry Concentration:** Generalist with a primary focus in
Aerospace/Defense, Automotive, Chemical Products, Consumer Products,
Electronics, High Technology, Oil/Gas, Transportation; **Function
Concentration:** Generalist with a primary focus in Engineering,
Finance/Accounting, General Management, Human Resources, Marketing,
Research and Development

**Bright, Timothy** — *Executive Recruiter*
MSI International
5215 North O'Connor Boulevard
Suite 1875
Irving, TX 75039
Telephone: (214) 869-3939
**Recruiter Classification:** Contingency; **Lowest/Average Salary:**
$30,000/$75,000; **Industry Concentration:** Generalist with a primary focus in
Manufacturing; **Function Concentration:** Generalist with a primary focus in
Administration, Engineering, Finance/Accounting, General Management,
Marketing, Sales

**Brindise, Michael J.** — *Partner*
Dynamic Search Systems, Inc.
3800 North Wilke Road, Suite 485
Arlington Heights, IL 60004
Telephone: (847) 259-3444
**Recruiter Classification:** Contingency; **Lowest/Average Salary:**
$30,000/$60,000; **Industry Concentration:** Generalist with a primary focus in
Information Technology; **Function Concentration:** Generalist

**Brink, James** — *Senior Vice President*
Noble & Associates Inc.
420 Madison Avenue
New York, NY 10017
Telephone: (212) 838-7020
**Recruiter Classification:** Contingency; **Lowest/Average Salary:**
$40,000/$90,000; **Industry Concentration:** Generalist; **Function
Concentration:** Marketing

**Brinson, Robert** — *Executive Recruiter*
MSI International
229 Peachtree Street, NE
Suite 1201
Atlanta, GA 30303
Telephone: (404) 659-5050
**Recruiter Classification:** Contingency; **Lowest/Average Salary:**
$30,000/$60,000; **Industry Concentration:** Generalist with a primary focus in
Financial Services; **Function Concentration:** Administration, Engineering,
Finance/Accounting, General Management, Marketing

**Briody, Steve** — *Manager Midwest Region*
Management Recruiters International, Inc.
Arlington Heights Office Center
3413-A North Kennicot Avenue
Arlington Heights, IL 60004
Telephone: (847) 590-8880
**Recruiter Classification:** Contingency; **Lowest/Average Salary:**
$30,000/$75,000; **Industry Concentration:** Generalist; **Function
Concentration:** Generalist

**Broadhurst, Austin** — *Managing Director*
Russell Reynolds Associates, Inc.
200 Park Avenue
New York, NY 10166-0002
Telephone: (212) 351-2000
**Recruiter Classification:** Retained; **Lowest/Average Salary:** $90,000/$90,000;
**Industry Concentration:** Healthcare/Hospitals; **Function Concentration:**
Generalist

**Brocaglia, Joyce** — *Vice President*
Alta Associates, Inc.
8 Bartles Corner Road, Suite 021
Flemington, NJ 08822
Telephone: (908) 806-8442
**Recruiter Classification:** Retained; **Lowest/Average Salary:** $50,000/$90,000;
**Industry Concentration:** Generalist with a primary focus in Chemical Products,
Entertainment, Financial Services, High Technology, Information Technology,
Insurance, Manufacturing, Pharmaceutical/Medical, Publishing/Media, Venture
Capital; **Function Concentration:** Finance/Accounting

**Brock, John** — *Managing Vice President*
Korn/Ferry International
1100 Louisiana, Suite 3400
Houston, TX 77002
Telephone: (713) 651-1834
**Recruiter Classification:** Retained; **Lowest/Average Salary:** $90,000/$90,000;
**Industry Concentration:** Generalist; **Function Concentration:** Generalist

**Brock, Rufus C.** — *Manager South Atlantic Region*
Management Recruiters International, Inc.
3623 Demetropolis Road, Suite 6-C
Mobile, AL 36693
Telephone: (334) 602-0104
**Recruiter Classification:** Contingency; **Lowest/Average Salary:**
$30,000/$75,000; **Industry Concentration:** Generalist; **Function
Concentration:** Generalist

**Brockman, Dan B.** — *Owner*
Dan B. Brockman Recruiters
P.O. Box 913
Barrington, IL 60011
Telephone: (847) 382-6015
**Recruiter Classification:** Contingency; **Lowest/Average Salary:**
$40,000/$50,000; **Industry Concentration:** Generalist; **Function
Concentration:** Engineering

**Brodie, Ricki R.** — *Executive Recruiter*
MSI International
200 Galleria Parkway
Suite 1610
Atlanta, GA 30339
Telephone: (404) 951-1208
**Recruiter Classification:** Contingency; **Lowest/Average Salary:**
$30,000/$60,000; **Industry Concentration:** Generalist with a primary focus in
Healthcare/Hospitals; **Function Concentration:** Administration, Engineering,
Finance/Accounting, General Management, Marketing

**Bronger, Patricia** — *Associate*
Source Services Corporation
500 108th Avenue NE, Suite 1780
Bellevue, WA 98004
Telephone: (206) 454-6400
**Recruiter Classification:** Contingency; **Lowest/Average Salary:**
$30,000/$50,000; **Industry Concentration:** Financial Services, Information
Technology; **Function Concentration:** Engineering, Finance/Accounting

**Brooks, Bernard E.** — *Partner*
Mruk & Partners/EMA Partners Int'l
675 Third Avenue, Suite 1805
New York, NY 10017
Telephone: (212) 983-7676
**Recruiter Classification:** Retained; **Lowest/Average Salary:** $75,000/$90,000;
**Industry Concentration:** Biotechnology, Education/Libraries,
Healthcare/Hospitals, Information Technology; **Function Concentration:**
Generalist

**Brooks, Charles** — *Recruiter*
Corporate Recruiters Ltd.
490-1140 West Pender
Vancouver, British Columbia, CANADA V6E 4G1
Telephone: (604) 687-5993
**Recruiter Classification:** Contingency; **Lowest/Average Salary:**
$40,000/$60,000; **Industry Concentration:** Aerospace/Defense, Electronics,
High Technology, Information Technology; **Function Concentration:**
Engineering

**Brooks, Kimberllay** — *Manager Electronic Engineering*
Corporate Recruiters Ltd.
490-1140 West Pender
Vancouver, British Columbia, CANADA V6E 4G1
Telephone: (604) 687-5993
**Recruiter Classification:** Contingency; **Lowest/Average Salary:**
$50,000/$60,000; **Industry Concentration:** Electronics; **Function
Concentration:** Engineering, Research and Development

**Brooks, Natalie** — *Principal*
Raymond Karsan Associates
348 Wall Street
Princeton, NJ 08540
Telephone: (609) 252-0999
**Recruiter Classification:** Contingency; **Lowest/Average Salary:**
$30,000/$90,000; **Industry Concentration:** Generalist with a primary focus in
Pharmaceutical/Medical; **Function Concentration:** Generalist with a primary
focus in Human Resources

**Brophy, Melissa** — *President*
Maximum Management Corp.
420 Lexington Avenue
Suite 2016
New York, NY 10170
Telephone: (212) 867-4646
**Recruiter Classification:** Contingency, Executive Temporary; **Lowest/Average
Salary:** $30,000/$75,000; **Industry Concentration:** Generalist with a primary
focus in Consumer Products, Entertainment, Financial Services, Information
Technology, Insurance, Manufacturing, Pharmaceutical/Medical,
Publishing/Media; **Function Concentration:** Human Resources

**Brovender, Claire** — *Software Engineering Recruiter*
Winter, Wyman & Company
950 Winter Street, Suite 3100
Waltham, MA 02154-1294
Telephone: (617) 890-7000
**Recruiter Classification:** Contingency; **Lowest/Average Salary:**
$40,000/$75,000; **Industry Concentration:** High Technology, Information
Technology, Publishing/Media; **Function Concentration:** Engineering

**Brown, Arlene** — *Co-Manager*
Management Recruiters International, Inc.
2600 Maitland Center Parkway, Suite 295
Maitland, FL 32751-7227
Telephone: (407) 660-0089
**Recruiter Classification:** Contingency; **Lowest/Average Salary:**
$30,000/$75,000; **Industry Concentration:** Generalist; **Function
Concentration:** Generalist

**Brown, Buzz** — *President*
Brown, Bernardy, Van Remmen, Inc.
12100 Wilshire Boulevard, Suite M-40
Los Angeles, CA 90025
Telephone: (310) 826-5777
**Recruiter Classification:** Contingency; **Lowest/Average Salary:**
$30,000/$75,000; **Industry Concentration:** Automotive, Consumer Products,
Electronics, Entertainment, Fashion (Retail/Apparel), Financial Services,
Healthcare/Hospitals, High Technology, Hospitality/Leisure, Non-Profit,
Publishing/Media; **Function Concentration:** Marketing

**Brown, Charlene N.** — *President*
Accent on Achievement, Inc.
3190 Rochester Road, Suite 104
Troy, MI 48083
Telephone: (810) 528-1390
**Recruiter Classification:** Contingency, Executive Temporary; **Lowest/Average
Salary:** $30,000/$50,000; **Industry Concentration:** Automotive, Consumer
Products, Financial Services, Healthcare/Hospitals, High Technology,
Information Technology, Manufacturing, Utilities/Nuclear; **Function
Concentration:** Administration, Finance/Accounting, Human Resources,
Marketing, Women/Minorities

**Brown, Clifford** — *Associate*
Source Services Corporation
111 Founders Plaza, Suite 1501E
Hartford, CT 06108
Telephone: (860) 528-0300
**Recruiter Classification:** Contingency; **Lowest/Average Salary:**
$30,000/$50,000; **Industry Concentration:** Financial Services, Information
Technology; **Function Concentration:** Engineering, Finance/Accounting

**Brown, D. Perry** — *Partner*
Don Richard Associates of Washington, D.C., Inc.
5 Choke Cherry Road, Suite 378
Rockville, MD 20850
Telephone: (301) 590-9800
**Recruiter Classification:** Contingency, Executive Temporary; **Lowest/Average
Salary:** $30,000/$60,000; **Industry Concentration:** Financial Services,
Healthcare/Hospitals, High Technology, Hospitality/Leisure, Manufacturing,
Non-Profit, Real Estate, Utilities/Nuclear; **Function Concentration:**
Finance/Accounting

**Brown, Daniel** — *Associate*
Source Services Corporation
500 108th Avenue NE, Suite 1780
Bellevue, WA 98004
Telephone: (206) 454-6400
**Recruiter Classification:** Contingency; **Lowest/Average Salary:**
$30,000/$50,000; **Industry Concentration:** Financial Services, Information
Technology; **Function Concentration:** Engineering, Finance/Accounting

**Brown, David** — *Managing Director*
Korn/Ferry International
237 Park Avenue
New York, NY 10017
Telephone: (212) 687-1834
**Recruiter Classification:** Retained; **Lowest/Average Salary:** $90,000/$90,000;
**Industry Concentration:** Generalist with a primary focus in Fashion
(Retail/Apparel); **Function Concentration:** Generalist

**Brown, David C.** — *Executive Director*
Russell Reynolds Associates, Inc.
200 South Wacker Drive
Suite 3600
Chicago, IL 60606
Telephone: (312) 993-9696
**Recruiter Classification:** Retained; **Lowest/Average Salary:** $90,000/$90,000;
**Industry Concentration:** Generalist; **Function Concentration:** Generalist

**Brown, Debra J.** — *Managing Director*
Norman Broadbent International, Inc.
200 Park Avenue, 20th Floor
New York, NY 10166
Telephone: (212) 953-6990
**Recruiter Classification:** Retained; **Lowest/Average Salary:** $90,000/$90,000;
**Industry Concentration:** Generalist with a primary focus in Financial Services;
**Function Concentration:** Generalist

**Brown, Floyd** — *Executive Recruiter*
Richard, Wayne and Roberts
24 Greenway Plaza, Suite 1304
Houston, TX 77046-2493
Telephone: (713) 629-6681
**Recruiter Classification:** Retained; **Lowest/Average Salary:** $40,000/$60,000;
**Industry Concentration:** Generalist; **Function Concentration:** Generalist

**Brown, Franklin Key** — *Executive Vice President and
Managing Director*
Handy HRM Corp.
250 Park Avenue
New York, NY 10177-0074
Telephone: (212) 557-0400
**Recruiter Classification:** Retained; **Lowest/Average Salary:** $90,000/$90,000;
**Industry Concentration:** Generalist with a primary focus in Board Services,
Financial Services; **Function Concentration:** Finance/Accounting, General
Management, Research and Development

**Brown, Hobson** — *President and CEO*
Russell Reynolds Associates, Inc.
200 Park Avenue
New York, NY 10166-0002
Telephone: (212) 351-2000
**Recruiter Classification:** Retained; **Lowest/Average Salary:** $90,000/$90,000;
**Industry Concentration:** Generalist; **Function Concentration:** Generalist

**Brown, Jeffrey W.** — *President*
Comprehensive Search
316 South Lewis Street
LaGrange, GA 30240
Telephone: (706) 884-3232
**Recruiter Classification:** Contingency, Executive Temporary; **Lowest/Average
Salary:** $50,000/$75,000; **Industry Concentration:** Consumer Products,
Fashion (Retail/Apparel), Hospitality/Leisure, Manufacturing, Public
Administration; **Function Concentration:** Generalist

**Brown, John T.** — *Manager Eastern Region*
Management Recruiters International, Inc.
Melrose Square, Suite 102
100 Melrose Avenue
Greenwich, CT 06830-6213
Telephone: (203) 861-2235
**Recruiter Classification:** Contingency; **Lowest/Average Salary:**
$30,000/$75,000; **Industry Concentration:** Generalist; **Function
Concentration:** Generalist

**Brown, Kelly A.** — *Associate*
Russell Reynolds Associates, Inc.
200 South Wacker Drive
Suite 3600
Chicago, IL 60606
Telephone: (312) 993-9696
**Recruiter Classification:** Retained; **Lowest/Average Salary:** $90,000/$90,000;
**Industry Concentration:** Generalist with a primary focus in Consumer
Products; **Function Concentration:** Generalist

**Brown, Kevin P.** — *Senior Consultant*
Raymond Karsan Associates
989 Old Eagle School Road, Suite 814
Wayne, PA 19087
Telephone: (610) 971-9171
**Recruiter Classification:** Contingency; **Lowest/Average Salary:**
$30,000/$90,000; **Industry Concentration:** Generalist with a primary focus in
Information Technology; **Function Concentration:** Generalist

**Brown, Larry C.** — *Vice President*
Horton International
10 Tower Lane
Avon, CT 06001
Telephone: (860) 674-8701
**Recruiter Classification:** Retained; **Lowest/Average Salary:** $90,000/$90,000;
**Industry Concentration:** Generalist with a primary focus in
Aerospace/Defense, Automotive, Biotechnology, Chemical Products,
Consumer Products, Electronics, Environmental, Financial Services,
Healthcare/Hospitals, High Technology, Information Technology, Insurance,
Manufacturing, Packaging, Pharmaceutical/Medical; **Function Concentration:**
Generalist with a primary focus in Administration, Finance/Accounting,
General Management, Human Resources, Marketing, Sales

**Brown, Lawrence Anthony** — *Executive Recruiter*
MSI International
229 Peachtree Street, NE
Suite 1201
Atlanta, GA 30303
Telephone: (404) 659-5050
Recruiter Classification: Contingency; Lowest/Average Salary:
$30,000/$60,000; Industry Concentration: Generalist with a primary focus in
Financial Services; Function Concentration: Generalist with a primary focus in
Administration, Engineering, Finance/Accounting, General Management,
Marketing, Sales

**Brown, Michael R.** — *Executive Recruiter*
MSI International
1050 Crown Pointe Parkway
Suite 1000
Atlanta, GA 30338
Telephone: (404) 394-2494
Recruiter Classification: Contingency; Lowest/Average Salary:
$30,000/$60,000; Industry Concentration: Generalist with a primary focus in
Manufacturing; Function Concentration: Administration, Engineering,
Finance/Accounting, General Management, Marketing

**Brown, Ronald** — *Executive Recruiter*
Richard, Wayne and Roberts
24 Greenway Plaza, Suite 1304
Houston, TX 77046-2493
Telephone: (713) 629-6681
Recruiter Classification: Retained; Lowest/Average Salary: $50,000/$90,000;
Industry Concentration: Generalist with a primary focus in Real Estate;
Function Concentration: Generalist

**Brown, S. Ross** — *Managing Partner*
Egon Zehnder International Inc.
100 Spear Street, Suite 1135
San Francisco, CA 94105
Telephone: (415) 904-7800
Recruiter Classification: Retained; Lowest/Average Salary: $90,000/$90,000;
Industry Concentration: Generalist with a primary focus in Biotechnology,
Financial Services, High Technology, Manufacturing, Pharmaceutical/Medical;
Function Concentration: Generalist

**Brown, Sandra E.** — *Executive Recruiter*
MSI International
2170 West State Road 434
Suite 454
Longwood, FL 32779
Telephone: (407) 788-7700
Recruiter Classification: Contingency; Lowest/Average Salary:
$30,000/$75,000; Industry Concentration: Generalist with a primary focus in
Manufacturing; Function Concentration: Generalist with a primary focus in
Engineering

**Brown, Steven** — *Associate*
Source Services Corporation
5429 LBJ Freeway, Suite 275
Dallas, TX 75240
Telephone: (214) 387-1600
Recruiter Classification: Contingency; Lowest/Average Salary:
$30,000/$50,000; Industry Concentration: Financial Services, Information
Technology; Function Concentration: Engineering, Finance/Accounting

**Brown, Tom** — *Co-Manager South Atlantic Region*
Management Recruiters International, Inc.
2600 Maitland Center Parkway, Suite 295
Maitland, FL 32751-7227
Telephone: (407) 660-0089
Recruiter Classification: Contingency; Lowest/Average Salary:
$30,000/$75,000; Industry Concentration: Generalist; Function
Concentration: Generalist

**Browndyke, Chip** — *Consultant*
Paul Ray Berndtson
One Allen Center
500 Dallas, Suite 3010
Houston, TX 77002
Telephone: (713) 309-1400
Recruiter Classification: Retained; Lowest/Average Salary: $90,000/$90,000;
Industry Concentration: Generalist; Function Concentration: Generalist

**Browne, Michael** — *Associate*
Source Services Corporation
20 Burlington Mall Road, Suite 405
Burlington, MA 01803
Telephone: (617) 272-5000
Recruiter Classification: Contingency; Lowest/Average Salary:
$30,000/$50,000; Industry Concentration: Financial Services, Information
Technology; Function Concentration: Engineering, Finance/Accounting

**Bruce, Michael C.** — *Director*
Spencer Stuart
10900 Wilshire Boulevard, Suite 800
Los Angeles, CA 90024-6524
Telephone: (310) 209-0610
Recruiter Classification: Retained; Lowest/Average Salary: $90,000/$90,000;
Industry Concentration: Consumer Products, Financial Services, High
Technology, Information Technology, Insurance, Real Estate; Function
Concentration: Generalist

**Brudno, Robert J.** — *Managing Director*
Savoy Partners, Ltd.
1620 L Street N.W., Suite 801
Washington, DC 20036
Telephone: (202) 887-0666
Recruiter Classification: Retained; Lowest/Average Salary: $90,000/$90,000;
Industry Concentration: Generalist with a primary focus in
Aerospace/Defense, Biotechnology, Board Services, Consumer Products,
Electronics, Environmental, Financial Services, High Technology, Information
Technology, Manufacturing, Pharmaceutical/Medical, Publishing/Media,
Venture Capital; Function Concentration: Generalist with a primary focus in
Administration, Engineering, Finance/Accounting, General Management,
Human Resources, Marketing, Sales, Women/Minorities

**Brunelle, Francis W.H.** — *Partner*
The Caldwell Partners Amrop International
Sixty-Four Prince Arthur Avenue
Toronto, Ontario, CANADA M5R 1B4
Telephone: (416) 920-7702
Recruiter Classification: Retained; Lowest/Average Salary: $/$90,000; Industry
Concentration: Generalist with a primary focus in Biotechnology, Consumer
Products, Education/Libraries, Healthcare/Hospitals, Non-Profit,
Pharmaceutical/Medical, Public Administration; Function Concentration:
Generalist

**Brunner, Terry** — *Associate*
Source Services Corporation
2000 Town Center, Suite 850
Southfield, MI 48075
Telephone: (810) 352-6520
Recruiter Classification: Contingency; Lowest/Average Salary:
$30,000/$50,000; Industry Concentration: Financial Services, Information
Technology; Function Concentration: Engineering, Finance/Accounting

**Bruno, David A.** — *Executive Vice President Retail/*
*Managing Director*
DHR International, Inc.
11811 North Tatum, Suite 3031
Phoenix, AZ 85020
Telephone: (602) 953-7810
Recruiter Classification: Retained; Lowest/Average Salary: $60,000/$90,000;
Industry Concentration: Generalist; Function Concentration: Generalist

**Bruno, Deborah F.** — *Vice President*
The Hindman Company
Browenton Place, Suite 110
2000 Warrington Way
Louisville, KY 40222
Telephone: (502) 426-4040
Recruiter Classification: Retained; Lowest/Average Salary: $50,000/$90,000;
Industry Concentration: Generalist with a primary focus in
Aerospace/Defense, Automotive, Chemical Products, Consumer Products,
Electronics, Financial Services, High Technology, Manufacturing, Oil/Gas,
Pharmaceutical/Medical, Transportation; Function Concentration: Generalist

**Brunson, Therese** — *Principal*
Kors Montgomery International
1980 Post Oak Boulevard, Suite 2280
Houston, TX 77042
Telephone: (713) 840-7101
Recruiter Classification: Retained; Lowest/Average Salary: $90,000/$90,000;
Industry Concentration: Energy, Information Technology; Function
Concentration: Engineering, General Management, Marketing, Sales

**Bryant, Christopher P.** — *Partner*
Ast/Bryant
2716 Ocean Park Boulevard, Suite 3001
Santa Monica, CA 90405
Telephone: (310) 314-2424
Recruiter Classification: Retained; Lowest/Average Salary: $75,000/$90,000;
Industry Concentration: Education/Libraries, Environmental,
Healthcare/Hospitals, Non-Profit; Function Concentration: Women/Minorities

**Bryant, Henry** — *Consultant Accounting and Finance*
D. Brown and Associates, Inc.
610 S.W. Alder, Suite 1111
Portland, OR 97205
Telephone: (503) 224-6860
Recruiter Classification: Contingency; Lowest/Average Salary:
$40,000/$50,000; Industry Concentration: Healthcare/Hospitals; Function
Concentration: Finance/Accounting

**Bryant, Richard D.** — *President*
Bryant Associates, Inc.
1390 The Point
Barrington, IL 60010
Telephone: (847) 382-0795
**Recruiter Classification:** Contingency; **Lowest/Average Salary:**
$40,000/$75,000; **Industry Concentration:** Generalist with a primary focus in
Aerospace/Defense, Automotive, Biotechnology, Chemical Products,
Consumer Products, Electronics, Energy, Environmental, Financial Services,
High Technology, Information Technology, Manufacturing, Oil/Gas,
Pharmaceutical/Medical; **Function Concentration:** Generalist with a primary
focus in Engineering, Finance/Accounting, General Management, Human
Resources, Marketing, Research and Development, Sales, Women/Minorities

**Bryant, Thomas** — *President*
Bryant Research
466 Old Hook Road, Suite 32
Emerson, NJ 07630
Telephone: (201) 599-0590
**Recruiter Classification:** Contingency; **Lowest/Average Salary:**
$50,000/$90,000; **Industry Concentration:** Biotechnology,
Pharmaceutical/Medical; **Function Concentration:** Research and Development

**Bryza, Robert M.** — *Chairman and President*
Robert Lowell International
12200 Park Central Drive, Suite 120
Dallas, TX 75251
Telephone: (214) 233-2270
**Recruiter Classification:** Retained; **Lowest/Average Salary:** $50,000/$60,000;
**Industry Concentration:** Generalist with a primary focus in
Aerospace/Defense, Automotive, Biotechnology, Chemical Products,
Consumer Products, Electronics, Energy, Healthcare/Hospitals, High
Technology, Information Technology, Manufacturing, Oil/Gas,
Pharmaceutical/Medical, Transportation; **Function Concentration:** Generalist
with a primary focus in Administration, Engineering, Finance/Accounting,
General Management, Human Resources, Marketing, Research and
Development, Sales, Women/Minorities

**Brzowski, John** — *Senior Associate*
Financial Search Corporation
2720 Des Plaines Avenue, Suite 106
Des Plaines, IL 60018
Telephone: (708) 297-4900
**Recruiter Classification:** Contingency; **Lowest/Average Salary:**
$30,000/$50,000; **Industry Concentration:** Generalist; **Function
Concentration:** Finance/Accounting

**Buchalter, Allyson** — *Senior Consultant*
The Whitney Group
850 Third Avenue, 11th Floor
New York, NY 10022
Telephone: (212) 508-3500
**Recruiter Classification:** Retained; **Lowest/Average Salary:** $75,000/$90,000;
**Industry Concentration:** Generalist with a primary focus in Financial Services,
Real Estate, Venture Capital; **Function Concentration:** Generalist with a
primary focus in Sales

**Buchsbaum, Deborah** — *Vice President*
Accountants on Call
Park 80 West, Plaza II, 9th Fl.
Garden State Parkway/I-80
Saddle Brook, NJ 07662
Telephone: (201) 843-0006
**Recruiter Classification:** Contingency; **Lowest/Average Salary:**
$20,000/$30,000; **Industry Concentration:** Generalist; **Function
Concentration:** Finance/Accounting

**Buck, Charles** — *President*
Charles Buck & Associates
400 East 59th Street
New York, NY 10022
Telephone: (212) 759-2356
**Recruiter Classification:** Retained; **Lowest/Average Salary:** $90,000/$90,000;
**Industry Concentration:** Generalist with a primary focus in Board Services,
Consumer Products, Fashion (Retail/Apparel), Publishing/Media; **Function
Concentration:** Generalist with a primary focus in Administration, General
Management, Human Resources, Marketing

**Buck, Walter J.** — *Senior Associate*
E.G. Jones Associates, Ltd.
1505 York Road
Lutherville, MD 21093
Telephone: (410) 337-4925
**Recruiter Classification:** Contingency; **Lowest/Average Salary:**
$40,000/$60,000; **Industry Concentration:** Packaging; **Function
Concentration:** Marketing

**Buckles, Donna** — *Recruiter*
Cochran, Cochran & Yale, Inc.
955 East Henrietta Road
Rochester, NY 14623
Telephone: (716) 424-6060
**Recruiter Classification:** Contingency; **Lowest/Average Salary:**
$40,000/$60,000; **Industry Concentration:** Generalist with a primary focus in
Automotive, Consumer Products, Electronics, High Technology, Manufacturing,
Packaging, Pharmaceutical/Medical; **Function Concentration:** Engineering

**Buda, Danny** — *General Manager*
Management Recruiters International, Inc.
Corporate Woods Building 40, Suite 920
9401 Indian Creek Parkway
Overland Park, KS 66210-2098
Telephone: (913) 661-9300
**Recruiter Classification:** Contingency; **Lowest/Average Salary:**
$30,000/$75,000; **Industry Concentration:** Generalist; **Function
Concentration:** Generalist

**Budill, Edward** — *Contract Recruiter*
Professional Search Consultants
3050 Post Oak Boulevard, Suite 1615
Houston, TX 77056
Telephone: (713) 960-9215
**Recruiter Classification:** Executive Temporary; **Lowest/Average Salary:**
$75,000/$75,000; **Industry Concentration:** Aerospace/Defense, Automotive,
Chemical Products, Information Technology, Manufacturing,
Pharmaceutical/Medical; **Function Concentration:** Engineering, General
Management, Marketing, Sales

**Bueschel, David A.** — *Principal*
Shepherd Bueschel & Provus, Inc.
401 North Michigan Avenue, Suite 3020
Chicago, IL 60611-5555
Telephone: (312) 832-3020
**Recruiter Classification:** Retained; **Lowest/Average Salary:** $90,000/$90,000;
**Industry Concentration:** Generalist with a primary focus in Automotive,
Electronics, Fashion (Retail/Apparel), High Technology, Information
Technology, Manufacturing, Non-Profit, Pharmaceutical/Medical; **Function
Concentration:** Generalist with a primary focus in Finance/Accounting,
General Management, Marketing, Sales

**Bulla, Steven W.** — *Manager Southwest Region*
Management Recruiters International, Inc.
10121 South Whitehouse Road
Fayetteville, AR 72701-9408
Telephone: (501) 582-4121
**Recruiter Classification:** Contingency; **Lowest/Average Salary:**
$30,000/$75,000; **Industry Concentration:** Generalist; **Function
Concentration:** Generalist

**Bullard, Roger C.** — *Managing Director*
Russell Reynolds Associates, Inc.
200 Park Avenue
New York, NY 10166-0002
Telephone: (212) 351-2000
**Recruiter Classification:** Retained; **Lowest/Average Salary:** $90,000/$90,000;
**Industry Concentration:** Generalist; **Function Concentration:** Generalist

**Bullock, Conni** — *Director Research*
Earley Kielty and Associates, Inc.
Two Pennsylvania Plaza
New York, NY 10121
Telephone: (212) 736-5626
**Recruiter Classification:** Retained; **Lowest/Average Salary:** $90,000/$90,000;
**Industry Concentration:** Generalist with a primary focus in Information
Technology; **Function Concentration:** Generalist with a primary focus in
Administration, Finance/Accounting, General Management, Human Resources,
Marketing, Research and Development, Sales, Women/Minorities

**Bump, Gerald J.** — *Executive Managing Director*
D.E. Foster Partners Inc.
303 Peachtree Street N.E., Suite 2000
Atlanta, GA 30308
Telephone: (404) 222-3440
**Recruiter Classification:** Retained; **Lowest/Average Salary:** $90,000/$90,000;
**Industry Concentration:** Generalist with a primary focus in Board Services,
Financial Services, Insurance, Manufacturing; **Function Concentration:**
Generalist with a primary focus in Finance/Accounting, General Management,
Human Resources, Marketing

**Bunker, Ralph L.** — *Manager Pacific Region*
Management Recruiters International, Inc.
697 Higuera, Suite B
San Luis Obispo, CA 93401
Telephone: (805) 541-1424
**Recruiter Classification:** Contingency; **Lowest/Average Salary:**
$30,000/$75,000; **Industry Concentration:** Generalist; **Function
Concentration:** Generalist

**Buntrock, George E.** — *Manager Southwest Region*
Management Recruiters International, Inc.
8131 LBJ Freeway, Suite 800
Dallas, TX 75251
Telephone: (214) 907-1010
**Recruiter Classification:** Contingency; **Lowest/Average Salary:**
$30,000/$75,000; **Industry Concentration:** Generalist; **Function Concentration:** Generalist

**Burch, Donald** — *Associate*
Source Services Corporation
925 Westchester Avenue, Suite 309
White Plains, NY 10604
Telephone: (914) 428-9100
**Recruiter Classification:** Contingency; **Lowest/Average Salary:**
$30,000/$50,000; **Industry Concentration:** Financial Services, Information
Technology; **Function Concentration:** Engineering, Finance/Accounting

**Burch, R. Stuart** — *Executive Director*
Russell Reynolds Associates, Inc.
1700 Pennsylvania Avenue N.W.
Suite 850
Washington, DC 20006
Telephone: (202) 628-2150
**Recruiter Classification:** Retained; **Lowest/Average Salary:** $90,000/$90,000;
**Industry Concentration:** Generalist with a primary focus in High Technology;
**Function Concentration:** Generalist

**Burchard, Stephen R.** — *President*
Burchard & Associates, Inc.
12977 North Outer Forty Drive
Suite 315
St. Louis, MO 63141
Telephone: (314) 878-2270
**Recruiter Classification:** Contingency; **Lowest/Average Salary:**
$40,000/$60,000; **Industry Concentration:** Generalist with a primary focus in
Fashion (Retail/Apparel), Financial Services, Healthcare/Hospitals,
Manufacturing; **Function Concentration:** Finance/Accounting, Human
Resources

**Burchill, Barb** — *President*
BGB Associates
P.O. Box 556
Itasca, IL 60143
Telephone: (630) 250-8993
**Recruiter Classification:** Contingency; **Lowest/Average Salary:**
$30,000/$60,000; **Industry Concentration:** Generalist with a primary focus in
Manufacturing; **Function Concentration:** Generalist with a primary focus in
Administration, Finance/Accounting, Human Resources

**Burchill, Greg** — *Principal*
BGB Associates
P.O. Box 556
Itasca, IL 60143
Telephone: (630) 250-8993
**Recruiter Classification:** Contingency; **Lowest/Average Salary:**
$30,000/$75,000; **Industry Concentration:** Generalist with a primary focus in
Aerospace/Defense, Automotive, Chemical Products, Consumer Products,
Electronics, Environmental, High Technology, Information Technology,
Manufacturing, Packaging, Pharmaceutical/Medical, Publishing/Media,
Transportation; **Function Concentration:** Generalist with a primary focus in
Engineering, Finance/Accounting, General Management, Human Resources,
Marketing, Sales, Women/Minorities

**Burden, Gene** — *Associate*
The Cherbonnier Group, Inc.
7986 138th Avenue S.E.
New Castle, WA 98059
Telephone: (206) 255-6383
**Recruiter Classification:** Retained; **Lowest/Average Salary:** $75,000/$90,000;
**Industry Concentration:** Generalist with a primary focus in Chemical Products,
Electronics, Energy, Environmental, Financial Services, Healthcare/Hospitals,
High Technology, Information Technology, Manufacturing, Oil/Gas,
Utilities/Nuclear, Venture Capital; **Function Concentration:** Generalist with a
primary focus in Administration, Engineering, Finance/Accounting, General
Management, Marketing, Research and Development, Sales

**Burfield, Elaine** — *Senior Vice President*
Skott/Edwards Consultants, Inc.
1776 On the Green
Morristown, NJ 07006
Telephone: (201) 644-0900
**Recruiter Classification:** Retained; **Lowest/Average Salary:** $75,000/$90,000;
**Industry Concentration:** Generalist with a primary focus in Biotechnology,
Board Services, Chemical Products, Financial Services, Healthcare/Hospitals,
Information Technology, Pharmaceutical/Medical; **Function Concentration:**
Generalist with a primary focus in Finance/Accounting, General Management,
Human Resources, Research and Development, Women/Minorities

**Burke, George M.** — *Partner*
The Burke Group
119 Hill Avenue
Manchester, MO 63011
Telephone: (314) 230-8100
**Recruiter Classification:** Contingency; **Lowest/Average Salary:**
$40,000/$60,000; **Industry Concentration:** Generalist with a primary focus in
Manufacturing; **Function Concentration:** Generalist with a primary focus in
Engineering, General Management, Research and Development

**Burke, J. Michael** — *Managing Director*
Merit Resource Group, Inc.
7950 Dublin Boulevard, Suite 205
Dublin, CA 94568
Telephone: (510) 828-4700
**Recruiter Classification:** Executive Temporary; **Lowest/Average Salary:**
$75,000/$90,000; **Industry Concentration:** Generalist; **Function
Concentration:** Human Resources

**Burke, John** — *President*
The Experts
200 Reservoir Street
Needham, MA 02194
Telephone: (617) 449-6700
**Recruiter Classification:** Executive Temporary; **Lowest/Average Salary:**
$50,000/$90,000; **Industry Concentration:** Generalist with a primary focus in
Consumer Products, Environmental, Financial Services, Healthcare/Hospitals,
High Technology, Information Technology, Manufacturing,
Pharmaceutical/Medical; **Function Concentration:** Generalist with a primary
focus in Administration, Engineering, Finance/Accounting, General
Management, Human Resources, Marketing, Research and Development, Sales

**Burke, Sally** — *Senior Associate*
Chaloner Associates
P.O. Box 1097, Back Bay Annex
Boston, MA 02117-1097
Telephone: (617) 451-5170
**Recruiter Classification:** Retained; **Lowest/Average Salary:** $/$75,000; **Industry
Concentration:** Generalist; **Function Concentration:** Generalist

**Burkholder, John A.** — *Manager Southwest Region*
Management Recruiters International, Inc.
15400 Knoll Trail, Suite 230
Dallas, TX 75248-3465
Telephone: (214) 960-1291
**Recruiter Classification:** Contingency; **Lowest/Average Salary:**
$30,000/$75,000; **Industry Concentration:** Generalist; **Function
Concentration:** Generalist

**Burkland, Skott B.** — *President*
Skott/Edwards Consultants, Inc.
1776 On the Green
Morristown, NJ 07006
Telephone: (201) 644-0900
**Recruiter Classification:** Retained; **Lowest/Average Salary:** $75,000/$90,000;
**Industry Concentration:** Biotechnology, Financial Services,
Healthcare/Hospitals, Venture Capital; **Function Concentration:** Generalist

**Burmaster, Holly** — *Software Quality Assurance Recruiter*
Winter, Wyman & Company
950 Winter Street, Suite 3100
Waltham, MA 02154-1294
Telephone: (617) 890-7000
**Recruiter Classification:** Contingency; **Lowest/Average Salary:**
$40,000/$75,000; **Industry Concentration:** Hospitality/Leisure, Information
Technology, Publishing/Media; **Function Concentration:** Generalist

**Burnett, Brendan G.** — *Principal*
Sullivan & Company
20 Exchange Place, 50th Floor
New York, NY 10005
Telephone: (212) 422-3000
**Recruiter Classification:** Retained; **Lowest/Average Salary:** $90,000/$90,000;
**Industry Concentration:** Generalist with a primary focus in Financial Services;
**Function Concentration:** Generalist

**Burnett, Rebecca J.** — *Executive Recruiter*
MSI International
200 Galleria Parkway
Suite 1610
Atlanta, GA 30339
Telephone: (404) 951-1208
**Recruiter Classification:** Contingency; **Lowest/Average Salary:**
$30,000/$60,000; **Industry Concentration:** Generalist with a primary focus in
Manufacturing; **Function Concentration:** Generalist with a primary focus in
Administration, Engineering, Finance/Accounting, General Management,
Marketing, Sales

**Burnette, Dennis W.** — *Principal*
Sanford Rose Associates
1580 Warsaw Road, Suite 101
Roswell, GA 30076
Telephone: (770) 643-4510
**Recruiter Classification:** Contingency; **Lowest/Average Salary:**
$30,000/$75,000; **Industry Concentration:** Generalist; **Function
Concentration:** Generalist

**Burns, Alan** — *Partner*
The Enns Partners Inc.
70 University Avenue, Suite 410, P.O. Box 14
Toronto, Ontario, CANADA M5J 2M4
Telephone: (416) 598-0012
**Recruiter Classification:** Retained; **Lowest/Average Salary:** $75,000/$90,000;
**Industry Concentration:** Generalist with a primary focus in
Aerospace/Defense, Board Services, Consumer Products, Electronics, Energy,
Financial Services, High Technology, Hospitality/Leisure, Manufacturing,
Pharmaceutical/Medical, Publishing/Media, Transportation, Venture Capital;
**Function Concentration:** Generalist with a primary focus in Administration,
Finance/Accounting, General Management, Human Resources, Marketing,
Sales

**Burns, Terence N.** — *Managing Director*
D.E. Foster Partners Inc.
Peat Marwick Plaza
303 East Wacker Drive, 26th Floor
Chicago, IL 60601-5255
Telephone: (312) 938-1201
**Recruiter Classification:** Retained; **Lowest/Average Salary:** $90,000/$90,000;
**Industry Concentration:** Generalist with a primary focus in Board Services,
Education/Libraries, Financial Services, Healthcare/Hospitals, Insurance,
Manufacturing, Non-Profit, Real Estate; **Function Concentration:** Generalist
with a primary focus in Administration, Finance/Accounting, General
Management, Human Resources, Marketing, Sales, Women/Minorities

**Burris, James C.** — *Executive Vice President*
Boyden
55 Madison Avenue
Suite 400
Morristown, NJ 07960
Telephone: (201) 267-0980
**Recruiter Classification:** Retained; **Lowest/Average Salary:** $75,000/$90,000;
**Industry Concentration:** Chemical Products; **Function Concentration:**
Generalist with a primary focus in Engineering, Finance/Accounting, General
Management, Human Resources, Marketing, Research and Development,
Sales, Women/Minorities

**Burton, Linda** — *Manager Eastern Region*
Management Recruiters International, Inc.
9515 Deereco Road, Suite 900
Baltimore, MD 21093
Telephone: (410) 252-6616
**Recruiter Classification:** Contingency; **Lowest/Average Salary:**
$30,000/$75,000; **Industry Concentration:** Generalist; **Function
Concentration:** Generalist

**Busch, Jack** — *President*
Busch International
One First Street, Suite 6
Los Altos, CA 94022-2754
Telephone: (415) 949-1115
**Recruiter Classification:** Retained; **Lowest/Average Salary:** $90,000/$90,000;
**Industry Concentration:** Biotechnology, Electronics, High Technology,
Information Technology, Venture Capital; **Function Concentration:** Generalist
with a primary focus in Engineering, Finance/Accounting, General
Management, Marketing, Research and Development, Sales

**Bush, Martha A.** — *Executive Recruiter*
MSI International
8521 Leesburg Pike, Suite 435
Vienna, VA 22182
Telephone: (703) 893-5669
**Recruiter Classification:** Contingency; **Lowest/Average Salary:**
$30,000/$75,000; **Industry Concentration:** Generalist with a primary focus in
Healthcare/Hospitals; **Function Concentration:** Generalist with a primary focus
in Administration, Engineering, Finance/Accounting, General Management,
Marketing, Sales

**Bush, R. Stuart** — *Managing Director/Area Manager*
Russell Reynolds Associates, Inc.
1900 Trammell Crow Center
2001 Ross Avenue
Dallas, TX 75201
Telephone: (214) 220-2033
**Recruiter Classification:** Retained; **Lowest/Average Salary:** $90,000/$90,000;
**Industry Concentration:** Financial Services, Healthcare/Hospitals; **Function
Concentration:** Generalist

**Busterna, Charles** — *Vice President*
The KPA Group
150 Broadway, Suite 1802
New York, NY 10038
Telephone: (212) 964-3640
**Recruiter Classification:** Contingency; **Lowest/Average Salary:**
$20,000/$40,000; **Industry Concentration:** Financial Services, High
Technology, Information Technology; **Function Concentration:** Administration,
Finance/Accounting, Human Resources, Marketing

**Butcher, Pascale** — *Executive Recruiter*
F-O-R-T-U-N-E Personnel Consultants of Manatee County
923 4th Street West
Palmetto, FL 34221
Telephone: (941) 729-3674
**Recruiter Classification:** Contingency; **Lowest/Average Salary:**
$30,000/$50,000; **Industry Concentration:** Automotive, Consumer Products,
Electronics, Financial Services, High Technology, Manufacturing; **Function
Concentration:** Finance/Accounting

**Butler, Kevin M.** — *Executive Director*
Russell Reynolds Associates, Inc.
200 Park Avenue
New York, NY 10166-0002
Telephone: (212) 351-2000
**Recruiter Classification:** Retained; **Lowest/Average Salary:** $90,000/$90,000;
**Industry Concentration:** Generalist with a primary focus in High Technology;
**Function Concentration:** Generalist

**Butler, Kirby B.** — *President*
The Butlers Company Insurance Recruiters
2753 State Road 580, Suite 103
Clearwater, FL 34621-3351
Telephone: (813) 725-1065
**Recruiter Classification:** Contingency; **Lowest/Average Salary:**
$50,000/$90,000; **Industry Concentration:** Insurance; **Function
Concentration:** Finance/Accounting, General Management, Human Resources,
Marketing, Research and Development, Sales

**Butterfass, Stanley** — *Principal*
Butterfass, Pepe & MacCallan Inc.
P.O. Box 721
Mahwah, NJ 07430
Telephone: (201) 512-3330
**Recruiter Classification:** Retained; **Lowest/Average Salary:** $60,000/$75,000;
**Industry Concentration:** Generalist with a primary focus in Financial Services,
Insurance, Venture Capital; **Function Concentration:** Generalist with a primary
focus in Finance/Accounting, Human Resources, Marketing, Women/Minorities

**Button, David R.** — *Principal*
The Button Group
1608 Emory Circle
Plano, TX 75093
Telephone: (214) 985-0619
**Recruiter Classification:** Retained, Contingency; **Lowest/Average Salary:**
$60,000/$90,000; **Industry Concentration:** Generalist with a primary focus in
Biotechnology, Board Services, Electronics, High Technology, Manufacturing,
Oil/Gas, Packaging, Pharmaceutical/Medical, Real Estate; **Function
Concentration:** Generalist with a primary focus in Engineering, General
Management, Marketing, Research and Development, Sales

**Buttrey, Daniel** — *Managing Director*
Source Services Corporation
100 North Tryon Street, Suite 3130
Charlotte, NC 28202
Telephone: (704) 333-8311
**Recruiter Classification:** Contingency; **Lowest/Average Salary:**
$30,000/$50,000; **Industry Concentration:** Financial Services, Information
Technology; **Function Concentration:** Engineering, Finance/Accounting

**Buzolits, Patrick** — *Associate*
Source Services Corporation
2000 Town Center, Suite 850
Southfield, MI 48075
Telephone: (810) 352-6520
**Recruiter Classification:** Contingency; **Lowest/Average Salary:**
$30,000/$50,000; **Industry Concentration:** Financial Services, Information
Technology; **Function Concentration:** Engineering, Finance/Accounting

**Bye, Randy** — *Managing Partner*
Romac & Associates
3200 Beechleaf Court
Suite 409
Raleigh, NC 27625
Telephone: (919) 878-4454
**Recruiter Classification:** Executive Temporary; **Lowest/Average Salary:**
$/$60,000; **Industry Concentration:** Financial Services, Healthcare/Hospitals,
High Technology, Hospitality/Leisure, Information Technology, Insurance;
**Function Concentration:** Finance/Accounting

**Byrnes, Thomas A.** — *President*
Thomas A. Byrnes Associates
148 East Avenue, Suite 2L
Norwalk, CT 06851
Telephone: (203) 838-9936
**Recruiter Classification:** Retained; **Lowest/Average Salary:** $90,000/$90,000;
**Industry Concentration:** Generalist with a primary focus in Board Services,
Consumer Products, Financial Services, Insurance; **Function Concentration:**
Generalist with a primary focus in Finance/Accounting, General Management,
Human Resources, Marketing, Research and Development, Sales,
Women/Minorities

**Cafero, Les** — *Associate*
Source Services Corporation
425 California Street, Suite 1200
San Francisco, CA 94104
Telephone: (415) 434-2410
**Recruiter Classification:** Contingency; **Lowest/Average Salary:**
$30,000/$50,000; **Industry Concentration:** Financial Services, Information
Technology; **Function Concentration:** Engineering, Finance/Accounting

**Cahill, James P.** — *Vice President*
Thorndike Deland Associates
275 Madison Avenue, Suite 1300
New York, NY 10016
Telephone: (212) 661-6200
**Recruiter Classification:** Retained; **Lowest/Average Salary:** $90,000/$90,000;
**Industry Concentration:** Generalist with a primary focus in Consumer
Products, Entertainment, Financial Services, Healthcare/Hospitals, High
Technology, Information Technology, Publishing/Media; **Function
Concentration:** Generalist

**Cahill, Peter M.** — *President*
Peter M. Cahill Associates, Inc.
P.O. Box 401, 100 Main Street
Southington, CT 06489
Telephone: (203) 628-3963
**Recruiter Classification:** Contingency; **Lowest/Average Salary:**
$60,000/$50,000; **Industry Concentration:** Generalist with a primary focus in
Aerospace/Defense, Automotive, Chemical Products, Consumer Products,
Electronics, High Technology, Manufacturing, Packaging,
Pharmaceutical/Medical; **Function Concentration:** Generalist with a primary
focus in Engineering, General Management, Human Resources, Marketing,
Research and Development, Sales

**Cahoon, D.B.** — *Principal*
Sanford Rose Associates
12 Minneakoning Road, Suite 4
Flemington, NJ 08822-5729
Telephone: (908) 788-1788
**Recruiter Classification:** Contingency; **Lowest/Average Salary:**
$30,000/$75,000; **Industry Concentration:** Generalist; **Function
Concentration:** Generalist

**Cahouet, Frank** — *Senior Associate*
Korn/Ferry International
Presidential Plaza
900 19th Street, N.W.
Washington, DC 20006
Telephone: (202) 822-9444
**Recruiter Classification:** Retained; **Lowest/Average Salary:** $90,000/$90,000;
**Industry Concentration:** Generalist; **Function Concentration:** Generalist

**Caldemeyer, Marjorie L.** — *Manager Central Region*
Management Recruiters International, Inc.
101 Court Street
Suite 209, Riverside 1
Evansville, IN 47708
Telephone: (812) 464-9155
**Recruiter Classification:** Contingency; **Lowest/Average Salary:**
$30,000/$75,000; **Industry Concentration:** Generalist; **Function
Concentration:** Generalist

**Caldwell, C. Douglas** — *Chairman*
The Caldwell Partners Amrop International
Sixty-Four Prince Arthur Avenue
Toronto, Ontario, CANADA M5R 1B4
Telephone: (416) 920-7702
**Recruiter Classification:** Retained; **Lowest/Average Salary:** $/$90,000; **Industry
Concentration:** Generalist with a primary focus in Education/Libraries,
Entertainment, Financial Services, Insurance, Non-Profit, Oil/Gas, Public
Administration, Real Estate; **Function Concentration:** Generalist

**Caldwell, Robert** — *President*
Robert Caldwell & Associates
12021 Wilshire Boulevard, Suite 650
Los Angeles, CA 90025
Telephone: (310) 454-1946
**Recruiter Classification:** Retained; **Lowest/Average Salary:** $90,000/$90,000;
**Industry Concentration:** Generalist; **Function Concentration:** Generalist

**Caldwell, William R.** — *Partner*
Pearson, Caldwell & Farnsworth, Inc.
One California Street, Suite 1950
San Francisco, CA 94111
Telephone: (415) 982-0300
**Recruiter Classification:** Retained; **Lowest/Average Salary:** $90,000/$90,000;
**Industry Concentration:** Financial Services; **Function Concentration:**
Administration, Finance/Accounting, General Management, Human Resources,
Marketing, Sales

**Calivas, Kay** — *Recruiter*
A.J. Burton Group, Inc.
120 East Baltimore Street, Suite 2220
Baltimore, MD 21202
Telephone: (410) 752-5244
**Recruiter Classification:** Contingency; **Lowest/Average Salary:**
$40,000/$60,000; **Industry Concentration:** Financial Services; **Function
Concentration:** Finance/Accounting

**Call, David** — *Manager Technical Recruitment*
Cochran, Cochran & Yale, Inc.
955 East Henrietta Road
Rochester, NY 14623
Telephone: (716) 424-6060
**Recruiter Classification:** Contingency; **Lowest/Average Salary:**
$40,000/$60,000; **Industry Concentration:** Generalist with a primary focus in
Automotive, Consumer Products, High Technology, Manufacturing, Packaging,
Pharmaceutical/Medical; **Function Concentration:** Engineering, General
Management, Women/Minorities

**Callahan, Wanda** — *Recruiter*
Cochran, Cochran & Yale, Inc.
955 East Henrietta Road
Rochester, NY 14623
Telephone: (716) 424-6060
**Recruiter Classification:** Contingency; **Lowest/Average Salary:**
$40,000/$60,000; **Industry Concentration:** Generalist with a primary focus in
Consumer Products, Electronics, Financial Services, High Technology,
Packaging, Pharmaceutical/Medical, Publishing/Media; **Function
Concentration:** Marketing, Sales, Women/Minorities

**Callan, Robert M.** — *Partner*
Callan Associates, Ltd.
1550 Spring Road
Oak Brook, IL 60521
Telephone: (708) 832-7080
**Recruiter Classification:** Retained; **Lowest/Average Salary:** $90,000/$90,000;
**Industry Concentration:** Generalist with a primary focus in Aerospace/Defense,
Automotive, Biotechnology, Chemical Products, Consumer Products,
Electronics, Energy, Environmental, Fashion (Retail/Apparel), Financial Services,
High Technology, Information Technology, Manufacturing, Oil/Gas; **Function
Concentration:** Generalist with a primary focus in Administration, Engineering,
Finance/Accounting, General Management, Human Resources, Marketing,
Research and Development, Sales, Women/Minorities

**Callaway, Lisa** — *Associate*
Korn/Ferry International
One Palmer Square
Princeton, NJ 08542
Telephone: (609) 921-8811
**Recruiter Classification:** Retained; **Lowest/Average Salary:** $90,000/$90,000;
**Industry Concentration:** Generalist; **Function Concentration:** Generalist

**Callaway, Thomas H.** — *Executive Director*
Russell Reynolds Associates, Inc.
101 California Street
Suite 3140
San Francisco, CA 94111
Telephone: (415) 352-3300
**Recruiter Classification:** Retained; **Lowest/Average Salary:** $90,000/$90,000;
**Industry Concentration:** Generalist; **Function Concentration:** Generalist

**Callen, John H.** — *Managing Director*
Ward Howell International, Inc.
99 Park Avenue, Suite 2000
New York, NY 10016-1699
Telephone: (212) 697-3730
**Recruiter Classification:** Retained; **Lowest/Average Salary:** $75,000/$90,000;
**Industry Concentration:** Consumer Products, Fashion (Retail/Apparel),
Information Technology; **Function Concentration:** Generalist with a primary
focus in General Management

**Callihan, Diana L.** — *Vice President*
Search Northwest Associates
10117 SE Sunnyside, Suite F-727
Clackamas, OR 97015
Telephone: (503) 654-1487
**Recruiter Classification:** Contingency; **Lowest/Average Salary:**
$30,000/$75,000; **Industry Concentration:** Biotechnology, Oil/Gas,
Pharmaceutical/Medical; **Function Concentration:** Administration,
Engineering, General Management, Research and Development

**Came, Paul E.** — *Partner*
Paul Ray Berndtson
10 South Riverside Plaza
Suite 720
Chicago, IL 60606
Telephone: (312) 876-0730
**Recruiter Classification:** Retained; **Lowest/Average Salary:** $90,000/$90,000;
**Industry Concentration:** Generalist with a primary focus in
Healthcare/Hospitals, Manufacturing; **Function Concentration:** Generalist

**Camp, David K.** — *Manager North Atlantic Region*
Management Recruiters International, Inc.
624 Matthews Mint Hill Road, Suite 224
Matthews, NC 28105
Telephone: (704) 841-8850
**Recruiter Classification:** Contingency; **Lowest/Average Salary:**
$30,000/$75,000; **Industry Concentration:** Generalist; **Function
Concentration:** Generalist

**Campbell, E.** — *Associate*
Source Services Corporation
120 East Baltimore Street, Suite 1950
Baltimore, MD 21202
Telephone: (410) 727-4050
**Recruiter Classification:** Contingency; **Lowest/Average Salary:**
$30,000/$50,000; **Industry Concentration:** Financial Services, Information
Technology; **Function Concentration:** Engineering, Finance/Accounting

**Campbell, Gary** — *Branch Manager*
Romac & Associates
Three Ravinia Drive
Suite 1460
Atlanta, GA 30346
Telephone: (404) 604-3880
**Recruiter Classification:** Executive Temporary; **Lowest/Average Salary:**
$/$60,000; **Industry Concentration:** Financial Services, Healthcare/Hospitals,
High Technology, Hospitality/Leisure, Information Technology, Insurance;
**Function Concentration:** Finance/Accounting

**Campbell, Jeff** — *Associate*
Source Services Corporation
425 California Street, Suite 1200
San Francisco, CA 94104
Telephone: (415) 434-2410
**Recruiter Classification:** Contingency; **Lowest/Average Salary:**
$30,000/$50,000; **Industry Concentration:** Financial Services, Information
Technology; **Function Concentration:** Engineering, Finance/Accounting

**Campbell, Margaret** — *Manager*
Coopers & Lybrand Consulting
145 King Street West
Toronto, Ontario, CANADA M5H 1V8
Telephone: (416) 869-1130
**Recruiter Classification:** Retained; **Lowest/Average Salary:** $60,000/$90,000;
**Industry Concentration:** Generalist; **Function Concentration:** Generalist

**Campbell, Patricia A.** — *Managing Director*
The Onstott Group, Inc.
60 William Street
Wellesley, MA 02181
Telephone: (617) 235-3050
**Recruiter Classification:** Retained; **Lowest/Average Salary:** $90,000/$90,000;
**Industry Concentration:** Generalist with a primary focus in Consumer
Products, Financial Services, High Technology, Information Technology,
Publishing/Media; **Function Concentration:** Generalist with a primary focus in
General Management, Human Resources, Marketing, Sales, Women/Minorities

**Campbell, Robert Scott** — *Principal*
Wellington Management Group
117 South 17th Street, Suite 1625
Philadelphia, PA 19103
Telephone: (215) 569-8900
**Recruiter Classification:** Retained; **Lowest/Average Salary:** $75,000/$90,000;
**Industry Concentration:** Generalist with a primary focus in Biotechnology,
Chemical Products, Consumer Products, Healthcare/Hospitals, High
Technology, Information Technology, Manufacturing, Oil/Gas; **Function
Concentration:** Generalist with a primary focus in Administration,
Finance/Accounting, General Management, Human Resources, Marketing,
Research and Development, Sales

**Campbell, Sandy T.** — *Co-Manager*
Management Recruiters International, Inc.
61 Cherry Street
Milford, CT 06460-3414
Telephone: (203) 876-8755
**Recruiter Classification:** Contingency; **Lowest/Average Salary:**
$30,000/$75,000; **Industry Concentration:** Generalist; **Function
Concentration:** Generalist

**Campbell, Stephen P.** — *Senior Vice President*
DHR International, Inc.
10 South Riverside Plaza, Suite 2220
Chicago, IL 60606
Telephone: (312) 782-1581
**Recruiter Classification:** Retained; **Lowest/Average Salary:** $60,000/$90,000;
**Industry Concentration:** Generalist; **Function Concentration:** Generalist

**Campbell, Thomas J.** — *Partner*
Heidrick & Struggles, Inc.
2740 Sand Hill Road
Menlo Park, CA 94025
Telephone: (415) 854-9300
**Recruiter Classification:** Retained; **Lowest/Average Salary:** $75,000/$90,000;
**Industry Concentration:** Generalist with a primary focus in Financial Services;
**Function Concentration:** Generalist

**Campbell, W. Ross** — *Consultant*
Egon Zehnder International Inc.
1 First Canadian Place
P.O. Box 179
Toronto, Ontario, CANADA M5X 1C7
Telephone: (416) 364-0222
**Recruiter Classification:** Retained; **Lowest/Average Salary:** $90,000/$90,000;
**Industry Concentration:** Generalist with a primary focus in Biotechnology,
Financial Services, High Technology, Manufacturing, Pharmaceutical/Medical;
**Function Concentration:** Generalist

**Campeas, David E.** — *Co-Manager*
Management Recruiters International, Inc.
1170 Route 22 East
Bridgewater, NJ 08807-1786
Telephone: (908) 725-2595
**Recruiter Classification:** Contingency; **Lowest/Average Salary:** $30,000/$75,000;
**Industry Concentration:** Generalist; **Function Concentration:** Generalist

**Canan, Bruce** — *Vice President Candidate Relations*
The Nielsen Healthcare Group
P.O. Box 30220
Cincinnati, OH 45230
Telephone: (513) 232-2209
**Recruiter Classification:** Executive Temporary; **Lowest/Average Salary:**
$20,000/$50,000; **Industry Concentration:** Healthcare/Hospitals; **Function
Concentration:** Generalist

**Cannavino, John J.** — *President*
Financial Resource Associates, Inc.
105 West Orange Street
Altamonte Springs, FL 32714
Telephone: (407) 869-7000
**Recruiter Classification:** Contingency; **Lowest/Average Salary:**
$40,000/$60,000; **Industry Concentration:** Financial Services; **Function
Concentration:** Generalist with a primary focus in Finance/Accounting

**Cannavo, Louise** — *Managing Director*
The Whitney Group
850 Third Avenue, 11th Floor
New York, NY 10022
Telephone: (212) 508-3500
**Recruiter Classification:** Retained; **Lowest/Average Salary:** $75,000/$90,000;
**Industry Concentration:** Generalist with a primary focus in Financial Services,
Real Estate, Venture Capital; **Function Concentration:** Generalist with a
primary focus in Sales

**Cannon, Alexis** — *Associate Partner*
Richard, Wayne and Roberts
24 Greenway Plaza, Suite 1304
Houston, TX 77046-2493
Telephone: (713) 629-6681
**Recruiter Classification:** Retained; **Lowest/Average Salary:** $50,000/$90,000;
**Industry Concentration:** Generalist with a primary focus in Financial Services;
**Function Concentration:** Generalist with a primary focus in
Finance/Accounting

**Cannon, Alicia** — *Branch Manager*
Accountants on Call
Princeton Corporate Center
5 Independence Way
Princeton, NJ 08540
Telephone: (609) 452-7117
**Recruiter Classification:** Contingency; **Lowest/Average Salary:** $20,000/$30,000;
**Industry Concentration:** Generalist; **Function Concentration:** Finance/Accounting

**Cannon, Alicia** — *Branch Manager*
Accountants on Call
505 Thornall Street
Edison, NJ 08837
Telephone: (908) 321-1700
**Recruiter Classification:** Contingency; **Lowest/Average Salary:**
$20,000/$30,000; **Industry Concentration:** Generalist; **Function
Concentration:** Finance/Accounting

**Cantor, Bill** — *President*
Cantor Concern Staffing Options, Inc.
330 West 58th Street
Suite 216
New York, NY 10019
Telephone: (212) 333-3000
**Recruiter Classification:** Executive Temporary; **Lowest/Average Salary:** $40,000/$50,000

**Cantus, Jane Scott** — *Senior Associate*
Korn/Ferry International
Presidential Plaza
900 19th Street, N.W.
Washington, DC 20006
Telephone: (202) 822-9444
**Recruiter Classification:** Retained; **Lowest/Average Salary:** $90,000/$90,000; **Industry Concentration:** Generalist; **Function Concentration:** Generalist

**Capanna, Pat A.** — *Manager Midwest Region*
Management Recruiters International, Inc.
1800 Parmenter Street, Suite 200
Middleton, WI 53562-3137
Telephone: (608) 831-1717
**Recruiter Classification:** Contingency; **Lowest/Average Salary:** $30,000/$75,000; **Industry Concentration:** Generalist; **Function Concentration:** Generalist

**Capeloto, Robert** — *Consultant*
Korn/Ferry International
600 University Street, Suite 3111
Seattle, WA 98101
Telephone: (206) 447-1834
**Recruiter Classification:** Retained; **Lowest/Average Salary:** $90,000/$90,000; **Industry Concentration:** Generalist; **Function Concentration:** Generalist

**Capizzi, Salvatore** — *Accounting and Finance Recruiter*
Winter, Wyman & Company
950 Winter Street, Suite 3100
Waltham, MA 02154-1294
Telephone: (617) 890-7000
**Recruiter Classification:** Contingency; **Lowest/Average Salary:** $20,000/$50,000; **Industry Concentration:** Generalist; **Function Concentration:** Finance/Accounting

**Caplan, Deborah** — *Director*
Price Waterhouse
1 First Canadian Place, Box 190, Suite 3300
Toronto, Ontario, CANADA M5X 1H7
Telephone: (416) 863-1133
**Recruiter Classification:** Retained; **Lowest/Average Salary:** $60,000/$90,000; **Industry Concentration:** Generalist; **Function Concentration:** Generalist

**Cappe, Richard R.** — *President*
Roberts Ryan and Bentley
1107 Kenilworth Drive, Suite 208
Towson, MD 21204
Telephone: (410) 321-6600
**Recruiter Classification:** Retained; **Lowest/Average Salary:** $90,000/$90,000; **Industry Concentration:** Energy, Financial Services, Information Technology, Insurance; **Function Concentration:** Administration, General Management

**Carabelli, Paula** — *Shareholder*
Witt/Kieffer, Ford, Hadelman & Lloyd
1920 Main Street, Suite 310
Irvine, CA 92714
Telephone: (714) 851-5070
**Recruiter Classification:** Retained; **Lowest/Average Salary:** $75,000/$90,000; **Industry Concentration:** Healthcare/Hospitals; **Function Concentration:** Generalist with a primary focus in General Management

**Carey, Dennis C.** — *Managing Director*
Spencer Stuart
2005 Market Street, Suite 2350
Philadelphia, PA 19103
Telephone: (215) 851-6200
**Recruiter Classification:** Retained; **Lowest/Average Salary:** $90,000/$90,000; **Industry Concentration:** Generalist with a primary focus in Board Services; **Function Concentration:** Generalist with a primary focus in General Management

**Cargill, Jim B.** — *Manager Pacific Region*
Management Recruiters International, Inc.
276 Kingsbury Square, Suite 213, P.O. Box 4766
Stateline, NV 89449
Telephone: (702) 588-7388
**Recruiter Classification:** Contingency; **Lowest/Average Salary:** $30,000/$75,000; **Industry Concentration:** Generalist; **Function Concentration:** Generalist

**Cargo, Catherine** — *Executive Recruiter*
MSI International
8521 Leesburg Pike, Suite 435
Vienna, VA 22182
Telephone: (703) 893-5669
**Recruiter Classification:** Contingency; **Lowest/Average Salary:** $30,000/$75,000; **Industry Concentration:** Generalist with a primary focus in Healthcare/Hospitals; **Function Concentration:** Generalist with a primary focus in Administration, Engineering, Finance/Accounting, General Management, Marketing, Sales

**Carideo, Joseph** — *Partner*
Thorndike Deland Associates
275 Madison Avenue, Suite 1300
New York, NY 10016
Telephone: (212) 661-6200
**Recruiter Classification:** Retained; **Lowest/Average Salary:** $75,000/$90,000; **Industry Concentration:** Generalist with a primary focus in Board Services, Consumer Products, Entertainment, Fashion (Retail/Apparel), Financial Services, Healthcare/Hospitals, Hospitality/Leisure, Information Technology, Insurance, Manufacturing, Pharmaceutical/Medical, Publishing/Media, Venture Capital; **Function Concentration:** Generalist with a primary focus in Finance/Accounting, General Management, Human Resources, Marketing, Sales

**Carlson, Eric** — *Associate*
Source Services Corporation
500 108th Avenue NE, Suite 1780
Bellevue, WA 98004
Telephone: (206) 454-6400
**Recruiter Classification:** Contingency; **Lowest/Average Salary:** $30,000/$50,000; **Industry Concentration:** Financial Services, Information Technology; **Function Concentration:** Engineering, Finance/Accounting

**Carlson, Judith** — *Financial Recruiter*
Bowman & Marshall, Inc.
P.O. Box 25503
Overland Park, KS 66225
Telephone: (913) 648-3332
**Recruiter Classification:** Retained; **Lowest/Average Salary:** $30,000/$50,000; **Industry Concentration:** Automotive, Chemical Products, Consumer Products, Fashion (Retail/Apparel), Financial Services, Insurance, Manufacturing, Packaging, Pharmaceutical/Medical, Publishing/Media; **Function Concentration:** Finance/Accounting

**Carlson, Sharon A.** — *Executive Vice President*
Assisting Professionals, Inc.
2000 North Woodward, Suite 250
Bloomfield Hills, MI 48304-2255
Telephone: (810) 647-9800
**Recruiter Classification:** Executive Temporary; **Lowest/Average Salary:** $50,000/$75,000; **Industry Concentration:** Generalist; **Function Concentration:** Generalist

**Carnal, Rick** — *Associate*
Source Services Corporation
3 Summit Park Drive, Suite 550
Independence, OH 44131
Telephone: (216) 328-5900
**Recruiter Classification:** Contingency; **Lowest/Average Salary:** $30,000/$50,000; **Industry Concentration:** Financial Services, Information Technology; **Function Concentration:** Engineering, Finance/Accounting

**Carpenter, Harold G.** — *Physician Recruiter*
MSI International
201 St. Charles Avenue
Suite 2205
New Orleans, LA 70170
Telephone: (504) 522-6700
**Recruiter Classification:** Contingency; **Lowest/Average Salary:** $30,000/$60,000; **Industry Concentration:** Generalist with a primary focus in Healthcare/Hospitals; **Function Concentration:** Generalist with a primary focus in Administration, Engineering, Finance/Accounting, General Management, Marketing, Sales

**Carpenter, James J.** — *Managing Director*
Russell Reynolds Associates, Inc.
200 Park Avenue
New York, NY 10166-0002
Telephone: (212) 351-2000
**Recruiter Classification:** Retained; **Lowest/Average Salary:** $90,000/$90,000; **Industry Concentration:** Generalist with a primary focus in Consumer Products; **Function Concentration:** Generalist

**Carr, W. Lyles** — *Senior Vice President*
The McCormick Group, Inc.
1400 Wilson Boulevard
Arlington, VA 22209
Telephone: (703) 841-1700
**Recruiter Classification:** Retained, Contingency; **Lowest/Average Salary:** $75,000/$90,000; **Industry Concentration:** Generalist; **Function Concentration:** Generalist

**Carrara, Gilbert J.** — *Principal*
Korn/Ferry International
One Palmer Square
Princeton, NJ 08542
Telephone: (609) 921-8811
**Recruiter Classification:** Retained; **Lowest/Average Salary:** $90,000/$90,000;
**Industry Concentration:** Generalist with a primary focus in
Healthcare/Hospitals; **Function Concentration:** Generalist

**Carrick, Kenneth D.** — *Consultant*
Coleman Lew & Associates, Inc.
326 West Tenth Street
Charlotte, NC 28202
Telephone: (704) 377-0362
**Recruiter Classification:** Retained; **Lowest/Average Salary:** $/$90,000; **Industry Concentration:** Generalist; **Function Concentration:** Generalist

**Carrigan, Denise** — *Co-Manager Southwest Region*
Management Recruiters International, Inc.
8700 Crownhill, Suite 701
San Antonio, TX 78209
Telephone: (210) 829-8666
**Recruiter Classification:** Contingency; **Lowest/Average Salary:** $30,000/$75,000;
**Industry Concentration:** Generalist; **Function Concentration:** Generalist

**Carrigan, Maureen** — *Senior Consultant*
R.D. Gatti & Associates, Incorporated
266 Main Street, Suite 21
Medfield, MA 02052
Telephone: (508) 359-4153
**Recruiter Classification:** Contingency; **Lowest/Average Salary:**
$40,000/$75,000; **Industry Concentration:** Generalist; **Function Concentration:** Human Resources

**Carrillo, Jose** — *Managing Partner*
Amrop International
Av. Lazaro Cardenas, 2400 PTE
Edificio Los Soles, P.D. 2
Garza Garcia, N.L., MEXICO 66270
Telephone: (528) 363-2529
**Recruiter Classification:** Retained, Contingency; **Lowest/Average Salary:**
$75,000/$90,000; **Industry Concentration:** Generalist; **Function Concentration:** Generalist

**Carrott, Gregory T.** — *Consultant*
Egon Zehnder International Inc.
One First National Plaza
21 South Clark Street, Suite 3300
Chicago, IL 60603-2006
Telephone: (312) 782-4500
**Recruiter Classification:** Retained; **Lowest/Average Salary:** $90,000/$90,000;
**Industry Concentration:** Generalist with a primary focus in Biotechnology,
Financial Services, High Technology, Manufacturing, Pharmaceutical/Medical;
**Function Concentration:** Generalist

**Cartella, Janet** — *Co-Manager*
Management Recruiters International, Inc.
Highway 5, Southport Building, P.O. Box 1509
Laurie, MO 65038-1509
Telephone: (573) 374-9338
**Recruiter Classification:** Contingency; **Lowest/Average Salary:**
$30,000/$75,000; **Industry Concentration:** Generalist; **Function Concentration:** Generalist

**Cartella, Mike** — *Co-Manager Midwest Region*
Management Recruiters International, Inc.
Highway 5, Southport Building, P.O. Box 1509
Laurie, MO 65038-1509
Telephone: (573) 374-9338
**Recruiter Classification:** Contingency; **Lowest/Average Salary:**
$30,000/$75,000; **Industry Concentration:** Generalist; **Function Concentration:** Generalist

**Carter, Carolyn** — *Associate Consultant*
Thomas Mangum Company
500 East Del Mar Boulevard, Suite 19
Pasadena, CA 91101
Telephone: (818) 577-2070
**Recruiter Classification:** Retained; **Lowest/Average Salary:** $75,000/$90,000;
**Industry Concentration:** Generalist; **Function Concentration:** Generalist

**Carter, Christine C.** — *Vice President*
Health Care Dimensions
7150 Campus Drive, Suite 320
Colorado Springs, CO 80920
Telephone: (800) 373-3401
**Recruiter Classification:** Contingency; **Lowest/Average Salary:**
$40,000/$75,000; **Industry Concentration:** Healthcare/Hospitals, Insurance;
**Function Concentration:** Generalist with a primary focus in Administration,
Finance/Accounting, General Management, Human Resources, Marketing,
Research and Development, Sales

**Carter, D. Michael** — *Manager Midwest Region*
Management Recruiters International, Inc.
1740 Bell School Road
Cherry Valley, IL 61016-9337
Telephone: (815) 399-1942
**Recruiter Classification:** Contingency; **Lowest/Average Salary:** $30,000/$75,000;
**Industry Concentration:** Generalist; **Function Concentration:** Generalist

**Carter, Guy W.** — *Manager North Atlantic Region*
Management Recruiters International, Inc.
P.O. Box 639
Travelers Rest, SC 29690-0639
Telephone: (864) 834-0643
**Recruiter Classification:** Contingency; **Lowest/Average Salary:**
$30,000/$75,000; **Industry Concentration:** Generalist; **Function Concentration:** Generalist

**Carter, I. Wayne** — *Partner*
Heidrick & Struggles, Inc.
300 South Grand Avenue, Suite 2400
Los Angeles, CA 90071
Telephone: (213) 625-8811
**Recruiter Classification:** Retained; **Lowest/Average Salary:** $75,000/$90,000;
**Industry Concentration:** Generalist with a primary focus in High Technology;
**Function Concentration:** Generalist

**Carter, Jon F.** — *Consultant*
Egon Zehnder International Inc.
100 Spear Street, Suite 1135
San Francisco, CA 94105
Telephone: (415) 904-7800
**Recruiter Classification:** Retained; **Lowest/Average Salary:** $90,000/$90,000;
**Industry Concentration:** Generalist with a primary focus in Biotechnology,
Financial Services, High Technology, Manufacturing, Pharmaceutical/Medical;
**Function Concentration:** Generalist

**Carter, Kitte H.** — *Manager South Atlantic Region*
Management Recruiters International, Inc.
1406 Hays Street, Suite 7
Tallahassee, FL 32301-2843
Telephone: (904) 656-8444
**Recruiter Classification:** Contingency; **Lowest/Average Salary:**
$30,000/$75,000; **Industry Concentration:** Generalist; **Function Concentration:** Generalist

**Carter, Linda** — *Associate*
Source Services Corporation
5429 LBJ Freeway, Suite 275
Dallas, TX 75240
Telephone: (214) 387-1600
**Recruiter Classification:** Contingency; **Lowest/Average Salary:**
$30,000/$50,000; **Industry Concentration:** Financial Services, Information
Technology; **Function Concentration:** Engineering, Finance/Accounting

**Caruso, Kathy** — *Manager Executive Search*
Accounting Resources, Inc.
8744 Frederick Street
Omaha, NE 68124-3068
Telephone: (402) 397-3308
**Recruiter Classification:** Contingency; **Lowest/Average Salary:**
$75,000/$90,000; **Industry Concentration:** Generalist with a primary focus in
Automotive, Consumer Products, Financial Services, Insurance, Manufacturing,
Publishing/Media, Transportation; **Function Concentration:**
Finance/Accounting

**Carvalho-Esteves, Maria** — *Associate*
Source Services Corporation
379 Thornall Street
Edison, NJ 08837
Telephone: (908) 494-2800
**Recruiter Classification:** Contingency; **Lowest/Average Salary:**
$30,000/$50,000; **Industry Concentration:** Financial Services, Information
Technology; **Function Concentration:** Engineering, Finance/Accounting

**Carver, Graham** — *Partner*
Cambridge Management Planning
2323 Yonge Street, Suite 203
Toronto, Ontario, CANADA M4P 2C9
Telephone: (416) 484-8408
**Recruiter Classification:** Retained, Executive Temporary; **Lowest/Average
Salary:** $75,000/$90,000; **Industry Concentration:** Generalist; **Function Concentration:** Generalist

**Carzo, Frank L.** — *Executive Director*
Russell Reynolds Associates, Inc.
1700 Pennsylvania Avenue N.W.
Suite 850
Washington, DC 20006
Telephone: (202) 628-2150
**Recruiter Classification:** Retained; **Lowest/Average Salary:** $90,000/$90,000;
**Industry Concentration:** Generalist; **Function Concentration:** Generalist

**Casal, Daniel G.** — *Executive Recruiter*
Bonifield Associates
3003E Lincoln Drive West
Marlton, NJ 08053
Telephone: (609) 596-3300
**Recruiter Classification:** Contingency; **Lowest/Average Salary:**
$40,000/$50,000; **Industry Concentration:** Financial Services, Insurance; **Function Concentration:** Generalist with a primary focus in Administration, Finance/Accounting, General Management, Marketing, Research and Development, Sales

**Case, David** — *President*
Case Executive Search
15008 Kercheval Avenue
Grosse Pointe Park, MI 48236
Telephone: (313) 331-6095
**Recruiter Classification:** Contingency; **Lowest/Average Salary:**
$30,000/$50,000; **Industry Concentration:** Automotive, Manufacturing, Transportation; **Function Concentration:** Engineering, Women/Minorities

**Casey, Darren** — *Consultant*
Parfitt Recruiting and Consulting
1540 140th Avenue NE #201
Bellevue, WA 98005
Telephone: (206) 646-6300
**Recruiter Classification:** Contingency; **Lowest/Average Salary:**
$30,000/$75,000; **Industry Concentration:** Generalist; **Function Concentration:** Finance/Accounting, General Management

**Casey, Jean** — *Manager Research*
Peter W. Ambler Company
14651 Dallas Parkway, Suite 402
Dallas, TX 75240
Telephone: (214) 404-8712
**Recruiter Classification:** Retained; **Lowest/Average Salary:** $50,000/$90,000; **Industry Concentration:** Generalist with a primary focus in Board Services, Chemical Products, Consumer Products, Fashion (Retail/Apparel), Manufacturing, Packaging, Real Estate, Transportation; **Function Concentration:** Generalist with a primary focus in Administration, General Management, Human Resources, Marketing, Sales

**Cashen, Anthony B.** — *Senior Partner*
Lamalie Amrop International
200 Park Avenue
New York, NY 10166-0136
Telephone: (212) 953-7900
**Recruiter Classification:** Retained; **Lowest/Average Salary:** $90,000/$90,000; **Industry Concentration:** Generalist with a primary focus in Financial Services; **Function Concentration:** Generalist with a primary focus in Finance/Accounting, General Management

**Cashman, Tracy** — *Information Technology Recruiter*
Winter, Wyman & Company
950 Winter Street, Suite 3100
Waltham, MA 02154-1294
Telephone: (617) 890-7000
**Recruiter Classification:** Contingency; **Lowest/Average Salary:**
$30,000/$60,000; **Industry Concentration:** Information Technology; **Function Concentration:** Generalist

**Cass, Kathryn H.** — *Assistant Vice President*
Don Richard Associates of Tidewater, Inc.
4701 Columbus Street, Suite 102
Virginia Beach, VA 23462
Telephone: (757) 518-8600
**Recruiter Classification:** Contingency, Executive Temporary; **Lowest/Average Salary:** $20,000/$30,000; **Industry Concentration:** Generalist; **Function Concentration:** Generalist with a primary focus in Administration, Finance/Accounting, General Management, Human Resources

**Cassie, Ronald L.** — *President*
The Cassie Group
2906 William Penn Highway
Easton, PA 18045
Telephone: (610) 250-7010
**Recruiter Classification:** Retained; **Lowest/Average Salary:** $75,000/$90,000; **Industry Concentration:** Biotechnology, Pharmaceutical/Medical; **Function Concentration:** Administration, Engineering, Finance/Accounting, General Management, Human Resources, Marketing, Sales, Women/Minorities

**Cast, Donald** — *Executive Recruiter*
Dunhill Search International
59 Elm Street
New Haven, CT 06510
Telephone: (203) 562-0511
**Recruiter Classification:** Contingency; **Lowest/Average Salary:**
$30,000/$60,000; **Industry Concentration:** Chemical Products, High Technology, Information Technology, Manufacturing; **Function Concentration:** Engineering

**Castine, Michael P.** — *Senior Director*
Spencer Stuart
277 Park Avenue, 29th Floor
New York, NY 10172
Telephone: (212) 336-0200
**Recruiter Classification:** Retained; **Lowest/Average Salary:** $90,000/$90,000; **Industry Concentration:** Generalist with a primary focus in Board Services, Financial Services, Information Technology, Non-Profit; **Function Concentration:** Generalist with a primary focus in Finance/Accounting

**Castle, Lisa** — *Associate*
Source Services Corporation
379 Thornall Street
Edison, NJ 08837
Telephone: (908) 494-2800
**Recruiter Classification:** Contingency; **Lowest/Average Salary:**
$30,000/$50,000; **Industry Concentration:** Financial Services, Information Technology; **Function Concentration:** Engineering, Finance/Accounting

**Cattanach, Bruce B.** — *Vice President*
Horton International
33 Sloan Street
Roswell, GA 30075
Telephone: (770) 640-1533
**Recruiter Classification:** Retained; **Lowest/Average Salary:** $90,000/$90,000; **Industry Concentration:** Generalist with a primary focus in Financial Services, High Technology, Information Technology, Manufacturing, Venture Capital; **Function Concentration:** Generalist with a primary focus in Administration, Finance/Accounting, General Management, Human Resources, Sales

**Caudill, Nancy** — *Managing Director*
Webb, Johnson Associates, Inc.
280 Park Avenue, 43rd Floor
New York, NY 10017
Telephone: (212) 661-3700
**Recruiter Classification:** Retained; **Lowest/Average Salary:** $90,000/$90,000; **Industry Concentration:** Generalist with a primary focus in Biotechnology, Chemical Products, Financial Services, Healthcare/Hospitals, High Technology, Non-Profit, Pharmaceutical/Medical; **Function Concentration:** Generalist

**Causey, Andrea C.** — *Executive Recruiter*
MSI International
1900 North 18th Street
Suite 303
Monroe, LA 71201
Telephone: (318) 324-0406
**Recruiter Classification:** Contingency; **Lowest/Average Salary:**
$30,000/$60,000; **Industry Concentration:** Generalist with a primary focus in Healthcare/Hospitals, Pharmaceutical/Medical; **Function Concentration:** Generalist with a primary focus in Administration, Engineering, Finance/Accounting, General Management, Marketing, Sales

**Cavanagh, Michael J.** — *President*
Michael J. Cavanagh and Associates
30 St. Clair West
Toronto, Ontario, CANADA M4V 3A1
Telephone: (416) 324-9661
**Recruiter Classification:** Retained; **Lowest/Average Salary:** $75,000/$90,000; **Industry Concentration:** Generalist with a primary focus in Aerospace/Defense, Automotive, Board Services, Consumer Products, Electronics, Healthcare/Hospitals, Information Technology, Manufacturing, Non-Profit, Packaging, Pharmaceutical/Medical, Real Estate, Transportation, Venture Capital; **Function Concentration:** Generalist with a primary focus in Administration, Engineering, Finance/Accounting, General Management, Human Resources, Marketing

**Caver, Michael D.** — *Partner*
Heidrick & Struggles, Inc.
125 South Wacker Drive
Suite 2800
Chicago, IL 60606-4590
Telephone: (312) 372-8811
**Recruiter Classification:** Retained; **Lowest/Average Salary:** $75,000/$90,000; **Industry Concentration:** Generalist with a primary focus in Healthcare/Hospitals; **Function Concentration:** Generalist

**Caviness, Susan** — *Senior Associate*
Korn/Ferry International
120 South Riverside Plaza
Suite 918
Chicago, IL 60606
Telephone: (312) 726-1841
**Recruiter Classification:** Retained; **Lowest/Average Salary:** $90,000/$90,000; **Industry Concentration:** Generalist; **Function Concentration:** Generalist

**Cavolina, Michael** — *Managing Director*
Carver Search Consultants
9303 East Bullard, Suite 1
Clovis, CA 93611-8211
Telephone: (209) 298-7791
Recruiter Classification: Contingency; Lowest/Average Salary:
$50,000/$75,000; Industry Concentration: Generalist with a primary focus in
Biotechnology, Environmental, Healthcare/Hospitals, High Technology,
Manufacturing, Pharmaceutical/Medical; Function Concentration: Engineering,
General Management, Marketing, Research and Development, Sales

**Cavriani, Randolph** — *Account Executive*
Search West, Inc.
3401 Centrelake Drive
Suite 690
Ontario, CA 91761-1207
Telephone: (909) 986-1966
Recruiter Classification: Contingency; Lowest/Average Salary:
$40,000/$60,000; Industry Concentration: Generalist; Function
Concentration: Marketing, Sales

**Celentano, James** — *Senior Associate*
Korn/Ferry International
237 Park Avenue
New York, NY 10017
Telephone: (212) 687-1834
Recruiter Classification: Retained; Lowest/Average Salary: $90,000/$90,000;
Industry Concentration: Generalist; Function Concentration: Generalist

**Celenza, Catherine** — *Executive Recruiter*
CPS Inc.
303 Congress Street, 5th Floor
Boston, MA 02210
Telephone: (617) 439-7950
Recruiter Classification: Contingency; Lowest/Average Salary:
$30,000/$50,000; Industry Concentration: Generalist with a primary focus in
Automotive, Biotechnology, Chemical Products, Consumer Products, High
Technology, Insurance, Manufacturing, Oil/Gas, Packaging,
Pharmaceutical/Medical; Function Concentration: Engineering, Research and
Development, Sales, Women/Minorities

**Cellers, Darrell L.** — *Co-Manager*
Management Recruiters International, Inc.
Northtown Office Building, Suite 910 North
4407 Division Street
Spokane, WA 99207-1613
Telephone: (509) 484-0084
Recruiter Classification: Contingency; Lowest/Average Salary:
$30,000/$75,000; Industry Concentration: Generalist; Function
Concentration: Generalist

**Cellers, Marsha** — *Co-Manager Pacific Region*
Management Recruiters International, Inc.
Northtown Office Building, Suite 910 North
4407 Division Street
Spokane, WA 99207-1613
Telephone: (509) 484-0084
Recruiter Classification: Contingency; Lowest/Average Salary:
$30,000/$75,000; Industry Concentration: Generalist; Function
Concentration: Generalist

**Cendejas, Stella** — *Manager Pacific Region*
Management Recruiters International, Inc.
150 South Robles Avenue, Suite 865
Pasadena, CA 91101
Telephone: (818) 683-7580
Recruiter Classification: Contingency; Lowest/Average Salary:
$30,000/$75,000; Industry Concentration: Generalist; Function
Concentration: Generalist

**Center, Linda** — *President*
The Search Center Inc.
1155 Dairy Ashford, Suite 404
Houston, TX 77079
Telephone: (713) 589-8303
Recruiter Classification: Contingency; Lowest/Average Salary:
$75,000/$90,000; Industry Concentration: Energy; Function Concentration:
Marketing

**Cerasoli, Philip A.** — *President*
Experience-On-Tap Inc.
175 Strafford Avenue, Suite 1
Wayne, PA 19087
Telephone: (610) 825-7416
Recruiter Classification: Executive Temporary; Industry Concentration:
Generalist; Function Concentration: Generalist

**Ceresi, Carole** — *Co-Manager*
Management Recruiters International, Inc.
Bay Head Commons
106 Bridge Avenue
Bay Head, NJ 08742
Telephone: (908) 714-1300
Recruiter Classification: Contingency; Lowest/Average Salary:
$30,000/$75,000; Industry Concentration: Generalist; Function
Concentration: Generalist

**Ceresi, Robert P.** — *Co-Manager Eastern Region*
Management Recruiters International, Inc.
Bay Head Commons
106 Bridge Avenue
Bay Head, NJ 08742
Telephone: (908) 714-1300
Recruiter Classification: Contingency; Lowest/Average Salary:
$30,000/$75,000; Industry Concentration: Generalist; Function
Concentration: Generalist

**Cersosimo, Rocco** — *Associate*
Source Services Corporation
Foster Plaza VI
681 Anderson Drive, 2nd Floor
Pittsburgh, PA 15220
Telephone: (412) 928-8300
Recruiter Classification: Contingency; Lowest/Average Salary:
$30,000/$50,000; Industry Concentration: Financial Services, Information
Technology; Function Concentration: Engineering, Finance/Accounting

**Ceryak, George V.** — *Co-Manager Central Region*
Management Recruiters International, Inc.
11611 North Meridian Street, Suite 100
Carmel, IN 46032
Telephone: (317) 582-0202
Recruiter Classification: Contingency; Lowest/Average Salary:
$30,000/$75,000; Industry Concentration: Generalist; Function
Concentration: Generalist

**Cesafsky, Barry R.** — *Partner*
Lamalie Amrop International
225 West Wacker Drive
Chicago, IL 60606-1229
Telephone: (312) 782-3113
Recruiter Classification: Retained; Lowest/Average Salary: $90,000/$90,000;
Industry Concentration: Generalist with a primary focus in
Healthcare/Hospitals, Information Technology; Function Concentration:
Generalist with a primary focus in Administration

**Chadick, Susan L.** — *Managing Director*
Gould, McCoy & Chadick Incorporated
300 Park Avenue, Suite 20F
New York, NY 10022
Telephone: (212) 688-8671
Recruiter Classification: Retained; Lowest/Average Salary: $90,000/$90,000;
Industry Concentration: Generalist; Function Concentration: Generalist

**Chalk, Charles J.** — *President*
GKR Americas, Inc.
100 Galleria Parkway, Suite 1100
Atlanta, GA 30339
Telephone: (770) 955-9550
Recruiter Classification: Retained; Lowest/Average Salary: $90,000/$90,000;
Industry Concentration: Generalist; Function Concentration: Generalist

**Chaloner, Edward** — *Principal*
Chaloner Associates
P.O. Box 1097, Back Bay Annex
Boston, MA 02117-1097
Telephone: (617) 451-5170
Recruiter Classification: Retained; Lowest/Average Salary: $/$75,000; Industry
Concentration: Generalist; Function Concentration: Generalist

**Chamberland, Roland R.** — *Manager Pacific Region*
Management Recruiters International, Inc.
Petaluma Marina, Suite 225
765 Baywood Drive
Petaluma, CA 94954-5388
Telephone: (707) 769-2955
Recruiter Classification: Contingency; Lowest/Average Salary:
$30,000/$75,000; Industry Concentration: Generalist; Function
Concentration: Generalist

**Chamberlin, Brooks T.** — *Managing Director*
Korn/Ferry International
237 Park Avenue
New York, NY 10017
Telephone: (212) 687-1834
Recruiter Classification: Retained; Lowest/Average Salary: $90,000/$90,000;
Industry Concentration: Generalist with a primary focus in Financial Services,
Insurance; Function Concentration: Generalist

**Chambers, Robert** — *Manager*
The Wentworth Company, Inc.
The Arcade Building
479 West Sixth Street
San Pedro, CA 90731
Telephone: (800) 995-9678
**Recruiter Classification:** Retained; **Lowest/Average Salary:** $/$90,000; **Industry Concentration:** Generalist; **Function Concentration:** Generalist

**Champoux, Yves** — *Partner*
Ward Howell International, Inc.
420 McGill Street, Room 400
Montreal, Quebec, CANADA H2Y 2G1
Telephone: (514) 397-9655
**Recruiter Classification:** Retained; **Lowest/Average Salary:** $75,000/$90,000; **Industry Concentration:** Generalist; **Function Concentration:** Generalist

**Chan, Margaret** — *Managing Director*
Webb, Johnson Associates, Inc.
280 Park Avenue, 43rd Floor
New York, NY 10017
Telephone: (212) 661-3700
**Recruiter Classification:** Retained; **Lowest/Average Salary:** $90,000/$90,000; **Industry Concentration:** Generalist with a primary focus in Biotechnology, Chemical Products, Financial Services, Healthcare/Hospitals, High Technology, Non-Profit, Pharmaceutical/Medical; **Function Concentration:** Generalist

**Chandler, Cynthia** — *Associate*
Kenzer Corp.
Fifth Street Tower, Suite 1330
150 South Fifth Street
Minneapolis, MN 55402
Telephone: (612) 332-7700
**Recruiter Classification:** Retained; **Lowest/Average Salary:** $50,000/$90,000; **Industry Concentration:** Generalist; **Function Concentration:** Generalist

**Chandler, Robert C.** — *Managing Director*
Ward Howell International, Inc.
3350 Peachtree Road N.E.
Suite 1600
Atlanta, GA 30326
Telephone: (404) 261-6532
**Recruiter Classification:** Retained; **Lowest/Average Salary:** $75,000/$90,000; **Industry Concentration:** Healthcare/Hospitals; **Function Concentration:** Generalist with a primary focus in Administration, General Management

**Chappell, Peter** — *Managing Director*
The Bankers Group
10 South Riverside Plaza, Suite 1424
Chicago, IL 60606
Telephone: (312) 930-9456
**Recruiter Classification:** Contingency; **Lowest/Average Salary:** $50,000/$75,000; **Industry Concentration:** Generalist with a primary focus in Automotive, Financial Services, High Technology, Information Technology, Insurance, Venture Capital; **Function Concentration:** Generalist with a primary focus in Administration, Finance/Accounting, General Management, Human Resources, Marketing, Sales, Women/Minorities

**Chargar, Frances** — *Manager Transportation*
Hunt Ltd.
21 West 38th Street
New York, NY 10018
Telephone: (212) 997-2299
**Recruiter Classification:** Contingency; **Lowest/Average Salary:** $30,000/$50,000; **Industry Concentration:** Automotive, Chemical Products, Consumer Products, Fashion (Retail/Apparel), Manufacturing, Pharmaceutical/Medical, Publishing/Media, Transportation; **Function Concentration:** Generalist

**Charles, Ronald D.** — *Partner*
The Caldwell Partners Amrop International
Sixty-Four Prince Arthur Avenue
Toronto, Ontario, CANADA M5R 1B4
Telephone: (416) 920-7702
**Recruiter Classification:** Retained; **Lowest/Average Salary:** $/$90,000; **Industry Concentration:** Generalist with a primary focus in Biotechnology, Board Services, Consumer Products, Financial Services, Hospitality/Leisure, Insurance, Pharmaceutical/Medical, Public Administration; **Function Concentration:** Generalist

**Chase, James** — *Associate*
Source Services Corporation
1500 West Park Drive, Suite 390
Westborough, MA 01581
Telephone: (508) 366-2600
**Recruiter Classification:** Contingency; **Lowest/Average Salary:** $30,000/$50,000; **Industry Concentration:** Financial Services, Information Technology; **Function Concentration:** Engineering, Finance/Accounting

**Chase, Kevin** — *Consultant*
Paul Ray Berndtson
101 Park Avenue, 41st Floor
New York, NY 10178
Telephone: (212) 370-1316
**Recruiter Classification:** Retained; **Lowest/Average Salary:** $90,000/$90,000; **Industry Concentration:** Generalist; **Function Concentration:** Generalist

**Chatterjie, Alok** — *Executive Recruiter*
MSI International
8521 Leesburg Pike, Suite 435
Vienna, VA 22182
Telephone: (703) 893-5669
**Recruiter Classification:** Contingency; **Lowest/Average Salary:** $30,000/$75,000; **Industry Concentration:** Financial Services, Healthcare/Hospitals, High Technology, Information Technology, Manufacturing; **Function Concentration:** Generalist with a primary focus in Administration, Engineering, Finance/Accounting, General Management, Marketing, Sales

**Chattin, Norma Anne** — *Branch Manager*
Accountants on Call
701 East Franklin Street, Suite 1408
Richmond, VA 23219
Telephone: (804) 225-0200
**Recruiter Classification:** Contingency; **Lowest/Average Salary:** $20,000/$30,000; **Industry Concentration:** Generalist; **Function Concentration:** Finance/Accounting

**Chauvin, Ralph A.** — *Partner*
The Caldwell Partners Amrop International
Sixty-Four Prince Arthur Avenue
Toronto, Ontario, CANADA M5R 1B4
Telephone: (416) 920-7702
**Recruiter Classification:** Retained; **Lowest/Average Salary:** $/$90,000; **Industry Concentration:** Generalist with a primary focus in Board Services, Chemical Products, Consumer Products, Fashion (Retail/Apparel), Insurance, Non-Profit, Public Administration, Transportation; **Function Concentration:** Generalist

**Chavous, C. Crawford** — *Consultant*
Phillips Resource Group
330 Pelham Road, Building A
Greenville, SC 29615
Telephone: (864) 271-6350
**Recruiter Classification:** Contingency; **Lowest/Average Salary:** $40,000/$50,000; **Industry Concentration:** Generalist with a primary focus in Chemical Products, Electronics, Environmental, High Technology, Information Technology, Manufacturing, Packaging, Utilities/Nuclear; **Function Concentration:** Generalist with a primary focus in Administration, Engineering, General Management, Human Resources, Marketing, Research and Development, Sales, Women/Minorities

**Cheadle, Neil E.** — *Managing Director*
The IMC Group of Companies Ltd.
P.O. Box 2954
Olympic Valley, CA 96146
Telephone: (916) 581-0102
**Recruiter Classification:** Retained; **Lowest/Average Salary:** $75,000/$90,000; **Industry Concentration:** Entertainment, Hospitality/Leisure; **Function Concentration:** Generalist

**Cheah, Victor** — *Associate*
Source Services Corporation
20 Burlington Mall Road, Suite 405
Burlington, MA 01803
Telephone: (617) 272-5000
**Recruiter Classification:** Contingency; **Lowest/Average Salary:** $30,000/$50,000; **Industry Concentration:** Financial Services, Information Technology; **Function Concentration:** Engineering, Finance/Accounting

**Cherbonnier, L. Michael** — *President*
The Cherbonnier Group, Inc.
3050 Post Oak Boulevard, Suite 1600
Houston, TX 77056
Telephone: (713) 688-4701
**Recruiter Classification:** Retained; **Lowest/Average Salary:** $75,000/$90,000; **Industry Concentration:** Generalist with a primary focus in Biotechnology, Board Services, Chemical Products, Electronics, Energy, Environmental, Financial Services, Healthcare/Hospitals, High Technology, Information Technology, Manufacturing, Oil/Gas, Utilities/Nuclear, Venture Capital; **Function Concentration:** Generalist with a primary focus in Administration, Engineering, Finance/Accounting, General Management, Human Resources, Marketing, Research and Development, Sales

**Cherbonnier, L. Michael** — *President*
TCG International, Inc.
471 North Post Oak Lane
Houston, TX 77024
Telephone: (713) 960-9511
Recruiter Classification: Executive Temporary; **Lowest/Average Salary:**
$75,000/$90,000; **Industry Concentration:** Generalist with a primary focus in
Board Services, Chemical Products, Electronics, Energy, High Technology,
Information Technology, Oil/Gas, Venture Capital; **Function Concentration:**
Generalist with a primary focus in Engineering, Finance/Accounting, General
Management, Marketing, Research and Development, Sales

**Chermak, Carolyn A.** — *Manager Eastern Region*
Management Recruiters International, Inc.
P.O. Box 1530
Greenwood Lake, NY 10925-1530
Telephone: (914) 477-9509
Recruiter Classification: Contingency; **Lowest/Average Salary:** $30,000/$75,000;
**Industry Concentration:** Generalist; **Function Concentration:** Generalist

**Chesla, Garry** — *Account Executive*
Executive Referral Services, Inc.
8770 West Bryn Mawr, Suite 110
Chicago, IL 60631
Telephone: (312) 693-6622
Recruiter Classification: Contingency; **Lowest/Average Salary:**
$30,000/$50,000; **Industry Concentration:** Fashion (Retail/Apparel); **Function
Concentration:** Finance/Accounting, General Management, Human Resources,
Women/Minorities

**Chewning, Ed** — *Co-Manager North Atlantic Region*
Management Recruiters International, Inc.
2037 St. Matthews Road
Orangeburg, SC 29118
Telephone: (803) 531-4101
Recruiter Classification: Contingency; **Lowest/Average Salary:** $30,000/$75,000;
**Industry Concentration:** Generalist; **Function Concentration:** Generalist

**Chilla, Mary** — *Associate*
Kenzer Corp.
6033 West Century Boulevard, Suite 808
Los Angeles, CA 90045
Telephone: (310) 417-8577
Recruiter Classification: Retained; **Lowest/Average Salary:** $50,000/$90,000;
**Industry Concentration:** Generalist; **Function Concentration:** Generalist

**Chitvanni, Andrew** — *Director*
National Restaurant Search, Inc.
910 West Lake Street, Suite 108
Roselle, IL 60172
Telephone: (708) 924-1800
Recruiter Classification: Retained; **Lowest/Average Salary:** $40,000/$50,000;
**Industry Concentration:** Hospitality/Leisure; **Function Concentration:** Generalist

**Chitvanni, John** — *President*
National Restaurant Search, Inc.
910 West Lake Street, Suite 108
Roselle, IL 60172
Telephone: (708) 924-1800
Recruiter Classification: Retained; **Lowest/Average Salary:** $75,000/$90,000;
**Industry Concentration:** Hospitality/Leisure; **Function Concentration:** Generalist

**Cho, Ui** — *Executive Recruiter*
Richard, Wayne and Roberts
24 Greenway Plaza, Suite 1304
Houston, TX 77046-2493
Telephone: (713) 629-6681
Recruiter Classification: Retained; **Lowest/Average Salary:** $50,000/$90,000;
**Industry Concentration:** Generalist with a primary focus in Financial Services;
**Function Concentration:** Generalist with a primary focus in Finance/Accounting

**Chojnacki, Bindi** — *Senior Consultant*
Raymond Karsan Associates
989 Old Eagle School Road, Suite 814
Wayne, PA 19087
Telephone: (610) 971-9171
Recruiter Classification: Contingency; **Lowest/Average Salary:**
$30,000/$90,000; **Industry Concentration:** Generalist; **Function
Concentration:** Generalist

**Chorman, Marilyn A.** — *Director Research/Recruiter*
Hite Executive Search
6515 Chase Drive
P.O. Box 43217
Cleveland, OH 44143
Telephone: (216) 461-1600
Recruiter Classification: Retained; **Lowest/Average Salary:** $90,000/$90,000;
**Industry Concentration:** Generalist with a primary focus in Education/Libraries,
Information Technology; **Function Concentration:** Generalist with a primary
focus in Administration, General Management, Human Resources,
Women/Minorities

**Chrisman, Timothy R.** — *Chief Executive Officer*
Chrisman & Company, Incorporated
350 South Figueroa Street, Suite 550
Los Angeles, CA 90071
Telephone: (213) 620-1192
Recruiter Classification: Retained; **Lowest/Average Salary:** $75,000/$90,000;
**Industry Concentration:** Generalist; **Function Concentration:** Generalist

**Christensen, Lois** — *Co-Manager*
Management Recruiters International, Inc.
Route 3, Box 138-A, Sunset Drive
Albion, IL 62806
Telephone: (618) 445-2333
Recruiter Classification: Contingency; **Lowest/Average Salary:**
$30,000/$75,000; **Industry Concentration:** Generalist; **Function
Concentration:** Generalist

**Christensen, Thomas C.** — *Co-Manager Midwest Region*
Management Recruiters International, Inc.
Route 3, Box 138-A, Sunset Drive
Albion, IL 62806
Telephone: (618) 445-2333
Recruiter Classification: Contingency; **Lowest/Average Salary:**
$30,000/$75,000; **Industry Concentration:** Generalist; **Function
Concentration:** Generalist

**Christenson, H. Alan** — *Managing Partner*
Christenson & Hutchison
466 Southern Boulevard
Chatham, NJ 07928
Telephone: (201) 966-1600
Recruiter Classification: Retained; **Lowest/Average Salary:** $75,000/$90,000;
**Industry Concentration:** Generalist with a primary focus in Financial Services,
Healthcare/Hospitals, Insurance, Manufacturing, Non-Profit, Public
Administration, Real Estate; **Function Concentration:** Generalist with a primary
focus in Finance/Accounting, General Management, Marketing, Sales

**Christian, Jeffrey E.** — *President and CEO*
Christian & Timbers
One Corporate Exchange
25825 Science Park Drive, Suite 400
Cleveland, OH 44122
Telephone: (216) 464-8710
Recruiter Classification: Retained; **Lowest/Average Salary:** $90,000/$90,000;
**Industry Concentration:** Board Services, Electronics, Entertainment, High
Technology, Information Technology, Manufacturing, Venture Capital; **Function
Concentration:** Engineering, General Management, Marketing, Research and
Development, Sales, Women/Minorities

**Christian, Kevin** — *Co-Manager Southwest Region*
Management Recruiters International, Inc.
6950 East Belleview, Suite 201
Englewood, CO 80111-1626
Telephone: (303) 267-0600
Recruiter Classification: Contingency; **Lowest/Average Salary:**
$30,000/$75,000; **Industry Concentration:** Generalist; **Function
Concentration:** Generalist

**Christiana, Jack** — *Executive Recruiter*
Richard, Wayne and Roberts
24 Greenway Plaza, Suite 1304
Houston, TX 77046-2493
Telephone: (713) 629-6681
Recruiter Classification: Retained; **Lowest/Average Salary:** $50,000/$90,000;
**Industry Concentration:** Generalist; **Function Concentration:** Generalist

**Christiansen, Amy** — *Executive Recruiter*
CPS Inc.
One Westbrook Corporate Centre, Suite 600
Westchester, IL 60154
Telephone: (708) 531-8370
Recruiter Classification: Contingency; **Lowest/Average Salary:**
$30,000/$50,000; **Industry Concentration:** Generalist with a primary focus in
Automotive, Biotechnology, Chemical Products, Consumer Products, High
Technology, Insurance, Manufacturing, Oil/Gas, Packaging,
Pharmaceutical/Medical; **Function Concentration:** Engineering, Research and
Development, Sales, Women/Minorities

**Christiansen, Doug** — *Executive Recruiter*
CPS Inc.
One Westbrook Corporate Centre, Suite 600
Westchester, IL 60154
Telephone: (708) 531-8370
Recruiter Classification: Contingency; **Lowest/Average Salary:**
$30,000/$50,000; **Industry Concentration:** Generalist with a primary focus in
Automotive, Biotechnology, Chemical Products, Consumer Products, High
Technology, Insurance, Manufacturing, Oil/Gas, Packaging,
Pharmaceutical/Medical; **Function Concentration:** Engineering, Research and
Development, Sales, Women/Minorities

**Christie, Ian** — *Associate*
The Caldwell Partners Amrop International
999 West Hastings Street
Suite 750
Vancouver, British Columbia, CANADA V6C 2W2
Telephone: (604) 669-3550
**Recruiter Classification:** Retained; **Lowest/Average Salary:** $/$90,000; **Industry Concentration:** Generalist; **Function Concentration:** Generalist

**Christman, Joel** — *Associate*
Source Services Corporation
525 Vine Street, Suite 2250
Cincinnati, OH 45202
Telephone: (513) 651-3303
**Recruiter Classification:** Contingency; **Lowest/Average Salary:** $30,000/$50,000; **Industry Concentration:** Financial Services, Information Technology; **Function Concentration:** Engineering, Finance/Accounting

**Christoff, Matthew J.** — *Director*
Spencer Stuart
401 North Michigan Avenue, Suite 3400
Chicago, IL 60611-4244
Telephone: (312) 822-0080
**Recruiter Classification:** Retained; **Lowest/Average Salary:** $90,000/$90,000; **Industry Concentration:** Generalist with a primary focus in Consumer Products, Information Technology; **Function Concentration:** Generalist with a primary focus in General Management, Marketing

**Christy, Michael T.** — *Managing Partner*
Heidrick & Struggles, Inc.
8000 Towers Crescent Drive, Suite 555
Vienna, VA 22182
Telephone: (703) 761-4830
**Recruiter Classification:** Retained; **Lowest/Average Salary:** $75,000/$90,000; **Industry Concentration:** Generalist with a primary focus in High Technology, Utilities/Nuclear; **Function Concentration:** Generalist

**Chronopoulos, Dennis** — *Associate*
Source Services Corporation
20 Burlington Mall Road, Suite 405
Burlington, MA 01803
Telephone: (617) 272-5000
**Recruiter Classification:** Contingency; **Lowest/Average Salary:** $30,000/$50,000; **Industry Concentration:** Financial Services, Information Technology; **Function Concentration:** Engineering, Finance/Accounting

**Chua, Jackie** — *Consultant*
Keith Bagg & Associates Inc.
36 Toronto Street, Suite 520
Toronto, Ontario, CANADA M5C 2C5
Telephone: (416) 863-1800
**Recruiter Classification:** Contingency, Executive Temporary; **Lowest/Average Salary:** $40,000/$60,000; **Industry Concentration:** Consumer Products, Financial Services, Insurance, Pharmaceutical/Medical; **Function Concentration:** Administration, Marketing

**Cicchino, William M.** — *Principal*
Lamalie Amrop International
200 Park Avenue
New York, NY 10166-0136
Telephone: (212) 953-7900
**Recruiter Classification:** Retained; **Lowest/Average Salary:** $90,000/$90,000; **Industry Concentration:** Generalist; **Function Concentration:** Generalist

**Cinco, Larry** — *Manager*
Management Recruiters International, Inc.
134 Fifth Avenue, Suite 208
Indialantic, FL 32903
Telephone: (407) 951-7644
**Recruiter Classification:** Contingency; **Lowest/Average Salary:** $30,000/$75,000; **Industry Concentration:** Generalist; **Function Concentration:** Generalist

**Cinco, Susan M.** — *Manager South Atlantic Region*
Management Recruiters International, Inc.
134 Fifth Avenue, Suite 208
Indialantic, FL 32903
Telephone: (407) 951-7644
**Recruiter Classification:** Contingency; **Lowest/Average Salary:** $30,000/$75,000; **Industry Concentration:** Generalist; **Function Concentration:** Generalist

**Cinquemano, Teri** — *Coordinator Clerical Staffing*
Accounting Personnel Consultants
210 Baronne Street, Suite 920
New Orleans, LA 70112
Telephone: (504) 581-7800
**Recruiter Classification:** Contingency, Executive Temporary; **Lowest/Average Salary:** $20,000/$20,000; **Industry Concentration:** Generalist; **Function Concentration:** Finance/Accounting

**Citarella, Richard A.** — *Vice President*
A.T. Kearney, Inc.
1100 Abernathy Road, Suite 900
Atlanta, GA 30328-5603
Telephone: (770) 393-9900
**Recruiter Classification:** Retained; **Lowest/Average Salary:** $90,000/$90,000; **Industry Concentration:** Generalist with a primary focus in Financial Services, Manufacturing; **Function Concentration:** Generalist with a primary focus in Finance/Accounting, Marketing, Sales

**Citera, Tom** — *Associate Recruiter*
Howe-Lewis International
521 Fifth Avenue, 36th Floor
New York, NY 10175
Telephone: (212) 697-5000
**Recruiter Classification:** Retained; **Lowest/Average Salary:** $90,000/$90,000; **Industry Concentration:** Education/Libraries, Healthcare/Hospitals, Non-Profit; **Function Concentration:** Generalist with a primary focus in General Management, Marketing, Women/Minorities

**Citrin, James M.** — *Director*
Spencer Stuart
Financial Centre
695 East Main Street
Stamford, CT 06901
Telephone: (203) 324-6333
**Recruiter Classification:** Retained; **Lowest/Average Salary:** $90,000/$90,000; **Industry Concentration:** Generalist with a primary focus in Entertainment, Financial Services, Publishing/Media; **Function Concentration:** Generalist

**Citrin, Lea** — *Executive Vice President*
K.L. Whitney Company
6 Aspen Drive
North Caldwell, NJ 07006
Telephone: (201) 228-7124
**Recruiter Classification:** Retained; **Lowest/Average Salary:** $75,000/$90,000; **Industry Concentration:** Financial Services; **Function Concentration:** Marketing, Sales

**Cizek, John T.** — *Principal*
Cizek Associates, Inc.
2021 Midwest Road, Suite 200
Oak Brook, IL 60521
Telephone: (708) 953-8570
**Recruiter Classification:** Retained; **Lowest/Average Salary:** $75,000/$90,000; **Industry Concentration:** Generalist with a primary focus in Aerospace/Defense, Automotive, Board Services, Consumer Products, Electronics, Financial Services, Healthcare/Hospitals, High Technology, Manufacturing, Pharmaceutical/Medical, Publishing/Media; **Function Concentration:** Generalist with a primary focus in Administration, Engineering, Finance/Accounting, General Management, Human Resources, Marketing, Research and Development, Sales

**Cizek, Marti J.** — *President*
Cizek Associates, Inc.
2390 East Camelback Road, Suite 300
Phoenix, AZ 85016
Telephone: (602) 553-1066
**Recruiter Classification:** Retained; **Lowest/Average Salary:** $75,000/$90,000; **Industry Concentration:** Generalist with a primary focus in Aerospace/Defense, Board Services, Consumer Products, Electronics, Financial Services, Healthcare/Hospitals, High Technology, Manufacturing, Non-Profit; **Function Concentration:** Generalist with a primary focus in Administration, Engineering, Finance/Accounting, General Management, Human Resources, Marketing, Research and Development, Sales, Women/Minorities

**Clanton, Diane** — *President*
Clanton & Co.
1095 North Main Street, Suite M
Orange, CA 92667
Telephone: (714) 532-5652
**Recruiter Classification:** Contingency; **Lowest/Average Salary:** $30,000/$50,000; **Industry Concentration:** Manufacturing; **Function Concentration:** Sales

**Clarey, Jack R.** — *Partner*
Clarey & Andrews, Inc.
1200 Shermer Road, Suite 108
Northbrook, IL 60062
Telephone: (847) 498-2870
**Recruiter Classification:** Retained; **Lowest/Average Salary:** $90,000/$90,000; **Industry Concentration:** Generalist with a primary focus in Automotive, Consumer Products, Electronics, Healthcare/Hospitals, High Technology, Manufacturing, Pharmaceutical/Medical; **Function Concentration:** Generalist with a primary focus in Administration, Finance/Accounting, General Management, Human Resources

**Clarey, William A.** — *Associate/Consultant*
Preng & Associates, Inc.
2925 Briarpark, Suite 1111
Houston, TX 77042
Telephone: (713) 266-2600
**Recruiter Classification:** Retained; **Lowest/Average Salary:** $75,000/$90,000; **Industry Concentration:** Generalist with a primary focus in Chemical Products, Energy, Environmental, Information Technology, Oil/Gas, Utilities/Nuclear; **Function Concentration:** Generalist with a primary focus in Engineering, Finance/Accounting, General Management, Human Resources, Research and Development

**Clark, Bruce M.** — *Executive Vice President*
IMCOR, Inc.
100 Prospect Street, North Tower
Stamford, CT 06901
Telephone: (203) 975-8000
**Recruiter Classification:** Executive Temporary; **Lowest/Average Salary:** $75,000/$90,000; **Industry Concentration:** Generalist; **Function Concentration:** Generalist

**Clark, Donald B.** — *Industry Leader - Financial Services*
Paul Ray Berndtson
10 South Riverside Plaza
Suite 720
Chicago, IL 60606
Telephone: (312) 876-0730
**Recruiter Classification:** Retained; **Lowest/Average Salary:** $90,000/$90,000; **Industry Concentration:** Financial Services, Manufacturing; **Function Concentration:** Generalist

**Clark, Elliot H.** — *Principal*
Raymond Karsan Associates
989 Old Eagle School Road, Suite 814
Wayne, PA 19087
Telephone: (610) 971-9171
**Recruiter Classification:** Contingency; **Lowest/Average Salary:** $30,000/$90,000; **Industry Concentration:** Generalist with a primary focus in Biotechnology, Pharmaceutical/Medical; **Function Concentration:** Generalist

**Clark, Evan** — *Vice President*
The Whitney Group
850 Third Avenue, 11th Floor
New York, NY 10022
Telephone: (212) 508-3500
**Recruiter Classification:** Retained; **Lowest/Average Salary:** $75,000/$90,000; **Industry Concentration:** Generalist with a primary focus in Financial Services, Real Estate, Venture Capital; **Function Concentration:** Generalist with a primary focus in Sales

**Clark, Gary** — *Managing Director*
MRG Search & Placement Inc.
2693 Whitney Avenue
Hamden, CT 06518
Telephone: (203) 230-1088
**Recruiter Classification:** Contingency; **Lowest/Average Salary:** $40,000/$90,000

**Clark, James** — *Manager/Lab Recruiter*
CPS Inc.
363 East Lincoln Highway, Suite E
DeKalb, IL 60115
Telephone: (815) 756-1221
**Recruiter Classification:** Contingency; **Lowest/Average Salary:** $30,000/$50,000; **Industry Concentration:** Generalist with a primary focus in Automotive, Biotechnology, Chemical Products, Consumer Products, High Technology, Insurance, Manufacturing, Oil/Gas, Packaging, Pharmaceutical/Medical; **Function Concentration:** Engineering, Research and Development, Sales, Women/Minorities

**Clark, James D.** — *Manager South Atlantic Region*
Management Recruiters International, Inc.
603-A East Government Street
Pensacola, FL 32501
Telephone: (904) 434-6500
**Recruiter Classification:** Contingency; **Lowest/Average Salary:** $30,000/$75,000; **Industry Concentration:** Generalist; **Function Concentration:** Generalist

**Clark, John Edward** — *Manager South Atlantic Region*
Management Recruiters International, Inc.
Sanlando Center, Suite 320
2170 West State Road 434
Longwood, FL 32779-4990
Telephone: (407) 865-7979
**Recruiter Classification:** Contingency; **Lowest/Average Salary:** $30,000/$75,000; **Industry Concentration:** Generalist; **Function Concentration:** Generalist

**Clark, Linda** — *Associate*
Kenzer Corp.
Triwest Plaza
3030 LBJ Freeway, Suite 1430
Dallas, TX 75234
Telephone: (214) 620-7776
**Recruiter Classification:** Retained; **Lowest/Average Salary:** $50,000/$90,000; **Industry Concentration:** Generalist; **Function Concentration:** Generalist

**Clark, Ronda** — *Co-Manager*
Management Recruiters International, Inc.
2510 Fairview Avenue East
Seattle, WA 98102
Telephone: (206) 328-0936
**Recruiter Classification:** Contingency; **Lowest/Average Salary:** $30,000/$75,000; **Industry Concentration:** Generalist; **Function Concentration:** Generalist

**Clark, Steven** — *Partner*
D.A. Kreuter Associates, Inc.
1100 East Hector Street, Suite 388
Conshohocken, PA 19428
Telephone: (610) 834-1100
**Recruiter Classification:** Retained; **Lowest/Average Salary:** $60,000/$90,000; **Industry Concentration:** Financial Services, Insurance; **Function Concentration:** General Management, Marketing, Sales

**Clark, W. Christopher** — *Partner*
Heidrick & Struggles, Inc.
One Peachtree Center
303 Peachtree Street, NE, Suite 3100
Atlanta, GA 30308
Telephone: (404) 577-2410
**Recruiter Classification:** Retained; **Lowest/Average Salary:** $75,000/$90,000; **Industry Concentration:** Generalist with a primary focus in Healthcare/Hospitals; **Function Concentration:** Generalist

**Claude, Abe** — *Partner*
Paul Ray Berndtson
101 Park Avenue, 41st Floor
New York, NY 10178
Telephone: (212) 370-1316
**Recruiter Classification:** Retained; **Lowest/Average Salary:** $90,000/$90,000; **Industry Concentration:** Healthcare/Hospitals; **Function Concentration:** Generalist

**Clauhsen, Elizabeth A.** — *Senior Vice President*
Savoy Partners, Ltd.
1620 L Street N.W., Suite 801
Washington, DC 20036
Telephone: (202) 887-0666
**Recruiter Classification:** Retained; **Lowest/Average Salary:** $90,000/$90,000; **Industry Concentration:** Generalist with a primary focus in Aerospace/Defense, Biotechnology, Board Services, Consumer Products, Electronics, Environmental, Financial Services, High Technology, Information Technology, Manufacturing, Pharmaceutical/Medical, Publishing/Media, Venture Capital; **Function Concentration:** Generalist with a primary focus in Administration, Engineering, Finance/Accounting, General Management, Human Resources, Marketing, Sales, Women/Minorities

**Clawson, Bob** — *Managing Director*
Source Services Corporation
3701 West Algonquin Road, Suite 380
Rolling Meadows, IL 60008
Telephone: (847) 392-0244
**Recruiter Classification:** Contingency; **Lowest/Average Salary:** $30,000/$50,000; **Industry Concentration:** Financial Services, Information Technology; **Function Concentration:** Engineering, Finance/Accounting

**Clawson, Robert** — *Managing Director*
Source Services Corporation
150 South Wacker Drive, Suite 400
Chicago, IL 60606
Telephone: (312) 346-7000
**Recruiter Classification:** Contingency; **Lowest/Average Salary:** $30,000/$50,000; **Industry Concentration:** Financial Services, Information Technology; **Function Concentration:** Engineering, Finance/Accounting

**Clayborne, Paul** — *Manager Manufacturing and Engineering*
Prestige Inc.
P.O. Box 421
Reedsburg, WI 53959
Telephone: (608) 524-4032
**Recruiter Classification:** Contingency; **Lowest/Average Salary:** $50,000/$90,000; **Industry Concentration:** Manufacturing; **Function Concentration:** Generalist

**Cleary, Thomas R.** — *Search Consultant*
ARJay & Associates
875 Walnut Street, Suite 150
Cary, NC 27511
Telephone: (919) 469-5540
**Recruiter Classification:** Contingency; **Lowest/Average Salary:** $40,000/$90,000; **Industry Concentration:** Aerospace/Defense, Automotive; **Function Concentration:** Generalist with a primary focus in Engineering, General Management, Marketing, Research and Development, Sales

**Cleeve, Coleen** — *Senior Associate*
Howe-Lewis International
521 Fifth Avenue, 36th Floor
New York, NY 10175
Telephone: (212) 697-5000
**Recruiter Classification:** Retained; **Lowest/Average Salary:** $90,000/$90,000; **Industry Concentration:** Education/Libraries, Healthcare/Hospitals, Non-Profit; **Function Concentration:** Generalist with a primary focus in General Management, Human Resources, Marketing, Women/Minorities

**Clegg, Cynthia** — *Vice President*
Horton International
10 Tower Lane
Avon, CT 06001
Telephone: (860) 674-8701
**Recruiter Classification:** Retained; **Lowest/Average Salary:** $90,000/$90,000; **Industry Concentration:** Generalist with a primary focus in Aerospace/Defense, Consumer Products, Financial Services, Insurance, Manufacturing; **Function Concentration:** Generalist with a primary focus in Engineering, Finance/Accounting, General Management, Human Resources, Marketing

**Clemens, William B.** — *Managing Director*
Norman Broadbent International, Inc.
200 Park Avenue, 20th Floor
New York, NY 10166
Telephone: (212) 953-6990
**Recruiter Classification:** Retained; **Lowest/Average Salary:** $90,000/$90,000; **Industry Concentration:** Generalist with a primary focus in Financial Services, Insurance; **Function Concentration:** Generalist with a primary focus in Administration, Finance/Accounting, General Management

**Clemens, William B.** — *Managing Director*
Norman Broadbent International, Inc.
100 Prospect Street
Stamford, CT 06901
Telephone: (203) 353-8070
**Recruiter Classification:** Retained; **Lowest/Average Salary:** $90,000/$90,000; **Industry Concentration:** Generalist with a primary focus in Financial Services, Insurance; **Function Concentration:** Generalist with a primary focus in Administration, Finance/Accounting, General Management

**Clement, Norman** — *Vice President*
Korn/Ferry International
1800 Century Park East, Suite 900
Los Angeles, CA 90067
Telephone: (310) 552-1834
**Recruiter Classification:** Retained; **Lowest/Average Salary:** $90,000/$90,000; **Industry Concentration:** Generalist with a primary focus in Board Services; **Function Concentration:** Generalist

**Cline, Mark** — *Manager Operations*
NYCOR Search, Inc.
4930 West 77th Street, Suite 300
Minneapolis, MN 55435
Telephone: (612) 831-6444
**Recruiter Classification:** Contingency; **Lowest/Average Salary:** $40,000/$75,000; **Industry Concentration:** Generalist with a primary focus in Biotechnology, Chemical Products, Electronics, High Technology, Information Technology, Manufacturing; **Function Concentration:** Engineering, Research and Development

**Clingan, Bob H.** — *Co-Manager Eastern Region*
Management Recruiters International, Inc.
One Marine Midland Plaza, Suite 603
Binghamton, NY 13901-3216
Telephone: (607) 722-2243
**Recruiter Classification:** Contingency; **Lowest/Average Salary:** $30,000/$75,000; **Industry Concentration:** Generalist; **Function Concentration:** Generalist

**Close, E. Wade** — *Managing Director*
Boyden
Allegheny Tower, Suite 2405
625 Stanwix Street
Pittsburgh, PA 15222-1423
Telephone: (412) 391-3020
**Recruiter Classification:** Retained; **Lowest/Average Salary:** $75,000/$90,000; **Industry Concentration:** Generalist; **Function Concentration:** Generalist with a primary focus in Engineering, Finance/Accounting, General Management, Human Resources, Marketing, Research and Development, Sales, Women/Minorities

**Clovis, James R.** — *Senior Vice President*
Handy HRM Corp.
250 Park Avenue
New York, NY 10177-0074
Telephone: (212) 557-0400
**Recruiter Classification:** Retained; **Lowest/Average Salary:** $90,000/$90,000; **Industry Concentration:** Generalist with a primary focus in Financial Services, Non-Profit; **Function Concentration:** Administration, General Management, Human Resources

**Cobb, Lynn A.** — *Manager*
Management Recruiters International, Inc.
124-B East Laurel Street
Springfield, IL 62704-3946
Telephone: (217) 544-2051
**Recruiter Classification:** Contingency; **Lowest/Average Salary:** $30,000/$75,000; **Industry Concentration:** Generalist; **Function Concentration:** Generalist

**Cobb, Mark A.** — *Manager Midwest Region*
Management Recruiters International, Inc.
124-B East Laurel Street
Springfield, IL 62704-3946
Telephone: (217) 544-2051
**Recruiter Classification:** Contingency; **Lowest/Average Salary:** $30,000/$75,000; **Industry Concentration:** Generalist; **Function Concentration:** Generalist

**Cocchiaro, Richard** — *Regional President*
Romac & Associates
20 North Wacker Drive
Suite 2420
Chicago, IL 60606
Telephone: (312) 263-0902
**Recruiter Classification:** Executive Temporary; **Lowest/Average Salary:** $/$60,000; **Industry Concentration:** Financial Services, Healthcare/Hospitals, High Technology, Hospitality/Leisure, Information Technology, Insurance; **Function Concentration:** Finance/Accounting

**Cocconi, Alan** — *Associate*
Source Services Corporation
150 South Wacker Drive, Suite 400
Chicago, IL 60606
Telephone: (312) 346-7000
**Recruiter Classification:** Contingency; **Lowest/Average Salary:** $30,000/$50,000; **Industry Concentration:** Financial Services, Information Technology; **Function Concentration:** Engineering, Finance/Accounting

**Cochran, Corinne** — *Principal*
Early Cochran & Olson, Inc.
401 North Michigan, Suite 515
Chicago, IL 60611-4205
Telephone: (312) 595-4200
**Recruiter Classification:** Retained; **Lowest/Average Salary:** $90,000/$90,000; **Industry Concentration:** Generalist; **Function Concentration:** Generalist

**Cochran, Hale** — *Partner*
Fenwick Partners
57 Bedford Street, Suite 101
Lexington, MA 02173
Telephone: (617) 862-3370
**Recruiter Classification:** Retained; **Lowest/Average Salary:** $90,000/$90,000; **Industry Concentration:** Board Services, Electronics, High Technology, Information Technology; **Function Concentration:** Engineering, Finance/Accounting, General Management, Marketing, Research and Development, Sales

**Cochrun, James** — *Associate*
Source Services Corporation
9020 Capital of Texas Highway
Building I, Suite 337
Austin, TX 78759
Telephone: (512) 345-7473
**Recruiter Classification:** Contingency; **Lowest/Average Salary:** $30,000/$50,000; **Industry Concentration:** Financial Services, Information Technology; **Function Concentration:** Engineering, Finance/Accounting

**Coelyn, Ronald H.** — *Director*
Spencer Stuart
10900 Wilshire Boulevard, Suite 800
Los Angeles, CA 90024-6524
Telephone: (310) 209-0610
**Recruiter Classification:** Retained; **Lowest/Average Salary:** $90,000/$90,000; **Industry Concentration:** Generalist; **Function Concentration:** Generalist

**Coff, Scott** — *Partner*
Johnson Smith & Knisely Accord
100 Park Avenue, 15th Floor
New York, NY 10017
Telephone: (212) 885-9100
**Recruiter Classification:** Retained; **Lowest/Average Salary:** $90,000/$90,000; **Industry Concentration:** Generalist; **Function Concentration:** Generalist

**Coffey, Patty** — *Information Technology Recruiter*
Winter, Wyman & Company
950 Winter Street, Suite 3100
Waltham, MA 02154-1294
Telephone: (617) 890-7000
Recruiter Classification: Contingency; Lowest/Average Salary:
$30,000/$60,000; Industry Concentration: Generalist with a primary focus in
Information Technology; Function Concentration: Generalist

**Coffman, Brian** — *Vice President*
Kossuth & Associates, Inc.
800 Bellevue Way N.E., Suite 400
Bellevue, WA 98004
Telephone: (206) 450-9050
Recruiter Classification: Retained; Lowest/Average Salary: $50,000/$90,000;
Industry Concentration: High Technology, Information Technology, Venture
Capital; Function Concentration: Generalist with a primary focus in
Administration, Engineering, Finance/Accounting, General Management, Human
Resources, Marketing, Research and Development, Sales, Women/Minorities

**Cohen, Kasumi** — *Principal*
Korn/Ferry International
The Transamerica Pyramid
600 Montgomery Street
San Francisco, CA 94111
Telephone: (415) 956-1834
Recruiter Classification: Retained; Lowest/Average Salary: $90,000/$90,000;
Industry Concentration: Generalist; Function Concentration: Generalist

**Cohen, Luis Lezama** — *Partner*
Paul Ray Berndtson
Palo Santo No. 6
Colonia Lomas Altas
Mexico City, D.F., MEXICO 11950
Telephone: (525) 259-6010
Recruiter Classification: Retained; Lowest/Average Salary: $90,000/$90,000;
Industry Concentration: Generalist with a primary focus in Insurance,
Publishing/Media; Function Concentration: Generalist

**Cohen, Michael R.** — *Chief Executive Officer*
Intech Summit Group, Inc.
5075 Shoreham Place, Suite 280
San Diego, CA 92122
Telephone: (619) 452-2100
Recruiter Classification: Retained; Lowest/Average Salary: $75,000/$90,000;
Industry Concentration: Generalist with a primary focus in Financial Services,
Healthcare/Hospitals, High Technology, Information Technology, Insurance,
Manufacturing; Function Concentration: Generalist with a primary focus in
Administration, Engineering, Finance/Accounting, General Management,
Marketing, Research and Development, Sales

**Cohen, Pamela** — *Legal Consultant*
TOPAZ Legal Solutions
383 Northfield Avenue
West Orange, NJ 07052
Telephone: (201) 669-7300
Recruiter Classification: Executive Temporary; Lowest/Average Salary:
$40,000/$75,000; Industry Concentration: Chemical Products, Consumer
Products, Electronics, Entertainment, Environmental, Financial Services, High
Technology, Manufacturing; Function Concentration: Generalist with a
primary focus in Women/Minorities

**Cohen, Pamela** — *Legal Consultant*
TOPAZ International, Inc.
383 Northfield Avenue
West Orange, NJ 07052
Telephone: (201) 669-7300
Recruiter Classification: Contingency; Lowest/Average Salary:
$40,000/$75,000; Industry Concentration: Chemical Products, Consumer
Products, Electronics, Entertainment, Financial Services, High Technology,
Manufacturing, Pharmaceutical/Medical; Function Concentration: Generalist
with a primary focus in Women/Minorities

**Cohen, Richard** — *Manager Eastern Region*
Management Recruiters International, Inc.
1650 Broadway, Suite 410
New York, NY 10019
Telephone: (212) 974-7676
Recruiter Classification: Contingency; Lowest/Average Salary: $30,000/$75,000;
Industry Concentration: Generalist; Function Concentration: Generalist

**Cohen, Robert C.** — *President*
Intech Summit Group, Inc.
5075 Shoreham Place, Suite 280
San Diego, CA 92122
Telephone: (619) 452-2100
Recruiter Classification: Retained; Lowest/Average Salary: $75,000/$90,000;
Industry Concentration: Generalist with a primary focus in Aerospace/Defense,
Financial Services, Healthcare/Hospitals, High Technology, Information
Technology, Insurance; Function Concentration: Generalist with a primary
focus in Administration, Engineering, Finance/Accounting, General
Management, Marketing, Research and Development, Sales

**Colasanto, Frank M.** — *Principal*
W.R. Rosato & Associates, Inc.
71 Broadway, Suite 1601
New York, NY 10006
Telephone: (212) 509-5700
Recruiter Classification: Retained; Lowest/Average Salary: $90,000/$90,000;
Industry Concentration: Financial Services, High Technology, Information
Technology; Function Concentration: Administration, Marketing, Research and
Development, Sales

**Colavito, Joseph W.** — *Principal*
Lamalie Amrop International
191 Peachtree Street N.E.
Atlanta, GA 30303
Telephone: (404) 688-0800
Recruiter Classification: Retained; Lowest/Average Salary: $90,000/$90,000;
Industry Concentration: Generalist; Function Concentration: Generalist

**Colborne, Janis M.** — *Associate*
AJM Professional Services
803 West Big Beaver Road, Suite 357
Troy, MI 48084-4734
Telephone: (810) 244-2222
Recruiter Classification: Contingency; Lowest/Average Salary: $30,000/$60,000;
Industry Concentration: Generalist with a primary focus in Financial Services,
Healthcare/Hospitals, Information Technology, Insurance, Manufacturing;
Function Concentration: Generalist with a primary focus in Finance/Accounting

**Cole, Elizabeth** — *Department Manager*
MSI International
8521 Leesburg Pike, Suite 435
Vienna, VA 22182
Telephone: (703) 893-5669
Recruiter Classification: Contingency; Lowest/Average Salary:
$30,000/$60,000; Industry Concentration: Generalist with a primary focus in
Healthcare/Hospitals; Function Concentration: Administration, Engineering,
Finance/Accounting, General Management, Marketing

**Cole, Kevin** — *Partner*
Don Richard Associates of Washington, D.C., Inc.
8180 Greensboro Drive, Suite 1020
McLean, VA 22102
Telephone: (703) 827-5990
Recruiter Classification: Contingency, Executive Temporary; Lowest/Average
Salary: $40,000/$60,000; Industry Concentration: Aerospace/Defense,
Automotive, Financial Services, Healthcare/Hospitals, High Technology,
Hospitality/Leisure, Real Estate; Function Concentration: Finance/Accounting

**Cole, Les C.** — *Manager Eastern Region*
Management Recruiters International, Inc.
Building 3, Unit C
154 West Street
Cromwell, CT 06416-2425
Telephone: (860) 635-0612
Recruiter Classification: Contingency; Lowest/Average Salary: $30,000/$75,000;
Industry Concentration: Generalist; Function Concentration: Generalist

**Cole, Ronald J.** — *Chairman*
Cole, Warren & Long, Inc.
2 Penn Center, Suite 312
Philadelphia, PA 19102
Telephone: (215) 563-0701
Recruiter Classification: Retained; Lowest/Average Salary: $90,000/$90,000;
Industry Concentration: Generalist; Function Concentration: Generalist

**Cole, Rosalie** — *Associate*
Source Services Corporation
150 South Wacker Drive, Suite 400
Chicago, IL 60606
Telephone: (312) 346-7000
Recruiter Classification: Contingency; Lowest/Average Salary:
$30,000/$50,000; Industry Concentration: Financial Services, Information
Technology; Function Concentration: Engineering, Finance/Accounting

**Cole, Sharon A.** — *Associate*
AJM Professional Services
803 West Big Beaver Road, Suite 357
Troy, MI 48084-4734
Telephone: (810) 244-2222
Recruiter Classification: Contingency; Lowest/Average Salary:
$30,000/$60,000; Industry Concentration: Generalist with a primary focus in
Financial Services, Healthcare/Hospitals, High Technology, Information
Technology, Insurance, Manufacturing

**Colella, Thomas V.** — *Vice President*
Korn/Ferry International
303 Peachtree Street N.E.
Suite 1600
Atlanta, GA 30308
Telephone: (404) 577-7542
Recruiter Classification: Retained; Lowest/Average Salary: $90,000/$90,000;
Industry Concentration: Generalist; Function Concentration: Generalist

**Coleman, Gregory** — *Associate/Executive Recruiter*
Strategic Associates, Inc.
13915 Burnet Road, Suite 304
Austin, TX 78728
Telephone: (512) 218-8222
**Recruiter Classification:** Contingency; **Lowest/Average Salary:**
$40,000/$50,000; **Industry Concentration:** Consumer Products,
Manufacturing; **Function Concentration:** General Management, Human
Resources

**Coleman, J. Gregory** — *Managing Director*
Korn/Ferry International
237 Park Avenue
New York, NY 10017
Telephone: (212) 687-1834
**Recruiter Classification:** Retained; **Lowest/Average Salary:** $90,000/$90,000;
**Industry Concentration:** Generalist with a primary focus in Financial Services;
**Function Concentration:** Generalist

**Coleman, J. Kevin** — *President*
J. Kevin Coleman & Associates, Inc.
P.O. Box 70747
Pasadena, CA 91117
Telephone: (818) 792-0533
**Recruiter Classification:** Retained; **Lowest/Average Salary:** $60,000/$90,000;
**Industry Concentration:** Generalist with a primary focus in
Aerospace/Defense, Entertainment, High Technology, Manufacturing, Venture
Capital; **Function Concentration:** Generalist with a primary focus in
Engineering, Finance/Accounting, General Management, Human Resources,
Marketing

**Coleman, John A.** — *Senior Vice President/Director*
Canny, Bowen Inc.
200 Park Avenue
New York, NY 10166
Telephone: (212) 949-6611
**Recruiter Classification:** Retained; **Lowest/Average Salary:** $90,000/$90,000;
**Industry Concentration:** Generalist with a primary focus in Biotechnology,
Entertainment, Financial Services, Venture Capital; **Function Concentration:**
Generalist with a primary focus in Finance/Accounting, General Management

**Coleman, Michael M.** — *Founder and Partner*
Coleman Legal Search Consultants
1435 Walnut Street, 3rd Floor
Philadelphia, PA 19102
Telephone: (215) 864-2700
**Recruiter Classification:** Contingency; **Lowest/Average Salary:**
$60,000/$75,000; **Function Concentration:** Generalist

**Coleman, Neil F.** — *Manager North Atlantic Region*
Management Recruiters International, Inc.
City Center, Suite 305
211 South Center
Statesville, NC 28677
Telephone: (704) 871-9890
**Recruiter Classification:** Contingency; **Lowest/Average Salary:**
$30,000/$75,000; **Industry Concentration:** Generalist; **Function
Concentration:** Generalist

**Coleman, Scott A.** — *Associate*
Kenzer Corp.
Fifth Street Tower, Suite 1330
150 South Fifth Street
Minneapolis, MN 55402
Telephone: (612) 332-7700
**Recruiter Classification:** Retained; **Lowest/Average Salary:** $50,000/$90,000;
**Industry Concentration:** Generalist; **Function Concentration:** Generalist

**Collard, Joseph A.** — *Senior Director*
Spencer Stuart
1111 Bagby, Suite 1616
Houston, TX 77002-2594
Telephone: (713) 225-1621
**Recruiter Classification:** Retained; **Lowest/Average Salary:**
$90,000/$90,000; **Industry Concentration:** Generalist with a primary focus
in Board Services, Chemical Products, Energy, Environmental,
Healthcare/Hospitals, Insurance, Manufacturing, Non-Profit, Oil/Gas, Public
Administration, Real Estate, Transportation, Utilities/Nuclear; **Function
Concentration:** Generalist with a primary focus in Engineering,
Finance/Accounting, General Management, Human Resources, Marketing,
Sales

**Collier, David** — *Recruiter*
Parfitt Recruiting and Consulting/PRO TEM
1540 140th Avenue, N.E., Suite 201
Bellevue, WA 98005
Telephone: (206) 646-6300
**Recruiter Classification:** Executive Temporary; **Lowest/Average Salary:**
$30,000/$60,000; **Industry Concentration:** Generalist; **Function
Concentration:** Finance/Accounting, General Management, Human Resources,
Marketing, Sales

**Colling, Douglas** — *Principal*
KPMG Management Consulting
2300 Yonge Street
Toronto, Ontario, CANADA M4P 1G2
Telephone: (416) 482-5786
**Recruiter Classification:** Executive Temporary; **Lowest/Average Salary:**
$75,000/$90,000; **Industry Concentration:** Generalist with a primary focus in
Automotive, Consumer Products, Electronics, High Technology, Information
Technology, Non-Profit, Packaging, Publishing/Media; **Function
Concentration:** Generalist with a primary focus in Administration, Engineering,
Finance/Accounting, General Management, Human Resources, Marketing,
Research and Development, Sales

**Colling, Douglas** — *Principal*
KPMG Executive Search
P.O. Box 31, Stn. Commerce Court
Toronto, Ontario, CANADA M5L 1B2
Telephone: (416) 777-8500
**Recruiter Classification:** Retained; **Lowest/Average Salary:** $75,000/$90,000;
**Industry Concentration:** Generalist; **Function Concentration:** Generalist

**Collins, Mollie P.** — *Partner*
Belvedere Partners
100 Larkspur Landing Circle, Suite 120
Larkspur, CA 94939
Telephone: (415) 925-9959
**Recruiter Classification:** Retained; **Lowest/Average Salary:** $75,000/$90,000;
**Industry Concentration:** Board Services, Non-Profit; **Function Concentration:**
Administration, Women/Minorities

**Collins, Robert** — *President*
Financial Search Corporation
2720 Des Plaines Avenue, Suite 106
Des Plaines, IL 60018
Telephone: (708) 297-4900
**Recruiter Classification:** Contingency; **Lowest/Average Salary:**
$30,000/$50,000; **Industry Concentration:** Generalist; **Function
Concentration:** Finance/Accounting

**Collins, Scott** — *Associate*
Source Services Corporation
5343 North 16th Street, Suite 270
Phoenix, AZ 85016
Telephone: (602) 230-0220
**Recruiter Classification:** Contingency; **Lowest/Average Salary:**
$30,000/$50,000; **Industry Concentration:** Financial Services, Information
Technology; **Function Concentration:** Engineering, Finance/Accounting

**Collins, Stephen** — *Managing Director*
The Johnson Group, Inc.
1 World Trade Center, Suite 4517
New York, NY 10048-0202
Telephone: (212) 775-0036
**Recruiter Classification:** Contingency; **Lowest/Average Salary:**
$60,000/$75,000; **Industry Concentration:** Financial Services; **Function
Concentration:** Finance/Accounting, Women/Minorities

**Collins, Tom** — *Vice President*
J.B. Homer Associates, Inc.
Graybar Building
420 Lexington Avenue, Suite 2328
New York, NY 10170
Telephone: (212) 697-3300
**Recruiter Classification:** Retained; **Lowest/Average Salary:** $90,000/$90,000;
**Industry Concentration:** Generalist with a primary focus in Information
Technology; **Function Concentration:** Generalist

**Collis, Gerald** — *Executive Recruiter*
TSS Consulting, Ltd.
2425 East Camelback Road
Suite 375
Phoenix, AZ 85016
Telephone: (602) 955-7000
**Recruiter Classification:** Contingency; **Lowest/Average Salary:**
$60,000/$75,000; **Industry Concentration:** Aerospace/Defense, Electronics,
High Technology; **Function Concentration:** Engineering, General Management,
Marketing

**Collis, Martin** — *Consultant*
E.L. Shore & Associates Ltd.
2 St. Clair Avenue, Suite 1201
Toronto, Ontario, CANADA M4T 2T5
Telephone: (416) 928-9399
**Recruiter Classification:** Retained; **Lowest/Average Salary:** $60,000/$90,000;
**Industry Concentration:** Generalist with a primary focus in Automotive,
Chemical Products, Consumer Products, Environmental, Financial Services,
Insurance, Manufacturing, Non-Profit; **Function Concentration:** Generalist

**Colman, Michael** — *President*
Executive Placement Consultants, Inc.
2700 River Road, Suite 107
Des Plaines, IL 60018
Telephone: (847) 298-6445
**Recruiter Classification:** Contingency; **Lowest/Average Salary:**
$40,000/$75,000; **Industry Concentration:** Generalist with a primary focus in
Consumer Products, Financial Services, Healthcare/Hospitals, Information
Technology, Manufacturing, Packaging, Pharmaceutical/Medical,
Transportation; **Function Concentration:** Finance/Accounting, Human
Resources, Women/Minorities

**Colosimo, Chris** — *Executive Recruiter*
Richard, Wayne and Roberts
24 Greenway Plaza, Suite 1304
Houston, TX 77046-2493
Telephone: (713) 629-6681
**Recruiter Classification:** Retained; **Lowest/Average Salary:** $50,000/$90,000;
**Industry Concentration:** Generalist; **Function Concentration:** Generalist with a
primary focus in Engineering

**Coltrane, Michael** — *Executive Recruiter*
Richard, Wayne and Roberts
4625 South Wendler Drive
Suite 111
Tempe, AZ 85282
Telephone: (602) 438-1496
**Recruiter Classification:** Retained; **Lowest/Average Salary:** $50,000/$90,000;
**Industry Concentration:** Generalist; **Function Concentration:** Generalist

**Colucci, Bart A.** — *President*
Colucci, Blendow and Johnson, Inc.
445 Greenbrier Road
Half Moon Bay, CA 94019
Telephone: (415) 712-0103
**Recruiter Classification:** Retained; **Lowest/Average Salary:** $60,000/$90,000;
**Industry Concentration:** Biotechnology, Healthcare/Hospitals,
Pharmaceutical/Medical; **Function Concentration:** Generalist with a primary
focus in Administration, Engineering, Finance/Accounting, General
Management, Human Resources, Marketing, Research and Development, Sales

**Comai, Christine** — *Associate*
Source Services Corporation
2000 Town Center, Suite 850
Southfield, MI 48075
Telephone: (810) 352-6520
**Recruiter Classification:** Contingency; **Lowest/Average Salary:**
$30,000/$50,000; **Industry Concentration:** Financial Services, Information
Technology; **Function Concentration:** Engineering, Finance/Accounting

**Combs, Stephen L.** — *Managing Director*
Juntunen-Combs-Poirier
600 Montgomery Street, 2nd Floor
San Francisco, CA 94111
Telephone: (415) 291-1699
**Recruiter Classification:** Retained; **Lowest/Average Salary:** $90,000/$90,000;
**Industry Concentration:** Consumer Products, Electronics, Entertainment, High
Technology, Information Technology, Publishing/Media; **Function
Concentration:** Generalist with a primary focus in Engineering, General
Management, Marketing, Research and Development, Sales

**Combs, Thomas** — *Associate*
Source Services Corporation
161 Ottawa NW, Suite 409D
Grand Rapids, MI 49503
Telephone: (616) 451-2400
**Recruiter Classification:** Contingency; **Lowest/Average Salary:**
$30,000/$50,000; **Industry Concentration:** Financial Services, Information
Technology; **Function Concentration:** Engineering, Finance/Accounting

**Commersoli, Al** — *Branch Manager*
Executive Referral Services, Inc.
8770 West Bryn Mawr, Suite 110
Chicago, IL 60631
Telephone: (312) 693-6622
**Recruiter Classification:** Contingency; **Lowest/Average Salary:**
$30,000/$50,000; **Industry Concentration:** Fashion (Retail/Apparel),
Hospitality/Leisure, Information Technology; **Function Concentration:**
Finance/Accounting, Human Resources, Women/Minorities

**Cona, Joseph A.** — *President*
Cona Personnel Search
625 South Second Avenue
Springfield, IL 62704-2500
Telephone: (217) 522-3933
**Recruiter Classification:** Contingency; **Lowest/Average Salary:**
$20,000/$50,000; **Industry Concentration:** Generalist with a primary focus in
Environmental, Financial Services, Information Technology, Insurance,
Manufacturing; **Function Concentration:** Generalist with a primary focus in
Administration, Engineering, Finance/Accounting, General Management

**Conard, Rodney J.** — *President*
Conard Associates, Inc.
74 Northeastern Boulevard, Suite 22A
Nashua, NH 03062
Telephone: (603) 886-0600
**Recruiter Classification:** Retained; **Lowest/Average Salary:** $90,000/$90,000;
**Industry Concentration:** Generalist with a primary focus in Education/Libraries,
Energy, Financial Services, Healthcare/Hospitals, High Technology,
Manufacturing; **Function Concentration:** Generalist with a primary focus in
Finance/Accounting, General Management

**Condit, Madeleine** — *Vice President*
Korn/Ferry International
120 South Riverside Plaza
Suite 918
Chicago, IL 60606
Telephone: (312) 726-1841
**Recruiter Classification:** Retained; **Lowest/Average Salary:** $90,000/$90,000;
**Industry Concentration:** Generalist with a primary focus in Non-Profit;
**Function Concentration:** Generalist

**Cone, Dan P.** — *Manager North Atlantic Region*
Management Recruiters International, Inc.
P.O. Box 699
Bunn, NC 27508
Telephone: (919) 269-6612
**Recruiter Classification:** Contingency; **Lowest/Average Salary:**
$30,000/$75,000; **Industry Concentration:** Generalist; **Function
Concentration:** Generalist

**Coneys, Bridget** — *Associate*
Source Services Corporation
8614 Westwood Center, Suite 750
Vienna, VA 22182
Telephone: (703) 790-5610
**Recruiter Classification:** Contingency; **Lowest/Average Salary:**
$30,000/$50,000; **Industry Concentration:** Financial Services, Information
Technology; **Function Concentration:** Engineering, Finance/Accounting

**Connaghan, Linda** — *Financial Recruiter*
Bowman & Marshall, Inc.
P.O. Box 25503
Overland Park, KS 66225
Telephone: (913) 648-3332
**Recruiter Classification:** Contingency; **Lowest/Average Salary:**
$30,000/$50,000; **Industry Concentration:** Automotive, Chemical Products,
Consumer Products, Fashion (Retail/Apparel), Financial Services, Insurance,
Manufacturing, Packaging, Pharmaceutical/Medical, Publishing/Media;
**Function Concentration:** Finance/Accounting

**Connelly, Heather** — *Partner*
The Caldwell Partners Amrop International
Sixty-Four Prince Arthur Avenue
Toronto, Ontario, CANADA M5R 1B4
Telephone: (416) 920-7702
**Recruiter Classification:** Retained; **Lowest/Average Salary:** $/$90,000; **Industry
Concentration:** Generalist; **Function Concentration:** Generalist

**Connelly, Kevin M.** — *Director*
Spencer Stuart
401 North Michigan Avenue, Suite 3400
Chicago, IL 60611-4244
Telephone: (312) 822-0080
**Recruiter Classification:** Retained; **Lowest/Average Salary:** $90,000/$90,000;
**Industry Concentration:** Generalist with a primary focus in Automotive,
Financial Services, Manufacturing, Venture Capital; **Function Concentration:**
Generalist with a primary focus in Administration, Finance/Accounting,
General Management

**Connelly, Laura J.** — *Manager Central Region*
Management Recruiters International, Inc.
2 Chatham Center
112 Washington Place, Suite 1570
Pittsburgh, PA 15219-3427
Telephone: (412) 566-2100
**Recruiter Classification:** Contingency; **Lowest/Average Salary:**
$30,000/$75,000; **Industry Concentration:** Generalist; **Function
Concentration:** Generalist

**Connelly, Scott** — *Recruiter*
Technical Connections Inc.
11400 Olympic Boulevard, Suite 770
Los Angeles, CA 90064
Telephone: (310) 479-8830
**Recruiter Classification:** Contingency; **Lowest/Average Salary:**
$40,000/$60,000; **Industry Concentration:** High Technology, Information
Technology; **Function Concentration:** Generalist

**Connelly, Thomas A.** — *Vice President*
Korn/Ferry International
200 South Biscayne Boulevard, Suite 2790
Miami, FL 33131
Telephone: (305) 579-1266
Recruiter Classification: Retained; Lowest/Average Salary: $90,000/$90,000;
Industry Concentration: Generalist with a primary focus in Hospitality/Leisure;
Function Concentration: Generalist

**Conner, John** — *Recruiter*
Flex Execs Management Solutions
16350 South 105th Court
Orland Park, IL 60462
Telephone: (708) 460-8500
Recruiter Classification: Executive Temporary; Lowest/Average Salary:
$40,000/$50,000; Industry Concentration: Generalist; Function
Concentration: Generalist with a primary focus in Finance/Accounting,
General Management, Human Resources, Marketing, Sales

**Conners, Theresa** — *Consultant Healthcare Search*
D. Brown and Associates, Inc.
610 S.W. Alder, Suite 1111
Portland, OR 97205
Telephone: (503) 224-6860
Recruiter Classification: Contingency; Lowest/Average Salary: $40,000/$50,000;
Industry Concentration: Healthcare/Hospitals

**Connet, Mel** — *Partner*
Heidrick & Struggles, Inc.
2740 Sand Hill Road
Menlo Park, CA 94025
Telephone: (415) 854-9300
Recruiter Classification: Retained; Lowest/Average Salary: $75,000/$90,000;
Industry Concentration: Generalist; Function Concentration: Generalist

**Connolly, Cathryn** — *Associate/Executive Recruiter*
Strategic Associates, Inc.
13915 Burnet Road, Suite 304
Austin, TX 78728
Telephone: (512) 218-8222
Recruiter Classification: Contingency; Lowest/Average Salary:
$50,000/$60,000; Industry Concentration: Electronics, High Technology,
Information Technology, Manufacturing; Function Concentration: General
Management, Women/Minorities

**Connolly, Michael R.** — *Manager Pacific Region*
Management Recruiters International, Inc.
7092 Sylvan Lane
Anderson, CA 96007
Telephone: (916) 365-6974
Recruiter Classification: Contingency; Lowest/Average Salary: $30,000/$75,000;
Industry Concentration: Generalist; Function Concentration: Generalist

**Connor, Michele** — *Executive Recruiter*
Abraham & London, Ltd.
7 Old Sherman Turnpike, Suite 209
Danbury, CT 06810
Telephone: (203) 730-4000
Recruiter Classification: Contingency; Lowest/Average Salary:
$40,000/$75,000; Industry Concentration: High Technology, Information
Technology; Function Concentration: Marketing, Sales

**Connors, Claire** — *Senior Associate*
Korn/Ferry International
Presidential Plaza
900 19th Street, N.W.
Washington, DC 20006
Telephone: (202) 822-9444
Recruiter Classification: Retained; Lowest/Average Salary: $90,000/$90,000;
Industry Concentration: Generalist; Function Concentration: Generalist

**Conover, Jo** — *Principal*
TASA International
430 Cowper Street, Suite 206
Palo Alto, CA 94301
Telephone: (415) 323-0202
Recruiter Classification: Retained; Lowest/Average Salary: $90,000/$90,000;
Industry Concentration: Generalist; Function Concentration: Generalist

**Conway, William P.** — *Executive Recruiter*
Phillips Resource Group
330 Pelham Road, Building A
Greenville, SC 29615
Telephone: (864) 271-6350
Recruiter Classification: Contingency; Lowest/Average Salary:
$40,000/$50,000; Industry Concentration: Chemical Products, Electronics,
Environmental, High Technology, Information Technology, Manufacturing,
Packaging, Utilities/Nuclear; Function Concentration: Generalist with a
primary focus in Administration, Engineering, General Management, Human
Resources, Marketing, Research and Development, Sales, Women/Minorities

**Cook, Charlene** — *Associate*
Source Services Corporation
15260 Ventura Boulevard, Suite 380
Sherman Oaks, CA 91403
Telephone: (818) 905-1500
Recruiter Classification: Contingency; Lowest/Average Salary:
$30,000/$50,000; Industry Concentration: Financial Services, Information
Technology; Function Concentration: Engineering, Finance/Accounting

**Cook, Dan** — *Manager Midwest Region*
Management Recruiters International, Inc.
3400 Dundee Road, Suite 340
Northbrook, IL 60062
Telephone: (847) 509-9000
Recruiter Classification: Contingency; Lowest/Average Salary:
$30,000/$75,000; Industry Concentration: Generalist; Function
Concentration: Generalist

**Cook, Dennis** — *Principal*
Korn/Ferry International
Scotia Plaza
40 King Street West
Toronto, Ontario, CANADA M5H 3Y2
Telephone: (416) 366-1300
Recruiter Classification: Retained; Lowest/Average Salary: $90,000/$90,000;
Industry Concentration: Generalist; Function Concentration: Generalist

**Cook, Nancy L.** — *Executive Vice President*
The Diversified Search Companies
2005 Market Street, Suite 3300
Philadelphia, PA 19103
Telephone: (215) 732-6666
Recruiter Classification: Retained; Lowest/Average Salary: $90,000/$90,000;
Industry Concentration: Generalist; Function Concentration: Generalist

**Cook, Patricia** — *Partner*
Heidrick & Struggles, Inc.
245 Park Avenue, Suite 4300
New York, NY 10167-0152
Telephone: (212) 867-9876
Recruiter Classification: Retained; Lowest/Average Salary: $75,000/$90,000;
Industry Concentration: Generalist; Function Concentration: Generalist

**Cooke, Jeffrey R.** — *Consultant*
Jonas, Walters & Assoc., Inc.
1110 North Old World Third St., Suite 510
Milwaukee, WI 53203-1102
Telephone: (414) 291-2828
Recruiter Classification: Retained; Lowest/Average Salary: $60,000/$90,000;
Industry Concentration: Generalist with a primary focus in Automotive,
Consumer Products, Electronics, High Technology, Information Technology,
Manufacturing; Function Concentration: Generalist with a primary focus in
Administration, Engineering, Finance/Accounting, General Management,
Human Resources, Marketing, Research and Development, Sales

**Cooke, Katherine H.** — *Vice President*
Horton International
10 Tower Lane
Avon, CT 06001
Telephone: (860) 674-8701
Recruiter Classification: Retained; Lowest/Average Salary: $90,000/$90,000;
Industry Concentration: Generalist with a primary focus in Consumer
Products, Energy, Financial Services, High Technology, Insurance,
Manufacturing, Publishing/Media; Function Concentration: Generalist with a
primary focus in Finance/Accounting, General Management, Human
Resources, Marketing, Sales

**Cooksey, Ben** — *Manager Southwest Region*
Management Recruiters International, Inc.
14133 Memorial Drive, Suite 2
Houston, TX 77079
Telephone: (713) 497-1444
Recruiter Classification: Contingency; Lowest/Average Salary:
$30,000/$75,000; Industry Concentration: Generalist; Function
Concentration: Generalist

**Coon, David** — *Vice President*
Don Richard Associates of Richmond, Inc.
7275 Glen Forest Drive, Suite 200
Richmond, VA 23226
Telephone: (804) 282-6300
Recruiter Classification: Contingency; Lowest/Average Salary:
$20,000/$30,000; Industry Concentration: Generalist; Function
Concentration: Finance/Accounting

**Cooper, Bill** — *Manager North Atlantic Region*
Management Recruiters International, Inc.
Kensington Place, Suite 520
7405 Shallowford Road
Chattanooga, TN 37421-2662
Telephone: (423) 894-5500
**Recruiter Classification:** Contingency; **Lowest/Average Salary:** $30,000/$75,000;
**Industry Concentration:** Generalist; **Function Concentration:** Generalist

**Cooper, David C.** — *President/Consultant*
David C. Cooper and Associates, Inc.
Five Concourse Parkway, Suite 2700
Atlanta, GA 30328
Telephone: (770) 395-0014
**Recruiter Classification:** Contingency, Executive Temporary; **Lowest/Average Salary:** $20,000/$40,000; **Industry Concentration:** Generalist; **Function Concentration:** Finance/Accounting

**Cooper, Larry W.** — *Manager North Atlantic Region*
Management Recruiters International, Inc.
5901-C Peachtree-Dunwoody Road, Suite 370
Atlanta, GA 30328-5342
Telephone: (770) 394-1300
**Recruiter Classification:** Contingency; **Lowest/Average Salary:** $30,000/$75,000;
**Industry Concentration:** Generalist; **Function Concentration:** Generalist

**Cooper, William** — *Account Executive*
Search West, Inc.
750 The City Drive South
Suite 100
Orange, CA 92668-4940
Telephone: (714) 748-0400
**Recruiter Classification:** Contingency; **Lowest/Average Salary:** $40,000/$60,000; **Industry Concentration:** Information Technology; **Function Concentration:** Generalist

**Copeland, Linda K.** — *Manager Southwest Region*
Management Recruiters International, Inc.
400 North Sam Houston Parkway East, Suite 312
Houston, TX 77060-3548
Telephone: (713) 999-5700
**Recruiter Classification:** Contingency; **Lowest/Average Salary:** $30,000/$75,000;
**Industry Concentration:** Generalist; **Function Concentration:** Generalist

**Cordaro, Concetta** — *Vice President*
Flynn, Hannock, Incorporated
1001 Farmington Avenue
West Hartford, CT 06107
Telephone: (860) 521-5005
**Recruiter Classification:** Retained; **Lowest/Average Salary:** $75,000/$90,000;
**Industry Concentration:** Generalist with a primary focus in Consumer Products,
Financial Services, Healthcare/Hospitals, Insurance, Manufacturing; **Function Concentration:** Generalist with a primary focus in Finance/Accounting, General Management, Human Resources, Marketing, Women/Minorities

**Corey, Michael J.** — *Managing Director*
Ward Howell International, Inc.
401 East Host Drive
Lake Geneva, WI 53147
Telephone: (414) 249-5200
**Recruiter Classification:** Retained; **Lowest/Average Salary:** $75,000/$90,000;
**Industry Concentration:** Generalist; **Function Concentration:** Generalist

**Corey, Michael J.** — *Shareholder*
Witt/Kieffer, Ford, Hadelman & Lloyd
2015 Spring Road, Suite 510
Oak Brook, IL 60521
Telephone: (708) 990-1370
**Recruiter Classification:** Retained; **Lowest/Average Salary:** $75,000/$90,000;
**Industry Concentration:** Healthcare/Hospitals; **Function Concentration:** Generalist with a primary focus in General Management

**Corey, Patrick M.** — *Managing Director*
Ward Howell International, Inc.
401 East Host Drive
Lake Geneva, WI 53147
Telephone: (414) 249-5200
**Recruiter Classification:** Retained; **Lowest/Average Salary:** $75,000/$90,000;
**Industry Concentration:** Generalist; **Function Concentration:** Generalist

**Cornehlsen, James H.** — *Partner*
Lamalie Amrop International
200 Park Avenue
New York, NY 10166-0136
Telephone: (212) 953-7900
**Recruiter Classification:** Retained; **Lowest/Average Salary:** $90,000/$90,000;
**Industry Concentration:** Generalist with a primary focus in Publishing/Media;
**Function Concentration:** Generalist with a primary focus in
Finance/Accounting, General Management, Marketing, Sales

**Cornfoot, Jim L.** — *Co-Manager*
Management Recruiters International, Inc.
8700 Crownhill, Suite 701
San Antonio, TX 78209
Telephone: (210) 829-8666
**Recruiter Classification:** Contingency; **Lowest/Average Salary:**
$30,000/$75,000; **Industry Concentration:** Generalist; **Function Concentration:** Generalist

**Corrigan, Gerald F.** — *Managing Partner*
The Corrigan Group
1333 Ocean Avenue
Santa Monica, CA 90401
Telephone: (310) 260-9488
**Recruiter Classification:** Retained; **Lowest/Average Salary:** $90,000/$90,000;
**Industry Concentration:** Generalist with a primary focus in Consumer
Products, Education/Libraries, Entertainment, Healthcare/Hospitals, Information
Technology, Manufacturing, Non-Profit, Publishing/Media; **Function Concentration:** Generalist with a primary focus in Administration,
Finance/Accounting, General Management, Human Resources, Marketing,
Sales

**Corso, Glen S.** — *Director*
Chartwell Partners International, Inc.
275 Battery Street, Suite 2180
San Francisco, CA 94111
Telephone: (415) 296-0600
**Recruiter Classification:** Retained; **Lowest/Average Salary:** $90,000/$90,000;
**Industry Concentration:** Financial Services, Real Estate; **Function Concentration:** Generalist with a primary focus in Administration,
Finance/Accounting, General Management, Marketing, Women/Minorities

**Corwin, J. Blade** — *Vice President*
Seitchik Corwin and Seitchik, Inc.
3443 Clay Street
San Francisco, CA 94118-2008
Telephone: (415) 928-5717
**Recruiter Classification:** Retained; **Lowest/Average Salary:** $40,000/$90,000;
**Industry Concentration:** Fashion (Retail/Apparel); **Function Concentration:** Generalist

**Costa, Cynthia A.** — *Executive Recruiter*
MSI International
229 Peachtree Street, NE
Suite 1201
Atlanta, GA 30303
Telephone: (404) 659-5050
**Recruiter Classification:** Contingency; **Lowest/Average Salary:**
$30,000/$75,000; **Industry Concentration:** Generalist with a primary focus in
Healthcare/Hospitals; **Function Concentration:** Generalist with a primary focus
in Administration, Engineering, Finance/Accounting, General Management,
Marketing, Sales

**Costa, Frances** — *Vice President*
Gilbert Tweed/INESA
415 Madison Avenue
New York, NY 10017
Telephone: (212) 758-3000
**Recruiter Classification:** Retained; **Lowest/Average Salary:** $90,000/$90,000;
**Industry Concentration:** Generalist; **Function Concentration:** Generalist

**Costello, Andrea L.** — *Vice President*
Gallin Associates
P.O. Box 13106
Clearwater, FL 34621
Telephone: (813) 724-8303
**Recruiter Classification:** Retained; **Lowest/Average Salary:** $50,000/$60,000;
**Industry Concentration:** Chemical Products, Environmental, Oil/Gas; **Function Concentration:** Engineering, Women/Minorities

**Costello, Jack** — *Senior Associate*
Gallin Associates
P.O. Box 13106
Clearwater, FL 34621
Telephone: (813) 724-8303
**Recruiter Classification:** Retained; **Lowest/Average Salary:** $50,000/$60,000;
**Industry Concentration:** Chemical Products, Environmental; **Function Concentration:** Engineering

**Costick, Kathryn J.** — *Vice President*
John Sibbald Associates, Inc.
8725 West Higgins Road, Suite 575
Chicago, IL 60631
Telephone: (312) 693-0575
**Recruiter Classification:** Retained; **Lowest/Average Salary:** $75,000/$75,000;
**Industry Concentration:** Entertainment, Fashion (Retail/Apparel),
Hospitality/Leisure, Non-Profit; **Function Concentration:** Administration,
General Management, Human Resources, Women/Minorities

**Coston, Bruce G.** — *Physician Recruiter*
MSI International
201 St. Charles Avenue
Suite 2205
New Orleans, LA 70170
Telephone: (504) 522-6700
**Recruiter Classification:** Contingency; **Lowest/Average Salary:**
$30,000/$60,000; **Industry Concentration:** Generalist with a primary focus in
Healthcare/Hospitals; **Function Concentration:** Generalist with a primary focus
in Administration, Engineering, Finance/Accounting, General Management,
Marketing, Sales

**Cotter, L.L.** — *Managing Director*
IMCOR, Inc.
12201 Merit Drive, Suite 170
Dallas, TX 75251
Telephone: (214) 239-7760
**Recruiter Classification:** Executive Temporary; **Lowest/Average Salary:**
$75,000/$90,000; **Industry Concentration:** Generalist; **Function
Concentration:** Generalist

**Cotterell, Dirk A.** — *Manager Pacific Region*
Management Recruiters International, Inc.
6600 South 1100 East, Suite 420
Salt Lake City, UT 84121-2400
Telephone: (801) 264-9800
**Recruiter Classification:** Contingency; **Lowest/Average Salary:**
$30,000/$75,000; **Industry Concentration:** Generalist; **Function
Concentration:** Generalist

**Cottick, Ron** — *Manager South Atlantic Region*
Management Recruiters International, Inc.
500 North Westshore Boulevard, Suite 540
Tampa, FL 33609
Telephone: (813) 281-2353
**Recruiter Classification:** Contingency; **Lowest/Average Salary:**
$30,000/$75,000; **Industry Concentration:** Generalist; **Function
Concentration:** Generalist

**Cottingham, R.L.** — *Director Legal Search*
Marvin L. Silcott & Associates, Inc.
7557 Rambler Road, Suite 1336
Dallas, TX 75231
Telephone: (214) 369-7802
**Recruiter Classification:** Contingency; **Lowest/Average Salary:**
$60,000/$90,000; **Industry Concentration:** Generalist with a primary focus in
Biotechnology, Chemical Products, Electronics, Energy, High Technology,
Manufacturing, Oil/Gas, Pharmaceutical/Medical; **Function Concentration:**
Generalist with a primary focus in Administration

**Cotugno, James** — *Associate*
Source Services Corporation
1 Gatehall Drive, Suite 250
Parsippany, NJ 07054
Telephone: (201) 267-3222
**Recruiter Classification:** Contingency; **Lowest/Average Salary:**
$30,000/$50,000; **Industry Concentration:** Financial Services, Information
Technology; **Function Concentration:** Engineering, Finance/Accounting

**Coughlin, Stephen** — *Associate*
Source Services Corporation
100 North Tryon Street, Suite 3130
Charlotte, NC 28202
Telephone: (704) 333-8311
**Recruiter Classification:** Contingency; **Lowest/Average Salary:**
$30,000/$50,000; **Industry Concentration:** Financial Services, Information
Technology; **Function Concentration:** Engineering, Finance/Accounting

**Coulman, Karen** — *Executive Recruiter*
CPS Inc.
One Westbrook Corporate Centre, Suite 600
Westchester, IL 60154
Telephone: (708) 531-8370
**Recruiter Classification:** Contingency; **Lowest/Average Salary:**
$30,000/$50,000; **Industry Concentration:** Generalist with a primary focus in
Automotive, Biotechnology, Chemical Products, Consumer Products, High
Technology, Insurance, Manufacturing, Oil/Gas, Packaging,
Pharmaceutical/Medical; **Function Concentration:** Engineering, Research and
Development, Sales, Women/Minorities

**Courtney, Brendan A.J.** — *Recruiter*
A.J. Burton Group, Inc.
120 East Baltimore Street, Suite 2220
Baltimore, MD 21202
Telephone: (410) 752-5244
**Recruiter Classification:** Contingency; **Lowest/Average Salary:**
$40,000/$75,000; **Industry Concentration:** Financial Services; **Function
Concentration:** Finance/Accounting

**Cowan, Roberta** — *Search Consultant*
Drew Associates International
77 Park Street
Montclair, NJ 07042
Telephone: (201) 746-8877
**Recruiter Classification:** Retained; **Lowest/Average Salary:** $60,000/$90,000;
**Industry Concentration:** Healthcare/Hospitals, Pharmaceutical/Medical;
**Function Concentration:** Generalist

**Cowling, Wes** — *Manager Eastern Region*
Management Recruiters International, Inc.
10 Mall Way
Simsbury, CT 06070-2244
Telephone: (860) 651-9306
**Recruiter Classification:** Contingency; **Lowest/Average Salary:**
$30,000/$75,000; **Industry Concentration:** Generalist; **Function
Concentration:** Generalist

**Cox, James O.** — *Manager*
MSI International
1050 Crown Pointe Parkway
Suite 1000
Atlanta, GA 30338
Telephone: (404) 394-2494
**Recruiter Classification:** Contingency; **Lowest/Average Salary:**
$30,000/$60,000; **Industry Concentration:** Generalist with a primary focus in
Manufacturing; **Function Concentration:** Administration, Engineering,
Finance/Accounting, General Management, Marketing

**Cox, Mark M.** — *Shareholder*
Witt/Kieffer, Ford, Hadelman & Lloyd
2015 Spring Road, Suite 510
Oak Brook, IL 60521
Telephone: (708) 990-1370
**Recruiter Classification:** Retained; **Lowest/Average Salary:** $75,000/$90,000;
**Industry Concentration:** Healthcare/Hospitals; **Function Concentration:**
Generalist with a primary focus in General Management

**Cox, William** — *Vice President*
E.J. Ashton & Associates, Ltd.
P.O. Box 1048
Lake Zurich, IL 60047-1048
Telephone: (847) 540-9922
**Recruiter Classification:** Contingency; **Lowest/Average Salary:**
$30,000/$60,000; **Industry Concentration:** Insurance; **Function
Concentration:** Generalist with a primary focus in Administration,
Finance/Accounting, General Management, Marketing, Sales

**Coyle, Hugh F.** — *Recruiter*
A.J. Burton Group, Inc.
120 East Baltimore Street, Suite 2220
Baltimore, MD 21202
Telephone: (410) 752-5244
**Recruiter Classification:** Contingency, Executive Temporary; **Lowest/Average
Salary:** $40,000/$75,000; **Industry Concentration:** Financial Services;
**Function Concentration:** Finance/Accounting

**Cozzillio, Larry** — *Vice President/General Manager*
The Andre Group, Inc.
500 North Gulph Road, Suite 210
King of Prussia, PA 19406
Telephone: (610) 337-0600
**Recruiter Classification:** Retained; **Lowest/Average Salary:** $75,000/$90,000;
**Industry Concentration:** Generalist; **Function Concentration:** Generalist with a
primary focus in Human Resources

**Crabtree, Bonnie** — *Vice President*
Korn/Ferry International
303 Peachtree Street N.E.
Suite 1600
Atlanta, GA 30308
Telephone: (404) 577-7542
**Recruiter Classification:** Retained; **Lowest/Average Salary:** $90,000/$90,000;
**Industry Concentration:** Generalist with a primary focus in
Healthcare/Hospitals; **Function Concentration:** Generalist

**Cragg, Barbara R.** — *Consultant*
Southwestern Professional Services
2451 Atrium Way
Nashville, TN 37214
Telephone: (615) 391-2722
**Recruiter Classification:** Contingency; **Lowest/Average Salary:**
$30,000/$50,000; **Industry Concentration:** Generalist with a primary focus in
Hospitality/Leisure, Insurance, Pharmaceutical/Medical, Publishing/Media;
**Function Concentration:** Generalist with a primary focus in Engineering,
Human Resources, Sales, Women/Minorities

**Cram, Noel** — *Vice President*
R.P. Barone Associates
57 Green Street
Woodbridge, NJ 07095
Telephone: (908) 634-4300
**Recruiter Classification:** Contingency; **Lowest/Average Salary:**
$30,000/$75,000; **Industry Concentration:** Aerospace/Defense, Electronics,
Information Technology, Manufacturing; **Function Concentration:** Engineering,
Research and Development

**Cramer, Barbara Lee** — *Physician Recruiter*
Physicians Search, Inc.
1224 Katella Avenue, Suite 202
Orange, CA 92667-5045
Telephone: (714) 288-8350
**Recruiter Classification:** Contingency; **Lowest/Average Salary:**
$90,000/$90,000; **Industry Concentration:** Biotechnology,
Healthcare/Hospitals, Pharmaceutical/Medical

**Cramer, Katherine M.** — *Vice President*
Pendleton James and Associates, Inc.
One International Place
Boston, MA 02110
Telephone: (617) 261-9696
**Recruiter Classification:** Retained; **Lowest/Average Salary:** $90,000/$90,000;
**Industry Concentration:** Generalist; **Function Concentration:** Generalist

**Cramer, Paul J.** — *Partner*
C/R Associates
1231 Delaware Avenue
Buffalo, NY 14209
Telephone: (716) 884-1734
**Recruiter Classification:** Contingency; **Lowest/Average Salary:**
$20,000/$50,000; **Industry Concentration:** Generalist with a primary focus in
Aerospace/Defense, Consumer Products, Financial Services,
Healthcare/Hospitals, Manufacturing, Real Estate; **Function Concentration:**
Administration, Finance/Accounting, Human Resources

**Crane, Howard C.** — *Director*
Chartwell Partners International, Inc.
275 Battery Street, Suite 2180
San Francisco, CA 94111
Telephone: (415) 296-0600
**Recruiter Classification:** Retained; **Lowest/Average Salary:** $90,000/$90,000;
**Industry Concentration:** Generalist with a primary focus in Consumer
Products, Electronics, Financial Services, High Technology, Hospitality/Leisure,
Information Technology, Insurance, Publishing/Media; **Function
Concentration:** Generalist with a primary focus in Finance/Accounting,
General Management, Human Resources, Marketing, Sales

**Crath, Paul F.** — *Partner*
Price Waterhouse
1 First Canadian Place, Box 190, Suite 3300
Toronto, Ontario, CANADA M5X 1H7
Telephone: (416) 863-1133
**Recruiter Classification:** Retained; **Lowest/Average Salary:** $75,000/$90,000;
**Industry Concentration:** Generalist with a primary focus in Automotive, Board
Services, Consumer Products, Education/Libraries, Energy, Environmental,
Financial Services, High Technology, Manufacturing, Oil/Gas, Packaging, Real
Estate, Transportation, Venture Capital; **Function Concentration:** Generalist
with a primary focus in Administration, Engineering, Finance/Accounting,
General Management, Human Resources, Marketing, Research and
Development, Sales

**Crawford, Cassondra** — *Associate*
Don Richard Associates of Washington, D.C., Inc.
1020 19th Street, NW, Suite 650
Washington, DC 20036
Telephone: (202) 463-7210
**Recruiter Classification:** Contingency; **Lowest/Average Salary:**
$20,000/$30,000; **Industry Concentration:** Aerospace/Defense, Financial
Services, Healthcare/Hospitals, Non-Profit, Real Estate; **Function
Concentration:** Finance/Accounting

**Crawford, Dick B.** — *Co-Manager*
Management Recruiters International, Inc.
2037 St. Matthews Road
Orangeburg, SC 29118
Telephone: (803) 531-4101
**Recruiter Classification:** Contingency; **Lowest/Average Salary:** $30,000/$75,000;
**Industry Concentration:** Generalist; **Function Concentration:** Generalist

**Crean, Jeremiah N.** — *Recruiter*
Bryant Research
466 Old Hook Road, Suite 32
Emerson, NJ 07630
Telephone: (201) 599-0590
**Recruiter Classification:** Contingency; **Lowest/Average Salary:**
$50,000/$90,000; **Industry Concentration:** Biotechnology,
Pharmaceutical/Medical; **Function Concentration:** Research and Development

**Creger, Elizabeth** — *Account Executive*
Search West, Inc.
100 Pine Street, Suite 2500
San Francisco, CA 94111-5203
Telephone: (415) 788-1770
**Recruiter Classification:** Contingency; **Lowest/Average Salary:**
$40,000/$60,000; **Industry Concentration:** Real Estate; **Function
Concentration:** Administration, Finance/Accounting, Marketing, Sales

**Crigler, Jim** — *Manager Midwest Region*
Management Recruiters International, Inc.
157 West 3rd Street, Suite 100
Winona, MN 55987
Telephone: (507) 452-2700
**Recruiter Classification:** Contingency; **Lowest/Average Salary:**
$30,000/$75,000; **Industry Concentration:** Generalist; **Function
Concentration:** Generalist

**Cripe, Joyce** — *Senior Principal*
Mixtec Group
31255 Cedar Valley Drive
Suite 300-327
Westlake Village, CA 91362
Telephone: (818) 889-8819
**Recruiter Classification:** Contingency; **Lowest/Average Salary:**
$60,000/$90,000; **Industry Concentration:** Healthcare/Hospitals; **Function
Concentration:** Generalist with a primary focus in General Management,
Research and Development

**Crist, Peter** — *President*
Crist Partners, Ltd.
303 West Madison, Suite 2650
Chicago, IL 60606
Telephone: (312) 920-0609
**Recruiter Classification:** Retained; **Lowest/Average Salary:** $90,000/$90,000;
**Industry Concentration:** Generalist with a primary focus in Automotive, Board
Services, Chemical Products, Consumer Products, Financial Services,
Insurance, Manufacturing, Venture Capital; **Function Concentration:** Generalist
with a primary focus in Finance/Accounting, General Management

**Critchley, Walter** — *President*
Cochran, Cochran & Yale, Inc.
955 East Henrietta Road
Rochester, NY 14623
Telephone: (716) 424-6060
**Recruiter Classification:** Contingency; **Lowest/Average Salary:**
$40,000/$60,000; **Industry Concentration:** Generalist with a primary focus in
Biotechnology, Consumer Products, Electronics, Financial Services, High
Technology, Manufacturing, Packaging, Pharmaceutical/Medical; **Function
Concentration:** General Management, Human Resources, Marketing, Research
and Development, Sales, Women/Minorities

**Critchley, Walter** — *Vice President*
Temporary Accounting Personnel, Inc.
955 East Henrietta Road
Rochester, NY 14623
Telephone: (716) 427-9930
**Recruiter Classification:** Executive Temporary; **Lowest/Average Salary:**
$20,000/$30,000; **Industry Concentration:** Generalist with a primary focus in
Financial Services; **Function Concentration:** Finance/Accounting, Human
Resources

**Cronin, Dolores** — *President*
Corporate Careers, Inc.
1500 Quail Street, Suite 290
Newport Beach, CA 92660
Telephone: (714) 476-7007
**Recruiter Classification:** Contingency; **Lowest/Average Salary:**
$30,000/$60,000

**Cronin, Richard J.** — *President*
Hodge-Cronin & Associates, Inc.
9575 West Higgins Road, Suite 904
Rosemont, IL 60018
Telephone: (847) 692-2041
**Recruiter Classification:** Retained; **Lowest/Average Salary:** $90,000/$90,000;
**Industry Concentration:** Generalist with a primary focus in Automotive,
Chemical Products, Electronics, Manufacturing, Packaging, Public
Administration, Publishing/Media; **Function Concentration:** Generalist

**Crowder, Edward W.** — *President*
Crowder & Company
2050 North Woodward Avenue, Suite 335
Bloomfield Hills, MI 48304
Telephone: (810) 645-0909
**Recruiter Classification:** Retained; **Lowest/Average Salary:** $90,000/$90,000;
**Industry Concentration:** Generalist with a primary focus in Automotive,
Electronics, Manufacturing, Packaging, Transportation; **Function
Concentration:** Generalist with a primary focus in Engineering,
Finance/Accounting, General Management, Human Resources, Marketing,
Sales, Women/Minorities

**Crowell, Elizabeth** — *Research Manager*
H.M. Long International, Ltd.
237 Park Avenue, 21st Floor
New York, NY 10017
Telephone: (212) 725-5150
**Recruiter Classification:** Retained; **Lowest/Average Salary:** $90,000/$90,000;
**Industry Concentration:** Generalist with a primary focus in Biotechnology,
Consumer Products, Electronics, Financial Services, Pharmaceutical/Medical;
**Function Concentration:** Generalist with a primary focus in Administration,
Engineering, General Management, Human Resources, Marketing, Research
and Development

**Crownover, Kathryn L.** — *Executive Recruiter*
MSI International
800 Gessner, Suite 1220
Houston, TX 77024
Telephone: (713) 722-0050
**Recruiter Classification:** Contingency; **Lowest/Average Salary:**
$30,000/$75,000; **Industry Concentration:** Generalist with a primary focus in
Healthcare/Hospitals; **Function Concentration:** Generalist with a primary focus
in Administration, Engineering, Finance/Accounting, General Management,
Marketing, Sales

**Crumbaker, Robert H.** — *Partner*
Lamalie Amrop International
Key Tower, 127 Public Square
Cleveland, OH 44114-1216
Telephone: (216) 694-3000
**Recruiter Classification:** Retained; **Lowest/Average Salary:** $90,000/$90,000;
**Industry Concentration:** Generalist; **Function Concentration:** Generalist with a
primary focus in Finance/Accounting, General Management

**Crump, William G.** — *Partner*
Paul Ray Berndtson
101 Park Avenue, 41st Floor
New York, NY 10178
Telephone: (212) 370-1316
**Recruiter Classification:** Retained; **Lowest/Average Salary:** $90,000/$90,000;
**Industry Concentration:** Generalist with a primary focus in Information
Technology; **Function Concentration:** Generalist

**Crumpley, Jim** — *President*
Jim Crumpley & Associates
1200 East Woodhurst Drive
Suite B-400
Springfield, MO 65804
Telephone: (417) 882-7555
**Recruiter Classification:** Contingency; **Lowest/Average Salary:**
$30,000/$60,000; **Industry Concentration:** Biotechnology, Consumer
Products, Pharmaceutical/Medical; **Function Concentration:** Engineering,
Research and Development

**Crumpton, Marc** — *Consultant/Director*
Logix Partners
1601 Trapelo Road
Waltham, MA 02154
Telephone: (617) 890-0500
**Recruiter Classification:** Retained; **Lowest/Average Salary:** $60,000/$75,000;
**Industry Concentration:** High Technology, Information Technology; **Function
Concentration:** Engineering

**Crumpton, Marc** — *Consultant/Director*
Logix, Inc.
1601 Trapelo Road
Waltham, MA 02154
Telephone: (617) 890-0500
**Recruiter Classification:** Retained; **Lowest/Average Salary:** $60,000/$75,000;
**Industry Concentration:** High Technology, Information Technology; **Function
Concentration:** Engineering

**Crumpton, Marc** — *Consultant*
Walden Associates
1601 Trapelo Road
Waltham, MA 02154
Telephone: (617) 890-8885
**Recruiter Classification:** Retained; **Lowest/Average Salary:** $90,000/$90,000;
**Industry Concentration:** High Technology, Information Technology; **Function
Concentration:** General Management

**Cruse, O.D.** — *Managing Director*
Spencer Stuart
1717 Main Street, Suite 5300
Dallas, TX 75201-4605
Telephone: (214) 658-1777
**Recruiter Classification:** Retained; **Lowest/Average Salary:** $90,000/$90,000;
**Industry Concentration:** Aerospace/Defense, Board Services, Electronics, High
Technology, Information Technology, Manufacturing, Venture Capital; **Function
Concentration:** Engineering, Finance/Accounting, General Management,
Marketing, Research and Development, Sales, Women/Minorities

**Cruz, Catherine** — *Office Manager/Legal Consultant*
TOPAZ International, Inc.
383 Northfield Avenue
West Orange, NJ 07052
Telephone: (201) 669-7300
**Recruiter Classification:** Contingency; **Lowest/Average Salary:**
$40,000/$75,000; **Industry Concentration:** Chemical Products, Consumer
Products, Electronics, Entertainment, Financial Services, High Technology,
Manufacturing, Pharmaceutical/Medical; **Function Concentration:** Generalist
with a primary focus in Women/Minorities

**Cruz, Catherine** — *Office Manager/Legal Consultant*
TOPAZ Legal Solutions
383 Northfield Avenue
West Orange, NJ 07052
Telephone: (201) 669-7300
**Recruiter Classification:** Executive Temporary; **Lowest/Average Salary:**
$40,000/$75,000; **Industry Concentration:** Chemical Products, Consumer
Products, Electronics, Entertainment, Environmental, Financial Services, High
Technology, Manufacturing; **Function Concentration:** Generalist with a
primary focus in Women/Minorities

**Crystal, Jonathan A.** — *Senior Director*
Spencer Stuart
1111 Bagby, Suite 1616
Houston, TX 77002-2594
Telephone: (713) 225-1621
**Recruiter Classification:** Retained; **Lowest/Average Salary:** $90,000/$90,000;
**Industry Concentration:** Generalist with a primary focus in Board Services,
Energy, Financial Services, Healthcare/Hospitals, Insurance, Manufacturing,
Oil/Gas, Real Estate; **Function Concentration:** Generalist with a primary focus
in Administration, Finance/Accounting, General Management, Marketing,
Sales, Women/Minorities

**Csorba, Les** — *Vice President*
A.T. Kearney, Inc.
3050 Post Oak Boulevard, Suite 570
Houston, TX 77056
Telephone: (713) 621-9967
**Recruiter Classification:** Retained; **Lowest/Average Salary:** $90,000/$90,000;
**Industry Concentration:** Generalist; **Function Concentration:** Generalist

**Cuddy, Brian C.** — *Managing Partner*
Romac & Associates
125 Summer Street, Suite 1450
Boston, MA 02110
Telephone: (617) 439-4300
**Recruiter Classification:** Executive Temporary; **Lowest/Average Salary:**
$/$60,000; **Industry Concentration:** Financial Services, Healthcare/Hospitals,
High Technology, Hospitality/Leisure, Information Technology, Insurance;
**Function Concentration:** Finance/Accounting

**Cuddy, Patricia** — *Associate*
Source Services Corporation
379 Thornall Street
Edison, NJ 08837
Telephone: (908) 494-2800
**Recruiter Classification:** Contingency; **Lowest/Average Salary:**
$30,000/$50,000; **Industry Concentration:** Financial Services, Information
Technology; **Function Concentration:** Engineering, Finance/Accounting

**Cuellar, Paulina Robles** — *Partner*
Paul Ray Berndtson
Palo Santo No. 6
Colonia Lomas Altas
Mexico City, D.F., MEXICO 11950
Telephone: (525) 259-6010
**Recruiter Classification:** Retained; **Lowest/Average Salary:** $90,000/$90,000;
**Industry Concentration:** Generalist with a primary focus in Consumer
Products; **Function Concentration:** Generalist

**Cuellar, Scott R.** — *Associate*
Russell Reynolds Associates, Inc.
200 South Wacker Drive
Suite 3600
Chicago, IL 60606
Telephone: (312) 993-9696
**Recruiter Classification:** Retained; **Lowest/Average Salary:** $90,000/$90,000;
**Industry Concentration:** Generalist; **Function Concentration:** Generalist

**Culotta, Jonathan** — *Managing Director*
MRG Search & Placement Inc.
2693 Whitney Avenue
Hamden, CT 06518
Telephone: (203) 230-1088
**Recruiter Classification:** Contingency; **Lowest/Average Salary:**
$40,000/$90,000

**Culp, Thomas C.** — *Senior Vice President*
The Diversified Search Companies
2005 Market Street, Suite 3300
Philadelphia, PA 19103
Telephone: (215) 732-6666
**Recruiter Classification:** Retained; **Lowest/Average Salary:** $90,000/$90,000;
**Industry Concentration:** Generalist; **Function Concentration:** Generalist

**Cummings, Harry J.** — *Principal*
Sanford Rose Associates
5237 Darrow Road, Suite 6
Hudson, OH 44236
Telephone: (216) 653-3325
**Recruiter Classification:** Contingency; **Lowest/Average Salary:**
$30,000/$75,000; **Industry Concentration:** Generalist with a primary focus in
Chemical Products; **Function Concentration:** Generalist

**Cundick, Jeff L.** — *Manager Pacific Region*
Management Recruiters International, Inc.
367 Civic Drive, Suite 7
Pleasant Hill, CA 94523
Telephone: (510) 602-4600
**Recruiter Classification:** Contingency; **Lowest/Average Salary:** $30,000/$75,000;
**Industry Concentration:** Generalist; **Function Concentration:** Generalist

**Cunneff, Harry J.** — *Manager Midwest Region*
Management Recruiters International, Inc.
191 East Deerpath, Suite 302
Lake Forest, IL 60045-1950
Telephone: (708) 604-9000
**Recruiter Classification:** Contingency; **Lowest/Average Salary:** $30,000/$75,000;
**Industry Concentration:** Generalist; **Function Concentration:** Generalist

**Cunningham, Claudia** — *Senior Associate*
Korn/Ferry International
One Landmark Square
Stamford, CT 06901
Telephone: (203) 359-3350
**Recruiter Classification:** Retained; **Lowest/Average Salary:** $90,000/$90,000;
**Industry Concentration:** Generalist; **Function Concentration:** Generalist

**Cunningham, Lawrence** — *Consultant*
Howard Fischer Associates, Inc.
1800 John F. Kennedy Boulevard, 7th Floor
Philadelphia, PA 19103
Telephone: (215) 568-8363
**Recruiter Classification:** Retained; **Lowest/Average Salary:** $90,000/$90,000;
**Industry Concentration:** Generalist; **Function Concentration:** Generalist

**Cunningham, Robert Y.** — *Director Consulting Services*
Goodrich & Sherwood Associates, Inc.
521 Fifth Avenue
New York, NY 10175
Telephone: (212) 697-4131
**Recruiter Classification:** Retained; **Lowest/Average Salary:** $60,000/$90,000;
**Industry Concentration:** Generalist with a primary focus in Biotechnology,
Board Services, Chemical Products, Consumer Products, Financial Services,
Healthcare/Hospitals, Information Technology, Insurance, Manufacturing,
Oil/Gas, Publishing/Media, Venture Capital; **Function Concentration:**
Generalist with a primary focus in Administration, Finance/Accounting,
General Management, Human Resources, Marketing, Sales

**Cunningham, Sheila** — *Director/Recruiter*
Adams & Associates International
978 Hampton Park
Barrington, IL 60010
Telephone: (847) 304-5300
**Recruiter Classification:** Retained; **Lowest/Average Salary:** $75,000/$75,000;
**Industry Concentration:** Generalist with a primary focus in High Technology,
Information Technology, Pharmaceutical/Medical; **Function Concentration:**
Generalist with a primary focus in Engineering, General Management, Marketing

**Cuomo, Frank** — *President*
Frank Cuomo and Associates, Inc.
111 Brook Street
Scarsdale, NY 10583
Telephone: (914) 723-8001
**Recruiter Classification:** Contingency; **Lowest/Average Salary:**
$30,000/$75,000; **Industry Concentration:** Chemical Products, Energy,
Environmental, High Technology, Manufacturing; **Function Concentration:**
Engineering, General Management, Marketing, Sales

**Curlett, Lisa** — *Senior Associate*
Korn/Ferry International
237 Park Avenue
New York, NY 10017
Telephone: (212) 687-1834
**Recruiter Classification:** Retained; **Lowest/Average Salary:** $90,000/$90,000;
**Industry Concentration:** Generalist; **Function Concentration:** Generalist

**Curren, Camella** — *Associate*
Source Services Corporation
4170 Ashford Dunwoody Road, Suite 285
Atlanta, GA 30319
Telephone: (404) 255-2045
**Recruiter Classification:** Contingency; **Lowest/Average Salary:**
$30,000/$50,000; **Industry Concentration:** Financial Services, Information
Technology; **Function Concentration:** Engineering, Finance/Accounting

**Currence, Anna** — *Associate*
Kenzer Corp.
777 Third Avenue, 26th Floor
New York, NY 10017
Telephone: (212) 308-4300
**Recruiter Classification:** Retained; **Lowest/Average Salary:** $50,000/$90,000;
**Industry Concentration:** Generalist; **Function Concentration:** Generalist

**Currie, Lawrence S.** — *Executive Recruiter*
MSI International
1050 Crown Pointe Parkway
Suite 1000
Atlanta, GA 30338
Telephone: (404) 394-2494
**Recruiter Classification:** Contingency; **Lowest/Average Salary:** $30,000/$75,000;
**Industry Concentration:** Generalist with a primary focus in Manufacturing;
**Function Concentration:** Generalist with a primary focus in Administration,
Engineering, Finance/Accounting, General Management, Marketing, Sales

**Curtis, Ellissa** — *Recruiter*
Cochran, Cochran & Yale, Inc.
955 East Henrietta Road
Rochester, NY 14623
Telephone: (716) 424-6060
**Recruiter Classification:** Contingency; **Lowest/Average Salary:**
$40,000/$60,000; **Industry Concentration:** Financial Services; **Function
Concentration:** Finance/Accounting, Women/Minorities

**Cushman, Judith** — *President*
Marshall Consultants/West
P.O. Box 1749
Seattle, WA 98111
Telephone: (206) 392-8660
**Recruiter Classification:** Retained; **Lowest/Average Salary:** $30,000/$90,000;
**Industry Concentration:** Generalist with a primary focus in Energy, High
Technology; **Function Concentration:** Generalist

**Cutka, Matthew** — *Associate*
Source Services Corporation
2029 Century Park East, Suite 1350
Los Angeles, CA 90067
Telephone: (310) 277-8092
**Recruiter Classification:** Contingency; **Lowest/Average Salary:**
$30,000/$50,000; **Industry Concentration:** Financial Services, Information
Technology; **Function Concentration:** Engineering, Finance/Accounting

**Cyphers, Ralph R.** — *Senior Associate/Executive Recruiter*
Strategic Associates, Inc.
13915 Burnet Road, Suite 304
Austin, TX 78728
Telephone: (512) 218-8222
**Recruiter Classification:** Contingency; **Lowest/Average Salary:**
$90,000/$90,000; **Industry Concentration:** High Technology, Information
Technology, Manufacturing; **Function Concentration:** General Management

**Czajkowski, John** — *Manager Eastern Region*
Management Recruiters International, Inc.
2083 West Street, Suite 5A
Annapolis, MD 21401-3030
Telephone: (410) 841-6600
**Recruiter Classification:** Contingency; **Lowest/Average Salary:** $30,000/$75,000;
**Industry Concentration:** Generalist; **Function Concentration:** Generalist

**Czamanske, Paul W.** — *President and CEO*
Executive Interim Management, Inc.
401 South Woodward Avenue
Suite 460
Birmingham, MI 48009-6613
Telephone: (810) 540-9110
**Recruiter Classification:** Executive Temporary; **Lowest/Average Salary:**
$75,000/$90,000; **Industry Concentration:** Generalist; **Function
Concentration:** Generalist

**Czamanske, Paul W.** — *President and CEO*
Compass Group Ltd.
401 South Woodward Avenue, Suite 460
Birmingham, MI 48009-6613
Telephone: (810) 540-9110
**Recruiter Classification:** Retained; **Lowest/Average Salary:** $75,000/$90,000;
**Industry Concentration:** Automotive, Chemical Products, Education/Libraries,
Electronics, Information Technology, Manufacturing, Transportation; **Function
Concentration:** Engineering, Finance/Accounting, General Management, Human
Resources, Marketing, Research and Development, Sales, Women/Minorities

**Czamanske, Peter M.** — *Director Research and Administration*
Executive Interim Management, Inc.
401 South Woodward Avenue
Suite 460
Birmingham, MI 48009-6613
Telephone: (810) 540-9110
**Recruiter Classification:** Executive Temporary; **Lowest/Average Salary:** $75,000/$90,000; **Industry Concentration:** Generalist; **Function Concentration:** Generalist

**Czepiel, Susan** — *Executive Recruiter*
CPS Inc.
303 Congress Street, 5th Floor
Boston, MA 02210
Telephone: (617) 439-7950
**Recruiter Classification:** Contingency; **Lowest/Average Salary:** $30,000/$50,000; **Industry Concentration:** Generalist with a primary focus in Automotive, Biotechnology, Chemical Products, Consumer Products, High Technology, Insurance, Manufacturing, Oil/Gas, Packaging, Pharmaceutical/Medical; **Function Concentration:** Engineering, Research and Development, Sales, Women/Minorities

**D'Alessio, Gary A.** — *President*
Chicago Legal Search, Ltd.
33 North Dearborn Street, Suite 2302
Chicago, IL 60602-3109
Telephone: (312) 251-2580
**Recruiter Classification:** Contingency; **Lowest/Average Salary:** $40,000/$90,000; **Industry Concentration:** Consumer Products, Electronics, Energy, Entertainment, Environmental, Healthcare/Hospitals, High Technology, Information Technology, Non-Profit, Oil/Gas, Pharmaceutical/Medical, Venture Capital; **Function Concentration:** Women/Minorities

**D'Ambrosio, Nicholas** — *Senior Partner*
Alexander Ross Inc.
280 Madison Avenue
New York, NY 10016
Telephone: (212) 889-9333
**Recruiter Classification:** Retained; **Lowest/Average Salary:** $75,000/$90,000; **Industry Concentration:** Generalist; **Function Concentration:** Human Resources

**D'Angelo, Ron E.** — *Manager Eastern Region*
Management Recruiters International, Inc.
201 North Charles Street, Suite 2208
Baltimore, MD 21201-4102
Telephone: (410) 385-0300
**Recruiter Classification:** Contingency; **Lowest/Average Salary:** $30,000/$75,000; **Industry Concentration:** Generalist; **Function Concentration:** Generalist

**D'Elia, Arthur P.** — *Vice President*
Korn/Ferry International
237 Park Avenue
New York, NY 10017
Telephone: (212) 687-1834
**Recruiter Classification:** Retained; **Lowest/Average Salary:** $90,000/$90,000; **Industry Concentration:** Generalist with a primary focus in Financial Services; **Function Concentration:** Generalist

**D'Eramo, Tony P.** — *Co-Owner*
Management Recruiters International, Inc.
Bartlett, Suite 800
36 East Fourth Street
Cincinnati, OH 45202-2451
Telephone: (513) 651-5500
**Recruiter Classification:** Contingency; **Lowest/Average Salary:** $30,000/$75,000; **Industry Concentration:** Generalist; **Function Concentration:** Generalist

**Dabich, Thomas M.** — *Vice President*
Robert Harkins Associates, Inc.
P.O. Box 236
1248 West Main Street
Ephrata, PA 17522
Telephone: (717) 733-9664
**Recruiter Classification:** Contingency; **Lowest/Average Salary:** $40,000/$50,000; **Industry Concentration:** Generalist with a primary focus in Automotive, Chemical Products, Consumer Products, Electronics, Financial Services, Manufacturing, Packaging, Pharmaceutical/Medical; **Function Concentration:** Generalist with a primary focus in Finance/Accounting

**Dach, Bradley M.** — *Manager Midwest Region*
Management Recruiters International, Inc.
Country Club Estates
1812 24 Avenue West, Suite 304, P.O. Box 1400
Spencer, IA 51301
Telephone: (712) 262-2701
**Recruiter Classification:** Contingency; **Lowest/Average Salary:** $30,000/$75,000; **Industry Concentration:** Generalist; **Function Concentration:** Generalist

**Daily, John C.** — *Executive Vice President*
Handy HRM Corp.
250 Park Avenue
New York, NY 10177-0074
Telephone: (212) 557-0400
**Recruiter Classification:** Retained; **Lowest/Average Salary:** $90,000/$90,000; **Industry Concentration:** Generalist with a primary focus in High Technology; **Function Concentration:** General Management, Research and Development

**Dalton, Bret** — *Associate*
Robert W. Dingman Company, Inc.
32129 West Lindero Canyon Road
Suite 206
Westlake Village, CA 91361
Telephone: (818) 991-5950
**Recruiter Classification:** Retained; **Lowest/Average Salary:** $90,000/$90,000; **Industry Concentration:** Generalist with a primary focus in Consumer Products, High Technology, Non-Profit, Publishing/Media; **Function Concentration:** Generalist with a primary focus in Finance/Accounting, General Management, Marketing, Sales

**Dalton, David R.** — *Executive Recruiter*
MSI International
800 Gessner, Suite 1220
Houston, TX 77024
Telephone: (713) 722-0050
**Recruiter Classification:** Contingency; **Lowest/Average Salary:** $30,000/$75,000; **Industry Concentration:** Generalist with a primary focus in Healthcare/Hospitals; **Function Concentration:** Generalist with a primary focus in Administration, Engineering, Finance/Accounting, General Management, Marketing, Sales

**Damon, Richard E.** — *President*
Damon & Associates, Inc.
7515 Greenville Avenue, Suite 900
Dallas, TX 75231
Telephone: (214) 696-6990
**Recruiter Classification:** Contingency; **Lowest/Average Salary:** $30,000/$50,000; **Industry Concentration:** Generalist with a primary focus in Manufacturing; **Function Concentration:** General Management, Marketing, Sales

**Damon, Robert A.** — *Managing Director*
Spencer Stuart
277 Park Avenue, 29th Floor
New York, NY 10172
Telephone: (212) 336-0200
**Recruiter Classification:** Retained; **Lowest/Average Salary:** $90,000/$90,000; **Industry Concentration:** Generalist with a primary focus in Automotive, Consumer Products, Entertainment, Manufacturing, Transportation; **Function Concentration:** Generalist with a primary focus in General Management, Marketing, Sales

**Dandurand, Jeff J.** — *Executive Vice President/ Managing Director*
DHR International, Inc.
Two Galleria Tower
13455 Noel Road, Suite 1000
Dallas, TX 75240
Telephone: (214) 774-4555
**Recruiter Classification:** Retained; **Lowest/Average Salary:** $60,000/$90,000; **Industry Concentration:** Generalist; **Function Concentration:** Generalist

**Danforth, Monica** — *Specialist Contract Recruiting*
Search Consultants International, Inc.
4545 Post Oak Place, Suite 208
Houston, TX 77027
Telephone: (713) 622-9188
**Recruiter Classification:** Contingency, Executive Temporary; **Lowest/Average Salary:** $60,000/$75,000; **Industry Concentration:** Chemical Products, Energy, Environmental, Manufacturing, Oil/Gas; **Function Concentration:** Engineering, General Management, Marketing

**Danforth, W. Michael** — *Executive Vice President*
Hyde Danforth Wold & Co.
5950 Berkshire Lane, Suite 1600
Dallas, TX 75225
Telephone: (214) 691-5966
**Recruiter Classification:** Retained; **Lowest/Average Salary:** $50,000/$75,000; **Industry Concentration:** Generalist with a primary focus in Information Technology, Insurance, Publishing/Media, Transportation; **Function Concentration:** Generalist

**Daniel, Beverly** — *Partner*
Foy, Schneid & Daniel, Inc.
555 Madison Avenue, 12th Floor
New York, NY 10022
Telephone: (212) 980-2525
**Recruiter Classification:** Retained; **Lowest/Average Salary:** $60,000/$90,000; **Industry Concentration:** Generalist with a primary focus in Chemical Products, Consumer Products, Energy, Environmental, Information Technology, Pharmaceutical/Medical; **Function Concentration:** Generalist with a primary focus in Engineering, Finance/Accounting, General Management, Human Resources, Marketing

**Daniel, David S.** — *Director*
Spencer Stuart
277 Park Avenue, 29th Floor
New York, NY 10172
Telephone: (212) 336-0200
**Recruiter Classification:** Retained; **Lowest/Average Salary:** $90,000/$90,000;
**Industry Concentration:** Generalist with a primary focus in Consumer
Products, Fashion (Retail/Apparel); **Function Concentration:** Generalist

**Daniels, Alfred** — *Managing Director*
Alfred Daniels & Associates
5795 Waverly Avenue
La Jolla, CA 92037
Telephone: (619) 459-4009
**Recruiter Classification:** Contingency; **Lowest/Average Salary:** $75,000/$90,000;
**Industry Concentration:** Financial Services; **Function Concentration:** Generalist
with a primary focus in Administration, Finance/Accounting, General
Management, Marketing, Research and Development, Sales

**Daniels, David** — *Account Executive*
Search West, Inc.
1888 Century Park East
Suite 2050
Los Angeles, CA 90067-1736
Telephone: (310) 284-8888
**Recruiter Classification:** Contingency; **Lowest/Average Salary:** $40,000/$60,000;
**Industry Concentration:** Healthcare/Hospitals; **Function Concentration:** General
Management, Marketing, Research and Development, Sales

**Daniels, Leonard** — *President*
Placement Associates Inc.
136 East 57th Street
New York, NY 10022
Telephone: (212) 980-5969
**Recruiter Classification:** Retained; **Lowest/Average Salary:** $40,000/$90,000;
**Industry Concentration:** Generalist; **Function Concentration:** Marketing

**Dankberg, Iris** — *Associate*
Source Services Corporation
4170 Ashford Dunwoody Road, Suite 285
Atlanta, GA 30319
Telephone: (404) 255-2045
**Recruiter Classification:** Contingency; **Lowest/Average Salary:**
$30,000/$50,000; **Industry Concentration:** Financial Services, Information
Technology; **Function Concentration:** Engineering, Finance/Accounting

**Dankowski, Thomas A.** — *President*
Dankowski and Associates, Inc.
6479 Stoney Ridge Road, Suite 200NE
No. Ridgeville, OH 44039
Telephone: (216) 327-8717
**Recruiter Classification:** Retained; **Lowest/Average Salary:** $50,000/$75,000;
**Industry Concentration:** Generalist; **Function Concentration:** Human Resources

**Dannenberg, Richard A.** — *Principal*
Roberts Ryan and Bentley
1107 Kenilworth Drive, Suite 208
Towson, MD 21204
Telephone: (410) 321-6600
**Recruiter Classification:** Retained; **Lowest/Average Salary:** $90,000/$90,000;
**Industry Concentration:** Financial Services, Insurance, **Function
Concentration:** Administration, Marketing

**Danoff, Audrey** — *Recruiter*
Don Richard Associates of Tidewater, Inc.
4701 Columbus Street, Suite 102
Virginia Beach, VA 23462
Telephone: (757) 518-8600
**Recruiter Classification:** Contingency, Executive Temporary; **Lowest/Average
Salary:** $20,000/$30,000; **Industry Concentration:** Generalist with a primary
focus in Consumer Products, Fashion (Retail/Apparel), Hospitality/Leisure,
Information Technology, Manufacturing, Packaging, Publishing/Media;
**Function Concentration:** Marketing, Sales

**Darcy, Pat** — *Consultant*
Paul Ray Berndtson
101 Park Avenue, 41st Floor
New York, NY 10178
Telephone: (212) 370-1316
**Recruiter Classification:** Retained; **Lowest/Average Salary:** $90,000/$90,000;
**Industry Concentration:** Generalist; **Function Concentration:** Generalist

**Darnell, Nadine** — *Vice President*
Brennan Associates
P.O. Box 29026
Dallas, TX 75229
Telephone: (214) 351-6005
**Recruiter Classification:** Contingency; **Lowest/Average Salary:**
$50,000/$60,000; **Industry Concentration:** Manufacturing; **Function
Concentration:** Engineering, Sales

**Darter, Steven M.** — *President*
People Management Northeast Incorporated
One Darling Drive, Avon Park South
Avon, CT 06001
Telephone: (860) 678-8900
**Recruiter Classification:** Retained; **Lowest/Average Salary:** $75,000/$90,000;
**Industry Concentration:** Generalist with a primary focus in Financial Services,
Healthcare/Hospitals, Information Technology, Insurance, Manufacturing;
**Function Concentration:** Generalist

**Daughety, Mac M.** — *Co-Manager*
Management Recruiters International, Inc.
Village Square Mall, Suite 1
Highway 258 North, P.O. Box 219
Kinston, NC 28502-0219
Telephone: (919) 527-9191
**Recruiter Classification:** Contingency; **Lowest/Average Salary:** $30,000/$75,000;
**Industry Concentration:** Generalist; **Function Concentration:** Generalist

**Daum, Julie** — *Director*
Spencer Stuart
277 Park Avenue, 29th Floor
New York, NY 10172
Telephone: (212) 336-0200
**Recruiter Classification:** Retained; **Lowest/Average Salary:** $90,000/$90,000;
**Industry Concentration:** Generalist with a primary focus in Board Services;
**Function Concentration:** Women/Minorities

**Dautenhahn, Thomas** — *Principal*
Sanford Rose Associates
114 1/2 North West Street
Lima, OH 45801
Telephone: (419) 227-5740
**Recruiter Classification:** Contingency; **Lowest/Average Salary:**
$30,000/$75,000; **Industry Concentration:** Generalist with a primary focus in
Automotive; **Function Concentration:** Generalist

**David, Dodie** — *Vice President*
Sullivan & Associates
344 North Woodward, Suite 304
Birmingham, MI 48009
Telephone: (810) 258-0616
**Recruiter Classification:** Retained; **Lowest/Average Salary:** $90,000/$90,000;
**Industry Concentration:** Generalist; **Function Concentration:** Generalist

**David, Jennifer** — *Consultant*
Gilbert Tweed/INESA
415 Madison Avenue
New York, NY 10017
Telephone: (212) 758-3000
**Recruiter Classification:** Retained; **Lowest/Average Salary:** $90,000/$90,000;
**Industry Concentration:** Generalist; **Function Concentration:** Generalist

**David, Paul** — *Principal*
Ward Howell International, Inc.
401 East Host Drive
Lake Geneva, WI 53147
Telephone: (414) 249-5200
**Recruiter Classification:** Retained; **Lowest/Average Salary:** $75,000/$90,000;
**Industry Concentration:** Generalist; **Function Concentration:** Generalist

**Davidson, Arthur J.** — *Partner*
Lamalie Amrop International
225 West Wacker Drive
Chicago, IL 60606-1229
Telephone: (312) 782-3113
**Recruiter Classification:** Retained; **Lowest/Average Salary:** $90,000/$90,000;
**Industry Concentration:** Generalist with a primary focus in Automotive,
Transportation; **Function Concentration:** Generalist with a primary focus in
Finance/Accounting, General Management

**Davis, Bernel** — *Physician Recruiter*
MSI International
201 St. Charles Avenue
Suite 2205
New Orleans, LA 70170
Telephone: (504) 522-6700
**Recruiter Classification:** Contingency; **Lowest/Average Salary:** $30,000/$60,000;
**Industry Concentration:** Generalist with a primary focus in Healthcare/Hospitals;
**Function Concentration:** Generalist with a primary focus in Administration,
Engineering, Finance/Accounting, General Management, Marketing, Sales

**Davis, Bert** — *President*
Bert Davis Executive Search, Inc.
425 Madison Avenue
New York, NY 10017
Telephone: (212) 838-4000
**Recruiter Classification:** Contingency; **Lowest/Average Salary:** $/$60,000;
**Industry Concentration:** Information Technology, Publishing/Media; **Function
Concentration:** Finance/Accounting, General Management, Marketing,
Research and Development, Sales, Women/Minorities

**Davis, C. Scott** — *Associate*
Source Services Corporation
7730 East Bellview Avenue, Suite 302
Englewood, CO 80111
Telephone: (303) 773-3700
**Recruiter Classification:** Contingency; **Lowest/Average Salary:**
$30,000/$50,000; **Industry Concentration:** Financial Services, Information
Technology; **Function Concentration:** Engineering, Finance/Accounting

**Davis, Dana** — *Accounting and Finance Recruiter*
Winter, Wyman & Company
950 Winter Street, Suite 3100
Waltham, MA 02154-1294
Telephone: (617) 890-7000
**Recruiter Classification:** Contingency; **Lowest/Average Salary:**
$20,000/$50,000; **Industry Concentration:** Generalist; **Function
Concentration:** Finance/Accounting

**Davis, Elease** — *Associate*
Source Services Corporation
525 Vine Street, Suite 2250
Cincinnati, OH 45202
Telephone: (513) 651-3303
**Recruiter Classification:** Contingency; **Lowest/Average Salary:**
$30,000/$50,000; **Industry Concentration:** Financial Services, Information
Technology; **Function Concentration:** Engineering, Finance/Accounting

**Davis, Evelyn C.** — *Senior Vice President*
EFL Associates
7101 College Boulevard, Suite 550
Overland Park, KS 66210-1891
Telephone: (913) 451-8866
**Recruiter Classification:** Retained; **Lowest/Average Salary:** $60,000/$90,000;
**Industry Concentration:** Generalist; **Function Concentration:** Generalist

**Davis, G. Gordon** — *President*
Davis & Company
3419 Via Lido, Suite 615
Newport Beach, CA 92663
Telephone: (714) 376-6995
**Recruiter Classification:** Retained; **Lowest/Average Salary:** $50,000/$75,000;
**Industry Concentration:** Generalist with a primary focus in
Aerospace/Defense, Automotive, Biotechnology, Chemical Products,
Consumer Products, Electronics, Environmental, High Technology, Information
Technology, Manufacturing, Packaging, Transportation, Venture Capital;
**Function Concentration:** Generalist with a primary focus in Administration,
Engineering, Finance/Accounting, General Management, Human Resources,
Marketing, Research and Development, Sales

**Davis, Joan** — *Executive Recruiter*
MSI International
5215 North O'Connor Boulevard
Suite 1875
Irving, TX 75039
Telephone: (214) 869-3939
**Recruiter Classification:** Contingency; **Lowest/Average Salary:**
$30,000/$75,000; **Industry Concentration:** Generalist with a primary focus in
Financial Services; **Function Concentration:** Generalist with a primary focus in
Finance/Accounting

**Davis, Joel C.** — *Executive Recruiter*
MSI International
2170 West State Road 434
Suite 454
Longwood, FL 32779
Telephone: (407) 788-7700
**Recruiter Classification:** Contingency; **Lowest/Average Salary:**
$30,000/$75,000; **Industry Concentration:** Generalist with a primary focus in
Manufacturing; **Function Concentration:** Generalist with a primary focus in
Engineering

**Davis, John** — *Consultant*
John J. Davis & Associates, Inc.
521 Fifth Avenue, Suite 1740
New York, NY 10175
Telephone: (212) 286-9489
**Recruiter Classification:** Retained; **Lowest/Average Salary:** $90,000/$90,000;
**Industry Concentration:** Information Technology; **Function Concentration:**
Generalist

**Davis, John J.** — *President*
John J. Davis & Associates, Inc.
P.O. Box G
Short Hills, NJ 07078
Telephone: (201) 467-8339
**Recruiter Classification:** Retained; **Lowest/Average Salary:** $90,000/$90,000;
**Industry Concentration:** Information Technology; **Function Concentration:**
Generalist

**Davis, Ken R.** — *General Manager*
Management Recruiters International, Inc.
9515 Deereco Road, Suite 900
Baltimore, MD 21093
Telephone: (410) 252-6616
**Recruiter Classification:** Contingency; **Lowest/Average Salary:**
$30,000/$75,000; **Industry Concentration:** Generalist; **Function
Concentration:** Generalist

**Davis, Orlin R.** — *Partner*
Heidrick & Struggles, Inc.
245 Park Avenue, Suite 4300
New York, NY 10167-0152
Telephone: (212) 867-9876
**Recruiter Classification:** Retained; **Lowest/Average Salary:** $75,000/$90,000;
**Industry Concentration:** Generalist with a primary focus in Consumer
Products, Publishing/Media; **Function Concentration:** Generalist

**Davis, Robert** — *Senior Associate*
CG & Associates
P.O. Box 11160
Pittsburgh, PA 15237
Telephone: (412) 935-1288
**Recruiter Classification:** Contingency; **Lowest/Average Salary:**
$30,000/$60,000; **Industry Concentration:** Real Estate; **Function
Concentration:** Generalist with a primary focus in Administration, Engineering,
Finance/Accounting, General Management

**Davison, Kristin** — *Senior Associate*
Korn/Ferry International
120 South Riverside Plaza
Suite 918
Chicago, IL 60606
Telephone: (312) 726-1841
**Recruiter Classification:** Retained; **Lowest/Average Salary:** $90,000/$90,000;
**Industry Concentration:** Generalist; **Function Concentration:** Generalist

**Davison, Patricia E.** — *Principal*
Lamalie Amrop International
Thanksgiving Tower
1601 Elm Street
Dallas, TX 75201-4768
Telephone: (214) 754-0019
**Recruiter Classification:** Retained; **Lowest/Average Salary:** $90,000/$90,000;
**Industry Concentration:** Generalist with a primary focus in High Technology;
**Function Concentration:** Generalist with a primary focus in
Finance/Accounting, General Management, Marketing, Sales

**Davitt, John** — *Senior Associate*
Korn/Ferry International
One Landmark Square
Stamford, CT 06901
Telephone: (203) 359-3350
**Recruiter Classification:** Retained; **Lowest/Average Salary:** $90,000/$90,000;
**Industry Concentration:** Generalist; **Function Concentration:** Generalist

**Dawson, Joe** — *Executive Recruiter*
S.C. International, Ltd.
1430 Branding Lane, Suite 119
Downers Grove, IL 60515
Telephone: (708) 963-3033
**Recruiter Classification:** Contingency; **Lowest/Average Salary:**
$30,000/$50,000; **Industry Concentration:** Information Technology, Insurance;
**Function Concentration:** Administration, Human Resources

**Dawson, William** — *Associate*
Source Services Corporation
8614 Westwood Center, Suite 750
Vienna, VA 22182
Telephone: (703) 790-5610
**Recruiter Classification:** Contingency; **Lowest/Average Salary:**
$30,000/$50,000; **Industry Concentration:** Financial Services, Information
Technology; **Function Concentration:** Engineering, Finance/Accounting

**de Bardin, Francesca** — *President*
F.L. Taylor & Company, Inc.
300 East 34th Street
New York, NY 10016
Telephone: (212) 679-4674
**Recruiter Classification:** Retained; **Lowest/Average Salary:** $75,000/$90,000;
**Industry Concentration:** Generalist with a primary focus in Fashion
(Retail/Apparel), Financial Services, Healthcare/Hospitals, Hospitality/Leisure,
Publishing/Media; **Function Concentration:** Generalist with a primary focus in
Human Resources, Marketing, Sales

**de Cholnoky, Andrea** — *Senior Director*
Spencer Stuart
277 Park Avenue, 29th Floor
New York, NY 10172
Telephone: (212) 336-0200
**Recruiter Classification:** Retained; **Lowest/Average Salary:** $90,000/$90,000;
**Industry Concentration:** Financial Services; **Function Concentration:**
Generalist with a primary focus in Administration, Finance/Accounting,
General Management, Research and Development, Sales

**De Kesel, Herman** — *Managing Partner*
TASA International
430 Cowper Street, Suite 206
Palo Alto, CA 94301
Telephone: (415) 323-0202
**Recruiter Classification:** Retained; **Lowest/Average Salary:** $90,000/$90,000;
**Industry Concentration:** Generalist; **Function Concentration:** Generalist

**De Moch, Betty** — *Account Executive*
Search West, Inc.
3401 Centrelake Drive
Suite 690
Ontario, CA 91761-1207
Telephone: (909) 986-1966
**Recruiter Classification:** Contingency; **Lowest/Average Salary:**
$40,000/$60,000; **Industry Concentration:** Generalist; **Function
Concentration:** Generalist

**de Palacios, Jeannette C.** — *President*
J. Palacios & Associates, Inc.
P.O. Box 362437
San Juan, PR 00936-2437
Telephone: (787) 723-6433
**Recruiter Classification:** Retained; **Lowest/Average Salary:** $50,000/$75,000;
**Industry Concentration:** Chemical Products, Financial Services,
Pharmaceutical/Medical; **Function Concentration:** Generalist with a primary
focus in Engineering, Finance/Accounting, General Management, Human
Resources, Marketing, Sales

**de Regt, John** — *Partner*
Heidrick & Struggles, Inc.
Greenwich Office Park #3
Greenwich, CT 06831
Telephone: (203) 629-3200
**Recruiter Classification:** Retained; **Lowest/Average Salary:** $75,000/$90,000;
**Industry Concentration:** Generalist with a primary focus in Utilities/Nuclear;
**Function Concentration:** Generalist

**de Tuede, Catherine** — *Senior Associate*
Thomas A. Byrnes Associates
148 East Avenue, Suite 2L
Norwalk, CT 06851
Telephone: (203) 838-9936
**Recruiter Classification:** Retained; **Lowest/Average Salary:** $90,000/$90,000;
**Industry Concentration:** Generalist with a primary focus in Consumer
Products, Financial Services, Insurance; **Function Concentration:** Generalist
with a primary focus in General Management, Human Resources, Marketing,
Sales, Women/Minorities

**Deal, Chuck H.** — *Manager North Atlantic Region*
Management Recruiters International, Inc.
1501 South York Road
Gastonia, NC 28052-6137
Telephone: (704) 868-8080
**Recruiter Classification:** Contingency; **Lowest/Average Salary:**
$30,000/$75,000; **Industry Concentration:** Generalist; **Function
Concentration:** Generalist

**Deal, Leslie** — *Research Associate*
Bryant Research
466 Old Hook Road, Suite 32
Emerson, NJ 07630
Telephone: (201) 599-0590
**Recruiter Classification:** Contingency; **Lowest/Average Salary:**
$50,000/$90,000; **Industry Concentration:** Biotechnology,
Pharmaceutical/Medical; **Function Concentration:** Research and Development

**Debrueys, Lee G.** — *Physician Recruiter*
MSI International
201 St. Charles Avenue
Suite 2205
New Orleans, LA 70170
Telephone: (504) 522-6700
**Recruiter Classification:** Contingency; **Lowest/Average Salary:**
$30,000/$75,000; **Industry Concentration:** Generalist with a primary focus in
Healthcare/Hospitals, Pharmaceutical/Medical; **Function Concentration:**
Generalist with a primary focus in Administration, Engineering,
Finance/Accounting, General Management, Marketing, Sales

**Debus, Wayne** — *Associate*
Source Services Corporation
5343 North 16th Street, Suite 270
Phoenix, AZ 85016
Telephone: (602) 230-0220
**Recruiter Classification:** Contingency; **Lowest/Average Salary:**
$30,000/$50,000; **Industry Concentration:** Financial Services, Information
Technology; **Function Concentration:** Engineering, Finance/Accounting

**Deck, Jack** — *Managing Director*
Source Services Corporation
One CityPlace, Suite 170
St. Louis, MO 63141
Telephone: (314) 432-4500
**Recruiter Classification:** Contingency; **Lowest/Average Salary:**
$30,000/$50,000; **Industry Concentration:** Financial Services, Information
Technology; **Function Concentration:** Engineering, Finance/Accounting

**Decker, Richard** — *Consultant Information Systems Search*
D. Brown and Associates, Inc.
610 S.W. Alder, Suite 1111
Portland, OR 97205
Telephone: (503) 224-6860
**Recruiter Classification:** Contingency; **Lowest/Average Salary:**
$40,000/$50,000; **Industry Concentration:** Information Technology

**DeCorrevont, James** — *President*
DeCorrevont & Associates
225 Country Club Drive
Largo, FL 34641
Telephone: (312) 642-9300
**Recruiter Classification:** Contingency; **Lowest/Average Salary:**
$40,000/$90,000; **Industry Concentration:** Generalist with a primary focus in
Financial Services, Healthcare/Hospitals, High Technology, Information
Technology, Insurance, Non-Profit; **Function Concentration:** Generalist with a
primary focus in Administration, Finance/Accounting, Human Resources,
Marketing, Sales, Women/Minorities

**DeCorrevont, James** — *President*
DeCorrevont & Associates
1122 North Clark Street
Chicago, IL 60610
Telephone: (312) 642-9300
**Recruiter Classification:** Contingency; **Lowest/Average Salary:**
$40,000/$90,000; **Industry Concentration:** Generalist with a primary focus in
Financial Services, Healthcare/Hospitals, High Technology, Information
Technology, Insurance, Non-Profit; **Function Concentration:** Generalist with a
primary focus in Administration, Finance/Accounting, Human Resources,
Marketing, Sales, Women/Minorities

**DeCosta, Michael** — *Senior Associate*
Korn/Ferry International
One International Place
Boston, MA 02110-1800
Telephone: (617) 345-0200
**Recruiter Classification:** Retained; **Lowest/Average Salary:** $90,000/$90,000;
**Industry Concentration:** Generalist; **Function Concentration:** Generalist

**Deering, Joseph** — *Recruiter*
U.S. Envirosearch
445 Union Boulevard, Suite 225
Lakewood, CO 80228
Telephone: (303) 980-6600
**Recruiter Classification:** Contingency; **Lowest/Average Salary:**
$30,000/$60,000; **Industry Concentration:** Environmental; **Function
Concentration:** Generalist with a primary focus in Administration, Engineering,
Finance/Accounting, General Management, Marketing, Sales,
Women/Minorities

**DeFrancesco, Mary Ellen** — *Vice President and Principal*
The Onstott Group, Inc.
60 William Street
Wellesley, MA 02181
Telephone: (617) 235-3050
**Recruiter Classification:** Retained; **Lowest/Average Salary:** $90,000/$90,000;
**Industry Concentration:** Generalist with a primary focus in Biotechnology,
Board Services, Chemical Products, Healthcare/Hospitals,
Pharmaceutical/Medical; **Function Concentration:** Generalist with a primary
focus in Finance/Accounting, General Management, Human Resources,
Marketing, Research and Development, Sales

**DeFuniak, William S.** — *Managing Partner*
DeFuniak & Edwards
1602 Hidden Hills Trail
Long Beach, IN 46360
Telephone: (219) 878-9790
**Recruiter Classification:** Retained; **Lowest/Average Salary:** $50,000/$90,000;
**Industry Concentration:** Insurance; **Function Concentration:** General
Management

**DeGioia, Joseph** — *President*
JDG Associates, Ltd.
1700 Research Boulevard
Rockville, MD 20850
Telephone: (301) 340-2210
**Recruiter Classification:** Contingency; **Lowest/Average Salary:**
$50,000/$90,000; **Industry Concentration:** Aerospace/Defense, Electronics,
Environmental, Healthcare/Hospitals, High Technology, Information
Technology, Manufacturing, Transportation; **Function Concentration:**
Generalist with a primary focus in Administration, Engineering,
Finance/Accounting, Research and Development

**DeHart, Donna** — *Vice President*
Tower Consultants, Ltd.
771 East Lancaster Avenue
Villanova, PA 19085
Telephone: (610) 519-1700
**Recruiter Classification:** Retained; **Lowest/Average Salary:** $90,000/$90,000;
**Industry Concentration:** Generalist with a primary focus in Consumer
Products, Healthcare/Hospitals, Insurance, Non-Profit,
Pharmaceutical/Medical; **Function Concentration:** Administration, General
Management, Human Resources, Marketing, Sales, Women/Minorities

**Dejong, Jack C.** — *Co-Manager*
Management Recruiters International, Inc.
6303 East Tanque Verde Road, Suite 230
Tucson, AZ 85715
Telephone: (520) 885-1560
**Recruiter Classification:** Contingency; **Lowest/Average Salary:**
$30,000/$75,000; **Industry Concentration:** Generalist; **Function**
**Concentration:** Generalist

**Del Pino, William** — *Insurance Consultant*
National Search, Inc.
2816 University Drive
Coral Springs, FL 33071
Telephone: (800) 935-4355
**Recruiter Classification:** Contingency; **Lowest/Average Salary:**
$30,000/$50,000; **Industry Concentration:** Healthcare/Hospitals, Insurance,
Pharmaceutical/Medical; **Function Concentration:** Generalist with a primary
focus in Administration, Finance/Accounting, General Management, Human
Resources, Marketing, Research and Development, Sales, Women/Minorities

**Del Prete, Karen** — *Vice President*
Gilbert Tweed/INESA
415 Madison Avenue
New York, NY 10017
Telephone: (212) 758-3000
**Recruiter Classification:** Retained; **Lowest/Average Salary:** $90,000/$90,000;
**Industry Concentration:** Generalist with a primary focus in Automotive,
Biotechnology, Chemical Products, Environmental, Financial Services,
Healthcare/Hospitals, High Technology, Information Technology,
Manufacturing, Packaging, Pharmaceutical/Medical, Venture Capital; **Function**
**Concentration:** Generalist

**Del'Ange, Gabrielle N.** — *Physician Recruiter*
MSI International
230 Peachtree Street, N.E.
Suite 1550
Atlanta, GA 30303
Telephone: (404) 653-7360
**Recruiter Classification:** Contingency; **Lowest/Average Salary:**
$30,000/$75,000; **Industry Concentration:** Generalist with a primary focus in
Healthcare/Hospitals, Pharmaceutical/Medical; **Function Concentration:**
Generalist with a primary focus in Administration, Engineering,
Finance/Accounting, General Management, Marketing, Sales

**Delaney, Patrick** — *Account Executive*
Search West, Inc.
340 North Westlake Boulevard
Suite 200
Westlake Village, CA 91362-3761
Telephone: (805) 496-6811
**Recruiter Classification:** Contingency; **Lowest/Average Salary:**
$40,000/$60,000; **Industry Concentration:** Manufacturing; **Function**
**Concentration:** Engineering, Research and Development

**Delaney, Patrick J.** — *Principal*
Sensible Solutions, Inc.
239 West Coolidge Avenue
Barrington, IL 60010
Telephone: (847) 382-0070
**Recruiter Classification:** Retained, Executive Temporary; **Lowest/Average**
**Salary:** $60,000/$90,000; **Industry Concentration:** Generalist with a primary
focus in Electronics, Financial Services, Healthcare/Hospitals, High
Technology, Information Technology, Non-Profit, Transportation; **Function**
**Concentration:** Generalist with a primary focus in Administration, Engineering,
Finance/Accounting, General Management, Human Resources, Marketing,
Sales

**Delin, Norm** — *Manager Midwest Region*
Management Recruiters International, Inc.
6110 Bluecircle Drive, Suite 290
Minnetonka, MN 55343-9132
Telephone: (612) 932-9400
**Recruiter Classification:** Contingency; **Lowest/Average Salary:**
$30,000/$75,000; **Industry Concentration:** Generalist; **Function**
**Concentration:** Generalist

**Della Monica, Vincent** — *Account Executive*
Search West, Inc.
340 North Westlake Boulevard
Suite 200
Westlake Village, CA 91362-3761
Telephone: (805) 496-6811
**Recruiter Classification:** Contingency; **Lowest/Average Salary:**
$40,000/$60,000; **Industry Concentration:** Insurance; **Function**
**Concentration:** Administration, Marketing

**Delman, Charles** — *Vice President*
Korn/Ferry International
237 Park Avenue
New York, NY 10017
Telephone: (212) 687-1834
**Recruiter Classification:** Retained; **Lowest/Average Salary:** $90,000/$90,000;
**Industry Concentration:** Generalist with a primary focus in Financial Services;
**Function Concentration:** Generalist

**Delmonico, Laura** — *Recruiter*
A.J. Burton Group, Inc.
120 East Baltimore Street, Suite 2220
Baltimore, MD 21202
Telephone: (410) 752-5244
**Recruiter Classification:** Contingency; **Lowest/Average Salary:**
$30,000/$40,000; **Industry Concentration:** Consumer Products,
Healthcare/Hospitals, Manufacturing, Real Estate; **Function Concentration:**
Finance/Accounting

**DelNegro, Anthony T.** — *Executive Vice President/*
*Managing Director*
DHR International, Inc.
Two Pomperaug Office Park, Suite 206C
Southbury, CT 06488
Telephone: (203) 262-8740
**Recruiter Classification:** Retained; **Lowest/Average Salary:** $60,000/$90,000;
**Industry Concentration:** Generalist; **Function Concentration:** Generalist

**DelNegro, Anthony T.** — *Executive Vice President/*
*Managing Director*
DHR International, Inc.
300 Park Avenue, Suite 1761
New York, NY 10022
Telephone: (212) 572-6266
**Recruiter Classification:** Retained; **Lowest/Average Salary:** $60,000/$90,000;
**Industry Concentration:** Generalist; **Function Concentration:** Generalist

**DeLong, Art** — *Vice President*
Richard Kader & Associates
343 West Bagley Road, Suite 209
Berea, OH 44017
Telephone: (216) 891-1700
**Recruiter Classification:** Contingency; **Lowest/Average Salary:**
$40,000/$50,000; **Industry Concentration:** Generalist with a primary focus in
Chemical Products, Consumer Products, Environmental, High Technology,
Manufacturing; **Function Concentration:** Generalist with a primary focus in
General Management, Human Resources, Marketing, Research and
Development, Sales, Women/Minorities

**Delvani-Hart, Angela** — *Executive Recruiter*
F-O-R-T-U-N-E Personnel Consultants of Nashua, Inc.
505 West Hollis Street, Suite 208
Nashua, NH 03062
Telephone: (603) 880-4900
**Recruiter Classification:** Contingency; **Lowest/Average Salary:**
$40,000/$50,000; **Industry Concentration:** Biotechnology, Manufacturing,
Pharmaceutical/Medical; **Function Concentration:** Engineering

**DeMarco, Robert** — *Managing Director*
Source Services Corporation
1500 West Park Drive, Suite 390
Westborough, MA 01581
Telephone: (508) 366-2600
**Recruiter Classification:** Contingency; **Lowest/Average Salary:**
$30,000/$50,000; **Industry Concentration:** Financial Services, Information
Technology; **Function Concentration:** Engineering, Finance/Accounting

**DeMario, William** — *Area Manager*
Accountants on Call
3500 West Olive Avenue, Suite 550
Burbank, CA 91505
Telephone: (818) 845-6600
**Recruiter Classification:** Contingency; **Lowest/Average Salary:**
$20,000/$30,000; **Industry Concentration:** Generalist; **Function Concentration:** Finance/Accounting

**deMartino, Cathy** — *Vice President*
Lucas Associates
5901-A Peachtree-Dunwoody Road
Suite 525
Atlanta, GA 30328
Telephone: (404) 901-5570
**Recruiter Classification:** Contingency; **Lowest/Average Salary:**
$50,000/$75,000; **Industry Concentration:** Biotechnology, Chemical Products, Consumer Products, Healthcare/Hospitals, Manufacturing, Packaging, Pharmaceutical/Medical, Transportation; **Function Concentration:** Engineering, General Management, Marketing, Sales

**Demchak, James P.** — *Partner*
Sandhurst Associates
4851 LBJ Freeway, Suite 601
Dallas, TX 75244
Telephone: (214) 458-1212
**Recruiter Classification:** Retained; **Lowest/Average Salary:** $75,000/$90,000; **Industry Concentration:** Generalist with a primary focus in Consumer Products, Education/Libraries, Entertainment, Financial Services, Healthcare/Hospitals, High Technology, Hospitality/Leisure, Insurance, Manufacturing, Pharmaceutical/Medical, Real Estate, Transportation; **Function Concentration:** Generalist with a primary focus in Finance/Accounting, Human Resources, Marketing, Sales

**Dennen, Bob E.** — *Co-Manager*
Management Recruiters International, Inc.
2001 West Main Street, Suite 185
Stamford, CT 06902-4517
Telephone: (203) 324-2232
**Recruiter Classification:** Contingency; **Lowest/Average Salary:**
$30,000/$75,000; **Industry Concentration:** Generalist; **Function Concentration:** Generalist

**Dennen, Lorraine T.** — *Co-Manager Eastern Region*
Management Recruiters International, Inc.
2001 West Main Street, Suite 185
Stamford, CT 06902-4517
Telephone: (203) 324-2232
**Recruiter Classification:** Contingency; **Lowest/Average Salary:**
$30,000/$75,000; **Industry Concentration:** Generalist; **Function Concentration:** Generalist

**Denney, Edward B.** — *Associate*
Denney & Company Incorporated
P.O. Box 382681
Cambridge, MA 02238-2681
Telephone: (617) 864-1006
**Recruiter Classification:** Retained; **Lowest/Average Salary:** $90,000/$90,000; **Industry Concentration:** Generalist; **Function Concentration:** Generalist

**Denney, Thomas L.** — *President*
Denney & Company Incorporated
P.O. Box 22156
Pittsburgh, PA 15222
Telephone: (412) 441-9636
**Recruiter Classification:** Retained; **Lowest/Average Salary:** $90,000/$90,000; **Industry Concentration:** Generalist; **Function Concentration:** Generalist

**Densmore, Geraldine** — *Senior Consultant*
Michael Stern Associates Inc.
70 University Avenue, Suite 370
Toronto, Ontario, CANADA M5J 2M4
Telephone: (416) 593-0100
**Recruiter Classification:** Retained; **Lowest/Average Salary:** $75,000/$90,000; **Industry Concentration:** Generalist; **Function Concentration:** Generalist with a primary focus in Finance/Accounting, General Management, Human Resources, Marketing, Sales

**Denson, Marsha** — *Consultant - L.A. Retail*
Evie Kreisler & Associates, Inc.
865 South Figueroa, Suite 950
Los Angeles, CA 90017
Telephone: (213) 622-8994
**Recruiter Classification:** Contingency; **Lowest/Average Salary:**
$30,000/$75,000; **Industry Concentration:** Fashion (Retail/Apparel); **Function Concentration:** Generalist

**DeSanto, Constance E.** — *Consultant*
Paul Ray Berndtson
191 Peachtree Tower, Suite 3800
191 Peachtree Street, NE
Atlanta, GA 30303-1757
Telephone: (404) 215-4600
**Recruiter Classification:** Retained; **Lowest/Average Salary:** $90,000/$90,000; **Industry Concentration:** Generalist; **Function Concentration:** Generalist

**Desgrosellier, Gary P.** — *President*
Personnel Unlimited/Executive Search
25 West Nora
Spokane, WA 99205
Telephone: (509) 326-8880
**Recruiter Classification:** Contingency; **Lowest/Average Salary:**
$30,000/$60,000; **Industry Concentration:** Generalist with a primary focus in Chemical Products, Consumer Products, Healthcare/Hospitals, High Technology, Insurance, Manufacturing, Packaging, Pharmaceutical/Medical; **Function Concentration:** Generalist with a primary focus in Engineering, Finance/Accounting, Human Resources, Marketing, Sales

**Desgrosellier, Shawn** — *Executive Recruiter*
Personnel Unlimited/Executive Search
25 West Nora
Spokane, WA 99205
Telephone: (509) 326-8880
**Recruiter Classification:** Contingency; **Lowest/Average Salary:**
$30,000/$60,000; **Industry Concentration:** Generalist; **Function Concentration:** Finance/Accounting

**Desir, Etheline** — *Consultant*
Tyler & Company
1000 Abernathy Road N.E.
Suite 1400
Atlanta, GA 30328-5655
Telephone: (770) 396-3939
**Recruiter Classification:** Retained; **Lowest/Average Salary:** $60,000/$90,000; **Industry Concentration:** Healthcare/Hospitals, Insurance; **Function Concentration:** Generalist

**Desmond, Dennis** — *Executive Vice President/Partner*
Beall & Company, Inc.
535 Colonial Park Drive
Roswell, GA 30075
Telephone: (404) 992-0900
**Recruiter Classification:** Retained; **Lowest/Average Salary:** $90,000/$90,000; **Industry Concentration:** Generalist with a primary focus in Biotechnology, Board Services, Financial Services, Healthcare/Hospitals, High Technology, Insurance, Pharmaceutical/Medical, Real Estate, Venture Capital; **Function Concentration:** Generalist with a primary focus in Administration, Engineering, Finance/Accounting, General Management, Human Resources, Marketing, Research and Development, Sales

**Desmond, Mary** — *Associate*
Source Services Corporation
150 South Wacker Drive, Suite 400
Chicago, IL 60606
Telephone: (312) 346-7000
**Recruiter Classification:** Contingency; **Lowest/Average Salary:**
$30,000/$50,000; **Industry Concentration:** Financial Services, Information Technology; **Function Concentration:** Engineering, Finance/Accounting

**Detore, Robert R.** — *President and CEO*
Drew Associates International
77 Park Street
Montclair, NJ 07042
Telephone: (201) 746-8877
**Recruiter Classification:** Retained; **Lowest/Average Salary:** $60,000/$90,000; **Industry Concentration:** Healthcare/Hospitals, Pharmaceutical/Medical; **Function Concentration:** Generalist

**Dever, Mary** — *Associate*
Source Services Corporation
505 East 200 South, Suite 300
Salt Lake City, UT 84102
Telephone: (801) 328-0011
**Recruiter Classification:** Contingency; **Lowest/Average Salary:**
$30,000/$50,000; **Industry Concentration:** Financial Services, Information Technology; **Function Concentration:** Engineering, Finance/Accounting

**Devito, Alice** — *Associate*
Source Services Corporation
925 Westchester Avenue, Suite 309
White Plains, NY 10604
Telephone: (914) 428-9100
**Recruiter Classification:** Contingency; **Lowest/Average Salary:**
$30,000/$50,000; **Industry Concentration:** Financial Services, Information Technology; **Function Concentration:** Engineering, Finance/Accounting

**deVry, Kimberly A.** — *Executive Recruiter*
Tower Consultants, Ltd.
771 East Lancaster Avenue
Villanova, PA 19085
Telephone: (610) 519-1700
**Recruiter Classification:** Retained; **Lowest/Average Salary:** $60,000/$90,000; **Industry Concentration:** Generalist with a primary focus in Consumer Products, Fashion (Retail/Apparel), Financial Services, Healthcare/Hospitals, Hospitality/Leisure, Insurance, Manufacturing; **Function Concentration:** Administration, Human Resources, Women/Minorities

**deWilde, David M.** — *Managing Director*
Chartwell Partners International, Inc.
275 Battery Street, Suite 2180
San Francisco, CA 94111
Telephone: (415) 296-0600
**Recruiter Classification:** Retained; **Lowest/Average Salary:** $90,000/$90,000; **Industry Concentration:** Generalist with a primary focus in Board Services, Consumer Products, Financial Services, High Technology, Information Technology, Insurance, Real Estate, Transportation, Venture Capital; **Function Concentration:** Finance/Accounting, General Management, Human Resources, Marketing, Women/Minorities

**Dewing, Jesse J.** — *Consultant/Recruiter*
Don Richard Associates of Charlotte
2650 One First Union Center
301 South College Street
Charlotte, NC 28202-6000
Telephone: (704) 377-6447
**Recruiter Classification:** Contingency; **Lowest/Average Salary:** $30,000/$50,000; **Industry Concentration:** Financial Services; **Function Concentration:** Finance/Accounting

**Di Filippo, Thomas** — *Associate*
Source Services Corporation
20 Burlington Mall Road, Suite 405
Burlington, MA 01803
Telephone: (617) 272-5000
**Recruiter Classification:** Contingency; **Lowest/Average Salary:** $30,000/$50,000; **Industry Concentration:** Financial Services, Information Technology; **Function Concentration:** Engineering, Finance/Accounting

**Diamond, Peter** — *Principal*
Korn/Ferry International
3950 Lincoln Plaza
500 North Akard Street
Dallas, TX 75201
Telephone: (214) 954-1834
**Recruiter Classification:** Retained; **Lowest/Average Salary:** $90,000/$90,000; **Industry Concentration:** Generalist; **Function Concentration:** Generalist

**Diaz, Del J.** — *Manager South Atlantic Region*
Management Recruiters International, Inc.
815 Northwest 57th Avenue, Suite 110
Miami, FL 33126
Telephone: (305) 264-4212
**Recruiter Classification:** Contingency; **Lowest/Average Salary:** $30,000/$75,000; **Industry Concentration:** Generalist; **Function Concentration:** Generalist

**Diaz-Joslyn, Mabel** — *Executive Recruiter*
Walker Communications
1212 Avenue of the Americas
New York, NY 10036
Telephone: (212) 944-0011
**Recruiter Classification:** Retained; **Lowest/Average Salary:** $75,000/$90,000; **Industry Concentration:** Publishing/Media; **Function Concentration:** Generalist with a primary focus in Finance/Accounting, General Management, Marketing, Research and Development, Sales, Women/Minorities

**Dickerson, Scot** — *Vice President*
Key Employment Services
1001 Office Park Road, Suite 320
West Des Moines, IA 50265-2567
Telephone: (515) 224-0446
**Recruiter Classification:** Contingency; **Lowest/Average Salary:** $30,000/$75,000; **Industry Concentration:** Insurance; **Function Concentration:** General Management

**Dickey, Arlene** — *Associate*
Kenzer Corp.
6033 West Century Boulevard, Suite 808
Los Angeles, CA 90045
Telephone: (310) 417-8577
**Recruiter Classification:** Retained; **Lowest/Average Salary:** $50,000/$90,000; **Industry Concentration:** Generalist; **Function Concentration:** Generalist

**Dickey, Chet W.** — *President and CEO*
Bowden & Company, Inc.
5000 Rockside Road, Suite 550
Cleveland, OH 44131
Telephone: (216) 447-1800
**Recruiter Classification:** Retained; **Lowest/Average Salary:** $90,000/$90,000; **Industry Concentration:** Generalist with a primary focus in Aerospace/Defense, Automotive, Chemical Products, Consumer Products, Energy, Financial Services, Healthcare/Hospitals, High Technology, Information Technology, Insurance, Manufacturing, Non-Profit, Packaging, Transportation, Venture Capital; **Function Concentration:** Generalist

**Dickinson, Peter K.** — *Consultant*
Shepherd Bueschel & Provus, Inc.
401 North Michigan Avenue, Suite 3020
Chicago, IL 60611-5555
Telephone: (312) 832-3020
**Recruiter Classification:** Retained; **Lowest/Average Salary:** $90,000/$90,000; **Industry Concentration:** Generalist; **Function Concentration:** Generalist

**Dickstein, Joel** — *Manager South Atlantic Region*
Management Recruiters International, Inc.
1500 NW 49th Street, Suite 500
Fort Lauderdale, FL 33309
Telephone: (954) 776-4477
**Recruiter Classification:** Contingency; **Lowest/Average Salary:** $30,000/$75,000; **Industry Concentration:** Generalist; **Function Concentration:** Generalist

**Diduca, Tom A.** — *Co-Manager Midwest Region*
Management Recruiters International, Inc.
Kensington Center
479 Business Center Drive, Suite 104
Mount Prospect, IL 60056-6037
Telephone: (847) 298-8780
**Recruiter Classification:** Contingency; **Lowest/Average Salary:** $30,000/$75,000; **Industry Concentration:** Generalist; **Function Concentration:** Generalist

**Dieck, Daniel W.** — *Vice President*
Dieck, Mueller & Associates, Inc.
1017 Orchard Drive
Seymour, WI 54165
Telephone: (414) 833-7600
**Recruiter Classification:** Retained; **Lowest/Average Salary:** $75,000/$90,000; **Industry Concentration:** Chemical Products, Consumer Products, Manufacturing, Packaging; **Function Concentration:** Generalist

**Dieckmann, Ralph E.** — *President*
Dieckmann & Associates, Ltd.
180 North Stetson, Suite 5555
Two Prudential Plaza
Chicago, IL 60601
Telephone: (312) 819-5900
**Recruiter Classification:** Retained; **Lowest/Average Salary:** $90,000/$90,000; **Industry Concentration:** Generalist with a primary focus in Financial Services, Information Technology, Insurance, Manufacturing; **Function Concentration:** Generalist with a primary focus in Finance/Accounting, General Management, Human Resources, Women/Minorities

**Diers, Gary** — *Associate*
Source Services Corporation
10220 SW Greenburg Road, Suite 625
Portland, OR 97223
Telephone: (503) 768-4546
**Recruiter Classification:** Contingency; **Lowest/Average Salary:** $30,000/$50,000; **Industry Concentration:** Financial Services, Information Technology; **Function Concentration:** Engineering, Finance/Accounting

**Dietz, David S.** — *Manager*
MSI International
201 St. Charles Avenue
Suite 2205
New Orleans, LA 70170
Telephone: (504) 522-6700
**Recruiter Classification:** Contingency; **Lowest/Average Salary:** $30,000/$60,000; **Industry Concentration:** Generalist with a primary focus in Financial Services, Healthcare/Hospitals, High Technology, Information Technology, Manufacturing; **Function Concentration:** Generalist with a primary focus in Administration, Engineering, Finance/Accounting, General Management, Marketing, Sales

**DiGiovanni, Charles** — *President*
Penn Search
687 West Lancaster Avenue
Strafford, PA 19087
Telephone: (610) 964-8820
**Recruiter Classification:** Contingency; **Lowest/Average Salary:** $30,000/$60,000; **Industry Concentration:** Generalist with a primary focus in Chemical Products, Financial Services, Healthcare/Hospitals, Hospitality/Leisure, Insurance, Manufacturing, Packaging; **Function Concentration:** Finance/Accounting

**DiMarchi, Paul** — *President*
DiMarchi Partners, Inc.
1225 17th Street, Suite 1460
Denver, CO 80202
Telephone: (303) 292-9300
**Recruiter Classification:** Retained; **Lowest/Average Salary:** $75,000/$90,000;
**Industry Concentration:** Generalist with a primary focus in Biotechnology,
Chemical Products, Consumer Products, Electronics, Healthcare/Hospitals,
High Technology, Information Technology, Manufacturing,
Pharmaceutical/Medical, Publishing/Media, Real Estate, Venture Capital;
**Function Concentration:** Generalist with a primary focus in
Finance/Accounting, General Management, Marketing, Research and
Development, Sales

**Dingman, Bruce** — *President*
Robert W. Dingman Company, Inc.
32129 West Lindero Canyon Road
Suite 206
Westlake Village, CA 91361
Telephone: (818) 991-5950
**Recruiter Classification:** Retained; **Lowest/Average Salary:** $90,000/$90,000;
**Industry Concentration:** Generalist with a primary focus in
Aerospace/Defense, Automotive, Consumer Products, Education/Libraries,
Electronics, Healthcare/Hospitals, High Technology, Hospitality/Leisure,
Manufacturing, Non-Profit, Oil/Gas, Packaging, Pharmaceutical/Medical,
Publishing/Media; **Function Concentration:** Generalist with a primary focus in
Administration, Finance/Accounting, General Management, Human Resources,
Marketing, Sales

**Dingman, Robert W.** — *Chairman*
Robert W. Dingman Company, Inc.
32129 West Lindero Canyon Road
Suite 206
Westlake Village, CA 91361
Telephone: (818) 991-5950
**Recruiter Classification:** Retained; **Lowest/Average Salary:** $90,000/$90,000;
**Industry Concentration:** Aerospace/Defense, Automotive, Consumer Products,
Education/Libraries, Electronics, Healthcare/Hospitals, High Technology,
Hospitality/Leisure, Manufacturing, Non-Profit, Oil/Gas, Packaging,
Pharmaceutical/Medical, Publishing/Media; **Function Concentration:**
Generalist with a primary focus in Administration, Finance/Accounting,
General Management, Human Resources, Marketing, Sales

**Dinse, Beth** — *Manager Pacific Region*
Management Recruiters International, Inc.
Capital Place
915 L Street, Suite 110
Sacramento, CA 95814
Telephone: (916) 442-9116
**Recruiter Classification:** Contingency; **Lowest/Average Salary:**
$30,000/$75,000; **Industry Concentration:** Generalist; **Function
Concentration:** Generalist

**Dinte, Paul** — *President and CEO*
Dinte Resources, Incorporated
8300 Greensboro Drive
Suite 880
McLean, VA 22102
Telephone: (703) 448-3300
**Recruiter Classification:** Executive Temporary; **Lowest/Average Salary:**
$75,000/$90,000; **Industry Concentration:** Generalist with a primary focus in
Aerospace/Defense, Electronics, Entertainment, Financial Services, High
Technology, Information Technology, Insurance, Publishing/Media; **Function
Concentration:** Generalist

**Dinwiddie, Jill** — *Partner*
Belvedere Partners
100 Larkspur Landing Circle, Suite 120
Larkspur, CA 94939
Telephone: (415) 925-9959
**Recruiter Classification:** Retained; **Lowest/Average Salary:** $75,000/$90,000;
**Industry Concentration:** Board Services, Non-Profit; **Function Concentration:**
Administration

**Dipaolo, Jeff** — *Manager Central Region*
Management Recruiters International, Inc.
7550 Lucerne Drive, Suite 205
Cleveland, OH 44130
Telephone: (216) 243-5151
**Recruiter Classification:** Contingency; **Lowest/Average Salary:**
$30,000/$75,000; **Industry Concentration:** Generalist; **Function
Concentration:** Generalist

**DiPiazza, Joseph** — *Senior Vice President*
Boyden
375 Park Avenue, Suite 1509
New York, NY 10152
Telephone: (212) 980-6480
**Recruiter Classification:** Retained; **Lowest/Average Salary:** $75,000/$90,000;
**Industry Concentration:** Financial Services; **Function Concentration:**
Finance/Accounting

**DiSalvo, Fred** — *Vice President*
The Cambridge Group Ltd
161A John Jefferson Road
Williamsburg, VA 23185
Telephone: Unpublished
**Recruiter Classification:** Contingency; **Lowest/Average Salary:**
$90,000/$90,000; **Industry Concentration:** Generalist with a primary focus in
Biotechnology, Entertainment, Fashion (Retail/Apparel), Financial Services,
High Technology, Information Technology, Manufacturing; **Function
Concentration:** Finance/Accounting, General Management, Human Resources,
Marketing, Sales

**Diskin, Rochelle** — *Account Executive*
Search West, Inc.
340 North Westlake Boulevard
Suite 200
Westlake Village, CA 91362-3761
Telephone: (805) 496-6811
**Recruiter Classification:** Contingency; **Lowest/Average Salary:**
$40,000/$60,000; **Industry Concentration:** Biotechnology, Chemical Products,
Electronics, Entertainment, Financial Services, Healthcare/Hospitals,
Manufacturing, Oil/Gas; **Function Concentration:** Administration,
Finance/Accounting, Marketing

**Dittmar, Richard** — *Associate*
Source Services Corporation
4200 West Cypress Street, Suite 101
Tampa, FL 33607
Telephone: (813) 879-2221
**Recruiter Classification:** Contingency; **Lowest/Average Salary:**
$30,000/$50,000; **Industry Concentration:** Financial Services, Information
Technology; **Function Concentration:** Engineering, Finance/Accounting

**Divine, Robert S.** — *Principal*
O'Shea, Divine & Company, Inc.
610 Newport Center Drive, Suite 1040
Newport Beach, CA 92660
Telephone: (714) 720-9070
**Recruiter Classification:** Retained; **Lowest/Average Salary:** $75,000/$90,000;
**Industry Concentration:** Generalist with a primary focus in Board Services,
Chemical Products, Consumer Products, Education/Libraries, Electronics,
Financial Services, High Technology, Manufacturing, Non-Profit, Packaging,
Pharmaceutical/Medical, Public Administration, Publishing/Media, Real Estate;
**Function Concentration:** Generalist with a primary focus in Administration,
Engineering, Finance/Accounting, General Management, Human Resources,
Marketing, Research and Development, Sales

**Dixon, Aris** — *Executive Recruiter*
CPS Inc.
One Westbrook Corporate Centre, Suite 600
Westchester, IL 60154
Telephone: (708) 531-8370
**Recruiter Classification:** Contingency; **Lowest/Average Salary:**
$30,000/$50,000; **Industry Concentration:** Generalist with a primary focus in
Automotive, Biotechnology, Chemical Products, Consumer Products, High
Technology, Insurance, Manufacturing, Oil/Gas, Packaging,
Pharmaceutical/Medical; **Function Concentration:** Engineering, Research and
Development, Sales, Women/Minorities

**Dixon, C.R.** — *Administrative Manager*
A la carte International
3330 Pacific Avenue, Suite 500
Virginia Beach, VA 23451
Telephone: (804) 425-6111
**Recruiter Classification:** Retained; **Lowest/Average Salary:** $60,000/$90,000;
**Industry Concentration:** Generalist with a primary focus in Consumer
Products, Environmental, Manufacturing; **Function Concentration:** Generalist
with a primary focus in General Management, Human Resources, Marketing,
Research and Development

**Djandji, Guy N.** — *Partner*
Belle Isle, Djandji Inc.
1200 McGill College Avenue
Suite 2250
Montreal, Quebec, CANADA H3B 4G7
Telephone: (514) 878-1991
**Recruiter Classification:** Retained; **Lowest/Average Salary:** $75,000/$90,000;
**Industry Concentration:** Generalist; **Function Concentration:** Generalist

**Do, Sonnie** — *Executive Recruiter*
Whitney & Associates, Inc.
920 Second Avenue South, Suite 625
Minneapolis, MN 55402-4035
Telephone: (612) 338-5600
**Recruiter Classification:** Contingency; **Lowest/Average Salary:**
$20,000/$50,000; **Industry Concentration:** Generalist with a primary focus in
Biotechnology, Consumer Products, Electronics, Financial Services,
Healthcare/Hospitals, High Technology, Information Technology, Insurance,
Manufacturing, Packaging, Pharmaceutical/Medical, Publishing/Media, Real
Estate, Transportation, Venture Capital; **Function Concentration:**
Finance/Accounting

**Doan, Lisa** — *Vice President*
Rhodes Associates
555 Fifth Avenue
New York, NY 10017
Telephone: (212) 983-2000
**Recruiter Classification:** Retained; **Lowest/Average Salary:** $90,000/$90,000;
**Industry Concentration:** Financial Services, Insurance, Real Estate, Venture
Capital; **Function Concentration:** Generalist

**Dobrow, Samuel** — *Associate*
Source Services Corporation
4170 Ashford Dunwoody Road, Suite 285
Atlanta, GA 30319
Telephone: (404) 255-2045
**Recruiter Classification:** Contingency; **Lowest/Average Salary:**
$30,000/$50,000; **Industry Concentration:** Financial Services, Information
Technology; **Function Concentration:** Engineering, Finance/Accounting

**Doele, Donald C.** — *Vice President*
Goodrich & Sherwood Associates, Inc.
One Independence Way
Princeton, NJ 08540
Telephone: (609) 452-0202
**Recruiter Classification:** Retained; **Lowest/Average Salary:** $60,000/$90,000;
**Industry Concentration:** Generalist with a primary focus in Board Services,
Chemical Products, Consumer Products, Financial Services,
Healthcare/Hospitals, Information Technology, Insurance, Manufacturing,
Oil/Gas, Publishing/Media, Venture Capital; **Function Concentration:**
Generalist with a primary focus in Administration, Finance/Accounting,
General Management, Human Resources, Marketing, Sales

**Dolezal, Dave** — *Consultant*
Evie Kreisler & Associates, Inc.
2575 Peachtree Road, Suite 300
Atlanta, GA 30305
Telephone: (404) 262-0599
**Recruiter Classification:** Contingency; **Lowest/Average Salary:**
$30,000/$75,000; **Industry Concentration:** Fashion (Retail/Apparel); **Function
Concentration:** Generalist

**Doliva, Lauren M.** — *Partner*
Heidrick & Struggles, Inc.
Four Embarcadero Center, Suite 3570
San Francisco, CA 94111
Telephone: (415) 981-2854
**Recruiter Classification:** Retained; **Lowest/Average Salary:** $75,000/$90,000;
**Industry Concentration:** Generalist with a primary focus in Education/Libraries,
Healthcare/Hospitals, Non-Profit; **Function Concentration:** Generalist

**Doman, Matthew** — *Executive Recruiter*
S.C. International, Ltd.
1430 Branding Lane, Suite 119
Downers Grove, IL 60515
Telephone: (708) 963-3033
**Recruiter Classification:** Contingency; **Lowest/Average Salary:**
$30,000/$50,000; **Industry Concentration:** Information Technology, Insurance;
**Function Concentration:** Administration, Human Resources

**Domann, William A.** — *President*
The Domann Organization
P.O. Box 1717
Glen Ellen, CA 95442
Telephone: (800) 923-6626
**Recruiter Classification:** Retained; **Lowest/Average Salary:** $60,000/$90,000;
**Industry Concentration:** Biotechnology, Pharmaceutical/Medical; **Function
Concentration:** General Management, Research and Development

**Domenico, Alfred J.** — *President*
Domenico/Bowman Associates
23861 El Toro Road, Suite 700
Lake Forest, CA 92630
Telephone: (714) 588-2390
**Recruiter Classification:** Contingency; **Lowest/Average Salary:**
$75,000/$90,000; **Industry Concentration:** Hospitality/Leisure; **Function
Concentration:** Generalist

**Dominguez, Carl** — *Partner*
Heidrick & Struggles, Inc.
1301 K Street N.W., Suite 500 East
Washington, DC 20005
Telephone: (202) 289-4450
**Recruiter Classification:** Retained; **Lowest/Average Salary:** $75,000/$90,000;
**Industry Concentration:** Generalist; **Function Concentration:** Generalist

**Donahie, Stephen** — *Account Executive*
Search West, Inc.
340 North Westlake Boulevard
Suite 200
Westlake Village, CA 91362-3761
Telephone: (805) 496-6811
**Recruiter Classification:** Contingency; **Lowest/Average Salary:**
$40,000/$60,000; **Industry Concentration:** Generalist; **Function
Concentration:** Marketing, Sales

**Donahue, Debora** — *Associate*
Source Services Corporation
505 East 200 South, Suite 300
Salt Lake City, UT 84102
Telephone: (801) 328-0011
**Recruiter Classification:** Contingency; **Lowest/Average Salary:**
$30,000/$50,000; **Industry Concentration:** Financial Services, Information
Technology; **Function Concentration:** Engineering, Finance/Accounting

**Donnelly, George J.** — *Vice Chairman International*
Ward Howell International, Inc.
1000 Louisiana Street
Suite 3150
Houston, TX 77002
Telephone: (713) 655-7155
**Recruiter Classification:** Retained; **Lowest/Average Salary:** $75,000/$90,000;
**Industry Concentration:** Generalist with a primary focus in Consumer
Products, Energy, Financial Services; **Function Concentration:** Generalist with
a primary focus in General Management

**Donnelly, Patti** — *Associate*
Source Services Corporation
150 South Warner Road, Suite 238
King of Prussia, PA 19406
Telephone: (610) 341-1960
**Recruiter Classification:** Contingency; **Lowest/Average Salary:**
$30,000/$50,000; **Industry Concentration:** Financial Services, Information
Technology; **Function Concentration:** Engineering, Finance/Accounting

**Donovan, Jerry E.** — *Manager Eastern Region*
Management Recruiters International, Inc.
5001-A Lee Highway, Suite 102
Arlington, VA 22207-2538
Telephone: (703) 276-1135
**Recruiter Classification:** Contingency; **Lowest/Average Salary:**
$30,000/$75,000; **Industry Concentration:** Generalist; **Function
Concentration:** Generalist

**Doody, Michael F.** — *Shareholder*
Witt/Kieffer, Ford, Hadelman & Lloyd
2015 Spring Road, Suite 510
Oak Brook, IL 60521
Telephone: (708) 990-1370
**Recruiter Classification:** Retained; **Lowest/Average Salary:** $75,000/$90,000;
**Industry Concentration:** Healthcare/Hospitals; **Function Concentration:**
Generalist with a primary focus in Administration, Finance/Accounting,
General Management, Human Resources, Marketing

**Dooley, James L.** — *Manager North Atlantic Region*
Management Recruiters International, Inc.
1051 Johnnie Dodds Boulevard, Suite B
Mount Pleasant, SC 29464
Telephone: (803) 856-0544
**Recruiter Classification:** Contingency; **Lowest/Average Salary:**
$30,000/$75,000; **Industry Concentration:** Generalist; **Function
Concentration:** Generalist

**Doran, Mary Ann** — *Associate*
Kenzer Corp.
Triwest Plaza
3030 LBJ Freeway, Suite 1430
Dallas, TX 75234
Telephone: (214) 620-7776
**Recruiter Classification:** Retained; **Lowest/Average Salary:** $50,000/$90,000;
**Industry Concentration:** Generalist; **Function Concentration:** Generalist

**Dorfner, Martin** — *Associate*
Source Services Corporation
Foster Plaza VI
681 Anderson Drive, 2nd Floor
Pittsburgh, PA 15220
Telephone: (412) 928-8300
**Recruiter Classification:** Contingency; **Lowest/Average Salary:**
$30,000/$50,000; **Industry Concentration:** Financial Services, Information
Technology; **Function Concentration:** Engineering, Finance/Accounting

**Dornblut, Cindy** — *Marketing and Recruitment Support Specialist*
Ashton Computer Professionals Inc.
#1498 - 1090 West Georgia Street
Vancouver, British Columbia, CANADA V6E 3V7
Telephone: (604) 688-1134
**Recruiter Classification:** Contingency; **Lowest/Average Salary:**
$30,000/$60,000; **Industry Concentration:** Electronics, High Technology, Manufacturing; **Function Concentration:** Engineering, Marketing, Research and Development, Sales

**Dorsey, Jim** — *Executive Recruiter*
Ryan, Miller & Associates Inc.
4601 Wilshire Boulevard, Suite 225
Los Angeles, CA 90010
Telephone: (213) 938-4768
**Recruiter Classification:** Contingency; **Lowest/Average Salary:**
$60,000/$75,000; **Industry Concentration:** Consumer Products, Financial Services, High Technology, Manufacturing, Real Estate; **Function Concentration:** Generalist

**Dotson, M. Ileen** — *Principal*
Dotson & Associates
412 East 55th Street, Suite 8A
New York, NY 10022
Telephone: (212) 593-4274
**Recruiter Classification:** Contingency; **Lowest/Average Salary:**
$75,000/$90,000; **Industry Concentration:** Generalist with a primary focus in Consumer Products, Financial Services, Healthcare/Hospitals, High Technology, Information Technology, Insurance, Pharmaceutical/Medical, Publishing/Media; **Function Concentration:** General Management, Marketing, Sales, Women/Minorities

**Dougherty, Bridget L.** — *Associate*
Wellington Management Group
117 South 17th Street, Suite 1625
Philadelphia, PA 19103
Telephone: (215) 569-8900
**Recruiter Classification:** Retained; **Lowest/Average Salary:** $75,000/$75,000; **Industry Concentration:** Generalist with a primary focus in High Technology, Information Technology, Publishing/Media, Venture Capital; **Function Concentration:** Generalist with a primary focus in Engineering, General Management, Human Resources, Marketing, Sales, Women/Minorities

**Dougherty, Janice** — *Principal*
The McCormick Group, Inc.
2405 Grand Avenue, Suite 500
Kansas City, MO 64108
Telephone: (816) 374-7641
**Recruiter Classification:** Retained, Contingency; **Lowest/Average Salary:**
$60,000/$75,000; **Industry Concentration:** Consumer Products, Entertainment; **Function Concentration:** Generalist with a primary focus in Finance/Accounting, General Management, Marketing, Sales

**Dougherty, Lawrence J.** — *Manager North Atlantic Region*
Management Recruiters International, Inc.
3113 Roswell Road, Suite 203, P.O. Box 72527
Marietta, GA 30007-2527
Telephone: (770) 509-9055
**Recruiter Classification:** Contingency; **Lowest/Average Salary:**
$30,000/$75,000; **Industry Concentration:** Generalist; **Function Concentration:** Generalist

**Douglas, Anne** — *Manager Housewares and Giftware*
Prestige Inc.
P.O. Box 421
Reedsburg, WI 53959
Telephone: (608) 524-4032
**Recruiter Classification:** Contingency; **Lowest/Average Salary:**
$50,000/$90,000; **Industry Concentration:** Consumer Products; **Function Concentration:** Generalist

**Douglas, Barbara L.** — *Director*
David C. Cooper and Associates, Inc.
Five Concourse Parkway, Suite 2700
Atlanta, GA 30328
Telephone: (770) 395-0014
**Recruiter Classification:** Contingency, Executive Temporary; **Lowest/Average Salary:** $20,000/$40,000; **Industry Concentration:** Generalist; **Function Concentration:** Finance/Accounting

**Doukas, Jon A.** — *Principal and Senior Consultant*
Professional Bank Services, Inc. D/B/A Executive Search, Inc.
Suite 305, 6200 Dutchman's Lane
Louisville, KY 40205
Telephone: (502) 451-6633
**Recruiter Classification:** Retained; **Lowest/Average Salary:** $20,000/$90,000; **Industry Concentration:** Financial Services; **Function Concentration:** Generalist with a primary focus in Administration, Finance/Accounting, General Management, Human Resources

**Dow, Lori** — *Managing Partner*
Davidson, Laird & Associates
29260 Franklin, Suite 110
Southfield, MI 48034
Telephone: (810) 358-2160
**Recruiter Classification:** Contingency; **Lowest/Average Salary:**
$60,000/$75,000; **Industry Concentration:** Generalist with a primary focus in Automotive, Consumer Products, Environmental, High Technology, Manufacturing; **Function Concentration:** Generalist with a primary focus in Administration, Engineering, Finance/Accounting, General Management, Human Resources, Sales, Women/Minorities

**Dowell, Mary K.** — *Principal*
Professional Search Associates
12459 Lewis Street, Suite 102
Garden Grove, CA 92640-6606
Telephone: (714) 740-0919
**Recruiter Classification:** Contingency; **Lowest/Average Salary:**
$40,000/$75,000; **Industry Concentration:** Generalist with a primary focus in Consumer Products, Entertainment, Financial Services, Information Technology, Manufacturing, Real Estate; **Function Concentration:** Finance/Accounting, General Management, Human Resources, Marketing, Sales

**Dowlatzadch, Homayoun** — *Associate*
Source Services Corporation
4510 Executive Drive, Suite 200
San Diego, CA 92121
Telephone: (619) 552-0300
**Recruiter Classification:** Contingency; **Lowest/Average Salary:**
$30,000/$50,000; **Industry Concentration:** Financial Services, Information Technology; **Function Concentration:** Engineering, Finance/Accounting

**Downs, James L.** — *Principal*
Sanford Rose Associates
2915 Providence Road
Suite 300
Charlotte, NC 28211
Telephone: (704) 366-0730
**Recruiter Classification:** Contingency; **Lowest/Average Salary:**
$30,000/$75,000; **Industry Concentration:** Generalist with a primary focus in Financial Services; **Function Concentration:** Generalist

**Downs, William** — *Associate*
Source Services Corporation
4170 Ashford Dunwoody Road, Suite 285
Atlanta, GA 30319
Telephone: (404) 255-2045
**Recruiter Classification:** Contingency; **Lowest/Average Salary:**
$30,000/$50,000; **Industry Concentration:** Financial Services, Information Technology; **Function Concentration:** Engineering, Finance/Accounting

**Dowrick, Jeanne A.** — *Manager*
Longshore & Simmons, Inc.
Plymouth Corporate Center
625 Ridge Pike, Suite 410
Conshohocken, PA 19428-3216
Telephone: (610) 941-3400
**Recruiter Classification:** Retained; **Lowest/Average Salary:** $50,000/$90,000; **Industry Concentration:** Healthcare/Hospitals; **Function Concentration:** Generalist

**Doyle, Bobby** — *Executive Recruiter*
Richard, Wayne and Roberts
24 Greenway Plaza, Suite 1304
Houston, TX 77046-2493
Telephone: (713) 629-6681
**Recruiter Classification:** Retained; **Lowest/Average Salary:** $50,000/$90,000; **Industry Concentration:** Generalist with a primary focus in High Technology; **Function Concentration:** Generalist with a primary focus in Engineering

**Doyle, John P.** — *Partner*
Paul Ray Berndtson
10 South Riverside Plaza
Suite 720
Chicago, IL 60606
Telephone: (312) 876-0730
**Recruiter Classification:** Retained; **Lowest/Average Salary:** $90,000/$90,000; **Industry Concentration:** Consumer Products, Financial Services; **Function Concentration:** Generalist with a primary focus in Human Resources

**Doyle, Marie** — *Senior Consultant*
Spectra International Inc.
6991 East Camelback Road, Suite B-305
Scottsdale, AZ 85251
Telephone: (602) 481-0411
**Recruiter Classification:** Contingency; **Lowest/Average Salary:**
$50,000/$60,000; **Industry Concentration:** Electronics; **Function Concentration:** Engineering

**Dreifus, Donald** — *Account Executive*
Search West, Inc.
1888 Century Park East
Suite 2050
Los Angeles, CA 90067-1736
Telephone: (310) 284-8888
Recruiter Classification: Contingency; **Lowest/Average Salary:**
$40,000/$60,000; **Industry Concentration:** Generalist with a primary focus in
Chemical Products, Consumer Products, Electronics, Financial Services, High
Technology, Information Technology, Manufacturing, Transportation; **Function
Concentration:** Generalist with a primary focus in Administration,
Finance/Accounting, General Management, Marketing

**Dremely, Mark** — *Associate Partner*
Richard, Wayne and Roberts
24 Greenway Plaza, Suite 1304
Houston, TX 77046-2493
Telephone: (713) 629-6681
Recruiter Classification: Retained; **Lowest/Average Salary:** $50,000/$90,000;
**Industry Concentration:** Generalist with a primary focus in Real Estate;
**Function Concentration:** Generalist

**Drennan, Ronald** — *Partner*
Ward Howell International, Inc.
420 McGill Street, Room 400
Montreal, Quebec, CANADA H2Y 2G1
Telephone: (514) 397-9655
Recruiter Classification: Retained; **Lowest/Average Salary:** $75,000/$90,000;
**Industry Concentration:** Generalist; **Function Concentration:** Generalist

**Dreslinski, Robert S.** — *Specialist Automotive*
Sharrow & Associates
24735 Van Dyke
Center Line, MI 48015
Telephone: (810) 759-6910
Recruiter Classification: Contingency; **Lowest/Average Salary:**
$40,000/$60,000; **Industry Concentration:** Automotive, Manufacturing;
**Function Concentration:** Engineering

**Dresser, Amy K.** — *Consultant*
David C. Cooper and Associates, Inc.
Five Concourse Parkway, Suite 2700
Atlanta, GA 30328
Telephone: (770) 395-0014
Recruiter Classification: Contingency, Executive Temporary; **Lowest/Average
Salary:** $20,000/$40,000; **Industry Concentration:** Generalist; **Function
Concentration:** Finance/Accounting

**Dressler, Ralph** — *Senior Consultant*
Romac & Associates
1040 North Kings Highway
Suite 624
Cherry Hill, NJ 08034
Telephone: (609) 482-9677
Recruiter Classification: Executive Temporary; **Lowest/Average Salary:**
$/$60,000; **Industry Concentration:** Financial Services, Healthcare/Hospitals,
High Technology, Hospitality/Leisure, Information Technology, Insurance;
**Function Concentration:** Finance/Accounting

**Drexler, Robert** — *President*
Robert Drexler Associates, Inc.
210 River Street
Hackensack, NJ 07601
Telephone: (201) 342-0200
Recruiter Classification: Retained; **Lowest/Average Salary:** $50,000/$90,000;
**Industry Concentration:** Aerospace/Defense, Biotechnology, Chemical
Products, Electronics, Energy, Environmental, High Technology, Oil/Gas,
Packaging, Pharmaceutical/Medical, Transportation, Utilities/Nuclear; **Function
Concentration:** Engineering, General Management, Research and
Development

**Driscoll, Donald L.** — *Manager North Atlantic Region*
Management Recruiters International, Inc.
Boone Business Park, Suite 4
1064 Meadowview Drive
Boone, NC 28607-4855
Telephone: (704) 264-6066
Recruiter Classification: Contingency; **Lowest/Average Salary:**
$30,000/$75,000; **Industry Concentration:** Generalist; **Function
Concentration:** Generalist

**Dromeshauser, Peter** — *President*
Dromeshauser Associates
20 William Street
Wellesley, MA 02181
Telephone: (617) 239-0222
Recruiter Classification: Retained; **Lowest/Average Salary:** $90,000/$90,000;
**Industry Concentration:** Electronics, Financial Services, High Technology,
Information Technology, Manufacturing, Venture Capital; **Function
Concentration:** General Management, Marketing, Sales

**Drown, Clifford F.** — *Manager Southwest Region*
Management Recruiters International, Inc.
5959 West Loop South, Suite 380
Bellaire, TX 77401
Telephone: (713) 665-6660
Recruiter Classification: Contingency; **Lowest/Average Salary:**
$30,000/$75,000; **Industry Concentration:** Generalist; **Function
Concentration:** Generalist

**Drummond-Hay, Peter** — *Managing Director*
Russell Reynolds Associates, Inc.
200 Park Avenue
New York, NY 10166-0002
Telephone: (212) 351-2000
Recruiter Classification: Retained; **Lowest/Average Salary:** $90,000/$90,000;
**Industry Concentration:** Generalist with a primary focus in Financial Services;
**Function Concentration:** Generalist

**Drury, James J.** — *Managing Director*
Spencer Stuart
401 North Michigan Avenue, Suite 3400
Chicago, IL 60611-4244
Telephone: (312) 822-0080
Recruiter Classification: Retained; **Lowest/Average Salary:** $90,000/$90,000;
**Industry Concentration:** Generalist with a primary focus in
Aerospace/Defense, Automotive, Board Services, Consumer Products,
Electronics, Entertainment, Fashion (Retail/Apparel), High Technology,
Manufacturing, Packaging, Publishing/Media, Transportation, Venture Capital;
**Function Concentration:** Generalist with a primary focus in Administration,
Finance/Accounting, General Management, Human Resources, Marketing,
Sales

**DuBois, Joseph W.** — *President*
Horizon Medical Search of New Hampshire
8 Grenada Circle
Nashua, NH 03062-1429
Telephone: (603) 598-6611
Recruiter Classification: Contingency; **Lowest/Average Salary:**
$40,000/$50,000; **Industry Concentration:** Healthcare/Hospitals,
Pharmaceutical/Medical

**Duckworth, Donald R.** — *Partner*
Paul Ray Berndtson
191 Peachtree Tower, Suite 3800
191 Peachtree Street, NE
Atlanta, GA 30303-1757
Telephone: (404) 215-4600
Recruiter Classification: Retained; **Lowest/Average Salary:** $90,000/$90,000;
**Industry Concentration:** Energy; **Function Concentration:** Generalist with a
primary focus in General Management

**Ducruet, Linda K.** — *Consultant*
Heidrick & Struggles, Inc.
Greenwich Office Park #3
Greenwich, CT 06831
Telephone: (203) 629-3200
Recruiter Classification: Retained; **Lowest/Average Salary:** $75,000/$90,000;
**Industry Concentration:** Generalist with a primary focus in Financial Services;
**Function Concentration:** Generalist with a primary focus in
Finance/Accounting

**Dudley, Craig J.** — *Managing Partner*
Paul Ray Berndtson
Palo Santo No. 6
Colonia Lomas Altas
Mexico City, D.F., MEXICO 11950
Telephone: (525) 259-6010
Recruiter Classification: Retained; **Lowest/Average Salary:** $90,000/$90,000;
**Industry Concentration:** Generalist with a primary focus in Financial Services;
**Function Concentration:** Generalist

**Dudley, Robert** — *Principal*
Sanford Rose Associates
580 Broadway, Suite 226
Laguna Beach, CA 92651
Telephone: (714) 497-5728
Recruiter Classification: Contingency; **Lowest/Average Salary:**
$30,000/$75,000; **Industry Concentration:** Generalist with a primary focus in
Automotive, Chemical Products, Transportation; **Function Concentration:**
Generalist

**Duelks, John** — *Associate*
Source Services Corporation
4170 Ashford Dunwoody Road, Suite 285
Atlanta, GA 30319
Telephone: (404) 255-2045
Recruiter Classification: Contingency; **Lowest/Average Salary:**
$30,000/$50,000; **Industry Concentration:** Financial Services, Information
Technology; **Function Concentration:** Engineering, Finance/Accounting

**Dugan, John H.** — *President*
J.H. Dugan and Associates, Inc.
225 Crossroads Boulevard, Suite 416
Carmel, CA 93923
Telephone: (408) 625-5880
Recruiter Classification: Retained; Lowest/Average Salary: $50,000/$75,000;
Industry Concentration: Chemical Products, Packaging; Function
Concentration: Engineering, General Management, Marketing, Research and
Development, Sales, Women/Minorities

**Duggan, James P.** — *Vice President*
Slayton International, Inc.
181 West Madison Street, Suite 4510
Chicago, IL 60602
Telephone: (312) 456-0080
Recruiter Classification: Retained; Lowest/Average Salary: $90,000/$90,000;
Industry Concentration: Generalist with a primary focus in Biotechnology,
High Technology, Information Technology, Manufacturing, Packaging, Venture
Capital; Function Concentration: Generalist with a primary focus in
Engineering, General Management, Sales

**Duke, Larry G.** — *Manager North Atlantic Region*
Management Recruiters International, Inc.
8604 Cliff Cameron Drive, Suite 105
Charlotte, NC 28269
Telephone: (704) 548-9200
Recruiter Classification: Contingency; Lowest/Average Salary:
$30,000/$75,000; Industry Concentration: Generalist; Function
Concentration: Generalist

**Dukes, Ronald** — *Partner*
Heidrick & Struggles, Inc.
125 South Wacker Drive
Suite 2800
Chicago, IL 60606-4590
Telephone: (312) 372-8811
Recruiter Classification: Retained; Lowest/Average Salary: $75,000/$90,000;
Industry Concentration: Generalist; Function Concentration: Generalist

**Dulet, Donna** — *Recruiter*
Bryant Research
466 Old Hook Road, Suite 32
Emerson, NJ 07630
Telephone: (201) 599-0590
Recruiter Classification: Contingency; Lowest/Average Salary:
$50,000/$90,000; Industry Concentration: Biotechnology,
Pharmaceutical/Medical; Function Concentration: Research and Development

**Duley, Richard I.** — *Vice President/General Manager*
ARJay & Associates
875 Walnut Street, Suite 150
Cary, NC 27511
Telephone: (919) 469-5540
Recruiter Classification: Contingency; Lowest/Average Salary:
$40,000/$90,000; Industry Concentration: Generalist with a primary focus in
Automotive, Consumer Products, Electronics, Energy, Hospitality/Leisure,
Manufacturing, Utilities/Nuclear; Function Concentration: Generalist with a
primary focus in Engineering, Finance/Accounting, General Management,
Human Resources, Marketing, Research and Development, Sales

**Dumesnil, Curtis** — *Executive Recruiter*
Richard, Wayne and Roberts
24 Greenway Plaza, Suite 1304
Houston, TX 77046-2493
Telephone: (713) 629-6681
Recruiter Classification: Retained; Lowest/Average Salary: $40,000/$60,000;
Industry Concentration: Generalist with a primary focus in Information
Technology; Function Concentration: Generalist

**Dunbar, Geoffrey T.** — *Partner*
Heidrick & Struggles, Inc.
300 South Grand Avenue, Suite 2400
Los Angeles, CA 90071
Telephone: (213) 625-8811
Recruiter Classification: Retained; Lowest/Average Salary: $75,000/$90,000;
Industry Concentration: Generalist with a primary focus in High Technology;
Function Concentration: Generalist

**Duncan, Dana** — *Associate*
Source Services Corporation
5429 LBJ Freeway, Suite 275
Dallas, TX 75240
Telephone: (214) 387-1600
Recruiter Classification: Contingency; Lowest/Average Salary:
$30,000/$50,000; Industry Concentration: Financial Services, Information
Technology; Function Concentration: Engineering, Finance/Accounting

**Dunford, Michael S.** — *Vice President*
Korn/Ferry International
120 South Riverside Plaza
Suite 918
Chicago, IL 60606
Telephone: (312) 726-1841
Recruiter Classification: Retained; Lowest/Average Salary: $90,000/$90,000;
Industry Concentration: Generalist; Function Concentration: Generalist

**Dunkel, David L.** — *Managing Partner*
Romac & Associates
120 Hyde Park Place
Suite 200
Tampa, FL 33606
Telephone: (813) 229-5575
Recruiter Classification: Executive Temporary; Lowest/Average Salary:
$/$60,000; Industry Concentration: Financial Services, Healthcare/Hospitals,
High Technology, Hospitality/Leisure, Information Technology, Insurance;
Function Concentration: Finance/Accounting

**Dunlevie, Craig** — *Vice President*
Korn/Ferry International
303 Peachtree Street N.E.
Suite 1600
Atlanta, GA 30308
Telephone: (404) 577-7542
Recruiter Classification: Retained; Lowest/Average Salary: $90,000/$90,000;
Industry Concentration: Generalist; Function Concentration: Generalist

**Dunlop, Eric** — *Information Technology Recruiter*
Southwestern Professional Services
2451 Atrium Way
Nashville, TN 37214
Telephone: (615) 391-2722
Recruiter Classification: Contingency; Lowest/Average Salary:
$40,000/$60,000; Industry Concentration: High Technology, Information
Technology; Function Concentration: Sales

**Dunlow, Aimee** — *Associate*
Source Services Corporation
5429 LBJ Freeway, Suite 275
Dallas, TX 75240
Telephone: (214) 387-1600
Recruiter Classification: Contingency; Lowest/Average Salary:
$30,000/$50,000; Industry Concentration: Financial Services, Information
Technology; Function Concentration: Engineering, Finance/Accounting

**Dunman, Betsy L.** — *President*
Crawford & Crofford
15327 NW 60th Avenue, Suite 240
Miami Lakes, FL 33014
Telephone: (305) 820-0855
Recruiter Classification: Contingency, Executive Temporary; Lowest/Average
Salary: $30,000/$60,000; Industry Concentration: Generalist with a primary
focus in Electronics, Financial Services, High Technology, Information
Technology, Insurance, Manufacturing, Oil/Gas, Packaging; Function
Concentration: Generalist with a primary focus in Administration, Engineering,
Finance/Accounting, General Management, Marketing, Research and
Development, Sales

**Dunn, Ed L.** — *Manager Eastern Region*
Management Recruiters International, Inc.
120 Genesee Street, Suite 602, P.O. Box 711
Auburn, NY 13021
Telephone: (315) 487-5428
Recruiter Classification: Contingency; Lowest/Average Salary:
$30,000/$75,000; Industry Concentration: Generalist; Function
Concentration: Generalist

**Dunn, Kathleen** — *Vice President*
A.T. Kearney, Inc.
Miami Center, Suite 3180
201 South Biscayne Boulevard
Miami, FL 33131
Telephone: (305) 577-0046
Recruiter Classification: Retained; Lowest/Average Salary: $90,000/$90,000;
Industry Concentration: Generalist; Function Concentration: Generalist

**Dunn, Mary Helen** — *Partner*
Paul Ray Berndtson
101 Park Avenue, 41st Floor
New York, NY 10178
Telephone: (212) 370-1316
Recruiter Classification: Retained; Lowest/Average Salary: $90,000/$90,000;
Industry Concentration: Financial Services, Real Estate; Function
Concentration: Generalist

**Dupont, Rick** — *Chief Financial Officer*
Source Services Corporation
5580 LBJ Freeway, Suite 300
Dallas, TX 75240
Telephone: (214) 385-3002
**Recruiter Classification:** Contingency; **Lowest/Average Salary:**
$30,000/$50,000; **Industry Concentration:** Financial Services, Information
Technology; **Function Concentration:** Engineering, Finance/Accounting

**Durakis, Charles A.** — *Chairman*
C.A. Durakis Associates, Inc.
66 Bayberry Lane
Westport, CT 06880
Telephone: (203) 255-5567
**Recruiter Classification:** Retained; **Lowest/Average Salary:** $90,000/$90,000;
**Industry Concentration:** Generalist; **Function Concentration:** Generalist

**Durakis, Charles A.** — *Chairman*
C.A. Durakis Associates, Inc.
3003 Gulfshore Boulevard North
Naples, FL 33940
Telephone: (941) 261-9277
**Recruiter Classification:** Retained; **Lowest/Average Salary:** $90,000/$90,000;
**Industry Concentration:** Generalist; **Function Concentration:** Generalist

**Durakis, Charles A.** — *President*
C.A. Durakis Associates, Inc.
5550 Sterret Place, Suite 302
Columbia, MD 21044
Telephone: (410) 740-5590
**Recruiter Classification:** Retained; **Lowest/Average Salary:** $90,000/$90,000;
**Industry Concentration:** Generalist; **Function Concentration:** Generalist

**Durand, Francois** — *Partner*
Ward Howell International, Inc.
420 McGill Street, Room 400
Montreal, Quebec, CANADA H2Y 2G1
Telephone: (514) 397-9655
**Recruiter Classification:** Retained; **Lowest/Average Salary:** $75,000/$90,000;
**Industry Concentration:** Generalist; **Function Concentration:** Generalist

**Durant, Jane** — *Accounting and Finance Recruiter*
Winter, Wyman & Company
950 Winter Street, Suite 3100
Waltham, MA 02154-1294
Telephone: (617) 890-7000
**Recruiter Classification:** Contingency; **Lowest/Average Salary:**
$20,000/$50,000; **Industry Concentration:** Generalist; **Function
Concentration:** Finance/Accounting

**Dussick, Vince** — *President*
Dussick Management Associates
149 Durham Road
Madison, CT 06443
Telephone: (203) 245-9311
**Recruiter Classification:** Contingency; **Lowest/Average Salary:**
$50,000/$60,000; **Industry Concentration:** Generalist with a primary focus in
Consumer Products, High Technology, Information Technology, Packaging,
Pharmaceutical/Medical; **Function Concentration:** Generalist with a primary
focus in Marketing, Research and Development, Sales, Women/Minorities

**Dwyer, Julie** — *Executive Recruiter*
CPS Inc.
One Westbrook Corporate Centre, Suite 600
Westchester, IL 60154
Telephone: (708) 531-8370
**Recruiter Classification:** Contingency; **Lowest/Average Salary:**
$30,000/$50,000; **Industry Concentration:** Generalist with a primary focus in
Automotive, Biotechnology, Chemical Products, Consumer Products, High
Technology, Insurance, Manufacturing, Oil/Gas, Packaging,
Pharmaceutical/Medical; **Function Concentration:** Engineering, Research and
Development, Sales, Women/Minorities

**Dykeman, James J.** — *Manager Pacific Region*
Management Recruiters International, Inc.
Globe Building, Suite 312
9725 SE 36th Street
Mercer Island, WA 98040-3896
Telephone: (206) 232-0204
**Recruiter Classification:** Contingency; **Lowest/Average Salary:** $30,000/$75,000;
**Industry Concentration:** Generalist; **Function Concentration:** Generalist

**Dykstra, Nicolette** — *Executive Recruiter*
CPS Inc.
One Westbrook Corporate Centre, Suite 600
Westchester, IL 60154
Telephone: (708) 531-8370
**Recruiter Classification:** Contingency; **Lowest/Average Salary:**
$30,000/$50,000; **Industry Concentration:** Generalist with a primary focus in
Automotive, Biotechnology, Chemical Products, Consumer Products, High
Technology, Insurance, Manufacturing, Oil/Gas, Packaging,
Pharmaceutical/Medical; **Function Concentration:** Engineering, Research and
Development, Sales, Women/Minorities

**Eagan, Karen L.** — *Manager*
Management Recruiters International, Inc.
350 Crown Point Circle, Suite 125
Grass Valley, CA 95945
Telephone: (916) 273-0200
**Recruiter Classification:** Contingency; **Lowest/Average Salary:**
$30,000/$75,000; **Industry Concentration:** Generalist; **Function
Concentration:** Generalist

**Eagan, Ridge** — *Manager Pacific Region*
Management Recruiters International, Inc.
350 Crown Point Circle, Suite 125
Grass Valley, CA 95945
Telephone: (916) 273-0200
**Recruiter Classification:** Contingency; **Lowest/Average Salary:**
$30,000/$75,000; **Industry Concentration:** Generalist; **Function
Concentration:** Generalist

**Earhart, William D.** — *Principal*
Sanford Rose Associates
6230 Busch Boulevard
Suite 418
Columbus, OH 43229
Telephone: (614) 436-3778
**Recruiter Classification:** Contingency; **Lowest/Average Salary:**
$30,000/$75,000; **Industry Concentration:** Generalist with a primary focus in
High Technology; **Function Concentration:** Generalist

**Earle, Paul W.** — *Senior Director*
Spencer Stuart
401 North Michigan Avenue, Suite 3400
Chicago, IL 60611-4244
Telephone: (312) 822-0080
**Recruiter Classification:** Retained; **Lowest/Average Salary:** $90,000/$90,000;
**Industry Concentration:** Healthcare/Hospitals; **Function Concentration:**
Generalist with a primary focus in Administration, Finance/Accounting,
General Management, Human Resources, Marketing, Research and
Development, Sales, Women/Minorities

**Early, Alice C.** — *Managing Director*
Russell Reynolds Associates, Inc.
200 Park Avenue
New York, NY 10166-0002
Telephone: (212) 351-2000
**Recruiter Classification:** Retained; **Lowest/Average Salary:** $90,000/$90,000;
**Industry Concentration:** Generalist with a primary focus in Financial Services;
**Function Concentration:** Generalist

**Early, Bert H.** — *Principal*
Early Cochran & Olson, Inc.
401 North Michigan, Suite 515
Chicago, IL 60611-4205
Telephone: (312) 595-4200
**Recruiter Classification:** Retained; **Lowest/Average Salary:** $90,000/$90,000;
**Industry Concentration:** Generalist; **Function Concentration:** Generalist

**Eason, James** — *Vice President/Manager*
JRL Executive Recruiters
2187 Hopkins Terrace
Duluth, GA 30136
Telephone: (404) 446-1291
**Recruiter Classification:** Executive Temporary; **Lowest/Average Salary:**
$30,000/$60,000; **Industry Concentration:** Automotive, Chemical Products,
Consumer Products, Energy, Environmental, Manufacturing, Packaging,
Pharmaceutical/Medical, Transportation, Utilities/Nuclear; **Function
Concentration:** Engineering, General Management, Human Resources,
Research and Development

**Eason, Larry E.** — *President*
JRL Executive Recruiters
2700 Rockcreek Parkway, Suite 303
North Kansas City, MO 64117-2519
Telephone: (816) 471-4022
**Recruiter Classification:** Executive Temporary; **Lowest/Average Salary:**
$30,000/$60,000; **Industry Concentration:** Automotive, Chemical Products,
Consumer Products, Energy, Environmental, Manufacturing, Packaging,
Pharmaceutical/Medical, Transportation, Utilities/Nuclear; **Function
Concentration:** Engineering, General Management, Human Resources,
Research and Development

**Eastham, Marvene M.** — *Shareholder*
Witt/Kieffer, Ford, Hadelman & Lloyd
10375 Richmond Avenue, Suite 1625
Houston, TX 77042
Telephone: (713) 266-6779
**Recruiter Classification:** Retained; **Lowest/Average Salary:** $75,000/$90,000;
**Industry Concentration:** Healthcare/Hospitals; **Function Concentration:**
Generalist with a primary focus in Administration, Finance/Accounting,
General Management, Human Resources, Marketing

**Eatman, Fred** — *Manager North Atlantic Region*
Management Recruiters International, Inc.
1319 South Glenburnie Road
New Bern, NC 28562-2605
Telephone: (919) 633-1900
**Recruiter Classification:** Contingency; **Lowest/Average Salary:** $30,000/$75,000;
**Industry Concentration:** Generalist; **Function Concentration:** Generalist

**Eatmon, Michael** — *Recruiter*
U.S. Envirosearch
445 Union Boulevard, Suite 225
Lakewood, CO 80228
Telephone: (303) 980-6600
**Recruiter Classification:** Contingency; **Lowest/Average Salary:** $30,000/$60,000;
**Industry Concentration:** Environmental; **Function Concentration:** Generalist
with a primary focus in Administration, Engineering, Finance/Accounting,
General Management, Marketing, Sales, Women/Minorities

**Ebeling, John A.** — *Vice President*
Gilbert Tweed/INESA
155 Prospect Avenue
West Orange, NJ 07052
Telephone: (201) 731-3033
**Recruiter Classification:** Retained; **Lowest/Average Salary:** $90,000/$90,000;
**Industry Concentration:** Generalist with a primary focus in Consumer Products,
Electronics, Financial Services, Healthcare/Hospitals, High Technology,
Information Technology, Manufacturing, Pharmaceutical/Medical; **Function
Concentration:** Generalist with a primary focus in General Management, Human
Resources, Marketing, Research and Development, Sales, Women/Minorities

**Eberly, Carrie** — *Executive Recruiter*
Accounting Resources, Inc.
8744 Frederick Street
Omaha, NE 68124-3068
Telephone: (402) 397-3308
**Recruiter Classification:** Contingency; **Lowest/Average Salary:**
$40,000/$75,000; **Industry Concentration:** Generalist with a primary focus in
Automotive, Financial Services, Manufacturing, Packaging, Publishing/Media,
Transportation; **Function Concentration:** Finance/Accounting

**Eckhart, Ken** — *Director*
Spencer Stuart
One Atlantic Center, Suite 3230
1201 West Peachtree Street
Atlanta, GA 30309
Telephone: (404) 892-2800
**Recruiter Classification:** Retained; **Lowest/Average Salary:** $90,000/$90,000;
**Industry Concentration:** Generalist; **Function Concentration:** Generalist

**Edell, David E.** — *President*
The Development Resource Group Incorporated
104 East 40th Street, Suite 806
New York, NY 10016
Telephone: (212) 983-1600
**Recruiter Classification:** Retained; **Lowest/Average Salary:** $60,000/$90,000;
**Industry Concentration:** Board Services, Education/Libraries,
Healthcare/Hospitals, Non-Profit, Public Administration; **Function
Concentration:** General Management

**Eden, Brooks D.** — *President and CEO*
Eden & Associates, Inc.
794 North Valley Road
Paoli, PA 19301
Telephone: (610) 889-9993
**Recruiter Classification:** Contingency, Executive Temporary; **Lowest/Average
Salary:** $50,000/$90,000; **Industry Concentration:** Generalist; **Function
Concentration:** Generalist with a primary focus in Administration, Engineering,
General Management, Human Resources, Marketing

**Eden, Dianne** — *President*
Steeple Associates
45 Park Place South, Suite 210
Morristown, NJ 07960
Telephone: (201) 644-2477
**Recruiter Classification:** Contingency; **Lowest/Average Salary:**
$50,000/$60,000; **Industry Concentration:** Generalist; **Function Concentration:**
Generalist with a primary focus in Administration, Finance/Accounting, General
Management, Human Resources, Marketing, Sales

**Eden, Don F.** — *Manager Central Region*
Management Recruiters International, Inc.
37677 Professional Center Drive, Suite 100-C
Livonia, MI 48154-1138
Telephone: (313) 953-9590
**Recruiter Classification:** Contingency; **Lowest/Average Salary:**
$30,000/$75,000; **Industry Concentration:** Generalist; **Function
Concentration:** Generalist

**Eden, Earl M.** — *Chairman*
Eden & Associates, Inc.
794 North Valley Road
Paoli, PA 19301
Telephone: (610) 889-9993
**Recruiter Classification:** Contingency, Executive Temporary; **Lowest/Average
Salary:** $50,000/$90,000; **Industry Concentration:** Generalist with a primary
focus in Board Services; **Function Concentration:** Generalist with a primary
focus in Administration, General Management

**Edmond, Bruce** — *Technical Recruiter*
Corporate Recruiters Ltd.
490-1140 West Pender
Vancouver, British Columbia, CANADA V6E 4G1
Telephone: (604) 687-5993
**Recruiter Classification:** Contingency; **Lowest/Average Salary:**
$40,000/$60,000; **Industry Concentration:** Chemical Products, Energy,
Environmental, Manufacturing; **Function Concentration:** Engineering, General
Management, Marketing, Research and Development, Sales

**Edwards, Dorothy** — *Manager*
MSI International
800 Gessner, Suite 1220
Houston, TX 77024
Telephone: (713) 722-0050
**Recruiter Classification:** Contingency; **Lowest/Average Salary:**
$30,000/$75,000; **Industry Concentration:** Generalist with a primary focus in
Financial Services, Healthcare/Hospitals, High Technology, Information
Technology, Manufacturing; **Function Concentration:** Generalist with a
primary focus in Administration, Engineering, Finance/Accounting, General
Management, Marketing, Sales

**Edwards, Douglas W.** — *Consultant*
Egon Zehnder International Inc.
One Atlantic Center, Suite 3000
1201 West Peachtree Street N.E.
Atlanta, GA 30309
Telephone: (404) 875-3000
**Recruiter Classification:** Retained; **Lowest/Average Salary:** $90,000/$90,000;
**Industry Concentration:** Generalist with a primary focus in Biotechnology,
Financial Services, High Technology, Manufacturing, Pharmaceutical/Medical;
**Function Concentration:** Generalist

**Edwards, Randolph J.** — *Managing Partner*
DeFuniak & Edwards
960 Fell Street, Suite 317
Baltimore, MD 21231
Telephone: (410) 732-1521
**Recruiter Classification:** Retained; **Lowest/Average Salary:** $50,000/$90,000;
**Industry Concentration:** Insurance; **Function Concentration:** General
Management

**Edwards, Robert** — *Recruiter*
J.P. Canon Associates
225 Broadway, Suite 3602
New York, NY 10007
Telephone: (212) 233-3131
**Recruiter Classification:** Contingency; **Lowest/Average Salary:**
$30,000/$60,000; **Industry Concentration:** Generalist; **Function
Concentration:** Generalist with a primary focus in Engineering

**Edwards, Verba L.** — *President and CEO*
Wing Tips & Pumps, Inc.
P.O. Box 99580
Troy, MI 48099
Telephone: (810) 641-0980
**Recruiter Classification:** Contingency; **Lowest/Average Salary:** $20,000/$60,000;
**Industry Concentration:** Generalist with a primary focus in Aerospace/Defense,
Automotive, Consumer Products, Electronics, Environmental, Financial Services,
High Technology, Hospitality/Leisure, Information Technology, Insurance,
Manufacturing, Oil/Gas, Packaging, Pharmaceutical/Medical; **Function
Concentration:** Generalist with a primary focus in Administration, Engineering,
Finance/Accounting, General Management, Human Resources, Marketing,
Research and Development, Sales, Women/Minorities

**Eggena, Roger** — *Executive Recruiter*
Phillips Resource Group
Ridgeway Business Park
3125 Ashley Phosphate Road, Suite 106
North Charleston, SC 29418
Telephone: (803) 552-8840
**Recruiter Classification:** Contingency; **Lowest/Average Salary:**
$40,000/$50,000; **Industry Concentration:** Chemical Products, Electronics,
Environmental, High Technology, Information Technology, Manufacturing,
Packaging; **Function Concentration:** Administration, Engineering,
Finance/Accounting, General Management, Human Resources, Marketing,
Research and Development, Sales

**Eggert, Scott** — *Associate*
Source Services Corporation
1105 Schrock Road, Suite 510
Columbus, OH 43229
Telephone: (614) 846-3311
Recruiter Classification: Contingency; Lowest/Average Salary:
$30,000/$50,000; Industry Concentration: Financial Services, Information
Technology; Function Concentration: Engineering, Finance/Accounting

**Ehrenzeller, Tony A.** — *Manager Eastern Region*
Management Recruiters International, Inc.
4400 Fair Lakes Court, Suite 103
Fairfax, VA 22033
Telephone: (703) 222-8220
Recruiter Classification: Contingency; Lowest/Average Salary:
$30,000/$75,000; Industry Concentration: Generalist; Function
Concentration: Generalist

**Ehrgott, Elizabeth** — *Associate Director*
The Ascher Group
25 Pompton Avenue, Suite 310
Verona, NJ 07044
Telephone: (201) 239-6116
Recruiter Classification: Executive Temporary; Lowest/Average Salary:
$50,000/$90,000; Industry Concentration: Generalist with a primary focus in
Consumer Products, Fashion (Retail/Apparel), Financial Services, Information
Technology, Insurance, Manufacturing, Pharmaceutical/Medical,
Publishing/Media; Function Concentration: Generalist with a primary focus in
Administration, Finance/Accounting, General Management, Human Resources,
Marketing, Women/Minorities

**Ehrhart, Jennifer** — *Executive Recruiter/Manager*
ADOW's Executeam
10921 Reed Hartman Highway, Suite 225
Blue Ash, OH 45242-2830
Telephone: (513) 891-5335
Recruiter Classification: Executive Temporary; Industry Concentration:
Generalist with a primary focus in Chemical Products, Electronics, Financial
Services, High Technology, Information Technology, Manufacturing, Packaging,
Utilities/Nuclear; Function Concentration: Generalist with a primary focus in
Administration, Engineering, Finance/Accounting, General Management,
Human Resources, Marketing, Women/Minorities

**Eibeler, C.** — *Vice President*
Amherst Personnel Group Inc.
550 West Old Country Road
Hicksville, NY 11801
Telephone: (516) 433-7610
Recruiter Classification: Contingency; Lowest/Average Salary:
$20,000/$50,000; Industry Concentration: Generalist with a primary focus in
Consumer Products, Fashion (Retail/Apparel), Healthcare/Hospitals,
Hospitality/Leisure, Pharmaceutical/Medical; Function Concentration:
Generalist with a primary focus in Marketing, Sales, Women/Minorities

**Eilertson, Douglas R.** — *Vice President*
Sanford Rose Associates
265 South Main Street, Suite 100
Akron, OH 44308
Telephone: (330) 762-7162
Recruiter Classification: Contingency; Lowest/Average Salary:
$30,000/$75,000; Industry Concentration: Generalist; Function
Concentration: Generalist

**Einsele, Neil** — *Agribusiness Recruiter*
Agra Placements International Ltd.
2200 North Kickapoo, Suite 2
Lincoln, IL 62656
Telephone: (217) 735-4373
Recruiter Classification: Contingency; Lowest/Average Salary:
$20,000/$30,000; Industry Concentration: Generalist with a primary focus in
Biotechnology, Chemical Products, Energy, Financial Services, Manufacturing;
Function Concentration: Administration, Engineering, Finance/Accounting,
General Management, Human Resources, Marketing, Research and
Development, Sales

**Eiseman, Joe** — *Managing Director*
Source Services Corporation
1 Gatehall Drive, Suite 250
Parsippany, NJ 07054
Telephone: (201) 267-3222
Recruiter Classification: Contingency; Lowest/Average Salary:
$30,000/$50,000; Industry Concentration: Financial Services, Information
Technology; Function Concentration: Engineering, Finance/Accounting

**Eiseman, Joe** — *Managing Director*
Source Services Corporation
925 Westchester Avenue, Suite 309
White Plains, NY 10604
Telephone: (914) 428-9100
Recruiter Classification: Contingency; Lowest/Average Salary:
$30,000/$50,000; Industry Concentration: Financial Services, Information
Technology; Function Concentration: Engineering, Finance/Accounting

**Eiseman, Joe** — *Managing Director*
Source Services Corporation
15 Essex Road, Suite 201
Paramus, NJ 07652
Telephone: (201) 845-3900
Recruiter Classification: Contingency; Lowest/Average Salary:
$30,000/$50,000; Industry Concentration: Financial Services, Information
Technology; Function Concentration: Engineering, Finance/Accounting

**Eisert, Robert M.** — *Principal*
Sanford Rose Associates
5230 Old York Road, Suite 2
P.O. Box 1017
Buckingham, PA 18912-1017
Telephone: (215) 794-5570
Recruiter Classification: Contingency; Lowest/Average Salary:
$30,000/$75,000; Industry Concentration: Generalist; Function
Concentration: Generalist

**El-Darwish, Jill** — *Technical Documentation and Technical
Training Recruiter*
Winter, Wyman & Company
950 Winter Street, Suite 3100
Waltham, MA 02154-1294
Telephone: (617) 890-7000
Recruiter Classification: Contingency; Lowest/Average Salary:
$30,000/$50,000; Industry Concentration: Generalist; Function
Concentration: Generalist

**Elam, Bill J.** — *Manager Midwest Region*
Management Recruiters International, Inc.
Greentree Court, Suite 434
210 Gateway
Lincoln, NE 68505-2438
Telephone: (402) 467-5534
Recruiter Classification: Contingency; Lowest/Average Salary:
$30,000/$75,000; Industry Concentration: Generalist; Function
Concentration: Generalist

**Eldredge, L. Lincoln** — *Partner*
Lamalie Amrop International
Thanksgiving Tower
1601 Elm Street
Dallas, TX 75201-4768
Telephone: (214) 754-0019
Recruiter Classification: Retained; Lowest/Average Salary: $90,000/$90,000;
Industry Concentration: Generalist with a primary focus in Non-Profit;
Function Concentration: Generalist with a primary focus in
Finance/Accounting, General Management, Human Resources, Marketing,
Research and Development, Sales

**Elliott, A. Larry** — *Partner*
Heidrick & Struggles, Inc.
8000 Towers Crescent Drive, Suite 555
Vienna, VA 22182
Telephone: (703) 761-4830
Recruiter Classification: Retained; Lowest/Average Salary: $75,000/$90,000;
Industry Concentration: Generalist with a primary focus in High Technology;
Function Concentration: Generalist

**Elliott, David H.** — *Partner*
Heidrick & Struggles, Inc.
Four Embarcadero Center, Suite 3570
San Francisco, CA 94111
Telephone: (415) 981-2854
Recruiter Classification: Retained; Lowest/Average Salary: $75,000/$90,000;
Industry Concentration: Generalist with a primary focus in High Technology;
Function Concentration: Generalist

**Elliott, Mark P.** — *Senior Partner*
Lamalie Amrop International
Key Tower, 127 Public Square
Cleveland, OH 44114-1216
Telephone: (216) 694-3000
Recruiter Classification: Retained; Lowest/Average Salary: $90,000/$90,000;
Industry Concentration: Generalist; Function Concentration: Generalist with a
primary focus in General Management, Human Resources, Marketing, Sales

**Ellis, David** — *Recruiter/Co-Owner*
Don Richard Associates of Georgia, Inc.
3475 Lenox Road, Suite 210
Atlanta, GA 30326
Telephone: (404) 231-3688
**Recruiter Classification:** Executive Temporary; **Lowest/Average Salary:** $/$75,000; **Industry Concentration:** Financial Services; **Function Concentration:** Finance/Accounting, Human Resources

**Ellis, Milton** — *Manager*
Accountants on Call
1101 Kermit Drive, Suite 600
Nashville, TN 37217
Telephone: (615) 399-0200
**Recruiter Classification:** Contingency; **Lowest/Average Salary:** $20,000/$30,000; **Industry Concentration:** Generalist; **Function Concentration:** Finance/Accounting

**Ellis, Patricia** — *Associate*
Source Services Corporation
7730 East Bellview Avenue, Suite 302
Englewood, CO 80111
Telephone: (303) 773-3700
**Recruiter Classification:** Contingency; **Lowest/Average Salary:** $30,000/$50,000; **Industry Concentration:** Financial Services, Information Technology; **Function Concentration:** Engineering, Finance/Accounting

**Ellis, Ronald A.** — *Manager South Atlantic Region*
Management Recruiters International, Inc.
Reynolds Plaza, Suite 410N
1061 East Indiantown Road
Jupiter, FL 33477
Telephone: (407) 743-7772
**Recruiter Classification:** Contingency; **Lowest/Average Salary:** $30,000/$75,000; **Industry Concentration:** Generalist; **Function Concentration:** Generalist

**Ellis, Ted K.** — *Vice President - Bristol/Southeast*
The Hindman Company
325 Springlake Road
Bristol, VA 24201
Telephone: (540) 669-5006
**Recruiter Classification:** Retained; **Lowest/Average Salary:** $50,000/$90,000; **Industry Concentration:** Generalist with a primary focus in Aerospace/Defense, Automotive, Chemical Products, Consumer Products, Electronics, Financial Services, High Technology, Manufacturing, Oil/Gas, Pharmaceutical/Medical, Transportation; **Function Concentration:** Generalist

**Ellis, William** — *President*
Interspace Interactive Inc.
521 Fifth Avenue
New York, NY 10017
Telephone: (212) 867-6661
**Recruiter Classification:** Contingency; **Lowest/Average Salary:** $50,000/$60,000; **Industry Concentration:** Generalist with a primary focus in Consumer Products, Financial Services, Information Technology; **Function Concentration:** Generalist with a primary focus in Engineering, Finance/Accounting, General Management, Human Resources, Marketing, Sales, Women/Minorities

**Ellison, Richard** — *Principal*
Sanford Rose Associates
545 North Broad Street
Suite 2
Canfield, OH 44406-9204
Telephone: (216) 533-9270
**Recruiter Classification:** Contingency; **Lowest/Average Salary:** $30,000/$75,000; **Industry Concentration:** Generalist with a primary focus in Information Technology; **Function Concentration:** Generalist

**Elster, Irv** — *Executive Vice President*
Spectrum Search Associates, Inc.
1888 Century Park East, Suite 320
Los Angeles, CA 90067
Telephone: (310) 286-6921
**Recruiter Classification:** Contingency; **Lowest/Average Salary:** $30,000/$50,000; **Industry Concentration:** Financial Services; **Function Concentration:** Finance/Accounting

**Elston, William S.** — *Executive Vice President/ Managing Director*
DHR International, Inc.
Two Sawgrass Village Drive, Suite 4
Ponte Vedra Beach, FL 32082
Telephone: (904) 273-4656
**Recruiter Classification:** Retained; **Lowest/Average Salary:** $60,000/$90,000; **Industry Concentration:** Generalist; **Function Concentration:** Generalist

**Elwell, Richard F.** — *President*
Elwell & Associates Inc.
301 East Liberty, Suite 535
Ann Arbor, MI 48104
Telephone: (313) 662-8775
**Recruiter Classification:** Retained; **Lowest/Average Salary:** $75,000/$90,000; **Industry Concentration:** Generalist; **Function Concentration:** Generalist

**Elwell, Stephen R.** — *Senior Consultant*
Elwell & Associates Inc.
301 East Liberty, Suite 535
Ann Arbor, MI 48104
Telephone: (313) 662-8775
**Recruiter Classification:** Retained; **Lowest/Average Salary:** $75,000/$90,000; **Industry Concentration:** Generalist; **Function Concentration:** Generalist

**Emerson, Randall** — *Managing Director*
Source Services Corporation
111 Monument Circle, Suite 3930
Indianapolis, IN 46204
Telephone: (317) 631-2900
**Recruiter Classification:** Contingency; **Lowest/Average Salary:** $30,000/$50,000; **Industry Concentration:** Financial Services, Information Technology; **Function Concentration:** Engineering, Finance/Accounting

**Emmott, Carol B.** — *Director*
Spencer Stuart
525 Market Street, Suite 3700
San Francisco, CA 94105
Telephone: (415) 495-4141
**Recruiter Classification:** Retained; **Lowest/Average Salary:** $90,000/$90,000; **Industry Concentration:** Education/Libraries, Healthcare/Hospitals, Non-Profit, Pharmaceutical/Medical; **Function Concentration:** Generalist with a primary focus in Administration, Finance/Accounting, General Management, Human Resources, Marketing, Sales

**Empey, David G.** — *Manager Southwest Region*
Management Recruiters International, Inc.
Clocktower Building, Suite 23
2195 North State Highway 83
Franktown, CO 80116-9664
Telephone: (303) 660-0766
**Recruiter Classification:** Contingency; **Lowest/Average Salary:** $30,000/$75,000; **Industry Concentration:** Generalist; **Function Concentration:** Generalist

**Endres, Robert** — *Principal*
Sanford Rose Associates
2132 Salt Air Drive
Santa Ana, CA 92705
Telephone: (714) 730-6864
**Recruiter Classification:** Contingency; **Lowest/Average Salary:** $30,000/$75,000; **Industry Concentration:** Generalist with a primary focus in Manufacturing; **Function Concentration:** Generalist

**Enfield, Jerry J.** — *Vice President*
Executive Manning Corporation
3000 N.E. 30th Place, Suite 405/402/411
Fort Lauderdale, FL 33306
Telephone: (954) 561-5100
**Recruiter Classification:** Retained; **Lowest/Average Salary:** $75,000/$90,000; **Industry Concentration:** Generalist with a primary focus in Aerospace/Defense, Automotive, Chemical Products, Consumer Products, Electronics, High Technology, Manufacturing, Pharmaceutical/Medical; **Function Concentration:** Generalist

**Engelgau, Elvita P.** — *Co-Manager Pacific Region*
Management Recruiters International, Inc.
2020 Lloyd Center
Portland, OR 97232-1376
Telephone: (503) 287-8701
**Recruiter Classification:** Contingency; **Lowest/Average Salary:** $30,000/$75,000; **Industry Concentration:** Generalist; **Function Concentration:** Generalist

**Engelgau, Larry P.** — *Co-Manager*
Management Recruiters International, Inc.
2020 Lloyd Center
Portland, OR 97232-1376
Telephone: (503) 287-8701
**Recruiter Classification:** Contingency; **Lowest/Average Salary:** $30,000/$75,000; **Industry Concentration:** Generalist; **Function Concentration:** Generalist

**England, Mark** — *Vice President*
Austin-McGregor International
12005 Ford Road, Suite 160
Dallas, TX 75234-7247
Telephone: (214) 488-0500
**Recruiter Classification:** Retained; **Lowest/Average Salary:** $50,000/$90,000;
**Industry Concentration:** Generalist with a primary focus in Automotive, Board
Services, Chemical Products, Consumer Products, Electronics, Entertainment,
Healthcare/Hospitals, High Technology, Hospitality/Leisure, Manufacturing,
Pharmaceutical/Medical, Publishing/Media, Venture Capital; **Function
Concentration:** Generalist with a primary focus in Engineering,
Finance/Accounting, General Management, Human Resources, Marketing,
Research and Development, Sales, Women/Minorities

**Engle, Bryan** — *Managing Director*
Source Services Corporation
120 East Baltimore Street, Suite 1950
Baltimore, MD 21202
Telephone: (410) 727-4050
**Recruiter Classification:** Contingency; **Lowest/Average Salary:**
$30,000/$50,000; **Industry Concentration:** Financial Services, Information
Technology; **Function Concentration:** Engineering, Finance/Accounting

**Engman, Steven T.** — *Partner*
Lamalie Amrop International
Thanksgiving Tower
1601 Elm Street
Dallas, TX 75201-4768
Telephone: (214) 754-0019
**Recruiter Classification:** Retained; **Lowest/Average Salary:** $90,000/$90,000;
**Industry Concentration:** Generalist with a primary focus in
Healthcare/Hospitals; **Function Concentration:** Generalist with a primary focus
in Finance/Accounting, General Management, Marketing, Sales

**Enns, George** — *Partner*
The Enns Partners Inc.
70 University Avenue, Suite 410, P.O. Box 14
Toronto, Ontario, CANADA M5J 2M4
Telephone: (416) 598-0012
**Recruiter Classification:** Retained; **Lowest/Average Salary:** $75,000/$90,000;
**Industry Concentration:** Generalist with a primary focus in Aerospace/Defense,
Board Services, Consumer Products, Electronics, Energy, Financial Services,
High Technology, Hospitality/Leisure, Manufacturing, Pharmaceutical/Medical,
Publishing/Media, Transportation, Venture Capital; **Function Concentration:**
Generalist with a primary focus in Administration, Finance/Accounting, General
Management, Human Resources, Marketing, Sales

**Ensminger, Barbara** — *Manager North Atlantic Region*
Management Recruiters International, Inc.
Suite H, Plaza 153 Building
5211 Highway 153
Chattanooga, TN 37343
Telephone: (423) 877-4040
**Recruiter Classification:** Contingency; **Lowest/Average Salary:** $30,000/$75,000;
**Industry Concentration:** Generalist; **Function Concentration:** Generalist

**Ensminger, Chub** — *Manager*
Management Recruiters International, Inc.
Suite H, Plaza 153 Building
5211 Highway 153
Chattanooga, TN 37343
Telephone: (423) 877-4040
**Recruiter Classification:** Contingency; **Lowest/Average Salary:** $30,000/$75,000;
**Industry Concentration:** Generalist; **Function Concentration:** Generalist

**Epstein, Kathy** — *Vice President*
Canny, Bowen Inc.
10 Post Office Square, Suite 960
Boston, MA 02109
Telephone: (617) 292-6242
**Recruiter Classification:** Retained; **Lowest/Average Salary:** $90,000/$90,000;
**Industry Concentration:** Generalist; **Function Concentration:** Generalist

**Erbes, Roysi** — *Senior Associate*
Korn/Ferry International
1800 Century Park East, Suite 900
Los Angeles, CA 90067
Telephone: (310) 552-1834
**Recruiter Classification:** Retained; **Lowest/Average Salary:** $90,000/$90,000;
**Industry Concentration:** Generalist; **Function Concentration:** Generalist

**Erder, Debra** — *Vice President*
Canny, Bowen Inc.
200 Park Avenue
New York, NY 10166
Telephone: (212) 949-6611
**Recruiter Classification:** Retained; **Lowest/Average Salary:** $90,000/$90,000;
**Industry Concentration:** Generalist; **Function Concentration:** Generalist

**Erickson, Elaine** — *Executive Vice President*
Kenzer Corp.
777 Third Avenue, 26th Floor
New York, NY 10017
Telephone: (212) 308-4300
**Recruiter Classification:** Retained; **Lowest/Average Salary:** $50,000/$90,000;
**Industry Concentration:** Consumer Products, Entertainment, Financial
Services, Packaging, Venture Capital; **Function Concentration:** Generalist with
a primary focus in Administration, Finance/Accounting, General Management,
Human Resources, Marketing, Research and Development, Sales

**Erickson, Mary R.** — *President*
Mary R. Erickson & Associates, Inc.
8300 Norman Center Drive, Suite 545
Minneapolis, MN 55437
Telephone: (612) 893-1010
**Recruiter Classification:** Retained; **Lowest/Average Salary:** $90,000/$90,000;
**Industry Concentration:** Generalist; **Function Concentration:** Generalist

**Erlanger, Richard A.** — *President*
Erlanger Associates Inc.
Two Pickwick Plaza
Greenwich, CT 06830
Telephone: (203) 629-5410
**Recruiter Classification:** Retained; **Lowest/Average Salary:** $90,000/$90,000;
**Industry Concentration:** Generalist; **Function Concentration:** Generalist

**Erlien, Nancy B.** — *Executive Recruiter*
Jacobson Associates
150 North Wacker Drive
Suite 1120
Chicago, IL 60606
Telephone: (312) 726-1578
**Recruiter Classification:** Contingency; **Lowest/Average Salary:**
$20,000/$50,000; **Industry Concentration:** Insurance; **Function
Concentration:** Generalist

**Erstling, Gregory** — *Principal*
Normyle/Erstling Health Search Group
350 West Passaic Street
Rochelle Park, NJ 07662
Telephone: (201) 843-6009
**Recruiter Classification:** Contingency; **Lowest/Average Salary:**
$40,000/$75,000; **Industry Concentration:** Biotechnology,
Healthcare/Hospitals, Pharmaceutical/Medical; **Function Concentration:**
General Management, Marketing, Sales

**Ervin, Darlene** — *Executive Recruiter*
CPS Inc.
One Westbrook Corporate Centre, Suite 600
Westchester, IL 60154
Telephone: (708) 531-8370
**Recruiter Classification:** Contingency; **Lowest/Average Salary:**
$30,000/$50,000; **Industry Concentration:** Generalist with a primary focus in
Automotive, Biotechnology, Chemical Products, Consumer Products, High
Technology, Insurance, Manufacturing, Oil/Gas, Packaging,
Pharmaceutical/Medical; **Function Concentration:** Engineering, Research and
Development, Sales, Women/Minorities

**Ervin, James** — *Account Executive*
Search West, Inc.
3401 Centrelake Drive
Suite 690
Ontario, CA 91761-1207
Telephone: (909) 986-1966
**Recruiter Classification:** Contingency; **Lowest/Average Salary:**
$40,000/$60,000; **Industry Concentration:** Generalist; **Function
Concentration:** Marketing, Sales

**Ervin, Russell** — *Associate*
Source Services Corporation
10220 SW Greenburg Road, Suite 625
Portland, OR 97223
Telephone: (503) 768-4546
**Recruiter Classification:** Contingency; **Lowest/Average Salary:**
$30,000/$50,000; **Industry Concentration:** Financial Services, Information
Technology; **Function Concentration:** Engineering, Finance/Accounting

**Erwin, Lee** — *Agribusiness Recruiter*
Agra Placements International Ltd.
4949 Pleasant Suite 1, West 50th Place III
West Des Moines, IA 50266-5494
Telephone: (515) 225-6562
**Recruiter Classification:** Contingency; **Lowest/Average Salary:**
$20,000/$30,000; **Industry Concentration:** Generalist with a primary focus in
Biotechnology, Chemical Products, Energy, Financial Services, Manufacturing;
**Function Concentration:** Administration, Engineering, Finance/Accounting,
General Management, Human Resources, Marketing, Research and
Development, Sales

**Eskra, Michael D.** — *Principal*
Sanford Rose Associates
222 East Main Street
Port Washington, WI 53074
Telephone: (414) 268-1750
**Recruiter Classification:** Contingency; **Lowest/Average Salary:**
$30,000/$75,000; **Industry Concentration:** Generalist; **Function Concentration:** Generalist

**Esty, Greg C.** — *Manager Pacific Region*
Management Recruiters International, Inc.
50 Shadow Ridge, Suite 103
P.O. Box 680337
Park City, UT 84068-0337
Telephone: (801) 647-5670
**Recruiter Classification:** Contingency; **Lowest/Average Salary:**
$30,000/$75,000; **Industry Concentration:** Generalist; **Function Concentration:** Generalist

**Eton, Steven** — *Account Executive*
Search West, Inc.
750 The City Drive South
Suite 100
Orange, CA 92668-4940
Telephone: (714) 748-0400
**Recruiter Classification:** Contingency; **Lowest/Average Salary:**
$40,000/$60,000; **Industry Concentration:** Manufacturing; **Function Concentration:** Engineering, General Management, Marketing, Sales

**Etter, Duane A.** — *Manager*
Accounting & Bookkeeping Personnel, Inc.
4400 East Broadway, Suite 600
Tucson, AZ 85711
Telephone: (602) 323-3600
**Recruiter Classification:** Contingency, Executive Temporary; **Lowest/Average Salary:** $20,000/$40,000; **Industry Concentration:** Generalist; **Function Concentration:** Finance/Accounting

**Eustis, Lucy R.** — *Unit Manager*
MSI International
201 St. Charles Avenue
Suite 2205
New Orleans, LA 70170
Telephone: (504) 522-6700
**Recruiter Classification:** Contingency; **Lowest/Average Salary:**
$30,000/$60,000; **Industry Concentration:** Generalist with a primary focus in Financial Services, Healthcare/Hospitals, High Technology, Information Technology, Manufacturing; **Function Concentration:** Generalist with a primary focus in Administration, Engineering, Finance/Accounting, General Management, Marketing, Sales

**Evan-Cook, James W.** — *Executive Recruiter*
Jacobson Associates
150 North Wacker Drive
Suite 1120
Chicago, IL 60606
Telephone: (312) 726-1578
**Recruiter Classification:** Contingency; **Lowest/Average Salary:**
$20,000/$50,000; **Industry Concentration:** Insurance; **Function Concentration:** Generalist

**Evans, Jeffrey** — *Vice President*
Sullivan & Associates
344 North Woodward, Suite 304
Birmingham, MI 48009
Telephone: (810) 258-0616
**Recruiter Classification:** Retained; **Lowest/Average Salary:** $90,000/$90,000; **Industry Concentration:** Generalist; **Function Concentration:** Generalist

**Evans, Robert M.** — *Executive Recruiter*
TASA International
1428 Franklin Street
P.O. Box 604
Columbus, IN 47202
Telephone: (812) 376-9061
**Recruiter Classification:** Retained; **Lowest/Average Salary:** $90,000/$90,000; **Industry Concentration:** Generalist; **Function Concentration:** Generalist

**Evans, Timothy** — *Associate*
Source Services Corporation
1500 West Park Drive, Suite 390
Westborough, MA 01581
Telephone: (508) 366-2600
**Recruiter Classification:** Contingency; **Lowest/Average Salary:**
$30,000/$50,000; **Industry Concentration:** Financial Services, Information Technology; **Function Concentration:** Engineering, Finance/Accounting

**Ezersky, Jane E.** — *Associate*
Highland Search Group, L.L.C.
565 Fifth Avenue, 22nd Floor
New York, NY 10017
Telephone: (212) 328-1113
**Recruiter Classification:** Retained; **Lowest/Average Salary:** $90,000/$90,000; **Industry Concentration:** Financial Services; **Function Concentration:** Generalist with a primary focus in Finance/Accounting, General Management, Sales, Women/Minorities

**Fabbro, Vivian** — *Vice President*
A.T. Kearney, Inc.
222 West Adams Street
Chicago, IL 60606
Telephone: (312) 648-0111
**Recruiter Classification:** Retained; **Lowest/Average Salary:** $90,000/$90,000; **Industry Concentration:** Generalist with a primary focus in Financial Services, Manufacturing; **Function Concentration:** Generalist with a primary focus in Finance/Accounting

**Faber, Jill** — *Vice President/Managing Director*
A.T. Kearney, Inc.
Park One, Suite 135
2141 East Highland
Phoenix, AZ 85016
Telephone: (602) 994-3032
**Recruiter Classification:** Retained; **Lowest/Average Salary:**
$90,000/$90,000; **Industry Concentration:** Generalist with a primary focus in Chemical Products, Healthcare/Hospitals; **Function Concentration:** Generalist with a primary focus in Administration, Human Resources, Marketing, Sales

**Fagan, Mark** — *Manager North Atlantic Region*
Management Recruiters International, Inc.
Pelham Links Professional Park
201 Old Boiling Springs Road, Suite D
Greer, SC 29650-4227
Telephone: (803) 987-9258
**Recruiter Classification:** Contingency; **Lowest/Average Salary:** $30,000/$75,000; **Industry Concentration:** Generalist; **Function Concentration:** Generalist

**Fagerstrom, Jon** — *Associate*
Source Services Corporation
4510 Executive Drive, Suite 200
San Diego, CA 92121
Telephone: (619) 552-0300
**Recruiter Classification:** Contingency; **Lowest/Average Salary:**
$30,000/$50,000; **Industry Concentration:** Financial Services, Information Technology; **Function Concentration:** Engineering, Finance/Accounting

**Fahlin, Kelly** — *Information Technology Recruiter*
Winter, Wyman & Company
950 Winter Street, Suite 3100
Waltham, MA 02154-1294
Telephone: (617) 890-7000
**Recruiter Classification:** Contingency; **Lowest/Average Salary:**
$30,000/$60,000; **Industry Concentration:** Generalist with a primary focus in Information Technology; **Function Concentration:** Generalist

**Fair, Donna** — *Manager Quality Assurance*
ProResource, Inc.
500 Ohio Savings Plaza
1801 East Ninth Street, Suite 500
Cleveland, OH 44114
Telephone: (216) 579-1515
**Recruiter Classification:** Executive Temporary; **Lowest/Average Salary:**
$30,000/$75,000; **Industry Concentration:** Generalist; **Function Concentration:** Generalist with a primary focus in Engineering, Finance/Accounting, General Management, Human Resources, Marketing, Research and Development

**Fairlie, Suzanne F.** — *President*
ProSearch, Inc.
610 West Germantown Pike, Suite 120
Plymouth Meeting, PA 19462
Telephone: (610) 834-8260
**Recruiter Classification:** Contingency; **Lowest/Average Salary:**
$40,000/$60,000; **Industry Concentration:** High Technology, Information Technology; **Function Concentration:** Women/Minorities

**Fales, Scott** — *Associate*
Source Services Corporation
161 Ottawa NW, Suite 409D
Grand Rapids, MI 49503
Telephone: (616) 451-2400
**Recruiter Classification:** Contingency; **Lowest/Average Salary:**
$30,000/$50,000; **Industry Concentration:** Financial Services, Information Technology; **Function Concentration:** Engineering, Finance/Accounting

**Falk, John** — *Vice President*
D.S. Allen Associates, Inc.
4 Commerce Park Sq., Suite 222
24200 Chagrin Boulevard
Beachwood, OH 44122
Telephone: (216) 831-1701
**Recruiter Classification:** Contingency; **Lowest/Average Salary:** $/$90,000;
**Industry Concentration:** Generalist with a primary focus in Entertainment, High
Technology, Information Technology ; **Function Concentration:** Generalist with
a primary focus in Engineering, General Management, Marketing

**Fancher, Robert L.** — *Vice President*
Bason Associates Inc.
11311 Cornell Park Drive
Cincinnati, OH 45242
Telephone: (513) 469-9881
**Recruiter Classification:** Retained; **Lowest/Average Salary:** $60,000/$90,000;
**Industry Concentration:** Generalist with a primary focus in Automotive,
Biotechnology, Board Services, Chemical Products, Consumer Products,
Environmental, Fashion (Retail/Apparel), Financial Services, Healthcare/Hospitals,
High Technology, Insurance, Manufacturing, Packaging, Pharmaceutical/Medical,
Public Administration; **Function Concentration:** Generalist with a primary focus in
Administration, Engineering, Finance/Accounting, General Management, Human
Resources, Marketing, Research and Development, Sales

**Fanning, Paul** — *Associate*
Source Services Corporation
15260 Ventura Boulevard, Suite 380
Sherman Oaks, CA 91403
Telephone: (818) 905-1500
**Recruiter Classification:** Contingency; **Lowest/Average Salary:**
$30,000/$50,000; **Industry Concentration:** Financial Services, Information
Technology; **Function Concentration:** Engineering, Finance/Accounting

**Farber, Susan** — *Consultant*
Heidrick & Struggles, Inc.
125 South Wacker Drive
Suite 2800
Chicago, IL 60606-4590
Telephone: (312) 372-8811
**Recruiter Classification:** Retained; **Lowest/Average Salary:** $75,000/$90,000;
**Industry Concentration:** Generalist with a primary focus in High Technology;
**Function Concentration:** Generalist

**Farish, John G.** — *Partner*
Paul Ray Berndtson
191 Peachtree Tower, Suite 3800
191 Peachtree Street, NE
Atlanta, GA 30303-1757
Telephone: (404) 215-4600
**Recruiter Classification:** Retained; **Lowest/Average Salary:** $90,000/$90,000;
**Industry Concentration:** Manufacturing, Real Estate; **Function Concentration:**
Generalist

**Farkas, Denny P.** — *Manager Eastern Region*
Management Recruiters International, Inc.
Peachtree Office Plaza
1815 Schadt Avenue, Suite 4
Whitehall, PA 18052-3761
Telephone: (610) 740-9200
**Recruiter Classification:** Contingency; **Lowest/Average Salary:**
$30,000/$75,000; **Industry Concentration:** Generalist; **Function
Concentration:** Generalist

**Farler, Wiley** — *Managing Director*
Source Services Corporation
Foster Plaza VI
681 Anderson Drive, 2nd Floor
Pittsburgh, PA 15220
Telephone: (412) 928-8300
**Recruiter Classification:** Contingency; **Lowest/Average Salary:**
$30,000/$50,000; **Industry Concentration:** Financial Services, Information
Technology; **Function Concentration:** Engineering, Finance/Accounting

**Farley, Antoinette L.** — *Consultant*
Witt/Kieffer, Ford, Hadelman & Lloyd
2015 Spring Road, Suite 510
Oak Brook, IL 60521
Telephone: (708) 990-1370
**Recruiter Classification:** Retained; **Lowest/Average Salary:** $75,000/$90,000;
**Industry Concentration:** Healthcare/Hospitals; **Function Concentration:**
Generalist with a primary focus in Administration, Finance/Accounting,
General Management, Human Resources, Marketing

**Farley, Leon A.** — *Managing Partner*
Leon A. Farley Associates
468 Jackson Street
San Francisco, CA 94111
Telephone: (415) 989-0989
**Recruiter Classification:** Retained; **Lowest/Average Salary:** $90,000/$90,000;
**Industry Concentration:** Generalist with a primary focus in Board Services,
Electronics, Financial Services, High Technology, Information Technology,
Manufacturing; **Function Concentration:** Generalist with a primary focus in
Engineering, Finance/Accounting, General Management, Human Resources,
Marketing, Sales

**Farnsworth, John A.** — *Partner*
Pearson, Caldwell & Farnsworth, Inc.
One California Street, Suite 1950
San Francisco, CA 94111
Telephone: (415) 982-0300
**Recruiter Classification:** Retained; **Lowest/Average Salary:** $90,000/$90,000;
**Industry Concentration:** Financial Services; **Function Concentration:**
Administration, Finance/Accounting, General Management, Human Resources,
Marketing, Sales

**Farrar, Carolyn** — *Principal*
Sanford Rose Associates
5407 East Riverview
Springfield, MO 65809
Telephone: (417) 887-0484
**Recruiter Classification:** Contingency; **Lowest/Average Salary:** $30,000/$75,000;
**Industry Concentration:** Generalist; **Function Concentration:** Generalist

**Farrar, Gary** — *Principal*
Sanford Rose Associates
5407 East Riverview
Springfield, MO 65809
Telephone: (417) 887-0484
**Recruiter Classification:** Contingency; **Lowest/Average Salary:** $30,000/$75,000;
**Industry Concentration:** Generalist; **Function Concentration:** Generalist

**Farrell, Barbara** — *Recruiter*
The Barack Group, Inc.
885 Third Avenue
New York, NY 10022
Telephone: (212) 230-3280
**Recruiter Classification:** Retained; **Lowest/Average Salary:** $75,000/$90,000;
**Industry Concentration:** Consumer Products, Entertainment; **Function
Concentration:** General Management, Marketing

**Farrow, Jerry M.** — *Managing Partner*
McCormack & Farrow
695 Town Center Drive
Suite 660
Costa Mesa, CA 92626
Telephone: (714) 549-7222
**Recruiter Classification:** Retained; **Lowest/Average Salary:** $90,000/$90,000;
**Industry Concentration:** Generalist with a primary focus in Aerospace/Defense,
Board Services, Electronics, Energy, Financial Services, Healthcare/Hospitals,
High Technology, Information Technology, Manufacturing, Non-Profit, Oil/Gas,
Venture Capital; **Function Concentration:** Generalist with a primary focus in
Administration, Engineering, Finance/Accounting, General Management,
Human Resources, Marketing, Sales

**Farthing, Andrew R.** — *Contract Manager*
Parfitt Recruiting and Consulting
1540 140th Avenue NE #201
Bellevue, WA 98005
Telephone: (206) 646-6300
**Recruiter Classification:** Contingency; **Lowest/Average Salary:**
$30,000/$75,000; **Industry Concentration:** Generalist with a primary focus in
Information Technology; **Function Concentration:** Engineering

**Faure, Nicole** — *Consultant*
The Caldwell Partners Amrop International
1840 Sherbrooke Street West
Montreal, Quebec, CANADA H3H 1E4
Telephone: (514) 935-6969
**Recruiter Classification:** Retained; **Lowest/Average Salary:** $/$90,000; **Industry
Concentration:** Generalist with a primary focus in Consumer Products,
Environmental, Packaging, Transportation; **Function Concentration:** Generalist

**Fawcett, Anne M.** — *President/Managing Partner*
The Caldwell Partners Amrop International
Sixty-Four Prince Arthur Avenue
Toronto, Ontario, CANADA M5R 1B4
Telephone: (416) 920-7702
**Recruiter Classification:** Retained; **Lowest/Average Salary:** $/$90,000; **Industry
Concentration:** Generalist with a primary focus in Aerospace/Defense, Board
Services, Consumer Products, Education/Libraries, Financial Services, Non-
Profit, Public Administration, Real Estate; **Function Concentration:** Generalist

**Fazekas, John A.** — *Senior Associate*
Korn/Ferry International
One International Place
Boston, MA 02110-1800
Telephone: (617) 345-0200
**Recruiter Classification:** Retained; **Lowest/Average Salary:** $90,000/$90,000;
**Industry Concentration:** Generalist; **Function Concentration:** Generalist

**Fechheimer, Peter** — *Associate*
Source Services Corporation
1290 Oakmead Parkway, Suite 318
Sunnyvale, CA 94086
Telephone: (408) 738-8440
**Recruiter Classification:** Contingency; **Lowest/Average Salary:**
$30,000/$50,000; **Industry Concentration:** Financial Services, Information
Technology; **Function Concentration:** Engineering, Finance/Accounting

**Feder, Gwen** — *Consultant*
Egon Zehnder International Inc.
55 East 59th Street, 14th Floor
New York, NY 10022
Telephone: (212) 838-9199
**Recruiter Classification:** Retained; **Lowest/Average Salary:** $90,000/$90,000;
**Industry Concentration:** Generalist with a primary focus in Biotechnology,
Financial Services, High Technology, Manufacturing, Pharmaceutical/Medical;
**Function Concentration:** Generalist

**Federman, Jack R.** — *Principal*
W.R. Rosato & Associates, Inc.
71 Broadway, Suite 1601
New York, NY 10006
Telephone: (212) 509-5700
**Recruiter Classification:** Retained; **Lowest/Average Salary:** $90,000/$90,000;
**Industry Concentration:** Financial Services, High Technology, Information
Technology; **Function Concentration:** Administration, Marketing, Research and
Development, Sales

**Fee, J. Curtis** — *Senior Director*
Spencer Stuart
401 North Michigan Avenue, Suite 3400
Chicago, IL 60611-4244
Telephone: (312) 822-0080
**Recruiter Classification:** Retained; **Lowest/Average Salary:** $90,000/$90,000;
**Industry Concentration:** Generalist with a primary focus in Automotive, Board
Services, Consumer Products, Financial Services, Manufacturing; **Function
Concentration:** Generalist with a primary focus in Finance/Accounting,
General Management

**Felderman, Kenneth I.** — *Partner*
Lamalie Amrop International
Key Tower, 127 Public Square
Cleveland, OH 44114-1216
Telephone: (216) 694-3000
**Recruiter Classification:** Retained; **Lowest/Average Salary:** $90,000/$90,000;
**Industry Concentration:** Generalist; **Function Concentration:** Generalist with a
primary focus in General Management, Research and Development

**Feldman, Abe** — *President*
A.E. Feldman Associates
445 Northern Boulevard
Great Neck, NY 11021
Telephone: (516) 466-4708
**Recruiter Classification:** Contingency, Executive Temporary; **Lowest/Average
Salary:** $50,000/$90,000; **Industry Concentration:** Generalist with a primary
focus in Consumer Products, Entertainment, Fashion (Retail/Apparel), Financial
Services, High Technology, Publishing/Media, Venture Capital; **Function
Concentration:** Generalist with a primary focus in Administration,
Finance/Accounting, General Management, Human Resources, Marketing,
Sales, Women/Minorities

**Feldman, Kimberley** — *Consultant*
Atlantic Search Group, Inc.
One Liberty Square
Boston, MA 02109
Telephone: (617) 426-9700
**Recruiter Classification:** Contingency; **Lowest/Average Salary:**
$20,000/$60,000; **Industry Concentration:** Generalist with a primary focus in
Biotechnology, Consumer Products, Electronics, Financial Services,
Information Technology, Manufacturing, Real Estate; **Function Concentration:**
Finance/Accounting

**Felton, Meg** — *Senior Associate*
Korn/Ferry International
237 Park Avenue
New York, NY 10017
Telephone: (212) 687-1834
**Recruiter Classification:** Retained; **Lowest/Average Salary:** $90,000/$90,000;
**Industry Concentration:** Generalist with a primary focus in Fashion
(Retail/Apparel); **Function Concentration:** Generalist

**Fennel, P.J.** — *Partner*
Heidrick & Struggles, Inc.
BCE Place, 161 Bay Street, Suite 2310
P.O. Box 601
Toronto, Ontario, CANADA M5J 2S1
Telephone: (416) 361-4700
**Recruiter Classification:** Retained; **Lowest/Average Salary:** $75,000/$90,000;
**Industry Concentration:** Generalist; **Function Concentration:** Generalist

**Ferguson, Kenneth** — *Associate*
Source Services Corporation
4170 Ashford Dunwoody Road, Suite 285
Atlanta, GA 30319
Telephone: (404) 255-2045
**Recruiter Classification:** Contingency; **Lowest/Average Salary:**
$30,000/$50,000; **Industry Concentration:** Financial Services, Information
Technology; **Function Concentration:** Engineering, Finance/Accounting

**Ferguson, Lauren** — *Account Executive*
Search West, Inc.
1888 Century Park East
Suite 2050
Los Angeles, CA 90067-1736
Telephone: (310) 284-8888
**Recruiter Classification:** Contingency; **Lowest/Average Salary:**
$40,000/$60,000; **Industry Concentration:** Biotechnology; **Function
Concentration:** Engineering, Research and Development

**Ferguson, Robert** — *Vice President/General Manager*
Bill Hahn Group, Inc.
2052 Highway 35
Suites 203, 204
Wall, NJ 07719
Telephone: (908) 449-9302
**Recruiter Classification:** Contingency; **Lowest/Average Salary:**
$50,000/$75,000; **Industry Concentration:** Biotechnology,
Pharmaceutical/Medical; **Function Concentration:** Generalist

**Ferneborg, Jay W.** — *Vice President/Partner*
Ferneborg & Associates, Inc.
1450 Fashion Island Boulevard, Suite 650
San Mateo, CA 94404
Telephone: (415) 577-0100
**Recruiter Classification:** Retained; **Lowest/Average Salary:** $90,000/$90,000;
**Industry Concentration:** Generalist with a primary focus in Biotechnology,
Consumer Products, Electronics, Entertainment, Financial Services, High
Technology, Hospitality/Leisure, Information Technology, Manufacturing,
Publishing/Media, Real Estate, Transportation, Venture Capital; **Function
Concentration:** Generalist with a primary focus in Administration,
Finance/Accounting, General Management, Human Resources, Marketing,
Sales

**Ferneborg, John R.** — *President*
Ferneborg & Associates, Inc.
1450 Fashion Island Boulevard, Suite 650
San Mateo, CA 94404
Telephone: (415) 577-0100
**Recruiter Classification:** Retained; **Lowest/Average Salary:** $90,000/$90,000;
**Industry Concentration:** Generalist with a primary focus in Biotechnology,
Consumer Products, Electronics, Entertainment, Financial Services, High
Technology, Hospitality/Leisure, Information Technology, Manufacturing,
Publishing/Media, Real Estate, Transportation, Venture Capital; **Function
Concentration:** Generalist with a primary focus in Administration,
Finance/Accounting, General Management, Human Resources, Marketing,
Sales

**Ferrara, David M.** — *Vice President*
Intech Summit Group, Inc.
5075 Shoreham Place, Suite 280
San Diego, CA 92122
Telephone: (619) 452-2100
**Recruiter Classification:** Retained; **Lowest/Average Salary:** $90,000/$90,000;
**Industry Concentration:** Financial Services, Healthcare/Hospitals, High
Technology, Information Technology, Manufacturing; **Function Concentration:**
Administration, General Management, Research and Development

**Ferrari, S. Jay** — *President/Senior Partner*
Ferrari Search Group
16781 Chagrin Boulevard, Suite 164
Cleveland, OH 44120
Telephone: (216) 491-1122
**Recruiter Classification:** Retained; **Lowest/Average Salary:** $60,000/$75,000;
**Industry Concentration:** Generalist with a primary focus in Financial Services,
Insurance, Publishing/Media, Venture Capital; **Function Concentration:**
Finance/Accounting, General Management, Human Resources, Marketing,
Sales, Women/Minorities

**Ferris, Sheri Rae** — *Branch Manager*
Accountants on Call
Quadrangle Building, Suite 690
2828 Routh Street
Dallas, TX 75201
Telephone: (214) 979-9001
**Recruiter Classification:** Contingency; **Lowest/Average Salary:**
$20,000/$30,000; **Industry Concentration:** Generalist; **Function Concentration:** Finance/Accounting

**Ferry, Richard M.** — *Chairman and CEO*
Korn/Ferry International
1800 Century Park East, Suite 900
Los Angeles, CA 90067
Telephone: (310) 552-1834
**Recruiter Classification:** Retained; **Lowest/Average Salary:** $90,000/$90,000;
**Industry Concentration:** Generalist with a primary focus in Board Services;
**Function Concentration:** Generalist

**Feyder, Michael** — *Vice President*
A.T. Kearney, Inc.
Biltmore Tower
500 South Grand Avenue
Los Angeles, CA 90071
Telephone: (213) 689-6800
**Recruiter Classification:** Retained; **Lowest/Average Salary:** $90,000/$90,000;
**Industry Concentration:** Generalist with a primary focus in Automotive,
Entertainment, High Technology, Hospitality/Leisure; **Function Concentration:**
Generalist with a primary focus in General Management, Marketing, Sales

**Field, Andrew** — *Associate*
Source Services Corporation
7730 East Bellview Avenue, Suite 302
Englewood, CO 80111
Telephone: (303) 773-3700
**Recruiter Classification:** Contingency; **Lowest/Average Salary:**
$30,000/$50,000; **Industry Concentration:** Financial Services, Information
Technology; **Function Concentration:** Engineering, Finance/Accounting

**Fienberg, Chester** — *President*
Drummond Associates, Inc.
50 Broadway, Suite 1201
New York, NY 10004
Telephone: (212) 248-1120
**Recruiter Classification:** Contingency; **Lowest/Average Salary:**
$40,000/$75,000; **Industry Concentration:** Financial Services, Information
Technology; **Function Concentration:** Finance/Accounting

**Fifield, George C.** — *Managing Partner*
Egon Zehnder International Inc.
California Plaza, Suite 2625
300 South Grand Avenue
Los Angeles, CA 90071
Telephone: (213) 621-8900
**Recruiter Classification:** Retained; **Lowest/Average Salary:** $90,000/$90,000;
**Industry Concentration:** Generalist with a primary focus in Biotechnology,
Financial Services, High Technology, Manufacturing, Pharmaceutical/Medical;
**Function Concentration:** Generalist

**Filko, Gary** — *Manager Eastern Region*
Management Recruiters International, Inc.
2141 Downyflake Lane
Allentown, PA 18103-4774
Telephone: (610) 797-8863
**Recruiter Classification:** Contingency; **Lowest/Average Salary:** $30,000/$75,000;
**Industry Concentration:** Generalist; **Function Concentration:** Generalist

**Fill, Clifford G.** — *President*
D.S.A. - Dixie Search Associates
501 Village Trace, Building 9
Marietta, GA 30067
Telephone: (770) 850-0250
**Recruiter Classification:** Contingency; **Lowest/Average Salary:**
$30,000/$50,000; **Industry Concentration:** Biotechnology, Consumer
Products, Hospitality/Leisure, Manufacturing, Packaging, Transportation;
**Function Concentration:** Generalist with a primary focus in Engineering,
Finance/Accounting, General Management, Human Resources, Marketing,
Research and Development, Sales

**Fill, Ellyn H.** — *Senior Vice President*
D.S.A. - Dixie Search Associates
501 Village Trace, Building 9
Marietta, GA 30067
Telephone: (770) 850-0250
**Recruiter Classification:** Contingency; **Lowest/Average Salary:**
$30,000/$50,000; **Industry Concentration:** Biotechnology, Consumer
Products, Hospitality/Leisure, Manufacturing, Packaging, Transportation;
**Function Concentration:** Generalist with a primary focus in Engineering,
Finance/Accounting, General Management, Human Resources, Marketing,
Research and Development, Sales

**Fincher, Richard P.** — *President*
Phase II Management
25 Stonybrook Road
Westport, CT 06880
Telephone: (203) 226-7252
**Recruiter Classification:** Retained; **Lowest/Average Salary:** $60,000/$90,000;
**Industry Concentration:** Generalist with a primary focus in Automotive,
Consumer Products, Electronics, Healthcare/Hospitals, Information
Technology, Manufacturing, Packaging, Pharmaceutical/Medical; **Function
Concentration:** Generalist with a primary focus in Engineering,
Finance/Accounting, General Management, Marketing, Research and
Development, Sales

**Fingers, David** — *Branch Manager*
Bradford & Galt, Inc.
8575 West 110th Street, Suite 302
Overland Park, KS 66210
Telephone: (913) 663-1264
**Recruiter Classification:** Contingency; **Lowest/Average Salary:**
$30,000/$30,000; **Industry Concentration:** Generalist with a primary focus in
Information Technology; **Function Concentration:** Generalist

**Finkel, Leslie** — *Managing Director*
Source Services Corporation
150 South Warner Road, Suite 238
King of Prussia, PA 19406
Telephone: (610) 341-1960
**Recruiter Classification:** Contingency; **Lowest/Average Salary:**
$30,000/$50,000; **Industry Concentration:** Financial Services, Information
Technology; **Function Concentration:** Engineering, Finance/Accounting

**Finn, Andrew** — *Accounting and Finance Recruiter*
Winter, Wyman & Company
950 Winter Street, Suite 3100
Waltham, MA 02154-1294
Telephone: (617) 890-7000
**Recruiter Classification:** Contingency; **Lowest/Average Salary:**
$20,000/$50,000; **Industry Concentration:** Generalist; **Function
Concentration:** Finance/Accounting

**Finn, Jacquelyn** — *Partner*
Jacquelyn Finn & Susan Schneider Associates, Inc.
1730 Rhode Island Avenue, NW
Suite 1212
Washington, DC 20036
Telephone: (202) 822-8400
**Recruiter Classification:** Contingency; **Function Concentration:** Generalist

**Finnerty, James** — *Associate*
Source Services Corporation
20 Burlington Mall Road, Suite 405
Burlington, MA 01803
Telephone: (617) 272-5000
**Recruiter Classification:** Contingency; **Lowest/Average Salary:**
$30,000/$50,000; **Industry Concentration:** Financial Services, Information
Technology; **Function Concentration:** Engineering, Finance/Accounting

**Fiore, Richard** — *Senior Consultant*
Search Consultants International, Inc.
4545 Post Oak Place, Suite 208
Houston, TX 77027
Telephone: (713) 622-9188
**Recruiter Classification:** Contingency, Executive Temporary;
**Lowest/Average Salary:** $60,000/$75,000; **Industry Concentration:**
Chemical Products, Energy, Environmental, Manufacturing, Oil/Gas;
**Function Concentration:** Engineering, General Management, Marketing,
Research and Development

**Fioretti, Kim** — *Assistant Branch Manager*
Accountants on Call
99 Summer Street, Suite 1610
Boston, MA 02110
Telephone: (617) 345-0440
**Recruiter Classification:** Contingency; **Lowest/Average Salary:**
$20,000/$30,000; **Industry Concentration:** Generalist; **Function
Concentration:** Finance/Accounting

**Fischer, Adam** — *Consultant*
Howard Fischer Associates, Inc.
1800 John F. Kennedy Boulevard, 7th Floor
Philadelphia, PA 19103
Telephone: (215) 568-8363
**Recruiter Classification:** Retained; **Lowest/Average Salary:** $90,000/$90,000;
**Industry Concentration:** Generalist; **Function Concentration:** Generalist

**Fischer, Howard M.** — *President*
Howard Fischer Associates, Inc.
1800 John F. Kennedy Boulevard, 7th Floor
Philadelphia, PA 19103
Telephone: (215) 568-8363
**Recruiter Classification:** Retained; **Lowest/Average Salary:** $90,000/$90,000;
**Industry Concentration:** Generalist; **Function Concentration:** Generalist

**Fischer, Janet L.** — *Partner*
Boyden
2 Prudential Plaza, Suite 5050
180 North Stetson Avenue
Chicago, IL 60601
Telephone: (312) 565-1300
**Recruiter Classification:** Retained; **Lowest/Average Salary:** $75,000/$90,000;
**Industry Concentration:** Financial Services; **Function Concentration:**
Generalist with a primary focus in Engineering, Finance/Accounting, General
Management, Human Resources, Marketing, Research and Development,
Sales, Women/Minorities

**Fischer, John C.** — *Managing Director*
Horton International
10 Tower Lane
Avon, CT 06001
Telephone: (860) 674-8701
**Recruiter Classification:** Retained; **Lowest/Average Salary:** $90,000/$90,000;
**Industry Concentration:** Generalist with a primary focus in Biotechnology,
Chemical Products, Consumer Products, Electronics, High Technology,
Information Technology, Manufacturing, Pharmaceutical/Medical, Venture
Capital; **Function Concentration:** Generalist with a primary focus in
Finance/Accounting, General Management, Human Resources

**Fishback, Joren** — *President*
Derek Associates, Inc.
P.O. Box 13
Mendon, MA 01756-0013
Telephone: (508) 883-2289
**Recruiter Classification:** Contingency; **Lowest/Average Salary:**
$40,000/$60,000; **Industry Concentration:** Environmental; **Function
Concentration:** Engineering, Marketing, Sales

**Fisher, Earl L.** — *Manager Midwest Region*
Management Recruiters International, Inc.
546 Avenue A, Suite 7, P.O. Box A
Plattsmouth, NE 68048
Telephone: (402) 296-2792
**Recruiter Classification:** Contingency; **Lowest/Average Salary:** $30,000/$75,000;
**Industry Concentration:** Generalist; **Function Concentration:** Generalist

**Fisher, Neal** — *Principal*
Fisher Personnel Management Services
1219 Morningside Drive
Manhattan Beach, CA 90266
Telephone: (310) 546-7507
**Recruiter Classification:** Retained; **Lowest/Average Salary:** $50,000/$75,000;
**Industry Concentration:** Generalist with a primary focus in
Aerospace/Defense, Automotive, Board Services, Consumer Products,
Electronics, Financial Services, High Technology, Manufacturing, Packaging,
Transportation, Venture Capital; **Function Concentration:** Generalist with a
primary focus in Engineering, Finance/Accounting, General Management,
Human Resources, Marketing, Research and Development, Sales

**Fitch, Lori** — *Associate*
R. Parker and Associates, Inc.
551 5th Avenue, Suite 222
New York, NY 10176
Telephone: (212) 661-8074
**Recruiter Classification:** Retained; **Lowest/Average Salary:** $50,000/$75,000;
**Industry Concentration:** Generalist with a primary focus in Consumer
Products, Fashion (Retail/Apparel); **Function Concentration:** Generalist with a
primary focus in General Management, Marketing, Sales

**Fitzgerald, Brian** — *Associate*
Source Services Corporation
5429 LBJ Freeway, Suite 275
Dallas, TX 75240
Telephone: (214) 387-1600
**Recruiter Classification:** Contingency; **Lowest/Average Salary:**
$30,000/$50,000; **Industry Concentration:** Financial Services, Information
Technology; **Function Concentration:** Engineering, Finance/Accounting

**Fixler, Eugene** — *President*
Ariel Recruitment Associates
440 West 53rd Street, Suite 126
New York, NY 10019
Telephone: (212) 765-8300
**Recruiter Classification:** Contingency; **Lowest/Average Salary:**
$50,000/$75,000; **Industry Concentration:** Entertainment, Publishing/Media;
**Function Concentration:** Generalist with a primary focus in Administration,
Finance/Accounting, General Management, Human Resources, Marketing, Sales

**Flanagan, Dale M.** — *Partner*
Lamalie Amrop International
200 Park Avenue
New York, NY 10166-0136
Telephone: (212) 953-7900
**Recruiter Classification:** Retained; **Lowest/Average Salary:** $90,000/$90,000;
**Industry Concentration:** Generalist; **Function Concentration:** Generalist with a
primary focus in Finance/Accounting, General Management, Marketing, Sales

**Flanagan, Robert M.** — *President*
Robert M. Flanagan & Associates, Ltd.
Fields Lane
North Salem, NY 10560
Telephone: (914) 277-7210
**Recruiter Classification:** Retained; **Lowest/Average Salary:** $90,000/$90,000;
**Industry Concentration:** Generalist with a primary focus in Consumer
Products, Fashion (Retail/Apparel), Financial Services, Information Technology,
Insurance, Packaging, Publishing/Media; **Function Concentration:** Generalist
with a primary focus in Administration, Finance/Accounting, Human
Resources, Marketing, Sales

**Flanders, Karen** — *Regional Manager*
Advanced Information Management
900 Wilshire Boulevard, Suite 1424
Los Angeles, CA 90017
Telephone: (213) 243-9236
**Recruiter Classification:** Contingency; **Lowest/Average Salary:**
$20,000/$40,000; **Industry Concentration:** Information Technology; **Function
Concentration:** Human Resources, Research and Development,
Women/Minorities

**Flannery, Peter** — *Vice President*
Jonas, Walters & Assoc., Inc.
1110 North Old World Third St., Suite 510
Milwaukee, WI 53203-1102
Telephone: (414) 291-2828
**Recruiter Classification:** Retained; **Lowest/Average Salary:** $60,000/$90,000;
**Industry Concentration:** Generalist with a primary focus in Consumer
Products, Electronics, Healthcare/Hospitals, High Technology, Insurance,
Manufacturing, Non-Profit, Publishing/Media; **Function Concentration:**
Generalist with a primary focus in Administration, Engineering,
Finance/Accounting, General Management, Human Resources, Marketing,
Research and Development, Sales

**Flash, James** — *Vice President*
Richard Kader & Associates
343 West Bagley Road, Suite 209
Berea, OH 44017
Telephone: (216) 891-1700
**Recruiter Classification:** Contingency; **Lowest/Average Salary:** $40,000/$50,000;
**Industry Concentration:** Generalist; **Function Concentration:** Generalist

**Flask, A. Paul** — *Managing Director*
Korn/Ferry International
120 South Riverside Plaza
Suite 918
Chicago, IL 60606
Telephone: (312) 726-1841
**Recruiter Classification:** Retained; **Lowest/Average Salary:** $90,000/$90,000;
**Industry Concentration:** Generalist; **Function Concentration:** Generalist

**Fleck, George** — *Vice President*
Canny, Bowen Inc.
1177 High Ridge Road
Stamford, CT 06905
Telephone: (203) 321-1248
**Recruiter Classification:** Retained; **Lowest/Average Salary:** $90,000/$90,000;
**Industry Concentration:** Generalist; **Function Concentration:** Generalist

**Fleming, Joseph M.** — *Managing Director*
IMCOR, Inc.
233 South Wacker Drive, Suite 8000
Chicago, IL 60606
Telephone: (312) 876-2534
**Recruiter Classification:** Executive Temporary; **Lowest/Average Salary:**
$75,000/$90,000; **Industry Concentration:** Generalist; **Function
Concentration:** Generalist

**Fleming, Marco** — *Executive Recruiter*
MSI International
2170 West State Road 434
Suite 454
Longwood, FL 32779
Telephone: (407) 788-7700
**Recruiter Classification:** Contingency; **Lowest/Average Salary:**
$30,000/$60,000; **Industry Concentration:** Generalist with a primary focus in
Financial Services; **Function Concentration:** Generalist with a primary focus in
Administration, Engineering, Finance/Accounting, General Management,
Marketing, Sales

**Fleming, Richard** — *Senior Associate*
R.D. Gatti & Associates, Incorporated
266 Main Street, Suite 21
Medfield, MA 02052
Telephone: (508) 359-4153
**Recruiter Classification:** Contingency; **Lowest/Average Salary:**
$40,000/$75,000; **Industry Concentration:** Generalist; **Function Concentration:** Human Resources

**Fleming, Richard L.** — *Partner*
TASA International
7061 South Tamiami Trail
Sarasota, FL 34231
Telephone: (941) 922-8856
**Recruiter Classification:** Retained; **Lowest/Average Salary:** $90,000/$90,000; **Industry Concentration:** Generalist; **Function Concentration:** Generalist

**Fletcher, Karen** — *Vice President*
Don Richard Associates of Tidewater, Inc.
4701 Columbus Street, Suite 102
Virginia Beach, VA 23462
Telephone: (757) 518-8600
**Recruiter Classification:** Contingency, Executive Temporary; **Lowest/Average Salary:** $20,000/$30,000; **Industry Concentration:** Generalist; **Function Concentration:** Administration, Finance/Accounting

**Flickinger, Susan V.** — *Senior Associate*
Korn/Ferry International
The Transamerica Pyramid
600 Montgomery Street
San Francisco, CA 94111
Telephone: (415) 956-1834
**Recruiter Classification:** Retained; **Lowest/Average Salary:** $90,000/$90,000; **Industry Concentration:** Generalist with a primary focus in Healthcare/Hospitals; **Function Concentration:** Generalist

**Flink, Debra** — *Partner*
Heidrick & Struggles, Inc.
245 Park Avenue, Suite 4300
New York, NY 10167-0152
Telephone: (212) 867-9876
**Recruiter Classification:** Retained; **Lowest/Average Salary:** $75,000/$90,000; **Industry Concentration:** Generalist; **Function Concentration:** Generalist

**Flink, Debra K.** — *Managing Director*
Russell Reynolds Associates, Inc.
200 Park Avenue
New York, NY 10166-0002
Telephone: (212) 351-2000
**Recruiter Classification:** Retained; **Lowest/Average Salary:** $90,000/$90,000; **Industry Concentration:** Generalist with a primary focus in Financial Services; **Function Concentration:** Generalist

**Flinn, Richard A.** — *Associate*
Denney & Company Incorporated
P.O. Box 22156
Pittsburgh, PA 15222
Telephone: (412) 391-3746
**Recruiter Classification:** Retained; **Lowest/Average Salary:** $90,000/$90,000; **Industry Concentration:** Generalist; **Function Concentration:** Generalist

**Flora, Dodi** — *Regional Director*
Crawford & Crofford
15327 NW 60th Avenue, Suite 240
Miami Lakes, FL 33014
Telephone: (305) 820-0855
**Recruiter Classification:** Contingency, Executive Temporary; **Lowest/Average Salary:** $30,000/$60,000; **Industry Concentration:** Chemical Products, Consumer Products, Education/Libraries, Electronics, Energy, Financial Services, Healthcare/Hospitals, High Technology, Insurance, Manufacturing, Pharmaceutical/Medical, Real Estate, Transportation; **Function Concentration:** Administration, Engineering, Finance/Accounting, General Management, Human Resources, Sales

**Flores, Agustin** — *Partner*
Ward Howell International, Inc.
Rexer Seleccion de Ejecutivos, S.C.
Blvd. Adolfo Lopez Mateos 20, Col. San Angel Inn
Mexico City, D.F., MEXICO 01060
Telephone: (525) 550-9180
**Recruiter Classification:** Retained; **Lowest/Average Salary:** $75,000/$90,000; **Industry Concentration:** Consumer Products, Financial Services, Information Technology; **Function Concentration:** Generalist

**Florio, Robert** — *Associate*
Source Services Corporation
525 Vine Street, Suite 2250
Cincinnati, OH 45202
Telephone: (513) 651-3303
**Recruiter Classification:** Contingency; **Lowest/Average Salary:** $30,000/$50,000; **Industry Concentration:** Financial Services, Information Technology; **Function Concentration:** Engineering, Finance/Accounting

**Flowers, Hayden** — *Executive Recruiter*
Southwestern Professional Services
101 West Renner Road, Suite 230
Richardson, TX 75082
Telephone: (214) 705-9500
**Recruiter Classification:** Contingency; **Lowest/Average Salary:** $30,000/$75,000; **Industry Concentration:** Electronics, Information Technology; **Function Concentration:** Engineering

**Flowers, John E.** — *Sole Proprietor*
Balfour Associates
P.O. Box 173
Lansdowne, PA 19050
Telephone: (610) 259-3314
**Recruiter Classification:** Contingency; **Lowest/Average Salary:** $20,000/$50,000; **Industry Concentration:** Generalist with a primary focus in Publishing/Media; **Function Concentration:** Engineering, General Management, Human Resources, Marketing, Sales

**Flynn, Brian** — *Senior Associate*
Korn/Ferry International
One International Place
Boston, MA 02110-1800
Telephone: (617) 345-0200
**Recruiter Classification:** Retained; **Lowest/Average Salary:** $90,000/$90,000; **Industry Concentration:** Generalist; **Function Concentration:** Generalist

**Flynn, Jack** — *Managing Partner*
Executive Search Consultants Corporation
8 South Michigan Avenue, Suite 1205
Chicago, IL 60603
Telephone: (312) 251-8400
**Recruiter Classification:** Contingency; **Lowest/Average Salary:** $40,000/$60,000; **Industry Concentration:** Financial Services, Insurance; **Function Concentration:** Administration, General Management

**Fogarty, Deirdre** — *Consultant*
Paul Ray Berndtson
101 Park Avenue, 41st Floor
New York, NY 10178
Telephone: (212) 370-1316
**Recruiter Classification:** Retained; **Lowest/Average Salary:** $90,000/$90,000; **Industry Concentration:** Generalist; **Function Concentration:** Generalist

**Fogarty, Michael** — *Executive Recruiter*
CPS Inc.
One Westbrook Corporate Centre, Suite 600
Westchester, IL 60154
Telephone: (708) 531-8370
**Recruiter Classification:** Contingency; **Lowest/Average Salary:** $30,000/$50,000; **Industry Concentration:** Generalist with a primary focus in Automotive, Biotechnology, Chemical Products, Consumer Products, High Technology, Insurance, Manufacturing, Oil/Gas, Packaging, Pharmaceutical/Medical; **Function Concentration:** Engineering, Research and Development, Sales, Women/Minorities

**Fogelgren, Stephen W.** — *Senior Vice President Operations*
Management Recruiters International, Inc.
200 Public Square, 31st Floor
Cleveland, OH 44114-2301
Telephone: (216) 696-1122
**Recruiter Classification:** Contingency; **Lowest/Average Salary:** $30,000/$75,000; **Industry Concentration:** Generalist; **Function Concentration:** Generalist

**Foley, Eileen** — *Information Technology Recruiter*
Winter, Wyman & Company
950 Winter Street, Suite 3100
Waltham, MA 02154-1294
Telephone: (617) 890-7000
**Recruiter Classification:** Contingency; **Lowest/Average Salary:** $30,000/$60,000; **Industry Concentration:** Generalist with a primary focus in Information Technology; **Function Concentration:** Generalist

**Foley, John J.** — *Managing Director*
Executive Outsourcing International
16528 Calle Pulido, Suite 101
San Diego, CA 92128
Telephone: (619) 487-0390
**Recruiter Classification:** Executive Temporary; **Lowest/Average Salary:** $75,000/$90,000; **Industry Concentration:** Generalist; **Function Concentration:** Generalist

**Folkerth, Gene** — *President*
Gene Folkerth & Associates, Inc.
970 Patriot Square
Dayton, OH 45459-4042
Telephone: (513) 291-2722
**Recruiter Classification:** Executive Temporary; **Lowest/Average Salary:** $40,000/$75,000; **Industry Concentration:** Generalist with a primary focus in Automotive, Chemical Products, Consumer Products, Electronics, Manufacturing; **Function Concentration:** Generalist with a primary focus in Engineering, Human Resources, Research and Development

**Follmer, Gary** — *Agribusiness Recruiter/Manager*
Agra Placements International Ltd.
4949 Pleasant Suite 1, West 50th Place III
West Des Moines, IA 50266-5494
Telephone: (515) 225-6562
**Recruiter Classification:** Contingency; **Lowest/Average Salary:**
$20,000/$30,000; **Industry Concentration:** Generalist with a primary focus in
Biotechnology, Chemical Products, Energy, Financial Services, Manufacturing;
**Function Concentration:** Administration, Engineering, Finance/Accounting,
General Management, Human Resources, Marketing, Research and
Development, Sales

**Follrath, Noel** — *Consultant*
Paul Ray Berndtson
191 Peachtree Tower, Suite 3800
191 Peachtree Street, NE
Atlanta, GA 30303-1757
Telephone: (404) 215-4600
**Recruiter Classification:** Retained; **Lowest/Average Salary:** $90,000/$90,000;
**Industry Concentration:** Generalist; **Function Concentration:** Generalist

**Fone, Carol** — *Consultant/Market Research*
Walden Associates
1601 Trapelo Road
Waltham, MA 02154
Telephone: (617) 890-8885
**Recruiter Classification:** Retained; **Lowest/Average Salary:** $90,000/$90,000;
**Industry Concentration:** High Technology, Information Technology; **Function
Concentration:** General Management

**Fonfa, Ann** — *Consultant*
S.R. Wolman Associates, Inc.
133 East 35th Street
New York, NY 10016
Telephone: (212) 685-2692
**Recruiter Classification:** Retained; **Lowest/Average Salary:** $50,000/$90,000;
**Industry Concentration:** Generalist with a primary focus in Consumer Products,
Entertainment, Fashion (Retail/Apparel); **Function Concentration:** Generalist
with a primary focus in Administration, General Management, Human
Resources, Marketing, Research and Development, Sales, Women/Minorities

**Foote, Leland W.** — *President*
L.W. Foote Company
110-110th Avenue N.E.
Suite 680
Bellevue, WA 98004-5840
Telephone: (206) 451-1660
**Recruiter Classification:** Retained; **Lowest/Average Salary:** $75,000/$75,000;
**Industry Concentration:** Generalist with a primary focus in Biotechnology,
Consumer Products, Electronics, Fashion (Retail/Apparel),
Healthcare/Hospitals, High Technology, Manufacturing, Venture Capital;
**Function Concentration:** Generalist

**Foote, Ray P.** — *Managing Partner*
Heidrick & Struggles, Inc.
Greenwich Office Park #3
Greenwich, CT 06831
Telephone: (203) 629-3200
**Recruiter Classification:** Retained; **Lowest/Average Salary:** $75,000/$90,000;
**Industry Concentration:** Generalist with a primary focus in Board Services,
Financial Services; **Function Concentration:** Generalist

**Forbes, Kay Koob** — *Principal*
Sanford Rose Associates
8042 Robin Hill Road
P.O. Box 1106
Newburgh, IN 47629
Telephone: (812) 853-9325
**Recruiter Classification:** Contingency; **Lowest/Average Salary:** $30,000/$75,000;
**Industry Concentration:** Generalist; **Function Concentration:** Generalist

**Forbes, Kenneth P.** — *Principal*
Sanford Rose Associates
8042 Robin Hill Road
P.O. Box 1106
Newburgh, IN 47629
Telephone: (812) 853-9325
**Recruiter Classification:** Contingency; **Lowest/Average Salary:** $30,000/$75,000;
**Industry Concentration:** Generalist; **Function Concentration:** Generalist

**Ford, J. Daniel** — *Shareholder*
Witt/Kieffer, Ford, Hadelman & Lloyd
2015 Spring Road, Suite 510
Oak Brook, IL 60521
Telephone: (708) 990-1370
**Recruiter Classification:** Retained; **Lowest/Average Salary:** $75,000/$90,000;
**Industry Concentration:** Healthcare/Hospitals; **Function Concentration:**
Generalist with a primary focus in Administration, Finance/Accounting,
General Management, Human Resources, Marketing

**Ford, Sandra D.** — *Managing Director*
Phillips & Ford, Inc.
485 Devon Park Drive, Suite 110
Wayne, PA 19087
Telephone: (610) 975-9007
**Recruiter Classification:** Retained; **Lowest/Average Salary:** $90,000/$90,000;
**Industry Concentration:** Biotechnology, Financial Services, High Technology,
Information Technology, Insurance; **Function Concentration:** Finance/Accounting,
General Management, Human Resources, Marketing, Women/Minorities

**Foreman, David C.** — *Senior Associate*
Koontz, Jeffries & Associates, Inc.
18-22 Bank Street
Summit, NJ 07901
Telephone: (908) 598-1900
**Recruiter Classification:** Retained; **Lowest/Average Salary:** $60,000/$90,000;
**Industry Concentration:** Generalist with a primary focus in Aerospace/Defense,
Automotive, Biotechnology, Chemical Products, Consumer Products,
Electronics, Environmental, Financial Services, Healthcare/Hospitals, High
Technology, Manufacturing, Pharmaceutical/Medical; **Function Concentration:**
Generalist with a primary focus in Administration, Engineering,
Finance/Accounting, General Management, Human Resources, Marketing,
Research and Development, Sales, Women/Minorities

**Foreman, Kathryn A.** — *Partner*
Paul Ray Berndtson
2029 Century Park East
Suite 1000
Los Angeles, CA 90067
Telephone: (310) 557-2828
**Recruiter Classification:** Retained; **Lowest/Average Salary:** $90,000/$90,000;
**Industry Concentration:** Generalist; **Function Concentration:** Generalist

**Foreman, Rebecca** — *Associate*
Aubin International
Somerset Court, 281 Winter Street
Waltham, MA 02154
Telephone: (617) 890-1722
**Recruiter Classification:** Retained; **Lowest/Average Salary:** $90,000/$90,000;
**Industry Concentration:** Generalist with a primary focus in High Technology,
Venture Capital; **Function Concentration:** Generalist

**Forest, Adam** — *Partner*
McCormack & Associates
5042 Wilshire Boulevard, Suite 505
Los Angeles, CA 90036
Telephone: (213) 549-9200
**Recruiter Classification:** Retained; **Lowest/Average Salary:** $75,000/$90,000;
**Industry Concentration:** Environmental, Information Technology, Non-Profit,
Transportation; **Function Concentration:** Engineering, Finance/Accounting,
General Management, Human Resources, Marketing, Sales, Women/Minorities

**Forestier, Lois** — *Associate*
Source Services Corporation
2 Penn Plaza, Suite 1176
New York, NY 10121
Telephone: (212) 760-2200
**Recruiter Classification:** Contingency; **Lowest/Average Salary:**
$30,000/$50,000; **Industry Concentration:** Financial Services, Information
Technology; **Function Concentration:** Engineering, Finance/Accounting

**Forgosh, Jack H.** — *Senior Consultant*
Raymond Karsan Associates
989 Old Eagle School Road, Suite 814
Wayne, PA 19087
Telephone: (610) 971-9171
**Recruiter Classification:** Contingency; **Lowest/Average Salary:**
$30,000/$90,000; **Industry Concentration:** Generalist with a primary focus in
Insurance; **Function Concentration:** Generalist

**Forman, Donald R.** — *Director*
Stanton Chase International
5050 Quorum Drive, Suite 330
Dallas, TX 75240
Telephone: (214) 404-8411
**Recruiter Classification:** Retained; **Lowest/Average Salary:** $75,000/$90,000;
**Industry Concentration:** Generalist with a primary focus in Chemical Products,
Consumer Products, Environmental, High Technology, Manufacturing;
**Function Concentration:** Generalist with a primary focus in Administration,
Engineering, Marketing, Sales

**Fosnot, Bob** — *Co-Manager*
Management Recruiters International, Inc.
115 Hidden Valley Road
McMurray, PA 15317
Telephone: (412) 942-4100
**Recruiter Classification:** Contingency; **Lowest/Average Salary:**
$30,000/$75,000; **Industry Concentration:** Generalist; **Function
Concentration:** Generalist

**Fosnot, Mike** — *Co-Manager Central Region*
Management Recruiters International, Inc.
115 Hidden Valley Road
McMurray, PA 15317
Telephone: (412) 942-4100
**Recruiter Classification:** Contingency; **Lowest/Average Salary:**
$30,000/$75,000; **Industry Concentration:** Generalist; **Function
Concentration:** Generalist

**Fossett, Gary J.** — *Chief Executive Officer*
John Michael Associates
102 Elden Street, Suite 12
Herndon, VA 22070-4809
Telephone: (703) 471-6300
**Recruiter Classification:** Contingency; **Lowest/Average Salary:**
$75,000/$90,000

**Foster, Bradley** — *Associate*
Source Services Corporation
2000 Town Center, Suite 850
Southfield, MI 48075
Telephone: (810) 352-6520
**Recruiter Classification:** Contingency; **Lowest/Average Salary:**
$30,000/$50,000; **Industry Concentration:** Financial Services, Information
Technology; **Function Concentration:** Engineering, Finance/Accounting

**Foster, Brian Scott** — *Banking Recruiting Manager*
Don Richard Associates of Charlotte
2650 One First Union Center
301 South College Street
Charlotte, NC 28202-6000
Telephone: (704) 377-6447
**Recruiter Classification:** Contingency, Executive Temporary; **Lowest/Average
Salary:** $30,000/$50,000; **Industry Concentration:** Financial Services;
**Function Concentration:** Finance/Accounting

**Foster, Drew B.** — *Manager North Atlantic Region*
Management Recruiters International, Inc.
The Bristol Building, Suite 331
7003 Chadwick Drive
Brentwood, TN 37027-5232
Telephone: (615) 373-1111
**Recruiter Classification:** Contingency; **Lowest/Average Salary:**
$30,000/$75,000; **Industry Concentration:** Generalist; **Function
Concentration:** Generalist

**Foster, Duke** — *Senior Officer*
Korn/Ferry International
One Landmark Square
Stamford, CT 06901
Telephone: (203) 359-3350
**Recruiter Classification:** Retained; **Lowest/Average Salary:** $90,000/$90,000;
**Industry Concentration:** Generalist; **Function Concentration:** Generalist

**Foster, Dwight E.** — *Chairman/Executive Managing Director*
D.E. Foster Partners Inc.
570 Lexington Avenue, 14th Floor
New York, NY 10022
Telephone: (212) 872-6232
**Recruiter Classification:** Retained; **Lowest/Average Salary:** $90,000/$90,000;
**Industry Concentration:** Generalist with a primary focus in Chemical Products,
Consumer Products, Electronics, Financial Services, Insurance, Manufacturing;
**Function Concentration:** Finance/Accounting, General Management

**Foster, John** — *Associate*
Source Services Corporation
8614 Westwood Center, Suite 750
Vienna, VA 22182
Telephone: (703) 790-5610
**Recruiter Classification:** Contingency; **Lowest/Average Salary:**
$30,000/$50,000; **Industry Concentration:** Financial Services, Information
Technology; **Function Concentration:** Engineering, Finance/Accounting

**Foster, Michael** — *Principal*
Sanford Rose Associates
35 South Main Street, Third Floor
Hanover, NH 03755
Telephone: (603) 643-4101
**Recruiter Classification:** Contingency; **Lowest/Average Salary:**
$30,000/$75,000; **Industry Concentration:** Generalist; **Function
Concentration:** Generalist

**Foster, Robert** — *Principal*
Korn/Ferry International
237 Park Avenue
New York, NY 10017
Telephone: (212) 687-1834
**Recruiter Classification:** Retained; **Lowest/Average Salary:** $90,000/$90,000;
**Industry Concentration:** Generalist; **Function Concentration:** Generalist

**Foster, Torrey N.** — *Associate*
Lynch Miller Moore Partners, Inc.
10 South Wacker Drive, Suite 2935
Chicago, IL 60606
Telephone: (312) 876-1505
**Recruiter Classification:** Retained; **Lowest/Average Salary:** $75,000/$90,000;
**Industry Concentration:** Generalist with a primary focus in Consumer
Products; **Function Concentration:** Generalist with a primary focus in
Marketing, Sales

**Fotia, Frank** — *Principal*
JDG Associates, Ltd.
1700 Research Boulevard
Rockville, MD 20850
Telephone: (301) 340-2210
**Recruiter Classification:** Contingency; **Lowest/Average Salary:**
$50,000/$90,000; **Industry Concentration:** Aerospace/Defense, Financial
Services, Healthcare/Hospitals, High Technology, Information Technology;
**Function Concentration:** Engineering, Finance/Accounting, Research and
Development

**Fotino, Anne** — *Recruiter*
Normyle/Erstling Health Search Group
350 West Passaic Street
Rochelle Park, NJ 07662
Telephone: (201) 843-6009
**Recruiter Classification:** Contingency; **Lowest/Average Salary:**
$20,000/$40,000; **Industry Concentration:** Biotechnology,
Healthcare/Hospitals, Pharmaceutical/Medical; **Function Concentration:**
General Management, Marketing, Sales

**Fountain, Ray** — *Manager North Atlantic Region*
Management Recruiters International, Inc.
Rivergate Center II, Suite 311
4975 Lacross Road
North Charleston, SC 29406-6525
Telephone: (803) 744-5888
**Recruiter Classification:** Contingency; **Lowest/Average Salary:**
$30,000/$75,000; **Industry Concentration:** Generalist; **Function
Concentration:** Generalist

**Fovhez, Michael J.P.** — *Director Corporate Staffing*
Sloan & Associates
1769 Jamestown Road
Williamsburg, VA 23185
Telephone: (757) 220-1111
**Recruiter Classification:** Contingency; **Lowest/Average Salary:**
$60,000/$75,000; **Industry Concentration:** Consumer Products; **Function
Concentration:** Marketing, Research and Development, Sales

**Fowler, Jim** — *Agri-Business Consultant*
First Search America, Inc.
P.O. Box 85
Ardmore, TN 38449
Telephone: (205) 423-8800
**Recruiter Classification:** Contingency; **Lowest/Average Salary:**
$30,000/$60,000; **Industry Concentration:** Manufacturing,
Pharmaceutical/Medical; **Function Concentration:** Generalist with a primary
focus in Administration, Engineering, Finance/Accounting, General
Management, Marketing, Research and Development, Sales

**Fowler, Susan B.** — *Managing Director*
Russell Reynolds Associates, Inc.
200 Park Avenue
New York, NY 10166-0002
Telephone: (212) 351-2000
**Recruiter Classification:** Retained; **Lowest/Average Salary:** $90,000/$90,000;
**Industry Concentration:** Generalist with a primary focus in Financial Services;
**Function Concentration:** Generalist

**Fowler, Thomas A.** — *Vice President - Dallas/Southwest*
The Hindman Company
Suite 200, The Tower at Williams Square
5215 North O'Connor Road
Irving, TX 75039
Telephone: (214) 868-9122
**Recruiter Classification:** Retained; **Lowest/Average Salary:** $50,000/$90,000;
**Industry Concentration:** Generalist; **Function Concentration:** Generalist

**Fox, Amanda C.** — *Partner*
Paul Ray Berndtson
10 South Riverside Plaza
Suite 720
Chicago, IL 60606
Telephone: (312) 876-0730
**Recruiter Classification:** Retained; **Lowest/Average Salary:** $90,000/$90,000;
**Industry Concentration:** Generalist with a primary focus in Financial Services,
Healthcare/Hospitals, Insurance, Manufacturing; **Function Concentration:**
Generalist with a primary focus in Finance/Accounting, Human Resources

**Fox, Lucie** — *Associate*
Allard Associates
44 Montgomery Street, Suite 500
San Francisco, CA 94104
Telephone: (415) 433-0500
**Recruiter Classification:** Retained; **Lowest/Average Salary:** $60,000/$90,000;
**Industry Concentration:** Generalist with a primary focus in Financial Services;
**Function Concentration:** Generalist with a primary focus in Administration,
General Management, Marketing, Research and Development, Sales

**Foy, James** — *Partner*
Foy, Schneid & Daniel, Inc.
555 Madison Avenue, 12th Floor
New York, NY 10022
Telephone: (212) 980-2525
**Recruiter Classification:** Retained; **Lowest/Average Salary:** $60,000/$90,000;
**Industry Concentration:** Generalist with a primary focus in Consumer
Products, Hospitality/Leisure, Packaging; **Function Concentration:** Generalist
with a primary focus in General Management, Human Resources

**Foy, Richard** — *Senior Vice President Finance and*
*Administration*
Boyden
364 Elwood Avenue
Hawthorne, NY 10532-1239
Telephone: (914) 747-0093
**Recruiter Classification:** Retained; **Lowest/Average Salary:** $75,000/$90,000;
**Industry Concentration:** Non-Profit; **Function Concentration:** Generalist with a
primary focus in Engineering, Finance/Accounting, General Management,
Human Resources, Marketing, Research and Development, Sales,
Women/Minorities

**Francis, Brad** — *Managing Director*
Source Services Corporation
7730 East Bellview Avenue, Suite 302
Englewood, CO 80111
Telephone: (303) 773-3700
**Recruiter Classification:** Contingency; **Lowest/Average Salary:**
$30,000/$50,000; **Industry Concentration:** Financial Services, Information
Technology; **Function Concentration:** Engineering, Finance/Accounting

**Francis, David P.** — *Partner*
Heidrick & Struggles, Inc.
245 Park Avenue, Suite 4300
New York, NY 10167-0152
Telephone: (212) 867-9876
**Recruiter Classification:** Retained; **Lowest/Average Salary:** $75,000/$90,000;
**Industry Concentration:** Generalist with a primary focus in High Technology;
**Function Concentration:** Generalist

**Francis, Dwaine** — *Managing Partner*
Francis & Associates
6923 Vista Drive
West Des Moines, IA 50266
Telephone: (515) 221-9800
**Recruiter Classification:** Retained; **Lowest/Average Salary:** $90,000/$90,000;
**Industry Concentration:** Generalist; **Function Concentration:** Generalist

**Francis, Joseph** — *Vice President*
Hospitality International
23 West 73rd Street, Suite 100
New York, NY 10023
Telephone: (212) 769-8800
**Recruiter Classification:** Contingency; **Lowest/Average Salary:**
$40,000/$60,000; **Industry Concentration:** Entertainment,
Healthcare/Hospitals, Hospitality/Leisure, Information Technology; **Function
Concentration:** Finance/Accounting, General Management, Human Resources,
Marketing, Sales, Women/Minorities

**Francis, Kay** — *Managing Partner*
Francis & Associates
6923 Vista Drive
West Des Moines, IA 50266
Telephone: (515) 221-9800
**Recruiter Classification:** Retained; **Lowest/Average Salary:** $90,000/$90,000;
**Industry Concentration:** Generalist; **Function Concentration:** Generalist

**Frank, Valerie S.** — *Executive Vice President*
Norman Roberts & Associates, Inc.
1800 Century Park East, Suite 430
Los Angeles, CA 90067
Telephone: (310) 552-1112
**Recruiter Classification:** Retained; **Lowest/Average Salary:** $60,000/$90,000;
**Industry Concentration:** Education/Libraries, Energy, Environmental,
Healthcare/Hospitals, Information Technology, Non-Profit, Public
Administration, Real Estate, Transportation; **Function Concentration:** Generalist
with a primary focus in Administration, Engineering, Finance/Accounting,
General Management, Human Resources, Marketing, Women/Minorities

**Franklin, Cecilia** — *Co-Manager Southwest Region*
Management Recruiters International, Inc.
P.O. Box 3553
Baton Rouge, LA 70821-3553
Telephone: (504) 383-1234
**Recruiter Classification:** Contingency; **Lowest/Average Salary:** $30,000/$75,000;
**Industry Concentration:** Generalist; **Function Concentration:** Generalist

**Franklin, Cleve** — *Co-Manager*
Management Recruiters International, Inc.
P.O. Box 3553
Baton Rouge, LA 70821-3553
Telephone: (504) 383-1234
**Recruiter Classification:** Contingency; **Lowest/Average Salary:** $30,000/$75,000;
**Industry Concentration:** Generalist; **Function Concentration:** Generalist

**Franklin, John W.** — *Managing Director*
Russell Reynolds Associates, Inc.
1700 Pennsylvania Avenue N.W.
Suite 850
Washington, DC 20006
Telephone: (202) 628-2150
**Recruiter Classification:** Retained; **Lowest/Average Salary:** $90,000/$90,000;
**Industry Concentration:** Healthcare/Hospitals, Non-Profit; **Function
Concentration:** Generalist

**Franquemont, William R.** — *Executive Vice President*
EFL Associates
8777 East Via de Ventura, Suite 100
Scottsdale, AZ 85258
Telephone: (602) 483-0496
**Recruiter Classification:** Retained; **Lowest/Average Salary:** $60,000/$90,000;
**Industry Concentration:** Generalist; **Function Concentration:** Generalist

**Frantino, Michael** — *Associate*
Source Services Corporation
379 Thornall Street
Edison, NJ 08837
Telephone: (908) 494-2800
**Recruiter Classification:** Contingency; **Lowest/Average Salary:**
$30,000/$50,000; **Industry Concentration:** Financial Services, Information
Technology; **Function Concentration:** Engineering, Finance/Accounting

**Franzino, Michael** — *Partner*
TASA International
750 Lexington Avenue
Suite 1800
New York, NY 10022
Telephone: (212) 486-1490
**Recruiter Classification:** Retained; **Lowest/Average Salary:** $90,000/$90,000;
**Industry Concentration:** Generalist; **Function Concentration:** Generalist

**Frazier, John** — *Recruiter*
Cochran, Cochran & Yale, Inc.
955 East Henrietta Road
Rochester, NY 14623
Telephone: (716) 424-6060
**Recruiter Classification:** Contingency; **Lowest/Average Salary:**
$40,000/$60,000; **Industry Concentration:** Generalist with a primary focus in
Automotive, Consumer Products, Healthcare/Hospitals, High Technology,
Manufacturing, Packaging, Pharmaceutical/Medical, Publishing/Media;
**Function Concentration:** Generalist with a primary focus in Engineering,
Finance/Accounting, General Management, Human Resources, Marketing,
Research and Development, Sales, Women/Minorities

**Frazier, Steven M.** — *Principal*
Sanford Rose Associates
75 James Way
Southampton, PA 18966
Telephone: (215) 953-7433
**Recruiter Classification:** Contingency; **Lowest/Average Salary:** $30,000/$75,000;
**Industry Concentration:** Generalist; **Function Concentration:** Generalist

**Freda, Louis A.** — *Senior Vice President*
DHR International, Inc.
10 South Riverside Plaza, Suite 2220
Chicago, IL 60606
Telephone: (312) 782-1581
**Recruiter Classification:** Retained; **Lowest/Average Salary:** $60,000/$90,000;
**Industry Concentration:** Generalist; **Function Concentration:** Generalist

**Frederick, Dianne** — *Associate*
Source Services Corporation
525 Vine Street, Suite 2250
Cincinnati, OH 45202
Telephone: (513) 651-3303
**Recruiter Classification:** Contingency; **Lowest/Average Salary:**
$30,000/$50,000; **Industry Concentration:** Financial Services, Information
Technology; **Function Concentration:** Engineering, Finance/Accounting

**Fredericks, Ward A.** — *Chairman*
Mixtec Group
31255 Cedar Valley Drive
Suite 300-327
Westlake Village, CA 91362
Telephone: (818) 889-8819
**Recruiter Classification:** Contingency; **Lowest/Average Salary:**
$60,000/$90,000; **Industry Concentration:** High Technology; **Function Concentration:** Generalist with a primary focus in Administration, General Management, Marketing

**Freedman, Glenn** — *Accounting and Finance Recruiter*
Winter, Wyman & Company
950 Winter Street, Suite 3100
Waltham, MA 02154-1294
Telephone: (617) 890-7000
**Recruiter Classification:** Contingency; **Lowest/Average Salary:**
$20,000/$50,000; **Industry Concentration:** Generalist; **Function Concentration:** Finance/Accounting

**Freedman, Howard** — *Vice President*
Korn/Ferry International
237 Park Avenue
New York, NY 10017
Telephone: (212) 687-1834
**Recruiter Classification:** Retained; **Lowest/Average Salary:** $90,000/$90,000;
**Industry Concentration:** Generalist with a primary focus in Financial Services;
**Function Concentration:** Generalist

**Freeh, Thomas** — *Managing Director*
Source Services Corporation
4170 Ashford Dunwoody Road, Suite 285
Atlanta, GA 30319
Telephone: (404) 255-2045
**Recruiter Classification:** Contingency; **Lowest/Average Salary:**
$30,000/$50,000; **Industry Concentration:** Financial Services, Information
Technology; **Function Concentration:** Engineering, Finance/Accounting

**Freemon, Ted** — *Manager Southwest Region*
Management Recruiters International, Inc.
800 West Airport Freeway, Suite 1015
Irving, TX 75062-6312
Telephone: (214) 554-7966
**Recruiter Classification:** Contingency; **Lowest/Average Salary:**
$30,000/$75,000; **Industry Concentration:** Generalist; **Function Concentration:** Generalist

**Freier, Bruce** — *President*
Executive Referral Services, Inc.
8770 West Bryn Mawr, Suite 110
Chicago, IL 60631
Telephone: (312) 693-6622
**Recruiter Classification:** Contingency; **Lowest/Average Salary:**
$30,000/$50,000; **Industry Concentration:** Generalist with a primary focus in
Biotechnology, Entertainment, Fashion (Retail/Apparel), Healthcare/Hospitals,
Hospitality/Leisure, Pharmaceutical/Medical, Venture Capital; **Function Concentration:** Finance/Accounting, General Management, Marketing,
Women/Minorities

**French, Ted** — *Senior Consultant*
Spectra International Inc.
6991 East Camelback Road, Suite B-305
Scottsdale, AZ 85251
Telephone: (602) 481-0411
**Recruiter Classification:** Contingency; **Lowest/Average Salary:**
$30,000/$50,000; **Industry Concentration:** Fashion (Retail/Apparel); **Function Concentration:** General Management, Sales

**French, William G.** — *Managing Director Europe*
Preng & Associates, Inc.
2925 Briarpark, Suite 1111
Houston, TX 77042
Telephone: (713) 266-2600
**Recruiter Classification:** Retained; **Lowest/Average Salary:** $75,000/$90,000;
**Industry Concentration:** Generalist with a primary focus in
Aerospace/Defense, Chemical Products, Consumer Products, Energy,
Environmental, Financial Services, High Technology, Information Technology,
Manufacturing, Oil/Gas, Pharmaceutical/Medical, Transportation,
Utilities/Nuclear; **Function Concentration:** Generalist with a primary focus in
Administration, Engineering, Finance/Accounting, General Management,
Human Resources, Marketing, Research and Development, Sales

**Frerichs, April** — *Executive Recruiter*
Ryan, Miller & Associates Inc.
4601 Wilshire Boulevard, Suite 225
Los Angeles, CA 90010
Telephone: (213) 938-4768
**Recruiter Classification:** Contingency; **Lowest/Average Salary:**
$40,000/$50,000; **Industry Concentration:** Generalist with a primary focus in
Financial Services; **Function Concentration:** Generalist with a primary focus in
Finance/Accounting

**Freud, John W.** — *Partner*
Paul Ray Berndtson
One Allen Center
500 Dallas, Suite 3010
Houston, TX 77002
Telephone: (713) 309-1400
**Recruiter Classification:** Retained; **Lowest/Average Salary:** $90,000/$90,000;
**Industry Concentration:** Energy; **Function Concentration:** Generalist

**Friar, Timothy K.** — *Vice President*
Korn/Ferry International
One Landmark Square
Stamford, CT 06901
Telephone: (203) 359-3350
**Recruiter Classification:** Retained; **Lowest/Average Salary:** $90,000/$90,000;
**Industry Concentration:** Generalist; **Function Concentration:** Generalist

**Fribush, Richard** — *Recruiter*
A.J. Burton Group, Inc.
120 East Baltimore Street, Suite 2220
Baltimore, MD 21202
Telephone: (410) 752-5244
**Recruiter Classification:** Contingency; **Lowest/Average Salary:**
$40,000/$60,000; **Industry Concentration:** Financial Services, Insurance, Real
Estate, Transportation, Venture Capital; **Function Concentration:**
Finance/Accounting

**Friedman, Deborah** — *Associate*
Source Services Corporation
425 California Street, Suite 1200
San Francisco, CA 94104
Telephone: (415) 434-2410
**Recruiter Classification:** Contingency; **Lowest/Average Salary:**
$30,000/$50,000; **Industry Concentration:** Financial Services, Information
Technology; **Function Concentration:** Engineering, Finance/Accounting

**Friedman, Donna L.** — *President*
Tower Consultants, Ltd.
771 East Lancaster Avenue
Villanova, PA 19085
Telephone: (610) 519-1700
**Recruiter Classification:** Retained; **Lowest/Average Salary:**
$90,000/$90,000; **Industry Concentration:** Generalist with a primary focus
in Consumer Products, Fashion (Retail/Apparel), Financial Services,
Healthcare/Hospitals, High Technology, Hospitality/Leisure, Insurance,
Manufacturing; **Function Concentration:** Human Resources,
Women/Minorities

**Friedman, Helen E.** — *Partner*
McCormack & Farrow
695 Town Center Drive
Suite 660
Costa Mesa, CA 92626
Telephone: (714) 549-7222
**Recruiter Classification:** Retained; **Lowest/Average Salary:** $75,000/$90,000;
**Industry Concentration:** Generalist with a primary focus in Financial Services,
Healthcare/Hospitals, Information Technology, Manufacturing, Oil/Gas,
Packaging, Pharmaceutical/Medical, Transportation; **Function Concentration:**
Generalist with a primary focus in Engineering, Finance/Accounting, General
Management, Human Resources, Marketing, Research and Development,
Sales, Women/Minorities

**Friedman, Janet** — *Executive Recruiter*
Litchfield & Willis Inc.
3900 Essex at Weslayan
Suite 650
Houston, TX 77027
Telephone: (713) 439-8200
**Recruiter Classification:** Executive Temporary; **Lowest/Average Salary:**
$50,000/$60,000; **Industry Concentration:** Generalist; **Function Concentration:** Generalist

**Friedman, Lesley M.** — *President*
Special Counsel International
19 West 34th Street
New York, NY 10001
Telephone: (800) 659-9456
**Recruiter Classification:** Executive Temporary; **Lowest/Average Salary:**
$60,000/$90,000

**Friedman, Marcie W.** — *Consultant*
Coleman Legal Search Consultants
1435 Walnut Street, 3rd Floor
Philadelphia, PA 19102
Telephone: (215) 864-2700
**Recruiter Classification:** Contingency; **Lowest/Average Salary:**
$60,000/$75,000; **Function Concentration:** Generalist

**Friel, Thomas J.** — *Partner*
Heidrick & Struggles, Inc.
2740 Sand Hill Road
Menlo Park, CA 94025
Telephone: (415) 854-9300
Recruiter Classification: Retained; **Lowest/Average Salary:** $75,000/$90,000;
**Industry Concentration:** Generalist with a primary focus in High Technology;
**Function Concentration:** Generalist

**Frieze, Stanley B.** — *President*
Stanley B. Frieze Company
45 Shore Park Road
Great Neck, NY 11023
Telephone: (516) 487-1959
Recruiter Classification: Executive Temporary; **Lowest/Average Salary:**
$90,000/$90,000; **Industry Concentration:** Generalist; **Function
Concentration:** Generalist

**Frock, Suzanne D.** — *Principal*
Brandjes Associates
16 South Calvert Street
Suite 500
Baltimore, MD 21202
Telephone: (410) 547-6886
Recruiter Classification: Contingency; **Lowest/Average Salary:**
$50,000/$75,000; **Industry Concentration:** Financial Services; **Function
Concentration:** Generalist with a primary focus in Administration,
Finance/Accounting, General Management, Human Resources, Marketing,
Research and Development

**Fruchtman, Gary K.** — *Manager Central Region*
Management Recruiters International, Inc.
The Westgate Building, Suite 360
3450 West Central Avenue
Toledo, OH 43606
Telephone: (419) 537-1100
Recruiter Classification: Contingency; **Lowest/Average Salary:** $30,000/$75,000;
**Industry Concentration:** Generalist; **Function Concentration:** Generalist

**Frumess, Gregory** — *Managing Director Financial Services
Practice*
D.E. Foster Partners Inc.
570 Lexington Avenue, 14th Floor
New York, NY 10022
Telephone: (212) 872-6232
Recruiter Classification: Retained; **Lowest/Average Salary:** $90,000/$90,000;
**Industry Concentration:** Financial Services, Insurance; **Function
Concentration:** Finance/Accounting

**Fry, Edmund L.** — *Consultant*
Witt/Kieffer, Ford, Hadelman & Lloyd
10375 Richmond Avenue, Suite 1625
Houston, TX 77042
Telephone: (713) 266-6779
Recruiter Classification: Retained; **Lowest/Average Salary:** $75,000/$90,000;
**Industry Concentration:** Healthcare/Hospitals; **Function Concentration:**
Generalist with a primary focus in General Management

**Fry, John M.** — *President*
The Fry Group, Inc.
18 East 41st Street, Suite 1705
New York, NY 10017
Telephone: (212) 532-8100
Recruiter Classification: Contingency; **Lowest/Average Salary:** $30,000/$50,000;
**Industry Concentration:** Generalist; **Function Concentration:** Generalist

**Frye, Garland V.** — *Partner*
Schuyler, Frye & Baker, Inc.
1100 Abernathy Road N.E., Suite 1825
Atlanta, GA 30328
Telephone: (770) 804-1996
Recruiter Classification: Retained; **Lowest/Average Salary:** $90,000/$90,000;
**Industry Concentration:** Generalist; **Function Concentration:** Generalist

**Fueglein, Hugo** — *Senior Associate*
Korn/Ferry International
One Landmark Square
Stamford, CT 06901
Telephone: (203) 359-3350
Recruiter Classification: Retained; **Lowest/Average Salary:** $90,000/$90,000;
**Industry Concentration:** Generalist; **Function Concentration:** Generalist

**Fuhrman, Dennis** — *Managing Director*
Source Services Corporation
500 108th Avenue NE, Suite 1780
Bellevue, WA 98004
Telephone: (206) 454-6400
Recruiter Classification: Contingency; **Lowest/Average Salary:**
$30,000/$50,000; **Industry Concentration:** Financial Services, Information
Technology; **Function Concentration:** Engineering, Finance/Accounting

**Fuhrman, Katherine** — *Executive Recruiter*
Richard, Wayne and Roberts
24 Greenway Plaza, Suite 1304
Houston, TX 77046-2493
Telephone: (713) 629-6681
Recruiter Classification: Retained; **Lowest/Average Salary:** $40,000/$60,000;
**Industry Concentration:** Generalist with a primary focus in
Healthcare/Hospitals; **Function Concentration:** Generalist with a primary focus
in Finance/Accounting

**Fujino, Rickey** — *Associate*
Source Services Corporation
1290 Oakmead Parkway, Suite 318
Sunnyvale, CA 94086
Telephone: (408) 738-8440
Recruiter Classification: Contingency; **Lowest/Average Salary:**
$30,000/$50,000; **Industry Concentration:** Financial Services, Information
Technology; **Function Concentration:** Engineering, Finance/Accounting

**Fulger, Herbert** — *Associate*
Source Services Corporation
3 Summit Park Drive, Suite 550
Independence, OH 44131
Telephone: (216) 328-5900
Recruiter Classification: Contingency; **Lowest/Average Salary:**
$30,000/$50,000; **Industry Concentration:** Financial Services, Information
Technology; **Function Concentration:** Engineering, Finance/Accounting

**Fuller, Craig L.** — *Managing Director*
Korn/Ferry International
Presidential Plaza
900 19th Street, N.W.
Washington, DC 20006
Telephone: (202) 822-9444
Recruiter Classification: Retained; **Lowest/Average Salary:** $90,000/$90,000;
**Industry Concentration:** Generalist; **Function Concentration:** Generalist

**Fuller, Ev** — *Co-Manager North Atlantic Region*
Management Recruiters International, Inc.
5701 Westpark Drive, Suite 110
Charlotte, NC 28217
Telephone: (704) 525-9270
Recruiter Classification: Contingency; **Lowest/Average Salary:**
$30,000/$75,000; **Industry Concentration:** Generalist; **Function
Concentration:** Generalist

**Fuller, Robert L.** — *Executive Recruiter*
Litchfield & Willis Inc.
3900 Essex at Weslayan
Suite 650
Houston, TX 77027
Telephone: (713) 439-8200
Recruiter Classification: Executive Temporary; **Lowest/Average Salary:**
$50,000/$60,000; **Industry Concentration:** Generalist; **Function
Concentration:** Generalist

**Fulton, Christine N.** — *Research Assistant*
Highland Search Group, L.L.C.
565 Fifth Avenue, 22nd Floor
New York, NY 10017
Telephone: (212) 328-1113
Recruiter Classification: Retained; **Lowest/Average Salary:** $90,000/$90,000;
**Industry Concentration:** Financial Services, Real Estate, Venture Capital;
**Function Concentration:** Generalist with a primary focus in
Finance/Accounting, General Management, Human Resources, Research and
Development, Sales, Women/Minorities

**Funk, Robert William** — *Managing Vice President*
Korn/Ferry International
3950 Lincoln Plaza
500 North Akard Street
Dallas, TX 75201
Telephone: (214) 954-1834
Recruiter Classification: Retained; **Lowest/Average Salary:** $90,000/$90,000;
**Industry Concentration:** Generalist with a primary focus in Education/Libraries;
**Function Concentration:** Generalist

**Furlong, James W.** — *President*
Furlong Search, Inc.
634 East Main Street
Hillsboro, OR 97123
Telephone: (503) 640-3221
Recruiter Classification: Retained; **Lowest/Average Salary:** $90,000/$90,000;
**Industry Concentration:** Electronics, High Technology, Venture Capital;
**Function Concentration:** Generalist with a primary focus in Engineering,
Finance/Accounting, General Management, Marketing, Research and
Development, Sales

**Furlong, James W.** — *President*
Furlong Search, Inc.
19312 Romar Street
Northridge, CA 91324
Telephone: (818) 885-7044
**Recruiter Classification:** Retained; **Lowest/Average Salary:** $90,000/$90,000;
**Industry Concentration:** Electronics, High Technology, Venture Capital;
**Function Concentration:** Generalist with a primary focus in Engineering,
Finance/Accounting, General Management, Marketing, Research and
Development, Sales

**Furlong, James W.** — *President*
Furlong Search, Inc.
550 Tyndall Street, Suite 11
Los Altos, CA 94022
Telephone: (415) 856-8484
**Recruiter Classification:** Retained; **Lowest/Average Salary:** $90,000/$90,000;
**Industry Concentration:** Electronics, High Technology, Venture Capital;
**Function Concentration:** Generalist with a primary focus in Engineering,
Finance/Accounting, General Management, Marketing, Research and
Development, Sales

**Futornick, Bill** — *Consultant*
Paul Ray Berndtson
2029 Century Park East
Suite 1000
Los Angeles, CA 90067
Telephone: (310) 557-2828
**Recruiter Classification:** Retained; **Lowest/Average Salary:** $90,000/$90,000;
**Industry Concentration:** Generalist; **Function Concentration:** Generalist

**Fyhrie, David** — *Associate*
Source Services Corporation
3701 West Algonquin Road, Suite 380
Rolling Meadows, IL 60008
Telephone: (847) 392-0244
**Recruiter Classification:** Contingency; **Lowest/Average Salary:**
$30,000/$50,000; **Industry Concentration:** Financial Services, Information
Technology; **Function Concentration:** Engineering, Finance/Accounting

**Gabbay, Steve** — *Placement Manager*
Accounting & Bookkeeping Personnel, Inc.
1702 East Highland, Suite 200
Phoenix, AZ 85016
Telephone: (602) 277-3700
**Recruiter Classification:** Contingency; **Lowest/Average Salary:**
$20,000/$30,000; **Industry Concentration:** Generalist; **Function
Concentration:** Finance/Accounting

**Gabel, Gregory N.** — *Vice President*
Canny, Bowen Inc.
200 Park Avenue
New York, NY 10166
Telephone: (212) 949-6611
**Recruiter Classification:** Retained; **Lowest/Average Salary:** $90,000/$90,000;
**Industry Concentration:** Generalist with a primary focus in Consumer
Products, Fashion (Retail/Apparel), Financial Services, Hospitality/Leisure,
Manufacturing; **Function Concentration:** Generalist with a primary focus in
General Management, Human Resources, Marketing, Sales, Women/Minorities

**Gabler, Howard A.** — *President*
G.Z. Stephens Inc.
One World Trade Center
Suite 1527
New York, NY 10048
Telephone: (212) 321-3040
**Recruiter Classification:** Retained; **Lowest/Average Salary:** $90,000/$90,000;
**Industry Concentration:** Financial Services; **Function Concentration:** Generalist

**Gabriel, David L.** — *Managing Director*
The Arcus Group
100 North Central (At Main), Suite 1200
Dallas, TX 75201
Telephone: (214) 744-2100
**Recruiter Classification:** Retained; **Lowest/Average Salary:** $90,000/$90,000;
**Industry Concentration:** Generalist with a primary focus in Biotechnology,
Chemical Products, Consumer Products, Financial Services, High Technology,
Information Technology, Manufacturing, Transportation, Venture Capital;
**Function Concentration:** Generalist with a primary focus in Engineering,
Finance/Accounting, General Management, Human Resources, Marketing,
Women/Minorities

**Gadison, William** — *Executive Recruiter*
Richard, Wayne and Roberts
24 Greenway Plaza, Suite 1304
Houston, TX 77046-2493
Telephone: (713) 629-6681
**Recruiter Classification:** Retained; **Lowest/Average Salary:** $40,000/$60,000;
**Industry Concentration:** Generalist with a primary focus in Electronics, High
Technology; **Function Concentration:** Generalist

**Gaffney, Denise O'Grady** — *Senior Recruiter*
Isaacson, Miller
334 Boylston Street, Suite 500
Boston, MA 02111
Telephone: (617) 262-6500
**Recruiter Classification:** Retained; **Lowest/Average Salary:** $75,000/$90,000;
**Industry Concentration:** Generalist with a primary focus in
Healthcare/Hospitals; **Function Concentration:** Administration,
Finance/Accounting, General Management, Human Resources,
Women/Minorities

**Gaffney, Keith** — *Managing Director Executive Search*
Gaffney Management Consultants
35 North Brandon Drive
Glendale Heights, IL 60139-2087
Telephone: (708) 307-3380
**Recruiter Classification:** Retained; **Lowest/Average Salary:** $60,000/$90,000;
**Industry Concentration:** Generalist with a primary focus in
Aerospace/Defense, Automotive, Chemical Products, Electronics, High
Technology, Manufacturing, Transportation, Venture Capital; **Function
Concentration:** Generalist with a primary focus in Engineering, General
Management, Research and Development, Women/Minorities

**Gaffney, Megan** — *Associate*
Source Services Corporation
8614 Westwood Center, Suite 750
Vienna, VA 22182
Telephone: (703) 790-5610
**Recruiter Classification:** Contingency; **Lowest/Average Salary:**
$30,000/$50,000; **Industry Concentration:** Financial Services, Information
Technology; **Function Concentration:** Engineering, Finance/Accounting

**Gaffney, William** — *President*
Gaffney Management Consultants
35 North Brandon Drive
Glendale Heights, IL 60139-2087
Telephone: (708) 307-3380
**Recruiter Classification:** Retained; **Lowest/Average Salary:** $60,000/$90,000;
**Industry Concentration:** Generalist with a primary focus in
Aerospace/Defense, Automotive, Chemical Products, Electronics, High
Technology, Manufacturing, Transportation, Venture Capital; **Function
Concentration:** Generalist with a primary focus in Engineering, General
Management, Research and Development, Women/Minorities

**Gagan, Joan** — *Senior Vice President*
Gilbert Tweed/INESA
415 Madison Avenue
New York, NY 10017
Telephone: (212) 758-3000
**Recruiter Classification:** Retained; **Lowest/Average Salary:** $75,000/$90,000;
**Industry Concentration:** Generalist; **Function Concentration:** Generalist

**Gaillard, Bill** — *Manager North Atlantic Region*
Management Recruiters International, Inc.
835 Highland Avenue, SE
Hickory, NC 28602-1140
Telephone: (704) 324-2020
**Recruiter Classification:** Contingency; **Lowest/Average Salary:**
$30,000/$75,000; **Industry Concentration:** Generalist; **Function
Concentration:** Generalist

**Gaimster, Ann** — *Senior Vice President*
The Diversified Search Companies
2005 Market Street, Suite 3300
Philadelphia, PA 19103
Telephone: (215) 732-6666
**Recruiter Classification:** Retained; **Lowest/Average Salary:** $90,000/$90,000;
**Industry Concentration:** Generalist; **Function Concentration:** Generalist

**Gaines, Jay** — *President*
Jay Gaines & Company, Inc.
450 Park Avenue
New York, NY 10022
Telephone: (212) 308-9222
**Recruiter Classification:** Retained; **Lowest/Average Salary:** $90,000/$90,000;
**Industry Concentration:** Generalist with a primary focus in Financial Services,
Information Technology, Publishing/Media; **Function Concentration:**
Finance/Accounting, General Management, Human Resources, Marketing,
Sales

**Gaines, Ronni L.** — *President*
TOPAZ Legal Solutions
383 Northfield Avenue
West Orange, NJ 07052
Telephone: (201) 669-7300
**Recruiter Classification:** Executive Temporary; **Lowest/Average Salary:**
$40,000/$75,000; **Industry Concentration:** Chemical Products, Consumer
Products, Electronics, Entertainment, Environmental, Financial Services, High
Technology, Manufacturing; **Function Concentration:** Generalist with a
primary focus in Women/Minorities

**Gaines, Ronni L.** — *Partner*
TOPAZ International, Inc.
383 Northfield Avenue
West Orange, NJ 07052
Telephone: (201) 669-7300
**Recruiter Classification:** Contingency; **Lowest/Average Salary:**
$40,000/$75,000; **Industry Concentration:** Chemical Products, Consumer
Products, Electronics, Entertainment, Financial Services, High Technology,
Manufacturing, Pharmaceutical/Medical; **Function Concentration:** Generalist
with a primary focus in Women/Minorities

**Galante, Suzanne M.** — *Vice President*
Vlcek & Company, Inc.
620 Newport Center Drive
Suite 1100
Newport Beach, CA 92660
Telephone: (714) 752-0661
**Recruiter Classification:** Retained; **Lowest/Average Salary:** $75,000/$90,000;
**Industry Concentration:** Generalist with a primary focus in Biotechnology,
Chemical Products, Consumer Products, Electronics, Entertainment, Financial
Services, Healthcare/Hospitals, Hospitality/Leisure, Information Technology,
Manufacturing, Packaging, Pharmaceutical/Medical, Publishing/Media;
**Function Concentration:** Generalist with a primary focus in Administration,
Engineering, Finance/Accounting, General Management, Human Resources,
Marketing, Research and Development, Sales, Women/Minorities

**Gale, Rhoda E.** — *Senior Associate*
E.G. Jones Associates, Ltd.
1505 York Road
Lutherville, MD 21093
Telephone: (410) 337-4925
**Recruiter Classification:** Contingency; **Lowest/Average Salary:**
$40,000/$60,000; **Industry Concentration:** Biotechnology, Environmental,
High Technology; **Function Concentration:** Engineering, Marketing, Research
and Development, Sales

**Galinski, Paul** — *Assistant Vice President*
E.J. Ashton & Associates, Ltd.
P.O. Box 1048
Lake Zurich, IL 60047-1048
Telephone: (847) 540-9922
**Recruiter Classification:** Contingency; **Lowest/Average Salary:**
$30,000/$60,000; **Industry Concentration:** Insurance; **Function
Concentration:** Generalist with a primary focus in Administration,
Finance/Accounting, General Management, Marketing, Sales

**Gallagher, David W.** — *Senior Partner, Practice Leader
(Consumer Products)*
Lamalie Amrop International
191 Peachtree Street N.E.
Atlanta, GA 30303
Telephone: (404) 688-0800
**Recruiter Classification:** Retained; **Lowest/Average Salary:** $90,000/$90,000;
**Industry Concentration:** Generalist with a primary focus in Consumer
Products; **Function Concentration:** Generalist with a primary focus in
Finance/Accounting, General Management, Marketing, Sales

**Gallagher, Jim** — *Co-Manager Central Region*
Management Recruiters International, Inc.
2589 Washington Road, Suite 435
Pittsburgh, PA 15241
Telephone: (412) 831-7290
**Recruiter Classification:** Contingency; **Lowest/Average Salary:**
$30,000/$75,000; **Industry Concentration:** Generalist; **Function
Concentration:** Generalist

**Gallagher, Marilyn** — *Executive Vice President*
Hogan Acquisitions
7205 Chagrin Road #3
Chagrin Falls, OH 44023
Telephone: (216) 247-9600
**Recruiter Classification:** Retained; **Lowest/Average Salary:** $90,000/$90,000;
**Industry Concentration:** Generalist with a primary focus in Automotive,
Chemical Products, Consumer Products, Environmental, Fashion
(Retail/Apparel), Financial Services, High Technology, Information Technology,
Insurance, Manufacturing, Packaging, Publishing/Media, Transportation,
Venture Capital; **Function Concentration:** Generalist with a primary focus in
Administration, Engineering, Finance/Accounting, General Management,
Marketing

**Gallagher, Sallie** — *Co-Manager*
Management Recruiters International, Inc.
2589 Washington Road, Suite 435
Pittsburgh, PA 15241
Telephone: (412) 831-7290
**Recruiter Classification:** Contingency; **Lowest/Average Salary:**
$30,000/$75,000; **Industry Concentration:** Generalist; **Function
Concentration:** Generalist

**Gallagher, Terence M.** — *Chief Operating Officer*
Battalia Winston International
120 Wood Avenue, South
Iselin, NJ 08830
Telephone: (908) 549-2002
**Recruiter Classification:** Retained; **Lowest/Average Salary:** $90,000/$90,000;
**Industry Concentration:** Generalist with a primary focus in
Aerospace/Defense, Automotive, Board Services, Chemical Products,
Consumer Products, Electronics, Energy, Environmental, Fashion
(Retail/Apparel), Financial Services, Healthcare/Hospitals, High Technology,
Information Technology, Insurance, Manufacturing; **Function Concentration:**
Generalist with a primary focus in Administration, Finance/Accounting,
General Management, Human Resources, Marketing, Sales, Women/Minorities

**Gallin, Larry** — *President*
Gallin Associates
P.O. Box 13106
Clearwater, FL 34621
Telephone: (813) 724-8303
**Recruiter Classification:** Retained; **Lowest/Average Salary:** $50,000/$60,000;
**Industry Concentration:** Chemical Products, Environmental, Oil/Gas,
Pharmaceutical/Medical; **Function Concentration:** Engineering, General
Management, Marketing, Research and Development, Sales

**Galvani, Frank J.** — *Physician Recruiter*
MSI International
230 Peachtree Street, N.E.
Suite 1550
Atlanta, GA 30303
Telephone: (404) 653-7360
**Recruiter Classification:** Contingency; **Lowest/Average Salary:**
$30,000/$60,000; **Industry Concentration:** Generalist with a primary focus in
Healthcare/Hospitals; **Function Concentration:** Administration, Engineering,
Finance/Accounting, General Management, Marketing

**Gamble, Ira** — *Associate*
Source Services Corporation
1290 Oakmead Parkway, Suite 318
Sunnyvale, CA 94086
Telephone: (408) 738-8440
**Recruiter Classification:** Contingency; **Lowest/Average Salary:**
$30,000/$50,000; **Industry Concentration:** Financial Services, Information
Technology; **Function Concentration:** Engineering, Finance/Accounting

**Gandee, Bob** — *General Manager*
Management Recruiters International, Inc.
7550 Lucerne Drive, Suite 205
Cleveland, OH 44130
Telephone: (216) 243-5151
**Recruiter Classification:** Contingency; **Lowest/Average Salary:**
$30,000/$75,000; **Industry Concentration:** Generalist; **Function
Concentration:** Generalist

**Gandee, Bob** — *General Manager Central Region*
Management Recruiters International, Inc.
Tower East, Suite 703
20600 Chagrin Boulevard
Cleveland, OH 44122
Telephone: (216) 561-6776
**Recruiter Classification:** Contingency; **Lowest/Average Salary:**
$30,000/$75,000; **Industry Concentration:** Generalist; **Function
Concentration:** Generalist

**Gandee, John R.** — *Manager Southwest Region*
Management Recruiters International, Inc.
The Churchill Building, Suite 120
10707 Corporate Drive
Stafford, TX 77477-4001
Telephone: (713) 240-0220
**Recruiter Classification:** Contingency; **Lowest/Average Salary:**
$30,000/$75,000; **Industry Concentration:** Generalist; **Function
Concentration:** Generalist

**Gantar, Donna** — *Consultant*
Howard Fischer Associates, Inc.
1800 John F. Kennedy Boulevard, 7th Floor
Philadelphia, PA 19103
Telephone: (215) 568-8363
**Recruiter Classification:** Retained; **Lowest/Average Salary:** $90,000/$90,000;
**Industry Concentration:** Generalist; **Function Concentration:** Generalist

**Garcia, Joseph** — *Manager Pacific Region*
Management Recruiters International, Inc.
235 North Freeport Drive, Suite 6
Nogales, AZ 85621-2423
Telephone: (520) 281-9440
**Recruiter Classification:** Contingency; **Lowest/Average Salary:**
$30,000/$75,000; **Industry Concentration:** Generalist; **Function
Concentration:** Generalist

**Garcia, Samuel K.** — *Technical Recruiter*
Southwestern Professional Services
2451 Atrium Way
Nashville, TN 37214
Telephone: (615) 391-2722
**Recruiter Classification:** Contingency; **Lowest/Average Salary:**
$30,000/$50,000; **Industry Concentration:** Automotive, Consumer Products,
Healthcare/Hospitals, Information Technology, Manufacturing, Transportation;
**Function Concentration:** Engineering, Sales

**Gardiner, E. Nicholas P.** — *President*
Gardiner International
101 East 52nd Street
New York, NY 10022
Telephone: (212) 838-0707
**Recruiter Classification:** Retained; **Lowest/Average Salary:** $90,000/$90,000;
**Industry Concentration:** Generalist with a primary focus in Chemical Products,
Energy, Entertainment, Financial Services, Information Technology, Insurance,
Oil/Gas, Publishing/Media, Transportation; **Function Concentration:** Generalist
with a primary focus in Finance/Accounting, General Management

**Gardner, Catherine** — *Medical Recruiter*
Aureus Group
8744 Frederick Street
Omaha, NE 68124-3068
Telephone: (402) 397-2980
**Recruiter Classification:** Contingency; **Lowest/Average Salary:**
$30,000/$40,000; **Industry Concentration:** Healthcare/Hospitals; **Function**
**Concentration:** Administration, General Management

**Gardner, Dina** — *Accounting and Finance Recruiter*
Winter, Wyman & Company
950 Winter Street, Suite 3100
Waltham, MA 02154-1294
Telephone: (617) 890-7000
**Recruiter Classification:** Contingency; **Lowest/Average Salary:**
$20,000/$50,000; **Industry Concentration:** Generalist; **Function**
**Concentration:** Finance/Accounting

**Gardner, J.W.** — *General Manager Southwest Region*
Management Recruiters International, Inc.
1755 Lelia Drive, Suite 102
Jackson, MS 39216
Telephone: (601) 366-4488
**Recruiter Classification:** Contingency; **Lowest/Average Salary:**
$30,000/$75,000; **Industry Concentration:** Generalist; **Function**
**Concentration:** Generalist

**Gardner, John T.** — *Partner*
Heidrick & Struggles, Inc.
125 South Wacker Drive
Suite 2800
Chicago, IL 60606-4590
Telephone: (312) 372-8811
**Recruiter Classification:** Retained; **Lowest/Average Salary:** $75,000/$90,000;
**Industry Concentration:** Generalist with a primary focus in Consumer
Products; **Function Concentration:** Generalist

**Gardner, Michael** — *Associate*
Source Services Corporation
2 Penn Plaza, Suite 1176
New York, NY 10121
Telephone: (212) 760-2200
**Recruiter Classification:** Contingency; **Lowest/Average Salary:**
$30,000/$50,000; **Industry Concentration:** Financial Services, Information
Technology; **Function Concentration:** Engineering, Finance/Accounting

**Gardner, Ned** — *Senior Account Manager*
The Paladin Companies, Inc.
875 North Michigan Avenue, Suite 3218
Chicago, IL 60611
Telephone: (312) 654-2600
**Recruiter Classification:** Executive Temporary; **Lowest/Average Salary:**
$50,000/$90,000; **Industry Concentration:** Generalist; **Function**
**Concentration:** Marketing

**Gardy, Susan H.** — *Consultant*
Paul Ray Berndtson
101 Park Avenue, 41st Floor
New York, NY 10178
Telephone: (212) 370-1316
**Recruiter Classification:** Retained; **Lowest/Average Salary:** $90,000/$90,000;
**Industry Concentration:** Generalist; **Function Concentration:** Generalist

**Gares, Conrad** — *Executive Recruiter*
TSS Consulting, Ltd.
2425 East Camelback Road
Suite 375
Phoenix, AZ 85016
Telephone: (602) 955-7000
**Recruiter Classification:** Contingency; **Lowest/Average Salary:**
$60,000/$75,000; **Industry Concentration:** Aerospace/Defense, Electronics,
High Technology; **Function Concentration:** Engineering, General Management,
Marketing

**Garfinkle, Steven M.** — *Managing Director*
Battalia Winston International
20 William Street
Wellesley Hills, MA 02181
Telephone: (617) 239-1400
**Recruiter Classification:** Retained; **Lowest/Average Salary:** $90,000/$90,000;
**Industry Concentration:** Generalist with a primary focus in Automotive,
Biotechnology, Board Services, Chemical Products, Consumer Products,
Electronics, Financial Services, Healthcare/Hospitals, High Technology,
Information Technology, Insurance, Manufacturing, Non-Profit, Packaging,
Pharmaceutical/Medical, Publishing/Media; **Function Concentration:**
Generalist with a primary focus in Engineering, Finance/Accounting, General
Management, Human Resources, Marketing, Research and Development,
Sales, Women/Minorities

**Gargalli, Claire W.** — *Vice Chairman*
The Diversified Search Companies
2005 Market Street, Suite 3300
Philadelphia, PA 19103
Telephone: (215) 732-6666
**Recruiter Classification:** Retained; **Lowest/Average Salary:** $90,000/$90,000;
**Industry Concentration:** Generalist; **Function Concentration:** Generalist

**Gariano, Robert J.** — *Executive Director*
Russell Reynolds Associates, Inc.
200 South Wacker Drive
Suite 3600
Chicago, IL 60606
Telephone: (312) 993-9696
**Recruiter Classification:** Retained; **Lowest/Average Salary:** $90,000/$90,000;
**Industry Concentration:** Generalist; **Function Concentration:** Generalist

**Garman, Herb C.** — *Co-Manager Pacific Region*
Management Recruiters International, Inc.
6303 East Tanque Verde Road, Suite 230
Tucson, AZ 85715
Telephone: (520) 885-1560
**Recruiter Classification:** Contingency; **Lowest/Average Salary:**
$30,000/$75,000; **Industry Concentration:** Generalist; **Function**
**Concentration:** Generalist

**Garner, Ann** — *Manager*
Accountants on Call
100 Howe Avenue, Suite 210 North
Sacramento, CA 95825
Telephone: (916) 483-6666
**Recruiter Classification:** Contingency; **Lowest/Average Salary:**
$20,000/$30,000; **Industry Concentration:** Generalist; **Function**
**Concentration:** Finance/Accounting

**Garner, Ronald** — *Manager*
Accountants on Call
100 Howe Avenue, Suite 210 North
Sacramento, CA 95825
Telephone: (916) 483-6666
**Recruiter Classification:** Contingency; **Lowest/Average Salary:**
$20,000/$30,000; **Industry Concentration:** Generalist; **Function**
**Concentration:** Finance/Accounting

**Garrett, Donald L.** — *Principal*
Garrett Associates Inc.
P.O. Box 190189
Atlanta, GA 31119-0189
Telephone: (404) 364-0001
**Recruiter Classification:** Retained; **Lowest/Average Salary:** $50,000/$90,000;
**Industry Concentration:** Healthcare/Hospitals; **Function Concentration:**
Generalist with a primary focus in Administration, Engineering,
Finance/Accounting, General Management, Human Resources, Marketing,
Research and Development, Sales, Women/Minorities

**Garrett, Linda M.** — *Principal*
Garrett Associates Inc.
P.O. Box 190189
Atlanta, GA 31119-0189
Telephone: (404) 364-0001
**Recruiter Classification:** Retained; **Lowest/Average Salary:** $50,000/$90,000;
**Industry Concentration:** Healthcare/Hospitals; **Function Concentration:**
Generalist with a primary focus in Administration, Engineering,
Finance/Accounting, General Management, Human Resources, Marketing,
Research and Development, Sales, Women/Minorities

**Garrett, Mark** — *Associate*
Source Services Corporation
One CityPlace, Suite 170
St. Louis, MO 63141
Telephone: (314) 432-4500
**Recruiter Classification:** Contingency; **Lowest/Average Salary:**
$30,000/$50,000; **Industry Concentration:** Financial Services, Information
Technology; **Function Concentration:** Engineering, Finance/Accounting

**Garrity, Irene** — *Manager Eastern Region*
Management Recruiters International, Inc.
Westborough Office Park
2000 West Park Drive
Westborough, MA 01581-3901
Telephone: (508) 366-9900
**Recruiter Classification:** Contingency; **Lowest/Average Salary:**
$30,000/$75,000; **Industry Concentration:** Generalist; **Function
Concentration:** Generalist

**Gaskins, Kim** — *Associate*
Kenzer Corp.
1600 Parkwood Circle NW, Suite 310
Atlanta, GA 30339
Telephone: (770) 955-7210
**Recruiter Classification:** Retained; **Lowest/Average Salary:** $50,000/$90,000;
**Industry Concentration:** Generalist; **Function Concentration:** Generalist

**Gates, Douglas H.** — *Senior Vice President*
Skott/Edwards Consultants, Inc.
500 Fifth Avenue, 26th Floor
New York, NY 10110
Telephone: (212) 382-1166
**Recruiter Classification:** Retained; **Lowest/Average Salary:** $75,000/$90,000;
**Industry Concentration:** Generalist with a primary focus in Consumer
Products, Packaging; **Function Concentration:** Generalist

**Gates, Will** — *Senior Associate*
Korn/Ferry International
1800 Century Park East, Suite 900
Los Angeles, CA 90067
Telephone: (310) 552-1834
**Recruiter Classification:** Retained; **Lowest/Average Salary:** $90,000/$90,000;
**Industry Concentration:** Generalist; **Function Concentration:** Generalist

**Gatti, Robert D.** — *President*
R.D. Gatti & Associates, Incorporated
266 Main Street, Suite 21
Medfield, MA 02052
Telephone: (508) 359-4153
**Recruiter Classification:** Contingency; **Lowest/Average Salary:**
$40,000/$75,000; **Industry Concentration:** Generalist; **Function
Concentration:** Human Resources

**Gauny, Brian** — *Principal*
Merit Resource Group, Inc.
7950 Dublin Boulevard, Suite 205
Dublin, CA 94568
Telephone: (510) 828-4700
**Recruiter Classification:** Executive Temporary; **Lowest/Average Salary:**
$75,000/$90,000; **Industry Concentration:** Generalist; **Function
Concentration:** Human Resources

**Gauss, James W.** — *Shareholder*
Witt/Kieffer, Ford, Hadelman & Lloyd
1920 Main Street, Suite 310
Irvine, CA 92714
Telephone: (714) 851-5070
**Recruiter Classification:** Retained; **Lowest/Average Salary:** $75,000/$90,000;
**Industry Concentration:** Healthcare/Hospitals; **Function Concentration:**
Generalist with a primary focus in General Management

**Gauthier, Robert C.** — *Managing Director*
Columbia Consulting Group
20 South Charles Street, 9th Floor
Baltimore, MD 21201
Telephone: (410) 385-2525
**Recruiter Classification:** Retained; **Lowest/Average Salary:** $75,000/$90,000;
**Industry Concentration:** Generalist with a primary focus in Automotive,
Consumer Products, Electronics, Financial Services, Healthcare/Hospitals, High
Technology, Information Technology, Insurance, Manufacturing, Packaging,
Pharmaceutical/Medical, Publishing/Media; **Function Concentration:**
Generalist with a primary focus in Finance/Accounting, General Management,
Human Resources, Marketing, Research and Development

**Gaxiola, Alejandro** — *Associate*
Smith Search, S.C.
Fray Juan de Zumarraga 710
Col. Chapalita
Guadalajara, Jal., MEXICO 54030
Telephone: (523) 647-2470
**Recruiter Classification:** Retained; **Lowest/Average Salary:** $75,000/$90,000;
**Industry Concentration:** Generalist; **Function Concentration:** Generalist

**Geiger, Jan** — *Outplacement Manager*
Wilcox, Bertoux & Miller
100 Howe Avenue, Suite 155N
Sacramento, CA 95825
Telephone: (916) 977-3700
**Recruiter Classification:** Contingency; **Lowest/Average Salary:**
$40,000/$75,000; **Industry Concentration:** Biotechnology, Board Services,
Financial Services, Healthcare/Hospitals, Information Technology, Non-Profit;
**Function Concentration:** Administration, Finance/Accounting, General
Management

**Gelfman, David** — *Account Executive*
Career Management International
197 Route 18
East Brunswick, NJ 08816
Telephone: (908) 937-4800
**Recruiter Classification:** Retained; **Lowest/Average Salary:** $30,000/$50,000;
**Industry Concentration:** Fashion (Retail/Apparel); **Function Concentration:**
Generalist with a primary focus in General Management, Human Resources,
Marketing, Sales

**Gelinas, Lynn** — *Consultant Physician Search*
D. Brown and Associates, Inc.
610 S.W. Alder, Suite 1111
Portland, OR 97205
Telephone: (503) 224-6860
**Recruiter Classification:** Contingency; **Lowest/Average Salary:**
$90,000/$90,000; **Industry Concentration:** Healthcare/Hospitals

**Gennawey, Robert** — *Managing Director*
Source Services Corporation
One Park Plaza, Suite 560
Irvine, CA 92714
Telephone: (714) 660-1666
**Recruiter Classification:** Contingency; **Lowest/Average Salary:**
$30,000/$50,000; **Industry Concentration:** Financial Services, Information
Technology; **Function Concentration:** Engineering, Finance/Accounting

**Genser, Elaina S.** — *Partner*
Witt/Kieffer, Ford, Hadelman & Lloyd
2000 Powell Street, Suite 1645
Emeryville, CA 94608
Telephone: (510) 420-1370
**Recruiter Classification:** Retained; **Lowest/Average Salary:** $75,000/$90,000;
**Industry Concentration:** Healthcare/Hospitals; **Function Concentration:**
Generalist with a primary focus in General Management

**George, Delores F.** — *President and Owner*
Delores F. George Human Resource Management &
Consulting Industry
269 Hamilton Street, Suite 1
Worcester, MA 01604
Telephone: (508) 754-3451
**Recruiter Classification:** Contingency; **Lowest/Average Salary:** $/$50,000;
**Industry Concentration:** Generalist with a primary focus in Biotechnology,
Electronics, Environmental, Financial Services, Healthcare/Hospitals, High
Technology, Hospitality/Leisure, Information Technology, Insurance,
Manufacturing, Pharmaceutical/Medical, Public Administration,
Publishing/Media, Real Estate, Transportation; **Function Concentration:**
Generalist with a primary focus in Administration, Finance/Accounting,
General Management, Human Resources, Marketing, Research and
Development, Sales, Women/Minorities

**George, Scott** — *Medical Recruiter*
Aureus Group
8744 Frederick Street
Omaha, NE 68124-3068
Telephone: (402) 397-2980
**Recruiter Classification:** Contingency; **Lowest/Average Salary:**
$30,000/$40,000; **Industry Concentration:** Healthcare/Hospitals; **Function
Concentration:** General Management

**Gerber, Mark J.** — *Associate*
Wellington Management Group
117 South 17th Street, Suite 1625
Philadelphia, PA 19103
Telephone: (215) 569-8900
**Recruiter Classification:** Retained; **Lowest/Average Salary:** $75,000/$90,000;
**Industry Concentration:** Generalist with a primary focus in Chemical Products,
Financial Services, Healthcare/Hospitals; **Function Concentration:** Generalist with
a primary focus in Administration, Finance/Accounting, General Management

**Gerbosi, Karen** — *Vice President Records Management*
Hernand & Partners
770 Tamalpais Drive, Suite 204
Corte Madera, CA 94925
Telephone: (415) 927-7000
**Recruiter Classification:** Executive Temporary; **Industry Concentration:** High Technology, Information Technology; **Function Concentration:** Engineering

**Gerevas, Ronald E.** — *Managing Director*
Spencer Stuart
525 Market Street, Suite 3700
San Francisco, CA 94105
Telephone: (415) 495-4141
**Recruiter Classification:** Retained; **Lowest/Average Salary:** $90,000/$90,000; **Industry Concentration:** Generalist with a primary focus in Consumer Products, Entertainment, Hospitality/Leisure, Manufacturing, Non-Profit, Real Estate; **Function Concentration:** Generalist with a primary focus in Administration, General Management, Human Resources, Marketing, Sales

**Gerevas, Ronald E.** — *Managing Director*
Spencer Stuart
10900 Wilshire Boulevard, Suite 800
Los Angeles, CA 90024-6524
Telephone: (310) 209-0610
**Recruiter Classification:** Retained; **Lowest/Average Salary:** $90,000/$90,000; **Industry Concentration:** Generalist with a primary focus in Consumer Products, Entertainment, Hospitality/Leisure, Manufacturing, Non-Profit, Real Estate; **Function Concentration:** Generalist with a primary focus in Administration, General Management, Human Resources, Marketing, Sales

**Germain, Valerie** — *Managing Director*
Jay Gaines & Company, Inc.
450 Park Avenue
New York, NY 10022
Telephone: (212) 308-9222
**Recruiter Classification:** Retained; **Lowest/Average Salary:** $90,000/$90,000; **Industry Concentration:** Financial Services, Information Technology; **Function Concentration:** General Management, Marketing, Sales

**Germaine, Debra** — *Partner*
Fenwick Partners
57 Bedford Street, Suite 101
Lexington, MA 02173
Telephone: (617) 862-3370
**Recruiter Classification:** Retained; **Lowest/Average Salary:** $90,000/$90,000; **Industry Concentration:** Board Services, Electronics, High Technology, Information Technology; **Function Concentration:** Generalist

**Gerson, Russ D.** — *Managing Director*
Webb, Johnson Associates, Inc.
280 Park Avenue, 43rd Floor
New York, NY 10017
Telephone: (212) 661-3700
**Recruiter Classification:** Retained; **Lowest/Average Salary:** $90,000/$90,000; **Industry Concentration:** Generalist with a primary focus in Biotechnology, Chemical Products, Financial Services, Healthcare/Hospitals, High Technology, Non-Profit, Pharmaceutical/Medical; **Function Concentration:** Generalist

**Gerst, Tom J.** — *Manager Central Region*
Management Recruiters International, Inc.
1900 West Market Street
Akron, OH 44313-6927
Telephone: (330) 867-2900
**Recruiter Classification:** Contingency; **Lowest/Average Salary:** $30,000/$75,000; **Industry Concentration:** Generalist; **Function Concentration:** Generalist

**Gerstl, Ronald** — *Managing Director*
Maxecon Executive Search Consultants
9500 South Dadeland Boulevard, Suite 601
Miami, FL 33156
Telephone: (305) 670-1933
**Recruiter Classification:** Retained; **Lowest/Average Salary:** $75,000/$90,000; **Industry Concentration:** Generalist with a primary focus in Consumer Products; **Function Concentration:** Generalist with a primary focus in Finance/Accounting, General Management

**Gettys, James R.** — *President*
International Staffing Consultants, Inc.
500 Newport Center Drive, Suite 300
Newport Beach, CA 92660-7003
Telephone: (714) 721-7990
**Recruiter Classification:** Contingency, Executive Temporary; **Lowest/Average Salary:** $50,000/$75,000; **Industry Concentration:** Generalist with a primary focus in Chemical Products, Energy, Environmental, Oil/Gas, Utilities/Nuclear; **Function Concentration:** Generalist with a primary focus in Administration, Engineering, Finance/Accounting, Human Resources

**Getzkin, Helen** — *Senior Associate*
Korn/Ferry International
4816 IDS Center
Minneapolis, MN 55402
Telephone: (612) 333-1834
**Recruiter Classification:** Retained; **Lowest/Average Salary:** $90,000/$90,000; **Industry Concentration:** Generalist; **Function Concentration:** Generalist

**Giacalone, Louis** — *Associate*
Allard Associates
70 Pine Street, 60th Floor
New York, NY 10270
Telephone: (212) 770-7170
**Recruiter Classification:** Retained; **Lowest/Average Salary:** $60,000/$75,000; **Industry Concentration:** Financial Services; **Function Concentration:** Generalist with a primary focus in Administration, General Management, Marketing, Sales, Women/Minorities

**Gibb, Jeffrey B.** — *Consultant*
Coleman Legal Search Consultants
1435 Walnut Street, 3rd Floor
Philadelphia, PA 19102
Telephone: (215) 864-2700
**Recruiter Classification:** Contingency; **Lowest/Average Salary:** $60,000/$75,000; **Function Concentration:** Generalist

**Gibbons, Betsy** — *Partner*
The Caldwell Partners Amrop International
999 West Hastings Street
Suite 750
Vancouver, British Columbia, CANADA V6C 2W2
Telephone: (604) 669-3550
**Recruiter Classification:** Retained; **Lowest/Average Salary:** $/$90,000; **Industry Concentration:** Generalist; **Function Concentration:** Generalist

**Gibbs, John S.** — *Director*
Spencer Stuart
277 Park Avenue, 29th Floor
New York, NY 10172
Telephone: (212) 336-0200
**Recruiter Classification:** Retained; **Lowest/Average Salary:** $90,000/$90,000; **Industry Concentration:** Generalist with a primary focus in Board Services, Consumer Products, Electronics, Energy, Financial Services, High Technology, Hospitality/Leisure, Insurance, Manufacturing, Oil/Gas, Utilities/Nuclear, Venture Capital; **Function Concentration:** Generalist with a primary focus in Administration, Finance/Accounting, General Management, Human Resources, Marketing, Sales

**Gibson, Bruce** — *President*
Gibson & Company Inc.
250 North Sunnyslope Road, Suite 300
Brookfield, WI 53005
Telephone: (414) 785-8100
**Recruiter Classification:** Retained; **Lowest/Average Salary:** $90,000/$90,000; **Industry Concentration:** Generalist with a primary focus in Consumer Products, Education/Libraries, Electronics, Entertainment, Fashion (Retail/Apparel), Healthcare/Hospitals, Packaging; **Function Concentration:** Generalist

**Giella, Thomas J.** — *Vice President*
Korn/Ferry International
120 South Riverside Plaza
Suite 918
Chicago, IL 60606
Telephone: (312) 726-1841
**Recruiter Classification:** Retained; **Lowest/Average Salary:** $90,000/$90,000; **Industry Concentration:** Generalist with a primary focus in Healthcare/Hospitals; **Function Concentration:** Generalist

**Giesy, John** — *Associate*
Source Services Corporation
1105 Schrock Road, Suite 510
Columbus, OH 43229
Telephone: (614) 846-3311
**Recruiter Classification:** Contingency; **Lowest/Average Salary:** $30,000/$50,000; **Industry Concentration:** Financial Services, Information Technology; **Function Concentration:** Engineering, Finance/Accounting

**Gikas, Bill** — *Vice President*
Tarnow International
150 Morris Avenue
Springfield, NJ 07081
Telephone: (201) 376-3900
**Recruiter Classification:** Retained; **Lowest/Average Salary:** $90,000/$90,000; **Industry Concentration:** Generalist; **Function Concentration:** Generalist

**Gilbert, Carol** — *Principal*
Korn/Ferry International
1800 Century Park East, Suite 900
Los Angeles, CA 90067
Telephone: (310) 552-1834
**Recruiter Classification:** Retained; **Lowest/Average Salary:** $90,000/$90,000;
**Industry Concentration:** Generalist with a primary focus in
Healthcare/Hospitals; **Function Concentration:** Generalist

**Gilbert, Elaine** — *Vice President*
Herbert Mines Associates, Inc.
399 Park Avenue, 27th Floor
New York, NY 10022
Telephone: (212) 355-0909
**Recruiter Classification:** Retained; **Lowest/Average Salary:** $75,000/$90,000;
**Industry Concentration:** Board Services, Consumer Products, Fashion
(Retail/Apparel); **Function Concentration:** Generalist with a primary focus in
Finance/Accounting, General Management, Human Resources, Marketing,
Sales

**Gilbert, Jerry** — *Member Advisory Board*
Gilbert & Van Campen International
Graybar Building, 420 Lexington Avenue
New York, NY 10170
Telephone: (212) 661-2122
**Recruiter Classification:** Retained; **Lowest/Average Salary:** $90,000/$90,000;
**Industry Concentration:** Generalist with a primary focus in Fashion
(Retail/Apparel), Financial Services, High Technology, Manufacturing,
Pharmaceutical/Medical, Public Administration, Real Estate, Venture Capital;
**Function Concentration:** Generalist with a primary focus in
Finance/Accounting, General Management, Human Resources, Marketing,
Sales, Women/Minorities

**Gilbert, Keith A.** — *Co-Manager Pacific Region*
Management Recruiters International, Inc.
575 Price Street, Suite 313
Pismo Beach, CA 93449-2553
Telephone: (805) 773-2816
**Recruiter Classification:** Contingency; **Lowest/Average Salary:**
$30,000/$75,000; **Industry Concentration:** Generalist; **Function
Concentration:** Generalist

**Gilbert, Mary** — *Co-Manager*
Management Recruiters International, Inc.
575 Price Street, Suite 313
Pismo Beach, CA 93449-2553
Telephone: (805) 773-2816
**Recruiter Classification:** Contingency; **Lowest/Average Salary:** $30,000/$75,000;
**Industry Concentration:** Generalist; **Function Concentration:** Generalist

**Gilbert, Patricia G.** — *Associate*
Lynch Miller Moore Partners, Inc.
10 South Wacker Drive, Suite 2935
Chicago, IL 60606
Telephone: (312) 876-1505
**Recruiter Classification:** Retained; **Lowest/Average Salary:** $75,000/$90,000;
**Industry Concentration:** Generalist with a primary focus in Financial Services,
Manufacturing, Venture Capital; **Function Concentration:** Generalist with a
primary focus in Finance/Accounting, General Management, Human Resources

**Gilbert, Robert** — *Manager*
U.S. Envirosearch
445 Union Boulevard, Suite 225
Lakewood, CO 80228
Telephone: (303) 980-6600
**Recruiter Classification:** Contingency; **Lowest/Average Salary:**
$75,000/$90,000; **Industry Concentration:** Environmental; **Function
Concentration:** Generalist with a primary focus in Administration, Engineering,
Finance/Accounting, General Management, Marketing, Sales,
Women/Minorities

**Gilchrist, Carl C.** — *Partner*
Paul Ray Berndtson
191 Peachtree Tower, Suite 3800
191 Peachtree Street, NE
Atlanta, GA 30303-1757
Telephone: (404) 215-4600
**Recruiter Classification:** Retained; **Lowest/Average Salary:** $90,000/$90,000;
**Industry Concentration:** Generalist; **Function Concentration:** Generalist

**Gilchrist, Robert J.** — *Vice President*
Horton International
10 Tower Lane
Avon, CT 06001
Telephone: (860) 674-8701
**Recruiter Classification:** Retained; **Lowest/Average Salary:** $90,000/$90,000;
**Industry Concentration:** Generalist with a primary focus in
Aerospace/Defense, Automotive, Chemical Products, Consumer Products,
Electronics, Energy, High Technology, Information Technology, Manufacturing;
**Function Concentration:** Engineering, General Management, Research and
Development

**Giles, Joe L.** — *President*
Joe L. Giles and Associates, Inc.
18105 Parkside Street
Detroit, MI 48221
Telephone: (313) 864-0022
**Recruiter Classification:** Contingency; **Lowest/Average Salary:**
$30,000/$50,000; **Industry Concentration:** Generalist with a primary focus in
Aerospace/Defense, Automotive, Biotechnology, Consumer Products,
Electronics, Healthcare/Hospitals, High Technology, Information Technology,
Manufacturing, Pharmaceutical/Medical, Transportation; **Function
Concentration:** Engineering, Finance/Accounting, Human Resources, Research
and Development, Women/Minorities

**Gilinsky, David** — *Associate*
Source Services Corporation
3 Summit Park Drive, Suite 550
Independence, OH 44131
Telephone: (216) 328-5900
**Recruiter Classification:** Contingency; **Lowest/Average Salary:**
$30,000/$50,000; **Industry Concentration:** Financial Services, Information
Technology; **Function Concentration:** Engineering, Finance/Accounting

**Gill, Patricia** — *Managing Principal*
Columbia Consulting Group
P.O. Box 1483
Princeton, NJ 08542-1483
Telephone: (609) 466-8900
**Recruiter Classification:** Retained; **Lowest/Average Salary:** $75,000/$90,000;
**Industry Concentration:** Generalist with a primary focus in Consumer
Products, Electronics, Environmental, Financial Services, Healthcare/Hospitals,
High Technology, Information Technology, Insurance, Manufacturing,
Pharmaceutical/Medical, Publishing/Media, Transportation, Venture Capital;
**Function Concentration:** Generalist with a primary focus in
Finance/Accounting, General Management, Human Resources, Marketing,
Research and Development, Sales, Women/Minorities

**Gill, Susan** — *Consultant*
Plummer & Associates, Inc.
30 Myano Lane, Suite 36
Stamford, CT 06902
Telephone: (203) 965-7878
**Recruiter Classification:** Retained, Executive Temporary; **Lowest/Average
Salary:** $90,000/$90,000; **Industry Concentration:** Board Services, Consumer
Products, Entertainment, Fashion (Retail/Apparel), Financial Services,
Manufacturing, Venture Capital; **Function Concentration:** Generalist with a
primary focus in Administration, Finance/Accounting, General Management,
Marketing

**Gillespie, Kathleen M.** — *Consultant*
Witt/Kieffer, Ford, Hadelman & Lloyd
2015 Spring Road, Suite 510
Oak Brook, IL 60521
Telephone: (708) 990-1370
**Recruiter Classification:** Retained; **Lowest/Average Salary:** $75,000/$90,000;
**Industry Concentration:** Healthcare/Hospitals; **Function Concentration:**
Generalist with a primary focus in General Management

**Gillespie, Thomas** — *Contract Recruiter*
Professional Search Consultants
3050 Post Oak Boulevard, Suite 1615
Houston, TX 77056
Telephone: (713) 960-9215
**Recruiter Classification:** Executive Temporary; **Lowest/Average Salary:**
$50,000/$60,000; **Industry Concentration:** Generalist with a primary focus in
Biotechnology, Chemical Products, Energy, Environmental, Financial Services,
Healthcare/Hospitals, High Technology, Manufacturing, Oil/Gas; **Function
Concentration:** Generalist with a primary focus in Engineering, Human
Resources, Sales

**Gilliam, Dale** — *Co-Manager Pacific Region*
Management Recruiters International, Inc.
North 1212 Washington, Suite 300
Spokane, WA 99201
Telephone: (509) 324-3333
**Recruiter Classification:** Contingency; **Lowest/Average Salary:**
$30,000/$75,000; **Industry Concentration:** Generalist; **Function
Concentration:** Generalist

**Gillies, Margaret** — *Manager*
KPMG Executive Search
P.O. Box 31, Stn. Commerce Court
Toronto, Ontario, CANADA M5L 1B2
Telephone: (416) 777-8500
**Recruiter Classification:** Retained; **Lowest/Average Salary:** $75,000/$90,000;
**Industry Concentration:** Generalist; **Function Concentration:** Generalist

**Gilmartin, William** — *Associate*
Hockett Associates, Inc.
P.O. Box 1765
Los Altos, CA 94023
Telephone: (415) 941-8815
**Recruiter Classification:** Retained; **Lowest/Average Salary:** $90,000/$90,000;
**Industry Concentration:** Generalist with a primary focus in Biotechnology,
Board Services, Electronics, Entertainment, Environmental, High Technology,
Information Technology, Pharmaceutical/Medical, Venture Capital; **Function
Concentration:** Generalist with a primary focus in Engineering,
Finance/Accounting, General Management, Marketing, Research and
Development, Sales

**Gilmore, David A.** — *Vice President*
Elwell & Associates Inc.
301 East Liberty, Suite 535
Ann Arbor, MI 48104
Telephone: (313) 662-8775
**Recruiter Classification:** Retained; **Lowest/Average Salary:** $75,000/$90,000;
**Industry Concentration:** Generalist; **Function Concentration:** Generalist

**Gilmore, Jerry W.** — *Co-Manager*
Management Recruiters International, Inc.
44084 Riverside Parkway, Suite 170
Leesburg, VA 22075-5102
Telephone: (703) 729-5600
**Recruiter Classification:** Contingency; **Lowest/Average Salary:**
$30,000/$75,000; **Industry Concentration:** Generalist; **Function
Concentration:** Generalist

**Gilmore, Lori** — *Executive Recruiter*
CPS Inc.
One Westbrook Corporate Centre, Suite 600
Westchester, IL 60154
Telephone: (708) 531-8370
**Recruiter Classification:** Contingency; **Lowest/Average Salary:**
$30,000/$50,000; **Industry Concentration:** Generalist with a primary focus in
Automotive, Biotechnology, Chemical Products, Consumer Products, High
Technology, Insurance, Manufacturing, Oil/Gas, Packaging,
Pharmaceutical/Medical; **Function Concentration:** Engineering, Research and
Development, Sales, Women/Minorities

**Gilmore, Pam** — *Co-Manager Eastern Region*
Management Recruiters International, Inc.
44084 Riverside Parkway, Suite 170
Leesburg, VA 22075-5102
Telephone: (703) 729-5600
**Recruiter Classification:** Contingency; **Lowest/Average Salary:**
$30,000/$75,000; **Industry Concentration:** Generalist; **Function
Concentration:** Generalist

**Gilreath, James M.** — *President*
Gilreath Weatherby, Inc.
P.O. Box 1483 - Three Hidden Ledge Road
Manchester-by-the-Sea, MA 01944
Telephone: (508) 526-8771
**Recruiter Classification:** Retained; **Lowest/Average Salary:** $75,000/$90,000;
**Industry Concentration:** Generalist with a primary focus in
Aerospace/Defense, Consumer Products, High Technology, Manufacturing,
Venture Capital; **Function Concentration:** Generalist with a primary focus in
Engineering, Finance/Accounting, General Management, Human Resources,
Marketing

**Ginsberg, Sheldon M.** — *President*
Lloyd Prescott Associates, Inc.
One Presidents Plaza, Ste. 115
4902 Eisenhower Boulevard
Tampa, FL 33634
Telephone: (813) 881-1110
**Recruiter Classification:** Contingency; **Lowest/Average Salary:**
$60,000/$90,000; **Industry Concentration:** Generalist; **Function
Concentration:** Generalist

**Gionta, Michael E.** — *Manager Eastern Region*
Management Recruiters International, Inc.
711 Middletown Road
Colchester, CT 06415
Telephone: (860) 267-0680
**Recruiter Classification:** Contingency; **Lowest/Average Salary:**
$30,000/$75,000; **Industry Concentration:** Generalist; **Function
Concentration:** Generalist

**Gipson, Jeffrey** — *Vice President*
Bradford & Galt, Inc.
12400 Olive Boulevard, Suite 430
St. Louis, MO 63141
Telephone: (314) 434-9200
**Recruiter Classification:** Contingency; **Lowest/Average Salary:**
$30,000/$30,000; **Industry Concentration:** Generalist; **Function
Concentration:** Generalist

**Girsinger, Linda** — *Recruiter*
Industrial Recruiters Associates, Inc.
20 Hurlbut Street, 1st Floor
West Hartford, CT 06110
Telephone: (860) 953-3643
**Recruiter Classification:** Contingency; **Lowest/Average Salary:**
$30,000/$50,000; **Industry Concentration:** Generalist with a primary focus in
Consumer Products, Environmental, Transportation; **Function Concentration:**
Generalist with a primary focus in Women/Minorities

**Gitlin, Bernardo** — *Consultant*
Boyden
Paseo de la Reforma 509
110. Piso, Cuauhtemoc
Mexico City, D.F., MEXICO 06500
Telephone: (525) 553-7777
**Recruiter Classification:** Retained; **Lowest/Average Salary:** $90,000/$90,000;
**Industry Concentration:** Generalist with a primary focus in Fashion
(Retail/Apparel); **Function Concentration:** Generalist

**Glacy, Kurt** — *Software Engineering Recruiter*
Winter, Wyman & Company
950 Winter Street, Suite 3100
Waltham, MA 02154-1294
Telephone: (617) 890-7000
**Recruiter Classification:** Contingency; **Lowest/Average Salary:**
$40,000/$75,000; **Industry Concentration:** High Technology, Information
Technology, Publishing/Media; **Function Concentration:** Engineering

**Gladstone, Arthur** — *Vice President*
Executive Referral Services, Inc.
8770 West Bryn Mawr, Suite 110
Chicago, IL 60631
Telephone: (312) 693-6622
**Recruiter Classification:** Contingency; **Lowest/Average Salary:**
$30,000/$50,000; **Industry Concentration:** Biotechnology, Financial Services,
Healthcare/Hospitals, High Technology, Pharmaceutical/Medical; **Function
Concentration:** Finance/Accounting, General Management, Human Resources,
Marketing, Research and Development, Sales

**Gladstone, Martin J.** — *Executiver Recruiter*
MSI International
229 Peachtree Street, NE
Suite 1201
Atlanta, GA 30303
Telephone: (404) 659-5050
**Recruiter Classification:** Contingency; **Lowest/Average Salary:**
$30,000/$75,000; **Industry Concentration:** Generalist with a primary focus in
Information Technology; **Function Concentration:** Generalist with a primary
focus in Administration, Engineering, Finance/Accounting, General
Management, Marketing, Sales

**Glancey, Thomas F.** — *President*
Gordon Wahls Company
P.O. Box 905
610 East Baltimore Pike
Media, PA 19063
Telephone: (610) 565-0800
**Recruiter Classification:** Contingency; **Lowest/Average Salary:**
$30,000/$60,000; **Industry Concentration:** Packaging, Publishing/Media;
**Function Concentration:** Generalist with a primary focus in Administration,
Engineering, Finance/Accounting, General Management, Marketing, Sales

**Glass, Lori** — *Vice President*
The Executive Source
55 Fifth Avenue, 19th Floor
New York, NY 10003
Telephone: (212) 691-5505
**Recruiter Classification:** Executive Temporary; **Lowest/Average Salary:**
$75,000/$90,000; **Industry Concentration:** Generalist with a primary focus in
Financial Services, Insurance, Venture Capital; **Function Concentration:**
Human Resources

**Glass, Sharon** — *Director*
Logix, Inc.
1601 Trapelo Road
Waltham, MA 02154
Telephone: (617) 890-0500
**Recruiter Classification:** Retained; **Lowest/Average Salary:** $60,000/$75,000;
**Industry Concentration:** High Technology; **Function Concentration:**
Engineering

**Glass, Sharon** — *Consultant/Director*
Logix Partners
1601 Trapelo Road
Waltham, MA 02154
Telephone: (617) 890-0500
**Recruiter Classification:** Retained; **Lowest/Average Salary:** $60,000/$75,000;
**Industry Concentration:** High Technology; **Function Concentration:**
Engineering

**Glatman, Marcia** — *President*
HRD Consultants, Inc.
60 Walnut Avenue
Clark, NJ 07066
Telephone: (908) 815-7825
**Recruiter Classification:** Retained; **Lowest/Average Salary:** $90,000/$90,000;
**Industry Concentration:** Generalist; **Function Concentration:** Human
Resources

**Glaza, Ron** — *Manager Pacific Region*
Management Recruiters International, Inc.
Quintana Plaza
365 Quintana Road, Suite D
Morro Bay, CA 93442-2000
Telephone: (805) 772-1964
**Recruiter Classification:** Contingency; **Lowest/Average Salary:**
$30,000/$75,000; **Industry Concentration:** Generalist; **Function
Concentration:** Generalist

**Gleason-Lianopolis, Helen W.** — *Manager South Atlantic Region*
Management Recruiters International, Inc.
1305 South Michigan Avenue, P.O. Box 7711
Clearwater, FL 34618-7711
Telephone: (813) 791-3277
**Recruiter Classification:** Contingency; **Lowest/Average Salary:**
$30,000/$75,000; **Industry Concentration:** Generalist; **Function
Concentration:** Generalist

**Gleckman, Mark** — *Branch Manager/Accounting and Finance Recruiter*
Winter, Wyman & Company
101 Federal Street, 27th Floor
Boston, MA 02110-1800
Telephone: (617) 951-2700
**Recruiter Classification:** Contingency; **Lowest/Average Salary:**
$20,000/$50,000; **Industry Concentration:** Generalist; **Function
Concentration:** Finance/Accounting

**Glennie, Francisco** — *Partner*
Ward Howell International, Inc.
Rexer Seleccion de Ejecutivos, S.C.
Blvd. Adolfo Lopez Mateos 20, Col. San Angel Inn
Mexico City, D.F., MEXICO 01060
Telephone: (525) 550-9180
**Recruiter Classification:** Retained; **Lowest/Average Salary:** $75,000/$90,000;
**Industry Concentration:** Automotive, Consumer Products; **Function
Concentration:** Generalist with a primary focus in Human Resources

**Glickman, Leenie** — *Associate*
Source Services Corporation
20 Burlington Mall Road, Suite 405
Burlington, MA 01803
Telephone: (617) 272-5000
**Recruiter Classification:** Contingency; **Lowest/Average Salary:**
$30,000/$50,000; **Industry Concentration:** Financial Services, Information
Technology; **Function Concentration:** Engineering, Finance/Accounting

**Gloss, Frederick C.** — *President*
F. Gloss International
1595 Spring Hill Road, Suite 350
Vienna, VA 22182
Telephone: (703) 847-0010
**Recruiter Classification:** Retained; **Lowest/Average Salary:** $60,000/$75,000;
**Industry Concentration:** Aerospace/Defense, High Technology, Information
Technology; **Function Concentration:** Engineering, General Management,
Marketing, Research and Development, Sales

**Glueck, Sharon** — *Owner*
Career Temps, Inc.
6710 Main Street, Suite 234
Miami Lakes, FL 33014
Telephone: (305) 558-1700
**Recruiter Classification:** Executive Temporary; **Lowest/Average Salary:**
$20,000/$30,000; **Industry Concentration:** Generalist; **Function
Concentration:** Finance/Accounting, Human Resources

**Gluzman, Arthur** — *Associate*
Source Services Corporation
2000 Town Center, Suite 850
Southfield, MI 48075
Telephone: (810) 352-6520
**Recruiter Classification:** Contingency; **Lowest/Average Salary:**
$30,000/$50,000; **Industry Concentration:** Financial Services, Information
Technology; **Function Concentration:** Engineering, Finance/Accounting

**Gnatowski, Bruce** — *Associate*
Source Services Corporation
8614 Westwood Center, Suite 750
Vienna, VA 22182
Telephone: (703) 790-5610
**Recruiter Classification:** Contingency; **Lowest/Average Salary:**
$30,000/$50,000; **Industry Concentration:** Financial Services, Information
Technology; **Function Concentration:** Engineering, Finance/Accounting

**Goar, Duane R.** — *Partner*
Sandhurst Associates
4851 LBJ Freeway, Suite 601
Dallas, TX 75244
Telephone: (214) 458-1212
**Recruiter Classification:** Retained; **Lowest/Average Salary:** $75,000/$90,000;
**Industry Concentration:** Generalist with a primary focus in Consumer
Products, Education/Libraries, Entertainment, Financial Services,
Healthcare/Hospitals, High Technology, Hospitality/Leisure, Insurance,
Manufacturing, Pharmaceutical/Medical, Real Estate, Transportation; **Function
Concentration:** Generalist with a primary focus in Finance/Accounting, Human
Resources, Marketing, Sales

**Gobert, Larry** — *Chief Operating Officer*
Professional Search Consultants
3050 Post Oak Boulevard, Suite 1615
Houston, TX 77056
Telephone: (713) 960-9215
**Recruiter Classification:** Executive Temporary; **Lowest/Average Salary:**
$75,000/$75,000; **Industry Concentration:** Generalist with a primary focus in
Chemical Products, Electronics, Energy, Environmental, Financial Services,
Healthcare/Hospitals, High Technology, Oil/Gas, Venture Capital; **Function
Concentration:** Generalist with a primary focus in Finance/Accounting,
General Management

**Goebel, George A.** — *Vice President*
John Kurosky & Associates
3 Corporate Park Drive, Suite 210
Irvine, CA 92714
Telephone: (714) 851-6370
**Recruiter Classification:** Retained; **Lowest/Average Salary:** $60,000/$90,000;
**Industry Concentration:** Chemical Products, Environmental,
Pharmaceutical/Medical; **Function Concentration:** Generalist

**Goedtke, Steven** — *Consultant*
Southwestern Professional Services
2451 Atrium Way
Nashville, TN 37214
Telephone: (615) 391-2722
**Recruiter Classification:** Contingency; **Lowest/Average Salary:**
$30,000/$50,000; **Industry Concentration:** Generalist with a primary focus in
Education/Libraries, Electronics, Fashion (Retail/Apparel), Financial Services,
High Technology, Information Technology, Insurance, Manufacturing; **Function
Concentration:** Sales

**Goicoechea, Lydia** — *Co-Manager Southwest Region*
Management Recruiters International, Inc.
7550 Interstate Highway 10 West, Suite 1230
San Antonio, TX 78229
Telephone: (210) 525-1800
**Recruiter Classification:** Contingency; **Lowest/Average Salary:**
$30,000/$75,000; **Industry Concentration:** Generalist; **Function
Concentration:** Generalist

**Goicoechea, Sam** — *Co-Manager*
Management Recruiters International, Inc.
7550 Interstate Highway 10 West, Suite 1230
San Antonio, TX 78229
Telephone: (210) 525-1800
**Recruiter Classification:** Contingency; **Lowest/Average Salary:**
$30,000/$75,000; **Industry Concentration:** Generalist; **Function
Concentration:** Generalist

**Gold, Stacey** — *Research Associate*
Earley Kielty and Associates, Inc.
Two Pennsylvania Plaza
New York, NY 10121
Telephone: (212) 736-5626
**Recruiter Classification:** Retained; **Lowest/Average Salary:** $90,000/$90,000;
**Industry Concentration:** Generalist with a primary focus in Information
Technology; **Function Concentration:** Generalist with a primary focus in
Administration, Finance/Accounting, General Management, Human Resources,
Marketing, Research and Development, Sales, Women/Minorities

**Gold, Stanley** — *Account Executive*
Search West, Inc.
100 Pine Street, Suite 2500
San Francisco, CA 94111-5203
Telephone: (415) 788-1770
**Recruiter Classification:** Contingency; **Lowest/Average Salary:**
$40,000/$60,000; **Industry Concentration:** Manufacturing; **Function
Concentration:** Engineering, Research and Development

**Goldberg, Bret** — *Director Restaurant and Fast Food Division*
Roth Young Personnel Service of Boston, Inc.
200 Boston Avenue, Suite 2300
Medford, MA 02155
Telephone: (617) 395-3600
**Recruiter Classification:** Contingency; **Lowest/Average Salary:**
$30,000/$30,000; **Function Concentration:** Finance/Accounting, General
Management, Human Resources, Marketing, Sales

**Goldberg, Susan C.** — *President*
Susan C. Goldberg Associates
65 LaSalle Road
West Hartford, CT 06107
Telephone: (860) 236-4597
**Recruiter Classification:** Contingency; **Lowest/Average Salary:**
$40,000/$60,000; **Industry Concentration:** Aerospace/Defense, High
Technology, Insurance, Manufacturing; **Function Concentration:**
Finance/Accounting

**Goldenberg, Sheryl** — *Director Research/Associate*
Neail Behringer Consultants
24 East 38th Street
New York, NY 10016
Telephone: (212) 689-7555
**Recruiter Classification:** Retained; **Lowest/Average Salary:** $40,000/$75,000;
**Industry Concentration:** Generalist with a primary focus in Fashion
(Retail/Apparel), Healthcare/Hospitals; **Function Concentration:** Generalist
with a primary focus in Administration, General Management, Marketing

**Goldenberg, Susan** — *Senior Associate*
Grant Cooper and Associates
795 Office Parkway, Suite 117
St. Louis, MO 63141
Telephone: (314) 567-4690
**Recruiter Classification:** Retained; **Lowest/Average Salary:** $60,000/$90,000;
**Industry Concentration:** Generalist with a primary focus in Board Services,
Chemical Products, Consumer Products, Electronics, Fashion (Retail/Apparel),
Financial Services, Healthcare/Hospitals, High Technology, Information
Technology, Insurance, Manufacturing, Non-Profit, Packaging, Venture Capital;
**Function Concentration:** Generalist with a primary focus in Administration,
Engineering, Finance/Accounting, General Management, Human Resources,
Marketing, Research and Development, Sales

**Goldfarb-Lee, Terry** — *Principal*
O'Shea, Divine & Company, Inc.
610 Newport Center Drive, Suite 1040
Newport Beach, CA 92660
Telephone: (714) 720-9070
**Recruiter Classification:** Retained; **Lowest/Average Salary:** $75,000/$90,000;
**Industry Concentration:** Generalist; **Function Concentration:** Generalist

**Golding, Robert L.** — *Managing Partner*
Lamalie Amrop International
Chevron Tower
1301 McKinney Street
Houston, TX 77010-3034
Telephone: (713) 739-8602
**Recruiter Classification:** Retained; **Lowest/Average Salary:** $90,000/$90,000;
**Industry Concentration:** Generalist; **Function Concentration:** Generalist

**Goldman, Elaine** — *Legal Recruiter*
Phyllis Hawkins & Associates, Inc.
3550 North Central Avenue, Suite 1400
Phoenix, AZ 85012
Telephone: (602) 263-0248
**Recruiter Classification:** Contingency; **Lowest/Average Salary:**
$60,000/$90,000

**Goldman, Michael L.** — *President/Executive Recruiter*
Strategic Associates, Inc.
13915 Burnet Road, Suite 304
Austin, TX 78728
Telephone: (512) 218-8222
**Recruiter Classification:** Contingency; **Lowest/Average Salary:**
$60,000/$75,000; **Industry Concentration:** Automotive, Chemical Products,
Consumer Products, Electronics, High Technology, Information Technology,
Manufacturing, Pharmaceutical/Medical; **Function Concentration:** General
Management, Women/Minorities

**Goldsmith, Fred J.** — *President*
Fred J. Goldsmith Associates
14056 Margate Street
Sherman Oaks, CA 91401
Telephone: (818) 783-3931
**Recruiter Classification:** Retained; **Lowest/Average Salary:** $60,000/$75,000;
**Industry Concentration:** Generalist with a primary focus in Aerospace/Defense,
Consumer Products, Electronics, Energy, Fashion (Retail/Apparel), High
Technology, Manufacturing, Oil/Gas, Transportation; **Function Concentration:**
Generalist with a primary focus in Engineering, Finance/Accounting, General
Management, Human Resources, Marketing, Sales

**Goldsmith, Phillip R.** — *Executive Vice President and COO*
The Diversified Search Companies
2005 Market Street, Suite 3300
Philadelphia, PA 19103
Telephone: (215) 732-6666
**Recruiter Classification:** Retained; **Lowest/Average Salary:** $90,000/$90,000;
**Industry Concentration:** Generalist; **Function Concentration:** Generalist

**Goldson, Bob** — *Principal*
The McCormick Group, Inc.
20 Walnut Street, Suite 308
Wellesley Hills, MA 02181
Telephone: (617) 239-1233
**Recruiter Classification:** Retained; **Lowest/Average Salary:** $60,000/$75,000;
**Industry Concentration:** Insurance, Pharmaceutical/Medical; **Function
Concentration:** Generalist

**Goldstein, Gary** — *President*
The Whitney Group
850 Third Avenue, 11th Floor
New York, NY 10022
Telephone: (212) 508-3500
**Recruiter Classification:** Retained; **Lowest/Average Salary:** $75,000/$90,000;
**Industry Concentration:** Generalist with a primary focus in Financial Services,
Real Estate, Venture Capital; **Function Concentration:** Generalist with a
primary focus in Sales

**Goldstein, Steve** — *Senior Vice President*
R. Parker and Associates, Inc.
551 5th Avenue, Suite 222
New York, NY 10176
Telephone: (212) 661-8074
**Recruiter Classification:** Retained; **Lowest/Average Salary:** $50,000/$75,000;
**Industry Concentration:** Generalist with a primary focus in Consumer
Products, Fashion (Retail/Apparel); **Function Concentration:** Generalist with a
primary focus in General Management, Marketing, Sales

**Gomez, Paul** — *Director Utility Search Services*
ARJay & Associates
875 Walnut Street, Suite 150
Cary, NC 27511
Telephone: (919) 469-5540
**Recruiter Classification:** Contingency; **Lowest/Average Salary:**
$40,000/$90,000; **Industry Concentration:** Generalist with a primary focus in
Utilities/Nuclear; **Function Concentration:** Generalist with a primary focus in
Engineering, Finance/Accounting, General Management, Human Resources,
Marketing, Research and Development, Sales

**Gonye, Peter K.** — *Consultant*
Egon Zehnder International Inc.
55 East 59th Street, 14th Floor
New York, NY 10022
Telephone: (212) 838-9199
**Recruiter Classification:** Retained; **Lowest/Average Salary:** $90,000/$90,000;
**Industry Concentration:** Generalist with a primary focus in Biotechnology,
Financial Services, High Technology, Manufacturing, Pharmaceutical/Medical;
**Function Concentration:** Generalist

**Gonzalez, Naomi** — *Director Research*
McManners Associates, Inc.
400 East 54th Street, 16th Floor
New York, NY 10022
Telephone: (212) 980-7140
**Recruiter Classification:** Retained; **Lowest/Average Salary:** $90,000/$90,000;
**Industry Concentration:** Generalist with a primary focus in Manufacturing;
**Function Concentration:** Generalist

**Gonzalez, Romulo H.** — *Vice President*
Korn/Ferry International
Daniel Zambrano 525
Col. Chepe Vera
Monterrey, N.L., MEXICO 11000
Telephone: (528) 348-4355
**Recruiter Classification:** Retained; **Lowest/Average Salary:** $90,000/$90,000;
**Industry Concentration:** Generalist; **Function Concentration:** Generalist

**Gonzalez de Coindreau, Alicia M.** — *Junior Associate*
Korn/Ferry International
Daniel Zambrano 525
Col. Chepe Vera
Monterrey, N.L., MEXICO 11000
Telephone: (528) 348-4355
**Recruiter Classification:** Retained; **Lowest/Average Salary:** $90,000/$90,000;
**Industry Concentration:** Generalist; **Function Concentration:** Generalist

**Gonzalez de la Rocha, Sergio** — *Principal*
Korn/Ferry International
Daniel Zambrano 525
Col. Chepe Vera
Monterrey, N.L., MEXICO 11000
Telephone: (528) 348-4355
**Recruiter Classification:** Retained; **Lowest/Average Salary:** $90,000/$90,000;
**Industry Concentration:** Generalist; **Function Concentration:** Generalist

**Gonzalez-Miller, Laura** — *Co-Owner/Manager*
Management Recruiters International, Inc.
Prestwick Pointe
5250 East US 36, Suite 730
Danville, IN 46122-9771
Telephone: (317) 745-2284
**Recruiter Classification:** Contingency; **Lowest/Average Salary:** $30,000/$75,000;
**Industry Concentration:** Generalist; **Function Concentration:** Generalist

**Gooch, Randy** — *Executive Recruiter*
Richard, Wayne and Roberts
24 Greenway Plaza, Suite 1304
Houston, TX 77046-2493
Telephone: (713) 629-6681
**Recruiter Classification:** Retained; **Lowest/Average Salary:** $40,000/$60,000;
**Industry Concentration:** Generalist with a primary focus in
Healthcare/Hospitals; **Function Concentration:** Generalist with a primary focus
in Administration, General Management, Marketing

**Good, Bob B.** — *Co-Manager*
Management Recruiters International, Inc.
2600 South Minnesota Avenue, Suite 202
Sioux Falls, SD 57105-4731
Telephone: (605) 334-9291
**Recruiter Classification:** Contingency; **Lowest/Average Salary:** $30,000/$75,000;
**Industry Concentration:** Generalist; **Function Concentration:** Generalist

**Good, Dave J.** — *Co-Manager Midwest Region*
Management Recruiters International, Inc.
2600 South Minnesota Avenue, Suite 202
Sioux Falls, SD 57105-4731
Telephone: (605) 334-9291
**Recruiter Classification:** Contingency; **Lowest/Average Salary:** $30,000/$75,000;
**Industry Concentration:** Generalist; **Function Concentration:** Generalist

**Goodere, Greg** — *Associate*
Splaine & Associates, Inc.
15951 Los Gatos Boulevard
Los Gatos, CA 95032
Telephone: (408) 354-3664
**Recruiter Classification:** Retained; **Lowest/Average Salary:** $90,000/$90,000;
**Industry Concentration:** Generalist with a primary focus in Electronics, High
Technology; **Function Concentration:** Generalist

**Goodman, Dawn M.** — *Project Associate*
Bason Associates Inc.
11311 Cornell Park Drive
Cincinnati, OH 45242
Telephone: (513) 469-9881
**Recruiter Classification:** Retained; **Lowest/Average Salary:** $60,000/$90,000;
**Industry Concentration:** Generalist with a primary focus in Automotive,
Biotechnology, Board Services, Chemical Products, Consumer Products,
Environmental, Fashion (Retail/Apparel), Financial Services, Healthcare/Hospitals,
High Technology, Insurance, Manufacturing, Packaging, Pharmaceutical/Medical,
Public Administration; **Function Concentration:** Generalist with a primary focus in
Administration, Engineering, Finance/Accounting, General Management, Human
Resources, Marketing, Research and Development, Sales

**Goodman, Julie** — *Account Executive*
Search West, Inc.
750 The City Drive South
Suite 100
Orange, CA 92668-4940
Telephone: (714) 748-0400
**Recruiter Classification:** Contingency; **Lowest/Average Salary:**
$40,000/$60,000; **Industry Concentration:** Financial Services; **Function
Concentration:** Administration, Finance/Accounting

**Goodman, Victor** — *President*
Anderson Sterling Associates
18623 Ventura Boulevard, Suite 207
Tarzana, CA 91356
Telephone: (818) 996-0921
**Recruiter Classification:** Executive Temporary; **Lowest/Average Salary:**
$30,000/$60,000; **Industry Concentration:** Biotechnology, Consumer
Products, Electronics, High Technology, Information Technology,
Manufacturing, Pharmaceutical/Medical; **Function Concentration:** Engineering,
Finance/Accounting, General Management, Human Resources, Marketing,
Research and Development, Sales, Women/Minorities

**Goodridge, Benjamin** — *Executive Recruiter*
S.C. International, Ltd.
1430 Branding Lane, Suite 119
Downers Grove, IL 60515
Telephone: (708) 963-3033
**Recruiter Classification:** Contingency; **Lowest/Average Salary:**
$30,000/$50,000; **Industry Concentration:** Information Technology, Insurance;
**Function Concentration:** Administration, Human Resources

**Goodspeed, Peter W.** — *Consultant*
Witt/Kieffer, Ford, Hadelman & Lloyd
8117 Preston Road, Suite 690
Dallas, TX 75225
Telephone: (214) 739-1370
**Recruiter Classification:** Retained; **Lowest/Average Salary:** $75,000/$90,000;
**Industry Concentration:** Healthcare/Hospitals; **Function Concentration:**
Generalist with a primary focus in General Management

**Goodwin, Gary** — *Associate*
Source Services Corporation
2 Penn Plaza, Suite 1176
New York, NY 10121
Telephone: (212) 760-2200
**Recruiter Classification:** Contingency; **Lowest/Average Salary:**
$30,000/$50,000; **Industry Concentration:** Financial Services, Information
Technology; **Function Concentration:** Engineering, Finance/Accounting

**Goodwin, Joe D.** — *Managing Partner*
Lamalie Amrop International
191 Peachtree Street N.E.
Atlanta, GA 30303
Telephone: (404) 688-0800
**Recruiter Classification:** Retained; **Lowest/Average Salary:** $90,000/$90,000;
**Industry Concentration:** Generalist; **Function Concentration:** Generalist with a
primary focus in Finance/Accounting, General Management

**Goodwin, Melissa** — *Associate*
Financial Search Corporation
2720 Des Plaines Avenue, Suite 106
Des Plaines, IL 60018
Telephone: (708) 297-4900
**Recruiter Classification:** Contingency; **Lowest/Average Salary:**
$30,000/$50,000; **Industry Concentration:** Generalist; **Function
Concentration:** Finance/Accounting

**Goodwin, Tom** — *President*
Goodwin & Company
1320 19th Street N.W., Suite 801
Washington, DC 20036
Telephone: (202) 785-9292
**Recruiter Classification:** Retained; **Lowest/Average Salary:** $50,000/$75,000;
**Industry Concentration:** Generalist; **Function Concentration:** Generalist

**Gordon, Elliot** — *Vice President*
Korn/Ferry International
1300 Dove Street
Suite 300
Newport Beach, CA 92660
Telephone: (714) 851-1834
**Recruiter Classification:** Retained; **Lowest/Average Salary:** $90,000/$90,000;
**Industry Concentration:** Generalist with a primary focus in High Technology;
**Function Concentration:** Generalist

**Gordon, Gene** — *Consultant*
The McCormick Group, Inc.
20 Walnut Street, Suite 308
Wellesley Hills, MA 02181
Telephone: (617) 239-1233
**Recruiter Classification:** Retained; **Lowest/Average Salary:** $60,000/$75,000;
**Industry Concentration:** Generalist; **Function Concentration:** Generalist

**Gordon, Gerald L.** — *Senior Associate*
E.G. Jones Associates, Ltd.
1505 York Road
Lutherville, MD 21093
Telephone: (410) 337-4925
**Recruiter Classification:** Contingency; **Lowest/Average Salary:**
$20,000/$50,000; **Industry Concentration:** Generalist with a primary focus in
Automotive, Consumer Products, Entertainment, Financial Services,
Healthcare/Hospitals, Hospitality/Leisure, Information Technology,
Manufacturing, Pharmaceutical/Medical, Real Estate, Transportation; **Function
Concentration:** Generalist with a primary focus in Administration,
Finance/Accounting, General Management, Marketing, Sales

**Gordon, Gloria** — *Vice President*
A.T. Kearney, Inc.
Biltmore Tower
500 South Grand Avenue
Los Angeles, CA 90071
Telephone: (213) 689-6800
**Recruiter Classification:** Retained; **Lowest/Average Salary:** $90,000/$90,000;
**Industry Concentration:** Generalist with a primary focus in Information
Technology; **Function Concentration:** Generalist

**Gordon, Jacqueline** — *Consultant*
Evie Kreisler & Associates, Inc.
2575 Peachtree Road, Suite 300
Atlanta, GA 30305
Telephone: (404) 262-0599
**Recruiter Classification:** Contingency; **Lowest/Average Salary:**
$30,000/$75,000; **Industry Concentration:** Fashion (Retail/Apparel); **Function
Concentration:** Generalist

**Gordon, Teri** — *Director*
Don Richard Associates of Washington, D.C., Inc.
8180 Greensboro Drive, Suite 1020
McLean, VA 22102
Telephone: (703) 827-5990
**Recruiter Classification:** Executive Temporary; **Lowest/Average Salary:**
$20,000/$30,000; **Industry Concentration:** Financial Services, High
Technology, Non-Profit, Real Estate; **Function Concentration:** Administration,
Finance/Accounting, Human Resources

**Gordon, Trina D.** — *Partner*
Boyden
2 Prudential Plaza, Suite 5050
180 North Stetson Avenue
Chicago, IL 60601
Telephone: (312) 565-1300
**Recruiter Classification:** Retained; **Lowest/Average Salary:** $75,000/$90,000;
**Industry Concentration:** Generalist; **Function Concentration:** Generalist with a
primary focus in Engineering, Finance/Accounting, General Management,
Human Resources, Marketing, Research and Development, Sales,
Women/Minorities

**Gore, Les** — *Managing Partner*
Executive Search International
60 Walnut Street
Wellesley, MA 02181
Telephone: (617) 239-0303
**Recruiter Classification:** Retained; **Lowest/Average Salary:** $75,000/$90,000;
**Industry Concentration:** Consumer Products, Entertainment, Fashion
(Retail/Apparel), High Technology; **Function Concentration:** Generalist

**Gorfinkle, Gayle** — *Partner*
Executive Search International
60 Walnut Street
Wellesley, MA 02181
Telephone: (617) 239-0303
**Recruiter Classification:** Retained; **Lowest/Average Salary:** $75,000/$90,000;
**Industry Concentration:** Automotive, Chemical Products, Consumer Products,
Electronics, Fashion (Retail/Apparel), High Technology, Manufacturing,
Packaging, Pharmaceutical/Medical, Transportation, Venture Capital; **Function
Concentration:** Generalist

**Gorman, Patrick** — *Associate*
Source Services Corporation
425 California Street, Suite 1200
San Francisco, CA 94104
Telephone: (415) 434-2410
**Recruiter Classification:** Contingency; **Lowest/Average Salary:**
$30,000/$50,000; **Industry Concentration:** Financial Services, Information
Technology; **Function Concentration:** Engineering, Finance/Accounting

**Gorman, T. Patrick** — *Vice President*
Techsearch Services, Inc.
6 Hachaliah Brown Drive
Somers, NY 10589
Telephone: (914) 277-2727
**Recruiter Classification:** Contingency; **Lowest/Average Salary:**
$50,000/$75,000; **Industry Concentration:** Financial Services, High
Technology, Information Technology; **Function Concentration:**
Finance/Accounting

**Gossage, Wayne** — *Principal*
Gossage Regan Associates, Inc.
25 West 43rd Street, Suite 812
New York, NY 10036
Telephone: (212) 869-3348
**Recruiter Classification:** Retained; **Lowest/Average Salary:** $50,000/$60,000;
**Industry Concentration:** Education/Libraries; **Function Concentration:**
Generalist

**Gosselin, Jocelyne** — *Researcher*
The Caldwell Partners Amrop International
1840 Sherbrooke Street West
Montreal, Quebec, CANADA H3H 1E4
Telephone: (514) 935-6969
**Recruiter Classification:** Retained; **Lowest/Average Salary:** $/$90,000; **Industry
Concentration:** Generalist; **Function Concentration:** Generalist

**Gostin, Howard I.** — *Principal*
Sanford Rose Associates
1000 Century Plaza, Suite 309
10630 Little Patuxent Parkway
Columbia, MD 21044
Telephone: (301) 596-4000
**Recruiter Classification:** Contingency; **Lowest/Average Salary:**
$30,000/$75,000; **Industry Concentration:** Generalist; **Function
Concentration:** Generalist

**Gostyla, Rick** — *Senior Director*
Spencer Stuart
3000 Sand Hill Road
Building 2, Suite 175
Menlo Park, CA 94025
Telephone: (415) 688-1285
**Recruiter Classification:** Retained; **Lowest/Average Salary:** $90,000/$90,000;
**Industry Concentration:** Electronics, High Technology, Information
Technology; **Function Concentration:** Administration, Engineering,
Finance/Accounting, General Management, Human Resources, Marketing,
Research and Development, Sales

**Gottenberg, Norbert A.** — *Managing Director*
Norman Broadbent International, Inc.
200 Park Avenue, 20th Floor
New York, NY 10166
Telephone: (212) 953-6990
**Recruiter Classification:** Retained; **Lowest/Average Salary:** $90,000/$90,000;
**Industry Concentration:** Generalist with a primary focus in Information
Technology; **Function Concentration:** Generalist with a primary focus in
General Management

**Gould, Adam** — *Director/Multimedia*
Logix, Inc.
1601 Trapelo Road
Waltham, MA 02154
Telephone: (617) 890-0500
**Recruiter Classification:** Retained; **Lowest/Average Salary:** $60,000/$75,000;
**Industry Concentration:** High Technology; **Function Concentration:**
Engineering

**Gould, Adam** — *Consultant/Director*
Logix Partners
1601 Trapelo Road
Waltham, MA 02154
Telephone: (617) 890-0500
**Recruiter Classification:** Retained; **Lowest/Average Salary:** $60,000/$75,000;
**Industry Concentration:** High Technology; **Function Concentration:**
Engineering

**Gould, Dana** — *Senior Consultant*
Logix, Inc.
1601 Trapelo Road
Waltham, MA 02154
Telephone: (617) 890-0500
**Recruiter Classification:** Retained; **Lowest/Average Salary:** $60,000/$75,000;
**Industry Concentration:** High Technology, Information Technology; **Function
Concentration:** Engineering, Research and Development

**Gould, Dana** — *Senior Consultant*
Logix Partners
1601 Trapelo Road
Waltham, MA 02154
Telephone: (617) 890-0500
**Recruiter Classification:** Retained; **Lowest/Average Salary:** $60,000/$75,000;
**Industry Concentration:** High Technology, Information Technology; **Function
Concentration:** Engineering

**Gould, William E.** — *Managing Director*
Gould, McCoy & Chadick Incorporated
300 Park Avenue, Suite 20F
New York, NY 10022
Telephone: (212) 688-8671
**Recruiter Classification:** Retained; **Lowest/Average Salary:** $90,000/$90,000;
**Industry Concentration:** Generalist; **Function Concentration:** Generalist

**Gourlay, Debra** — *Associate*
Rene Plessner Associates, Inc.
375 Park Avenue
New York, NY 10152
Telephone: (212) 421-3490
**Recruiter Classification:** Retained; **Lowest/Average Salary:** $75,000/$90,000;
**Industry Concentration:** Generalist with a primary focus in
Aerospace/Defense, Consumer Products, Fashion (Retail/Apparel), Insurance,
Pharmaceutical/Medical; **Function Concentration:** Generalist with a primary
focus in Administration, Finance/Accounting, General Management, Human
Resources, Marketing, Research and Development, Sales

**Gourley, Timothy** — *Associate*
Source Services Corporation
155 Federal Street, Suite 410
Boston, MA 02110
Telephone: (617) 482-8211
**Recruiter Classification:** Contingency; **Lowest/Average Salary:**
$30,000/$50,000; **Industry Concentration:** Financial Services, Information
Technology; **Function Concentration:** Engineering, Finance/Accounting

**Govig, Dick A.** — *General Manager*
Management Recruiters International, Inc.
Bank of America Building, Suite 935-6900 East
Camelback Road
Scottsdale, AZ 85251
Telephone: (602) 941-1515
**Recruiter Classification:** Contingency; **Lowest/Average Salary:**
$30,000/$75,000; **Industry Concentration:** Generalist; **Function
Concentration:** Generalist

**Govig, Todd** — *Manager Pacific Region*
Management Recruiters International, Inc.
Bank of America Building, Suite 935-6900 East
Camelback Road
Scottsdale, AZ 85251
Telephone: (602) 941-1515
**Recruiter Classification:** Contingency; **Lowest/Average Salary:**
$30,000/$75,000; **Industry Concentration:** Generalist; **Function
Concentration:** Generalist

**Gow, Roderick C.** — *Managing Partner*
Lamalie Amrop International
200 Park Avenue
New York, NY 10166-0136
Telephone: (212) 953-7900
**Recruiter Classification:** Retained; **Lowest/Average Salary:** $90,000/$90,000;
**Industry Concentration:** Generalist with a primary focus in Board Services,
Financial Services, Insurance, Venture Capital; **Function Concentration:**
Generalist with a primary focus in Finance/Accounting, General Management,
Marketing, Sales

**Goyette, Marc L.** — *Manager Pacific Region*
Management Recruiters International, Inc.
16040 Christensen Road
Suite 316, Building 1
Seattle, WA 98188
Telephone: (206) 242-7484
**Recruiter Classification:** Contingency; **Lowest/Average Salary:**
$30,000/$75,000; **Industry Concentration:** Generalist; **Function
Concentration:** Generalist

**Gozarina, Linda** — *General Manager*
Noble & Associates Inc.
1685 7th Avenue
San Francisco, CA 94122
Telephone: (415) 664-9776
**Recruiter Classification:** Contingency; **Lowest/Average Salary:**
$40,000/$90,000; **Industry Concentration:** Generalist; **Function
Concentration:** Marketing

**Grabeel, Frank** — *Manager North Atlantic Region*
Management Recruiters International, Inc.
Westgate Professional Building, Suite 3
2609 W. Andrew Johnson Highway
Morristown, TN 37814-3213
Telephone: (423) 587-3701
**Recruiter Classification:** Contingency; **Lowest/Average Salary:**
$30,000/$75,000; **Industry Concentration:** Generalist; **Function
Concentration:** Generalist

**Grado, Eduardo** — *Associate*
Source Services Corporation
5429 LBJ Freeway, Suite 275
Dallas, TX 75240
Telephone: (214) 387-1600
**Recruiter Classification:** Contingency; **Lowest/Average Salary:**
$30,000/$50,000; **Industry Concentration:** Financial Services, Information
Technology; **Function Concentration:** Engineering, Finance/Accounting

**Grady, James** — *Account Executive*
Search West, Inc.
100 Pine Street, Suite 2500
San Francisco, CA 94111-5203
Telephone: (415) 788-1770
**Recruiter Classification:** Contingency; **Lowest/Average Salary:**
$40,000/$60,000; **Industry Concentration:** Automotive, Chemical Products,
Consumer Products, Electronics, Environmental, High Technology,
Manufacturing, Packaging; **Function Concentration:** Administration,
Marketing, Sales

**Grady, Richard F.** — *Medical Director*
Drew Associates International
77 Park Street
Montclair, NJ 07042
Telephone: (201) 746-8877
**Recruiter Classification:** Retained; **Lowest/Average Salary:** $60,000/$90,000;
**Industry Concentration:** Healthcare/Hospitals, Pharmaceutical/Medical;
**Function Concentration:** Generalist

**Graf, Debra** — *Associate*
Kenzer Corp.
777 Third Avenue, 26th Floor
New York, NY 10017
Telephone: (212) 308-4300
**Recruiter Classification:** Retained; **Lowest/Average Salary:** $50,000/$90,000;
**Industry Concentration:** Generalist; **Function Concentration:** Generalist

**Graff, Jack** — *Associate*
Source Services Corporation
5343 North 16th Street, Suite 270
Phoenix, AZ 85016
Telephone: (602) 230-0220
**Recruiter Classification:** Contingency; **Lowest/Average Salary:**
$30,000/$50,000; **Industry Concentration:** Financial Services, Information
Technology; **Function Concentration:** Engineering, Finance/Accounting

**Graham, Craig** — *Partner*
Ward Howell International, Inc.
141 Adelaide Street West
Suite 1800
Toronto, Ontario, CANADA M5H 3L5
Telephone: (416) 862-1273
**Recruiter Classification:** Retained; **Lowest/Average Salary:** $75,000/$90,000;
**Industry Concentration:** Fashion (Retail/Apparel), Financial Services,
Information Technology; **Function Concentration:** Generalist

**Graham, Dale** — *Executive Recruiter*
CPS Inc.
One Westbrook Corporate Centre, Suite 600
Westchester, IL 60154
Telephone: (708) 531-8370
**Recruiter Classification:** Contingency; **Lowest/Average Salary:**
$30,000/$50,000; **Industry Concentration:** Generalist with a primary focus in
Automotive, Biotechnology, Chemical Products, Consumer Products, High
Technology, Insurance, Manufacturing, Oil/Gas, Packaging,
Pharmaceutical/Medical; **Function Concentration:** Engineering, Research and
Development, Sales, Women/Minorities

**Graham, Elizabeth** — *Senior Associate*
Korn/Ferry International
120 South Riverside Plaza
Suite 918
Chicago, IL 60606
Telephone: (312) 726-1841
**Recruiter Classification:** Retained; **Lowest/Average Salary:** $90,000/$90,000;
**Industry Concentration:** Generalist; **Function Concentration:** Generalist

**Graham, Robert** — *Partner*
Cambridge Management Planning
2323 Yonge Street, Suite 203
Toronto, Ontario, CANADA M4P 2C9
Telephone: (416) 484-8408
**Recruiter Classification:** Retained, Executive Temporary; **Lowest/Average
Salary:** $75,000/$90,000; **Industry Concentration:** Generalist; **Function
Concentration:** Generalist

**Graham, Robert W.** — *Senior Partner*
The Westminster Group, Inc.
40 Westminster Street
Providence, RI 02903
Telephone: (401) 273-9300
**Recruiter Classification:** Retained; **Lowest/Average Salary:** $90,000/$90,000;
**Industry Concentration:** Generalist; **Function Concentration:** Generalist

**Graham, Shannon** — *Associate*
Source Services Corporation
7730 East Bellview Avenue, Suite 302
Englewood, CO 80111
Telephone: (303) 773-3700
**Recruiter Classification:** Contingency; **Lowest/Average Salary:**
$30,000/$50,000; **Industry Concentration:** Financial Services, Information
Technology; **Function Concentration:** Engineering, Finance/Accounting

**Grand, Gordon** — *Managing Director*
Russell Reynolds Associates, Inc.
200 Park Avenue
New York, NY 10166-0002
Telephone: (212) 351-2000
**Recruiter Classification:** Retained; **Lowest/Average Salary:** $90,000/$90,000;
**Industry Concentration:** Generalist with a primary focus in Financial Services;
**Function Concentration:** Generalist

**Grandinetti, Suzanne** — *Associate*
Source Services Corporation
1500 West Park Drive, Suite 390
Westborough, MA 01581
Telephone: (508) 366-2600
**Recruiter Classification:** Contingency; **Lowest/Average Salary:**
$30,000/$50,000; **Industry Concentration:** Financial Services, Information
Technology; **Function Concentration:** Engineering, Finance/Accounting

**Granger, Lisa D.** — *Recruiter*
D.S.A. - Dixie Search Associates
501 Village Trace, Building 9
Marietta, GA 30067
Telephone: (770) 850-0250
**Recruiter Classification:** Contingency; **Lowest/Average Salary:**
$30,000/$50,000; **Industry Concentration:** Biotechnology, Consumer
Products, Hospitality/Leisure, Manufacturing, Packaging, Transportation;
**Function Concentration:** Generalist with a primary focus in Engineering,
Finance/Accounting, General Management, Human Resources, Marketing,
Research and Development, Sales

**Grant, Carol** — *Vice President*
Hitchens & Foster, Inc.
Pines Office Center
One The Pines Court
St. Louis, MO 63141
Telephone: (314) 453-0800
**Recruiter Classification:** Contingency; **Lowest/Average Salary:**
$90,000/$90,000; **Industry Concentration:** Healthcare/Hospitals; **Function**
**Concentration:** General Management

**Grantham, John** — *President*
Grantham & Co., Inc.
114 Old Durham Road
Chapel Hill, NC 27514
Telephone: (919) 932-5650
**Recruiter Classification:** Retained; **Lowest/Average Salary:** $75,000/$90,000;
**Industry Concentration:** Generalist with a primary focus in
Aerospace/Defense, Automotive, Chemical Products, Consumer Products,
Financial Services, Healthcare/Hospitals, Information Technology,
Manufacturing, Non-Profit, Packaging, Pharmaceutical/Medical,
Publishing/Media, Transportation; **Function Concentration:** Generalist with a
primary focus in Finance/Accounting, General Management, Human
Resources, Marketing, Research and Development, Sales

**Grantham, Philip H.** — *Managing Principal*
Columbia Consulting Group
20 South Charles Street, 9th Floor
Baltimore, MD 21201
Telephone: (410) 385-2525
**Recruiter Classification:** Retained; **Lowest/Average Salary:** $75,000/$90,000;
**Industry Concentration:** Generalist with a primary focus in Biotechnology,
Consumer Products, Electronics, Financial Services, Healthcare/Hospitals, High
Technology, Hospitality/Leisure, Information Technology, Insurance,
Manufacturing, Pharmaceutical/Medical, Venture Capital; **Function**
**Concentration:** Generalist with a primary focus in Engineering,
Finance/Accounting, General Management, Human Resources, Marketing,
Research and Development

**Grasch, Jerry E.** — *Vice President*
The Hindman Company
Browenton Place, Suite 110
2000 Warrington Way
Louisville, KY 40222
Telephone: (502) 426-4040
**Recruiter Classification:** Retained; **Lowest/Average Salary:** $50,000/$90,000;
**Industry Concentration:** Generalist; **Function Concentration:** Generalist

**Grassl, Peter O.** — *President*
Bowman & Marshall, Inc.
P.O. Box 25503
Overland Park, KS 66225
Telephone: (913) 648-3332
**Recruiter Classification:** Contingency; **Lowest/Average Salary:**
$30,000/$50,000; **Industry Concentration:** Automotive, Chemical Products,
Consumer Products, Fashion (Retail/Apparel), Financial Services, Insurance,
Manufacturing, Packaging, Pharmaceutical/Medical, Publishing/Media;
**Function Concentration:** Finance/Accounting

**Graue, Monica** — *Principal*
Korn/Ferry International
Montes Urales 641
Lomas De Chapultepec
Mexico City, D.F., MEXICO 11000
Telephone: (525) 202-0046
**Recruiter Classification:** Retained; **Lowest/Average Salary:** $90,000/$90,000;
**Industry Concentration:** Generalist; **Function Concentration:** Generalist

**Graver, Merialee** — *Clerical Recruiter*
Accounting Personnel Consultants
210 Baronne Street, Suite 920
New Orleans, LA 70112
Telephone: (504) 581-7800
**Recruiter Classification:** Contingency; **Lowest/Average Salary:**
$20,000/$20,000; **Industry Concentration:** Generalist; **Function**
**Concentration:** Administration

**Graves, Rosemarie** — *Partner*
Don Richard Associates of Washington, D.C., Inc.
8201 Corporate Drive, Suite 620
Landover, MD 20785
Telephone: (301) 474-3900
**Recruiter Classification:** Contingency, Executive Temporary; **Lowest/Average**
**Salary:** $40,000/$60,000; **Industry Concentration:** Aerospace/Defense,
Automotive, Financial Services, Healthcare/Hospitals, High Technology,
Hospitality/Leisure, Real Estate; **Function Concentration:** Finance/Accounting

**Gray, Annie** — *President and CEO*
Annie Gray Associates, Inc./The Executive Search Firm
12400 Olive Boulevard, Suite 555
St. Louis, MO 63141
Telephone: (314) 275-4405
**Recruiter Classification:** Retained; **Lowest/Average Salary:** $75,000/$90,000;
**Industry Concentration:** Generalist with a primary focus in Board Services,
Consumer Products, Education/Libraries, Entertainment, Financial Services,
Hospitality/Leisure, Manufacturing, Non-Profit, Publishing/Media; **Function**
**Concentration:** Generalist with a primary focus in Administration, General
Management, Human Resources

**Gray, David** — *Senior Associate*
CG & Associates
P.O. Box 11160
Pittsburgh, PA 15237
Telephone: (412) 935-1288
**Recruiter Classification:** Contingency; **Lowest/Average Salary:**
$30,000/$60,000; **Industry Concentration:** Real Estate; **Function**
**Concentration:** Generalist with a primary focus in Administration, Engineering,
Finance/Accounting, General Management

**Gray, Heather** — *Associate*
Source Services Corporation
520 Post Oak Boulevard, Suite 700
Houston, TX 77027
Telephone: (713) 439-1077
**Recruiter Classification:** Contingency; **Lowest/Average Salary:**
$30,000/$50,000; **Industry Concentration:** Financial Services, Information
Technology; **Function Concentration:** Engineering, Finance/Accounting

**Gray, Lisa** — *Consultant*
Evie Kreisler & Associates, Inc.
2575 Peachtree Road, Suite 300
Atlanta, GA 30305
Telephone: (404) 262-0599
**Recruiter Classification:** Contingency; **Lowest/Average Salary:**
$30,000/$75,000; **Industry Concentration:** Fashion (Retail/Apparel); **Function**
**Concentration:** Generalist

**Gray, Mark** — *Vice President*
Executive Referral Services, Inc.
8770 West Bryn Mawr, Suite 110
Chicago, IL 60631
Telephone: (312) 693-6622
**Recruiter Classification:** Contingency; **Lowest/Average Salary:**
$30,000/$50,000; **Industry Concentration:** Entertainment, Hospitality/Leisure,
Venture Capital; **Function Concentration:** Administration, Finance/Accounting,
General Management, Human Resources, Marketing, Research and
Development, Sales, Women/Minorities

**Gray, Russell** — *Associate*
Source Services Corporation
1290 Oakmead Parkway, Suite 318
Sunnyvale, CA 94086
Telephone: (408) 738-8440
**Recruiter Classification:** Contingency; **Lowest/Average Salary:**
$30,000/$50,000; **Industry Concentration:** Financial Services, Information
Technology; **Function Concentration:** Engineering, Finance/Accounting

**Gray, Russell E.** — *Vice President*
Horton International
33 Sloan Street
Roswell, GA 30075
Telephone: (770) 640-1533
**Recruiter Classification:** Retained; **Lowest/Average Salary:** $90,000/$90,000;
**Industry Concentration:** Generalist; **Function Concentration:** Generalist

**Grayson, E.C.** — *Senior Director*
Spencer Stuart
525 Market Street, Suite 3700
San Francisco, CA 94105
Telephone: (415) 495-4141
**Recruiter Classification:** Retained; **Lowest/Average Salary:** $90,000/$90,000;
**Industry Concentration:** Generalist with a primary focus in Financial Services;
**Function Concentration:** Generalist

**Graziano, Lisa** — *Associate*
Source Services Corporation
1 Gatehall Drive, Suite 250
Parsippany, NJ 07054
Telephone: (201) 267-3222
**Recruiter Classification:** Contingency; **Lowest/Average Salary:**
$30,000/$50,000; **Industry Concentration:** Financial Services, Information
Technology; **Function Concentration:** Engineering, Finance/Accounting

**Grebenschikoff, Jennifer R.** — *Vice President*
Physician Executive Management Center
4014 Gunn Highway, Suite 160
Tampa, FL 33624
Telephone: (813) 963-1800
**Recruiter Classification:** Retained; **Lowest/Average Salary:** $90,000/$90,000;
**Industry Concentration:** Healthcare/Hospitals, Insurance; **Function
Concentration:** General Management

**Grebenstein, Charles R.** — *Senior Vice President*
Skott/Edwards Consultants, Inc.
1776 On the Green
Morristown, NJ 07006
Telephone: (201) 644-0900
**Recruiter Classification:** Retained; **Lowest/Average Salary:** $75,000/$90,000;
**Industry Concentration:** Generalist with a primary focus in Biotechnology,
Chemical Products, Energy, Environmental, Healthcare/Hospitals, High
Technology, Pharmaceutical/Medical; **Function Concentration:** Generalist with
a primary focus in Engineering, General Management, Research and
Development

**Greco, Maria** — *Senior Consultant*
R L Plimpton Associates
5655 South Yosemite Street, Suite 410
Greenwood Village, CO 80111
Telephone: (303) 771-1311
**Recruiter Classification:** Retained; **Lowest/Average Salary:** $40,000/$75,000;
**Industry Concentration:** Generalist; **Function Concentration:** Generalist

**Greco, Patricia** — *Co-Managing Director*
Howe-Lewis International
521 Fifth Avenue, 36th Floor
New York, NY 10175
Telephone: (212) 697-5000
**Recruiter Classification:** Retained; **Lowest/Average Salary:** $90,000/$90,000;
**Industry Concentration:** Board Services, Education/Libraries,
Healthcare/Hospitals, Insurance, Non-Profit; **Function Concentration:** General
Management, Human Resources, Marketing, Women/Minorities

**Greebe, Neil** — *Recruiter Consumer Sales*
Flowers & Associates
1446 South Reynolds, Suite 112
P.O. Box 538
Maumee, OH 43537
Telephone: (419) 893-4816
**Recruiter Classification:** Contingency; **Lowest/Average Salary:**
$30,000/$50,000; **Industry Concentration:** Generalist with a primary focus in
Automotive, Consumer Products, Hospitality/Leisure, Manufacturing; **Function
Concentration:** Generalist with a primary focus in Administration, Marketing,
Sales

**Green, Jane** — *Executive Recruiter*
Phillips Resource Group
330 Pelham Road, Building A
Greenville, SC 29615
Telephone: (864) 271-6350
**Recruiter Classification:** Contingency; **Lowest/Average Salary:**
$40,000/$50,000; **Industry Concentration:** Chemical Products, Electronics,
Environmental, High Technology, Information Technology, Manufacturing,
Packaging; **Function Concentration:** Administration, Engineering,
Finance/Accounting, General Management, Human Resources, Marketing,
Research and Development, Sales

**Green, Jean** — *Vice President*
Broward-Dobbs, Inc.
1532 Dunwoody Village Parkway, Suite 200
Atlanta, GA 30338
Telephone: (770) 399-0744
**Recruiter Classification:** Contingency; **Lowest/Average Salary:**
$40,000/$50,000; **Industry Concentration:** Generalist with a primary focus in
Aerospace/Defense, Chemical Products, Electronics, Environmental, High
Technology, Information Technology, Manufacturing; **Function Concentration:**
Engineering, Human Resources

**Green, Marc** — *Executive Recruiter*
TSS Consulting, Ltd.
2425 East Camelback Road
Suite 375
Phoenix, AZ 85016
Telephone: (602) 955-7000
**Recruiter Classification:** Contingency; **Lowest/Average Salary:** $60,000/$75,000;
**Industry Concentration:** Aerospace/Defense, Electronics, High Technology;
**Function Concentration:** Engineering, General Management, Marketing

**Greenberg, Ruth** — *Associate*
Kenzer Corp.
777 Third Avenue, 26th Floor
New York, NY 10017
Telephone: (212) 308-4300
**Recruiter Classification:** Retained; **Lowest/Average Salary:** $50,000/$90,000;
**Industry Concentration:** Generalist; **Function Concentration:** Generalist

**Greene, Brian** — *Temp-to-Perm Accounting Recruiter*
Winter, Wyman & Company
950 Winter Street, Suite 3100
Waltham, MA 02154-1294
Telephone: (617) 890-7000
**Recruiter Classification:** Contingency; **Lowest/Average Salary:**
$20,000/$50,000; **Industry Concentration:** Generalist; **Function
Concentration:** Finance/Accounting

**Greene, C. Edward** — *President*
Don Richard Associates of Tidewater, Inc.
4701 Columbus Street, Suite 102
Virginia Beach, VA 23462
Telephone: (757) 518-8600
**Recruiter Classification:** Contingency, Executive Temporary; **Lowest/Average
Salary:** $20,000/$50,000; **Industry Concentration:** Generalist; **Function
Concentration:** Finance/Accounting

**Greene, Frederick J.** — *Managing Director*
Boyden
Embarcadero Center West Tower
275 Battery St., Suite 420
San Francisco, CA 94111
Telephone: (415) 981-7900
**Recruiter Classification:** Retained; **Lowest/Average Salary:** $75,000/$90,000;
**Industry Concentration:** Generalist; **Function Concentration:** Generalist with a
primary focus in Engineering, Finance/Accounting, General Management,
Human Resources, Marketing, Research and Development, Sales,
Women/Minorities

**Greene, Luke** — *President*
Broward-Dobbs, Inc.
1532 Dunwoody Village Parkway, Suite 200
Atlanta, GA 30338
Telephone: (770) 399-0744
**Recruiter Classification:** Contingency; **Lowest/Average Salary:**
$40,000/$60,000; **Industry Concentration:** Generalist with a primary focus in
Chemical Products, Energy, Environmental, High Technology, Manufacturing,
Oil/Gas, Pharmaceutical/Medical, Real Estate; **Function Concentration:**
Engineering

**Greene, Neal** — *Associate*
Kenzer Corp.
6033 West Century Boulevard, Suite 808
Los Angeles, CA 90045
Telephone: (310) 417-8577
**Recruiter Classification:** Retained; **Lowest/Average Salary:** $50,000/$90,000;
**Industry Concentration:** Generalist; **Function Concentration:** Generalist

**Greene, Neal B.** — *Consultant*
Vera L. Rast Partners, Inc.
One South Wacker Drive, Suite 3890
Chicago, IL 60606
Telephone: (312) 629-0339
**Recruiter Classification:** Contingency; **Lowest/Average Salary:**
$50,000/$90,000

**Greene, Wallace** — *Senior Associate*
Korn/Ferry International
237 Park Avenue
New York, NY 10017
Telephone: (212) 687-1834
**Recruiter Classification:** Retained; **Lowest/Average Salary:** $90,000/$90,000;
**Industry Concentration:** Generalist; **Function Concentration:** Generalist

**Greenfield, Art** — *Manager Corporate Administration*
*Eastern Region*
Management Recruiters International, Inc.
607 Boylston Street, Suite 603
Boston, MA 02116
Telephone: (617) 262-5050
**Recruiter Classification:** Contingency; **Lowest/Average Salary:**
$30,000/$75,000; **Industry Concentration:** Generalist; **Function
Concentration:** Generalist

**Greenspan, Phillip D.** — *Executive Vice President/*
*Managing Director*
DHR International, Inc.
10 South Riverside Plaza, Suite 2220
Chicago, IL 60606
Telephone: (312) 782-1581
**Recruiter Classification:** Retained; **Lowest/Average Salary:** $60,000/$90,000;
**Industry Concentration:** Generalist; **Function Concentration:** Generalist

**Greenwald, Jane K.** — *Managing Director*
Gilbert Tweed/INESA
155 Prospect Avenue
West Orange, NJ 07052
Telephone: (201) 731-3033
**Recruiter Classification:** Retained; **Lowest/Average Salary:** $90,000/$90,000;
**Industry Concentration:** Generalist; **Function Concentration:** Generalist

**Greenwood, Janet** — *Partner*
Heidrick & Struggles, Inc.
1301 K Street N.W., Suite 500 East
Washington, DC 20005
Telephone: (202) 289-4450
**Recruiter Classification:** Retained; **Lowest/Average Salary:** $75,000/$90,000;
**Industry Concentration:** Generalist with a primary focus in Education/Libraries,
Non-Profit; **Function Concentration:** Generalist

**Gregg, Pat** — *Manager Pacific Region*
Management Recruiters International, Inc.
One City Boulevard West, Suite 710
Orange, CA 92668-3157
Telephone: (714) 978-0500
**Recruiter Classification:** Contingency; **Lowest/Average Salary:**
$30,000/$75,000; **Industry Concentration:** Generalist; **Function
Concentration:** Generalist

**Gregor, Joie A.** — *Partner*
Heidrick & Struggles, Inc.
600 Superior Avenue East
Suite 2500
Cleveland, OH 44114
Telephone: (216) 241-7410
**Recruiter Classification:** Retained; **Lowest/Average Salary:** $75,000/$90,000;
**Industry Concentration:** Generalist with a primary focus in High Technology;
**Function Concentration:** Generalist

**Gregory, Gary A.** — *Vice President*
John Kurosky & Associates
3 Corporate Park Drive, Suite 210
Irvine, CA 92714
Telephone: (714) 851-6370
**Recruiter Classification:** Retained; **Lowest/Average Salary:** $60,000/$90,000;
**Industry Concentration:** Generalist; **Function Concentration:** Generalist

**Gregory, Mark** — *Vice President/Area Manager*
Accountants on Call
The Carillon Bldg., Suite 908
227 West Trade Street
Charlotte, NC 28202
Telephone: (704) 376-0006
**Recruiter Classification:** Contingency; **Lowest/Average Salary:**
$20,000/$30,000; **Industry Concentration:** Generalist; **Function
Concentration:** Finance/Accounting

**Gregory, Quintard** — *Vice President*
Korn/Ferry International
The Transamerica Pyramid
600 Montgomery Street
San Francisco, CA 94111
Telephone: (415) 956-1834
**Recruiter Classification:** Retained; **Lowest/Average Salary:** $90,000/$90,000;
**Industry Concentration:** Generalist; **Function Concentration:** Generalist

**Gregory, Stephen** — *Consultant*
Don Richard Associates of Richmond, Inc.
7275 Glen Forest Drive, Suite 200
Richmond, VA 23226
Telephone: (804) 282-6300
**Recruiter Classification:** Contingency; **Lowest/Average Salary:** $30,000/$50,000;
**Industry Concentration:** Information Technology

**Grenier, Glorianne** — *Executive Recruiter*
CPS Inc.
One Westbrook Corporate Centre, Suite 600
Westchester, IL 60154
Telephone: (708) 531-8370
**Recruiter Classification:** Contingency; **Lowest/Average Salary:**
$30,000/$50,000; **Industry Concentration:** Generalist with a primary focus in
Automotive, Biotechnology, Chemical Products, Consumer Products, High
Technology, Insurance, Manufacturing, Oil/Gas, Packaging,
Pharmaceutical/Medical; **Function Concentration:** Engineering, Research and
Development, Sales, Women/Minorities

**Gresia, Paul** — *Associate*
Source Services Corporation
8614 Westwood Center, Suite 750
Vienna, VA 22182
Telephone: (703) 790-5610
**Recruiter Classification:** Contingency; **Lowest/Average Salary:**
$30,000/$50,000; **Industry Concentration:** Financial Services, Information
Technology; **Function Concentration:** Engineering, Finance/Accounting

**Grey, Cort** — *Consultant*
The McCormick Group, Inc.
1400 Wilson Boulevard
Arlington, VA 22209
Telephone: (703) 841-1700
**Recruiter Classification:** Retained; **Lowest/Average Salary:** $60,000/$75,000;
**Industry Concentration:** Generalist with a primary focus in Consumer Products;
**Function Concentration:** Generalist with a primary focus in Marketing, Sales

**Grey, Fred** — *Director/Executive Recruiter*
J.B. Homer Associates, Inc.
Graybar Building
420 Lexington Avenue, Suite 2328
New York, NY 10170
Telephone: (212) 697-3300
**Recruiter Classification:** Retained; **Lowest/Average Salary:** $90,000/$90,000;
**Industry Concentration:** Generalist with a primary focus in Information
Technology; **Function Concentration:** Generalist

**Grieco, Joseph** — *Vice President*
Goodrich & Sherwood Associates, Inc.
521 Fifth Avenue
New York, NY 10175
Telephone: (212) 697-4131
**Recruiter Classification:** Retained; **Lowest/Average Salary:** $60,000/$90,000;
**Industry Concentration:** Generalist; **Function Concentration:** Generalist

**Griesedieck, Joseph E.** — *Regional Director U.S.*
Spencer Stuart
525 Market Street, Suite 3700
San Francisco, CA 94105
Telephone: (415) 495-4141
**Recruiter Classification:** Retained; **Lowest/Average Salary:** $90,000/$90,000;
**Industry Concentration:** Generalist with a primary focus in Board Services,
Consumer Products, Fashion (Retail/Apparel), Manufacturing; **Function
Concentration:** Generalist with a primary focus in General Management,
Marketing

**Griffen, Leslie G.** — *Senior Vice President*
EFL Associates
7101 College Boulevard, Suite 550
Overland Park, KS 66210-1891
Telephone: (913) 451-8866
**Recruiter Classification:** Retained; **Lowest/Average Salary:** $60,000/$90,000;
**Industry Concentration:** Generalist; **Function Concentration:** Generalist

**Griffin, Gilroye A.** — *Partner*
Paul Ray Berndtson
101 Park Avenue, 41st Floor
New York, NY 10178
Telephone: (212) 370-1316
**Recruiter Classification:** Retained; **Lowest/Average Salary:** $90,000/$90,000;
**Industry Concentration:** Generalist; **Function Concentration:** Generalist

**Griffin, John A.** — *Partner*
Heidrick & Struggles, Inc.
1 Houston Center
1221 McKinney Street, Suite 3050
Houston, TX 77010
Telephone: (713) 237-9000
Recruiter Classification: Retained; Lowest/Average Salary: $75,000/$90,000;
Industry Concentration: Generalist; Function Concentration: Generalist

**Grimes, G.D.** — *Co-Manager Central Region*
Management Recruiters International, Inc.
546 Park Street, Suite 300
Bowling Green, KY 42101
Telephone: (502) 782-3820
Recruiter Classification: Contingency; Lowest/Average Salary:
$30,000/$75,000; Industry Concentration: Generalist; Function
Concentration: Generalist

**Grimm, Peter G.** — *Vice Chairman*
Nordeman Grimm, Inc.
717 Fifth Avenue, 26th Floor
New York, NY 10022
Telephone: (212) 935-1000
Recruiter Classification: Retained; Lowest/Average Salary: $90,000/$90,000;
Industry Concentration: Generalist; Function Concentration: Generalist

**Grinnell, Janis R.** — *Associate*
Physicians Search, Inc.
1224 Katella Avenue, Suite 202
Orange, CA 92667-5045
Telephone: (714) 288-8350
Recruiter Classification: Contingency; Lowest/Average Salary:
$90,000/$90,000; Industry Concentration: Biotechnology,
Healthcare/Hospitals, Pharmaceutical/Medical

**Groban, Jack** — *Vice President/Managing Director*
A.T. Kearney, Inc.
Biltmore Tower
500 South Grand Avenue
Los Angeles, CA 90071
Telephone: (213) 689-6800
Recruiter Classification: Retained; Lowest/Average Salary: $90,000/$90,000;
Industry Concentration: Generalist with a primary focus in Entertainment,
Financial Services, Information Technology, Manufacturing, Non-Profit;
Function Concentration: Generalist with a primary focus in
Finance/Accounting

**Groner, David** — *Associate*
Source Services Corporation
150 South Wacker Drive, Suite 400
Chicago, IL 60606
Telephone: (312) 346-7000
Recruiter Classification: Contingency; Lowest/Average Salary:
$30,000/$50,000; Industry Concentration: Financial Services, Information
Technology; Function Concentration: Engineering, Finance/Accounting

**Groom, Charles C.** — *Principal*
CG & Associates
P.O. Box 11160
Pittsburgh, PA 15237
Telephone: (412) 935-1288
Recruiter Classification: Contingency; Lowest/Average Salary:
$30,000/$60,000; Industry Concentration: Real Estate; Function
Concentration: Generalist with a primary focus in Administration, Engineering,
Finance/Accounting, General Management

**Groover, David** — *Unit Manager*
MSI International
200 Galleria Parkway
Suite 1610
Atlanta, GA 30339
Telephone: (404) 951-1208
Recruiter Classification: Contingency; Lowest/Average Salary:
$30,000/$60,000; Industry Concentration: Generalist with a primary focus in
High Technology; Function Concentration: Administration, Engineering,
Finance/Accounting, General Management, Marketing

**Groover, Howard J.** — *Vice President*
John Kurosky & Associates
3 Corporate Park Drive, Suite 210
Irvine, CA 92714
Telephone: (714) 851-6370
Recruiter Classification: Retained; Lowest/Average Salary: $60,000/$90,000;
Industry Concentration: Generalist; Function Concentration: Generalist

**Gross, Barbara** — *Consultant*
S. Reyman & Associates Ltd.
20 North Michigan Avenue, Suite 520
Chicago, IL 60602
Telephone: (312) 580-0808
Recruiter Classification: Retained; Lowest/Average Salary: $75,000/$90,000;
Industry Concentration: Generalist; Function Concentration: Generalist

**Gross, Howard** — *Vice President*
Herbert Mines Associates, Inc.
399 Park Avenue, 27th Floor
New York, NY 10022
Telephone: (212) 355-0909
Recruiter Classification: Retained; Lowest/Average Salary: $75,000/$90,000;
Industry Concentration: Board Services, Consumer Products, Fashion
(Retail/Apparel); Function Concentration: Generalist with a primary focus in
Finance/Accounting, General Management, Human Resources, Marketing, Sales

**Gross, Kathy** — *Vice President*
Evie Kreisler & Associates, Inc.
1460 Broadway, 3rd Floor
New York, NY 10036
Telephone: (212) 921-8999
Recruiter Classification: Contingency; Lowest/Average Salary:
$30,000/$75,000; Industry Concentration: Fashion (Retail/Apparel); Function
Concentration: Generalist

**Grossman, James** — *Associate*
Source Services Corporation
10300 West 103rd Street, Suite 101
Overland Park, KS 66214
Telephone: (913) 888-8885
Recruiter Classification: Contingency; Lowest/Average Salary:
$30,000/$50,000; Industry Concentration: Financial Services, Information
Technology; Function Concentration: Engineering, Finance/Accounting

**Grossman, Martin** — *Associate*
Source Services Corporation
15600 N.W. 67th Avenue, Suite 210
Miami Lakes, FL 33014
Telephone: (305) 556-8000
Recruiter Classification: Contingency; Lowest/Average Salary:
$30,000/$50,000; Industry Concentration: Financial Services, Information
Technology; Function Concentration: Engineering, Finance/Accounting

**Groves, Jim** — *Co-Manager*
Management Recruiters International, Inc.
2510 Fairview Avenue East
Seattle, WA 98102
Telephone: (206) 328-0936
Recruiter Classification: Contingency; Lowest/Average Salary: $30,000/$75,000;
Industry Concentration: Generalist; Function Concentration: Generalist

**Grumulaitis, Leo** — *Associate*
Source Services Corporation
5429 LBJ Freeway, Suite 275
Dallas, TX 75240
Telephone: (214) 387-1600
Recruiter Classification: Contingency; Lowest/Average Salary:
$30,000/$50,000; Industry Concentration: Financial Services, Information
Technology; Function Concentration: Engineering, Finance/Accounting

**Grushkin, Joel T.** — *Senior Vice President/Managing Director*
DHR International, Inc.
12526 High Bluff Drive, Suite 300
San Diego, CA 92130
Telephone: (619) 792-3611
Recruiter Classification: Retained; Lowest/Average Salary: $60,000/$90,000;
Industry Concentration: Generalist; Function Concentration: Generalist

**Grzybowski, Jill** — *Executive Recruiter*
CPS Inc.
One Westbrook Corporate Centre, Suite 600
Westchester, IL 60154
Telephone: (708) 531-8370
Recruiter Classification: Contingency; Lowest/Average Salary:
$30,000/$50,000; Industry Concentration: Generalist with a primary focus in
Automotive, Biotechnology, Chemical Products, Consumer Products, High
Technology, Insurance, Manufacturing, Oil/Gas, Packaging,
Pharmaceutical/Medical; Function Concentration: Engineering, Research and
Development, Sales, Women/Minorities

**Guberman, Robert P.** — *Vice President*
A.T. Kearney, Inc.
225 Reinekers Lane
Alexandria, VA 22314
Telephone: (703) 739-4624
Recruiter Classification: Retained; Lowest/Average Salary: $90,000/$90,000;
Industry Concentration: Generalist with a primary focus in High Technology,
Utilities/Nuclear; Function Concentration: Generalist with a primary focus in
General Management

**Guc, Stephen** — *Associate*
Source Services Corporation
2000 Town Center, Suite 850
Southfield, MI 48075
Telephone: (810) 352-6520
**Recruiter Classification:** Contingency; **Lowest/Average Salary:**
$30,000/$50,000; **Industry Concentration:** Financial Services, Information
Technology; **Function Concentration:** Engineering, Finance/Accounting

**Gude, John S.** — *Partner*
Boyden
2 Prudential Plaza, Suite 5050
180 North Stetson Avenue
Chicago, IL 60601
Telephone: (312) 565-1300
**Recruiter Classification:** Retained; **Lowest/Average Salary:** $75,000/$90,000;
**Industry Concentration:** Generalist; **Function Concentration:** Generalist with a
primary focus in Engineering, Finance/Accounting, General Management,
Human Resources, Marketing, Research and Development, Sales,
Women/Minorities

**Gulley, Marylyn** — *Physician Recruiter*
MSI International
201 St. Charles Avenue
Suite 2205
New Orleans, LA 70170
Telephone: (504) 522-6700
**Recruiter Classification:** Contingency; **Lowest/Average Salary:**
$30,000/$60,000; **Industry Concentration:** Generalist with a primary focus in
Healthcare/Hospitals; **Function Concentration:** Generalist with a primary focus
in Administration, Engineering, Finance/Accounting, General Management,
Marketing, Sales

**Gurley, Herschel** — *Manager North Atlantic Region*
Management Recruiters International, Inc.
212 Starling Avenue, Suite 201
Martinsville, VA 24112-3844
Telephone: (540) 632-2355
**Recruiter Classification:** Contingency; **Lowest/Average Salary:** $30,000/$75,000;
**Industry Concentration:** Generalist; **Function Concentration:** Generalist

**Gurtin, Kay L.** — *Managing Partner*
Executive Options, Ltd.
910 Skokie Boulevard
Suite 210
Northbrook, IL 60068
Telephone: (708) 291-4322
**Recruiter Classification:** Executive Temporary; **Lowest/Average Salary:**
$40,000/$60,000; **Industry Concentration:** Generalist with a primary focus in
Consumer Products, Financial Services, Healthcare/Hospitals, Manufacturing,
Non-Profit, Packaging, Real Estate; **Function Concentration:** Generalist with a
primary focus in Finance/Accounting, General Management, Human
Resources, Marketing, Women/Minorities

**Gustafson, Eric P.** — *Principal*
Korn/Ferry International
237 Park Avenue
New York, NY 10017
Telephone: (212) 687-1834
**Recruiter Classification:** Retained; **Lowest/Average Salary:** $90,000/$90,000;
**Industry Concentration:** Generalist; **Function Concentration:** Generalist

**Gustafson, Jeremy** — *Vice President Operations*
The Paladin Companies, Inc.
875 North Michigan Avenue, Suite 3218
Chicago, IL 60611
Telephone: (312) 654-2600
**Recruiter Classification:** Executive Temporary; **Lowest/Average Salary:**
$50,000/$90,000; **Industry Concentration:** Generalist; **Function
Concentration:** Marketing

**Gustafson, Richard P.** — *Partner*
Heidrick & Struggles, Inc.
125 South Wacker Drive
Suite 2800
Chicago, IL 60606-4590
Telephone: (312) 372-8811
**Recruiter Classification:** Retained; **Lowest/Average Salary:** $75,000/$90,000;
**Industry Concentration:** Generalist with a primary focus in
Healthcare/Hospitals; **Function Concentration:** Generalist

**Guthrie, Stuart** — *Associate*
Source Services Corporation
One Park Plaza, Suite 560
Irvine, CA 92714
Telephone: (714) 660-1666
**Recruiter Classification:** Contingency; **Lowest/Average Salary:**
$30,000/$50,000; **Industry Concentration:** Financial Services, Information
Technology; **Function Concentration:** Engineering, Finance/Accounting

**Gutknecht, Steven** — *Executive Recruiter*
Jacobson Associates
150 North Wacker Drive
Suite 1120
Chicago, IL 60606
Telephone: (312) 726-1578
**Recruiter Classification:** Contingency; **Lowest/Average Salary:**
$20,000/$50,000; **Industry Concentration:** High Technology, Insurance;
**Function Concentration:** Generalist

**Gwin, Ric** — *Senior Consultant*
Southwestern Professional Services
9485 Regency Square Boulevard, Suite 110
Jacksonville, FL 32225
Telephone: (904) 725-9200
**Recruiter Classification:** Contingency; **Lowest/Average Salary:**
$30,000/$40,000; **Industry Concentration:** Healthcare/Hospitals,
Hospitality/Leisure, Real Estate; **Function Concentration:** Generalist

**Haas, Margaret P.** — *President*
Haas International, Inc.
443 West 24th Street
New York, NY 10011
Telephone: (212) 741-2457
**Recruiter Classification:** Retained; **Lowest/Average Salary:** $40,000/$90,000;
**Industry Concentration:** Financial Services, High Technology, Information
Technology; **Function Concentration:** Administration, Finance/Accounting,
General Management, Human Resources, Marketing, Sales

**Haberman, Joseph C.** — *Vice President*
A.T. Kearney, Inc.
225 Reinekers Lane
Alexandria, VA 22314
Telephone: (703) 739-4624
**Recruiter Classification:** Retained; **Lowest/Average Salary:** $90,000/$90,000;
**Industry Concentration:** Generalist with a primary focus in Financial Services,
Manufacturing; **Function Concentration:** Generalist with a primary focus in
Finance/Accounting, General Management, Human Resources

**Hacker-Taylor, Dianna** — *Associate*
Source Services Corporation
525 Vine Street, Suite 2250
Cincinnati, OH 45202
Telephone: (513) 651-3303
**Recruiter Classification:** Contingency; **Lowest/Average Salary:**
$30,000/$50,000; **Industry Concentration:** Financial Services, Information
Technology; **Function Concentration:** Engineering, Finance/Accounting

**Hackett, Don F.** — *Manager North Atlantic Region*
Management Recruiters International, Inc.
231 North Main Street
Mount Airy, NC 27030-3809
Telephone: (910) 719-2250
**Recruiter Classification:** Contingency; **Lowest/Average Salary:**
$30,000/$75,000; **Industry Concentration:** Generalist; **Function
Concentration:** Generalist

**Haddad, Charles** — *Managing Partner*
Romac & Associates
1770 Kirby Parkway
Suite 216
Memphis, TN 38138-7405
Telephone: (901) 756-6050
**Recruiter Classification:** Executive Temporary; **Lowest/Average Salary:**
$/$60,000; **Industry Concentration:** Financial Services, Healthcare/Hospitals,
High Technology, Hospitality/Leisure, Information Technology, Insurance;
**Function Concentration:** Finance/Accounting

**Hadelman, Jordan M.** — *President*
Witt/Kieffer, Ford, Hadelman & Lloyd
2015 Spring Road, Suite 510
Oak Brook, IL 60521
Telephone: (708) 990-1370
**Recruiter Classification:** Retained; **Lowest/Average Salary:** $75,000/$90,000;
**Industry Concentration:** Healthcare/Hospitals; **Function Concentration:**
Generalist with a primary focus in Administration, Finance/Accounting,
General Management, Human Resources, Marketing

**Hadfield, Sheri** — *Consultant*
Paul Ray Berndtson
One Allen Center
500 Dallas, Suite 3010
Houston, TX 77002
Telephone: (713) 309-1400
**Recruiter Classification:** Retained; **Lowest/Average Salary:** $90,000/$90,000;
**Industry Concentration:** Generalist; **Function Concentration:** Generalist

**Hagerthy, Michael J.** — *Regional Director*
IMCOR, Inc.
23133 Hawthorne Boulevard, Suite 311
Torrance, CA 90505
Telephone: (310) 791-2033
**Recruiter Classification:** Executive Temporary; **Lowest/Average Salary:** $75,000/$90,000; **Industry Concentration:** Generalist; **Function Concentration:** Generalist

**Hagler, Holly** — *Consultant*
Heidrick & Struggles, Inc.
2200 Ross Avenue, Suite 4700E
Dallas, TX 75201-2787
Telephone: (214) 220-2130
**Recruiter Classification:** Retained; **Lowest/Average Salary:** $75,000/$90,000; **Industry Concentration:** Generalist; **Function Concentration:** Generalist

**Hahn, William R.** — *President*
Bill Hahn Group, Inc.
2052 Highway 35
Suites 203, 204
Wall, NJ 07719
Telephone: (908) 449-9302
**Recruiter Classification:** Contingency; **Lowest/Average Salary:** $75,000/$90,000; **Industry Concentration:** Biotechnology, Pharmaceutical/Medical; **Function Concentration:** General Management, Marketing

**Haider, Martin** — *Associate*
Source Services Corporation
7730 East Bellview Avenue, Suite 302
Englewood, CO 80111
Telephone: (303) 773-3700
**Recruiter Classification:** Contingency; **Lowest/Average Salary:** $30,000/$50,000; **Industry Concentration:** Financial Services, Information Technology; **Function Concentration:** Engineering, Finance/Accounting

**Haigler, Lisa S.** — *Consultant*
Don Richard Associates of Charlotte
2650 One First Union Center
301 South College Street
Charlotte, NC 28202-6000
Telephone: (704) 377-6447
**Recruiter Classification:** Contingency; **Lowest/Average Salary:** $20,000/$30,000; **Industry Concentration:** Generalist; **Function Concentration:** Generalist with a primary focus in Finance/Accounting

**Hailes, Brian** — *Executive Director*
Russell Reynolds Associates, Inc.
The Hurt Building
50 Hurt Plaza, Suite 600
Atlanta, GA 30303
Telephone: (404) 577-3000
**Recruiter Classification:** Retained; **Lowest/Average Salary:** $90,000/$90,000; **Industry Concentration:** Generalist with a primary focus in High Technology; **Function Concentration:** Generalist

**Hailey, H.M.** — *Vice President Operations*
Damon & Associates, Inc.
7515 Greenville Avenue, Suite 900
Dallas, TX 75231
Telephone: (214) 696-6990
**Recruiter Classification:** Contingency; **Lowest/Average Salary:** $30,000/$50,000; **Industry Concentration:** Generalist with a primary focus in Electronics, Financial Services, High Technology, Information Technology, Packaging; **Function Concentration:** General Management, Marketing, Sales

**Halbeck, Bruce N.** — *Executive Director*
Russell Reynolds Associates, Inc.
200 South Wacker Drive
Suite 3600
Chicago, IL 60606
Telephone: (312) 993-9696
**Recruiter Classification:** Retained; **Lowest/Average Salary:** $90,000/$90,000; **Industry Concentration:** Generalist; **Function Concentration:** Generalist

**Halek, Frederick D.** — *Principal*
Sanford Rose Associates
3816-21 South New Hope Road
Gastonia, NC 28056
Telephone: (704) 824-0895
**Recruiter Classification:** Contingency; **Lowest/Average Salary:** $30,000/$75,000; **Industry Concentration:** Generalist with a primary focus in Manufacturing; **Function Concentration:** Generalist

**Hales, Daphne** — *Associate*
Source Services Corporation
4170 Ashford Dunwoody Road, Suite 285
Atlanta, GA 30319
Telephone: (404) 255-2045
**Recruiter Classification:** Contingency; **Lowest/Average Salary:** $30,000/$50,000; **Industry Concentration:** Financial Services, Information Technology; **Function Concentration:** Engineering, Finance/Accounting

**Hall, Debbie** — *Co-Manager*
Management Recruiters International, Inc.
2800 Bush River Road, Suite 4
Columbia, SC 29210-5698
Telephone: (803) 772-0300
**Recruiter Classification:** Contingency; **Lowest/Average Salary:** $30,000/$75,000; **Industry Concentration:** Generalist; **Function Concentration:** Generalist

**Hall, Earl R.** — *Co-Manager Southwest Region*
Management Recruiters International, Inc.
Redding Building, Suite 314
1701 Centerview Drive
Little Rock, AR 72211-4313
Telephone: (501) 224-0801
**Recruiter Classification:** Contingency; **Lowest/Average Salary:** $30,000/$75,000; **Industry Concentration:** Generalist; **Function Concentration:** Generalist

**Hall, George** — *Manager*
Coopers & Lybrand Consulting
1809 Barrington Street, Suite 600
Halifax, Nova Scotia, CANADA B3J 3K8
Telephone: (902) 425-6190
**Recruiter Classification:** Retained; **Lowest/Average Salary:** $60,000/$90,000; **Industry Concentration:** Generalist; **Function Concentration:** Generalist

**Hall, Marty B.** — *Executive Vice President*
Catlin-Wells & White
5413 Patterson Avenue
Suite 200
Richmond, VA 23226
Telephone: (804) 288-8800
**Recruiter Classification:** Contingency; **Lowest/Average Salary:** $50,000/$60,000; **Industry Concentration:** High Technology, Information Technology; **Function Concentration:** Generalist

**Hall, Noel K.** — *Co-Manager*
Management Recruiters International, Inc.
Redding Building, Suite 314
1701 Centerview Drive
Little Rock, AR 72211-4313
Telephone: (501) 224-0801
**Recruiter Classification:** Contingency; **Lowest/Average Salary:** $30,000/$75,000; **Industry Concentration:** Generalist; **Function Concentration:** Generalist

**Hall, Peter V.** — *Managing Director*
Chartwell Partners International, Inc.
275 Battery Street, Suite 2180
San Francisco, CA 94111
Telephone: (415) 296-0600
**Recruiter Classification:** Retained; **Lowest/Average Salary:** $90,000/$90,000; **Industry Concentration:** Generalist with a primary focus in Board Services, Financial Services, Information Technology, Real Estate, Venture Capital; **Function Concentration:** Generalist with a primary focus in Finance/Accounting, General Management, Marketing, Sales, Women/Minorities

**Hall, Robert** — *Recruiter*
Don Richard Associates of Tidewater, Inc.
4701 Columbus Street, Suite 102
Virginia Beach, VA 23462
Telephone: (757) 518-8600
**Recruiter Classification:** Contingency, Executive Temporary; **Lowest/Average Salary:** $30,000/$40,000; **Industry Concentration:** Generalist with a primary focus in Chemical Products, Electronics, Energy, High Technology, Information Technology, Manufacturing, Publishing/Media; **Function Concentration:** Generalist with a primary focus in Engineering, Research and Development

**Hall, Roger** — *Co-Manager North Atlantic Region*
Management Recruiters International, Inc.
2800 Bush River Road, Suite 4
Columbia, SC 29210-5698
Telephone: (803) 772-0300
**Recruiter Classification:** Contingency; **Lowest/Average Salary:** $30,000/$75,000; **Industry Concentration:** Generalist; **Function Concentration:** Generalist

**Hall, Thomas H.** — *Senior Officer*
Korn/Ferry International
303 Peachtree Street N.E.
Suite 1600
Atlanta, GA 30308
Telephone: (404) 577-7542
**Recruiter Classification:** Retained; **Lowest/Average Salary:** $90,000/$90,000;
**Industry Concentration:** Generalist; **Function Concentration:** Generalist

**Halladay, Patti** — *Principal*
Intersource, Ltd.
1010 Mopac Circle, Suite 200
Austin, TX 78746
Telephone: (512) 306-1422
**Recruiter Classification:** Retained; **Lowest/Average Salary:** $40,000/$75,000;
**Industry Concentration:** Generalist with a primary focus in Financial Services,
High Technology; **Function Concentration:** Finance/Accounting, Human
Resources

**Hallagan, Robert E.** — *President and CEO*
Heidrick & Struggles, Inc.
One Post Office Square
Boston, MA 02109-0199
Telephone: (617) 423-1140
**Recruiter Classification:** Retained; **Lowest/Average Salary:** $75,000/$90,000;
**Industry Concentration:** Generalist with a primary focus in Financial Services;
**Function Concentration:** Generalist

**Hallam, Andy J.** — *Co-Manager*
Management Recruiters International, Inc.
300 Weyman Plaza, Suite 140
Pittsburgh, PA 15236
Telephone: (412) 885-5222
**Recruiter Classification:** Contingency; **Lowest/Average Salary:**
$30,000/$75,000; **Industry Concentration:** Generalist; **Function
Concentration:** Generalist

**Haller, Mark** — *Associate*
Source Services Corporation
525 Vine Street, Suite 2250
Cincinnati, OH 45202
Telephone: (513) 651-3303
**Recruiter Classification:** Contingency; **Lowest/Average Salary:**
$30,000/$50,000; **Industry Concentration:** Financial Services, Information
Technology; **Function Concentration:** Engineering, Finance/Accounting

**Hallock, Peter B.** — *Senior Vice President*
Goodrich & Sherwood Associates, Inc.
401 Merritt Seven Corporate Park
Norwalk, CT 06851
Telephone: (203) 847-2525
**Recruiter Classification:** Retained; **Lowest/Average Salary:** $60,000/$90,000;
**Industry Concentration:** Generalist with a primary focus in Board Services,
Chemical Products, Consumer Products, Financial Services,
Healthcare/Hospitals, Information Technology, Insurance, Manufacturing,
Oil/Gas, Publishing/Media, Venture Capital; **Function Concentration:**
Generalist with a primary focus in Administration, Finance/Accounting,
General Management, Human Resources, Marketing, Sales

**Halstead, Frederick A.** — *Managing Director*
Ward Howell International, Inc.
1601 Elm Street, Suite 900
Thanksgiving Tower
Dallas, TX 75201
Telephone: (214) 749-0099
**Recruiter Classification:** Retained; **Lowest/Average Salary:** $75,000/$90,000;
**Industry Concentration:** Healthcare/Hospitals; **Function Concentration:**
Generalist with a primary focus in Finance/Accounting

**Halvorsen, Jeanne M.** — *Vice President and Partner*
Kittleman & Associates
300 South Wacker Drive, Suite 1710
Chicago, IL 60606
Telephone: (312) 986-1166
**Recruiter Classification:** Retained; **Lowest/Average Salary:** $50,000/$75,000;
**Industry Concentration:** Healthcare/Hospitals, Non-Profit; **Function
Concentration:** Finance/Accounting, General Management, Marketing,
Women/Minorities

**Halvorsen, Kara** — *Regional Director*
Chrisman & Company, Incorporated
44 Montgomery Street, Suite 2360
San Francisco, CA 94104
Telephone: (415) 352-1200
**Recruiter Classification:** Retained; **Lowest/Average Salary:** $75,000/$90,000;
**Industry Concentration:** Financial Services, Venture Capital; **Function
Concentration:** Generalist with a primary focus in Finance/Accounting,
General Management, Human Resources

**Halyburton, Robert R.** — *President*
The Halyburton Co., Inc.
6201 Fairview Road, Suite 200
Charlotte, NC 28210
Telephone: (704) 556-9892
**Recruiter Classification:** Retained; **Lowest/Average Salary:** $50,000/$90,000;
**Industry Concentration:** Generalist with a primary focus in Manufacturing,
Non-Profit, Public Administration; **Function Concentration:** Generalist with a
primary focus in General Management, Marketing, Sales

**Hamar, Rolie C.** — *Vice President*
Accountants on Call
Canada Trust Tower, BCE Place
161 Bay St., Suite 4530
Toronto, Ontario, CANADA M5J 2S1
Telephone: (416) 363-7747
**Recruiter Classification:** Contingency; **Lowest/Average Salary:**
$20,000/$30,000; **Industry Concentration:** Generalist; **Function
Concentration:** Finance/Accounting

**Hamdan, Mark** — *President*
Careernet of Florida, Inc.
1320 South Dixie Highway, Suite 821
Coral Gables, FL 33146
Telephone: (305) 665-5627
**Recruiter Classification:** Contingency; **Lowest/Average Salary:**
$30,000/$50,000; **Industry Concentration:** Generalist; **Function
Concentration:** Generalist with a primary focus in Engineering,
Finance/Accounting, General Management, Human Resources, Marketing,
Sales

**Hamer, Thurston** — *Senior Officer*
Korn/Ferry International
Montes Urales 641
Lomas De Chapultepec
Mexico City, D.F., MEXICO 11000
Telephone: (525) 202-0046
**Recruiter Classification:** Retained; **Lowest/Average Salary:** $90,000/$90,000;
**Industry Concentration:** Generalist; **Function Concentration:** Generalist

**Hamilton, John R.** — *Vice President*
A.T. Kearney, Inc.
1200 Bank One Center
600 Superior Avenue, East
Cleveland, OH 44114-2650
Telephone: (216) 241-6880
**Recruiter Classification:** Retained; **Lowest/Average Salary:** $90,000/$90,000;
**Industry Concentration:** Generalist; **Function Concentration:** Generalist

**Hamilton, Timothy** — *Partner*
The Caldwell Partners Amrop International
400 Third Avenue S.W.
Suite 3450
Calgary, Alberta, CANADA T2P 4H2
Telephone: (403) 265-8780
**Recruiter Classification:** Retained; **Lowest/Average Salary:** $/$90,000; **Industry
Concentration:** Generalist with a primary focus in Board Services, Consumer
Products, Education/Libraries, Energy, Environmental, Healthcare/Hospitals,
Non-Profit, Public Administration; **Function Concentration:** Generalist

**Hamm, Gary** — *Associate*
Source Services Corporation
5429 LBJ Freeway, Suite 275
Dallas, TX 75240
Telephone: (214) 387-1600
**Recruiter Classification:** Contingency; **Lowest/Average Salary:**
$30,000/$50,000; **Industry Concentration:** Financial Services, Information
Technology; **Function Concentration:** Engineering, Finance/Accounting

**Hamm, Gary P.** — *Consultant*
Witt/Kieffer, Ford, Hadelman & Lloyd
1920 Main Street, Suite 310
Irvine, CA 92714
Telephone: (714) 851-5070
**Recruiter Classification:** Retained; **Lowest/Average Salary:** $75,000/$90,000;
**Industry Concentration:** Healthcare/Hospitals; **Function Concentration:**
Generalist with a primary focus in General Management

**Hamm, Mary Kay** — *Managing Partner*
Romac & Associates
530 East Swedesford Road
Suite 202
Valley Forge, PA 19087
Telephone: (215) 687-6107
**Recruiter Classification:** Executive Temporary; **Lowest/Average Salary:**
$/$60,000; **Industry Concentration:** Financial Services, Healthcare/Hospitals,
High Technology, Hospitality/Leisure, Information Technology, Insurance;
**Function Concentration:** Finance/Accounting

**Hammes, Betsy** — *Senior Technical Recruiter*
Search Enterprises, Inc.
160 Quail Ridge Drive
Westmont, IL 60559
Telephone: (708) 654-2300
**Recruiter Classification:** Contingency; **Lowest/Average Salary:**
$20,000/$50,000; **Industry Concentration:** Chemical Products, Oil/Gas;
**Function Concentration:** Engineering

**Hancock, Deborah L.** — *Administrative Division Consultant*
Morgan Hunter Corp.
6800 College Boulevard, Suite 550
Overland Park, KS 66211
Telephone: (913) 491-3434
**Recruiter Classification:** Contingency; **Lowest/Average Salary:**
$20,000/$30,000; **Industry Concentration:** Generalist; **Function
Concentration:** Generalist with a primary focus in Administration

**Hancock, Mimi** — *Executive Director*
Russell Reynolds Associates, Inc.
101 California Street
Suite 3140
San Francisco, CA 94111
Telephone: (415) 352-3300
**Recruiter Classification:** Retained; **Lowest/Average Salary:** $90,000/$90,000;
**Industry Concentration:** Generalist with a primary focus in
Healthcare/Hospitals; **Function Concentration:** Generalist

**Hand, Jean** — *Manager South Atlantic Region*
Management Recruiters International, Inc.
Lighthouse Point
4020 Park Street
St. Petersburg, FL 33709-4034
Telephone: (813) 345-8811
**Recruiter Classification:** Contingency; **Lowest/Average Salary:**
$30,000/$75,000; **Industry Concentration:** Generalist; **Function
Concentration:** Generalist

**Hanford, Michael** — *Vice President*
Richard Kader & Associates
343 West Bagley Road, Suite 209
Berea, OH 44017
Telephone: (216) 891-1700
**Recruiter Classification:** Contingency; **Lowest/Average Salary:**
$40,000/$50,000; **Industry Concentration:** Generalist with a primary focus in
Consumer Products, Healthcare/Hospitals, Pharmaceutical/Medical; **Function
Concentration:** Generalist with a primary focus in General Management,
Human Resources, Marketing, Research and Development, Sales,
Women/Minorities

**Hanley, Maureen E.** — *Vice President*
Gilbert Tweed/INESA
155 Prospect Avenue
West Orange, NJ 07052
Telephone: (201) 731-3033
**Recruiter Classification:** Retained; **Lowest/Average Salary:** $90,000/$90,000;
**Industry Concentration:** Generalist with a primary focus in Education/Libraries,
Financial Services, Healthcare/Hospitals, High Technology, Information
Technology; **Function Concentration:** Generalist with a primary focus in
Finance/Accounting, General Management, Human Resources, Marketing,
Sales

**Hanley, Steven** — *Associate*
Source Services Corporation
8614 Westwood Center, Suite 750
Vienna, VA 22182
Telephone: (703) 790-5610
**Recruiter Classification:** Contingency; **Lowest/Average Salary:**
$30,000/$50,000; **Industry Concentration:** Financial Services, Information
Technology; **Function Concentration:** Engineering, Finance/Accounting

**Hanna, Dwight** — *President*
Cadillac Associates
100 South Sunrise Way, Suite 353
Palm Springs, CA 92262
Telephone: (619) 327-0920
**Recruiter Classification:** Contingency; **Lowest/Average Salary:**
$60,000/$75,000; **Industry Concentration:** Healthcare/Hospitals, High
Technology, Pharmaceutical/Medical; **Function Concentration:** Generalist

**Hanna, Remon** — *Associate*
Source Services Corporation
2029 Century Park East, Suite 1350
Los Angeles, CA 90067
Telephone: (310) 277-8092
**Recruiter Classification:** Contingency; **Lowest/Average Salary:**
$30,000/$50,000; **Industry Concentration:** Financial Services, Information
Technology; **Function Concentration:** Engineering, Finance/Accounting

**Hanna, Rodney** — *Principal*
Merit Resource Group, Inc.
7950 Dublin Boulevard, Suite 205
Dublin, CA 94568
Telephone: (510) 828-4700
**Recruiter Classification:** Executive Temporary; **Lowest/Average Salary:**
$75,000/$90,000; **Industry Concentration:** Generalist; **Function
Concentration:** Human Resources

**Hannock, Elwin W.** — *President*
Flynn, Hannock, Incorporated
1001 Farmington Avenue
West Hartford, CT 06107
Telephone: (860) 521-5005
**Recruiter Classification:** Retained, Executive Temporary; **Lowest/Average
Salary:** $75,000/$90,000; **Industry Concentration:** Generalist with a primary
focus in Consumer Products, Financial Services, Healthcare/Hospitals,
Insurance, Manufacturing, Pharmaceutical/Medical; **Function Concentration:**
Generalist with a primary focus in General Management, Human Resources

**Hanrahan, Kevin R.** — *Managing Director*
Russell Reynolds Associates, Inc.
200 South Wacker Drive
Suite 3600
Chicago, IL 60606
Telephone: (312) 993-9696
**Recruiter Classification:** Retained; **Lowest/Average Salary:** $90,000/$90,000;
**Industry Concentration:** Generalist with a primary focus in Consumer
Products; **Function Concentration:** Generalist

**Hansen, Bente K.** — *Vice President*
DHR International, Inc.
12526 High Bluff Drive, Suite 300
San Diego, CA 92130
Telephone: (619) 792-3611
**Recruiter Classification:** Retained; **Lowest/Average Salary:** $60,000/$90,000;
**Industry Concentration:** Generalist; **Function Concentration:** Generalist

**Hansen, Charles A.** — *Manager South Atlantic Region*
Management Recruiters International, Inc.
3840-1 Williamsburg Park Boulevard
Jacksonville, FL 32257-5586
Telephone: (904) 448-5200
**Recruiter Classification:** Contingency; **Lowest/Average Salary:**
$30,000/$75,000; **Industry Concentration:** Generalist; **Function
Concentration:** Generalist

**Hansen, David G.** — *Executive Vice President*
Ott & Hansen, Inc.
136 South Oak Knoll, Suite 300
Pasadena, CA 91101
Telephone: (818) 578-0551
**Recruiter Classification:** Retained; **Lowest/Average Salary:** $75,000/$90,000;
**Industry Concentration:** Generalist with a primary focus in
Aerospace/Defense, Chemical Products, Consumer Products, Energy, High
Technology, Hospitality/Leisure, Manufacturing, Non-Profit, Transportation,
Venture Capital; **Function Concentration:** Generalist with a primary focus in
Engineering, Finance/Accounting, General Management, Human Resources,
Marketing

**Hansen, Erik Lars** — *Vice President*
Korn/Ferry International
1800 Century Park East, Suite 900
Los Angeles, CA 90067
Telephone: (310) 552-1834
**Recruiter Classification:** Retained; **Lowest/Average Salary:** $90,000/$90,000;
**Industry Concentration:** Generalist; **Function Concentration:** Generalist

**Hansen, Jan** — *Co-Manager Southwest Region*
Management Recruiters International, Inc.
3 Cielo Center, Suite 650
1250 Capital of Texas Highway South
Austin, TX 78746-2605
Telephone: (512) 327-8292
**Recruiter Classification:** Contingency; **Lowest/Average Salary:**
$30,000/$75,000; **Industry Concentration:** Generalist; **Function
Concentration:** Generalist

**Hansen, Martin L.** — *Co-Manager*
Management Recruiters International, Inc.
3 Cielo Center, Suite 650
1250 Capital of Texas Highway South
Austin, TX 78746-2605
Telephone: (512) 327-8292
**Recruiter Classification:** Contingency; **Lowest/Average Salary:**
$30,000/$75,000; **Industry Concentration:** Generalist; **Function
Concentration:** Generalist

**Hansen, Ty E.** — *Chairman and CEO*
Blake, Hansen & Nye, Limited
1920 Bayshore Drive
Englewood, FL 34223
Telephone: (941) 475-1300
**Recruiter Classification:** Retained; **Lowest/Average Salary:** $75,000/$90,000;
**Industry Concentration:** Generalist; **Function Concentration:** Generalist with a
primary focus in Engineering, Finance/Accounting, General Management,
Human Resources, Marketing, Sales

**Hanson, Carrie** — *Recruiter*
U.S. Envirosearch
445 Union Boulevard, Suite 225
Lakewood, CO 80228
Telephone: (303) 980-6600
**Recruiter Classification:** Contingency; **Lowest/Average Salary:** $30,000/$60,000;
**Industry Concentration:** Environmental; **Function Concentration:** Generalist
with a primary focus in Administration, Engineering, Finance/Accounting,
General Management, Marketing, Sales, Women/Minorities

**Hanson, Grant M.** — *Associate Director*
Goodrich & Sherwood Associates, Inc.
6 Century Drive
Parsippany, NJ 07054
Telephone: (201) 455-7100
**Recruiter Classification:** Retained; **Lowest/Average Salary:** $60,000/$90,000;
**Industry Concentration:** Generalist with a primary focus in Biotechnology,
Board Services, Chemical Products, Consumer Products, Financial Services,
Healthcare/Hospitals, Information Technology, Insurance, Manufacturing,
Oil/Gas, Publishing/Media, Venture Capital; **Function Concentration:**
Generalist with a primary focus in Administration, Finance/Accounting,
General Management, Human Resources, Marketing, Sales

**Hanson, Jeremy** — *Senior Associate*
Korn/Ferry International
4816 IDS Center
Minneapolis, MN 55402
Telephone: (612) 333-1834
**Recruiter Classification:** Retained; **Lowest/Average Salary:** $90,000/$90,000;
**Industry Concentration:** Generalist; **Function Concentration:** Generalist

**Hanson, Lee** — *Consultant*
Heidrick & Struggles, Inc.
Four Embarcadero Center, Suite 3570
San Francisco, CA 94111
Telephone: (415) 981-2854
**Recruiter Classification:** Retained; **Lowest/Average Salary:** $75,000/$90,000;
**Industry Concentration:** Generalist with a primary focus in Financial Services,
High Technology; **Function Concentration:** Generalist with a primary focus in
Finance/Accounting

**Hanson, Paul L.** — *Managing Director*
Ward Howell International, Inc.
401 East Host Drive
Lake Geneva, WI 53147
Telephone: (414) 249-5200
**Recruiter Classification:** Retained; **Lowest/Average Salary:** $75,000/$90,000;
**Industry Concentration:** Generalist; **Function Concentration:** Generalist

**Hanson, Russell V.** — *Manager Midwest Region*
Management Recruiters International, Inc.
911 North Lynndale Drive
Appleton, WI 54914
Telephone: (414) 731-5221
**Recruiter Classification:** Contingency; **Lowest/Average Salary:** $30,000/$75,000;
**Industry Concentration:** Generalist; **Function Concentration:** Generalist

**Harap, David** — *Senior Associate*
Korn/Ferry International
1300 Dove Street
Suite 300
Newport Beach, CA 92660
Telephone: (714) 851-1834
**Recruiter Classification:** Retained; **Lowest/Average Salary:** $90,000/$90,000;
**Industry Concentration:** Generalist with a primary focus in
Healthcare/Hospitals, Pharmaceutical/Medical; **Function Concentration:**
Generalist

**Harbaugh, Paul J.** — *Executive Vice President*
International Management Advisors, Inc.
516 Fifth Avenue
New York, NY 10036-7501
Telephone: (212) 758-7770
**Recruiter Classification:** Retained; **Lowest/Average Salary:** $75,000/$90,000;
**Industry Concentration:** Generalist with a primary focus in
Aerospace/Defense, Automotive, Biotechnology, Chemical Products,
Consumer Products, Electronics, Energy, Financial Services,
Healthcare/Hospitals, High Technology, Hospitality/Leisure, Manufacturing,
Non-Profit, Oil/Gas; **Function Concentration:** Generalist with a primary focus
in Engineering, Finance/Accounting, General Management, Human Resources,
Marketing, Research and Development, Women/Minorities

**Harbert, David O.** — *Partner*
Sweeney Harbert & Mummert, Inc.
777 South Harbour Island Boulevard, Suite 130
Tampa, FL 33602
Telephone: (813) 229-5360
**Recruiter Classification:** Retained; **Lowest/Average Salary:** $90,000/$90,000;
**Industry Concentration:** Generalist with a primary focus in Board Services,
Energy, Financial Services, Information Technology, Manufacturing, Non-Profit,
Transportation; **Function Concentration:** Generalist with a primary focus in
Administration, Finance/Accounting, General Management, Human Resources,
Marketing, Research and Development, Sales

**Hard, Sally Ann** — *Associate*
Ast/Bryant
One Atlantic Street
Stamford, CT 06901
Telephone: (203) 975-7188
**Recruiter Classification:** Retained; **Lowest/Average Salary:** $75,000/$90,000;
**Industry Concentration:** Education/Libraries, Environmental, Non-Profit;
**Function Concentration:** Women/Minorities

**Hardbrod, Herbert** — *Manager Eastern Region*
Management Recruiters International, Inc.
984 Route 9, Suite 5
Parlin, NJ 08859-2033
Telephone: (908) 727-8300
**Recruiter Classification:** Contingency; **Lowest/Average Salary:**
$30,000/$75,000; **Industry Concentration:** Generalist; **Function
Concentration:** Generalist

**Hardison, Richard L.** — *President*
Hardison & Company
4975 Preston Park Boulevard, Suite 150
Plano, TX 75093
Telephone: (214) 985-6990
**Recruiter Classification:** Retained; **Lowest/Average Salary:** $90,000/$90,000;
**Industry Concentration:** Generalist with a primary focus in Chemical Products,
Electronics, Energy, Financial Services, High Technology, Hospitality/Leisure,
Information Technology, Manufacturing, Oil/Gas, Packaging, Real Estate,
Venture Capital; **Function Concentration:** Generalist with a primary focus in
Engineering, Finance/Accounting, General Management, Human Resources,
Marketing, Research and Development, Sales, Women/Minorities

**Hardwick, Michael** — *Manager North Atlantic Region*
Management Recruiters International, Inc.
1431 Richland Avenue West, P.O. Box 730
Aiken, SC 29801
Telephone: (803) 648-1361
**Recruiter Classification:** Contingency; **Lowest/Average Salary:**
$30,000/$75,000; **Industry Concentration:** Generalist; **Function
Concentration:** Generalist

**Hardy, Thomas G.** — *Senior Director*
Spencer Stuart
277 Park Avenue, 29th Floor
New York, NY 10172
Telephone: (212) 336-0200
**Recruiter Classification:** Retained; **Lowest/Average Salary:** $90,000/$90,000;
**Industry Concentration:** Generalist with a primary focus in Biotechnology,
Consumer Products, Venture Capital; **Function Concentration:** Generalist

**Harelick, Arthur S.** — *Office of the President*
Ashway, Ltd.
295 Madison Avenue
New York, NY 10017
Telephone: (212) 679-3300
**Recruiter Classification:** Contingency; **Lowest/Average Salary:**
$30,000/$90,000; **Industry Concentration:** Biotechnology, Environmental,
High Technology, Insurance; **Function Concentration:** General Management

**Harfenist, Harry** — *President*
Parker Page Group
12550 Biscayne Boulevard
Suite 209
Miami, FL 33181
Telephone: (305) 892-2822
**Recruiter Classification:** Executive Temporary; **Lowest/Average Salary:**
$30,000/$75,000; **Industry Concentration:** Generalist with a primary focus in
Biotechnology, Electronics, Environmental, Financial Services, High
Technology, Hospitality/Leisure, Manufacturing, Pharmaceutical/Medical;
**Function Concentration:** Generalist

**Hargis, N. Leann** — *Senior Associate*
Montgomery Resources, Inc.
555 Montgomery Street, Suite 1650
San Francisco, CA 94111
Telephone: (415) 956-4242
**Recruiter Classification:** Contingency; **Lowest/Average Salary:**
$30,000/$60,000; **Industry Concentration:** Consumer Products, Financial
Services, High Technology, Insurance, Manufacturing, Real Estate, Venture
Capital; **Function Concentration:** Finance/Accounting

**Harkins, Robert E.** — *President*
Robert Harkins Associates, Inc.
P.O. Box 236
1248 West Main Street
Ephrata, PA 17522
Telephone: (717) 733-9664
**Recruiter Classification:** Contingency; **Lowest/Average Salary:**
$40,000/$50,000; **Industry Concentration:** Generalist with a primary focus in
Automotive, Chemical Products, Consumer Products, Electronics,
Environmental, Manufacturing, Packaging, Pharmaceutical/Medical; **Function
Concentration:** Engineering, General Management, Human Resources

**Harlow, John** — *Managing Director*
Korn/Ferry International
2180 Sand Hill Road
Menlo Park, CA 94025
Telephone: (415) 529-1834
**Recruiter Classification:** Retained; **Lowest/Average Salary:** $90,000/$90,000;
**Industry Concentration:** Generalist; **Function Concentration:** Generalist

**Harmon, Tony** — *Consultant*
Mixtec Group
31255 Cedar Valley Drive
Suite 300-327
Westlake Village, CA 91362
Telephone: (818) 889-8819
**Recruiter Classification:** Contingency; **Lowest/Average Salary:**
$60,000/$90,000; **Industry Concentration:** Hospitality/Leisure; **Function
Concentration:** Generalist with a primary focus in Marketing, Sales

**Haro, Adolfo Medina** — *Consultant*
Egon Zehnder International Inc.
Paseo de las Palmas No. 405-703
Co. Lomas de Chapultepec
Mexico City, D.F., MEXICO 11000
Telephone: (525) 540-7635
**Recruiter Classification:** Retained; **Lowest/Average Salary:** $90,000/$90,000;
**Industry Concentration:** Generalist with a primary focus in Biotechnology,
Financial Services, High Technology, Manufacturing, Pharmaceutical/Medical;
**Function Concentration:** Generalist

**Harp, Kimberly** — *Associate*
Source Services Corporation
7730 East Bellview Avenue, Suite 302
Englewood, CO 80111
Telephone: (303) 773-3700
**Recruiter Classification:** Contingency; **Lowest/Average Salary:**
$30,000/$50,000; **Industry Concentration:** Financial Services, Information
Technology; **Function Concentration:** Engineering, Finance/Accounting

**Harrell, L. Parker** — *Managing Director*
Korn/Ferry International
Presidential Plaza
900 19th Street, N.W.
Washington, DC 20006
Telephone: (202) 822-9444
**Recruiter Classification:** Retained; **Lowest/Average Salary:** $90,000/$90,000;
**Industry Concentration:** Generalist with a primary focus in Financial Services;
**Function Concentration:** Generalist

**Harreus, Charles F.** — *Principal*
Harreus & Associates
2250 Vineyard Road
Novato, CA 94947
Telephone: (415) 898-7879
**Recruiter Classification:** Retained; **Lowest/Average Salary:** $75,000/$90,000;
**Industry Concentration:** Consumer Products; **Function Concentration:**
Marketing

**Harrington, Chip** — *Manager North Atlantic Region*
Management Recruiters International, Inc.
West Oak Square
2811 Reidville Road, Suite 21
Spartanburg, SC 29301-5650
Telephone: (864) 587-1045
**Recruiter Classification:** Contingency; **Lowest/Average Salary:**
$30,000/$75,000; **Industry Concentration:** Generalist; **Function
Concentration:** Generalist

**Harrington, Joan** — *Manager North Atlantic Region*
Management Recruiters International, Inc.
P.O. Box 5320
Florence, SC 29501-3322
Telephone: (803) 664-1112
**Recruiter Classification:** Contingency; **Lowest/Average Salary:**
$30,000/$75,000; **Industry Concentration:** Generalist; **Function
Concentration:** Generalist

**Harrington, Robert J.** — *Principal*
Sanford Rose Associates
3405H West Wendover Avenue
Greensboro, NC 27407
Telephone: (910) 852-3003
**Recruiter Classification:** Contingency; **Lowest/Average Salary:** $30,000/$75,000;
**Industry Concentration:** Generalist; **Function Concentration:** Generalist

**Harris, Andrew** — *President*
Harris Heery & Associates
40 Richards Avenue
One Norwalk West
Norwalk, CT 06854
Telephone: (203) 857-0808
**Recruiter Classification:** Retained; **Lowest/Average Salary:** $75,000/$90,000;
**Industry Concentration:** Consumer Products; **Function Concentration:**
Marketing

**Harris, Bruce** — *Executive Vice President*
ProResource, Inc.
500 Ohio Savings Plaza
1801 East Ninth Street, Suite 500
Cleveland, OH 44114
Telephone: (216) 579-1515
**Recruiter Classification:** Executive Temporary; **Lowest/Average Salary:**
$30,000/$75,000; **Industry Concentration:** Generalist; **Function
Concentration:** Generalist with a primary focus in Engineering,
Finance/Accounting, General Management, Human Resources, Marketing,
Research and Development

**Harris, Ethel S.** — *Manager Administrative Services*
Don Richard Associates of Charlotte
2650 One First Union Center
301 South College Street
Charlotte, NC 28202-6000
Telephone: (704) 377-6447
**Recruiter Classification:** Contingency, Executive Temporary; **Lowest/Average
Salary:** $30,000/$30,000; **Industry Concentration:** Generalist with a primary
focus in Environmental, Manufacturing, Real Estate; **Function Concentration:**
Generalist with a primary focus in Administration, General Management,
Human Resources

**Harris, Jack** — *Partner*
Baker, Harris & Partners Limited
130 Adelaide Street West, Suite 2710
Toronto, Ontario, CANADA M5H 3P5
Telephone: (416) 947-1990
**Recruiter Classification:** Retained; **Lowest/Average Salary:** $75,000/$90,000;
**Industry Concentration:** Generalist with a primary focus in Automotive,
Chemical Products, Consumer Products, Financial Services, Manufacturing,
Non-Profit; **Function Concentration:** Generalist with a primary focus in
Finance/Accounting, Human Resources

**Harris, Jack L.** — *Co-Owner/Manager*
Management Recruiters International, Inc.
7190 West Houghton Lake Drive, Suite 109
Houghton, MI 48629
Telephone: (517) 422-5700
**Recruiter Classification:** Contingency; **Lowest/Average Salary:**
$30,000/$75,000; **Industry Concentration:** Generalist; **Function
Concentration:** Generalist

**Harris, Julia** — *Managing Director*
The Whitney Group
850 Third Avenue, 11th Floor
New York, NY 10022
Telephone: (212) 508-3500
**Recruiter Classification:** Retained; **Lowest/Average Salary:** $75,000/$90,000;
**Industry Concentration:** Generalist with a primary focus in Financial Services,
Real Estate, Venture Capital; **Function Concentration:** Generalist with a
primary focus in Sales

**Harris, Melissa** — *Consultant*
Paul Ray Berndtson
2029 Century Park East
Suite 1000
Los Angeles, CA 90067
Telephone: (310) 557-2828
**Recruiter Classification:** Retained; **Lowest/Average Salary:** $90,000/$90,000;
**Industry Concentration:** Generalist; **Function Concentration:** Generalist

**Harris, Vicki M.** — *Co-Owner/Manager*
Management Recruiters International, Inc.
7190 West Houghton Lake Drive, Suite 109
Houghton, MI 48629
Telephone: (517) 422-5700
**Recruiter Classification:** Contingency; **Lowest/Average Salary:**
$30,000/$75,000; **Industry Concentration:** Generalist; **Function
Concentration:** Generalist

**Harrison, Joel** — *Managing Partner*
D.A. Kreuter Associates, Inc.
1100 East Hector Street, Suite 388
Conshohocken, PA 19428
Telephone: (610) 834-1100
**Recruiter Classification:** Retained; **Lowest/Average Salary:** $60,000/$90,000;
**Industry Concentration:** Financial Services, Insurance; **Function
Concentration:** General Management, Marketing, Sales

**Harrison, Patricia** — *Associate*
Source Services Corporation
5429 LBJ Freeway, Suite 275
Dallas, TX 75240
Telephone: (214) 387-1600
**Recruiter Classification:** Contingency; **Lowest/Average Salary:**
$30,000/$50,000; **Industry Concentration:** Financial Services, Information
Technology; **Function Concentration:** Engineering, Finance/Accounting

**Harrison, Priscilla** — *Executive Recruiter*
Phillips Resource Group
330 Pelham Road, Building A
Greenville, SC 29615
Telephone: (864) 271-6350
**Recruiter Classification:** Contingency; **Lowest/Average Salary:**
$40,000/$50,000; **Industry Concentration:** Chemical Products, Electronics,
Environmental, High Technology, Information Technology, Manufacturing,
Packaging; **Function Concentration:** Administration, Engineering,
Finance/Accounting, General Management, Human Resources, Marketing,
Research and Development, Sales

**Harshman, Donald** — *Senior Vice President*
The Stevenson Group of New Jersey
560 Sylvan Avenue
Englewood Cliffs, NJ 07632
Telephone: (201) 568-1900
**Recruiter Classification:** Retained; **Lowest/Average Salary:** $75,000/$90,000;
**Industry Concentration:** Generalist with a primary focus in Chemical Products,
Consumer Products, Fashion (Retail/Apparel), Financial Services, Information
Technology, Pharmaceutical/Medical; **Function Concentration:** Generalist with
a primary focus in Finance/Accounting, General Management, Human
Resources, Marketing, Sales

**Hart, Andrew D.** — *Managing Director*
Russell Reynolds Associates, Inc.
200 Park Avenue
New York, NY 10166-0002
Telephone: (212) 351-2000
**Recruiter Classification:** Retained; **Lowest/Average Salary:** $90,000/$90,000;
**Industry Concentration:** Financial Services, Healthcare/Hospitals; **Function
Concentration:** Generalist

**Hart, Crystal** — *Associate*
Source Services Corporation
One Park Plaza, Suite 560
Irvine, CA 92714
Telephone: (714) 660-1666
**Recruiter Classification:** Contingency; **Lowest/Average Salary:**
$30,000/$50,000; **Industry Concentration:** Financial Services, Information
Technology; **Function Concentration:** Engineering, Finance/Accounting

**Hart, David** — *Executive Vice President*
Hadley Lockwood, Inc.
17 State Street, 38th Floor
New York, NY 10004
Telephone: (212) 785-4405
**Recruiter Classification:** Retained; **Lowest/Average Salary:** $90,000/$90,000;
**Industry Concentration:** Financial Services; **Function Concentration:**
Generalist

**Hart, James** — *Associate*
Source Services Corporation
One CityPlace, Suite 170
St. Louis, MO 63141
Telephone: (314) 432-4500
**Recruiter Classification:** Contingency; **Lowest/Average Salary:**
$30,000/$50,000; **Industry Concentration:** Financial Services, Information
Technology; **Function Concentration:** Engineering, Finance/Accounting

**Hart, Robert T.** — *Director*
D.E. Foster Partners Inc.
Stamford Square, 3001 Summer Street, 5th Floor
Stamford, CT 06905
Telephone: (203) 406-8247
**Recruiter Classification:** Retained; **Lowest/Average Salary:** $90,000/$90,000;
**Industry Concentration:** Generalist with a primary focus in Biotechnology,
Chemical Products, Consumer Products, Education/Libraries, Financial
Services, Healthcare/Hospitals, Information Technology, Manufacturing,
Packaging, Pharmaceutical/Medical; **Function Concentration:** Generalist with
a primary focus in Administration, Finance/Accounting, General Management,
Human Resources, Marketing, Research and Development, Sales,
Women/Minorities

**Hart, Susan S.** — *Senior Director*
Spencer Stuart
Financial Centre
695 East Main Street
Stamford, CT 06901
Telephone: (203) 324-6333
**Recruiter Classification:** Retained; **Lowest/Average Salary:** $90,000/$90,000;
**Industry Concentration:** Consumer Products, Fashion (Retail/Apparel);
**Function Concentration:** Generalist

**Hartnett, Katy** — *Senior Account Manager*
The Paladin Companies, Inc.
875 North Michigan Avenue, Suite 3218
Chicago, IL 60611
Telephone: (312) 654-2600
**Recruiter Classification:** Executive Temporary; **Lowest/Average Salary:**
$50,000/$90,000; **Industry Concentration:** Generalist; **Function
Concentration:** Marketing

**Harty, Shirley Cox** — *Consultant*
Paul Ray Berndtson
191 Peachtree Tower, Suite 3800
191 Peachtree Street, NE
Atlanta, GA 30303-1757
Telephone: (404) 215-4600
**Recruiter Classification:** Retained; **Lowest/Average Salary:** $90,000/$90,000;
**Industry Concentration:** Generalist with a primary focus in Financial Services;
**Function Concentration:** Generalist

**Hartzman, Deborah** — *Regional Manager*
Advanced Information Management
900 Wilshire Boulevard, Suite 1424
Los Angeles, CA 90017
Telephone: (213) 243-9236
**Recruiter Classification:** Contingency; **Lowest/Average Salary:**
$20,000/$40,000; **Industry Concentration:** Information Technology; **Function
Concentration:** Human Resources, Women/Minorities

**Harvey, Jill** — *Physician Recruiter*
MSI International
230 Peachtree Street, N.E.
Suite 1550
Atlanta, GA 30303
Telephone: (404) 653-7360
**Recruiter Classification:** Contingency; **Lowest/Average Salary:** $30,000/$60,000;
**Industry Concentration:** Generalist with a primary focus in Healthcare/Hospitals;
**Function Concentration:** Generalist with a primary focus in Administration,
Engineering, Finance/Accounting, General Management, Marketing, Sales

**Harvey, John K.** — *Manager North Atlantic Region*
Management Recruiters International, Inc.
21 North Main Street, Suite 204
Alpharetta, GA 30201-1620
Telephone: (770) 664-5512
**Recruiter Classification:** Contingency; **Lowest/Average Salary:** $30,000/$75,000;
**Industry Concentration:** Generalist; **Function Concentration:** Generalist

**Harvey, Joy** — *Placement Specialist*
Key Employment Services
1001 Office Park Road, Suite 320
West Des Moines, IA 50265-2567
Telephone: (515) 224-0446
**Recruiter Classification:** Contingency; **Lowest/Average Salary:**
$30,000/$75,000; **Industry Concentration:** Generalist; **Function
Concentration:** Marketing, Sales

**Harvey, Mike** — *President*
Advanced Executive Resources
3040 Charlevoix Drive, SE
Grand Rapids, MI 49546
Telephone: (616) 942-4030
**Recruiter Classification:** Retained; **Lowest/Average Salary:** $30,000/$50,000;
**Industry Concentration:** Generalist with a primary focus in
Aerospace/Defense, Automotive, Chemical Products, Consumer Products,
Electronics, Energy, Environmental, Financial Services, Healthcare/Hospitals,
High Technology, Information Technology, Manufacturing, Packaging, Real
Estate; **Function Concentration:** Generalist with a primary focus in
Engineering, Finance/Accounting, General Management, Human Resources,
Marketing, Research and Development, Sales, Women/Minorities

**Harvey, Richard** — *Director*
Price Waterhouse
2401 Toronto Dominion Tower
Edmonton Centre
Edmonton, Alberta, CANADA T5J 2Z1
Telephone: (403) 493-8200
**Recruiter Classification:** Retained; **Lowest/Average Salary:** $75,000/$75,000;
**Industry Concentration:** Generalist with a primary focus in Board Services,
Energy, Financial Services, Healthcare/Hospitals, High Technology,
Manufacturing, Non-Profit, Oil/Gas; **Function Concentration:** Generalist with a
primary focus in Administration, Engineering, Finance/Accounting, General
Management, Human Resources, Marketing, Sales

**Harwood, Brian** — *Associate*
Source Services Corporation
111 Founders Plaza, Suite 1501E
Hartford, CT 06108
Telephone: (860) 528-0300
Recruiter Classification: Contingency; **Lowest/Average Salary:**
$30,000/$50,000; **Industry Concentration:** Financial Services, Information
Technology; **Function Concentration:** Engineering, Finance/Accounting

**Haselby, James** — *Associate*
Source Services Corporation
10300 West 103rd Street, Suite 101
Overland Park, KS 66214
Telephone: (913) 888-8885
Recruiter Classification: Contingency; **Lowest/Average Salary:**
$30,000/$50,000; **Industry Concentration:** Financial Services, Information
Technology; **Function Concentration:** Engineering, Finance/Accounting

**Hasler, Betty** — *Partner*
Heidrick & Struggles, Inc.
Four Embarcadero Center, Suite 3570
San Francisco, CA 94111
Telephone: (415) 981-2854
Recruiter Classification: Retained; **Lowest/Average Salary:** $75,000/$90,000;
**Industry Concentration:** Generalist; **Function Concentration:** Generalist

**Hasten, Lawrence** — *Associate*
Source Services Corporation
15260 Ventura Boulevard, Suite 380
Sherman Oaks, CA 91403
Telephone: (818) 905-1500
Recruiter Classification: Contingency; **Lowest/Average Salary:**
$30,000/$50,000; **Industry Concentration:** Financial Services, Information
Technology; **Function Concentration:** Engineering, Finance/Accounting

**Hatcher, Joe B.** — *Director Presidential Search Division*
Ast/Bryant
916 Heather Circle
Conway, AR 72032
Telephone: (501) 513-0206
Recruiter Classification: Retained; **Lowest/Average Salary:** $75,000/$90,000;
**Industry Concentration:** Education/Libraries, Environmental, Non-Profit;
**Function Concentration:** Women/Minorities

**Hauck, Fred P.** — *Vice President*
The Cassie Group
12 Running Brook Road
Bridgewater, NJ 08807
Telephone: (908) 429-1335
Recruiter Classification: Retained; **Lowest/Average Salary:** $75,000/$90,000;
**Industry Concentration:** Biotechnology, Pharmaceutical/Medical; **Function
Concentration:** General Management, Research and Development,
Women/Minorities

**Haughton, Michael** — *Senior Vice President*
DeFrain, Mayer, Lee & Burgess LLC
6900 College Boulevard
Overland Park, KS 66211
Telephone: (913) 345-0500
Recruiter Classification: Retained; **Lowest/Average Salary:** $50,000/$90,000;
**Industry Concentration:** Generalist with a primary focus in Automotive,
Chemical Products, Consumer Products, Electronics, Energy, Environmental,
Financial Services, Healthcare/Hospitals, High Technology, Insurance,
Manufacturing, Non-Profit, Oil/Gas, Real Estate; **Function Concentration:**
Generalist with a primary focus in Engineering, Finance/Accounting, General
Management, Human Resources, Marketing, Sales

**Hauser, David E.** — *Principal*
Lamalie Amrop International
191 Peachtree Street N.E.
Atlanta, GA 30303
Telephone: (404) 688-0800
Recruiter Classification: Retained; **Lowest/Average Salary:**
$90,000/$90,000; **Industry Concentration:** Generalist; **Function
Concentration:** Generalist

**Hauser, Jack** — *Principal*
Andcor Human Resources
539 East Lake Street
Wayzata, MN 55391
Telephone: (612) 821-1000
Recruiter Classification: Retained; **Lowest/Average Salary:**
$40,000/$75,000; **Industry Concentration:** Generalist; **Function
Concentration:** Generalist

**Hauser, Martha** — *Director*
Spencer Stuart
One Atlantic Center, Suite 3230
1201 West Peachtree Street
Atlanta, GA 30309
Telephone: (404) 892-2800
Recruiter Classification: Retained; **Lowest/Average Salary:** $90,000/$90,000;
**Industry Concentration:** Education/Libraries, Healthcare/Hospitals, Insurance,
Pharmaceutical/Medical, Public Administration; **Function Concentration:**
Generalist with a primary focus in Finance/Accounting, General Management,
Human Resources, Sales, Women/Minorities

**Hauswirth, Jeffrey M.** — *Director*
Spencer Stuart
One University Avenue
Suite 801
Toronto, Ontario, CANADA M5J 2P1
Telephone: (416) 361-0311
Recruiter Classification: Retained; **Lowest/Average Salary:** $90,000/$90,000;
**Industry Concentration:** Generalist with a primary focus in
Aerospace/Defense, Automotive, Entertainment, High Technology, Information
Technology, Manufacturing, Real Estate; **Function Concentration:** Generalist
with a primary focus in Engineering, General Management, Human Resources,
Marketing, Research and Development, Sales

**Hauver, Scott** — *Consultant*
Logix Partners
1601 Trapelo Road
Waltham, MA 02154
Telephone: (617) 890-0500
Recruiter Classification: Retained; **Lowest/Average Salary:** $60,000/$75,000;
**Industry Concentration:** High Technology; **Function Concentration:** Engineering

**Havas, Judy** — *Partner*
Heidrick & Struggles, Inc.
300 South Grand Avenue, Suite 2400
Los Angeles, CA 90071
Telephone: (213) 625-8811
Recruiter Classification: Retained; **Lowest/Average Salary:** $75,000/$90,000;
**Industry Concentration:** Generalist with a primary focus in Consumer
Products, Publishing/Media; **Function Concentration:** Generalist

**Havener, Donald Clarke** — *Partner*
The Abbott Group, Inc.
530 College Parkway, Suite N
Annapolis, MD 21401
Telephone: (410) 757-4100
Recruiter Classification: Retained; **Lowest/Average Salary:** $90,000/$90,000;
**Industry Concentration:** Generalist with a primary focus in
Aerospace/Defense, Chemical Products, Electronics, Energy, Environmental,
Financial Services, High Technology, Information Technology, Manufacturing,
Non-Profit, Publishing/Media, Transportation, Venture Capital; **Function
Concentration:** Generalist with a primary focus in Engineering,
Finance/Accounting, General Management, Human Resources, Marketing,
Research and Development, Sales, Women/Minorities

**Hawfield, Sam G.** — *Manager North Atlantic Region*
Management Recruiters International, Inc.
19501 Highway 73 West, Suite 20
Cornelius, NC 28031
Telephone: (704) 896-1916
Recruiter Classification: Contingency; **Lowest/Average Salary:** $30,000/$75,000;
**Industry Concentration:** Generalist; **Function Concentration:** Generalist

**Hawkins, John T.W.** — *Managing Director*
Russell Reynolds Associates, Inc.
1700 Pennsylvania Avenue N.W.
Suite 850
Washington, DC 20006
Telephone: (202) 628-2150
Recruiter Classification: Retained; **Lowest/Average Salary:** $90,000/$90,000;
**Industry Concentration:** Generalist with a primary focus in
Healthcare/Hospitals; **Function Concentration:** Generalist

**Hawkins, Kirk V.** — *Co-Manager Midwest Region*
Management Recruiters International, Inc.
3400 SW Van Buren
Topeka, KS 66611
Telephone: (913) 267-5430
Recruiter Classification: Contingency; **Lowest/Average Salary:**
$30,000/$75,000; **Industry Concentration:** Generalist; **Function
Concentration:** Generalist

**Hawkins, Phyllis** — *Managing Director/Legal Recruiter*
Phyllis Hawkins & Associates, Inc.
3550 North Central Avenue, Suite 1400
Phoenix, AZ 85012
Telephone: (602) 263-0248
Recruiter Classification: Contingency; **Lowest/Average Salary:**
$60,000/$90,000

**Hawkins, W. Davis** — *Director*
Spencer Stuart
277 Park Avenue, 29th Floor
New York, NY 10172
Telephone: (212) 336-0200
**Recruiter Classification:** Retained; **Lowest/Average Salary:** $90,000/$90,000;
**Industry Concentration:** Financial Services; **Function Concentration:**
Finance/Accounting

**Hawksworth, A. Dwight** — *President/Owner*
A.D. & Associates Executive Search, Inc.
5589 Woodsong Drive, Suite 100
Atlanta, GA 30338
Telephone: (770) 393-0021
**Recruiter Classification:** Contingency; **Lowest/Average Salary:**
$40,000/$50,000; **Industry Concentration:** Generalist with a primary focus in
Electronics, Financial Services, High Technology, Information Technology,
Manufacturing; **Function Concentration:** Generalist with a primary focus in
Engineering, Finance/Accounting, General Management, Human Resources,
Marketing, Research and Development, Sales, Women/Minorities

**Hay, Ian** — *Principal*
Korn/Ferry International
Scotia Plaza
40 King Street West
Toronto, Ontario, CANADA M5H 3Y2
Telephone: (416) 366-1300
**Recruiter Classification:** Retained; **Lowest/Average Salary:** $90,000/$90,000;
**Industry Concentration:** Generalist; **Function Concentration:** Generalist

**Hay, William E.** — *President*
William E. Hay & Company
20 South Clark Street, Suite 2305
Chicago, IL 60603
Telephone: (312) 782-6510
**Recruiter Classification:** Retained; **Lowest/Average Salary:** $50,000/$75,000;
**Industry Concentration:** Generalist with a primary focus in Financial Services,
Hospitality/Leisure, Information Technology, Insurance, Manufacturing, Non-
Profit, Public Administration, Transportation; **Function Concentration:**
Generalist with a primary focus in Administration, Finance/Accounting,
General Management, Human Resources, Marketing, Women/Minorities

**Hayden, Dale** — *Principal*
Sanford Rose Associates
3500 Brooktree Center, Suite 220
Wexford, PA 15090
Telephone: (412) 934-2261
**Recruiter Classification:** Contingency; **Lowest/Average Salary:**
$30,000/$75,000; **Industry Concentration:** Generalist; **Function
Concentration:** Generalist

**Hayden, John** — *Partner*
Johnson Smith & Knisely Accord
100 Park Avenue, 15th Floor
New York, NY 10017
Telephone: (212) 885-9100
**Recruiter Classification:** Retained; **Lowest/Average Salary:** $90,000/$90,000;
**Industry Concentration:** Generalist; **Function Concentration:** Generalist

**Hayden, Lynn** — *Managing Director*
Erlanger Associates Inc.
Phillips Pt.-777 S. Flagler Dr.
Suite 800 West
West Palm Beach, FL 33401
Telephone: (407) 820-9461
**Recruiter Classification:** Retained; **Lowest/Average Salary:** $90,000/$90,000;
**Industry Concentration:** Generalist; **Function Concentration:** Generalist

**Hayes, Lee** — *Associate*
Source Services Corporation
3701 West Algonquin Road, Suite 380
Rolling Meadows, IL 60008
Telephone: (847) 392-0244
**Recruiter Classification:** Contingency; **Lowest/Average Salary:**
$30,000/$50,000; **Industry Concentration:** Financial Services, Information
Technology; **Function Concentration:** Engineering, Finance/Accounting

**Hayes, Stacy** — *Consultant*
The McCormick Group, Inc.
1400 Wilson Boulevard
Arlington, VA 22209
Telephone: (703) 841-1700
**Recruiter Classification:** Retained; **Lowest/Average Salary:** $40,000/$60,000;
**Industry Concentration:** High Technology, Information Technology; **Function
Concentration:** Engineering, Marketing, Sales

**Hayes, Stephen A.** — *Executive Vice President/
Managing Director*
DHR International, Inc.
1155 Connecticut Avenue, Suite 505
Washington, DC 20036
Telephone: (202) 429-6578
**Recruiter Classification:** Retained; **Lowest/Average Salary:** $60,000/$90,000;
**Industry Concentration:** Generalist; **Function Concentration:** Generalist

**Haystead, Steve** — *Executive Recruiter*
Advanced Executive Resources
3040 Charlevoix Drive, SE
Grand Rapids, MI 49546
Telephone: (616) 942-4030
**Recruiter Classification:** Retained; **Lowest/Average Salary:** $30,000/$50,000;
**Industry Concentration:** Generalist with a primary focus in
Aerospace/Defense, Automotive, Chemical Products, Consumer Products,
Electronics, Energy, Environmental, Financial Services, Healthcare/Hospitals,
High Technology, Information Technology, Manufacturing, Packaging, Real
Estate; **Function Concentration:** Generalist with a primary focus in
Engineering, Finance/Accounting, General Management, Human Resources,
Marketing, Research and Development, Sales, Women/Minorities

**Hazelton, Lisa M.** — *Vice President*
Health Care Dimensions
7150 Campus Drive, Suite 320
Colorado Springs, CO 80920
Telephone: (800) 373-3401
**Recruiter Classification:** Contingency; **Lowest/Average Salary:**
$40,000/$75,000; **Industry Concentration:** Healthcare/Hospitals, Insurance;
**Function Concentration:** Generalist with a primary focus in Administration,
Finance/Accounting, General Management, Marketing, Sales

**Hazerjian, Cynthia** — *Executive Recruiter*
CPS Inc.
303 Congress Street, 5th Floor
Boston, MA 02210
Telephone: (617) 439-7950
**Recruiter Classification:** Contingency; **Lowest/Average Salary:**
$30,000/$50,000; **Industry Concentration:** Generalist with a primary focus in
Automotive, Biotechnology, Chemical Products, Consumer Products, High
Technology, Insurance, Manufacturing, Oil/Gas, Packaging,
Pharmaceutical/Medical; **Function Concentration:** Engineering, Research and
Development, Sales, Women/Minorities

**Heafey, Bill** — *Executive Recruiter*
CPS Inc.
One Westbrook Corporate Centre, Suite 600
Westchester, IL 60154
Telephone: (708) 531-8370
**Recruiter Classification:** Contingency; **Lowest/Average Salary:**
$30,000/$50,000; **Industry Concentration:** Generalist with a primary focus in
Automotive, Biotechnology, Chemical Products, Consumer Products, High
Technology, Insurance, Manufacturing, Oil/Gas, Packaging,
Pharmaceutical/Medical; **Function Concentration:** Engineering, Research and
Development, Sales, Women/Minorities

**Heagy, Linda H.** — *Partner*
Paul Ray Berndtson
10 South Riverside Plaza
Suite 720
Chicago, IL 60606
Telephone: (312) 876-0730
**Recruiter Classification:** Retained; **Lowest/Average Salary:** $90,000/$90,000;
**Industry Concentration:** Generalist; **Function Concentration:** Generalist

**Healey, Joseph T.** — *Associate*
Highland Search Group, L.L.C.
565 Fifth Avenue, 22nd Floor
New York, NY 10017
Telephone: (212) 328-1113
**Recruiter Classification:** Retained; **Lowest/Average Salary:** $90,000/$90,000;
**Industry Concentration:** Financial Services; **Function Concentration:**
Generalist with a primary focus in Finance/Accounting, General Management,
Human Resources, Sales

**Healy, Vanda K.** — *Co-Owner*
Management Recruiters International, Inc.
13000 West Bluemound Road, Suite 310
Elm Grove, WI 53122-2650
Telephone: (414) 797-7500
**Recruiter Classification:** Contingency; **Lowest/Average Salary:**
$30,000/$75,000; **Industry Concentration:** Generalist; **Function
Concentration:** Generalist

**Healy, William C.** — *Co-Owner*
Management Recruiters International, Inc.
13000 West Bluemound Road, Suite 310
Elm Grove, WI 53122-2650
Telephone: (414) 797-7500
**Recruiter Classification:** Contingency; **Lowest/Average Salary:**
$30,000/$75,000; **Industry Concentration:** Generalist; **Function Concentration:** Generalist

**Heath, Jeffrey A.** — *Manager Eastern Region*
Management Recruiters International, Inc.
370 Lexington Avenue, Suite 412
New York, NY 10017
Telephone: (212) 972-7300
**Recruiter Classification:** Contingency; **Lowest/Average Salary:**
$30,000/$75,000; **Industry Concentration:** Generalist; **Function Concentration:** Generalist

**Heavey, John** — *Manager Consumer Products*
Prestige Inc.
P.O. Box 421
Reedsburg, WI 53959
Telephone: (608) 524-4032
**Recruiter Classification:** Contingency; **Lowest/Average Salary:**
$50,000/$90,000; **Industry Concentration:** Consumer Products; **Function Concentration:** Generalist

**Hebard, Roy** — *Vice President*
Korn/Ferry International
120 South Riverside Plaza
Suite 918
Chicago, IL 60606
Telephone: (312) 726-1841
**Recruiter Classification:** Retained; **Lowest/Average Salary:** $90,000/$90,000;
**Industry Concentration:** Generalist with a primary focus in Consumer
Products; **Function Concentration:** Generalist

**Hebel, Robert W.** — *President*
R.W. Hebel Associates
4833 Spicewood Springs Road, Suite 202
Austin, TX 78759-8404
Telephone: (512) 338-9691
**Recruiter Classification:** Retained; **Lowest/Average Salary:** $90,000/$90,000;
**Industry Concentration:** Biotechnology, Pharmaceutical/Medical; **Function Concentration:** Generalist with a primary focus in Engineering,
Finance/Accounting, General Management, Human Resources, Marketing,
Research and Development, Sales

**Hebert, Guy J.** — *Director*
Spencer Stuart
1981 Avenue McGill College
Montreal, Quebec, CANADA H3A 2Y1
Telephone: (514) 288-3377
**Recruiter Classification:** Retained; **Lowest/Average Salary:** $90,000/$90,000;
**Industry Concentration:** Generalist; **Function Concentration:** Generalist

**Hecker, Henry C.** — *Executive Vice President*
Hogan Acquisitions
7205 Chagrin Road #3
Chagrin Falls, OH 44023
Telephone: (216) 247-9600
**Recruiter Classification:** Retained; **Lowest/Average Salary:** $90,000/$90,000;
**Industry Concentration:** Generalist with a primary focus in Automotive,
Chemical Products, Consumer Products, Environmental, Fashion
(Retail/Apparel), Financial Services, High Technology, Information Technology,
Insurance, Manufacturing, Packaging, Publishing/Media, Transportation,
Venture Capital; **Function Concentration:** Generalist with a primary focus in
Administration, Engineering, Finance/Accounting, General Management,
Marketing

**Heckscher, Cindy P.** — *Executive Vice President*
The Diversified Search Companies
2005 Market Street, Suite 3300
Philadelphia, PA 19103
Telephone: (215) 732-6666
**Recruiter Classification:** Retained; **Lowest/Average Salary:** $90,000/$90,000;
**Industry Concentration:** Generalist; **Function Concentration:** Generalist

**Hedlund, David** — *President*
Hedlund Corporation
One IBM Plaza, Suite 2618
Chicago, IL 60611
Telephone: (312) 755-1400
**Recruiter Classification:** Contingency; **Lowest/Average Salary:**
$75,000/$90,000

**Heery, William** — *Vice President*
Harris Heery & Associates
40 Richards Avenue
One Norwalk West
Norwalk, CT 06854
Telephone: (203) 857-0808
**Recruiter Classification:** Retained; **Lowest/Average Salary:** $75,000/$90,000;
**Industry Concentration:** Consumer Products; **Function Concentration:**
Marketing

**Heideman, Mary Marren** — *Vice President*
DeFrain, Mayer, Lee & Burgess LLC
6900 College Boulevard
Overland Park, KS 66211
Telephone: (913) 345-0500
**Recruiter Classification:** Retained; **Lowest/Average Salary:** $60,000/$90,000;
**Industry Concentration:** Generalist with a primary focus in Consumer
Products, Fashion (Retail/Apparel), Hospitality/Leisure, Non-Profit; **Function Concentration:** Generalist with a primary focus in Administration, Human
Resources

**Heidrick, Gardner W.** — *Chairman*
The Heidrick Partners, Inc.
20 North Wacker Drive
Suite 2850
Chicago, IL 60606-3171
Telephone: (312) 845-9700
**Recruiter Classification:** Retained; **Lowest/Average Salary:** $90,000/$90,000;
**Industry Concentration:** Generalist; **Function Concentration:** Generalist

**Heidrick, Robert L.** — *President*
The Heidrick Partners, Inc.
20 North Wacker Drive
Suite 2850
Chicago, IL 60606-3171
Telephone: (312) 845-9700
**Recruiter Classification:** Retained; **Lowest/Average Salary:** $90,000/$90,000;
**Industry Concentration:** Generalist; **Function Concentration:** Generalist

**Heiken, Barbara E.** — *President*
Randell-Heiken, Inc.
The Lincoln Building
60 East 42nd Street, Suite 2022
New York, NY 10165
Telephone: (212) 490-1313
**Recruiter Classification:** Retained; **Lowest/Average Salary:** $60,000/$90,000;
**Industry Concentration:** Generalist with a primary focus in Consumer
Products, Financial Services, Healthcare/Hospitals, High Technology,
Information Technology, Insurance, Manufacturing, Oil/Gas,
Pharmaceutical/Medical, Publishing/Media; **Function Concentration:**
Generalist with a primary focus in General Management, Human Resources,
Marketing, Sales, Women/Minorities

**Heinrich, Scott** — *Associate*
Source Services Corporation
500 108th Avenue NE, Suite 1780
Bellevue, WA 98004
Telephone: (206) 454-6400
**Recruiter Classification:** Contingency; **Lowest/Average Salary:**
$30,000/$50,000; **Industry Concentration:** Financial Services, Information
Technology; **Function Concentration:** Engineering, Finance/Accounting

**Heintz, William** — *Managing Director - Produce*
Mixtec Group
13626 Tierra Spur
Salinas, CA 93908
Telephone: (408) 484-9391
**Recruiter Classification:** Contingency; **Lowest/Average Salary:**
$60,000/$90,000; **Function Concentration:** Generalist with a primary focus in
Administration, General Management, Marketing, Research and Development,
Sales

**Heiser, Charles S.** — *Vice President*
The Cassie Group
P.O. Box 2282
Valley Center, CA 92082-2282
Telephone: (619) 751-2174
**Recruiter Classification:** Retained; **Lowest/Average Salary:** $75,000/$90,000;
**Industry Concentration:** Pharmaceutical/Medical; **Function Concentration:**
Administration, Engineering, Finance/Accounting, General Management,
Human Resources, Marketing, Sales, Women/Minorities

**Heisser, Robert** — *Co-Manager*
Management Recruiters International, Inc.
6950 East Belleview, Suite 201
Englewood, CO 80111-1626
Telephone: (303) 267-0600
**Recruiter Classification:** Contingency; **Lowest/Average Salary:**
$30,000/$75,000; **Industry Concentration:** Generalist; **Function Concentration:** Generalist

**Heldenbrand, Paul** — *Principal*
The McCormick Group, Inc.
1400 Wilson Boulevard
Arlington, VA 22209
Telephone: (703) 841-1700
**Recruiter Classification:** Retained; **Lowest/Average Salary:** $90,000/$90,000; **Industry Concentration:** Generalist; **Function Concentration:** Generalist

**Helgeson, Burton H.** — *Senior Consultant*
Norm Sanders Associates
2 Village Court
Hazlet, NJ 07730
Telephone: (908) 264-3700
**Recruiter Classification:** Retained; **Lowest/Average Salary:** $90,000/$90,000; **Industry Concentration:** Information Technology; **Function Concentration:** Generalist

**Hellebusch, Jerry** — *President*
Morgan Hunter Corp.
6800 College Boulevard, Suite 550
Overland Park, KS 66211
Telephone: (913) 491-3434
**Recruiter Classification:** Contingency; **Lowest/Average Salary:** $20,000/$30,000; **Industry Concentration:** Consumer Products, Financial Services, Healthcare/Hospitals, Insurance, Manufacturing, Packaging, Publishing/Media, Real Estate; **Function Concentration:** Finance/Accounting

**Heller, Steven A.** — *Vice President*
Martin H. Bauman Associates, Inc.
375 Park Avenue, Suite 2002
New York, NY 10152
Telephone: (212) 752-6580
**Recruiter Classification:** Retained; **Lowest/Average Salary:** $90,000/$90,000; **Industry Concentration:** Generalist with a primary focus in Chemical Products, Consumer Products, Financial Services, Manufacturing, Transportation, Venture Capital; **Function Concentration:** Generalist

**Hellinger, Audrey** — *Vice President*
Martin H. Bauman Associates, Inc.
625 North Michigan Avenue, Suite 500
Chicago, IL 60611-3108
Telephone: (312) 751-5407
**Recruiter Classification:** Retained; **Lowest/Average Salary:** $90,000/$90,000; **Industry Concentration:** Generalist with a primary focus in Board Services, Chemical Products, Consumer Products, Financial Services, Manufacturing, Transportation, Venture Capital; **Function Concentration:** Generalist with a primary focus in Administration, Engineering, Finance/Accounting, General Management, Human Resources, Marketing, Research and Development, Sales, Women/Minorities

**Helmholz, Steven W.** — *Principal*
Korn/Ferry International
237 Park Avenue
New York, NY 10017
Telephone: (212) 687-1834
**Recruiter Classification:** Retained; **Lowest/Average Salary:** $90,000/$90,000; **Industry Concentration:** Generalist; **Function Concentration:** Generalist

**Helminiak, Audrey** — *Executive Recruiter*
Gaffney Management Consultants
35 North Brandon Drive
Glendale Heights, IL 60139-2087
Telephone: (708) 307-3380
**Recruiter Classification:** Retained; **Lowest/Average Salary:** $60,000/$90,000; **Industry Concentration:** Generalist with a primary focus in Automotive, Electronics, High Technology, Manufacturing, Transportation, Venture Capital; **Function Concentration:** Generalist with a primary focus in Engineering, General Management, Human Resources, Marketing, Research and Development, Sales, Women/Minorities

**Helt, Wally A.** — *Manager Eastern Region*
Management Recruiters International, Inc.
The Farm Complex
Box 220-64B
Montoursville, PA 17754
Telephone: (717) 368-2277
**Recruiter Classification:** Contingency; **Lowest/Average Salary:** $30,000/$75,000; **Industry Concentration:** Generalist; **Function Concentration:** Generalist

**Hemer, Craig** — *Senior Consultant*
Tanton Mitchell/Paul Ray Berndtson
710-1050 West Pender Street
Vancouver, British Columbia, CANADA V6E 3S7
Telephone: (604) 685-0261
**Recruiter Classification:** Retained; **Lowest/Average Salary:** $75,000/$90,000; **Industry Concentration:** Generalist; **Function Concentration:** Generalist

**Hemingway, Stuart C.** — *Vice President and Associate*
Robison & Associates
1350 First Citizens Plaza
128 South Tryon Street
Charlotte, NC 28202
Telephone: (704) 376-0059
**Recruiter Classification:** Retained; **Lowest/Average Salary:** $50,000/$90,000; **Industry Concentration:** Generalist with a primary focus in Education/Libraries, Energy, Environmental, Information Technology, Insurance, Manufacturing, Non-Profit, Real Estate, Transportation; **Function Concentration:** Generalist with a primary focus in General Management, Human Resources, Marketing, Women/Minorities

**Henard, John B.** — *Partner*
Lamalie Amrop International
Northdale Plaza, 3903 Northdale Boulevard
Tampa, FL 33624-1864
Telephone: (813) 961-7494
**Recruiter Classification:** Retained; **Lowest/Average Salary:** $90,000/$90,000; **Industry Concentration:** Generalist with a primary focus in Consumer Products, High Technology; **Function Concentration:** Generalist with a primary focus in General Management, Marketing, Sales

**Henderson, Cathy** — *Manager Pacific Region*
Management Recruiters International, Inc.
15 Seascape Village
Aptos, CA 95003
Telephone: (408) 688-5200
**Recruiter Classification:** Contingency; **Lowest/Average Salary:** $30,000/$75,000; **Industry Concentration:** Generalist; **Function Concentration:** Generalist

**Henderson, Dale** — *Manager*
Management Recruiters International, Inc.
15 Seascape Village
Aptos, CA 95003
Telephone: (408) 688-5200
**Recruiter Classification:** Contingency; **Lowest/Average Salary:** $30,000/$75,000; **Industry Concentration:** Generalist; **Function Concentration:** Generalist

**Henderson, John** — *Placement Specialist*
Key Employment Services
1001 Office Park Road, Suite 320
West Des Moines, IA 50265-2567
Telephone: (515) 224-0446
**Recruiter Classification:** Contingency; **Lowest/Average Salary:** $30,000/$75,000; **Industry Concentration:** Generalist; **Function Concentration:** Generalist with a primary focus in Finance/Accounting

**Henderson, Marc** — *Manager Retail Chains and Department Stores*
Prestige Inc.
P.O. Box 421
Reedsburg, WI 53959
Telephone: (608) 524-4032
**Recruiter Classification:** Contingency; **Lowest/Average Salary:** $50,000/$90,000; **Industry Concentration:** Consumer Products; **Function Concentration:** Generalist

**Henderson, William D.** — *Managing Director*
Russell Reynolds Associates, Inc.
200 Park Avenue
New York, NY 10166-0002
Telephone: (212) 351-2000
**Recruiter Classification:** Retained; **Lowest/Average Salary:** $90,000/$90,000; **Industry Concentration:** Generalist; **Function Concentration:** Generalist

**Hendon, Jill** — *Associate*
Korn/Ferry International
303 Peachtree Street N.E.
Suite 1600
Atlanta, GA 30308
Telephone: (404) 577-7542
**Recruiter Classification:** Retained; **Lowest/Average Salary:** $90,000/$90,000; **Industry Concentration:** Generalist; **Function Concentration:** Generalist

**Hendrickson, David L.** — *Partner*
Heidrick & Struggles, Inc.
Greenwich Office Park #3
Greenwich, CT 06831
Telephone: (203) 629-3200
**Recruiter Classification:** Retained; **Lowest/Average Salary:** $75,000/$90,000; **Industry Concentration:** Generalist with a primary focus in Consumer Products, High Technology; **Function Concentration:** Generalist

**Hendrickson, Gary E.** — *Manager Pacific Region*
Management Recruiters International, Inc.
150 Clovis Avenue, Suite 205
Clovis, CA 93612-1152
Telephone: (209) 299-7992
**Recruiter Classification:** Contingency; **Lowest/Average Salary:**
$30,000/$75,000; **Industry Concentration:** Generalist; **Function Concentration:** Generalist

**Hendriks, Warren K.** — *Executive Vice President*
DHR International, Inc.
10 South Riverside Plaza, Suite 2220
Chicago, IL 60606
Telephone: (312) 782-1581
**Recruiter Classification:** Retained; **Lowest/Average Salary:** $60,000/$90,000;
**Industry Concentration:** Generalist; **Function Concentration:** Generalist

**Hendrixson, Ron** — *Senior Associate*
Korn/Ferry International
601 South Figueroa
Suite 1900
Los Angeles, CA 90017
Telephone: (213) 624-6600
**Recruiter Classification:** Retained; **Lowest/Average Salary:** $90,000/$90,000;
**Industry Concentration:** Generalist; **Function Concentration:** Generalist

**Heneghan, Donald A.** — *Partner*
Allerton Heneghan & O'Neill
70 West Madison Street, Suite 2015
Chicago, IL 60602
Telephone: (312) 263-1075
**Recruiter Classification:** Retained; **Lowest/Average Salary:** $75,000/$90,000;
**Industry Concentration:** Generalist with a primary focus in Automotive,
Consumer Products, High Technology, Hospitality/Leisure, Information
Technology, Manufacturing, Packaging, Transportation; **Function
Concentration:** Generalist with a primary focus in Finance/Accounting,
General Management, Human Resources, Marketing, Research and
Development, Women/Minorities

**Henkel, John J.** — *Co-Owner*
Management Recruiters International, Inc.
Valley View Center, Suite 125
5307 South 92nd Street
Hales Corners, WI 53130
Telephone: (414) 529-8020
**Recruiter Classification:** Contingency; **Lowest/Average Salary:**
$30,000/$75,000; **Industry Concentration:** Generalist; **Function
Concentration:** Generalist

**Henkel, John J.** — *Co-Owner/Manager Midwest Region*
Management Recruiters International, Inc.
8338 Corporate Drive, Suite 300
Racine, WI 53406
Telephone: (414) 886-8000
**Recruiter Classification:** Contingency; **Lowest/Average Salary:**
$30,000/$75,000; **Industry Concentration:** Generalist; **Function
Concentration:** Generalist

**Henn, George W.** — *President*
G.W. Henn & Company
42 East Gay Street, Suite 1312
Columbus, OH 43215-3119
Telephone: (614) 469-9666
**Recruiter Classification:** Retained; **Lowest/Average Salary:** $75,000/$90,000;
**Industry Concentration:** Generalist with a primary focus in Automotive,
Financial Services, Information Technology, Insurance, Manufacturing,
Pharmaceutical/Medical; **Function Concentration:** Generalist

**Henneberry, Ward** — *Associate*
Source Services Corporation
500 108th Avenue NE, Suite 1780
Bellevue, WA 98004
Telephone: (206) 454-6400
**Recruiter Classification:** Contingency; **Lowest/Average Salary:**
$30,000/$50,000; **Industry Concentration:** Financial Services, Information
Technology; **Function Concentration:** Engineering, Finance/Accounting

**Hennessy, Robert D.** — *Senior Associate*
Korn/Ferry International
2 Logan Square, Suite 2530
Philadelphia, PA 19103
Telephone: (215) 496-6666
**Recruiter Classification:** Retained; **Lowest/Average Salary:** $90,000/$90,000;
**Industry Concentration:** Generalist; **Function Concentration:** Generalist

**Hennig, Sandra M.** — *Executive Recruiter*
MSI International
229 Peachtree Street, NE
Suite 1201
Atlanta, GA 30303
Telephone: (404) 659-5050
**Recruiter Classification:** Contingency; **Lowest/Average Salary:**
$30,000/$60,000; **Industry Concentration:** Generalist with a primary focus in
Financial Services; **Function Concentration:** Administration, Engineering,
Finance/Accounting, General Management, Marketing

**Henry, Patrick** — *Executive Recruiter*
F-O-R-T-U-N-E Personnel Consultants of Huntsville, Inc.
3311 Bob Wallace Avenue, Suite 204
Huntsville, AL 35805
Telephone: (205) 534-7282
**Recruiter Classification:** Contingency, Executive Temporary; **Lowest/Average
Salary:** $30,000/$60,000; **Industry Concentration:** Electronics, High
Technology, Information Technology; **Function Concentration:** Generalist with
a primary focus in Engineering

**Henshaw, Robert** — *Executive Recruiter*
F-O-R-T-U-N-E Personnel Consultants of Huntsville, Inc.
3311 Bob Wallace Avenue, Suite 204
Huntsville, AL 35805
Telephone: (205) 534-7282
**Recruiter Classification:** Contingency, Executive Temporary; **Lowest/Average
Salary:** $30,000/$50,000; **Industry Concentration:** Generalist with a primary
focus in Automotive, Consumer Products, Electronics, Environmental,
Manufacturing; **Function Concentration:** Engineering, General Management,
Human Resources

**Hensley, Bert** — *Principal*
Korn/Ferry International
1800 Century Park East, Suite 900
Los Angeles, CA 90067
Telephone: (310) 552-1834
**Recruiter Classification:** Retained; **Lowest/Average Salary:** $90,000/$90,000;
**Industry Concentration:** Generalist; **Function Concentration:** Generalist

**Hensley, Gayla** — *Principal*
Atlantic Search Group, Inc.
One Liberty Square
Boston, MA 02109
Telephone: (617) 426-9700
**Recruiter Classification:** Contingency; **Lowest/Average Salary:**
$20,000/$60,000; **Industry Concentration:** Generalist with a primary focus in
Biotechnology, Consumer Products, Electronics, Financial Services, High
Technology, Information Technology, Manufacturing, Real Estate; **Function
Concentration:** Finance/Accounting

**Hergenrather, Edmund R.** — *Chairman*
Hergenrather & Company
P.O. Box 1100
Solvang, CA 93463
Telephone: (805) 686-2018
**Recruiter Classification:** Retained; **Lowest/Average Salary:** $60,000/$90,000;
**Industry Concentration:** Generalist; **Function Concentration:** Generalist

**Hergenrather, Richard A.** — *President and CEO*
Hergenrather & Company
401 West Charlton Avenue
Spokane, WA 99208-7246
Telephone: (509) 466-6700
**Recruiter Classification:** Retained; **Lowest/Average Salary:** $60,000/$90,000;
**Industry Concentration:** Generalist; **Function Concentration:** Generalist

**Herget, James P.** — *Senior Partner*
Lamalie Amrop International
Key Tower, 127 Public Square
Cleveland, OH 44114-1216
Telephone: (216) 694-3000
**Recruiter Classification:** Retained; **Lowest/Average Salary:** $90,000/$90,000;
**Industry Concentration:** Generalist; **Function Concentration:** Generalist with a
primary focus in Finance/Accounting, General Management, Human
Resources, Marketing, Research and Development, Sales

**Herman, Beth** — *Area Vice President*
Accountants on Call
3355 Lenox Road, Suite 630
Atlanta, GA 30326
Telephone: (404) 261-4800
**Recruiter Classification:** Contingency; **Lowest/Average Salary:**
$20,000/$30,000; **Industry Concentration:** Generalist; **Function
Concentration:** Finance/Accounting

**Herman, Eugene J.** — *Executive Vice President*
Earley Kielty and Associates, Inc.
Two Pennsylvania Plaza
New York, NY 10121
Telephone: (212) 736-5626
**Recruiter Classification:** Retained; **Lowest/Average Salary:** $90,000/$90,000;
**Industry Concentration:** Generalist with a primary focus in Information
Technology; **Function Concentration:** Generalist with a primary focus in
Administration, Finance/Accounting, General Management, Human Resources,
Marketing, Research and Development, Sales, Women/Minorities

**Herman, Pat** — *Executive Recruiter*
Whitney & Associates, Inc.
920 Second Avenue South, Suite 625
Minneapolis, MN 55402-4035
Telephone: (612) 338-5600
**Recruiter Classification:** Contingency; **Lowest/Average Salary:**
$20,000/$50,000; **Industry Concentration:** Generalist with a primary focus in
Biotechnology, Consumer Products, Electronics, Financial Services,
Healthcare/Hospitals, High Technology, Information Technology, Insurance,
Manufacturing, Packaging, Pharmaceutical/Medical, Publishing/Media, Real
Estate, Transportation, Venture Capital; **Function Concentration:**
Finance/Accounting

**Hermanson, Shelley** — *Recruiter*
Ells Personnel System Inc.
9900 Bren Road East, Suite 105 Opus Center
Minnetonka, MN 55343
Telephone: (612) 932-9933
**Recruiter Classification:** Contingency; **Lowest/Average Salary:**
$20,000/$20,000; **Industry Concentration:** Generalist with a primary focus in
Consumer Products, Transportation; **Function Concentration:** Administration,
Women/Minorities

**Hermsmeyer, Rex** — *President*
Hitchens & Foster, Inc.
Pines Office Center
One The Pines Court
St. Louis, MO 63141
Telephone: (314) 453-0800
**Recruiter Classification:** Contingency; **Lowest/Average Salary:**
$90,000/$90,000; **Industry Concentration:** Healthcare/Hospitals; **Function
Concentration:** General Management

**Hernand, Warren L.** — *President*
Hernand & Partners
770 Tamalpais Drive, Suite 204
Corte Madera, CA 94925
Telephone: (415) 927-7000
**Recruiter Classification:** Executive Temporary; **Industry Concentration:**
High Technology, Information Technology; **Function Concentration:**
Engineering

**Hernandez, Luis A.** — *President*
CoEnergy, Inc.
5065 Westheimer, Suite 815E
Houston, TX 77056
Telephone: (713) 960-1868
**Recruiter Classification:** Contingency; **Lowest/Average Salary:**
$60,000/$90,000; **Industry Concentration:** Energy; **Function Concentration:**
Generalist with a primary focus in Engineering, Marketing

**Hernandez, Ruben** — *Associate*
Source Services Corporation
15600 N.W. 67th Avenue, Suite 210
Miami Lakes, FL 33014
Telephone: (305) 556-8000
**Recruiter Classification:** Contingency; **Lowest/Average Salary:**
$30,000/$50,000; **Industry Concentration:** Financial Services, Information
Technology; **Function Concentration:** Engineering, Finance/Accounting

**Heroux, David** — *Associate*
Source Services Corporation
15260 Ventura Boulevard, Suite 380
Sherman Oaks, CA 91403
Telephone: (818) 905-1500
**Recruiter Classification:** Contingency; **Lowest/Average Salary:**
$30,000/$50,000; **Industry Concentration:** Financial Services, Information
Technology; **Function Concentration:** Engineering, Finance/Accounting

**Herrmann, Jerry C.** — *Manager Midwest Region*
Management Recruiters International, Inc.
Alpine Centre South, Penthouse
2435 Kimberly Road
Bettendorf, IA 52722
Telephone: (319) 359-3503
**Recruiter Classification:** Contingency; **Lowest/Average Salary:**
$30,000/$75,000; **Industry Concentration:** Generalist; **Function
Concentration:** Generalist

**Herrod, Vicki** — *Branch Manager*
Accountants on Call
Bank One Center/Twr., Ste. 3510
111 Monument Circle
Indianapolis, IN 46204
Telephone: (317) 686-0001
**Recruiter Classification:** Contingency; **Lowest/Average Salary:**
$20,000/$30,000; **Industry Concentration:** Generalist; **Function
Concentration:** Finance/Accounting

**Hertan, Richard L.** — *President and COO*
Executive Manning Corporation
3000 N.E. 30th Place, Suite 405/402/411
Fort Lauderdale, FL 33306
Telephone: (954) 561-5100
**Recruiter Classification:** Retained; **Lowest/Average Salary:** $75,000/$90,000;
**Industry Concentration:** Generalist with a primary focus in
Aerospace/Defense, Automotive, Chemical Products, Consumer Products,
Electronics, High Technology, Manufacturing, Pharmaceutical/Medical;
**Function Concentration:** Generalist

**Hertan, Wiliam A.** — *Chairman and CEO*
Executive Manning Corporation
3000 N.E. 30th Place, Suite 405/402/411
Fort Lauderdale, FL 33306
Telephone: (954) 561-5100
**Recruiter Classification:** Retained; **Lowest/Average Salary:** $75,000/$90,000;
**Industry Concentration:** Generalist with a primary focus in
Aerospace/Defense, Automotive, Chemical Products, Consumer Products,
Electronics, High Technology, Manufacturing, Pharmaceutical/Medical;
**Function Concentration:** Generalist

**Hertlein, James N.J.** — *Consultant*
Boyden/Zay & Company
Three Allen Center
333 Clay Street, Suite 3810
Houston, TX 77002
Telephone: (713) 655-0123
**Recruiter Classification:** Retained; **Lowest/Average Salary:** $90,000/$90,000;
**Industry Concentration:** Generalist with a primary focus in Chemical Products,
Energy, High Technology, Information Technology, Oil/Gas; **Function
Concentration:** Generalist with a primary focus in Engineering, General
Management, Human Resources

**Hertner, Herbert H.** — *President*
H. Hertner Associates, Inc.
6600 Cowpen Road, Suite 220
Miami Lakes, FL 33014
Telephone: (305) 556-8882
**Recruiter Classification:** Contingency; **Lowest/Average Salary:**
$50,000/$90,000

**Hertner, Pamela R.** — *Search Consultant*
H. Hertner Associates, Inc.
6600 Cowpen Road, Suite 220
Miami Lakes, FL 33014
Telephone: (305) 556-8882
**Recruiter Classification:** Contingency; **Lowest/Average Salary:**
$50,000/$60,000

**Herz, Stanley** — *Principal*
Stanley Herz and Company, Inc.
Mill Pond Office Complex, Suite 103
Somers, NY 10589
Telephone: (914) 277-7500
**Recruiter Classification:** Retained; **Lowest/Average Salary:** $90,000/$90,000;
**Industry Concentration:** Generalist; **Function Concentration:** General
Management

**Herzog, Sarah** — *Associate*
Source Services Corporation
One Park Plaza, Suite 560
Irvine, CA 92714
Telephone: (714) 660-1666
**Recruiter Classification:** Contingency; **Lowest/Average Salary:**
$30,000/$50,000; **Industry Concentration:** Financial Services, Information
Technology; **Function Concentration:** Engineering, Finance/Accounting

**Hess, David B.** — *Principal*
Sanford Rose Associates
201B Rosser Avenue, Suite 201
Waynesboro, VA 22980-3351
Telephone: (540) 943-8400
**Recruiter Classification:** Contingency; **Lowest/Average Salary:**
$30,000/$75,000; **Industry Concentration:** Generalist; **Function
Concentration:** Generalist

**Hess, James C.** — *Executive Vice President*
The Diversified Search Companies
2005 Market Street, Suite 3300
Philadelphia, PA 19103
Telephone: (215) 732-6666
Recruiter Classification: Retained; Lowest/Average Salary: $90,000/$90,000;
Industry Concentration: Generalist; Function Concentration: Generalist

**Hess, Patricia** — *Principal*
Sanford Rose Associates
201B Rosser Avenue, Suite 201
Waynesboro, VA 22980-3351
Telephone: (540) 943-8400
Recruiter Classification: Contingency; Lowest/Average Salary:
$30,000/$75,000; Industry Concentration: Generalist; Function
Concentration: Generalist

**Hessel, Gregory** — *Senior Associate*
Korn/Ferry International
3950 Lincoln Plaza
500 North Akard Street
Dallas, TX 75201
Telephone: (214) 954-1834
Recruiter Classification: Retained; Lowest/Average Salary: $90,000/$90,000;
Industry Concentration: Generalist; Function Concentration: Generalist

**Hetherman, Margaret F.** — *Director Research*
Highland Search Group, L.L.C.
565 Fifth Avenue, 22nd Floor
New York, NY 10017
Telephone: (212) 328-1113
Recruiter Classification: Retained; Lowest/Average Salary: $90,000/$90,000;
Industry Concentration: Financial Services, Real Estate, Venture Capital;
Function Concentration: Generalist with a primary focus in
Finance/Accounting, General Management, Human Resources, Research and
Development, Sales

**Hettinger, Susan** — *Associate*
Kenzer Corp.
Fifth Street Tower, Suite 1330
150 South Fifth Street
Minneapolis, MN 55402
Telephone: (612) 332-7700
Recruiter Classification: Retained; Lowest/Average Salary: $50,000/$90,000;
Industry Concentration: Generalist; Function Concentration: Generalist

**Hetzel, William G.** — *President*
The Hetzel Group, Inc.
1601 Colonial Parkway
Inverness, IL 60067
Telephone: (708) 776-7000
Recruiter Classification: Retained; Lowest/Average Salary: $90,000/$90,000;
Industry Concentration: Generalist; Function Concentration: Generalist

**Heuerman, James N.** — *Senior Officer*
Korn/Ferry International
The Transamerica Pyramid
600 Montgomery Street
San Francisco, CA 94111
Telephone: (415) 956-1834
Recruiter Classification: Retained; Lowest/Average Salary: $90,000/$90,000;
Industry Concentration: Generalist with a primary focus in
Healthcare/Hospitals; Function Concentration: Generalist

**Hewitt, Rives D.** — *Principal*
The Dalley Hewitt Company
1401 Peachtree Street, Suite 500
Atlanta, GA 30309
Telephone: (404) 885-6642
Recruiter Classification: Retained; Lowest/Average Salary: $50,000/$90,000;
Industry Concentration: Generalist with a primary focus in Consumer
Products, Financial Services, Healthcare/Hospitals, Information Technology,
Insurance, Pharmaceutical/Medical; Function Concentration: Generalist with a
primary focus in Finance/Accounting, General Management, Human
Resources, Marketing

**Hickman, Andrew** — *Senior Associate*
Korn/Ferry International
3950 Lincoln Plaza
500 North Akard Street
Dallas, TX 75201
Telephone: (214) 954-1834
Recruiter Classification: Retained; Lowest/Average Salary: $90,000/$90,000;
Industry Concentration: Generalist; Function Concentration: Generalist

**Hicks, Albert M.** — *President*
Phillips Resource Group
330 Pelham Road, Building A
Greenville, SC 29615
Telephone: (864) 271-6350
Recruiter Classification: Contingency; Lowest/Average Salary:
$40,000/$50,000; Industry Concentration: Generalist with a primary focus in
Chemical Products, Electronics, Environmental, High Technology, Information
Technology, Manufacturing, Packaging, Utilities/Nuclear; Function
Concentration: Generalist with a primary focus in Administration, Engineering,
General Management, Human Resources, Marketing, Research and
Development, Sales, Women/Minorities

**Hicks, James L.** — *Executive Recruiter*
MSI International
229 Peachtree Street, NE
Suite 1201
Atlanta, GA 30303
Telephone: (404) 659-5050
Recruiter Classification: Contingency; Lowest/Average Salary:
$30,000/$75,000; Industry Concentration: Generalist with a primary focus in
Healthcare/Hospitals, Pharmaceutical/Medical; Function Concentration:
Generalist with a primary focus in Administration, Engineering,
Finance/Accounting, General Management, Marketing, Sales

**Hicks, Mike** — *Executive Recruiter*
Damon & Associates, Inc.
7515 Greenville Avenue, Suite 900
Dallas, TX 75231
Telephone: (214) 696-6990
Recruiter Classification: Contingency; Lowest/Average Salary:
$30,000/$75,000; Industry Concentration: Electronics, High Technology;
Function Concentration: Generalist

**Hicks, Nancy** — *Consultant*
Paul Ray Berndtson
2029 Century Park East
Suite 1000
Los Angeles, CA 90067
Telephone: (310) 557-2828
Recruiter Classification: Retained; Lowest/Average Salary: $90,000/$90,000;
Industry Concentration: Generalist; Function Concentration: Generalist

**Hicks, Timothy C.** — *Vice President*
Korn/Ferry International
120 South Riverside Plaza
Suite 918
Chicago, IL 60606
Telephone: (312) 726-1841
Recruiter Classification: Retained; Lowest/Average Salary: $90,000/$90,000;
Industry Concentration: Generalist with a primary focus in Consumer
Products; Function Concentration: Generalist

**Hidalgo, Rhonda** — *Executive Recruiter*
Richard, Wayne and Roberts
24 Greenway Plaza, Suite 1304
Houston, TX 77046-2493
Telephone: (713) 629-6681
Recruiter Classification: Retained; Lowest/Average Salary: $40,000/$60,000;
Industry Concentration: Generalist; Function Concentration: Generalist

**Hiebert, Wilf** — *Manager*
KPMG Executive Search
400-128 Fourth Avenue South
Saskatoon, Saskatchewan, CANADA S7K 1M8
Telephone: (306) 934-6280
Recruiter Classification: Retained; Lowest/Average Salary: $75,000/$90,000;
Industry Concentration: Generalist; Function Concentration: Generalist

**Higdon, Henry G.** — *Managing Director*
Higdon Prince Inc.
230 Park Avenue, Suite 1455
New York, NY 10169
Telephone: (212) 986-4662
Recruiter Classification: Retained; Lowest/Average Salary: $90,000/$90,000;
Industry Concentration: Generalist with a primary focus in Board Services,
Energy, Financial Services, Oil/Gas, Venture Capital; Function Concentration:
Generalist with a primary focus in Administration, Finance/Accounting,
General Management, Human Resources, Marketing, Women/Minorities

**Higgins, David** — *Executive Vice President/*
*Managing Director*
DHR International, Inc.
3200 West End Avenue
Nashville, TN 37203
Telephone: (615) 783-1690
Recruiter Classification: Retained; Lowest/Average Salary: $60,000/$90,000;
Industry Concentration: Generalist; Function Concentration: Generalist

**Higgins, Donna** — *Consultant*
Howard Fischer Associates, Inc.
1800 John F. Kennedy Boulevard, 7th Floor
Philadelphia, PA 19103
Telephone: (215) 568-8363
**Recruiter Classification:** Retained; **Lowest/Average Salary:** $90,000/$90,000;
**Industry Concentration:** Generalist; **Function Concentration:** Generalist

**Higgins, John B.** — *President*
Higgins Associates, Inc.
108 Wilmot Road, Suite 250
Deerfield, IL 60015
Telephone: (708) 940-4800
**Recruiter Classification:** Retained; **Lowest/Average Salary:** $90,000/$90,000;
**Industry Concentration:** Generalist; **Function Concentration:** Generalist with a
primary focus in Finance/Accounting, General Management

**Hight, Susan** — *Associate*
Source Services Corporation
150 South Warner Road, Suite 238
King of Prussia, PA 19406
Telephone: (610) 341-1960
**Recruiter Classification:** Contingency; **Lowest/Average Salary:**
$30,000/$50,000; **Industry Concentration:** Financial Services, Information
Technology; **Function Concentration:** Engineering, Finance/Accounting

**Hilbert, Laurence** — *Managing Director*
Source Services Corporation
9020 Capital of Texas Highway
Building I, Suite 337
Austin, TX 78759
Telephone: (512) 345-7473
**Recruiter Classification:** Contingency; **Lowest/Average Salary:**
$30,000/$50,000; **Industry Concentration:** Financial Services, Information
Technology; **Function Concentration:** Engineering, Finance/Accounting

**Hildebrand, Thomas B.** — *President*
Professional Resources Group, Inc.
1331 50th Street, Suite 102
West Des Moines, IA 50266-1602
Telephone: (515) 222-0248
**Recruiter Classification:** Executive Temporary; **Industry Concentration:**
Generalist with a primary focus in Financial Services, Healthcare/Hospitals,
Information Technology, Insurance, Manufacturing, Public Administration;
**Function Concentration:** Generalist with a primary focus in Administration,
Finance/Accounting, General Management, Human Resources, Marketing

**Hilgenberg, Thomas** — *Associate*
Source Services Corporation
1233 North Mayfair Road, Suite 300
Milwaukee, WI 53226
Telephone: (414) 774-6700
**Recruiter Classification:** Contingency; **Lowest/Average Salary:**
$30,000/$50,000; **Industry Concentration:** Financial Services, Information
Technology; **Function Concentration:** Engineering, Finance/Accounting

**Hill, Emery** — *Manager*
MSI International
4801 Independence Boulevard
Suite 408
Charlotte, NC 28212
Telephone: (704) 535-6610
**Recruiter Classification:** Contingency; **Lowest/Average Salary:**
$30,000/$60,000; **Industry Concentration:** Generalist with a primary focus in
Financial Services, Healthcare/Hospitals, High Technology, Information
Technology, Manufacturing; **Function Concentration:** Generalist with a
primary focus in Administration, Engineering, Finance/Accounting, General
Management, Marketing, Sales

**Hill, Mike** — *Vice President*
Tyler & Company
1521 North Cooper Street, Suite 200
Dallas, TX 76011
Telephone: (817) 460-4242
**Recruiter Classification:** Retained; **Lowest/Average Salary:** $75,000/$90,000;
**Industry Concentration:** Healthcare/Hospitals; **Function Concentration:**
Generalist

**Hill, Randall W.** — *Partner*
Heidrick & Struggles, Inc.
300 South Grand Avenue, Suite 2400
Los Angeles, CA 90071
Telephone: (213) 625-8811
**Recruiter Classification:** Retained; **Lowest/Average Salary:** $75,000/$90,000;
**Industry Concentration:** Generalist with a primary focus in Financial Services;
**Function Concentration:** Generalist

**Hillen, Skip** — *Vice President*
The McCormick Group, Inc.
20 Walnut Street, Suite 308
Wellesley Hills, MA 02181
Telephone: (617) 239-1233
**Recruiter Classification:** Retained, Contingency; **Lowest/Average Salary:**
$50,000/$75,000; **Industry Concentration:** Generalist with a primary focus in
High Technology, Information Technology, Insurance, Manufacturing,
Transportation; **Function Concentration:** Generalist with a primary focus in
Engineering, General Management, Human Resources, Marketing, Sales

**Hiller, Steve** — *Consultant*
The McCormick Group, Inc.
20 Walnut Street, Suite 308
Wellesley Hills, MA 02181
Telephone: (617) 239-1233
**Recruiter Classification:** Retained; **Lowest/Average Salary:** $40,000/$75,000;
**Industry Concentration:** Insurance; **Function Concentration:** Generalist

**Hilliker, Alan D.** — *Consultant*
Egon Zehnder International Inc.
55 East 59th Street, 14th Floor
New York, NY 10022
Telephone: (212) 838-9199
**Recruiter Classification:** Retained; **Lowest/Average Salary:** $90,000/$90,000;
**Industry Concentration:** Generalist with a primary focus in Biotechnology,
Financial Services, High Technology, Manufacturing, Pharmaceutical/Medical;
**Function Concentration:** Generalist

**Hillyer, Carolyn** — *Associate*
Source Services Corporation
10300 West 103rd Street, Suite 101
Overland Park, KS 66214
Telephone: (913) 888-8885
**Recruiter Classification:** Contingency; **Lowest/Average Salary:**
$30,000/$50,000; **Industry Concentration:** Financial Services, Information
Technology; **Function Concentration:** Engineering, Finance/Accounting

**Hillyer, Robert L.** — *Executive Recruiter*
Executive Manning Corporation
3000 N.E. 30th Place, Suite 405/402/411
Fort Lauderdale, FL 33306
Telephone: (954) 561-5100
**Recruiter Classification:** Retained; **Lowest/Average Salary:** $75,000/$90,000;
**Industry Concentration:** Generalist with a primary focus in
Aerospace/Defense, Automotive, Chemical Products, Consumer Products,
Electronics, High Technology, Manufacturing, Pharmaceutical/Medical;
**Function Concentration:** Generalist

**Hilton, Diane** — *Executive Recruiter*
Richard, Wayne and Roberts
24 Greenway Plaza, Suite 1304
Houston, TX 77046-2493
Telephone: (713) 629-6681
**Recruiter Classification:** Retained; **Lowest/Average Salary:** $50,000/$90,000;
**Industry Concentration:** Generalist with a primary focus in Environmental;
**Function Concentration:** Generalist with a primary focus in Engineering

**Hilyard, Paul J.** — *Executive Recruiter*
MSI International
5215 North O'Connor Boulevard
Suite 1875
Irving, TX 75039
Telephone: (214) 869-3939
**Recruiter Classification:** Contingency; **Lowest/Average Salary:**
$30,000/$75,000; **Industry Concentration:** Generalist with a primary focus in
Healthcare/Hospitals, Pharmaceutical/Medical; **Function Concentration:**
Generalist with a primary focus in Administration, Engineering,
Finance/Accounting, General Management, Marketing, Sales

**Hindman, Neil C.** — *President*
The Hindman Company
Browenton Place, Suite 110
2000 Warrington Way
Louisville, KY 40222
Telephone: (502) 426-4040
**Recruiter Classification:** Retained; **Lowest/Average Salary:** $50,000/$90,000;
**Industry Concentration:** Generalist with a primary focus in
Aerospace/Defense, Automotive, Chemical Products, Consumer Products,
Electronics, Financial Services, High Technology, Manufacturing, Oil/Gas,
Pharmaceutical/Medical, Transportation; **Function Concentration:** Generalist

**Hingers, Marilyn H.** — *Manager Eastern Region*
Management Recruiters International, Inc.
1100 Wayne Avenue, Suite 710
Silver Spring, MD 20910
Telephone: (301) 589-5400
**Recruiter Classification:** Contingency; **Lowest/Average Salary:**
$30,000/$75,000; **Industry Concentration:** Generalist; **Function
Concentration:** Generalist

**Hinkle, Dee** — *Vice President/Senior Recruiter*
Bradford & Galt, Inc.
12400 Olive Boulevard, Suite 430
St. Louis, MO 63141
Telephone: (314) 434-9200
**Recruiter Classification:** Contingency; **Lowest/Average Salary:**
$30,000/$30,000; **Industry Concentration:** Generalist; **Function Concentration:** Generalist

**Hinojosa, Oscar** — *Associate*
Source Services Corporation
5429 LBJ Freeway, Suite 275
Dallas, TX 75240
Telephone: (214) 387-1600
**Recruiter Classification:** Contingency; **Lowest/Average Salary:**
$30,000/$50,000; **Industry Concentration:** Financial Services, Information Technology; **Function Concentration:** Engineering, Finance/Accounting

**Hirsch, Julia C.** — *Senior Vice President*
Boyden
Embarcadero Center West Tower
275 Battery St., Suite 420
San Francisco, CA 94111
Telephone: (415) 981-7900
**Recruiter Classification:** Retained; **Lowest/Average Salary:** $75,000/$90,000;
**Industry Concentration:** Non-Profit; **Function Concentration:** Generalist with a primary focus in Engineering, Finance/Accounting, General Management, Human Resources, Marketing, Research and Development, Sales, Women/Minorities

**Hirschbein, Don L.** — *Manager Pacific Region*
Management Recruiters International, Inc.
111 Anza Boulevard, Suite 109
Burlingame, CA 94010
Telephone: (415) 548-4800
**Recruiter Classification:** Contingency; **Lowest/Average Salary:**
$30,000/$75,000; **Industry Concentration:** Generalist; **Function Concentration:** Generalist

**Hirschey, K. David** — *Principal*
Andcor Human Resources
539 East Lake Street
Wayzata, MN 55391
Telephone: (612) 821-1000
**Recruiter Classification:** Retained; **Lowest/Average Salary:** $40,000/$75,000;
**Industry Concentration:** Generalist; **Function Concentration:** Generalist

**Hite, William A.** — *President*
Hite Executive Search
6515 Chase Drive
P.O. Box 43217
Cleveland, OH 44143
Telephone: (216) 461-1600
**Recruiter Classification:** Retained; **Lowest/Average Salary:** $90,000/$90,000;
**Industry Concentration:** Generalist with a primary focus in Aerospace/Defense, Automotive, Board Services, Manufacturing, Non-Profit, Public Administration, Publishing/Media, Transportation; **Function Concentration:** Generalist

**Hites, Susan** — *Branch Supervisor*
Accountants on Call
111 Westport Plaza, Suite 512
St. Louis, MO 63146
Telephone: (314) 576-0006
**Recruiter Classification:** Contingency; **Lowest/Average Salary:**
$20,000/$30,000; **Industry Concentration:** Generalist; **Function Concentration:** Finance/Accounting

**Hnatuik, Ivan** — *Recruiter*
Corporate Recruiters Ltd.
490-1140 West Pender
Vancouver, British Columbia, CANADA V6E 4G1
Telephone: (604) 687-5993
**Recruiter Classification:** Contingency; **Lowest/Average Salary:**
$40,000/$60,000; **Industry Concentration:** Generalist with a primary focus in High Technology, Information Technology; **Function Concentration:** Marketing, Sales

**Hoagland, John H.** — *Associate*
Pendleton James and Associates, Inc.
One International Place
Boston, MA 02110
Telephone: (617) 261-9696
**Recruiter Classification:** Retained; **Lowest/Average Salary:** $90,000/$90,000;
**Industry Concentration:** Generalist; **Function Concentration:** Generalist

**Hobart, John N.** — *Partner*
Paul Ray Berndtson
301 Commerce Street, Suite 2300
Fort Worth, TX 76102
Telephone: (817) 334-0500
**Recruiter Classification:** Retained; **Lowest/Average Salary:** $90,000/$90,000;
**Industry Concentration:** Consumer Products, Energy, Financial Services; **Function Concentration:** Generalist

**Hobson, Mary L.** — *Vice President*
EFL Associates
7120 East Orchard, Suite 240
Englewood, CO 80111
Telephone: (303) 779-1724
**Recruiter Classification:** Retained; **Lowest/Average Salary:** $60,000/$90,000;
**Industry Concentration:** Generalist; **Function Concentration:** Generalist

**Hockett, William** — *Principal*
Hockett Associates, Inc.
P.O. Box 1765
Los Altos, CA 94023
Telephone: (415) 941-8815
**Recruiter Classification:** Retained; **Lowest/Average Salary:** $90,000/$90,000;
**Industry Concentration:** Generalist with a primary focus in Biotechnology, Board Services, Entertainment, Environmental, High Technology, Information Technology, Pharmaceutical/Medical, Venture Capital; **Function Concentration:** Generalist with a primary focus in Engineering, Finance/Accounting, General Management, Marketing, Research and Development, Sales

**Hodge, Jeff** — *Managing Partner*
Heidrick & Struggles, Inc.
Four Embarcadero Center, Suite 3570
San Francisco, CA 94111
Telephone: (415) 981-2854
**Recruiter Classification:** Retained; **Lowest/Average Salary:** $75,000/$90,000;
**Industry Concentration:** Generalist with a primary focus in Financial Services; **Function Concentration:** Generalist with a primary focus in Finance/Accounting

**Hodges, Robert J.** — *Senior Vice President*
Sampson Neill & Wilkins Inc.
543 Valley Road
Upper Montclair, NJ 07043
Telephone: (201) 783-9600
**Recruiter Classification:** Retained; **Lowest/Average Salary:** $75,000/$90,000;
**Industry Concentration:** Biotechnology, Pharmaceutical/Medical; **Function Concentration:** Engineering, General Management, Marketing, Research and Development, Sales

**Hodgson, Judy H.** — *Co-Owner/Manager Midwest Region*
Management Recruiters International, Inc.
Camdenton Professional Building
583-A East Highway 54, P.O. Box 1197
Camdenton, MO 65020-9004
Telephone: (573) 346-4833
**Recruiter Classification:** Contingency; **Lowest/Average Salary:**
$30,000/$75,000; **Industry Concentration:** Generalist; **Function Concentration:** Generalist

**Hodgson, Robert D.** — *Co-Owner/Manager*
Management Recruiters International, Inc.
Camdenton Professional Building
583-A East Highway 54, P.O. Box 1197
Camdenton, MO 65020-9004
Telephone: (573) 346-4833
**Recruiter Classification:** Contingency; **Lowest/Average Salary:**
$30,000/$75,000; **Industry Concentration:** Generalist; **Function Concentration:** Generalist

**Hoevel, Michael J.** — *Partner*
Poirier, Hoevel & Co.
12400 Wilshire Boulevard, Suite 1250
Los Angeles, CA 90025
Telephone: (310) 207-3427
**Recruiter Classification:** Retained; **Lowest/Average Salary:** $75,000/$90,000;
**Industry Concentration:** Aerospace/Defense, Automotive, Consumer Products, Electronics, Entertainment, Fashion (Retail/Apparel), Financial Services, High Technology, Information Technology, Insurance, Manufacturing, Packaging, Publishing/Media; **Function Concentration:** Generalist with a primary focus in Administration, Finance/Accounting, General Management, Human Resources, Marketing, Sales, Women/Minorities

**Hoffman, Brian** — *Information Technology Recruiter*
Winter, Wyman & Company
950 Winter Street, Suite 3100
Waltham, MA 02154-1294
Telephone: (617) 890-7000
**Recruiter Classification:** Contingency; **Lowest/Average Salary:**
$30,000/$60,000; **Industry Concentration:** Generalist with a primary focus in Information Technology; **Function Concentration:** Generalist

**Hoffman, Mark** — *Manager Pacific Region*
Management Recruiters International, Inc.
2000 Powell Street, Suite 1200
Emeryville, CA 94608
Telephone: (510) 658-1405
Recruiter Classification: Contingency; Lowest/Average Salary:
$30,000/$75,000; Industry Concentration: Generalist; Function
Concentration: Generalist

**Hoffman, Sharon L.** — *Branch Manager*
Accountants on Call
Telephone: (410) 685-5700
Recruiter Classification: Contingency; Lowest/Average Salary:
$20,000/$30,000; Industry Concentration: Generalist; Function
Concentration: Finance/Accounting

**Hoffman, Stephen** — *Managing Director*
Source Services Corporation
1290 Oakmead Parkway, Suite 318
Sunnyvale, CA 94086
Telephone: (408) 738-8440
Recruiter Classification: Contingency; Lowest/Average Salary:
$30,000/$50,000; Industry Concentration: Financial Services, Information
Technology; Function Concentration: Engineering, Finance/Accounting

**Hoffmann, David H.** — *Chairman and CEO*
DHR International, Inc.
8182 Maryland Avenue, Suite 200
Clayton, MO 63105
Telephone: (314) 725-1191
Recruiter Classification: Retained; Lowest/Average Salary: $60,000/$90,000;
Industry Concentration: Generalist; Function Concentration: Generalist

**Hoffmann, David H.** — *Chairman and CEO*
DHR International, Inc.
10 South Riverside Plaza, Suite 2220
Chicago, IL 60606
Telephone: (312) 782-1581
Recruiter Classification: Retained; Lowest/Average Salary: $60,000/$90,000;
Industry Concentration: Generalist; Function Concentration: Generalist

**Hoffmeir, Patricia A.** — *Principal*
Gilbert Tweed/INESA
3411 Silverside Road, Suite 100
Wilmington, DE 19810
Telephone: (302) 479-5144
Recruiter Classification: Retained; Lowest/Average Salary: $75,000/$90,000;
Industry Concentration: Healthcare/Hospitals; Function Concentration:
Administration, Finance/Accounting, General Management, Marketing,
Research and Development

**Hofner, Andrew** — *Associate*
Source Services Corporation
150 South Wacker Drive, Suite 400
Chicago, IL 60606
Telephone: (312) 346-7000
Recruiter Classification: Contingency; Lowest/Average Salary:
$30,000/$50,000; Industry Concentration: Financial Services, Information
Technology; Function Concentration: Engineering, Finance/Accounting

**Hogan, Edward** — *Principal*
Sanford Rose Associates
P.O. Box 475
Hockessin, DE 19707
Telephone: (302) 239-9340
Recruiter Classification: Contingency; Lowest/Average Salary:
$30,000/$75,000; Industry Concentration: Generalist with a primary focus in
Chemical Products; Function Concentration: Generalist

**Hogan, Larry H.** — *President and CEO*
Hogan Acquisitions
7205 Chagrin Road #3
Chagrin Falls, OH 44023
Telephone: (216) 247-9600
Recruiter Classification: Retained; Lowest/Average Salary: $90,000/$90,000;
Industry Concentration: Generalist with a primary focus in Automotive,
Chemical Products, Consumer Products, Environmental, Fashion
(Retail/Apparel), Financial Services, High Technology, Information Technology,
Insurance, Manufacturing, Packaging, Publishing/Media, Transportation,
Venture Capital; Function Concentration: Generalist with a primary focus in
Administration, Engineering, Finance/Accounting, General Management,
Marketing

**Hohlstein, Jeff G.** — *Co-Manager Southwest Region*
Management Recruiters International, Inc.
301 Hesters Crossing, Suite 110
Round Rock, TX 78681-6914
Telephone: (512) 310-1918
Recruiter Classification: Contingency; Lowest/Average Salary:
$30,000/$75,000; Industry Concentration: Generalist; Function
Concentration: Generalist

**Hohlstein, Jodi** — *Co-Manager*
Management Recruiters International, Inc.
301 Hesters Crossing, Suite 110
Round Rock, TX 78681-6914
Telephone: (512) 310-1918
Recruiter Classification: Contingency; Lowest/Average Salary:
$30,000/$75,000; Industry Concentration: Generalist; Function
Concentration: Generalist

**Holden, Bradley J.** — *Vice President*
Korn/Ferry International
120 South Riverside Plaza
Suite 918
Chicago, IL 60606
Telephone: (312) 726-1841
Recruiter Classification: Retained; Lowest/Average Salary: $90,000/$90,000;
Industry Concentration: Generalist; Function Concentration: Generalist

**Holden, Richard** — *Executive Recruiter*
Hornberger Management Company
One Commerce Center, 7th Floor
Wilmington, DE 19801
Telephone: (302) 573-2541
Recruiter Classification: Retained; Lowest/Average Salary: $90,000/$90,000;
Industry Concentration: Real Estate; Function Concentration: Generalist

**Holden, Richard B.** — *President*
Ames Personnel Consultants, Inc.
P.O. Box 651
Brunswick, ME 04011
Telephone: (207) 729-5158
Recruiter Classification: Executive Temporary; Lowest/Average Salary:
$30,000/$60,000; Industry Concentration: Generalist with a primary focus in
Chemical Products, Environmental, High Technology, Manufacturing,
Packaging, Utilities/Nuclear; Function Concentration: Generalist with a
primary focus in Engineering, Finance/Accounting, General Management,
Human Resources, Marketing, Research and Development, Sales

**Holland, Dave G.** — *Co-Manager North Atlantic Region*
Management Recruiters International, Inc.
104 East College Avenue, P.O. Box 1405
Boiling Springs, NC 28017-1405
Telephone: (704) 434-0211
Recruiter Classification: Contingency; Lowest/Average Salary:
$30,000/$75,000; Industry Concentration: Generalist; Function
Concentration: Generalist

**Holland, John H.** — *Director Western Area*
Sloan & Associates
1769 Jamestown Road
Williamsburg, VA 23185
Telephone: (757) 220-1111
Recruiter Classification: Contingency; Lowest/Average Salary:
$60,000/$75,000; Industry Concentration: Consumer Products; Function
Concentration: Marketing, Research and Development, Sales

**Holland, Kathleen** — *Legal Consultant*
TOPAZ International, Inc.
383 Northfield Avenue
West Orange, NJ 07052
Telephone: (201) 669-7300
Recruiter Classification: Contingency; Lowest/Average Salary:
$40,000/$75,000; Industry Concentration: Chemical Products, Consumer
Products, Electronics, Entertainment, Financial Services, High Technology,
Manufacturing, Pharmaceutical/Medical; Function Concentration: Generalist
with a primary focus in Women/Minorities

**Holland, Kathleen** — *Legal Consultant*
TOPAZ Legal Solutions
383 Northfield Avenue
West Orange, NJ 07052
Telephone: (201) 669-7300
Recruiter Classification: Executive Temporary; Lowest/Average Salary:
$40,000/$75,000; Industry Concentration: Chemical Products, Consumer
Products, Electronics, Entertainment, Environmental, Financial Services, High
Technology, Manufacturing; Function Concentration: Generalist with a
primary focus in Women/Minorities

**Holland, Richard G.** — *Manager North Atlantic Region*
Management Recruiters International, Inc.
2625 Cumberland Parkway, Suite 485
Atlanta, GA 30339-3911
Telephone: (770) 433-8330
Recruiter Classification: Contingency; Lowest/Average Salary:
$30,000/$75,000; Industry Concentration: Generalist; Function
Concentration: Generalist

**Hollinger, Bill A.** — *Co-Manager*
Management Recruiters International, Inc.
1151 SW 30th Street, Suite D
Palm City, FL 34990
Telephone: (407) 287-9700
**Recruiter Classification:** Contingency; **Lowest/Average Salary:**
$30,000/$75,000; **Industry Concentration:** Generalist; **Function Concentration:** Generalist

**Hollinger, Lois** — *Co-Manager South Atlantic Region*
Management Recruiters International, Inc.
1151 SW 30th Street, Suite D
Palm City, FL 34990
Telephone: (407) 287-9700
**Recruiter Classification:** Contingency; **Lowest/Average Salary:**
$30,000/$75,000; **Industry Concentration:** Generalist; **Function Concentration:** Generalist

**Hollingsworth, Leslie** — *Managing Director*
Brad Marks International
1888 Century Park East
Suite 1040
Los Angeles, CA 90067
Telephone: (310) 286-0600
**Recruiter Classification:** Retained; **Lowest/Average Salary:** $60,000/$75,000;
**Industry Concentration:** Entertainment; **Function Concentration:** Generalist

**Hollins, Howard D.** — *Executive Recruiter*
MSI International
1900 North 18th Street
Suite 303
Monroe, LA 71201
Telephone: (318) 324-0406
**Recruiter Classification:** Contingency; **Lowest/Average Salary:**
$30,000/$75,000; **Industry Concentration:** Generalist with a primary focus in
Healthcare/Hospitals, High Technology, Pharmaceutical/Medical; **Function
Concentration:** Generalist with a primary focus in Administration, Engineering,
Finance/Accounting, General Management, Marketing, Sales

**Holloway, Linda** — *Co-Manager*
Management Recruiters International, Inc.
1117 North Donnelly Street
Mount Dora, FL 32757-4259
Telephone: (904) 383-7101
**Recruiter Classification:** Contingency; **Lowest/Average Salary:**
$30,000/$75,000; **Industry Concentration:** Generalist; **Function
Concentration:** Generalist

**Holloway, Roger M.** — *Co-Manager South Atlantic Region*
Management Recruiters International, Inc.
1117 North Donnelly Street
Mount Dora, FL 32757-4259
Telephone: (904) 383-7101
**Recruiter Classification:** Contingency; **Lowest/Average Salary:**
$30,000/$75,000; **Industry Concentration:** Generalist; **Function
Concentration:** Generalist

**Holmes, Lawrence J.** — *Managing Director*
Columbia Consulting Group
20 South Charles Street, 9th Floor
Baltimore, MD 21201
Telephone: (410) 385-2525
**Recruiter Classification:** Retained; **Lowest/Average Salary:** $75,000/$90,000;
**Industry Concentration:** Generalist with a primary focus in
Aerospace/Defense, Electronics, Financial Services, High Technology,
Hospitality/Leisure, Information Technology, Insurance, Manufacturing,
Pharmaceutical/Medical; **Function Concentration:** Generalist with a primary
focus in Engineering, General Management, Marketing, Research and
Development, Sales

**Holmes, Len** — *Manager Pacific Region*
Management Recruiters International, Inc.
6124 Motor Avenue SW
Lakewood, WA 98499-1529
Telephone: (206) 582-8488
**Recruiter Classification:** Contingency; **Lowest/Average Salary:**
$30,000/$75,000; **Industry Concentration:** Generalist; **Function
Concentration:** Generalist

**Holodnak, William A.** — *President*
J. Robert Scott
27 State Street
Boston, MA 02109
Telephone: (617) 720-2770
**Recruiter Classification:** Retained; **Lowest/Average Salary:** $75,000/$90,000;
**Industry Concentration:** Generalist with a primary focus in Biotechnology,
Chemical Products, Electronics, Financial Services, Healthcare/Hospitals, High
Technology, Information Technology, Pharmaceutical/Medical; **Function
Concentration:** Generalist with a primary focus in Finance/Accounting,
General Management, Human Resources

**Holt, Carol** — *Consultant*
Bartholdi & Company, Inc.
2465 Freetown Drive
Reston, VA 22091
Telephone: (703) 476-5519
**Recruiter Classification:** Retained; **Lowest/Average Salary:** $60,000/$90,000;
**Industry Concentration:** High Technology, Information Technology, Venture
Capital; **Function Concentration:** Generalist with a primary focus in
Engineering, Finance/Accounting, General Management, Marketing, Research
and Development, Sales

**Holt, Doug C.** — *Manager North Atlantic Region*
Management Recruiters International, Inc.
1117 Trotwood Avenue, Suite 201
Columbia, TN 38401-3033
Telephone: (615) 388-5586
**Recruiter Classification:** Contingency; **Lowest/Average Salary:**
$30,000/$75,000; **Industry Concentration:** Generalist; **Function
Concentration:** Generalist

**Holtz, Gene** — *Agribusiness Recruiter*
Agra Placements International Ltd.
16 East Fifth Street, Berkshire Court
Peru, IN 46970
Telephone: (317) 472-1988
**Recruiter Classification:** Contingency; **Lowest/Average Salary:**
$20,000/$30,000; **Industry Concentration:** Generalist with a primary focus in
Biotechnology, Chemical Products, Energy, Environmental, Financial Services,
Manufacturing; **Function Concentration:** Administration, Engineering,
Finance/Accounting, General Management, Human Resources, Marketing,
Research and Development, Sales

**Holupka, Gary F.** — *Co-Manager Central Region*
Management Recruiters International, Inc.
4840 McKnight Road
Pittsburgh, PA 15237-3413
Telephone: (412) 364-0282
**Recruiter Classification:** Contingency; **Lowest/Average Salary:**
$30,000/$75,000; **Industry Concentration:** Generalist; **Function
Concentration:** Generalist

**Holupka, Patricia Lampl** — *Co-Manager*
Management Recruiters International, Inc.
4840 McKnight Road
Pittsburgh, PA 15237-3413
Telephone: (412) 364-0282
**Recruiter Classification:** Contingency; **Lowest/Average Salary:**
$30,000/$75,000; **Industry Concentration:** Generalist; **Function
Concentration:** Generalist

**Holzberger, Georges L.** — *Partner*
Highland Search Group, L.L.C.
565 Fifth Avenue, 22nd Floor
New York, NY 10017
Telephone: (212) 328-1113
**Recruiter Classification:** Retained; **Lowest/Average Salary:** $90,000/$90,000;
**Industry Concentration:** Financial Services, Venture Capital; **Function
Concentration:** Generalist with a primary focus in Finance/Accounting,
General Management, Human Resources, Sales

**Homer, Judy B.** — *President*
J.B. Homer Associates, Inc.
Graybar Building
420 Lexington Avenue, Suite 2328
New York, NY 10170
Telephone: (212) 697-3300
**Recruiter Classification:** Retained; **Lowest/Average Salary:** $90,000/$90,000;
**Industry Concentration:** Generalist with a primary focus in Information
Technology; **Function Concentration:** Generalist

**Homrich, Patricia J.** — *Vice President/Consultant*
David C. Cooper and Associates, Inc.
Five Concourse Parkway, Suite 2700
Atlanta, GA 30328
Telephone: (770) 395-0014
**Recruiter Classification:** Contingency; **Lowest/Average Salary:**
$20,000/$40,000; **Industry Concentration:** Generalist; **Function
Concentration:** Finance/Accounting

**Honer, Paul** — *Partner*
Johnson Smith & Knisely Accord
100 Park Avenue, 15th Floor
New York, NY 10017
Telephone: (212) 885-9100
**Recruiter Classification:** Retained; **Lowest/Average Salary:** $90,000/$90,000;
**Industry Concentration:** Generalist; **Function Concentration:** Generalist

**Honey, W. Michael M.** — *Partner*
O'Callaghan Honey/Paul Ray Berndtson, Inc.
400-400 Fifth Avenue S.W.
Calgary, Alberta, CANADA T2P 0L6
Telephone: (403) 269-3277
**Recruiter Classification:** Retained; **Lowest/Average Salary:** $90,000/$90,000;
**Industry Concentration:** Generalist with a primary focus in Energy, Financial
Services, Oil/Gas; **Function Concentration:** Generalist

**Hooker, Lisa** — *Partner*
Paul Ray Berndtson
101 Park Avenue, 41st Floor
New York, NY 10178
Telephone: (212) 370-1316
**Recruiter Classification:** Retained; **Lowest/Average Salary:** $90,000/$90,000;
**Industry Concentration:** Information Technology; **Function Concentration:**
Generalist

**Hopgood, Earl** — *Principal*
JDG Associates, Ltd.
1700 Research Boulevard
Rockville, MD 20850
Telephone: (301) 340-2210
**Recruiter Classification:** Contingency; **Lowest/Average Salary:**
$50,000/$90,000; **Industry Concentration:** Aerospace/Defense, Biotechnology,
Electronics, High Technology, Information Technology,
Pharmaceutical/Medical; **Function Concentration:** Engineering, General
Management, Marketing, Research and Development

**Hopkins, Chester A.** — *Senior Vice President*
Handy HRM Corp.
250 Park Avenue
New York, NY 10177-0074
Telephone: (212) 557-0400
**Recruiter Classification:** Retained; **Lowest/Average Salary:** $90,000/$90,000;
**Industry Concentration:** Generalist with a primary focus in Entertainment,
Manufacturing, Publishing/Media; **Function Concentration:** Generalist with a
primary focus in General Management

**Hopkinson, Dana** — *Banking and Investment Services
Recruiter*
Winter, Wyman & Company
101 Federal Street, 27th Floor
Boston, MA 02110-1800
Telephone: (617) 951-2700
**Recruiter Classification:** Contingency; **Lowest/Average Salary:**
$30,000/$60,000; **Industry Concentration:** Financial Services, Venture Capital;
**Function Concentration:** Finance/Accounting

**Hoppert, Phil** — *Director Research/Recruiter*
Wargo and Co., Inc.
850 Elm Grove Road
Elm Grove, WI 53122
Telephone: (414) 785-1211
**Recruiter Classification:** Retained; **Lowest/Average Salary:** $50,000/$90,000;
**Industry Concentration:** Generalist with a primary focus in Automotive,
Biotechnology, Consumer Products, Electronics, Financial Services,
Healthcare/Hospitals, High Technology, Information Technology, Insurance,
Manufacturing, Pharmaceutical/Medical, Publishing/Media, Transportation;
**Function Concentration:** Generalist with a primary focus in Engineering,
Finance/Accounting, General Management, Human Resources, Marketing,
Research and Development, Sales

**Horgan, Thomas F.** — *Partner*
Nadzam, Lusk, Horgan & Associates, Inc.
3211 Scott Boulevard
Suite 205
Santa Clara, CA 95054-3091
Telephone: (408) 727-6601
**Recruiter Classification:** Retained; **Lowest/Average Salary:** $90,000/$90,000;
**Industry Concentration:** Generalist with a primary focus in
Aerospace/Defense, Electronics, High Technology, Information Technology,
Manufacturing; **Function Concentration:** Generalist

**Hornberger, Frederick C.** — *President*
Hornberger Management Company
One Commerce Center, 7th Floor
Wilmington, DE 19801
Telephone: (302) 573-2541
**Recruiter Classification:** Retained; **Lowest/Average Salary:** $90,000/$90,000;
**Industry Concentration:** Real Estate; **Function Concentration:** Generalist

**Horner, Gregory** — *Corporate Recruiter*
Corporate Recruiters Ltd.
490-1140 West Pender
Vancouver, British Columbia, CANADA V6E 4G1
Telephone: (604) 687-5993
**Recruiter Classification:** Contingency; **Lowest/Average Salary:**
$50,000/$75,000; **Industry Concentration:** Electronics, High Technology,
Information Technology; **Function Concentration:** Marketing, Sales

**Horton, Robert H.** — *President*
Horton International
10 Tower Lane
Avon, CT 06001
Telephone: (860) 674-8701
**Recruiter Classification:** Retained; **Lowest/Average Salary:** $90,000/$90,000;
**Industry Concentration:** Generalist with a primary focus in
Aerospace/Defense, Automotive, Chemical Products, Consumer Products,
Electronics, Financial Services, High Technology, Information Technology,
Insurance, Manufacturing, Publishing/Media, Venture Capital; **Function
Concentration:** Generalist with a primary focus in General Management

**Horwitz, Sandy** — *Associate*
Kenzer Corp.
777 Third Avenue, 26th Floor
New York, NY 10017
Telephone: (212) 308-4300
**Recruiter Classification:** Retained; **Lowest/Average Salary:** $50,000/$90,000;
**Industry Concentration:** Generalist; **Function Concentration:** Generalist

**Hoskins, Charles R.** — *Managing Partner*
Heidrick & Struggles, Inc.
76 South Laura Street, Suite 2110
Jacksonville, FL 32202
Telephone: (904) 355-6674
**Recruiter Classification:** Retained; **Lowest/Average Salary:** $75,000/$90,000;
**Industry Concentration:** Generalist with a primary focus in Financial Services;
**Function Concentration:** Generalist

**Hostetter, Kristi** — *Associate*
Source Services Corporation
1105 Schrock Road, Suite 510
Columbus, OH 43229
Telephone: (614) 846-3311
**Recruiter Classification:** Contingency; **Lowest/Average Salary:**
$30,000/$50,000; **Industry Concentration:** Financial Services, Information
Technology; **Function Concentration:** Engineering, Finance/Accounting

**Houchins, Gene E.** — *Manager North Atlantic Region*
Management Recruiters International, Inc.
1776 Peachtree Street NW, Suite 306 South
P.O. Box 18636
Atlanta, GA 31126-0636
Telephone: (404) 874-3636
**Recruiter Classification:** Contingency; **Lowest/Average Salary:**
$30,000/$75,000; **Industry Concentration:** Generalist; **Function
Concentration:** Generalist

**Houchins, William N.** — *Vice President*
Christian & Timbers
10480 Little Patuxent Parkway, Suite 500
Columbia, MD 21044
Telephone: (410) 740-5651
**Recruiter Classification:** Retained; **Lowest/Average Salary:** $90,000/$90,000;
**Industry Concentration:** Electronics, Healthcare/Hospitals, High Technology,
Information Technology, Manufacturing, Pharmaceutical/Medical, Venture
Capital; **Function Concentration:** Generalist with a primary focus in
Engineering, General Management, Marketing

**Houterloot, Tim** — *Associate*
Source Services Corporation
111 Monument Circle, Suite 3930
Indianapolis, IN 46204
Telephone: (317) 631-2900
**Recruiter Classification:** Contingency; **Lowest/Average Salary:**
$30,000/$50,000; **Industry Concentration:** Financial Services, Information
Technology; **Function Concentration:** Engineering, Finance/Accounting

**Houtz, Kenneth** — *Executive Vice President*
Houtz-Strawn Associates, Inc.
11402 Bee Caves Road, West
Austin, TX 78733
Telephone: (512) 263-1131
**Recruiter Classification:** Retained; **Lowest/Average Salary:** $90,000/$90,000;
**Industry Concentration:** Biotechnology, Pharmaceutical/Medical; **Function
Concentration:** General Management, Marketing, Research and Development

**Houver, Scott** — *Consultant*
Logix, Inc.
1601 Trapelo Road
Waltham, MA 02154
Telephone: (617) 890-0500
**Recruiter Classification:** Retained; **Lowest/Average Salary:** $60,000/$75,000;
**Industry Concentration:** High Technology; **Function Concentration:**
Engineering

**Hovey, Dick** — *Manager Midwest Region*
Management Recruiters International, Inc.
100¹/₂ East Jackson
Centerville, IA 52544-1708
Telephone: (515) 437-1115
**Recruiter Classification:** Contingency; **Lowest/Average Salary:**
$30,000/$75,000; **Industry Concentration:** Generalist; **Function Concentration:** Generalist

**Howard, Brian E.** — *Co-Manager Midwest Region*
Management Recruiters International, Inc.
7600 West 110th Street, Suite 204
Overland Park, KS 66210
Telephone: (913) 663-2323
**Recruiter Classification:** Contingency; **Lowest/Average Salary:**
$30,000/$75,000; **Industry Concentration:** Generalist; **Function Concentration:** Generalist

**Howard, Jill** — *Vice President*
Health Care Dimensions
7150 Campus Drive, Suite 320
Colorado Springs, CO 80920
Telephone: (800) 373-3401
**Recruiter Classification:** Contingency; **Lowest/Average Salary:**
$40,000/$75,000; **Industry Concentration:** Healthcare/Hospitals, Insurance; **Function Concentration:** Generalist with a primary focus in Administration, Finance/Accounting, General Management, Marketing, Sales

**Howard, Kathy S.** — *Co-Manager*
Management Recruiters International, Inc.
7600 West 110th Street, Suite 204
Overland Park, KS 66210
Telephone: (913) 663-2323
**Recruiter Classification:** Contingency; **Lowest/Average Salary:**
$30,000/$75,000; **Industry Concentration:** Generalist; **Function Concentration:** Generalist

**Howard, Leon** — *Executive Recruiter*
Richard, Wayne and Roberts
24 Greenway Plaza, Suite 1304
Houston, TX 77046-2493
Telephone: (713) 629-6681
**Recruiter Classification:** Retained; **Lowest/Average Salary:** $50,000/$90,000;
**Industry Concentration:** Generalist with a primary focus in Financial Services;
**Function Concentration:** Generalist with a primary focus in Finance/Accounting

**Howard, Marybeth** — *Manager*
Accounting & Bookkeeping Personnel, Inc.
1702 East Highland, Suite 200
Phoenix, AZ 85016
Telephone: (602) 277-3700
**Recruiter Classification:** Contingency, Executive Temporary; **Lowest/Average Salary:** $20,000/$60,000; **Industry Concentration:** Generalist; **Function Concentration:** Finance/Accounting

**Howard, Richard H.** — *Manager Pacific Region*
Management Recruiters International, Inc.
2150 Shattuck Avenue, Suite 704
Berkeley, CA 94704-1306
Telephone: (510) 486-8100
**Recruiter Classification:** Contingency; **Lowest/Average Salary:**
$30,000/$75,000; **Industry Concentration:** Generalist; **Function Concentration:** Generalist

**Howard, Susy** — *Consultant*
The McCormick Group, Inc.
1400 Wilson Boulevard
Arlington, VA 22209
Telephone: (703) 841-1700
**Recruiter Classification:** Retained; **Lowest/Average Salary:** $40,000/$60,000;
**Industry Concentration:** Generalist with a primary focus in Financial Services, Insurance; **Function Concentration:** Generalist

**Howe, Theodore** — *General Manager*
Romac & Associates
Commerce Tower, Suite 1700
P.O. Box 13264
Kansas City, MO 64199
Telephone: (816) 221-1020
**Recruiter Classification:** Executive Temporary; **Lowest/Average Salary:**
$/$60,000; **Industry Concentration:** Financial Services, Healthcare/Hospitals, High Technology, Hospitality/Leisure, Information Technology, Insurance; **Function Concentration:** Finance/Accounting

**Howe, Vance A.** — *Managing Director*
Ward Howell International, Inc.
2525 E. Arizona Biltmore Circle
Suite 124
Phoenix, AZ 85016
Telephone: (602) 955-3800
**Recruiter Classification:** Retained; **Lowest/Average Salary:** $75,000/$90,000;
**Industry Concentration:** Generalist with a primary focus in Education/Libraries, Fashion (Retail/Apparel), Financial Services, Manufacturing, Publishing/Media, Utilities/Nuclear; **Function Concentration:** Generalist

**Howe, William S.** — *Partner*
Kenny, Kindler, Hunt & Howe
1 Dag Hammarskjold Plaza
New York, NY 10017
Telephone: (212) 355-5560
**Recruiter Classification:** Retained; **Lowest/Average Salary:** $90,000/$90,000;
**Industry Concentration:** Generalist; **Function Concentration:** Generalist

**Howell, Robert B.** — *Principal*
Atlantic Search Group, Inc.
One Liberty Square
Boston, MA 02109
Telephone: (617) 426-9700
**Recruiter Classification:** Contingency; **Lowest/Average Salary:**
$20,000/$60,000; **Industry Concentration:** Generalist with a primary focus in Biotechnology, Consumer Products, Electronics, Financial Services, Information Technology, Manufacturing, Real Estate; **Function Concentration:** Finance/Accounting

**Howell, Robert B.** — *Principal*
Atlantic Search Group, Inc.
One Liberty Square
Boston, MA 02109
Telephone: (617) 426-9700
**Recruiter Classification:** Contingency; **Lowest/Average Salary:**
$20,000/$60,000; **Industry Concentration:** Generalist with a primary focus in Biotechnology, Consumer Products, Electronics, Financial Services, High Technology, Information Technology, Manufacturing, Real Estate; **Function Concentration:** Finance/Accounting

**Hoyda, Louis A.** — *Partner*
Thorndike Deland Associates
275 Madison Avenue, Suite 1300
New York, NY 10016
Telephone: (212) 661-6200
**Recruiter Classification:** Retained; **Lowest/Average Salary:** $75,000/$90,000;
**Industry Concentration:** Generalist with a primary focus in Board Services, Consumer Products, Entertainment, Fashion (Retail/Apparel), Financial Services, Healthcare/Hospitals, Hospitality/Leisure, Information Technology, Insurance, Manufacturing, Pharmaceutical/Medical, Publishing/Media, Venture Capital; **Function Concentration:** Generalist with a primary focus in Finance/Accounting, General Management, Human Resources, Marketing, Sales

**Hubert, David L.** — *Director Operations*
ARJay & Associates
3286 Clower Street, Suite A-202
Snellville, GA 30278
Telephone: (404) 979-3799
**Recruiter Classification:** Contingency; **Lowest/Average Salary:**
$40,000/$90,000; **Industry Concentration:** Generalist with a primary focus in Electronics, Energy, Manufacturing; **Function Concentration:** Engineering, Finance/Accounting

**Hucko, Donald S.** — *Senior Vice President*
Jonas, Walters & Assoc., Inc.
1110 North Old World Third St., Suite 510
Milwaukee, WI 53203-1102
Telephone: (414) 291-2828
**Recruiter Classification:** Retained; **Lowest/Average Salary:** $60,000/$90,000;
**Industry Concentration:** Generalist with a primary focus in Board Services, Consumer Products, Manufacturing, Publishing/Media; **Function Concentration:** Generalist with a primary focus in Administration, Engineering, Finance/Accounting, General Management, Human Resources, Marketing, Research and Development, Sales

**Hudson, Kevin** — *Senior Consultant*
Raymond Karsan Associates
989 Old Eagle School Road, Suite 814
Wayne, PA 19087
Telephone: (610) 971-9171
**Recruiter Classification:** Contingency; **Lowest/Average Salary:**
$30,000/$90,000; **Industry Concentration:** Generalist with a primary focus in Chemical Products; **Function Concentration:** Generalist

**Hudson, Reginald M.** — *President*
Search Bureau International
P.O. Box 377608
Chicago, IL 60637
Telephone: (708) 210-1834
**Recruiter Classification:** Contingency; **Lowest/Average Salary:**
$40,000/$60,000; **Industry Concentration:** Generalist with a primary focus in
Aerospace/Defense, Consumer Products, Financial Services,
Healthcare/Hospitals, High Technology, Information Technology, Insurance,
Real Estate; **Function Concentration:** Generalist with a primary focus in
Engineering, Finance/Accounting, General Management, Human Resources,
Marketing, Research and Development, Sales, Women/Minorities

**Hudson, William** — *Vice President*
Robert Sage Recruiting
127 East Windsor
Elkhart, IN 46514
Telephone: (219) 264-1126
**Recruiter Classification:** Contingency; **Lowest/Average Salary:**
$30,000/$75,000; **Industry Concentration:** Automotive; **Function
Concentration:** Generalist

**Hughes, Barbara** — *Associate*
Source Services Corporation
1290 Oakmead Parkway, Suite 318
Sunnyvale, CA 94086
Telephone: (408) 738-8440
**Recruiter Classification:** Contingency; **Lowest/Average Salary:**
$30,000/$50,000; **Industry Concentration:** Financial Services, Information
Technology; **Function Concentration:** Engineering, Finance/Accounting

**Hughes, Cathy N.** — *Recruiter*
The Ogdon Partnership
375 Park Avenue, Suite 2409
New York, NY 10152-0175
Telephone: (212) 308-1600
**Recruiter Classification:** Retained; **Lowest/Average Salary:** $90,000/$90,000;
**Industry Concentration:** Generalist with a primary focus in Consumer
Products, Entertainment, Fashion (Retail/Apparel), Information Technology,
Manufacturing, Publishing/Media, Venture Capital; **Function Concentration:**
Generalist with a primary focus in Administration, Finance/Accounting,
General Management, Human Resources, Marketing, Sales, Women/Minorities

**Hughes, David** — *Recruiter*
Southwestern Professional Services
2451 Atrium Way
Nashville, TN 37214
Telephone: (615) 391-2722
**Recruiter Classification:** Contingency; **Lowest/Average Salary:**
$20,000/$20,000; **Industry Concentration:** Insurance; **Function
Concentration:** Sales

**Hughes, Donald J.** — *Managing Partner*
Hughes & Company
3682 King Street
P.O. Box 16944
Alexandria, VA 22303-0944
Telephone: (703) 379-2499
**Recruiter Classification:** Retained; **Lowest/Average Salary:** $60,000/$90,000;
**Industry Concentration:** Consumer Products, Hospitality/Leisure, Information
Technology; **Function Concentration:** General Management, Human
Resources, Marketing, Sales

**Hughes, James J.** — *Vice President*
R.P. Barone Associates
57 Green Street
Woodbridge, NJ 07095
Telephone: (908) 634-4300
**Recruiter Classification:** Contingency; **Lowest/Average Salary:**
$30,000/$75,000; **Industry Concentration:** Generalist with a primary focus in
Aerospace/Defense, Automotive, Chemical Products, Electronics, Energy,
Environmental, Manufacturing, Oil/Gas, Packaging, Pharmaceutical/Medical;
**Function Concentration:** Generalist with a primary focus in Engineering,
General Management, Marketing

**Hughes, Kendall G.** — *Principal*
Hughes & Associates
718 Oakwood Trail
Fort Worth, TX 76112
Telephone: (817) 496-3650
**Recruiter Classification:** Contingency; **Lowest/Average Salary:**
$30,000/$60,000; **Industry Concentration:** Insurance; **Function
Concentration:** Generalist

**Hughes, Kevin R.** — *Senior Vice President*
Handy HRM Corp.
250 Park Avenue
New York, NY 10177-0074
Telephone: (212) 557-0400
**Recruiter Classification:** Retained; **Lowest/Average Salary:** $90,000/$90,000;
**Industry Concentration:** Generalist with a primary focus in Financial Services,
High Technology; **Function Concentration:** Finance/Accounting, Human
Resources

**Hughes, Pat** — *Associate*
Kenzer Corp.
777 Third Avenue, 26th Floor
New York, NY 10017
Telephone: (212) 308-4300
**Recruiter Classification:** Retained; **Lowest/Average Salary:** $50,000/$90,000;
**Industry Concentration:** Generalist; **Function Concentration:** Generalist

**Hughes, Randall** — *Associate*
Source Services Corporation
4200 West Cypress Street, Suite 101
Tampa, FL 33607
Telephone: (813) 879-2221
**Recruiter Classification:** Contingency; **Lowest/Average Salary:**
$30,000/$50,000; **Industry Concentration:** Financial Services, Information
Technology; **Function Concentration:** Engineering, Finance/Accounting

**Hulce, Colleen** — *Vice President*
Korn/Ferry International
1800 Century Park East, Suite 900
Los Angeles, CA 90067
Telephone: (310) 552-1834
**Recruiter Classification:** Retained; **Lowest/Average Salary:** $90,000/$90,000;
**Industry Concentration:** Generalist; **Function Concentration:** Generalist

**Hull, Chuck** — *Software Engineering Recruiter*
Winter, Wyman & Company
950 Winter Street, Suite 3100
Waltham, MA 02154-1294
Telephone: (617) 890-7000
**Recruiter Classification:** Contingency; **Lowest/Average Salary:**
$40,000/$75,000; **Industry Concentration:** High Technology, Information
Technology, Publishing/Media; **Function Concentration:** Engineering

**Hult, Dana** — *Associate*
Source Services Corporation
71 Spit Brook Road, Suite 305
Nashua, NH 03060
Telephone: (603) 888-7650
**Recruiter Classification:** Contingency; **Lowest/Average Salary:**
$30,000/$50,000; **Industry Concentration:** Financial Services, Information
Technology; **Function Concentration:** Engineering, Finance/Accounting

**Hume, David** — *Manager Permanent Placement*
Bradford & Galt, Inc.
12400 Olive Boulevard, Suite 430
St. Louis, MO 63141
Telephone: (314) 434-9200
**Recruiter Classification:** Contingency; **Lowest/Average Salary:**
$30,000/$30,000; **Industry Concentration:** Generalist; **Function
Concentration:** Generalist

**Humphrey, Joan** — *Executive Recruiter*
Abraham & London, Ltd.
7 Old Sherman Turnpike, Suite 209
Danbury, CT 06810
Telephone: (203) 730-4000
**Recruiter Classification:** Contingency; **Lowest/Average Salary:**
$40,000/$75,000; **Industry Concentration:** High Technology, Information
Technology; **Function Concentration:** Marketing, Sales

**Humphrey, Titus** — *Associate*
Source Services Corporation
1290 Oakmead Parkway, Suite 318
Sunnyvale, CA 94086
Telephone: (408) 738-8440
**Recruiter Classification:** Contingency; **Lowest/Average Salary:**
$30,000/$50,000; **Industry Concentration:** Financial Services, Information
Technology; **Function Concentration:** Engineering, Finance/Accounting

**Humphreys, Sidney** — *Managing Vice President*
Korn/Ferry International
Scotia Plaza
40 King Street West
Toronto, Ontario, CANADA M5H 3Y2
Telephone: (416) 366-1300
**Recruiter Classification:** Retained; **Lowest/Average Salary:** $90,000/$90,000;
**Industry Concentration:** Generalist; **Function Concentration:** Generalist

**Hunt, James E.** — *Partner*
Kenny, Kindler, Hunt & Howe
1 Dag Hammarskjold Plaza
New York, NY 10017
Telephone: (212) 355-5560
**Recruiter Classification:** Retained; **Lowest/Average Salary:** $90,000/$90,000;
**Industry Concentration:** Generalist; **Function Concentration:** Generalist

**Hunt, Thomas** — *Physician Recruiter*
MSI International
201 St. Charles Avenue
Suite 2205
New Orleans, LA 70170
Telephone: (504) 522-6700
**Recruiter Classification:** Contingency; **Lowest/Average Salary:**
$30,000/$60,000; **Industry Concentration:** Generalist with a primary focus in
Healthcare/Hospitals; **Function Concentration:** Generalist with a primary focus
in Administration, Engineering, Finance/Accounting, General Management,
Marketing, Sales

**Hunter, Durant A.** — *President*
Pendleton James and Associates, Inc.
One International Place
Boston, MA 02110
Telephone: (617) 261-9696
**Recruiter Classification:** Retained; **Lowest/Average Salary:** $90,000/$90,000;
**Industry Concentration:** Generalist; **Function Concentration:** Generalist

**Hunter, Gabe** — *Executive Recruiter*
Phillips Resource Group
330 Pelham Road, Building A
Greenville, SC 29615
Telephone: (864) 271-6350
**Recruiter Classification:** Contingency; **Lowest/Average Salary:**
$40,000/$50,000; **Industry Concentration:** Generalist with a primary focus in
Chemical Products, Electronics, Environmental, High Technology, Information
Technology, Manufacturing, Packaging, Utilities/Nuclear; **Function
Concentration:** Generalist with a primary focus in Administration, Engineering,
General Management, Human Resources, Marketing, Research and
Development, Sales, Women/Minorities

**Hunter, John B.** — *Vice President*
John Sibbald Associates, Inc.
8725 West Higgins Road, Suite 575
Chicago, IL 60631
Telephone: (312) 693-0575
**Recruiter Classification:** Retained; **Lowest/Average Salary:** $75,000/$90,000;
**Industry Concentration:** Consumer Products, Environmental,
Hospitality/Leisure, Non-Profit; **Function Concentration:** Administration,
General Management, Human Resources

**Hunter, Patricia** — *Associate*
Kenzer Corp.
6033 West Century Boulevard, Suite 808
Los Angeles, CA 90045
Telephone: (310) 417-8577
**Recruiter Classification:** Retained; **Lowest/Average Salary:** $50,000/$90,000;
**Industry Concentration:** Generalist; **Function Concentration:** Generalist

**Hunter, Sharon W.** — *Manager Southwest Region*
Management Recruiters International, Inc.
1401 Walnut Street, Suite 301, P.O. Box 4657
Boulder, CO 80306-4657
Telephone: (303) 447-9900
**Recruiter Classification:** Contingency; **Lowest/Average Salary:**
$30,000/$75,000; **Industry Concentration:** Generalist; **Function
Concentration:** Generalist

**Hunter, Steven** — *President*
Diamond Tax Recruiting
Two Pennsylvania Plaza, Suite 1985
New York, NY 10121
Telephone: (212) 695-4220
**Recruiter Classification:** Contingency; **Lowest/Average Salary:**
$50,000/$75,000; **Industry Concentration:** Consumer Products, Electronics,
Entertainment, Financial Services, High Technology, Manufacturing,
Publishing/Media; **Function Concentration:** Finance/Accounting

**Hunter, Sue J.** — *Vice President*
Robison & Associates
1350 First Citizens Plaza
128 South Tryon Street
Charlotte, NC 28202
Telephone: (704) 376-0059
**Recruiter Classification:** Retained; **Lowest/Average Salary:** $50,000/$90,000;
**Industry Concentration:** Generalist with a primary focus in Consumer
Products, Education/Libraries, Energy, Financial Services, Hospitality/Leisure,
Non-Profit, Real Estate; **Function Concentration:** Generalist with a primary
focus in Administration, Engineering, General Management, Human
Resources, Marketing, Sales

**Huntoon, Cliff** — *Executive Recruiter*
Richard, Wayne and Roberts
24 Greenway Plaza, Suite 1304
Houston, TX 77046-2493
Telephone: (713) 629-6681
**Recruiter Classification:** Retained; **Lowest/Average Salary:** $50,000/$90,000;
**Industry Concentration:** Generalist with a primary focus in High Technology;
**Function Concentration:** Generalist with a primary focus in Engineering

**Huntting, Lisa** — *President*
Professional Alternatives, Inc.
601 Lakeshore Parkway, Suite 1050
Minneapolis, MN 55305-5219
Telephone: (612) 449-5180
**Recruiter Classification:** Executive Temporary; **Lowest/Average Salary:**
$30,000/$40,000; **Industry Concentration:** Generalist; **Function
Concentration:** Generalist with a primary focus in Finance/Accounting, Human
Resources, Marketing

**Hurd, J. Nicholas** — *Managing Director/Area Manager*
Russell Reynolds Associates, Inc.
Old City Hall, 45 School Street
Boston, MA 02108
Telephone: (617) 523-1111
**Recruiter Classification:** Retained; **Lowest/Average Salary:** $90,000/$90,000;
**Industry Concentration:** Generalist with a primary focus in Financial Services;
**Function Concentration:** Generalist

**Hurley, Helen** — *Co-Manager Midwest Region*
Management Recruiters International, Inc.
4617 Morningside Avenue
Sioux City, IA 51106-2943
Telephone: (712) 276-8454
**Recruiter Classification:** Contingency; **Lowest/Average Salary:**
$30,000/$75,000; **Industry Concentration:** Generalist; **Function
Concentration:** Generalist

**Hurley, Janeen** — *Software Engineering Recruiter*
Winter, Wyman & Company
950 Winter Street, Suite 3100
Waltham, MA 02154-1294
Telephone: (617) 890-7000
**Recruiter Classification:** Contingency; **Lowest/Average Salary:**
$40,000/$75,000; **Industry Concentration:** High Technology, Information
Technology, Publishing/Media; **Function Concentration:** Engineering

**Hursey, Bruce** — *Manager Southwest Region*
Management Recruiters International, Inc.
1401 Hudson Lane, Suite 135
Monroe, LA 71201-2184
Telephone: (318) 322-2200
**Recruiter Classification:** Contingency; **Lowest/Average Salary:**
$30,000/$75,000; **Industry Concentration:** Generalist; **Function
Concentration:** Generalist

**Hurst, Joan E.** — *Senior Associate*
Korn/Ferry International
303 Peachtree Street N.E.
Suite 1600
Atlanta, GA 30308
Telephone: (404) 577-7542
**Recruiter Classification:** Retained; **Lowest/Average Salary:** $90,000/$90,000;
**Industry Concentration:** Generalist; **Function Concentration:** Generalist

**Hurt, Thomas E.** — *Co-Owner/Manager Midwest Region*
Management Recruiters International, Inc.
Valley View Center, Suite 125
5307 South 92nd Street
Hales Corners, WI 53130
Telephone: (414) 529-8020
**Recruiter Classification:** Contingency; **Lowest/Average Salary:**
$30,000/$75,000; **Industry Concentration:** Generalist; **Function
Concentration:** Generalist

**Hurt, Thomas E.** — *Co-Owner*
Management Recruiters International, Inc.
8338 Corporate Drive, Suite 300
Racine, WI 53406
Telephone: (414) 886-8000
**Recruiter Classification:** Contingency; **Lowest/Average Salary:**
$30,000/$75,000; **Industry Concentration:** Generalist; **Function
Concentration:** Generalist

**Hurtado, Jaime** — *Associate*
Source Services Corporation
879 West 190th Street, Suite 250
Los Angeles, CA 90248
Telephone: (310) 323-6633
**Recruiter Classification:** Contingency; **Lowest/Average Salary:**
$30,000/$50,000; **Industry Concentration:** Financial Services, Information
Technology; **Function Concentration:** Engineering, Finance/Accounting

**Huss, Juli** — *Branch Manager*
Accountants on Call
200 North LaSalle Street, Suite 2830
Chicago, IL 60601
Telephone: (312) 782-7788
Recruiter Classification: Contingency; Lowest/Average Salary:
$20,000/$30,000; Industry Concentration: Generalist; Function
Concentration: Finance/Accounting

**Hussey, Wayne** — *Consultant Associate*
Krecklo & Associates Inc.
Scotia Plaza, Suite 4900
40 King Street West
Toronto, Ontario, CANADA M5H 4A2
Telephone: (416) 777-6799
Recruiter Classification: Retained; Lowest/Average Salary: $75,000/$90,000;
Industry Concentration: Information Technology

**Hutchinson, Loretta M.** — *President*
Hutchinson Resources International
573 76th Street
Brooklyn, NY 11209
Telephone: (718) 748-5056
Recruiter Classification: Retained; Lowest/Average Salary: $75,000/$90,000;
Industry Concentration: Generalist with a primary focus in
Aerospace/Defense, Chemical Products, Consumer Products, Electronics,
Financial Services, High Technology, Manufacturing, Pharmaceutical/Medical;
Function Concentration: Generalist

**Hutchison, Richard H.** — *Executive Recruiter*
Rurak & Associates, Inc.
1350 Connecticut Avenue N.W.
Suite 801
Washington, DC 20036
Telephone: (202) 293-7603
Recruiter Classification: Retained; Lowest/Average Salary: $90,000/$90,000;
Industry Concentration: Generalist with a primary focus in
Aerospace/Defense, Electronics, Healthcare/Hospitals, High Technology,
Information Technology, Manufacturing, Non-Profit, Pharmaceutical/Medical;
Function Concentration: Generalist with a primary focus in
Finance/Accounting, General Management, Human Resources, Marketing,
Research and Development, Sales

**Hutchison, William K.** — *Partner*
Christenson & Hutchison
466 Southern Boulevard
Chatham, NJ 07928
Telephone: (201) 966-1600
Recruiter Classification: Retained; Lowest/Average Salary: $75,000/$90,000;
Industry Concentration: Generalist with a primary focus in Financial Services,
Healthcare/Hospitals, Insurance, Manufacturing, Non-Profit, Public
Administration, Real Estate; Function Concentration: Generalist with a primary
focus in Finance/Accounting, General Management, Marketing, Sales

**Huttner, Leah** — *Associate*
Korn/Ferry International
2 Logan Square, Suite 2530
Philadelphia, PA 19103
Telephone: (215) 496-6666
Recruiter Classification: Retained; Lowest/Average Salary: $90,000/$90,000;
Industry Concentration: Generalist; Function Concentration: Generalist

**Hutton, Thomas J.** — *Vice President*
The Thomas Tucker Company
425 California Street, Suite 2502
San Francisco, CA 94104
Telephone: (415) 693-5900
Recruiter Classification: Retained; Lowest/Average Salary: $90,000/$90,000;
Industry Concentration: Aerospace/Defense, Electronics, Information
Technology, Manufacturing; Function Concentration: Engineering, General
Management, Research and Development

**Hwang, Yvette** — *Executive Recruiter*
MSI International
6345 Balboa Boulevard
Suite 335
Encino, CA 91316
Telephone: (818) 342-0222
Recruiter Classification: Contingency; Lowest/Average Salary:
$30,000/$75,000; Industry Concentration: Generalist with a primary focus in
Healthcare/Hospitals, Pharmaceutical/Medical; Function Concentration:
Generalist with a primary focus in Administration, Engineering,
Finance/Accounting, General Management, Marketing, Sales

**Hyde, Mark D.** — *Physician Recruiter*
MSI International
230 Peachtree Street, N.E.
Suite 1550
Atlanta, GA 30303
Telephone: (404) 653-7360
Recruiter Classification: Contingency; Lowest/Average Salary:
$30,000/$60,000; Industry Concentration: Generalist with a primary focus in
Healthcare/Hospitals; Function Concentration: Generalist with a primary focus
in Administration, Engineering, Finance/Accounting, General Management,
Marketing, Sales

**Hyde, Tom G.** — *Manager North Atlantic Region*
Management Recruiters International, Inc.
2414 Taylor Close, P.O. Box 4094
Murfreesboro, TN 37133-4094
Telephone: (615) 890-7623
Recruiter Classification: Contingency; Lowest/Average Salary:
$30,000/$75,000; Industry Concentration: Generalist; Function
Concentration: Generalist

**Hyde, W. Jerry** — *President*
Hyde Danforth Wold & Co.
5950 Berkshire Lane, Suite 1600
Dallas, TX 75225
Telephone: (214) 691-5966
Recruiter Classification: Retained; Lowest/Average Salary: $50,000/$75,000;
Industry Concentration: Generalist with a primary focus in Consumer
Products, Energy, Healthcare/Hospitals, Manufacturing, Oil/Gas; Function
Concentration: Generalist with a primary focus in Administration, Engineering,
Finance/Accounting, General Management, Human Resources, Marketing,
Sales

**Hykes, Don A.** — *Vice President/Managing Director*
A.T. Kearney, Inc.
8500 Normandale Lake Boulevard
Suite 1630
Minneapolis, MN 55437
Telephone: (612) 921-8436
Recruiter Classification: Retained; Lowest/Average Salary: $90,000/$90,000;
Industry Concentration: Generalist with a primary focus in Chemical Products,
High Technology, Manufacturing, Pharmaceutical/Medical; Function
Concentration: Generalist with a primary focus in Administration, Engineering,
Finance/Accounting, General Management, Human Resources, Marketing,
Research and Development, Sales

**Hylas, Lisa** — *Associate*
Source Services Corporation
15600 N.W. 67th Avenue, Suite 210
Miami Lakes, FL 33014
Telephone: (305) 556-8000
Recruiter Classification: Contingency; Lowest/Average Salary:
$30,000/$50,000; Industry Concentration: Financial Services, Information
Technology; Function Concentration: Engineering, Finance/Accounting

**Hypes, Richard G.** — *Partner*
Lynch Miller Moore Partners, Inc.
10 South Wacker Drive, Suite 2935
Chicago, IL 60606
Telephone: (312) 876-1505
Recruiter Classification: Retained; Lowest/Average Salary: $75,000/$90,000;
Industry Concentration: Generalist with a primary focus in Consumer
Products, Financial Services, Manufacturing, Venture Capital; Function
Concentration: Generalist with a primary focus in Finance/Accounting,
General Management

**Iacovelli, Heather** — *Executive Recruiter*
CPS Inc.
One Westbrook Corporate Centre, Suite 600
Westchester, IL 60154
Telephone: (708) 531-8370
Recruiter Classification: Contingency; Lowest/Average Salary:
$30,000/$50,000; Industry Concentration: Generalist with a primary focus in
Automotive, Biotechnology, Chemical Products, Consumer Products, High
Technology, Insurance, Manufacturing, Oil/Gas, Packaging,
Pharmaceutical/Medical; Function Concentration: Engineering, Research and
Development, Sales, Women/Minorities

**Iammatteo, Enzo** — *Consultant*
Keith Bagg & Associates Inc.
36 Toronto Street, Suite 520
Toronto, Ontario, CANADA M5C 2C5
Telephone: (416) 863-1800
Recruiter Classification: Contingency; Lowest/Average Salary:
$40,000/$60,000; Industry Concentration: Biotechnology, Chemical Products,
Consumer Products, Electronics, High Technology, Manufacturing,
Pharmaceutical/Medical; Function Concentration: Administration,
Engineering, Finance/Accounting, General Management, Marketing, Research
and Development, Sales

**Iannacone, Kelly** — *Executive Recruiter*
Abraham & London, Ltd.
7 Old Sherman Turnpike, Suite 209
Danbury, CT 06810
Telephone: (203) 730-4000
**Recruiter Classification:** Contingency, Executive Temporary; **Lowest/Average Salary:** $40,000/$75,000; **Industry Concentration:** High Technology, Information Technology; **Function Concentration:** Marketing, Sales

**Ide, Ian** — *Information Technology Recruiter*
Winter, Wyman & Company
950 Winter Street, Suite 3100
Waltham, MA 02154-1294
Telephone: (617) 890-7000
**Recruiter Classification:** Contingency; **Lowest/Average Salary:** $30,000/$60,000; **Industry Concentration:** Generalist with a primary focus in Information Technology; **Function Concentration:** Generalist

**Ikle, A. Donald** — *Managing Director*
Ward Howell International, Inc.
99 Park Avenue, Suite 2000
New York, NY 10016-1699
Telephone: (212) 697-3730
**Recruiter Classification:** Retained; **Lowest/Average Salary:** $75,000/$90,000; **Industry Concentration:** Insurance; **Function Concentration:** Generalist with a primary focus in General Management

**Illsley, Hugh G.** — *Managing Partner*
Ward Howell International, Inc.
141 Adelaide Street West
Suite 1800
Toronto, Ontario, CANADA M5H 3L5
Telephone: (416) 862-1273
**Recruiter Classification:** Retained; **Lowest/Average Salary:** $75,000/$90,000; **Industry Concentration:** Automotive, Financial Services, Insurance, Real Estate; **Function Concentration:** Generalist

**Imely, Larry** — *Vice President*
Christian & Timbers
One Corporate Exchange
25825 Science Park Drive, Suite 400
Cleveland, OH 44122
Telephone: (216) 464-8710
**Recruiter Classification:** Retained; **Lowest/Average Salary:** $90,000/$90,000; **Industry Concentration:** Generalist with a primary focus in Entertainment, Environmental, Financial Services, High Technology, Information Technology; **Function Concentration:** Generalist with a primary focus in Finance/Accounting, General Management, Marketing, Research and Development, Sales

**Imhof, Kirk** — *Associate*
Source Services Corporation
505 East 200 South, Suite 300
Salt Lake City, UT 84102
Telephone: (801) 328-0011
**Recruiter Classification:** Contingency; **Lowest/Average Salary:** $30,000/$50,000; **Industry Concentration:** Financial Services, Information Technology; **Function Concentration:** Engineering, Finance/Accounting

**Incitti, Lance M.** — *Manager Eastern Region*
Management Recruiters International, Inc.
191 Woodport Road, Suite 201
Sparta, NJ 07871-2641
Telephone: (201) 729-1888
**Recruiter Classification:** Contingency; **Lowest/Average Salary:** $30,000/$75,000; **Industry Concentration:** Generalist; **Function Concentration:** Generalist

**Indiveri, Peter** — *Associate*
Kenzer Corp.
777 Third Avenue, 26th Floor
New York, NY 10017
Telephone: (212) 308-4300
**Recruiter Classification:** Retained; **Lowest/Average Salary:** $50,000/$90,000; **Industry Concentration:** Generalist; **Function Concentration:** Generalist

**Infantino, James** — *Manager Eastern Region*
Management Recruiters International, Inc.
2 Church Street, P.O. Box 218
Madrid, NY 13660
Telephone: (315) 322-0222
**Recruiter Classification:** Contingency; **Lowest/Average Salary:** $30,000/$75,000; **Industry Concentration:** Generalist; **Function Concentration:** Generalist

**Infinger, Ronald E.** — *Vice President and Associate*
Robison & Associates
1350 First Citizens Plaza
128 South Tryon Street
Charlotte, NC 28202
Telephone: (704) 376-0059
**Recruiter Classification:** Retained; **Lowest/Average Salary:** $50,000/$90,000; **Industry Concentration:** Generalist with a primary focus in Energy, Information Technology, Non-Profit; **Function Concentration:** Generalist with a primary focus in Engineering, Finance/Accounting, General

**Ingalls, Joseph M.** — *Vice President*
John Kurosky & Associates
3 Corporate Park Drive, Suite 210
Irvine, CA 92714
Telephone: (714) 851-6370
**Recruiter Classification:** Retained; **Lowest/Average Salary:** $60,000/$90,000; **Industry Concentration:** Electronics, High Technology, Manufacturing; **Function Concentration:** Generalist

**Inger, Barry** — *Associate*
Source Services Corporation
20 Burlington Mall Road, Suite 405
Burlington, MA 01803
Telephone: (617) 272-5000
**Recruiter Classification:** Contingency; **Lowest/Average Salary:** $30,000/$50,000; **Industry Concentration:** Financial Services, Information Technology; **Function Concentration:** Engineering, Finance/Accounting

**Inglis, William** — *Vice President*
Korn/Ferry International
601 South Figueroa
Suite 1900
Los Angeles, CA 90017
Telephone: (213) 624-6600
**Recruiter Classification:** Retained; **Lowest/Average Salary:** $90,000/$90,000; **Industry Concentration:** Generalist with a primary focus in Financial Services; **Function Concentration:** Generalist

**Ingram, D. John** — *Partner*
Ingram & Aydelotte Inc.
430 Park Avenue, Suite 700
New York, NY 10022
Telephone: (212) 319-7777
**Recruiter Classification:** Retained; **Lowest/Average Salary:** $90,000/$90,000; **Industry Concentration:** Generalist with a primary focus in Board Services, Consumer Products, Energy, Entertainment, Financial Services, Insurance, Manufacturing, Publishing/Media, Transportation, Venture Capital; **Function Concentration:** Generalist with a primary focus in Finance/Accounting, General Management, Human Resources, Marketing

**Inguagiato, Gregory** — *Manager*
MSI International
6345 Balboa Boulevard
Suite 335
Encino, CA 91316
Telephone: (818) 342-0222
**Recruiter Classification:** Contingency; **Lowest/Average Salary:** $30,000/$60,000; **Industry Concentration:** Generalist with a primary focus in Financial Services, Healthcare/Hospitals, High Technology, Information Technology, Manufacturing; **Function Concentration:** Generalist with a primary focus in Administration, Engineering, Finance/Accounting, General Management, Marketing, Sales

**Inskeep, Thomas** — *Associate*
Source Services Corporation
150 South Warner Road, Suite 238
King of Prussia, PA 19406
Telephone: (610) 341-1960
**Recruiter Classification:** Contingency; **Lowest/Average Salary:** $30,000/$50,000; **Industry Concentration:** Financial Services, Information Technology; **Function Concentration:** Engineering, Finance/Accounting

**Intravaia, Salvatore** — *Associate*
Source Services Corporation
2 Penn Plaza, Suite 1176
New York, NY 10121
Telephone: (212) 760-2200
**Recruiter Classification:** Contingency; **Lowest/Average Salary:** $30,000/$50,000; **Industry Concentration:** Financial Services, Information Technology; **Function Concentration:** Engineering, Finance/Accounting

**Inzinna, Dennis** — *Executive Vice President*
AlternaStaff
1155 Avenue of the Americas, 15th Floor
New York, NY 10036
Telephone: (212) 302-1141
**Recruiter Classification:** Executive Temporary; **Lowest/Average Salary:** $30,000/$60,000; **Industry Concentration:** Automotive, Biotechnology, Chemical Products, Electronics, High Technology, Manufacturing, Oil/Gas, Packaging, Pharmaceutical/Medical; **Function Concentration:** Engineering, General Management, Human Resources, Research and Development

**Inzitari, Gloria** — *Office Manager*
Accountants on Call
100 Constitution Plaza, Suite 957
Hartford, CT 06103
Telephone: (203) 246-4200
Recruiter Classification: Contingency; Lowest/Average Salary:
$20,000/$30,000; Industry Concentration: Generalist; Function
Concentration: Finance/Accounting

**Irish, Alan** — *Executive Recruiter*
CPS Inc.
One Westbrook Corporate Centre, Suite 600
Westchester, IL 60154
Telephone: (708) 531-8370
Recruiter Classification: Contingency; Lowest/Average Salary:
$30,000/$50,000; Industry Concentration: Generalist with a primary focus in
Automotive, Biotechnology, Chemical Products, Consumer Products, High
Technology, Insurance, Manufacturing, Oil/Gas, Packaging,
Pharmaceutical/Medical; Function Concentration: Engineering, Research and
Development, Sales, Women/Minorities

**Irvine, Robert** — *Consultant*
Keith Bagg & Associates Inc.
36 Toronto Street, Suite 520
Toronto, Ontario, CANADA M5C 2C5
Telephone: (416) 863-1800
Recruiter Classification: Contingency; Lowest/Average Salary:
$40,000/$60,000; Industry Concentration: Biotechnology, Chemical Products,
Consumer Products, Electronics, High Technology, Manufacturing,
Pharmaceutical/Medical; Function Concentration: Administration,
Engineering, Finance/Accounting, General Management, Marketing, Research
and Development, Sales

**Irwin, Mark** — *Associate*
Source Services Corporation
10220 SW Greenburg Road, Suite 625
Portland, OR 97223
Telephone: (503) 768-4546
Recruiter Classification: Contingency; Lowest/Average Salary:
$30,000/$50,000; Industry Concentration: Financial Services, Information
Technology; Function Concentration: Engineering, Finance/Accounting

**Isaacson, John** — *Managing Director*
Isaacson, Miller
334 Boylston Street, Suite 500
Boston, MA 02111
Telephone: (617) 262-6500
Recruiter Classification: Retained; Lowest/Average Salary: $75,000/$90,000;
Industry Concentration: Generalist with a primary focus in Education/Libraries,
Healthcare/Hospitals, Non-Profit, Publishing/Media; Function Concentration:
Administration, Finance/Accounting, General Management, Human Resources,
Women/Minorities

**Isenberg, Peter** — *Manager Central Region*
Management Recruiters International, Inc.
15209 Herriman Boulevard
Noblesville, IN 46060-4230
Telephone: (317) 773-4323
Recruiter Classification: Contingency; Lowest/Average Salary:
$30,000/$75,000; Industry Concentration: Generalist; Function
Concentration: Generalist

**Israel, Stephen** — *Vice President*
Korn/Ferry International
237 Park Avenue
New York, NY 10017
Telephone: (212) 687-1834
Recruiter Classification: Retained; Lowest/Average Salary:
$90,000/$90,000; Industry Concentration: Generalist; Function
Concentration: Generalist

**Issacs, Judith A.** — *Senior Associate*
Grant Cooper and Associates
795 Office Parkway, Suite 117
St. Louis, MO 63141
Telephone: (314) 567-4690
Recruiter Classification: Retained; Lowest/Average Salary: $60,000/$90,000;
Industry Concentration: Generalist with a primary focus in Board Services,
Consumer Products, Electronics, Financial Services, Healthcare/Hospitals,
Manufacturing, Non-Profit, Pharmaceutical/Medical; Function Concentration:
Generalist with a primary focus in Administration, Engineering,
Finance/Accounting, General Management, Human Resources, Marketing,
Sales

**Ives, Richard K.** — *Partner*
Wilkinson & Ives
One Bush Street, Suite 550
San Francisco, CA 94104
Telephone: (415) 834-3100
Recruiter Classification: Retained; Lowest/Average Salary: $90,000/$90,000;
Industry Concentration: Generalist with a primary focus in Board Services,
Electronics, Financial Services, High Technology, Information Technology,
Insurance, Manufacturing, Utilities/Nuclear, Venture Capital; Function
Concentration: Generalist with a primary focus in Engineering,
Finance/Accounting, General Management, Human Resources, Marketing,
Research and Development, Sales

**Ivey, Deborah M.** — *Physician Recruiter*
MSI International
201 St. Charles Avenue
Suite 2205
New Orleans, LA 70170
Telephone: (504) 522-6700
Recruiter Classification: Contingency; Lowest/Average Salary:
$30,000/$60,000; Industry Concentration: Generalist with a primary focus in
Healthcare/Hospitals; Function Concentration: Generalist with a primary focus
in Administration, Engineering, Finance/Accounting, General Management,
Marketing, Sales

**Jable, Maria C.** — *Recruiter*
Bryant Research
466 Old Hook Road, Suite 32
Emerson, NJ 07630
Telephone: (201) 599-0590
Recruiter Classification: Contingency; Lowest/Average Salary:
$50,000/$90,000; Industry Concentration: Biotechnology,
Pharmaceutical/Medical; Function Concentration: Research and
Development

**Jablo, Steven** — *Principal*
Dieckmann & Associates, Ltd.
180 North Stetson, Suite 5555
Two Prudential Plaza
Chicago, IL 60601
Telephone: (312) 819-5900
Recruiter Classification: Retained; Lowest/Average Salary: $75,000/$90,000;
Industry Concentration: Generalist with a primary focus in Chemical Products,
Electronics, Manufacturing, Packaging; Function Concentration: Generalist
with a primary focus in Engineering, General Management, Marketing,
Research and Development

**Jackowitz, Todd** — *Vice President*
J. Robert Scott
27 State Street
Boston, MA 02109
Telephone: (617) 720-2770
Recruiter Classification: Retained; Lowest/Average Salary: $75,000/$90,000;
Industry Concentration: Generalist with a primary focus in Biotechnology,
Chemical Products, Electronics, Financial Services, High Technology,
Information Technology, Pharmaceutical/Medical; Function Concentration:
Generalist

**Jackson, Barry** — *Recruiter*
Morgan Hunter Corp.
6800 College Boulevard, Suite 550
Overland Park, KS 66211
Telephone: (913) 491-3434
Recruiter Classification: Contingency; Lowest/Average Salary:
$30,000/$40,000; Industry Concentration: Information Technology; Function
Concentration: Generalist

**Jackson, Bruce** — *Senior Vice President*
Noble & Associates Inc.
420 Madison Avenue
New York, NY 10017
Telephone: (212) 838-7020
Recruiter Classification: Contingency; Lowest/Average Salary:
$40,000/$90,000; Industry Concentration: Generalist; Function
Concentration: Marketing

**Jackson, Carol** — *Manager*
The Wentworth Company, Inc.
The Arcade Building
479 West Sixth Street
San Pedro, CA 90731
Telephone: (800) 995-9678
Recruiter Classification: Retained; Lowest/Average Salary: $/$90,000; Industry
Concentration: Generalist; Function Concentration: Generalist

**Jackson, Clarke H.** — *Partner*
The Caldwell Partners Amrop International
999 West Hastings Street
Suite 750
Vancouver, British Columbia, CANADA V6C 2W2
Telephone: (604) 669-3550
**Recruiter Classification:** Retained; **Lowest/Average Salary:** $/$90,000; **Industry Concentration:** Generalist with a primary focus in Biotechnology, Energy, Environmental, Manufacturing, Publishing/Media, Transportation; **Function Concentration:** Generalist

**Jackson, Clay** — *Consultant*
Paul Ray Berndtson
One Allen Center
500 Dallas, Suite 3010
Houston, TX 77002
Telephone: (713) 309-1400
**Recruiter Classification:** Retained; **Lowest/Average Salary:** $90,000/$90,000; **Industry Concentration:** Generalist; **Function Concentration:** Generalist

**Jackson, James Greg** — *Senior Associate*
Korn/Ferry International
One Landmark Square
Stamford, CT 06901
Telephone: (203) 359-3350
**Recruiter Classification:** Retained; **Lowest/Average Salary:** $90,000/$90,000; **Industry Concentration:** Generalist; **Function Concentration:** Generalist

**Jackson, Pam** — *Marketing Representative*
Accounting Personnel Consultants
210 Baronne Street, Suite 920
New Orleans, LA 70112
Telephone: (504) 581-7800
**Recruiter Classification:** Contingency; **Lowest/Average Salary:** $20,000/$20,000; **Industry Concentration:** Generalist; **Function Concentration:** Administration

**Jackson, W.T.** — *Vice President*
Sampson Neill & Wilkins Inc.
543 Valley Road
Upper Montclair, NJ 07043
Telephone: (201) 783-9600
**Recruiter Classification:** Retained; **Lowest/Average Salary:** $75,000/$90,000; **Industry Concentration:** Biotechnology, Environmental, Pharmaceutical/Medical; **Function Concentration:** Engineering, General Management, Marketing, Research and Development, Sales

**Jacob, Don C.** — *Manager Southwest Region*
Management Recruiters International, Inc.
2301 North Central Expressway, Suite 250
Plano, TX 75075
Telephone: (214) 422-3311
**Recruiter Classification:** Contingency; **Lowest/Average Salary:** $30,000/$75,000; **Industry Concentration:** Generalist; **Function Concentration:** Generalist

**Jacobs, James W.** — *Associate*
Callan Associates, Ltd.
1550 Spring Road
Oak Brook, IL 60521
Telephone: (708) 832-7080
**Recruiter Classification:** Retained; **Lowest/Average Salary:** $90,000/$90,000; **Industry Concentration:** Generalist; **Function Concentration:** Generalist

**Jacobs, Judith** — *President/Recruiter*
The Rubicon Group
P.O. Box 2159
Scottsdale, AZ 85252-2159
Telephone: (602) 423-9280
**Recruiter Classification:** Contingency; **Lowest/Average Salary:** $30,000/$50,000; **Industry Concentration:** Hospitality/Leisure; **Function Concentration:** Administration, Finance/Accounting, General Management, Human Resources, Marketing, Sales

**Jacobs, Klaus** — *President*
TASA International
750 Lexington Avenue
Suite 1800
New York, NY 10022
Telephone: (212) 486-1490
**Recruiter Classification:** Retained; **Lowest/Average Salary:** $90,000/$90,000; **Industry Concentration:** Generalist; **Function Concentration:** Generalist

**Jacobs, Martin J.** — *Executive Vice President/Recruiter*
The Rubicon Group
P.O. Box 2159
Scottsdale, AZ 85252-2159
Telephone: (602) 423-9280
**Recruiter Classification:** Contingency; **Lowest/Average Salary:** $30,000/$60,000; **Industry Concentration:** Generalist with a primary focus in Aerospace/Defense, Biotechnology, Chemical Products, Electronics, Environmental, Financial Services, Healthcare/Hospitals, High Technology, Information Technology, Insurance, Manufacturing, Pharmaceutical/Medical; **Function Concentration:** Generalist with a primary focus in Administration, Engineering, Finance/Accounting, General Management, Marketing, Research and Development

**Jacobs, Mike** — *Principal*
Thorne, Brieger Associates Inc.
11 East 44th Street
New York, NY 10017
Telephone: (212) 682-5424
**Recruiter Classification:** Retained; **Lowest/Average Salary:** $90,000/$90,000; **Industry Concentration:** Generalist with a primary focus in Chemical Products, Consumer Products, Electronics, Fashion (Retail/Apparel), Financial Services, Insurance, Manufacturing; **Function Concentration:** Generalist with a primary focus in Administration, Engineering, Finance/Accounting, General Management, Human Resources, Marketing, Research and Development, Sales

**Jacobson, Al** — *Partner*
KPMG Executive Search
Suite 2610, Canada Trust Tower
10104-103 Avenue
Edmonton, Alberta, CANADA T5J 0H8
Telephone: (403) 429-1700
**Recruiter Classification:** Retained; **Lowest/Average Salary:** $75,000/$90,000; **Industry Concentration:** Generalist; **Function Concentration:** Generalist

**Jacobson, David N.** — *President*
Jacobson Associates
150 North Wacker Drive
Suite 1120
Chicago, IL 60606
Telephone: (312) 726-1578
**Recruiter Classification:** Contingency; **Lowest/Average Salary:** $20,000/$50,000; **Industry Concentration:** Insurance; **Function Concentration:** Generalist

**Jacobson, Donald** — *Vice President*
Hunt Advisory Services
21 West 38th Street
New York, NY 10018
Telephone: (212) 997-2299
**Recruiter Classification:** Executive Temporary; **Lowest/Average Salary:** $50,000/$60,000; **Industry Concentration:** Automotive, Chemical Products, Consumer Products, Fashion (Retail/Apparel), Manufacturing, Pharmaceutical/Medical, Publishing/Media, Transportation; **Function Concentration:** General Management

**Jacobson, Donald** — *Vice President*
Hunt Ltd.
21 West 38th Street
New York, NY 10018
Telephone: (212) 997-2299
**Recruiter Classification:** Contingency; **Lowest/Average Salary:** $30,000/$60,000; **Industry Concentration:** Automotive, Chemical Products, Consumer Products, Fashion (Retail/Apparel), Manufacturing, Packaging, Publishing/Media, Transportation; **Function Concentration:** Generalist

**Jacobson, Eric K.** — *Manager Southwest Region*
Management Recruiters International, Inc.
8445 Freeport Parkway, Suite 330
Irving, TX 75063
Telephone: (214) 929-2222
**Recruiter Classification:** Contingency; **Lowest/Average Salary:** $30,000/$75,000; **Industry Concentration:** Generalist; **Function Concentration:** Generalist

**Jacobson, Gregory** — *Executive Recruiter*
Jacobson Associates
1785 The Exchange, Suite 320
Atlanta, GA 30339
Telephone: (404) 952-3877
**Recruiter Classification:** Contingency; **Lowest/Average Salary:** $20,000/$50,000; **Industry Concentration:** Insurance; **Function Concentration:** Generalist

**Jacobson, Hayley** — *Associate*
Source Services Corporation
2 Penn Plaza, Suite 1176
New York, NY 10121
Telephone: (212) 760-2200
**Recruiter Classification:** Contingency; **Lowest/Average Salary:** $30,000/$50,000; **Industry Concentration:** Financial Services, Information Technology; **Function Concentration:** Engineering, Finance/Accounting

**Jacobson, Jewel** — *Vice President*
Jacobson Associates
150 North Wacker Drive
Suite 1120
Chicago, IL 60606
Telephone: (312) 726-1578
**Recruiter Classification:** Contingency; **Lowest/Average Salary:** $20,000/$50,000; **Industry Concentration:** Insurance; **Function Concentration:** Generalist

**Jacobson, Robert E.** — *Manager Central Region*
Management Recruiters International, Inc.
9700 Rockside Road, Suite 490
Cleveland, OH 44125-6264
Telephone: (216) 642-5788
**Recruiter Classification:** Contingency; **Lowest/Average Salary:**
$30,000/$75,000; **Industry Concentration:** Generalist; **Function Concentration:** Generalist

**Jadick, Theodore N.** — *Partner*
Heidrick & Struggles, Inc.
245 Park Avenue, Suite 4300
New York, NY 10167-0152
Telephone: (212) 867-9876
**Recruiter Classification:** Retained; **Lowest/Average Salary:** $75,000/$90,000;
**Industry Concentration:** Generalist with a primary focus in Board Services,
Healthcare/Hospitals; **Function Concentration:** Generalist

**Jadulang, Vincent** — *Associate*
Source Services Corporation
One Park Plaza, Suite 560
Irvine, CA 92714
Telephone: (714) 660-1666
**Recruiter Classification:** Contingency; **Lowest/Average Salary:**
$30,000/$50,000; **Industry Concentration:** Financial Services, Information
Technology; **Function Concentration:** Engineering, Finance/Accounting

**Jaedike, Eldron** — *Recruiter*
Prestige Inc.
P.O. Box 421
Reedsburg, WI 53959
Telephone: (608) 524-4032
**Recruiter Classification:** Contingency; **Lowest/Average Salary:**
$50,000/$90,000; **Industry Concentration:** Automotive, Consumer Products,
Financial Services, Healthcare/Hospitals, Insurance, Manufacturing; **Function Concentration:** Generalist

**Jaffe, Mark** — *Partner*
Wyatt & Jaffe
9900 Bren Road East, Suite 550
Minnetonka, MN 55343-9668
Telephone: (612) 945-0099
**Recruiter Classification:** Retained; **Lowest/Average Salary:** $75,000/$90,000;
**Industry Concentration:** Biotechnology, Board Services, Electronics, High
Technology; **Function Concentration:** Generalist with a primary focus in
Engineering, General Management, Human Resources, Marketing, Research
and Development

**Jambor, Hilary L.** — *Senior Associate*
Korn/Ferry International
120 South Riverside Plaza
Suite 918
Chicago, IL 60606
Telephone: (312) 726-1841
**Recruiter Classification:** Retained; **Lowest/Average Salary:** $90,000/$90,000;
**Industry Concentration:** Generalist; **Function Concentration:** Generalist

**James, Allison A.** — *Executive Recruiter*
MSI International
201 St. Charles Avenue
Suite 2205
New Orleans, LA 70170
Telephone: (504) 522-6700
**Recruiter Classification:** Contingency; **Lowest/Average Salary:**
$30,000/$75,000; **Industry Concentration:** Generalist with a primary focus in
Healthcare/Hospitals, Pharmaceutical/Medical; **Function Concentration:**
Generalist with a primary focus in Administration, Engineering,
Finance/Accounting, General Management, Marketing, Sales

**James, Bruce** — *Recruiter*
Roberson and Company
10752 North 89th Place, Suite 202
Scottsdale, AZ 85260
Telephone: (602) 391-3200
**Recruiter Classification:** Contingency; **Lowest/Average Salary:**
$40,000/$50,000; **Industry Concentration:** Generalist with a primary focus in
Aerospace/Defense, Automotive, Chemical Products, Consumer Products,
Electronics, High Technology, Information Technology, Manufacturing,
Packaging, Pharmaceutical/Medical, Publishing/Media, Transportation;
**Function Concentration:** Generalist with a primary focus in Administration,
Engineering, General Management, Human Resources, Marketing, Sales

**James, E. Pendleton** — *Chairman*
Pendleton James and Associates, Inc.
200 Park Avenue, Suite 4520
New York, NY 10166
Telephone: (212) 557-1599
**Recruiter Classification:** Retained; **Lowest/Average Salary:** $90,000/$90,000;
**Industry Concentration:** Generalist; **Function Concentration:** Generalist

**James, Jane** — *Vice President*
Canny, Bowen Inc.
200 Park Avenue
New York, NY 10166
Telephone: (212) 949-6611
**Recruiter Classification:** Retained; **Lowest/Average Salary:** $90,000/$90,000;
**Industry Concentration:** Generalist; **Function Concentration:** Generalist

**James, Michele** — *Principal*
Korn/Ferry International
237 Park Avenue
New York, NY 10017
Telephone: (212) 687-1834
**Recruiter Classification:** Retained; **Lowest/Average Salary:** $90,000/$90,000;
**Industry Concentration:** Generalist; **Function Concentration:** Generalist

**James, Richard** — *President*
Criterion Executive Search, Inc.
5420 Bay Center Drive, Suite 101
Tampa, FL 33609-3402
Telephone: (813) 286-2000
**Recruiter Classification:** Contingency; **Lowest/Average Salary:**
$40,000/$90,000; **Industry Concentration:** Generalist with a primary focus in
Electronics, Financial Services, High Technology, Information Technology,
Insurance, Manufacturing, Packaging; **Function Concentration:** Generalist with
a primary focus in Administration, Engineering, Finance/Accounting, Research
and Development, Women/Minorities

**Janecek, Robert** — *Co-Manager Midwest Region*
Management Recruiters International, Inc.
The Underwriter's Exchange Building
828 North Broadway, Suite 850
Milwaukee, WI 53202
Telephone: (414) 226-2420
**Recruiter Classification:** Contingency; **Lowest/Average Salary:** $30,000/$75,000;
**Industry Concentration:** Generalist; **Function Concentration:** Generalist

**Janis, Laurence** — *Partner*
Integrated Search Solutions Group, LLC
33 Main Street
Port Washington, NY 11050
Telephone: (516) 767-3030
**Recruiter Classification:** Retained; **Lowest/Average Salary:** $90,000/$90,000;
**Industry Concentration:** Generalist with a primary focus in High Technology,
Information Technology; **Function Concentration:** Generalist with a primary
focus in Human Resources, Marketing, Sales

**Jansen, Douglas L.** — *President*
Search Northwest Associates
10117 SE Sunnyside, Suite F-727
Clackamas, OR 97015
Telephone: (503) 654-1487
**Recruiter Classification:** Contingency; **Lowest/Average Salary:**
$40,000/$75,000; **Industry Concentration:** Automotive, Electronics, High
Technology, Packaging; **Function Concentration:** Engineering, Research and
Development

**Januleski, Geoff** — *Associate*
Source Services Corporation
150 South Warner Road, Suite 238
King of Prussia, PA 19406
Telephone: (610) 341-1960
**Recruiter Classification:** Contingency; **Lowest/Average Salary:**
$30,000/$50,000; **Industry Concentration:** Financial Services, Information
Technology; **Function Concentration:** Engineering, Finance/Accounting

**Jayne, Edward R.** — *Consultant*
Heidrick & Struggles, Inc.
8000 Towers Crescent Drive, Suite 555
Vienna, VA 22182
Telephone: (703) 761-4830
**Recruiter Classification:** Retained; **Lowest/Average Salary:** $75,000/$90,000;
**Industry Concentration:** Generalist; **Function Concentration:** Generalist

**Jeanes, Marshall M.** — *Vice Chairman*
IMCOR, Inc.
475 Park Avenue South
New York, NY 10016
Telephone: (212) 213-3600
**Recruiter Classification:** Executive Temporary; **Lowest/Average Salary:**
$75,000/$90,000; **Industry Concentration:** Generalist; **Function Concentration:** Generalist

**Jeffers, Carol S.** — *Vice President*
John Sibbald Associates, Inc.
8725 West Higgins Road, Suite 575
Chicago, IL 60631
Telephone: (312) 693-0575
**Recruiter Classification:** Retained; **Lowest/Average Salary:** $75,000/$90,000;
**Industry Concentration:** Environmental, Fashion (Retail/Apparel),
Hospitality/Leisure, Non-Profit; **Function Concentration:** Administration,
General Management, Women/Minorities

**Jelley, Sarah L.** — *Associate*
Pendleton James and Associates, Inc.
200 Park Avenue, Suite 4520
New York, NY 10166
Telephone: (212) 557-1599
**Recruiter Classification:** Retained; **Lowest/Average Salary:** $90,000/$90,000;
**Industry Concentration:** Generalist; **Function Concentration:** Generalist

**Jeltema, John** — *Associate*
Source Services Corporation
One Park Plaza, Suite 560
Irvine, CA 92714
Telephone: (714) 660-1666
**Recruiter Classification:** Contingency; **Lowest/Average Salary:**
$30,000/$50,000; **Industry Concentration:** Financial Services, Information
Technology; **Function Concentration:** Engineering, Finance/Accounting

**Jenkins, Jeffrey N.** — *Principal*
Sanford Rose Associates
6116 North Central Expressway, Suite 301
Dallas, TX 75206
Telephone: (214) 739-8962
**Recruiter Classification:** Contingency; **Lowest/Average Salary:**
$30,000/$75,000; **Industry Concentration:** Generalist; **Function
Concentration:** Generalist

**Jensen, Christine K.** — *Vice President*
John Kurosky & Associates
3 Corporate Park Drive, Suite 210
Irvine, CA 92714
Telephone: (714) 851-6370
**Recruiter Classification:** Retained; **Lowest/Average Salary:** $60,000/$90,000;
**Industry Concentration:** Information Technology; **Function Concentration:**
Generalist

**Jensen, Debra** — *Recruiter*
Flex Execs Management Solutions
16350 South 105th Court
Orland Park, IL 60462
Telephone: (708) 460-8500
**Recruiter Classification:** Executive Temporary; **Lowest/Average Salary:**
$40,000/$50,000; **Industry Concentration:** Generalist; **Function
Concentration:** Generalist with a primary focus in Finance/Accounting,
General Management, Human Resources, Marketing, Sales

**Jensen, Robert** — *Associate*
Source Services Corporation
3701 West Algonquin Road, Suite 380
Rolling Meadows, IL 60008
Telephone: (847) 392-0244
**Recruiter Classification:** Contingency; **Lowest/Average Salary:**
$30,000/$50,000; **Industry Concentration:** Financial Services, Information
Technology; **Function Concentration:** Engineering, Finance/Accounting

**Jensen, Stephanie** — *Recruiter*
Don Richard Associates of Tidewater, Inc.
4701 Columbus Street, Suite 102
Virginia Beach, VA 23462
Telephone: (757) 518-8600
**Recruiter Classification:** Contingency; **Lowest/Average Salary:**
$30,000/$40,000; **Industry Concentration:** Generalist with a primary focus in
Aerospace/Defense, Automotive, Biotechnology, Chemical Products,
Consumer Products, Electronics, Energy, Environmental, Healthcare/Hospitals,
High Technology, Information Technology, Manufacturing, Oil/Gas, Packaging;
**Function Concentration:** Engineering

**Jernigan, Alice** — *Director Operations*
Ariel Recruitment Associates
440 West 53rd Street, Suite 126
New York, NY 10019
Telephone: (212) 765-8300
**Recruiter Classification:** Contingency; **Lowest/Average Salary:**
$50,000/$75,000; **Industry Concentration:** Entertainment, Publishing/Media;
**Function Concentration:** Generalist with a primary focus in Administration,
Finance/Accounting, General Management, Human Resources, Marketing,
Sales

**Jernigan, Susan N.** — *Executive Recruiter*
Sockwell & Associates
227 West Trade Street, Suite 1930
Charlotte, NC 28202
Telephone: (704) 372-1865
**Recruiter Classification:** Retained; **Lowest/Average Salary:** $90,000/$90,000;
**Industry Concentration:** Generalist with a primary focus in Education/Libraries,
Financial Services, Healthcare/Hospitals, Non-Profit, Real Estate; **Function
Concentration:** Generalist with a primary focus in Administration,
Finance/Accounting, General Management, Human Resources, Marketing,
Sales

**Jessamy, Howard T.** — *Consultant*
Witt/Kieffer, Ford, Hadelman & Lloyd
4550 Montgomery Avenue
Bethesda, MD 20814
Telephone: (301) 654-5070
**Recruiter Classification:** Retained; **Lowest/Average Salary:** $75,000/$90,000;
**Industry Concentration:** Healthcare/Hospitals; **Function Concentration:**
General Management

**Jilka, Daniel L.** — *Co-Manager Pacific Region*
Management Recruiters International, Inc.
2510 Fairview Avenue East
Seattle, WA 98102
Telephone: (206) 328-0936
**Recruiter Classification:** Contingency; **Lowest/Average Salary:**
$30,000/$75,000; **Industry Concentration:** Generalist; **Function
Concentration:** Generalist

**Jimenez, Gil C.** — *Manager Southwest Region*
Management Recruiters International, Inc.
4100 Piedras Drive East, Suite 204
San Antonio, TX 78228-1426
Telephone: (210) 733-1074
**Recruiter Classification:** Contingency; **Lowest/Average Salary:** $30,000/$75,000;
**Industry Concentration:** Generalist; **Function Concentration:** Generalist

**Joffe, Barry** — *Director Executive Search Consulting*
Bason Associates Inc.
11311 Cornell Park Drive
Cincinnati, OH 45242
Telephone: (513) 469-9881
**Recruiter Classification:** Retained; **Lowest/Average Salary:** $60,000/$90,000;
**Industry Concentration:** Generalist with a primary focus in Automotive,
Biotechnology, Board Services, Chemical Products, Consumer Products,
Environmental, Fashion (Retail/Apparel), Financial Services, Healthcare/Hospitals,
High Technology, Insurance, Manufacturing, Packaging, Pharmaceutical/Medical,
Public Administration; **Function Concentration:** Generalist with a primary focus in
Administration, Engineering, Finance/Accounting, General Management, Human
Resources, Marketing, Research and Development, Sales

**Johasky, Tom K.** — *Manager South Atlantic Region*
Management Recruiters International, Inc.
1700 East Las OLas Boulevard, Penthouse 5
Fort Lauderdale, FL 33301
Telephone: (954) 525-0355
**Recruiter Classification:** Contingency; **Lowest/Average Salary:**
$30,000/$75,000; **Industry Concentration:** Generalist; **Function
Concentration:** Generalist

**Johnson, Brian** — *Recruiter*
A.J. Burton Group, Inc.
120 East Baltimore Street, Suite 2220
Baltimore, MD 21202
Telephone: (410) 752-5244
**Recruiter Classification:** Contingency; **Lowest/Average Salary:**
$20,000/$30,000; **Industry Concentration:** Consumer Products,
Healthcare/Hospitals, Insurance, Manufacturing; **Function Concentration:**
Finance/Accounting

**Johnson, David** — *Executive Recruiter*
Gaffney Management Consultants
35 North Brandon Drive
Glendale Heights, IL 60139-2087
Telephone: (708) 307-3380
**Recruiter Classification:** Retained; **Lowest/Average Salary:** $60,000/$90,000;
**Industry Concentration:** Generalist with a primary focus in
Aerospace/Defense, Automotive, Electronics, High Technology, Manufacturing,
Transportation, Venture Capital; **Function Concentration:** Generalist with a
primary focus in Engineering, Finance/Accounting, General Management,
Human Resources, Marketing, Research and Development, Sales,
Women/Minorities

**Johnson, Dennis R.** — *Manager Pacific Region*
Management Recruiters International, Inc.
2709 Jahn Avenue, N.W., Suite H-11
Gig Harbor, WA 98335
Telephone: (206) 858-9991
**Recruiter Classification:** Contingency; **Lowest/Average Salary:**
$30,000/$75,000; **Industry Concentration:** Generalist; **Function
Concentration:** Generalist

**Johnson, Douglas** — *Executive Recruiter*
Quality Search
P.O. Box 752294
Dayton, OH 45475-2294
Telephone: (500) 442-1305
**Recruiter Classification:** Contingency; **Lowest/Average Salary:**
$30,000/$50,000; **Industry Concentration:** Automotive, Biotechnology,
Chemical Products, Electronics, Environmental, High Technology, Information
Technology, Manufacturing, Oil/Gas, Packaging, Pharmaceutical/Medical;
**Function Concentration:** Engineering, General Management, Human
Resources, Marketing, Research and Development, Sales, Women/Minorities

**Johnson, Greg** — *Managing Director*
Source Services Corporation
525 Vine Street, Suite 2250
Cincinnati, OH 45202
Telephone: (513) 651-3303
**Recruiter Classification:** Contingency; **Lowest/Average Salary:**
$30,000/$50,000; **Industry Concentration:** Financial Services, Information
Technology; **Function Concentration:** Engineering, Finance/Accounting

**Johnson, Harold E.** — *Managing Director*
Norman Broadbent International, Inc.
200 Park Avenue, 20th Floor
New York, NY 10166
Telephone: (212) 953-6990
**Recruiter Classification:** Retained; **Lowest/Average Salary:** $90,000/$90,000;
**Industry Concentration:** Generalist; **Function Concentration:** Generalist with a
primary focus in General Management, Human Resources

**Johnson, Janet** — *Recruiter*
Normyle/Erstling Health Search Group
350 West Passaic Street
Rochelle Park, NJ 07662
Telephone: (201) 843-6009
**Recruiter Classification:** Contingency; **Lowest/Average Salary:**
$30,000/$50,000; **Industry Concentration:** Biotechnology,
Healthcare/Hospitals, Pharmaceutical/Medical; **Function Concentration:**
General Management, Marketing, Sales

**Johnson, John F.** — *Chairman*
Lamalie Amrop International
Key Tower, 127 Public Square
Cleveland, OH 44114-1216
Telephone: (216) 694-3000
**Recruiter Classification:** Retained; **Lowest/Average Salary:** $90,000/$90,000;
**Industry Concentration:** Generalist with a primary focus in Automotive, Board
Services, Packaging; **Function Concentration:** Generalist with a primary focus
in Finance/Accounting, General Management, Human Resources

**Johnson, John W.** — *Managing Director*
Webb, Johnson Associates, Inc.
280 Park Avenue, 43rd Floor
New York, NY 10017
Telephone: (212) 661-3700
**Recruiter Classification:** Retained; **Lowest/Average Salary:** $90,000/$90,000;
**Industry Concentration:** Generalist with a primary focus in Biotechnology,
Chemical Products, Financial Services, Healthcare/Hospitals, High Technology,
Manufacturing, Non-Profit, Pharmaceutical/Medical; **Function Concentration:**
Generalist with a primary focus in Administration, Engineering,
Finance/Accounting, General Management, Human Resources, Marketing,
Research and Development, Sales

**Johnson, Julie** — *Staffing Consultant*
International Staffing Consultants, Inc.
500 Newport Center Drive, Suite 300
Newport Beach, CA 92660-7003
Telephone: (714) 721-7990
**Recruiter Classification:** Contingency; **Lowest/Average Salary:**
$30,000/$75,000; **Industry Concentration:** Consumer Products, High
Technology, Oil/Gas; **Function Concentration:** Human Resources, Marketing,
Sales

**Johnson, Kathleen A.** — *Executive Director/Consultant*
Barton Raben, Inc.
One Riverway, Suite 2500
Houston, TX 77056
Telephone: (713) 961-9111
**Recruiter Classification:** Retained; **Lowest/Average Salary:** $75,000/$90,000;
**Industry Concentration:** Generalist with a primary focus in Automotive, Board
Services, Consumer Products, Electronics, Energy, Environmental, Financial
Services, High Technology, Oil/Gas, Transportation, Venture Capital; **Function
Concentration:** Generalist with a primary focus in Administration,
Finance/Accounting, General Management, Human Resources, Marketing,
Sales

**Johnson, Keith** — *Managing Partner*
Romac & Associates
760 Pillsbury Center
200 South Sixth Street
Minneapolis, MN 55402
Telephone: (612) 334-5990
**Recruiter Classification:** Executive Temporary; **Lowest/Average Salary:**
$/$60,000; **Industry Concentration:** Financial Services, Healthcare/Hospitals,
High Technology, Hospitality/Leisure, Information Technology, Insurance;
**Function Concentration:** Finance/Accounting

**Johnson, Maxene** — *Vice President*
Norman Roberts & Associates, Inc.
1800 Century Park East, Suite 430
Los Angeles, CA 90067
Telephone: (310) 552-1112
**Recruiter Classification:** Retained; **Lowest/Average Salary:** $60,000/$90,000;
**Industry Concentration:** Education/Libraries, Healthcare/Hospitals, Non-Profit,
Public Administration; **Function Concentration:** Generalist with a primary
focus in Administration, General Managemen

**Johnson, Michael E.** — *Vice President*
Sharrow & Associates
24735 Van Dyke
Center Line, MI 48015
Telephone: (810) 759-6910
**Recruiter Classification:** Contingency; **Lowest/Average Salary:**
$30,000/$50,000; **Industry Concentration:** Automotive, Manufacturing;
**Function Concentration:** Engineering, Research and Development

**Johnson, Pete** — *Recruiter*
Morgan Hunter Corp.
6800 College Boulevard, Suite 550
Overland Park, KS 66211
Telephone: (913) 491-3434
**Recruiter Classification:** Contingency; **Lowest/Average Salary:**
$30,000/$40,000; **Industry Concentration:** Information Technology; **Function
Concentration:** Generalist

**Johnson, Peter** — *Software Engineering Recruiter*
Winter, Wyman & Company
950 Winter Street, Suite 3100
Waltham, MA 02154-1294
Telephone: (617) 890-7000
**Recruiter Classification:** Contingency; **Lowest/Average Salary:**
$40,000/$75,000; **Industry Concentration:** High Technology, Information
Technology, Publishing/Media; **Function Concentration:** Engineering

**Johnson, Priscilla** — *President*
The Johnson Group, Inc.
1 World Trade Center, Suite 4517
New York, NY 10048-0202
Telephone: (212) 775-0036
**Recruiter Classification:** Contingency; **Lowest/Average Salary:**
$60,000/$75,000; **Industry Concentration:** Generalist with a primary focus in
Board Services, Entertainment, Financial Services, Insurance, Manufacturing,
Pharmaceutical/Medical, Publishing/Media; **Function Concentration:**
Generalist with a primary focus in Finance/Accounting, General Management,
Human Resources, Marketing, Sales, Women/Minorities

**Johnson, Robert J.** — *President*
Quality Search
P.O. Box 752294
Dayton, OH 45475-2294
Telephone: (500) 442-1305
**Recruiter Classification:** Contingency; **Lowest/Average Salary:**
$30,000/$50,000; **Industry Concentration:** Automotive, Biotechnology,
Chemical Products, Electronics, Environmental, High Technology, Information
Technology, Manufacturing, Oil/Gas, Packaging, Pharmaceutical/Medical;
**Function Concentration:** Engineering, General Management, Human
Resources, Marketing, Research and Development, Sales, Women/Minorities

**Johnson, Rocky** — *Vice President/Managing Director*
A.T. Kearney, Inc.
Lincoln Plaza, Suite 4170
500 North Akard Street
Dallas, TX 75201
Telephone: (214) 969-0010
**Recruiter Classification:** Retained; **Lowest/Average Salary:** $90,000/$90,000;
**Industry Concentration:** Generalist with a primary focus in High Technology,
Hospitality/Leisure, Manufacturing, Transportation; **Function Concentration:**
Generalist with a primary focus in General Management

**Johnson, Ron L.** — *Manager Pacific Region*
Management Recruiters International, Inc.
114 East Shaw, Suite 207
Fresno, CA 93710
Telephone: (209) 226-5578
**Recruiter Classification:** Contingency; **Lowest/Average Salary:**
$30,000/$75,000; **Industry Concentration:** Generalist; **Function
Concentration:** Generalist

**Johnson, Ronald S.** — *President*
Ronald S. Johnson Associates, Inc.
11661 San Vicente Boulevard, Suite 400
Los Angeles, CA 90049
Telephone: (310) 820-5855
**Recruiter Classification:** Retained; **Lowest/Average Salary:** $90,000/$90,000;
**Industry Concentration:** Generalist with a primary focus in Biotechnology,
Board Services, Electronics, Environmental, High Technology, Information
Technology, Venture Capital; **Function Concentration:** Generalist

**Johnson, S. Hope** — *Vice President*
The Interface Group, Ltd./Boyden
2828 Pennsylvania Avenue, N.W., Suite 305
Washington, DC 20007
Telephone: (202) 342-7200
**Recruiter Classification:** Retained; **Lowest/Average Salary:** $75,000/$90,000;
**Industry Concentration:** Generalist with a primary focus in Biotechnology,
Consumer Products, Energy, Environmental, Healthcare/Hospitals, High
Technology, Information Technology, Manufacturing, Non-Profit,
Pharmaceutical/Medical, Publishing/Media; **Function Concentration:**
Generalist with a primary focus in Administration, General Management,
Human Resources, Marketing, Research and Development, Women/Minorities

**Johnson, Shirley E.** — *Vice President*
The Heidrick Partners, Inc.
20 North Wacker Drive
Suite 2850
Chicago, IL 60606-3171
Telephone: (312) 845-9700
**Recruiter Classification:** Retained; **Lowest/Average Salary:** $90,000/$90,000;
**Industry Concentration:** Generalist; **Function Concentration:** Generalist

**Johnson, Stephanie** — *Consultant*
Carver Search Consultants
9303 East Bullard, Suite 1
Clovis, CA 93611-8211
Telephone: (209) 298-7791
**Recruiter Classification:** Contingency; **Lowest/Average Salary:**
$50,000/$60,000; **Industry Concentration:** Generalist; **Function
Concentration:** General Management, Marketing, Sales

**Johnson, Walt W.** — *Co-Manager Pacific Region*
Management Recruiters International, Inc.
3070 South Bristol Street, Suite 400
Costa Mesa, CA 92626
Telephone: (714) 668-7470
**Recruiter Classification:** Contingency; **Lowest/Average Salary:**
$30,000/$75,000; **Industry Concentration:** Generalist; **Function
Concentration:** Generalist

**Johnston, Cindy** — *Manager Central Region*
Management Recruiters International, Inc.
Chagrin Plaza East, Suite 140
23811 Chagrin Boulevard
Shaker Heights, OH 44122
Telephone: (216) 292-1072
**Recruiter Classification:** Contingency; **Lowest/Average Salary:**
$30,000/$75,000; **Industry Concentration:** Generalist; **Function
Concentration:** Generalist

**Johnston, James R.** — *Principal*
The Stevenson Group of Delaware Inc.
836 Farmington Avenue, Suite 223
West Hartford, CT 06119
Telephone: (860) 232-3393
**Recruiter Classification:** Retained; **Lowest/Average Salary:** $75,000/$90,000;
**Industry Concentration:** Chemical Products, Consumer Products, Electronics,
Financial Services, Insurance, Pharmaceutical/Medical; **Function
Concentration:** Generalist

**Johnston, Philip D.** — *Consultant*
Egon Zehnder International Inc.
1 Place Ville-Marie, Suite 3310
Montreal, Quebec, CANADA H3B 3N2
Telephone: (514) 876-4249
**Recruiter Classification:** Retained; **Lowest/Average Salary:** $90,000/$90,000;
**Industry Concentration:** Generalist; **Function Concentration:** Generalist

**Johnstone, Grant** — *Associate*
Source Services Corporation
520 Post Oak Boulevard, Suite 700
Houston, TX 77027
Telephone: (713) 439-1077
**Recruiter Classification:** Contingency; **Lowest/Average Salary:**
$30,000/$50,000; **Industry Concentration:** Financial Services, Information
Technology; **Function Concentration:** Engineering, Finance/Accounting

**Jones, B.J.** — *Principal*
Intersource, Ltd.
515 East Carefree Highway
P.O. Box 42033438
Phoenix, AZ 80080
Telephone: (602) 780-4540
**Recruiter Classification:** Retained; **Lowest/Average Salary:** $30,000/$75,000;
**Industry Concentration:** Generalist with a primary focus in Financial Services,
High Technology; **Function Concentration:** Human Resources

**Jones, Barbara J.** — *Senior Vice President*
Kaye-Bassman International Corp.
18333 Preston Road, Suite 500
Dallas, TX 75252
Telephone: (214) 931-5242
**Recruiter Classification:** Executive Temporary; **Lowest/Average Salary:**
$40,000/$60,000; **Industry Concentration:** Biotechnology, Chemical Products,
Financial Services, Healthcare/Hospitals, High Technology, Information
Technology, Pharmaceutical/Medical, Transportation; **Function Concentration:**
Generalist

**Jones, Dale E.** — *Principal*
Lamalie Amrop International
191 Peachtree Street N.E.
Atlanta, GA 30303
Telephone: (404) 688-0800
**Recruiter Classification:** Retained; **Lowest/Average Salary:** $90,000/$90,000;
**Industry Concentration:** Generalist; **Function Concentration:** Generalist

**Jones, Daniel F.** — *Principal*
Atlantic Search Group, Inc.
One Liberty Square
Boston, MA 02109
Telephone: (617) 426-9700
**Recruiter Classification:** Contingency; **Lowest/Average Salary:**
$20,000/$60,000; **Industry Concentration:** Generalist with a primary focus in
Biotechnology, Consumer Products, Electronics, Financial Services, High
Technology, Information Technology, Manufacturing, Real Estate; **Function
Concentration:** Finance/Accounting

**Jones, Don** — *Associate*
Kenzer Corp.
Triwest Plaza
3030 LBJ Freeway, Suite 1430
Dallas, TX 75234
Telephone: (214) 620-7776
**Recruiter Classification:** Retained; **Lowest/Average Salary:** $50,000/$90,000;
**Industry Concentration:** Generalist; **Function Concentration:** Generalist

**Jones, Donald K.** — *Managing Director*
Russell Reynolds Associates, Inc.
1700 Pennsylvania Avenue N.W.
Suite 850
Washington, DC 20006
Telephone: (202) 628-2150
**Recruiter Classification:** Retained; **Lowest/Average Salary:** $90,000/$90,000;
**Industry Concentration:** Generalist with a primary focus in High Technology;
**Function Concentration:** Generalist

**Jones, Edgar** — *Vice President*
A.T. Kearney, Inc.
Miami Center, Suite 3180
201 South Biscayne Boulevard
Miami, FL 33131
Telephone: (305) 577-0046
**Recruiter Classification:** Retained; **Lowest/Average Salary:** $90,000/$90,000;
**Industry Concentration:** Generalist; **Function Concentration:** Generalist

**Jones, Edward G.** — *President*
E.G. Jones Associates, Ltd.
1505 York Road
Lutherville, MD 21093
Telephone: (410) 337-4925
**Recruiter Classification:** Contingency; **Lowest/Average Salary:**
$90,000/$90,000; **Industry Concentration:** Venture Capital; **Function
Concentration:** Generalist

**Jones, Francis E.** — *President*
Earley Kielty and Associates, Inc.
One Landmark Square
Stamford, CT 06901
Telephone: (203) 324-6723
**Recruiter Classification:** Retained; **Lowest/Average Salary:** $90,000/$90,000;
**Industry Concentration:** Generalist with a primary focus in Information
Technology; **Function Concentration:** Generalist with a primary focus in
Administration, Finance/Accounting, General Management, Human Resources,
Marketing, Research and Development, Sales, Women/Minorities

**Jones, Gary** — *Consultant/Recruiter*
BGB Associates
P.O. Box 556
Itasca, IL 60143
Telephone: (630) 250-8993
**Recruiter Classification:** Contingency; **Lowest/Average Salary:**
$20,000/$50,000; **Industry Concentration:** Generalist with a primary focus in
Aerospace/Defense, Automotive, Chemical Products, Consumer Products,
Energy, Environmental, Information Technology, Manufacturing, Oil/Gas,
Packaging, Pharmaceutical/Medical, Transportation; **Function Concentration:**
Generalist with a primary focus in Administration, Engineering,
Finance/Accounting, General Management, Human Resources, Marketing,
Sales, Women/Minorities

**Jones, Herschel** — *Vice President*
Korn/Ferry International
600 University Street, Suite 3111
Seattle, WA 98101
Telephone: (206) 447-1834
**Recruiter Classification:** Retained; **Lowest/Average Salary:** $90,000/$90,000;
**Industry Concentration:** Generalist with a primary focus in Financial Services;
**Function Concentration:** Generalist

**Jones, Jeffrey** — *Principal*
AJM Professional Services
803 West Big Beaver Road, Suite 357
Troy, MI 48084-4734
Telephone: (810) 244-2222
**Recruiter Classification:** Contingency; **Lowest/Average Salary:**
$30,000/$60,000; **Industry Concentration:** Generalist with a primary focus in
Financial Services, Healthcare/Hospitals, Information Technology, Insurance,
Manufacturing; **Function Concentration:** Generalist with a primary focus in
Finance/Accounting

**Jones, Jonathan C.** — *Recruiter*
The Ogdon Partnership
375 Park Avenue, Suite 2409
New York, NY 10152-0175
Telephone: (212) 308-1600
**Recruiter Classification:** Retained; **Lowest/Average Salary:** $75,000/$90,000;
**Industry Concentration:** Generalist with a primary focus in Consumer
Products, Financial Services, Information Technology, Insurance,
Publishing/Media; **Function Concentration:** Generalist with a primary focus in
Administration, Finance/Accounting, General Management, Human Resources,
Marketing, Sales

**Jones, Judy M.** — *Manager North Atlantic Region*
Management Recruiters International, Inc.
P.O. Box 17054
Winston-Salem, NC 27116-7054
Telephone: (910) 723-0484
**Recruiter Classification:** Contingency; **Lowest/Average Salary:**
$30,000/$75,000; **Industry Concentration:** Generalist; **Function**
**Concentration:** Generalist

**Jones, Mike R.** — *Manager*
Management Recruiters International, Inc.
P.O. Box 17054
Winston-Salem, NC 27116-7054
Telephone: (910) 723-0484
**Recruiter Classification:** Contingency; **Lowest/Average Salary:**
$30,000/$75,000; **Industry Concentration:** Generalist; **Function**
**Concentration:** Generalist

**Jones, Rodney** — *Associate*
Source Services Corporation
379 Thornall Street
Edison, NJ 08837
Telephone: (908) 494-2800
**Recruiter Classification:** Contingency; **Lowest/Average Salary:**
$30,000/$50,000; **Industry Concentration:** Financial Services, Information
Technology; **Function Concentration:** Engineering, Finance/Accounting

**Jones, Ronald T.** — *President*
ARJay & Associates
3286 Clower Street, Suite A-202
Snellville, GA 30278
Telephone: (404) 979-3799
**Recruiter Classification:** Contingency; **Lowest/Average Salary:**
$40,000/$90,000; **Industry Concentration:** Generalist with a primary focus in
Automotive, Consumer Products, Electronics, Energy, Environmental,
Manufacturing, Utilities/Nuclear; **Function Concentration:** Generalist with a
primary focus in Engineering, Finance/Accounting, General Management,
Human Resources, Marketing, Research and Development, Sales

**Jones, Suzanne English** — *Consultant*
Vera L. Rast Partners, Inc.
One South Wacker Drive, Suite 3890
Chicago, IL 60606
Telephone: (312) 629-0339
**Recruiter Classification:** Contingency; **Lowest/Average Salary:**
$50,000/$90,000

**Jordan, Stephen T.** — *Partner*
Paul Ray Berndtson
2200 Ross Avenue, Suite 4500W
Dallas, TX 75201
Telephone: (214) 969-7620
**Recruiter Classification:** Retained; **Lowest/Average Salary:** $90,000/$90,000;
**Industry Concentration:** Generalist with a primary focus in Financial Services;
**Function Concentration:** Generalist

**Jose, Bill O.** — *General Manager*
Management Recruiters International, Inc.
Plaza Building, Suite 208
100 Crossways Park West
Woodbury, NY 11797
Telephone: (516) 364-9290
**Recruiter Classification:** Contingency; **Lowest/Average Salary:**
$30,000/$75,000; **Industry Concentration:** Generalist; **Function**
**Concentration:** Generalist

**Jose, Bill O.** — *Co-Manager*
Management Recruiters International, Inc.
Flying Point Office Park, Suite 207
33 Flying Point Road
Southampton, NY 11968-5244
Telephone: (516) 287-5030
**Recruiter Classification:** Contingency; **Lowest/Average Salary:**
$30,000/$75,000; **Industry Concentration:** Generalist; **Function**
**Concentration:** Generalist

**Joubert, Pierre E.** — *Consultant*
Boyden
1250, boul. Rene-Levesque ouest
Bureau 4110
Montreal, Quebec, CANADA H3B 4W8
Telephone: (514) 935-4560
**Recruiter Classification:** Retained; **Lowest/Average Salary:** $75,000/$90,000;
**Industry Concentration:** Generalist; **Function Concentration:** Generalist with a
primary focus in Engineering, Finance/Accounting, General Management,
Human Resources, Marketing, Research and Development, Sales,
Women/Minorities

**Joyce, James** — *Director Medical Division*
Sharrow & Associates
P.O. Box 515
Angola, IN 46703
Telephone: (800) 344-5032
**Recruiter Classification:** Contingency; **Lowest/Average Salary:**
$30,000/$40,000; **Industry Concentration:** Healthcare/Hospitals

**Joyce, Sheila M.** — *Partner*
Verkamp-Joyce Associates, Inc.
Westwood of Lisle, Suite 600
2443 Warrenville Road
Lisle, IL 60532
Telephone: (708) 955-3750
**Recruiter Classification:** Retained; **Lowest/Average Salary:** $75,000/$90,000;
**Industry Concentration:** Generalist; **Function Concentration:** Generalist

**Joyce, William J.** — *Principal*
The Guild Corporation
8260 Greensboro Drive, Suite 460
McLean, VA 22102
Telephone: (703) 761-4023
**Recruiter Classification:** Contingency; **Lowest/Average Salary:**
$40,000/$50,000; **Industry Concentration:** Aerospace/Defense, Electronics,
High Technology, Information Technology; **Function Concentration:**
Engineering, Finance/Accounting, General Management, Research and
Development

**Joys, David S.** — *Partner*
Heidrick & Struggles, Inc.
245 Park Avenue, Suite 4300
New York, NY 10167-0152
Telephone: (212) 867-9876
**Recruiter Classification:** Retained; **Lowest/Average Salary:** $75,000/$90,000;
**Industry Concentration:** Generalist with a primary focus in Financial Services;
**Function Concentration:** Generalist

**Jozwik, Peter** — *Managing Director*
The Search Firm, Inc.
595 Market Street, Suite 1400
San Francisco, CA 94105
Telephone: (415) 777-3900
**Recruiter Classification:** Contingency; **Lowest/Average Salary:**
$40,000/$75,000; **Industry Concentration:** Electronics, High Technology,
Information Technology

**Juarez, Maria Elena** — *Partner*
Amrop International
Amberes #4, 2 Pia, Colonia Juarez
Mexico City, D.F., MEXICO 06600
Telephone: (525) 208-3977
**Recruiter Classification:** Retained, Contingency; **Lowest/Average Salary:**
$75,000/$90,000; **Industry Concentration:** Generalist; **Function**
**Concentration:** Generalist

**Judd, Susan** — *Senior Associate*
Korn/Ferry International
1800 Century Park East, Suite 900
Los Angeles, CA 90067
Telephone: (310) 552-1834
**Recruiter Classification:** Retained; **Lowest/Average Salary:** $90,000/$90,000;
**Industry Concentration:** Generalist with a primary focus in
Healthcare/Hospitals; **Function Concentration:** Generalist

**Judge, Alfred L.** — *President*
The Cambridge Group Ltd
830 Post Road East
Westport, CT 06880
Telephone: (203) 226-4243
**Recruiter Classification:** Contingency; **Lowest/Average Salary:**
$40,000/$75,000; **Industry Concentration:** Healthcare/Hospitals, High
Technology, Information Technology; **Function Concentration:** Administration,
Finance/Accounting

**Judy, William** — *Account Executive*
Search West, Inc.
750 The City Drive South
Suite 100
Orange, CA 92668-4940
Telephone: (714) 748-0400
**Recruiter Classification:** Contingency; **Lowest/Average Salary:**
$40,000/$60,000; **Industry Concentration:** Aerospace/Defense, Automotive,
Consumer Products; **Function Concentration:** Marketing, Sales

**Juelis, John J.** — *Vice President*
Peeney Associates
141 South Avenue
Fanwood, NJ 07023
Telephone: (908) 322-2324
**Recruiter Classification:** Retained; **Lowest/Average Salary:** $60,000/$90,000;
**Industry Concentration:** Generalist with a primary focus in Automotive,
Electronics, Financial Services, Manufacturing, Pharmaceutical/Medical;
**Function Concentration:** Generalist with a primary focus in Administration,
Engineering, Finance/Accounting, General Management, Human Resources,
Marketing, Research and Development, Sales, Women/Minorities

**Juhan, Louise B.** — *Senior Associate*
Korn/Ferry International
303 Peachtree Street N.E.
Suite 1600
Atlanta, GA 30308
Telephone: (404) 577-7542
**Recruiter Classification:** Retained; **Lowest/Average Salary:** $90,000/$90,000;
**Industry Concentration:** Generalist; **Function Concentration:** Generalist

**Juratovac, Michael** — *Senior Associate*
Montgomery Resources, Inc.
555 Montgomery Street, Suite 1650
San Francisco, CA 94111
Telephone: (415) 956-4242
**Recruiter Classification:** Contingency; **Lowest/Average Salary:**
$30,000/$60,000; **Industry Concentration:** Consumer Products, Financial
Services, High Technology, Insurance, Manufacturing, Real Estate, Venture
Capital; **Function Concentration:** Finance/Accounting

**Juska, Frank** — *Vice President*
Rusher, Loscavio & LoPresto
180 Montgomery Street, Suite 1616
San Francisco, CA 94104-4239
Telephone: (415) 765-6600
**Recruiter Classification:** Retained; **Lowest/Average Salary:** $75,000/$90,000;
**Industry Concentration:** Electronics, Financial Services, High Technology,
Information Technology, Manufacturing, Oil/Gas, Venture Capital; **Function
Concentration:** Administration, Engineering, General Management

**Justiss, Ted W.** — *Consultant*
David C. Cooper and Associates, Inc.
Five Concourse Parkway, Suite 2700
Atlanta, GA 30328
Telephone: (770) 395-0014
**Recruiter Classification:** Contingency; **Lowest/Average Salary:**
$20,000/$40,000; **Industry Concentration:** Generalist; **Function
Concentration:** Finance/Accounting

**Kacyn, Louis J.** — *Consultant*
Egon Zehnder International Inc.
One First National Plaza
21 South Clark Street, Suite 3300
Chicago, IL 60603-2006
Telephone: (312) 782-4500
**Recruiter Classification:** Retained; **Lowest/Average Salary:** $90,000/$90,000;
**Industry Concentration:** Generalist with a primary focus in Biotechnology,
Financial Services, High Technology, Manufacturing, Pharmaceutical/Medical;
**Function Concentration:** Generalist

**Kader, Richard** — *President*
Richard Kader & Associates
343 West Bagley Road, Suite 209
Berea, OH 44017
Telephone: (216) 891-1700
**Recruiter Classification:** Contingency; **Lowest/Average Salary:**
$50,000/$60,000; **Industry Concentration:** Generalist with a primary focus in
Biotechnology, Chemical Products, Consumer Products, Environmental,
Financial Services, Manufacturing, Packaging, Pharmaceutical/Medical;
**Function Concentration:** Generalist with a primary focus in Administration,
Engineering, Finance/Accounting, Marketing, Sales, Women/Minorities

**Kadin, Tom** — *Associate*
Kenzer Corp.
777 Third Avenue, 26th Floor
New York, NY 10017
Telephone: (212) 308-4300
**Recruiter Classification:** Retained; **Lowest/Average Salary:** $50,000/$90,000;
**Industry Concentration:** Generalist; **Function Concentration:** Generalist

**Kahn, P. Frederick** — *Managing Partner*
Heidrick & Struggles, Inc.
125 South Wacker Drive
Suite 2800
Chicago, IL 60606-4590
Telephone: (312) 372-8811
**Recruiter Classification:** Retained; **Lowest/Average Salary:** $75,000/$90,000;
**Industry Concentration:** Generalist with a primary focus in Consumer
Products; **Function Concentration:** Generalist

**Kaiser, Donald J.** — *President*
Dunhill Search International
59 Elm Street
New Haven, CT 06510
Telephone: (203) 562-0511
**Recruiter Classification:** Contingency; **Lowest/Average Salary:**
$30,000/$60,000; **Industry Concentration:** Generalist with a primary focus in
Chemical Products, Consumer Products, Financial Services, High Technology,
Information Technology, Manufacturing, Pharmaceutical/Medical; **Function
Concentration:** Administration, Engineering, Finance/Accounting, General
Management, Human Resources, Marketing, Sales

**Kaiser, Irene** — *Vice President*
Dunhill Search International
59 Elm Street
New Haven, CT 06510
Telephone: (203) 562-0511
**Recruiter Classification:** Contingency; **Lowest/Average Salary:**
$30,000/$60,000; **Industry Concentration:** Generalist with a primary focus in
Chemical Products, Consumer Products, Financial Services, Manufacturing,
Pharmaceutical/Medical; **Function Concentration:** Generalist with a primary
focus in Administration, Human Resources

**Kaiser, James G.** — *International Recruiter*
Dunhill Search International
59 Elm Street
New Haven, CT 06510
Telephone: (203) 562-0511
**Recruiter Classification:** Contingency; **Lowest/Average Salary:**
$30,000/$60,000; **Industry Concentration:** Generalist with a primary focus in
Automotive, Chemical Products, Consumer Products, Manufacturing; **Function
Concentration:** Generalist with a primary focus in Administration, Human
Resources, Marketing

**Kalb, Lenny** — *Account Executive*
Career Management International
197 Route 18
East Brunswick, NJ 08816
Telephone: (908) 937-4800
**Recruiter Classification:** Retained; **Lowest/Average Salary:** $20,000/$40,000;
**Industry Concentration:** Fashion (Retail/Apparel); **Function Concentration:**
Generalist with a primary focus in Human Resources

**Kalinowski, David** — *Search Consultant*
Jacobson Associates
Five Neshaminy Interplex
Suite 113
Trevose, PA 19053
Telephone: (215) 639-5860
**Recruiter Classification:** Contingency; **Lowest/Average Salary:**
$20,000/$40,000; **Industry Concentration:** Financial Services, Insurance;
**Function Concentration:** Generalist with a primary focus in Administration,
Finance/Accounting, General Management, Marketing, Research and
Development, Sales

**Kalus, Lisa** — *President*
Lisa Kalus & Associates, Inc.
26 Broadway, Suite 400
New York, NY 10004
Telephone: (212) 837-7889
**Recruiter Classification:** Contingency; **Lowest/Average Salary:**
$30,000/$50,000; **Industry Concentration:** Real Estate; **Function
Concentration:** Engineering

**Kampmann, Sara** — *Managing Director West Coast
Operations*
Johnson Smith & Knisely Accord
233 Sansome Street, Suite 1108
San Francisco, CA 94104
Telephone: (415) 397-0846
**Recruiter Classification:** Retained; **Lowest/Average Salary:** $90,000/$90,000;
**Industry Concentration:** Generalist; **Function Concentration:** Generalist

**Kanal, David S.** — *Partner*
Johnson Smith & Knisely Accord
100 Park Avenue, 15th Floor
New York, NY 10017
Telephone: (212) 885-9100
**Recruiter Classification:** Retained; **Lowest/Average Salary:** $90,000/$90,000;
**Industry Concentration:** Consumer Products, Fashion (Retail/Apparel);
**Function Concentration:** Finance/Accounting, General Management, Human
Resources, Marketing, Sales

**Kane, Frank** — *Recruiter*
A.J. Burton Group, Inc.
35 Wisconsin Circle, Suite 250
Chevy Chase, MD 20815
Telephone: (301) 654-0082
**Recruiter Classification:** Contingency, Executive Temporary; **Lowest/Average
Salary:** $20,000/$30,000; **Industry Concentration:** Financial Services;
**Function Concentration:** Finance/Accounting

**Kanovsky, Gerald** — *Chairman*
Career Consulting Group, Inc.
1100 Summer Street
Stamford, CT 06905
Telephone: (203) 975-8800
**Recruiter Classification:** Contingency; **Lowest/Average Salary:**
$40,000/$75,000; **Industry Concentration:** Consumer Products, Financial
Services, Information Technology, Manufacturing, Publishing/Media; **Function
Concentration:** Marketing, Sales

**Kanovsky, Marlene** — *President*
Career Consulting Group, Inc.
1100 Summer Street
Stamford, CT 06905
Telephone: (203) 975-8800
**Recruiter Classification:** Contingency; **Lowest/Average Salary:**
$40,000/$50,000; **Industry Concentration:** Consumer Products, Financial
Services, Information Technology, Manufacturing, Publishing/Media; **Function
Concentration:** Marketing, Sales

**Kanrich, Susan Azaria** — *Director*
AlternaStaff
1155 Avenue of the Americas, 15th Floor
New York, NY 10036
Telephone: (212) 302-1141
**Recruiter Classification:** Executive Temporary; **Lowest/Average Salary:**
$30,000/$60,000; **Industry Concentration:** Automotive, Biotechnology,
Chemical Products, Electronics, High Technology, Manufacturing, Oil/Gas,
Packaging, Pharmaceutical/Medical; **Function Concentration:** Engineering,
General Management, Human Resources, Research and Development

**Kantor, Richard** — *Account Executive*
Search West, Inc.
340 North Westlake Boulevard
Suite 200
Westlake Village, CA 91362-3761
Telephone: (805) 496-6811
**Recruiter Classification:** Contingency; **Lowest/Average Salary:**
$40,000/$60,000; **Industry Concentration:** Financial Services; **Function
Concentration:** Administration, Finance/Accounting

**Kaplan, Alexandra** — *Principal*
J.M. Eagle Partners Ltd.
10140 North Port Washington Rd.
Mequon, WI 53092
Telephone: (414) 241-1113
**Recruiter Classification:** Contingency; **Lowest/Average Salary:** $/$90,000;
**Industry Concentration:** Biotechnology, Electronics, Healthcare/Hospitals,
High Technology, Information Technology, Pharmaceutical/Medical; **Function
Concentration:** Generalist

**Kaplan, Gary** — *President*
Gary Kaplan & Associates
201 South Lake Avenue
Suite 600
Pasadena, CA 91101
Telephone: (818) 796-8100
**Recruiter Classification:** Retained; **Lowest/Average Salary:** $60,000/$90,000;
**Industry Concentration:** Generalist with a primary focus in Consumer
Products, Education/Libraries, Electronics, Entertainment, Environmental,
Fashion (Retail/Apparel), Financial Services, Healthcare/Hospitals, High
Technology, Hospitality/Leisure, Information Technology, Manufacturing, Non-
Profit; **Function Concentration:** Generalist with a primary focus in
Administration, Finance/Accounting, General Management, Human Resources,
Marketing, Research and Development, Sales

**Kaplan, Marc** — *Associate*
Gary Kaplan & Associates
201 South Lake Avenue
Suite 600
Pasadena, CA 91101
Telephone: (818) 796-8100
**Recruiter Classification:** Retained; **Lowest/Average Salary:** $60,000/$90,000;
**Industry Concentration:** Generalist with a primary focus in Consumer
Products, Education/Libraries, Electronics, Entertainment, Environmental,
Fashion (Retail/Apparel), Financial Services, Healthcare/Hospitals, High
Technology, Hospitality/Leisure, Information Technology, Manufacturing, Non-
Profit; **Function Concentration:** Generalist with a primary focus in
Administration, Finance/Accounting, General Management, Human Resources,
Marketing, Research and Development, Sales

**Kaplan, Traci** — *Associate*
Source Services Corporation
8614 Westwood Center, Suite 750
Vienna, VA 22182
Telephone: (703) 790-5610
**Recruiter Classification:** Contingency; **Lowest/Average Salary:**
$30,000/$50,000; **Industry Concentration:** Financial Services, Information
Technology; **Function Concentration:** Engineering, Finance/Accounting

**Kaplowitz, Marji** — *Executive Recruiter*
Richard, Wayne and Roberts
24 Greenway Plaza, Suite 1304
Houston, TX 77046-2493
Telephone: (713) 629-6681
**Recruiter Classification:** Retained; **Lowest/Average Salary:** $40,000/$60,000;
**Industry Concentration:** Generalist; **Function Concentration:** Generalist

**Kaptain, John** — *Chief Executive Officer*
Blau Kaptain Schroeder
12 Roszel Road, Suite C-101
Princeton, NJ 08540
Telephone: (609) 520-8400
**Recruiter Classification:** Retained; **Lowest/Average Salary:** $75,000/$75,000;
**Industry Concentration:** Biotechnology, Healthcare/Hospitals,
Pharmaceutical/Medical, Venture Capital; **Function Concentration:** General
Management, Marketing, Research and Development

**Kapur, Sharmila** — *Senior Associate*
Korn/Ferry International
237 Park Avenue
New York, NY 10017
Telephone: (212) 687-1834
**Recruiter Classification:** Retained; **Lowest/Average Salary:** $90,000/$90,000;
**Industry Concentration:** Generalist; **Function Concentration:** Generalist

**Karalis, William** — *Executive Recruiter*
CPS Inc.
One Westbrook Corporate Centre, Suite 600
Westchester, IL 60154
Telephone: (708) 531-8370
**Recruiter Classification:** Contingency; **Lowest/Average Salary:**
$30,000/$50,000; **Industry Concentration:** Generalist with a primary focus in
Automotive, Biotechnology, Chemical Products, Consumer Products, High
Technology, Insurance, Manufacturing, Oil/Gas, Packaging,
Pharmaceutical/Medical; **Function Concentration:** Engineering, Research and
Development, Sales, Women/Minorities

**Karr, Cynthia L.** — *Vice President*
Howard Karr & Associates, Inc.
1777 Borel Place, Suite 408
San Mateo, CA 94402
Telephone: (415) 574-5277
**Recruiter Classification:** Retained; **Lowest/Average Salary:** $75,000/$90,000;
**Industry Concentration:** Generalist; **Function Concentration:**
Finance/Accounting

**Karr, Howard L.** — *President*
Howard Karr & Associates, Inc.
1777 Borel Place, Suite 408
San Mateo, CA 94402
Telephone: (415) 574-5277
**Recruiter Classification:** Retained; **Lowest/Average Salary:** $90,000/$90,000; **Industry Concentration:** Generalist; **Function Concentration:** Finance/Accounting

**Karsan, N.S.** — *Principal*
Raymond Karsan Associates
989 Old Eagle School Road, Suite 814
Wayne, PA 19087
Telephone: (610) 971-9171
**Recruiter Classification:** Contingency; **Lowest/Average Salary:** $30,000/$90,000; **Industry Concentration:** Generalist; **Function Concentration:** Generalist

**Kashinsky, Richard J.** — *Manager Pacific Region*
Management Recruiters International, Inc.
494 Alvarado Street, Suite F
Monterey, CA 93940-2717
Telephone: (408) 649-0737
**Recruiter Classification:** Contingency; **Lowest/Average Salary:** $30,000/$75,000; **Industry Concentration:** Generalist; **Function Concentration:** Generalist

**Kashiwagi, Keiko** — *Director Research*
The Repovich-Reynolds Group
709 East Colorado Boulevard, Suite 200
Pasadena, CA 91101
Telephone: (818) 585-9455
**Recruiter Classification:** Retained; **Lowest/Average Salary:** $75,000/$90,000; **Industry Concentration:** Generalist; **Function Concentration:** Marketing

**Kasmouski, Steve** — *Software Engineering Recruiter*
Winter, Wyman & Company
950 Winter Street, Suite 3100
Waltham, MA 02154-1294
Telephone: (617) 890-7000
**Recruiter Classification:** Contingency; **Lowest/Average Salary:** $40,000/$75,000; **Industry Concentration:** High Technology, Information Technology, Publishing/Media; **Function Concentration:** Engineering

**Kasprzyk, Michael** — *Associate*
Source Services Corporation
8614 Westwood Center, Suite 750
Vienna, VA 22182
Telephone: (703) 790-5610
**Recruiter Classification:** Contingency; **Lowest/Average Salary:** $30,000/$50,000; **Industry Concentration:** Financial Services, Information Technology; **Function Concentration:** Engineering, Finance/Accounting

**Kassouf, Connie** — *Vice President*
The Whitney Group
850 Third Avenue, 11th Floor
New York, NY 10022
Telephone: (212) 508-3500
**Recruiter Classification:** Retained; **Lowest/Average Salary:** $75,000/$90,000; **Industry Concentration:** Generalist with a primary focus in Financial Services, Real Estate, Venture Capital; **Function Concentration:** Generalist with a primary focus in Sales

**Katz, Art E.** — *Manager North Atlantic Region*
Management Recruiters International, Inc.
30 Woodstock Street
Roswell, GA 30075-3546
Telephone: (770) 998-1555
**Recruiter Classification:** Contingency; **Lowest/Average Salary:** $30,000/$75,000; **Industry Concentration:** Generalist; **Function Concentration:** Generalist

**Katz, Cyndi** — *Account Executive*
Search West, Inc.
1888 Century Park East
Suite 2050
Los Angeles, CA 90067-1736
Telephone: (310) 284-8888
**Recruiter Classification:** Contingency; **Lowest/Average Salary:** $40,000/$60,000; **Industry Concentration:** Generalist with a primary focus in Biotechnology, Consumer Products, Electronics, Energy, Entertainment, Financial Services, Healthcare/Hospitals, Manufacturing; **Function Concentration:** Administration

**Katz, Robert L.** — *Physician Recruiter*
MSI International
230 Peachtree Street, N.E.
Suite 1550
Atlanta, GA 30303
Telephone: (404) 653-7360
**Recruiter Classification:** Contingency; **Lowest/Average Salary:** $30,000/$60,000; **Industry Concentration:** Generalist with a primary focus in Healthcare/Hospitals; **Function Concentration:** Generalist with a primary focus in Administration, Engineering, Finance/Accounting, General Management, Marketing, Sales

**Katz, Rosalind N.** — *Vice President*
ExecuScope Division of Russell Staffing Resources, Inc.
120 Montgomery Street, 3rd Floor
San Francisco, CA 94104
Telephone: (415) 781-1444
**Recruiter Classification:** Executive Temporary; **Lowest/Average Salary:** $20,000/$60,000; **Industry Concentration:** Generalist; **Function Concentration:** Generalist

**Kaufman, Stuart** — *Co-Manager Eastern Region*
Management Recruiters International, Inc.
98 Cutter Mill Road, Suite 234 South
Great Neck, NY 11021-3006
Telephone: (516) 482-4000
**Recruiter Classification:** Contingency; **Lowest/Average Salary:** $30,000/$75,000; **Industry Concentration:** Generalist; **Function Concentration:** Generalist

**Kaufmann, Robert C.** — *Director*
Spencer Stuart
Financial Centre
695 East Main Street
Stamford, CT 06901
Telephone: (203) 324-6333
**Recruiter Classification:** Retained; **Lowest/Average Salary:** $90,000/$90,000; **Industry Concentration:** Generalist; **Function Concentration:** Generalist

**Kaun, Loren A.** — *Manager Pacific Region*
Management Recruiters International, Inc.
16027 Ventura Boulevard, Suite 320
Encino, CA 91436-2740
Telephone: (818) 906-3155
**Recruiter Classification:** Contingency; **Lowest/Average Salary:** $30,000/$75,000; **Industry Concentration:** Generalist; **Function Concentration:** Generalist

**Kayajian, Bob A.** — *Manager Eastern Region*
Management Recruiters International, Inc.
435 New Karner Road
Albany, NY 12205-3833
Telephone: (518) 464-1461
**Recruiter Classification:** Contingency; **Lowest/Average Salary:** $30,000/$75,000; **Industry Concentration:** Generalist; **Function Concentration:** Generalist

**Kaye, Jeff** — *Co-Manager*
Management Recruiters International, Inc.
18333 Preston Road, Suite 500
Dallas, TX 75252
Telephone: (214) 931-5242
**Recruiter Classification:** Contingency; **Lowest/Average Salary:** $30,000/$75,000; **Industry Concentration:** Generalist; **Function Concentration:** Generalist

**Kaye, Jeffrey** — *President and COO*
Kaye-Bassman International Corp.
18333 Preston Road, Suite 500
Dallas, TX 75252
Telephone: (214) 931-5242
**Recruiter Classification:** Executive Temporary; **Lowest/Average Salary:** $40,000/$60,000; **Industry Concentration:** Biotechnology, Chemical Products, Financial Services, Healthcare/Hospitals, High Technology, Information Technology, Pharmaceutical/Medical, Transportation; **Function Concentration:** Generalist

**Kaye, Jerry** — *Managing Director*
Ward Howell International, Inc.
16255 Ventura Boulevard
Suite 400
Encino, CA 91436-2394
Telephone: (818) 905-6010
**Recruiter Classification:** Retained; **Lowest/Average Salary:** $75,000/$90,000; **Industry Concentration:** Generalist; **Function Concentration:** Generalist

**Kean, Marjorie** — *Vice President*
Korn/Ferry International
200 South Biscayne Boulevard, Suite 2790
Miami, FL 33131
Telephone: (305) 579-1266
**Recruiter Classification:** Retained; **Lowest/Average Salary:** $90,000/$90,000;
**Industry Concentration:** Generalist; **Function Concentration:** Generalist

**Keating, Anne F.** — *Principal*
Korn/Ferry International
237 Park Avenue
New York, NY 10017
Telephone: (212) 687-1834
**Recruiter Classification:** Retained; **Lowest/Average Salary:** $90,000/$90,000;
**Industry Concentration:** Generalist; **Function Concentration:** Generalist

**Keating, Pierson** — *Partner*
Nordeman Grimm, Inc.
717 Fifth Avenue, 26th Floor
New York, NY 10022
Telephone: (212) 935-1000
**Recruiter Classification:** Retained; **Lowest/Average Salary:** $90,000/$90,000;
**Industry Concentration:** Generalist; **Function Concentration:** Generalist

**Keefe, Donald J.** — *Managing Partner*
TASA International
Hurstbourne Place
9300 Shelbyville Road
Louisville, KY 40222
Telephone: (502) 426-3500
**Recruiter Classification:** Retained; **Lowest/Average Salary:** $90,000/$90,000;
**Industry Concentration:** Generalist; **Function Concentration:** Generalist

**Keefer, Russell R.** — *Specialist Legal*
Sharrow & Associates
24735 Van Dyke
Center Line, MI 48015
Telephone: (810) 759-6910
**Recruiter Classification:** Contingency; **Lowest/Average Salary:**
$40,000/$75,000; **Industry Concentration:** Biotechnology,
Pharmaceutical/Medical

**Keegen, Joanne** — *Consultant*
Evie Kreisler & Associates, Inc.
333 North Michigan Avenue, Suite 818
Chicago, IL 60601
Telephone: (312) 251-0077
**Recruiter Classification:** Contingency; **Lowest/Average Salary:**
$30,000/$75,000; **Industry Concentration:** Fashion (Retail/Apparel); **Function
Concentration:** Generalist

**Keen, Robert** — *Manager North Atlantic Region*
Management Recruiters International, Inc.
1201 Hampton Street, Suite 2B
P.O. Box 50785
Columbia, SC 29250-0785
Telephone: (803) 254-1334
**Recruiter Classification:** Contingency; **Lowest/Average Salary:**
$30,000/$75,000; **Industry Concentration:** Generalist; **Function
Concentration:** Generalist

**Keesom, W. Peter** — *Consultant*
Boyden/Zay & Company
Two Midtown Plaza, Suite 1740
1360 Peachtree Street, NE
Atlanta, GA 30309
Telephone: (404) 876-9986
**Recruiter Classification:** Retained; **Lowest/Average Salary:** $90,000/$90,000;
**Industry Concentration:** Generalist with a primary focus in Chemical Products,
Manufacturing, Pharmaceutical/Medical; **Function Concentration:** Generalist
with a primary focus in Engineering, Finance/Accounting, General
Management, Human Resources, Marketing, Research and Development, Sales

**Keeton, Susan G.** — *Office Support Recruiter*
The Corporate Connection, Ltd.
7202 Glen Forest Drive
Richmond, VA 23226
Telephone: (804) 288-8844
**Recruiter Classification:** Contingency; **Lowest/Average Salary:**
$20,000/$30,000; **Industry Concentration:** Generalist with a primary focus in
Aerospace/Defense, Chemical Products, Consumer Products, Environmental,
Financial Services, Information Technology, Insurance, Manufacturing, Non-
Profit, Pharmaceutical/Medical, Transportation; **Function Concentration:**
Generalist

**Kehoe, Mike** — *Executive Recruiter*
CPS Inc.
One Westbrook Corporate Centre, Suite 600
Westchester, IL 60154
Telephone: (708) 531-8370
**Recruiter Classification:** Contingency; **Lowest/Average Salary:**
$30,000/$50,000; **Industry Concentration:** Generalist with a primary focus in
Automotive, Biotechnology, Chemical Products, Consumer Products, High
Technology, Insurance, Manufacturing, Oil/Gas, Packaging,
Pharmaceutical/Medical; **Function Concentration:** Engineering, Research and
Development, Sales, Women/Minorities

**Keitel, Robert S.** — *Vice President*
A.T. Kearney, Inc.
3 Lagoon Drive, Suite 160
Redwood City, CA 94065
Telephone: (415) 637-6600
**Recruiter Classification:** Retained; **Lowest/Average Salary:** $90,000/$90,000;
**Industry Concentration:** Generalist with a primary focus in Chemical Products,
Entertainment, Fashion (Retail/Apparel), Financial Services, High Technology,
Pharmaceutical/Medical; **Function Concentration:** Generalist with a primary
focus in General Management

**Keith, Stephanie** — *Recruiter*
Southwestern Professional Services
9485 Regency Square Boulevard, Suite 110
Jacksonville, FL 32225
Telephone: (904) 464-0400
**Recruiter Classification:** Contingency; **Lowest/Average Salary:**
$40,000/$60,000; **Industry Concentration:** Financial Services, High
Technology; **Function Concentration:** Finance/Accounting

**Keller, Barbara** — *Consultant*
Barton Raben, Inc.
One Riverway, Suite 2500
Houston, TX 77056
Telephone: (713) 961-9111
**Recruiter Classification:** Retained; **Lowest/Average Salary:** $75,000/$90,000;
**Industry Concentration:** Generalist with a primary focus in Consumer
Products, Electronics, Fashion (Retail/Apparel), High Technology, Information
Technology, Non-Profit, Publishing/Media; **Function Concentration:** Generalist
with a primary focus in Administration, Finance/Accounting, General
Management, Marketing, Sales

**Keller, Lorraine L.** — *Manager Southwest Region*
Management Recruiters International, Inc.
P.O. Box 27258
Austin, TX 78755-2258
Telephone: (512) 338-0880
**Recruiter Classification:** Contingency; **Lowest/Average Salary:**
$30,000/$75,000; **Industry Concentration:** Generalist; **Function
Concentration:** Generalist

**Keller, Peggy** — *Consultant*
The McCormick Group, Inc.
20 Walnut Street, Suite 308
Wellesley Hills, MA 02181
Telephone: (617) 239-1233
**Recruiter Classification:** Retained; **Lowest/Average Salary:** $50,000/$60,000;
**Industry Concentration:** Insurance; **Function Concentration:** Generalist

**Kellerhals, Gloria** — *Manager Southwest Region*
Management Recruiters International, Inc.
Suite 125, 14 Sheridan Park
8771 Wolff Court
Westminster, CO 80030-3683
Telephone: (303) 650-8870
**Recruiter Classification:** Contingency; **Lowest/Average Salary:**
$30,000/$75,000; **Industry Concentration:** Generalist; **Function
Concentration:** Generalist

**Kelley, Randall D.** — *Director*
Spencer Stuart
1717 Main Street, Suite 5300
Dallas, TX 75201-4605
Telephone: (214) 658-1777
**Recruiter Classification:** Retained; **Lowest/Average Salary:** $90,000/$90,000;
**Industry Concentration:** Generalist; **Function Concentration:** Generalist

**Kelly, Claudia L.** — *Managing Director*
Spencer Stuart
Financial Centre
695 East Main Street
Stamford, CT 06901
Telephone: (203) 324-6333
**Recruiter Classification:** Retained; **Lowest/Average Salary:** $90,000/$90,000;
**Industry Concentration:** Generalist with a primary focus in Board Services,
Consumer Products, Entertainment, Financial Services, Publishing/Media;
**Function Concentration:** Generalist with a primary focus in
Finance/Accounting, Marketing, Women/Minorities

**Kelly, Donna J.** — *Vice President Placement*
Accountants Executive Search
535 Fifth Avenue, Suite 1200
New York, NY 10017
Telephone: (212) 682-5900
**Recruiter Classification:** Executive Temporary; **Lowest/Average Salary:**
$40,000/$60,000; **Industry Concentration:** Generalist with a primary focus in
Consumer Products, Entertainment, Fashion (Retail/Apparel), Financial
Services, Non-Profit, Public Administration, Publishing/Media, Real Estate;
**Function Concentration:** Finance/Accounting

**Kelly, Elizabeth Ann** — *Associate*
Wellington Management Group
117 South 17th Street, Suite 1625
Philadelphia, PA 19103
Telephone: (215) 569-8900
**Recruiter Classification:** Retained; **Lowest/Average Salary:** $75,000/$90,000;
**Industry Concentration:** Generalist with a primary focus in Biotechnology,
Chemical Products, Consumer Products, Healthcare/Hospitals, High
Technology, Information Technology, Manufacturing, Oil/Gas; **Function
Concentration:** Generalist with a primary focus in Administration,
Finance/Accounting, General Management, Human Resources, Marketing,
Research and Development, Sales

**Kelly, Kevin B.** — *Executive Director*
Russell Reynolds Associates, Inc.
The Hurt Building
50 Hurt Plaza, Suite 600
Atlanta, GA 30303
Telephone: (404) 577-3000
**Recruiter Classification:** Retained; **Lowest/Average Salary:** $90,000/$90,000;
**Industry Concentration:** Generalist; **Function Concentration:** Generalist

**Kelly, Michael T.** — *Managing Director/Area Manager*
Russell Reynolds Associates, Inc.
2500 Sand Hill Road, Suite 105
Menlo Park, CA 94025
Telephone: (415) 233-2400
**Recruiter Classification:** Retained; **Lowest/Average Salary:** $90,000/$90,000;
**Industry Concentration:** Generalist; **Function Concentration:** Generalist

**Kelly, Michael T.** — *Managing Director*
Russell Reynolds Associates, Inc.
3050 Norwest Center
90 South Seventh Street
Minneapolis, MN 55402
Telephone: (612) 332-6966
**Recruiter Classification:** Retained; **Lowest/Average Salary:** $90,000/$90,000;
**Industry Concentration:** Generalist with a primary focus in
Healthcare/Hospitals; **Function Concentration:** Generalist

**Kelly, Peter W.** — *Partner*
R. Rollo Associates
725 South Figueroa Street, Suite 3230
Los Angeles, CA 90017
Telephone: (213) 892-7845
**Recruiter Classification:** Retained; **Lowest/Average Salary:** $90,000/$90,000;
**Industry Concentration:** Generalist with a primary focus in
Aerospace/Defense, Consumer Products, Energy, Financial Services,
Healthcare/Hospitals, Hospitality/Leisure, Insurance, Manufacturing, Non-
Profit, Oil/Gas, Real Estate, Transportation, Venture Capital; **Function
Concentration:** Generalist

**Kelly, Robert** — *Associate*
Source Services Corporation
100 North Tryon Street, Suite 3130
Charlotte, NC 28202
Telephone: (704) 333-8311
**Recruiter Classification:** Contingency; **Lowest/Average Salary:**
$30,000/$50,000; **Industry Concentration:** Financial Services, Information
Technology; **Function Concentration:** Engineering, Finance/Accounting

**Kelly, Roy P.** — *Manager Eastern Region*
Management Recruiters International, Inc.
19 Tanner Street
Haddonfield, NJ 08033
Telephone: (609) 428-2233
**Recruiter Classification:** Contingency; **Lowest/Average Salary:**
$30,000/$75,000; **Industry Concentration:** Generalist; **Function
Concentration:** Generalist

**Kelly, Sheri** — *Associate/Executive Recruiter*
Strategic Associates, Inc.
13915 Burnet Road, Suite 304
Austin, TX 78728
Telephone: (512) 218-8222
**Recruiter Classification:** Contingency; **Lowest/Average Salary:**
$50,000/$60,000; **Industry Concentration:** Consumer Products, Electronics,
High Technology, Information Technology, Manufacturing, Transportation;
**Function Concentration:** General Management, Women/Minorities

**Kelly, Susan D.** — *President*
S.D. Kelly & Associates, Inc.
990 Washington Street
Dedham, MA 02026
Telephone: (617) 326-8038
**Recruiter Classification:** Contingency; **Lowest/Average Salary:**
$60,000/$75,000; **Industry Concentration:** Electronics, High Technology;
**Function Concentration:** Engineering, General Management, Marketing, Sales

**Kelsey, Micki** — *Recruiter*
Davidson, Laird & Associates
29260 Franklin, Suite 110
Southfield, MI 48034
Telephone: (810) 358-2160
**Recruiter Classification:** Contingency; **Lowest/Average Salary:**
$30,000/$50,000; **Industry Concentration:** Automotive, Manufacturing;
**Function Concentration:** Generalist with a primary focus in Engineering,
Women/Minorities

**Kelso, Patricia C.** — *Associate Partner*
Barton Raben, Inc.
One Riverway, Suite 2500
Houston, TX 77056
Telephone: (713) 961-9111
**Recruiter Classification:** Retained; **Lowest/Average Salary:** $75,000/$90,000;
**Industry Concentration:** Generalist with a primary focus in Consumer
Products, Financial Services, Information Technology, Manufacturing; **Function
Concentration:** Generalist with a primary focus in Finance/Accounting, Human
Resources, Marketing

**Kemp, M. Scott** — *President*
M. Scott Kemp & Associates
7305 Deep Run Drive, Suite 620
Bloomfield Hills, MI 48301
Telephone: (810) 646-6464
**Recruiter Classification:** Retained; **Lowest/Average Salary:** $90,000/$90,000;
**Industry Concentration:** Generalist; **Function Concentration:** Generalist

**Kendall, Steven W.** — *Manager North Atlantic Region*
Management Recruiters International, Inc.
685 Thornton Way
Lithia Springs, GA 30057-1579
Telephone: (770) 948-5560
**Recruiter Classification:** Contingency; **Lowest/Average Salary:**
$30,000/$75,000; **Industry Concentration:** Generalist; **Function
Concentration:** Generalist

**Kendrick, M. Steven** — *Principal*
Lamalie Amrop International
Thanksgiving Tower
1601 Elm Street
Dallas, TX 75201-4768
Telephone: (214) 754-0019
**Recruiter Classification:** Retained; **Lowest/Average Salary:** $90,000/$90,000;
**Industry Concentration:** Generalist; **Function Concentration:** Generalist

**Kennedy, Craig** — *Associate*
Source Services Corporation
10220 SW Greenburg Road, Suite 625
Portland, OR 97223
Telephone: (503) 768-4546
**Recruiter Classification:** Contingency; **Lowest/Average Salary:**
$30,000/$50,000; **Industry Concentration:** Financial Services, Information
Technology; **Function Concentration:** Engineering, Finance/Accounting

**Kennedy, Michael** — *Senior Partner*
The Danbrook Group, Inc.
14180 Dallas Parkway, Suite 400
Dallas, TX 75240
Telephone: (214) 392-0057
**Recruiter Classification:** Contingency; **Lowest/Average Salary:**
$30,000/$50,000; **Industry Concentration:** Insurance; **Function
Concentration:** Generalist with a primary focus in Administration,
Finance/Accounting, General Management, Marketing, Sales

**Kennedy, Paul** — *Associate*
Source Services Corporation
One Park Plaza, Suite 560
Irvine, CA 92714
Telephone: (714) 660-1666
**Recruiter Classification:** Contingency; **Lowest/Average Salary:**
$30,000/$50,000; **Industry Concentration:** Financial Services, Information
Technology; **Function Concentration:** Engineering, Finance/Accounting

**Kennedy, Walter** — *Managing Director*
Source Services Corporation
8500 Normandale Lake, Suite 955
Bloomington, MN 55437
Telephone: (612) 835-5100
**Recruiter Classification:** Contingency; **Lowest/Average Salary:**
$30,000/$50,000; **Industry Concentration:** Financial Services, Information
Technology; **Function Concentration:** Engineering, Finance/Accounting

**Kennedy, Walter** — *Managing Director*
Source Services Corporation
80 South 8th Street
Minneapolis, MN 55402
Telephone: (612) 332-6460
**Recruiter Classification:** Contingency; **Lowest/Average Salary:**
$30,000/$50,000; **Industry Concentration:** Financial Services, Information
Technology; **Function Concentration:** Engineering, Finance/Accounting

**Kennedy, Walter** — *Branch Manager*
Romac & Associates
111 North Orange Avenue
Suite 1150
Orlando, FL 32801
Telephone: (407) 843-0765
**Recruiter Classification:** Executive Temporary; **Lowest/Average Salary:**
$/$60,000; **Industry Concentration:** Financial Services, Healthcare/Hospitals,
High Technology, Hospitality/Leisure, Information Technology, Insurance;
**Function Concentration:** Finance/Accounting

**Kennedy-Radmer, Carol** — *Area Manager*
Accountants on Call
515 North Sixth Street, Suite 2002
St. Louis, MO 63101
Telephone: (314) 436-0500
**Recruiter Classification:** Contingency; **Lowest/Average Salary:**
$20,000/$30,000; **Industry Concentration:** Generalist; **Function
Concentration:** Finance/Accounting

**Kenney, Jeanne** — *Associate*
Source Services Corporation
425 California Street, Suite 1200
San Francisco, CA 94104
Telephone: (415) 434-2410
**Recruiter Classification:** Contingency; **Lowest/Average Salary:**
$30,000/$50,000; **Industry Concentration:** Financial Services, Information
Technology; **Function Concentration:** Engineering, Finance/Accounting

**Kenny, Roger M.** — *Partner*
Kenny, Kindler, Hunt & Howe
1 Dag Hammarskjold Plaza
New York, NY 10017
Telephone: (212) 355-5560
**Recruiter Classification:** Retained; **Lowest/Average Salary:** $90,000/$90,000;
**Industry Concentration:** Generalist; **Function Concentration:** Generalist

**Kent, Melvin** — *President*
Melvin Kent & Associates, Inc.
6477 Quarry Lane, Suite 100
Dublin, OH 43017
Telephone: (614) 798-9501
**Recruiter Classification:** Retained; **Lowest/Average Salary:** $60,000/$90,000;
**Industry Concentration:** Generalist; **Function Concentration:** Generalist

**Kent, Vickey** — *Vice President*
Professional Alternatives, Inc.
601 Lakeshore Parkway, Suite 1050
Minneapolis, MN 55305-5219
Telephone: (612) 449-5180
**Recruiter Classification:** Executive Temporary; **Lowest/Average Salary:**
$30,000/$40,000; **Industry Concentration:** Generalist; **Function
Concentration:** Generalist with a primary focus in Finance/Accounting, Human
Resources, Marketing

**Kenzer, Robert D.** — *Chairman*
Kenzer Corp.
777 Third Avenue, 26th Floor
New York, NY 10017
Telephone: (212) 308-4300
**Recruiter Classification:** Retained; **Lowest/Average Salary:** $50,000/$90,000;
**Industry Concentration:** Consumer Products, Entertainment, Financial
Services, Packaging, Venture Capital; **Function Concentration:** Generalist with
a primary focus in Administration, Finance/Accounting, General Management,
Human Resources, Marketing, Research and Development, Sales

**Keogh, James** — *Principal*
Sanford Rose Associates
2625 Butterfield Road
Suite 107W
Oak Brook, IL 60521
Telephone: (708) 574-9405
**Recruiter Classification:** Contingency; **Lowest/Average Salary:**
$30,000/$75,000; **Industry Concentration:** Generalist with a primary focus in
Chemical Products, Financial Services; **Function Concentration:** Generalist

**Kepler, Charles W.** — *Managing Director*
Russell Reynolds Associates, Inc.
200 South Wacker Drive
Suite 3600
Chicago, IL 60606
Telephone: (312) 993-9696
**Recruiter Classification:** Retained; **Lowest/Average Salary:** $90,000/$90,000;
**Function Concentration:** Generalist

**Kerester, Jonathon** — *Account Executive*
Cadillac Associates
8033 Sunset Boulevard, Suite 5200
Los Angeles, CA 90046
Telephone: (213) 385-9111
**Recruiter Classification:** Contingency; **Lowest/Average Salary:**
$60,000/$75,000; **Industry Concentration:** Generalist with a primary focus in
Healthcare/Hospitals, High Technology; **Function Concentration:** Generalist

**Kern, Ann P.** — *Vice President*
Korn/Ferry International
237 Park Avenue
New York, NY 10017
Telephone: (212) 687-1834
**Recruiter Classification:** Retained; **Lowest/Average Salary:** $90,000/$90,000;
**Industry Concentration:** Generalist with a primary focus in Non-Profit;
**Function Concentration:** Generalist

**Kern, Jerry L.** — *Executive Vice President*
ADOW's Executeam
2734 Chancellor Drive, Suite 102
Crestview Hills, KY 41017-3443
Telephone: (606) 344-8600
**Recruiter Classification:** Executive Temporary; **Industry Concentration:**
Generalist with a primary focus in Chemical Products, Consumer Products,
Electronics, Financial Services, High Technology, Information Technology,
Manufacturing, Packaging; **Function Concentration:** Generalist with a primary
focus in Administration, Engineering, Finance/Accounting, General
Management, Human Resources, Marketing, Research and Development,
Women/Minorities

**Kern, Kathleen G.** — *President*
ADOW's Executeam
36 East Fourth Street, Suite 1020
Cincinnati, OH 45202-3810
Telephone: (513) 721-2369
**Recruiter Classification:** Executive Temporary; **Industry Concentration:**
Generalist with a primary focus in Chemical Products, Consumer Products,
Electronics, Financial Services, High Technology, Information Technology,
Manufacturing, Packaging; **Function Concentration:** Generalist with a primary
focus in Administration, Engineering, Finance/Accounting, General
Management, Human Resources, Marketing, Women/Minorities

**Kerr, John** — *Account Executive*
Search West, Inc.
3401 Centrelake Drive
Suite 690
Ontario, CA 91761-1207
Telephone: (909) 986-1966
**Recruiter Classification:** Contingency; **Lowest/Average Salary:**
$40,000/$60,000; **Industry Concentration:** Chemical Products, Manufacturing;
**Function Concentration:** Engineering, Research and Development

**Kershaw, Lisa** — *Consultant*
Tanton Mitchell/Paul Ray Berndtson
710-1050 West Pender Street
Vancouver, British Columbia, CANADA V6E 3S7
Telephone: (604) 685-0261
**Recruiter Classification:** Retained; **Lowest/Average Salary:** $75,000/$90,000;
**Industry Concentration:** Generalist with a primary focus in Consumer
Products, Education/Libraries, Financial Services, Healthcare/Hospitals, High
Technology, Insurance, Manufacturing, Public Administration, Transportation;
**Function Concentration:** Generalist with a primary focus in Administration,
Finance/Accounting, General Management, Human Resources, Marketing,
Sales

**Kerth, Norman** — *Accounting and Finance Recruiter*
Accounting Personnel Consultants
210 Baronne Street, Suite 920
New Orleans, LA 70112
Telephone: (504) 581-7800
**Recruiter Classification:** Contingency, Executive Temporary; **Lowest/Average Salary:** $20,000/$20,000; **Industry Concentration:** Generalist; **Function Concentration:** Administration, Finance/Accounting

**Keshishian, Gregory** — *Senior Vice President Executive Compensation*
Handy HRM Corp.
250 Park Avenue
New York, NY 10177-0074
Telephone: (212) 557-0400
**Recruiter Classification:** Retained; **Lowest/Average Salary:** $90,000/$90,000; **Industry Concentration:** Generalist; **Function Concentration:** Generalist

**Kettwig, David A.** — *Vice President*
A.T. Kearney, Inc.
222 West Adams Street
Chicago, IL 60606
Telephone: (312) 648-0111
**Recruiter Classification:** Retained; **Lowest/Average Salary:** $90,000/$90,000; **Industry Concentration:** Generalist with a primary focus in Financial Services, Manufacturing; **Function Concentration:** Generalist with a primary focus in Finance/Accounting, General Management, Human Resources, Marketing, Sales

**Kick, James W.** — *Principal*
The Prairie Group
One Westbrook Corporate Center
Suite 300
Westchester, IL 60154
Telephone: (708) 449-7710
**Recruiter Classification:** Contingency; **Lowest/Average Salary:** $50,000/$75,000; **Industry Concentration:** Generalist; **Function Concentration:** Finance/Accounting, Marketing, Sales

**Kiedel, Michelle** — *Human Resources Contracts Recruiter*
Winter, Wyman & Company
950 Winter Street, Suite 3100
Waltham, MA 02154-1294
Telephone: (617) 890-7000
**Recruiter Classification:** Contingency; **Lowest/Average Salary:** $30,000/$50,000; **Industry Concentration:** Generalist; **Function Concentration:** Human Resources

**Kieffer, Michael C.** — *Chairman*
Witt/Kieffer, Ford, Hadelman & Lloyd
2015 Spring Road, Suite 510
Oak Brook, IL 60521
Telephone: (708) 990-1370
**Recruiter Classification:** Retained; **Lowest/Average Salary:** $75,000/$90,000; **Industry Concentration:** Healthcare/Hospitals, Venture Capital; **Function Concentration:** Generalist with a primary focus in Administration, Finance/Accounting, General Management, Human Resources, Marketing

**Kielty, John L.** — *Chairman*
Earley Kielty and Associates, Inc.
Two Pennsylvania Plaza
New York, NY 10121
Telephone: (212) 736-5626
**Recruiter Classification:** Retained; **Lowest/Average Salary:** $90,000/$90,000; **Industry Concentration:** Generalist with a primary focus in Information Technology; **Function Concentration:** Generalist with a primary focus in Administration, Finance/Accounting, General Management, Human Resources, Marketing, Research and Development, Sales, Women/Minorities

**Kilcoyne, Pat** — *Executive Recruiter*
CPS Inc.
One Westbrook Corporate Centre, Suite 600
Westchester, IL 60154
Telephone: (708) 531-8370
**Recruiter Classification:** Contingency; **Lowest/Average Salary:** $30,000/$50,000; **Industry Concentration:** Generalist with a primary focus in Automotive, Biotechnology, Chemical Products, Consumer Products, High Technology, Insurance, Manufacturing, Oil/Gas, Packaging, Pharmaceutical/Medical; **Function Concentration:** Engineering, Research and Development, Sales, Women/Minorities

**Kilcullen, Brian A.** — *Partner*
D.A. Kreuter Associates, Inc.
1100 East Hector Street, Suite 388
Conshohocken, PA 19428
Telephone: (610) 834-1100
**Recruiter Classification:** Retained; **Lowest/Average Salary:** $60,000/$90,000; **Industry Concentration:** Financial Services, Insurance; **Function Concentration:** General Management, Marketing, Sales

**Kile, Robert W.** — *Vice President*
Rusher, Loscavio & LoPresto
180 Montgomery Street, Suite 1616
San Francisco, CA 94104-4239
Telephone: (415) 765-6600
**Recruiter Classification:** Retained; **Lowest/Average Salary:** $75,000/$75,000; **Industry Concentration:** Insurance, Non-Profit; **Function Concentration:** Administration, General Management

**Kiley, Phyllis** — *Senior Insurance Consultant*
National Search, Inc.
2816 University Drive
Coral Springs, FL 33071
Telephone: (800) 935-4355
**Recruiter Classification:** Contingency; **Lowest/Average Salary:** $30,000/$50,000; **Industry Concentration:** Healthcare/Hospitals, Insurance, Pharmaceutical/Medical; **Function Concentration:** Generalist with a primary focus in Administration, Finance/Accounting, General Management, Human Resources, Marketing, Research and Development, Sales, Women/Minorities

**Kiliper, Catherine G.** — *Senior Associate*
Korn/Ferry International
237 Park Avenue
New York, NY 10017
Telephone: (212) 687-1834
**Recruiter Classification:** Retained; **Lowest/Average Salary:** $90,000/$90,000; **Industry Concentration:** Generalist with a primary focus in Consumer Products; **Function Concentration:** Generalist

**Kincannon, Kelly** — *President*
Kincannon & Reed
2106-C Gallows Road
Vienna, VA 22182
Telephone: (703) 761-4046
**Recruiter Classification:** Retained; **Lowest/Average Salary:** $90,000/$90,000; **Industry Concentration:** Biotechnology; **Function Concentration:** Generalist

**Kindler, Peter A.** — *Partner*
Kenny, Kindler, Hunt & Howe
1 Dag Hammarskjold Plaza
New York, NY 10017
Telephone: (212) 355-5560
**Recruiter Classification:** Retained; **Lowest/Average Salary:** $90,000/$90,000; **Industry Concentration:** Generalist; **Function Concentration:** Generalist

**King, Bill** — *Vice President Administration*
The McCormick Group, Inc.
1400 Wilson Boulevard
Arlington, VA 22209
Telephone: (703) 841-1700
**Recruiter Classification:** Retained; **Lowest/Average Salary:** $50,000/$90,000; **Industry Concentration:** Biotechnology, Consumer Products, Financial Services, High Technology, Information Technology, Insurance, Publishing/Media, Real Estate; **Function Concentration:** Engineering, Finance/Accounting, General Management, Human Resources, Marketing, Sales

**King, Byron L.** — *Manager North Atlantic Region*
Management Recruiters International, Inc.
Shiloh Church Road, Highway 127 North
P.O. Box 6077
Hickory, NC 28603
Telephone: (704) 495-8233
**Recruiter Classification:** Contingency; **Lowest/Average Salary:** $30,000/$75,000; **Industry Concentration:** Generalist; **Function Concentration:** Generalist

**King, Gary A.** — *Manager South Atlantic Region*
Management Recruiters International, Inc.
4012 Gunn Highway, Suite 140
Tampa, FL 33624-4724
Telephone: (813) 264-7165
**Recruiter Classification:** Contingency; **Lowest/Average Salary:** $30,000/$75,000; **Industry Concentration:** Generalist; **Function Concentration:** Generalist

**King, James B.** — *Managing Partner*
The Westminster Group, Inc.
40 Westminster Street
Providence, RI 02903
Telephone: (401) 273-9300
**Recruiter Classification:** Retained; **Lowest/Average Salary:** $90,000/$90,000; **Industry Concentration:** Generalist; **Function Concentration:** Generalist

**King, Joyce L.** — *Executive Recruiter*
MSI International
200 Galleria Parkway
Suite 1610
Atlanta, GA 30339
Telephone: (404) 951-1208
**Recruiter Classification:** Contingency; **Lowest/Average Salary:**
$30,000/$60,000; **Industry Concentration:** Generalist with a primary focus in
Healthcare/Hospitals; **Function Concentration:** Administration, Engineering,
Finance/Accounting, General Management, Marketing

**King, Richard M.** — *Managing Partner*
Kittleman & Associates
300 South Wacker Drive, Suite 1710
Chicago, IL 60606
Telephone: (312) 986-1166
**Recruiter Classification:** Retained; **Lowest/Average Salary:** $50,000/$75,000;
**Industry Concentration:** Healthcare/Hospitals, Non-Profit; **Function
Concentration:** Finance/Accounting, General Management, Marketing,
Women/Minorities

**King, Shannon** — *Associate*
Source Services Corporation
4510 Executive Drive, Suite 200
San Diego, CA 92121
Telephone: (619) 552-0300
**Recruiter Classification:** Contingency; **Lowest/Average Salary:**
$30,000/$50,000; **Industry Concentration:** Financial Services, Information
Technology; **Function Concentration:** Engineering, Finance/Accounting

**King, Stephen C.** — *Consultant*
Boyden/Zay & Company
Three Allen Center
333 Clay Street, Suite 3810
Houston, TX 77002
Telephone: (713) 655-0123
**Recruiter Classification:** Retained; **Lowest/Average Salary:** $90,000/$90,000;
**Industry Concentration:** Generalist with a primary focus in Energy, Financial
Services, Oil/Gas; **Function Concentration:** Generalist with a primary focus in
Finance/Accounting, General Management

**King, Steven** — *Office of the President*
Ashway, Ltd.
295 Madison Avenue
New York, NY 10017
Telephone: (212) 679-3300
**Recruiter Classification:** Contingency; **Lowest/Average Salary:**
$30,000/$90,000; **Industry Concentration:** Biotechnology, Environmental,
High Technology, Insurance; **Function Concentration:** General Management

**King, Thomas** — *Recruiter*
Morgan Hunter Corp.
6800 College Boulevard, Suite 550
Overland Park, KS 66211
Telephone: (913) 491-3434
**Recruiter Classification:** Contingency; **Lowest/Average Salary:**
$20,000/$30,000; **Industry Concentration:** Generalist with a primary focus in
Consumer Products, Financial Services, Healthcare/Hospitals, Manufacturing,
Oil/Gas, Public Administration, Real Estate; **Function Concentration:**
Finance/Accounting

**Kingdom, Scott** — *Managing Director*
Korn/Ferry International
120 South Riverside Plaza
Suite 918
Chicago, IL 60606
Telephone: (312) 726-1841
**Recruiter Classification:** Retained; **Lowest/Average Salary:** $90,000/$90,000;
**Industry Concentration:** Generalist; **Function Concentration:** Generalist

**Kingore, William C.** — *Executive Vice President*
DHR International, Inc.
10 South Riverside Plaza, Suite 2220
Chicago, IL 60606
Telephone: (312) 782-1581
**Recruiter Classification:** Retained; **Lowest/Average Salary:** $60,000/$90,000;
**Industry Concentration:** Generalist; **Function Concentration:** Generalist

**Kingsley, Kate** — *Principal*
Korn/Ferry International
The Transamerica Pyramid
600 Montgomery Street
San Francisco, CA 94111
Telephone: (415) 956-1834
**Recruiter Classification:** Retained; **Lowest/Average Salary:** $90,000/$90,000;
**Industry Concentration:** Generalist with a primary focus in
Healthcare/Hospitals; **Function Concentration:** Generalist

**Kinley, David** — *Partner*
The Caldwell Partners Amrop International
Sixty-Four Prince Arthur Avenue
Toronto, Ontario, CANADA M5R 1B4
Telephone: (416) 920-7702
**Recruiter Classification:** Retained; **Lowest/Average Salary:** $/$90,000; **Industry
Concentration:** Generalist; **Function Concentration:** Generalist

**Kinley, Kathy** — *Senior Vice President*
Intech Summit Group, Inc.
5075 Shoreham Place, Suite 280
San Diego, CA 92122
Telephone: (619) 452-2100
**Recruiter Classification:** Retained; **Lowest/Average Salary:** $75,000/$90,000;
**Industry Concentration:** Consumer Products, Insurance, Manufacturing,
Oil/Gas; **Function Concentration:** Human Resources, Women/Minorities

**Kinney, Carol** — *Associate*
Dussick Management Associates
149 Durham Road
Madison, CT 06443
Telephone: (203) 245-9311
**Recruiter Classification:** Contingency; **Lowest/Average Salary:**
$50,000/$60,000; **Industry Concentration:** Generalist with a primary focus in
Consumer Products, High Technology, Information Technology, Packaging,
Pharmaceutical/Medical; **Function Concentration:** Generalist with a primary
focus in Marketing, Research and Development, Sales, Women/Minorities

**Kinser, Richard E.** — *President*
Richard Kinser & Associates
919 Third Avenue, 10th Floor
New York, NY 10022
Telephone: (212) 593-5429
**Recruiter Classification:** Retained; **Lowest/Average Salary:** $90,000/$90,000;
**Industry Concentration:** Generalist with a primary focus in Board Services,
Chemical Products, Consumer Products, Electronics, Energy, Environmental,
Financial Services, High Technology, Insurance, Manufacturing, Oil/Gas,
Packaging, Real Estate, Transportation; **Function Concentration:** Generalist
with a primary focus in Administration, Engineering, Finance/Accounting,
General Management, Human Resources, Marketing, Research and
Development

**Kinsey, Joanne** — *Recruiter*
Eastridge InfoTech
2355 Northside Drive, Suite 180
San Diego, CA 92108
Telephone: (619) 260-2048
**Recruiter Classification:** Contingency; **Lowest/Average Salary:**
$40,000/$60,000; **Industry Concentration:** High Technology, Information
Technology

**Kirby, James E.** — *Manager North Atlantic Region*
Management Recruiters International, Inc.
274 North Marietta Parkway NE, Suite C
Marietta, GA 30060-1456
Telephone: (770) 423-1443
**Recruiter Classification:** Contingency; **Lowest/Average Salary:**
$30,000/$75,000; **Industry Concentration:** Generalist; **Function
Concentration:** Generalist

**Kirchgessner, Ken F.** — *General Manager*
Management Recruiters International, Inc.
603-A East Government Street
Pensacola, FL 32501
Telephone: (904) 434-6500
**Recruiter Classification:** Contingency; **Lowest/Average Salary:**
$30,000/$75,000; **Industry Concentration:** Generalist; **Function
Concentration:** Generalist

**Kirchner, Michael** — *Principal*
American Medical Consultants
471 Lexington Avenue, Suite 100
Fort Lauderdale, FL 33325
Telephone: (954) 424-8777
**Recruiter Classification:** Contingency; **Lowest/Average Salary:**
$75,000/$90,000; **Industry Concentration:** Healthcare/Hospitals; **Function
Concentration:** Generalist

**Kirkpatrick, Robert L.** — *Vice President*
Reese Associates
10475 Perry Highway
Wexford, PA 15090
Telephone: (412) 935-8644
**Recruiter Classification:** Retained; **Lowest/Average Salary:** $75,000/$90,000;
**Industry Concentration:** Generalist with a primary focus in
Aerospace/Defense, Automotive, Chemical Products, Consumer Products,
Energy, Environmental, Manufacturing; **Function Concentration:** Generalist
with a primary focus in Engineering, Finance/Accounting, General
Management, Human Resources, Marketing, Research and Development, Sales

**Kirschman, David R.** — *President*
Physician Executive Management Center
4014 Gunn Highway, Suite 160
Tampa, FL 33624
Telephone: (813) 963-1800
**Recruiter Classification:** Retained; **Lowest/Average Salary:** $90,000/$90,000;
**Industry Concentration:** Healthcare/Hospitals, Insurance; **Function Concentration:** General Management

**Kirschner, Alan** — *Associate*
Source Services Corporation
2 Penn Plaza, Suite 1176
New York, NY 10121
Telephone: (212) 760-2200
**Recruiter Classification:** Contingency; **Lowest/Average Salary:**
$30,000/$50,000; **Industry Concentration:** Financial Services, Information
Technology; **Function Concentration:** Engineering, Finance/Accounting

**Kirschner, John** — *Manager Southwest Region*
Management Recruiters International, Inc.
Sherman Plaza, Suite 420
1888 Sherman Street
Denver, CO 80203-1159
Telephone: (303) 832-5250
**Recruiter Classification:** Contingency; **Lowest/Average Salary:**
$30,000/$75,000; **Industry Concentration:** Generalist; **Function Concentration:** Generalist

**Kishbaugh, Herbert S.** — *President*
Kishbaugh Associates International
2 Elm Square
Andover, MA 01810
Telephone: (508) 475-7224
**Recruiter Classification:** Retained; **Lowest/Average Salary:** $75,000/$90,000;
**Industry Concentration:** Generalist with a primary focus in Automotive,
Chemical Products, Consumer Products, Financial Services, High Technology,
Information Technology, Manufacturing, Packaging; **Function Concentration:**
Generalist with a primary focus in Administration, Finance/Accounting,
General Management, Human Resources, Marketing, Research and
Development, Sales

**Kissel, Jim R.** — *Manager South Atlantic Region*
Management Recruiters International, Inc.
Northlake Corporate Park
8895 North Military Trail, Suite 301B
Palm Beach Gardens, FL 33410-6239
Telephone: (407) 622-8110
**Recruiter Classification:** Contingency; **Lowest/Average Salary:**
$30,000/$75,000; **Industry Concentration:** Generalist; **Function Concentration:** Generalist

**Kister, Edward A.** — *Managing Director*
Pendleton James and Associates, Inc.
200 Park Avenue, Suite 4520
New York, NY 10166
Telephone: (212) 557-1599
**Recruiter Classification:** Retained; **Lowest/Average Salary:** $90,000/$90,000;
**Industry Concentration:** Generalist; **Function Concentration:** Generalist

**Kixmiller, David B.** — *Managing Partner*
Heidrick & Struggles, Inc.
2740 Sand Hill Road
Menlo Park, CA 94025
Telephone: (415) 854-9300
**Recruiter Classification:** Retained; **Lowest/Average Salary:** $75,000/$90,000;
**Industry Concentration:** Generalist with a primary focus in Education/Libraries,
Healthcare/Hospitals, High Technology, Non-Profit; **Function Concentration:**
Generalist

**Kizer, Jay R.** — *Partner*
Paul Ray Berndtson
301 Commerce Street, Suite 2300
Fort Worth, TX 76102
Telephone: (817) 334-0500
**Recruiter Classification:** Retained; **Lowest/Average Salary:** $90,000/$90,000;
**Industry Concentration:** Generalist with a primary focus in Consumer
Products, Pharmaceutical/Medical; **Function Concentration:** Generalist

**Kkorzyniewski, Nicole** — *Executive Recruiter*
CPS Inc.
One Westbrook Corporate Centre, Suite 600
Westchester, IL 60154
Telephone: (708) 531-8370
**Recruiter Classification:** Contingency; **Lowest/Average Salary:**
$30,000/$50,000; **Industry Concentration:** Generalist with a primary focus in
Automotive, Biotechnology, Chemical Products, Consumer Products, High
Technology, Insurance, Manufacturing, Oil/Gas, Packaging,
Pharmaceutical/Medical; **Function Concentration:** Engineering, Research and
Development, Sales, Women/Minorities

**Klages, Constance W.** — *President*
International Management Advisors, Inc.
516 Fifth Avenue
New York, NY 10036-7501
Telephone: (212) 758-7770
**Recruiter Classification:** Retained; **Lowest/Average Salary:** $75,000/$90,000;
**Industry Concentration:** Generalist with a primary focus in
Aerospace/Defense, Automotive, Biotechnology, Chemical Products,
Consumer Products, Electronics, Energy, Financial Services,
Healthcare/Hospitals, High Technology, Hospitality/Leisure, Manufacturing,
Non-Profit, Oil/Gas; **Function Concentration:** Generalist with a primary focus
in Engineering, Finance/Accounting, General Management, Human Resources,
Marketing, Research and Development, Women/Minorities

**Klauck, James J.** — *Managing Director*
Horton International
10 Tower Lane
Avon, CT 06001
Telephone: (860) 674-8701
**Recruiter Classification:** Retained; **Lowest/Average Salary:** $90,000/$90,000;
**Industry Concentration:** Generalist with a primary focus in
Aerospace/Defense, Automotive, Chemical Products, Electronics, Energy, High
Technology, Manufacturing; **Function Concentration:** Generalist with a
primary focus in Administration, Engineering, General Management, Human
Resources, Marketing, Research and Development, Sales

**Klavens, Cecile J.** — *President*
The Pickwick Group, Inc.
One Washington Street, Suite 111
Wellesley, MA 02181
Telephone: (617) 235-6222
**Recruiter Classification:** Executive Temporary; **Lowest/Average Salary:**
$40,000/$60,000; **Industry Concentration:** Generalist with a primary focus in
Biotechnology, Consumer Products, Electronics, Financial Services,
Healthcare/Hospitals, High Technology, Information Technology, Non-Profit;
**Function Concentration:** Generalist with a primary focus in
Finance/Accounting, General Management, Human Resources, Marketing,
Women/Minorities

**Klavins, Larissa R.** — *Principal*
Dieckmann & Associates, Ltd.
180 North Stetson, Suite 5555
Two Prudential Plaza
Chicago, IL 60601
Telephone: (312) 819-5900
**Recruiter Classification:** Retained; **Lowest/Average Salary:** $75,000/$90,000;
**Industry Concentration:** Generalist with a primary focus in Consumer
Products, Environmental, Fashion (Retail/Apparel); **Function Concentration:**
Generalist with a primary focus in Finance/Accounting, General Management

**Klein, Brandon** — *Recruiter*
A.J. Burton Group, Inc.
120 East Baltimore Street, Suite 2220
Baltimore, MD 21202
Telephone: (410) 752-5244
**Recruiter Classification:** Contingency; **Lowest/Average Salary:**
$40,000/$60,000; **Industry Concentration:** Financial Services; **Function Concentration:** Finance/Accounting

**Klein, Gary Ethan** — *Managing Director*
Klein, Landau, Romm & North
1725 K Street NW, Suite 602
Washington, DC 20006
Telephone: (202) 728-0100
**Recruiter Classification:** Contingency; **Lowest/Average Salary:**
$50,000/$90,000

**Klein, Gary I.** — *Managing Director*
Johnson Smith & Knisely Accord
100 Park Avenue, 15th Floor
New York, NY 10017
Telephone: (212) 885-9100
**Recruiter Classification:** Retained; **Lowest/Average Salary:** $90,000/$90,000;
**Industry Concentration:** Publishing/Media; **Function Concentration:**
Administration, Engineering, Finance/Accounting, General Management,
Human Resources, Marketing, Sales, Women/Minorities

**Klein, Gregory A.** — *Vice President*
A.T. Kearney, Inc.
222 West Adams Street
Chicago, IL 60606
Telephone: (312) 648-0111
**Recruiter Classification:** Retained; **Lowest/Average Salary:** $90,000/$90,000;
**Industry Concentration:** Generalist with a primary focus in Manufacturing;
**Function Concentration:** Generalist with a primary focus in Engineering,
Finance/Accounting, General Management, Human Resources, Marketing,
Research and Development, Sales

**Klein, Jill S.** — *Consultant*
David C. Cooper and Associates, Inc.
Five Concourse Parkway, Suite 2700
Atlanta, GA 30328
Telephone: (770) 395-0014
**Recruiter Classification:** Contingency; **Lowest/Average Salary:** $20,000/$40,000; **Industry Concentration:** Generalist; **Function Concentration:** Finance/Accounting

**Kleinstein, Jonah A.** — *President*
The Kleinstein Group
33 Wood Avenue South
Metro Park Plaza
Iselin, NJ 08830
Telephone: (908) 494-7500
**Recruiter Classification:** Retained; **Lowest/Average Salary:** $60,000/$90,000; **Industry Concentration:** Generalist with a primary focus in Biotechnology, Consumer Products, Electronics, Financial Services, Insurance, Manufacturing, Non-Profit, Pharmaceutical/Medical; **Function Concentration:** Generalist

**Kleinstein, Scott** — *Associate*
Source Services Corporation
150 South Wacker Drive, Suite 400
Chicago, IL 60606
Telephone: (312) 346-7000
**Recruiter Classification:** Contingency; **Lowest/Average Salary:** $30,000/$50,000; **Industry Concentration:** Financial Services, Information Technology; **Function Concentration:** Engineering, Finance/Accounting

**Kline, James O.** — *Manager North Atlantic Region*
Management Recruiters International, Inc.
9050 Executive Park Drive, Suite 16
Knoxville, TN 37923-4693
Telephone: (423) 694-1628
**Recruiter Classification:** Contingency; **Lowest/Average Salary:** $30,000/$75,000; **Industry Concentration:** Generalist; **Function Concentration:** Generalist

**Klock, Lawrence S.** — *Managing Director*
Russell Reynolds Associates, Inc.
200 South Wacker Drive
Suite 3600
Chicago, IL 60606
Telephone: (312) 993-9696
**Recruiter Classification:** Retained; **Lowest/Average Salary:** $90,000/$90,000; **Industry Concentration:** Generalist with a primary focus in Utilities/Nuclear; **Function Concentration:** Generalist

**Kloess, Janice Sciulli** — *Recruiter*
David C. Cooper and Associates, Inc.
Five Concourse Parkway, Suite 2700
Atlanta, GA 30328
Telephone: (770) 395-0014
**Recruiter Classification:** Contingency; **Lowest/Average Salary:** $20,000/$40,000; **Industry Concentration:** Generalist; **Function Concentration:** Finance/Accounting

**Klopfenstein, Edward L.** — *Vice President*
Crowder & Company
2050 North Woodward Avenue, Suite 335
Bloomfield Hills, MI 48304
Telephone: (810) 645-0909
**Recruiter Classification:** Retained; **Lowest/Average Salary:** $75,000/$75,000; **Industry Concentration:** Generalist with a primary focus in Automotive, Electronics, Manufacturing, Packaging, Transportation; **Function Concentration:** Generalist with a primary focus in Engineering, Finance/Accounting, General Management, Human Resources, Marketing, Sales, Women/Minorities

**Klopmeyerr, Vanessa** — *Associate*
Kenzer Corp.
6033 West Century Boulevard, Suite 808
Los Angeles, CA 90045
Telephone: (310) 417-8577
**Recruiter Classification:** Retained; **Lowest/Average Salary:** $50,000/$90,000; **Industry Concentration:** Generalist; **Function Concentration:** Generalist

**Klos, Larry** — *Manager Southwest Region*
Management Recruiters International, Inc.
5001 Kee Brook Drive
Arlington, TX 76017
Telephone: (817) 572-2131
**Recruiter Classification:** Contingency; **Lowest/Average Salary:** $30,000/$75,000; **Industry Concentration:** Generalist; **Function Concentration:** Generalist

**Kluber, Bruce** — *Executive Recruiter*
Richard, Wayne and Roberts
24 Greenway Plaza, Suite 1304
Houston, TX 77046-2493
Telephone: (713) 629-6681
**Recruiter Classification:** Retained; **Lowest/Average Salary:** $40,000/$60,000; **Industry Concentration:** Generalist; **Function Concentration:** Generalist

**Klumpjan, Sonja** — *Executive Recruiter*
CPS Inc.
One Westbrook Corporate Centre, Suite 600
Westchester, IL 60154
Telephone: (708) 531-8370
**Recruiter Classification:** Contingency; **Lowest/Average Salary:** $30,000/$50,000; **Industry Concentration:** Generalist with a primary focus in Automotive, Biotechnology, Chemical Products, Consumer Products, High Technology, Insurance, Manufacturing, Oil/Gas, Packaging, Pharmaceutical/Medical; **Function Concentration:** Engineering, Research and Development, Sales, Women/Minorities

**Klusman, Edwin** — *Associate*
Source Services Corporation
2000 Town Center, Suite 850
Southfield, MI 48075
Telephone: (810) 352-6520
**Recruiter Classification:** Contingency; **Lowest/Average Salary:** $30,000/$50,000; **Industry Concentration:** Financial Services, Information Technology; **Function Concentration:** Engineering, Finance/Accounting

**Knapp, Ronald A.** — *President*
Knapp Consultants
184 Old Ridgefield Road
Wilton, CT 06897
Telephone: (203) 762-0790
**Recruiter Classification:** Retained; **Lowest/Average Salary:** $90,000/$90,000; **Industry Concentration:** Generalist with a primary focus in Aerospace/Defense, Electronics, High Technology, Information Technology, Manufacturing; **Function Concentration:** Generalist

**Knecht, Luke D.** — *Executive Director*
Russell Reynolds Associates, Inc.
200 South Wacker Drive
Suite 3600
Chicago, IL 60606
Telephone: (312) 993-9696
**Recruiter Classification:** Retained; **Lowest/Average Salary:** $90,000/$90,000; **Industry Concentration:** Generalist; **Function Concentration:** Generalist

**Knight, Gwen** — *Executive Recruiter*
Richard, Wayne and Roberts
24 Greenway Plaza, Suite 1304
Houston, TX 77046-2493
Telephone: (713) 629-6681
**Recruiter Classification:** Retained; **Lowest/Average Salary:** $50,000/$90,000; **Industry Concentration:** Generalist with a primary focus in Financial Services; **Function Concentration:** Generalist with a primary focus in Finance/Accounting

**Knight, Kim L.** — *Principal*
Telford, Adams & Alexander/The Knight Company
11775 Clark Street
Post Office Box 1133
Arcadia, CA 91077
Telephone: (818) 359-4848
**Recruiter Classification:** Retained; **Lowest/Average Salary:** $50,000/$75,000; **Industry Concentration:** Generalist with a primary focus in Financial Services; **Function Concentration:** Generalist with a primary focus in Finance/Accounting, General Management, Human Resources

**Knight, Lisa** — *Partner*
Ward Howell International, Inc.
141 Adelaide Street West
Suite 1800
Toronto, Ontario, CANADA M5H 3L5
Telephone: (416) 862-1273
**Recruiter Classification:** Retained; **Lowest/Average Salary:** $75,000/$90,000; **Industry Concentration:** Generalist; **Function Concentration:** Generalist

**Knight, Liz** — *Consultant*
Plummer & Associates, Inc.
30 Myano Lane, Suite 36
Stamford, CT 06902
Telephone: (203) 965-7878
**Recruiter Classification:** Retained, Executive Temporary; **Lowest/Average Salary:** $90,000/$90,000; **Industry Concentration:** Entertainment, Fashion (Retail/Apparel), Manufacturing, Venture Capital; **Function Concentration:** Generalist

**Knight, Russell** — *Executive Recruiter*
Hornberger Management Company
One Commerce Center, 7th Floor
Wilmington, DE 19801
Telephone: (302) 573-2541
**Recruiter Classification:** Retained; **Lowest/Average Salary:** $90,000/$90,000;
**Industry Concentration:** Real Estate; **Function Concentration:** Generalist

**Knisely, Gary** — *Chief Executive Officer*
Johnson Smith & Knisely Accord
100 Park Avenue, 15th Floor
New York, NY 10017
Telephone: (212) 885-9100
**Recruiter Classification:** Retained; **Lowest/Average Salary:** $90,000/$90,000;
**Industry Concentration:** Generalist with a primary focus in Board Services,
Consumer Products, Entertainment, Financial Services, Non-Profit,
Publishing/Media, Venture Capital; **Function Concentration:** Generalist with a
primary focus in Administration, Finance/Accounting, General Management,
Human Resources, Marketing, Research and Development, Sales,
Women/Minorities

**Knoll, Robert** — *Associate*
Source Services Corporation
One CityPlace, Suite 170
St. Louis, MO 63141
Telephone: (314) 432-4500
**Recruiter Classification:** Contingency; **Lowest/Average Salary:**
$30,000/$50,000; **Industry Concentration:** Financial Services, Information
Technology; **Function Concentration:** Engineering, Finance/Accounting

**Knotts, Jerry** — *Senior Principal*
Mixtec Group
31255 Cedar Valley Drive
Suite 300-327
Westlake Village, CA 91362
Telephone: (818) 889-8819
**Recruiter Classification:** Contingency; **Lowest/Average Salary:**
$60,000/$90,000; **Industry Concentration:** High Technology; **Function
Concentration:** Generalist with a primary focus in Administration, Engineering,
Finance/Accounting, General Management, Research and Development

**Knox, Andrew** — *Vice President*
Korn/Ferry International
601 South Figueroa
Suite 1900
Los Angeles, CA 90017
Telephone: (213) 624-6600
**Recruiter Classification:** Retained; **Lowest/Average Salary:** $90,000/$90,000;
**Industry Concentration:** Generalist; **Function Concentration:** Generalist

**Knutson, Rebecca J.** — *Manager Midwest Region*
Management Recruiters International, Inc.
Weston Plaza
4203 Schofield Avenue, Suite 3B, P.O. Box 1165
Wausau, WI 54402-1165
Telephone: (715) 359-6715
**Recruiter Classification:** Contingency; **Lowest/Average Salary:**
$30,000/$75,000; **Industry Concentration:** Generalist; **Function
Concentration:** Generalist

**Kobayashi, Raelen** — *Manager Research*
The Repovich-Reynolds Group
709 East Colorado Boulevard, Suite 200
Pasadena, CA 91101
Telephone: (818) 585-9455
**Recruiter Classification:** Retained; **Lowest/Average Salary:** $75,000/$90,000;
**Industry Concentration:** Generalist; **Function Concentration:** Marketing

**Koblentz, Joel M.** — *Managing Partner*
Egon Zehnder International Inc.
One Atlantic Center, Suite 3000
1201 West Peachtree Street N.E.
Atlanta, GA 30309
Telephone: (404) 875-3000
**Recruiter Classification:** Retained; **Lowest/Average Salary:** $90,000/$90,000;
**Industry Concentration:** Generalist with a primary focus in Biotechnology,
Financial Services, High Technology, Manufacturing, Pharmaceutical/Medical;
**Function Concentration:** Generalist

**Kochert, Don** — *Executive Recruiter*
Summerfield Associates, Inc.
6555 Quince Road, Suite 311
Memphis, TN 38119
Telephone: (901) 753-7068
**Recruiter Classification:** Contingency; **Lowest/Average Salary:**
$30,000/$40,000; **Industry Concentration:** Generalist with a primary focus in
Manufacturing; **Function Concentration:** Engineering, General Management,
Human Resources

**Kochmer, Sheila** — *Co-Manager*
Management Recruiters International, Inc.
Village Center
639 Northern Boulevard, P.O. Box 648
Chinchilla, PA 18410-0648
Telephone: (717) 587-9909
**Recruiter Classification:** Contingency; **Lowest/Average Salary:**
$30,000/$75,000; **Industry Concentration:** Generalist; **Function
Concentration:** Generalist

**Kochmer, Victor** — *Co-Manager Eastern Region*
Management Recruiters International, Inc.
Village Center
639 Northern Boulevard, P.O. Box 648
Chinchilla, PA 18410-0648
Telephone: (717) 587-9909
**Recruiter Classification:** Contingency; **Lowest/Average Salary:**
$30,000/$75,000; **Industry Concentration:** Generalist; **Function
Concentration:** Generalist

**Koczak, John** — *Associate*
Source Services Corporation
525 Vine Street, Suite 2250
Cincinnati, OH 45202
Telephone: (513) 651-3303
**Recruiter Classification:** Contingency; **Lowest/Average Salary:**
$30,000/$50,000; **Industry Concentration:** Financial Services, Information
Technology; **Function Concentration:** Engineering, Finance/Accounting

**Koehler, Cathy** — *Recruiter*
Ells Personnel System Inc.
9900 Bren Road East, Suite 105 Opus Center
Minnetonka, MN 55343
Telephone: (612) 932-9933
**Recruiter Classification:** Contingency; **Lowest/Average Salary:**
$20,000/$30,000; **Industry Concentration:** Healthcare/Hospitals,
Pharmaceutical/Medical; **Function Concentration:** Administration,
Finance/Accounting, General Management, Human Resources

**Koehler, Frank R.** — *Principal*
The Koehler Group
P.O. Box 18156
Philadelphia, PA 19116
Telephone: (215) 673-8315
**Recruiter Classification:** Contingency; **Lowest/Average Salary:**
$60,000/$75,000; **Industry Concentration:** Generalist with a primary focus in
Chemical Products, Consumer Products, Electronics, Financial Services,
Healthcare/Hospitals, High Technology, Information Technology, Insurance,
Manufacturing, Oil/Gas, Packaging, Pharmaceutical/Medical,
Publishing/Media, Utilities/Nuclear; **Function Concentration:** Human
Resources

**Koenig, Joel S.** — *Executive Director*
Russell Reynolds Associates, Inc.
333 South Grand Avenue
Suite 3500
Los Angeles, CA 90071
Telephone: (213) 253-4400
**Recruiter Classification:** Retained; **Lowest/Average Salary:** $90,000/$90,000;
**Industry Concentration:** Generalist with a primary focus in Entertainment;
**Function Concentration:** Generalist

**Kohn, Adam P.** — *Vice President*
Christian & Timbers
One Corporate Exchange
25825 Science Park Drive, Suite 400
Cleveland, OH 44122
Telephone: (216) 464-8710
**Recruiter Classification:** Retained; **Lowest/Average Salary:** $90,000/$90,000;
**Industry Concentration:** Generalist with a primary focus in Chemical Products,
Environmental, High Technology, Venture Capital; **Function Concentration:**
Generalist with a primary focus in Engineering, Finance/Accounting, General
Management, Marketing, Research and Development, Sales,
Women/Minorities

**Kohn, Carole** — *Associate*
Kenzer Corp.
Triwest Plaza
3030 LBJ Freeway, Suite 1430
Dallas, TX 75234
Telephone: (214) 620-7776
**Recruiter Classification:** Retained; **Lowest/Average Salary:** $50,000/$90,000;
**Industry Concentration:** Generalist; **Function Concentration:** Generalist

**Kohn, Thomas C.** — *President*
Reflex Services, Inc.
Manor Oak Two, Suite 344
1910 Cochran Road
Pittsburgh, PA 15220
Telephone: (412) 341-8842
**Recruiter Classification:** Executive Temporary; **Lowest/Average Salary:**
$40,000/$60,000; **Industry Concentration:** Generalist; **Function
Concentration:** Generalist

**Kohonoski, Michael M.** — *Principal*
The Guild Corporation
8260 Greensboro Drive, Suite 460
McLean, VA 22102
Telephone: (703) 761-4023
**Recruiter Classification:** Contingency; **Lowest/Average Salary:**
$40,000/$50,000; **Industry Concentration:** Aerospace/Defense, Electronics,
High Technology, Information Technology; **Function Concentration:**
Engineering, Finance/Accounting, General Management, Research and
Development

**Kolburne, Barbara** — *Director North American
Communications*
D.E. Foster Partners Inc.
570 Lexington Avenue, 14th Floor
New York, NY 10022
Telephone: (212) 872-6232
**Recruiter Classification:** Retained; **Lowest/Average Salary:** $90,000/$90,000;
**Industry Concentration:** Generalist; **Function Concentration:** Generalist

**Kolder, Thomas R.** — *Associate*
Russell Reynolds Associates, Inc.
200 South Wacker Drive
Suite 3600
Chicago, IL 60606
Telephone: (312) 993-9696
**Recruiter Classification:** Retained; **Lowest/Average Salary:** $90,000/$90,000;
**Industry Concentration:** Generalist; **Function Concentration:** Generalist

**Koletic, Rudy E.** — *Manager South Atlantic Region*
Management Recruiters International, Inc.
2909 Bay to Bay Boulevard, Suite 302
Tampa, FL 33629
Telephone: (813) 831-7611
**Recruiter Classification:** Contingency; **Lowest/Average Salary:**
$30,000/$75,000; **Industry Concentration:** Generalist; **Function
Concentration:** Generalist

**Kolke, Rick** — *Executive Recruiter*
Richard, Wayne and Roberts
24 Greenway Plaza, Suite 1304
Houston, TX 77046-2493
Telephone: (713) 629-6681
**Recruiter Classification:** Retained; **Lowest/Average Salary:** $40,000/$60,000;
**Industry Concentration:** Generalist with a primary focus in Chemical Products,
Manufacturing; **Function Concentration:** Generalist with a primary focus in
Sales

**Kondra, Vernon J.** — *Director Operations*
The Douglas Reiter Company, Inc.
1221 S.W. Yamhill, Suite 301A
Portland, OR 97205
Telephone: (503) 228-6916
**Recruiter Classification:** Executive Temporary; **Lowest/Average Salary:**
$75,000/$90,000; **Industry Concentration:** Generalist with a primary focus in
Aerospace/Defense, Biotechnology, Board Services, Energy, Financial Services,
Healthcare/Hospitals, High Technology, Manufacturing; **Function
Concentration:** Generalist with a primary focus in Administration, Engineering,
Finance/Accounting, General Management, Human Resources, Marketing

**Konker, David N.** — *Managing Director*
Russell Reynolds Associates, Inc.
1900 Trammell Crow Center
2001 Ross Avenue
Dallas, TX 75201
Telephone: (214) 220-2033
**Recruiter Classification:** Retained; **Lowest/Average Salary:** $90,000/$90,000;
**Industry Concentration:** Generalist with a primary focus in Financial Services;
**Function Concentration:** Generalist

**Konkolski, Laurie** — *Office Manager*
The Paladin Companies, Inc.
875 North Michigan Avenue, Suite 3218
Chicago, IL 60611
Telephone: (312) 654-2600
**Recruiter Classification:** Executive Temporary; **Lowest/Average Salary:**
$50,000/$90,000; **Industry Concentration:** Generalist; **Function
Concentration:** Marketing

**Koontz, Donald N.** — *President*
Koontz, Jeffries & Associates, Inc.
18-22 Bank Street
Summit, NJ 07901
Telephone: (908) 598-1900
**Recruiter Classification:** Retained; **Lowest/Average Salary:** $75,000/$90,000;
**Industry Concentration:** Generalist with a primary focus in Automotive,
Biotechnology, Chemical Products, Consumer Products, Electronics,
Environmental, Financial Services, Healthcare/Hospitals, High Technology,
Manufacturing, Pharmaceutical/Medical; **Function Concentration:** Generalist
with a primary focus in Administration, Engineering, Finance/Accounting,
General Management, Human Resources, Marketing, Research and
Development, Sales, Women/Minorities

**Kopsick, Joseph M.** — *Senior Director*
Spencer Stuart
401 North Michigan Avenue, Suite 3400
Chicago, IL 60611-4244
Telephone: (312) 822-0080
**Recruiter Classification:** Retained; **Lowest/Average Salary:** $90,000/$90,000;
**Industry Concentration:** Generalist with a primary focus in Automotive,
Chemical Products, Consumer Products, Manufacturing,
Pharmaceutical/Medical, Publishing/Media, Transportation, Venture Capital;
**Function Concentration:** Generalist with a primary focus in Engineering,
Finance/Accounting, General Management, Human Resources, Marketing,
Research and Development, Sales

**Korkuch, Sandy** — *Executive Vice President*
Barone-O'Hara Associates
29 Emmons Drive
Princeton, NJ 08540
Telephone: (609) 452-1980
**Recruiter Classification:** Retained; **Lowest/Average Salary:** $60,000/$90,000;
**Industry Concentration:** Pharmaceutical/Medical; **Function Concentration:**
Generalist with a primary focus in Engineering, General Management,
Marketing, Research and Development, Sales

**Kornfeld, Warren** — *Manager Eastern Region*
Management Recruiters International, Inc.
Plaza Building, Suite 208
100 Crossways Park West
Woodbury, NY 11797
Telephone: (516) 364-9290
**Recruiter Classification:** Contingency; **Lowest/Average Salary:**
$30,000/$75,000; **Industry Concentration:** Generalist; **Function
Concentration:** Generalist

**Kors, R. Paul** — *President*
Kors Montgomery International
1980 Post Oak Boulevard, Suite 2280
Houston, TX 77042
Telephone: (713) 840-7101
**Recruiter Classification:** Retained; **Lowest/Average Salary:** $90,000/$90,000;
**Industry Concentration:** Energy, Information Technology; **Function
Concentration:** Engineering, General Management, Marketing, Sales

**Kossuth, David** — *Vice President*
Kossuth & Associates, Inc.
800 Bellevue Way N.E., Suite 400
Bellevue, WA 98004
Telephone: (206) 450-9050
**Recruiter Classification:** Retained; **Lowest/Average Salary:** $50,000/$90,000;
**Industry Concentration:** Board Services, Consumer Products, Electronics,
Environmental, High Technology, Information Technology, Venture Capital;
**Function Concentration:** Generalist with a primary focus in Administration,
Engineering, Finance/Accounting, General Management, Human Resources,
Marketing, Research and Development, Sales, Women/Minorities

**Kossuth, Jane** — *President*
Kossuth & Associates, Inc.
800 Bellevue Way N.E., Suite 400
Bellevue, WA 98004
Telephone: (206) 450-9050
**Recruiter Classification:** Retained; **Lowest/Average Salary:** $50,000/$90,000;
**Industry Concentration:** Board Services, Consumer Products, Electronics, High
Technology, Information Technology, Venture Capital; **Function Concentration:**
Generalist with a primary focus in Administration, Engineering,
Finance/Accounting, General Management, Human Resources, Marketing,
Research and Development, Sales, Women/Minorities

**Kotick, Madeline** — *Consultant*
The Stevenson Group of New Jersey
560 Sylvan Avenue
Englewood Cliffs, NJ 07632
Telephone: (201) 568-1900
**Recruiter Classification:** Retained; **Lowest/Average Salary:** $75,000/$90,000;
**Industry Concentration:** Generalist with a primary focus in Chemical Products,
Consumer Products, Fashion (Retail/Apparel), Financial Services, Information
Technology, Pharmaceutical/Medical; **Function Concentration:** Generalist with
a primary focus in Finance/Accounting, General Management, Human
Resources, Marketing, Sales

**Kotler, Herman** — *Co-Manager*
Management Recruiters International, Inc.
98 Cutter Mill Road, Suite 234 South
Great Neck, NY 11021-3006
Telephone: (516) 482-4000
**Recruiter Classification:** Contingency; **Lowest/Average Salary:**
$30,000/$75,000; **Industry Concentration:** Generalist; **Function
Concentration:** Generalist

**Kotler, Jerry R.** — *Co-Manager Central Region*
Management Recruiters International, Inc.
West First Plaza, Suite 304
333 West First Street
Dayton, OH 45402
Telephone: (513) 228-8271
**Recruiter Classification:** Contingency; **Lowest/Average Salary:**
$30,000/$75,000; **Industry Concentration:** Generalist; **Function
Concentration:** Generalist

**Kouble, Tim** — *Consultant*
Logix, Inc.
1601 Trapelo Road
Waltham, MA 02154
Telephone: (617) 890-0500
**Recruiter Classification:** Retained; **Lowest/Average Salary:** $60,000/$75,000;
**Industry Concentration:** High Technology, Information Technology; **Function
Concentration:** Engineering

**Kouble, Tim** — *Consultant*
Logix Partners
1601 Trapelo Road
Waltham, MA 02154
Telephone: (617) 890-0500
**Recruiter Classification:** Retained; **Lowest/Average Salary:** $60,000/$75,000;
**Industry Concentration:** High Technology, Information Technology; **Function
Concentration:** Engineering

**Kozlowski, Elaine K.** — *Manager Central Region*
Management Recruiters International, Inc.
Parklane Towers West, Suite 1224
Three Parklane Boulevard
Dearborn, MI 48126-2502
Telephone: (313) 336-6650
**Recruiter Classification:** Contingency; **Lowest/Average Salary:**
$30,000/$75,000; **Industry Concentration:** Generalist; **Function
Concentration:** Generalist

**Kracker, Robert** — *Account Executive*
Search West, Inc.
340 North Westlake Boulevard
Suite 200
Westlake Village, CA 91362-3761
Telephone: (805) 496-6811
**Recruiter Classification:** Contingency; **Lowest/Average Salary:**
$40,000/$60,000; **Industry Concentration:** Fashion (Retail/Apparel); **Function
Concentration:** Administration

**Kramer, Desni** — *Co-Manager Southwest Region*
Management Recruiters International, Inc.
Brookhollow North, Suite 460
1660 South Stemmons
Lewisviile, TX 75067
Telephone: (214) 434-9612
**Recruiter Classification:** Contingency; **Lowest/Average Salary:**
$30,000/$75,000; **Industry Concentration:** Generalist; **Function
Concentration:** Generalist

**Kramer, Donald** — *President*
Dunhill Personnel of Tampa, Inc.
4350 West Cypress Street, Suite 814
Tampa, FL 33607
Telephone: (813) 872-8118
**Recruiter Classification:** Contingency; **Lowest/Average Salary:**
$20,000/$40,000; **Industry Concentration:** Financial Services,
Healthcare/Hospitals, Insurance, Manufacturing; **Function Concentration:**
Finance/Accounting

**Kramer, Peter** — *Vice President*
Dunhill Personnel of Tampa, Inc.
4350 West Cypress Street, Suite 814
Tampa, FL 33607
Telephone: (813) 872-8118
**Recruiter Classification:** Contingency; **Lowest/Average Salary:**
$20,000/$40,000; **Industry Concentration:** Financial Services,
Healthcare/Hospitals, Insurance, Manufacturing; **Function Concentration:**
Finance/Accounting

**Kratz, Steve** — *Senior Vice President*
Tyler & Company
1000 Abernathy Road N.E.
Suite 1400
Atlanta, GA 30328-5655
Telephone: (770) 396-3939
**Recruiter Classification:** Retained; **Lowest/Average Salary:** $60,000/$90,000;
**Industry Concentration:** Healthcare/Hospitals, Insurance; **Function
Concentration:** Generalist

**Kraus, Kathy** — *Vice President*
Evie Kreisler & Associates, Inc.
333 North Michigan Avenue, Suite 818
Chicago, IL 60601
Telephone: (312) 251-0077
**Recruiter Classification:** Contingency; **Lowest/Average Salary:**
$30,000/$75,000; **Industry Concentration:** Fashion (Retail/Apparel); **Function
Concentration:** Generalist

**Krauser, H. James** — *Senior Director*
Spencer Stuart
Financial Centre
695 East Main Street
Stamford, CT 06901
Telephone: (203) 324-6333
**Recruiter Classification:** Retained; **Lowest/Average Salary:** $90,000/$90,000;
**Industry Concentration:** Financial Services, Insurance, Real Estate, Venture
Capital; **Function Concentration:** Generalist with a primary focus in
Finance/Accounting, General Management

**Krecklo, Brian Douglas** — *President*
Krecklo & Associates Inc.
1115 Sherbrooke Street West
Montreal, Quebec, CANADA H3A 1H3
Telephone: (514) 281-9999
**Recruiter Classification:** Retained; **Lowest/Average Salary:** $75,000/$90,000;
**Industry Concentration:** Information Technology

**Kreisman, Charlotte** — *Associate*
Kenzer Corp.
777 Third Avenue, 26th Floor
New York, NY 10017
Telephone: (212) 308-4300
**Recruiter Classification:** Retained; **Lowest/Average Salary:** $50,000/$90,000;
**Industry Concentration:** Generalist; **Function Concentration:** Generalist

**Krejci, Stanley L.** — *President*
The Interface Group, Ltd./Boyden
2828 Pennsylvania Avenue, N.W., Suite 305
Washington, DC 20007
Telephone: (202) 342-7200
**Recruiter Classification:** Retained; **Lowest/Average Salary:** $75,000/$90,000;
**Industry Concentration:** Generalist with a primary focus in
Aerospace/Defense, Electronics, Energy, Financial Services,
Healthcare/Hospitals, High Technology, Information Technology,
Manufacturing, Pharmaceutical/Medical, Public Administration, Venture
Capital; **Function Concentration:** Generalist with a primary focus in
Finance/Accounting, General Management, Human Resources, Marketing,
Women/Minorities

**Krell, Richard B.** — *Managing Director/Area Manager*
Russell Reynolds Associates, Inc.
333 South Grand Avenue
Suite 3500
Los Angeles, CA 90071
Telephone: (213) 253-4400
**Recruiter Classification:** Retained; **Lowest/Average Salary:** $90,000/$90,000;
**Industry Concentration:** Generalist; **Function Concentration:** Generalist

**Kreps, Charles D.** — *Managing Partner*
Normyle/Erstling Health Search Group
350 West Passaic Street
Rochelle Park, NJ 07662
Telephone: (201) 843-6009
**Recruiter Classification:** Contingency; **Lowest/Average Salary:**
$30,000/$60,000; **Industry Concentration:** Biotechnology,
Healthcare/Hospitals, Pharmaceutical/Medical; **Function Concentration:**
General Management, Marketing, Sales

**Kreuter, Daniel A.** — *President*
D.A. Kreuter Associates, Inc.
1100 East Hector Street, Suite 388
Conshohocken, PA 19428
Telephone: (610) 834-1100
**Recruiter Classification:** Retained; **Lowest/Average Salary:** $60,000/$90,000;
**Industry Concentration:** Financial Services, Insurance; **Function
Concentration:** General Management, Marketing, Sales

**Kreutz, Gary L.** — *President*
Kreutz Consulting Group, Inc.
585 North Bank Lane, Suite 2000
Lake Forest, IL 60045
Telephone: (847) 234-9115
**Recruiter Classification:** Retained; **Lowest/Average Salary:** $75,000/$90,000;
**Industry Concentration:** Generalist with a primary focus in Automotive,
Consumer Products, Financial Services, Healthcare/Hospitals, High
Technology, Information Technology, Pharmaceutical/Medical,
Publishing/Media; **Function Concentration:** General Management, Marketing,
Research and Development, Women/Minorities

**Krick, Terry L.** — *Senior Associate*
Financial Resource Associates, Inc.
105 West Orange Street
Altamonte Springs, FL 32714
Telephone: (407) 869-7000
**Recruiter Classification:** Contingency; **Lowest/Average Salary:**
$40,000/$60,000; **Industry Concentration:** Financial Services; **Function
Concentration:** Generalist with a primary focus in Finance/Accounting

**Krieger, Dennis F.** — *Managing Director*
Seiden Krieger Associates, Inc.
375 Park Avenue
New York, NY 10152
Telephone: (212) 688-8383
**Recruiter Classification:** Retained; **Lowest/Average Salary:** $90,000/$90,000;
**Industry Concentration:** Generalist with a primary focus in Manufacturing;
**Function Concentration:** Generalist with a primary focus in Administration,
Finance/Accounting, General Management, Human Resources, Marketing

**Kring, Kenneth L.** — *Senior Director*
Spencer Stuart
2005 Market Street, Suite 2350
Philadelphia, PA 19103
Telephone: (215) 851-6200
**Recruiter Classification:** Retained; **Lowest/Average Salary:** $90,000/$90,000;
**Industry Concentration:** Generalist with a primary focus in Board Services,
Financial Services, Information Technology, Insurance, Publishing/Media;
**Function Concentration:** Generalist with a primary focus in Administration,
Finance/Accounting, General Management, Human Resources, Marketing,
Sales, Women/Minorities

**Krinsky, Ira W.** — *Managing Vice President*
Korn/Ferry International
1800 Century Park East, Suite 900
Los Angeles, CA 90067
Telephone: (310) 552-1834
**Recruiter Classification:** Retained; **Lowest/Average Salary:** $90,000/$90,000;
**Industry Concentration:** Generalist with a primary focus in Education/Libraries;
**Function Concentration:** Generalist

**Krochenski, Caren S.** — *Co-Manager*
Management Recruiters International, Inc.
1610 Woodstead Court, Suite 495
Woodlands, TX 77380-3404
Telephone: (713) 363-9494
**Recruiter Classification:** Contingency; **Lowest/Average Salary:**
$30,000/$75,000; **Industry Concentration:** Generalist; **Function
Concentration:** Generalist

**Krochenski, Lynette** — *Co-Manager Southwest Region*
Management Recruiters International, Inc.
1610 Woodstead Court, Suite 495
Woodlands, TX 77380-3404
Telephone: (713) 363-9494
**Recruiter Classification:** Contingency; **Lowest/Average Salary:**
$30,000/$75,000; **Industry Concentration:** Generalist; **Function
Concentration:** Generalist

**Krohn, Eileen** — *Consultant*
The Stevenson Group of New Jersey
560 Sylvan Avenue
Englewood Cliffs, NJ 07632
Telephone: (201) 568-1900
**Recruiter Classification:** Retained; **Lowest/Average Salary:** $75,000/$90,000;
**Industry Concentration:** Generalist with a primary focus in Chemical Products,
Consumer Products, Fashion (Retail/Apparel), Financial Services, Information
Technology, Pharmaceutical/Medical; **Function Concentration:** Generalist with
a primary focus in Finance/Accounting, General Management, Human
Resources, Marketing, Sales

**Kropp, Randy** — *Recruiter*
Ells Personnel System Inc.
9900 Bren Road East, Suite 105 Opus Center
Minnetonka, MN 55343
Telephone: (612) 932-9933
**Recruiter Classification:** Contingency; **Lowest/Average Salary:**
$20,000/$30,000; **Industry Concentration:** Healthcare/Hospitals,
Pharmaceutical/Medical; **Function Concentration:** Administration,
Finance/Accounting, General Management, Human Resources

**Krostangel, Thomas** — *Executive Recruiter*
Personnel Unlimited/Executive Search
25 West Nora
Spokane, WA 99205
Telephone: (509) 326-8880
**Recruiter Classification:** Contingency; **Lowest/Average Salary:**
$30,000/$60,000; **Industry Concentration:** Generalist; **Function
Concentration:** Sales

**Kruchoski, Jan** — *Branch Manager*
Accountants on Call
Plaza VII Building, Suite 2312
45 South Seventh Street
Minneapolis, MN 55402
Telephone: (612) 341-9900
**Recruiter Classification:** Contingency; **Lowest/Average Salary:**
$20,000/$30,000; **Industry Concentration:** Generalist; **Function
Concentration:** Finance/Accounting

**Krull, Joan R.** — *Senior Consultant*
Lawstaf Legal Search, Inc.
1201 West Peachtree Street, Suite 4830
Atlanta, GA 30309
Telephone: (404) 872-6672
**Recruiter Classification:** Contingency, Executive Temporary; **Lowest/Average
Salary:** $40,000/$60,000

**Kruse, Kevin** — *Principal*
Korn/Ferry International
237 Park Avenue
New York, NY 10017
Telephone: (212) 687-1834
**Recruiter Classification:** Retained; **Lowest/Average Salary:** $90,000/$90,000;
**Industry Concentration:** Generalist with a primary focus in Fashion
(Retail/Apparel); **Function Concentration:** Generalist

**Krutzsch, Linda** — *Vice President*
Accountants on Call
Park 80 West, Plaza II, 9th Fl.
Garden State Parkway/I-80
Saddle Brook, NJ 07662
Telephone: (201) 843-0006
**Recruiter Classification:** Contingency; **Lowest/Average Salary:**
$20,000/$30,000; **Industry Concentration:** Generalist; **Function
Concentration:** Finance/Accounting

**Kucewicz, William** — *Account Executive*
Search West, Inc.
1888 Century Park East
Suite 2050
Los Angeles, CA 90067-1736
Telephone: (310) 284-8888
**Recruiter Classification:** Contingency; **Lowest/Average Salary:**
$40,000/$60,000; **Industry Concentration:** Generalist with a primary focus in
Aerospace/Defense, Energy, Fashion (Retail/Apparel), Hospitality/Leisure,
Insurance, Pharmaceutical/Medical, Publishing/Media, Real Estate; **Function
Concentration:** Generalist with a primary focus in Administration

**Kuehnling, William A.** — *Principal*
Sanford Rose Associates
4450 Belden Village Street NW, Suite 209
Canton, OH 44718
Telephone: (330) 649-9100
**Recruiter Classification:** Contingency; **Lowest/Average Salary:**
$30,000/$75,000; **Industry Concentration:** Generalist; **Function
Concentration:** Generalist

**Kuhl, Debra** — *Consultant*
Paul Ray Berndtson
191 Peachtree Tower, Suite 3800
191 Peachtree Street, NE
Atlanta, GA 30303-1757
Telephone: (404) 215-4600
**Recruiter Classification:** Retained; **Lowest/Average Salary:** $90,000/$90,000;
**Industry Concentration:** Generalist; **Function Concentration:** Generalist

**Kuhl, Teresa** — *Executive Recruiter*
Don Richard Associates of Tampa, Inc.
100 North Tampa Street, Suite 1925
Tampa, FL 33602
Telephone: (813) 221-7930
**Recruiter Classification:** Contingency, Executive Temporary; **Lowest/Average
Salary:** $20,000/$50,000; **Industry Concentration:** Generalist with a primary
focus in Financial Services, Healthcare/Hospitals, High Technology,
Hospitality/Leisure, Publishing/Media; **Function Concentration:** Generalist
with a primary focus in Administration, Finance/Accounting, Human
Resources, Research and Development

**Kuhnle, John H.** — *Managing Vice President*
Korn/Ferry International
Presidential Plaza
900 19th Street, N.W.
Washington, DC 20006
Telephone: (202) 822-9444
**Recruiter Classification:** Retained; **Lowest/Average Salary:** $90,000/$90,000; **Industry Concentration:** Generalist with a primary focus in Education/Libraries; **Function Concentration:** Generalist

**Kuhns, David** — *Partner*
Paul Ray Berndtson
101 Park Avenue, 41st Floor
New York, NY 10178
Telephone: (212) 370-1316
**Recruiter Classification:** Retained; **Lowest/Average Salary:** $90,000/$90,000; **Industry Concentration:** Generalist; **Function Concentration:** Generalist

**Kuntz, Bill** — *Manager Central Region*
Management Recruiters International, Inc.
8200 Haverstick Road, Suite 240
Indianapolis, IN 46240-2472
Telephone: (317) 257-5411
**Recruiter Classification:** Contingency; **Lowest/Average Salary:** $30,000/$75,000; **Industry Concentration:** Generalist; **Function Concentration:** Generalist

**Kunzer, William J.** — *President*
Kunzer Associates, Ltd.
1415 West 22nd Street
Oak Brook, IL 60521
Telephone: (708) 574-0010
**Recruiter Classification:** Retained; **Lowest/Average Salary:** $50,000/$90,000; **Industry Concentration:** Generalist; **Function Concentration:** Generalist

**Kuo, Linda** — *Senior Associate*
Montgomery Resources, Inc.
555 Montgomery Street, Suite 1650
San Francisco, CA 94111
Telephone: (415) 956-4242
**Recruiter Classification:** Contingency; **Lowest/Average Salary:** $30,000/$60,000; **Industry Concentration:** Consumer Products, Financial Services, High Technology, Insurance, Manufacturing, Real Estate, Venture Capital; **Function Concentration:** Finance/Accounting

**Kuper, Keith D.** — *Associate*
Christenson & Hutchison
466 Southern Boulevard
Chatham, NJ 07928
Telephone: (201) 966-1600
**Recruiter Classification:** Retained; **Lowest/Average Salary:** $75,000/$90,000; **Industry Concentration:** Generalist with a primary focus in Financial Services, Healthcare/Hospitals, Insurance, Manufacturing, Non-Profit, Public Administration, Real Estate; **Function Concentration:** Generalist with a primary focus in Finance/Accounting, General Management, Marketing, Sales

**Kurosky, John** — *President/Principal*
John Kurosky & Associates
3 Corporate Park Drive, Suite 210
Irvine, CA 92714
Telephone: (714) 851-6370
**Recruiter Classification:** Retained; **Lowest/Average Salary:** $60,000/$90,000; **Industry Concentration:** Generalist; **Function Concentration:** Generalist

**Kurtz, Michael E.** — *President Consulting and Training Division*
MDR Associates, Inc.
12774 Flat Meadow Lane
Herndon, VA 22071
Telephone: (703) 620-9475
**Recruiter Classification:** Retained; **Lowest/Average Salary:** $90,000/$90,000; **Industry Concentration:** Healthcare/Hospitals; **Function Concentration:** Generalist

**Kurz, Dick A.** — *Manager Midwest Region*
Management Recruiters International, Inc.
1400 East Touhy Avenue, Suite 160
Des Plaines, IL 60018-3374
Telephone: (847) 297-7102
**Recruiter Classification:** Contingency; **Lowest/Average Salary:** $30,000/$75,000; **Industry Concentration:** Generalist; **Function Concentration:** Generalist

**Kush, Max** — *Manager Eastern Region*
Management Recruiters International, Inc.
Easton Center Square
6 South Third Street, Suite 304
Easton, PA 18042-4572
Telephone: (610) 258-0490
**Recruiter Classification:** Contingency; **Lowest/Average Salary:** $30,000/$75,000; **Industry Concentration:** Generalist; **Function Concentration:** Generalist

**Kusin, Melanie B.** — *Partner*
Heidrick & Struggles, Inc.
245 Park Avenue, Suite 4300
New York, NY 10167-0152
Telephone: (212) 867-9876
**Recruiter Classification:** Retained; **Lowest/Average Salary:** $75,000/$90,000; **Industry Concentration:** Generalist; **Function Concentration:** Generalist

**Kuypers, Arnold** — *Partner (Practice Leader - Healthcare)*
Lamalie Amrop International
Thanksgiving Tower
1601 Elm Street
Dallas, TX 75201-4768
Telephone: (214) 754-0019
**Recruiter Classification:** Retained; **Lowest/Average Salary:** $90,000/$90,000; **Industry Concentration:** Generalist with a primary focus in Healthcare/Hospitals; **Function Concentration:** Generalist with a primary focus in Finance/Accounting, General Management, Human Resources, Marketing

**Kuzmick, John** — *Branch Manager*
Accountants on Call
Park One, 2111 East Highland, Suite B-360
Phoenix, AZ 85016
Telephone: (602) 957-1200
**Recruiter Classification:** Contingency; **Lowest/Average Salary:** $20,000/$30,000; **Industry Concentration:** Generalist; **Function Concentration:** Finance/Accounting

**Kvasnicka, Jay Allen** — *Consultant Accounting and Finance*
Morgan Hunter Corp.
6800 College Boulevard, Suite 550
Overland Park, KS 66211
Telephone: (913) 491-3434
**Recruiter Classification:** Contingency; **Lowest/Average Salary:** $30,000/$50,000; **Industry Concentration:** Generalist with a primary focus in Financial Services; **Function Concentration:** Finance/Accounting

**La Chance, Ronald** — *Associate*
Source Services Corporation
15600 N.W. 67th Avenue, Suite 210
Miami Lakes, FL 33014
Telephone: (305) 556-8000
**Recruiter Classification:** Contingency; **Lowest/Average Salary:** $30,000/$50,000; **Industry Concentration:** Financial Services, Information Technology; **Function Concentration:** Engineering, Finance/Accounting

**La Grow, Ronald E.** — *Managing Director*
DHR International, Inc.
19200 Von Karman, Suite 500
Irvine, CA 92715
Telephone: (714) 622-5520
**Recruiter Classification:** Retained; **Lowest/Average Salary:** $60,000/$90,000; **Industry Concentration:** Generalist; **Function Concentration:** Generalist

**Laba, Marvin** — *President*
Marvin Laba & Associates
6255 Sunset Boulevard, Suite 617
Los Angeles, CA 90028
Telephone: (213) 464-1355
**Recruiter Classification:** Retained; **Lowest/Average Salary:** $40,000/$75,000; **Industry Concentration:** Consumer Products, Fashion (Retail/Apparel), Financial Services, Manufacturing; **Function Concentration:** Generalist with a primary focus in Finance/Accounting, General Management, Human Resources, Marketing, Sales

**Laba, Stuart M.** — *Senior Vice President*
Marvin Laba & Associates
250 Ridgedale Avenue, Suite #A-1
Florham Park, NJ 07932
Telephone: (201) 966-2888
**Recruiter Classification:** Retained; **Lowest/Average Salary:** $40,000/$75,000; **Industry Concentration:** Generalist with a primary focus in Consumer Products, Fashion (Retail/Apparel), Financial Services, Manufacturing; **Function Concentration:** Generalist with a primary focus in Finance/Accounting, General Management, Human Resources, Marketing, Sales

**Labadie, Ernie B.** — *Manager South Atlantic Region*
Management Recruiters International, Inc.
370 West Camino Gardens Boulevard, Suite 200
Boca Raton, FL 33432
Telephone: (407) 393-3991
**Recruiter Classification:** Contingency; **Lowest/Average Salary:** $30,000/$75,000; **Industry Concentration:** Generalist; **Function Concentration:** Generalist

**Labrecque, Bernard F.** — *Partner*
Laurendeau, Labrecque/Paul Ray Berndtson, Inc.
1250 West Rene-Levesque Boulevard
Suite 3925
Montreal, Quebec, CANADA H3B 4W8
Telephone: (514) 937-1000
**Recruiter Classification:** Retained; **Lowest/Average Salary:** $90,000/$90,000;
**Industry Concentration:** Generalist with a primary focus in Financial Services,
Pharmaceutical/Medical

**Lachance, Roger** — *Partner*
Laurendeau, Labrecque/Paul Ray Berndtson, Inc.
1250 West Rene-Levesque Boulevard
Suite 3925
Montreal, Quebec, CANADA H3B 4W8
Telephone: (514) 937-1000
**Recruiter Classification:** Retained; **Lowest/Average Salary:** $90,000/$90,000;
**Industry Concentration:** Generalist with a primary focus in Financial Services,
Pharmaceutical/Medical; **Function Concentration:** Generalist

**LaCharite, Danielle** — *Office Manager*
The Guild Corporation
8260 Greensboro Drive, Suite 460
McLean, VA 22102
Telephone: (703) 761-4023
**Recruiter Classification:** Contingency; **Lowest/Average Salary:**
$40,000/$50,000; **Industry Concentration:** Aerospace/Defense, Electronics,
High Technology, Information Technology; **Function Concentration:**
Engineering, Finance/Accounting, General Management, Research and
Development

**Lachenauer, Bruce J.** — *Consultant*
Heidrick & Struggles, Inc.
125 South Wacker Drive
Suite 2800
Chicago, IL 60606-4590
Telephone: (312) 372-8811
**Recruiter Classification:** Retained; **Lowest/Average Salary:** $75,000/$90,000;
**Industry Concentration:** Generalist; **Function Concentration:** Generalist

**Laderman, David** — *Manager*
Romac & Associates
530 East Swedesford Road
Suite 202
Wayne, PA 19087
Telephone: (215) 687-6107
**Recruiter Classification:** Executive Temporary; **Lowest/Average Salary:**
$/$60,000; **Industry Concentration:** Financial Services, Healthcare/Hospitals,
High Technology, Hospitality/Leisure, Information Technology, Insurance;
**Function Concentration:** Finance/Accounting

**LaFaye, Susan** — *Physician Recruiter*
MSI International
201 St. Charles Avenue
Suite 2205
New Orleans, LA 70170
Telephone: (504) 522-6700
**Recruiter Classification:** Contingency; **Lowest/Average Salary:**
$30,000/$75,000; **Industry Concentration:** Generalist with a primary focus in
Healthcare/Hospitals, Pharmaceutical/Medical; **Function Concentration:**
Generalist with a primary focus in Administration, Engineering,
Finance/Accounting, General Management, Marketing, Sales

**Laird, Cheryl** — *Executive Recruiter*
CPS Inc.
One Westbrook Corporate Centre, Suite 600
Westchester, IL 60154
Telephone: (708) 531-8370
**Recruiter Classification:** Contingency; **Lowest/Average Salary:**
$30,000/$50,000; **Industry Concentration:** Generalist with a primary focus in
Automotive, Biotechnology, Chemical Products, Consumer Products, High
Technology, Insurance, Manufacturing, Oil/Gas, Packaging,
Pharmaceutical/Medical; **Function Concentration:** Engineering, Research and
Development, Sales, Women/Minorities

**Laird, Meri** — *President*
Davidson, Laird & Associates
29260 Franklin, Suite 110
Southfield, MI 48034
Telephone: (810) 358-2160
**Recruiter Classification:** Contingency; **Lowest/Average Salary:**
$40,000/$60,000; **Industry Concentration:** Automotive, Manufacturing;
**Function Concentration:** Generalist with a primary focus in Engineering,
General Management, Research and Development, Sales, Women/Minorities

**Lajous, Luz** — *Managing Director/Country Manager*
Russell Reynolds Associates, Inc.
Arquimedes 130-3
Colonia Polanco
Mexico City, D.F., MEXICO 11560
Telephone: (525) 281-0440
**Recruiter Classification:** Retained; **Lowest/Average Salary:** $90,000/$90,000;
**Industry Concentration:** Generalist; **Function Concentration:** Generalist

**Lake, Phillip R.** — *President*
U.S. Envirosearch
445 Union Boulevard, Suite 225
Lakewood, CO 80228
Telephone: (303) 980-6600
**Recruiter Classification:** Contingency; **Lowest/Average Salary:**
$40,000/$60,000; **Industry Concentration:** Environmental; **Function
Concentration:** Generalist with a primary focus in Administration, Engineering,
Finance/Accounting, General Management, Marketing, Sales,
Women/Minorities

**Lalonde, Joel** — *Co-Manager Pacific Region*
Management Recruiters International, Inc.
Copper Point
4530 South Eastern, Suite A-12
Las Vegas, NV 89119-6181
Telephone: (702) 733-1818
**Recruiter Classification:** Contingency; **Lowest/Average Salary:**
$30,000/$75,000; **Industry Concentration:** Generalist; **Function
Concentration:** Generalist

**Lamb, Angus K.** — *Principal*
Raymond Karsan Associates
200 West Cummings Park, Suite 7000
Woburn, MA 01801
Telephone: (617) 273-4022
**Recruiter Classification:** Contingency; **Lowest/Average Salary:**
$30,000/$90,000; **Industry Concentration:** Generalist with a primary focus in
Biotechnology, Chemical Products, Environmental, Healthcare/Hospitals,
Information Technology, Insurance, Manufacturing, Pharmaceutical/Medical;
**Function Concentration:** Generalist

**Lamb, Lynn M.** — *Executive Recruiter*
F-O-R-T-U-N-E Personnel Consultants of Huntsville, Inc.
3311 Bob Wallace Avenue, Suite 204
Huntsville, AL 35805
Telephone: (205) 534-7282
**Recruiter Classification:** Contingency, Executive Temporary; **Lowest/Average
Salary:** $30,000/$50,000; **Industry Concentration:** Generalist with a primary
focus in Automotive, Consumer Products, Electronics, High Technology,
Manufacturing; **Function Concentration:** Generalist with a primary focus in
Engineering, General Management

**Lamb, Peter S.** — *Banking and Trust Recruiter*
Executive Resource, Inc.
553 South Industrial Drive
P.O. Box 356
Hartland, WI 53029-0356
Telephone: (414) 369-2540
**Recruiter Classification:** Contingency; **Lowest/Average Salary:**
$40,000/$60,000; **Industry Concentration:** Financial Services; **Function
Concentration:** Generalist with a primary focus in Finance/Accounting

**Lambert, Robert J.** — *Consultant*
Heidrick & Struggles, Inc.
300 South Grand Avenue, Suite 2400
Los Angeles, CA 90071
Telephone: (213) 625-8811
**Recruiter Classification:** Retained; **Lowest/Average Salary:** $75,000/$90,000;
**Industry Concentration:** Generalist; **Function Concentration:** Generalist

**Lambert, William** — *Associate*
Source Services Corporation
525 Vine Street, Suite 2250
Cincinnati, OH 45202
Telephone: (513) 651-3303
**Recruiter Classification:** Contingency; **Lowest/Average Salary:**
$30,000/$50,000; **Industry Concentration:** Financial Services, Information
Technology; **Function Concentration:** Engineering, Finance/Accounting

**Lamia, Michael** — *Associate*
Source Services Corporation
15600 N.W. 67th Avenue, Suite 210
Miami Lakes, FL 33014
Telephone: (305) 556-8000
**Recruiter Classification:** Contingency; **Lowest/Average Salary:**
$30,000/$50,000; **Industry Concentration:** Financial Services, Information
Technology; **Function Concentration:** Engineering, Finance/Accounting

**Lampl, Joni** — *Manager Central Region*
Management Recruiters International, Inc.
P.O. Box 69
Sewickley, PA 15143-0069
Telephone: (412) 741-5805
**Recruiter Classification:** Contingency; **Lowest/Average Salary:** $30,000/$75,000; **Industry Concentration:** Generalist; **Function Concentration:** Generalist

**Lampl, Lisa** — *Co-Manager*
Management Recruiters International, Inc.
180 East 7th Street
Erickson Building, Unit D, P.O. Box 599
Ketchum, ID 83340-0599
Telephone: (208) 726-8005
**Recruiter Classification:** Contingency; **Lowest/Average Salary:** $30,000/$75,000; **Industry Concentration:** Generalist; **Function Concentration:** Generalist

**Lampl, Mark** — *Vice President*
Korn/Ferry International
237 Park Avenue
New York, NY 10017
Telephone: (212) 687-1834
**Recruiter Classification:** Retained; **Lowest/Average Salary:** $90,000/$90,000; **Industry Concentration:** Generalist with a primary focus in Manufacturing; **Function Concentration:** Generalist

**Lampl, Richard** — *General Manager*
Management Recruiters International, Inc.
P.O. Box 69
Sewickley, PA 15143-0069
Telephone: (412) 741-5805
**Recruiter Classification:** Contingency; **Lowest/Average Salary:** $30,000/$75,000; **Industry Concentration:** Generalist; **Function Concentration:** Generalist

**Lampl, Tom W.** — *Co-Manager Pacific Region*
Management Recruiters International, Inc.
180 East 7th Street
Erickson Building, Unit D, P.O. Box 599
Ketchum, ID 83340-0599
Telephone: (208) 726-8005
**Recruiter Classification:** Contingency; **Lowest/Average Salary:** $30,000/$75,000; **Industry Concentration:** Generalist; **Function Concentration:** Generalist

**Lamson-Gran, Jill** — *Executive Recruiter*
Accounting Resources, Inc.
8744 Frederick Street
Omaha, NE 68124-3068
Telephone: (402) 397-3308
**Recruiter Classification:** Contingency; **Lowest/Average Salary:** $40,000/$75,000; **Industry Concentration:** Generalist with a primary focus in Automotive, Consumer Products, Electronics, Financial Services, High Technology, Manufacturing, Packaging, Pharmaceutical/Medical, Publishing/Media; **Function Concentration:** Finance/Accounting

**Lanctot, William D.** — *Partner*
Corporate Resources Professional Placement
4205 Lancaster Lane, Suite 107
Plymouth, MN 55441
Telephone: (612) 550-9222
**Recruiter Classification:** Contingency; **Lowest/Average Salary:** $40,000/$60,000; **Industry Concentration:** Electronics, High Technology, Manufacturing; **Function Concentration:** Engineering, Research and Development

**Land, Shaun** — *Manager Communications*
Dunhill Professional Search of Irvine, Inc.
9 Executive Circle, Suite 240
Irvine, CA 92714
Telephone: (714) 474-6666
**Recruiter Classification:** Contingency; **Lowest/Average Salary:** $50,000/$90,000; **Industry Concentration:** Electronics, High Technology, Manufacturing, Venture Capital; **Function Concentration:** Generalist with a primary focus in Engineering, General Management, Marketing, Research and Development, Sales

**Landan, Joy** — *Executive Recruiter*
Jacobson Associates
150 North Wacker Drive
Suite 1120
Chicago, IL 60606
Telephone: (312) 726-1578
**Recruiter Classification:** Contingency; **Lowest/Average Salary:** $20,000/$50,000; **Industry Concentration:** Insurance; **Function Concentration:** Generalist

**Landau, David** — *Managing Director*
Klein, Landau, Romm & North
1725 K Street NW, Suite 602
Washington, DC 20006
Telephone: (202) 728-0100
**Recruiter Classification:** Contingency; **Lowest/Average Salary:** $50,000/$90,000

**Landon, Susan J.** — *Partner*
Lamalie Amrop International
200 Park Avenue
New York, NY 10166-0136
Telephone: (212) 953-7900
**Recruiter Classification:** Retained; **Lowest/Average Salary:** $90,000/$90,000; **Industry Concentration:** Generalist; **Function Concentration:** Generalist with a primary focus in General Management

**Landry, Leo G.** — *Executive Recruiter*
MSI International
2170 West State Road 434
Suite 454
Longwood, FL 32779
Telephone: (407) 788-7700
**Recruiter Classification:** Contingency; **Lowest/Average Salary:** $30,000/$75,000; **Industry Concentration:** Generalist with a primary focus in Manufacturing; **Function Concentration:** Generalist with a primary focus in Engineering

**Lane, Doug** — *Co-Manager*
Management Recruiters International, Inc.
The Underwriter's Exchange Building
828 North Broadway, Suite 850
Milwaukee, WI 53202
Telephone: (414) 226-2420
**Recruiter Classification:** Contingency; **Lowest/Average Salary:** $30,000/$75,000; **Industry Concentration:** Generalist; **Function Concentration:** Generalist

**Lane, Sheri** — *Executive Recruiter*
Ryan, Miller & Associates Inc.
4601 Wilshire Boulevard, Suite 225
Los Angeles, CA 90010
Telephone: (213) 938-4768
**Recruiter Classification:** Contingency; **Lowest/Average Salary:** $40,000/$50,000; **Industry Concentration:** Generalist with a primary focus in Entertainment; **Function Concentration:** Finance/Accounting

**Lang, Vicki J.** — *Corporate Search Consultant*
Morgan Hunter Corp.
6800 College Boulevard, Suite 550
Overland Park, KS 66211
Telephone: (913) 491-3434
**Recruiter Classification:** Contingency; **Lowest/Average Salary:** $30,000/$50,000; **Industry Concentration:** Generalist; **Function Concentration:** Administration, Human Resources

**Langan, Marion** — *Consultant*
Logix Partners
1601 Trapelo Road
Waltham, MA 02154
Telephone: (617) 890-0500
**Recruiter Classification:** Retained; **Lowest/Average Salary:** $60,000/$75,000; **Industry Concentration:** High Technology, Information Technology; **Function Concentration:** Engineering

**Langan, Marion** — *Consultant*
Logix, Inc.
1601 Trapelo Road
Waltham, MA 02154
Telephone: (617) 890-0500
**Recruiter Classification:** Retained; **Lowest/Average Salary:** $60,000/$75,000; **Industry Concentration:** High Technology, Information Technology; **Function Concentration:** Research and Development

**Langer, Joel A.** — *President*
Langer Associates, Inc.
188 East Post Road
White Plains, NY 10601
Telephone: (914) 684-0505
**Recruiter Classification:** Retained; **Lowest/Average Salary:** $75,000/$90,000; **Industry Concentration:** Generalist with a primary focus in Chemical Products, Consumer Products, Entertainment, Financial Services, Packaging, Pharmaceutical/Medical, Publishing/Media; **Function Concentration:** Generalist with a primary focus in Administration, Finance/Accounting, General Management, Human Resources, Marketing, Research and Development

**Langford, Robert W.** — *President*
F-O-R-T-U-N-E Personnel Consultants of Huntsville, Inc.
3311 Bob Wallace Avenue, Suite 204
Huntsville, AL 35805
Telephone: (205) 534-7282
**Recruiter Classification:** Contingency, Executive Temporary; **Lowest/Average Salary:** $30,000/$50,000; **Industry Concentration:** Electronics, High Technology; **Function Concentration:** Engineering, General Management, Sales

**Lankford, Charles** — *Executive Recruiter*
MSI International
5215 North O'Connor Boulevard
Suite 1875
Irving, TX 75039
Telephone: (214) 869-3939
**Recruiter Classification:** Contingency; **Lowest/Average Salary:** $30,000/$60,000; **Industry Concentration:** Generalist with a primary focus in Healthcare/Hospitals; **Function Concentration:** Generalist with a primary focus in Administration, Engineering, Finance/Accounting, General Management, Marketing, Sales

**Lannamann, Richard S.** — *Managing Director*
Russell Reynolds Associates, Inc.
200 Park Avenue
New York, NY 10166-0002
Telephone: (212) 351-2000
**Recruiter Classification:** Retained; **Lowest/Average Salary:** $90,000/$90,000; **Industry Concentration:** Generalist with a primary focus in Financial Services; **Function Concentration:** Generalist

**Lapat, Aaron D.** — *Associate*
J. Robert Scott
27 State Street
Boston, MA 02109
Telephone: (617) 720-2770
**Recruiter Classification:** Retained; **Lowest/Average Salary:** $75,000/$90,000; **Industry Concentration:** Generalist with a primary focus in Biotechnology, Chemical Products, Electronics, Financial Services, High Technology, Information Technology, Pharmaceutical/Medical; **Function Concentration:** Generalist

**Lapham, Lawrence L.** — *President*
Lawrence L. Lapham Inc.
80 Park Avenue, Suite 3K
New York, NY 10016
Telephone: (212) 599-0644
**Recruiter Classification:** Retained; **Lowest/Average Salary:** $90,000/$90,000; **Industry Concentration:** Generalist; **Function Concentration:** Generalist

**LaPierre, Louis** — *Managing Partner*
Romac & Associates
183 Middle Street, 3rd Floor
P.O. Box 7040
Portland, ME 04112
Telephone: (207) 773-4749
**Recruiter Classification:** Executive Temporary; **Lowest/Average Salary:** $/$60,000; **Industry Concentration:** Financial Services, Healthcare/Hospitals, High Technology, Hospitality/Leisure, Information Technology, Insurance; **Function Concentration:** Finance/Accounting

**Lapointe, Fabien** — *Associate*
Source Services Corporation
1500 West Park Drive, Suite 390
Westborough, MA 01581
Telephone: (508) 366-2600
**Recruiter Classification:** Contingency; **Lowest/Average Salary:** $30,000/$50,000; **Industry Concentration:** Financial Services, Information Technology; **Function Concentration:** Engineering, Finance/Accounting

**Lareau, Belle** — *Co-Manager*
Management Recruiters International, Inc.
Flying Point Office Park, Suite 207
33 Flying Point Road
Southampton, NY 11968-5244
Telephone: (516) 287-5030
**Recruiter Classification:** Contingency; **Lowest/Average Salary:** $30,000/$75,000; **Industry Concentration:** Generalist; **Function Concentration:** Generalist

**Lareau, Jerry A.** — *Co-Manager*
Management Recruiters International, Inc.
Flying Point Office Park, Suite 207
33 Flying Point Road
Southampton, NY 11968-5244
Telephone: (516) 287-5030
**Recruiter Classification:** Contingency; **Lowest/Average Salary:** $30,000/$75,000; **Industry Concentration:** Generalist; **Function Concentration:** Generalist

**Larkin, Kathleen** — *Human Resources Recruiter*
Winter, Wyman & Company
950 Winter Street, Suite 3100
Waltham, MA 02154-1294
Telephone: (617) 890-7000
**Recruiter Classification:** Contingency; **Lowest/Average Salary:** $30,000/$50,000; **Industry Concentration:** Generalist; **Function Concentration:** Human Resources

**Larsen, Bruce** — *Manager Insurance/Healthcare and Banking*
Prestige Inc.
P.O. Box 421
Reedsburg, WI 53959
Telephone: (608) 524-4032
**Recruiter Classification:** Contingency; **Lowest/Average Salary:** $50,000/$90,000; **Industry Concentration:** Financial Services, Healthcare/Hospitals, Insurance; **Function Concentration:** Generalist

**Larsen, Jack B.** — *President*
Jack B. Larsen & Associates
334 West Eighth Street
Erie, PA 16502
Telephone: (814) 459-3725
**Recruiter Classification:** Executive Temporary; **Lowest/Average Salary:** $30,000/$50,000; **Industry Concentration:** Generalist with a primary focus in Automotive, Electronics, High Technology; **Function Concentration:** Generalist with a primary focus in Engineering, Finance/Accounting, General Management, Human Resources, Sales

**Larsen, Richard F.** — *President*
Larsen, Zilliacus & Associates, Inc.
601 West Fifth Street, Suite 710
Los Angeles, CA 90071
Telephone: (213) 243-0033
**Recruiter Classification:** Retained; **Lowest/Average Salary:** $75,000/$90,000; **Industry Concentration:** Generalist with a primary focus in Education/Libraries, Financial Services, Information Technology, Non-Profit, Publishing/Media, Real Estate, Venture Capital; **Function Concentration:** Generalist with a primary focus in Finance/Accounting, General Management, Human Resources, Sales

**Larsen, William G.** — *Vice President Finance and Administration*
The Paladin Companies, Inc.
One Market Plaza, 41st Floor
Spear Street Tower
San Francisco, CA 94105
Telephone: (415) 495-0900
**Recruiter Classification:** Executive Temporary; **Lowest/Average Salary:** $40,000/$75,000; **Industry Concentration:** Generalist; **Function Concentration:** Marketing

**Larson, Paul W.** — *Partner*
Paul Ray Berndtson
2029 Century Park East
Suite 1000
Los Angeles, CA 90067
Telephone: (310) 557-2828
**Recruiter Classification:** Retained; **Lowest/Average Salary:** $90,000/$90,000; **Industry Concentration:** Generalist with a primary focus in Biotechnology, Pharmaceutical/Medical; **Function Concentration:** Generalist

**Lasher, Charles M.** — *President*
Lasher Associates
1200 South Pine Island Road, Suite 370
Fort Lauderdale, FL 33324-4402
Telephone: (305) 472-5658
**Recruiter Classification:** Retained; **Lowest/Average Salary:** $75,000/$90,000; **Industry Concentration:** Generalist with a primary focus in Biotechnology, Board Services, Electronics, Financial Services, High Technology, Information Technology, Insurance, Manufacturing, Non-Profit, Pharmaceutical/Medical, Publishing/Media, Real Estate, Venture Capital; **Function Concentration:** Generalist with a primary focus in Engineering, Finance/Accounting, General Management, Human Resources, Marketing, Research and Development, Sales

**Laskin, Sandy** — *Associate*
Source Services Corporation
925 Westchester Avenue, Suite 309
White Plains, NY 10604
Telephone: (914) 428-9100
**Recruiter Classification:** Contingency; **Lowest/Average Salary:** $30,000/$50,000; **Industry Concentration:** Financial Services, Information Technology; **Function Concentration:** Engineering, Finance/Accounting

**Lasse, Daniel C.** — *Manager Midwest Region*
Management Recruiters International, Inc.
10 East State Avenue
St. Charles, IL 60174
Telephone: (708) 377-6466
**Recruiter Classification:** Contingency; **Lowest/Average Salary:** $30,000/$75,000; **Industry Concentration:** Generalist; **Function Concentration:** Generalist

**Latino, Irene K.** — *Principal*
Ward Howell International, Inc.
One Landmark Square
Suite 1810
Stamford, CT 06901
Telephone: (203) 964-1481
**Recruiter Classification:** Retained; **Lowest/Average Salary:** $75,000/$90,000;
**Industry Concentration:** Generalist; **Function Concentration:** Generalist

**LaTraverse, Jean J.** — *Partner*
Belle Isle, Djandji Inc.
1200 McGill College Avenue
Suite 2250
Montreal, Quebec, CANADA H3B 4G7
Telephone: (514) 878-1991
**Recruiter Classification:** Retained; **Lowest/Average Salary:** $75,000/$90,000;
**Industry Concentration:** Generalist; **Function Concentration:** Generalist

**Latterell, Jeffrey D.** — *Vice President*
Smith & Latterell (HRS, Inc.)
P.O. Box 4499
Pittsburgh, PA 15205
Telephone: (412) 331-4700
**Recruiter Classification:** Retained; **Lowest/Average Salary:** $75,000/$75,000;
**Industry Concentration:** Generalist with a primary focus in Manufacturing;
**Function Concentration:** Generalist with a primary focus in Engineering

**Laub, Stuart R.** — *President*
Abraham & London, Ltd.
7 Old Sherman Turnpike, Suite 209
Danbury, CT 06810
Telephone: (203) 730-4000
**Recruiter Classification:** Contingency, Executive Temporary; **Lowest/Average
Salary:** $40,000/$75,000; **Industry Concentration:** High Technology,
Information Technology; **Function Concentration:** Marketing, Sales

**Laubitz, Chris** — *Partner*
The Caldwell Partners Amrop International
Sixty-Four Prince Arthur Avenue
Toronto, Ontario, CANADA M5R 1B4
Telephone: (416) 920-7702
**Recruiter Classification:** Retained; **Lowest/Average Salary:** $/$90,000; **Industry
Concentration:** Generalist; **Function Concentration:** Generalist

**Lauderback, David R.** — *Vice President*
A.T. Kearney, Inc.
1200 Bank One Center
600 Superior Avenue, East
Cleveland, OH 44114-2650
Telephone: (216) 241-6880
**Recruiter Classification:** Retained; **Lowest/Average Salary:** $90,000/$90,000;
**Industry Concentration:** Generalist with a primary focus in Chemical Products,
Financial Services, High Technology, Non-Profit, Pharmaceutical/Medical;
**Function Concentration:** Generalist with a primary focus in
Finance/Accounting, General Management, Marketing, Sales

**Lauerman, Fred J.** — *President*
Development Search Specialists
W1072 First National Bank Bldg.
St. Paul, MN 55101-1312
Telephone: (612) 224-3750
**Recruiter Classification:** Retained; **Lowest/Average Salary:** $50,000/$75,000;
**Industry Concentration:** Non-Profit; **Function Concentration:** Human
Resources

**Laurendeau, Jean L.** — *Partner*
Laurendeau, Labrecque/Paul Ray Berndtson, Inc.
1250 West Rene-Levesque Boulevard
Suite 3925
Montreal, Quebec, CANADA H3B 4W8
Telephone: (514) 937-1000
**Recruiter Classification:** Retained; **Lowest/Average Salary:** $90,000/$90,000;
**Industry Concentration:** Generalist with a primary focus in Financial Services,
Pharmaceutical/Medical; **Function Concentration:** Generalist

**Lautz, Lindsay A.** — *Partner*
Wilkinson & Ives
One Bush Street, Suite 550
San Francisco, CA 94104
Telephone: (415) 834-3100
**Recruiter Classification:** Retained; **Lowest/Average Salary:** $90,000/$90,000;
**Industry Concentration:** Generalist with a primary focus in Board Services,
Consumer Products, Electronics, Entertainment, High Technology,
Hospitality/Leisure, Information Technology, Publishing/Media; **Function
Concentration:** Generalist with a primary focus in Administration, Engineering,
Finance/Accounting, General Management, Human Resources, Marketing,
Sales, Women/Minorities

**LaValle, Michael** — *Managing Partner*
Romac & Associates
Two Piedmont Plaza, Suite 701
2000 West First Street
Winston-Salem, NC 27104-4206
Telephone: (919) 725-1933
**Recruiter Classification:** Executive Temporary; **Lowest/Average Salary:**
$/$60,000; **Industry Concentration:** Financial Services, Healthcare/Hospitals,
High Technology, Hospitality/Leisure, Information Technology, Insurance;
**Function Concentration:** Finance/Accounting

**Lavender, Jane** — *Consultant*
Paul Ray Berndtson
2200 Ross Avenue, Suite 4500W
Dallas, TX 75201
Telephone: (214) 969-7620
**Recruiter Classification:** Retained; **Lowest/Average Salary:** $90,000/$90,000;
**Industry Concentration:** Generalist; **Function Concentration:** Generalist

**Laverty, William** — *Associate*
Source Services Corporation
525 Vine Street, Suite 2250
Cincinnati, OH 45202
Telephone: (513) 651-3303
**Recruiter Classification:** Contingency; **Lowest/Average Salary:**
$30,000/$50,000; **Industry Concentration:** Financial Services, Information
Technology; **Function Concentration:** Engineering, Finance/Accounting

**Lawler, Tim M.** — *Manager Midwest Region*
Management Recruiters International, Inc.
601 East Henry Clay
Milwaukee, WI 53217-5646
Telephone: (414) 963-2520
**Recruiter Classification:** Contingency; **Lowest/Average Salary:**
$30,000/$75,000; **Industry Concentration:** Generalist; **Function
Concentration:** Generalist

**Lawner, Harvey** — *President*
Walden Associates
1601 Trapelo Road
Waltham, MA 02154
Telephone: (617) 890-8885
**Recruiter Classification:** Retained; **Lowest/Average Salary:** $90,000/$90,000;
**Industry Concentration:** High Technology, Information Technology; **Function
Concentration:** General Management

**Lawrance, Susanne** — *Specialist Insurance/Legal*
Sharrow & Associates
24735 Van Dyke
Center Line, MI 48015
Telephone: (810) 759-6910
**Recruiter Classification:** Contingency; **Lowest/Average Salary:**
$20,000/$40,000; **Industry Concentration:** Insurance; **Function
Concentration:** Administration, General Management, Sales

**Lawrence, David** — *Agribusiness Recruiter*
Agra Placements International Ltd.
16 East Fifth Street, Berkshire Court
Peru, IN 46970
Telephone: (317) 472-1988
**Recruiter Classification:** Contingency; **Lowest/Average Salary:**
$20,000/$30,000; **Industry Concentration:** Generalist with a primary focus in
Biotechnology, Chemical Products, Energy, Financial Services, Manufacturing;
**Function Concentration:** Administration, Engineering, Finance/Accounting,
General Management, Human Resources, Marketing, Research and
Development, Sales

**Lawson, Bettye N.** — *Executive Recruiter*
MSI International
1900 North 18th Street
Suite 303
Monroe, LA 71201
Telephone: (318) 324-0406
**Recruiter Classification:** Contingency; **Lowest/Average Salary:**
$30,000/$75,000; **Industry Concentration:** Generalist with a primary focus in
Healthcare/Hospitals, Pharmaceutical/Medical; **Function Concentration:**
Generalist with a primary focus in Administration, Engineering,
Finance/Accounting, General Management, Marketing, Sales

**Lawson, Debra** — *Manager Central Region*
Management Recruiters International, Inc.
300 River Place, Suite 3000
Detroit, MI 48207
Telephone: (313) 568-4200
**Recruiter Classification:** Contingency; **Lowest/Average Salary:**
$30,000/$75,000; **Industry Concentration:** Generalist; **Function
Concentration:** Generalist

**Lawson, Ron S.** — *Manager Central Region*
Management Recruiters International, Inc.
213 St. George Street
Richmond, KY 40475
Telephone: (606) 624-3535
**Recruiter Classification:** Contingency; **Lowest/Average Salary:**
$30,000/$75,000; **Industry Concentration:** Generalist; **Function Concentration:** Generalist

**Layton, Bradford** — *President*
Bradford & Galt, Inc.
12400 Olive Boulevard, Suite 430
St. Louis, MO 63141
Telephone: (314) 434-9200
**Recruiter Classification:** Contingency; **Lowest/Average Salary:**
$30,000/$30,000; **Industry Concentration:** Generalist; **Function Concentration:** Generalist

**Layton, Patrick R.** — *Executive Recruiter*
MSI International
5215 North O'Connor Boulevard
Suite 1875
Irving, TX 75039
Telephone: (214) 869-3939
**Recruiter Classification:** Contingency; **Lowest/Average Salary:**
$30,000/$75,000; **Industry Concentration:** Generalist with a primary focus in Environmental; **Function Concentration:** Generalist with a primary focus in Administration, Engineering, Finance/Accounting, General Management, Marketing, Sales

**Lazar, Miriam** — *Associate*
Source Services Corporation
120 East Baltimore Street, Suite 1950
Baltimore, MD 21202
Telephone: (410) 727-4050
**Recruiter Classification:** Contingency; **Lowest/Average Salary:**
$30,000/$50,000; **Industry Concentration:** Financial Services, Information Technology; **Function Concentration:** Engineering, Finance/Accounting

**Lazaro, Alicia C.** — *Managing Director*
The Whitney Group
850 Third Avenue, 11th Floor
New York, NY 10022
Telephone: (212) 508-3500
**Recruiter Classification:** Retained; **Lowest/Average Salary:** $75,000/$90,000;
**Industry Concentration:** Generalist with a primary focus in Financial Services, Real Estate, Venture Capital; **Function Concentration:** Generalist with a primary focus in Sales

**Leahy, Jan** — *Executive Recruiter*
CPS Inc.
One Westbrook Corporate Centre, Suite 600
Westchester, IL 60154
Telephone: (708) 531-8370
**Recruiter Classification:** Contingency; **Lowest/Average Salary:**
$30,000/$50,000; **Industry Concentration:** Generalist with a primary focus in Automotive, Biotechnology, Chemical Products, Consumer Products, High Technology, Insurance, Manufacturing, Oil/Gas, Packaging, Pharmaceutical/Medical; **Function Concentration:** Engineering, Research and Development, Sales, Women/Minorities

**Leben, Sally** — *Consultant Healthcare Search*
D. Brown and Associates, Inc.
610 S.W. Alder, Suite 1111
Portland, OR 97205
Telephone: (503) 224-6860
**Recruiter Classification:** Contingency; **Lowest/Average Salary:**
$40,000/$50,000; **Industry Concentration:** Healthcare/Hospitals

**Leblanc, Danny** — *Associate*
Source Services Corporation
5429 LBJ Freeway, Suite 275
Dallas, TX 75240
Telephone: (214) 387-1600
**Recruiter Classification:** Contingency; **Lowest/Average Salary:**
$30,000/$50,000; **Industry Concentration:** Financial Services, Information Technology; **Function Concentration:** Engineering, Finance/Accounting

**Lebo, Terry** — *Agribusiness Recruiter*
Agra Placements International Ltd.
4949 Pleasant Suite 1, West 50th Place III
West Des Moines, IA 50266-5494
Telephone: (515) 225-6562
**Recruiter Classification:** Contingency; **Lowest/Average Salary:**
$20,000/$30,000; **Industry Concentration:** Generalist with a primary focus in Biotechnology, Chemical Products, Energy, Financial Services, Manufacturing; **Function Concentration:** Administration, Engineering, Finance/Accounting, General Management, Human Resources, Marketing, Research and Development, Sales

**Lebovits, Neil** — *Vice President/Branch Manager*
Accountants on Call
The Atrium, East 80 Route 4, Suite 430
Paramus, NJ 07652
Telephone: (201) 843-8882
**Recruiter Classification:** Contingency; **Lowest/Average Salary:**
$20,000/$30,000; **Industry Concentration:** Generalist; **Function Concentration:** Finance/Accounting

**Lechner, David B.** — *Manager South Atlantic Region*
Management Recruiters International, Inc.
7737 Holiday Drive
Sarasota, FL 34231
Telephone: (941) 923-3671
**Recruiter Classification:** Contingency; **Lowest/Average Salary:**
$30,000/$75,000; **Industry Concentration:** Generalist; **Function Concentration:** Generalist

**LeComte, Andre** — *Consultant*
Egon Zehnder International Inc.
1 Place Ville-Marie, Suite 3310
Montreal, Quebec, CANADA H3B 3N2
Telephone: (514) 876-4249
**Recruiter Classification:** Retained; **Lowest/Average Salary:** $90,000/$90,000;
**Industry Concentration:** Generalist with a primary focus in Biotechnology, Financial Services, High Technology, Manufacturing, Pharmaceutical/Medical; **Function Concentration:** Generalist

**Lee, Barbara A.** — *Co-Manager South Atlantic Region*
Management Recruiters International, Inc.
4231 Walnut Bend, Suite 1-D
Jacksonville, FL 32257
Telephone: (904) 260-4444
**Recruiter Classification:** Contingency; **Lowest/Average Salary:**
$30,000/$75,000; **Industry Concentration:** Generalist; **Function Concentration:** Generalist

**Lee, Donna M.** — *Vice President*
Kincannon & Reed
2106-C Gallows Road
Vienna, VA 22182
Telephone: (703) 761-4046
**Recruiter Classification:** Retained; **Lowest/Average Salary:** $90,000/$90,000;
**Industry Concentration:** Biotechnology; **Function Concentration:** Generalist

**Lee, Everett** — *Associate*
Source Services Corporation
5429 LBJ Freeway, Suite 275
Dallas, TX 75240
Telephone: (214) 387-1600
**Recruiter Classification:** Contingency; **Lowest/Average Salary:**
$30,000/$50,000; **Industry Concentration:** Financial Services, Information Technology; **Function Concentration:** Engineering, Finance/Accounting

**Lee, Janice** — *Executive Recruiter*
Summerfield Associates, Inc.
6555 Quince Road, Suite 311
Memphis, TN 38119
Telephone: (901) 753-7068
**Recruiter Classification:** Contingency; **Lowest/Average Salary:**
$30,000/$40,000; **Industry Concentration:** Generalist with a primary focus in Information Technology; **Function Concentration:** Human Resources

**Lee, Robert E.** — *Co-Manager*
Management Recruiters International, Inc.
4231 Walnut Bend, Suite 1-D
Jacksonville, FL 32257
Telephone: (904) 260-4444
**Recruiter Classification:** Contingency; **Lowest/Average Salary:**
$30,000/$75,000; **Industry Concentration:** Generalist; **Function Concentration:** Generalist

**Lee, Rodger A.** — *Principal*
Sanford Rose Associates
8941 Upper Lando Lane
Park City, UT 84098
Telephone: (801) 647-9755
**Recruiter Classification:** Contingency; **Lowest/Average Salary:**
$30,000/$75,000; **Industry Concentration:** Generalist; **Function Concentration:** Generalist

**Lee, Roger** — *Partner*
Montgomery Resources, Inc.
555 Montgomery Street, Suite 1650
San Francisco, CA 94111
Telephone: (415) 956-4242
**Recruiter Classification:** Contingency, Executive Temporary; **Lowest/Average Salary:** $30,000/$60,000; **Industry Concentration:** Generalist with a primary focus in Consumer Products, Financial Services, High Technology, Insurance, Manufacturing, Real Estate, Venture Capital; **Function Concentration:** Finance/Accounting

**Leetma, Imbi** — *Principal*
Stanton Chase International
10866 Wilshire Boulevard
Suite 870
Los Angeles, CA 90024
Telephone: (310) 474-1029
**Recruiter Classification:** Retained; **Lowest/Average Salary:** $75,000/$90,000; **Industry Concentration:** Generalist with a primary focus in Board Services, Consumer Products, Energy, Healthcare/Hospitals, Hospitality/Leisure, Insurance, Oil/Gas, Pharmaceutical/Medical, Publishing/Media, Venture Capital; **Function Concentration:** Generalist with a primary focus in Finance/Accounting, General Management, Human Resources, Marketing, Sales

**Lefebvre, Jean-Pierre** — *Partner*
Ward Howell International, Inc.
420 McGill Street, Room 400
Montreal, Quebec, CANADA H2Y 2G1
Telephone: (514) 397-9655
**Recruiter Classification:** Retained; **Lowest/Average Salary:** $75,000/$90,000; **Industry Concentration:** Generalist; **Function Concentration:** Generalist

**Leff, Lisa A.** — *President*
Berger and Leff
One Sansome Street, Suite 2100
San Francisco, CA 94104
Telephone: (415) 951-4750
**Recruiter Classification:** Contingency; **Lowest/Average Salary:** $40,000/$75,000; **Industry Concentration:** Generalist with a primary focus in Biotechnology, Electronics, Fashion (Retail/Apparel), Financial Services, Healthcare/Hospitals, High Technology, Information Technology, Manufacturing, Pharmaceutical/Medical, Real Estate; **Function Concentration:** Finance/Accounting

**Lehnst, Joh L.** — *Manager Midwest Region*
Management Recruiters International, Inc.
600 Court Street, P.O. Box 1136
Williamsburg, IA 52361-1136
Telephone: (319) 668-2881
**Recruiter Classification:** Contingency; **Lowest/Average Salary:** $30,000/$75,000; **Industry Concentration:** Generalist; **Function Concentration:** Generalist

**Leigh, Daniel S.** — *Branch Manager*
Accountants on Call
900-505 Burrard Street
Vancouver, British Columbia, CANADA V7X 1M4
Telephone: (604) 669-9096
**Recruiter Classification:** Contingency; **Lowest/Average Salary:** $20,000/$30,000; **Industry Concentration:** Generalist; **Function Concentration:** Finance/Accounting

**Leigh, Rebecca** — *Associate*
Source Services Corporation
9020 Capital of Texas Highway
Building I, Suite 337
Austin, TX 78759
Telephone: (512) 345-7473
**Recruiter Classification:** Contingency; **Lowest/Average Salary:** $30,000/$50,000; **Industry Concentration:** Financial Services, Information Technology; **Function Concentration:** Engineering, Finance/Accounting

**Leighton, Mark** — *Associate*
Source Services Corporation
1500 West Park Drive, Suite 390
Westborough, MA 01581
Telephone: (508) 366-2600
**Recruiter Classification:** Contingency; **Lowest/Average Salary:** $30,000/$50,000; **Industry Concentration:** Financial Services, Information Technology; **Function Concentration:** Engineering, Finance/Accounting

**Leininger, Dennis** — *Executive Vice President/ General Manager*
Key Employment Services
1001 Office Park Road, Suite 320
West Des Moines, IA 50265-2567
Telephone: (515) 224-0446
**Recruiter Classification:** Contingency; **Lowest/Average Salary:** $30,000/$75,000; **Industry Concentration:** Consumer Products, Financial Services, Information Technology, Insurance; **Function Concentration:** Engineering, Finance/Accounting, General Management, Human Resources, Marketing, Research and Development, Sales, Women/Minorities

**Lejeune, Jeanette** — *Executive Recruiter*
F-O-R-T-U-N-E Personnel Consultants of Huntsville, Inc.
3311 Bob Wallace Avenue, Suite 204
Huntsville, AL 35805
Telephone: (205) 534-7282
**Recruiter Classification:** Contingency; **Lowest/Average Salary:** $30,000/$50,000; **Industry Concentration:** Generalist with a primary focus in Aerospace/Defense, Automotive, Consumer Products, Electronics, Financial Services, High Technology, Information Technology, Manufacturing; **Function Concentration:** Administration, Finance/Accounting, Research and Development

**Leland, Paul** — *Vice President*
McInturff & Associates, Inc.
209 West Central Street
Natick, MA 01760
Telephone: (617) 237-0220
**Recruiter Classification:** Contingency; **Lowest/Average Salary:** $50,000/$50,000; **Industry Concentration:** Aerospace/Defense, Consumer Products, Electronics, Energy, High Technology, Information Technology, Manufacturing, Transportation; **Function Concentration:** General Management

**LeMay, Steven E.** — *President*
Saber Consultants
5300 Hollister, Suite 100
Houston, TX 77040
Telephone: (713) 462-6900
**Recruiter Classification:** Retained; **Lowest/Average Salary:** $40,000/$75,000; **Function Concentration:** Generalist

**Lemke, Peter K.** — *President*
EFL Associates
7101 College Boulevard, Suite 550
Overland Park, KS 66210-1891
Telephone: (913) 451-8866
**Recruiter Classification:** Retained; **Lowest/Average Salary:** $60,000/$90,000; **Industry Concentration:** Generalist; **Function Concentration:** Generalist

**LemMou, Paul** — *Staffing Consultant*
International Staffing Consultants, Inc.
500 Newport Center Drive, Suite 300
Newport Beach, CA 92660-7003
Telephone: (714) 721-7990
**Recruiter Classification:** Executive Temporary; **Lowest/Average Salary:** $50,000/$75,000; **Industry Concentration:** Generalist with a primary focus in Chemical Products, Energy, Environmental, High Technology, Information Technology, Oil/Gas; **Function Concentration:** Engineering

**Lemon, Kay** — *Manager Pacific Region*
Management Recruiters International, Inc.
150 Clovis Avenue, Suite 104
Clovis, CA 93612
Telephone: (209) 297-5900
**Recruiter Classification:** Contingency; **Lowest/Average Salary:** $30,000/$75,000; **Industry Concentration:** Generalist; **Function Concentration:** Generalist

**Lence, Julie Anne** — *Senior Physicians Consultant*
Spectra International Inc.
6991 East Camelback Road, Suite B-305
Scottsdale, AZ 85251
Telephone: (602) 481-0411
**Recruiter Classification:** Contingency; **Lowest/Average Salary:** $90,000/$90,000; **Industry Concentration:** Healthcare/Hospitals

**Lence, Julie Anne** — *Unit Manager*
MSI International
201 St. Charles Avenue
Suite 2205
New Orleans, LA 70170
Telephone: (504) 522-6700
**Recruiter Classification:** Contingency; **Lowest/Average Salary:** $30,000/$60,000; **Industry Concentration:** Generalist with a primary focus in Financial Services, Healthcare/Hospitals, High Technology, Information Technology, Manufacturing; **Function Concentration:** Generalist with a primary focus in Administration, Engineering, Finance/Accounting, General Management, Marketing, Sales

**Lenga, Bobbie** — *Associate*
Kenzer Corp.
625 North Michigan Avenue, Suite 1244
Chicago, IL 60611
Telephone: (312) 266-0976
**Recruiter Classification:** Retained; **Lowest/Average Salary:** $50,000/$90,000; **Industry Concentration:** Generalist; **Function Concentration:** Generalist

**Lenkaitis, Lewis F.** — *Vice President/Managing Director*
A.T. Kearney, Inc.
1200 Bank One Center
600 Superior Avenue, East
Cleveland, OH 44114-2650
Telephone: (216) 241-6880
**Recruiter Classification:** Retained; **Lowest/Average Salary:** $90,000/$90,000; **Industry Concentration:** Generalist with a primary focus in High Technology, Manufacturing; **Function Concentration:** Generalist with a primary focus in Administration, Engineering, General Management, Human Resources, Marketing, Research and Development, Sales

**Lennon, Roslyn J.** — *Consultant*
Heidrick & Struggles, Inc.
125 South Wacker Drive
Suite 2800
Chicago, IL 60606-4590
Telephone: (312) 372-8811
**Recruiter Classification:** Retained; **Lowest/Average Salary:** $75,000/$90,000; **Industry Concentration:** Generalist with a primary focus in Healthcare/Hospitals; **Function Concentration:** Generalist

**Lennox, Charles** — *Director*
Price Waterhouse
1 First Canadian Place, Box 190, Suite 3300
Toronto, Ontario, CANADA M5X 1H7
Telephone: (416) 863-1133
**Recruiter Classification:** Retained; **Lowest/Average Salary:** $60,000/$90,000; **Industry Concentration:** Generalist with a primary focus in Financial Services, Healthcare/Hospitals, High Technology, Information Technology, Manufacturing, Oil/Gas, Pharmaceutical/Medical; **Function Concentration:** Generalist

**Leon, Jeffrey J.** — *Managing Director*
Russell Reynolds Associates, Inc.
200 Park Avenue
New York, NY 10166-0002
Telephone: (212) 351-2000
**Recruiter Classification:** Retained; **Lowest/Average Salary:** $90,000/$90,000; **Industry Concentration:** Generalist with a primary focus in Information Technology; **Function Concentration:** Generalist

**Leonard, Linda** — *Senior Associate*
Harris Heery & Associates
40 Richards Avenue
One Norwalk West
Norwalk, CT 06854
Telephone: (203) 857-0808
**Recruiter Classification:** Retained; **Lowest/Average Salary:** $75,000/$90,000; **Industry Concentration:** Consumer Products, Fashion (Retail/Apparel), Financial Services, Insurance, Publishing/Media; **Function Concentration:** General Management, Marketing

**Lerner, Alyssa** — *Associate Recruiter*
Klein, Landau, Romm & North
1725 K Street NW, Suite 602
Washington, DC 20006
Telephone: (202) 728-0100
**Recruiter Classification:** Contingency; **Lowest/Average Salary:** $50,000/$90,000

**Lerner, Joel S.** — *Principal*
Sanford Rose Associates
2100 Gardiner Lane, Suite 107
Louisville, KY 40205
Telephone: (502) 451-4444
**Recruiter Classification:** Contingency; **Lowest/Average Salary:** $30,000/$75,000; **Industry Concentration:** Generalist; **Function Concentration:** Generalist

**Leske, Lucy A.** — *Vice President*
Educational Management Network
98 Old South Road
Nantucket, MA 02554
Telephone: (508) 228-6700
**Recruiter Classification:** Retained; **Lowest/Average Salary:** $60,000/$90,000; **Industry Concentration:** Education/Libraries, Non-Profit; **Function Concentration:** Administration, Finance/Accounting, Human Resources

**Leske, Lucy Apthorp** — *Vice President*
Educational Management Network
98 Old South Road
Nantucket, MA 02554
Telephone: (508) 228-6700
**Recruiter Classification:** Retained; **Lowest/Average Salary:** $60,000/$90,000; **Industry Concentration:** Education/Libraries, Non-Profit; **Function Concentration:** Generalist with a primary focus in Administration, Finance/Accounting, Human Resources

**LesKovec, Charles S.** — *Vice President Recruitment*
MDR Associates, Inc.
9360 Sunset Drive, Suite 250
Miami, FL 33173
Telephone: (305) 271-9213
**Recruiter Classification:** Retained; **Lowest/Average Salary:** $90,000/$90,000; **Industry Concentration:** Healthcare/Hospitals; **Function Concentration:** Generalist

**Leslie, William H.** — *Consultant*
Boyden/Zay & Company
Two Midtown Plaza, Suite 1740
1360 Peachtree Street, NE
Atlanta, GA 30309
Telephone: (404) 876-9986
**Recruiter Classification:** Retained; **Lowest/Average Salary:** $90,000/$90,000; **Industry Concentration:** Generalist with a primary focus in Chemical Products, Consumer Products, Financial Services, Insurance, Manufacturing, Packaging, Public Administration, Venture Capital; **Function Concentration:** Generalist with a primary focus in Administration, Engineering, Finance/Accounting, General Management, Human Resources, Marketing

**Leszynski, Edward** — *Business Manager*
ProResource, Inc.
520 South Main Street, Suite 2541
Akron, OH 44311
Telephone: (216) 434-6700
**Recruiter Classification:** Executive Temporary; **Lowest/Average Salary:** $30,000/$75,000; **Industry Concentration:** Generalist; **Function Concentration:** Generalist with a primary focus in Engineering, Finance/Accounting, General Management, Human Resources, Marketing, Research and Development

**Letcher, Harvey D.** — *Partner*
Sandhurst Associates
4851 LBJ Freeway, Suite 601
Dallas, TX 75244
Telephone: (214) 458-1212
**Recruiter Classification:** Retained; **Lowest/Average Salary:** $75,000/$90,000; **Industry Concentration:** Generalist with a primary focus in Consumer Products, Education/Libraries, Entertainment, Financial Services, Healthcare/Hospitals, High Technology, Hospitality/Leisure, Insurance, Manufacturing, Pharmaceutical/Medical, Real Estate, Transportation; **Function Concentration:** Generalist with a primary focus in Finance/Accounting, Human Resources, Marketing, Sales

**Letson, Susan** — *Principal*
KPMG Executive Search
Suite 1507, Purdy's Wharf
Tower One
Halifax, Nova Scotia, CANADA B3J 3N2
Telephone: (902) 492-6000
**Recruiter Classification:** Retained; **Lowest/Average Salary:** $75,000/$90,000; **Industry Concentration:** Generalist; **Function Concentration:** Generalist

**Lettrii, Mary** — *Director Research*
BioQuest, Inc.
100 Spear Street, Suite 1125
San Francisco, CA 94105
Telephone: (415) 777-2422
**Recruiter Classification:** Retained; **Lowest/Average Salary:** $75,000/$90,000; **Industry Concentration:** Biotechnology, Pharmaceutical/Medical; **Function Concentration:** Engineering, Finance/Accounting, General Management, Marketing, Research and Development, Sales

**Levenson, Laurel** — *Managing Director*
Source Services Corporation
4510 Executive Drive, Suite 200
San Diego, CA 92121
Telephone: (619) 552-0300
**Recruiter Classification:** Contingency; **Lowest/Average Salary:** $30,000/$50,000; **Industry Concentration:** Financial Services, Information Technology; **Function Concentration:** Engineering, Finance/Accounting

**Levine, Alan M.** — *President*
MB Inc. Interim Executive Division
505 Fifth Avenue
New York, NY 10017
Telephone: (212) 661-4937
**Recruiter Classification:** Executive Temporary; **Lowest/Average Salary:** $75,000/$90,000; **Industry Concentration:** Generalist with a primary focus in Consumer Products, Financial Services, Pharmaceutical/Medical; **Function Concentration:** Finance/Accounting, General Management, Marketing, Sales

**Levine, Irwin** — *Associate*
Source Services Corporation
2 Penn Plaza, Suite 1176
New York, NY 10121
Telephone: (212) 760-2200
**Recruiter Classification:** Contingency; **Lowest/Average Salary:** $30,000/$50,000; **Industry Concentration:** Financial Services, Information Technology; **Function Concentration:** Engineering, Finance/Accounting

**Levine, Lois** — *Medical Consultant*
National Search, Inc.
2816 University Drive
Coral Springs, FL 33071
Telephone: (800) 935-4355
**Recruiter Classification:** Contingency; **Lowest/Average Salary:**
$30,000/$50,000; **Industry Concentration:** Healthcare/Hospitals, Insurance,
Pharmaceutical/Medical; **Function Concentration:** Generalist with a primary
focus in Administration, Finance/Accounting, General Management, Human
Resources, Marketing, Research and Development, Sales, Women/Minorities

**Levinson, Lauren** — *Partner*
The Danbrook Group, Inc.
14180 Dallas Parkway, Suite 400
Dallas, TX 75240
Telephone: (214) 392-0057
**Recruiter Classification:** Contingency; **Lowest/Average Salary:**
$30,000/$50,000; **Industry Concentration:** Insurance; **Function
Concentration:** Generalist with a primary focus in Administration,
Finance/Accounting, General Management, Marketing, Sales

**Levitt, Bob** — *Manager Eastern Region*
Management Recruiters International, Inc.
33 Walt Whitman Road, Suite 107
Huntington Station, NY 11746-3627
Telephone: (516) 385-0633
**Recruiter Classification:** Contingency; **Lowest/Average Salary:**
$30,000/$75,000; **Industry Concentration:** Generalist; **Function
Concentration:** Generalist

**Levitt, Muriel A.** — *Vice President*
D.S. Allen Associates, Inc.
7 Pointe San Pablo, Suite 400
Laguna Niguel, CA 92677
Telephone: (714) 363-1505
**Recruiter Classification:** Contingency; **Lowest/Average Salary:** $/$90,000;
**Industry Concentration:** Generalist with a primary focus in Entertainment,
High Technology, Information ; **Function Concentration:** Generalist with a
primary focus in Engineering, General Management, Marketing

**Levy, Carlotta** — *Consultant - L.A. Wholesale*
Evie Kreisler & Associates, Inc.
865 South Figueroa, Suite 950
Los Angeles, CA 90017
Telephone: (213) 622-8994
**Recruiter Classification:** Contingency; **Lowest/Average Salary:**
$30,000/$75,000; **Industry Concentration:** Fashion (Retail/Apparel); **Function
Concentration:** Generalist

**Lew, Charles E.** — *President*
Coleman Lew & Associates, Inc.
326 West Tenth Street
Charlotte, NC 28202
Telephone: (704) 377-0362
**Recruiter Classification:** Retained; **Lowest/Average Salary:** $/$90,000; **Industry
Concentration:** Generalist; **Function Concentration:** Generalist

**Lewicki, Christopher** — *Manager*
MSI International
8521 Leesburg Pike, Suite 435
Vienna, VA 22182
Telephone: (703) 893-5669
**Recruiter Classification:** Contingency; **Lowest/Average Salary:**
$30,000/$60,000; **Industry Concentration:** Generalist with a primary focus in
Financial Services, Healthcare/Hospitals, High Technology, Information
Technology, Manufacturing; **Function Concentration:** Administration,
Engineering, Finance/Accounting, General Management, Marketing

**Lewis, Charles G.** — *Principal*
Longshore & Simmons, Inc.
Plymouth Corporate Center
625 Ridge Pike, Suite 410
Conshohocken, PA 19428-3216
Telephone: (610) 941-3400
**Recruiter Classification:** Retained; **Lowest/Average Salary:** $50,000/$90,000;
**Industry Concentration:** Healthcare/Hospitals; **Function Concentration:**
Generalist

**Lewis, Daniel** — *Associate*
Source Services Corporation
2000 Town Center, Suite 850
Southfield, MI 48075
Telephone: (810) 352-6520
**Recruiter Classification:** Contingency; **Lowest/Average Salary:**
$30,000/$50,000; **Industry Concentration:** Financial Services, Information
Technology; **Function Concentration:** Engineering, Finance/Accounting

**Lewis, Gretchen S.** — *Partner*
Heidrick & Struggles, Inc.
2740 Sand Hill Road
Menlo Park, CA 94025
Telephone: (415) 854-9300
**Recruiter Classification:** Retained; **Lowest/Average Salary:** $75,000/$90,000;
**Industry Concentration:** Generalist with a primary focus in High Technology;
**Function Concentration:** Generalist

**Lewis, John** — *Co-Manager*
Management Recruiters International, Inc.
5701 Westpark Drive, Suite 110
Charlotte, NC 28217
Telephone: (704) 525-9270
**Recruiter Classification:** Contingency; **Lowest/Average Salary:**
$30,000/$75,000; **Industry Concentration:** Generalist; **Function
Concentration:** Generalist

**Lewis, Jon A.** — *Associate*
Sandhurst Associates
4851 LBJ Freeway, Suite 601
Dallas, TX 75244
Telephone: (212) 458-1212
**Recruiter Classification:** Retained; **Lowest/Average Salary:** $75,000/$90,000;
**Industry Concentration:** Generalist with a primary focus in Consumer
Products, Education/Libraries, Entertainment, Financial Services,
Healthcare/Hospitals, High Technology, Hospitality/Leisure, Information
Technology, Insurance, Manufacturing, Pharmaceutical/Medical, Real Estate,
Transportation, Venture Capital; **Function Concentration:** Generalist with a
primary focus in Administration, Finance/Accounting, General Management,
Human Resources, Marketing, Sales

**Lewis, Marc D.** — *Senior Vice President*
Handy HRM Corp.
250 Park Avenue
New York, NY 10177-0074
Telephone: (212) 557-0400
**Recruiter Classification:** Retained; **Lowest/Average Salary:** $90,000/$90,000;
**Industry Concentration:** Generalist with a primary focus in Financial Services,
High Technology, Real Estate, Venture Capital; **Function Concentration:**
Generalist with a primary focus in Finance/Accounting, General Management

**Lewis, Mark** — *Manager Eastern Region*
Management Recruiters International, Inc.
22 Liberty Street, P.O. Box 728
Bath, NY 14810-0728
Telephone: (607) 776-5316
**Recruiter Classification:** Contingency; **Lowest/Average Salary:**
$30,000/$75,000; **Industry Concentration:** Generalist; **Function
Concentration:** Generalist

**Lewis, Richard A.** — *Consultant*
Cole, Warren & Long, Inc.
2 Penn Center, Suite 312
Philadelphia, PA 19102
Telephone: (215) 563-0701
**Recruiter Classification:** Retained; **Lowest/Average Salary:** $90,000/$90,000;
**Industry Concentration:** Generalist; **Function Concentration:** Generalist

**Lewis, Sandee** — *Sales Consultant*
Southwestern Professional Services
2451 Atrium Way
Nashville, TN 37214
Telephone: (615) 391-2722
**Recruiter Classification:** Contingency; **Lowest/Average Salary:**
$30,000/$40,000; **Industry Concentration:** Generalist; **Function
Concentration:** Sales

**Lewis, Sean** — *Leasing/Finance Specialist*
Southwestern Professional Services
2451 Atrium Way
Nashville, TN 37214
Telephone: (615) 391-2722
**Recruiter Classification:** Contingency; **Lowest/Average Salary:**
$90,000/$90,000; **Industry Concentration:** Generalist with a primary focus in
Financial Services; **Function Concentration:** Sales

**Lewis, Susan** — *Consultant*
Logix, Inc.
1601 Trapelo Road
Waltham, MA 02154
Telephone: (617) 890-0500
**Recruiter Classification:** Retained; **Lowest/Average Salary:** $60,000/$75,000;
**Industry Concentration:** High Technology; **Function Concentration:**
Engineering

**Lewis, Susan** — *Consultant*
Logix Partners
1601 Trapelo Road
Waltham, MA 02154
Telephone: (617) 890-0500
**Recruiter Classification:** Retained; **Lowest/Average Salary:** $60,000/$75,000;
**Industry Concentration:** High Technology; **Function Concentration:** Engineering

**Libes, Dory** — *Senior Vice President*
Accountants on Call
Park 80 West, Plaza II, 9th Fl.
Garden State Parkway/I-80
Saddle Brook, NJ 07662
Telephone: (201) 843-0006
**Recruiter Classification:** Contingency; **Lowest/Average Salary:**
$20,000/$30,000; **Industry Concentration:** Generalist; **Function
Concentration:** Finance/Accounting

**Libes, Mark S.** — *Manager*
Accountants on Call
1600 Market Street, Suite 1418
Philadelphia, PA 19103
Telephone: (215) 568-5600
**Recruiter Classification:** Contingency; **Lowest/Average Salary:** $20,000/$30,000;
**Industry Concentration:** Generalist; **Function Concentration:** Finance/Accounting

**Libes, Mark S.** — *Manager*
Accountants on Call
Valley Forge Plaza, Suite 1005
1150 First Avenue
King of Prussia, PA 19406
Telephone: (610) 337-8500
**Recruiter Classification:** Contingency; **Lowest/Average Salary:**
$20,000/$30,000; **Industry Concentration:** Generalist; **Function
Concentration:** Finance/Accounting

**Libes, Mark S.** — *Manager*
Accountants on Call
Telephone: (609) 596-9200
**Recruiter Classification:** Contingency; **Lowest/Average Salary:**
$20,000/$30,000; **Industry Concentration:** Generalist; **Function
Concentration:** Finance/Accounting

**Libes, Stewart C.** — *President*
Accountants on Call
Park 80 West, Plaza II, 9th Fl.
Garden State Parkway/I-80
Saddle Brook, NJ 07662
Telephone: (201) 843-0006
**Recruiter Classification:** Contingency; **Lowest/Average Salary:**
$20,000/$30,000; **Industry Concentration:** Generalist; **Function
Concentration:** Finance/Accounting

**Lichtenauer, William E.** — *President*
Britt Associates, Inc.
2709 Black Road
Joliet, IL 60435
Telephone: (815) 744-7200
**Recruiter Classification:** Contingency; **Lowest/Average Salary:**
$30,000/$60,000; **Industry Concentration:** Generalist

**Lichtenstein, Ben** — *Senior Partner*
Alexander Ross Inc.
280 Madison Avenue
New York, NY 10016
Telephone: (212) 889-9333
**Recruiter Classification:** Retained; **Lowest/Average Salary:** $75,000/$90,000;
**Industry Concentration:** Generalist; **Function Concentration:** Human Resources

**Lieb, Donald F.** — *Managing Director*
Russell Reynolds Associates, Inc.
1900 Trammell Crow Center
2001 Ross Avenue
Dallas, TX 75201
Telephone: (214) 220-2033
**Recruiter Classification:** Retained; **Lowest/Average Salary:** $90,000/$90,000;
**Industry Concentration:** Generalist with a primary focus in Energy; **Function
Concentration:** Generalist

**Lieberman, Beverly** — *President*
Halbrecht Lieberman Associates, Inc.
1200 Summer Street
Stamford, CT 06905
Telephone: (203) 327-5630
**Recruiter Classification:** Retained; **Lowest/Average Salary:** $90,000/$90,000;
**Industry Concentration:** High Technology, Information Technology; **Function
Concentration:** Generalist

**Liebowitz, Michael E.** — *Associate*
Highland Search Group, L.L.C.
565 Fifth Avenue, 22nd Floor
New York, NY 10017
Telephone: (212) 328-1113
**Recruiter Classification:** Retained; **Lowest/Average Salary:** $90,000/$90,000;
**Industry Concentration:** Financial Services; **Function Concentration:**
Generalist with a primary focus in Finance/Accounting, General Management,
Sales

**Liebross, Eric** — *Associate*
Source Services Corporation
1 Gatehall Drive, Suite 250
Parsippany, NJ 07054
Telephone: (201) 267-3222
**Recruiter Classification:** Contingency; **Lowest/Average Salary:**
$30,000/$50,000; **Industry Concentration:** Financial Services, Information
Technology; **Function Concentration:** Engineering, Finance/Accounting

**Lightner, Shayne** — *Senior Associate*
Korn/Ferry International
1800 Century Park East, Suite 900
Los Angeles, CA 90067
Telephone: (310) 552-1834
**Recruiter Classification:** Retained; **Lowest/Average Salary:** $90,000/$90,000;
**Industry Concentration:** Generalist with a primary focus in Entertainment;
**Function Concentration:** Generalist

**Liles, J.D.** — *Manager North Atlantic Region*
Management Recruiters International, Inc.
P.O. Box 5330
Emerald Isle, NC 28594
Telephone: (919) 354-7600
**Recruiter Classification:** Contingency; **Lowest/Average Salary:**
$30,000/$75,000; **Industry Concentration:** Generalist; **Function
Concentration:** Generalist

**Lin, Felix** — *Associate*
Source Services Corporation
879 West 190th Street, Suite 250
Los Angeles, CA 90248
Telephone: (310) 323-6633
**Recruiter Classification:** Contingency; **Lowest/Average Salary:**
$30,000/$50,000; **Industry Concentration:** Financial Services, Information
Technology; **Function Concentration:** Engineering, Finance/Accounting

**Lincoln, Thomas C.** — *President*
Oppedisano & Company, Inc.
370 Lexington Avenue, Suite 1200
New York, NY 10017
Telephone: (212) 696-0144
**Recruiter Classification:** Retained; **Lowest/Average Salary:** $/$90,000; **Industry
Concentration:** Financial Services; **Function Concentration:** Generalist with a
primary focus in Finance/Accounting

**Lindberg, Eric J.** — *President and CEO*
MSI International
2500 Marquis One Tower
245 Peachtree Center Ave.
Atlanta, GA 30303
Telephone: (404) 659-5236
**Recruiter Classification:** Contingency; **Lowest/Average Salary:**
$30,000/$60,000; **Industry Concentration:** Generalist with a primary focus in
Financial Services, Healthcare/Hospitals, High Technology, Information
Technology, Manufacturing; **Function Concentration:** Generalist with a
primary focus in Administration, Engineering, Finance/Accounting, General
Management, Marketing, Sales

**Linde, Rick** — *Vice President*
Battalia Winston International
300 Park Avenue
New York, NY 10022
Telephone: (212) 308-8080
**Recruiter Classification:** Retained; **Lowest/Average Salary:** $90,000/$90,000;
**Industry Concentration:** Generalist with a primary focus in Consumer
Products, Entertainment, Healthcare/Hospitals, Manufacturing, Non-Profit,
Pharmaceutical/Medical, Publishing/Media, Real Estate; **Function
Concentration:** Generalist with a primary focus in Finance/Accounting,
General Management, Human Resources, Marketing, Sales

**Lindegren, Joan** — *Human Resources Contracts Recruiter*
Winter, Wyman & Company
950 Winter Street, Suite 3100
Waltham, MA 02154-1294
Telephone: (617) 890-7000
**Recruiter Classification:** Contingency; **Lowest/Average Salary:**
$30,000/$50,000; **Industry Concentration:** Generalist; **Function
Concentration:** Human Resources

**Lindenmuth, Mary** — *Account Executive*
Search West, Inc.
750 The City Drive South
Suite 100
Orange, CA 92668-4940
Telephone: (714) 748-0400
**Recruiter Classification:** Contingency; **Lowest/Average Salary:** $40,000/$60,000; **Industry Concentration:** Biotechnology, Chemical Products, Consumer Products, Electronics, Fashion (Retail/Apparel), High Technology, Manufacturing, Pharmaceutical/Medical; **Function Concentration:** Administration, Finance/Accounting, General Management

**Lindholst, Kai** — *Managing Partner*
Egon Zehnder International Inc.
One First National Plaza
21 South Clark Street, Suite 3300
Chicago, IL 60603-2006
Telephone: (312) 782-4500
**Recruiter Classification:** Retained; **Lowest/Average Salary:** $90,000/$90,000; **Industry Concentration:** Generalist with a primary focus in Biotechnology, Financial Services, High Technology, Manufacturing, Pharmaceutical/Medical; **Function Concentration:** Generalist

**Lindsay, M. Evan** — *Partner*
Heidrick & Struggles, Inc.
One Peachtree Center
303 Peachtree Street, NE, Suite 3100
Atlanta, GA 30308
Telephone: (404) 577-2410
**Recruiter Classification:** Retained; **Lowest/Average Salary:** $75,000/$90,000; **Industry Concentration:** Generalist with a primary focus in Financial Services, Healthcare/Hospitals; **Function Concentration:** Generalist

**Lindsay, Mary** — *Senior Consultant*
Norm Sanders Associates
2 Village Court
Hazlet, NJ 07730
Telephone: (908) 264-3700
**Recruiter Classification:** Retained; **Lowest/Average Salary:** $90,000/$90,000; **Industry Concentration:** Information Technology; **Function Concentration:** Generalist

**Line, Joseph T.** — *Vice President*
Sharrow & Associates
24735 Van Dyke
Center Line, MI 48015
Telephone: (810) 759-6910
**Recruiter Classification:** Contingency; **Lowest/Average Salary:** $30,000/$50,000; **Industry Concentration:** Aerospace/Defense, Automotive, Chemical Products, Consumer Products, Electronics, Energy, Fashion (Retail/Apparel), Healthcare/Hospitals, High Technology, Hospitality/Leisure, Insurance, Manufacturing, Pharmaceutical/Medical, Real Estate, Transportation

**Lineback, Pam** — *Manager Southwest Region*
Management Recruiters International, Inc.
13101 Preston Road, Suite 560
Dallas, TX 75240
Telephone: (214) 788-1515
**Recruiter Classification:** Contingency; **Lowest/Average Salary:** $30,000/$75,000; **Industry Concentration:** Generalist; **Function Concentration:** Generalist

**Lineback, Robert** — *General Manager*
Management Recruiters International, Inc.
13101 Preston Road, Suite 560
Dallas, TX 75240
Telephone: (214) 788-1515
**Recruiter Classification:** Contingency; **Lowest/Average Salary:** $30,000/$75,000; **Industry Concentration:** Generalist; **Function Concentration:** Generalist

**Lineback, Robert** — *Manager Southwest Region*
Management Recruiters International, Inc.
13101 Preston Road, Suite 560
Dallas, TX 75240
Telephone: (214) 788-1515
**Recruiter Classification:** Contingency; **Lowest/Average Salary:** $30,000/$75,000; **Industry Concentration:** Generalist; **Function Concentration:** Generalist

**Linton, Leonard M.** — *President*
Byron Leonard International, Inc.
2659 Townsgate Road, Suite 100
Westlake Village, CA 91361
Telephone: (805) 373-7500
**Recruiter Classification:** Retained; **Lowest/Average Salary:** $60,000/$90,000; **Industry Concentration:** Generalist with a primary focus in Aerospace/Defense, Biotechnology, Electronics, Financial Services, Healthcare/Hospitals, High Technology, Information Technology, Manufacturing; **Function Concentration:** Generalist with a primary focus in Administration, Engineering, Finance/Accounting, General Management, Human Resources, Marketing, Research and Development, Sales

**Lipe, Jerold L.** — *Vice President*
Compass Group Ltd.
Two Mid-America Plaza, Suite 800 South
Oakbrook Terrace, IL 60181
Telephone: (708) 954-2255
**Recruiter Classification:** Retained; **Lowest/Average Salary:** $75,000/$90,000; **Industry Concentration:** Automotive, Chemical Products, Education/Libraries, Electronics, Information Technology, Manufacturing, Transportation; **Function Concentration:** Engineering, General Management, Human Resources, Sales, Women/Minorities

**Lippman, Lloyd A.** — *President*
Career Management International
197 Route 18
East Brunswick, NJ 08816
Telephone: (908) 937-4800
**Recruiter Classification:** Retained; **Lowest/Average Salary:** $75,000/$90,000; **Industry Concentration:** Fashion (Retail/Apparel); **Function Concentration:** Generalist with a primary focus in Administration, Finance/Accounting, General Management, Human Resources, Marketing

**Lipuma, Thomas** — *Associate*
Source Services Corporation
1 Gatehall Drive, Suite 250
Parsippany, NJ 07054
Telephone: (201) 267-3222
**Recruiter Classification:** Contingency; **Lowest/Average Salary:** $30,000/$50,000; **Industry Concentration:** Financial Services, Information Technology; **Function Concentration:** Engineering, Finance/Accounting

**Lissy, Elaine** — *Consultant*
Paul Ray Berndtson
2029 Century Park East
Suite 1000
Los Angeles, CA 90067
Telephone: (310) 557-2828
**Recruiter Classification:** Retained; **Lowest/Average Salary:** $90,000/$90,000; **Industry Concentration:** Generalist; **Function Concentration:** Generalist

**Litchfield, Barbara H.** — *Principal*
Litchfield & Willis Inc.
3900 Essex at Weslayan
Suite 650
Houston, TX 77027
Telephone: (713) 439-8200
**Recruiter Classification:** Executive Temporary; **Lowest/Average Salary:** $50,000/$60,000; **Industry Concentration:** Generalist; **Function Concentration:** Generalist

**Litt-Peck, Michelle** — *Senior Consultant*
The Whitney Group
850 Third Avenue, 11th Floor
New York, NY 10022
Telephone: (212) 508-3500
**Recruiter Classification:** Retained; **Lowest/Average Salary:** $75,000/$90,000; **Industry Concentration:** Generalist with a primary focus in Financial Services, Real Estate, Venture Capital; **Function Concentration:** Generalist with a primary focus in Sales

**Little, Elizabeth A.** — *Associate*
Financial Resource Associates, Inc.
105 West Orange Street
Altamonte Springs, FL 32714
Telephone: (407) 869-7000
**Recruiter Classification:** Contingency; **Lowest/Average Salary:** $40,000/$60,000; **Industry Concentration:** Financial Services, Information Technology; **Function Concentration:** Finance/Accounting, Sales

**Little, Gary** — *Agribusiness Recruiter*
Agra Placements International Ltd.
2200 North Kickapoo, Suite 2
Lincoln, IL 62656
Telephone: (217) 735-4373
**Recruiter Classification:** Contingency; **Lowest/Average Salary:** $20,000/$30,000; **Industry Concentration:** Generalist with a primary focus in Biotechnology, Chemical Products, Energy, Financial Services, Manufacturing; **Function Concentration:** Administration, Engineering, Finance/Accounting, General Management, Human Resources, Marketing, Research and Development, Sales

**Little, Suzaane** — *Executive Recruiter*
Don Richard Associates of Tampa, Inc.
100 North Tampa Street, Suite 1925
Tampa, FL 33602
Telephone: (813) 221-7930
**Recruiter Classification:** Contingency, Executive Temporary; **Lowest/Average Salary:** $20,000/$50,000; **Industry Concentration:** Generalist with a primary focus in Fashion (Retail/Apparel), Financial Services, Hospitality/Leisure, Information Technology, Publishing/Media, Real Estate, Transportation, Utilities/Nuclear; **Function Concentration:** Generalist with a primary focus in Administration, Finance/Accounting

**Littman, Stephen** — *Managing Partner*
Rhodes Associates
555 Fifth Avenue
New York, NY 10017
Telephone: (212) 983-2000
**Recruiter Classification:** Retained; **Lowest/Average Salary:** $90,000/$90,000;
**Industry Concentration:** Financial Services, Insurance, Real Estate, Venture
Capital; **Function Concentration:** Generalist

**Livesay, Christopher C.** — *Physician Recruiter*
MSI International
6345 Balboa Boulevard
Suite 335
Encino, CA 91316
Telephone: (818) 342-0222
**Recruiter Classification:** Contingency; **Lowest/Average Salary:**
$30,000/$75,000; **Industry Concentration:** Generalist with a primary focus in
Healthcare/Hospitals, Pharmaceutical/Medical; **Function Concentration:**
Generalist with a primary focus in Administration, Engineering,
Finance/Accounting, General Management, Marketing, Sales

**Livingston, Peter R.** — *President*
Livingston, Robert and Company Inc.
Two Greenwich Plaza
Greenwich, CT 06830
Telephone: (203) 622-4901
**Recruiter Classification:** Retained; **Lowest/Average Salary:** $90,000/$90,000;
**Industry Concentration:** Generalist with a primary focus in Chemical Products,
Consumer Products, Fashion (Retail/Apparel), Financial Services, High
Technology, Pharmaceutical/Medical; **Function Concentration:** Generalist

**Livolsi, Sebastian F.** — *Manager Eastern Region*
Management Recruiters International, Inc.
225 Main Street, Suite 204
Northport, NY 11768
Telephone: (516) 261-0400
**Recruiter Classification:** Contingency; **Lowest/Average Salary:**
$30,000/$75,000; **Industry Concentration:** Generalist; **Function
Concentration:** Generalist

**Llaguno, Juan F.** — *Managing Director*
Korn/Ferry International
Daniel Zambrano 525
Col. Chepe Vera
Monterrey, N.L., MEXICO 11000
Telephone: (528) 348-4355
**Recruiter Classification:** Retained; **Lowest/Average Salary:** $90,000/$90,000;
**Industry Concentration:** Generalist; **Function Concentration:** Generalist

**Lloyd, John S.** — *Vice Chairman*
Witt/Kieffer, Ford, Hadelman & Lloyd
2015 Spring Road, Suite 510
Oak Brook, IL 60521
Telephone: (708) 990-1370
**Recruiter Classification:** Retained; **Lowest/Average Salary:** $75,000/$90,000;
**Industry Concentration:** Healthcare/Hospitals; **Function Concentration:**
Generalist with a primary focus in General Management, Human Resources

**Loeb, Stephen H.** — *President*
Grant Cooper and Associates
795 Office Parkway, Suite 117
St. Louis, MO 63141
Telephone: (314) 567-4690
**Recruiter Classification:** Retained; **Lowest/Average Salary:** $60,000/$90,000;
**Industry Concentration:** Generalist with a primary focus in Board Services,
Consumer Products, Electronics, Financial Services, Healthcare/Hospitals,
Manufacturing, Non-Profit, Pharmaceutical/Medical; **Function Concentration:**
Generalist with a primary focus in Administration, Engineering,
Finance/Accounting, General Management, Human Resources, Marketing, Sales

**Loewenstein, Victor H.** — *Managing Partner*
Egon Zehnder International Inc.
55 East 59th Street, 14th Floor
New York, NY 10022
Telephone: (212) 838-9199
**Recruiter Classification:** Retained; **Lowest/Average Salary:** $90,000/$90,000;
**Industry Concentration:** Generalist with a primary focus in Biotechnology,
Financial Services, High Technology, Manufacturing, Pharmaceutical/Medical;
**Function Concentration:** Generalist

**Lofthouse, Cindy** — *Executive Recruiter*
CPS Inc.
One Westbrook Corporate Centre, Suite 600
Westchester, IL 60154
Telephone: (708) 531-8370
**Recruiter Classification:** Contingency; **Lowest/Average Salary:**
$30,000/$50,000; **Industry Concentration:** Generalist with a primary focus in
Automotive, Biotechnology, Chemical Products, Consumer Products, High
Technology, Insurance, Manufacturing, Oil/Gas, Packaging,
Pharmaceutical/Medical; **Function Concentration:** Engineering, Research and
Development, Sales, Women/Minorities

**Logan, Valarie A.** — *Manager Research and Recruiting*
D.S.A. - Dixie Search Associates
501 Village Trace, Building 9
Marietta, GA 30067
Telephone: (770) 850-0250
**Recruiter Classification:** Contingency; **Lowest/Average Salary:**
$30,000/$50,000; **Industry Concentration:** Biotechnology, Consumer
Products, Hospitality/Leisure, Manufacturing, Packaging, Transportation;
**Function Concentration:** Generalist with a primary focus in Engineering,
Finance/Accounting, General Management, Human Resources, Marketing,
Research and Development, Sales

**Logue, Kenneth F.** — *Principal*
Logue & Rice Inc.
8000 Towers Crescent Drive
Suite 650
Vienna, VA 22182-2700
Telephone: (703) 761-4261
**Recruiter Classification:** Contingency; **Lowest/Average Salary:**
$40,000/$90,000; **Industry Concentration:** Generalist with a primary focus in
Education/Libraries; **Function Concentration:** Generalist with a primary focus
in Administration, Finance/Accounting, General Management, Human
Resources, Women/Minorities

**Lombardi, Nancy W.** — *Vice President*
WTW Associates
675 Third Avenue, Suite 2808
New York, NY 10017
Telephone: (212) 972-6990
**Recruiter Classification:** Retained; **Lowest/Average Salary:** $75,000/$90,000;
**Industry Concentration:** Generalist with a primary focus in Entertainment,
Financial Services; **Function Concentration:** Generalist

**London, Gregory J.** — *Executive Recruiter*
MSI International
229 Peachtree Street, NE
Suite 1201
Atlanta, GA 30303
Telephone: (404) 659-5050
**Recruiter Classification:** Contingency; **Lowest/Average Salary:**
$30,000/$75,000; **Industry Concentration:** Generalist with a primary focus in
Healthcare/Hospitals, Pharmaceutical/Medical; **Function Concentration:**
Generalist with a primary focus in Administration, Engineering,
Finance/Accounting, General Management, Marketing, Sales

**Lonergan, Mark W.** — *Partner*
Heidrick & Struggles, Inc.
2740 Sand Hill Road
Menlo Park, CA 94025
Telephone: (415) 854-9300
**Recruiter Classification:** Retained; **Lowest/Average Salary:** $75,000/$90,000;
**Industry Concentration:** Generalist with a primary focus in High Technology;
**Function Concentration:** Generalist

**Long, Benjamin H.** — *President*
Travaille Executive Search
1730 Rhode Island Avenue NW, Suite 401
Washington, DC 20036
Telephone: (202) 463-6342
**Recruiter Classification:** Contingency; **Lowest/Average Salary:**
$50,000/$90,000; **Industry Concentration:** Generalist with a primary focus in
Aerospace/Defense, Automotive, Biotechnology, Environmental, High
Technology, Publishing/Media; **Function Concentration:** Marketing

**Long, Helga** — *President*
H.M. Long International, Ltd.
237 Park Avenue, 21st Floor
New York, NY 10017
Telephone: (212) 725-5150
**Recruiter Classification:** Retained; **Lowest/Average Salary:** $90,000/$90,000;
**Industry Concentration:** Generalist with a primary focus in Biotechnology,
Consumer Products, Electronics, Financial Services, Pharmaceutical/Medical;
**Function Concentration:** Generalist with a primary focus in Administration,
Engineering, General Management, Human Resources, Marketing, Research
and Development

**Long, John** — *Associate*
Source Services Corporation
4200 West Cypress Street, Suite 101
Tampa, FL 33607
Telephone: (813) 879-2221
**Recruiter Classification:** Contingency; **Lowest/Average Salary:**
$30,000/$50,000; **Industry Concentration:** Financial Services, Information
Technology; **Function Concentration:** Engineering, Finance/Accounting

**Long, John P.** — *Managing Director*
John J. Davis & Associates, Inc.
521 Fifth Avenue, Suite 1740
New York, NY 10175
Telephone: (212) 286-9489
**Recruiter Classification:** Retained; **Lowest/Average Salary:** $90,000/$90,000;
**Industry Concentration:** Information Technology; **Function Concentration:**
Generalist with a primary focus in General Management

**Long, Mark** — *Associate*
Source Services Corporation
111 Monument Circle, Suite 3930
Indianapolis, IN 46204
Telephone: (317) 631-2900
**Recruiter Classification:** Contingency; **Lowest/Average Salary:**
$30,000/$50,000; **Industry Concentration:** Financial Services, Information
Technology; **Function Concentration:** Engineering, Finance/Accounting

**Long, Melanie** — *Senior Medical Consultant*
National Search, Inc.
2816 University Drive
Coral Springs, FL 33071
Telephone: (800) 935-4355
**Recruiter Classification:** Contingency; **Lowest/Average Salary:**
$30,000/$50,000; **Industry Concentration:** Healthcare/Hospitals, Insurance,
Pharmaceutical/Medical; **Function Concentration:** Generalist with a primary
focus in Administration, Finance/Accounting, General Management, Human
Resources, Marketing, Research and Development, Sales,
Women/Minorities

**Long, Thomas** — *Managing Partner*
Egon Zehnder International Inc.
1 First Canadian Place
P.O. Box 179
Toronto, Ontario, CANADA M5X 1C7
Telephone: (416) 364-0222
**Recruiter Classification:** Retained; **Lowest/Average Salary:** $90,000/$90,000;
**Industry Concentration:** Generalist with a primary focus in Biotechnology,
Financial Services, High Technology, Manufacturing, Pharmaceutical/Medical;
**Function Concentration:** Generalist

**Long, William G.** — *President*
McDonald, Long & Associates, Inc.
670 White Plains Road
Scarsdale, NY 10583
Telephone: (914) 723-5400
**Recruiter Classification:** Retained, Executive Temporary; **Lowest/Average
Salary:** $75,000/$90,000; **Industry Concentration:** Generalist with a primary
focus in Chemical Products, Consumer Products, Electronics, Financial
Services, High Technology, Information Technology, Insurance, Manufacturing,
Non-Profit, Pharmaceutical/Medical, Publishing/Media, Real Estate, Venture
Capital; **Function Concentration:** Generalist with a primary focus in
Administration, Engineering, Finance/Accounting, General Management,
Human Resources, Marketing, Sales, Women/Minorities

**Longmore, Marilyn** — *Vice President*
Richard Kader & Associates
343 West Bagley Road, Suite 209
Berea, OH 44017
Telephone: (216) 891-1700
**Recruiter Classification:** Contingency; **Lowest/Average Salary:**
$40,000/$50,000; **Industry Concentration:** Generalist with a primary focus in
Consumer Products, Healthcare/Hospitals, Pharmaceutical/Medical; **Function
Concentration:** Generalist with a primary focus in Marketing, Sales,
Women/Minorities

**Longoria, Janine** — *Associate*
Russell Reynolds Associates, Inc.
200 South Wacker Drive
Suite 3600
Chicago, IL 60606
Telephone: (312) 993-9696
**Recruiter Classification:** Retained; **Lowest/Average Salary:** $90,000/$90,000;
**Industry Concentration:** Generalist; **Function Concentration:** Generalist

**Longshore, George F.** — *President*
Longshore & Simmons, Inc.
Plymouth Corporate Center
625 Ridge Pike, Suite 410
Conshohocken, PA 19428-3216
Telephone: (610) 941-3400
**Recruiter Classification:** Retained; **Lowest/Average Salary:** $50,000/$90,000;
**Industry Concentration:** Healthcare/Hospitals; **Function Concentration:**
Generalist

**Lonneke, John W.** — *Executive Recruiter*
MSI International
5215 North O'Connor Boulevard
Suite 1875
Irving, TX 75039
Telephone: (214) 869-3939
**Recruiter Classification:** Contingency; **Lowest/Average Salary:**
$30,000/$75,000; **Industry Concentration:** Generalist with a primary focus in
Financial Services; **Function Concentration:** Generalist with a primary focus in
Finance/Accounting

**Loomis, Ruth L.** — *Associate*
Ast/Bryant
2716 Ocean Park Boulevard, Suite 3001
Santa Monica, CA 90405
Telephone: (310) 314-2424
**Recruiter Classification:** Retained; **Lowest/Average Salary:** $75,000/$90,000;
**Industry Concentration:** Education/Libraries, Environmental,
Healthcare/Hospitals, Non-Profit; **Function Concentration:** Women/Minorities

**Loper, Doris** — *Regional Manager*
Mortgage & Financial Personnel Services
5850 Canoga Avenue, Suite 400
Woodland Hills, CA 91367
Telephone: (818) 710-7133
**Recruiter Classification:** Contingency, Executive Temporary; **Lowest/Average
Salary:** $30,000/$40,000; **Industry Concentration:** Financial Services,
Insurance; **Function Concentration:** Finance/Accounting

**Lopez, Manney C.** — *Manager Pacific Region*
Management Recruiters International, Inc.
61419 South Highway 97, Suite V
Bend, OR 97702-2103
Telephone: (541) 383-8550
**Recruiter Classification:** Contingency; **Lowest/Average Salary:**
$30,000/$75,000; **Industry Concentration:** Generalist; **Function
Concentration:** Generalist

**Lopis, Roberta** — *Executive Recruiter*
Richard, Wayne and Roberts
24 Greenway Plaza, Suite 1304
Houston, TX 77046-2493
Telephone: (713) 629-6681
**Recruiter Classification:** Retained; **Lowest/Average Salary:** $50,000/$90,000;
**Industry Concentration:** Generalist with a primary focus in Financial Services;
**Function Concentration:** Generalist with a primary focus in
Finance/Accounting

**LoPresto, Robert L.** — *President - High Technology*
Rusher, Loscavio & LoPresto
2479 Bayshore Road, Suite 700
Palo Alto, CA 94303
Telephone: (415) 494-0883
**Recruiter Classification:** Retained; **Lowest/Average Salary:** $90,000/$90,000;
**Industry Concentration:** Biotechnology, Board Services, Electronics, High
Technology, Information Technology, Manufacturing, Venture Capital; **Function
Concentration:** Administration, Engineering, General Management, Marketing,
Research and Development, Sales

**Lord, Anthony W.G.** — *Managing Director*
Ward Howell International, Inc.
99 Park Avenue, Suite 2000
New York, NY 10016-1699
Telephone: (212) 697-3730
**Recruiter Classification:** Retained; **Lowest/Average Salary:** $75,000/$90,000;
**Industry Concentration:** Generalist; **Function Concentration:** Generalist

**Lorenz, Paula** — *Associate*
Kenzer Corp.
625 North Michigan Avenue, Suite 1244
Chicago, IL 60611
Telephone: (312) 266-0976
**Recruiter Classification:** Retained; **Lowest/Average Salary:** $50,000/$90,000;
**Industry Concentration:** Generalist; **Function Concentration:** Generalist

**Loria, Frank** — *President*
Accounting Personnel Consultants
210 Baronne Street, Suite 920
New Orleans, LA 70112
Telephone: (504) 581-7800
**Recruiter Classification:** Contingency, Executive Temporary; **Lowest/Average
Salary:** $20,000/$20,000; **Industry Concentration:** Generalist with a primary
focus in Chemical Products, Healthcare/Hospitals, Hospitality/Leisure, Oil/Gas;
**Function Concentration:** Administration, Engineering, Finance/Accounting,
General Management, Human Resources, Research and Development

**Loscavio, J. Michael** — *Executive Vice President*
Rusher, Loscavio & LoPresto
180 Montgomery Street, Suite 1616
San Francisco, CA 94104-4239
Telephone: (415) 765-6600
**Recruiter Classification:** Retained; **Lowest/Average Salary:** $75,000/$90,000; **Industry Concentration:** Generalist with a primary focus in Biotechnology, Board Services, Chemical Products, Financial Services, Insurance, Manufacturing, Non-Profit, Oil/Gas; **Function Concentration:** Generalist with a primary focus in General Management, Research and Development

**Lotufo, Donald A.** — *Managing Partner*
D.A.L. Associates, Inc.
2777 Summer Street
Stamford, CT 06905
Telephone: (203) 961-8777
**Recruiter Classification:** Retained; **Lowest/Average Salary:** $75,000/$90,000; **Industry Concentration:** Generalist with a primary focus in Biotechnology, Chemical Products, Consumer Products, Electronics, Financial Services, Healthcare/Hospitals, High Technology, Information Technology, Manufacturing, Packaging, Pharmaceutical/Medical; **Function Concentration:** Generalist with a primary focus in Administration, Engineering, Finance/Accounting, General Management, Human Resources, Marketing, Research and Development, Sales

**Lotz, R. James** — *Chairman*
International Management Advisors, Inc.
516 Fifth Avenue
New York, NY 10036-7501
Telephone: (212) 758-7770
**Recruiter Classification:** Retained; **Lowest/Average Salary:** $75,000/$90,000; **Industry Concentration:** Generalist with a primary focus in Aerospace/Defense, Automotive, Biotechnology, Chemical Products, Consumer Products, Electronics, Energy, Financial Services, Healthcare/Hospitals, High Technology, Hospitality/Leisure, Manufacturing, Non-Profit, Oil/Gas; **Function Concentration:** Generalist with a primary focus in Engineering, Finance/Accounting, General Management, Human Resources, Marketing, Research and Development, Women/Minorities

**Louden, Leo** — *Software Quality Assurance Recruiter*
Winter, Wyman & Company
950 Winter Street, Suite 3100
Waltham, MA 02154-1294
Telephone: (617) 890-7000
**Recruiter Classification:** Contingency; **Lowest/Average Salary:** $40,000/$75,000; **Industry Concentration:** Hospitality/Leisure, Information Technology, Publishing/Media; **Function Concentration:** Generalist

**Lovas, W. Carl** — *Managing Partner*
Lovas Stanley/Paul Ray Berndtson Inc.
Royal Bank Plaza, South Tower, Suite 3150
200 Bay Street, P.O. Box 125
Toronto, Ontario, CANADA M5J 2J3
Telephone: (416) 366-1990
**Recruiter Classification:** Retained; **Lowest/Average Salary:** $90,000/$90,000; **Industry Concentration:** Generalist with a primary focus in Financial Services, High Technology; **Function Concentration:** Generalist with a primary focus in Finance/Accounting, General Management

**Love, David M.** — *Partner*
Paul Ray Berndtson
2200 Ross Avenue, Suite 4500W
Dallas, TX 75201
Telephone: (214) 969-7620
**Recruiter Classification:** Retained; **Lowest/Average Salary:** $90,000/$90,000; **Industry Concentration:** Education/Libraries, Healthcare/Hospitals, High Technology, Hospitality/Leisure, Public Administration; **Function Concentration:** Generalist

**Love, Nolanda** — *Consultant - L.A. Retail*
Evie Kreisler & Associates, Inc.
865 South Figueroa, Suite 950
Los Angeles, CA 90017
Telephone: (213) 622-8994
**Recruiter Classification:** Contingency; **Lowest/Average Salary:** $30,000/$75,000; **Industry Concentration:** Fashion (Retail/Apparel); **Function Concentration:** Generalist

**Lovell, Robert W.** — *Vice President*
John Kurosky & Associates
3 Corporate Park Drive, Suite 210
Irvine, CA 92714
Telephone: (714) 851-6370
**Recruiter Classification:** Retained; **Lowest/Average Salary:** $60,000/$90,000; **Industry Concentration:** Generalist; **Function Concentration:** Engineering, Research and Development

**Lovely, Edward** — *Senior Vice President*
The Stevenson Group of New Jersey
560 Sylvan Avenue
Englewood Cliffs, NJ 07632
Telephone: (201) 568-1900
**Recruiter Classification:** Retained; **Lowest/Average Salary:** $75,000/$90,000; **Industry Concentration:** Generalist with a primary focus in Chemical Products, Consumer Products, Fashion (Retail/Apparel), Financial Services, Information Technology, Pharmaceutical/Medical; **Function Concentration:** Generalist with a primary focus in Finance/Accounting, General Management, Human Resources, Marketing, Sales

**Loving, Vikki** — *President*
Intersource, Ltd.
72 Sloan Street
Roswell, GA 30075
Telephone: (770) 645-0015
**Recruiter Classification:** Retained, Contingency; **Lowest/Average Salary:** $90,000/$90,000; **Industry Concentration:** Generalist with a primary focus in Consumer Products, Electronics, Financial Services, Healthcare/Hospitals, High Technology, Hospitality/Leisure, Information Technology, Insurance, Manufacturing, Pharmaceutical/Medical; **Function Concentration:** Finance/Accounting, Human Resources, Women/Minorities

**Low, Linda** — *Executive Vice President*
The Development Resource Group Incorporated
1629 K Street, NW, Suite 802
Washington, DC 20006
Telephone: (202) 223-6528
**Recruiter Classification:** Retained; **Lowest/Average Salary:** $60,000/$90,000; **Industry Concentration:** Board Services, Education/Libraries, Healthcare/Hospitals, Non-Profit, Public Administration; **Function Concentration:** General Management

**Lowry, W. Randall** — *Partner*
Paul Ray Berndtson
One Allen Center
500 Dallas, Suite 3010
Houston, TX 77002
Telephone: (713) 309-1400
**Recruiter Classification:** Retained; **Lowest/Average Salary:** $90,000/$90,000; **Industry Concentration:** Energy; **Function Concentration:** Generalist

**Lowther, Marsha** — *Regional Vice President/Branch Manager*
Accountants on Call
525 University Avenue, Suite 23
Palo Alto, CA 94301
Telephone: (415) 328-8400
**Recruiter Classification:** Contingency; **Lowest/Average Salary:** $20,000/$30,000; **Industry Concentration:** Generalist; **Function Concentration:** Finance/Accounting

**Lubawski, James** — *Managing Director*
Ward Howell International, Inc.
300 South Wacker Drive
Suite 2940
Chicago, IL 60606
Telephone: (312) 236-2211
**Recruiter Classification:** Retained; **Lowest/Average Salary:** $75,000/$90,000; **Industry Concentration:** Generalist; **Function Concentration:** Generalist

**Lucarelli, Joan** — *Vice President and Principal*
The Onstott Group, Inc.
60 William Street
Wellesley, MA 02181
Telephone: (617) 235-3050
**Recruiter Classification:** Retained; **Lowest/Average Salary:** $90,000/$90,000; **Industry Concentration:** Generalist with a primary focus in Board Services, Financial Services, High Technology, Information Technology, Manufacturing, Publishing/Media; **Function Concentration:** Generalist with a primary focus in Engineering, Finance/Accounting, General Management, Human Resources, Marketing, Research and Development, Sales, Women/Minorities

**Lucas, Charles C.** — *Associate*
The McAulay Firm
Nations Bank Corporate Center, Suite 3140
100 North Tryon Street
Charlotte, NC 28202
Telephone: (704) 342-1880
**Recruiter Classification:** Retained; **Lowest/Average Salary:** $75,000/$90,000; **Industry Concentration:** Generalist; **Function Concentration:** Generalist

**Lucas, J. Curtis** — *Vice President*
Korn/Ferry International
120 South Riverside Plaza
Suite 918
Chicago, IL 60606
Telephone: (312) 726-1841
**Recruiter Classification:** Retained; **Lowest/Average Salary:** $90,000/$90,000; **Industry Concentration:** Generalist with a primary focus in Healthcare/Hospitals; **Function Concentration:** Generalist

**Lucas, Ronnie L.** — *Manager*
MSI International
5215 North O'Connor Boulevard
Suite 1875
Irving, TX 75039
Telephone: (214) 869-3939
**Recruiter Classification:** Contingency; **Lowest/Average Salary:** $30,000/$75,000; **Industry Concentration:** Generalist with a primary focus in Financial Services, Healthcare/Hospitals, High Technology, Information Technology, Manufacturing; **Function Concentration:** Generalist with a primary focus in Administration, Engineering, Finance/Accounting, General Management, Marketing, Sales

**Lucas, Thomas A.** — *Manager Eastern Region*
Management Recruiters International, Inc.
Constitution Place
325 Chestnut Street, Suite 1106
Philadelphia, PA 19106
Telephone: (215) 829-1900
**Recruiter Classification:** Contingency; **Lowest/Average Salary:** $30,000/$75,000; **Industry Concentration:** Generalist; **Function Concentration:** Generalist

**Luce, Daniel** — *Managing Director*
Source Services Corporation
520 Post Oak Boulevard, Suite 700
Houston, TX 77027
Telephone: (713) 439-1077
**Recruiter Classification:** Contingency; **Lowest/Average Salary:** $30,000/$50,000; **Industry Concentration:** Financial Services, Information Technology; **Function Concentration:** Engineering, Finance/Accounting

**Luce, Paul M.** — *Manager Southwest Region*
Management Recruiters International, Inc.
3527 Ridgelake Drive, P.O. Box 6605
Metairie, LA 70009
Telephone: (504) 831-7333
**Recruiter Classification:** Contingency; **Lowest/Average Salary:** $30,000/$75,000; **Industry Concentration:** Generalist; **Function Concentration:** Generalist

**Lucht, John** — *President*
The John Lucht Consultancy Inc.
The Olympic Tower
641 Fifth Avenue
New York, NY 10022
Telephone: (212) 935-4660
**Recruiter Classification:** Retained; **Lowest/Average Salary:** $90,000/$90,000; **Industry Concentration:** Generalist with a primary focus in Board Services, Chemical Products, Consumer Products, Education/Libraries, Electronics, Entertainment, Fashion (Retail/Apparel), Financial Services, High Technology, Information Technology, Insurance, Non-Profit, Publishing/Media, Venture Capital; **Function Concentration:** Generalist with a primary focus in Administration, Engineering, Finance/Accounting, General Management, Human Resources, Marketing, Research and Development, Sales, Women/Minorities

**Lucien, David** — *Engineering and Technical Recruiter*
Accounting Personnel Consultants
210 Baronne Street, Suite 920
New Orleans, LA 70112
Telephone: (504) 581-7800
**Recruiter Classification:** Contingency, Executive Temporary; **Lowest/Average Salary:** $20,000/$20,000; **Industry Concentration:** Generalist; **Function Concentration:** Engineering

**Ludder, Mark** — *Associate*
Source Services Corporation
8614 Westwood Center, Suite 750
Vienna, VA 22182
Telephone: (703) 790-5610
**Recruiter Classification:** Contingency; **Lowest/Average Salary:** $30,000/$50,000; **Industry Concentration:** Financial Services, Information Technology; **Function Concentration:** Engineering, Finance/Accounting

**Ludlow, Michael** — *Associate*
Source Services Corporation
One Park Plaza, Suite 560
Irvine, CA 92714
Telephone: (714) 660-1666
**Recruiter Classification:** Contingency; **Lowest/Average Salary:** $30,000/$50,000; **Industry Concentration:** Financial Services, Information Technology; **Function Concentration:** Engineering, Finance/Accounting

**Luke, A. Wayne** — *Managing Partner*
Heidrick & Struggles, Inc.
One Peachtree Center
303 Peachtree Street, NE, Suite 3100
Atlanta, GA 30308
Telephone: (404) 577-2410
**Recruiter Classification:** Retained; **Lowest/Average Salary:** $75,000/$90,000; **Industry Concentration:** Generalist with a primary focus in High Technology; **Function Concentration:** Generalist

**Lumsby, George N.** — *Senior Consultant*
International Management Advisors, Inc.
516 Fifth Avenue
New York, NY 10036-7501
Telephone: (212) 758-7770
**Recruiter Classification:** Retained; **Lowest/Average Salary:** $75,000/$90,000; **Industry Concentration:** Generalist with a primary focus in Aerospace/Defense, Automotive, Biotechnology, Chemical Products, Consumer Products, Electronics, Energy, Financial Services, Healthcare/Hospitals, High Technology, Hospitality/Leisure, Manufacturing, Non-Profit, Oil/Gas; **Function Concentration:** Generalist with a primary focus in Engineering, Finance/Accounting, General Management, Human Resources, Marketing, Research and Development, Women/Minorities

**Lumsby, George N.** — *Vice President*
Boyden
375 Park Avenue, Suite 1509
New York, NY 10152
Telephone: (212) 980-6480
**Recruiter Classification:** Retained; **Lowest/Average Salary:** $75,000/$90,000; **Industry Concentration:** Generalist; **Function Concentration:** Generalist

**Lundburg, Kirk** — *Managing Director*
Accountemps (division of Robert Half International)
2884 Sand Hill Road
Menlo Park, CA 94025
Telephone: (415) 854-9700
**Recruiter Classification:** Executive Temporary; **Industry Concentration:** Generalist; **Function Concentration:** Finance/Accounting

**Lundy, Martin** — *Associate*
Source Services Corporation
20 Burlington Mall Road, Suite 405
Burlington, MA 01803
Telephone: (617) 272-5000
**Recruiter Classification:** Contingency; **Lowest/Average Salary:** $30,000/$50,000; **Industry Concentration:** Financial Services, Information Technology; **Function Concentration:** Engineering, Finance/Accounting

**Lunn, Jerry D.** — *Executive Vice President/Managing Director*
DHR International, Inc.
Seville-on-the-Plaza
500 Nichols Road, Suite 430
Kansas City, MO 64112
Telephone: (816) 756-2965
**Recruiter Classification:** Retained; **Lowest/Average Salary:** $60,000/$90,000; **Industry Concentration:** Generalist; **Function Concentration:** Generalist

**Lusk, Theodore E.** — *Partner*
Nadzam, Lusk, Horgan & Associates, Inc.
3211 Scott Boulevard
Suite 205
Santa Clara, CA 95054-3091
Telephone: (408) 727-6601
**Recruiter Classification:** Retained; **Lowest/Average Salary:** $90,000/$90,000; **Industry Concentration:** Generalist; **Function Concentration:** Generalist

**Lussier, Grant P.** — *Partner*
Heidrick & Struggles, Inc.
Torre Chapultepec, Ruben Dario No. 281 Ofna. 1403
Col. Bosque de Chapultepec
Mexico City, D.F., MEXICO 11580
Telephone: (525) 280-5200
**Recruiter Classification:** Retained; **Lowest/Average Salary:** $75,000/$90,000; **Industry Concentration:** Generalist with a primary focus in Financial Services, High Technology; **Function Concentration:** Generalist

**Lynch, Anita F.** — *Co-Manager Eastern Region*
Management Recruiters International, Inc.
80 West Welsh Pool Road, Suite 101
Exton, PA 19341-1233
Telephone: (610) 363-5455
**Recruiter Classification:** Contingency; **Lowest/Average Salary:** $30,000/$75,000; **Industry Concentration:** Generalist; **Function Concentration:** Generalist

**Lynch, Charles J.** — *Vice President*
F-O-R-T-U-N-E Personnel Consultants of Nashua, Inc.
505 West Hollis Street, Suite 208
Nashua, NH 03062
Telephone: (603) 880-4900
**Recruiter Classification:** Contingency; **Lowest/Average Salary:**
$40,000/$60,000; **Industry Concentration:** Biotechnology, Manufacturing,
Pharmaceutical/Medical; **Function Concentration:** Generalist

**Lynch, John** — *Partner*
Blackshaw, Olmstead & Lynch
60 Arch Street
Greenwich, CT 06830
Telephone: (203) 869-7727
**Recruiter Classification:** Retained; **Lowest/Average Salary:** $75,000/$90,000;
**Industry Concentration:** Generalist; **Function Concentration:** Generalist

**Lynch, John F.** — *Co-Manager*
Management Recruiters International, Inc.
80 West Welsh Pool Road, Suite 101
Exton, PA 19341-1233
Telephone: (610) 363-5455
**Recruiter Classification:** Contingency; **Lowest/Average Salary:**
$30,000/$75,000; **Industry Concentration:** Generalist; **Function
Concentration:** Generalist

**Lynch, Michael C.** — *Partner*
Lynch Miller Moore Partners, Inc.
10 South Wacker Drive, Suite 2935
Chicago, IL 60606
Telephone: (312) 876-1505
**Recruiter Classification:** Retained; **Lowest/Average Salary:** $75,000/$90,000;
**Industry Concentration:** Generalist with a primary focus in Consumer
Products, Fashion (Retail/Apparel), Financial Services, Insurance,
Manufacturing, Venture Capital; **Function Concentration:** Generalist with a
primary focus in Finance/Accounting, General Management

**Lynch, Sean E.** — *Senior Consultant*
Raymond Karsan Associates
989 Old Eagle School Road, Suite 814
Wayne, PA 19087
Telephone: (610) 971-9171
**Recruiter Classification:** Contingency; **Lowest/Average Salary:**
$30,000/$90,000; **Industry Concentration:** Generalist with a primary focus in
Insurance; **Function Concentration:** Generalist

**Lynn, Donald** — *Vice President*
Frank Cuomo and Associates, Inc.
111 Brook Street
Scarsdale, NY 10583
Telephone: (914) 723-8001
**Recruiter Classification:** Contingency; **Lowest/Average Salary:**
$30,000/$75,000; **Industry Concentration:** Chemical Products, Energy,
Environmental, High Technology, Manufacturing; **Function Concentration:**
Engineering, General Management, Marketing, Sales

**Lyons, Denis B.K.** — *Senior Director*
Spencer Stuart
277 Park Avenue, 29th Floor
New York, NY 10172
Telephone: (212) 336-0200
**Recruiter Classification:** Retained; **Lowest/Average Salary:** $90,000/$90,000;
**Industry Concentration:** Generalist with a primary focus in Consumer
Products, Financial Services; **Function Concentration:** Generalist with a
primary focus in Finance/Accounting, General Management

**Lyons, Jane A.** — *Senior Vice President*
Rhodes Associates
555 Fifth Avenue
New York, NY 10017
Telephone: (212) 983-2000
**Recruiter Classification:** Retained; **Lowest/Average Salary:** $90,000/$90,000;
**Industry Concentration:** Financial Services, Insurance, Real Estate, Venture
Capital; **Function Concentration:** Generalist

**Lyons, Margaret** — *Consultant*
Paul Ray Berndtson
10 South Riverside Plaza
Suite 720
Chicago, IL 60606
Telephone: (312) 876-0730
**Recruiter Classification:** Retained; **Lowest/Average Salary:** $90,000/$90,000;
**Industry Concentration:** Generalist; **Function Concentration:** Generalist

**Lyons, Mary Fran** — *Managing Director/Consultant*
Witt/Kieffer, Ford, Hadelman & Lloyd
8000 Maryland Avenue, Suite 1080
St. Louis, MO 63105
Telephone: (314) 862-1370
**Recruiter Classification:** Retained; **Lowest/Average Salary:** $75,000/$90,000;
**Industry Concentration:** Healthcare/Hospitals, Pharmaceutical/Medical;
**Function Concentration:** Generalist

**Lyons, Michael** — *Associate*
Source Services Corporation
4510 Executive Drive, Suite 200
San Diego, CA 92121
Telephone: (619) 552-0300
**Recruiter Classification:** Contingency; **Lowest/Average Salary:**
$30,000/$50,000; **Industry Concentration:** Financial Services, Information
Technology; **Function Concentration:** Engineering, Finance/Accounting

**Lyons, Michele R.** — *Vice President*
R. Rollo Associates
725 South Figueroa Street, Suite 3230
Los Angeles, CA 90017
Telephone: (213) 892-7845
**Recruiter Classification:** Retained; **Lowest/Average Salary:** $90,000/$90,000;
**Industry Concentration:** Generalist with a primary focus in
Aerospace/Defense, Consumer Products, Energy, Financial Services,
Healthcare/Hospitals, Hospitality/Leisure, Insurance, Manufacturing, Non-
Profit, Oil/Gas, Real Estate, Transportation, Venture Capital; **Function
Concentration:** Generalist

**Lyttle, Jordene** — *Consultant*
The Caldwell Partners Amrop International
Sixty-Four Prince Arthur Avenue
Toronto, Ontario, CANADA M5R 1B4
Telephone: (416) 920-7702
**Recruiter Classification:** Retained; **Lowest/Average Salary:** $/$90,000; **Industry
Concentration:** Generalist; **Function Concentration:** Generalist

**MacArthur, Lauren** — *Technical Documentation and
Technical Training Recruiter*
Winter, Wyman & Company
950 Winter Street, Suite 3100
Waltham, MA 02154-1294
Telephone: (617) 890-7000
**Recruiter Classification:** Contingency; **Lowest/Average Salary:**
$30,000/$50,000; **Industry Concentration:** Generalist; **Function
Concentration:** Generalist

**MacCallan, Deirdre** — *Principal*
Butterfass, Pepe & MacCallan Inc.
P.O. Box 721
Mahwah, NJ 07430
Telephone: (201) 512-3330
**Recruiter Classification:** Retained; **Lowest/Average Salary:** $60,000/$75,000;
**Industry Concentration:** Generalist with a primary focus in Financial Services,
Insurance; **Function Concentration:** Generalist with a primary focus in
Finance/Accounting, Women/Minorities

**MacCarthy, Ann** — *Managing Principal*
Columbia Consulting Group
230 Park Avenue, Suite 456
New York, NY 10169
Telephone: (212) 983-2525
**Recruiter Classification:** Retained; **Lowest/Average Salary:** $75,000/$90,000;
**Industry Concentration:** Generalist with a primary focus in Consumer
Products, Fashion (Retail/Apparel), Healthcare/Hospitals, High Technology,
Information Technology, Manufacturing, Publishing/Media; **Function
Concentration:** Generalist with a primary focus in Administration,
Finance/Accounting, General Management, Human Resources, Marketing,
Sales

**Macdonald, G. William** — *President*
The Macdonald Group, Inc.
301 Route 17, Suite 800
Rutherford, NJ 07070
Telephone: (201) 939-2312
**Recruiter Classification:** Retained; **Lowest/Average Salary:** $75,000/$90,000;
**Industry Concentration:** Generalist with a primary focus in Biotechnology,
Financial Services, Healthcare/Hospitals, High Technology, Information
Technology, Manufacturing, Pharmaceutical/Medical, Venture Capital;
**Function Concentration:** Generalist with a primary focus in General
Management, Human Resources, Research and Development

**Macdonald, Robert W.** — *Managing Director/Area Manager*
Russell Reynolds Associates, Inc.
3050 Norwest Center
90 South Seventh Street
Minneapolis, MN 55402
Telephone: (612) 332-6966
**Recruiter Classification:** Retained; **Lowest/Average Salary:**
$90,000/$90,000; **Industry Concentration:** Generalist; **Function
Concentration:** Generalist

**MacDougall, Andrew J.** — *Managing Director*
Spencer Stuart
One University Avenue
Suite 801
Toronto, Ontario, CANADA M5J 2P1
Telephone: (416) 361-0311
Recruiter Classification: Retained; Lowest/Average Salary: $90,000/$90,000;
Industry Concentration: Automotive, Board Services, Chemical Products,
Entertainment, Financial Services, High Technology, Information Technology,
Insurance, Manufacturing, Packaging, Publishing/Media, Real Estate,
Transportation, Utilities/Nuclear; Function Concentration: Generalist

**MacEachern, David** — *Director*
Spencer Stuart
One University Avenue
Suite 801
Toronto, Ontario, CANADA M5J 2P1
Telephone: (416) 361-0311
Recruiter Classification: Retained; Lowest/Average Salary: $60,000/$75,000;
Industry Concentration: Generalist with a primary focus in Automotive,
Chemical Products, Consumer Products, Information Technology,
Manufacturing; Function Concentration: Generalist with a primary focus in
Engineering, General Management, Human Resources

**MacGregor, Malcolm** — *Managing Director*
Boyden
Allegheny Tower, Suite 2405
625 Stanwix Street
Pittsburgh, PA 15222-1423
Telephone: (412) 391-3020
Recruiter Classification: Retained; Lowest/Average Salary: $75,000/$90,000;
Industry Concentration: Generalist; Function Concentration: Generalist with a
primary focus in Engineering, Finance/Accounting, General Management,
Human Resources, Marketing, Research and Development, Sales,
Women/Minorities

**Machi, Mike T.** — *Manager Pacific Region*
Management Recruiters International, Inc.
4125 Mohr Avenue, Suite M
Pleasanton, CA 94566-4740
Telephone: (510) 462-8579
Recruiter Classification: Contingency; Lowest/Average Salary:
$30,000/$75,000; Industry Concentration: Generalist; Function
Concentration: Generalist

**MacIntyre, Lisa W.** — *Managing Director*
Russell Reynolds Associates, Inc.
200 Park Avenue
New York, NY 10166-0002
Telephone: (212) 351-2000
Recruiter Classification: Retained; Lowest/Average Salary: $90,000/$90,000;
Industry Concentration: Generalist with a primary focus in Financial Services;
Function Concentration: Generalist

**MacJadyen, David J.** — *President East Coast*
Sharrow & Associates
15800 Perkins Lane
Mitchellville, MD 20716
Telephone: (800) 823-1001
Recruiter Classification: Contingency; Lowest/Average Salary:
$30,000/$60,000; Function Concentration: Administration, Engineering,
General Management, Marketing, Sales

**MacKay, Malcolm** — *Managing Director*
Russell Reynolds Associates, Inc.
200 Park Avenue
New York, NY 10166-0002
Telephone: (212) 351-2000
Recruiter Classification: Retained; Lowest/Average Salary: $90,000/$90,000;
Industry Concentration: Non-Profit; Function Concentration: Generalist

**Mackenna, Kathy** — *Consultant*
Plummer & Associates, Inc.
30 Myano Lane, Suite 36
Stamford, CT 06902
Telephone: (203) 965-7878
Recruiter Classification: Retained; Lowest/Average Salary: $90,000/$90,000;
Industry Concentration: Generalist with a primary focus in Board Services,
Consumer Products, Electronics, Entertainment, Fashion (Retail/Apparel),
Manufacturing, Venture Capital; Function Concentration: Generalist with a
primary focus in Administration, Finance/Accounting, General Management,
Human Resources, Marketing

**Mackenzie, Robert A.** — *Manager Eastern Region*
Management Recruiters International, Inc.
Arra Realty Complex, Route 209
P.O. Box 386
Stone Ridge, NY 12484-0386
Telephone: (914) 339-1300
Recruiter Classification: Contingency; Lowest/Average Salary:
$30,000/$75,000; Industry Concentration: Generalist; Function
Concentration: Generalist

**Mackey-Ross, Christine** — *Consultant*
Witt/Kieffer, Ford, Hadelman & Lloyd
8000 Maryland Avenue, Suite 1080
St. Louis, MO 63105
Telephone: (314) 862-1370
Recruiter Classification: Retained; Lowest/Average Salary: $75,000/$90,000;
Industry Concentration: Healthcare/Hospitals; Function Concentration:
General Management

**Mackin, Michael** — *Consultant*
D. Brown and Associates, Inc.
610 S.W. Alder, Suite 1111
Portland, OR 97205
Telephone: (503) 224-6860
Recruiter Classification: Contingency; Lowest/Average Salary:
$50,000/$75,000; Industry Concentration: Healthcare/Hospitals; Function
Concentration: Sales

**Mackinlay, Marcelo D.** — *Partner*
Heidrick & Struggles, Inc.
BCE Place, 161 Bay Street, Suite 2310
P.O. Box 601
Toronto, Ontario, CANADA M5J 2S1
Telephone: (416) 361-4700
Recruiter Classification: Retained; Lowest/Average Salary: $75,000/$90,000;
Industry Concentration: Generalist with a primary focus in Financial Services;
Function Concentration: Generalist

**MacKinnon, Helen** — *President*
Technical Connections Inc.
11400 Olympic Boulevard, Suite 770
Los Angeles, CA 90064
Telephone: (310) 479-8830
Recruiter Classification: Contingency; Lowest/Average Salary:
$40,000/$60,000; Industry Concentration: High Technology, Information
Technology

**MacLane, Bruce W.** — *Senior Associate*
Korn/Ferry International
303 Peachtree Street N.E.
Suite 1600
Atlanta, GA 30308
Telephone: (404) 577-7542
Recruiter Classification: Retained; Lowest/Average Salary: $90,000/$90,000;
Industry Concentration: Generalist; Function Concentration: Generalist

**MacLean, B.A.** — *Vice Chairman*
The Diversified Search Companies
2005 Market Street, Suite 3300
Philadelphia, PA 19103
Telephone: (215) 732-6666
Recruiter Classification: Retained; Lowest/Average Salary: $90,000/$90,000;
Industry Concentration: Generalist; Function Concentration: Generalist

**MacLeod, Jill C.** — *Consultant*
Lovas Stanley/Paul Ray Berndtson Inc.
Royal Bank Plaza, South Tower, Suite 3150
200 Bay Street, P.O. Box 125
Toronto, Ontario, CANADA M5J 2J3
Telephone: (416) 366-1990
Recruiter Classification: Retained; Lowest/Average Salary: $60,000/$75,000;
Industry Concentration: Generalist; Function Concentration: Generalist

**MacMillan, James** — *Associate*
Source Services Corporation
100 North Tryon Street, Suite 3130
Charlotte, NC 28202
Telephone: (704) 333-8311
Recruiter Classification: Contingency; Lowest/Average Salary:
$30,000/$50,000; Industry Concentration: Financial Services, Information
Technology; Function Concentration: Engineering, Finance/Accounting

**MacPherson, Holly** — *Associate*
Source Services Corporation
425 California Street, Suite 1200
San Francisco, CA 94104
Telephone: (415) 434-2410
Recruiter Classification: Contingency; Lowest/Average Salary:
$30,000/$50,000; Industry Concentration: Financial Services, Information
Technology; Function Concentration: Engineering, Finance/Accounting

**Macrides, Michael** — *Associate*
Source Services Corporation
20 Burlington Mall Road, Suite 405
Burlington, MA 01803
Telephone: (617) 272-5000
**Recruiter Classification:** Contingency; **Lowest/Average Salary:**
$30,000/$50,000; **Industry Concentration:** Financial Services, Information
Technology; **Function Concentration:** Engineering, Finance/Accounting

**Madaras, Debra** — *Associate*
Financial Resource Associates, Inc.
105 West Orange Street
Altamonte Springs, FL 32714
Telephone: (407) 869-7000
**Recruiter Classification:** Contingency; **Lowest/Average Salary:**
$40,000/$60,000; **Industry Concentration:** Financial Services; **Function
Concentration:** Finance/Accounting

**Mader, Stephen P.** — *Vice President*
Christian & Timbers
24 New England Executive Park
Burlington, MA 01803
Telephone: (617) 229-9515
**Recruiter Classification:** Retained; **Lowest/Average Salary:** $90,000/$90,000;
**Industry Concentration:** Electronics, High Technology, Information
Technology, Manufacturing, Venture Capital; **Function Concentration:**
Generalist with a primary focus in Administration, Engineering,
Finance/Accounting, General Management, Human Resources, Marketing,
Research and Development, Sales

**Maer, Harry** — *Vice President, New York*
Kenzer Corp.
777 Third Avenue, 26th Floor
New York, NY 10017
Telephone: (212) 308-4300
**Recruiter Classification:** Retained; **Lowest/Average Salary:** $50,000/$90,000;
**Industry Concentration:** Consumer Products, Entertainment, Financial
Services, Packaging, Venture Capital; **Function Concentration:** Generalist with
a primary focus in Administration, Finance/Accounting, General Management,
Human Resources, Marketing, Research and Development, Sales

**Magee, Charles** — *Co-Manager*
Management Recruiters International, Inc.
920 Pierremont, Suite 112
Shreveport, LA 71106-8794
Telephone: (318) 865-8411
**Recruiter Classification:** Contingency; **Lowest/Average Salary:**
$30,000/$75,000; **Industry Concentration:** Generalist; **Function
Concentration:** Generalist

**Magee, Charles R.** — *Senior Search Consultant*
Dieck, Mueller & Associates, Inc.
1017 Orchard Drive
Seymour, WI 54165
Telephone: (414) 833-7600
**Recruiter Classification:** Retained; **Lowest/Average Salary:** $75,000/$90,000;
**Industry Concentration:** Chemical Products, Consumer Products,
Manufacturing, Packaging; **Function Concentration:** Generalist

**Magee, Gerri** — *Co-Manager Southwest Region*
Management Recruiters International, Inc.
920 Pierremont, Suite 112
Shreveport, LA 71106-8794
Telephone: (318) 865-8411
**Recruiter Classification:** Contingency; **Lowest/Average Salary:**
$30,000/$75,000; **Industry Concentration:** Generalist; **Function
Concentration:** Generalist

**Magee, Harrison R.** — *Vice President*
Bowden & Company, Inc.
5000 Rockside Road, Suite 550
Cleveland, OH 44131
Telephone: (216) 447-1800
**Recruiter Classification:** Retained; **Lowest/Average Salary:** $90,000/$90,000;
**Industry Concentration:** Generalist with a primary focus in
Aerospace/Defense, Automotive, Chemical Products, Consumer Products,
Energy, Financial Services, Healthcare/Hospitals, High Technology, Information
Technology, Insurance, Manufacturing, Non-Profit, Packaging, Transportation,
Venture Capital; **Function Concentration:** Generalist

**Maggio, Mary** — *Associate*
Source Services Corporation
925 Westchester Avenue, Suite 309
White Plains, NY 10604
Telephone: (914) 428-9100
**Recruiter Classification:** Contingency; **Lowest/Average Salary:**
$30,000/$50,000; **Industry Concentration:** Financial Services, Information
Technology; **Function Concentration:** Engineering, Finance/Accounting

**Magnani, Susan** — *Vice President*
The Search Center Inc.
1155 Dairy Ashford, Suite 404
Houston, TX 77079
Telephone: (713) 589-8303
**Recruiter Classification:** Contingency; **Lowest/Average Salary:**
$75,000/$90,000; **Industry Concentration:** Chemical Products, Energy;
**Function Concentration:** Marketing

**Magnusen, Hank F.** — *Manager Eastern Region*
Management Recruiters International, Inc.
American House Annex
298 Route 519, Box 244
Hope, NJ 07844-0244
Telephone: (908) 459-5798
**Recruiter Classification:** Contingency; **Lowest/Average Salary:**
$30,000/$75,000; **Industry Concentration:** Generalist; **Function
Concentration:** Generalist

**Mahaney, Joann** — *Consultant*
Heidrick & Struggles, Inc.
2740 Sand Hill Road
Menlo Park, CA 94025
Telephone: (415) 854-9300
**Recruiter Classification:** Retained; **Lowest/Average Salary:** $75,000/$90,000;
**Industry Concentration:** Generalist with a primary focus in High Technology;
**Function Concentration:** Generalist

**Maher, William J.** — *Senior Managing Director*
Johnson Smith & Knisely Accord
100 Park Avenue, 15th Floor
New York, NY 10017
Telephone: (212) 885-9100
**Recruiter Classification:** Retained; **Lowest/Average Salary:** $90,000/$90,000;
**Industry Concentration:** Consumer Products, Fashion (Retail/Apparel),
Manufacturing; **Function Concentration:** Administration, Engineering,
Finance/Accounting, General Management, Human Resources, Marketing,
Research and Development, Sales

**Mahmoud, Sophia** — *Associate*
Source Services Corporation
425 California Street, Suite 1200
San Francisco, CA 94104
Telephone: (415) 434-2410
**Recruiter Classification:** Contingency; **Lowest/Average Salary:**
$30,000/$50,000; **Industry Concentration:** Financial Services, Information
Technology; **Function Concentration:** Engineering, Finance/Accounting

**Mahr, Toni** — *Recruiter*
K. Russo Associates
2 Greenwich Plaza, Suite 100
Greenwich, CT 06830
Telephone: (203) 622-3903
**Recruiter Classification:** Retained; **Lowest/Average Salary:** $30,000/$90,000;
**Industry Concentration:** Consumer Products, Entertainment, Financial
Services, Insurance, Manufacturing, Pharmaceutical/Medical,
Publishing/Media; **Function Concentration:** Human Resources

**Maibach, Lisa W.** — *Managing Director*
Russell Reynolds Associates, Inc.
101 California Street
Suite 3140
San Francisco, CA 94111
Telephone: (415) 352-3300
**Recruiter Classification:** Retained; **Lowest/Average Salary:** $90,000/$90,000;
**Industry Concentration:** Generalist with a primary focus in Consumer
Products; **Function Concentration:** Generalist

**Maiers, Robert** — *Placement Specialist*
Key Employment Services
1001 Office Park Road, Suite 320
West Des Moines, IA 50265-2567
Telephone: (515) 224-0446
**Recruiter Classification:** Contingency; **Lowest/Average Salary:**
$30,000/$75,000; **Industry Concentration:** Generalist; **Function
Concentration:** Engineering

**Mainwaring, Andrew Brian** — *Senior Consultant*
Executive Search Consultants Corporation
8 South Michigan Avenue, Suite 1205
Chicago, IL 60603
Telephone: (312) 251-8400
**Recruiter Classification:** Contingency; **Lowest/Average Salary:**
$40,000/$60,000; **Industry Concentration:** Generalist with a primary focus in
Aerospace/Defense, Automotive, Education/Libraries, Insurance,
Pharmaceutical/Medical, Utilities/Nuclear; **Function Concentration:** Generalist
with a primary focus in Administration, Finance/Accounting, Human
Resources, Women/Minorities

**Mairn, Todd** — *Associate*
Source Services Corporation
161 Ottawa NW, Suite 409D
Grand Rapids, MI 49503
Telephone: (616) 451-2400
**Recruiter Classification:** Contingency; **Lowest/Average Salary:**
$30,000/$50,000; **Industry Concentration:** Financial Services, Information
Technology; **Function Concentration:** Engineering, Finance/Accounting

**Maitland, Thomas M.** — *Senior Vice President*
DHR International, Inc.
Denver Tech Center
7900 East Union Avenue, Suite 1100
Denver, CO 80237
Telephone: (303) 694-5360
**Recruiter Classification:** Retained; **Lowest/Average Salary:** $60,000/$90,000;
**Industry Concentration:** Generalist; **Function Concentration:** Generalist

**Mak, I. Paul** — *Partner*
Thomas A. Byrnes Associates
148 East Avenue, Suite 2L
Norwalk, CT 06851
Telephone: (203) 838-9936
**Recruiter Classification:** Retained; **Lowest/Average Salary:** $90,000/$90,000;
**Industry Concentration:** Generalist with a primary focus in Consumer
Products, Financial Services, Insurance; **Function Concentration:** Generalist
with a primary focus in Finance/Accounting, General Management, Human
Resources, Marketing, Sales, Women/Minorities

**Makrianes, James K.** — *Managing Director*
Webb, Johnson Associates, Inc.
280 Park Avenue, 43rd Floor
New York, NY 10017
Telephone: (212) 661-3700
**Recruiter Classification:** Retained; **Lowest/Average Salary:** $90,000/$90,000;
**Industry Concentration:** Generalist with a primary focus in Biotechnology,
Chemical Products, Financial Services, Healthcare/Hospitals, High Technology,
Non-Profit, Pharmaceutical/Medical; **Function Concentration:** Generalist

**Malcolm, Doug C.** — *Co-Manager North Atlantic Region*
Management Recruiters International, Inc.
2814 New Spring Road, Suite 217
Atlanta, GA 30339
Telephone: (404) 436-3464
**Recruiter Classification:** Contingency; **Lowest/Average Salary:**
$30,000/$75,000; **Industry Concentration:** Generalist; **Function
Concentration:** Generalist

**Malcolm, Rod** — *Partner*
The Enns Partners Inc.
70 University Avenue, Suite 410, P.O. Box 14
Toronto, Ontario, CANADA M5J 2M4
Telephone: (416) 598-0012
**Recruiter Classification:** Retained; **Lowest/Average Salary:** $75,000/$90,000;
**Industry Concentration:** Generalist with a primary focus in
Aerospace/Defense, Board Services, Consumer Products, Electronics, Energy,
Financial Services, High Technology, Hospitality/Leisure, Manufacturing,
Pharmaceutical/Medical, Publishing/Media, Transportation, Venture Capital;
**Function Concentration:** Generalist with a primary focus in Administration,
Finance/Accounting, General Management, Human Resources, Marketing,
Sales

**Malcom, John W.** — *Managing Director*
Johnson Smith & Knisely Accord
100 Park Avenue, 15th Floor
New York, NY 10017
Telephone: (212) 885-9100
**Recruiter Classification:** Retained; **Lowest/Average Salary:** $90,000/$90,000;
**Industry Concentration:** Entertainment, Publishing/Media; **Function
Concentration:** Generalist with a primary focus in General Management,
Human Resources, Marketing, Sales, Women/Minorities

**Malfetti, Jim L.** — *Co-Manager*
Management Recruiters International, Inc.
Mountainside Crossing
1104 Springfield Avenue
Mountainside, NJ 07092
Telephone: (908) 789-9400
**Recruiter Classification:** Contingency; **Lowest/Average Salary:**
$30,000/$75,000; **Industry Concentration:** Generalist; **Function
Concentration:** Generalist

**Malfetti, Ro** — *Co-Manager Eastern Region*
Management Recruiters International, Inc.
Mountainside Crossing
1104 Springfield Avenue
Mountainside, NJ 07092
Telephone: (908) 789-9400
**Recruiter Classification:** Contingency; **Lowest/Average Salary:**
$30,000/$75,000; **Industry Concentration:** Generalist; **Function
Concentration:** Generalist

**Mallin, Ellen** — *Vice President*
Howard Fischer Associates, Inc.
1800 John F. Kennedy Boulevard, 7th Floor
Philadelphia, PA 19103
Telephone: (215) 568-8363
**Recruiter Classification:** Retained; **Lowest/Average Salary:** $90,000/$90,000;
**Industry Concentration:** Generalist; **Function Concentration:** Generalist

**Mallipudi, Anand** — *Principal*
Raymond Karsan Associates
500 East Calaveras Boulevard, Suite 332
Milpitas, CA 95035
Telephone: (408) 262-6154
**Recruiter Classification:** Contingency; **Lowest/Average Salary:**
$30,000/$90,000; **Industry Concentration:** Generalist with a primary focus in
Biotechnology, Chemical Products, Environmental, Healthcare/Hospitals,
Information Technology, Insurance, Manufacturing, Pharmaceutical/Medical;
**Function Concentration:** Generalist

**Malone, George V.** — *Senior Vice President*
Boyden
55 Madison Avenue
Suite 400
Morristown, NJ 07960
Telephone: (201) 267-0980
**Recruiter Classification:** Retained; **Lowest/Average Salary:** $75,000/$90,000;
**Industry Concentration:** Financial Services; **Function Concentration:**
Generalist with a primary focus in Engineering, Finance/Accounting, General
Management, Human Resources, Marketing, Research and Development,
Sales, Women/Minorities

**Malone, Tom S.** — *Co-Manager*
Management Recruiters International, Inc.
One Blue Hill Plaza, Suite 1428
P.O. Box 1603
Pearl River, NY 10965-8603
Telephone: (914) 735-7015
**Recruiter Classification:** Contingency; **Lowest/Average Salary:**
$30,000/$75,000; **Industry Concentration:** Generalist; **Function
Concentration:** Generalist

**Manassero, Henri J.P.** — *Partner Hospitality*
International Management Advisors, Inc.
516 Fifth Avenue
New York, NY 10036-7501
Telephone: (212) 758-7770
**Recruiter Classification:** Retained; **Lowest/Average Salary:** $75,000/$90,000;
**Industry Concentration:** Generalist with a primary focus in
Aerospace/Defense, Automotive, Biotechnology, Chemical Products,
Consumer Products, Electronics, Energy, Financial Services,
Healthcare/Hospitals, High Technology, Hospitality/Leisure, Manufacturing,
Non-Profit, Oil/Gas; **Function Concentration:** Generalist with a primary focus
in Engineering, Finance/Accounting, General Management, Human Resources,
Marketing, Research and Development, Women/Minorities

**Mancino, Gene** — *President*
Blau Kaptain Schroeder
12 Roszel Road, Suite C-101
Princeton, NJ 08540
Telephone: (609) 520-8400
**Recruiter Classification:** Retained; **Lowest/Average Salary:** $75,000/$75,000;
**Industry Concentration:** Biotechnology, Healthcare/Hospitals,
Pharmaceutical/Medical, Venture Capital; **Function Concentration:** General
Management, Marketing, Research and Development

**Mancos, Barbara** — *Branch Manager*
Accountants on Call
3333 North Mayfair Road, Suite 112
Wauwatosa, WI 53222
Telephone: (414) 771-1900
**Recruiter Classification:** Contingency; **Lowest/Average Salary:**
$20,000/$30,000; **Industry Concentration:** Generalist; **Function
Concentration:** Finance/Accounting

**Manes, Kathy** — *Account Executive*
Dunhill Professional Search of Irvine, Inc.
9 Executive Circle, Suite 240
Irvine, CA 92714
Telephone: (714) 474-6666
**Recruiter Classification:** Contingency; **Lowest/Average Salary:**
$30,000/$40,000; **Function Concentration:** Sales

**Mangum, Jackie** — *Consultant*
Thomas Mangum Company
500 East Del Mar Boulevard, Suite 19
Pasadena, CA 91101
Telephone: (818) 577-2070
**Recruiter Classification:** Retained; **Lowest/Average Salary:** $75,000/$90,000;
**Industry Concentration:** Generalist; **Function Concentration:** Generalist

**Mangum, William T.** — *President*
Thomas Mangum Company
500 East Del Mar Boulevard, Suite 19
Pasadena, CA 91101
Telephone: (818) 577-2070
**Recruiter Classification:** Retained; **Lowest/Average Salary:** $75,000/$90,000;
**Industry Concentration:** Generalist with a primary focus in Automotive,
Biotechnology, Chemical Products, Consumer Products, Electronics, Energy,
Environmental, Financial Services, High Technology, Hospitality/Leisure,
Information Technology, Manufacturing, Packaging, Pharmaceutical/Medical;
**Function Concentration:** Generalist

**Mann, Carol** — *Recruiter*
Bryant Research
466 Old Hook Road, Suite 32
Emerson, NJ 07630
Telephone: (201) 599-0590
**Recruiter Classification:** Contingency; **Lowest/Average Salary:**
$50,000/$90,000; **Industry Concentration:** Biotechnology,
Pharmaceutical/Medical; **Function Concentration:** Research and Development

**Mann, Douglas G.** — *Principal*
Ward Howell International, Inc.
401 East Host Drive
Lake Geneva, WI 53147
Telephone: (414) 249-5200
**Recruiter Classification:** Retained; **Lowest/Average Salary:** $75,000/$90,000;
**Industry Concentration:** Generalist; **Function Concentration:** Generalist

**Manning, Jerry A.** — *Manager Pacific Region*
Management Recruiters International, Inc.
533 26th Street, Suite 203-B
Ogden, UT 84401
Telephone: (801) 621-1777
**Recruiter Classification:** Contingency; **Lowest/Average Salary:**
$30,000/$75,000; **Industry Concentration:** Generalist; **Function
Concentration:** Generalist

**Manning, Robert A.** — *General Manager North Atlantic
Region*
Management Recruiters International, Inc.
Alford Building
121 Tarboro Street, P.O. Box 1186
Rocky Mount, NC 27802-1186
Telephone: (919) 442-8000
**Recruiter Classification:** Contingency; **Lowest/Average Salary:**
$30,000/$75,000; **Industry Concentration:** Generalist; **Function
Concentration:** Generalist

**Manns, Alex** — *Executive Recruiter*
Crawford & Crofford
15327 NW 60th Avenue, Suite 240
Miami Lakes, FL 33014
Telephone: (305) 820-0855
**Recruiter Classification:** Contingency; **Lowest/Average Salary:**
$20,000/$50,000; **Industry Concentration:** Generalist with a primary focus in
Chemical Products, Consumer Products, Electronics, Environmental, Financial
Services, Healthcare/Hospitals, High Technology, Information Technology,
Manufacturing, Packaging, Pharmaceutical/Medical, Public Administration,
Transportation; **Function Concentration:** Generalist with a primary focus in
Administration, Engineering, Finance/Accounting, General Management,
Human Resources, Marketing, Sales

**Mansfield, Chris** — *Consultant*
Paul Ray Berndtson
10 South Riverside Plaza
Suite 720
Chicago, IL 60606
Telephone: (312) 876-0730
**Recruiter Classification:** Retained; **Lowest/Average Salary:** $90,000/$90,000;
**Industry Concentration:** Generalist; **Function Concentration:** Generalist

**Mansford, Keith** — *Chairman Bio-Pharmaceutical Division*
Howard Fischer Associates, Inc.
1800 John F. Kennedy Boulevard, 7th Floor
Philadelphia, PA 19103
Telephone: (215) 568-8363
**Recruiter Classification:** Retained; **Lowest/Average Salary:** $90,000/$90,000;
**Industry Concentration:** Biotechnology, Pharmaceutical/Medical; **Function
Concentration:** Generalist

**Manthey, Merv** — *Principal*
KPMG Executive Search
Suite 750
205 Fifth Avenue S.W.
Calgary, Alberta, CANADA T2P 2V7
Telephone: (403) 691-8300
**Recruiter Classification:** Retained; **Lowest/Average Salary:** $75,000/$90,000;
**Industry Concentration:** Generalist; **Function Concentration:** Generalist

**Manzo, Renee** — *Consultant*
Atlantic Search Group, Inc.
One Liberty Square
Boston, MA 02109
Telephone: (617) 426-9700
**Recruiter Classification:** Contingency; **Lowest/Average Salary:**
$20,000/$60,000; **Industry Concentration:** Generalist with a primary focus in
Biotechnology, Consumer Products, Electronics, Financial Services,
Information Technology, Manufacturing, Real Estate; **Function Concentration:**
Finance/Accounting

**Manzo, Romero** — *Principal*
The Prairie Group
One Westbrook Corporate Center
Suite 300
Westchester, IL 60154
Telephone: (708) 449-7710
**Recruiter Classification:** Contingency; **Lowest/Average Salary:**
$50,000/$75,000; **Industry Concentration:** Generalist; **Function
Concentration:** Human Resources

**Maphet, Harriet** — *Vice President*
The Stevenson Group of New Jersey
560 Sylvan Avenue
Englewood Cliffs, NJ 07632
Telephone: (201) 568-1900
**Recruiter Classification:** Retained; **Lowest/Average Salary:** $75,000/$90,000;
**Industry Concentration:** Generalist with a primary focus in Chemical Products,
Consumer Products, Fashion (Retail/Apparel), Financial Services, Information
Technology, Pharmaceutical/Medical; **Function Concentration:** Generalist with
a primary focus in Finance/Accounting, General Management, Human
Resources, Marketing, Sales

**Marchette, Steve** — *Director*
Juntunen-Combs-Poirier
600 Montgomery Street, 2nd Floor
San Francisco, CA 94111
Telephone: (415) 291-1699
**Recruiter Classification:** Retained; **Lowest/Average Salary:** $90,000/$90,000;
**Industry Concentration:** Consumer Products, Electronics, Entertainment, High
Technology, Information Technology, Publishing/Media; **Function
Concentration:** Generalist with a primary focus in Engineering, General
Management, Marketing, Research and Development, Sales

**Marcus, Jane B.** — *Executive Director*
Russell Reynolds Associates, Inc.
200 South Wacker Drive
Suite 3600
Chicago, IL 60606
Telephone: (312) 993-9696
**Recruiter Classification:** Retained; **Lowest/Average Salary:** $90,000/$90,000;
**Industry Concentration:** Generalist; **Function Concentration:** Generalist

**Margolis, Michael** — *Executive Recruiter*
Spectra International Inc.
6991 East Camelback Road, Suite B-305
Scottsdale, AZ 85251
Telephone: (602) 481-0411
**Recruiter Classification:** Contingency; **Lowest/Average Salary:**
$30,000/$75,000

**Marino, Chester** — *Recruiter*
Cochran, Cochran & Yale, Inc.
955 East Henrietta Road
Rochester, NY 14623
Telephone: (716) 424-6060
**Recruiter Classification:** Contingency; **Lowest/Average Salary:**
$40,000/$60,000; **Industry Concentration:** Generalist with a primary focus in
Automotive, Consumer Products, High Technology, Information Technology,
Manufacturing, Packaging, Pharmaceutical/Medical, Publishing/Media;
**Function Concentration:** Engineering, Research and Development,
Women/Minorities

**Marino, Jory J.** — *Principal*
Sullivan & Company
20 Exchange Place, 50th Floor
New York, NY 10005
Telephone: (212) 422-3000
**Recruiter Classification:** Retained; **Lowest/Average Salary:** $90,000/$90,000;
**Industry Concentration:** Generalist with a primary focus in Financial Services;
**Function Concentration:** Generalist

**Marion, Bradford B.** — *Principal*
Lamalie Amrop International
225 West Wacker Drive
Chicago, IL 60606-1229
Telephone: (312) 782-3113
**Recruiter Classification:** Retained; **Lowest/Average Salary:** $90,000/$90,000;
**Industry Concentration:** Generalist; **Function Concentration:** Generalist with a
primary focus in Finance/Accounting, General Management, Human
Resources, Marketing, Sales

**Marion, Michael** — *Recruiter*
S.D. Kelly & Associates, Inc.
990 Washington Street
Dedham, MA 02026
Telephone: (617) 326-8038
**Recruiter Classification:** Contingency; **Lowest/Average Salary:**
$50,000/$60,000; **Industry Concentration:** Electronics, High Technology,
Manufacturing; **Function Concentration:** Engineering, General Management,
Marketing, Sales

**Mark, John L.** — *Principal*
J.L. Mark Associates, Inc.
2000 Arapahoe Street, Suite 505
Denver, CO 80205
Telephone: (303) 292-0360
**Recruiter Classification:** Retained; **Lowest/Average Salary:** $/$90,000; **Industry
Concentration:** Generalist with a primary focus in Consumer Products,
Financial Services, High Technology, Information Technology, Manufacturing,
Publishing/Media, Transportation; **Function Concentration:** Generalist

**Marks, Brad** — *Chairman and CEO*
Brad Marks International
1888 Century Park East
Suite 1040
Los Angeles, CA 90067
Telephone: (310) 286-0600
**Recruiter Classification:** Retained; **Lowest/Average Salary:** $60,000/$75,000;
**Industry Concentration:** Entertainment; **Function Concentration:** Generalist

**Marks, Ira** — *Principal*
Strategic Alternatives
3 Portola Road
Portola Valley, CA 94028
Telephone: (415) 851-2211
**Recruiter Classification:** Retained; **Lowest/Average Salary:** $75,000/$90,000;
**Industry Concentration:** Generalist with a primary focus in Board Services,
Consumer Products, Electronics, High Technology, Information Technology,
Publishing/Media, Venture Capital; **Function Concentration:** Generalist with a
primary focus in Engineering, General Management, Marketing, Research and
Development, Sales, Women/Minorities

**Marks, Paula** — *Senior Partner*
Alexander Ross Inc.
280 Madison Avenue
New York, NY 10016
Telephone: (212) 889-9333
**Recruiter Classification:** Retained; **Lowest/Average Salary:** $75,000/$90,000;
**Industry Concentration:** Generalist; **Function Concentration:** Human
Resources

**Marks, Russell E.** — *Managing Director*
Webb, Johnson Associates, Inc.
280 Park Avenue, 43rd Floor
New York, NY 10017
Telephone: (212) 661-3700
**Recruiter Classification:** Retained; **Lowest/Average Salary:** $90,000/$90,000;
**Industry Concentration:** Generalist with a primary focus in Biotechnology,
Chemical Products, Financial Services, Healthcare/Hospitals, High Technology,
Manufacturing, Non-Profit, Pharmaceutical/Medical; **Function Concentration:**
Generalist with a primary focus in Administration, Engineering,
Finance/Accounting, General Management, Human Resources, Marketing,
Research and Development, Sales

**Marks, Sarah J.** — *Principal*
The Executive Source
55 Fifth Avenue, 19th Floor
New York, NY 10003
Telephone: (212) 691-5505
**Recruiter Classification:** Executive Temporary; **Lowest/Average Salary:**
$75,000/$90,000; **Industry Concentration:** Financial Services, Insurance,
Venture Capital; **Function Concentration:** Human Resources

**Marlow, William** — *Vice President Technology*
Straube Associates
Willows Professional Park
855 Turnpike Street
North Andover, MA 01845-6105
Telephone: (508) 687-1993
**Recruiter Classification:** Retained; **Lowest/Average Salary:** $60,000/$90,000;
**Industry Concentration:** Generalist with a primary focus in Electronics,
Healthcare/Hospitals, High Technology, Manufacturing; **Function
Concentration:** Generalist with a primary focus in Engineering,
Finance/Accounting, General Management, Human Resources, Marketing,
Women/Minorities

**Marra, John** — *Partner*
Marra Peters & Partners
Millburn Esplanade
Millburn, NJ 07041
Telephone: (201) 376-8999
**Recruiter Classification:** Retained; **Lowest/Average Salary:** $/$90,000; **Industry
Concentration:** Generalist with a primary focus in Biotechnology, Consumer
Products, Entertainment, Financial Services, Information Technology,
Manufacturing, Pharmaceutical/Medical; **Function Concentration:** Generalist
with a primary focus in Administration, Engineering, Finance/Accounting,
General Management, Human Resources, Marketing, Research and
Development, Sales

**Marra, John** — *Partner*
Marra Peters & Partners
7040 West Palmetto Park Road, Suite 145
Boca Raton, FL 33433
Telephone: (407) 347-7778
**Recruiter Classification:** Retained; **Lowest/Average Salary:** $/$90,000; **Industry
Concentration:** Generalist with a primary focus in Biotechnology, Consumer
Products, Entertainment, Financial Services, Information Technology,
Manufacturing, Pharmaceutical/Medical; **Function Concentration:** Generalist
with a primary focus in Administration, Engineering, Finance/Accounting,
General Management, Human Resources, Marketing, Research and
Development, Sales

**Marriott, Gloria A.** — *Co-Manager North Atlantic Region*
Management Recruiters International, Inc.
236 Public Square, Suite 201
Franklin, TN 37064-2520
Telephone: (615) 791-4391
**Recruiter Classification:** Contingency; **Lowest/Average Salary:**
$30,000/$75,000; **Industry Concentration:** Generalist; **Function
Concentration:** Generalist

**Marriott, Roger** — *Co-Manager*
Management Recruiters International, Inc.
236 Public Square, Suite 201
Franklin, TN 37064-2520
Telephone: (615) 791-4391
**Recruiter Classification:** Contingency; **Lowest/Average Salary:**
$30,000/$75,000; **Industry Concentration:** Generalist; **Function
Concentration:** Generalist

**Marshall, Gerald** — *Consultant*
Blair/Tech Recruiters
77 Milltown Road
East Brunswick, NJ 08816
Telephone: (908) 390-5550
**Recruiter Classification:** Contingency; **Lowest/Average Salary:**
$40,000/$60,000; **Industry Concentration:** Biotechnology, Chemical Products,
Consumer Products, Environmental, Manufacturing, Packaging,
Pharmaceutical/Medical; **Function Concentration:** Engineering, Research and
Development

**Marshall, John** — *Manager*
Accountants on Call
700 Ackerman Road
Columbus, OH 43202
Telephone: (614) 267-7200
**Recruiter Classification:** Contingency; **Lowest/Average Salary:**
$20,000/$30,000; **Industry Concentration:** Generalist; **Function
Concentration:** Finance/Accounting

**Marshall, Larry** — *President and CEO*
Marshall Consultants, Inc.
360 East 65th Street
New York, NY 10021
Telephone: (212) 628-8400
**Recruiter Classification:** Retained; **Lowest/Average Salary:** $75,000/$90,000;
**Industry Concentration:** Generalist; **Function Concentration:** Marketing

**Marshall, Neill P.** — *Consultant*
Witt/Kieffer, Ford, Hadelman & Lloyd
8117 Preston Road, Suite 690
Dallas, TX 75225
Telephone: (214) 739-1370
**Recruiter Classification:** Retained; **Lowest/Average Salary:** $75,000/$90,000;
**Industry Concentration:** Healthcare/Hospitals; **Function Concentration:**
Generalist with a primary focus in General Management

**Marsteller, Franklin D.** — *Director*
Spencer Stuart
2005 Market Street, Suite 2350
Philadelphia, PA 19103
Telephone: (215) 851-6200
**Recruiter Classification:** Retained; **Lowest/Average Salary:** $90,000/$90,000;
**Industry Concentration:** Financial Services, Insurance; **Function
Concentration:** Generalist

**Martens, Maxine** — *Vice President*
Rene Plessner Associates, Inc.
375 Park Avenue
New York, NY 10152
Telephone: (212) 421-3490
**Recruiter Classification:** Retained; **Lowest/Average Salary:** $75,000/$90,000;
**Industry Concentration:** Generalist with a primary focus in Consumer
Products, Fashion (Retail/Apparel), Packaging, Publishing/Media; **Function
Concentration:** Generalist with a primary focus in Administration,
Finance/Accounting, General Management, Human Resources, Marketing,
Sales

**Martin, Al** — *Associate*
KPMG Executive Search
800-200 Graham Avenue
Winnipeg, Manitoba, CANADA R3C 4M1
Telephone: (204) 944-1014
**Recruiter Classification:** Retained; **Lowest/Average Salary:** $75,000/$90,000;
**Industry Concentration:** Generalist; **Function Concentration:** Generalist

**Martin, Bette** — *Manager Customer Relations*
R.D. Gatti & Associates, Incorporated
266 Main Street, Suite 21
Medfield, MA 02052
Telephone: (508) 359-4153
**Recruiter Classification:** Contingency; **Lowest/Average Salary:**
$40,000/$75,000; **Industry Concentration:** Generalist; **Function
Concentration:** Human Resources

**Martin, Charles E.** — *Co-Manager South Atlantic Region*
Management Recruiters International, Inc.
Chase Commerce Park, Building 100
3821 Lorna Road, Suite 108
Birmingham, AL 35244-1035
Telephone: (205) 444-9116
**Recruiter Classification:** Contingency; **Lowest/Average Salary:**
$30,000/$75,000; **Industry Concentration:** Generalist; **Function
Concentration:** Generalist

**Martin, David** — *Associate*
The Guild Corporation
8260 Greensboro Drive, Suite 460
McLean, VA 22102
Telephone: (703) 761-4023
**Recruiter Classification:** Contingency; **Lowest/Average Salary:**
$40,000/$50,000; **Industry Concentration:** Aerospace/Defense, Electronics,
High Technology, Information Technology; **Function Concentration:** Generalist
with a primary focus in Engineering, Finance/Accounting, General
Management, Research and Development

**Martin, Ellen** — *Account Executive*
Hunt Ltd.
21 West 38th Street
New York, NY 10018
Telephone: (212) 997-2299
**Recruiter Classification:** Contingency; **Lowest/Average Salary:**
$40,000/$50,000; **Industry Concentration:** Automotive, Chemical Products,
Consumer Products, Fashion (Retail/Apparel), Manufacturing,
Pharmaceutical/Medical, Publishing/Media, Transportation; **Function
Concentration:** Generalist

**Martin, Geary D.** — *Consultant*
Boyden/Zay & Company
Two Midtown Plaza, Suite 1740
1360 Peachtree Street, NE
Atlanta, GA 30309
Telephone: (404) 876-9986
**Recruiter Classification:** Retained; **Lowest/Average Salary:** $90,000/$90,000;
**Industry Concentration:** Generalist with a primary focus in
Aerospace/Defense, Consumer Products, Environmental, Fashion
(Retail/Apparel), Manufacturing; **Function Concentration:** Generalist with a
primary focus in Engineering, Finance/Accounting, General Management,
Marketing, Research and Development, Sales

**Martin, James** — *Senior Consultant - Datacommunications*
Spectra International Inc.
6991 East Camelback Road, Suite B-305
Scottsdale, AZ 85251
Telephone: (602) 481-0411
**Recruiter Classification:** Contingency; **Lowest/Average Salary:**
$50,000/$60,000; **Function Concentration:** Engineering

**Martin, John G.** — *Principal*
Lamalie Amrop International
Thanksgiving Tower
1601 Elm Street
Dallas, TX 75201-4768
Telephone: (214) 754-0019
**Recruiter Classification:** Retained; **Lowest/Average Salary:**
$90,000/$90,000; **Industry Concentration:** Generalist; **Function
Concentration:** Generalist

**Martin, Jon** — *Consultant*
Egon Zehnder International Inc.
1 First Canadian Place
P.O. Box 179
Toronto, Ontario, CANADA M5X 1C7
Telephone: (416) 364-0222
**Recruiter Classification:** Retained; **Lowest/Average Salary:** $90,000/$90,000;
**Industry Concentration:** Generalist with a primary focus in Biotechnology,
Financial Services, High Technology, Manufacturing, Pharmaceutical/Medical;
**Function Concentration:** Generalist

**Martin, Ken** — *Director*
Spencer Stuart
2005 Market Street, Suite 2350
Philadelphia, PA 19103
Telephone: (215) 851-6200
**Recruiter Classification:** Retained; **Lowest/Average Salary:** $90,000/$90,000;
**Industry Concentration:** Generalist; **Function Concentration:** Generalist

**Martin, Kenneth** — *Accounting and Finance Recruiter*
Winter, Wyman & Company
101 Federal Street, 27th Floor
Boston, MA 02110-1800
Telephone: (617) 951-2700
**Recruiter Classification:** Contingency; **Lowest/Average Salary:**
$20,000/$50,000; **Industry Concentration:** Generalist; **Function
Concentration:** Finance/Accounting

**Martin, Lynne Koll** — *Managing Director*
Boyden
Embarcadero Center West Tower
275 Battery St., Suite 420
San Francisco, CA 94111
Telephone: (415) 981-7900
**Recruiter Classification:** Retained; **Lowest/Average Salary:** $75,000/$90,000;
**Industry Concentration:** Generalist; **Function Concentration:** Generalist with a
primary focus in Engineering, Finance/Accounting, General Management,
Human Resources, Marketing, Research and Development, Sales,
Women/Minorities

**Martin, Mary Lou** — *Associate*
Neail Behringer Consultants
24 East 38th Street
New York, NY 10016
Telephone: (212) 689-7555
**Recruiter Classification:** Retained; **Lowest/Average Salary:** $40,000/$75,000;
**Industry Concentration:** Healthcare/Hospitals; **Function Concentration:**
Generalist with a primary focus in Administration, General Management,
Human Resources

**Martin, Nancy A.** — *Partner*
Educational Management Network
98 Old South Road
Nantucket, MA 02554
Telephone: (508) 228-6700
**Recruiter Classification:** Retained; **Lowest/Average Salary:** $60,000/$90,000;
**Industry Concentration:** Education/Libraries, Non-Profit; **Function
Concentration:** Generalist with a primary focus in Administration,
Finance/Accounting, Human Resources

**Martin, Pat A.** — *Co-Manager*
Management Recruiters International, Inc.
Chase Commerce Park, Building 100
3821 Lorna Road, Suite 108
Birmingham, AL 35244-1035
Telephone: (205) 444-9116
**Recruiter Classification:** Contingency; **Lowest/Average Salary:**
$30,000/$75,000; **Industry Concentration:** Generalist; **Function
Concentration:** Generalist

**Martin, Paula** — *Executive Recruiter*
MSI International
8521 Leesburg Pike, Suite 435
Vienna, VA 22182
Telephone: (703) 893-5669
**Recruiter Classification:** Contingency; **Lowest/Average Salary:**
$30,000/$60,000; **Industry Concentration:** Generalist with a primary focus in
Healthcare/Hospitals; **Function Concentration:** Administration, Engineering,
Finance/Accounting, General Management, Marketing

**Martin, Rande L.** — *Manager Central Region*
Management Recruiters International, Inc.
Forest Park Building, Suite 101
2519 East Main Street
Richmond, IN 47374-5864
Telephone: (317) 935-3356
**Recruiter Classification:** Contingency; **Lowest/Average Salary:**
$30,000/$75,000; **Industry Concentration:** Generalist; **Function
Concentration:** Generalist

**Martines, James** — *Specialist Chemicals*
Sharrow & Associates
24735 Van Dyke
Center Line, MI 48015
Telephone: (810) 759-6910
**Recruiter Classification:** Contingency; **Lowest/Average Salary:**
$30,000/$50,000; **Industry Concentration:** Automotive, Biotechnology,
Chemical Products, Consumer Products, Environmental; **Function
Concentration:** Engineering

**Marumoto, William H.** — *Managing Director*
The Interface Group, Ltd./Boyden
2828 Pennsylvania Avenue, N.W., Suite 305
Washington, DC 20007
Telephone: (202) 342-7200
**Recruiter Classification:** Retained; **Lowest/Average Salary:** $75,000/$90,000;
**Industry Concentration:** Generalist with a primary focus in
Aerospace/Defense, Board Services, Consumer Products, Energy, Financial
Services, Healthcare/Hospitals, Non-Profit, Pharmaceutical/Medical,
Publishing/Media, Utilities/Nuclear, Venture Capital; **Function Concentration:**
Generalist with a primary focus in Administration, Finance/Accounting,
General Management, Human Resources, Marketing, Women/Minorities

**Marwil, Jennifer** — *Associate*
Source Services Corporation
One South Main Street, Suite 1440
Dayton, OH 45402
Telephone: (513) 461-4660
**Recruiter Classification:** Contingency; **Lowest/Average Salary:**
$30,000/$50,000; **Industry Concentration:** Financial Services, Information
Technology; **Function Concentration:** Engineering, Finance/Accounting

**Marx, Dennis R.** — *Chief Operating Officer*
DHR International, Inc.
10 South Riverside Plaza, Suite 2220
Chicago, IL 60606
Telephone: (312) 782-1581
**Recruiter Classification:** Retained; **Lowest/Average Salary:** $60,000/$90,000;
**Industry Concentration:** Generalist; **Function Concentration:** Generalist

**Marye, George** — *Executive Recruiter*
Damon & Associates, Inc.
7515 Greenville Avenue, Suite 900
Dallas, TX 75231
Telephone: (214) 696-6990
**Recruiter Classification:** Contingency; **Lowest/Average Salary:**
$40,000/$60,000; **Industry Concentration:** Generalist with a primary focus in
High Technology, Information Technology; **Function Concentration:** Sales

**Maschal, Charles E.** — *President*
Maschal/Connors, Inc.
306 South Bay Avenue, P.O. Box 1301
Beach Haven, NJ 08008
Telephone: (609) 492-3400
**Recruiter Classification:** Retained; **Lowest/Average Salary:** $90,000/$90,000;
**Industry Concentration:** Generalist with a primary focus in Manufacturing;
**Function Concentration:** Generalist with a primary focus in Administration,
Engineering, Finance/Accounting, General Management, Human Resources,
Marketing, Research and Development, Sales

**Mashack, Ted M.** — *Manager Eastern Region*
Management Recruiters International, Inc.
678 Louis Drive
Warminster, PA 18974
Telephone: (215) 675-6440
**Recruiter Classification:** Contingency; **Lowest/Average Salary:**
$30,000/$75,000; **Industry Concentration:** Generalist; **Function
Concentration:** Generalist

**Mashakas, Elizabeth** — *Legal Consultant*
TOPAZ International, Inc.
383 Northfield Avenue
West Orange, NJ 07052
Telephone: (201) 669-7300
**Recruiter Classification:** Contingency; **Lowest/Average Salary:**
$40,000/$75,000; **Industry Concentration:** Chemical Products, Consumer
Products, Electronics, Entertainment, Financial Services, High Technology,
Manufacturing, Pharmaceutical/Medical; **Function Concentration:** Generalist
with a primary focus in Women/Minorities

**Mashakas, Elizabeth** — *Legal Consultant*
TOPAZ Legal Solutions
383 Northfield Avenue
West Orange, NJ 07052
Telephone: (201) 669-7300
**Recruiter Classification:** Executive Temporary; **Lowest/Average Salary:**
$40,000/$75,000; **Industry Concentration:** Chemical Products, Consumer
Products, Electronics, Entertainment, Environmental, Financial Services, High
Technology, Manufacturing; **Function Concentration:** Generalist with a
primary focus in Women/Minorities

**Maslan, Neal L.** — *Managing Director*
Ward Howell International, Inc.
16255 Ventura Boulevard
Suite 400
Encino, CA 91436-2394
Telephone: (818) 905-6010
**Recruiter Classification:** Retained; **Lowest/Average Salary:** $75,000/$90,000;
**Industry Concentration:** Biotechnology, Healthcare/Hospitals; **Function
Concentration:** Generalist with a primary focus in General Management

**Mason, Eileen** — *Co-Manager*
Management Recruiters International, Inc.
Soho Office Center, Suite 500
712 Broadway
Kansas City, MO 64105
Telephone: (816) 221-2377
**Recruiter Classification:** Contingency; **Lowest/Average Salary:**
$30,000/$75,000; **Industry Concentration:** Generalist; **Function
Concentration:** Generalist

**Mason, Marlene** — *Vice President*
Richard Kader & Associates
343 West Bagley Road, Suite 209
Berea, OH 44017
Telephone: (216) 891-1700
**Recruiter Classification:** Contingency; **Lowest/Average Salary:**
$40,000/$50,000; **Industry Concentration:** Generalist; **Function
Concentration:** Generalist

**Mason, William E.** — *Executive Vice President*
John Kurosky & Associates
3 Corporate Park Drive, Suite 210
Irvine, CA 92714
Telephone: (714) 851-6370
**Recruiter Classification:** Retained; **Lowest/Average Salary:** $60,000/$90,000;
**Industry Concentration:** Generalist with a primary focus in
Aerospace/Defense, Chemical Products, Electronics, High Technology,
Manufacturing, Pharmaceutical/Medical; **Function Concentration:** Generalist
with a primary focus in Engineering, Finance/Accounting, General
Management, Research and Development

**Masse, Laurence R.** — *Managing Director*
Ward Howell International, Inc.
1300 Grove Avenue, Suite 100
Barrington, IL 60010
Telephone: (847) 382-2206
**Recruiter Classification:** Retained; **Lowest/Average Salary:** $90,000/$90,000;
**Industry Concentration:** Aerospace/Defense, Automotive, Manufacturing;
**Function Concentration:** Generalist

**Massey, H. Heath** — *Vice President and Associate*
Robison & Associates
1350 First Citizens Plaza
128 South Tryon Street
Charlotte, NC 28202
Telephone: (704) 376-0059
**Recruiter Classification:** Retained; **Lowest/Average Salary:** $50,000/$90,000;
**Industry Concentration:** Generalist with a primary focus in Chemical Products,
Consumer Products, Energy, Financial Services, Manufacturing, Non-Profit,
Public Administration, Transportation; **Function Concentration:** Generalist with
a primary focus in Engineering, Finance/Accounting, General Management,
Human Resources, Sales

**Massey, R. Bruce** — *Partner*
Bruce Massey & Partners Inc.
330 Bay Street, Suite 1104
Toronto, Ontario, CANADA M5H 2S8
Telephone: (416) 861-0077
**Recruiter Classification:** Retained; **Lowest/Average Salary:** $90,000/$90,000;
**Industry Concentration:** Generalist; **Function Concentration:** Generalist with a
primary focus in Administration, Engineering, Finance/Accounting, General
Management, Human Resources, Marketing, Research and Development

**Massung, Larry J.** — *Manager Pacific Region*
Management Recruiters International, Inc.
Cottontree Square, Building 11-I
2230 N. at University Parkway
Provo, UT 84604-1509
Telephone: (801) 375-0777
**Recruiter Classification:** Contingency; **Lowest/Average Salary:**
$30,000/$75,000; **Industry Concentration:** Generalist; **Function
Concentration:** Generalist

**Mastandrea, Pat** — *Partner*
Johnson Smith & Knisely Accord
100 Park Avenue, 15th Floor
New York, NY 10017
Telephone: (212) 885-9100
**Recruiter Classification:** Retained; **Lowest/Average Salary:** $90,000/$90,000;
**Industry Concentration:** Generalist; **Function Concentration:** Generalist

**Matheny, Robert P.** — *Executive Recruiter*
MSI International
1900 North 18th Street
Suite 303
Monroe, LA 71201
Telephone: (318) 324-0406
**Recruiter Classification:** Contingency; **Lowest/Average Salary:**
$30,000/$75,000; **Industry Concentration:** Generalist with a primary focus in
Healthcare/Hospitals, Pharmaceutical/Medical; **Function Concentration:**
Generalist with a primary focus in Administration, Engineering,
Finance/Accounting, General Management, Marketing, Sales

**Mather, David R.** — *Vice President*
Christian & Timbers
20823 Stevens Creek Boulevard, Suite 250
Cupertino, CA 95014
Telephone: (408) 446-5440
**Recruiter Classification:** Retained; **Lowest/Average Salary:** $90,000/$90,000;
**Industry Concentration:** Generalist with a primary focus in Financial Services,
High Technology, Information Technology, Manufacturing, Venture Capital;
**Function Concentration:** Generalist with a primary focus in Administration,
Engineering, Finance/Accounting, General Management, Human Resources,
Marketing, Research and Development, Sales, Women/Minorities

**Mathias, Douglas** — *Managing Director*
Source Services Corporation
10220 SW Greenburg Road, Suite 625
Portland, OR 97223
Telephone: (503) 768-4546
**Recruiter Classification:** Contingency; **Lowest/Average Salary:**
$30,000/$50,000; **Industry Concentration:** Financial Services, Information
Technology; **Function Concentration:** Engineering, Finance/Accounting

**Mathias, Kathy** — *Managing Director*
Stone Murphy & Olson
5500 Wayzata Boulevard
Suite 1020
Minneapolis, MN 55416
Telephone: (612) 591-2300
**Recruiter Classification:** Retained; **Lowest/Average Salary:** $60,000/$75,000;
**Industry Concentration:** Generalist with a primary focus in Environmental,
Financial Services, Insurance, Manufacturing, Non-Profit; **Function
Concentration:** Generalist

**Mathias, William J.** — *Associate/Consultant*
Preng & Associates, Inc.
2925 Briarpark, Suite 1111
Houston, TX 77042
Telephone: (713) 266-2600
**Recruiter Classification:** Retained; **Lowest/Average Salary:** $75,000/$90,000;
**Industry Concentration:** Generalist with a primary focus in Biotechnology,
Chemical Products, Education/Libraries, Energy, Environmental,
Healthcare/Hospitals, Information Technology, Oil/Gas, Real Estate; **Function
Concentration:** Generalist with a primary focus in Engineering,
Finance/Accounting, General Management, Human Resources, Research and
Development

**Mathis, Carrie** — *Associate*
Source Services Corporation
5429 LBJ Freeway, Suite 275
Dallas, TX 75240
Telephone: (214) 387-1600
**Recruiter Classification:** Contingency; **Lowest/Average Salary:**
$30,000/$50,000; **Industry Concentration:** Financial Services, Information
Technology; **Function Concentration:** Engineering, Finance/Accounting

**Matthews, James M.** — *Senior Associate*
Stanton Chase International
100 East Pratt Street
Suite 2530
Baltimore, MD 21202
Telephone: (410) 528-8400
**Recruiter Classification:** Retained; **Lowest/Average Salary:** $75,000/$90,000;
**Industry Concentration:** Generalist; **Function Concentration:** Generalist

**Matthews, John C.** — *Manager North Atlantic Region*
Management Recruiters International, Inc.
2 East Church Street, 3rd Floor
P.O. Box 107
Martinsville, VA 24114-0107
Telephone: (703) 638-2000
**Recruiter Classification:** Contingency; **Lowest/Average Salary:**
$30,000/$75,000; **Industry Concentration:** Generalist; **Function
Concentration:** Generalist

**Matthews, Mary E.** — *Principal*
Nordeman Grimm, Inc.
717 Fifth Avenue, 26th Floor
New York, NY 10022
Telephone: (212) 935-1000
**Recruiter Classification:** Retained; **Lowest/Average Salary:** $90,000/$90,000;
**Industry Concentration:** Generalist; **Function Concentration:** Generalist

**Matthews, Nadie** — *Branch Manager*
Accountants on Call
7677 Oakport Street, Suite 180
Oakland, CA 94621
Telephone: (510) 633-1665
**Recruiter Classification:** Contingency; **Lowest/Average Salary:**
$20,000/$30,000; **Industry Concentration:** Generalist; **Function
Concentration:** Finance/Accounting

**Matthews, William A.** — *Partner*
Heidrick & Struggles, Inc.
One Peachtree Center
303 Peachtree Street, NE, Suite 3100
Atlanta, GA 30308
Telephone: (404) 577-2410
**Recruiter Classification:** Retained; **Lowest/Average Salary:** $75,000/$90,000;
**Industry Concentration:** Generalist; **Function Concentration:** Generalist

**Matti, Suzy** — *Recruiter*
Southwestern Professional Services
9485 Regency Square Boulevard, Suite 110
Jacksonville, FL 32225
Telephone: (904) 464-0400
**Recruiter Classification:** Contingency; **Lowest/Average Salary:**
$30,000/$60,000; **Industry Concentration:** Generalist with a primary focus in
Healthcare/Hospitals, Information Technology, Pharmaceutical/Medical,
Publishing/Media; **Function Concentration:** Marketing, Sales

**Mattingly, Kathleen** — *Managing Director*
Source Services Corporation
2850 National City Tower
Louisville, KY 40202
Telephone: (502) 581-9900
**Recruiter Classification:** Contingency; **Lowest/Average Salary:**
$30,000/$50,000; **Industry Concentration:** Financial Services, Information
Technology; **Function Concentration:** Engineering, Finance/Accounting

**Mattox, Robert D.** — *Director*
Spencer Stuart
One Atlantic Center, Suite 3230
1201 West Peachtree Street
Atlanta, GA 30309
Telephone: (404) 892-2800
**Recruiter Classification:** Retained; **Lowest/Average Salary:** $90,000/$90,000;
**Industry Concentration:** Generalist; **Function Concentration:** Generalist

**Matueny, Robert** — *Executive Recruiter*
Ryan, Miller & Associates Inc.
4601 Wilshire Boulevard, Suite 225
Los Angeles, CA 90010
Telephone: (213) 938-4768
**Recruiter Classification:** Contingency; **Lowest/Average Salary:**
$40,000/$50,000; **Industry Concentration:** Consumer Products, Electronics,
Entertainment, Financial Services, Manufacturing, Publishing/Media; **Function
Concentration:** Finance/Accounting

**Mauer, Kristin** — *Senior Associate*
Montgomery Resources, Inc.
555 Montgomery Street, Suite 1650
San Francisco, CA 94111
Telephone: (415) 956-4242
**Recruiter Classification:** Contingency; **Lowest/Average Salary:**
$30,000/$60,000; **Industry Concentration:** Consumer Products, Financial
Services, High Technology, Insurance, Manufacturing, Real Estate, Venture
Capital; **Function Concentration:** Finance/Accounting

**Maurizio, Michael** — *Manager Eastern Region*
Management Recruiters International, Inc.
10 Main Street, Suite 202
Whitesboro, NY 13492
Telephone: (315) 768-3322
**Recruiter Classification:** Contingency; **Lowest/Average Salary:**
$30,000/$75,000; **Industry Concentration:** Generalist; **Function
Concentration:** Generalist

**Max, Bruno** — *President*
RBR Associates, Inc.
P.O. Box 602
Silver Spring, MD 20901
Telephone: (301) 681-3443
**Recruiter Classification:** Contingency; **Lowest/Average Salary:**
$75,000/$75,000; **Industry Concentration:** Environmental; **Function
Concentration:** Engineering, General Management, Marketing, Sales

**Maxwell, Carol** — *Consultant*
Paul Ray Berndtson
10 South Riverside Plaza
Suite 720
Chicago, IL 60606
Telephone: (312) 876-0730
**Recruiter Classification:** Retained; **Lowest/Average Salary:** $90,000/$90,000; **Industry Concentration:** Generalist; **Function Concentration:** Generalist

**Maxwell, John** — *Associate*
Source Services Corporation
1500 West Park Drive, Suite 390
Westborough, MA 01581
Telephone: (508) 366-2600
**Recruiter Classification:** Contingency; **Lowest/Average Salary:** $30,000/$50,000; **Industry Concentration:** Financial Services, Information Technology; **Function Concentration:** Engineering, Finance/Accounting

**May, Peter** — *Senior Principal*
Mixtec Group
31255 Cedar Valley Drive
Suite 300-327
Westlake Village, CA 91362
Telephone: (818) 889-8819
**Recruiter Classification:** Contingency; **Lowest/Average Salary:** $60,000/$90,000; **Industry Concentration:** Electronics, High Technology, Hospitality/Leisure; **Function Concentration:** Generalist with a primary focus in Administration, Engineering, Finance/Accounting, General Management, Marketing, Research and Development, Sales

**Mayer, Thomas** — *Associate*
Source Services Corporation
3 Summit Park Drive, Suite 550
Independence, OH 44131
Telephone: (216) 328-5900
**Recruiter Classification:** Contingency; **Lowest/Average Salary:** $30,000/$50,000; **Industry Concentration:** Financial Services, Information Technology; **Function Concentration:** Engineering, Finance/Accounting

**Mayes, Kay H.** — *Director*
John Shell Associates, Inc.
115 Atrium Way, Suite 122
Columbia, SC 29223
Telephone: (803) 788-6619
**Recruiter Classification:** Contingency, Executive Temporary; **Lowest/Average Salary:** $20,000/$40,000; **Industry Concentration:** Generalist with a primary focus in Environmental, Financial Services, Healthcare/Hospitals, High Technology, Information Technology, Insurance, Manufacturing, Packaging, Real Estate; **Function Concentration:** Finance/Accounting

**Mayland, Tina** — *Executive Director*
Russell Reynolds Associates, Inc.
The Hurt Building
50 Hurt Plaza, Suite 600
Atlanta, GA 30303
Telephone: (404) 577-3000
**Recruiter Classification:** Retained; **Lowest/Average Salary:** $90,000/$90,000; **Industry Concentration:** Generalist with a primary focus in High Technology; **Function Concentration:** Generalist

**Maynard, Raun** — *Branch Manager*
Accountants on Call
21800 Oxnard Street, Suite 750
Woodland Hills, CA 91367
Telephone: (818) 992-7676
**Recruiter Classification:** Contingency; **Lowest/Average Salary:** $20,000/$30,000; **Industry Concentration:** Generalist; **Function Concentration:** Finance/Accounting

**Mazor, Elly** — *Consultant*
Howard Fischer Associates, Inc.
1800 John F. Kennedy Boulevard, 7th Floor
Philadelphia, PA 19103
Telephone: (215) 568-8363
**Recruiter Classification:** Retained; **Lowest/Average Salary:** $90,000/$90,000; **Industry Concentration:** Generalist; **Function Concentration:** Generalist

**Mazza, David B.** — *Partner*
Mazza & Riley, Inc.
55 William Street, Suite 120
Wellesley, MA 02181-4000
Telephone: (617) 235-7724
**Recruiter Classification:** Retained; **Lowest/Average Salary:** $90,000/$90,000; **Industry Concentration:** Generalist with a primary focus in Consumer Products, Financial Services, High Technology, Information Technology, Venture Capital; **Function Concentration:** Generalist with a primary focus in Finance/Accounting, General Management, Marketing, Sales

**Mazza, Leslie P.** — *Senior Vice President and Director Research*
The Diversified Search Companies
2005 Market Street, Suite 3300
Philadelphia, PA 19103
Telephone: (215) 732-6666
**Recruiter Classification:** Retained; **Lowest/Average Salary:** $90,000/$90,000; **Industry Concentration:** Generalist; **Function Concentration:** Generalist

**Mazzitelli, Teresa A.** — *President*
The Mazzitelli Group, Ltd.
603 East Lake Street, Suite 200K
Wayzata, MN 55391
Telephone: (612) 449-9490
**Recruiter Classification:** Retained; **Lowest/Average Salary:** $60,000/$90,000; **Industry Concentration:** Generalist; **Function Concentration:** Generalist

**Mazzocchi, Jonathan** — *Accounting and Finance Recruiter*
Winter, Wyman & Company
950 Winter Street, Suite 3100
Waltham, MA 02154-1294
Telephone: (617) 890-7000
**Recruiter Classification:** Contingency; **Lowest/Average Salary:** $20,000/$50,000; **Industry Concentration:** Generalist; **Function Concentration:** Finance/Accounting

**McAleavy, Steve** — *Consultant*
Search Consultants International, Inc.
4545 Post Oak Place, Suite 208
Houston, TX 77027
Telephone: (713) 622-9188
**Recruiter Classification:** Contingency; **Lowest/Average Salary:** $60,000/$75,000; **Industry Concentration:** Utilities/Nuclear; **Function Concentration:** Marketing

**McAlpine, Bruce** — *Consultant Finance and Accounting*
Keith Bagg & Associates Inc.
36 Toronto Street, Suite 520
Toronto, Ontario, CANADA M5C 2C5
Telephone: (416) 863-1800
**Recruiter Classification:** Contingency, Executive Temporary; **Lowest/Average Salary:** $40,000/$60,000; **Industry Concentration:** Automotive, Biotechnology, Consumer Products, Electronics, Financial Services, Healthcare/Hospitals, Manufacturing, Pharmaceutical/Medical; **Function Concentration:** Finance/Accounting

**McAndrews, Kathy** — *Executive Recruiter*
CPS Inc.
One Westbrook Corporate Centre, Suite 600
Westchester, IL 60154
Telephone: (708) 531-8370
**Recruiter Classification:** Contingency; **Lowest/Average Salary:** $30,000/$50,000; **Industry Concentration:** Generalist with a primary focus in Automotive, Biotechnology, Chemical Products, Consumer Products, High Technology, Insurance, Manufacturing, Oil/Gas, Packaging, Pharmaceutical/Medical; **Function Concentration:** Engineering, Research and Development, Sales, Women/Minorities

**McAteer, Thomas** — *Partner*
Montgomery Resources, Inc.
555 Montgomery Street, Suite 1650
San Francisco, CA 94111
Telephone: (415) 956-4242
**Recruiter Classification:** Contingency, Executive Temporary; **Lowest/Average Salary:** $30,000/$60,000; **Industry Concentration:** Generalist with a primary focus in Consumer Products, Financial Services, High Technology, Insurance, Manufacturing, Real Estate, Venture Capital; **Function Concentration:** Finance/Accounting

**McAulay, A.L.** — *Principal*
The McAulay Firm
Nations Bank Corporate Center, Suite 3140
100 North Tryon Street
Charlotte, NC 28202
Telephone: (704) 342-1880
**Recruiter Classification:** Retained; **Lowest/Average Salary:** $75,000/$90,000; **Industry Concentration:** Generalist; **Function Concentration:** Generalist

**McBride, Jonathan E.** — *President*
McBride Associates, Inc.
1511 K Street N.W., Suite 819
Washington, DC 20005
Telephone: (202) 638-1150
**Recruiter Classification:** Retained; **Lowest/Average Salary:** $90,000/$90,000; **Industry Concentration:** Generalist with a primary focus in Biotechnology, Environmental, Financial Services, Healthcare/Hospitals, High Technology, Insurance, Manufacturing, Non-Profit, Pharmaceutical/Medical, Venture Capital; **Function Concentration:** Generalist with a primary focus in Administration, Finance/Accounting, General Management, Human Resources, Marketing, Research and Development, Sales

**McBryde, Marnie** — *Senior Director*
Spencer Stuart
277 Park Avenue, 29th Floor
New York, NY 10172
Telephone: (212) 336-0200
**Recruiter Classification:** Retained; **Lowest/Average Salary:** $50,000/$75,000; **Industry Concentration:** Generalist with a primary focus in Consumer Products, Fashion (Retail/Apparel), Financial Services; **Function Concentration:** Generalist with a primary focus in Finance/Accounting, General Management, Marketing, Sales

**McBurney, Kevin** — *Partner*
The Caldwell Partners Amrop International
999 West Hastings Street
Suite 750
Vancouver, British Columbia, CANADA V6C 2W2
Telephone: (604) 669-3550
**Recruiter Classification:** Retained; **Lowest/Average Salary:** $/$90,000; **Industry Concentration:** Generalist with a primary focus in Aerospace/Defense, Energy, Environmental, Hospitality/Leisure; **Function Concentration:** Generalist

**McCabe, Christopher** — *Consultant*
Raymond Karsan Associates
2001 Westside Drive, Suite 130
Alpharetta, GA 30201
Telephone: (770) 442-8771
**Recruiter Classification:** Contingency; **Lowest/Average Salary:** $30,000/$90,000; **Industry Concentration:** Generalist with a primary focus in Biotechnology, Chemical Products, Environmental, Healthcare/Hospitals, Information Technology, Insurance, Manufacturing, Pharmaceutical/Medical; **Function Concentration:** Generalist

**McCallister, Jane T.** — *Consultant*
Heidrick & Struggles, Inc.
245 Park Avenue, Suite 4300
New York, NY 10167-0152
Telephone: (212) 867-9876
**Recruiter Classification:** Retained; **Lowest/Average Salary:** $75,000/$90,000; **Industry Concentration:** Generalist with a primary focus in Healthcare/Hospitals; **Function Concentration:** Generalist

**McCallister, Richard A.** — *Managing Director*
Boyden
2 Prudential Plaza, Suite 5050
180 North Stetson Avenue
Chicago, IL 60601
Telephone: (312) 565-1300
**Recruiter Classification:** Retained; **Lowest/Average Salary:** $75,000/$90,000; **Industry Concentration:** Board Services, Financial Services; **Function Concentration:** Generalist with a primary focus in Engineering, Finance/Accounting, General Management, Human Resources, Marketing, Research and Development, Sales, Women/Minorities

**McCandless, Hugh** — *Executive Vice President*
Marshall Consultants, Inc.
360 East 65th Street
New York, NY 10021
Telephone: (212) 628-8400
**Recruiter Classification:** Retained; **Lowest/Average Salary:** $20,000/$50,000; **Industry Concentration:** Generalist; **Function Concentration:** Marketing

**McCann, Cornelia B.** — *Director*
Spencer Stuart
2005 Market Street, Suite 2350
Philadelphia, PA 19103
Telephone: (215) 851-6200
**Recruiter Classification:** Retained; **Lowest/Average Salary:** $90,000/$90,000; **Industry Concentration:** Board Services, Financial Services, Information Technology, Publishing/Media, Venture Capital; **Function Concentration:** Generalist

**McCarthy, David R.** — *Director*
Spencer Stuart
2005 Market Street, Suite 2350
Philadelphia, PA 19103
Telephone: (215) 851-6200
**Recruiter Classification:** Retained; **Lowest/Average Salary:** $90,000/$90,000; **Industry Concentration:** Board Services, Education/Libraries, Non-Profit; **Function Concentration:** Generalist with a primary focus in General Management, Women/Minorities

**McCarthy, Laura** — *Associate*
Source Services Corporation
8614 Westwood Center, Suite 750
Vienna, VA 22182
Telephone: (703) 790-5610
**Recruiter Classification:** Contingency; **Lowest/Average Salary:** $30,000/$50,000; **Industry Concentration:** Financial Services, Information Technology; **Function Concentration:** Engineering, Finance/Accounting

**McCartney, Paul** — *Managing Director*
Korn/Ferry International
3950 Lincoln Plaza
500 North Akard Street
Dallas, TX 75201
Telephone: (214) 954-1834
**Recruiter Classification:** Retained; **Lowest/Average Salary:** $90,000/$90,000; **Industry Concentration:** Generalist; **Function Concentration:** Generalist

**McCarty, J. Rucker** — *Partner*
Heidrick & Struggles, Inc.
One Peachtree Center
303 Peachtree Street, NE, Suite 3100
Atlanta, GA 30308
Telephone: (404) 577-2410
**Recruiter Classification:** Retained; **Lowest/Average Salary:** $75,000/$90,000; **Industry Concentration:** Generalist with a primary focus in Financial Services; **Function Concentration:** Generalist

**McClain, Michael D.** — *Executive Vice President/ Managing Director*
DHR International, Inc.
1888 Century Park East, Suite 1917
Los Angeles, CA 90067
Telephone: (310) 284-3131
**Recruiter Classification:** Retained; **Lowest/Average Salary:** $60,000/$90,000; **Industry Concentration:** Generalist; **Function Concentration:** Generalist

**McClearen, Bruce** — *Vice President*
Tyler & Company
1000 Abernathy Road N.E.
Suite 1400
Atlanta, GA 30328-5655
Telephone: (770) 396-3939
**Recruiter Classification:** Retained; **Lowest/Average Salary:** $60,000/$90,000; **Industry Concentration:** Healthcare/Hospitals, Insurance; **Function Concentration:** Generalist

**McClement, John** — *Principal*
Korn/Ferry International
237 Park Avenue
New York, NY 10017
Telephone: (212) 687-1834
**Recruiter Classification:** Retained; **Lowest/Average Salary:** $90,000/$90,000; **Industry Concentration:** Generalist with a primary focus in Financial Services; **Function Concentration:** Generalist

**McCloskey, Frank** — *Vice President*
Korn/Ferry International
120 South Riverside Plaza
Suite 918
Chicago, IL 60606
Telephone: (312) 726-1841
**Recruiter Classification:** Retained; **Lowest/Average Salary:** $90,000/$90,000; **Industry Concentration:** Generalist; **Function Concentration:** Generalist

**McClure, James K.** — *Vice President*
Korn/Ferry International
One International Place
Boston, MA 02110-1800
Telephone: (617) 345-0200
**Recruiter Classification:** Retained; **Lowest/Average Salary:** $90,000/$90,000; **Industry Concentration:** Generalist with a primary focus in High Technology; **Function Concentration:** Generalist

**McComas, Kelly E.** — *Director*
The Guild Corporation
8260 Greensboro Drive, Suite 460
McLean, VA 22102
Telephone: (703) 761-4023
**Recruiter Classification:** Contingency; **Lowest/Average Salary:** $40,000/$50,000; **Industry Concentration:** Aerospace/Defense, Electronics, High Technology, Information Technology; **Function Concentration:** Engineering, Finance/Accounting, General Management, Research and Development

**McConnell, Greg** — *Branch Manager/Information Technology Recruiter*
Winter, Wyman & Company
1100 Circle 75 Parkway, Suite 800
Atlanta, GA 30339
Telephone: (770) 933-1525
**Recruiter Classification:** Contingency; **Lowest/Average Salary:** $30,000/$60,000; **Industry Concentration:** Generalist with a primary focus in Consumer Products, Financial Services, Healthcare/Hospitals, High Technology, Information Technology, Insurance, Manufacturing, Pharmaceutical/Medical, Publishing/Media, Real Estate; **Function Concentration:** Generalist

**McConnell, Rod** — *Consultant*
The McCormick Group, Inc.
1400 Wilson Boulevard
Arlington, VA 22209
Telephone: (703) 841-1700
**Recruiter Classification:** Retained, Contingency; **Lowest/Average Salary:** $60,000/$75,000; **Industry Concentration:** Biotechnology; **Function Concentration:** Generalist

**McCool, Anne G.** — *Senior Vice President*
Sullivan & Company
20 Exchange Place, 50th Floor
New York, NY 10005
Telephone: (212) 422-3000
**Recruiter Classification:** Retained; **Lowest/Average Salary:** $90,000/$90,000; **Industry Concentration:** Generalist with a primary focus in Financial Services; **Function Concentration:** Generalist

**McCorkle, Sam B.** — *President*
Morton, McCorkle & Associates, Inc.
2190 South Mason Road, Suite 309
St. Louis, MO 63131-1637
Telephone: (314) 984-9494
**Recruiter Classification:** Retained; **Lowest/Average Salary:** $60,000/$90,000; **Industry Concentration:** Generalist with a primary focus in Biotechnology, Chemical Products, Environmental, Manufacturing, Packaging; **Function Concentration:** Generalist with a primary focus in Engineering, General Management, Human Resources, Marketing, Sales

**McCormack, Joseph A.** — *Managing Partner*
McCormack & Associates
5042 Wilshire Boulevard, Suite 505
Los Angeles, CA 90036
Telephone: (213) 549-9200
**Recruiter Classification:** Retained; **Lowest/Average Salary:** $60,000/$90,000; **Industry Concentration:** Generalist with a primary focus in Board Services, Healthcare/Hospitals, Non-Profit, Public Administration; **Function Concentration:** Generalist with a primary focus in General Management, Women/Minorities

**McCormack, William Reed** — *Executive Recruiter*
MSI International
1050 Crown Pointe Parkway
Suite 1000
Atlanta, GA 30338
Telephone: (404) 394-2494
**Recruiter Classification:** Contingency; **Lowest/Average Salary:** $30,000/$60,000; **Industry Concentration:** Generalist with a primary focus in Manufacturing; **Function Concentration:** Administration, Engineering, Finance/Accounting, General Management, Marketing

**McCormick, Brian** — *Executive Vice President*
The McCormick Group, Inc.
1400 Wilson Boulevard
Arlington, VA 22209
Telephone: (703) 841-1700
**Recruiter Classification:** Retained; **Lowest/Average Salary:** $50,000/$90,000; **Industry Concentration:** Biotechnology, Consumer Products, Financial Services, High Technology, Information Technology, Insurance, Publishing/Media, Real Estate; **Function Concentration:** Engineering, Finance/Accounting, General Management, Human Resources, Marketing, Sales

**McCormick, Cyndi** — *Accounting and Finance Recruiter*
Winter, Wyman & Company
950 Winter Street, Suite 3100
Waltham, MA 02154-1294
Telephone: (617) 890-7000
**Recruiter Classification:** Contingency; **Lowest/Average Salary:** $20,000/$50,000; **Industry Concentration:** Generalist; **Function Concentration:** Finance/Accounting

**McCormick, Joseph** — *Associate*
Source Services Corporation
111 Founders Plaza, Suite 1501E
Hartford, CT 06108
Telephone: (860) 528-0300
**Recruiter Classification:** Contingency; **Lowest/Average Salary:** $30,000/$50,000; **Industry Concentration:** Financial Services, Information Technology; **Function Concentration:** Engineering, Finance/Accounting

**McCormick, William J.** — *Chief Executive Officer*
The McCormick Group, Inc.
4024 Plank Road
Fredericksburg, VA 22407
Telephone: (703) 786-9777
**Recruiter Classification:** Retained, Contingency; **Lowest/Average Salary:** $60,000/$90,000; **Industry Concentration:** Generalist with a primary focus in High Technology, Information Technology, Real Estate; **Function Concentration:** Generalist with a primary focus in Engineering, Finance/Accounting, General Management, Marketing, Research and Development, Sales

**McCoy, Horacio** — *President Latin America*
Korn/Ferry International
Montes Urales 641
Lomas De Chapultepec
Mexico City, D.F., MEXICO 11000
Telephone: (525) 202-0046
**Recruiter Classification:** Retained; **Lowest/Average Salary:** $90,000/$90,000; **Industry Concentration:** Generalist; **Function Concentration:** Generalist

**McCoy, Millington F.** — *Managing Director*
Gould, McCoy & Chadick Incorporated
300 Park Avenue, Suite 20F
New York, NY 10022
Telephone: (212) 688-8671
**Recruiter Classification:** Retained; **Lowest/Average Salary:** $90,000/$90,000; **Industry Concentration:** Generalist; **Function Concentration:** Generalist

**McCreary, Charles** — *President*
Austin-McGregor International
12005 Ford Road, Suite 160
Dallas, TX 75234-7247
Telephone: (214) 488-0500
**Recruiter Classification:** Retained; **Lowest/Average Salary:** $50,000/$90,000; **Industry Concentration:** Generalist with a primary focus in Automotive, Board Services, Chemical Products, Consumer Products, Electronics, Entertainment, Healthcare/Hospitals, High Technology, Hospitality/Leisure, Manufacturing, Pharmaceutical/Medical, Publishing/Media, Venture Capital; **Function Concentration:** Generalist with a primary focus in Engineering, Finance/Accounting, General Management, Human Resources, Marketing, Research and Development, Sales, Women/Minorities

**McCullough, Joe** — *Co-Owner/Manager Central Region*
Management Recruiters International, Inc.
Bartlett, Suite 800
36 East Fourth Street
Cincinnati, OH 45202-2451
Telephone: (513) 651-5500
**Recruiter Classification:** Contingency; **Lowest/Average Salary:** $30,000/$75,000; **Industry Concentration:** Generalist; **Function Concentration:** Generalist

**McCurdy, Mark** — *Research Consultant*
Summerfield Associates, Inc.
6555 Quince Road, Suite 311
Memphis, TN 38119
Telephone: (901) 753-7068
**Recruiter Classification:** Contingency; **Lowest/Average Salary:** $30,000/$50,000; **Industry Concentration:** Generalist with a primary focus in Information Technology; **Function Concentration:** Generalist

**McCutcheon, C. Scott** — *Vice President*
John Kurosky & Associates
3 Corporate Park Drive, Suite 210
Irvine, CA 92714
Telephone: (714) 851-6370
**Recruiter Classification:** Retained; **Lowest/Average Salary:** $60,000/$90,000; **Industry Concentration:** Generalist; **Function Concentration:** Finance/Accounting

**McDaniel, Debra A.** — *Director Recruitment*
Simpson Associates
Trump Parc
106 Central Park South
New York, NY 10019
Telephone: (212) 767-0006
**Recruiter Classification:** Contingency; **Lowest/Average Salary:** $60,000/$90,000; **Industry Concentration:** Fashion (Retail/Apparel); **Function Concentration:** Finance/Accounting, Human Resources, Marketing, Sales

**McDermott, Richard A.** — *Partner*
Paul Ray Berndtson
10 South Riverside Plaza
Suite 720
Chicago, IL 60606
Telephone: (312) 876-0730
**Recruiter Classification:** Retained; **Lowest/Average Salary:** $90,000/$90,000; **Industry Concentration:** Insurance, Transportation; **Function Concentration:** Generalist

**McDonald, Gary E.** — *Horticulture Recruiter*
Agra Placements International Ltd.
2200 North Kickapoo, Suite 2
Lincoln, IL 62656
Telephone: (217) 735-4373
**Recruiter Classification:** Contingency; **Lowest/Average Salary:** $20,000/$30,000; **Industry Concentration:** Generalist with a primary focus in Biotechnology, Chemical Products, Energy, Financial Services, Manufacturing; **Function Concentration:** Administration, Engineering, Finance/Accounting, General Management, Human Resources, Marketing, Research and Development, Sales

**McDonald, John R.** — *President*
TSS Consulting, Ltd.
2425 East Camelback Road
Suite 375
Phoenix, AZ 85016
Telephone: (602) 955-7000
**Recruiter Classification:** Contingency; **Lowest/Average Salary:**
$60,000/$75,000; **Industry Concentration:** Aerospace/Defense, Electronics,
High Technology; **Function Concentration:** Engineering, General Management,
Marketing

**McDonald, Scott A.** — *Partner*
McDonald Associates International
234 Washington Road
Rye, NH 03870
Telephone: (603) 433-6295
**Recruiter Classification:** Retained; **Lowest/Average Salary:** $60,000/$90,000;
**Industry Concentration:** Generalist with a primary focus in Automotive,
Biotechnology, Consumer Products, Electronics, Financial Services,
Healthcare/Hospitals, High Technology, Information Technology, Insurance,
Manufacturing, Pharmaceutical/Medical, Utilities/Nuclear; **Function
Concentration:** Generalist with a primary focus in Administration, Engineering,
Finance/Accounting, General Management, Marketing, Sales,
Women/Minorities

**McDonald, Stanleigh B.** — *Partner*
McDonald Associates International
1290 N. Western Avenue
Suite 209
Lake Forest, IL 60045
Telephone: (708) 234-6889
**Recruiter Classification:** Retained; **Lowest/Average Salary:** $60,000/$90,000;
**Industry Concentration:** Generalist with a primary focus in Automotive,
Biotechnology, Consumer Products, Electronics, Financial Services,
Healthcare/Hospitals, High Technology, Information Technology, Insurance,
Manufacturing, Pharmaceutical/Medical, Utilities/Nuclear; **Function
Concentration:** Generalist with a primary focus in Administration, Engineering,
Finance/Accounting, General Management, Human Resources, Marketing,
Sales, Women/Minorities

**McDonnell, Julie** — *Owner*
Technical Personnel of Minnesota
5354 Parkdale Drive, Suite 104
Minneapolis, MN 55416
Telephone: (612) 544-8550
**Recruiter Classification:** Contingency; **Lowest/Average Salary:**
$20,000/$50,000; **Industry Concentration:** Generalist with a primary focus in
Automotive, Biotechnology, Chemical Products, Electronics, High Technology,
Information Technology, Manufacturing, Packaging, Pharmaceutical/Medical;
**Function Concentration:** Generalist with a primary focus in Administration,
Engineering, Finance/Accounting, General Management, Human Resources,
Marketing, Research and Development, Sales

**McElhaney, Ron** — *Co-Manager South Atlantic Region*
Management Recruiters International, Inc.
2431 Habersham Street, P.O. Box 22548
Savannah, GA 31403-2548
Telephone: (912) 232-0132
**Recruiter Classification:** Contingency; **Lowest/Average Salary:**
$30,000/$75,000; **Industry Concentration:** Generalist; **Function
Concentration:** Generalist

**McElhaney, Ronald W.** — *General Manager*
Management Recruiters International, Inc.
2431 Habersham Street, P.O. Box 22548
Savannah, GA 31403-2548
Telephone: (912) 232-0132
**Recruiter Classification:** Contingency; **Lowest/Average Salary:**
$30,000/$75,000; **Industry Concentration:** Generalist; **Function
Concentration:** Generalist

**McElroy, John** — *Manager Pacific Region*
Management Recruiters International, Inc.
8221-C 44th Avenue West, Suite M
Mulkilteo, WA 98275-2847
Telephone: (206) 348-0113
**Recruiter Classification:** Contingency; **Lowest/Average Salary:**
$30,000/$75,000; **Industry Concentration:** Generalist; **Function
Concentration:** Generalist

**McEwan, Paul** — *Executive Recruiter*
Richard, Wayne and Roberts
24 Greenway Plaza, Suite 1304
Houston, TX 77046-2493
Telephone: (713) 629-6681
**Recruiter Classification:** Retained; **Lowest/Average Salary:** $40,000/$60,000;
**Industry Concentration:** Generalist with a primary focus in Chemical Products,
Manufacturing; **Function Concentration:** Generalist with a primary focus in
Sales

**McEwen, Al** — *Manager Southwest Region*
Management Recruiters International, Inc.
Popular Plaza Building
224 South Second Street, Suite G
Rogers, AR 72756-4511
Telephone: (501) 621-0706
**Recruiter Classification:** Contingency; **Lowest/Average Salary:** $30,000/$75,000;
**Industry Concentration:** Generalist; **Function Concentration:** Generalist

**McFadden, Ashton S.** — *Consulting Associate*
Johnson Smith & Knisely Accord
100 Park Avenue, 15th Floor
New York, NY 10017
Telephone: (212) 885-9100
**Recruiter Classification:** Retained; **Lowest/Average Salary:** $90,000/$90,000;
**Industry Concentration:** Financial Services, Information Technology,
Insurance, Real Estate, Venture Capital; **Function Concentration:** Generalist
with a primary focus in Administration, Finance/Accounting, General
Management, Human Resources, Marketing, Research and Development, Sales

**McFeely, Clarence E.** — *Partner*
McFeely Wackerle Shulman
20 North Wacker Drive, Suite 3110
Chicago, IL 60606
Telephone: (312) 641-2977
**Recruiter Classification:** Retained; **Lowest/Average Salary:** $90,000/$90,000;
**Industry Concentration:** Generalist; **Function Concentration:** Generalist with a
primary focus in Administration

**McGahey, Patricia M.** — *Consultant*
Witt/Kieffer, Ford, Hadelman & Lloyd
4550 Montgomery Avenue
Bethesda, MD 20814
Telephone: (301) 654-5070
**Recruiter Classification:** Retained; **Lowest/Average Salary:** $75,000/$90,000;
**Industry Concentration:** Healthcare/Hospitals; **Function Concentration:**
Generalist with a primary focus in General Management

**McGann, Paul L.** — *Vice President*
The Cassie Group
1824 Willow Oak Drive
Palm Harbor, FL 34683
Telephone: (813) 785-4092
**Recruiter Classification:** Retained; **Lowest/Average Salary:** $75,000/$90,000;
**Industry Concentration:** Biotechnology, Pharmaceutical/Medical; **Function
Concentration:** Administration, Engineering, Marketing, Research and
Development, Sales, Women/Minorities

**McGill, Robert** — *Partner*
The Caldwell Partners Amrop International
Sixty-Four Prince Arthur Avenue
Toronto, Ontario, CANADA M5R 1B4
Telephone: (416) 920-7702
**Recruiter Classification:** Retained; **Lowest/Average Salary:** $/$90,000; **Industry
Concentration:** Generalist; **Function Concentration:** Generalist

**McGinnis, Rita** — *Associate*
Source Services Corporation
5429 LBJ Freeway, Suite 275
Dallas, TX 75240
Telephone: (214) 387-1600
**Recruiter Classification:** Contingency; **Lowest/Average Salary:**
$30,000/$50,000; **Industry Concentration:** Financial Services, Information
Technology; **Function Concentration:** Engineering, Finance/Accounting

**McGoldrick, Terrence** — *Associate*
Source Services Corporation
One South Main Street, Suite 1440
Dayton, OH 45402
Telephone: (513) 461-4660
**Recruiter Classification:** Contingency; **Lowest/Average Salary:**
$30,000/$50,000; **Industry Concentration:** Financial Services, Information
Technology; **Function Concentration:** Engineering, Finance/Accounting

**McGonigle, Kevin M.** — *Consultant*
Egon Zehnder International Inc.
One Atlantic Center, Suite 3000
1201 West Peachtree Street N.E.
Atlanta, GA 30309
Telephone: (404) 875-3000
**Recruiter Classification:** Retained; **Lowest/Average Salary:** $90,000/$90,000;
**Industry Concentration:** Generalist; **Function Concentration:** Generalist

**McGovern, Terence** — *Managing Director*
Korn/Ferry International
One Landmark Square
Stamford, CT 06901
Telephone: (203) 359-3350
**Recruiter Classification:** Retained; **Lowest/Average Salary:** $90,000/$90,000;
**Industry Concentration:** Generalist with a primary focus in Manufacturing;
**Function Concentration:** Generalist

**McGrath, Robert E.** — *President*
Robert E. McGrath & Associates
256 Post Road East
Westport, CT 06880
Telephone: (203) 221-8335
**Recruiter Classification:** Retained; **Lowest/Average Salary:** $90,000/$90,000;
**Industry Concentration:** Chemical Products, Consumer Products,
Education/Libraries, Environmental, Manufacturing, Packaging; **Function
Concentration:** Engineering, Marketing

**McGrath, Thomas F.** — *Partner*
Spriggs & Company, Inc.
1701 East Lake Avenue
Suite 265
Glenview, IL 60025
Telephone: (708) 657-7181
**Recruiter Classification:** Retained; **Lowest/Average Salary:** $90,000/$90,000;
**Industry Concentration:** Consumer Products, Fashion (Retail/Apparel);
**Function Concentration:** General Management, Human Resources, Marketing,
Sales

**McGue, Marsha S.** — *Associate*
Kenzer Corp.
1600 Parkwood Circle NW, Suite 310
Atlanta, GA 30339
Telephone: (770) 955-7210
**Recruiter Classification:** Retained; **Lowest/Average Salary:** $50,000/$90,000;
**Industry Concentration:** Generalist; **Function Concentration:** Generalist

**McGuigan, Walter J.** — *Senior Consultant*
Norm Sanders Associates
2 Village Court
Hazlet, NJ 07730
Telephone: (908) 264-3700
**Recruiter Classification:** Retained; **Lowest/Average Salary:** $90,000/$90,000;
**Industry Concentration:** Information Technology; **Function Concentration:**
Generalist

**McGuire, Bud** — *Account Executive*
Search West, Inc.
750 The City Drive South
Suite 100
Orange, CA 92668-4940
Telephone: (714) 748-0400
**Recruiter Classification:** Contingency; **Lowest/Average Salary:**
$40,000/$60,000; **Industry Concentration:** Chemical Products, Manufacturing,
Packaging; **Function Concentration:** Engineering, General Management,
Research and Development

**McGuire, Corey** — *Associate*
Peter W. Ambler Company
14651 Dallas Parkway, Suite 402
Dallas, TX 75240
Telephone: (214) 404-8712
**Recruiter Classification:** Retained; **Lowest/Average Salary:** $50,000/$90,000;
**Industry Concentration:** Generalist with a primary focus in Board Services,
Chemical Products, Consumer Products, Education/Libraries, Electronics,
Fashion (Retail/Apparel), Manufacturing, Non-Profit, Oil/Gas, Packaging,
Pharmaceutical/Medical, Real Estate, Transportation; **Function Concentration:**
Generalist with a primary focus in Engineering, General Management, Human
Resources, Marketing, Sales

**McGuire, D.** — *Associate*
The Gabriel Group
1515 Market Street, Suite 504
Philadelphia, PA 19102
Telephone: (215) 496-9990
**Recruiter Classification:** Retained; **Lowest/Average Salary:** $75,000/$75,000;
**Industry Concentration:** Generalist; **Function Concentration:** Generalist

**McGuire, John J.** — *Vice President*
Robert Sage Recruiting
127 East Windsor
Elkhart, IN 46514
Telephone: (219) 264-1126
**Recruiter Classification:** Contingency; **Lowest/Average Salary:**
$30,000/$75,000; **Industry Concentration:** Automotive; **Function
Concentration:** Generalist

**McHugh, Keith** — *Associate*
Source Services Corporation
879 West 190th Street, Suite 250
Los Angeles, CA 90248
Telephone: (310) 323-6633
**Recruiter Classification:** Contingency; **Lowest/Average Salary:**
$30,000/$50,000; **Industry Concentration:** Financial Services, Information
Technology; **Function Concentration:** Engineering, Finance/Accounting

**McHugh, Margaret** — *Senior Associate*
Korn/Ferry International
237 Park Avenue
New York, NY 10017
Telephone: (212) 687-1834
**Recruiter Classification:** Retained; **Lowest/Average Salary:** $90,000/$90,000;
**Industry Concentration:** Generalist; **Function Concentration:** Generalist

**McIntosh, Arthur** — *Associate*
Source Services Corporation
5429 LBJ Freeway, Suite 275
Dallas, TX 75240
Telephone: (214) 387-1600
**Recruiter Classification:** Contingency; **Lowest/Average Salary:**
$30,000/$50,000; **Industry Concentration:** Financial Services, Information
Technology; **Function Concentration:** Engineering, Finance/Accounting

**McIntosh, Tad** — *Associate*
Source Services Corporation
5429 LBJ Freeway, Suite 275
Dallas, TX 75240
Telephone: (214) 387-1600
**Recruiter Classification:** Contingency; **Lowest/Average Salary:**
$30,000/$50,000; **Industry Concentration:** Financial Services, Information
Technology; **Function Concentration:** Engineering, Finance/Accounting

**McInturff, Robert** — *President*
McInturff & Associates, Inc.
209 West Central Street
Natick, MA 01760
Telephone: (617) 237-0220
**Recruiter Classification:** Contingency; **Lowest/Average Salary:**
$50,000/$50,000; **Industry Concentration:** Aerospace/Defense, Consumer
Products, Electronics, Energy, High Technology, Information Technology,
Manufacturing, Transportation; **Function Concentration:** General Management

**McIntyre, Alex D.** — *Vice President*
Norman Roberts & Associates, Inc.
1800 Century Park East, Suite 430
Los Angeles, CA 90067
Telephone: (310) 552-1112
**Recruiter Classification:** Retained; **Lowest/Average Salary:** $60,000/$90,000;
**Industry Concentration:** Public Administration; **Function Concentration:**
Generalist with a primary focus in Administration, Engineering,
Finance/Accounting, General Management, Human Resources,
Women/Minorities

**McIntyre, Joel** — *Regional Manager*
Phillips Resource Group
2031-A Carolina Place
P.O. Box 609
Fort Mill, SC 29715
Telephone: (803) 548-6918
**Recruiter Classification:** Contingency; **Lowest/Average Salary:**
$40,000/$50,000; **Industry Concentration:** Generalist with a primary focus in
Chemical Products, Electronics, Environmental, High Technology, Information
Technology, Manufacturing, Packaging, Utilities/Nuclear; **Function
Concentration:** Generalist with a primary focus in Administration, Engineering,
General Management, Human Resources, Marketing, Research and
Development, Sales, Women/Minorities

**McKay, W. John** — *Partner*
O'Callaghan Honey/Paul Ray Berndtson, Inc.
400-400 Fifth Avenue S.W.
Calgary, Alberta, CANADA T2P 0L6
Telephone: (403) 269-3277
**Recruiter Classification:** Retained; **Lowest/Average Salary:** $90,000/$90,000;
**Industry Concentration:** Generalist with a primary focus in Energy, Oil/Gas;
**Function Concentration:** Generalist

**McKell, Linda** — *President*
Advanced Information Management
444 Castro Street, Suite 320
Mountain View, CA 94041
Telephone: (415) 965-7799
**Recruiter Classification:** Contingency; **Lowest/Average Salary:**
$20,000/$40,000; **Industry Concentration:** Information Technology; **Function
Concentration:** Human Resources, Women/Minorities

**McKie, Miles L.** — *Managing Director*
Russell Reynolds Associates, Inc.
200 South Wacker Drive
Suite 3600
Chicago, IL 60606
Telephone: (312) 993-9696
**Recruiter Classification:** Retained; **Lowest/Average Salary:** $90,000/$90,000;
**Industry Concentration:** Generalist with a primary focus in Consumer
Products; **Function Concentration:** Generalist

**McKinney, Julia** — *Associate*
Source Services Corporation
100 North Tryon Street, Suite 3130
Charlotte, NC 28202
Telephone: (704) 333-8311
**Recruiter Classification:** Contingency; **Lowest/Average Salary:**
$30,000/$50,000; **Industry Concentration:** Financial Services, Information
Technology; **Function Concentration:** Engineering, Finance/Accounting

**McKinnis, Paul D.** — *Partner*
Paul Ray Berndtson
191 Peachtree Tower, Suite 3800
191 Peachtree Street, NE
Atlanta, GA 30303-1757
Telephone: (404) 215-4600
**Recruiter Classification:** Retained; **Lowest/Average Salary:** $90,000/$90,000;
**Industry Concentration:** Board Services, Financial Services, Manufacturing,
Real Estate, Utilities/Nuclear; **Function Concentration:** Generalist

**McKnight, Amy E.** — *Director*
Chartwell Partners International, Inc.
275 Battery Street, Suite 2180
San Francisco, CA 94111
Telephone: (415) 296-0600
**Recruiter Classification:** Retained; **Lowest/Average Salary:** $90,000/$90,000;
**Industry Concentration:** Generalist with a primary focus in Consumer
Products, Financial Services, High Technology, Transportation; **Function
Concentration:** Generalist with a primary focus in Finance/Accounting,
Marketing, Sales

**McKnight, Lourdes D.** — *Principal*
Sanford Rose Associates
753 East El Camino Real, Suite A
Sunnyvale, CA 94087
Telephone: (408) 730-5833
**Recruiter Classification:** Contingency; **Lowest/Average Salary:**
$30,000/$75,000; **Industry Concentration:** Generalist; **Function
Concentration:** Generalist

**McLane, Brad** — *Consultant*
Egon Zehnder International Inc.
One First National Plaza
21 South Clark Street, Suite 3300
Chicago, IL 60603-2006
Telephone: (312) 782-4500
**Recruiter Classification:** Retained; **Lowest/Average Salary:** $90,000/$90,000;
**Industry Concentration:** Generalist; **Function Concentration:** Generalist

**McLane, Thomas L.** — *Managing Director*
Russell Reynolds Associates, Inc.
200 Park Avenue
New York, NY 10166-0002
Telephone: (212) 351-2000
**Recruiter Classification:** Retained; **Lowest/Average Salary:** $90,000/$90,000;
**Industry Concentration:** Generalist; **Function Concentration:** Generalist

**McLaughlin, John** — *Managing Partner*
Romac & Associates
180 Montgomery Street
Suite 1860
San Francisco, CA 94104
Telephone: (415) 788-2815
**Recruiter Classification:** Executive Temporary; **Lowest/Average Salary:**
$/$60,000; **Industry Concentration:** Financial Services, Healthcare/Hospitals,
High Technology, Hospitality/Leisure, Information Technology, Insurance;
**Function Concentration:** Finance/Accounting

**McLaughlin, John** — *Managing Partner*
TASA International
750 Lexington Avenue
Suite 1800
New York, NY 10022
Telephone: (212) 486-1490
**Recruiter Classification:** Retained; **Lowest/Average Salary:** $90,000/$90,000;
**Industry Concentration:** Generalist; **Function Concentration:** Generalist

**McLean, B. Keith** — *Partner*
Price Waterhouse
1 First Canadian Place, Box 190, Suite 3300
Toronto, Ontario, CANADA M5X 1H7
Telephone: (416) 863-1133
**Recruiter Classification:** Retained; **Lowest/Average Salary:** $90,000/$90,000;
**Industry Concentration:** Generalist with a primary focus in Automotive, Board
Services, Chemical Products, Consumer Products, Education/Libraries,
Entertainment, Healthcare/Hospitals, Hospitality/Leisure, Insurance, Non-Profit,
Pharmaceutical/Medical, Public Administration, Publishing/Media; **Function
Concentration:** Generalist

**McLean, Chris** — *Associate*
Chaloner Associates
P.O. Box 1097, Back Bay Annex
Boston, MA 02117-1097
Telephone: (617) 451-5170
**Recruiter Classification:** Retained; **Lowest/Average Salary:** $/$75,000; **Industry
Concentration:** Generalist; **Function Concentration:** Generalist

**McLean, E. Peter** — *Senior Director*
Spencer Stuart
277 Park Avenue, 29th Floor
New York, NY 10172
Telephone: (212) 336-0200
**Recruiter Classification:** Retained; **Lowest/Average Salary:** $90,000/$90,000;
**Industry Concentration:** Generalist with a primary focus in Financial Services,
Publishing/Media; **Function Concentration:** Generalist with a primary focus in
Finance/Accounting, General Management

**McLeish, Robert H.** — *Partner*
Executive Search International
60 Walnut Street
Wellesley, MA 02181
Telephone: (617) 239-0303
**Recruiter Classification:** Retained; **Lowest/Average Salary:** $75,000/$90,000;
**Industry Concentration:** Energy, High Technology, Utilities/Nuclear; **Function
Concentration:** Generalist

**McMahan, Stephen** — *Managing Director*
Source Services Corporation
71 Spit Brook Road, Suite 305
Nashua, NH 03060
Telephone: (603) 888-7650
**Recruiter Classification:** Contingency; **Lowest/Average Salary:**
$30,000/$50,000; **Industry Concentration:** Financial Services, Information
Technology; **Function Concentration:** Engineering, Finance/Accounting

**McMahan, Stephen** — *Managing Director*
Source Services Corporation
155 Federal Street, Suite 410
Boston, MA 02110
Telephone: (617) 482-8211
**Recruiter Classification:** Contingency; **Lowest/Average Salary:**
$30,000/$50,000; **Industry Concentration:** Financial Services, Information
Technology; **Function Concentration:** Engineering, Finance/Accounting

**McMahon, Mark J.** — *Vice President/Managing Director*
A.T. Kearney, Inc.
One Landmark Square, Suite 426
Stamford, CT 06901
Telephone: (203) 969-2222
**Recruiter Classification:** Retained; **Lowest/Average Salary:** $90,000/$90,000;
**Industry Concentration:** Generalist with a primary focus in
Aerospace/Defense, Fashion (Retail/Apparel), High Technology, Manufacturing;
**Function Concentration:** Generalist

**McManamon, Tim** — *Partner*
Rogers-McManamon Executive Search
33781 Via Cascada
San Juan Capistrano, CA 92675
Telephone: (714) 496-1614
**Recruiter Classification:** Retained; **Lowest/Average Salary:** $60,000/$90,000;
**Industry Concentration:** High Technology, Information Technology; **Function
Concentration:** Generalist with a primary focus in Engineering, Marketing,
Research and Development

**McManners, Donald E.** — *President*
McManners Associates, Inc.
400 East 54th Street, 16th Floor
New York, NY 10022
Telephone: (212) 980-7140
**Recruiter Classification:** Retained; **Lowest/Average Salary:** $90,000/$90,000;
**Industry Concentration:** Generalist with a primary focus in Manufacturing;
**Function Concentration:** Generalist

**McManus, Paul** — *Principal*
Aubin International
Somerset Court, 281 Winter Street
Waltham, MA 02154
Telephone: (617) 890-1722
**Recruiter Classification:** Retained; **Lowest/Average Salary:** $90,000/$90,000;
**Industry Concentration:** Generalist with a primary focus in High Technology,
Venture Capital; **Function Concentration:** Generalist

**McMillin, Bob** — *Director*
Price Waterhouse
601 West Hastings Street
Suite 1400
Vancouver, British Columbia, CANADA V6B 5A5
Telephone: (604) 682-4711
Recruiter Classification: Retained; Lowest/Average Salary: $75,000/$75,000;
Industry Concentration: Generalist with a primary focus in Biotechnology,
Board Services, Education/Libraries, Energy, Environmental, Financial Services,
High Technology, Insurance, Pharmaceutical/Medical; Function Concentration:
Generalist with a primary focus in Administration, Engineering,
Finance/Accounting, General Management, Human Resources, Marketing, Sales

**McNamara, Gerard P.** — *Consultant*
Heidrick & Struggles, Inc.
600 Superior Avenue East
Suite 2500
Cleveland, OH 44114
Telephone: (216) 241-7410
Recruiter Classification: Retained; Lowest/Average Salary: $75,000/$90,000;
Industry Concentration: Generalist with a primary focus in Financial Services;
Function Concentration: Generalist

**McNamara, Timothy C.** — *Managing Director*
Columbia Consulting Group
20 South Charles Street, 9th Floor
Baltimore, MD 21201
Telephone: (410) 385-2525
Recruiter Classification: Retained; Lowest/Average Salary: $75,000/$90,000;
Industry Concentration: Generalist with a primary focus in Aerospace/Defense,
Biotechnology, Board Services, Financial Services, Healthcare/Hospitals, High
Technology, Information Technology, Insurance, Manufacturing, Non-Profit,
Pharmaceutical/Medical, Publishing/Media, Transportation; Function
Concentration: Generalist with a primary focus in Engineering,
Finance/Accounting, Marketing, Research and Development, Women/Minorities

**McNamee, Erin** — *Recruiter*
Technical Connections Inc.
11400 Olympic Boulevard, Suite 770
Los Angeles, CA 90064
Telephone: (310) 479-8830
Recruiter Classification: Contingency; Lowest/Average Salary:
$40,000/$60,000; Industry Concentration: High Technology, Information
Technology; Function Concentration: Generalist

**McNear, Jeffrey E.** — *Operations Manager/Barrettemps
Search Division*
Barrett Partners
100 North LaSalle Street, Suite 1420
Chicago, IL 60602
Telephone: (312) 443-8877
Recruiter Classification: Contingency; Lowest/Average Salary:
$30,000/$50,000; Industry Concentration: Automotive, Biotechnology,
Chemical Products, Consumer Products, Environmental, Financial Services,
Healthcare/Hospitals, Information Technology, Insurance, Manufacturing,
Packaging, Publishing/Media, Real Estate, Transportation; Function
Concentration: Engineering, Finance/Accounting

**McNerney, Kevin A.** — *Partner*
Heidrick & Struggles, Inc.
8000 Towers Crescent Drive, Suite 555
Vienna, VA 22182
Telephone: (703) 761-4830
Recruiter Classification: Retained; Lowest/Average Salary: $75,000/$90,000;
Industry Concentration: Generalist with a primary focus in High Technology;
Function Concentration: Generalist

**McNichol, John** — *President*
McNichol Associates
620 Chestnut Street, Suite 1031
Philadelphia, PA 19106
Telephone: (215) 922-4142
Recruiter Classification: Retained; Lowest/Average Salary: $75,000/$90,000;
Industry Concentration: Environmental, Healthcare/Hospitals, High
Technology, Pharmaceutical/Medical, Transportation; Function Concentration:
Generalist with a primary focus in Administration, Engineering,
Finance/Accounting, General Management, Human Resources, Marketing,
Research and Development, Sales, Women/Minorities

**McNichols, Walter B.** — *Vice President*
Gary Kaplan & Associates
201 South Lake Avenue
Suite 600
Pasadena, CA 91101
Telephone: (818) 796-8100
Recruiter Classification: Retained; Lowest/Average Salary: $60,000/$90,000;
Industry Concentration: Generalist with a primary focus in Consumer
Products, Education/Libraries, Electronics, Entertainment, Environmental,
Fashion (Retail/Apparel), Financial Services, Healthcare/Hospitals, High
Technology, Hospitality/Leisure, Information Technology, Manufacturing, Non-
Profit; Function Concentration: Generalist with a primary focus in
Administration, Finance/Accounting, General Management, Human Resources,
Marketing, Research and Development, Sales

**McNulty, Neil P.** — *Manager North Atlantic Region*
Management Recruiters International, Inc.
River Creek Executive Center, Suite 101
1577 Wilroy Road
Suffolk, VA 23434
Telephone: (804) 538-1519
Recruiter Classification: Contingency; Lowest/Average Salary:
$30,000/$75,000; Industry Concentration: Generalist; Function
Concentration: Generalist

**McPherson, Stephen M.** — *Managing Director*
Ward Howell International, Inc.
99 Park Avenue, Suite 2000
New York, NY 10016-1699
Telephone: (212) 697-3730
Recruiter Classification: Retained; Lowest/Average Salary: $75,000/$90,000;
Industry Concentration: Fashion (Retail/Apparel), Financial Services, Non-
Profit; Function Concentration: Generalist

**McPoyle, Thomas C.** — *Principal*
Sanford Rose Associates
57 West Timonium Road
Suite 310
Timonium, MD 21093
Telephone: (410) 561-5244
Recruiter Classification: Contingency; Lowest/Average Salary:
$30,000/$75,000; Industry Concentration: Generalist with a primary focus in
Electronics; Function Concentration: Generalist

**McQuoid, David** — *Vice President*
A.T. Kearney, Inc.
8500 Normandale Lake Boulevard
Suite 1630
Minneapolis, MN 55437
Telephone: (612) 921-8436
Recruiter Classification: Retained; Lowest/Average Salary: $90,000/$90,000;
Industry Concentration: Generalist with a primary focus in Financial Services,
Manufacturing, Publishing/Media; Function Concentration: Generalist with a
primary focus in Administration, Finance/Accounting, Human Resources

**McRae, O. Jon** — *President*
Jon McRae & Associates, Inc.
1930 North Druid Hills Road, NE
Suite 200
Atlanta, GA 30319
Telephone: (404) 325-3252
Recruiter Classification: Retained; Lowest/Average Salary: $90,000/$90,000;
Industry Concentration: Education/Libraries, Non-Profit; Function
Concentration: Administration, Finance/Accounting, General Management

**McRoberts, Dana L.** — *Co-Manager Southwest Region*
Management Recruiters International, Inc.
Executive Center, Suite 200
555 Republic Drive
Plano, TX 75074
Telephone: (214) 516-4227
Recruiter Classification: Contingency; Lowest/Average Salary:
$30,000/$75,000; Industry Concentration: Generalist; Function
Concentration: Generalist

**McSherry, James F.** — *Senior Vice President Midwest Region*
Battalia Winston International
180 North Wacker Drive, Suite 600
Chicago, IL 60606
Telephone: (312) 704-0050
Recruiter Classification: Retained; Lowest/Average Salary: $90,000/$90,000;
Industry Concentration: Generalist with a primary focus in Board Services,
Chemical Products, Consumer Products, High Technology, Information
Technology, Insurance, Manufacturing, Non-Profit, Venture Capital; Function
Concentration: Generalist with a primary focus in General Management,
Human Resources, Sales, Women/Minorities

**McSherry, Terrence J.** — *Consultant*
Paul Ray Berndtson
10 South Riverside Plaza
Suite 720
Chicago, IL 60606
Telephone: (312) 876-0730
Recruiter Classification: Retained; Lowest/Average Salary: $90,000/$90,000;
Industry Concentration: Consumer Products, Manufacturing; Function
Concentration: Generalist

**McThrall, David** — *Executive Recruiter*
TSS Consulting, Ltd.
2425 East Camelback Road
Suite 375
Phoenix, AZ 85016
Telephone: (602) 955-7000
Recruiter Classification: Contingency; Lowest/Average Salary: $60,000/$75,000;
Industry Concentration: Aerospace/Defense, Electronics, High Technology;
Function Concentration: Engineering, General Management, Marketing

**Mead, James D.** — *President*
James Mead & Company
164 Kings Highway North
Westport, CT 06880
Telephone: (203) 454-5544
**Recruiter Classification:** Retained; **Lowest/Average Salary:** $90,000/$90,000;
**Industry Concentration:** Generalist with a primary focus in Consumer
Products, Publishing/Media; **Function Concentration:** General Management,
Marketing, Sales

**Meadley, Ronald J.** — *Manager Central Region*
Management Recruiters International, Inc.
McKay Tower
146 Monroe Center, Suite 1126
Grand Rapids, MI 49503
Telephone: (616) 336-8484
**Recruiter Classification:** Contingency; **Lowest/Average Salary:**
$30,000/$75,000; **Industry Concentration:** Generalist; **Function
Concentration:** Generalist

**Meagher, Patricia G.** — *Director*
Spencer Stuart
401 North Michigan Avenue, Suite 3400
Chicago, IL 60611-4244
Telephone: (312) 822-0080
**Recruiter Classification:** Retained; **Lowest/Average Salary:** $90,000/$90,000;
**Industry Concentration:** Generalist with a primary focus in
Aerospace/Defense, Automotive, Consumer Products, Healthcare/Hospitals,
Insurance, Manufacturing, Packaging, Pharmaceutical/Medical; **Function
Concentration:** Generalist with a primary focus in Administration,
Finance/Accounting, General Management, Human Resources, Marketing,
Sales, Women/Minorities

**Means, Wallace** — *Manager North Atlantic Region*
Management Recruiters International, Inc.
660 Westinghouse Boulevard, Suite 108
Charlotte, NC 28273-6303
Telephone: (704) 588-9300
**Recruiter Classification:** Contingency; **Lowest/Average Salary:**
$30,000/$75,000; **Industry Concentration:** Generalist; **Function
Concentration:** Generalist

**Meany, Brian** — *Vice President*
Herbert Mines Associates, Inc.
399 Park Avenue, 27th Floor
New York, NY 10022
Telephone: (212) 355-0909
**Recruiter Classification:** Retained; **Lowest/Average Salary:** $75,000/$90,000;
**Industry Concentration:** Board Services, Consumer Products, Fashion
(Retail/Apparel); **Function Concentration:** Generalist with a primary focus in
Finance/Accounting, General Management, Human Resources, Marketing,
Sales

**Meara, Helen** — *Associate*
Source Services Corporation
5 Independence Way
Princeton, NJ 08540
Telephone: (609) 452-7277
**Recruiter Classification:** Contingency; **Lowest/Average Salary:**
$30,000/$50,000; **Industry Concentration:** Financial Services, Information
Technology; **Function Concentration:** Engineering, Finance/Accounting

**Medinger, Ronald B.** — *Managing Director*
IMCOR, Inc.
100 Prospect Street, North Tower
Stamford, CT 06901
Telephone: (203) 975-8000
**Recruiter Classification:** Executive Temporary; **Lowest/Average Salary:**
$75,000/$90,000; **Industry Concentration:** Generalist; **Function
Concentration:** Generalist

**Medoff, Lynn** — *Vice President*
C.A. Durakis Associates, Inc.
66 Bayberry Lane
Westport, CT 06880
Telephone: (203) 255-5567
**Recruiter Classification:** Retained; **Lowest/Average Salary:** $90,000/$90,000;
**Industry Concentration:** Generalist; **Function Concentration:** Generalist

**Medtlie, Peder M.** — *Manager Midwest Region*
Management Recruiters International, Inc.
13000 West Bluemound Road, Suite 310
Elm Grove, WI 53122-2650
Telephone: (414) 797-7500
**Recruiter Classification:** Contingency; **Lowest/Average Salary:**
$30,000/$75,000; **Industry Concentration:** Generalist; **Function
Concentration:** Generalist

**Meehan, John** — *Associate*
Source Services Corporation
8614 Westwood Center, Suite 750
Vienna, VA 22182
Telephone: (703) 790-5610
**Recruiter Classification:** Contingency; **Lowest/Average Salary:**
$30,000/$50,000; **Industry Concentration:** Financial Services, Information
Technology; **Function Concentration:** Engineering, Finance/Accounting

**Meehan, Robert** — *Recruiter*
A.J. Burton Group, Inc.
120 East Baltimore Street, Suite 2220
Baltimore, MD 21202
Telephone: (410) 752-5244
**Recruiter Classification:** Contingency; **Lowest/Average Salary:**
$40,000/$60,000; **Industry Concentration:** Financial Services; **Function
Concentration:** Finance/Accounting

**Mefford, Bob** — *Executive Recruiter*
Executive Manning Corporation
3000 N.E. 30th Place, Suite 405/402/411
Fort Lauderdale, FL 33306
Telephone: (954) 561-5100
**Recruiter Classification:** Retained; **Lowest/Average Salary:** $75,000/$90,000;
**Industry Concentration:** Generalist with a primary focus in
Aerospace/Defense, Automotive, Chemical Products, Consumer Products,
Electronics, High Technology, Manufacturing, Pharmaceutical/Medical;
**Function Concentration:** Generalist

**Mehrbrodt, Al W.** — *Manager Pacific Region*
Management Recruiters International, Inc.
7148 Armstrong Parkway
Santa Barbara, CA 93117-2921
Telephone: (805) 968-3624
**Recruiter Classification:** Contingency; **Lowest/Average Salary:**
$30,000/$75,000; **Industry Concentration:** Generalist; **Function
Concentration:** Generalist

**Meier, J. Dale** — *Principal*
Grant Cooper and Associates
795 Office Parkway, Suite 117
St. Louis, MO 63141
Telephone: (314) 567-4690
**Recruiter Classification:** Retained; **Lowest/Average Salary:** $60,000/$90,000;
**Industry Concentration:** Generalist with a primary focus in Board Services,
Consumer Products, Financial Services, Healthcare/Hospitals,
Non-Profit, Pharmaceutical/Medical; **Function Concentration:** Generalist with
a primary focus in Administration, Engineering, Finance/Accounting, General
Management, Human Resources, Marketing, Sales

**Meiland, A. Daniel** — *Consultant*
Egon Zehnder International Inc.
55 East 59th Street, 14th Floor
New York, NY 10022
Telephone: (212) 838-9199
**Recruiter Classification:** Retained; **Lowest/Average Salary:** $90,000/$90,000;
**Industry Concentration:** Generalist with a primary focus in Biotechnology,
Financial Services, High Technology, Manufacturing, Pharmaceutical/Medical;
**Function Concentration:** Generalist

**Meister, Connie** — *Manager Southwest Region*
Management Recruiters International, Inc.
1008 East 21st Street
Cheyenne, WY 82001-3910
Telephone: (307) 635-8731
**Recruiter Classification:** Contingency; **Lowest/Average Salary:**
$30,000/$75,000; **Industry Concentration:** Generalist; **Function
Concentration:** Generalist

**Meister, Verle** — *Manager*
Management Recruiters International, Inc.
1008 East 21st Street
Cheyenne, WY 82001-3910
Telephone: (307) 635-8731
**Recruiter Classification:** Contingency; **Lowest/Average Salary:**
$30,000/$75,000; **Industry Concentration:** Generalist; **Function
Concentration:** Generalist

**Meitz, Bob L.** — *Manager Eastern Region*
Management Recruiters International, Inc.
129 Willowbrook Lane
West Chester, PA 19382-5571
Telephone: (610) 436-6556
**Recruiter Classification:** Contingency; **Lowest/Average Salary:**
$30,000/$75,000; **Industry Concentration:** Generalist; **Function
Concentration:** Generalist

**Meltzer, Andrea Y.** — *Managing Partner*
Executive Options, Ltd.
910 Skokie Boulevard
Suite 210
Northbrook, IL 60068
Telephone: (708) 291-4322
**Recruiter Classification:** Executive Temporary; **Lowest/Average Salary:**
$40,000/$60,000; **Industry Concentration:** Generalist with a primary focus in
Consumer Products, Financial Services, Healthcare/Hospitals, Manufacturing,
Non-Profit, Packaging, Real Estate; **Function Concentration:** Generalist with a
primary focus in Finance/Accounting, General Management, Human
Resources, Marketing, Women/Minorities

**Mendelson, Jeffrey** — *Associate*
Source Services Corporation
2 Penn Plaza, Suite 1176
New York, NY 10121
Telephone: (212) 760-2200
**Recruiter Classification:** Contingency; **Lowest/Average Salary:**
$30,000/$50,000; **Industry Concentration:** Financial Services, Information
Technology; **Function Concentration:** Engineering, Finance/Accounting

**Mendoza, Guadalupe** — *Partner*
Ward Howell International, Inc.
Rexer Seleccion de Ejecutivos, S.C.
Blvd. Adolfo Lopez Mateos 20, Col. San Angel Inn
Mexico City, D.F., MEXICO 01060
Telephone: (525) 550-9180
**Recruiter Classification:** Retained; **Lowest/Average Salary:** $75,000/$90,000;
**Industry Concentration:** Consumer Products, Financial Services, Insurance;
**Function Concentration:** Generalist

**Mendoza-Green, Robin** — *Associate*
Source Services Corporation
1 Gatehall Drive, Suite 250
Parsippany, NJ 07054
Telephone: (201) 267-3222
**Recruiter Classification:** Contingency; **Lowest/Average Salary:**
$30,000/$50,000; **Industry Concentration:** Financial Services, Information
Technology; **Function Concentration:** Engineering, Finance/Accounting

**Menendez, Todd** — *Executive Recruiter*
Don Richard Associates of Tampa, Inc.
100 North Tampa Street, Suite 1925
Tampa, FL 33602
Telephone: (813) 221-7930
**Recruiter Classification:** Contingency, Executive Temporary; **Lowest/Average
Salary:** $20,000/$50,000; **Industry Concentration:** Generalist with a primary
focus in Information Technology, Manufacturing; **Function Concentration:**
Generalist with a primary focus in Finance/Accounting, Human Resources

**Menk, Carl W.** — *Chairman*
Canny, Bowen Inc.
200 Park Avenue
New York, NY 10166
Telephone: (212) 949-6611
**Recruiter Classification:** Retained; **Lowest/Average Salary:** $90,000/$90,000;
**Industry Concentration:** Generalist with a primary focus in
Aerospace/Defense, Board Services, Consumer Products, Entertainment,
Insurance, Manufacturing, Pharmaceutical/Medical; **Function Concentration:**
Generalist with a primary focus in General Management, Human Resources

**Merkuris, Jennifer** — *Medical Recruiter*
Aureus Group
8744 Frederick Street
Omaha, NE 68124-3068
Telephone: (402) 397-2980
**Recruiter Classification:** Contingency; **Lowest/Average Salary:**
$30,000/$40,000; **Industry Concentration:** Healthcare/Hospitals; **Function
Concentration:** General Management

**Merrifield, Gary** — *Branch Manager*
Accountants on Call
Chiquita Center
250 East Fifth Street, Suite 1630
Cincinnati, OH 45202
Telephone: (513) 381-4545
**Recruiter Classification:** Contingency; **Lowest/Average Salary:**
$20,000/$30,000; **Industry Concentration:** Generalist; **Function
Concentration:** Finance/Accounting

**Merrigan, Eileen M.** — *Partner*
Lamalie Amrop International
200 Park Avenue
New York, NY 10166-0136
Telephone: (212) 953-7900
**Recruiter Classification:** Retained; **Lowest/Average Salary:** $90,000/$90,000;
**Industry Concentration:** Generalist with a primary focus in Education/Libraries,
Financial Services; **Function Concentration:** Generalist with a primary focus in
Finance/Accounting, Marketing, Sales

**Merriman, Mark** — *Manager Southwest Region*
Management Recruiters International, Inc.
13 South Tejon Street, Suite 501
Colorado Springs, CO 80903
Telephone: (719) 575-0500
**Recruiter Classification:** Contingency; **Lowest/Average Salary:** $30,000/$75,000;
**Industry Concentration:** Generalist; **Function Concentration:** Generalist

**Mertensotto, Chuck H.** — *Executive Recruiter*
Whitney & Associates, Inc.
920 Second Avenue South, Suite 625
Minneapolis, MN 55402-4035
Telephone: (612) 338-5600
**Recruiter Classification:** Contingency, Executive Temporary; **Lowest/Average
Salary:** $20,000/$50,000; **Industry Concentration:** Generalist with a primary
focus in Biotechnology, Consumer Products, Electronics, Financial Services,
Healthcare/Hospitals, High Technology, Information Technology, Insurance,
Manufacturing, Packaging, Pharmaceutical/Medical, Publishing/Media, Real
Estate, Transportation, Venture Capital; **Function Concentration:**
Finance/Accounting

**Meschke, Jason M.** — *Senior Vice President*
EFL Associates
7101 College Boulevard, Suite 550
Overland Park, KS 66210-1891
Telephone: (913) 451-8866
**Recruiter Classification:** Retained; **Lowest/Average Salary:** $60,000/$90,000;
**Industry Concentration:** Generalist; **Function Concentration:** Generalist

**Messett, William J.** — *President*
Messett Associates, Inc.
7700 North Kendall Drive, Suite 304
Miami, FL 33156
Telephone: (305) 275-1000
**Recruiter Classification:** Retained; **Lowest/Average Salary:** $75,000/$90,000;
**Industry Concentration:** Generalist with a primary focus in Biotechnology,
Chemical Products, Consumer Products, Electronics, Financial Services,
Healthcare/Hospitals, High Technology, Hospitality/Leisure, Insurance,
Manufacturing, Non-Profit, Oil/Gas, Pharmaceutical/Medical, Real Estate;
**Function Concentration:** Generalist with a primary focus in Administration,
Finance/Accounting, General Management, Human Resources, Marketing,
Women/Minorities

**Messina, Kenneth** — *Vice President*
Chestnut Hill Partners
20 William Street, Suite 240
Wellesley, MA 02181
Telephone: (617) 239-1400
**Recruiter Classification:** Retained; **Lowest/Average Salary:** $90,000/$90,000;
**Industry Concentration:** Generalist; **Function Concentration:** Generalist

**Messina, Marco** — *Associate*
Source Services Corporation
500 108th Avenue NE, Suite 1780
Bellevue, WA 98004
Telephone: (206) 454-6400
**Recruiter Classification:** Contingency; **Lowest/Average Salary:**
$30,000/$50,000; **Industry Concentration:** Financial Services, Information
Technology; **Function Concentration:** Engineering, Finance/Accounting

**Mestepey, John** — *Vice President/Managing Director*
A.T. Kearney, Inc.
Miami Center, Suite 3180
201 South Biscayne Boulevard
Miami, FL 33131
Telephone: (305) 577-0046
**Recruiter Classification:** Retained; **Lowest/Average Salary:** $90,000/$90,000;
**Industry Concentration:** Generalist with a primary focus in Automotive,
Education/Libraries, Entertainment, Financial Services, Hospitality/Leisure,
Non-Profit, Publishing/Media, Utilities/Nuclear; **Function Concentration:**
Generalist with a primary focus in Administration, Finance/Accounting,
General Management, Human Resources, Marketing, Sales

**Mestre, Mercedes** — *Vice President*
Korn/Ferry International
237 Park Avenue
New York, NY 10017
Telephone: (212) 687-1834
**Recruiter Classification:** Retained; **Lowest/Average Salary:** $90,000/$90,000;
**Industry Concentration:** Generalist; **Function Concentration:** Generalist

**Metz, Alex** — *President*
Hunt Ltd.
21 West 38th Street
New York, NY 10018
Telephone: (212) 997-2299
**Recruiter Classification:** Contingency; **Lowest/Average Salary:**
$75,000/$75,000; **Industry Concentration:** Automotive, Chemical Products,
Consumer Products, Fashion (Retail/Apparel), Manufacturing, Packaging,
Publishing/Media, Transportation; **Function Concentration:** Generalist with a
primary focus in General Management

**Metz, Dan K.** — *Managing Director*
Russell Reynolds Associates, Inc.
101 California Street
Suite 3140
San Francisco, CA 94111
Telephone: (415) 352-3300
**Recruiter Classification:** Retained; **Lowest/Average Salary:** $90,000/$90,000;
**Industry Concentration:** Generalist with a primary focus in High Technology;
**Function Concentration:** Generalist

**Meyer, Fred R.** — *Manager Eastern Region*
Management Recruiters International, Inc.
1414 Millard Street, Suite 102
Bethlehem, PA 18018-2632
Telephone: (610) 974-9770
**Recruiter Classification:** Contingency; **Lowest/Average Salary:** $30,000/$75,000;
**Industry Concentration:** Generalist; **Function Concentration:** Generalist

**Meyer, Marjorie** — *Area Vice President*
Accountants on Call
Park One, 2111 East Highland, Suite B-360
Phoenix, AZ 85016
Telephone: (602) 957-1200
**Recruiter Classification:** Contingency; **Lowest/Average Salary:**
$20,000/$30,000; **Industry Concentration:** Generalist; **Function
Concentration:** Finance/Accounting

**Meyer, Michael F.** — *Shareholder*
Witt/Kieffer, Ford, Hadelman & Lloyd
432 North 44th Street
Suite 360
Phoenix, AZ 85008
Telephone: (602) 267-1370
**Recruiter Classification:** Retained; **Lowest/Average Salary:** $75,000/$90,000;
**Industry Concentration:** Healthcare/Hospitals, Insurance; **Function
Concentration:** Generalist with a primary focus in General Management,
Human Resources

**Meyer, Stacey** — *Senior Associate*
Gary Kaplan & Associates
201 South Lake Avenue
Suite 600
Pasadena, CA 91101
Telephone: (818) 796-8100
**Recruiter Classification:** Retained; **Lowest/Average Salary:** $60,000/$90,000;
**Industry Concentration:** Generalist with a primary focus in Consumer
Products, Education/Libraries, Electronics, Entertainment, Environmental,
Fashion (Retail/Apparel), Financial Services, Healthcare/Hospitals, High
Technology, Hospitality/Leisure, Information Technology, Manufacturing, Non-
Profit; **Function Concentration:** Generalist with a primary focus in
Administration, Finance/Accounting, General Management, Human Resources,
Marketing, Research and Development, Sales

**Meyer, William** — *Agribusiness Recruiter*
Agra Placements International Ltd.
2200 North Kickapoo, Suite 2
Lincoln, IL 62656
Telephone: (217) 735-4373
**Recruiter Classification:** Contingency; **Lowest/Average Salary:** $20,000/$30,000;
**Industry Concentration:** Generalist with a primary focus in Biotechnology,
Chemical Products, Energy, Financial Services, Manufacturing; **Function
Concentration:** Administration, Engineering, Finance/Accounting, General
Management, Human Resources, Marketing, Research and Development, Sales

**Meyers, Maurice R.** — *Manager Pacific Region*
Management Recruiters International, Inc.
19 East Cirus, Suite 201
Redlands, CA 92373
Telephone: (909) 335-2055
**Recruiter Classification:** Contingency; **Lowest/Average Salary:** $30,000/$75,000;
**Industry Concentration:** Generalist; **Function Concentration:** Generalist

**Meyers, Mel** — *Executive Vice President/Managing Director*
DHR International, Inc.
700 Ackerman Road, Suite 600
Columbus, OH 43202
Telephone: (614) 265-8213
**Recruiter Classification:** Retained; **Lowest/Average Salary:** $60,000/$90,000;
**Industry Concentration:** Generalist; **Function Concentration:** Generalist

**Meyers, Steven** — *Senior Associate*
Montgomery Resources, Inc.
555 Montgomery Street, Suite 1650
San Francisco, CA 94111
Telephone: (415) 956-4242
**Recruiter Classification:** Contingency, Executive Temporary; **Lowest/Average
Salary:** $30,000/$60,000; **Industry Concentration:** Generalist with a primary
focus in Consumer Products, Financial Services, High Technology, Insurance,
Manufacturing, Real Estate, Venture Capital; **Function Concentration:**
Finance/Accounting

**Meza, Anna** — *Executive Recruiter*
Richard, Wayne and Roberts
24 Greenway Plaza, Suite 1304
Houston, TX 77046-2493
Telephone: (713) 629-6681
**Recruiter Classification:** Retained; **Lowest/Average Salary:** $50,000/$90,000;
**Industry Concentration:** Generalist with a primary focus in Financial Services;
**Function Concentration:** Generalist with a primary focus in
Finance/Accounting

**Michaels, Joseph** — *Executive Recruiter*
CPS Inc.
One Westbrook Corporate Centre, Suite 600
Westchester, IL 60154
Telephone: (708) 531-8370
**Recruiter Classification:** Contingency; **Lowest/Average Salary:**
$30,000/$50,000; **Industry Concentration:** Generalist with a primary focus in
Automotive, Biotechnology, Chemical Products, Consumer Products, High
Technology, Insurance, Manufacturing, Oil/Gas, Packaging,
Pharmaceutical/Medical; **Function Concentration:** Engineering, Research and
Development, Sales, Women/Minorities

**Michaels, Stewart** — *Partner*
TOPAZ International, Inc.
383 Northfield Avenue
West Orange, NJ 07052
Telephone: (201) 669-7300
**Recruiter Classification:** Contingency; **Lowest/Average Salary:**
$40,000/$75,000; **Industry Concentration:** Chemical Products, Consumer
Products, Electronics, Entertainment, Financial Services, High Technology,
Manufacturing, Pharmaceutical/Medical; **Function Concentration:** Generalist
with a primary focus in Women/Minorities

**Michaels, Stewart** — *Partner*
TOPAZ Legal Solutions
383 Northfield Avenue
West Orange, NJ 07052
Telephone: (201) 669-7300
**Recruiter Classification:** Executive Temporary; **Lowest/Average Salary:**
$40,000/$75,000; **Industry Concentration:** Chemical Products, Consumer
Products, Electronics, Entertainment, Environmental, Financial Services, High
Technology, Manufacturing; **Function Concentration:** Generalist with a
primary focus in Women/Minorities

**Middleton, Alfred E.** — *Vice President*
The Neil Michael Group, Inc.
305 Madison Avenue, Suite 902
New York, NY 10165
Telephone: (212) 986-3790
**Recruiter Classification:** Retained; **Lowest/Average Salary:** $90,000/$90,000;
**Industry Concentration:** Biotechnology, Healthcare/Hospitals,
Pharmaceutical/Medical; **Function Concentration:** Generalist

**Mierzwinski, John** — *Director Sales*
Industrial Recruiters Associates, Inc.
20 Hurlbut Street, 1st Floor
West Hartford, CT 06110
Telephone: (860) 953-3643
**Recruiter Classification:** Contingency; **Lowest/Average Salary:**
$30,000/$50,000; **Industry Concentration:** Generalist with a primary focus in
Aerospace/Defense, Biotechnology, Chemical Products, Electronics,
Environmental, High Technology, Manufacturing, Packaging; **Function
Concentration:** Generalist with a primary focus in Engineering,
Finance/Accounting, General Management, Marketing, Research and
Development, Sales, Women/Minorities

**Miesemer, Arthur C.** — *Executive Recruiter*
MSI International
8521 Leesburg Pike, Suite 435
Vienna, VA 22182
Telephone: (703) 893-5669
**Recruiter Classification:** Contingency; **Lowest/Average Salary:**
$30,000/$75,000; **Industry Concentration:** Generalist with a primary focus in
Healthcare/Hospitals; **Function Concentration:** Generalist with a primary focus
in Administration, Engineering, Finance/Accounting, General Management,
Marketing, Sales

**Mikula, Linda** — *Vice President Life Sciences*
Schweichler Associates, Inc.
200 Tamal Vista, Building 200, Suite 100
Corte Madera, CA 94925
Telephone: (415) 924-7200
**Recruiter Classification:** Retained; **Lowest/Average Salary:** $90,000/$90,000;
**Industry Concentration:** Biotechnology, High Technology,
Pharmaceutical/Medical; **Function Concentration:** General Management,
Marketing, Research and Development, Sales

**Miles, Kenneth T.** — *Executive Recruiter*
MSI International
6151 Powers Ferry Road, Suite 540
Atlanta, GA 30339
Telephone: (404) 850-6465
**Recruiter Classification:** Contingency; **Lowest/Average Salary:**
$30,000/$75,000; **Industry Concentration:** Generalist with a primary focus in
Electronics, High Technology; **Function Concentration:** Generalist with a
primary focus in Administration, Engineering, Finance/Accounting, General
Management, Marketing, Sales

**Miles, Marybeth** — *Information Technology Recruiter*
Winter, Wyman & Company
950 Winter Street, Suite 3100
Waltham, MA 02154-1294
Telephone: (617) 890-7000
**Recruiter Classification:** Contingency; **Lowest/Average Salary:**
$30,000/$60,000; **Industry Concentration:** Information Technology; **Function
Concentration:** Generalist

**Milius, Kent L.** — *Manager Southwest Region*
Management Recruiters International, Inc.
9350 East Arapahoe Road, Suite 480
Englewood, CO 80112
Telephone: (303) 799-8188
**Recruiter Classification:** Contingency; **Lowest/Average Salary:**
$30,000/$75,000; **Industry Concentration:** Generalist; **Function
Concentration:** Generalist

**Milkint, Margaret Resce** — *Executive Vice President*
Jacobson Associates
150 North Wacker Drive
Suite 1120
Chicago, IL 60606
Telephone: (312) 726-1578
**Recruiter Classification:** Contingency; **Lowest/Average Salary:**
$20,000/$50,000; **Industry Concentration:** Insurance; **Function
Concentration:** Generalist

**Mill, Christopher A.** — *President Paladin - San Francisco*
The Paladin Companies, Inc.
One Market Plaza, 41st Floor
Spear Street Tower
San Francisco, CA 94105
Telephone: (415) 495-0900
**Recruiter Classification:** Executive Temporary; **Lowest/Average Salary:**
$40,000/$75,000; **Industry Concentration:** Generalist; **Function
Concentration:** Marketing

**Miller, Andrew S.** — *Manager Eastern Region*
Management Recruiters International, Inc.
76 Floral Avenue
New Providence, NJ 07974-1511
Telephone: (908) 771-0600
**Recruiter Classification:** Contingency; **Lowest/Average Salary:**
$30,000/$75,000; **Industry Concentration:** Generalist; **Function
Concentration:** Generalist

**Miller, Arnie** — *Managing Director*
Isaacson, Miller
334 Boylston Street, Suite 500
Boston, MA 02111
Telephone: (617) 262-6500
**Recruiter Classification:** Retained; **Lowest/Average Salary:** $75,000/$90,000;
**Industry Concentration:** Generalist with a primary focus in Non-Profit, Public
Administration, Transportation; **Function Concentration:** Administration,
Finance/Accounting, General Management, Human Resources,
Women/Minorities

**Miller, Benjamin J.** — *Executive Recruiter*
MSI International
5215 North O'Connor Boulevard
Suite 1875
Irving, TX 75039
Telephone: (214) 869-3939
**Recruiter Classification:** Contingency; **Lowest/Average Salary:**
$30,000/$60,000; **Industry Concentration:** Generalist with a primary focus in
Healthcare/Hospitals; **Function Concentration:** Generalist with a primary focus
in Administration, Engineering, Finance/Accounting, General Management,
Marketing, Sales

**Miller, Bert E.** — *Co-Owner/Manager Central Region*
Management Recruiters International, Inc.
Prestwick Pointe
5250 East US 36, Suite 730
Danville, IN 46122-9771
Telephone: (317) 745-2284
**Recruiter Classification:** Contingency; **Lowest/Average Salary:**
$30,000/$75,000; **Industry Concentration:** Generalist; **Function
Concentration:** Generalist

**Miller, Brett** — *Consultant*
The McCormick Group, Inc.
1400 Wilson Boulevard
Arlington, VA 22209
Telephone: (703) 841-1700
**Recruiter Classification:** Retained; **Lowest/Average Salary:** $40,000/$60,000;
**Industry Concentration:** High Technology, Information Technology; **Function
Concentration:** Marketing, Sales

**Miller, David** — *Recruiter*
Temporary Accounting Personnel, Inc.
955 East Henrietta Road
Rochester, NY 14623
Telephone: (716) 427-9930
**Recruiter Classification:** Executive Temporary; **Lowest/Average Salary:**
$20,000/$30,000; **Industry Concentration:** Generalist with a primary focus in
Financial Services; **Function Concentration:** Finance/Accounting, Human
Resources

**Miller, Diane D.** — *Vice President*
Wilcox, Bertoux & Miller
100 Howe Avenue, Suite 155N
Sacramento, CA 95825
Telephone: (916) 977-3700
**Recruiter Classification:** Contingency; **Lowest/Average Salary:**
$50,000/$90,000; **Industry Concentration:** Board Services, Non-Profit;
**Function Concentration:** Administration, General Management

**Miller, Elaine** — *Account Executive*
Search West, Inc.
340 North Westlake Boulevard
Suite 200
Westlake Village, CA 91362-3761
Telephone: (805) 496-6811
**Recruiter Classification:** Contingency; **Lowest/Average Salary:**
$40,000/$60,000; **Industry Concentration:** Biotechnology,
Pharmaceutical/Medical; **Function Concentration:** Engineering, Research and
Development

**Miller, George N.** — *Senior Associate*
Hite Executive Search
6515 Chase Drive
P.O. Box 43217
Cleveland, OH 44143
Telephone: (216) 461-1600
**Recruiter Classification:** Retained; **Lowest/Average Salary:** $90,000/$90,000;
**Industry Concentration:** Generalist with a primary focus in Consumer
Products, Information Technology, Manufacturing, Packaging; **Function
Concentration:** Generalist with a primary focus in Administration, Human
Resources

**Miller, Harold B.** — *Executive Recruiter*
MSI International
1050 Crown Pointe Parkway
Suite 1000
Atlanta, GA 30338
Telephone: (404) 394-2494
**Recruiter Classification:** Contingency; **Lowest/Average Salary:**
$30,000/$60,000; **Industry Concentration:** Generalist with a primary focus in
Financial Services; **Function Concentration:** Finance/Accounting

**Miller, Joanna** — *Vice President*
Korn/Ferry International
One Landmark Square
Stamford, CT 06901
Telephone: (203) 359-3350
**Recruiter Classification:** Retained; **Lowest/Average Salary:** $90,000/$90,000;
**Industry Concentration:** Generalist; **Function Concentration:** Generalist

**Miller, Julie** — *Recruiting Consultant*
Southwestern Professional Services
2451 Atrium Way
Nashville, TN 37214
Telephone: (615) 391-2722
**Recruiter Classification:** Contingency; **Lowest/Average Salary:**
$30,000/$60,000; **Industry Concentration:** Generalist with a primary focus in
Pharmaceutical/Medical; **Function Concentration:** Generalist with a primary
focus in Sales

**Miller, Kenneth A.** — *President*
Computer Network Resources, Inc.
28231 Tinajo
Mission Viejo, CA 92692
Telephone: (714) 951-5929
**Recruiter Classification:** Contingency; **Lowest/Average Salary:**
$60,000/$75,000; **Industry Concentration:** Financial Services,
Healthcare/Hospitals, High Technology, Information Technology, Insurance;
**Function Concentration:** Sales

**Miller, Larry** — *Associate*
Source Services Corporation
4200 West Cypress Street, Suite 101
Tampa, FL 33607
Telephone: (813) 879-2221
**Recruiter Classification:** Contingency; **Lowest/Average Salary:**
$30,000/$50,000; **Industry Concentration:** Financial Services, Information
Technology; **Function Concentration:** Engineering, Finance/Accounting

**Miller, Laura** — *Coordinator Bookkeeping and Temporary
Staffing*
Accounting Personnel Consultants
210 Baronne Street, Suite 920
New Orleans, LA 70112
Telephone: (504) 581-7800
**Recruiter Classification:** Contingency, Executive Temporary; **Lowest/Average
Salary:** $20,000/$20,000; **Industry Concentration:** Generalist; **Function
Concentration:** Administration, Finance/Accounting

**Miller, Michael R.** — *Partner*
Lynch Miller Moore Partners, Inc.
10 South Wacker Drive, Suite 2935
Chicago, IL 60606
Telephone: (312) 876-1505
**Recruiter Classification:** Retained; **Lowest/Average Salary:** $75,000/$90,000;
**Industry Concentration:** Generalist with a primary focus in Biotechnology,
Manufacturing, Packaging, Pharmaceutical/Medical, Venture Capital; **Function
Concentration:** Generalist with a primary focus in Finance/Accounting,
General Management

**Miller, Paul McG.** — *Partner*
Lamalie Amrop International
225 West Wacker Drive
Chicago, IL 60606-1229
Telephone: (312) 782-3113
**Recruiter Classification:** Retained; **Lowest/Average Salary:** $90,000/$90,000;
**Industry Concentration:** Generalist with a primary focus in Utilities/Nuclear;
**Function Concentration:** Generalist with a primary focus in General
Management, Marketing, Sales

**Miller, Roy** — *Partner*
The Enns Partners Inc.
70 University Avenue, Suite 410, P.O. Box 14
Toronto, Ontario, CANADA M5J 2M4
Telephone: (416) 598-0012
**Recruiter Classification:** Retained; **Lowest/Average Salary:** $75,000/$90,000;
**Industry Concentration:** Generalist with a primary focus in
Aerospace/Defense, Board Services, Consumer Products, Electronics, Energy,
Financial Services, High Technology, Hospitality/Leisure, Manufacturing,
Pharmaceutical/Medical, Publishing/Media, Transportation, Venture Capital;
**Function Concentration:** Generalist with a primary focus in Administration,
Finance/Accounting, General Management, Human Resources, Marketing,
Sales

**Miller, Russel E.** — *Executive Vice President*
ARJay & Associates
875 Walnut Street, Suite 150
Cary, NC 27511
Telephone: (919) 469-5540
**Recruiter Classification:** Contingency; **Lowest/Average Salary:**
$40,000/$90,000; **Industry Concentration:** Generalist with a primary focus in
Automotive, Electronics, Energy, Environmental, Manufacturing,
Utilities/Nuclear; **Function Concentration:** Generalist with a primary focus in
Engineering, Finance/Accounting, General Management, Human Resources,
Marketing, Research and Development, Sales

**Miller, Timothy** — *Associate*
Source Services Corporation
3 Summit Park Drive, Suite 550
Independence, OH 44131
Telephone: (216) 328-5900
**Recruiter Classification:** Contingency; **Lowest/Average Salary:**
$30,000/$50,000; **Industry Concentration:** Financial Services, Information
Technology; **Function Concentration:** Engineering, Finance/Accounting

**Milligan, Dale** — *Associate*
Source Services Corporation
4170 Ashford Dunwoody Road, Suite 285
Atlanta, GA 30319
Telephone: (404) 255-2045
**Recruiter Classification:** Contingency; **Lowest/Average Salary:**
$30,000/$50,000; **Industry Concentration:** Financial Services, Information
Technology; **Function Concentration:** Engineering, Finance/Accounting

**Millonzi, Joel C.** — *Senior Managing Director*
Johnson Smith & Knisely Accord
100 Park Avenue, 15th Floor
New York, NY 10017
Telephone: (212) 885-9100
**Recruiter Classification:** Retained; **Lowest/Average Salary:** $90,000/$90,000;
**Industry Concentration:** Financial Services, Insurance, Real Estate, Venture
Capital; **Function Concentration:** Generalist with a primary focus in
Administration, Finance/Accounting, General Management, Human Resources,
Marketing, Research and Development, Sales

**Mills, John** — *Associate*
Source Services Corporation
1105 Schrock Road, Suite 510
Columbus, OH 43229
Telephone: (614) 846-3311
**Recruiter Classification:** Contingency; **Lowest/Average Salary:**
$30,000/$50,000; **Industry Concentration:** Financial Services, Information
Technology; **Function Concentration:** Engineering, Finance/Accounting

**Milne, Robert P.** — *Consultant*
Boyden/Zay & Company
Two Midtown Plaza, Suite 1740
1360 Peachtree Street, NE
Atlanta, GA 30309
Telephone: (404) 876-9986
**Recruiter Classification:** Retained; **Lowest/Average Salary:** $90,000/$90,000;
**Industry Concentration:** Environmental, Information Technology; **Function
Concentration:** Generalist

**Milner, Carol** — *Associate*
Source Services Corporation
One CityPlace, Suite 170
St. Louis, MO 63141
Telephone: (314) 432-4500
**Recruiter Classification:** Contingency; **Lowest/Average Salary:**
$30,000/$50,000; **Industry Concentration:** Financial Services, Information
Technology; **Function Concentration:** Engineering, Finance/Accounting

**Milo, Bill** — *Manager Eastern Region*
Management Recruiters International, Inc.
3901 North Front, Suite 1A
Harrisburg, PA 17110-1536
Telephone: (717) 238-3995
**Recruiter Classification:** Contingency; **Lowest/Average Salary:**
$30,000/$75,000; **Industry Concentration:** Generalist; **Function
Concentration:** Generalist

**Milstein, Bonnie** — *Executive Vice President*
Marvin Laba & Associates
6255 Sunset Boulevard, Suite 617
Los Angeles, CA 90028
Telephone: (213) 464-1355
**Recruiter Classification:** Retained; **Lowest/Average Salary:** $40,000/$75,000;
**Industry Concentration:** Consumer Products, Fashion (Retail/Apparel),
Financial Services, Manufacturing; **Function Concentration:** Generalist with a
primary focus in Finance/Accounting, General Management, Human
Resources, Marketing, Sales

**Milton, Suzanne** — *Vice President*
Marra Peters & Partners
Millburn Esplanade
Millburn, NJ 07041
Telephone: (201) 376-8999
**Recruiter Classification:** Retained; **Lowest/Average Salary:** $/$90,000; **Industry
Concentration:** Generalist with a primary focus in Biotechnology, Consumer
Products, Entertainment, Financial Services, Information Technology,
Manufacturing, Pharmaceutical/Medical; **Function Concentration:** Generalist
with a primary focus in Administration, Engineering, Finance/Accounting,
General Management, Human Resources, Marketing, Research and
Development, Sales

**Mines, Herbert T.** — *Chairman and CEO*
Herbert Mines Associates, Inc.
399 Park Avenue, 27th Floor
New York, NY 10022
Telephone: (212) 355-0909
**Recruiter Classification:** Retained; **Lowest/Average Salary:** $75,000/$90,000;
**Industry Concentration:** Board Services, Consumer Products, Fashion
(Retail/Apparel); **Function Concentration:** Generalist with a primary focus in
Finance/Accounting, General Management, Human Resources, Marketing, Sales

**Miras, Cliff** — *Managing Director*
Source Services Corporation
5 Independence Way
Princeton, NJ 08540
Telephone: (609) 452-7277
**Recruiter Classification:** Contingency; **Lowest/Average Salary:**
$30,000/$50,000; **Industry Concentration:** Financial Services, Information
Technology; **Function Concentration:** Engineering, Finance/Accounting

**Miras, Cliff** — *Managing Director*
Source Services Corporation
379 Thornall Street
Edison, NJ 08837
Telephone: (908) 494-2800
**Recruiter Classification:** Contingency; **Lowest/Average Salary:**
$30,000/$50,000; **Industry Concentration:** Financial Services, Information
Technology; **Function Concentration:** Engineering, Finance/Accounting

**Mirtz, P. John** — *Partner*
Mirtz Morice, Inc.
One Dock Street
Stamford, CT 06902
Telephone: (203) 964-9266
**Recruiter Classification:** Retained; **Lowest/Average Salary:** $90,000/$90,000;
**Industry Concentration:** Generalist with a primary focus in Board Services,
Chemical Products, Consumer Products, Electronics, Financial Services,
Insurance, Manufacturing, Pharmaceutical/Medical; **Function Concentration:**
Generalist

**Mitchell, F. Wayne** — *Vice President*
Korn/Ferry International
3950 Lincoln Plaza
500 North Akard Street
Dallas, TX 75201
Telephone: (214) 954-1834
**Recruiter Classification:** Retained; **Lowest/Average Salary:** $90,000/$90,000;
**Industry Concentration:** Generalist with a primary focus in High Technology;
**Function Concentration:** Generalist

**Mitchell, John** — *Managing Partner*
Romac & Associates
Plaza of the Americas
700 North Pear St. #940
Dallas, TX 75201
Telephone: (214) 720-0050
**Recruiter Classification:** Executive Temporary; **Lowest/Average Salary:**
$/$60,000; **Industry Concentration:** Financial Services, Healthcare/Hospitals,
High Technology, Hospitality/Leisure, Information Technology, Insurance;
**Function Concentration:** Finance/Accounting

**Mitchell, John R.** — *Manager Central Region*
Management Recruiters International, Inc.
3145 Henry Street, Suite 203
Muskegon, MI 49441
Telephone: (616) 755-6486
**Recruiter Classification:** Contingency; **Lowest/Average Salary:**
$30,000/$75,000; **Industry Concentration:** Generalist; **Function
Concentration:** Generalist

**Mitchell, John T.** — *Industry Leader - Healthcare*
Paul Ray Berndtson
191 Peachtree Tower, Suite 3800
191 Peachtree Street, NE
Atlanta, GA 30303-1757
Telephone: (404) 215-4600
**Recruiter Classification:** Retained; **Lowest/Average Salary:** $90,000/$90,000;
**Industry Concentration:** Healthcare/Hospitals, Manufacturing; **Function
Concentration:** Generalist

**Mitchell, Katie** — *Consultant*
Paul Ray Berndtson
2200 Ross Avenue, Suite 4500W
Dallas, TX 75201
Telephone: (214) 969-7620
**Recruiter Classification:** Retained; **Lowest/Average Salary:** $90,000/$90,000;
**Industry Concentration:** Generalist; **Function Concentration:** Generalist

**Mitchell, Kim** — *Executive Recruiter*
Richard, Wayne and Roberts
24 Greenway Plaza, Suite 1304
Houston, TX 77046-2493
Telephone: (713) 629-6681
**Recruiter Classification:** Retained; **Lowest/Average Salary:** $40,000/$60,000;
**Industry Concentration:** Generalist; **Function Concentration:** Generalist

**Mitchell, Kyle R.** — *Partner*
Tanton Mitchell/Paul Ray Berndtson
710-1050 West Pender Street
Vancouver, British Columbia, CANADA V6E 3S7
Telephone: (604) 685-0261
**Recruiter Classification:** Retained; **Lowest/Average Salary:** $75,000/$90,000;
**Industry Concentration:** Generalist with a primary focus in
Healthcare/Hospitals, Non-Profit; **Function Concentration:** Generalist with a
primary focus in General Management

**Mitchell, Norman F.** — *Vice President*
A.T. Kearney, Inc.
1100 Abernathy Road, Suite 900
Atlanta, GA 30328-5603
Telephone: (770) 393-9900
**Recruiter Classification:** Retained; **Lowest/Average Salary:** $90,000/$90,000;
**Industry Concentration:** Generalist with a primary focus in
Healthcare/Hospitals, Manufacturing; **Function Concentration:** Generalist with
a primary focus in Engineering, Research and Development

**Mitchell, Thomas M.** — *Managing Partner*
Heidrick & Struggles, Inc.
300 South Grand Avenue, Suite 2400
Los Angeles, CA 90071
Telephone: (213) 625-8811
**Recruiter Classification:** Retained; **Lowest/Average Salary:** $75,000/$90,000;
**Industry Concentration:** Generalist; **Function Concentration:** Generalist

**Mitros, George N.** — *Advisor*
Mixtec Group
31255 Cedar Valley Drive
Suite 300-327
Westlake Village, CA 91362
Telephone: (818) 889-8819
**Recruiter Classification:** Contingency; **Lowest/Average Salary:**
$60,000/$90,000; **Industry Concentration:** Hospitality/Leisure; **Function
Concentration:** Generalist with a primary focus in Marketing, Research and
Development, Sales

**Mitton, Bill** — *Executive Vice President*
Executive Resource, Inc.
553 South Industrial Drive
P.O. Box 356
Hartland, WI 53029-0356
Telephone: (414) 369-2540
**Recruiter Classification:** Contingency; **Lowest/Average Salary:**
$30,000/$50,000; **Industry Concentration:** Generalist with a primary focus in
Automotive, Chemical Products, Consumer Products, Electronics, Fashion
(Retail/Apparel), High Technology, Manufacturing, Oil/Gas,
Packaging, Pharmaceutical/Medical; **Function Concentration:**
Finance/Accounting, Human Resources

**Mittwol, Myles** — *Associate*
Source Services Corporation
1 Gatehall Drive, Suite 250
Parsippany, NJ 07054
Telephone: (201) 267-3222
**Recruiter Classification:** Contingency; **Lowest/Average Salary:**
$30,000/$50,000; **Industry Concentration:** Financial Services, Information
Technology; **Function Concentration:** Engineering, Finance/Accounting

**Mochwart, Donald** — *Vice President*
Drummond Associates, Inc.
50 Broadway, Suite 1201
New York, NY 10004
Telephone: (212) 248-1120
**Recruiter Classification:** Contingency; **Lowest/Average Salary:**
$40,000/$75,000; **Industry Concentration:** Financial Services, Information
Technology; **Function Concentration:** Finance/Accounting

**Mockler, Nadine** — *Partner*
Part Time Resources, Inc.
399 East Putnam Avenue
Cos Cob, CT 06807
Telephone: (203) 629-3255
**Recruiter Classification:** Executive Temporary; **Lowest/Average Salary:**
$20,000/$50,000; **Industry Concentration:** Generalist; **Function
Concentration:** Generalist with a primary focus in Administration,
Finance/Accounting, General Management, Human Resources, Marketing,
Research and Development, Sales

**Moeller, Ed J.** — *Manager Central Region*
Management Recruiters International, Inc.
550 Stephenson Highway, Suite 407
Troy, MI 48083-1152
Telephone: (810) 585-4200
**Recruiter Classification:** Contingency; **Lowest/Average Salary:**
$30,000/$75,000; **Industry Concentration:** Generalist; **Function
Concentration:** Generalist

**Moerbe, Ed H.** — *Managing Director*
Stanton Chase International
5050 Quorum Drive, Suite 330
Dallas, TX 75240
Telephone: (214) 404-8411
**Recruiter Classification:** Retained; **Lowest/Average Salary:** $75,000/$90,000;
**Industry Concentration:** Generalist with a primary focus in Chemical Products,
Consumer Products, Environmental, High Technology, Manufacturing;
**Function Concentration:** Generalist with a primary focus in Administration,
Engineering, Marketing, Sales

**Moga, Michael** — *Principal*
Korn/Ferry International
Scotia Plaza
40 King Street West
Toronto, Ontario, CANADA M5H 3Y2
Telephone: (416) 366-1300
**Recruiter Classification:** Retained; **Lowest/Average Salary:** $90,000/$90,000;
**Industry Concentration:** Generalist; **Function Concentration:** Generalist

**Mogul, Gene** — *President*
Mogul Consultants, Inc.
380 North Broadway, Suite 208
Jericho, NY 11753-2109
Telephone: (516) 822-4363
**Recruiter Classification:** Contingency; **Lowest/Average Salary:**
$40,000/$75,000; **Industry Concentration:** Electronics, Financial Services,
High Technology, Information Technology, Insurance, Manufacturing,
Transportation; **Function Concentration:** Generalist with a primary focus in
Engineering, General Management, Marketing, Research and Development,
Sales

**Mohan, Jack** — *Manager Eastern Region*
Management Recruiters International, Inc.
Bay Bank Tower, Suite 1822
1500 Main Street
Springfield, MA 01115
Telephone: (413) 781-1550
**Recruiter Classification:** Contingency; **Lowest/Average Salary:**
$30,000/$75,000; **Industry Concentration:** Generalist; **Function**
**Concentration:** Generalist

**Mohan, Jack** — *General Manager*
Management Recruiters International, Inc.
607 Boylston Street, Suite 603
Boston, MA 02116
Telephone: (617) 262-5050
**Recruiter Classification:** Contingency; **Lowest/Average Salary:**
$30,000/$75,000; **Industry Concentration:** Generalist; **Function**
**Concentration:** Generalist

**Mohr, Brian** — *Executive Recruiter*
CPS Inc.
One Westbrook Corporate Centre, Suite 600
Westchester, IL 60154
Telephone: (708) 531-8370
**Recruiter Classification:** Contingency; **Lowest/Average Salary:**
$30,000/$50,000; **Industry Concentration:** Generalist with a primary focus in
Automotive, Biotechnology, Chemical Products, Consumer Products, High
Technology, Insurance, Manufacturing, Oil/Gas, Packaging,
Pharmaceutical/Medical; **Function Concentration:** Engineering, Research and
Development, Sales, Women/Minorities

**Moliski, Robert** — *Senior Associate*
Korn/Ferry International
120 South Riverside Plaza
Suite 918
Chicago, IL 60606
Telephone: (312) 726-1841
**Recruiter Classification:** Retained; **Lowest/Average Salary:** $90,000/$90,000;
**Industry Concentration:** Generalist; **Function Concentration:** Generalist

**Molitor, John L.** — *Manager Accounting/Financial Search*
*Division*
Barrett Partners
100 North LaSalle Street, Suite 1420
Chicago, IL 60602
Telephone: (312) 443-8877
**Recruiter Classification:** Contingency; **Lowest/Average Salary:**
$30,000/$50,000; **Industry Concentration:** Automotive, Biotechnology,
Chemical Products, Consumer Products, Environmental, Financial Services,
Healthcare/Hospitals, Information Technology, Insurance, Manufacturing,
Packaging, Publishing/Media, Real Estate, Transportation; **Function**
**Concentration:** Engineering, Finance/Accounting

**Mollichelli, David** — *Associate*
Source Services Corporation
One Park Plaza, Suite 560
Irvine, CA 92714
Telephone: (714) 660-1666
**Recruiter Classification:** Contingency; **Lowest/Average Salary:**
$30,000/$50,000; **Industry Concentration:** Financial Services, Information
Technology; **Function Concentration:** Engineering, Finance/Accounting

**Molnar, Robert A.** — *Partner*
Johnson Smith & Knisely Accord
100 Park Avenue, 15th Floor
New York, NY 10017
Telephone: (212) 885-9100
**Recruiter Classification:** Retained; **Lowest/Average Salary:** $90,000/$90,000;
**Industry Concentration:** Board Services, Chemical Products, Consumer
Products, Electronics, Entertainment, Financial Services, Healthcare/Hospitals,
High Technology, Information Technology, Insurance, Manufacturing,
Publishing/Media, Venture Capital; **Function Concentration:** Generalist

**Momtaz, Heba** — *Consultant - L.A. Retail*
Evie Kreisler & Associates, Inc.
865 South Figueroa, Suite 950
Los Angeles, CA 90017
Telephone: (213) 622-8994
**Recruiter Classification:** Contingency; **Lowest/Average Salary:**
$30,000/$75,000; **Industry Concentration:** Fashion (Retail/Apparel); **Function**
**Concentration:** Generalist

**Monaghan, Jill** — *Consultant*
Paul Ray Berndtson
191 Peachtree Tower, Suite 3800
191 Peachtree Street, NE
Atlanta, GA 30303-1757
Telephone: (404) 215-4600
**Recruiter Classification:** Retained; **Lowest/Average Salary:** $90,000/$90,000;
**Industry Concentration:** Generalist; **Function Concentration:** Generalist

**Monahan, B. Roderick** — *Partner*
Lamalie Amrop International
Thanksgiving Tower
1601 Elm Street
Dallas, TX 75201-4768
Telephone: (214) 754-0019
**Recruiter Classification:** Retained; **Lowest/Average Salary:** $90,000/$90,000;
**Industry Concentration:** Generalist; **Function Concentration:** Generalist

**Mondragon, Philip** — *Vice President and Partner*
Boyden
Paseo de la Reforma 509
110. Piso, Cuauhtemoc
Mexico City, D.F., MEXICO 06500
Telephone: (525) 553-7777
**Recruiter Classification:** Retained; **Lowest/Average Salary:** $75,000/$90,000;
**Industry Concentration:** Generalist; **Function Concentration:** Generalist with a
primary focus in Engineering, Finance/Accounting, General Management,
Human Resources, Marketing, Research and Development, Sales,
Women/Minorities

**Monogenis, Emanuel N.** — *Partner*
Heidrick & Struggles, Inc.
245 Park Avenue, Suite 4300
New York, NY 10167-0152
Telephone: (212) 867-9876
**Recruiter Classification:** Retained; **Lowest/Average Salary:** $75,000/$90,000;
**Industry Concentration:** Generalist with a primary focus in Financial Services;
**Function Concentration:** Generalist

**Monroe, Kenneth D.** — *Principal*
Sanford Rose Associates
2623 McCormick Drive, Suite 104
Clearwater, FL 34619-1041
Telephone: (813) 796-2201
**Recruiter Classification:** Contingency; **Lowest/Average Salary:**
$30,000/$75,000; **Industry Concentration:** Generalist; **Function**
**Concentration:** Generalist

**Montgomery, Catherine C.** — *Vice President*
Boyden
55 Madison Avenue
Suite 400
Morristown, NJ 07960
Telephone: (201) 267-0980
**Recruiter Classification:** Retained; **Lowest/Average Salary:** $75,000/$90,000;
**Industry Concentration:** Generalist; **Function Concentration:** Generalist with a
primary focus in Engineering, Finance/Accounting, General Management,
Human Resources, Marketing, Research and Development, Sales,
Women/Minorities

**Montgomery, James M.** — *President*
Houze, Shourds & Montgomery, Inc.
Greater L.A. World Trade Center, Suite 1840
Long Beach, CA 90831-1840
Telephone: (310) 495-6495
**Recruiter Classification:** Retained; **Lowest/Average Salary:** $90,000/$90,000;
**Industry Concentration:** Generalist with a primary focus in
Aerospace/Defense, Consumer Products, Electronics, Environmental, High
Technology, Manufacturing, Venture Capital; **Function Concentration:**
Generalist with a primary focus in Finance/Accounting, General Management,
Human Resources, Marketing, Women/Minorities

**Montigny, Paul F.** — *General Manager*
Management Recruiters International, Inc.
9700 Rockside Road, Suite 490
Cleveland, OH 44125-6264
Telephone: (216) 642-5788
**Recruiter Classification:** Contingency; **Lowest/Average Salary:**
$30,000/$75,000; **Industry Concentration:** Generalist; **Function Concentration:** Generalist

**Mooney, Kelly** — *Consultant*
Paul Ray Berndtson
301 Commerce Street, Suite 2300
Fort Worth, TX 76102
Telephone: (817) 334-0500
**Recruiter Classification:** Retained; **Lowest/Average Salary:** $90,000/$90,000;
**Industry Concentration:** Generalist; **Function Concentration:** Generalist

**Mooney, Matt** — *Consultant*
Paul Ray Berndtson
191 Peachtree Tower, Suite 3800
191 Peachtree Street, NE
Atlanta, GA 30303-1757
Telephone: (404) 215-4600
**Recruiter Classification:** Retained; **Lowest/Average Salary:** $90,000/$90,000;
**Industry Concentration:** Generalist; **Function Concentration:** Generalist

**Mooney, Penny P.** — *Principal*
Ward Howell International, Inc.
One Landmark Square
Suite 1810
Stamford, CT 06901
Telephone: (203) 964-1481
**Recruiter Classification:** Retained; **Lowest/Average Salary:** $75,000/$90,000;
**Industry Concentration:** Generalist; **Function Concentration:** Generalist

**Moore, Anne** — *Principal*
KPMG Executive Search
500-777 Dunsmuir Street
Vancouver, British Columbia, CANADA V7Y 1K5
Telephone: (604) 691-3000
**Recruiter Classification:** Retained; **Lowest/Average Salary:** $75,000/$90,000;
**Industry Concentration:** Generalist; **Function Concentration:** Generalist

**Moore, Craig** — *Associate*
Source Services Corporation
20 Burlington Mall Road, Suite 405
Burlington, MA 01803
Telephone: (617) 272-5000
**Recruiter Classification:** Contingency; **Lowest/Average Salary:**
$30,000/$50,000; **Industry Concentration:** Financial Services, Information Technology; **Function Concentration:** Engineering, Finance/Accounting

**Moore, David S.** — *Partner*
Lynch Miller Moore Partners, Inc.
10 South Wacker Drive, Suite 2935
Chicago, IL 60606
Telephone: (312) 876-1505
**Recruiter Classification:** Retained; **Lowest/Average Salary:** $75,000/$90,000;
**Industry Concentration:** Generalist with a primary focus in Automotive, Electronics, High Technology, Information Technology, Manufacturing; **Function Concentration:** Generalist with a primary focus in Finance/Accounting, General Management

**Moore, Denise** — *Executive Recruiter*
Jonas, Walters & Assoc., Inc.
1110 North Old World Third St., Suite 510
Milwaukee, WI 53203-1102
Telephone: (414) 291-2828
**Recruiter Classification:** Retained; **Lowest/Average Salary:** $60,000/$90,000;
**Industry Concentration:** Generalist with a primary focus in Consumer Products, Electronics, Healthcare/Hospitals, High Technology, Insurance, Manufacturing, Non-Profit, Publishing/Media; **Function Concentration:** Generalist with a primary focus in Administration, Engineering, Finance/Accounting, General Management, Human Resources, Marketing, Research and Development, Sales

**Moore, Dianna** — *Associate*
Source Services Corporation
2850 National City Tower
Louisville, KY 40202
Telephone: (502) 581-9900
**Recruiter Classification:** Contingency; **Lowest/Average Salary:**
$30,000/$50,000; **Industry Concentration:** Financial Services, Information Technology; **Function Concentration:** Engineering, Finance/Accounting

**Moore, Janice E.** — *Executive Recruiter*
MSI International
1050 Crown Pointe Parkway
Suite 1000
Atlanta, GA 30338
Telephone: (404) 394-2494
**Recruiter Classification:** Contingency; **Lowest/Average Salary:**
$30,000/$75,000; **Industry Concentration:** Generalist with a primary focus in Financial Services; **Function Concentration:** Generalist with a primary focus in Finance/Accounting

**Moore, Lemuel R.** — *Executive Recruiter*
MSI International
6151 Powers Ferry Road, Suite 540
Atlanta, GA 30339
Telephone: (404) 850-6465
**Recruiter Classification:** Contingency; **Lowest/Average Salary:**
$30,000/$75,000; **Industry Concentration:** Generalist with a primary focus in Electronics, High Technology; **Function Concentration:** Generalist with a primary focus in Administration, Engineering, Finance/Accounting, General Management, Marketing, Sales

**Moore, Lynn W.** — *Manager South Atlantic Region*
Management Recruiters International, Inc.
3005 26th Street West, Suite C
Bradenton, FL 34205
Telephone: (941) 753-5837
**Recruiter Classification:** Contingency; **Lowest/Average Salary:**
$30,000/$75,000; **Industry Concentration:** Generalist; **Function Concentration:** Generalist

**Moore, Mark** — *Chairman and CEO*
Wheeler, Moore & Elam Co.
14800 Quorum Drive, Suite 200
Dallas, TX 75240
Telephone: (214) 386-8806
**Recruiter Classification:** Retained; **Lowest/Average Salary:** $50,000/$75,000;
**Industry Concentration:** Generalist with a primary focus in Aerospace/Defense, Biotechnology, Chemical Products, Electronics, High Technology, Information Technology, Manufacturing, Oil/Gas, Pharmaceutical/Medical; **Function Concentration:** Generalist with a primary focus in Administration, Engineering, Finance/Accounting, General Management, Human Resources, Marketing, Research and Development, Sales

**Moore, Michael** — *Recruiter*
Agra Placements International Ltd.
4949 Pleasant Suite 1, West 50th Place III
West Des Moines, IA 50266-5494
Telephone: (515) 225-6562
**Recruiter Classification:** Contingency; **Lowest/Average Salary:**
$20,000/$30,000; **Industry Concentration:** Generalist with a primary focus in Biotechnology, Chemical Products, Energy, Financial Services, Manufacturing; **Function Concentration:** Generalist with a primary focus in Administration, Engineering, Finance/Accounting, General Management, Human Resources, Marketing, Research and Development, Sales, Women/Minorities

**Moore, Mike** — *Co-Manager*
Management Recruiters International, Inc.
Copper Point
4530 South Eastern, Suite A-12
Las Vegas, NV 89119-6181
Telephone: (702) 733-1818
**Recruiter Classification:** Contingency; **Lowest/Average Salary:**
$30,000/$75,000; **Industry Concentration:** Generalist; **Function Concentration:** Generalist

**Moore, Richard C.E.** — *Managing Director/Country Manager*
Russell Reynolds Associates, Inc.
Scotia Plaza
40 King Street West, Suite 3500
Toronto, Ontario, CANADA M5H 3Y2
Telephone: (416) 364-3355
**Recruiter Classification:** Retained; **Lowest/Average Salary:** $90,000/$90,000;
**Industry Concentration:** Generalist; **Function Concentration:** Generalist

**Moore, Suzanne** — *Associate*
Source Services Corporation
8614 Westwood Center, Suite 750
Vienna, VA 22182
Telephone: (703) 790-5610
**Recruiter Classification:** Contingency; **Lowest/Average Salary:**
$30,000/$50,000; **Industry Concentration:** Financial Services, Information Technology; **Function Concentration:** Engineering, Finance/Accounting

**Moore, Thomas** — *Technical Recruiter*
Aureus Group
8744 Frederick Street
Omaha, NE 68124-3068
Telephone: (402) 397-2980
**Recruiter Classification:** Contingency; **Lowest/Average Salary:**
$30,000/$60,000; **Industry Concentration:** Electronics, Manufacturing,
Packaging; **Function Concentration:** Engineering

**Moors, Donald** — *Partner*
Coopers & Lybrand Consulting
801 Brunswick House
44 Chipman Hill
Saint John, New Brunswick, CANADA E2L 4B9
Telephone: (506) 632-1810
**Recruiter Classification:** Retained; **Lowest/Average Salary:** $60,000/$90,000;
**Industry Concentration:** Generalist; **Function Concentration:** Generalist

**Moran, Carla** — *Placement Specialist*
Key Employment Services
1001 Office Park Road, Suite 320
West Des Moines, IA 50265-2567
Telephone: (515) 224-0446
**Recruiter Classification:** Contingency; **Lowest/Average Salary:**
$30,000/$75,000; **Industry Concentration:** Generalist; **Function
Concentration:** Marketing, Sales

**Moran, Douglas** — *Associate*
Source Services Corporation
10220 SW Greenburg Road, Suite 625
Portland, OR 97223
Telephone: (503) 768-4546
**Recruiter Classification:** Contingency; **Lowest/Average Salary:**
$30,000/$50,000; **Industry Concentration:** Financial Services, Information
Technology; **Function Concentration:** Engineering, Finance/Accounting

**Moran, Gail** — *Senior Account Manager*
Comprehensive Search
316 South Lewis Street
LaGrange, GA 30240
Telephone: (706) 884-3232
**Recruiter Classification:** Contingency; **Lowest/Average Salary:**
$40,000/$50,000; **Industry Concentration:** Generalist with a primary focus in
Fashion (Retail/Apparel), Hospitality/Leisure, Manufacturing, Real Estate;
**Function Concentration:** Generalist with a primary focus in Administration,
General Management, Marketing

**Moran, Gayle** — *Associate*
Dussick Management Associates
149 Durham Road
Madison, CT 06443
Telephone: (203) 245-9311
**Recruiter Classification:** Contingency; **Lowest/Average Salary:**
$50,000/$60,000; **Industry Concentration:** Generalist with a primary focus in
Consumer Products, High Technology, Information Technology, Packaging,
Pharmaceutical/Medical; **Function Concentration:** Generalist with a primary
focus in Marketing, Research and Development, Sales, Women/Minorities

**Moran, Robert** — *Vice President*
A.T. Kearney, Inc.
Miami Center, Suite 3180
201 South Biscayne Boulevard
Miami, FL 33131
Telephone: (305) 577-0046
**Recruiter Classification:** Retained; **Lowest/Average Salary:** $90,000/$90,000;
**Industry Concentration:** Generalist with a primary focus in Chemical Products,
Healthcare/Hospitals, Pharmaceutical/Medical; **Function Concentration:**
Generalist with a primary focus in Administration, Engineering, Human
Resources, Research and Development

**Moran, Thomas F.** — *Managing Director*
Ward Howell International, Inc.
401 East Host Drive
Lake Geneva, WI 53147
Telephone: (414) 249-5200
**Recruiter Classification:** Retained; **Lowest/Average Salary:** $75,000/$90,000;
**Industry Concentration:** Generalist; **Function Concentration:** Generalist

**Morato, Rene** — *Associate*
Source Services Corporation
15600 N.W. 67th Avenue, Suite 210
Miami Lakes, FL 33014
Telephone: (305) 556-8000
**Recruiter Classification:** Contingency; **Lowest/Average Salary:**
$30,000/$50,000; **Industry Concentration:** Financial Services, Information
Technology; **Function Concentration:** Engineering, Finance/Accounting

**Moretti, Denise** — *Associate*
Source Services Corporation
150 South Warner Road, Suite 238
King of Prussia, PA 19406
Telephone: (610) 341-1960
**Recruiter Classification:** Contingency; **Lowest/Average Salary:**
$30,000/$50,000; **Industry Concentration:** Financial Services, Information
Technology; **Function Concentration:** Engineering, Finance/Accounting

**Morgan, Beverly** — *Human Resources Recruiter*
Winter, Wyman & Company
950 Winter Street, Suite 3100
Waltham, MA 02154-1294
Telephone: (617) 890-7000
**Recruiter Classification:** Contingency; **Lowest/Average Salary:**
$30,000/$50,000; **Industry Concentration:** Generalist; **Function
Concentration:** Human Resources

**Morgan, Christopher** — *Consultant*
Paul Ray Berndtson
10 South Riverside Plaza
Suite 720
Chicago, IL 60606
Telephone: (312) 876-0730
**Recruiter Classification:** Retained; **Lowest/Average Salary:** $90,000/$90,000;
**Industry Concentration:** Generalist; **Function Concentration:** Generalist

**Morgan, David G.** — *Principal*
Morgan Stampfl, Inc.
6 West 32nd Street
New York, NY 10001
Telephone: (212) 643-7165
**Recruiter Classification:** Contingency; **Lowest/Average Salary:**
$50,000/$90,000; **Industry Concentration:** Financial Services; **Function
Concentration:** Finance/Accounting

**Morgan, Donald T.** — *Vice President*
MSI International
1050 Crown Pointe Parkway
Suite 1000
Atlanta, GA 30338
Telephone: (404) 394-2494
**Recruiter Classification:** Contingency; **Lowest/Average Salary:**
$30,000/$60,000; **Industry Concentration:** Generalist with a primary focus in
Financial Services; **Function Concentration:** Finance/Accounting

**Morgan, Gary** — *Insurance Consultant*
National Search, Inc.
2816 University Drive
Coral Springs, FL 33071
Telephone: (800) 935-4355
**Recruiter Classification:** Contingency; **Lowest/Average Salary:**
$30,000/$50,000; **Industry Concentration:** Healthcare/Hospitals, Insurance,
Pharmaceutical/Medical; **Function Concentration:** Generalist with a primary
focus in Administration, Finance/Accounting, General Management, Human
Resources, Marketing, Research and Development, Sales, Women/Minorities

**Morgan, Richard J.** — *Chairman*
Morgan Samuels Co., Inc.
9171 Wilshire Boulevard
Suite 428
Beverly Hills, CA 90210
Telephone: (310) 278-9660
**Recruiter Classification:** Retained; **Lowest/Average Salary:** $90,000/$90,000;
**Industry Concentration:** Environmental, Manufacturing; **Function
Concentration:** Generalist

**Morgan, Richard S.** — *Partner*
Lovas Stanley/Paul Ray Berndtson Inc.
155 Queen Street, Suite 900
Ottawa, Ontario, CANADA K1P 6L1
Telephone: (613) 786-3191
**Recruiter Classification:** Retained; **Lowest/Average Salary:** $50,000/$75,000;
**Industry Concentration:** Generalist with a primary focus in
Aerospace/Defense, High Technology, Hospitality/Leisure, Information
Technology, Publishing/Media; **Function Concentration:** Generalist with a
primary focus in General Management, Human Resources, Marketing,
Research and Development, Sales

**Morgan, Vincent S.** — *Partner*
Johnson Smith & Knisely Accord
100 Park Avenue, 15th Floor
New York, NY 10017
Telephone: (212) 885-9100
**Recruiter Classification:** Retained; **Lowest/Average Salary:** $90,000/$90,000;
**Industry Concentration:** Electronics, High Technology, Information
Technology; **Function Concentration:** Generalist with a primary focus in
Engineering, General Management, Marketing, Research and Development,
Sales

**Moriarty, Mike** — *Associate*
Source Services Corporation
2850 National City Tower
Louisville, KY 40202
Telephone: (502) 581-9900
**Recruiter Classification:** Contingency; **Lowest/Average Salary:**
$30,000/$50,000; **Industry Concentration:** Financial Services, Information
Technology; **Function Concentration:** Engineering, Finance/Accounting

**Morice, James L.** — *Partner*
Mirtz Morice, Inc.
One Dock Street
Stamford, CT 06902
Telephone: (203) 964-9266
**Recruiter Classification:** Retained; **Lowest/Average Salary:** $90,000/$90,000;
**Industry Concentration:** Generalist with a primary focus in Board Services,
Chemical Products, Consumer Products, Electronics, Financial Services,
Insurance, Manufacturing, Pharmaceutical/Medical; **Function Concentration:**
Generalist

**Morin, Michelle** — *Director*
Spencer Stuart
One University Avenue
Suite 801
Toronto, Ontario, CANADA M5J 2P1
Telephone: (416) 361-0311
**Recruiter Classification:** Retained; **Lowest/Average Salary:** $90,000/$90,000;
**Industry Concentration:** Generalist; **Function Concentration:** Generalist

**Morrill, Nancy** — *Information Technology Recruiter*
Winter, Wyman & Company
950 Winter Street, Suite 3100
Waltham, MA 02154-1294
Telephone: (617) 890-7000
**Recruiter Classification:** Contingency; **Lowest/Average Salary:**
$30,000/$60,000; **Industry Concentration:** Generalist with a primary focus in
Information Technology; **Function Concentration:** Generalist

**Morris, David A.** — *Partner*
Heidrick & Struggles, Inc.
1 Houston Center
1221 McKinney Street, Suite 3050
Houston, TX 77010
Telephone: (713) 237-9000
**Recruiter Classification:** Retained; **Lowest/Average Salary:** $75,000/$90,000;
**Industry Concentration:** Generalist with a primary focus in Financial Services;
**Function Concentration:** Generalist

**Morris, David W.** — *Managing Director*
WTW Associates
675 Third Avenue, Suite 2808
New York, NY 10017
Telephone: (212) 972-6990
**Recruiter Classification:** Retained; **Lowest/Average Salary:** $75,000/$90,000;
**Industry Concentration:** Generalist with a primary focus in Entertainment,
Financial Services; **Function Concentration:** Generalist

**Morris, Kristine A.** — *Partner*
Morris & Berger
201 South Lake Avenue, Suite 700
Pasadena, CA 91101
Telephone: (818) 795-0522
**Recruiter Classification:** Retained; **Lowest/Average Salary:** $60,000/$90,000;
**Industry Concentration:** Generalist with a primary focus in Biotechnology,
Board Services, Chemical Products, Education/Libraries, Electronics,
Environmental, Financial Services, Healthcare/Hospitals, High Technology,
Information Technology, Manufacturing, Non-Profit, Packaging,
Pharmaceutical/Medical, Public Administration, Real Estate; **Function
Concentration:** Generalist

**Morris, Paul T.** — *President*
The Morris Group
1024 East Lancaster Avenue
P.O. Box 188
Bryn Mawr, PA 19010-0188
Telephone: (610) 520-0100
**Recruiter Classification:** Contingency; **Lowest/Average Salary:**
$40,000/$75,000; **Industry Concentration:** Generalist with a primary focus in
Biotechnology, Consumer Products, Financial Services, Insurance,
Pharmaceutical/Medical; **Function Concentration:** Human Resources,
Marketing, Research and Development, Sales, Women/Minorities

**Morris, Scott** — *Associate*
Source Services Corporation
1105 Schrock Road, Suite 510
Columbus, OH 43229
Telephone: (614) 846-3311
**Recruiter Classification:** Contingency; **Lowest/Average Salary:**
$30,000/$50,000; **Industry Concentration:** Financial Services, Information
Technology; **Function Concentration:** Engineering, Finance/Accounting

**Morrison, Janis L.** — *Vice President*
Garrett Associates Inc.
P.O. Box 190189
Atlanta, GA 31119-0189
Telephone: (404) 364-0001
**Recruiter Classification:** Retained; **Lowest/Average Salary:** $50,000/$90,000;
**Industry Concentration:** Healthcare/Hospitals; **Function Concentration:**
Generalist with a primary focus in Administration, Engineering,
Finance/Accounting, General Management, Human Resources, Marketing,
Research and Development, Sales, Women/Minorities

**Morrow, Melanie** — *Associate*
Source Services Corporation
3 Summit Park Drive, Suite 550
Independence, OH 44131
Telephone: (216) 328-5900
**Recruiter Classification:** Contingency; **Lowest/Average Salary:**
$30,000/$50,000; **Industry Concentration:** Financial Services, Information
Technology; **Function Concentration:** Engineering, Finance/Accounting

**Morrow, Miles** — *Vice President*
Key Employment Services
1001 Office Park Road, Suite 320
West Des Moines, IA 50265-2567
Telephone: (515) 224-0446
**Recruiter Classification:** Contingency; **Lowest/Average Salary:**
$30,000/$75,000; **Industry Concentration:** Generalist; **Function
Concentration:** Finance/Accounting

**Morse, Aaron H.** — *Co-Manager Pacific Region*
Management Recruiters International, Inc.
215 Fidalgo Avenue, Suite 101
Kenai, AK 99611-7798
Telephone: (907) 283-5633
**Recruiter Classification:** Contingency; **Lowest/Average Salary:**
$30,000/$75,000; **Industry Concentration:** Generalist; **Function
Concentration:** Generalist

**Morse, Jeannine** — *Co-Manager*
Management Recruiters International, Inc.
215 Fidalgo Avenue, Suite 101
Kenai, AK 99611-7798
Telephone: (907) 283-5633
**Recruiter Classification:** Contingency; **Lowest/Average Salary:**
$30,000/$75,000; **Industry Concentration:** Generalist; **Function
Concentration:** Generalist

**Morse, Stephen W.** — *Manager Eastern Region*
Management Recruiters International, Inc.
101 Dyer Street, Suite 5-A
Providence, RI 02903-3904
Telephone: (401) 274-2810
**Recruiter Classification:** Contingency; **Lowest/Average Salary:**
$30,000/$75,000; **Industry Concentration:** Generalist; **Function
Concentration:** Generalist

**Morse, Steve** — *General Manager Eastern Region*
Management Recruiters International, Inc.
639 Granite Street
Braintree, MA 02184
Telephone: (617) 848-1666
**Recruiter Classification:** Contingency; **Lowest/Average Salary:**
$30,000/$75,000; **Industry Concentration:** Generalist; **Function
Concentration:** Generalist

**Morton, Robert C.** — *Senior Consultant*
Morton, McCorkle & Associates, Inc.
2190 South Mason Road, Suite 309
St. Louis, MO 63131-1637
Telephone: (314) 984-9494
**Recruiter Classification:** Retained; **Lowest/Average Salary:** $60,000/$90,000;
**Industry Concentration:** Generalist with a primary focus in Board Services,
Chemical Products, Energy, Environmental, Insurance, Non-Profit, Packaging,
Venture Capital; **Function Concentration:** Generalist with a primary focus in
Engineering, Finance/Accounting, General Management, Human Resources,
Marketing, Research and Development, Sales

**Morton, Sheila Ann** — *Northeast Area Recruiter*
Sloan & Associates
1769 Jamestown Road
Williamsburg, VA 23185
Telephone: (757) 220-1111
**Recruiter Classification:** Contingency; **Lowest/Average Salary:**
$60,000/$75,000; **Industry Concentration:** Consumer Products; **Function
Concentration:** Marketing, Research and Development, Sales

**Moschel, Evie** — *Senior Consultant*
S. Reyman & Associates Ltd.
20 North Michigan Avenue, Suite 520
Chicago, IL 60602
Telephone: (312) 580-0808
**Recruiter Classification:** Retained; **Lowest/Average Salary:** $75,000/$90,000;
**Industry Concentration:** Generalist; **Function Concentration:** Generalist

**Moseley, Monroe** — *Senior Recruiter*
Isaacson, Miller
334 Boylston Street, Suite 500
Boston, MA 02111
Telephone: (617) 262-6500
**Recruiter Classification:** Retained; **Lowest/Average Salary:** $75,000/$90,000;
**Industry Concentration:** Generalist; **Function Concentration:** Administration,
Finance/Accounting, General Management, Human Resources,
Women/Minorities

**Moses, Brenda** — *Consultant*
Paul Ray Berndtson
One Allen Center
500 Dallas, Suite 3010
Houston, TX 77002
Telephone: (713) 309-1400
**Recruiter Classification:** Retained; **Lowest/Average Salary:** $90,000/$90,000;
**Industry Concentration:** Generalist; **Function Concentration:** Generalist

**Moses, Jerry** — *President*
J.M. Eagle Partners Ltd.
10140 North Port Washington Rd.
Mequon, WI 53092
Telephone: (414) 241-1113
**Recruiter Classification:** Contingency; **Lowest/Average Salary:** $/$90,000;
**Industry Concentration:** Biotechnology, Electronics, Healthcare/Hospitals,
High Technology, Information Technology, Pharmaceutical/Medical; **Function
Concentration:** Generalist

**Moss, Ethan** — *Executive Recruiter*
Richard, Wayne and Roberts
24 Greenway Plaza, Suite 1304
Houston, TX 77046-2493
Telephone: (713) 629-6681
**Recruiter Classification:** Retained; **Lowest/Average Salary:** $50,000/$90,000;
**Industry Concentration:** Generalist; **Function Concentration:** Generalist

**Mott, Greg** — *Associate*
Source Services Corporation
5429 LBJ Freeway, Suite 275
Dallas, TX 75240
Telephone: (214) 387-1600
**Recruiter Classification:** Contingency; **Lowest/Average Salary:**
$30,000/$50,000; **Industry Concentration:** Financial Services, Information
Technology; **Function Concentration:** Engineering, Finance/Accounting

**Mouchet, Marcus** — *Partner*
Commonwealth Consultants
4840 Roswell Road
Atlanta, GA 30342
Telephone: (404) 256-0000
**Recruiter Classification:** Contingency; **Lowest/Average Salary:**
$30,000/$90,000; **Industry Concentration:** High Technology; **Function
Concentration:** Sales

**Mowatt, Virginia C.** — *Executive Vice President*
DHR International, Inc.
10 South Riverside Plaza, Suite 2220
Chicago, IL 60606
Telephone: (312) 782-1581
**Recruiter Classification:** Retained; **Lowest/Average Salary:** $60,000/$90,000;
**Industry Concentration:** Generalist; **Function Concentration:** Generalist

**Moxley, John H.** — *Managing Director*
Korn/Ferry International
1800 Century Park East, Suite 900
Los Angeles, CA 90067
Telephone: (310) 552-1834
**Recruiter Classification:** Retained; **Lowest/Average Salary:** $90,000/$90,000;
**Industry Concentration:** Generalist with a primary focus in
Healthcare/Hospitals; **Function Concentration:** Generalist

**Moyer, David S.** — *President*
Moyer, Sherwood Associates, Inc.
65 High Ridge Road, Suite 502
Stamford, CT 06905
Telephone: (203) 656-2220
**Recruiter Classification:** Retained; **Lowest/Average Salary:** $75,000/$90,000;
**Industry Concentration:** Generalist; **Function Concentration:** Marketing

**Moynihan, Kerry** — *Vice President*
Korn/Ferry International
Presidential Plaza
900 19th Street, N.W.
Washington, DC 20006
Telephone: (202) 822-9444
**Recruiter Classification:** Retained; **Lowest/Average Salary:** $90,000/$90,000;
**Industry Concentration:** Generalist; **Function Concentration:** Generalist

**Moyse, Richard G.** — *Principal*
Thorndike Deland Associates
275 Madison Avenue, Suite 1300
New York, NY 10016
Telephone: (212) 661-6200
**Recruiter Classification:** Retained; **Lowest/Average Salary:** $90,000/$90,000;
**Industry Concentration:** Generalist with a primary focus in Consumer
Products, Entertainment, Financial Services, Healthcare/Hospitals, Information
Technology, Insurance, Publishing/Media; **Function Concentration:** Generalist
with a primary focus in Sales

**Mruk, Edwin S.** — *Partner*
Mruk & Partners/EMA Partners Int'l
675 Third Avenue, Suite 1805
New York, NY 10017
Telephone: (212) 983-7676
**Recruiter Classification:** Retained; **Lowest/Average Salary:** $75,000/$90,000;
**Industry Concentration:** Board Services, Energy, Entertainment, Oil/Gas;
**Function Concentration:** Generalist

**Msidment, Roger** — *Associate*
Source Services Corporation
10300 West 103rd Street, Suite 101
Overland Park, KS 66214
Telephone: (913) 888-8885
**Recruiter Classification:** Contingency; **Lowest/Average Salary:**
$30,000/$50,000; **Industry Concentration:** Financial Services, Information
Technology; **Function Concentration:** Engineering, Finance/Accounting

**Mueller, Colleen** — *Associate*
Source Services Corporation
5429 LBJ Freeway, Suite 275
Dallas, TX 75240
Telephone: (214) 387-1600
**Recruiter Classification:** Contingency; **Lowest/Average Salary:**
$30,000/$50,000; **Industry Concentration:** Financial Services, Information
Technology; **Function Concentration:** Engineering, Finance/Accounting

**Mueller, Michael S.** — *President*
Dieck, Mueller & Associates, Inc.
1017 Orchard Drive
Seymour, WI 54165
Telephone: (414) 833-7600
**Recruiter Classification:** Retained; **Lowest/Average Salary:** $75,000/$90,000;
**Industry Concentration:** Chemical Products, Manufacturing, Packaging;
**Function Concentration:** Generalist

**Mueller-Maerki, Fortunat F.** — *Consultant*
Egon Zehnder International Inc.
55 East 59th Street, 14th Floor
New York, NY 10022
Telephone: (212) 838-9199
**Recruiter Classification:** Retained; **Lowest/Average Salary:** $90,000/$90,000;
**Industry Concentration:** Generalist with a primary focus in Biotechnology,
Financial Services, High Technology, Manufacturing, Pharmaceutical/Medical;
**Function Concentration:** Generalist

**Muendel, H. Edward** — *Managing Director*
Stanton Chase International
100 East Pratt Street
Suite 2530
Baltimore, MD 21202
Telephone: (410) 528-8400
**Recruiter Classification:** Retained; **Lowest/Average Salary:** $75,000/$90,000;
**Industry Concentration:** Generalist with a primary focus in Biotechnology,
Chemical Products, Consumer Products, Electronics, Energy, Environmental,
Financial Services, Healthcare/Hospitals, High Technology, Hospitality/Leisure,
Manufacturing, Oil/Gas, Pharmaceutical/Medical, Venture Capital; **Function
Concentration:** Generalist with a primary focus in Administration, Engineering,
Finance/Accounting, General Management, Human Resources, Marketing,
Research and Development, Sales

**Mulcahey, Bob T.** — *Manager Eastern Region*
Management Recruiters International, Inc.
Stuyvesant Plaza
One Executive Park Drive
Albany, NY 12203-3707
Telephone: (518) 438-7722
**Recruiter Classification:** Contingency; **Lowest/Average Salary:**
$30,000/$75,000; **Industry Concentration:** Generalist; **Function
Concentration:** Generalist

**Mullane, Patrick** — *Associate*
Kenzer Corp.
625 North Michigan Avenue, Suite 1244
Chicago, IL 60611
Telephone: (312) 266-0976
**Recruiter Classification:** Retained; **Lowest/Average Salary:** $50,000/$90,000;
**Industry Concentration:** Generalist; **Function Concentration:** Generalist

**Mullen, Edward** — *Vice President*
Korn/Ferry International
1800 Century Park East, Suite 900
Los Angeles, CA 90067
Telephone: (310) 552-1834
**Recruiter Classification:** Retained; **Lowest/Average Salary:** $90,000/$90,000;
**Industry Concentration:** Generalist; **Function Concentration:** Generalist

**Muller, Charles A.** — *Principal*
AJM Professional Services
803 West Big Beaver Road, Suite 357
Troy, MI 48084-4734
Telephone: (810) 244-2222
**Recruiter Classification:** Contingency; **Lowest/Average Salary:**
$30,000/$60,000; **Industry Concentration:** Generalist with a primary focus in
Financial Services, Healthcare/Hospitals, Information Technology, Insurance,
Manufacturing; **Function Concentration:** Finance/Accounting

**Muller, Sonja** — *Partner*
TASA International
750 Lexington Avenue
Suite 1800
New York, NY 10022
Telephone: (212) 486-1490
**Recruiter Classification:** Retained; **Lowest/Average Salary:** $90,000/$90,000;
**Industry Concentration:** Generalist; **Function Concentration:** Generalist

**Mulligan, Robert P.** — *Vice President/Managing Director*
William Willis Worldwide Inc.
164 Mason Street
Greenwich, CT 06830-6611
Telephone: (203) 661-4500
**Recruiter Classification:** Retained; **Lowest/Average Salary:** $90,000/$90,000;
**Industry Concentration:** Generalist with a primary focus in Chemical Products,
Consumer Products, Electronics, Environmental; **Function Concentration:**
Generalist with a primary focus in Administration, Engineering, General
Management, Human Resources, Marketing, Research and Development

**Mullings, Joe S.** — *Manager South Atlantic Region*
Management Recruiters International, Inc.
8181 NW 154th Street, Suite 250
Miami Lakes, FL 33016
Telephone: (305) 828-2887
**Recruiter Classification:** Contingency; **Lowest/Average Salary:**
$30,000/$75,000; **Industry Concentration:** Generalist; **Function
Concentration:** Generalist

**Mummert, Dennis D.** — *Partner*
Sweeney Harbert & Mummert, Inc.
777 South Harbour Island Boulevard, Suite 130
Tampa, FL 33602
Telephone: (813) 229-5360
**Recruiter Classification:** Retained; **Lowest/Average Salary:** $90,000/$90,000;
**Industry Concentration:** Generalist with a primary focus in Consumer
Products, Entertainment; **Function Concentration:** Generalist with a primary
focus in Finance/Accounting, General Management, Human Resources,
Marketing, Research and Development, Sales

**Munguia, Rebecca** — *Executive Recruiter*
Richard, Wayne and Roberts
24 Greenway Plaza, Suite 1304
Houston, TX 77046-2493
Telephone: (713) 629-6681
**Recruiter Classification:** Retained; **Lowest/Average Salary:** $40,000/$60,000;
**Industry Concentration:** Generalist with a primary focus in
Healthcare/Hospitals; **Function Concentration:** Generalist with a primary focus
in Finance/Accounting

**Murin, Rose Mary** — *Recruiter*
U.S. Envirosearch
445 Union Boulevard, Suite 225
Lakewood, CO 80228
Telephone: (303) 980-6600
**Recruiter Classification:** Contingency; **Lowest/Average Salary:**
$30,000/$75,000; **Industry Concentration:** Environmental; **Function
Concentration:** Generalist with a primary focus in Administration, Engineering,
Finance/Accounting, General Management, Marketing, Sales,
Women/Minorities

**Murlas, Kim** — *Senior Vice President*
DHR International, Inc.
10 South Riverside Plaza, Suite 2220
Chicago, IL 60606
Telephone: (312) 782-1581
**Recruiter Classification:** Retained; **Lowest/Average Salary:** $60,000/$90,000;
**Industry Concentration:** Generalist; **Function Concentration:** Generalist

**Murphey, James F.** — *Manager North Atlantic Region*
Management Recruiters International, Inc.
4092 Foxwood Drive, Suite 102
Virginia Beach, VA 23462-5259
Telephone: (804) 474-2752
**Recruiter Classification:** Contingency; **Lowest/Average Salary:**
$30,000/$75,000; **Industry Concentration:** Generalist; **Function
Concentration:** Generalist

**Murphy, Carrie** — *Consultant*
Paul Ray Berndtson
10 South Riverside Plaza
Suite 720
Chicago, IL 60606
Telephone: (312) 876-0730
**Recruiter Classification:** Retained; **Lowest/Average Salary:** $90,000/$90,000;
**Industry Concentration:** Generalist; **Function Concentration:** Generalist

**Murphy, Corinne** — *Associate*
Source Services Corporation
100 North Tryon Street, Suite 3130
Charlotte, NC 28202
Telephone: (704) 333-8311
**Recruiter Classification:** Contingency; **Lowest/Average Salary:**
$30,000/$50,000; **Industry Concentration:** Financial Services, Information
Technology; **Function Concentration:** Engineering, Finance/Accounting

**Murphy, Cornelius J.** — *Senior Vice President*
Goodrich & Sherwood Associates, Inc.
250 Mill Street
Rochester, NY 14614
Telephone: (716) 777-4060
**Recruiter Classification:** Retained; **Lowest/Average Salary:** $60,000/$90,000;
**Industry Concentration:** Generalist with a primary focus in Board Services,
Chemical Products, Consumer Products, Financial Services,
Healthcare/Hospitals, Information Technology, Insurance, Manufacturing,
Oil/Gas, Publishing/Media, Venture Capital; **Function Concentration:**
Generalist with a primary focus in Administration, Finance/Accounting,
General Management, Human Resources, Marketing, Sales

**Murphy, Gary J.** — *Partner*
Stone Murphy & Olson
5500 Wayzata Boulevard
Suite 1020
Minneapolis, MN 55416
Telephone: (612) 591-2300
**Recruiter Classification:** Retained; **Lowest/Average Salary:** $60,000/$75,000;
**Industry Concentration:** Generalist with a primary focus in Electronics, Energy,
Financial Services, High Technology, Insurance, Manufacturing,
Publishing/Media; **Function Concentration:** Generalist with a primary focus in
Engineering, Finance/Accounting, General Management, Human Resources,
Marketing, Women/Minorities

**Murphy, James** — *Associate*
Source Services Corporation
4170 Ashford Dunwoody Road, Suite 285
Atlanta, GA 30319
Telephone: (404) 255-2045
**Recruiter Classification:** Contingency; **Lowest/Average Salary:**
$30,000/$50,000; **Industry Concentration:** Financial Services, Information
Technology; **Function Concentration:** Engineering, Finance/Accounting

**Murphy, Karen S.** — *Managing Partner*
Flex Execs Management Solutions
16350 South 105th Court
Orland Park, IL 60462
Telephone: (708) 460-8500
**Recruiter Classification:** Executive Temporary; **Lowest/Average Salary:**
$40,000/$50,000; **Industry Concentration:** Generalist; **Function
Concentration:** Generalist with a primary focus in Finance/Accounting,
General Management, Human Resources, Marketing, Sales

**Murphy, Patrick** — *Executive Recruiter*
Richard, Wayne and Roberts
4625 South Wendler Drive
Suite 111
Tempe, AZ 85282
Telephone: (602) 438-1496
**Recruiter Classification:** Retained; **Lowest/Average Salary:** $50,000/$90,000;
**Industry Concentration:** Generalist; **Function Concentration:** Generalist

**Murphy, Patrick J.** — *President*
P.J. Murphy & Associates, Inc.
735 North Water Street
Milwaukee, WI 53202
Telephone: (414) 277-9777
**Recruiter Classification:** Retained; **Lowest/Average Salary:** $60,000/$90,000;
**Industry Concentration:** Generalist with a primary focus in Board Services,
Financial Services, Healthcare/Hospitals, Information Technology,
Manufacturing; **Function Concentration:** Generalist with a primary focus in
Administration, Finance/Accounting, General Management, Human Resources,
Marketing, Sales

**Murphy, Timothy D.** — *Executive Recruiter*
MSI International
200 Galleria Parkway
Suite 1610
Atlanta, GA 30339
Telephone: (404) 951-1208
**Recruiter Classification:** Contingency; **Lowest/Average Salary:**
$30,000/$60,000; **Industry Concentration:** Generalist with a primary focus in
High Technology; **Function Concentration:** Administration, Engineering,
Finance/Accounting, General Management, Marketing

**Murphy, Wendy** — *Human Resources Recruiter*
Winter, Wyman & Company
950 Winter Street, Suite 3100
Waltham, MA 02154-1294
Telephone: (617) 890-7000
**Recruiter Classification:** Contingency; **Lowest/Average Salary:**
$30,000/$50,000; **Industry Concentration:** Generalist; **Function
Concentration:** Human Resources

**Murray, Cathy M.** — *Senior Consultant*
EFL Associates
7101 College Boulevard, Suite 550
Overland Park, KS 66210-1891
Telephone: (913) 451-8866
**Recruiter Classification:** Retained; **Lowest/Average Salary:** $60,000/$90,000;
**Industry Concentration:** Generalist; **Function Concentration:** Generalist

**Murray, Virginia** — *Partner*
Baker, Harris & Partners Limited
130 Adelaide Street West, Suite 2710
Toronto, Ontario, CANADA M5H 3P5
Telephone: (416) 947-1990
**Recruiter Classification:** Retained; **Lowest/Average Salary:** $60,000/$75,000;
**Industry Concentration:** Generalist with a primary focus in
Aerospace/Defense, Energy, Financial Services, Information Technology, Non-
Profit, Oil/Gas; **Function Concentration:** Generalist with a primary focus in
Finance/Accounting, Human Resources, Women/Minorities

**Murry, John** — *Associate*
Source Services Corporation
20 Burlington Mall Road, Suite 405
Burlington, MA 01803
Telephone: (617) 272-5000
**Recruiter Classification:** Contingency; **Lowest/Average Salary:**
$30,000/$50,000; **Industry Concentration:** Financial Services, Information
Technology; **Function Concentration:** Engineering, Finance/Accounting

**Mursuli, Meredith** — *Consultant*
Lasher Associates
1200 South Pine Island Road, Suite 370
Fort Lauderdale, FL 33324-4402
Telephone: (305) 472-5658
**Recruiter Classification:** Retained; **Lowest/Average Salary:** $75,000/$90,000;
**Industry Concentration:** Generalist with a primary focus in Biotechnology,
Board Services, Electronics, Financial Services, High Technology, Information
Technology, Insurance, Manufacturing, Non-Profit, Pharmaceutical/Medical,
Publishing/Media, Real Estate, Venture Capital; **Function Concentration:**
Generalist with a primary focus in Engineering, Finance/Accounting, General
Management, Human Resources, Marketing, Research and Development, Sales

**Mustin, Joyce M.** — *Vice President and Partner*
J: Blakslee International, Ltd.
49 Hillside Avenue
Mill Valley, CA 94941
Telephone: (415) 389-7300
**Recruiter Classification:** Retained; **Lowest/Average Salary:** $90,000/$90,000;
**Industry Concentration:** Biotechnology, Board Services,
Pharmaceutical/Medical, Venture Capital; **Function Concentration:** Generalist
with a primary focus in Engineering, Finance/Accounting, General
Management, Human Resources, Marketing, Research and Development,
Women/Minorities

**Myatt, James S.** — *Principal*
Sanford Rose Associates
101 East Victoria Street
Suite 22
Santa Barbara, CA 93101
Telephone: (805) 966-1846
**Recruiter Classification:** Contingency; **Lowest/Average Salary:**
$30,000/$75,000; **Industry Concentration:** Generalist with a primary focus in
Aerospace/Defense, Electronics, High Technology; **Function Concentration:**
Generalist

**Mydlach, Renee** — *Senior Section Manager*
CPS Inc.
One Westbrook Corporate Centre, Suite 600
Westchester, IL 60154
Telephone: (708) 531-8370
**Recruiter Classification:** Contingency; **Lowest/Average Salary:**
$30,000/$50,000; **Industry Concentration:** Generalist with a primary focus in
Automotive, Biotechnology, Chemical Products, Consumer Products, High
Technology, Insurance, Manufacturing, Oil/Gas, Packaging,
Pharmaceutical/Medical; **Function Concentration:** Engineering, Research and
Development, Sales, Women/Minorities

**Myers, Kay** — *Recruiter*
Signature Staffing
6800 College Boulevard, Suite 550
Overland Park, KS 66211
Telephone: (913) 338-2020
**Recruiter Classification:** Executive Temporary; **Lowest/Average Salary:**
$30,000/$40,000; **Industry Concentration:** Generalist with a primary focus in
Electronics, Financial Services, Healthcare/Hospitals, Insurance, Public
Administration, Publishing/Media, Transportation; **Function Concentration:**
Generalist with a primary focus in Finance/Accounting, Marketing

**Myrick, Marilou** — *President and CEO*
ProResource, Inc.
100 East Campus View Boulevard, Suite 250
Columbus, OH 43235
Telephone: (614) 438-7551
**Recruiter Classification:** Executive Temporary; **Lowest/Average Salary:**
$30,000/$75,000; **Industry Concentration:** Generalist; **Function
Concentration:** Generalist with a primary focus in Engineering,
Finance/Accounting, General Management, Human Resources, Marketing,
Research and Development

**Myrick, Marilou** — *President and CEO*
ProResource, Inc.
500 Ohio Savings Plaza
1801 East Ninth Street, Suite 500
Cleveland, OH 44114
Telephone: (216) 579-1515
**Recruiter Classification:** Executive Temporary; **Lowest/Average Salary:**
$30,000/$75,000; **Industry Concentration:** Generalist; **Function
Concentration:** Generalist with a primary focus in Engineering,
Finance/Accounting, General Management, Human Resources, Marketing,
Research and Development

**Nabers, Karen** — *Associate*
Source Services Corporation
9020 Capital of Texas Highway
Building I, Suite 337
Austin, TX 78759
Telephone: (512) 345-7473
**Recruiter Classification:** Contingency; **Lowest/Average Salary:**
$30,000/$50,000; **Industry Concentration:** Financial Services, Information
Technology; **Function Concentration:** Engineering, Finance/Accounting

**Nadherny, Christopher C.** — *Senior Director*
Spencer Stuart
401 North Michigan Avenue, Suite 3400
Chicago, IL 60611-4244
Telephone: (312) 822-0080
**Recruiter Classification:** Retained; **Lowest/Average Salary:** $90,000/$90,000;
**Industry Concentration:** Generalist with a primary focus in Chemical Products,
Consumer Products, Fashion (Retail/Apparel), High Technology,
Manufacturing; **Function Concentration:** Generalist with a primary focus in
Finance/Accounting, General Management, Human Resources, Marketing,
Sales

**Nadherny, Ferdinand** — *Managing Director*
Russell Reynolds Associates, Inc.
200 South Wacker Drive
Suite 3600
Chicago, IL 60606
Telephone: (312) 993-9696
**Recruiter Classification:** Retained; **Lowest/Average Salary:** $90,000/$90,000;
**Industry Concentration:** Generalist; **Function Concentration:** Generalist

**Nadzam, Richard** — *Partner*
Nadzam, Lusk, Horgan & Associates, Inc.
3211 Scott Boulevard
Suite 205
Santa Clara, CA 95054-3091
Telephone: (408) 727-6601
Recruiter Classification: Retained; Lowest/Average Salary: $90,000/$90,000;
Industry Concentration: Generalist; Function Concentration: Generalist

**Naff, Budd B.** — *Manager Pacific Region*
Management Recruiters International, Inc.
Alderwood Business Center
19109 36th Avenue West, Suite 206
Lynnwood, WA 98036-5767
Telephone: (206) 778-1212
Recruiter Classification: Contingency; Lowest/Average Salary:
$30,000/$75,000; Industry Concentration: Generalist; Function
Concentration: Generalist

**Nagle, Charles L.** — *Senior Vice President*
Tyler & Company
1000 Abernathy Road N.E.
Suite 1400
Atlanta, GA 30328-5655
Telephone: (770) 396-3939
Recruiter Classification: Retained; Lowest/Average Salary: $60,000/$90,000;
Industry Concentration: Healthcare/Hospitals, Insurance; Function
Concentration: Generalist

**Nagler, Leon G.** — *Managing Director*
Nagler, Robins & Poe, Inc.
65 William Street
Wellesley Hills, MA 02181
Telephone: (617) 431-1330
Recruiter Classification: Retained; Lowest/Average Salary: $75,000/$90,000;
Industry Concentration: Generalist with a primary focus in Biotechnology,
Chemical Products, Consumer Products, Electronics, Environmental, Financial
Services, Healthcare/Hospitals, High Technology, Information Technology,
Manufacturing, Non-Profit, Publishing/Media, Venture Capital; Function
Concentration: Generalist with a primary focus in Administration, Engineering,
Finance/Accounting, General Management, Human Resources, Marketing,
Research and Development, Sales

**Nagy, Les** — *Managing Director*
Source Services Corporation
255 Consumers Road, Suite 404
North York, Ontario, CANADA M2J 1R1
Telephone: (416) 495-1551
Recruiter Classification: Contingency; Lowest/Average Salary:
$30,000/$50,000; Industry Concentration: Financial Services, Information
Technology; Function Concentration: Engineering, Finance/Accounting

**Nahas, Caroline W.** — *Senior Officer*
Korn/Ferry International
1800 Century Park East, Suite 900
Los Angeles, CA 90067
Telephone: (310) 552-1834
Recruiter Classification: Retained; Lowest/Average Salary: $90,000/$90,000;
Industry Concentration: Generalist with a primary focus in Board Services;
Function Concentration: Generalist

**Nahas, Robert** — *Vice President*
Herbert Mines Associates, Inc.
399 Park Avenue, 27th Floor
New York, NY 10022
Telephone: (212) 355-0909
Recruiter Classification: Retained; Lowest/Average Salary: $75,000/$90,000;
Industry Concentration: Board Services, Fashion (Retail/Apparel); Function
Concentration: Generalist with a primary focus in Finance/Accounting,
General Management, Human Resources, Marketing, Sales

**Nakatsuka, Walt** — *Consultant*
Evie Kreisler & Associates, Inc.
333 North Michigan Avenue, Suite 818
Chicago, IL 60601
Telephone: (312) 251-0077
Recruiter Classification: Contingency; Lowest/Average Salary:
$30,000/$75,000; Industry Concentration: Fashion (Retail/Apparel); Function
Concentration: Generalist

**Napier, Ginger L.** — *Associate/Consultant*
Preng & Associates, Inc.
2925 Briarpark, Suite 1111
Houston, TX 77042
Telephone: (713) 266-2600
Recruiter Classification: Retained; Lowest/Average Salary: $75,000/$90,000;
Industry Concentration: Generalist with a primary focus in Chemical Products,
Energy, Environmental, Information Technology, Oil/Gas, Utilities/Nuclear;
Function Concentration: Generalist with a primary focus in Engineering,
Finance/Accounting, General Management, Human Resources,
Women/Minorities

**Nass, Martin D.** — *Partner (Practice Leader - Real Estate)*
Lamalie Amrop International
200 Park Avenue
New York, NY 10166-0136
Telephone: (212) 953-7900
Recruiter Classification: Retained; Lowest/Average Salary: $90,000/$90,000;
Industry Concentration: Generalist with a primary focus in Financial Services,
Real Estate; Function Concentration: Generalist with a primary focus in
Finance/Accounting, General Management

**Nathan, Catherine R.** — *Managing Director*
Ward Howell International, Inc.
99 Park Avenue, Suite 2000
New York, NY 10016-1699
Telephone: (212) 697-3730
Recruiter Classification: Retained; Lowest/Average Salary: $75,000/$90,000;
Industry Concentration: Generalist; Function Concentration: Generalist

**Nathan, Gerri** — *Associate*
R.D. Gatti & Associates, Incorporated
266 Main Street, Suite 21
Medfield, MA 02052
Telephone: (508) 359-4153
Recruiter Classification: Contingency; Lowest/Average Salary:
$40,000/$75,000; Industry Concentration: Generalist; Function
Concentration: Human Resources

**Nathanson, Barry F.** — *President*
Barry Nathanson Associates
40 Cutter Mill Road
Great Neck, NY 11021
Telephone: (516) 482-7222
Recruiter Classification: Retained; Lowest/Average Salary: $90,000/$90,000;
Industry Concentration: Generalist with a primary focus in Financial Services;
Function Concentration: Generalist with a primary focus in Administration,
Finance/Accounting, General Management, Human Resources, Marketing,
Research and Development, Sales

**Naughtin, Terri** — *Principal*
Andcor Human Resources
539 East Lake Street
Wayzata, MN 55391
Telephone: (612) 821-1000
Recruiter Classification: Retained; Lowest/Average Salary: $40,000/$75,000;
Industry Concentration: Generalist; Function Concentration: Generalist

**Nazzaro, Samuel G.** — *Vice President*
Boyden
Allegheny Tower, Suite 2405
625 Stanwix Street
Pittsburgh, PA 15222-1423
Telephone: (412) 391-3020
Recruiter Classification: Retained; Lowest/Average Salary: $75,000/$90,000;
Industry Concentration: Healthcare/Hospitals; Function Concentration:
Generalist with a primary focus in Engineering, Finance/Accounting, General
Management, Human Resources, Marketing, Research and Development,
Sales, Women/Minorities

**Neblett, Jon** — *Consultant*
Don Richard Associates of Richmond, Inc.
7275 Glen Forest Drive, Suite 200
Richmond, VA 23226
Telephone: (804) 282-6300
Recruiter Classification: Contingency; Lowest/Average Salary:
$20,000/$40,000; Industry Concentration: Generalist; Function
Concentration: Finance/Accounting

**Necessary, Rick** — *Associate*
Source Services Corporation
111 Monument Circle, Suite 3930
Indianapolis, IN 46204
Telephone: (317) 631-2900
Recruiter Classification: Contingency; Lowest/Average Salary:
$30,000/$50,000; Industry Concentration: Financial Services, Information
Technology; Function Concentration: Engineering, Finance/Accounting

**Neckanoff, Sharon** — *Account Executive*
Search West, Inc.
340 North Westlake Boulevard
Suite 200
Westlake Village, CA 91362-3761
Telephone: (805) 496-6811
Recruiter Classification: Contingency; Lowest/Average Salary:
$40,000/$60,000; Industry Concentration: Financial Services; Function
Concentration: Administration, Finance/Accounting

**Nederpelt, Jack H.B.** — *Executive Director*
Russell Reynolds Associates, Inc.
Scotia Plaza
40 King Street West, Suite 3500
Toronto, Ontario, CANADA M5H 3Y2
Telephone: (416) 364-3355
**Recruiter Classification:** Retained; **Lowest/Average Salary:** $90,000/$90,000;
**Industry Concentration:** Generalist; **Function Concentration:** Generalist

**Needham, Karen** — *Associate*
Source Services Corporation
111 Founders Plaza, Suite 1501E
Hartford, CT 06108
Telephone: (860) 528-0300
**Recruiter Classification:** Contingency; **Lowest/Average Salary:**
$30,000/$50,000; **Industry Concentration:** Financial Services, Information
Technology; **Function Concentration:** Engineering, Finance/Accounting

**Neelin, Sharon** — *Consultant*
The Caldwell Partners Amrop International
Sixty-Four Prince Arthur Avenue
Toronto, Ontario, CANADA M5R 1B4
Telephone: (416) 920-7702
**Recruiter Classification:** Retained; **Lowest/Average Salary:** $/$90,000; **Industry
Concentration:** Generalist with a primary focus in Consumer Products,
Electronics, Financial Services, High Technology, Information Technology,
Insurance, Manufacturing, Packaging; **Function Concentration:** Generalist

**Neely, Alan S.** — *Managing Director*
Korn/Ferry International
303 Peachtree Street N.E.
Suite 1600
Atlanta, GA 30308
Telephone: (404) 577-7542
**Recruiter Classification:** Retained; **Lowest/Average Salary:** $90,000/$90,000;
**Industry Concentration:** Generalist with a primary focus in High Technology;
**Function Concentration:** Generalist

**Neff, Herbert** — *Associate*
Source Services Corporation
15600 N.W. 67th Avenue, Suite 210
Miami Lakes, FL 33014
Telephone: (305) 556-8000
**Recruiter Classification:** Contingency; **Lowest/Average Salary:**
$30,000/$50,000; **Industry Concentration:** Financial Services, Information
Technology; **Function Concentration:** Engineering, Finance/Accounting

**Neff, Thomas J.** — *President*
Spencer Stuart
277 Park Avenue, 29th Floor
New York, NY 10172
Telephone: (212) 336-0200
**Recruiter Classification:** Retained; **Lowest/Average Salary:** $90,000/$90,000;
**Industry Concentration:** Generalist with a primary focus in Board Services,
Consumer Products, Fashion (Retail/Apparel), Financial Services, High
Technology, Insurance, Manufacturing, Pharmaceutical/Medical,
Publishing/Media, Transportation, Venture Capital; **Function Concentration:**
Generalist with a primary focus in General Management

**Neher, Robert L.** — *Executive Vice President*
Intech Summit Group, Inc.
5075 Shoreham Place, Suite 280
San Diego, CA 92122
Telephone: (619) 452-2100
**Recruiter Classification:** Retained; **Lowest/Average Salary:** $90,000/$90,000;
**Industry Concentration:** Board Services, Education/Libraries,
Healthcare/Hospitals, High Technology, Information Technology, Non-Profit,
Public Administration; **Function Concentration:** Administration, General
Management

**Nehiley, Jack J.** — *Manager Eastern Region*
Management Recruiters International, Inc.
607 Boylston Street, Suite 700
Boston, MA 02116
Telephone: (617) 262-5050
**Recruiter Classification:** Contingency; **Lowest/Average Salary:**
$30,000/$75,000; **Industry Concentration:** Generalist; **Function
Concentration:** Generalist

**Neidhart, Craig C.** — *Partner*
TNS Partners, Inc.
12655 North Central Expressway
Suite 900
Dallas, TX 75243
Telephone: (214) 991-3555
**Recruiter Classification:** Retained; **Lowest/Average Salary:** $75,000/$90,000;
**Industry Concentration:** Generalist with a primary focus in
Aerospace/Defense, Consumer Products, Electronics, Energy, Financial
Services, High Technology, Information Technology, Manufacturing, Oil/Gas,
Packaging, Real Estate, Transportation; **Function Concentration:** Generalist

**Neil, Colleen Ellen** — *Senior Associate*
Korn/Ferry International
Scotia Plaza
40 King Street West
Toronto, Ontario, CANADA M5H 3Y2
Telephone: (416) 366-1300
**Recruiter Classification:** Retained; **Lowest/Average Salary:** $90,000/$90,000;
**Industry Concentration:** Generalist; **Function Concentration:** Generalist

**Neill, Wellden K.** — *Executive Vice President*
Sampson Neill & Wilkins Inc.
543 Valley Road
Upper Montclair, NJ 07043
Telephone: (201) 783-9600
**Recruiter Classification:** Retained; **Lowest/Average Salary:** $75,000/$90,000;
**Industry Concentration:** Insurance, Pharmaceutical/Medical; **Function
Concentration:** Engineering, General Management, Marketing, Research and
Development, Sales

**Nein, Lawrence F.** — *Managing Partner*
Lamalie Amrop International
225 West Wacker Drive
Chicago, IL 60606-1229
Telephone: (312) 782-3113
**Recruiter Classification:** Retained; **Lowest/Average Salary:** $90,000/$90,000;
**Industry Concentration:** Generalist; **Function Concentration:** Generalist with a
primary focus in Finance/Accounting, General Management

**Nekervis, Nancy** — *Consultant - L.A. Retail*
Evie Kreisler & Associates, Inc.
865 South Figueroa, Suite 950
Los Angeles, CA 90017
Telephone: (213) 622-8994
**Recruiter Classification:** Contingency; **Lowest/Average Salary:**
$30,000/$75,000; **Industry Concentration:** Fashion (Retail/Apparel); **Function
Concentration:** Generalist

**Nelson, Barbara** — *Partner*
Herman Smith Executive Initiatives Inc.
Suite 3600, 161 Bay Street, Box 629
Toronto, Ontario, CANADA M5J 2S1
Telephone: (416) 862-8830
**Recruiter Classification:** Retained; **Lowest/Average Salary:** $60,000/$90,000;
**Industry Concentration:** Generalist with a primary focus in
Aerospace/Defense, Energy, High Technology, Hospitality/Leisure, Information
Technology, Non-Profit, Packaging, Public Administration, Publishing/Media;
**Function Concentration:** Engineering, Finance/Accounting, General
Management, Human Resources, Marketing, Sales, Women/Minorities

**Nelson, Garry A.** — *Partner*
Rhodes Associates
555 Fifth Avenue
New York, NY 10017
Telephone: (212) 983-2000
**Recruiter Classification:** Retained; **Lowest/Average Salary:** $90,000/$90,000;
**Industry Concentration:** Financial Services, Insurance, Real Estate, Venture
Capital; **Function Concentration:** Generalist

**Nelson, Hitch** — *Associate*
Source Services Corporation
1290 Oakmead Parkway, Suite 318
Sunnyvale, CA 94086
Telephone: (408) 738-8440
**Recruiter Classification:** Contingency; **Lowest/Average Salary:**
$30,000/$50,000; **Industry Concentration:** Financial Services, Information
Technology; **Function Concentration:** Engineering, Finance/Accounting

**Nelson, Mary** — *Associate*
Source Services Corporation
8614 Westwood Center, Suite 750
Vienna, VA 22182
Telephone: (703) 790-5610
**Recruiter Classification:** Contingency; **Lowest/Average Salary:**
$30,000/$50,000; **Industry Concentration:** Financial Services, Information
Technology; **Function Concentration:** Engineering, Finance/Accounting

**Nelson, Rick J.** — *Co-Manager*
Management Recruiters International, Inc.
3070 South Bristol Street, Suite 400
Costa Mesa, CA 92626
Telephone: (714) 668-7470
**Recruiter Classification:** Contingency; **Lowest/Average Salary:**
$30,000/$75,000; **Industry Concentration:** Generalist; **Function
Concentration:** Generalist

**Nelson, Steve** — *Consultant*
The McCormick Group, Inc.
1400 Wilson Boulevard
Arlington, VA 22209
Telephone: (703) 841-1700
**Recruiter Classification:** Retained; **Lowest/Average Salary:** $90,000/$90,000; **Industry Concentration:** Generalist; **Function Concentration:** Generalist

**Nelson-Folkersen, Jeffrey** — *Associate*
Source Services Corporation
4200 West Cypress Street, Suite 101
Tampa, FL 33607
Telephone: (813) 879-2221
**Recruiter Classification:** Contingency; **Lowest/Average Salary:** $30,000/$50,000; **Industry Concentration:** Financial Services, Information Technology; **Function Concentration:** Engineering, Finance/Accounting

**Neman, Nancy** — *Legal Recruiter*
Phyllis Hawkins & Associates, Inc.
31017 Westwood
Farmington Hills, MI 48331
Telephone: (810) 661-8900
**Recruiter Classification:** Contingency; **Lowest/Average Salary:** $60,000/$75,000

**Nephew, Robert** — *Vice President*
Christian & Timbers
24 New England Executive Park
Burlington, MA 01803
Telephone: (617) 229-9515
**Recruiter Classification:** Retained; **Lowest/Average Salary:** $90,000/$90,000; **Industry Concentration:** Healthcare/Hospitals, High Technology, Information Technology, Manufacturing, Venture Capital; **Function Concentration:** Generalist with a primary focus in Engineering, Finance/Accounting, General Management, Marketing, Sales

**Neri, Gene** — *Executive Recruiter*
S.C. International, Ltd.
1430 Branding Lane, Suite 119
Downers Grove, IL 60515
Telephone: (708) 963-3033
**Recruiter Classification:** Contingency; **Lowest/Average Salary:** $30,000/$50,000; **Industry Concentration:** Information Technology, Insurance; **Function Concentration:** Administration, Human Resources

**Nesbit, Robert G.** — *Manager*
Korn/Ferry International
237 Park Avenue
New York, NY 10017
Telephone: (212) 687-1834
**Recruiter Classification:** Retained; **Lowest/Average Salary:** $90,000/$90,000; **Industry Concentration:** Generalist with a primary focus in Fashion (Retail/Apparel); **Function Concentration:** Generalist

**Neuberth, Jeffrey G.** — *Senior Vice President/Director*
Canny, Bowen Inc.
200 Park Avenue
New York, NY 10166
Telephone: (212) 949-6611
**Recruiter Classification:** Retained; **Lowest/Average Salary:** $90,000/$90,000; **Industry Concentration:** Generalist with a primary focus in Board Services, Electronics, Energy, Financial Services, Healthcare/Hospitals, High Technology, Information Technology, Insurance, Manufacturing, Non-Profit, Oil/Gas, Publishing/Media, Transportation, Utilities/Nuclear; **Function Concentration:** Generalist with a primary focus in Administration, Engineering, Finance/Accounting, General Management, Human Resources, Marketing, Sales, Women/Minorities

**Neuffer, Bob P.** — *Manager Eastern Region*
Management Recruiters International, Inc.
220 White Plains Road
Tarrytown, NY 10591
Telephone: (914) 524-9400
**Recruiter Classification:** Contingency; **Lowest/Average Salary:** $30,000/$75,000; **Industry Concentration:** Generalist; **Function Concentration:** Generalist

**Neumann, Joan** — *Associate*
Gossage Regan Associates, Inc.
25 West 43rd Street, Suite 812
New York, NY 10036
Telephone: (212) 869-3348
**Recruiter Classification:** Retained; **Lowest/Average Salary:** $50,000/$60,000; **Industry Concentration:** Generalist with a primary focus in Education/Libraries; **Function Concentration:** Generalist

**Neumann, Pete** — *Co-Manager*
Management Recruiters International, Inc.
27972 Meadow Drive, Suite 110
Evergreen, CO 80439
Telephone: (303) 670-2002
**Recruiter Classification:** Contingency; **Lowest/Average Salary:** $30,000/$75,000; **Industry Concentration:** Generalist; **Function Concentration:** Generalist

**Neumann, Vicki A.** — *Co-Manager Southwest Region*
Management Recruiters International, Inc.
27972 Meadow Drive, Suite 110
Evergreen, CO 80439
Telephone: (303) 670-2002
**Recruiter Classification:** Contingency; **Lowest/Average Salary:** $30,000/$75,000; **Industry Concentration:** Generalist; **Function Concentration:** Generalist

**Neuwald, Debrah** — *Associate*
Source Services Corporation
1233 North Mayfair Road, Suite 300
Milwaukee, WI 53226
Telephone: (414) 774-6700
**Recruiter Classification:** Contingency; **Lowest/Average Salary:** $30,000/$50,000; **Industry Concentration:** Financial Services, Information Technology; **Function Concentration:** Engineering, Finance/Accounting

**Neuwiler, Mark D.** — *Director Recruitment*
Saber Consultants
5300 Hollister, Suite 100
Houston, TX 77040
Telephone: (713) 462-6900
**Lowest/Average Salary:** $50,000/$75,000; **Function Concentration:** Generalist

**Nevins, Patricia** — *Vice President*
Rhodes Associates
555 Fifth Avenue
New York, NY 10017
Telephone: (212) 983-2000
**Recruiter Classification:** Retained; **Lowest/Average Salary:** $90,000/$90,000; **Industry Concentration:** Financial Services, Insurance, Real Estate, Venture Capital; **Function Concentration:** Generalist

**Newbold, Michael** — *Agribusiness Recruiter*
Agra Placements International Ltd.
2200 North Kickapoo, Suite 2
Lincoln, IL 62656
Telephone: (217) 735-4373
**Recruiter Classification:** Contingency; **Lowest/Average Salary:** $20,000/$30,000; **Industry Concentration:** Generalist with a primary focus in Biotechnology, Chemical Products, Energy, Financial Services, Manufacturing; **Function Concentration:** Administration, Engineering, Finance/Accounting, General Management, Human Resources, Marketing, Research and Development, Sales

**Newcorn, Andrew R.** — *Consultant*
The Neil Michael Group, Inc.
305 Madison Avenue, Suite 902
New York, NY 10165
Telephone: (212) 986-3790
**Recruiter Classification:** Retained; **Lowest/Average Salary:** $90,000/$90,000; **Industry Concentration:** Biotechnology, Healthcare/Hospitals, Pharmaceutical/Medical; **Function Concentration:** Generalist

**Newlon, Jay** — *Senior Consultant*
Logix, Inc.
1601 Trapelo Road
Waltham, MA 02154
Telephone: (617) 890-0500
**Recruiter Classification:** Retained; **Lowest/Average Salary:** $60,000/$75,000; **Industry Concentration:** Information Technology; **Function Concentration:** Engineering

**Newman, Arthur I.** — *Senior Partner (Practice Leader - Energy/Natural Resources)*
Lamalie Amrop International
Chevron Tower
1301 McKinney Street
Houston, TX 77010-3034
Telephone: (713) 739-8602
**Recruiter Classification:** Retained; **Lowest/Average Salary:** $90,000/$90,000; **Industry Concentration:** Generalist with a primary focus in Energy; **Function Concentration:** Generalist with a primary focus in General Management

**Newman, Jose L.** — *Managing Partner*
Ward Howell International, Inc.
Rexer Seleccion de Ejecutivos, S.C.
Blvd. Adolfo Lopez Mateos 20, Col. San Angel Inn
Mexico City, D.F., MEXICO 01060
Telephone: (525) 550-9180
**Recruiter Classification:** Retained; **Lowest/Average Salary:** $75,000/$90,000;
**Industry Concentration:** Consumer Products, Financial Services,
Publishing/Media; **Function Concentration:** Generalist

**Newman, Lynn** — *Associate*
Kishbaugh Associates International
2 Elm Square
Andover, MA 01810
Telephone: (508) 475-7224
**Recruiter Classification:** Retained; **Lowest/Average Salary:** $75,000/$90,000;
**Industry Concentration:** Generalist with a primary focus in Chemical Products,
Consumer Products, Financial Services, High Technology, Information
Technology, Manufacturing; **Function Concentration:** Generalist with a
primary focus in Finance/Accounting, General Management, Marketing,
Research and Development, Sales

**Newman, Mark** — *Consultant*
Cole, Warren & Long, Inc.
2 Penn Center, Suite 312
Philadelphia, PA 19102
Telephone: (215) 563-0701
**Recruiter Classification:** Retained; **Lowest/Average Salary:** $90,000/$90,000;
**Industry Concentration:** Generalist; **Function Concentration:** Generalist

**Newman, Maryann** — *Associate*
The Gabriel Group
1515 Market Street, Suite 504
Philadelphia, PA 19102
Telephone: (215) 496-9990
**Recruiter Classification:** Retained; **Lowest/Average Salary:** $75,000/$75,000;
**Industry Concentration:** Generalist; **Function Concentration:** Generalist

**Newton, Jay** — *Senior Consultant*
Logix Partners
1601 Trapelo Road
Waltham, MA 02154
Telephone: (617) 890-0500
**Recruiter Classification:** Retained; **Lowest/Average Salary:** $60,000/$75,000;
**Industry Concentration:** Information Technology; **Function Concentration:**
Engineering

**Newton, Stephen D.** — *Managing Director/Area Manager*
Russell Reynolds Associates, Inc.
First Interstate Bank Plaza
1000 Louisiana Street, Suite 4800
Houston, TX 77002-5095
Telephone: (713) 658-1776
**Recruiter Classification:** Retained; **Lowest/Average Salary:** $90,000/$90,000;
**Industry Concentration:** Generalist; **Function Concentration:** Generalist

**Nicastro, Kelley P.** — *Director Research*
A la carte International
3330 Pacific Avenue, Suite 500
Virginia Beach, VA 23451
Telephone: (804) 425-6111
**Recruiter Classification:** Retained; **Lowest/Average Salary:** $60,000/$90,000;
**Industry Concentration:** Consumer Products, Manufacturing; **Function
Concentration:** Generalist with a primary focus in General Management,
Marketing, Research and Development, Sales, Women/Minorities

**Nichols, Nancy S.** — *Partner*
Heidrick & Struggles, Inc.
245 Park Avenue, Suite 4300
New York, NY 10167-0152
Telephone: (212) 867-9876
**Recruiter Classification:** Retained; **Lowest/Average Salary:** $75,000/$90,000;
**Industry Concentration:** Generalist; **Function Concentration:** Generalist

**Nicol, Peg** — *Consultant*
Evie Kreisler & Associates, Inc.
1460 Broadway, 3rd Floor
New York, NY 10036
Telephone: (212) 921-8999
**Recruiter Classification:** Contingency; **Lowest/Average Salary:**
$30,000/$75,000; **Industry Concentration:** Fashion (Retail/Apparel); **Function
Concentration:** Generalist

**Nielsen, Bruce** — *President*
The Nielsen Healthcare Group
P.O. Box 3734
St. Louis, MO 63122
Telephone: (314) 984-0910
**Recruiter Classification:** Executive Temporary; **Lowest/Average Salary:**
$20,000/$50,000; **Industry Concentration:** Healthcare/Hospitals; **Function
Concentration:** Generalist

**Nielsen, Eric C.** — *Associate*
Russell Reynolds Associates, Inc.
First Interstate Bank Plaza
1000 Louisiana Street, Suite 4800
Houston, TX 77002-5095
Telephone: (713) 658-1776
**Recruiter Classification:** Retained; **Lowest/Average Salary:** $90,000/$90,000;
**Industry Concentration:** Generalist with a primary focus in Energy; **Function
Concentration:** Generalist

**Nielsen, Sue** — *Recruiter*
Ells Personnel System Inc.
9900 Bren Road East, Suite 105 Opus Center
Minnetonka, MN 55343
Telephone: (612) 932-9933
**Recruiter Classification:** Contingency; **Lowest/Average Salary:**
$20,000/$20,000; **Industry Concentration:** Generalist with a primary focus in
Consumer Products, Insurance, Publishing/Media, Transportation; **Function
Concentration:** Generalist with a primary focus in Administration,
Finance/Accounting, Human Resources, Women/Minorities

**Nitti, Jacqueline** — *Senior Service Coordinator*
ALTCO Temporary Services
100 Menlo Park
Edison, NJ 08837
Telephone: (908) 549-6100
**Recruiter Classification:** Executive Temporary; **Lowest/Average Salary:**
$20,000/$30,000; **Industry Concentration:** Generalist; **Function
Concentration:** Finance/Accounting, Human Resources, Marketing,
Women/Minorities

**Nixon, Sarah** — *Researcher*
The Caldwell Partners Amrop International
Sixty-Four Prince Arthur Avenue
Toronto, Ontario, CANADA M5R 1B4
Telephone: (416) 920-7702
**Recruiter Classification:** Retained; **Lowest/Average Salary:** $/$90,000; **Industry
Concentration:** Generalist; **Function Concentration:** Generalist

**Noble, Donald H.** — *Principal*
Noble & Associates Inc.
420 Madison Avenue
New York, NY 10017
Telephone: (212) 838-7020
**Recruiter Classification:** Contingency; **Lowest/Average Salary:**
$40,000/$90,000; **Industry Concentration:** Generalist; **Function
Concentration:** Marketing

**Noble, Jeffrey M.** — *Co-Manager*
Management Recruiters International, Inc.
West First Plaza, Suite 304
333 West First Street
Dayton, OH 45402
Telephone: (513) 228-8271
**Recruiter Classification:** Contingency; **Lowest/Average Salary:**
$30,000/$75,000; **Industry Concentration:** Generalist; **Function
Concentration:** Generalist

**Nocero, John** — *Business Manager Technical Services*
ProResource, Inc.
500 Ohio Savings Plaza
1801 East Ninth Street, Suite 500
Cleveland, OH 44114
Telephone: (216) 579-1515
**Recruiter Classification:** Executive Temporary; **Lowest/Average Salary:**
$30,000/$75,000; **Industry Concentration:** Generalist; **Function
Concentration:** Generalist with a primary focus in Engineering,
Finance/Accounting, General Management, Human Resources, Marketing,
Research and Development

**Noguchi, Yoshi** — *Industry Leader - Technology*
Paul Ray Berndtson
One Park Plaza, Suite 420
Irvine, CA 92714
Telephone: (714) 476-8844
**Recruiter Classification:** Retained; **Lowest/Average Salary:** $90,000/$90,000;
**Industry Concentration:** Biotechnology, High Technology; **Function
Concentration:** Generalist

**Nolan, Jean M.** — *Recruiter*
S.D. Kelly & Associates, Inc.
990 Washington Street
Dedham, MA 02026
Telephone: (617) 326-8038
**Recruiter Classification:** Contingency; **Lowest/Average Salary:**
$50,000/$60,000; **Industry Concentration:** Electronics, High Technology;
**Function Concentration:** Engineering, Marketing, Sales

**Nolan, Michael W.** — *Manager*
Accounting & Bookkeeping Personnel, Inc.
1702 East Highland, Suite 200
Phoenix, AZ 85016
Telephone: (602) 277-3700
**Recruiter Classification:** Contingency, Executive Temporary; **Lowest/Average Salary:** $20,000/$60,000; **Industry Concentration:** Generalist; **Function Concentration:** Finance/Accounting

**Nolan, Robert** — *Associate*
Source Services Corporation
150 South Warner Road, Suite 238
King of Prussia, PA 19406
Telephone: (610) 341-1960
**Recruiter Classification:** Contingency; **Lowest/Average Salary:** $30,000/$50,000; **Industry Concentration:** Financial Services, Information Technology; **Function Concentration:** Engineering, Finance/Accounting

**Nold, Robert** — *Recruiter*
Roberson and Company
10752 North 89th Place, Suite 202
Scottsdale, AZ 85260
Telephone: (602) 391-3200
**Recruiter Classification:** Contingency; **Lowest/Average Salary:** $40,000/$50,000; **Industry Concentration:** Generalist with a primary focus in Aerospace/Defense, Automotive, High Technology; **Function Concentration:** Generalist with a primary focus in Administration, Engineering, Human Resources, Marketing, Sales

**Nolen, Shannon** — *Associate*
Source Services Corporation
2029 Century Park East, Suite 1350
Los Angeles, CA 90067
Telephone: (310) 277-8092
**Recruiter Classification:** Contingency; **Lowest/Average Salary:** $30,000/$50,000; **Industry Concentration:** Financial Services, Information Technology; **Function Concentration:** Engineering, Finance/Accounting

**Noll, Robert J.** — *Vice President*
The Hindman Company
Browenton Place, Suite 110
2000 Warrington Way
Louisville, KY 40222
Telephone: (502) 426-4040
**Recruiter Classification:** Retained; **Lowest/Average Salary:** $50,000/$90,000; **Industry Concentration:** Generalist with a primary focus in Aerospace/Defense, Automotive, Chemical Products, Consumer Products, Electronics, Financial Services, High Technology, Manufacturing, Oil/Gas, Pharmaceutical/Medical, Transportation; **Function Concentration:** Generalist

**Noorani, Frank** — *Manager Eastern Region*
Management Recruiters International, Inc.
272 Main Street
Metuchen, NJ 08840-2429
Telephone: (908) 767-1025
**Recruiter Classification:** Contingency; **Lowest/Average Salary:** $30,000/$75,000; **Industry Concentration:** Generalist; **Function Concentration:** Generalist

**Nordeman, Jacques C.** — *Chairman*
Nordeman Grimm, Inc.
717 Fifth Avenue, 26th Floor
New York, NY 10022
Telephone: (212) 935-1000
**Recruiter Classification:** Retained; **Lowest/Average Salary:** $90,000/$90,000; **Industry Concentration:** Generalist; **Function Concentration:** Generalist

**Nordland, Martin N.** — *Vice President*
Horton International
33 Sloan Street
Roswell, GA 30075
Telephone: (770) 640-1533
**Recruiter Classification:** Retained; **Lowest/Average Salary:** $90,000/$90,000; **Industry Concentration:** Generalist with a primary focus in Biotechnology, Chemical Products, Consumer Products, Healthcare/Hospitals, High Technology, Hospitality/Leisure, Manufacturing, Non-Profit, Packaging, Pharmaceutical/Medical, Transportation; **Function Concentration:** Generalist with a primary focus in Administration, Engineering, Finance/Accounting, General Management, Human Resources, Marketing, Research and Development

**Norman, Randy** — *Executive Recruiter*
Austin-McGregor International
12005 Ford Road, Suite 160
Dallas, TX 75234-7247
Telephone: (214) 488-0500
**Recruiter Classification:** Retained; **Lowest/Average Salary:** $50,000/$90,000; **Industry Concentration:** Generalist with a primary focus in Automotive, Board Services, Chemical Products, Consumer Products, Electronics, Entertainment, Healthcare/Hospitals, High Technology, Hospitality/Leisure, Manufacturing, Pharmaceutical/Medical, Publishing/Media, Venture Capital; **Function Concentration:** Generalist with a primary focus in Engineering, Finance/Accounting, General Management, Human Resources, Marketing, Research and Development, Sales, Women/Minorities

**Normann, Amy** — *Research Associate*
Robert M. Flanagan & Associates, Ltd.
Fields Lane
North Salem, NY 10560
Telephone: (914) 277-7210
**Recruiter Classification:** Retained; **Lowest/Average Salary:** $90,000/$90,000; **Industry Concentration:** Generalist with a primary focus in Consumer Products, Fashion (Retail/Apparel), Financial Services, Information Technology, Insurance, Packaging, Publishing/Media; **Function Concentration:** Generalist with a primary focus in Administration, Finance/Accounting, Human Resources, Marketing, Sales

**Norris, Ken** — *Vice President*
A.T. Kearney, Inc.
Miami Center, Suite 3180
201 South Biscayne Boulevard
Miami, FL 33131
Telephone: (305) 577-0046
**Recruiter Classification:** Retained; **Lowest/Average Salary:** $90,000/$90,000; **Industry Concentration:** Generalist; **Function Concentration:** Generalist

**Norris, Ken** — *Vice President*
Boyden
Allegheny Tower, Suite 2405
625 Stanwix Street
Pittsburgh, PA 15222-1423
Telephone: (412) 391-3020
**Recruiter Classification:** Retained; **Lowest/Average Salary:** $90,000/$90,000; **Industry Concentration:** Generalist; **Function Concentration:** Generalist

**Norsell, Paul E.** — *President*
Paul Norsell & Associates, Inc.
P.O. Box 6686
Auburn, CA 95604-6686
Telephone: (916) 269-0121
**Recruiter Classification:** Retained; **Lowest/Average Salary:** $90,000/$90,000; **Industry Concentration:** Generalist with a primary focus in Biotechnology, Consumer Products, Electronics, Energy, Financial Services, High Technology, Manufacturing, Pharmaceutical/Medical; **Function Concentration:** Generalist with a primary focus in Administration, Engineering, Finance/Accounting, General Management, Human Resources, Marketing, Research and Development, Salès

**North, Liz** — *Managing Director*
Klein, Landau, Romm & North
1725 K Street NW, Suite 602
Washington, DC 20006
Telephone: (202) 728-0100
**Recruiter Classification:** Contingency; **Lowest/Average Salary:** $50,000/$90,000

**Norton, Douglas** — *Principal*
Korn/Ferry International
Presidential Plaza
900 19th Street, N.W.
Washington, DC 20006
Telephone: (202) 822-9444
**Recruiter Classification:** Retained; **Lowest/Average Salary:** $90,000/$90,000; **Industry Concentration:** Generalist with a primary focus in Healthcare/Hospitals; **Function Concentration:** Generalist

**Norton, George F.** — *Consultant*
Heidrick & Struggles, Inc.
76 South Laura Street, Suite 2110
Jacksonville, FL 32202
Telephone: (904) 355-6674
**Recruiter Classification:** Retained; **Lowest/Average Salary:** $75,000/$90,000; **Industry Concentration:** Generalist; **Function Concentration:** Generalist

**Norton, James B.** — *Executive Director*
GKR Americas, Inc.
100 Galleria Parkway, Suite 1100
Atlanta, GA 30339
Telephone: (770) 955-9550
**Recruiter Classification:** Retained; **Lowest/Average Salary:** $90,000/$90,000; **Industry Concentration:** Generalist; **Function Concentration:** Generalist

**Nosal, David** — *Managing Director*
Korn/Ferry International
The Transamerica Pyramid
600 Montgomery Street
San Francisco, CA 94111
Telephone: (415) 956-1834
**Recruiter Classification:** Retained; **Lowest/Average Salary:** $90,000/$90,000; **Industry Concentration:** Generalist; **Function Concentration:** Generalist

**Nosal, David A.** — *Partner*
Heidrick & Struggles, Inc.
Four Embarcadero Center, Suite 3570
San Francisco, CA 94111
Telephone: (415) 981-2854
**Recruiter Classification:** Retained; **Lowest/Average Salary:** $75,000/$90,000;
**Industry Concentration:** Generalist with a primary focus in High Technology,
Utilities/Nuclear; **Function Concentration:** Generalist

**Nosky, Richard E.** — *Managing Director*
Ward Howell International, Inc.
2525 E. Arizona Biltmore Circle
Suite 124
Phoenix, AZ 85016
Telephone: (602) 955-3800
**Recruiter Classification:** Retained; **Lowest/Average Salary:** $75,000/$90,000;
**Industry Concentration:** Information Technology, Utilities/Nuclear; **Function
Concentration:** Generalist

**Novak, William J.** — *Managing Director*
Ward Howell International, Inc.
1601 Elm Street, Suite 900
Thanksgiving Tower
Dallas, TX 75201
Telephone: (214) 749-0099
**Recruiter Classification:** Retained; **Lowest/Average Salary:** $75,000/$90,000;
**Industry Concentration:** Generalist; **Function Concentration:** Generalist

**Noyes, Kathleen M.** — *Executive Director*
Russell Reynolds Associates, Inc.
200 Park Avenue
New York, NY 10166-0002
Telephone: (212) 351-2000
**Recruiter Classification:** Retained; **Lowest/Average Salary:** $90,000/$90,000;
**Industry Concentration:** Generalist; **Function Concentration:** Generalist

**Nunziata, Fred** — *Executive Vice President*
Eden & Associates, Inc.
794 North Valley Road
Paoli, PA 19301
Telephone: (610) 889-9993
**Recruiter Classification:** Contingency, Executive Temporary; **Lowest/Average
Salary:** $75,000/$90,000; **Industry Concentration:** Generalist; **Function
Concentration:** Generalist with a primary focus in Finance/Accounting,
Marketing

**Nunziata, Peter** — *Consultant*
Atlantic Search Group, Inc.
One Liberty Square
Boston, MA 02109
Telephone: (617) 426-9700
**Recruiter Classification:** Contingency; **Lowest/Average Salary:**
$20,000/$60,000; **Industry Concentration:** Generalist with a primary focus in
Biotechnology, Consumer Products, Electronics, Financial Services,
Information Technology, Manufacturing, Real Estate; **Function Concentration:**
Finance/Accounting

**Nutter, Roger** — *Principal*
Raymond Karsan Associates
100 Merchant Street, Suite 220
Cincinnati, OH 45246
Telephone: (513) 771-7979
**Recruiter Classification:** Contingency; **Lowest/Average Salary:**
$30,000/$90,000; **Industry Concentration:** Generalist with a primary focus in
Biotechnology, Chemical Products, Environmental, Healthcare/Hospitals,
Information Technology, Insurance, Manufacturing, Pharmaceutical/Medical;
**Function Concentration:** Generalist

**Nye, David S.** — *President*
Blake, Hansen & Nye, Limited
1155 Connecticut Avenue N.W.
Suite 300
Washington, DC 20036
Telephone: (202) 429-6611
**Recruiter Classification:** Retained; **Lowest/Average Salary:** $75,000/$90,000;
**Industry Concentration:** Generalist; **Function Concentration:** Generalist with a
primary focus in Administration, Finance/Accounting, General Management,
Human Resources

**Nyhan, Alan** — *Manager Eastern Region*
Management Recruiters International, Inc.
187 St. Paul Street, Suite 4
Burlington, VT 05401-4689
Telephone: (802) 865-0541
**Recruiter Classification:** Contingency; **Lowest/Average Salary:**
$30,000/$75,000; **Industry Concentration:** Generalist; **Function
Concentration:** Generalist

**Nymark, John** — *Vice President*
NYCOR Search, Inc.
4930 West 77th Street, Suite 300
Minneapolis, MN 55435
Telephone: (612) 831-6444
**Recruiter Classification:** Contingency; **Lowest/Average Salary:**
$40,000/$75,000; **Industry Concentration:** Generalist with a primary focus in
Chemical Products, Electronics, High Technology, Information Technology,
Manufacturing; **Function Concentration:** Engineering, Research and
Development

**Nymark, Paul** — *President*
NYCOR Search, Inc.
4930 West 77th Street, Suite 300
Minneapolis, MN 55435
Telephone: (612) 831-6444
**Recruiter Classification:** Contingency; **Lowest/Average Salary:**
$40,000/$75,000; **Industry Concentration:** Generalist with a primary focus in
Biotechnology, Chemical Products, Electronics, High Technology, Information
Technology, Manufacturing; **Function Concentration:** Engineering, Research
and Development

**O'Brien, Anne Lim** — *Consultant*
Heidrick & Struggles, Inc.
245 Park Avenue, Suite 4300
New York, NY 10167-0152
Telephone: (212) 867-9876
**Recruiter Classification:** Retained; **Lowest/Average Salary:** $75,000/$90,000;
**Industry Concentration:** Generalist with a primary focus in Board Services;
**Function Concentration:** Generalist with a primary focus in General
Management

**O'Brien, Debbie A.** — *Co-Manager Eastern Region*
Management Recruiters International, Inc.
10 Anderson Road, Suite 7
Bernardsville, NJ 07924-2319
Telephone: (908) 204-0070
**Recruiter Classification:** Contingency; **Lowest/Average Salary:**
$30,000/$75,000; **Industry Concentration:** Generalist; **Function
Concentration:** Generalist

**O'Brien, John G.** — *Consultant*
CanMed Consultants Inc.
62 Queen Street South
Mississauga, Ontario, CANADA L5M 1K4
Telephone: (905) 567-1080
**Recruiter Classification:** Executive Temporary; **Lowest/Average Salary:**
$40,000/$75,000; **Industry Concentration:** Biotechnology,
Healthcare/Hospitals, Pharmaceutical/Medical; **Function Concentration:**
Finance/Accounting, General Management, Human Resources, Marketing,
Research and Development, Sales

**O'Brien, Lori** — *Consultant*
Paul Ray Berndtson
One Allen Center
500 Dallas, Suite 3010
Houston, TX 77002
Telephone: (713) 309-1400
**Recruiter Classification:** Retained; **Lowest/Average Salary:** $90,000/$90,000;
**Industry Concentration:** Generalist; **Function Concentration:** Generalist

**O'Brien, Maggie** — *Regional Manager*
Advanced Information Management
900 Wilshire Boulevard, Suite 1424
Los Angeles, CA 90017
Telephone: (213) 243-9236
**Recruiter Classification:** Contingency; **Lowest/Average Salary:**
$20,000/$40,000; **Industry Concentration:** Information Technology; **Function
Concentration:** Human Resources, Research and Development,
Women/Minorities

**O'Brien, Marlon W.A.** — *Co-Manager*
Management Recruiters International, Inc.
10 Anderson Road, Suite 7
Bernardsville, NJ 07924-2319
Telephone: (908) 204-0070
**Recruiter Classification:** Contingency; **Lowest/Average Salary:**
$30,000/$75,000; **Industry Concentration:** Generalist; **Function
Concentration:** Generalist

**O'Brien, Susan** — *Associate*
Source Services Corporation
1105 Schrock Road, Suite 510
Columbus, OH 43229
Telephone: (614) 846-3311
**Recruiter Classification:** Contingency; **Lowest/Average Salary:**
$30,000/$50,000; **Industry Concentration:** Financial Services, Information
Technology; **Function Concentration:** Engineering, Finance/Accounting

**O'Callaghan, Terry K.** — *Partner*
O'Callaghan Honey/Paul Ray Berndtson, Inc.
400-400 Fifth Avenue S.W.
Calgary, Alberta, CANADA T2P 0L6
Telephone: (403) 269-3277
**Recruiter Classification:** Retained; **Lowest/Average Salary:** $90,000/$90,000;
**Industry Concentration:** Generalist with a primary focus in Energy, Oil/Gas,
Real Estate; **Function Concentration:** Generalist

**O'Connell, Bridget** — *Area Manager*
Accountants on Call
3400 Dundee Road, Suite 260
Northbrook, IL 60062
Telephone: (708) 205-0800
**Recruiter Classification:** Contingency; **Lowest/Average Salary:**
$20,000/$30,000; **Industry Concentration:** Generalist; **Function
Concentration:** Finance/Accounting

**O'Connell, Mary** — *Executive Recruiter*
CPS Inc.
303 Congress Street, 5th Floor
Boston, MA 02210
Telephone: (617) 439-7950
**Recruiter Classification:** Contingency; **Lowest/Average Salary:**
$30,000/$50,000; **Industry Concentration:** Generalist with a primary focus in
Automotive, Biotechnology, Chemical Products, Consumer Products, High
Technology, Insurance, Manufacturing, Oil/Gas, Packaging,
Pharmaceutical/Medical; **Function Concentration:** Engineering, Research and
Development, Sales, Women/Minorities

**O'Connell, Michael** — *Partner*
Ryan, Miller & Associates Inc.
4601 Wilshire Boulevard, Suite 225
Los Angeles, CA 90010
Telephone: (213) 938-4768
**Recruiter Classification:** Contingency, Executive Temporary; **Lowest/Average
Salary:** $60,000/$60,000; **Industry Concentration:** Financial Services;
**Function Concentration:** Finance/Accounting

**O'Connell, William** — *Accounting and Finance Recruiter*
Winter, Wyman & Company
101 Federal Street, 27th Floor
Boston, MA 02110-1800
Telephone: (617) 951-2700
**Recruiter Classification:** Contingency; **Lowest/Average Salary:**
$20,000/$50,000; **Industry Concentration:** Generalist; **Function
Concentration:** Finance/Accounting

**O'Donnell, James H.** — *Physician Recruiter*
MSI International
230 Peachtree Street, N.E.
Suite 1550
Atlanta, GA 30303
Telephone: (404) 653-7360
**Recruiter Classification:** Contingency; **Lowest/Average Salary:**
$30,000/$75,000; **Industry Concentration:** Generalist with a primary focus in
Healthcare/Hospitals, Pharmaceutical/Medical; **Function Concentration:**
Generalist with a primary focus in Administration, Engineering,
Finance/Accounting, General Management, Marketing, Sales

**O'Donnell, Timothy** — *Principal*
Ward Howell International, Inc.
401 East Host Drive
Lake Geneva, WI 53147
Telephone: (414) 249-5200
**Recruiter Classification:** Retained; **Lowest/Average Salary:** $75,000/$90,000;
**Industry Concentration:** Generalist; **Function Concentration:** Generalist

**O'Donnell, Timothy W.** — *Vice President*
Boyden
2 Prudential Plaza, Suite 5050
180 North Stetson Avenue
Chicago, IL 60601
Telephone: (312) 565-1300
**Recruiter Classification:** Retained; **Lowest/Average Salary:** $75,000/$90,000;
**Industry Concentration:** Generalist; **Function Concentration:** Generalist with a
primary focus in Engineering, Finance/Accounting, General Management,
Human Resources, Marketing, Research and Development, Sales,
Women/Minorities

**O'Gorman, David J.** — *Senior Vice President*
DHR International, Inc.
10 South Riverside Plaza, Suite 2220
Chicago, IL 60606
Telephone: (312) 782-1581
**Recruiter Classification:** Retained; **Lowest/Average Salary:** $60,000/$90,000;
**Industry Concentration:** Generalist; **Function Concentration:** Generalist

**O'Halloran, Robert** — *Executive Recruiter*
MSI International
1050 Crown Pointe Parkway
Suite 1000
Atlanta, GA 30338
Telephone: (404) 394-2494
**Recruiter Classification:** Contingency; **Lowest/Average Salary:**
$30,000/$75,000; **Industry Concentration:** Generalist with a primary focus in
Financial Services; **Function Concentration:** Generalist with a primary focus in
Finance/Accounting

**O'Hara, Daniel M.** — *Partner*
Lynch Miller Moore Partners, Inc.
10 South Wacker Drive, Suite 2935
Chicago, IL 60606
Telephone: (312) 876-1505
**Recruiter Classification:** Retained; **Lowest/Average Salary:** $75,000/$90,000;
**Industry Concentration:** Generalist with a primary focus in Automotive,
Biotechnology, Board Services, Consumer Products, Fashion (Retail/Apparel),
Financial Services, Healthcare/Hospitals, High Technology, Information
Technology, Manufacturing, Pharmaceutical/Medical, Real Estate,
Transportation, Venture Capital; **Function Concentration:** Generalist with a
primary focus in Administration, Finance/Accounting, General Management,
Human Resources, Marketing, Research and Development, Sales

**O'Hara, James J.** — *Executive Vice President*
Barone-O'Hara Associates
29 Emmons Drive
Princeton, NJ 08540
Telephone: (609) 452-1980
**Recruiter Classification:** Retained; **Lowest/Average Salary:** $60,000/$90,000;
**Industry Concentration:** Pharmaceutical/Medical; **Function Concentration:**
Generalist with a primary focus in Engineering, General Management,
Marketing, Research and Development, Sales

**O'Maley, Kimberlee** — *Director*
Spencer Stuart
525 Market Street, Suite 3700
San Francisco, CA 94105
Telephone: (415) 495-4141
**Recruiter Classification:** Retained; **Lowest/Average Salary:** $90,000/$90,000;
**Industry Concentration:** Generalist with a primary focus in Consumer
Products, Entertainment, Financial Services, High Technology,
Publishing/Media; **Function Concentration:** Generalist with a primary focus in
Finance/Accounting, General Management, Marketing, Sales

**O'Malley, Robert** — *Senior Consultant*
Raymond Karsan Associates
989 Old Eagle School Road, Suite 814
Wayne, PA 19087
Telephone: (610) 971-9171
**Recruiter Classification:** Contingency; **Lowest/Average Salary:**
$30,000/$90,000; **Industry Concentration:** Generalist; **Function
Concentration:** Generalist

**O'Meally, Diane** — *Senior Vice President*
Accountants on Call
3500 West Olive Avenue, Suite 550
Burbank, CA 91505
Telephone: (818) 845-6600
**Recruiter Classification:** Contingency; **Lowest/Average Salary:**
$20,000/$30,000; **Industry Concentration:** Generalist; **Function
Concentration:** Finance/Accounting

**O'Neill, David** — *Vice President*
Korn/Ferry International
The Transamerica Pyramid
600 Montgomery Street
San Francisco, CA 94111
Telephone: (415) 956-1834
**Recruiter Classification:** Retained; **Lowest/Average Salary:** $90,000/$90,000;
**Industry Concentration:** Generalist with a primary focus in
Healthcare/Hospitals; **Function Concentration:** Generalist

**O'Neill, James P.** — *Partner*
Allerton Heneghan & O'Neill
70 West Madison Street, Suite 2015
Chicago, IL 60602
Telephone: (312) 263-1075
**Recruiter Classification:** Retained; **Lowest/Average Salary:** $75,000/$90,000;
**Industry Concentration:** Generalist with a primary focus in Automotive,
Financial Services, Insurance, Manufacturing, Non-Profit; **Function
Concentration:** Generalist with a primary focus in Finance/Accounting,
General Management, Human Resources, Marketing, Women/Minorities

**O'Neill, Karen** — *Manager IT Recruitment Services*
Ashton Computer Professionals Inc.
#1498 - 1090 West Georgia Street
Vancouver, British Columbia, CANADA V6E 3V7
Telephone: (604) 688-1134
**Recruiter Classification:** Contingency; **Lowest/Average Salary:**
$30,000/$60,000; **Industry Concentration:** Information Technology; **Function Concentration:** Generalist

**O'Neill, Stephen A.** — *Senior Associate*
Harris Heery & Associates
40 Richards Avenue
One Norwalk West
Norwalk, CT 06854
Telephone: (203) 857-0808
**Recruiter Classification:** Retained; **Lowest/Average Salary:** $75,000/$90,000;
**Industry Concentration:** Consumer Products, Fashion (Retail/Apparel),
Financial Services, Insurance, Publishing/Media; **Function Concentration:**
Finance/Accounting, General Management, Marketing

**O'Reilly, Bill** — *Manager Central Region*
Management Recruiters International, Inc.
4050 Executive Park Drive, Suite 125
Cincinnati, OH 45241-2020
Telephone: (513) 769-4747
**Recruiter Classification:** Contingency; **Lowest/Average Salary:**
$30,000/$75,000; **Industry Concentration:** Generalist; **Function Concentration:** Generalist

**O'Reilly, Jack** — *Managing Director*
Catalyx Group
4040 Campbell Avenue, Second Floor
Menlo Park, CA 94025
Telephone: (415) 325-4032
**Recruiter Classification:** Retained; **Lowest/Average Salary:** $90,000/$90,000;
**Industry Concentration:** Biotechnology, Board Services, High Technology,
Information Technology, Pharmaceutical/Medical, Publishing/Media, Venture
Capital; **Function Concentration:** Generalist with a primary focus in General
Management, Research and Development

**O'Shea, Laurie A.** — *Vice President*
The Heidrick Partners, Inc.
20 North Wacker Drive
Suite 2850
Chicago, IL 60606-3171
Telephone: (312) 845-9700
**Recruiter Classification:** Retained; **Lowest/Average Salary:** $90,000/$90,000;
**Industry Concentration:** Generalist; **Function Concentration:** Generalist

**O'Shea, Timothy J.** — *Partner*
Heidrick & Struggles, Inc.
300 South Grand Avenue, Suite 2400
Los Angeles, CA 90071
Telephone: (213) 625-8811
**Recruiter Classification:** Retained; **Lowest/Average Salary:** $75,000/$90,000;
**Industry Concentration:** Generalist; **Function Concentration:** Generalist

**O'Such, Tracy** — *Associate*
Bishop Partners
708 Third Avenue
New York, NY 10017
Telephone: (212) 986-3419
**Recruiter Classification:** Retained; **Lowest/Average Salary:** $90,000/$90,000;
**Industry Concentration:** Entertainment, Information Technology,
Publishing/Media; **Function Concentration:** Generalist with a primary focus in
General Management, Marketing, Sales, Women/Minorities

**O'Toole, Dennis P.** — *President*
Dennis P. O'Toole & Associates Inc.
1865 Palmer Avenue, Suite 210
Larchmont, NY 10538
Telephone: (914) 833-3712
**Recruiter Classification:** Retained; **Lowest/Average Salary:** $75,000/$90,000;
**Industry Concentration:** Generalist with a primary focus in Entertainment,
Hospitality/Leisure; **Function Concentration:** Generalist with a primary focus in
Administration, Engineering, Finance/Accounting, General Management,
Human Resources, Marketing, Sales

**Oakes, Meg B.** — *Vice President*
D.P. Parker and Associates
372 Washington Street
Wellesley, MA 02181
Telephone: (617) 237-1220
**Recruiter Classification:** Retained; **Lowest/Average Salary:** $75,000/$90,000;
**Industry Concentration:** Generalist with a primary focus in
Aerospace/Defense, Automotive, Biotechnology, Chemical Products; **Function
Concentration:** Engineering, General Management, Marketing, Research and
Development

**Oakley, Mitch** — *Manager North Atlantic Region*
Management Recruiters International, Inc.
324 West Wendover, Suite 230
Greensboro, NC 27408
Telephone: (910) 378-1818
**Recruiter Classification:** Contingency; **Lowest/Average Salary:**
$30,000/$75,000; **Industry Concentration:** Generalist; **Function Concentration:** Generalist

**Oaks, Robert** — *Account Executive*
Search West, Inc.
3401 Centrelake Drive
Suite 690
Ontario, CA 91761-1207
Telephone: (909) 986-1966
**Recruiter Classification:** Contingency; **Lowest/Average Salary:**
$40,000/$60,000; **Industry Concentration:** Manufacturing; **Function
Concentration:** Engineering, Research and Development

**Oberg, Roy** — *Division Manager - Packaging*
The Danbrook Group, Inc.
14180 Dallas Parkway, Suite 400
Dallas, TX 75240
Telephone: (214) 392-0057
**Recruiter Classification:** Contingency; **Lowest/Average Salary:**
$30,000/$50,000; **Industry Concentration:** Generalist with a primary focus in
Packaging; **Function Concentration:** Generalist with a primary focus in
Engineering, General Management, Sales

**Oberting, Dave W.** — *Manager North Atlantic Region*
Management Recruiters International, Inc.
One Pine Brook Plaza, Suite 110
9101 Southern Pine Boulevard
Charlotte, NC 28273
Telephone: (704) 523-3377
**Recruiter Classification:** Contingency; **Lowest/Average Salary:**
$30,000/$75,000; **Industry Concentration:** Generalist; **Function Concentration:** Generalist

**Oberting, David J.** — *Manager Central Region*
Management Recruiters International, Inc.
800 East Broad Street
Columbus, OH 43205
Telephone: (614) 252-6200
**Recruiter Classification:** Contingency; **Lowest/Average Salary:**
$30,000/$75,000; **Industry Concentration:** Generalist; **Function Concentration:** Generalist

**Occhiboi, Emil** — *Associate*
Source Services Corporation
925 Westchester Avenue, Suite 309
White Plains, NY 10604
Telephone: (914) 428-9100
**Recruiter Classification:** Contingency; **Lowest/Average Salary:**
$30,000/$50,000; **Industry Concentration:** Financial Services, Information
Technology; **Function Concentration:** Engineering, Finance/Accounting

**Ocon, Olga** — *Principal*
Busch International
One First Street, Suite 6
Los Altos, CA 94022-2754
Telephone: (415) 949-1115
**Recruiter Classification:** Retained; **Lowest/Average Salary:** $90,000/$90,000;
**Industry Concentration:** Biotechnology, Electronics, High Technology,
Information Technology, Venture Capital; **Function Concentration:** Generalist
with a primary focus in Engineering, Finance/Accounting, General
Management, Marketing, Research and Development, Sales

**Oddo, Judith** — *Representative Marketing*
Accounting Personnel Consultants
210 Baronne Street, Suite 920
New Orleans, LA 70112
Telephone: (504) 581-7800
**Recruiter Classification:** Contingency, Executive Temporary; **Lowest/Average
Salary:** $20,000/$20,000; **Industry Concentration:** Generalist; **Function
Concentration:** Administration, Engineering, Finance/Accounting

**Odom, Philip** — *Executive Recruiter*
Richard, Wayne and Roberts
24 Greenway Plaza, Suite 1304
Houston, TX 77046-2493
Telephone: (713) 629-6681
**Recruiter Classification:** Retained; **Lowest/Average Salary:** $50,000/$90,000;
**Industry Concentration:** Generalist with a primary focus in Information
Technology; **Function Concentration:** Generalist

**Ogden, Dayton** — *Chief Executive Officer*
Spencer Stuart
Financial Centre
695 East Main Street
Stamford, CT 06901
Telephone: (203) 324-6333
**Recruiter Classification:** Retained; **Lowest/Average Salary:** $90,000/$90,000;
**Industry Concentration:** Generalist with a primary focus in Board Services,
Financial Services, Real Estate, Transportation; **Function Concentration:**
Generalist with a primary focus in General Management

**Ogdon, Thomas H.** — *President*
The Ogdon Partnership
375 Park Avenue, Suite 2409
New York, NY 10152-0175
Telephone: (212) 308-1600
**Recruiter Classification:** Retained; **Lowest/Average Salary:** $90,000/$90,000;
**Industry Concentration:** Generalist with a primary focus in Board Services,
Consumer Products, Entertainment, Fashion (Retail/Apparel), Financial
Services, Information Technology, Insurance, Publishing/Media, Venture
Capital; **Function Concentration:** Generalist with a primary focus in
Administration, Finance/Accounting, General Management, Human Resources,
Marketing, Research and Development, Sales

**Ogilvie, Kit** — *Vice President Bio-Pharmaceutical Division*
Howard Fischer Associates, Inc.
1800 John F. Kennedy Boulevard, 7th Floor
Philadelphia, PA 19103
Telephone: (215) 568-8363
**Recruiter Classification:** Retained; **Lowest/Average Salary:** $90,000/$90,000;
**Industry Concentration:** Biotechnology, Pharmaceutical/Medical; **Function
Concentration:** Generalist

**Ohman, Gregory L.** — *Partner*
Pearson, Caldwell & Farnsworth, Inc.
250 Park Avenue, 17th Floor
New York, NY 10177
Telephone: (212) 983-5850
**Recruiter Classification:** Retained; **Lowest/Average Salary:** $90,000/$90,000;
**Industry Concentration:** Financial Services; **Function Concentration:**
Administration, Finance/Accounting, General Management, Human Resources,
Marketing, Sales

**Olesky, Beth Green** — *Managing Director/Area Manager*
Russell Reynolds Associates, Inc.
200 Park Avenue
New York, NY 10166-0002
Telephone: (212) 351-2000
**Recruiter Classification:** Retained; **Lowest/Average Salary:** $90,000/$90,000;
**Industry Concentration:** Generalist; **Function Concentration:** Generalist

**Olin, Robyn** — *Executive Recruiter*
Richard, Wayne and Roberts
24 Greenway Plaza, Suite 1304
Houston, TX 77046-2493
Telephone: (713) 629-6681
**Recruiter Classification:** Retained; **Lowest/Average Salary:** $50,000/$90,000;
**Industry Concentration:** Generalist with a primary focus in Financial Services;
**Function Concentration:** Generalist with a primary focus in
Finance/Accounting

**Olivares, Rebecca** — *Consultant*
Paul Ray Berndtson
2029 Century Park East
Suite 1000
Los Angeles, CA 90067
Telephone: (310) 557-2828
**Recruiter Classification:** Retained; **Lowest/Average Salary:** $90,000/$90,000;
**Industry Concentration:** Generalist; **Function Concentration:** Generalist

**Oliver, Phoebe** — *Vice President*
Seiden Krieger Associates, Inc.
375 Park Avenue
New York, NY 10152
Telephone: (212) 688-8383
**Recruiter Classification:** Retained; **Lowest/Average Salary:** $90,000/$90,000;
**Industry Concentration:** Generalist with a primary focus in Manufacturing;
**Function Concentration:** Generalist with a primary focus in Administration,
Finance/Accounting, General Management, Human Resources, Marketing

**Oliverio, Anthony P.** — *Manager Central Region*
Management Recruiters International, Inc.
1587 East Washington Street
Charleston, WV 25311-2505
Telephone: (304) 344-5632
**Recruiter Classification:** Contingency; **Lowest/Average Salary:**
$30,000/$75,000; **Industry Concentration:** Generalist; **Function
Concentration:** Generalist

**Oller, Jose E.** — *Managing Director*
Ward Howell International, Inc.
1601 Elm Street, Suite 900
Thanksgiving Tower
Dallas, TX 75201
Telephone: (214) 749-0099
**Recruiter Classification:** Retained; **Lowest/Average Salary:** $75,000/$90,000;
**Industry Concentration:** Manufacturing, Transportation; **Function
Concentration:** Generalist with a primary focus in Administration, General
Management, Human Resources, Marketing

**Ollinger, Charles D.** — *Partner*
Heidrick & Struggles, Inc.
One Post Office Square
Boston, MA 02109-0199
Telephone: (617) 423-1140
**Recruiter Classification:** Retained; **Lowest/Average Salary:** $75,000/$90,000;
**Industry Concentration:** Generalist with a primary focus in Consumer
Products; **Function Concentration:** Generalist

**Olmstead, George T.** — *Partner*
Blackshaw, Olmstead & Lynch
1010 Monarch Plaza
3414 Peachtree Road N.E.
Atlanta, GA 30326
Telephone: (404) 261-7770
**Recruiter Classification:** Retained; **Lowest/Average Salary:** $75,000/$90,000;
**Industry Concentration:** Generalist with a primary focus in Entertainment,
Fashion (Retail/Apparel), Information Technology; **Function Concentration:**
Generalist with a primary focus in Finance/Accounting, General Management,
Human Resources, Marketing

**Olsen, Carl** — *Vice President/Managing Director*
A.T. Kearney, Inc.
3 Lagoon Drive, Suite 160
Redwood City, CA 94065
Telephone: (415) 637-6600
**Recruiter Classification:** Retained; **Lowest/Average Salary:** $90,000/$90,000;
**Industry Concentration:** Generalist with a primary focus in
Aerospace/Defense, High Technology, Manufacturing,
Pharmaceutical/Medical; **Function Concentration:** Generalist with a primary
focus in Engineering, General Management, Marketing, Research and
Development, Sales

**Olsen, David** — *Technical Recruiter*
Search Enterprises South, Inc.
10100 West Sample Road
Coral Springs, FL 33065
Telephone: (305) 755-3121
**Recruiter Classification:** Contingency; **Lowest/Average Salary:**
$40,000/$50,000; **Industry Concentration:** Chemical Products, Consumer
Products, Oil/Gas; **Function Concentration:** Engineering

**Olsen, David G.** — *Vice President*
Handy HRM Corp.
250 Park Avenue
New York, NY 10177-0074
Telephone: (212) 557-0400
**Recruiter Classification:** Retained; **Lowest/Average Salary:** $90,000/$90,000;
**Industry Concentration:** High Technology; **Function Concentration:** General
Management

**Olsen, Robert** — *Associate*
Source Services Corporation
150 South Wacker Drive, Suite 400
Chicago, IL 60606
Telephone: (312) 346-7000
**Recruiter Classification:** Contingency; **Lowest/Average Salary:**
$30,000/$50,000; **Industry Concentration:** Financial Services, Information
Technology; **Function Concentration:** Engineering, Finance/Accounting

**Olsen, Robert F.** — *President*
Robert Connelly and Associates Incorporated
P.O. Box 24028
Minneapolis, MN 55424
Telephone: (612) 925-3039
**Recruiter Classification:** Retained; **Lowest/Average Salary:** $50,000/$75,000;
**Industry Concentration:** Real Estate; **Function Concentration:** Engineering

**Olsen, Theodore J.** — *Vice President*
Senior Careers Executive Search
257 Park Avenue South
New York, NY 10010
Telephone: (212) 529-6660
**Recruiter Classification:** Retained; **Lowest/Average Salary:** $50,000/$75,000;
**Industry Concentration:** Generalist; **Function Concentration:** Generalist

**Olson, A. Andrew** — *Partner*
Paul Ray Berndtson
10 South Riverside Plaza
Suite 720
Chicago, IL 60606
Telephone: (312) 876-0730
**Recruiter Classification:** Retained; **Lowest/Average Salary:** $90,000/$90,000;
**Industry Concentration:** High Technology; **Function Concentration:** Generalist

**Olson, B. Tucker** — *Principal*
Early Cochran & Olson, Inc.
401 North Michigan, Suite 515
Chicago, IL 60611-4205
Telephone: (312) 595-4200
**Recruiter Classification:** Retained; **Lowest/Average Salary:** $90,000/$90,000;
**Industry Concentration:** Generalist; **Function Concentration:** Generalist

**Olson, Cherene** — *Resource Manager Computer Graphics Design and Production*
The Paladin Companies, Inc.
875 North Michigan Avenue, Suite 3218
Chicago, IL 60611
Telephone: (312) 654-2600
**Recruiter Classification:** Executive Temporary; **Lowest/Average Salary:**
$40,000/$60,000; **Industry Concentration:** Generalist

**Olson, Nels** — *Senior Associate*
Korn/Ferry International
Presidential Plaza
900 19th Street, N.W.
Washington, DC 20006
Telephone: (202) 822-9444
**Recruiter Classification:** Retained; **Lowest/Average Salary:** $90,000/$90,000;
**Industry Concentration:** Generalist; **Function Concentration:** Generalist

**Ongirski, Richard P.** — *Principal*
Raymond Karsan Associates
989 Old Eagle School Road, Suite 814
Wayne, PA 19087
Telephone: (610) 971-9171
**Recruiter Classification:** Contingency; **Lowest/Average Salary:**
$30,000/$90,000; **Industry Concentration:** Generalist with a primary focus in
Insurance; **Function Concentration:** Generalist

**Onstott, Joseph E.** — *Managing Director*
The Onstott Group, Inc.
60 William Street
Wellesley, MA 02181
Telephone: (617) 235-3050
**Recruiter Classification:** Retained; **Lowest/Average Salary:** $90,000/$90,000;
**Industry Concentration:** Generalist with a primary focus in Board Services,
Chemical Products, Consumer Products, Financial Services, High Technology,
Information Technology, Manufacturing, Publishing/Media, Venture Capital;
**Function Concentration:** Generalist with a primary focus in
Finance/Accounting, General Management, Marketing, Sales

**Oppedisano, Edward** — *Chairman and CEO*
Oppedisano & Company, Inc.
370 Lexington Avenue, Suite 1200
New York, NY 10017
Telephone: (212) 696-0144
**Recruiter Classification:** Retained; **Lowest/Average Salary:** $/$90,000; **Industry Concentration:** Financial Services; **Function Concentration:** Generalist with a primary focus in Finance/Accounting

**Oppenheim, Jeffrey** — *Director Food Service/Supermarkets*
Roth Young Personnel Service of Boston, Inc.
200 Boston Avenue, Suite 2300
Medford, MA 02155
Telephone: (617) 395-3600
**Recruiter Classification:** Contingency; **Lowest/Average Salary:**
$40,000/$60,000; **Function Concentration:** General Management, Marketing,
Research and Development, Sales

**Oppenheim, Norman J.** — *President*
F-O-R-T-U-N-E Personnel Consultants of Nashua, Inc.
505 West Hollis Street, Suite 208
Nashua, NH 03062
Telephone: (603) 880-4900
**Recruiter Classification:** Contingency; **Lowest/Average Salary:**
$40,000/$60,000; **Industry Concentration:** Biotechnology,
Pharmaceutical/Medical; **Function Concentration:** Generalist

**Oppenheimer, Janet** — *Consultant*
Paul Ray Berndtson
10 South Riverside Plaza
Suite 720
Chicago, IL 60606
Telephone: (312) 876-0730
**Recruiter Classification:** Retained; **Lowest/Average Salary:** $90,000/$90,000;
**Industry Concentration:** Generalist; **Function Concentration:** Generalist

**Orkin, Ralph** — *Principal*
Sanford Rose Associates
26250 Euclid Avenue, Suite 629
Euclid, OH 44132
Telephone: (216) 731-0005
**Recruiter Classification:** Contingency; **Lowest/Average Salary:**
$30,000/$75,000; **Industry Concentration:** Generalist with a primary focus in
Financial Services, High Technology; **Function Concentration:** Generalist

**Orkin, Sheilah** — *Principal*
Sanford Rose Associates
26250 Euclid Avenue, Suite 629
Euclid, OH 44132
Telephone: (216) 731-0005
**Recruiter Classification:** Contingency; **Lowest/Average Salary:**
$30,000/$75,000; **Industry Concentration:** Generalist with a primary focus in
Financial Services, High Technology; **Function Concentration:** Generalist

**Orner, Ted A.** — *Managing Director*
Russell Reynolds Associates, Inc.
First Interstate Bank Plaza
1000 Louisiana Street, Suite 4800
Houston, TX 77002-5095
Telephone: (713) 658-1776
**Recruiter Classification:** Retained; **Lowest/Average Salary:** $90,000/$90,000;
**Industry Concentration:** Energy; **Function Concentration:** Generalist

**Orr, Don** — *President*
Orr Executive Search
5125 North 16th Street, Suite B-223
Phoenix, AZ 85016
Telephone: (602) 274-2170
**Recruiter Classification:** Contingency; **Lowest/Average Salary:**
$40,000/$60,000; **Industry Concentration:** Generalist; **Function
Concentration:** Generalist

**Orr, Stacie** — *Associate*
Source Services Corporation
155 Federal Street, Suite 410
Boston, MA 02110
Telephone: (617) 482-8211
**Recruiter Classification:** Contingency; **Lowest/Average Salary:**
$30,000/$50,000; **Industry Concentration:** Financial Services, Information
Technology; **Function Concentration:** Engineering, Finance/Accounting

**Orr, Steve** — *Co-Manager Midwest Region*
Management Recruiters International, Inc.
Soho Office Center, Suite 500
712 Broadway
Kansas City, MO 64105
Telephone: (816) 221-2377
**Recruiter Classification:** Contingency; **Lowest/Average Salary:**
$30,000/$75,000; **Industry Concentration:** Generalist; **Function
Concentration:** Generalist

**Osborn, Jim** — *Consultant*
Southwestern Professional Services
2451 Atrium Way
Nashville, TN 37214
Telephone: (615) 391-2722
**Recruiter Classification:** Contingency; **Lowest/Average Salary:**
$30,000/$30,000; **Industry Concentration:** Generalist with a primary focus in
Consumer Products, Healthcare/Hospitals, Information Technology; **Function
Concentration:** General Management

**Osinski, Martin H.** — *Principal*
American Medical Consultants
11625 Southwest 110 Road
Miami, FL 33176
Telephone: (305) 271-9225
**Recruiter Classification:** Contingency; **Lowest/Average Salary:**
$75,000/$90,000; **Industry Concentration:** Healthcare/Hospitals

**Oster, Joan** — *Manager Eastern Region*
Management Recruiters International, Inc.
140 Sherman Street
Fairfield, CT 06430-5849
Telephone: (203) 255-2299
**Recruiter Classification:** Contingency; **Lowest/Average Salary:**
$30,000/$75,000; **Industry Concentration:** Generalist; **Function
Concentration:** Generalist

**Oster, Rush R.** — *Manager*
Management Recruiters International, Inc.
140 Sherman Street
Fairfield, CT 06430-5849
Telephone: (203) 255-2299
**Recruiter Classification:** Contingency; **Lowest/Average Salary:**
$30,000/$75,000; **Industry Concentration:** Generalist; **Function Concentration:** Generalist

**Oswald, Mark G.** — *Vice President*
Canny, Bowen Inc.
10 Post Office Square, Suite 960
Boston, MA 02109
Telephone: (617) 292-6242
**Recruiter Classification:** Retained; **Lowest/Average Salary:** $90,000/$90,000;
**Industry Concentration:** Generalist with a primary focus in Consumer
Products, Fashion (Retail/Apparel), Financial Services, Hospitality/Leisure,
Manufacturing; **Function Concentration:** Generalist with a primary focus in
General Management, Human Resources, Marketing, Sales, Women/Minorities

**Ott, George W.** — *President and CEO*
Ott & Hansen, Inc.
136 South Oak Knoll, Suite 300
Pasadena, CA 91101
Telephone: (818) 578-0551
**Recruiter Classification:** Retained; **Lowest/Average Salary:** $75,000/$90,000;
**Industry Concentration:** Generalist with a primary focus in
Aerospace/Defense, Board Services, Consumer Products, Manufacturing, Non-
Profit, Real Estate; **Function Concentration:** Generalist with a primary focus in
Administration, Finance/Accounting, General Management, Human Resources,
Women/Minorities

**Ottenritter, Chris** — *Executive Recruiter*
CPS Inc.
One Westbrook Corporate Centre, Suite 600
Westchester, IL 60154
Telephone: (708) 531-8370
**Recruiter Classification:** Contingency; **Lowest/Average Salary:**
$30,000/$50,000; **Industry Concentration:** Generalist with a primary focus in
Automotive, Biotechnology, Chemical Products, Consumer Products, High
Technology, Insurance, Manufacturing, Oil/Gas, Packaging,
Pharmaceutical/Medical; **Function Concentration:** Engineering, Research and
Development, Sales, Women/Minorities

**Otto, Karen E.** — *Consultant*
Witt/Kieffer, Ford, Hadelman & Lloyd
2015 Spring Road, Suite 510
Oak Brook, IL 60521
Telephone: (708) 990-1370
**Recruiter Classification:** Retained; **Lowest/Average Salary:** $75,000/$90,000;
**Industry Concentration:** Healthcare/Hospitals; **Function Concentration:**
Generalist with a primary focus in General Management

**Ouellette, Christopher** — *Associate*
Source Services Corporation
155 Federal Street, Suite 410
Boston, MA 02110
Telephone: (617) 482-8211
**Recruiter Classification:** Contingency; **Lowest/Average Salary:**
$30,000/$50,000; **Industry Concentration:** Financial Services, Information
Technology; **Function Concentration:** Engineering, Finance/Accounting

**Owen, Christopher** — *Associate*
Source Services Corporation
8614 Westwood Center, Suite 750
Vienna, VA 22182
Telephone: (703) 790-5610
**Recruiter Classification:** Contingency; **Lowest/Average Salary:**
$30,000/$50,000; **Industry Concentration:** Financial Services, Information
Technology; **Function Concentration:** Engineering, Finance/Accounting

**Owen, Jamie L.** — *Manager Pacific Region*
Management Recruiters International, Inc.
100 Corporate Pointe, Suite 380
Culver City, CA 90230
Telephone: (310) 670-3040
**Recruiter Classification:** Contingency; **Lowest/Average Salary:**
$30,000/$75,000; **Industry Concentration:** Generalist; **Function Concentration:** Generalist

**Owen, John** — *Assistant Vice President*
Key Employment Services
1001 Office Park Road, Suite 320
West Des Moines, IA 50265-2567
Telephone: (515) 224-0446
**Recruiter Classification:** Contingency; **Lowest/Average Salary:**
$30,000/$75,000; **Industry Concentration:** Generalist; **Function Concentration:** Engineering

**Owens, Ken** — *Executive Recruiter*
F-O-R-T-U-N-E Personnel Consultants of Huntsville, Inc.
3311 Bob Wallace Avenue, Suite 204
Huntsville, AL 35805
Telephone: (205) 534-7282
**Recruiter Classification:** Contingency; **Lowest/Average Salary:**
$30,000/$50,000; **Industry Concentration:** Automotive, Consumer Products,
High Technology, Manufacturing, Transportation; **Function Concentration:**
Engineering, General Management, Marketing, Sales

**Owens, LaMonte** — *President/Owner*
LaMonte Owens & Company
805 East Willow Grove Avenue
P.O. Box 27742
Philadelphia, PA 19118
Telephone: (215) 248-0500
**Recruiter Classification:** Retained, Contingency; **Lowest/Average Salary:**
$/$50,000; **Industry Concentration:** Generalist; **Function Concentration:**
Generalist with a primary focus in Women/Minorities

**Owens, Reggie R.** — *Associate*
The Gabriel Group
1515 Market Street, Suite 504
Philadelphia, PA 19102
Telephone: (215) 496-9990
**Recruiter Classification:** Retained; **Lowest/Average Salary:** $90,000/$90,000;
**Industry Concentration:** Generalist; **Function Concentration:** Generalist

**Pace, Susan A.** — *Vice President*
Horton International
10 Tower Lane
Avon, CT 06001
Telephone: (860) 674-8701
**Recruiter Classification:** Retained; **Lowest/Average Salary:** $90,000/$90,000;
**Industry Concentration:** Generalist with a primary focus in Automotive,
Chemical Products, Education/Libraries, Financial Services,
Healthcare/Hospitals, Information Technology, Insurance, Manufacturing, Non-
Profit, Pharmaceutical/Medical; **Function Concentration:** Generalist with a
primary focus in Finance/Accounting, Human Resources, Marketing, Sales

**Pacheco, Ricardo** — *Partner*
Amrop International
Av. Lazaro Cardenas, 2400 PTE
Edificio Los Soles, P.D. 2
Garza Garcia, N.L., MEXICO 66270
Telephone: (528) 363-2529
**Recruiter Classification:** Retained, Contingency; **Lowest/Average Salary:**
$75,000/$75,000; **Industry Concentration:** Generalist; **Function Concentration:** Generalist

**Pachowitz, John** — *Associate*
Source Services Corporation
1233 North Mayfair Road, Suite 300
Milwaukee, WI 53226
Telephone: (414) 774-6700
**Recruiter Classification:** Contingency; **Lowest/Average Salary:**
$30,000/$50,000; **Industry Concentration:** Financial Services, Information
Technology; **Function Concentration:** Engineering, Finance/Accounting

**Pacini, Lauren R.** — *Vice President*
Hite Executive Search
6515 Chase Drive
P.O. Box 43217
Cleveland, OH 44143
Telephone: (216) 461-1600
**Recruiter Classification:** Retained; **Lowest/Average Salary:** $90,000/$90,000;
**Industry Concentration:** Generalist with a primary focus in Biotechnology,
Chemical Products, Electronics, Energy, Healthcare/Hospitals, High
Technology, Information Technology, Pharmaceutical/Medical; **Function
Concentration:** Generalist with a primary focus in Administration, Engineering,
General Management, Marketing, Sales

**Padilla, Jose Sanchez** — *Consultant*
Egon Zehnder International Inc.
Paseo de las Palmas No. 405-703
Co. Lomas de Chapultepec
Mexico City, D.F., MEXICO 11000
Telephone: (525) 540-7635
**Recruiter Classification:** Retained; **Lowest/Average Salary:** $90,000/$90,000;
**Industry Concentration:** Generalist with a primary focus in Biotechnology,
Financial Services, High Technology, Manufacturing, Pharmaceutical/Medical;
**Function Concentration:** Generalist

**Pagan, Vernon R.** — *Manager North Atlantic Region*
Management Recruiters International, Inc.
Elizabeth Square, Suite D
2406 North Main Street, P.O. Box 2874
Anderson, SC 29622
Telephone: (864) 225-1258
**Recruiter Classification:** Contingency; **Lowest/Average Salary:**
$30,000/$75,000; **Industry Concentration:** Generalist; **Function Concentration:** Generalist

**Page, G. Schuyler** — *Vice President*
A.T. Kearney, Inc.
Lincoln Plaza, Suite 4170
500 North Akard Street
Dallas, TX 75201
Telephone: (214) 969-0010
**Recruiter Classification:** Retained; **Lowest/Average Salary:** $90,000/$90,000;
**Industry Concentration:** Generalist with a primary focus in Financial Services,
High Technology, Non-Profit, Transportation; **Function Concentration:**
Generalist with a primary focus in Finance/Accounting

**Page, Linda** — *Executive Recruiter*
Jonas, Walters & Assoc., Inc.
1110 North Old World Third St., Suite 510
Milwaukee, WI 53203-1102
Telephone: (414) 291-2828
**Recruiter Classification:** Retained; **Lowest/Average Salary:** $60,000/$90,000;
**Industry Concentration:** Generalist with a primary focus in Consumer
Products, Electronics, Healthcare/Hospitals, High Technology, Insurance,
Manufacturing, Non-Profit, Publishing/Media; **Function Concentration:**
Generalist with a primary focus in Administration, Engineering,
Finance/Accounting, General Management, Human Resources, Marketing,
Research and Development, Sales

**Page, Linda M.** — *Senior Recruiter*
Wargo and Co., Inc.
850 Elm Grove Road
Elm Grove, WI 53122
Telephone: (414) 785-1211
**Recruiter Classification:** Retained; **Lowest/Average Salary:** $50,000/$90,000;
**Industry Concentration:** Generalist with a primary focus in Automotive,
Biotechnology, Consumer Products, Electronics, Financial Services,
Healthcare/Hospitals, High Technology, Information Technology, Insurance,
Manufacturing, Pharmaceutical/Medical, Publishing/Media, Transportation;
**Function Concentration:** Generalist with a primary focus in Engineering,
Finance/Accounting, General Management, Human Resources, Marketing,
Research and Development, Sales

**Palazio, Carla** — *Vice President*
A.T. Kearney, Inc.
Miami Center, Suite 3180
201 South Biscayne Boulevard
Miami, FL 33131
Telephone: (305) 577-0046
**Recruiter Classification:** Retained; **Lowest/Average Salary:** $90,000/$90,000;
**Industry Concentration:** Generalist with a primary focus in Financial Services;
**Function Concentration:** Generalist with a primary focus in
Finance/Accounting, General Management

**Paliwoda, William** — *Associate*
Source Services Corporation
925 Westchester Avenue, Suite 309
White Plains, NY 10604
Telephone: (914) 428-9100
**Recruiter Classification:** Contingency; **Lowest/Average Salary:**
$30,000/$50,000; **Industry Concentration:** Financial Services, Information
Technology; **Function Concentration:** Engineering, Finance/Accounting

**Palma, Frank R.** — *Executive Vice President*
Goodrich & Sherwood Associates, Inc.
6 Century Drive
Parsippany, NJ 07054
Telephone: (201) 455-7100
**Recruiter Classification:** Retained; **Lowest/Average Salary:** $60,000/$90,000;
**Industry Concentration:** Generalist with a primary focus in Board Services,
Chemical Products, Consumer Products, Financial Services,
Healthcare/Hospitals, Information Technology, Insurance, Manufacturing,
Oil/Gas, Publishing/Media, Venture Capital; **Function Concentration:**
Generalist with a primary focus in Administration, Finance/Accounting,
General Management, Human Resources, Marketing, Sales

**Palmer, Carlton A.** — *Senior Vice President/Partner*
Beall & Company, Inc.
535 Colonial Park Drive
Roswell, GA 30075
Telephone: (404) 992-0900
**Recruiter Classification:** Retained; **Lowest/Average Salary:** $90,000/$90,000;
**Industry Concentration:** Generalist with a primary focus in Biotechnology,
Board Services, Financial Services, Healthcare/Hospitals, High Technology,
Insurance, Pharmaceutical/Medical, Real Estate, Venture Capital; **Function
Concentration:** Generalist with a primary focus in Administration, Engineering,
Finance/Accounting, General Management, Human Resources, Marketing,
Research and Development, Sales

**Palmer, James H.** — *Vice President*
The Hindman Company
Browenton Place, Suite 110
2000 Warrington Way
Louisville, KY 40222
Telephone: (502) 426-4040
**Recruiter Classification:** Retained; **Lowest/Average Salary:** $50,000/$90,000;
**Industry Concentration:** Generalist with a primary focus in
Aerospace/Defense, Automotive, Chemical Products, Consumer Products,
Electronics, Financial Services, High Technology, Manufacturing, Oil/Gas,
Pharmaceutical/Medical, Transportation; **Function Concentration:** Generalist

**Palmer, Melissa** — *Executive Recruiter*
Don Richard Associates of Tampa, Inc.
100 North Tampa Street, Suite 1925
Tampa, FL 33602
Telephone: (813) 221-7930
**Recruiter Classification:** Contingency, Executive Temporary; **Lowest/Average
Salary:** $20,000/$50,000; **Industry Concentration:** Generalist with a primary
focus in Automotive, High Technology, Hospitality/Leisure, Manufacturing,
Packaging, Publishing/Media, Real Estate; **Function Concentration:** Generalist
with a primary focus in Administration, Finance/Accounting

**Palmieri, Cathryn C.** — *Vice President*
Korn/Ferry International
237 Park Avenue
New York, NY 10017
Telephone: (212) 687-1834
**Recruiter Classification:** Retained; **Lowest/Average Salary:** $90,000/$90,000;
**Industry Concentration:** Generalist with a primary focus in Financial Services;
**Function Concentration:** Generalist

**Palmlund, David W.** — *Managing Partner*
Lamalie Amrop International
Thanksgiving Tower
1601 Elm Street
Dallas, TX 75201-4768
Telephone: (214) 754-0019
**Recruiter Classification:** Retained; **Lowest/Average Salary:** $90,000/$90,000;
**Industry Concentration:** Generalist with a primary focus in Consumer
Products, Entertainment, Hospitality/Leisure, Transportation; **Function
Concentration:** Generalist with a primary focus in Finance/Accounting,
General Management, Marketing, Research and Development, Sales

**Pamplin, LaShana** — *Manager Research*
The Repovich-Reynolds Group
709 East Colorado Boulevard, Suite 200
Pasadena, CA 91101
Telephone: (818) 585-9455
**Recruiter Classification:** Retained; **Lowest/Average Salary:** $75,000/$90,000;
**Industry Concentration:** Generalist; **Function Concentration:** Marketing

**Panetta, Timothy** — *Partner*
Commonwealth Consultants
4840 Roswell Road
Atlanta, GA 30342
Telephone: (404) 256-0000
**Recruiter Classification:** Contingency; **Lowest/Average Salary:**
$30,000/$90,000; **Industry Concentration:** High Technology; **Function
Concentration:** Sales

**Paolotti, Susan** — *Associate*
Kenzer Corp.
777 Third Avenue, 26th Floor
New York, NY 10017
Telephone: (212) 308-4300
**Recruiter Classification:** Retained; **Lowest/Average Salary:** $50,000/$90,000;
**Industry Concentration:** Generalist; **Function Concentration:** Generalist

**Papayanopulos, Manuel** — *Vice President*
Korn/Ferry International
Montes Urales 641
Lomas De Chapultepec
Mexico City, D.F., MEXICO 11000
Telephone: (525) 202-0046
**Recruiter Classification:** Retained; **Lowest/Average Salary:** $90,000/$90,000;
**Industry Concentration:** Generalist; **Function Concentration:** Generalist

**Papciak, Dennis J.** — *President*
Accounting Personnel Associates, Inc.
2100 Wharton Street, Suite 710
Pittsburgh, PA 15203-1942
Telephone: (412) 481-6015
**Recruiter Classification:** Contingency; **Lowest/Average Salary:**
$20,000/$50,000; **Industry Concentration:** Consumer Products, Financial
Services, High Technology, Information Technology, Manufacturing; **Function
Concentration:** Administration, Finance/Accounting, Women/Minorities

**Papciak, Dennis J.** — *President*
Temporary Accounting Personnel
2100 Wharton Street
Suite 710
Pittsburgh, PA 15203-1942
Telephone: (412) 488-9155
**Recruiter Classification:** Executive Temporary; **Industry Concentration:** Generalist with a primary focus in Financial Services, Healthcare/Hospitals, High Technology, Hospitality/Leisure, Manufacturing, Real Estate; **Function Concentration:** Administration, Finance/Accounting

**Papilsky, Alice** — *Vice President*
HRD Consultants, Inc.
60 Walnut Avenue
Clark, NJ 07066
Telephone: (908) 815-7825
**Recruiter Classification:** Retained; **Lowest/Average Salary:** $90,000/$90,000; **Industry Concentration:** Generalist; **Function Concentration:** Human Resources

**Pappalardo, Charles** — *Consultant*
Christian & Timbers
One Corporate Exchange
25825 Science Park Drive, Suite 400
Cleveland, OH 44122
Telephone: (216) 464-8710
**Recruiter Classification:** Retained; **Lowest/Average Salary:** $90,000/$90,000; **Industry Concentration:** Generalist; **Function Concentration:** Generalist

**Pappas, Jim** — *Manager*
Search Dynamics, Inc.
9420 West Foster Avenue, Suite 200
Chicago, IL 60656-1006
Telephone: (312) 992-3900
**Recruiter Classification:** Contingency; **Lowest/Average Salary:** $40,000/$50,000; **Industry Concentration:** Aerospace/Defense, Automotive, Chemical Products, Electronics, Energy, Environmental, Healthcare/Hospitals, High Technology, Information Technology, Manufacturing, Oil/Gas, Pharmaceutical/Medical, Transportation, Utilities/Nuclear; **Function Concentration:** Administration, Engineering, General Management, Marketing, Research and Development, Sales

**Pappas, Timothy C.** — *Vice President*
Jonas, Walters & Assoc., Inc.
1110 North Old World Third St., Suite 510
Milwaukee, WI 53203-1102
Telephone: (414) 291-2828
**Recruiter Classification:** Retained; **Lowest/Average Salary:** $60,000/$90,000; **Industry Concentration:** Generalist with a primary focus in Aerospace/Defense, Automotive, Chemical Products, Consumer Products, Electronics, Manufacturing; **Function Concentration:** Generalist with a primary focus in Administration, Engineering, Finance/Accounting, General Management, Human Resources, Marketing, Research and Development, Sales

**Paradise, Malcolm** — *Associate*
Source Services Corporation
71 Spit Brook Road, Suite 305
Nashua, NH 03060
Telephone: (603) 888-7650
**Recruiter Classification:** Contingency; **Lowest/Average Salary:** $30,000/$50,000; **Industry Concentration:** Financial Services, Information Technology; **Function Concentration:** Engineering, Finance/Accounting

**Parbs, Michael** — *Area Director*
Accountants on Call
8000 Towers Crescent Drive, Suite 240
Vienna, VA 22182
Telephone: (703) 448-7500
**Recruiter Classification:** Contingency; **Lowest/Average Salary:** $20,000/$30,000; **Industry Concentration:** Generalist; **Function Concentration:** Finance/Accounting

**Parbs, Michael** — *Area Director*
Accountants on Call
Telephone: (410) 685-5700
**Recruiter Classification:** Contingency; **Lowest/Average Salary:** $20,000/$30,000; **Industry Concentration:** Generalist; **Function Concentration:** Finance/Accounting

**Pardo, Maria Elena** — *Partner*
Smith Search, S.C.
Barranca del Muerto No. 472, Col. Alpes
Mexico City, D.F., MEXICO 01010
Telephone: (525) 593-8766
**Recruiter Classification:** Retained; **Lowest/Average Salary:** $50,000/$75,000; **Industry Concentration:** Generalist; **Function Concentration:** Generalist

**Parent, Martine L.** — *Consultant*
O'Callaghan Honey/Paul Ray Berndtson, Inc.
400-400 Fifth Avenue S.W.
Calgary, Alberta, CANADA T2P 0L6
Telephone: (403) 269-3277
**Recruiter Classification:** Retained; **Lowest/Average Salary:** $60,000/$75,000; **Industry Concentration:** Oil/Gas; **Function Concentration:** Engineering, Human Resources

**Parente, James** — *Associate*
Source Services Corporation
925 Westchester Avenue, Suite 309
White Plains, NY 10604
Telephone: (914) 428-9100
**Recruiter Classification:** Contingency; **Lowest/Average Salary:** $30,000/$50,000; **Industry Concentration:** Financial Services, Information Technology; **Function Concentration:** Engineering, Finance/Accounting

**Parfitt, William C.** — *President*
Parfitt Recruiting and Consulting/PRO TEM
1540 140th Avenue, N.E., Suite 201
Bellevue, WA 98005
Telephone: (206) 646-6300
**Recruiter Classification:** Executive Temporary; **Lowest/Average Salary:** $30,000/$60,000; **Industry Concentration:** Generalist; **Function Concentration:** Finance/Accounting, General Management, Human Resources, Marketing, Sales

**Parfitt, William C.** — *President*
Parfitt Recruiting and Consulting
1540 140th Avenue NE #201
Bellevue, WA 98005
Telephone: (206) 646-6300
**Recruiter Classification:** Contingency; **Lowest/Average Salary:** $30,000/$75,000; **Industry Concentration:** Generalist with a primary focus in Information Technology; **Function Concentration:** Generalist

**Paris, Stephen** — *Executive Recruiter*
Richard, Wayne and Roberts
24 Greenway Plaza, Suite 1304
Houston, TX 77046-2493
Telephone: (713) 629-6681
**Recruiter Classification:** Retained; **Lowest/Average Salary:** $40,000/$60,000; **Industry Concentration:** Generalist with a primary focus in Information Technology; **Function Concentration:** Generalist

**Park, Cleve A.** — *Manager South Atlantic Region*
Management Recruiters International, Inc.
200 Public Square, 31st Floor
Cleveland, OH 44114-2301
Telephone: (205) 404-0855
**Recruiter Classification:** Contingency; **Lowest/Average Salary:** $30,000/$75,000; **Industry Concentration:** Generalist; **Function Concentration:** Generalist

**Park, Dabney G.** — *Senior Partner*
Mark Stanley & Company
2121 Ponce de Leon Boulevard #630
P.O. Box 149071
Coral Gables, FL 33114
Telephone: (305) 444-1612
**Recruiter Classification:** Retained; **Lowest/Average Salary:** $75,000/$90,000; **Industry Concentration:** Generalist with a primary focus in Consumer Products, Environmental, Financial Services, Healthcare/Hospitals, High Technology, Pharmaceutical/Medical, Real Estate; **Function Concentration:** Generalist with a primary focus in Finance/Accounting, General Management, Human Resources, Sales

**Parker, David P.** — *President*
D.P. Parker and Associates
372 Washington Street
Wellesley, MA 02181
Telephone: (617) 237-1220
**Recruiter Classification:** Retained; **Lowest/Average Salary:** $75,000/$90,000; **Industry Concentration:** Generalist with a primary focus in Aerospace/Defense, Automotive, Biotechnology, Chemical Products; **Function Concentration:** Engineering, General Management, Marketing, Research and Development

**Parker, Murray B.** — *President*
The Borton Wallace Company
3083 Noble Court
Boulder, CO 80301
Telephone: (303) 546-6618
**Recruiter Classification:** Retained; **Lowest/Average Salary:** $50,000/$75,000; **Industry Concentration:** Chemical Products, Consumer Products, Manufacturing, Packaging; **Function Concentration:** Engineering, Research and Development

**Parker, P. Grant** — *Principal*
Raymond Karsan Associates
989 Old Eagle School Road, Suite 814
Wayne, PA 19087
Telephone: (610) 971-9171
**Recruiter Classification:** Contingency; **Lowest/Average Salary:**
$30,000/$90,000; **Industry Concentration:** Generalist with a primary focus in
Insurance; **Function Concentration:** Generalist

**Parker, Roberta** — *President*
R. Parker and Associates, Inc.
551 5th Avenue, Suite 222
New York, NY 10176
Telephone: (212) 661-8074
**Recruiter Classification:** Retained; **Lowest/Average Salary:** $50,000/$75,000;
**Industry Concentration:** Generalist with a primary focus in Consumer
Products, Fashion (Retail/Apparel); **Function Concentration:** Generalist with a
primary focus in General Management, Marketing, Sales

**Parker, Stephen B.** — *Managing Director*
Russell Reynolds Associates, Inc.
The Hurt Building
50 Hurt Plaza, Suite 600
Atlanta, GA 30303
Telephone: (404) 577-3000
**Recruiter Classification:** Retained; **Lowest/Average Salary:** $90,000/$90,000;
**Industry Concentration:** Generalist; **Function Concentration:** Generalist

**Parkin, Myrna** — *Recruiter*
S.D. Kelly & Associates, Inc.
990 Washington Street
Dedham, MA 02026
Telephone: (617) 326-8038
**Recruiter Classification:** Contingency; **Lowest/Average Salary:**
$60,000/$75,000; **Industry Concentration:** Electronics, High Technology;
**Function Concentration:** Engineering, General Management, Marketing, Sales

**Parr, James A.** — *Partner*
KPMG Management Consulting
2300 Yonge Street
Toronto, Ontario, CANADA M4P 1G2
Telephone: (416) 482-5786
**Recruiter Classification:** Executive Temporary; **Lowest/Average Salary:**
$75,000/$90,000; **Industry Concentration:** Generalist with a primary focus in
Automotive, Consumer Products, Electronics, High Technology, Information
Technology, Non-Profit, Packaging, Publishing/Media; **Function
Concentration:** Generalist with a primary focus in Administration, Engineering,
Finance/Accounting, General Management, Human Resources, Marketing,
Research and Development, Sales

**Parr, James A.** — *Partner-In-Charge, Executive Search*
KPMG Executive Search
P.O. Box 31, Stn. Commerce Court
Toronto, Ontario, CANADA M5L 1B2
Telephone: (416) 777-8500
**Recruiter Classification:** Retained; **Lowest/Average Salary:** $75,000/$90,000;
**Industry Concentration:** Generalist; **Function Concentration:** Generalist

**Parris, Ed** — *Manager North Atlantic Region*
Management Recruiters International, Inc.
113 Court Street
Pickens, SC 29671-2372
Telephone: (803) 878-1113
**Recruiter Classification:** Contingency; **Lowest/Average Salary:**
$30,000/$75,000; **Industry Concentration:** Generalist; **Function
Concentration:** Generalist

**Parroco, Jason** — *Associate*
Source Services Corporation
2850 National City Tower
Louisville, KY 40202
Telephone: (502) 581-9900
**Recruiter Classification:** Contingency; **Lowest/Average Salary:**
$30,000/$50,000; **Industry Concentration:** Financial Services, Information
Technology; **Function Concentration:** Engineering, Finance/Accounting

**Parry, Heather** — *Executive Recruiter*
Richard, Wayne and Roberts
24 Greenway Plaza, Suite 1304
Houston, TX 77046-2493
Telephone: (713) 629-6681
**Recruiter Classification:** Retained; **Lowest/Average Salary:** $40,000/$60,000;
**Industry Concentration:** Generalist with a primary focus in Information
Technology; **Function Concentration:** Generalist

**Parry, William H.** — *Vice President*
Horton International
24405 Chestnut Street, Suite 107
Santa Clarita, CA 91321
Telephone: (805) 222-2272
**Recruiter Classification:** Retained; **Lowest/Average Salary:** $90,000/$90,000;
**Industry Concentration:** Generalist with a primary focus in
Aerospace/Defense, Automotive, Chemical Products, Electronics, Financial
Services, Insurance, Manufacturing, Pharmaceutical/Medical; **Function
Concentration:** Generalist with a primary focus in General Management,
Human Resources, Marketing, Research and Development, Sales

**Pasahow, David** — *Managing Partner*
Heidrick & Struggles, Inc.
BCE Place, 161 Bay Street, Suite 2310
P.O. Box 601
Toronto, Ontario, CANADA M5J 2S1
Telephone: (416) 361-4700
**Recruiter Classification:** Retained; **Lowest/Average Salary:** $75,000/$90,000;
**Industry Concentration:** Generalist; **Function Concentration:** Generalist

**Pastrana, Dario** — *Managing Partner*
Egon Zehnder International Inc.
Paseo de las Palmas No. 405-703
Co. Lomas de Chapultepec
Mexico City, D.F., MEXICO 11000
Telephone: (525) 540-7635
**Recruiter Classification:** Retained; **Lowest/Average Salary:** $90,000/$90,000;
**Industry Concentration:** Generalist with a primary focus in Biotechnology,
Financial Services, High Technology, Manufacturing, Pharmaceutical/Medical;
**Function Concentration:** Generalist

**Patel, Shailesh** — *Associate*
Source Services Corporation
925 Westchester Avenue, Suite 309
White Plains, NY 10604
Telephone: (914) 428-9100
**Recruiter Classification:** Contingency; **Lowest/Average Salary:**
$30,000/$50,000; **Industry Concentration:** Financial Services, Information
Technology; **Function Concentration:** Engineering, Finance/Accounting

**Patence, David W.** — *Senior Vice President*
Handy HRM Corp.
250 Park Avenue
New York, NY 10177-0074
Telephone: (212) 557-0400
**Recruiter Classification:** Retained; **Lowest/Average Salary:** $90,000/$90,000;
**Industry Concentration:** Generalist with a primary focus in Consumer
Products, Financial Services, High Technology; **Function Concentration:**
Generalist with a primary focus in Administration, Finance/Accounting,
General Management, Human Resources, Marketing, Sales

**Paternie, Patrick** — *Associate*
Source Services Corporation
One Park Plaza, Suite 560
Irvine, CA 92714
Telephone: (714) 660-1666
**Recruiter Classification:** Contingency; **Lowest/Average Salary:**
$30,000/$50,000; **Industry Concentration:** Financial Services, Information
Technology; **Function Concentration:** Engineering, Finance/Accounting

**Patlovich, Michael J.** — *Shareholder*
Witt/Kieffer, Ford, Hadelman & Lloyd
25 Burlington Mall Road, 6th Floor
Burlington, MA 01803
Telephone: (617) 272-8899
**Recruiter Classification:** Retained; **Lowest/Average Salary:** $75,000/$90,000;
**Industry Concentration:** Healthcare/Hospitals; **Function Concentration:**
Generalist with a primary focus in General Management

**Patrick, Donald R.** — *Principal*
Sanford Rose Associates
3525 Holcomb Bridge Road
Suite 2B
Norcross, GA 30092
Telephone: (404) 449-7200
**Recruiter Classification:** Contingency; **Lowest/Average Salary:**
$30,000/$75,000; **Industry Concentration:** Generalist with a primary focus in
High Technology; **Function Concentration:** Generalist

**Patterson, Brenda** — *Manager Central Region*
Management Recruiters International, Inc.
3905 Vincennes Road, Suite 301
Indianapolis, IN 46268
Telephone: (317) 228-3300
**Recruiter Classification:** Contingency; **Lowest/Average Salary:**
$30,000/$75,000; **Industry Concentration:** Generalist; **Function
Concentration:** Generalist

**Patton, Claudette W.** — *Search Consultant*
H. Hertner Associates, Inc.
6600 Cowpen Road, Suite 220
Miami Lakes, FL 33014
Telephone: (305) 556-8882
**Recruiter Classification:** Contingency; **Lowest/Average Salary:**
$50,000/$75,000

**Patton, Mitchell** — *President*
Patton/Perry Associates, Inc.
112 South Tryon Street, Suite 500
Charlotte, NC 28202
Telephone: (704) 376-4292
**Recruiter Classification:** Retained; **Lowest/Average Salary:** $50,000/$90,000;
**Industry Concentration:** Generalist with a primary focus in Consumer
Products, Education/Libraries, Energy, Financial Services, Healthcare/Hospitals,
Information Technology, Insurance, Manufacturing, Non-Profit, Public
Administration, Publishing/Media, Transportation, Utilities/Nuclear, Venture
Capital; **Function Concentration:** Generalist with a primary focus in
Administration, Finance/Accounting, General Management, Human Resources,
Marketing, Sales

**Paul, Kathleen** — *Associate*
Source Services Corporation
One CityPlace, Suite 170
St. Louis, MO 63141
Telephone: (314) 432-4500
**Recruiter Classification:** Contingency; **Lowest/Average Salary:**
$30,000/$50,000; **Industry Concentration:** Financial Services, Information
Technology; **Function Concentration:** Engineering, Finance/Accounting

**Paul, Linda** — *Consultant*
Gilbert Tweed/INESA
155 Prospect Avenue
West Orange, NJ 07052
Telephone: (201) 731-3033
**Recruiter Classification:** Retained; **Lowest/Average Salary:** $90,000/$90,000;
**Industry Concentration:** Generalist; **Function Concentration:** Generalist

**Paul, Lisa D.** — *Resource Manager*
Merit Resource Group, Inc.
7950 Dublin Boulevard, Suite 205
Dublin, CA 94568
Telephone: (510) 828-4700
**Recruiter Classification:** Executive Temporary; **Lowest/Average Salary:**
$75,000/$90,000; **Industry Concentration:** Generalist with a primary focus in
Consumer Products, Electronics, Entertainment, Financial Services,
Manufacturing, Oil/Gas, Transportation, Venture Capital; **Function
Concentration:** Generalist with a primary focus in Human Resources

**Pawlik, Cynthia** — *Consultant*
Paul Ray Berndtson
10 South Riverside Plaza
Suite 720
Chicago, IL 60606
Telephone: (312) 876-0730
**Recruiter Classification:** Retained; **Lowest/Average Salary:** $90,000/$90,000;
**Industry Concentration:** Generalist; **Function Concentration:** Generalist

**Paxton, James W.** — *Principal*
Stanton Chase International
100 East Pratt Street
Suite 2530
Baltimore, MD 21202
Telephone: (410) 528-8400
**Recruiter Classification:** Retained; **Lowest/Average Salary:** $75,000/$90,000;
**Industry Concentration:** Generalist; **Function Concentration:** Generalist

**Payette, Pierre** — *Consultant*
Egon Zehnder International Inc.
1 Place Ville-Marie, Suite 3310
Montreal, Quebec, CANADA H3B 3N2
Telephone: (514) 876-4249
**Recruiter Classification:** Retained; **Lowest/Average Salary:** $90,000/$90,000;
**Industry Concentration:** Generalist with a primary focus in Biotechnology,
Financial Services, High Technology, Manufacturing, Pharmaceutical/Medical;
**Function Concentration:** Generalist

**Payne, Mary A.** — *Co-Manager Midwest Region*
Management Recruiters International, Inc.
1661 Florine Boulevard
St. Charles, MO 63303
Telephone: (314) 441-3235
**Recruiter Classification:** Contingency; **Lowest/Average Salary:**
$30,000/$75,000; **Industry Concentration:** Generalist; **Function
Concentration:** Generalist

**Payne, Robert** — *Accounting and Finance Recruiter*
Winter, Wyman & Company
950 Winter Street, Suite 3100
Waltham, MA 02154-1294
Telephone: (617) 890-7000
**Recruiter Classification:** Contingency; **Lowest/Average Salary:**
$20,000/$50,000; **Industry Concentration:** Generalist; **Function
Concentration:** Finance/Accounting

**Payne, Tom H.** — *Co-Manager*
Management Recruiters International, Inc.
1661 Florine Boulevard
St. Charles, MO 63303
Telephone: (314) 441-3235
**Recruiter Classification:** Contingency; **Lowest/Average Salary:**
$30,000/$75,000; **Industry Concentration:** Generalist; **Function
Concentration:** Generalist

**Paynter, Sandra L.** — *Partner*
Ward Howell International, Inc.
141 Adelaide Street West
Suite 1800
Toronto, Ontario, CANADA M5H 3L5
Telephone: (416) 862-1273
**Recruiter Classification:** Retained; **Lowest/Average Salary:** $75,000/$90,000;
**Industry Concentration:** Financial Services, Insurance, Manufacturing;
**Function Concentration:** Generalist

**Peal, Matthew** — *Associate*
Source Services Corporation
161 Ottawa NW, Suite 409D
Grand Rapids, MI 49503
Telephone: (616) 451-2400
**Recruiter Classification:** Contingency; **Lowest/Average Salary:**
$30,000/$50,000; **Industry Concentration:** Financial Services, Information
Technology; **Function Concentration:** Engineering, Finance/Accounting

**Pearcy, Marsha G.** — *Executive Director*
Russell Reynolds Associates, Inc.
1700 Pennsylvania Avenue N.W.
Suite 850
Washington, DC 20006
Telephone: (202) 628-2150
**Recruiter Classification:** Retained; **Lowest/Average Salary:** $90,000/$90,000;
**Industry Concentration:** Generalist; **Function Concentration:** Generalist

**Pearson, John R.** — *Partner*
Pearson, Caldwell & Farnsworth, Inc.
One California Street, Suite 1950
San Francisco, CA 94111
Telephone: (415) 982-0300
**Recruiter Classification:** Retained; **Lowest/Average Salary:** $90,000/$90,000;
**Industry Concentration:** Financial Services; **Function Concentration:**
Administration, Finance/Accounting, General Management, Human Resources,
Marketing, Sales

**Pearson, Robert L.** — *President and CEO*
Lamalie Amrop International
225 West Wacker Drive
Chicago, IL 60606-1229
Telephone: (312) 782-3113
**Recruiter Classification:** Retained; **Lowest/Average Salary:** $90,000/$90,000;
**Industry Concentration:** Generalist with a primary focus in Board Services,
Consumer Products, High Technology; **Function Concentration:** Generalist
with a primary focus in Finance/Accounting, General Management, Human
Resources, Marketing, Sales

**Peasback, David R.** — *Vice Chairman and CEO*
Canny, Bowen Inc.
200 Park Avenue
New York, NY 10166
Telephone: (212) 949-6611
**Recruiter Classification:** Retained; **Lowest/Average Salary:** $90,000/$90,000;
**Industry Concentration:** Generalist; **Function Concentration:** Generalist with a
primary focus in Engineering, Finance/Accounting, General Management,
Human Resources, Women/Minorities

**Pease, Edward** — *President/Co-Owner*
Don Richard Associates of Georgia, Inc.
3475 Lenox Road, Suite 210
Atlanta, GA 30326
Telephone: (404) 231-3688
**Recruiter Classification:** Executive Temporary; **Lowest/Average Salary:**
$/$75,000; **Industry Concentration:** Financial Services; **Function
Concentration:** Finance/Accounting, Human Resources

**Pease, Samuel C.** — *Partner*
Heidrick & Struggles, Inc.
One Post Office Square
Boston, MA 02109-0199
Telephone: (617) 423-1140
**Recruiter Classification:** Retained; **Lowest/Average Salary:** $75,000/$90,000;
**Industry Concentration:** Generalist with a primary focus in Consumer
Products; **Function Concentration:** Generalist

**Peck, David W.** — *Principal*
The Peck Consultancy
17 West 54th Street
New York, NY 10019
Telephone: (212) 757-2688
**Recruiter Classification:** Retained; **Lowest/Average Salary:** $75,000/$90,000;
**Industry Concentration:** Biotechnology, Board Services, Consumer Products,
Education/Libraries, Environmental, Non-Profit, Pharmaceutical/Medical;
**Function Concentration:** Generalist

**Peckenpaugh, Ann D.** — *Vice President*
Schweichler Associates, Inc.
200 Tamal Vista, Building 200, Suite 100
Corte Madera, CA 94925
Telephone: (415) 924-7200
**Recruiter Classification:** Retained; **Lowest/Average Salary:** $90,000/$90,000;
**Industry Concentration:** Electronics, High Technology, Information
Technology; **Function Concentration:** Engineering, Finance/Accounting,
General Management, Marketing, Research and Development, Sales,
Women/Minorities

**Pecot, Jack L.** — *Manager Southwest Region*
Management Recruiters International, Inc.
106 Village Square, Suite 2
Slidell, LA 70458
Telephone: (504) 847-1900
**Recruiter Classification:** Contingency; **Lowest/Average Salary:**
$30,000/$75,000; **Industry Concentration:** Generalist; **Function
Concentration:** Generalist

**Pederson, Terre** — *Executive Recruiter*
Richard, Wayne and Roberts
24 Greenway Plaza, Suite 1304
Houston, TX 77046-2493
Telephone: (713) 629-6681
**Recruiter Classification:** Retained; **Lowest/Average Salary:** $50,000/$90,000;
**Industry Concentration:** Generalist with a primary focus in Information
Technology; **Function Concentration:** Generalist

**Pedley, Jill** — *Executive Recruiter*
CPS Inc.
One Westbrook Corporate Centre, Suite 600
Westchester, IL 60154
Telephone: (708) 531-8370
**Recruiter Classification:** Contingency; **Lowest/Average Salary:**
$30,000/$50,000; **Industry Concentration:** Generalist with a primary focus in
Automotive, Biotechnology, Chemical Products, Consumer Products, High
Technology, Insurance, Manufacturing, Oil/Gas, Packaging,
Pharmaceutical/Medical; **Function Concentration:** Engineering, Research and
Development, Sales, Women/Minorities

**Peeney, James D.** — *President*
Peeney Associates
141 South Avenue
Fanwood, NJ 07023
Telephone: (908) 322-2324
**Recruiter Classification:** Retained; **Lowest/Average Salary:** $60,000/$90,000;
**Industry Concentration:** Generalist with a primary focus in Automotive,
Electronics, Financial Services, Healthcare/Hospitals, Manufacturing, Non-
Profit, Pharmaceutical/Medical; **Function Concentration:** Generalist with a
primary focus in Administration, Engineering, Finance/Accounting, General
Management, Human Resources, Marketing, Research and Development,
Sales, Women/Minorities

**Pelisson, Charles** — *Vice President*
Marra Peters & Partners
Millburn Esplanade
Millburn, NJ 07041
Telephone: (201) 376-8999
**Recruiter Classification:** Retained; **Lowest/Average Salary:** $/$90,000; **Industry
Concentration:** Generalist with a primary focus in Biotechnology, Consumer
Products, Entertainment, Financial Services, Information Technology,
Manufacturing, Pharmaceutical/Medical; **Function Concentration:** Generalist
with a primary focus in Administration, Engineering, Finance/Accounting,
General Management, Human Resources, Marketing, Research and
Development, Sales

**Pelkey, Chris** — *Consultant*
The McCormick Group, Inc.
1400 Wilson Boulevard
Arlington, VA 22209
Telephone: (703) 841-1700
**Recruiter Classification:** Retained; **Lowest/Average Salary:** $40,000/$60,000;
**Industry Concentration:** High Technology, Information Technology; **Function
Concentration:** Engineering, Marketing, Sales

**Pelletier, Jacques F.** — *President*
Roth Young Personnel Service of Boston, Inc.
200 Boston Avenue, Suite 2300
Medford, MA 02155
Telephone: (617) 395-3600
**Recruiter Classification:** Contingency; **Lowest/Average Salary:**
$40,000/$75,000; **Industry Concentration:** Hospitality/Leisure; **Function
Concentration:** Finance/Accounting, General Management, Human Resources,
Marketing, Sales

**Pelton, Margaret** — *Director*
Price Waterhouse
1 First Canadian Place, Box 190, Suite 3300
Toronto, Ontario, CANADA M5X 1H7
Telephone: (416) 863-1133
**Recruiter Classification:** Retained; **Lowest/Average Salary:** $75,000/$75,000;
**Industry Concentration:** Healthcare/Hospitals; **Function Concentration:**
Generalist with a primary focus in Women/Minorities

**Penfield, G. Jeff** — *Co-Manager*
Management Recruiters International, Inc.
Canyon Lake Plaza, Suite 14
2374 Connie Drive
Canyon Lake, TX 78133
Telephone: (210) 964-4071
**Recruiter Classification:** Contingency; **Lowest/Average Salary:**
$30,000/$75,000; **Industry Concentration:** Generalist; **Function
Concentration:** Generalist

**Penfield, Marian** — *Co-Manager Southwest Region*
Management Recruiters International, Inc.
Canyon Lake Plaza, Suite 14
2374 Connie Drive
Canyon Lake, TX 78133
Telephone: (210) 964-4071
**Recruiter Classification:** Contingency; **Lowest/Average Salary:**
$30,000/$75,000; **Industry Concentration:** Generalist; **Function
Concentration:** Generalist

**Peniche, Pedro** — *Associate*
Amrop International
Amberes #4, 2 Pia, Colonia Juarez
Mexico City, D.F., MEXICO 06600
Telephone: (525) 208-3977
**Recruiter Classification:** Retained; **Lowest/Average Salary:** $75,000/$90,000;
**Industry Concentration:** Generalist; **Function Concentration:** Generalist

**Pepe, Leonida** — *Principal*
Butterfass, Pepe & MacCallan Inc.
P.O. Box 721
Mahwah, NJ 07430
Telephone: (201) 512-3330
**Recruiter Classification:** Retained; **Lowest/Average Salary:** $60,000/$75,000;
**Industry Concentration:** Generalist with a primary focus in Financial Services,
Insurance, Real Estate, Venture Capital; **Function Concentration:** Generalist
with a primary focus in Finance/Accounting, Human Resources, Marketing,
Women/Minorities

**Percifield, J. Michael** — *Manager Central Region*
Management Recruiters International, Inc.
1405 Jackson Street, Suite A, P.O. Box 2234
Columbus, IN 47201
Telephone: (812) 372-5500
**Recruiter Classification:** Contingency; **Lowest/Average Salary:**
$30,000/$75,000; **Industry Concentration:** Generalist; **Function
Concentration:** Generalist

**Percival, Chris** — *Senior Legal Search Consultant*
Chicago Legal Search, Ltd.
33 North Dearborn Street, Suite 2302
Chicago, IL 60602-3109
Telephone: (312) 251-2580
**Recruiter Classification:** Contingency; **Lowest/Average Salary:**
$40,000/$90,000; **Industry Concentration:** Consumer Products, Electronics,
Energy, Entertainment, Environmental, Healthcare/Hospitals, High Technology,
Information Technology, Non-Profit, Oil/Gas, Pharmaceutical/Medical, Venture
Capital; **Function Concentration:** Women/Minorities

**Peretz, Jamie** — *Principal*
Nordeman Grimm, Inc.
717 Fifth Avenue, 26th Floor
New York, NY 10022
Telephone: (212) 935-1000
**Recruiter Classification:** Retained; **Lowest/Average Salary:** $90,000/$90,000;
**Industry Concentration:** Generalist; **Function Concentration:** Generalist

**Perez, Christina** — *Director Hispanic Division*
Orr Executive Search
5125 North 16th Street, Suite B-223
Phoenix, AZ 85016
Telephone: (602) 274-2170
**Recruiter Classification:** Contingency; **Lowest/Average Salary:**
$40,000/$60,000; **Industry Concentration:** Generalist with a primary focus in
Consumer Products, Entertainment, Healthcare/Hospitals, Hospitality/Leisure;
**Function Concentration:** Generalist with a primary focus in General
Management, Marketing, Research and Development, Sales,
Women/Minorities

**Perkey, Richard** — *Vice President*
Korn/Ferry International
303 Peachtree Street N.E.
Suite 1600
Atlanta, GA 30308
Telephone: (404) 577-7542
**Recruiter Classification:** Retained; **Lowest/Average Salary:** $90,000/$90,000;
**Industry Concentration:** Generalist with a primary focus in Financial Services;
**Function Concentration:** Generalist

**Perkins, Bob** — *Executive Recruiter*
Richard, Wayne and Roberts
24 Greenway Plaza, Suite 1304
Houston, TX 77046-2493
Telephone: (713) 629-6681
**Recruiter Classification:** Retained; **Lowest/Average Salary:** $40,000/$60,000;
**Industry Concentration:** Generalist with a primary focus in Chemical Products,
Environmental, Oil/Gas; **Function Concentration:** Generalist with a primary
focus in Engineering

**Perkins, Daphne** — *Executive Recruiter*
CPS Inc.
One Westbrook Corporate Centre, Suite 600
Westchester, IL 60154
Telephone: (708) 531-8370
**Recruiter Classification:** Contingency; **Lowest/Average Salary:**
$30,000/$50,000; **Industry Concentration:** Generalist with a primary focus in
Automotive, Biotechnology, Chemical Products, Consumer Products, High
Technology, Insurance, Manufacturing, Oil/Gas, Packaging,
Pharmaceutical/Medical; **Function Concentration:** Engineering, Research and
Development, Sales, Women/Minorities

**Perlman, Tali** — *Consultant*
Coleman Legal Search Consultants
1435 Walnut Street, 3rd Floor
Philadelphia, PA 19102
Telephone: (215) 864-2700
**Recruiter Classification:** Contingency; **Lowest/Average Salary:**
$60,000/$75,000; **Function Concentration:** Generalist

**Perron, Daniel** — *Branch Manager*
Accountants on Call
One Alhambra Plaza, Suite 1435
Coral Gables, FL 33134
Telephone: (305) 443-9333
**Recruiter Classification:** Contingency; **Lowest/Average Salary:**
$20,000/$30,000; **Industry Concentration:** Generalist; **Function
Concentration:** Finance/Accounting

**Perry, Carolyn** — *Associate*
Source Services Corporation
1 Gatehall Drive, Suite 250
Parsippany, NJ 07054
Telephone: (201) 267-3222
**Recruiter Classification:** Contingency; **Lowest/Average Salary:**
$30,000/$50,000; **Industry Concentration:** Financial Services, Information
Technology; **Function Concentration:** Engineering, Finance/Accounting

**Perry, Darrell L.** — *Manager North Atlantic Region*
Management Recruiters International, Inc.
P.O. Box 8
Louisburg, NC 27549-0008
Telephone: (919) 496-2153
**Recruiter Classification:** Contingency; **Lowest/Average Salary:**
$30,000/$75,000; **Industry Concentration:** Generalist; **Function
Concentration:** Generalist

**Perry, Richard** — *Vice President/Consultant*
McManners Associates, Inc.
400 East 54th Street, 16th Floor
New York, NY 10022
Telephone: (212) 980-7140
**Recruiter Classification:** Retained; **Lowest/Average Salary:** $90,000/$90,000;
**Industry Concentration:** Generalist with a primary focus in Manufacturing;
**Function Concentration:** Generalist

**Perry, Robert H.** — *President*
R.H. Perry & Associates, Inc.
2607 31st Street N.W.
Washington, DC 20008
Telephone: (202) 965-6464
**Recruiter Classification:** Retained; **Lowest/Average Salary:** $60,000/$75,000;
**Industry Concentration:** Generalist; **Function Concentration:** Generalist

**Perry, Wayne B.** — *Partner*
Bruce Massey & Partners Inc.
330 Bay Street, Suite 1104
Toronto, Ontario, CANADA M5H 2S8
Telephone: (416) 861-0077
**Recruiter Classification:** Retained; **Lowest/Average Salary:** $90,000/$90,000;
**Industry Concentration:** Generalist; **Function Concentration:** Generalist with a
primary focus in Administration, Engineering, Finance/Accounting, General
Management, Human Resources, Marketing, Research and Development

**Perryman, Ben** — *Consultant*
Paul Ray Berndtson
301 Commerce Street, Suite 2300
Fort Worth, TX 76102
Telephone: (817) 334-0500
**Recruiter Classification:** Retained; **Lowest/Average Salary:** $90,000/$90,000;
**Industry Concentration:** Generalist; **Function Concentration:** Generalist

**Persico, Victor J.** — *Manager Midwest Region*
Management Recruiters International, Inc.
College Drive Office Center
7804 West College Drive
Palos Heights, IL 60463
Telephone: (708) 361-8778
**Recruiter Classification:** Contingency; **Lowest/Average Salary:**
$30,000/$75,000; **Industry Concentration:** Generalist; **Function
Concentration:** Generalist

**Persinger, Andrea J.** — *Consultant*
John Michael Associates
102 Elden Street, Suite 12
Herndon, VA 22070-4809
Telephone: (703) 471-6300
**Recruiter Classification:** Contingency; **Lowest/Average Salary:**
$75,000/$90,000

**Persky, Barry** — *President*
Barry Persky & Company, Inc.
P.O. Box 1286
Weston, CT 06883-0286
Telephone: (203) 454-4500
**Recruiter Classification:** Retained; **Lowest/Average Salary:** $60,000/$90,000;
**Industry Concentration:** Generalist with a primary focus in Consumer
Products, Electronics, Energy, Environmental, Fashion (Retail/Apparel),
Healthcare/Hospitals, High Technology, Information Technology,
Manufacturing, Non-Profit, Pharmaceutical/Medical, Publishing/Media,
Transportation, Utilities/Nuclear; **Function Concentration:** Generalist with a
primary focus in Administration, Engineering, Finance/Accounting, General
Management, Human Resources, Marketing, Research and Development, Sales

**Pessin, Mark** — *Consultant*
Evie Kreisler & Associates, Inc.
2720 Stemmons Freeway, Suite 812
Dallas, TX 75207
Telephone: (214) 631-8994
**Recruiter Classification:** Contingency; **Lowest/Average Salary:**
$30,000/$75,000; **Industry Concentration:** Fashion (Retail/Apparel); **Function
Concentration:** Generalist

**Peternell, Melanie** — *Division Supervisor*
Signature Staffing
6800 College Boulevard, Suite 550
Overland Park, KS 66211
Telephone: (913) 338-2020
**Recruiter Classification:** Executive Temporary; **Lowest/Average Salary:**
$30,000/$40,000; **Industry Concentration:** Generalist with a primary focus in
Electronics, Financial Services, Healthcare/Hospitals, Insurance, Public
Administration, Publishing/Media, Transportation; **Function Concentration:**
Generalist with a primary focus in Finance/Accounting, Marketing

**Peternich, Tracy** — *Vice President*
Simpson Associates
Trump Parc
106 Central Park South
New York, NY 10019
Telephone: (212) 767-0006
**Recruiter Classification:** Contingency; **Lowest/Average Salary:**
$60,000/$90,000; **Industry Concentration:** Fashion (Retail/Apparel); **Function Concentration:** General Management, Human Resources, Marketing, Women/Minorities

**Peters, James N.** — *Vice President*
TNS Partners, Inc.
12655 North Central Expressway
Suite 900
Dallas, TX 75243
Telephone: (214) 991-3555
**Recruiter Classification:** Retained; **Lowest/Average Salary:** $75,000/$90,000;
**Industry Concentration:** Generalist with a primary focus in
Aerospace/Defense, Chemical Products, Consumer Products, Electronics,
Environmental, Fashion (Retail/Apparel), Financial Services, High Technology,
Information Technology, Manufacturing, Packaging, Transportation, Venture
Capital; **Function Concentration:** Generalist with a primary focus in
Administration, Engineering, Finance/Accounting, General Management,
Human Resources, Marketing, Sales

**Peters, Kevin** — *Associate*
Source Services Corporation
879 West 190th Street, Suite 250
Los Angeles, CA 90248
Telephone: (310) 323-6633
**Recruiter Classification:** Contingency; **Lowest/Average Salary:**
$30,000/$50,000; **Industry Concentration:** Financial Services, Information
Technology; **Function Concentration:** Engineering, Finance/Accounting

**Peters, Todd** — *Recruiter*
Morgan Hunter Corp.
6800 College Boulevard, Suite 550
Overland Park, KS 66211
Telephone: (913) 491-3434
**Recruiter Classification:** Contingency; **Lowest/Average Salary:**
$20,000/$40,000; **Industry Concentration:** Generalist; **Function Concentration:** Finance/Accounting

**Petersen, Richard** — *Associate*
Source Services Corporation
5343 North 16th Street, Suite 270
Phoenix, AZ 85016
Telephone: (602) 230-0220
**Recruiter Classification:** Contingency; **Lowest/Average Salary:**
$30,000/$50,000; **Industry Concentration:** Financial Services, Information
Technology; **Function Concentration:** Engineering, Finance/Accounting

**Peterson, Bruce** — *Principal*
Korn/Ferry International
1100 Louisiana, Suite 3400
Houston, TX 77002
Telephone: (713) 651-1834
**Recruiter Classification:** Retained; **Lowest/Average Salary:** $90,000/$90,000;
**Industry Concentration:** Generalist; **Function Concentration:** Generalist

**Peterson, Dave A.** — *Co-Manager South Atlantic Region*
Management Recruiters International, Inc.
505 Beachland Boulevard, Suite 1256
Vero Beach, FL 32963
Telephone: (407) 234-8686
**Recruiter Classification:** Contingency; **Lowest/Average Salary:**
$30,000/$75,000; **Industry Concentration:** Generalist; **Function Concentration:** Generalist

**Peterson, Diana K.** — *Co-Manager*
Management Recruiters International, Inc.
505 Beachland Boulevard, Suite 1256
Vero Beach, FL 32963
Telephone: (407) 234-8686
**Recruiter Classification:** Contingency; **Lowest/Average Salary:**
$30,000/$75,000; **Industry Concentration:** Generalist; **Function Concentration:** Generalist

**Peterson, John** — *Executive Recruiter*
CPS Inc.
One Westbrook Corporate Centre, Suite 600
Westchester, IL 60154
Telephone: (708) 531-8370
**Recruiter Classification:** Contingency; **Lowest/Average Salary:**
$30,000/$50,000; **Industry Concentration:** Generalist with a primary focus in
Automotive, Biotechnology, Chemical Products, Consumer Products, High
Technology, Insurance, Manufacturing, Oil/Gas, Packaging,
Pharmaceutical/Medical; **Function Concentration:** Engineering, Research and
Development, Sales, Women/Minorities

**Peterson, John A.** — *Co-Manager Central Region*
Management Recruiters International, Inc.
2491 Cedar Park Drive
Holt, MI 48842-2184
Telephone: (517) 694-1153
**Recruiter Classification:** Contingency; **Lowest/Average Salary:**
$30,000/$75,000; **Industry Concentration:** Generalist; **Function Concentration:** Generalist

**Peterson, Priscilla J.** — *Co-Manager*
Management Recruiters International, Inc.
2491 Cedar Park Drive
Holt, MI 48842-2184
Telephone: (517) 694-1153
**Recruiter Classification:** Contingency; **Lowest/Average Salary:**
$30,000/$75,000; **Industry Concentration:** Generalist; **Function Concentration:** Generalist

**Petrides, Andrew S.** — *Director Manufacturing Search Services*
ARJay & Associates
875 Walnut Street, Suite 150
Cary, NC 27511
Telephone: (919) 469-5540
**Recruiter Classification:** Contingency; **Lowest/Average Salary:**
$40,000/$90,000; **Industry Concentration:** Generalist with a primary focus in
Manufacturing; **Function Concentration:** Generalist with a primary focus in
Engineering, General Management

**Pettersson, Tara L.** — *Partner*
Lamalie Amrop International
Chevron Tower
1301 McKinney Street
Houston, TX 77010-3034
Telephone: (713) 739-8602
**Recruiter Classification:** Retained; **Lowest/Average Salary:** $90,000/$90,000;
**Industry Concentration:** Generalist; **Function Concentration:** Generalist with a
primary focus in General Management, Human Resources, Marketing, Sales

**Pettibone, Linda** — *Vice President*
Herbert Mines Associates, Inc.
399 Park Avenue, 27th Floor
New York, NY 10022
Telephone: (212) 355-0909
**Recruiter Classification:** Retained; **Lowest/Average Salary:** $75,000/$90,000;
**Industry Concentration:** Board Services, Consumer Products, Fashion
(Retail/Apparel); **Function Concentration:** Generalist with a primary focus in
Finance/Accounting, General Management, Human Resources, Marketing,
Sales

**Pettway, Samuel H.** — *Director*
Spencer Stuart
One Atlantic Center, Suite 3230
1201 West Peachtree Street
Atlanta, GA 30309
Telephone: (404) 892-2800
**Recruiter Classification:** Retained; **Lowest/Average Salary:** $90,000/$90,000;
**Industry Concentration:** Board Services, Consumer Products, Fashion
(Retail/Apparel), Financial Services, Hospitality/Leisure, Non-Profit, Venture
Capital; **Function Concentration:** Administration, Finance/Accounting, General
Management, Human Resources, Marketing, Sales, Women/Minorities

**Petty, J. Scott** — *Associate*
The Arcus Group
15915 Katy Freeway, Suite 635
Houston, TX 77094
Telephone: (713) 578-3100
**Recruiter Classification:** Retained; **Lowest/Average Salary:** $90,000/$90,000;
**Industry Concentration:** Generalist with a primary focus in Biotechnology,
Chemical Products, Consumer Products, Financial Services, High Technology,
Information Technology, Manufacturing; **Function Concentration:** Generalist
with a primary focus in Engineering, Finance/Accounting, Human Resources,
Marketing

**Peyton, Leslie** — *Vice President*
Korn/Ferry International
237 Park Avenue
New York, NY 10017
Telephone: (212) 687-1834
**Recruiter Classification:** Retained; **Lowest/Average Salary:** $90,000/$90,000;
**Industry Concentration:** Generalist; **Function Concentration:** Generalist

**Pfannkuche, Anthony V.** — *Senior Director*
Spencer Stuart
10900 Wilshire Boulevard, Suite 800
Los Angeles, CA 90024-6524
Telephone: (310) 209-0610
**Recruiter Classification:** Retained; **Lowest/Average Salary:** $40,000/$60,000;
**Industry Concentration:** Healthcare/Hospitals, Information Technology,
Venture Capital; **Function Concentration:** Generalist with a primary focus in
Finance/Accounting, General Management

**Pfau, Madelaine** — *Partner*
Heidrick & Struggles, Inc.
2200 Ross Avenue, Suite 4700E
Dallas, TX 75201-2787
Telephone: (214) 220-2130
**Recruiter Classification:** Retained; **Lowest/Average Salary:** $75,000/$90,000;
**Industry Concentration:** Generalist with a primary focus in Financial Services,
High Technology; **Function Concentration:** Generalist

**Pfeiffer, Irene** — *Director*
Price Waterhouse
Esso Plaza - East Tower
1200 425 First Street S.W.
Calgary, Alberta, CANADA T2P 3V7
Telephone: (403) 267-1200
**Recruiter Classification:** Retained; **Lowest/Average Salary:** $75,000/$75,000;
**Industry Concentration:** Generalist with a primary focus in Board Services,
Chemical Products, Energy, Financial Services, Healthcare/Hospitals, High
Technology, Manufacturing, Oil/Gas; **Function Concentration:** Generalist with
a primary focus in Administration, Engineering, Finance/Accounting, General
Management, Human Resources, Marketing, Sales

**Pfeiffer, Leonard** — *Vice President*
Korn/Ferry International
Presidential Plaza
900 19th Street, N.W.
Washington, DC 20006
Telephone: (202) 822-9444
**Recruiter Classification:** Retained; **Lowest/Average Salary:** $90,000/$90,000;
**Industry Concentration:** Generalist; **Function Concentration:** Generalist

**Pfister, Shelli** — *Manager Temporary Personnel Division*
Jack B. Larsen & Associates
334 West Eighth Street
Erie, PA 16502
Telephone: (814) 459-3725
**Recruiter Classification:** Executive Temporary; **Lowest/Average Salary:**
$30,000/$50,000; **Industry Concentration:** Generalist with a primary focus in
Automotive, Electronics, High Technology; **Function Concentration:** Generalist
with a primary focus in Engineering, Finance/Accounting, General
Management, Human Resources, Sales

**Phelps, Gene L.** — *Partner*
McCormack & Farrow
695 Town Center Drive
Suite 660
Costa Mesa, CA 92626
Telephone: (714) 549-7222
**Recruiter Classification:** Retained; **Lowest/Average Salary:** $90,000/$90,000;
**Industry Concentration:** Generalist with a primary focus in Automotive, Board
Services, Consumer Products, Electronics, Entertainment, Hospitality/Leisure,
Manufacturing, Non-Profit, Transportation, Venture Capital; **Function
Concentration:** Generalist with a primary focus in General Management,
Human Resources, Marketing, Sales, Women/Minorities

**Philips, Ann** — *Manager North Atlantic Region*
Management Recruiters International, Inc.
5102 Chapel Hill-Durham Boulevard, Suite 112
Durham, NC 27707
Telephone: (919) 489-6521
**Recruiter Classification:** Contingency; **Lowest/Average Salary:**
$30,000/$75,000; **Industry Concentration:** Generalist; **Function
Concentration:** Generalist

**Phillips, Anna W.** — *Shareholder*
Witt/Kieffer, Ford, Hadelman & Lloyd
4550 Montgomery Avenue
Bethesda, MD 20814
Telephone: (301) 654-5070
**Recruiter Classification:** Retained; **Lowest/Average Salary:** $75,000/$90,000;
**Industry Concentration:** Healthcare/Hospitals; **Function Concentration:**
Generalist with a primary focus in General Management

**Phillips, Bill** — *Executive Recruiter*
Dunhill Search International
59 Elm Street
New Haven, CT 06510
Telephone: (203) 562-0511
**Recruiter Classification:** Contingency; **Lowest/Average Salary:**
$30,000/$60,000; **Industry Concentration:** Chemical Products, High
Technology, Information Technology, Manufacturing; **Function Concentration:**
Engineering

**Phillips, Donald** — *Manager*
Accountants on Call
2699 Lee Road, Suite 525
Winter Park, FL 32789
Telephone: (407) 629-2999
**Recruiter Classification:** Contingency; **Lowest/Average Salary:**
$20,000/$30,000; **Industry Concentration:** Generalist; **Function
Concentration:** Finance/Accounting

**Phillips, Donald L.** — *Principal*
O'Shea, Divine & Company, Inc.
610 Newport Center Drive, Suite 1040
Newport Beach, CA 92660
Telephone: (714) 720-9070
**Recruiter Classification:** Retained; **Lowest/Average Salary:** $75,000/$90,000;
**Industry Concentration:** Generalist with a primary focus in Automotive, Board
Services, Consumer Products, Education/Libraries, Entertainment,
Environmental, Financial Services, High Technology, Hospitality/Leisure,
Manufacturing, Oil/Gas, Real Estate, Transportation, Utilities/Nuclear; **Function
Concentration:** Generalist with a primary focus in Administration, Engineering,
Finance/Accounting, General Management, Human Resources, Marketing,
Sales, Women/Minorities

**Phillips, James L.** — *Partner*
Highland Search Group, L.L.C.
565 Fifth Avenue, 22nd Floor
New York, NY 10017
Telephone: (212) 328-1113
**Recruiter Classification:** Retained; **Lowest/Average Salary:** $90,000/$90,000;
**Industry Concentration:** Financial Services, Insurance, Real Estate, Venture
Capital; **Function Concentration:** Generalist with a primary focus in
Finance/Accounting, General Management, Human Resources, Sales

**Phillips, Richard K.** — *Executive Vice President*
Handy HRM Corp.
250 Park Avenue
New York, NY 10177-0074
Telephone: (212) 557-0400
**Recruiter Classification:** Retained; **Lowest/Average Salary:** $90,000/$90,000;
**Industry Concentration:** Generalist with a primary focus in Financial Services,
Venture Capital; **Function Concentration:** Finance/Accounting, General
Management, Research and Development

**Phillips, Scott K.** — *Managing Director*
Phillips & Ford, Inc.
485 Devon Park Drive, Suite 110
Wayne, PA 19087
Telephone: (610) 975-9007
**Recruiter Classification:** Retained; **Lowest/Average Salary:** $90,000/$90,000;
**Industry Concentration:** Biotechnology, Healthcare/Hospitals, High
Technology, Information Technology, Insurance, Pharmaceutical/Medical,
Venture Capital; **Function Concentration:** Finance/Accounting, General
Management, Human Resources, Marketing

**Phillips, Whitney** — *Senior Associate*
Korn/Ferry International
1800 Century Park East, Suite 900
Los Angeles, CA 90067
Telephone: (310) 552-1834
**Recruiter Classification:** Retained; **Lowest/Average Salary:** $90,000/$90,000;
**Industry Concentration:** Generalist; **Function Concentration:** Generalist

**Pickens, Barbara** — *Managing Director*
Johnson Smith & Knisely Accord
100 Park Avenue, 15th Floor
New York, NY 10017
Telephone: (212) 885-9100
**Recruiter Classification:** Retained; **Lowest/Average Salary:** $90,000/$90,000;
**Industry Concentration:** Consumer Products; **Function Concentration:** General
Management, Human Resources, Marketing, Sales

**Pickering, Dale** — *President*
Agri-Tech Personnel, Inc.
3113 Northeast 69th Street
Kansas City, MO 64119
Telephone: (816) 453-7200
**Recruiter Classification:** Contingency; **Lowest/Average Salary:**
$30,000/$75,000; **Industry Concentration:** Biotechnology, Chemical Products,
Consumer Products, Environmental, Manufacturing, Packaging,
Pharmaceutical/Medical, Transportation; **Function Concentration:**
Administration, Engineering, Finance/Accounting, General Management,
Human Resources, Marketing, Research and Development, Sales

**Pickering, Dorothy C.** — *Vice President*
Livingston, Robert and Company Inc.
Two Greenwich Plaza
Greenwich, CT 06830
Telephone: (203) 622-4902
**Recruiter Classification:** Retained; **Lowest/Average Salary:** $90,000/$90,000;
**Industry Concentration:** Generalist with a primary focus in Consumer
Products, Entertainment, Fashion (Retail/Apparel), Financial Services,
Publishing/Media; **Function Concentration:** Generalist

**Pickford, Stephen T.** — *President*
The Corporate Staff, Inc.
177 Bovet Road, Suite 600
San Mateo, CA 94402
Telephone: (415) 344-2613
**Recruiter Classification:** Executive Temporary; **Lowest/Average Salary:**
$40,000/$75,000; **Industry Concentration:** Generalist with a primary focus in
Consumer Products, Financial Services, Healthcare/Hospitals, High
Technology, Information Technology, Insurance, Non-Profit,
Pharmaceutical/Medical; **Function Concentration:** Generalist with a primary
focus in Administration, Finance/Accounting, General Management, Human
Resources, Marketing, Sales

**Pieh, Jerry** — *Senior Recruiter*
Isaacson, Miller
334 Boylston Street, Suite 500
Boston, MA 02111
Telephone: (617) 262-6500
**Recruiter Classification:** Retained; **Lowest/Average Salary:** $75,000/$90,000;
**Industry Concentration:** Generalist; **Function Concentration:** Generalist

**Pierce, Matthew** — *Associate*
Source Services Corporation
One Park Plaza, Suite 560
Irvine, CA 92714
Telephone: (714) 660-1666
**Recruiter Classification:** Contingency; **Lowest/Average Salary:**
$30,000/$50,000; **Industry Concentration:** Financial Services, Information
Technology; **Function Concentration:** Engineering, Finance/Accounting

**Pierce, Nicholas J.** — *Partner*
Paul Ray Berndtson
191 Peachtree Tower, Suite 3800
191 Peachtree Street, NE
Atlanta, GA 30303-1757
Telephone: (404) 215-4600
**Recruiter Classification:** Retained; **Lowest/Average Salary:** $90,000/$90,000;
**Industry Concentration:** Consumer Products, Manufacturing; **Function
Concentration:** Generalist

**Pierce, Richard** — *Managing Director*
Russell Reynolds Associates, Inc.
200 South Wacker Drive
Suite 3600
Chicago, IL 60606
Telephone: (312) 993-9696
**Recruiter Classification:** Retained; **Lowest/Average Salary:** $90,000/$90,000;
**Industry Concentration:** Generalist; **Function Concentration:** Generalist

**Pierpont, Elizabeth H.** — *Associate*
Russell Reynolds Associates, Inc.
200 Park Avenue
New York, NY 10166-0002
Telephone: (212) 351-2000
**Recruiter Classification:** Retained; **Lowest/Average Salary:** $90,000/$90,000;
**Industry Concentration:** Generalist with a primary focus in Financial Services;
**Function Concentration:** Generalist

**Piers, Robert L.** — *Partner*
TASA International
1428 Franklin Street
P.O. Box 604
Columbus, IN 47202
Telephone: (812) 376-9061
**Recruiter Classification:** Retained; **Lowest/Average Salary:** $90,000/$90,000;
**Industry Concentration:** Generalist; **Function Concentration:** Generalist

**Pierson, Edward J.** — *Partner*
Johnson Smith & Knisely Accord
100 Park Avenue, 15th Floor
New York, NY 10017
Telephone: (212) 885-9100
**Recruiter Classification:** Retained; **Lowest/Average Salary:** $90,000/$90,000;
**Industry Concentration:** Financial Services, Insurance, Venture Capital;
**Function Concentration:** Generalist with a primary focus in Administration,
Finance/Accounting, General Management, Human Resources, Marketing,
Sales, Women/Minorities

**Pike, Dick F.** — *Manager North Atlantic Region*
Management Recruiters International, Inc.
336 Holly Hill Lane
Burlington, NC 27215-5209
Telephone: (910) 584-1444
**Recruiter Classification:** Contingency; **Lowest/Average Salary:**
$30,000/$75,000; **Industry Concentration:** Generalist; **Function
Concentration:** Generalist

**Pillow, Charles** — *Associate*
Source Services Corporation
5429 LBJ Freeway, Suite 275
Dallas, TX 75240
Telephone: (214) 387-1600
**Recruiter Classification:** Contingency; **Lowest/Average Salary:**
$30,000/$50,000; **Industry Concentration:** Financial Services, Information
Technology; **Function Concentration:** Engineering, Finance/Accounting

**Pimentel, Alberto** — *Senior Associate*
Korn/Ferry International
1800 Century Park East, Suite 900
Los Angeles, CA 90067
Telephone: (310) 552-1834
**Recruiter Classification:** Retained; **Lowest/Average Salary:** $90,000/$90,000;
**Industry Concentration:** Generalist; **Function Concentration:** Generalist

**Pineda, Rosanna** — *Associate*
Source Services Corporation
2 Penn Plaza, Suite 1176
New York, NY 10121
Telephone: (212) 760-2200
**Recruiter Classification:** Contingency; **Lowest/Average Salary:**
$30,000/$50,000; **Industry Concentration:** Financial Services, Information
Technology; **Function Concentration:** Engineering, Finance/Accounting

**Pinkman, Karen N.** — *Vice President*
Skott/Edwards Consultants, Inc.
500 Fifth Avenue, 26th Floor
New York, NY 10110
Telephone: (212) 382-1166
**Recruiter Classification:** Retained; **Lowest/Average Salary:** $75,000/$90,000;
**Industry Concentration:** Generalist with a primary focus in Biotechnology,
Board Services, Consumer Products, Entertainment, Fashion (Retail/Apparel),
Financial Services, Hospitality/Leisure, Information Technology, Manufacturing,
Pharmaceutical/Medical, Publishing/Media, Venture Capital; **Function
Concentration:** Administration, Finance/Accounting, General Management,
Human Resources, Marketing, Sales, Women/Minorities

**Pinson, Liz A.** — *Manager Central Region*
Management Recruiters International, Inc.
800 Diederich Boulevard, Suite B
Russell, KY 41169-1807
Telephone: (606) 833-0294
**Recruiter Classification:** Contingency; **Lowest/Average Salary:**
$30,000/$75,000; **Industry Concentration:** Generalist; **Function
Concentration:** Generalist

**Pinson, Stephanie L.** — *President*
Gilbert Tweed/INESA
155 Prospect Avenue
West Orange, NJ 07052
Telephone: (201) 731-3033
**Recruiter Classification:** Retained; **Lowest/Average Salary:** $90,000/$90,000;
**Industry Concentration:** Generalist with a primary focus in Biotechnology,
Chemical Products, Consumer Products, Healthcare/Hospitals, High
Technology, Hospitality/Leisure, Information Technology, Insurance,
Manufacturing, Non-Profit, Pharmaceutical/Medical, Public Administration,
Transportation; **Function Concentration:** Generalist

**Pirhalla, Denise** — *Associate*
Kenzer Corp.
1600 Parkwood Circle NW, Suite 310
Atlanta, GA 30339
Telephone: (770) 955-7210
**Recruiter Classification:** Retained; **Lowest/Average Salary:** $50,000/$90,000;
**Industry Concentration:** Generalist; **Function Concentration:** Generalist

**Pirro, Sheri** — *Associate*
Source Services Corporation
1105 Schrock Road, Suite 510
Columbus, OH 43229
Telephone: (614) 846-3311
**Recruiter Classification:** Contingency; **Lowest/Average Salary:**
$30,000/$50,000; **Industry Concentration:** Financial Services, Information
Technology; **Function Concentration:** Engineering, Finance/Accounting

**Pistole, Ingrid** — *Executive Recruiter*
Richard, Wayne and Roberts
24 Greenway Plaza, Suite 1304
Houston, TX 77046-2404
Telephone: (713) 629-6681
**Recruiter Classification:** Retained; **Lowest/Average Salary:** $50,000/$90,000;
**Industry Concentration:** Generalist with a primary focus in Information
Technology; **Function Concentration:** Generalist

**Pitcher, Brian D.** — *Associate*
Skott/Edwards Consultants, Inc.
1776 On the Green
Morristown, NJ 07006
Telephone: (201) 644-0900
**Recruiter Classification:** Retained; **Lowest/Average Salary:** $75,000/$90,000; **Industry Concentration:** Generalist with a primary focus in Biotechnology, Pharmaceutical/Medical; **Function Concentration:** Generalist with a primary focus in Administration, Engineering, Finance/Accounting, General Management, Human Resources, Marketing, Research and Development, Sales, Women/Minorities

**Pitchford, Jim J.** — *Manager Pacific Region*
Management Recruiters International, Inc.
2633-A Parkmount Lane SW, Suite B
Olympia, WA 98502
Telephone: (360) 357-9996
**Recruiter Classification:** Contingency; **Lowest/Average Salary:** $30,000/$75,000; **Industry Concentration:** Generalist; **Function Concentration:** Generalist

**Pittard, Patrick S.** — *North American Managing Partner*
Heidrick & Struggles, Inc.
One Peachtree Center
303 Peachtree Street, NE, Suite 3100
Atlanta, GA 30308
Telephone: (404) 577-2410
**Recruiter Classification:** Retained; **Lowest/Average Salary:** $75,000/$90,000; **Industry Concentration:** Generalist with a primary focus in Education/Libraries, Financial Services, Non-Profit; **Function Concentration:** Generalist

**Pitto, Lili** — *Vice President*
Ryan, Miller & Associates Inc.
790 East Colorado, Suite 506
Pasadena, CA 91101
Telephone: (818) 568-3100
**Recruiter Classification:** Contingency; **Lowest/Average Salary:** $40,000/$75,000; **Industry Concentration:** Financial Services; **Function Concentration:** Generalist with a primary focus in Finance/Accounting

**Pitts, Charles** — *President*
Contemporary Management Services, Inc.
60 Pointe Circle
Greenville, SC 29615
Telephone: (864) 235-5271
**Recruiter Classification:** Contingency; **Lowest/Average Salary:** $30,000/$50,000; **Industry Concentration:** Generalist with a primary focus in Automotive, Chemical Products, Consumer Products, Electronics, Environmental, Manufacturing, Packaging, Pharmaceutical/Medical; **Function Concentration:** Generalist with a primary focus in Engineering

**Pizzariello, Ann Marie** — *Vice President*
Conex Incorporated
919 Third Avenue, 18th Floor
New York, NY 10022
Telephone: (212) 371-3737
**Recruiter Classification:** Retained; **Lowest/Average Salary:** $60,000/$90,000; **Industry Concentration:** Generalist; **Function Concentration:** Generalist

**Plagge, Cheryl L.** — *Manager Midwest Region*
Management Recruiters International, Inc.
Westside Offices, Suite 102
1312 Fourth Street SW
Mason City, IA 50401
Telephone: (515) 424-1680
**Recruiter Classification:** Contingency; **Lowest/Average Salary:** $30,000/$75,000; **Industry Concentration:** Generalist; **Function Concentration:** Generalist

**Plant, Jerry** — *Associate*
Source Services Corporation
1 Gatehall Drive, Suite 250
Parsippany, NJ 07054
Telephone: (201) 267-3222
**Recruiter Classification:** Contingency; **Lowest/Average Salary:** $30,000/$50,000; **Industry Concentration:** Financial Services, Information Technology; **Function Concentration:** Engineering, Finance/Accounting

**Platte, John D.** — *Managing Director*
Russell Reynolds Associates, Inc.
200 Park Avenue
New York, NY 10166-0002
Telephone: (212) 351-2000
**Recruiter Classification:** Retained; **Lowest/Average Salary:** $90,000/$90,000; **Industry Concentration:** Generalist with a primary focus in Financial Services; **Function Concentration:** Generalist

**Plazza, Richard C.** — *Principal*
The Executive Source
55 Fifth Avenue, 19th Floor
New York, NY 10003
Telephone: (212) 691-5505
**Recruiter Classification:** Executive Temporary; **Lowest/Average Salary:** $75,000/$90,000; **Industry Concentration:** Generalist with a primary focus in Financial Services, Insurance, Venture Capital; **Function Concentration:** Human Resources

**Plecash, Bob** — *Manager Eastern Region*
Management Recruiters International, Inc.
FarmBrook Park
1625 Rochester Road
Farmington, NY 14425
Telephone: (716) 398-2099
**Recruiter Classification:** Contingency; **Lowest/Average Salary:** $30,000/$75,000; **Industry Concentration:** Generalist; **Function Concentration:** Generalist

**Plessner, Rene** — *President*
Rene Plessner Associates, Inc.
375 Park Avenue
New York, NY 10152
Telephone: (212) 421-3490
**Recruiter Classification:** Retained; **Lowest/Average Salary:** $75,000/$90,000; **Industry Concentration:** Generalist with a primary focus in Aerospace/Defense, Consumer Products, Fashion (Retail/Apparel), Insurance, Manufacturing, Packaging; **Function Concentration:** Generalist with a primary focus in Administration, Finance/Accounting, General Management, Human Resources, Marketing, Research and Development, Sales

**Plimpton, Ralph L.** — *President*
R L Plimpton Associates
5655 South Yosemite Street, Suite 410
Greenwood Village, CO 80111
Telephone: (303) 771-1311
**Recruiter Classification:** Retained; **Lowest/Average Salary:** $40,000/$75,000; **Industry Concentration:** Generalist with a primary focus in Biotechnology, Electronics, Energy, Environmental, Financial Services, Healthcare/Hospitals, High Technology, Information Technology, Insurance, Oil/Gas, Pharmaceutical/Medical; **Function Concentration:** Finance/Accounting, General Management, Human Resources, Research and Development

**Plotner, George A.** — *Manager Central Region*
Management Recruiters International, Inc.
North Towne Professional Plaza
1054 North University Boulevard
Middletown, OH 45042-3300
Telephone: (513) 420-1800
**Recruiter Classification:** Contingency; **Lowest/Average Salary:** $30,000/$75,000; **Industry Concentration:** Generalist; **Function Concentration:** Generalist

**Plummer, John** — *President*
Plummer & Associates, Inc.
30 Myano Lane, Suite 36
Stamford, CT 06902
Telephone: (203) 965-7878
**Recruiter Classification:** Retained, Executive Temporary; **Lowest/Average Salary:** $90,000/$90,000; **Industry Concentration:** Board Services, Consumer Products, Electronics, Entertainment, Fashion (Retail/Apparel), Information Technology, Manufacturing, Venture Capital; **Function Concentration:** Generalist with a primary focus in Finance/Accounting, General Management, Human Resources, Marketing

**Plummer, Winkie Donovan** — *Vice President/Consultant*
McManners Associates, Inc.
400 East 54th Street, 16th Floor
New York, NY 10022
Telephone: (212) 980-7140
**Recruiter Classification:** Retained; **Lowest/Average Salary:** $90,000/$90,000; **Industry Concentration:** Generalist with a primary focus in Aerospace/Defense, Automotive, Biotechnology, Entertainment, Fashion (Retail/Apparel), Pharmaceutical/Medical, Publishing/Media, Transportation; **Function Concentration:** Generalist

**Pocs, Martin M.** — *Executive Vice President*
DHR International, Inc.
Denver Tech Center
7900 East Union Avenue, Suite 1100
Denver, CO 80237
Telephone: (303) 694-5360
**Recruiter Classification:** Retained; **Lowest/Average Salary:** $60,000/$90,000; **Industry Concentration:** Generalist; **Function Concentration:** Generalist

**Podway, Hope** — *Account Executive*
Search West, Inc.
1888 Century Park East
Suite 2050
Los Angeles, CA 90067-1736
Telephone: (310) 284-8888
**Recruiter Classification:** Contingency; **Lowest/Average Salary:**
$40,000/$60,000; **Industry Concentration:** Biotechnology,
Healthcare/Hospitals; **Function Concentration:** Marketing, Sales

**Poe, James B.** — *Managing Director*
Nagler, Robins & Poe, Inc.
65 William Street
Wellesley Hills, MA 02181
Telephone: (617) 431-1330
**Recruiter Classification:** Retained; **Lowest/Average Salary:** $75,000/$90,000;
**Industry Concentration:** Environmental, Financial Services, High Technology,
Information Technology; **Function Concentration:** Engineering,
Finance/Accounting, General Management, Human Resources, Marketing

**Poirier, Frank** — *Principal*
Juntunen-Combs-Poirier
600 Montgomery Street, 2nd Floor
San Francisco, CA 94111
Telephone: (415) 291-1699
**Recruiter Classification:** Retained; **Lowest/Average Salary:** $90,000/$90,000;
**Industry Concentration:** Consumer Products, Electronics, Entertainment, High
Technology, Information Technology, Publishing/Media; **Function
Concentration:** Generalist with a primary focus in Engineering, General
Management, Marketing, Research and Development, Sales

**Poirier, Roland** — *Partner*
Poirier, Hoevel & Co.
12400 Wilshire Boulevard, Suite 1250
Los Angeles, CA 90025
Telephone: (310) 207-3427
**Recruiter Classification:** Retained; **Lowest/Average Salary:** $75,000/$90,000;
**Industry Concentration:** Generalist with a primary focus in
Aerospace/Defense, Automotive, Consumer Products, Electronics,
Entertainment, Fashion (Retail/Apparel), Financial Services, High Technology,
Information Technology, Insurance, Manufacturing, Packaging,
Publishing/Media; **Function Concentration:** Generalist with a primary focus in
Administration, Finance/Accounting, General Management, Human Resources,
Marketing, Sales, Women/Minorities

**Polacek, Frank** — *President*
Search Enterprises South, Inc.
10100 West Sample Road
Coral Springs, FL 33065
Telephone: (305) 755-3121
**Recruiter Classification:** Contingency; **Lowest/Average Salary:**
$40,000/$50,000; **Industry Concentration:** Chemical Products, Consumer
Products, Oil/Gas; **Function Concentration:** Engineering

**Polachi, Charles A.** — *Partner*
Fenwick Partners
57 Bedford Street, Suite 101
Lexington, MA 02173
Telephone: (617) 862-3370
**Recruiter Classification:** Retained; **Lowest/Average Salary:** $90,000/$90,000;
**Industry Concentration:** Board Services, Electronics, High Technology,
Information Technology; **Function Concentration:** Generalist

**Polachi, Peter V.** — *Partner*
Fenwick Partners
57 Bedford Street, Suite 101
Lexington, MA 02173
Telephone: (617) 862-3370
**Recruiter Classification:** Retained; **Lowest/Average Salary:** $90,000/$90,000;
**Industry Concentration:** Board Services, Electronics, High Technology,
Information Technology; **Function Concentration:** Generalist

**Poloni, James A.** — *Manager Pacific Region*
Management Recruiters International, Inc.
703 Broadway Street, Suite 500
Vancouver, WA 98660
Telephone: (360) 695-4688
**Recruiter Classification:** Contingency; **Lowest/Average Salary:**
$30,000/$75,000; **Industry Concentration:** Generalist; **Function
Concentration:** Generalist

**Polvere, Gary T.** — *Manager Midwest Region*
Management Recruiters International, Inc.
406 North Hough Street
Barrington, IL 60010
Telephone: (847) 382-5544
**Recruiter Classification:** Contingency; **Lowest/Average Salary:**
$30,000/$75,000; **Industry Concentration:** Generalist; **Function
Concentration:** Generalist

**Pomerance, Mark** — *Executive Recruiter*
CPS Inc.
One Westbrook Corporate Centre, Suite 600
Westchester, IL 60154
Telephone: (708) 531-8370
**Recruiter Classification:** Contingency; **Lowest/Average Salary:**
$30,000/$50,000; **Industry Concentration:** Generalist with a primary focus in
Automotive, Biotechnology, Chemical Products, Consumer Products, High
Technology, Insurance, Manufacturing, Oil/Gas, Packaging,
Pharmaceutical/Medical; **Function Concentration:** Engineering, Research and
Development, Sales, Women/Minorities

**Pomeroy, T. Lee** — *Consultant*
Egon Zehnder International Inc.
55 East 59th Street, 14th Floor
New York, NY 10022
Telephone: (212) 838-9199
**Recruiter Classification:** Retained; **Lowest/Average Salary:** $90,000/$90,000;
**Industry Concentration:** Generalist with a primary focus in Biotechnology,
Financial Services, High Technology, Manufacturing, Pharmaceutical/Medical;
**Function Concentration:** Generalist

**Pompeo, Paul** — *Account Executive*
Search West, Inc.
100 Pine Street, Suite 2500
San Francisco, CA 94111-5203
Telephone: (415) 788-1770
**Recruiter Classification:** Contingency; **Lowest/Average Salary:**
$40,000/$60,000; **Industry Concentration:** Electronics, Energy, Manufacturing;
**Function Concentration:** Engineering, Marketing, Sales

**Poore, Larry D.** — *Managing Director*
Ward Howell International, Inc.
300 South Wacker Drive
Suite 2940
Chicago, IL 60606
Telephone: (312) 236-2211
**Recruiter Classification:** Retained; **Lowest/Average Salary:** $75,000/$90,000;
**Industry Concentration:** Generalist with a primary focus in Chemical Products,
Consumer Products, Healthcare/Hospitals, Information Technology,
Manufacturing, Oil/Gas; **Function Concentration:** Generalist with a primary
focus in Human Resources, Women/Minorities

**Pope, John S.** — *Executive Vice President*
DHR International, Inc.
10 South Riverside Plaza, Suite 2220
Chicago, IL 60606
Telephone: (312) 782-1581
**Recruiter Classification:** Retained; **Lowest/Average Salary:** $60,000/$90,000;
**Industry Concentration:** Generalist; **Function Concentration:** Generalist

**Poracky, John W.** — *Partner*
M. Wood Company
10 North Dearborn Street, Suite 700
Chicago, IL 60602
Telephone: (312) 368-0633
**Recruiter Classification:** Retained; **Lowest/Average Salary:** $60,000/$90,000;
**Industry Concentration:** Generalist with a primary focus in Consumer
Products, Financial Services, Information Technology, Insurance; **Function
Concentration:** Generalist with a primary focus in Finance/Accounting,
General Management, Sales

**Porada, Stephen D.** — *President*
CAP Inc.
P.O. Box 82
Tennent, NJ 07763
Telephone: (908) 446-0383
**Recruiter Classification:** Contingency; **Lowest/Average Salary:**
$30,000/$50,000; **Industry Concentration:** Chemical Products, Electronics,
Environmental, Manufacturing, Oil/Gas, Packaging, Pharmaceutical/Medical;
**Function Concentration:** Engineering, General Management, Marketing

**Porter, Albert** — *Vice President*
The Experts
200 Reservoir Street
Needham, MA 02194
Telephone: (617) 449-6700
**Recruiter Classification:** Executive Temporary; **Lowest/Average Salary:**
$50,000/$90,000; **Industry Concentration:** Generalist with a primary focus in
Consumer Products, Environmental, Financial Services, Healthcare/Hospitals,
High Technology, Information Technology, Manufacturing,
Pharmaceutical/Medical; **Function Concentration:** Generalist with a primary
focus in Administration, Engineering, Finance/Accounting, General
Management, Human Resources, Marketing, Research and Development, Sales

**Porter, Donald** — *President*
Amherst Personnel Group Inc.
550 West Old Country Road
Hicksville, NY 11801
Telephone: (516) 433-7610
**Recruiter Classification:** Contingency; **Lowest/Average Salary:**
$20,000/$50,000; **Industry Concentration:** Generalist with a primary focus in
Consumer Products, Fashion (Retail/Apparel), Healthcare/Hospitals,
Hospitality/Leisure, Pharmaceutical/Medical; **Function Concentration:**
Generalist with a primary focus in Marketing, Sales, Women/Minorities

**Porter, Ken** — *Senior Vice President*
Tourism Development International
P.O. Box 22323
Fort Lauderdale, FL 33335
Telephone: (305) 764-3949
**Recruiter Classification:** Retained, Executive Temporary; **Lowest/Average
Salary:** $90,000/$90,000; **Industry Concentration:** Generalist with a primary
focus in Board Services, Hospitality/Leisure, Transportation; **Function
Concentration:** General Management

**Porter, Nanci** — *Director*
Eastridge InfoTech
2355 Northside Drive, Suite 180
San Diego, CA 92108
Telephone: (619) 260-2048
**Recruiter Classification:** Contingency; **Lowest/Average Salary:**
$40,000/$60,000; **Industry Concentration:** Chemical Products, Energy,
Environmental, Oil/Gas; **Function Concentration:** Engineering, Sales

**Posner, Gary J.** — *Partner*
Educational Management Network
5143 North Stanford Drive
Nashville, TN 37215
Telephone: (615) 665-3388
**Recruiter Classification:** Retained; **Lowest/Average Salary:** $60,000/$90,000;
**Industry Concentration:** Education/Libraries, Non-Profit; **Function Concentration:**
Generalist with a primary focus in Administration, Finance/Accounting, Human
Resources

**Poster, Lawrence D.** — *Managing Director*
Catalyx Group
One Harkness Plaza, Suite 300
61 West 62nd Street
New York, NY 10023
Telephone: (212) 956-3525
**Recruiter Classification:** Retained; **Lowest/Average Salary:** $90,000/$90,000;
**Industry Concentration:** Biotechnology, Board Services, Healthcare/Hospitals,
High Technology, Information Technology, Pharmaceutical/Medical,
Publishing/Media, Venture Capital; **Function Concentration:** Generalist with a
primary focus in General Management, Research and Development

**Postles, Doris W.** — *Vice President*
Longshore & Simmons, Inc.
Plymouth Corporate Center
625 Ridge Pike, Suite 410
Conshohocken, PA 19428-3216
Telephone: (610) 941-3400
**Recruiter Classification:** Retained; **Lowest/Average Salary:** $50,000/$90,000;
**Industry Concentration:** Healthcare/Hospitals; **Function Concentration:**
Generalist

**Potenza, Gregory** — *Senior Principal*
Mixtec Group
31255 Cedar Valley Drive
Suite 300-327
Westlake Village, CA 91362
Telephone: (818) 889-8819
**Recruiter Classification:** Contingency; **Lowest/Average Salary:**
$60,000/$90,000; **Industry Concentration:** Healthcare/Hospitals; **Function
Concentration:** Generalist with a primary focus in Administration,
Finance/Accounting, General Management, Marketing

**Pototo, Brian** — *Associate*
Source Services Corporation
1500 West Park Drive, Suite 390
Westborough, MA 01581
Telephone: (508) 366-2600
**Recruiter Classification:** Contingency; **Lowest/Average Salary:**
$30,000/$50,000; **Industry Concentration:** Financial Services, Information
Technology; **Function Concentration:** Engineering, Finance/Accounting

**Potter, Douglas C.** — *Director*
Stanton Chase International
5050 Quorum Drive, Suite 330
Dallas, TX 75240
Telephone: (214) 404-8411
**Recruiter Classification:** Retained; **Lowest/Average Salary:** $75,000/$90,000;
**Industry Concentration:** Generalist with a primary focus in Chemical Products,
Consumer Products, Environmental, High Technology, Manufacturing;
**Function Concentration:** Generalist with a primary focus in Administration,
Engineering, Marketing, Sales

**Potter, Steven B.** — *Partner*
Highland Search Group, L.L.C.
565 Fifth Avenue, 22nd Floor
New York, NY 10017
Telephone: (212) 328-1113
**Recruiter Classification:** Retained; **Lowest/Average Salary:** $90,000/$90,000;
**Industry Concentration:** Financial Services, Real Estate, Venture Capital;
**Function Concentration:** Generalist with a primary focus in
Finance/Accounting, General Management, Human Resources, Sales

**Powell, Danny** — *Associate*
Source Services Corporation
520 Post Oak Boulevard, Suite 700
Houston, TX 77027
Telephone: (713) 439-1077
**Recruiter Classification:** Contingency; **Lowest/Average Salary:**
$30,000/$50,000; **Industry Concentration:** Financial Services, Information
Technology; **Function Concentration:** Engineering, Finance/Accounting

**Powell, Gregory** — *Associate*
Source Services Corporation
8614 Westwood Center, Suite 750
Vienna, VA 22182
Telephone: (703) 790-5610
**Recruiter Classification:** Contingency; **Lowest/Average Salary:**
$30,000/$50,000; **Industry Concentration:** Financial Services, Information
Technology; **Function Concentration:** Engineering, Finance/Accounting

**Powell, Leslie** — *Vice President*
Rhodes Associates
555 Fifth Avenue
New York, NY 10017
Telephone: (212) 983-2000
**Recruiter Classification:** Retained; **Lowest/Average Salary:** $90,000/$90,000;
**Industry Concentration:** Financial Services, Insurance, Real Estate, Venture
Capital; **Function Concentration:** Generalist

**Powell, Lloyd** — *Principal*
KPMG Executive Search
100 New Gower Street
Suite 800
St. John's, Newfoundland, CANADA A1C 6K3
Telephone: (709) 722-5804
**Recruiter Classification:** Retained; **Lowest/Average Salary:** $75,000/$90,000;
**Industry Concentration:** Generalist; **Function Concentration:** Generalist

**Powell, Marie** — *Vice President*
Kenzer Corp.
1600 Parkwood Circle NW, Suite 310
Atlanta, GA 30339
Telephone: (770) 955-7210
**Recruiter Classification:** Retained; **Lowest/Average Salary:** $50,000/$90,000;
**Industry Concentration:** Generalist; **Function Concentration:** Generalist

**Power, Michael** — *Associate*
Source Services Corporation
3701 West Algonquin Road, Suite 380
Rolling Meadows, IL 60008
Telephone: (847) 392-0244
**Recruiter Classification:** Contingency; **Lowest/Average Salary:**
$30,000/$50,000; **Industry Concentration:** Financial Services, Information
Technology; **Function Concentration:** Engineering, Finance/Accounting

**Powers-Johnson, Allyson** — *Consultant*
Johnson Smith & Knisely Accord
100 Park Avenue, 15th Floor
New York, NY 10017
Telephone: (212) 885-9100
**Recruiter Classification:** Retained; **Lowest/Average Salary:** $90,000/$90,000;
**Industry Concentration:** Generalist; **Function Concentration:** Generalist

**Prados, Daniel** — *Accounting and Finance Recruiter*
Accounting Personnel Consultants
210 Baronne Street, Suite 920
New Orleans, LA 70112
Telephone: (504) 581-7800
**Recruiter Classification:** Contingency, Executive Temporary; **Lowest/Average
Salary:** $20,000/$20,000; **Industry Concentration:** Generalist; **Function
Concentration:** Administration, Finance/Accounting

**Pratt, Michael W.** — *Manager Midwest Region*
Management Recruiters International, Inc.
707 Cycare Plaza
Dubuque, IA 52001-6824
Telephone: (319) 583-1554
**Recruiter Classification:** Contingency; **Lowest/Average Salary:**
$30,000/$75,000; **Industry Concentration:** Generalist; **Function
Concentration:** Generalist

**Pregeant, David** — *Associate*
Source Services Corporation
1290 Oakmead Parkway, Suite 318
Sunnyvale, CA 94086
Telephone: (408) 738-8440
**Recruiter Classification:** Contingency; **Lowest/Average Salary:**
$30,000/$50,000; **Industry Concentration:** Financial Services, Information
Technology; **Function Concentration:** Engineering, Finance/Accounting

**Prencipe, V. Michael** — *Principal*
Raymond Karsan Associates
1500 North Beauregard Street, Suite 110
Alexandria, VA 22311
Telephone: (703) 845-1114
**Recruiter Classification:** Contingency; **Lowest/Average Salary:**
$30,000/$90,000; **Industry Concentration:** Biotechnology, Chemical Products,
Environmental, Healthcare/Hospitals, Information Technology, Insurance,
Manufacturing, Pharmaceutical/Medical; **Function Concentration:** Generalist

**Preng, David E.** — *President*
Preng & Associates, Inc.
2925 Briarpark, Suite 1111
Houston, TX 77042
Telephone: (713) 266-2600
**Recruiter Classification:** Retained; **Lowest/Average Salary:** $75,000/$90,000;
**Industry Concentration:** Generalist with a primary focus in Chemical Products,
Energy, Environmental, Information Technology, Oil/Gas, Utilities/Nuclear;
**Function Concentration:** Generalist with a primary focus in Engineering,
Finance/Accounting, General Management, Human Resources, Research and
Development

**Prentiss, Michael C.** — *Manager Eastern Region*
Management Recruiters International, Inc.
8710 Preston Place
Chevy Chase, MD 20815
Telephone: (301) 654-9282
**Recruiter Classification:** Contingency; **Lowest/Average Salary:**
$30,000/$75,000; **Industry Concentration:** Generalist; **Function
Concentration:** Generalist

**Preschlack, Jack E.** — *Senior Director*
Spencer Stuart
401 North Michigan Avenue, Suite 3400
Chicago, IL 60611-4244
Telephone: (312) 822-0080
**Recruiter Classification:** Retained; **Lowest/Average Salary:** $75,000/$90,000;
**Industry Concentration:** Generalist with a primary focus in Automotive, Board
Services, High Technology, Information Technology, Manufacturing, Venture
Capital; **Function Concentration:** Generalist with a primary focus in General
Management

**Press, Fred** — *President*
Adept Tech Recruiting
219 Glendale Road
Scarsdale, NY 10583
Telephone: Unpublished
**Recruiter Classification:** Contingency; **Lowest/Average Salary:**
$30,000/$50,000; **Industry Concentration:** Generalist with a primary focus in
Financial Services, Healthcare/Hospitals, Information Technology; **Function
Concentration:** Generalist with a primary focus in Finance/Accounting

**Preusse, Eric** — *Associate*
Source Services Corporation
1500 West Park Drive, Suite 390
Westborough, MA 01581
Telephone: (508) 366-2600
**Recruiter Classification:** Contingency; **Lowest/Average Salary:**
$30,000/$50,000; **Industry Concentration:** Financial Services, Information
Technology; **Function Concentration:** Engineering, Finance/Accounting

**Price, Andrew G.** — *Associate*
The Thomas Tucker Company
425 California Street, Suite 2502
San Francisco, CA 94104
Telephone: (415) 693-5900
**Recruiter Classification:** Retained; **Lowest/Average Salary:** $90,000/$90,000;
**Industry Concentration:** Generalist with a primary focus in
Aerospace/Defense, Board Services, Electronics, Financial Services, High
Technology, Information Technology, Manufacturing, Venture Capital; **Function
Concentration:** Generalist with a primary focus in Engineering, Human
Resources, Marketing, Research and Development

**Price, Carl** — *Associate*
Source Services Corporation
3701 West Algonquin Road, Suite 380
Rolling Meadows, IL 60008
Telephone: (847) 392-0244
**Recruiter Classification:** Contingency; **Lowest/Average Salary:**
$30,000/$50,000; **Industry Concentration:** Financial Services, Information
Technology; **Function Concentration:** Engineering, Finance/Accounting

**Price, P. Anthony** — *Managing Director/Area Manager*
Russell Reynolds Associates, Inc.
101 California Street
Suite 3140
San Francisco, CA 94111
Telephone: (415) 352-3300
**Recruiter Classification:** Retained; **Lowest/Average Salary:** $90,000/$90,000;
**Industry Concentration:** Generalist with a primary focus in
Healthcare/Hospitals, High Technology; **Function Concentration:** Generalist

**Priem, Windle B.** — *President North America*
Korn/Ferry International
237 Park Avenue
New York, NY 10017
Telephone: (212) 687-1834
**Recruiter Classification:** Retained; **Lowest/Average Salary:** $90,000/$90,000;
**Industry Concentration:** Generalist with a primary focus in Financial Services;
**Function Concentration:** Generalist

**Priftis, Anthony** — *Vice President*
Evie Kreisler & Associates, Inc.
2720 Stemmons Freeway, Suite 812
Dallas, TX 75207
Telephone: (214) 631-8994
**Recruiter Classification:** Contingency; **Lowest/Average Salary:**
$30,000/$75,000; **Industry Concentration:** Fashion (Retail/Apparel); **Function
Concentration:** Generalist

**Prince, Marilyn L.** — *Managing Director*
Higdon Prince Inc.
230 Park Avenue, Suite 1455
New York, NY 10169
Telephone: (212) 986-4662
**Recruiter Classification:** Retained; **Lowest/Average Salary:** $90,000/$90,000;
**Industry Concentration:** Financial Services, Venture Capital; **Function
Concentration:** Generalist with a primary focus in Administration,
Finance/Accounting, General Management, Marketing, Sales,
Women/Minorities

**Prior, Donald** — *Consultant*
The Caldwell Partners Amrop International
999 West Hastings Street
Suite 750
Vancouver, British Columbia, CANADA V6C 2W2
Telephone: (604) 669-3550
**Recruiter Classification:** Retained; **Lowest/Average Salary:** $/$90,000; **Industry
Concentration:** Generalist with a primary focus in Entertainment,
Environmental, High Technology, Information Technology, Manufacturing,
Oil/Gas, Real Estate; **Function Concentration:** Generalist

**Probert, William W.** — *Partner*
Ward Howell International, Inc.
141 Adelaide Street West
Suite 1800
Toronto, Ontario, CANADA M5H 3L5
Telephone: (416) 862-1273
**Recruiter Classification:** Retained; **Lowest/Average Salary:** $75,000/$90,000;
**Industry Concentration:** Generalist with a primary focus in Automotive,
Consumer Products, Financial Services, Oil/Gas, Packaging,
Pharmaceutical/Medical; **Function Concentration:** Generalist

**Proct, Nina** — *Vice President*
Martin H. Bauman Associates, Inc.
375 Park Avenue, Suite 2002
New York, NY 10152
Telephone: (212) 752-6580
**Recruiter Classification:** Retained; **Lowest/Average Salary:** $90,000/$90,000;
**Industry Concentration:** Generalist with a primary focus in Board Services,
Chemical Products, Consumer Products, Financial Services, Manufacturing,
Transportation, Venture Capital; **Function Concentration:** Generalist with a
primary focus in Administration, Engineering, Finance/Accounting, General
Management, Human Resources, Marketing, Research and Development,
Sales, Women/Minorities

**Proctor, Robert A.** — *Partner*
Heidrick & Struggles, Inc.
245 Park Avenue, Suite 4300
New York, NY 10167-0152
Telephone: (212) 867-9876
**Recruiter Classification:** Retained; **Lowest/Average Salary:** $75,000/$90,000;
**Industry Concentration:** Generalist; **Function Concentration:** Generalist

**Prosser, Shane** — *Consultant*
Search Consultants International, Inc.
4545 Post Oak Place, Suite 208
Houston, TX 77027
Telephone: (713) 622-9188
**Recruiter Classification:** Contingency, Executive Temporary; **Lowest/Average
Salary:** $60,000/$75,000; **Industry Concentration:** Chemical Products, Energy,
Environmental, Manufacturing, Oil/Gas; **Function Concentration:** Engineering,
General Management, Marketing, Research and Development

**Provost, Ed** — *Co-Manager Pacific Region*
Management Recruiters International, Inc.
24681 La PLaza Drive, Suite 105
Dana Point, CA 92629
Telephone: (714) 443-2800
**Recruiter Classification:** Contingency; **Lowest/Average Salary:**
$30,000/$75,000; **Industry Concentration:** Generalist; **Function
Concentration:** Generalist

**Provost, Vicky L.** — *Co-Manager*
Management Recruiters International, Inc.
24681 La PLaza Drive, Suite 105
Dana Point, CA 92629
Telephone: (714) 443-2800
**Recruiter Classification:** Contingency; **Lowest/Average Salary:**
$30,000/$75,000; **Industry Concentration:** Generalist; **Function
Concentration:** Generalist

**Provus, Barbara L.** — *Principal*
Shepherd Bueschel & Provus, Inc.
401 North Michigan Avenue, Suite 3020
Chicago, IL 60611-5555
Telephone: (312) 832-3020
**Recruiter Classification:** Retained; **Lowest/Average Salary:** $90,000/$90,000;
**Industry Concentration:** Generalist with a primary focus in Biotechnology,
Consumer Products, Fashion (Retail/Apparel), Information Technology,
Manufacturing, Pharmaceutical/Medical, Venture Capital; **Function
Concentration:** Generalist with a primary focus in Human Resources,
Marketing, Sales

**Pryde, Marcia P.** — *Vice President/Managing Director*
A.T. Kearney, Inc.
One Tabor Center, Suite 950
1200 Seventeenth Street
Denver, CO 80202
Telephone: (303) 572-6175
**Recruiter Classification:** Retained; **Lowest/Average Salary:** $90,000/$90,000;
**Industry Concentration:** Generalist with a primary focus in High Technology,
Manufacturing; **Function Concentration:** Generalist with a primary focus in
Finance/Accounting, General Management, Marketing, Sales

**Pryor, Keith** — *Executive Vice President*
The Diversified Search Companies
2005 Market Street, Suite 3300
Philadelphia, PA 19103
Telephone: (215) 732-6666
**Recruiter Classification:** Retained; **Lowest/Average Salary:** $90,000/$90,000;
**Industry Concentration:** Generalist; **Function Concentration:** Generalist

**Puente, Fred J.** — *Manager Eastern Region*
Management Recruiters International, Inc.
132 East Main Street, Suite 300
Salisbury, MD 21801-4921
Telephone: (410) 548-4473
**Recruiter Classification:** Contingency; **Lowest/Average Salary:**
$30,000/$75,000; **Industry Concentration:** Generalist; **Function
Concentration:** Generalist

**Pugh, Judith Geist** — *Senior Vice President*
InterimManagement Solutions, Inc.
6464 South Quebec Street
Englewood, CO 80111
Telephone: (303) 290-9500
**Recruiter Classification:** Executive Temporary; **Lowest/Average Salary:**
$50,000/$90,000; **Industry Concentration:** Entertainment, Information
Technology; **Function Concentration:** Generalist with a primary focus in
Administration, Finance/Accounting, Marketing

**Pugliese, Vincent** — *Account Executive*
Search West, Inc.
1888 Century Park East
Suite 2050
Los Angeles, CA 90067-1736
Telephone: (310) 284-8888
**Recruiter Classification:** Contingency; **Lowest/Average Salary:**
$40,000/$60,000; **Industry Concentration:** Chemical Products, Environmental,
Manufacturing; **Function Concentration:** Engineering, General Management,
Sales

**Pugrant, Mark A.** — *Managing Director*
Grant/Morgan Associates, Inc.
7500 Old Georgetown Road
Suite 710
Bethesda, MD 20814
Telephone: (301) 718-8888
**Recruiter Classification:** Contingency; **Lowest/Average Salary:**
$30,000/$50,000; **Industry Concentration:** Entertainment, Financial Services,
High Technology, Manufacturing, Real Estate; **Function Concentration:**
Administration, Finance/Accounting

**Putrim, Tom** — *Consultant*
Paul Ray Berndtson
101 Park Avenue, 41st Floor
New York, NY 10178
Telephone: (212) 370-1316
**Recruiter Classification:** Retained; **Lowest/Average Salary:** $90,000/$90,000;
**Industry Concentration:** Generalist; **Function Concentration:** Generalist

**Quatrone, Olivia S.** — *Consultant*
Heidrick & Struggles, Inc.
245 Park Avenue, Suite 4300
New York, NY 10167-0152
Telephone: (212) 867-9876
**Recruiter Classification:** Retained; **Lowest/Average Salary:** $75,000/$90,000;
**Industry Concentration:** Generalist with a primary focus in Fashion
(Retail/Apparel); **Function Concentration:** Generalist

**Quick, Roger A.** — *President*
Norman Broadbent International, Inc.
233 South Wacker Drive
Chicago, IL 60606
Telephone: (312) 876-3300
**Recruiter Classification:** Retained; **Lowest/Average Salary:** $90,000/$90,000;
**Industry Concentration:** Generalist with a primary focus in Biotechnology,
Consumer Products, Healthcare/Hospitals, Hospitality/Leisure; **Function
Concentration:** Generalist with a primary focus in Administration, General
Management

**Quinlan, Lynne** — *Software Engineering Recruiter*
Winter, Wyman & Company
950 Winter Street, Suite 3100
Waltham, MA 02154-1294
Telephone: (617) 890-7000
**Recruiter Classification:** Contingency; **Lowest/Average Salary:**
$40,000/$75,000; **Industry Concentration:** High Technology, Information
Technology, Publishing/Media; **Function Concentration:** Engineering

**Quinn, Frank A.** — *Manager North Atlantic Region*
Management Recruiters International, Inc.
2101 Sardis Road North, Suite 205
Charlotte, NC 28227
Telephone: (704) 849-9200
**Recruiter Classification:** Contingency; **Lowest/Average Salary:**
$30,000/$75,000; **Industry Concentration:** Generalist; **Function
Concentration:** Generalist

**Quinn, John** — *Consultant*
Paul Ray Berndtson
10 South Riverside Plaza
Suite 720
Chicago, IL 60606
Telephone: (312) 876-0730
**Recruiter Classification:** Retained; **Lowest/Average Salary:** $90,000/$90,000;
**Industry Concentration:** Generalist; **Function Concentration:** Generalist

**Quinn, Nola** — *Recruiter*
Technical Connections Inc.
11400 Olympic Boulevard, Suite 770
Los Angeles, CA 90064
Telephone: (310) 479-8830
**Recruiter Classification:** Contingency; **Lowest/Average Salary:**
$40,000/$60,000; **Industry Concentration:** High Technology, Information
Technology; **Function Concentration:** Generalist

**Quitel, Scott M.** — *Manager Eastern Region*
Management Recruiters International, Inc.
161 Leverington Avenue, Suite 102
Philadelphia, PA 19127
Telephone: (215) 482-6881
**Recruiter Classification:** Contingency; **Lowest/Average Salary:**
$30,000/$75,000; **Industry Concentration:** Generalist; **Function
Concentration:** Generalist

**Raab, Julie** — *Director National Accounts*
Dunhill Professional Search of Irvine, Inc.
9 Executive Circle, Suite 240
Irvine, CA 92714
Telephone: (714) 474-6666
**Recruiter Classification:** Contingency; **Lowest/Average Salary:**
$40,000/$60,000; **Industry Concentration:** Electronics, High Technology,
Manufacturing, Transportation; **Function Concentration:** Generalist with a
primary focus in Engineering, General Management, Marketing, Research and
Development, Sales, Women/Minorities

**Rabe, William** — *Executive Vice President*
Sales Executives Inc.
755 West Big Beaver Road, Suite 2107
Troy, MI 48084
Telephone: (810) 362-1900
**Recruiter Classification:** Contingency; **Lowest/Average Salary:**
$50,000/$90,000; **Industry Concentration:** Chemical Products, Electronics,
Pharmaceutical/Medical; **Function Concentration:** General Management,
Marketing, Sales

**Raben, Steven** — *Partner*
Paul Ray Berndtson
One Allen Center
500 Dallas, Suite 3010
Houston, TX 77002
Telephone: (713) 309-1400
**Recruiter Classification:** Retained; **Lowest/Average Salary:** $90,000/$90,000;
**Industry Concentration:** Energy; **Function Concentration:** Generalist

**Rabinowitz, Peter A.** — *President*
P.A.R. Associates Inc.
60 State Street, Suite 1040
Boston, MA 02109-2706
Telephone: (617) 367-0320
**Recruiter Classification:** Retained; **Lowest/Average Salary:** $90,000/$90,000;
**Industry Concentration:** Generalist with a primary focus in Board Services,
Education/Libraries, Energy, Environmental, Financial Services,
Healthcare/Hospitals, High Technology, Hospitality/Leisure, Information
Technology, Insurance, Manufacturing, Non-Profit, Pharmaceutical/Medical,
Real Estate; **Function Concentration:** Generalist with a primary focus in
Administration, Finance/Accounting, General Management, Marketing,
Women/Minorities

**Rachels, John W.** — *Senior Consultant*
Southwestern Professional Services
2451 Atrium Way
Nashville, TN 37214
Telephone: (615) 391-2722
**Recruiter Classification:** Contingency; **Lowest/Average Salary:**
$50,000/$50,000; **Industry Concentration:** Generalist with a primary focus in
Information Technology, Manufacturing, Packaging, Publishing/Media;
**Function Concentration:** Sales

**Rackley, Eugene M.** — *Partner*
Heidrick & Struggles, Inc.
One Peachtree Center
303 Peachtree Street, NE, Suite 3100
Atlanta, GA 30308
Telephone: (404) 577-2410
**Recruiter Classification:** Retained; **Lowest/Average Salary:** $75,000/$90,000;
**Industry Concentration:** Generalist with a primary focus in Education/Libraries,
Financial Services, Healthcare/Hospitals, Non-Profit; **Function Concentration:**
Generalist

**Radawicz, Angela** — *Principal Researcher*
Mixtec Group
31255 Cedar Valley Drive
Suite 300-327
Westlake Village, CA 91362
Telephone: (818) 889-8819
**Recruiter Classification:** Contingency; **Lowest/Average Salary:**
$60,000/$90,000; **Function Concentration:** Generalist with a primary focus in
Administration, Engineering, Finance/Accounting, General Management,
Human Resources, Marketing, Research and Development, Sales

**Radden, David B.** — *Partner*
Paul Ray Berndtson
2029 Century Park East
Suite 1000
Los Angeles, CA 90067
Telephone: (310) 557-2828
**Recruiter Classification:** Retained; **Lowest/Average Salary:** $90,000/$90,000;
**Industry Concentration:** High Technology; **Function Concentration:**
Generalist

**Radford-Oster, Deborah** — *Administrative Placement
Consultant*
Morgan Hunter Corp.
6800 College Boulevard, Suite 550
Overland Park, KS 66211
Telephone: (913) 491-3434
**Recruiter Classification:** Contingency; **Lowest/Average Salary:**
$20,000/$30,000; **Industry Concentration:** Generalist; **Function
Concentration:** Generalist with a primary focus in Administration

**Radice, Joseph** — *Partner*
Hospitality International
23 West 73rd Street, Suite 100
New York, NY 10023
Telephone: (212) 769-8800
**Recruiter Classification:** Contingency; **Lowest/Average Salary:**
$40,000/$60,000; **Industry Concentration:** Entertainment,
Healthcare/Hospitals, Hospitality/Leisure, Information Technology; **Function
Concentration:** Finance/Accounting, General Management, Human Resources,
Marketing, Sales, Women/Minorities

**Raffin, Robert P.** — *Manager South Atlantic Region*
Management Recruiters International, Inc.
9500 Koger Boulevard, Suite 203
St. Petersburg, FL 33702
Telephone: (813) 577-2116
**Recruiter Classification:** Contingency; **Lowest/Average Salary:**
$30,000/$75,000; **Industry Concentration:** Generalist; **Function
Concentration:** Generalist

**Raheja, Marc C.** — *President*
CanMed Consultants Inc.
62 Queen Street South
Mississauga, Ontario, CANADA L5M 1K4
Telephone: (905) 567-1080
**Recruiter Classification:** Executive Temporary; **Lowest/Average Salary:**
$40,000/$75,000; **Industry Concentration:** Biotechnology,
Healthcare/Hospitals, Pharmaceutical/Medical; **Function Concentration:**
Finance/Accounting, General Management, Human Resources, Marketing,
Research and Development, Sales

**Raiber, Laurie Altman** — *Director Interactive Media Practice*
The IMC Group of Companies Ltd.
14 East 60th Street, Suite 1200
New York, NY 10022
Telephone: (212) 838-9535
**Recruiter Classification:** Retained; **Lowest/Average Salary:** $75,000/$90,000;
**Industry Concentration:** Entertainment, Information Technology,
Publishing/Media; **Function Concentration:** Generalist with a primary focus in
General Management, Marketing, Research and Development, Sales

**Ralston, Doug O.** — *Manager North Atlantic Region*
Management Recruiters International, Inc.
9465 Main Street, Suite 210
Woodstock, GA 30188-3700
Telephone: (770) 592-9550
**Recruiter Classification:** Contingency; **Lowest/Average Salary:**
$30,000/$75,000; **Industry Concentration:** Generalist; **Function
Concentration:** Generalist

**Ramler, Carolyn S.** — *Vice President*
The Corporate Connection, Ltd.
7202 Glen Forest Drive
Richmond, VA 23226
Telephone: (804) 288-8844
**Recruiter Classification:** Contingency; **Lowest/Average Salary:**
$20,000/$50,000; **Industry Concentration:** Generalist with a primary focus in
Aerospace/Defense, Biotechnology, Financial Services, Healthcare/Hospitals,
High Technology, Information Technology, Insurance, Manufacturing; **Function
Concentration:** Generalist

**Ramsey, John H.** — *President*
Mark Stanley & Company
2121 Ponce de Leon Boulevard #630
P.O. Box 149071
Coral Gables, FL 33114
Telephone: (305) 444-1612
**Recruiter Classification:** Retained; **Lowest/Average Salary:** $75,000/$90,000;
**Industry Concentration:** Generalist with a primary focus in Consumer
Products, Environmental, Financial Services, Healthcare/Hospitals, High
Technology, Pharmaceutical/Medical, Real Estate; **Function Concentration:**
Generalist with a primary focus in Finance/Accounting, General Management,
Human Resources, Sales

**Ranberger, Mike J.** — *Manager Eastern Region*
Management Recruiters International, Inc.
8807 Sudley Road, Suite 208
Manassas, VA 22110-4719
Telephone: (703) 330-1830
**Recruiter Classification:** Contingency; **Lowest/Average Salary:**
$30,000/$75,000; **Industry Concentration:** Generalist; **Function
Concentration:** Generalist

**Randell, James E.** — *Chief Executive Officer*
Randell-Heiken, Inc.
The Lincoln Building
60 East 42nd Street, Suite 2022
New York, NY 10165
Telephone: (212) 490-1313
**Recruiter Classification:** Retained; **Lowest/Average Salary:** $60,000/$90,000;
**Industry Concentration:** Generalist with a primary focus in Consumer Products,
Financial Services, Healthcare/Hospitals, High Technology, Information
Technology, Insurance, Manufacturing, Oil/Gas, Pharmaceutical/Medical,
Publishing/Media; **Function Concentration:** Generalist with a primary focus in
General Management, Human Resources, Marketing, Sales, Women/Minorities

**Range, Mary Jane** — *Partner*
Ingram & Aydelotte Inc.
430 Park Avenue, Suite 700
New York, NY 10022
Telephone: (212) 319-7777
**Recruiter Classification:** Retained; **Lowest/Average Salary:** $90,000/$90,000;
**Industry Concentration:** High Technology, Information Technology, Insurance,
Manufacturing, Pharmaceutical/Medical; **Function Concentration:** General
Management

**Rapoport, William** — *Consultant*
Blair/Tech Recruiters
77 Milltown Road
East Brunswick, NJ 08816
Telephone: (908) 390-5550
**Recruiter Classification:** Contingency; **Lowest/Average Salary:** $40,000/$60,000;
**Industry Concentration:** Biotechnology, Chemical Products, Consumer Products,
Environmental, Manufacturing, Packaging, Pharmaceutical/Medical; **Function
Concentration:** Engineering, Research and Development

**Rasmussen, Timothy** — *Associate*
Source Services Corporation
1233 North Mayfair Road, Suite 300
Milwaukee, WI 53226
Telephone: (414) 774-6700
**Recruiter Classification:** Contingency; **Lowest/Average Salary:**
$30,000/$50,000; **Industry Concentration:** Financial Services, Information
Technology; **Function Concentration:** Engineering, Finance/Accounting

**Rast, Vera L.** — *President/Consultant*
Vera L. Rast Partners, Inc.
One South Wacker Drive, Suite 3890
Chicago, IL 60606
Telephone: (312) 629-0339
**Recruiter Classification:** Contingency; **Lowest/Average Salary:**
$50,000/$90,000

**Ratajczak, Paul** — *Managing Director*
Source Services Corporation
15260 Ventura Boulevard, Suite 380
Sherman Oaks, CA 91403
Telephone: (818) 905-1500
**Recruiter Classification:** Contingency; **Lowest/Average Salary:**
$30,000/$50,000; **Industry Concentration:** Financial Services, Information
Technology; **Function Concentration:** Engineering, Finance/Accounting

**Rathborne, Kenneth J.** — *Principal*
Blair/Tech Recruiters
77 Milltown Road
East Brunswick, NJ 08816
Telephone: (908) 390-5550
**Recruiter Classification:** Contingency; **Lowest/Average Salary:** $40,000/$60,000;
**Industry Concentration:** Biotechnology, Chemical Products, Consumer Products,
Environmental, Manufacturing, Packaging, Pharmaceutical/Medical; **Function
Concentration:** Engineering, Research and Development

**Ratigan, Charles C.** — *Partner*
Heidrick & Struggles, Inc.
125 South Wacker Drive
Suite 2800
Chicago, IL 60606-4590
Telephone: (312) 372-8811
**Recruiter Classification:** Retained; **Lowest/Average Salary:** $75,000/$90,000;
**Industry Concentration:** Generalist with a primary focus in Publishing/Media;
**Function Concentration:** Generalist

**Rattner, Kenneth L.** — *Partner*
Heidrick & Struggles, Inc.
125 South Wacker Drive
Suite 2800
Chicago, IL 60606-4590
Telephone: (312) 372-8811
**Recruiter Classification:** Retained; **Lowest/Average Salary:** $75,000/$90,000;
**Industry Concentration:** Generalist with a primary focus in
Healthcare/Hospitals; **Function Concentration:** Generalist

**Rauch, Ben** — *Managing Director*
Korn/Ferry International
237 Park Avenue
New York, NY 10017
Telephone: (212) 687-1834
**Recruiter Classification:** Retained; **Lowest/Average Salary:** $90,000/$90,000;
**Industry Concentration:** Generalist; **Function Concentration:** Generalist

**Rauch, Carl W.** — *Vice President*
Physicians Search, Inc.
1224 Katella Avenue, Suite 202
Orange, CA 92667-5045
Telephone: (714) 288-8350
**Recruiter Classification:** Contingency; **Lowest/Average Salary:**
$90,000/$90,000; **Industry Concentration:** Biotechnology,
Healthcare/Hospitals, Pharmaceutical/Medical, Real Estate; **Function
Concentration:** Administration

**Rauch, Cliff** — *President*
Physicians Search, Inc.
1224 Katella Avenue, Suite 202
Orange, CA 92667-5045
Telephone: (714) 288-8350
**Recruiter Classification:** Contingency; **Lowest/Average Salary:**
$90,000/$90,000; **Industry Concentration:** Biotechnology,
Healthcare/Hospitals, Pharmaceutical/Medical, Real Estate; **Function
Concentration:** Administration

**Ravenel, Lavinia** — *Executive Recruiter*
MSI International
229 Peachtree Street, NE
Suite 1201
Atlanta, GA 30303
Telephone: (404) 659-5050
**Recruiter Classification:** Contingency; **Lowest/Average Salary:**
$30,000/$75,000; **Industry Concentration:** Generalist with a primary focus in
Financial Services; **Function Concentration:** Generalist with a primary focus in
Finance/Accounting

**Ravit, Alan** — *Executive Vice President*
Career Management International
197 Route 18
East Brunswick, NJ 08816
Telephone: (908) 937-4800
**Recruiter Classification:** Retained; **Lowest/Average Salary:** $75,000/$90,000;
**Industry Concentration:** Fashion (Retail/Apparel)

**Ray, Breck** — *Industry Leader - Energy and Utilities*
Paul Ray Berndtson
301 Commerce Street, Suite 2300
Fort Worth, TX 76102
Telephone: (817) 334-0500
**Recruiter Classification:** Retained; **Lowest/Average Salary:** $90,000/$90,000;
**Industry Concentration:** Generalist with a primary focus in Energy,
Utilities/Nuclear; **Function Concentration:** Generalist

**Ray, Marianne C.** — *Partner*
Callan Associates, Ltd.
1550 Spring Road
Oak Brook, IL 60521
Telephone: (708) 832-7080
**Recruiter Classification:** Retained; **Lowest/Average Salary:** $90,000/$90,000;
**Industry Concentration:** Generalist with a primary focus in
Aerospace/Defense, Automotive, Biotechnology, Chemical Products,
Consumer Products, Electronics, Energy, Environmental, Fashion
(Retail/Apparel), Financial Services, High Technology, Information Technology,
Manufacturing, Oil/Gas; **Function Concentration:** Generalist with a primary
focus in Administration, Engineering, Finance/Accounting, General
Management, Human Resources, Marketing, Research and Development,
Sales, Women/Minorities

**Ray, Paul R.** — *Chairman*
Paul Ray Berndtson
301 Commerce Street, Suite 2300
Fort Worth, TX 76102
Telephone: (817) 334-0500
**Recruiter Classification:** Retained; **Lowest/Average Salary:** $90,000/$90,000;
**Industry Concentration:** Aerospace/Defense, Board Services, Consumer
Products; **Function Concentration:** Generalist

**Ray, Paul R.** — *President and CEO*
Paul Ray Berndtson
301 Commerce Street, Suite 2300
Fort Worth, TX 76102
Telephone: (817) 334-0500
**Recruiter Classification:** Retained; **Lowest/Average Salary:** $90,000/$90,000;
**Industry Concentration:** Consumer Products, Non-Profit, Public
Administration; **Function Concentration:** Generalist

**Raymond, Allan H.** — *Managing Vice President*
Korn/Ferry International
4816 IDS Center
Minneapolis, MN 55402
Telephone: (612) 333-1834
**Recruiter Classification:** Retained; **Lowest/Average Salary:** $90,000/$90,000;
**Industry Concentration:** Generalist; **Function Concentration:** Generalist

**Raymond, Anne** — *Recruiter*
Anderson Sterling Associates
18623 Ventura Boulevard, Suite 207
Tarzana, CA 91356
Telephone: (818) 996-0921
**Recruiter Classification:** Executive Temporary; **Lowest/Average Salary:**
$30,000/$60,000; **Industry Concentration:** Biotechnology, Consumer
Products, Electronics, High Technology, Information Technology,
Manufacturing, Pharmaceutical/Medical; **Function Concentration:** Engineering,
Finance/Accounting, General Management, Human Resources, Marketing,
Research and Development, Sales, Women/Minorities

**Raymond, Barry** — *Principal*
Raymond Karsan Associates
989 Old Eagle School Road, Suite 814
Wayne, PA 19087
Telephone: (610) 971-9171
**Recruiter Classification:** Contingency; **Lowest/Average Salary:**
$30,000/$90,000; **Industry Concentration:** Generalist; **Function
Concentration:** Generalist

**Raymond, Jean** — *Partner*
The Caldwell Partners Amrop International
1840 Sherbrooke Street West
Montreal, Quebec, CANADA H3H 1E4
Telephone: (514) 935-6969
**Recruiter Classification:** Retained; **Lowest/Average Salary:** $/$90,000; **Industry
Concentration:** Generalist with a primary focus in Biotechnology, Consumer
Products, Financial Services, Manufacturing, Packaging,
Pharmaceutical/Medical, Public Administration; **Function Concentration:**
Generalist

**Reagan, Paul W.** — *Manager Pacific Region*
Management Recruiters International, Inc.
33 South King Street, Suite 514
Honolulu, HI 96813
Telephone: (808) 521-0387
**Recruiter Classification:** Contingency; **Lowest/Average Salary:**
$30,000/$75,000; **Industry Concentration:** Generalist; **Function
Concentration:** Generalist

**Reardon, Joseph** — *Associate*
Source Services Corporation
155 Federal Street, Suite 410
Boston, MA 02110
Telephone: (617) 482-8211
**Recruiter Classification:** Contingency; **Lowest/Average Salary:**
$30,000/$50,000; **Industry Concentration:** Financial Services, Information
Technology; **Function Concentration:** Engineering, Finance/Accounting

**Recsetar, Steven** — *Executive Vice President*
DHR International, Inc.
10 South Riverside Plaza, Suite 2220
Chicago, IL 60606
Telephone: (312) 782-1581
**Recruiter Classification:** Retained; **Lowest/Average Salary:** $60,000/$90,000;
**Industry Concentration:** Generalist; **Function Concentration:** Generalist

**Reddick, David C.** — *Managing Director*
Horton International
33 Sloan Street
Roswell, GA 30075
Telephone: (770) 640-1533
**Recruiter Classification:** Retained; **Lowest/Average Salary:** $90,000/$90,000;
**Industry Concentration:** Generalist with a primary focus in Consumer
Products, Environmental, Financial Services, Healthcare/Hospitals, High
Technology, Pharmaceutical/Medical; **Function Concentration:** Generalist with
a primary focus in Finance/Accounting, General Management, Human
Resources, Marketing, Sales

**Reddicks, Nate** — *Account Executive*
Search West, Inc.
3401 Centrelake Drive
Suite 690
Ontario, CA 91761-1207
Telephone: (909) 986-1966
**Recruiter Classification:** Contingency; **Lowest/Average Salary:**
$40,000/$60,000; **Industry Concentration:** Manufacturing, Packaging;
**Function Concentration:** Engineering, Research and Development, Sales

**Redding, Denise** — *Administrative Assistant*
The Douglas Reiter Company, Inc.
1221 S.W. Yamhill, Suite 301A
Portland, OR 97205
Telephone: (503) 228-6916
**Recruiter Classification:** Executive Temporary; **Lowest/Average Salary:**
$75,000/$90,000; **Industry Concentration:** Generalist with a primary focus in
Aerospace/Defense, Biotechnology, Board Services, Energy, Financial Services,
Healthcare/Hospitals, High Technology, Manufacturing; **Function
Concentration:** Generalist with a primary focus in Administration, Engineering,
Finance/Accounting, General Management, Human Resources, Marketing

**Redler, Rhonda** — *Executive Medical Consultant*
National Search, Inc.
2816 University Drive
Coral Springs, FL 33071
Telephone: (800) 935-4355
**Recruiter Classification:** Contingency; **Lowest/Average Salary:**
$30,000/$50,000; **Industry Concentration:** Healthcare/Hospitals, Insurance,
Pharmaceutical/Medical; **Function Concentration:** Generalist with a primary
focus in Administration, Finance/Accounting, General Management, Human
Resources, Marketing, Research and Development, Sales, Women/Minorities

**Redmond, Andrea** — *Managing Director/Area Co-Manager*
Russell Reynolds Associates, Inc.
200 South Wacker Drive
Suite 3600
Chicago, IL 60606
Telephone: (312) 993-9696
**Recruiter Classification:** Retained; **Lowest/Average Salary:** $90,000/$90,000;
**Industry Concentration:** Generalist with a primary focus in Financial Services;
**Function Concentration:** Generalist

**Redwood, Guy W.** — *Partner*
Bruce Massey & Partners Inc.
330 Bay Street, Suite 1104
Toronto, Ontario, CANADA M5H 2S8
Telephone: (416) 861-0077
**Recruiter Classification:** Retained; **Lowest/Average Salary:** $90,000/$90,000;
**Industry Concentration:** Generalist; **Function Concentration:** Generalist with a
primary focus in Administration, Engineering, Finance/Accounting, General
Management, Human Resources, Marketing, Research and Development

**Reece, Christopher S.** — *Managing Partner*
Reece & Mruk Partners
75 Second Avenue
Needham, MA 02194-2800
Telephone: (617) 449-3603
**Recruiter Classification:** Retained; **Lowest/Average Salary:** $75,000/$90,000;
**Industry Concentration:** Generalist with a primary focus in Biotechnology,
Board Services, Electronics, Financial Services, High Technology, Information
Technology, Insurance, Manufacturing, Venture Capital; **Function
Concentration:** Generalist with a primary focus in Administration,
Finance/Accounting, General Management, Human Resources, Marketing,
Research and Development, Sales, Women/Minorities

**Reed, David Q.** — *Manager Central Region*
Management Recruiters International, Inc.
G-5524 South Saginaw
Flint, MI 48507
Telephone: (810) 695-0120
**Recruiter Classification:** Contingency; **Lowest/Average Salary:**
$30,000/$75,000; **Industry Concentration:** Generalist; **Function
Concentration:** Generalist

**Reed, Ruthann** — *Technical Recruiter*
Spectra International Inc.
6991 East Camelback Road, Suite B-305
Scottsdale, AZ 85251
Telephone: (602) 481-0411
**Recruiter Classification:** Contingency; **Lowest/Average Salary:**
$40,000/$60,000; **Industry Concentration:** Generalist with a primary focus in
High Technology, Information Technology; **Function Concentration:** Generalist
with a primary focus in Engineering, Marketing, Research and Development

**Reed, Susan** — *Associate*
Source Services Corporation
379 Thornall Street
Edison, NJ 08837
Telephone: (908) 494-2800
**Recruiter Classification:** Contingency; **Lowest/Average Salary:**
$30,000/$50,000; **Industry Concentration:** Financial Services, Information
Technology; **Function Concentration:** Engineering, Finance/Accounting

**Reed, William D.** — *Executive Director*
Russell Reynolds Associates, Inc.
Old City Hall, 45 School Street
Boston, MA 02108
Telephone: (617) 523-1111
**Recruiter Classification:** Retained; **Lowest/Average Salary:** $90,000/$90,000;
**Industry Concentration:** Generalist; **Function Concentration:** Generalist

**Reeder, Michael S.** — *Senior Partner*
Lamalie Amrop International
191 Peachtree Street N.E.
Atlanta, GA 30303
Telephone: (404) 688-0800
**Recruiter Classification:** Retained; **Lowest/Average Salary:** $90,000/$90,000;
**Industry Concentration:** Generalist with a primary focus in
Healthcare/Hospitals, Insurance; **Function Concentration:** Generalist with a
primary focus in General Management, Marketing, Sales

**Reese, Charles D.** — *President*
Reese Associates
10475 Perry Highway
Wexford, PA 15090
Telephone: (412) 935-8644
**Recruiter Classification:** Retained; **Lowest/Average Salary:** $75,000/$90,000;
**Industry Concentration:** Manufacturing; **Function Concentration:** Generalist

**Reeves, Ron C.** — *Manager Midwest Region*
Management Recruiters International, Inc.
472 North McLean Boulevard, Suite 201
Elgin, IL 60123
Telephone: (847) 697-2201
**Recruiter Classification:** Contingency; **Lowest/Average Salary:**
$30,000/$75,000; **Industry Concentration:** Generalist; **Function
Concentration:** Generalist

**Reeves, William B.** — *Managing Director*
Spencer Stuart
One Atlantic Center, Suite 3230
1201 West Peachtree Street
Atlanta, GA 30309
Telephone: (404) 892-2800
**Recruiter Classification:** Retained; **Lowest/Average Salary:** $90,000/$90,000;
**Industry Concentration:** Board Services, Consumer Products, Financial
Services, Insurance, Real Estate; **Function Concentration:** Generalist with a
primary focus in Finance/Accounting, General Management, Human
Resources, Marketing

**Referente, Gwen** — *Executive Recruiter*
Richard, Wayne and Roberts
24 Greenway Plaza, Suite 1304
Houston, TX 77046-2493
Telephone: (713) 629-6681
**Recruiter Classification:** Retained; **Lowest/Average Salary:** $40,000/$60,000;
**Industry Concentration:** Generalist with a primary focus in Information
Technology; **Function Concentration:** Generalist

**Regan, Muriel** — *Principal*
Gossage Regan Associates, Inc.
25 West 43rd Street, Suite 812
New York, NY 10036
Telephone: (212) 869-3348
**Recruiter Classification:** Retained; **Lowest/Average Salary:** $50,000/$60,000;
**Industry Concentration:** Education/Libraries; **Function Concentration:**
Generalist

**Regan, Thomas J.** — *Vice President*
Tower Consultants, Ltd.
4650 N.E. Spinnaker Point
Stuart, FL 34996
Telephone: (407) 225-3595
**Recruiter Classification:** Retained; **Lowest/Average Salary:** $90,000/$90,000;
**Industry Concentration:** Generalist; **Function Concentration:** Administration,
Human Resources, Women/Minorities

**Regehly, Herbert L.** — *President*
The IMC Group of Companies Ltd.
14 East 60th Street, Suite 1200
New York, NY 10022
Telephone: (212) 838-9535
**Recruiter Classification:** Retained; **Lowest/Average Salary:** $75,000/$90,000;
**Industry Concentration:** Entertainment, Hospitality/Leisure, Transportation;
**Function Concentration:** Engineering, Finance/Accounting, General
Management, Human Resources, Marketing, Research and Development, Sales

**Regeuye, Peter J.** — *Director*
Accountants Executive Search
535 Fifth Avenue, Suite 1200
New York, NY 10017
Telephone: (212) 682-5900
**Recruiter Classification:** Executive Temporary; **Lowest/Average Salary:**
$40,000/$60,000; **Industry Concentration:** Generalist with a primary focus in
Consumer Products, Entertainment, Fashion (Retail/Apparel), Financial
Services, Non-Profit, Public Administration, Publishing/Media, Real Estate;
**Function Concentration:** Finance/Accounting

**Reid, Gary** — *Partner*
KPMG Executive Search
World Exchange Plaza
45 O'Connor Street
Ottawa, Ontario, CANADA K1P 1A4
Telephone: (613) 560-0011
**Recruiter Classification:** Retained; **Lowest/Average Salary:** $75,000/$90,000;
**Industry Concentration:** Generalist; **Function Concentration:** Generalist

**Reid, Katherine** — *Associate*
Source Services Corporation
150 South Warner Road, Suite 238
King of Prussia, PA 19406
Telephone: (610) 341-1960
**Recruiter Classification:** Contingency; **Lowest/Average Salary:**
$30,000/$50,000; **Industry Concentration:** Financial Services, Information
Technology; **Function Concentration:** Engineering, Finance/Accounting

**Reid, Scott** — *Associate*
Source Services Corporation
Foster Plaza VI
681 Anderson Drive, 2nd Floor
Pittsburgh, PA 15220
Telephone: (412) 928-8300
**Recruiter Classification:** Contingency; **Lowest/Average Salary:**
$30,000/$50,000; **Industry Concentration:** Financial Services, Information
Technology; **Function Concentration:** Engineering, Finance/Accounting

**Reilly, John** — *Consultant*
The McCormick Group, Inc.
1400 Wilson Boulevard
Arlington, VA 22209
Telephone: (703) 841-1700
**Recruiter Classification:** Retained; **Lowest/Average Salary:** $60,000/$90,000;
**Industry Concentration:** Financial Services; **Function Concentration:**
Generalist

**Reilly, Robert E.** — *President*
DHR International, Inc.
10 South Riverside Plaza, Suite 2220
Chicago, IL 60606
Telephone: (312) 782-1581
**Recruiter Classification:** Retained; **Lowest/Average Salary:** $60,000/$90,000;
**Industry Concentration:** Generalist; **Function Concentration:** Generalist

**Reimenschneider, Donald** — *Consultant*
Evie Kreisler & Associates, Inc.
2575 Peachtree Road, Suite 300
Atlanta, GA 30305
Telephone: (404) 262-0599
**Recruiter Classification:** Contingency; **Lowest/Average Salary:**
$30,000/$75,000; **Industry Concentration:** Fashion (Retail/Apparel); **Function
Concentration:** Generalist

**Reimer, Marvin** — *Manager Southwest Region*
Management Recruiters International, Inc.
Building 1500, Suite B
8100 East 22nd Street North
Wichita, KS 67226
Telephone: (316) 682-8239
**Recruiter Classification:** Contingency; **Lowest/Average Salary:**
$30,000/$75,000; **Industry Concentration:** Generalist; **Function
Concentration:** Generalist

**Reinhart, Jeaneen** — *Branch Manager*
Accountants on Call
Two Union Square, 601 Union Street
Seattle, WA 98101
Telephone: (206) 467-0700
**Recruiter Classification:** Contingency; **Lowest/Average Salary:**
$20,000/$30,000; **Industry Concentration:** Generalist; **Function
Concentration:** Finance/Accounting

**Reiser, Ellen** — *Principal*
Thorndike Deland Associates
275 Madison Avenue, Suite 1300
New York, NY 10016
Telephone: (212) 661-6200
**Recruiter Classification:** Retained; **Lowest/Average Salary:** $75,000/$90,000;
**Industry Concentration:** Generalist with a primary focus in Board Services,
Consumer Products, Entertainment, Fashion (Retail/Apparel), Financial
Services, Healthcare/Hospitals, Hospitality/Leisure, Information Technology,
Insurance, Manufacturing, Pharmaceutical/Medical, Publishing/Media, Venture
Capital; **Function Concentration:** Generalist with a primary focus in
Finance/Accounting, General Management, Human Resources, Marketing,
Sales

**Reisig, Alexsandra** — *Vice President*
John Kurosky & Associates
3 Corporate Park Drive, Suite 210
Irvine, CA 92714
Telephone: (714) 851-6370
**Recruiter Classification:** Retained; **Lowest/Average Salary:** $60,000/$90,000;
**Industry Concentration:** Generalist

**Reiss, Matt** — *Insurance Consultant*
National Search, Inc.
2816 University Drive
Coral Springs, FL 33071
Telephone: (800) 935-4355
**Recruiter Classification:** Contingency; **Lowest/Average Salary:**
$30,000/$50,000; **Industry Concentration:** Healthcare/Hospitals, Insurance,
Pharmaceutical/Medical; **Function Concentration:** Generalist with a primary
focus in Administration, Finance/Accounting, General Management, Human
Resources, Marketing, Research and Development, Sales, Women/Minorities

**Reiter, Douglas** — *President*
The Douglas Reiter Company, Inc.
1221 S.W. Yamhill, Suite 301A
Portland, OR 97205
Telephone: (503) 228-6916
**Recruiter Classification:** Executive Temporary; **Lowest/Average Salary:**
$75,000/$90,000; **Industry Concentration:** Generalist with a primary focus in
Aerospace/Defense, Biotechnology, Board Services, Energy, Financial Services,
Healthcare/Hospitals, High Technology, Manufacturing; **Function
Concentration:** Generalist with a primary focus in Administration, Engineering,
Finance/Accounting, General Management, Human Resources, Marketing

**Reiter, Harold D.** — *President and COO*
Herbert Mines Associates, Inc.
399 Park Avenue, 27th Floor
New York, NY 10022
Telephone: (212) 355-0909
**Recruiter Classification:** Retained; **Lowest/Average Salary:** $75,000/$90,000;
**Industry Concentration:** Board Services, Consumer Products, Fashion
(Retail/Apparel); **Function Concentration:** Generalist with a primary focus in
Finance/Accounting, General Management, Human Resources, Marketing,
Sales

**Reitkopp, Ellen** — *Co-Manager Eastern Region*
Management Recruiters International, Inc.
6849 Old Dominion Drive, Suite 225
McLean, VA 22101
Telephone: (703) 442-4842
**Recruiter Classification:** Contingency; **Lowest/Average Salary:**
$30,000/$75,000; **Industry Concentration:** Generalist; **Function
Concentration:** Generalist

**Reitkopp, Howard H.** — *Co-Manager*
Management Recruiters International, Inc.
6849 Old Dominion Drive, Suite 225
McLean, VA 22101
Telephone: (703) 442-4842
**Recruiter Classification:** Contingency; **Lowest/Average Salary:**
$30,000/$75,000; **Industry Concentration:** Generalist; **Function
Concentration:** Generalist

**Remick, Tierney Boyd** — *Associate*
Russell Reynolds Associates, Inc.
200 South Wacker Drive
Suite 3600
Chicago, IL 60606
Telephone: (312) 993-9696
**Recruiter Classification:** Retained; **Lowest/Average Salary:** $90,000/$90,000;
**Industry Concentration:** Generalist; **Function Concentration:** Generalist

**Rendl, Ric** — *Executive Recruiter*
CPS Inc.
One Westbrook Corporate Centre, Suite 600
Westchester, IL 60154
Telephone: (708) 531-8370
**Recruiter Classification:** Contingency; **Lowest/Average Salary:**
$30,000/$50,000; **Industry Concentration:** Generalist with a primary focus in
Automotive, Biotechnology, Chemical Products, Consumer Products, High
Technology, Insurance, Manufacturing, Oil/Gas, Packaging,
Pharmaceutical/Medical; **Function Concentration:** Engineering, Research and
Development, Sales, Women/Minorities

**Renfroe, Ann-Marie** — *Associate*
Source Services Corporation
1 Gatehall Drive, Suite 250
Parsippany, NJ 07054
Telephone: (201) 267-3222
**Recruiter Classification:** Contingency; **Lowest/Average Salary:**
$30,000/$50,000; **Industry Concentration:** Financial Services, Information
Technology; **Function Concentration:** Engineering, Finance/Accounting

**Renick, Cynthia L.** — *Manager Insurance/Risk Management
Division*
Morgan Hunter Corp.
6800 College Boulevard, Suite 550
Overland Park, KS 66211
Telephone: (913) 491-3434
**Recruiter Classification:** Contingency; **Lowest/Average Salary:**
$30,000/$60,000; **Industry Concentration:** Insurance; **Function
Concentration:** Administration, Engineering, General Management, Human
Resources, Marketing, Sales, Women/Minorities

**Renick, Paula** — *Associate*
Kenzer Corp.
777 Third Avenue, 26th Floor
New York, NY 10017
Telephone: (212) 308-4300
**Recruiter Classification:** Retained; **Lowest/Average Salary:** $50,000/$90,000;
**Industry Concentration:** Generalist; **Function Concentration:** Generalist

**Rennell, Thomas** — *Associate*
Source Services Corporation
1500 West Park Drive, Suite 390
Westborough, MA 01581
Telephone: (508) 366-2600
**Recruiter Classification:** Contingency; **Lowest/Average Salary:**
$30,000/$50,000; **Industry Concentration:** Financial Services, Information
Technology; **Function Concentration:** Engineering, Finance/Accounting

**Renner, Sandra L.** — *Senior Consultant*
Spectra International Inc.
6991 East Camelback Road, Suite B-305
Scottsdale, AZ 85251
Telephone: (602) 481-0411
**Recruiter Classification:** Contingency; **Lowest/Average Salary:**
$20,000/$50,000; **Industry Concentration:** Generalist with a primary focus in
Automotive, Consumer Products, Electronics, Financial Services, High
Technology, Insurance, Manufacturing, Oil/Gas, Pharmaceutical/Medical,
Publishing/Media; **Function Concentration:** Finance/Accounting

**Reno, Geri** — *Vice President*
Corporate Careers, Inc.
1500 Quail Street, Suite 290
Newport Beach, CA 92660
Telephone: (714) 476-7007
**Recruiter Classification:** Contingency; **Lowest/Average Salary:**
$30,000/$60,000

**Renteria, Elizabeth** — *Associate*
Source Services Corporation
15260 Ventura Boulevard, Suite 380
Sherman Oaks, CA 91403
Telephone: (818) 905-1500
**Recruiter Classification:** Contingency; **Lowest/Average Salary:**
$30,000/$50,000; **Industry Concentration:** Financial Services, Information
Technology; **Function Concentration:** Engineering, Finance/Accounting

**Renwick, David** — *Vice President*
John Kurosky & Associates
3 Corporate Park Drive, Suite 210
Irvine, CA 92714
Telephone: (714) 851-6370
**Recruiter Classification:** Retained; **Lowest/Average Salary:** $60,000/$90,000;
**Industry Concentration:** Electronics, High Technology; **Function
Concentration:** Engineering, Marketing, Sales

**Resnic, Alan** — *Associate*
Source Services Corporation
155 Federal Street, Suite 410
Boston, MA 02110
Telephone: (617) 482-8211
**Recruiter Classification:** Contingency; **Lowest/Average Salary:**
$30,000/$50,000; **Industry Concentration:** Financial Services, Information
Technology; **Function Concentration:** Engineering, Finance/Accounting

**Ressler, Dan R.** — *Manager South Atlantic Region*
Management Recruiters International, Inc.
1300 Third Street South, Suite 301-A
Naples, FL 33940-7239
Telephone: (813) 261-8800
**Recruiter Classification:** Contingency; **Lowest/Average Salary:**
$30,000/$75,000; **Industry Concentration:** Generalist; **Function
Concentration:** Generalist

**Reticker, Peter** — *Unit Manager*
MSI International
229 Peachtree Street, NE
Suite 1201
Atlanta, GA 30303
Telephone: (404) 659-5050
**Recruiter Classification:** Contingency; **Lowest/Average Salary:**
$30,000/$60,000; **Industry Concentration:** Generalist with a primary focus in
Financial Services, Healthcare/Hospitals; **Function Concentration:**
Administration, Engineering, Finance/Accounting, General Management,
Marketing

**Reyes, Randolph G.** — *Manager Eastern Region*
Management Recruiters International, Inc.
5550 Sterrett Place
Suite 314-K&M, Lakefront-N
Columbia, MD 21044
Telephone: (410) 715-1141
**Recruiter Classification:** Contingency; **Lowest/Average Salary:**
$30,000/$75,000; **Industry Concentration:** Generalist; **Function
Concentration:** Generalist

**Reyman, Susan** — *President*
S. Reyman & Associates Ltd.
20 North Michigan Avenue, Suite 520
Chicago, IL 60602
Telephone: (312) 580-0808
**Recruiter Classification:** Retained; **Lowest/Average Salary:** $75,000/$90,000;
**Industry Concentration:** Generalist with a primary focus in Automotive,
Consumer Products, Electronics, Fashion (Retail/Apparel), Financial Services,
Healthcare/Hospitals, Insurance, Manufacturing, Packaging,
Pharmaceutical/Medical, Transportation; **Function Concentration:** Generalist
with a primary focus in Administration, Engineering, Finance/Accounting,
General Management, Human Resources, Marketing, Sales

**Reynes, Tony** — *Partner*
Tesar-Reynes, Inc.
500 North Michigan Avenue
Chicago, IL 60611
Telephone: (312) 661-0700
**Recruiter Classification:** Retained; **Lowest/Average Salary:** $50,000/$75,000;
**Industry Concentration:** Automotive, Consumer Products, High Technology,
Hospitality/Leisure, Publishing/Media; **Function Concentration:** Marketing

**Reynolds, Bud O.** — *Manager Southwest Region*
Management Recruiters International, Inc.
10 Boulder Crescent, Suite 302-B
Colorado Springs, CO 80903
Telephone: (719) 389-0600
**Recruiter Classification:** Contingency; **Lowest/Average Salary:**
$30,000/$75,000; **Industry Concentration:** Generalist; **Function
Concentration:** Generalist

**Reynolds, Catherine** — *Information Technology Recruiter*
Winter, Wyman & Company
101 Federal Street, 27th Floor
Boston, MA 02110-1800
Telephone: (617) 951-2700
**Recruiter Classification:** Contingency; **Lowest/Average Salary:**
$30,000/$60,000; **Industry Concentration:** Generalist with a primary focus in
Information Technology; **Function Concentration:** Generalist

**Reynolds, Gregory P.** — *Vice President - Account Executive*
Roberts Ryan and Bentley
7315 Wisconsin Avenue, Suite 333E
Bethesda, MD 20814
Telephone: (301) 469-3150
**Recruiter Classification:** Retained; **Lowest/Average Salary:** $90,000/$90,000;
**Industry Concentration:** Generalist with a primary focus in Energy, Information
Technology, Insurance; **Function Concentration:** Generalist with a primary
focus in Administration, Engineering, General Management, Marketing,
Women/Minorities

**Reynolds, Juli Ann** — *Vice President*
Korn/Ferry International
One International Place
Boston, MA 02110-1800
Telephone: (617) 345-0200
**Recruiter Classification:** Retained; **Lowest/Average Salary:** $90,000/$90,000;
**Industry Concentration:** Generalist with a primary focus in
Healthcare/Hospitals; **Function Concentration:** Generalist

**Reynolds, Laura** — *Associate*
Source Services Corporation
7730 East Bellview Avenue, Suite 302
Englewood, CO 80111
Telephone: (303) 773-3700
**Recruiter Classification:** Contingency; **Lowest/Average Salary:**
$30,000/$50,000; **Industry Concentration:** Financial Services, Information
Technology; **Function Concentration:** Engineering, Finance/Accounting

**Reynolds, Smooch S.** — *President*
The Repovich-Reynolds Group
709 East Colorado Boulevard, Suite 200
Pasadena, CA 91101
Telephone: (818) 585-9455
**Recruiter Classification:** Retained; **Lowest/Average Salary:** $75,000/$90,000;
**Industry Concentration:** Generalist; **Function Concentration:** Marketing

**Reynolds, Susan F.** — *Consultant*
Heidrick & Struggles, Inc.
300 South Grand Avenue, Suite 2400
Los Angeles, CA 90071
Telephone: (213) 625-8811
**Recruiter Classification:** Retained; **Lowest/Average Salary:** $75,000/$90,000;
**Industry Concentration:** Generalist; **Function Concentration:** Generalist

**Rheude, Jim** — *Co-Manager*
Management Recruiters International, Inc.
11611 North Meridian Street, Suite 100
Carmel, IN 46032
Telephone: (317) 582-0202
**Recruiter Classification:** Contingency; **Lowest/Average Salary:**
$30,000/$75,000; **Industry Concentration:** Generalist; **Function
Concentration:** Generalist

**Rhoades, Michael** — *Associate*
Source Services Corporation
One South Main Street, Suite 1440
Dayton, OH 45402
Telephone: (513) 461-4660
**Recruiter Classification:** Contingency; **Lowest/Average Salary:**
$30,000/$50,000; **Industry Concentration:** Financial Services, Information
Technology; **Function Concentration:** Engineering, Finance/Accounting

**Rice, Douglas** — *Agribusiness Recruiter/Manager*
Agra Placements International Ltd.
16 East Fifth Street, Berkshire Court
Peru, IN 46970
Telephone: (317) 472-1988
**Recruiter Classification:** Contingency; **Lowest/Average Salary:**
$20,000/$30,000; **Industry Concentration:** Generalist with a primary focus in
Biotechnology, Chemical Products, Energy, Financial Services, Manufacturing;
**Function Concentration:** Administration, Engineering, Finance/Accounting,
General Management, Human Resources, Marketing, Research and
Development, Sales

**Rice, Jim K.** — *Manager Southwest Region*
Management Recruiters International, Inc.
494 South Seguin
New Braunfels, TX 78130-7938
Telephone: (210) 629-6290
**Recruiter Classification:** Contingency; **Lowest/Average Salary:**
$30,000/$75,000; **Industry Concentration:** Generalist; **Function
Concentration:** Generalist

**Rice, John** — *Consultant*
Paul Ray Berndtson
301 Commerce Street, Suite 2300
Fort Worth, TX 76102
Telephone: (817) 334-0500
**Recruiter Classification:** Retained; **Lowest/Average Salary:** $90,000/$90,000;
**Industry Concentration:** Generalist; **Function Concentration:** Generalist

**Rice, Marie** — *Senior Consultant*
Jay Gaines & Company, Inc.
450 Park Avenue
New York, NY 10022
Telephone: (212) 308-9222
**Recruiter Classification:** Retained; **Lowest/Average Salary:** $90,000/$90,000;
**Industry Concentration:** Financial Services, High Technology,
Publishing/Media; **Function Concentration:** Finance/Accounting, General
Management, Human Resources, Marketing, Sales

**Rice, Raymond D.** — *President*
Logue & Rice Inc.
8000 Towers Crescent Drive
Suite 650
Vienna, VA 22182-2700
Telephone: (703) 761-4261
**Recruiter Classification:** Contingency; **Lowest/Average Salary:**
$40,000/$90,000; **Industry Concentration:** Generalist with a primary focus in
Biotechnology, Board Services, Financial Services, High Technology,
Information Technology, Venture Capital; **Function Concentration:** Generalist
with a primary focus in Administration, Finance/Accounting, General
Management, Human Resources, Women/Minorities

**Rich, Kenneth M.** — *Geographic Manager/Partner*
Paul Ray Berndtson
101 Park Avenue, 41st Floor
New York, NY 10178
Telephone: (212) 370-1316
**Recruiter Classification:** Retained; **Lowest/Average Salary:** $90,000/$90,000;
**Industry Concentration:** Financial Services; **Function Concentration:**
Generalist

**Rich, Lyttleton** — *Executive Recruiter*
Sockwell & Associates
227 West Trade Street, Suite 1930
Charlotte, NC 28202
Telephone: (704) 372-1865
**Recruiter Classification:** Retained; **Lowest/Average Salary:** $90,000/$90,000;
**Industry Concentration:** Generalist with a primary focus in Education/Libraries,
Financial Services, Healthcare/Hospitals, Non-Profit, Real Estate; **Function
Concentration:** Generalist with a primary focus in Administration,
Finance/Accounting, General Management, Human Resources, Marketing,
Sales

**Richard, Albert L.** — *President*
Human Resources Inc.
311 Centre Street, Suite 206
Fernandina Beach, FL 32034
Telephone: (904) 277-2535
**Recruiter Classification:** Retained; **Lowest/Average Salary:** $90,000/$90,000;
**Industry Concentration:** Healthcare/Hospitals, High Technology, Information
Technology, Manufacturing; **Function Concentration:** Generalist

**Richard, Ryan** — *Consultant*
Logix Partners
1601 Trapelo Road
Waltham, MA 02154
Telephone: (617) 890-0500
**Recruiter Classification:** Retained; **Lowest/Average Salary:** $60,000/$75,000;
**Industry Concentration:** Information Technology; **Function Concentration:**
Engineering

**Richard, Ryan** — *Consultant*
Logix, Inc.
1601 Trapelo Road
Waltham, MA 02154
Telephone: (617) 890-0500
**Recruiter Classification:** Retained; **Lowest/Average Salary:** $60,000/$75,000;
**Industry Concentration:** Information Technology; **Function Concentration:**
Engineering

**Richards, Robert A.** — *Southern Area Recruiter*
Sloan & Associates
1769 Jamestown Road
Williamsburg, VA 23185
Telephone: (757) 220-1111
**Recruiter Classification:** Contingency; **Lowest/Average Salary:**
$60,000/$75,000; **Industry Concentration:** Consumer Products; **Function
Concentration:** Marketing, Research and Development, Sales

**Richards, Sharon** — *Recruiter*
The Barack Group, Inc.
885 Third Avenue
New York, NY 10022
Telephone: (212) 230-3280
**Recruiter Classification:** Retained; **Lowest/Average Salary:** $75,000/$90,000;
**Industry Concentration:** Consumer Products, Entertainment; **Function
Concentration:** General Management, Marketing

**Richards, Wes** — *Consultant*
Heidrick & Struggles, Inc.
2740 Sand Hill Road
Menlo Park, CA 94025
Telephone: (415) 854-9300
**Recruiter Classification:** Retained; **Lowest/Average Salary:** $75,000/$90,000;
**Industry Concentration:** Generalist; **Function Concentration:** Generalist

**Richardson, David M.** — *Executive Vice President/Managing
Director*
DHR International, Inc.
248 Lorraine Avenue, 4th Floor
Upper Montclair, NJ 07043
Telephone: (201) 746-2100
**Recruiter Classification:** Retained; **Lowest/Average Salary:** $60,000/$90,000;
**Industry Concentration:** Generalist; **Function Concentration:** Generalist

**Richardson, J. Rick** — *Senior Director*
Spencer Stuart
Financial Centre
695 East Main Street
Stamford, CT 06901
Telephone: (203) 324-6333
**Recruiter Classification:** Retained; **Lowest/Average Salary:** $90,000/$90,000;
**Industry Concentration:** Generalist with a primary focus in Consumer
Products, Financial Services; **Function Concentration:** Generalist with a
primary focus in General Management, Marketing

**Richardson, Paul C.** — *Vice President*
Korn/Ferry International
One Landmark Square
Stamford, CT 06901
Telephone: (203) 359-3350
**Recruiter Classification:** Retained; **Lowest/Average Salary:** $90,000/$90,000;
**Industry Concentration:** Generalist; **Function Concentration:** Generalist

**Richardson, Tony R.** — *Manager Central Region*
Management Recruiters International, Inc.
500 Country Pine Lane, Suite 1
Battle Creek, MI 49015-4282
Telephone: (616) 979-3939
**Recruiter Classification:** Contingency; **Lowest/Average Salary:**
$30,000/$75,000; **Industry Concentration:** Generalist; **Function
Concentration:** Generalist

**Riederer, Larry** — *Executive Recruiter*
CPS Inc.
One Westbrook Corporate Centre, Suite 600
Westchester, IL 60154
Telephone: (708) 531-8370
**Recruiter Classification:** Contingency; **Lowest/Average Salary:**
$30,000/$50,000; **Industry Concentration:** Generalist with a primary focus in
Automotive, Biotechnology, Chemical Products, Consumer Products, High
Technology, Insurance, Manufacturing, Oil/Gas, Packaging,
Pharmaceutical/Medical; **Function Concentration:** Engineering, Research and
Development, Sales, Women/Minorities

**Rieger, Louis J.** — *Managing Director*
Spencer Stuart
1111 Bagby, Suite 1616
Houston, TX 77002-2594
Telephone: (713) 225-1621
**Recruiter Classification:** Retained; **Lowest/Average Salary:** $90,000/$90,000;
**Industry Concentration:** Generalist with a primary focus in Automotive, Board
Services, Chemical Products, Consumer Products, Energy, Environmental,
Financial Services, Healthcare/Hospitals, Information Technology,
Manufacturing, Non-Profit, Oil/Gas, Transportation, Venture Capital; **Function
Concentration:** Generalist with a primary focus in Administration,
Finance/Accounting, General Management, Human Resources, Marketing,
Women/Minorities

**Riggs, David T.** — *Co-Manager North Atlantic Region*
Management Recruiters International, Inc.
3700 Crestwood Parkway, Suite 320
Duluth, GA 30136
Telephone: (770) 925-2266
**Recruiter Classification:** Contingency; **Lowest/Average Salary:**
$30,000/$75,000; **Industry Concentration:** Generalist; **Function
Concentration:** Generalist

**Riggs, Lena** — *Co-Manager*
Management Recruiters International, Inc.
3700 Crestwood Parkway, Suite 320
Duluth, GA 30136
Telephone: (770) 925-2266
**Recruiter Classification:** Contingency; **Lowest/Average Salary:**
$30,000/$75,000; **Industry Concentration:** Generalist; **Function
Concentration:** Generalist

**Rijke, R. Fred** — *Partner*
TASA International
750 Lexington Avenue
Suite 1800
New York, NY 10022
Telephone: (212) 486-1490
**Recruiter Classification:** Retained; **Lowest/Average Salary:** $90,000/$90,000;
**Industry Concentration:** Generalist; **Function Concentration:** Generalist

**Riley, Elizabeth G.** — *Partner*
Mazza & Riley, Inc.
55 William Street, Suite 120
Wellesley, MA 02181-4000
Telephone: (617) 235-7724
**Recruiter Classification:** Retained; **Lowest/Average Salary:** $90,000/$90,000;
**Industry Concentration:** Generalist with a primary focus in Entertainment,
High Technology, Information Technology, Publishing/Media, Venture Capital;
**Function Concentration:** Generalist with a primary focus in
Finance/Accounting, General Management, Marketing, Sales

**Riley, James** — *Director Security and Loss Prevention*
Hunt Ltd.
21 West 38th Street
New York, NY 10018
Telephone: (212) 997-2299
**Recruiter Classification:** Contingency; **Lowest/Average Salary:**
$40,000/$60,000; **Industry Concentration:** Automotive, Chemical Products,
Consumer Products, Fashion (Retail/Apparel), Manufacturing,
Pharmaceutical/Medical, Publishing/Media, Transportation; **Function**
**Concentration:** Generalist

**Riley, Jeffrey K.** — *Senior Vice President*
EFL Associates
7120 East Orchard, Suite 240
Englewood, CO 80111
Telephone: (303) 779-1724
**Recruiter Classification:** Retained; **Lowest/Average Salary:** $60,000/$90,000;
**Industry Concentration:** Generalist; **Function Concentration:** Generalist

**Rimmel, James E.** — *Vice President - Cleveland/Northeast*
The Hindman Company
123 Lakhani Lane
Canfield, OH 44406
Telephone: (330) 533-5450
**Recruiter Classification:** Retained; **Lowest/Average Salary:** $50,000/$90,000;
**Industry Concentration:** Generalist with a primary focus in
Aerospace/Defense, Automotive, Chemical Products, Consumer Products,
Electronics, Financial Services, High Technology, Manufacturing, Oil/Gas,
Pharmaceutical/Medical, Transportation; **Function Concentration:** Generalist

**Rimmele, Michael** — *Vice President*
The Bankers Group
10 South Riverside Plaza, Suite 1424
Chicago, IL 60606
Telephone: (312) 930-9456
**Recruiter Classification:** Contingency; **Lowest/Average Salary:**
$50,000/$75,000; **Industry Concentration:** Generalist with a primary focus in
Automotive, Financial Services, High Technology, Information Technology,
Insurance, Venture Capital; **Function Concentration:** Generalist with a primary
focus in Administration, Finance/Accounting, General Management, Human
Resources, Marketing, Sales, Women/Minorities

**Rinaldi, Michael D.** — *Vice President*
D.P. Parker and Associates
372 Washington Street
Wellesley, MA 02181
Telephone: (617) 237-1220
**Recruiter Classification:** Retained; **Lowest/Average Salary:** $75,000/$90,000;
**Industry Concentration:** Generalist with a primary focus in
Aerospace/Defense, Automotive, Biotechnology, Chemical Products; **Function**
**Concentration:** Engineering, General Management, Marketing, Research and
Development

**Ring, Paul R.** — *Principal*
Sanford Rose Associates
5335 Far Hills Avenue, Suite 120
Dayton, OH 45429
Telephone: (513) 291-5770
**Recruiter Classification:** Contingency; **Lowest/Average Salary:**
$30,000/$75,000; **Industry Concentration:** Generalist; **Function**
**Concentration:** Generalist

**Rinker, Jim** — *Commercial Finance Specialist*
Southwestern Professional Services
2451 Atrium Way
Nashville, TN 37214
Telephone: (615) 391-2722
**Recruiter Classification:** Contingency; **Lowest/Average Salary:**
$40,000/$50,000; **Industry Concentration:** Automotive, Financial Services,
Insurance, Venture Capital; **Function Concentration:** Administration,
Finance/Accounting, General Management, Marketing, Sales

**Rio, Monica** — *Manager Central Region*
Management Recruiters International, Inc.
P.O. Box 31495
Independence, OH 44131-0495
Telephone: (216) 621-5522
**Recruiter Classification:** Contingency; **Lowest/Average Salary:**
$30,000/$75,000; **Industry Concentration:** Generalist; **Function**
**Concentration:** Generalist

**Rios, Vince** — *Managing Director*
Source Services Corporation
1 Corporate Drive, Suite 215
Shelton, CT 06484
Telephone: (203) 944-9001
**Recruiter Classification:** Contingency; **Lowest/Average Salary:**
$30,000/$50,000; **Industry Concentration:** Financial Services, Information
Technology; **Function Concentration:** Engineering, Finance/Accounting

**Rios, Vincent** — *Managing Director*
Source Services Corporation
2 Penn Plaza, Suite 1176
New York, NY 10121
Telephone: (212) 760-2200
**Recruiter Classification:** Contingency; **Lowest/Average Salary:**
$30,000/$50,000; **Industry Concentration:** Financial Services, Information
Technology; **Function Concentration:** Engineering, Finance/Accounting

**Rippey, George E.** — *Partner*
Heidrick & Struggles, Inc.
Greenwich Office Park #3
Greenwich, CT 06831
Telephone: (203) 629-3200
**Recruiter Classification:** Retained; **Lowest/Average Salary:** $75,000/$90,000;
**Industry Concentration:** Generalist with a primary focus in Consumer
Products, High Technology; **Function Concentration:** Generalist

**Rittenberg, Richard S.** — *Managing Director*
D.E. Foster Partners Inc.
Stamford Square, 3001 Summer Street, 5th Floor
Stamford, CT 06905
Telephone: (203) 406-8247
**Recruiter Classification:** Retained; **Lowest/Average Salary:** $90,000/$90,000;
**Industry Concentration:** Generalist; **Function Concentration:** Generalist

**Rivard, Dick** — *Manager North Atlantic Region*
Management Recruiters International, Inc.
5390 Peachtree Industrial Boulevard, Suite 200
Norcross, GA 30071-1593
Telephone: (770) 825-0003
**Recruiter Classification:** Contingency; **Lowest/Average Salary:**
$30,000/$75,000; **Industry Concentration:** Generalist; **Function**
**Concentration:** Generalist

**Rivas, Alberto F.** — *Managing Director*
Boyden
Paseo de la Reforma 509
110. Piso, Cuauhtemoc
Mexico City, D.F., MEXICO 06500
Telephone: (525) 553-7777
**Recruiter Classification:** Retained; **Lowest/Average Salary:** $75,000/$90,000;
**Industry Concentration:** Generalist; **Function Concentration:** Generalist with a
primary focus in Engineering, Finance/Accounting, General Management,
Human Resources, Marketing, Research and Development, Sales,
Women/Minorities

**Rivera, Elba R.** — *Senior Consultant*
Raymond Karsan Associates
989 Old Eagle School Road, Suite 814
Wayne, PA 19087
Telephone: (610) 971-9171
**Recruiter Classification:** Contingency; **Lowest/Average Salary:**
$30,000/$90,000; **Industry Concentration:** Generalist with a primary focus in
Insurance; **Function Concentration:** Generalist

**Rivers, Geri** — *Executive Recruiter*
Chrisman & Company, Incorporated
350 South Figueroa Street, Suite 550
Los Angeles, CA 90071
Telephone: (213) 620-1192
**Recruiter Classification:** Retained; **Lowest/Average Salary:** $75,000/$90,000;
**Industry Concentration:** Generalist with a primary focus in
Aerospace/Defense, Consumer Products, Energy, Financial Services, Oil/Gas;
**Function Concentration:** Generalist with a primary focus in Engineering,
General Management

**Rizk, Nyla** — *Director*
Spencer Stuart
3000 Sand Hill Road
Building 2, Suite 175
Menlo Park, CA 94025
Telephone: (415) 688-1285
**Recruiter Classification:** Retained; **Lowest/Average Salary:** $90,000/$90,000;
**Industry Concentration:** Generalist; **Function Concentration:** Generalist

**Rizzo, L. Donald** — *President*
R.P. Barone Associates
57 Green Street
Woodbridge, NJ 07095
Telephone: (908) 634-4300
**Recruiter Classification:** Contingency; **Lowest/Average Salary:**
$30,000/$75,000; **Industry Concentration:** Generalist with a primary focus in
Aerospace/Defense, Biotechnology, Chemical Products, Electronics, Energy,
Environmental, Information Technology, Oil/Gas, Packaging,
Pharmaceutical/Medical; **Function Concentration:** Generalist with a primary
focus in Engineering, General Management, Marketing, Research and
Development, Sales

**Roach, Ronald R.** — *Principal*
Sanford Rose Associates
2004 Lowell Avenue, Suite 2-L
Erie, PA 16505
Telephone: (814) 835-7117
**Recruiter Classification:** Contingency; **Lowest/Average Salary:**
$30,000/$75,000; **Industry Concentration:** Generalist; **Function Concentration:** Generalist

**Robb, Tammy** — *Associate*
Source Services Corporation
10300 West 103rd Street, Suite 101
Overland Park, KS 66214
Telephone: (913) 888-8885
**Recruiter Classification:** Contingency; **Lowest/Average Salary:**
$30,000/$50,000; **Industry Concentration:** Financial Services, Information Technology; **Function Concentration:** Engineering, Finance/Accounting

**Robert, Diana** — *Principal*
Korn/Ferry International
303 Peachtree Street N.E.
Suite 1600
Atlanta, GA 30308
Telephone: (404) 577-7542
**Recruiter Classification:** Retained; **Lowest/Average Salary:** $90,000/$90,000; **Industry Concentration:** Generalist; **Function Concentration:** Generalist

**Roberts, Carl R.** — *Vice President/Director*
Southwestern Professional Services
2451 Atrium Way
Nashville, TN 37214
Telephone: (615) 391-2722
**Recruiter Classification:** Contingency; **Lowest/Average Salary:**
$20,000/$40,000; **Industry Concentration:** Generalist with a primary focus in Consumer Products, Financial Services, Information Technology, Insurance, Manufacturing, Pharmaceutical/Medical, Publishing/Media, Real Estate; **Function Concentration:** Generalist with a primary focus in Finance/Accounting, Sales

**Roberts, Clifford** — *Technical Recruiter*
Search Enterprises, Inc.
160 Quail Ridge Drive
Westmont, IL 60559
Telephone: (708) 654-2300
**Recruiter Classification:** Contingency; **Lowest/Average Salary:**
$20,000/$50,000; **Industry Concentration:** Chemical Products; **Function Concentration:** Engineering

**Roberts, Derek J.** — *Partner*
Ward Howell International, Inc.
141 Adelaide Street West
Suite 1800
Toronto, Ontario, CANADA M5H 3L5
Telephone: (416) 862-1273
**Recruiter Classification:** Retained; **Lowest/Average Salary:** $75,000/$90,000; **Industry Concentration:** Fashion (Retail/Apparel), Financial Services, Insurance, Packaging; **Function Concentration:** Generalist

**Roberts, Gary** — *Vice President*
A.T. Kearney, Inc.
One Tabor Center, Suite 950
1200 Seventeenth Street
Denver, CO 80202
Telephone: (303) 572-6175
**Recruiter Classification:** Retained; **Lowest/Average Salary:** $90,000/$90,000; **Industry Concentration:** Generalist; **Function Concentration:** Generalist

**Roberts, Jane** — *Consultant*
Paul Ray Berndtson
191 Peachtree Tower, Suite 3800
191 Peachtree Street, NE
Atlanta, GA 30303-1757
Telephone: (404) 215-4600
**Recruiter Classification:** Retained; **Lowest/Average Salary:** $90,000/$90,000; **Industry Concentration:** Generalist; **Function Concentration:** Generalist

**Roberts, Kenneth** — *Actuarial Specialist*
The Rubicon Group
P.O. Box 2159
Scottsdale, AZ 85252-2159
Telephone: (602) 423-9280
**Recruiter Classification:** Contingency; **Lowest/Average Salary:**
$40,000/$60,000; **Industry Concentration:** Insurance; **Function Concentration:** Generalist with a primary focus in Administration, Finance/Accounting, Research and Development

**Roberts, Mitch** — *Senior Vice President*
A.E. Feldman Associates
445 Northern Boulevard
Great Neck, NY 11021
Telephone: (516) 466-4708
**Recruiter Classification:** Contingency, Executive Temporary; **Lowest/Average Salary:** $50,000/$90,000; **Industry Concentration:** Generalist with a primary focus in Consumer Products, Electronics, Entertainment, Fashion (Retail/Apparel), Financial Services, High Technology, Publishing/Media, Venture Capital; **Function Concentration:** Generalist with a primary focus in Administration, Finance/Accounting, General Management, Human Resources, Marketing, Research and Development, Sales, Women/Minorities

**Roberts, Nick P.** — *President*
Spectrum Search Associates, Inc.
1888 Century Park East, Suite 320
Los Angeles, CA 90067
Telephone: (310) 286-6921
**Recruiter Classification:** Contingency; **Lowest/Average Salary:**
$40,000/$60,000; **Industry Concentration:** Generalist with a primary focus in Biotechnology, Consumer Products, Education/Libraries, Electronics, Entertainment, Environmental, Financial Services, Healthcare/Hospitals, High Technology, Information Technology, Insurance, Manufacturing, Pharmaceutical/Medical, Real Estate; **Function Concentration:** Generalist with a primary focus in Administration, Finance/Accounting, General Management, Human Resources

**Roberts, Norman C.** — *President*
Norman Roberts & Associates, Inc.
1800 Century Park East, Suite 430
Los Angeles, CA 90067
Telephone: (310) 552-1112
**Recruiter Classification:** Retained; **Lowest/Average Salary:** $60,000/$90,000; **Industry Concentration:** Education/Libraries, Energy, Environmental, Healthcare/Hospitals, Information Technology, Non-Profit, Public Administration, Real Estate, Transportation; **Function Concentration:** Generalist with a primary focus in Administration, Engineering, Finance/Accounting, General Management, Human Resources, Marketing, Women/Minorities

**Roberts, Raymond R.** — *Physician Recruiter*
MSI International
201 St. Charles Avenue
Suite 2205
New Orleans, LA 70170
Telephone: (504) 522-6700
**Recruiter Classification:** Contingency; **Lowest/Average Salary:**
$30,000/$60,000; **Industry Concentration:** Generalist with a primary focus in Healthcare/Hospitals; **Function Concentration:** Generalist with a primary focus in Administration, Engineering, Finance/Accounting, General Management, Marketing, Sales

**Roberts, Richard F.** — *Manager Pacific Region*
Management Recruiters International, Inc.
11925 Wilshire Boulevard, Suite 211
Los Angeles, CA 90025
Telephone: (310) 473-0803
**Recruiter Classification:** Contingency; **Lowest/Average Salary:**
$30,000/$75,000; **Industry Concentration:** Generalist; **Function Concentration:** Generalist

**Roberts, Scott B.** — *President*
Wargo and Co., Inc.
850 Elm Grove Road
Elm Grove, WI 53122
Telephone: (414) 785-1211
**Recruiter Classification:** Retained; **Lowest/Average Salary:** $50,000/$90,000; **Industry Concentration:** Generalist with a primary focus in Automotive, Biotechnology, Consumer Products, Electronics, Financial Services, Healthcare/Hospitals, High Technology, Information Technology, Insurance, Manufacturing, Pharmaceutical/Medical, Publishing/Media, Transportation; **Function Concentration:** Generalist with a primary focus in Engineering, Finance/Accounting, General Management, Human Resources, Marketing, Research and Development, Sales

**Roberts, William** — *Recruiter*
Cochran, Cochran & Yale, Inc.
955 East Henrietta Road
Rochester, NY 14623
Telephone: (716) 424-6060
**Recruiter Classification:** Contingency; **Lowest/Average Salary:**
$40,000/$60,000; **Industry Concentration:** Generalist with a primary focus in Automotive, Chemical Products, Consumer Products, Electronics, High Technology, Manufacturing, Packaging, Pharmaceutical/Medical; **Function Concentration:** Marketing, Sales, Women/Minorities

**Robertson, Bruce J.** — *Managing Director*
Norman Broadbent International, Inc.
200 Park Avenue, 20th Floor
New York, NY 10166
Telephone: (212) 953-6990
**Recruiter Classification:** Retained; **Lowest/Average Salary:** $90,000/$90,000;
**Industry Concentration:** Generalist with a primary focus in Consumer Products;
**Function Concentration:** Generalist with a primary focus in Marketing

**Robertson, John H.C.** — *Principal*
Sanford Rose Associates
650 East Carmel Drive
Suite 450
Carmel, IN 46032
Telephone: (317) 848-9987
**Recruiter Classification:** Contingency; **Lowest/Average Salary:**
$30,000/$75,000; **Industry Concentration:** Generalist with a primary focus in
Automotive, Manufacturing; **Function Concentration:** Generalist

**Robertson, Sherry** — *Associate*
Source Services Corporation
5343 North 16th Street, Suite 270
Phoenix, AZ 85016
Telephone: (602) 230-0220
**Recruiter Classification:** Contingency; **Lowest/Average Salary:**
$30,000/$50,000; **Industry Concentration:** Financial Services, Information
Technology; **Function Concentration:** Engineering, Finance/Accounting

**Robertson, William R.** — *Managing Director*
Ward Howell International, Inc.
3350 Peachtree Road N.E.
Suite 1600
Atlanta, GA 30326
Telephone: (404) 261-6532
**Recruiter Classification:** Retained; **Lowest/Average Salary:** $75,000/$90,000;
**Industry Concentration:** Consumer Products, Manufacturing, Packaging,
Pharmaceutical/Medical; **Function Concentration:** Generalist with a primary
focus in Finance/Accounting, General Management

**Robertson, William W.** — *Vice President Legal Search*
Marvin L. Silcott & Associates, Inc.
7557 Rambler Road, Suite 1336
Dallas, TX 75231
Telephone: (214) 369-7802
**Recruiter Classification:** Contingency; **Lowest/Average Salary:** $75,000/$90,000;
**Industry Concentration:** Generalist; **Function Concentration:** Generalist

**Robinette, Paul** — *Account Executive*
Hernand & Partners
3949 Freshwind Circle
Westlake Village, CA 91361
Telephone: (310) 203-0149
**Recruiter Classification:** Executive Temporary; **Industry Concentration:**
High Technology, Information Technology; **Function Concentration:**
Engineering

**Robins, Jeri N.** — *Managing Director*
Nagler, Robins & Poe, Inc.
65 William Street
Wellesley Hills, MA 02181
Telephone: (617) 431-1330
**Recruiter Classification:** Retained; **Lowest/Average Salary:** $75,000/$90,000;
**Industry Concentration:** Generalist with a primary focus in Biotechnology,
Chemical Products, Consumer Products, Electronics, Financial Services, High
Technology, Information Technology, Manufacturing, Public Administration,
Publishing/Media, Real Estate; **Function Concentration:** Generalist with a
primary focus in Engineering, Finance/Accounting, General Management,
Human Resources, Marketing, Sales, Women/Minorities

**Robinson, Adrienne** — *Senior Consultant*
R L Plimpton Associates
5655 South Yosemite Street, Suite 410
Greenwood Village, CO 80111
Telephone: (303) 771-1311
**Recruiter Classification:** Retained; **Lowest/Average Salary:** $40,000/$75,000;
**Industry Concentration:** Generalist; **Function Concentration:** Generalist

**Robinson, Bruce** — *President*
Bruce Robinson Associates
Harmon Cove Towers
Suite 8, A/L Level
Secaucus, NJ 07094
Telephone: (201) 617-9595
**Recruiter Classification:** Retained; **Lowest/Average Salary:** $75,000/$90,000;
**Industry Concentration:** Generalist with a primary focus in Biotechnology,
Board Services, Chemical Products, Consumer Products, Education/Libraries,
Entertainment, Financial Services, High Technology, Insurance, Manufacturing,
Non-Profit, Pharmaceutical/Medical, Publishing/Media, Utilities/Nuclear;
**Function Concentration:** Generalist with a primary focus in Administration,
Engineering, Finance/Accounting, General Management, Human Resources,
Marketing, Research and Development, Sales, Women/Minorities

**Robinson, Eric B.** — *Vice President/Partner*
Bruce Robinson Associates
Harmon Cove Towers
Suite 8, A/L Level
Secaucus, NJ 07094
Telephone: (201) 617-9595
**Recruiter Classification:** Retained; **Lowest/Average Salary:** $75,000/$90,000;
**Industry Concentration:** Generalist with a primary focus in Chemical Products,
Consumer Products, Entertainment, Financial Services, Healthcare/Hospitals,
Information Technology, Insurance, Manufacturing, Pharmaceutical/Medical,
Publishing/Media, Venture Capital; **Function Concentration:** Generalist with a
primary focus in Women/Minorities

**Robinson, Tonya** — *Associate*
Source Services Corporation
2850 National City Tower
Louisville, KY 40202
Telephone: (502) 581-9900
**Recruiter Classification:** Contingency; **Lowest/Average Salary:**
$30,000/$50,000; **Industry Concentration:** Financial Services, Information
Technology; **Function Concentration:** Engineering, Finance/Accounting

**Robison, John H.** — *Chairman and President*
Robison & Associates
1350 First Citizens Plaza
128 South Tryon Street
Charlotte, NC 28202
Telephone: (704) 376-0059
**Recruiter Classification:** Retained; **Lowest/Average Salary:** $50,000/$90,000;
**Industry Concentration:** Generalist with a primary focus in Consumer
Products, Energy, Entertainment, Financial Services, Information Technology,
Insurance, Manufacturing, Non-Profit, Packaging, Public Administration, Real
Estate, Transportation, Venture Capital; **Function Concentration:** Generalist
with a primary focus in Administration, Engineering, Finance/Accounting,
General Management, Human Resources, Marketing, Research and
Development, Sales

**Robson, Ridgely** — *Data Processing Recruiter*
Accounting Personnel Consultants
210 Baronne Street, Suite 920
New Orleans, LA 70112
Telephone: (504) 581-7800
**Recruiter Classification:** Contingency; **Lowest/Average Salary:**
$30,000/$50,000; **Industry Concentration:** Generalist; **Function
Concentration:** Generalist

**Roche, Gerard R.** — *Chairman*
Heidrick & Struggles, Inc.
245 Park Avenue, Suite 4300
New York, NY 10167-0152
Telephone: (212) 867-9876
**Recruiter Classification:** Retained; **Lowest/Average Salary:** $75,000/$90,000;
**Industry Concentration:** Generalist; **Function Concentration:** Generalist

**Rockwell, Bruce** — *Managing Director*
Source Services Corporation
One South Main Street, Suite 1440
Dayton, OH 45402
Telephone: (513) 461-4660
**Recruiter Classification:** Contingency; **Lowest/Average Salary:**
$30,000/$50,000; **Industry Concentration:** Financial Services, Information
Technology; **Function Concentration:** Engineering, Finance/Accounting

**Rodebaugh, Karen** — *Co-Manager Eastern Region*
Management Recruiters International, Inc.
2233 Dutch Gold Drive
Lancaster, PA 17601-1997
Telephone: (717) 397-6444
**Recruiter Classification:** Contingency; **Lowest/Average Salary:**
$30,000/$75,000; **Industry Concentration:** Generalist; **Function
Concentration:** Generalist

**Rodebaugh, Thomas L.** — *Co-Manager*
Management Recruiters International, Inc.
2233 Dutch Gold Drive
Lancaster, PA 17601-1997
Telephone: (717) 397-6444
**Recruiter Classification:** Contingency; **Lowest/Average Salary:**
$30,000/$75,000; **Industry Concentration:** Generalist; **Function
Concentration:** Generalist

**Rodetsky, Laurie** — *Representative Marketing*
Bradford & Galt, Inc.
12400 Olive Boulevard, Suite 430
St. Louis, MO 63141
Telephone: (314) 434-9200
**Recruiter Classification:** Contingency; **Lowest/Average Salary:**
$30,000/$30,000; **Industry Concentration:** Generalist; **Function
Concentration:** Generalist

**Rodgers, John** — *Agribusiness Recruiter*
Agra Placements International Ltd.
16 East Fifth Street, Berkshire Court
Peru, IN 46970
Telephone: (317) 472-1988
**Recruiter Classification:** Contingency; **Lowest/Average Salary:**
$20,000/$30,000; **Industry Concentration:** Generalist with a primary focus in
Biotechnology, Chemical Products, Energy, Financial Services, Manufacturing;
**Function Concentration:** Administration, Engineering, Finance/Accounting,
General Management, Human Resources, Marketing, Research and
Development, Sales

**Rodgers, Kathi** — *President*
St. Lawrence International, Inc.
6432 Baird Avenue
Syracuse, NY 13206
Telephone: (315) 432-4588
**Recruiter Classification:** Executive Temporary; **Lowest/Average Salary:**
$30,000/$50,000; **Industry Concentration:** Generalist with a primary focus in
Aerospace/Defense, Automotive, Consumer Products, Manufacturing,
Packaging; **Function Concentration:** Generalist with a primary focus in
Administration, Engineering, General Management, Human Resources,
Marketing, Research and Development, Sales

**Rodgers, Sarah J.** — *Manager Eastern Region*
Management Recruiters International, Inc.
440 County Road 513, Suite 207
Califon, NJ 07830
Telephone: (908) 832-6455
**Recruiter Classification:** Contingency; **Lowest/Average Salary:**
$30,000/$75,000; **Industry Concentration:** Generalist; **Function
Concentration:** Generalist

**Rodney, Brett** — *Physician Recruiter*
MSI International
6345 Balboa Boulevard
Suite 335
Encino, CA 91316
Telephone: (818) 342-0222
**Recruiter Classification:** Contingency; **Lowest/Average Salary:**
$30,000/$60,000; **Industry Concentration:** Generalist with a primary focus in
Healthcare/Hospitals; **Function Concentration:** Generalist with a primary focus
in Administration, Engineering, Finance/Accounting, General Management,
Marketing, Sales

**Rodriguez, Carlos R.** — *Manager South Atlantic Region*
Management Recruiters International, Inc.
General Computer Building
1590 Ponce de Leon, Suite 112
Rio Piedras, PR 00926-2702
Telephone: (809) 766-4055
**Recruiter Classification:** Contingency; **Lowest/Average Salary:**
$30,000/$75,000; **Industry Concentration:** Generalist; **Function
Concentration:** Generalist

**Rodriguez, Josie** — *Associate*
R. Parker and Associates, Inc.
551 5th Avenue, Suite 222
New York, NY 10176
Telephone: (212) 661-8074
**Recruiter Classification:** Retained; **Lowest/Average Salary:** $50,000/$75,000;
**Industry Concentration:** Generalist with a primary focus in Consumer
Products, Fashion (Retail/Apparel); **Function Concentration:** Generalist with a
primary focus in General Management, Marketing, Sales

**Rodriguez, Manuel** — *Associate*
Source Services Corporation
15600 N.W. 67th Avenue, Suite 210
Miami Lakes, FL 33014
Telephone: (305) 556-8000
**Recruiter Classification:** Contingency; **Lowest/Average Salary:**
$30,000/$50,000; **Industry Concentration:** Financial Services, Information
Technology; **Function Concentration:** Engineering, Finance/Accounting

**Rodriguez, Steven** — *Director*
Spencer Stuart
10900 Wilshire Boulevard, Suite 800
Los Angeles, CA 90024-6524
Telephone: (310) 209-0610
**Recruiter Classification:** Retained; **Lowest/Average Salary:** $90,000/$90,000;
**Industry Concentration:** Generalist; **Function Concentration:** Generalist

**Roehrig, Kurt W.** — *Associate*
AJM Professional Services
803 West Big Beaver Road, Suite 357
Troy, MI 48084-4734
Telephone: (810) 244-2222
**Recruiter Classification:** Contingency; **Lowest/Average Salary:**
$30,000/$60,000; **Industry Concentration:** Generalist with a primary focus in
Financial Services, Healthcare/Hospitals, High Technology, Information
Technology, Insurance, Manufacturing

**Roethlein, John** — *Co-Manager*
Management Recruiters International, Inc.
6262 North Swan Road, Suite 125
Tucson, AZ 85718-3600
Telephone: (520) 529-6818
**Recruiter Classification:** Contingency; **Lowest/Average Salary:** $30,000/$75,000;
**Industry Concentration:** Generalist; **Function Concentration:** Generalist

**Roethlein, Lorian E.** — *Co-Manager Pacific Region*
Management Recruiters International, Inc.
6262 North Swan Road, Suite 125
Tucson, AZ 85718-3600
Telephone: (520) 529-6818
**Recruiter Classification:** Contingency; **Lowest/Average Salary:** $30,000/$75,000;
**Industry Concentration:** Generalist; **Function Concentration:** Generalist

**Rogan, John P.** — *Managing Director*
Russell Reynolds Associates, Inc.
200 Park Avenue
New York, NY 10166-0002
Telephone: (212) 351-2000
**Recruiter Classification:** Retained; **Lowest/Average Salary:** $90,000/$90,000;
**Industry Concentration:** Generalist with a primary focus in Financial Services;
**Function Concentration:** Generalist

**Rogers, Gay** — *Partner*
Rogers-McManamon Executive Search
33781 Via Cascada
San Juan Capistrano, CA 92675
Telephone: (714) 496-1614
**Recruiter Classification:** Retained; **Lowest/Average Salary:** $60,000/$90,000;
**Industry Concentration:** High Technology, Information Technology; **Function
Concentration:** Generalist

**Rogers, Leah** — *Vice President*
Dinte Resources, Incorporated
8300 Greensboro Drive
Suite 880
McLean, VA 22102
Telephone: (703) 448-3300
**Recruiter Classification:** Executive Temporary; **Lowest/Average Salary:**
$75,000/$90,000; **Industry Concentration:** Generalist with a primary focus in
Environmental, Financial Services, Healthcare/Hospitals, High Technology,
Information Technology, Non-Profit, Oil/Gas, Transportation; **Function
Concentration:** Generalist

**Rohan, James E.** — *Senior Partner*
J.P. Canon Associates
225 Broadway, Suite 3602
New York, NY 10007
Telephone: (212) 233-3131
**Recruiter Classification:** Contingency; **Lowest/Average Salary:**
$30,000/$60,000; **Industry Concentration:** Generalist with a primary focus in
Information Technology; **Function Concentration:** Generalist

**Rohan, Kevin A.** — *Recruiter*
J.P. Canon Associates
225 Broadway, Suite 3602
New York, NY 10007
Telephone: (212) 233-3131
**Recruiter Classification:** Contingency; **Lowest/Average Salary:** $30,000/$50,000;
**Industry Concentration:** Generalist; **Function Concentration:** Generalist

**Rojas-Magnon, Carlos** — *Managing Partner*
Amrop International
Amberes #4, 2 Pia, Colonia Juarez
Mexico City, D.F., MEXICO 06600
Telephone: (525) 208-3977
**Recruiter Classification:** Retained, Contingency; **Lowest/Average Salary:**
$90,000/$90,000; **Industry Concentration:** Generalist; **Function
Concentration:** Generalist

**Roll, Bill** — *Manager Southwest Region*
Management Recruiters International, Inc.
1333 Corporate Drive, Suite 211
Irving, TX 75038
Telephone: (214) 550-2424
**Recruiter Classification:** Contingency; **Lowest/Average Salary:** $30,000/$75,000;
**Industry Concentration:** Generalist; **Function Concentration:** Generalist

**Rollins, Scott** — *President*
S.C. International, Ltd.
1430 Branding Lane, Suite 119
Downers Grove, IL 60515
Telephone: (708) 963-3033
**Recruiter Classification:** Contingency; **Lowest/Average Salary:**
$30,000/$50,000; **Industry Concentration:** Information Technology, Insurance;
**Function Concentration:** Administration, Human Resources

**Rollo, Robert S.** — *Partner*
R. Rollo Associates
725 South Figueroa Street, Suite 3230
Los Angeles, CA 90017
Telephone: (213) 892-7845
**Recruiter Classification:** Retained; **Lowest/Average Salary:** $90,000/$90,000;
**Industry Concentration:** Generalist with a primary focus in
Aerospace/Defense, Consumer Products, Energy, Financial Services,
Healthcare/Hospitals, Hospitality/Leisure, Insurance, Manufacturing, Non-
Profit, Oil/Gas, Real Estate, Transportation, Venture Capital; **Function
Concentration:** Generalist

**Romaine, Stanley J.** — *Principal*
Mixtec Group
31255 Cedar Valley Drive
Suite 300-327
Westlake Village, CA 91362
Telephone: (818) 889-8819
**Recruiter Classification:** Contingency; **Lowest/Average Salary:**
$60,000/$90,000; **Industry Concentration:** Hospitality/Leisure; **Function
Concentration:** Generalist with a primary focus in Administration,
Finance/Accounting, General Management, Marketing, Sales

**Romanchek, Walter R.** — *Principal*
Wellington Management Group
117 South 17th Street, Suite 1625
Philadelphia, PA 19103
Telephone: (215) 569-8900
**Recruiter Classification:** Retained; **Lowest/Average Salary:** $75,000/$90,000;
**Industry Concentration:** Generalist with a primary focus in Biotechnology,
Chemical Products, Consumer Products, Healthcare/Hospitals, High
Technology, Information Technology, Manufacturing, Oil/Gas; **Function
Concentration:** Generalist with a primary focus in Administration,
Finance/Accounting, General Management, Human Resources, Marketing,
Research and Development, Sales

**Romanello, Daniel P.** — *Senior Director*
Spencer Stuart
Financial Centre
695 East Main Street
Stamford, CT 06901
Telephone: (203) 324-6333
**Recruiter Classification:** Retained; **Lowest/Average Salary:** $90,000/$90,000;
**Industry Concentration:** Electronics, High Technology, Information
Technology, Venture Capital; **Function Concentration:** Generalist with a
primary focus in Engineering, Finance/Accounting, General Management,
Human Resources, Marketing, Research and Development, Sales

**Romaniw, Michael J.** — *President*
A la carte International
1617 South Pacific Coast Highway, Suite C
Redondo Beach, CA 90217
Telephone: (800) 446-3037
**Recruiter Classification:** Retained; **Lowest/Average Salary:** $60,000/$90,000;
**Industry Concentration:** Generalist with a primary focus in Consumer
Products, Hospitality/Leisure; **Function Concentration:** Generalist with a
primary focus in General Management, Human Resources, Marketing,
Research and Development, Sales

**Romaniw, Michael J.** — *President*
A la carte International
3330 Pacific Avenue, Suite 500
Virginia Beach, VA 23451
Telephone: (804) 425-6111
**Recruiter Classification:** Retained; **Lowest/Average Salary:** $60,000/$90,000;
**Industry Concentration:** Generalist with a primary focus in Consumer
Products, Hospitality/Leisure; **Function Concentration:** Generalist with a
primary focus in General Management, Human Resources, Marketing,
Research and Development, Sales

**Romaniw, Michael J.** — *President*
A la carte International
Aguascalientes No. 199 Piso 6
Col. Hipodromo Condesa
Mexico City, D.F., MEXICO 06700
Telephone: (525) 584-0288
**Recruiter Classification:** Retained; **Lowest/Average Salary:** $60,000/$90,000;
**Industry Concentration:** Generalist with a primary focus in Consumer
Products, Hospitality/Leisure; **Function Concentration:** Generalist with a
primary focus in General Management, Human Resources, Marketing,
Research and Development, Sales

**Romano, Darren G.** — *Senior Associate*
Korn/Ferry International
One Landmark Square
Stamford, CT 06901
Telephone: (203) 359-3350
**Recruiter Classification:** Retained; **Lowest/Average Salary:** $90,000/$90,000;
**Industry Concentration:** Generalist; **Function Concentration:** Generalist

**Romanowicz, Jill** — *Consultant*
Howard Fischer Associates, Inc.
1800 John F. Kennedy Boulevard, 7th Floor
Philadelphia, PA 19103
Telephone: (215) 568-8363
**Recruiter Classification:** Retained; **Lowest/Average Salary:** $90,000/$90,000;
**Industry Concentration:** Generalist; **Function Concentration:** Generalist

**Romm, Barry** — *Managing Director*
Klein, Landau, Romm & North
1725 K Street NW, Suite 602
Washington, DC 20006
Telephone: (202) 728-0100
**Recruiter Classification:** Contingency; **Lowest/Average Salary:**
$50,000/$90,000

**Romo, Dorothy** — *Consultant Physician Search*
D. Brown and Associates, Inc.
610 S.W. Alder, Suite 1111
Portland, OR 97205
Telephone: (503) 224-6860
**Recruiter Classification:** Contingency; **Lowest/Average Salary:** $90,000/$90,000;
**Industry Concentration:** Healthcare/Hospitals

**Ropella, Patrick B.** — *President*
Ropella & Associates
1307 East Road Five
Edgerton, WI 53534
Telephone: (608) 884-9250
**Recruiter Classification:** Retained; **Lowest/Average Salary:** $75,000/$90,000;
**Industry Concentration:** Chemical Products; **Function Concentration:**
Engineering, General Management, Marketing, Research and Development, Sales

**Ropes, John** — *President*
Ropes Associates, Inc.
333 North New River Drive East
Fort Lauderdale, FL 33301
Telephone: (305) 525-6600
**Recruiter Classification:** Retained; **Lowest/Average Salary:** $90,000/$90,000;
**Industry Concentration:** Financial Services, Hospitality/Leisure, Real Estate;
**Function Concentration:** Generalist

**Rorech, Maureen** — *Division Vice President*
Romac & Associates
120 Hyde Park Place
Suite 200
Tampa, FL 33606
Telephone: (813) 229-5575
**Recruiter Classification:** Executive Temporary; **Lowest/Average Salary:**
$/$60,000; **Industry Concentration:** Financial Services, Healthcare/Hospitals,
High Technology, Hospitality/Leisure, Information Technology, Insurance;
**Function Concentration:** Finance/Accounting

**Rosato, William R.** — *President*
W.R. Rosato & Associates, Inc.
71 Broadway, Suite 1601
New York, NY 10006
Telephone: (212) 509-5700
**Recruiter Classification:** Retained; **Lowest/Average Salary:** $90,000/$90,000;
**Industry Concentration:** Financial Services, High Technology, Information
Technology; **Function Concentration:** Administration, Marketing, Research and
Development, Sales

**Rose, Sanford M.** — *Principal*
Sanford Rose Associates
265 South Main Street, Suite 200
Akron, OH 44308
Telephone: (330) 762-6211
**Recruiter Classification:** Contingency; **Lowest/Average Salary:** $30,000/$75,000;
**Industry Concentration:** Generalist; **Function Concentration:** Generalist

**Rosemarin, Gloria J.** — *President*
Barrington Hart, Inc.
20 North Wacker Drive, Suite 2710
Chicago, IL 60606
Telephone: (312) 332-3344
**Recruiter Classification:** Retained; **Lowest/Average Salary:** $40,000/$75,000;
**Industry Concentration:** Generalist with a primary focus in Financial Services;
**Function Concentration:** Generalist with a primary focus in
Finance/Accounting, General Management, Marketing, Sales

**Rosen, Elayne** — *Senior Vice President*
Noble & Associates Inc.
420 Madison Avenue
New York, NY 10017
Telephone: (212) 838-7020
**Recruiter Classification:** Contingency; **Lowest/Average Salary:**
$40,000/$90,000; **Industry Concentration:** Generalist; **Function
Concentration:** Marketing

**Rosen, Mark** — *Accounting and Finance Recruiter*
Winter, Wyman & Company
101 Federal Street, 27th Floor
Boston, MA 02110-1800
Telephone: (617) 951-2700
**Recruiter Classification:** Contingency; **Lowest/Average Salary:**
$20,000/$50,000; **Industry Concentration:** Generalist; **Function Concentration:** Finance/Accounting

**Rosen, Mitchell** — *Associate*
Source Services Corporation
1290 Oakmead Parkway, Suite 318
Sunnyvale, CA 94086
Telephone: (408) 738-8440
**Recruiter Classification:** Contingency; **Lowest/Average Salary:**
$30,000/$50,000; **Industry Concentration:** Financial Services, Information Technology; **Function Concentration:** Engineering, Finance/Accounting

**Rosen, Salene** — *Research Associate*
Bryant Research
466 Old Hook Road, Suite 32
Emerson, NJ 07630
Telephone: (201) 599-0590
**Recruiter Classification:** Contingency; **Lowest/Average Salary:**
$50,000/$90,000; **Industry Concentration:** Biotechnology, Pharmaceutical/Medical; **Function Concentration:** Research and Development

**Rosenberg, Esther** — *Co-Managing Director*
Howe-Lewis International
521 Fifth Avenue, 36th Floor
New York, NY 10175
Telephone: (212) 697-5000
**Recruiter Classification:** Retained; **Lowest/Average Salary:** $90,000/$90,000;
**Industry Concentration:** Board Services, Education/Libraries,
Healthcare/Hospitals, Non-Profit; **Function Concentration:** Generalist with a primary focus in General Management, Marketing, Women/Minorities

**Rosenfeld, Martin J.** — *Principal*
Sanford Rose Associates
25900 Greenfield Road
Suite 236
Oak Park, MI 48237
Telephone: (810) 968-3210
**Recruiter Classification:** Contingency; **Lowest/Average Salary:**
$30,000/$75,000; **Industry Concentration:** Generalist with a primary focus in Automotive, Healthcare/Hospitals; **Function Concentration:** Generalist

**Rosenstein, Michele** — *Associate*
Source Services Corporation
120 East Baltimore Street, Suite 1950
Baltimore, MD 21202
Telephone: (410) 727-4050
**Recruiter Classification:** Contingency; **Lowest/Average Salary:**
$30,000/$50,000; **Industry Concentration:** Financial Services, Information Technology; **Function Concentration:** Engineering, Finance/Accounting

**Rosenthal, Andrea** — *Senior Associate*
Korn/Ferry International
1800 Century Park East, Suite 900
Los Angeles, CA 90067
Telephone: (310) 552-1834
**Recruiter Classification:** Retained; **Lowest/Average Salary:** $90,000/$90,000;
**Industry Concentration:** Generalist; **Function Concentration:** Generalist

**Rosenthal, Charles** — *Senior Medical Consultant*
National Search, Inc.
2816 University Drive
Coral Springs, FL 33071
Telephone: (800) 935-4355
**Recruiter Classification:** Contingency; **Lowest/Average Salary:**
$30,000/$50,000; **Industry Concentration:** Healthcare/Hospitals, Insurance, Pharmaceutical/Medical; **Function Concentration:** Generalist with a primary focus in Administration, Finance/Accounting, General Management, Human Resources, Marketing, Research and Development, Sales, Women/Minorities

**Rosenwald, Tom H.** — *Partner*
Heidrick & Struggles, Inc.
245 Park Avenue, Suite 4300
New York, NY 10167-0152
Telephone: (212) 867-9876
**Recruiter Classification:** Retained; **Lowest/Average Salary:** $75,000/$90,000;
**Industry Concentration:** Generalist with a primary focus in Consumer Products, Healthcare/Hospitals; **Function Concentration:** Generalist

**Rosica, John** — *Manager Pacific Region*
Management Recruiters International, Inc.
2055 Gateway Place, Suite 420
San Jose, CA 95110
Telephone: (408) 453-9999
**Recruiter Classification:** Contingency; **Lowest/Average Salary:**
$30,000/$75,000; **Industry Concentration:** Generalist; **Function Concentration:** Generalist

**Ross, Garland E.** — *Manager Midwest Region*
Management Recruiters International, Inc.
Cadillac Square, Suite 1
444 South Adams Street
Green Bay, WI 54301
Telephone: (414) 437-4353
**Recruiter Classification:** Contingency; **Lowest/Average Salary:**
$30,000/$75,000; **Industry Concentration:** Generalist; **Function Concentration:** Generalist

**Ross, John** — *Associate*
Morgan Stampfl, Inc.
6 West 32nd Street
New York, NY 10001
Telephone: (212) 643-7165
**Recruiter Classification:** Contingency; **Lowest/Average Salary:**
$50,000/$90,000; **Industry Concentration:** Financial Services; **Function Concentration:** Finance/Accounting

**Ross, Lawrence** — *Consultant*
Lovas Stanley/Paul Ray Berndtson Inc.
Royal Bank Plaza, South Tower, Suite 3150
200 Bay Street, P.O. Box 125
Toronto, Ontario, CANADA M5J 2J3
Telephone: (416) 366-1990
**Recruiter Classification:** Retained; **Lowest/Average Salary:** $75,000/$90,000;
**Industry Concentration:** Generalist with a primary focus in Aerospace/Defense, Automotive, Consumer Products, Financial Services, High Technology, Information Technology, Manufacturing; **Function Concentration:** Generalist with a primary focus in Finance/Accounting, General Management, Human Resources, Marketing, Sales

**Ross, Marc A.** — *Recruiter*
Flowers & Associates
1446 South Reynolds, Suite 112
P.O. Box 538
Maumee, OH 43537
Telephone: (419) 893-4816
**Recruiter Classification:** Contingency; **Lowest/Average Salary:**
$30,000/$50,000; **Industry Concentration:** Generalist with a primary focus in Automotive, Manufacturing; **Function Concentration:** Generalist with a primary focus in Engineering, General Management, Sales

**Ross, Mark S.** — *Partner*
Herman Smith Executive Initiatives Inc.
Suite 3600, 161 Bay Street, Box 629
Toronto, Ontario, CANADA M5J 2S1
Telephone: (416) 862-8830
**Recruiter Classification:** Retained; **Lowest/Average Salary:** $60,000/$90,000;
**Industry Concentration:** Generalist with a primary focus in Aerospace/Defense, Consumer Products, Education/Libraries, Entertainment, Financial Services, High Technology, Information Technology, Manufacturing, Pharmaceutical/Medical, Public Administration, Real Estate, Transportation; **Function Concentration:** Generalist with a primary focus in Engineering, Finance/Accounting, General Management, Human Resources, Marketing

**Ross, Martin B.** — *Managing Director*
Ward Howell International, Inc.
16255 Ventura Boulevard
Suite 400
Encino, CA 91436-2394
Telephone: (818) 905-6010
**Recruiter Classification:** Retained; **Lowest/Average Salary:** $75,000/$90,000;
**Industry Concentration:** Education/Libraries, Healthcare/Hospitals; **Function Concentration:** Generalist with a primary focus in General Management, Research and Development

**Ross, Sheila L.** — *Partner*
Ward Howell International, Inc.
141 Adelaide Street West
Suite 1800
Toronto, Ontario, CANADA M5H 3L5
Telephone: (416) 862-1273
**Recruiter Classification:** Retained; **Lowest/Average Salary:** $75,000/$90,000;
**Industry Concentration:** Fashion (Retail/Apparel), Financial Services, Insurance; **Function Concentration:** Generalist

**Ross, William J.** — *President*
Flowers & Associates
1446 South Reynolds, Suite 112
P.O. Box 538
Maumee, OH 43537
Telephone: (419) 893-4816
**Recruiter Classification:** Contingency; **Lowest/Average Salary:**
$30,000/$50,000; **Industry Concentration:** Generalist with a primary focus in
Automotive, High Technology, Manufacturing; **Function Concentration:**
Generalist with a primary focus in Administration, Engineering,
Finance/Accounting, General Management, Sales

**Rossi, George A.** — *Managing Partner*
Heidrick & Struggles, Inc.
One Post Office Square
Boston, MA 02109-0199
Telephone: (617) 423-1140
**Recruiter Classification:** Retained; **Lowest/Average Salary:** $75,000/$90,000;
**Industry Concentration:** Generalist with a primary focus in High Technology;
**Function Concentration:** Generalist

**Rossi, Silvio** — *Consultant*
Keith Bagg & Associates Inc.
36 Toronto Street, Suite 520
Toronto, Ontario, CANADA M5C 2C5
Telephone: (416) 863-1800
**Recruiter Classification:** Contingency; **Lowest/Average Salary:**
$40,000/$60,000; **Industry Concentration:** Biotechnology, Chemical Products,
Consumer Products, Electronics, High Technology, Manufacturing,
Pharmaceutical/Medical; **Function Concentration:** Administration,
Engineering, Finance/Accounting, General Management, Marketing, Research
and Development, Sales

**Rossi, Thomas** — *Manager*
Southwestern Professional Services
2451 Atrium Way
Nashville, TN 37214
Telephone: (615) 391-2722
**Recruiter Classification:** Contingency; **Lowest/Average Salary:**
$40,000/$75,000; **Industry Concentration:** Healthcare/Hospitals, High
Technology, Information Technology; **Function Concentration:**
Finance/Accounting, Sales

**Rossman, Paul R.** — *Co-Manager Central Region*
Management Recruiters International, Inc.
300 Weyman Plaza, Suite 140
Pittsburgh, PA 15236
Telephone: (412) 885-5222
**Recruiter Classification:** Contingency; **Lowest/Average Salary:**
$30,000/$75,000; **Industry Concentration:** Generalist; **Function
Concentration:** Generalist

**Rotella, Marshall W.** — *President*
The Corporate Connection, Ltd.
7202 Glen Forest Drive
Richmond, VA 23226
Telephone: (804) 288-8844
**Recruiter Classification:** Contingency; **Lowest/Average Salary:**
$20,000/$50,000; **Industry Concentration:** Generalist with a primary focus in
Aerospace/Defense, Biotechnology, Financial Services, Healthcare/Hospitals,
High Technology, Information Technology, Insurance, Manufacturing; **Function
Concentration:** Generalist

**Roth, Robert J.** — *Partner*
Williams, Roth & Krueger Inc.
20 North Wacker Drive
Chicago, IL 60606
Telephone: (312) 977-0800
**Recruiter Classification:** Retained; **Lowest/Average Salary:** $90,000/$90,000;
**Industry Concentration:** Generalist with a primary focus in
Aerospace/Defense, Board Services, Consumer Products, Electronics, Financial
Services, High Technology, Information Technology, Manufacturing; **Function
Concentration:** Generalist with a primary focus in Administration, Engineering,
Finance/Accounting, General Management, Human Resources, Marketing,
Research and Development, Sales

**Roth, William** — *Senior Associate*
Harris Heery & Associates
40 Richards Avenue
One Norwalk West
Norwalk, CT 06854
Telephone: (203) 857-0808
**Recruiter Classification:** Retained; **Lowest/Average Salary:** $75,000/$90,000;
**Industry Concentration:** Consumer Products, Fashion (Retail/Apparel),
Financial Services, Insurance, Publishing/Media; **Function Concentration:**
General Management, Marketing

**Rothenberg, Paul** — *Senior Consultant*
The McCormick Group, Inc.
1400 Wilson Boulevard
Arlington, VA 22209
Telephone: (703) 841-1700
**Recruiter Classification:** Retained; **Lowest/Average Salary:** $90,000/$90,000;
**Industry Concentration:** Generalist; **Function Concentration:** Generalist

**Rothenbush, Clayton** — *Managing Director*
Source Services Corporation
1105 Schrock Road, Suite 510
Columbus, OH 43229
Telephone: (614) 846-3311
**Recruiter Classification:** Contingency; **Lowest/Average Salary:**
$30,000/$50,000; **Industry Concentration:** Financial Services, Information
Technology; **Function Concentration:** Engineering, Finance/Accounting

**Rothfeld, Robert** — *Vice President*
A.E. Feldman Associates
445 Northern Boulevard
Great Neck, NY 11021
Telephone: (516) 466-4708
**Recruiter Classification:** Contingency, Executive Temporary; **Lowest/Average
Salary:** $50,000/$90,000; **Industry Concentration:** Generalist with a primary
focus in Consumer Products, Electronics, Entertainment, Environmental,
Fashion (Retail/Apparel), Financial Services, Publishing/Media, Venture Capital;
**Function Concentration:** Generalist with a primary focus in Administration,
Finance/Accounting, General Management, Marketing, Sales,
Women/Minorities

**Rothman, Jeffrey** — *Director Business Development*
ProResource, Inc.
301 Grant Street, Suite 1500
Pittsburgh, PA 15219
Telephone: (412) 255-3741
**Recruiter Classification:** Executive Temporary; **Lowest/Average Salary:**
$30,000/$75,000; **Industry Concentration:** Generalist; **Function
Concentration:** Generalist with a primary focus in Engineering,
Finance/Accounting, General Management, Human Resources, Marketing,
Research and Development

**Rothschild, John S.** — *Partner*
Heidrick & Struggles, Inc.
125 South Wacker Drive
Suite 2800
Chicago, IL 60606-4590
Telephone: (312) 372-8811
**Recruiter Classification:** Retained; **Lowest/Average Salary:** $75,000/$90,000;
**Industry Concentration:** Generalist with a primary focus in High Technology;
**Function Concentration:** Generalist

**Rothwell, Amy** — *Consultant*
Howard Fischer Associates, Inc.
1800 John F. Kennedy Boulevard, 7th Floor
Philadelphia, PA 19103
Telephone: (215) 568-8363
**Recruiter Classification:** Retained; **Lowest/Average Salary:** $90,000/$90,000;
**Industry Concentration:** Generalist; **Function Concentration:** Generalist

**Rottblatt, Michael** — *Vice President*
Korn/Ferry International
One Landmark Square
Stamford, CT 06901
Telephone: (203) 359-3350
**Recruiter Classification:** Retained; **Lowest/Average Salary:** $90,000/$90,000;
**Industry Concentration:** Generalist with a primary focus in High Technology;
**Function Concentration:** Generalist

**Roussel, Vicki** — *Consultant*
Logix Partners
1601 Trapelo Road
Waltham, MA 02154
Telephone: (617) 890-0500
**Recruiter Classification:** Retained; **Lowest/Average Salary:** $60,000/$75,000;
**Industry Concentration:** High Technology; **Function Concentration:**
Engineering

**Roussel, Vicki J.** — *Consultant*
Logix, Inc.
1601 Trapelo Road
Waltham, MA 02154
Telephone: (617) 890-0500
**Recruiter Classification:** Retained; **Lowest/Average Salary:** $60,000/$75,000;
**Industry Concentration:** High Technology; **Function Concentration:**
Engineering

**Rowe, Thomas A.** — *Principal*
Korn/Ferry International
237 Park Avenue
New York, NY 10017
Telephone: (212) 687-1834
**Recruiter Classification:** Retained; **Lowest/Average Salary:** $90,000/$90,000;
**Industry Concentration:** Generalist with a primary focus in Financial Services;
**Function Concentration:** Generalist with a primary focus in
Finance/Accounting

**Rowe, William D.** — *Vice Chairman/Executive Managing Director*
D.E. Foster Partners Inc.
200 Crescent Court, Suite 300
Dallas, TX 75201-1885
Telephone: (214) 754-2241
**Recruiter Classification:** Retained; **Lowest/Average Salary:** $90,000/$90,000;
**Industry Concentration:** Board Services, Financial Services,
Healthcare/Hospitals, High Technology, Hospitality/Leisure, Insurance, Venture
Capital; **Function Concentration:** Generalist with a primary focus in
Finance/Accounting, General Management, Human Resources

**Rowell, Roger** — *Vice President*
Halbrecht Lieberman Associates, Inc.
1200 Summer Street
Stamford, CT 06905
Telephone: (203) 327-5630
**Recruiter Classification:** Retained; **Lowest/Average Salary:** $90,000/$90,000;
**Industry Concentration:** High Technology, Information Technology; **Function
Concentration:** Generalist

**Rowells, Michael** — *Physician Recruiter*
MSI International
201 St. Charles Avenue
Suite 2205
New Orleans, LA 70170
Telephone: (504) 522-6700
**Recruiter Classification:** Contingency; **Lowest/Average Salary:**
$30,000/$60,000; **Industry Concentration:** Generalist with a primary focus in
Healthcare/Hospitals; **Function Concentration:** Generalist with a primary focus
in Administration, Engineering, Finance/Accounting, General Management,
Marketing, Sales

**Rowenhorst, Brenda** — *President*
The Bren Group
7320 East Shoeman Lane
Scottsdale, AZ 85251
Telephone: (602) 970-1091
**Recruiter Classification:** Contingency; **Lowest/Average Salary:**
$20,000/$40,000; **Industry Concentration:** Hospitality/Leisure; **Function
Concentration:** Generalist

**Rowland, James** — *Associate*
Source Services Corporation
10300 West 103rd Street, Suite 101
Overland Park, KS 66214
Telephone: (913) 888-8885
**Recruiter Classification:** Contingency; **Lowest/Average Salary:**
$30,000/$50,000; **Industry Concentration:** Financial Services, Information
Technology; **Function Concentration:** Engineering, Finance/Accounting

**Roy, Gary P.** — *Manager Southwest Region*
Management Recruiters International, Inc.
Memport Office Park, Suite 4
3441 West Memorial Road
Oklahoma City, OK 73134
Telephone: (405) 752-8848
**Recruiter Classification:** Contingency; **Lowest/Average Salary:**
$30,000/$75,000; **Industry Concentration:** Generalist; **Function
Concentration:** Generalist

**Rozan, Naomi** — *Managing Director*
Comprehensive Search
316 South Lewis Street
LaGrange, GA 30240
Telephone: (706) 884-3232
**Recruiter Classification:** Contingency, Executive Temporary; **Lowest/Average
Salary:** $30,000/$60,000; **Industry Concentration:** Consumer Products,
Fashion (Retail/Apparel), Hospitality/Leisure, Manufacturing, Non-Profit, Public
Administration, Real Estate; **Function Concentration:** Generalist

**Rozentsvayg, Michael** — *Consultant*
Logix Partners
1601 Trapelo Road
Waltham, MA 02154
Telephone: (617) 890-0500
**Recruiter Classification:** Retained; **Lowest/Average Salary:** $60,000/$75,000;
**Industry Concentration:** High Technology, Information Technology; **Function
Concentration:** Engineering

**Rozentsvayg, Michael** — *Consultant*
Logix, Inc.
1601 Trapelo Road
Waltham, MA 02154
Telephone: (617) 890-0500
**Recruiter Classification:** Retained; **Lowest/Average Salary:** $60,000/$75,000;
**Industry Concentration:** High Technology, Information Technology; **Function
Concentration:** Engineering

**Rozner, Burton L.** — *President*
Oliver & Rozner Associates, Inc.
598 Madison Avenue
New York, NY 10022
Telephone: (212) 688-1850
**Recruiter Classification:** Retained; **Lowest/Average Salary:** $90,000/$90,000;
**Industry Concentration:** Generalist with a primary focus in Biotechnology,
Chemical Products, Electronics, Healthcare/Hospitals, High Technology,
Manufacturing, Pharmaceutical/Medical, Transportation; **Function
Concentration:** Generalist

**Rubin, Marcey S.** — *Associate*
Kenzer Corp.
625 North Michigan Avenue, Suite 1244
Chicago, IL 60611
Telephone: (312) 266-0976
**Recruiter Classification:** Retained; **Lowest/Average Salary:** $50,000/$90,000;
**Industry Concentration:** Generalist; **Function Concentration:** Generalist

**Rubinstein, Alan J.** — *Legal Search Consultant*
Chicago Legal Search, Ltd.
33 North Dearborn Street, Suite 2302
Chicago, IL 60602-3109
Telephone: (312) 251-2580
**Recruiter Classification:** Contingency; **Lowest/Average Salary:**
$40,000/$90,000; **Industry Concentration:** Consumer Products, Electronics,
Energy, Entertainment, Environmental, Healthcare/Hospitals, High Technology,
Information Technology, Non-Profit, Oil/Gas, Pharmaceutical/Medical, Venture
Capital; **Function Concentration:** Women/Minorities

**Rubinstein, Walter** — *Recruiter*
Technical Connections Inc.
11400 Olympic Boulevard, Suite 770
Los Angeles, CA 90064
Telephone: (310) 479-8830
**Recruiter Classification:** Contingency; **Lowest/Average Salary:**
$40,000/$60,000; **Industry Concentration:** High Technology, Information
Technology; **Function Concentration:** Generalist

**Rudin, Harold** — *Co-Manager Central Region*
Management Recruiters International, Inc.
4011 West Jefferson Boulevard
Fort Wayne, IN 46804-6853
Telephone: (219) 459-1123
**Recruiter Classification:** Contingency; **Lowest/Average Salary:**
$30,000/$75,000; **Industry Concentration:** Generalist; **Function
Concentration:** Generalist

**Rudin, Myra** — *Co-Manager*
Management Recruiters International, Inc.
4011 West Jefferson Boulevard
Fort Wayne, IN 46804-6853
Telephone: (219) 459-1123
**Recruiter Classification:** Contingency; **Lowest/Average Salary:**
$30,000/$75,000; **Industry Concentration:** Generalist; **Function
Concentration:** Generalist

**Rudolph, Arlyn B.** — *Manager Midwest Region*
Management Recruiters International, Inc.
The Edgewood, Suite B
1807 East Edgewood
Springfield, MO 65804
Telephone: (417) 882-6220
**Recruiter Classification:** Contingency; **Lowest/Average Salary:**
$30,000/$75,000; **Industry Concentration:** Generalist; **Function
Concentration:** Generalist

**Rudolph, Kenneth** — *Associate*
Kossuth & Associates, Inc.
800 Bellevue Way N.E., Suite 400
Bellevue, WA 98004
Telephone: (206) 450-9050
**Recruiter Classification:** Retained; **Lowest/Average Salary:** $50,000/$90,000;
**Industry Concentration:** High Technology, Information Technology, Venture
Capital; **Function Concentration:** Generalist with a primary focus in
Administration, Engineering, Finance/Accounting, General Management,
Human Resources, Marketing, Research and Development, Sales,
Women/Minorities

**Rudzinsky, Howard** — *Vice President/Senior Recruiter*
Louis Rudzinsky Associates
394 Lowell Street, P.O. Box 640
Lexington, MA 02173
Telephone: (617) 862-6727
**Recruiter Classification:** Contingency; **Lowest/Average Salary:**
$20,000/$50,000; **Industry Concentration:** Aerospace/Defense, Electronics,
High Technology; **Function Concentration:** Generalist with a primary focus in
Engineering, General Management, Marketing, Research and Development,
Sales

**Rudzinsky, Jeffrey** — *Vice President/Senior Recruiter*
Louis Rudzinsky Associates
394 Lowell Street, P.O. Box 640
Lexington, MA 02173
Telephone: (617) 862-6727
**Recruiter Classification:** Contingency; **Lowest/Average Salary:**
$30,000/$60,000; **Industry Concentration:** Aerospace/Defense, Electronics,
High Technology, Information Technology; **Function Concentration:** Generalist
with a primary focus in Engineering, Research and Development

**Ruello, Brenda L.** — *Partner*
Heidrick & Struggles, Inc.
245 Park Avenue, Suite 4300
New York, NY 10167-0152
Telephone: (212) 867-9876
**Recruiter Classification:** Retained; **Lowest/Average Salary:** $75,000/$90,000;
**Industry Concentration:** Generalist with a primary focus in Consumer
Products, Fashion (Retail/Apparel); **Function Concentration:** Generalist

**Rumson, Barbara** — *Co-Manager North Atlantic Region*
Management Recruiters International, Inc.
22 South Park Square, Suite 302
Asheville, NC 28801
Telephone: (704) 258-9646
**Recruiter Classification:** Contingency; **Lowest/Average Salary:**
$30,000/$75,000; **Industry Concentration:** Generalist; **Function
Concentration:** Generalist

**Rumson, Paul** — *Director Hospitality Division*
Roth Young Personnel Service of Boston, Inc.
200 Boston Avenue, Suite 2300
Medford, MA 02155
Telephone: (617) 395-3600
**Recruiter Classification:** Contingency; **Lowest/Average Salary:**
$30,000/$50,000; **Industry Concentration:** Hospitality/Leisure; **Function
Concentration:** Finance/Accounting, General Management, Human Resources,
Marketing, Sales

**Rumson, Paul M.** — *Co-Manager*
Management Recruiters International, Inc.
22 South Park Square, Suite 302
Asheville, NC 28801
Telephone: (704) 258-9646
**Recruiter Classification:** Contingency; **Lowest/Average Salary:**
$30,000/$75,000; **Industry Concentration:** Generalist; **Function
Concentration:** Generalist

**Runge, Gary** — *Senior Technical Recruiter*
Search Enterprises South, Inc.
10100 West Sample Road
Coral Springs, FL 33065
Telephone: (305) 755-3121
**Recruiter Classification:** Contingency; **Lowest/Average Salary:**
$40,000/$50,000; **Industry Concentration:** Chemical Products, Consumer
Products, Oil/Gas; **Function Concentration:** Engineering

**Runquist, U.W.** — *Managing Director*
Webb, Johnson Associates, Inc.
280 Park Avenue, 43rd Floor
New York, NY 10017
Telephone: (212) 661-3700
**Recruiter Classification:** Retained; **Lowest/Average Salary:** $90,000/$90,000;
**Industry Concentration:** Generalist with a primary focus in Biotechnology,
Chemical Products, Financial Services, Healthcare/Hospitals, High Technology,
Non-Profit, Pharmaceutical/Medical; **Function Concentration:** Generalist

**Rupert, Jim** — *Co-Manager*
Management Recruiters International, Inc.
4617 Morningside Avenue
Sioux City, IA 51106-2943
Telephone: (712) 276-8454
**Recruiter Classification:** Contingency; **Lowest/Average Salary:**
$30,000/$75,000; **Industry Concentration:** Generalist; **Function
Concentration:** Generalist

**Rurak, Zbigniew T.** — *President*
Rurak & Associates, Inc.
1350 Connecticut Avenue N.W.
Suite 801
Washington, DC 20036
Telephone: (202) 293-7603
**Recruiter Classification:** Retained; **Lowest/Average Salary:** $90,000/$90,000;
**Industry Concentration:** Generalist with a primary focus in
Aerospace/Defense, Biotechnology, Consumer Products, Electronics,
Environmental, Healthcare/Hospitals, High Technology, Hospitality/Leisure,
Information Technology, Non-Profit, Venture Capital; **Function Concentration:**
Generalist with a primary focus in Engineering, Finance/Accounting, General
Management, Human Resources, Marketing, Research and Development, Sales

**Ruschak, Randy R.** — *Manager Eastern Region*
Management Recruiters International, Inc.
1200 South Church Street, Suite 20, Village Ii
Mount Laurel, NJ 08054
Telephone: (609) 727-0005
**Recruiter Classification:** Contingency; **Lowest/Average Salary:**
$30,000/$75,000; **Industry Concentration:** Generalist; **Function
Concentration:** Generalist

**Rusher, William H.** — *President*
Rusher, Loscavio & LoPresto
180 Montgomery Street, Suite 1616
San Francisco, CA 94104-4239
Telephone: (415) 765-6600
**Recruiter Classification:** Retained; **Lowest/Average Salary:** $90,000/$90,000;
**Industry Concentration:** Generalist with a primary focus in Insurance;
**Function Concentration:** Generalist with a primary focus in Administration,
Engineering, Marketing, Sales

**Russell, Carol** — *President*
ExecuScope Division of Russell Staffing Resources, Inc.
120 Montgomery Street, 3rd Floor
San Francisco, CA 94104
Telephone: (415) 781-1444
**Recruiter Classification:** Executive Temporary; **Lowest/Average Salary:**
$20,000/$60,000; **Industry Concentration:** Generalist; **Function
Concentration:** Generalist

**Russell, Richard A.** — *Vice President*
Executive Search Consultants Corporation
8 South Michigan Avenue, Suite 1205
Chicago, IL 60603
Telephone: (312) 251-8400
**Recruiter Classification:** Contingency; **Lowest/Average Salary:**
$50,000/$75,000; **Industry Concentration:** Generalist with a primary focus in
Financial Services, Hospitality/Leisure, Insurance, Non-Profit; **Function
Concentration:** Generalist with a primary focus in Administration, General
Management, Human Resources

**Russell, Robin E.** — *Vice President*
Kenzer Corp.
6033 West Century Boulevard, Suite 808
Los Angeles, CA 90045
Telephone: (310) 417-8577
**Recruiter Classification:** Retained; **Lowest/Average Salary:** $50,000/$90,000;
**Industry Concentration:** Consumer Products, Entertainment, Financial
Services, Packaging, Venture Capital; **Function Concentration:** Generalist with
a primary focus in Administration, Finance/Accounting, General Management,
Human Resources, Marketing, Research and Development, Sales

**Russell, Sam** — *Associate Director*
The Guild Corporation
8260 Greensboro Drive, Suite 460
McLean, VA 22102
Telephone: (703) 761-4023
**Recruiter Classification:** Contingency; **Lowest/Average Salary:**
$40,000/$50,000; **Industry Concentration:** Aerospace/Defense, Electronics,
High Technology, Information Technology; **Function Concentration:** Generalist
with a primary focus in Engineering, Finance/Accounting, General
Management, Research and Development

**Russell, Susan Anne** — *President*
Executive Search Consultants Corporation
8 South Michigan Avenue, Suite 1205
Chicago, IL 60603
Telephone: (312) 251-8400
**Recruiter Classification:** Contingency; **Lowest/Average Salary:**
$75,000/$90,000; **Industry Concentration:** Generalist with a primary focus in
Board Services, Education/Libraries, Fashion (Retail/Apparel),
Healthcare/Hospitals, Hospitality/Leisure, Non-Profit; **Function Concentration:**
Generalist with a primary focus in Administration, General Management

**Russo, Karen** — *President*
K. Russo Associates
2 Greenwich Plaza, Suite 100
Greenwich, CT 06830
Telephone: (203) 622-3903
**Recruiter Classification:** Retained; **Lowest/Average Salary:** $30,000/$90,000; **Industry Concentration:** Consumer Products, Entertainment, Financial Services, Insurance, Manufacturing, Pharmaceutical/Medical, Publishing/Media; **Function Concentration:** Human Resources

**Russo, Karen** — *Executive Recruiter*
Maximum Management Corp.
420 Lexington Avenue
Suite 2016
New York, NY 10170
Telephone: (212) 867-4646
**Recruiter Classification:** Contingency, Executive Temporary; **Lowest/Average Salary:** $30,000/$75,000; **Industry Concentration:** Generalist with a primary focus in Consumer Products, Entertainment, Financial Services, Information Technology, Insurance, Manufacturing, Pharmaceutical/Medical, Publishing/Media; **Function Concentration:** Human Resources

**Rust, John R.** — *Executive Vice President*
DHR International, Inc.
10 South Riverside Plaza, Suite 2220
Chicago, IL 60606
Telephone: (312) 782-1581
**Recruiter Classification:** Retained; **Lowest/Average Salary:** $60,000/$90,000; **Industry Concentration:** Generalist; **Function Concentration:** Generalist

**Rustad, Binth** — *Vice President*
Educational Management Network
98 Old South Road
Nantucket, MA 02554
Telephone: (508) 228-6700
**Recruiter Classification:** Retained; **Lowest/Average Salary:** $60,000/$90,000; **Industry Concentration:** Education/Libraries, Non-Profit; **Function Concentration:** Generalist with a primary focus in Administration, Finance/Accounting, Human Resources

**Rustin, Beth** — *Vice President*
The Whitney Group
850 Third Avenue, 11th Floor
New York, NY 10022
Telephone: (212) 508-3500
**Recruiter Classification:** Retained; **Lowest/Average Salary:** $75,000/$90,000; **Industry Concentration:** Generalist with a primary focus in Financial Services, Real Estate, Venture Capital; **Function Concentration:** Generalist with a primary focus in Sales

**Ryan, David** — *Associate*
Source Services Corporation
150 South Wacker Drive, Suite 400
Chicago, IL 60606
Telephone: (312) 346-7000
**Recruiter Classification:** Contingency; **Lowest/Average Salary:** $30,000/$50,000; **Industry Concentration:** Financial Services, Information Technology; **Function Concentration:** Engineering, Finance/Accounting

**Ryan, Joseph W.** — *Associate*
Skott/Edwards Consultants, Inc.
1776 On the Green
Morristown, NJ 07006
Telephone: (201) 644-0900
**Recruiter Classification:** Retained; **Lowest/Average Salary:** $75,000/$90,000; **Industry Concentration:** Generalist; **Function Concentration:** Generalist

**Ryan, Kathleen** — *Associate*
Source Services Corporation
10300 West 103rd Street, Suite 101
Overland Park, KS 66214
Telephone: (913) 888-8885
**Recruiter Classification:** Contingency; **Lowest/Average Salary:** $30,000/$50,000; **Industry Concentration:** Financial Services, Information Technology; **Function Concentration:** Engineering, Finance/Accounting

**Ryan, Lee** — *President*
Ryan, Miller & Associates Inc.
4601 Wilshire Boulevard, Suite 225
Los Angeles, CA 90010
Telephone: (213) 938-4768
**Recruiter Classification:** Contingency; **Lowest/Average Salary:** $40,000/$75,000; **Industry Concentration:** Consumer Products, Entertainment, Financial Services, Healthcare/Hospitals, High Technology, Information Technology, Manufacturing, Real Estate; **Function Concentration:** Administration, Finance/Accounting, Human Resources

**Ryan, Mark** — *Associate*
Source Services Corporation
One CityPlace, Suite 170
St. Louis, MO 63141
Telephone: (314) 432-4500
**Recruiter Classification:** Contingency; **Lowest/Average Salary:** $30,000/$50,000; **Industry Concentration:** Financial Services, Information Technology; **Function Concentration:** Engineering, Finance/Accounting

**Ryan, Mary L.** — *Manager Recruitment*
Summerfield Associates, Inc.
6555 Quince Road, Suite 311
Memphis, TN 38119
Telephone: (901) 753-7068
**Recruiter Classification:** Contingency; **Lowest/Average Salary:** $30,000/$40,000; **Industry Concentration:** Generalist with a primary focus in Information Technology; **Function Concentration:** Generalist

**Ryckaert, Terri** — *Associate*
Financial Search Corporation
2720 Des Plaines Avenue, Suite 106
Des Plaines, IL 60018
Telephone: (708) 297-4900
**Recruiter Classification:** Contingency; **Lowest/Average Salary:** $30,000/$50,000; **Industry Concentration:** Generalist; **Function Concentration:** Finance/Accounting

**Sabados, Terri** — *General Manager*
Management Recruiters International, Inc.
167 Avenue at the Common, Suite 7
Shrewsbury, NJ 07702
Telephone: (908) 542-9332
**Recruiter Classification:** Contingency; **Lowest/Average Salary:** $30,000/$75,000; **Industry Concentration:** Generalist; **Function Concentration:** Generalist

**Sabat, Lori S.** — *President*
Alta Associates, Inc.
8 Bartles Corner Road, Suite 021
Flemington, NJ 08822
Telephone: (908) 806-8442
**Recruiter Classification:** Retained; **Lowest/Average Salary:** $50,000/$90,000; **Industry Concentration:** Generalist with a primary focus in Chemical Products, Consumer Products, Entertainment, Financial Services, High Technology, Information Technology, Insurance, Manufacturing, Pharmaceutical/Medical, Publishing/Media; **Function Concentration:** Finance/Accounting

**Sacerdote, John** — *Principal*
Raymond Karsan Associates
200 West Cummings Park, Suite 7000
Woburn, MA 01801
Telephone: (617) 273-4022
**Recruiter Classification:** Contingency; **Lowest/Average Salary:** $30,000/$90,000; **Industry Concentration:** Generalist with a primary focus in Biotechnology, Chemical Products, Environmental, Healthcare/Hospitals, Information Technology, Insurance, Manufacturing, Pharmaceutical/Medical; **Function Concentration:** Generalist with a primary focus in Administration, Engineering, Finance/Accounting, General Management, Human Resources, Marketing, Research and Development, Sales, Women/Minorities

**Sackmary, Marcia** — *Principal*
Sanford Rose Associates
4210 Spicewood Springs Road, Suite 211
Austin, TX 78759
Telephone: (512) 418-8444
**Recruiter Classification:** Contingency; **Lowest/Average Salary:** $30,000/$75,000; **Industry Concentration:** Generalist; **Function Concentration:** Generalist

**Sackmary, Steven** — *Principal*
Sanford Rose Associates
4210 Spicewood Springs Road, Suite 211
Austin, TX 78759
Telephone: (512) 418-8444
**Recruiter Classification:** Contingency; **Lowest/Average Salary:** $30,000/$75,000; **Industry Concentration:** Generalist; **Function Concentration:** Generalist

**Sadaj, Michael** — *Managing Director*
Source Services Corporation
505 East 200 South, Suite 300
Salt Lake City, UT 84102
Telephone: (801) 328-0011
**Recruiter Classification:** Contingency; **Lowest/Average Salary:** $30,000/$50,000; **Industry Concentration:** Financial Services, Information Technology; **Function Concentration:** Engineering, Finance/Accounting

**Safnuk, Donald** — *President*
Corporate Recruiters Ltd.
490-1140 West Pender
Vancouver, British Columbia, CANADA V6E 4G1
Telephone: (604) 687-5993
**Recruiter Classification:** Contingency; **Lowest/Average Salary:**
$90,000/$90,000; **Industry Concentration:** High Technology; **Function
Concentration:** General Management

**Sahagian, John** — *Associate*
Human Resources Inc.
203 South Main Street
Providence, RI 02903
Telephone: (401) 861-2550
**Recruiter Classification:** Retained; **Lowest/Average Salary:** $90,000/$90,000;
**Industry Concentration:** Healthcare/Hospitals, High Technology, Information
Technology, Manufacturing; **Function Concentration:** Generalist

**Sahe, Mark** — *Branch Manager*
Accountants on Call
One Tabor Center, Suite 2160
1200 17th Street
Denver, CO 80202
Telephone: (303) 571-1110
**Recruiter Classification:** Contingency; **Lowest/Average Salary:**
$20,000/$30,000; **Industry Concentration:** Generalist; **Function
Concentration:** Finance/Accounting

**Sahlas, Chrissy** — *Executive Recruiter*
CPS Inc.
One Westbrook Corporate Centre, Suite 600
Westchester, IL 60154
Telephone: (708) 531-8370
**Recruiter Classification:** Contingency; **Lowest/Average Salary:**
$30,000/$50,000; **Industry Concentration:** Generalist with a primary focus in
Automotive, Biotechnology, Chemical Products, Consumer Products, High
Technology, Insurance, Manufacturing, Oil/Gas, Packaging,
Pharmaceutical/Medical; **Function Concentration:** Engineering, Research and
Development, Sales, Women/Minorities

**Salet, Michael** — *Associate*
Source Services Corporation
4170 Ashford Dunwoody Road, Suite 285
Atlanta, GA 30319
Telephone: (404) 255-2045
**Recruiter Classification:** Contingency; **Lowest/Average Salary:**
$30,000/$50,000; **Industry Concentration:** Financial Services, Information
Technology; **Function Concentration:** Engineering, Finance/Accounting

**Saletra, Andrew** — *Executive Recruiter*
CPS Inc.
One Westbrook Corporate Centre, Suite 600
Westchester, IL 60154
Telephone: (708) 531-8370
**Recruiter Classification:** Contingency; **Lowest/Average Salary:**
$30,000/$50,000; **Industry Concentration:** Generalist with a primary focus in
Automotive, Biotechnology, Chemical Products, Consumer Products, High
Technology, Insurance, Manufacturing, Oil/Gas, Packaging,
Pharmaceutical/Medical; **Function Concentration:** Engineering, Research and
Development, Sales, Women/Minorities

**Salikof, Allen B.** — *Co-Manager*
Management Recruiters International, Inc.
11 Penn Center, Suite 1717
1835 Market Street
Philadelphia, PA 19103
Telephone: (215) 567-1448
**Recruiter Classification:** Contingency; **Lowest/Average Salary:**
$30,000/$75,000; **Industry Concentration:** Generalist; **Function
Concentration:** Generalist

**Salikof, Kaye R.** — *Co-Manager Eastern Region*
Management Recruiters International, Inc.
11 Penn Center, Suite 1717
1835 Market Street
Philadelphia, PA 19103
Telephone: (215) 567-1448
**Recruiter Classification:** Contingency; **Lowest/Average Salary:**
$30,000/$75,000; **Industry Concentration:** Generalist; **Function
Concentration:** Generalist

**Salinger, Helen** — *Consultant*
Gilbert Tweed/INESA
415 Madison Avenue
New York, NY 10017
Telephone: (212) 758-3000
**Recruiter Classification:** Retained; **Lowest/Average Salary:** $90,000/$90,000;
**Industry Concentration:** Generalist; **Function Concentration:** Generalist

**Salvagno, Michael J.** — *Executive Vice President*
The Cambridge Group Ltd
830 Post Road East
Westport, CT 06880
Telephone: (203) 226-4243
**Recruiter Classification:** Contingency; **Lowest/Average Salary:**
$40,000/$75,000; **Industry Concentration:** Healthcare/Hospitals, High
Technology, Information Technology; **Function Concentration:** Administration,
Finance/Accounting

**Samet, Saul** — *Vice President*
Fisher-Todd Associates
535 Fifth Avenue, Suite 710
New York, NY 10017
Telephone: (212) 986-9052
**Recruiter Classification:** Contingency; **Lowest/Average Salary:**
$50,000/$75,000; **Industry Concentration:** Consumer Products,
Pharmaceutical/Medical; **Function Concentration:** Generalist with a primary
focus in Marketing

**Sammons, James A.** — *Director Retail and Wholesale
Manufacturing Divisions*
Prestige Inc.
P.O. Box 421
Reedsburg, WI 53959
Telephone: (608) 524-4032
**Recruiter Classification:** Contingency; **Lowest/Average Salary:**
$50,000/$90,000; **Industry Concentration:** Manufacturing; **Function
Concentration:** Generalist

**Sampson, Martin C.** — *President*
Sampson Neill & Wilkins Inc.
543 Valley Road
Upper Montclair, NJ 07043
Telephone: (201) 783-9600
**Recruiter Classification:** Retained; **Lowest/Average Salary:** $75,000/$90,000;
**Industry Concentration:** Board Services, Pharmaceutical/Medical, Venture
Capital; **Function Concentration:** Engineering, General Management,
Marketing, Research and Development, Sales

**Samsel, Randy** — *Managing Director*
Source Services Corporation
3 Summit Park Drive, Suite 550
Independence, OH 44131
Telephone: (216) 328-5900
**Recruiter Classification:** Contingency; **Lowest/Average Salary:**
$30,000/$50,000; **Industry Concentration:** Financial Services, Information
Technology; **Function Concentration:** Engineering, Finance/Accounting

**Samuels, Lewis J.** — *President*
Morgan Samuels Co., Inc.
9171 Wilshire Boulevard
Suite 428
Beverly Hills, CA 90210
Telephone: (310) 278-9660
**Recruiter Classification:** Retained; **Lowest/Average Salary:** $90,000/$90,000;
**Industry Concentration:** Environmental, Manufacturing; **Function
Concentration:** Generalist

**Samuelson, Robert** — *Associate*
Source Services Corporation
520 Post Oak Boulevard, Suite 700
Houston, TX 77027
Telephone: (713) 439-1077
**Recruiter Classification:** Contingency; **Lowest/Average Salary:**
$30,000/$50,000; **Industry Concentration:** Financial Services, Information
Technology; **Function Concentration:** Engineering, Finance/Accounting

**Sanchez, William** — *Associate*
Source Services Corporation
425 California Street, Suite 1200
San Francisco, CA 94104
Telephone: (415) 434-2410
**Recruiter Classification:** Contingency; **Lowest/Average Salary:**
$30,000/$50,000; **Industry Concentration:** Financial Services, Information
Technology; **Function Concentration:** Engineering, Finance/Accounting

**Sandbloom, Kenneth** — *Technical Recruiter*
Search Enterprises South, Inc.
10100 West Sample Road
Coral Springs, FL 33065
Telephone: (305) 755-3121
**Recruiter Classification:** Contingency; **Lowest/Average Salary:**
$40,000/$50,000; **Industry Concentration:** Chemical Products, Consumer
Products, Oil/Gas; **Function Concentration:** Engineering

**Sanders, Dave A.** — *Manager Pacific Region*
Management Recruiters International, Inc.
775 Sunrise Avenue, Suite 220
Roseville, CA 95661-4523
Telephone: (916) 781-8110
**Recruiter Classification:** Contingency; **Lowest/Average Salary:**
$30,000/$75,000; **Industry Concentration:** Generalist; **Function
Concentration:** Generalist

**Sanders, Natalie** — *Executive Recruiter*
CPS Inc.
One Westbrook Corporate Centre, Suite 600
Westchester, IL 60154
Telephone: (708) 531-8370
**Recruiter Classification:** Contingency; **Lowest/Average Salary:**
$30,000/$50,000; **Industry Concentration:** Generalist with a primary focus in
Automotive, Biotechnology, Chemical Products, Consumer Products, High
Technology, Insurance, Manufacturing, Oil/Gas, Packaging,
Pharmaceutical/Medical; **Function Concentration:** Engineering, Research and
Development, Sales, Women/Minorities

**Sanders, Norman D.** — *Managing Director*
Norm Sanders Associates
2 Village Court
Hazlet, NJ 07730
Telephone: (908) 264-3700
**Recruiter Classification:** Retained; **Lowest/Average Salary:** $90,000/$90,000;
**Industry Concentration:** Information Technology; **Function Concentration:**
Generalist

**Sanders, Spencer H.** — *Senior Vice President*
Battalia Winston International
300 Park Avenue
New York, NY 10022
Telephone: (212) 308-8080
**Recruiter Classification:** Retained; **Lowest/Average Salary:** $90,000/$90,000;
**Industry Concentration:** Generalist with a primary focus in Automotive, Board
Services, Chemical Products, Manufacturing, Pharmaceutical/Medical, Venture
Capital; **Function Concentration:** Generalist with a primary focus in
Engineering, Finance/Accounting, General Management, Human Resources,
Marketing, Research and Development, Sales

**Sanderson, Jeffrey M.** — *Senior Vice President*
Sullivan & Company
20 Exchange Place, 50th Floor
New York, NY 10005
Telephone: (212) 422-3000
**Recruiter Classification:** Retained; **Lowest/Average Salary:** $90,000/$90,000;
**Industry Concentration:** Generalist with a primary focus in Financial Services;
**Function Concentration:** Generalist

**Sandor, Richard J.** — *Vice President*
Flynn, Hannock, Incorporated
P.O. Box 8027
Stamford, CT 06905
Telephone: (203) 357-0009
**Recruiter Classification:** Retained, Executive Temporary; **Lowest/Average
Salary:** $75,000/$90,000; **Industry Concentration:** Generalist with a primary
focus in Consumer Products, Financial Services, Healthcare/Hospitals,
Insurance, Manufacturing, Pharmaceutical/Medical; **Function Concentration:**
Generalist with a primary focus in Human Resources

**Saner, Harold** — *Branch Manager*
Romac & Associates
1060 North Kings Highway
Suite 653
Cherry Hill, NJ 08034
Telephone: (609) 779-9077
**Recruiter Classification:** Executive Temporary; **Lowest/Average Salary:**
$/$60,000; **Industry Concentration:** Financial Services, Healthcare/Hospitals,
High Technology, Hospitality/Leisure, Information Technology, Insurance;
**Function Concentration:** Finance/Accounting

**Sanford, David** — *Human Resources Recruiter*
Winter, Wyman & Company
950 Winter Street, Suite 3100
Waltham, MA 02154-1294
Telephone: (617) 890-7000
**Recruiter Classification:** Contingency; **Lowest/Average Salary:**
$30,000/$50,000; **Industry Concentration:** Generalist; **Function
Concentration:** Human Resources

**Sangster, Jeffrey** — *President*
F-O-R-T-U-N-E Personnel Consultants of Manatee County
923 4th Street West
Palmetto, FL 34221
Telephone: (941) 729-3674
**Recruiter Classification:** Contingency; **Lowest/Average Salary:**
$30,000/$60,000; **Industry Concentration:** Automotive, Consumer Products,
Electronics, High Technology, Manufacturing; **Function Concentration:**
Engineering, General Management, Research and Development

**Santiago, Benefrido** — *Associate*
Source Services Corporation
879 West 190th Street, Suite 250
Los Angeles, CA 90248
Telephone: (310) 323-6633
**Recruiter Classification:** Contingency; **Lowest/Average Salary:**
$30,000/$50,000; **Industry Concentration:** Financial Services, Information
Technology; **Function Concentration:** Engineering, Finance/Accounting

**Sapers, Mark** — *Associate*
Source Services Corporation
71 Spit Brook Road, Suite 305
Nashua, NH 03060
Telephone: (603) 888-7650
**Recruiter Classification:** Contingency; **Lowest/Average Salary:**
$30,000/$50,000; **Industry Concentration:** Financial Services, Information
Technology; **Function Concentration:** Engineering, Finance/Accounting

**Saposhnik, Doron** — *Associate*
Source Services Corporation
2029 Century Park East, Suite 1350
Los Angeles, CA 90067
Telephone: (310) 277-8092
**Recruiter Classification:** Contingency; **Lowest/Average Salary:**
$30,000/$50,000; **Industry Concentration:** Financial Services, Information
Technology; **Function Concentration:** Engineering, Finance/Accounting

**Sapperstein, Jerry S.** — *President*
CFO Associates, Inc.
1055 Parsippany Boulevard
Suite 501
Parsippany, NJ 07054
Telephone: (201) 402-2005
**Recruiter Classification:** Executive Temporary; **Lowest/Average Salary:**
$90,000/$90,000; **Industry Concentration:** Generalist with a primary focus in
Consumer Products, Manufacturing; **Function Concentration:** Administration,
Finance/Accounting, General Management, Marketing, Sales

**Sarafa, Sam N.** — *Manager Central Region*
Management Recruiters International, Inc.
The Plymouth Building
2929 Plymouth Road, Suitre 209
Ann Arbor, MI 48105-3293
Telephone: (313) 769-1720
**Recruiter Classification:** Contingency; **Lowest/Average Salary:**
$30,000/$75,000; **Industry Concentration:** Generalist; **Function
Concentration:** Generalist

**Sardella, Sharon** — *Associate*
Source Services Corporation
1500 West Park Drive, Suite 390
Westborough, MA 01581
Telephone: (508) 366-2600
**Recruiter Classification:** Contingency; **Lowest/Average Salary:**
$30,000/$50,000; **Industry Concentration:** Financial Services, Information
Technology; **Function Concentration:** Engineering, Finance/Accounting

**Sarn, Allan G.** — *President*
Allan Sarn Associates Inc.
230 Park Avenue, Suite 1522
New York, NY 10169
Telephone: (212) 687-0600
**Recruiter Classification:** Retained; **Lowest/Average Salary:** $75,000/$90,000;
**Industry Concentration:** Generalist with a primary focus in
Aerospace/Defense, Consumer Products, Energy, Entertainment,
Environmental, Financial Services, High Technology, Information Technology,
Insurance, Manufacturing, Pharmaceutical/Medical, Publishing/Media, Real
Estate, Utilities/Nuclear; **Function Concentration:** Human Resources

**Sathe, Mark A.** — *President*
Sathe & Associates, Inc.
5821 Cedar Lake Road
Minneapolis, MN 55416
Telephone: (612) 546-2100
**Recruiter Classification:** Retained; **Lowest/Average Salary:** $60,000/$75,000;
**Industry Concentration:** Biotechnology, Consumer Products, Entertainment,
Financial Services, Hospitality/Leisure, Insurance, Manufacturing, Real Estate;
**Function Concentration:** Generalist with a primary focus in Administration,
Engineering, Finance/Accounting, General Management, Human Resources,
Marketing, Sales

**Sauer, Harry J.** — *Managing Partner*
Romac & Associates
1700 Market Street
Suite 2702
Philadelphia, PA 19103
Telephone: (215) 568-6810
**Recruiter Classification:** Executive Temporary; **Lowest/Average Salary:**
$/$60,000; **Industry Concentration:** Financial Services, Healthcare/Hospitals,
High Technology, Hospitality/Leisure, Information Technology, Insurance;
**Function Concentration:** Finance/Accounting

**Sauer, Robert C.** — *Partner*
Heidrick & Struggles, Inc.
600 Superior Avenue East
Suite 2500
Cleveland, OH 44114
Telephone: (216) 241-7410
**Recruiter Classification:** Retained; **Lowest/Average Salary:** $75,000/$90,000;
**Industry Concentration:** Generalist with a primary focus in
Healthcare/Hospitals, High Technology; **Function Concentration:** Generalist

**Savage, Edward J.** — *Managing Director*
Stanton Chase International
10866 Wilshire Boulevard
Suite 870
Los Angeles, CA 90024
Telephone: (310) 474-1029
**Recruiter Classification:** Retained; **Lowest/Average Salary:** $75,000/$90,000;
**Industry Concentration:** Generalist with a primary focus in Board Services,
Consumer Products, Energy, Healthcare/Hospitals, Hospitality/Leisure,
Insurance, Oil/Gas, Pharmaceutical/Medical, Publishing/Media, Venture
Capital; **Function Concentration:** Generalist with a primary focus in
Finance/Accounting, General Management, Human Resources, Marketing,
Sales

**Savage, Julie** — *Accounting and Finance Recruiter*
Winter, Wyman & Company
101 Federal Street, 27th Floor
Boston, MA 02110-1800
Telephone: (617) 951-2700
**Recruiter Classification:** Contingency; **Lowest/Average Salary:**
$20,000/$50,000; **Industry Concentration:** Generalist; **Function
Concentration:** Finance/Accounting

**Savard, Robert F.** — *Account Executive*
The Stevenson Group of Delaware Inc.
836 Farmington Avenue, Suite 223
West Hartford, CT 06119
Telephone: (860) 232-3393
**Recruiter Classification:** Retained; **Lowest/Average Salary:** $75,000/$90,000;
**Industry Concentration:** Chemical Products, Consumer Products, Electronics,
Financial Services, Insurance, Pharmaceutical/Medical; **Function
Concentration:** Generalist

**Savela, Edward** — *Associate*
Source Services Corporation
4170 Ashford Dunwoody Road, Suite 285
Atlanta, GA 30319
Telephone: (404) 255-2045
**Recruiter Classification:** Retained; **Lowest/Average Salary:**
$30,000/$50,000; **Industry Concentration:** Financial Services, Information
Technology; **Function Concentration:** Engineering, Finance/Accounting

**Savereid, Lisa** — *Senior Recruiter*
Isaacson, Miller
334 Boylston Street, Suite 500
Boston, MA 02111
Telephone: (617) 262-6500
**Recruiter Classification:** Retained; **Lowest/Average Salary:** $75,000/$90,000;
**Industry Concentration:** Generalist; **Function Concentration:** Generalist

**Sawhill, Louise B.** — *Partner*
Paul Ray Berndtson
191 Peachtree Tower, Suite 3800
191 Peachtree Street, NE
Atlanta, GA 30303-1757
Telephone: (404) 215-4600
**Recruiter Classification:** Retained; **Lowest/Average Salary:** $90,000/$90,000;
**Industry Concentration:** Generalist with a primary focus in
Healthcare/Hospitals, Pharmaceutical/Medical; **Function Concentration:**
Generalist

**Sawhook, Danny** — *Executive Recruiter*
Richard, Wayne and Roberts
24 Greenway Plaza, Suite 1304
Houston, TX 77046-2493
Telephone: (713) 629-6681
**Recruiter Classification:** Retained; **Lowest/Average Salary:** $40,000/$60,000;
**Industry Concentration:** Generalist; **Function Concentration:** Generalist

**Sawyer, Deborah A.** — *Consultant*
Heidrick & Struggles, Inc.
One Peachtree Center
303 Peachtree Street, NE, Suite 3100
Atlanta, GA 30308
Telephone: (404) 577-2410
**Recruiter Classification:** Retained; **Lowest/Average Salary:** $75,000/$90,000;
**Industry Concentration:** Generalist with a primary focus in High Technology;
**Function Concentration:** Generalist

**Sawyer, Patricia L.** — *Partner*
Smith & Sawyer Inc.
230 Park Avenue, 33rd Floor
New York, NY 10169
Telephone: (212) 490-4390
**Recruiter Classification:** Retained; **Lowest/Average Salary:** $90,000/$90,000;
**Industry Concentration:** Generalist with a primary focus in Consumer
Products, Financial Services, Healthcare/Hospitals, High Technology,
Information Technology, Manufacturing, Publishing/Media, Venture Capital;
**Function Concentration:** Generalist with a primary focus in
Finance/Accounting, General Management, Human Resources, Marketing,
Sales, Women/Minorities

**Saxner, David** — *Principal*
DSA, Inc.
Three First National Plaza, Suite 1400
Chicago, IL 60602
Telephone: (312) 201-0964
**Recruiter Classification:** Retained; **Lowest/Average Salary:** $60,000/$90,000;
**Industry Concentration:** Real Estate; **Function Concentration:** Generalist with
a primary focus in Engineering, Finance/Accounting

**Saydah, Robert F.** — *Partner*
Heidrick & Struggles, Inc.
Four Embarcadero Center, Suite 3570
San Francisco, CA 94111
Telephone: (415) 981-2854
**Recruiter Classification:** Retained; **Lowest/Average Salary:** $75,000/$90,000;
**Industry Concentration:** Generalist with a primary focus in
Healthcare/Hospitals; **Function Concentration:** Generalist

**Sayers, Bruce D.** — *Partner*
Brackin & Sayers Associates
1000 McKnight Park Drive, Suite 1001
Pittsburgh, PA 15237
Telephone: (412) 367-4644
**Recruiter Classification:** Contingency; **Lowest/Average Salary:** $30,000/$60,000;
**Industry Concentration:** Generalist with a primary focus in Chemical Products,
Consumer Products, Electronics, Energy, Financial Services,
Healthcare/Hospitals, High Technology, Information Technology, Manufacturing,
Packaging, Pharmaceutical/Medical, Publishing/Media, Transportation; **Function
Concentration:** Generalist with a primary focus in Administration,
Finance/Accounting, General Management, Human Resources, Marketing, Sales

**Saylor, Bill E.** — *Manager Pacific Region*
Management Recruiters International, Inc.
535 Dock Street, Suite 111
Tacoma, WA 98402-4614
Telephone: (206) 572-7542
**Recruiter Classification:** Contingency; **Lowest/Average Salary:** $30,000/$75,000;
**Industry Concentration:** Generalist; **Function Concentration:** Generalist

**Scalamera, Tom** — *Executive Recruiter*
CPS Inc.
One Westbrook Corporate Centre, Suite 600
Westchester, IL 60154
Telephone: (708) 531-8370
**Recruiter Classification:** Contingency; **Lowest/Average Salary:**
$30,000/$50,000; **Industry Concentration:** Generalist with a primary focus in
Automotive, Biotechnology, Chemical Products, Consumer Products, High
Technology, Insurance, Manufacturing, Oil/Gas, Packaging,
Pharmaceutical/Medical; **Function Concentration:** Engineering, Research and
Development, Sales, Women/Minorities

**Scarbrough, Debbi** — *President/Atlanta*
Evie Kreisler & Associates, Inc.
2575 Peachtree Road, Suite 300
Atlanta, GA 30305
Telephone: (404) 262-0599
**Recruiter Classification:** Contingency; **Lowest/Average Salary:**
$30,000/$75,000; **Industry Concentration:** Fashion (Retail/Apparel); **Function
Concentration:** Generalist

**Schaad, Carl A.** — *Partner*
Heidrick & Struggles, Inc.
One Post Office Square
Boston, MA 02109-0199
Telephone: (617) 423-1140
**Recruiter Classification:** Retained; **Lowest/Average Salary:** $75,000/$90,000;
**Industry Concentration:** Generalist with a primary focus in Biotechnology,
Healthcare/Hospitals, High Technology; **Function Concentration:** Generalist

**Schachter, Laura J.** — *President*
Professional Placement Associates, Inc.
14 Rye Ridge Plaza
Rye Brook, NY 10573
Telephone: (914) 251-1000
**Recruiter Classification:** Contingency; **Lowest/Average Salary:**
$40,000/$75,000; **Industry Concentration:** Healthcare/Hospitals; **Function
Concentration:** Administration, Human Resources

**Schaefer, Brett** — *Branch Manager*
Accountants on Call
5550 LBJ Freeway, Suite 310
Dallas, TX 75240
Telephone: (214) 980-4184
**Recruiter Classification:** Contingency; **Lowest/Average Salary:**
$20,000/$30,000; **Industry Concentration:** Generalist; **Function Concentration:** Finance/Accounting

**Schaefer, Frederic M.** — *Vice President*
A.T. Kearney, Inc.
One Tabor Center, Suite 950
1200 Seventeenth Street
Denver, CO 80202
Telephone: (303) 572-6175
**Recruiter Classification:** Retained; **Lowest/Average Salary:** $90,000/$90,000;
**Industry Concentration:** Generalist with a primary focus in Chemical Products,
Financial Services, High Technology, Manufacturing, Non-Profit,
Pharmaceutical/Medical, Transportation; **Function Concentration:** Generalist
with a primary focus in General Management, Marketing, Sales

**Schaefer, Robert** — *Senior Technical Recruiter*
Search Enterprises, Inc.
160 Quail Ridge Drive
Westmont, IL 60559
Telephone: (708) 654-2300
**Recruiter Classification:** Contingency; **Lowest/Average Salary:**
$20,000/$50,000; **Industry Concentration:** Biotechnology, Consumer
Products, Pharmaceutical/Medical; **Function Concentration:** Engineering,
General Management, Research and Development

**Schaller, F. William** — *Principal*
Sanford Rose Associates
7919 Pebble Beach Drive, Suite 209
Citrus Heights, CA 95610
Telephone: (916) 864-4888
**Recruiter Classification:** Contingency; **Lowest/Average Salary:**
$30,000/$75,000; **Industry Concentration:** Generalist; **Function Concentration:** Generalist

**Schaller, Karen** — *Principal*
Sanford Rose Associates
7919 Pebble Beach Drive, Suite 209
Citrus Heights, CA 95610
Telephone: (916) 864-4888
**Recruiter Classification:** Contingency; **Lowest/Average Salary:**
$30,000/$75,000; **Industry Concentration:** Generalist; **Function Concentration:** Generalist

**Schappell, Marc P.** — *Consultant*
Egon Zehnder International Inc.
55 East 59th Street, 14th Floor
New York, NY 10022
Telephone: (212) 838-9199
**Recruiter Classification:** Retained; **Lowest/Average Salary:** $90,000/$90,000;
**Industry Concentration:** Generalist with a primary focus in Biotechnology,
Financial Services, High Technology, Manufacturing, Pharmaceutical/Medical;
**Function Concentration:** Generalist

**Scharett, Carol** — *Specialist Recruitment*
St. Lawrence International, Inc.
6432 Baird Avenue
Syracuse, NY 13206
Telephone: (315) 432-4588
**Recruiter Classification:** Executive Temporary; **Lowest/Average Salary:**
$30,000/$50,000; **Industry Concentration:** Generalist with a primary focus in
Aerospace/Defense, Automotive, Consumer Products, Manufacturing,
Packaging; **Function Concentration:** Generalist with a primary focus in
Administration, Engineering, General Management, Human Resources,
Marketing, Research and Development, Sales

**Scharringhausen, Michael** — *Vice President*
Saber Consultants
5300 Hollister, Suite 100
Houston, TX 77040
Telephone: (713) 462-6900
**Recruiter Classification:** Retained; **Lowest/Average Salary:** $40,000/$60,000;
**Function Concentration:** Generalist

**Schedra, Sharon** — *Research Associate*
Earley Kielty and Associates, Inc.
Two Pennsylvania Plaza
New York, NY 10121
Telephone: (212) 736-5626
**Recruiter Classification:** Retained; **Lowest/Average Salary:** $90,000/$90,000;
**Industry Concentration:** Generalist with a primary focus in Information
Technology; **Function Concentration:** Generalist with a primary focus in
Administration, Finance/Accounting, General Management, Human Resources,
Marketing, Research and Development, Sales, Women/Minorities

**Schegg, Paul** — *Managing Director*
Goodrich & Sherwood Associates, Inc.
4 Armstrong Road
Building #2, 3rd Floor
Shelton, CT 06484
Telephone: (203) 944-2828
**Recruiter Classification:** Retained; **Lowest/Average Salary:** $60,000/$90,000;
**Industry Concentration:** Generalist; **Function Concentration:** Generalist

**Scheidt, Sandi** — *Consultant*
Paul Ray Berndtson
191 Peachtree Tower, Suite 3800
191 Peachtree Street, NE
Atlanta, GA 30303-1757
Telephone: (404) 215-4600
**Recruiter Classification:** Retained; **Lowest/Average Salary:** $90,000/$90,000;
**Industry Concentration:** Generalist; **Function Concentration:** Generalist

**Scheidt, Sandra L.** — *Vice President*
The Heidrick Partners, Inc.
20 North Wacker Drive
Suite 2850
Chicago, IL 60606-3171
Telephone: (312) 845-9700
**Recruiter Classification:** Retained; **Lowest/Average Salary:** $90,000/$90,000;
**Industry Concentration:** Generalist; **Function Concentration:** Generalist

**Scherck, Henry J.** — *Managing Director*
Ward Howell International, Inc.
99 Park Avenue, Suite 2000
New York, NY 10016-1699
Telephone: (212) 697-3730
**Recruiter Classification:** Retained; **Lowest/Average Salary:** $75,000/$90,000;
**Industry Concentration:** Biotechnology, Chemical Products, Consumer
Products, Financial Services, Pharmaceutical/Medical; **Function
Concentration:** Generalist

**Schiavone, Mary Rose** — *Vice President*
Canny, Bowen Inc.
200 Park Avenue
New York, NY 10166
Telephone: (212) 949-6611
**Recruiter Classification:** Retained; **Lowest/Average Salary:** $90,000/$90,000;
**Industry Concentration:** Generalist with a primary focus in Biotechnology,
Board Services, Chemical Products, Electronics, Entertainment, Fashion
(Retail/Apparel), High Technology, Hospitality/Leisure, Information Technology,
Packaging, Pharmaceutical/Medical, Venture Capital; **Function Concentration:**
Generalist with a primary focus in Administration, Engineering,
Finance/Accounting, Marketing, Research and Development, Sales,
Women/Minorities

**Schiffer, Stewart** — *Senior Vice President/Search Consultant*
Career Management International
197 Route 18
East Brunswick, NJ 08816
Telephone: (908) 937-4800
**Recruiter Classification:** Retained; **Lowest/Average Salary:** $40,000/$75,000;
**Industry Concentration:** Fashion (Retail/Apparel); **Function Concentration:**
Generalist with a primary focus in Finance/Accounting, Human Resources,
Marketing

**Schlanger, Ruth** — *Associate Partner*
Richard, Wayne and Roberts
24 Greenway Plaza, Suite 1304
Houston, TX 77046-2493
Telephone: (713) 629-6681
**Recruiter Classification:** Retained; **Lowest/Average Salary:** $50,000/$90,000;
**Industry Concentration:** Generalist; **Function Concentration:** Generalist

**Schlecht, Nancy** — *Partner*
Morgan Samuels Co., Inc.
9171 Wilshire Boulevard
Suite 428
Beverly Hills, CA 90210
Telephone: (310) 278-9660
**Recruiter Classification:** Retained; **Lowest/Average Salary:** $90,000/$90,000;
**Industry Concentration:** Environmental, Manufacturing; **Function
Concentration:** Generalist

**Schlosser, John R.** — *Partner*
Heidrick & Struggles, Inc.
300 South Grand Avenue, Suite 2400
Los Angeles, CA 90071
Telephone: (213) 625-8811
**Recruiter Classification:** Retained; **Lowest/Average Salary:** $75,000/$90,000;
**Industry Concentration:** Generalist with a primary focus in
Healthcare/Hospitals; **Function Concentration:** Generalist

**Schlpma, Christine** — *Executive Recruiter*
Advanced Executive Resources
3040 Charlevoix Drive, SE
Grand Rapids, MI 49546
Telephone: (616) 942-4030
**Recruiter Classification:** Retained; **Lowest/Average Salary:** $30,000/$50,000;
**Industry Concentration:** Generalist with a primary focus in
Aerospace/Defense, Automotive, Chemical Products, Consumer Products,
Electronics, Energy, Environmental, Financial Services, Healthcare/Hospitals,
High Technology, Manufacturing, Packaging, Real Estate; **Function**
**Concentration:** Generalist with a primary focus in Engineering,
Finance/Accounting, General Management, Human Resources, Marketing,
Research and Development, Sales, Women/Minorities

**Schmidt, Frank B.** — *President*
F.B. Schmidt International
30423 Canwood Place, Suite 239
Agoura Hills, CA 91301
Telephone: (818) 706-0500
**Recruiter Classification:** Retained; **Lowest/Average Salary:** $60,000/$90,000;
**Industry Concentration:** Consumer Products, Entertainment, Financial
Services, Information Technology, Pharmaceutical/Medical; **Function**
**Concentration:** Marketing

**Schmidt, Jeri E.** — *Senior Vice President*
Blake, Hansen & Nye, Limited
151 West 74th Street, Suite 3A
New York, NY 10023
Telephone: (212) 874-4933
**Recruiter Classification:** Retained; **Lowest/Average Salary:** $75,000/$90,000;
**Industry Concentration:** Generalist; **Function Concentration:** Generalist with a
primary focus in Engineering, Finance/Accounting, General Management,
Human Resources, Marketing, Research and Development, Sales

**Schmidt, Michelle C.** — *Principal*
Sanford Rose Associates
300 Mariners Plaza, Suite 321-A
Mandeville, LA 70448
Telephone: (504) 674-5050
**Recruiter Classification:** Contingency; **Lowest/Average Salary:**
$30,000/$75,000; **Industry Concentration:** Generalist; **Function**
**Concentration:** Generalist

**Schmidt, Paul** — *Partner*
Paul Ray Berndtson
10 South Riverside Plaza
Suite 720
Chicago, IL 60606
Telephone: (312) 876-0730
**Recruiter Classification:** Retained; **Lowest/Average Salary:** $90,000/$90,000;
**Industry Concentration:** Generalist; **Function Concentration:** Generalist

**Schmidt, Peter R.** — *President*
Boyden
55 Madison Avenue
Suite 400
Morristown, NJ 07960
Telephone: (201) 267-0980
**Recruiter Classification:** Retained; **Lowest/Average Salary:** $90,000/$90,000;
**Industry Concentration:** Generalist with a primary focus in High Technology;
**Function Concentration:** Generalist

**Schmidt, Peter R.** — *President*
Boyden
375 Park Avenue, Suite 1509
New York, NY 10152
Telephone: (212) 980-6480
**Recruiter Classification:** Retained; **Lowest/Average Salary:** $75,000/$90,000;
**Industry Concentration:** Board Services, High Technology; **Function**
**Concentration:** Generalist with a primary focus in Engineering,
Finance/Accounting, General Management, Human Resources, Marketing,
Research and Development, Sales, Women/Minorities

**Schmidt, Robert C.** — *Manager Eastern Region*
Management Recruiters International, Inc.
57 Danbury Road
Wilton, CT 06897-4439
Telephone: (203) 834-1111
**Recruiter Classification:** Contingency; **Lowest/Average Salary:**
$30,000/$75,000; **Industry Concentration:** Generalist; **Function**
**Concentration:** Generalist

**Schmidt, Timothy G.** — *Principal*
Sanford Rose Associates
300 Mariners Plaza, Suite 321-A
Mandeville, LA 70448
Telephone: (504) 674-5050
**Recruiter Classification:** Contingency; **Lowest/Average Salary:**
$30,000/$75,000; **Industry Concentration:** Generalist; **Function**
**Concentration:** Generalist

**Schmidt, William C.** — *Senior Vice President*
Christian & Timbers
One Corporate Exchange
25825 Science Park Drive, Suite 400
Cleveland, OH 44122
Telephone: (216) 464-8710
**Recruiter Classification:** Retained; **Lowest/Average Salary:** $90,000/$90,000;
**Industry Concentration:** Generalist with a primary focus in Consumer
Products, Electronics, Venture Capital; **Function Concentration:** Generalist
with a primary focus in Engineering, General Management, Marketing

**Schneider, James** — *Managing Director*
The Search Firm, Inc.
595 Market Street, Suite 1400
San Francisco, CA 94105
Telephone: (415) 777-3900
**Recruiter Classification:** Contingency; **Lowest/Average Salary:**
$40,000/$75,000; **Industry Concentration:** Electronics, High Technology,
Information Technology

**Schneider, Margo** — *Account Executive*
Search West, Inc.
340 North Westlake Boulevard
Suite 200
Westlake Village, CA 91362-3761
Telephone: (805) 496-6811
**Recruiter Classification:** Contingency; **Lowest/Average Salary:**
$40,000/$60,000; **Industry Concentration:** Publishing/Media; **Function**
**Concentration:** Administration, Marketing

**Schneider, Perry** — *Agribusiness Recruiter/Manager*
Agra Placements International Ltd.
2200 North Kickapoo, Suite 2
Lincoln, IL 62656
Telephone: (217) 735-4373
**Recruiter Classification:** Contingency; **Lowest/Average Salary:**
$20,000/$30,000; **Industry Concentration:** Generalist with a primary focus in
Biotechnology, Chemical Products, Energy, Financial Services, Manufacturing;
**Function Concentration:** Administration, Engineering, Finance/Accounting,
General Management, Human Resources, Marketing, Research and
Development, Sales

**Schneider, Susan** — *Partner*
Jacquelyn Finn & Susan Schneider Associates, Inc.
1730 Rhode Island Avenue, NW
Suite 1212
Washington, DC 20036
Telephone: (202) 822-8400
**Recruiter Classification:** Contingency; **Industry Concentration:** Generalist;
**Function Concentration:** Generalist

**Schneider, Thomas P.** — *Vice President*
WTW Associates
675 Third Avenue, Suite 2808
New York, NY 10017
Telephone: (212) 972-6990
**Recruiter Classification:** Retained; **Lowest/Average Salary:** $75,000/$90,000;
**Industry Concentration:** Generalist with a primary focus in Entertainment,
Financial Services; **Function Concentration:** Generalist

**Schneider, Tom J.** — *Manager Southwest Region*
Management Recruiters International, Inc.
2500 Louisiana Boulevard, NE, Suite 506
Albuquerque, NM 87110-4319
Telephone: (505) 875-0920
**Recruiter Classification:** Contingency; **Lowest/Average Salary:**
$30,000/$75,000; **Industry Concentration:** Generalist; **Function**
**Concentration:** Generalist

**Schneider, Victor** — *Manager*
Accountants on Call
1650 Spruce Street, Suite 210
Riverside, CA 92507
Telephone: (909) 686-2100
**Recruiter Classification:** Contingency; **Lowest/Average Salary:**
$20,000/$30,000; **Industry Concentration:** Generalist; **Function**
**Concentration:** Finance/Accounting

**Schneiderman, Gerald** — *President*
Management Resource Associates, Inc.
P.O. Box 3266
Boca Raton, FL 33427
Telephone: (561) 852-5650
**Recruiter Classification:** Contingency; **Lowest/Average Salary:**
$50,000/$90,000; **Industry Concentration:** Generalist with a primary focus in
Aerospace/Defense, Consumer Products, Electronics, Financial Services, High
Technology, Information Technology, Manufacturing; **Function Concentration:**
Generalist with a primary focus in Engineering, Finance/Accounting, General
Management, Human Resources, Marketing, Research and Development, Sales

**Schneidermeyer, Phil** — *Principal*
Korn/Ferry International
One Landmark Square
Stamford, CT 06901
Telephone: (203) 359-3350
**Recruiter Classification:** Retained; **Lowest/Average Salary:** $90,000/$90,000;
**Industry Concentration:** Generalist; **Function Concentration:** Generalist

**Schneirov, Miriam A.** — *Partner*
Coleman Legal Search Consultants
1435 Walnut Street, 3rd Floor
Philadelphia, PA 19102
Telephone: (215) 864-2700
**Recruiter Classification:** Contingency; **Lowest/Average Salary:**
$60,000/$75,000; **Function Concentration:** Generalist

**Schnierow, Beryl** — *Associate*
Tesar-Reynes, Inc.
500 North Michigan Avenue
Chicago, IL 60611
Telephone: (312) 661-0700
**Recruiter Classification:** Retained; **Lowest/Average Salary:**
$50,000/$75,000; **Industry Concentration:** Automotive, Consumer
Products, High Technology, Hospitality/Leisure, Publishing/Media; **Function
Concentration:** Marketing

**Schoen, Stephen G.** — *Executive Director*
MDR Associates, Inc.
9360 Sunset Drive, Suite 250
Miami, FL 33173
Telephone: (305) 271-9213
**Recruiter Classification:** Retained; **Lowest/Average Salary:** $90,000/$90,000;
**Industry Concentration:** Healthcare/Hospitals; **Function Concentration:**
Generalist

**Schoenwetter, Carrie** — *Manager Midwest Region*
Management Recruiters International, Inc.
7550 France Avenue South, Suite 180
Minneapolis, MN 55435
Telephone: (612) 830-1420
**Recruiter Classification:** Contingency; **Lowest/Average Salary:**
$30,000/$75,000; **Industry Concentration:** Generalist; **Function
Concentration:** Generalist

**Schoettle, Michael B.** — *Partner*
Heidrick & Struggles, Inc.
300 South Grand Avenue, Suite 2400
Los Angeles, CA 90071
Telephone: (213) 625-8811
**Recruiter Classification:** Retained; **Lowest/Average Salary:** $75,000/$90,000;
**Industry Concentration:** Generalist with a primary focus in High Technology;
**Function Concentration:** Generalist

**Schoff, Frank J.** — *Manager North Atlantic Region*
Management Recruiters International, Inc.
Coldwell Banker Melton Office
Route 276 Sherwood Forest, P.O. Box 399
Cedar Mountain, NC 28718
Telephone: (704) 884-4118
**Recruiter Classification:** Contingency; **Lowest/Average Salary:**
$30,000/$75,000; **Industry Concentration:** Generalist; **Function
Concentration:** Generalist

**Schonberg, Alan R.** — *President and CEO*
Management Recruiters International, Inc.
200 Public Square, 31st Floor
Cleveland, OH 44114-2301
Telephone: (216) 696-1122
**Recruiter Classification:** Contingency; **Lowest/Average Salary:**
$30,000/$75,000; **Industry Concentration:** Generalist; **Function
Concentration:** Generalist

**Schoppergrell, Holly** — *Consultant*
Don Richard Associates of Charlotte
2650 One First Union Center
301 South College Street
Charlotte, NC 28202-6000
Telephone: (704) 377-6447
**Recruiter Classification:** Contingency; **Lowest/Average Salary:**
$30,000/$40,000; **Industry Concentration:** Generalist; **Function
Concentration:** Finance/Accounting

**Schor, Neil D.** — *Associate*
Kenzer Corp.
1600 Parkwood Circle NW, Suite 310
Atlanta, GA 30339
Telephone: (770) 955-7210
**Recruiter Classification:** Retained; **Lowest/Average Salary:** $50,000/$90,000;
**Industry Concentration:** Generalist; **Function Concentration:** Generalist

**Schostak, Glen** — *Principal*
Korn/Ferry International
One Palmer Square
Princeton, NJ 08542
Telephone: (609) 921-8811
**Recruiter Classification:** Retained; **Lowest/Average Salary:** $90,000/$90,000;
**Industry Concentration:** Generalist; **Function Concentration:** Generalist

**Schramm, Walter M.** — *Consultant*
Executive Outsourcing International
1920 Main Street, Suite 520
Irvine, CA 92714
Telephone: (714) 282-7158
**Recruiter Classification:** Executive Temporary; **Lowest/Average Salary:**
$75,000/$90,000; **Industry Concentration:** Generalist; **Function
Concentration:** Generalist

**Schreiber, Stuart M.** — *Managing Partner*
Heidrick & Struggles, Inc.
245 Park Avenue, Suite 4300
New York, NY 10167-0152
Telephone: (212) 867-9876
**Recruiter Classification:** Retained; **Lowest/Average Salary:** $75,000/$90,000;
**Industry Concentration:** Generalist with a primary focus in Consumer
Products, Financial Services; **Function Concentration:** Generalist

**Schrenzel, Benjamin** — *Consultant*
Parfitt Recruiting and Consulting
1540 140th Avenue NE #201
Bellevue, WA 98005
Telephone: (206) 646-6300
**Recruiter Classification:** Contingency; **Lowest/Average Salary:**
$30,000/$75,000; **Industry Concentration:** Generalist with a primary focus in
Information Technology; **Function Concentration:** Engineering

**Schroeder, James** — *Associate*
Source Services Corporation
One South Main Street, Suite 1440
Dayton, OH 45402
Telephone: (513) 461-4660
**Recruiter Classification:** Contingency; **Lowest/Average Salary:**
$30,000/$50,000; **Industry Concentration:** Financial Services, Information
Technology; **Function Concentration:** Engineering, Finance/Accounting

**Schroeder, James L.** — *Senior Associate*
Korn/Ferry International
120 South Riverside Plaza
Suite 918
Chicago, IL 60606
Telephone: (312) 726-1841
**Recruiter Classification:** Retained; **Lowest/Average Salary:** $90,000/$90,000;
**Industry Concentration:** Generalist; **Function Concentration:** Generalist

**Schroeder, John W.** — *Senior Director*
Spencer Stuart
1717 Main Street, Suite 5300
Dallas, TX 75201-4605
Telephone: (214) 658-1777
**Recruiter Classification:** Retained; **Lowest/Average Salary:** $90,000/$90,000;
**Industry Concentration:** Generalist with a primary focus in Consumer
Products, Fashion (Retail/Apparel), Financial Services, Hospitality/Leisure,
Insurance, Manufacturing, Packaging, Publishing/Media, Real Estate,
Transportation, Venture Capital; **Function Concentration:** Generalist with a
primary focus in Finance/Accounting, General Management, Human
Resources, Marketing, Women/Minorities

**Schroeder, Lee** — *Partner*
Blau Kaptain Schroeder
800 FirsTier Bank Building
Lincoln, NE 68508
Telephone: (402) 434-1494
**Recruiter Classification:** Retained; **Lowest/Average Salary:** $75,000/$75,000;
**Industry Concentration:** Biotechnology, Healthcare/Hospitals,
Pharmaceutical/Medical, Venture Capital; **Function Concentration:** General
Management, Marketing, Research and Development

**Schroeder, Steven J.** — *Vice President Medical Products
Group*
Blau Kaptain Schroeder
3900 Juan Tabo N.E., Suite 22
Albuquerque, NM 87111
Telephone: (505) 271-0702
**Recruiter Classification:** Retained; **Lowest/Average Salary:** $75,000/$90,000;
**Industry Concentration:** Biotechnology, Healthcare/Hospitals,
Pharmaceutical/Medical, Venture Capital; **Function Concentration:**
Engineering, General Management, Marketing, Research and Development,
Sales

**Schroeder, Victoria** — *Consultant*
Paul Ray Berndtson
10 South Riverside Plaza
Suite 720
Chicago, IL 60606
Telephone: (312) 876-0730
**Recruiter Classification:** Retained; **Lowest/Average Salary:** $90,000/$90,000;
**Industry Concentration:** Generalist; **Function Concentration:** Generalist

**Schuckman, Louis** — *Manager Executive Search*
Accountants on Call
2099 Gateway Place, Suite 440
San Jose, CA 95110
Telephone: (408) 437-9779
**Recruiter Classification:** Contingency; **Lowest/Average Salary:**
$20,000/$30,000; **Industry Concentration:** Generalist; **Function
Concentration:** Finance/Accounting

**Schueneman, David** — *Executive Recruiter*
CPS Inc.
One Westbrook Corporate Centre, Suite 600
Westchester, IL 60154
Telephone: (708) 531-8370
**Recruiter Classification:** Contingency; **Lowest/Average Salary:**
$30,000/$50,000; **Industry Concentration:** Generalist with a primary focus in
Automotive, Biotechnology, Chemical Products, Consumer Products, High
Technology, Insurance, Manufacturing, Oil/Gas, Packaging,
Pharmaceutical/Medical; **Function Concentration:** Engineering, Research and
Development, Sales, Women/Minorities

**Schuette, Dorothy** — *Senior Associate*
Harris Heery & Associates
40 Richards Avenue
One Norwalk West
Norwalk, CT 06854
Telephone: (203) 857-0808
**Recruiter Classification:** Retained; **Lowest/Average Salary:** $75,000/$90,000;
**Industry Concentration:** Consumer Products, Fashion (Retail/Apparel),
Financial Services, Insurance, Publishing/Media; **Function Concentration:**
General Management, Marketing

**Schulte, Bernard** — *Managing Director*
Korn/Ferry International
The Transamerica Pyramid
600 Montgomery Street
San Francisco, CA 94111
Telephone: (415) 956-1834
**Recruiter Classification:** Retained; **Lowest/Average Salary:** $90,000/$90,000;
**Industry Concentration:** Generalist; **Function Concentration:** Generalist

**Schultz, Randy** — *Associate*
Source Services Corporation
1233 North Mayfair Road, Suite 300
Milwaukee, WI 53226
Telephone: (414) 774-6700
**Recruiter Classification:** Contingency; **Lowest/Average Salary:**
$30,000/$50,000; **Industry Concentration:** Financial Services, Information
Technology; **Function Concentration:** Engineering, Finance/Accounting

**Schultz, Roger C.** — *Manager Eastern Region*
Management Recruiters International, Inc.
2139 Silas Deane Highway
Rocky Hill, CT 06067-2336
Telephone: (860) 563-1268
**Recruiter Classification:** Contingency; **Lowest/Average Salary:**
$30,000/$75,000; **Industry Concentration:** Generalist; **Function
Concentration:** Generalist

**Schuyler, Lambert** — *Partner*
Schuyler, Frye & Baker, Inc.
1100 Abernathy Road N.E., Suite 1825
Atlanta, GA 30328
Telephone: (770) 804-1996
**Recruiter Classification:** Retained; **Lowest/Average Salary:** $90,000/$90,000;
**Industry Concentration:** Generalist; **Function Concentration:** Generalist

**Schwalbach, Robert** — *Associate*
Source Services Corporation
1290 Oakmead Parkway, Suite 318
Sunnyvale, CA 94086
Telephone: (408) 738-8440
**Recruiter Classification:** Contingency; **Lowest/Average Salary:**
$30,000/$50,000; **Industry Concentration:** Financial Services, Information
Technology; **Function Concentration:** Engineering, Finance/Accounting

**Schwam, Carol** — *Vice President*
A.E. Feldman Associates
445 Northern Boulevard
Great Neck, NY 11021
Telephone: (516) 466-4708
**Recruiter Classification:** Contingency; **Lowest/Average Salary:**
$50,000/$75,000; **Industry Concentration:** Generalist with a primary focus in
Publishing/Media; **Function Concentration:** Generalist with a primary focus in
Administration, Engineering, Finance/Accounting, General Management,
Human Resources, Marketing, Research and Development, Sales,
Women/Minorities

**Schwartz, Carole** — *Vice President*
A.T. Kearney, Inc.
153 East 53rd Street
New York, NY 10022
Telephone: (212) 751-7040
**Recruiter Classification:** Retained; **Lowest/Average Salary:** $90,000/$90,000;
**Industry Concentration:** Generalist with a primary focus in Chemical Products,
Financial Services, Manufacturing, Pharmaceutical/Medical, Transportation;
**Function Concentration:** Generalist with a primary focus in Administration,
Finance/Accounting, Human Resources, Marketing, Sales

**Schwartz, Harry** — *Executive Recruiter*
Jacobson Associates
1785 The Exchange, Suite 320
Atlanta, GA 30339
Telephone: (404) 952-3877
**Recruiter Classification:** Contingency; **Lowest/Average Salary:**
$20,000/$50,000; **Industry Concentration:** Insurance; **Function
Concentration:** Generalist

**Schwartz, Jay S.** — *Manager North Atlantic Region*
Management Recruiters International, Inc.
Brookfield Building, Suite 406
6620 West Broad Street
Richmond, VA 23230
Telephone: (804) 285-2071
**Recruiter Classification:** Contingency; **Lowest/Average Salary:**
$30,000/$75,000; **Industry Concentration:** Generalist; **Function
Concentration:** Generalist

**Schwartz, Stephen D.** — *Manager Eastern Region*
Management Recruiters International, Inc.
200 Park Avenue South, Suite 1510
New York, NY 10003-1503
Telephone: (212) 505-5530
**Recruiter Classification:** Contingency; **Lowest/Average Salary:**
$30,000/$75,000; **Industry Concentration:** Generalist; **Function
Concentration:** Generalist

**Schwartz, Susan** — *Principal*
Korn/Ferry International
237 Park Avenue
New York, NY 10017
Telephone: (212) 687-1834
**Recruiter Classification:** Retained; **Lowest/Average Salary:** $90,000/$90,000;
**Industry Concentration:** Generalist with a primary focus in Financial Services;
**Function Concentration:** Generalist

**Schwartz, Vincent P.** — *Vice President*
Slayton International, Inc.
181 West Madison Street, Suite 4510
Chicago, IL 60602
Telephone: (312) 456-0080
**Recruiter Classification:** Retained; **Lowest/Average Salary:** $90,000/$90,000;
**Industry Concentration:** Electronics, High Technology, Information
Technology, Venture Capital; **Function Concentration:** Generalist

**Schwarzkopf, A. Renee** — *Consultant*
David C. Cooper and Associates, Inc.
Five Concourse Parkway, Suite 2700
Atlanta, GA 30328
Telephone: (770) 395-0014
**Recruiter Classification:** Contingency, Executive Temporary; **Lowest/Average
Salary:** $20,000/$40,000; **Industry Concentration:** Generalist; **Function
Concentration:** Finance/Accounting

**Schweichler, Lee J.** — *President*
Schweichler Associates, Inc.
200 Tamal Vista, Building 200, Suite 100
Corte Madera, CA 94925
Telephone: (415) 924-7200
**Recruiter Classification:** Retained; **Lowest/Average Salary:** $90,000/$90,000;
**Industry Concentration:** Electronics, High Technology, Information
Technology, Venture Capital; **Function Concentration:** Engineering,
Finance/Accounting, General Management, Human Resources, Marketing,
Research and Development, Sales

**Schwinden, William** — *Associate*
Source Services Corporation
500 108th Avenue NE, Suite 1780
Bellevue, WA 98004
Telephone: (206) 454-6400
**Recruiter Classification:** Contingency; **Lowest/Average Salary:**
$30,000/$50,000; **Industry Concentration:** Financial Services, Information
Technology; **Function Concentration:** Engineering, Finance/Accounting

**Scimone, James** — *Managing Director*
Source Services Corporation
15600 N.W. 67th Avenue, Suite 210
Miami Lakes, FL 33014
Telephone: (305) 556-8000
**Recruiter Classification:** Contingency; **Lowest/Average Salary:**
$30,000/$50,000; **Industry Concentration:** Financial Services, Information
Technology; **Function Concentration:** Engineering, Finance/Accounting

**Scimone, Jim** — *Managing Director*
Source Services Corporation
701 West Cypress Creek Road, Suite 202
Ft. Lauderdale, FL 33309
Telephone: (954) 771-0777
**Recruiter Classification:** Contingency; **Lowest/Average Salary:**
$30,000/$50,000; **Industry Concentration:** Financial Services, Information
Technology; **Function Concentration:** Engineering, Finance/Accounting

**Scoff, Barry** — *Associate*
Source Services Corporation
379 Thornall Street
Edison, NJ 08837
Telephone: (908) 494-2800
**Recruiter Classification:** Contingency; **Lowest/Average Salary:**
$30,000/$50,000; **Industry Concentration:** Financial Services, Information
Technology; **Function Concentration:** Engineering, Finance/Accounting

**Scognamillo, Sandra V.** — *Consultant*
Witt/Kieffer, Ford, Hadelman & Lloyd
1920 Main Street, Suite 310
Irvine, CA 92714
Telephone: (714) 851-5070
**Recruiter Classification:** Retained; **Lowest/Average Salary:** $75,000/$90,000;
**Industry Concentration:** Healthcare/Hospitals; **Function Concentration:**
Generalist with a primary focus in General Management

**Scothon, Alan** — *Managing Partner*
Romac & Associates
6130 Westford Road
Dayton, OH 45426
Telephone: (513) 854-5719
**Recruiter Classification:** Executive Temporary; **Lowest/Average Salary:**
$/$60,000; **Industry Concentration:** Financial Services, Healthcare/Hospitals,
High Technology, Hospitality/Leisure, Information Technology, Insurance;
**Function Concentration:** Finance/Accounting

**Scott, Alison** — *Senior Associate*
Korn/Ferry International
2180 Sand Hill Road
Menlo Park, CA 94025
Telephone: (415) 529-1834
**Recruiter Classification:** Retained; **Lowest/Average Salary:** $90,000/$90,000;
**Industry Concentration:** Generalist; **Function Concentration:** Generalist

**Scott, Evan** — *Partner*
Howard Fischer Associates, Inc.
1800 John F. Kennedy Boulevard, 7th Floor
Philadelphia, PA 19103
Telephone: (215) 568-8363
**Recruiter Classification:** Retained; **Lowest/Average Salary:** $90,000/$90,000;
**Industry Concentration:** Generalist; **Function Concentration:** Generalist

**Scott, George W.** — *Senior Consultant*
Raymond Karsan Associates
989 Old Eagle School Road, Suite 814
Wayne, PA 19087
Telephone: (610) 971-9171
**Recruiter Classification:** Contingency; **Lowest/Average Salary:**
$30,000/$90,000; **Industry Concentration:** Generalist; **Function
Concentration:** Generalist

**Scott, Jack** — *Principal*
Korn/Ferry International
The Transamerica Pyramid
600 Montgomery Street
San Francisco, CA 94111
Telephone: (415) 956-1834
**Recruiter Classification:** Retained; **Lowest/Average Salary:** $90,000/$90,000;
**Industry Concentration:** Generalist; **Function Concentration:** Generalist

**Scott, Mark S.** — *Principal*
The Prairie Group
One Westbrook Corporate Center
Suite 300
Westchester, IL 60154
Telephone: (708) 449-7710
**Recruiter Classification:** Contingency; **Lowest/Average Salary:**
$50,000/$75,000; **Industry Concentration:** Generalist; **Function
Concentration:** Human Resources

**Scott, Ron** — *Vice President*
Richard Kader & Associates
343 West Bagley Road, Suite 209
Berea, OH 44017
Telephone: (216) 891-1700
**Recruiter Classification:** Contingency; **Lowest/Average Salary:**
$40,000/$50,000; **Industry Concentration:** Generalist; **Function
Concentration:** Generalist

**Scranton, Lisa** — *Recruiter*
A.J. Burton Group, Inc.
120 East Baltimore Street, Suite 2220
Baltimore, MD 21202
Telephone: (410) 752-5244
**Recruiter Classification:** Contingency; **Lowest/Average Salary:**
$40,000/$60,000; **Industry Concentration:** Consumer Products, Energy,
Financial Services, Insurance, Manufacturing

**Scrivines, Hank** — *Vice President*
Search Northwest Associates
10117 SE Sunnyside, Suite F-727
Clackamas, OR 97015
Telephone: (503) 654-1487
**Recruiter Classification:** Contingency; **Lowest/Average Salary:**
$30,000/$75,000; **Industry Concentration:** Biotechnology, Chemical Products,
Energy, Environmental, Oil/Gas, Utilities/Nuclear; **Function Concentration:**
Engineering, General Management, Research and Development

**Scroggins, Stephen R.** — *Managing Director*
Russell Reynolds Associates, Inc.
200 Park Avenue
New York, NY 10166-0002
Telephone: (212) 351-2000
**Recruiter Classification:** Retained; **Lowest/Average Salary:** $90,000/$90,000;
**Industry Concentration:** Generalist with a primary focus in Financial Services;
**Function Concentration:** Generalist

**Scullin, Richard** — *Account Executive*
Eden & Associates, Inc.
794 North Valley Road
Paoli, PA 19301
Telephone: (610) 889-9993
**Recruiter Classification:** Contingency, Executive Temporary; **Lowest/Average
Salary:** $60,000/$90,000; **Industry Concentration:** Generalist; **Function
Concentration:** Generalist with a primary focus in Women/Minorities

**Seals, Sonny** — *Vice President*
A.T. Kearney, Inc.
1100 Abernathy Road, Suite 900
Atlanta, GA 30328-5603
Telephone: (770) 393-9900
**Recruiter Classification:** Retained; **Lowest/Average Salary:** $90,000/$90,000;
**Industry Concentration:** Generalist with a primary focus in Entertainment,
Fashion (Retail/Apparel); **Function Concentration:** Generalist with a primary
focus in General Management, Marketing, Sales

**Seamon, Kenneth** — *Associate*
Source Services Corporation
3 Summit Park Drive, Suite 550
Independence, OH 44131
Telephone: (216) 328-5900
**Recruiter Classification:** Contingency; **Lowest/Average Salary:**
$30,000/$50,000; **Industry Concentration:** Financial Services, Information
Technology; **Function Concentration:** Engineering, Finance/Accounting

**Sears, Kirk** — *Manager North Atlantic Region*
Management Recruiters International, Inc.
4929 North Main Street, Suite 104
Acworth, GA 30101
Telephone: (770) 966-1772
**Recruiter Classification:** Contingency; **Lowest/Average Salary:**
$30,000/$75,000; **Industry Concentration:** Generalist; **Function
Concentration:** Generalist

**Sears, Rick** — *Manager Eastern Region*
Management Recruiters International, Inc.
22 West Pomfret Street
Carlisle, PA 17013-3216
Telephone: (717) 249-2626
**Recruiter Classification:** Contingency; **Lowest/Average Salary:**
$30,000/$75,000; **Industry Concentration:** Generalist; **Function**
**Concentration:** Generalist

**Seco, William** — *Managing Partner*
Seco & Zetto Associates, Inc.
P.O. Box 225
Harrington Park, NJ 07640
Telephone: (201) 784-0674
**Recruiter Classification:** Contingency; **Lowest/Average Salary:**
$60,000/$75,000; **Industry Concentration:** Generalist with a primary focus in
Financial Services, High Technology, Information Technology; **Function**
**Concentration:** Generalist with a primary focus in Marketing, Sales,
Women/Minorities

**Seebeck, Robert F.** — *Managing Director*
Russell Reynolds Associates, Inc.
200 South Wacker Drive
Suite 3600
Chicago, IL 60606
Telephone: (312) 993-9696
**Recruiter Classification:** Retained; **Lowest/Average Salary:** $90,000/$90,000;
**Industry Concentration:** Board Services; **Function Concentration:** Generalist

**Seefeld, David** — *Co-Manager*
Management Recruiters International, Inc.
North 1212 Washington, Suite 300
Spokane, WA 99201
Telephone: (509) 324-3333
**Recruiter Classification:** Contingency; **Lowest/Average Salary:**
$30,000/$75,000; **Industry Concentration:** Generalist; **Function**
**Concentration:** Generalist

**Segal, Eric B.** — *President*
Kenzer Corp.
777 Third Avenue, 26th Floor
New York, NY 10017
Telephone: (212) 308-4300
**Recruiter Classification:** Retained; **Lowest/Average Salary:** $50,000/$90,000;
**Industry Concentration:** Consumer Products, Entertainment, Financial
Services, Packaging, Venture Capital; **Function Concentration:** Generalist with
a primary focus in Administration, Finance/Accounting, General Management,
Human Resources, Marketing, Research and Development, Sales

**Seibert, Nancy** — *Consultant*
Tyler & Company
1000 Abernathy Road N.E.
Suite 1400
Atlanta, GA 30328-5655
Telephone: (770) 396-3939
**Recruiter Classification:** Retained; **Lowest/Average Salary:** $60,000/$90,000;
**Industry Concentration:** Healthcare/Hospitals, Insurance; **Function**
**Concentration:** Generalist

**Seiden, Steven A.** — *President*
Seiden Krieger Associates, Inc.
375 Park Avenue
New York, NY 10152
Telephone: (212) 688-8383
**Recruiter Classification:** Retained; **Lowest/Average Salary:** $90,000/$90,000;
**Industry Concentration:** Generalist with a primary focus in Manufacturing;
**Function Concentration:** Generalist with a primary focus in Administration,
Finance/Accounting, General Management, Human Resources, Marketing

**Seitchik, Jack** — *President*
Seitchik Corwin and Seitchik, Inc.
3443 Clay Street
San Francisco, CA 94118-2008
Telephone: (415) 928-5717
**Recruiter Classification:** Retained; **Lowest/Average Salary:** $40,000/$90,000;
**Industry Concentration:** Fashion (Retail/Apparel); **Function Concentration:**
Generalist

**Seitchik, William** — *Vice President*
Seitchik Corwin and Seitchik, Inc.
330 East 38th Street, Suite 5P
New York, NY 10016
Telephone: (212) 370-3592
**Recruiter Classification:** Retained; **Lowest/Average Salary:** $40,000/$90,000;
**Industry Concentration:** Fashion (Retail/Apparel); **Function Concentration:**
Generalist

**Seitz, Charles J.** — *Associate*
Neail Behringer Consultants
24 East 38th Street
New York, NY 10016
Telephone: (212) 689-7555
**Recruiter Classification:** Retained; **Lowest/Average Salary:** $50,000/$75,000;
**Industry Concentration:** Fashion (Retail/Apparel), Manufacturing; **Function**
**Concentration:** Generalist with a primary focus in Administration,
Finance/Accounting, General Management, Marketing, Sales

**Sekera, Roger I.** — *Vice President/Managing Director*
A.T. Kearney, Inc.
225 Reinekers Lane
Alexandria, VA 22314
Telephone: (703) 739-4624
**Recruiter Classification:** Retained; **Lowest/Average Salary:** $90,000/$90,000;
**Industry Concentration:** Generalist with a primary focus in
Healthcare/Hospitals, Manufacturing; **Function Concentration:** Generalist with
a primary focus in Administration, Finance/Accounting, General Management,
Human Resources, Marketing, Sales

**Selbach, Barbara** — *Director*
Spencer Stuart
277 Park Avenue, 29th Floor
New York, NY 10172
Telephone: (212) 336-0200
**Recruiter Classification:** Retained; **Lowest/Average Salary:** $90,000/$90,000;
**Industry Concentration:** Financial Services; **Function Concentration:**
Finance/Accounting, Marketing

**Selbst, Denise** — *Executive Recruiter*
Richard, Wayne and Roberts
24 Greenway Plaza, Suite 1304
Houston, TX 77046-2493
Telephone: (713) 629-6681
**Recruiter Classification:** Retained; **Lowest/Average Salary:** $40,000/$60,000;
**Industry Concentration:** Generalist; **Function Concentration:** Generalist

**Selker, Gregory L.** — *Vice President*
Christian & Timbers
One Corporate Exchange
25825 Science Park Drive, Suite 400
Cleveland, OH 44122
Telephone: (216) 464-8710
**Recruiter Classification:** Retained; **Lowest/Average Salary:** $90,000/$90,000;
**Industry Concentration:** Board Services, Electronics, High Technology,
Information Technology, Venture Capital; **Function Concentration:**
Engineering, General Management, Marketing, Research and Development,
Sales, Women/Minorities

**Selko, Philip W.** — *Executive Vice President*
Hogan Acquisitions
7205 Chagrin Road #3
Chagrin Falls, OH 44023
Telephone: (216) 247-9600
**Recruiter Classification:** Retained; **Lowest/Average Salary:** $90,000/$90,000;
**Industry Concentration:** Generalist with a primary focus in Automotive,
Chemical Products, Consumer Products, Environmental, Fashion
(Retail/Apparel), Financial Services, High Technology, Information Technology,
Insurance, Manufacturing, Packaging, Publishing/Media, Transportation,
Venture Capital; **Function Concentration:** Generalist with a primary focus in
Administration, Engineering, Finance/Accounting, General Management,
Marketing

**Sell, David** — *Associate*
Source Services Corporation
7730 East Bellview Avenue, Suite 302
Englewood, CO 80111
Telephone: (303) 773-3700
**Recruiter Classification:** Contingency; **Lowest/Average Salary:**
$30,000/$50,000; **Industry Concentration:** Financial Services, Information
Technology; **Function Concentration:** Engineering, Finance/Accounting

**Sellery, Robert A.** — *Managing Director*
Robert Sellery Associates, Ltd.
1155 Connecticut Avenue, N.W.
Washington, DC 20036
Telephone: (202) 331-0090
**Recruiter Classification:** Retained; **Lowest/Average Salary:** $40,000/$75,000;
**Industry Concentration:** Non-Profit

**Seltzer, Deborah Coogan** — *Consultant*
Paul Ray Berndtson
191 Peachtree Tower, Suite 3800
191 Peachtree Street, NE
Atlanta, GA 30303-1757
Telephone: (404) 215-4600
**Recruiter Classification:** Retained; **Lowest/Average Salary:** $90,000/$90,000;
**Industry Concentration:** Generalist; **Function Concentration:** Generalist

**Selvaggi, Esther** — *Associate*
Source Services Corporation
150 South Warner Road, Suite 238
King of Prussia, PA 19406
Telephone: (610) 341-1960
**Recruiter Classification:** Contingency; **Lowest/Average Salary:**
$30,000/$50,000; **Industry Concentration:** Financial Services, Information
Technology; **Function Concentration:** Engineering, Finance/Accounting

**Semmes, John R.** — *Manager North Atlantic Region*
Management Recruiters International, Inc.
951 South McPherson Church Road, Suite 105
Fayetteville, NC 28303
Telephone: (910) 483-2555
**Recruiter Classification:** Contingency; **Lowest/Average Salary:**
$30,000/$75,000; **Industry Concentration:** Generalist; **Function
Concentration:** Generalist

**Semple, David** — *Associate*
Source Services Corporation
4170 Ashford Dunwoody Road, Suite 285
Atlanta, GA 30319
Telephone: (404) 255-2045
**Recruiter Classification:** Contingency; **Lowest/Average Salary:**
$30,000/$50,000; **Industry Concentration:** Financial Services, Information
Technology; **Function Concentration:** Engineering, Finance/Accounting

**Semyan, John K.** — *Partner*
TNS Partners, Inc.
12655 North Central Expressway
Suite 900
Dallas, TX 75243
Telephone: (214) 991-3555
**Recruiter Classification:** Retained; **Lowest/Average Salary:** $90,000/$90,000;
**Industry Concentration:** Generalist with a primary focus in Board Services,
Consumer Products, Fashion (Retail/Apparel), Financial Services, High
Technology, Information Technology, Manufacturing, Pharmaceutical/Medical,
Publishing/Media, Venture Capital; **Function Concentration:** Generalist with a
primary focus in Finance/Accounting, General Management, Human
Resources, Marketing, Sales

**Sennello, Gendra** — *Insurance Consultant*
National Search, Inc.
2816 University Drive
Coral Springs, FL 33071
Telephone: (800) 935-4355
**Recruiter Classification:** Contingency; **Lowest/Average Salary:**
$30,000/$50,000; **Industry Concentration:** Healthcare/Hospitals, Insurance,
Pharmaceutical/Medical; **Function Concentration:** Generalist with a primary
focus in Administration, Finance/Accounting, General Management, Human
Resources, Marketing, Research and Development, Sales, Women/Minorities

**Serba, Kerri** — *Associate*
Source Services Corporation
155 Federal Street, Suite 410
Boston, MA 02110
Telephone: (617) 482-8211
**Recruiter Classification:** Contingency; **Lowest/Average Salary:**
$30,000/$50,000; **Industry Concentration:** Financial Services, Information
Technology; **Function Concentration:** Engineering, Finance/Accounting

**Serio, Judith A.** — *President*
Lawstaf Legal Search, Inc.
1201 West Peachtree Street, Suite 4830
Atlanta, GA 30309
Telephone: (404) 872-6672
**Recruiter Classification:** Contingency, Executive Temporary; **Lowest/Average
Salary:** $40,000/$60,000

**Serota, Joel** — *Associate*
Kenzer Corp.
777 Third Avenue, 26th Floor
New York, NY 10017
Telephone: (212) 308-4300
**Recruiter Classification:** Retained; **Lowest/Average Salary:** $50,000/$90,000;
**Industry Concentration:** Generalist; **Function Concentration:** Generalist

**Serwat, Leonard A.** — *Senior Director*
Spencer Stuart
401 North Michigan Avenue, Suite 3400
Chicago, IL 60611-4244
Telephone: (312) 822-0080
**Recruiter Classification:** Retained; **Lowest/Average Salary:** $90,000/$90,000;
**Industry Concentration:** Generalist with a primary focus in Automotive, Board
Services, Consumer Products, Environmental, Manufacturing, Packaging,
Transportation; **Function Concentration:** Generalist with a primary focus in
Administration, Finance/Accounting, General Management, Human Resources,
Marketing, Sales, Women/Minorities

**Sessa, Beth** — *Executive Recruiter*
Richard, Wayne and Roberts
24 Greenway Plaza, Suite 1304
Houston, TX 77046-2493
Telephone: (713) 629-6681
**Recruiter Classification:** Retained; **Lowest/Average Salary:** $50,000/$90,000;
**Industry Concentration:** Generalist with a primary focus in
Healthcare/Hospitals; **Function Concentration:** Generalist

**Sessa, Vincent J.** — *Partner*
Integrated Search Solutions Group, LLC
33 Main Street
Port Washington, NY 11050
Telephone: (516) 767-3030
**Recruiter Classification:** Retained; **Lowest/Average Salary:** $90,000/$90,000;
**Industry Concentration:** Generalist with a primary focus in High Technology,
Information Technology; **Function Concentration:** Generalist with a primary
focus in Human Resources, Marketing, Sales

**Settles, Barbara Z.** — *Partner*
Lamalie Amrop International
Thanksgiving Tower
1601 Elm Street
Dallas, TX 75201-4768
Telephone: (214) 754-0019
**Recruiter Classification:** Retained; **Lowest/Average Salary:** $90,000/$90,000;
**Industry Concentration:** Generalist; **Function Concentration:** Generalist with a
primary focus in General Management, Human Resources, Marketing, Sales

**Sevilla, Claudio A.** — *General Manager*
Crawford & Crofford
15327 NW 60th Avenue, Suite 240
Miami Lakes, FL 33014
Telephone: (305) 820-0855
**Recruiter Classification:** Contingency; **Lowest/Average Salary:**
$30,000/$50,000; **Industry Concentration:** Generalist with a primary focus in
Biotechnology, Chemical Products, Electronics, Energy, Financial Services,
Healthcare/Hospitals, Information Technology, Manufacturing, Oil/Gas,
Packaging, Pharmaceutical/Medical; **Function Concentration:** Generalist with
a primary focus in Administration, Engineering, Finance/Accounting, General
Management, Marketing, Research and Development, Sales

**Sewell, Danny J.** — *Manager North Atlantic Region*
Management Recruiters International, Inc.
Building J, Suite 101
120 North Franklin
Rocky Mount, NC 27804-5448
Telephone: (919) 446-3456
**Recruiter Classification:** Contingency; **Lowest/Average Salary:**
$30,000/$75,000; **Industry Concentration:** Generalist; **Function
Concentration:** Generalist

**Seweloh, Theodore W.** — *Partner*
The Heidrick Partners, Inc.
20 North Wacker Drive
Suite 2850
Chicago, IL 60606-3171
Telephone: (312) 845-9700
**Recruiter Classification:** Retained; **Lowest/Average Salary:** $90,000/$90,000;
**Industry Concentration:** Generalist; **Function Concentration:** Generalist

**Shabot, David** — *Vice President*
Korn/Ferry International
One International Place
Boston, MA 02110-1800
Telephone: (617) 345-0200
**Recruiter Classification:** Retained; **Lowest/Average Salary:** $90,000/$90,000;
**Industry Concentration:** Generalist with a primary focus in
Healthcare/Hospitals; **Function Concentration:** Generalist

**Shackleford, David** — *Associate*
Source Services Corporation
150 South Warner Road, Suite 238
King of Prussia, PA 19406
Telephone: (610) 341-1960
**Recruiter Classification:** Contingency; **Lowest/Average Salary:**
$30,000/$50,000; **Industry Concentration:** Financial Services, Information
Technology; **Function Concentration:** Engineering, Finance/Accounting

**Shake, Samuel D.** — *Vice President*
DHR International, Inc.
Two Sawgrass Village Drive, Suite 4
Ponte Vedra Beach, FL 32082
Telephone: (904) 273-4656
**Recruiter Classification:** Retained; **Lowest/Average Salary:** $60,000/$90,000;
**Industry Concentration:** Generalist; **Function Concentration:** Generalist

**Shamir, Ben** — *Recruiter*
S.D. Kelly & Associates, Inc.
990 Washington Street
Dedham, MA 02026
Telephone: (617) 326-8038
**Recruiter Classification:** Contingency; **Lowest/Average Salary:**
$50,000/$60,000; **Industry Concentration:** Electronics, High Technology,
Manufacturing; **Function Concentration:** Engineering, General Management,
Marketing, Sales

**Shanks, Jennifer** — *Associate*
Source Services Corporation
2029 Century Park East, Suite 1350
Los Angeles, CA 90067
Telephone: (310) 277-8092
**Recruiter Classification:** Contingency; **Lowest/Average Salary:**
$30,000/$50,000; **Industry Concentration:** Financial Services, Information
Technology; **Function Concentration:** Engineering, Finance/Accounting

**Shapanka, Samuel** — *Associate*
Source Services Corporation
2 Penn Plaza, Suite 1176
New York, NY 10121
Telephone: (212) 760-2200
**Recruiter Classification:** Contingency; **Lowest/Average Salary:**
$30,000/$50,000; **Industry Concentration:** Financial Services, Information
Technology; **Function Concentration:** Engineering, Finance/Accounting

**Shapiro, Elaine** — *Executive Recruiter*
CPS Inc.
303 Congress Street, 5th Floor
Boston, MA 02210
Telephone: (617) 439-7950
**Recruiter Classification:** Contingency; **Lowest/Average Salary:**
$30,000/$50,000; **Industry Concentration:** Generalist with a primary focus in
Automotive, Biotechnology, Chemical Products, Consumer Products, High
Technology, Insurance, Manufacturing, Oil/Gas, Packaging,
Pharmaceutical/Medical; **Function Concentration:** Engineering, Research and
Development, Sales, Women/Minorities

**Sharf, Bernard** — *Co-President*
Search Associates, Inc.
5900 Sepulveda Boulevard, Suite 104
Van Nuys, CA 91411
Telephone: (818) 989-2200
**Recruiter Classification:** Contingency; **Lowest/Average Salary:**
$30,000/$60,000; **Industry Concentration:** Entertainment; **Function
Concentration:** Women/Minorities

**Sharp, Paul S.** — *Manager North Atlantic Region*
Management Recruiters International, Inc.
1960 Electric Road, Suite B
Roanoke, VA 24018-2200
Telephone: (540) 989-1676
**Recruiter Classification:** Contingency; **Lowest/Average Salary:**
$30,000/$75,000; **Industry Concentration:** Generalist; **Function
Concentration:** Generalist

**Shattuck, Merrill B.** — *President*
M.B. Shattuck and Associates, Inc.
100 Bush Street, Suite 1675
San Francisco, CA 94104
Telephone: (415) 421-6264
**Recruiter Classification:** Retained; **Lowest/Average Salary:** $75,000/$90,000;
**Industry Concentration:** Generalist with a primary focus in Consumer
Products, Electronics, High Technology, Information Technology,
Manufacturing, Non-Profit; **Function Concentration:** Generalist with a primary
focus in Administration, Engineering, Human Resources, Marketing, Research
and Development

**Shaw, Eric D.** — *Manager Pacific Region*
Management Recruiters International, Inc.
290 East Verdugo, Suite 101
Burbank, CA 91502
Telephone: (818) 563-4230
**Recruiter Classification:** Contingency; **Lowest/Average Salary:**
$30,000/$75,000; **Industry Concentration:** Generalist; **Function
Concentration:** Generalist

**Shaw, Ken** — *Executive Recruiter*
Hornberger Management Company
One Commerce Center, 7th Floor
Wilmington, DE 19801
Telephone: (302) 573-2541
**Recruiter Classification:** Retained; **Lowest/Average Salary:** $90,000/$90,000;
**Industry Concentration:** Real Estate; **Function Concentration:** Generalist

**Shawhan, Heather** — *Associate*
Source Services Corporation
879 West 190th Street, Suite 250
Los Angeles, CA 90248
Telephone: (310) 323-6633
**Recruiter Classification:** Contingency; **Lowest/Average Salary:**
$30,000/$50,000; **Industry Concentration:** Financial Services, Information
Technology; **Function Concentration:** Engineering, Finance/Accounting

**Shea, Christopher J.** — *Partner*
Ingram & Aydelotte Inc.
430 Park Avenue, Suite 700
New York, NY 10022
Telephone: (212) 319-7777
**Recruiter Classification:** Retained; **Lowest/Average Salary:** $90,000/$90,000;
**Industry Concentration:** Energy, Entertainment, Financial Services, High
Technology, Information Technology, Publishing/Media; **Function
Concentration:** Finance/Accounting

**Shea, John** — *Senior Consultant*
ALTCO Temporary Services
100 Menlo Park
Edison, NJ 08837
Telephone: (908) 549-6100
**Recruiter Classification:** Executive Temporary; **Lowest/Average Salary:**
$30,000/$60,000; **Industry Concentration:** Consumer Products, Packaging,
Pharmaceutical/Medical; **Function Concentration:** Engineering, Research and
Development, Women/Minorities

**Shea, John** — *Senior Search Consultant*
The ALTCO Group
100 Menlo Park
Edison, NJ 08837
Telephone: (908) 549-6100
**Recruiter Classification:** Contingency; **Lowest/Average Salary:**
$50,000/$60,000; **Industry Concentration:** Consumer Products, Packaging,
Pharmaceutical/Medical; **Function Concentration:** Engineering, Human
Resources, Research and Development

**Shea, Kathleen M.** — *President*
The Penn Partners, Incorporated
117 South 17th Street, Suite 400
Philadelphia, PA 19103
Telephone: (215) 568-9285
**Recruiter Classification:** Retained; **Lowest/Average Salary:** $60,000/$90,000;
**Industry Concentration:** Generalist with a primary focus in Biotechnology,
Chemical Products, Electronics, Financial Services, Healthcare/Hospitals, High
Technology, Manufacturing, Pharmaceutical/Medical; **Function Concentration:**
Generalist

**Shearer, Gary F.** — *Manager South Atlantic Region*
Management Recruiters International, Inc.
9240 Bonita Beach Road, Suite 3307
Bonita Springs, FL 33923
Telephone: (941) 495-7885
**Recruiter Classification:** Contingency; **Lowest/Average Salary:**
$30,000/$75,000; **Industry Concentration:** Generalist; **Function
Concentration:** Generalist

**Sheedy, Edward J.** — *Principal*
Dieckmann & Associates, Ltd.
180 North Stetson, Suite 5555
Two Prudential Plaza
Chicago, IL 60601
Telephone: (312) 819-5900
**Recruiter Classification:** Retained; **Lowest/Average Salary:** $75,000/$90,000;
**Industry Concentration:** Generalist with a primary focus in Biotechnology,
Electronics, Healthcare/Hospitals, High Technology, Information Technology,
Pharmaceutical/Medical; **Function Concentration:** Generalist with a primary
focus in Finance/Accounting, General Management, Human Resources,
Marketing

**Sheehan, Arthur** — *Manager*
Management Recruiters International, Inc.
558 SE Port St. Lucie Boulevard
Port St. Lucie, FL 34984
Telephone: (407) 879-2400
**Recruiter Classification:** Contingency; **Lowest/Average Salary:**
$30,000/$75,000; **Industry Concentration:** Generalist; **Function
Concentration:** Generalist

**Sheehan, Patricia** — *Manager South Atlantic Region*
Management Recruiters International, Inc.
558 SE Port St. Lucie Boulevard
Port St. Lucie, FL 34984
Telephone: (407) 879-2400
**Recruiter Classification:** Contingency; **Lowest/Average Salary:**
$30,000/$75,000; **Industry Concentration:** Generalist; **Function
Concentration:** Generalist

**Sheets, Russel** — *Branch Manager*
Accountants on Call
700 Ackerman Road
Columbus, OH 43202
Telephone: (614) 267-7200
**Recruiter Classification:** Contingency; **Lowest/Average Salary:**
$20,000/$30,000; **Industry Concentration:** Generalist; **Function Concentration:** Finance/Accounting

**Shell, John C.** — *President*
John Shell Associates, Inc.
115 Atrium Way, Suite 122
Columbia, SC 29223
Telephone: (803) 788-6619
**Recruiter Classification:** Contingency, Executive Temporary; **Lowest/Average Salary:** $20,000/$40,000; **Industry Concentration:** Generalist with a primary focus in Environmental, Financial Services, Healthcare/Hospitals, High Technology, Information Technology, Insurance, Manufacturing, Packaging, Real Estate; **Function Concentration:** Finance/Accounting

**Shelton, Jonathan** — *Associate*
Source Services Corporation
1105 Schrock Road, Suite 510
Columbus, OH 43229
Telephone: (614) 846-3311
**Recruiter Classification:** Contingency; **Lowest/Average Salary:**
$30,000/$50,000; **Industry Concentration:** Financial Services, Information Technology; **Function Concentration:** Engineering, Finance/Accounting

**Shelton, Sandra** — *Insurance Consultant*
National Search, Inc.
2816 University Drive
Coral Springs, FL 33071
Telephone: (800) 935-4355
**Recruiter Classification:** Contingency; **Lowest/Average Salary:**
$30,000/$50,000; **Industry Concentration:** Healthcare/Hospitals, Insurance, Pharmaceutical/Medical; **Function Concentration:** Generalist with a primary focus in Administration, Finance/Accounting, General Management, Human Resources, Marketing, Research and Development, Sales, Women/Minorities

**Shemin, Grace** — *Executive Recruiter*
Maximum Management Corp.
420 Lexington Avenue
Suite 2016
New York, NY 10170
Telephone: (212) 867-4646
**Recruiter Classification:** Contingency, Executive Temporary; **Lowest/Average Salary:** $30,000/$75,000; **Industry Concentration:** Generalist with a primary focus in Consumer Products, Entertainment, Financial Services, Information Technology, Insurance, Manufacturing, Pharmaceutical/Medical, Publishing/Media; **Function Concentration:** Human Resources

**Shen, Eugene Y.** — *Managing Director*
The Whitney Group
850 Third Avenue, 11th Floor
New York, NY 10022
Telephone: (212) 508-3500
**Recruiter Classification:** Retained; **Lowest/Average Salary:** $75,000/$90,000;
**Industry Concentration:** Generalist with a primary focus in Financial Services, Real Estate, Venture Capital; **Function Concentration:** Generalist with a primary focus in Sales

**Shenfield, Peter** — *Partner*
Baker, Harris & Partners Limited
130 Adelaide Street West, Suite 2710
Toronto, Ontario, CANADA M5H 3P5
Telephone: (416) 947-1990
**Recruiter Classification:** Retained; **Lowest/Average Salary:** $50,000/$60,000;
**Industry Concentration:** Generalist with a primary focus in Aerospace/Defense, Consumer Products, Entertainment, Environmental, Fashion (Retail/Apparel), High Technology, Information Technology, Manufacturing, Non-Profit, Publishing/Media; **Function Concentration:** Generalist with a primary focus in Administration, Engineering, Finance/Accounting, General Management, Human Resources, Marketing

**Shepard, Michael J.** — *Group Vice President*
MSI International
2500 Marquis One Tower
245 Peachtree Center Ave.
Atlanta, GA 30303
Telephone: (404) 659-5236
**Recruiter Classification:** Contingency; **Lowest/Average Salary:**
$30,000/$60,000; **Industry Concentration:** Generalist with a primary focus in Financial Services, Healthcare/Hospitals, High Technology, Information Technology, Manufacturing; **Function Concentration:** Generalist with a primary focus in Administration, Engineering, Finance/Accounting, General Management, Marketing, Sales

**Shepherd, Daniel M.** — *Principal*
Shepherd Bueschel & Provus, Inc.
401 North Michigan Avenue, Suite 3020
Chicago, IL 60611-5555
Telephone: (312) 832-3020
**Recruiter Classification:** Retained; **Lowest/Average Salary:** $90,000/$90,000;
**Industry Concentration:** Generalist with a primary focus in Board Services, Chemical Products, Consumer Products, Environmental, Healthcare/Hospitals, High Technology, Pharmaceutical/Medical, Publishing/Media; **Function Concentration:** Generalist with a primary focus in Finance/Accounting, General Management, Marketing, Sales

**Shepherd, Gail L.** — *Consultant*
Shepherd Bueschel & Provus, Inc.
401 North Michigan Avenue, Suite 3020
Chicago, IL 60611-5555
Telephone: (312) 832-3020
**Recruiter Classification:** Retained; **Lowest/Average Salary:** $90,000/$90,000;
**Industry Concentration:** Generalist; **Function Concentration:** Generalist

**Sher, Lawrence** — *Managing Director*
M.A. Churchill & Associates, Inc.
Morelyn Plaza
1111 Street Road
Southampton, PA 18966
Telephone: (215) 953-0300
**Recruiter Classification:** Contingency; **Lowest/Average Salary:**
$50,000/$75,000; **Industry Concentration:** Financial Services, Insurance;
**Function Concentration:** Marketing, Research and Development, Sales

**Sherburne, Zachary** — *Branch Manager*
Accountants on Call
Telephone: (213) 689-4606
**Recruiter Classification:** Contingency; **Lowest/Average Salary:**
$20,000/$30,000; **Industry Concentration:** Generalist; **Function Concentration:** Finance/Accounting

**Sheridan, Kenneth T.** — *Co-Manager Southwest Region*
Management Recruiters International, Inc.
17111 Fawnbrook Drive
San Antonio, TX 78248
Telephone: (210) 979-0671
**Recruiter Classification:** Contingency; **Lowest/Average Salary:**
$30,000/$75,000; **Industry Concentration:** Generalist; **Function Concentration:** Generalist

**Sheridan, Theresa** — *Co-Manager*
Management Recruiters International, Inc.
17111 Fawnbrook Drive
San Antonio, TX 78248
Telephone: (210) 979-0671
**Recruiter Classification:** Contingency; **Lowest/Average Salary:**
$30,000/$75,000; **Industry Concentration:** Generalist; **Function Concentration:** Generalist

**Sherman, Daniel A.** — *Vice President*
Goodwin & Company
1320 19th Street N.W., Suite 801
Washington, DC 20036
Telephone: (202) 785-9292
**Recruiter Classification:** Retained; **Lowest/Average Salary:** $50,000/$75,000;
**Industry Concentration:** Generalist; **Function Concentration:** Generalist

**Sherman, Robert R.** — *President*
Mortgage & Financial Personnel Services
5850 Canoga Avenue, Suite 400
Woodland Hills, CA 91367
Telephone: (818) 710-7133
**Recruiter Classification:** Contingency, Executive Temporary; **Lowest/Average Salary:** $40,000/$60,000; **Industry Concentration:** Financial Services, Insurance; **Function Concentration:** Finance/Accounting

**Sherrill, Lee S.** — *Co-Manager*
Management Recruiters International, Inc.
104 East College Avenue, P.O. Box 1405
Boiling Springs, NC 28017-1405
Telephone: (704) 434-0211
**Recruiter Classification:** Contingency; **Lowest/Average Salary:**
$30,000/$75,000; **Industry Concentration:** Generalist; **Function Concentration:** Generalist

**Sherry, Joan** — *Senior Associate*
Korn/Ferry International
237 Park Avenue
New York, NY 10017
Telephone: (212) 687-1834
**Recruiter Classification:** Retained; **Lowest/Average Salary:** $90,000/$90,000;
**Industry Concentration:** Generalist with a primary focus in Non-Profit;
**Function Concentration:** Generalist

**Shervey, Brent C.** — *Consultant*
O'Callaghan Honey/Paul Ray Berndtson, Inc.
400-400 Fifth Avenue S.W.
Calgary, Alberta, CANADA T2P 0L6
Telephone: (403) 269-3277
**Recruiter Classification:** Retained; **Lowest/Average Salary:** $75,000/$90,000;
**Industry Concentration:** Generalist with a primary focus in Education/Libraries,
Energy, Environmental, Financial Services, Non-Profit, Oil/Gas, Public
Administration, Publishing/Media; **Function Concentration:** Generalist with a
primary focus in Administration, Finance/Accounting, General Management,
Human Resources, Marketing

**Sherwin, Thomas** — *Executive Vice President*
Barone-O'Hara Associates
P.O. Box 2883
Framingham, MA 01701-0410
Telephone: (508) 877-2775
**Recruiter Classification:** Retained; **Lowest/Average Salary:** $60,000/$90,000;
**Industry Concentration:** Pharmaceutical/Medical; **Function Concentration:**
Generalist with a primary focus in Engineering, General Management,
Marketing, Research and Development, Sales

**Sherwood, Andrew** — *Chairman*
Goodrich & Sherwood Associates, Inc.
521 Fifth Avenue
New York, NY 10175
Telephone: (212) 697-4131
**Recruiter Classification:** Retained; **Lowest/Average Salary:** $60,000/$90,000;
**Industry Concentration:** Generalist with a primary focus in Biotechnology,
Board Services, Chemical Products, Consumer Products, Financial Services,
Healthcare/Hospitals, Information Technology, Insurance, Manufacturing,
Oil/Gas, Publishing/Media, Venture Capital; **Function Concentration:**
Generalist with a primary focus in Administration, Finance/Accounting,
General Management, Human Resources, Marketing, Sales

**Shield, Nancy** — *Vice President*
Maximum Management Corp.
420 Lexington Avenue
Suite 2016
New York, NY 10170
Telephone: (212) 867-4646
**Recruiter Classification:** Contingency, Executive Temporary; **Lowest/Average
Salary:** $30,000/$75,000; **Industry Concentration:** Generalist with a primary
focus in Consumer Products, Entertainment, Financial Services, Information
Technology, Insurance, Manufacturing, Pharmaceutical/Medical,
Publishing/Media; **Function Concentration:** Human Resources

**Shimp, David J.** — *Partner*
Lamalie Amrop International
225 West Wacker Drive
Chicago, IL 60606-1229
Telephone: (312) 782-3113
**Recruiter Classification:** Retained; **Lowest/Average Salary:** $90,000/$90,000;
**Industry Concentration:** Generalist with a primary focus in High Technology,
Information Technology; **Function Concentration:** Generalist with a primary
focus in General Management, Marketing, Sales

**Shipherd, John T.** — *Vice President*
The Cassie Group
38 Beekman Place
Madison, CT 06443
Telephone: (203) 245-0423
**Recruiter Classification:** Retained; **Lowest/Average Salary:** $75,000/$90,000;
**Industry Concentration:** Pharmaceutical/Medical; **Function Concentration:**
Administration, Engineering, Finance/Accounting, General Management,
Human Resources, Marketing, Sales, Women/Minorities

**Shirilla, Robert M.** — *Senior Vice President*
F.B. Schmidt International
30423 Canwood Place, Suite 239
Agoura Hills, CA 91301
Telephone: (818) 706-0500
**Recruiter Classification:** Retained; **Lowest/Average Salary:** $60,000/$90,000;
**Industry Concentration:** Consumer Products, Entertainment, Financial
Services, Information Technology, Pharmaceutical/Medical; **Function
Concentration:** Marketing

**Shockey, William** — *Principal*
Korn/Ferry International
237 Park Avenue
New York, NY 10017
Telephone: (212) 687-1834
**Recruiter Classification:** Retained; **Lowest/Average Salary:** $90,000/$90,000;
**Industry Concentration:** Generalist with a primary focus in Publishing/Media;
**Function Concentration:** Generalist

**Shoemaker, Fred W.** — *Executive Recruiter*
MSI International
2170 West State Road 434
Suite 454
Longwood, FL 32779
Telephone: (407) 788-7700
**Recruiter Classification:** Contingency; **Lowest/Average Salary:**
$30,000/$75,000; **Industry Concentration:** Generalist with a primary focus in
Manufacturing; **Function Concentration:** Generalist with a primary focus in
Engineering

**Shoemaker, Larry C.** — *President*
Shoemaker & Associates
1862 Independence Square, Suite A
Atlanta, GA 30338
Telephone: (770) 395-7225
**Recruiter Classification:** Retained; **Lowest/Average Salary:** $60,000/$90,000;
**Industry Concentration:** Generalist with a primary focus in Consumer
Products, Manufacturing, Packaging, Pharmaceutical/Medical; **Function
Concentration:** Generalist with a primary focus in Administration, Engineering,
Finance/Accounting, General Management, Human Resources, Marketing,
Research and Development, Sales, Women/Minorities

**Shontell, William** — *Senior Director*
Don Richard Associates of Washington, D.C., Inc.
8180 Greensboro Drive, Suite 1020
McLean, VA 22102
Telephone: (703) 827-5990
**Recruiter Classification:** Contingency; **Lowest/Average Salary:**
$50,000/$60,000; **Industry Concentration:** Aerospace/Defense, High
Technology, Publishing/Media; **Function Concentration:** Finance/Accounting

**Shore, Earl L.** — *President*
E.L. Shore & Associates Ltd.
2 St. Clair Avenue, Suite 1201
Toronto, Ontario, CANADA M4T 2T5
Telephone: (416) 928-9399
**Recruiter Classification:** Retained; **Lowest/Average Salary:** $60,000/$90,000;
**Industry Concentration:** Generalist with a primary focus in Automotive,
Chemical Products, Consumer Products, Environmental, Financial Services,
Insurance, Manufacturing, Non-Profit; **Function Concentration:** Generalist

**Shourds, Mary E.** — *Executive Vice President*
Houze, Shourds & Montgomery, Inc.
Greater L.A. World Trade Center, Suite 1840
Long Beach, CA 90831-1840
Telephone: (310) 495-6495
**Recruiter Classification:** Retained; **Lowest/Average Salary:** $90,000/$90,000;
**Industry Concentration:** Generalist with a primary focus in Automotive,
Consumer Products, Electronics, Energy, Financial Services, High Technology,
Information Technology, Manufacturing; **Function Concentration:** Generalist

**Shulman, Barry** — *Principal*
Shulman Associates
796 Elizabeth Street
San Francisco, CA 94114
Telephone: (415) 648-1790
**Recruiter Classification:** Retained; **Lowest/Average Salary:** $60,000/$90,000;
**Industry Concentration:** High Technology; **Function Concentration:** Marketing

**Shulman, Melvin** — *Partner*
McFeely Wackerle Shulman
425 California Street
Suite 2502
San Francisco, CA 94104
Telephone: (415) 398-3488
**Recruiter Classification:** Retained; **Lowest/Average Salary:** $90,000/$90,000;
**Industry Concentration:** Generalist; **Function Concentration:** Generalist with a
primary focus in Administration

**Shultz, Deborah M.** — *Vice President West Coast Operations*
Blau Kaptain Schroeder
4660 La Jolla Drive, Suite 500
La Jolla, CA 92122
Telephone: (619) 535-4835
**Recruiter Classification:** Retained; **Lowest/Average Salary:** $75,000/$75,000;
**Industry Concentration:** Biotechnology, Healthcare/Hospitals,
Pharmaceutical/Medical, Venture Capital; **Function Concentration:** General
Management, Marketing, Research and Development

**Shultz, Susan F.** — *President*
SSA Executive Search International
4350 Camelback Road
Suite 8200
Phoenix, AZ 85018
Telephone: (602) 998-1744
**Recruiter Classification:** Retained; **Lowest/Average Salary:** $50,000/$75,000;
**Industry Concentration:** Generalist; **Function Concentration:** Generalist with a
primary focus in Women/Minorities

**Sibbald, John R.** — *President*
John Sibbald Associates, Inc.
8725 West Higgins Road, Suite 575
Chicago, IL 60631
Telephone: (312) 693-0575
**Recruiter Classification:** Retained; **Lowest/Average Salary:** $90,000/$90,000;
**Industry Concentration:** Generalist with a primary focus in Biotechnology,
Board Services, Chemical Products, Consumer Products, Entertainment,
Fashion (Retail/Apparel), Financial Services, Hospitality/Leisure,
Manufacturing, Non-Profit, Pharmaceutical/Medical, Publishing/Media,
Transportation; **Function Concentration:** Generalist with a primary focus in
Engineering, Finance/Accounting, General Management, Human Resources,
Marketing, Research and Development, Sales, Women/Minorities

**Sibul, Shelly Remen** — *Legal Search Consultant*
Chicago Legal Search, Ltd.
33 North Dearborn Street, Suite 2302
Chicago, IL 60602-3109
Telephone: (312) 251-2580
**Recruiter Classification:** Contingency; **Lowest/Average Salary:**
$40,000/$90,000; **Industry Concentration:** Consumer Products, Electronics,
Energy, Entertainment, Environmental, Healthcare/Hospitals, High Technology,
Information Technology, Non-Profit, Oil/Gas, Pharmaceutical/Medical, Venture
Capital; **Function Concentration:** Women/Minorities

**Siegel, Fred** — *President*
Conex Incorporated
919 Third Avenue, 18th Floor
New York, NY 10022
Telephone: (212) 371-3737
**Recruiter Classification:** Retained; **Lowest/Average Salary:** $60,000/$90,000;
**Industry Concentration:** Generalist; **Function Concentration:** Generalist

**Siegel, Pamela** — *Recruiter*
Executive Options, Ltd.
910 Skokie Boulevard
Suite 210
Northbrook, IL 60068
Telephone: (708) 291-4322
**Recruiter Classification:** Executive Temporary; **Lowest/Average Salary:**
$30,000/$50,000; **Industry Concentration:** Generalist with a primary focus in
Consumer Products, Financial Services, Healthcare/Hospitals, Manufacturing,
Non-Profit, Packaging, Real Estate; **Function Concentration:** Generalist with a
primary focus in Finance/Accounting, General Management, Human
Resources, Marketing, Women/Minorities

**Siegel, RitaSue** — *President*
RitaSue Siegel Resources Inc.
20 East 46th Street, 14th Floor
New York, NY 10017-2417
Telephone: (212) 682-2100
**Recruiter Classification:** Retained; **Lowest/Average Salary:** $30,000/$90,000;
**Industry Concentration:** Generalist; **Function Concentration:** Engineering,
Marketing, Sales

**Sierra, Rafael A.** — *Partner*
Lamalie Amrop International
191 Peachtree Street N.E.
Atlanta, GA 30303
Telephone: (404) 688-0800
**Recruiter Classification:** Retained; **Lowest/Average Salary:** $90,000/$90,000;
**Industry Concentration:** Generalist with a primary focus in
Healthcare/Hospitals; **Function Concentration:** Generalist with a primary focus
in General Management, Marketing, Sales

**Signer, Julie** — *Executive Recruiter*
CPS Inc.
One Westbrook Corporate Centre, Suite 600
Westchester, IL 60154
Telephone: (708) 531-8370
**Recruiter Classification:** Contingency; **Lowest/Average Salary:**
$30,000/$50,000; **Industry Concentration:** Generalist with a primary focus in
Automotive, Biotechnology, Chemical Products, Consumer Products, High
Technology, Insurance, Manufacturing, Oil/Gas, Packaging,
Pharmaceutical/Medical; **Function Concentration:** Engineering, Research and
Development, Sales, Women/Minorities

**Sigurdson, Eric J.** — *Associate*
Russell Reynolds Associates, Inc.
200 South Wacker Drive
Suite 3600
Chicago, IL 60606
Telephone: (312) 993-9696
**Recruiter Classification:** Retained; **Lowest/Average Salary:** $90,000/$90,000;
**Industry Concentration:** Generalist; **Function Concentration:** Generalist

**Siker, Paul W.** — *Principal*
The Guild Corporation
8260 Greensboro Drive, Suite 460
McLean, VA 22102
Telephone: (703) 761-4023
**Recruiter Classification:** Contingency; **Lowest/Average Salary:**
$40,000/$50,000; **Industry Concentration:** Aerospace/Defense, Electronics,
High Technology, Information Technology; **Function Concentration:**
Engineering, Finance/Accounting, General Management, Research and
Development

**Silcott, Marvin L.** — *President/Executive Recruiter*
Marvin L. Silcott & Associates, Inc.
7557 Rambler Road, Suite 1336
Dallas, TX 75231
Telephone: (214) 369-7802
**Recruiter Classification:** Contingency; **Lowest/Average Salary:**
$60,000/$90,000; **Industry Concentration:** Generalist with a primary focus in
Aerospace/Defense, Biotechnology, Chemical Products, Electronics, Energy,
Manufacturing, Oil/Gas, Pharmaceutical/Medical; **Function Concentration:**
Engineering, Human Resources, Research and Development,
Women/Minorities

**Silkiner, David S.** — *Consultant*
Paul Ray Berndtson
191 Peachtree Tower, Suite 3800
191 Peachtree Street, NE
Atlanta, GA 30303-1757
Telephone: (404) 215-4600
**Recruiter Classification:** Retained; **Lowest/Average Salary:** $90,000/$90,000;
**Industry Concentration:** High Technology, Utilities/Nuclear; **Function
Concentration:** Generalist

**Sill, Igor M.** — *Managing Partner*
Geneva Group International
Four Embarcadero Center, Suite 3470
San Francisco, CA 94111
Telephone: (415) 433-4646
**Recruiter Classification:** Retained; **Lowest/Average Salary:** $90,000/$90,000;
**Industry Concentration:** Biotechnology, Board Services, High Technology,
Pharmaceutical/Medical, Venture Capital; **Function Concentration:** Engineering,
General Management, Marketing, Research and Development, Sales

**Sill, Igor M.** — *Managing Partner*
Geneva Group International
375 Forest Avenue
Palo Alto, CA 94303
Telephone: Unpublished
**Recruiter Classification:** Retained; **Lowest/Average Salary:** $90,000/$90,000;
**Industry Concentration:** Biotechnology, Board Services, High Technology,
Pharmaceutical/Medical, Venture Capital; **Function Concentration:** Engineering,
General Management, Marketing, Research and Development, Sales

**Silvas, Stephen D.** — *President*
Roberson and Company
10752 North 89th Place, Suite 202
Scottsdale, AZ 85260
Telephone: (602) 391-3200
**Recruiter Classification:** Contingency; **Lowest/Average Salary:**
$40,000/$60,000; **Industry Concentration:** Generalist with a primary focus in
Automotive, Chemical Products, Electronics, Financial Services,
Healthcare/Hospitals, High Technology, Information Technology,
Manufacturing, Transportation; **Function Concentration:** Generalist with a
primary focus in Engineering, Finance/Accounting, General Management,
Human Resources, Sales

**Silver, Kit** — *Associate*
Source Services Corporation
1290 Oakmead Parkway, Suite 318
Sunnyvale, CA 94086
Telephone: (408) 738-8440
**Recruiter Classification:** Contingency; **Lowest/Average Salary:**
$30,000/$50,000; **Industry Concentration:** Financial Services, Information
Technology; **Function Concentration:** Engineering, Finance/Accounting

**Silver, Lee A.** — *President*
L.A. Silver Associates, Inc.
463 Worcester Road
Framingham, MA 01701
Telephone: (508) 879-2603
**Recruiter Classification:** Contingency; **Lowest/Average Salary:**
$75,000/$75,000; **Industry Concentration:** Generalist with a primary focus in
Chemical Products, Consumer Products, Electronics, Environmental,
Healthcare/Hospitals, High Technology, Information Technology,
Publishing/Media; **Function Concentration:** Generalist with a primary focus in
Administration, Engineering, Finance/Accounting, General Management,
Human Resources, Marketing, Research and Development, Sales

**Silverberg, Alisa** — *Branch Manager*
Accountants on Call
450 Harmon Meadow Boulevard, Third Floor
Secaucus, NJ 07094
Telephone: (201) 330-0080
**Recruiter Classification:** Contingency; **Lowest/Average Salary:**
$20,000/$30,000; **Industry Concentration:** Generalist; **Function
Concentration:** Finance/Accounting

**Silverman, Paul M.** — *President*
The Marshall Group
1900 East Golf Road, Suite M100
Schaumburg, IL 60173
Telephone: (708) 330-0009
**Recruiter Classification:** Executive Temporary; **Lowest/Average Salary:**
$50,000/$90,000; **Industry Concentration:** Generalist with a primary focus in
Electronics, Environmental, Financial Services, Manufacturing, Packaging;
**Function Concentration:** Generalist

**Silverstein, Michael L.** — *Manager North Atlantic Region*
Management Recruiters International, Inc.
233 12th Street, Suite 818-A
Columbus, GA 31901
Telephone: (706) 571-9611
**Recruiter Classification:** Contingency; **Lowest/Average Salary:**
$30,000/$75,000; **Industry Concentration:** Generalist; **Function
Concentration:** Generalist

**Silverstein, Rita** — *Branch Manager*
Accountants on Call
354 Eisenhower Parkway
Livingston, NJ 07039
Telephone: (201) 533-0600
**Recruiter Classification:** Contingency; **Lowest/Average Salary:**
$20,000/$30,000; **Industry Concentration:** Generalist; **Function
Concentration:** Finance/Accounting

**Simankov, Dmitry** — *Consultant*
Logix, Inc.
1601 Trapelo Road
Waltham, MA 02154
Telephone: (617) 890-0500
**Recruiter Classification:** Retained; **Lowest/Average Salary:** $60,000/$75,000;
**Industry Concentration:** High Technology, Information Technology; **Function
Concentration:** Engineering

**Simmonds, David** — *Principal*
Coopers & Lybrand Consulting
2700 Oxford Tower
10235-101 Street
Edmonton, Alberta, CANADA T5J 3N5
Telephone: (403) 421-3111
**Recruiter Classification:** Retained; **Lowest/Average Salary:** $60,000/$90,000;
**Industry Concentration:** Generalist; **Function Concentration:** Generalist

**Simmons, Anneta** — *Executive Recruiter*
F-O-R-T-U-N-E Personnel Consultants of Huntsville, Inc.
3311 Bob Wallace Avenue, Suite 204
Huntsville, AL 35805
Telephone: (205) 534-7282
**Recruiter Classification:** Contingency; **Lowest/Average Salary:**
$30,000/$50,000; **Industry Concentration:** Automotive, Electronics, High
Technology, Information Technology, Manufacturing; **Function Concentration:**
Marketing, Sales

**Simmons, Deborah** — *Associate*
Source Services Corporation
10220 SW Greenburg Road, Suite 625
Portland, OR 97223
Telephone: (503) 768-4546
**Recruiter Classification:** Contingency; **Lowest/Average Salary:**
$30,000/$50,000; **Industry Concentration:** Financial Services, Information
Technology; **Function Concentration:** Engineering, Finance/Accounting

**Simmons, Gerald J.** — *President*
Handy HRM Corp.
250 Park Avenue
New York, NY 10177-0074
Telephone: (212) 557-0400
**Recruiter Classification:** Retained; **Lowest/Average Salary:** $90,000/$90,000;
**Industry Concentration:** Generalist with a primary focus in Board Services,
Chemical Products, High Technology, Information Technology, Non-Profit,
Packaging, Transportation; **Function Concentration:** Generalist with a primary
focus in General Management, Marketing, Sales

**Simmons, Jeffrey** — *Associate*
Kenzer Corp.
6033 West Century Boulevard, Suite 808
Los Angeles, CA 90045
Telephone: (310) 417-8577
**Recruiter Classification:** Retained; **Lowest/Average Salary:** $50,000/$90,000;
**Industry Concentration:** Generalist; **Function Concentration:** Generalist

**Simmons, Sandra K.** — *Department Manager*
MSI International
229 Peachtree Street, NE
Suite 1201
Atlanta, GA 30303
Telephone: (404) 659-5050
**Recruiter Classification:** Contingency; **Lowest/Average Salary:**
$30,000/$60,000; **Industry Concentration:** Generalist with a primary focus in
Financial Services, High Technology; **Function Concentration:** Administration,
Engineering, Finance/Accounting, General Management, Marketing

**Simmons, Tom** — *Director*
Spencer Stuart
1111 Bagby, Suite 1616
Houston, TX 77002-2594
Telephone: (713) 225-1621
**Recruiter Classification:** Retained; **Lowest/Average Salary:** $90,000/$90,000;
**Industry Concentration:** Generalist; **Function Concentration:** Generalist

**Simmons, Vicki** — *Executive Recruiter*
Richard, Wayne and Roberts
24 Greenway Plaza, Suite 1304
Houston, TX 77046-2493
Telephone: (713) 629-6681
**Recruiter Classification:** Retained; **Lowest/Average Salary:** $30,000/$60,000;
**Industry Concentration:** Generalist; **Function Concentration:** Generalist with a
primary focus in Human Resources

**Simon, Bernard** — *Manager*
Accountants on Call
100 Constitution Plaza, Suite 957
Hartford, CT 06103
Telephone: (203) 246-4200
**Recruiter Classification:** Contingency; **Lowest/Average Salary:**
$20,000/$30,000; **Industry Concentration:** Generalist; **Function
Concentration:** Finance/Accounting

**Simon, Bernard** — *Manager*
Accountants on Call
535 Fifth Avenue
New York, NY 10017
Telephone: (212) 953-7400
**Recruiter Classification:** Contingency; **Lowest/Average Salary:**
$20,000/$30,000; **Industry Concentration:** Generalist; **Function
Concentration:** Finance/Accounting

**Simon, John** — *Vice President*
John J. Davis & Associates, Inc.
521 Fifth Avenue, Suite 1740
New York, NY 10175
Telephone: (212) 286-9489
**Recruiter Classification:** Retained; **Lowest/Average Salary:** $90,000/$90,000;
**Industry Concentration:** Information Technology; **Function Concentration:**
Generalist

**Simon, Penny B.** — *Partner*
Paul Ray Berndtson
101 Park Avenue, 41st Floor
New York, NY 10178
Telephone: (212) 370-1316
**Recruiter Classification:** Retained; **Lowest/Average Salary:** $90,000/$90,000;
**Industry Concentration:** Financial Services, Real Estate; **Function
Concentration:** Generalist

**Simon, William** — *Managing Vice President*
Korn/Ferry International
1800 Century Park East, Suite 900
Los Angeles, CA 90067
Telephone: (310) 552-1834
**Recruiter Classification:** Retained; **Lowest/Average Salary:** $90,000/$90,000;
**Industry Concentration:** Generalist with a primary focus in Entertainment;
**Function Concentration:** Generalist

**Simpson, Kent T.** — *Manager Central Region*
Management Recruiters International, Inc.
Alumni Office Park
2350 Sterlington Road
Lexington, KY 40502
Telephone: (606) 273-5665
**Recruiter Classification:** Contingency; **Lowest/Average Salary:**
$30,000/$75,000; **Industry Concentration:** Generalist; **Function
Concentration:** Generalist

**Sims, John** — *Manager Midwest Region*
Management Recruiters International, Inc.
Fifth Street Business Center
806 Fifth Street, Suite 209
Coralville, IA 52241
Telephone: (319) 354-4320
**Recruiter Classification:** Contingency; **Lowest/Average Salary:**
$30,000/$75,000; **Industry Concentration:** Generalist; **Function**
**Concentration:** Generalist

**Sinclair, Amy** — *Executive Recruiter*
Fisher Personnel Management Services
1219 Morningside Drive
Manhattan Beach, CA 90266
Telephone: (310) 546-7507
**Recruiter Classification:** Retained; **Lowest/Average Salary:** $50,000/$75,000;
**Industry Concentration:** Generalist with a primary focus in Automotive,
Electronics, High Technology, Information Technology, Manufacturing,
Publishing/Media; **Function Concentration:** Generalist with a primary focus in
Administration, Engineering, General Management, Human Resources,
Marketing, Sales, Women/Minorities

**Sinclair, Tom** — *Director Executive Search*
Coopers & Lybrand Consulting
145 King Street West
Toronto, Ontario, CANADA M5H 1V8
Telephone: (416) 869-1130
**Recruiter Classification:** Retained; **Lowest/Average Salary:** $60,000/$90,000;
**Industry Concentration:** Generalist; **Function Concentration:** Generalist

**Sindler, Jay** — *Recruiter*
A.J. Burton Group, Inc.
120 East Baltimore Street, Suite 2220
Baltimore, MD 21202
Telephone: (410) 752-5244
**Recruiter Classification:** Contingency; **Lowest/Average Salary:**
$40,000/$60,000; **Industry Concentration:** Consumer Products, Energy,
Financial Services, Insurance, Manufacturing

**Sine, Mark** — *Vice President*
Hospitality International
181 Port Watson Street
Cortland, NY 13045
Telephone: (607) 756-8550
**Recruiter Classification:** Contingency; **Lowest/Average Salary:**
$40,000/$60,000; **Industry Concentration:** Entertainment,
Healthcare/Hospitals, Hospitality/Leisure; **Function Concentration:**
Finance/Accounting, General Management, Human Resources, Marketing,
Sales, Women/Minorities

**Singer, Glenn** — *Consultant*
Witt/Kieffer, Ford, Hadelman & Lloyd
1920 Main Street, Suite 310
Irvine, CA 92714
Telephone: (714) 851-5070
**Recruiter Classification:** Retained; **Lowest/Average Salary:** $75,000/$90,000;
**Industry Concentration:** Healthcare/Hospitals; **Function Concentration:**
General Management

**Singleton, Robin** — *Senior Vice President*
Tyler & Company
1000 Abernathy Road N.E.
Suite 1400
Atlanta, GA 30328-5655
Telephone: (770) 396-3939
**Recruiter Classification:** Retained; **Lowest/Average Salary:** $60,000/$90,000;
**Industry Concentration:** Healthcare/Hospitals, Insurance; **Function**
**Concentration:** Generalist

**Sirena, Evelyn** — *Associate*
Source Services Corporation
925 Westchester Avenue, Suite 309
White Plains, NY 10604
Telephone: (914) 428-9100
**Recruiter Classification:** Contingency; **Lowest/Average Salary:**
$30,000/$50,000; **Industry Concentration:** Financial Services, Information
Technology; **Function Concentration:** Engineering, Finance/Accounting

**Sitarski, Stan** — *Vice President*
Howard Fischer Associates, Inc.
1800 John F. Kennedy Boulevard, 7th Floor
Philadelphia, PA 19103
Telephone: (215) 568-8363
**Recruiter Classification:** Retained; **Lowest/Average Salary:** $90,000/$90,000;
**Industry Concentration:** Generalist; **Function Concentration:** Generalist

**Sjogren, Dennis** — *Agribusiness Recruiter*
Agra Placements International Ltd.
Valley Office Park, Suite 214
10800 Lyndale Avenue South
Minneapolis, MN 55420
Telephone: (612) 881-3692
**Recruiter Classification:** Contingency; **Lowest/Average Salary:**
$20,000/$30,000; **Industry Concentration:** Generalist with a primary focus in
Biotechnology, Chemical Products, Energy, Financial Services, Manufacturing;
**Function Concentration:** Administration, Engineering, Finance/Accounting,
General Management, Human Resources, Marketing, Research and
Development, Sales

**Skinner, Aimee** — *Recruiter*
Don Richard Associates of Tidewater, Inc.
4701 Columbus Street, Suite 102
Virginia Beach, VA 23462
Telephone: (757) 518-8600
**Recruiter Classification:** Contingency; **Lowest/Average Salary:**
$30,000/$40,000; **Industry Concentration:** Generalist; **Function**
**Concentration:** Finance/Accounting

**Skirbe, Douglas** — *Vice President*
Rhodes Associates
555 Fifth Avenue
New York, NY 10017
Telephone: (212) 983-2000
**Recruiter Classification:** Retained; **Lowest/Average Salary:** $90,000/$90,000;
**Industry Concentration:** Financial Services, Insurance, Real Estate, Venture
Capital; **Function Concentration:** Generalist

**Sklover, Bruce** — *President*
Professional Assignments of New York, Inc.
31 East 32nd Street, Suite 300
New York, NY 10016
Telephone: (212) 481-8484
**Recruiter Classification:** Executive Temporary; **Lowest/Average Salary:**
$40,000/$75,000; **Industry Concentration:** Generalist with a primary focus in
Publishing/Media; **Function Concentration:** Generalist with a primary focus in
Administration, Human Resources, Marketing

**Skunda, Donna M.** — *Vice President*
Allerton Heneghan & O'Neill
70 West Madison Street, Suite 2015
Chicago, IL 60602
Telephone: (312) 263-1075
**Recruiter Classification:** Retained; **Lowest/Average Salary:** $75,000/$90,000;
**Industry Concentration:** Generalist with a primary focus in Automotive,
Consumer Products, Electronics, Financial Services, High Technology,
Manufacturing, Pharmaceutical/Medical, Publishing/Media, Transportation;
**Function Concentration:** Generalist with a primary focus in Engineering,
Finance/Accounting, General Management, Marketing, Research and
Development, Women/Minorities

**Slater, Ronald E.** — *Vice President*
A.T. Kearney, Inc.
222 West Adams Street
Chicago, IL 60606
Telephone: (312) 648-0111
**Recruiter Classification:** Retained; **Lowest/Average Salary:** $90,000/$90,000;
**Industry Concentration:** Generalist with a primary focus in Automotive,
Chemical Products, Pharmaceutical/Medical, Publishing/Media, Transportation,
Utilities/Nuclear; **Function Concentration:** Generalist with a primary focus in
Engineering, Marketing, Research and Development, Sales

**Slaughter, Katherine T.** — *Vice President*
Compass Group Ltd.
401 South Woodward Avenue, Suite 460
Birmingham, MI 48009-6613
Telephone: (810) 540-9110
**Recruiter Classification:** Retained; **Lowest/Average Salary:** $75,000/$90,000;
**Industry Concentration:** Generalist with a primary focus in Automotive,
Chemical Products, Education/Libraries, Manufacturing, Transportation;
**Function Concentration:** Administration, Engineering, General Management,
Human Resources, Marketing, Research and Development, Sales,
Women/Minorities

**Slayton, Richard C.** — *President*
Slayton International, Inc.
181 West Madison Street, Suite 4510
Chicago, IL 60602
Telephone: (312) 456-0080
**Recruiter Classification:** Retained; **Lowest/Average Salary:** $90,000/$90,000;
**Industry Concentration:** Aerospace/Defense, Automotive, Board Services,
Chemical Products, Electronics, Information Technology, Manufacturing,
Transportation, Venture Capital; **Function Concentration:** Engineering,
Finance/Accounting, General Management, Human Resources, Marketing,
Research and Development

**Slayton, Richard S.** — *Vice President*
Slayton International, Inc.
181 West Madison Street, Suite 4510
Chicago, IL 60602
Telephone: (312) 456-0080
**Recruiter Classification:** Retained; **Lowest/Average Salary:** $90,000/$90,000;
**Industry Concentration:** Automotive, Information Technology, Manufacturing,
Transportation; **Function Concentration:** Generalist

**Sloan, Michael D.** — *President*
Sloan & Associates
1769 Jamestown Road
Williamsburg, VA 23185
Telephone: (757) 220-1111
**Recruiter Classification:** Contingency; **Lowest/Average Salary:**
$90,000/$90,000; **Industry Concentration:** Consumer Products; **Function
Concentration:** Marketing, Research and Development, Sales

**Sloan, Scott** — *Associate*
Source Services Corporation
150 South Wacker Drive, Suite 400
Chicago, IL 60606
Telephone: (312) 346-7000
**Recruiter Classification:** Contingency; **Lowest/Average Salary:**
$30,000/$50,000; **Industry Concentration:** Financial Services, Information
Technology; **Function Concentration:** Engineering, Finance/Accounting

**Slocum, Ann Marie** — *Vice President*
K.L. Whitney Company
6 Aspen Drive
North Caldwell, NJ 07006
Telephone: (201) 228-7124
**Recruiter Classification:** Retained; **Lowest/Average Salary:** $75,000/$90,000;
**Industry Concentration:** Financial Services; **Function Concentration:**
Marketing, Sales

**Slosar, John M.** — *Senior Vice President/Director*
Canny, Bowen Inc.
200 Park Avenue
New York, NY 10166
Telephone: (212) 949-6611
**Recruiter Classification:** Retained; **Lowest/Average Salary:** $90,000/$90,000;
**Industry Concentration:** Automotive, Electronics, Information Technology,
Manufacturing, Transportation; **Function Concentration:** Administration,
Engineering, Finance/Accounting, Human Resources

**Small, Ellyn** — *Regional Vice President*
Accountants on Call
One Alhambra Plaza, Suite 1435
Coral Gables, FL 33134
Telephone: (305) 443-9333
**Recruiter Classification:** Contingency; **Lowest/Average Salary:** $20,000/$30,000;
**Industry Concentration:** Generalist; **Function Concentration:** Finance/Accounting

**Smead, Michelle M.** — *Vice President*
A.T. Kearney, Inc.
222 West Adams Street
Chicago, IL 60606
Telephone: (312) 648-0111
**Recruiter Classification:** Retained; **Lowest/Average Salary:** $90,000/$90,000;
**Industry Concentration:** Generalist with a primary focus in Chemical Products,
Financial Services, High Technology, Manufacturing, Non-Profit,
Pharmaceutical/Medical, Transportation; **Function Concentration:** Generalist
with a primary focus in Administration, Finance/Accounting, General
Management, Human Resources, Marketing, Sales

**Smirnov, Tatiana** — *Vice President*
Allan Sarn Associates Inc.
230 Park Avenue, Suite 1522
New York, NY 10169
Telephone: (212) 687-0600
**Recruiter Classification:** Retained; **Lowest/Average Salary:** $75,000/$90,000;
**Industry Concentration:** Generalist with a primary focus in
Aerospace/Defense, Consumer Products, Energy, Entertainment,
Environmental, Financial Services, High Technology, Information Technology,
Insurance, Manufacturing, Pharmaceutical/Medical, Publishing/Media, Real
Estate, Utilities/Nuclear; **Function Concentration:** Human Resources

**Smith, Adam M.** — *Vice President*
The Abbott Group, Inc.
530 College Parkway, Suite N
Annapolis, MD 21401
Telephone: (410) 757-4100
**Recruiter Classification:** Retained; **Lowest/Average Salary:** $90,000/$90,000;
**Industry Concentration:** Generalist with a primary focus in Aerospace/Defense,
Biotechnology, Board Services, Chemical Products, Electronics, Energy,
Entertainment, Environmental, Financial Services, Healthcare/Hospitals, High
Technology, Information Technology, Manufacturing, Non-Profit,
Publishing/Media, Venture Capital; **Function Concentration:** Generalist with a
primary focus in Engineering, Finance/Accounting, General Management, Human
Resources, Marketing, Research and Development, Sales, Women/Minorities

**Smith, Ana Luz** — *Associate*
Smith Search, S.C.
Bosques de Versalles #76
Colinas del Bosque 2a Secc.
Villa Corregidora, Qro., MEXICO
Telephone: (524) 228-1414
**Recruiter Classification:** Retained; **Lowest/Average Salary:** $50,000/$75,000;
**Industry Concentration:** Generalist; **Function Concentration:** Generalist

**Smith, Barry S.** — *Co-Manager Eastern Region*
Management Recruiters International, Inc.
1170 Route 22 East
Bridgewater, NJ 08807-1786
Telephone: (908) 725-2595
**Recruiter Classification:** Contingency; **Lowest/Average Salary:**
$30,000/$75,000; **Industry Concentration:** Generalist; **Function
Concentration:** Generalist

**Smith, Brant** — *Partner*
Smith Hanley Associates
99 Park Avenue
New York, NY 10016
Telephone: (212) 687-9696
**Recruiter Classification:** Contingency; **Lowest/Average Salary:**
$75,000/$90,000; **Industry Concentration:** Financial Services; **Function
Concentration:** Finance/Accounting

**Smith, Carroll V.** — *Manager Midwest Region*
Management Recruiters International, Inc.
Hayes Block Building
20 East Milwaukee Street, Suite 304
Janesville, WI 53545-3061
Telephone: (608) 752-2125
**Recruiter Classification:** Contingency; **Lowest/Average Salary:**
$30,000/$75,000; **Industry Concentration:** Generalist; **Function
Concentration:** Generalist

**Smith, Cheryl** — *Consultant*
KPMG Executive Search
P.O. Box 31, Stn. Commerce Court
Toronto, Ontario, CANADA M5L 1B2
Telephone: (416) 777-8500
**Recruiter Classification:** Retained; **Lowest/Average Salary:** $75,000/$90,000;
**Industry Concentration:** Generalist; **Function Concentration:** Generalist

**Smith, Cheryl** — *Senior Consultant*
Barton Raben, Inc.
One Riverway, Suite 2500
Houston, TX 77056
Telephone: (713) 961-9111
**Recruiter Classification:** Retained; **Lowest/Average Salary:** $75,000/$90,000;
**Industry Concentration:** Generalist with a primary focus in Consumer
Products, Financial Services, High Technology, Information Technology,
Oil/Gas; **Function Concentration:** Generalist with a primary focus in
Finance/Accounting, Human Resources, Marketing, Sales

**Smith, Cheryl** — *Corporate Accountant*
ProResource, Inc.
500 Ohio Savings Plaza
1801 East Ninth Street, Suite 500
Cleveland, OH 44114
Telephone: (216) 579-1515
**Recruiter Classification:** Executive Temporary; **Lowest/Average Salary:**
$30,000/$75,000; **Industry Concentration:** Generalist; **Function
Concentration:** Generalist with a primary focus in Engineering,
Finance/Accounting, General Management, Human Resources, Marketing,
Research and Development

**Smith, Clawson** — *Managing Director*
Ward Howell International, Inc.
One Landmark Square
Suite 1810
Stamford, CT 06901
Telephone: (203) 964-1481
**Recruiter Classification:** Retained; **Lowest/Average Salary:** $75,000/$90,000;
**Industry Concentration:** Generalist; **Function Concentration:** Generalist

**Smith, David P.** — *President*
Smith & Latterell (HRS, Inc.)
P.O. Box 4499
Pittsburgh, PA 15205
Telephone: (412) 331-4700
**Recruiter Classification:** Retained; **Lowest/Average Salary:** $90,000/$90,000;
**Industry Concentration:** Generalist with a primary focus in Board Services,
Chemical Products, Electronics, Environmental, Financial Services, High
Technology, Information Technology, Manufacturing, Non-Profit, Venture
Capital; **Function Concentration:** Generalist with a primary focus in
Engineering, Finance/Accounting, General Management, Human Resources,
Marketing, Research and Development, Sales, Women/Minorities

**Smith, Douglas M.** — *Managing Director*
Ward Howell International, Inc.
1300 Grove Avenue, Suite 100
Barrington, IL 60010
Telephone: (847) 382-2206
**Recruiter Classification:** Retained; **Lowest/Average Salary:** $90,000/$90,000;
**Industry Concentration:** Automotive, Consumer Products, Environmental,
Manufacturing; **Function Concentration:** Generalist with a primary focus in
General Management

**Smith, Eric E.** — *Manager Southwest Region*
Management Recruiters International, Inc.
1335 Regents Park Drive, Suite 150
Houston, TX 77058
Telephone: (713) 286-9977
**Recruiter Classification:** Contingency; **Lowest/Average Salary:**
$30,000/$75,000; **Industry Concentration:** Generalist; **Function
Concentration:** Generalist

**Smith, Ethan L.** — *Associate*
Highland Search Group, L.L.C.
565 Fifth Avenue, 22nd Floor
New York, NY 10017
Telephone: (212) 328-1113
**Recruiter Classification:** Retained; **Lowest/Average Salary:** $90,000/$90,000;
**Industry Concentration:** Financial Services, Real Estate, Venture Capital;
**Function Concentration:** Generalist with a primary focus in
Finance/Accounting, General Management, Human Resources, Sales

**Smith, Gin-Nie** — *Manager North Atlantic Region*
Management Recruiters International, Inc.
110 Scott
High Point, NC 27262-7832
Telephone: (910) 869-1200
**Recruiter Classification:** Contingency; **Lowest/Average Salary:**
$30,000/$75,000; **Industry Concentration:** Generalist; **Function
Concentration:** Generalist

**Smith, Grant** — *Director*
Price Waterhouse
601 West Hastings Street
Suite 1400
Vancouver, British Columbia, CANADA V6B 5A5
Telephone: (604) 682-4711
**Recruiter Classification:** Retained; **Lowest/Average Salary:** $75,000/$75,000;
**Industry Concentration:** Generalist with a primary focus in Education/Libraries,
Energy, Healthcare/Hospitals, High Technology, Hospitality/Leisure,
Manufacturing, Non-Profit, Pharmaceutical/Medical; **Function Concentration:**
Generalist with a primary focus in Administration, Engineering,
Finance/Accounting, General Management, Human Resources, Marketing,
Sales

**Smith, Herbert C.** — *President*
H C Smith Ltd.
20600 Chagrin Boulevard, Suite 200
Shaker Heights, OH 44122
Telephone: (216) 752-9966
**Recruiter Classification:** Retained; **Lowest/Average Salary:** $75,000/$75,000;
**Industry Concentration:** Generalist; **Function Concentration:** Generalist

**Smith, Herman D.** — *Manager North Atlantic Region*
Management Recruiters International, Inc.
1925 Ebenezer Road
Rock Hill, SC 29732-1068
Telephone: (803) 324-5181
**Recruiter Classification:** Contingency; **Lowest/Average Salary:**
$30,000/$75,000; **Industry Concentration:** Generalist; **Function
Concentration:** Generalist

**Smith, Herman M.** — *President*
Herman Smith Executive Initiatives Inc.
Suite 3600, 161 Bay Street, Box 629
Toronto, Ontario, CANADA M5J 2S1
Telephone: (416) 862-8830
**Recruiter Classification:** Retained; **Lowest/Average Salary:** $90,000/$90,000;
**Industry Concentration:** Generalist with a primary focus in
Aerospace/Defense, Financial Services, High Technology, Information
Technology, Manufacturing, Non-Profit, Oil/Gas, Public Administration,
Publishing/Media, Real Estate, Transportation; **Function Concentration:**
Generalist with a primary focus in General Management, Human Resources,
Research and Development

**Smith, Ian** — *Staffing Consultant*
International Staffing Consultants, Inc.
500 Newport Center Drive, Suite 300
Newport Beach, CA 92660-7003
Telephone: (714) 721-7990
**Recruiter Classification:** Contingency; **Lowest/Average Salary:**
$50,000/$75,000; **Industry Concentration:** Oil/Gas; **Function Concentration:**
Engineering

**Smith, John E.** — *President*
Smith Search, S.C.
Barranca del Muerto No. 472, Col. Alpes
Mexico City, D.F., MEXICO 01010
Telephone: (525) 593-8766
**Recruiter Classification:** Retained; **Lowest/Average Salary:** $75,000/$90,000;
**Industry Concentration:** Generalist; **Function Concentration:** Generalist

**Smith, John F.** — *Vice President*
The Penn Partners, Incorporated
117 South 17th Street, Suite 400
Philadelphia, PA 19103
Telephone: (215) 568-9285
**Recruiter Classification:** Retained; **Lowest/Average Salary:** $60,000/$90,000;
**Industry Concentration:** Generalist with a primary focus in Biotechnology,
Chemical Products, Electronics, Financial Services, Healthcare/Hospitals, High
Technology, Manufacturing, Pharmaceutical/Medical; **Function Concentration:**
Generalist

**Smith, Kevin** — *Executive Recruiter*
F-O-R-T-U-N-E Personnel Consultants of Manatee County
923 4th Street West
Palmetto, FL 34221
Telephone: (941) 729-3674
**Recruiter Classification:** Contingency; **Lowest/Average Salary:**
$30,000/$50,000; **Industry Concentration:** Automotive, Consumer Products,
Electronics, High Technology, Manufacturing; **Function Concentration:**
Engineering

**Smith, Lawrence** — *Associate*
Source Services Corporation
One South Main Street, Suite 1440
Dayton, OH 45402
Telephone: (513) 461-4660
**Recruiter Classification:** Contingency; **Lowest/Average Salary:**
$30,000/$50,000; **Industry Concentration:** Financial Services, Information
Technology; **Function Concentration:** Engineering, Finance/Accounting

**Smith, Margaret A.** — *Physician Recruiter*
MSI International
201 St. Charles Avenue
Suite 2205
New Orleans, LA 70170
Telephone: (504) 522-6700
**Recruiter Classification:** Contingency; **Lowest/Average Salary:**
$30,000/$60,000; **Industry Concentration:** Generalist with a primary focus in
Healthcare/Hospitals; **Function Concentration:** Generalist with a primary focus
in Administration, Engineering, Finance/Accounting, General Management,
Marketing, Sales

**Smith, Mark L.** — *Managing Vice President*
Korn/Ferry International
One International Place
Boston, MA 02110-1800
Telephone: (617) 345-0200
**Recruiter Classification:** Retained; **Lowest/Average Salary:** $90,000/$90,000;
**Industry Concentration:** Generalist; **Function Concentration:** Generalist

**Smith, Marvin E.** — *Search Manager*
Parfitt Recruiting and Consulting
1540 140th Avenue NE #201
Bellevue, WA 98005
Telephone: (206) 646-6300
**Recruiter Classification:** Contingency; **Lowest/Average Salary:**
$30,000/$75,000; **Industry Concentration:** Generalist with a primary focus in
Manufacturing; **Function Concentration:** Finance/Accounting, General
Management, Human Resources

**Smith, Matthew** — *Vice President*
Korn/Ferry International
120 South Riverside Plaza
Suite 918
Chicago, IL 60606
Telephone: (312) 726-1841
**Recruiter Classification:** Retained; **Lowest/Average Salary:** $90,000/$90,000;
**Industry Concentration:** Generalist; **Function Concentration:** Generalist

**Smith, Melanie F.** — *Principal*
The Heidrick Partners, Inc.
20 North Wacker Drive
Suite 2850
Chicago, IL 60606-3171
Telephone: (312) 845-9700
**Recruiter Classification:** Retained; **Lowest/Average Salary:** $90,000/$90,000;
**Industry Concentration:** Generalist; **Function Concentration:** Generalist

**Smith, Mike W.** — *Manager Central Region*
Management Recruiters International, Inc.
105 Citation, Suite A
Danville, KY 40422-9200
Telephone: (606) 236-0506
**Recruiter Classification:** Contingency; **Lowest/Average Salary:**
$30,000/$75,000; **Industry Concentration:** Generalist; **Function Concentration:** Generalist

**Smith, Monica L.** — *President*
Analysts Resources, Inc.
75 Maiden Lane
New York, NY 10038
Telephone: (212) 755-2777
**Recruiter Classification:** Contingency; **Lowest/Average Salary:**
$75,000/$90,000; **Industry Concentration:** Financial Services, Venture Capital; **Function Concentration:** Generalist with a primary focus in Finance/Accounting, Marketing, Sales

**Smith, Perry V.** — *Manager Southwest Region*
Management Recruiters International, Inc.
Twin Towers North, Suite 1025N
8585 Stemmons Freeway
Dallas, TX 75247
Telephone: (214) 638-2300
**Recruiter Classification:** Contingency; **Lowest/Average Salary:**
$30,000/$75,000; **Industry Concentration:** Generalist; **Function Concentration:** Generalist

**Smith, R. Michael** — *Senior Partner*
Smith James Group, Inc.
11660 Alpharetta Highway, Suite 515
Roswell, GA 30076
Telephone: (770) 667-0212
**Recruiter Classification:** Retained; **Lowest/Average Salary:** $40,000/$75,000;
**Industry Concentration:** Generalist with a primary focus in Aerospace/Defense, Consumer Products, Electronics, Financial Services, High Technology; **Function Concentration:** Generalist

**Smith, Rebecca Ruben** — *Executive Vice President*
H C Smith Ltd.
20600 Chagrin Boulevard, Suite 200
Shaker Heights, OH 44122
Telephone: (216) 752-9966
**Recruiter Classification:** Retained; **Lowest/Average Salary:** $75,000/$75,000;
**Industry Concentration:** Generalist; **Function Concentration:** Generalist

**Smith, Richard** — *Executive Recruiter*
S.C. International, Ltd.
1430 Branding Lane, Suite 119
Downers Grove, IL 60515
Telephone: (708) 963-3033
**Recruiter Classification:** Contingency; **Lowest/Average Salary:**
$30,000/$50,000; **Industry Concentration:** Information Technology, Insurance; **Function Concentration:** Administration, Human Resources

**Smith, Robert L.** — *Partner*
Smith & Sawyer Inc.
230 Park Avenue, 33rd Floor
New York, NY 10169
Telephone: (212) 490-4390
**Recruiter Classification:** Retained; **Lowest/Average Salary:** $90,000/$90,000;
**Industry Concentration:** Generalist with a primary focus in Consumer Products, Fashion (Retail/Apparel), Financial Services, High Technology, Information Technology, Manufacturing; **Function Concentration:** Generalist with a primary focus in Finance/Accounting, General Management, Human Resources, Marketing, Sales

**Smith, Scott B.** — *Principal*
Ward Howell International, Inc.
401 East Host Drive
Lake Geneva, WI 53147
Telephone: (414) 249-5200
**Recruiter Classification:** Retained; **Lowest/Average Salary:** $75,000/$90,000;
**Industry Concentration:** Generalist; **Function Concentration:** Generalist

**Smith, Shellie L.** — *Vice President*
The Heidrick Partners, Inc.
20 North Wacker Drive
Suite 2850
Chicago, IL 60606-3171
Telephone: (312) 845-9700
**Recruiter Classification:** Retained; **Lowest/Average Salary:** $90,000/$90,000;
**Industry Concentration:** Generalist; **Function Concentration:** Generalist

**Smith, Steve L.** — *General Manager*
Management Recruiters International, Inc.
110 Scott
High Point, NC 27262-7832
Telephone: (910) 869-1200
**Recruiter Classification:** Contingency; **Lowest/Average Salary:**
$30,000/$75,000; **Industry Concentration:** Generalist; **Function Concentration:** Generalist

**Smith, Timothy** — *Associate*
Source Services Corporation
155 Federal Street, Suite 410
Boston, MA 02110
Telephone: (617) 482-8211
**Recruiter Classification:** Contingency; **Lowest/Average Salary:**
$30,000/$50,000; **Industry Concentration:** Financial Services, Information Technology; **Function Concentration:** Engineering, Finance/Accounting

**Smith, Toni S.** — *Senior Director*
Spencer Stuart
401 North Michigan Avenue, Suite 3400
Chicago, IL 60611-4244
Telephone: (312) 822-0080
**Recruiter Classification:** Retained; **Lowest/Average Salary:** $90,000/$90,000;
**Industry Concentration:** Non-Profit; **Function Concentration:** General Management

**Smith, W. Guice** — *Senior Consultant*
Southwestern Professional Services
2451 Atrium Way
Nashville, TN 37214
Telephone: (615) 391-2722
**Recruiter Classification:** Contingency; **Lowest/Average Salary:**
$40,000/$90,000; **Industry Concentration:** Financial Services; **Function Concentration:** Finance/Accounting

**Smock, Cynthia** — *Associate*
Source Services Corporation
Foster Plaza VI
681 Anderson Drive, 2nd Floor
Pittsburgh, PA 15220
Telephone: (412) 928-8300
**Recruiter Classification:** Contingency; **Lowest/Average Salary:**
$30,000/$50,000; **Industry Concentration:** Financial Services, Information Technology; **Function Concentration:** Engineering, Finance/Accounting

**Smoller, Howard** — *Associate*
Source Services Corporation
2 Penn Plaza, Suite 1176
New York, NY 10121
Telephone: (212) 760-2200
**Recruiter Classification:** Contingency; **Lowest/Average Salary:**
$30,000/$50,000; **Industry Concentration:** Financial Services, Information Technology; **Function Concentration:** Engineering, Finance/Accounting

**Smyth, Brendan** — *Director Recruitment*
Simpson Associates
Trump Parc
106 Central Park South
New York, NY 10019
Telephone: (212) 767-0006
**Recruiter Classification:** Contingency; **Lowest/Average Salary:**
$60,000/$90,000; **Industry Concentration:** Fashion (Retail/Apparel); **Function Concentration:** Finance/Accounting, Human Resources, Marketing, Sales

**Snedden, Al** — *Manager Midwest Region*
Management Recruiters International, Inc.
707 North East Street, Suite 4
Bloomington, IL 61701
Telephone: (309) 452-1844
**Recruiter Classification:** Contingency; **Lowest/Average Salary:**
$30,000/$75,000; **Industry Concentration:** Generalist; **Function Concentration:** Generalist

**Snelgrove, Geiger** — *Manager Operations*
National Search, Inc.
2816 University Drive
Coral Springs, FL 33071
Telephone: (800) 935-4355
**Recruiter Classification:** Contingency; **Lowest/Average Salary:**
$30,000/$50,000; **Industry Concentration:** Healthcare/Hospitals, Insurance, Pharmaceutical/Medical; **Function Concentration:** Generalist with a primary focus in Administration, Finance/Accounting, General Management, Human Resources, Marketing, Research and Development, Sales, Women/Minorities

**Snellbaker, Mary W.** — *Manager Central Region*
Management Recruiters International, Inc.
225 West Adrian Street, P.O. Box 3
Blissfield, MI 49228-0003
Telephone: (517) 486-2167
**Recruiter Classification:** Contingency; **Lowest/Average Salary:**
$30,000/$75,000; **Industry Concentration:** Generalist; **Function Concentration:** Generalist

**Snider, George R.** — *President*
Sanford Rose Associates
265 South Main Street, Suite 100
Akron, OH 44308
Telephone: (330) 762-7162
**Recruiter Classification:** Contingency; **Lowest/Average Salary:**
$30,000/$75,000; **Industry Concentration:** Generalist; **Function Concentration:** Generalist

**Snodgrass, Stephen** — *Vice President Executive Search*
DeFrain, Mayer, Lee & Burgess LLC
6900 College Boulevard
Overland Park, KS 66211
Telephone: (913) 345-0500
**Recruiter Classification:** Retained; **Lowest/Average Salary:** $50,000/$75,000; **Industry Concentration:** Generalist with a primary focus in Consumer Products, Energy, Financial Services, Healthcare/Hospitals, Insurance, Manufacturing, Non-Profit, Oil/Gas, Pharmaceutical/Medical, Publishing/Media, Real Estate, Transportation; **Function Concentration:** Generalist with a primary focus in Administration, Engineering, Finance/Accounting, General Management, Human Resources, Marketing, Sales

**Snook, Maria P.** — *Co-Manager*
Management Recruiters International, Inc.
111 NW Railroad Street
Enfield, NC 27823-1334
Telephone: (919) 445-4251
**Recruiter Classification:** Contingency; **Lowest/Average Salary:**
$30,000/$75,000; **Industry Concentration:** Generalist; **Function Concentration:** Generalist

**Snook, Marvin G.** — *Co-Manager North Atlantic Region*
Management Recruiters International, Inc.
111 NW Railroad Street
Enfield, NC 27823-1334
Telephone: (919) 445-4251
**Recruiter Classification:** Contingency; **Lowest/Average Salary:**
$30,000/$75,000; **Industry Concentration:** Generalist; **Function Concentration:** Generalist

**Snowden, Charles** — *Associate*
Source Services Corporation
8614 Westwood Center, Suite 750
Vienna, VA 22182
Telephone: (703) 790-5610
**Recruiter Classification:** Contingency; **Lowest/Average Salary:**
$30,000/$50,000; **Industry Concentration:** Financial Services, Information Technology; **Function Concentration:** Engineering, Finance/Accounting

**Snowhite, Rebecca** — *Associate*
Source Services Corporation
525 Vine Street, Suite 2250
Cincinnati, OH 45202
Telephone: (513) 651-3303
**Recruiter Classification:** Contingency; **Lowest/Average Salary:**
$30,000/$50,000; **Industry Concentration:** Financial Services, Information Technology; **Function Concentration:** Engineering, Finance/Accounting

**Snyder, C. Edward** — *Managing Director*
Horton International
666 Fifth Avenue, 37th Floor
New York, NY 10103
Telephone: (212) 541-3900
**Recruiter Classification:** Retained; **Lowest/Average Salary:** $90,000/$90,000; **Industry Concentration:** Generalist; **Function Concentration:** Generalist

**Snyder, James F.** — *President*
Snyder & Company
35 Old Avon Village, Suite 185
Avon, CT 06001-3822
Telephone: (860) 521-9760
**Recruiter Classification:** Retained; **Lowest/Average Salary:** $90,000/$90,000; **Industry Concentration:** Generalist with a primary focus in Aerospace/Defense, Automotive, Biotechnology, Board Services, Chemical Products, Consumer Products, Electronics, Financial Services, Healthcare/Hospitals, High Technology, Information Technology, Insurance, Manufacturing, Pharmaceutical/Medical; **Function Concentration:** Generalist with a primary focus in Administration, Engineering, Finance/Accounting, General Management, Human Resources, Marketing, Research and Development, Sales

**Snyder, Thomas J.** — *Director*
Spencer Stuart
401 North Michigan Avenue, Suite 3400
Chicago, IL 60611-4244
Telephone: (312) 822-0080
**Recruiter Classification:** Retained; **Lowest/Average Salary:** $90,000/$90,000; **Industry Concentration:** Generalist with a primary focus in Consumer Products, Fashion (Retail/Apparel), Manufacturing, Packaging; **Function Concentration:** Generalist with a primary focus in General Management, Marketing, Sales

**Sobczak, Ronald** — *Senior Technical Recruiter*
Search Enterprises, Inc.
160 Quail Ridge Drive
Westmont, IL 60559
Telephone: (708) 654-2300
**Recruiter Classification:** Contingency; **Lowest/Average Salary:**
$20,000/$50,000; **Industry Concentration:** Biotechnology, Chemical Products, Consumer Products, Packaging; **Function Concentration:** Engineering

**Sochacki, Michael** — *Associate*
Source Services Corporation
161 Ottawa NW, Suite 409D
Grand Rapids, MI 49503
Telephone: (616) 451-2400
**Recruiter Classification:** Contingency; **Lowest/Average Salary:**
$30,000/$50,000; **Industry Concentration:** Financial Services, Information Technology; **Function Concentration:** Engineering, Finance/Accounting

**Sockwell, J. Edgar** — *Partner*
Sockwell & Associates
227 West Trade Street, Suite 1930
Charlotte, NC 28202
Telephone: (704) 372-1865
**Recruiter Classification:** Retained; **Lowest/Average Salary:** $90,000/$90,000; **Industry Concentration:** Generalist with a primary focus in Education/Libraries, Financial Services, Healthcare/Hospitals, Non-Profit, Real Estate; **Function Concentration:** Generalist with a primary focus in Administration, Finance/Accounting, General Management, Human Resources, Marketing, Sales

**Soggs, Cheryl Pavick** — *Vice President*
A.T. Kearney, Inc.
1100 Abernathy Road, Suite 900
Atlanta, GA 30328-5603
Telephone: (770) 393-9900
**Recruiter Classification:** Retained; **Lowest/Average Salary:** $90,000/$90,000; **Industry Concentration:** Generalist with a primary focus in Chemical Products, Entertainment, Healthcare/Hospitals, Hospitality/Leisure, Manufacturing, Pharmaceutical/Medical, Utilities/Nuclear; **Function Concentration:** Generalist with a primary focus in Administration, Engineering, General Management, Human Resources, Marketing, Research and Development, Sales

**Sola, George L.** — *Vice President*
A.T. Kearney, Inc.
222 West Adams Street
Chicago, IL 60606
Telephone: (312) 648-0111
**Recruiter Classification:** Retained; **Lowest/Average Salary:** $90,000/$90,000; **Industry Concentration:** Generalist with a primary focus in High Technology, Manufacturing; **Function Concentration:** Generalist with a primary focus in Engineering, General Management, Marketing, Research and Development, Sales

**Solomon, Christina** — *Executive Recruiter*
Richard, Wayne and Roberts
24 Greenway Plaza, Suite 1304
Houston, TX 77046-2493
Telephone: (713) 629-6681
**Recruiter Classification:** Retained; **Lowest/Average Salary:** $40,000/$60,000; **Industry Concentration:** Generalist with a primary focus in Electronics, High Technology; **Function Concentration:** Generalist

**Solomon Ph.D., Neil M.** — *President*
The Neil Michael Group, Inc.
305 Madison Avenue, Suite 902
New York, NY 10165
Telephone: (212) 986-3790
**Recruiter Classification:** Retained; **Lowest/Average Salary:** $90,000/$90,000; **Industry Concentration:** Biotechnology, Healthcare/Hospitals, Pharmaceutical/Medical; **Function Concentration:** Generalist

**Solters, Jeanne** — *Associate*
The Guild Corporation
8260 Greensboro Drive, Suite 460
McLean, VA 22102
Telephone: (703) 761-4023
**Recruiter Classification:** Contingency; **Lowest/Average Salary:**
$40,000/$50,000; **Industry Concentration:** Aerospace/Defense, Electronics, High Technology, Information Technology; **Function Concentration:** Generalist with a primary focus in Engineering, Finance/Accounting, General Management, Research and Development

**Somers, Donald A.** — *Manager Central Region*
Management Recruiters International, Inc.
8090 Market Street, Suite 2
Boardman, OH 44512-6216
Telephone: (330) 726-6656
**Recruiter Classification:** Contingency; **Lowest/Average Salary:**
$30,000/$75,000; **Industry Concentration:** Generalist; **Function Concentration:** Generalist

**Somers, Scott D.** — *Industry Leader - Business Services*
Paul Ray Berndtson
2029 Century Park East
Suite 1000
Los Angeles, CA 90067
Telephone: (310) 557-2828
**Recruiter Classification:** Retained; **Lowest/Average Salary:** $90,000/$90,000;
**Function Concentration:** Generalist

**Song, Louis** — *Associate*
Source Services Corporation
4510 Executive Drive, Suite 200
San Diego, CA 92121
Telephone: (619) 552-0300
**Recruiter Classification:** Contingency; **Lowest/Average Salary:**
$30,000/$50,000; **Industry Concentration:** Financial Services, Information
Technology; **Function Concentration:** Engineering, Finance/Accounting

**Songy, Al** — *Vice President*
U.S. Envirosearch
445 Union Boulevard, Suite 225
Lakewood, CO 80228
Telephone: (303) 980-6600
**Recruiter Classification:** Contingency; **Lowest/Average Salary:**
$30,000/$60,000; **Industry Concentration:** Environmental; **Function Concentration:** Generalist with a primary focus in Administration, Engineering,
Finance/Accounting, General Management, Marketing, Sales,
Women/Minorities

**Sorg, Leslie** — *Senior Consultant*
The McCormick Group, Inc.
1400 Wilson Boulevard
Arlington, VA 22209
Telephone: (703) 841-1700
**Recruiter Classification:** Retained, Contingency; **Lowest/Average Salary:**
$50,000/$75,000; **Industry Concentration:** Generalist; **Function Concentration:** Human Resources

**Sorgen, Jay** — *Associate*
Source Services Corporation
2 Penn Plaza, Suite 1176
New York, NY 10121
Telephone: (212) 760-2200
**Recruiter Classification:** Contingency; **Lowest/Average Salary:**
$30,000/$50,000; **Industry Concentration:** Financial Services, Information
Technology; **Function Concentration:** Engineering, Finance/Accounting

**Sostilio, Louis** — *Associate*
Source Services Corporation
155 Federal Street, Suite 410
Boston, MA 02110
Telephone: (617) 482-8211
**Recruiter Classification:** Contingency; **Lowest/Average Salary:**
$30,000/$50,000; **Industry Concentration:** Financial Services, Information
Technology; **Function Concentration:** Engineering, Finance/Accounting

**Soth, Mark H.** — *Manager Midwest Region*
Management Recruiters International, Inc.
508 North Second Street, Suite 104
Fairfield, IA 52556
Telephone: (515) 469-5811
**Recruiter Classification:** Contingency; **Lowest/Average Salary:** $30,000/$75,000;
**Industry Concentration:** Generalist; **Function Concentration:** Generalist

**Southerland, Keith C.** — *Shareholder*
Witt/Kieffer, Ford, Hadelman & Lloyd
8117 Preston Road, Suite 690
Dallas, TX 75225
Telephone: (214) 739-1370
**Recruiter Classification:** Retained; **Lowest/Average Salary:** $75,000/$90,000;
**Industry Concentration:** Healthcare/Hospitals; **Function Concentration:**
Generalist with a primary focus in General Management

**Soutouras, James** — *Senior Partner*
Smith James Group, Inc.
11660 Alpharetta Highway, Suite 515
Roswell, GA 30076
Telephone: (770) 667-0212
**Recruiter Classification:** Retained; **Lowest/Average Salary:** $40,000/$75,000;
**Industry Concentration:** Generalist with a primary focus in
Aerospace/Defense, Consumer Products, Electronics, Financial Services, High
Technology; **Function Concentration:** Generalist

**Sowerbutt, Richard S.** — *Vice President*
Hite Executive Search
6515 Chase Drive
P.O. Box 43217
Cleveland, OH 44143
Telephone: (216) 461-1600
**Recruiter Classification:** Retained; **Lowest/Average Salary:** $90,000/$90,000;
**Industry Concentration:** Generalist with a primary focus in Chemical Products,
Energy, Environmental, High Technology; **Function Concentration:** Generalist
with a primary focus in Engineering, General Management, Marketing,
Research and Development, Sales

**Spadavecchia, Jennifer** — *Associate*
Alta Associates, Inc.
8 Bartles Corner Road, Suite 021
Flemington, NJ 08822
Telephone: (908) 806-8442
**Recruiter Classification:** Retained; **Lowest/Average Salary:** $40,000/$75,000;
**Industry Concentration:** Generalist with a primary focus in Chemical Products,
Entertainment, High Technology, Information Technology, Insurance,
Manufacturing, Oil/Gas, Pharmaceutical/Medical, Publishing/Media,
Transportation; **Function Concentration:** Finance/Accounting

**Spangenberg, J. Brand** — *Chairman*
The Brand Company, Inc.
8402 Red Bay Court
Vero Beach, FL 32963
Telephone: (407) 231-1807
**Recruiter Classification:** Retained; **Lowest/Average Salary:** $75,000/$90,000;
**Industry Concentration:** Generalist; **Function Concentration:** Generalist

**Spangenberg, Sigrid** — *Vice President*
The Brand Company, Inc.
8402 Red Bay Court
Vero Beach, FL 32963
Telephone: (407) 231-1807
**Recruiter Classification:** Retained; **Lowest/Average Salary:** $75,000/$90,000;
**Industry Concentration:** Generalist; **Function Concentration:** Generalist

**Spangler, Lloyd** — *Executive Vice President*
Cole, Warren & Long, Inc.
2 Penn Center, Suite 312
Philadelphia, PA 19102
Telephone: (215) 563-0701
**Recruiter Classification:** Retained; **Lowest/Average Salary:** $90,000/$90,000;
**Industry Concentration:** Generalist; **Function Concentration:** Generalist

**Spann, Richard E.** — *Managing Principal*
Goodrich & Sherwood Associates, Inc.
401 Merritt Seven Corporate Park
Norwalk, CT 06851
Telephone: (203) 847-2525
**Recruiter Classification:** Retained; **Lowest/Average Salary:** $60,000/$90,000;
**Industry Concentration:** Generalist with a primary focus in Board Services,
Chemical Products, Consumer Products, Financial Services,
Healthcare/Hospitals, Information Technology, Insurance, Manufacturing,
Oil/Gas, Publishing/Media, Venture Capital; **Function Concentration:**
Generalist with a primary focus in Administration, Finance/Accounting,
General Management, Human Resources, Marketing, Sales

**Spanninger, Mark J.** — *Director*
The Guild Corporation
8260 Greensboro Drive, Suite 460
McLean, VA 22102
Telephone: (703) 761-4023
**Recruiter Classification:** Contingency; **Lowest/Average Salary:**
$40,000/$50,000; **Industry Concentration:** Aerospace/Defense, Electronics,
High Technology, Information Technology; **Function Concentration:**
Engineering, Finance/Accounting, General Management, Research and
Development

**Speck, Michael J.** — *Partner*
Lovas Stanley/Paul Ray Berndtson Inc.
Royal Bank Plaza, South Tower, Suite 3150
200 Bay Street, P.O. Box 125
Toronto, Ontario, CANADA M5J 2J3
Telephone: (416) 366-1990
**Recruiter Classification:** Retained; **Lowest/Average Salary:** $60,000/$75,000;
**Industry Concentration:** Generalist with a primary focus in Consumer
Products, Pharmaceutical/Medical; **Function Concentration:** Generalist with a
primary focus in Finance/Accounting, General Management, Marketing, Sales

**Spector, Michael** — *Associate*
Source Services Corporation
5343 North 16th Street, Suite 270
Phoenix, AZ 85016
Telephone: (602) 230-0220
**Recruiter Classification:** Contingency; **Lowest/Average Salary:**
$30,000/$50,000; **Industry Concentration:** Financial Services, Information
Technology; **Function Concentration:** Engineering, Finance/Accounting

**Spellacy, James P.** — *Manager Central Region*
Management Recruiters International, Inc.
Liberty Center, Suite 110
34100 Center Ridge Road
North Ridgeville, OH 44039-3220
Telephone: (216) 327-2800
**Recruiter Classification:** Contingency; **Lowest/Average Salary:**
$30,000/$75,000; **Industry Concentration:** Generalist; **Function Concentration:** Generalist

**Spellman, Frances** — *Associate*
Kenzer Corp.
625 North Michigan Avenue, Suite 1244
Chicago, IL 60611
Telephone: (312) 266-0976
**Recruiter Classification:** Retained; **Lowest/Average Salary:** $50,000/$90,000;
**Industry Concentration:** Generalist; **Function Concentration:** Generalist

**Spence, Gene L.** — *Partner*
Heidrick & Struggles, Inc.
245 Park Avenue, Suite 4300
New York, NY 10167-0152
Telephone: (212) 867-9876
**Recruiter Classification:** Retained; **Lowest/Average Salary:** $75,000/$90,000;
**Industry Concentration:** Generalist with a primary focus in High Technology;
**Function Concentration:** Generalist

**Spence, Joseph T.** — *Managing Director/Area Manager*
Russell Reynolds Associates, Inc.
The Hurt Building
50 Hurt Plaza, Suite 600
Atlanta, GA 30303
Telephone: (404) 577-3000
**Recruiter Classification:** Retained; **Lowest/Average Salary:** $90,000/$90,000;
**Industry Concentration:** Generalist; **Function Concentration:** Generalist

**Spencer, Frank** — *Associate*
Kenzer Corp.
777 Third Avenue, 26th Floor
New York, NY 10017
Telephone: (212) 308-4300
**Recruiter Classification:** Retained; **Lowest/Average Salary:** $50,000/$90,000;
**Industry Concentration:** Generalist; **Function Concentration:** Generalist

**Spencer, John** — *Managing Director*
Source Services Corporation
2029 Century Park East, Suite 1350
Los Angeles, CA 90067
Telephone: (310) 277-8092
**Recruiter Classification:** Contingency; **Lowest/Average Salary:**
$30,000/$50,000; **Industry Concentration:** Financial Services, Information
Technology; **Function Concentration:** Engineering, Finance/Accounting

**Spencer, John** — *Managing Director*
Source Services Corporation
879 West 190th Street, Suite 250
Los Angeles, CA 90248
Telephone: (310) 323-6633
**Recruiter Classification:** Contingency; **Lowest/Average Salary:**
$30,000/$50,000; **Industry Concentration:** Financial Services, Information
Technology; **Function Concentration:** Engineering, Finance/Accounting

**Sperry, Elizabeth B.** — *Senior Associate*
Korn/Ferry International
120 South Riverside Plaza
Suite 918
Chicago, IL 60606
Telephone: (312) 726-1841
**Recruiter Classification:** Retained; **Lowest/Average Salary:** $90,000/$90,000;
**Industry Concentration:** Generalist; **Function Concentration:** Generalist

**Spicer, Merrilyn** — *Account Executive*
Search West, Inc.
750 The City Drive South
Suite 100
Orange, CA 92668-4940
Telephone: (714) 748-0400
**Recruiter Classification:** Contingency; **Lowest/Average Salary:**
$40,000/$60,000; **Industry Concentration:** Manufacturing; **Function Concentration:** Administration, Finance/Accounting, General Management

**Spicher, John** — *Manager National Accounts*
M.A. Churchill & Associates, Inc.
Morelyn Plaza
1111 Street Road
Southampton, PA 18966
Telephone: (215) 953-0300
**Recruiter Classification:** Contingency; **Lowest/Average Salary:**
$50,000/$75,000; **Industry Concentration:** Financial Services, Insurance;
**Function Concentration:** Marketing, Research and Development, Sales

**Spiegel, Deborah** — *Associate*
Kenzer Corp.
777 Third Avenue, 26th Floor
New York, NY 10017
Telephone: (212) 308-4300
**Recruiter Classification:** Retained; **Lowest/Average Salary:** $50,000/$90,000;
**Industry Concentration:** Generalist; **Function Concentration:** Generalist

**Spiegel, Gay** — *Senior Vice President*
L.A. Silver Associates, Inc.
463 Worcester Road
Framingham, MA 01701
Telephone: (508) 879-2603
**Recruiter Classification:** Contingency; **Lowest/Average Salary:**
$75,000/$75,000; **Industry Concentration:** Generalist with a primary focus in
Chemical Products, Consumer Products, Electronics, Environmental,
Healthcare/Hospitals, High Technology, Information Technology,
Publishing/Media; **Function Concentration:** Generalist with a primary focus in
Administration, Engineering, Finance/Accounting, General Management,
Human Resources, Marketing, Research and Development, Sales

**Spitz, Grant** — *Partner*
The Caldwell Partners Amrop International
999 West Hastings Street
Suite 750
Vancouver, British Columbia, CANADA V6C 2W2
Telephone: (604) 669-3550
**Recruiter Classification:** Retained; **Lowest/Average Salary:** $/$90,000; **Industry Concentration:** Generalist with a primary focus in Board Services,
Environmental, Financial Services, High Technology; **Function Concentration:**
Generalist

**Spitz, Richard** — *Senior Associate*
Korn/Ferry International
1800 Century Park East, Suite 900
Los Angeles, CA 90067
Telephone: (310) 552-1834
**Recruiter Classification:** Retained; **Lowest/Average Salary:** $90,000/$90,000;
**Industry Concentration:** Generalist; **Function Concentration:** Generalist

**Splaine, Charles** — *President*
Splaine & Associates, Inc.
15951 Los Gatos Boulevard
Los Gatos, CA 95032
Telephone: (408) 354-3664
**Recruiter Classification:** Retained; **Lowest/Average Salary:** $90,000/$90,000;
**Industry Concentration:** Generalist with a primary focus in Electronics, High
Technology; **Function Concentration:** Generalist

**Sponseller, Vern** — *Vice President*
Richard Kader & Associates
343 West Bagley Road, Suite 209
Berea, OH 44017
Telephone: (216) 891-1700
**Recruiter Classification:** Contingency; **Lowest/Average Salary:**
$40,000/$50,000; **Industry Concentration:** Generalist with a primary focus in
Consumer Products, Financial Services, Hospitality/Leisure, Manufacturing;
**Function Concentration:** Generalist with a primary focus in
Finance/Accounting, Sales

**Spoutz, Paul** — *Associate*
Source Services Corporation
7730 East Bellview Avenue, Suite 302
Englewood, CO 80111
Telephone: (303) 773-3700
**Recruiter Classification:** Contingency; **Lowest/Average Salary:**
$30,000/$50,000; **Industry Concentration:** Financial Services, Information
Technology; **Function Concentration:** Engineering, Finance/Accounting

**Sprague, David** — *Vice President*
Michael Stern Associates Inc.
70 University Avenue, Suite 370
Toronto, Ontario, CANADA M5J 2M4
Telephone: (416) 593-0100
**Recruiter Classification:** Retained; **Lowest/Average Salary:** $75,000/$90,000;
**Industry Concentration:** Generalist; **Function Concentration:** Generalist with a
primary focus in Finance/Accounting, General Management, Human
Resources, Marketing, Sales

**Sprau, Collin L.** — *Partner*
Paul Ray Berndtson
10 South Riverside Plaza
Suite 720
Chicago, IL 60606
Telephone: (312) 876-0730
**Recruiter Classification:** Retained; **Lowest/Average Salary:** $90,000/$90,000;
**Industry Concentration:** Generalist with a primary focus in Information
Technology; **Function Concentration:** Generalist with a primary focus in
Finance/Accounting, Marketing, Sales

**Spriggs, Robert D.** — *Partner*
Spriggs & Company, Inc.
1701 East Lake Avenue
Suite 265
Glenview, IL 60025
Telephone: (708) 657-7181
**Recruiter Classification:** Retained; **Lowest/Average Salary:** $90,000/$90,000;
**Industry Concentration:** Generalist with a primary focus in Chemical Products,
Consumer Products, Electronics, Energy, Financial Services, High Technology,
Information Technology, Manufacturing, Pharmaceutical/Medical,
Publishing/Media, Transportation, Venture Capital; **Function Concentration:**
Generalist with a primary focus in Administration, Engineering,
Finance/Accounting, General Management, Human Resources, Marketing,
Research and Development, Sales

**Springer, Mark H.** — *President*
M.H. Springer & Associates Incorporated
5855 Topanga Canyon Boulevard, Suite 230
Woodland Hills, CA 91367
Telephone: (818) 710-8955
**Recruiter Classification:** Retained; **Lowest/Average Salary:** $90,000/$90,000;
**Industry Concentration:** Financial Services; **Function Concentration:**
Generalist

**Sprowls, Linda** — *Assistant Recruiter*
Allard Associates
39811 Sharon Avenue
Davis, CA 95616
Telephone: (916) 757-1649
**Recruiter Classification:** Retained; **Lowest/Average Salary:** $60,000/$90,000;
**Industry Concentration:** Generalist with a primary focus in Financial Services;
**Function Concentration:** Generalist with a primary focus in Administration,
General Management, Marketing, Research and Development, Sales

**Srolis, Robert B.** — *Senior Consultant*
Raymond Karsan Associates
989 Old Eagle School Road, Suite 814
Wayne, PA 19087
Telephone: (610) 971-9171
**Recruiter Classification:** Contingency; **Lowest/Average Salary:**
$30,000/$90,000; **Industry Concentration:** Generalist; **Function
Concentration:** Generalist

**St. Denis, Robert A.** — *Principal*
Sanford Rose Associates
444 South Willow, Suite 11
Effingham, IL 62401
Telephone: (217) 342-3928
**Recruiter Classification:** Contingency; **Lowest/Average Salary:**
$30,000/$75,000; **Industry Concentration:** Generalist with a primary focus in
Publishing/Media; **Function Concentration:** Generalist

**St. John, J. Burke** — *Partner*
Heidrick & Struggles, Inc.
245 Park Avenue, Suite 4300
New York, NY 10167-0152
Telephone: (212) 867-9876
**Recruiter Classification:** Retained; **Lowest/Average Salary:** $75,000/$90,000;
**Industry Concentration:** Generalist; **Function Concentration:** Generalist

**St. Martin, Peter** — *Associate*
Source Services Corporation
4170 Ashford Dunwoody Road, Suite 285
Atlanta, GA 30319
Telephone: (404) 255-2045
**Recruiter Classification:** Contingency; **Lowest/Average Salary:**
$30,000/$50,000; **Industry Concentration:** Financial Services, Information
Technology; **Function Concentration:** Engineering, Finance/Accounting

**Staats, Dave** — *Technical Recruiting Manager*
Southwestern Professional Services
2451 Atrium Way
Nashville, TN 37214
Telephone: (615) 391-2722
**Recruiter Classification:** Contingency; **Lowest/Average Salary:**
$40,000/$60,000; **Industry Concentration:** Aerospace/Defense, High
Technology, Information Technology; **Function Concentration:** Engineering,
Research and Development

**Stack, James K.** — *Managing Director*
Boyden
Embarcadero Center West Tower
275 Battery St., Suite 420
San Francisco, CA 94111
Telephone: (415) 981-7900
**Recruiter Classification:** Retained; **Lowest/Average Salary:** $75,000/$90,000;
**Industry Concentration:** Generalist; **Function Concentration:** Generalist with a
primary focus in Engineering, Finance/Accounting, General Management,
Human Resources, Marketing, Research and Development, Sales,
Women/Minorities

**Stack, Richard** — *Associate*
Source Services Corporation
2 Penn Plaza, Suite 1176
New York, NY 10121
Telephone: (212) 760-2200
**Recruiter Classification:** Contingency; **Lowest/Average Salary:**
$30,000/$50,000; **Industry Concentration:** Financial Services, Information
Technology; **Function Concentration:** Engineering, Finance/Accounting

**Stackhouse, P. John** — *Consultant*
Heidrick & Struggles, Inc.
BCE Place, 161 Bay Street, Suite 2310
P.O. Box 601
Toronto, Ontario, CANADA M5J 2S1
Telephone: (416) 361-4700
**Recruiter Classification:** Retained; **Lowest/Average Salary:** $75,000/$90,000;
**Industry Concentration:** Generalist with a primary focus in High Technology;
**Function Concentration:** Generalist

**Staehely, Janna** — *Recruiter*
Southwestern Professional Services
2451 Atrium Way
Nashville, TN 37214
Telephone: (615) 391-2722
**Recruiter Classification:** Contingency; **Lowest/Average Salary:**
$50,000/$75,000; **Industry Concentration:** Information Technology; **Function
Concentration:** Engineering

**Stafford, Charles B.** — *Manager Pacific Region*
Management Recruiters International, Inc.
5011 Golden Foothill Parkway, Suite 2
El Dorado Hills, CA 95762
Telephone: (916) 933-6903
**Recruiter Classification:** Contingency; **Lowest/Average Salary:**
$30,000/$75,000; **Industry Concentration:** Generalist; **Function
Concentration:** Generalist

**Stafford, Susan** — *Vice President*
Hospitality International
181 Port Watson Street
Cortland, NY 13045
Telephone: (607) 756-8550
**Recruiter Classification:** Contingency; **Lowest/Average Salary:**
$40,000/$60,000; **Industry Concentration:** Entertainment,
Healthcare/Hospitals, Hospitality/Leisure; **Function Concentration:**
Finance/Accounting, General Management, Human Resources, Marketing,
Sales, Women/Minorities

**Stahl, Cynthia** — *Consultant*
Plummer & Associates, Inc.
30 Myano Lane, Suite 36
Stamford, CT 06902
Telephone: (203) 965-7878
**Recruiter Classification:** Retained, Executive Temporary; **Lowest/Average
Salary:** $90,000/$90,000; **Industry Concentration:** Fashion (Retail/Apparel),
Manufacturing, Venture Capital; **Function Concentration:** Generalist with a
primary focus in General Management

**Stampfl, Eric** — *Principal*
Morgan Stampfl, Inc.
6 West 32nd Street
New York, NY 10001
Telephone: (212) 643-7165
**Recruiter Classification:** Contingency; **Lowest/Average Salary:**
$50,000/$90,000; **Industry Concentration:** Financial Services; **Function
Concentration:** Finance/Accounting

**Standard, Gail** — *Vice President*
Comprehensive Search
316 South Lewis Street
LaGrange, GA 30240
Telephone: (706) 884-3232
**Recruiter Classification:** Contingency, Executive Temporary; **Lowest/Average
Salary:** $30,000/$60,000; **Industry Concentration:** Consumer Products,
Fashion (Retail/Apparel), Hospitality/Leisure, Manufacturing; **Function
Concentration:** Generalist

**Stanislaw, Robert J.** — *Executive Vice President/
Managing Director*
DHR International, Inc.
405 North Calhoun Road, P.O. Box 589
Brookfield, WI 53005
Telephone: (414) 784-8590
**Recruiter Classification:** Retained; **Lowest/Average Salary:** $60,000/$90,000;
**Industry Concentration:** Generalist; **Function Concentration:** Generalist

**Stanley, Paul R.A.** — *Partner*
Lovas Stanley/Paul Ray Berndtson Inc.
Royal Bank Plaza, South Tower, Suite 3150
200 Bay Street, P.O. Box 125
Toronto, Ontario, CANADA M5J 2J3
Telephone: (416) 366-1990
**Recruiter Classification:** Retained; **Lowest/Average Salary:** $75,000/$90,000;
**Industry Concentration:** Generalist with a primary focus in Board Services,
Healthcare/Hospitals, High Technology, Non-Profit; **Function Concentration:**
Generalist with a primary focus in Finance/Accounting, General Management,
Human Resources, Research and Development

**Stanley, Wade** — *General Manager North Atlantic Region*
Management Recruiters International, Inc.
5509 Creedmoor Road, Suite 206
Raleigh, NC 27612-6314
Telephone: (919) 781-0400
**Recruiter Classification:** Contingency; **Lowest/Average Salary:** $30,000/$75,000;
**Industry Concentration:** Generalist; **Function Concentration:** Generalist

**Stark, Gary L.** — *Co-Manager*
Management Recruiters International, Inc.
Kensington Center
479 Business Center Drive, Suite 104
Mount Prospect, IL 60056-6037
Telephone: (847) 298-8780
**Recruiter Classification:** Contingency; **Lowest/Average Salary:** $30,000/$75,000;
**Industry Concentration:** Generalist; **Function Concentration:** Generalist

**Stark, Jeff** — *Principal*
Thorne, Brieger Associates Inc.
11 East 44th Street
New York, NY 10017
Telephone: (212) 682-5424
**Recruiter Classification:** Retained; **Lowest/Average Salary:** $90,000/$90,000;
**Industry Concentration:** Generalist with a primary focus in
Aerospace/Defense, Chemical Products, Consumer Products, Electronics,
Financial Services, Healthcare/Hospitals, Insurance, Manufacturing,
Pharmaceutical/Medical; **Function Concentration:** Generalist with a primary
focus in Administration, Engineering, Finance/Accounting, General
Management, Human Resources, Marketing, Research and Development, Sales

**Starner, William S.** — *Partner*
Fenwick Partners
57 Bedford Street, Suite 101
Lexington, MA 02173
Telephone: (617) 862-3370
**Recruiter Classification:** Retained; **Lowest/Average Salary:** $90,000/$90,000;
**Industry Concentration:** Board Services, Electronics, High Technology,
Information Technology; **Function Concentration:** Generalist

**Starr, Anna** — *Executive Recruiter*
Richard, Wayne and Roberts
24 Greenway Plaza, Suite 1304
Houston, TX 77046-2493
Telephone: (713) 629-6681
**Recruiter Classification:** Retained; **Lowest/Average Salary:** $40,000/$60,000;
**Industry Concentration:** Generalist with a primary focus in Chemical Products,
Environmental, Oil/Gas; **Function Concentration:** Generalist with a primary
focus in Engineering

**Statson, Dale E.** — *President*
Sales Executives Inc.
755 West Big Beaver Road, Suite 2107
Troy, MI 48084
Telephone: (810) 362-1900
**Recruiter Classification:** Contingency; **Lowest/Average Salary:** $50,000/$90,000;
**Industry Concentration:** Chemical Products, Electronics, Pharmaceutical/Medical;
**Function Concentration:** General Management, Marketing, Sales

**Steck, Frank T.** — *Vice President*
A.T. Kearney, Inc.
222 West Adams Street
Chicago, IL 60606
Telephone: (312) 648-0111
**Recruiter Classification:** Retained; **Lowest/Average Salary:** $90,000/$90,000;
**Industry Concentration:** Generalist with a primary focus in Automotive, Fashion
(Retail/Apparel), Manufacturing, Transportation; **Function Concentration:**
Generalist with a primary focus in General Management, Marketing, Sales

**Steele, Kevin** — *President*
Winter, Wyman & Company
950 Winter Street, Suite 3100
Waltham, MA 02154-1294
Telephone: (617) 890-7000
**Recruiter Classification:** Contingency; **Lowest/Average Salary:**
$40,000/$75,000; **Industry Concentration:** Generalist with a primary focus in
Information Technology; **Function Concentration:** Generalist

**Steenerson, Thomas L.** — *Executive Recruiter*
MSI International
1050 Crown Pointe Parkway
Suite 1000
Atlanta, GA 30338
Telephone: (404) 394-2494
**Recruiter Classification:** Contingency; **Lowest/Average Salary:**
$30,000/$75,000; **Industry Concentration:** Generalist with a primary focus in
Manufacturing; **Function Concentration:** Generalist with a primary focus in
Administration, Engineering, Finance/Accounting, General Management,
Marketing, Sales

**Stein, Neil A.** — *Vice President*
R.H. Perry & Associates, Inc.
2607 31st Street N.W.
Washington, DC 20008
Telephone: (202) 965-6464
**Recruiter Classification:** Retained; **Lowest/Average Salary:** $60,000/$75,000;
**Industry Concentration:** Generalist; **Function Concentration:** Generalist

**Stein, Terry W.** — *Vice President*
Stewart, Stein and Scott, Ltd.
1000 Shelard Parkway, Suite 606
Minneapolis, MN 55426
Telephone: (612) 595-4456
**Recruiter Classification:** Retained; **Lowest/Average Salary:** $60,000/$90,000;
**Industry Concentration:** Generalist with a primary focus in
Aerospace/Defense, Biotechnology, Chemical Products, Consumer Products,
Electronics, Energy, Financial Services, Healthcare/Hospitals, High Technology,
Information Technology, Insurance, Manufacturing, Pharmaceutical/Medical,
Transportation; **Function Concentration:** Generalist with a primary focus in
Finance/Accounting, General Management, Human Resources, Marketing,
Research and Development, Sales, Women/Minorities

**Steinem, Andy** — *Principal*
Dahl-Morrow International
12110 Sunset Hills Road
Suite 450
Reston, VA 22090
Telephone: (703) 648-1594
**Recruiter Classification:** Executive Temporary; **Lowest/Average Salary:**
$75,000/$90,000; **Industry Concentration:** Generalist with a primary focus in
Aerospace/Defense, Electronics, High Technology, Information Technology,
Venture Capital; **Function Concentration:** Generalist

**Steinem, Barbara** — *President*
Dahl-Morrow International
12110 Sunset Hills Road
Suite 450
Reston, VA 22090
Telephone: (703) 648-1594
**Recruiter Classification:** Executive Temporary; **Lowest/Average Salary:**
$75,000/$90,000; **Industry Concentration:** Generalist with a primary focus in
Aerospace/Defense, Electronics, High Technology, Information Technology,
Venture Capital; **Function Concentration:** Generalist

**Steinman, Stephen** — *President and CEO*
The Stevenson Group of New Jersey
560 Sylvan Avenue
Englewood Cliffs, NJ 07632
Telephone: (201) 568-1900
**Recruiter Classification:** Retained; **Lowest/Average Salary:** $75,000/$90,000;
**Industry Concentration:** Generalist with a primary focus in Chemical Products,
Consumer Products, Fashion (Retail/Apparel), Financial Services, Information
Technology, Pharmaceutical/Medical; **Function Concentration:** Generalist with
a primary focus in Finance/Accounting, General Management, Human
Resources, Marketing, Sales

**Stemphoski, Ronald L.** — *Executive Vice President*
The Diversified Search Companies
2005 Market Street, Suite 3300
Philadelphia, PA 19103
Telephone: (215) 732-6666
**Recruiter Classification:** Retained; **Lowest/Average Salary:** $90,000/$90,000;
**Industry Concentration:** Generalist; **Function Concentration:** Generalist

**Stenberg, Edward** — *Materials Management and
Manufacturing Recruiter*
Winter, Wyman & Company
950 Winter Street, Suite 3100
Waltham, MA 02154-1294
Telephone: (617) 890-7000
**Recruiter Classification:** Contingency; **Lowest/Average Salary:**
$30,000/$50,000; **Industry Concentration:** Aerospace/Defense, Consumer
Products, Electronics, High Technology, Information Technology,
Manufacturing; **Function Concentration:** Generalist

**Stenholm, Gilbert R.** — *Senior Director*
Spencer Stuart
401 North Michigan Avenue, Suite 3400
Chicago, IL 60611-4244
Telephone: (312) 822-0080
**Recruiter Classification:** Retained; **Lowest/Average Salary:** $60,000/$90,000;
**Industry Concentration:** Board Services, Consumer Products, Entertainment,
Fashion (Retail/Apparel), Hospitality/Leisure, Pharmaceutical/Medical;
**Function Concentration:** Generalist with a primary focus in
Finance/Accounting, General Management, Human Resources, Marketing,
Research and Development, Sales

**Stephanian, Armand A.** — *Consultant*
Paul Ray Berndtson
2029 Century Park East
Suite 1000
Los Angeles, CA 90067
Telephone: (310) 557-2828
**Recruiter Classification:** Retained; **Lowest/Average Salary:** $90,000/$90,000;
**Industry Concentration:** Generalist with a primary focus in Biotechnology,
Pharmaceutical/Medical; **Function Concentration:** Generalist

**Stephens, Andrew** — *Associate*
Source Services Corporation
8614 Westwood Center, Suite 750
Vienna, VA 22182
Telephone: (703) 790-5610
**Recruiter Classification:** Contingency; **Lowest/Average Salary:**
$30,000/$50,000; **Industry Concentration:** Financial Services, Information
Technology; **Function Concentration:** Engineering, Finance/Accounting

**Stephens, John** — *Associate*
Source Services Corporation
15600 N.W. 67th Avenue, Suite 210
Miami Lakes, FL 33014
Telephone: (305) 556-8000
**Recruiter Classification:** Contingency; **Lowest/Average Salary:**
$30,000/$50,000; **Industry Concentration:** Financial Services, Information
Technology; **Function Concentration:** Engineering, Finance/Accounting

**Stephens, Roberto Salinas** — *Associate*
Smith Search, S.C.
Barranca del Muerto No. 472, Col. Alpes
Mexico City, D.F., MEXICO 01010
Telephone: (525) 593-8766
**Recruiter Classification:** Retained; **Lowest/Average Salary:** $75,000/$90,000;
**Industry Concentration:** Generalist; **Function Concentration:** Generalist

**Stephenson, Craig** — *Senior Associate*
Korn/Ferry International
237 Park Avenue
New York, NY 10017
Telephone: (212) 687-1834
**Recruiter Classification:** Retained; **Lowest/Average Salary:** $90,000/$90,000;
**Industry Concentration:** Generalist; **Function Concentration:** Generalist

**Stephenson, Don L.** — *President*
Ells Personnel System Inc.
9900 Bren Road East, Suite 105 Opus Center
Minnetonka, MN 55343
Telephone: (612) 932-9933
**Recruiter Classification:** Contingency; **Lowest/Average Salary:**
$20,000/$40,000; **Industry Concentration:** Generalist with a primary focus in
Electronics, Environmental, Healthcare/Hospitals, High Technology,
Information Technology, Manufacturing, Pharmaceutical/Medical; **Function
Concentration:** Generalist with a primary focus in Administration, Engineering,
Research and Development

**Stephenson, Mike** — *Consultant*
Evie Kreisler & Associates, Inc.
2720 Stemmons Freeway, Suite 812
Dallas, TX 75207
Telephone: (214) 631-8994
**Recruiter Classification:** Contingency; **Lowest/Average Salary:**
$30,000/$75,000; **Industry Concentration:** Fashion (Retail/Apparel); **Function
Concentration:** Generalist

**Sterling, Cheryl E.** — *Manager Central Region*
Management Recruiters International, Inc.
Suite 20, Mentor 306 Building
8039 Broadmoor Road
Mentor, OH 44060
Telephone: (216) 946-2355
**Recruiter Classification:** Contingency; **Lowest/Average Salary:**
$30,000/$75,000; **Industry Concentration:** Generalist; **Function
Concentration:** Generalist

**Sterling, Jay** — *Senior Vice President*
Earley Kielty and Associates, Inc.
Two Pennsylvania Plaza
New York, NY 10121
Telephone: (212) 736-5626
**Recruiter Classification:** Retained; **Lowest/Average Salary:** $90,000/$90,000;
**Industry Concentration:** Generalist with a primary focus in Information
Technology; **Function Concentration:** Generalist with a primary focus in
Administration, Finance/Accounting, General Management, Human Resources,
Marketing, Research and Development, Sales, Women/Minorities

**Sterling, Ronald** — *General Manager*
Management Recruiters International, Inc.
Suite 20, Mentor 306 Building
8039 Broadmoor Road
Mentor, OH 44060
Telephone: (216) 946-2355
**Recruiter Classification:** Contingency; **Lowest/Average Salary:**
$30,000/$75,000; **Industry Concentration:** Generalist; **Function
Concentration:** Generalist

**Sterling, Sally M.** — *Partner*
Heidrick & Struggles, Inc.
1301 K Street N.W., Suite 500 East
Washington, DC 20005
Telephone: (202) 289-4450
**Recruiter Classification:** Retained; **Lowest/Average Salary:** $75,000/$90,000;
**Industry Concentration:** Generalist with a primary focus in Education/Libraries,
Healthcare/Hospitals, Non-Profit; **Function Concentration:** Generalist

**Stern, Leslie W.** — *Principal*
Sullivan & Company
20 Exchange Place, 50th Floor
New York, NY 10005
Telephone: (212) 422-3000
**Recruiter Classification:** Retained; **Lowest/Average Salary:** $90,000/$90,000;
**Industry Concentration:** Generalist with a primary focus in Financial Services;
**Function Concentration:** Generalist

**Stern, Michael I.** — *President*
Michael Stern Associates Inc.
70 University Avenue, Suite 370
Toronto, Ontario, CANADA M5J 2M4
Telephone: (416) 593-0100
**Recruiter Classification:** Retained; **Lowest/Average Salary:** $75,000/$90,000;
**Industry Concentration:** Generalist; **Function Concentration:** Generalist with a
primary focus in Finance/Accounting, General Management, Human
Resources, Marketing, Sales

**Stern, Ronni** — *Associate*
Kenzer Corp.
625 North Michigan Avenue, Suite 1244
Chicago, IL 60611
Telephone: (312) 266-0976
**Recruiter Classification:** Retained; **Lowest/Average Salary:** $50,000/$90,000;
**Industry Concentration:** Generalist; **Function Concentration:** Generalist

**Stern, Stephen** — *Executive Recruiter*
CPS Inc.
One Westbrook Corporate Centre, Suite 600
Westchester, IL 60154
Telephone: (708) 531-8370
**Recruiter Classification:** Contingency; **Lowest/Average Salary:**
$30,000/$50,000; **Industry Concentration:** Generalist with a primary focus in
Automotive, Biotechnology, Chemical Products, Consumer Products, High
Technology, Insurance, Manufacturing, Oil/Gas, Packaging,
Pharmaceutical/Medical; **Function Concentration:** Engineering, Research and
Development, Sales, Women/Minorities

**Sterner, Doug** — *Executive Recruiter*
CPS Inc.
One Westbrook Corporate Centre, Suite 600
Westchester, IL 60154
Telephone: (708) 531-8370
**Recruiter Classification:** Contingency; **Lowest/Average Salary:**
$30,000/$50,000; **Industry Concentration:** Generalist with a primary focus in
Automotive, Biotechnology, Chemical Products, Consumer Products, High
Technology, Insurance, Manufacturing, Oil/Gas, Packaging,
Pharmaceutical/Medical; **Function Concentration:** Engineering, Research and
Development, Sales, Women/Minorities

**Sternlicht, Marvin H.** — *Manager*
Accountants on Call
2777 Summer Street
Stamford, CT 06905
Telephone: (203) 327-5100
**Recruiter Classification:** Contingency; **Lowest/Average Salary:**
$20,000/$30,000; **Industry Concentration:** Generalist; **Function
Concentration:** Finance/Accounting

**Sternlicht, Marvin H.** — *Manager*
Accountants on Call
Telephone: (914) 968-1100
**Recruiter Classification:** Contingency; **Lowest/Average Salary:**
$20,000/$30,000; **Industry Concentration:** Generalist; **Function**
**Concentration:** Finance/Accounting

**Stevens, David** — *Partner*
Johnson Smith & Knisely Accord
100 Park Avenue, 15th Floor
New York, NY 10017
Telephone: (212) 885-9100
**Recruiter Classification:** Retained; **Lowest/Average Salary:** $90,000/$90,000;
**Industry Concentration:** Generalist; **Function Concentration:** Generalist

**Stevens, Glenn** — *Senior Associate*
Korn/Ferry International
237 Park Avenue
New York, NY 10017
Telephone: (212) 687-1834
**Recruiter Classification:** Retained; **Lowest/Average Salary:** $90,000/$90,000;
**Industry Concentration:** Generalist with a primary focus in Financial Services;
**Function Concentration:** Generalist with a primary focus in
Finance/Accounting

**Stevens, Robin** — *Consultant*
Paul Ray Berndtson
191 Peachtree Tower, Suite 3800
191 Peachtree Street, NE
Atlanta, GA 30303-1757
Telephone: (404) 215-4600
**Recruiter Classification:** Retained; **Lowest/Average Salary:** $90,000/$90,000;
**Industry Concentration:** Generalist; **Function Concentration:** Generalist

**Stevens, Tracey** — *Associate*
Don Richard Associates of Washington, D.C., Inc.
1020 19th Street, NW, Suite 650
Washington, DC 20036
Telephone: (202) 463-7210
**Recruiter Classification:** Contingency; **Lowest/Average Salary:**
$20,000/$30,000; **Industry Concentration:** Aerospace/Defense, Financial
Services, Healthcare/Hospitals, Non-Profit, Real Estate; **Function**
**Concentration:** Finance/Accounting

**Stevenson, Jani** — *Senior Vice President*
Howard Fischer Associates, Inc.
1800 John F. Kennedy Boulevard, 7th Floor
Philadelphia, PA 19103
Telephone: (215) 568-8363
**Recruiter Classification:** Retained; **Lowest/Average Salary:** $90,000/$90,000;
**Industry Concentration:** Generalist; **Function Concentration:** Generalist

**Stevenson, Julianne M.** — *Executive Director*
Russell Reynolds Associates, Inc.
Old City Hall, 45 School Street
Boston, MA 02108
Telephone: (617) 523-1111
**Recruiter Classification:** Retained; **Lowest/Average Salary:** $90,000/$90,000;
**Industry Concentration:** Generalist; **Function Concentration:** Generalist

**Stevenson, Terry** — *Consultant*
Bartholdi & Company, Inc.
P.O. Box 947
Leadville, CO 80461
Telephone: (719) 486-2918
**Recruiter Classification:** Retained; **Lowest/Average Salary:** $60,000/$90,000;
**Industry Concentration:** High Technology, Information Technology; **Function**
**Concentration:** Generalist with a primary focus in Engineering,
Finance/Accounting, General Management, Marketing, Research and
Development, Sales

**Stewart, Clifford** — *Associate*
Morgan Stampfl, Inc.
6 West 32nd Street
New York, NY 10001
Telephone: (212) 643-7165
**Recruiter Classification:** Contingency; **Lowest/Average Salary:**
$50,000/$90,000; **Industry Concentration:** Financial Services; **Function**
**Concentration:** Finance/Accounting

**Stewart, Jan J.** — *Consultant*
Egon Zehnder International Inc.
1 First Canadian Place
P.O. Box 179
Toronto, Ontario, CANADA M5X 1C7
Telephone: (416) 364-0222
**Recruiter Classification:** Retained; **Lowest/Average Salary:** $90,000/$90,000;
**Industry Concentration:** Generalist with a primary focus in Biotechnology,
Financial Services, High Technology, Manufacturing, Pharmaceutical/Medical;
**Function Concentration:** Generalist

**Stewart, Jeffrey O.** — *President*
Stewart, Stein and Scott, Ltd.
1000 Shelard Parkway, Suite 606
Minneapolis, MN 55426
Telephone: (612) 595-4455
**Recruiter Classification:** Retained; **Lowest/Average Salary:** $60,000/$90,000;
**Industry Concentration:** Generalist with a primary focus in
Aerospace/Defense, Biotechnology, Chemical Products, Consumer Products,
Electronics, Energy, Financial Services, Healthcare/Hospitals, High Technology,
Information Technology, Insurance, Manufacturing, Pharmaceutical/Medical,
Transportation; **Function Concentration:** Generalist with a primary focus in
Finance/Accounting, General Management, Human Resources, Marketing,
Research and Development, Sales

**Stewart, Ross M.** — *Managing Director*
Human Resources Network Partners Inc.
Two Galleria Tower
13455 Noel Road, 10th Floor
Dallas, TX 75240
Telephone: (214) 702-7932
**Recruiter Classification:** Retained; **Lowest/Average Salary:** $60,000/$90,000;
**Industry Concentration:** Generalist with a primary focus in Board Services,
Chemical Products, Electronics, Environmental, Financial Services, High
Technology, Information Technology, Manufacturing, Oil/Gas, Transportation,
Venture Capital; **Function Concentration:** Generalist with a primary focus in
Administration, Engineering, Finance/Accounting, General Management,
Human Resources, Marketing, Research and Development, Sales,
Women/Minorities

**Stewart, Steve** — *Manager North Atlantic Region*
Management Recruiters International, Inc.
Northlake Square
1726 Montreal Circle, Suite G
Tucker, GA 30084-6809
Telephone: (770) 621-0677
**Recruiter Classification:** Contingency; **Lowest/Average Salary:**
$30,000/$75,000; **Industry Concentration:** Generalist; **Function**
**Concentration:** Generalist

**Stewart, Wilf** — *Principal*
KPMG Executive Search
P.O. Box 31, Stn. Commerce Court
Toronto, Ontario, CANADA M5L 1B2
Telephone: (416) 777-8500
**Recruiter Classification:** Retained; **Lowest/Average Salary:** $75,000/$90,000;
**Industry Concentration:** Generalist; **Function Concentration:** Generalist

**Stiles, Jack D.** — *Principal*
Sanford Rose Associates
10200 SW Eastridge, Suite 200
Portland, OR 97225
Telephone: (503) 297-9191
**Recruiter Classification:** Contingency; **Lowest/Average Salary:**
$30,000/$75,000; **Industry Concentration:** Generalist with a primary focus in
Consumer Products, High Technology, Packaging; **Function Concentration:**
Generalist

**Stiles, Judy** — *Director/Recruiter*
MedQuest Associates
9250 East Costilla Avenue, Suite 600
Englewood, CO 80112
Telephone: (303) 790-2009
**Recruiter Classification:** Contingency; **Lowest/Average Salary:**
$30,000/$75,000; **Industry Concentration:** Biotechnology, Electronics,
Healthcare/Hospitals, High Technology, Manufacturing,
Pharmaceutical/Medical; **Function Concentration:** Engineering, General
Management, Marketing, Research and Development, Sales

**Stiles, Timothy** — *Senior Associate*
Sanford Rose Associates
10200 SW Eastridge, Suite 200
Portland, OR 97225
Telephone: (503) 297-9191
**Recruiter Classification:** Contingency; **Lowest/Average Salary:**
$30,000/$75,000; **Industry Concentration:** Generalist with a primary focus in
Consumer Products, High Technology, Packaging; **Function Concentration:**
Generalist

**Stinson, R.J.** — *Vice President*
Sampson Neill & Wilkins Inc.
543 Valley Road
Upper Montclair, NJ 07043
Telephone: (201) 783-9600
**Recruiter Classification:** Retained; **Lowest/Average Salary:** $75,000/$90,000;
**Industry Concentration:** Board Services, Pharmaceutical/Medical, Venture
Capital; **Function Concentration:** Engineering, General Management,
Marketing, Research and Development, Sales

**Stirn, Bradley A.** — *Managing Director*
Spencer Stuart
3000 Sand Hill Road
Building 2, Suite 175
Menlo Park, CA 94025
Telephone: (415) 688-1285
**Recruiter Classification:** Retained; **Lowest/Average Salary:** $90,000/$90,000; **Industry Concentration:** High Technology, Information Technology; **Function Concentration:** Generalist

**Stivk, Barbara A.** — *General Manager*
Thornton Resources
9800 McKnight Road
Pittsburgh, PA 15237
Telephone: (412) 364-2111
**Recruiter Classification:** Contingency, Executive Temporary; **Lowest/Average Salary:** $40,000/$50,000; **Industry Concentration:** Generalist with a primary focus in Board Services, Consumer Products, Financial Services, Non-Profit; **Function Concentration:** Generalist with a primary focus in General Management, Human Resources,

**Stoessel, Robert J.** — *Manager Southwest Region*
Management Recruiters International, Inc.
1009 West Randol Mill Road, Suite 209
Arlington, TX 76012
Telephone: (817) 469-6161
**Recruiter Classification:** Contingency; **Lowest/Average Salary:** $30,000/$75,000; **Industry Concentration:** Generalist; **Function Concentration:** Generalist

**Stokes, John** — *Consultant*
Nordeman Grimm, Inc.
717 Fifth Avenue, 26th Floor
New York, NY 10022
Telephone: (212) 935-1000
**Recruiter Classification:** Retained; **Lowest/Average Salary:** $90,000/$90,000; **Industry Concentration:** Generalist; **Function Concentration:** Generalist

**Stoll, Steven G.** — *Managing Partner*
Sharrow & Associates
8100 Burlington Pike
Suite 336
Florence, KY 41042
Telephone: (606) 282-0111
**Recruiter Classification:** Contingency; **Lowest/Average Salary:** $30,000/$50,000; **Industry Concentration:** Real Estate; **Function Concentration:** Administration, Finance/Accounting, Marketing, Sales

**Stoltz, Dick** — *General Manager Central Region*
Management Recruiters International, Inc.
1900 East Dublin-Granville, Suite 110B
Columbus, OH 43229-3374
Telephone: (614) 794-3200
**Recruiter Classification:** Contingency; **Lowest/Average Salary:** $30,000/$75,000; **Industry Concentration:** Generalist; **Function Concentration:** Generalist

**Stone, Kayla** — *Senior Associate*
Korn/Ferry International
3950 Lincoln Plaza
500 North Akard Street
Dallas, TX 75201
Telephone: (214) 954-1834
**Recruiter Classification:** Retained; **Lowest/Average Salary:** $90,000/$90,000; **Industry Concentration:** Generalist; **Function Concentration:** Generalist

**Stone, Robert Ryder** — *Partner*
Lamalie Amrop International
200 Park Avenue
New York, NY 10166-0136
Telephone: (212) 953-7900
**Recruiter Classification:** Retained; **Lowest/Average Salary:** $90,000/$90,000; **Industry Concentration:** Generalist with a primary focus in Financial Services; **Function Concentration:** Generalist with a primary focus in General Management, Marketing, Sales

**Stone, Susan L.** — *President*
Stone Enterprises Ltd.
645 North Michigan Avenue, Suite 800
Chicago, IL 60611
Telephone: (312) 404-9300
**Recruiter Classification:** Contingency; **Lowest/Average Salary:** $30,000/$90,000; **Industry Concentration:** Generalist with a primary focus in Automotive, Chemical Products, Consumer Products, Electronics, Financial Services, Healthcare/Hospitals, High Technology, Information Technology, Manufacturing, Packaging, Pharmaceutical/Medical, Transportation; **Function Concentration:** Generalist with a primary focus in Engineering, Finance/Accounting, Marketing, Research and Development, Sales

**Stoneham, Herbert E.C.** — *Chairman*
Stoneham Associates Corp.
Royal Bank Plaza, South Tower
200 Bay Street, Suite 2930
Toronto, Ontario, CANADA M5J 2J3
Telephone: (416) 362-0852
**Recruiter Classification:** Retained; **Lowest/Average Salary:** $90,000/$90,000; **Industry Concentration:** Generalist with a primary focus in Consumer Products, Entertainment, Fashion (Retail/Apparel), Financial Services, Packaging, Transportation; **Function Concentration:** Generalist

**Storbeck, Shelly** — *Vice President*
A.T. Kearney, Inc.
225 Reinekers Lane
Alexandria, VA 22314
Telephone: (703) 739-4624
**Recruiter Classification:** Retained; **Lowest/Average Salary:** $90,000/$90,000; **Industry Concentration:** Generalist with a primary focus in Education/Libraries; **Function Concentration:** Generalist

**Storm, Deborah** — *Associate*
Source Services Corporation
150 South Warner Road, Suite 238
King of Prussia, PA 19406
Telephone: (610) 341-1960
**Recruiter Classification:** Contingency; **Lowest/Average Salary:** $30,000/$50,000; **Industry Concentration:** Financial Services, Information Technology; **Function Concentration:** Engineering, Finance/Accounting

**Storment, John H.** — *Manager Pacific Region*
Management Recruiters International, Inc.
Waimea Town Plaza, Suite 10, P.O. Box 2908
Kailua-Kona, HI 96745
Telephone: (808) 885-7503
**Recruiter Classification:** Contingency; **Lowest/Average Salary:** $30,000/$75,000; **Industry Concentration:** Generalist; **Function Concentration:** Generalist

**Stouffer, Dale** — *Agribusiness Recruiter*
Agra Placements International Ltd.
16 East Fifth Street, Berkshire Court
Peru, IN 46970
Telephone: (317) 472-1988
**Recruiter Classification:** Contingency; **Lowest/Average Salary:** $20,000/$30,000; **Industry Concentration:** Generalist with a primary focus in Biotechnology, Chemical Products, Energy, Financial Services, Manufacturing; **Function Concentration:** Administration, Engineering, Finance/Accounting, General Management, Human Resources, Marketing, Research and Development, Sales

**Stouffer, Kenneth** — *Consultant*
Keith Bagg & Associates Inc.
36 Toronto Street, Suite 520
Toronto, Ontario, CANADA M5C 2C5
Telephone: (416) 863-1800
**Recruiter Classification:** Contingency, Executive Temporary; **Lowest/Average Salary:** $40,000/$60,000; **Industry Concentration:** Automotive, Biotechnology, Consumer Products, Electronics, Financial Services, Healthcare/Hospitals, Manufacturing, Pharmaceutical/Medical; **Function Concentration:** Finance/Accounting

**Stoy, Roger M.** — *Managing Partner*
Heidrick & Struggles, Inc.
1301 K Street N.W., Suite 500 East
Washington, DC 20005
Telephone: (202) 289-4450
**Recruiter Classification:** Retained; **Lowest/Average Salary:** $75,000/$90,000; **Industry Concentration:** Generalist with a primary focus in Financial Services; **Function Concentration:** Generalist

**Strain, Stephen R.** — *Senior Director*
Spencer Stuart
3000 Sand Hill Road
Building 2, Suite 175
Menlo Park, CA 94025
Telephone: (415) 688-1285
**Recruiter Classification:** Retained; **Lowest/Average Salary:** $90,000/$90,000; **Industry Concentration:** Electronics, High Technology, Information Technology, Manufacturing; **Function Concentration:** Generalist

**Strander, Dervin** — *Associate*
Source Services Corporation
5429 LBJ Freeway, Suite 275
Dallas, TX 75240
Telephone: (214) 387-1600
**Recruiter Classification:** Contingency; **Lowest/Average Salary:** $30,000/$50,000; **Industry Concentration:** Financial Services, Information Technology; **Function Concentration:** Engineering, Finance/Accounting

**Strassman, Mark** — *Managing Partner*
Don Richard Associates of Washington, D.C., Inc.
1020 19th Street, NW, Suite 650
Washington, DC 20036
Telephone: (202) 463-7210
**Recruiter Classification:** Contingency, Executive Temporary; **Lowest/Average Salary:** $60,000/$75,000; **Industry Concentration:** Financial Services, High Technology, Information Technology, Non-Profit, Real Estate; **Function Concentration:** Finance/Accounting

**Stratman, Sandy L.** — *Co-Manager Eastern Region*
Management Recruiters International, Inc.
61 Cherry Street
Milford, CT 06460-3414
Telephone: (203) 876-8755
**Recruiter Classification:** Contingency; **Lowest/Average Salary:** $30,000/$75,000; **Industry Concentration:** Generalist; **Function Concentration:** Generalist

**Stratmeyer, Karin Bergwall** — *President*
Princeton Entrepreneurial Resources
600 Alexander Road, P.O. Box 2051
Princeton, NJ 08543
Telephone: (609) 243-0010
**Recruiter Classification:** Executive Temporary; **Lowest/Average Salary:** $75,000/$90,000; **Industry Concentration:** Generalist with a primary focus in Biotechnology, Consumer Products, Electronics, Healthcare/Hospitals, Information Technology, Pharmaceutical/Medical, Venture Capital; **Function Concentration:** Generalist with a primary focus in Finance/Accounting, General Management, Human Resources, Marketing

**Straube, Stanley H.** — *President*
Straube Associates
Willows Professional Park
855 Turnpike Street
North Andover, MA 01845-6105
Telephone: (508) 687-1993
**Recruiter Classification:** Retained; **Lowest/Average Salary:** $60,000/$90,000; **Industry Concentration:** Generalist with a primary focus in Consumer Products, Environmental, Fashion (Retail/Apparel), Financial Services, Hospitality/Leisure, Publishing/Media; **Function Concentration:** Generalist with a primary focus in Engineering, Finance/Accounting, General Management, Human Resources, Marketing, Women/Minorities

**Strawn, William** — *President*
Houtz-Strawn Associates, Inc.
11402 Bee Caves Road, West
Austin, TX 78733
Telephone: (512) 263-1131
**Recruiter Classification:** Retained; **Lowest/Average Salary:** $90,000/$90,000; **Industry Concentration:** Biotechnology, Pharmaceutical/Medical; **Function Concentration:** General Management, Marketing, Research and Development

**Strayhorn, Larry** — *Co-Manager Midwest Region*
Management Recruiters International, Inc.
Meridian Business Campus/Tech Center
600 North Commons Drive, Suite 101
Aurora, IL 60504-4155
Telephone: (708) 851-4164
**Recruiter Classification:** Contingency; **Lowest/Average Salary:** $30,000/$75,000; **Industry Concentration:** Generalist; **Function Concentration:** Generalist

**Strayhorn, Patricia** — *Co-Manager*
Management Recruiters International, Inc.
Meridian Business Campus/Tech Center
600 North Commons Drive, Suite 101
Aurora, IL 60504-4155
Telephone: (708) 851-4164
**Recruiter Classification:** Contingency; **Lowest/Average Salary:** $30,000/$75,000; **Industry Concentration:** Generalist; **Function Concentration:** Generalist

**Stricker, Sidney G.** — *Chairman and Founder*
Stricker & Zagor
342 Madison Avenue, Suite 926
New York, NY 10173
Telephone: (212) 983-0388
**Recruiter Classification:** Retained; **Lowest/Average Salary:** $90,000/$90,000; **Industry Concentration:** Generalist with a primary focus in Consumer Products, Entertainment, Fashion (Retail/Apparel), Financial Services, Healthcare/Hospitals, Hospitality/Leisure, Packaging; **Function Concentration:** Generalist with a primary focus in Administration, Finance/Accounting, General Management, Human Resources, Marketing, Research and Development, Sales

**Stringer, Dann P.** — *Senior Managing Director*
D.E. Foster Partners Inc.
2001 M Street N.W.
Washington, DC 20036
Telephone: (202) 739-8749
**Recruiter Classification:** Retained; **Lowest/Average Salary:** $90,000/$90,000; **Industry Concentration:** Generalist with a primary focus in Aerospace/Defense, Board Services, Chemical Products, Consumer Products, Electronics, Financial Services, High Technology, Information Technology, Manufacturing, Non-Profit, Oil/Gas, Pharmaceutical/Medical; **Function Concentration:** Generalist with a primary focus in Administration, Finance/Accounting, General Management, Marketing, Women/Minorities

**Strobo, Ray S.** — *Manager North Atlantic Region*
Management Recruiters International, Inc.
530 Highway 321 North, Suite 303
Lenoir City, TN 37771-8914
Telephone: (423) 986-3000
**Recruiter Classification:** Contingency; **Lowest/Average Salary:** $30,000/$75,000; **Industry Concentration:** Generalist; **Function Concentration:** Generalist

**Strobridge, Richard P.** — *Vice President*
F.L. Taylor & Company, Inc.
300 East 34th Street
New York, NY 10016
Telephone: (212) 679-4674
**Recruiter Classification:** Retained; **Lowest/Average Salary:** $75,000/$90,000; **Industry Concentration:** Generalist with a primary focus in Fashion (Retail/Apparel), Financial Services, Healthcare/Hospitals, Hospitality/Leisure, Publishing/Media; **Function Concentration:** Generalist with a primary focus in Human Resources, Marketing, Sales

**Strom, Mark N.** — *President*
Search Advisors International Corp.
777 South Harbour Island Boulevard
Suite 925
Tampa, FL 33602
Telephone: (813) 221-7555
**Recruiter Classification:** Retained; **Lowest/Average Salary:** $75,000/$90,000; **Industry Concentration:** Generalist with a primary focus in Aerospace/Defense, Automotive, Chemical Products, Consumer Products, Electronics, Fashion (Retail/Apparel), Financial Services, High Technology, Hospitality/Leisure, Information Technology, Insurance, Manufacturing, Pharmaceutical/Medical, Public Administration; **Function Concentration:** Generalist with a primary focus in Administration, Engineering, Finance/Accounting, General Management, Human Resources, Marketing, Research and Development, Sales, Women/Minorities

**Strong, Duane K.** — *President*
Executive Resource, Inc.
553 South Industrial Drive
P.O. Box 356
Hartland, WI 53029-0356
Telephone: (414) 369-2540
**Recruiter Classification:** Contingency; **Lowest/Average Salary:** $40,000/$50,000; **Industry Concentration:** Automotive, Consumer Products, Manufacturing; **Function Concentration:** Engineering, General Management, Research and Development

**Strong, Robert W.** — *Chief Operating Officer/Recruiter*
The Barack Group, Inc.
885 Third Avenue
New York, NY 10022
Telephone: (212) 230-3280
**Recruiter Classification:** Retained; **Lowest/Average Salary:** $75,000/$90,000; **Industry Concentration:** Consumer Products, Entertainment; **Function Concentration:** General Management, Marketing

**Stroup, Jonathan C.** — *Consultant*
Egon Zehnder International Inc.
One Atlantic Center, Suite 3000
1201 West Peachtree Street N.E.
Atlanta, GA 30309
Telephone: (404) 875-3000
**Recruiter Classification:** Retained; **Lowest/Average Salary:** $90,000/$90,000; **Industry Concentration:** Generalist; **Function Concentration:** Generalist

**Struzziero, Ralph E.** — *President*
Romac & Associates
183 Middle Street, 3rd Floor
P.O. Box 7040
Portland, ME 04112
Telephone: (207) 773-4749
**Recruiter Classification:** Executive Temporary; **Lowest/Average Salary:** $/$60,000; **Industry Concentration:** Financial Services, Healthcare/Hospitals, High Technology, Hospitality/Leisure, Information Technology, Insurance; **Function Concentration:** Finance/Accounting

**Stuart, Karen M.** — *Sales Representative*
Reflex Services, Inc.
Manor Oak Two, Suite 344
1910 Cochran Road
Pittsburgh, PA 15220
Telephone: (412) 341-8842
**Recruiter Classification:** Executive Temporary; **Lowest/Average Salary:**
$40,000/$60,000; **Industry Concentration:** Generalist; **Function
Concentration:** Generalist

**Stubberfield, Lee** — *Manager Eastern Region*
Management Recruiters International, Inc.
7240 Parkway Drive, Suite 150
Hanover, MD 21076
Telephone: (410) 712-0770
**Recruiter Classification:** Contingency; **Lowest/Average Salary:**
$30,000/$75,000; **Industry Concentration:** Generalist; **Function
Concentration:** Generalist

**Stubbs, Judy N.** — *Partner*
Lamalie Amrop International
Thanksgiving Tower
1601 Elm Street
Dallas, TX 75201-4768
Telephone: (214) 754-0019
**Recruiter Classification:** Retained; **Lowest/Average Salary:** $90,000/$90,000;
**Industry Concentration:** Generalist; **Function Concentration:** Generalist with a
primary focus in Administration, Finance/Accounting, General Management,
Human Resources, Marketing, Research and Development, Sales

**Sturges, J.S.** — *Managing Director*
Contract Professionals
P.O. Box 2498
New York, NY 10008-2498
Telephone: (212) 353-2525
**Recruiter Classification:** Executive Temporary; **Lowest/Average Salary:**
$40,000/$60,000; **Industry Concentration:** Generalist; **Function
Concentration:** Generalist

**Sturtz, James W.** — *Vice President*
Compass Group Ltd.
401 South Woodward Avenue, Suite 460
Birmingham, MI 48009-6613
Telephone: (810) 540-9110
**Recruiter Classification:** Retained; **Lowest/Average Salary:** $75,000/$90,000;
**Industry Concentration:** Automotive, Chemical Products, Electronics,
Information Technology, Manufacturing, Transportation; **Function
Concentration:** Engineering, General Management, Human Resources,
Marketing, Research and Development, Sales, Women/Minorities

**Stutt, Brian** — *Executive Recruiter*
Richard, Wayne and Roberts
24 Greenway Plaza, Suite 1304
Houston, TX 77046-2493
Telephone: (713) 629-6681
**Recruiter Classification:** Retained; **Lowest/Average Salary:** $40,000/$60,000;
**Industry Concentration:** Generalist with a primary focus in
Healthcare/Hospitals; **Function Concentration:** Generalist with a primary focus
in Administration, General Management, Marketing

**Suit-Terry, J.A.** — *Manager Southwest Region*
Management Recruiters International, Inc.
Western Tower, Suite 207E
5350 South Western Avenue
Oklahoma City, OK 73109
Telephone: (405) 634-8200
**Recruiter Classification:** Contingency; **Lowest/Average Salary:**
$30,000/$75,000; **Industry Concentration:** Generalist; **Function
Concentration:** Generalist

**Sullivan, Brian M.** — *President*
Sullivan & Company
20 Exchange Place, 50th Floor
New York, NY 10005
Telephone: (212) 422-3000
**Recruiter Classification:** Retained; **Lowest/Average Salary:** $90,000/$90,000;
**Industry Concentration:** Generalist with a primary focus in Financial Services;
**Function Concentration:** Generalist

**Sullivan, Catherine** — *Senior Associate*
Korn/Ferry International
601 South Figueroa
Suite 1900
Los Angeles, CA 90017
Telephone: (213) 624-6600
**Recruiter Classification:** Retained; **Lowest/Average Salary:** $90,000/$90,000;
**Industry Concentration:** Generalist with a primary focus in Non-Profit;
**Function Concentration:** Generalist

**Sullivan, Dennis** — *President*
Sullivan & Associates
344 North Woodward, Suite 304
Birmingham, MI 48009
Telephone: (810) 258-0616
**Recruiter Classification:** Retained; **Lowest/Average Salary:** $90,000/$90,000;
**Industry Concentration:** Generalist; **Function Concentration:** Generalist

**Sullivan, James** — *General Manager*
Search Enterprises, Inc.
160 Quail Ridge Drive
Westmont, IL 60559
Telephone: (708) 654-2300
**Recruiter Classification:** Contingency; **Lowest/Average Salary:**
$20,000/$50,000; **Industry Concentration:** Biotechnology, Consumer
Products, Pharmaceutical/Medical; **Function Concentration:** Engineering,
General Management, Research and Development

**Sullivan, Joseph J.** — *President*
Joe Sullivan & Associates, Inc.
44210 County Road 48
P.O. Box 612
Southold, NY 11971
Telephone: (516) 765-5050
**Recruiter Classification:** Retained; **Lowest/Average Salary:** $75,000/$90,000;
**Industry Concentration:** Entertainment; **Function Concentration:** Generalist

**Sullivan, Kay** — *Principal*
Rusher, Loscavio & LoPresto
2479 Bayshore Road, Suite 700
Palo Alto, CA 94303
Telephone: (415) 494-0883
**Recruiter Classification:** Retained; **Lowest/Average Salary:** $75,000/$90,000;
**Industry Concentration:** Electronics, Financial Services, High Technology,
Manufacturing; **Function Concentration:** General Management, Human
Resources, Marketing, Research and Development, Sales, Women/Minorities

**Sullivan, Robert** — *Principal*
Korn/Ferry International
One International Place
Boston, MA 02110-1800
Telephone: (617) 345-0200
**Recruiter Classification:** Retained; **Lowest/Average Salary:** $90,000/$90,000;
**Industry Concentration:** Generalist; **Function Concentration:** Generalist

**Summerfield-Beall, Dotty** — *President*
Summerfield Associates, Inc.
6555 Quince Road, Suite 311
Memphis, TN 38119
Telephone: (901) 753-7068
**Recruiter Classification:** Contingency; **Lowest/Average Salary:**
$40,000/$50,000; **Industry Concentration:** Generalist with a primary focus in
Information Technology; **Function Concentration:** General Management,
Human Resources, Women/Minorities

**Summerlin, Gerald** — *Manager North Atlantic Region*
Management Recruiters International, Inc.
108 South Market Street, Suite D
Madison, NC 27025-2124
Telephone: (910) 427-6153
**Recruiter Classification:** Contingency; **Lowest/Average Salary:**
$30,000/$75,000; **Industry Concentration:** Generalist; **Function
Concentration:** Generalist

**Summers, Burke** — *Senior Consultant*
The McCormick Group, Inc.
1400 Wilson Boulevard
Arlington, VA 22209
Telephone: (703) 841-1700
**Recruiter Classification:** Retained, Contingency; **Lowest/Average Salary:**
$30,000/$60,000; **Industry Concentration:** Consumer Products, Fashion
(Retail/Apparel); **Function Concentration:** Generalist with a primary focus in
Finance/Accounting, General Management, Marketing, Sales

**Sumurdy, Melinda** — *Vice President*
Kenzer Corp.
Triwest Plaza
3030 LBJ Freeway, Suite 1430
Dallas, TX 75234
Telephone: (214) 620-7776
**Recruiter Classification:** Retained; **Lowest/Average Salary:** $50,000/$90,000;
**Industry Concentration:** Consumer Products, Entertainment, Financial
Services, Packaging, Venture Capital; **Function Concentration:** Generalist with
a primary focus in Administration, Finance/Accounting, General Management,
Human Resources, Marketing, Research and Development, Sales

**Sur, William K.** — *Senior Vice President/Director*
Canny, Bowen Inc.
200 Park Avenue
New York, NY 10166
Telephone: (212) 949-6611
**Recruiter Classification:** Retained; **Lowest/Average Salary:** $90,000/$90,000;
**Industry Concentration:** Generalist with a primary focus in Biotechnology,
Board Services, Chemical Products, Consumer Products, Electronics,
Entertainment, Fashion (Retail/Apparel), High Technology, Hospitality/Leisure,
Information Technology, Manufacturing, Packaging, Pharmaceutical/Medical,
Venture Capital; **Function Concentration:** Generalist with a primary focus in
Administration, Engineering, Finance/Accounting, General Management,
Human Resources, Marketing, Research and Development, Sales,
Women/Minorities

**Susoreny, Samali** — *Associate*
Source Services Corporation
5429 LBJ Freeway, Suite 275
Dallas, TX 75240
Telephone: (214) 387-1600
**Recruiter Classification:** Contingency; **Lowest/Average Salary:**
$30,000/$50,000; **Industry Concentration:** Financial Services, Information
Technology; **Function Concentration:** Engineering, Finance/Accounting

**Sussman, Lynda** — *Vice President*
Gilbert Tweed/INESA
415 Madison Avenue
New York, NY 10017
Telephone: (212) 758-3000
**Recruiter Classification:** Retained; **Lowest/Average Salary:** $90,000/$90,000;
**Industry Concentration:** Generalist with a primary focus in
Aerospace/Defense, Consumer Products, Electronics, Financial Services, High
Technology, Hospitality/Leisure, Insurance; **Function Concentration:** Generalist
with a primary focus in Engineering, Finance/Accounting, General
Management, Human Resources, Women/Minorities

**Sutter, Howard** — *Managing Partner*
Romac & Associates
5900 North Andrews Avenue
Suite 900
Fort Lauderdale, FL 33309
Telephone: (305) 928-0811
**Recruiter Classification:** Executive Temporary; **Lowest/Average Salary:**
$/$60,000; **Industry Concentration:** Financial Services, Healthcare/Hospitals,
High Technology, Hospitality/Leisure, Information Technology, Insurance;
**Function Concentration:** Finance/Accounting

**Sutter, Terry A.** — *Associate*
Russell Reynolds Associates, Inc.
1900 Trammell Crow Center
2001 Ross Avenue
Dallas, TX 75201
Telephone: (214) 220-2033
**Recruiter Classification:** Retained; **Lowest/Average Salary:** $90,000/$90,000;
**Industry Concentration:** Generalist; **Function Concentration:** Generalist

**Sutton, Robert J.** — *Partner*
The Caldwell Partners Amrop International
400 Third Avenue S.W.
Suite 3450
Calgary, Alberta, CANADA T2P 4H2
Telephone: (403) 265-8780
**Recruiter Classification:** Retained; **Lowest/Average Salary:** $/$90,000; **Industry
Concentration:** Generalist with a primary focus in Chemical Products, Energy,
Environmental, High Technology, Hospitality/Leisure, Oil/Gas,
Utilities/Nuclear; **Function Concentration:** Generalist

**Swan, Richard A.** — *Shareholder*
Witt/Kieffer, Ford, Hadelman & Lloyd
1920 Main Street, Suite 310
Irvine, CA 92714
Telephone: (714) 851-5070
**Recruiter Classification:** Retained; **Lowest/Average Salary:** $75,000/$90,000;
**Industry Concentration:** Healthcare/Hospitals; **Function Concentration:**
Generalist with a primary focus in Administration, Finance/Accounting,
General Management, Human Resources, Marketing

**Swanner, William** — *Managing Director*
Source Services Corporation
2000 Town Center, Suite 850
Southfield, MI 48075
Telephone: (810) 352-6520
**Recruiter Classification:** Contingency; **Lowest/Average Salary:**
$30,000/$50,000; **Industry Concentration:** Financial Services, Information
Technology; **Function Concentration:** Engineering, Finance/Accounting

**Swanson, Dick** — *Principal*
Raymond Karsan Associates
200 West Cummings Park, Suite 7000
Woburn, MA 01801
Telephone: (617) 273-4022
**Recruiter Classification:** Contingency; **Lowest/Average Salary:**
$30,000/$90,000; **Industry Concentration:** Generalist with a primary focus in
Biotechnology, Chemical Products, Environmental, Healthcare/Hospitals,
Information Technology, Insurance, Manufacturing, Pharmaceutical/Medical;
**Function Concentration:** Generalist with a primary focus in Administration,
Engineering, Finance/Accounting, General Management, Human Resources,
Marketing, Research and Development, Sales, Women/Minorities

**Swanson, Jarl** — *Senior Vice President*
The Gabriel Group
1515 Market Street, Suite 504
Philadelphia, PA 19102
Telephone: (215) 496-9990
**Recruiter Classification:** Retained; **Lowest/Average Salary:** $75,000/$75,000;
**Industry Concentration:** Generalist; **Function Concentration:** Generalist

**Swanson, Kris** — *Managing Partner*
Flex Execs Management Solutions
16350 South 105th Court
Orland Park, IL 60462
Telephone: (708) 460-8500
**Recruiter Classification:** Executive Temporary; **Lowest/Average Salary:**
$40,000/$50,000; **Industry Concentration:** Generalist; **Function
Concentration:** Generalist with a primary focus in Finance/Accounting,
General Management, Human Resources, Marketing, Sales

**Swaringen, Mac** — *Manager North Atlantic Region*
Management Recruiters International, Inc.
305 South Main Street
Kannapolis, NC 28081
Telephone: (704) 938-6144
**Recruiter Classification:** Contingency; **Lowest/Average Salary:**
$30,000/$75,000; **Industry Concentration:** Generalist; **Function
Concentration:** Generalist

**Swatts, Stone** — *Executive Recruiter*
F-O-R-T-U-N-E Personnel Consultants of Huntsville, Inc.
3311 Bob Wallace Avenue, Suite 204
Huntsville, AL 35805
Telephone: (205) 534-7282
**Recruiter Classification:** Contingency; **Lowest/Average Salary:**
$30,000/$50,000; **Industry Concentration:** Aerospace/Defense, Automotive,
Consumer Products, Electronics, High Technology, Information Technology,
Manufacturing, Pharmaceutical/Medical; **Function Concentration:** Engineering,
General Management, Marketing, Research and Development, Sales

**Sweeney, Anne** — *Associate*
Source Services Corporation
525 Vine Street, Suite 2250
Cincinnati, OH 45202
Telephone: (513) 651-3303
**Recruiter Classification:** Contingency; **Lowest/Average Salary:**
$30,000/$50,000; **Industry Concentration:** Financial Services, Information
Technology; **Function Concentration:** Engineering, Finance/Accounting

**Sweeney, James W.** — *Partner*
Sweeney Harbert & Mummert, Inc.
777 South Harbour Island Boulevard, Suite 130
Tampa, FL 33602
Telephone: (813) 229-5360
**Recruiter Classification:** Retained; **Lowest/Average Salary:** $90,000/$90,000;
**Industry Concentration:** Generalist with a primary focus in Biotechnology,
Chemical Products, Electronics, High Technology, Pharmaceutical/Medical;
**Function Concentration:** Generalist with a primary focus in
Finance/Accounting, General Management, Human Resources, Marketing,
Research and Development, Sales

**Sweeney, Sean K.** — *Executive Recruiter*
Bonifield Associates
3003E Lincoln Drive West
Marlton, NJ 08053
Telephone: (609) 596-3300
**Recruiter Classification:** Contingency; **Lowest/Average Salary:**
$40,000/$60,000; **Industry Concentration:** Financial Services, Insurance;
**Function Concentration:** Generalist with a primary focus in Administration,
Finance/Accounting, General Management, Marketing, Research and
Development, Sales

**Sweet, Charles W.** — *President*
A.T. Kearney, Inc.
222 West Adams Street
Chicago, IL 60606
Telephone: (312) 648-0111
**Recruiter Classification:** Retained; **Lowest/Average Salary:** $90,000/$90,000;
**Industry Concentration:** Generalist with a primary focus in Board Services,
Manufacturing; **Function Concentration:** Generalist

**Sweet, Randall** — *Associate*
Source Services Corporation
150 South Wacker Drive, Suite 400
Chicago, IL 60606
Telephone: (312) 346-7000
**Recruiter Classification:** Contingency; **Lowest/Average Salary:**
$30,000/$50,000; **Industry Concentration:** Financial Services, Information
Technology; **Function Concentration:** Engineering, Finance/Accounting

**Swick, Jan** — *Executive Recruiter*
TSS Consulting, Ltd.
2425 East Camelback Road
Suite 375
Phoenix, AZ 85016
Telephone: (602) 955-7000
**Recruiter Classification:** Contingency; **Lowest/Average Salary:**
$60,000/$75,000; **Industry Concentration:** Aerospace/Defense, Electronics,
High Technology; **Function Concentration:** Engineering, General Management,
Marketing

**Swidler, J. Robert** — *Managing Partner*
Egon Zehnder International Inc.
1 Place Ville-Marie, Suite 3310
Montreal, Quebec, CANADA H3B 3N2
Telephone: (514) 876-4249
**Recruiter Classification:** Retained; **Lowest/Average Salary:** $90,000/$90,000;
**Industry Concentration:** Generalist with a primary focus in Biotechnology,
Financial Services, High Technology, Manufacturing, Pharmaceutical/Medical;
**Function Concentration:** Generalist

**Swystun, Karen** — *Director*
Price Waterhouse
2200 One Lombard Place
Winnipeg, Manitoba, CANADA R3B 0X7
Telephone: (204) 943-7321
**Recruiter Classification:** Retained; **Lowest/Average Salary:** $60,000/$90,000;
**Industry Concentration:** Generalist; **Function Concentration:** Generalist

**Sykes, Hugh L.** — *Manager North Atlantic Region*
Management Recruiters International, Inc.
322 East Center Avenue
Mooresville, NC 28115
Telephone: (704) 664-4997
**Recruiter Classification:** Contingency; **Lowest/Average Salary:**
$30,000/$75,000; **Industry Concentration:** Generalist; **Function
Concentration:** Generalist

**Szafran, Jack** — *Recruiter*
U.S. Envirosearch
445 Union Boulevard, Suite 225
Lakewood, CO 80228
Telephone: (303) 980-6600
**Recruiter Classification:** Contingency; **Lowest/Average Salary:**
$30,000/$60,000; **Industry Concentration:** Environmental; **Function
Concentration:** Generalist with a primary focus in Administration, Engineering,
Finance/Accounting, General Management, Marketing, Sales,
Women/Minorities

**Szubielski, Ellen** — *Researcher*
Klein, Landau, Romm & North
1725 K Street NW, Suite 602
Washington, DC 20006
Telephone: (202) 728-0100
**Recruiter Classification:** Contingency; **Lowest/Average Salary:**
$50,000/$90,000

**Tabisz, Susanne** — *Account Executive*
Executive Referral Services, Inc.
8770 West Bryn Mawr, Suite 110
Chicago, IL 60631
Telephone: (312) 693-6622
**Recruiter Classification:** Contingency; **Lowest/Average Salary:**
$30,000/$50,000; **Industry Concentration:** Generalist; **Function
Concentration:** Finance/Accounting, General Management

**Taft, David G.** — *President*
Techsearch Services, Inc.
6 Hachaliah Brown Drive
Somers, NY 10589
Telephone: (914) 277-2727
**Recruiter Classification:** Contingency; **Lowest/Average Salary:**
$50,000/$75,000; **Industry Concentration:** Financial Services, High
Technology, Information Technology; **Function Concentration:**
Finance/Accounting

**Taft, Steven D.** — *Associate*
The Guild Corporation
8260 Greensboro Drive, Suite 460
McLean, VA 22102
Telephone: (703) 761-4023
**Recruiter Classification:** Contingency; **Lowest/Average Salary:**
$40,000/$50,000; **Industry Concentration:** Aerospace/Defense, Electronics,
High Technology, Information Technology; **Function Concentration:**
Engineering, Finance/Accounting, General Management, Research and
Development

**Takacs, Gloria** — *Manager*
Gilbert & Van Campen International
393 Lake Shore Drive
Operations Center
Belvidere, NJ 07840
Telephone: (908) 475-2222
**Recruiter Classification:** Retained; **Lowest/Average Salary:** $90,000/$90,000;
**Industry Concentration:** Generalist; **Function Concentration:** Generalist with a
primary focus in Finance/Accounting, General Management, Human
Resources, Marketing, Sales, Women/Minorities

**Talbot, Matt T.** — *Manager Eastern Region*
Management Recruiters International, Inc.
520 Stokes Road, Building B, Suite B-6
Medford, NJ 08055
Telephone: (609) 654-9109
**Recruiter Classification:** Contingency; **Lowest/Average Salary:**
$30,000/$75,000; **Industry Concentration:** Generalist; **Function
Concentration:** Generalist

**Talbot, Norman** — *Manager*
Management Recruiters International, Inc.
520 Stokes Road, Building B, Suite B-6
Medford, NJ 08055
Telephone: (609) 654-9109
**Recruiter Classification:** Contingency; **Lowest/Average Salary:**
$30,000/$75,000; **Industry Concentration:** Generalist; **Function
Concentration:** Generalist

**Tallent, Diane** — *Consultant - L.A. Wholesale*
Evie Kreisler & Associates, Inc.
865 South Figueroa, Suite 950
Los Angeles, CA 90017
Telephone: (213) 622-8994
**Recruiter Classification:** Contingency; **Lowest/Average Salary:**
$30,000/$75,000; **Industry Concentration:** Fashion (Retail/Apparel); **Function
Concentration:** Generalist

**Tames, Rodolfo** — *Associate*
Amrop International
Amberes #4, 2 Pia, Colonia Juarez
Mexico City, D.F., MEXICO 06600
Telephone: (525) 208-3977
**Recruiter Classification:** Retained, Contingency; **Lowest/Average Salary:**
$75,000/$90,000; **Industry Concentration:** Generalist; **Function
Concentration:** Generalist

**Tanabe, Sharon** — *Senior Associate*
Korn/Ferry International
1800 Century Park East, Suite 900
Los Angeles, CA 90067
Telephone: (310) 552-1834
**Recruiter Classification:** Retained; **Lowest/Average Salary:** $90,000/$90,000;
**Industry Concentration:** Generalist; **Function Concentration:** Generalist

**Tanenbaum, Ray** — *Associate*
Kenzer Corp.
777 Third Avenue, 26th Floor
New York, NY 10017
Telephone: (212) 308-4300
**Recruiter Classification:** Retained; **Lowest/Average Salary:** $50,000/$90,000;
**Industry Concentration:** Generalist; **Function Concentration:** Generalist

**Tankson, Dawn** — *Associate*
Source Services Corporation
1 Gatehall Drive, Suite 250
Parsippany, NJ 07054
Telephone: (201) 267-3222
**Recruiter Classification:** Contingency; **Lowest/Average Salary:**
$30,000/$50,000; **Industry Concentration:** Financial Services, Information
Technology; **Function Concentration:** Engineering, Finance/Accounting

**Tanner, Frank** — *Associate*
Source Services Corporation
520 Post Oak Boulevard, Suite 700
Houston, TX 77027
Telephone: (713) 439-1077
**Recruiter Classification:** Contingency; **Lowest/Average Salary:**
$30,000/$50,000; **Industry Concentration:** Financial Services, Information
Technology; **Function Concentration:** Engineering, Finance/Accounting

**Tanner, Gary** — *Associate*
Source Services Corporation
505 East 200 South, Suite 300
Salt Lake City, UT 84102
Telephone: (801) 328-0011
**Recruiter Classification:** Contingency; **Lowest/Average Salary:** $30,000/$50,000; **Industry Concentration:** Financial Services, Information Technology; **Function Concentration:** Engineering, Finance/Accounting

**Tanton, John E.** — *Partner*
Tanton Mitchell/Paul Ray Berndtson
710-1050 West Pender Street
Vancouver, British Columbia, CANADA V6E 3S7
Telephone: (604) 685-0261
**Recruiter Classification:** Retained; **Lowest/Average Salary:** $75,000/$90,000; **Industry Concentration:** Generalist with a primary focus in Energy, High Technology, Manufacturing; **Function Concentration:** Generalist

**Tappan, Michael A.** — *Managing Director*
Ward Howell International, Inc.
99 Park Avenue, Suite 2000
New York, NY 10016-1699
Telephone: (212) 697-3730
**Recruiter Classification:** Retained; **Lowest/Average Salary:** $75,000/$90,000; **Industry Concentration:** Consumer Products, Electronics, Financial Services, Insurance, Non-Profit; **Function Concentration:** Generalist

**Tardugno, Carl** — *Manager Eastern Region*
Management Recruiters International, Inc.
Executive Building, Suite 205
1721 Black River Road
Rome, NY 13440
Telephone: (315) 339-6342
**Recruiter Classification:** Contingency; **Lowest/Average Salary:** $30,000/$75,000; **Industry Concentration:** Generalist; **Function Concentration:** Generalist

**Targovnik, Andrew** — *Branch Manager*
Accountants on Call
The Jericho Atrium, Suite 144
500 North Broadway
Jericho, NY 11753
Telephone: (516) 935-0050
**Recruiter Classification:** Contingency; **Lowest/Average Salary:** $20,000/$30,000; **Industry Concentration:** Generalist; **Function Concentration:** Finance/Accounting

**Tate, Robert H.** — *Partner*
Paul Ray Berndtson
10 South Riverside Plaza
Suite 720
Chicago, IL 60606
Telephone: (312) 876-0730
**Recruiter Classification:** Retained; **Lowest/Average Salary:** $90,000/$90,000; **Industry Concentration:** Generalist with a primary focus in Consumer Products; **Function Concentration:** Generalist

**Taylor, Charles E.** — *Managing Partner*
Lamalie Amrop International
Key Tower, 127 Public Square
Cleveland, OH 44114-1216
Telephone: (216) 694-3000
**Recruiter Classification:** Retained; **Lowest/Average Salary:** $90,000/$90,000; **Industry Concentration:** Generalist with a primary focus in Education/Libraries, Public Administration; **Function Concentration:** Generalist with a primary focus in General Management

**Taylor, Conrad G.** — *Manager*
MSI International
6151 Powers Ferry Road, Suite 540
Atlanta, GA 30339
Telephone: (404) 850-6465
**Recruiter Classification:** Contingency; **Lowest/Average Salary:** $30,000/$75,000; **Industry Concentration:** Generalist with a primary focus in Financial Services, Healthcare/Hospitals, High Technology, Information Technology, Manufacturing; **Function Concentration:** Generalist with a primary focus in Administration, Engineering, Finance/Accounting, General Management, Marketing, Sales

**Taylor, Ernest A.** — *Managing Director*
Ward Howell International, Inc.
3350 Peachtree Road N.E.
Suite 1600
Atlanta, GA 30326
Telephone: (404) 261-6532
**Recruiter Classification:** Retained; **Lowest/Average Salary:** $75,000/$90,000; **Industry Concentration:** Generalist with a primary focus in Education/Libraries, Fashion (Retail/Apparel), Financial Services, Healthcare/Hospitals, Real Estate; **Function Concentration:** Generalist with a primary focus in General Management, Marketing, Sales

**Taylor, Kenneth W.** — *Consultant*
Egon Zehnder International Inc.
One First National Plaza
21 South Clark Street, Suite 3300
Chicago, IL 60603-2006
Telephone: (312) 782-4500
**Recruiter Classification:** Retained; **Lowest/Average Salary:** $90,000/$90,000; **Industry Concentration:** Generalist with a primary focus in Biotechnology, Financial Services, High Technology, Manufacturing, Pharmaceutical/Medical; **Function Concentration:** Generalist

**Taylor, Richard** — *Senior Associate*
Korn/Ferry International
237 Park Avenue
New York, NY 10017
Telephone: (212) 687-1834
**Recruiter Classification:** Retained; **Lowest/Average Salary:** $90,000/$90,000; **Industry Concentration:** Generalist; **Function Concentration:** Generalist

**Taylor, Walt W.** — *Manager South Atlantic Region*
Management Recruiters International, Inc.
996-B Laguna Drive
Venice, FL 34285-1207
Telephone: (813) 484-3900
**Recruiter Classification:** Contingency; **Lowest/Average Salary:** $30,000/$75,000; **Industry Concentration:** Generalist; **Function Concentration:** Generalist

**Taylor-Gordon, Elaine** — *Associate*
Kenzer Corp.
777 Third Avenue, 26th Floor
New York, NY 10017
Telephone: (212) 308-4300
**Recruiter Classification:** Retained; **Lowest/Average Salary:** $50,000/$90,000; **Industry Concentration:** Generalist; **Function Concentration:** Generalist

**Teas, John** — *Sales Recruiter*
Southwestern Professional Services
2451 Atrium Way
Nashville, TN 37214
Telephone: (615) 391-2722
**Recruiter Classification:** Contingency; **Lowest/Average Salary:** $30,000/$40,000; **Industry Concentration:** Healthcare/Hospitals, Pharmaceutical/Medical; **Function Concentration:** Generalist with a primary focus in Administration, Marketing, Sales

**Teger, Stella** — *Associate*
Source Services Corporation
2 Penn Plaza, Suite 1176
New York, NY 10121
Telephone: (212) 760-2200
**Recruiter Classification:** Contingency; **Lowest/Average Salary:** $30,000/$50,000; **Industry Concentration:** Financial Services, Information Technology; **Function Concentration:** Engineering, Finance/Accounting

**Teinert, Jay** — *Executive Recruiter*
Damon & Associates, Inc.
7515 Greenville Avenue, Suite 900
Dallas, TX 75231
Telephone: (214) 696-6990
**Recruiter Classification:** Contingency; **Lowest/Average Salary:** $30,000/$60,000; **Industry Concentration:** Consumer Products, Healthcare/Hospitals, Pharmaceutical/Medical; **Function Concentration:** Generalist with a primary focus in Administration, General Management, Human Resources, Marketing, Research and Development, Sales

**Telford, John H.** — *Managing Principal*
Telford, Adams & Alexander/Telford & Co., Inc.
650 Town Center Drive, Suite 850A
Costa Mesa, CA 92626
Telephone: (714) 850-4354
**Recruiter Classification:** Retained; **Lowest/Average Salary:** $75,000/$90,000; **Industry Concentration:** Generalist with a primary focus in Consumer Products, Financial Services, Healthcare/Hospitals, High Technology, Information Technology, Manufacturing, Non-Profit, Pharmaceutical/Medical, Public Administration, Real Estate, Transportation; **Function Concentration:** Generalist

**Tello, Fernando** — *Vice President*
Korn/Ferry International
Montes Urales 641
Lomas De Chapultepec
Mexico City, D.F., MEXICO 11000
Telephone: (525) 202-0046
**Recruiter Classification:** Retained; **Lowest/Average Salary:** $90,000/$90,000; **Industry Concentration:** Generalist; **Function Concentration:** Generalist

**Temple, John D.** — *Vice President*
The Hindman Company
Browenton Place, Suite 110
2000 Warrington Way
Louisville, KY 40222
Telephone: (502) 426-4040
**Recruiter Classification:** Retained; **Lowest/Average Salary:** $50,000/$90,000;
**Industry Concentration:** Generalist; **Function Concentration:** Generalist

**Templin, Robert E.** — *Principal*
Gilbert Tweed/INESA
3411 Silverside Road, Suite 100
Wilmington, DE 19810
Telephone: (302) 479-5144
**Recruiter Classification:** Retained; **Lowest/Average Salary:** $75,000/$90,000;
**Industry Concentration:** Healthcare/Hospitals, Pharmaceutical/Medical;
**Function Concentration:** Administration, Finance/Accounting, General
Management, Human Resources, Marketing, Research and Development

**ten Cate, Herman H.** — *President*
Stoneham Associates Corp.
Royal Bank Plaza, South Tower
200 Bay Street, Suite 2930
Toronto, Ontario, CANADA M5J 2J3
Telephone: (416) 362-0852
**Recruiter Classification:** Retained; **Lowest/Average Salary:** $90,000/$90,000;
**Industry Concentration:** Generalist with a primary focus in Consumer
Products, Entertainment, Fashion (Retail/Apparel), Financial Services,
Packaging, Transportation; **Function Concentration:** Generalist

**Tenero, Kymberly** — *Associate*
Source Services Corporation
111 Founders Plaza, Suite 1501E
Hartford, CT 06108
Telephone: (860) 528-0300
**Recruiter Classification:** Contingency; **Lowest/Average Salary:**
$30,000/$50,000; **Industry Concentration:** Financial Services, Information
Technology; **Function Concentration:** Engineering, Finance/Accounting

**Terry, Douglas** — *Executive Recruiter*
Jacobson Associates
150 North Wacker Drive
Suite 1120
Chicago, IL 60606
Telephone: (312) 726-1578
**Recruiter Classification:** Contingency; **Lowest/Average Salary:**
$20,000/$50,000; **Industry Concentration:** Insurance; **Function
Concentration:** Generalist

**Tesar, Bob** — *Partner*
Tesar-Reynes, Inc.
500 North Michigan Avenue
Chicago, IL 60611
Telephone: (312) 661-0700
**Recruiter Classification:** Retained; **Lowest/Average Salary:** $50,000/$75,000;
**Industry Concentration:** Automotive, Consumer Products, High Technology,
Hospitality/Leisure, Publishing/Media; **Function Concentration:** Marketing

**Tessin, Cy** — *Manager Central Region*
Management Recruiters International, Inc.
Briarwood Valley Office Plaza, Suite 200
4021 West Main Street
Kalamazoo, MI 49007-2746
Telephone: (616) 381-1153
**Recruiter Classification:** Contingency; **Lowest/Average Salary:**
$30,000/$75,000; **Industry Concentration:** Generalist; **Function
Concentration:** Generalist

**Teter, Sandra** — *Division Manager - Accounting*
The Danbrook Group, Inc.
14180 Dallas Parkway, Suite 400
Dallas, TX 75240
Telephone: (214) 392-0057
**Recruiter Classification:** Contingency; **Lowest/Average Salary:**
$30,000/$50,000; **Industry Concentration:** Financial Services; **Function
Concentration:** Generalist with a primary focus in Administration,
Finance/Accounting, General Management, Sales

**Theard, Susan** — *Branch Manager*
Romac & Associates
650 Poydras Street, Suite 2523
New Orleans, LA 70130
Telephone: (504) 522-6611
**Recruiter Classification:** Executive Temporary; **Lowest/Average Salary:**
$/$60,000; **Industry Concentration:** Financial Services, Healthcare/Hospitals,
High Technology, Hospitality/Leisure, Information Technology, Insurance;
**Function Concentration:** Finance/Accounting

**Theobald, David B.** — *President*
Theobald & Associates
1750 Montgomery Street
San Francisco, CA 94111
Telephone: (415) 883-6007
**Recruiter Classification:** Retained; **Lowest/Average Salary:** $90,000/$90,000;
**Industry Concentration:** Generalist with a primary focus in
Aerospace/Defense, Automotive, Biotechnology, Chemical Products,
Consumer Products, Electronics, Fashion (Retail/Apparel), Financial Services,
Healthcare/Hospitals, High Technology, Information Technology,
Manufacturing, Packaging, Pharmaceutical/Medical; **Function Concentration:**
Generalist with a primary focus in Engineering, Finance/Accounting, General
Management, Human Resources, Marketing, Sales

**Thielman, Joseph** — *President*
Barrett Partners
100 North LaSalle Street, Suite 1420
Chicago, IL 60602
Telephone: (312) 443-8877
**Recruiter Classification:** Contingency; **Lowest/Average Salary:**
$30,000/$50,000; **Industry Concentration:** Automotive, Biotechnology,
Chemical Products, Consumer Products, Environmental, Financial Services,
Healthcare/Hospitals, Information Technology, Insurance, Manufacturing,
Packaging, Publishing/Media, Real Estate, Transportation; **Function
Concentration:** Engineering, Finance/Accounting

**Thies, Gary** — *Recruiter*
S.D. Kelly & Associates, Inc.
990 Washington Street
Dedham, MA 02026
Telephone: (617) 326-8038
**Recruiter Classification:** Contingency; **Lowest/Average Salary:**
$50,000/$60,000; **Industry Concentration:** Electronics, Energy, High
Technology; **Function Concentration:** Engineering, General Management,
Marketing, Sales

**Thiras, Ted** — *Senior Principal*
Mixtec Group
31255 Cedar Valley Drive
Suite 300-327
Westlake Village, CA 91362
Telephone: (818) 889-8819
**Recruiter Classification:** Contingency; **Lowest/Average Salary:**
$60,000/$90,000; **Function Concentration:** Generalist with a primary focus
in Administration, Finance/Accounting, General Management, Marketing,
Sales

**Tholke, William E.** — *President*
Canny, Bowen Inc.
1177 High Ridge Road
Stamford, CT 06905
Telephone: (203) 321-1248
**Recruiter Classification:** Retained; **Lowest/Average Salary:** $90,000/$90,000;
**Industry Concentration:** Generalist with a primary focus in Automotive,
Biotechnology, Board Services, Chemical Products, Electronics, Entertainment,
Fashion (Retail/Apparel), Financial Services, High Technology,
Hospitality/Leisure, Non-Profit, Pharmaceutical/Medical, Venture Capital;
**Function Concentration:** Generalist with a primary focus in Administration,
Engineering, Finance/Accounting, General Management, Human Resources,
Marketing, Research and Development, Sales, Women/Minorities

**Thomas, Bill** — *General Manager*
Management Recruiters International, Inc.
Village Square Mall, Suite 1
Highway 258 North, P.O. Box 219
Kinston, NC 28502-0219
Telephone: (919) 527-9191
**Recruiter Classification:** Contingency; **Lowest/Average Salary:**
$30,000/$75,000; **Industry Concentration:** Generalist; **Function
Concentration:** Generalist

**Thomas, Cheryl M.** — *Executive Recruiter*
CPS Inc.
One Westbrook Corporate Centre, Suite 600
Westchester, IL 60154
Telephone: (708) 531-8370
**Recruiter Classification:** Contingency; **Lowest/Average Salary:**
$30,000/$50,000; **Industry Concentration:** Generalist with a primary focus in
Automotive, Biotechnology, Chemical Products, Consumer Products, High
Technology, Insurance, Manufacturing, Oil/Gas, Packaging,
Pharmaceutical/Medical; **Function Concentration:** Engineering, Research and
Development, Sales, Women/Minorities

**Thomas, Christine S.** — *Consultant*
Lovas Stanley/Paul Ray Berndtson Inc.
Royal Bank Plaza, South Tower, Suite 3150
200 Bay Street, P.O. Box 125
Toronto, Ontario, CANADA M5J 2J3
Telephone: (416) 366-1990
**Recruiter Classification:** Retained; **Lowest/Average Salary:** $50,000/$75,000;
**Industry Concentration:** Generalist with a primary focus in Entertainment,
Healthcare/Hospitals; **Function Concentration:** Generalist with a primary focus
in General Management, Human Resources, Marketing, Sales

**Thomas, Donald** — *Principal*
Mixtec Group
75-355 St. Andrews
Indian Wells, CA 92210
Telephone: (619) 773-0717
**Recruiter Classification:** Contingency; **Lowest/Average Salary:**
$60,000/$90,000; **Industry Concentration:** Electronics, High Technology,
Information Technology; **Function Concentration:** Generalist with a primary
focus in Administration, Engineering, General Management, Research and
Development

**Thomas, Ian** — *International Staffing Consultant*
International Staffing Consultants, Inc.
500 Newport Center Drive, Suite 300
Newport Beach, CA 92660-7003
Telephone: (714) 721-7990
**Recruiter Classification:** Contingency, Executive Temporary; **Lowest/Average
Salary:** $50,000/$75,000; **Industry Concentration:** Generalist with a primary
focus in Chemical Products, Energy, Environmental, Oil/Gas, Utilities/Nuclear;
**Function Concentration:** Generalist with a primary focus in Engineering

**Thomas, Jeffrey** — *President*
Fairfaxx Corporation
17 High Street
Norwalk, CT 06851
Telephone: (203) 838-8300
**Recruiter Classification:** Retained; **Lowest/Average Salary:** $60,000/$90,000;
**Industry Concentration:** Consumer Products, Entertainment, Fashion
(Retail/Apparel), Venture Capital; **Function Concentration:** Generalist with a
primary focus in Engineering, Finance/Accounting, General Management,
Human Resources, Marketing, Sales

**Thomas, John T.** — *Managing Director*
Ward Howell International, Inc.
300 South Wacker Drive
Suite 2940
Chicago, IL 60606
Telephone: (312) 236-2211
**Recruiter Classification:** Retained; **Lowest/Average Salary:** $75,000/$90,000;
**Industry Concentration:** Consumer Products, Manufacturing,
Pharmaceutical/Medical; **Function Concentration:** Generalist with a primary
focus in General Management, Marketing, Sales

**Thomas, Kim** — *Executive Recruiter*
CPS Inc.
One Westbrook Corporate Centre, Suite 600
Westchester, IL 60154
Telephone: (708) 531-8370
**Recruiter Classification:** Contingency; **Lowest/Average Salary:**
$30,000/$50,000; **Industry Concentration:** Generalist with a primary focus in
Automotive, Biotechnology, Chemical Products, Consumer Products, High
Technology, Insurance, Manufacturing, Oil/Gas, Packaging,
Pharmaceutical/Medical; **Function Concentration:** Engineering, Research and
Development, Sales, Women/Minorities

**Thomas, Kurt J.** — *Vice President*
P.J. Murphy & Associates, Inc.
735 North Water Street
Milwaukee, WI 53202
Telephone: (414) 277-9777
**Recruiter Classification:** Retained; **Lowest/Average Salary:** $60,000/$90,000;
**Industry Concentration:** Generalist with a primary focus in Board Services,
Financial Services, Healthcare/Hospitals, Information Technology,
Manufacturing; **Function Concentration:** Generalist with a primary focus in
Administration, Finance/Accounting, General Management, Human Resources,
Marketing, Sales

**Thomas, Terry** — *President*
Montague Enterprises
1630 Tiburon Boulevard
Tiburon, CA 94920
Telephone: (415) 435-5123
**Recruiter Classification:** Retained; **Lowest/Average Salary:** $90,000/$90,000;
**Industry Concentration:** Biotechnology, Board Services, Consumer Products,
Financial Services, High Technology, Pharmaceutical/Medical, Venture Capital;
**Function Concentration:** Generalist with a primary focus in
Finance/Accounting, General Management

**Thomas, William** — *Senior Principal*
Mixtec Group
31255 Cedar Valley Drive
Suite 300-327
Westlake Village, CA 91362
Telephone: (818) 889-8819
**Recruiter Classification:** Contingency; **Lowest/Average Salary:** $60,000/$90,000;
**Industry Concentration:** High Technology; **Function Concentration:** Generalist
with a primary focus in Administration, General Management

**Thompson, Brett** — *Recruiting Manager*
Southwestern Professional Services
2451 Atrium Way
Nashville, TN 37214
Telephone: (615) 391-2722
**Recruiter Classification:** Contingency; **Lowest/Average Salary:**
$30,000/$60,000; **Industry Concentration:** Publishing/Media; **Function
Concentration:** Human Resources, Marketing, Sales

**Thompson, Carlton W.** — *Senior Director*
Spencer Stuart
Financial Centre
695 East Main Street
Stamford, CT 06901
Telephone: (203) 324-6333
**Recruiter Classification:** Retained; **Lowest/Average Salary:** $90,000/$90,000;
**Industry Concentration:** Entertainment, Publishing/Media; **Function
Concentration:** Generalist with a primary focus in General Management

**Thompson, Dave** — *Director West Coast Operations*
Battalia Winston International
One Sansome Street, Suite 2100
Citicorp Center
San Francisco, CA 94104
Telephone: (415) 984-3180
**Recruiter Classification:** Retained; **Lowest/Average Salary:** $90,000/$90,000;
**Industry Concentration:** Financial Services, Healthcare/Hospitals, Information
Technology, Manufacturing; **Function Concentration:** Generalist with a
primary focus in General Management, Human Resources, Marketing, Sales

**Thompson, James R.** — *Vice President*
Gordon Wahls Company
P.O. Box 905
610 East Baltimore Pike
Media, PA 19063
Telephone: (610) 565-0800
**Recruiter Classification:** Contingency; **Lowest/Average Salary:**
$30,000/$60,000; **Industry Concentration:** Packaging, Publishing/Media;
**Function Concentration:** Generalist with a primary focus in Administration,
Engineering, Finance/Accounting, General Management, Marketing, Sales

**Thompson, Jim E.** — *Manager Southwest Region*
Management Recruiters International, Inc.
8214 Westchester Avenue, Suite 500
Dallas, TX 75225
Telephone: (214) 692-3520
**Recruiter Classification:** Contingency; **Lowest/Average Salary:** $30,000/$75,000;
**Industry Concentration:** Generalist; **Function Concentration:** Generalist

**Thompson, John R.** — *Executive Recruiter*
MSI International
229 Peachtree Street, NE
Suite 1201
Atlanta, GA 30303
Telephone: (404) 659-5050
**Recruiter Classification:** Contingency; **Lowest/Average Salary:**
$30,000/$60,000; **Industry Concentration:** Generalist with a primary focus in
Financial Services; **Function Concentration:** Administration, Engineering,
Finance/Accounting, General Management, Marketing

**Thompson, John T.** — *Vice Chairman*
Heidrick & Struggles, Inc.
2740 Sand Hill Road
Menlo Park, CA 94025
Telephone: (415) 854-9300
**Recruiter Classification:** Retained; **Lowest/Average Salary:** $75,000/$90,000;
**Industry Concentration:** Generalist; **Function Concentration:** Generalist

**Thompson, Kenneth L.** — *Partner*
McCormack & Farrow
695 Town Center Drive
Suite 660
Costa Mesa, CA 92626
Telephone: (714) 549-7222
**Recruiter Classification:** Retained; **Lowest/Average Salary:** $75,000/$90,000;
**Industry Concentration:** Generalist with a primary focus in
Aerospace/Defense, Financial Services, Healthcare/Hospitals, High
Technology, Information Technology, Manufacturing, Pharmaceutical/Medical,
Publishing/Media, Transportation; **Function Concentration:** Generalist with a
primary focus in Administration, Engineering, Finance/Accounting, General
Management, Human Resources, Marketing, Research and Development

**Thompson, Leslie** — *Associate*
Source Services Corporation
879 West 190th Street, Suite 250
Los Angeles, CA 90248
Telephone: (310) 323-6633
**Recruiter Classification:** Contingency; **Lowest/Average Salary:**
$30,000/$50,000; **Industry Concentration:** Financial Services, Information
Technology; **Function Concentration:** Engineering, Finance/Accounting

**Thompson, Timothy W.** — *Vice President*
Korn/Ferry International
One Landmark Square
Stamford, CT 06901
Telephone: (203) 359-3350
**Recruiter Classification:** Retained; **Lowest/Average Salary:** $90,000/$90,000;
**Industry Concentration:** Generalist; **Function Concentration:** Generalist

**Thomson, Alexander G.** — *Associate*
Russell Reynolds Associates, Inc.
Old City Hall, 45 School Street
Boston, MA 02108
Telephone: (617) 523-1111
**Recruiter Classification:** Retained; **Lowest/Average Salary:** $90,000/$90,000;
**Industry Concentration:** Generalist with a primary focus in Financial Services;
**Function Concentration:** Generalist

**Thornton, John C.** — *President*
Thornton Resources
9800 McKnight Road
Pittsburgh, PA 15237
Telephone: (412) 364-2111
**Recruiter Classification:** Contingency, Executive Temporary; **Lowest/Average
Salary:** $40,000/$50,000; **Industry Concentration:** Generalist with a primary
focus in Board Services, Consumer Products, Financial Services, Non-Profit;
**Function Concentration:** Generalist with a primary focus in General
Management, Human Resources

**Thorpe, David L.** — *President*
IMCOR, Inc.
100 Prospect Street, North Tower
Stamford, CT 06901
Telephone: (203) 975-8000
**Recruiter Classification:** Executive Temporary; **Lowest/Average Salary:**
$75,000/$90,000; **Industry Concentration:** Generalist; **Function
Concentration:** Generalist

**Thrower, Tom S.** — *Manager Pacific Region*
Management Recruiters International, Inc.
480 Roland Way, Suite 103
Oakland, CA 94621-2065
Telephone: (510) 635-7901
**Recruiter Classification:** Contingency; **Lowest/Average Salary:**
$30,000/$75,000; **Industry Concentration:** Generalist; **Function
Concentration:** Generalist

**Thrower, Troy** — *Associate*
Source Services Corporation
2029 Century Park East, Suite 1350
Los Angeles, CA 90067
Telephone: (310) 277-8092
**Recruiter Classification:** Contingency; **Lowest/Average Salary:**
$30,000/$50,000; **Industry Concentration:** Financial Services, Information
Technology; **Function Concentration:** Engineering, Finance/Accounting

**Tice, Diane** — *Branch Manager*
Accountants on Call
17700 Castleton Street, Suite 265
City of Industry, CA 91748
Telephone: (818) 912-0090
**Recruiter Classification:** Contingency; **Lowest/Average Salary:**
$20,000/$30,000; **Industry Concentration:** Generalist; **Function
Concentration:** Finance/Accounting

**Tierney, Eileen** — *Senior Vice President*
The Whitney Group
850 Third Avenue, 11th Floor
New York, NY 10022
Telephone: (212) 508-3500
**Recruiter Classification:** Retained; **Lowest/Average Salary:** $75,000/$90,000;
**Industry Concentration:** Generalist with a primary focus in Financial Services,
Real Estate, Venture Capital; **Function Concentration:** Generalist with a
primary focus in Sales

**Tilley, Kyle** — *Associate*
Source Services Corporation
10300 West 103rd Street, Suite 101
Overland Park, KS 66214
Telephone: (913) 888-8885
**Recruiter Classification:** Contingency; **Lowest/Average Salary:**
$30,000/$50,000; **Industry Concentration:** Financial Services, Information
Technology; **Function Concentration:** Engineering, Finance/Accounting

**Tillman, J. Robert** — *Executive Director*
Russell Reynolds Associates, Inc.
200 South Wacker Drive
Suite 3600
Chicago, IL 60606
Telephone: (312) 993-9696
**Recruiter Classification:** Retained; **Lowest/Average Salary:** $90,000/$90,000;
**Industry Concentration:** Generalist with a primary focus in Financial Services;
**Function Concentration:** Generalist

**Timms, Alan R.** — *Senior Vice President/Managing Director*
DHR International, Inc.
44 Montgomery Street, Fifth Floor
San Francisco, CA 94104
Telephone: (415) 955-2787
**Recruiter Classification:** Retained; **Lowest/Average Salary:** $60,000/$90,000;
**Industry Concentration:** Generalist; **Function Concentration:** Generalist

**Timoney, Laura** — *Vice President*
Bishop Partners
708 Third Avenue
New York, NY 10017
Telephone: (212) 986-3419
**Recruiter Classification:** Retained; **Lowest/Average Salary:** $90,000/$90,000;
**Industry Concentration:** Entertainment, Information Technology,
Publishing/Media; **Function Concentration:** Generalist with a primary focus in
General Management, Marketing, Sales, Women/Minorities

**Tingle, Trina A.** — *Executive Recruiter*
MSI International
1050 Crown Pointe Parkway
Suite 1000
Atlanta, GA 30338
Telephone: (404) 394-2494
**Recruiter Classification:** Contingency; **Lowest/Average Salary:**
$30,000/$75,000; **Industry Concentration:** Generalist with a primary focus in
Financial Services; **Function Concentration:** Generalist with a primary focus in
Finance/Accounting

**Tinucci, Crystal M.** — *Consultant*
Witt/Kieffer, Ford, Hadelman & Lloyd
2015 Spring Road, Suite 510
Oak Brook, IL 60521
Telephone: (708) 990-1370
**Recruiter Classification:** Retained; **Lowest/Average Salary:** $75,000/$90,000;
**Industry Concentration:** Healthcare/Hospitals; **Function Concentration:**
Generalist with a primary focus in General Management

**Tipp, George** — *Executive Director Healthcare*
Intech Summit Group, Inc.
5075 Shoreham Place, Suite 280
San Diego, CA 92122
Telephone: (619) 452-2100
**Recruiter Classification:** Retained; **Lowest/Average Salary:** $75,000/$90,000;
**Industry Concentration:** Healthcare/Hospitals, Information Technology;
**Function Concentration:** Administration, General Management, Marketing,
Sales

**Tipping, William M.** — *Managing Director*
Ward Howell International, Inc.
3350 Peachtree Road N.E.
Suite 1600
Atlanta, GA 30326
Telephone: (404) 261-6532
**Recruiter Classification:** Retained; **Lowest/Average Salary:** $75,000/$90,000;
**Industry Concentration:** Consumer Products, Education/Libraries, Non-Profit,
Utilities/Nuclear; **Function Concentration:** Generalist with a primary focus in
Women/Minorities

**Titterington, Catherine F.** — *Physician Recruiter*
MSI International
201 St. Charles Avenue
Suite 2205
New Orleans, LA 70170
Telephone: (504) 522-6700
**Recruiter Classification:** Contingency; **Lowest/Average Salary:**
$30,000/$60,000; **Industry Concentration:** Generalist with a primary focus in
Healthcare/Hospitals; **Function Concentration:** Generalist with a primary focus
in Administration, Engineering, Finance/Accounting, General Management,
Marketing, Sales

**Titus, Dave** — *Manager South Atlantic Region*
Management Recruiters International, Inc.
160 East Summerling Street, Suite 208
Bartow, FL 33830
Telephone: (941) 533-0505
**Recruiter Classification:** Contingency; **Lowest/Average Salary:**
$30,000/$75,000; **Industry Concentration:** Generalist; **Function
Concentration:** Generalist

**To, Raymond** — *Technical Recruiter*
Corporate Recruiters Ltd.
490-1140 West Pender
Vancouver, British Columbia, CANADA V6E 4G1
Telephone: (604) 687-5993
Recruiter Classification: Contingency; **Lowest/Average Salary:**
$30,000/$50,000; Industry Concentration: Electronics, High Technology;
Function Concentration: Engineering, Research and Development

**Tobin, Christopher** — *Associate*
Source Services Corporation
One South Main Street, Suite 1440
Dayton, OH 45402
Telephone: (513) 461-4660
Recruiter Classification: Contingency; **Lowest/Average Salary:**
$30,000/$50,000; Industry Concentration: Financial Services, Information
Technology; Function Concentration: Engineering, Finance/Accounting

**Tobin, Jim** — *Senior Consultant*
Barton Raben, Inc.
One Riverway, Suite 2500
Houston, TX 77056
Telephone: (713) 961-9111
Recruiter Classification: Retained; **Lowest/Average Salary:** $75,000/$90,000;
Industry Concentration: Generalist with a primary focus in Electronics,
Information Technology, Oil/Gas; Function Concentration: Generalist with a
primary focus in Administration, Engineering, Finance/Accounting, Human
Resources

**Tobin, William** — *Vice President*
Korn/Ferry International
Presidential Plaza
900 19th Street, N.W.
Washington, DC 20006
Telephone: (202) 822-9444
Recruiter Classification: Retained; **Lowest/Average Salary:** $90,000/$90,000;
Industry Concentration: Generalist with a primary focus in
Aerospace/Defense; Function Concentration: Generalist

**Tokarcik, Patricia** — *Executive Vice President*
ProResource, Inc.
500 Ohio Savings Plaza
1801 East Ninth Street, Suite 500
Cleveland, OH 44114
Telephone: (216) 579-1515
Recruiter Classification: Executive Temporary; **Lowest/Average Salary:**
$30,000/$75,000; Industry Concentration: Generalist; **Function**
Concentration: Generalist with a primary focus in Engineering,
Finance/Accounting, General Management, Human Resources, Marketing,
Research and Development

**Tokash, Ronald E.** — *Executive Recruiter*
MSI International
8521 Leesburg Pike, Suite 435
Vienna, VA 22182
Telephone: (703) 893-5669
Recruiter Classification: Contingency; **Lowest/Average Salary:**
$30,000/$60,000; Industry Concentration: Generalist with a primary focus in
Healthcare/Hospitals; Function Concentration: Administration, Engineering,
Finance/Accounting, General Management, Marketing

**Tolle, David W.** — *Manager Midwest Region*
Management Recruiters International, Inc.
1405 Lafayette Avenue, Box 461
Mattoon, IL 61938
Telephone: (217) 235-9393
Recruiter Classification: Contingency; **Lowest/Average Salary:**
$30,000/$75,000; Industry Concentration: Generalist; **Function**
Concentration: Generalist

**Toms, Evangeline** — *Associate*
Nordeman Grimm, Inc.
717 Fifth Avenue, 26th Floor
New York, NY 10022
Telephone: (212) 935-1000
Recruiter Classification: Retained; **Lowest/Average Salary:** $90,000/$90,000;
Industry Concentration: Generalist; Function Concentration: Generalist

**Tonjuk, Tina** — *Manager Associate Relations*
The Paladin Companies, Inc.
875 North Michigan Avenue, Suite 3218
Chicago, IL 60611
Telephone: (312) 654-2600
Recruiter Classification: Executive Temporary; **Lowest/Average Salary:**
$50,000/$90,000; Industry Concentration: Generalist; **Function**
Concentration: Marketing

**Toole, Mary** — *Co-Manager Pacific Region*
Management Recruiters International, Inc.
23461 South Pointe Drive, Suite 390
Laguna Hills, CA 92653
Telephone: (714) 768-9112
Recruiter Classification: Contingency; **Lowest/Average Salary:**
$30,000/$75,000; Industry Concentration: Generalist; **Function**
Concentration: Generalist

**Toole, Tom J.** — *Co-Manager*
Management Recruiters International, Inc.
23461 South Pointe Drive, Suite 390
Laguna Hills, CA 92653
Telephone: (714) 768-9112
Recruiter Classification: Contingency; **Lowest/Average Salary:**
$30,000/$75,000; Industry Concentration: Generalist; **Function**
Concentration: Generalist

**Tootsey, Mark A.** — *Recruiter*
A.J. Burton Group, Inc.
35 Wisconsin Circle, Suite 250
Chevy Chase, MD 20815
Telephone: (301) 654-0082
Recruiter Classification: Contingency, Executive Temporary; **Lowest/Average
Salary:** $40,000/$60,000; Industry Concentration: Education/Libraries, Energy,
Fashion (Retail/Apparel), Financial Services, Healthcare/Hospitals,
Manufacturing, Venture Capital; Function Concentration: Finance/Accounting

**Torbert, Laura** — *Vice President*
Temporary Accounting Personnel Inc.
1801 Broadway, Suite 810
Denver, CO 80202
Telephone: (303) 297-8367
Recruiter Classification: Executive Temporary; **Lowest/Average Salary:**
$30,000/$40,000; Industry Concentration: Generalist; **Function**
Concentration: Administration, Finance/Accounting, Women/Minorities

**Toson, James** — *Manager Automotive Aftermarket*
Prestige Inc.
P.O. Box 421
Reedsburg, WI 53959
Telephone: (608) 524-4032
Recruiter Classification: Contingency; **Lowest/Average Salary:**
$50,000/$90,000; Industry Concentration: Automotive; **Function**
Concentration: Generalist

**Tovrog, Dan** — *Executive Recruiter*
CPS Inc.
One Westbrook Corporate Centre, Suite 600
Westchester, IL 60154
Telephone: (708) 531-8370
Recruiter Classification: Contingency; **Lowest/Average Salary:**
$30,000/$50,000; Industry Concentration: Generalist with a primary focus in
Automotive, Biotechnology, Chemical Products, Consumer Products, High
Technology, Insurance, Manufacturing, Oil/Gas, Packaging,
Pharmaceutical/Medical; Function Concentration: Engineering, Research and
Development, Sales, Women/Minorities

**Tracey, Garvis** — *Placement Specialist*
Key Employment Services
1001 Office Park Road, Suite 320
West Des Moines, IA 50265-2567
Telephone: (515) 224-0446
Recruiter Classification: Contingency; **Lowest/Average Salary:**
$30,000/$75,000; Industry Concentration: Generalist; **Function**
Concentration: Generalist

**Tracey, Jack** — *President*
Management Assistance Group, Inc.
10 North Main Street
West Hartford, CT 06107
Telephone: (203) 523-0000
Recruiter Classification: Executive Temporary; **Lowest/Average Salary:**
$40,000/$60,000; Industry Concentration: Generalist with a primary focus in
Aerospace/Defense, Biotechnology, Consumer Products, Financial Services,
Healthcare/Hospitals, Insurance, Manufacturing, Real Estate; **Function**
Concentration: Generalist with a primary focus in Administration, Engineering,
Finance/Accounting, General Management, Human Resources, Marketing,
Research and Development, Sales

**Tracy, Ronald O.** — *Consultant*
Egon Zehnder International Inc.
One First National Plaza
21 South Clark Street, Suite 3300
Chicago, IL 60603-2006
Telephone: (312) 782-4500
Recruiter Classification: Retained; **Lowest/Average Salary:** $90,000/$90,000;
Industry Concentration: Generalist with a primary focus in Biotechnology,
Financial Services, High Technology, Manufacturing, Pharmaceutical/Medical;
Function Concentration: Generalist·

**Trapp, Ed** — *Manager Pacific Region*
Management Recruiters International, Inc.
1025 Ridgeview Drive, Suite 100
Reno, NV 89509
Telephone: (702) 826-5243
**Recruiter Classification:** Contingency; **Lowest/Average Salary:**
$30,000/$75,000; **Industry Concentration:** Generalist; **Function
Concentration:** Generalist

**Trautman, William E.** — *Vice President*
A.T. Kearney, Inc.
153 East 53rd Street
New York, NY 10022
Telephone: (212) 751-7040
**Recruiter Classification:** Retained; **Lowest/Average Salary:** $90,000/$90,000;
**Industry Concentration:** Generalist; **Function Concentration:** Generalist

**Trautman, William E.** — *Senior Vice President*
Boyden
375 Park Avenue, Suite 1509
New York, NY 10152
Telephone: (212) 980-6480
**Recruiter Classification:** Retained; **Lowest/Average Salary:** $75,000/$90,000;
**Industry Concentration:** Generalist with a primary focus in Financial Services;
**Function Concentration:** Generalist with a primary focus in
Finance/Accounting

**Travis, Ed** — *General Manager*
Management Recruiters International, Inc.
Meramec Valley Center
200 Fabricator Drive
Fenton, MO 63026
Telephone: (314) 349-4455
**Recruiter Classification:** Contingency; **Lowest/Average Salary:**
$30,000/$75,000; **Industry Concentration:** Generalist; **Function
Concentration:** Generalist

**Trefzer, Kristie** — *Associate*
Source Services Corporation
150 South Wacker Drive, Suite 400
Chicago, IL 60606
Telephone: (312) 346-7000
**Recruiter Classification:** Contingency; **Lowest/Average Salary:**
$30,000/$50,000; **Industry Concentration:** Financial Services, Information
Technology; **Function Concentration:** Engineering, Finance/Accounting

**Trent, Alex** — *Consultant*
Vera L. Rast Partners, Inc.
One South Wacker Drive, Suite 3890
Chicago, IL 60606
Telephone: (312) 629-0339
**Recruiter Classification:** Contingency; **Lowest/Average Salary:**
$50,000/$90,000

**Trewhella, Michael** — *Managing Director*
Source Services Corporation
161 Ottawa NW, Suite 409D
Grand Rapids, MI 49503
Telephone: (616) 451-2400
**Recruiter Classification:** Contingency; **Lowest/Average Salary:**
$30,000/$50,000; **Industry Concentration:** Financial Services, Information
Technology; **Function Concentration:** Engineering, Finance/Accounting

**Tribbett, Charles A.** — *Managing Director/Area Co-Manager*
Russell Reynolds Associates, Inc.
200 South Wacker Drive
Suite 3600
Chicago, IL 60606
Telephone: (312) 993-9696
**Recruiter Classification:** Retained; **Lowest/Average Salary:** $90,000/$90,000;
**Industry Concentration:** Generalist; **Function Concentration:** Generalist

**Trice, Renee** — *Associate*
Source Services Corporation
Foster Plaza VI
681 Anderson Drive, 2nd Floor
Pittsburgh, PA 15220
Telephone: (412) 928-8300
**Recruiter Classification:** Contingency; **Lowest/Average Salary:**
$30,000/$50,000; **Industry Concentration:** Financial Services, Information
Technology; **Function Concentration:** Engineering, Finance/Accounting

**Trieschmann, Daniel** — *Associate*
Source Services Corporation
One CityPlace, Suite 170
St. Louis, MO 63141
Telephone: (314) 432-4500
**Recruiter Classification:** Contingency; **Lowest/Average Salary:**
$30,000/$50,000; **Industry Concentration:** Financial Services, Information
Technology; **Function Concentration:** Engineering, Finance/Accounting

**Trimble, Patricia** — *Associate*
Source Services Corporation
15260 Ventura Boulevard, Suite 380
Sherman Oaks, CA 91403
Telephone: (818) 905-1500
**Recruiter Classification:** Contingency; **Lowest/Average Salary:**
$30,000/$50,000; **Industry Concentration:** Financial Services, Information
Technology; **Function Concentration:** Engineering, Finance/Accounting

**Trimble, Rhonda** — *Associate*
Source Services Corporation
7730 East Bellview Avenue, Suite 302
Englewood, CO 80111
Telephone: (303) 773-3700
**Recruiter Classification:** Contingency; **Lowest/Average Salary:**
$30,000/$50,000; **Industry Concentration:** Financial Services, Information
Technology; **Function Concentration:** Engineering, Finance/Accounting

**Tripp, William J.** — *General Manager*
Management Recruiters International, Inc.
Parklane Towers West, Suite 1224
Three Parklane Boulevard
Dearborn, MI 48126-2502
Telephone: (313) 336-6650
**Recruiter Classification:** Contingency; **Lowest/Average Salary:**
$30,000/$75,000; **Industry Concentration:** Generalist; **Function
Concentration:** Generalist

**Trivedi, Jay** — *Senior Technical Recruiter*
Search Enterprises, Inc.
160 Quail Ridge Drive
Westmont, IL 60559
Telephone: (708) 654-2300
**Recruiter Classification:** Contingency; **Lowest/Average Salary:**
$20,000/$50,000; **Industry Concentration:** Chemical Products; **Function
Concentration:** Engineering

**Trosin, Walter R.** — *Partner*
Johnson Smith & Knisely Accord
100 Park Avenue, 15th Floor
New York, NY 10017
Telephone: (212) 885-9100
**Recruiter Classification:** Retained; **Lowest/Average Salary:** $90,000/$90,000;
**Industry Concentration:** Biotechnology, Healthcare/Hospitals,
Pharmaceutical/Medical; **Function Concentration:** Generalist with a primary
focus in Administration, Engineering, General Management, Human
Resources, Marketing, Research and Development, Sales, Women/Minorities

**Trott, Kathryn** — *Partner*
Allard Associates
44 Montgomery Street, Suite 500
San Francisco, CA 94104
Telephone: (415) 433-0500
**Recruiter Classification:** Retained; **Lowest/Average Salary:** $60,000/$90,000;
**Industry Concentration:** Financial Services; **Function Concentration:**
Generalist with a primary focus in Administration, General Management,
Marketing, Research and Development, Sales, Women/Minorities

**Trott, Kathryn** — *Partner*
Allard Associates
39811 Sharon Avenue
Davis, CA 95616
Telephone: (916) 757-1649
**Recruiter Classification:** Retained; **Lowest/Average Salary:** $60,000/$75,000;
**Industry Concentration:** Financial Services; **Function Concentration:**
Generalist with a primary focus in Administration, General Management,
Marketing, Sales, Women/Minorities

**Troup, Roger** — *Consultant*
The McCormick Group, Inc.
1400 Wilson Boulevard
Arlington, VA 22209
Telephone: (703) 841-1700
**Recruiter Classification:** Retained; **Lowest/Average Salary:** $40,000/$75,000;
**Industry Concentration:** Insurance; **Function Concentration:** Human
Resources

**Truax, Kevin** — *Placement Specialist*
Key Employment Services
1001 Office Park Road, Suite 320
West Des Moines, IA 50265-2567
Telephone: (515) 224-0446
**Recruiter Classification:** Contingency; **Lowest/Average Salary:**
$30,000/$75,000; **Industry Concentration:** Insurance; **Function
Concentration:** General Management

**Trueblood, Brian G.** — *Vice President*
TNS Partners, Inc.
12655 North Central Expressway
Suite 900
Dallas, TX 75243
Telephone: (214) 991-3555
**Recruiter Classification:** Retained; **Lowest/Average Salary:** $90,000/$90,000;
**Industry Concentration:** Generalist with a primary focus in
Aerospace/Defense, Automotive, Biotechnology, Consumer Products,
Electronics, Financial Services, High Technology, Information Technology,
Manufacturing, Publishing/Media, Transportation, Venture Capital; **Function
Concentration:** Generalist with a primary focus in Administration, Engineering,
Finance/Accounting, General Management, Human Resources, Marketing,
Sales

**Truemper, Dean** — *Executive Recruiter*
CPS Inc.
One Westbrook Corporate Centre, Suite 600
Westchester, IL 60154
Telephone: (708) 531-8370
**Recruiter Classification:** Contingency; **Lowest/Average Salary:**
$30,000/$50,000; **Industry Concentration:** Generalist with a primary focus in
Automotive, Biotechnology, Chemical Products, Consumer Products, High
Technology, Insurance, Manufacturing, Oil/Gas, Packaging,
Pharmaceutical/Medical; **Function Concentration:** Engineering, Research and
Development, Sales, Women/Minorities

**Truex, John F.** — *Vice President*
Morton, McCorkle & Associates, Inc.
2190 South Mason Road, Suite 309
St. Louis, MO 63131-1637
Telephone: (314) 984-9494
**Recruiter Classification:** Retained; **Lowest/Average Salary:** $30,000/$40,000;
**Industry Concentration:** Generalist with a primary focus in Chemical Products,
Consumer Products, Education/Libraries, Financial Services,
Healthcare/Hospitals, Hospitality/Leisure, Manufacturing, Non-Profit,
Pharmaceutical/Medical, Public Administration, Transportation; **Function
Concentration:** Generalist with a primary focus in Administration, Engineering,
Finance/Accounting, General Management, Human Resources, Marketing,
Sales, Women/Minorities

**Truitt, Thomas B.** — *Senior Manager*
Southwestern Professional Services
2451 Atrium Way
Nashville, TN 37214
Telephone: (615) 391-2722
**Recruiter Classification:** Contingency; **Lowest/Average Salary:**
$60,000/$90,000; **Industry Concentration:** Aerospace/Defense, Automotive,
Chemical Products, Consumer Products, Electronics, Energy, Financial
Services, Healthcare/Hospitals, High Technology, Information Technology,
Manufacturing, Oil/Gas, Packaging, Transportation; **Function Concentration:**
Engineering, Finance/Accounting, General Management

**Truvillion, Mary** — *Branch Manager*
Accountants on Call
911 Main Street, Suite 620
Commerce Tower
Kansas City, MO 64105
Telephone: (816) 421-7774
**Recruiter Classification:** Contingency; **Lowest/Average Salary:**
$20,000/$30,000; **Industry Concentration:** Generalist; **Function
Concentration:** Finance/Accounting

**Tryon, Katey** — *Senior Vice President - Practice Leader*
DeFrain, Mayer, Lee & Burgess LLC
6900 College Boulevard
Overland Park, KS 66211
Telephone: (913) 345-0500
**Recruiter Classification:** Retained; **Lowest/Average Salary:** $60,000/$90,000;
**Industry Concentration:** Generalist with a primary focus in Automotive,
Chemical Products, Consumer Products, Electronics, Energy, Environmental,
Financial Services, Healthcare/Hospitals, High Technology, Insurance,
Manufacturing, Non-Profit, Oil/Gas, Real Estate; **Function Concentration:**
Generalist with a primary focus in Engineering, Finance/Accounting, General
Management, Human Resources, Marketing, Sales

**Tscelli, Maureen** — *Associate*
Source Services Corporation
155 Federal Street, Suite 410
Boston, MA 02110
Telephone: (617) 482-8211
**Recruiter Classification:** Contingency; **Lowest/Average Salary:**
$30,000/$50,000; **Industry Concentration:** Financial Services, Information
Technology; **Function Concentration:** Engineering, Finance/Accounting

**Tschan, Stephen** — *Associate*
Source Services Corporation
3 Summit Park Drive, Suite 550
Independence, OH 44131
Telephone: (216) 328-5900
**Recruiter Classification:** Contingency; **Lowest/Average Salary:**
$30,000/$50,000; **Industry Concentration:** Financial Services, Information
Technology; **Function Concentration:** Engineering, Finance/Accounting

**Tucci, Joseph** — *Executive Vice President*
Fairfaxx Corporation
17 High Street
Norwalk, CT 06851
Telephone: (203) 838-8300
**Recruiter Classification:** Retained; **Lowest/Average Salary:** $60,000/$90,000;
**Industry Concentration:** Generalist with a primary focus in Consumer Products,
Entertainment, Fashion (Retail/Apparel), Venture Capital; **Function
Concentration:** Generalist with a primary focus in Engineering,
Finance/Accounting, General Management, Human Resources, Marketing, Sales

**Tucker, Thomas A.** — *Principal*
The Thomas Tucker Company
425 California Street, Suite 2502
San Francisco, CA 94104
Telephone: (415) 693-5900
**Recruiter Classification:** Retained; **Lowest/Average Salary:** $90,000/$90,000;
**Industry Concentration:** Generalist with a primary focus in Board Services,
Consumer Products, Electronics, Energy, Entertainment, Financial Services,
High Technology, Information Technology, Manufacturing, Oil/Gas,
Publishing/Media, Utilities/Nuclear, Venture Capital; **Function Concentration:**
Generalist with a primary focus in Engineering, Finance/Accounting, General
Management, Human Resources, Marketing, Research and Development

**Tufenkjian, Richard** — *Vice President*
C.A. Durakis Associates, Inc.
620 Massachusetts Avenue
Cambridge, MA 02138
Telephone: (617) 497-7769
**Recruiter Classification:** Retained; **Lowest/Average Salary:** $90,000/$90,000;
**Industry Concentration:** Generalist; **Function Concentration:** Generalist

**Tullberg, Tina** — *Executive Recruiter*
CPS Inc.
One Westbrook Corporate Centre, Suite 600
Westchester, IL 60154
Telephone: (708) 531-8370
**Recruiter Classification:** Contingency; **Lowest/Average Salary:**
$30,000/$50,000; **Industry Concentration:** Generalist with a primary focus in
Automotive, Biotechnology, Chemical Products, Consumer Products, High
Technology, Insurance, Manufacturing, Oil/Gas, Packaging,
Pharmaceutical/Medical; **Function Concentration:** Engineering, Research and
Development, Sales, Women/Minorities

**Tully, Thomas** — *Technical Recruiter*
Search Enterprises, Inc.
160 Quail Ridge Drive
Westmont, IL 60559
Telephone: (708) 654-2300
**Recruiter Classification:** Contingency; **Lowest/Average Salary:** $20,000/$50,000;
**Industry Concentration:** Chemical Products; **Function Concentration:** Engineering

**Tunney, William** — *Vice President*
Grant Cooper and Associates
795 Office Parkway, Suite 117
St. Louis, MO 63141
Telephone: (314) 567-4690
**Recruiter Classification:** Retained; **Lowest/Average Salary:** $60,000/$90,000;
**Industry Concentration:** Generalist with a primary focus in Board Services,
Consumer Products, Electronics, Healthcare/Hospitals,
Manufacturing, Non-Profit, Pharmaceutical/Medical; **Function Concentration:**
Generalist with a primary focus in Administration, Engineering,
Finance/Accounting, General Management, Human Resources, Marketing, Sales

**Turnblacer, John** — *President*
The Gabriel Group
1515 Market Street, Suite 504
Philadelphia, PA 19102
Telephone: (215) 496-9990
**Recruiter Classification:** Retained; **Lowest/Average Salary:** $90,000/$90,000;
**Industry Concentration:** Generalist; **Function Concentration:** Generalist

**Turner, Allan W.** — *Co-Manager*
Management Recruiters International, Inc.
Village Square Mall, Suite 1
Highway 258 North, P.O. Box 219
Kinston, NC 28502-0219
Telephone: (919) 527-9191
**Recruiter Classification:** Contingency; **Lowest/Average Salary:**
$30,000/$75,000; **Industry Concentration:** Generalist; **Function
Concentration:** Generalist

**Turner, Brad** — *Manager Midwest Region*
Management Recruiters International, Inc.
8700 Monrovia, Suite 213
Lenexa, KS 66215-3500
Telephone: (913) 533-6602
**Recruiter Classification:** Contingency; **Lowest/Average Salary:** $30,000/$75,000;
**Industry Concentration:** Generalist; **Function Concentration:** Generalist

**Turner, Edward K.** — *President*
Don Richard Associates of Charlotte
2650 One First Union Center
301 South College Street
Charlotte, NC 28202-6000
Telephone: (704) 377-6447
**Recruiter Classification:** Contingency, Executive Temporary; **Lowest/Average
Salary:** $75,000/$75,000; **Industry Concentration:** Energy, Entertainment,
Financial Services, Healthcare/Hospitals, High Technology, Hospitality/Leisure,
Information Technology, Insurance, Manufacturing, Packaging,
Publishing/Media, Real Estate, Transportation; **Function Concentration:**
Finance/Accounting, General Management, Human Resources

**Turner, Elaine** — *Consultant*
Witt/Kieffer, Ford, Hadelman & Lloyd
1920 Main Street, Suite 310
Irvine, CA 92714
Telephone: (714) 851-5070
**Recruiter Classification:** Retained; **Lowest/Average Salary:** $75,000/$90,000;
**Industry Concentration:** Healthcare/Hospitals; **Function Concentration:**
Generalist

**Turner, Marilyn** — *President*
Temporary Accounting Personnel Inc.
1801 Broadway, Suite 810
Denver, CO 80202
Telephone: (303) 297-8367
**Recruiter Classification:** Executive Temporary; **Lowest/Average Salary:**
$30,000/$40,000; **Industry Concentration:** Generalist; **Function
Concentration:** Administration, Finance/Accounting, Women/Minorities

**Turner, Michael** — *President*
Rocky Mountain Recruiters, Inc.
1801 Broadway, Suite 810
Denver, CO 80202
Telephone: (303) 296-2000
**Recruiter Classification:** Contingency; **Lowest/Average Salary:**
$30,000/$50,000; **Industry Concentration:** Generalist; **Function
Concentration:** Finance/Accounting

**Turner, Raymond** — *Managing Director*
Source Services Corporation
111 Founders Plaza, Suite 1501E
Hartford, CT 06108
Telephone: (860) 528-0300
**Recruiter Classification:** Contingency; **Lowest/Average Salary:**
$30,000/$50,000; **Industry Concentration:** Financial Services, Information
Technology; **Function Concentration:** Engineering, Finance/Accounting

**Tursi, Deborah J.** — *Sales Recruiter*
The Corporate Connection, Ltd.
7202 Glen Forest Drive
Richmond, VA 23226
Telephone: (804) 288-8844
**Recruiter Classification:** Contingency; **Lowest/Average Salary:**
$20,000/$30,000; **Industry Concentration:** Aerospace/Defense, Chemical
Products, Consumer Products, Environmental, Financial Services, Information
Technology, Insurance, Manufacturing, Non-Profit, Pharmaceutical/Medical,
Transportation; **Function Concentration:** Sales

**Tutwiler, Stephen** — *President*
Don Richard Associates of Tampa, Inc.
100 North Tampa Street, Suite 1925
Tampa, FL 33602
Telephone: (813) 221-7930
**Recruiter Classification:** Contingency, Executive Temporary; **Lowest/Average
Salary:** $20,000/$50,000; **Industry Concentration:** Generalist with a primary
focus in Aerospace/Defense, Energy, Entertainment, Environmental, Financial
Services, Insurance, Manufacturing, Pharmaceutical/Medical; **Function
Concentration:** Generalist with a primary focus in Finance/Accounting,
General Management

**Tweed, Janet** — *Chief Executive Officer*
Gilbert Tweed/INESA
415 Madison Avenue
New York, NY 10017
Telephone: (212) 758-3000
**Recruiter Classification:** Retained; **Lowest/Average Salary:** $90,000/$90,000;
**Industry Concentration:** Generalist with a primary focus in Automotive,
Biotechnology, Chemical Products, Consumer Products, Entertainment,
Financial Services, Healthcare/Hospitals, High Technology, Manufacturing,
Packaging, Pharmaceutical/Medical, Real Estate, Transportation, Venture
Capital; **Function Concentration:** Generalist with a primary focus in
Engineering, Finance/Accounting, General Management, Human Resources,
Marketing, Research and Development, Sales

**Twiste, Craig** — *Senior Consultant*
Raymond Karsan Associates
3725 National Drive, Suite 115
Raleigh, NC 27612
Telephone: (919) 571-1690
**Recruiter Classification:** Contingency; **Lowest/Average Salary:**
$30,000/$90,000; **Industry Concentration:** Generalist with a primary focus in
Biotechnology, Chemical Products, Environmental, Healthcare/Hospitals,
Information Technology, Insurance, Manufacturing, Pharmaceutical/Medical;
**Function Concentration:** Generalist

**Twomey, James** — *Managing Director*
Source Services Corporation
20 Burlington Mall Road, Suite 405
Burlington, MA 01803
Telephone: (617) 272-5000
**Recruiter Classification:** Contingency; **Lowest/Average Salary:**
$30,000/$50,000; **Industry Concentration:** Financial Services, Information
Technology; **Function Concentration:** Engineering, Finance/Accounting

**Tydings, Mary C.** — *Executive Director*
Russell Reynolds Associates, Inc.
1700 Pennsylvania Avenue N.W.
Suite 850
Washington, DC 20006
Telephone: (202) 628-2150
**Recruiter Classification:** Retained; **Lowest/Average Salary:** $90,000/$90,000;
**Industry Concentration:** Generalist with a primary focus in Non-Profit;
**Function Concentration:** Generalist

**Tyler, J. Larry** — *President*
Tyler & Company
1000 Abernathy Road N.E.
Suite 1400
Atlanta, GA 30328-5655
Telephone: (770) 396-3939
**Recruiter Classification:** Retained; **Lowest/Average Salary:** $60,000/$90,000;
**Industry Concentration:** Healthcare/Hospitals, Insurance; **Function
Concentration:** Generalist

**Tyler, Jackie** — *Associate*
Kenzer Corp.
625 North Michigan Avenue, Suite 1244
Chicago, IL 60611
Telephone: (312) 266-0976
**Recruiter Classification:** Retained; **Lowest/Average Salary:** $50,000/$90,000;
**Industry Concentration:** Generalist; **Function Concentration:** Generalist

**Tyler, Janet** — *Branch Supervisor*
Accountants on Call
5000 Birch Street, Suite 550
Newport Beach, CA 92660
Telephone: (714) 955-0100
**Recruiter Classification:** Contingency; **Lowest/Average Salary:**
$20,000/$30,000; **Industry Concentration:** Generalist; **Function
Concentration:** Finance/Accounting

**Tyson, Richard L.** — *President*
Bonifield Associates
3003E Lincoln Drive West
Marlton, NJ 08053
Telephone: (609) 596-3300
**Recruiter Classification:** Contingency; **Lowest/Average Salary:**
$40,000/$60,000; **Industry Concentration:** Financial Services, Insurance;
**Function Concentration:** Generalist with a primary focus in Administration,
Finance/Accounting, General Management, Marketing, Research and
Development, Sales

**Uhl, Jack N.** — *Manager Central Region*
Management Recruiters International, Inc.
Boyce Plaza One
1035 Boyce Road, Suite 120
Upper St. Clair, PA 15241
Telephone: (412) 257-9585
**Recruiter Classification:** Contingency; **Lowest/Average Salary:**
$30,000/$75,000; **Industry Concentration:** Generalist; **Function
Concentration:** Generalist

**Ulbert, Nancy** — *Director Data Processing/MIS*
Aureus Group
8744 Frederick Street
Omaha, NE 68124-3068
Telephone: (402) 397-2980
**Recruiter Classification:** Contingency; **Lowest/Average Salary:**
$30,000/$50,000; **Industry Concentration:** Consumer Products, Electronics,
Energy, Fashion (Retail/Apparel), Financial Services, Healthcare/Hospitals,
High Technology, Hospitality/Leisure, Information Technology, Insurance,
Manufacturing, Pharmaceutical/Medical, Publishing/Media, Transportation;
**Function Concentration:** Administration, Engineering, Finance/Accounting,
General Management, Human Resources

**Unger, Mike A.** — *Manager Eastern Region*
Management Recruiters International, Inc.
210 West Front Street, Suite 102
Red Bank, NJ 07701-0871
Telephone: (908) 530-0600
**Recruiter Classification:** Contingency; **Lowest/Average Salary:** $30,000/$75,000; **Industry Concentration:** Generalist; **Function Concentration:** Generalist

**Unger, Paul T.** — *Vice President*
A.T. Kearney, Inc.
225 Reinekers Lane
Alexandria, VA 22314
Telephone: (703) 739-4624
**Recruiter Classification:** Retained; **Lowest/Average Salary:** $90,000/$90,000; **Industry Concentration:** Generalist with a primary focus in Aerospace/Defense, Healthcare/Hospitals, Information Technology; **Function Concentration:** Generalist with a primary focus in Administration, Engineering, Human Resources, Marketing, Research and Development, Sales

**Unger, Stephen A.** — *Senior Director*
Spencer Stuart
10900 Wilshire Boulevard, Suite 800
Los Angeles, CA 90024-6524
Telephone: (310) 209-0610
**Recruiter Classification:** Retained; **Lowest/Average Salary:** $90,000/$90,000; **Industry Concentration:** Entertainment, Hospitality/Leisure; **Function Concentration:** Generalist with a primary focus in Administration, Finance/Accounting, General Management, Human Resources, Marketing, Research and Development, Sales

**Uniacke, Keith J.** — *Manager Central Region*
Management Recruiters International, Inc.
The Ohio Building
113 North Ohio Avenue, Suite 400
Sidney, OH 45365
Telephone: (513) 497-7080
**Recruiter Classification:** Contingency; **Lowest/Average Salary:** $30,000/$75,000; **Industry Concentration:** Generalist; **Function Concentration:** Generalist

**Unterberg, Edward L.** — *Managing Director*
Russell Reynolds Associates, Inc.
200 South Wacker Drive
Suite 3600
Chicago, IL 60606
Telephone: (312) 993-9696
**Recruiter Classification:** Retained; **Lowest/Average Salary:** $90,000/$90,000; **Industry Concentration:** High Technology; **Function Concentration:** Generalist

**Utroska, Donald R.** — *Partner*
Lamalie Amrop International
225 West Wacker Drive
Chicago, IL 60606-1229
Telephone: (312) 782-3113
**Recruiter Classification:** Retained; **Lowest/Average Salary:** $90,000/$90,000; **Industry Concentration:** Generalist with a primary focus in Biotechnology, Chemical Products, Healthcare/Hospitals, High Technology, Manufacturing; **Function Concentration:** Generalist with a primary focus in General Management, Marketing

**Uzzel, Linda** — *Associate*
Source Services Corporation
One South Main Street, Suite 1440
Dayton, OH 45402
Telephone: (513) 461-4660
**Recruiter Classification:** Contingency; **Lowest/Average Salary:** $30,000/$50,000; **Industry Concentration:** Financial Services, Information Technology; **Function Concentration:** Engineering, Finance/Accounting

**Vacca, Domenic** — *Managing Partner*
Romac & Associates
1300 North Market Street
Suite 501
Wilmington, DE 19801
Telephone: (302) 658-6181
**Recruiter Classification:** Executive Temporary; **Lowest/Average Salary:** $/$60,000; **Industry Concentration:** Financial Services, Healthcare/Hospitals, High Technology, Hospitality/Leisure, Information Technology, Insurance; **Function Concentration:** Finance/Accounting

**Vachon, David A.** — *Associate*
McNichol Associates
620 Chestnut Street, Suite 1031
Philadelphia, PA 19106
Telephone: (215) 922-4142
**Recruiter Classification:** Retained; **Lowest/Average Salary:** $75,000/$90,000; **Industry Concentration:** Environmental, Healthcare/Hospitals, High Technology, Pharmaceutical/Medical, Transportation; **Function Concentration:** Generalist with a primary focus in Administration, Engineering, Finance/Accounting, General Management, Human Resources, Marketing, Research and Development, Sales, Women/Minorities

**Vainblat, Galina** — *Consultant*
Foy, Schneid & Daniel, Inc.
555 Madison Avenue, 12th Floor
New York, NY 10022
Telephone: (212) 980-2525
**Recruiter Classification:** Retained; **Lowest/Average Salary:** $60,000/$90,000; **Industry Concentration:** Generalist with a primary focus in Chemical Products, Consumer Products, Energy, Environmental, Information Technology, Pharmaceutical/Medical; **Function Concentration:** Generalist with a primary focus in Engineering, Finance/Accounting, General Management, Human Resources, Marketing

**Vairo, Leonard A.** — *Vice President*
Christian & Timbers
24 New England Executive Park
Burlington, MA 01803
Telephone: (617) 229-9515
**Recruiter Classification:** Retained; **Lowest/Average Salary:** $90,000/$90,000; **Industry Concentration:** Generalist; **Function Concentration:** Generalist

**Valdes, Ma. Elena** — *Vice President*
Korn/Ferry International
Montes Urales 641
Lomas De Chapultepec
Mexico City, D.F., MEXICO 11000
Telephone: (525) 202-0046
**Recruiter Classification:** Retained; **Lowest/Average Salary:** $90,000/$90,000; **Industry Concentration:** Generalist; **Function Concentration:** Generalist

**Valenta, Joseph** — *Director*
Princeton Entrepreneurial Resources
600 Alexander Road, P.O. Box 2051
Princeton, NJ 08543
Telephone: (609) 243-0010
**Recruiter Classification:** Executive Temporary; **Lowest/Average Salary:** $75,000/$90,000; **Industry Concentration:** Generalist with a primary focus in Biotechnology, Consumer Products, Electronics, Healthcare/Hospitals, Information Technology, Pharmaceutical/Medical, Venture Capital; **Function Concentration:** Generalist with a primary focus in Finance/Accounting, General Management, Human Resources, Marketing

**Valente, Joe J.** — *Co-Manager Midwest Region*
Management Recruiters International, Inc.
Tower Business Center
28 South Water Street, Suite 201
Batavia, IL 60510-2486
Telephone: (708) 406-8003
**Recruiter Classification:** Contingency; **Lowest/Average Salary:** $30,000/$75,000; **Industry Concentration:** Generalist; **Function Concentration:** Generalist

**Valente, Sam** — *Co-Manager*
Management Recruiters International, Inc.
Tower Business Center
28 South Water Street, Suite 201
Batavia, IL 60510-2486
Telephone: (708) 406-8003
**Recruiter Classification:** Contingency; **Lowest/Average Salary:** $30,000/$75,000; **Industry Concentration:** Generalist; **Function Concentration:** Generalist

**Valle, Javier** — *Vice President/Managing Director*
A.T. Kearney, Inc.
Ruben Dario 281-Piso 17
Col. Bosques de Chapultepec
Mexico City D.F., MEXICO 11580
Telephone: (525) 282-0050
**Recruiter Classification:** Retained; **Lowest/Average Salary:** $90,000/$90,000; **Industry Concentration:** Generalist; **Function Concentration:** Generalist

**Van Alstine, Catherine** — *Partner*
Tanton Mitchell/Paul Ray Berndtson
710-1050 West Pender Street
Vancouver, British Columbia, CANADA V6E 3S7
Telephone: (604) 685-0261
**Recruiter Classification:** Retained; **Lowest/Average Salary:** $75,000/$90,000; **Industry Concentration:** Generalist with a primary focus in Consumer Products, Financial Services; **Function Concentration:** Generalist with a primary focus in Finance/Accounting, Marketing, Sales

**Van Alstyne, Susan** — *Executive Recruiter*
Richard, Wayne and Roberts
24 Greenway Plaza, Suite 1304
Houston, TX 77046-2493
Telephone: (713) 629-6681
**Recruiter Classification:** Retained; **Lowest/Average Salary:** $40,000/$60,000; **Industry Concentration:** Generalist with a primary focus in Healthcare/Hospitals; **Function Concentration:** Generalist with a primary focus in Finance/Accounting

**Van Campen, Jerry** — *Vice President Research and Development*
Gilbert & Van Campen International
Graybar Building, 420 Lexington Avenue
New York, NY 10170
Telephone: (212) 661-2122
**Recruiter Classification:** Retained; **Lowest/Average Salary:** $90,000/$90,000; **Industry Concentration:** Generalist with a primary focus in Chemical Products, Consumer Products, Electronics, Financial Services, High Technology, Manufacturing, Pharmaceutical/Medical; **Function Concentration:** Generalist with a primary focus in Finance/Accounting, General Management, Human Resources, Marketing, Sales, Women/Minorities

**Van Campen, Stephen B.** — *President and CEO*
Gilbert & Van Campen International
Graybar Building, 420 Lexington Avenue
New York, NY 10170
Telephone: (212) 661-2122
**Recruiter Classification:** Retained; **Lowest/Average Salary:** $90,000/$90,000; **Industry Concentration:** Generalist; **Function Concentration:** Generalist

**Van Clieaf, Mark** — *Managing Director*
MVC Associates International
36 Toronto Street, Suite 850
Toronto, Ontario, CANADA M5C 2C5
Telephone: (416) 489-1917
**Recruiter Classification:** Retained; **Lowest/Average Salary:** $50,000/$90,000; **Industry Concentration:** Generalist with a primary focus in Aerospace/Defense, Automotive, Consumer Products, Energy, Entertainment, Financial Services, High Technology, Information Technology, Manufacturing, Pharmaceutical/Medical, Publishing/Media, Real Estate, Venture Capital; **Function Concentration:** Generalist with a primary focus in General Management, Human Resources

**van de Wetering, Shirley** — *Associate*
The Caldwell Partners Amrop International
400 Third Avenue S.W.
Suite 3450
Calgary, Alberta, CANADA T2P 4H2
Telephone: (403) 265-8780
**Recruiter Classification:** Retained; **Lowest/Average Salary:** $/$90,000; **Industry Concentration:** Generalist; **Function Concentration:** Generalist

**Van Horn, Carol** — *Vice President Retail Division*
R. Parker and Associates, Inc.
551 5th Avenue, Suite 222
New York, NY 10176
Telephone: (212) 661-8074
**Recruiter Classification:** Retained; **Lowest/Average Salary:** $50,000/$75,000; **Industry Concentration:** Generalist with a primary focus in Consumer Products, Fashion (Retail/Apparel); **Function Concentration:** Generalist with a primary focus in General Management, Marketing, Sales

**Van Norman, Ben** — *Associate*
Source Services Corporation
425 California Street, Suite 1200
San Francisco, CA 94104
Telephone: (415) 434-2410
**Recruiter Classification:** Contingency; **Lowest/Average Salary:** $30,000/$50,000; **Industry Concentration:** Financial Services, Information Technology; **Function Concentration:** Engineering, Finance/Accounting

**Van Nus, Robert** — *Principal*
Coopers & Lybrand Consulting
1111 West Hastings Street
Vancouver, British Columbia, CANADA V6E 3L2
Telephone: (604) 661-5700
**Recruiter Classification:** Retained; **Lowest/Average Salary:** $60,000/$90,000; **Industry Concentration:** Generalist; **Function Concentration:** Generalist

**Van Remmen, Roger** — *Partner*
Brown, Bernardy, Van Remmen, Inc.
12100 Wilshire Boulevard, Suite M-40
Los Angeles, CA 90025
Telephone: (310) 826-5777
**Recruiter Classification:** Contingency; **Lowest/Average Salary:** $30,000/$75,000; **Industry Concentration:** Automotive, Consumer Products, Electronics, Entertainment, Fashion (Retail/Apparel), Financial Services, Healthcare/Hospitals, High Technology, Hospitality/Leisure, Non-Profit, Publishing/Media; **Function Concentration:** Marketing

**Van Someren, Chris** — *Principal*
Korn/Ferry International
237 Park Avenue
New York, NY 10017
Telephone: (212) 687-1834
**Recruiter Classification:** Retained; **Lowest/Average Salary:** $90,000/$90,000; **Industry Concentration:** Generalist; **Function Concentration:** Generalist

**van Someren, Christian** — *Consultant*
Johnson Smith & Knisely Accord
100 Park Avenue, 15th Floor
New York, NY 10017
Telephone: (212) 885-9100
**Recruiter Classification:** Retained; **Lowest/Average Salary:** $90,000/$90,000; **Industry Concentration:** Consumer Products; **Function Concentration:** Generalist with a primary focus in General Management, Human Resources, Marketing, Sales

**Van Steenkiste, Julie** — *Recruiter*
Davidson, Laird & Associates
29260 Franklin, Suite 110
Southfield, MI 48034
Telephone: (810) 358-2160
**Recruiter Classification:** Contingency; **Lowest/Average Salary:** $30,000/$50,000; **Industry Concentration:** Generalist with a primary focus in Automotive, Consumer Products, Electronics, Manufacturing; **Function Concentration:** Generalist with a primary focus in Engineering, Finance/Accounting, Research and Development

**Van Wick, Mike** — *Manager Southwest Region*
Management Recruiters International, Inc.
2506 Lakeland Drive, Suite 408
Jackson, MS 39208-9752
Telephone: (601) 936-7900
**Recruiter Classification:** Contingency; **Lowest/Average Salary:** $30,000/$75,000; **Industry Concentration:** Generalist; **Function Concentration:** Generalist

**Vande-Water, Katie** — *Vice President*
J. Robert Scott
27 State Street
Boston, MA 02109
Telephone: (617) 720-2770
**Recruiter Classification:** Retained; **Lowest/Average Salary:** $75,000/$90,000; **Industry Concentration:** Generalist with a primary focus in Biotechnology, Chemical Products, Electronics, Financial Services, High Technology, Information Technology, Pharmaceutical/Medical; **Function Concentration:** Generalist

**Vandenbulcke, Cynthia** — *Associate*
Source Services Corporation
2029 Century Park East, Suite 1350
Los Angeles, CA 90067
Telephone: (310) 277-8092
**Recruiter Classification:** Contingency; **Lowest/Average Salary:** $30,000/$50,000; **Industry Concentration:** Financial Services, Information Technology; **Function Concentration:** Engineering, Finance/Accounting

**Vann, Dianne** — *Senior Associate*
The Button Group
1608 Emory Circle
Plano, TX 75093
Telephone: (214) 985-0619
**Recruiter Classification:** Retained, Contingency; **Lowest/Average Salary:** $60,000/$90,000; **Industry Concentration:** Generalist with a primary focus in Biotechnology, Board Services, Electronics, High Technology, Manufacturing, Oil/Gas, Packaging, Pharmaceutical/Medical, Real Estate; **Function Concentration:** Generalist with a primary focus in Engineering, General Management, Marketing, Research and Development, Sales

**Varian, Veronica** — *Co-Manager Eastern Region*
Management Recruiters International, Inc.
One Blue Hill Plaza, Suite 1428
P.O. Box 1603
Pearl River, NY 10965-8603
Telephone: (914) 735-7015
**Recruiter Classification:** Contingency; **Lowest/Average Salary:** $30,000/$75,000; **Industry Concentration:** Generalist; **Function Concentration:** Generalist

**Varney, Monique** — *Associate*
Source Services Corporation
500 108th Avenue NE, Suite 1780
Bellevue, WA 98004
Telephone: (206) 454-6400
**Recruiter Classification:** Contingency; **Lowest/Average Salary:** $30,000/$50,000; **Industry Concentration:** Financial Services, Information Technology; **Function Concentration:** Engineering, Finance/Accounting

**Varrichio, Michael** — *Managing Director*
Source Services Corporation
5429 LBJ Freeway, Suite 275
Dallas, TX 75240
Telephone: (214) 387-1600
**Recruiter Classification:** Contingency; **Lowest/Average Salary:** $30,000/$50,000; **Industry Concentration:** Financial Services, Information Technology; **Function Concentration:** Engineering, Finance/Accounting

**Vaughan, David B.** — *President*
Dunhill Professional Search of Irvine, Inc.
9 Executive Circle, Suite 240
Irvine, CA 92714
Telephone: (714) 474-6666
**Recruiter Classification:** Contingency; **Lowest/Average Salary:**
$40,000/$60,000; **Industry Concentration:** Aerospace/Defense, Consumer
Products, Manufacturing; **Function Concentration:** Generalist with a primary
focus in Engineering, Human Resources, Marketing, Sales

**Vautour, Eric L.** — *Managing Director/Area Manager*
Russell Reynolds Associates, Inc.
1700 Pennsylvania Avenue N.W.
Suite 850
Washington, DC 20006
Telephone: (202) 628-2150
**Recruiter Classification:** Retained; **Lowest/Average Salary:** $90,000/$90,000;
**Industry Concentration:** Generalist; **Function Concentration:** Generalist

**Velez, Hector** — *Associate*
Source Services Corporation
8614 Westwood Center, Suite 750
Vienna, VA 22182
Telephone: (703) 790-5610
**Recruiter Classification:** Contingency; **Lowest/Average Salary:**
$30,000/$50,000; **Industry Concentration:** Financial Services, Information
Technology; **Function Concentration:** Engineering, Finance/Accounting

**Velline, Ena A.** — *Consultant*
Paul Ray Berndtson
2029 Century Park East
Suite 1000
Los Angeles, CA 90067
Telephone: (310) 557-2828
**Recruiter Classification:** Retained; **Lowest/Average Salary:** $90,000/$90,000;
**Industry Concentration:** Generalist with a primary focus in Information
Technology; **Function Concentration:** Generalist

**Velten, Mark** — *Manager Transportation and Inventory
Control Division*
Hunt Ltd.
21 West 38th Street
New York, NY 10018
Telephone: (212) 997-2299
**Recruiter Classification:** Contingency; **Lowest/Average Salary:**
$40,000/$50,000; **Industry Concentration:** Automotive, Chemical Products,
Consumer Products, Fashion (Retail/Apparel), Manufacturing,
Pharmaceutical/Medical, Publishing/Media, Transportation; **Function
Concentration:** Generalist

**Velten, Mark** — *Director*
Hunt Advisory Services
21 West 38th Street
New York, NY 10018
Telephone: (212) 997-2299
**Recruiter Classification:** Executive Temporary; **Lowest/Average Salary:**
$20,000/$30,000; **Industry Concentration:** Automotive, Chemical Products,
Consumer Products, Fashion (Retail/Apparel), Manufacturing,
Pharmaceutical/Medical, Publishing/Media, Transportation; **Function
Concentration:** General Management

**Venable, William W.** — *Vice President*
Thorndike Deland Associates
275 Madison Avenue, Suite 1300
New York, NY 10016
Telephone: (212) 661-6200
**Recruiter Classification:** Retained; **Lowest/Average Salary:** $75,000/$90,000;
**Industry Concentration:** Generalist with a primary focus in Board Services,
Consumer Products, Entertainment, Fashion (Retail/Apparel), Financial
Services, Healthcare/Hospitals, Hospitality/Leisure, Information Technology,
Insurance, Manufacturing, Pharmaceutical/Medical, Publishing/Media, Venture
Capital; **Function Concentration:** Generalist with a primary focus in
Finance/Accounting, General Management, Human Resources, Marketing,
Sales

**Vennat, Manon** — *Managing Director*
Spencer Stuart
1981 Avenue McGill College
Montreal, Quebec, CANADA H3A 2Y1
Telephone: (514) 288-3377
**Recruiter Classification:** Retained; **Lowest/Average Salary:** $90,000/$90,000;
**Industry Concentration:** Generalist with a primary focus in
Aerospace/Defense, Board Services, Electronics, Fashion (Retail/Apparel), High
Technology, Information Technology, Manufacturing, Non-Profit, Public
Administration; **Function Concentration:** Generalist with a primary focus in
Administration, Finance/Accounting, General Management, Human Resources,
Marketing, Women/Minorities

**Vergara, Gail H.** — *Senior Director*
Spencer Stuart
401 North Michigan Avenue, Suite 3400
Chicago, IL 60611-4244
Telephone: (312) 822-0080
**Recruiter Classification:** Retained; **Lowest/Average Salary:** $90,000/$90,000;
**Industry Concentration:** Biotechnology, Healthcare/Hospitals, Insurance,
Pharmaceutical/Medical; **Function Concentration:** Generalist with a primary
focus in Administration, Finance/Accounting, General Management, Human
Resources, Marketing, Research and Development, Women/Minorities

**Vergari, Jane** — *Senior Vice President*
Herbert Mines Associates, Inc.
399 Park Avenue, 27th Floor
New York, NY 10022
Telephone: (212) 355-0909
**Recruiter Classification:** Retained; **Lowest/Average Salary:** $75,000/$90,000;
**Industry Concentration:** Board Services, Consumer Products, Fashion
(Retail/Apparel); **Function Concentration:** Generalist with a primary focus in
Finance/Accounting, General Management, Human Resources, Marketing,
Sales

**Verkamp, James Franklin** — *Partner*
Verkamp-Joyce Associates, Inc.
Westwood of Lisle, Suite 600
2443 Warrenville Road
Lisle, IL 60532
Telephone: (708) 955-3750
**Recruiter Classification:** Retained; **Lowest/Average Salary:** $75,000/$90,000;
**Industry Concentration:** Generalist; **Function Concentration:** Generalist

**Vermillion, Mike W.** — *Manager Midwest Region*
Management Recruiters International, Inc.
7400 University, Suite D
Clive, IA 50325-1336
Telephone: (515) 255-1242
**Recruiter Classification:** Contingency; **Lowest/Average Salary:**
$30,000/$75,000; **Industry Concentration:** Generalist; **Function
Concentration:** Generalist

**Vernon, Jack H.** — *Managing Director*
Russell Reynolds Associates, Inc.
Old City Hall, 45 School Street
Boston, MA 02108
Telephone: (617) 523-1111
**Recruiter Classification:** Retained; **Lowest/Average Salary:** $90,000/$90,000;
**Industry Concentration:** Generalist with a primary focus in
Healthcare/Hospitals; **Function Concentration:** Generalist

**Verrill-Schlager, Martha** — *Senior Associate*
Korn/Ferry International
Presidential Plaza
900 19th Street, N.W.
Washington, DC 20006
Telephone: (202) 822-9444
**Recruiter Classification:** Retained; **Lowest/Average Salary:** $90,000/$90,000;
**Industry Concentration:** Generalist with a primary focus in Education/Libraries;
**Function Concentration:** Generalist

**Vet, Jan** — *Vice President*
Korn/Ferry International
1800 Century Park East, Suite 900
Los Angeles, CA 90067
Telephone: (310) 552-1834
**Recruiter Classification:** Retained; **Lowest/Average Salary:** $90,000/$90,000;
**Industry Concentration:** Generalist; **Function Concentration:** Generalist

**Vierkant, Nona E.** — *Co-Manager Midwest Region*
Management Recruiters International, Inc.
1903 South Broadway
Rochester, MN 55904-7924
Telephone: (507) 282-2400
**Recruiter Classification:** Contingency; **Lowest/Average Salary:**
$30,000/$75,000; **Industry Concentration:** Generalist; **Function
Concentration:** Generalist

**Vierkant, Robert** — *Co-Manager*
Management Recruiters International, Inc.
1903 South Broadway
Rochester, MN 55904-7924
Telephone: (507) 282-2400
**Recruiter Classification:** Contingency; **Lowest/Average Salary:**
$30,000/$75,000; **Industry Concentration:** Generalist; **Function
Concentration:** Generalist

**Viglino, Victor P.** — *Senior Vice President/Managing Director*
DHR International, Inc.
2810 East Oakland Park Boulevard, Suite 304
Fort Lauderdale, FL 33306
Telephone: (305) 564-6110
Recruiter Classification: Retained; Lowest/Average Salary:
$60,000/$90,000; Industry Concentration: Generalist; Function
Concentration: Generalist

**Vilella, Paul** — *Managing Director*
Source Services Corporation
1111 19th Street NW, Suite 620
Washington, DC 20036
Telephone: (202) 822-0100
Recruiter Classification: Contingency; Lowest/Average Salary:
$30,000/$50,000; Industry Concentration: Financial Services, Information
Technology; Function Concentration: Engineering, Finance/Accounting

**Villareal, Morey** — *President*
Villareal & Associates, Inc.
427 South Boston, Suite 215
Tulsa, OK 74103
Telephone: (918) 584-0808
Recruiter Classification: Retained; Lowest/Average Salary: $30,000/$75,000;
Industry Concentration: Generalist; Function Concentration: Generalist

**Villella, Paul** — *Managing Director*
Source Services Corporation
8614 Westwood Center, Suite 750
Vienna, VA 22182
Telephone: (703) 790-5610
Recruiter Classification: Contingency; Lowest/Average Salary:
$30,000/$50,000; Industry Concentration: Financial Services, Information
Technology; Function Concentration: Engineering, Finance/Accounting

**Vincelette, Kathy A.** — *Senior Consultant*
Raymond Karsan Associates
989 Old Eagle School Road, Suite 814
Wayne, PA 19087
Telephone: (610) 971-9171
Recruiter Classification: Contingency; Lowest/Average Salary:
$30,000/$90,000; Industry Concentration: Generalist with a primary focus in
Insurance; Function Concentration: Generalist

**Vinett-Hessel, Deidre** — *Associate*
Source Services Corporation
9020 Capital of Texas Highway
Building I, Suite 337
Austin, TX 78759
Telephone: (512) 345-7473
Recruiter Classification: Contingency; Lowest/Average Salary:
$30,000/$50,000; Industry Concentration: Financial Services, Information
Technology; Function Concentration: Engineering, Finance/Accounting

**Vinnedge, Sandra** — *Recruiter*
U.S. Envirosearch
445 Union Boulevard, Suite 225
Lakewood, CO 80228
Telephone: (303) 980-6600
Recruiter Classification: Contingency; Lowest/Average Salary:
$30,000/$60,000; Industry Concentration: Environmental; Function
Concentration: Generalist with a primary focus in Administration, Engineering,
Finance/Accounting, General Management, Marketing, Sales,
Women/Minorities

**Violette, Bradley** — *Area Vice President*
Accountants on Call
Telephone: (410) 685-5700
Recruiter Classification: Contingency; Lowest/Average Salary:
$20,000/$30,000; Industry Concentration: Generalist; Function
Concentration: Finance/Accounting

**Virgili, Franca** — *Consultant*
Johnson Smith & Knisely Accord
1888 Century Park East, Suite 1900
Los Angeles, CA 90067
Telephone: (310) 284-3238
Recruiter Classification: Retained; Lowest/Average Salary: $90,000/$90,000;
Industry Concentration: Biotechnology, Entertainment, Fashion
(Retail/Apparel), Oil/Gas, Pharmaceutical/Medical, Publishing/Media;
Function Concentration: Generalist with a primary focus in General
Management, Human Resources, Marketing, Research and Development,
Sales

**Visnich, L. Christine** — *Director Executive Search Consulting*
Bason Associates Inc.
11311 Cornell Park Drive
Cincinnati, OH 45242
Telephone: (513) 469-9881
Recruiter Classification: Retained; Lowest/Average Salary: $60,000/$90,000;
Industry Concentration: Generalist with a primary focus in Automotive,
Biotechnology, Board Services, Chemical Products, Consumer Products,
Environmental, Fashion (Retail/Apparel), Financial Services, Healthcare/Hospitals,
High Technology, Insurance, Manufacturing, Packaging, Pharmaceutical/Medical,
Public Administration; Function Concentration: Generalist with a primary focus in
Administration, Engineering, Finance/Accounting, General Management, Human
Resources, Marketing, Research and Development, Sales

**Visokey, Dale M.** — *Managing Director*
Russell Reynolds Associates, Inc.
200 South Wacker Drive
Suite 3600
Chicago, IL 60606
Telephone: (312) 993-9696
Recruiter Classification: Retained; Lowest/Average Salary: $90,000/$90,000;
Industry Concentration: Generalist; Function Concentration: Generalist

**Visotsky, Thomas** — *President*
Don Richard Associates of Richmond, Inc.
7275 Glen Forest Drive, Suite 200
Richmond, VA 23226
Telephone: (804) 282-6300
Recruiter Classification: Contingency, Executive Temporary; Lowest/Average
Salary: $30,000/$40,000; Industry Concentration: Generalist; Function
Concentration: Finance/Accounting

**Viviano, Cathleen** — *Associate*
Source Services Corporation
10300 West 103rd Street, Suite 101
Overland Park, KS 66214
Telephone: (913) 888-8885
Recruiter Classification: Contingency; Lowest/Average Salary:
$30,000/$50,000; Industry Concentration: Financial Services, Information
Technology; Function Concentration: Engineering, Finance/Accounting

**Vlasek, Ray D.** — *Manager Southwest Region*
Management Recruiters International, Inc.
3003 LBJ Freeway, Suite 220-E
Dallas, TX 75234-7771
Telephone: (214) 488-1133
Recruiter Classification: Contingency; Lowest/Average Salary:
$30,000/$75,000; Industry Concentration: Generalist; Function
Concentration: Generalist

**Vlcek, Thomas J.** — *President*
Vlcek & Company, Inc.
620 Newport Center Drive
Suite 1100
Newport Beach, CA 92660
Telephone: (714) 752-0661
Recruiter Classification: Retained; Lowest/Average Salary: $75,000/$90,000;
Industry Concentration: Generalist with a primary focus in Biotechnology,
Chemical Products, Consumer Products, Electronics, Entertainment, Financial
Services, Healthcare/Hospitals, Hospitality/Leisure, Information Technology,
Manufacturing, Packaging, Pharmaceutical/Medical, Publishing/Media;
Function Concentration: Generalist with a primary focus in Administration,
Engineering, Finance/Accounting, General Management, Human Resources,
Marketing, Research and Development, Sales, Women/Minorities

**Vogel, Emil** — *President*
Tarnow International
150 Morris Avenue
Springfield, NJ 07081
Telephone: (201) 376-3900
Recruiter Classification: Retained; Lowest/Average Salary: $90,000/$90,000;
Industry Concentration: Generalist; Function Concentration: Generalist

**Vogel, Michael S.** — *President*
Vogel Associates
P.O. Box 269X
Huntingdon Valley, PA 19006-0269
Telephone: (215) 938-1700
Recruiter Classification: Contingency; Lowest/Average Salary:
$40,000/$60,000; Industry Concentration: Generalist with a primary focus in
Aerospace/Defense, Chemical Products, Consumer Products, High Technology,
Manufacturing, Oil/Gas, Packaging, Pharmaceutical/Medical; Function
Concentration: Human Resources

**Vognsen, Rikke** — *Principal*
DSA, Inc.
Three First National Plaza, Suite 1400
Chicago, IL 60602
Telephone: (312) 201-0964
**Recruiter Classification:** Retained; **Lowest/Average Salary:** $60,000/$90,000;
**Industry Concentration:** Real Estate; **Function Concentration:** Generalist with
a primary focus in Engineering, Finance/Accounting

**Vogus, Jerry** — *Senior Partner*
Cumberland Group Inc.
608 South Washington Street, Suite 101
Naperville, IL 60540
Telephone: (708) 416-9494
**Recruiter Classification:** Contingency; **Lowest/Average Salary:**
$40,000/$75,000; **Industry Concentration:** Manufacturing; **Function
Concentration:** Engineering, Marketing, Sales

**Voigt, John A.** — *Managing Partner*
Romac & Associates
4350 North Fairfax Drive
Suite 400
Arlington, VA 22203
Telephone: (703) 351-7600
**Recruiter Classification:** Executive Temporary; **Lowest/Average Salary:**
$/$60,000; **Industry Concentration:** Financial Services, Healthcare/Hospitals,
High Technology, Hospitality/Leisure, Information Technology, Insurance;
**Function Concentration:** Finance/Accounting

**Vojta, Marilyn B.** — *Associate*
James Mead & Company
164 Kings Highway North
Westport, CT 06880
Telephone: (203) 454-5544
**Recruiter Classification:** Retained; **Lowest/Average Salary:** $90,000/$90,000;
**Industry Concentration:** Generalist with a primary focus in Consumer
Products, Publishing/Media; **Function Concentration:** General Management,
Marketing, Sales

**Volk, Richard** — *Executive Recruiter*
MSI International
229 Peachtree Street, NE
Suite 1201
Atlanta, GA 30303
Telephone: (404) 659-5050
**Recruiter Classification:** Contingency; **Lowest/Average Salary:**
$30,000/$75,000; **Industry Concentration:** Healthcare/Hospitals,
Pharmaceutical/Medical; **Function Concentration:** Generalist with a primary
focus in Administration, Engineering, Finance/Accounting, General
Management, Marketing, Sales

**Volz, Scott** — *General Manager*
Management Recruiters International, Inc.
835 Highland Avenue, SE
Hickory, NC 28602-1140
Telephone: (704) 324-2020
**Recruiter Classification:** Contingency; **Lowest/Average Salary:**
$30,000/$75,000; **Industry Concentration:** Generalist; **Function
Concentration:** Generalist

**Von Der Ahe, Christopher** — *Vice President*
Korn/Ferry International
1800 Century Park East, Suite 900
Los Angeles, CA 90067
Telephone: (310) 552-1834
**Recruiter Classification:** Retained; **Lowest/Average Salary:** $90,000/$90,000;
**Industry Concentration:** Generalist; **Function Concentration:** Generalist

**von der Linden, James A.** — *Associate*
Pendleton James and Associates, Inc.
One International Place
Boston, MA 02110
Telephone: (617) 261-9696
**Recruiter Classification:** Retained; **Lowest/Average Salary:** $90,000/$90,000;
**Industry Concentration:** Generalist; **Function Concentration:** Generalist

**von Seldeneck, Judith M.** — *Chairman, President and CEO*
The Diversified Search Companies
2005 Market Street, Suite 3300
Philadelphia, PA 19103
Telephone: (215) 732-6666
**Recruiter Classification:** Retained; **Lowest/Average Salary:** $90,000/$90,000;
**Industry Concentration:** Generalist; **Function Concentration:** Generalist

**von Stein, Scott** — *Partner*
Wilkinson & Ives
One Bush Street, Suite 550
San Francisco, CA 94104
Telephone: (415) 834-3100
**Recruiter Classification:** Retained; **Lowest/Average Salary:** $90,000/$90,000;
**Industry Concentration:** Generalist with a primary focus in Board Services,
Consumer Products, Electronics, Entertainment, Financial Services, High
Technology, Information Technology, Insurance, Manufacturing,
Publishing/Media, Transportation, Utilities/Nuclear, Venture Capital; **Function
Concentration:** Generalist

**Vossler, James** — *Recruiter*
A.J. Burton Group, Inc.
35 Wisconsin Circle, Suite 250
Chevy Chase, MD 20815
Telephone: (301) 654-0082
**Recruiter Classification:** Contingency; **Lowest/Average Salary:**
$30,000/$40,000; **Industry Concentration:** Energy, Manufacturing, Real Estate,
Utilities/Nuclear; **Function Concentration:** Finance/Accounting

**Wackerle, Frederick W.** — *Partner*
McFeely Wackerle Shulman
20 North Wacker Drive, Suite 3110
Chicago, IL 60606
Telephone: (312) 641-2977
**Recruiter Classification:** Retained; **Lowest/Average Salary:** $90,000/$90,000;
**Industry Concentration:** Generalist; **Function Concentration:** Generalist with a
primary focus in Administration

**Wade, Christy** — *Associate*
Source Services Corporation
520 Post Oak Boulevard, Suite 700
Houston, TX 77027
Telephone: (713) 439-1077
**Recruiter Classification:** Contingency; **Lowest/Average Salary:**
$30,000/$50,000; **Industry Concentration:** Financial Services, Information
Technology; **Function Concentration:** Engineering, Finance/Accounting

**Waggoner, Lisa** — *Senior Partner*
Intersource, Ltd.
72 Sloan Street
Roswell, GA 30075
Telephone: (770) 645-0015
**Recruiter Classification:** Retained, Contingency; **Lowest/Average Salary:**
$50,000/$75,000; **Industry Concentration:** Generalist with a primary focus in
Consumer Products, Electronics, Financial Services, Healthcare/Hospitals, High
Technology, Hospitality/Leisure, Information Technology, Manufacturing;
**Function Concentration:** Finance/Accounting, Human Resources,
Women/Minorities

**Wagman, Marc E.** — *Manager Midwest Region*
Management Recruiters International, Inc.
Corporate Woods Building 40, Suite 920
9401 Indian Creek Parkway
Overland Park, KS 66210-2098
Telephone: (913) 661-9300
**Recruiter Classification:** Contingency; **Lowest/Average Salary:**
$30,000/$75,000; **Industry Concentration:** Generalist; **Function
Concentration:** Generalist

**Wagner, Robert** — *Principal*
Korn/Ferry International
1800 Century Park East, Suite 900
Los Angeles, CA 90067
Telephone: (310) 552-1834
**Recruiter Classification:** Retained; **Lowest/Average Salary:** $90,000/$90,000;
**Industry Concentration:** Generalist; **Function Concentration:** Generalist

**Waindle, Maureen** — *Consultant*
Paul Ray Berndtson
191 Peachtree Tower, Suite 3800
191 Peachtree Street, NE
Atlanta, GA 30303-1757
Telephone: (404) 215-4600
**Recruiter Classification:** Retained; **Lowest/Average Salary:** $90,000/$90,000;
**Industry Concentration:** Generalist; **Function Concentration:** Generalist

**Wait, Kristin** — *Principal*
Korn/Ferry International
237 Park Avenue
New York, NY 10017
Telephone: (212) 687-1834
**Recruiter Classification:** Retained; **Lowest/Average Salary:** $90,000/$90,000;
**Industry Concentration:** Generalist; **Function Concentration:** Generalist

**Waitkus, Karen** — *Senior Executive Recruiter*
Richard, Wayne and Roberts
24 Greenway Plaza, Suite 1304
Houston, TX 77046-2493
Telephone: (713) 629-6681
**Recruiter Classification:** Retained; **Lowest/Average Salary:** $50,000/$90,000;
**Industry Concentration:** Generalist with a primary focus in Financial Services;
**Function Concentration:** Generalist with a primary focus in
Finance/Accounting

**Wakefield, Scott** — *Insurance Consultant*
National Search, Inc.
2816 University Drive
Coral Springs, FL 33071
Telephone: (800) 935-4355
**Recruiter Classification:** Contingency; **Lowest/Average Salary:**
$30,000/$50,000; **Industry Concentration:** Healthcare/Hospitals, Insurance,
Pharmaceutical/Medical; **Function Concentration:** Generalist with a primary
focus in Administration, Finance/Accounting, General Management, Human
Resources, Marketing, Research and Development, Sales, Women/Minorities

**Wakeham, Robin** — *Senior Associate*
Korn/Ferry International
One International Place
Boston, MA 02110-1800
Telephone: (617) 345-0200
**Recruiter Classification:** Retained; **Lowest/Average Salary:** $90,000/$90,000;
**Industry Concentration:** Generalist; **Function Concentration:** Generalist

**Walburger, Gary** — *Vice President*
Korn/Ferry International
1800 Century Park East, Suite 900
Los Angeles, CA 90067
Telephone: (310) 552-1834
**Recruiter Classification:** Retained; **Lowest/Average Salary:** $90,000/$90,000;
**Industry Concentration:** Generalist; **Function Concentration:** Generalist

**Waldman, Noah H.** — *Partner*
Lamalie Amrop International
191 Peachtree Street N.E.
Atlanta, GA 30303
Telephone: (404) 688-0800
**Recruiter Classification:** Retained; **Lowest/Average Salary:** $90,000/$90,000;
**Industry Concentration:** Generalist with a primary focus in
Healthcare/Hospitals, Insurance; **Function Concentration:** Generalist with a
primary focus in Administration, Finance/Accounting, General Management,
Marketing, Sales

**Waldoch, D. Mark** — *Consultant*
Barnes Development Group, LLC
1017 West Glen Oaks Lane, Suite 108
Mequon, WI 53092
Telephone: (414) 241-8468
**Recruiter Classification:** Retained; **Lowest/Average Salary:** $50,000/$75,000;
**Industry Concentration:** Automotive, Board Services, Chemical Products,
Electronics, Healthcare/Hospitals, Information Technology, Insurance,
Manufacturing, Non-Profit, Packaging, Pharmaceutical/Medical,
Transportation; **Function Concentration:** Generalist with a primary focus in
Administration, Engineering, Finance/Accounting, General Management,
Human Resources, Marketing, Research and Development, Sales

**Waldon, Jeffrey** — *Manager*
Accountants on Call
1715 North Westshore Boulevard
Suite 753, Westshore Ctr.
Tampa, FL 33607
Telephone: (813) 289-0051
**Recruiter Classification:** Contingency; **Lowest/Average Salary:** $20,000/$30,000;
**Industry Concentration:** Generalist; **Function Concentration:** Finance/Accounting

**Waldon, Maita** — *Manager*
Accountants on Call
1715 North Westshore Boulevard
Suite 753, Westshore Ctr.
Tampa, FL 33607
Telephone: (813) 289-0051
**Recruiter Classification:** Contingency; **Lowest/Average Salary:** $20,000/$30,000;
**Industry Concentration:** Generalist; **Function Concentration:** Finance/Accounting

**Waldrop, Gary R.** — *Manager*
MSI International
230 Peachtree Street, N.E.
Suite 1550
Atlanta, GA 30303
Telephone: (404) 653-7360
**Recruiter Classification:** Contingency; **Lowest/Average Salary:**
$30,000/$60,000; **Industry Concentration:** Generalist with a primary focus in
Financial Services, Healthcare/Hospitals, High Technology, Information
Technology, Manufacturing; **Function Concentration:** Generalist with a
primary focus in Administration, Engineering, Finance/Accounting, General
Management, Marketing, Sales

**Walker, Ann** — *Associate*
Source Services Corporation
111 Monument Circle, Suite 3930
Indianapolis, IN 46204
Telephone: (317) 631-2900
**Recruiter Classification:** Contingency; **Lowest/Average Salary:**
$30,000/$50,000; **Industry Concentration:** Financial Services, Information
Technology; **Function Concentration:** Engineering, Finance/Accounting

**Walker, Craig H.** — *Recruiter*
A.J. Burton Group, Inc.
120 East Baltimore Street, Suite 2220
Baltimore, MD 21202
Telephone: (410) 752-5244
**Recruiter Classification:** Contingency; **Lowest/Average Salary:**
$40,000/$75,000; **Industry Concentration:** Consumer Products, Energy,
Hospitality/Leisure, Insurance, Manufacturing, Real Estate, Transportation;
**Function Concentration:** Finance/Accounting

**Walker, Don** — *Executive Recruiter*
Richard, Wayne and Roberts
24 Greenway Plaza, Suite 1304
Houston, TX 77046-2493
Telephone: (713) 629-6681
**Recruiter Classification:** Retained; **Lowest/Average Salary:** $40,000/$60,000;
**Industry Concentration:** Generalist; **Function Concentration:** Generalist with a
primary focus in Finance/Accounting

**Walker, Ewing J.** — *Managing Director*
Ward Howell International, Inc.
1000 Louisiana Street
Suite 3150
Houston, TX 77002
Telephone: (713) 655-7155
**Recruiter Classification:** Retained; **Lowest/Average Salary:** $90,000/$90,000;
**Industry Concentration:** Chemical Products, Energy, Environmental, Financial
Services, High Technology, Insurance, Oil/Gas, Utilities/Nuclear, Venture
Capital; **Function Concentration:** Administration, Engineering,
Finance/Accounting, General Management, Human Resources, Marketing,
Women/Minorities

**Walker, Judy** — *Executive Recruiter*
Richard, Wayne and Roberts
24 Greenway Plaza, Suite 1304
Houston, TX 77046-2493
Telephone: (713) 629-6681
**Recruiter Classification:** Retained; **Lowest/Average Salary:** $40,000/$60,000;
**Industry Concentration:** Generalist with a primary focus in Chemical Products,
Environmental, Oil/Gas; **Function Concentration:** Generalist with a primary
focus in Engineering

**Walker, Martin S.** — *Chairman*
Walker Communications
1212 Avenue of the Americas
New York, NY 10036
Telephone: (212) 944-0011
**Recruiter Classification:** Retained; **Lowest/Average Salary:** $75,000/$90,000;
**Industry Concentration:** Publishing/Media; **Function Concentration:** Generalist
with a primary focus in Finance/Accounting, General Management, Marketing,
Research and Development, Sales, Women/Minorities

**Walker, Richard** — *Staff Manager*
Bradford & Galt, Inc.
1211 West 22nd Street, Suite 417
Oak Brook, IL 60521
Telephone: (708) 990-4644
**Recruiter Classification:** Contingency; **Lowest/Average Salary:**
$30,000/$30,000; **Industry Concentration:** Generalist with a primary focus in
Information Technology; **Function Concentration:** Generalist

**Walker, Ronald H.** — *Managing Director*
Korn/Ferry International
Presidential Plaza
900 19th Street, N.W.
Washington, DC 20006
Telephone: (202) 822-9444
**Recruiter Classification:** Retained; **Lowest/Average Salary:** $90,000/$90,000;
**Industry Concentration:** Generalist with a primary focus in Board Services;
**Function Concentration:** Generalist

**Walker, Rose** — *Associate*
Source Services Corporation
One Park Plaza, Suite 560
Irvine, CA 92714
Telephone: (714) 660-1666
**Recruiter Classification:** Contingency; **Lowest/Average Salary:**
$30,000/$50,000; **Industry Concentration:** Financial Services, Information
Technology; **Function Concentration:** Engineering, Finance/Accounting

**Wall, David** — *Consultant*
Southwestern Professional Services
2451 Atrium Way
Nashville, TN 37214
Telephone: (615) 391-2722
**Recruiter Classification:** Contingency; **Lowest/Average Salary:**
$30,000/$50,000; **Industry Concentration:** Generalist with a primary focus in
Healthcare/Hospitals, Pharmaceutical/Medical, Publishing/Media; **Function
Concentration:** Generalist with a primary focus in Human Resources,
Marketing, Sales

**Wallace, Alec** — *Partner*
Tanton Mitchell/Paul Ray Berndtson
710-1050 West Pender Street
Vancouver, British Columbia, CANADA V6E 3S7
Telephone: (604) 685-0261
**Recruiter Classification:** Retained; **Lowest/Average Salary:** $75,000/$90,000;
**Industry Concentration:** Generalist with a primary focus in Financial Services,
Healthcare/Hospitals, Non-Profit; **Function Concentration:** Generalist with a
primary focus in Finance/Accounting, General Management, Human
Resources

**Wallace, Charles E.** — *Managing Partner*
Heidrick & Struggles, Inc.
600 Superior Avenue East
Suite 2500
Cleveland, OH 44114
Telephone: (216) 241-7410
**Recruiter Classification:** Retained; **Lowest/Average Salary:** $75,000/$90,000;
**Industry Concentration:** Generalist; **Function Concentration:** Generalist

**Wallace, Dennis M.** — *Principal*
Sanford Rose Associates
333 East State Street
Rockford, IL 61104-1012
Telephone: (815) 964-4080
**Recruiter Classification:** Contingency; **Lowest/Average Salary:**
$30,000/$75,000; **Industry Concentration:** Generalist with a primary focus in
Automotive, Manufacturing; **Function Concentration:** Generalist

**Wallace, Mark J.** — *Co-Manager*
Management Recruiters International, Inc.
One Marine Midland Plaza, Suite 603
Binghamton, NY 13901-3216
Telephone: (607) 722-2243
**Recruiter Classification:** Contingency; **Lowest/Average Salary:**
$30,000/$75,000; **Industry Concentration:** Generalist; **Function
Concentration:** Generalist

**Wallace, Toby** — *Associate*
Source Services Corporation
5429 LBJ Freeway, Suite 275
Dallas, TX 75240
Telephone: (214) 387-1600
**Recruiter Classification:** Contingency; **Lowest/Average Salary:**
$30,000/$50,000; **Industry Concentration:** Financial Services, Information
Technology; **Function Concentration:** Engineering, Finance/Accounting

**Wallis, Barry** — *Senior Representative Marketing*
Bradford & Galt, Inc.
12400 Olive Boulevard, Suite 430
St. Louis, MO 63141
Telephone: (314) 434-9200
**Recruiter Classification:** Contingency; **Lowest/Average Salary:**
$30,000/$30,000; **Industry Concentration:** Generalist; **Function
Concentration:** Generalist

**Walsh, Patty** — *Executive Recruiter*
Abraham & London, Ltd.
237 Danbury Road
Wilton, CT 06897
Telephone: (203) 834-2500
**Recruiter Classification:** Contingency, Executive Temporary; **Lowest/Average
Salary:** $40,000/$75,000; **Industry Concentration:** High Technology,
Information Technology; **Function Concentration:** Marketing, Sales

**Walter, Mary Ann** — *Director*
Spencer Stuart
525 Market Street, Suite 3700
San Francisco, CA 94105
Telephone: (414) 495-4141
**Recruiter Classification:** Retained; **Lowest/Average Salary:** $90,000/$90,000;
**Industry Concentration:** Generalist; **Function Concentration:** Generalist

**Walters, William F.** — *President*
Jonas, Walters & Assoc., Inc.
1110 North Old World Third St., Suite 510
Milwaukee, WI 53203-1102
Telephone: (414) 291-2828
**Recruiter Classification:** Retained; **Lowest/Average Salary:** $60,000/$90,000;
**Industry Concentration:** Generalist with a primary focus in Automotive,
Chemical Products, Consumer Products, Electronics, High Technology,
Manufacturing, Publishing/Media; **Function Concentration:** Generalist with a
primary focus in Administration, Engineering, Finance/Accounting, General
Management, Human Resources, Marketing, Research and Development, Sales

**Walther, Linda S.** — *Executive Recruiter*
MSI International
2170 West State Road 434
Suite 454
Longwood, FL 32779
Telephone: (407) 788-7700
**Recruiter Classification:** Contingency; **Lowest/Average Salary:**
$30,000/$60,000; **Industry Concentration:** Generalist with a primary focus in
Healthcare/Hospitals; **Function Concentration:** Generalist with a primary focus
in Administration, Engineering, Finance/Accounting, General Management,
Marketing, Sales

**Walton, Bruce H.** — *Partner*
Heidrick & Struggles, Inc.
One Post Office Square
Boston, MA 02109-0199
Telephone: (617) 423-1140
**Recruiter Classification:** Retained; **Lowest/Average Salary:** $75,000/$90,000;
**Industry Concentration:** Generalist with a primary focus in High Technology;
**Function Concentration:** Generalist

**Walton, James H.** — *Manager Central Region*
Management Recruiters International, Inc.
1435 Rombach Avenue, Suite 7A
P.O. Box 863
Wilmington, OH 45177-0863
Telephone: (513) 383-1355
**Recruiter Classification:** Contingency; **Lowest/Average Salary:**
$30,000/$75,000; **Industry Concentration:** Generalist; **Function
Concentration:** Generalist

**Walton, Terry P.** — *Partner*
Heidrick & Struggles, Inc.
76 South Laura Street, Suite 2110
Jacksonville, FL 32202
Telephone: (904) 355-6674
**Recruiter Classification:** Retained; **Lowest/Average Salary:** $75,000/$90,000;
**Industry Concentration:** Generalist with a primary focus in Consumer
Products; **Function Concentration:** Generalist

**Wanless, Theresa** — *Associate*
The Caldwell Partners Amrop International
Sixty-Four Prince Arthur Avenue
Toronto, Ontario, CANADA M5R 1B4
Telephone: (416) 920-7702
**Recruiter Classification:** Retained; **Lowest/Average Salary:** $/$90,000; **Industry
Concentration:** Generalist; **Function Concentration:** Generalist

**Ward, Les** — *President*
Source Services Corporation
5580 LBJ Freeway, Suite 300
Dallas, TX 75240
Telephone: (214) 385-3002
**Recruiter Classification:** Contingency; **Lowest/Average Salary:**
$30,000/$50,000; **Industry Concentration:** Financial Services, Information
Technology; **Function Concentration:** Engineering, Finance/Accounting

**Ward, Madeleine** — *Principal*
LTM Associates
1112 Elizabeth
Naperville, IL 60540
Telephone: (708) 961-3331
**Recruiter Classification:** Contingency; **Lowest/Average Salary:**
$50,000/$90,000; **Industry Concentration:** Financial Services, High
Technology, Information Technology, Venture Capital; **Function Concentration:**
Finance/Accounting, General Management, Sales

**Ward, Robert** — *Associate*
Source Services Corporation
One Park Plaza, Suite 560
Irvine, CA 92714
Telephone: (714) 660-1666
**Recruiter Classification:** Contingency; **Lowest/Average Salary:**
$30,000/$50,000; **Industry Concentration:** Financial Services, Information
Technology; **Function Concentration:** Engineering, Finance/Accounting

**Ward, Ted** — *Vice President*
Korn/Ferry International
237 Park Avenue
New York, NY 10017
Telephone: (212) 687-1834
**Recruiter Classification:** Retained; **Lowest/Average Salary:** $90,000/$90,000;
**Industry Concentration:** Generalist with a primary focus in Financial Services;
**Function Concentration:** Generalist

**Ward, William F.** — *Partner*
Heidrick & Struggles, Inc.
2200 Ross Avenue, Suite 4700E
Dallas, TX 75201-2787
Telephone: (214) 220-2130
**Recruiter Classification:** Retained; **Lowest/Average Salary:** $75,000/$90,000;
**Industry Concentration:** Generalist with a primary focus in
Healthcare/Hospitals; **Function Concentration:** Generalist

**Wardell, Charles W.B.** — *Partner*
Lamalie Amrop International
200 Park Avenue
New York, NY 10166-0136
Telephone: (212) 953-7900
**Recruiter Classification:** Retained; **Lowest/Average Salary:** $90,000/$90,000;
**Industry Concentration:** Generalist; **Function Concentration:** Generalist with a
primary focus in General Management, Marketing, Sales

**Ware, John C.** — *Senior Director*
Spencer Stuart
3000 Sand Hill Road
Building 2, Suite 175
Menlo Park, CA 94025
Telephone: (415) 688-1285
**Recruiter Classification:** Retained; **Lowest/Average Salary:** $90,000/$90,000;
**Industry Concentration:** Entertainment, High Technology, Information
Technology, Publishing/Media; **Function Concentration:** Generalist with a
primary focus in General Management, Marketing, Research and Development

**Wargo, G. Rick** — *Vice President*
A.T. Kearney, Inc.
222 West Adams Street
Chicago, IL 60606
Telephone: (312) 648-0111
**Recruiter Classification:** Retained; **Lowest/Average Salary:** $90,000/$90,000;
**Industry Concentration:** Generalist with a primary focus in High Technology;
**Function Concentration:** Generalist with a primary focus in Administration,
Engineering, General Management, Human Resources, Marketing, Research
and Development, Sales

**Waring, David C.** — *Executive Director*
Russell Reynolds Associates, Inc.
200 South Wacker Drive
Suite 3600
Chicago, IL 60606
Telephone: (312) 993-9696
**Recruiter Classification:** Retained; **Lowest/Average Salary:** $90,000/$90,000;
**Industry Concentration:** Generalist; **Function Concentration:** Generalist

**Warnock, Phyl** — *Associate*
Source Services Corporation
505 East 200 South, Suite 300
Salt Lake City, UT 84102
Telephone: (801) 328-0011
**Recruiter Classification:** Contingency; **Lowest/Average Salary:**
$30,000/$50,000; **Industry Concentration:** Financial Services, Information
Technology; **Function Concentration:** Engineering, Finance/Accounting

**Warren, Lester A.** — *Manager Southwest Region*
Management Recruiters International, Inc.
7602 University Boulevard, Suite 125
Lubbock, TX 79423
Telephone: (806) 745-8755
**Recruiter Classification:** Contingency; **Lowest/Average Salary:**
$30,000/$75,000; **Industry Concentration:** Generalist; **Function
Concentration:** Generalist

**Warren, Linda** — *Manager Convenience Stores*
Prestige Inc.
P.O. Box 421
Reedsburg, WI 53959
Telephone: (608) 524-4032
**Recruiter Classification:** Contingency; **Lowest/Average Salary:**
$50,000/$90,000; **Industry Concentration:** Consumer Products; **Function
Concentration:** Generalist

**Warren, Richard B.** — *President*
Cole, Warren & Long, Inc.
2 Penn Center, Suite 312
Philadelphia, PA 19102
Telephone: (215) 563-0701
**Recruiter Classification:** Retained; **Lowest/Average Salary:** $90,000/$90,000;
**Industry Concentration:** Generalist; **Function Concentration:** Generalist

**Warren, Sylvia W.** — *Partner*
Thorndike Deland Associates
275 Madison Avenue, Suite 1300
New York, NY 10016
Telephone: (212) 661-6200
**Recruiter Classification:** Retained; **Lowest/Average Salary:** $75,000/$90,000;
**Industry Concentration:** Generalist with a primary focus in Board Services,
Consumer Products, Entertainment, Fashion (Retail/Apparel), Financial
Services, Healthcare/Hospitals, Hospitality/Leisure, Information Technology,
Insurance, Manufacturing, Pharmaceutical/Medical, Publishing/Media, Venture
Capital; **Function Concentration:** Generalist with a primary focus in
Finance/Accounting, General Management, Human Resources, Marketing,
Sales

**Warter, Mark** — *Senior Recruiter*
Isaacson, Miller
334 Boylston Street, Suite 500
Boston, MA 02111
Telephone: (617) 262-6500
**Recruiter Classification:** Retained; **Lowest/Average Salary:** $75,000/$90,000;
**Industry Concentration:** Generalist with a primary focus in Information
Technology, Publishing/Media, Venture Capital; **Function Concentration:**
Administration, Finance/Accounting, General Management, Human Resources,
Women/Minorities

**Wasp, Warren T.** — *President*
WTW Associates
675 Third Avenue, Suite 2808
New York, NY 10017
Telephone: (212) 972-6990
**Recruiter Classification:** Retained; **Lowest/Average Salary:** $75,000/$90,000;
**Industry Concentration:** Generalist with a primary focus in Entertainment,
Financial Services; **Function Concentration:** Generalist

**Wasserman, Harvey** — *President*
Churchill and Affiliates, Inc.
1200 Bustleton Pike, Suite 3
Feasterville, PA 19053
Telephone: (215) 364-8070
**Recruiter Classification:** Contingency; **Lowest/Average Salary:**
$60,000/$90,000; **Industry Concentration:** High Technology; **Function
Concentration:** Engineering, Marketing, Sales

**Wassill, Larry** — *Recruiter*
Corporate Recruiters Ltd.
490-1140 West Pender
Vancouver, British Columbia, CANADA V6E 4G1
Telephone: (604) 687-5993
**Recruiter Classification:** Contingency; **Lowest/Average Salary:**
$40,000/$60,000; **Industry Concentration:** Electronics, High Technology,
Manufacturing, Transportation; **Function Concentration:** General Management,
Sales

**Wasson, Thomas W.** — *Senior Director*
Spencer Stuart
Financial Centre
695 East Main Street
Stamford, CT 06901
Telephone: (203) 324-6333
**Recruiter Classification:** Retained; **Lowest/Average Salary:** $90,000/$90,000;
**Industry Concentration:** Consumer Products, Financial Services, High
Technology, Information Technology, Insurance, Manufacturing,
Pharmaceutical/Medical; **Function Concentration:** Generalist

**Waters, Peter D.** — *Vice President*
John Kurosky & Associates
3 Corporate Park Drive, Suite 210
Irvine, CA 92714
Telephone: (714) 851-6370
**Recruiter Classification:** Retained; **Lowest/Average Salary:** $60,000/$90,000;
**Industry Concentration:** Pharmaceutical/Medical; **Function Concentration:**
Engineering, General Management, Marketing, Research and Development,
Sales

**Watkins, Jeffrey P.** — *Consultant*
Paul Ray Berndtson
191 Peachtree Tower, Suite 3800
191 Peachtree Street, NE
Atlanta, GA 30303-1757
Telephone: (404) 215-4600
**Recruiter Classification:** Retained; **Lowest/Average Salary:** $90,000/$90,000;
**Industry Concentration:** Generalist; **Function Concentration:** Generalist

**Watkins, Thomas M.** — *Partner*
Lamalie Amrop International
Thanksgiving Tower
1601 Elm Street
Dallas, TX 75201-4768
Telephone: (214) 754-0019
**Recruiter Classification:** Retained; **Lowest/Average Salary:** $90,000/$90,000;
**Industry Concentration:** Generalist with a primary focus in Education/Libraries,
Financial Services; **Function Concentration:** Generalist with a primary focus in
Finance/Accounting, General Management, Human Resources, Marketing

**Watson, James** — *Vice President*
MSI International
1050 Crown Pointe Parkway
Suite 1000
Atlanta, GA 30338
Telephone: (404) 394-2494
**Recruiter Classification:** Contingency; **Lowest/Average Salary:**
$30,000/$60,000; **Industry Concentration:** Generalist with a primary focus in
Financial Services, Healthcare/Hospitals, High Technology, Information
Technology, Manufacturing; **Function Concentration:** Administration,
Engineering, Finance/Accounting, General Management, Marketing

**Watson, Peggy** — *Regional Manager*
Advanced Information Management
444 Castro Street, Suite 320
Mountain View, CA 94041
Telephone: (415) 965-7799
**Recruiter Classification:** Contingency; **Lowest/Average Salary:**
$20,000/$40,000; **Industry Concentration:** Education/Libraries, Information
Technology; **Function Concentration:** Human Resources, Women/Minorities

**Watson, Stephen** — *Partner*
Paul Ray Berndtson
2200 Ross Avenue, Suite 4500W
Dallas, TX 75201
Telephone: (214) 969-7620
**Recruiter Classification:** Retained; **Lowest/Average Salary:** $90,000/$90,000;
**Industry Concentration:** High Technology; **Function Concentration:** Generalist

**Watson, Wally** — *Manager Southwest Region*
Management Recruiters International, Inc.
5495 Winchester Road, Suite 5
Memphis, TN 38115-4607
Telephone: (901) 794-3130
**Recruiter Classification:** Contingency; **Lowest/Average Salary:**
$30,000/$75,000; **Industry Concentration:** Generalist; **Function
Concentration:** Generalist

**Watt, Jennifer** — *Consultant*
The McCormick Group, Inc.
1400 Wilson Boulevard
Arlington, VA 22209
Telephone: (703) 841-1700
**Recruiter Classification:** Retained; **Lowest/Average Salary:** $90,000/$90,000;
**Industry Concentration:** Generalist; **Function Concentration:** Generalist

**Watters, John T.** — *Vice President/Managing Director*
DHR International, Inc.
201 East Kennedy Boulevard, Suite 1400
Tampa, FL 33602
Telephone: (813) 222-8940
**Recruiter Classification:** Retained; **Lowest/Average Salary:** $60,000/$90,000;
**Industry Concentration:** Generalist; **Function Concentration:** Generalist

**Wattier, David** — *Placement Specialist*
Key Employment Services
1001 Office Park Road, Suite 320
West Des Moines, IA 50265-2567
Telephone: (515) 224-0446
**Recruiter Classification:** Contingency; **Lowest/Average Salary:**
$30,000/$75,000; **Industry Concentration:** Generalist; **Function
Concentration:** Generalist

**Waxman, Bruce** — *Partner*
Ryan, Miller & Associates Inc.
4601 Wilshire Boulevard, Suite 225
Los Angeles, CA 90010
Telephone: (213) 938-4768
**Recruiter Classification:** Contingency; **Lowest/Average Salary:**
$50,000/$60,000; **Industry Concentration:** Generalist with a primary focus in
Consumer Products, Entertainment, Fashion (Retail/Apparel), Real Estate;
**Function Concentration:** Generalist with a primary focus in
Finance/Accounting

**Waxman, Kathleen** — *Branch Manager*
Accountants on Call
2175 North California Boulevard, Suite 615
Walnut Creek, CA 94596
Telephone: (510) 937-1000
**Recruiter Classification:** Contingency; **Lowest/Average Salary:**
$20,000/$30,000; **Industry Concentration:** Generalist; **Function
Concentration:** Finance/Accounting

**Waymire, Pamela** — *Associate*
Source Services Corporation
One South Main Street, Suite 1440
Dayton, OH 45402
Telephone: (513) 461-4660
**Recruiter Classification:** Contingency; **Lowest/Average Salary:**
$30,000/$50,000; **Industry Concentration:** Financial Services, Information
Technology; **Function Concentration:** Engineering, Finance/Accounting

**Wayne, Cary S.** — *President*
ProSearch Inc.
2550 SOM Center Road
Suite 320
Willoughby Hills, OH 44094
Telephone: (216) 585-9099
**Recruiter Classification:** Contingency; **Lowest/Average Salary:**
$40,000/$75,000; **Industry Concentration:** Aerospace/Defense, Automotive,
Chemical Products, Energy, Environmental, Financial Services, High
Technology, Information Technology; **Function Concentration:** Administration,
Engineering, Finance/Accounting, General Management, Human Resources,
Marketing, Research and Development, Sales

**Wayne, Victoria P.** — *Principal*
Korn/Ferry International
The Transamerica Pyramid
600 Montgomery Street
San Francisco, CA 94111
Telephone: (415) 956-1834
**Recruiter Classification:** Retained; **Lowest/Average Salary:** $90,000/$90,000;
**Industry Concentration:** Generalist; **Function Concentration:** Generalist

**Webb, Don W.** — *Co-Manager*
Management Recruiters International, Inc.
415 East Walnut Avenue, Suite 314
Dalton, GA 30721-4406
Telephone: (706) 226-8550
**Recruiter Classification:** Contingency; **Lowest/Average Salary:**
$30,000/$75,000; **Industry Concentration:** Generalist; **Function
Concentration:** Generalist

**Webb, George H.** — *Managing Director*
Webb, Johnson Associates, Inc.
280 Park Avenue, 43rd Floor
New York, NY 10017
Telephone: (212) 661-3700
**Recruiter Classification:** Retained; **Lowest/Average Salary:** $90,000/$90,000;
**Industry Concentration:** Generalist with a primary focus in Biotechnology,
Chemical Products, Financial Services, Healthcare/Hospitals, High Technology,
Manufacturing, Non-Profit, Pharmaceutical/Medical; **Function Concentration:**
Generalist with a primary focus in Administration, Engineering,
Finance/Accounting, General Management, Human Resources, Marketing,
Research and Development, Sales

**Webb, Pat A.** — *Manager Eastern Region*
Management Recruiters International, Inc.
201 Thomas Johnson Drive, Suite 202
Frederick, MD 21702
Telephone: (301) 663-0600
**Recruiter Classification:** Contingency; **Lowest/Average Salary:**
$30,000/$75,000; **Industry Concentration:** Generalist; **Function
Concentration:** Generalist

**Webb, Shawn K.** — *Executive Recruiter*
MSI International
200 Galleria Parkway
Suite 1610
Atlanta, GA 30339
Telephone: (404) 951-1208
**Recruiter Classification:** Contingency; **Lowest/Average Salary:**
$30,000/$75,000; **Industry Concentration:** Generalist with a primary focus in
Manufacturing; **Function Concentration:** Generalist with a primary focus in
Administration, Engineering, Finance/Accounting, General Management,
Marketing, Sales

**Webb, Verna F.** — *Co-Manager North Atlantic Region*
Management Recruiters International, Inc.
415 East Walnut Avenue, Suite 314
Dalton, GA 30721-4406
Telephone: (706) 226-8550
**Recruiter Classification:** Contingency; **Lowest/Average Salary:**
$30,000/$75,000; **Industry Concentration:** Generalist; **Function
Concentration:** Generalist

**Webber, Edward** — *Associate*
Source Services Corporation
155 Federal Street, Suite 410
Boston, MA 02110
Telephone: (617) 482-8211
**Recruiter Classification:** Contingency; **Lowest/Average Salary:**
$30,000/$50,000; **Industry Concentration:** Financial Services, Information
Technology; **Function Concentration:** Engineering, Finance/Accounting

**Weber, Fred** — *Managing Director*
J.B. Homer Associates, Inc.
Graybar Building
420 Lexington Avenue, Suite 2328
New York, NY 10170
Telephone: (212) 697-3300
**Recruiter Classification:** Retained; **Lowest/Average Salary:** $90,000/$90,000;
**Industry Concentration:** Generalist with a primary focus in Information
Technology; **Function Concentration:** Generalist

**Weber, Fritz** — *Manager Midwest Region*
Management Recruiters International, Inc.
Brenton Financial Center, Suite 400
150 1st Avenue N.E.
Cedar Rapids, IA 52401
Telephone: (319) 366-8441
**Recruiter Classification:** Contingency; **Lowest/Average Salary:**
$30,000/$75,000; **Industry Concentration:** Generalist; **Function
Concentration:** Generalist

**Weber, James K.** — *Manager South Atlantic Region*
Management Recruiters International, Inc.
2121 Ponce De Leon Boulevard, Suite 940
Coral Gables, FL 33134
Telephone: (305) 444-1200
**Recruiter Classification:** Contingency; **Lowest/Average Salary:**
$30,000/$75,000; **Industry Concentration:** Generalist; **Function
Concentration:** Generalist

**Weber, Jurgen** — *Principal*
BioQuest, Inc.
100 Spear Street, Suite 1125
San Francisco, CA 94105
Telephone: (415) 777-2422
**Recruiter Classification:** Retained; **Lowest/Average Salary:** $75,000/$90,000;
**Industry Concentration:** Biotechnology, Pharmaceutical/Medical; **Function
Concentration:** Engineering, Finance/Accounting, General Management,
Marketing, Research and Development, Sales

**Weber, Machelle** — *Consultant*
Paul Ray Berndtson
10 South Riverside Plaza
Suite 720
Chicago, IL 60606
Telephone: (312) 876-0730
**Recruiter Classification:** Retained; **Lowest/Average Salary:** $90,000/$90,000;
**Industry Concentration:** Generalist; **Function Concentration:** Generalist

**Webster, Robert C.** — *President*
The Lawsmiths of Northern California, Inc.
2443 Fillmore Street, Suite 319
San Francisco, CA 94115
Telephone: (415) 929-1090
**Recruiter Classification:** Executive Temporary

**Weed, William H.** — *Partner*
Paul Ray Berndtson
101 Park Avenue, 41st Floor
New York, NY 10178
Telephone: (212) 370-1316
**Recruiter Classification:** Retained; **Lowest/Average Salary:** $90,000/$90,000;
**Industry Concentration:** Consumer Products, Environmental,
Healthcare/Hospitals, Real Estate; **Function Concentration:** Generalist

**Weeks, Glenn** — *Associate*
Source Services Corporation
5343 North 16th Street, Suite 270
Phoenix, AZ 85016
Telephone: (602) 230-0220
**Recruiter Classification:** Contingency; **Lowest/Average Salary:**
$30,000/$50,000; **Industry Concentration:** Financial Services, Information
Technology; **Function Concentration:** Engineering, Finance/Accounting

**Weidener, Andrew E.** — *Industry Leader - Consumer Products*
Paul Ray Berndtson
191 Peachtree Tower, Suite 3800
191 Peachtree Street, NE
Atlanta, GA 30303-1757
Telephone: (404) 215-4600
**Recruiter Classification:** Retained; **Lowest/Average Salary:** $90,000/$90,000;
**Industry Concentration:** Consumer Products; **Function Concentration:**
Generalist

**Weiler, Tom** — *Consultant*
Executive Placement Consultants, Inc.
2700 River Road, Suite 107
Des Plaines, IL 60018
Telephone: (847) 298-6445
**Recruiter Classification:** Contingency; **Lowest/Average Salary:**
$30,000/$40,000; **Industry Concentration:** Generalist with a primary focus in
Information Technology; **Function Concentration:** Generalist

**Wein, Michael S.** — *Chairman*
InterimManagement Solutions, Inc.
6464 South Quebec Street
Englewood, CO 80111
Telephone: (303) 290-9500
**Recruiter Classification:** Executive Temporary; **Lowest/Average Salary:**
$50,000/$90,000; **Industry Concentration:** Electronics, Entertainment, High
Technology, Information Technology; **Function Concentration:** Generalist with
a primary focus in Administration, Engineering, Finance/Accounting, General
Management, Marketing, Research and Development, Sales

**Wein, Michael S.** — *President*
Media Management Resources, Inc.
6464 South Quebec Street
Englewood, CO 80111
Telephone: (303) 290-9800
**Recruiter Classification:** Contingency; **Lowest/Average Salary:**
$50,000/$75,000; **Industry Concentration:** Entertainment, High Technology,
Information Technology, Publishing/Media, Venture Capital; **Function
Concentration:** Administration, Engineering, General Management, Marketing,
Research and Development, Sales, Women/Minorities

**Wein, William** — *Associate*
InterimManagement Solutions, Inc.
6464 South Quebec Street
Englewood, CO 80111
Telephone: (303) 290-9500
**Recruiter Classification:** Executive Temporary; **Lowest/Average Salary:**
$50,000/$90,000; **Industry Concentration:** High Technology, Information
Technology, Publishing/Media; **Function Concentration:** Generalist with a
primary focus in Administration, Engineering, General Management,
Marketing, Sales

**Wein, William** — *Vice President*
Media Management Resources, Inc.
6464 South Quebec Street
Englewood, CO 80111
Telephone: (303) 290-9800
**Recruiter Classification:** Contingency; **Lowest/Average Salary:**
$50,000/$75,000; **Industry Concentration:** Entertainment, High Technology,
Information Technology, Publishing/Media, Venture Capital; **Function
Concentration:** Administration, Engineering, General Management, Marketing,
Research and Development, Sales, Women/Minorities

**Weinberg, Melvin** — *Managing Partner*
Romac & Associates
1001 Craig Road, Suite 260
St. Louis, MO 63146
Telephone: (314) 569-9898
**Recruiter Classification:** Executive Temporary; **Lowest/Average Salary:**
$/$60,000; **Industry Concentration:** Financial Services, Healthcare/Hospitals,
High Technology, Hospitality/Leisure, Information Technology, Insurance;
**Function Concentration:** Finance/Accounting

**Weiner, Arlene** — *Principal*
Sanford Rose Associates
394 South Milledge Avenue
Athens, GA 30605
Telephone: (706) 548-3942
**Recruiter Classification:** Contingency; **Lowest/Average Salary:**
$30,000/$75,000; **Industry Concentration:** Generalist with a primary focus in
Manufacturing, Pharmaceutical/Medical; **Function Concentration:** Generalist

**Weiner, Arthur** — *Principal*
Sanford Rose Associates
394 South Milledge Avenue
Athens, GA 30605
Telephone: (706) 548-3942
**Recruiter Classification:** Contingency; **Lowest/Average Salary:**
$30,000/$75,000; **Industry Concentration:** Generalist with a primary focus in
Manufacturing, Pharmaceutical/Medical; **Function Concentration:** Generalist

**Weintraub, Lynn** — *Director Associates/San Francisco*
The Paladin Companies, Inc.
One Market Plaza, 41st Floor
Spear Street Tower
San Francisco, CA 94105
Telephone: (415) 495-0900
**Recruiter Classification:** Executive Temporary; **Lowest/Average Salary:**
$40,000/$75,000; **Industry Concentration:** Generalist; **Function Concentration:** Marketing

**Weir, Norma** — *Consultant*
Paul Ray Berndtson
10 South Riverside Plaza
Suite 720
Chicago, IL 60606
Telephone: (312) 876-0730
**Recruiter Classification:** Retained; **Lowest/Average Salary:** $90,000/$90,000;
**Industry Concentration:** Generalist; **Function Concentration:** Generalist

**Weis, Theodore** — *Associate*
Source Services Corporation
5343 North 16th Street, Suite 270
Phoenix, AZ 85016
Telephone: (602) 230-0220
**Recruiter Classification:** Contingency; **Lowest/Average Salary:**
$30,000/$50,000; **Industry Concentration:** Financial Services, Information
Technology; **Function Concentration:** Engineering, Finance/Accounting

**Weisler, Nancy** — *Executive Insurance Consultant*
National Search, Inc.
2816 University Drive
Coral Springs, FL 33071
Telephone: (800) 935-4355
**Recruiter Classification:** Contingency; **Lowest/Average Salary:**
$30,000/$50,000; **Industry Concentration:** Healthcare/Hospitals, Insurance,
Pharmaceutical/Medical; **Function Concentration:** Generalist with a primary
focus in Administration, Finance/Accounting, General Management, Human
Resources, Marketing, Research and Development, Sales, Women/Minorities

**Weiss, Elizabeth** — *Associate*
Source Services Corporation
5429 LBJ Freeway, Suite 275
Dallas, TX 75240
Telephone: (214) 387-1600
**Recruiter Classification:** Contingency; **Lowest/Average Salary:**
$30,000/$50,000; **Industry Concentration:** Financial Services, Information
Technology; **Function Concentration:** Engineering, Finance/Accounting

**Weiss, Jeffrey** — *Account Executive*
Search West, Inc.
1888 Century Park East
Suite 2050
Los Angeles, CA 90067-1736
Telephone: (310) 284-8888
**Recruiter Classification:** Contingency; **Lowest/Average Salary:** $40,000/$60,000;
**Industry Concentration:** Biotechnology, Healthcare/Hospitals; **Function Concentration:** Engineering, General Management, Research and Development

**Weiss, Karen** — *Director International Client Services*
D.E. Foster Partners Inc.
570 Lexington Avenue, 14th Floor
New York, NY 10022
Telephone: (212) 872-6232
**Recruiter Classification:** Retained; **Lowest/Average Salary:** $90,000/$90,000;
**Industry Concentration:** Generalist; **Function Concentration:** Generalist

**Weissman-Rosenthal, Abbe** — *President*
ALW Research International
60 Canterbury Road
Chatham, NJ 07928
Telephone: (201) 701-9700
**Recruiter Classification:** Retained; **Lowest/Average Salary:** $60,000/$75,000;
**Industry Concentration:** Generalist with a primary focus in
Aerospace/Defense, Automotive, Biotechnology, Board Services, Chemical
Products, Consumer Products, Electronics, Energy, Environmental,
Healthcare/Hospitals, High Technology, Manufacturing, Non-Profit, Oil/Gas,
Pharmaceutical/Medical, Publishing/Media; **Function Concentration:**
Generalist with a primary focus in Engineering, General Management, Human
Resources, Marketing, Research and Development, Sales, Women/Minorities

**Weisz, Laura** — *Recruiter*
Anderson Sterling Associates
18623 Ventura Boulevard, Suite 207
Tarzana, CA 91356
Telephone: (818) 996-0921
**Recruiter Classification:** Executive Temporary; **Lowest/Average Salary:**
$30,000/$60,000; **Industry Concentration:** Biotechnology, Consumer
Products, Electronics, High Technology, Information Technology,
Manufacturing, Pharmaceutical/Medical; **Function Concentration:** Engineering,
Finance/Accounting, General Management, Human Resources, Marketing,
Research and Development, Sales, Women/Minorities

**Welch, Dale** — *Software Engineering Recruiter*
Winter, Wyman & Company
950 Winter Street, Suite 3100
Waltham, MA 02154-1294
Telephone: (617) 890-7000
**Recruiter Classification:** Contingency; **Lowest/Average Salary:**
$40,000/$75,000; **Industry Concentration:** High Technology, Information
Technology, Publishing/Media; **Function Concentration:** Engineering

**Welch, David** — *Senior Recruiter*
Isaacson, Miller
334 Boylston Street, Suite 500
Boston, MA 02111
Telephone: (617) 262-6500
**Recruiter Classification:** Retained; **Lowest/Average Salary:** $75,000/$90,000;
**Industry Concentration:** Generalist with a primary focus in Education/Libraries,
Healthcare/Hospitals; **Function Concentration:** Administration,
Finance/Accounting, General Management, Human Resources,
Women/Minorities

**Welch, Robert H.** — *Partner*
Heidrick & Struggles, Inc.
245 Park Avenue, Suite 4300
New York, NY 10167-0152
Telephone: (212) 867-9876
**Recruiter Classification:** Retained; **Lowest/Average Salary:** $75,000/$90,000;
**Industry Concentration:** Generalist with a primary focus in Utilities/Nuclear;
**Function Concentration:** Generalist

**Welch, Sarah** — *Principal*
Korn/Ferry International
One International Place
Boston, MA 02110-1800
Telephone: (617) 345-0200
**Recruiter Classification:** Retained; **Lowest/Average Salary:** $90,000/$90,000;
**Industry Concentration:** Generalist; **Function Concentration:** Generalist

**Weller, Paul S.** — *Senior Partner*
Mark Stanley & Company
1629 K Street N.W.
Washington, DC 20006-1602
Telephone: (202) 785-6711
**Recruiter Classification:** Retained; **Lowest/Average Salary:** $75,000/$90,000;
**Industry Concentration:** Generalist with a primary focus in Consumer
Products, Environmental, Financial Services, Healthcare/Hospitals, High
Technology, Pharmaceutical/Medical, Real Estate; **Function Concentration:**
Generalist with a primary focus in Finance/Accounting, General Management,
Human Resources, Sales

**Wellman, Michael** — *Managing Director*
Korn/Ferry International
237 Park Avenue
New York, NY 10017
Telephone: (212) 687-1834
**Recruiter Classification:** Retained; **Lowest/Average Salary:** $90,000/$90,000;
**Industry Concentration:** Generalist; **Function Concentration:** Generalist

**Welsh, Jason** — *Recruiter*
Ells Personnel System Inc.
9900 Bren Road East, Suite 105 Opus Center
Minnetonka, MN 55343
Telephone: (612) 932-9933
**Recruiter Classification:** Contingency; **Lowest/Average Salary:**
$40,000/$50,000; **Industry Concentration:** Manufacturing; **Function Concentration:** Engineering

**Wendorff, Tom** — *Associate*
Kenzer Corp.
777 Third Avenue, 26th Floor
New York, NY 10017
Telephone: (212) 308-4300
**Recruiter Classification:** Retained; **Lowest/Average Salary:** $50,000/$90,000;
**Industry Concentration:** Generalist; **Function Concentration:** Generalist

**Wentworth, John** — *President*
The Wentworth Company, Inc.
The Arcade Building
479 West Sixth Street
San Pedro, CA 90731
Telephone: (800) 995-9678
**Recruiter Classification:** Retained; **Lowest/Average Salary:** $/$90,000; **Industry Concentration:** Generalist; **Function Concentration:** Generalist

**Wentz, Terry M.** — *Manager South Atlantic Region*
Management Recruiters International, Inc.
916 Main Street, Suite 2000, P.O. Box 1455
Perry, GA 31069
Telephone: (912) 988-4444
**Recruiter Classification:** Contingency; **Lowest/Average Salary:**
$30,000/$75,000; **Industry Concentration:** Generalist; **Function Concentration:** Generalist

**Wenz, Alexander** — *Associate*
Source Services Corporation
4510 Executive Drive, Suite 200
San Diego, CA 92121
Telephone: (619) 552-0300
**Recruiter Classification:** Contingency; **Lowest/Average Salary:**
$30,000/$50,000; **Industry Concentration:** Financial Services, Information
Technology; **Function Concentration:** Engineering, Finance/Accounting

**Werner, Bonnie** — *Senior Consultant*
H.M. Long International, Ltd.
237 Park Avenue, 21st Floor
New York, NY 10017
Telephone: (212) 725-5150
**Recruiter Classification:** Retained; **Lowest/Average Salary:** $90,000/$90,000;
**Industry Concentration:** Generalist with a primary focus in Biotechnology,
Consumer Products, Electronics, Financial Services, Pharmaceutical/Medical;
**Function Concentration:** Generalist with a primary focus in Administration,
Engineering, General Management, Human Resources, Marketing, Research
and Development

**Wert, Marty** — *Consultant*
Parfitt Recruiting and Consulting
1540 140th Avenue NE #201
Bellevue, WA 98005
Telephone: (206) 646-6300
**Recruiter Classification:** Contingency; **Lowest/Average Salary:**
$30,000/$75,000; **Industry Concentration:** Generalist with a primary focus in
Information Technology; **Function Concentration:** Generalist

**Wertel, Ronald E.** — *Vice President*
Gordon Wahls Company
P.O. Box 905
610 East Baltimore Pike
Media, PA 19063
Telephone: (610) 565-0800
**Recruiter Classification:** Contingency; **Lowest/Average Salary:**
$30,000/$60,000; **Industry Concentration:** Packaging, Publishing/Media;
**Function Concentration:** Generalist with a primary focus in Administration,
Engineering, Finance/Accounting, General Management, Marketing, Sales

**Wertheim, M. Chris** — *Consultant*
Witt/Kieffer, Ford, Hadelman & Lloyd
432 North 44th Street
Suite 360
Phoenix, AZ 85008
Telephone: (602) 267-1370
**Recruiter Classification:** Retained; **Lowest/Average Salary:** $75,000/$90,000;
**Industry Concentration:** Healthcare/Hospitals; **Function Concentration:**
Generalist

**Wesley, Terry R.** — *Manager Central Region*
Management Recruiters International, Inc.
Euclid Office Plaza, Suite 811
26250 Euclid Avenue
Cleveland, OH 44132-3674
Telephone: (216) 261-7696
**Recruiter Classification:** Contingency; **Lowest/Average Salary:**
$30,000/$75,000; **Industry Concentration:** Generalist; **Function
Concentration:** Generalist

**Wessel, Michael J.** — *Senior Consultant*
Spectra International Inc.
6991 East Camelback Road, Suite B-305
Scottsdale, AZ 85251
Telephone: (602) 481-0411
**Recruiter Classification:** Contingency; **Lowest/Average Salary:**
$30,000/$50,000; **Industry Concentration:** Fashion (Retail/Apparel); **Function
Concentration:** Generalist

**Wessling, Jerry** — *Associate*
Source Services Corporation
One South Main Street, Suite 1440
Dayton, OH 45402
Telephone: (513) 461-4660
**Recruiter Classification:** Contingency; **Lowest/Average Salary:**
$30,000/$50,000; **Industry Concentration:** Financial Services, Information
Technology; **Function Concentration:** Engineering, Finance/Accounting

**West, Nancy** — *Vice President*
Health Care Dimensions
7150 Campus Drive, Suite 320
Colorado Springs, CO 80920
Telephone: (800) 373-3401
**Recruiter Classification:** Contingency; **Lowest/Average Salary:**
$40,000/$75,000; **Industry Concentration:** Healthcare/Hospitals, Insurance;
**Function Concentration:** Generalist with a primary focus in Administration,
Finance/Accounting, General Management, Marketing, Sales

**West, Vikki Lynn** — *Placement Manager*
Accounting & Bookkeeping Personnel, Inc.
1702 East Highland, Suite 200
Phoenix, AZ 85016
Telephone: (602) 277-3700
**Recruiter Classification:** Contingency, Executive Temporary; **Lowest/Average
Salary:** $20,000/$50,000; **Industry Concentration:** Generalist; **Function
Concentration:** Finance/Accounting

**Westberry, David M.** — *Partner*
Lamalie Amrop International
Thanksgiving Tower
1601 Elm Street
Dallas, TX 75201-4768
Telephone: (214) 754-0019
**Recruiter Classification:** Retained; **Lowest/Average Salary:** $90,000/$90,000;
**Industry Concentration:** Generalist; **Function Concentration:** Generalist

**Westerfield, Putney** — *Managing Director*
Boyden
Embarcadero Center West Tower
275 Battery St., Suite 420
San Francisco, CA 94111
Telephone: (415) 981-7900
**Recruiter Classification:** Retained; **Lowest/Average Salary:** $75,000/$90,000;
**Industry Concentration:** Generalist; **Function Concentration:** Generalist with a
primary focus in Engineering, Finance/Accounting, General Management,
Human Resources, Marketing, Research and Development, Sales,
Women/Minorities

**Weston, Corinne F.** — *Director Research*
D.A. Kreuter Associates, Inc.
1100 East Hector Street, Suite 388
Conshohocken, PA 19428
Telephone: (610) 834-1100
**Recruiter Classification:** Retained; **Lowest/Average Salary:** $60,000/$90,000;
**Industry Concentration:** Financial Services, Insurance; **Function
Concentration:** General Management, Marketing, Sales

**Wexler, Rona** — *Executive Vice President*
Ariel Recruitment Associates
440 West 53rd Street, Suite 126
New York, NY 10019
Telephone: (212) 765-8300
**Recruiter Classification:** Contingency; **Lowest/Average Salary:**
$50,000/$75,000; **Industry Concentration:** Entertainment, Publishing/Media;
**Function Concentration:** Generalist with a primary focus in Administration,
Finance/Accounting, General Management, Human Resources, Marketing,
Sales

**Whalen, Kathleen** — *Vice President*
The Nielsen Healthcare Group
P.O. Box 3734
St. Louis, MO 63122
Telephone: (314) 984-0910
**Recruiter Classification:** Executive Temporary; **Lowest/Average Salary:**
$20,000/$50,000; **Industry Concentration:** Healthcare/Hospitals; **Function
Concentration:** Generalist

**Whaley, Robert B.** — *Partner*
TASA International
750 Lexington Avenue
Suite 1800
New York, NY 10022
Telephone: (212) 486-1490
**Recruiter Classification:** Retained; **Lowest/Average Salary:** $90,000/$90,000;
**Industry Concentration:** Generalist; **Function Concentration:** Generalist

**Wheatley, William** — *Senior Recruiter*
Drummond Associates, Inc.
50 Broadway, Suite 1201
New York, NY 10004
Telephone: (212) 248-1120
**Recruiter Classification:** Contingency; **Lowest/Average Salary:**
$40,000/$75,000; **Industry Concentration:** Financial Services, Information
Technology; **Function Concentration:** Finance/Accounting

**Wheel, Eric** — *Manager Pacific Region*
Management Recruiters International, Inc.
591 Redwood Highway, Suite 2225
Mill Valley, CA 94941
Telephone: (415) 383-7044
**Recruiter Classification:** Contingency; **Lowest/Average Salary:**
$30,000/$75,000; **Industry Concentration:** Generalist; **Function
Concentration:** Generalist

**Wheeler, Gerard H.** — *Recruiter*
A.J. Burton Group, Inc.
120 East Baltimore Street, Suite 2220
Baltimore, MD 21202
Telephone: (410) 752-5244
**Recruiter Classification:** Contingency; **Lowest/Average Salary:**
$40,000/$60,000; **Industry Concentration:** Consumer Products, Energy, Financial Services, Insurance, Manufacturing; **Function Concentration:**
Finance/Accounting

**Wheeler, Mary T.** — *Partner*
Lamalie Amrop International
200 Park Avenue
New York, NY 10166-0136
Telephone: (212) 953-7900
**Recruiter Classification:** Retained; **Lowest/Average Salary:** $90,000/$90,000;
**Industry Concentration:** Generalist with a primary focus in Non-Profit;
**Function Concentration:** Generalist with a primary focus in
Finance/Accounting

**Whitaker, Charles** — *Consultant*
Evie Kreisler & Associates, Inc.
2720 Stemmons Freeway, Suite 812
Dallas, TX 75207
Telephone: (214) 631-8994
**Recruiter Classification:** Contingency; **Lowest/Average Salary:**
$30,000/$75,000; **Industry Concentration:** Fashion (Retail/Apparel); **Function Concentration:** Generalist

**Whitcomb, Nancy C.** — *Consultant Associate*
Educational Management Network
98 Old South Road
Nantucket, MA 02554
Telephone: (508) 228-6700
**Recruiter Classification:** Retained; **Lowest/Average Salary:** $60,000/$90,000;
**Industry Concentration:** Education/Libraries, Non-Profit; **Function Concentration:** Generalist with a primary focus in Administration,
Finance/Accounting, Human Resources

**White, Jeffrey E.** — *Director Recruitment*
Simpson Associates
Trump Parc
106 Central Park South
New York, NY 10019
Telephone: (212) 767-0006
**Recruiter Classification:** Contingency; **Lowest/Average Salary:**
$60,000/$90,000; **Industry Concentration:** Fashion (Retail/Apparel); **Function Concentration:** Finance/Accounting, Human Resources, Marketing, Sales

**White, Jonathan** — *Director*
Spencer Stuart
525 Market Street, Suite 3700
San Francisco, CA 94105
Telephone: (415) 495-4141
**Recruiter Classification:** Retained; **Lowest/Average Salary:** $90,000/$90,000;
**Industry Concentration:** Generalist; **Function Concentration:** Generalist

**White, Jonathan O.** — *Vice President*
The Badger Group
4125 Blackhawk Plaza Circle, Suite 270
Danville, CA 94506
Telephone: (510) 736-5553
**Recruiter Classification:** Retained; **Lowest/Average Salary:** $90,000/$90,000;
**Industry Concentration:** Generalist with a primary focus in Consumer Products, Electronics, Financial Services, Healthcare/Hospitals, High Technology, Information Technology, Manufacturing; **Function Concentration:** Generalist with a primary focus in Engineering, Finance/Accounting, General Management, Marketing, Research and Development, Sales

**White, Kimberly** — *Account Executive*
Executive Referral Services, Inc.
8770 West Bryn Mawr, Suite 110
Chicago, IL 60631
Telephone: (312) 693-6622
**Recruiter Classification:** Contingency; **Lowest/Average Salary:**
$30,000/$50,000; **Industry Concentration:** Fashion (Retail/Apparel),
Hospitality/Leisure; **Function Concentration:** Finance/Accounting, General Management, Human Resources, Sales

**White, Patricia D.** — *Physician Recruiter*
MSI International
230 Peachtree Street, N.E.
Suite 1550
Atlanta, GA 30303
Telephone: (404) 653-7360
**Recruiter Classification:** Contingency; **Lowest/Average Salary:**
$30,000/$75,000; **Industry Concentration:** Generalist with a primary focus in Healthcare/Hospitals, Pharmaceutical/Medical; **Function Concentration:**
Generalist with a primary focus in Administration, Engineering,
Finance/Accounting, General Management, Marketing, Sales

**White, Richard B.** — *Senior Director*
Spencer Stuart
Financial Centre
695 East Main Street
Stamford, CT 06901
Telephone: (203) 324-6333
**Recruiter Classification:** Retained; **Lowest/Average Salary:** $90,000/$90,000;
**Industry Concentration:** Generalist with a primary focus in Consumer Products, Financial Services, Venture Capital; **Function Concentration:**
Generalist with a primary focus in General Management, Marketing, Sales

**White, William C.** — *President*
Venture Resources Inc.
2659 Townsgate Road, Suite 119
Westlake Village, CA 91361
Telephone: (805) 371-3600
**Recruiter Classification:** Retained; **Lowest/Average Salary:** $90,000/$90,000;
**Industry Concentration:** Biotechnology, Electronics, High Technology, Information Technology, Venture Capital; **Function Concentration:** Generalist with a primary focus in Engineering, Finance/Accounting, General Management, Human Resources, Marketing, Research and Development, Sales

**Whitfield, Jack** — *Associate*
Source Services Corporation
1233 North Mayfair Road, Suite 300
Milwaukee, WI 53226
Telephone: (414) 774-6700
**Recruiter Classification:** Contingency; **Lowest/Average Salary:**
$30,000/$50,000; **Industry Concentration:** Financial Services, Information Technology; **Function Concentration:** Engineering, Finance/Accounting

**Whiting, Anthony** — *Consulting Associate*
Johnson Smith & Knisely Accord
100 Park Avenue, 15th Floor
New York, NY 10017
Telephone: (212) 885-9100
**Recruiter Classification:** Retained; **Lowest/Average Salary:** $90,000/$90,000;
**Industry Concentration:** Financial Services, Insurance, Real Estate, Venture Capital; **Function Concentration:** Generalist with a primary focus in Administration, Finance/Accounting, General Management, Human Resources, Marketing, Research and Development, Sales

**Whitley, Sue Ann** — *Principal*
Roberts Ryan and Bentley
245 Dean Lane
Grosse Pointe, MI 48236
Telephone: (313) 882-9967
**Recruiter Classification:** Retained; **Lowest/Average Salary:** $90,000/$90,000;
**Industry Concentration:** Healthcare/Hospitals, Insurance; **Function Concentration:** Generalist with a primary focus in Human Resources, Marketing, Sales

**Whitley, Tom H.** — *General Manager*
Management Recruiters International, Inc.
305 South Main Street
Kannapolis, NC 28081
Telephone: (704) 938-6144
**Recruiter Classification:** Contingency; **Lowest/Average Salary:**
$30,000/$75,000; **Industry Concentration:** Generalist; **Function Concentration:** Generalist

**Whitney, David L.** — *President*
Whitney & Associates, Inc.
920 Second Avenue South, Suite 625
Minneapolis, MN 55402-4035
Telephone: (612) 338-5600
**Recruiter Classification:** Contingency, Executive Temporary; **Lowest/Average Salary:** $20,000/$50,000; **Industry Concentration:** Generalist with a primary focus in Biotechnology, Consumer Products, Electronics, Financial Services, Healthcare/Hospitals, High Technology, Information Technology, Insurance, Manufacturing, Packaging, Pharmaceutical/Medical, Publishing/Media, Real Estate, Transportation, Venture Capital; **Function Concentration:**
Finance/Accounting

**Whitney, Kenneth L.** — *Chief Executive Officer*
K.L. Whitney Company
6 Aspen Drive
North Caldwell, NJ 07006
Telephone: (201) 228-7124
**Recruiter Classification:** Retained; **Lowest/Average Salary:** $75,000/$90,000;
**Industry Concentration:** Financial Services; **Function Concentration:**
Marketing, Sales

**Whittall, Barbara** — *Partner*
Heidrick & Struggles, Inc.
BCE Place, 161 Bay Street, Suite 2310
P.O. Box 601
Toronto, Ontario, CANADA M5J 2S1
Telephone: (416) 361-4700
**Recruiter Classification:** Retained; **Lowest/Average Salary:** $75,000/$90,000;
**Industry Concentration:** Generalist with a primary focus in Consumer
Products, Healthcare/Hospitals; **Function Concentration:** Generalist

**Whitton, Paula L.** — *Associate*
Pearson, Caldwell & Farnsworth, Inc.
250 Park Avenue, 17th Floor
New York, NY 10177
Telephone: (212) 983-5850
**Recruiter Classification:** Retained; **Lowest/Average Salary:** $90,000/$90,000;
**Industry Concentration:** Financial Services; **Function Concentration:**
Administration, Finance/Accounting, General Management, Human Resources,
Marketing, Sales

**Wichansky, Mark** — *Executive Recruiter*
TSS Consulting, Ltd.
2425 East Camelback Road
Suite 375
Phoenix, AZ 85016
Telephone: (602) 955-7000
**Recruiter Classification:** Contingency; **Lowest/Average Salary:** $60,000/$75,000;
**Industry Concentration:** Aerospace/Defense, Electronics, High Technology;
**Function Concentration:** Engineering, General Management, Marketing

**Wichlei, Alan** — *Senior Recruiter*
Isaacson, Miller
334 Boylston Street, Suite 500
Boston, MA 02111
Telephone: (617) 262-6500
**Recruiter Classification:** Retained; **Lowest/Average Salary:** $75,000/$90,000;
**Industry Concentration:** Generalist; **Function Concentration:** Administration,
Finance/Accounting, General Management, Human Resources,
Women/Minorities

**Wicklund, Grant** — *Partner*
Heidrick & Struggles, Inc.
2200 Ross Avenue, Suite 4700E
Dallas, TX 75201-2787
Telephone: (214) 220-2130
**Recruiter Classification:** Retained; **Lowest/Average Salary:** $75,000/$90,000;
**Industry Concentration:** Generalist with a primary focus in
Healthcare/Hospitals; **Function Concentration:** Generalist

**Wieder, Thomas A.** — *Manager Eastern Region*
Management Recruiters International, Inc.
77 North Centre Avenue, Suite 211
Rockville Centre, NY 11571
Telephone: (516) 536-3111
**Recruiter Classification:** Contingency; **Lowest/Average Salary:** $30,000/$75,000;
**Industry Concentration:** Generalist; **Function Concentration:** Generalist

**Wieland, Patrick** — *Staff Manager*
Bradford & Galt, Inc.
12400 Olive Boulevard, Suite 430
St. Louis, MO 63141
Telephone: (314) 434-9200
**Recruiter Classification:** Contingency; **Lowest/Average Salary:** $30,000/$30,000;
**Industry Concentration:** Generalist; **Function Concentration:** Generalist

**Wier, Daniel** — *Managing Director Western Region*
Horton International
333 South Grand Avenue, Suite 2980
Los Angeles, CA 90071
Telephone: (213) 628-2580
**Recruiter Classification:** Retained; **Lowest/Average Salary:** $90,000/$90,000;
**Industry Concentration:** Generalist with a primary focus in
Aerospace/Defense, Board Services, Consumer Products, Education/Libraries,
Electronics, Energy, Entertainment, Environmental, Financial Services, High
Technology, Manufacturing, Non-Profit, Oil/Gas, Publishing/Media, Real
Estate, Transportation, Venture Capital; **Function Concentration:** Generalist
with a primary focus in Administration, Engineering, Finance/Accounting,
General Management, Human Resources, Marketing, Sales, Women/Minorities

**Wierichs, Jeffrey C.** — *Principal*
TASA International
750 Lexington Avenue
Suite 1800
New York, NY 10022
Telephone: (212) 486-1490
**Recruiter Classification:** Retained; **Lowest/Average Salary:** $90,000/$90,000;
**Industry Concentration:** Generalist; **Function Concentration:** Generalist

**Wilbanks, George R.** — *Managing Director*
Russell Reynolds Associates, Inc.
200 Park Avenue
New York, NY 10166-0002
Telephone: (212) 351-2000
**Recruiter Classification:** Retained; **Lowest/Average Salary:** $90,000/$90,000;
**Industry Concentration:** Generalist with a primary focus in Financial Services;
**Function Concentration:** Generalist

**Wilcox, Fred T.** — *President*
Wilcox, Bertoux & Miller
100 Howe Avenue, Suite 155N
Sacramento, CA 95825
Telephone: (916) 977-3700
**Recruiter Classification:** Contingency; **Lowest/Average Salary:**
$50,000/$90,000; **Industry Concentration:** Board Services, Financial Services,
Information Technology; **Function Concentration:** Administration,
Finance/Accounting, General Management

**Wilcox, Jan** — *Associate*
Kenzer Corp.
777 Third Avenue, 26th Floor
New York, NY 10017
Telephone: (212) 308-4300
**Recruiter Classification:** Retained; **Lowest/Average Salary:** $50,000/$90,000;
**Industry Concentration:** Generalist; **Function Concentration:** Generalist

**Wilcox, Karen** — *Senior Recruiter*
Isaacson, Miller
334 Boylston Street, Suite 500
Boston, MA 02111
Telephone: (617) 262-6500
**Recruiter Classification:** Retained; **Lowest/Average Salary:** $75,000/$90,000;
**Industry Concentration:** Generalist with a primary focus in Environmental,
Non-Profit; **Function Concentration:** Administration, Finance/Accounting,
General Management, Human Resources, Women/Minorities

**Wilder, Barry** — *Partner*
Rhodes Associates
555 Fifth Avenue
New York, NY 10017
Telephone: (212) 983-2000
**Recruiter Classification:** Retained; **Lowest/Average Salary:** $90,000/$90,000;
**Industry Concentration:** Financial Services, Insurance, Real Estate, Venture
Capital; **Function Concentration:** Generalist

**Wilder, Richard B.** — *Managing Principal*
Columbia Consulting Group
10725 East Cholla Lane
Scottsdale, AZ 85259
Telephone: (602) 451-1180
**Recruiter Classification:** Retained; **Lowest/Average Salary:** $75,000/$90,000;
**Industry Concentration:** Generalist with a primary focus in Biotechnology,
Consumer Products, Financial Services, Healthcare/Hospitals, High
Technology, Hospitality/Leisure, Information Technology, Insurance,
Manufacturing, Publishing/Media, Venture Capital; **Function Concentration:**
Generalist with a primary focus in Finance/Accounting, General Management,
Human Resources, Marketing

**Wile, Harold** — *Associate*
Kenzer Corp.
1600 Parkwood Circle NW, Suite 310
Atlanta, GA 30339
Telephone: (770) 955-7210
**Recruiter Classification:** Retained; **Lowest/Average Salary:** $50,000/$90,000;
**Industry Concentration:** Generalist; **Function Concentration:** Generalist

**Wilensky, Joel H.** — *President*
Joel H. Wilensky Associates, Inc.
22 Union Avenue
P.O. Box 155
Sudbury, MA 01776
Telephone: (508) 443-5176
**Recruiter Classification:** Contingency; **Lowest/Average Salary:**
$50,000/$90,000; **Industry Concentration:** Fashion (Retail/Apparel); **Function
Concentration:** Finance/Accounting

**Wilkie, Glenn** — *Vice President*
Korn/Ferry International
Scotia Plaza
40 King Street West
Toronto, Ontario, CANADA M5H 3Y2
Telephone: (416) 366-1300
**Recruiter Classification:** Retained; **Lowest/Average Salary:** $90,000/$90,000;
**Industry Concentration:** Generalist; **Function Concentration:** Generalist

**Wilkins, Walter K.** — *Senior Vice President*
Sampson Neill & Wilkins Inc.
543 Valley Road
Upper Montclair, NJ 07043
Telephone: (201) 783-9600
**Recruiter Classification:** Retained; **Lowest/Average Salary:** $75,000/$90,000;
**Industry Concentration:** Healthcare/Hospitals, Pharmaceutical/Medical;
**Function Concentration:** Engineering, General Management, Marketing,
Research and Development, Sales

**Wilkinson, Barbara** — *Associate*
Beall & Company, Inc.
535 Colonial Park Drive
Roswell, GA 30075
Telephone: (404) 992-0900
**Recruiter Classification:** Retained; **Lowest/Average Salary:** $90,000/$90,000;
**Industry Concentration:** Generalist with a primary focus in Biotechnology,
Board Services, Financial Services, Healthcare/Hospitals, High Technology,
Insurance, Pharmaceutical/Medical, Real Estate, Venture Capital; **Function
Concentration:** Generalist with a primary focus in Administration, Engineering,
Finance/Accounting, General Management, Human Resources, Marketing,
Research and Development, Sales

**Wilkinson, William R.** — *Partner*
Wilkinson & Ives
One Bush Street, Suite 550
San Francisco, CA 94104
Telephone: (415) 834-3100
**Recruiter Classification:** Retained; **Lowest/Average Salary:** $90,000/$90,000;
**Industry Concentration:** Generalist with a primary focus in
Aerospace/Defense, Board Services, Consumer Products, Energy, High
Technology, Insurance, Manufacturing, Non-Profit, Packaging, Transportation,
Venture Capital; **Function Concentration:** Generalist with a primary focus in
Administration, Engineering, Finance/Accounting, General Management,
Human Resources, Marketing, Research and Development, Sales

**Willbrandt, Curt** — *Associate*
Source Services Corporation
161 Ottawa NW, Suite 409D
Grand Rapids, MI 49503
Telephone: (616) 451-2400
**Recruiter Classification:** Contingency; **Lowest/Average Salary:**
$30,000/$50,000; **Industry Concentration:** Financial Services, Information
Technology; **Function Concentration:** Engineering, Finance/Accounting

**Willcox, David R.** — *Managing Director*
Senior Careers Executive Search
257 Park Avenue South
New York, NY 10010
Telephone: (212) 529-6660
**Recruiter Classification:** Retained, Executive Temporary; **Lowest/Average
Salary:** $50,000/$75,000; **Industry Concentration:** Generalist; **Function
Concentration:** Generalist

**Williams, Alexander H.** — *Shareholder*
Witt/Kieffer, Ford, Hadelman & Lloyd
Three Park Avenue, 29th Floor
New York, NY 10016
Telephone: (212) 686-2676
**Recruiter Classification:** Retained; **Lowest/Average Salary:** $75,000/$90,000;
**Industry Concentration:** Healthcare/Hospitals; **Function Concentration:**
Generalist with a primary focus in Administration, Finance/Accounting,
General Management, Human Resources, Marketing

**Williams, Angie** — *Executive Recruiter*
Whitney & Associates, Inc.
920 Second Avenue South, Suite 625
Minneapolis, MN 55402-4035
Telephone: (612) 338-5600
**Recruiter Classification:** Contingency, Executive Temporary; **Lowest/Average
Salary:** $20,000/$50,000; **Industry Concentration:** Generalist with a primary
focus in Biotechnology, Consumer Products, Electronics, Financial Services,
Healthcare/Hospitals, High Technology, Information Technology, Insurance,
Manufacturing, Packaging, Pharmaceutical/Medical, Publishing/Media, Real
Estate, Transportation, Venture Capital; **Function Concentration:**
Finance/Accounting

**Williams, Barbara** — *Associate*
Kenzer Corp.
625 North Michigan Avenue, Suite 1244
Chicago, IL 60611
Telephone: (312) 266-0976
**Recruiter Classification:** Retained; **Lowest/Average Salary:** $50,000/$90,000;
**Industry Concentration:** Generalist; **Function Concentration:** Generalist

**Williams, Brad** — *Information Technology Recruiter*
Winter, Wyman & Company
950 Winter Street, Suite 3100
Waltham, MA 02154-1294
Telephone: (617) 890-7000
**Recruiter Classification:** Contingency; **Lowest/Average Salary:**
$30,000/$60,000; **Industry Concentration:** Generalist with a primary focus in
Information Technology; **Function Concentration:** Generalist

**Williams, Dave** — *Consultant*
The McCormick Group, Inc.
1400 Wilson Boulevard
Arlington, VA 22209
Telephone: (703) 841-1700
**Recruiter Classification:** Retained; **Lowest/Average Salary:** $40,000/$60,000;
**Industry Concentration:** Generalist with a primary focus in High Technology,
Information Technology, Real Estate; **Function Concentration:** Engineering,
Marketing, Sales

**Williams, Ellen** — *Senior Associate*
Korn/Ferry International
One Landmark Square
Stamford, CT 06901
Telephone: (203) 359-3350
**Recruiter Classification:** Retained; **Lowest/Average Salary:** $90,000/$90,000;
**Industry Concentration:** Generalist; **Function Concentration:** Generalist

**Williams, Gary L.** — *Consultant*
Barnes Development Group, LLC
1017 West Glen Oaks Lane, Suite 108
Mequon, WI 53092
Telephone: (414) 241-8468
**Recruiter Classification:** Retained; **Lowest/Average Salary:** $50,000/$75,000;
**Industry Concentration:** Generalist with a primary focus in Automotive, Board
Services, Chemical Products, Electronics, Healthcare/Hospitals, Information
Technology, Insurance, Manufacturing, Non-Profit, Packaging,
Pharmaceutical/Medical, Transportation; **Function Concentration:** Generalist
with a primary focus in Administration, Engineering, Finance/Accounting,
General Management, Human Resources, Marketing, Research and
Development, Sales

**Williams, Harry D.** — *Search Consultant*
Jacobson Associates
Five Neshaminy Interplex
Suite 113
Trevose, PA 19053
Telephone: (215) 639-5860
**Recruiter Classification:** Contingency; **Lowest/Average Salary:**
$20,000/$40,000; **Industry Concentration:** Financial Services, Insurance;
**Function Concentration:** Generalist with a primary focus in Administration,
Finance/Accounting, General Management, Marketing, Research and
Development, Sales

**Williams, John** — *Associate*
Source Services Corporation
2850 National City Tower
Louisville, KY 40202
Telephone: (502) 581-9900
**Recruiter Classification:** Contingency; **Lowest/Average Salary:**
$30,000/$50,000; **Industry Concentration:** Financial Services, Information
Technology; **Function Concentration:** Engineering, Finance/Accounting

**Williams, Kenneth C.** — *Manager Midwest Region*
Management Recruiters International, Inc.
2110 North Market Street, Suite 112
Champaign, IL 61821-1306
Telephone: (217) 398-0050
**Recruiter Classification:** Contingency; **Lowest/Average Salary:**
$30,000/$75,000; **Industry Concentration:** Generalist; **Function
Concentration:** Generalist

**Williams, Larry** — *Manager Midwest Region*
Management Recruiters International, Inc.
684 SE Bayberry Lane, Suite 104
Lee's Summit, MO 64063
Telephone: (816) 246-6636
**Recruiter Classification:** Contingency; **Lowest/Average Salary:**
$30,000/$75,000; **Industry Concentration:** Generalist; **Function
Concentration:** Generalist

**Williams, Laura** — *Consultant*
Paul Ray Berndtson
One Allen Center
500 Dallas, Suite 3010
Houston, TX 77002
Telephone: (713) 309-1400
**Recruiter Classification:** Retained; **Lowest/Average Salary:** $90,000/$90,000;
**Industry Concentration:** Generalist; **Function Concentration:** Generalist

**Williams, Laurelle N.** — *Manager*
MSI International
1900 North 18th Street
Suite 303
Monroe, LA 71201
Telephone: (318) 324-0406
**Recruiter Classification:** Contingency; **Lowest/Average Salary:**
$30,000/$60,000; **Industry Concentration:** Generalist with a primary focus in
Healthcare/Hospitals, Pharmaceutical/Medical; **Function Concentration:**
Generalist with a primary focus in Administration, Engineering,
Finance/Accounting, General Management, Marketing, Sales

**Williams, Lis** — *Recruiter*
Executive Options, Ltd.
910 Skokie Boulevard
Suite 210
Northbrook, IL 60068
Telephone: (708) 291-4322
**Recruiter Classification:** Executive Temporary; **Lowest/Average Salary:**
$30,000/$50,000; **Industry Concentration:** Generalist with a primary focus in
Consumer Products, Financial Services, Healthcare/Hospitals, Manufacturing,
Non-Profit, Packaging, Real Estate; **Function Concentration:** Generalist with a
primary focus in Finance/Accounting, General Management, Human
Resources, Marketing, Women/Minorities

**Williams, Lynn** — *Principal*
Korn/Ferry International
One Landmark Square
Stamford, CT 06901
Telephone: (203) 359-3350
**Recruiter Classification:** Retained; **Lowest/Average Salary:** $90,000/$90,000;
**Industry Concentration:** Generalist; **Function Concentration:** Generalist

**Williams, Michelle Cruz** — *Senior Recruiter*
Isaacson, Miller
334 Boylston Street, Suite 500
Boston, MA 02111
Telephone: (617) 262-6500
**Recruiter Classification:** Retained; **Lowest/Average Salary:** $75,000/$90,000;
**Industry Concentration:** Generalist; **Function Concentration:** Administration,
Finance/Accounting, General Management, Human Resources,
Women/Minorities

**Williams, Nicole** — *Executive Recruiter*
Richard, Wayne and Roberts
24 Greenway Plaza, Suite 1304
Houston, TX 77046-2493
Telephone: (713) 629-6681
**Recruiter Classification:** Retained; **Lowest/Average Salary:** $40,000/$60,000;
**Industry Concentration:** Generalist with a primary focus in Real Estate;
**Function Concentration:** Generalist

**Williams, Richard** — *Vice President*
Blackshaw, Olmstead & Lynch
1010 Monarch Plaza
3414 Peachtree Road N.E.
Atlanta, GA 30326
Telephone: (404) 261-7770
**Recruiter Classification:** Retained; **Lowest/Average Salary:** $75,000/$90,000;
**Industry Concentration:** Generalist; **Function Concentration:** Generalist

**Williams, Roger K.** — *Partner*
Williams, Roth & Krueger Inc.
20 North Wacker Drive
Chicago, IL 60606
Telephone: (312) 977-0800
**Recruiter Classification:** Retained; **Lowest/Average Salary:** $90,000/$90,000;
**Industry Concentration:** Generalist with a primary focus in Automotive,
Biotechnology, Board Services, Chemical Products, Consumer Products,
Electronics, Financial Services, Healthcare/Hospitals, High Technology,
Information Technology, Manufacturing, Pharmaceutical/Medical,
Transportation, Venture Capital; **Function Concentration:** Generalist with a
primary focus in Administration, Engineering, Finance/Accounting, General
Management, Human Resources, Marketing, Research and Development, Sales

**Williams, Scott D.** — *Partner*
Heidrick & Struggles, Inc.
2200 Ross Avenue, Suite 4700E
Dallas, TX 75201-2787
Telephone: (214) 220-2130
**Recruiter Classification:** Retained; **Lowest/Average Salary:** $75,000/$90,000;
**Industry Concentration:** Generalist with a primary focus in High Technology;
**Function Concentration:** Generalist

**Williams, Walter E.** — *Senior Vice President/Director*
Canny, Bowen Inc.
10 Post Office Square, Suite 960
Boston, MA 02109
Telephone: (617) 292-6242
**Recruiter Classification:** Retained; **Lowest/Average Salary:** $90,000/$90,000;
**Industry Concentration:** Generalist with a primary focus in Biotechnology,
Consumer Products, Financial Services, Healthcare/Hospitals, High
Technology, Hospitality/Leisure, Information Technology; **Function
Concentration:** Generalist with a primary focus in Finance/Accounting,
General Management, Human Resources, Marketing, Sales

**Williamson, Frank** — *Manager Central Region*
Management Recruiters International, Inc.
3925 Reed Boulevard, Suite 200
Murrysville, PA 15668-1852
Telephone: (412) 325-4011
**Recruiter Classification:** Contingency; **Lowest/Average Salary:**
$30,000/$75,000; **Industry Concentration:** Generalist; **Function
Concentration:** Generalist

**Willis, William H.** — *President/Managing Director*
William Willis Worldwide Inc.
164 Mason Street
Greenwich, CT 06830-6611
Telephone: (203) 661-4500
**Recruiter Classification:** Retained; **Lowest/Average Salary:** $90,000/$90,000;
**Industry Concentration:** Generalist with a primary focus in Biotechnology,
Board Services, Chemical Products, Consumer Products, Financial Services,
High Technology, Insurance, Manufacturing, Non-Profit, Oil/Gas,
Pharmaceutical/Medical, Publishing/Media, Real Estate, Venture Capital;
**Function Concentration:** Generalist with a primary focus in Administration,
Finance/Accounting, General Management, Human Resources, Marketing,
Research and Development, Sales

**Willner, Nannette** — *Vice President*
S.R. Wolman Associates, Inc.
133 East 35th Street
New York, NY 10016
Telephone: (212) 685-2692
**Recruiter Classification:** Retained; **Lowest/Average Salary:** $50,000/$90,000;
**Industry Concentration:** Consumer Products, Entertainment, Fashion
(Retail/Apparel); **Function Concentration:** Generalist with a primary focus in
Administration, General Management, Human Resources, Marketing, Research
and Development, Sales, Women/Minorities

**Wilson, Derrick** — *Senior Manager Accounts*
Thornton Resources
9800 McKnight Road
Pittsburgh, PA 15237
Telephone: (412) 364-2111
**Recruiter Classification:** Contingency, Executive Temporary; **Lowest/Average
Salary:** $40,000/$50,000; **Industry Concentration:** Generalist with a primary
focus in Board Services, Consumer Products, Financial Services, Non-Profit;
**Function Concentration:** Generalist with a primary focus in General
Management, Human Resources

**Wilson, Helen S.** — *Senior Vice President*
The Diversified Search Companies
2005 Market Street, Suite 3300
Philadelphia, PA 19103
Telephone: (215) 732-6666
**Recruiter Classification:** Retained; **Lowest/Average Salary:** $90,000/$90,000;
**Industry Concentration:** Generalist; **Function Concentration:** Generalist

**Wilson, John C.** — *Managing Director*
Russell Reynolds Associates, Inc.
101 California Street
Suite 3140
San Francisco, CA 94111
Telephone: (415) 352-3300
**Recruiter Classification:** Retained; **Lowest/Average Salary:** $90,000/$90,000;
**Industry Concentration:** Generalist with a primary focus in Consumer
Products, Financial Services; **Function Concentration:** Generalist

**Wilson, Joyce** — *Associate*
Source Services Corporation
One Park Plaza, Suite 560
Irvine, CA 92714
Telephone: (714) 660-1666
**Recruiter Classification:** Contingency; **Lowest/Average Salary:**
$30,000/$50,000; **Industry Concentration:** Financial Services, Information
Technology; **Function Concentration:** Engineering, Finance/Accounting

**Wilson, Patricia L.** — *Partner*
Leon A. Farley Associates
468 Jackson Street
San Francisco, CA 94111
Telephone: (415) 989-0989
**Recruiter Classification:** Retained; **Lowest/Average Salary:** $90,000/$90,000; **Industry Concentration:** Generalist with a primary focus in Board Services, Consumer Products, Electronics, Financial Services, High Technology, Information Technology, Manufacturing; **Function Concentration:** Generalist with a primary focus in Administration, Finance/Accounting, General Management, Human Resources, Marketing, Sales, Women/Minorities

**Wilson, Robert J.** — *Consultant*
Coleman Lew & Associates, Inc.
326 West Tenth Street
Charlotte, NC 28202
Telephone: (704) 377-0362
**Recruiter Classification:** Retained; **Lowest/Average Salary:** $/$90,000; **Industry Concentration:** Generalist; **Function Concentration:** Generalist

**Wilson, Thomas H.** — *Partner*
Lamalie Amrop International
Chevron Tower
1301 McKinney Street
Houston, TX 77010-3034
Telephone: (713) 739-8602
**Recruiter Classification:** Retained; **Lowest/Average Salary:** $90,000/$90,000; **Industry Concentration:** Generalist; **Function Concentration:** Generalist with a primary focus in Finance/Accounting

**Wimer, Thomas W.** — *Senior Vice President*
DHR International, Inc.
11811 North Tatum, Suite 3031
Phoenix, AZ 85020
Telephone: (602) 953-7810
**Recruiter Classification:** Retained; **Lowest/Average Salary:** $60,000/$90,000; **Industry Concentration:** Generalist; **Function Concentration:** Generalist

**Windle, Mary** — *Vice President - L.A. Retail*
Evie Kreisler & Associates, Inc.
865 South Figueroa, Suite 950
Los Angeles, CA 90017
Telephone: (213) 622-8994
**Recruiter Classification:** Contingency; **Lowest/Average Salary:** $30,000/$75,000; **Industry Concentration:** Fashion (Retail/Apparel); **Function Concentration:** Generalist

**Winfrey, James** — *Vice President*
Korn/Ferry International
1100 Louisiana, Suite 3400
Houston, TX 77002
Telephone: (713) 651-1834
**Recruiter Classification:** Retained; **Lowest/Average Salary:** $90,000/$90,000; **Industry Concentration:** Generalist; **Function Concentration:** Generalist

**Wingate, Mary** — *Associate*
Source Services Corporation
5429 LBJ Freeway, Suite 275
Dallas, TX 75240
Telephone: (214) 387-1600
**Recruiter Classification:** Contingency; **Lowest/Average Salary:** $30,000/$50,000; **Industry Concentration:** Financial Services, Information Technology; **Function Concentration:** Engineering, Finance/Accounting

**Winitz, Joel** — *President*
GSW Consulting Group, Inc.
5510 Morehouse Drive, Suite 260
San Diego, CA 92121-3722
Telephone: (619) 457-7500
**Recruiter Classification:** Retained; **Lowest/Average Salary:** $60,000/$90,000; **Industry Concentration:** Generalist with a primary focus in Biotechnology, Consumer Products, Electronics, Energy, Entertainment, Environmental, Financial Services, Healthcare/Hospitals, High Technology, Information Technology, Pharmaceutical/Medical, Publishing/Media; **Function Concentration:** Generalist with a primary focus in Engineering, Finance/Accounting, General Management, Marketing, Research and Development, Sales

**Winitz, Marla** — *Vice President*
GSW Consulting Group, Inc.
5510 Morehouse Drive, Suite 260
San Diego, CA 92121-3722
Telephone: (619) 457-7500
**Recruiter Classification:** Retained; **Lowest/Average Salary:** $60,000/$90,000; **Industry Concentration:** Generalist with a primary focus in Biotechnology, Consumer Products, Electronics, Energy, Entertainment, Environmental, Financial Services, Healthcare/Hospitals, High Technology, Information Technology, Pharmaceutical/Medical, Publishing/Media; **Function Concentration:** Generalist with a primary focus in Engineering, Finance/Accounting, General Management, Marketing, Research and Development, Sales

**Winkowski, Stephen** — *Associate*
Source Services Corporation
20 Burlington Mall Road, Suite 405
Burlington, MA 01803
Telephone: (617) 272-5000
**Recruiter Classification:** Contingency; **Lowest/Average Salary:** $30,000/$50,000; **Industry Concentration:** Financial Services, Information Technology; **Function Concentration:** Engineering, Finance/Accounting

**Winnewisser, William E.** — *President*
Accounting & Computer Personnel
200 Salina Meadows Parkway, Suite 180
Syracuse, NY 13221
Telephone: (315) 457-8000
**Recruiter Classification:** Contingency; **Lowest/Average Salary:** $20,000/$40,000; **Industry Concentration:** Generalist with a primary focus in Biotechnology, Chemical Products, Consumer Products, Electronics, Environmental, Financial Services, High Technology, Hospitality/Leisure, Information Technology, Insurance, Manufacturing, Pharmaceutical/Medical, Transportation, Utilities/Nuclear; **Function Concentration:** Finance/Accounting, General Management

**Winnicki, Kimberly** — *Associate*
Source Services Corporation
120 East Baltimore Street, Suite 1950
Baltimore, MD 21202
Telephone: (410) 727-4050
**Recruiter Classification:** Contingency; **Lowest/Average Salary:** $30,000/$50,000; **Industry Concentration:** Financial Services, Information Technology; **Function Concentration:** Engineering, Finance/Accounting

**Winograd, Glenn** — *Vice President/Division Manager*
Criterion Executive Search, Inc.
5420 Bay Center Drive, Suite 101
Tampa, FL 33609-3402
Telephone: (813) 286-2000
**Recruiter Classification:** Contingency; **Lowest/Average Salary:** $40,000/$90,000; **Industry Concentration:** Generalist with a primary focus in Automotive, Biotechnology, Electronics, Financial Services, Healthcare/Hospitals, High Technology, Information Technology, Insurance, Manufacturing, Packaging; **Function Concentration:** Generalist with a primary focus in Engineering, Finance/Accounting, General Management, Research and Development, Women/Minorities

**Winslow, Lawrence J.** — *Executive Vice President/ Managing Director*
DHR International, Inc.
Denver Tech Center
7900 East Union Avenue, Suite 1100
Denver, CO 80237
Telephone: (303) 694-5360
**Recruiter Classification:** Retained; **Lowest/Average Salary:** $60,000/$90,000; **Industry Concentration:** Generalist; **Function Concentration:** Generalist

**Winston, Dale** — *President*
Battalia Winston International
300 Park Avenue
New York, NY 10022
Telephone: (212) 308-8080
**Recruiter Classification:** Retained; **Lowest/Average Salary:** $90,000/$90,000; **Industry Concentration:** Generalist with a primary focus in Board Services, Consumer Products, Electronics, Healthcare/Hospitals, Information Technology, Manufacturing, Non-Profit, Pharmaceutical/Medical, Venture Capital; **Function Concentration:** Generalist with a primary focus in Engineering, Finance/Accounting, General Management, Human Resources, Marketing, Research and Development, Sales, Women/Minorities

**Winston, Susan** — *Executive Recruiter*
CPS Inc.
One Westbrook Corporate Centre, Suite 600
Westchester, IL 60154
Telephone: (708) 531-8370
**Recruiter Classification:** Contingency; **Lowest/Average Salary:** $30,000/$50,000; **Industry Concentration:** Generalist with a primary focus in Automotive, Biotechnology, Chemical Products, Consumer Products, High Technology, Insurance, Manufacturing, Oil/Gas, Packaging, Pharmaceutical/Medical; **Function Concentration:** Engineering, Research and Development, Sales, Women/Minorities

**Winter, Peter** — *Managing Director and Director Canada*
Catalyx Group
20 Stonepark Lane
Nepean, Ontario, CANADA K2H 9P4
Telephone: (613) 726-7379
**Recruiter Classification:** Retained; **Lowest/Average Salary:** $90,000/$90,000; **Industry Concentration:** Biotechnology, Healthcare/Hospitals, Pharmaceutical/Medical, Publishing/Media; **Function Concentration:** Generalist with a primary focus in General Management, Research and Development

**Winter, Robert** — *Vice President*
The Whitney Group
850 Third Avenue, 11th Floor
New York, NY 10022
Telephone: (212) 508-3500
**Recruiter Classification:** Retained; **Lowest/Average Salary:** $75,000/$90,000;
**Industry Concentration:** Generalist with a primary focus in Financial Services,
Real Estate, Venture Capital; **Function Concentration:** Generalist with a
primary focus in Sales

**Wirtshafter, Linda** — *Senior Associate*
Grant Cooper and Associates
795 Office Parkway, Suite 117
St. Louis, MO 63141
Telephone: (314) 567-4690
**Recruiter Classification:** Retained; **Lowest/Average Salary:** $60,000/$90,000;
**Industry Concentration:** Generalist with a primary focus in Consumer
Products, Electronics, Financial Services, Healthcare/Hospitals, Manufacturing,
Non-Profit; **Function Concentration:** Generalist

**Wisch, Steven C.** — *Director*
MB Inc. Interim Executive Division
505 Fifth Avenue
New York, NY 10017
Telephone: (212) 661-4937
**Recruiter Classification:** Executive Temporary; **Lowest/Average Salary:**
$50,000/$90,000; **Industry Concentration:** Generalist with a primary focus in
Consumer Products, Financial Services, Pharmaceutical/Medical; **Function
Concentration:** Finance/Accounting, General Management, Human Resources,
Marketing, Sales

**Wise, Anne** — *Recruiter*
U.S. Envirosearch
445 Union Boulevard, Suite 225
Lakewood, CO 80228
Telephone: (303) 980-6600
**Recruiter Classification:** Contingency; **Lowest/Average Salary:**
$30,000/$60,000; **Industry Concentration:** Environmental; **Function
Concentration:** Generalist with a primary focus in Administration, Engineering,
Finance/Accounting, General Management, Marketing, Sales,
Women/Minorities

**Wise, J. Herbert** — *Partner*
Sandhurst Associates
4851 LBJ Freeway, Suite 601
Dallas, TX 75244
Telephone: (212) 458-1212
**Recruiter Classification:** Retained; **Lowest/Average Salary:** $75,000/$90,000;
**Industry Concentration:** Generalist with a primary focus in Consumer
Products, Education/Libraries, Entertainment, Financial Services,
Healthcare/Hospitals, High Technology, Hospitality/Leisure, Insurance,
Manufacturing, Pharmaceutical/Medical, Real Estate, Transportation; **Function
Concentration:** Generalist with a primary focus in Finance/Accounting, Human
Resources, Marketing, Sales

**Wise, Ronald L.** — *Manager North Atlantic Region*
Management Recruiters International, Inc.
406 Line Creek Road, Suite B
Peachtree City, GA 30269
Telephone: (770) 486-0603
**Recruiter Classification:** Contingency; **Lowest/Average Salary:**
$30,000/$75,000; **Industry Concentration:** Generalist; **Function
Concentration:** Generalist

**Wiseman, Bonnie** — *Consultant*
Witt/Kieffer, Ford, Hadelman & Lloyd
2015 Spring Road, Suite 510
Oak Brook, IL 60521
Telephone: (708) 990-1370
**Recruiter Classification:** Retained; **Lowest/Average Salary:** $75,000/$90,000;
**Industry Concentration:** Healthcare/Hospitals; **Function Concentration:**
Generalist with a primary focus in General Management

**Witte, David L.** — *Chief Executive Officer*
Ward Howell International, Inc.
99 Park Avenue, Suite 2000
New York, NY 10016-1699
Telephone: (212) 697-3730
**Recruiter Classification:** Retained; **Lowest/Average Salary:** $90,000/$90,000;
**Industry Concentration:** Aerospace/Defense, Automotive, Chemical Products,
Consumer Products, Energy, Information Technology, Manufacturing, Oil/Gas;
**Function Concentration:** Generalist with a primary focus in Administration,
Engineering, General Management

**Wittenberg, Laura L.** — *Associate*
Boyden
2 Prudential Plaza, Suite 5050
180 North Stetson Avenue
Chicago, IL 60601
Telephone: (312) 565-1300
**Recruiter Classification:** Retained; **Lowest/Average Salary:** $75,000/$90,000;
**Industry Concentration:** Generalist; **Function Concentration:** Generalist with a
primary focus in Engineering, Finance/Accounting, General Management,
Human Resources, Marketing, Research and Development, Sales,
Women/Minorities

**Witzgall, William** — *Associate*
Source Services Corporation
525 Vine Street, Suite 2250
Cincinnati, OH 45202
Telephone: (513) 651-3303
**Recruiter Classification:** Contingency; **Lowest/Average Salary:**
$30,000/$50,000; **Industry Concentration:** Financial Services, Information
Technology; **Function Concentration:** Engineering, Finance/Accounting

**Wold, Ted W.** — *Secretary*
Hyde Danforth Wold & Co.
5950 Berkshire Lane, Suite 1600
Dallas, TX 75225
Telephone: (214) 691-5966
**Recruiter Classification:** Retained; **Lowest/Average Salary:** $50,000/$75,000;
**Industry Concentration:** Generalist; **Function Concentration:** Generalist

**Wolf, Craig** — *Medical Recruiter*
Aureus Group
8744 Frederick Street
Omaha, NE 68124-3068
Telephone: (402) 397-2980
**Recruiter Classification:** Contingency; **Lowest/Average Salary:**
$30,000/$40,000; **Industry Concentration:** Healthcare/Hospitals; **Function
Concentration:** General Management

**Wolf, Donald** — *Associate*
Source Services Corporation
111 Founders Plaza, Suite 1501E
Hartford, CT 06108
Telephone: (860) 528-0300
**Recruiter Classification:** Contingency; **Lowest/Average Salary:**
$30,000/$50,000; **Industry Concentration:** Financial Services, Information
Technology; **Function Concentration:** Engineering, Finance/Accounting

**Wolf, Stephen M.** — *Principal*
Byron Leonard International, Inc.
2659 Townsgate Road, Suite 100
Westlake Village, CA 91361
Telephone: (805) 373-7500
**Recruiter Classification:** Retained; **Lowest/Average Salary:** $60,000/$90,000;
**Industry Concentration:** Generalist with a primary focus in Biotechnology,
Consumer Products, Electronics, Entertainment, Financial Services, High
Technology, Information Technology, Insurance, Pharmaceutical/Medical;
**Function Concentration:** Generalist with a primary focus in Administration,
Finance/Accounting, General Management, Human Resources, Marketing,
Research and Development, Sales

**Wolfe, David** — *Associate*
Kenzer Corp.
777 Third Avenue, 26th Floor
New York, NY 10017
Telephone: (212) 308-4300
**Recruiter Classification:** Retained; **Lowest/Average Salary:** $50,000/$90,000;
**Industry Concentration:** Generalist; **Function Concentration:** Generalist

**Wolfe, Peter** — *Managing Director*
Source Services Corporation
4200 West Cypress Street, Suite 101
Tampa, FL 33607
Telephone: (813) 879-2221
**Recruiter Classification:** Contingency; **Lowest/Average Salary:**
$30,000/$50,000; **Industry Concentration:** Financial Services, Information
Technology; **Function Concentration:** Engineering, Finance/Accounting

**Wolfram, David A.** — *Senior Vice President*
EFL Associates
7101 College Boulevard, Suite 550
Overland Park, KS 66210-1891
Telephone: (913) 451-8866
**Recruiter Classification:** Retained; **Lowest/Average Salary:** $60,000/$90,000;
**Industry Concentration:** Generalist; **Function Concentration:** Generalist

**Wollman, Harry** — *Consultant*
Howard Fischer Associates, Inc.
1800 John F. Kennedy Boulevard, 7th Floor
Philadelphia, PA 19103
Telephone: (215) 568-8363
**Recruiter Classification:** Retained; **Lowest/Average Salary:** $90,000/$90,000;
**Industry Concentration:** Healthcare/Hospitals; **Function Concentration:**
Generalist

**Wolman, Stephen R.** — *President*
S.R. Wolman Associates, Inc.
133 East 35th Street
New York, NY 10016
Telephone: (212) 685-2692
**Recruiter Classification:** Retained; **Lowest/Average Salary:** $50,000/$90,000;
**Industry Concentration:** Generalist with a primary focus in Consumer
Products, Entertainment, Fashion (Retail/Apparel); **Function Concentration:**
Generalist with a primary focus in Administration, General Management,
Human Resources, Marketing, Research and Development, Sales,
Women/Minorities

**Wolters, Tony A.** — *Manager Southwest Region*
Management Recruiters International, Inc.
5801 East 41st Street, Suite 440
Tulsa, OK 74135-5614
Telephone: (918) 663-6744
**Recruiter Classification:** Contingency; **Lowest/Average Salary:**
$30,000/$75,000; **Industry Concentration:** Generalist; **Function
Concentration:** Generalist

**Womack, Joseph** — *Vice President*
The Bankers Group
10 South Riverside Plaza, Suite 1424
Chicago, IL 60606
Telephone: (312) 930-9456
**Recruiter Classification:** Contingency; **Lowest/Average Salary:**
$50,000/$75,000; **Industry Concentration:** Generalist with a primary focus in
Automotive, Financial Services, High Technology, Information Technology,
Insurance, Venture Capital; **Function Concentration:** Generalist with a primary
focus in Administration, Finance/Accounting, General Management, Human
Resources, Marketing, Sales, Women/Minorities

**Wood, Allison** — *Senior Associate*
Korn/Ferry International
3950 Lincoln Plaza
500 North Akard Street
Dallas, TX 75201
Telephone: (214) 954-1834
**Recruiter Classification:** Retained; **Lowest/Average Salary:** $90,000/$90,000;
**Industry Concentration:** Generalist; **Function Concentration:** Generalist

**Wood, Gary** — *Associate*
Source Services Corporation
3 Summit Park Drive, Suite 550
Independence, OH 44131
Telephone: (216) 328-5900
**Recruiter Classification:** Contingency; **Lowest/Average Salary:**
$30,000/$50,000; **Industry Concentration:** Financial Services, Information
Technology; **Function Concentration:** Engineering, Finance/Accounting

**Wood, John S.** — *Consultant*
Egon Zehnder International Inc.
55 East 59th Street, 14th Floor
New York, NY 10022
Telephone: (212) 838-9199
**Recruiter Classification:** Retained; **Lowest/Average Salary:** $90,000/$90,000;
**Industry Concentration:** Generalist with a primary focus in Biotechnology,
Financial Services, High Technology, Manufacturing, Pharmaceutical/Medical;
**Function Concentration:** Generalist

**Wood, Martin F.** — *Principal*
Lamalie Amrop International
Key Tower, 127 Public Square
Cleveland, OH 44114-1216
Telephone: (216) 694-3000
**Recruiter Classification:** Retained; **Lowest/Average Salary:** $90,000/$90,000;
**Industry Concentration:** Generalist; **Function Concentration:** Generalist with a
primary focus in Finance/Accounting, General Management, Marketing, Sales

**Wood, Milton M.** — *President*
M. Wood Company
10 North Dearborn Street, Suite 700
Chicago, IL 60602
Telephone: (312) 368-0633
**Recruiter Classification:** Retained; **Lowest/Average Salary:** $60,000/$90,000;
**Industry Concentration:** Generalist with a primary focus in Automotive,
Consumer Products, Financial Services, Healthcare/Hospitals, Information
Technology, Insurance; **Function Concentration:** Generalist with a primary
focus in General Management, Human Resources, Marketing, Sales

**Wood, Steven N.** — *Senior Vice President/Managing Director*
DHR International, Inc.
8182 Maryland Avenue, Suite 200
Clayton, MO 63105
Telephone: (314) 725-1191
**Recruiter Classification:** Retained; **Lowest/Average Salary:** $60,000/$90,000;
**Industry Concentration:** Generalist; **Function Concentration:** Generalist

**Woodruff, Mark S.** — *Manager Southwest Region*
Management Recruiters International, Inc.
402 Linwood Drive, Suite 1
Paragould, AR 72450-4027
Telephone: (501) 236-1800
**Recruiter Classification:** Contingency; **Lowest/Average Salary:**
$30,000/$75,000; **Industry Concentration:** Generalist; **Function
Concentration:** Generalist

**Woodrum, Robert L.** — *Vice President*
Korn/Ferry International
237 Park Avenue
New York, NY 10017
Telephone: (212) 687-1834
**Recruiter Classification:** Retained; **Lowest/Average Salary:** $90,000/$90,000;
**Industry Concentration:** Generalist; **Function Concentration:** Generalist

**Woods, Craig** — *Associate*
Source Services Corporation
One Park Plaza, Suite 560
Irvine, CA 92714
Telephone: (714) 660-1666
**Recruiter Classification:** Contingency; **Lowest/Average Salary:**
$30,000/$50,000; **Industry Concentration:** Financial Services, Information
Technology; **Function Concentration:** Engineering, Finance/Accounting

**Woodward, Lee** — *Co-President*
Search Associates, Inc.
5900 Sepulveda Boulevard, Suite 104
Van Nuys, CA 91411
Telephone: (818) 989-2200
**Recruiter Classification:** Contingency; **Lowest/Average Salary:**
$30,000/$50,000; **Industry Concentration:** Electronics, High Technology;
**Function Concentration:** Research and Development, Women/Minorities

**Woody, Jacqueline K.** — *Medical Services Director*
Aureus Group
8744 Frederick Street
Omaha, NE 68124-3068
Telephone: (402) 397-2980
**Recruiter Classification:** Contingency; **Lowest/Average Salary:**
$40,000/$50,000; **Industry Concentration:** Healthcare/Hospitals; **Function
Concentration:** Administration, General Management

**Wooller, Edmund A.M.** — *President*
Windsor International
3350 Cumberland Circle, Suite 1900
Atlanta, GA 30339-3363
Telephone: (770) 438-2300
**Recruiter Classification:** Retained; **Lowest/Average Salary:** $40,000/$75,000;
**Industry Concentration:** Generalist with a primary focus in Financial Services,
Information Technology, Manufacturing, Non-Profit; **Function Concentration:**
Generalist with a primary focus in Administration, Finance/Accounting,
General Management, Marketing, Sales

**Woollett, James** — *Vice President*
Rusher, Loscavio & LoPresto
2479 Bayshore Road, Suite 700
Palo Alto, CA 94303
Telephone: (415) 494-0883
**Recruiter Classification:** Retained; **Lowest/Average Salary:** $75,000/$75,000;
**Industry Concentration:** Biotechnology, Electronics, High Technology,
Information Technology, Manufacturing; **Function Concentration:** Generalist
with a primary focus in Administration, Engineering, General Management,
Marketing, Research and Development, Sales

**Woomer, Jerome** — *Associate*
Source Services Corporation
7730 East Bellview Avenue, Suite 302
Englewood, CO 80111
Telephone: (303) 773-3700
**Recruiter Classification:** Contingency; **Lowest/Average Salary:**
$30,000/$50,000; **Industry Concentration:** Financial Services, Information
Technology; **Function Concentration:** Engineering, Finance/Accounting

**Workman, David** — *Associate*
Source Services Corporation
2850 National City Tower
Louisville, KY 40202
Telephone: (502) 581-9900
**Recruiter Classification:** Contingency; **Lowest/Average Salary:**
$30,000/$50,000; **Industry Concentration:** Financial Services, Information
Technology; **Function Concentration:** Engineering, Finance/Accounting

**Worth, Janet M.** — *Consultant*
Witt/Kieffer, Ford, Hadelman & Lloyd
8117 Preston Road, Suite 690
Dallas, TX 75225
Telephone: (214) 739-1370
**Recruiter Classification:** Retained; **Lowest/Average Salary:** $75,000/$90,000;
**Industry Concentration:** Healthcare/Hospitals; **Function Concentration:**
Generalist with a primary focus in General Management

**Wotipka, Lee** — *Account Executive*
Search West, Inc.
3401 Centrelake Drive
Suite 690
Ontario, CA 91761-1207
Telephone: (909) 986-1966
**Recruiter Classification:** Contingency; **Lowest/Average Salary:**
$40,000/$60,000; **Industry Concentration:** Manufacturing; **Function
Concentration:** Engineering, Research and Development

**Wozniak, Bernard D.** — *Principal*
Sanford Rose Associates
8252 South Harvard, Suite 151
Tulsa, OK 74137
Telephone: (918) 494-0909
**Recruiter Classification:** Contingency; **Lowest/Average Salary:**
$30,000/$75,000; **Industry Concentration:** Generalist; **Function
Concentration:** Generalist

**Wozniak, Jane K.** — *Principal*
Sanford Rose Associates
8252 South Harvard, Suite 151
Tulsa, OK 74137
Telephone: (918) 494-0909
**Recruiter Classification:** Contingency; **Lowest/Average Salary:**
$30,000/$75,000; **Industry Concentration:** Generalist; **Function
Concentration:** Generalist

**Wren, Jay** — *President*
Jay Wren & Associates
6355 Riverside Boulevard, Suite P
Sacramento, CA 95831
Telephone: (916) 394-2920
**Recruiter Classification:** Contingency; **Lowest/Average Salary:**
$30,000/$90,000; **Industry Concentration:** Consumer Products, Information
Technology; **Function Concentration:** Marketing, Sales

**Wren, Shelly J.** — *Executive Assistant to President*
Sloan & Associates
1769 Jamestown Road
Williamsburg, VA 23185
Telephone: (757) 220-1111
**Recruiter Classification:** Contingency; **Lowest/Average Salary:**
$60,000/$75,000; **Industry Concentration:** Consumer Products; **Function
Concentration:** Marketing, Research and Development, Sales

**Wright, Anne B.** — *Manager North Atlantic Region*
Management Recruiters International, Inc.
3 Turnberry Wood
130 Applecross Road at Braemar, P.O. Box 4834
Pinehurst, NC 28374
Telephone: (910) 695-3300
**Recruiter Classification:** Contingency; **Lowest/Average Salary:**
$30,000/$75,000; **Industry Concentration:** Generalist; **Function
Concentration:** Generalist

**Wright, Carl A.J.** — *President*
A.J. Burton Group, Inc.
120 East Baltimore Street, Suite 2220
Baltimore, MD 21202
Telephone: (410) 752-5244
**Recruiter Classification:** Contingency, Executive Temporary; **Lowest/Average
Salary:** $40,000/$75,000; **Industry Concentration:** Consumer Products,
Education/Libraries, Energy, Financial Services, Insurance; **Function
Concentration:** Finance/Accounting

**Wright, Charles D.** — *Senior Vice President*
Goodrich & Sherwood Associates, Inc.
401 Merritt Seven Corporate Park
Norwalk, CT 06851
Telephone: (203) 847-2525
**Recruiter Classification:** Retained; **Lowest/Average Salary:** $60,000/$90,000;
**Industry Concentration:** Generalist with a primary focus in Board Services,
Chemical Products, Consumer Products, Entertainment, Financial Services,
Healthcare/Hospitals, Information Technology, Insurance, Manufacturing,
Oil/Gas, Publishing/Media, Venture Capital; **Function Concentration:**
Generalist with a primary focus in Administration, Finance/Accounting,
General Management, Human Resources, Marketing, Sales

**Wright, Doug** — *General Manager*
Management Recruiters International, Inc.
3 Turnberry Wood
130 Applecross Road at Braemar, P.O. Box 4834
Pinehurst, NC 28374
Telephone: (910) 695-3300
**Recruiter Classification:** Contingency; **Lowest/Average Salary:** $30,000/$75,000;
**Industry Concentration:** Generalist; **Function Concentration:** Generalist

**Wright, Leslie** — *Vice President*
The Stevenson Group of New Jersey
560 Sylvan Avenue
Englewood Cliffs, NJ 07632
Telephone: (201) 568-1900
**Recruiter Classification:** Retained; **Lowest/Average Salary:** $75,000/$90,000;
**Industry Concentration:** Generalist with a primary focus in Chemical Products,
Consumer Products, Fashion (Retail/Apparel), Financial Services, Information
Technology, Pharmaceutical/Medical; **Function Concentration:** Generalist with
a primary focus in Finance/Accounting, General Management, Human
Resources, Marketing, Sales

**Wright, Linus** — *Consultant*
Paul Ray Berndtson
2200 Ross Avenue, Suite 4500W
Dallas, TX 75201
Telephone: (214) 969-7620
**Recruiter Classification:** Retained; **Lowest/Average Salary:** $90,000/$90,000;
**Industry Concentration:** Education/Libraries; **Function Concentration:** Generalist

**Wrynn, Robert F.** — *Physician Recruiter*
MSI International
230 Peachtree Street, N.E.
Suite 1550
Atlanta, GA 30303
Telephone: (404) 653-7360
**Recruiter Classification:** Contingency; **Lowest/Average Salary:** $30,000/$60,000;
**Industry Concentration:** Generalist with a primary focus in Healthcare/Hospitals;
**Function Concentration:** Generalist with a primary focus in Administration,
Engineering, Finance/Accounting, General Management, Marketing, Sales

**Wujciak, Sandra** — *Area Vice President*
Accountants on Call
Plaza VII Building, Suite 2312
45 South Seventh Street
Minneapolis, MN 55402
Telephone: (612) 341-9900
**Recruiter Classification:** Contingency; **Lowest/Average Salary:** $20,000/$30,000;
**Industry Concentration:** Generalist; **Function Concentration:** Finance/Accounting

**Wyatt, James** — *President*
Wyatt & Jaffe
9900 Bren Road East, Suite 550
Minnetonka, MN 55343-9668
Telephone: (612) 945-0099
**Recruiter Classification:** Retained; **Lowest/Average Salary:** $75,000/$90,000;
**Industry Concentration:** Biotechnology, Board Services, Electronics,
Healthcare/Hospitals, High Technology, Information Technology,
Manufacturing, Pharmaceutical/Medical; **Function Concentration:** Generalist
with a primary focus in General Management, Human Resources, Marketing,
Research and Development, Sales

**Wyatt, Janice** — *Vice President*
Korn/Ferry International
One International Place
Boston, MA 02110-1800
Telephone: (617) 345-0200
**Recruiter Classification:** Retained; **Lowest/Average Salary:** $90,000/$90,000;
**Industry Concentration:** Generalist with a primary focus in
Healthcare/Hospitals; **Function Concentration:** Generalist

**Wycoff-Viola, Amy** — *Associate*
Source Services Corporation
150 South Wacker Drive, Suite 400
Chicago, IL 60606
Telephone: (312) 346-7000
**Recruiter Classification:** Contingency; **Lowest/Average Salary:**
$30,000/$50,000; **Industry Concentration:** Financial Services, Information
Technology; **Function Concentration:** Engineering, Finance/Accounting

**Wylie, Pamela** — *Executive Recruiter*
M.A. Churchill & Associates, Inc.
Morelyn Plaza
1111 Street Road
Southampton, PA 18966
Telephone: (215) 953-0300
**Recruiter Classification:** Contingency; **Lowest/Average Salary:**
$50,000/$75,000; **Industry Concentration:** Financial Services, Insurance;
**Function Concentration:** Marketing, Research and Development, Sales

**Wynkoop, Mary** — *Vice President*
Tyler & Company
1000 Abernathy Road N.E.
Suite 1400
Atlanta, GA 30328-5655
Telephone: (770) 396-3939
**Recruiter Classification:** Retained; **Lowest/Average Salary:** $60,000/$90,000;
**Industry Concentration:** Healthcare/Hospitals, Insurance; **Function Concentration:** Generalist

**Wyser-Pratte, Anne** — *Partner*
Heidrick & Struggles, Inc.
245 Park Avenue, Suite 4300
New York, NY 10167-0152
Telephone: (212) 867-9876
**Recruiter Classification:** Retained; **Lowest/Average Salary:** $75,000/$90,000;
**Industry Concentration:** Generalist with a primary focus in Biotechnology,
Healthcare/Hospitals; **Function Concentration:** Generalist

**Yamada, Steven** — *Principal*
Korn/Ferry International
The Transamerica Pyramid
600 Montgomery Street
San Francisco, CA 94111
Telephone: (415) 956-1834
**Recruiter Classification:** Retained; **Lowest/Average Salary:** $90,000/$90,000;
**Industry Concentration:** Generalist; **Function Concentration:** Generalist

**Yamvaketis, Stephen** — *Vice President*
John Kurosky & Associates
3 Corporate Park Drive, Suite 210
Irvine, CA 92714
Telephone: (714) 851-6370
**Recruiter Classification:** Retained; **Lowest/Average Salary:** $60,000/$90,000;
**Industry Concentration:** Generalist; **Function Concentration:** Generalist

**Yang, George** — *Recruiter*
Technical Connections Inc.
11400 Olympic Boulevard, Suite 770
Los Angeles, CA 90064
Telephone: (310) 479-8830
**Recruiter Classification:** Contingency; **Lowest/Average Salary:**
$40,000/$60,000; **Industry Concentration:** High Technology, Information
Technology; **Function Concentration:** Generalist

**Yard, Allan S.** — *Recruiter*
Bryant Research
466 Old Hook Road, Suite 32
Emerson, NJ 07630
Telephone: (201) 599-0590
**Recruiter Classification:** Contingency; **Lowest/Average Salary:**
$50,000/$90,000; **Industry Concentration:** Biotechnology,
Pharmaceutical/Medical; **Function Concentration:** Research and Development

**Yeaton, Robert** — *Associate*
Source Services Corporation
1500 West Park Drive, Suite 390
Westborough, MA 01581
Telephone: (508) 366-2600
**Recruiter Classification:** Contingency; **Lowest/Average Salary:**
$30,000/$50,000; **Industry Concentration:** Financial Services, Information
Technology; **Function Concentration:** Engineering, Finance/Accounting

**Yilmaz, Muriel** — *Vice President*
Dinte Resources, Incorporated
8300 Greensboro Drive
Suite 880
McLean, VA 22102
Telephone: (703) 448-3300
**Recruiter Classification:** Executive Temporary; **Lowest/Average Salary:**
$75,000/$90,000; **Industry Concentration:** Generalist with a primary focus in
Biotechnology, Consumer Products, Healthcare/Hospitals, Hospitality/Leisure,
Non-Profit, Pharmaceutical/Medical, Public Administration, Real Estate;
**Function Concentration:** Generalist

**Yoon, Kyung** — *Consultant*
Heidrick & Struggles, Inc.
2740 Sand Hill Road
Menlo Park, CA 94025
Telephone: (415) 854-9300
**Recruiter Classification:** Retained; **Lowest/Average Salary:** $75,000/$90,000;
**Industry Concentration:** Generalist; **Function Concentration:** Generalist

**Youlano, John** — *Executive Recruiter*
Personnel Unlimited/Executive Search
25 West Nora
Spokane, WA 99205
Telephone: (509) 326-8880
**Recruiter Classification:** Contingency; **Lowest/Average Salary:**
$30,000/$60,000; **Industry Concentration:** Generalist; **Function
Concentration:** Engineering

**Young, Alexander** — *Vice President*
Messett Associates, Inc.
7700 North Kendall Drive, Suite 304
Miami, FL 33156
Telephone: (305) 275-1000
**Recruiter Classification:** Retained; **Lowest/Average Salary:** $75,000/$90,000;
**Industry Concentration:** Generalist with a primary focus in Biotechnology,
Chemical Products, Consumer Products, Electronics, Financial Services,
Healthcare/Hospitals, High Technology, Hospitality/Leisure, Insurance,
Manufacturing, Non-Profit, Oil/Gas, Pharmaceutical/Medical, Real Estate;
**Function Concentration:** Generalist with a primary focus in Administration,
Finance/Accounting, General Management, Human Resources, Marketing,
Women/Minorities

**Young, Arthur L.** — *Manager Eastern Region*
Management Recruiters International, Inc.
Waterloo Executive Plaza
4 Waterloo Road
Stanhope, NJ 07874
Telephone: (201) 691-2020
**Recruiter Classification:** Contingency; **Lowest/Average Salary:**
$30,000/$75,000; **Industry Concentration:** Generalist; **Function
Concentration:** Generalist

**Young, Charles E.** — *Manager Manufacturing Division*
Flowers & Associates
1446 South Reynolds, Suite 112
P.O. Box 538
Maumee, OH 43537
Telephone: (419) 893-4816
**Recruiter Classification:** Contingency; **Lowest/Average Salary:**
$30,000/$50,000; **Industry Concentration:** Generalist with a primary focus in
Aerospace/Defense, Automotive, Manufacturing; **Function Concentration:**
Generalist with a primary focus in Engineering, General Management

**Young, Heather** — *Director*
The Guild Corporation
8260 Greensboro Drive, Suite 460
McLean, VA 22102
Telephone: (703) 761-4023
**Recruiter Classification:** Contingency; **Lowest/Average Salary:**
$40,000/$50,000; **Industry Concentration:** Aerospace/Defense, Electronics,
High Technology, Information Technology; **Function Concentration:**
Engineering, Finance/Accounting, General Management, Research and
Development

**Young, Laurie** — *Partner*
Part Time Resources, Inc.
399 East Putnam Avenue
Cos Cob, CT 06807
Telephone: (203) 629-3255
**Recruiter Classification:** Executive Temporary; **Lowest/Average Salary:**
$20,000/$50,000; **Industry Concentration:** Generalist; **Function
Concentration:** Generalist with a primary focus in Administration,
Finance/Accounting, General Management, Human Resources, Marketing,
Research and Development, Sales

**Young, Lesley** — *Account Executive*
Search West, Inc.
340 North Westlake Boulevard
Suite 200
Westlake Village, CA 91362-3761
Telephone: (805) 496-6811
**Recruiter Classification:** Contingency; **Lowest/Average Salary:**
$40,000/$60,000; **Industry Concentration:** Information Technology; **Function
Concentration:** Marketing, Sales

**Young, Mark** — *Managing Director*
D.E. Foster Partners Inc.
One Biscayne Tower
2 South Biscayne Boulevard, Suite 2900
Miami, FL 33131
Telephone: (305) 577-3684
**Recruiter Classification:** Retained; **Lowest/Average Salary:** $90,000/$90,000;
**Industry Concentration:** Generalist; **Function Concentration:** Generalist

**Young, Mimi** — *Consultant Associate*
Educational Management Network
98 Old South Road
Nantucket, MA 02554
Telephone: (508) 228-6700
**Recruiter Classification:** Retained; **Lowest/Average Salary:** $60,000/$90,000;
**Industry Concentration:** Education/Libraries, Non-Profit; **Function
Concentration:** Generalist with a primary focus in Administration,
Finance/Accounting, Human Resources

**Young, Nick** — *Director*
Spencer Stuart
Financial Centre
695 East Main Street
Stamford, CT 06901
Telephone: (203) 324-6333
Recruiter Classification: Retained; Lowest/Average Salary: $90,000/$90,000;
Industry Concentration: Generalist; Function Concentration: Generalist

**Young, Susan M.** — *Co-Manager*
Management Recruiters International, Inc.
42 Court Street
Morristown, NJ 07960-5154
Telephone: (201) 984-0700
Recruiter Classification: Contingency; Lowest/Average Salary:
$30,000/$75,000; Industry Concentration: Generalist; Function
Concentration: Generalist

**Young, Van G.** — *Consultant*
Heidrick & Struggles, Inc.
245 Park Avenue, Suite 4300
New York, NY 10167-0152
Telephone: (212) 867-9876
Recruiter Classification: Retained; Lowest/Average Salary: $75,000/$90,000;
Industry Concentration: Generalist; Function Concentration: Generalist

**Young, Wayne T.** — *Co-Manager Eastern Region*
Management Recruiters International, Inc.
42 Court Street
Morristown, NJ 07960-5154
Telephone: (201) 984-0700
Recruiter Classification: Contingency; Lowest/Average Salary:
$30,000/$75,000; Industry Concentration: Generalist; Function
Concentration: Generalist

**Youngberg, David** — *Managing Director*
Source Services Corporation
1233 North Mayfair Road, Suite 300
Milwaukee, WI 53226
Telephone: (414) 774-6700
Recruiter Classification: Contingency; Lowest/Average Salary:
$30,000/$50,000; Industry Concentration: Financial Services, Information
Technology; Function Concentration: Engineering, Finance/Accounting

**Youngs, Donald L.** — *Partner*
Youngs & Company
P.O. Box 43635
Seven Points, TX 75143
Telephone: (903) 432-4646
Recruiter Classification: Retained; Lowest/Average Salary: $90,000/$90,000;
Industry Concentration: Generalist with a primary focus in Chemical Products,
Consumer Products, Manufacturing, Oil/Gas; Function Concentration:
Generalist with a primary focus in Administration, Finance/Accounting,
General Management

**Yowe, Mark** — *Consultant*
Heidrick & Struggles, Inc.
Four Embarcadero Center, Suite 3570
San Francisco, CA 94111
Telephone: (415) 981-2854
Recruiter Classification: Retained; Lowest/Average Salary: $75,000/$90,000;
Industry Concentration: Generalist with a primary focus in
Healthcare/Hospitals; Function Concentration: Generalist

**Yturbe, Rafael** — *Executive Director*
Russell Reynolds Associates, Inc.
Arquimedes 130-3
Colonia Polanco
Mexico City, D.F., MEXICO 11560
Telephone: (525) 281-0440
Recruiter Classification: Retained; Lowest/Average Salary: $90,000/$90,000;
Industry Concentration: Generalist; Function Concentration: Generalist

**Zaffrann, Craig S.** — *Vice President*
P.J. Murphy & Associates, Inc.
735 North Water Street
Milwaukee, WI 53202
Telephone: (414) 277-9777
Recruiter Classification: Retained; Lowest/Average Salary: $60,000/$90,000;
Industry Concentration: Generalist with a primary focus in Board Services,
Financial Services, Healthcare/Hospitals, Information Technology,
Manufacturing; Function Concentration: Generalist with a primary focus in
Administration, Finance/Accounting, General Management, Human Resources,
Marketing, Sales

**Zahradka, James F.** — *Vice President*
P.J. Murphy & Associates, Inc.
735 North Water Street
Milwaukee, WI 53202
Telephone: (414) 277-9777
Recruiter Classification: Retained; Lowest/Average Salary: $60,000/$90,000;
Industry Concentration: Generalist with a primary focus in Board Services,
Financial Services, Healthcare/Hospitals, Information Technology,
Manufacturing; Function Concentration: Generalist with a primary focus in
Administration, Finance/Accounting, General Management, Human Resources,
Marketing, Sales

**Zak, Adam** — *President*
Adams & Associates International
978 Hampton Park
Barrington, IL 60010
Telephone: (847) 304-5300
Recruiter Classification: Retained; Lowest/Average Salary: $75,000/$75,000;
Industry Concentration: Generalist with a primary focus in Automotive, Board
Services, Manufacturing, Venture Capital; Function Concentration: General
Management

**Zaleta, Andrew R.** — *Vice President*
A.T. Kearney, Inc.
222 West Adams Street
Chicago, IL 60606
Telephone: (312) 648-0111
Recruiter Classification: Retained; Lowest/Average Salary: $90,000/$90,000;
Industry Concentration: Generalist; Function Concentration: Generalist

**Zander, Barry W.** — *Executive Recruiter*
MSI International
6345 Balboa Boulevard
Suite 335
Encino, CA 91316
Telephone: (818) 342-0222
Recruiter Classification: Contingency; Lowest/Average Salary:
$30,000/$75,000; Industry Concentration: Generalist with a primary focus in
Healthcare/Hospitals, Pharmaceutical/Medical; Function Concentration:
Generalist with a primary focus in Administration, Engineering,
Finance/Accounting, General Management, Marketing, Sales

**Zanotti, Les V.** — *General Manager*
Management Recruiters International, Inc.
7171 West Mercy Road, Suite 252
Omaha, NE 68106-2696
Telephone: (402) 397-8320
Recruiter Classification: Contingency; Lowest/Average Salary:
$30,000/$75,000; Industry Concentration: Generalist; Function
Concentration: Generalist

**Zaring, David J.** — *Manager South Atlantic Region*
Management Recruiters International, Inc.
1001 East Baker Street, Suite 202
Plant City, FL 33566-3700
Telephone: (813) 754-6340
Recruiter Classification: Contingency; Lowest/Average Salary:
$30,000/$75,000; Industry Concentration: Generalist; Function
Concentration: Generalist

**Zarkin, Norman** — *President*
The Zarkin Group, Inc.
550 Mamaroneck Avenue
Harrison, NY 10528-1636
Telephone: (914) 777-0500
Recruiter Classification: Retained; Lowest/Average Salary: $50,000/$90,000;
Industry Concentration: Generalist with a primary focus in Manufacturing,
Real Estate; Function Concentration: General Management, Human Resources,
Marketing, Sales

**Zarkin, Norman** — *Managing Partner*
Rhodes Associates
555 Fifth Avenue
New York, NY 10017
Telephone: (212) 983-2000
Recruiter Classification: Retained; Lowest/Average Salary: $90,000/$90,000;
Industry Concentration: Financial Services, Insurance, Real Estate, Venture
Capital; Function Concentration: Generalist

**Zarnoski, Hank** — *Vice President Technical Recruitment*
Dunhill Search International
59 Elm Street
New Haven, CT 06510
Telephone: (203) 562-0511
Recruiter Classification: Contingency; Lowest/Average Salary:
$30,000/$60,000; Industry Concentration: Chemical Products, High
Technology, Information Technology, Manufacturing; Function Concentration:
Engineering, General Management

**Zaslav, Debra M.** — *Principal*
Telford, Adams & Alexander/Telford & Co., Inc.
650 Town Center Drive, Suite 850A
Costa Mesa, CA 92626
Telephone: (714) 850-4354
**Recruiter Classification:** Retained; **Lowest/Average Salary:** $75,000/$90,000;
**Industry Concentration:** Generalist with a primary focus in Consumer Products,
Financial Services, Healthcare/Hospitals, High Technology, Information
Technology, Manufacturing, Non-Profit, Pharmaceutical/Medical, Public
Administration, Real Estate, Transportation; **Function Concentration:** Generalist

**Zatman, Allen** — *Technical Recruiter*
Search Enterprises South, Inc.
10100 West Sample Road
Coral Springs, FL 33065
Telephone: (305) 755-3121
**Recruiter Classification:** Contingency; **Lowest/Average Salary:**
$40,000/$50,000; **Industry Concentration:** Chemical Products, Consumer
Products, Oil/Gas; **Function Concentration:** Engineering

**Zatzick, Michael** — *Account Executive*
Search West, Inc.
1888 Century Park East
Suite 2050
Los Angeles, CA 90067-1736
Telephone: (310) 284-8888
**Recruiter Classification:** Contingency; **Lowest/Average Salary:**
$40,000/$60,000; **Industry Concentration:** Electronics, High Technology;
**Function Concentration:** Engineering, Research and Development, Sales

**Zavala, Lorenzo** — *Executive Director*
Russell Reynolds Associates, Inc.
Arquimedes 130-3
Colonia Polanco
Mexico City, D.F., MEXICO 11560
Telephone: (525) 281-0440
**Recruiter Classification:** Retained; **Lowest/Average Salary:** $90,000/$90,000;
**Industry Concentration:** Generalist with a primary focus in Financial Services;
**Function Concentration:** Generalist

**Zavat, Marc** — *Senior Consultant*
Ryan, Miller & Associates Inc.
790 East Colorado, Suite 506
Pasadena, CA 91101
Telephone: (818) 568-3100
**Recruiter Classification:** Contingency; **Lowest/Average Salary:**
$40,000/$75,000; **Industry Concentration:** Financial Services; **Function
Concentration:** Finance/Accounting

**Zavrel, Mark** — *Associate*
Source Services Corporation
8614 Westwood Center, Suite 750
Vienna, VA 22182
Telephone: (703) 790-5610
**Recruiter Classification:** Contingency; **Lowest/Average Salary:**
$30,000/$50,000; **Industry Concentration:** Financial Services, Information
Technology; **Function Concentration:** Engineering, Finance/Accounting

**Zawicki, David** — *Manager Eastern Region*
Management Recruiters International, Inc.
750 Hamburg Turnpike, Suite 203
Pompton Lakes, NJ 07442-1418
Telephone: (201) 831-7778
**Recruiter Classification:** Contingency; **Lowest/Average Salary:**
$30,000/$75,000; **Industry Concentration:** Generalist; **Function
Concentration:** Generalist

**Zay, Thomas C.** — *President/Consultant*
Boyden/Zay & Company
Two Midtown Plaza, Suite 1740
1360 Peachtree Street, NE
Atlanta, GA 30309
Telephone: (404) 876-9986
**Recruiter Classification:** Retained; **Lowest/Average Salary:** $90,000/$90,000;
**Industry Concentration:** Generalist with a primary focus in Consumer
Products, Fashion (Retail/Apparel), Financial Services, Healthcare/Hospitals;
**Function Concentration:** Generalist with a primary focus in Engineering,
General Management, Marketing

**Zay, Thomas C.** — *Managing Director*
Boyden/Zay & Company
Three Allen Center
333 Clay Street, Suite 3810
Houston, TX 77002
Telephone: (713) 655-0123
**Recruiter Classification:** Retained; **Lowest/Average Salary:** $90,000/$90,000;
**Industry Concentration:** Generalist with a primary focus in Chemical Products,
Consumer Products, Energy, Financial Services, Insurance; **Function
Concentration:** Generalist with a primary focus in Finance/Accounting,
General Management, Human Resources, Marketing

**Zee, Wanda** — *Vice President*
Tesar-Reynes, Inc.
500 North Michigan Avenue
Chicago, IL 60611
Telephone: (312) 661-0700
**Recruiter Classification:** Retained; **Lowest/Average Salary:** $50,000/$75,000;
**Industry Concentration:** Automotive, Consumer Products, High Technology,
Hospitality/Leisure, Publishing/Media; **Function Concentration:** Marketing

**Zegel, Gary** — *Associate*
Source Services Corporation
155 Federal Street, Suite 410
Boston, MA 02110
Telephone: (617) 482-8211
**Recruiter Classification:** Contingency; **Lowest/Average Salary:**
$30,000/$50,000; **Industry Concentration:** Financial Services, Information
Technology; **Function Concentration:** Engineering, Finance/Accounting

**Zell, David M.** — *President and CEO*
Logix Partners
1601 Trapelo Road
Waltham, MA 02154
Telephone: (617) 890-0500
**Recruiter Classification:** Retained; **Lowest/Average Salary:** $60,000/$75,000;
**Industry Concentration:** High Technology, Information Technology; **Function
Concentration:** Engineering

**Zellner, Paul A.** — *Partner*
Paul Ray Berndtson
10 South Riverside Plaza
Suite 720
Chicago, IL 60606
Telephone: (312) 876-0730
**Recruiter Classification:** Retained; **Lowest/Average Salary:** $90,000/$90,000;
**Industry Concentration:** Generalist; **Function Concentration:** Generalist

**Zenzer, Anne** — *Shareholder*
Witt/Kieffer, Ford, Hadelman & Lloyd
2015 Spring Road, Suite 510
Oak Brook, IL 60521
Telephone: (708) 990-1370
**Recruiter Classification:** Retained; **Lowest/Average Salary:** $75,000/$90,000;
**Industry Concentration:** Healthcare/Hospitals; **Function Concentration:**
Generalist with a primary focus in General Management

**Zera, Ronald J.** — *Director*
Spencer Stuart
1717 Main Street, Suite 5300
Dallas, TX 75201-4605
Telephone: (214) 658-1777
**Recruiter Classification:** Retained; **Lowest/Average Salary:** $90,000/$90,000;
**Industry Concentration:** Non-Profit; **Function Concentration:** Administration,
Engineering, Finance/Accounting, General Management, Human Resources,
Marketing, Research and Development, Sales, Women/Minorities

**Zerkle, John P.** — *Manager Eastern Region*
Management Recruiters International, Inc.
5 Great Valley Parkway, P.O. Box 1803
Southeastern, PA 19399-1803
Telephone: (610) 648-3888
**Recruiter Classification:** Contingency; **Lowest/Average Salary:** $30,000/$75,000;
**Industry Concentration:** Generalist; **Function Concentration:** Generalist

**Zerkle, John P.** — *Manager Eastern Region*
Management Recruiters International, Inc.
2500 Office Center
Maryland Road, Suite 612
Willow Grove, PA 19090
Telephone: (215) 657-6250
**Recruiter Classification:** Contingency; **Lowest/Average Salary:** $30,000/$75,000;
**Industry Concentration:** Generalist; **Function Concentration:** Generalist

**Zetter, Roger** — *Director Logistic Division*
Hunt Ltd.
21 West 38th Street
New York, NY 10018
Telephone: (212) 997-2299
**Recruiter Classification:** Contingency; **Lowest/Average Salary:**
$50,000/$60,000; **Industry Concentration:** Automotive, Chemical Products,
Consumer Products, Electronics, Manufacturing, Pharmaceutical/Medical,
Publishing/Media, Transportation; **Function Concentration:** Generalist

**Zetto, Kathryn** — *Vice President/Partner*
Seco & Zetto Associates, Inc.
P.O. Box 225
Harrington Park, NJ 07640
Telephone: (201) 784-0674
**Recruiter Classification:** Contingency; **Lowest/Average Salary:** $60,000/$60,000;
**Industry Concentration:** Generalist with a primary focus in Financial Services,
High Technology, Information Technology; **Function Concentration:** Generalist
with a primary focus in Marketing, Sales, Women/Minorities

**Zila, Laurie M.** — *Manager Client Services*
Princeton Entrepreneurial Resources
600 Alexander Road, P.O. Box 2051
Princeton, NJ 08543
Telephone: (609) 243-0010
**Recruiter Classification:** Executive Temporary; **Lowest/Average Salary:**
$75,000/$90,000; **Industry Concentration:** Generalist with a primary focus in
Biotechnology, Consumer Products, Electronics, Healthcare/Hospitals,
Information Technology, Pharmaceutical/Medical, Venture Capital; **Function
Concentration:** Generalist with a primary focus in Finance/Accounting,
General Management, Human Resources, Marketing

**Zilliacus, Patrick W.** — *Treasurer and Secretary*
Larsen, Zilliacus & Associates, Inc.
601 West Fifth Street, Suite 710
Los Angeles, CA 90071
Telephone: (213) 243-0033
**Recruiter Classification:** Retained; **Lowest/Average Salary:** $60,000/$90,000;
**Industry Concentration:** Generalist with a primary focus in
Aerospace/Defense, Automotive, Biotechnology, Electronics,
Healthcare/Hospitals, Manufacturing, Packaging, Pharmaceutical/Medical;
**Function Concentration:** Generalist with a primary focus in Engineering,
General Management, Marketing, Research and Development,
Women/Minorities

**Ziluck, Scott W.** — *Manager Eastern Region*
Management Recruiters International, Inc.
Suite 705, Executive House
1040 North Kings Highway
Cherry Hill, NJ 08034-1908
Telephone: (609) 667-3381
**Recruiter Classification:** Contingency; **Lowest/Average Salary:**
$30,000/$75,000; **Industry Concentration:** Generalist; **Function
Concentration:** Generalist

**Zimbal, Mark** — *Associate*
Source Services Corporation
1233 North Mayfair Road, Suite 300
Milwaukee, WI 53226
Telephone: (414) 774-6700
**Recruiter Classification:** Contingency; **Lowest/Average Salary:**
$30,000/$50,000; **Industry Concentration:** Financial Services, Information
Technology; **Function Concentration:** Engineering, Finance/Accounting

**Zimmerman, Joan C.** — *Executive Vice President*
G.Z. Stephens Inc.
One World Trade Center
Suite 1527
New York, NY 10048
Telephone: (212) 321-3040
**Recruiter Classification:** Retained; **Lowest/Average Salary:** $90,000/$90,000;
**Industry Concentration:** Financial Services; **Function Concentration:**
Generalist

**Zimont, Scott** — *Associate*
Source Services Corporation
520 Post Oak Boulevard, Suite 700
Houston, TX 77027
Telephone: (713) 439-1077
**Recruiter Classification:** Contingency; **Lowest/Average Salary:**
$30,000/$50,000; **Industry Concentration:** Financial Services, Information
Technology; **Function Concentration:** Engineering, Finance/Accounting

**Zingaro, Ron** — *President*
Zingaro and Company
4200 Green Cliffs Road
Austin, TX 78746
Telephone: (512) 327-7277
**Recruiter Classification:** Retained; **Lowest/Average Salary:** $90,000/$90,000;
**Industry Concentration:** Biotechnology, Healthcare/Hospitals,
Pharmaceutical/Medical; **Function Concentration:** Engineering,
Finance/Accounting, General Management, Human Resources, Marketing,
Research and Development, Sales

**Zinn, Donald** — *Vice President and Managing Director*
Bishop Partners
708 Third Avenue
New York, NY 10017
Telephone: (212) 986-3419
**Recruiter Classification:** Retained; **Lowest/Average Salary:** $90,000/$90,000;
**Industry Concentration:** Entertainment, Information Technology,
Publishing/Media; **Function Concentration:** Generalist with a primary focus in
General Management, Marketing, Sales, Women/Minorities

**Zivic, Janis M.** — *Director*
Spencer Stuart
525 Market Street, Suite 3700
San Francisco, CA 94105
Telephone: (415) 495-4141
**Recruiter Classification:** Retained; **Lowest/Average Salary:** $90,000/$90,000;
**Industry Concentration:** Generalist with a primary focus in Biotechnology,
Board Services, Education/Libraries, Entertainment, Environmental, Financial
Services, Healthcare/Hospitals, Hospitality/Leisure, Non-Profit,
Pharmaceutical/Medical, Public Administration, Publishing/Media; **Function
Concentration:** Generalist with a primary focus in Administration, Engineering,
Finance/Accounting, General Management, Human Resources, Research and
Development, Women/Minorities

**Zona, Henry F.** — *President*
Zona & Associates, Inc.
26 Broadway, Suite 400
New York, NY 10004
Telephone: (212) 837-7878
**Recruiter Classification:** Contingency; **Lowest/Average Salary:**
$50,000/$60,000; **Industry Concentration:** Financial Services, Insurance;
**Function Concentration:** Generalist with a primary focus in Administration,
Finance/Accounting, General Management, Human Resources, Marketing,
Research and Development, Sales

**Zonis, Hildy R.** — *Manager Placement*
Accountants Executive Search
535 Fifth Avenue, Suite 1200
New York, NY 10017
Telephone: (212) 682-5900
**Recruiter Classification:** Executive Temporary; **Lowest/Average Salary:**
$40,000/$60,000; **Industry Concentration:** Generalist with a primary focus in
Consumer Products, Entertainment, Fashion (Retail/Apparel), Financial
Services, Non-Profit, Public Administration, Publishing/Media, Real Estate;
**Function Concentration:** Finance/Accounting

**Zoppo, Dorathea** — *Executive Director Scientific Recruitment*
Bill Hahn Group, Inc.
2052 Highway 35
Suites 203, 204
Wall, NJ 07719
Telephone: (908) 449-9302
**Recruiter Classification:** Contingency; **Lowest/Average Salary:**
$50,000/$75,000; **Industry Concentration:** Biotechnology,
Pharmaceutical/Medical; **Function Concentration:** Generalist with a primary
focus in Research and Development

**Zucchiatti, Elizabeth** — *Researcher*
The Caldwell Partners Amrop International
Sixty-Four Prince Arthur Avenue
Toronto, Ontario, CANADA M5R 1B4
Telephone: (416) 920-7702
**Recruiter Classification:** Retained; **Lowest/Average Salary:** $/$90,000; **Industry
Concentration:** Generalist; **Function Concentration:** Generalist

**Zucker, Nancy** — *Executive Recruiter*
Maximum Management Corp.
420 Lexington Avenue
Suite 2016
New York, NY 10170
Telephone: (212) 867-4646
**Recruiter Classification:** Contingency, Executive Temporary; **Lowest/Average
Salary:** $30,000/$75,000; **Industry Concentration:** Generalist with a primary
focus in Consumer Products, Entertainment, Financial Services, Information
Technology, Insurance, Manufacturing, Pharmaceutical/Medical,
Publishing/Media; **Function Concentration:** Human Resources

**Zwiff, Jeffrey G.** — *Partner*
Johnson Smith & Knisely Accord
100 Park Avenue, 15th Floor
New York, NY 10017
Telephone: (212) 885-9100
**Recruiter Classification:** Retained; **Lowest/Average Salary:** $90,000/$90,000;
**Industry Concentration:** Consumer Products, Entertainment, Financial
Services, Information Technology, Insurance, Venture Capital; **Function
Concentration:** Generalist with a primary focus in Administration,
Finance/Accounting, General Management, Marketing, Research and
Development, Sales

# Industry Specialization Index by Recruiter

# Industry Specialization Index by Recruiter

This index is arranged into 30 business sectors, including the generalist category, and provides a breakdown of the primary and secondary lines of industry specializations of each executive recruiter. Many recruiters have multiple listings in this index depending on the various specializations in which they are engaged. *Recruiters listed in the generalist category serve all industry specializations.*

1. Generalist
2. Aerospace/Defense
3. Automotive
4. Biotechnology
5. Board Services
6. Chemical Products
7. Consumer Products
8. Education/Libraries
9. Electronics
10. Energy
11. Entertainment
12. Environmental
13. Fashion (Retail/Apparel)
14. Financial Services
15. Healthcare/Hospitals
16. High Technology
17. Hospitality/Leisure
18. Information Technology
19. Insurance
20. Manufacturing
21. Non-Profit
22. Oil/Gas
23. Packaging
24. Pharmaceutical/Medical
25. Public Administration
26. Publishing/Media
27. Real Estate
28. Transportation
29. Utilities/Nuclear
30. Venture Capital

## 1. Generalist

Abbatiello, Christine Murphy — *Winter, Wyman & Company*
Abbott, Peter — *The Abbott Group, Inc.*
Abe, Sherman — *Korn/Ferry International*
Abell, Vincent W. — *MSI International*
Abernathy, Donald E. — *Don Richard Associates of Charlotte*
Abruzzo, James — *A.T. Kearney, Inc.*
Adams, Amy — *Richard, Wayne and Roberts*
Adams, Gary — *Management Recruiters International, Inc.*
Adams, Jeffrey C. — *Telford, Adams & Alexander/Jeffrey C. Adams & Co., Inc.*
Adelson, Duane — *Stanton Chase International*
Aki, Alvin W. — *MSI International*
Akin, Gary K. — *Management Recruiters International, Inc.*
Akin, J.R. — *J.R. Akin & Company Inc.*
Albanese, Matt J. — *Management Recruiters International, Inc.*
Albores, Sergio — *Management Recruiters International, Inc.*
Albrecht, Franke M. — *Management Recruiters International, Inc.*
Albright, Cindy — *Summerfield Associates, Inc.*
Alden, Brian R. — *MSI International*
Alderman, Douglas — *Management Recruiters International, Inc.*
Alekel, Karren — *ALW Research International*
Alexander, Craig R. — *Management Recruiters International, Inc.*
Alexander, John T. — *Telford, Adams & Alexander/Human Resource Services*
Alfano, Anthony J. — *Russell Reynolds Associates, Inc.*
Allen, Donald — *D.S. Allen Associates, Inc.*
Allen, Douglas — *Sullivan & Associates*
Allen, John L. — *Heidrick & Struggles, Inc.*
Allen, Rita B. — *R.D. Gatti & Associates, Incorporated*
Allerton, Donald T. — *Allerton Heneghan & O'Neill*
Alley, Glenwood — *Management Recruiters International, Inc.*
Alpeyrie, Jean-Louis — *Heidrick & Struggles, Inc.*
Alphonse-Charles, Maureen — *Pendleton James and Associates, Inc.*
Altreuter, Rose — *The ALTCO Group*
Ambler, Peter W. — *Peter W. Ambler Company*
Ameen, Edward N. — *Management Recruiters International, Inc.*
Ames, George C. — *Ames O'Neill Associates*
Ancona, Donald J. — *Management Recruiters International, Inc.*
Anderson, David C. — *Heidrick & Struggles, Inc.*
Anderson, Dennis — *Andcor Human Resources*
Anderson, Glenn G. — *Lamalie Amrop International*
Anderson, Janet — *Professional Alternatives, Inc.*
Anderson, Jim L. — *Management Recruiters International, Inc.*
Anderson, Richard — *Grant Cooper and Associates*
Anderson, Shawn — *Temporary Accounting Personnel, Inc.*
Anderson, Thomas — *Paul J. Biestek Associates, Inc.*
Andre, Richard — *The Andre Group, Inc.*
Andrews, J. Douglas — *Clarey & Andrews, Inc.*
Andrews, Laura L. — *Stricker & Zagor*
Andrick, Patty — *CPS Inc.*
Andujo, Michele M. — *Chrisman & Company, Incorporated*
Angel, Steven R. — *Management Recruiters International, Inc.*
Anglade, Jennifer — *Korn/Ferry International*
Angott, Mark R. — *Management Recruiters International, Inc.*
Ankeney, Dan R. — *Management Recruiters International, Inc.*
Annesi, Jerry — *Management Recruiters International, Inc.*
Anterasian, Kathy — *Egon Zehnder International Inc.*
Appleton, Diane — *Management Recruiters International, Inc.*
Archer, John W. — *Russell Reynolds Associates, Inc.*
Archer, Sandra F. — *Ryan, Miller & Associates Inc.*
Ardi, Dana B. — *Paul Ray Berndtson*
Argentin, Jo — *Executive Placement Consultants, Inc.*
Arnold, David — *Christian & Timbers*
Arnold, David J. — *Heidrick & Struggles, Inc.*
Arnold, Janet N. — *Management Recruiters International, Inc.*
Arnold, Sheridan J. — *William B. Arnold Associates*
Arnold, William B. — *William B. Arnold Associates*
Aronin, Michael — *Fisher-Todd Associates*
Arons, Richard — *Korn/Ferry International*
Arozarena, Elaine — *Russell Reynolds Associates, Inc.*
Arrington, Renee — *Paul Ray Berndtson*
Arseneault, Daniel S. — *MSI International*
Artimovich, Lee J. — *Korn/Ferry International*
Ascher, Susan P. — *The Ascher Group*
Aslaksen, James G. — *Lamalie Amrop International*
Asquith, Peter S. — *Ames Personnel Consultants, Inc.*
Aston, Kathy — *Marra Peters & Partners*
Atkins, Laurie — *Battalia Winston International*
Atkinson, S. Graham — *Raymond Karsan Associates*
Aubin, Richard E. — *Aubin International*
Aydelotte, G. Thomas — *Ingram & Aydelotte Inc.*
Azzani, Eunice — *Korn/Ferry International*
Bacher, Philip J. — *Handy HRM Corp.*
Bachmeier, Kevin — *Agra Placements International Ltd.*
Bacigalupo, Terry — *Management Recruiters International, Inc.*
Bacon, Michael — *Management Recruiters International, Inc.*
Bacorn, Debra — *Accountants on Call*

Badger, Fred H. — *The Badger Group*
Bagley, James W. — *Russell Reynolds Associates, Inc.*
Bagwell, Bruce — *Intersource, Ltd.*
Bailey, Joseph W. — *Russell Reynolds Associates, Inc.*
Bailey, Linda S. — *Kenzer Corp.*
Bailey, Lisa — *Nordeman Grimm, Inc.*
Bailey, William A. — *TNS Partners, Inc.*
Baillou, Astrid — *Richard Kinser & Associates*
Baird, John — *Professional Search Consultants*
Baker, Charles E. — *Kenzer Corp.*
Baker, Gary M. — *Cochran, Cochran & Yale, Inc.*
Baker, Gary M. — *Temporary Accounting Personnel, Inc.*
Baker, Gerry — *Baker, Harris & Partners Limited*
Baker, Jerry H. — *Schuyler, Frye & Baker, Inc.*
Baker, Jim — *Southwestern Professional Services*
Baker, Kerry — *Management Recruiters International, Inc.*
Baker, Walter U. — *Lamalie Amrop International*
Baker-Greene, Edward — *Isaacson, Miller*
Bakker, Robert E. — *Management Recruiters International, Inc.*
Balch, Randy — *CPS Inc.*
Baldi, Virgil — *Korn/Ferry International*
Baldock, Robert G. — *Lovas Stanley/Paul Ray Berndtson Inc.*
Baldwin, Keith R. — *The Baldwin Group*
Ballantine, Caroline B. — *Heidrick & Struggles, Inc.*
Ballenger, Michael — *Heidrick & Struggles, Inc.*
Ban, Jean T. — *The Paladin Companies, Inc.*
Ban, Michael P. — *The Paladin Companies, Inc.*
Banker, Judith G. — *R.D. Gatti & Associates, Incorporated*
Banks, Renate — *Management Recruiters International, Inc.*
Baran, Helena — *Michael J. Cavanagh and Associates*
Baranski, David J. — *Management Recruiters International, Inc.*
Baranski, Glenda A. — *Management Recruiters International, Inc.*
Barao, Thomas — *Korn/Ferry International*
Barber, Toni L. — *MSI International*
Barger, H. Carter — *Barger & Sargeant, Inc.*
Bargholz, Harry — *Management Recruiters International, Inc.*
Barick, Bradford L. — *Management Recruiters International, Inc.*
Barick, Linda R. — *Management Recruiters International, Inc.*
Barilone, John — *Search West, Inc.*
Barker, Mary J. — *Management Recruiters International, Inc.*
Barker, Mary J. — *Management Recruiters International, Inc.*
Barlow, Ken H. — *The Cherbonnier Group, Inc.*
Barnes, Richard E. — *Barnes Development Group, LLC*
Barnes, Roanne L. — *Barnes Development Group, LLC*
Barnett, Barney O. — *Management Recruiters International, Inc.*
Barnett, Kim M. — *Management Recruiters International, Inc.*
Barnett-Flint, Juliet — *Heidrick & Struggles, Inc.*
Barnette, Dennis A. — *Heidrick & Struggles, Inc.*
Barnum, Toni M. — *Stone Murphy & Olson*
Baron, Harvey J. — *Management Recruiters International, Inc.*
Baron, Jon C. — *MSI International*
Baron, Len — *Industrial Recruiters Associates, Inc.*
Barowsky, Diane M. — *Lamalie Amrop International*
Barrett, Betsy — *Russell Reynolds Associates, Inc.*
Barrett, Dan E. — *Management Recruiters International, Inc.*
Barrett, J. David — *Heidrick & Struggles, Inc.*
Barrucci, Jim — *Winter, Wyman & Company*
Barton, Gary R. — *Barton Raben, Inc.*
Bascom, Roger C. — *Management Recruiters International, Inc.*
Bascom, Shirley R. — *Management Recruiters International, Inc.*
Bason, Maurice L. — *Bason Associates Inc.*
Bassler, John P. — *Korn/Ferry International*
Bassman, Bob W. — *Management Recruiters International, Inc.*
Bassman, Sandy M. — *Management Recruiters International, Inc.*
Bastoky, Bruce M. — *January Management Group, Inc.*
Bates, Nina — *Allard Associates*
Battalia, O. William — *Battalia Winston International*
Battistoni, Bea — *Accountants on Call*
Battistoni, Bea — *Accountants on Call*
Bauer, Bob — *Management Recruiters International, Inc.*
Baugh, Amy — *Richard, Wayne and Roberts*
Bauman, Martin H. — *Martin H. Bauman Associates, Inc.*
Bawulski, Fred B. — *Management Recruiters International, Inc.*
Baxter, Robert — *Korn/Ferry International*
Beal, Richard D. — *A.T. Kearney, Inc.*
Beall, Charles P. — *Beall & Company, Inc.*
Beals, Calvin H. — *Management Recruiters International, Inc.*
Bean, Bob — *Management Recruiters International, Inc.*
Bearman, Linda — *Grant Cooper and Associates*
Beatty, Jane — *Paul Ray Berndtson*
Beaudin, Elizabeth C. — *Callan Associates, Ltd.*
Beaudine, Frank R. — *Eastman & Beaudine*
Beaudine, Frank R. — *Eastman & Beaudine*
Beaudine, Robert E. — *Eastman & Beaudine*
Beaupre, Joseph — *Price Waterhouse*
Beaver, Bentley H. — *The Onstott Group, Inc.*
Beaver, Robert W. — *Executive Manning Corporation*
Beck, Jerry — *Financial Search Corporation*

Beckvold, John B. — *Atlantic Search Group, Inc.*
Bedford, Jennifer — *Korn/Ferry International*
Beer, John — *People Management Northeast Incorporated*
Beerman, Joan — *Kenzer Corp.*
Beeson, William B. — *Lawrence-Leiter and Company*
Beir, Ellen Haupt — *Korn/Ferry International*
Belden, Charles P. — *Raymond Karsan Associates*
Bell, Cathy — *Management Recruiters International, Inc.*
Bell, Danny — *Management Recruiters International, Inc.*
Bell, Jeffrey G. — *Norman Broadbent International, Inc.*
Bell, Lindy — *F-O-R-T-U-N-E Personnel Consultants of Huntsville, Inc.*
Bell, Lisa — *Winter, Wyman & Company*
Bell, Michael — *Spencer Stuart*
Bellano, Robert W. — *Stanton Chase International*
Belle Isle, Charles — *Belle Isle, Djandji Inc.*
Bellshaw, David — *Isaacson, Miller*
Bellview, Louis P. — *Management Recruiters International, Inc.*
Bellview, Sibyl M. — *Management Recruiters International, Inc.*
Benabou, Donna — *Kenzer Corp.*
Bennett, Jo — *Battalia Winston International*
Bennett, Joan — *Adams & Associates International*
Bennett, Richard T. — *Isaacson, Miller*
Benson, Kate — *Rene Plessner Associates, Inc.*
Bentley, David W. — *Nordeman Grimm, Inc.*
Berarducci, Arthur — *Heidrick & Struggles, Inc.*
Berenblum, Marvin B. — *Heidrick & Struggles, Inc.*
Bergen, Anthony M. — *CFO Associates, Inc.*
Berger, Emanuel — *Isaacson, Miller*
Berger, Jay V. — *Morris & Berger*
Berk-Levine, Margo — *MB Inc. Interim Executive Division*
Berlet, William — *KPMG Executive Search*
Berlin, Marc — *Accountants on Call*
Berman, Kenneth D. — *MSI International*
Bermea, Jose — *Gaffney Management Consultants*
Berne, Marlene — *The Whitney Group*
Bernstein, Charles Page — *Paul Ray Berndtson*
Berrong, Barbie H. — *Management Recruiters International, Inc.*
Berrong, Ray — *Management Recruiters International, Inc.*
Berry, Chuck — *Management Recruiters International, Inc.*
Berry, Harold B. — *The Hindman Company*
Berry, John R. — *Heidrick & Struggles, Inc.*
Bertok, Ken — *The Wentworth Company, Inc.*
Bertsch, Phil L. — *Management Recruiters International, Inc.*
Bertsch, Phil L. — *Management Recruiters International, Inc.*
Besen, Douglas — *Besen Associates Inc.*
Bethmann, James M. — *Russell Reynolds Associates, Inc.*
Bicknese, Elizabeth — *Heidrick & Struggles, Inc.*
Biestek, Paul J. — *Paul J. Biestek Associates, Inc.*
Biggins, J. Veronica — *Heidrick & Struggles, Inc.*
Biggins, Joseph — *Winter, Wyman & Company*
Billingsly, Dorothy M. — *DHR International, Inc.*
Billington, Brian — *Billington & Associates*
Billington, William H. — *Spriggs & Company, Inc.*
Bilz, Deirdre — *Johnson Smith & Knisely Accord*
Bird, Len L. — *Management Recruiters International, Inc.*
Bishop, B. Susan — *DHR International, Inc.*
Bishop, Barbara — *The Executive Source*
Bishop, James F. — *Burke, O'Brien & Bishop Associates, Inc.*
Bishop, Sandy — *Management Recruiters International, Inc.*
Biskin, Donald — *Heidrick & Struggles, Inc.*
Bitar, Edward — *The Interface Group, Ltd./Boyden*
Bizick, Ron — *Management Recruiters International, Inc.*
Black, Douglas E. — *MSI International*
Black, Frank S. — *Management Recruiters International, Inc.*
Black, James L. — *DHR International, Inc.*
Black, Nancy C. — *Assisting Professionals, Inc.*
Blackmon, Sharon — *The Abbott Group, Inc.*
Blackshaw, Brian M. — *Blackshaw, Olmstead & Lynch*
Bladon, Andrew — *Don Richard Associates of Tampa, Inc.*
Blair, Kelly A. — *The Caldwell Partners Amrop International*
Blanton, Thomas — *Blanton and Company*
Blecksmith, Edward — *Korn/Ferry International*
Blessing, Marc L. — *Management Recruiters International, Inc.*
Bliley, Jerry — *Spencer Stuart*
Bloom, Howard C. — *The Howard C. Bloom Co.*
Bloom, Joyce — *The Howard C. Bloom Co.*
Bloomer, James E. — *L.W. Foote Company*
Bloomfield, Mary — *R.D. Gatti & Associates, Incorporated*
Blue, C. David — *Management Recruiters International, Inc.*
Blumenthal, Deborah — *Paul Ray Berndtson*
Blumenthal, Paula — *J.P. Canon Associates*
Boal, Robert A. — *Management Recruiters International, Inc.*
Bodnar, Beverly — *Management Recruiters International, Inc.*
Bodnar, Robert J. — *Management Recruiters International, Inc.*
Bodner, Marilyn — *Bodner, Inc.*
Boehmer, Jack — *KPMG Executive Search*
Boerkoel, Timothy B. — *Russell Reynolds Associates, Inc.*

Bohn, Steve J. — *MSI International*
Bole, J. Jeffrey — *William J. Christopher Associates, Inc.*
Bolger, Thomas — *Korn/Ferry International*
Bolls, Rich — *Management Recruiters International, Inc.*
Bommarito, Bob C. — *Management Recruiters International, Inc.*
Bond, James L. — *People Management Northeast Incorporated*
Bonnell, William R. — *Bonnell Associates Ltd.*
Bonner, Rodney D. — *Management Recruiters International, Inc.*
Boone, James E. — *Korn/Ferry International*
Booth, Otis — *A.T. Kearney, Inc.*
Bopray, Pat — *Personnel Unlimited/Executive Search*
Borel, David P. — *Management Recruiters International, Inc.*
Borenstine, Alvin — *Synergistics Associates Ltd.*
Borland, James — *Goodrich & Sherwood Associates, Inc.*
Borman, Theodore H. — *Lamalie Amrop International*
Bormann, Cindy Ann — *MSI International*
Bos, Marijo — *Russell Reynolds Associates, Inc.*
Bostic, James E. — *Phillips Resource Group*
Bostick, Tim — *Paul Ray Berndtson*
Bothereau, Elizabeth A. — *Kenzer Corp.*
Boucher, Greg — *Southwestern Professional Services*
Bouer, Judy — *Baker Scott & Company*
Bourbeau, Paul J. — *Boyden*
Bourbonnais, Jean-Pierre — *Ward Howell International, Inc.*
Bourque, Jack J. — *Management Recruiters International, Inc.*
Bourrie, Sharon D. — *Chartwell Partners International, Inc.*
Bovich, Maryann C. — *Higdon Prince Inc.*
Bowen, Tad — *Executive Search International*
Bowen, William J. — *Heidrick & Struggles, Inc.*
Boxberger, Michael D. — *Korn/Ferry International*
Boyd, Michael — *Accountants on Call*
Boyd, Sara — *Accountants on Call*
Boyd, Sara — *Accountants on Call*
Boyer, Dennis M. — *Heidrick & Struggles, Inc.*
Boyer, Heath C. — *Spencer Stuart*
Boyle, Russell E. — *Egon Zehnder International Inc.*
Brackin, James B. — *Brackin & Sayers Associates*
Bradshaw, John W. — *A.T. Kearney, Inc.*
Bradshaw, Monte — *Christian & Timbers*
Brady, Robert — *CPS Inc.*
Brand, John E. — *Management Recruiters International, Inc.*
Brand, Karen M. — *Management Recruiters International, Inc.*
Brandeis, Richard — *CPS Inc.*
Brandt, Brian S. — *The Paladin Companies, Inc.*
Brassard, Phillipe — *KPMG Executive Search*
Bratches, Howard — *Thorndike Deland Associates*
Breault, Larry J. — *Management Recruiters International, Inc.*
Brennan, Patrick J. — *Handy HRM Corp.*
Brennan, Vincent F. — *Korn/Ferry International*
Brennecke, Richard C. — *Management Recruiters International, Inc.*
Brennen, Richard J. — *Spencer Stuart*
Brenner, Michael — *Lamalie Amrop International*
Brent, Art — *Goodrich & Sherwood Associates, Inc.*
Brenzel, John A. — *TASA International*
Brieger, Steve — *Thorne, Brieger Associates Inc.*
Briggs, Adam — *Horton International*
Bright, Timothy — *MSI International*
Brindise, Michael J. — *Dynamic Search Systems, Inc.*
Brink, James — *Noble & Associates Inc.*
Brinson, Robert — *MSI International*
Briody, Steve — *Management Recruiters International, Inc.*
Brocaglia, Joyce — *Alta Associates, Inc.*
Brock, John — *Korn/Ferry International*
Brock, Rufus C. — *Management Recruiters International, Inc.*
Brockman, Dan B. — *Dan B. Brockman Recruiters*
Brodie, Ricki R. — *MSI International*
Brooks, Natalie — *Raymond Karsan Associates*
Brophy, Melissa — *Maximum Management Corp.*
Brown, Arlene — *Management Recruiters International, Inc.*
Brown, David — *Korn/Ferry International*
Brown, David C. — *Russell Reynolds Associates, Inc.*
Brown, Debra J. — *Norman Broadbent International, Inc.*
Brown, Floyd — *Richard, Wayne and Roberts*
Brown, Franklin Key — *Handy HRM Corp.*
Brown, Hobson — *Russell Reynolds Associates, Inc.*
Brown, John T. — *Management Recruiters International, Inc.*
Brown, Kelly A. — *Russell Reynolds Associates, Inc.*
Brown, Kevin P. — *Raymond Karsan Associates*
Brown, Larry C. — *Horton International*
Brown, Lawrence Anthony — *MSI International*
Brown, Michael R. — *MSI International*
Brown, Ronald — *Richard, Wayne and Roberts*
Brown, S. Ross — *Egon Zehnder International Inc.*
Brown, Sandra E. — *MSI International*
Brown, Tom — *Management Recruiters International, Inc.*
Browndyke, Chip — *Paul Ray Berndtson*
Brudno, Robert J. — *Savoy Partners, Ltd.*

Brunelle, Francis W.H. — *The Caldwell Partners Amrop International*
Bruno, David A. — *DHR International, Inc.*
Bruno, Deborah F. — *The Hindman Company*
Bryant, Richard D. — *Bryant Associates, Inc.*
Bryza, Robert M. — *Robert Lowell International*
Brzowski, John — *Financial Search Corporation*
Buchalter, Allyson — *The Whitney Group*
Buchsbaum, Deborah — *Accountants on Call*
Buck, Charles — *Charles Buck & Associates*
Buckles, Donna — *Cochran, Cochran & Yale, Inc.*
Buda, Danny — *Management Recruiters International, Inc.*
Bueschel, David A. — *Shepherd Bueschel & Provus, Inc.*
Bulla, Steven W. — *Management Recruiters International, Inc.*
Bullard, Roger C. — *Russell Reynolds Associates, Inc.*
Bullock, Conni — *Earley Kielty and Associates, Inc.*
Bump, Gerald J. — *D.E. Foster Partners Inc.*
Bunker, Ralph L. — *Management Recruiters International, Inc.*
Buntrock, George E. — *Management Recruiters International, Inc.*
Burch, R. Stuart — *Russell Reynolds Associates, Inc.*
Burchard, Stephen R. — *Burchard & Associates, Inc.*
Burchill, Barb — *BGB Associates*
Burchill, Greg — *BGB Associates*
Burden, Gene — *The Cherbonnier Group, Inc.*
Burfield, Elaine — *Skott/Edwards Consultants, Inc.*
Burke, George M. — *The Burke Group*
Burke, J. Michael — *Merit Resource Group, Inc.*
Burke, John — *The Experts*
Burke, Sally — *Chaloner Associates*
Burkholder, John A. — *Management Recruiters International, Inc.*
Burnett, Brendan G. — *Sullivan & Company*
Burnett, Rebecca J. — *MSI International*
Burnette, Dennis W. — *Sanford Rose Associates*
Burns, Alan — *The Enns Partners Inc.*
Burns, Terence N. — *D.E. Foster Partners Inc.*
Burton, Linda — *Management Recruiters International, Inc.*
Bush, Martha A. — *MSI International*
Butler, Kevin M. — *Russell Reynolds Associates, Inc.*
Butterfass, Stanley — *Butterfass, Pepe & MacCallan Inc.*
Button, David R. — *The Button Group*
Byrnes, Thomas A. — *Thomas A. Byrnes Associates*
Cahill, James P. — *Thorndike Deland Associates*
Cahill, Peter M. — *Peter M. Cahill Associates, Inc.*
Cahoon, D.B. — *Sanford Rose Associates*
Cahouet, Frank — *Korn/Ferry International*
Caldemeyer, Marjorie L. — *Management Recruiters International, Inc.*
Caldwell, C. Douglas — *The Caldwell Partners Amrop International*
Caldwell, Robert — *Robert Caldwell & Associates*
Call, David — *Cochran, Cochran & Yale, Inc.*
Callahan, Wanda — *Cochran, Cochran & Yale, Inc.*
Callan, Robert M. — *Callan Associates, Ltd.*
Callaway, Lisa — *Korn/Ferry International*
Callaway, Thomas H. — *Russell Reynolds Associates, Inc.*
Came, Paul E. — *Paul Ray Berndtson*
Camp, David K. — *Management Recruiters International, Inc.*
Campbell, Margaret — *Coopers & Lybrand Consulting*
Campbell, Patricia A. — *The Onstott Group, Inc.*
Campbell, Robert Scott — *Wellington Management Group*
Campbell, Sandy T. — *Management Recruiters International, Inc.*
Campbell, Stephen P. — *DHR International, Inc.*
Campbell, Thomas J. — *Heidrick & Struggles, Inc.*
Campbell, W. Ross — *Egon Zehnder International Inc.*
Campeas, David E. — *Management Recruiters International, Inc.*
Cannavo, Louise — *The Whitney Group*
Cannon, Alexis — *Richard, Wayne and Roberts*
Cannon, Alicia — *Accountants on Call*
Cannon, Alicia — *Accountants on Call*
Cantus, Jane Scott — *Korn/Ferry International*
Capanna, Pat A. — *Management Recruiters International, Inc.*
Capeloto, Robert — *Korn/Ferry International*
Capizzi, Salvatore — *Winter, Wyman & Company*
Caplan, Deborah — *Price Waterhouse*
Carey, Dennis C. — *Spencer Stuart*
Cargill, Jim B. — *Management Recruiters International, Inc.*
Cargo, Catherine — *MSI International*
Carideo, Joseph — *Thorndike Deland Associates*
Carlson, Sharon A. — *Assisting Professionals, Inc.*
Carpenter, Harold G. — *MSI International*
Carpenter, James J. — *Russell Reynolds Associates, Inc.*
Carr, W. Lyles — *The McCormick Group, Inc.*
Carrara, Gilbert J. — *Korn/Ferry International*
Carrick, Kenneth D. — *Coleman Lew & Associates, Inc.*
Carrigan, Denise — *Management Recruiters International, Inc.*
Carrigan, Maureen — *R.D. Gatti & Associates, Incorporated*
Carrillo, Jose — *Amrop International*
Carrott, Gregory T. — *Egon Zehnder International Inc.*
Cartella, Janet — *Management Recruiters International, Inc.*

Cartella, Mike — *Management Recruiters International, Inc.*
Carter, Carolyn — *Thomas Mangum Company*
Carter, D. Michael — *Management Recruiters International, Inc.*
Carter, Guy W. — *Management Recruiters International, Inc.*
Carter, I. Wayne — *Heidrick & Struggles, Inc.*
Carter, Jon F. — *Egon Zehnder International Inc.*
Carter, Kitte H. — *Management Recruiters International, Inc.*
Caruso, Kathy — *Accounting Resources, Inc.*
Carver, Graham — *Cambridge Management Planning*
Carzo, Frank L. — *Russell Reynolds Associates, Inc.*
Casey, Darren — *Parfitt Recruiting and Consulting*
Casey, Jean — *Peter W. Ambler Company*
Cashen, Anthony B. — *Lamalie Amrop International*
Cass, Kathryn H. — *Don Richard Associates of Tidewater, Inc.*
Castine, Michael P. — *Spencer Stuart*
Cattanach, Bruce B. — *Horton International*
Caudill, Nancy — *Webb, Johnson Associates, Inc.*
Causey, Andrea C. — *MSI International*
Cavanagh, Michael J. — *Michael J. Cavanagh and Associates*
Caver, Michael D. — *Heidrick & Struggles, Inc.*
Caviness, Susan — *Korn/Ferry International*
Cavolina, Michael — *Carver Search Consultants*
Cavriani, Randolph — *Search West, Inc.*
Celentano, James — *Korn/Ferry International*
Celenza, Catherine — *CPS Inc.*
Cellers, Darrell L. — *Management Recruiters International, Inc.*
Cellers, Marsha — *Management Recruiters International, Inc.*
Cendejas, Stella — *Management Recruiters International, Inc.*
Cerasoli, Philip A. — *Experience-On-Tap Inc.*
Ceresi, Carole — *Management Recruiters International, Inc.*
Ceresi, Robert P. — *Management Recruiters International, Inc.*
Ceryak, George V. — *Management Recruiters International, Inc.*
Cesafsky, Barry R. — *Lamalie Amrop International*
Chadick, Susan L. — *Gould, McCoy & Chadick Incorporated*
Chalk, Charles J. — *GKR Americas, Inc.*
Chaloner, Edward — *Chaloner Associates*
Chamberland, Roland R. — *Management Recruiters International, Inc.*
Chamberlin, Brooks T. — *Korn/Ferry International*
Chambers, Robert — *The Wentworth Company, Inc.*
Champoux, Yves — *Ward Howell International, Inc.*
Chan, Margaret — *Webb, Johnson Associates, Inc.*
Chandler, Cynthia — *Kenzer Corp.*
Chappell, Peter — *The Bankers Group*
Charles, Ronald D. — *The Caldwell Partners Amrop International*
Chase, Kevin — *Paul Ray Berndtson*
Chattin, Norma Anne — *Accountants on Call*
Chauvin, Ralph A. — *The Caldwell Partners Amrop International*
Chavous, C. Crawford — *Phillips Resource Group*
Cherbonnier, L. Michael — *TCG International, Inc.*
Cherbonnier, L. Michael — *The Cherbonnier Group, Inc.*
Chermak, Carolyn A. — *Management Recruiters International, Inc.*
Chewning, Ed — *Management Recruiters International, Inc.*
Chilla, Mary — *Kenzer Corp.*
Cho, Ui — *Richard, Wayne and Roberts*
Chojnacki, Bindi — *Raymond Karsan Associates*
Chorman, Marilyn A. — *Hite Executive Search*
Chrisman, Timothy R. — *Chrisman & Company, Incorporated*
Christensen, Lois — *Management Recruiters International, Inc.*
Christensen, Thomas C. — *Management Recruiters International, Inc.*
Christenson, H. Alan — *Christenson & Hutchison*
Christian, Kevin — *Management Recruiters International, Inc.*
Christiana, Jack — *Richard, Wayne and Roberts*
Christiansen, Amy — *CPS Inc.*
Christiansen, Doug — *CPS Inc.*
Christie, Ian — *The Caldwell Partners Amrop International*
Christoff, Matthew J. — *Spencer Stuart*
Christy, Michael T. — *Heidrick & Struggles, Inc.*
Cicchino, William M. — *Lamalie Amrop International*
Cinco, Larry — *Management Recruiters International, Inc.*
Cinco, Susan M. — *Management Recruiters International, Inc.*
Cinquemano, Teri — *Accounting Personnel Consultants*
Citarella, Richard A. — *A.T. Kearney, Inc.*
Citrin, James M. — *Spencer Stuart*
Cizek, John T. — *Cizek Associates, Inc.*
Cizek, Marti J. — *Cizek Associates, Inc.*
Clarey, Jack R. — *Clarey & Andrews, Inc.*
Clarey, William A. — *Preng & Associates, Inc.*
Clark, Bruce M. — *IMCOR, Inc.*
Clark, Elliot H. — *Raymond Karsan Associates*
Clark, Evan — *The Whitney Group*
Clark, James — *CPS Inc.*
Clark, James D. — *Management Recruiters International, Inc.*
Clark, John Edward — *Management Recruiters International, Inc.*
Clark, Linda — *Kenzer Corp.*
Clark, Ronda — *Management Recruiters International, Inc.*
Clark, W. Christopher — *Heidrick & Struggles, Inc.*
Clauhsen, Elizabeth A. — *Savoy Partners, Ltd.*

Clegg, Cynthia — *Horton International*
Clemens, William B. — *Norman Broadbent International, Inc.*
Clemens, William B. — *Norman Broadbent International, Inc.*
Clement, Norman — *Korn/Ferry International*
Cline, Mark — *NYCOR Search, Inc.*
Clingan, Bob H. — *Management Recruiters International, Inc.*
Close, E. Wade — *Boyden*
Clovis, James R. — *Handy HRM Corp.*
Cobb, Lynn A. — *Management Recruiters International, Inc.*
Cobb, Mark A. — *Management Recruiters International, Inc.*
Cochran, Corinne — *Early Cochran & Olson, Inc.*
Coelyn, Ronald H. — *Spencer Stuart*
Coff, Scott — *Johnson Smith & Knisely Accord*
Coffey, Patty — *Winter, Wyman & Company*
Cohen, Kasumi — *Korn/Ferry International*
Cohen, Luis Lezama — *Paul Ray Berndtson*
Cohen, Michael R. — *Intech Summit Group, Inc.*
Cohen, Richard — *Management Recruiters International, Inc.*
Cohen, Robert C. — *Intech Summit Group, Inc.*
Colavito, Joseph W. — *Lamalie Amrop International*
Colborne, Janis M. — *AJM Professional Services*
Cole, Elizabeth — *MSI International*
Cole, Les C. — *Management Recruiters International, Inc.*
Cole, Ronald J. — *Cole, Warren & Long, Inc.*
Cole, Sharon A. — *AJM Professional Services*
Colella, Thomas V. — *Korn/Ferry International*
Coleman, J. Gregory — *Korn/Ferry International*
Coleman, J. Kevin — *J. Kevin Coleman & Associates, Inc.*
Coleman, John A. — *Canny, Bowen Inc.*
Coleman, Neil F. — *Management Recruiters International, Inc.*
Coleman, Scott A. — *Kenzer Corp.*
Collard, Joseph A. — *Spencer Stuart*
Collier, David — *Parfitt Recruiting and Consulting/PRO TEM*
Colling, Douglas — *KPMG Executive Search*
Colling, Douglas — *KPMG Management Consulting*
Collins, Robert — *Financial Search Corporation*
Collins, Tom — *J.B. Homer Associates, Inc.*
Collis, Martin — *E.L. Shore & Associates Ltd.*
Colman, Michael — *Executive Placement Consultants, Inc.*
Colosimo, Chris — *Richard, Wayne and Roberts*
Coltrane, Michael — *Richard, Wayne and Roberts*
Cona, Joseph A. — *Cona Personnel Search*
Conard, Rodney J. — *Conard Associates, Inc.*
Condit, Madeleine — *Korn/Ferry International*
Cone, Dan P. — *Management Recruiters International, Inc.*
Connelly, Heather — *The Caldwell Partners Amrop International*
Connelly, Kevin M. — *Spencer Stuart*
Connelly, Laura J. — *Management Recruiters International, Inc.*
Connelly, Thomas A. — *Korn/Ferry International*
Conner, John — *Flex Execs Management Solutions*
Connet, Mel — *Heidrick & Struggles, Inc.*
Connolly, Michael R. — *Management Recruiters International, Inc.*
Connors, Claire — *Korn/Ferry International*
Conover, Jo — *TASA International*
Cook, Dan — *Management Recruiters International, Inc.*
Cook, Dennis — *Korn/Ferry International*
Cook, Nancy L. — *The Diversified Search Companies*
Cook, Patricia — *Heidrick & Struggles, Inc.*
Cooke, Jeffrey R. — *Jonas, Walters & Assoc., Inc.*
Cooke, Katherine H. — *Horton International*
Cooksey, Ben — *Management Recruiters International, Inc.*
Coon, David — *Don Richard Associates of Richmond, Inc.*
Cooper, Bill — *Management Recruiters International, Inc.*
Cooper, David C. — *David C. Cooper and Associates, Inc.*
Cooper, Larry W. — *Management Recruiters International, Inc.*
Copeland, Linda K. — *Management Recruiters International, Inc.*
Cordaro, Concetta — *Flynn, Hannock, Incorporated*
Corey, Michael J. — *Ward Howell International, Inc.*
Corey, Patrick M. — *Ward Howell International, Inc.*
Cornehlsen, James H. — *Lamalie Amrop International*
Cornfoot, Jim L. — *Management Recruiters International, Inc.*
Corrigan, Gerald F. — *The Corrigan Group*
Costa, Cynthia A. — *MSI International*
Costa, Frances — *Gilbert Tweed/INESA*
Coston, Bruce G. — *MSI International*
Cotter, L.L. — *IMCOR, Inc.*
Cotterell, Dirk A. — *Management Recruiters International, Inc.*
Cottick, Ron — *Management Recruiters International, Inc.*
Cottingham, R.L. — *Marvin L. Silcott & Associates, Inc.*
Coulman, Karen — *CPS Inc.*
Cowling, Wes — *Management Recruiters International, Inc.*
Cox, James O. — *MSI International*
Cozzillio, Larry — *The Andre Group, Inc.*
Crabtree, Bonnie — *Korn/Ferry International*
Cragg, Barbara R. — *Southwestern Professional Services*
Cramer, Katherine M. — *Pendleton James and Associates, Inc.*
Cramer, Paul J. — *C/R Associates*
Crane, Howard C. — *Chartwell Partners International, Inc.*

Crath, Paul F. — *Price Waterhouse*
Crawford, Dick B. — *Management Recruiters International, Inc.*
Crigler, Jim — *Management Recruiters International, Inc.*
Crist, Peter — *Crist Partners, Ltd.*
Critchley, Walter — *Cochran, Cochran & Yale, Inc.*
Critchley, Walter — *Temporary Accounting Personnel, Inc.*
Cronin, Richard J. — *Hodge-Cronin & Associates, Inc.*
Crowder, Edward W. — *Crowder & Company*
Crowell, Elizabeth — *H.M. Long International, Ltd.*
Crownover, Kathryn L. — *MSI International*
Crumbaker, Robert H. — *Lamalie Amrop International*
Crump, William G. — *Paul Ray Berndtson*
Crystal, Jonathan A. — *Spencer Stuart*
Csorba, Les — *A.T. Kearney, Inc.*
Cuellar, Paulina Robles — *Paul Ray Berndtson*
Cuellar, Scott R. — *Russell Reynolds Associates, Inc.*
Culp, Thomas C. — *The Diversified Search Companies*
Cummings, Harry J. — *Sanford Rose Associates*
Cundick, Jeff L. — *Management Recruiters International, Inc.*
Cunneff, Harry J. — *Management Recruiters International, Inc.*
Cunningham, Claudia — *Korn/Ferry International*
Cunningham, Lawrence — *Howard Fischer Associates, Inc.*
Cunningham, Robert Y. — *Goodrich & Sherwood Associates, Inc.*
Cunningham, Sheila — *Adams & Associates International*
Curlett, Lisa — *Korn/Ferry International*
Currence, Anna — *Kenzer Corp.*
Currie, Lawrence S. — *MSI International*
Cushman, Judith — *Marshall Consultants/West*
Czajkowski, John — *Management Recruiters International, Inc.*
Czamanske, Paul W. — *Executive Interim Management, Inc.*
Czamanske, Peter M. — *Executive Interim Management, Inc.*
Czepiel, Susan — *CPS Inc.*
D'Ambrosio, Nicholas — *Alexander Ross Inc.*
D'Angelo, Ron E. — *Management Recruiters International, Inc.*
D'Elia, Arthur P. — *Korn/Ferry International*
D'Eramo, Tony P. — *Management Recruiters International, Inc.*
Dabich, Thomas M. — *Robert Harkins Associates, Inc.*
Dach, Bradley M. — *Management Recruiters International, Inc.*
Daily, John C. — *Handy HRM Corp.*
Dalton, Bret — *Robert W. Dingman Company, Inc.*
Dalton, David R. — *MSI International*
Damon, Richard E. — *Damon & Associates, Inc.*
Damon, Robert A. — *Spencer Stuart*
Dandurand, Jeff J. — *DHR International, Inc.*
Danforth, W. Michael — *Hyde Danforth Wold & Co.*
Daniel, Beverly — *Foy, Schneid & Daniel, Inc.*
Daniel, David S. — *Spencer Stuart*
Daniels, Leonard — *Placement Associates Inc.*
Dankowski, Thomas A. — *Dankowski and Associates, Inc.*
Danoff, Audrey — *Don Richard Associates of Tidewater, Inc.*
Darcy, Pat — *Paul Ray Berndtson*
Darter, Steven M. — *People Management Northeast Incorporated*
Daughety, Mac M. — *Management Recruiters International, Inc.*
Daum, Julie — *Spencer Stuart*
Dautenhahn, Thomas — *Sanford Rose Associates*
David, Dodie — *Sullivan & Associates*
David, Jennifer — *Gilbert Tweed/INESA*
David, Paul — *Ward Howell International, Inc.*
Davidson, Arthur J. — *Lamalie Amrop International*
Davis, Bernel — *MSI International*
Davis, Dana — *Winter, Wyman & Company*
Davis, Evelyn C. — *EFL Associates*
Davis, G. Gordon — *Davis & Company*
Davis, Joan — *MSI International*
Davis, Joel C. — *MSI International*
Davis, Ken R. — *Management Recruiters International, Inc.*
Davis, Orlin R. — *Heidrick & Struggles, Inc.*
Davison, Kristin — *Korn/Ferry International*
Davison, Patricia E. — *Lamalie Amrop International*
Davitt, John — *Korn/Ferry International*
de Bardin, Francesca — *F.L. Taylor & Company, Inc.*
De Kesel, Herman — *TASA International*
De Moch, Betty — *Search West, Inc.*
de Regt, John — *Heidrick & Struggles, Inc.*
de Tuede, Catherine — *Thomas A. Byrnes Associates*
Deal, Chuck H. — *Management Recruiters International, Inc.*
Debrueys, Lee G. — *MSI International*
DeCorrevont, James — *DeCorrevont & Associates*
DeCorrevont, James — *DeCorrevont & Associates*
DeCosta, Michael — *Korn/Ferry International*
DeFrancesco, Mary Ellen — *The Onstott Group, Inc.*
DeHart, Donna — *Tower Consultants, Ltd.*
Dejong, Jack C. — *Management Recruiters International, Inc.*
Del Prete, Karen — *Gilbert Tweed/INESA*
Del'Ange, Gabrielle N. — *MSI International*
Delaney, Patrick J. — *Sensible Solutions, Inc.*
Delin, Norm — *Management Recruiters International, Inc.*
Delman, Charles — *Korn/Ferry International*

DelNegro, Anthony T. — *DHR International, Inc.*
DelNegro, Anthony T. — *DHR International, Inc.*
DeLong, Art — *Richard Kader & Associates*
DeMario, William — *Accountants on Call*
Demchak, James P. — *Sandhurst Associates*
Dennen, Bob E. — *Management Recruiters International, Inc.*
Dennen, Lorraine T. — *Management Recruiters International, Inc.*
Denney, Edward B. — *Denney & Company Incorporated*
Denney, Thomas L. — *Denney & Company Incorporated*
Densmore, Geraldine — *Michael Stern Associates Inc.*
DeSanto, Constance E. — *Paul Ray Berndtson*
Desgrosellier, Gary P. — *Personnel Unlimited/Executive Search*
Desgrosellier, Shawn — *Personnel Unlimited/Executive Search*
Desmond, Dennis — *Beall & Company, Inc.*
deVry, Kimberly A. — *Tower Consultants, Ltd.*
deWilde, David M. — *Chartwell Partners International, Inc.*
Diamond, Peter — *Korn/Ferry International*
Diaz, Del J. — *Management Recruiters International, Inc.*
Dickey, Arlene — *Kenzer Corp.*
Dickey, Chet W. — *Bowden & Company, Inc.*
Dickinson, Peter K. — *Shepherd Bueschel & Provus, Inc.*
Dickstein, Joel — *Management Recruiters International, Inc.*
Diduca, Tom A. — *Management Recruiters International, Inc.*
Dieckmann, Ralph E. — *Dieckmann & Associates, Ltd.*
Dietz, David S. — *MSI International*
DiGiovanni, Charles — *Penn Search*
DiMarchi, Paul — *DiMarchi Partners, Inc.*
Dingman, Bruce — *Robert W. Dingman Company, Inc.*
Dinse, Beth — *Management Recruiters International, Inc.*
Dinte, Paul — *Dinte Resources, Incorporated*
Dipaolo, Jeff — *Management Recruiters International, Inc.*
DiSalvo, Fred — *The Cambridge Group Ltd*
Divine, Robert S. — *O'Shea, Divine & Company, Inc.*
Dixon, Aris — *CPS Inc.*
Dixon, C.R. — *A la carte International*
Djandji, Guy N. — *Belle Isle, Djandji Inc.*
Do, Sonnie — *Whitney & Associates, Inc.*
Doele, Donald C. — *Goodrich & Sherwood Associates, Inc.*
Doliva, Lauren M. — *Heidrick & Struggles, Inc.*
Dominguez, Carl — *Heidrick & Struggles, Inc.*
Donahie, Stephen — *Search West, Inc.*
Donnelly, George J. — *Ward Howell International, Inc.*
Donovan, Jerry E. — *Management Recruiters International, Inc.*
Dooley, James L. — *Management Recruiters International, Inc.*
Doran, Mary Ann — *Kenzer Corp.*
Dotson, M. Ileen — *Dotson & Associates*
Dougherty, Bridget L. — *Wellington Management Group*
Dougherty, Lawrence J. — *Management Recruiters International, Inc.*
Douglas, Barbara L. — *David C. Cooper and Associates, Inc.*
Dow, Lori — *Davidson, Laird & Associates*
Dowell, Mary K. — *Professional Search Associates*
Downs, James L. — *Sanford Rose Associates*
Doyle, Bobby — *Richard, Wayne and Roberts*
Dreifus, Donald — *Search West, Inc.*
Dremely, Mark — *Richard, Wayne and Roberts*
Drennan, Ronald — *Ward Howell International, Inc.*
Dresser, Amy K. — *David C. Cooper and Associates, Inc.*
Driscoll, Donald L. — *Management Recruiters International, Inc.*
Drown, Clifford F. — *Management Recruiters International, Inc.*
Drummond-Hay, Peter — *Russell Reynolds Associates, Inc.*
Drury, James J. — *Spencer Stuart*
Ducruet, Linda K. — *Heidrick & Struggles, Inc.*
Dudley, Craig J. — *Paul Ray Berndtson*
Dudley, Robert — *Sanford Rose Associates*
Duggan, James P. — *Slayton International, Inc.*
Duke, Larry G. — *Management Recruiters International, Inc.*
Dukes, Ronald — *Heidrick & Struggles, Inc.*
Duley, Richard I. — *ARJay & Associates*
Dumesnil, Curtis — *Richard, Wayne and Roberts*
Dunbar, Geoffrey T. — *Heidrick & Struggles, Inc.*
Dunford, Michael S. — *Korn/Ferry International*
Dunlevie, Craig — *Korn/Ferry International*
Dunman, Betsy L. — *Crawford & Crofford*
Dunn, Ed L. — *Management Recruiters International, Inc.*
Dunn, Kathleen — *A.T. Kearney, Inc.*
Durakis, Charles A. — *C.A. Durakis Associates, Inc.*
Durakis, Charles A. — *C.A. Durakis Associates, Inc.*
Durakis, Charles A. — *C.A. Durakis Associates, Inc.*
Durand, Francois — *Ward Howell International, Inc.*
Durant, Jane — *Winter, Wyman & Company*
Dussick, Vince — *Dussick Management Associates*
Dwyer, Julie — *CPS Inc.*
Dykeman, James J. — *Management Recruiters International, Inc.*
Dykstra, Nicolette — *CPS Inc.*
Eagan, Karen L. — *Management Recruiters International, Inc.*
Eagan, Ridge — *Management Recruiters International, Inc.*
Earhart, William D. — *Sanford Rose Associates*
Early, Alice C. — *Russell Reynolds Associates, Inc.*

Early, Bert H. — *Early Cochran & Olson, Inc.*
Eatman, Fred — *Management Recruiters International, Inc.*
Ebeling, John A. — *Gilbert Tweed/INESA*
Eberly, Carrie — *Accounting Resources, Inc.*
Eckhart, Ken — *Spencer Stuart*
Eden, Brooks D. — *Eden & Associates, Inc.*
Eden, Dianne — *Steeple Associates*
Eden, Don F. — *Management Recruiters International, Inc.*
Eden, Earl M. — *Eden & Associates, Inc.*
Edwards, Dorothy — *MSI International*
Edwards, Douglas W. — *Egon Zehnder International Inc.*
Edwards, Robert — *J.P. Canon Associates*
Edwards, Verba L. — *Wing Tips & Pumps, Inc.*
Ehrenzeller, Tony A. — *Management Recruiters International, Inc.*
Ehrgott, Elizabeth — *The Ascher Group*
Ehrhart, Jennifer — *ADOW's Executeam*
Eibeler, C. — *Amherst Personnel Group Inc.*
Eilertson, Douglas R. — *Sanford Rose Associates*
Einsele, Neil — *Agra Placements International Ltd.*
Eisert, Robert M. — *Sanford Rose Associates*
El-Darwish, Jill — *Winter, Wyman & Company*
Elam, Bill J. — *Management Recruiters International, Inc.*
Eldredge, L. Lincoln — *Lamalie Amrop International*
Elliott, A. Larry — *Heidrick & Struggles, Inc.*
Elliott, David H. — *Heidrick & Struggles, Inc.*
Elliott, Mark P. — *Lamalie Amrop International*
Ellis, Milton — *Accountants on Call*
Ellis, Ronald A. — *Management Recruiters International, Inc.*
Ellis, Ted K. — *The Hindman Company*
Ellis, William — *Interspace Interactive Inc.*
Ellison, Richard — *Sanford Rose Associates*
Elston, William S. — *DHR International, Inc.*
Elwell, Richard F. — *Elwell & Associates Inc.*
Elwell, Stephen R. — *Elwell & Associates Inc.*
Empey, David G. — *Management Recruiters International, Inc.*
Endres, Robert — *Sanford Rose Associates*
Enfield, Jerry J. — *Executive Manning Corporation*
Engelgau, Elvita P. — *Management Recruiters International, Inc.*
Engelgau, Larry P. — *Management Recruiters International, Inc.*
England, Mark — *Austin-McGregor International*
Engman, Steven T. — *Lamalie Amrop International*
Enns, George — *The Enns Partners Inc.*
Ensminger, Barbara — *Management Recruiters International, Inc.*
Ensminger, Chub — *Management Recruiters International, Inc.*
Epstein, Kathy — *Canny, Bowen Inc.*
Erbes, Roysi — *Korn/Ferry International*
Erder, Debra — *Canny, Bowen Inc.*
Erickson, Mary R. — *Mary R. Erickson & Associates, Inc.*
Erlanger, Richard A. — *Erlanger Associates Inc.*
Ervin, Darlene — *CPS Inc.*
Ervin, James — *Search West, Inc.*
Erwin, Lee — *Agra Placements International Ltd.*
Eskra, Michael D. — *Sanford Rose Associates*
Esty, Greg C. — *Management Recruiters International, Inc.*
Etter, Duane A. — *Accounting & Bookkeeping Personnel, Inc.*
Eustis, Lucy R. — *MSI International*
Evans, Jeffrey — *Sullivan & Associates*
Evans, Robert M. — *TASA International*
Fabbro, Vivian — *A.T. Kearney, Inc.*
Faber, Jill — *A.T. Kearney, Inc.*
Fagan, Mark — *Management Recruiters International, Inc.*
Fahlin, Kelly — *Winter, Wyman & Company*
Fair, Donna — *ProResource, Inc.*
Falk, John — *D.S. Allen Associates, Inc.*
Fancher, Robert L. — *Bason Associates Inc.*
Farber, Susan — *Heidrick & Struggles, Inc.*
Farkas, Denny P. — *Management Recruiters International, Inc.*
Farley, Leon A. — *Leon A. Farley Associates*
Farrar, Carolyn — *Sanford Rose Associates*
Farrar, Gary — *Sanford Rose Associates*
Farrow, Jerry M. — *McCormack & Farrow*
Farthing, Andrew R. — *Parfitt Recruiting and Consulting*
Faure, Nicole — *The Caldwell Partners Amrop International*
Fawcett, Anne M. — *The Caldwell Partners Amrop International*
Fazekas, John A. — *Korn/Ferry International*
Feder, Gwen — *Egon Zehnder International Inc.*
Fee, J. Curtis — *Spencer Stuart*
Felderman, Kenneth I. — *Lamalie Amrop International*
Feldman, Abe — *A.E. Feldman Associates*
Feldman, Kimberley — *Atlantic Search Group, Inc.*
Felton, Meg — *Korn/Ferry International*
Fennel, P.J. — *Heidrick & Struggles, Inc.*
Ferneborg, Jay W. — *Ferneborg & Associates, Inc.*
Ferneborg, John R. — *Ferneborg & Associates, Inc.*
Ferrari, S. Jay — *Ferrari Search Group*
Ferris, Sheri Rae — *Accountants on Call*
Ferry, Richard M. — *Korn/Ferry International*
Feyder, Michael — *A.T. Kearney, Inc.*

Fifield, George C. — *Egon Zehnder International Inc.*
Filko, Gary — *Management Recruiters International, Inc.*
Fincher, Richard P. — *Phase II Management*
Fingers, David — *Bradford & Galt, Inc.*
Finn, Andrew — *Winter, Wyman & Company*
Fioretti, Kim — *Accountants on Call*
Fischer, Adam — *Howard Fischer Associates, Inc.*
Fischer, Howard M. — *Howard Fischer Associates, Inc.*
Fischer, John C. — *Horton International*
Fisher, Earl L. — *Management Recruiters International, Inc.*
Fisher, Neal — *Fisher Personnel Management Services*
Fitch, Lori — *R. Parker and Associates, Inc.*
Flanagan, Dale M. — *Lamalie Amrop International*
Flanagan, Robert M. — *Robert M. Flanagan & Associates, Ltd.*
Flannery, Peter — *Jonas, Walters & Assoc., Inc.*
Flash, James — *Richard Kader & Associates*
Flask, A. Paul — *Korn/Ferry International*
Fleck, George — *Canny, Bowen Inc.*
Fleming, Joseph M. — *IMCOR, Inc.*
Fleming, Marco — *MSI International*
Fleming, Richard — *R.D. Gatti & Associates, Incorporated*
Fleming, Richard L. — *TASA International*
Fletcher, Karen — *Don Richard Associates of Tidewater, Inc.*
Flickinger, Susan V. — *Korn/Ferry International*
Flink, Debra — *Heidrick & Struggles, Inc.*
Flink, Debra K. — *Russell Reynolds Associates, Inc.*
Flinn, Richard A. — *Denney & Company Incorporated*
Flowers, John E. — *Balfour Associates*
Flynn, Brian — *Korn/Ferry International*
Fogarty, Deirdre — *Paul Ray Berndtson*
Fogarty, Michael — *CPS Inc.*
Fogelgren, Stephen W. — *Management Recruiters International, Inc.*
Foley, Eileen — *Winter, Wyman & Company*
Foley, John J. — *Executive Outsourcing International*
Folkerth, Gene — *Gene Folkerth & Associates, Inc.*
Follmer, Gary — *Agra Placements International Ltd.*
Follrath, Noel — *Paul Ray Berndtson*
Fonfa, Ann — *S.R. Wolman Associates, Inc.*
Foote, Leland W. — *L.W. Foote Company*
Foote, Ray P. — *Heidrick & Struggles, Inc.*
Forbes, Kay Koob — *Sanford Rose Associates*
Forbes, Kenneth P. — *Sanford Rose Associates*
Foreman, David C. — *Koontz, Jeffries & Associates, Inc.*
Foreman, Kathryn A. — *Paul Ray Berndtson*
Foreman, Rebecca — *Aubin International*
Forgosh, Jack H. — *Raymond Karsan Associates*
Forman, Donald R. — *Stanton Chase International*
Fosnot, Bob — *Management Recruiters International, Inc.*
Fosnot, Mike — *Management Recruiters International, Inc.*
Foster, Drew B. — *Management Recruiters International, Inc.*
Foster, Duke — *Korn/Ferry International*
Foster, Dwight E. — *D.E. Foster Partners Inc.*
Foster, Michael — *Sanford Rose Associates*
Foster, Robert — *Korn/Ferry International*
Foster, Torrey N. — *Lynch Miller Moore Partners, Inc.*
Fountain, Ray — *Management Recruiters International, Inc.*
Fowler, Susan B. — *Russell Reynolds Associates, Inc.*
Fowler, Thomas A. — *The Hindman Company*
Fox, Amanda C. — *Paul Ray Berndtson*
Fox, Lucie — *Allard Associates*
Foy, James — *Foy, Schneid & Daniel, Inc.*
Francis, David P. — *Heidrick & Struggles, Inc.*
Francis, Dwaine — *Francis & Associates*
Francis, Kay — *Francis & Associates*
Franklin, Cecilia — *Management Recruiters International, Inc.*
Franklin, Cleve — *Management Recruiters International, Inc.*
Franquemont, William R. — *EFL Associates*
Franzino, Michael — *TASA International*
Frazier, John — *Cochran, Cochran & Yale, Inc.*
Frazier, Steven M. — *Sanford Rose Associates*
Freda, Louis A. — *DHR International, Inc.*
Freedman, Glenn — *Winter, Wyman & Company*
Freedman, Howard — *Korn/Ferry International*
Freemon, Ted — *Management Recruiters International, Inc.*
Freier, Bruce — *Executive Referral Services, Inc.*
French, William G. — *Preng & Associates, Inc.*
Frerichs, April — *Ryan, Miller & Associates Inc.*
Friar, Timothy K. — *Korn/Ferry International*
Friedman, Donna L. — *Tower Consultants, Ltd.*
Friedman, Helen E. — *McCormack & Farrow*
Friedman, Janet — *Litchfield & Willis Inc.*
Friel, Thomas J. — *Heidrick & Struggles, Inc.*
Frieze, Stanley B. — *Stanley B. Frieze Company*
Fruchtman, Gary K. — *Management Recruiters International, Inc.*
Fry, John M. — *The Fry Group, Inc.*
Frye, Garland V. — *Schuyler, Frye & Baker, Inc.*
Fueglein, Hugo — *Korn/Ferry International*

Fuhrman, Katherine — *Richard, Wayne and Roberts*
Fuller, Craig L. — *Korn/Ferry International*
Fuller, Ev — *Management Recruiters International, Inc.*
Fuller, Robert L. — *Litchfield & Willis Inc.*
Funk, Robert William — *Korn/Ferry International*
Futornick, Bill — *Paul Ray Berndtson*
Gabbay, Steve — *Accounting & Bookkeeping Personnel, Inc.*
Gabel, Gregory N. — *Canny, Bowen Inc.*
Gabriel, David L. — *The Arcus Group*
Gadison, William — *Richard, Wayne and Roberts*
Gaffney, Denise O'Grady — *Isaacson, Miller*
Gaffney, Keith — *Gaffney Management Consultants*
Gaffney, William — *Gaffney Management Consultants*
Gagan, Joan — *Gilbert Tweed/INESA*
Gaillard, Bill — *Management Recruiters International, Inc.*
Gaimster, Ann — *The Diversified Search Companies*
Gaines, Jay — *Jay Gaines & Company, Inc.*
Galante, Suzanne M. — *Vlcek & Company, Inc.*
Gallagher, David W. — *Lamalie Amrop International*
Gallagher, Jim — *Management Recruiters International, Inc.*
Gallagher, Marilyn — *Hogan Acquisitions*
Gallagher, Sallie — *Management Recruiters International, Inc.*
Gallagher, Terence M. — *Battalia Winston International*
Galvani, Frank J. — *MSI International*
Gandee, Bob — *Management Recruiters International, Inc.*
Gandee, Bob — *Management Recruiters International, Inc.*
Gandee, John R. — *Management Recruiters International, Inc.*
Gantar, Donna — *Howard Fischer Associates, Inc.*
Garcia, Joseph — *Management Recruiters International, Inc.*
Gardiner, E. Nicholas P. — *Gardiner International*
Gardner, Dina — *Winter, Wyman & Company*
Gardner, J.W. — *Management Recruiters International, Inc.*
Gardner, John T. — *Heidrick & Struggles, Inc.*
Gardner, Ned — *The Paladin Companies, Inc.*
Gardy, Susan H. — *Paul Ray Berndtson*
Garfinkle, Steven M. — *Battalia Winston International*
Gargalli, Claire W. — *The Diversified Search Companies*
Gariano, Robert J. — *Russell Reynolds Associates, Inc.*
Garman, Herb C. — *Management Recruiters International, Inc.*
Garner, Ann — *Accountants on Call*
Garner, Ronald — *Accountants on Call*
Garrity, Irene — *Management Recruiters International, Inc.*
Gaskins, Kim — *Kenzer Corp.*
Gates, Douglas H. — *Skott/Edwards Consultants, Inc.*
Gates, Will — *Korn/Ferry International*
Gatti, Robert D. — *R.D. Gatti & Associates, Incorporated*
Gauny, Brian — *Merit Resource Group, Inc.*
Gauthier, Robert C. — *Columbia Consulting Group*
Gaxiola, Alejandro — *Smith Search, S.C.*
George, Delores F. — *Delores F. George Human Resource Management & Consulting Industry*
Gerber, Mark J. — *Wellington Management Group*
Gerevas, Ronald E. — *Spencer Stuart*
Gerevas, Ronald E. — *Spencer Stuart*
Gerson, Russ D. — *Webb, Johnson Associates, Inc.*
Gerst, Tom J. — *Management Recruiters International, Inc.*
Gerstl, Ronald — *Maxecon Executive Search Consultants*
Gettys, James R. — *International Staffing Consultants, Inc.*
Getzkin, Helen — *Korn/Ferry International*
Gibbons, Betsy — *The Caldwell Partners Amrop International*
Gibbs, John S. — *Spencer Stuart*
Gibson, Bruce — *Gibson & Company Inc.*
Giella, Thomas J. — *Korn/Ferry International*
Gikas, Bill — *Tarnow International*
Gilbert, Carol — *Korn/Ferry International*
Gilbert, Jerry — *Gilbert & Van Campen International*
Gilbert, Keith A. — *Management Recruiters International, Inc.*
Gilbert, Mary — *Management Recruiters International, Inc.*
Gilbert, Patricia G. — *Lynch Miller Moore Partners, Inc.*
Gilchrist, Carl C. — *Paul Ray Berndtson*
Gilchrist, Robert J. — *Horton International*
Giles, Joe L. — *Joe L. Giles and Associates, Inc.*
Gill, Patricia — *Columbia Consulting Group*
Gillespie, Thomas — *Professional Search Consultants*
Gilliam, Dale — *Management Recruiters International, Inc.*
Gillies, Margarett — *KPMG Executive Search*
Gilmartin, William — *Hockett Associates, Inc.*
Gilmore, David A. — *Elwell & Associates Inc.*
Gilmore, Jerry W. — *Management Recruiters International, Inc.*
Gilmore, Lori — *CPS Inc.*
Gilmore, Pam — *Management Recruiters International, Inc.*
Gilreath, James M. — *Gilreath Weatherby, Inc.*
Ginsberg, Sheldon M. — *Lloyd Prescott Associates, Inc.*
Gionta, Michael E. — *Management Recruiters International, Inc.*
Gipson, Jeffrey — *Bradford & Galt, Inc.*
Girsinger, Linda — *Industrial Recruiters Associates, Inc.*
Gitlin, Bernardo — *Boyden*

Gladstone, Martin J. — *MSI International*
Glass, Lori — *The Executive Source*
Glatman, Marcia — *HRD Consultants, Inc.*
Glaza, Ron — *Management Recruiters International, Inc.*
Gleason-Lianopolis, Helen W. — *Management Recruiters International, Inc.*
Gleckman, Mark — *Winter, Wyman & Company*
Glueck, Sharon — *Career Temps, Inc.*
Goar, Duane R. — *Sandhurst Associates*
Gobert, Larry — *Professional Search Consultants*
Goedtke, Steven — *Southwestern Professional Services*
Goicoechea, Lydia — *Management Recruiters International, Inc.*
Goicoechea, Sam — *Management Recruiters International, Inc.*
Gold, Stacey — *Earley Kielty and Associates, Inc.*
Goldenberg, Sheryl — *Neail Behringer Consultants*
Goldenberg, Susan — *Grant Cooper and Associates*
Goldfarb-Lee, Terry — *O'Shea, Divine & Company, Inc.*
Golding, Robert L. — *Lamalie Amrop International*
Goldsmith, Fred J. — *Fred J. Goldsmith Associates*
Goldsmith, Phillip R. — *The Diversified Search Companies*
Goldstein, Gary — *The Whitney Group*
Goldstein, Steve — *R. Parker and Associates, Inc.*
Gomez, Paul — *ARJay & Associates*
Gonye, Peter K. — *Egon Zehnder International Inc.*
Gonzalez de Coindreau, Alicia M. — *Korn/Ferry International*
Gonzalez de la Rocha, Sergio — *Korn/Ferry International*
Gonzalez, Naomi — *McManners Associates, Inc.*
Gonzalez, Romulo H. — *Korn/Ferry International*
Gonzalez-Miller, Laura — *Management Recruiters International, Inc.*
Gooch, Randy — *Richard, Wayne and Roberts*
Good, Bob B. — *Management Recruiters International, Inc.*
Good, Dave J. — *Management Recruiters International, Inc.*
Goodere, Greg — *Splaine & Associates, Inc.*
Goodman, Dawn M. — *Bason Associates Inc.*
Goodwin, Joe D. — *Lamalie Amrop International*
Goodwin, Melissa — *Financial Search Corporation*
Goodwin, Tom — *Goodwin & Company*
Gordon, Elliot — *Korn/Ferry International*
Gordon, Gene — *The McCormick Group, Inc.*
Gordon, Gerald L. — *E.G. Jones Associates, Ltd.*
Gordon, Gloria — *A.T. Kearney, Inc.*
Gordon, Trina D. — *Boyden*
Gosselin, Jocelyne — *The Caldwell Partners Amrop International*
Gostin, Howard I. — *Sanford Rose Associates*
Gottenberg, Norbert A. — *Norman Broadbent International, Inc.*
Gould, William E. — *Gould, McCoy & Chadick Incorporated*
Gourlay, Debra — *Rene Plessner Associates, Inc.*
Govig, Dick A. — *Management Recruiters International, Inc.*
Govig, Todd — *Management Recruiters International, Inc.*
Gow, Roderick C. — *Lamalie Amrop International*
Goyette, Marc L. — *Management Recruiters International, Inc.*
Gozarina, Linda — *Noble & Associates Inc.*
Grabeel, Frank — *Management Recruiters International, Inc.*
Graf, Debra — *Kenzer Corp.*
Graham, Dale — *CPS Inc.*
Graham, Elizabeth — *Korn/Ferry International*
Graham, Robert — *Cambridge Management Planning*
Graham, Robert W. — *The Westminster Group, Inc.*
Grand, Gordon — *Russell Reynolds Associates, Inc.*
Grantham, John — *Grantham & Co., Inc.*
Grantham, Philip H. — *Columbia Consulting Group*
Grasch, Jerry E. — *The Hindman Company*
Graue, Monica — *Korn/Ferry International*
Graver, Merialee — *Accounting Personnel Consultants*
Gray, Annie — *Annie Gray Associates, Inc./The Executive Search Firm*
Gray, Russell E. — *Horton International*
Grayson, E.C. — *Spencer Stuart*
Grebenstein, Charles R. — *Skott/Edwards Consultants, Inc.*
Greco, Maria — *R L Plimpton Associates*
Greebe, Neil — *Flowers & Associates*
Green, Jean — *Broward-Dobbs, Inc.*
Greenberg, Ruth — *Kenzer Corp.*
Greene, Brian — *Winter, Wyman & Company*
Greene, C. Edward — *Don Richard Associates of Tidewater, Inc.*
Greene, Frederick J. — *Boyden*
Greene, Luke — *Broward-Dobbs, Inc.*
Greene, Neal — *Kenzer Corp.*
Greene, Wallace — *Korn/Ferry International*
Greenfield, Art — *Management Recruiters International, Inc.*
Greenspan, Phillip D. — *DHR International, Inc.*
Greenwall, Jane K. — *Gilbert Tweed/INESA*
Greenwood, Janet — *Heidrick & Struggles, Inc.*
Gregg, Pat — *Management Recruiters International, Inc.*
Gregor, Joie A. — *Heidrick & Struggles, Inc.*
Gregory, Gary A. — *John Kurosky & Associates*
Gregory, Mark — *Accountants on Call*

Gregory, Quintard — *Korn/Ferry International*
Grenier, Glorianne — *CPS Inc.*
Grey, Cort — *The McCormick Group, Inc.*
Grey, Fred — *J.B. Homer Associates, Inc.*
Grieco, Joseph — *Goodrich & Sherwood Associates, Inc.*
Griesedieck, Joseph E. — *Spencer Stuart*
Griffen, Leslie G. — *EFL Associates*
Griffin, Gilroye A. — *Paul Ray Berndtson*
Griffin, John A. — *Heidrick & Struggles, Inc.*
Grimes, G.D. — *Management Recruiters International, Inc.*
Grimm, Peter G. — *Nordeman Grimm, Inc.*
Groban, Jack — *A.T. Kearney, Inc.*
Groover, David — *MSI International*
Groover, Howard J. — *John Kurosky & Associates*
Gross, Barbara — *S. Reyman & Associates Ltd.*
Groves, Jim — *Management Recruiters International, Inc.*
Grushkin, Joel T. — *DHR International, Inc.*
Grzybowski, Jill — *CPS Inc.*
Guberman, Robert P. — *A.T. Kearney, Inc.*
Gude, John S. — *Boyden*
Gulley, Marylyn — *MSI International*
Gurley, Herschel — *Management Recruiters International, Inc.*
Gurtin, Kay L. — *Executive Options, Ltd.*
Gustafson, Eric P. — *Korn/Ferry International*
Gustafson, Jeremy — *The Paladin Companies, Inc.*
Gustafson, Richard P. — *Heidrick & Struggles, Inc.*
Haberman, Joseph C. — *A.T. Kearney, Inc.*
Hackett, Don F. — *Management Recruiters International, Inc.*
Hadfield, Sheri — *Paul Ray Berndtson*
Hagerthy, Michael J. — *IMCOR, Inc.*
Hagler, Holly — *Heidrick & Struggles, Inc.*
Haigler, Lisa S. — *Don Richard Associates of Charlotte*
Hailes, Brian — *Russell Reynolds Associates, Inc.*
Hailey, H.M. — *Damon & Associates, Inc.*
Halbeck, Bruce N. — *Russell Reynolds Associates, Inc.*
Halek, Frederick D. — *Sanford Rose Associates*
Hall, Debbie — *Management Recruiters International, Inc.*
Hall, Earl R. — *Management Recruiters International, Inc.*
Hall, George — *Coopers & Lybrand Consulting*
Hall, Noel K. — *Management Recruiters International, Inc.*
Hall, Peter V. — *Chartwell Partners International, Inc.*
Hall, Robert — *Don Richard Associates of Tidewater, Inc.*
Hall, Roger — *Management Recruiters International, Inc.*
Hall, Thomas H. — *Korn/Ferry International*
Halladay, Patti — *Intersource, Ltd.*
Hallagan, Robert E. — *Heidrick & Struggles, Inc.*
Hallam, Andy J. — *Management Recruiters International, Inc.*
Hallock, Peter B. — *Goodrich & Sherwood Associates, Inc.*
Halyburton, Robert R. — *The Halyburton Co., Inc.*
Hamar, Rolie C. — *Accountants on Call*
Hamdan, Mark — *Careernet of Florida, Inc.*
Hamer, Thurston — *Korn/Ferry International*
Hamilton, John R. — *A.T. Kearney, Inc.*
Hamilton, Timothy — *The Caldwell Partners Amrop International*
Hancock, Deborah L. — *Morgan Hunter Corp.*
Hancock, Mimi — *Russell Reynolds Associates, Inc.*
Hand, Jean — *Management Recruiters International, Inc.*
Hanford, Michael — *Richard Kader & Associates*
Hanley, Maureen E. — *Gilbert Tweed/INESA*
Hanna, Rodney — *Merit Resource Group, Inc.*
Hannock, Elwin W. — *Flynn, Hannock, Incorporated*
Hanrahan, Kevin R. — *Russell Reynolds Associates, Inc.*
Hansen, Bente K. — *DHR International, Inc.*
Hansen, Charles A. — *Management Recruiters International, Inc.*
Hansen, David G. — *Ott & Hansen, Inc.*
Hansen, Erik Lars — *Korn/Ferry International*
Hansen, Jan — *Management Recruiters International, Inc.*
Hansen, Martin L. — *Management Recruiters International, Inc.*
Hansen, Ty E. — *Blake, Hansen & Nye, Limited*
Hanson, Grant M. — *Goodrich & Sherwood Associates, Inc.*
Hanson, Jeremy — *Korn/Ferry International*
Hanson, Lee — *Heidrick & Struggles, Inc.*
Hanson, Paul L. — *Ward Howell International, Inc.*
Hanson, Russell V. — *Management Recruiters International, Inc.*
Harap, David — *Korn/Ferry International*
Harbaugh, Paul J. — *International Management Advisors, Inc.*
Harbert, David O. — *Sweeney Harbert & Mummert, Inc.*
Hardbrod, Herbert — *Management Recruiters International, Inc.*
Hardison, Richard L. — *Hardison & Company*
Hardwick, Michael — *Management Recruiters International, Inc.*
Hardy, Thomas G. — *Spencer Stuart*
Harfenist, Harry — *Parker Page Group*
Harkins, Robert E. — *Robert Harkins Associates, Inc.*
Harlow, John — *Korn/Ferry International*
Haro, Adolfo Medina — *Egon Zehnder International Inc.*
Harrell, L. Parker — *Korn/Ferry International*
Harrington, Chip — *Management Recruiters International, Inc.*
Harrington, Joan — *Management Recruiters International, Inc.*

Harrington, Robert J. — *Sanford Rose Associates*
Harris, Bruce — *ProResource, Inc.*
Harris, Ethel S. — *Don Richard Associates of Charlotte*
Harris, Jack — *Baker, Harris & Partners Limited*
Harris, Jack L. — *Management Recruiters International, Inc.*
Harris, Julia — *The Whitney Group*
Harris, Melissa — *Paul Ray Berndtson*
Harris, Vicki M. — *Management Recruiters International, Inc.*
Harshman, Donald — *The Stevenson Group of New Jersey*
Hart, Robert T. — *D.E. Foster Partners Inc.*
Hartnett, Katy — *The Paladin Companies, Inc.*
Harty, Shirley Cox — *Paul Ray Berndtson*
Harvey, Jill — *MSI International*
Harvey, John K. — *Management Recruiters International, Inc.*
Harvey, Joy — *Key Employment Services*
Harvey, Mike — *Advanced Executive Resources*
Harvey, Richard — *Price Waterhouse*
Hasler, Betty — *Heidrick & Struggles, Inc.*
Haughton, Michael — *DeFrain, Mayer, Lee & Burgess LLC*
Hauser, David E. — *Lamalie Amrop International*
Hauser, Jack — *Andcor Human Resources*
Hauswirth, Jeffrey M. — *Spencer Stuart*
Havas, Judy — *Heidrick & Struggles, Inc.*
Havener, Donald Clarke — *The Abbott Group, Inc.*
Hawfield, Sam G. — *Management Recruiters International, Inc.*
Hawkins, John T.W. — *Russell Reynolds Associates, Inc.*
Hawkins, Kirk V. — *Management Recruiters International, Inc.*
Hawksworth, A. Dwight — *A.D. & Associates Executive Search, Inc.*
Hay, Ian — *Korn/Ferry International*
Hay, William E. — *William E. Hay & Company*
Hayden, Dale — *Sanford Rose Associates*
Hayden, John — *Johnson Smith & Knisely Accord*
Hayden, Lynn — *Erlanger Associates Inc.*
Hayes, Stephen A. — *DHR International, Inc.*
Haystead, Steve — *Advanced Executive Resources*
Hazerjian, Cynthia — *CPS Inc.*
Heafey, Bill — *CPS Inc.*
Heagy, Linda H. — *Paul Ray Berndtson*
Healy, Vanda K. — *Management Recruiters International, Inc.*
Healy, William C. — *Management Recruiters International, Inc.*
Heath, Jeffrey A. — *Management Recruiters International, Inc.*
Hebard, Roy — *Korn/Ferry International*
Hebert, Guy J. — *Spencer Stuart*
Hecker, Henry C. — *Hogan Acquisitions*
Heckscher, Cindy P. — *The Diversified Search Companies*
Heideman, Mary Marren — *DeFrain, Mayer, Lee & Burgess LLC*
Heidrick, Gardner W. — *The Heidrick Partners, Inc.*
Heidrick, Robert L. — *The Heidrick Partners, Inc.*
Heiken, Barbara E. — *Randell-Heiken, Inc.*
Heisser, Robert — *Management Recruiters International, Inc.*
Heldenbrand, Paul — *The McCormick Group, Inc.*
Heller, Steven A. — *Martin H. Bauman Associates, Inc.*
Hellinger, Audrey — *Martin H. Bauman Associates, Inc.*
Helmholz, Steven W. — *Korn/Ferry International*
Helminiak, Audrey — *Gaffney Management Consultants*
Helt, Wally A. — *Management Recruiters International, Inc.*
Hemer, Craig — *Tanton Mitchell/Paul Ray Berndtson*
Hemingway, Stuart C. — *Robison & Associates*
Henard, John B. — *Lamalie Amrop International*
Henderson, Cathy — *Management Recruiters International, Inc.*
Henderson, Dale — *Management Recruiters International, Inc.*
Henderson, John — *Key Employment Services*
Henderson, William D. — *Russell Reynolds Associates, Inc.*
Hendon, Jill — *Korn/Ferry International*
Hendrickson, David L. — *Heidrick & Struggles, Inc.*
Hendrickson, Gary E. — *Management Recruiters International, Inc.*
Hendriks, Warren K. — *DHR International, Inc.*
Hendrixson, Ron — *Korn/Ferry International*
Heneghan, Donald A. — *Allerton Heneghan & O'Neill*
Henkel, John J. — *Management Recruiters International, Inc.*
Henkel, John J. — *Management Recruiters International, Inc.*
Henn, George W. — *G.W. Henn & Company*
Hennessy, Robert D. — *Korn/Ferry International*
Hennig, Sandra M. — *MSI International*
Henshaw, Robert — *F-O-R-T-U-N-E Personnel Consultants of Huntsville, Inc.*
Hensley, Bert — *Korn/Ferry International*
Hensley, Gayla — *Atlantic Search Group, Inc.*
Hergenrather, Edmund R. — *Hergenrather & Company*
Hergenrather, Richard A. — *Hergenrather & Company*
Herget, James P. — *Lamalie Amrop International*
Herman, Beth — *Accountants on Call*
Herman, Eugene J. — *Earley Kielty and Associates, Inc.*
Herman, Pat — *Whitney & Associates, Inc.*
Hermanson, Shelley — *Ells Personnel System Inc.*
Herrmann, Jerry C. — *Management Recruiters International, Inc.*
Herrod, Vicki — *Accountants on Call*
Hertan, Richard L. — *Executive Manning Corporation*

Hertan, Wiliam A. — *Executive Manning Corporation*
Hertlein, James N.J. — *Boyden/Zay & Company*
Herz, Stanley — *Stanley Herz and Company, Inc.*
Hess, David B. — *Sanford Rose Associates*
Hess, James C. — *The Diversified Search Companies*
Hess, Patricia — *Sanford Rose Associates*
Hessel, Gregory — *Korn/Ferry International*
Hettinger, Susan — *Kenzer Corp.*
Hetzel, William G. — *The Hetzel Group, Inc.*
Heuerman, James N. — *Korn/Ferry International*
Hewitt, Rives D. — *The Dalley Hewitt Company*
Hickman, Andrew — *Korn/Ferry International*
Hicks, Albert M. — *Phillips Resource Group*
Hicks, James L. — *MSI International*
Hicks, Nancy — *Paul Ray Berndtson*
Hicks, Timothy C. — *Korn/Ferry International*
Hidalgo, Rhonda — *Richard, Wayne and Roberts*
Hiebert, Wilf — *KPMG Executive Search*
Higdon, Henry G. — *Higdon Prince Inc.*
Higgins, David — *DHR International, Inc.*
Higgins, Donna — *Howard Fischer Associates, Inc.*
Higgins, John B. — *Higgins Associates, Inc.*
Hildebrand, Thomas B. — *Professional Resources Group, Inc.*
Hill, Emery — *MSI International*
Hill, Randall W. — *Heidrick & Struggles, Inc.*
Hillen, Skip — *The McCormick Group, Inc.*
Hilliker, Alan D. — *Egon Zehnder International Inc.*
Hillyer, Robert L. — *Executive Manning Corporation*
Hilton, Diane — *Richard, Wayne and Roberts*
Hilyard, Paul J. — *MSI International*
Hindman, Neil C. — *The Hindman Company*
Hingers, Marilyn H. — *Management Recruiters International, Inc.*
Hinkle, Dee — *Bradford & Galt, Inc.*
Hirschbein, Don L. — *Management Recruiters International, Inc.*
Hirschey, K. David — *Andcor Human Resources*
Hite, William A. — *Hite Executive Search*
Hites, Susan — *Accountants on Call*
Hnatuik, Ivan — *Corporate Recruiters Ltd.*
Hoagland, John H. — *Pendleton James and Associates, Inc.*
Hobson, Mary L. — *EFL Associates*
Hockett, William — *Hockett Associates, Inc.*
Hodge, Jeff — *Heidrick & Struggles, Inc.*
Hodgson, Judy H. — *Management Recruiters International, Inc.*
Hodgson, Robert D. — *Management Recruiters International, Inc.*
Hoffman, Brian — *Winter, Wyman & Company*
Hoffman, Mark — *Management Recruiters International, Inc.*
Hoffman, Sharon L. — *Accountants on Call*
Hoffmann, David H. — *DHR International, Inc.*
Hoffmann, David H. — *DHR International, Inc.*
Hogan, Edward — *Sanford Rose Associates*
Hogan, Larry H. — *Hogan Acquisitions*
Hohlstein, Jeff G. — *Management Recruiters International, Inc.*
Hohlstein, Jodi — *Management Recruiters International, Inc.*
Holden, Bradley J. — *Korn/Ferry International*
Holden, Richard B. — *Ames Personnel Consultants, Inc.*
Holland, Dave G. — *Management Recruiters International, Inc.*
Holland, Richard G. — *Management Recruiters International, Inc.*
Hollinger, Bill A. — *Management Recruiters International, Inc.*
Hollinger, Lois — *Management Recruiters International, Inc.*
Hollins, Howard D. — *MSI International*
Holloway, Linda — *Management Recruiters International, Inc.*
Holloway, Roger M. — *Management Recruiters International, Inc.*
Holmes, Lawrence J. — *Columbia Consulting Group*
Holmes, Len — *Management Recruiters International, Inc.*
Holodnak, William A. — *J. Robert Scott*
Holt, Doug C. — *Management Recruiters International, Inc.*
Holtz, Gene — *Agra Placements International Ltd.*
Holupka, Gary F. — *Management Recruiters International, Inc.*
Holupka, Patricia Lampl — *Management Recruiters International, Inc.*
Homer, Judy B. — *J.B. Homer Associates, Inc.*
Homrich, Patricia J. — *David C. Cooper and Associates, Inc.*
Honer, Paul — *Johnson Smith & Knisely Accord*
Honey, W. Michael M. — *O'Callaghan Honey/Paul Ray Berndtson, Inc.*
Hopkins, Chester A. — *Handy HRM Corp.*
Hoppert, Phil — *Wargo and Co., Inc.*
Horgan, Thomas F. — *Nadzam, Lusk, Horgan & Associates, Inc.*
Horton, Robert H. — *Horton International*
Horwitz, Sandy — *Kenzer Corp.*
Hoskins, Charles R. — *Heidrick & Struggles, Inc.*
Houchins, Gene E. — *Management Recruiters International, Inc.*
Hovey, Dick — *Management Recruiters International, Inc.*
Howard, Brian E. — *Management Recruiters International, Inc.*
Howard, Kathy S. — *Management Recruiters International, Inc.*
Howard, Leon — *Richard, Wayne and Roberts*
Howard, Marybeth — *Accounting & Bookkeeping Personnel, Inc.*
Howard, Richard H. — *Management Recruiters International, Inc.*
Howard, Susy — *The McCormick Group, Inc.*

Howe, Vance A. — *Ward Howell International, Inc.*
Howe, William S. — *Kenny, Kindler, Hunt & Howe*
Howell, Robert B. — *Atlantic Search Group, Inc.*
Howell, Robert B. — *Atlantic Search Group, Inc.*
Hoyda, Louis A. — *Thorndike Deland Associates*
Hubert, David L. — *ARJay & Associates*
Hucko, Donald S. — *Jonas, Walters & Assoc., Inc.*
Hudson, Kevin — *Raymond Karsan Associates*
Hudson, Reginald M. — *Search Bureau International*
Hughes, Cathy N. — *The Ogdon Partnership*
Hughes, James J. — *R.P. Barone Associates*
Hughes, Kevin R. — *Handy HRM Corp.*
Hughes, Pat — *Kenzer Corp.*
Hulce, Colleen — *Korn/Ferry International*
Hume, David — *Bradford & Galt, Inc.*
Humphreys, Sidney — *Korn/Ferry International*
Hunt, James E. — *Kenny, Kindler, Hunt & Howe*
Hunt, Thomas — *MSI International*
Hunter, Durant A. — *Pendleton James and Associates, Inc.*
Hunter, Gabe — *Phillips Resource Group*
Hunter, Patricia — *Kenzer Corp.*
Hunter, Sharon W. — *Management Recruiters International, Inc.*
Hunter, Sue J. — *Robison & Associates*
Huntoon, Cliff — *Richard, Wayne and Roberts*
Huntting, Lisa — *Professional Alternatives, Inc.*
Hurd, J. Nicholas — *Russell Reynolds Associates, Inc.*
Hurley, Helen — *Management Recruiters International, Inc.*
Hursey, Bruce — *Management Recruiters International, Inc.*
Hurst, Joan E. — *Korn/Ferry International*
Hurt, Thomas E. — *Management Recruiters International, Inc.*
Hurt, Thomas E. — *Management Recruiters International, Inc.*
Huss, Juli — *Accountants on Call*
Hutchinson, Loretta M. — *Hutchinson Resources International*
Hutchison, Richard H. — *Rurak & Associates, Inc.*
Hutchison, William K. — *Christenson & Hutchison*
Huttner, Leah — *Korn/Ferry International*
Hwang, Yvette — *MSI International*
Hyde, Mark D. — *MSI International*
Hyde, Tom G. — *Management Recruiters International, Inc.*
Hyde, W. Jerry — *Hyde Danforth Wold & Co.*
Hykes, Don A. — *A.T. Kearney, Inc.*
Hypes, Richard G. — *Lynch Miller Moore Partners, Inc.*
Iacovelli, Heather — *CPS Inc.*
Ide, Ian — *Winter, Wyman & Company*
Imely, Larry — *Christian & Timbers*
Incitti, Lance M. — *Management Recruiters International, Inc.*
Indiveri, Peter — *Kenzer Corp.*
Infantino, James — *Management Recruiters International, Inc.*
Infinger, Ronald E. — *Robison & Associates*
Inglis, William — *Korn/Ferry International*
Ingram, D. John — *Ingram & Aydelotte Inc.*
Inguagiato, Gregory — *MSI International*
Inzitari, Gloria — *Accountants on Call*
Irish, Alan — *CPS Inc.*
Isaacson, John — *Isaacson, Miller*
Isenberg, Peter — *Management Recruiters International, Inc.*
Israel, Stephen — *Korn/Ferry International*
Issacs, Judith A. — *Grant Cooper and Associates*
Ives, Richard K. — *Wilkinson & Ives*
Ivey, Deborah M. — *MSI International*
Jablo, Steven — *Dieckmann & Associates, Ltd.*
Jackowitz, Todd — *J. Robert Scott*
Jackson, Bruce — *Noble & Associates Inc.*
Jackson, Carol — *The Wentworth Company, Inc.*
Jackson, Clarke H. — *The Caldwell Partners Amrop International*
Jackson, Clay — *Paul Ray Berndtson*
Jackson, James Greg — *Korn/Ferry International*
Jackson, Pam — *Accounting Personnel Consultants*
Jacob, Don C. — *Management Recruiters International, Inc.*
Jacobs, James W. — *Callan Associates, Ltd.*
Jacobs, Klaus — *TASA International*
Jacobs, Martin J. — *The Rubicon Group*
Jacobs, Mike — *Thorne, Brieger Associates Inc.*
Jacobson, Al — *KPMG Executive Search*
Jacobson, Eric K. — *Management Recruiters International, Inc.*
Jacobson, Robert E. — *Management Recruiters International, Inc.*
Jadick, Theodore N. — *Heidrick & Struggles, Inc.*
Jambor, Hilary L. — *Korn/Ferry International*
James, Allison A. — *MSI International*
James, Bruce — *Roberson and Company*
James, E. Pendleton — *Pendleton James and Associates, Inc.*
James, Jane — *Canny, Bowen Inc.*
James, Michele — *Korn/Ferry International*
James, Richard — *Criterion Executive Search, Inc.*
Janecek, Robert — *Management Recruiters International, Inc.*
Janis, Laurence — *Integrated Search Solutions Group, LLC*
Jayne, Edward R. — *Heidrick & Struggles, Inc.*
Jeanes, Marshall M. — *IMCOR, Inc.*

Jelley, Sarah L. — *Pendleton James and Associates, Inc.*
Jenkins, Jeffrey N. — *Sanford Rose Associates*
Jensen, Debra — *Flex Execs Management Solutions*
Jensen, Stephanie — *Don Richard Associates of Tidewater, Inc.*
Jernigan, Susan N. — *Sockwell & Associates*
Jilka, Daniel L. — *Management Recruiters International, Inc.*
Jimenez, Gil C. — *Management Recruiters International, Inc.*
Joffe, Barry — *Bason Associates Inc.*
Johasky, Tom K. — *Management Recruiters International, Inc.*
Johnson, David — *Gaffney Management Consultants*
Johnson, Dennis R. — *Management Recruiters International, Inc.*
Johnson, Harold E. — *Norman Broadbent International, Inc.*
Johnson, John F. — *Lamalie Amrop International*
Johnson, John W. — *Webb, Johnson Associates, Inc.*
Johnson, Kathleen A. — *Barton Raben, Inc.*
Johnson, Priscilla — *The Johnson Group, Inc.*
Johnson, Rocky — *A.T. Kearney, Inc.*
Johnson, Ron L. — *Management Recruiters International, Inc.*
Johnson, Ronald S. — *Ronald S. Johnson Associates, Inc.*
Johnson, S. Hope — *The Interface Group, Ltd./Boyden*
Johnson, Shirley E. — *The Heidrick Partners, Inc.*
Johnson, Stephanie — *Carver Search Consultants*
Johnson, Walt W. — *Management Recruiters International, Inc.*
Johnston, Cindy — *Management Recruiters International, Inc.*
Johnston, Philip D. — *Egon Zehnder International Inc.*
Jones, B.J. — *Intersource, Ltd.*
Jones, Dale E. — *Lamalie Amrop International*
Jones, Daniel F. — *Atlantic Search Group, Inc.*
Jones, Don — *Kenzer Corp.*
Jones, Donald K. — *Russell Reynolds Associates, Inc.*
Jones, Edgar — *A.T. Kearney, Inc.*
Jones, Francis E. — *Earley Kielty and Associates, Inc.*
Jones, Gary — *BGB Associates*
Jones, Herschel — *Korn/Ferry International*
Jones, Jeffrey — *AJM Professional Services*
Jones, Jonathan C. — *The Ogdon Partnership*
Jones, Judy M. — *Management Recruiters International, Inc.*
Jones, Mike R. — *Management Recruiters International, Inc.*
Jones, Ronald T. — *ARJay & Associates*
Jordan, Stephen T. — *Paul Ray Berndtson*
Jose, Bill O. — *Management Recruiters International, Inc.*
Jose, Bill O. — *Management Recruiters International, Inc.*
Joubert, Pierre E. — *Boyden*
Joyce, Sheila M. — *Verkamp-Joyce Associates, Inc.*
Joys, David S. — *Heidrick & Struggles, Inc.*
Juarez, Maria Elena — *Amrop International*
Judd, Susan — *Korn/Ferry International*
Juelis, John J. — *Peeney Associates*
Juhan, Louise B. — *Korn/Ferry International*
Justiss, Ted W. — *David C. Cooper and Associates, Inc.*
Kacyn, Louis J. — *Egon Zehnder International Inc.*
Kader, Richard — *Richard Kader & Associates*
Kadin, Tom — *Kenzer Corp.*
Kahn, P. Frederick — *Heidrick & Struggles, Inc.*
Kaiser, Donald J. — *Dunhill Search International*
Kaiser, Irene — *Dunhill Search International*
Kaiser, James G. — *Dunhill Search International*
Kampmann, Sara — *Johnson Smith & Knisely Accord*
Kaplan, Gary — *Gary Kaplan & Associates*
Kaplan, Marc — *Gary Kaplan & Associates*
Kaplowitz, Marji — *Richard, Wayne and Roberts*
Kapur, Sharmila — *Korn/Ferry International*
Karalis, William — *CPS Inc.*
Karr, Cynthia L. — *Howard Karr & Associates, Inc.*
Karr, Howard L. — *Howard Karr & Associates, Inc.*
Karsan, N.S. — *Raymond Karsan Associates*
Kashinsky, Richard J. — *Management Recruiters International, Inc.*
Kashiwagi, Keiko — *The Repovich-Reynolds Group*
Kassouf, Connie — *The Whitney Group*
Katz, Art E. — *Management Recruiters International, Inc.*
Katz, Cyndi — *Search West, Inc.*
Katz, Robert L. — *MSI International*
Katz, Rosalind N. — *ExecuScope Division of Russell Staffing Resources, Inc.*
Kaufman, Stuart — *Management Recruiters International, Inc.*
Kaufmann, Robert C. — *Spencer Stuart*
Kaun, Loren A. — *Management Recruiters International, Inc.*
Kayajian, Bob A. — *Management Recruiters International, Inc.*
Kaye, Jeff — *Management Recruiters International, Inc.*
Kaye, Jerry — *Ward Howell International, Inc.*
Kean, Marjorie — *Korn/Ferry International*
Keating, Anne F. — *Korn/Ferry International*
Keating, Pierson — *Nordeman Grimm, Inc.*
Keefe, Donald J. — *TASA International*
Keen, Robert — *Management Recruiters International, Inc.*
Keesom, W. Peter — *Boyden/Zay & Company*
Keeton, Susan G. — *The Corporate Connection, Ltd.*
Kehoe, Mike — *CPS Inc.*

Keitel, Robert S. — *A.T. Kearney, Inc.*
Keller, Barbara — *Barton Raben, Inc.*
Keller, Lorraine L. — *Management Recruiters International, Inc.*
Kellerhals, Gloria — *Management Recruiters International, Inc.*
Kelley, Randall D. — *Spencer Stuart*
Kelly, Claudia L. — *Spencer Stuart*
Kelly, Donna J. — *Accountants Executive Search*
Kelly, Elizabeth Ann — *Wellington Management Group*
Kelly, Kevin B. — *Russell Reynolds Associates, Inc.*
Kelly, Michael T. — *Russell Reynolds Associates, Inc.*
Kelly, Michael T. — *Russell Reynolds Associates, Inc.*
Kelly, Peter W. — *R. Rollo Associates*
Kelly, Roy P. — *Management Recruiters International, Inc.*
Kelso, Patricia C. — *Barton Raben, Inc.*
Kemp, M. Scott — *M. Scott Kemp & Associates*
Kendall, Steven W. — *Management Recruiters International, Inc.*
Kendrick, M. Steven — *Lamalie Amrop International*
Kennedy-Radmer, Carol — *Accountants on Call*
Kenny, Roger M. — *Kenny, Kindler, Hunt & Howe*
Kent, Melvin — *Melvin Kent & Associates, Inc.*
Kent, Vickey — *Professional Alternatives, Inc.*
Keogh, James — *Sanford Rose Associates*
Kerester, Jonathon — *Cadillac Associates*
Kern, Ann P. — *Korn/Ferry International*
Kern, Jerry L. — *ADOW's Executeam*
Kern, Kathleen G. — *ADOW's Executeam*
Kershaw, Lisa — *Tanton Mitchell/Paul Ray Berndtson*
Kerth, Norman — *Accounting Personnel Consultants*
Keshishian, Gregory — *Handy HRM Corp.*
Kettwig, David A. — *A.T. Kearney, Inc.*
Kick, James W. — *The Prairie Group*
Kiedel, Michelle — *Winter, Wyman & Company*
Kielty, John L. — *Earley Kielty and Associates, Inc.*
Kilcoyne, Pat — *CPS Inc.*
Kiliper, Catherine G. — *Korn/Ferry International*
Kindler, Peter A. — *Kenny, Kindler, Hunt & Howe*
King, Byron L. — *Management Recruiters International, Inc.*
King, Gary A. — *Management Recruiters International, Inc.*
King, James B. — *The Westminster Group, Inc.*
King, Joyce L. — *MSI International*
King, Stephen C. — *Boyden/Zay & Company*
King, Thomas — *Morgan Hunter Corp.*
Kingdom, Scott — *Korn/Ferry International*
Kingore, William C. — *DHR International, Inc.*
Kingsley, Kate — *Korn/Ferry International*
Kinley, David — *The Caldwell Partners Amrop International*
Kinney, Carol — *Dussick Management Associates*
Kinser, Richard E. — *Richard Kinser & Associates*
Kirby, James E. — *Management Recruiters International, Inc.*
Kirchgessner, Ken F. — *Management Recruiters International, Inc.*
Kirkpatrick, Robert L. — *Reese Associates*
Kirschner, John — *Management Recruiters International, Inc.*
Kishbaugh, Herbert S. — *Kishbaugh Associates International*
Kissel, Jim R. — *Management Recruiters International, Inc.*
Kister, Edward A. — *Pendleton James and Associates, Inc.*
Kixmiller, David B. — *Heidrick & Struggles, Inc.*
Kizer, Jay R. — *Paul Ray Berndtson*
Kkorzyniewski, Nicole — *CPS Inc.*
Klages, Constance W. — *International Management Advisors, Inc.*
Klauck, James J. — *Horton International*
Klavens, Cecile J. — *The Pickwick Group, Inc.*
Klavins, Laura R. — *Dieckmann & Associates, Ltd.*
Klein, Gregory A. — *A.T. Kearney, Inc.*
Klein, Jill S. — *David C. Cooper and Associates, Inc.*
Kleinstein, Jonah A. — *The Kleinstein Group*
Kline, James O. — *Management Recruiters International, Inc.*
Klock, Lawrence S. — *Russell Reynolds Associates, Inc.*
Kloess, Janice Sciulli — *David C. Cooper and Associates, Inc.*
Klopfenstein, Edward L. — *Crowder & Company*
Klopmeyerr, Vanessa — *Kenzer Corp.*
Klos, Larry — *Management Recruiters International, Inc.*
Kluber, Bruce — *Richard, Wayne and Roberts*
Klumpjan, Sonja — *CPS Inc.*
Knapp, Ronald A. — *Knapp Consultants*
Knecht, Luke D. — *Russell Reynolds Associates, Inc.*
Knight, Gwen — *Richard, Wayne and Roberts*
Knight, Kim L. — *Telford, Adams & Alexander/The Knight Company*
Knight, Lisa — *Ward Howell International, Inc.*
Knisely, Gary — *Johnson Smith & Knisely Accord*
Knox, Andrew — *Korn/Ferry International*
Knutson, Rebecca J. — *Management Recruiters International, Inc.*
Kobayashi, Raelen — *The Repovich-Reynolds Group*
Koblentz, Joel M. — *Egon Zehnder International Inc.*
Kochert, Don — *Summerfield Associates, Inc.*
Kochmer, Sheila — *Management Recruiters International, Inc.*
Kochmer, Victor — *Management Recruiters International, Inc.*
Koehler, Frank R. — *The Koehler Group*
Koenig, Joel S. — *Russell Reynolds Associates, Inc.*

Kohn, Adam P. — *Christian & Timbers*
Kohn, Carole — *Kenzer Corp.*
Kohn, Thomas C. — *Reflex Services, Inc.*
Kolburne, Barbara — *D.E. Foster Partners Inc.*
Kolder, Thomas R. — *Russell Reynolds Associates, Inc.*
Koletic, Rudy E. — *Management Recruiters International, Inc.*
Kolke, Rick — *Richard, Wayne and Roberts*
Kondra, Vernon J. — *The Douglas Reiter Company, Inc.*
Konker, David N. — *Russell Reynolds Associates, Inc.*
Konkolski, Laurie — *The Paladin Companies, Inc.*
Koontz, Donald N. — *Koontz, Jeffries & Associates, Inc.*
Kopsick, Joseph M. — *Spencer Stuart*
Kornfeld, Warren — *Management Recruiters International, Inc.*
Kotick, Madeline — *The Stevenson Group of New Jersey*
Kotler, Herman — *Management Recruiters International, Inc.*
Kotler, Jerry R. — *Management Recruiters International, Inc.*
Kozlowski, Elaine K. — *Management Recruiters International, Inc.*
Kramer, Desni — *Management Recruiters International, Inc.*
Kreisman, Charlotte — *Kenzer Corp.*
Krejci, Stanley L. — *The Interface Group, Ltd./Boyden*
Krell, Richard B. — *Russell Reynolds Associates, Inc.*
Kreutz, Gary L. — *Kreutz Consulting Group, Inc.*
Krieger, Dennis F. — *Seiden Krieger Associates, Inc.*
Kring, Kenneth L. — *Spencer Stuart*
Krinsky, Ira W. — *Korn/Ferry International*
Krochenski, Caren S. — *Management Recruiters International, Inc.*
Krochenski, Lynette — *Management Recruiters International, Inc.*
Krohn, Eileen — *The Stevenson Group of New Jersey*
Krostangel, Thomas — *Personnel Unlimited/Executive Search*
Kruchoski, Jan — *Accountants on Call*
Kruse, Kevin — *Korn/Ferry International*
Krutzsch, Linda — *Accountants on Call*
Kucewicz, William — *Search West, Inc.*
Kuehnling, William A. — *Sanford Rose Associates*
Kuhl, Debra — *Paul Ray Berndtson*
Kuhl, Teresa — *Don Richard Associates of Tampa, Inc.*
Kuhnle, John H. — *Korn/Ferry International*
Kuhns, David — *Paul Ray Berndtson*
Kuntz, Bill — *Management Recruiters International, Inc.*
Kunzer, William J. — *Kunzer Associates, Ltd.*
Kuper, Keith D. — *Christenson & Hutchison*
Kurosky, John — *John Kurosky & Associates*
Kurz, Dick A. — *Management Recruiters International, Inc.*
Kush, Max — *Management Recruiters International, Inc.*
Kusin, Melanie B. — *Heidrick & Struggles, Inc.*
Kuypers, Arnold — *Lamalie Amrop International*
Kuzmick, John — *Accountants on Call*
Kvasnicka, Jay Allen — *Morgan Hunter Corp.*
La Grow, Ronald E. — *DHR International, Inc.*
Laba, Stuart M. — *Marvin Laba & Associates*
Labadie, Ernie B. — *Management Recruiters International, Inc.*
Labrecque, Bernard F. — *Laurendeau, Labrecque/Paul Ray Berndtson, Inc.*
Lachance, Roger — *Laurendeau, Labrecque/Paul Ray Berndtson, Inc.*
Lachenauer, Bruce J. — *Heidrick & Struggles, Inc.*
LaFaye, Susan — *MSI International*
Laird, Cheryl — *CPS Inc.*
Lajous, Luz — *Russell Reynolds Associates, Inc.*
Lalonde, Joel — *Management Recruiters International, Inc.*
Lamb, Angus K. — *Raymond Karsan Associates*
Lamb, Lynn M. — *F-O-R-T-U-N-E Personnel Consultants of Huntsville, Inc.*
Lambert, Robert J. — *Heidrick & Struggles, Inc.*
Lampl, Joni — *Management Recruiters International, Inc.*
Lampl, Lisa — *Management Recruiters International, Inc.*
Lampl, Mark — *Korn/Ferry International*
Lampl, Richard — *Management Recruiters International, Inc.*
Lampl, Tom W. — *Management Recruiters International, Inc.*
Lamson-Gran, Jill — *Accounting Resources, Inc.*
Landon, Susan J. — *Lamalie Amrop International*
Landry, Leo G. — *MSI International*
Lane, Doug — *Management Recruiters International, Inc.*
Lane, Sheri — *Ryan, Miller & Associates Inc.*
Lang, Vicki J. — *Morgan Hunter Corp.*
Langer, Joel A. — *Langer Associates, Inc.*
Lankford, Charles — *MSI International*
Lannamann, Richard S. — *Russell Reynolds Associates, Inc.*
Lapat, Aaron D. — *J. Robert Scott*
Lapham, Lawrence L. — *Lawrence L. Lapham Inc.*
Lareau, Belle — *Management Recruiters International, Inc.*
Lareau, Jerry A. — *Management Recruiters International, Inc.*
Larkin, Kathleen — *Winter, Wyman & Company*
Larsen, Jack B. — *Jack B. Larsen & Associates*
Larsen, Richard F. — *Larsen, Zilliacus & Associates, Inc.*
Larsen, William G. — *The Paladin Companies, Inc.*
Larson, Paul W. — *Paul Ray Berndtson*
Lasher, Charles M. — *Lasher Associates*
Lasse, Daniel C. — *Management Recruiters International, Inc.*

Mancos, Barbara — *Accountants on Call*
Mangum, Jackie — *Thomas Mangum Company*
Mangum, William T. — *Thomas Mangum Company*
Mann, Douglas G. — *Ward Howell International, Inc.*
Manning, Jerry A. — *Management Recruiters International, Inc.*
Manning, Robert A. — *Management Recruiters International, Inc.*
Manns, Alex — *Crawford & Crofford*
Mansfield, Chris — *Paul Ray Berndtson*
Manthey, Merv — *KPMG Executive Search*
Manzo, Renee — *Atlantic Search Group, Inc.*
Manzo, Romero — *The Prairie Group*
Maphet, Harriet — *The Stevenson Group of New Jersey*
Marcus, Jane B. — *Russell Reynolds Associates, Inc.*
Marino, Chester — *Cochran, Cochran & Yale, Inc.*
Marino, Jory J. — *Sullivan & Company*
Marion, Bradford B. — *Lamalie Amrop International*
Mark, John L. — *J.L. Mark Associates, Inc.*
Marks, Ira — *Strategic Alternatives*
Marks, Paula — *Alexander Ross Inc.*
Marks, Russell E. — *Webb, Johnson Associates, Inc.*
Marlow, William — *Straube Associates*
Marra, John — *Marra Peters & Partners*
Marra, John — *Marra Peters & Partners*
Marriott, Gloria A. — *Management Recruiters International, Inc.*
Marriott, Roger — *Management Recruiters International, Inc.*
Marshall, John — *Accountants on Call*
Marshall, Larry — *Marshall Consultants, Inc.*
Martens, Maxine — *Rene Plessner Associates, Inc.*
Martin, Al — *KPMG Executive Search*
Martin, Bette — *R.D. Gatti & Associates, Incorporated*
Martin, Charles E. — *Management Recruiters International, Inc.*
Martin, Geary D. — *Boyden/Zay & Company*
Martin, John G. — *Lamalie Amrop International*
Martin, Jon — *Egon Zehnder International Inc.*
Martin, Ken — *Spencer Stuart*
Martin, Kenneth — *Winter, Wyman & Company*
Martin, Lynne Koll — *Boyden*
Martin, Pat A. — *Management Recruiters International, Inc.*
Martin, Paula — *MSI International*
Martin, Rande L. — *Management Recruiters International, Inc.*
Marumoto, William H. — *The Interface Group, Ltd./Boyden*
Marx, Dennis R. — *DHR International, Inc.*
Marye, George — *Damon & Associates, Inc.*
Maschal, Charles E. — *Maschal/Connors, Inc.*
Mashack, Ted M. — *Management Recruiters International, Inc.*
Mason, Eileen — *Management Recruiters International, Inc.*
Mason, Marlene — *Richard Kader & Associates*
Mason, William E. — *John Kurosky & Associates*
Massey, H. Heath — *Robison & Associates*
Massey, R. Bruce — *Bruce Massey & Partners Inc.*
Massung, Larry J. — *Management Recruiters International, Inc.*
Mastandrea, Pat — *Johnson Smith & Knisely Accord*
Matheny, Robert P. — *MSI International*
Mather, David R. — *Christian & Timbers*
Mathias, Kathy — *Stone Murphy & Olson*
Mathias, William J. — *Preng & Associates, Inc.*
Matthews, James M. — *Stanton Chase International*
Matthews, John C. — *Management Recruiters International, Inc.*
Matthews, Mary E. — *Nordeman Grimm, Inc.*
Matthews, Nadie — *Accountants on Call*
Matthews, William A. — *Heidrick & Struggles, Inc.*
Matti, Suzy — *Southwestern Professional Services*
Mattox, Robert D. — *Spencer Stuart*
Maurizio, Michael — *Management Recruiters International, Inc.*
Maxwell, Carol — *Paul Ray Berndtson*
Mayes, Kay H. — *John Shell Associates, Inc.*
Mayland, Tina — *Russell Reynolds Associates, Inc.*
Maynard, Raun — *Accountants on Call*
Mazor, Elly — *Howard Fischer Associates, Inc.*
Mazza, David B. — *Mazza & Riley, Inc.*
Mazza, Leslie P. — *The Diversified Search Companies*
Mazzitelli, Teresa A. — *The Mazzitelli Group, Ltd.*
Mazzocchi, Jonathan — *Winter, Wyman & Company*
McAndrews, Kathy — *CPS Inc.*
McAteer, Thomas — *Montgomery Resources, Inc.*
McAulay, A.L. — *The McAulay Firm*
McBride, Jonathan E. — *McBride Associates, Inc.*
McBryde, Marnie — *Spencer Stuart*
McBurney, Kevin — *The Caldwell Partners Amrop International*
McCabe, Christopher — *Raymond Karsan Associates*
McCallister, Jane T. — *Heidrick & Struggles, Inc.*
McCandless, Hugh — *Marshall Consultants, Inc.*
McCartney, Paul — *Korn/Ferry International*
McCarty, J. Rucker — *Heidrick & Struggles, Inc.*
McClain, Michael D. — *DHR International, Inc.*
McClement, John — *Korn/Ferry International*
McCloskey, Frank — *Korn/Ferry International*
McClure, James K. — *Korn/Ferry International*

McConnell, Greg — *Winter, Wyman & Company*
McCool, Anne G. — *Sullivan & Company*
McCorkle, Sam B. — *Morton, McCorkle & Associates, Inc.*
McCormack, Joseph A. — *McCormack & Associates*
McCormack, William Reed — *MSI International*
McCormick, Cyndi — *Winter, Wyman & Company*
McCormick, William J. — *The McCormick Group, Inc.*
McCoy, Horacio — *Korn/Ferry International*
McCoy, Millington F. — *Gould, McCoy & Chadick Incorporated*
McCreary, Charles — *Austin-McGregor International*
McCullough, Joe — *Management Recruiters International, Inc.*
McCurdy, Mark — *Summerfield Associates, Inc.*
McCutcheon, C. Scott — *John Kurosky & Associates*
McDonald, Gary E. — *Agra Placements International Ltd.*
McDonald, Scott A. — *McDonald Associates International*
McDonald, Stanleigh B. — *McDonald Associates International*
McDonnell, Julie — *Technical Personnel of Minnesota*
McElhaney, Ron — *Management Recruiters International, Inc.*
McElhaney, Ronald W. — *Management Recruiters International, Inc.*
McElroy, John — *Management Recruiters International, Inc.*
McEwan, Paul — *Richard, Wayne and Roberts*
McEwen, Al — *Management Recruiters International, Inc.*
McFeely, Clarence E. — *McFeely Wackerle Shulman*
McGill, Robert — *The Caldwell Partners Amrop International*
McGonigle, Kevin M. — *Egon Zehnder International Inc.*
McGovern, Terence — *Korn/Ferry International*
McGue, Marsha S. — *Kenzer Corp.*
McGuire, Corey — *Peter W. Ambler Company*
McGuire, D. — *The Gabriel Group*
McHugh, Margaret — *Korn/Ferry International*
McIntyre, Joel — *Phillips Resource Group*
McKay, W. John — *O'Callaghan Honey/Paul Ray Berndtson, Inc.*
McKie, Miles L. — *Russell Reynolds Associates, Inc.*
McKnight, Amy E. — *Chartwell Partners International, Inc.*
McKnight, Lourdes D. — *Sanford Rose Associates*
McLane, Brad — *Egon Zehnder International Inc.*
McLane, Thomas L. — *Russell Reynolds Associates, Inc.*
McLaughlin, John — *TASA International*
McLean, B. Keith — *Price Waterhouse*
McLean, Chris — *Chaloner Associates*
McLean, E. Peter — *Spencer Stuart*
McMahon, Mark J. — *A.T. Kearney, Inc.*
McManners, Donald E. — *McManners Associates, Inc.*
McManus, Paul — *Aubin International*
McMillin, Bob — *Price Waterhouse*
McNamara, Gerard P. — *Heidrick & Struggles, Inc.*
McNamara, Timothy C. — *Columbia Consulting Group*
McNerney, Kevin A. — *Heidrick & Struggles, Inc.*
McNichols, Walter B. — *Gary Kaplan & Associates*
McNulty, Neil P. — *Management Recruiters International, Inc.*
McPoyle, Thomas C. — *Sanford Rose Associates*
McQuoid, David — *A.T. Kearney, Inc.*
McRoberts, Dana L. — *Management Recruiters International, Inc.*
McSherry, James F. — *Battalia Winston International*
Mead, James D. — *James Mead & Company*
Meadley, Ronald J. — *Management Recruiters International, Inc.*
Meagher, Patricia G. — *Spencer Stuart*
Means, Wallace — *Management Recruiters International, Inc.*
Medinger, Ronald B. — *IMCOR, Inc.*
Medoff, Lynn — *C.A. Durakis Associates, Inc.*
Medtlie, Peder M. — *Management Recruiters International, Inc.*
Mefford, Bob — *Executive Manning Corporation*
Mehrbrodt, Al W. — *Management Recruiters International, Inc.*
Meier, J. Dale — *Grant Cooper and Associates*
Meiland, A. Daniel — *Egon Zehnder International Inc.*
Meister, Connie — *Management Recruiters International, Inc.*
Meister, Verle — *Management Recruiters International, Inc.*
Meitz, Bob L. — *Management Recruiters International, Inc.*
Meltzer, Andrea Y. — *Executive Options, Ltd.*
Menendez, Todd — *Don Richard Associates of Tampa, Inc.*
Menk, Carl W. — *Canny, Bowen Inc.*
Merrifield, Gary — *Accountants on Call*
Merrigan, Eileen M. — *Lamalie Amrop International*
Merriman, Mark — *Management Recruiters International, Inc.*
Mertensotto, Chuck H. — *Whitney & Associates, Inc.*
Meschke, Jason M. — *EFL Associates*
Messett, William J. — *Messett Associates, Inc.*
Messina, Kenneth — *Chestnut Hill Partners*
Mestepey, John — *A.T. Kearney, Inc.*
Mestre, Mercedes — *Korn/Ferry International*
Metz, Dan K. — *Russell Reynolds Associates, Inc.*
Meyer, Fred R. — *Management Recruiters International, Inc.*
Meyer, Marjorie — *Accountants on Call*
Meyer, Stacey — *Gary Kaplan & Associates*
Meyer, William — *Agra Placements International Ltd.*
Meyers, Maurice R. — *Management Recruiters International, Inc.*
Meyers, Mel — *DHR International, Inc.*
Meyers, Steven — *Montgomery Resources, Inc.*

Meza, Anna — *Richard, Wayne and Roberts*
Michaels, Joseph — *CPS Inc.*
Mierzwinski, John — *Industrial Recruiters Associates, Inc.*
Miesemer, Arthur C. — *MSI International*
Miles, Kenneth T. — *MSI International*
Milius, Kent L. — *Management Recruiters International, Inc.*
Mill, Christopher A. — *The Paladin Companies, Inc.*
Miller, Andrew S. — *Management Recruiters International, Inc.*
Miller, Arnie — *Isaacson, Miller*
Miller, Benjamin J. — *MSI International*
Miller, Bert E. — *Management Recruiters International, Inc.*
Miller, David — *Temporary Accounting Personnel, Inc.*
Miller, George N. — *Hite Executive Search*
Miller, Harold B. — *MSI International*
Miller, Joanna — *Korn/Ferry International*
Miller, Julie — *Southwestern Professional Services*
Miller, Laura — *Accounting Personnel Consultants*
Miller, Michael R. — *Lynch Miller Moore Partners, Inc.*
Miller, Paul McG. — *Lamalie Amrop International*
Miller, Roy — *The Enns Partners Inc.*
Miller, Russel E. — *ARJay & Associates*
Milo, Bill — *Management Recruiters International, Inc.*
Milton, Suzanne — *Marra Peters & Partners*
Mirtz, P. John — *Mirtz Morice, Inc.*
Mitchell, F. Wayne — *Korn/Ferry International*
Mitchell, John R. — *Management Recruiters International, Inc.*
Mitchell, Katie — *Paul Ray Berndtson*
Mitchell, Kim — *Richard, Wayne and Roberts*
Mitchell, Kyle R. — *Tanton Mitchell/Paul Ray Berndtson*
Mitchell, Norman F. — *A.T. Kearney, Inc.*
Mitchell, Thomas M. — *Heidrick & Struggles, Inc.*
Mitton, Bill — *Executive Resource, Inc.*
Mockler, Nadine — *Part Time Resources, Inc.*
Moeller, Ed J. — *Management Recruiters International, Inc.*
Moerbe, Ed H. — *Stanton Chase International*
Moga, Michael — *Korn/Ferry International*
Mohan, Jack — *Management Recruiters International, Inc.*
Mohan, Jack — *Management Recruiters International, Inc.*
Mohr, Brian — *CPS Inc.*
Moliski, Robert — *Korn/Ferry International*
Monaghan, Jill — *Paul Ray Berndtson*
Monahan, B. Roderick — *Lamalie Amrop International*
Mondragon, Philip — *Boyden*
Monogenis, Emanuel N. — *Heidrick & Struggles, Inc.*
Monroe, Kenneth D. — *Sanford Rose Associates*
Montgomery, Catherine C. — *Boyden*
Montgomery, James M. — *Houze, Shourds & Montgomery, Inc.*
Montigny, Paul F. — *Management Recruiters International, Inc.*
Mooney, Kelly — *Paul Ray Berndtson*
Mooney, Matt — *Paul Ray Berndtson*
Mooney, Penny P. — *Ward Howell International, Inc.*
Moore, Anne — *KPMG Executive Search*
Moore, David S. — *Lynch Miller Moore Partners, Inc.*
Moore, Denise — *Jonas, Walters & Assoc., Inc.*
Moore, Janice E. — *MSI International*
Moore, Lemuel R. — *MSI International*
Moore, Lynn W. — *Management Recruiters International, Inc.*
Moore, Mark — *Wheeler, Moore & Elam Co.*
Moore, Michael — *Agra Placements International Ltd.*
Moore, Mike — *Management Recruiters International, Inc.*
Moore, Richard C.E. — *Russell Reynolds Associates, Inc.*
Moors, Donald — *Coopers & Lybrand Consulting*
Moran, Carla — *Key Employment Services*
Moran, Gail — *Comprehensive Search*
Moran, Gayle — *Dussick Management Associates*
Moran, Robert — *A.T. Kearney, Inc.*
Moran, Thomas F. — *Ward Howell International, Inc.*
Morgan, Beverly — *Winter, Wyman & Company*
Morgan, Christopher — *Paul Ray Berndtson*
Morgan, Donald T. — *MSI International*
Morgan, Richard S. — *Lovas Stanley/Paul Ray Berndtson Inc.*
Morice, James L. — *Mirtz Morice, Inc.*
Morin, Michelle — *Spencer Stuart*
Morrill, Nancy — *Winter, Wyman & Company*
Morris, David A. — *Heidrick & Struggles, Inc.*
Morris, David W. — *WTW Associates*
Morris, Kristine A. — *Morris & Berger*
Morris, Paul T. — *The Morris Group*
Morrow, Miles — *Key Employment Services*
Morse, Aaron H. — *Management Recruiters International, Inc.*
Morse, Jeannine — *Management Recruiters International, Inc.*
Morse, Stephen W. — *Management Recruiters International, Inc.*
Morse, Steve — *Management Recruiters International, Inc.*
Morton, Robert C. — *Morton, McCorkle & Associates, Inc.*
Moschel, Evie — *S. Reyman & Associates Ltd.*
Moseley, Monroe — *Isaacson, Miller*
Moses, Brenda — *Paul Ray Berndtson*
Moss, Ethan — *Richard, Wayne and Roberts*

Mowatt, Virginia C. — *DHR International, Inc.*
Moxley, John H. — *Korn/Ferry International*
Moyer, David S. — *Moyer, Sherwood Associates, Inc.*
Moynihan, Kerry — *Korn/Ferry International*
Moyse, Richard G. — *Thorndike Deland Associates*
Mueller-Maerki, Fortunat F. — *Egon Zehnder International Inc.*
Muendel, H. Edward — *Stanton Chase International*
Mulcahey, Bob T. — *Management Recruiters International, Inc.*
Mullane, Patrick — *Kenzer Corp.*
Mullen, Edward — *Korn/Ferry International*
Muller, Charles A. — *AJM Professional Services*
Muller, Sonja — *TASA International*
Mulligan, Robert P. — *William Willis Worldwide Inc.*
Mullings, Joe S. — *Management Recruiters International, Inc.*
Mummert, Dennis D. — *Sweeney Harbert & Mummert, Inc.*
Munguia, Rebecca — *Richard, Wayne and Roberts*
Murlas, Kim — *DHR International, Inc.*
Murphey, James F. — *Management Recruiters International, Inc.*
Murphy, Carrie — *Paul Ray Berndtson*
Murphy, Cornelius J. — *Goodrich & Sherwood Associates, Inc.*
Murphy, Gary J. — *Stone Murphy & Olson*
Murphy, Karen S. — *Flex Execs Management Solutions*
Murphy, Patrick — *Richard, Wayne and Roberts*
Murphy, Patrick J. — *P.J. Murphy & Associates, Inc.*
Murphy, Timothy D. — *MSI International*
Murphy, Wendy — *Winter, Wyman & Company*
Murray, Cathy M. — *EFL Associates*
Murray, Virginia — *Baker, Harris & Partners Limited*
Mursuli, Meredith — *Lasher Associates*
Myatt, James S. — *Sanford Rose Associates*
Mydlach, Renee — *CPS Inc.*
Myers, Kay — *Signature Staffing*
Myrick, Marilou — *ProResource, Inc.*
Myrick, Marilou — *ProResource, Inc.*
Nadherny, Christopher C. — *Spencer Stuart*
Nadherny, Ferdinand — *Russell Reynolds Associates, Inc.*
Nadzam, Richard — *Nadzam, Lusk, Horgan & Associates, Inc.*
Naff, Budd B. — *Management Recruiters International, Inc.*
Nagler, Leon G. — *Nagler, Robins & Poe, Inc.*
Nahas, Caroline W. — *Korn/Ferry International*
Napier, Ginger L. — *Preng & Associates, Inc.*
Nass, Martin D. — *Lamalie Amrop International*
Nathan, Catherine R. — *Ward Howell International, Inc.*
Nathan, Gerri — *R.D. Gatti & Associates, Incorporated*
Nathanson, Barry F. — *Barry Nathanson Associates*
Naughtin, Terri — *Andcor Human Resources*
Neblett, Jon — *Don Richard Associates of Richmond, Inc.*
Nederpelt, Jack H.B. — *Russell Reynolds Associates, Inc.*
Neelin, Sharon — *The Caldwell Partners Amrop International*
Neely, Alan S. — *Korn/Ferry International*
Neff, Thomas J. — *Spencer Stuart*
Nehiley, Jack J. — *Management Recruiters International, Inc.*
Neidhart, Craig C. — *TNS Partners, Inc.*
Neil, Colleen Ellen — *Korn/Ferry International*
Nein, Lawrence F. — *Lamalie Amrop International*
Nelson, Barbara — *Herman Smith Executive Initiatives Inc.*
Nelson, Rick J. — *Management Recruiters International, Inc.*
Nelson, Steve — *The McCormick Group, Inc.*
Nesbit, Robert G. — *Korn/Ferry International*
Neuberth, Jeffrey G. — *Canny, Bowen Inc.*
Neuffer, Bob P. — *Management Recruiters International, Inc.*
Neumann, Joan — *Gossage Regan Associates, Inc.*
Neumann, Pete — *Management Recruiters International, Inc.*
Neumann, Vicki A. — *Management Recruiters International, Inc.*
Newbold, Michael — *Agra Placements International Ltd.*
Newman, Arthur I. — *Lamalie Amrop International*
Newman, Lynn — *Kishbaugh Associates International*
Newman, Mark — *Cole, Warren & Long, Inc.*
Newman, Maryann — *The Gabriel Group*
Newton, Stephen D. — *Russell Reynolds Associates, Inc.*
Nichols, Nancy S. — *Heidrick & Struggles, Inc.*
Nielsen, Eric C. — *Russell Reynolds Associates, Inc.*
Nielsen, Sue — *Ells Personnel System Inc.*
Nitti, Jacqueline — *ALTCO Temporary Services*
Nixon, Sarah — *The Caldwell Partners Amrop International*
Noble, Donald H. — *Noble & Associates Inc.*
Noble, Jeffrey M. — *Management Recruiters International, Inc.*
Nocero, John — *ProResource, Inc.*
Nolan, Michael W. — *Accounting & Bookkeeping Personnel, Inc.*
Nold, Robert — *Roberson and Company*
Noll, Robert J. — *The Hindman Company*
Noorani, Frank — *Management Recruiters International, Inc.*
Nordeman, Jacques C. — *Nordeman Grimm, Inc.*
Nordland, Martin N. — *Horton International*
Norman, Randy — *Austin-McGregor International*
Normann, Amy — *Robert M. Flanagan & Associates, Ltd.*
Norris, Ken — *A.T. Kearney, Inc.*
Norris, Ken — *Boyden*

Norsell, Paul E. — *Paul Norsell & Associates, Inc.*
Norton, Douglas — *Korn/Ferry International*
Norton, George F. — *Heidrick & Struggles, Inc.*
Norton, James B. — *GKR Americas, Inc.*
Nosal, David — *Korn/Ferry International*
Nosal, David A. — *Heidrick & Struggles, Inc.*
Novak, William J. — *Ward Howell International, Inc.*
Noyes, Kathleen M. — *Russell Reynolds Associates, Inc.*
Nunziata, Fred — *Eden & Associates, Inc.*
Nunziata, Peter — *Atlantic Search Group, Inc.*
Nutter, Roger — *Raymond Karsan Associates*
Nye, David S. — *Blake, Hansen & Nye, Limited*
Nyhan, Alan — *Management Recruiters International, Inc.*
Nymark, John — *NYCOR Search, Inc.*
Nymark, Paul — *NYCOR Search, Inc.*
O'Brien, Anne Lim — *Heidrick & Struggles, Inc.*
O'Brien, Debbie A. — *Management Recruiters International, Inc.*
O'Brien, Lori — *Paul Ray Berndtson*
O'Brien, Marlon W.A. — *Management Recruiters International, Inc.*
O'Callaghan, Terry K. — *O'Callaghan Honey/Paul Ray Berndtson, Inc.*
O'Connell, Bridget — *Accountants on Call*
O'Connell, Mary — *CPS Inc.*
O'Connell, William — *Winter, Wyman & Company*
O'Donnell, James H. — *MSI International*
O'Donnell, Timothy — *Ward Howell International, Inc.*
O'Donnell, Timothy W. — *Boyden*
O'Gorman, David J. — *DHR International, Inc.*
O'Halloran, Robert — *MSI International*
O'Hara, Daniel M. — *Lynch Miller Moore Partners, Inc.*
O'Maley, Kimberlee — *Spencer Stuart*
O'Malley, Robert — *Raymond Karsan Associates*
O'Meally, Diane — *Accountants on Call*
O'Neill, David — *Korn/Ferry International*
O'Neill, James P. — *Allerton Heneghan & O'Neill*
O'Reilly, Bill — *Management Recruiters International, Inc.*
O'Shea, Laurie A. — *The Heidrick Partners, Inc.*
O'Shea, Timothy J. — *Heidrick & Struggles, Inc.*
O'Toole, Dennis P. — *Dennis P. O'Toole & Associates Inc.*
Oakes, Meg B. — *D.P. Parker and Associates*
Oakley, Mitch — *Management Recruiters International, Inc.*
Oberg, Roy — *The Danbrook Group, Inc.*
Oberting, Dave W. — *Management Recruiters International, Inc.*
Oberting, David J. — *Management Recruiters International, Inc.*
Oddo, Judith — *Accounting Personnel Consultants*
Odom, Philip — *Richard, Wayne and Roberts*
Ogden, Dayton — *Spencer Stuart*
Ogden, Thomas H. — *The Ogdon Partnership*
Olesky, Beth Green — *Russell Reynolds Associates, Inc.*
Olin, Robyn — *Richard, Wayne and Roberts*
Olivares, Rebecca — *Paul Ray Berndtson*
Oliver, Phoebe — *Seiden Krieger Associates, Inc.*
Oliverio, Anthony P. — *Management Recruiters International, Inc.*
Ollinger, Charles D. — *Heidrick & Struggles, Inc.*
Olmstead, George T. — *Blackshaw, Olmstead & Lynch*
Olsen, Carl — *A.T. Kearney, Inc.*
Olsen, Theodore J. — *Senior Careers Executive Search*
Olson, B. Tucker — *Early Cochran & Olson, Inc.*
Olson, Cherene — *The Paladin Companies, Inc.*
Olson, Nels — *Korn/Ferry International*
Ongirski, Richard P. — *Raymond Karsan Associates*
Onstott, Joseph E. — *The Onstott Group, Inc.*
Oppenheimer, Janet — *Paul Ray Berndtson*
Orkin, Ralph — *Sanford Rose Associates*
Orkin, Sheilah — *Sanford Rose Associates*
Orr, Don — *Orr Executive Search*
Orr, Steve — *Management Recruiters International, Inc.*
Osborn, Jim — *Southwestern Professional Services*
Oster, Joan — *Management Recruiters International, Inc.*
Oster, Rush R. — *Management Recruiters International, Inc.*
Oswald, Mark G. — *Canny, Bowen Inc.*
Ott, George W. — *Ott & Hansen, Inc.*
Ottenritter, Chris — *CPS Inc.*
Owen, Jamie L. — *Management Recruiters International, Inc.*
Owen, John — *Key Employment Services*
Owens, LaMonte — *LaMonte Owens & Company*
Owens, Reggie R. — *The Gabriel Group*
Pace, Susan A. — *Horton International*
Pacheco, Ricardo — *Amrop International*
Pacini, Lauren R. — *Hite Executive Search*
Padilla, Jose Sanchez — *Egon Zehnder International Inc.*
Pagan, Vernon R. — *Management Recruiters International, Inc.*
Page, G. Schuyler — *A.T. Kearney, Inc.*
Page, Linda — *Jonas, Walters & Assoc., Inc.*
Page, Linda M. — *Wargo and Co., Inc.*
Palazio, Carla — *A.T. Kearney, Inc.*
Palma, Frank R. — *Goodrich & Sherwood Associates, Inc.*
Palmer, Carlton A. — *Beall & Company, Inc.*

Palmer, James H. — *The Hindman Company*
Palmer, Melissa — *Don Richard Associates of Tampa, Inc.*
Palmieri, Cathryn C. — *Korn/Ferry International*
Palmlund, David W. — *Lamalie Amrop International*
Pamplin, LaShana — *The Repovich-Reynolds Group*
Paolotti, Susan — *Kenzer Corp.*
Papayanopulos, Manuel — *Korn/Ferry International*
Papciak, Dennis J. — *Temporary Accounting Personnel*
Papilsky, Alice — *HRD Consultants, Inc.*
Pappalardo, Charles — *Christian & Timbers*
Pappas, Timothy C. — *Jonas, Walters & Assoc., Inc.*
Parbs, Michael — *Accountants on Call*
Parbs, Michael — *Accountants on Call*
Pardo, Maria Elena — *Smith Search, S.C.*
Parfitt, William C. — *Parfitt Recruiting and Consulting/PRO TEM*
Parfitt, William C. — *Parfitt Recruiting and Consulting*
Paris, Stephen — *Richard, Wayne and Roberts*
Park, Cleve A. — *Management Recruiters International, Inc.*
Park, Dabney G. — *Mark Stanley & Company*
Parker, David P. — *D.P. Parker and Associates*
Parker, P. Grant — *Raymond Karsan Associates*
Parker, Roberta — *R. Parker and Associates, Inc.*
Parker, Stephen B. — *Russell Reynolds Associates, Inc.*
Parr, James A. — *KPMG Executive Search*
Parr, James A. — *KPMG Management Consulting*
Parris, Ed — *Management Recruiters International, Inc.*
Parry, Heather — *Richard, Wayne and Roberts*
Parry, William H. — *Horton International*
Pasahow, David — *Heidrick & Struggles, Inc.*
Pastrana, Dario — *Egon Zehnder International Inc.*
Patence, David W. — *Handy HRM Corp.*
Patrick, Donald R. — *Sanford Rose Associates*
Patterson, Brenda — *Management Recruiters International, Inc.*
Patton, Mitchell — *Patton/Perry Associates, Inc.*
Paul, Linda — *Gilbert Tweed/INESA*
Paul, Lisa D. — *Merit Resource Group, Inc.*
Pawlik, Cynthia — *Paul Ray Berndtson*
Paxton, James W. — *Stanton Chase International*
Payette, Pierre — *Egon Zehnder International Inc.*
Payne, Mary A. — *Management Recruiters International, Inc.*
Payne, Robert — *Winter, Wyman & Company*
Payne, Tom H. — *Management Recruiters International, Inc.*
Pearcy, Marsha G. — *Russell Reynolds Associates, Inc.*
Pearson, Robert L. — *Lamalie Amrop International*
Peasback, David R. — *Canny, Bowen Inc.*
Pease, Samuel C. — *Heidrick & Struggles, Inc.*
Pecot, Jack L. — *Management Recruiters International, Inc.*
Pederson, Terre — *Richard, Wayne and Roberts*
Pedley, Jill — *CPS Inc.*
Peeney, James D. — *Peeney Associates*
Pelisson, Charles — *Marra Peters & Partners*
Penfield, G. Jeff — *Management Recruiters International, Inc.*
Penfield, Marian — *Management Recruiters International, Inc.*
Peniche, Pedro — *Amrop International*
Pepe, Leonida — *Butterfass, Pepe & MacCallan Inc.*
Percifield, J. Michael — *Management Recruiters International, Inc.*
Peretz, Jamie — *Nordeman Grimm, Inc.*
Perez, Christina — *Orr Executive Search*
Perkey, Richard — *Korn/Ferry International*
Perkins, Bob — *Richard, Wayne and Roberts*
Perkins, Daphne — *CPS Inc.*
Perron, Daniel — *Accountants on Call*
Perry, Darrell L. — *Management Recruiters International, Inc.*
Perry, Richard — *McManners Associates, Inc.*
Perry, Robert H. — *R.H. Perry & Associates, Inc.*
Perry, Wayne B. — *Bruce Massey & Partners Inc.*
Perryman, Ben — *Paul Ray Berndtson*
Persico, Victor J. — *Management Recruiters International, Inc.*
Persky, Barry — *Barry Persky & Company, Inc.*
Peternell, Melanie — *Signature Staffing*
Peters, James N. — *TNS Partners, Inc.*
Peters, Todd — *Morgan Hunter Corp.*
Peterson, Bruce — *Korn/Ferry International*
Peterson, Dave A. — *Management Recruiters International, Inc.*
Peterson, Diana K. — *Management Recruiters International, Inc.*
Peterson, John — *CPS Inc.*
Peterson, John A. — *Management Recruiters International, Inc.*
Peterson, Priscilla J. — *Management Recruiters International, Inc.*
Petrides, Andrew S. — *ARJay & Associates*
Pettersson, Tara L. — *Lamalie Amrop International*
Petty, J. Scott — *The Arcus Group*
Peyton, Leslie — *Korn/Ferry International*
Pfau, Madelaine — *Heidrick & Struggles, Inc.*
Pfeiffer, Irene — *Price Waterhouse*
Pfeiffer, Leonard — *Korn/Ferry International*
Pfister, Shelli — *Jack B. Larsen & Associates*
Phelps, Gene L. — *McCormack & Farrow*
Philips, Ann — *Management Recruiters International, Inc.*

Phillips, Donald — *Accountants on Call*
Phillips, Donald L. — *O'Shea, Divine & Company, Inc.*
Phillips, Richard K. — *Handy HRM Corp.*
Phillips, Whitney — *Korn/Ferry International*
Pickering, Dorothy C. — *Livingston, Robert and Company Inc.*
Pickford, Stephen T. — *The Corporate Staff, Inc.*
Pieh, Jerry — *Isaacson, Miller*
Pierce, Richard — *Russell Reynolds Associates, Inc.*
Pierpont, Elizabeth H. — *Russell Reynolds Associates, Inc.*
Piers, Robert L. — *TASA International*
Pike, Dick F. — *Management Recruiters International, Inc.*
Pimentel, Alberto — *Korn/Ferry International*
Pinkman, Karen N. — *Skott/Edwards Consultants, Inc.*
Pinson, Liz A. — *Management Recruiters International, Inc.*
Pinson, Stephanie L. — *Gilbert Tweed/INESA*
Pirhalla, Denise — *Kenzer Corp.*
Pistole, Ingrid — *Richard, Wayne and Roberts*
Pitcher, Brian D. — *Skott/Edwards Consultants, Inc.*
Pitchford, Jim J. — *Management Recruiters International, Inc.*
Pittard, Patrick S. — *Heidrick & Struggles, Inc.*
Pitts, Charles — *Contemporary Management Services, Inc.*
Pizzariello, Ann Marie — *Conex Incorporated*
Plagge, Cheryl L. — *Management Recruiters International, Inc.*
Platte, John D. — *Russell Reynolds Associates, Inc.*
Plazza, Richard C. — *The Executive Source*
Plecash, Bob — *Management Recruiters International, Inc.*
Plessner, Rene — *Rene Plessner Associates, Inc.*
Plimpton, Ralph L. — *R L Plimpton Associates*
Plotner, George A. — *Management Recruiters International, Inc.*
Plummer, Winkie Donovan — *McManners Associates, Inc.*
Pocs, Martin M. — *DHR International, Inc.*
Poirier, Roland — *Poirier, Hoevel & Co.*
Poloni, James A. — *Management Recruiters International, Inc.*
Polvere, Gary T. — *Management Recruiters International, Inc.*
Pomerance, Mark — *CPS Inc.*
Pomeroy, T. Lee — *Egon Zehnder International Inc.*
Poore, Larry D. — *Ward Howell International, Inc.*
Pope, John S. — *DHR International, Inc.*
Poracky, John W. — *M. Wood Company*
Porter, Albert — *The Experts*
Porter, Donald — *Amherst Personnel Group Inc.*
Porter, Ken — *Tourism Development International*
Potter, Douglas C. — *Stanton Chase International*
Powell, Lloyd — *KPMG Executive Search*
Powell, Marie — *Kenzer Corp.*
Powers-Johnson, Allyson — *Johnson Smith & Knisely Accord*
Prados, Daniel — *Accounting Personnel Consultants*
Pratt, Michael W. — *Management Recruiters International, Inc.*
Preng, David E. — *Preng & Associates, Inc.*
Prentiss, Michael C. — *Management Recruiters International, Inc.*
Preschlack, Jack E. — *Spencer Stuart*
Press, Fred — *Adept Tech Recruiting*
Price, Andrew G. — *The Thomas Tucker Company*
Price, P. Anthony — *Russell Reynolds Associates, Inc.*
Priem, Windle B. — *Korn/Ferry International*
Prior, Donald — *The Caldwell Partners Amrop International*
Probert, William W. — *Ward Howell International, Inc.*
Proct, Nina — *Martin H. Bauman Associates, Inc.*
Proctor, Robert A. — *Heidrick & Struggles, Inc.*
Provost, Ed — *Management Recruiters International, Inc.*
Provost, Vicky L. — *Management Recruiters International, Inc.*
Provus, Barbara L. — *Shepherd Bueschel & Provus, Inc.*
Pryde, Marcia P. — *A.T. Kearney, Inc.*
Pryor, Keith — *The Diversified Search Companies*
Puente, Fred J. — *Management Recruiters International, Inc.*
Putrim, Tom — *Paul Ray Berndtson*
Quatrone, Olivia S. — *Heidrick & Struggles, Inc.*
Quick, Roger A. — *Norman Broadbent International, Inc.*
Quinn, Frank A. — *Management Recruiters International, Inc.*
Quinn, John — *Paul Ray Berndtson*
Quitel, Scott M. — *Management Recruiters International, Inc.*
Rabinowitz, Peter A. — *P.A.R. Associates Inc.*
Rachels, John W. — *Southwestern Professional Services*
Rackley, Eugene M. — *Heidrick & Struggles, Inc.*
Radford-Oster, Deborah — *Morgan Hunter Corp.*
Raffin, Robert P. — *Management Recruiters International, Inc.*
Ralston, Doug O. — *Management Recruiters International, Inc.*
Ramler, Carolyn S. — *The Corporate Connection, Ltd.*
Ramsey, John H. — *Mark Stanley & Company*
Ranberger, Mike J. — *Management Recruiters International, Inc.*
Randell, James E. — *Randell-Heiken, Inc.*
Ratigan, Charles C. — *Heidrick & Struggles, Inc.*
Rattner, Kenneth L. — *Heidrick & Struggles, Inc.*
Rauch, Ben — *Korn/Ferry International*
Ravenel, Lavinia — *MSI International*
Ray, Breck — *Paul Ray Berndtson*
Ray, Marianne C. — *Callan Associates, Ltd.*
Raymond, Allan H. — *Korn/Ferry International*

Raymond, Barry — *Raymond Karsan Associates*
Raymond, Jean — *The Caldwell Partners Amrop International*
Reagan, Paul W. — *Management Recruiters International, Inc.*
Recsetar, Steven — *DHR International, Inc.*
Reddick, David C. — *Horton International*
Redding, Denise — *The Douglas Reiter Company, Inc.*
Redmond, Andrea — *Russell Reynolds Associates, Inc.*
Redwood, Guy W. — *Bruce Massey & Partners Inc.*
Reece, Christopher S. — *Reece & Mruk Partners*
Reed, David Q. — *Management Recruiters International, Inc.*
Reed, Ruthann — *Spectra International Inc.*
Reed, William D. — *Russell Reynolds Associates, Inc.*
Reeder, Michael S. — *Lamalie Amrop International*
Reeves, Ron C. — *Management Recruiters International, Inc.*
Referente, Gwen — *Richard, Wayne and Roberts*
Regan, Thomas J. — *Tower Consultants, Ltd.*
Regeuye, Peter J. — *Accountants Executive Search*
Reid, Gary — *KPMG Executive Search*
Reilly, Robert E. — *DHR International, Inc.*
Reimer, Marvin — *Management Recruiters International, Inc.*
Reinhart, Jeaneen — *Accountants on Call*
Reiser, Ellen — *Thorndike Deland Associates*
Reisig, Alexsandra — *John Kurosky & Associates*
Reiter, Douglas — *The Douglas Reiter Company, Inc.*
Reitkopp, Ellen — *Management Recruiters International, Inc.*
Reitkopp, Howard H. — *Management Recruiters International, Inc.*
Remick, Tierney Boyd — *Russell Reynolds Associates, Inc.*
Rendl, Ric — *CPS Inc.*
Renick, Paula — *Kenzer Corp.*
Renner, Sandra L. — *Spectra International Inc.*
Ressler, Dan R. — *Management Recruiters International, Inc.*
Reticker, Peter — *MSI International*
Reyes, Randolph G. — *Management Recruiters International, Inc.*
Reyman, Susan — *S. Reyman & Associates Ltd.*
Reynolds, Bud O. — *Management Recruiters International, Inc.*
Reynolds, Catherine — *Winter, Wyman & Company*
Reynolds, Gregory P. — *Roberts Ryan and Bentley*
Reynolds, Juli Ann — *Korn/Ferry International*
Reynolds, Smooch S. — *The Repovich-Reynolds Group*
Reynolds, Susan F. — *Heidrick & Struggles, Inc.*
Rheude, Jim — *Management Recruiters International, Inc.*
Rice, Douglas — *Agra Placements International Ltd.*
Rice, Jim K. — *Management Recruiters International, Inc.*
Rice, John — *Paul Ray Berndtson*
Rice, Raymond D. — *Logue & Rice Inc.*
Rich, Lyttleton — *Sockwell & Associates*
Richards, Wes — *Heidrick & Struggles, Inc.*
Richardson, David M. — *DHR International, Inc.*
Richardson, J. Rick — *Spencer Stuart*
Richardson, Paul C. — *Korn/Ferry International*
Richardson, Tony R. — *Management Recruiters International, Inc.*
Riederer, Larry — *CPS Inc.*
Rieger, Louis J. — *Spencer Stuart*
Riggs, David T. — *Management Recruiters International, Inc.*
Riggs, Lena — *Management Recruiters International, Inc.*
Rijke, R. Fred — *TASA International*
Riley, Elizabeth G. — *Mazza & Riley, Inc.*
Riley, Jeffrey K. — *EFL Associates*
Rimmel, James E. — *The Hindman Company*
Rimmele, Michael — *The Bankers Group*
Rinaldi, Michael D. — *D.P. Parker and Associates*
Ring, Paul R. — *Sanford Rose Associates*
Rio, Monica — *Management Recruiters International, Inc.*
Rippey, George E. — *Heidrick & Struggles, Inc.*
Rittenberg, Richard S. — *D.E. Foster Partners Inc.*
Rivard, Dick — *Management Recruiters International, Inc.*
Rivas, Alberto F. — *Boyden*
Rivera, Elba R. — *Raymond Karsan Associates*
Rivers, Geri — *Chrisman & Company, Incorporated*
Rizk, Nyla — *Spencer Stuart*
Rizzo, L. Donald — *R.P. Barone Associates*
Roach, Ronald R. — *Sanford Rose Associates*
Robert, Diana — *Korn/Ferry International*
Roberts, Carl R. — *Southwestern Professional Services*
Roberts, Gary — *A.T. Kearney, Inc.*
Roberts, Jane — *Paul Ray Berndtson*
Roberts, Mitch — *A.E. Feldman Associates*
Roberts, Nick P. — *Spectrum Search Associates, Inc.*
Roberts, Raymond R. — *MSI International*
Roberts, Richard F. — *Management Recruiters International, Inc.*
Roberts, Scott B. — *Wargo and Co., Inc.*
Roberts, William — *Cochran, Cochran & Yale, Inc.*
Robertson, Bruce J. — *Norman Broadbent International, Inc.*
Robertson, John H.C. — *Sanford Rose Associates*
Robertson, William W. — *Marvin L. Silcott & Associates, Inc.*
Robins, Jeri N. — *Nagler, Robins & Poe, Inc.*
Robinson, Adrienne — *R L Plimpton Associates*
Robinson, Bruce — *Bruce Robinson Associates*

Robinson, Eric B. — *Bruce Robinson Associates*
Robison, John H. — *Robison & Associates*
Robson, Ridgely — *Accounting Personnel Consultants*
Roche, Gerard R. — *Heidrick & Struggles, Inc.*
Rodebaugh, Karen — *Management Recruiters International, Inc.*
Rodebaugh, Thomas L. — *Management Recruiters International, Inc.*
Rodetsky, Laurie — *Bradford & Galt, Inc.*
Rodgers, John — *Agra Placements International Ltd.*
Rodgers, Kathi — *St. Lawrence International, Inc.*
Rodgers, Sarah J. — *Management Recruiters International, Inc.*
Rodney, Brett — *MSI International*
Rodriguez, Carlos R. — *Management Recruiters International, Inc.*
Rodriguez, Josie — *R. Parker and Associates, Inc.*
Rodriguez, Steven — *Spencer Stuart*
Roehrig, Kurt W. — *AJM Professional Services*
Roethlein, John — *Management Recruiters International, Inc.*
Roethlein, Lorian E. — *Management Recruiters International, Inc.*
Rogan, John P. — *Russell Reynolds Associates, Inc.*
Rogers, Leah — *Dinte Resources, Incorporated*
Rohan, James E. — *J.P. Canon Associates*
Rohan, Kevin A. — *J.P. Canon Associates*
Rojas-Magnon, Carlos — *Amrop International*
Roll, Bill — *Management Recruiters International, Inc.*
Rollo, Robert S. — *R. Rollo Associates*
Romanchek, Walter R. — *Wellington Management Group*
Romaniw, Michael J. — *A la carte International*
Romaniw, Michael J. — *A la carte International*
Romaniw, Michael J. — *A la carte International*
Romano, Darren G. — *Korn/Ferry International*
Romanowicz, Jill — *Howard Fischer Associates, Inc.*
Rose, Sanford M. — *Sanford Rose Associates*
Rosemarin, Gloria J. — *Barrington Hart, Inc.*
Rosen, Elayne — *Noble & Associates Inc.*
Rosen, Mark — *Winter, Wyman & Company*
Rosenfeld, Martin J. — *Sanford Rose Associates*
Rosenthal, Andrea — *Korn/Ferry International*
Rosenwald, Tom H. — *Heidrick & Struggles, Inc.*
Rosica, John — *Management Recruiters International, Inc.*
Ross, Garland E. — *Management Recruiters International, Inc.*
Ross, Lawrence — *Lovas Stanley/Paul Ray Berndtson Inc.*
Ross, Marc A. — *Flowers & Associates*
Ross, Mark S. — *Herman Smith Executive Initiatives Inc.*
Ross, William J. — *Flowers & Associates*
Rossi, George A. — *Heidrick & Struggles, Inc.*
Rossman, Paul R. — *Management Recruiters International, Inc.*
Rotella, Marshall W. — *The Corporate Connection, Ltd.*
Roth, Robert J. — *Williams, Roth & Krueger Inc.*
Rothenberg, Paul — *The McCormick Group, Inc.*
Rothfeld, Robert — *A.E. Feldman Associates*
Rothman, Jeffrey — *ProResource, Inc.*
Rothschild, John S. — *Heidrick & Struggles, Inc.*
Rothwell, Amy — *Howard Fischer Associates, Inc.*
Rottblatt, Michael — *Korn/Ferry International*
Rowe, Thomas A. — *Korn/Ferry International*
Rowells, Michael — *MSI International*
Roy, Gary P. — *Management Recruiters International, Inc.*
Rozner, Burton L. — *Oliver & Rozner Associates, Inc.*
Rubin, Marcey S. — *Kenzer Corp.*
Rudin, Harold — *Management Recruiters International, Inc.*
Rudin, Myra — *Management Recruiters International, Inc.*
Rudolph, Arlyn B. — *Management Recruiters International, Inc.*
Ruello, Brenda L. — *Heidrick & Struggles, Inc.*
Rumson, Barbara — *Management Recruiters International, Inc.*
Rumson, Paul M. — *Management Recruiters International, Inc.*
Runquist, U.W. — *Webb, Johnson Associates, Inc.*
Rupert, Jim — *Management Recruiters International, Inc.*
Rurak, Zbigniew T. — *Rurak & Associates, Inc.*
Ruschak, Randy R. — *Management Recruiters International, Inc.*
Rusher, William H. — *Rusher, Loscavio & LoPresto*
Russell, Carol — *ExecuScope Division of Russell Staffing Resources, Inc.*
Russell, Richard A. — *Executive Search Consultants Corporation*
Russell, Susan Anne — *Executive Search Consultants Corporation*
Russo, Karen — *Maximum Management Corp.*
Rust, John R. — *DHR International, Inc.*
Rustin, Beth — *The Whitney Group*
Ryan, Joseph W. — *Skott/Edwards Consultants, Inc.*
Ryan, Mary L. — *Summerfield Associates, Inc.*
Ryckaert, Terri — *Financial Search Corporation*
Sabados, Terri — *Management Recruiters International, Inc.*
Sabat, Lori S. — *Alta Associates, Inc.*
Sacerdote, John — *Raymond Karsan Associates*
Sackmary, Marcia — *Sanford Rose Associates*
Sackmary, Steven — *Sanford Rose Associates*
Sahe, Mark — *Accountants on Call*
Sahlas, Chrissy — *CPS Inc.*
Saletra, Andrew — *CPS Inc.*
Salikof, Allen B. — *Management Recruiters International, Inc.*

Salikof, Kaye R. — *Management Recruiters International, Inc.*
Salinger, Helen — *Gilbert Tweed/INESA*
Sanders, Dave A. — *Management Recruiters International, Inc.*
Sanders, Natalie — *CPS Inc.*
Sanders, Spencer H. — *Battalia Winston International*
Sanderson, Jeffrey M. — *Sullivan & Company*
Sandor, Richard J. — *Flynn, Hannock, Incorporated*
Sanford, David — *Winter, Wyman & Company*
Sapperstein, Jerry S. — *CFO Associates, Inc.*
Sarafa, Sam N. — *Management Recruiters International, Inc.*
Sarn, Allan G. — *Allan Sarn Associates Inc.*
Sauer, Robert C. — *Heidrick & Struggles, Inc.*
Savage, Edward J. — *Stanton Chase International*
Savage, Julie — *Winter, Wyman & Company*
Savereid, Lisa — *Isaacson, Miller*
Sawhill, Louise B. — *Paul Ray Berndtson*
Sawhook, Danny — *Richard, Wayne and Roberts*
Sawyer, Deborah A. — *Heidrick & Struggles, Inc.*
Sawyer, Patricia L. — *Smith & Sawyer Inc.*
Saydah, Robert F. — *Heidrick & Struggles, Inc.*
Sayers, Bruce D. — *Brackin & Sayers Associates*
Saylor, Bill E. — *Management Recruiters International, Inc.*
Scalamera, Tom — *CPS Inc.*
Schaad, Carl A. — *Heidrick & Struggles, Inc.*
Schaefer, Brett — *Accountants on Call*
Schaefer, Frederic M. — *A.T. Kearney, Inc.*
Schaller, F. William — *Sanford Rose Associates*
Schaller, Karen — *Sanford Rose Associates*
Schappell, Marc P. — *Egon Zehnder International Inc.*
Scharett, Carol — *St. Lawrence International, Inc.*
Schedra, Sharon — *Earley Kielty and Associates, Inc.*
Schegg, Paul — *Goodrich & Sherwood Associates, Inc.*
Scheidt, Sandi — *Paul Ray Berndtson*
Scheidt, Sandra L. — *The Heidrick Partners, Inc.*
Schiavone, Mary Rose — *Canny, Bowen Inc.*
Schlanger, Ruth — *Richard, Wayne and Roberts*
Schlosser, John R. — *Heidrick & Struggles, Inc.*
Schlpma, Christine — *Advanced Executive Resources*
Schmidt, Jeri E. — *Blake, Hansen & Nye, Limited*
Schmidt, Michelle C. — *Sanford Rose Associates*
Schmidt, Paul — *Paul Ray Berndtson*
Schmidt, Peter R. — *Boyden*
Schmidt, Robert C. — *Management Recruiters International, Inc.*
Schmidt, Timothy G. — *Sanford Rose Associates*
Schmidt, William C. — *Christian & Timbers*
Schneider, Perry — *Agra Placements International Ltd.*
Schneider, Susan — *Jacquelyn Finn & Susan Schneider Associates, Inc.*
Schneider, Thomas P. — *WTW Associates*
Schneider, Tom J. — *Management Recruiters International, Inc.*
Schneider, Victor — *Accountants on Call*
Schneiderman, Gerald — *Management Resource Associates, Inc.*
Schneidermeyer, Phil — *Korn/Ferry International*
Schoenwetter, Carrie — *Management Recruiters International, Inc.*
Schoettle, Michael B. — *Heidrick & Struggles, Inc.*
Schoff, Frank J. — *Management Recruiters International, Inc.*
Schonberg, Alan R. — *Management Recruiters International, Inc.*
Schoppergrell, Holly — *Don Richard Associates of Charlotte*
Schor, Neil D. — *Kenzer Corp.*
Schostak, Glen — *Korn/Ferry International*
Schramm, Walter M. — *Executive Outsourcing International*
Schreiber, Stuart M. — *Heidrick & Struggles, Inc.*
Schrenzel, Benjamin — *Parfitt Recruiting and Consulting*
Schroeder, James L. — *Korn/Ferry International*
Schroeder, John W. — *Spencer Stuart*
Schroeder, Victoria — *Paul Ray Berndtson*
Schuckman, Louis — *Accountants on Call*
Schueneman, David — *CPS Inc.*
Schulte, Bernard — *Korn/Ferry International*
Schultz, Roger C. — *Management Recruiters International, Inc.*
Schuyler, Lambert — *Schuyler, Frye & Baker, Inc.*
Schwam, Carol — *A.E. Feldman Associates*
Schwartz, Carole — *A.T. Kearney, Inc.*
Schwartz, Jay S. — *Management Recruiters International, Inc.*
Schwartz, Stephen D. — *Management Recruiters International, Inc.*
Schwartz, Susan — *Korn/Ferry International*
Schwarzkopf, A. Renee — *David C. Cooper and Associates, Inc.*
Scott, Alison — *Korn/Ferry International*
Scott, Evan — *Howard Fischer Associates, Inc.*
Scott, George W. — *Raymond Karsan Associates*
Scott, Jack — *Korn/Ferry International*
Scott, Mark S. — *The Prairie Group*
Scott, Ron — *Richard Kader & Associates*
Scroggins, Stephen R. — *Russell Reynolds Associates, Inc.*
Scullin, Richard — *Eden & Associates, Inc.*
Seals, Sonny — *A.T. Kearney, Inc.*
Sears, Kirk — *Management Recruiters International, Inc.*
Sears, Rick — *Management Recruiters International, Inc.*

Seco, William — *Seco & Zetto Associates, Inc.*
Seefeld, David — *Management Recruiters International, Inc.*
Seiden, Steven A. — *Seiden Krieger Associates, Inc.*
Sekera, Roger I. — *A.T. Kearney, Inc.*
Selbst, Denise — *Richard, Wayne and Roberts*
Selko, Philip W. — *Hogan Acquisitions*
Seltzer, Deborah Coogan — *Paul Ray Berndtson*
Semmes, John R. — *Management Recruiters International, Inc.*
Semyan, John K. — *TNS Partners, Inc.*
Serota, Joel — *Kenzer Corp.*
Serwat, Leonard A. — *Spencer Stuart*
Sessa, Beth — *Richard, Wayne and Roberts*
Sessa, Vincent J. — *Integrated Search Solutions Group, LLC*
Settles, Barbara Z. — *Lamalie Amrop International*
Sevilla, Claudio A. — *Crawford & Crofford*
Sewell, Danny J. — *Management Recruiters International, Inc.*
Seweloh, Theodore W. — *The Heidrick Partners, Inc.*
Shabot, David — *Korn/Ferry International*
Shake, Samuel D. — *DHR International, Inc.*
Shapiro, Elaine — *CPS Inc.*
Sharp, Paul S. — *Management Recruiters International, Inc.*
Shattuck, Merrill B. — *M.B. Shattuck and Associates, Inc.*
Shaw, Eric D. — *Management Recruiters International, Inc.*
Shea, Kathleen M. — *The Penn Partners, Incorporated*
Shearer, Gary F. — *Management Recruiters International, Inc.*
Sheedy, Edward J. — *Dieckmann & Associates, Ltd.*
Sheehan, Arthur — *Management Recruiters International, Inc.*
Sheehan, Patricia — *Management Recruiters International, Inc.*
Sheets, Russel — *Accountants on Call*
Shell, John C. — *John Shell Associates, Inc.*
Shemin, Grace — *Maximum Management Corp.*
Shen, Eugene Y. — *The Whitney Group*
Shenfield, Peter — *Baker, Harris & Partners Limited*
Shepard, Michael J. — *MSI International*
Shepherd, Daniel M. — *Shepherd Bueschel & Provus, Inc.*
Shepherd, Gail L. — *Shepherd Bueschel & Provus, Inc.*
Sherburne, Zachary — *Accountants on Call*
Sheridan, Kenneth T. — *Management Recruiters International, Inc.*
Sheridan, Theresa — *Management Recruiters International, Inc.*
Sherman, Daniel A. — *Goodwin & Company*
Sherrill, Lee S. — *Management Recruiters International, Inc.*
Sherry, Joan — *Korn/Ferry International*
Shervey, Brent C. — *O'Callaghan Honey/Paul Ray Berndtson, Inc.*
Sherwood, Andrew — *Goodrich & Sherwood Associates, Inc.*
Shield, Nancy — *Maximum Management Corp.*
Shimp, David J. — *Lamalie Amrop International*
Shockey, William — *Korn/Ferry International*
Shoemaker, Fred W. — *MSI International*
Shoemaker, Larry C. — *Shoemaker & Associates*
Shore, Earl L. — *E.L. Shore & Associates Ltd.*
Shourds, Mary E. — *Houze, Shourds & Montgomery, Inc.*
Shulman, Melvin — *McFeely Wackerle Shulman*
Shultz, Susan F. — *SSA Executive Search International*
Sibbald, John R. — *John Sibbald Associates, Inc.*
Siegel, Fred — *Conex Incorporated*
Siegel, Pamela — *Executive Options, Ltd.*
Siegel, RitaSue — *RitaSue Siegel Resources Inc.*
Sierra, Rafael A. — *Lamalie Amrop International*
Signer, Julie — *CPS Inc.*
Sigurdson, Eric J. — *Russell Reynolds Associates, Inc.*
Silcott, Marvin L. — *Marvin L. Silcott & Associates, Inc.*
Silvas, Stephen D. — *Roberson and Company*
Silver, Lee A. — *L.A. Silver Associates, Inc.*
Silverberg, Alisa — *Accountants on Call*
Silverman, Paul M. — *The Marshall Group*
Silverstein, Michael L. — *Management Recruiters International, Inc.*
Silverstein, Rita — *Accountants on Call*
Simmonds, David — *Coopers & Lybrand Consulting*
Simmons, Gerald J. — *Handy HRM Corp.*
Simmons, Jeffrey — *Kenzer Corp.*
Simmons, Sandra K. — *MSI International*
Simmons, Tom — *Spencer Stuart*
Simmons, Vicki — *Richard, Wayne and Roberts*
Simon, Bernard — *Accountants on Call*
Simon, Bernard — *Accountants on Call*
Simon, William — *Korn/Ferry International*
Simpson, Kent T. — *Management Recruiters International, Inc.*
Sims, John — *Management Recruiters International, Inc.*
Sinclair, Amy — *Fisher Personnel Management Services*
Sinclair, Tom — *Coopers & Lybrand Consulting*
Sitarski, Stan — *Howard Fischer Associates, Inc.*
Sjogren, Dennis — *Agra Placements International Ltd.*
Skinner, Aimee — *Don Richard Associates of Tidewater, Inc.*
Sklover, Bruce — *Professional Assignments of New York, Inc.*
Skunda, Donna M. — *Allerton Heneghan & O'Neill*
Slater, Ronald E. — *A.T. Kearney, Inc.*
Slaughter, Katherine T. — *Compass Group Ltd.*
Small, Ellyn — *Accountants on Call*

Smead, Michelle M. — *A.T. Kearney, Inc.*
Smirnov, Tatiana — *Allan Sarn Associates Inc.*
Smith, Adam M. — *The Abbott Group, Inc.*
Smith, Ana Luz — *Smith Search, S.C.*
Smith, Barry S. — *Management Recruiters International, Inc.*
Smith, Carroll V. — *Management Recruiters International, Inc.*
Smith, Cheryl — *Barton Raben, Inc.*
Smith, Cheryl — *KPMG Executive Search*
Smith, Cheryl — *ProResource, Inc.*
Smith, Clawson — *Ward Howell International, Inc.*
Smith, David P. — *Smith & Latterell (HRS, Inc.)*
Smith, Eric E. — *Management Recruiters International, Inc.*
Smith, Gin-Nie — *Management Recruiters International, Inc.*
Smith, Grant — *Price Waterhouse*
Smith, Herbert C. — *H C Smith Ltd.*
Smith, Herman D. — *Management Recruiters International, Inc.*
Smith, Herman M. — *Herman Smith Executive Initiatives Inc.*
Smith, John E. — *Smith Search, S.C.*
Smith, John F. — *The Penn Partners, Incorporated*
Smith, Margaret A. — *MSI International*
Smith, Mark L. — *Korn/Ferry International*
Smith, Marvin E. — *Parfitt Recruiting and Consulting*
Smith, Matthew — *Korn/Ferry International*
Smith, Melanie F. — *The Heidrick Partners, Inc.*
Smith, Mike W. — *Management Recruiters International, Inc.*
Smith, Perry V. — *Management Recruiters International, Inc.*
Smith, R. Michael — *Smith James Group, Inc.*
Smith, Rebecca Ruben — *H C Smith Ltd.*
Smith, Robert L. — *Smith & Sawyer Inc.*
Smith, Scott B. — *Ward Howell International, Inc.*
Smith, Shellie L. — *The Heidrick Partners, Inc.*
Smith, Steve L. — *Management Recruiters International, Inc.*
Snedden, Al — *Management Recruiters International, Inc.*
Snellbaker, Mary W. — *Management Recruiters International, Inc.*
Snider, George R. — *Sanford Rose Associates*
Snodgrass, Stephen — *DeFrain, Mayer, Lee & Burgess LLC*
Snook, Maria P. — *Management Recruiters International, Inc.*
Snook, Marvin G. — *Management Recruiters International, Inc.*
Snyder, C. Edward — *Horton International*
Snyder, James F. — *Snyder & Company*
Snyder, Thomas J. — *Spencer Stuart*
Sockwell, J. Edgar — *Sockwell & Associates*
Soggs, Cheryl Pavick — *A.T. Kearney, Inc.*
Sola, George L. — *A.T. Kearney, Inc.*
Solomon, Christina — *Richard, Wayne and Roberts*
Somers, Donald A. — *Management Recruiters International, Inc.*
Sorg, Leslie — *The McCormick Group, Inc.*
Soth, Mark H. — *Management Recruiters International, Inc.*
Soutouras, James — *Smith James Group, Inc.*
Sowerbutt, Richard S. — *Hite Executive Search*
Spadavecchia, Jennifer — *Alta Associates, Inc.*
Spangenberg, J. Brand — *The Brand Company, Inc.*
Spangenberg, Sigrid — *The Brand Company, Inc.*
Spangler, Lloyd — *Cole, Warren & Long, Inc.*
Spann, Richard E. — *Goodrich & Sherwood Associates, Inc.*
Speck, Michael J. — *Lovas Stanley/Paul Ray Berndtson Inc.*
Spellacy, James P. — *Management Recruiters International, Inc.*
Spellman, Frances — *Kenzer Corp.*
Spence, Gene L. — *Heidrick & Struggles, Inc.*
Spence, Joseph T. — *Russell Reynolds Associates, Inc.*
Spencer, Frank — *Kenzer Corp.*
Sperry, Elizabeth B. — *Korn/Ferry International*
Spiegel, Deborah — *Kenzer Corp.*
Spiegel, Gay — *L.A. Silver Associates, Inc.*
Spitz, Grant — *The Caldwell Partners Amrop International*
Spitz, Richard — *Korn/Ferry International*
Splaine, Charles — *Splaine & Associates, Inc.*
Sponseller, Vern — *Richard Kader & Associates*
Sprague, David — *Michael Stern Associates Inc.*
Sprau, Collin L. — *Paul Ray Berndtson*
Spriggs, Robert D. — *Spriggs & Company, Inc.*
Sprowls, Linda — *Allard Associates*
Srolis, Robert B. — *Raymond Karsan Associates*
St. Denis, Robert A. — *Sanford Rose Associates*
St. John, J. Burke — *Heidrick & Struggles, Inc.*
Stack, James K. — *Boyden*
Stackhouse, P. John — *Heidrick & Struggles, Inc.*
Stafford, Charles B. — *Management Recruiters International, Inc.*
Stanislaw, Robert J. — *DHR International, Inc.*
Stanley, Paul R.A. — *Lovas Stanley/Paul Ray Berndtson Inc.*
Stanley, Wade — *Management Recruiters International, Inc.*
Stark, Gary L. — *Management Recruiters International, Inc.*
Stark, Jeff — *Thorne, Brieger Associates Inc.*
Starr, Anna — *Richard, Wayne and Roberts*
Steck, Frank T. — *A.T. Kearney, Inc.*
Steele, Kevin — *Winter, Wyman & Company*
Steenerson, Thomas L. — *MSI International*
Stein, Neil A. — *R.H. Perry & Associates, Inc.*

Stein, Terry W. — *Stewart, Stein and Scott, Ltd.*
Steinem, Andy — *Dahl-Morrow International*
Steinem, Barbara — *Dahl-Morrow International*
Steinman, Stephen — *The Stevenson Group of New Jersey*
Stemphoski, Ronald L. — *The Diversified Search Companies*
Stephanian, Armand A. — *Paul Ray Berndtson*
Stephens, Roberto Salinas — *Smith Search, S.C.*
Stephenson, Craig — *Korn/Ferry International*
Stephenson, Don L. — *Ells Personnel System Inc.*
Sterling, Cheryl E. — *Management Recruiters International, Inc.*
Sterling, Jay — *Earley Kielty and Associates, Inc.*
Sterling, Ronald — *Management Recruiters International, Inc.*
Sterling, Sally M. — *Heidrick & Struggles, Inc.*
Stern, Leslie W. — *Sullivan & Company*
Stern, Michael I. — *Michael Stern Associates Inc.*
Stern, Ronni — *Kenzer Corp.*
Stern, Stephen — *CPS Inc.*
Sterner, Doug — *CPS Inc.*
Sternlicht, Marvin H. — *Accountants on Call*
Sternlicht, Marvin H. — *Accountants on Call*
Stevens, David — *Johnson Smith & Knisely Accord*
Stevens, Glenn — *Korn/Ferry International*
Stevens, Robin — *Paul Ray Berndtson*
Stevenson, Jani — *Howard Fischer Associates, Inc.*
Stevenson, Julianne M. — *Russell Reynolds Associates, Inc.*
Stewart, Jan J. — *Egon Zehnder International Inc.*
Stewart, Jeffrey O. — *Stewart, Stein and Scott, Ltd.*
Stewart, Ross M. — *Human Resources Network Partners Inc.*
Stewart, Steve — *Management Recruiters International, Inc.*
Stewart, Wilf — *KPMG Executive Search*
Stiles, Jack D. — *Sanford Rose Associates*
Stiles, Timothy — *Sanford Rose Associates*
Stivk, Barbara A. — *Thornton Resources*
Stoessel, Robert J. — *Management Recruiters International, Inc.*
Stokes, John — *Nordeman Grimm, Inc.*
Stoltz, Dick — *Management Recruiters International, Inc.*
Stone, Kayla — *Korn/Ferry International*
Stone, Robert Ryder — *Lamalie Amrop International*
Stone, Susan L. — *Stone Enterprises Ltd.*
Stoneham, Herbert E.C. — *Stoneham Associates Corp.*
Storbeck, Shelly — *A.T. Kearney, Inc.*
Storment, John H. — *Management Recruiters International, Inc.*
Stouffer, Dale — *Agra Placements International Ltd.*
Stoy, Roger M. — *Heidrick & Struggles, Inc.*
Stratman, Sandy L. — *Management Recruiters International, Inc.*
Stratmeyer, Karin Bergwall — *Princeton Entrepreneurial Resources*
Straube, Stanley H. — *Straube Associates*
Strayhorn, Larry — *Management Recruiters International, Inc.*
Strayhorn, Patricia — *Management Recruiters International, Inc.*
Stricker, Sidney G. — *Stricker & Zagor*
Stringer, Dann P. — *D.E. Foster Partners Inc.*
Strobo, Ray S. — *Management Recruiters International, Inc.*
Strobridge, Richard P. — *F.L. Taylor & Company, Inc.*
Strom, Mark N. — *Search Advisors International Corp.*
Stroup, Jonathan C. — *Egon Zehnder International Inc.*
Stuart, Karen M. — *Reflex Services, Inc.*
Stubberfield, Lee — *Management Recruiters International, Inc.*
Stubbs, Judy N. — *Lamalie Amrop International*
Sturges, J.S. — *Contract Professionals*
Stutt, Brian — *Richard, Wayne and Roberts*
Suit-Terry, J.A. — *Management Recruiters International, Inc.*
Sullivan, Brian M. — *Sullivan & Company*
Sullivan, Catherine — *Korn/Ferry International*
Sullivan, Dennis — *Sullivan & Associates*
Sullivan, Robert — *Korn/Ferry International*
Summerfield-Beall, Dotty — *Summerfield Associates, Inc.*
Summerlin, Gerald — *Management Recruiters International, Inc.*
Sur, William K. — *Canny, Bowen Inc.*
Sussman, Lynda — *Gilbert Tweed/INESA*
Sutter, Terry A. — *Russell Reynolds Associates, Inc.*
Sutton, Robert J. — *The Caldwell Partners Amrop International*
Swanson, Dick — *Raymond Karsan Associates*
Swanson, Jarl — *The Gabriel Group*
Swanson, Kris — *Flex Execs Management Solutions*
Swaringen, Mac — *Management Recruiters International, Inc.*
Sweeney, James W. — *Sweeney Harbert & Mummert, Inc.*
Sweet, Charles W. — *A.T. Kearney, Inc.*
Swidler, J. Robert — *Egon Zehnder International Inc.*
Swystun, Karen — *Price Waterhouse*
Sykes, Hugh L. — *Management Recruiters International, Inc.*
Tabisz, Susanne — *Executive Referral Services, Inc.*
Takacs, Gloria — *Gilbert & Van Campen International*
Talbot, Matt T. — *Management Recruiters International, Inc.*
Talbot, Norman — *Management Recruiters International, Inc.*
Tames, Rodolfo — *Amrop International*
Tanabe, Sharon — *Korn/Ferry International*
Tanenbaum, Ray — *Kenzer Corp.*
Tanton, John E. — *Tanton Mitchell/Paul Ray Berndtson*

Tardugno, Carl — *Management Recruiters International, Inc.*
Targovnik, Andrew — *Accountants on Call*
Tate, Robert H. — *Paul Ray Berndtson*
Taylor, Charles E. — *Lamalie Amrop International*
Taylor, Conrad G. — *MSI International*
Taylor, Ernest A. — *Ward Howell International, Inc.*
Taylor, Kenneth W. — *Egon Zehnder International Inc.*
Taylor, Richard — *Korn/Ferry International*
Taylor, Walt W. — *Management Recruiters International, Inc.*
Taylor-Gordon, Elaine — *Kenzer Corp.*
Telford, John H. — *Telford, Adams & Alexander/Telford & Co., Inc.*
Tello, Fernando — *Korn/Ferry International*
Temple, John D. — *The Hindman Company*
ten Cate, Herman H. — *Stoneham Associates Corp.*
Tessin, Cy — *Management Recruiters International, Inc.*
Theobald, David B. — *Theobald & Associates*
Tholke, William E. — *Canny, Bowen Inc.*
Thomas, Bill — *Management Recruiters International, Inc.*
Thomas, Cheryl M. — *CPS Inc.*
Thomas, Christine S. — *Lovas Stanley/Paul Ray Berndtson Inc.*
Thomas, Ian — *International Staffing Consultants, Inc.*
Thomas, Kim — *CPS Inc.*
Thomas, Kurt J. — *P.J. Murphy & Associates, Inc.*
Thompson, Jim E. — *Management Recruiters International, Inc.*
Thompson, John R. — *MSI International*
Thompson, John T. — *Heidrick & Struggles, Inc.*
Thompson, Kenneth L. — *McCormack & Farrow*
Thompson, Timothy W. — *Korn/Ferry International*
Thomson, Alexander G. — *Russell Reynolds Associates, Inc.*
Thornton, John C. — *Thornton Resources*
Thorpe, David L. — *IMCOR, Inc.*
Thrower, Tom S. — *Management Recruiters International, Inc.*
Tice, Diane — *Accountants on Call*
Tierney, Eileen — *The Whitney Group*
Tillman, J. Robert — *Russell Reynolds Associates, Inc.*
Timms, Alan R. — *DHR International, Inc.*
Tingle, Trina A. — *MSI International*
Titterington, Catherine F. — *MSI International*
Titus, Dave — *Management Recruiters International, Inc.*
Tobin, Jim — *Barton Raben, Inc.*
Tobin, William — *Korn/Ferry International*
Tokarcik, Patricia — *ProResource, Inc.*
Tokash, Ronald E. — *MSI International*
Tolle, David W. — *Management Recruiters International, Inc.*
Toms, Evangeline — *Nordeman Grimm, Inc.*
Tonjuk, Tina — *The Paladin Companies, Inc.*
Toole, Mary — *Management Recruiters International, Inc.*
Toole, Tom J. — *Management Recruiters International, Inc.*
Torbert, Laura — *Temporary Accounting Personnel Inc.*
Tovrog, Dan — *CPS Inc.*
Tracey, Garvis — *Key Employment Services*
Tracey, Jack — *Management Assistance Group, Inc.*
Tracy, Ronald O. — *Egon Zehnder International Inc.*
Trapp, Ed — *Management Recruiters International, Inc.*
Trautman, William E. — *A.T. Kearney, Inc.*
Trautman, William E. — *Boyden*
Travis, Ed — *Management Recruiters International, Inc.*
Tribbett, Charles A. — *Russell Reynolds Associates, Inc.*
Tripp, William J. — *Management Recruiters International, Inc.*
Trueblood, Brian G. — *TNS Partners, Inc.*
Truemper, Dean — *CPS Inc.*
Truex, John F. — *Morton, McCorkle & Associates, Inc.*
Truvillion, Mary — *Accountants on Call*
Tryon, Katey — *DeFrain, Mayer, Lee & Burgess LLC*
Tucci, Joseph — *Fairfaxx Corporation*
Tucker, Thomas A. — *The Thomas Tucker Company*
Tufenkjian, Richard — *C.A. Durakis Associates, Inc.*
Tullberg, Tina — *CPS Inc.*
Tunney, William — *Grant Cooper and Associates*
Turnblacer, John — *The Gabriel Group*
Turner, Allan W. — *Management Recruiters International, Inc.*
Turner, Brad — *Management Recruiters International, Inc.*
Turner, Marilyn — *Temporary Accounting Personnel Inc.*
Turner, Michael — *Rocky Mountain Recruiters, Inc.*
Tutwiler, Stephen — *Don Richard Associates of Tampa, Inc.*
Tweed, Janet — *Gilbert Tweed/INESA*
Twiste, Craig — *Raymond Karsan Associates*
Tydings, Mary C. — *Russell Reynolds Associates, Inc.*
Tyler, Jackie — *Kenzer Corp.*
Tyler, Janet — *Accountants on Call*
Uhl, Jack N. — *Management Recruiters International, Inc.*
Unger, Mike A. — *Management Recruiters International, Inc.*
Unger, Paul T. — *A.T. Kearney, Inc.*
Uniacke, Keith J. — *Management Recruiters International, Inc.*
Utroska, Donald R. — *Lamalie Amrop International*
Vainblat, Galina — *Foy, Schneid & Daniel, Inc.*
Vairo, Leonard A. — *Christian & Timbers*
Valdes, Ma. Elena — *Korn/Ferry International*

Wilson, Robert J. — *Coleman Lew & Associates, Inc.*
Wilson, Thomas H. — *Lamalie Amrop International*
Wimer, Thomas W. — *DHR International, Inc.*
Winfrey, James — *Korn/Ferry International*
Winitz, Joel — *GSW Consulting Group, Inc.*
Winitz, Marla — *GSW Consulting Group, Inc.*
Winnewisser, William E. — *Accounting & Computer Personnel*
Winograd, Glenn — *Criterion Executive Search, Inc.*
Winslow, Lawrence J. — *DHR International, Inc.*
Winston, Dale — *Battalia Winston International*
Winston, Susan — *CPS Inc.*
Winter, Robert — *The Whitney Group*
Wirtshafter, Linda — *Grant Cooper and Associates*
Wisch, Steven C. — *MB Inc. Interim Executive Division*
Wise, J. Herbert — *Sandhurst Associates*
Wise, Ronald L. — *Management Recruiters International, Inc.*
Wittenberg, Laura L. — *Boyden*
Wold, Ted W. — *Hyde Danforth Wold & Co.*
Wolf, Stephen M. — *Byron Leonard International, Inc.*
Wolfe, David — *Kenzer Corp.*
Wolfram, David A. — *EFL Associates*
Wolman, Stephen R. — *S.R. Wolman Associates, Inc.*
Wolters, Tony A. — *Management Recruiters International, Inc.*
Womack, Joseph — *The Bankers Group*
Wood, Allison — *Korn/Ferry International*
Wood, John S. — *Egon Zehnder International Inc.*
Wood, Martin F. — *Lamalie Amrop International*
Wood, Milton M. — *M. Wood Company*
Wood, Steven N. — *DHR International, Inc.*
Woodruff, Mark S. — *Management Recruiters International, Inc.*
Woodrum, Robert L. — *Korn/Ferry International*
Wooller, Edmund A.M. — *Windsor International*
Wozniak, Bernard D. — *Sanford Rose Associates*
Wozniak, Jane K. — *Sanford Rose Associates*
Wright, Anne B. — *Management Recruiters International, Inc.*
Wright, Charles D. — *Goodrich & Sherwood Associates, Inc.*
Wright, Doug — *Management Recruiters International, Inc.*
Wright, Leslie — *The Stevenson Group of New Jersey*
Wrynn, Robert F. — *MSI International*
Wujciak, Sandra — *Accountants on Call*
Wyatt, Janice — *Korn/Ferry International*
Wyser-Pratte, Anne — *Heidrick & Struggles, Inc.*
Yamada, Steven — *Korn/Ferry International*
Yamvaketis, Stephen — *John Kurosky & Associates*
Yilmaz, Muriel — *Dinte Resources, Incorporated*
Yoon, Kyung — *Heidrick & Struggles, Inc.*
Youlano, John — *Personnel Unlimited/Executive Search*
Young, Alexander — *Messett Associates, Inc.*
Young, Arthur L. — *Management Recruiters International, Inc.*
Young, Charles E. — *Flowers & Associates*
Young, Laurie — *Part Time Resources, Inc.*
Young, Mark — *D.E. Foster Partners Inc.*
Young, Nick — *Spencer Stuart*
Young, Susan M. — *Management Recruiters International, Inc.*
Young, Van G. — *Heidrick & Struggles, Inc.*
Young, Wayne T. — *Management Recruiters International, Inc.*
Youngs, Donald L. — *Youngs & Company*
Yowe, Mark — *Heidrick & Struggles, Inc.*
Yturbe, Rafael — *Russell Reynolds Associates, Inc.*
Zaffrann, Craig S. — *P.J. Murphy & Associates, Inc.*
Zahradka, James F. — *P.J. Murphy & Associates, Inc.*
Zak, Adam — *Adams & Associates International*
Zaleta, Andrew R. — *A.T. Kearney, Inc.*
Zander, Barry W. — *MSI International*
Zanotti, Les V. — *Management Recruiters International, Inc.*
Zaring, David J. — *Management Recruiters International, Inc.*
Zarkin, Norman — *The Zarkin Group, Inc.*
Zaslav, Debra M. — *Telford, Adams & Alexander/Telford & Co., Inc.*
Zavala, Lorenzo — *Russell Reynolds Associates, Inc.*
Zawicki, David — *Management Recruiters International, Inc.*
Zay, Thomas C. — *Boyden/Zay & Company*
Zay, Thomas C. — *Boyden/Zay & Company*
Zellner, Paul A. — *Paul Ray Berndtson*
Zerkle, John P. — *Management Recruiters International, Inc.*
Zerkle, John P. — *Management Recruiters International, Inc.*
Zetto, Kathryn — *Seco & Zetto Associates, Inc.*
Zila, Laurie M. — *Princeton Entrepreneurial Resources*
Zilliacus, Patrick W. — *Larsen, Zilliacus & Associates, Inc.*
Ziluck, Scott W. — *Management Recruiters International, Inc.*
Zivic, Janis M. — *Spencer Stuart*
Zonis, Hildy R. — *Accountants Executive Search*
Zucchiatti, Elizabeth — *The Caldwell Partners Amrop International*
Zucker, Nancy — *Maximum Management Corp.*

## 2. Aerospace/Defense

Abbott, Peter — *The Abbott Group, Inc.*
Ainsworth, Lawrence — *Search West, Inc.*
Akin, J.R. — *J.R. Akin & Company Inc.*

Alekel, Karren — *ALW Research International*
Allred, J. Michael — *Spencer Stuart*
Altreuter, Rose — *The ALTCO Group*
Ames, George C. — *Ames O'Neill Associates*
Apostle, George — *Search Dynamics, Inc.*
Bailey, William A. — *TNS Partners, Inc.*
Baird, John — *Professional Search Consultants*
Baldwin, Keith R. — *The Baldwin Group*
Baran, Helena — *Michael J. Cavanagh and Associates*
Baron, Len — *Industrial Recruiters Associates, Inc.*
Beall, Charles P. — *Beall & Company, Inc.*
Beaudin, Elizabeth C. — *Callan Associates, Ltd.*
Beaver, Robert W. — *Executive Manning Corporation*
Belfrey, Edward — *Dunhill Professional Search of Irvine, Inc.*
Benson, Kate — *Rene Plessner Associates, Inc.*
Bermea, Jose — *Gaffney Management Consultants*
Berry, Harold B. — *The Hindman Company*
Blackmon, Sharon — *The Abbott Group, Inc.*
Blecker, Jay — *TSS Consulting, Ltd.*
Blim, Barbara — *JDG Associates, Ltd.*
Boccella, Ralph — *Susan C. Goldberg Associates*
Boczany, William J. — *The Guild Corporation*
Booth, Otis — *A.T. Kearney, Inc.*
Briggs, Adam — *Horton International*
Brooks, Charles — *Corporate Recruiters Ltd.*
Brown, Larry C. — *Horton International*
Brudno, Robert J. — *Savoy Partners, Ltd.*
Bruno, Deborah F. — *The Hindman Company*
Bryant, Richard D. — *Bryant Associates, Inc.*
Bryza, Robert M. — *Robert Lowell International*
Budill, Edward — *Professional Search Consultants*
Burchill, Greg — *BGB Associates*
Burns, Alan — *The Enns Partners Inc.*
Cahill, Peter M. — *Peter M. Cahill Associates, Inc.*
Callan, Robert M. — *Callan Associates, Ltd.*
Cavanagh, Michael J. — *Michael J. Cavanagh and Associates*
Cizek, John T. — *Cizek Associates, Inc.*
Cizek, Marti J. — *Cizek Associates, Inc.*
Clauhsen, Elizabeth A. — *Savoy Partners, Ltd.*
Cleary, Thomas R. — *ARJay & Associates*
Clegg, Cynthia — *Horton International*
Cohen, Robert C. — *Intech Summit Group, Inc.*
Cole, Kevin — *Don Richard Associates of Washington, D.C., Inc.*
Coleman, J. Kevin — *J. Kevin Coleman & Associates, Inc.*
Collis, Gerald — *TSS Consulting, Ltd.*
Cram, Noel — *R.P. Barone Associates*
Cramer, Paul J. — *C/R Associates*
Crawford, Cassondra — *Don Richard Associates of Washington, D.C., Inc.*
Cruse, O.D. — *Spencer Stuart*
Davis, G. Gordon — *Davis & Company*
DeGioia, Joseph — *JDG Associates, Ltd.*
Dickey, Chet W. — *Bowden & Company, Inc.*
Dingman, Bruce — *Robert W. Dingman Company, Inc.*
Dingman, Robert W. — *Robert W. Dingman Company, Inc.*
Dinte, Paul — *Dinte Resources, Incorporated*
Drexler, Robert — *Robert Drexler Associates, Inc.*
Drury, James J. — *Spencer Stuart*
Edwards, Verba L. — *Wing Tips & Pumps, Inc.*
Ellis, Ted K. — *The Hindman Company*
Enfield, Jerry L. — *Executive Manning Corporation*
Enns, George — *The Enns Partners Inc.*
Farrow, Jerry M. — *McCormack & Farrow*
Fawcett, Anne M. — *The Caldwell Partners Amrop International*
Fisher, Neal — *Fisher Personnel Management Services*
Foreman, David C. — *Koontz, Jeffries & Associates, Inc.*
Fotia, Frank — *JDG Associates, Ltd.*
French, William G. — *Preng & Associates, Inc.*
Gaffney, Keith — *Gaffney Management Consultants*
Gaffney, William — *Gaffney Management Consultants*
Gallagher, Terence M. — *Battalia Winston International*
Gares, Conrad — *TSS Consulting, Ltd.*
Gilchrist, Robert J. — *Horton International*
Giles, Joe L. — *Joe L. Giles and Associates, Inc.*
Gilreath, James M. — *Gilreath Weatherby, Inc.*
Gloss, Frederick C. — *F. Gloss International*
Goldberg, Susan C. — *Susan C. Goldberg Associates*
Goldsmith, Fred J. — *Fred J. Goldsmith Associates*
Gourlay, Debra — *Rene Plessner Associates, Inc.*
Grantham, John — *Grantham & Co., Inc.*
Graves, Rosemarie — *Don Richard Associates of Washington, D.C., Inc.*
Green, Jean — *Broward-Dobbs, Inc.*
Green, Marc — *TSS Consulting, Ltd.*
Hansen, David G. — *Ott & Hansen, Inc.*
Harbaugh, Paul J. — *International Management Advisors, Inc.*
Harvey, Mike — *Advanced Executive Resources*
Hauswirth, Jeffrey M. — *Spencer Stuart*

### 3. Automotive

Barnes, Richard E. — *Barnes Development Group, LLC*
Barnes, Roanne L. — *Barnes Development Group, LLC*
Baron, Len — *Industrial Recruiters Associates, Inc.*
Bason, Maurice L. — *Bason Associates Inc.*
Beaudin, Elizabeth C. — *Callan Associates, Ltd.*
Beaver, Robert W. — *Executive Manning Corporation*
Bell, Lindy — *F-O-R-T-U-N-E Personnel Consultants of Huntsville, Inc.*
Bermea, Jose — *Gaffney Management Consultants*
Berry, Harold B. — *The Hindman Company*
Biestek, Paul J. — *Paul J. Biestek Associates, Inc.*
Bladon, Andrew — *Don Richard Associates of Tampa, Inc.*
Bliley, Jerry — *Spencer Stuart*
Brackenbury, Robert — *Bowman & Marshall, Inc.*
Brady, Colin S. — *Ward Howell International, Inc.*
Brady, Robert — *CPS Inc.*
Brandeis, Richard — *CPS Inc.*
Brennan, Jerry — *Brennan Associates*
Brennan, Timothy — *Brennan Associates*
Brenner, Mary — *Prestige Inc.*
Briggs, Adam — *Horton International*
Brown, Buzz — *Brown, Bernardy, Van Remmen, Inc.*
Brown, Charlene N. — *Accent on Achievement, Inc.*
Brown, Larry C. — *Horton International*
Bruno, Deborah F. — *The Hindman Company*
Bryant, Richard D. — *Bryant Associates, Inc.*
Bryza, Robert M. — *Robert Lowell International*
Buckles, Donna — *Cochran, Cochran & Yale, Inc.*
Budill, Edward — *Professional Search Consultants*
Bueschel, David A. — *Shepherd Bueschel & Provus, Inc.*
Burchill, Greg — *BGB Associates*
Butcher, Pascale — *F-O-R-T-U-N-E Personnel Consultants of Manatee County*
Cahill, Peter M. — *Peter M. Cahill Associates, Inc.*
Call, David — *Cochran, Cochran & Yale, Inc.*
Callan, Robert M. — *Callan Associates, Ltd.*
Carlson, Judith — *Bowman & Marshall, Inc.*
Caruso, Kathy — *Accounting Resources, Inc.*
Case, David — *Case Executive Search*
Cavanagh, Michael J. — *Michael J. Cavanagh and Associates*
Celenza, Catherine — *CPS Inc.*
Chappell, Peter — *The Bankers Group*
Chargar, Frances — *Hunt Ltd.*
Christiansen, Amy — *CPS Inc.*
Christiansen, Doug — *CPS Inc.*
Cizek, John T. — *Cizek Associates, Inc.*
Clarey, Jack R. — *Clarey & Andrews, Inc.*
Clark, James — *CPS Inc.*
Cleary, Thomas R. — *ARJay & Associates*
Cole, Kevin — *Don Richard Associates of Washington, D.C., Inc.*
Colling, Douglas — *KPMG Management Consulting*
Collis, Martin — *E.L. Shore & Associates Ltd.*
Connaghan, Linda — *Bowman & Marshall, Inc.*
Connelly, Kevin M. — *Spencer Stuart*
Cooke, Jeffrey R. — *Jonas, Walters & Assoc., Inc.*
Coulman, Karen — *CPS Inc.*
Crath, Paul F. — *Price Waterhouse*
Crist, Peter — *Crist Partners, Ltd.*
Cronin, Richard J. — *Hodge-Cronin & Associates, Inc.*
Crowder, Edward W. — *Crowder & Company*
Czamanske, Paul W. — *Compass Group Ltd.*
Czepiel, Susan — *CPS Inc.*
Dabich, Thomas M. — *Robert Harkins Associates, Inc.*
Damon, Robert A. — *Spencer Stuart*
Dautenhahn, Thomas — *Sanford Rose Associates*
Davidson, Arthur J. — *Lamalie Amrop International*
Davis, G. Gordon — *Davis & Company*
Del Prete, Karen — *Gilbert Tweed/INESA*
Dickey, Chet W. — *Bowden & Company, Inc.*
Dingman, Bruce — *Robert W. Dingman Company, Inc.*
Dingman, Robert W. — *Robert W. Dingman Company, Inc.*
Dixon, Aris — *CPS Inc.*
Dow, Lori — *Davidson, Laird & Associates*
Dreslinski, Robert S. — *Sharrow & Associates*
Drury, James J. — *Spencer Stuart*
Dudley, Robert — *Sanford Rose Associates*
Duley, Richard I. — *ARJay & Associates*
Dwyer, Julie — *CPS Inc.*
Dykstra, Nicolette — *CPS Inc.*
Eason, James — *JRL Executive Recruiters*
Eason, Larry E. — *JRL Executive Recruiters*
Eberly, Carrie — *Accounting Resources, Inc.*
Edwards, Verba L. — *Wing Tips & Pumps, Inc.*
Ellis, Ted K. — *The Hindman Company*
Enfield, Jerry J. — *Executive Manning Corporation*
England, Mark — *Austin-McGregor International*
Ervin, Darlene — *CPS Inc.*
Fancher, Robert L. — *Bason Associates Inc.*

Fee, J. Curtis — *Spencer Stuart*
Feyder, Michael — *A.T. Kearney, Inc.*
Fincher, Richard P. — *Phase II Management*
Fisher, Neal — *Fisher Personnel Management Services*
Fogarty, Michael — *CPS Inc.*
Folkerth, Gene — *Gene Folkerth & Associates, Inc.*
Foreman, David C. — *Koontz, Jeffries & Associates, Inc.*
Frazier, John — *Cochran, Cochran & Yale, Inc.*
Gaffney, Keith — *Gaffney Management Consultants*
Gaffney, William — *Gaffney Management Consultants*
Gallagher, Marilyn — *Hogan Acquisitions*
Gallagher, Terence M. — *Battalia Winston International*
Garcia, Samuel K. — *Southwestern Professional Services*
Garfinkle, Steven M. — *Battalia Winston International*
Gauthier, Robert C. — *Columbia Consulting Group*
Gilchrist, Robert J. — *Horton International*
Giles, Joe L. — *Joe L. Giles and Associates, Inc.*
Gilmore, Lori — *CPS Inc.*
Glennie, Francisco — *Ward Howell International, Inc.*
Goldman, Michael L. — *Strategic Associates, Inc.*
Goodman, Dawn M. — *Bason Associates Inc.*
Gordon, Gerald L. — *E.G. Jones Associates, Ltd.*
Gorfinkle, Gayle — *Executive Search International*
Grady, James — *Search West, Inc.*
Graham, Dale — *CPS Inc.*
Grantham, John — *Grantham & Co., Inc.*
Grassl, Peter O. — *Bowman & Marshall, Inc.*
Graves, Rosemarie — *Don Richard Associates of Washington, D.C., Inc.*
Greebe, Neil — *Flowers & Associates*
Grenier, Glorianne — *CPS Inc.*
Grzybowski, Jill — *CPS Inc.*
Harbaugh, Paul J. — *International Management Advisors, Inc.*
Harkins, Robert E. — *Robert Harkins Associates, Inc.*
Harris, Jack — *Baker, Harris & Partners Limited*
Harvey, Mike — *Advanced Executive Resources*
Haughton, Michael — *DeFrain, Mayer, Lee & Burgess LLC*
Hauswirth, Jeffrey M. — *Spencer Stuart*
Haystead, Steve — *Advanced Executive Resources*
Hazerjian, Cynthia — *CPS Inc.*
Heafey, Bill — *CPS Inc.*
Hecker, Henry C. — *Hogan Acquisitions*
Helminiak, Audrey — *Gaffney Management Consultants*
Heneghan, Donald A. — *Allerton Heneghan & O'Neill*
Henn, George W. — *G.W. Henn & Company*
Henshaw, Robert — *F-O-R-T-U-N-E Personnel Consultants of Huntsville, Inc.*
Hertan, Richard L. — *Executive Manning Corporation*
Hertan, Wiliam A. — *Executive Manning Corporation*
Hillyer, Robert L. — *Executive Manning Corporation*
Hindman, Neil O. — *The Hindman Company*
Hite, William A. — *Hite Executive Search*
Hoevel, Michael J. — *Poirier, Hoevel & Co.*
Hogan, Larry H. — *Hogan Acquisitions*
Hoppert, Phil — *Wargo and Co., Inc.*
Horton, Robert H. — *Horton International*
Hudson, William — *Robert Sage Recruiting*
Hughes, James J. — *R.P. Barone Associates*
Iacovelli, Heather — *CPS Inc.*
Illsley, Hugh G. — *Ward Howell International, Inc.*
Inzinna, Dennis — *AlternaStaff*
Irish, Alan — *CPS Inc.*
Jacobson, Donald — *Hunt Advisory Services*
Jacobson, Donald — *Hunt Ltd.*
Jaedike, Eldron — *Prestige Inc.*
James, Bruce — *Roberson and Company*
Jansen, Douglas L. — *Search Northwest Associates*
Jensen, Stephanie — *Don Richard Associates of Tidewater, Inc.*
Joffe, Barry — *Bason Associates Inc.*
Johnson, David — *Gaffney Management Consultants*
Johnson, Douglas — *Quality Search*
Johnson, John F. — *Lamalie Amrop International*
Johnson, Kathleen A. — *Barton Raben, Inc.*
Johnson, Michael E. — *Sharrow & Associates*
Johnson, Robert J. — *Quality Search*
Jones, Gary — *BGB Associates*
Jones, Ronald T. — *ARJay & Associates*
Judy, William — *Search West, Inc.*
Juelis, John J. — *Peeney Associates*
Kaiser, James G. — *Dunhill Search International*
Kanrich, Susan Azaria — *AlternaStaff*
Karalis, William — *CPS Inc.*
Kehoe, Mike — *CPS Inc.*
Kelsey, Micki — *Davidson, Laird & Associates*
Kilcoyne, Pat — *CPS Inc.*
Kirkpatrick, Robert L. — *Reese Associates*
Kishbaugh, Herbert S. — *Kishbaugh Associates International*
Kkorzyniewski, Nicole — *CPS Inc.*

Womack, Joseph — *The Bankers Group*
Wood, Milton M. — *M. Wood Company*
Young, Charles E. — *Flowers & Associates*
Zak, Adam — *Adams & Associates International*
Zee, Wanda — *Tesar-Reynes, Inc.*
Zetter, Roger — *Hunt Ltd.*
Zilliacus, Patrick W. — *Larsen, Zilliacus & Associates, Inc.*

## 4. Biotechnology

Abby, Daniel — *Bill Hahn Group, Inc.*
Albers, Joan — *Carver Search Consultants*
Alekel, Karren — *ALW Research International*
Allerton, Donald T. — *Allerton Heneghan & O'Neill*
Altreuter, Rose — *The ALTCO Group*
Ambert, Amadol — *Bryant Research*
Ames, George C. — *Ames O'Neill Associates*
Anderson, Roger J. — *BioQuest, Inc.*
Anderson, Thomas — *Paul J. Biestek Associates, Inc.*
Andrick, Patty — *CPS Inc.*
Arnold, Jerry — *Houtz-Strawn Associates, Inc.*
Aronin, Michael — *Fisher-Todd Associates*
Aston, Kathy — *Marra Peters & Partners*
Atkinson, S. Graham — *Raymond Karsan Associates*
Austin, Jessica L. — *D.S.A. - Dixie Search Associates*
Bachmeier, Kevin — *Agra Placements International Ltd.*
Bailey, William A. — *TNS Partners, Inc.*
Baird, Blaine T. — *Physicians Search, Inc.*
Baker, Gary M. — *Cochran, Cochran & Yale, Inc.*
Balch, Randy — *CPS Inc.*
Baron, Len — *Industrial Recruiters Associates, Inc.*
Bason, Maurice L. — *Bason Associates Inc.*
Bassman, Robert — *Kaye-Bassman International Corp.*
Bassman, Sandy — *Kaye-Bassman International Corp.*
Beaudin, Elizabeth C. — *Callan Associates, Ltd.*
Beckvold, John B. — *Atlantic Search Group, Inc.*
Belford, Paul — *JDG Associates, Ltd.*
Berger, Jay V. — *Morris & Berger*
Besen, Douglas — *Besen Associates Inc.*
Biestek, Paul J. — *Paul J. Biestek Associates, Inc.*
Billotti, Lisa — *Bryant Research*
Blakslee, Jan H. — *J: Blakslee International, Ltd.*
Blanton, Thomas — *Blanton and Company*
Bloomer, James E. — *L.W. Foote Company*
Boccuzi, Joseph H. — *Spencer Stuart*
Borman, Theodore H. — *Lamalie Amrop International*
Bovich, Maryann C. — *Higdon Prince Inc.*
Boyle, Russell E. — *Egon Zehnder International Inc.*
Braak, Diana — *Kincannon & Reed*
Brady, Robert — *CPS Inc.*
Brandeis, Richard — *CPS Inc.*
Brazil, Kathy — *Bryant Research*
Brieger, Steve — *Thorne, Brieger Associates Inc.*
Brooks, Bernard E. — *Mruk & Partners/EMA Partners Int'l*
Brown, Larry C. — *Horton International*
Brown, S. Ross — *Egon Zehnder International Inc.*
Brudno, Robert J. — *Savoy Partners, Ltd.*
Brunelle, Francis W.H. — *The Caldwell Partners Amrop International*
Bryant, Richard D. — *Bryant Associates, Inc.*
Bryant, Thomas — *Bryant Research*
Bryza, Robert M. — *Robert Lowell International*
Burfield, Elaine — *Skott/Edwards Consultants, Inc.*
Burkland, Skott B. — *Skott/Edwards Consultants, Inc.*
Busch, Jack — *Busch International*
Button, David R. — *The Button Group*
Callan, Robert M. — *Callan Associates, Ltd.*
Callihan, Diana L. — *Search Northwest Associates*
Campbell, Robert Scott — *Wellington Management Group*
Campbell, W. Ross — *Egon Zehnder International Inc.*
Carrott, Gregory T. — *Egon Zehnder International Inc.*
Carter, Jon F. — *Egon Zehnder International Inc.*
Cassie, Ronald L. — *The Cassie Group*
Caudill, Nancy — *Webb, Johnson Associates, Inc.*
Cavolina, Michael — *Carver Search Consultants*
Celenza, Catherine — *CPS Inc.*
Chan, Margaret — *Webb, Johnson Associates, Inc.*
Charles, Ronald D. — *The Caldwell Partners Amrop International*
Cherbonnier, L. Michael — *The Cherbonnier Group, Inc.*
Christiansen, Amy — *CPS Inc.*
Christiansen, Doug — *CPS Inc.*
Clark, Elliot H. — *Raymond Karsan Associates*
Clark, James — *CPS Inc.*
Clauhsen, Elizabeth A. — *Savoy Partners, Ltd.*
Cline, Mark — *NYCOR Search, Inc.*
Coleman, John A. — *Canny, Bowen Inc.*
Colucci, Bart A. — *Colucci, Blendow and Johnson, Inc.*
Cottingham, R.L. — *Marvin L. Silcott & Associates, Inc.*
Coulman, Karen — *CPS Inc.*
Cramer, Barbara Lee — *Physicians Search, Inc.*

Crean, Jeremiah N. — *Bryant Research*
Critchley, Walter — *Cochran, Cochran & Yale, Inc.*
Crowell, Elizabeth — *H.M. Long International, Ltd.*
Crumpley, Jim — *Jim Crumpley & Associates*
Cunningham, Robert Y. — *Goodrich & Sherwood Associates, Inc.*
Czepiel, Susan — *CPS Inc.*
Davis, G. Gordon — *Davis & Company*
Deal, Leslie — *Bryant Research*
DeFrancesco, Mary Ellen — *The Onstott Group, Inc.*
Del Prete, Karen — *Gilbert Tweed/INESA*
Delvani-Hart, Angela — *F-O-R-T-U-N-E Personnel Consultants of Nashua, Inc.*
deMartino, Cathy — *Lucas Associates*
Desmond, Dennis — *Beall & Company, Inc.*
DiMarchi, Paul — *DiMarchi Partners, Inc.*
DiSalvo, Fred — *The Cambridge Group Ltd*
Diskin, Rochelle — *Search West, Inc.*
Dixon, Aris — *CPS Inc.*
Do, Sonnie — *Whitney & Associates, Inc.*
Domann, William A. — *The Domann Organization*
Drexler, Robert — *Robert Drexler Associates, Inc.*
Duggan, James P. — *Slayton International, Inc.*
Dulet, Donna — *Bryant Research*
Dwyer, Julie — *CPS Inc.*
Dykstra, Nicolette — *CPS Inc.*
Edwards, Douglas W. — *Egon Zehnder International Inc.*
Einsele, Neil — *Agra Placements International Ltd.*
Erstling, Gregory — *Normyle/Erstling Health Search Group*
Ervin, Darlene — *CPS Inc.*
Erwin, Lee — *Agra Placements International Ltd.*
Fancher, Robert L. — *Bason Associates Inc.*
Feder, Gwen — *Egon Zehnder International Inc.*
Feldman, Kimberley — *Atlantic Search Group, Inc.*
Ferguson, Lauren — *Search West, Inc.*
Ferguson, Robert — *Bill Hahn Group, Inc.*
Ferneborg, Jay W. — *Ferneborg & Associates, Inc.*
Ferneborg, John R. — *Ferneborg & Associates, Inc.*
Fifield, George C. — *Egon Zehnder International Inc.*
Fill, Clifford G. — *D.S.A. - Dixie Search Associates*
Fill, Ellyn H. — *D.S.A. - Dixie Search Associates*
Fischer, John C. — *Horton International*
Fogarty, Michael — *CPS Inc.*
Follmer, Gary — *Agra Placements International Ltd.*
Foote, Leland W. — *L.W. Foote Company*
Ford, Sandra D. — *Phillips & Ford, Inc.*
Foreman, David C. — *Koontz, Jeffries & Associates, Inc.*
Fotino, Anne — *Normyle/Erstling Health Search Group*
Freier, Bruce — *Executive Referral Services, Inc.*
Gabriel, David L. — *The Arcus Group*
Galante, Suzanne M. — *Vlcek & Company, Inc.*
Gale, Rhoda E. — *E.G. Jones Associates, Ltd.*
Garfinkle, Steven M. — *Battalia Winston International*
Geiger, Jan — *Wilcox, Bertoux & Miller*
George, Delores F. — *Delores F. George Human Resource Management & Consulting Industry*
Gerson, Russ D. — *Webb, Johnson Associates, Inc.*
Giles, Joe L. — *Joe L. Giles and Associates, Inc.*
Gillespie, Thomas — *Professional Search Consultants*
Gilmartin, William — *Hockett Associates, Inc.*
Gilmore, Lori — *CPS Inc.*
Gladstone, Arthur — *Executive Referral Services, Inc.*
Gonye, Peter K. — *Egon Zehnder International Inc.*
Goodman, Dawn M. — *Bason Associates Inc.*
Goodman, Victor — *Anderson Sterling Associates*
Graham, Dale — *CPS Inc.*
Granger, Lisa D. — *D.S.A. - Dixie Search Associates*
Grantham, Philip H. — *Columbia Consulting Group*
Grebenstein, Charles R. — *Skott/Edwards Consultants, Inc.*
Grenier, Glorianne — *CPS Inc.*
Grinnell, Janis R. — *Physicians Search, Inc.*
Grzybowski, Jill — *CPS Inc.*
Hahn, William R. — *Bill Hahn Group, Inc.*
Hanson, Grant M. — *Goodrich & Sherwood Associates, Inc.*
Harbaugh, Paul J. — *International Management Advisors, Inc.*
Hardy, Thomas G. — *Spencer Stuart*
Harelick, Arthur S. — *Ashway, Ltd.*
Harfenist, Harry — *Parker Page Group*
Haro, Adolfo Medina — *Egon Zehnder International Inc.*
Hart, Robert T. — *D.E. Foster Partners Inc.*
Hauck, Fred P. — *The Cassie Group*
Hazerjian, Cynthia — *CPS Inc.*
Heafey, Bill — *CPS Inc.*
Hebel, Robert W. — *R.W. Hebel Associates*
Hensley, Gayla — *Atlantic Search Group, Inc.*
Herman, Pat — *Whitney & Associates, Inc.*
Hilliker, Alan D. — *Egon Zehnder International Inc.*
Hockett, William — *Hockett Associates, Inc.*
Hodges, Robert J. — *Sampson Neill & Wilkins Inc.*

Pomerance, Mark — *CPS Inc.*
Pomeroy, T. Lee — *Egon Zehnder International Inc.*
Poster, Lawrence D. — *Catalyx Group*
Prencipe, V. Michael — *Raymond Karsan Associates*
Provus, Barbara L. — *Shepherd Bueschel & Provus, Inc.*
Quick, Roger A. — *Norman Broadbent International, Inc.*
Raheja, Marc C. — *CanMed Consultants Inc.*
Ramler, Carolyn S. — *The Corporate Connection, Ltd.*
Rapoport, William — *Blair/Tech Recruiters*
Rathborne, Kenneth J. — *Blair/Tech Recruiters*
Rauch, Carl W. — *Physicians Search, Inc.*
Rauch, Cliff — *Physicians Search, Inc.*
Ray, Marianne C. — *Callan Associates, Ltd.*
Raymond, Anne — *Anderson Sterling Associates*
Raymond, Jean — *The Caldwell Partners Amrop International*
Redding, Denise — *The Douglas Reiter Company, Inc.*
Reece, Christopher S. — *Reece & Mruk Partners*
Reiter, Douglas — *The Douglas Reiter Company, Inc.*
Rendl, Ric — *CPS Inc.*
Rice, Douglas — *Agra Placements International Ltd.*
Rice, Raymond D. — *Logue & Rice Inc.*
Riederer, Larry — *CPS Inc.*
Rinaldi, Michael D. — *D.P. Parker and Associates*
Rizzo, L. Donald — *R.P. Barone Associates*
Roberts, Nick P. — *Spectrum Search Associates, Inc.*
Roberts, Scott B. — *Wargo and Co., Inc.*
Robins, Jeri N. — *Nagler, Robins & Poe, Inc.*
Robinson, Bruce — *Bruce Robinson Associates*
Rodgers, John — *Agra Placements International Ltd.*
Romanchek, Walter R. — *Wellington Management Group*
Rosen, Salene — *Bryant Research*
Rossi, Silvio — *Keith Bagg & Associates Inc.*
Rotella, Marshall W. — *The Corporate Connection, Ltd.*
Rozner, Burton L. — *Oliver & Rozner Associates, Inc.*
Runquist, U.W. — *Webb, Johnson Associates, Inc.*
Rurak, Zbigniew T. — *Rurak & Associates, Inc.*
Sacerdote, John — *Raymond Karsan Associates*
Sahlas, Chrissy — *CPS Inc.*
Saletra, Andrew — *CPS Inc.*
Sanders, Natalie — *CPS Inc.*
Sathe, Mark A. — *Sathe & Associates, Inc.*
Scalamera, Tom — *CPS Inc.*
Schaad, Carl A. — *Heidrick & Struggles, Inc.*
Schaefer, Robert — *Search Enterprises, Inc.*
Schappell, Marc P. — *Egon Zehnder International Inc.*
Scherck, Henry J. — *Ward Howell International, Inc.*
Schiavone, Mary Rose — *Canny, Bowen Inc.*
Schneider, Perry — *Agra Placements International Ltd.*
Schroeder, Lee — *Blau Kaptain Schroeder*
Schroeder, Steven J. — *Blau Kaptain Schroeder*
Schueneman, David — *CPS Inc.*
Scrivines, Hank — *Search Northwest Associates*
Sevilla, Claudio A. — *Crawford & Crofford*
Shapiro, Elaine — *CPS Inc.*
Shea, Kathleen M. — *The Penn Partners, Incorporated*
Sheedy, Edward J. — *Dieckmann & Associates, Ltd.*
Sherwood, Andrew — *Goodrich & Sherwood Associates, Inc.*
Shultz, Deborah M. — *Blau Kaptain Schroeder*
Sibbald, John R. — *John Sibbald Associates, Inc.*
Signer, Julie — *CPS Inc.*
Silcott, Marvin L. — *Marvin L. Silcott & Associates, Inc.*
Sill, Igor M. — *Geneva Group International*
Sill, Igor M. — *Geneva Group International*
Sjogren, Dennis — *Agra Placements International Ltd.*
Smith, Adam M. — *The Abbott Group, Inc.*
Smith, John F. — *The Penn Partners, Incorporated*
Snyder, James F. — *Snyder & Company*
Sobczak, Ronald — *Search Enterprises, Inc.*
Solomon Ph.D., Neil M. — *The Neil Michael Group, Inc.*
Stein, Terry W. — *Stewart, Stein and Scott, Ltd.*
Stephanian, Armand A. — *Paul Ray Berndtson*
Stern, Stephen — *CPS Inc.*
Sterner, Doug — *CPS Inc.*
Stewart, Jan J. — *Egon Zehnder International Inc.*
Stewart, Jeffrey O. — *Stewart, Stein and Scott, Ltd.*
Stiles, Judy — *MedQuest Associates*
Stouffer, Dale — *Agra Placements International Ltd.*
Stouffer, Kenneth — *Keith Bagg & Associates Inc.*
Stratmeyer, Karin Bergwall — *Princeton Entrepreneurial Resources*
Strawn, William — *Houtz-Strawn Associates, Inc.*
Sullivan, James — *Search Enterprises, Inc.*
Sur, William K. — *Canny, Bowen Inc.*
Swanson, Dick — *Raymond Karsan Associates*
Sweeney, James W. — *Sweeney Harbert & Mummert, Inc.*
Swidler, J. Robert — *Egon Zehnder International Inc.*
Taylor, Kenneth W. — *Egon Zehnder International Inc.*
Theobald, David B. — *Theobald & Associates*
Thielman, Joseph — *Barrett Partners*

Tholke, William E. — *Canny, Bowen Inc.*
Thomas, Cheryl M. — *CPS Inc.*
Thomas, Kim — *CPS Inc.*
Thomas, Terry — *Montague Enterprises*
Tovrog, Dan — *CPS Inc.*
Tracey, Jack — *Management Assistance Group, Inc.*
Tracy, Ronald O. — *Egon Zehnder International Inc.*
Trosin, Walter R. — *Johnson Smith & Knisely Accord*
Trueblood, Brian G. — *TNS Partners, Inc.*
Truemper, Dean — *CPS Inc.*
Tullberg, Tina — *CPS Inc.*
Tweed, Janet — *Gilbert Tweed/INESA*
Twiste, Craig — *Raymond Karsan Associates*
Utroska, Donald R. — *Lamalie Amrop International*
Valenta, Joseph — *Princeton Entrepreneurial Resources*
Vande-Water, Katie — *J. Robert Scott*
Vann, Dianne — *The Button Group*
Vergara, Gail H. — *Spencer Stuart*
Virgili, Franca — *Johnson Smith & Knisely Accord*
Visnich, L. Christine — *Bason Associates Inc.*
Vlcek, Thomas J. — *Vlcek & Company, Inc.*
Webb, George H. — *Webb, Johnson Associates, Inc.*
Weber, Jurgen — *BioQuest, Inc.*
Weiss, Jeffrey — *Search West, Inc.*
Weissman-Rosenthal, Abbe — *ALW Research International*
Weisz, Laura — *Anderson Sterling Associates*
Werner, Bonnie — *H.M. Long International, Ltd.*
White, William C. — *Venture Resources Inc.*
Whitney, David L. — *Whitney & Associates, Inc.*
Wilder, Richard B. — *Columbia Consulting Group*
Wilkinson, Barbara — *Beall & Company, Inc.*
Williams, Angie — *Whitney & Associates, Inc.*
Williams, Roger K. — *Williams, Roth & Krueger Inc.*
Williams, Walter E. — *Canny, Bowen Inc.*
Willis, William H. — *William Willis Worldwide Inc.*
Winitz, Joel — *GSW Consulting Group, Inc.*
Winitz, Marla — *GSW Consulting Group, Inc.*
Winnewisser, William E. — *Accounting & Computer Personnel*
Winograd, Glenn — *Criterion Executive Search, Inc.*
Winston, Susan — *CPS Inc.*
Winter, Peter — *Catalyx Group*
Wolf, Stephen M. — *Byron Leonard International, Inc.*
Wood, John S. — *Egon Zehnder International Inc.*
Woollett, James — *Rusher, Loscavio & LoPresto*
Wyatt, James — *Wyatt & Jaffe*
Wyser-Pratte, Anne — *Heidrick & Struggles, Inc.*
Yard, Allan S. — *Bryant Research*
Yilmaz, Muriel — *Dinte Resources, Incorporated*
Young, Alexander — *Messett Associates, Inc.*
Zila, Laurie M. — *Princeton Entrepreneurial Resources*
Zilliacus, Patrick W. — *Larsen, Zilliacus & Associates, Inc.*
Zingaro, Ron — *Zingaro and Company*
Zivic, Janis M. — *Spencer Stuart*
Zoppo, Dorathea — *Bill Hahn Group, Inc.*

## 5. Board Services

Alekel, Karren — *ALW Research International*
Ambler, Peter W. — *Peter W. Ambler Company*
Anderson, Richard — *Grant Cooper and Associates*
Aubin, Richard E. — *Aubin International*
Aydelotte, G. Thomas — *Ingram & Aydelotte Inc.*
Baillou, Astrid — *Richard Kinser & Associates*
Baran, Helena — *Michael J. Cavanagh and Associates*
Barnes, Richard E. — *Barnes Development Group, LLC*
Barnes, Roanne L. — *Barnes Development Group, LLC*
Barton, Gary R. — *Barton Raben, Inc.*
Bason, Maurice L. — *Bason Associates Inc.*
Bauman, Martin H. — *Martin H. Bauman Associates, Inc.*
Bearman, Linda — *Grant Cooper and Associates*
Bellano, Robert W. — *Stanton Chase International*
Bennett, Jo — *Battalia Winston International*
Berger, Jay V. — *Morris & Berger*
Billington, William H. — *Spriggs & Company, Inc.*
Blakslee, Jan H. — *J: Blakslee International, Ltd.*
Bliley, Jerry — *Spencer Stuart*
Booth, Otis — *A.T. Kearney, Inc.*
Borland, James — *Goodrich & Sherwood Associates, Inc.*
Bourrie, Sharon D. — *Chartwell Partners International, Inc.*
Bovich, Maryann C. — *Higdon Prince Inc.*
Boxberger, Michael D. — *Korn/Ferry International*
Bratches, Howard — *Thorndike Deland Associates*
Brown, Franklin Key — *Handy HRM Corp.*
Brudno, Robert J. — *Savoy Partners, Ltd.*
Buck, Charles — *Charles Buck & Associates*
Bump, Gerald J. — *D.E. Foster Partners Inc.*
Burfield, Elaine — *Skott/Edwards Consultants, Inc.*
Burns, Alan — *The Enns Partners Inc.*
Burns, Terence N. — *D.E. Foster Partners Inc.*

Button, David R. — *The Button Group*
Byrnes, Thomas A. — *Thomas A. Byrnes Associates*
Carey, Dennis C. — *Spencer Stuart*
Carideo, Joseph — *Thorndike Deland Associates*
Casey, Jean — *Peter W. Ambler Company*
Castine, Michael P. — *Spencer Stuart*
Cavanagh, Michael J. — *Michael J. Cavanagh and Associates*
Charles, Ronald D. — *The Caldwell Partners Amrop International*
Chauvin, Ralph A. — *The Caldwell Partners Amrop International*
Cherbonnier, L. Michael — *TCG International, Inc.*
Cherbonnier, L. Michael — *The Cherbonnier Group, Inc.*
Christian, Jeffrey E. — *Christian & Timbers*
Cizek, John T. — *Cizek Associates, Inc.*
Cizek, Marti J. — *Cizek Associates, Inc.*
Clauhsen, Elizabeth A. — *Savoy Partners, Ltd.*
Clement, Norman — *Korn/Ferry International*
Cochran, Hale — *Fenwick Partners*
Collard, Joseph A. — *Spencer Stuart*
Collins, Mollie P. — *Belvedere Partners*
Crath, Paul F. — *Price Waterhouse*
Crist, Peter — *Crist Partners, Ltd.*
Cruse, O.D. — *Spencer Stuart*
Crystal, Jonathan A. — *Spencer Stuart*
Cunningham, Robert Y. — *Goodrich & Sherwood Associates, Inc.*
Daum, Julie — *Spencer Stuart*
DeFrancesco, Mary Ellen — *The Onstott Group, Inc.*
Desmond, Dennis — *Beall & Company, Inc.*
deWilde, David M. — *Chartwell Partners International, Inc.*
Dinwiddie, Jim — *Belvedere Partners*
Divine, Robert S. — *O'Shea, Divine & Company, Inc.*
Doele, Donald C. — *Goodrich & Sherwood Associates, Inc.*
Drury, James J. — *Spencer Stuart*
Edell, David E. — *The Development Resource Group Incorporated*
Eden, Earl M. — *Eden & Associates, Inc.*
England, Mark — *Austin-McGregor International*
Enns, George — *The Enns Partners Inc.*
Fancher, Robert L. — *Bason Associates Inc.*
Farley, Leon A. — *Leon A. Farley Associates*
Farrow, Jerry M. — *McCormack & Farrow*
Fawcett, Anne M. — *The Caldwell Partners Amrop International*
Fee, J. Curtis — *Spencer Stuart*
Ferry, Richard M. — *Korn/Ferry International*
Fisher, Neal — *Fisher Personnel Management Services*
Foote, Ray P. — *Heidrick & Struggles, Inc.*
Gallagher, Terence M. — *Battalia Winston International*
Garfinkle, Steven M. — *Battalia Winston International*
Geiger, Jan — *Wilcox, Bertoux & Miller*
Germaine, Debra — *Fenwick Partners*
Gibbs, John S. — *Spencer Stuart*
Gilbert, Elaine — *Herbert Mines Associates, Inc.*
Gill, Susan — *Plummer & Associates, Inc.*
Gilmartin, William — *Hockett Associates, Inc.*
Goldenberg, Susan — *Grant Cooper and Associates*
Goodman, Dawn M. — *Bason Associates Inc.*
Gow, Roderick C. — *Lamalie Amrop International*
Gray, Annie — *Annie Gray Associates, Inc./The Executive Search Firm*
Greco, Patricia — *Howe-Lewis International*
Griesedieck, Joseph E. — *Spencer Stuart*
Gross, Howard — *Herbert Mines Associates, Inc.*
Hall, Peter V. — *Chartwell Partners International, Inc.*
Hallock, Peter B. — *Goodrich & Sherwood Associates, Inc.*
Hamilton, Timothy — *The Caldwell Partners Amrop International*
Hanson, Grant M. — *Goodrich & Sherwood Associates, Inc.*
Harbert, David O. — *Sweeney Harbert & Mummert, Inc.*
Harvey, Richard — *Price Waterhouse*
Hellinger, Audrey — *Martin H. Bauman Associates, Inc.*
Higdon, Henry G. — *Higdon Prince Inc.*
Hite, William A. — *Hite Executive Search*
Hockett, William — *Hockett Associates, Inc.*
Hoyda, Louis A. — *Thorndike Deland Associates*
Hucko, Donald S. — *Jonas, Walters & Assoc., Inc.*
Ingram, D. John — *Ingram & Aydelotte Inc.*
Issacs, Judith A. — *Grant Cooper and Associates*
Ives, Richard K. — *Wilkinson & Ives*
Jadick, Theodore N. — *Heidrick & Struggles, Inc.*
Jaffe, Mark — *Wyatt & Jaffe*
Joffe, Barry — *Bason Associates Inc.*
Johnson, John F. — *Lamalie Amrop International*
Johnson, Kathleen A. — *Barton Raben, Inc.*
Johnson, Priscilla — *The Johnson Group, Inc.*
Johnson, Ronald S. — *Ronald S. Johnson Associates, Inc.*
Kelly, Claudia L. — *Spencer Stuart*
Kinser, Richard E. — *Richard Kinser & Associates*
Knisely, Gary — *Johnson Smith & Knisely Accord*
Kondra, Vernon J. — *The Douglas Reiter Company, Inc.*
Kossuth, David — *Kossuth & Associates, Inc.*
Kossuth, Jane — *Kossuth & Associates, Inc.*

Kring, Kenneth L. — *Spencer Stuart*
Lasher, Charles M. — *Lasher Associates*
Lautz, Lindsay A. — *Wilkinson & Ives*
Leetma, Imbi — *Stanton Chase International*
Loeb, Stephen H. — *Grant Cooper and Associates*
LoPresto, Robert L. — *Rusher, Loscavio & LoPresto*
Loscavio, J. Michael — *Rusher, Loscavio & LoPresto*
Low, Linda — *The Development Resource Group Incorporated*
Lucarelli, Joan — *The Onstott Group, Inc.*
Lucht, John — *The John Lucht Consultancy Inc.*
MacDougall, Andrew J. — *Spencer Stuart*
Mackenna, Kathy — *Plummer & Associates, Inc.*
Malcolm, Rod — *The Enns Partners Inc.*
Marks, Ira — *Strategic Alternatives*
Marumoto, William H. — *The Interface Group, Ltd./Boyden*
McCallister, Richard A. — *Boyden*
McCann, Cornelia B. — *Spencer Stuart*
McCarthy, David R. — *Spencer Stuart*
McCormack, Joseph A. — *McCormack & Associates*
McCreary, Charles — *Austin-McGregor International*
McGuire, Corey — *Peter W. Ambler Company*
McKinnis, Paul D. — *Paul Ray Berndtson*
McLean, B. Keith — *Price Waterhouse*
McMillin, Bob — *Price Waterhouse*
McNamara, Timothy C. — *Columbia Consulting Group*
McSherry, James F. — *Battalia Winston International*
Meany, Brian — *Herbert Mines Associates, Inc.*
Meier, J. Dale — *Grant Cooper and Associates*
Menk, Carl W. — *Canny, Bowen Inc.*
Miller, Diane D. — *Wilcox, Bertoux & Miller*
Miller, Roy — *The Enns Partners Inc.*
Mines, Herbert T. — *Herbert Mines Associates, Inc.*
Mirtz, P. John — *Mirtz Morice, Inc.*
Molnar, Robert A. — *Johnson Smith & Knisely Accord*
Morice, James L. — *Mirtz Morice, Inc.*
Morris, Kristine A. — *Morris & Berger*
Morton, Robert C. — *Morton, McCorkle & Associates, Inc.*
Mruk, Edwin S. — *Mruk & Partners/EMA Partners Int'l*
Murphy, Cornelius J. — *Goodrich & Sherwood Associates, Inc.*
Murphy, Patrick J. — *P.J. Murphy & Associates, Inc.*
Mursuli, Meredith — *Lasher Associates*
Mustin, Joyce M. — *J: Blakslee International, Ltd.*
Nahas, Caroline W. — *Korn/Ferry International*
Nahas, Robert — *Herbert Mines Associates, Inc.*
Neff, Thomas J. — *Spencer Stuart*
Neher, Robert L. — *Intech Summit Group, Inc.*
Neuberth, Jeffrey G. — *Canny, Bowen Inc.*
Norman, Randy — *Austin-McGregor International*
O'Brien, Anne Lim — *Heidrick & Struggles, Inc.*
O'Hara, Daniel M. — *Lynch Miller Moore Partners, Inc.*
O'Reilly, Jack — *Catalyx Group*
Ogden, Dayton — *Spencer Stuart*
Ogdon, Thomas H. — *The Ogdon Partnership*
Onstott, Joseph E. — *The Onstott Group, Inc.*
Ott, George W. — *Ott & Hansen, Inc.*
Palma, Frank R. — *Goodrich & Sherwood Associates, Inc.*
Palmer, Carlton A. — *Beall & Company, Inc.*
Pearson, Robert L. — *Lamalie Amrop International*
Peck, David W. — *The Peck Consultancy*
Pettibone, Linda — *Herbert Mines Associates, Inc.*
Pettway, Samuel H. — *Spencer Stuart*
Pfeiffer, Irene — *Price Waterhouse*
Phelps, Gene L. — *McCormack & Farrow*
Phillips, Donald L. — *O'Shea, Divine & Company, Inc.*
Pinkman, Karen N. — *Skott/Edwards Consultants, Inc.*
Plummer, John — *Plummer & Associates, Inc.*
Polachi, Charles A. — *Fenwick Partners*
Polachi, Peter V. — *Fenwick Partners*
Porter, Ken — *Tourism Development International*
Poster, Lawrence D. — *Catalyx Group*
Preschlack, Jack E. — *Spencer Stuart*
Price, Andrew G. — *The Thomas Tucker Company*
Proct, Nina — *Martin H. Bauman Associates, Inc.*
Rabinowitz, Peter A. — *P.A.R. Associates Inc.*
Ray, Paul R. — *Paul Ray Berndtson*
Redding, Denise — *The Douglas Reiter Company, Inc.*
Reece, Christopher S. — *Reece & Mruk Partners*
Reeves, William B. — *Spencer Stuart*
Reiser, Ellen — *Thorndike Deland Associates*
Reiter, Douglas — *The Douglas Reiter Company, Inc.*
Reiter, Harold D. — *Herbert Mines Associates, Inc.*
Rice, Raymond D. — *Logue & Rice Inc.*
Rieger, Louis J. — *Spencer Stuart*
Robinson, Bruce — *Bruce Robinson Associates*
Rosenberg, Esther — *Howe-Lewis International*
Roth, Robert J. — *Williams, Roth & Krueger Inc.*
Rowe, William D. — *D.E. Foster Partners Inc.*
Russell, Susan Anne — *Executive Search Consultants Corporation*

Sampson, Martin C. — *Sampson Neill & Wilkins Inc.*
Sanders, Spencer H. — *Battalia Winston International*
Savage, Edward J. — *Stanton Chase International*
Schiavone, Mary Rose — *Canny, Bowen Inc.*
Schmidt, Peter R. — *Boyden*
Seebeck, Robert F. — *Russell Reynolds Associates, Inc.*
Selker, Gregory L. — *Christian & Timbers*
Semyan, John K. — *TNS Partners, Inc.*
Serwat, Leonard A. — *Spencer Stuart*
Shepherd, Daniel M. — *Shepherd Bueschel & Provus, Inc.*
Sherwood, Andrew — *Goodrich & Sherwood Associates, Inc.*
Sibbald, John R. — *John Sibbald Associates, Inc.*
Sill, Igor M. — *Geneva Group International*
Sill, Igor M. — *Geneva Group International*
Simmons, Gerald J. — *Handy HRM Corp.*
Slayton, Richard C. — *Slayton International, Inc.*
Smith, Adam M. — *The Abbott Group, Inc.*
Smith, David P. — *Smith & Latterell (HRS, Inc.)*
Snyder, James F. — *Snyder & Company*
Spann, Richard E. — *Goodrich & Sherwood Associates, Inc.*
Spitz, Grant — *The Caldwell Partners Amrop International*
Stanley, Paul R.A. — *Lovas Stanley/Paul Ray Berndtson Inc.*
Starner, William S. — *Fenwick Partners*
Stenholm, Gilbert R. — *Spencer Stuart*
Stewart, Ross M. — *Human Resources Network Partners Inc.*
Stinson, R.J. — *Sampson Neill & Wilkins Inc.*
Stivk, Barbara A. — *Thornton Resources*
Stringer, Dann P. — *D.E. Foster Partners Inc.*
Sur, William K. — *Canny, Bowen Inc.*
Sweet, Charles W. — *A.T. Kearney, Inc.*
Tholke, William E. — *Canny, Bowen Inc.*
Thomas, Kurt J. — *P.J. Murphy & Associates, Inc.*
Thomas, Terry — *Montague Enterprises*
Thornton, John C. — *Thornton Resources*
Tucker, Thomas A. — *The Thomas Tucker Company*
Tunney, William — *Grant Cooper and Associates*
Vann, Dianne — *The Button Group*
Venable, William W. — *Thorndike Deland Associates*
Vennat, Manon — *Spencer Stuart*
Vergari, Jane — *Herbert Mines Associates, Inc.*
Visnich, L. Christine — *Bason Associates Inc.*
von Stein, Scott — *Wilkinson & Ives*
Waldoch, D. Mark — *Barnes Development Group, LLC*
Walker, Ronald H. — *Korn/Ferry International*
Warren, Sylvia W. — *Thorndike Deland Associates*
Weissman-Rosenthal, Abbe — *ALW Research International*
Wier, Daniel — *Horton International*
Wilcox, Fred T. — *Wilcox, Bertoux & Miller*
Wilkinson, Barbara — *Beall & Company, Inc.*
Wilkinson, William R. — *Wilkinson & Ives*
Williams, Gary L. — *Barnes Development Group, LLC*
Williams, Roger K. — *Williams, Roth & Krueger Inc.*
Willis, William H. — *William Willis Worldwide Inc.*
Wilson, Derrick — *Thornton Resources*
Wilson, Patricia L. — *Leon A. Farley Associates*
Winston, Dale — *Battalia Winston International*
Wright, Charles D. — *Goodrich & Sherwood Associates, Inc.*
Wyatt, James — *Wyatt & Jaffe*
Zaffrann, Craig S. — *P.J. Murphy & Associates, Inc.*
Zahradka, James F. — *P.J. Murphy & Associates, Inc.*
Zak, Adam — *Adams & Associates International*
Zivic, Janis M. — *Spencer Stuart*

## 6. Chemical Products

Abbott, Peter — *The Abbott Group, Inc.*
Ainsworth, Lawrence — *Search West, Inc.*
Alekel, Karren — *ALW Research International*
Altreuter, Rose — *The ALTCO Group*
Ambler, Peter W. — *Peter W. Ambler Company*
Anderson, Thomas — *Paul J. Biestek Associates, Inc.*
Andrick, Patty — *CPS Inc.*
Angell, Tryg R. — *Tryg R. Angell Ltd.*
Apostle, George — *Search Dynamics, Inc.*
Arms, Douglas — *TOPAZ International, Inc.*
Arms, Douglas — *TOPAZ Legal Solutions*
Aslaksen, James G. — *Lamalie Amrop International*
Asquith, Peter S. — *Ames Personnel Consultants, Inc.*
Atkinson, S. Graham — *Raymond Karsan Associates*
Bachmeier, Kevin — *Agra Placements International Ltd.*
Bagg, Keith — *Keith Bagg & Associates Inc.*
Bailey, David O. — *Paul Ray Berndtson*
Baird, David W. — *D.W. Baird & Associates*
Baird, John — *Professional Search Consultants*
Baitler, Simon C. — *The Stevenson Group of Delaware Inc.*
Baker, Judith — *Search Consultants International, Inc.*
Baker, S. Joseph — *Search Consultants International, Inc.*
Balch, Randy — *CPS Inc.*
Baldwin, Keith R. — *The Baldwin Group*

Barlow, Ken H. — *The Cherbonnier Group, Inc.*
Barnes, Richard E. — *Barnes Development Group, LLC*
Barnes, Roanne L. — *Barnes Development Group, LLC*
Baron, Len — *Industrial Recruiters Associates, Inc.*
Bason, Maurice L. — *Bason Associates Inc.*
Bassman, Robert — *Kaye-Bassman International Corp.*
Bassman, Sandy — *Kaye-Bassman International Corp.*
Battalia, O. William — *Battalia Winston International*
Bauman, Martin H. — *Martin H. Bauman Associates, Inc.*
Beaudin, Elizabeth C. — *Callan Associates, Ltd.*
Beaver, Bentley H. — *The Onstott Group, Inc.*
Beaver, Robert W. — *Executive Manning Corporation*
Bennett, Jo — *Battalia Winston International*
Berger, Jay V. — *Morris & Berger*
Bermea, Jose — *Gaffney Management Consultants*
Berry, Harold B. — *The Hindman Company*
Besen, Douglas — *Besen Associates Inc.*
Biestek, Paul J. — *Paul J. Biestek Associates, Inc.*
Blanton, Thomas — *Blanton and Company*
Borland, James — *Goodrich & Sherwood Associates, Inc.*
Borman, Theodore H. — *Lamalie Amrop International*
Bostic, James E. — *Phillips Resource Group*
Boyer, Heath C. — *Spencer Stuart*
Brackenbury, Robert — *Bowman & Marshall, Inc.*
Brackin, James B. — *Brackin & Sayers Associates*
Brady, Colin S. — *Ward Howell International, Inc.*
Brady, Robert — *CPS Inc.*
Brandeis, Richard — *CPS Inc.*
Brentari, Michael — *Search Consultants International, Inc.*
Brieger, Steve — *Thorne, Brieger Associates Inc.*
Briggs, Adam — *Horton International*
Brocaglia, Joyce — *Alta Associates, Inc.*
Brown, Larry C. — *Horton International*
Bruno, Deborah F. — *The Hindman Company*
Bryant, Richard D. — *Bryant Associates, Inc.*
Bryza, Robert M. — *Robert Lowell International*
Budill, Edward — *Professional Search Consultants*
Burchill, Greg — *BGB Associates*
Burden, Gene — *The Cherbonnier Group, Inc.*
Burfield, Elaine — *Skott/Edwards Consultants, Inc.*
Burris, James C. — *Boyden*
Cahill, Peter M. — *Peter M. Cahill Associates, Inc.*
Callan, Robert M. — *Callan Associates, Ltd.*
Campbell, Robert Scott — *Wellington Management Group*
Carlson, Judith — *Bowman & Marshall, Inc.*
Casey, Jean — *Peter W. Ambler Company*
Cast, Donald — *Dunhill Search International*
Caudill, Nancy — *Webb, Johnson Associates, Inc.*
Celenza, Catherine — *CPS Inc.*
Chan, Margaret — *Webb, Johnson Associates, Inc.*
Chargar, Frances — *Hunt Ltd.*
Chauvin, Ralph A. — *The Caldwell Partners Amrop International*
Chavous, C. Crawford — *Phillips Resource Group*
Cherbonnier, L. Michael — *TCG International, Inc.*
Cherbonnier, L. Michael — *The Cherbonnier Group, Inc.*
Christiansen, Amy — *CPS Inc.*
Christiansen, Doug — *CPS Inc.*
Clarey, William A. — *Preng & Associates, Inc.*
Clark, James — *CPS Inc.*
Cline, Mark — *NYCOR Search, Inc.*
Cohen, Pamela — *TOPAZ International, Inc.*
Cohen, Pamela — *TOPAZ Legal Solutions*
Collard, Joseph A. — *Spencer Stuart*
Collis, Martin — *E.L. Shore & Associates Ltd.*
Connaghan, Linda — *Bowman & Marshall, Inc.*
Conway, William P. — *Phillips Resource Group*
Costello, Andrea L. — *Gallin Associates*
Costello, Jack — *Gallin Associates*
Cottingham, R.L. — *Marvin L. Silcott & Associates, Inc.*
Coulman, Karen — *CPS Inc.*
Crist, Peter — *Crist Partners, Ltd.*
Cronin, Richard J. — *Hodge-Cronin & Associates, Inc.*
Cruz, Catherine — *TOPAZ International, Inc.*
Cruz, Catherine — *TOPAZ Legal Solutions*
Cummings, Harry J. — *Sanford Rose Associates*
Cunningham, Robert Y. — *Goodrich & Sherwood Associates, Inc.*
Cuomo, Frank — *Frank Cuomo and Associates, Inc.*
Czamanske, Paul W. — *Compass Group Ltd.*
Czepiel, Susan — *CPS Inc.*
Dabich, Thomas M. — *Robert Harkins Associates, Inc.*
Danforth, Monica — *Search Consultants International, Inc.*
Daniel, Beverly — *Foy, Schneid & Daniel, Inc.*
Davis, G. Gordon — *Davis & Company*
de Palacios, Jeannette C. — *J. Palacios & Associates, Inc.*
DeFrancesco, Mary Ellen — *The Onstott Group, Inc.*
Del Prete, Karen — *Gilbert Tweed/INESA*
DeLong, Art — *Richard Kader & Associates*
deMartino, Cathy — *Lucas Associates*

Desgrosellier, Gary P. — *Personnel Unlimited/Executive Search*
Dickey, Chet W. — *Bowden & Company, Inc.*
Dieck, Daniel W. — *Dieck, Mueller & Associates, Inc.*
DiGiovanni, Charles — *Penn Search*
DiMarchi, Paul — *DiMarchi Partners, Inc.*
Diskin, Rochelle — *Search West, Inc.*
Divine, Robert S. — *O'Shea, Divine & Company, Inc.*
Dixon, Aris — *CPS Inc.*
Doele, Donald C. — *Goodrich & Sherwood Associates, Inc.*
Dreifus, Donald — *Search West, Inc.*
Drexler, Robert — *Robert Drexler Associates, Inc.*
Dudley, Robert — *Sanford Rose Associates*
Dugan, John H. — *J.H. Dugan and Associates, Inc.*
Dwyer, Julie — *CPS Inc.*
Dykstra, Nicolette — *CPS Inc.*
Eason, James — *JRL Executive Recruiters*
Eason, Larry E. — *JRL Executive Recruiters*
Edmond, Bruce — *Corporate Recruiters Ltd.*
Eggena, Roger — *Phillips Resource Group*
Ehrhart, Jennifer — *ADOW's Executeam*
Einsele, Neil — *Agra Placements International Ltd.*
Ellis, Ted K. — *The Hindman Company*
Enfield, Jerry J. — *Executive Manning Corporation*
England, Mark — *Austin-McGregor International*
Ervin, Darlene — *CPS Inc.*
Erwin, Lee — *Agra Placements International Ltd.*
Faber, Jill — *A.T. Kearney, Inc.*
Fancher, Robert L. — *Bason Associates Inc.*
Fiore, Richard — *Search Consultants International, Inc.*
Fischer, John C. — *Horton International*
Flora, Dodi — *Crawford & Crofford*
Fogarty, Michael — *CPS Inc.*
Folkerth, Gene — *Gene Folkerth & Associates, Inc.*
Follmer, Gary — *Agra Placements International Ltd.*
Foreman, David C. — *Koontz, Jeffries & Associates, Inc.*
Forman, Donald R. — *Stanton Chase International*
Foster, Dwight E. — *D.E. Foster Partners Inc.*
French, William G. — *Preng & Associates, Inc.*
Gabriel, David L. — *The Arcus Group*
Gaffney, Keith — *Gaffney Management Consultants*
Gaffney, William — *Gaffney Management Consultants*
Gaines, Ronni L. — *TOPAZ International, Inc.*
Gaines, Ronni L. — *TOPAZ Legal Solutions*
Galante, Suzanne M. — *Vlcek & Company, Inc.*
Gallagher, Marilyn — *Hogan Acquisitions*
Gallagher, Terence M. — *Battalia Winston International*
Gallin, Larry — *Gallin Associates*
Gardiner, E. Nicholas P. — *Gardiner International*
Garfinkle, Steven M. — *Battalia Winston International*
Gerber, Mark J. — *Wellington Management Group*
Gerson, Russ D. — *Webb, Johnson Associates, Inc.*
Gettys, James R. — *International Staffing Consultants, Inc.*
Gilchrist, Robert J. — *Horton International*
Gillespie, Thomas — *Professional Search Consultants*
Gilmore, Lori — *CPS Inc.*
Gobert, Larry — *Professional Search Consultants*
Goebel, George A. — *John Kurosky & Associates*
Goldenberg, Susan — *Grant Cooper and Associates*
Goldman, Michael L. — *Strategic Associates, Inc.*
Goodman, Dawn M. — *Bason Associates Inc.*
Gorfinkle, Gayle — *Executive Search International*
Grady, James — *Search West, Inc.*
Graham, Dale — *CPS Inc.*
Grantham, John — *Grantham & Co., Inc.*
Grassl, Peter O. — *Bowman & Marshall, Inc.*
Grebenstein, Charles R. — *Skott/Edwards Consultants, Inc.*
Green, Jane — *Phillips Resource Group*
Green, Jean — *Broward-Dobbs, Inc.*
Greene, Luke — *Broward-Dobbs, Inc.*
Grenier, Glorianne — *CPS Inc.*
Grzybowski, Jill — *CPS Inc.*
Hall, Barbara — *Don Richard Associates of Tidewater, Inc.*
Hallock, Peter B. — *Goodrich & Sherwood Associates, Inc.*
Hammes, Betsy — *Search Enterprises, Inc.*
Hansen, David G. — *Ott & Hansen, Inc.*
Hanson, Grant M. — *Goodrich & Sherwood Associates, Inc.*
Harbaugh, Paul J. — *International Management Advisors, Inc.*
Hardison, Richard L. — *Hardison & Company*
Harkins, Robert E. — *Robert Harkins Associates, Inc.*
Harris, Jack — *Baker, Harris & Partners Limited*
Harrison, Priscilla — *Phillips Resource Group*
Harshman, Donald — *The Stevenson Group of New Jersey*
Hart, Robert T. — *D.E. Foster Partners Inc.*
Harvey, Mike — *Advanced Executive Resources*
Haughton, Michael — *DeFrain, Mayer, Lee & Burgess LLC*
Havener, Donald Clarke — *The Abbott Group, Inc.*
Haystead, Steve — *Advanced Executive Resources*
Hazerjian, Cynthia — *CPS Inc.*

Heafey, Bill — *CPS Inc.*
Hecker, Henry C. — *Hogan Acquisitions*
Heller, Steven A. — *Martin H. Bauman Associates, Inc.*
Hellinger, Audrey — *Martin H. Bauman Associates, Inc.*
Hertan, Richard L. — *Executive Manning Corporation*
Hertan, Wiliam A. — *Executive Manning Corporation*
Hertlein, James N.J. — *Boyden/Zay & Company*
Hicks, Albert M. — *Phillips Resource Group*
Hillyer, Robert L. — *Executive Manning Corporation*
Hindman, Neil C. — *The Hindman Company*
Hogan, Edward — *Sanford Rose Associates*
Hogan, Larry H. — *Hogan Acquisitions*
Holden, Richard B. — *Ames Personnel Consultants, Inc.*
Holland, Kathleen — *TOPAZ International, Inc.*
Holland, Kathleen — *TOPAZ Legal Solutions*
Holodnak, William A. — *J. Robert Scott*
Holtz, Gene — *Agra Placements International Ltd.*
Horton, Robert H. — *Horton International*
Hudson, Kevin — *Raymond Karsan Associates*
Hughes, James J. — *R.P. Barone Associates*
Hunter, Gabe — *Phillips Resource Group*
Hutchinson, Loretta M. — *Hutchinson Resources International*
Hykes, Don A. — *A.T. Kearney, Inc.*
Iacovelli, Heather — *CPS Inc.*
Iammatteo, Enzo — *Keith Bagg & Associates Inc.*
Inzinna, Dennis — *AlternaStaff*
Irish, Alan — *CPS Inc.*
Irvine, Robert — *Keith Bagg & Associates Inc.*
Jablo, Steven — *Dieckmann & Associates, Ltd.*
Jackowitz, Todd — *J. Robert Scott*
Jacobs, Martin J. — *The Rubicon Group*
Jacobs, Mike — *Thorne, Brieger Associates Inc.*
Jacobson, Donald — *Hunt Advisory Services*
Jacobson, Donald — *Hunt Ltd.*
James, Bruce — *Roberson and Company*
Jensen, Stephanie — *Don Richard Associates of Tidewater, Inc.*
Joffe, Barry — *Bason Associates Inc.*
Johnson, Douglas — *Quality Search*
Johnson, John W. — *Webb, Johnson Associates, Inc.*
Johnson, Robert J. — *Quality Search*
Johnston, James R. — *The Stevenson Group of Delaware Inc.*
Jones, Barbara J. — *Kaye-Bassman International Corp.*
Jones, Gary — *BGB Associates*
Kader, Richard — *Richard Kader & Associates*
Kaiser, Donald J. — *Dunhill Search International*
Kaiser, Irene — *Dunhill Search International*
Kaiser, James G. — *Dunhill Search International*
Kanrich, Susan Azaria — *AlternaStaff*
Karalis, William — *CPS Inc.*
Kaye, Jeffrey — *Kaye-Bassman International Corp.*
Keesom, W. Peter — *Boyden/Zay & Company*
Keeton, Susan G. — *The Corporate Connection, Ltd.*
Kehoe, Mike — *CPS Inc.*
Keitel, Robert S. — *A.T. Kearney, Inc.*
Kelly, Elizabeth Ann — *Wellington Management Group*
Keogh, James — *Sanford Rose Associates*
Kern, Jerry L. — *ADOW's Executeam*
Kern, Kathleen G. — *ADOW's Executeam*
Kerr, John — *Search West, Inc.*
Kilcoyne, Pat — *CPS Inc.*
Kinser, Richard E. — *Richard Kinser & Associates*
Kirkpatrick, Robert L. — *Reese Associates*
Kishbaugh, Herbert S. — *Kishbaugh Associates International*
Kkorzyniewski, Nicole — *CPS Inc.*
Klages, Constance W. — *International Management Advisors, Inc.*
Klauck, James J. — *Horton International*
Klumpjan, Sonja — *CPS Inc.*
Koehler, Frank R. — *The Koehler Group*
Kohn, Adam P. — *Christian & Timbers*
Kolke, Rick — *Richard, Wayne and Roberts*
Koontz, Donald N. — *Koontz, Jeffries & Associates, Inc.*
Kopsick, Joseph M. — *Spencer Stuart*
Kotick, Madeline — *The Stevenson Group of New Jersey*
Krohn, Eileen — *The Stevenson Group of New Jersey*
Laird, Cheryl — *CPS Inc.*
Lamb, Angus K. — *Raymond Karsan Associates*
Langer, Joel A. — *Langer Associates, Inc.*
Lapat, Aaron D. — *J. Robert Scott*
Lauderback, David R. — *A.T. Kearney, Inc.*
Lawrence, David — *Agra Placements International Ltd.*
Leahy, Jan — *CPS Inc.*
Lebo, Terry — *Agra Placements International Ltd.*
LemMou, Paul — *International Staffing Consultants, Inc.*
Leslie, William H. — *Boyden/Zay & Company*
Lindenmuth, Mary — *Search West, Inc.*
Line, Joseph T. — *Sharrow & Associates*
Lipe, Jerold L. — *Compass Group Ltd.*
Little, Gary — *Agra Placements International Ltd.*

Livingston, Peter R. — *Livingston, Robert and Company Inc.*
Lofthouse, Cindy — *CPS Inc.*
Long, William G. — *McDonald, Long & Associates, Inc.*
Loria, Frank — *Accounting Personnel Consultants*
Loscavio, J. Michael — *Rusher, Loscavio & LoPresto*
Lotufo, Donald A. — *D.A.L. Associates, Inc.*
Lotz, R. James — *International Management Advisors, Inc.*
Lovely, Edward — *The Stevenson Group of New Jersey*
Lucht, John — *The John Lucht Consultancy Inc.*
Lumsby, George N. — *International Management Advisors, Inc.*
Lynn, Donald — *Frank Cuomo and Associates, Inc.*
MacDougall, Andrew J. — *Spencer Stuart*
MacEachern, David — *Spencer Stuart*
Magee, Charles R. — *Dieck, Mueller & Associates, Inc.*
Magee, Harrison R. — *Bowden & Company, Inc.*
Magnani, Susan — *The Search Center Inc.*
Makrianes, James K. — *Webb, Johnson Associates, Inc.*
Mallipudi, Anand — *Raymond Karsan Associates*
Manassero, Henri J.P. — *International Management Advisors, Inc.*
Mangum, William T. — *Thomas Mangum Company*
Manns, Alex — *Crawford & Crofford*
Maphet, Harriet — *The Stevenson Group of New Jersey*
Marks, Russell E. — *Webb, Johnson Associates, Inc.*
Marshall, Gerald — *Blair/Tech Recruiters*
Martin, Ellen — *Hunt Ltd.*
Martines, James — *Sharrow & Associates*
Mashakas, Elizabeth — *TOPAZ International, Inc.*
Mashakas, Elizabeth — *TOPAZ Legal Solutions*
Mason, William E. — *John Kurosky & Associates*
Massey, H. Heath — *Robison & Associates*
Mathias, William J. — *Preng & Associates, Inc.*
McAndrews, Kathy — *CPS Inc.*
McCabe, Christopher — *Raymond Karsan Associates*
McCorkle, Sam B. — *Morton, McCorkle & Associates, Inc.*
McCreary, Charles — *Austin-McGregor International*
McDonald, Gary E. — *Agra Placements International Ltd.*
McDonnell, Julie — *Technical Personnel of Minnesota*
McEwan, Paul — *Richard, Wayne and Roberts*
McGrath, Robert E. — *Robert E. McGrath & Associates*
McGuire, Bud — *Search West, Inc.*
McGuire, Corey — *Peter W. Ambler Company*
McIntyre, Joel — *Phillips Resource Group*
McLean, B. Keith — *Price Waterhouse*
McNear, Jeffrey E. — *Barrett Partners*
McSherry, James F. — *Battalia Winston International*
Mefford, Bob — *Executive Manning Corporation*
Messett, William J. — *Messett Associates, Inc.*
Metz, Alex — *Hunt Ltd.*
Meyer, William — *Agra Placements International Ltd.*
Michaels, Joseph — *CPS Inc.*
Michaels, Stewart — *TOPAZ International, Inc.*
Michaels, Stewart — *TOPAZ Legal Solutions*
Mierzwinski, John — *Industrial Recruiters Associates, Inc.*
Mirtz, P. John — *Mirtz Morice, Inc.*
Mitton, Bill — *Executive Resource, Inc.*
Moerbe, Ed H. — *Stanton Chase International*
Mohr, Brian — *CPS Inc.*
Molitor, John L. — *Barrett Partners*
Molnar, Robert A. — *Johnson Smith & Knisely Accord*
Moore, Mark — *Wheeler, Moore & Elam Co.*
Moore, Michael — *Agra Placements International Ltd.*
Moran, Robert — *A.T. Kearney, Inc.*
Morice, James L. — *Mirtz Morice, Inc.*
Morris, Kristine A. — *Morris & Berger*
Morton, Robert C. — *Morton, McCorkle & Associates, Inc.*
Mueller, Michael S. — *Dieck, Mueller & Associates, Inc.*
Muendel, H. Edward — *Stanton Chase International*
Mulligan, Robert P. — *William Willis Worldwide Inc.*
Murphy, Cornelius J. — *Goodrich & Sherwood Associates, Inc.*
Mydlach, Renee — *CPS Inc.*
Nadherny, Christopher C. — *Spencer Stuart*
Nagler, Leon G. — *Nagler, Robins & Poe, Inc.*
Napier, Ginger L. — *Preng & Associates, Inc.*
Newbold, Michael — *Agra Placements International Ltd.*
Newman, Lynn — *Kishbaugh Associates International*
Noll, Robert J. — *The Hindman Company*
Nordland, Martin N. — *Horton International*
Norman, Randy — *Austin-McGregor International*
Nutter, Roger — *Raymond Karsan Associates*
Nymark, John — *NYCOR Search, Inc.*
Nymark, Paul — *NYCOR Search, Inc.*
O'Connell, Mary — *CPS Inc.*
Oakes, Meg B. — *D.P. Parker and Associates*
Olsen, David — *Search Enterprises South, Inc.*
Onstott, Joseph E. — *The Onstott Group, Inc.*
Ottenritter, Chris — *CPS Inc.*
Pace, Susan A. — *Horton International*
Pacini, Lauren R. — *Hite Executive Search*

Palma, Frank R. — *Goodrich & Sherwood Associates, Inc.*
Palmer, James H. — *The Hindman Company*
Pappas, Jim — *Search Dynamics, Inc.*
Pappas, Timothy C. — *Jonas, Walters & Assoc., Inc.*
Parker, David P. — *D.P. Parker and Associates*
Parker, Murray B. — *The Borton Wallace Company*
Parry, William H. — *Horton International*
Pedley, Jill — *CPS Inc.*
Perkins, Bob — *Richard, Wayne and Roberts*
Perkins, Daphne — *CPS Inc.*
Peters, James N. — *TNS Partners, Inc.*
Peterson, John — *CPS Inc.*
Petty, J. Scott — *The Arcus Group*
Pfeiffer, Irene — *Price Waterhouse*
Phillips, Bill — *Dunhill Search International*
Pickering, Dale — *Agri-Tech Personnel, Inc.*
Pinson, Stephanie L. — *Gilbert Tweed/INESA*
Pitts, Charles — *Contemporary Management Services, Inc.*
Polacek, Frank — *Search Enterprises South, Inc.*
Pomerance, Mark — *CPS Inc.*
Poore, Larry D. — *Ward Howell International, Inc.*
Porada, Stephen D. — *CAP Inc.*
Porter, Nanci — *Eastridge InfoTech*
Potter, Douglas C. — *Stanton Chase International*
Prencipe, V. Michael — *Raymond Karsan Associates*
Preng, David E. — *Preng & Associates, Inc.*
Proct, Nina — *Martin H. Bauman Associates, Inc.*
Prosser, Shane — *Search Consultants International, Inc.*
Pugliese, Vincent — *Search West, Inc.*
Rabe, William — *Sales Executives Inc.*
Rapoport, William — *Blair/Tech Recruiters*
Rathborne, Kenneth J. — *Blair/Tech Recruiters*
Ray, Marianne C. — *Callan Associates, Ltd.*
Rendl, Ric — *CPS Inc.*
Rice, Douglas — *Agra Placements International Ltd.*
Riederer, Larry — *CPS Inc.*
Rieger, Louis J. — *Spencer Stuart*
Riley, James — *Hunt Ltd.*
Rimmel, James E. — *The Hindman Company*
Rinaldi, Michael D. — *D.P. Parker and Associates*
Rizzo, L. Donald — *R.P. Barone Associates*
Roberts, Clifford — *Search Enterprises, Inc.*
Roberts, William — *Cochran, Cochran & Yale, Inc.*
Robins, Jeri N. — *Nagler, Robins & Poe, Inc.*
Robinson, Bruce — *Bruce Robinson Associates*
Robinson, Eric B. — *Bruce Robinson Associates*
Rodgers, John — *Agra Placements International Ltd.*
Romanchek, Walter R. — *Wellington Management Group*
Ropella, Patrick B. — *Ropella & Associates*
Rossi, Silvio — *Keith Bagg & Associates Inc.*
Rozner, Burton L. — *Oliver & Rozner Associates, Inc.*
Runge, Gary — *Search Enterprises South, Inc.*
Runquist, U.W. — *Webb, Johnson Associates, Inc.*
Sabat, Lori S. — *Alta Associates, Inc.*
Sacerdote, John — *Raymond Karsan Associates*
Sahlas, Chrissy — *CPS Inc.*
Saletra, Andrew — *CPS Inc.*
Sandbloom, Kenneth — *Search Enterprises South, Inc.*
Sanders, Natalie — *CPS Inc.*
Sanders, Spencer H. — *Battalia Winston International*
Savard, Robert F. — *The Stevenson Group of Delaware Inc.*
Sayers, Bruce D. — *Brackin & Sayers Associates*
Scalamera, Tom — *CPS Inc.*
Schaefer, Frederic M. — *A.T. Kearney, Inc.*
Scherck, Henry J. — *Ward Howell International, Inc.*
Schiavone, Mary Rose — *Canny, Bowen Inc.*
Schlpma, Christine — *Advanced Executive Resources*
Schneider, Perry — *Agra Placements International Ltd.*
Schueneman, David — *CPS Inc.*
Schwartz, Carole — *A.T. Kearney, Inc.*
Scrivines, Hank — *Search Northwest Associates*
Selko, Philip W. — *Hogan Acquisitions*
Sevilla, Claudio A. — *Crawford & Crofford*
Shapiro, Elaine — *CPS Inc.*
Shea, Kathleen M. — *The Penn Partners, Incorporated*
Shepherd, Daniel M. — *Shepherd Bueschel & Provus, Inc.*
Sherwood, Andrew — *Goodrich & Sherwood Associates, Inc.*
Shore, Earl L. — *E.L. Shore & Associates Ltd.*
Sibbald, John R. — *John Sibbald Associates, Inc.*
Signer, Julie — *CPS Inc.*
Silcott, Marvin L. — *Marvin L. Silcott & Associates, Inc.*
Silvas, Stephen D. — *Roberson and Company*
Silver, Lee A. — *L.A. Silver Associates, Inc.*
Simmons, Gerald J. — *Handy HRM Corp.*
Sjogren, Dennis — *Agra Placements International Ltd.*
Slater, Ronald E. — *A.T. Kearney, Inc.*
Slaughter, Katherine T. — *Compass Group Ltd.*
Slayton, Richard C. — *Slayton International, Inc.*

Smead, Michelle M. — *A.T. Kearney, Inc.*
Smith, Adam M. — *The Abbott Group, Inc.*
Smith, David P. — *Smith & Latterell (HRS, Inc.)*
Smith, John F. — *The Penn Partners, Incorporated*
Snyder, James F. — *Snyder & Company*
Sobczak, Ronald — *Search Enterprises, Inc.*
Soggs, Cheryl Pavick — *A.T. Kearney, Inc.*
Sowerbutt, Richard S. — *Hite Executive Search*
Spadavecchia, Jennifer — *Alta Associates, Inc.*
Spann, Richard E. — *Goodrich & Sherwood Associates, Inc.*
Spiegel, Gay — *L.A. Silver Associates, Inc.*
Spriggs, Robert D. — *Spriggs & Company, Inc.*
Stark, Jeff — *Thorne, Brieger Associates Inc.*
Starr, Anna — *Richard, Wayne and Roberts*
Statson, Dale E. — *Sales Executives Inc.*
Stein, Terry W. — *Stewart, Stein and Scott, Ltd.*
Steinman, Stephen — *The Stevenson Group of New Jersey*
Stern, Stephen — *CPS Inc.*
Sterner, Doug — *CPS Inc.*
Stewart, Jeffrey O. — *Stewart, Stein and Scott, Ltd.*
Stewart, Ross M. — *Human Resources Network Partners Inc.*
Stone, Susan L. — *Stone Enterprises Ltd.*
Stouffer, Dale — *Agra Placements International Ltd.*
Stringer, Dann P. — *D.E. Foster Partners Inc.*
Strom, Mark N. — *Search Advisors International Corp.*
Sturtz, James W. — *Compass Group Ltd.*
Sur, William K. — *Canny, Bowen Inc.*
Sutton, Robert J. — *The Caldwell Partners Amrop International*
Swanson, Dick — *Raymond Karsan Associates*
Sweeney, James W. — *Sweeney Harbert & Mummert, Inc.*
Theobald, David B. — *Theobald & Associates*
Thielman, Joseph — *Barrett Partners*
Tholke, William E. — *Canny, Bowen Inc.*
Thomas, Cheryl M. — *CPS Inc.*
Thomas, Ian — *International Staffing Consultants, Inc.*
Thomas, Kim — *CPS Inc.*
Tovrog, Dan — *CPS Inc.*
Trivedi, Jay — *Search Enterprises, Inc.*
Truemper, Dean — *CPS Inc.*
Truex, John F. — *Morton, McCorkle & Associates, Inc.*
Truitt, Thomas B. — *Southwestern Professional Services*
Tryon, Katey — *DeFrain, Mayer, Lee & Burgess LLC*
Tullberg, Tina — *CPS Inc.*
Tully, Thomas — *Search Enterprises, Inc.*
Tursi, Deborah J. — *The Corporate Connection, Ltd.*
Tweed, Janet — *Gilbert Tweed/INESA*
Twiste, Craig — *Raymond Karsan Associates*
Utroska, Donald R. — *Lamalie Amrop International*
Vainblat, Galina — *Foy, Schneid & Daniel, Inc.*
Van Campen, Jerry — *Gilbert & Van Campen International*
Vande-Water, Katie — *J. Robert Scott*
Velten, Mark — *Hunt Advisory Services*
Velten, Mark — *Hunt Ltd.*
Visnich, L. Christine — *Bason Associates Inc.*
Vlcek, Thomas J. — *Vlcek & Company, Inc.*
Vogel, Michael S. — *Vogel Associates*
Waldoch, D. Mark — *Barnes Development Group, LLC*
Walker, Ewing J. — *Ward Howell International, Inc.*
Walker, Judy — *Richard, Wayne and Roberts*
Walters, William F. — *Jonas, Walters & Assoc., Inc.*
Wayne, Cary S. — *ProSearch Inc.*
Webb, George H. — *Webb, Johnson Associates, Inc.*
Weissman-Rosenthal, Abbe — *ALW Research International*
Williams, Gary L. — *Barnes Development Group, LLC*
Williams, Roger K. — *Williams, Roth & Krueger Inc.*
Willis, William H. — *William Willis Worldwide Inc.*
Winnewisser, William E. — *Accounting & Computer Personnel*
Winston, Susan — *CPS Inc.*
Witte, David L. — *Ward Howell International, Inc.*
Wright, Charles D. — *Goodrich & Sherwood Associates, Inc.*
Wright, Leslie — *The Stevenson Group of New Jersey*
Young, Alexander — *Messett Associates, Inc.*
Youngs, Donald L. — *Youngs & Company*
Zarnoski, Hank — *Dunhill Search International*
Zatman, Allen — *Search Enterprises South, Inc.*
Zay, Thomas C. — *Boyden/Zay & Company*
Zetter, Roger — *Hunt Ltd.*

## 7. Consumer Products

Abbatiello, Christine Murphy — *Winter, Wyman & Company*
Abby, Daniel — *Bill Hahn Group, Inc.*
Adams, Jeffrey C. — *Telford, Adams & Alexander/Jeffrey C. Adams & Co., Inc.*
Alekel, Karren — *ALW Research International*
Allgire, Mary L. — *Kenzer Corp.*
Altreuter, Ken — *ALTCO Temporary Services*
Altreuter, Kenneth — *The ALTCO Group*
Altreuter, Rose — *ALTCO Temporary Services*

Altreuter, Rose — *The ALTCO Group*
Ambler, Peter W. — *Peter W. Ambler Company*
Amsterdam, Gail E. — *D.E. Foster Partners Inc.*
Anderson, Richard — *Grant Cooper and Associates*
Anderson, Thomas — *Paul J. Biestek Associates, Inc.*
Andrews, J. Douglas — *Clarey & Andrews, Inc.*
Andrews, Laura L. — *Stricker & Zagor*
Andrick, Patty — *CPS Inc.*
Apostle, George — *Search Dynamics, Inc.*
Aquavella, Charles P. — *CPA & Associates*
Argentin, Jo — *Executive Placement Consultants, Inc.*
Arms, Douglas — *TOPAZ International, Inc.*
Arms, Douglas — *TOPAZ Legal Solutions*
Arnold, David — *Christian & Timbers*
Arnold, David J. — *Heidrick & Struggles, Inc.*
Aronin, Michael — *Fisher-Todd Associates*
Ascher, Susan P. — *The Ascher Group*
Aston, Kathy — *Marra Peters & Partners*
Atkeson, George G. — *Ward Howell International, Inc.*
Atkins, Laurie — *Battalia Winston International*
Austin, Jessica L. — *D.S.A. - Dixie Search Associates*
Aydelotte, G. Thomas — *Ingram & Aydelotte Inc.*
Badger, Fred H. — *The Badger Group*
Bagwell, Bruce — *Intersource, Ltd.*
Bailey, David O. — *Paul Ray Berndtson*
Baitler, Simon C. — *The Stevenson Group of Delaware Inc.*
Baker, Gary M. — *Cochran, Cochran & Yale, Inc.*
Balch, Randy — *CPS Inc.*
Baltin, Carrie — *Search West, Inc.*
Barack, Brianne — *The Barack Group, Inc.*
Baran, Helena — *Michael J. Cavanagh and Associates*
Barger, H. Carter — *Barger & Sargeant, Inc.*
Barton, Gary R. — *Barton Raben, Inc.*
Bason, Maurice L. — *Bason Associates Inc.*
Bassler, John P. — *Korn/Ferry International*
Battalia, O. William — *Battalia Winston International*
Bauman, Martin H. — *Martin H. Bauman Associates, Inc.*
Beall, Charles P. — *Beall & Company, Inc.*
Bearman, Linda — *Grant Cooper and Associates*
Beaudin, Elizabeth C. — *Callan Associates, Ltd.*
Beaver, Bentley H. — *The Onstott Group, Inc.*
Beaver, Robert W. — *Executive Manning Corporation*
Beckvold, John B. — *Atlantic Search Group, Inc.*
Beeson, William B. — *Lawrence-Leiter and Company*
Bell, Lindy — *F-O-R-T-U-N-E Personnel Consultants of Huntsville, Inc.*
Bellano, Robert W. — *Stanton Chase International*
Bennett, Delora — *Genesis Personnel Service, Inc.*
Bennett, Jo — *Battalia Winston International*
Benson, Kate — *Rene Plessner Associates, Inc.*
Berenblum, Marvin B. — *Heidrick & Struggles, Inc.*
Bergen, Anthony M. — *CFO Associates, Inc.*
Berk-Levine, Margo — *MB Inc. Interim Executive Division*
Berry, Harold B. — *The Hindman Company*
Besen, Douglas — *Besen Associates Inc.*
Bettick, Michael J. — *A.J. Burton Group, Inc.*
Biestek, Paul J. — *Paul J. Biestek Associates, Inc.*
Billington, Brian — *Billington & Associates*
Billington, William H. — *Spriggs & Company, Inc.*
Bitar, Edward — *The Interface Group, Ltd./Boyden*
Blair, Kelly A. — *The Caldwell Partners Amrop International*
Boerkoel, Timothy B. — *Russell Reynolds Associates, Inc.*
Borland, James — *Goodrich & Sherwood Associates, Inc.*
Bos, Marijo — *Russell Reynolds Associates, Inc.*
Bourrie, Sharon D. — *Chartwell Partners International, Inc.*
Bovich, Maryann C. — *Higdon Prince Inc.*
Boyer, Dennis M. — *Heidrick & Struggles, Inc.*
Boyer, Heath C. — *Spencer Stuart*
Brackenbury, Robert — *Bowman & Marshall, Inc.*
Brackin, James B. — *Brackin & Sayers Associates*
Brady, Robert — *CPS Inc.*
Brandeis, Richard — *CPS Inc.*
Bratches, Howard — *Thorndike Deland Associates*
Brenner, Mary — *Prestige Inc.*
Brieger, Steve — *Thorne, Brieger Associates Inc.*
Briggs, Adam — *Horton International*
Brophy, Melissa — *Maximum Management Corp.*
Brown, Buzz — *Brown, Bernardy, Van Remmen, Inc.*
Brown, Charlene N. — *Accent on Achievement, Inc.*
Brown, Jeffrey W. — *Comprehensive Search*
Brown, Kelly A. — *Russell Reynolds Associates, Inc.*
Brown, Larry C. — *Horton International*
Bruce, Michael C. — *Spencer Stuart*
Brudno, Robert J. — *Savoy Partners, Ltd.*
Brunelle, Francis W.H. — *The Caldwell Partners Amrop International*
Bruno, Deborah F. — *The Hindman Company*
Bryant, Richard D. — *Bryant Associates, Inc.*

Bryza, Robert M. — *Robert Lowell International*
Buck, Charles — *Charles Buck & Associates*
Buckles, Donna — *Cochran, Cochran & Yale, Inc.*
Burchill, Greg — *BGB Associates*
Burke, John — *The Experts*
Burns, Alan — *The Enns Partners Inc.*
Butcher, Pascale — *F-O-R-T-U-N-E Personnel Consultants of Manatee County*
Byrnes, Thomas A. — *Thomas A. Byrnes Associates*
Cahill, James P. — *Thorndike Deland Associates*
Cahill, Peter M. — *Peter M. Cahill Associates, Inc.*
Call, David — *Cochran, Cochran & Yale, Inc.*
Callahan, Wanda — *Cochran, Cochran & Yale, Inc.*
Callan, Robert M. — *Callan Associates, Ltd.*
Callen, John H. — *Ward Howell International, Inc.*
Campbell, Patricia A. — *The Onstott Group, Inc.*
Campbell, Robert Scott — *Wellington Management Group*
Carideo, Joseph — *Thorndike Deland Associates*
Carlson, Judith — *Bowman & Marshall, Inc.*
Carpenter, James J. — *Russell Reynolds Associates, Inc.*
Caruso, Kathy — *Accounting Resources, Inc.*
Casey, Jean — *Peter W. Ambler Company*
Cavanagh, Michael J. — *Michael J. Cavanagh and Associates*
Celenza, Catherine — *CPS Inc.*
Chargar, Frances — *Hunt Ltd.*
Charles, Ronald D. — *The Caldwell Partners Amrop International*
Chauvin, Ralph A. — *The Caldwell Partners Amrop International*
Christiansen, Amy — *CPS Inc.*
Christiansen, Doug — *CPS Inc.*
Christoff, Matthew J. — *Spencer Stuart*
Chua, Jackie — *Keith Bagg & Associates Inc.*
Cizek, John T. — *Cizek Associates, Inc.*
Cizek, Marti J. — *Cizek Associates, Inc.*
Clarey, Jack R. — *Clarey & Andrews, Inc.*
Clark, James — *CPS Inc.*
Clauhsen, Elizabeth A. — *Savoy Partners, Ltd.*
Clegg, Cynthia — *Horton International*
Cohen, Pamela — *TOPAZ International, Inc.*
Cohen, Pamela — *TOPAZ Legal Solutions*
Coleman, Gregory — *Strategic Associates, Inc.*
Colling, Douglas — *KPMG Management Consulting*
Collis, Martin — *E.L. Shore & Associates Ltd.*
Colman, Michael — *Executive Placement Consultants, Inc.*
Combs, Stephen L. — *Juntunen-Combs-Poirier*
Connaghan, Linda — *Bowman & Marshall, Inc.*
Cooke, Jeffrey R. — *Jonas, Walters & Assoc., Inc.*
Cooke, Katherine H. — *Horton International*
Cordaro, Concetta — *Flynn, Hannock, Incorporated*
Corrigan, Gerald F. — *The Corrigan Group*
Coulman, Karen — *CPS Inc.*
Cramer, Paul J. — *C/R Associates*
Crane, Howard C. — *Chartwell Partners International, Inc.*
Crath, Paul F. — *Price Waterhouse*
Crist, Peter — *Crist Partners, Ltd.*
Critchley, Walter — *Cochran, Cochran & Yale, Inc.*
Crowell, Elizabeth — *H.M. Long International, Ltd.*
Crumpley, Jim — *Jim Crumpley & Associates*
Cruz, Catherine — *TOPAZ International, Inc.*
Cruz, Catherine — *TOPAZ Legal Solutions*
Cuellar, Paulina Robles — *Paul Ray Berndtson*
Cunningham, Robert Y. — *Goodrich & Sherwood Associates, Inc.*
Czepiel, James — *CPS Inc.*
D'Alessio, Gary A. — *Chicago Legal Search, Ltd.*
Dabich, Thomas M. — *Robert Harkins Associates, Inc.*
Dalton, Bret — *Robert W. Dingman Company, Inc.*
Damon, Robert A. — *Spencer Stuart*
Daniel, Beverly — *Foy, Schneid & Daniel, Inc.*
Daniel, David S. — *Spencer Stuart*
Danoff, Audrey — *Don Richard Associates of Tidewater, Inc.*
Davis, G. Gordon — *Davis & Company*
Davis, Orlin R. — *Heidrick & Struggles, Inc.*
de Tuede, Catherine — *Thomas A. Byrnes Associates*
DeHart, Donna — *Tower Consultants, Ltd.*
Delmonico, Laura — *A.J. Burton Group, Inc.*
DeLong, Art — *Richard Kader & Associates*
deMartino, Cathy — *Lucas Associates*
Demchak, James P. — *Sandhurst Associates*
Desgrosellier, Gary P. — *Personnel Unlimited/Executive Search*
deVry, Kimberly A. — *Tower Consultants, Ltd.*
deWilde, David M. — *Chartwell Partners International, Inc.*
Dickey, Chet W. — *Bowden & Company, Inc.*
Dieck, Daniel W. — *Dieck, Mueller & Associates, Inc.*
DiMarchi, Paul — *DiMarchi Partners, Inc.*
Dingman, Bruce — *Robert W. Dingman Company, Inc.*
Dingman, Robert W. — *Robert W. Dingman Company, Inc.*
Divine, Robert S. — *O'Shea, Divine & Company, Inc.*
Dixon, Aris — *CPS Inc.*
Dixon, C.R. — *A la carte International*

Do, Sonnie — *Whitney & Associates, Inc.*
Doele, Donald C. — *Goodrich & Sherwood Associates, Inc.*
Donnelly, George J. — *Ward Howell International, Inc.*
Dorsey, Jim — *Ryan, Miller & Associates Inc.*
Dotson, M. Ileen — *Dotson & Associates*
Dougherty, Janice — *The McCormick Group, Inc.*
Douglas, Anne — *Prestige Inc.*
Dow, Lori — *Davidson, Laird & Associates*
Dowell, Mary K. — *Professional Search Associates*
Doyle, John P. — *Paul Ray Berndtson*
Dreifus, Donald — *Search West, Inc.*
Drury, James J. — *Spencer Stuart*
Duley, Richard I. — *ARJay & Associates*
Dussick, Vince — *Dussick Management Associates*
Dwyer, Julie — *CPS Inc.*
Dykstra, Nicolette — *CPS Inc.*
Eason, James — *JRL Executive Recruiters*
Eason, Larry E. — *JRL Executive Recruiters*
Ebeling, John A. — *Gilbert Tweed/INESA*
Edwards, Verba L. — *Wing Tips & Pumps, Inc.*
Ehrgott, Elizabeth — *The Ascher Group*
Eibeler, C. — *Amherst Personnel Group Inc.*
Ellis, Ted K. — *The Hindman Company*
Ellis, William — *Interspace Interactive Inc.*
Enfield, Jerry J. — *Executive Manning Corporation*
England, Mark — *Austin-McGregor International*
Enns, George — *The Enns Partners Inc.*
Erickson, Elaine — *Kenzer Corp.*
Ervin, Darlene — *CPS Inc.*
Fancher, Robert L. — *Bason Associates Inc.*
Farrell, Barbara — *The Barack Group, Inc.*
Faure, Nicole — *The Caldwell Partners Amrop International*
Fawcett, Anne M. — *The Caldwell Partners Amrop International*
Fee, J. Curtis — *Spencer Stuart*
Feldman, Abe — *A.E. Feldman Associates*
Feldman, Kimberley — *Atlantic Search Group, Inc.*
Ferneborg, Jay W. — *Ferneborg & Associates, Inc.*
Ferneborg, John R. — *Ferneborg & Associates, Inc.*
Fill, Clifford G. — *D.S.A. - Dixie Search Associates*
Fill, Ellyn H. — *D.S.A. - Dixie Search Associates*
Fincher, Richard P. — *Phase II Management*
Fischer, John C. — *Horton International*
Fisher, Neal — *Fisher Personnel Management Services*
Fitch, Lori — *R. Parker and Associates, Inc.*
Flanagan, Robert M. — *Robert M. Flanagan & Associates, Ltd.*
Flannery, Peter — *Jonas, Walters & Assoc., Inc.*
Flora, Dodi — *Crawford & Crofford*
Flores, Agustin — *Ward Howell International, Inc.*
Fogarty, Michael — *CPS Inc.*
Folkerth, Gene — *Gene Folkerth & Associates, Inc.*
Fonfa, Ann — *S.R. Wolman Associates, Inc.*
Foote, Leland W. — *L.W. Foote Company*
Foreman, David C. — *Koontz, Jeffries & Associates, Inc.*
Forman, Donald R. — *Stanton Chase International*
Foster, Dwight E. — *D.E. Foster Partners Inc.*
Foster, Torrey N. — *Lynch Miller Moore Partners, Inc.*
Fovhez, Michael J.P. — *Sloan & Associates*
Foy, James — *Foy, Schneid & Daniel, Inc.*
Frazier, John — *Cochran, Cochran & Yale, Inc.*
French, William G. — *Preng & Associates, Inc.*
Friedman, Donna L. — *Tower Consultants, Ltd.*
Gabel, Gregory N. — *Canny, Bowen Inc.*
Gabriel, David L. — *The Arcus Group*
Gaines, Ronni L. — *TOPAZ International, Inc.*
Gaines, Ronni L. — *TOPAZ Legal Solutions*
Galante, Suzanne M. — *Vlcek & Company, Inc.*
Gallagher, David W. — *Lamalie Amrop International*
Gallagher, Marilyn — *Hogan Acquisitions*
Gallagher, Terence M. — *Battalia Winston International*
Garcia, Samuel K. — *Southwestern Professional Services*
Gardner, John T. — *Heidrick & Struggles, Inc.*
Garfinkle, Steven M. — *Battalia Winston International*
Gates, Douglas H. — *Skott/Edwards Consultants, Inc.*
Gauthier, Robert C. — *Columbia Consulting Group*
Gerevas, Ronald E. — *Spencer Stuart*
Gerevas, Ronald E. — *Spencer Stuart*
Gerstl, Ronald — *Maxecon Executive Search Consultants*
Gibbs, John S. — *Spencer Stuart*
Gibson, Bruce — *Gibson & Company Inc.*
Gilbert, Elaine — *Herbert Mines Associates, Inc.*
Gilchrist, Robert J. — *Horton International*
Giles, Joe L. — *Joe L. Giles and Associates, Inc.*
Gill, Patricia — *Columbia Consulting Group*
Gill, Susan — *Plummer & Associates, Inc.*
Gilmore, Lori — *CPS Inc.*
Gilreath, James M. — *Gilreath Weatherby, Inc.*
Girsinger, Linda — *Industrial Recruiters Associates, Inc.*
Glennie, Francisco — *Ward Howell International, Inc.*

Goar, Duane R. — *Sandhurst Associates*
Goldenberg, Susan — *Grant Cooper and Associates*
Goldman, Michael L. — *Strategic Associates, Inc.*
Goldsmith, Fred J. — *Fred J. Goldsmith Associates*
Goldstein, Steve — *R. Parker and Associates, Inc.*
Goodman, Dawn M. — *Bason Associates Inc.*
Goodman, Victor — *Anderson Sterling Associates*
Gordon, Gerald L. — *E.G. Jones Associates, Ltd.*
Gore, Les — *Executive Search International*
Gorfinkle, Gayle — *Executive Search International*
Gourlay, Debra — *Rene Plessner Associates, Inc.*
Grady, James — *Search West, Inc.*
Graham, Dale — *CPS Inc.*
Granger, Lisa D. — *D.S.A. - Dixie Search Associates*
Grantham, John — *Grantham & Co., Inc.*
Grantham, Philip H. — *Columbia Consulting Group*
Grassl, Peter O. — *Bowman & Marshall, Inc.*
Gray, Annie — *Annie Gray Associates, Inc./The Executive Search Firm*
Greebe, Neil — *Flowers & Associates*
Grenier, Glorianne — *CPS Inc.*
Grey, Cort — *The McCormick Group, Inc.*
Griesedieck, Joseph E. — *Spencer Stuart*
Gross, Howard — *Herbert Mines Associates, Inc.*
Grzybowski, Jill — *CPS Inc.*
Gurtin, Kay L. — *Executive Options, Ltd.*
Hallock, Peter B. — *Goodrich & Sherwood Associates, Inc.*
Hamilton, Timothy — *The Caldwell Partners Amrop International*
Hanford, Michael — *Richard Kader & Associates*
Hannock, Elwin W. — *Flynn, Hannock, Incorporated*
Hanrahan, Kevin R. — *Russell Reynolds Associates, Inc.*
Hansen, David G. — *Ott & Hansen, Inc.*
Hanson, Grant M. — *Goodrich & Sherwood Associates, Inc.*
Harbaugh, Paul J. — *International Management Advisors, Inc.*
Hardy, Thomas G. — *Spencer Stuart*
Hargis, N. Leann — *Montgomery Resources, Inc.*
Harkins, Robert E. — *Robert Harkins Associates, Inc.*
Harreus, Charles F. — *Harreus & Associates*
Harris, Andrew — *Harris Heery & Associates*
Harris, Jack — *Baker, Harris & Partners Limited*
Harshman, Donald — *The Stevenson Group of New Jersey*
Hart, Robert T. — *D.E. Foster Partners Inc.*
Hart, Susan S. — *Spencer Stuart*
Harvey, Mike — *Advanced Executive Resources*
Haughton, Michael — *DeFrain, Mayer, Lee & Burgess LLC*
Havas, Judy — *Heidrick & Struggles, Inc.*
Haystead, Steve — *Advanced Executive Resources*
Hazerjian, Cynthia — *CPS Inc.*
Heafey, Bill — *CPS Inc.*
Heavey, John — *Prestige Inc.*
Hebard, Roy — *Korn/Ferry International*
Hecker, Henry C. — *Hogan Acquisitions*
Heery, William — *Harris Heery & Associates*
Heideman, Mary Marren — *DeFrain, Mayer, Lee & Burgess LLC*
Heiken, Barbara E. — *Randell-Heiken, Inc.*
Hellebusch, Jerry — *Morgan Hunter Corp.*
Heller, Steven A. — *Martin H. Bauman Associates, Inc.*
Hellinger, Audrey — *Martin H. Bauman Associates, Inc.*
Henard, John B. — *Lamalie Amrop International*
Henderson, Marc — *Prestige Inc.*
Hendrickson, David L. — *Heidrick & Struggles, Inc.*
Heneghan, Donald A. — *Allerton Heneghan & O'Neill*
Henshaw, Robert — *F-O-R-T-U-N-E Personnel Consultants of Huntsville, Inc.*
Hensley, Gayla — *Atlantic Search Group, Inc.*
Herman, Pat — *Whitney & Associates, Inc.*
Hermanson, Shelley — *Ells Personnel System Inc.*
Hertan, Richard L. — *Executive Manning Corporation*
Hertan, Wiliam A. — *Executive Manning Corporation*
Hewitt, Rives D. — *The Dalley Hewitt Company*
Hicks, Timothy C. — *Korn/Ferry International*
Hillyer, Robert L. — *Executive Manning Corporation*
Hindman, Neil C. — *The Hindman Company*
Hobart, John N. — *Paul Ray Berndtson*
Hoevel, Michael J. — *Poirier, Hoevel & Co.*
Hogan, Larry H. — *Hogan Acquisitions*
Holland, John H. — *Sloan & Associates*
Holland, Kathleen — *TOPAZ International, Inc.*
Holland, Kathleen — *TOPAZ Legal Solutions*
Hoppert, Phil — *Wargo and Co., Inc.*
Horton, Robert H. — *Horton International*
Howell, Robert B. — *Atlantic Search Group, Inc.*
Howell, Robert B. — *Atlantic Search Group, Inc.*
Hoyda, Louis A. — *Thorndike Deland Associates*
Hucko, Donald S. — *Jonas, Walters & Assoc., Inc.*
Hudson, Reginald M. — *Search Bureau International*
Hughes, Cathy N. — *The Ogdon Partnership*
Hughes, Donald J. — *Hughes & Company*

Hunter, John B. — *John Sibbald Associates, Inc.*
Hunter, Steven — *Diamond Tax Recruiting*
Hunter, Sue J. — *Robison & Associates*
Hutchinson, Loretta M. — *Hutchinson Resources International*
Hyde, W. Jerry — *Hyde Danforth Wold & Co.*
Hypes, Richard G. — *Lynch Miller Moore Partners, Inc.*
Iacovelli, Heather — *CPS Inc.*
Iammatteo, Enzo — *Keith Bagg & Associates Inc.*
Ingram, D. John — *Ingram & Aydelotte Inc.*
Irish, Alan — *CPS Inc.*
Irvine, Robert — *Keith Bagg & Associates Inc.*
Issacs, Judith A. — *Grant Cooper and Associates*
Jacobs, Mike — *Thorne, Brieger Associates Inc.*
Jacobson, Donald — *Hunt Advisory Services*
Jacobson, Donald — *Hunt Ltd.*
Jaedike, Eldron — *Prestige Inc.*
James, Bruce — *Roberson and Company*
Jensen, Stephanie — *Don Richard Associates of Tidewater, Inc.*
Joffe, Barry — *Bason Associates Inc.*
Johnson, Brian — *A.J. Burton Group, Inc.*
Johnson, Julie — *International Staffing Consultants, Inc.*
Johnson, Kathleen A. — *Barton Raben, Inc.*
Johnson, S. Hope — *The Interface Group, Ltd./Boyden*
Johnston, James R. — *The Stevenson Group of Delaware Inc.*
Jones, Daniel F. — *Atlantic Search Group, Inc.*
Jones, Gary — *BGB Associates*
Jones, Jonathan C. — *The Ogdon Partnership*
Jones, Ronald T. — *ARJay & Associates*
Judy, William — *Search West, Inc.*
Juratovac, Michael — *Montgomery Resources, Inc.*
Kader, Richard — *Richard Kader & Associates*
Kahn, P. Frederick — *Heidrick & Struggles, Inc.*
Kaiser, Donald J. — *Dunhill Search International*
Kaiser, Irene — *Dunhill Search International*
Kaiser, James G. — *Dunhill Search International*
Kanal, David S. — *Johnson Smith & Knisely Accord*
Kanovsky, Gerald — *Career Consulting Group, Inc.*
Kanovsky, Marlene — *Career Consulting Group, Inc.*
Kaplan, Gary — *Gary Kaplan & Associates*
Kaplan, Marc — *Gary Kaplan & Associates*
Karalis, William — *CPS Inc.*
Katz, Cyndi — *Search West, Inc.*
Keeton, Susan G. — *The Corporate Connection, Ltd.*
Kehoe, Mike — *CPS Inc.*
Keller, Barbara — *Barton Raben, Inc.*
Kelly, Claudia L. — *Spencer Stuart*
Kelly, Donna J. — *Accountants Executive Search*
Kelly, Elizabeth Ann — *Wellington Management Group*
Kelly, Peter W. — *R. Rollo Associates*
Kelly, Sheri — *Strategic Associates, Inc.*
Kelso, Patricia C. — *Barton Raben, Inc.*
Kenzer, Robert D. — *Kenzer Corp.*
Kern, Jerry L. — *ADOW's Executeam*
Kern, Kathleen G. — *ADOW's Executeam*
Kershaw, Lisa — *Tanton Mitchell/Paul Ray Berndtson*
Kilcoyne, Pat — *CPS Inc.*
Kiliper, Catherine G. — *Korn/Ferry International*
King, Bill — *The McCormick Group, Inc.*
King, Thomas — *Morgan Hunter Corp.*
Kinley, Kathy — *Intech Summit Group, Inc.*
Kinney, Carol — *Dussick Management Associates*
Kinser, Richard E. — *Richard Kinser & Associates*
Kirkpatrick, Robert L. — *Reese Associates*
Kishbaugh, Herbert S. — *Kishbaugh Associates International*
Kizer, Jay R. — *Paul Ray Berndtson*
Kkorzyniewski, Nicole — *CPS Inc.*
Klages, Constance W. — *International Management Advisors, Inc.*
Klavens, Cecile J. — *The Pickwick Group, Inc.*
Klavins, Larissa R. — *Dieckmann & Associates, Ltd.*
Kleinstein, Jonah A. — *The Kleinstein Group*
Klumpjan, Sonja — *CPS Inc.*
Knisely, Gary — *Johnson Smith & Knisely Accord*
Koehler, Frank R. — *The Koehler Group*
Koontz, Donald N. — *Koontz, Jeffries & Associates, Inc.*
Kopsick, Joseph M. — *Spencer Stuart*
Kossuth, David — *Kossuth & Associates, Inc.*
Kossuth, Jane — *Kossuth & Associates, Inc.*
Kotick, Madeline — *The Stevenson Group of New Jersey*
Kreutz, Gary L. — *Kreutz Consulting Group, Inc.*
Krohn, Eileen — *The Stevenson Group of New Jersey*
Kuo, Linda — *Montgomery Resources, Inc.*
Laba, Marvin — *Marvin Laba & Associates*
Laba, Stuart M. — *Marvin Laba & Associates*
Laird, Cheryl — *CPS Inc.*
Lamb, Lynn M. — *F-O-R-T-U-N-E Personnel Consultants of Huntsville, Inc.*
Lamson-Gran, Jill — *Accounting Resources, Inc.*
Langer, Joel A. — *Langer Associates, Inc.*

Lautz, Lindsay A. — *Wilkinson & Ives*
Leahy, Jan — *CPS Inc.*
Lee, Roger — *Montgomery Resources, Inc.*
Leetma, Imbi — *Stanton Chase International*
Leininger, Dennis — *Key Employment Services*
Lejeune, Jeanette — *F-O-R-T-U-N-E Personnel Consultants of Huntsville, Inc.*
Leland, Paul — *McInturff & Associates, Inc.*
Leonard, Linda — *Harris Heery & Associates*
Leslie, William H. — *Boyden/Zay & Company*
Letcher, Harvey D. — *Sandhurst Associates*
Levine, Alan M. — *MB Inc. Interim Executive Division*
Lewis, Jon A. — *Sandhurst Associates*
Linde, Rick — *Battalia Winston International*
Lindenmuth, Mary — *Search West, Inc.*
Line, Joseph T. — *Sharrow & Associates*
Livingston, Peter R. — *Livingston, Robert and Company Inc.*
Loeb, Stephen H. — *Grant Cooper and Associates*
Lofthouse, Cindy — *CPS Inc.*
Logan, Valarie A. — *D.S.A. - Dixie Search Associates*
Long, Helga — *H.M. Long International, Ltd.*
Long, William G. — *McDonald, Long & Associates, Inc.*
Longmore, Marilyn — *Richard Kader & Associates*
Lotufo, Donald A. — *D.A.L. Associates, Inc.*
Lotz, R. James — *International Management Advisors, Inc.*
Lovely, Edward — *The Stevenson Group of New Jersey*
Loving, Vikki — *Intersource, Ltd.*
Lucht, John — *The John Lucht Consultancy Inc.*
Lumsby, George N. — *International Management Advisors, Inc.*
Lynch, Michael C. — *Lynch Miller Moore Partners, Inc.*
Lyons, Denis B.K. — *Spencer Stuart*
Lyons, Michele R. — *R. Rollo Associates*
MacCarthy, Ann — *Columbia Consulting Group*
MacEachern, David — *Spencer Stuart*
Mackenna, Kathy — *Plummer & Associates, Inc.*
Maer, Harry — *Kenzer Corp.*
Magee, Charles R. — *Dieck, Mueller & Associates, Inc.*
Magee, Harrison R. — *Bowden & Company, Inc.*
Maher, William J. — *Johnson Smith & Knisely Accord*
Mahr, Toni — *K. Russo Associates*
Maibach, Lisa W. — *Russell Reynolds Associates, Inc.*
Mak, I. Paul — *Thomas A. Byrnes Associates*
Malcolm, Rod — *The Enns Partners Inc.*
Manassero, Henri J.P. — *International Management Advisors, Inc.*
Mangum, William T. — *Thomas Mangum Company*
Manns, Alex — *Crawford & Crofford*
Manzo, Renee — *Atlantic Search Group, Inc.*
Maphet, Harriet — *The Stevenson Group of New Jersey*
Marchette, Steve — *Juntunen-Combs-Poirier*
Marino, Chester — *Cochran, Cochran & Yale, Inc.*
Mark, John L. — *J.L. Mark Associates, Inc.*
Marks, Ira — *Strategic Alternatives*
Marra, John — *Marra Peters & Partners*
Marra, John — *Marra Peters & Partners*
Marshall, Gerald — *Blair/Tech Recruiters*
Martens, Maxine — *Rene Plessner Associates, Inc.*
Martin, Ellen — *Hunt Ltd.*
Martin, Geary D. — *Boyden/Zay & Company*
Martines, James — *Sharrow & Associates*
Marumoto, William H. — *The Interface Group, Ltd./Boyden*
Mashakas, Elizabeth — *TOPAZ International, Inc.*
Mashakas, Elizabeth — *TOPAZ Legal Solutions*
Massey, H. Heath — *Robison & Associates*
Matueny, Robert — *Ryan, Miller & Associates Inc.*
Mauer, Kristin — *Montgomery Resources, Inc.*
Mazza, David B. — *Mazza & Riley, Inc.*
McAlpine, Bruce — *Keith Bagg & Associates Inc.*
McAndrews, Kathy — *CPS Inc.*
McAteer, Thomas — *Montgomery Resources, Inc.*
McBryde, Marnie — *Spencer Stuart*
McConnell, Greg — *Winter, Wyman & Company*
McCormick, Brian — *The McCormick Group, Inc.*
McCreary, Charles — *Austin-McGregor International*
McDonald, Scott A. — *McDonald Associates International*
McDonald, Stanleigh B. — *McDonald Associates International*
McGrath, Robert E. — *Robert E. McGrath & Associates*
McGrath, Thomas F. — *Spriggs & Company, Inc.*
McGuire, Corey — *Peter W. Ambler Company*
McInturff, Robert — *McInturff & Associates, Inc.*
McKie, Miles L. — *Russell Reynolds Associates, Inc.*
McKnight, Amy E. — *Chartwell Partners International, Inc.*
McLean, B. Keith — *Price Waterhouse*
McNear, Jeffrey E. — *Barrett Partners*
McNichols, Walter B. — *Gary Kaplan & Associates*
McSherry, James F. — *Battalia Winston International*
McSherry, Terrence J. — *Paul Ray Berndtson*
Mead, James D. — *James Mead & Company*
Meagher, Patricia G. — *Spencer Stuart*

Meany, Brian — *Herbert Mines Associates, Inc.*
Mefford, Bob — *Executive Manning Corporation*
Meier, J. Dale — *Grant Cooper and Associates*
Meltzer, Andrea Y. — *Executive Options, Ltd.*
Mendoza, Guadalupe — *Ward Howell International, Inc.*
Menk, Carl W. — *Canny, Bowen Inc.*
Mertensotto, Chuck H. — *Whitney & Associates, Inc.*
Messett, William J. — *Messett Associates, Inc.*
Metz, Alex — *Hunt Ltd.*
Meyer, Stacey — *Gary Kaplan & Associates*
Meyers, Steven — *Montgomery Resources, Inc.*
Michaels, Joseph — *CPS Inc.*
Michaels, Stewart — *TOPAZ International, Inc.*
Michaels, Stewart — *TOPAZ Legal Solutions*
Miller, George N. — *Hite Executive Search*
Miller, Roy — *The Enns Partners Inc.*
Milstein, Bonnie — *Marvin Laba & Associates*
Milton, Suzanne — *Marra Peters & Partners*
Mines, Herbert T. — *Herbert Mines Associates, Inc.*
Mirtz, P. John — *Mirtz Morice, Inc.*
Mitton, Bill — *Executive Resource, Inc.*
Moerbe, Ed H. — *Stanton Chase International*
Mohr, Brian — *CPS Inc.*
Molitor, John L. — *Barrett Partners*
Molnar, Robert A. — *Johnson Smith & Knisely Accord*
Montgomery, James M. — *Houze, Shourds & Montgomery, Inc.*
Moore, Denise — *Jonas, Walters & Assoc., Inc.*
Moran, Gayle — *Dussick Management Associates*
Morice, James L. — *Mirtz Morice, Inc.*
Morris, Paul T. — *The Morris Group*
Morton, Sheila Ann — *Sloan & Associates*
Moyse, Richard G. — *Thorndike Deland Associates*
Muendel, H. Edward — *Stanton Chase International*
Mulligan, Robert P. — *William Willis Worldwide Inc.*
Mummert, Dennis D. — *Sweeney Harbert & Mummert, Inc.*
Murphy, Cornelius J. — *Goodrich & Sherwood Associates, Inc.*
Mydlach, Renee — *CPS Inc.*
Nadherny, Christopher C. — *Spencer Stuart*
Nagler, Leon G. — *Nagler, Robins & Poe, Inc.*
Neelin, Sharon — *The Caldwell Partners Amrop International*
Neff, Thomas J. — *Spencer Stuart*
Neidhart, Craig C. — *TNS Partners, Inc.*
Newman, Jose L. — *Ward Howell International, Inc.*
Newman, Lynn — *Kishbaugh Associates International*
Nicastro, Kelley P. — *A la carte International*
Nielsen, Sue — *Ells Personnel System Inc.*
Noll, Robert J. — *The Hindman Company*
Nordland, Martin N. — *Horton International*
Norman, Randy — *Austin-McGregor International*
Normann, Amy — *Robert M. Flanagan & Associates, Ltd.*
Norsell, Paul E. — *Paul Norsell & Associates, Inc.*
Nunziata, Peter — *Atlantic Search Group, Inc.*
O'Connell, Mary — *CPS Inc.*
O'Hara, Daniel M. — *Lynch Miller Moore Partners, Inc.*
O'Maley, Kimberlee — *Spencer Stuart*
O'Neill, Stephen A. — *Harris Heery & Associates*
Ogdon, Thomas H. — *The Ogdon Partnership*
Ollinger, Charles D. — *Heidrick & Struggles, Inc.*
Olsen, David — *Search Enterprises South, Inc.*
Onstott, Joseph E. — *The Onstott Group, Inc.*
Osborn, Jim — *Southwestern Professional Services*
Oswald, Mark G. — *Canny, Bowen Inc.*
Ott, George W. — *Ott & Hansen, Inc.*
Ottenritter, Chris — *CPS Inc.*
Owens, Ken — *F-O-R-T-U-N-E Personnel Consultants of Huntsville, Inc.*
Page, Linda — *Jonas, Walters & Assoc., Inc.*
Page, Linda M. — *Wargo and Co., Inc.*
Palma, Frank R. — *Goodrich & Sherwood Associates, Inc.*
Palmer, James H. — *The Hindman Company*
Palmlund, David W. — *Lamalie Amrop International*
Papciak, Dennis J. — *Accounting Personnel Associates, Inc.*
Pappas, Timothy C. — *Jonas, Walters & Assoc., Inc.*
Park, Dabney G. — *Mark Stanley & Company*
Parker, Murray B. — *The Borton Wallace Company*
Parker, Roberta — *R. Parker and Associates, Inc.*
Parr, James A. — *KPMG Management Consulting*
Patence, David W. — *Handy HRM Corp.*
Patton, Mitchell — *Patton/Perry Associates, Inc.*
Paul, Lisa D. — *Merit Resource Group, Inc.*
Pearson, Robert L. — *Lamalie Amrop International*
Pease, Samuel C. — *Heidrick & Struggles, Inc.*
Peck, David W. — *The Peck Consultancy*
Pedley, Jill — *CPS Inc.*
Pelisson, Charles — *Marra Peters & Partners*
Percival, Chris — *Chicago Legal Search, Ltd.*
Perez, Christina — *Orr Executive Search*
Perkins, Daphne — *CPS Inc.*

Stone, Susan L. — *Stone Enterprises Ltd.*
Stoneham, Herbert E.C. — *Stoneham Associates Corp.*
Stouffer, Kenneth — *Keith Bagg & Associates Inc.*
Stratmeyer, Karin Bergwall — *Princeton Entrepreneurial Resources*
Straube, Stanley H. — *Straube Associates*
Stricker, Sidney G. — *Stricker & Zagor*
Stringer, Dann P. — *D.E. Foster Partners Inc.*
Strom, Mark N. — *Search Advisors International Corp.*
Strong, Duane K. — *Executive Resource, Inc.*
Strong, Robert W. — *The Barack Group, Inc.*
Sullivan, James — *Search Enterprises, Inc.*
Summers, Burke — *The McCormick Group, Inc.*
Sumurdy, Melinda — *Kenzer Corp.*
Sur, William K. — *Canny, Bowen Inc.*
Sussman, Lynda — *Gilbert Tweed/INESA*
Swatts, Stone — *F-O-R-T-U-N-E Personnel Consultants of Huntsville, Inc.*
Tappan, Michael A. — *Ward Howell International, Inc.*
Tate, Robert H. — *Paul Ray Berndtson*
Teinert, Jay — *Damon & Associates, Inc.*
Telford, John H. — *Telford, Adams & Alexander/Telford & Co., Inc.*
ten Cate, Herman H. — *Stoneham Associates Corp.*
Tesar, Bob — *Tesar-Reynes, Inc.*
Theobald, David B. — *Theobald & Associates*
Thielman, Joseph — *Barrett Partners*
Thomas, Cheryl M. — *CPS Inc.*
Thomas, Jeffrey — *Fairfaxx Corporation*
Thomas, John T. — *Ward Howell International, Inc.*
Thomas, Kim — *CPS Inc.*
Thomas, Terry — *Montague Enterprises*
Thornton, John C. — *Thornton Resources*
Tipping, William M. — *Ward Howell International, Inc.*
Tovrog, Dan — *CPS Inc.*
Tracey, Jack — *Management Assistance Group, Inc.*
Trueblood, Brian G. — *TNS Partners, Inc.*
Truemper, Dean — *CPS Inc.*
Truex, John F. — *Morton, McCorkle & Associates, Inc.*
Truitt, Thomas B. — *Southwestern Professional Services*
Tryon, Katey — *DeFrain, Mayer, Lee & Burgess LLC*
Tucci, Joseph — *Fairfaxx Corporation*
Tucker, Thomas A. — *The Thomas Tucker Company*
Tullberg, Tina — *CPS Inc.*
Tunney, William — *Grant Cooper and Associates*
Tursi, Deborah J. — *The Corporate Connection, Ltd.*
Tweed, Janet — *Gilbert Tweed/INESA*
Ulbert, Nancy — *Aureus Group*
Vainblat, Galina — *Foy, Schneid & Daniel, Inc.*
Valenta, Joseph — *Princeton Entrepreneurial Resources*
Van Alstine, Catherine — *Tanton Mitchell/Paul Ray Berndtson*
Van Campen, Jerry — *Gilbert & Van Campen International*
Van Clieaf, Mark — *MVC Associates International*
Van Horn, Carol — *R. Parker and Associates, Inc.*
Van Remmen, Roger — *Brown, Bernardy, Van Remmen, Inc.*
van Someren, Christian — *Johnson Smith & Knisely Accord*
Van Steenkiste, Julie — *Davidson, Laird & Associates*
Vaughan, David B. — *Dunhill Professional Search of Irvine, Inc.*
Velten, Mark — *Hunt Advisory Services*
Velten, Mark — *Hunt Ltd.*
Venable, William W. — *Thorndike Deland Associates*
Vergari, Jane — *Herbert Mines Associates, Inc.*
Visnich, L. Christine — *Bason Associates Inc.*
Vlcek, Thomas J. — *Vlcek & Company, Inc.*
Vogel, Michael S. — *Vogel Associates*
Vojta, Marilyn B. — *James Mead & Company*
von Stein, Scott — *Wilkinson & Ives*
Waggoner, Lisa — *Intersource, Ltd.*
Walker, Craig H. — *A.J. Burton Group, Inc.*
Walters, William F. — *Jonas, Walters & Assoc., Inc.*
Walton, Terry P. — *Heidrick & Struggles, Inc.*
Warren, Linda — *Prestige Inc.*
Warren, Sylvia W. — *Thorndike Deland Associates*
Wasson, Thomas W. — *Spencer Stuart*
Waxman, Bruce — *Ryan, Miller & Associates Inc.*
Weed, William H. — *Paul Ray Berndtson*
Weidener, Andrew E. — *Paul Ray Berndtson*
Weissman-Rosenthal, Abbe — *ALW Research International*
Weisz, Laura — *Anderson Sterling Associates*
Weller, Paul S. — *Mark Stanley & Company*
Werner, Bonnie — *H.M. Long International, Ltd.*
Wheeler, Gerard H. — *A.J. Burton Group, Inc.*
White, Jonathan O. — *The Badger Group*
White, Richard B. — *Spencer Stuart*
Whitney, David L. — *Whitney & Associates, Inc.*
Whittall, Barbara — *Heidrick & Struggles, Inc.*
Wier, Daniel — *Horton International*
Wilder, Richard B. — *Columbia Consulting Group*
Wilkinson, William R. — *Wilkinson & Ives*
Williams, Angie — *Whitney & Associates, Inc.*

Williams, Lis — *Executive Options, Ltd.*
Williams, Roger K. — *Williams, Roth & Krueger Inc.*
Williams, Walter E. — *Canny, Bowen Inc.*
Willis, William H. — *William Willis Worldwide Inc.*
Willner, Nannette — *S.R. Wolman Associates, Inc.*
Wilson, Derrick — *Thornton Resources*
Wilson, John C. — *Russell Reynolds Associates, Inc.*
Wilson, Patricia L. — *Leon A. Farley Associates*
Winitz, Joel — *GSW Consulting Group, Inc.*
Winitz, Marla — *GSW Consulting Group, Inc.*
Winnewisser, William E. — *Accounting & Computer Personnel*
Winston, Dale — *Battalia Winston International*
Winston, Susan — *CPS Inc.*
Wirtshafter, Linda — *Grant Cooper and Associates*
Wisch, Steven C. — *MB Inc. Interim Executive Division*
Wise, J. Herbert — *Sandhurst Associates*
Witte, David L. — *Ward Howell International, Inc.*
Wolf, Stephen M. — *Byron Leonard International, Inc.*
Wolman, Stephen R. — *S.R. Wolman Associates, Inc.*
Wood, Milton M. — *M. Wood Company*
Wren, Jay — *Jay Wren & Associates*
Wren, Shelly J. — *Sloan & Associates*
Wright, Carl A.J. — *A.J. Burton Group, Inc.*
Wright, Charles D. — *Goodrich & Sherwood Associates, Inc.*
Wright, Leslie — *The Stevenson Group of New Jersey*
Yilmaz, Muriel — *Dinte Resources, Incorporated*
Young, Alexander — *Messett Associates, Inc.*
Youngs, Donald L. — *Youngs & Company*
Zaslav, Debra M. — *Telford, Adams & Alexander/Telford & Co., Inc.*
Zatman, Allen — *Search Enterprises South, Inc.*
Zay, Thomas C. — *Boyden/Zay & Company*
Zay, Thomas C. — *Boyden/Zay & Company*
Zee, Wanda — *Tesar-Reynes, Inc.*
Zetter, Roger — *Hunt Ltd.*
Zila, Laurie M. — *Princeton Entrepreneurial Resources*
Zonis, Hildy R. — *Accountants Executive Search*
Zucker, Nancy — *Maximum Management Corp.*
Zwiff, Jeffrey G. — *Johnson Smith & Knisely Accord*

## 8. Education/Libraries

Abruzzo, James — *A.T. Kearney, Inc.*
Alexander, John T. — *Telford, Adams & Alexander/Human Resource Services*
Antil, Pamela W. — *Norman Roberts & Associates, Inc.*
Ast, Steven T. — *Ast/Bryant*
Aydelotte, G. Thomas — *Ingram & Aydelotte Inc.*
Baker-Greene, Edward — *Isaacson, Miller*
Belford, Paul — *JDG Associates, Ltd.*
Berger, Emanuel — *Isaacson, Miller*
Berger, Jay V. — *Morris & Berger*
Bowen, William J. — *Heidrick & Struggles, Inc.*
Brooks, Bernard E. — *Mruk & Partners/EMA Partners Int'l*
Brunelle, Francis W.H. — *The Caldwell Partners Amrop International*
Bryant, Christopher P. — *Ast/Bryant*
Burns, Terence N. — *D.E. Foster Partners Inc.*
Caldwell, C. Douglas — *The Caldwell Partners Amrop International*
Chorman, Marilyn A. — *Hite Executive Search*
Citera, Tom — *Howe-Lewis International*
Cleeve, Coleen — *Howe-Lewis International*
Conard, Rodney J. — *Conard Associates, Inc.*
Corrigan, Gerald F. — *The Corrigan Group*
Crath, Paul F. — *Price Waterhouse*
Czamanske, Paul W. — *Compass Group Ltd.*
Demchak, James P. — *Sandhurst Associates*
Dingman, Bruce — *Robert W. Dingman Company, Inc.*
Dingman, Robert W. — *Robert W. Dingman Company, Inc.*
Divine, Robert S. — *O'Shea, Divine & Company, Inc.*
Doliva, Lauren M. — *Heidrick & Struggles, Inc.*
Edell, David E. — *The Development Resource Group Incorporated*
Emmott, Carol B. — *Spencer Stuart*
Fawcett, Anne M. — *The Caldwell Partners Amrop International*
Flora, Dodi — *Crawford & Crofford*
Frank, Valerie S. — *Norman Roberts & Associates, Inc.*
Funk, Robert William — *Korn/Ferry International*
Gibson, Bruce — *Gibson & Company Inc.*
Goar, Duane R. — *Sandhurst Associates*
Goedtke, Steven — *Southwestern Professional Services*
Gossage, Wayne — *Gossage Regan Associates, Inc.*
Gray, Annie — *Annie Gray Associates, Inc./The Executive Search Firm*
Greco, Patricia — *Howe-Lewis International*
Greenwood, Janet — *Heidrick & Struggles, Inc.*
Hamilton, Timothy — *The Caldwell Partners Amrop International*
Hanley, Maureen E. — *Gilbert Tweed/INESA*
Hard, Sally Ann — *Ast/Bryant*
Hart, Robert T. — *D.E. Foster Partners Inc.*
Hatcher, Joe B. — *Ast/Bryant*
Hauser, Martha — *Spencer Stuart*

Hemingway, Stuart C. — *Robison & Associates*
Howe, Vance A. — *Ward Howell International, Inc.*
Hunter, Sue J. — *Robison & Associates*
Isaacson, John — *Isaacson, Miller*
Jernigan, Susan N. — *Sockwell & Associates*
Johnson, Maxene — *Norman Roberts & Associates, Inc.*
Kaplan, Gary — *Gary Kaplan & Associates*
Kaplan, Marc — *Gary Kaplan & Associates*
Kershaw, Lisa — *Tanton Mitchell/Paul Ray Berndtson*
Kixmiller, David B. — *Heidrick & Struggles, Inc.*
Krinsky, Ira W. — *Korn/Ferry International*
Kuhnle, John H. — *Korn/Ferry International*
Larsen, Richard F. — *Larsen, Zilliacus & Associates, Inc.*
Leske, Lucy A. — *Educational Management Network*
Leske, Lucy Apthorp — *Educational Management Network*
Letcher, Harvey D. — *Sandhurst Associates*
Lewis, Jon A. — *Sandhurst Associates*
Lipe, Jerold L. — *Compass Group Ltd.*
Logue, Kenneth F. — *Logue & Rice Inc.*
Loomis, Ruth L. — *Ast/Bryant*
Love, David M. — *Paul Ray Berndtson*
Low, Linda — *The Development Resource Group Incorporated*
Lucht, John — *The John Lucht Consultancy Inc.*
Mainwaring, Andrew Brian — *Executive Search Consultants Corporation*
Martin, Nancy A. — *Educational Management Network*
Mathias, William J. — *Preng & Associates, Inc.*
McCarthy, David R. — *Spencer Stuart*
McGrath, Robert E. — *Robert E. McGrath & Associates*
McGuire, Corey — *Peter W. Ambler Company*
McLean, B. Keith — *Price Waterhouse*
McMillin, Bob — *Price Waterhouse*
McNichols, Walter B. — *Gary Kaplan & Associates*
McRae, O. Jon — *Jon McRae & Associates, Inc.*
Merrigan, Eileen M. — *Lamalie Amrop International*
Mestepey, John — *A.T. Kearney, Inc.*
Meyer, Stacey — *Gary Kaplan & Associates*
Morris, Kristine A. — *Morris & Berger*
Neher, Robert L. — *Intech Summit Group, Inc.*
Neumann, Joan — *Gossage Regan Associates, Inc.*
Pace, Susan A. — *Horton International*
Patton, Mitchell — *Patton/Perry Associates, Inc.*
Peck, David W. — *The Peck Consultancy*
Phillips, Donald L. — *O'Shea, Divine & Company, Inc.*
Pittard, Patrick S. — *Heidrick & Struggles, Inc.*
Posner, Gary J. — *Educational Management Network*
Rabinowitz, Peter A. — *P.A.R. Associates Inc.*
Rackley, Eugene M. — *Heidrick & Struggles, Inc.*
Regan, Muriel — *Gossage Regan Associates, Inc.*
Rich, Lyttleton — *Sockwell & Associates*
Roberts, Nick P. — *Spectrum Search Associates, Inc.*
Roberts, Norman C. — *Norman Roberts & Associates, Inc.*
Robinson, Bruce — *Bruce Robinson Associates*
Rosenberg, Esther — *Howe-Lewis International*
Ross, Mark S. — *Herman Smith Executive Initiatives Inc.*
Ross, Martin B. — *Ward Howell International, Inc.*
Russell, Susan Anne — *Executive Search Consultants Corporation*
Rustad, Binth — *Educational Management Network*
Shervey, Brent C. — *O'Callaghan Honey/Paul Ray Berndtson, Inc.*
Slaughter, Katherine T. — *Compass Group Ltd.*
Smith, Grant — *Price Waterhouse*
Sockwell, J. Edgar — *Sockwell & Associates*
Sterling, Sally M. — *Heidrick & Struggles, Inc.*
Storbeck, Shelly — *A.T. Kearney, Inc.*
Taylor, Charles E. — *Lamalie Amrop International*
Taylor, Ernest A. — *Ward Howell International, Inc.*
Tipping, William M. — *Ward Howell International, Inc.*
Tootsey, Mark A. — *A.J. Burton Group, Inc.*
Truex, John F. — *Morton, McCorkle & Associates, Inc.*
Verrill-Schlager, Martha — *Korn/Ferry International*
Watkins, Thomas M. — *Lamalie Amrop International*
Watson, Peggy — *Advanced Information Management*
Welch, David — *Isaacson, Miller*
Whitcomb, Nancy C. — *Educational Management Network*
Wier, Daniel — *Horton International*
Wise, J. Herbert — *Sandhurst Associates*
Wright, Carl A.J. — *A.J. Burton Group, Inc.*
Wright, Linus — *Paul Ray Berndtson*
Young, Mimi — *Educational Management Network*
Zivic, Janis M. — *Spencer Stuart*

## 9. Electronics

Abbott, Peter — *The Abbott Group, Inc.*
Ainsworth, Lawrence — *Search West, Inc.*
Akin, J.R. — *J.R. Akin & Company Inc.*
Alekel, Karren — *ALW Research International*
Allerton, Donald T. — *Allerton Heneghan & O'Neill*
Allred, J. Michael — *Spencer Stuart*

Altreuter, Rose — *ALTCO Temporary Services*
Altreuter, Rose — *The ALTCO Group*
Ambler, Peter W. — *Peter W. Ambler Company*
Ames, George C. — *Ames O'Neill Associates*
Anderson, Dean C. — *Corporate Resources Professional Placement*
Anderson, Richard — *Grant Cooper and Associates*
Anderson, Thomas — *Paul J. Biestek Associates, Inc.*
Andrews, J. Douglas — *Clarey & Andrews, Inc.*
Apostle, George — *Search Dynamics, Inc.*
Arms, Douglas — *TOPAZ International, Inc.*
Arms, Douglas — *TOPAZ Legal Solutions*
Arseneault, Daniel S. — *MSI International*
Ashton, Barbara L. — *Ashton Computer Professionals Inc.*
Atkins, Laurie — *Battalia Winston International*
Aubin, Richard E. — *Aubin International*
Badger, Fred H. — *The Badger Group*
Bagg, Keith — *Keith Bagg & Associates Inc.*
Bagwell, Bruce — *Intersource, Ltd.*
Bailey, William A. — *TNS Partners, Inc.*
Baitler, Simon C. — *The Stevenson Group of Delaware Inc.*
Baker, Gary M. — *Cochran, Cochran & Yale, Inc.*
Baker, Gerry — *Baker, Harris & Partners Limited*
Baldwin, Keith R. — *The Baldwin Group*
Baltin, Carrie — *Search West, Inc.*
Baran, Helena — *Michael J. Cavanagh and Associates*
Barlow, Ken H. — *The Cherbonnier Group, Inc.*
Barnes, Richard E. — *Barnes Development Group, LLC*
Barnes, Roanne L. — *Barnes Development Group, LLC*
Barnum, Toni M. — *Stone Murphy & Olson*
Baron, Len — *Industrial Recruiters Associates, Inc.*
Bartesch, Heinz — *The Search Firm, Inc.*
Barton, Gary R. — *Barton Raben, Inc.*
Battalia, O. William — *Battalia Winston International*
Bearman, Linda — *Grant Cooper and Associates*
Beaudin, Elizabeth C. — *Callan Associates, Ltd.*
Beaver, Bentley H. — *The Onstott Group, Inc.*
Beaver, Robert W. — *Executive Manning Corporation*
Beckvold, John B. — *Atlantic Search Group, Inc.*
Beeson, William B. — *Lawrence-Leiter and Company*
Belfrey, Edward — *Dunhill Professional Search of Irvine, Inc.*
Bennett, Jo — *Battalia Winston International*
Bennett, Joan — *Adams & Associates International*
Berger, Jay V. — *Morris & Berger*
Bermea, Jose — *Gaffney Management Consultants*
Berry, Harold B. — *The Hindman Company*
Biestek, Paul J. — *Paul J. Biestek Associates, Inc.*
Billington, William H. — *Spriggs & Company, Inc.*
Blackmon, Sharon — *The Abbott Group, Inc.*
Blanton, Thomas — *Blanton and Company*
Blecker, Jay — *TSS Consulting, Ltd.*
Bliley, Jerry — *Spencer Stuart*
Blim, Barbara — *JDG Associates, Ltd.*
Block, Randy — *Block & Associates*
Bloomer, James E. — *L.W. Foote Company*
Bluhm, Claudia — *Schweichler Associates, Inc.*
Boczany, William J. — *The Guild Corporation*
Bostic, James E. — *Phillips Resource Group*
Brackin, James B. — *Brackin & Sayers Associates*
Brieger, Steve — *Thorne, Brieger Associates Inc.*
Briggs, Adam — *Horton International*
Brooks, Charles — *Corporate Recruiters Ltd.*
Brooks, Kimberllay — *Corporate Recruiters Ltd.*
Brown, Buzz — *Brown, Bernardy, Van Remmen, Inc.*
Brown, Larry C. — *Horton International*
Brudno, Robert J. — *Savoy Partners, Ltd.*
Bruno, Deborah F. — *The Hindman Company*
Bryant, Richard D. — *Bryant Associates, Inc.*
Bryza, Robert M. — *Robert Lowell International*
Buckles, Donna — *Cochran, Cochran & Yale, Inc.*
Bueschel, David A. — *Shepherd Bueschel & Provus, Inc.*
Burchill, Greg — *BGB Associates*
Burden, Gene — *The Cherbonnier Group, Inc.*
Burns, Alan — *The Enns Partners Inc.*
Busch, Jack — *Busch International*
Butcher, Pascale — *F-O-R-T-U-N-E Personnel Consultants of Manatee County*
Button, David R. — *The Button Group*
Cahill, Peter M. — *Peter M. Cahill Associates, Inc.*
Callahan, Wanda — *Cochran, Cochran & Yale, Inc.*
Callan, Robert M. — *Callan Associates, Ltd.*
Cavanagh, Michael J. — *Michael J. Cavanagh and Associates*
Chavous, C. Crawford — *Phillips Resource Group*
Cherbonnier, L. Michael — *TCG International, Inc.*
Cherbonnier, L. Michael — *The Cherbonnier Group, Inc.*
Christian, Jeffrey E. — *Christian & Timbers*
Cizek, John T. — *Cizek Associates, Inc.*
Cizek, Marti J. — *Cizek Associates, Inc.*
Clarey, Jack R. — *Clarey & Andrews, Inc.*

Kaplan, Gary — *Gary Kaplan & Associates*
Kaplan, Marc — *Gary Kaplan & Associates*
Katz, Cyndi — *Search West, Inc.*
Keller, Barbara — *Barton Raben, Inc.*
Kelly, Sheri — *Strategic Associates, Inc.*
Kelly, Susan D. — *S.D. Kelly & Associates, Inc.*
Kern, Jerry L. — *ADOW's Executeam*
Kern, Kathleen G. — *ADOW's Executeam*
Kinser, Richard E. — *Richard Kinser & Associates*
Klages, Constance W. — *International Management Advisors, Inc.*
Klauck, James J. — *Horton International*
Klavens, Cecile J. — *The Pickwick Group, Inc.*
Kleinstein, Jonah A. — *The Kleinstein Group*
Klopfenstein, Edward L. — *Crowder & Company*
Knapp, Ronald A. — *Knapp Consultants*
Koehler, Frank R. — *The Koehler Group*
Kohonoski, Michael M. — *The Guild Corporation*
Koontz, Donald N. — *Koontz, Jeffries & Associates, Inc.*
Kossuth, David — *Kossuth & Associates, Inc.*
Kossuth, Jane — *Kossuth & Associates, Inc.*
Krejci, Stanley L. — *The Interface Group, Ltd./Boyden*
LaCharite, Danielle — *The Guild Corporation*
Lamb, Lynn M. — *F-O-R-T-U-N-E Personnel Consultants of Huntsville, Inc.*
Lamson-Gran, Jill — *Accounting Resources, Inc.*
Lanctot, William D. — *Corporate Resources Professional Placement*
Land, Shaun — *Dunhill Professional Search of Irvine, Inc.*
Langford, Robert W. — *F-O-R-T-U-N-E Personnel Consultants of Huntsville, Inc.*
Lapat, Aaron D. — *J. Robert Scott*
Larsen, Jack B. — *Jack B. Larsen & Associates*
Lasher, Charles M. — *Lasher Associates*
Lautz, Lindsay A. — *Wilkinson & Ives*
Leff, Lisa A. — *Berger and Leff*
Lejeune, Jeanette — *F-O-R-T-U-N-E Personnel Consultants of Huntsville, Inc.*
Leland, Paul — *McInturff & Associates, Inc.*
Lindenmuth, Mary — *Search West, Inc.*
Line, Joseph T. — *Sharrow & Associates*
Linton, Leonard M. — *Byron Leonard International, Inc.*
Lipe, Jerold L. — *Compass Group Ltd.*
Loeb, Stephen H. — *Grant Cooper and Associates*
Long, Helga — *H.M. Long International, Ltd.*
Long, William G. — *McDonald, Long & Associates, Inc.*
LoPresto, Robert L. — *Rusher, Loscavio & LoPresto*
Lotufo, Donald A. — *D.A.L. Associates, Inc.*
Lotz, R. James — *International Management Advisors, Inc.*
Loving, Vikki — *Intersource, Ltd.*
Lucht, John — *The John Lucht Consultancy Inc.*
Lumsby, George N. — *International Management Advisors, Inc.*
Mackenna, Kathy — *Plummer & Associates, Inc.*
Mader, Stephen P. — *Christian & Timbers*
Malcolm, Rod — *The Enns Partners Inc.*
Manassero, Henri J.P. — *International Management Advisors, Inc.*
Mangum, William T. — *Thomas Mangum Company*
Manns, Alex — *Crawford & Crofford*
Manzo, Renee — *Atlantic Search Group, Inc.*
Marchette, Steve — *Juntunen-Combs-Poirier*
Marion, Michael — *S.D. Kelly & Associates, Inc.*
Marks, Ira — *Strategic Alternatives*
Marlow, William — *Straube Associates*
Martin, David — *The Guild Corporation*
Mashakas, Elizabeth — *TOPAZ International, Inc.*
Mashakas, Elizabeth — *TOPAZ Legal Solutions*
Mason, William E. — *John Kurosky & Associates*
Matueny, Robert — *Ryan, Miller & Associates Inc.*
May, Peter — *Mixtec Group*
McAlpine, Bruce — *Keith Bagg & Associates Inc.*
McComas, Kelly E. — *The Guild Corporation*
McCreary, Charles — *Austin-McGregor International*
McDonald, John R. — *TSS Consulting, Ltd.*
McDonald, Scott A. — *McDonald Associates International*
McDonald, Stanleigh B. — *McDonald Associates International*
McDonnell, Julie — *Technical Personnel of Minnesota*
McGuire, Corey — *Peter W. Ambler Company*
McInturff, Robert — *McInturff & Associates, Inc.*
McIntyre, Joel — *Phillips Resource Group*
McNichols, Walter B. — *Gary Kaplan & Associates*
McPoyle, Thomas C. — *Sanford Rose Associates*
McThrall, David — *TSS Consulting, Ltd.*
Mefford, Bob — *Executive Manning Corporation*
Mertensotto, Chuck H. — *Whitney & Associates, Inc.*
Messett, William J. — *Messett Associates, Inc.*
Meyer, Stacey — *Gary Kaplan & Associates*
Michaels, Stewart — *TOPAZ International, Inc.*
Michaels, Stewart — *TOPAZ Legal Solutions*
Mierzwinski, John — *Industrial Recruiters Associates, Inc.*

Miles, Kenneth T. — *MSI International*
Miller, Roy — *The Enns Partners Inc.*
Miller, Russel E. — *ARJay & Associates*
Mirtz, P. John — *Mirtz Morice, Inc.*
Mitton, Bill — *Executive Resource, Inc.*
Mogul, Gene — *Mogul Consultants, Inc.*
Molnar, Robert A. — *Johnson Smith & Knisely Accord*
Montgomery, James M. — *Houze, Shourds & Montgomery, Inc.*
Moore, David S. — *Lynch Miller Moore Partners, Inc.*
Moore, Denise — *Jonas, Walters & Assoc., Inc.*
Moore, Lemuel R. — *MSI International*
Moore, Mark — *Wheeler, Moore & Elam Co.*
Moore, Thomas — *Aureus Group*
Morgan, Vincent S. — *Johnson Smith & Knisely Accord*
Morice, James L. — *Mirtz Morice, Inc.*
Morris, Kristine A. — *Morris & Berger*
Moses, Jerry — *J.M. Eagle Partners Ltd.*
Muendel, H. Edward — *Stanton Chase International*
Mulligan, Robert P. — *William Willis Worldwide Inc.*
Murphy, Gary J. — *Stone Murphy & Olson*
Mursuli, Meredith — *Lasher Associates*
Myatt, James S. — *Sanford Rose Associates*
Myers, Kay — *Signature Staffing*
Nagler, Leon G. — *Nagler, Robins & Poe, Inc.*
Neelin, Sharon — *The Caldwell Partners Amrop International*
Neidhart, Craig C. — *TNS Partners, Inc.*
Neuberth, Jeffrey G. — *Canny, Bowen Inc.*
Nolan, Jean M. — *S.D. Kelly & Associates, Inc.*
Noll, Robert J. — *The Hindman Company*
Norman, Randy — *Austin-McGregor International*
Norsell, Paul E. — *Paul Norsell & Associates, Inc.*
Nunziata, Peter — *Atlantic Search Group, Inc.*
Nymark, John — *NYCOR Search, Inc.*
Nymark, Paul — *NYCOR Search, Inc.*
Ocon, Olga — *Busch International*
Pacini, Lauren R. — *Hite Executive Search*
Page, Linda — *Jonas, Walters & Assoc., Inc.*
Page, Linda M. — *Wargo and Co., Inc.*
Palmer, James H. — *The Hindman Company*
Pappas, Jim — *Search Dynamics, Inc.*
Pappas, Timothy C. — *Jonas, Walters & Assoc., Inc.*
Parkin, Myrna — *S.D. Kelly & Associates, Inc.*
Parr, James A. — *KPMG Management Consulting*
Parry, William H. — *Horton International*
Paul, Lisa D. — *Merit Resource Group, Inc.*
Peckenpaugh, Ann D. — *Schweichler Associates, Inc.*
Peeney, James D. — *Peeney Associates*
Percival, Chris — *Chicago Legal Search, Ltd.*
Persky, Barry — *Barry Persky & Company, Inc.*
Peternell, Melanie — *Signature Staffing*
Peters, James N. — *TNS Partners, Inc.*
Pfister, Shelli — *Jack B. Larsen & Associates*
Phelps, Gene L. — *McCormack & Farrow*
Pitts, Charles — *Contemporary Management Services, Inc.*
Plimpton, Ralph L. — *R L Plimpton Associates*
Plummer, John — *Plummer & Associates, Inc.*
Poirier, Frank — *Juntunen-Combs-Poirier*
Poirier, Roland — *Poirier, Hoevel & Co.*
Polachi, Charles A. — *Fenwick Partners*
Polachi, Peter V. — *Fenwick Partners*
Pompeo, Paul — *Search West, Inc.*
Porada, Stephen D. — *CAP Inc.*
Price, Andrew G. — *The Thomas Tucker Company*
Raab, Julie — *Dunhill Professional Search of Irvine, Inc.*
Rabe, William — *Sales Executives Inc.*
Ray, Marianne C. — *Callan Associates, Ltd.*
Raymond, Anne — *Anderson Sterling Associates*
Reece, Christopher S. — *Reece & Mruk Partners*
Renner, Sandra L. — *Spectra International Inc.*
Renwick, David — *John Kurosky & Associates*
Reyman, Susan — *S. Reyman & Associates Ltd.*
Rimmel, James S. — *The Hindman Company*
Rizzo, L. Donald — *R.P. Barone Associates*
Roberts, Mitch — *A.E. Feldman Associates*
Roberts, Nick P. — *Spectrum Search Associates, Inc.*
Roberts, Scott B. — *Wargo and Co., Inc.*
Roberts, William — *Cochran, Cochran & Yale, Inc.*
Robins, Jeri N. — *Nagler, Robins & Poe, Inc.*
Romanello, Daniel P. — *Spencer Stuart*
Rossi, Silvio — *Keith Bagg & Associates Inc.*
Roth, Robert J. — *Williams, Roth & Krueger Inc.*
Rothfeld, Robert — *A.E. Feldman Associates*
Rozner, Burton L. — *Oliver & Rozner Associates, Inc.*
Rubinstein, Alan J. — *Chicago Legal Search, Ltd.*
Rudzinsky, Howard — *Louis Rudzinsky Associates*
Rudzinsky, Jeffrey — *Louis Rudzinsky Associates*
Rurak, Zbigniew T. — *Rurak & Associates, Inc.*
Russell, Sam — *The Guild Corporation*

Sangster, Jeffrey — *F-O-R-T-U-N-E Personnel Consultants of Manatee County*
Savard, Robert F. — *The Stevenson Group of Delaware Inc.*
Sayers, Bruce D. — *Brackin & Sayers Associates*
Schiavone, Mary Rose — *Canny, Bowen Inc.*
Schlpma, Christine — *Advanced Executive Resources*
Schmidt, William C. — *Christian & Timbers*
Schneider, James — *The Search Firm, Inc.*
Schneiderman, Gerald — *Management Resource Associates, Inc.*
Schwartz, Vincent P. — *Slayton International, Inc.*
Schweichler, Lee J. — *Schweichler Associates, Inc.*
Selker, Gregory L. — *Christian & Timbers*
Sevilla, Claudio A. — *Crawford & Crofford*
Shamir, Ben — *S.D. Kelly & Associates, Inc.*
Shattuck, Merrill B. — *M.B. Shattuck and Associates, Inc.*
Shea, Kathleen M. — *The Penn Partners, Incorporated*
Sheedy, Edward J. — *Dieckmann & Associates, Ltd.*
Shourds, Mary E. — *Houze, Shourds & Montgomery, Inc.*
Sibul, Shelly Remen — *Chicago Legal Search, Ltd.*
Siker, Paul W. — *The Guild Corporation*
Silcott, Marvin L. — *Marvin L. Silcott & Associates, Inc.*
Silvas, Stephen D. — *Roberson and Company*
Silver, Lee A. — *L.A. Silver Associates, Inc.*
Silverman, Paul M. — *The Marshall Group*
Simmons, Anneta — *F-O-R-T-U-N-E Personnel Consultants of Huntsville, Inc.*
Sinclair, Amy — *Fisher Personnel Management Services*
Skunda, Donna M. — *Allerton Heneghan & O'Neill*
Slayton, Richard C. — *Slayton International, Inc.*
Slosar, John M. — *Canny, Bowen Inc.*
Smith, Adam M. — *The Abbott Group, Inc.*
Smith, David P. — *Smith & Latterell (HRS, Inc.)*
Smith, John F. — *The Penn Partners, Incorporated*
Smith, Kevin — *F-O-R-T-U-N-E Personnel Consultants of Manatee County*
Smith, R. Michael — *Smith James Group, Inc.*
Snyder, James F. — *Snyder & Company*
Solomon, Christina — *Richard, Wayne and Roberts*
Solters, Jeanne — *The Guild Corporation*
Soutouras, James — *Smith James Group, Inc.*
Spanninger, Mark J. — *The Guild Corporation*
Spiegel, Gay — *L.A. Silver Associates, Inc.*
Splaine, Charles — *Splaine & Associates, Inc.*
Spriggs, Robert D. — *Spriggs & Company, Inc.*
Stark, Jeff — *Thorne, Brieger Associates Inc.*
Starner, William S. — *Fenwick Partners*
Statson, Dale E. — *Sales Executives Inc.*
Stein, Terry W. — *Stewart, Stein and Scott, Ltd.*
Steinem, Andy — *Dahl-Morrow International*
Steinem, Barbara — *Dahl-Morrow International*
Stenberg, Edward — *Winter, Wyman & Company*
Stephenson, Don L. — *Ells Personnel System Inc.*
Stewart, Jeffrey O. — *Stewart, Stein and Scott, Ltd.*
Stewart, Ross M. — *Human Resources Network Partners Inc.*
Stiles, Judy — *MedQuest Associates*
Stone, Susan L. — *Stone Enterprises Ltd.*
Stouffer, Kenneth — *Keith Bagg & Associates Inc.*
Strain, Stephen R. — *Spencer Stuart*
Stratmeyer, Karin Bergwall — *Princeton Entrepreneurial Resources*
Stringer, Dann P. — *D.E. Foster Partners Inc.*
Strom, Mark N. — *Search Advisors International Corp.*
Sturtz, James W. — *Compass Group Ltd.*
Sullivan, Kay — *Rusher, Loscavio & LoPresto*
Sur, William K. — *Canny, Bowen Inc.*
Sussman, Lynda — *Gilbert Tweed/INESA*
Swatts, Stone — *F-O-R-T-U-N-E Personnel Consultants of Huntsville, Inc.*
Sweeney, James W. — *Sweeney Harbert & Mummert, Inc.*
Swick, Jan — *TSS Consulting, Ltd.*
Taft, Steven D. — *The Guild Corporation*
Tappan, Michael A. — *Ward Howell International, Inc.*
Theobald, David B. — *Theobald & Associates*
Thies, Gary — *S.D. Kelly & Associates, Inc.*
Tholke, William E. — *Canny, Bowen Inc.*
Thomas, Donald — *Mixtec Group*
To, Raymond — *Corporate Recruiters Ltd.*
Tobin, Jim — *Barton Raben, Inc.*
Trueblood, Brian G. — *TNS Partners, Inc.*
Truitt, Thomas B. — *Southwestern Professional Services*
Tryon, Katey — *DeFrain, Mayer, Lee & Burgess LLC*
Tucker, Thomas A. — *The Thomas Tucker Company*
Tunney, William — *Grant Cooper and Associates*
Ulbert, Nancy — *Aureus Group*
Valenta, Joseph — *Princeton Entrepreneurial Resources*
Van Campen, Jerry — *Gilbert & Van Campen International*
Van Remmen, Roger — *Brown, Bernardy, Van Remmen, Inc.*
Van Steenkiste, Julie — *Davidson, Laird & Associates*
Vande-Water, Katie — *J. Robert Scott*

Vann, Dianne — *The Button Group*
Vennat, Manon — *Spencer Stuart*
Vlcek, Thomas J. — *Vlcek & Company, Inc.*
von Stein, Scott — *Wilkinson & Ives*
Waggoner, Lisa — *Intersource, Ltd.*
Waldoch, D. Mark — *Barnes Development Group, LLC*
Walters, William F. — *Jonas, Walters & Assoc., Inc.*
Wassill, Larry — *Corporate Recruiters Ltd.*
Wein, Michael S. — *InterimManagement Solutions, Inc.*
Weissman-Rosenthal, Abbe — *ALW Research International*
Weisz, Laura — *Anderson Sterling Associates*
Werner, Bonnie — *H.M. Long International, Ltd.*
White, Jonathan O. — *The Badger Group*
White, William C. — *Venture Resources Inc.*
Whitney, David L. — *Whitney & Associates, Inc.*
Wichansky, Mark — *TSS Consulting, Ltd.*
Wier, Daniel — *Horton International*
Williams, Angie — *Whitney & Associates, Inc.*
Williams, Gary L. — *Barnes Development Group, LLC*
Williams, Roger K. — *Williams, Roth & Krueger Inc.*
Wilson, Patricia L. — *Leon A. Farley Associates*
Winitz, Joel — *GSW Consulting Group, Inc.*
Winitz, Marla — *GSW Consulting Group, Inc.*
Winnewisser, William E. — *Accounting & Computer Personnel*
Winograd, Glenn — *Criterion Executive Search, Inc.*
Winston, Dale — *Battalia Winston International*
Wirtshafter, Linda — *Grant Cooper and Associates*
Wolf, Stephen M. — *Byron Leonard International, Inc.*
Woodward, Lee — *Search Associates, Inc.*
Woollett, James — *Rusher, Loscavio & LoPresto*
Wyatt, James — *Wyatt & Jaffe*
Young, Alexander — *Messett Associates, Inc.*
Young, Heather — *The Guild Corporation*
Zatzick, Michael — *Search West, Inc.*
Zetter, Roger — *Hunt Ltd.*
Zila, Laurie M. — *Princeton Entrepreneurial Resources*
Zilliacus, Patrick W. — *Larsen, Zilliacus & Associates, Inc.*

## 10. Energy

Alekel, Karren — *ALW Research International*
Ambler, Peter W. — *Peter W. Ambler Company*
Angell, Tryg R. — *Tryg R. Angell Ltd.*
Apostle, George — *Search Dynamics, Inc.*
Bachmeier, Kevin — *Agra Placements International Ltd.*
Baird, John — *Professional Search Consultants*
Baker, Judith — *Search Consultants International, Inc.*
Baker, S. Joseph — *Search Consultants International, Inc.*
Barlow, Ken H. — *The Cherbonnier Group, Inc.*
Barnum, Toni M. — *Stone Murphy & Olson*
Barton, Gary R. — *Barton Raben, Inc.*
Bean, Bill — *Professional Search Consultants*
Beaudin, Elizabeth C. — *Callan Associates, Ltd.*
Belford, Paul — *JDG Associates, Ltd.*
Bellano, Robert W. — *Stanton Chase International*
Bettick, Michael J. — *A.J. Burton Group, Inc.*
Bitar, Edward — *The Interface Group, Ltd./Boyden*
Bittman, Beth M. — *Norman Roberts & Associates, Inc.*
Blackmon, Sharon — *The Abbott Group, Inc.*
Bovich, Maryann C. — *Higdon Prince Inc.*
Boxberger, Michael D. — *Korn/Ferry International*
Brackin, James B. — *Brackin & Sayers Associates*
Bradshaw, John W. — *A.T. Kearney, Inc.*
Brentari, Michael — *Search Consultants International, Inc.*
Brunson, Therese — *Kors Montgomery International*
Bryant, Richard D. — *Bryant Associates, Inc.*
Bryza, Robert M. — *Robert Lowell International*
Burden, Gene — *The Cherbonnier Group, Inc.*
Burns, Alan — *The Enns Partners Inc.*
Callan, Robert M. — *Callan Associates, Ltd.*
Cappe, Richard R. — *Roberts Ryan and Bentley*
Center, Linda — *The Search Center Inc.*
Cherbonnier, L. Michael — *TCG International, Inc.*
Cherbonnier, L. Michael — *The Cherbonnier Group, Inc.*
Clarey, William A. — *Preng & Associates, Inc.*
Collard, Joseph A. — *Spencer Stuart*
Conard, Rodney J. — *Conard Associates, Inc.*
Cooke, Katherine H. — *Horton International*
Cottingham, R.L. — *Marvin L. Silcott & Associates, Inc.*
Crath, Paul F. — *Price Waterhouse*
Crystal, Jonathan A. — *Spencer Stuart*
Cuomo, Frank — *Frank Cuomo and Associates, Inc.*
Cushman, Judith — *Marshall Consultants/West*
D'Alessio, Gary A. — *Chicago Legal Search, Ltd.*
Danforth, Monica — *Search Consultants International, Inc.*
Daniel, Beverly — *Foy, Schneid & Daniel, Inc.*
Dickey, Chet W. — *Bowden & Company, Inc.*
Donnelly, George J. — *Ward Howell International, Inc.*
Drexler, Robert — *Robert Drexler Associates, Inc.*

Duckworth, Donald R. — *Paul Ray Berndtson*
Duley, Richard I. — *ARJay & Associates*
Eason, James — *JRL Executive Recruiters*
Eason, Larry E. — *JRL Executive Recruiters*
Edmond, Bruce — *Corporate Recruiters Ltd.*
Einsele, Neil — *Agra Placements International Ltd.*
Enns, George — *The Enns Partners Inc.*
Erwin, Lee — *Agra Placements International Ltd.*
Farrow, Jerry M. — *McCormack & Farrow*
Fiore, Richard — *Search Consultants International, Inc.*
Flora, Dodi — *Crawford & Crofford*
Follmer, Gary — *Agra Placements International Ltd.*
Frank, Valerie S. — *Norman Roberts & Associates, Inc.*
French, William G. — *Preng & Associates, Inc.*
Freud, John W. — *Paul Ray Berndtson*
Gallagher, Terence M. — *Battalia Winston International*
Gardiner, E. Nicholas P. — *Gardiner International*
Gettys, James R. — *International Staffing Consultants, Inc.*
Gibbs, John S. — *Spencer Stuart*
Gilchrist, Robert J. — *Horton International*
Gillespie, Thomas — *Professional Search Consultants*
Gobert, Larry — *Professional Search Consultants*
Goldsmith, Fred J. — *Fred J. Goldsmith Associates*
Grebenstein, Charles R. — *Skott/Edwards Consultants, Inc.*
Greene, Luke — *Broward-Dobbs, Inc.*
Hall, Robert — *Don Richard Associates of Tidewater, Inc.*
Hamilton, Timothy — *The Caldwell Partners Amrop International*
Hansen, David G. — *Ott & Hansen, Inc.*
Harbaugh, Paul J. — *International Management Advisors, Inc.*
Harbert, David O. — *Sweeney Harbert & Mummert, Inc.*
Hardison, Richard L. — *Hardison & Company*
Harvey, Mike — *Advanced Executive Resources*
Harvey, Richard — *Price Waterhouse*
Haughton, Michael — *DeFrain, Mayer, Lee & Burgess LLC*
Havener, Donald Clarke — *The Abbott Group, Inc.*
Haystead, Steve — *Advanced Executive Resources*
Hemingway, Stuart C. — *Robison & Associates*
Hernandez, Luis A. — *CoEnergy, Inc.*
Hertlein, James N.J. — *Boyden/Zay & Company*
Higdon, Henry G. — *Higdon Prince Inc.*
Hobart, John N. — *Paul Ray Berndtson*
Holtz, Gene — *Agra Placements International Ltd.*
Honey, W. Michael M. — *O'Callaghan Honey/Paul Ray Berndtson, Inc.*
Hubert, David L. — *ARJay & Associates*
Hughes, James J. — *R.P. Barone Associates*
Hunter, Sue J. — *Robison & Associates*
Hyde, W. Jerry — *Hyde Danforth Wold & Co.*
Infinger, Ronald E. — *Robison & Associates*
Ingram, D. John — *Ingram & Aydelotte Inc.*
Jackson, Clarke H. — *The Caldwell Partners Amrop International*
Jensen, Stephanie — *Don Richard Associates of Tidewater, Inc.*
Johnson, Kathleen A. — *Barton Raben, Inc.*
Johnson, S. Hope — *The Interface Group, Ltd./Boyden*
Jones, Gary — *BGB Associates*
Jones, Ronald T. — *ARJay & Associates*
Katz, Cyndi — *Search West, Inc.*
Kelly, Peter W. — *R. Rollo Associates*
King, Stephen C. — *Boyden/Zay & Company*
Kinser, Richard E. — *Richard Kinser & Associates*
Kirkpatrick, Robert L. — *Reese Associates*
Klages, Constance W. — *International Management Advisors, Inc.*
Klauck, James J. — *Horton International*
Kondra, Vernon J. — *The Douglas Reiter Company, Inc.*
Kors, R. Paul — *Kors Montgomery International*
Krejci, Stanley L. — *The Interface Group, Ltd./Boyden*
Kucewicz, William — *Search West, Inc.*
Lawrence, David — *Agra Placements International Ltd.*
Lebo, Terry — *Agra Placements International Ltd.*
Leetma, Imbi — *Stanton Chase International*
Leland, Paul — *McInturff & Associates, Inc.*
LemMou, Paul — *International Staffing Consultants, Inc.*
Lieb, Donald F. — *Russell Reynolds Associates, Inc.*
Line, Joseph T. — *Sharrow & Associates*
Little, Gary — *Agra Placements International Ltd.*
Lotz, R. James — *International Management Advisors, Inc.*
Lowry, W. Randall — *Paul Ray Berndtson*
Lumsby, George N. — *International Management Advisors, Inc.*
Lynn, Donald — *Frank Cuomo and Associates, Inc.*
Lyons, Michele R. — *R. Rollo Associates*
Magee, Harrison R. — *Bowden & Company, Inc.*
Magnani, Susan — *The Search Center Inc.*
Malcolm, Rod — *The Enns Partners Inc.*
Manassero, Henri J.P. — *International Management Advisors, Inc.*
Mangum, William T. — *Thomas Mangum Company*
Marumoto, William H. — *The Interface Group, Ltd./Boyden*
Massey, H. Heath — *Robison & Associates*
Mathias, William J. — *Preng & Associates, Inc.*

McBurney, Kevin — *The Caldwell Partners Amrop International*
McDonald, Gary E. — *Agra Placements International Ltd.*
McInturff, Robert — *McInturff & Associates, Inc.*
McKay, W. John — *O'Callaghan Honey/Paul Ray Berndtson, Inc.*
McLeish, Robert H. — *Executive Search International*
McMillin, Bob — *Price Waterhouse*
Meyer, William — *Agra Placements International Ltd.*
Miller, Roy — *The Enns Partners Inc.*
Miller, Russel E. — *ARJay & Associates*
Moore, Michael — *Agra Placements International Ltd.*
Morton, Robert C. — *Morton, McCorkle & Associates, Inc.*
Mruk, Edwin S. — *Mruk & Partners/EMA Partners Int'l*
Muendel, H. Edward — *Stanton Chase International*
Murphy, Gary J. — *Stone Murphy & Olson*
Murray, Virginia — *Baker, Harris & Partners Limited*
Napier, Ginger L. — *Preng & Associates, Inc.*
Neidhart, Craig C. — *TNS Partners, Inc.*
Nelson, Barbara — *Herman Smith Executive Initiatives Inc.*
Neuberth, Jeffrey G. — *Canny, Bowen Inc.*
Newbold, Michael — *Agra Placements International Ltd.*
Newman, Arthur I. — *Lamalie Amrop International*
Nielsen, Eric C. — *Russell Reynolds Associates, Inc.*
Norsell, Paul E. — *Paul Norsell & Associates, Inc.*
O'Callaghan, Terry K. — *O'Callaghan Honey/Paul Ray Berndtson, Inc.*
Orner, Ted A. — *Russell Reynolds Associates, Inc.*
Pacini, Lauren R. — *Hite Executive Search*
Pappas, Jim — *Search Dynamics, Inc.*
Patton, Mitchell — *Patton/Perry Associates, Inc.*
Percival, Chris — *Chicago Legal Search, Ltd.*
Persky, Barry — *Barry Persky & Company, Inc.*
Pfeiffer, Irene — *Price Waterhouse*
Plimpton, Ralph L. — *R L Plimpton Associates*
Pompeo, Paul — *Search West, Inc.*
Porter, Nanci — *Eastridge InfoTech*
Preng, David E. — *Preng & Associates, Inc.*
Prosser, Shane — *Search Consultants International, Inc.*
Raben, Steven — *Paul Ray Berndtson*
Rabinowitz, Peter A. — *P.A.R. Associates Inc.*
Ray, Breck — *Paul Ray Berndtson*
Ray, Marianne C. — *Callan Associates, Ltd.*
Redding, Denise — *The Douglas Reiter Company, Inc.*
Reiter, Douglas — *The Douglas Reiter Company, Inc.*
Reynolds, Gregory P. — *Roberts Ryan and Bentley*
Rice, Douglas — *Agra Placements International Ltd.*
Rieger, Louis J. — *Spencer Stuart*
Rivers, Geri — *Chrisman & Company, Incorporated*
Rizzo, L. Donald — *R.P. Barone Associates*
Roberts, Norman C. — *Norman Roberts & Associates, Inc.*
Robison, John H. — *Robison & Associates*
Rodgers, John — *Agra Placements International Ltd.*
Rollo, Robert S. — *R. Rollo Associates*
Rubinstein, Alan J. — *Chicago Legal Search, Ltd.*
Sarn, Allan G. — *Allan Sarn Associates Inc.*
Savage, Edward J. — *Stanton Chase International*
Sayers, Bruce D. — *Brackin & Sayers Associates*
Schlpma, Christine — *Advanced Executive Resources*
Schneider, Perry — *Agra Placements International Ltd.*
Scranton, Lisa — *A.J. Burton Group, Inc.*
Scrivines, Hank — *Search Northwest Associates*
Sevilla, Claudio A. — *Crawford & Crofford*
Shea, Christopher J. — *Ingram & Aydelotte Inc.*
Shervey, Brent C. — *O'Callaghan Honey/Paul Ray Berndtson, Inc.*
Shourds, Mary E. — *Houze, Shourds & Montgomery, Inc.*
Sibul, Shelly Remen — *Chicago Legal Search, Ltd.*
Silcott, Marvin L. — *Marvin L. Silcott & Associates, Inc.*
Sindler, Jay — *A.J. Burton Group, Inc.*
Sjogren, Dennis — *Agra Placements International Ltd.*
Smirnov, Tatiana — *Allan Sarn Associates Inc.*
Smith, Adam M. — *The Abbott Group, Inc.*
Smith, Grant — *Price Waterhouse*
Snodgrass, Stephen — *DeFrain, Mayer, Lee & Burgess LLC*
Sowerbutt, Richard S. — *Hite Executive Search*
Spriggs, Robert D. — *Spriggs & Company, Inc.*
Stein, Terry W. — *Stewart, Stein and Scott, Ltd.*
Stewart, Jeffrey O. — *Stewart, Stein and Scott, Ltd.*
Stouffer, Dale — *Agra Placements International Ltd.*
Sutton, Robert J. — *The Caldwell Partners Amrop International*
Tanton, John E. — *Tanton Mitchell/Paul Ray Berndtson*
Thies, Gary — *S.D. Kelly & Associates, Inc.*
Thomas, Ian — *International Staffing Consultants, Inc.*
Tootsey, Mark A. — *A.J. Burton Group, Inc.*
Truitt, Thomas B. — *Southwestern Professional Services*
Tryon, Katey — *DeFrain, Mayer, Lee & Burgess LLC*
Tucker, Thomas A. — *The Thomas Tucker Company*
Turner, Edward K. — *Don Richard Associates of Charlotte*
Tutwiler, Stephen — *Don Richard Associates of Tampa, Inc.*
Ulbert, Nancy — *Aureus Group*

Vainblat, Galina — *Foy, Schneid & Daniel, Inc.*
Van Clieaf, Mark — *MVC Associates International*
Vossler, James — *A.J. Burton Group, Inc.*
Walker, Craig H. — *A.J. Burton Group, Inc.*
Walker, Ewing J. — *Ward Howell International, Inc.*
Wayne, Cary S. — *ProSearch Inc.*
Weissman-Rosenthal, Abbe — *ALW Research International*
Wheeler, Gerard H. — *A.J. Burton Group, Inc.*
Wier, Daniel — *Horton International*
Wilkinson, William R. — *Wilkinson & Ives*
Winitz, Joel — *GSW Consulting Group, Inc.*
Winitz, Marla — *GSW Consulting Group, Inc.*
Witte, David L. — *Ward Howell International, Inc.*
Wright, Carl A.J. — *A.J. Burton Group, Inc.*
Zay, Thomas C. — *Boyden/Zay & Company*

## 11. Entertainment

Abruzzo, James — *A.T. Kearney, Inc.*
Adams, Ralda F. — *Hospitality International*
Allen, Donald — *D.S. Allen Associates, Inc.*
Allgire, Mary L. — *Kenzer Corp.*
Arms, Douglas — *TOPAZ International, Inc.*
Arms, Douglas — *TOPAZ Legal Solutions*
Aronin, Michael — *Fisher-Todd Associates*
Aston, Kathy — *Marra Peters & Partners*
Baillou, Astrid — *Richard Kinser & Associates*
Barack, Brianne — *The Barack Group, Inc.*
Berk-Levine, Margo — *MB Inc. Interim Executive Division*
Billington, Brian — *Billington & Associates*
Bishop, Susan — *Bishop Partners*
Bloomer, James E. — *L.W. Foote Company*
Bratches, Howard — *Thorndike Deland Associates*
Brocaglia, Joyce — *Alta Associates, Inc.*
Brophy, Melissa — *Maximum Management Corp.*
Brown, Buzz — *Brown, Bernardy, Van Remmen, Inc.*
Cahill, James P. — *Thorndike Deland Associates*
Caldwell, C. Douglas — *The Caldwell Partners Amrop International*
Carideo, Joseph — *Thorndike Deland Associates*
Cheadle, Neil E. — *The IMC Group of Companies Ltd.*
Christian, Jeffrey E. — *Christian & Timbers*
Citrin, James M. — *Spencer Stuart*
Cohen, Pamela — *TOPAZ International, Inc.*
Cohen, Pamela — *TOPAZ Legal Solutions*
Coleman, J. Kevin — *J. Kevin Coleman & Associates, Inc.*
Coleman, John A. — *Canny, Bowen Inc.*
Combs, Stephen L. — *Juntunen-Combs-Poirier*
Corrigan, Gerald F. — *The Corrigan Group*
Costick, Kathryn J. — *John Sibbald Associates, Inc.*
Cruz, Catherine — *TOPAZ International, Inc.*
Cruz, Catherine — *TOPAZ Legal Solutions*
D'Alessio, Gary A. — *Chicago Legal Search, Ltd.*
Damon, Robert A. — *Spencer Stuart*
Demchak, James P. — *Sandhurst Associates*
Dinte, Paul — *Dinte Resources, Incorporated*
DiSalvo, Fred — *The Cambridge Group Ltd*
Diskin, Rochelle — *Search West, Inc.*
Dougherty, Janice — *The McCormick Group, Inc.*
Dowell, Mary K. — *Professional Search Associates*
Drury, James J. — *Spencer Stuart*
England, Mark — *Austin-McGregor International*
Erickson, Elaine — *Kenzer Corp.*
Falk, John — *D.S. Allen Associates, Inc.*
Farrell, Barbara — *The Barack Group, Inc.*
Feldman, Abe — *A.E. Feldman Associates*
Ferneborg, Jay W. — *Ferneborg & Associates, Inc.*
Ferneborg, John R. — *Ferneborg & Associates, Inc.*
Feyder, Michael — *A.T. Kearney, Inc.*
Fixler, Eugene — *Ariel Recruitment Associates*
Fonfa, Ann — *S.R. Wolman Associates, Inc.*
Francis, Joseph — *Hospitality International*
Freier, Bruce — *Executive Referral Services, Inc.*
Gaines, Ronni L. — *TOPAZ International, Inc.*
Gaines, Ronni L. — *TOPAZ Legal Solutions*
Galante, Suzanne M. — *Vlcek & Company, Inc.*
Gardiner, E. Nicholas P. — *Gardiner International*
Gerevas, Ronald E. — *Spencer Stuart*
Gerevas, Ronald E. — *Spencer Stuart*
Gibson, Bruce — *Gibson & Company Inc.*
Gill, Susan — *Plummer & Associates, Inc.*
Gilmartin, William — *Hockett Associates, Inc.*
Goar, Duane R. — *Sandhurst Associates*
Gordon, Gerald L. — *E.G. Jones Associates, Ltd.*
Gore, Les — *Executive Search International*
Gray, Annie — *Annie Gray Associates, Inc./The Executive Search Firm*
Gray, Mark — *Executive Referral Services, Inc.*
Groban, Jack — *A.T. Kearney, Inc.*
Hauswirth, Jeffrey M. — *Spencer Stuart*

Hockett, William — *Hockett Associates, Inc.*
Hoevel, Michael J. — *Poirier, Hoevel & Co.*
Holland, Kathleen — *TOPAZ International, Inc.*
Holland, Kathleen — *TOPAZ Legal Solutions*
Hollingsworth, Leslie — *Brad Marks International*
Hopkins, Chester A. — *Handy HRM Corp.*
Hoyda, Louis A. — *Thorndike Deland Associates*
Hughes, Cathy N. — *The Ogdon Partnership*
Hunter, Steven — *Diamond Tax Recruiting*
Imely, Larry — *Christian & Timbers*
Ingram, D. John — *Ingram & Aydelotte Inc.*
Jernigan, Alice — *Ariel Recruitment Associates*
Johnson, Priscilla — *The Johnson Group, Inc.*
Kaplan, Gary — *Gary Kaplan & Associates*
Kaplan, Marc — *Gary Kaplan & Associates*
Katz, Cyndi — *Search West, Inc.*
Keitel, Robert S. — *A.T. Kearney, Inc.*
Kelly, Claudia L. — *Spencer Stuart*
Kelly, Donna J. — *Accountants Executive Search*
Kenzer, Robert D. — *Kenzer Corp.*
Knight, Liz — *Plummer & Associates, Inc.*
Knisely, Gary — *Johnson Smith & Knisely Accord*
Koenig, Joel S. — *Russell Reynolds Associates, Inc.*
Lane, Sheri — *Ryan, Miller & Associates Inc.*
Langer, Joel A. — *Langer Associates, Inc.*
Lautz, Lindsay A. — *Wilkinson & Ives*
Letcher, Harvey D. — *Sandhurst Associates*
Levitt, Muriel A. — *D.S. Allen Associates, Inc.*
Lewis, Jon A. — *Sandhurst Associates*
Lightner, Shayne — *Korn/Ferry International*
Linde, Rick — *Battalia Winston International*
Lombardi, Nancy W. — *WTW Associates*
Lucht, John — *The John Lucht Consultancy Inc.*
MacDougall, Andrew J. — *Spencer Stuart*
Mackenna, Kathy — *Plummer & Associates, Inc.*
Maer, Harry — *Kenzer Corp.*
Mahr, Toni — *K. Russo Associates*
Malcom, John W. — *Johnson Smith & Knisely Accord*
Marchette, Steve — *Juntunen-Combs-Poirier*
Marks, Brad — *Brad Marks International*
Marra, John — *Marra Peters & Partners*
Marra, John — *Marra Peters & Partners*
Mashakas, Elizabeth — *TOPAZ International, Inc.*
Mashakas, Elizabeth — *TOPAZ Legal Solutions*
Matueny, Robert — *Ryan, Miller & Associates Inc.*
McCreary, Charles — *Austin-McGregor International*
McLean, B. Keith — *Price Waterhouse*
McNichols, Walter B. — *Gary Kaplan & Associates*
Menk, Carl W. — *Canny, Bowen Inc.*
Mestepey, John — *A.T. Kearney, Inc.*
Meyer, Stacey — *Gary Kaplan & Associates*
Michaels, Stewart — *TOPAZ International, Inc.*
Michaels, Stewart — *TOPAZ Legal Solutions*
Milton, Suzanne — *Marra Peters & Partners*
Molnar, Robert A. — *Johnson Smith & Knisely Accord*
Morris, David W. — *WTW Associates*
Moyse, Richard G. — *Thorndike Deland Associates*
Mruk, Edwin S. — *Mruk & Partners/EMA Partners Int'l*
Mummert, Dennis D. — *Sweeney Harbert & Mummert, Inc.*
Norman, Randy — *Austin-McGregor International*
O'Maley, Kimberlee — *Spencer Stuart*
O'Such, Tracy — *Bishop Partners*
O'Toole, Dennis P. — *Dennis P. O'Toole & Associates Inc.*
Ogdon, Thomas H. — *The Ogdon Partnership*
Olmstead, George T. — *Blackshaw, Olmstead & Lynch*
Palmlund, David W. — *Lamalie Amrop International*
Paul, Lisa D. — *Merit Resource Group, Inc.*
Pelisson, Charles — *Marra Peters & Partners*
Percival, Chris — *Chicago Legal Search, Ltd.*
Perez, Christina — *Orr Executive Search*
Phelps, Gene L. — *McCormack & Farrow*
Phillips, Donald L. — *O'Shea, Divine & Company, Inc.*
Pickering, Dorothy C. — *Livingston, Robert and Company Inc.*
Pinkman, Karen N. — *Skott/Edwards Consultants, Inc.*
Plummer, John — *Plummer & Associates, Inc.*
Plummer, Winkie Donovan — *McManners Associates, Inc.*
Poirier, Frank — *Juntunen-Combs-Poirier*
Poirier, Roland — *Poirier, Hoevel & Co.*
Prior, Donald — *The Caldwell Partners Amrop International*
Pugh, Judith Geist — *InterimManagement Solutions, Inc.*
Pugrant, Mark A. — *Grant/Morgan Associates, Inc.*
Radice, Joseph — *Hospitality International*
Raiber, Laurie Altman — *The IMC Group of Companies Ltd.*
Regehly, Herbert L. — *The IMC Group of Companies Ltd.*
Regeuye, Peter J. — *Accountants Executive Search*
Reiser, Ellen — *Thorndike Deland Associates*
Richards, Sharon — *The Barack Group, Inc.*
Riley, Elizabeth G. — *Mazza & Riley, Inc.*

## 12. Environmental

Grebenstein, Charles R. — *Skott/Edwards Consultants, Inc.*
Green, Jane — *Phillips Resource Group*
Green, Jean — *Broward-Dobbs, Inc.*
Greene, Luke — *Broward-Dobbs, Inc.*
Hamilton, Timothy — *The Caldwell Partners Amrop International*
Hanson, Carrie — *U.S. Envirosearch*
Hard, Sally Ann — *Ast/Bryant*
Harelick, Arthur S. — *Ashway, Ltd.*
Harfenist, Harry — *Parker Page Group*
Harkins, Robert E. — *Robert Harkins Associates, Inc.*
Harris, Ethel S. — *Don Richard Associates of Charlotte*
Harrison, Priscilla — *Phillips Resource Group*
Harvey, Mike — *Advanced Executive Resources*
Hatcher, Joe B. — *Ast/Bryant*
Haughton, Michael — *DeFrain, Mayer, Lee & Burgess LLC*
Havener, Donald Clarke — *The Abbott Group, Inc.*
Haystead, Steve — *Advanced Executive Resources*
Hecker, Henry C. — *Hogan Acquisitions*
Hemingway, Stuart C. — *Robison & Associates*
Henshaw, Robert — *F-O-R-T-U-N-E Personnel Consultants of Huntsville, Inc.*
Hicks, Albert M. — *Phillips Resource Group*
Hilton, Diane — *Richard, Wayne and Roberts*
Hockett, William — *Hockett Associates, Inc.*
Hogan, Larry H. — *Hogan Acquisitions*
Holden, Richard B. — *Ames Personnel Consultants, Inc.*
Holland, Kathleen — *TOPAZ Legal Solutions*
Holtz, Gene — *Agra Placements International Ltd.*
Hughes, James J. — *R.P. Barone Associates*
Hunter, Gabe — *Phillips Resource Group*
Hunter, John B. — *John Sibbald Associates, Inc.*
Imely, Larry — *Christian & Timbers*
Jackson, Clarke H. — *The Caldwell Partners Amrop International*
Jackson, W.T. — *Sampson Neill & Wilkins Inc.*
Jacobs, Martin J. — *The Rubicon Group*
Jeffers, Carol S. — *John Sibbald Associates, Inc.*
Jensen, Stephanie — *Don Richard Associates of Tidewater, Inc.*
Joffe, Barry — *Bason Associates Inc.*
Johnson, Douglas — *Quality Search*
Johnson, Kathleen A. — *Barton Raben, Inc.*
Johnson, Robert J. — *Quality Search*
Johnson, Ronald S. — *Ronald S. Johnson Associates, Inc.*
Johnson, S. Hope — *The Interface Group, Ltd./Boyden*
Jones, Gary — *BGB Associates*
Jones, Ronald T. — *ARJay & Associates*
Kader, Richard — *Richard Kader & Associates*
Kaplan, Gary — *Gary Kaplan & Associates*
Kaplan, Marc — *Gary Kaplan & Associates*
Keeton, Susan G. — *The Corporate Connection, Ltd.*
King, Steven — *Ashway, Ltd.*
Kinser, Richard E. — *Richard Kinser & Associates*
Kirkpatrick, Robert L. — *Reese Associates*
Klavins, Larissa R. — *Dieckmann & Associates, Ltd.*
Kohn, Adam P. — *Christian & Timbers*
Koontz, Donald N. — *Koontz, Jeffries & Associates, Inc.*
Kossuth, David — *Kossuth & Associates, Inc.*
Lake, Phillip R. — *U.S. Envirosearch*
Lamb, Angus K. — *Raymond Karsan Associates*
Layton, Patrick R. — *MSI International*
LemMou, Paul — *International Staffing Consultants, Inc.*
Long, Benjamin H. — *Travaille Executive Search*
Loomis, Ruth L. — *Ast/Bryant*
Lynn, Diane — *Frank Cuomo and Associates, Inc.*
Mallipudi, Anand — *Raymond Karsan Associates*
Mangum, William T. — *Thomas Mangum Company*
Manns, Alex — *Crawford & Crofford*
Marshall, Gerald — *Blair/Tech Recruiters*
Martin, Geary D. — *Boyden/Zay & Company*
Martines, James — *Sharrow & Associates*
Mashakas, Elizabeth — *TOPAZ Legal Solutions*
Mathias, Kathy — *Stone Murphy & Olson*
Mathias, William J. — *Preng & Associates, Inc.*
Max, Bruno — *RBR Associates, Inc.*
Mayes, Kay H. — *John Shell Associates, Inc.*
McBride, Jonathan E. — *McBride Associates, Inc.*
McBurney, Kevin — *The Caldwell Partners Amrop International*
McCabe, Christopher — *Raymond Karsan Associates*
McCorkle, Sam B. — *Morton, McCorkle & Associates, Inc.*
McGrath, Robert E. — *Robert E. McGrath & Associates*
McIntyre, Joel — *Phillips Resource Group*
McMillin, Bob — *Price Waterhouse*
McNear, Jeffrey E. — *Barrett Partners*
McNichol, John — *McNichol Associates*
McNichols, Walter B. — *Gary Kaplan & Associates*
Meyer, Stacey — *Gary Kaplan & Associates*
Michaels, Stewart — *TOPAZ Legal Solutions*
Mierzwinski, John — *Industrial Recruiters Associates, Inc.*
Miller, Russel E. — *ARJay & Associates*

Milne, Robert P. — *Boyden/Zay & Company*
Moerbe, Ed H. — *Stanton Chase International*
Molitor, John L. — *Barrett Partners*
Montgomery, James M. — *Houze, Shourds & Montgomery, Inc.*
Morgan, Richard J. — *Morgan Samuels Co., Inc.*
Morris, Kristine A. — *Morris & Berger*
Morton, Robert C. — *Morton, McCorkle & Associates, Inc.*
Muendel, H. Edward — *Stanton Chase International*
Mulligan, Robert P. — *William Willis Worldwide Inc.*
Murin, Rose Mary — *U.S. Envirosearch*
Nagler, Leon G. — *Nagler, Robins & Poe, Inc.*
Napier, Ginger L. — *Preng & Associates, Inc.*
Nutter, Roger — *Raymond Karsan Associates*
Pappas, Jim — *Search Dynamics, Inc.*
Park, Dabney G. — *Mark Stanley & Company*
Peck, David W. — *The Peck Consultancy*
Percival, Chris — *Chicago Legal Search, Ltd.*
Perkins, Bob — *Richard, Wayne and Roberts*
Persky, Barry — *Barry Persky & Company, Inc.*
Peters, James N. — *TNS Partners, Inc.*
Phillips, Donald L. — *O'Shea, Divine & Company, Inc.*
Pickering, Dale — *Agri-Tech Personnel, Inc.*
Pitts, Charles — *Contemporary Management Services, Inc.*
Plimpton, Ralph L. — *R L Plimpton Associates*
Poe, James B. — *Nagler, Robins & Poe, Inc.*
Porada, Stephen D. — *CAP Inc.*
Porter, Albert — *The Experts*
Porter, Nanci — *Eastridge InfoTech*
Potter, Douglas C. — *Stanton Chase International*
Prencipe, V. Michael — *Raymond Karsan Associates*
Preng, David E. — *Preng & Associates, Inc.*
Prior, Donald — *The Caldwell Partners Amrop International*
Prosser, Shane — *Search Consultants International, Inc.*
Pugliese, Vincent — *Search West, Inc.*
Rabinowitz, Peter A. — *P.A.R. Associates Inc.*
Ramsey, John H. — *Mark Stanley & Company*
Rapoport, William — *Blair/Tech Recruiters*
Rathborne, Kenneth J. — *Blair/Tech Recruiters*
Ray, Marianne C. — *Callan Associates, Ltd.*
Reddick, David C. — *Horton International*
Rieger, Louis J. — *Spencer Stuart*
Rizzo, L. Donald — *R.P. Barone Associates*
Roberts, Nick P. — *Spectrum Search Associates, Inc.*
Roberts, Norman C. — *Norman Roberts & Associates, Inc.*
Rogers, Leah — *Dinte Resources, Incorporated*
Rothfeld, Robert — *A.E. Feldman Associates*
Rubinstein, Alan J. — *Chicago Legal Search, Ltd.*
Rurak, Zbigniew T. — *Rurak & Associates, Inc.*
Sacerdote, John — *Raymond Karsan Associates*
Samuels, Lewis J. — *Morgan Samuels Co., Inc.*
Sarn, Allan G. — *Allan Sarn Associates Inc.*
Schlecht, Nancy — *Morgan Samuels Co., Inc.*
Schlpma, Christine — *Advanced Executive Resources*
Scrivines, Hank — *Search Northwest Associates*
Selko, Philip W. — *Hogan Acquisitions*
Serwat, Leonard A. — *Spencer Stuart*
Shell, John C. — *John Shell Associates, Inc.*
Shenfield, Peter — *Baker, Harris & Partners Limited*
Shepherd, Daniel M. — *Shepherd Bueschel & Provus, Inc.*
Shervey, Brent C. — *O'Callaghan Honey/Paul Ray Berndtson, Inc.*
Shore, Earl L. — *E.L. Shore & Associates Ltd.*
Sibul, Shelly Remen — *Chicago Legal Search, Ltd.*
Silver, Lee A. — *L.A. Silver Associates, Inc.*
Silverman, Paul M. — *The Marshall Group*
Smirnov, Tatiana — *Allan Sarn Associates Inc.*
Smith, Adam M. — *The Abbott Group, Inc.*
Smith, David P. — *Smith & Latterell (HRS, Inc.)*
Smith, Douglas M. — *Ward Howell International, Inc.*
Songy, Al — *U.S. Envirosearch*
Sowerbutt, Richard S. — *Hite Executive Search*
Spiegel, Gay — *L.A. Silver Associates, Inc.*
Spitz, Grant — *The Caldwell Partners Amrop International*
Starr, Anna — *Richard, Wayne and Roberts*
Stephenson, Don L. — *Ells Personnel System Inc.*
Stewart, Ross M. — *Human Resources Network Partners Inc.*
Straube, Stanley H. — *Straube Associates*
Sutton, Robert J. — *The Caldwell Partners Amrop International*
Swanson, Dick — *Raymond Karsan Associates*
Szafran, Jack — *U.S. Envirosearch*
Thielman, Joseph — *Barrett Partners*
Thomas, Ian — *International Staffing Consultants, Inc.*
Tryon, Katey — *DeFrain, Mayer, Lee & Burgess LLC*
Tursi, Deborah J. — *The Corporate Connection, Ltd.*
Tutwiler, Stephen — *Don Richard Associates of Tampa, Inc.*
Twiste, Craig — *Raymond Karsan Associates*
Vachon, David A. — *McNichol Associates*
Vainblat, Galina — *Foy, Schneid & Daniel, Inc.*
Vinnedge, Sandra — *U.S. Envirosearch*

Nicol, Peg — Evie Kreisler & Associates, Inc.
Normann, Amy — Robert M. Flanagan & Associates, Ltd.
O'Hara, Daniel M. — Lynch Miller Moore Partners, Inc.
O'Neill, Stephen A. — Harris Heery & Associates
Ogdon, Thomas H. — The Ogdon Partnership
Olmstead, George T. — Blackshaw, Olmstead & Lynch
Oswald, Mark G. — Canny, Bowen Inc.
Parker, Roberta — R. Parker and Associates, Inc.
Persky, Barry — Barry Persky & Company, Inc.
Pessin, Mark — Evie Kreisler & Associates, Inc.
Peternich, Tracy — Simpson Associates
Peters, James N. — TNS Partners, Inc.
Pettibone, Linda — Herbert Mines Associates, Inc.
Pettway, Samuel H. — Spencer Stuart
Pickering, Dorothy C. — Livingston, Robert and Company Inc.
Pinkman, Karen N. — Skott/Edwards Consultants, Inc.
Plessner, Rene — Rene Plessner Associates, Inc.
Plummer, John — Plummer & Associates, Inc.
Plummer, Winkie Donovan — McManners Associates, Inc.
Poirier, Roland — Poirier, Hoevel & Co.
Porter, Donald — Amherst Personnel Group Inc.
Priftis, Anthony — Evie Kreisler & Associates, Inc.
Provus, Barbara L. — Shepherd Bueschel & Provus, Inc.
Quatrone, Olivia S. — Heidrick & Struggles, Inc.
Ravit, Alan — Career Management International
Ray, Marianne C. — Callan Associates, Ltd.
Regeuye, Peter J. — Accountants Executive Search
Reimenschneider, Donald — Evie Kreisler & Associates, Inc.
Reiser, Ellen — Thorndike Deland Associates
Reiter, Harold D. — Herbert Mines Associates, Inc.
Reyman, Susan — S. Reyman & Associates Ltd.
Riley, James — Hunt Ltd.
Roberts, Derek J. — Ward Howell International, Inc.
Roberts, Mitch — A.E. Feldman Associates
Rodriguez, Josie — R. Parker and Associates, Inc.
Ross, Sheila L. — Ward Howell International, Inc.
Roth, William — Harris Heery & Associates
Rothfeld, Robert — A.E. Feldman Associates
Rozan, Naomi — Comprehensive Search
Ruello, Brenda L. — Heidrick & Struggles, Inc.
Russell, Susan Anne — Executive Search Consultants Corporation
Scarbrough, Debbi — Evie Kreisler & Associates, Inc.
Schiavone, Mary Rose — Canny, Bowen Inc.
Schiffer, Stewart — Career Management International
Schroeder, John W. — Spencer Stuart
Schuette, Dorothy — Harris Heery & Associates
Seals, Sonny — A.T. Kearney, Inc.
Seitchik, Jack — Seitchik Corwin and Seitchik, Inc.
Seitchik, William — Seitchik Corwin and Seitchik, Inc.
Seitz, Charles J. — Neail Behringer Consultants
Selko, Philip W. — Hogan Acquisitions
Semyan, John K. — TNS Partners, Inc.
Shenfield, Peter — Baker, Harris & Partners Limited
Sibbald, John R. — John Sibbald Associates, Inc.
Smith, Robert L. — Smith & Sawyer Inc.
Smyth, Brendan — Simpson Associates
Snyder, Thomas J. — Spencer Stuart
Stahl, Cynthia — Plummer & Associates, Inc.
Standard, Gail — Comprehensive Search
Steck, Frank T. — A.T. Kearney, Inc.
Steinman, Stephen — The Stevenson Group of New Jersey
Stenholm, Gilbert R. — Spencer Stuart
Stephenson, Mike — Evie Kreisler & Associates, Inc.
Stoneham, Herbert E.C. — Stoneham Associates Corp.
Straube, Stanley H. — Straube Associates
Stricker, Sidney G. — Stricker & Zagor
Strobridge, Richard P. — F.L. Taylor & Company, Inc.
Strom, Mark N. — Search Advisors International Corp.
Summers, Burke — The McCormick Group, Inc.
Sur, William K. — Canny, Bowen Inc.
Tallent, Diane — Evie Kreisler & Associates, Inc.
Taylor, Ernest A. — Ward Howell International, Inc.
ten Cate, Herman H. — Stoneham Associates Corp.
Theobald, David B. — Theobald & Associates
Tholke, William E. — Canny, Bowen Inc.
Thomas, Jeffrey — Fairfaxx Corporation
Tootsey, Mark A. — A.J. Burton Group, Inc.
Tucci, Joseph — Fairfaxx Corporation
Ulbert, Nancy — Aureus Group
Van Horn, Carol — R. Parker and Associates, Inc.
Van Remmen, Roger — Brown, Bernardy, Van Remmen, Inc.
Velten, Mark — Hunt Advisory Services
Velten, Mark — Hunt Ltd.
Venable, William W. — Thorndike Deland Associates
Vennat, Manon — Spencer Stuart
Vergari, Jane — Herbert Mines Associates, Inc.
Virgili, Franca — Johnson Smith & Knisely Accord
Visnich, L. Christine — Bason Associates Inc.

Warren, Sylvia W. — Thorndike Deland Associates
Waxman, Bruce — Ryan, Miller & Associates Inc.
Wessel, Michael J. — Spectra International Inc.
Whitaker, Charles — Evie Kreisler & Associates, Inc.
White, Jeffrey E. — Simpson Associates
White, Kimberly — Executive Referral Services, Inc.
Wilensky, Joel H. — Joel H. Wilensky Associates, Inc.
Willner, Nannette — S.R. Wolman Associates, Inc.
Windle, Mary — Evie Kreisler & Associates, Inc.
Wolman, Stephen R. — S.R. Wolman Associates, Inc.
Wright, Leslie — The Stevenson Group of New Jersey
Zay, Thomas C. — Boyden/Zay & Company
Zonis, Hildy R. — Accountants Executive Search

## 14. Financial Services

Abbatiello, Christine Murphy — Winter, Wyman & Company
Abell, Vincent W. — MSI International
Abramson, Roye — Source Services Corporation
Ackerman, Larry R. — Spectrum Search Associates, Inc.
Adams, Amy — Richard, Wayne and Roberts
Adams, Jeffrey C. — Telford, Adams & Alexander/Jeffrey C. Adams & Co., Inc.
Adams, Len — The KPA Group
Albert, Richard — Source Services Corporation
Alexander, John T. — Telford, Adams & Alexander/Human Resource Services
Alfano, Anthony J. — Russell Reynolds Associates, Inc.
Alford, Holly — Source Services Corporation
Allard, Susan — Allard Associates
Allen, John L. — Heidrick & Struggles, Inc.
Allen, Scott — Chrisman & Company, Incorporated
Allgire, Mary L. — Kenzer Corp.
Allred, J. Michael — Spencer Stuart
Alringer, Marc — Source Services Corporation
Altreuter, Rose — ALTCO Temporary Services
Altreuter, Rose — The ALTCO Group
Ambler, Peter W. — Peter W. Ambler Company
Amico, Robert — Source Services Corporation
Anderson, Mary — Source Services Corporation
Anderson, Matthew — Source Services Corporation
Anderson, Richard — Grant Cooper and Associates
Anderson, Shawn — Temporary Accounting Personnel, Inc.
Andre, Jacques P. — Paul Ray Berndtson
Andrews, Laura L. — Stricker & Zagor
Anwar, Tarin — Jay Gaines & Company, Inc.
Archer, Sandra F. — Ryan, Miller & Associates Inc.
Argenio, Michelangelo — Spencer Stuart
Argentin, Jo — Executive Placement Consultants, Inc.
Arms, Douglas — TOPAZ International, Inc.
Arms, Douglas — TOPAZ Legal Solutions
Aronin, Michael — Fisher-Todd Associates
Aronow, Lawrence E. — Aronow Associates, Inc.
Ascher, Susan P. — The Ascher Group
Aston, Kathy — Marra Peters & Partners
Aydelotte, G. Thomas — Ingram & Aydelotte Inc.
Bachmeier, Kevin — Agra Placements International Ltd.
Bader, Sam — Bader Research Corporation
Badger, Fred H. — The Badger Group
Baer, Kenneth — Source Services Corporation
Bagg, Mary — Keith Bagg & Associates Inc.
Baglio, Robert — Source Services Corporation
Bagwell, Bruce — Intersource, Ltd.
Baier, Rebecca — Source Services Corporation
Bailey, William A. — TNS Partners, Inc.
Baitler, Simon C. — The Stevenson Group of Delaware Inc.
Baker, Gary M. — Cochran, Cochran & Yale, Inc.
Baker, Gary M. — Temporary Accounting Personnel, Inc.
Bakken, Mark — Source Services Corporation
Balchumas, Charles — Source Services Corporation
Baldock, Robert G. — Lovas Stanley/Paul Ray Berndtson Inc.
Baldwin, Keith R. — The Baldwin Group
Ballantine, Caroline B. — Heidrick & Struggles, Inc.
Balter, Sidney — Source Services Corporation
Banko, Scott — Source Services Corporation
Baranowski, Peter — Source Services Corporation
Barger, H. Carter — Barger & Sargeant, Inc.
Barlow, Ken H. — The Cherbonnier Group, Inc.
Barnaby, Richard — Source Services Corporation
Barnes, Roanne L. — Barnes Development Group, LLC
Barnette, Dennis A. — Heidrick & Struggles, Inc.
Barnum, Toni M. — Stone Murphy & Olson
Barrett, J. David — Heidrick & Struggles, Inc.
Bartels, Fredrick — Source Services Corporation
Bartfield, Philip — Source Services Corporation
Barton, Gary R. — Barton Raben, Inc.
Barton, James — Source Services Corporation
Bason, Maurice L. — Bason Associates Inc.
Bass, Nate — Jacobson Associates

Cohen, Michael R. — *Intech Summit Group, Inc.*
Cohen, Pamela — *TOPAZ International, Inc.*
Cohen, Pamela — *TOPAZ Legal Solutions*
Cohen, Robert C. — *Intech Summit Group, Inc.*
Colasanto, Frank M. — *W.R. Rosato & Associates, Inc.*
Colborne, Janis M. — *AJM Professional Services*
Cole, Kevin — *Don Richard Associates of Washington, D.C., Inc.*
Cole, Rosalie — *Source Services Corporation*
Cole, Sharon A. — *AJM Professional Services*
Coleman, J. Gregory — *Korn/Ferry International*
Coleman, John A. — *Canny, Bowen Inc.*
Collins, Scott — *Source Services Corporation*
Collins, Stephen — *The Johnson Group, Inc.*
Collis, Martin — *E.L. Shore & Associates Ltd.*
Colman, Michael — *Executive Placement Consultants, Inc.*
Comai, Christine — *Source Services Corporation*
Combs, Thomas — *Source Services Corporation*
Cona, Joseph A. — *Cona Personnel Search*
Conard, Rodney J. — *Conard Associates, Inc.*
Coneys, Bridget — *Source Services Corporation*
Connaghan, Linda — *Bowman & Marshall, Inc.*
Connelly, Kevin M. — *Spencer Stuart*
Cook, Charlene — *Source Services Corporation*
Cooke, Katherine H. — *Horton International*
Cordaro, Concetta — *Flynn, Hannock, Incorporated*
Corso, Glen S. — *Chartwell Partners International, Inc.*
Cotugno, James — *Source Services Corporation*
Coughlin, Stephen — *Source Services Corporation*
Courtney, Brendan A.J. — *A.J. Burton Group, Inc.*
Coyle, Hugh F. — *A.J. Burton Group, Inc.*
Cramer, Paul J. — *C/R Associates*
Crane, Howard C. — *Chartwell Partners International, Inc.*
Crath, Paul F. — *Price Waterhouse*
Crawford, Cassondra — *Don Richard Associates of Washington, D.C., Inc.*
Crist, Peter — *Crist Partners, Ltd.*
Critchley, Walter — *Cochran, Cochran & Yale, Inc.*
Critchley, Walter — *Temporary Accounting Personnel, Inc.*
Crowell, Elizabeth — *H.M. Long International, Ltd.*
Cruz, Catherine — *TOPAZ International, Inc.*
Cruz, Catherine — *TOPAZ Legal Solutions*
Crystal, Jonathan A. — *Spencer Stuart*
Cuddy, Brian C. — *Romac & Associates*
Cuddy, Patricia — *Source Services Corporation*
Cunningham, Robert Y. — *Goodrich & Sherwood Associates, Inc.*
Curren, Camella — *Source Services Corporation*
Curtis, Ellissa — *Cochran, Cochran & Yale, Inc.*
Cutka, Matthew — *Source Services Corporation*
D'Elia, Arthur P. — *Korn/Ferry International*
Dabich, Thomas M. — *Robert Harkins Associates, Inc.*
Daniels, Alfred — *Alfred Daniels & Associates*
Dankberg, Iris — *Source Services Corporation*
Dannenberg, Richard A. — *Roberts Ryan and Bentley*
Darter, Steven M. — *People Management Northeast Incorporated*
Davis, C. Scott — *Source Services Corporation*
Davis, Elease — *Source Services Corporation*
Davis, Joan — *MSI International*
Dawson, William — *Source Services Corporation*
de Bardin, Francesca — *F.L. Taylor & Company, Inc.*
de Cholnoky, Andrea — *Spencer Stuart*
de Palacios, Jeannette C. — *J. Palacios & Associates, Inc.*
de Tuede, Catherine — *Thomas A. Byrnes Associates*
Debus, Wayne — *Source Services Corporation*
Deck, Jack — *Source Services Corporation*
DeCorrevont, James — *DeCorrevont & Associates*
DeCorrevont, James — *DeCorrevont & Associates*
Del Prete, Karen — *Gilbert Tweed/INESA*
Delaney, Patrick J. — *Sensible Solutions, Inc.*
Delman, Charles — *Korn/Ferry International*
DeMarco, Robert — *Source Services Corporation*
Demchak, James P. — *Sandhurst Associates*
Desmond, Dennis — *Beall & Company, Inc.*
Desmond, Mary — *Source Services Corporation*
Dever, Mary — *Source Services Corporation*
Devito, Alice — *Source Services Corporation*
deVry, Kimberly A. — *Tower Consultants, Ltd.*
deWilde, David M. — *Chartwell Partners International, Inc.*
Dewing, Jesse J. — *Don Richard Associates of Charlotte*
Di Filippo, Thomas — *Source Services Corporation*
Dickey, Chet W. — *Bowden & Company, Inc.*
Dieckmann, Ralph E. — *Dieckmann & Associates, Ltd.*
Diers, Gary — *Source Services Corporation*
Dietz, David S. — *MSI International*
DiGiovanni, Charles — *Penn Search*
Dinte, Paul — *Dinte Resources, Incorporated*
DiPiazza, Joseph — *Boyden*
DiSalvo, Fred — *The Cambridge Group Ltd*
Diskin, Rochelle — *Search West, Inc.*

Dittmar, Richard — *Source Services Corporation*
Divine, Robert S. — *O'Shea, Divine & Company, Inc.*
Do, Sonnie — *Whitney & Associates, Inc.*
Doan, Lisa — *Rhodes Associates*
Dobrow, Samuel — *Source Services Corporation*
Doele, Donald C. — *Goodrich & Sherwood Associates, Inc.*
Donahue, Debora — *Source Services Corporation*
Donnelly, George J. — *Ward Howell International, Inc.*
Donnelly, Patti — *Source Services Corporation*
Dorfner, Martin — *Source Services Corporation*
Dorsey, Jim — *Ryan, Miller & Associates Inc.*
Dotson, M. Ileen — *Dotson & Associates*
Doukas, Jon A. — *Professional Bank Services, Inc. D/B/A Executive Search, Inc.*
Dowell, Mary K. — *Professional Search Associates*
Dowlatzadch, Homayoun — *Source Services Corporation*
Downs, James L. — *Sanford Rose Associates*
Downs, William — *Source Services Corporation*
Doyle, John P. — *Paul Ray Berndtson*
Dreifus, Donald — *Search West, Inc.*
Dressler, Ralph — *Romac & Associates*
Dromeshauser, Peter — *Dromeshauser Associates*
Drummond-Hay, Peter — *Russell Reynolds Associates, Inc.*
Ducruet, Linda K. — *Heidrick & Struggles, Inc.*
Dudley, Craig J. — *Paul Ray Berndtson*
Duelks, John — *Source Services Corporation*
Duncan, Dana — *Source Services Corporation*
Dunkel, David L. — *Romac & Associates*
Dunlow, Aimee — *Source Services Corporation*
Dunman, Betsy L. — *Crawford & Crofford*
Dunn, Mary Helen — *Paul Ray Berndtson*
Dupont, Rick — *Source Services Corporation*
Early, Alice C. — *Russell Reynolds Associates, Inc.*
Ebeling, John A. — *Gilbert Tweed/INESA*
Eberly, Carrie — *Accounting Resources, Inc.*
Edwards, Dorothy — *MSI International*
Edwards, Douglas W. — *Egon Zehnder International Inc.*
Edwards, Verba L. — *Wing Tips & Pumps, Inc.*
Eggert, Scott — *Source Services Corporation*
Ehrgott, Elizabeth — *The Ascher Group*
Ehrhart, Jennifer — *ADOW's Executeam*
Einsele, Neil — *Agra Placements International Ltd.*
Eiseman, Joe — *Source Services Corporation*
Eiseman, Joe — *Source Services Corporation*
Eiseman, Joe — *Source Services Corporation*
Ellis, David — *Don Richard Associates of Georgia, Inc.*
Ellis, Patricia — *Source Services Corporation*
Ellis, Ted K. — *The Hindman Company*
Ellis, William — *Interspace Interactive Inc.*
Elster, Irv — *Spectrum Search Associates, Inc.*
Emerson, Randall — *Source Services Corporation*
Engle, Bryan — *Source Services Corporation*
Enns, George — *The Enns Partners Inc.*
Erickson, Elaine — *Kenzer Corp.*
Ervin, Russell — *Source Services Corporation*
Erwin, Lee — *Agra Placements International Ltd.*
Eustis, Lucy R. — *MSI International*
Evans, Timothy — *Source Services Corporation*
Ezersky, Jane E. — *Highland Search Group, L.L.C.*
Fabbro, Vivian — *A.T. Kearney, Inc.*
Fagerstrom, Jon — *Source Services Corporation*
Fales, Scott — *Source Services Corporation*
Fancher, Robert L. — *Bason Associates Inc.*
Fanning, Paul — *Source Services Corporation*
Farler, Wiley — *Source Services Corporation*
Farley, Leon A. — *Leon A. Farley Associates*
Farnsworth, John A. — *Pearson, Caldwell & Farnsworth, Inc.*
Farrow, Jerry M. — *McCormack & Farrow*
Fawcett, Anne M. — *The Caldwell Partners Amrop International*
Fechheimer, Peter — *Source Services Corporation*
Feder, Gwen — *Egon Zehnder International Inc.*
Federman, Jack R. — *W.R. Rosato & Associates, Inc.*
Fee, J. Curtis — *Spencer Stuart*
Feldman, Abe — *A.E. Feldman Associates*
Feldman, Kimberley — *Atlantic Search Group, Inc.*
Ferguson, Kenneth — *Source Services Corporation*
Ferneborg, Jay W. — *Ferneborg & Associates, Inc.*
Ferneborg, John R. — *Ferneborg & Associates, Inc.*
Ferrara, David M. — *Intech Summit Group, Inc.*
Ferrari, S. Jay — *Ferrari Search Group*
Field, Andrew — *Source Services Corporation*
Fienberg, Chester — *Drummond Associates, Inc.*
Fifield, George C. — *Egon Zehnder International Inc.*
Finkel, Leslie — *Source Services Corporation*
Finnerty, James — *Source Services Corporation*
Fischer, Janet L. — *Boyden*
Fisher, Neal — *Fisher Personnel Management Services*
Fitzgerald, Brian — *Source Services Corporation*

Henneberry, Ward — *Source Services Corporation*
Hennig, Sandra M. — *MSI International*
Hensley, Gayla — *Atlantic Search Group, Inc.*
Herman, Pat — *Whitney & Associates, Inc.*
Hernandez, Ruben — *Source Services Corporation*
Heroux, David — *Source Services Corporation*
Herzog, Sarah — *Source Services Corporation*
Hetherman, Margaret F. — *Highland Search Group, L.L.C.*
Hewitt, Rives D. — *The Dalley Hewitt Company*
Higdon, Henry G. — *Higdon Prince Inc.*
Hight, Susan — *Source Services Corporation*
Hilbert, Laurence — *Source Services Corporation*
Hildebrand, Thomas B. — *Professional Resources Group, Inc.*
Hilgenberg, Thomas — *Source Services Corporation*
Hill, Emery — *MSI International*
Hill, Randall W. — *Heidrick & Struggles, Inc.*
Hilliker, Alan D. — *Egon Zehnder International Inc.*
Hillyer, Carolyn — *Source Services Corporation*
Hindman, Neil C. — *The Hindman Company*
Hinojosa, Oscar — *Source Services Corporation*
Hobart, John N. — *Paul Ray Berndtson*
Hodge, Jeff — *Heidrick & Struggles, Inc.*
Hoevel, Michael J. — *Poirier, Hoevel & Co.*
Hoffman, Stephen — *Source Services Corporation*
Hofner, Andrew — *Source Services Corporation*
Hogan, Larry H. — *Hogan Acquisitions*
Holland, Kathleen — *TOPAZ International, Inc.*
Holland, Kathleen — *TOPAZ Legal Solutions*
Holmes, Lawrence J. — *Columbia Consulting Group*
Holodnak, William A. — *J. Robert Scott*
Holtz, Gene — *Agra Placements International Ltd.*
Holzberger, Georges L. — *Highland Search Group, L.L.C.*
Honey, W. Michael M. — *O'Callaghan Honey/Paul Ray Berndtson, Inc.*
Hopkinson, Dana — *Winter, Wyman & Company*
Hoppert, Phil — *Wargo and Co., Inc.*
Horton, Robert H. — *Horton International*
Hoskins, Charles R. — *Heidrick & Struggles, Inc.*
Hostetter, Kristi — *Source Services Corporation*
Houterloot, Tim — *Source Services Corporation*
Howard, Leon — *Richard, Wayne and Roberts*
Howard, Susy — *The McCormick Group, Inc.*
Howe, Theodore — *Romac & Associates*
Howe, Vance A. — *Ward Howell International, Inc.*
Howell, Robert B. — *Atlantic Search Group, Inc.*
Howell, Robert B. — *Atlantic Search Group, Inc.*
Hoyda, Louis A. — *Thorndike Deland Associates*
Hudson, Reginald M. — *Search Bureau International*
Hughes, Barbara — *Source Services Corporation*
Hughes, Kevin R. — *Handy HRM Corp.*
Hughes, Randall — *Source Services Corporation*
Hult, Dana — *Source Services Corporation*
Humphrey, Titus — *Source Services Corporation*
Hunter, Steven — *Diamond Tax Recruiting*
Hunter, Sue J. — *Robison & Associates*
Hurd, J. Nicholas — *Russell Reynolds Associates, Inc.*
Hurtado, Jaime — *Source Services Corporation*
Hutchinson, Loretta M. — *Hutchinson Resources International*
Hutchison, William K. — *Christenson & Hutchison*
Hylas, Lisa — *Source Services Corporation*
Hypes, Richard G. — *Lynch Miller Moore Partners, Inc.*
Illsley, Hugh G. — *Ward Howell International, Inc.*
Imely, Larry — *Christian & Timbers*
Imhof, Kirk — *Source Services Corporation*
Inger, Barry — *Source Services Corporation*
Inglis, William — *Korn/Ferry International*
Ingram, D. John — *Ingram & Aydelotte Inc.*
Inguagiato, Gregory — *MSI International*
Inskeep, Thomas — *Source Services Corporation*
Intravaia, Salvatore — *Source Services Corporation*
Irwin, Mark — *Source Services Corporation*
Issacs, Judith A. — *Grant Cooper and Associates*
Ives, Richard K. — *Wilkinson & Ives*
Jackowitz, Todd — *J. Robert Scott*
Jacobs, Martin J. — *The Rubicon Group*
Jacobs, Mike — *Thorne, Brieger Associates Inc.*
Jacobson, Hayley — *Source Services Corporation*
Jadulang, Vincent — *Source Services Corporation*
Jaedike, Eldron — *Prestige Inc.*
James, Richard — *Criterion Executive Search, Inc.*
Januleski, Geoff — *Source Services Corporation*
Jeltema, John — *Source Services Corporation*
Jensen, Robert — *Source Services Corporation*
Jernigan, Susan N. — *Sockwell & Associates*
Joffe, Barry — *Bason Associates Inc.*
Johnson, Greg — *Source Services Corporation*
Johnson, John W. — *Webb, Johnson Associates, Inc.*
Johnson, Kathleen A. — *Barton Raben, Inc.*

Johnson, Keith — *Romac & Associates*
Johnson, Priscilla — *The Johnson Group, Inc.*
Johnston, James R. — *The Stevenson Group of Delaware Inc.*
Johnstone, Grant — *Source Services Corporation*
Jones, B.J. — *Intersource, Ltd.*
Jones, Barbara J. — *Kaye-Bassman International Corp.*
Jones, Daniel F. — *Atlantic Search Group, Inc.*
Jones, Herschel — *Korn/Ferry International*
Jones, Jeffrey — *AJM Professional Services*
Jones, Jonathan C. — *The Ogdon Partnership*
Jones, Rodney — *Source Services Corporation*
Jordan, Stephen T. — *Paul Ray Berndtson*
Joys, David S. — *Heidrick & Struggles, Inc.*
Juelis, John J. — *Peeney Associates*
Juratovac, Michael — *Montgomery Resources, Inc.*
Juska, Frank — *Rusher, Loscavio & LoPresto*
Kacyn, Louis J. — *Egon Zehnder International Inc.*
Kader, Richard — *Richard Kader & Associates*
Kaiser, Donald J. — *Dunhill Search International*
Kaiser, Irene — *Dunhill Search International*
Kalinowski, David — *Jacobson Associates*
Kane, Frank — *A.J. Burton Group, Inc.*
Kanovsky, Gerald — *Career Consulting Group, Inc.*
Kanovsky, Marlene — *Career Consulting Group, Inc.*
Kantor, Richard — *Search West, Inc.*
Kaplan, Gary — *Gary Kaplan & Associates*
Kaplan, Marc — *Gary Kaplan & Associates*
Kaplan, Traci — *Source Services Corporation*
Kasprzyk, Michael — *Source Services Corporation*
Kassouf, Connie — *The Whitney Group*
Katz, Cyndi — *Search West, Inc.*
Kaye, Jeffrey — *Kaye-Bassman International Corp.*
Keeton, Susan G. — *The Corporate Connection, Ltd.*
Keitel, Robert S. — *A.T. Kearney, Inc.*
Keith, Stephanie — *Southwestern Professional Services*
Kelly, Claudia L. — *Spencer Stuart*
Kelly, Donna J. — *Accountants Executive Search*
Kelly, Peter W. — *R. Rollo Associates*
Kelly, Robert — *Source Services Corporation*
Kelso, Patricia C. — *Barton Raben, Inc.*
Kennedy, Craig — *Source Services Corporation*
Kennedy, Paul — *Source Services Corporation*
Kennedy, Walter — *Romac & Associates*
Kennedy, Walter — *Source Services Corporation*
Kennedy, Walter — *Source Services Corporation*
Kenney, Jeanne — *Source Services Corporation*
Kenzer, Robert D. — *Kenzer Corp.*
Keogh, James — *Sanford Rose Associates*
Kern, Jerry L. — *ADOW's Executeam*
Kern, Kathleen G. — *ADOW's Executeam*
Kershaw, Lisa — *Tanton Mitchell/Paul Ray Berndtson*
Kettwig, David A. — *A.T. Kearney, Inc.*
Kilcullen, Brian A. — *D.A. Kreuter Associates, Inc.*
King, Bill — *The McCormick Group, Inc.*
King, Shannon — *Source Services Corporation*
King, Stephen C. — *Boyden/Zay & Company*
King, Thomas — *Morgan Hunter Corp.*
Kinser, Richard E. — *Richard Kinser & Associates*
Kirschner, Alan — *Source Services Corporation*
Kishbaugh, Herbert S. — *Kishbaugh Associates International*
Klages, Constance W. — *International Management Advisors, Inc.*
Klavens, Cecile J. — *The Pickwick Group, Inc.*
Klein, Brandon — *A.J. Burton Group, Inc.*
Kleinstein, Jonah A. — *The Kleinstein Group*
Kleinstein, Scott — *Source Services Corporation*
Klusman, Edwin — *Source Services Corporation*
Knight, Gwen — *Richard, Wayne and Roberts*
Knight, Kim L. — *Telford, Adams & Alexander/The Knight Company*
Knisely, Gary — *Johnson Smith & Knisely Accord*
Knoll, Robert — *Source Services Corporation*
Koblentz, Joel M. — *Egon Zehnder International Inc.*
Koczak, John — *Source Services Corporation*
Koehler, Frank R. — *The Koehler Group*
Kondra, Vernon J. — *The Douglas Reiter Company, Inc.*
Konker, David N. — *Russell Reynolds Associates, Inc.*
Koontz, Donald N. — *Koontz, Jeffries & Associates, Inc.*
Kotick, Madeline — *The Stevenson Group of New Jersey*
Kramer, Donald — *Dunhill Personnel of Tampa, Inc.*
Kramer, Peter — *Dunhill Personnel of Tampa, Inc.*
Krauser, H. James — *Spencer Stuart*
Krejci, Stanley L. — *The Interface Group, Ltd./Boyden*
Kreuter, Daniel A. — *D.A. Kreuter Associates, Inc.*
Kreutz, Gary L. — *Kreutz Consulting Group, Inc.*
Krick, Terry L. — *Financial Resource Associates, Inc.*
Kring, Kenneth L. — *Spencer Stuart*
Krohn, Eileen — *The Stevenson Group of New Jersey*
Kuhl, Teresa — *Don Richard Associates of Tampa, Inc.*

Kuo, Linda — *Montgomery Resources, Inc.*
Kuper, Keith D. — *Christenson & Hutchison*
Kvasnicka, Jay Allen — *Morgan Hunter Corp.*
La Chance, Ronald — *Source Services Corporation*
Laba, Marvin — *Marvin Laba & Associates*
Laba, Stuart M. — *Marvin Laba & Associates*
Labrecque, Bernard F. — *Laurendeau, Labrecque/Paul Ray Berndtson, Inc.*
Lachance, Roger — *Laurendeau, Labrecque/Paul Ray Berndtson, Inc.*
Laderman, David — *Romac & Associates*
Lamb, Peter S. — *Executive Resource, Inc.*
Lambert, William — *Source Services Corporation*
Lamia, Michael — *Source Services Corporation*
Lamson-Gran, Jill — *Accounting Resources, Inc.*
Langer, Joel A. — *Langer Associates, Inc.*
Lannamann, Richard S. — *Russell Reynolds Associates, Inc.*
Lapat, Aaron D. — *J. Robert Scott*
LaPierre, Louis — *Romac & Associates*
Lapointe, Fabien — *Source Services Corporation*
Larsen, Bruce — *Prestige Inc.*
Larsen, Richard F. — *Larsen, Zilliacus & Associates, Inc.*
Lasher, Charles M. — *Lasher Associates*
Laskin, Sandy — *Source Services Corporation*
Lauderback, David R. — *A.T. Kearney, Inc.*
Laurendeau, Jean L. — *Laurendeau, Labrecque/Paul Ray Berndtson, Inc.*
LaValle, Michael — *Romac & Associates*
Laverty, William — *Source Services Corporation*
Lawrence, David — *Agra Placements International Ltd.*
Lazar, Miriam — *Source Services Corporation*
Lazaro, Alicia C. — *The Whitney Group*
Leblanc, Danny — *Source Services Corporation*
Lebo, Terry — *Agra Placements International Ltd.*
LeComte, Andre — *Egon Zehnder International Inc.*
Lee, Everett — *Source Services Corporation*
Lee, Roger — *Montgomery Resources, Inc.*
Leff, Lisa A. — *Berger and Leff*
Leigh, Rebecca — *Source Services Corporation*
Leighton, Mark — *Source Services Corporation*
Leininger, Dennis — *Key Employment Services*
Lejeune, Jeanette — *F-O-R-T-U-N-E Personnel Consultants of Huntsville, Inc.*
Lence, Julie Anne — *MSI International*
Lennox, Charles — *Price Waterhouse*
Leonard, Linda — *Harris Heery & Associates*
Leslie, William H. — *Boyden/Zay & Company*
Letcher, Harvey D. — *Sandhurst Associates*
Levenson, Laurel — *Source Services Corporation*
Levine, Alan M. — *MB Inc. Interim Executive Division*
Levine, Irwin — *Source Services Corporation*
Lewicki, Christopher — *MSI International*
Lewis, Daniel — *Source Services Corporation*
Lewis, Jon A. — *Sandhurst Associates*
Lewis, Marc D. — *Handy HRM Corp.*
Lewis, Sean — *Southwestern Professional Services*
Liebowitz, Michael E. — *Highland Search Group, L.L.C.*
Liebross, Eric — *Source Services Corporation*
Lin, Felix — *Source Services Corporation*
Lincoln, Thomas C. — *Oppedisano & Company, Inc.*
Lindberg, Eric J. — *MSI International*
Lindholst, Kai — *Egon Zehnder International Inc.*
Lindsay, M. Evan — *Heidrick & Struggles, Inc.*
Linton, Leonard M. — *Byron Leonard International, Inc.*
Lipuma, Thomas — *Source Services Corporation*
Litt-Peck, Michelle — *The Whitney Group*
Little, Elizabeth A. — *Financial Resource Associates, Inc.*
Little, Gary — *Agra Placements International Ltd.*
Little, Suzaane — *Don Richard Associates of Tampa, Inc.*
Littman, Stephen — *Rhodes Associates*
Livingston, Peter R. — *Livingston, Robert and Company Inc.*
Loeb, Stephen H. — *Grant Cooper and Associates*
Loewenstein, Victor H. — *Egon Zehnder International Inc.*
Lombardi, Nancy W. — *WTW Associates*
Long, Helga — *H.M. Long International, Ltd.*
Long, John — *Source Services Corporation*
Long, Mark — *Source Services Corporation*
Long, Thomas — *Egon Zehnder International Inc.*
Long, William G. — *McDonald, Long & Associates, Inc.*
Lonneke, John W. — *MSI International*
Loper, Doris — *Mortgage & Financial Personnel Services*
Lopis, Roberta — *Richard, Wayne and Roberts*
Loscavio, J. Michael — *Rusher, Loscavio & LoPresto*
Lotufo, Donald A. — *D.A.L. Associates, Inc.*
Lotz, R. James — *International Management Advisors, Inc.*
Lovas, W. Carl — *Lovas Stanley/Paul Ray Berndtson Inc.*
Lovely, Edward — *The Stevenson Group of New Jersey*
Loving, Vikki — *Intersource, Ltd.*
Lucarelli, Joan — *The Onstott Group, Inc.*

Lucas, Ronnie L. — *MSI International*
Luce, Daniel — *Source Services Corporation*
Lucht, John — *The John Lucht Consultancy Inc.*
Ludder, Mark — *Source Services Corporation*
Ludlow, Michael — *Source Services Corporation*
Lumsby, George N. — *International Management Advisors, Inc.*
Lundy, Martin — *Source Services Corporation*
Lussier, Grant P. — *Heidrick & Struggles, Inc.*
Lynch, Michael C. — *Lynch Miller Moore Partners, Inc.*
Lyons, Denis B.K. — *Spencer Stuart*
Lyons, Jane A. — *Rhodes Associates*
Lyons, Michael — *Source Services Corporation*
Lyons, Michele R. — *R. Rollo Associates*
MacCallan, Deirdre — *Butterfass, Pepe & MacCallan Inc.*
Macdonald, G. William — *The Macdonald Group, Inc.*
MacDougall, Andrew J. — *Spencer Stuart*
MacIntyre, Lisa W. — *Russell Reynolds Associates, Inc.*
Mackinlay, Marcelo D. — *Heidrick & Struggles, Inc.*
MacMillan, James — *Source Services Corporation*
MacPherson, Holly — *Source Services Corporation*
Macrides, Michael — *Source Services Corporation*
Madaras, Debra — *Financial Resource Associates, Inc.*
Maer, Harry — *Kenzer Corp.*
Magee, Harrison R. — *Bowden & Company, Inc.*
Maggio, Mary — *Source Services Corporation*
Mahmoud, Sophia — *Source Services Corporation*
Mahr, Toni — *K. Russo Associates*
Mairn, Todd — *Source Services Corporation*
Mak, I. Paul — *Thomas A. Byrnes Associates*
Makrianes, James K. — *Webb, Johnson Associates, Inc.*
Malcolm, Rod — *The Enns Partners Inc.*
Malone, George V. — *Boyden*
Manassero, Henri J.P. — *International Management Advisors, Inc.*
Mangum, William T. — *Thomas Mangum Company*
Manns, Alex — *Crawford & Crofford*
Manzo, Renee — *Atlantic Search Group, Inc.*
Maphet, Harriet — *The Stevenson Group of New Jersey*
Marino, Jory J. — *Sullivan & Company*
Mark, John L. — *J.L. Mark Associates, Inc.*
Marks, Russell E. — *Webb, Johnson Associates, Inc.*
Marks, Sarah J. — *The Executive Source*
Marra, John — *Marra Peters & Partners*
Marra, John — *Marra Peters & Partners*
Marsteller, Franklin D. — *Spencer Stuart*
Martin, Jon — *Egon Zehnder International Inc.*
Marumoto, William H. — *The Interface Group, Ltd./Boyden*
Marwil, Jennifer — *Source Services Corporation*
Mashakas, Elizabeth — *TOPAZ International, Inc.*
Mashakas, Elizabeth — *TOPAZ Legal Solutions*
Massey, H. Heath — *Robison & Associates*
Mather, David R. — *Christian & Timbers*
Mathias, Douglas — *Source Services Corporation*
Mathias, Kathy — *Stone Murphy & Olson*
Mathis, Carrie — *Source Services Corporation*
Mattingly, Kathleen — *Source Services Corporation*
Matueny, Robert — *Ryan, Miller & Associates Inc.*
Mauer, Kristin — *Montgomery Resources, Inc.*
Maxwell, John — *Source Services Corporation*
Mayer, Thomas — *Source Services Corporation*
Mayes, Kay H. — *John Shell Associates, Inc.*
Mazza, David B. — *Mazza & Riley, Inc.*
McAlpine, Bruce — *Keith Bagg & Associates Inc.*
McAteer, Thomas — *Montgomery Resources, Inc.*
McBride, Jonathan E. — *McBride Associates, Inc.*
McBryde, Marnie — *Spencer Stuart*
McCallister, Richard A. — *Boyden*
McCann, Cornelia B. — *Spencer Stuart*
McCarthy, Laura — *Source Services Corporation*
McCarty, J. Rucker — *Heidrick & Struggles, Inc.*
McClement, John — *Korn/Ferry International*
McConnell, Greg — *Winter, Wyman & Company*
McCool, Anne G. — *Sullivan & Company*
McCormick, Brian — *The McCormick Group, Inc.*
McCormick, Joseph — *Source Services Corporation*
McDonald, Gary E. — *Agra Placements International Ltd.*
McDonald, Scott A. — *McDonald Associates International*
McDonald, Stanleigh B. — *McDonald Associates International*
McFadden, Ashton S. — *Johnson Smith & Knisely Accord*
McGinnis, Rita — *Source Services Corporation*
McGoldrick, Terrence — *Source Services Corporation*
McHugh, Keith — *Source Services Corporation*
McIntosh, Arthur — *Source Services Corporation*
McIntosh, Tad — *Source Services Corporation*
McKinney, Julia — *Source Services Corporation*
McKinnis, Paul D. — *Paul Ray Berndtson*
McKnight, Amy E. — *Chartwell Partners International, Inc.*
McLaughlin, John — *Romac & Associates*
McLean, E. Peter — *Spencer Stuart*

McMahan, Stephen — *Source Services Corporation*
McMahan, Stephen — *Source Services Corporation*
McMillin, Bob — *Price Waterhouse*
McNamara, Gerard P. — *Heidrick & Struggles, Inc.*
McNamara, Timothy C. — *Columbia Consulting Group*
McNear, Jeffrey E. — *Barrett Partners*
McNichols, Walter B. — *Gary Kaplan & Associates*
McPherson, Stephen M. — *Ward Howell International, Inc.*
McQuoid, David — *A.T. Kearney, Inc.*
Meara, Helen — *Source Services Corporation*
Meehan, John — *Source Services Corporation*
Meehan, Robert — *A.J. Burton Group, Inc.*
Meier, J. Dale — *Grant Cooper and Associates*
Meiland, A. Daniel — *Egon Zehnder International Inc.*
Meltzer, Andrea Y. — *Executive Options, Ltd.*
Mendelson, Jeffrey — *Source Services Corporation*
Mendoza, Guadalupe — *Ward Howell International, Inc.*
Mendoza-Green, Robin — *Source Services Corporation*
Merrigan, Eileen M. — *Lamalie Amrop International*
Mertensotto, Chuck H. — *Whitney & Associates, Inc.*
Messett, William J. — *Messett Associates, Inc.*
Messina, Marco — *Source Services Corporation*
Mestepey, John — *A.T. Kearney, Inc.*
Meyer, Stacey — *Gary Kaplan & Associates*
Meyer, William — *Agra Placements International Ltd.*
Meyers, Steven — *Montgomery Resources, Inc.*
Meza, Anna — *Richard, Wayne and Roberts*
Michaels, Stewart — *TOPAZ International, Inc.*
Michaels, Stewart — *TOPAZ Legal Solutions*
Miller, David — *Temporary Accounting Personnel, Inc.*
Miller, Harold B. — *MSI International*
Miller, Kenneth A. — *Computer Network Resources, Inc.*
Miller, Larry — *Source Services Corporation*
Miller, Roy — *The Enns Partners Inc.*
Miller, Timothy — *Source Services Corporation*
Milligan, Dale — *Source Services Corporation*
Millonzi, Joel C. — *Johnson Smith & Knisely Accord*
Mills, John — *Source Services Corporation*
Milner, Carol — *Source Services Corporation*
Milstein, Bonnie — *Marvin Laba & Associates*
Milton, Suzanne — *Marra Peters & Partners*
Miras, Cliff — *Source Services Corporation*
Miras, Cliff — *Source Services Corporation*
Mirtz, P. John — *Mirtz Morice, Inc.*
Mitchell, John — *Romac & Associates*
Mitton, Bill — *Executive Resource, Inc.*
Mittwol, Myles — *Source Services Corporation*
Mochwart, Donald — *Drummond Associates, Inc.*
Mogul, Gene — *Mogul Consultants, Inc.*
Molitor, John L. — *Barrett Partners*
Mollichelli, David — *Source Services Corporation*
Molnar, Robert A. — *Johnson Smith & Knisely Accord*
Monogenis, Emanuel N. — *Heidrick & Struggles, Inc.*
Moore, Craig — *Source Services Corporation*
Moore, Dianna — *Source Services Corporation*
Moore, Janice E. — *MSI International*
Moore, Michael — *Agra Placements International Ltd.*
Moore, Suzanne — *Source Services Corporation*
Moran, Douglas — *Source Services Corporation*
Morato, Rene — *Source Services Corporation*
Moretti, Denise — *Source Services Corporation*
Morgan, David G. — *Morgan Stampfl, Inc.*
Morgan, Donald T. — *MSI International*
Moriarty, Mike — *Source Services Corporation*
Morice, James L. — *Mirtz Morice, Inc.*
Morris, David A. — *Heidrick & Struggles, Inc.*
Morris, David W. — *WTW Associates*
Morris, Kristine A. — *Morris & Berger*
Morris, Paul T. — *The Morris Group*
Morris, Scott — *Source Services Corporation*
Morrow, Melanie — *Source Services Corporation*
Mott, Greg — *Source Services Corporation*
Moyse, Richard G. — *Thorndike Deland Associates*
Msidment, Roger — *Source Services Corporation*
Mueller, Colleen — *Source Services Corporation*
Mueller-Maerki, Fortunat F. — *Egon Zehnder International Inc.*
Muendel, H. Edward — *Stanton Chase International*
Muller, Charles A. — *AJM Professional Services*
Murphy, Corinne — *Source Services Corporation*
Murphy, Cornelius J. — *Goodrich & Sherwood Associates, Inc.*
Murphy, Gary J. — *Stone Murphy & Olson*
Murphy, James — *Source Services Corporation*
Murphy, Patrick J. — *P.J. Murphy & Associates, Inc.*
Murray, Virginia — *Baker, Harris & Partners Limited*
Murry, John — *Source Services Corporation*
Mursuli, Meredith — *Lasher Associates*
Myers, Kay — *Signature Staffing*
Nabers, Karen — *Source Services Corporation*

Nagler, Leon G. — *Nagler, Robins & Poe, Inc.*
Nagy, Les — *Source Services Corporation*
Nass, Martin D. — *Lamalie Amrop International*
Nathanson, Barry F. — *Barry Nathanson Associates*
Necessary, Rick — *Source Services Corporation*
Neckanoff, Sharon — *Search West, Inc.*
Needham, Karen — *Source Services Corporation*
Neelin, Sharon — *The Caldwell Partners Amrop International*
Neff, Herbert — *Source Services Corporation*
Neff, Thomas J. — *Spencer Stuart*
Neidhart, Craig C. — *TNS Partners, Inc.*
Nelson, Garry A. — *Rhodes Associates*
Nelson, Hitch — *Source Services Corporation*
Nelson, Mary — *Source Services Corporation*
Nelson-Folkersen, Jeffrey — *Source Services Corporation*
Neuberth, Jeffrey G. — *Canny, Bowen Inc.*
Neuwald, Debrah — *Source Services Corporation*
Nevins, Patricia — *Rhodes Associates*
Newbold, Michael — *Agra Placements International Ltd.*
Newman, Jose L. — *Ward Howell International, Inc.*
Newman, Lynn — *Kishbaugh Associates International*
Nolan, Robert — *Source Services Corporation*
Nolen, Shannon — *Source Services Corporation*
Noll, Robert J. — *The Hindman Company*
Normann, Amy — *Robert M. Flanagan & Associates, Ltd.*
Norsell, Paul E. — *Paul Norsell & Associates, Inc.*
Nunziata, Peter — *Atlantic Search Group, Inc.*
O'Brien, Susan — *Source Services Corporation*
O'Connell, Michael — *Ryan, Miller & Associates Inc.*
O'Halloran, Robert — *MSI International*
O'Hara, Daniel M. — *Lynch Miller Moore Partners, Inc.*
O'Maley, Kimberlee — *Spencer Stuart*
O'Neill, James P. — *Allerton Heneghan & O'Neill*
O'Neill, Stephen A. — *Harris Heery & Associates*
Occhiboi, Emil — *Source Services Corporation*
Ogden, Dayton — *Spencer Stuart*
Ogdon, Thomas H. — *The Ogdon Partnership*
Ohman, Gregory L. — *Pearson, Caldwell & Farnsworth, Inc.*
Olin, Robyn — *Richard, Wayne and Roberts*
Olsen, Robert — *Source Services Corporation*
Onstott, Joseph E. — *The Onstott Group, Inc.*
Oppedisano, Edward — *Oppedisano & Company, Inc.*
Orkin, Ralph — *Sanford Rose Associates*
Orkin, Sheilah — *Sanford Rose Associates*
Orr, Stacie — *Source Services Corporation*
Oswald, Mark G. — *Canny, Bowen Inc.*
Ouellette, Christopher — *Source Services Corporation*
Owen, Christopher — *Source Services Corporation*
Pace, Susan A. — *Horton International*
Pachowitz, John — *Source Services Corporation*
Padilla, Jose Sanchez — *Egon Zehnder International Inc.*
Page, G. Schuyler — *A.T. Kearney, Inc.*
Page, Linda M. — *Wargo and Co., Inc.*
Palazio, Carla — *A.T. Kearney, Inc.*
Paliwoda, William — *Source Services Corporation*
Palma, Frank R. — *Goodrich & Sherwood Associates, Inc.*
Palmer, Carlton A. — *Beall & Company, Inc.*
Palmer, James H. — *The Hindman Company*
Palmieri, Cathryn C. — *Korn/Ferry International*
Papciak, Dennis J. — *Accounting Personnel Associates, Inc.*
Papciak, Dennis J. — *Temporary Accounting Personnel*
Paradise, Malcolm — *Source Services Corporation*
Parente, James — *Source Services Corporation*
Park, Dabney G. — *Mark Stanley & Company*
Parroco, Jason — *Source Services Corporation*
Parry, William H. — *Horton International*
Pastrana, Dario — *Egon Zehnder International Inc.*
Patel, Shailesh — *Source Services Corporation*
Patence, David W. — *Handy HRM Corp.*
Paternie, Patrick — *Source Services Corporation*
Patton, Mitchell — *Patton/Perry Associates, Inc.*
Paul, Kathleen — *Source Services Corporation*
Paul, Lisa D. — *Merit Resource Group, Inc.*
Payette, Pierre — *Egon Zehnder International Inc.*
Paynter, Sandra L. — *Ward Howell International, Inc.*
Peal, Matthew — *Source Services Corporation*
Pearson, John R. — *Pearson, Caldwell & Farnsworth, Inc.*
Pease, Edward — *Don Richard Associates of Georgia, Inc.*
Peeney, James D. — *Peeney Associates*
Pelisson, Charles — *Marra Peters & Partners*
Pepe, Leonida — *Butterfass, Pepe & MacCallan Inc.*
Perkey, Richard — *Korn/Ferry International*
Perry, Carolyn — *Source Services Corporation*
Peternell, Melanie — *Signature Staffing*
Peters, James N. — *TNS Partners, Inc.*
Peters, Kevin — *Source Services Corporation*
Petersen, Richard — *Source Services Corporation*
Pettway, Samuel H. — *Spencer Stuart*

Petty, J. Scott — *The Arcus Group*
Pfau, Madelaine — *Heidrick & Struggles, Inc.*
Pfeiffer, Irene — *Price Waterhouse*
Phillips, Donald L. — *O'Shea, Divine & Company, Inc.*
Phillips, James L. — *Highland Search Group, L.L.C.*
Phillips, Richard K. — *Handy HRM Corp.*
Pickering, Dorothy C. — *Livingston, Robert and Company Inc.*
Pickford, Stephen T. — *The Corporate Staff, Inc.*
Pierce, Matthew — *Source Services Corporation*
Pierpont, Elizabeth H. — *Russell Reynolds Associates, Inc.*
Pierson, Edward J. — *Johnson Smith & Knisely Accord*
Pillow, Charles — *Source Services Corporation*
Pineda, Rosanna — *Source Services Corporation*
Pinkman, Karen N. — *Skott/Edwards Consultants, Inc.*
Pirro, Sheri — *Source Services Corporation*
Pittard, Patrick S. — *Heidrick & Struggles, Inc.*
Pitto, Lili — *Ryan, Miller & Associates Inc.*
Plant, Jerry — *Source Services Corporation*
Platte, John D. — *Russell Reynolds Associates, Inc.*
Plazza, Richard C. — *The Executive Source*
Plimpton, Ralph L. — *R L Plimpton Associates*
Poe, James B. — *Nagler, Robins & Poe, Inc.*
Poirier, Roland — *Poirier, Hoevel & Co.*
Pomeroy, T. Lee — *Egon Zehnder International Inc.*
Poracky, John W. — *M. Wood Company*
Porter, Albert — *The Experts*
Pototo, Brian — *Source Services Corporation*
Potter, Steven B. — *Highland Search Group, L.L.C.*
Powell, Danny — *Source Services Corporation*
Powell, Gregory — *Source Services Corporation*
Powell, Leslie — *Rhodes Associates*
Power, Michael — *Source Services Corporation*
Pregeant, David — *Source Services Corporation*
Press, Fred — *Adept Tech Recruiting*
Preusse, Eric — *Source Services Corporation*
Price, Andrew G. — *The Thomas Tucker Company*
Price, Carl — *Source Services Corporation*
Priem, Windle B. — *Korn/Ferry International*
Prince, Marilyn L. — *Higdon Prince Inc.*
Probert, William W. — *Ward Howell International, Inc.*
Proct, Nina — *Martin H. Bauman Associates, Inc.*
Pugrant, Mark A. — *Grant/Morgan Associates, Inc.*
Rabinowitz, Peter A. — *P.A.R. Associates Inc.*
Rackley, Eugene M. — *Heidrick & Struggles, Inc.*
Ramler, Carolyn S. — *The Corporate Connection, Ltd.*
Ramsey, John H. — *Mark Stanley & Company*
Randell, James E. — *Randell-Heiken, Inc.*
Rasmussen, Timothy — *Source Services Corporation*
Ratajczak, Paul — *Source Services Corporation*
Ravenel, Lavinia — *MSI International*
Ray, Marianne C. — *Callan Associates, Ltd.*
Raymond, Jean — *The Caldwell Partners Amrop International*
Reardon, Joseph — *Source Services Corporation*
Reddick, David C. — *Horton International*
Redding, Denise — *The Douglas Reiter Company, Inc.*
Redmond, Andrea — *Russell Reynolds Associates, Inc.*
Reece, Christopher S. — *Reece & Mruk Partners*
Reed, Susan — *Source Services Corporation*
Reeves, William B. — *Spencer Stuart*
Regeuye, Peter J. — *Accountants Executive Search*
Reid, Katherine — *Source Services Corporation*
Reid, Scott — *Source Services Corporation*
Reilly, John — *The McCormick Group, Inc.*
Reiser, Ellen — *Thorndike Deland Associates*
Reiter, Douglas — *The Douglas Reiter Company, Inc.*
Renfroe, Ann-Marie — *Source Services Corporation*
Rennell, Thomas — *Source Services Corporation*
Renner, Sandra L. — *Spectra International Inc.*
Renteria, Elizabeth — *Source Services Corporation*
Resnic, Alan — *Source Services Corporation*
Reticker, Peter — *MSI International*
Reyman, Susan — *S. Reyman & Associates Ltd.*
Reynolds, Laura — *Source Services Corporation*
Rhoades, Michael — *Source Services Corporation*
Rice, Douglas — *Agra Placements International Ltd.*
Rice, Marie — *Jay Gaines & Company, Inc.*
Rice, Raymond D. — *Logue & Rice Inc.*
Rich, Kenneth M. — *Paul Ray Berndtson*
Rich, Lyttleton — *Sockwell & Associates*
Richardson, J. Rick — *Spencer Stuart*
Rieger, Louis J. — *Spencer Stuart*
Rimmel, James E. — *The Hindman Company*
Rimmele, Michael — *The Bankers Group*
Rinker, Jim — *Southwestern Professional Services*
Rios, Vince — *Source Services Corporation*
Rios, Vincent — *Source Services Corporation*
Rivers, Geri — *Chrisman & Company, Incorporated*
Robb, Tammy — *Source Services Corporation*

Roberts, Carl R. — *Southwestern Professional Services*
Roberts, Derek J. — *Ward Howell International, Inc.*
Roberts, Mitch — *A.E. Feldman Associates*
Roberts, Nick P. — *Spectrum Search Associates, Inc.*
Roberts, Scott B. — *Wargo and Co., Inc.*
Robertson, Sherry — *Source Services Corporation*
Robins, Jeri N. — *Nagler, Robins & Poe, Inc.*
Robinson, Bruce — *Bruce Robinson Associates*
Robinson, Eric B. — *Bruce Robinson Associates*
Robinson, Tonya — *Source Services Corporation*
Robison, John H. — *Robison & Associates*
Rockwell, Bruce — *Source Services Corporation*
Rodgers, John — *Agra Placements International Ltd.*
Rodriguez, Manuel — *Source Services Corporation*
Roehrig, Kurt W. — *AJM Professional Services*
Rogan, John P. — *Russell Reynolds Associates, Inc.*
Rogers, Leah — *Dinte Resources, Incorporated*
Rollo, Robert S. — *R. Rollo Associates*
Ropes, John — *Ropes Associates, Inc.*
Rorech, Maureen — *Romac & Associates*
Rosato, William R. — *W.R. Rosato & Associates, Inc.*
Rosemarin, Gloria J. — *Barrington Hart, Inc.*
Rosen, Mitchell — *Source Services Corporation*
Rosenstein, Michele — *Source Services Corporation*
Ross, John — *Morgan Stampfl, Inc.*
Ross, Lawrence — *Lovas Stanley/Paul Ray Berndtson Inc.*
Ross, Mark S. — *Herman Smith Executive Initiatives Inc.*
Ross, Sheila L. — *Ward Howell International, Inc.*
Rotella, Marshall W. — *The Corporate Connection, Ltd.*
Roth, Robert J. — *Williams, Roth & Krueger Inc.*
Roth, William — *Harris Heery & Associates*
Rothenbush, Clayton — *Source Services Corporation*
Rothfeld, Robert — *A.E. Feldman Associates*
Rowe, Thomas A. — *Korn/Ferry International*
Rowe, William D. — *D.E. Foster Partners Inc.*
Rowland, James — *Source Services Corporation*
Runquist, U.W. — *Webb, Johnson Associates, Inc.*
Russell, Richard A. — *Executive Search Consultants Corporation*
Russell, Robin E. — *Kenzer Corp.*
Russo, Karen — *K. Russo Associates*
Russo, Karen — *Maximum Management Corp.*
Rustin, Beth — *The Whitney Group*
Ryan, David — *Source Services Corporation*
Ryan, Kathleen — *Source Services Corporation*
Ryan, Lee — *Ryan, Miller & Associates Inc.*
Ryan, Mark — *Source Services Corporation*
Sabat, Lori S. — *Alta Associates, Inc.*
Sadaj, Michael — *Source Services Corporation*
Salet, Michael — *Source Services Corporation*
Samsel, Randy — *Source Services Corporation*
Samuelson, Robert — *Source Services Corporation*
Sanchez, William — *Source Services Corporation*
Sanderson, Jeffrey M. — *Sullivan & Company*
Sandor, Richard J. — *Flynn, Hannock, Incorporated*
Saner, Harold — *Romac & Associates*
Santiago, Benefrido — *Source Services Corporation*
Sapers, Mark — *Source Services Corporation*
Saposhnik, Doron — *Source Services Corporation*
Sardella, Sharon — *Source Services Corporation*
Sarn, Allan G. — *Allan Sarn Associates Inc.*
Sathe, Mark A. — *Sathe & Associates, Inc.*
Sauer, Harry J. — *Romac & Associates*
Savard, Robert F. — *The Stevenson Group of Delaware Inc.*
Savela, Edward — *Source Services Corporation*
Sawyer, Patricia L. — *Smith & Sawyer Inc.*
Sayers, Bruce D. — *Brackin & Sayers Associates*
Schaefer, Frederic M. — *A.T. Kearney, Inc.*
Schappell, Marc P. — *Egon Zehnder International Inc.*
Scherck, Henry J. — *Ward Howell International, Inc.*
Schlpma, Christine — *Advanced Executive Resources*
Schmidt, Frank B. — *F.B. Schmidt International*
Schneider, Perry — *Agra Placements International Ltd.*
Schneider, Thomas P. — *WTW Associates*
Schneiderman, Gerald — *Management Resource Associates, Inc.*
Schreiber, Stuart M. — *Heidrick & Struggles, Inc.*
Schroeder, James — *Source Services Corporation*
Schroeder, John W. — *Spencer Stuart*
Schuette, Dorothy — *Harris Heery & Associates*
Schultz, Randy — *Source Services Corporation*
Schwalbach, Robert — *Source Services Corporation*
Schwartz, Carole — *A.T. Kearney, Inc.*
Schwartz, Susan — *Korn/Ferry International*
Schwinden, William — *Source Services Corporation*
Scimone, James — *Source Services Corporation*
Scimone, Jim — *Source Services Corporation*
Scoff, Barry — *Source Services Corporation*
Scothon, Alan — *Romac & Associates*
Scranton, Lisa — *A.J. Burton Group, Inc.*

Scroggins, Stephen R. — *Russell Reynolds Associates, Inc.*
Seamon, Kenneth — *Source Services Corporation*
Seco, William — *Seco & Zetto Associates, Inc.*
Segal, Eric B. — *Kenzer Corp.*
Selbach, Barbara — *Spencer Stuart*
Selko, Philip W. — *Hogan Acquisitions*
Sell, David — *Source Services Corporation*
Selvaggi, Esther — *Source Services Corporation*
Semple, David — *Source Services Corporation*
Semyan, John K. — *TNS Partners, Inc.*
Serba, Kerri — *Source Services Corporation*
Sevilla, Claudio A. — *Crawford & Crofford*
Shackleford, David — *Source Services Corporation*
Shanks, Jennifer — *Source Services Corporation*
Shapanka, Samuel — *Source Services Corporation*
Shawhan, Heather — *Source Services Corporation*
Shea, Christopher J. — *Ingram & Aydelotte Inc.*
Shea, Kathleen M. — *The Penn Partners, Incorporated*
Shell, John C. — *John Shell Associates, Inc.*
Shelton, Jonathan — *Source Services Corporation*
Shemin, Grace — *Maximum Management Corp.*
Shen, Eugene Y. — *The Whitney Group*
Shepard, Michael J. — *MSI International*
Sher, Lawrence — *M.A. Churchill & Associates, Inc.*
Sherman, Robert R. — *Mortgage & Financial Personnel Services*
Shervey, Brent C. — *O'Callaghan Honey/Paul Ray Berndtson, Inc.*
Sherwood, Andrew — *Goodrich & Sherwood Associates, Inc.*
Shield, Nancy — *Maximum Management Corp.*
Shirilla, Robert M. — *F.B. Schmidt International*
Shore, Earl L. — *E.L. Shore & Associates Ltd.*
Shourds, Mary E. — *Houze, Shourds & Montgomery, Inc.*
Sibbald, John R. — *John Sibbald Associates, Inc.*
Siegel, Pamela — *Executive Options, Ltd.*
Silvas, Stephen D. — *Roberson and Company*
Silver, Kit — *Source Services Corporation*
Silverman, Paul M. — *The Marshall Group*
Simmons, Deborah — *Source Services Corporation*
Simmons, Sandra K. — *MSI International*
Simon, Penny B. — *Paul Ray Berndtson*
Sindler, Jay — *A.J. Burton Group, Inc.*
Sirena, Evelyn — *Source Services Corporation*
Sjogren, Dennis — *Agra Placements International Ltd.*
Skirbe, Douglas — *Rhodes Associates*
Skunda, Donna M. — *Allerton Heneghan & O'Neill*
Sloan, Scott — *Source Services Corporation*
Slocum, Ann Marie — *K.L. Whitney Company*
Smead, Michelle M. — *A.T. Kearney, Inc.*
Smirnov, Tatiana — *Allan Sarn Associates Inc.*
Smith, Adam M. — *The Abbott Group, Inc.*
Smith, Brant — *Smith Hanley Associates*
Smith, Cheryl — *Barton Raben, Inc.*
Smith, David P. — *Smith & Latterell (HRS, Inc.)*
Smith, Ethan L. — *Highland Search Group, L.L.C.*
Smith, Herman M. — *Herman Smith Executive Initiatives Inc.*
Smith, John F. — *The Penn Partners, Incorporated*
Smith, Lawrence — *Source Services Corporation*
Smith, Monica L. — *Analysts Resources, Inc.*
Smith, R. Michael — *Smith James Group, Inc.*
Smith, Robert L. — *Smith & Sawyer Inc.*
Smith, Timothy — *Source Services Corporation*
Smith, W. Guice — *Southwestern Professional Services*
Smock, Cynthia — *Source Services Corporation*
Smoller, Howard — *Source Services Corporation*
Snodgrass, Stephen — *DeFrain, Mayer, Lee & Burgess LLC*
Snowden, Charles — *Source Services Corporation*
Snowhite, Rebecca — *Source Services Corporation*
Snyder, James F. — *Snyder & Company*
Sochacki, Michael — *Source Services Corporation*
Sockwell, J. Edgar — *Sockwell & Associates*
Song, Louis — *Source Services Corporation*
Sorgen, Jay — *Source Services Corporation*
Sostilio, Louis — *Source Services Corporation*
Soutouras, James — *Smith James Group, Inc.*
Spann, Richard E. — *Goodrich & Sherwood Associates, Inc.*
Spector, Michael — *Source Services Corporation*
Spencer, John — *Source Services Corporation*
Spencer, John — *Source Services Corporation*
Spicher, John — *M.A. Churchill & Associates, Inc.*
Spitz, Grant — *The Caldwell Partners Amrop International*
Sponseller, Vern — *Richard Kader & Associates*
Spoutz, Paul — *Source Services Corporation*
Spriggs, Robert D. — *Spriggs & Company, Inc.*
Springer, Mark H. — *M.H. Springer & Associates Incorporated*
Sprowls, Linda — *Allard Associates*
St. Martin, Peter — *Source Services Corporation*
Stack, Richard — *Source Services Corporation*
Stampfl, Eric — *Morgan Stampfl, Inc.*
Stark, Jeff — *Thorne, Brieger Associates Inc.*

Stein, Terry W. — *Stewart, Stein and Scott, Ltd.*
Steinman, Stephen — *The Stevenson Group of New Jersey*
Stephens, Andrew — *Source Services Corporation*
Stephens, John — *Source Services Corporation*
Stern, Leslie W. — *Sullivan & Company*
Stevens, Glenn — *Korn/Ferry International*
Stevens, Tracey — *Don Richard Associates of Washington, D.C., Inc.*
Stewart, Clifford — *Morgan Stampfl, Inc.*
Stewart, Jan J. — *Egon Zehnder International Inc.*
Stewart, Jeffrey O. — *Stewart, Stein and Scott, Ltd.*
Stewart, Ross M. — *Human Resources Network Partners Inc.*
Stivk, Barbara A. — *Thornton Resources*
Stone, Robert Ryder — *Lamalie Amrop International*
Stone, Susan L. — *Stone Enterprises Ltd.*
Stoneham, Herbert E.C. — *Stoneham Associates Corp.*
Storm, Deborah — *Source Services Corporation*
Stouffer, Dale — *Agra Placements International Ltd.*
Stouffer, Kenneth — *Keith Bagg & Associates Inc.*
Stoy, Roger M. — *Heidrick & Struggles, Inc.*
Strander, Dervin — *Source Services Corporation*
Strassman, Mark — *Don Richard Associates of Washington, D.C., Inc.*
Straube, Stanley H. — *Straube Associates*
Stricker, Sidney G. — *Stricker & Zagor*
Stringer, Dann P. — *D.E. Foster Partners Inc.*
Strobridge, Richard P. — *F.L. Taylor & Company, Inc.*
Strom, Mark N. — *Search Advisors International Corp.*
Struzziero, Ralph E. — *Romac & Associates*
Sullivan, Brian M. — *Sullivan & Company*
Sullivan, Kay — *Rusher, Loscavio & LoPresto*
Sumurdy, Melinda — *Kenzer Corp.*
Susoreny, Samali — *Source Services Corporation*
Sussman, Lynda — *Gilbert Tweed/INESA*
Sutter, Howard — *Romac & Associates*
Swanner, William — *Source Services Corporation*
Sweeney, Anne — *Source Services Corporation*
Sweeney, Sean K. — *Bonifield Associates*
Sweet, Randall — *Source Services Corporation*
Swidler, J. Robert — *Egon Zehnder International Inc.*
Taft, David G. — *Techsearch Services, Inc.*
Tankson, Dawn — *Source Services Corporation*
Tanner, Frank — *Source Services Corporation*
Tanner, Gary — *Source Services Corporation*
Tappan, Michael A. — *Ward Howell International, Inc.*
Taylor, Conrad G. — *MSI International*
Taylor, Ernest A. — *Ward Howell International, Inc.*
Taylor, Kenneth W. — *Egon Zehnder International Inc.*
Teger, Stella — *Allan Sarn Associates Inc.*
Telford, John H. — *Telford, Adams & Alexander/Telford & Co., Inc.*
ten Cate, Herman H. — *Stoneham Associates Corp.*
Tenero, Kymberly — *Source Services Corporation*
Teter, Sandra — *The Danbrook Group, Inc.*
Theard, Susan — *Romac & Associates*
Theobald, David B. — *Theobald & Associates*
Thielman, Joseph — *Barrett Partners*
Tholke, William E. — *Canny, Bowen Inc.*
Thomas, Kurt J. — *P.J. Murphy & Associates, Inc.*
Thomas, Terry — *Montague Enterprises*
Thompson, Dave — *Battalia Winston International*
Thompson, John R. — *MSI International*
Thompson, Kenneth L. — *McCormack & Farrow*
Thompson, Leslie — *Source Services Corporation*
Thomson, Alexander G. — *Russell Reynolds Associates, Inc.*
Thornton, John C. — *Thornton Resources*
Thrower, Troy — *Source Services Corporation*
Tierney, Eileen — *The Whitney Group*
Tilley, Kyle — *Source Services Corporation*
Tillman, J. Robert — *Russell Reynolds Associates, Inc.*
Tingle, Trina A. — *MSI International*
Tobin, Christopher — *Source Services Corporation*
Tootsey, Mark A. — *A.J. Burton Group, Inc.*
Tracey, Jack — *Management Assistance Group, Inc.*
Tracy, Ronald O. — *Egon Zehnder International Inc.*
Trautman, William E. — *Boyden*
Trefzer, Kristie — *Source Services Corporation*
Trewhella, Michael — *Source Services Corporation*
Trice, Renee — *Source Services Corporation*
Trieschmann, Daniel — *Source Services Corporation*
Trimble, Patricia — *Source Services Corporation*
Trimble, Rhonda — *Source Services Corporation*
Trott, Kathryn — *Allard Associates*
Trott, Kathryn — *Allard Associates*
Trueblood, Brian G. — *TNS Partners, Inc.*
Truex, John F. — *Morton, McCorkle & Associates, Inc.*
Truitt, Thomas B. — *Southwestern Professional Services*
Tryon, Katey — *DeFrain, Mayer, Lee & Burgess LLC*
Tscelli, Maureen — *Source Services Corporation*
Tschan, Stephen — *Source Services Corporation*

Tucker, Thomas A. — *The Thomas Tucker Company*
Tunney, William — *Grant Cooper and Associates*
Turner, Edward K. — *Don Richard Associates of Charlotte*
Turner, Raymond — *Source Services Corporation*
Tursi, Deborah J. — *The Corporate Connection, Ltd.*
Tutwiler, Stephen — *Don Richard Associates of Tampa, Inc.*
Tweed, Janet — *Gilbert Tweed/INESA*
Twomey, James — *Source Services Corporation*
Tyson, Richard L. — *Bonifield Associates*
Ulbert, Nancy — *Aureus Group*
Uzzel, Linda — *Source Services Corporation*
Vacca, Domenic — *Romac & Associates*
Van Alstine, Catherine — *Tanton Mitchell/Paul Ray Berndtson*
Van Campen, Jerry — *Gilbert & Van Campen International*
Van Clieaf, Mark — *MVC Associates International*
Van Norman, Ben — *Source Services Corporation*
Van Remmen, Roger — *Brown, Bernardy, Van Remmen, Inc.*
Vande-Water, Katie — *J. Robert Scott*
Vandenbulcke, Cynthia — *Source Services Corporation*
Varney, Monique — *Source Services Corporation*
Varrichio, Michael — *Source Services Corporation*
Velez, Hector — *Source Services Corporation*
Venable, William W. — *Thorndike Deland Associates*
Vilella, Paul — *Source Services Corporation*
Villella, Paul — *Source Services Corporation*
Vinett-Hessel, Deidre — *Source Services Corporation*
Visnich, L. Christine — *Bason Associates Inc.*
Viviano, Cathleen — *Source Services Corporation*
Vlcek, Thomas J. — *Vlcek & Company, Inc.*
Voigt, John A. — *Romac & Associates*
von Stein, Scott — *Wilkinson & Ives*
Wade, Christy — *Source Services Corporation*
Waggoner, Lisa — *Intersource, Ltd.*
Waitkus, Karen — *Richard, Wayne and Roberts*
Waldrop, Gary R. — *MSI International*
Walker, Ann — *Source Services Corporation*
Walker, Ewing J. — *Ward Howell International, Inc.*
Walker, Rose — *Source Services Corporation*
Wallace, Alec — *Tanton Mitchell/Paul Ray Berndtson*
Wallace, Toby — *Source Services Corporation*
Ward, Les — *Source Services Corporation*
Ward, Madeleine — *LTM Associates*
Ward, Robert — *Source Services Corporation*
Ward, Ted — *Korn/Ferry International*
Warnock, Phyl — *Source Services Corporation*
Warren, Sylvia W. — *Thorndike Deland Associates*
Wasp, Warren T. — *WTW Associates*
Wasson, Thomas W. — *Spencer Stuart*
Watkins, Thomas M. — *Lamalie Amrop International*
Watson, James — *MSI International*
Waymire, Pamela — *Source Services Corporation*
Wayne, Cary S. — *ProSearch Inc.*
Webb, George H. — *Webb, Johnson Associates, Inc.*
Webber, Edward — *Source Services Corporation*
Weeks, Glenn — *Source Services Corporation*
Weinberg, Melvin — *Romac & Associates*
Weis, Theodore — *Source Services Corporation*
Weiss, Elizabeth — *Source Services Corporation*
Weller, Paul S. — *Mark Stanley & Company*
Wenz, Alexander — *Source Services Corporation*
Werner, Bonnie — *H.M. Long International, Ltd.*
Wessling, Jerry — *Source Services Corporation*
Weston, Corinne F. — *D.A. Kreuter Associates, Inc.*
Wheatley, William — *Drummond Associates, Inc.*
Wheeler, Gerard H. — *A.J. Burton Group, Inc.*
White, Jonathan O. — *The Badger Group*
White, Richard B. — *Spencer Stuart*
Whitfield, Jack — *Source Services Corporation*
Whiting, Anthony — *Johnson Smith & Knisely Accord*
Whitney, David L. — *Whitney & Associates, Inc.*
Whitney, Kenneth L. — *K.L. Whitney Company*
Whitton, Paula L. — *Pearson, Caldwell & Farnsworth, Inc.*
Wier, Daniel — *Horton International*
Wilbanks, George R. — *Russell Reynolds Associates, Inc.*
Wilcox, Fred T. — *Wilcox, Bertoux & Miller*
Wilder, Barry — *Rhodes Associates*
Wilder, Richard B. — *Columbia Consulting Group*
Wilkinson, Barbara — *Beall & Company, Inc.*
Willbrandt, Curt — *Source Services Corporation*
Williams, Angie — *Whitney & Associates, Inc.*
Williams, Harry D. — *Jacobson Associates*
Williams, John — *Source Services Corporation*
Williams, Lis — *Executive Options, Ltd.*
Williams, Roger K. — *Williams, Roth & Krueger Inc.*
Williams, Walter E. — *Canny, Bowen Inc.*
Willis, William H. — *William Willis Worldwide Inc.*
Wilson, Derrick — *Thornton Resources*
Wilson, John C. — *Russell Reynolds Associates, Inc.*

Wilson, Joyce — *Source Services Corporation*
Wilson, Patricia L. — *Leon A. Farley Associates*
Wingate, Mary — *Source Services Corporation*
Winitz, Joel — *GSW Consulting Group, Inc.*
Winitz, Marla — *GSW Consulting Group, Inc.*
Winkowski, Stephen — *Source Services Corporation*
Winnewisser, William E. — *Accounting & Computer Personnel*
Winnicki, Kimberly — *Source Services Corporation*
Winograd, Glenn — *Criterion Executive Search, Inc.*
Winter, Robert — *The Whitney Group*
Wirtshafter, Linda — *Grant Cooper and Associates*
Wisch, Steven C. — *MB Inc. Interim Executive Division*
Wise, J. Herbert — *Sandhurst Associates*
Witzgall, William — *Source Services Corporation*
Wolf, Donald — *Source Services Corporation*
Wolf, Stephen M. — *Byron Leonard International, Inc.*
Wolfe, Peter — *Source Services Corporation*
Womack, Joseph — *The Bankers Group*
Wood, Gary — *Source Services Corporation*
Wood, John S. — *Egon Zehnder International Inc.*
Wood, Milton M. — *M. Wood Company*
Woods, Craig — *Source Services Corporation*
Wooller, Edmund A.M. — *Windsor International*
Woomer, Jerome — *Source Services Corporation*
Workman, David — *Source Services Corporation*
Wright, Carl A.J. — *A.J. Burton Group, Inc.*
Wright, Charles D. — *Goodrich & Sherwood Associates, Inc.*
Wright, Leslie — *The Stevenson Group of New Jersey*
Wycoff-Viola, Amy — *Source Services Corporation*
Wylie, Pamela — *M.A. Churchill & Associates, Inc.*
Yeaton, Robert — *Source Services Corporation*
Young, Alexander — *Messett Associates, Inc.*
Youngberg, David — *Source Services Corporation*
Zaffrann, Craig S. — *P.J. Murphy & Associates, Inc.*
Zahradka, James F. — *P.J. Murphy & Associates, Inc.*
Zarkin, Norman — *Rhodes Associates*
Zaslav, Debra M. — *Telford, Adams & Alexander/Telford & Co., Inc.*
Zavala, Lorenzo — *Russell Reynolds Associates, Inc.*
Zavat, Marc — *Ryan, Miller & Associates Inc.*
Zavrel, Mark — *Source Services Corporation*
Zay, Thomas C. — *Boyden/Zay & Company*
Zay, Thomas C. — *Boyden/Zay & Company*
Zegel, Gary — *Source Services Corporation*
Zetto, Kathryn — *Seco & Zetto Associates, Inc.*
Zimbal, Mark — *Source Services Corporation*
Zimmerman, Joan C. — *G.Z. Stephens Inc.*
Zimont, Scott — *Source Services Corporation*
Zivic, Janis M. — *Spencer Stuart*
Zona, Henry F. — *Zona & Associates, Inc.*
Zonis, Hildy R. — *Accountants Executive Search*
Zucker, Nancy — *Maximum Management Corp.*
Zwiff, Jeffrey G. — *Johnson Smith & Knisely Accord*

## 15. Healthcare/Hospitals

Abbatiello, Christine Murphy — *Winter, Wyman & Company*
Abell, Vincent W. — *MSI International*
Adams, Jeffrey C. — *Telford, Adams & Alexander/Jeffrey C. Adams & Co., Inc.*
Adams, Ralda F. — *Hospitality International*
Adkisson, Billy D. — *James Russell, Inc.*
Akin, J.R. — *J.R. Akin & Company Inc.*
Albers, Joan — *Carver Search Consultants*
Alekel, Karren — *ALW Research International*
Alexander, Raymond — *Howard Fischer Associates, Inc.*
Allen, Cynthia — *Roberson and Company*
Allen, David A. — *Intech Summit Group, Inc.*
Altieri, Robert J. — *Longshore & Simmons, Inc.*
Ambler, Peter W. — *Peter W. Ambler Company*
Anderson, Richard — *Grant Cooper and Associates*
Andrews, J. Douglas — *Clarey & Andrews, Inc.*
Apostle, George — *Search Dynamics, Inc.*
Archer, John W. — *Russell Reynolds Associates, Inc.*
Argentin, Jo — *Executive Placement Consultants, Inc.*
Aronin, Michael — *Fisher-Todd Associates*
Atkins, Laurie — *Battalia Winston International*
Atkinson, S. Graham — *Raymond Karsan Associates*
Aydelotte, G. Thomas — *Ingram & Aydelotte Inc.*
Badger, Fred H. — *The Badger Group*
Bagwell, Bruce — *Intersource, Ltd.*
Bailey, William A. — *TNS Partners, Inc.*
Baird, Blaine T. — *Physicians Search, Inc.*
Baird, John — *Professional Search Consultants*
Baker-Greene, Edward — *Isaacson, Miller*
Balkin, Linda E. — *Witt/Kieffer, Ford, Hadelman & Lloyd*
Ballein, Kathleen M. — *Witt/Kieffer, Ford, Hadelman & Lloyd*
Ballenger, Michael — *Heidrick & Struggles, Inc.*
Baran, Helena — *Michael J. Cavanagh and Associates*
Barger, H. Carter — *Barger & Sargeant, Inc.*

Barlow, Ken H. — *The Cherbonnier Group, Inc.*
Barnes, Richard E. — *Barnes Development Group, LLC*
Barnes, Roanne L. — *Barnes Development Group, LLC*
Baron, Jon C. — *MSI International*
Barowsky, Diane M. — *Lamalie Amrop International*
Barth, Cynthia P. — *Longshore & Simmons, Inc.*
Barthold, James A. — *McNichol Associates*
Bason, Maurice L. — *Bason Associates Inc.*
Bassman, Robert — *Kaye-Bassman International Corp.*
Bassman, Sandy — *Kaye-Bassman International Corp.*
Bates, Scott W. — *Kittleman & Associates*
Bearman, Linda — *Grant Cooper and Associates*
Beaulieu, Genie A. — *Romac & Associates*
Beck, Charlotte — *Witt/Kieffer, Ford, Hadelman & Lloyd*
Bellano, Robert W. — *Stanton Chase International*
Bennett, Delora — *Genesis Personnel Service, Inc.*
Bennett, Jo — *Battalia Winston International*
Berger, Emanuel — *Isaacson, Miller*
Berger, Jay V. — *Morris & Berger*
Berger, Judith E. — *MDR Associates, Inc.*
Berman, Kenneth D. — *MSI International*
Bettick, Michael J. — *A.J. Burton Group, Inc.*
Biddix, Maryanne — *Tyler & Company*
Billington, Brian — *Billington & Associates*
Biskin, Donald — *Heidrick & Struggles, Inc.*
Blake, Eileen — *Howard Fischer Associates, Inc.*
Blanton, Thomas — *Blanton and Company*
Bohn, Steve J. — *MSI International*
Bond, Robert J. — *Romac & Associates*
Bonnell, William R. — *Bonnell Associates Ltd.*
Book, Cheryl — *Aureus Group*
Borland, James — *Goodrich & Sherwood Associates, Inc.*
Borman, Theodore H. — *Lamalie Amrop International*
Bormann, Cindy Ann — *MSI International*
Bovich, Maryann C. — *Higdon Prince Inc.*
Bowen, Tad — *Executive Search International*
Bowen, William J. — *Heidrick & Struggles, Inc.*
Boyer, Heath C. — *Spencer Stuart*
Brackin, James B. — *Brackin & Sayers Associates*
Bratches, Howard — *Thorndike Deland Associates*
Brenner, Mary — *Prestige Inc.*
Brieger, Steve — *Thorne, Brieger Associates Inc.*
Broadhurst, Austin — *Russell Reynolds Associates, Inc.*
Brodie, Ricki R. — *MSI International*
Brooks, Bernard E. — *Mruk & Partners/EMA Partners Int'l*
Brown, Buzz — *Brown, Bernardy, Van Remmen, Inc.*
Brown, Charlene N. — *Accent on Achievement, Inc.*
Brown, D. Perry — *Don Richard Associates of Washington, D.C., Inc.*
Brown, Larry C. — *Horton International*
Brunelle, Francis W.H. — *The Caldwell Partners Amrop International*
Bryant, Christopher P. — *Ast/Bryant*
Bryant, Henry — *D. Brown and Associates, Inc.*
Bryza, Robert M. — *Robert Lowell International*
Burchard, Stephen R. — *Burchard & Associates, Inc.*
Burden, Gene — *The Cherbonnier Group, Inc.*
Burfield, Elaine — *Skott/Edwards Consultants, Inc.*
Burke, John — *The Experts*
Burkland, Skott B. — *Skott/Edwards Consultants, Inc.*
Burns, Terence N. — *D.E. Foster Partners Inc.*
Bush, Martha A. — *MSI International*
Bush, R. Stuart — *Russell Reynolds Associates, Inc.*
Bye, Randy — *Romac & Associates*
Cahill, James P. — *Thorndike Deland Associates*
Came, Paul E. — *Paul Ray Berndtson*
Campbell, Gary — *Romac & Associates*
Campbell, Robert Scott — *Wellington Management Group*
Canan, Bruce — *The Nielsen Healthcare Group*
Carabelli, Paula — *Witt/Kieffer, Ford, Hadelman & Lloyd*
Cargo, Catherine — *MSI International*
Carideo, Joseph — *Thorndike Deland Associates*
Carpenter, Harold G. — *MSI International*
Carrara, Gilbert J. — *Korn/Ferry International*
Carter, Christine C. — *Health Care Dimensions*
Caudill, Nancy — *Webb, Johnson Associates, Inc.*
Causey, Andrea C. — *MSI International*
Cavanagh, Michael J. — *Michael J. Cavanagh and Associates*
Caver, Michael D. — *Heidrick & Struggles, Inc.*
Cavolina, Michael — *Carver Search Consultants*
Cesafsky, Barry R. — *Lamalie Amrop International*
Chan, Margaret — *Webb, Johnson Associates, Inc.*
Chandler, Robert C. — *Ward Howell International, Inc.*
Chatterjie, Alok — *MSI International*
Cherbonnier, L. Michael — *The Cherbonnier Group, Inc.*
Christenson, H. Alan — *Christenson & Hutchison*
Citera, Tom — *Howe-Lewis International*
Cizek, John T. — *Cizek Associates, Inc.*
Cizek, Marti J. — *Cizek Associates, Inc.*

Clarey, Jack R. — *Clarey & Andrews, Inc.*
Clark, W. Christopher — *Heidrick & Struggles, Inc.*
Claude, Abe — *Paul Ray Berndtson*
Cleeve, Coleen — *Howe-Lewis International*
Cocchiaro, Richard — *Romac & Associates*
Cohen, Michael R. — *Intech Summit Group, Inc.*
Cohen, Robert C. — *Intech Summit Group, Inc.*
Colborne, Janis M. — *AJM Professional Services*
Cole, Elizabeth — *MSI International*
Cole, Kevin — *Don Richard Associates of Washington, D.C., Inc.*
Cole, Sharon A. — *AJM Professional Services*
Collard, Joseph A. — *Spencer Stuart*
Colman, Michael — *Executive Placement Consultants, Inc.*
Colucci, Bart A. — *Colucci, Blendow and Johnson, Inc.*
Conard, Rodney J. — *Conard Associates, Inc.*
Conners, Theresa — *D. Brown and Associates, Inc.*
Cordaro, Concetta — *Flynn, Hannock, Incorporated*
Corey, Michael J. — *Witt/Kieffer, Ford, Hadelman & Lloyd*
Corrigan, Gerald F. — *The Corrigan Group*
Costa, Cynthia A. — *MSI International*
Coston, Bruce G. — *MSI International*
Cowan, Roberta — *Drew Associates International*
Cox, Mark M. — *Witt/Kieffer, Ford, Hadelman & Lloyd*
Crabtree, Bonnie — *Korn/Ferry International*
Cramer, Barbara Lee — *Physicians Search, Inc.*
Cramer, Paul J. — *C/R Associates*
Crawford, Cassondra — *Don Richard Associates of Washington, D.C., Inc.*
Cripe, Joyce — *Mixtec Group*
Crownover, Kathryn L. — *MSI International*
Crystal, Jonathan A. — *Spencer Stuart*
Cuddy, Brian C. — *Romac & Associates*
Cunningham, Robert Y. — *Goodrich & Sherwood Associates, Inc.*
D'Alessio, Gary A. — *Chicago Legal Search, Ltd.*
Dalton, David R. — *MSI International*
Daniels, David — *Search West, Inc.*
Darter, Steven M. — *People Management Northeast Incorporated*
Davis, Bernel — *MSI International*
de Bardin, Francesca — *F.L. Taylor & Company, Inc.*
Debrueys, Lee G. — *MSI International*
DeCorrevont, James — *DeCorrevont & Associates*
DeCorrevont, James — *DeCorrevont & Associates*
DeFrancesco, Mary Ellen — *The Onstott Group, Inc.*
DeGioia, Joseph — *JDG Associates, Ltd.*
DeHart, Donna — *Tower Consultants, Ltd.*
Del Pino, William — *National Search, Inc.*
Del Prete, Karen — *Gilbert Tweed/INESA*
Del'Ange, Gabrielle N. — *MSI International*
Delaney, Patrick J. — *Sensible Solutions, Inc.*
Delmonico, Laura — *A.J. Burton Group, Inc.*
deMartino, Cathy — *Lucas Associates*
Demchak, James P. — *Sandhurst Associates*
Desgrosellier, Gary P. — *Personnel Unlimited/Executive Search*
Desir, Etheline — *Tyler & Company*
Desmond, Dennis — *Beall & Company, Inc.*
Detore, Robert R. — *Drew Associates International*
deVry, Kimberly A. — *Tower Consultants, Ltd.*
Dickey, Chet W. — *Bowden & Company, Inc.*
Dietz, David S. — *MSI International*
DiGiovanni, Charles — *Penn Search*
DiMarchi, Paul — *DiMarchi Partners, Inc.*
Dingman, Bruce — *Robert W. Dingman Company, Inc.*
Dingman, Robert W. — *Robert W. Dingman Company, Inc.*
Diskin, Rochelle — *Search West, Inc.*
Do, Sonnie — *Whitney & Associates, Inc.*
Doele, Donald C. — *Goodrich & Sherwood Associates, Inc.*
Doliva, Lauren M. — *Heidrick & Struggles, Inc.*
Doody, Michael F. — *Witt/Kieffer, Ford, Hadelman & Lloyd*
Dotson, M. Ileen — *Dotson & Associates*
Dowrick, Jeanne A. — *Longshore & Simmons, Inc.*
Dressler, Ralph — *Romac & Associates*
DuBois, Joseph W. — *Horizon Medical Search of New Hampshire*
Dunkel, David L. — *Romac & Associates*
Earle, Paul W. — *Spencer Stuart*
Eastham, Marvene M. — *Witt/Kieffer, Ford, Hadelman & Lloyd*
Ebeling, John A. — *Gilbert Tweed/INESA*
Edell, David E. — *The Development Resource Group Incorporated*
Edwards, Dorothy — *MSI International*
Eibeler, C. — *Amherst Personnel Group Inc.*
Emmott, Carol B. — *Spencer Stuart*
England, Mark — *Austin-McGregor International*
Engman, Steven T. — *Lamalie Amrop International*
Erstling, Gregory — *Normyle/Erstling Health Search Group*
Eustis, Lucy R. — *MSI International*
Faber, Jill — *A.T. Kearney, Inc.*
Fancher, Robert L. — *Bason Associates Inc.*
Farley, Antoinette L. — *Witt/Kieffer, Ford, Hadelman & Lloyd*
Farrow, Jerry M. — *McCormack & Farrow*

Ferrara, David M. — *Intech Summit Group, Inc.*
Fincher, Richard P. — *Phase II Management*
Flannery, Peter — *Jonas, Walters & Assoc., Inc.*
Flickinger, Susan V. — *Korn/Ferry International*
Flora, Dodi — *Crawford & Crofford*
Foote, Leland W. — *L.W. Foote Company*
Ford, J. Daniel — *Witt/Kieffer, Ford, Hadelman & Lloyd*
Foreman, David C. — *Koontz, Jeffries & Associates, Inc.*
Fotia, Frank — *JDG Associates, Ltd.*
Fotino, Anne — *Normyle/Erstling Health Search Group*
Fox, Amanda C. — *Paul Ray Berndtson*
Francis, Joseph — *Hospitality International*
Frank, Valerie S. — *Norman Roberts & Associates, Inc.*
Franklin, John W. — *Russell Reynolds Associates, Inc.*
Frazier, John — *Cochran, Cochran & Yale, Inc.*
Freier, Bruce — *Executive Referral Services, Inc.*
Friedman, Donna L. — *Tower Consultants, Ltd.*
Friedman, Helen E. — *McCormack & Farrow*
Fry, Edmund L. — *Witt/Kieffer, Ford, Hadelman & Lloyd*
Fuhrman, Katherine — *Richard, Wayne and Roberts*
Gaffney, Denise O'Grady — *Isaacson, Miller*
Galante, Suzanne M. — *Vlcek & Company, Inc.*
Gallagher, Terence M. — *Battalia Winston International*
Galvani, Frank J. — *MSI International*
Garcia, Samuel K. — *Southwestern Professional Services*
Gardner, Catherine — *Aureus Group*
Garfinkle, Steven M. — *Battalia Winston International*
Garrett, Donald L. — *Garrett Associates Inc.*
Garrett, Linda M. — *Garrett Associates Inc.*
Gauss, James W. — *Witt/Kieffer, Ford, Hadelman & Lloyd*
Gauthier, Robert C. — *Columbia Consulting Group*
Geiger, Jan — *Wilcox, Bertoux & Miller*
Gelinas, Lynn — *D. Brown and Associates, Inc.*
Genser, Elaina S. — *Witt/Kieffer, Ford, Hadelman & Lloyd*
George, Delores F. — *Delores F. George Human Resource Management & Consulting Industry*
George, Scott — *Aureus Group*
Gerber, Mark J. — *Wellington Management Group*
Gerson, Russ D. — *Webb, Johnson Associates, Inc.*
Gibson, Bruce — *Gibson & Company Inc.*
Giella, Thomas J. — *Korn/Ferry International*
Gilbert, Carol — *Korn/Ferry International*
Giles, Joe L. — *Joe L. Giles and Associates, Inc.*
Gill, Patricia — *Columbia Consulting Group*
Gillespie, Kathleen M. — *Witt/Kieffer, Ford, Hadelman & Lloyd*
Gillespie, Thomas — *Professional Search Consultants*
Gladstone, Arthur — *Executive Referral Services, Inc.*
Goar, Duane R. — *Sandhurst Associates*
Gobert, Larry — *Professional Search Consultants*
Goldenberg, Sheryl — *Neail Behringer Consultants*
Goldenberg, Susan — *Grant Cooper and Associates*
Gooch, Randy — *Richard, Wayne and Roberts*
Goodman, Dawn M. — *Bason Associates Inc.*
Goodspeed, Peter W. — *Witt/Kieffer, Ford, Hadelman & Lloyd*
Gordon, Gerald L. — *E.G. Jones Associates, Ltd.*
Grady, Richard F. — *Drew Associates International*
Grant, Carol — *Hitchens & Foster, Inc.*
Grantham, John — *Grantham & Co., Inc.*
Grantham, Philip H. — *Columbia Consulting Group*
Graves, Rosemarie — *Don Richard Associates of Washington, D.C., Inc.*
Grebenschikoff, Jennifer R. — *Physician Executive Management Center*
Grebenstein, Charles R. — *Skott/Edwards Consultants, Inc.*
Greco, Patricia — *Howe-Lewis International*
Grinnell, Janis R. — *Physicians Search, Inc.*
Gulley, Marylyn — *MSI International*
Gurtin, Kay L. — *Executive Options, Ltd.*
Gustafson, Richard P. — *Heidrick & Struggles, Inc.*
Gwin, Ric — *Southwestern Professional Services*
Haddad, Charles — *Romac & Associates*
Hadelman, Jordan M. — *Witt/Kieffer, Ford, Hadelman & Lloyd*
Hallock, Peter B. — *Goodrich & Sherwood Associates, Inc.*
Halstead, Frederick A. — *Ward Howell International, Inc.*
Halvorsen, Jeanne M. — *Kittleman & Associates*
Hamilton, Timothy — *The Caldwell Partners Amrop International*
Hamm, Gary P. — *Witt/Kieffer, Ford, Hadelman & Lloyd*
Hamm, Mary Kay — *Romac & Associates*
Hancock, Mimi — *Russell Reynolds Associates, Inc.*
Hanford, Michael — *Richard Kader & Associates*
Hanley, Maureen E. — *Gilbert Tweed/INESA*
Hanna, Dwight — *Cadillac Associates*
Hannock, Elwin W. — *Flynn, Hannock, Incorporated*
Hanson, Grant M. — *Goodrich & Sherwood Associates, Inc.*
Harap, David — *Korn/Ferry International*
Harbaugh, Paul J. — *International Management Advisors, Inc.*
Hart, Andrew D. — *Russell Reynolds Associates, Inc.*
Hart, Robert T. — *D.E. Foster Partners Inc.*

Harvey, Jill — *MSI International*
Harvey, Mike — *Advanced Executive Resources*
Harvey, Richard — *Price Waterhouse*
Haughton, Michael — *DeFrain, Mayer, Lee & Burgess LLC*
Hauser, Martha — *Spencer Stuart*
Hawkins, John T.W. — *Russell Reynolds Associates, Inc.*
Haystead, Steve — *Advanced Executive Resources*
Hazelton, Lisa M. — *Health Care Dimensions*
Heiken, Barbara E. — *Randell-Heiken, Inc.*
Hellebusch, Jerry — *Morgan Hunter Corp.*
Herman, Pat — *Whitney & Associates, Inc.*
Hermsmeyer, Rex — *Hitchens & Foster, Inc.*
Heuerman, James N. — *Korn/Ferry International*
Hewitt, Rives D. — *The Dalley Hewitt Company*
Hicks, James L. — *MSI International*
Hildebrand, Thomas B. — *Professional Resources Group, Inc.*
Hill, Emery — *MSI International*
Hill, Mike — *Tyler & Company*
Hilyard, Paul J. — *MSI International*
Hoffmeir, Patricia A. — *Gilbert Tweed/INESA*
Hollins, Howard D. — *MSI International*
Holodnak, William A. — *J. Robert Scott*
Hoppert, Phil — *Wargo and Co., Inc.*
Houchins, William N. — *Christian & Timbers*
Howard, Jill — *Health Care Dimensions*
Howe, Theodore — *Romac & Associates*
Hoyda, Louis A. — *Thorndike Deland Associates*
Hudson, Reginald M. — *Search Bureau International*
Hunt, Thomas — *MSI International*
Hutchison, Richard H. — *Rurak & Associates, Inc.*
Hutchison, William K. — *Christenson & Hutchison*
Hwang, Yvette — *MSI International*
Hyde, Mark D. — *MSI International*
Hyde, W. Jerry — *Hyde Danforth Wold & Co.*
Inguagiato, Gregory — *MSI International*
Isaacson, John — *Isaacson, Miller*
Issacs, Judith A. — *Grant Cooper and Associates*
Ivey, Deborah M. — *MSI International*
Jacobs, Martin J. — *The Rubicon Group*
Jadick, Theodore N. — *Heidrick & Struggles, Inc.*
Jaedike, Eldron — *Prestige Inc.*
James, Allison A. — *MSI International*
Jensen, Stephanie — *Don Richard Associates of Tidewater, Inc.*
Jernigan, Susan N. — *Sockwell & Associates*
Jessamy, Howard T. — *Witt/Kieffer, Ford, Hadelman & Lloyd*
Joffe, Barry — *Bason Associates Inc.*
Johnson, Brian — *A.J. Burton Group, Inc.*
Johnson, Janet — *Normyle/Erstling Health Search Group*
Johnson, John W. — *Webb, Johnson Associates, Inc.*
Johnson, Keith — *Romac & Associates*
Johnson, Maxene — *Norman Roberts & Associates, Inc.*
Johnson, S. Hope — *The Interface Group, Ltd./Boyden*
Jones, Barbara J. — *Kaye-Bassman International Corp.*
Jones, Jeffrey — *AJM Professional Services*
Joyce, James — *Sharrow & Associates*
Judd, Susan — *Korn/Ferry International*
Judge, Alfred L. — *The Cambridge Group Ltd*
Kaplan, Alexandra — *J.M. Eagle Partners Ltd.*
Kaplan, Gary — *Gary Kaplan & Associates*
Kaplan, Marc — *Gary Kaplan & Associates*
Kaptain, John — *Blau Kaptain Schroeder*
Katz, Cyndi — *Search West, Inc.*
Katz, Robert L. — *MSI International*
Kaye, Jeffrey — *Kaye-Bassman International Corp.*
Kelly, Elizabeth Ann — *Wellington Management Group*
Kelly, Michael T. — *Russell Reynolds Associates, Inc.*
Kelly, Peter W. — *R. Rollo Associates*
Kennedy, Walter — *Romac & Associates*
Kerester, Jonathon — *Cadillac Associates*
Kershaw, Lisa — *Tanton Mitchell/Paul Ray Berndtson*
Kieffer, Michael C. — *Witt/Kieffer, Ford, Hadelman & Lloyd*
Kiley, Phyllis — *National Search, Inc.*
King, Joyce L. — *MSI International*
King, Richard M. — *Kittleman & Associates*
King, Thomas — *Morgan Hunter Corp.*
Kingsley, Kate — *Korn/Ferry International*
Kirchner, Michael — *American Medical Consultants*
Kirschman, David R. — *Physician Executive Management Center*
Kixmiller, David B. — *Heidrick & Struggles, Inc.*
Klages, Constance W. — *International Management Advisors, Inc.*
Klavens, Cecile J. — *The Pickwick Group, Inc.*
Koehler, Cathy — *Ells Personnel System Inc.*
Koehler, Frank R. — *The Koehler Group*
Kondra, Vernon J. — *The Douglas Reiter Company, Inc.*
Koontz, Donald N. — *Koontz, Jeffries & Associates, Inc.*
Kramer, Donald — *Dunhill Personnel of Tampa, Inc.*
Kramer, Peter — *Dunhill Personnel of Tampa, Inc.*
Kratz, Steve — *Tyler & Company*

Krejci, Stanley L. — *The Interface Group, Ltd./Boyden*
Kreps, Charles D. — *Normyle/Erstling Health Search Group*
Kreutz, Gary L. — *Kreutz Consulting Group, Inc.*
Kropp, Randy — *Ells Personnel System Inc.*
Kuhl, Teresa — *Don Richard Associates of Tampa, Inc.*
Kuper, Keith D. — *Christenson & Hutchison*
Kurtz, Michael E. — *MDR Associates, Inc.*
Kuypers, Arnold — *Lamalie Amrop International*
Laderman, David — *Romac & Associates*
LaFaye, Susan — *MSI International*
Lamb, Angus K. — *Raymond Karsan Associates*
Lankford, Charles — *MSI International*
LaPierre, Louis — *Romac & Associates*
Larsen, Bruce — *Prestige Inc.*
LaValle, Michael — *Romac & Associates*
Lawson, Bettye N. — *MSI International*
Leben, Sally — *D. Brown and Associates, Inc.*
Leetma, Imbi — *Stanton Chase International*
Leff, Lisa A. — *Berger and Leff*
Lence, Julie Anne — *MSI International*
Lence, Julie Anne — *Spectra International Inc.*
Lennon, Roslyn J. — *Heidrick & Struggles, Inc.*
Lennox, Charles — *Price Waterhouse*
LesKovec, Charles S. — *MDR Associates, Inc.*
Letcher, Harvey D. — *Sandhurst Associates*
Levine, Lois — *National Search, Inc.*
Lewicki, Christopher — *MSI International*
Lewis, Charles G. — *Longshore & Simmons, Inc.*
Lewis, Jon A. — *Sandhurst Associates*
Lindberg, Eric J. — *MSI International*
Linde, Rick — *Battalia Winston International*
Lindsay, M. Evan — *Heidrick & Struggles, Inc.*
Line, Joseph T. — *Sharrow & Associates*
Linton, Leonard M. — *Byron Leonard International, Inc.*
Livesay, Christopher C. — *MSI International*
Lloyd, John S. — *Witt/Kieffer, Ford, Hadelman & Lloyd*
Loeb, Stephen H. — *Grant Cooper and Associates*
London, Gregory J. — *MSI International*
Long, Melanie — *National Search, Inc.*
Longmore, Marilyn — *Richard Kader & Associates*
Longshore, George F. — *Longshore & Simmons, Inc.*
Loomis, Ruth L. — *Ast/Bryant*
Loria, Frank — *Accounting Personnel Consultants*
Lotufo, Donald A. — *D.A.L. Associates, Inc.*
Lotz, R. James — *International Management Advisors, Inc.*
Love, David M. — *Paul Ray Berndtson*
Loving, Vikki — *Intersource, Ltd.*
Low, Linda — *The Development Resource Group Incorporated*
Lucas, J. Curtis — *Korn/Ferry International*
Lucas, Ronnie L. — *MSI International*
Lumsby, George N. — *International Management Advisors, Inc.*
Lyons, Mary Fran — *Witt/Kieffer, Ford, Hadelman & Lloyd*
Lyons, Michele R. — *R. Rollo Associates*
MacCarthy, Ann — *Columbia Consulting Group*
Macdonald, G. William — *The Macdonald Group, Inc.*
Mackey-Ross, Christine — *Witt/Kieffer, Ford, Hadelman & Lloyd*
Mackin, Michael — *D. Brown and Associates, Inc.*
Magee, Harrison R. — *Bowden & Company, Inc.*
Makrianes, James K. — *Webb, Johnson Associates, Inc.*
Mallipudi, Anand — *Raymond Karsan Associates*
Manassero, Henri J.P. — *International Management Advisors, Inc.*
Mancino, Gene — *Blau Kaptain Schroeder*
Manns, Alex — *Crawford & Crofford*
Marks, Russell E. — *Webb, Johnson Associates, Inc.*
Marlow, William — *Straube Associates*
Marshall, Neill P. — *Witt/Kieffer, Ford, Hadelman & Lloyd*
Martin, Mary Lou — *Neail Behringer Consultants*
Martin, Paula — *MSI International*
Marumoto, William H. — *The Interface Group, Ltd./Boyden*
Maslan, Neal L. — *Ward Howell International, Inc.*
Matheny, Robert P. — *MSI International*
Mathias, William J. — *Preng & Associates, Inc.*
Matti, Suzy — *Southwestern Professional Services*
Mayes, Kay H. — *John Shell Associates, Inc.*
McAlpine, Bruce — *Keith Bagg & Associates Inc.*
McBride, Jonathan E. — *McBride Associates, Inc.*
McCabe, Christopher — *Raymond Karsan Associates*
McCallister, Jane T. — *Heidrick & Struggles, Inc.*
McClearen, Bruce — *Tyler & Company*
McConnell, Greg — *Winter, Wyman & Company*
McCormack, Joseph A. — *McCormack & Associates*
McCreary, Charles — *Austin-McGregor International*
McDonald, Scott A. — *McDonald Associates International*
McDonald, Stanleigh B. — *McDonald Associates International*
McGahey, Patricia M. — *Witt/Kieffer, Ford, Hadelman & Lloyd*
McLaughlin, John — *Romac & Associates*
McLean, B. Keith — *Price Waterhouse*
McNamara, Timothy C. — *Columbia Consulting Group*

McNear, Jeffrey E. — *Barrett Partners*
McNichol, John — *McNichol Associates*
McNichols, Walter B. — *Gary Kaplan & Associates*
Meagher, Patricia G. — *Spencer Stuart*
Meier, J. Dale — *Grant Cooper and Associates*
Meltzer, Andrea Y. — *Executive Options, Ltd.*
Merkuris, Jennifer — *Aureus Group*
Mertensotto, Chuck H. — *Whitney & Associates, Inc.*
Messett, William J. — *Messett Associates, Inc.*
Meyer, Michael F. — *Witt/Kieffer, Ford, Hadelman & Lloyd*
Meyer, Stacey — *Gary Kaplan & Associates*
Middleton, Alfred E. — *The Neil Michael Group, Inc.*
Miesemer, Arthur C. — *MSI International*
Miller, Benjamin J. — *MSI International*
Miller, Kenneth A. — *Computer Network Resources, Inc.*
Mitchell, John — *Romac & Associates*
Mitchell, John T. — *Paul Ray Berndtson*
Mitchell, Kyle R. — *Tanton Mitchell/Paul Ray Berndtson*
Mitchell, Norman F. — *A.T. Kearney, Inc.*
Molitor, John L. — *Barrett Partners*
Molnar, Robert A. — *Johnson Smith & Knisely Accord*
Moore, Denise — *Jonas, Walters & Assoc., Inc.*
Moran, Robert — *A.T. Kearney, Inc.*
Morgan, Gary — *National Search, Inc.*
Morris, Kristine A. — *Morris & Berger*
Morrison, Janis L. — *Garrett Associates Inc.*
Moses, Jerry — *J.M. Eagle Partners Ltd.*
Moxley, John H. — *Korn/Ferry International*
Moyse, Richard G. — *Thorndike Deland Associates*
Muendel, H. Edward — *Stanton Chase International*
Muller, Charles A. — *AJM Professional Services*
Munguia, Rebecca — *Richard, Wayne and Roberts*
Murphy, Cornelius J. — *Goodrich & Sherwood Associates, Inc.*
Murphy, Patrick J. — *P.J. Murphy & Associates, Inc.*
Myers, Kay — *Signature Staffing*
Nagle, Charles L. — *Tyler & Company*
Nagler, Leon G. — *Nagler, Robins & Poe, Inc.*
Nazzaro, Samuel G. — *Boyden*
Neher, Robert L. — *Intech Summit Group, Inc.*
Nephew, Robert — *Christian & Timbers*
Neuberth, Jeffrey G. — *Canny, Bowen Inc.*
Newcorn, Andrew R. — *The Neil Michael Group, Inc.*
Nielsen, Bruce — *The Nielsen Healthcare Group*
Nordland, Martin N. — *Horton International*
Norman, Randy — *Austin-McGregor International*
Norton, Douglas — *Korn/Ferry International*
Nutter, Roger — *Raymond Karsan Associates*
O'Brien, John G. — *CanMed Consultants Inc.*
O'Donnell, James H. — *MSI International*
O'Hara, Daniel M. — *Lynch Miller Moore Partners, Inc.*
O'Neill, David — *Korn/Ferry International*
Osborn, Jim — *Southwestern Professional Services*
Osinski, Martin H. — *American Medical Consultants*
Otto, Karen E. — *Witt/Kieffer, Ford, Hadelman & Lloyd*
Pace, Susan A. — *Horton International*
Pacini, Lauren R. — *Hite Executive Search*
Page, Linda — *Jonas, Walters & Assoc., Inc.*
Page, Linda M. — *Wargo and Co., Inc.*
Palma, Frank R. — *Goodrich & Sherwood Associates, Inc.*
Palmer, Carlton A. — *Beall & Company, Inc.*
Papciak, Dennis J. — *Temporary Accounting Personnel*
Pappas, Jim — *Search Dynamics, Inc.*
Park, Dabney G. — *Mark Stanley & Company*
Patlovich, Michael J. — *Witt/Kieffer, Ford, Hadelman & Lloyd*
Patton, Mitchell — *Patton/Perry Associates, Inc.*
Peeney, James D. — *Peeney Associates*
Pelton, Margaret — *Price Waterhouse*
Percival, Chris — *Chicago Legal Search, Ltd.*
Perez, Christina — *Orr Executive Search*
Persky, Barry — *Barry Persky & Company, Inc.*
Peternell, Melanie — *Signature Staffing*
Pfannkuche, Anthony V. — *Spencer Stuart*
Pfeiffer, Irene — *Price Waterhouse*
Phillips, Anna W. — *Witt/Kieffer, Ford, Hadelman & Lloyd*
Phillips, Scott K. — *Phillips & Ford, Inc.*
Pickford, Stephen T. — *The Corporate Staff, Inc.*
Pinson, Stephanie L. — *Gilbert Tweed/INESA*
Plimpton, Ralph L. — *R L Plimpton Associates*
Podway, Hope — *Search West, Inc.*
Poore, Larry D. — *Ward Howell International, Inc.*
Porter, Albert — *The Experts*
Porter, Donald — *Amherst Personnel Group Inc.*
Poster, Lawrence D. — *Catalyx Group*
Postles, Doris W. — *Longshore & Simmons, Inc.*
Potenza, Gregory — *Mixtec Group*
Prencipe, V. Michael — *Raymond Karsan Associates*
Press, Fred — *Adept Tech Recruiting*
Price, P. Anthony — *Russell Reynolds Associates, Inc.*

Quick, Roger A. — *Norman Broadbent International, Inc.*
Rabinowitz, Peter A. — *P.A.R. Associates Inc.*
Rackley, Eugene M. — *Heidrick & Struggles, Inc.*
Radice, Joseph — *Hospitality International*
Raheja, Marc C. — *CanMed Consultants Inc.*
Ramler, Carolyn S. — *The Corporate Connection, Ltd.*
Ramsey, John H. — *Mark Stanley & Company*
Randell, James E. — *Randell-Heiken, Inc.*
Rattner, Kenneth L. — *Heidrick & Struggles, Inc.*
Rauch, Carl W. — *Physicians Search, Inc.*
Rauch, Cliff — *Physicians Search, Inc.*
Reddick, David C. — *Horton International*
Redding, Denise — *The Douglas Reiter Company, Inc.*
Redler, Rhonda — *National Search, Inc.*
Reeder, Michael S. — *Lamalie Amrop International*
Reiser, Ellen — *Thorndike Deland Associates*
Reiss, Matt — *National Search, Inc.*
Reiter, Douglas — *The Douglas Reiter Company, Inc.*
Reticker, Peter — *MSI International*
Reyman, Susan — *S. Reyman & Associates Ltd.*
Reynolds, Juli Ann — *Korn/Ferry International*
Rich, Lyttleton — *Sockwell & Associates*
Richard, Albert L. — *Human Resources Inc.*
Rieger, Louis J. — *Spencer Stuart*
Roberts, Nick P. — *Spectrum Search Associates, Inc.*
Roberts, Norman C. — *Norman Roberts & Associates, Inc.*
Roberts, Raymond R. — *MSI International*
Roberts, Scott B. — *Wargo and Co., Inc.*
Robinson, Eric B. — *Bruce Robinson Associates*
Rodney, Brett — *MSI International*
Roehrig, Kurt W. — *AJM Professional Services*
Rogers, Leah — *Dinte Resources, Incorporated*
Rollo, Robert S. — *R. Rollo Associates*
Romanchek, Walter R. — *Wellington Management Group*
Romo, Dorothy — *D. Brown and Associates, Inc.*
Rorech, Maureen — *Romac & Associates*
Rosenberg, Esther — *Howe-Lewis International*
Rosenfeld, Martin J. — *Sanford Rose Associates*
Rosenthal, Charles — *National Search, Inc.*
Rosenwald, Tom H. — *Heidrick & Struggles, Inc.*
Ross, Martin B. — *Ward Howell International, Inc.*
Rossi, Thomas — *Southwestern Professional Services*
Rotella, Marshall W. — *The Corporate Connection, Ltd.*
Rowe, William D. — *D.E. Foster Partners Inc.*
Rowells, Michael — *MSI International*
Rozner, Burton L. — *Oliver & Rozner Associates, Inc.*
Rubinstein, Alan J. — *Chicago Legal Search, Ltd.*
Runquist, U.W. — *Webb, Johnson Associates, Inc.*
Rurak, Zbigniew T. — *Rurak & Associates, Inc.*
Russell, Susan Anne — *Executive Search Consultants Corporation*
Ryan, Lee — *Ryan, Miller & Associates Inc.*
Sacerdote, John — *Raymond Karsan Associates*
Sahagian, John — *Human Resources Inc.*
Salvagno, Michael J. — *The Cambridge Group Ltd*
Sandor, Richard J. — *Flynn, Hannock, Incorporated*
Saner, Harold — *Romac & Associates*
Sauer, Harry J. — *Romac & Associates*
Sauer, Robert C. — *Heidrick & Struggles, Inc.*
Savage, Edward J. — *Stanton Chase International*
Sawhill, Louise B. — *Paul Ray Berndtson*
Sawyer, Patricia L. — *Smith & Sawyer Inc.*
Saydah, Robert F. — *Heidrick & Struggles, Inc.*
Sayers, Bruce D. — *Brackin & Sayers Associates*
Schaad, Carl A. — *Heidrick & Struggles, Inc.*
Schachter, Laura J. — *Professional Placement Associates, Inc.*
Schlosser, John R. — *Heidrick & Struggles, Inc.*
Schlpma, Christine — *Advanced Executive Resources*
Schoen, Stephen G. — *MDR Associates, Inc.*
Schroeder, Lee — *Blau Kaptain Schroeder*
Schroeder, Steven J. — *Blau Kaptain Schroeder*
Scognamillo, Sandra V. — *Witt/Kieffer, Ford, Hadelman & Lloyd*
Scothon, Alan — *Romac & Associates*
Seibert, Nancy — *Tyler & Company*
Sekera, Roger I. — *A.T. Kearney, Inc.*
Sennello, Gendra — *National Search, Inc.*
Sessa, Beth — *Richard, Wayne and Roberts*
Sevilla, Claudio A. — *Crawford & Crofford*
Shabot, David — *Korn/Ferry International*
Shea, Kathleen M. — *The Penn Partners, Incorporated*
Sheedy, Edward J. — *Dieckmann & Associates, Ltd.*
Shell, John C. — *John Shell Associates, Inc.*
Shelton, Sandra — *National Search, Inc.*
Shepard, Michael J. — *MSI International*
Shepherd, Daniel M. — *Shepherd Bueschel & Provus, Inc.*
Sherwood, Andrew — *Goodrich & Sherwood Associates, Inc.*
Shultz, Deborah M. — *Blau Kaptain Schroeder*
Sibul, Shelly Remen — *Chicago Legal Search, Ltd.*
Siegel, Pamela — *Executive Options, Ltd.*

Sierra, Rafael A. — *Lamalie Amrop International*
Silvas, Stephen D. — *Roberson and Company*
Silver, Lee A. — *L.A. Silver Associates, Inc.*
Sine, Mark — *Hospitality International*
Singer, Glenn — *Witt/Kieffer, Ford, Hadelman & Lloyd*
Singleton, Robin — *Tyler & Company*
Smith, Adam M. — *The Abbott Group, Inc.*
Smith, Grant — *Price Waterhouse*
Smith, John F. — *The Penn Partners, Incorporated*
Smith, Margaret L. — *MSI International*
Snelgrove, Geiger — *National Search, Inc.*
Snodgrass, Stephen — *DeFrain, Mayer, Lee & Burgess LLC*
Snyder, James F. — *Snyder & Company*
Sockwell, J. Edgar — *Sockwell & Associates*
Soggs, Cheryl Pavick — *A.T. Kearney, Inc.*
Solomon Ph.D., Neil M. — *The Neil Michael Group, Inc.*
Southerland, Keith C. — *Witt/Kieffer, Ford, Hadelman & Lloyd*
Spann, Richard E. — *Goodrich & Sherwood Associates, Inc.*
Spiegel, Gay — *L.A. Silver Associates, Inc.*
Stafford, Susan — *Hospitality International*
Stanley, Paul R.A. — *Lovas Stanley/Paul Ray Berndtson Inc.*
Stark, Jeff — *Thorne, Brieger Associates Inc.*
Stein, Terry W. — *Stewart, Stein and Scott, Ltd.*
Stephenson, Don L. — *Ells Personnel System Inc.*
Sterling, Sally M. — *Heidrick & Struggles, Inc.*
Stevens, Tracey — *Don Richard Associates of Washington, D.C., Inc.*
Stewart, Jeffrey O. — *Stewart, Stein and Scott, Ltd.*
Stiles, Judy — *MedQuest Associates*
Stone, Susan L. — *Stone Enterprises Ltd.*
Stouffer, Kenneth — *Keith Bagg & Associates Inc.*
Stratmeyer, Karin Bergwall — *Princeton Entrepreneurial Resources*
Stricker, Sidney G. — *Stricker & Zagor*
Strobridge, Richard P. — *F.L. Taylor & Company, Inc.*
Struzziero, Ralph E. — *Romac & Associates*
Stutt, Brian — *Richard, Wayne and Roberts*
Sutter, Howard — *Romac & Associates*
Swan, Richard A. — *Witt/Kieffer, Ford, Hadelman & Lloyd*
Swanson, Dick — *Raymond Karsan Associates*
Taylor, Conrad G. — *MSI International*
Taylor, Ernest A. — *Ward Howell International, Inc.*
Teas, John — *Southwestern Professional Services*
Teinert, Jay — *Damon & Associates, Inc.*
Telford, John H. — *Telford, Adams & Alexander/Telford & Co., Inc.*
Templin, Robert E. — *Gilbert Tweed/INESA*
Theard, Susan — *Romac & Associates*
Theobald, David B. — *Theobald & Associates*
Thielman, Joseph — *Barrett Partners*
Thomas, Christine S. — *Lovas Stanley/Paul Ray Berndtson Inc.*
Thomas, Kurt J. — *P.J. Murphy & Associates, Inc.*
Thompson, Dave — *Battalia Winston International*
Thompson, Kenneth L. — *McCormack & Farrow*
Tinucci, Crystal M. — *Witt/Kieffer, Ford, Hadelman & Lloyd*
Tipp, George — *Intech Summit Group, Inc.*
Titterington, Catherine F. — *MSI International*
Tokash, Ronald E. — *MSI International*
Tootsey, Mark A. — *A.J. Burton Group, Inc.*
Tracey, Jack — *Management Assistance Group, Inc.*
Trosin, Walter R. — *Johnson Smith & Knisely Accord*
Truex, John F. — *Morton, McCorkle & Associates, Inc.*
Truitt, Thomas B. — *Southwestern Professional Services*
Tryon, Katey — *DeFrain, Mayer, Lee & Burgess LLC*
Tunney, William — *Grant Cooper and Associates*
Turner, Edward K. — *Don Richard Associates of Charlotte*
Turner, Elaine — *Witt/Kieffer, Ford, Hadelman & Lloyd*
Tweed, Janet — *Gilbert Tweed/INESA*
Twiste, Craig — *Raymond Karsan Associates*
Tyler, J. Larry — *Tyler & Company*
Ulbert, Nancy — *Aureus Group*
Unger, Paul T. — *A.T. Kearney, Inc.*
Utroska, Donald R. — *Lamalie Amrop International*
Vacca, Domenic — *Romac & Associates*
Vachon, David A. — *McNichol Associates*
Valenta, Joseph — *Princeton Entrepreneurial Resources*
Van Alstyne, Susan — *Richard, Wayne and Roberts*
Van Remmen, Roger — *Brown, Bernardy, Van Remmen, Inc.*
Venable, William W. — *Thorndike Deland Associates*
Vergara, Gail H. — *Spencer Stuart*
Vernon, Jack H. — *Russell Reynolds Associates, Inc.*
Visnich, L. Christine — *Bason Associates Inc.*
Vlcek, Thomas J. — *Vlcek & Company, Inc.*
Voigt, John A. — *Romac & Associates*
Volk, Richard — *MSI International*
Waggoner, Lisa — *Intersource, Ltd.*
Wakefield, Scott — *National Search, Inc.*
Waldman, Noah H. — *Lamalie Amrop International*
Waldoch, D. Mark — *Barnes Development Group, LLC*
Waldrop, Gary R. — *MSI International*
Wall, David — *Southwestern Professional Services*

Wallace, Alec — *Tanton Mitchell/Paul Ray Berndtson*
Walther, Linda S. — *MSI International*
Ward, William F. — *Heidrick & Struggles, Inc.*
Warren, Sylvia W. — *Thorndike Deland Associates*
Watson, James — *MSI International*
Webb, George H. — *Webb, Johnson Associates, Inc.*
Weed, William H. — *Paul Ray Berndtson*
Weinberg, Melvin — *Romac & Associates*
Weisler, Nancy — *National Search, Inc.*
Weiss, Jeffrey — *Search West, Inc.*
Weissman-Rosenthal, Abbe — *ALW Research International*
Welch, David — *Isaacson, Miller*
Weller, Paul S. — *Mark Stanley & Company*
Wertheim, M. Chris — *Witt/Kieffer, Ford, Hadelman & Lloyd*
West, Nancy — *Health Care Dimensions*
Whalen, Kathleen — *The Nielsen Healthcare Group*
White, Jonathan O. — *The Badger Group*
White, Patricia D. — *MSI International*
Whitley, Sue Ann — *Roberts Ryan and Bentley*
Whitney, David L. — *Whitney & Associates, Inc.*
Whittall, Barbara — *Heidrick & Struggles, Inc.*
Wicklund, Grant — *Heidrick & Struggles, Inc.*
Wilder, Richard B. — *Columbia Consulting Group*
Wilkins, Walter K. — *Sampson Neill & Wilkins Inc.*
Wilkinson, Barbara — *Beall & Company, Inc.*
Williams, Alexander H. — *Witt/Kieffer, Ford, Hadelman & Lloyd*
Williams, Angie — *Whitney & Associates, Inc.*
Williams, Gary L. — *Barnes Development Group, LLC*
Williams, Laurelle N. — *MSI International*
Williams, Lis — *Executive Options, Ltd.*
Williams, Roger K. — *Williams, Roth & Krueger Inc.*
Williams, Walter E. — *Canny, Bowen Inc.*
Winitz, Joel — *GSW Consulting Group, Inc.*
Winitz, Marla — *GSW Consulting Group, Inc.*
Winograd, Glenn — *Criterion Executive Search, Inc.*
Winston, Dale — *Battalia Winston International*
Winter, Peter — *Catalyx Group*
Wirtshafter, Linda — *Grant Cooper and Associates*
Wise, J. Herbert — *Sandhurst Associates*
Wiseman, Bonnie — *Witt/Kieffer, Ford, Hadelman & Lloyd*
Wolf, Craig — *Aureus Group*
Wollman, Harry — *Howard Fischer Associates, Inc.*
Wood, Milton M. — *M. Wood Company*
Woody, Jacqueline K. — *Aureus Group*
Worth, Janet M. — *Witt/Kieffer, Ford, Hadelman & Lloyd*
Wright, Charles D. — *Goodrich & Sherwood Associates, Inc.*
Wrynn, Robert F. — *MSI International*
Wyatt, James — *Wyatt & Jaffe*
Wyatt, Janice — *Korn/Ferry International*
Wynkoop, Mary — *Tyler & Company*
Wyser-Pratte, Anne — *Heidrick & Struggles, Inc.*
Yilmaz, Muriel — *Dinte Resources, Incorporated*
Young, Alexander — *Messett Associates, Inc.*
Yowe, Mark — *Heidrick & Struggles, Inc.*
Zaffrann, Craig S. — *P.J. Murphy & Associates, Inc.*
Zahradka, James F. — *P.J. Murphy & Associates, Inc.*
Zander, Barry W. — *MSI International*
Zaslav, Debra M. — *Telford, Adams & Alexander/Telford & Co., Inc.*
Zay, Thomas C. — *Boyden/Zay & Company*
Zenzer, Anne — *Witt/Kieffer, Ford, Hadelman & Lloyd*
Zila, Laurie M. — *Princeton Entrepreneurial Resources*
Zilliacus, Patrick W. — *Larsen, Zilliacus & Associates, Inc.*
Zingaro, Ron — *Zingaro and Company*
Zivic, Janis M. — *Spencer Stuart*

## 16. High Technology

Abbatiello, Christine Murphy — *Winter, Wyman & Company*
Abbott, Peter — *The Abbott Group, Inc.*
Abell, Vincent W. — *MSI International*
Acquaviva, Jay — *Winter, Wyman & Company*
Adams, Jeffrey C. — *Telford, Adams & Alexander/Jeffrey C. Adams & Co., Inc.*
Ahearn, Jennifer — *Logix, Inc.*
Aheran, Jennifer — *Logix Partners*
Aiken, David — *Commonwealth Consultants*
Akin, J.R. — *J.R. Akin & Company Inc.*
Alekel, Karren — *ALW Research International*
Allen, Donald — *D.S. Allen Associates, Inc.*
Allerton, Donald T. — *Allerton Heneghan & O'Neill*
Allred, J. Michael — *Spencer Stuart*
Alpeyrie, Jean-Louis — *Heidrick & Struggles, Inc.*
Altreuter, Rose — *The ALTCO Group*
Ambler, Peter W. — *Peter W. Ambler Company*
Ames, George C. — *Ames O'Neill Associates*
Anderson, David C. — *Heidrick & Struggles, Inc.*
Anderson, Dean C. — *Corporate Resources Professional Placement*
Anderson, Thomas — *Paul J. Biestek Associates, Inc.*
Andrews, J. Douglas — *Clarey & Andrews, Inc.*

Andrick, Patty — *CPS Inc.*
Apostle, George — *Search Dynamics, Inc.*
Archer, Sandra F. — *Ryan, Miller & Associates Inc.*
Arms, Douglas — *TOPAZ International, Inc.*
Arms, Douglas — *TOPAZ Legal Solutions*
Arnold, David — *Christian & Timbers*
Arnson, Craig — *Hernand & Partners*
Arseneault, Daniel S. — *MSI International*
Ashton, Barbara L. — *Ashton Computer Professionals Inc.*
Asquith, Peter S. — *Ames Personnel Consultants, Inc.*
Atkins, Laurie — *Battalia Winston International*
Aubin, Richard E. — *Aubin International*
Badger, Fred H. — *The Badger Group*
Bagwell, Bruce — *Intersource, Ltd.*
Bailey, William A. — *TNS Partners, Inc.*
Baillou, Astrid — *Richard Kinser & Associates*
Baker, Gary M. — *Cochran, Cochran & Yale, Inc.*
Baker, Gerry — *Baker, Harris & Partners Limited*
Balch, Randy — *CPS Inc.*
Baldwin, Keith R. — *The Baldwin Group*
Baltin, Carrie — *Search West, Inc.*
Barbosa, Franklin J. — *Boyden*
Barger, H. Carter — *Barger & Sargeant, Inc.*
Barlow, Ken H. — *The Cherbonnier Group, Inc.*
Barnett-Flint, Juliet — *Heidrick & Struggles, Inc.*
Barnum, Toni M. — *Stone Murphy & Olson*
Baron, Len — *Industrial Recruiters Associates, Inc.*
Bartesch, Heinz — *The Search Firm, Inc.*
Barthold, James A. — *McNichol Associates*
Bartholdi, Ted — *Bartholdi & Company, Inc.*
Bartholdi, Theodore G. — *Bartholdi & Company, Inc.*
Barton, Gary R. — *Barton Raben, Inc.*
Bason, Maurice L. — *Bason Associates Inc.*
Bassman, Robert — *Kaye-Bassman International Corp.*
Bassman, Sandy — *Kaye-Bassman International Corp.*
Beal, Richard D. — *A.T. Kearney, Inc.*
Beall, Charles P. — *Beall & Company, Inc.*
Beaudin, Elizabeth C. — *Callan Associates, Ltd.*
Beaulieu, Genie A. — *Romac & Associates*
Beaver, Bentley H. — *The Onstott Group, Inc.*
Beaver, Robert W. — *Executive Manning Corporation*
Beckvold, John B. — *Atlantic Search Group, Inc.*
Bell, Lindy — *F-O-R-T-U-N-E Personnel Consultants of Huntsville, Inc.*
Bennett, Jo — *Battalia Winston International*
Bennett, Ness — *Technical Connections Inc.*
Berger, Jay V. — *Morris & Berger*
Bermea, Jose — *Gaffney Management Consultants*
Berry, Harold B. — *The Hindman Company*
Besen, Douglas — *Besen Associates Inc.*
Biestek, Paul J. — *Paul J. Biestek Associates, Inc.*
Bitar, Edward — *The Interface Group, Ltd./Boyden*
Blackmon, Sharon — *The Abbott Group, Inc.*
Bladon, Andrew — *Don Richard Associates of Tampa, Inc.*
Blecker, Jay — *TSS Consulting, Ltd.*
Bliley, Jerry — *Spencer Stuart*
Blim, Barbara — *JDG Associates, Ltd.*
Bloom, Howard C. — *Hernand & Partners*
Bloom, Joyce — *Hernand & Partners*
Bloomer, James E. — *L.W. Foote Company*
Bluhm, Claudia — *Schweichler Associates, Inc.*
Blunt, Peter — *Hernand & Partners*
Boccella, Ralph — *Susan C. Goldberg Associates*
Boczany, William J. — *The Guild Corporation*
Boesel, James — *Logix Partners*
Boesel, Jim — *Logix, Inc.*
Bohle, John B. — *Paul Ray Berndtson*
Bohn, Steve J. — *MSI International*
Bond, Allan — *Walden Associates*
Bond, Robert J. — *Romac & Associates*
Bormann, Cindy Ann — *MSI International*
Bostic, James E. — *Phillips Resource Group*
Bourrie, Sharon D. — *Chartwell Partners International, Inc.*
Bowen, Tad — *Executive Search International*
Boyle, Russell E. — *Egon Zehnder International Inc.*
Brackin, James B. — *Brackin & Sayers Associates*
Brady, Robert — *CPS Inc.*
Bragg, Garry — *The McCormick Group, Inc.*
Brandeis, Richard — *CPS Inc.*
Brennen, Richard J. — *Spencer Stuart*
Brieger, Steve — *Thorne, Brieger Associates Inc.*
Briggs, Adam — *Horton International*
Brocaglia, Joyce — *Alta Associates, Inc.*
Brooks, Charles — *Corporate Recruiters Ltd.*
Brovender, Claire — *Winter, Wyman & Company*
Brown, Buzz — *Brown, Bernardy, Van Remmen, Inc.*
Brown, Charlene N. — *Accent on Achievement, Inc.*
Brown, D. Perry — *Don Richard Associates of Washington, D.C., Inc.*

Brown, Larry C. — *Horton International*
Brown, S. Ross — *Egon Zehnder International Inc.*
Bruce, Michael C. — *Spencer Stuart*
Brudno, Robert J. — *Savoy Partners, Ltd.*
Bruno, Deborah F. — *The Hindman Company*
Bryant, Richard D. — *Bryant Associates, Inc.*
Bryza, Robert M. — *Robert Lowell International*
Buckles, Donna — *Cochran, Cochran & Yale, Inc.*
Bueschel, David A. — *Shepherd Bueschel & Provus, Inc.*
Burch, R. Stuart — *Russell Reynolds Associates, Inc.*
Burchill, Greg — *BGB Associates*
Burden, Gene — *The Cherbonnier Group, Inc.*
Burke, John — *The Experts*
Burns, Alan — *The Enns Partners Inc.*
Busch, Jack — *Busch International*
Busterna, Charles — *The KPA Group*
Butcher, Pascale — *F-O-R-T-U-N-E Personnel Consultants of Manatee County*
Butler, Kevin M. — *Russell Reynolds Associates, Inc.*
Button, David R. — *The Button Group*
Bye, Randy — *Romac & Associates*
Cahill, James P. — *Thorndike Deland Associates*
Cahill, Peter M. — *Peter M. Cahill Associates, Inc.*
Call, David — *Cochran, Cochran & Yale, Inc.*
Callahan, Wanda — *Cochran, Cochran & Yale, Inc.*
Callan, Robert M. — *Callan Associates, Ltd.*
Campbell, Gary — *Romac & Associates*
Campbell, Patricia A. — *The Onstott Group, Inc.*
Campbell, Robert Scott — *Wellington Management Group*
Campbell, W. Ross — *Egon Zehnder International Inc.*
Carrott, Gregory T. — *Egon Zehnder International Inc.*
Carter, I. Wayne — *Heidrick & Struggles, Inc.*
Carter, Jon F. — *Egon Zehnder International Inc.*
Cast, Donald — *Dunhill Search International*
Cattanach, Bruce B. — *Horton International*
Caudill, Nancy — *Webb, Johnson Associates, Inc.*
Cavolina, Michael — *Carver Search Consultants*
Celenza, Catherine — *CPS Inc.*
Chan, Margaret — *Webb, Johnson Associates, Inc.*
Chappell, Peter — *The Bankers Group*
Chatterjie, Alok — *MSI International*
Chavous, C. Crawford — *Phillips Resource Group*
Cherbonnier, L. Michael — *TCG International, Inc.*
Cherbonnier, L. Michael — *The Cherbonnier Group, Inc.*
Christian, Jeffrey E. — *Christian & Timbers*
Christiansen, Amy — *CPS Inc.*
Christiansen, Doug — *CPS Inc.*
Christy, Michael T. — *Heidrick & Struggles, Inc.*
Cizek, John T. — *Cizek Associates, Inc.*
Cizek, Marti J. — *Cizek Associates, Inc.*
Clarey, Jack R. — *Clarey & Andrews, Inc.*
Clark, James — *CPS Inc.*
Clauhsen, Elizabeth A. — *Savoy Partners, Ltd.*
Cline, Mark — *NYCOR Search, Inc.*
Cocchiaro, Richard — *Romac & Associates*
Cochran, Hale — *Fenwick Partners*
Coffman, Brian — *Kossuth & Associates, Inc.*
Cohen, Michael R. — *Intech Summit Group, Inc.*
Cohen, Pamela — *TOPAZ International, Inc.*
Cohen, Pamela — *TOPAZ Legal Solutions*
Cohen, Robert C. — *Intech Summit Group, Inc.*
Colasanto, Frank M. — *W.R. Rosato & Associates, Inc.*
Cole, Kevin — *Don Richard Associates of Washington, D.C., Inc.*
Cole, Sharon A. — *AJM Professional Services*
Coleman, J. Kevin — *J. Kevin Coleman & Associates, Inc.*
Colling, Douglas — *KPMG Management Consulting*
Collis, Gerald — *TSS Consulting, Ltd.*
Combs, Stephen L. — *Juntunen-Combs-Poirier*
Conard, Rodney J. — *Conard Associates, Inc.*
Connelly, Scott — *Technical Connections Inc.*
Connolly, Cathryn — *Strategic Associates, Inc.*
Connor, Michele — *Abraham & London, Ltd.*
Conway, William P. — *Phillips Resource Group*
Cooke, Jeffrey R. — *Jonas, Walters & Assoc., Inc.*
Cooke, Katherine H. — *Horton International*
Cottingham, R.L. — *Marvin L. Silcott & Associates, Inc.*
Coulman, Karen — *CPS Inc.*
Crane, Howard C. — *Chartwell Partners International, Inc.*
Crath, Paul F. — *Price Waterhouse*
Critchley, Walter — *Cochran, Cochran & Yale, Inc.*
Crumpton, Marc — *Logix Partners*
Crumpton, Marc — *Logix, Inc.*
Crumpton, Marc — *Walden Associates*
Cruse, O.D. — *Spencer Stuart*
Cruz, Catherine — *TOPAZ International, Inc.*
Cruz, Catherine — *TOPAZ Legal Solutions*
Cuddy, Brian C. — *Romac & Associates*
Cunningham, Sheila — *Adams & Associates International*

Cuomo, Frank — *Frank Cuomo and Associates, Inc.*
Cushman, Judith — *Marshall Consultants/West*
Cyphers, Ralph R. — *Strategic Associates, Inc.*
Czepiel, Susan — *CPS Inc.*
D'Alessio, Gary A. — *Chicago Legal Search, Ltd.*
Daily, John C. — *Handy HRM Corp.*
Dalton, Bret — *Robert W. Dingman Company, Inc.*
Davis, G. Gordon — *Davis & Company*
Davison, Patricia E. — *Lamalie Amrop International*
DeCorrevont, James — *DeCorrevont & Associates*
DeCorrevont, James — *DeCorrevont & Associates*
DeGioia, Joseph — *JDG Associates, Ltd.*
Del Prete, William — *Gilbert Tweed/INESA*
Delaney, Patrick J. — *Sensible Solutions, Inc.*
DeLong, Art — *Richard Kader & Associates*
Demchak, James P. — *Sandhurst Associates*
Desgrosellier, Gary P. — *Personnel Unlimited/Executive Search*
Desmond, Dennis — *Beall & Company, Inc.*
deWilde, David M. — *Chartwell Partners International, Inc.*
Dickey, Chet W. — *Bowden & Company, Inc.*
Dietz, David S. — *MSI International*
DiMarchi, Paul — *DiMarchi Partners, Inc.*
Dingman, Bruce — *Robert W. Dingman Company, Inc.*
Dingman, Robert W. — *Robert W. Dingman Company, Inc.*
Dinte, Paul — *Dinte Resources, Incorporated*
DiSalvo, Fred — *The Cambridge Group Ltd*
Divine, Robert S. — *O'Shea, Divine & Company, Inc.*
Dixon, Aris — *CPS Inc.*
Do, Sonnie — *Whitney & Associates, Inc.*
Dornblut, Cindy — *Ashton Computer Professionals Inc.*
Dorsey, Jim — *Ryan, Miller & Associates Inc.*
Dotson, M. Ileen — *Dotson & Associates*
Dougherty, Bridget L. — *Wellington Management Group*
Dow, Lori — *Davidson, Laird & Associates*
Doyle, Bobby — *Richard, Wayne and Roberts*
Dreifus, Donald — *Search West, Inc.*
Dressler, Ralph — *Romac & Associates*
Drexler, Robert — *Robert Drexler Associates, Inc.*
Dromeshauser, Peter — *Dromeshauser Associates*
Drury, James J. — *Spencer Stuart*
Duggan, James P. — *Slayton International, Inc.*
Dunbar, Geoffrey T. — *Heidrick & Struggles, Inc.*
Dunkel, David L. — *Romac & Associates*
Dunlop, Eric — *Southwestern Professional Services*
Dunman, Betsy L. — *Crawford & Crofford*
Dussick, Vince — *Dussick Management Associates*
Dwyer, Julie — *CPS Inc.*
Dykstra, Nicolette — *CPS Inc.*
Earhart, William D. — *Sanford Rose Associates*
Ebeling, John A. — *Gilbert Tweed/INESA*
Edwards, Dorothy — *MSI International*
Edwards, Douglas W. — *Egon Zehnder International Inc.*
Edwards, Verba L. — *Wing Tips & Pumps, Inc.*
Eggena, Roger — *Phillips Resource Group*
Ehrhart, Jennifer — *ADOW's Executeam*
Elliott, A. Larry — *Heidrick & Struggles, Inc.*
Elliott, David H. — *Heidrick & Struggles, Inc.*
Ellis, Ted K. — *The Hindman Company*
Enfield, Jerry J. — *Executive Manning Corporation*
England, Mark — *Austin-McGregor International*
Enns, George — *The Enns Partners Inc.*
Ervin, Darlene — *CPS Inc.*
Eustis, Lucy R. — *MSI International*
Fairlie, Suzanne F. — *ProSearch, Inc.*
Falk, John — *D.S. Allen Associates, Inc.*
Fancher, Robert L. — *Bason Associates Inc.*
Farber, Susan — *Heidrick & Struggles, Inc.*
Farley, Leon A. — *Leon A. Farley Associates*
Farrow, Jerry M. — *McCormack & Farrow*
Feder, Gwen — *Egon Zehnder International Inc.*
Federman, Jack R. — *W.R. Rosato & Associates, Inc.*
Feldman, Abe — *A.E. Feldman Associates*
Ferneborg, Jay W. — *Ferneborg & Associates, Inc.*
Ferneborg, John R. — *Ferneborg & Associates, Inc.*
Ferrara, David M. — *Intech Summit Group, Inc.*
Feyder, Michael — *A.T. Kearney, Inc.*
Fifield, George C. — *Egon Zehnder International Inc.*
Fischer, John C. — *Horton International*
Fisher, Neal — *Fisher Personnel Management Services*
Flannery, Peter — *Jonas, Walters & Assoc., Inc.*
Flora, Dodi — *Crawford & Crofford*
Fogarty, Michael — *CPS Inc.*
Fone, Carol — *Walden Associates*
Foote, Leland W. — *L.W. Foote Company*
Ford, Sandra D. — *Phillips & Ford, Inc.*
Foreman, David C. — *Koontz, Jeffries & Associates, Inc.*
Foreman, Rebecca — *Aubin International*
Forman, Donald R. — *Stanton Chase International*

Fotia, Frank — *JDG Associates, Ltd.*
Francis, David P. — *Heidrick & Struggles, Inc.*
Frazier, John — *Cochran, Cochran & Yale, Inc.*
Fredericks, Ward A. — *Mixtec Group*
French, William G. — *Preng & Associates, Inc.*
Friedman, Donna L. — *Tower Consultants, Ltd.*
Friel, Thomas J. — *Heidrick & Struggles, Inc.*
Furlong, James W. — *Furlong Search, Inc.*
Furlong, James W. — *Furlong Search, Inc.*
Furlong, James W. — *Furlong Search, Inc.*
Gabriel, David L. — *The Arcus Group*
Gadison, William — *Richard, Wayne and Roberts*
Gaffney, Keith — *Gaffney Management Consultants*
Gaffney, William — *Gaffney Management Consultants*
Gaines, Ronni L. — *TOPAZ International, Inc.*
Gaines, Ronni L. — *TOPAZ Legal Solutions*
Gale, Rhoda E. — *E.G. Jones Associates, Ltd.*
Gallagher, Marilyn — *Hogan Acquisitions*
Gallagher, Terence M. — *Battalia Winston International*
Gares, Conrad — *TSS Consulting, Ltd.*
Garfinkle, Steven M. — *Battalia Winston International*
Gauthier, Robert C. — *Columbia Consulting Group*
George, Delores F. — *Delores F. George Human Resource Management & Consulting Industry*
Gerbosi, Karen — *Hernand & Partners*
Germaine, Debra — *Fenwick Partners*
Gerson, Russ D. — *Webb, Johnson Associates, Inc.*
Gibbs, John S. — *Spencer Stuart*
Gibson, Bruce — *Gibson & Company Inc.*
Gilbert, Jerry — *Gilbert & Van Campen International*
Gilchrist, Robert J. — *Horton International*
Giles, Joe L. — *Joe L. Giles and Associates, Inc.*
Gill, Patricia — *Columbia Consulting Group*
Gillespie, Thomas — *Professional Search Consultants*
Gilmartin, William — *Hockett Associates, Inc.*
Gilmore, Lori — *CPS Inc.*
Gilreath, James M. — *Gilreath Weatherby, Inc.*
Glacy, Kurt — *Winter, Wyman & Company*
Gladstone, Arthur — *Executive Referral Services, Inc.*
Glass, Sharon — *Logix Partners*
Glass, Sharon — *Logix, Inc.*
Gloss, Frederick C. — *F. Gloss International*
Goar, Duane R. — *Sandhurst Associates*
Gobert, Larry — *Professional Search Consultants*
Goedtke, Steven — *Southwestern Professional Services*
Goldberg, Susan C. — *Susan C. Goldberg Associates*
Goldenberg, Susan — *Grant Cooper and Associates*
Goldman, Michael L. — *Strategic Associates, Inc.*
Goldsmith, Fred J. — *Fred J. Goldsmith Associates*
Gonye, Peter K. — *Egon Zehnder International Inc.*
Goodere, Greg — *Splaine & Associates, Inc.*
Goodman, Dawn M. — *Bason Associates Inc.*
Goodman, Victor — *Anderson Sterling Associates*
Gordon, Elliot — *Korn/Ferry International*
Gordon, Teri — *Don Richard Associates of Washington, D.C., Inc.*
Gore, Les — *Executive Search International*
Gorfinkle, Gayle — *Executive Search International*
Gorman, T. Patrick — *Techsearch Services, Inc.*
Gostyla, Rick — *Spencer Stuart*
Gould, Adam — *Logix Partners*
Gould, Adam — *Logix, Inc.*
Gould, Dana — *Logix Partners*
Gould, Dana — *Logix, Inc.*
Grady, James — *Search West, Inc.*
Graham, Dale — *CPS Inc.*
Grantham, Philip H. — *Columbia Consulting Group*
Graves, Rosemarie — *Don Richard Associates of Washington, D.C., Inc.*
Grebenstein, Charles R. — *Skott/Edwards Consultants, Inc.*
Green, Jane — *Phillips Resource Group*
Green, Jean — *Broward-Dobbs, Inc.*
Green, Marc — *TSS Consulting, Ltd.*
Greene, Luke — *Broward-Dobbs, Inc.*
Gregor, Joie A. — *Heidrick & Struggles, Inc.*
Grenier, Glorianne — *CPS Inc.*
Groover, David — *MSI International*
Grzybowski, Jill — *CPS Inc.*
Guberman, Robert P. — *A.T. Kearney, Inc.*
Gutknecht, Steven — *Jacobson Associates*
Haas, Margaret P. — *Haas International, Inc.*
Haddad, Charles — *Romac & Associates*
Hailes, Brian — *Russell Reynolds Associates, Inc.*
Hailey, H.M. — *Damon & Associates, Inc.*
Hall, Marty B. — *Catlin-Wells & White*
Hall, Robert — *Don Richard Associates of Tidewater, Inc.*
Halladay, Patti — *Intersource, Ltd.*
Hamm, Mary Kay — *Romac & Associates*
Hanley, Maureen E. — *Gilbert Tweed/INESA*

Hanna, Dwight — *Cadillac Associates*
Hansen, David G. — *Ott & Hansen, Inc.*
Hanson, Lee — *Heidrick & Struggles, Inc.*
Harbaugh, Paul J. — *International Management Advisors, Inc.*
Hardison, Richard L. — *Hardison & Company*
Harelick, Arthur S. — *Ashway, Ltd.*
Harfenist, Harry — *Parker Page Group*
Hargis, N. Leann — *Montgomery Resources, Inc.*
Haro, Adolfo Medina — *Egon Zehnder International Inc.*
Harrison, Priscilla — *Phillips Resource Group*
Harvey, Mike — *Advanced Executive Resources*
Harvey, Richard — *Price Waterhouse*
Haughton, Michael — *DeFrain, Mayer, Lee & Burgess LLC*
Hauswirth, Jeffrey M. — *Spencer Stuart*
Hauver, Scott — *Logix Partners*
Havener, Donald Clarke — *The Abbott Group, Inc.*
Hawksworth, A. Dwight — *A.D. & Associates Executive Search, Inc.*
Hayes, Stacy — *The McCormick Group, Inc.*
Haystead, Steve — *Advanced Executive Resources*
Hazerjian, Cynthia — *CPS Inc.*
Heafey, Bill — *CPS Inc.*
Hecker, Henry C. — *Hogan Acquisitions*
Heiken, Barbara E. — *Randell-Heiken, Inc.*
Helminiak, Audrey — *Gaffney Management Consultants*
Henard, John B. — *Lamalie Amrop International*
Hendrickson, David L. — *Heidrick & Struggles, Inc.*
Heneghan, Donald A. — *Allerton Heneghan & O'Neill*
Henry, Patrick — *F-O-R-T-U-N-E Personnel Consultants of Huntsville, Inc.*
Hensley, Gayla — *Atlantic Search Group, Inc.*
Herman, Pat — *Whitney & Associates, Inc.*
Hernand, Warren L. — *Hernand & Partners*
Hertan, Richard L. — *Executive Manning Corporation*
Hertan, Wiliam A. — *Executive Manning Corporation*
Hertlein, James N.J. — *Boyden/Zay & Company*
Hicks, Albert M. — *Phillips Resource Group*
Hicks, Mike — *Damon & Associates, Inc.*
Hill, Emery — *MSI International*
Hillen, Skip — *The McCormick Group, Inc.*
Hilliker, Alan D. — *Egon Zehnder International Inc.*
Hillyer, Robert L. — *Executive Manning Corporation*
Hindman, Neil C. — *The Hindman Company*
Hnatuik, Ivan — *Corporate Recruiters Ltd.*
Hockett, William — *Hockett Associates, Inc.*
Hoevel, Michael J. — *Poirier, Hoevel & Co.*
Hogan, Larry H. — *Hogan Acquisitions*
Holden, Richard B. — *Ames Personnel Consultants, Inc.*
Holland, Kathleen — *TOPAZ International, Inc.*
Holland, Kathleen — *TOPAZ Legal Solutions*
Hollins, Howard D. — *MSI International*
Holmes, Lawrence J. — *Columbia Consulting Group*
Holodnak, William A. — *J. Robert Scott*
Holt, Carol — *Bartholdi & Company, Inc.*
Hopgood, Earl — *JDG Associates, Ltd.*
Hoppert, Phil — *Wargo and Co., Inc.*
Horgan, Thomas F. — *Nadzam, Lusk, Horgan & Associates, Inc.*
Horner, Gregory — *Corporate Recruiters Ltd.*
Horton, Robert H. — *Horton International*
Houchins, William N. — *Christian & Timbers*
Houver, Scott — *Logix, Inc.*
Howe, Theodore — *Romac & Associates*
Howell, Robert B. — *Atlantic Search Group, Inc.*
Hudson, Reginald M. — *Search Bureau International*
Hughes, Kevin R. — *Handy HRM Corp.*
Hull, Chuck — *Winter, Wyman & Company*
Humphrey, Joan — *Abraham & London, Ltd.*
Hunter, Gabe — *Phillips Resource Group*
Hunter, Steven — *Diamond Tax Recruiting*
Huntoon, Cliff — *Richard, Wayne and Roberts*
Hurley, Janeen — *Winter, Wyman & Company*
Hutchinson, Loretta M. — *Hutchinson Resources International*
Hutchison, Richard H. — *Rurak & Associates, Inc.*
Hykes, Don A. — *A.T. Kearney, Inc.*
Iacovelli, Heather — *CPS Inc.*
Iammatteo, Enzo — *Keith Bagg & Associates Inc.*
Iannacone, Kelly — *Abraham & London, Ltd.*
Imely, Larry — *Christian & Timbers*
Ingalls, Joseph M. — *John Kurosky & Associates*
Inguagiato, Gregory — *MSI International*
Inzinna, Dennis — *AlternaStaff*
Irish, Alan — *CPS Inc.*
Irvine, Robert — *Keith Bagg & Associates Inc.*
Ives, Richard K. — *Wilkinson & Ives*
Jackowitz, Todd — *J. Robert Scott*
Jacobs, Martin J. — *The Rubicon Group*
Jaffe, Mark — *Wyatt & Jaffe*
James, Bruce — *Roberson and Company*
James, Richard — *Criterion Executive Search, Inc.*

McConnell, Greg — *Winter, Wyman & Company*
McCormick, Brian — *The McCormick Group, Inc.*
McCormick, William J. — *The McCormick Group, Inc.*
McCreary, Charles — *Austin-McGregor International*
McDonald, John R. — *TSS Consulting, Ltd.*
McDonald, Scott A. — *McDonald Associates International*
McDonald, Stanleigh B. — *McDonald Associates International*
McDonnell, Julie — *Technical Personnel of Minnesota*
McInturff, Robert — *McInturff & Associates, Inc.*
McIntyre, Joel — *Phillips Resource Group*
McKnight, Amy E. — *Chartwell Partners International, Inc.*
McLaughlin, John — *Romac & Associates*
McLeish, Robert H. — *Executive Search International*
McMahon, Mark J. — *A.T. Kearney, Inc.*
McManamon, Tim — *Rogers-McManamon Executive Search*
McManus, Paul — *Aubin International*
McMillin, Bob — *Price Waterhouse*
McNamara, Timothy C. — *Columbia Consulting Group*
McNamee, Erin — *Technical Connections Inc.*
McNerney, Kevin A. — *Heidrick & Struggles, Inc.*
McNichol, John — *McNichol Associates*
McNichols, Walter B. — *Gary Kaplan & Associates*
McSherry, James F. — *Battalia Winston International*
McThrall, David — *TSS Consulting, Ltd.*
Mefford, Bob — *Executive Manning Corporation*
Meiland, A. Daniel — *Egon Zehnder International Inc.*
Mertensotto, Chuck H. — *Whitney & Associates, Inc.*
Messett, William J. — *Messett Associates, Inc.*
Metz, Dan K. — *Russell Reynolds Associates, Inc.*
Meyer, Stacey — *Gary Kaplan & Associates*
Meyers, Steven — *Montgomery Resources, Inc.*
Michaels, Joseph — *CPS Inc.*
Michaels, Stewart — *TOPAZ International, Inc.*
Michaels, Stewart — *TOPAZ Legal Solutions*
Mierzwinski, John — *Industrial Recruiters Associates, Inc.*
Mikula, Linda — *Schweichler Associates, Inc.*
Miles, Kenneth T. — *MSI International*
Miller, Brett — *The McCormick Group, Inc.*
Miller, Kenneth A. — *Computer Network Resources, Inc.*
Miller, Roy — *The Enns Partners Inc.*
Mitchell, F. Wayne — *Korn/Ferry International*
Mitchell, John — *Romac & Associates*
Mitton, Bill — *Executive Resource, Inc.*
Moerbe, Ed H. — *Stanton Chase International*
Mogul, Gene — *Mogul Consultants, Inc.*
Mohr, Brian — *CPS Inc.*
Molnar, Robert A. — *Johnson Smith & Knisely Accord*
Montgomery, James M. — *Houze, Shourds & Montgomery, Inc.*
Moore, David S. — *Lynch Miller Moore Partners, Inc.*
Moore, Denise — *Jonas, Walters & Assoc., Inc.*
Moore, Lemuel R. — *MSI International*
Moore, Mark — *Wheeler, Moore & Elam Co.*
Moran, Gayle — *Dussick Management Associates*
Morgan, Richard S. — *Lovas Stanley/Paul Ray Berndtson Inc.*
Morgan, Vincent S. — *Johnson Smith & Knisely Accord*
Morris, Kristine A. — *Morris & Berger*
Moses, Jerry — *J.M. Eagle Partners Ltd.*
Mouchet, Marcus — *Commonwealth Consultants*
Mueller-Maerki, Fortunat F. — *Egon Zehnder International Inc.*
Muendel, H. Edward — *Stanton Chase International*
Murphy, Gary J. — *Stone Murphy & Olson*
Murphy, Timothy D. — *MSI International*
Mursuli, Meredith — *Lasher Associates*
Myatt, James S. — *Sanford Rose Associates*
Mydlach, Renee — *CPS Inc.*
Nadherny, Christopher C. — *Spencer Stuart*
Nagler, Leon G. — *Nagler, Robins & Poe, Inc.*
Neelin, Sharon — *The Caldwell Partners Amrop International*
Neely, Alan S. — *Korn/Ferry International*
Neff, Thomas J. — *Spencer Stuart*
Neher, Robert L. — *Intech Summit Group, Inc.*
Neidhart, Craig C. — *TNS Partners, Inc.*
Nelson, Barbara — *Herman Smith Executive Initiatives Inc.*
Nephew, Robert — *Christian & Timbers*
Neuberth, Jeffrey G. — *Canny, Bowen Inc.*
Newman, Lynn — *Kishbaugh Associates International*
Noguchi, Yoshi — *Paul Ray Berndtson*
Nolan, Jean M. — *S.D. Kelly & Associates, Inc.*
Nold, Robert — *Roberson and Company*
Noll, Robert J. — *The Hindman Company*
Nordland, Martin N. — *Horton International*
Norman, Randy — *Austin-McGregor International*
Norsell, Paul E. — *Paul Norsell & Associates, Inc.*
Nosal, David A. — *Heidrick & Struggles, Inc.*
Nymark, John — *NYCOR Search, Inc.*
Nymark, Paul — *NYCOR Search, Inc.*
O'Connell, Mary — *CPS Inc.*
O'Hara, Daniel M. — *Lynch Miller Moore Partners, Inc.*

O'Maley, Kimberlee — *Spencer Stuart*
O'Reilly, Jack — *Catalyx Group*
Ocon, Olga — *Busch International*
Olsen, Carl — *A.T. Kearney, Inc.*
Olsen, David G. — *Handy HRM Corp.*
Olson, A. Andrew — *Paul Ray Berndtson*
Onstott, Joseph E. — *The Onstott Group, Inc.*
Orkin, Ralph — *Sanford Rose Associates*
Orkin, Sheilah — *Sanford Rose Associates*
Ottenritter, Chris — *CPS Inc.*
Owens, Ken — *F-O-R-T-U-N-E Personnel Consultants of Huntsville, Inc.*
Pacini, Lauren R. — *Hite Executive Search*
Padilla, Jose Sanchez — *Egon Zehnder International Inc.*
Page, G. Schuyler — *A.T. Kearney, Inc.*
Page, Linda — *Jonas, Walters & Assoc., Inc.*
Page, Linda M. — *Wargo and Co., Inc.*
Palmer, Carlton A. — *Beall & Company, Inc.*
Palmer, James H. — *The Hindman Company*
Palmer, Melissa — *Don Richard Associates of Tampa, Inc.*
Panetta, Timothy — *Commonwealth Consultants*
Papciak, Dennis J. — *Accounting Personnel Associates, Inc.*
Papciak, Dennis J. — *Temporary Accounting Personnel*
Pappas, Jim — *Search Dynamics, Inc.*
Park, Dabney G. — *Mark Stanley & Company*
Parkin, Myrna — *S.D. Kelly & Associates, Inc.*
Parr, James A. — *KPMG Management Consulting*
Pastrana, Dario — *Egon Zehnder International Inc.*
Patence, David W. — *Handy HRM Corp.*
Patrick, Donald R. — *Sanford Rose Associates*
Payette, Pierre — *Egon Zehnder International Inc.*
Pearson, Robert L. — *Lamalie Amrop International*
Peckenpaugh, Ann D. — *Schweichler Associates, Inc.*
Pedley, Jill — *CPS Inc.*
Pelkey, Chris — *The McCormick Group, Inc.*
Percival, Chris — *Chicago Legal Search, Ltd.*
Perkins, Daphne — *CPS Inc.*
Persky, Barry — *Barry Persky & Company, Inc.*
Peters, James N. — *TNS Partners, Inc.*
Peterson, John — *CPS Inc.*
Petty, J. Scott — *The Arcus Group*
Pfau, Madelaine — *Heidrick & Struggles, Inc.*
Pfeiffer, Irene — *Price Waterhouse*
Pfister, Shelli — *Jack B. Larsen & Associates*
Phillips, Bill — *Dunhill Search International*
Phillips, Donald L. — *O'Shea, Divine & Company, Inc.*
Phillips, Scott K. — *Phillips & Ford, Inc.*
Pickford, Stephen T. — *The Corporate Staff, Inc.*
Pinson, Stephanie L. — *Gilbert Tweed/INESA*
Plimpton, Ralph L. — *R L Plimpton Associates*
Poe, James B. — *Nagler, Robins & Poe, Inc.*
Poirier, Frank — *Juntunen-Combs-Poirier*
Poirier, Roland — *Poirier, Hoevel & Co.*
Polachi, Charles A. — *Fenwick Partners*
Polachi, Peter V. — *Fenwick Partners*
Pomerance, Mark — *CPS Inc.*
Pomeroy, T. Lee — *Egon Zehnder International Inc.*
Porter, Albert — *The Experts*
Poster, Lawrence D. — *Catalyx Group*
Potter, Douglas C. — *Stanton Chase International*
Preschlack, Jack E. — *Spencer Stuart*
Price, Andrew G. — *The Thomas Tucker Company*
Price, P. Anthony — *Russell Reynolds Associates, Inc.*
Prior, Donald — *The Caldwell Partners Amrop International*
Pryde, Marcia P. — *A.T. Kearney, Inc.*
Pugrant, Mark A. — *Grant/Morgan Associates, Inc.*
Quinlan, Lynne — *Winter, Wyman & Company*
Quinn, Nola — *Technical Connections Inc.*
Raab, Julie — *Dunhill Professional Search of Irvine, Inc.*
Rabinowitz, Peter A. — *P.A.R. Associates Inc.*
Radden, David B. — *Paul Ray Berndtson*
Ramler, Carolyn S. — *The Corporate Connection, Ltd.*
Ramsey, John H. — *Mark Stanley & Company*
Randell, James E. — *Randell-Heiken, Inc.*
Range, Mary Jane — *Ingram & Aydelotte Inc.*
Ray, Marianne C. — *Callan Associates, Ltd.*
Raymond, Anne — *Anderson Sterling Associates*
Reddick, David C. — *Horton International*
Redding, Denise — *The Douglas Reiter Company, Inc.*
Reece, Christopher S. — *Reece & Mruk Partners*
Reed, Ruthann — *Spectra International Inc.*
Reiter, Douglas — *The Douglas Reiter Company, Inc.*
Rendl, Ric — *CPS Inc.*
Renner, Sandra L. — *Spectra International Inc.*
Renwick, David — *John Kurosky & Associates*
Reynes, Tony — *Tesar-Reynes, Inc.*
Rice, Marie — *Jay Gaines & Company, Inc.*
Rice, Raymond D. — *Logue & Rice Inc.*

Richard, Albert L. — *Human Resources Inc.*
Riederer, Larry — *CPS Inc.*
Riley, Elizabeth G. — *Mazza & Riley, Inc.*
Rimmel, James E. — *The Hindman Company*
Rimmele, Michael — *The Bankers Group*
Rippey, George E. — *Heidrick & Struggles, Inc.*
Roberts, Mitch — *A.E. Feldman Associates*
Roberts, Nick P. — *Spectrum Search Associates, Inc.*
Roberts, Scott B. — *Wargo and Co., Inc.*
Roberts, William — *Cochran, Cochran & Yale, Inc.*
Robinette, Paul — *Hernand & Partners*
Robins, Jeri N. — *Nagler, Robins & Poe, Inc.*
Robinson, Bruce — *Bruce Robinson Associates*
Roehrig, Kurt W. — *AJM Professional Services*
Rogers, Gay — *Rogers-McManamon Executive Search*
Rogers, Leah — *Dinte Resources, Incorporated*
Romanchek, Walter R. — *Wellington Management Group*
Romanello, Daniel P. — *Spencer Stuart*
Rorech, Maureen — *Romac & Associates*
Rosato, William R. — *W.R. Rosato & Associates, Inc.*
Ross, Lawrence — *Lovas Stanley/Paul Ray Berndtson Inc.*
Ross, Mark S. — *Herman Smith Executive Initiatives Inc.*
Ross, William J. — *Flowers & Associates*
Rossi, George A. — *Heidrick & Struggles, Inc.*
Rossi, Silvio — *Keith Bagg & Associates Inc.*
Rossi, Thomas — *Southwestern Professional Services*
Rotella, Marshall W. — *The Corporate Connection, Ltd.*
Roth, Robert J. — *Williams, Roth & Krueger Inc.*
Rothschild, John S. — *Heidrick & Struggles, Inc.*
Rottblatt, Michael — *Korn/Ferry International*
Roussel, Vicki — *Logix Partners*
Roussel, Vicki J. — *Logix, Inc.*
Rowe, William D. — *D.E. Foster Partners Inc.*
Rowell, Roger — *Halbrecht Lieberman Associates, Inc.*
Rozentsvayg, Michael — *Logix Partners*
Rozentsvayg, Michael — *Logix, Inc.*
Rozner, Burton L. — *Oliver & Rozner Associates, Inc.*
Rubinstein, Alan J. — *Chicago Legal Search, Ltd.*
Rubinstein, Walter — *Technical Connections Inc.*
Rudolph, Kenneth — *Kossuth & Associates, Inc.*
Rudzinsky, Howard — *Louis Rudzinsky Associates*
Rudzinsky, Jeffrey — *Louis Rudzinsky Associates*
Runquist, U.W. — *Webb, Johnson Associates, Inc.*
Rurak, Zbigniew T. — *Rurak & Associates, Inc.*
Russell, Sam — *The Guild Corporation*
Ryan, Lee — *Ryan, Miller & Associates Inc.*
Sabat, Lori S. — *Alta Associates, Inc.*
Safnuk, Donald — *Corporate Recruiters Ltd.*
Sahagian, John — *Human Resources Inc.*
Sahlas, Chrissy — *CPS Inc.*
Saletra, Andrew — *CPS Inc.*
Salvagno, Michael J. — *The Cambridge Group Ltd*
Sanders, Natalie — *CPS Inc.*
Saner, Harold — *Romac & Associates*
Sangster, Jeffrey — *F-O-R-T-U-N-E Personnel Consultants of Manatee County*
Sarn, Allan G. — *Allan Sarn Associates Inc.*
Sauer, Harry J. — *Romac & Associates*
Sauer, Robert C. — *Heidrick & Struggles, Inc.*
Sawyer, Deborah A. — *Heidrick & Struggles, Inc.*
Sawyer, Patricia L. — *Smith & Sawyer Inc.*
Sayers, Bruce D. — *Brackin & Sayers Associates*
Scalamera, Tom — *CPS Inc.*
Schaad, Carl A. — *Heidrick & Struggles, Inc.*
Schaefer, Frederic M. — *A.T. Kearney, Inc.*
Schappell, Marc P. — *Egon Zehnder International Inc.*
Schiavone, Mary Rose — *Canny, Bowen Inc.*
Schlpma, Christine — *Advanced Executive Resources*
Schmidt, Peter R. — *Boyden*
Schmidt, Peter R. — *Boyden*
Schneider, James — *The Search Firm, Inc.*
Schneiderman, Gerald — *Management Resource Associates, Inc.*
Schnierow, Beryl — *Tesar-Reynes, Inc.*
Schoettle, Michael B. — *Heidrick & Struggles, Inc.*
Schueneman, David — *CPS Inc.*
Schwartz, Vincent P. — *Slayton International, Inc.*
Schweichler, Lee J. — *Schweichler Associates, Inc.*
Scothon, Alan — *Romac & Associates*
Seco, William — *Seco & Zetto Associates, Inc.*
Selker, Gregory L. — *Christian & Timbers*
Selko, Philip W. — *Hogan Acquisitions*
Semyan, John K. — *TNS Partners, Inc.*
Sessa, Vincent J. — *Integrated Search Solutions Group, LLC*
Shamir, Ben — *S.D. Kelly & Associates, Inc.*
Shapiro, Elaine — *CPS Inc.*
Shattuck, Merrill B. — *M.B. Shattuck and Associates, Inc.*
Shea, Christopher J. — *Ingram & Aydelotte Inc.*
Shea, Kathleen M. — *The Penn Partners, Incorporated*

Sheedy, Edward J. — *Dieckmann & Associates, Ltd.*
Shell, John C. — *John Shell Associates, Inc.*
Shenfield, Peter — *Baker, Harris & Partners Limited*
Shepard, Michael J. — *MSI International*
Shepherd, Daniel M. — *Shepherd Bueschel & Provus, Inc.*
Shimp, David J. — *Lamalie Amrop International*
Shontell, William — *Don Richard Associates of Washington, D.C., Inc.*
Shourds, Mary E. — *Houze, Shourds & Montgomery, Inc.*
Shulman, Barry — *Shulman Associates*
Sibul, Shelly Remen — *Chicago Legal Search, Ltd.*
Signer, Julie — *CPS Inc.*
Siker, Paul W. — *The Guild Corporation*
Silkiner, David S. — *Paul Ray Berndtson*
Sill, Igor M. — *Geneva Group International*
Sill, Igor M. — *Geneva Group International*
Silvas, Stephen D. — *Roberson and Company*
Silver, Lee A. — *L.A. Silver Associates, Inc.*
Simankov, Dmitry — *Logix, Inc.*
Simmons, Anneta — *F-O-R-T-U-N-E Personnel Consultants of Huntsville, Inc.*
Simmons, Gerald J. — *Handy HRM Corp.*
Simmons, Sandra K. — *MSI International*
Sinclair, Amy — *Fisher Personnel Management Services*
Skunda, Donna M. — *Allerton Heneghan & O'Neill*
Smead, Michelle M. — *A.T. Kearney, Inc.*
Smirnov, Tatiana — *Allan Sarn Associates Inc.*
Smith, Adam M. — *The Abbott Group, Inc.*
Smith, Cheryl — *Barton Raben, Inc.*
Smith, David P. — *Smith & Latterell (HRS, Inc.)*
Smith, Grant — *Price Waterhouse*
Smith, Herman M. — *Herman Smith Executive Initiatives Inc.*
Smith, John F. — *The Penn Partners, Incorporated*
Smith, Kevin — *F-O-R-T-U-N-E Personnel Consultants of Manatee County*
Smith, R. Michael — *Smith James Group, Inc.*
Smith, Robert L. — *Smith & Sawyer Inc.*
Snyder, James F. — *Snyder & Company*
Sola, George L. — *A.T. Kearney, Inc.*
Solomon, Christina — *Richard, Wayne and Roberts*
Solters, Jeanne — *The Guild Corporation*
Soutouras, James — *Smith James Group, Inc.*
Sowerbutt, Richard S. — *Hite Executive Search*
Spadavecchia, Jennifer — *Alta Associates, Inc.*
Spanninger, Mark J. — *The Guild Corporation*
Spence, Gene L. — *Heidrick & Struggles, Inc.*
Spiegel, Gay — *L.A. Silver Associates, Inc.*
Spitz, Grant — *The Caldwell Partners Amrop International*
Splaine, Charles — *Splaine & Associates, Inc.*
Spriggs, Robert D. — *Spriggs & Company, Inc.*
Staats, Dave — *Southwestern Professional Services*
Stackhouse, P. John — *Heidrick & Struggles, Inc.*
Stanley, Paul R.A. — *Lovas Stanley/Paul Ray Berndtson Inc.*
Starner, William S. — *Fenwick Partners*
Stein, Terry W. — *Stewart, Stein and Scott, Ltd.*
Steinem, Andy — *Dahl-Morrow International*
Steinem, Barbara — *Dahl-Morrow International*
Stenberg, Edward — *Winter, Wyman & Company*
Stephenson, Don L. — *Ells Personnel System Inc.*
Stern, Stephen — *CPS Inc.*
Sterner, Doug — *CPS Inc.*
Stevenson, Terry — *Bartholdi & Company, Inc.*
Stewart, Jan J. — *Egon Zehnder International Inc.*
Stewart, Jeffrey O. — *Stewart, Stein and Scott, Ltd.*
Stewart, Ross M. — *Human Resources Network Partners Inc.*
Stiles, Jack D. — *Sanford Rose Associates*
Stiles, Judy — *MedQuest Associates*
Stiles, Timothy — *Sanford Rose Associates*
Stirn, Bradley A. — *Spencer Stuart*
Stone, Susan L. — *Stone Enterprises Ltd.*
Strain, Stephen R. — *Spencer Stuart*
Strassman, Mark — *Don Richard Associates of Washington, D.C., Inc.*
Stringer, Dann P. — *D.E. Foster Partners Inc.*
Strom, Mark N. — *Search Advisors International Corp.*
Struzziero, Ralph E. — *Romac & Associates*
Sullivan, Kay — *Rusher, Loscavio & LoPresto*
Sur, William K. — *Canny, Bowen Inc.*
Sussman, Lynda — *Gilbert Tweed/INESA*
Sutter, Howard — *Romac & Associates*
Sutton, Robert J. — *The Caldwell Partners Amrop International*
Swatts, Stone — *F-O-R-T-U-N-E Personnel Consultants of Huntsville, Inc.*
Sweeney, James W. — *Sweeney Harbert & Mummert, Inc.*
Swick, Jan — *TSS Consulting, Inc.*
Swidler, J. Robert — *Egon Zehnder International Inc.*
Taft, David G. — *Techsearch Services, Inc.*
Taft, Steven D. — *The Guild Corporation*
Tanton, John E. — *Tanton Mitchell/Paul Ray Berndtson*

Taylor, Conrad G. — *MSI International*
Taylor, Kenneth W. — *Egon Zehnder International Inc.*
Telford, John H. — *Telford, Adams & Alexander/Telford & Co., Inc.*
Tesar, Bob — *Tesar-Reynes, Inc.*
Theard, Susan — *Romac & Associates*
Theobald, David B. — *Theobald & Associates*
Thies, Gary — *S.D. Kelly & Associates, Inc.*
Tholke, William E. — *Canny, Bowen Inc.*
Thomas, Cheryl M. — *CPS Inc.*
Thomas, Donald — *Mixtec Group*
Thomas, Kim — *CPS Inc.*
Thomas, Terry — *Montague Enterprises*
Thomas, William — *Mixtec Group*
Thompson, Kenneth L. — *McCormack & Farrow*
To, Raymond — *Corporate Recruiters Ltd.*
Tovrog, Dan — *CPS Inc.*
Tracy, Ronald O. — *Egon Zehnder International Inc.*
Trueblood, Brian G. — *TNS Partners, Inc.*
Truemper, Dean — *CPS Inc.*
Truitt, Thomas B. — *Southwestern Professional Services*
Tryon, Katey — *DeFrain, Mayer, Lee & Burgess LLC*
Tucker, Thomas A. — *The Thomas Tucker Company*
Tullberg, Tina — *CPS Inc.*
Turner, Edward K. — *Don Richard Associates of Charlotte*
Tweed, Janet — *Gilbert Tweed/INESA*
Ulbert, Nancy — *Aureus Group*
Unterberg, Edward L. — *Russell Reynolds Associates, Inc.*
Utroska, Donald R. — *Lamalie Amrop International*
Vacca, Domenic — *Romac & Associates*
Vachon, David A. — *McNichol Associates*
Van Campen, Jerry — *Gilbert & Van Campen International*
Van Clieaf, Mark — *MVC Associates International*
Van Remmen, Roger — *Brown, Bernardy, Van Remmen, Inc.*
Vande-Water, Katie — *J. Robert Scott*
Vann, Dianne — *The Button Group*
Vennat, Manon — *Spencer Stuart*
Visnich, L. Christine — *Bason Associates Inc.*
Vogel, Michael S. — *Vogel Associates*
Voigt, John A. — *Romac & Associates*
von Stein, Scott — *Wilkinson & Ives*
Waggoner, Lisa — *Intersource, Ltd.*
Waldrop, Gary R. — *MSI International*
Walker, Ewing J. — *Ward Howell International, Inc.*
Walsh, Patty — *Abraham & London, Ltd.*
Walters, William F. — *Jonas, Walters & Assoc., Inc.*
Walton, Bruce H. — *Heidrick & Struggles, Inc.*
Ward, Madeleine — *LTM Associates*
Ware, John C. — *Spencer Stuart*
Wargo, G. Rick — *A.T. Kearney, Inc.*
Wasserman, Harvey — *Churchill and Affiliates, Inc.*
Wassill, Larry — *Corporate Recruiters Ltd.*
Wasson, Thomas W. — *Spencer Stuart*
Watson, James — *MSI International*
Watson, Stephen — *Paul Ray Berndtson*
Wayne, Cary S. — *ProSearch Inc.*
Webb, George H. — *Webb, Johnson Associates, Inc.*
Wein, Michael S. — *InterimManagement Solutions, Inc.*
Wein, Michael S. — *Media Management Resources, Inc.*
Wein, William — *InterimManagement Solutions, Inc.*
Wein, William — *Media Management Resources, Inc.*
Weinberg, Melvin — *Romac & Associates*
Weissman-Rosenthal, Abbe — *ALW Research International*
Weisz, Laura — *Anderson Sterling Associates*
Welch, Dale — *Winter, Wyman & Company*
Weller, Paul S. — *Mark Stanley & Company*
White, Jonathan O. — *The Badger Group*
White, William C. — *Venture Resources Inc.*
Whitney, David L. — *Whitney & Associates, Inc.*
Wichansky, Mark — *TSS Consulting, Ltd.*
Wier, Daniel — *Horton International*
Wilder, Richard B. — *Columbia Consulting Group*
Wilkinson, Barbara — *Beall & Company, Inc.*
Wilkinson, William R. — *Wilkinson & Ives*
Williams, Angie — *Whitney & Associates, Inc.*
Williams, Dave — *The McCormick Group, Inc.*
Williams, Roger K. — *Williams, Roth & Krueger Inc.*
Williams, Scott D. — *Heidrick & Struggles, Inc.*
Williams, Walter E. — *Canny, Bowen Inc.*
Willis, William H. — *William Willis Worldwide Inc.*
Wilson, Patricia L. — *Leon A. Farley Associates*
Winitz, Joel — *GSW Consulting Group, Inc.*
Winitz, Marla — *GSW Consulting Group, Inc.*
Winnewisser, William E. — *Accounting & Computer Personnel*
Winograd, Glenn — *Criterion Executive Search, Inc.*
Winston, Susan — *CPS Inc.*
Wise, J. Herbert — *Sandhurst Associates*
Wolf, Stephen M. — *Byron Leonard International, Inc.*
Womack, Joseph — *The Bankers Group*

Wood, John S. — *Egon Zehnder International Inc.*
Woodward, Lee — *Search Associates, Inc.*
Woollett, James — *Rusher, Loscavio & LoPresto*
Wyatt, James — *Wyatt & Jaffe*
Yang, George — *Technical Connections Inc.*
Young, Alexander — *Messett Associates, Inc.*
Young, Heather — *The Guild Corporation*
Zarnoski, Hank — *Dunhill Search International*
Zaslav, Debra M. — *Telford, Adams & Alexander/Telford & Co., Inc.*
Zatzick, Michael — *Search West, Inc.*
Zee, Wanda — *Tesar-Reynes, Inc.*
Zell, David M. — *Logix Partners*
Zetto, Kathryn — *Seco & Zetto Associates, Inc.*

## 17. Hospitality/Leisure

Adams, Ralda F. — *Hospitality International*
Agins, Ted — *National Restaurant Search, Inc.*
Andrews, Laura L. — *Stricker & Zagor*
Aquavella, Charles P. — *CPA & Associates*
Aronin, Michael — *Fisher-Todd Associates*
Austin, Jessica L. — *D.S.A. - Dixie Search Associates*
Bagwell, Bruce — *Intersource, Ltd.*
Bailey, William A. — *TNS Partners, Inc.*
Beaulieu, Genie A. — *Romac & Associates*
Bellano, Robert W. — *Stanton Chase International*
Berry, John R. — *Heidrick & Struggles, Inc.*
Billington, Brian — *Billington & Associates*
Blair, Kelly A. — *The Caldwell Partners Amrop International*
Bond, Robert J. — *Romac & Associates*
Boyer, Dennis M. — *Heidrick & Struggles, Inc.*
Bratches, Howard — *Thorndike Deland Associates*
Brown, Buzz — *Brown, Bernardy, Van Remmen, Inc.*
Brown, D. Perry — *Don Richard Associates of Washington, D.C., Inc.*
Brown, Jeffrey W. — *Comprehensive Search*
Burmaster, Holly — *Winter, Wyman & Company*
Burns, Alan — *The Enns Partners Inc.*
Bye, Randy — *Romac & Associates*
Campbell, Gary — *Romac & Associates*
Carideo, Joseph — *Thorndike Deland Associates*
Charles, Ronald D. — *The Caldwell Partners Amrop International*
Cheadle, Neil E. — *The IMC Group of Companies Ltd.*
Chitvanni, Andrew — *National Restaurant Search, Inc.*
Chitvanni, John — *National Restaurant Search, Inc.*
Cocchiaro, Richard — *Romac & Associates*
Cole, Kevin — *Don Richard Associates of Washington, D.C., Inc.*
Commersoli, Al — *Executive Referral Services, Inc.*
Connelly, Thomas A. — *Korn/Ferry International*
Costick, Kathryn J. — *John Sibbald Associates, Inc.*
Cragg, Barbara R. — *Southwestern Professional Services*
Crane, Howard C. — *Chartwell Partners International, Inc.*
Cuddy, Brian C. — *Romac & Associates*
Danoff, Audrey — *Don Richard Associates of Tidewater, Inc.*
de Bardin, Francesca — *F.L. Taylor & Company, Inc.*
Demchak, James P. — *Sandhurst Associates*
deVry, Kimberly A. — *Tower Consultants, Ltd.*
DiGiovanni, Charles — *Penn Search*
Dingman, Bruce — *Robert W. Dingman Company, Inc.*
Dingman, Robert W. — *Robert W. Dingman Company, Inc.*
Domenico, Alfred J. — *Domenico/Bowman Associates*
Dressler, Ralph — *Romac & Associates*
Duley, Richard I. — *ARJay & Associates*
Dunkel, David L. — *Romac & Associates*
Edwards, Verba L. — *Wing Tips & Pumps, Inc.*
Eibeler, C. — *Amherst Personnel Group Inc.*
England, Mark — *Austin-McGregor International*
Enns, George — *The Enns Partners Inc.*
Ferneborg, Jay W. — *Ferneborg & Associates, Inc.*
Ferneborg, John R. — *Ferneborg & Associates, Inc.*
Feyder, Michael — *A.T. Kearney, Inc.*
Fill, Clifford G. — *D.S.A. - Dixie Search Associates*
Fill, Ellyn H. — *D.S.A. - Dixie Search Associates*
Foy, James — *Foy, Schneid & Daniel, Inc.*
Francis, Joseph — *Hospitality International*
Freier, Bruce — *Executive Referral Services, Inc.*
Friedman, Donna L. — *Tower Consultants, Ltd.*
Gabel, Gregory N. — *Canny, Bowen Inc.*
Galante, Suzanne M. — *Vlcek & Company, Inc.*
George, Delores F. — *Delores F. George Human Resource Management & Consulting Industry*
Gerevas, Ronald E. — *Spencer Stuart*
Gerevas, Ronald E. — *Spencer Stuart*
Gibbs, John S. — *Spencer Stuart*
Goar, Duane R. — *Sandhurst Associates*
Gordon, Gerald L. — *E.G. Jones Associates, Ltd.*
Granger, Lisa D. — *D.S.A. - Dixie Search Associates*
Grantham, Philip H. — *Columbia Consulting Group*
Graves, Rosemarie — *Don Richard Associates of Washington, D.C., Inc.*

Gray, Annie — *Annie Gray Associates, Inc./The Executive Search Firm*
Gray, Mark — *Executive Referral Services, Inc.*
Greebe, Neil — *Flowers & Associates*
Gwin, Ric — *Southwestern Professional Services*
Haddad, Charles — *Romac & Associates*
Hamm, Mary Kay — *Romac & Associates*
Hansen, David G. — *Ott & Hansen, Inc.*
Harbaugh, Paul J. — *International Management Advisors, Inc.*
Hardison, Richard L. — *Hardison & Company*
Harfenist, Harry — *Parker Page Group*
Harmon, Tony — *Mixtec Group*
Hay, William E. — *William E. Hay & Company*
Heideman, Mary Marren — *DeFrain, Mayer, Lee & Burgess LLC*
Heneghan, Donald A. — *Allerton Heneghan & O'Neill*
Holmes, Lawrence J. — *Columbia Consulting Group*
Howe, Theodore — *Romac & Associates*
Hoyda, Louis A. — *Thorndike Deland Associates*
Hughes, Donald J. — *Hughes & Company*
Hunter, John B. — *John Sibbald Associates, Inc.*
Hunter, Sue J. — *Robison & Associates*
Jacobs, Judith — *The Rubicon Group*
Jeffers, Carol S. — *John Sibbald Associates, Inc.*
Johnson, Keith — *Romac & Associates*
Johnson, Rocky — *A.T. Kearney, Inc.*
Kaplan, Gary — *Gary Kaplan & Associates*
Kaplan, Marc — *Gary Kaplan & Associates*
Kelly, Peter W. — *R. Rollo Associates*
Kennedy, Walter — *Romac & Associates*
Klages, Constance W. — *International Management Advisors, Inc.*
Kucewicz, William — *Search West, Inc.*
Kuhl, Teresa — *Don Richard Associates of Tampa, Inc.*
Laderman, David — *Romac & Associates*
LaPierre, Louis — *Romac & Associates*
Lautz, Lindsay A. — *Wilkinson & Ives*
LaValle, Michael — *Romac & Associates*
Leetma, Imbi — *Stanton Chase International*
Letcher, Harvey D. — *Sandhurst Associates*
Lewis, Jon A. — *Sandhurst Associates*
Line, Joseph T. — *Sharrow & Associates*
Little, Suzaane — *Don Richard Associates of Tampa, Inc.*
Logan, Valarie A. — *D.S.A. - Dixie Search Associates*
Loria, Frank — *Accounting Personnel Consultants*
Lotz, R. James — *International Management Advisors, Inc.*
Louden, Leo — *Winter, Wyman & Company*
Love, David M. — *Paul Ray Berndtson*
Loving, Vikki — *Intersource, Ltd.*
Lumsby, George N. — *International Management Advisors, Inc.*
Lyons, Michele R. — *R. Rollo Associates*
Malcolm, Rod — *The Enns Partners Inc.*
Manassero, Henri J.P. — *International Management Advisors, Inc.*
Mangum, William T. — *Thomas Mangum Company*
May, Peter — *Mixtec Group*
McBurney, Kevin — *The Caldwell Partners Amrop International*
McCreary, Charles — *Austin-McGregor International*
McLaughlin, John — *Romac & Associates*
McLean, B. Keith — *Price Waterhouse*
McNichols, Walter B. — *Gary Kaplan & Associates*
Messett, William J. — *Messett Associates, Inc.*
Mestepey, John — *A.T. Kearney, Inc.*
Meyer, Stacey — *Gary Kaplan & Associates*
Miller, Roy — *The Enns Partners Inc.*
Mitchell, John — *Romac & Associates*
Mitros, George N. — *Mixtec Group*
Moran, Gail — *Comprehensive Search*
Morgan, Richard S. — *Lovas Stanley/Paul Ray Berndtson Inc.*
Muendel, H. Edward — *Stanton Chase International*
Mummert, Dennis D. — *Sweeney Harbert & Mummert, Inc.*
Nelson, Barbara — *Herman Smith Executive Initiatives Inc.*
Nordland, Martin N. — *Horton International*
Norman, Randy — *Austin-McGregor International*
O'Toole, Dennis P. — *Dennis P. O'Toole & Associates Inc.*
Oswald, Mark G. — *Canny, Bowen Inc.*
Palmer, Melissa — *Don Richard Associates of Tampa, Inc.*
Palmlund, David W. — *Lamalie Amrop International*
Papciak, Dennis J. — *Temporary Accounting Personnel*
Pelletier, Jacques F. — *Roth Young Personnel Service of Boston, Inc.*
Perez, Christina — *Orr Executive Search*
Pettway, Samuel H. — *Spencer Stuart*
Phelps, Gene L. — *McCormack & Farrow*
Phillips, Donald L. — *O'Shea, Divine & Company, Inc.*
Pinkman, Karen N. — *Skott/Edwards Consultants, Inc.*
Pinson, Stephanie L. — *Gilbert Tweed/INESA*
Porter, Donald — *Amherst Personnel Group Inc.*
Porter, Ken — *Tourism Development International*
Quick, Roger A. — *Norman Broadbent International, Inc.*
Rabinowitz, Peter A. — *P.A.R. Associates Inc.*
Radice, Joseph — *Hospitality International*

Regehly, Herbert L. — *The IMC Group of Companies Ltd.*
Reiser, Ellen — *Thorndike Deland Associates*
Reynes, Tony — *Tesar-Reynes, Inc.*
Rollo, Robert S. — *R. Rollo Associates*
Romaine, Stanley J. — *Mixtec Group*
Romaniw, Michael J. — *A la carte International*
Romaniw, Michael J. — *A la carte International*
Romaniw, Michael J. — *A la carte International*
Ropes, John — *Ropes Associates, Inc.*
Rorech, Maureen — *Romac & Associates*
Rowe, William D. — *D.E. Foster Partners Inc.*
Rowenhorst, Brenda — *The Bren Group*
Rozan, Naomi — *Comprehensive Search*
Rumson, Paul — *Roth Young Personnel Service of Boston, Inc.*
Rurak, Zbigniew T. — *Rurak & Associates, Inc.*
Russell, Richard A. — *Executive Search Consultants Corporation*
Russell, Susan Anne — *Executive Search Consultants Corporation*
Saner, Harold — *Romac & Associates*
Sathe, Mark A. — *Sathe & Associates, Inc.*
Sauer, Harry J. — *Romac & Associates*
Savage, Edward J. — *Stanton Chase International*
Schiavone, Mary Rose — *Canny, Bowen Inc.*
Schnierow, Beryl — *Tesar-Reynes, Inc.*
Schroeder, John W. — *Spencer Stuart*
Scothon, Alan — *Romac & Associates*
Sibbald, John R. — *John Sibbald Associates, Inc.*
Sine, Mark — *Hospitality International*
Smith, Grant — *Price Waterhouse*
Soggs, Cheryl Pavick — *A.T. Kearney, Inc.*
Sponseller, Vern — *Richard Kader & Associates*
Stafford, Susan — *Hospitality International*
Standard, Gail — *Comprehensive Search*
Stenholm, Gilbert R. — *Spencer Stuart*
Straube, Stanley H. — *Straube Associates*
Stricker, Sidney G. — *Stricker & Zagor*
Strobridge, Richard P. — *F.L. Taylor & Company, Inc.*
Strom, Mark N. — *Search Advisors International Corp.*
Struzziero, Ralph E. — *Romac & Associates*
Sur, William K. — *Canny, Bowen Inc.*
Sussman, Lynda — *Gilbert Tweed/INESA*
Sutter, Howard — *Romac & Associates*
Sutton, Robert J. — *The Caldwell Partners Amrop International*
Tesar, Bob — *Tesar-Reynes, Inc.*
Theard, Susan — *Romac & Associates*
Tholke, William E. — *Canny, Bowen Inc.*
Thomas, Christine S. — *Lovas Stanley/Paul Ray Berndtson Inc.*
Truex, John F. — *Morton, McCorkle & Associates, Inc.*
Turner, Edward K. — *Don Richard Associates of Charlotte*
Ulbert, Nancy — *Aureus Group*
Unger, Stephen A. — *Spencer Stuart*
Vacca, Domenic — *Romac & Associates*
Van Remmen, Roger — *Brown, Bernardy, Van Remmen, Inc.*
Venable, William W. — *Thorndike Deland Associates*
Vlcek, Thomas J. — *Vlcek & Company, Inc.*
Voigt, John A. — *Romac & Associates*
Waggoner, Lisa — *Intersource, Ltd.*
Walker, Craig H. — *A.J. Burton Group, Inc.*
Warren, Sylvia W. — *Thorndike Deland Associates*
Weinberg, Melvin — *Romac & Associates*
White, Kimberly — *Executive Referral Services, Inc.*
Wilder, Richard B. — *Columbia Consulting Group*
Williams, Walter E. — *Canny, Bowen Inc.*
Winnewisser, William E. — *Accounting & Computer Personnel*
Wise, J. Herbert — *Sandhurst Associates*
Yilmaz, Muriel — *Dinte Resources, Incorporated*
Young, Alexander — *Messett Associates, Inc.*
Zee, Wanda — *Tesar-Reynes, Inc.*
Zivic, Janis M. — *Spencer Stuart*

## 18. Information Technology

Abbatiello, Christine Murphy — *Winter, Wyman & Company*
Abbott, Peter — *The Abbott Group, Inc.*
Abell, Vincent W. — *MSI International*
Abramson, Roye — *Source Services Corporation*
Acquaviva, Jay — *Winter, Wyman & Company*
Adams, Jeffrey C. — *Telford, Adams & Alexander/Jeffrey C. Adams & Co., Inc.*
Adams, Len — *The KPA Group*
Akin, J.R. — *J.R. Akin & Company Inc.*
Albert, Richard — *Source Services Corporation*
Albright, Cindy — *Summerfield Associates, Inc.*
Alford, Holly — *Source Services Corporation*
Allen, Donald — *D.S. Allen Associates, Inc.*
Allen, Scott — *Chrisman & Company, Incorporated*
Allred, J. Michael — *Spencer Stuart*
Alringer, Marc — *Source Services Corporation*
Altreuter, Rose — *The ALTCO Group*
Ambler, Peter W. — *Peter W. Ambler Company*

Ames, George C. — *Ames O'Neill Associates*
Amico, Robert — *Source Services Corporation*
Anderson, Mary — *Source Services Corporation*
Anderson, Matthew — *Source Services Corporation*
Antil, Pamela W. — *Norman Roberts & Associates, Inc.*
Anwar, Tarin — *Jay Gaines & Company, Inc.*
Apostle, George — *Search Dynamics, Inc.*
Argentin, Jo — *Executive Placement Consultants, Inc.*
Arnold, David — *Christian & Timbers*
Arnson, Craig — *Hernand & Partners*
Aronin, Michael — *Fisher-Todd Associates*
Ascher, Susan P. — *The Ascher Group*
Ashton, Barbara L. — *Ashton Computer Professionals Inc.*
Aston, Kathy — *Marra Peters & Partners*
Atkinson, S. Graham — *Raymond Karsan Associates*
Aubin, Richard E. — *Aubin International*
Badger, Fred H. — *The Badger Group*
Baer, Kenneth — *Source Services Corporation*
Baglio, Robert — *Source Services Corporation*
Bagwell, Bruce — *Intersource, Ltd.*
Baier, Rebecca — *Source Services Corporation*
Bailey, David O. — *Paul Ray Berndtson*
Bailey, William A. — *TNS Partners, Inc.*
Baird, John — *Professional Search Consultants*
Baker, Gerry — *Baker, Harris & Partners Limited*
Bakken, Mark — *Source Services Corporation*
Balchumas, Charles — *Source Services Corporation*
Balter, Sidney — *Source Services Corporation*
Banko, Scott — *Source Services Corporation*
Baran, Helena — *Michael J. Cavanagh and Associates*
Baranowski, Peter — *Source Services Corporation*
Barlow, Ken H. — *The Cherbonnier Group, Inc.*
Barnaby, Richard — *Source Services Corporation*
Barnes, Richard E. — *Barnes Development Group, LLC*
Bartels, Fredrick — *Source Services Corporation*
Bartesch, Heinz — *The Search Firm, Inc.*
Bartfield, Philip — *Source Services Corporation*
Bartholdi, Ted — *Bartholdi & Company, Inc.*
Bartholdi, Theodore G. — *Bartholdi & Company, Inc.*
Barton, Gary R. — *Barton Raben, Inc.*
Barton, James — *Source Services Corporation*
Bassman, Robert — *Kaye-Bassman International Corp.*
Bassman, Sandy — *Kaye-Bassman International Corp.*
Battalia, O. William — *Battalia Winston International*
Batte, Carol — *Source Services Corporation*
Beaudin, Elizabeth C. — *Callan Associates, Ltd.*
Beaulieu, Genie A. — *Romac & Associates*
Beaver, Bentley H. — *The Onstott Group, Inc.*
Beaver, Robert — *Source Services Corporation*
Beck, Michael — *Don Richard Associates of Richmond, Inc.*
Beckvold, John B. — *Atlantic Search Group, Inc.*
Belden, Jeannette — *Source Services Corporation*
Bell, Lisa — *Winter, Wyman & Company*
Benjamin, Maurita — *Source Services Corporation*
Bennett, Ness — *Technical Connections Inc.*
Benson, Edward — *Source Services Corporation*
Berger, Jay V. — *Morris & Berger*
Berger, Jeffrey — *Source Services Corporation*
Bernard, Bryan — *Source Services Corporation*
Bernas, Sharon — *Source Services Corporation*
Betts, Suzette — *Source Services Corporation*
Bickett, Nicole — *Source Services Corporation*
Bidelman, Richard — *Source Services Corporation*
Biggins, Joseph — *Winter, Wyman & Company*
Biolsi, Joseph — *Source Services Corporation*
Birns, Douglas — *Source Services Corporation*
Bishop, Susan — *Bishop Partners*
Bitar, Edward — *The Interface Group, Ltd./Boyden*
Blackmon, Sharon — *The Abbott Group, Inc.*
Bladon, Andrew — *Don Richard Associates of Tampa, Inc.*
Bland, Walter — *Source Services Corporation*
Blanton, Thomas — *Blanton and Company*
Blassaras, Peggy — *Source Services Corporation*
Blickle, Michael — *Source Services Corporation*
Bliley, Jerry — *Spencer Stuart*
Blim, Barbara — *JDG Associates, Ltd.*
Bloch, Suzanne — *Source Services Corporation*
Blocher, John — *Source Services Corporation*
Bloom, Howard C. — *Hernand & Partners*
Bloom, Joyce — *Hernand & Partners*
Bluhm, Claudia — *Schweichler Associates, Inc.*
Blunt, Peter — *Hernand & Partners*
Boag, John — *Norm Sanders Associates*
Boczany, William J. — *The Guild Corporation*
Bohn, Steve J. — *MSI International*
Bond, Allan — *Walden Associates*
Bond, James L. — *People Management Northeast Incorporated*
Bond, Robert J. — *Romac & Associates*

Booth, Ronald — *Source Services Corporation*
Borenstine, Alvin — *Synergistics Associates Ltd.*
Borland, James — *Goodrich & Sherwood Associates, Inc.*
Bormann, Cindy Ann — *MSI International*
Bostic, James E. — *Phillips Resource Group*
Bosward, Allan — *Source Services Corporation*
Bourrie, Sharon D. — *Chartwell Partners International, Inc.*
Bovich, Maryann C. — *Higdon Prince Inc.*
Brackin, James B. — *Brackin & Sayers Associates*
Bragg, Garry — *The McCormick Group, Inc.*
Brassard, Gary — *Source Services Corporation*
Bratches, Howard — *Thorndike Deland Associates*
Bremer, Brian — *Source Services Corporation*
Brennen, Richard J. — *Spencer Stuart*
Brewster, Edward — *Source Services Corporation*
Brindise, Michael J. — *Dynamic Search Systems, Inc.*
Brocaglia, Joyce — *Alta Associates, Inc.*
Bronger, Patricia — *Source Services Corporation*
Brooks, Bernard E. — *Mruk & Partners/EMA Partners Int'l*
Brooks, Charles — *Corporate Recruiters Ltd.*
Brophy, Melissa — *Maximum Management Corp.*
Brovender, Claire — *Winter, Wyman & Company*
Brown, Charlene N. — *Accent on Achievement, Inc.*
Brown, Clifford — *Source Services Corporation*
Brown, Daniel — *Source Services Corporation*
Brown, Kevin P. — *Raymond Karsan Associates*
Brown, Larry C. — *Horton International*
Brown, Steven — *Source Services Corporation*
Browne, Michael — *Source Services Corporation*
Bruce, Michael C. — *Spencer Stuart*
Brudno, Robert J. — *Savoy Partners, Ltd.*
Brunner, Terry — *Source Services Corporation*
Brunson, Therese — *Kors Montgomery International*
Bryant, Richard D. — *Bryant Associates, Inc.*
Bryza, Robert M. — *Robert Lowell International*
Budill, Edward — *Professional Search Consultants*
Bueschel, David A. — *Shepherd Bueschel & Provus, Inc.*
Bullock, Conni — *Earley Kielty and Associates, Inc.*
Burch, Donald — *Source Services Corporation*
Burchill, Greg — *BGB Associates*
Burden, Gene — *The Cherbonnier Group, Inc.*
Burfield, Elaine — *Skott/Edwards Consultants, Inc.*
Burke, John — *The Experts*
Burmaster, Holly — *Winter, Wyman & Company*
Busch, Jack — *Busch International*
Busterna, Charles — *The KPA Group*
Buttrey, Daniel — *Source Services Corporation*
Buzolits, Patrick — *Source Services Corporation*
Bye, Randy — *Romac & Associates*
Cafero, Les — *Source Services Corporation*
Cahill, James P. — *Thorndike Deland Associates*
Callan, Robert M. — *Callan Associates, Ltd.*
Callen, John H. — *Ward Howell International, Inc.*
Campbell, E. — *Source Services Corporation*
Campbell, Gary — *Romac & Associates*
Campbell, Jeff — *Source Services Corporation*
Campbell, Patricia A. — *The Onstott Group, Inc.*
Campbell, Robert Scott — *Wellington Management Group*
Cappe, Richard R. — *Roberts Ryan and Bentley*
Carideo, Joseph — *Thorndike Deland Associates*
Carlson, Eric — *Source Services Corporation*
Carnal, Rick — *Source Services Corporation*
Carter, Linda — *Source Services Corporation*
Carvalho-Esteves, Maria — *Source Services Corporation*
Cashman, Tracy — *Winter, Wyman & Company*
Cast, Donald — *Dunhill Search International*
Castine, Michael P. — *Spencer Stuart*
Castle, Lisa — *Source Services Corporation*
Cattanach, Bruce B. — *Horton International*
Cavanagh, Michael J. — *Michael J. Cavanagh and Associates*
Cersosimo, Rocco — *Source Services Corporation*
Cesafsky, Barry R. — *Lamalie Amrop International*
Chappell, Peter — *The Bankers Group*
Chase, James — *Source Services Corporation*
Chatterjie, Alok — *MSI International*
Chavous, C. Crawford — *Phillips Resource Group*
Cheah, Victor — *Source Services Corporation*
Cherbonnier, L. Michael — *TCG International, Inc.*
Cherbonnier, L. Michael — *The Cherbonnier Group, Inc.*
Chorman, Marilyn A. — *Hite Executive Search*
Christian, Jeffrey E. — *Christian & Timbers*
Christman, Joel — *Source Services Corporation*
Christoff, Matthew J. — *Spencer Stuart*
Chronopoulos, Dennis — *Source Services Corporation*
Clarey, William A. — *Preng & Associates, Inc.*
Clauhsen, Elizabeth A. — *Savoy Partners, Ltd.*
Clawson, Bob — *Source Services Corporation*
Clawson, Robert — *Source Services Corporation*

Cline, Mark — *NYCOR Search, Inc.*
Cocchiaro, Richard — *Romac & Associates*
Cocconi, Alan — *Source Services Corporation*
Cochran, Hale — *Fenwick Partners*
Cochrun, James — *Source Services Corporation*
Coffey, Patty — *Winter, Wyman & Company*
Coffman, Brian — *Kossuth & Associates, Inc.*
Cohen, Michael R. — *Intech Summit Group, Inc.*
Cohen, Robert C. — *Intech Summit Group, Inc.*
Colasanto, Frank M. — *W.R. Rosato & Associates, Inc.*
Colborne, Janis M. — *AJM Professional Services*
Cole, Rosalie — *Source Services Corporation*
Cole, Sharon A. — *AJM Professional Services*
Colling, Douglas — *KPMG Management Consulting*
Collins, Scott — *Source Services Corporation*
Collins, Tom — *J.B. Homer Associates, Inc.*
Colman, Michael — *Executive Placement Consultants, Inc.*
Comai, Christine — *Source Services Corporation*
Combs, Stephen L. — *Juntunen-Combs-Poirier*
Combs, Thomas — *Source Services Corporation*
Commersoli, Al — *Executive Referral Services, Inc.*
Cona, Joseph A. — *Cona Personnel Search*
Coneys, Bridget — *Source Services Corporation*
Connelly, Scott — *Technical Connections Inc.*
Connolly, Cathryn — *Strategic Associates, Inc.*
Connor, Michele — *Abraham & London, Ltd.*
Conway, William P. — *Phillips Resource Group*
Cook, Charlene — *Source Services Corporation*
Cooke, Jeffrey R. — *Jonas, Walters & Assoc., Inc.*
Cooper, William — *Search West, Inc.*
Corrigan, Gerald F. — *The Corrigan Group*
Cotugno, James — *Source Services Corporation*
Coughlin, Stephen — *Source Services Corporation*
Cram, Noel — *R.P. Barone Associates*
Crane, Howard C. — *Chartwell Partners International, Inc.*
Crump, William G. — *Paul Ray Berndtson*
Crumpton, Marc — *Logix Partners*
Crumpton, Marc — *Logix, Inc.*
Crumpton, Marc — *Walden Associates*
Cruse, O.D. — *Spencer Stuart*
Cuddy, Brian C. — *Romac & Associates*
Cuddy, Patricia — *Source Services Corporation*
Cunningham, Robert Y. — *Goodrich & Sherwood Associates, Inc.*
Cunningham, Sheila — *Adams & Associates International*
Curren, Camella — *Source Services Corporation*
Cutka, Matthew — *Source Services Corporation*
Cyphers, Ralph R. — *Strategic Associates, Inc.*
Czamanske, Paul W. — *Compass Group Ltd.*
D'Alessio, Gary A. — *Chicago Legal Search, Ltd.*
Danforth, W. Michael — *Hyde Danforth Wold & Co.*
Daniel, Beverly — *Foy, Schneid & Daniel, Inc.*
Dankberg, Iris — *Source Services Corporation*
Danoff, Audrey — *Don Richard Associates of Tidewater, Inc.*
Darter, Steven M. — *People Management Northeast Incorporated*
Davis, Bert — *Bert Davis Executive Search, Inc.*
Davis, C. Scott — *Source Services Corporation*
Davis, Elease — *Source Services Corporation*
Davis, G. Gordon — *Davis & Company*
Davis, John — *John J. Davis & Associates, Inc.*
Davis, John J. — *John J. Davis & Associates, Inc.*
Dawson, Joe — *S.C. International, Ltd.*
Dawson, William — *Source Services Corporation*
Debus, Wayne — *Source Services Corporation*
Deck, Jack — *Source Services Corporation*
Decker, Richard — *D. Brown and Associates, Inc.*
DeCorrevont, James — *DeCorrevont & Associates*
DeCorrevont, James — *DeCorrevont & Associates*
DeGioia, Joseph — *JDG Associates, Ltd.*
Del Prete, Karen — *Gilbert Tweed/INESA*
Delaney, Patrick J. — *Sensible Solutions, Inc.*
DeMarco, Robert — *Source Services Corporation*
Desmond, Mary — *Source Services Corporation*
Dever, Mary — *Source Services Corporation*
Devito, Alice — *Source Services Corporation*
deWilde, David M. — *Chartwell Partners International, Inc.*
Di Filippo, Thomas — *Source Services Corporation*
Dickey, Chet W. — *Bowden & Company, Inc.*
Dieckmann, Ralph E. — *Dieckmann & Associates, Ltd.*
Diers, Gary — *Source Services Corporation*
Dietz, David S. — *MSI International*
DiMarchi, Paul — *DiMarchi Partners, Inc.*
Dinte, Paul — *Dinte Resources, Incorporated*
DiSalvo, Fred — *The Cambridge Group Ltd*
Dittmar, Richard — *Source Services Corporation*
Do, Sonnie — *Whitney & Associates, Inc.*
Dobrow, Samuel — *Source Services Corporation*
Doele, Donald C. — *Goodrich & Sherwood Associates, Inc.*
Doman, Matthew — *S.C. International, Ltd.*

Donahue, Debora — *Source Services Corporation*
Donnelly, Patti — *Source Services Corporation*
Dorfner, Martin — *Source Services Corporation*
Dotson, M. Ileen — *Dotson & Associates*
Dougherty, Bridget L. — *Wellington Management Group*
Dowell, Mary K. — *Professional Search Associates*
Dowlatzadch, Homayoun — *Source Services Corporation*
Downs, William — *Source Services Corporation*
Dreifus, Donald — *Search West, Inc.*
Dressler, Ralph — *Romac & Associates*
Dromeshauser, Peter — *Dromeshauser Associates*
Duelks, John — *Source Services Corporation*
Duggan, James P. — *Slayton International, Inc.*
Dumesnil, Curtis — *Richard, Wayne and Roberts*
Duncan, Dana — *Source Services Corporation*
Dunkel, David L. — *Romac & Associates*
Dunlop, Eric — *Southwestern Professional Services*
Dunlow, Aimee — *Source Services Corporation*
Dunman, Betsy L. — *Crawford & Crofford*
Dupont, Rick — *Source Services Corporation*
Dussick, Vince — *Dussick Management Associates*
Ebeling, John A. — *Gilbert Tweed/INESA*
Edwards, Dorothy — *MSI International*
Edwards, Verba L. — *Wing Tips & Pumps, Inc.*
Eggena, Roger — *Phillips Resource Group*
Eggert, Scott — *Source Services Corporation*
Ehrgott, Elizabeth — *The Ascher Group*
Ehrhart, Jennifer — *ADOW's Executeam*
Eiseman, Joe — *Source Services Corporation*
Eiseman, Joe — *Source Services Corporation*
Eiseman, Joe — *Source Services Corporation*
Ellis, Patricia — *Source Services Corporation*
Ellis, William — *Interspace Interactive Inc.*
Ellison, Richard — *Sanford Rose Associates*
Emerson, Randall — *Source Services Corporation*
Engle, Bryan — *Source Services Corporation*
Ervin, Russell — *Source Services Corporation*
Eustis, Lucy R. — *MSI International*
Evans, Timothy — *Source Services Corporation*
Fagerstrom, Jon — *Source Services Corporation*
Fahlin, Kelly — *Winter, Wyman & Company*
Fairlie, Suzanne F. — *ProSearch, Inc.*
Fales, Scott — *Source Services Corporation*
Falk, John — *D.S. Allen Associates, Inc.*
Fanning, Paul — *Source Services Corporation*
Farler, Wiley — *Source Services Corporation*
Farley, Leon A. — *Leon A. Farley Associates*
Farrow, Jerry M. — *McCormack & Farrow*
Farthing, Andrew R. — *Parfitt Recruiting and Consulting*
Fechheimer, Peter — *Source Services Corporation*
Federman, Jack R. — *W.R. Rosato & Associates, Inc.*
Feldman, Kimberley — *Atlantic Search Group, Inc.*
Ferguson, Kenneth — *Source Services Corporation*
Ferneborg, Jay W. — *Ferneborg & Associates, Inc.*
Ferneborg, John R. — *Ferneborg & Associates, Inc.*
Ferrara, David M. — *Intech Summit Group, Inc.*
Field, Andrew — *Source Services Corporation*
Fienberg, Chester — *Drummond Associates, Inc.*
Fincher, Richard P. — *Phase II Management*
Fingers, David — *Bradford & Galt, Inc.*
Finkel, Leslie — *Source Services Corporation*
Finnerty, James — *Source Services Corporation*
Fischer, John C. — *Horton International*
Fitzgerald, Brian — *Source Services Corporation*
Flanagan, Robert M. — *Robert M. Flanagan & Associates, Ltd.*
Flanders, Karen — *Advanced Information Management*
Flores, Agustin — *Ward Howell International, Inc.*
Florio, Robert — *Source Services Corporation*
Flowers, Bradley — *Southwestern Professional Services*
Foley, Eileen — *Winter, Wyman & Company*
Fone, Carol — *Walden Associates*
Ford, Sandra D. — *Phillips & Ford, Inc.*
Forest, Adam — *McCormack & Associates*
Forestier, Lois — *Source Services Corporation*
Foster, Bradley — *Source Services Corporation*
Foster, John — *Source Services Corporation*
Fotia, Frank — *JDG Associates, Ltd.*
Francis, Brad — *Source Services Corporation*
Francis, Joseph — *Hospitality International*
Frank, Valerie S. — *Norman Roberts & Associates, Inc.*
Frantino, Michael — *Source Services Corporation*
Frederick, Dianne — *Source Services Corporation*
Freeh, Thomas — *Source Services Corporation*
French, William G. — *Preng & Associates, Inc.*
Friedman, Deborah — *Source Services Corporation*
Friedman, Helen E. — *McCormack & Farrow*
Fuhrman, Dennis — *Source Services Corporation*
Fujino, Rickey — *Source Services Corporation*

Fulger, Herbert — *Source Services Corporation*
Fyhrie, David — *Source Services Corporation*
Gabriel, David L. — *The Arcus Group*
Gaffney, Megan — *Source Services Corporation*
Gaines, Jay — *Jay Gaines & Company, Inc.*
Galante, Suzanne M. — *Vlcek & Company, Inc.*
Gallagher, Marilyn — *Hogan Acquisitions*
Gallagher, Terence M. — *Battalia Winston International*
Gamble, Ira — *Source Services Corporation*
Garcia, Samuel K. — *Southwestern Professional Services*
Gardiner, E. Nicholas P. — *Gardiner International*
Gardner, Michael — *Source Services Corporation*
Garfinkle, Steven M. — *Battalia Winston International*
Garrett, Mark — *Source Services Corporation*
Gauthier, Robert C. — *Columbia Consulting Group*
Geiger, Jan — *Wilcox, Bertoux & Miller*
Gennawey, Robert — *Source Services Corporation*
George, Delores F. — *Delores F. George Human Resource Management & Consulting Industry*
Gerbosi, Karen — *Hernand & Partners*
Germain, Valerie — *Jay Gaines & Company, Inc.*
Germaine, Debra — *Fenwick Partners*
Giesy, John — *Source Services Corporation*
Gilchrist, Robert J. — *Horton International*
Giles, Joe L. — *Joe L. Giles and Associates, Inc.*
Gilinsky, David — *Source Services Corporation*
Gill, Patricia — *Columbia Consulting Group*
Gilmartin, William — *Hockett Associates, Inc.*
Glacy, Kurt — *Winter, Wyman & Company*
Gladstone, Martin J. — *MSI International*
Glickman, Leenie — *Source Services Corporation*
Gloss, Frederick C. — *F. Gloss International*
Gluzman, Arthur — *Source Services Corporation*
Gnatowski, Bruce — *Source Services Corporation*
Goedtke, Steven — *Southwestern Professional Services*
Gold, Stacey — *Earley Kielty and Associates, Inc.*
Goldenberg, Susan — *Grant Cooper and Associates*
Goldman, Michael L. — *Strategic Associates, Inc.*
Goodman, Victor — *Anderson Sterling Associates*
Goodridge, Benjamin — *S.C. International, Ltd.*
Goodwin, Gary — *Source Services Corporation*
Gordon, Gerald L. — *E.G. Jones Associates, Ltd.*
Gordon, Gloria — *A.T. Kearney, Inc.*
Gorman, Patrick — *Source Services Corporation*
Gorman, T. Patrick — *Techsearch Services, Inc.*
Gostyla, Rick — *Spencer Stuart*
Gottenberg, Norbert A. — *Norman Broadbent International, Inc.*
Gould, Dana — *Logix Partners*
Gould, Dana — *Logix, Inc.*
Gourley, Timothy — *Source Services Corporation*
Grado, Eduardo — *Source Services Corporation*
Graff, Jack — *Source Services Corporation*
Graham, Craig — *Ward Howell International, Inc.*
Graham, Shannon — *Source Services Corporation*
Grandinetti, Suzanne — *Source Services Corporation*
Grantham, John — *Grantham & Co., Inc.*
Grantham, Philip H. — *Columbia Consulting Group*
Gray, Heather — *Source Services Corporation*
Gray, Russell — *Source Services Corporation*
Graziano, Lisa — *Source Services Corporation*
Green, Jane — *Phillips Resource Group*
Green, Jean — *Broward-Dobbs, Inc.*
Gregory, Stephen — *Don Richard Associates of Richmond, Inc.*
Gresia, Paul — *Source Services Corporation*
Grey, Fred — *J.B. Homer Associates, Inc.*
Groban, Jack — *A.T. Kearney, Inc.*
Groner, David — *Source Services Corporation*
Grossman, James — *Source Services Corporation*
Grossman, Martin — *Source Services Corporation*
Grumulaitis, Leo — *Source Services Corporation*
Guc, Stephen — *Source Services Corporation*
Guthrie, Stuart — *Source Services Corporation*
Haas, Margaret P. — *Haas International, Inc.*
Hacker-Taylor, Dianna — *Source Services Corporation*
Haddad, Charles — *Romac & Associates*
Haider, Martin — *Source Services Corporation*
Hailey, H.M. — *Damon & Associates, Inc.*
Hales, Daphne — *Source Services Corporation*
Hall, Marty B. — *Catlin-Wells & White*
Hall, Peter V. — *Chartwell Partners International, Inc.*
Hall, Robert — *Don Richard Associates of Tidewater, Inc.*
Haller, Mark — *Source Services Corporation*
Hallock, Peter B. — *Goodrich & Sherwood Associates, Inc.*
Hamm, Gary — *Source Services Corporation*
Hamm, Mary Kay — *Romac & Associates*
Hanley, Maureen E. — *Gilbert Tweed/INESA*
Hanley, Steven — *Source Services Corporation*
Hanna, Remon — *Source Services Corporation*

Hanson, Grant M. — *Goodrich & Sherwood Associates, Inc.*
Harbert, David O. — *Sweeney Harbert & Mummert, Inc.*
Hardison, Richard L. — *Hardison & Company*
Harp, Kimberly — *Source Services Corporation*
Harrison, Patricia — *Source Services Corporation*
Harrison, Priscilla — *Phillips Resource Group*
Harshman, Donald — *The Stevenson Group of New Jersey*
Hart, Crystal — *Source Services Corporation*
Hart, James — *Source Services Corporation*
Hart, Robert T. — *D.E. Foster Partners Inc.*
Hartzman, Deborah — *Advanced Information Management*
Harvey, Mike — *Advanced Executive Resources*
Harwood, Brian — *Source Services Corporation*
Haselby, James — *Source Services Corporation*
Hasten, Lawrence — *Source Services Corporation*
Hauswirth, Jeffrey M. — *Spencer Stuart*
Havener, Donald Clarke — *The Abbott Group, Inc.*
Hawksworth, A. Dwight — *A.D. & Associates Executive Search, Inc.*
Hay, William E. — *William E. Hay & Company*
Hayes, Lee — *Source Services Corporation*
Hayes, Stacy — *The McCormick Group, Inc.*
Haystead, Steve — *Advanced Executive Resources*
Hecker, Henry C. — *Hogan Acquisitions*
Heiken, Barbara E. — *Randell-Heiken, Inc.*
Heinrich, Scott — *Source Services Corporation*
Helgeson, Burton H. — *Norm Sanders Associates*
Hemingway, Stuart C. — *Robison & Associates*
Heneghan, Donald A. — *Allerton Heneghan & O'Neill*
Henn, George W. — *G.W. Henn & Company*
Henneberry, Ward — *Source Services Corporation*
Henry, Patrick — *F-O-R-T-U-N-E Personnel Consultants of Huntsville, Inc.*
Hensley, Gayla — *Atlantic Search Group, Inc.*
Herman, Eugene J. — *Earley Kielty and Associates, Inc.*
Herman, Pat — *Whitney & Associates, Inc.*
Hernand, Warren L. — *Hernand & Partners*
Hernandez, Ruben — *Source Services Corporation*
Heroux, David — *Source Services Corporation*
Hertlein, James N.J. — *Boyden/Zay & Company*
Herzog, Sarah — *Source Services Corporation*
Hewitt, Rives D. — *The Dalley Hewitt Company*
Hicks, Albert M. — *Phillips Resource Group*
Hight, Susan — *Source Services Corporation*
Hilbert, Laurence — *Source Services Corporation*
Hildebrand, Thomas B. — *Professional Resources Group, Inc.*
Hilgenberg, Thomas — *Source Services Corporation*
Hill, Emery — *MSI International*
Hillen, Skip — *The McCormick Group, Inc.*
Hillyer, Carolyn — *Source Services Corporation*
Hinojosa, Oscar — *Source Services Corporation*
Hnatuik, Ivan — *Corporate Recruiters Ltd.*
Hockett, William — *Hockett Associates, Inc.*
Hoevel, Michael J. — *Poirier, Hoevel & Co.*
Hoffman, Brian — *Winter, Wyman & Company*
Hoffman, Stephen — *Source Services Corporation*
Hofner, Andrew — *Source Services Corporation*
Hogan, Larry H. — *Hogan Acquisitions*
Holmes, Lawrence J. — *Columbia Consulting Group*
Holodnak, William A. — *J. Robert Scott*
Holt, Carol — *Bartholdi & Company, Inc.*
Homer, Judy B. — *J.B. Homer Associates, Inc.*
Hooker, Lisa — *Paul Ray Berndtson*
Hopgood, Earl — *JDG Associates, Ltd.*
Hoppert, Phil — *Wargo and Co., Inc.*
Horgan, Thomas F. — *Nadzam, Lusk, Horgan & Associates, Inc.*
Horner, Gregory — *Corporate Recruiters Ltd.*
Horton, Robert H. — *Horton International*
Hostetter, Kristi — *Source Services Corporation*
Houchins, William N. — *Christian & Timbers*
Houterloot, Tim — *Source Services Corporation*
Howe, Theodore — *Romac & Associates*
Howell, Robert B. — *Atlantic Search Group, Inc.*
Howell, Robert B. — *Atlantic Search Group, Inc.*
Hoyda, Louis A. — *Thorndike Deland Associates*
Hudson, Reginald M. — *Search Bureau International*
Hughes, Barbara — *Source Services Corporation*
Hughes, Cathy N. — *The Ogdon Partnership*
Hughes, Donald J. — *Hughes & Company*
Hughes, Randall — *Source Services Corporation*
Hull, Chuck — *Winter, Wyman & Company*
Hult, Dana — *Source Services Corporation*
Humphrey, Joan — *Abraham & London, Ltd.*
Humphrey, Titus — *Source Services Corporation*
Hunter, Gabe — *Phillips Resource Group*
Hurley, Janeen — *Winter, Wyman & Company*
Hurtado, Jaime — *Source Services Corporation*
Hussey, Wayne — *Krecklo & Associates Inc.*
Hutchison, Richard H. — *Rurak & Associates, Inc.*

Hutton, Thomas J. — *The Thomas Tucker Company*
Hylas, Lisa — *Source Services Corporation*
Iannacone, Kelly — *Abraham & London, Ltd.*
Ide, Ian — *Winter, Wyman & Company*
Imely, Larry — *Christian & Timbers*
Imhof, Kirk — *Source Services Corporation*
Infinger, Ronald E. — *Robison & Associates*
Inger, Barry — *Source Services Corporation*
Inguagiato, Gregory — *MSI International*
Inskeep, Thomas — *Source Services Corporation*
Intravaia, Salvatore — *Source Services Corporation*
Irwin, Mark — *Source Services Corporation*
Ives, Richard K. — *Wilkinson & Ives*
Jackowitz, Todd — *J. Robert Scott*
Jackson, Barry — *Morgan Hunter Corp.*
Jacobs, Martin J. — *The Rubicon Group*
Jacobson, Hayley — *Source Services Corporation*
Jadulang, Vincent — *Source Services Corporation*
James, Bruce — *Roberson and Company*
James, Richard — *Criterion Executive Search, Inc.*
Janis, Laurence — *Integrated Search Solutions Group, LLC*
Januleski, Geoff — *Source Services Corporation*
Jeltema, John — *Source Services Corporation*
Jensen, Christine K. — *John Kurosky & Associates*
Jensen, Robert — *Source Services Corporation*
Jensen, Stephanie — *Don Richard Associates of Tidewater, Inc.*
Johnson, Douglas — *Quality Search*
Johnson, Greg — *Source Services Corporation*
Johnson, Keith — *Romac & Associates*
Johnson, Pete — *Morgan Hunter Corp.*
Johnson, Peter — *Winter, Wyman & Company*
Johnson, Robert J. — *Quality Search*
Johnson, Ronald S. — *Ronald S. Johnson Associates, Inc.*
Johnson, S. Hope — *The Interface Group, Ltd./Boyden*
Johnstone, Grant — *Source Services Corporation*
Jones, Barbara J. — *Kaye-Bassman International Corp.*
Jones, Daniel F. — *Atlantic Search Group, Inc.*
Jones, Francis E. — *Earley Kielty and Associates, Inc.*
Jones, Gary — *BGB Associates*
Jones, Jeffrey — *AJM Professional Services*
Jones, Jonathan C. — *The Ogdon Partnership*
Jones, Rodney — *Source Services Corporation*
Joyce, William J. — *The Guild Corporation*
Jozwik, Peter — *The Search Firm, Inc.*
Judge, Alfred L. — *The Cambridge Group Ltd*
Juska, Frank — *Rusher, Loscavio & LoPresto*
Kaiser, Donald J. — *Dunhill Search International*
Kanovsky, Gerald — *Career Consulting Group, Inc.*
Kanovsky, Marlene — *Career Consulting Group, Inc.*
Kaplan, Alexandra — *J.M. Eagle Partners Ltd.*
Kaplan, Gary — *Gary Kaplan & Associates*
Kaplan, Marc — *Gary Kaplan & Associates*
Kaplan, Traci — *Source Services Corporation*
Kasmouski, Steve — *Winter, Wyman & Company*
Kasprzyk, Michael — *Source Services Corporation*
Kaye, Jeffrey — *Kaye-Bassman International Corp.*
Keeton, Susan G. — *The Corporate Connection, Ltd.*
Keller, Barbara — *Barton Raben, Inc.*
Kelly, Elizabeth Ann — *Wellington Management Group*
Kelly, Robert — *Source Services Corporation*
Kelly, Sheri — *Strategic Associates, Inc.*
Kelso, Patricia C. — *Barton Raben, Inc.*
Kennedy, Craig — *Source Services Corporation*
Kennedy, Paul — *Source Services Corporation*
Kennedy, Walter — *Romac & Associates*
Kennedy, Walter — *Source Services Corporation*
Kennedy, Walter — *Source Services Corporation*
Kenney, Jeanne — *Source Services Corporation*
Kern, Jerry L. — *ADOW's Executeam*
Kern, Kathleen G. — *ADOW's Executeam*
Kielty, John L. — *Earley Kielty and Associates, Inc.*
King, Bill — *The McCormick Group, Inc.*
King, Shannon — *Source Services Corporation*
Kinney, Carol — *Dussick Management Associates*
Kinsey, Joanne — *Eastridge InfoTech*
Kirschner, Alan — *Source Services Corporation*
Kishbaugh, Herbert S. — *Kishbaugh Associates International*
Klavens, Cecile J. — *The Pickwick Group, Inc.*
Kleinstein, Scott — *Source Services Corporation*
Klusman, Edwin — *Source Services Corporation*
Knapp, Ronald A. — *Knapp Consultants*
Knoll, Robert — *Source Services Corporation*
Koczak, John — *Source Services Corporation*
Koehler, Frank R. — *The Koehler Group*
Kohonoski, Michael M. — *The Guild Corporation*
Kors, R. Paul — *Kors Montgomery International*
Kossuth, David — *Kossuth & Associates, Inc.*
Kossuth, Jane — *Kossuth & Associates, Inc.*

Kotick, Madeline — *The Stevenson Group of New Jersey*
Kouble, Tim — *Logix Partners*
Kouble, Tim — *Logix, Inc.*
Krecklo, Brian Douglas — *Krecklo & Associates Inc.*
Krejci, Stanley L. — *The Interface Group, Ltd./Boyden*
Kreutz, Gary L. — *Kreutz Consulting Group, Inc.*
Kring, Kenneth L. — *Spencer Stuart*
Krohn, Eileen — *The Stevenson Group of New Jersey*
La Chance, Ronald — *Source Services Corporation*
LaCharite, Danielle — *The Guild Corporation*
Laderman, David — *Romac & Associates*
Lamb, Angus K. — *Raymond Karsan Associates*
Lambert, William — *Source Services Corporation*
Lamia, Michael — *Source Services Corporation*
Langan, Marion — *Logix Partners*
Langan, Marion — *Logix, Inc.*
Lapat, Aaron D. — *J. Robert Scott*
LaPierre, Louis — *Romac & Associates*
Lapointe, Fabien — *Source Services Corporation*
Larsen, Richard F. — *Larsen, Zilliacus & Associates, Inc.*
Lasher, Charles M. — *Lasher Associates*
Laskin, Sandy — *Source Services Corporation*
Laub, Stuart R. — *Abraham & London, Ltd.*
Lautz, Lindsay A. — *Wilkinson & Ives*
LaValle, Michael — *Romac & Associates*
Laverty, William — *Source Services Corporation*
Lawner, Harvey — *Walden Associates*
Lazar, Miriam — *Source Services Corporation*
Leblanc, Danny — *Source Services Corporation*
Lee, Everett — *Source Services Corporation*
Lee, Janice — *Summerfield Associates, Inc.*
Leff, Lisa A. — *Berger and Leff*
Leigh, Rebecca — *Source Services Corporation*
Leighton, Mark — *Source Services Corporation*
Leininger, Dennis — *Key Employment Services*
Lejeune, Jeanette — *F-O-R-T-U-N-E Personnel Consultants of Huntsville, Inc.*
Leland, Paul — *McInturff & Associates, Inc.*
LemMou, Paul — *International Staffing Consultants, Inc.*
Lence, Julie Anne — *MSI International*
Lennox, Charles — *Price Waterhouse*
Leon, Jeffrey J. — *Russell Reynolds Associates, Inc.*
Levenson, Laurel — *Source Services Corporation*
Levine, Irwin — *Source Services Corporation*
Levitt, Muriel A. — *D.S. Allen Associates, Inc.*
Lewicki, Christopher — *MSI International*
Lewis, Daniel — *Source Services Corporation*
Lewis, Jon A. — *Sandhurst Associates*
Lieberman, Beverly — *Halbrecht Lieberman Associates, Inc.*
Liebross, Eric — *Source Services Corporation*
Lin, Felix — *Source Services Corporation*
Lindberg, Eric J. — *MSI International*
Lindsay, Mary — *Norm Sanders Associates*
Linton, Leonard M. — *Byron Leonard International, Inc.*
Lipe, Jerold L. — *Compass Group Ltd.*
Lipuma, Thomas — *Source Services Corporation*
Little, Elizabeth A. — *Financial Resource Associates, Inc.*
Little, Suzaane — *Don Richard Associates of Tampa, Inc.*
Long, John — *Source Services Corporation*
Long, John P. — *John J. Davis & Associates, Inc.*
Long, Mark — *Source Services Corporation*
Long, William G. — *McDonald, Long & Associates, Inc.*
LoPresto, Robert L. — *Rusher, Loscavio & LoPresto*
Lotufo, Donald A. — *D.A.L. Associates, Inc.*
Louden, Leo — *Winter, Wyman & Company*
Lovely, Edward — *The Stevenson Group of New Jersey*
Loving, Vikki — *Intersource, Ltd.*
Lucarelli, Joan — *The Onstott Group, Inc.*
Lucas, Ronnie L. — *MSI International*
Luce, Daniel — *Source Services Corporation*
Lucht, John — *The John Lucht Consultancy Inc.*
Ludder, Mark — *Source Services Corporation*
Ludlow, Michael — *Source Services Corporation*
Lundy, Martin — *Source Services Corporation*
Lyons, Michael — *Source Services Corporation*
MacCarthy, Ann — *Columbia Consulting Group*
Macdonald, G. William — *The Macdonald Group, Inc.*
MacDougall, Andrew J. — *Spencer Stuart*
MacEachern, David — *Spencer Stuart*
MacKinnon, Helen — *Technical Connections Inc.*
MacMillan, James — *Source Services Corporation*
MacPherson, Holly — *Source Services Corporation*
Macrides, Michael — *Source Services Corporation*
Mader, Stephen P. — *Christian & Timbers*
Magee, Harrison R. — *Bowden & Company, Inc.*
Maggio, Mary — *Source Services Corporation*
Mahmoud, Sophia — *Source Services Corporation*
Mairn, Todd — *Source Services Corporation*

Mallipudi, Anand — *Raymond Karsan Associates*
Mangum, William T. — *Thomas Mangum Company*
Manns, Alex — *Crawford & Crofford*
Manzo, Renee — *Atlantic Search Group, Inc.*
Maphet, Harriet — *The Stevenson Group of New Jersey*
Marchette, Steve — *Juntunen-Combs-Poirier*
Marino, Chester — *Cochran, Cochran & Yale, Inc.*
Mark, John L. — *J.L. Mark Associates, Inc.*
Marks, Ira — *Strategic Alternatives*
Marra, John — *Marra Peters & Partners*
Marra, John — *Marra Peters & Partners*
Martin, David — *The Guild Corporation*
Marwil, Jennifer — *Source Services Corporation*
Marye, George — *Damon & Associates, Inc.*
Mather, David R. — *Christian & Timbers*
Mathias, Douglas — *Source Services Corporation*
Mathias, William J. — *Preng & Associates, Inc.*
Mathis, Carrie — *Source Services Corporation*
Matti, Suzy — *Southwestern Professional Services*
Mattingly, Kathleen — *Source Services Corporation*
Maxwell, John — *Source Services Corporation*
Mayer, Thomas — *Source Services Corporation*
Mayes, Kay H. — *John Shell Associates, Inc.*
Mazza, David B. — *Mazza & Riley, Inc.*
McCabe, Christopher — *Raymond Karsan Associates*
McCann, Cornelia B. — *Spencer Stuart*
McCarthy, Laura — *Source Services Corporation*
McComas, Kelly E. — *The Guild Corporation*
McConnell, Greg — *Winter, Wyman & Company*
McCormick, Brian — *The McCormick Group, Inc.*
McCormick, Joseph — *Source Services Corporation*
McCormick, William J. — *The McCormick Group, Inc.*
McCurdy, Mark — *Summerfield Associates, Inc.*
McDonald, Scott A. — *McDonald Associates International*
McDonald, Stanleigh B. — *McDonald Associates International*
McDonnell, Julie — *Technical Personnel of Minnesota*
McFadden, Ashton S. — *Johnson Smith & Knisely Accord*
McGinnis, Rita — *Source Services Corporation*
McGoldrick, Terrence — *Source Services Corporation*
McGuigan, Walter J. — *Norm Sanders Associates*
McHugh, Keith — *Source Services Corporation*
McIntosh, Arthur — *Source Services Corporation*
McIntosh, Tad — *Source Services Corporation*
McInturff, Robert — *McInturff & Associates, Inc.*
McIntyre, Joel — *Phillips Resource Group*
McKell, Linda — *Advanced Information Management*
McKinney, Julia — *Source Services Corporation*
McLaughlin, John — *Romac & Associates*
McMahan, Stephen — *Source Services Corporation*
McMahan, Stephen — *Source Services Corporation*
McManamon, Tim — *Rogers-McManamon Executive Search*
McNamara, Timothy C. — *Columbia Consulting Group*
McNamee, Erin — *Technical Connections Inc.*
McNear, Jeffrey E. — *Barrett Partners*
McNichols, Walter B. — *Gary Kaplan & Associates*
McSherry, James F. — *Battalia Winston International*
Meara, Helen — *Source Services Corporation*
Meehan, John — *Source Services Corporation*
Mendelson, Jeffrey — *Source Services Corporation*
Mendoza-Green, Robin — *Source Services Corporation*
Menendez, Todd — *Don Richard Associates of Tampa, Inc.*
Mertensotto, Chuck H. — *Whitney & Associates, Inc.*
Messina, Marco — *Source Services Corporation*
Meyer, Stacey — *Gary Kaplan & Associates*
Miles, Marybeth — *Winter, Wyman & Company*
Miller, Brett — *The McCormick Group, Inc.*
Miller, George N. — *Hite Executive Search*
Miller, Kenneth A. — *Computer Network Resources, Inc.*
Miller, Larry — *Source Services Corporation*
Miller, Timothy — *Source Services Corporation*
Milligan, Dale — *Source Services Corporation*
Mills, John — *Source Services Corporation*
Milne, Robert P. — *Boyden/Zay & Company*
Milner, Carol — *Source Services Corporation*
Milton, Suzanne — *Marra Peters & Partners*
Miras, Cliff — *Source Services Corporation*
Miras, Cliff — *Source Services Corporation*
Mitchell, John — *Romac & Associates*
Mittwol, Myles — *Source Services Corporation*
Mochwart, Donald — *Drummond Associates, Inc.*
Mogul, Gene — *Mogul Consultants, Inc.*
Molitor, John L. — *Barrett Partners*
Mollichelli, David — *Source Services Corporation*
Molnar, Robert A. — *Johnson Smith & Knisely Accord*
Moore, Craig — *Source Services Corporation*
Moore, David S. — *Lynch Miller Moore Partners, Inc.*
Moore, Dianna — *Source Services Corporation*
Moore, Mark — *Wheeler, Moore & Elam Co.*

Moore, Suzanne — *Source Services Corporation*
Moran, Douglas — *Source Services Corporation*
Moran, Gayle — *Dussick Management Associates*
Morato, Rene — *Source Services Corporation*
Moretti, Denise — *Source Services Corporation*
Morgan, Richard S. — *Lovas Stanley/Paul Ray Berndtson Inc.*
Morgan, Vincent S. — *Johnson Smith & Knisely Accord*
Moriarty, Mike — *Source Services Corporation*
Morrill, Nancy — *Winter, Wyman & Company*
Morris, Kristine A. — *Morris & Berger*
Morris, Scott — *Source Services Corporation*
Morrow, Melanie — *Source Services Corporation*
Moses, Jerry — *J.M. Eagle Partners Ltd.*
Mott, Greg — *Source Services Corporation*
Moyse, Richard G. — *Thorndike Deland Associates*
Msidment, Roger — *Source Services Corporation*
Mueller, Colleen — *Source Services Corporation*
Muller, Charles A. — *AJM Professional Services*
Murphy, Corinne — *Source Services Corporation*
Murphy, Cornelius J. — *Goodrich & Sherwood Associates, Inc.*
Murphy, James — *Source Services Corporation*
Murphy, Patrick J. — *P.J. Murphy & Associates, Inc.*
Murray, Virginia — *Baker, Harris & Partners Limited*
Murry, John — *Source Services Corporation*
Mursuli, Meredith — *Lasher Associates*
Nabers, Karen — *Source Services Corporation*
Nagler, Leon G. — *Nagler, Robins & Poe, Inc.*
Nagy, Les — *Source Services Corporation*
Napier, Ginger L. — *Preng & Associates, Inc.*
Necessary, Rick — *Source Services Corporation*
Needham, Karen — *Source Services Corporation*
Neelin, Sharon — *The Caldwell Partners Amrop International*
Neff, Herbert — *Source Services Corporation*
Neher, Robert L. — *Intech Summit Group, Inc.*
Neidhart, Craig C. — *TNS Partners, Inc.*
Nelson, Barbara — *Herman Smith Executive Initiatives Inc.*
Nelson, Hitch — *Source Services Corporation*
Nelson, Mary — *Source Services Corporation*
Nelson-Folkersen, Jeffrey — *Source Services Corporation*
Nephew, Robert — *Christian & Timbers*
Neri, Gene — *S.C. International, Ltd.*
Neuberth, Jeffrey G. — *Canny, Bowen Inc.*
Neuwald, Debrah — *Source Services Corporation*
Newlon, Jay — *Logix, Inc.*
Newman, Lynn — *Kishbaugh Associates International*
Newton, Jay — *Logix Partners*
Nolan, Robert — *Source Services Corporation*
Nolen, Shannon — *Source Services Corporation*
Normann, Amy — *Robert M. Flanagan & Associates, Ltd.*
Nosky, Richard E. — *Ward Howell International, Inc.*
Nunziata, Peter — *Atlantic Search Group, Inc.*
Nutter, Roger — *Raymond Karsan Associates*
Nymark, John — *NYCOR Search, Inc.*
Nymark, Paul — *NYCOR Search, Inc.*
O'Brien, Maggie — *Advanced Information Management*
O'Brien, Susan — *Source Services Corporation*
O'Hara, Daniel M. — *Lynch Miller Moore Partners, Inc.*
O'Neill, Karen — *Ashton Computer Professionals Inc.*
O'Reilly, Jack — *Catalyx Group*
O'Such, Tracy — *Bishop Partners*
Occhiboi, Emil — *Source Services Corporation*
Ocon, Olga — *Busch International*
Odom, Philip — *Richard, Wayne and Roberts*
Ogden, Thomas H. — *The Ogdon Partnership*
Olmstead, George T. — *Blackshaw, Olmstead & Lynch*
Olsen, Robert — *Source Services Corporation*
Onstott, Joseph E. — *The Onstott Group, Inc.*
Orr, Stacie — *Source Services Corporation*
Osborn, Jim — *Southwestern Professional Services*
Ouellette, Christopher — *Source Services Corporation*
Owen, Christopher — *Source Services Corporation*
Pace, Susan A. — *Horton International*
Pachowitz, John — *Source Services Corporation*
Pacini, Lauren R. — *Hite Executive Search*
Page, Linda M. — *Wargo and Co., Inc.*
Paliwoda, William — *Source Services Corporation*
Palma, Frank R. — *Goodrich & Sherwood Associates, Inc.*
Papciak, Dennis J. — *Accounting Personnel Associates, Inc.*
Pappas, Jim — *Search Dynamics, Inc.*
Paradise, Malcolm — *Source Services Corporation*
Parente, James — *Source Services Corporation*
Parfitt, William C. — *Parfitt Recruiting and Consulting*
Paris, Stephen — *Richard, Wayne and Roberts*
Parr, James A. — *KPMG Management Consulting*
Parroco, Jason — *Source Services Corporation*
Parry, Heather — *Richard, Wayne and Roberts*
Patel, Shailesh — *Source Services Corporation*
Paternie, Patrick — *Source Services Corporation*

Patton, Mitchell — *Patton/Perry Associates, Inc.*
Paul, Kathleen — *Source Services Corporation*
Peal, Matthew — *Source Services Corporation*
Peckenpaugh, Ann D. — *Schweichler Associates, Inc.*
Pederson, Terre — *Richard, Wayne and Roberts*
Pelisson, Charles — *Marra Peters & Partners*
Pelkey, Chris — *The McCormick Group, Inc.*
Percival, Chris — *Chicago Legal Search, Ltd.*
Perry, Carolyn — *Source Services Corporation*
Persky, Barry — *Barry Persky & Company, Inc.*
Peters, James N. — *TNS Partners, Inc.*
Peters, Kevin — *Source Services Corporation*
Petersen, Richard — *Source Services Corporation*
Petty, J. Scott — *The Arcus Group*
Pfannkuche, Anthony V. — *Spencer Stuart*
Phillips, Bill — *Dunhill Search International*
Phillips, Scott K. — *Phillips & Ford, Inc.*
Pickford, Stephen T. — *The Corporate Staff, Inc.*
Pierce, Matthew — *Source Services Corporation*
Pillow, Charles — *Source Services Corporation*
Pineda, Rosanna — *Source Services Corporation*
Pinkman, Karen N. — *Skott/Edwards Consultants, Inc.*
Pinson, Stephanie L. — *Gilbert Tweed/INESA*
Pirro, Sheri — *Source Services Corporation*
Pistole, Ingrid — *Richard, Wayne and Roberts*
Plant, Jerry — *Source Services Corporation*
Plimpton, Ralph L. — *R L Plimpton Associates*
Plummer, John — *Plummer & Associates, Inc.*
Poe, James B. — *Nagler, Robins & Poe, Inc.*
Poirier, Frank — *Juntunen-Combs-Poirier*
Poirier, Roland — *Poirier, Hoevel & Co.*
Polachi, Charles A. — *Fenwick Partners*
Polachi, Peter V. — *Fenwick Partners*
Poore, Larry D. — *Ward Howell International, Inc.*
Poracky, John W. — *M. Wood Company*
Porter, Albert — *The Experts*
Poster, Lawrence D. — *Catalyx Group*
Pototo, Brian — *Source Services Corporation*
Powell, Danny — *Source Services Corporation*
Powell, Gregory — *Source Services Corporation*
Power, Michael — *Source Services Corporation*
Pregeant, David — *Source Services Corporation*
Prencipe, V. Michael — *Raymond Karsan Associates*
Preng, David E. — *Preng & Associates, Inc.*
Preschlack, Jack E. — *Spencer Stuart*
Press, Fred — *Adept Tech Recruiting*
Preusse, Eric — *Source Services Corporation*
Price, Andrew G. — *The Thomas Tucker Company*
Price, Carl — *Source Services Corporation*
Prior, Donald — *The Caldwell Partners Amrop International*
Provus, Barbara L. — *Shepherd Bueschel & Provus, Inc.*
Pugh, Judith Geist — *InterimManagement Solutions, Inc.*
Quinlan, Lynne — *Winter, Wyman & Company*
Quinn, Nola — *Technical Connections Inc.*
Rabinowitz, Peter A. — *P.A.R. Associates Inc.*
Rachels, John W. — *Southwestern Professional Services*
Radice, Joseph — *Hospitality International*
Raiber, Laurie Altman — *The IMC Group of Companies Ltd.*
Ramler, Carolyn S. — *The Corporate Connection, Ltd.*
Randell, James E. — *Randell-Heiken, Inc.*
Range, Mary Jane — *Ingram & Aydelotte Inc.*
Rasmussen, Timothy — *Source Services Corporation*
Ratajczak, Paul — *Source Services Corporation*
Ray, Marianne C. — *Callan Associates, Ltd.*
Raymond, Anne — *Anderson Sterling Associates*
Reardon, Joseph — *Source Services Corporation*
Reece, Christopher S. — *Reece & Mruk Partners*
Reed, Ruthann — *Spectra International Inc.*
Reed, Susan — *Source Services Corporation*
Referente, Gwen — *Richard, Wayne and Roberts*
Reid, Katherine — *Source Services Corporation*
Reid, Scott — *Source Services Corporation*
Reiser, Ellen — *Thorndike Deland Associates*
Renfroe, Ann-Marie — *Source Services Corporation*
Rennell, Thomas — *Source Services Corporation*
Renteria, Elizabeth — *Source Services Corporation*
Resnic, Alan — *Source Services Corporation*
Reynolds, Catherine — *Winter, Wyman & Company*
Reynolds, Gregory P. — *Roberts Ryan and Bentley*
Reynolds, Laura — *Source Services Corporation*
Rhoades, Michael — *Source Services Corporation*
Rice, Raymond D. — *Logue & Rice Inc.*
Richard, Albert L. — *Human Resources Inc.*
Richard, Ryan — *Logix Partners*
Richard, Ryan — *Logix, Inc.*
Rieger, Louis J. — *Spencer Stuart*
Riley, Elizabeth G. — *Mazza & Riley, Inc.*
Rimmele, Michael — *The Bankers Group*

Rios, Vince — *Source Services Corporation*
Rios, Vincent — *Source Services Corporation*
Rizzo, L. Donald — *R.P. Barone Associates*
Robb, Tammy — *Source Services Corporation*
Roberts, Carl R. — *Southwestern Professional Services*
Roberts, Nick P. — *Spectrum Search Associates, Inc.*
Roberts, Norman C. — *Norman Roberts & Associates, Inc.*
Roberts, Scott B. — *Wargo and Co., Inc.*
Robertson, Sherry — *Source Services Corporation*
Robinette, Paul — *Hernand & Partners*
Robins, Jeri N. — *Nagler, Robins & Poe, Inc.*
Robinson, Eric B. — *Bruce Robinson Associates*
Robinson, Tonya — *Source Services Corporation*
Robison, John H. — *Robison & Associates*
Rockwell, Bruce — *Source Services Corporation*
Rodriguez, Manuel — *Source Services Corporation*
Roehrig, Kurt W. — *AJM Professional Services*
Rogers, Gay — *Rogers-McManamon Executive Search*
Rogers, Leah — *Dinte Resources, Incorporated*
Rohan, James E. — *J.P. Canon Associates*
Rollins, Scott — *S.C. International, Ltd.*
Romanchek, Walter R. — *Wellington Management Group*
Romanello, Daniel P. — *Spencer Stuart*
Rorech, Maureen — *Romac & Associates*
Rosato, William R. — *W.R. Rosato & Associates, Inc.*
Rosen, Mitchell — *Source Services Corporation*
Rosenstein, Michele — *Source Services Corporation*
Ross, Lawrence — *Lovas Stanley/Paul Ray Berndtson Inc.*
Ross, Mark S. — *Herman Smith Executive Initiatives Inc.*
Rossi, Thomas — *Southwestern Professional Services*
Rotella, Marshall W. — *The Corporate Connection, Ltd.*
Roth, Robert J. — *Williams, Roth & Krueger Inc.*
Rothenbush, Clayton — *Source Services Corporation*
Rowell, Roger — *Halbrecht Lieberman Associates, Inc.*
Rowland, James — *Source Services Corporation*
Rozentsvayg, Michael — *Logix Partners*
Rozentsvayg, Michael — *Logix, Inc.*
Rubinstein, Alan J. — *Chicago Legal Search, Ltd.*
Rubinstein, Walter — *Technical Connections Inc.*
Rudolph, Kenneth — *Kossuth & Associates, Inc.*
Rudzinsky, Jeffrey — *Louis Rudzinsky Associates*
Rurak, Zbigniew T. — *Rurak & Associates, Inc.*
Russell, Sam — *The Guild Corporation*
Russo, Karen — *Maximum Management Corp.*
Ryan, David — *Source Services Corporation*
Ryan, Kathleen — *Source Services Corporation*
Ryan, Lee — *Ryan, Miller & Associates Inc.*
Ryan, Mark — *Source Services Corporation*
Ryan, Mary L. — *Summerfield Associates, Inc.*
Sabat, Lori S. — *Alta Associates, Inc.*
Sacerdote, John — *Raymond Karsan Associates*
Sadaj, Michael — *Source Services Corporation*
Sahagian, John — *Human Resources Inc.*
Salet, Michael — *Source Services Corporation*
Salvagno, Michael J. — *The Cambridge Group Ltd*
Samsel, Randy — *Source Services Corporation*
Samuelson, Robert — *Source Services Corporation*
Sanchez, William — *Source Services Corporation*
Sanders, Norman D. — *Norm Sanders Associates*
Saner, Harold — *Romac & Associates*
Santiago, Benefrido — *Source Services Corporation*
Sapers, Mark — *Source Services Corporation*
Saposhnik, Doron — *Source Services Corporation*
Sardella, Sharon — *Source Services Corporation*
Sarn, Allan G. — *Allan Sarn Associates Inc.*
Sauer, Harry J. — *Romac & Associates*
Savela, Edward — *Source Services Corporation*
Sawyer, Patricia L. — *Smith & Sawyer Inc.*
Sayers, Bruce D. — *Brackin & Sayers Associates*
Schedra, Sharon — *Earley Kielty and Associates, Inc.*
Schiavone, Mary Rose — *Canny, Bowen Inc.*
Schmidt, Frank B. — *F.B. Schmidt International*
Schneider, James — *The Search Firm, Inc.*
Schneiderman, Gerald — *Management Resource Associates, Inc.*
Schrenzel, Benjamin — *Parfitt Recruiting and Consulting*
Schroeder, James — *Source Services Corporation*
Schultz, Randy — *Source Services Corporation*
Schwalbach, Robert — *Source Services Corporation*
Schwartz, Vincent P. — *Slayton International, Inc.*
Schweichler, Lee J. — *Schweichler Associates, Inc.*
Schwinden, William — *Source Services Corporation*
Scimone, James — *Source Services Corporation*
Scimone, Jim — *Source Services Corporation*
Scoff, Barry — *Source Services Corporation*
Scothon, Alan — *Romac & Associates*
Seamon, Kenneth — *Source Services Corporation*
Seco, William — *Seco & Zetto Associates, Inc.*
Selker, Gregory L. — *Christian & Timbers*

Selko, Philip W. — *Hogan Acquisitions*
Sell, David — *Source Services Corporation*
Selvaggi, Esther — *Source Services Corporation*
Semple, David — *Source Services Corporation*
Semyan, John K. — *TNS Partners, Inc.*
Serba, Kerri — *Source Services Corporation*
Sessa, Vincent J. — *Integrated Search Solutions Group, LLC*
Sevilla, Claudio A. — *Crawford & Crofford*
Shackleford, David — *Source Services Corporation*
Shanks, Jennifer — *Source Services Corporation*
Shapanka, Samuel — *Source Services Corporation*
Shattuck, Merrill B. — *M.B. Shattuck and Associates, Inc.*
Shawhan, Heather — *Source Services Corporation*
Shea, Christopher J. — *Ingram & Aydelotte Inc.*
Sheedy, Edward J. — *Dieckmann & Associates, Ltd.*
Shell, John C. — *John Shell Associates, Inc.*
Shelton, Jonathan — *Source Services Corporation*
Shemin, Grace — *Maximum Management Corp.*
Shenfield, Peter — *Baker, Harris & Partners Limited*
Shepard, Michael J. — *MSI International*
Sherwood, Andrew — *Goodrich & Sherwood Associates, Inc.*
Shield, Nancy — *Maximum Management Corp.*
Shimp, David J. — *Lamalie Amrop International*
Shirilla, Robert M. — *F.B. Schmidt International*
Shourds, Mary E. — *Houze, Shourds & Montgomery, Inc.*
Sibul, Shelly Remen — *Chicago Legal Search, Ltd.*
Siker, Paul W. — *The Guild Corporation*
Silvas, Stephen D. — *Roberson and Company*
Silver, Kit — *Source Services Corporation*
Silver, Lee A. — *L.A. Silver Associates, Inc.*
Simankov, Dmitry — *Logix, Inc.*
Simmons, Anneta — *F-O-R-T-U-N-E Personnel Consultants of Huntsville, Inc.*
Simmons, Deborah — *Source Services Corporation*
Simmons, Gerald J. — *Handy HRM Corp.*
Simon, John — *John J. Davis & Associates, Inc.*
Sinclair, Amy — *Fisher Personnel Management Services*
Sirena, Evelyn — *Source Services Corporation*
Slayton, Richard C. — *Slayton International, Inc.*
Slayton, Richard S. — *Slayton International, Inc.*
Sloan, Scott — *Source Services Corporation*
Slosar, John M. — *Canny, Bowen Inc.*
Smirnov, Tatiana — *Allan Sarn Associates Inc.*
Smith, Adam M. — *The Abbott Group, Inc.*
Smith, Cheryl — *Barton Raben, Inc.*
Smith, David P. — *Smith & Latterell (HRS, Inc.)*
Smith, Herman M. — *Herman Smith Executive Initiatives Inc.*
Smith, Lawrence — *Source Services Corporation*
Smith, Richard — *S.C. International, Ltd.*
Smith, Robert L. — *Smith & Sawyer Inc.*
Smith, Timothy — *Source Services Corporation*
Smock, Cynthia — *Source Services Corporation*
Smoller, Howard — *Source Services Corporation*
Snowden, Charles — *Source Services Corporation*
Snowhite, Rebecca — *Source Services Corporation*
Snyder, James F. — *Snyder & Company*
Sochacki, Michael — *Source Services Corporation*
Solters, Jeanne — *The Guild Corporation*
Song, Louis — *Source Services Corporation*
Sorgen, Jay — *Source Services Corporation*
Sostilio, Louis — *Source Services Corporation*
Spadavecchia, Jennifer — *Alta Associates, Inc.*
Spann, Richard E. — *Goodrich & Sherwood Associates, Inc.*
Spanninger, Mark J. — *The Guild Corporation*
Spector, Michael — *Source Services Corporation*
Spencer, John — *Source Services Corporation*
Spencer, John — *Source Services Corporation*
Spiegel, Gay — *L.A. Silver Associates, Inc.*
Spoutz, Paul — *Source Services Corporation*
Sprau, Collin L. — *Paul Ray Berndtson*
Spriggs, Robert D. — *Spriggs & Company, Inc.*
St. Martin, Peter — *Source Services Corporation*
Staats, Dave — *Southwestern Professional Services*
Stack, Richard — *Source Services Corporation*
Staehely, Janna — *Southwestern Professional Services*
Starner, William S. — *Fenwick Partners*
Steele, Kevin — *Winter, Wyman & Company*
Stein, Terry W. — *Stewart, Stein and Scott, Ltd.*
Steinem, Andy — *Dahl-Morrow International*
Steinem, Barbara — *Dahl-Morrow International*
Steinman, Stephen — *The Stevenson Group of New Jersey*
Stenberg, Edward — *Winter, Wyman & Company*
Stephens, Andrew — *Source Services Corporation*
Stephens, John — *Source Services Corporation*
Stephenson, Don L. — *Ells Personnel System Inc.*
Sterling, Jay — *Earley Kielty and Associates, Inc.*
Stevenson, Terry — *Bartholdi & Company, Inc.*
Stewart, Jeffrey O. — *Stewart, Stein and Scott, Ltd.*

Stewart, Ross M. — *Human Resources Network Partners Inc.*
Stirn, Bradley A. — *Spencer Stuart*
Stone, Susan L. — *Stone Enterprises Ltd.*
Storm, Deborah — *Source Services Corporation*
Strain, Stephen R. — *Spencer Stuart*
Strander, Dervin — *Source Services Corporation*
Strassman, Mark — *Don Richard Associates of Washington, D.C., Inc.*
Stratmeyer, Karin Bergwall — *Princeton Entrepreneurial Resources*
Stringer, Dann P. — *D.E. Foster Partners Inc.*
Strom, Mark N. — *Search Advisors International Corp.*
Struzziero, Ralph E. — *Romac & Associates*
Sturtz, James W. — *Compass Group Ltd.*
Summerfield-Beall, Dotty — *Summerfield Associates, Inc.*
Sur, William K. — *Canny, Bowen Inc.*
Susoreny, Samali — *Source Services Corporation*
Sutter, Howard — *Romac & Associates*
Swanner, William — *Source Services Corporation*
Swanson, Dick — *Raymond Karsan Associates*
Swatts, Stone — *F-O-R-T-U-N-E Personnel Consultants of Huntsville, Inc.*
Sweeney, Anne — *Source Services Corporation*
Sweet, Randall — *Source Services Corporation*
Taft, David G. — *Techsearch Services, Inc.*
Taft, Steven D. — *The Guild Corporation*
Tankson, Dawn — *Source Services Corporation*
Tanner, Frank — *Source Services Corporation*
Tanner, Gary — *Source Services Corporation*
Taylor, Conrad G. — *MSI International*
Teger, Stella — *Source Services Corporation*
Telford, John H. — *Telford, Adams & Alexander/Telford & Co., Inc.*
Tenero, Kymberly — *Source Services Corporation*
Theard, Susan — *Romac & Associates*
Theobald, David B. — *Theobald & Associates*
Thielman, Joseph — *Barrett Partners*
Thomas, Donald — *Mixtec Group*
Thomas, Kurt J. — *P.J. Murphy & Associates, Inc.*
Thompson, Dave — *Battalia Winston International*
Thompson, Kenneth L. — *McCormack & Farrow*
Thompson, Leslie — *Source Services Corporation*
Thrower, Troy — *Source Services Corporation*
Tilley, Kyle — *Source Services Corporation*
Timoney, Laura — *Bishop Partners*
Tipp, George — *Intech Summit Group, Inc.*
Tobin, Christopher — *Source Services Corporation*
Tobin, Jim — *Barton Raben, Inc.*
Trefzer, Kristie — *Source Services Corporation*
Trewhella, Michael — *Source Services Corporation*
Trice, Renee — *Source Services Corporation*
Trieschmann, Daniel — *Source Services Corporation*
Trimble, Patricia — *Source Services Corporation*
Trimble, Rhonda — *Source Services Corporation*
Trueblood, Brian G. — *TNS Partners, Inc.*
Truitt, Thomas B. — *Southwestern Professional Services*
Tscelli, Maureen — *Source Services Corporation*
Tschan, Stephen — *Source Services Corporation*
Tucker, Thomas A. — *The Thomas Tucker Company*
Turner, Edward K. — *Don Richard Associates of Charlotte*
Turner, Raymond — *Source Services Corporation*
Tursi, Deborah J. — *The Corporate Connection, Ltd.*
Twiste, Craig — *Raymond Karsan Associates*
Twomey, James — *Source Services Corporation*
Ulbert, Nancy — *Aureus Group*
Unger, Paul T. — *A.T. Kearney, Inc.*
Uzzel, Linda — *Source Services Corporation*
Vacca, Domenic — *Romac & Associates*
Vainblat, Galina — *Foy, Schneid & Daniel, Inc.*
Valenta, Joseph — *Princeton Entrepreneurial Resources*
Van Clieaf, Mark — *MVC Associates International*
Van Norman, Ben — *Source Services Corporation*
Vande-Water, Katie — *J. Robert Scott*
Vandenbulcke, Cynthia — *Source Services Corporation*
Varney, Monique — *Source Services Corporation*
Varrichio, Michael — *Source Services Corporation*
Velez, Hector — *Source Services Corporation*
Velline, Ena A. — *Paul Ray Berndtson*
Venable, William W. — *Thorndike Deland Associates*
Vennat, Manon — *Spencer Stuart*
Vilella, Paul — *Source Services Corporation*
Villella, Paul — *Source Services Corporation*
Vinett-Hessel, Deidre — *Source Services Corporation*
Viviano, Cathleen — *Source Services Corporation*
Vlcek, Thomas J. — *Vlcek & Company, Inc.*
Voigt, John A. — *Romac & Associates*
von Stein, Scott — *Wilkinson & Ives*
Wade, Christy — *Source Services Corporation*
Waggoner, Lisa — *Intersource, Ltd.*
Waldoch, D. Mark — *Barnes Development Group, LLC*

Waldrop, Gary R. — *MSI International*
Walker, Ann — *Source Services Corporation*
Walker, Richard — *Bradford & Galt, Inc.*
Walker, Rose — *Source Services Corporation*
Wallace, Toby — *Source Services Corporation*
Walsh, Patty — *Abraham & London, Ltd.*
Ward, Les — *Source Services Corporation*
Ward, Madeleine — *LTM Associates*
Ward, Robert — *Source Services Corporation*
Ware, John C. — *Spencer Stuart*
Warnock, Phyl — *Source Services Corporation*
Warren, Sylvia W. — *Thorndike Deland Associates*
Warter, Mark — *Isaacson, Miller*
Wasson, Thomas W. — *Spencer Stuart*
Watson, James — *MSI International*
Watson, Peggy — *Advanced Information Management*
Waymire, Pamela — *Source Services Corporation*
Wayne, Cary S. — *ProSearch Inc.*
Webber, Edward — *Source Services Corporation*
Weber, Fred — *J.B. Homer Associates, Inc.*
Weeks, Glenn — *Source Services Corporation*
Weiler, Tom — *Executive Placement Consultants, Inc.*
Wein, Michael S. — *InterimManagement Solutions, Inc.*
Wein, Michael S. — *Media Management Resources, Inc.*
Wein, William — *InterimManagement Solutions, Inc.*
Wein, William — *Media Management Resources, Inc.*
Weinberg, Melvin — *Romac & Associates*
Weis, Theodore — *Source Services Corporation*
Weiss, Elizabeth — *Source Services Corporation*
Weisz, Laura — *Anderson Sterling Associates*
Welch, Dale — *Winter, Wyman & Company*
Wenz, Alexander — *Source Services Corporation*
Wert, Marty — *Parfitt Recruiting and Consulting*
Wessling, Jerry — *Source Services Corporation*
Wheatley, William — *Drummond Associates, Inc.*
White, Jonathan O. — *The Badger Group*
White, William C. — *Venture Resources Inc.*
Whitfield, Jack — *Source Services Corporation*
Whitney, David L. — *Whitney & Associates, Inc.*
Wilcox, Fred T. — *Wilcox, Bertoux & Miller*
Wilder, Richard B. — *Columbia Consulting Group*
Willbrandt, Curt — *Source Services Corporation*
Williams, Angie — *Whitney & Associates, Inc.*
Williams, Brad — *Winter, Wyman & Company*
Williams, Dave — *The McCormick Group, Inc.*
Williams, Gary L. — *Barnes Development Group, LLC*
Williams, John — *Source Services Corporation*
Williams, Roger K. — *Williams, Roth & Krueger Inc.*
Williams, Walter E. — *Canny, Bowen Inc.*
Wilson, Joyce — *Source Services Corporation*
Wilson, Patricia L. — *Leon A. Farley Associates*
Wingate, Mary — *Source Services Corporation*
Winitz, Joel — *GSW Consulting Group, Inc.*
Winitz, Marla — *GSW Consulting Group, Inc.*
Winkowski, Stephen — *Source Services Corporation*
Winnewisser, William E. — *Accounting & Computer Personnel*
Winnicki, Kimberly — *Source Services Corporation*
Winograd, Glenn — *Criterion Executive Search, Inc.*
Winston, Dale — *Battalia Winston International*
Witte, David L. — *Ward Howell International, Inc.*
Witzgall, William — *Source Services Corporation*
Wolf, Donald — *Source Services Corporation*
Wolf, Stephen M. — *Byron Leonard International, Inc.*
Wolfe, Peter — *Source Services Corporation*
Womack, Joseph — *The Bankers Group*
Wood, Gary — *Source Services Corporation*
Wood, Milton M. — *M. Wood Company*
Woods, Craig — *Source Services Corporation*
Wooller, Edmund A.M. — *Windsor International*
Woollett, James — *Rusher, Loscavio & LoPresto*
Woomer, Jerome — *Source Services Corporation*
Workman, David — *Source Services Corporation*
Wren, Jay — *Jay Wren & Associates*
Wright, Charles D. — *Goodrich & Sherwood Associates, Inc.*
Wright, Leslie — *The Stevenson Group of New Jersey*
Wyatt, James — *Wyatt & Jaffe*
Wycoff-Viola, Amy — *Source Services Corporation*
Yang, George — *Technical Connections Inc.*
Yeaton, Robert — *Source Services Corporation*
Young, Heather — *The Guild Corporation*
Young, Lesley — *Search West, Inc.*
Youngberg, David — *Source Services Corporation*
Zaffrann, Craig S. — *P.J. Murphy & Associates, Inc.*
Zahradka, James F. — *P.J. Murphy & Associates, Inc.*
Zarnoski, Hank — *Dunhill Search International*
Zaslav, Debra M. — *Telford, Adams & Alexander/Telford & Co., Inc.*
Zavrel, Mark — *Source Services Corporation*
Zegel, Gary — *Source Services Corporation*

Zell, David M. — *Logix Partners*
Zetto, Kathryn — *Seco & Zetto Associates, Inc.*
Zila, Laurie M. — *Princeton Entrepreneurial Resources*
Zimbal, Mark — *Source Services Corporation*
Zimont, Scott — *Source Services Corporation*
Zinn, Donald — *Bishop Partners*
Zucker, Nancy — *Maximum Management Corp.*
Zwiff, Jeffrey G. — *Johnson Smith & Knisely Accord*

## 19. Insurance

Abbatiello, Christine Murphy — *Winter, Wyman & Company*
Adams, Jeffrey C. — *Telford, Adams & Alexander/Jeffrey C. Adams & Co., Inc.*
Afforde, Sharon Gould — *Jacobson Associates*
Akin, J.R. — *J.R. Akin & Company Inc.*
Allen, Scott — *Chrisman & Company, Incorporated*
Altreuter, Rose — *The ALTCO Group*
Amato, Joseph — *Amato & Associates, Inc.*
Andrick, Patty — *CPS Inc.*
Ascher, Susan P. — *The Ascher Group*
Ashton, Edward J. — *E.J. Ashton & Associates, Ltd.*
Atkinson, S. Graham — *Raymond Karsan Associates*
Aydelotte, G. Thomas — *Ingram & Aydelotte Inc.*
Bagg, Mary — *Keith Bagg & Associates Inc.*
Baitler, Simon C. — *The Stevenson Group of Delaware Inc.*
Balch, Randy — *CPS Inc.*
Barger, H. Carter — *Barger & Sargeant, Inc.*
Barnes, Richard E. — *Barnes Development Group, LLC*
Barnes, Roanne L. — *Barnes Development Group, LLC*
Barnum, Toni M. — *Stone Murphy & Olson*
Bason, Maurice L. — *Bason Associates Inc.*
Bass, Nate — *Jacobson Associates*
Beaulieu, Genie A. — *Romac & Associates*
Beck, Barbara S. — *Rhodes Associates*
Beer, John — *People Management Northeast Incorporated*
Beeson, William B. — *Lawrence-Leiter and Company*
Belden, Charles P. — *Raymond Karsan Associates*
Bell, Michael — *Spencer Stuart*
Bellano, Robert W. — *Stanton Chase International*
Bennett, Jo — *Battalia Winston International*
Benson, Kate — *Rene Plessner Associates, Inc.*
Biddix, Maryanne — *Tyler & Company*
Bishop, Barbara — *The Executive Source*
Bogard, Nicholas C. — *The Onstott Group, Inc.*
Bond, Robert J. — *Romac & Associates*
Bonifield, Len — *Bonifield Associates*
Bonnell, William R. — *Bonnell Associates Ltd.*
Borden, Stuart — *M.A. Churchill & Associates, Inc.*
Borland, James — *Goodrich & Sherwood Associates, Inc.*
Bourrie, Sharon D. — *Chartwell Partners International, Inc.*
Brackenbury, Robert — *Bowman & Marshall, Inc.*
Brady, Robert — *CPS Inc.*
Brandeis, Richard — *CPS Inc.*
Bratches, Howard — *Thorndike Deland Associates*
Brenner, Mary — *Prestige Inc.*
Brocaglia, Joyce — *Alta Associates, Inc.*
Brophy, Melissa — *Maximum Management Corp.*
Brown, Larry C. — *Horton International*
Bruce, Michael C. — *Spencer Stuart*
Bump, Gerald J. — *D.E. Foster Partners Inc.*
Burns, Terence N. — *D.E. Foster Partners Inc.*
Butler, Kirby B. — *The Butlers Company Insurance Recruiters*
Butterfass, Stanley — *Butterfass, Pepe & MacCallan Inc.*
Bye, Randy — *Romac & Associates*
Byrnes, Thomas A. — *Thomas A. Byrnes Associates*
Caldwell, C. Douglas — *The Caldwell Partners Amrop International*
Campbell, Gary — *Romac & Associates*
Cappe, Richard R. — *Roberts Ryan and Bentley*
Carideo, Joseph — *Thorndike Deland Associates*
Carlson, Judith — *Bowman & Marshall, Inc.*
Carter, Christine C. — *Health Care Dimensions*
Caruso, Kathy — *Accounting Resources, Inc.*
Casal, Daniel G. — *Bonifield Associates*
Celenza, Catherine — *CPS Inc.*
Chamberlin, Brooks T. — *Korn/Ferry International*
Chappell, Peter — *The Bankers Group*
Charles, Ronald D. — *The Caldwell Partners Amrop International*
Chauvin, Ralph A. — *The Caldwell Partners Amrop International*
Christenson, H. Alan — *Christenson & Hutchison*
Christiansen, Amy — *CPS Inc.*
Christiansen, Doug — *CPS Inc.*
Chua, Jackie — *Keith Bagg & Associates Inc.*
Clark, James — *CPS Inc.*
Clark, Steven — *D.A. Kreuter Associates, Inc.*
Clegg, Cynthia — *Horton International*
Clemens, William B. — *Norman Broadbent International, Inc.*
Clemens, William B. — *Norman Broadbent International, Inc.*
Cocchiaro, Richard — *Romac & Associates*

Cohen, Luis Lezama — *Paul Ray Berndtson*
Cohen, Michael R. — *Intech Summit Group, Inc.*
Cohen, Robert C. — *Intech Summit Group, Inc.*
Colborne, Janis M. — *AJM Professional Services*
Cole, Sharon A. — *AJM Professional Services*
Collard, Joseph A. — *Spencer Stuart*
Collis, Martin — *E.L. Shore & Associates Ltd.*
Cona, Joseph A. — *Cona Personnel Search*
Connaghan, Linda — *Bowman & Marshall, Inc.*
Cooke, Katherine H. — *Horton International*
Cordaro, Concetta — *Flynn, Hannock, Incorporated*
Coulman, Karen — *CPS Inc.*
Cox, William — *E.J. Ashton & Associates, Ltd.*
Cragg, Barbara R. — *Southwestern Professional Services*
Crane, Howard C. — *Chartwell Partners International, Inc.*
Crist, Peter — *Crist Partners, Ltd.*
Crystal, Jonathan A. — *Spencer Stuart*
Cuddy, Brian C. — *Romac & Associates*
Cunningham, Robert Y. — *Goodrich & Sherwood Associates, Inc.*
Czepiel, Susan — *CPS Inc.*
Danforth, W. Michael — *Hyde Danforth Wold & Co.*
Dannenberg, Richard A. — *Roberts Ryan and Bentley*
Darter, Steven M. — *People Management Northeast Incorporated*
Dawson, Joe — *S.C. International, Ltd.*
de Tuede, Catherine — *Thomas A. Byrnes Associates*
DeCorrevont, James — *DeCorrevont & Associates*
DeCorrevont, James — *DeCorrevont & Associates*
DeFuniak, William S. — *DeFuniak & Edwards*
DeHart, Donna — *Tower Consultants, Ltd.*
Del Pino, William — *National Search, Inc.*
Della Monica, Vincent — *Search West, Inc.*
Demchak, James P. — *Sandhurst Associates*
Desgrosellier, Gary P. — *Personnel Unlimited/Executive Search*
Desir, Etheline — *Tyler & Company*
Desmond, Dennis — *Beall & Company, Inc.*
deVry, Kimberly A. — *Tower Consultants, Ltd.*
deWilde, David M. — *Chartwell Partners International, Inc.*
Dickerson, Scot — *Key Employment Services*
Dickey, Chet W. — *Bowden & Company, Inc.*
Dieckmann, Ralph E. — *Dieckmann & Associates, Ltd.*
DiGiovanni, Charles — *Penn Search*
Dinte, Paul — *Dinte Resources, Incorporated*
Dixon, Aris — *CPS Inc.*
Do, Sonnie — *Whitney & Associates, Inc.*
Doan, Lisa — *Rhodes Associates*
Doele, Donald C. — *Goodrich & Sherwood Associates, Inc.*
Doman, Matthew — *S.C. International, Ltd.*
Dotson, M. Ileen — *Dotson & Associates*
Dressler, Ralph — *Romac & Associates*
Dunkel, David L. — *Romac & Associates*
Dunman, Betsy L. — *Crawford & Crofford*
Dwyer, Julie — *CPS Inc.*
Dykstra, Nicolette — *CPS Inc.*
Edwards, Randolph J. — *DeFuniak & Edwards*
Edwards, Verba L. — *Wing Tips & Pumps, Inc.*
Ehrgott, Elizabeth — *The Ascher Group*
Erlien, Nancy B. — *Jacobson Associates*
Ervin, Darlene — *CPS Inc.*
Evan-Cook, James W. — *Jacobson Associates*
Fancher, Robert L. — *Bason Associates Inc.*
Ferrari, S. Jay — *Ferrari Search Group*
Flanagan, Robert M. — *Robert M. Flanagan & Associates, Ltd.*
Flannery, Peter — *Jonas, Walters & Assoc., Inc.*
Flora, Dodi — *Crawford & Crofford*
Flynn, Jack — *Executive Search Consultants Corporation*
Fogarty, Michael — *CPS Inc.*
Ford, Sandra D. — *Phillips & Ford, Inc.*
Forgosh, Jack H. — *Raymond Karsan Associates*
Foster, Dwight E. — *D.E. Foster Partners Inc.*
Fox, Amanda C. — *Paul Ray Berndtson*
Fribush, Richard — *A.J. Burton Group, Inc.*
Friedman, Donna L. — *Tower Consultants, Ltd.*
Frumess, Gregory — *D.E. Foster Partners Inc.*
Galinski, Paul — *E.J. Ashton & Associates, Ltd.*
Gallagher, Marilyn — *Hogan Acquisitions*
Gallagher, Terence M. — *Battalia Winston International*
Gardiner, E. Nicholas P. — *Gardiner International*
Garfinkle, Steven M. — *Battalia Winston International*
Gauthier, Robert C. — *Columbia Consulting Group*
George, Delores F. — *Delores F. George Human Resource Management & Consulting Industry*
Gibbs, John S. — *Spencer Stuart*
Gill, Patricia — *Columbia Consulting Group*
Gilmore, Lori — *CPS Inc.*
Glass, Lori — *The Executive Source*
Goar, Duane R. — *Sandhurst Associates*
Goedtke, Steven — *Southwestern Professional Services*
Goldberg, Susan C. — *Susan C. Goldberg Associates*

Goldenberg, Susan — *Grant Cooper and Associates*
Goldson, Bob — *The McCormick Group, Inc.*
Goodman, Dawn M. — *Bason Associates Inc.*
Goodridge, Benjamin — *S.C. International, Ltd.*
Gourlay, Debra — *Rene Plessner Associates, Inc.*
Gow, Roderick C. — *Lamalie Amrop International*
Graham, Dale — *CPS Inc.*
Grantham, Philip H. — *Columbia Consulting Group*
Grassl, Peter O. — *Bowman & Marshall, Inc.*
Grebenschikoff, Jennifer R. — *Physician Executive Management Center*
Greco, Patricia — *Howe-Lewis International*
Grenier, Glorianne — *CPS Inc.*
Grzybowski, Jill — *CPS Inc.*
Gutknecht, Steven — *Jacobson Associates*
Haddad, Charles — *Romac & Associates*
Hallock, Peter B. — *Goodrich & Sherwood Associates, Inc.*
Hamm, Mary Kay — *Romac & Associates*
Hannock, Elwin W. — *Flynn, Hannock, Incorporated*
Hanson, Grant M. — *Goodrich & Sherwood Associates, Inc.*
Harelick, Arthur S. — *Ashway, Ltd.*
Hargis, N. Leann — *Montgomery Resources, Inc.*
Harrison, Joel — *D.A. Kreuter Associates, Inc.*
Haughton, Michael — *DeFrain, Mayer, Lee & Burgess LLC*
Hauser, Martha — *Spencer Stuart*
Hay, William E. — *William E. Hay & Company*
Hazelton, Lisa M. — *Health Care Dimensions*
Hazerjian, Cynthia — *CPS Inc.*
Heafey, Bill — *CPS Inc.*
Hecker, Henry C. — *Hogan Acquisitions*
Heiken, Barbara E. — *Randell-Heiken, Inc.*
Hellebusch, Jerry — *Morgan Hunter Corp.*
Hemingway, Stuart C. — *Robison & Associates*
Henn, George W. — *G.W. Henn & Company*
Herman, Pat — *Whitney & Associates, Inc.*
Hewitt, Rives D. — *The Dalley Hewitt Company*
Hildebrand, Thomas B. — *Professional Resources Group, Inc.*
Hillen, Skip — *The McCormick Group, Inc.*
Hiller, Steve — *The McCormick Group, Inc.*
Hoevel, Michael J. — *Poirier, Hoevel & Co.*
Hogan, Larry H. — *Hogan Acquisitions*
Holmes, Lawrence J. — *Columbia Consulting Group*
Hoppert, Phil — *Wargo and Co., Inc.*
Horton, Robert H. — *Horton International*
Howard, Jill — *Health Care Dimensions*
Howard, Susy — *The McCormick Group, Inc.*
Howe, Theodore — *Romac & Associates*
Hoyda, Louis A. — *Thorndike Deland Associates*
Hudson, Reginald M. — *Search Bureau International*
Hughes, David — *Southwestern Professional Services*
Hughes, Kendall G. — *Hughes & Associates*
Hutchison, William K. — *Christenson & Hutchison*
Iacovelli, Heather — *CPS Inc.*
Ikle, A. Donald — *Ward Howell International, Inc.*
Illsley, Hugh G. — *Ward Howell International, Inc.*
Ingram, D. John — *Ingram & Aydelotte Inc.*
Irish, Alan — *CPS Inc.*
Ives, Richard K. — *Wilkinson & Ives*
Jacobs, Martin J. — *The Rubicon Group*
Jacobs, Mike — *Thorne, Brieger Associates Inc.*
Jacobson, David N. — *Jacobson Associates*
Jacobson, Gregory — *Jacobson Associates*
Jacobson, Jewel — *Jacobson Associates*
Jaedike, Eldron — *Prestige Inc.*
James, Richard — *Criterion Executive Search, Inc.*
Joffe, Barry — *Bason Associates Inc.*
Johnson, Brian — *A.J. Burton Group, Inc.*
Johnson, Keith — *Romac & Associates*
Johnson, Priscilla — *The Johnson Group, Inc.*
Johnston, James R. — *The Stevenson Group of Delaware Inc.*
Jones, Jeffrey — *AJM Professional Services*
Jones, Jonathan C. — *The Ogdon Partnership*
Juratovac, Michael — *Montgomery Resources, Inc.*
Kalinowski, David — *Jacobson Associates*
Karalis, William — *CPS Inc.*
Keeton, Susan G. — *The Corporate Connection, Ltd.*
Kehoe, Mike — *CPS Inc.*
Keller, Peggy — *The McCormick Group, Inc.*
Kelly, Peter W. — *R. Rollo Associates*
Kennedy, Michael — *The Danbrook Group, Inc.*
Kennedy, Walter — *Romac & Associates*
Kershaw, Lisa — *Tanton Mitchell/Paul Ray Berndtson*
Kilcoyne, Pat — *CPS Inc.*
Kilcullen, Brian A. — *D.A. Kreuter Associates, Inc.*
Kile, Robert W. — *Rusher, Loscavio & LoPresto*
Kiley, Phyllis — *National Search, Inc.*
King, Bill — *The McCormick Group, Inc.*
King, Steven — *Ashway, Ltd.*

Kinley, Kathy — *Intech Summit Group, Inc.*
Kinser, Richard E. — *Richard Kinser & Associates*
Kirschman, David R. — *Physician Executive Management Center*
Kkorzyniewski, Nicole — *CPS Inc.*
Kleinstein, Jonah A. — *The Kleinstein Group*
Klumpjan, Sonja — *CPS Inc.*
Koehler, Frank R. — *The Koehler Group*
Kramer, Donald — *Dunhill Personnel of Tampa, Inc.*
Kramer, Peter — *Dunhill Personnel of Tampa, Inc.*
Kratz, Steve — *Tyler & Company*
Krauser, H. James — *Spencer Stuart*
Kreuter, Daniel A. — *D.A. Kreuter Associates, Inc.*
Kring, Kenneth L. — *Spencer Stuart*
Kucewicz, William — *Search West, Inc.*
Kuo, Linda — *Montgomery Resources, Inc.*
Kuper, Keith D. — *Christenson & Hutchison*
Laderman, David — *Romac & Associates*
Laird, Cheryl — *CPS Inc.*
Lamb, Angus K. — *Raymond Karsan Associates*
Landan, Joy — *Jacobson Associates*
LaPierre, Louis — *Romac & Associates*
Larsen, Bruce — *Prestige Inc.*
Lasher, Charles M. — *Lasher Associates*
LaValle, Michael — *Romac & Associates*
Lawrance, Susanne — *Sharrow & Associates*
Leahy, Jan — *CPS Inc.*
Lee, Roger — *Montgomery Resources, Inc.*
Leetma, Imbi — *Stanton Chase International*
Leininger, Dennis — *Key Employment Services*
Leonard, Linda — *Harris Heery & Associates*
Leslie, William H. — *Boyden/Zay & Company*
Letcher, Harvey D. — *Sandhurst Associates*
Levine, Lois — *National Search, Inc.*
Levinson, Lauren — *The Danbrook Group, Inc.*
Lewis, Jon A. — *Sandhurst Associates*
Line, Joseph T. — *Sharrow & Associates*
Littman, Stephen — *Rhodes Associates*
Lofthouse, Cindy — *CPS Inc.*
Long, Melanie — *National Search, Inc.*
Long, William G. — *McDonald, Long & Associates, Inc.*
Loper, Doris — *Mortgage & Financial Personnel Services*
Loscavio, J. Michael — *Rusher, Loscavio & LoPresto*
Loving, Vikki — *Intersource, Ltd.*
Lucht, John — *The John Lucht Consultancy Inc.*
Lynch, Michael C. — *Lynch Miller Moore Partners, Inc.*
Lynch, Sean E. — *Raymond Karsan Associates*
Lyons, Jane A. — *Rhodes Associates*
Lyons, Michele R. — *R. Rollo Associates*
MacCallan, Deirdre — *Butterfass, Pepe & MacCallan Inc.*
MacDougall, Andrew J. — *Spencer Stuart*
Magee, Harrison R. — *Bowden & Company, Inc.*
Mahr, Toni — *K. Russo Associates*
Mainwaring, Andrew Brian — *Executive Search Consultants Corporation*
Mak, I. Paul — *Thomas A. Byrnes Associates*
Mallipudi, Anand — *Raymond Karsan Associates*
Marks, Sarah J. — *The Executive Source*
Marsteller, Franklin D. — *Spencer Stuart*
Mathias, Kathy — *Stone Murphy & Olson*
Mauer, Kristin — *Montgomery Resources, Inc.*
Mayes, Kay H. — *John Shell Associates, Inc.*
McAndrews, Kathy — *CPS Inc.*
McAteer, Thomas — *Montgomery Resources, Inc.*
McBride, Jonathan E. — *McBride Associates, Inc.*
McCabe, Christopher — *Raymond Karsan Associates*
McClearen, Bruce — *Tyler & Company*
McConnell, Greg — *Winter, Wyman & Company*
McCormick, Brian — *The McCormick Group, Inc.*
McDermott, Richard A. — *Paul Ray Berndtson*
McDonald, Scott A. — *McDonald Associates International*
McDonald, Stanleigh B. — *McDonald Associates International*
McFadden, Ashton S. — *Johnson Smith & Knisely Accord*
McLaughlin, John — *Romac & Associates*
McLean, B. Keith — *Price Waterhouse*
McMillin, Bob — *Price Waterhouse*
McNamara, Timothy C. — *Columbia Consulting Group*
McNear, Jeffrey E. — *Barrett Partners*
McSherry, James F. — *Battalia Winston International*
Meagher, Patricia G. — *Spencer Stuart*
Mendoza, Guadalupe — *Ward Howell International, Inc.*
Menk, Carl W. — *Canny, Bowen Inc.*
Mertensotto, Chuck H. — *Whitney & Associates, Inc.*
Messett, William J. — *Messett Associates, Inc.*
Meyer, Michael F. — *Witt/Kieffer, Ford, Hadelman & Lloyd*
Meyers, Steven — *Montgomery Resources, Inc.*
Michaels, Joseph — *CPS Inc.*
Milkint, Margaret Resce — *Jacobson Associates*
Miller, Kenneth A. — *Computer Network Resources, Inc.*

Millonzi, Joel C. — *Johnson Smith & Knisely Accord*
Mirtz, P. John — *Mirtz Morice, Inc.*
Mitchell, John — *Romac & Associates*
Mogul, Gene — *Mogul Consultants, Inc.*
Mohr, Brian — *CPS Inc.*
Molitor, John L. — *Barrett Partners*
Molnar, Robert A. — *Johnson Smith & Knisely Accord*
Moore, Denise — *Jonas, Walters & Assoc., Inc.*
Morgan, Gary — *National Search, Inc.*
Morice, James L. — *Mirtz Morice, Inc.*
Morris, Paul T. — *The Morris Group*
Morton, Robert C. — *Morton, McCorkle & Associates, Inc.*
Moyse, Richard G. — *Thorndike Deland Associates*
Muller, Charles A. — *AJM Professional Services*
Murphy, Cornelius J. — *Goodrich & Sherwood Associates, Inc.*
Murphy, Gary J. — *Stone Murphy & Olson*
Mursuli, Meredith — *Lasher Associates*
Mydlach, Renee — *CPS Inc.*
Myers, Kay — *Signature Staffing*
Nagle, Charles L. — *Tyler & Company*
Neelin, Sharon — *The Caldwell Partners Amrop International*
Neff, Thomas J. — *Spencer Stuart*
Neill, Wellden K. — *Sampson Neill & Wilkins Inc.*
Nelson, Garry A. — *Rhodes Associates*
Neri, Gene — *S.C. International, Ltd.*
Neuberth, Jeffrey G. — *Canny, Bowen Inc.*
Nevins, Patricia — *Rhodes Associates*
Nielsen, Sue — *Ells Personnel System Inc.*
Normann, Amy — *Robert M. Flanagan & Associates, Ltd.*
Nutter, Roger — *Raymond Karsan Associates*
O'Connell, Mary — *CPS Inc.*
O'Neill, James P. — *Allerton Heneghan & O'Neill*
O'Neill, Stephen A. — *Harris Heery & Associates*
Ogdon, Thomas H. — *The Ogdon Partnership*
Ongirski, Richard P. — *Raymond Karsan Associates*
Ottenritter, Chris — *CPS Inc.*
Pace, Susan A. — *Horton International*
Page, Linda — *Jonas, Walters & Assoc., Inc.*
Page, Linda M. — *Wargo and Co., Inc.*
Palma, Frank R. — *Goodrich & Sherwood Associates, Inc.*
Palmer, Carlton A. — *Beall & Company, Inc.*
Parker, P. Grant — *Raymond Karsan Associates*
Parry, William H. — *Horton International*
Patton, Mitchell — *Patton/Perry Associates, Inc.*
Paynter, Sandra L. — *Ward Howell International, Inc.*
Pedley, Jill — *CPS Inc.*
Pepe, Leonida — *Butterfass, Pepe & MacCallan Inc.*
Perkins, Daphne — *CPS Inc.*
Peternell, Melanie — *Signature Staffing*
Peterson, John — *CPS Inc.*
Phillips, James L. — *Highland Search Group, L.L.C.*
Phillips, Scott K. — *Phillips & Ford, Inc.*
Pickford, Stephen T. — *The Corporate Staff, Inc.*
Pierson, Edward J. — *Johnson Smith & Knisely Accord*
Pinson, Stephanie L. — *Gilbert Tweed/INESA*
Plazza, Richard C. — *The Executive Source*
Plessner, Rene — *Rene Plessner Associates, Inc.*
Plimpton, Ralph L. — *R L Plimpton Associates*
Poirier, Roland — *Poirier, Hoevel & Co.*
Pomerance, Mark — *CPS Inc.*
Poracky, John W. — *M. Wood Company*
Powell, Leslie — *Rhodes Associates*
Prencipe, V. Michael — *Raymond Karsan Associates*
Rabinowitz, Peter A. — *P.A.R. Associates Inc.*
Ramler, Carolyn S. — *The Corporate Connection, Ltd.*
Randell, James E. — *Randell-Heiken, Inc.*
Range, Mary Jane — *Ingram & Aydelotte Inc.*
Redler, Rhonda — *National Search, Inc.*
Reece, Christopher S. — *Reece & Mruk Partners*
Reeder, Michael S. — *Lamalie Amrop International*
Reeves, William B. — *Spencer Stuart*
Reiser, Ellen — *Thorndike Deland Associates*
Reiss, Matt — *National Search, Inc.*
Rendl, Ric — *CPS Inc.*
Renick, Cynthia L. — *Morgan Hunter Corp.*
Renner, Sandra L. — *Spectra International Inc.*
Reyman, Susan — *S. Reyman & Associates Ltd.*
Reynolds, Gregory P. — *Roberts Ryan and Bentley*
Riederer, Larry — *CPS Inc.*
Rimmele, Michael — *The Bankers Group*
Rinker, Jim — *Southwestern Professional Services*
Rivera, Elba R. — *Raymond Karsan Associates*
Roberts, Carl R. — *Southwestern Professional Services*
Roberts, Derek J. — *Ward Howell International, Inc.*
Roberts, Kenneth — *The Rubicon Group*
Roberts, Nick P. — *Spectrum Search Associates, Inc.*
Roberts, Scott B. — *Wargo and Co., Inc.*
Robinson, Bruce — *Bruce Robinson Associates*

Robinson, Eric B. — *Bruce Robinson Associates*
Robison, John H. — *Robison & Associates*
Roehrig, Kurt W. — *AJM Professional Services*
Rollins, Scott — *S.C. International, Ltd.*
Rollo, Robert S. — *R. Rollo Associates*
Rorech, Maureen — *Romac & Associates*
Rosenthal, Charles — *National Search, Inc.*
Ross, Sheila L. — *Ward Howell International, Inc.*
Rotella, Marshall W. — *The Corporate Connection, Ltd.*
Roth, William — *Harris Heery & Associates*
Rowe, William D. — *D.E. Foster Partners Inc.*
Rusher, William H. — *Rusher, Loscavio & LoPresto*
Russell, Richard A. — *Executive Search Consultants Corporation*
Russo, Karen — *K. Russo Associates*
Russo, Karen — *Maximum Management Corp.*
Sabat, Lori S. — *Alta Associates, Inc.*
Sacerdote, John — *Raymond Karsan Associates*
Sahlas, Chrissy — *CPS Inc.*
Saletra, Andrew — *CPS Inc.*
Sanders, Natalie — *CPS Inc.*
Sandor, Richard J. — *Flynn, Hannock, Incorporated*
Saner, Harold — *Romac & Associates*
Sarn, Allan G. — *Allan Sarn Associates Inc.*
Sathe, Mark A. — *Sathe & Associates, Inc.*
Sauer, Harry J. — *Romac & Associates*
Savage, Edward J. — *Stanton Chase International*
Savard, Robert F. — *The Stevenson Group of Delaware Inc.*
Scalamera, Tom — *CPS Inc.*
Schroeder, John W. — *Spencer Stuart*
Schueneman, David — *CPS Inc.*
Schuette, Dorothy — *Harris Heery & Associates*
Schwartz, Harry — *Jacobson Associates*
Scothon, Alan — *Romac & Associates*
Scranton, Lisa — *A.J. Burton Group, Inc.*
Seibert, Nancy — *Tyler & Company*
Selko, Philip W. — *Hogan Acquisitions*
Sennello, Gendra — *National Search, Inc.*
Shapiro, Elaine — *CPS Inc.*
Shell, John C. — *John Shell Associates, Inc.*
Shelton, Sandra — *National Search, Inc.*
Shemin, Grace — *Maximum Management Corp.*
Sher, Lawrence — *M.A. Churchill & Associates, Inc.*
Sherman, Robert R. — *Mortgage & Financial Personnel Services*
Sherwood, Andrew — *Goodrich & Sherwood Associates, Inc.*
Shield, Nancy — *Maximum Management Corp.*
Shore, Earl L. — *E.L. Shore & Associates Ltd.*
Signer, Julie — *CPS Inc.*
Sindler, Jay — *A.J. Burton Group, Inc.*
Singleton, Robin — *Tyler & Company*
Skirbe, Douglas — *Rhodes Associates*
Smirnov, Tatiana — *Allan Sarn Associates Inc.*
Smith, Richard — *S.C. International, Ltd.*
Snelgrove, Geiger — *National Search, Inc.*
Snodgrass, Stephen — *DeFrain, Mayer, Lee & Burgess LLC*
Snyder, James F. — *Snyder & Company*
Spadavecchia, Jennifer — *Alta Associates, Inc.*
Spann, Richard E. — *Goodrich & Sherwood Associates, Inc.*
Spicher, John — *M.A. Churchill & Associates, Inc.*
Stark, Jeff — *Thorne, Brieger Associates Inc.*
Stein, Terry W. — *Stewart, Stein and Scott, Ltd.*
Stern, Stephen — *CPS Inc.*
Sterner, Doug — *CPS Inc.*
Stewart, Jeffrey O. — *Stewart, Stein and Scott, Ltd.*
Strom, Mark N. — *Search Advisors International Corp.*
Struzziero, Ralph E. — *Romac & Associates*
Sussman, Lynda — *Gilbert Tweed/INESA*
Sutter, Howard — *Romac & Associates*
Swanson, Dick — *Raymond Karsan Associates*
Sweeney, Sean K. — *Bonifield Associates*
Tappan, Michael A. — *Ward Howell International, Inc.*
Terry, Douglas — *Jacobson Associates*
Theard, Susan — *Romac & Associates*
Thielman, Joseph — *Barrett Partners*
Thomas, Cheryl M. — *CPS Inc.*
Thomas, Kim — *CPS Inc.*
Tovrog, Dan — *CPS Inc.*
Tracey, Jack — *Management Assistance Group, Inc.*
Troup, Roger — *The McCormick Group, Inc.*
Truax, Kevin — *Key Employment Services*
Truemper, Dean — *CPS Inc.*
Tryon, Katey — *DeFrain, Mayer, Lee & Burgess LLC*
Tullberg, Tina — *CPS Inc.*
Turner, Edward K. — *Don Richard Associates of Charlotte*
Tursi, Deborah J. — *The Corporate Connection, Ltd.*
Tutwiler, Stephen — *Don Richard Associates of Tampa, Inc.*
Twiste, Craig — *Raymond Karsan Associates*
Tyler, J. Larry — *Tyler & Company*
Tyson, Richard L. — *Bonifield Associates*

Ulbert, Nancy — *Aureus Group*
Vacca, Domenic — *Romac & Associates*
Venable, William W. — *Thorndike Deland Associates*
Vergara, Gail H. — *Spencer Stuart*
Vincelette, Kathy A. — *Raymond Karsan Associates*
Visnich, L. Christine — *Bason Associates Inc.*
Voigt, John A. — *Romac & Associates*
von Stein, Scott — *Wilkinson & Ives*
Wakefield, Scott — *National Search, Inc.*
Waldman, Noah H. — *Lamalie Amrop International*
Waldoch, D. Mark — *Barnes Development Group, LLC*
Walker, Craig H. — *A.J. Burton Group, Inc.*
Walker, Ewing J. — *Ward Howell International, Inc.*
Warren, Sylvia W. — *Thorndike Deland Associates*
Wasson, Thomas W. — *Spencer Stuart*
Weinberg, Melvin — *Romac & Associates*
Weisler, Nancy — *National Search, Inc.*
West, Nancy — *Health Care Dimensions*
Weston, Corinne F. — *D.A. Kreuter Associates, Inc.*
Wheeler, Gerard H. — *A.J. Burton Group, Inc.*
Whiting, Anthony — *Johnson Smith & Knisely Accord*
Whitley, Sue Ann — *Roberts Ryan and Bentley*
Whitney, David L. — *Whitney & Associates, Inc.*
Wilder, Barry — *Rhodes Associates*
Wilder, Richard B. — *Columbia Consulting Group*
Wilkinson, Barbara — *Beall & Company, Inc.*
Wilkinson, William R. — *Wilkinson & Ives*
Williams, Angie — *Whitney & Associates, Inc.*
Williams, Gary L. — *Barnes Development Group, LLC*
Williams, Harry D. — *Jacobson Associates*
Willis, William H. — *William Willis Worldwide Inc.*
Winnewisser, William E. — *Accounting & Computer Personnel*
Winograd, Glenn — *Criterion Executive Search, Inc.*
Winston, Susan — *CPS Inc.*
Wise, J. Herbert — *Sandhurst Associates*
Wolf, Stephen M. — *Byron Leonard International, Inc.*
Womack, Joseph — *The Bankers Group*
Wood, Milton M. — *M. Wood Company*
Wright, Carl A.J. — *A.J. Burton Group, Inc.*
Wright, Charles D. — *Goodrich & Sherwood Associates, Inc.*
Wylie, Pamela — *M.A. Churchill & Associates, Inc.*
Wynkoop, Mary — *Tyler & Company*
Young, Alexander — *Messett Associates, Inc.*
Zarkin, Norman — *Rhodes Associates*
Zay, Thomas C. — *Boyden/Zay & Company*
Zona, Henry F. — *Zona & Associates, Inc.*
Zucker, Nancy — *Maximum Management Corp.*
Zwiff, Jeffrey G. — *Johnson Smith & Knisely Accord*

## 20. Manufacturing

Abbatiello, Christine Murphy — *Winter, Wyman & Company*
Abbott, Peter — *The Abbott Group, Inc.*
Abby, Daniel — *Bill Hahn Group, Inc.*
Abell, Vincent W. — *MSI International*
Adams, Jeffrey C. — *Telford, Adams & Alexander/Jeffrey C. Adams & Co., Inc.*
Aki, Alvin W. — *MSI International*
Akin, J.R. — *J.R. Akin & Company Inc.*
Alekel, Karren — *ALW Research International*
Altreuter, Rose — *ALTCO Temporary Services*
Altreuter, Rose — *The ALTCO Group*
Ambler, Peter W. — *Peter W. Ambler Company*
Ames, George C. — *Ames O'Neill Associates*
Anderson, Dean C. — *Corporate Resources Professional Placement*
Anderson, Richard — *Grant Cooper and Associates*
Andrews, J. Douglas — *Clarey & Andrews, Inc.*
Andrick, Patty — *CPS Inc.*
Angell, Tryg R. — *Tryg R. Angell Ltd.*
Apostle, George — *Search Dynamics, Inc.*
Aquavella, Charles P. — *CPA & Associates*
Argenio, Michelangelo — *Spencer Stuart*
Argentin, Jo — *Executive Placement Consultants, Inc.*
Ariail, C. Bowling — *Ariail & Associates*
Ariail, Randolph C. — *Ariail & Associates*
Arms, Douglas — *TOPAZ International, Inc.*
Arms, Douglas — *TOPAZ Legal Solutions*
Ascher, Susan P. — *The Ascher Group*
Asquith, Peter S. — *Ames Personnel Consultants, Inc.*
Aston, Kathy — *Marra Peters & Partners*
Atkins, Laurie — *Battalia Winston International*
Atkinson, S. Graham — *Raymond Karsan Associates*
Aubin, Richard E. — *Aubin International*
Austin, Jessica L. — *D.S.A. - Dixie Search Associates*
Bachmeier, Kevin — *Agra Placements International Ltd.*
Badger, Fred H. — *The Badger Group*
Bagg, Keith — *Keith Bagg & Associates Inc.*
Bagwell, Bruce — *Intersource, Ltd.*
Bailey, William A. — *TNS Partners, Inc.*

Baird, David W. — *D.W. Baird & Associates*
Baird, John — *Professional Search Consultants*
Baker, Gary M. — *Cochran, Cochran & Yale, Inc.*
Baker, Gerry — *Baker, Harris & Partners Limited*
Baker, Judith — *Search Consultants International, Inc.*
Baker, S. Joseph — *Search Consultants International, Inc.*
Balch, Randy — *CPS Inc.*
Baldwin, Keith R. — *The Baldwin Group*
Baltin, Carrie — *Search West, Inc.*
Baran, Helena — *Michael J. Cavanagh and Associates*
Barger, H. Carter — *Barger & Sargeant, Inc.*
Barlow, Ken H. — *The Cherbonnier Group, Inc.*
Barnes, Richard E. — *Barnes Development Group, LLC*
Barnes, Roanne L. — *Barnes Development Group, LLC*
Barnum, Toni M. — *Stone Murphy & Olson*
Baron, Len — *Industrial Recruiters Associates, Inc.*
Barton, Gary R. — *Barton Raben, Inc.*
Bason, Maurice L. — *Bason Associates, Inc.*
Bauman, Martin H. — *Martin H. Bauman Associates, Inc.*
Beal, Richard D. — *A.T. Kearney, Inc.*
Beall, Charles P. — *Beall & Company, Inc.*
Bean, Bill — *Professional Search Consultants*
Bearman, Linda — *Grant Cooper and Associates*
Beaudin, Elizabeth C. — *Callan Associates, Ltd.*
Beaver, Bentley H. — *The Onstott Group, Inc.*
Beaver, Robert W. — *Executive Manning Corporation*
Beckvold, John B. — *Atlantic Search Group, Inc.*
Beeson, William B. — *Lawrence-Leiter and Company*
Bell, Lindy — *F-O-R-T-U-N-E Personnel Consultants of Huntsville, Inc.*
Bennett, Jo — *Battalia Winston International*
Bergen, Anthony M. — *CFO Associates, Inc.*
Berger, Jay V. — *Morris & Berger*
Bermea, Jose — *Gaffney Management Consultants*
Berry, Harold B. — *The Hindman Company*
Besen, Douglas — *Besen Associates Inc.*
Bettick, Michael J. — *A.J. Burton Group, Inc.*
Billington, Brian — *Billington & Associates*
Billington, William H. — *Spriggs & Company, Inc.*
Bitar, Edward — *The Interface Group, Ltd./Boyden*
Black, Douglas E. — *MSI International*
Blanton, Thomas — *Blanton and Company*
Bliley, Jerry — *Spencer Stuart*
Bloomer, James E. — *L.W. Foote Company*
Boccella, Ralph — *Susan C. Goldberg Associates*
Bohn, Steve J. — *MSI International*
Booth, Otis — *A.T. Kearney, Inc.*
Borland, James — *Goodrich & Sherwood Associates, Inc.*
Bormann, Cindy Ann — *MSI International*
Bostic, James E. — *Phillips Resource Group*
Bovich, Maryann C. — *Higdon Prince Inc.*
Boyer, Heath C. — *Spencer Stuart*
Boyle, Russell E. — *Egon Zehnder International Inc.*
Brackenbury, Robert — *Bowman & Marshall, Inc.*
Brackin, James B. — *Brackin & Sayers Associates*
Brady, Colin S. — *Ward Howell International, Inc.*
Brady, Robert — *CPS Inc.*
Brandeis, Richard — *Search Consultants International, Inc.*
Bratches, Howard — *Thorndike Deland Associates*
Brennan, Jerry — *Brennan Associates*
Brennan, Timothy — *Brennan Associates*
Brenner, Mary — *Prestige Inc.*
Brentari, Michael — *Search Consultants International, Inc.*
Brieger, Steve — *Thorne, Brieger Associates Inc.*
Bright, Timothy — *MSI International*
Brocaglia, Joyce — *Alta Associates, Inc.*
Brooks, Charles — *Corporate Recruiters Ltd.*
Brophy, Melissa — *Maximum Management Corp.*
Brown, Charlene N. — *Accent on Achievement, Inc.*
Brown, D. Perry — *Don Richard Associates of Washington, D.C., Inc.*
Brown, Jeffrey W. — *Comprehensive Search*
Brown, Larry C. — *Horton International*
Brown, Michael R. — *MSI International*
Brown, S. Ross — *Egon Zehnder International Inc.*
Brown, Sandra E. — *MSI International*
Brudno, Robert J. — *Savoy Partners, Ltd.*
Bruno, Deborah F. — *The Hindman Company*
Bryant, Richard D. — *Bryant Associates, Inc.*
Bryza, Robert M. — *Robert Lowell International*
Buckles, Donna — *Cochran, Cochran & Yale, Inc.*
Budill, Edward — *Professional Search Consultants*
Bueschel, David A. — *Shepherd Bueschel & Provus, Inc.*
Bump, Gerald J. — *D.E. Foster Partners Inc.*
Burchard, Stephen R. — *Burchard & Associates, Inc.*
Burchill, Barb — *BGB Associates*
Burchill, Greg — *BGB Associates*
Burden, Gene — *The Cherbonnier Group, Inc.*
Burke, George M. — *The Burke Group*

Burke, John — *The Experts*
Burnett, Rebecca J. — *MSI International*
Burns, Alan — *The Enns Partners Inc.*
Burns, Terence N. — *D.E. Foster Partners Inc.*
Butcher, Pascale — *F-O-R-T-U-N-E Personnel Consultants of Manatee County*
Button, David R. — *The Button Group*
Cahill, Peter M. — *Peter M. Cahill Associates, Inc.*
Call, David — *Cochran, Cochran & Yale, Inc.*
Callan, Robert M. — *Callan Associates, Ltd.*
Came, Paul E. — *Paul Ray Berndtson*
Campbell, Robert Scott — *Wellington Management Group*
Campbell, W. Ross — *Egon Zehnder International Inc.*
Carideo, Joseph — *Thorndike Deland Associates*
Carlson, Judith — *Bowman & Marshall, Inc.*
Carrott, Gregory T. — *Egon Zehnder International Inc.*
Carter, Jon F. — *Egon Zehnder International Inc.*
Caruso, Kathy — *Accounting Resources, Inc.*
Case, David — *Case Executive Search*
Casey, Jean — *Peter W. Ambler Company*
Cast, Donald — *Dunhill Search International*
Cattanach, Bruce B. — *Horton International*
Cavanagh, Michael J. — *Michael J. Cavanagh and Associates*
Cavolina, Michael — *Carver Search Consultants*
Celenza, Catherine — *CPS Inc.*
Chargar, Frances — *Hunt Ltd.*
Chatterjie, Alok — *MSI International*
Chavous, C. Crawford — *Phillips Resource Group*
Cherbonnier, L. Michael — *The Cherbonnier Group, Inc.*
Christenson, H. Alan — *Christenson & Hutchison*
Christian, Jeffrey E. — *Christian & Timbers*
Christiansen, Amy — *CPS Inc.*
Christiansen, Doug — *CPS Inc.*
Citarella, Richard A. — *A.T. Kearney, Inc.*
Cizek, John T. — *Cizek Associates, Inc.*
Cizek, Marti J. — *Cizek Associates, Inc.*
Clanton, Diane — *Clanton & Co.*
Clarey, Jack R. — *Clarey & Andrews, Inc.*
Clark, Donald B. — *Paul Ray Berndtson*
Clark, James — *CPS Inc.*
Clauhsen, Elizabeth A. — *Savoy Partners, Ltd.*
Clayborne, Paul — *Prestige Inc.*
Clegg, Cynthia — *Horton International*
Cline, Mark — *NYCOR Search, Inc.*
Cohen, Michael R. — *Intech Summit Group, Inc.*
Cohen, Pamela — *TOPAZ International, Inc.*
Cohen, Pamela — *TOPAZ Legal Solutions*
Colborne, Janis M. — *AJM Professional Services*
Cole, Sharon A. — *AJM Professional Services*
Coleman, Gregory — *Strategic Associates, Inc.*
Coleman, J. Kevin — *J. Kevin Coleman & Associates, Inc.*
Collard, Joseph A. — *Spencer Stuart*
Collis, Martin — *E.L. Shore & Associates Ltd.*
Colman, Michael — *Executive Placement Consultants, Inc.*
Cona, Joseph A. — *Cona Personnel Search*
Conard, Rodney J. — *Conard Associates, Inc.*
Connaghan, Linda — *Bowman & Marshall, Inc.*
Connelly, Kevin M. — *Spencer Stuart*
Connolly, Cathryn — *Strategic Associates, Inc.*
Conway, William P. — *Phillips Resource Group*
Cooke, Jeffrey R. — *Jonas, Walters & Assoc., Inc.*
Cooke, Katherine H. — *Horton International*
Cordaro, Concetta — *Flynn, Hannock, Incorporated*
Corrigan, Gerald F. — *The Corrigan Group*
Cottingham, R.L. — *Marvin L. Silcott & Associates, Inc.*
Coulman, Karen — *CPS Inc.*
Cox, James O. — *MSI International*
Cram, Noel — *R.P. Barone Associates*
Cramer, Paul J. — *C/R Associates*
Crath, Paul F. — *Price Waterhouse*
Crist, Peter — *Crist Partners, Ltd.*
Critchley, Walter — *Cochran, Cochran & Yale, Inc.*
Cronin, Richard J. — *Hodge-Cronin & Associates, Inc.*
Crowder, Edward W. — *Crowder & Company*
Cruse, O.D. — *Spencer Stuart*
Cruz, Catherine — *TOPAZ International, Inc.*
Cruz, Catherine — *TOPAZ Legal Solutions*
Crystal, Jonathan A. — *Spencer Stuart*
Cunningham, Robert Y. — *Goodrich & Sherwood Associates, Inc.*
Cuomo, Frank — *Frank Cuomo and Associates, Inc.*
Currie, Lawrence S. — *MSI International*
Cyphers, Ralph R. — *Strategic Associates, Inc.*
Czamanske, Paul W. — *Compass Group Ltd.*
Czepiel, Susan — *CPS Inc.*
Dabich, Thomas M. — *Robert Harkins Associates, Inc.*
Damon, Richard E. — *Damon & Associates, Inc.*
Damon, Robert A. — *Spencer Stuart*
Danforth, Monica — *Search Consultants International, Inc.*

Danoff, Audrey — *Don Richard Associates of Tidewater, Inc.*
Darnell, Nadine — *Brennan Associates*
Darter, Steven M. — *People Management Northeast Incorporated*
Davis, G. Gordon — *Davis & Company*
Davis, Joel C. — *MSI International*
DeGioia, Joseph — *JDG Associates, Ltd.*
Del Prete, Karen — *Gilbert Tweed/INESA*
Delaney, Patrick — *Search West, Inc.*
Delmonico, Laura — *A.J. Burton Group, Inc.*
DeLong, Art — *Richard Kader & Associates*
Delvani-Hart, Angela — *F-O-R-T-U-N-E Personnel Consultants of Nashua, Inc.*
deMartino, Cathy — *Lucas Associates*
Demchak, James P. — *Sandhurst Associates*
Desgrosellier, Gary P. — *Personnel Unlimited/Executive Search*
deVry, Kimberly A. — *Tower Consultants, Ltd.*
Dickey, Chet W. — *Bowden & Company, Inc.*
Dieck, Daniel W. — *Dieck, Mueller & Associates, Inc.*
Dieckmann, Ralph E. — *Dieckmann & Associates, Ltd.*
Dietz, David S. — *MSI International*
DiGiovanni, Charles — *Penn Search*
DiMarchi, Paul — *DiMarchi Partners, Inc.*
Dingman, Bruce — *Robert W. Dingman Company, Inc.*
Dingman, Robert W. — *Robert W. Dingman Company, Inc.*
DiSalvo, Fred — *The Cambridge Group Ltd*
Diskin, Rochelle — *Search West, Inc.*
Divine, Robert S. — *O'Shea, Divine & Company, Inc.*
Dixon, Aris — *CPS Inc.*
Dixon, C.R. — *A la carte International*
Do, Sonnie — *Whitney & Associates, Inc.*
Doele, Donald C. — *Goodrich & Sherwood Associates, Inc.*
Dornblut, Cindy — *Ashton Computer Professionals Inc.*
Dorsey, Jim — *Ryan, Miller & Associates Inc.*
Dow, Lori — *Davidson, Laird & Associates*
Dowell, Mary K. — *Professional Search Associates*
Dreifus, Donald — *Search West, Inc.*
Dreslinski, Robert S. — *Sharrow & Associates*
Dromeshauser, Peter — *Dromeshauser Associates*
Drury, James J. — *Spencer Stuart*
Duggan, James P. — *Slayton International, Inc.*
Duley, Richard I. — *ARJay & Associates*
Dunman, Betsy L. — *Crawford & Crofford*
Dwyer, Julie — *CPS Inc.*
Dykstra, Nicolette — *CPS Inc.*
Eason, James — *JRL Executive Recruiters*
Eason, Larry E. — *JRL Executive Recruiters*
Ebeling, John A. — *Gilbert Tweed/INESA*
Eberly, Carrie — *Accounting Resources, Inc.*
Edmond, Bruce — *Corporate Recruiters Ltd.*
Edwards, Dorothy — *MSI International*
Edwards, Douglas W. — *Egon Zehnder International Inc.*
Edwards, Verba L. — *Wing Tips & Pumps, Inc.*
Eggena, Roger — *Phillips Resource Group*
Ehrgott, Elizabeth — *The Ascher Group*
Ehrhart, Jennifer — *ADOW's Executeam*
Einsele, Neil — *Agra Placements International Ltd.*
Ellis, Ted K. — *The Hindman Company*
Endres, Robert — *Sanford Rose Associates*
Enfield, Jerry J. — *Executive Manning Corporation*
England, Mark — *Austin-McGregor International*
Enns, George — *The Enns Partners Inc.*
Ervin, Darlene — *CPS Inc.*
Erwin, Lee — *Agra Placements International Ltd.*
Eton, Steven — *Search West, Inc.*
Eustis, Lucy R. — *MSI International*
Fabbro, Vivian — *A.T. Kearney, Inc.*
Fancher, Robert L. — *Bason Associates Inc.*
Farish, John G. — *Paul Ray Berndtson*
Farley, Leon A. — *Leon A. Farley Associates*
Farrow, Jerry M. — *McCormack & Farrow*
Feder, Gwen — *Egon Zehnder International Inc.*
Fee, J. Curtis — *Spencer Stuart*
Feldman, Kimberley — *Atlantic Search Group, Inc.*
Ferneborg, Jay W. — *Ferneborg & Associates, Inc.*
Ferneborg, John R. — *Ferneborg & Associates, Inc.*
Ferrara, David M. — *Intech Summit Group, Inc.*
Fifield, George C. — *Egon Zehnder International Inc.*
Fill, Clifford G. — *D.S.A. - Dixie Search Associates*
Fill, Ellyn H. — *D.S.A. - Dixie Search Associates*
Fincher, Richard P. — *Phase II Management*
Fiore, Richard — *Search Consultants International, Inc.*
Fischer, John C. — *Horton International*
Fisher, Neal — *Fisher Personnel Management Services*
Flannery, Peter — *Jonas, Walters & Assoc., Inc.*
Flora, Dodi — *Crawford & Crofford*
Fogarty, Michael — *CPS Inc.*
Folkerth, Gene — *Gene Folkerth & Associates, Inc.*
Follmer, Gary — *Agra Placements International Ltd.*

Foote, Leland W. — *L.W. Foote Company*
Foreman, David C. — *Koontz, Jeffries & Associates, Inc.*
Forman, Donald R. — *Stanton Chase International*
Foster, Dwight E. — *D.E. Foster Partners Inc.*
Fowler, Jim — *First Search America, Inc.*
Fox, Amanda C. — *Paul Ray Berndtson*
Frazier, John — *Cochran, Cochran & Yale, Inc.*
French, William G. — *Preng & Associates, Inc.*
Friedman, Donna L. — *Tower Consultants, Ltd.*
Friedman, Helen E. — *McCormack & Farrow*
Gabel, Gregory N. — *Canny, Bowen Inc.*
Gabriel, David L. — *The Arcus Group*
Gaffney, Keith — *Gaffney Management Consultants*
Gaffney, William — *Gaffney Management Consultants*
Gaines, Ronni L. — *TOPAZ International, Inc.*
Gaines, Ronni L. — *TOPAZ Legal Solutions*
Galante, Suzanne M. — *Vlcek & Company, Inc.*
Gallagher, Marilyn — *Hogan Acquisitions*
Gallagher, Terence M. — *Battalia Winston International*
Garcia, Samuel K. — *Southwestern Professional Services*
Garfinkle, Steven M. — *Battalia Winston International*
Gauthier, Robert C. — *Columbia Consulting Group*
George, Delores F. — *Delores F. George Human Resource Management & Consulting Industry*
Gerevas, Ronald E. — *Spencer Stuart*
Gerevas, Ronald E. — *Spencer Stuart*
Gibbs, John S. — *Spencer Stuart*
Gilbert, Jerry — *Gilbert & Van Campen International*
Gilbert, Patricia G. — *Lynch Miller Moore Partners, Inc.*
Gilchrist, Robert J. — *Horton International*
Giles, Joe L. — *Joe L. Giles and Associates, Inc.*
Gill, Patricia — *Columbia Consulting Group*
Gill, Susan — *Plummer & Associates, Inc.*
Gillespie, Thomas — *Professional Search Consultants*
Gilmore, Lori — *CPS Inc.*
Gilreath, James M. — *Gilreath Weatherby, Inc.*
Goar, Duane R. — *Sandhurst Associates*
Goedtke, Steven — *Southwestern Professional Services*
Gold, Stanley — *Search West, Inc.*
Goldberg, Susan C. — *Susan C. Goldberg Associates*
Goldenberg, Susan — *Grant Cooper and Associates*
Goldman, Michael L. — *Strategic Associates, Inc.*
Goldsmith, Fred J. — *Fred J. Goldsmith Associates*
Gonye, Peter K. — *Egon Zehnder International Inc.*
Gonzalez, Naomi — *McManners Associates, Inc.*
Goodman, Dawn M. — *Bason Associates Inc.*
Goodman, Victor — *Anderson Sterling Associates*
Gordon, Gerald L. — *E.G. Jones Associates, Ltd.*
Gorfinkle, Gayle — *Executive Search International*
Grady, James — *Search West, Inc.*
Graham, Dale — *CPS Inc.*
Granger, Lisa D. — *D.S.A. - Dixie Search Associates*
Grantham, John — *Grantham & Co., Inc.*
Grantham, Philip H. — *Columbia Consulting Group*
Grassl, Peter O. — *Bowman & Marshall, Inc.*
Gray, Annie — *Annie Gray Associates, Inc./The Executive Search Firm*
Greebe, Neil — *Flowers & Associates*
Green, Jane — *Phillips Resource Group*
Green, Jean — *Broward-Dobbs, Inc.*
Greene, Luke — *Broward-Dobbs, Inc.*
Grenier, Glorianne — *CPS Inc.*
Griesedieck, Joseph E. — *Spencer Stuart*
Groban, Jack — *A.T. Kearney, Inc.*
Grzybowski, Jill — *CPS Inc.*
Gurtin, Kay L. — *Executive Options, Ltd.*
Haberman, Joseph C. — *A.T. Kearney, Inc.*
Halek, Frederick D. — *Sanford Rose Associates*
Hall, Robert — *Don Richard Associates of Tidewater, Inc.*
Hallock, Peter B. — *Goodrich & Sherwood Associates, Inc.*
Halyburton, Robert R. — *The Halyburton Co., Inc.*
Hannock, Elwin W. — *Flynn, Hannock, Incorporated*
Hansen, David G. — *Ott & Hansen, Inc.*
Hanson, Grant M. — *Goodrich & Sherwood Associates, Inc.*
Harbaugh, Paul J. — *International Management Advisors, Inc.*
Harbert, David O. — *Sweeney Harbert & Mummert, Inc.*
Hardison, Richard L. — *Hardison & Company*
Harfenist, Harry — *Parker Page Group*
Hargis, N. Leann — *Montgomery Resources, Inc.*
Harkins, Robert E. — *Robert Harkins Associates, Inc.*
Haro, Adolfo Medina — *Egon Zehnder International Inc.*
Harris, Ethel S. — *Don Richard Associates of Charlotte*
Harris, Jack — *Baker, Harris & Partners Limited*
Harrison, Priscilla — *Phillips Resource Group*
Hart, Robert T. — *D.E. Foster Partners Inc.*
Harvey, Mike — *Advanced Executive Resources*
Harvey, Richard — *Price Waterhouse*
Haughton, Michael — *DeFrain, Mayer, Lee & Burgess LLC*

Hauswirth, Jeffrey M. — *Spencer Stuart*
Havener, Donald Clarke — *The Abbott Group, Inc.*
Hawksworth, A. Dwight — *A.D. & Associates Executive Search, Inc.*
Hay, William E. — *William E. Hay & Company*
Haystead, Steve — *Advanced Executive Resources*
Hazerjian, Cynthia — *CPS Inc.*
Heafey, Bill — *CPS Inc.*
Hecker, Henry C. — *Hogan Acquisitions*
Heiken, Barbara E. — *Randell-Heiken, Inc.*
Hellebusch, Jerry — *Morgan Hunter Corp.*
Heller, Steven A. — *Martin H. Bauman Associates, Inc.*
Hellinger, Audrey — *Martin H. Bauman Associates, Inc.*
Helminiak, Audrey — *Gaffney Management Consultants*
Hemingway, Stuart C. — *Robison & Associates*
Heneghan, Donald A. — *Allerton Heneghan & O'Neill*
Henn, George W. — *G.W. Henn & Company*
Henshaw, Robert — *F-O-R-T-U-N-E Personnel Consultants of Huntsville, Inc.*
Hensley, Gayla — *Atlantic Search Group, Inc.*
Herman, Pat — *Whitney & Associates, Inc.*
Hertan, Richard L. — *Executive Manning Corporation*
Hertan, Wiliam A. — *Executive Manning Corporation*
Hicks, Albert M. — *Phillips Resource Group*
Hildebrand, Thomas B. — *Professional Resources Group, Inc.*
Hill, Emery — *MSI International*
Hillen, Skip — *The McCormick Group, Inc.*
Hilliker, Alan D. — *Egon Zehnder International Inc.*
Hillyer, Robert L. — *Executive Manning Corporation*
Hindman, Neil C. — *The Hindman Company*
Hite, William A. — *Hite Executive Search*
Hoevel, Michael J. — *Poirier, Hoevel & Co.*
Hogan, Larry H. — *Hogan Acquisitions*
Holden, Richard B. — *Ames Personnel Consultants, Inc.*
Holland, Kathleen — *TOPAZ International, Inc.*
Holland, Kathleen — *TOPAZ Legal Solutions*
Holmes, Lawrence J. — *Columbia Consulting Group*
Holtz, Gene — *Agra Placements International Ltd.*
Hopkins, Chester A. — *Handy HRM Corp.*
Hoppert, Phil — *Wargo and Co., Inc.*
Horgan, Thomas F. — *Nadzam, Lusk, Horgan & Associates, Inc.*
Horton, Robert H. — *Horton International*
Houchins, William N. — *Christian & Timbers*
Howe, Vance A. — *Ward Howell International, Inc.*
Howell, Robert B. — *Atlantic Search Group, Inc.*
Howell, Robert B. — *Atlantic Search Group, Inc.*
Hoyda, Louis A. — *Thorndike Deland Associates*
Hubert, David L. — *ARJay & Associates*
Hucko, Donald S. — *Jonas, Walters & Assoc., Inc.*
Hughes, Cathy N. — *The Ogdon Partnership*
Hughes, James J. — *R.P. Barone Associates*
Hunter, Gabe — *Phillips Resource Group*
Hunter, Steven — *Diamond Tax Recruiting*
Hutchinson, Loretta M. — *Hutchinson Resources International*
Hutchison, Richard H. — *Rurak & Associates, Inc.*
Hutchison, William K. — *Christenson & Hutchison*
Hutton, Thomas J. — *The Thomas Tucker Company*
Hyde, W. Jerry — *Hyde Danforth Wold & Co.*
Hykes, Don A. — *A.T. Kearney, Inc.*
Hypes, Richard G. — *Lynch Miller Moore Partners, Inc.*
Iacovelli, Heather — *CPS Inc.*
Iammatteo, Enzo — *Keith Bagg & Associates Inc.*
Ingalls, Joseph M. — *John Kurosky & Associates*
Ingram, D. John — *Ingram & Aydelotte Inc.*
Inguagiato, Gregory — *MSI International*
Inzinna, Dennis — *AlternaStaff*
Irish, Alan — *CPS Inc.*
Irvine, Robert — *Keith Bagg & Associates Inc.*
Issacs, Judith A. — *Grant Cooper and Associates*
Ives, Richard K. — *Wilkinson & Ives*
Jablo, Steven — *Dieckmann & Associates, Ltd.*
Jackson, Clarke H. — *The Caldwell Partners Amrop International*
Jacobs, Martin J. — *The Rubicon Group*
Jacobs, Mike — *Thorne, Brieger Associates Inc.*
Jacobson, Donald — *Hunt Advisory Services*
Jacobson, Donald — *Hunt Ltd.*
Jaedike, Eldron — *Prestige Inc.*
James, Bruce — *Roberson and Company*
James, Richard — *Criterion Executive Search, Inc.*
Jensen, Stephanie — *Don Richard Associates of Tidewater, Inc.*
Joffe, Barry — *Bason Associates Inc.*
Johnson, Brian — *A.J. Burton Group, Inc.*
Johnson, David — *Gaffney Management Consultants*
Johnson, Douglas — *Quality Search*
Johnson, John W. — *Webb, Johnson Associates, Inc.*
Johnson, Michael E. — *Sharrow & Associates*
Johnson, Priscilla — *The Johnson Group, Inc.*
Johnson, Robert J. — *Quality Search*
Johnson, Rocky — *A.T. Kearney, Inc.*

Johnson, S. Hope — *The Interface Group, Ltd./Boyden*
Jones, Daniel F. — *Atlantic Search Group, Inc.*
Jones, Gary — *BGB Associates*
Jones, Jeffrey — *AJM Professional Services*
Jones, Ronald T. — *ARJay & Associates*
Juelis, John J. — *Peeney Associates*
Juratovac, Michael — *Montgomery Resources, Inc.*
Juska, Frank — *Rusher, Loscavio & LoPresto*
Kacyn, Louis J. — *Egon Zehnder International Inc.*
Kader, Richard — *Richard Kader & Associates*
Kaiser, Donald J. — *Dunhill Search International*
Kaiser, Irene — *Dunhill Search International*
Kaiser, James G. — *Dunhill Search International*
Kanovsky, Gerald — *Career Consulting Group, Inc.*
Kanovsky, Marlene — *Career Consulting Group, Inc.*
Kanrich, Susan Azaria — *AlternaStaff*
Kaplan, Gary — *Gary Kaplan & Associates*
Kaplan, Marc — *Gary Kaplan & Associates*
Karalis, William — *CPS Inc.*
Katz, Cyndi — *Search West, Inc.*
Keesom, W. Peter — *Boyden/Zay & Company*
Keeton, Susan G. — *The Corporate Connection, Ltd.*
Kehoe, Mike — *CPS Inc.*
Kelly, Elizabeth Ann — *Wellington Management Group*
Kelly, Peter W. — *R. Rollo Associates*
Kelly, Sheri — *Strategic Associates, Inc.*
Kelsey, Micki — *Davidson, Laird & Associates*
Kelso, Patricia C. — *Barton Raben, Inc.*
Kern, Jerry L. — *ADOW's Executeam*
Kern, Kathleen G. — *ADOW's Executeam*
Kerr, John — *Search West, Inc.*
Kershaw, Lisa — *Tanton Mitchell/Paul Ray Berndtson*
Kettwig, David A. — *A.T. Kearney, Inc.*
Kilcoyne, Pat — *CPS Inc.*
King, Thomas — *Morgan Hunter Corp.*
Kinley, Kathy — *Intech Summit Group, Inc.*
Kinser, Richard E. — *Richard Kinser & Associates*
Kirkpatrick, Robert L. — *Reese Associates*
Kishbaugh, Herbert S. — *Kishbaugh Associates International*
Kkorzyniewski, Nicole — *CPS Inc.*
Klages, Constance W. — *International Management Advisors, Inc.*
Klauck, James J. — *Horton International*
Klein, Gregory A. — *A.T. Kearney, Inc.*
Kleinstein, Jonah A. — *The Kleinstein Group*
Klopfenstein, Edward L. — *Crowder & Company*
Klumpjan, Sonja — *CPS Inc.*
Knapp, Ronald A. — *Knapp Consultants*
Knight, Liz — *Plummer & Associates, Inc.*
Koblentz, Joel M. — *Egon Zehnder International Inc.*
Kochert, Don — *Summerfield Associates, Inc.*
Koehler, Frank R. — *The Koehler Group*
Kolke, Rick — *Richard, Wayne and Roberts*
Kondra, Vernon J. — *The Douglas Reiter Company, Inc.*
Koontz, Donald N. — *Koontz, Jeffries & Associates, Inc.*
Kopsick, Joseph M. — *Spencer Stuart*
Kramer, Donald — *Dunhill Personnel of Tampa, Inc.*
Kramer, Peter — *Dunhill Personnel of Tampa, Inc.*
Krejci, Stanley V. — *The Interface Group, Ltd./Boyden*
Krieger, Dennis F. — *Seiden Krieger Associates, Inc.*
Kuo, Linda — *Montgomery Resources, Inc.*
Kuper, Keith D. — *Christenson & Hutchison*
Laba, Marvin — *Marvin Laba & Associates*
Laba, Stuart M. — *Marvin Laba & Associates*
Laird, Cheryl — *CPS Inc.*
Laird, Meri — *Davidson, Laird & Associates*
Lamb, Angus K. — *Raymond Karsan Associates*
Lamb, Lynn M. — *F-O-R-T-U-N-E Personnel Consultants of Huntsville, Inc.*
Lampl, Mark — *Korn/Ferry International*
Lamson-Gran, Jill — *Accounting Resources, Inc.*
Lanctot, William D. — *Corporate Resources Professional Placement*
Land, Shaun — *Dunhill Professional Search of Irvine, Inc.*
Landry, Leo G. — *MSI International*
Larsen, Jack B. — *Jack B. Larsen & Associates*
Lasher, Charles M. — *Lasher Associates*
Latterell, Jeffrey D. — *Smith & Latterell (HRS, Inc.)*
Lawrence, David — *Agra Placements International Ltd.*
Leahy, Jan — *CPS Inc.*
Lebo, Terry — *Agra Placements International Ltd.*
LeComte, Andre — *Egon Zehnder International Inc.*
Lee, Roger — *Montgomery Resources, Inc.*
Leff, Lisa A. — *Berger and Leff*
Leininger, Dennis — *Key Employment Services*
Lejeune, Jeanette — *F-O-R-T-U-N-E Personnel Consultants of Huntsville, Inc.*
Leland, Paul — *McInturff & Associates, Inc.*
Lence, Julie Anne — *MSI International*
Lenkaitis, Lewis F. — *A.T. Kearney, Inc.*

Lennox, Charles — *Price Waterhouse*
Leslie, William H. — *Boyden/Zay & Company*
Letcher, Harvey D. — *Sandhurst Associates*
Lewicki, Christopher — *MSI International*
Lewis, Jon A. — *Sandhurst Associates*
Lindberg, Eric J. — *MSI International*
Linde, Rick — *Battalia Winston International*
Lindenmuth, Mary — *Search West, Inc.*
Lindholst, Kai — *Egon Zehnder International Inc.*
Line, Joseph T. — *Sharrow & Associates*
Linton, Leonard M. — *Byron Leonard International, Inc.*
Lipe, Jerold L. — *Compass Group Ltd.*
Little, Gary — *Agra Placements International Ltd.*
Loeb, Stephen H. — *Grant Cooper and Associates*
Loewenstein, Victor H. — *Egon Zehnder International Inc.*
Lofthouse, Cindy — *CPS Inc.*
Logan, Valarie A. — *D.S.A. - Dixie Search Associates*
Long, Thomas — *Egon Zehnder International Inc.*
Long, William G. — *McDonald, Long & Associates, Inc.*
LoPresto, Robert L. — *Rusher, Loscavio & LoPresto*
Loscavio, J. Michael — *Rusher, Loscavio & LoPresto*
Lotufo, Donald A. — *D.A.L. Associates, Inc.*
Lotz, R. James — *International Management Advisors, Inc.*
Loving, Vikki — *Intersource, Ltd.*
Lucarelli, Joan — *The Onstott Group, Inc.*
Lucas, Ronnie L. — *MSI International*
Lumsby, George N. — *International Management Advisors, Inc.*
Lynch, Charles J. — *F-O-R-T-U-N-E Personnel Consultants of Nashua, Inc.*
Lynch, Michael C. — *Lynch Miller Moore Partners, Inc.*
Lynn, Donald — *Frank Cuomo and Associates, Inc.*
Lyons, Michele R. — *R. Rollo Associates*
MacCarthy, Ann — *Columbia Consulting Group*
Macdonald, G. William — *The Macdonald Group, Inc.*
MacDougall, Andrew J. — *Spencer Stuart*
MacEachern, David — *Spencer Stuart*
Mackenna, Kathy — *Plummer & Associates, Inc.*
Mader, Stephen P. — *Christian & Timbers*
Magee, Charles R. — *Dieck, Mueller & Associates, Inc.*
Magee, Harrison R. — *Bowden & Company, Inc.*
Maher, William J. — *Johnson Smith & Knisely Accord*
Mahr, Toni — *K. Russo Associates*
Malcolm, Rod — *The Enns Partners Inc.*
Mallipudi, Anand — *Raymond Karsan Associates*
Manassero, Henri J.P. — *International Management Advisors, Inc.*
Mangum, William T. — *Thomas Mangum Company*
Manns, Alex — *Crawford & Crofford*
Manzo, Renee — *Atlantic Search Group, Inc.*
Marino, Chester — *Cochran, Cochran & Yale, Inc.*
Marion, Michael — *S.D. Kelly & Associates, Inc.*
Mark, John L. — *J.L. Mark Associates, Inc.*
Marks, Russell E. — *Webb, Johnson Associates, Inc.*
Marlow, William — *Straube Associates*
Marra, John — *Marra Peters & Partners*
Marra, John — *Marra Peters & Partners*
Marshall, Gerald — *Blair/Tech Recruiters*
Martin, Ellen — *Hunt Ltd.*
Martin, Geary D. — *Boyden/Zay & Company*
Martin, Jon — *Egon Zehnder International Inc.*
Maschal, Charles E. — *Maschal/Connors, Inc.*
Mashakas, Elizabeth — *TOPAZ International, Inc.*
Mashakas, Elizabeth — *TOPAZ Legal Solutions*
Mason, William E. — *John Kurosky & Associates*
Masse, Laurence R. — *Ward Howell International, Inc.*
Massey, H. Heath — *Robison & Associates*
Mather, David R. — *Christian & Timbers*
Mathias, Kathy — *Stone Murphy & Olson*
Matueny, Robert — *Ryan, Miller & Associates Inc.*
Mauer, Kristin — *Montgomery Resources, Inc.*
Mayes, Kay H. — *John Shell Associates, Inc.*
McAlpine, Bruce — *Keith Bagg & Associates Inc.*
McAndrews, Kathy — *CPS Inc.*
McAteer, Thomas — *Montgomery Resources, Inc.*
McBride, Jonathan E. — *McBride Associates, Inc.*
McCabe, Christopher — *Raymond Karsan Associates*
McConnell, Greg — *Winter, Wyman & Company*
McCorkle, Sam B. — *Morton, McCorkle & Associates, Inc.*
McCormack, William Reed — *MSI International*
McCreary, Charles — *Austin-McGregor International*
McDonald, Gary E. — *Agra Placements International Ltd.*
McDonald, Scott A. — *McDonald Associates International*
McDonald, Stanleigh B. — *McDonald Associates International*
McDonnell, Julie — *Technical Personnel of Minnesota*
McEwan, Paul — *Richard, Wayne and Roberts*
McGovern, Terence — *Korn/Ferry International*
McGrath, Robert E. — *Robert E. McGrath & Associates*
McGuire, Bud — *Search West, Inc.*
McGuire, Corey — *Peter W. Ambler Company*

McInturff, Robert — *McInturff & Associates, Inc.*
McIntyre, Joel — *Phillips Resource Group*
McKinnis, Paul D. — *Paul Ray Berndtson*
McMahon, Mark J. — *A.T. Kearney, Inc.*
McManners, Donald E. — *McManners Associates, Inc.*
McNamara, Timothy C. — *Columbia Consulting Group*
McNear, Jeffrey E. — *Barrett Partners*
McNichols, Walter B. — *Gary Kaplan & Associates*
McQuoid, David — *A.T. Kearney, Inc.*
McSherry, James F. — *Battalia Winston International*
McSherry, Terrence J. — *Paul Ray Berndtson*
Meagher, Patricia G. — *Spencer Stuart*
Mefford, Bob — *Executive Manning Corporation*
Meier, J. Dale — *Grant Cooper and Associates*
Meiland, A. Daniel — *Egon Zehnder International Inc.*
Meltzer, Andrea Y. — *Executive Options, Ltd.*
Menendez, Todd — *Don Richard Associates of Tampa, Inc.*
Menk, Carl W. — *Canny, Bowen Inc.*
Mertensotto, Chuck H. — *Whitney & Associates, Inc.*
Messett, William J. — *Messett Associates, Inc.*
Metz, Alex — *Hunt Ltd.*
Meyer, Stacey — *Gary Kaplan & Associates*
Meyer, William — *Agra Placements International Ltd.*
Meyers, Steven — *Montgomery Resources, Inc.*
Michaels, Joseph — *CPS Inc.*
Michaels, Stewart — *TOPAZ International, Inc.*
Michaels, Stewart — *TOPAZ Legal Solutions*
Mierzwinski, John — *Industrial Recruiters Associates, Inc.*
Miller, George N. — *Hite Executive Search*
Miller, Michael R. — *Lynch Miller Moore Partners, Inc.*
Miller, Roy — *The Enns Partners Inc.*
Miller, Russel E. — *ARJay & Associates*
Milstein, Bonnie — *Marvin Laba & Associates*
Milton, Suzanne — *Marra Peters & Partners*
Mirtz, P. John — *Mirtz Morice, Inc.*
Mitchell, John T. — *Paul Ray Berndtson*
Mitchell, Norman F. — *A.T. Kearney, Inc.*
Mitton, Bill — *Executive Resource, Inc.*
Moerbe, Ed H. — *Stanton Chase International*
Mogul, Gene — *Mogul Consultants, Inc.*
Mohr, Brian — *CPS Inc.*
Molitor, John L. — *Barrett Partners*
Molnar, Robert A. — *Johnson Smith & Knisely Accord*
Montgomery, James M. — *Houze, Shourds & Montgomery, Inc.*
Moore, David S. — *Lynch Miller Moore Partners, Inc.*
Moore, Denise — *Jonas, Walters & Assoc., Inc.*
Moore, Mark — *Wheeler, Moore & Elam Co.*
Moore, Michael — *Agra Placements International Ltd.*
Moore, Thomas — *Aureus Group*
Moran, Gail — *Comprehensive Search*
Morgan, Richard J. — *Morgan Samuels Co., Inc.*
Morice, James L. — *Mirtz Morice, Inc.*
Morris, Kristine A. — *Morris & Berger*
Mueller, Michael S. — *Dieck, Mueller & Associates, Inc.*
Mueller-Maerki, Fortunat F. — *Egon Zehnder International Inc.*
Muendel, H. Edward — *Stanton Chase International*
Muller, Charles A. — *AJM Professional Services*
Murphy, Cornelius J. — *Goodrich & Sherwood Associates, Inc.*
Murphy, Gary J. — *Stone Murphy & Olson*
Murphy, Patrick J. — *P.J. Murphy & Associates, Inc.*
Mursuli, Meredith — *Lasher Associates*
Mydlach, Renee — *CPS Inc.*
Nadherny, Christopher C. — *Spencer Stuart*
Nagler, Leon G. — *Nagler, Robins & Poe, Inc.*
Neelin, Sharon — *The Caldwell Partners Amrop International*
Neff, Thomas J. — *Spencer Stuart*
Neidhart, Craig C. — *TNS Partners, Inc.*
Nephew, Robert — *Christian & Timbers*
Neuberth, Jeffrey G. — *Canny, Bowen Inc.*
Newbold, Michael — *Agra Placements International Ltd.*
Newman, Lynn — *Kishbaugh Associates International*
Nicastro, Kelley P. — *A la carte International*
Noll, Robert J. — *The Hindman Company*
Nordland, Martin N. — *Horton International*
Norman, Randy — *Austin-McGregor International*
Norsell, Paul E. — *Paul Norsell & Associates, Inc.*
Nunziata, Peter — *Atlantic Search Group, Inc.*
Nutter, Roger — *Raymond Karsan Associates*
Nymark, John — *NYCOR Search, Inc.*
Nymark, Paul — *NYCOR Search, Inc.*
O'Connell, Mary — *CPS Inc.*
O'Hara, Daniel M. — *Lynch Miller Moore Partners, Inc.*
O'Neill, James P. — *Allerton Heneghan & O'Neill*
Oaks, Robert — *Search West, Inc.*
Oliver, Phoebe — *Seiden Krieger Associates, Inc.*
Oller, Jose E. — *Ward Howell International, Inc.*
Olsen, Carl — *A.T. Kearney, Inc.*
Onstott, Joseph E. — *The Onstott Group, Inc.*

Oswald, Mark G. — *Canny, Bowen Inc.*
Ott, George W. — *Ott & Hansen, Inc.*
Ottenritter, Chris — *CPS Inc.*
Owens, Ken — *F-O-R-T-U-N-E Personnel Consultants of Huntsville, Inc.*
Pace, Susan A. — *Horton International*
Padilla, Jose Sanchez — *Egon Zehnder International Inc.*
Page, Linda — *Jonas, Walters & Assoc., Inc.*
Page, Linda M. — *Wargo and Co., Inc.*
Palma, Frank R. — *Goodrich & Sherwood Associates, Inc.*
Palmer, James H. — *The Hindman Company*
Palmer, Melissa — *Don Richard Associates of Tampa, Inc.*
Papciak, Dennis J. — *Accounting Personnel Associates, Inc.*
Papciak, Dennis J. — *Temporary Accounting Personnel*
Pappas, Jim — *Search Dynamics, Inc.*
Pappas, Timothy C. — *Jonas, Walters & Assoc., Inc.*
Parker, Murray B. — *The Borton Wallace Company*
Parry, William H. — *Horton International*
Pastrana, Dario — *Egon Zehnder International Inc.*
Patton, Mitchell — *Patton/Perry Associates, Inc.*
Paul, Lisa D. — *Merit Resource Group, Inc.*
Payette, Pierre — *Egon Zehnder International Inc.*
Paynter, Sandra L. — *Ward Howell International, Inc.*
Pedley, Jill — *CPS Inc.*
Peeney, James D. — *Peeney Associates*
Pelisson, Charles — *Marra Peters & Partners*
Perkins, Daphne — *CPS Inc.*
Perry, Richard — *McManners Associates, Inc.*
Persky, Barry — *Barry Persky & Company, Inc.*
Peters, James N. — *TNS Partners, Inc.*
Peterson, John — *CPS Inc.*
Petrides, Andrew S. — *ARJay & Associates*
Petty, J. Scott — *The Arcus Group*
Pfeiffer, Irene — *Price Waterhouse*
Pfister, Shelli — *Jack B. Larsen & Associates*
Phelps, Gene L. — *McCormack & Farrow*
Phillips, Bill — *Dunhill Search International*
Phillips, Donald L. — *O'Shea, Divine & Company, Inc.*
Pickering, Dale — *Agri-Tech Personnel, Inc.*
Pierce, Nicholas J. — *Paul Ray Berndtson*
Pinkman, Karen N. — *Skott/Edwards Consultants, Inc.*
Pinson, Stephanie L. — *Gilbert Tweed/INESA*
Pitts, Charles — *Contemporary Management Services, Inc.*
Plessner, Rene — *Rene Plessner Associates, Inc.*
Plummer, John — *Plummer & Associates, Inc.*
Poirier, Roland — *Poirier, Hoevel & Co.*
Pomerance, Mark — *CPS Inc.*
Pomeroy, T. Lee — *Egon Zehnder International Inc.*
Pompeo, Paul — *Search West, Inc.*
Poore, Larry D. — *Ward Howell International, Inc.*
Porada, Stephen D. — *CAP Inc.*
Porter, Albert — *The Experts*
Potter, Douglas C. — *Stanton Chase International*
Prencipe, V. Michael — *Raymond Karsan Associates*
Preschlack, Jack E. — *Spencer Stuart*
Price, Andrew G. — *The Thomas Tucker Company*
Prior, Donald — *The Caldwell Partners Amrop International*
Proct, Nina — *Martin H. Bauman Associates, Inc.*
Prosser, Shane — *Search Consultants International, Inc.*
Provus, Barbara L. — *Shepherd Bueschel & Provus, Inc.*
Pryde, Marcia P. — *A.T. Kearney, Inc.*
Pugliese, Vincent — *Search West, Inc.*
Pugrant, Mark A. — *Grant/Morgan Associates, Inc.*
Raab, Julie — *Dunhill Professional Search of Irvine, Inc.*
Rabinowitz, Peter A. — *P.A.R. Associates Inc.*
Rachels, John W. — *Southwestern Professional Services*
Ramler, Carolyn S. — *The Corporate Connection, Ltd.*
Randell, James E. — *Randell-Heiken, Inc.*
Range, Mary Jane — *Ingram & Aydelotte Inc.*
Rapoport, William — *Blair/Tech Recruiters*
Rathbone, Kenneth J. — *Blair/Tech Recruiters*
Ray, Marianne C. — *Callan Associates, Ltd.*
Raymond, Anne — *Anderson Sterling Associates*
Raymond, Jean — *The Caldwell Partners Amrop International*
Reddicks, Nate — *Search West, Inc.*
Redding, Denise — *The Douglas Reiter Company, Inc.*
Reece, Christopher S. — *Reece & Mruk Partners*
Reese, Charles D. — *Reese Associates*
Reiser, Ellen — *Thorndike Deland Associates*
Reiter, Douglas — *The Douglas Reiter Company, Inc.*
Rendl, Ric — *CPS Inc.*
Renner, Sandra L. — *Spectra International Inc.*
Reyman, Susan — *S. Reyman & Associates Ltd.*
Rice, Douglas — *Agra Placements International Ltd.*
Richard, Albert L. — *Human Resources Inc.*
Riederer, Larry — *CPS Inc.*
Rieger, Louis J. — *Spencer Stuart*
Riley, James — *Hunt Ltd.*

Rimmel, James E. — *The Hindman Company*
Roberts, Carl R. — *Southwestern Professional Services*
Roberts, Nick P. — *Spectrum Search Associates, Inc.*
Roberts, Scott B. — *Wargo and Co., Inc.*
Roberts, William — *Cochran, Cochran & Yale, Inc.*
Robertson, John H.C. — *Sanford Rose Associates*
Robertson, William R. — *Ward Howell International, Inc.*
Robins, Jeri N. — *Nagler, Robins & Poe, Inc.*
Robinson, Bruce — *Bruce Robinson Associates*
Robinson, Eric B. — *Bruce Robinson Associates*
Robison, John H. — *Robison & Associates*
Rodgers, John — *Agra Placements International Ltd.*
Rodgers, Kathi — *St. Lawrence International, Inc.*
Roehrig, Kurt W. — *AJM Professional Services*
Rollo, Robert S. — *R. Rollo Associates*
Romanchek, Walter R. — *Wellington Management Group*
Ross, Lawrence — *Lovas Stanley/Paul Ray Berndtson Inc.*
Ross, Marc A. — *Flowers & Associates*
Ross, Mark S. — *Herman Smith Executive Initiatives Inc.*
Ross, William J. — *Flowers & Associates*
Rossi, Silvio — *Keith Bagg & Associates Inc.*
Rotella, Marshall W. — *The Corporate Connection, Ltd.*
Roth, Robert J. — *Williams, Roth & Krueger Inc.*
Rozan, Naomi — *Comprehensive Search*
Rozner, Burton L. — *Oliver & Rozner Associates, Inc.*
Rudzinsky, Jeffrey — *Louis Rudzinsky Associates*
Russo, Karen — *K. Russo Associates*
Russo, Karen — *Maximum Management Corp.*
Ryan, Lee — *Ryan, Miller & Associates Inc.*
Sabat, Lori S. — *Alta Associates, Inc.*
Sacerdote, John — *Raymond Karsan Associates*
Sahagian, John — *Human Resources Inc.*
Sahlas, Chrissy — *CPS Inc.*
Saletra, Andrew — *CPS Inc.*
Sammons, James A. — *Prestige Inc.*
Samuels, Lewis J. — *Morgan Samuels Co., Inc.*
Sanders, Natalie — *CPS Inc.*
Sanders, Spencer H. — *Battalia Winston International*
Sandor, Richard J. — *Flynn, Hannock, Incorporated*
Sangster, Jeffrey — *F-O-R-T-U-N-E Personnel Consultants of Manatee County*
Sapperstein, Jerry S. — *CFO Associates, Inc.*
Sarn, Allan G. — *Allan Sarn Associates Inc.*
Sathe, Mark A. — *Sathe & Associates, Inc.*
Sawyer, Patricia L. — *Smith & Sawyer Inc.*
Sayers, Bruce D. — *Brackin & Sayers Associates*
Scalamera, Tom — *CPS Inc.*
Schaefer, Frederic M. — *A.T. Kearney, Inc.*
Schappell, Marc P. — *Egon Zehnder International Inc.*
Scharett, Carol — *St. Lawrence International, Inc.*
Schlecht, Nancy — *Morgan Samuels Co., Inc.*
Schlpma, Christine — *Advanced Executive Resources*
Schneider, Perry — *Agra Placements International Ltd.*
Schneiderman, Gerald — *Management Resource Associates, Inc.*
Schroeder, John W. — *Spencer Stuart*
Schueneman, David — *CPS Inc.*
Schwartz, Carole — *A.T. Kearney, Inc.*
Scranton, Lisa — *A.J. Burton Group, Inc.*
Seals, Sonny — *A.T. Kearney, Inc.*
Seiden, Steven A. — *Seiden Krieger Associates, Inc.*
Seitz, Charles J. — *Neail Behringer Consultants*
Sekera, Roger I. — *A.T. Kearney, Inc.*
Selko, Philip W. — *Hogan Acquisitions*
Semyan, John K. — *TNS Partners, Inc.*
Serwat, Leonard A. — *Spencer Stuart*
Sevilla, Claudio A. — *Crawford & Crofford*
Shamir, Ben — *S.D. Kelly & Associates, Inc.*
Shapiro, Elaine — *CPS Inc.*
Shattuck, Merrill B. — *M.B. Shattuck and Associates, Inc.*
Shea, Kathleen M. — *The Penn Partners, Incorporated*
Shell, John C. — *John Shell Associates, Inc.*
Shemin, Grace — *Maximum Management Corp.*
Shenfield, Peter — *Baker, Harris & Partners Limited*
Shepard, Michael J. — *MSI International*
Sherwood, Andrew — *Goodrich & Sherwood Associates, Inc.*
Shield, Nancy — *Maximum Management Corp.*
Shimp, David J. — *Lamalie Amrop International*
Shoemaker, Fred W. — *MSI International*
Shoemaker, Larry C. — *Shoemaker & Associates*
Shore, Earl L. — *E.L. Shore & Associates Ltd.*
Shourds, Mary E. — *Houze, Shourds & Montgomery, Inc.*
Sibbald, John R. — *John Sibbald Associates, Inc.*
Siegel, Pamela — *Executive Options, Ltd.*
Signer, Julie — *CPS Inc.*
Silcott, Marvin L. — *Marvin L. Silcott & Associates, Inc.*
Silvas, Stephen D. — *Roberson and Company*
Silverman, Paul M. — *The Marshall Group*

Simmons, Anneta — *F-O-R-T-U-N-E Personnel Consultants of Huntsville, Inc.*
Sinclair, Amy — *Fisher Personnel Management Services*
Sindler, Jay — *A.J. Burton Group, Inc.*
Sjogren, Dennis — *Agra Placements International Ltd.*
Skunda, Donna M. — *Allerton Heneghan & O'Neill*
Slaughter, Katherine T. — *Compass Group Ltd.*
Slayton, Richard C. — *Slayton International, Inc.*
Slayton, Richard S. — *Slayton International, Inc.*
Slosar, John M. — *Canny, Bowen Inc.*
Smead, Michelle M. — *A.T. Kearney, Inc.*
Smirnov, Tatiana — *Allan Sarn Associates Inc.*
Smith, Adam M. — *The Abbott Group, Inc.*
Smith, David P. — *Smith & Latterell (HRS, Inc.)*
Smith, Douglas M. — *Ward Howell International, Inc.*
Smith, Grant — *Price Waterhouse*
Smith, Herman M. — *Herman Smith Executive Initiatives Inc.*
Smith, John F. — *The Penn Partners, Incorporated*
Smith, Kevin — *F-O-R-T-U-N-E Personnel Consultants of Manatee County*
Smith, Marvin E. — *Parfitt Recruiting and Consulting*
Smith, Robert L. — *Smith & Sawyer Inc.*
Snodgrass, Stephen — *DeFrain, Mayer, Lee & Burgess LLC*
Snyder, James F. — *Snyder & Company*
Snyder, Thomas J. — *Spencer Stuart*
Soggs, Cheryl Pavick — *A.T. Kearney, Inc.*
Sola, George L. — *A.T. Kearney, Inc.*
Spadavecchia, Jennifer — *Alta Associates, Inc.*
Spann, Richard E. — *Goodrich & Sherwood Associates, Inc.*
Spicer, Merrilyn — *Search West, Inc.*
Sponseller, Vern — *Richard Kader & Associates*
Spriggs, Robert D. — *Spriggs & Company, Inc.*
Stahl, Cynthia — *Plummer & Associates, Inc.*
Standard, Gail — *Comprehensive Search*
Stark, Jeff — *Thorne, Brieger Associates Inc.*
Steck, Frank T. — *A.T. Kearney, Inc.*
Steenerson, Thomas L. — *MSI International*
Stein, Terry W. — *Stewart, Stein and Scott, Ltd.*
Stenberg, Edward — *Winter, Wyman & Company*
Stephenson, Don L. — *Ells Personnel System Inc.*
Stern, Stephen — *CPS Inc.*
Sterner, Doug — *CPS Inc.*
Stewart, Jan J. — *Egon Zehnder International Inc.*
Stewart, Jeffrey O. — *Stewart, Stein and Scott, Ltd.*
Stewart, Ross M. — *Human Resources Network Partners Inc.*
Stiles, Judy — *MedQuest Associates*
Stone, Susan L. — *Stone Enterprises Ltd.*
Stouffer, Dale — *Agra Placements International Ltd.*
Stouffer, Kenneth — *Keith Bagg & Associates Inc.*
Strain, Stephen R. — *Spencer Stuart*
Stringer, Dann P. — *D.E. Foster Partners Inc.*
Strom, Mark N. — *Search Advisors International Corp.*
Strong, Duane K. — *Executive Resource, Inc.*
Sturtz, James W. — *Compass Group Ltd.*
Sullivan, Kay — *Rusher, Loscavio & LoPresto*
Sur, William K. — *Canny, Bowen Inc.*
Swanson, Dick — *Raymond Karsan Associates*
Swatts, Stone — *F-O-R-T-U-N-E Personnel Consultants of Huntsville, Inc.*
Sweet, Charles W. — *A.T. Kearney, Inc.*
Swidler, J. Robert — *Egon Zehnder International Inc.*
Tanton, John E. — *Tanton Mitchell/Paul Ray Berndtson*
Taylor, Conrad G. — *MSI International*
Taylor, Kenneth W. — *Egon Zehnder International Inc.*
Telford, John H. — *Telford, Adams & Alexander/Telford & Co., Inc.*
Theobald, David B. — *Theobald & Associates*
Thielman, Joseph — *Barrett Partners*
Thomas, Cheryl M. — *CPS Inc.*
Thomas, John T. — *Ward Howell International, Inc.*
Thomas, Kim — *CPS Inc.*
Thomas, Kurt J. — *P.J. Murphy & Associates, Inc.*
Thompson, Dave — *Battalia Winston International*
Thompson, Kenneth L. — *McCormack & Farrow*
Tootsey, Mark A. — *A.J. Burton Group, Inc.*
Tovrog, Dan — *CPS Inc.*
Tracey, Jack — *Management Assistance Group, Inc.*
Tracy, Ronald O. — *Egon Zehnder International Inc.*
Trueblood, Brian G. — *TNS Partners, Inc.*
Truemper, Dean — *CPS Inc.*
Truex, John F. — *Morton, McCorkle & Associates, Inc.*
Truitt, Thomas B. — *Southwestern Professional Services*
Tryon, Katey — *DeFrain, Mayer, Lee & Burgess LLC*
Tucker, Thomas A. — *The Thomas Tucker Company*
Tullberg, Tina — *CPS Inc.*
Tunney, William — *Grant Cooper and Associates*
Turner, Edward K. — *Don Richard Associates of Charlotte*
Tursi, Deborah J. — *The Corporate Connection, Ltd.*
Tutwiler, Stephen — *Don Richard Associates of Tampa, Inc.*

Tweed, Janet — *Gilbert Tweed/INESA*
Twiste, Craig — *Raymond Karsan Associates*
Ulbert, Nancy — *Aureus Group*
Utroska, Donald R. — *Lamalie Amrop International*
Van Alstine, Catherine — *Tanton Mitchell/Paul Ray Berndtson*
Van Campen, Jerry — *Gilbert & Van Campen International*
Van Clieaf, Mark — *MVC Associates International*
Van Steenkiste, Julie — *Davidson, Laird & Associates*
Vann, Dianne — *The Button Group*
Vaughan, David B. — *Dunhill Professional Search of Irvine, Inc.*
Velten, Mark — *Hunt Advisory Services*
Velten, Mark — *Hunt Ltd.*
Venable, William W. — *Thorndike Deland Associates*
Vennat, Manon — *Spencer Stuart*
Visnich, L. Christine — *Bason Associates Inc.*
Vlcek, Thomas J. — *Vlcek & Company, Inc.*
Vogel, Michael S. — *Vogel Associates*
Vogus, Jerry — *Cumberland Group Inc.*
von Stein, Scott — *Wilkinson & Ives*
Vossler, James — *A.J. Burton Group, Inc.*
Waggoner, Lisa — *Intersource, Inc.*
Waldoch, D. Mark — *Barnes Development Group, LLC*
Waldrop, Gary R. — *MSI International*
Walker, Craig H. — *A.J. Burton Group, Inc.*
Wallace, Dennis M. — *Sanford Rose Associates*
Walters, William F. — *Jonas, Walters & Assoc., Inc.*
Warren, Sylvia W. — *Thorndike Deland Associates*
Wassill, Larry — *Corporate Recruiters Ltd.*
Wasson, Thomas W. — *Spencer Stuart*
Watson, James — *MSI International*
Webb, George H. — *Webb, Johnson Associates, Inc.*
Webb, Shawn K. — *MSI International*
Weiner, Arlene — *Sanford Rose Associates*
Weiner, Arthur — *Sanford Rose Associates*
Weissman-Rosenthal, Abbe — *ALW Research International*
Weisz, Laura — *Anderson Sterling Associates*
Welsh, Jason — *Ells Personnel System Inc.*
Wheeler, Gerard H. — *A.J. Burton Group, Inc.*
White, Jonathan O. — *The Badger Group*
Whitney, David L. — *Whitney & Associates, Inc.*
Wier, Daniel — *Horton International*
Wilder, Richard B. — *Columbia Consulting Group*
Wilkinson, William R. — *Wilkinson & Ives*
Williams, Angie — *Whitney & Associates, Inc.*
Williams, Gary L. — *Barnes Development Group, LLC*
Williams, Lis — *Executive Options, Ltd.*
Williams, Roger K. — *Williams, Roth & Krueger Inc.*
Willis, William H. — *William Willis Worldwide Inc.*
Wilson, Patricia L. — *Leon A. Farley Associates*
Winnewisser, William E. — *Accounting & Computer Personnel*
Winograd, Glenn — *Criterion Executive Search, Inc.*
Winston, Dale — *Battalia Winston International*
Winston, Susan — *CPS Inc.*
Wirtshafter, Linda — *Grant Cooper and Associates*
Wise, J. Herbert — *Sandhurst Associates*
Witte, David L. — *Ward Howell International, Inc.*
Wood, John S. — *Egon Zehnder International Inc.*
Wooller, Edmund A.M. — *Windsor International*
Woollett, James — *Rusher, Loscavio & LoPresto*
Wotipka, Lee — *Search West, Inc.*
Wright, Charles D. — *Goodrich & Sherwood Associates, Inc.*
Wyatt, James — *Wyatt & Jaffe*
Young, Alexander — *Messett Associates, Inc.*
Young, Charles E. — *Flowers & Associates*
Youngs, Donald L. — *Youngs & Company*
Zaffrann, Craig S. — *P.J. Murphy & Associates, Inc.*
Zahradka, James F. — *P.J. Murphy & Associates, Inc.*
Zak, Adam — *Adams & Associates International*
Zarkin, Norman — *The Zarkin Group, Inc.*
Zarnoski, Hank — *Dunhill Search International*
Zaslav, Debra M. — *Telford, Adams & Alexander/Telford & Co., Inc.*
Zetter, Roger — *Hunt Ltd.*
Zilliacus, Patrick W. — *Larsen, Zilliacus & Associates, Inc.*
Zucker, Nancy — *Maximum Management Corp.*

## 21. Non-Profit

Abbott, Peter — *The Abbott Group, Inc.*
Abruzzo, James — *A.T. Kearney, Inc.*
Adams, Jeffrey C. — *Telford, Adams & Alexander/Jeffrey C. Adams & Co., Inc.*
Alekel, Karren — *ALW Research International*
Altreuter, Rose — *The ALTCO Group*
Ambler, Peter W. — *Peter W. Ambler Company*
Anderson, Richard — *Grant Cooper and Associates*
Ast, Steven T. — *Ast/Bryant*
Bagg, Mary — *Keith Bagg & Associates Inc.*
Baker, Jim — *Southwestern Professional Services*

Baker-Greene, Edward — *Isaacson, Miller*
Baldwin, Keith R. — *The Baldwin Group*
Baran, Helena — *Michael J. Cavanagh and Associates*
Barnes, Richard E. — *Barnes Development Group, LLC*
Barnes, Roanne L. — *Barnes Development Group, LLC*
Bates, Scott W. — *Kittleman & Associates*
Bearman, Linda — *Grant Cooper and Associates*
Beeson, William B. — *Lawrence-Leiter and Company*
Belford, Paul — *JDG Associates, Ltd.*
Bell, Michael — *Spencer Stuart*
Bennett, Jo — *Battalia Winston International*
Berger, Emanuel — *Isaacson, Miller*
Berger, Jay V. — *Morris & Berger*
Biggins, J. Veronica — *Heidrick & Struggles, Inc.*
Billington, Brian — *Billington & Associates*
Bitar, Edward — *The Interface Group, Ltd./Boyden*
Blackmon, Sharon — *The Abbott Group, Inc.*
Blair, Kelly A. — *The Caldwell Partners Amrop International*
Booth, Otis — *A.T. Kearney, Inc.*
Bowen, William J. — *Heidrick & Struggles, Inc.*
Brooks, Bernard E. — *Mruk & Partners/EMA Partners Int'l*
Brown, Buzz — *Brown, Bernardy, Van Remmen, Inc.*
Brown, D. Perry — *Don Richard Associates of Washington, D.C., Inc.*
Brunelle, Francis W.H. — *The Caldwell Partners Amrop International*
Bryant, Christopher P. — *Ast/Bryant*
Bueschel, David A. — *Shepherd Bueschel & Provus, Inc.*
Burns, Terence N. — *D.E. Foster Partners Inc.*
Caldwell, C. Douglas — *The Caldwell Partners Amrop International*
Castine, Michael P. — *Spencer Stuart*
Caudill, Nancy — *Webb, Johnson Associates, Inc.*
Cavanagh, Michael J. — *Michael J. Cavanagh and Associates*
Chan, Margaret — *Webb, Johnson Associates, Inc.*
Chauvin, Ralph A. — *The Caldwell Partners Amrop International*
Christenson, H. Alan — *Christenson & Hutchison*
Citera, Tom — *Howe-Lewis International*
Cizek, Marti J. — *Cizek Associates, Inc.*
Cleeve, Coleen — *Howe-Lewis International*
Clovis, James R. — *Handy HRM Corp.*
Collard, Joseph A. — *Spencer Stuart*
Colling, Douglas — *KPMG Management Consulting*
Collins, Mollie P. — *Belvedere Partners*
Collis, Martin — *E.L. Shore & Associates Ltd.*
Condit, Madeleine — *Korn/Ferry International*
Corrigan, Gerald F. — *The Corrigan Group*
Costick, Kathryn J. — *John Sibbald Associates, Inc.*
Crawford, Cassondra — *Don Richard Associates of Washington, D.C., Inc.*
D'Alessio, Gary A. — *Chicago Legal Search, Ltd.*
Dalton, Bret — *Robert W. Dingman Company, Inc.*
DeCorrevont, James — *DeCorrevont & Associates*
DeCorrevont, James — *DeCorrevont & Associates*
DeHart, Donna — *Tower Consultants, Ltd.*
Delaney, Patrick J. — *Sensible Solutions, Inc.*
Dickey, Chet W. — *Bowden & Company, Inc.*
Dingman, Bruce — *Robert W. Dingman Company, Inc.*
Dingman, Robert W. — *Robert W. Dingman Company, Inc.*
Dinwiddie, Jill — *Belvedere Partners*
Divine, Robert S. — *O'Shea, Divine & Company, Inc.*
Doliva, Lauren M. — *Heidrick & Struggles, Inc.*
Edell, David E. — *The Development Resource Group Incorporated*
Eldredge, L. Lincoln — *Lamalie Amrop International*
Emmott, Carol B. — *Spencer Stuart*
Farrow, Jerry M. — *McCormack & Farrow*
Fawcett, Anne M. — *The Caldwell Partners Amrop International*
Flannery, Peter — *Jonas, Walters & Assoc., Inc.*
Forest, Adam — *McCormack & Associates*
Foy, Richard — *Boyden*
Frank, Valerie S. — *Norman Roberts & Associates, Inc.*
Franklin, John W. — *Russell Reynolds Associates, Inc.*
Garfinkle, Steven M. — *Battalia Winston International*
Geiger, Jan — *Wilcox, Bertoux & Miller*
Gerevas, Ronald E. — *Spencer Stuart*
Gerevas, Ronald E. — *Spencer Stuart*
Gerson, Russ D. — *Webb, Johnson Associates, Inc.*
Goldenberg, Susan — *Grant Cooper and Associates*
Gordon, Teri — *Don Richard Associates of Washington, D.C., Inc.*
Grantham, John — *Grantham & Co., Inc.*
Gray, Annie — *Annie Gray Associates, Inc./The Executive Search Firm*
Greco, Patricia — *Howe-Lewis International*
Greenwood, Janet — *Heidrick & Struggles, Inc.*
Groban, Jack — *A.T. Kearney, Inc.*
Gurtin, Kay L. — *Executive Options, Ltd.*
Halvorsen, Jeanne M. — *Kittleman & Associates*
Halyburton, Robert R. — *The Halyburton Co., Inc.*
Hamilton, Timothy — *The Caldwell Partners Amrop International*
Hansen, David G. — *Ott & Hansen, Inc.*
Harbaugh, Paul J. — *International Management Advisors, Inc.*

Harbert, David O. — *Sweeney Harbert & Mummert, Inc.*
Hard, Sally Ann — *Ast/Bryant*
Harris, Jack — *Baker, Harris & Partners Limited*
Harvey, Richard — *Price Waterhouse*
Hatcher, Joe B. — *Ast/Bryant*
Haughton, Michael — *DeFrain, Mayer, Lee & Burgess LLC*
Havener, Donald Clarke — *The Abbott Group, Inc.*
Hay, William E. — *William E. Hay & Company*
Heideman, Mary Marren — *DeFrain, Mayer, Lee & Burgess LLC*
Hemingway, Stuart C. — *Robison & Associates*
Hirsch, Julia C. — *Boyden*
Hite, William A. — *Hite Executive Search*
Hunter, John B. — *John Sibbald Associates, Inc.*
Hunter, Sue J. — *Robison & Associates*
Hutchison, Richard H. — *Rurak & Associates, Inc.*
Hutchison, William K. — *Christenson & Hutchison*
Infinger, Ronald E. — *Robison & Associates*
Isaacson, John — *Isaacson, Miller*
Issacs, Judith A. — *Grant Cooper and Associates*
Jeffers, Carol S. — *John Sibbald Associates, Inc.*
Jernigan, Susan N. — *Sockwell & Associates*
Johnson, John W. — *Webb, Johnson Associates, Inc.*
Johnson, Maxene — *Norman Roberts & Associates, Inc.*
Johnson, S. Hope — *The Interface Group, Ltd./Boyden*
Kaplan, Gary — *Gary Kaplan & Associates*
Kaplan, Marc — *Gary Kaplan & Associates*
Keeton, Susan G. — *The Corporate Connection, Ltd.*
Keller, Barbara — *Barton Raben, Inc.*
Kelly, Donna J. — *Accountants Executive Search*
Kelly, Peter W. — *R. Rollo Associates*
Kern, Ann P. — *Korn/Ferry International*
Kile, Robert W. — *Rusher, Loscavio & LoPresto*
King, Richard M. — *Kittleman & Associates*
Kixmiller, David B. — *Heidrick & Struggles, Inc.*
Klages, Constance W. — *International Management Advisors, Inc.*
Klavens, Cecile J. — *The Pickwick Group, Inc.*
Kleinstein, Jonah A. — *The Kleinstein Group*
Knisely, Gary — *Johnson Smith & Knisely Accord*
Kuper, Keith D. — *Christenson & Hutchison*
Larsen, Richard F. — *Larsen, Zilliacus & Associates, Inc.*
Lasher, Charles M. — *Lasher Associates*
Lauderback, David R. — *A.T. Kearney, Inc.*
Lauerman, Fred J. — *Development Search Specialists*
Leske, Lucy A. — *Educational Management Network*
Leske, Lucy Apthorp — *Educational Management Network*
Linde, Rick — *Battalia Winston International*
Loeb, Stephen H. — *Grant Cooper and Associates*
Long, William G. — *McDonald, Long & Associates, Inc.*
Loomis, Ruth L. — *Ast/Bryant*
Loscavio, J. Michael — *Rusher, Loscavio & LoPresto*
Lotz, R. James — *International Management Advisors, Inc.*
Low, Linda — *The Development Resource Group Incorporated*
Lucht, John — *The John Lucht Consultancy Inc.*
Lumsby, George N. — *International Management Advisors, Inc.*
Lyons, Michele R. — *R. Rollo Associates*
MacKay, Malcolm — *Russell Reynolds Associates, Inc.*
Magee, Harrison R. — *Bowden & Company, Inc.*
Makrianes, James K. — *Webb, Johnson Associates, Inc.*
Manassero, Henri J.P. — *International Management Advisors, Inc.*
Marks, Russell E. — *Webb, Johnson Associates, Inc.*
Martin, Nancy A. — *Educational Management Network*
Marumoto, William H. — *The Interface Group, Ltd./Boyden*
Massey, M. Heath — *Robison & Associates*
Mathias, Kathy — *Stone Murphy & Olson*
McBride, Jonathan E. — *McBride Associates, Inc.*
McCarthy, David R. — *Spencer Stuart*
McCormack, Joseph A. — *McCormack & Associates*
McGuire, Corey — *Peter W. Ambler Company*
McLean, B. Keith — *Price Waterhouse*
McNamara, Timothy C. — *Columbia Consulting Group*
McNichols, Walter B. — *Gary Kaplan & Associates*
McPherson, Stephen M. — *Ward Howell International, Inc.*
McRae, O. Jon — *Jon McRae & Associates, Inc.*
McSherry, James F. — *Battalia Winston International*
Meier, J. Dale — *Grant Cooper and Associates*
Meltzer, Andrea Y. — *Executive Options, Ltd.*
Messett, William J. — *Messett Associates, Inc.*
Mestepey, John — *A.T. Kearney, Inc.*
Meyer, Stacey — *Gary Kaplan & Associates*
Miller, Arnie — *Isaacson, Miller*
Miller, Diane D. — *Wilcox, Bertoux & Miller*
Mitchell, Kyle R. — *Tanton Mitchell/Paul Ray Berndtson*
Moore, Denise — *Jonas, Walters & Assoc., Inc.*
Morris, Kristine A. — *Morris & Berger*
Morton, Robert C. — *Morton, McCorkle & Associates, Inc.*
Murray, Virginia — *Baker, Harris & Partners Limited*
Mursuli, Meredith — *Lasher Associates*
Nagler, Leon G. — *Nagler, Robins & Poe, Inc.*

Neher, Robert L. — *Intech Summit Group, Inc.*
Nelson, Barbara — *Herman Smith Executive Initiatives Inc.*
Neuberth, Jeffrey G. — *Canny, Bowen Inc.*
Nordland, Martin N. — *Horton International*
O'Neill, James P. — *Allerton Heneghan & O'Neill*
Ott, George W. — *Ott & Hansen, Inc.*
Pace, Susan A. — *Horton International*
Page, G. Schuyler — *A.T. Kearney, Inc.*
Page, Linda — *Jonas, Walters & Assoc., Inc.*
Parr, James A. — *KPMG Management Consulting*
Patton, Mitchell — *Patton/Perry Associates, Inc.*
Peck, David W. — *The Peck Consultancy*
Peeney, James D. — *Peeney Associates*
Percival, Chris — *Chicago Legal Search, Ltd.*
Persky, Barry — *Barry Persky & Company, Inc.*
Pettway, Samuel H. — *Spencer Stuart*
Phelps, Gene L. — *McCormack & Farrow*
Pickford, Stephen T. — *The Corporate Staff, Inc.*
Pinson, Stephanie L. — *Gilbert Tweed/INESA*
Pittard, Patrick S. — *Heidrick & Struggles, Inc.*
Posner, Gary J. — *Educational Management Network*
Rabinowitz, Peter A. — *P.A.R. Associates Inc.*
Rackley, Eugene M. — *Heidrick & Struggles, Inc.*
Ray, Paul R. — *Paul Ray Berndtson*
Regeuye, Peter J. — *Accountants Executive Search*
Rich, Lyttleton — *Sockwell & Associates*
Rieger, Louis J. — *Spencer Stuart*
Roberts, Norman C. — *Norman Roberts & Associates, Inc.*
Robinson, Bruce — *Bruce Robinson Associates*
Robison, John H. — *Robison & Associates*
Rogers, Leah — *Dinte Resources, Incorporated*
Rollo, Robert S. — *R. Rollo Associates*
Rosenberg, Esther — *Howe-Lewis International*
Rozan, Naomi — *Comprehensive Search*
Rubinstein, Alan J. — *Chicago Legal Search, Ltd.*
Runquist, U.W. — *Webb, Johnson Associates, Inc.*
Rurak, Zbigniew T. — *Rurak & Associates, Inc.*
Russell, Richard A. — *Executive Search Consultants Corporation*
Russell, Susan Anne — *Executive Search Consultants Corporation*
Rustad, Binth — *Educational Management Network*
Schaefer, Frederic M. — *A.T. Kearney, Inc.*
Sellery, Robert A. — *Robert Sellery Associates, Ltd.*
Shattuck, Merrill B. — *M.B. Shattuck and Associates, Inc.*
Shenfield, Peter — *Baker, Harris & Partners Limited*
Sherry, Joan — *Korn/Ferry International*
Shervey, Brent C. — *O'Callaghan Honey/Paul Ray Berndtson, Inc.*
Shore, Earl L. — *E.L. Shore & Associates Ltd.*
Sibbald, John R. — *John Sibbald Associates, Inc.*
Sibul, Shelly Remen — *Chicago Legal Search, Ltd.*
Siegel, Pamela — *Executive Options, Ltd.*
Simmons, Gerald J. — *Handy HRM Corp.*
Smead, Michelle M. — *A.T. Kearney, Inc.*
Smith, Adam M. — *The Abbott Group, Inc.*
Smith, David P. — *Smith & Latterell (HRS, Inc.)*
Smith, Grant — *Price Waterhouse*
Smith, Herman M. — *Herman Smith Executive Initiatives Inc.*
Smith, Toni S. — *Spencer Stuart*
Snodgrass, Stephen — *DeFrain, Mayer, Lee & Burgess LLC*
Sockwell, J. Edgar — *Sockwell & Associates*
Stanley, Paul R.A. — *Lovas Stanley/Paul Ray Berndtson Inc.*
Sterling, Sally M. — *Heidrick & Struggles, Inc.*
Stevens, Tracey — *Don Richard Associates of Washington, D.C., Inc.*
Stivk, Barbara A. — *Thornton Resources*
Strassman, Mark — *Don Richard Associates of Washington, D.C., Inc.*
Stringer, Dann P. — *D.E. Foster Partners Inc.*
Sullivan, Catherine — *Korn/Ferry International*
Tappan, Michael A. — *Ward Howell International, Inc.*
Telford, John H. — *Telford, Adams & Alexander/Telford & Co., Inc.*
Tholke, William E. — *Canny, Bowen Inc.*
Thornton, John C. — *Thornton Resources*
Tipping, William M. — *Ward Howell International, Inc.*
Truex, John F. — *Morton, McCorkle & Associates, Inc.*
Tryon, Katey — *DeFrain, Mayer, Lee & Burgess LLC*
Tunney, William — *Grant Cooper and Associates*
Tursi, Deborah J. — *The Corporate Connection, Ltd.*
Tydings, Mary C. — *Russell Reynolds Associates, Inc.*
Van Remmen, Roger — *Brown, Bernardy, Van Remmen, Inc.*
Vennat, Manon — *Spencer Stuart*
Waldoch, D. Mark — *Barnes Development Group, LLC*
Wallace, Alec — *Tanton Mitchell/Paul Ray Berndtson*
Webb, George H. — *Webb, Johnson Associates, Inc.*
Weissman-Rosenthal, Abbe — *ALW Research International*
Wheeler, Mary T. — *Lamalie Amrop International*
Whitcomb, Nancy C. — *Educational Management Network*
Wier, Daniel — *Horton International*
Wilcox, Karen — *Isaacson, Miller*
Wilkinson, William R. — *Wilkinson & Ives*
Williams, Gary L. — *Barnes Development Group, LLC*

Williams, Lis — *Executive Options, Ltd.*
Willis, William H. — *William Willis Worldwide Inc.*
Wilson, Derrick — *Thornton Resources*
Winston, Dale — *Battalia Winston International*
Wirtshafter, Linda — *Grant Cooper and Associates*
Wooller, Edmund A.M. — *Windsor International*
Yilmaz, Muriel — *Dinte Resources, Incorporated*
Young, Alexander — *Messett Associates, Inc.*
Young, Mimi — *Educational Management Network*
Zaslav, Debra M. — *Telford, Adams & Alexander/Telford & Co., Inc.*
Zera, Ronald J. — *Spencer Stuart*
Zivic, Janis M. — *Spencer Stuart*
Zonis, Hildy R. — *Accountants Executive Search*

## 22. Oil/Gas

Alekel, Karren — *ALW Research International*
Ambler, Peter W. — *Peter W. Ambler Company*
Andrick, Patty — *CPS Inc.*
Angell, Tryg R. — *Tryg R. Angell Ltd.*
Apostle, George — *Search Dynamics, Inc.*
Bailey, William A. — *TNS Partners, Inc.*
Baird, John — *Professional Search Consultants*
Baker, Judith — *Search Consultants International, Inc.*
Baker, S. Joseph — *Search Consultants International, Inc.*
Balch, Randy — *CPS Inc.*
Barlow, Ken H. — *The Cherbonnier Group, Inc.*
Beaudin, Elizabeth C. — *Callan Associates, Ltd.*
Bellano, Robert W. — *Stanton Chase International*
Berry, Harold B. — *The Hindman Company*
Booth, Otis — *A.T. Kearney, Inc.*
Borland, James — *Goodrich & Sherwood Associates, Inc.*
Bovich, Maryann C. — *Higdon Prince Inc.*
Brady, Robert — *CPS Inc.*
Brandeis, Richard — *CPS Inc.*
Brentari, Michael — *Search Consultants International, Inc.*
Briggs, Adam — *Horton International*
Bruno, Deborah F. — *The Hindman Company*
Bryant, Richard D. — *Bryant Associates, Inc.*
Bryza, Robert M. — *Robert Lowell International*
Burden, Gene — *The Cherbonnier Group, Inc.*
Button, David R. — *The Button Group*
Caldwell, C. Douglas — *The Caldwell Partners Amrop International*
Callan, Robert M. — *Callan Associates, Ltd.*
Callihan, Diana L. — *Search Northwest Associates*
Campbell, Robert Scott — *Wellington Management Group*
Celenza, Catherine — *CPS Inc.*
Cherbonnier, L. Michael — *TCG International, Inc.*
Cherbonnier, L. Michael — *The Cherbonnier Group, Inc.*
Christiansen, Amy — *CPS Inc.*
Christiansen, Doug — *CPS Inc.*
Clarey, William A. — *Preng & Associates, Inc.*
Clark, James — *CPS Inc.*
Collard, Joseph A. — *Spencer Stuart*
Costello, Andrea L. — *Gallin Associates*
Cottingham, R.L. — *Marvin L. Silcott & Associates, Inc.*
Coulman, Karen — *CPS Inc.*
Crath, Paul F. — *Price Waterhouse*
Crystal, Jonathan A. — *Spencer Stuart*
Cunningham, Robert Y. — *Goodrich & Sherwood Associates, Inc.*
Czepiel, Susan — *CPS Inc.*
D'Alessio, Gary A. — *Chicago Legal Search, Ltd.*
Danforth, Monica — *Search Consultants International, Inc.*
Dingman, Bruce — *Robert W. Dingman Company, Inc.*
Dingman, Robert W. — *Robert W. Dingman Company, Inc.*
Diskin, Rochelle — *Search West, Inc.*
Dixon, Aris — *CPS Inc.*
Doele, Donald C. — *Goodrich & Sherwood Associates, Inc.*
Donnelly, George J. — *Ward Howell International, Inc.*
Drexler, Robert — *Robert Drexler Associates, Inc.*
Dunman, Betsy L. — *Crawford & Crofford*
Dwyer, Julie — *CPS Inc.*
Dykstra, Nicolette — *CPS Inc.*
Edwards, Verba L. — *Wing Tips & Pumps, Inc.*
Ellis, Ted K. — *The Hindman Company*
Ervin, Darlene — *CPS Inc.*
Farrow, Jerry M. — *McCormack & Farrow*
Fiore, Richard — *Search Consultants International, Inc.*
Fogarty, Michael — *CPS Inc.*
French, William G. — *Preng & Associates, Inc.*
Friedman, Helen E. — *McCormack & Farrow*
Gallin, Larry — *Gallin Associates*
Gardiner, E. Nicholas P. — *Gardiner International*
Gettys, James R. — *International Staffing Consultants, Inc.*
Gibbs, John S. — *Spencer Stuart*
Gillespie, Thomas — *Professional Search Consultants*
Gilmore, Lori — *CPS Inc.*
Gobert, Larry — *Professional Search Consultants*

Goldsmith, Fred J. — *Fred J. Goldsmith Associates*
Graham, Dale — *CPS Inc.*
Greene, Luke — *Broward-Dobbs, Inc.*
Grenier, Glorianne — *CPS Inc.*
Grzybowski, Jill — *CPS Inc.*
Hallock, Peter B. — *Goodrich & Sherwood Associates, Inc.*
Hammes, Betsy — *Search Enterprises, Inc.*
Hanson, Grant M. — *Goodrich & Sherwood Associates, Inc.*
Harbaugh, Paul J. — *International Management Advisors, Inc.*
Hardison, Richard L. — *Hardison & Company*
Harvey, Richard — *Price Waterhouse*
Haughton, Michael — *DeFrain, Mayer, Lee & Burgess LLC*
Hazerjian, Cynthia — *CPS Inc.*
Heafey, Bill — *CPS Inc.*
Heiken, Barbara E. — *Randell-Heiken, Inc.*
Hertlein, James N.J. — *Boyden/Zay & Company*
Higdon, Henry G. — *Higdon Prince Inc.*
Hindman, Neil C. — *The Hindman Company*
Honey, W. Michael M. — *O'Callaghan Honey/Paul Ray Berndtson, Inc.*
Hughes, James J. — *R.P. Barone Associates*
Hyde, W. Jerry — *Hyde Danforth Wold & Co.*
Iacovelli, Heather — *CPS Inc.*
Inzinna, Dennis — *AlternaStaff*
Irish, Alan — *CPS Inc.*
Jensen, Stephanie — *Don Richard Associates of Tidewater, Inc.*
Johnson, Douglas — *Quality Search*
Johnson, Julie — *International Staffing Consultants, Inc.*
Johnson, Kathleen A. — *Barton Raben, Inc.*
Johnson, Robert J. — *Quality Search*
Jones, Gary — *BGB Associates*
Juska, Frank — *Rusher, Loscavio & LoPresto*
Kanrich, Susan Azaria — *AlternaStaff*
Karalis, William — *CPS Inc.*
Kehoe, Mike — *CPS Inc.*
Kelly, Elizabeth Ann — *Wellington Management Group*
Kelly, Peter W. — *R. Rollo Associates*
Kilcoyne, Pat — *CPS Inc.*
King, Stephen C. — *Boyden/Zay & Company*
King, Thomas — *Morgan Hunter Corp.*
Kinley, Kathy — *Intech Summit Group, Inc.*
Kinser, Richard E. — *Richard Kinser & Associates*
Kkorzyniewski, Nicole — *CPS Inc.*
Klages, Constance W. — *International Management Advisors, Inc.*
Klumpjan, Sonja — *CPS Inc.*
Koehler, Frank R. — *The Koehler Group*
Laird, Cheryl — *CPS Inc.*
Leahy, Jan — *CPS Inc.*
Leetma, Imbi — *Stanton Chase International*
LemMou, Paul — *International Staffing Consultants, Inc.*
Lennox, Charles — *Price Waterhouse*
Lofthouse, Cindy — *CPS Inc.*
Loria, Frank — *Accounting Personnel Consultants*
Loscavio, J. Michael — *Rusher, Loscavio & LoPresto*
Lotz, R. James — *International Management Advisors, Inc.*
Lumsby, George N. — *International Management Advisors, Inc.*
Lyons, Michele R. — *R. Rollo Associates*
Manassero, Henri J.P. — *International Management Advisors, Inc.*
Mathias, William J. — *Preng & Associates, Inc.*
McAndrews, Kathy — *CPS Inc.*
McGuire, Corey — *Peter W. Ambler Company*
McKay, W. John — *O'Callaghan Honey/Paul Ray Berndtson, Inc.*
Messett, William J. — *Messett Associates, Inc.*
Michaels, Joseph — *CPS Inc.*
Mitton, Bill — *Executive Resource, Inc.*
Mohr, Brian — *CPS Inc.*
Moore, Mark — *Wheeler, Moore & Elam Co.*
Mruk, Edwin S. — *Mruk & Partners/EMA Partners Int'l*
Muendel, H. Edward — *Stanton Chase International*
Murphy, Cornelius J. — *Goodrich & Sherwood Associates, Inc.*
Murray, Virginia — *Baker, Harris & Partners Limited*
Mydlach, Renee — *CPS Inc.*
Napier, Ginger L. — *Preng & Associates, Inc.*
Neidhart, Craig C. — *TNS Partners, Inc.*
Neuberth, Jeffrey G. — *Canny, Bowen Inc.*
Noll, Robert J. — *The Hindman Company*
O'Callaghan, Terry K. — *O'Callaghan Honey/Paul Ray Berndtson, Inc.*
O'Connell, Mary — *CPS Inc.*
Olsen, David — *Search Enterprises South, Inc.*
Ottenritter, Chris — *CPS Inc.*
Palma, Frank R. — *Goodrich & Sherwood Associates, Inc.*
Palmer, James H. — *The Hindman Company*
Pappas, Jim — *Search Dynamics, Inc.*
Parent, Martine L. — *O'Callaghan Honey/Paul Ray Berndtson, Inc.*
Paul, Lisa D. — *Merit Resource Group, Inc.*
Pedley, Jill — *CPS Inc.*
Percival, Chris — *Chicago Legal Search, Ltd.*

Perkins, Bob — *Richard, Wayne and Roberts*
Perkins, Daphne — *CPS Inc.*
Peterson, John — *CPS Inc.*
Pfeiffer, Irene — *Price Waterhouse*
Phillips, Donald L. — *O'Shea, Divine & Company, Inc.*
Plimpton, Ralph L. — *R L Plimpton Associates*
Polacek, Frank — *Search Enterprises South, Inc.*
Pomerance, Mark — *CPS Inc.*
Poore, Larry D. — *Ward Howell International, Inc.*
Porada, Stephen D. — *CAP Inc.*
Porter, Nanci — *Eastridge InfoTech*
Preng, David E. — *Preng & Associates, Inc.*
Prior, Donald — *The Caldwell Partners Amrop International*
Probert, William W. — *Ward Howell International, Inc.*
Prosser, Shane — *Search Consultants International, Inc.*
Randell, James E. — *Randell-Heiken, Inc.*
Ray, Marianne C. — *Callan Associates, Ltd.*
Rendl, Ric — *CPS Inc.*
Renner, Sandra L. — *Spectra International Inc.*
Riederer, Larry — *CPS Inc.*
Rieger, Louis J. — *Spencer Stuart*
Rimmel, James E. — *The Hindman Company*
Rivers, Geri — *Chrisman & Company, Incorporated*
Rizzo, L. Donald — *R.P. Barone Associates*
Rogers, Leah — *Dinte Resources, Incorporated*
Rollo, Robert S. — *R. Rollo Associates*
Romanchek, Walter R. — *Wellington Management Group*
Rubinstein, Alan J. — *Chicago Legal Search, Ltd.*
Runge, Gary — *Search Enterprises South, Inc.*
Sahlas, Chrissy — *CPS Inc.*
Saletra, Andrew — *CPS Inc.*
Sandbloom, Kenneth — *Search Enterprises South, Inc.*
Sanders, Natalie — *CPS Inc.*
Savage, Edward J. — *Stanton Chase International*
Scalamera, Tom — *CPS Inc.*
Schueneman, David — *CPS Inc.*
Scrivines, Hank — *Search Northwest Associates*
Sevilla, Claudio A. — *Crawford & Crofford*
Shapiro, Elaine — *CPS Inc.*
Shervey, Brent C. — *O'Callaghan Honey/Paul Ray Berndtson, Inc.*
Sherwood, Andrew — *Goodrich & Sherwood Associates, Inc.*
Sibul, Shelly Remen — *Chicago Legal Search, Ltd.*
Signer, Julie — *CPS Inc.*
Silcott, Marvin L. — *Marvin L. Silcott & Associates, Inc.*
Smith, Cheryl — *Barton Raben, Inc.*
Smith, Herman M. — *Herman Smith Executive Initiatives Inc.*
Smith, Ian — *International Staffing Consultants, Inc.*
Snodgrass, Stephen — *DeFrain, Mayer, Lee & Burgess LLC*
Spadavecchia, Jennifer — *Alta Associates, Inc.*
Spann, Richard E. — *Goodrich & Sherwood Associates, Inc.*
Starr, Anna — *Richard, Wayne and Roberts*
Stern, Stephen — *CPS Inc.*
Sterner, Doug — *CPS Inc.*
Stewart, Ross M. — *Human Resources Network Partners Inc.*
Stringer, Dann P. — *D.E. Foster Partners Inc.*
Sutton, Robert J. — *The Caldwell Partners Amrop International*
Thomas, Cheryl M. — *CPS Inc.*
Thomas, Ian — *International Staffing Consultants, Inc.*
Thomas, Kim — *CPS Inc.*
Tobin, Jim — *Barton Raben, Inc.*
Tovrog, Dan — *CPS Inc.*
Truemper, Dean — *CPS Inc.*
Truitt, Thomas B. — *Southwestern Professional Services*
Tryon, Katey — *DeFrain, Mayer, Lee & Burgess LLC*
Tucker, Thomas A. — *The Thomas Tucker Company*
Tullberg, Tina — *CPS Inc.*
Vann, Dianne — *The Button Group*
Virgili, Franca — *Johnson Smith & Knisely Accord*
Vogel, Michael S. — *Vogel Associates*
Walker, Ewing J. — *Ward Howell International, Inc.*
Walker, Judy — *Richard, Wayne and Roberts*
Weissman-Rosenthal, Abbe — *ALW Research International*
Wier, Daniel — *Horton International*
Willis, William H. — *William Willis Worldwide Inc.*
Winston, Susan — *CPS Inc.*
Witte, David L. — *Ward Howell International, Inc.*
Wright, Charles D. — *Goodrich & Sherwood Associates, Inc.*
Young, Alexander — *Messett Associates, Inc.*
Youngs, Donald L. — *Youngs & Company*
Zatman, Allen — *Search Enterprises South, Inc.*

## 23. Packaging

Abbott, Peter — *The Abbott Group, Inc.*
Allgire, Mary L. — *Kenzer Corp.*
Altreuter, Ken — *ALTCO Temporary Services*
Altreuter, Kenneth — *The ALTCO Group*
Altreuter, Rose — *ALTCO Temporary Services*
Altreuter, Rose — *The ALTCO Group*

Ambler, Peter W. — *Peter W. Ambler Company*
Andrews, Laura L. — *Stricker & Zagor*
Andrick, Patty — *CPS Inc.*
Angell, Tryg R. — *Tryg R. Angell Ltd.*
Argentin, Jo — *Executive Placement Consultants, Inc.*
Asquith, Peter S. — *Ames Personnel Consultants, Inc.*
Austin, Jessica L. — *D.S.A. - Dixie Search Associates*
Bailey, William A. — *TNS Partners, Inc.*
Baker, Gary M. — *Cochran, Cochran & Yale, Inc.*
Balch, Randy — *CPS Inc.*
Baran, Helena — *Michael J. Cavanagh and Associates*
Barnes, Roanne L. — *Barnes Development Group, LLC*
Baron, Len — *Industrial Recruiters Associates, Inc.*
Barton, Gary R. — *Barton Raben, Inc.*
Bason, Maurice L. — *Bason Associates Inc.*
Bennett, Joan — *Adams & Associates International*
Berger, Jay V. — *Morris & Berger*
Blanton, Thomas — *Blanton and Company*
Bliley, Jerry — *Spencer Stuart*
Bole, J. Jeffrey — *William J. Christopher Associates, Inc.*
Bostic, James E. — *Phillips Resource Group*
Bovich, Maryann C. — *Higdon Prince Inc.*
Boyer, Heath C. — *Spencer Stuart*
Brackenbury, Robert — *Bowman & Marshall, Inc.*
Brackin, James B. — *Brackin & Sayers Associates*
Brady, Robert — *CPS Inc.*
Brandeis, Richard — *CPS Inc.*
Brieger, Steve — *Thorne, Brieger Associates Inc.*
Brown, Larry C. — *Horton International*
Buck, Walter J. — *E.G. Jones Associates, Ltd.*
Buckles, Donna — *Cochran, Cochran & Yale, Inc.*
Burchill, Greg — *BGB Associates*
Button, David R. — *The Button Group*
Cahill, Peter M. — *Peter M. Cahill Associates, Inc.*
Call, David — *Cochran, Cochran & Yale, Inc.*
Callahan, Wanda — *Cochran, Cochran & Yale, Inc.*
Carlson, Judith — *Bowman & Marshall, Inc.*
Casey, Jean — *Peter W. Ambler Company*
Cavanagh, Michael J. — *Michael J. Cavanagh and Associates*
Celenza, Catherine — *CPS Inc.*
Chavous, C. Crawford — *Phillips Resource Group*
Christiansen, Amy — *CPS Inc.*
Christiansen, Doug — *CPS Inc.*
Clark, James — *CPS Inc.*
Colling, Douglas — *KPMG Management Consulting*
Colman, Michael — *Executive Placement Consultants, Inc.*
Connaghan, Linda — *Bowman & Marshall, Inc.*
Conway, William P. — *Phillips Resource Group*
Coulman, Karen — *CPS Inc.*
Crath, Paul F. — *Price Waterhouse*
Critchley, Walter — *Cochran, Cochran & Yale, Inc.*
Cronin, Richard J. — *Hodge-Cronin & Associates, Inc.*
Crowder, Edward W. — *Crowder & Company*
Czepiel, Susan — *CPS Inc.*
Dabich, Thomas M. — *Robert Harkins Associates, Inc.*
Danoff, Audrey — *Don Richard Associates of Tidewater, Inc.*
Davis, G. Gordon — *Davis & Company*
Del Prete, Karen — *Gilbert Tweed/INESA*
deMartino, Cathy — *Lucas Associates*
Desgrosellier, Gary P. — *Personnel Unlimited/Executive Search*
Dickey, Chet W. — *Bowden & Company, Inc.*
Dieck, Daniel W. — *Dieck, Mueller & Associates, Inc.*
DiGiovanni, Charles — *Penn Search*
Dingman, Bruce — *Robert W. Dingman Company, Inc.*
Dingman, Robert W. — *Robert W. Dingman Company, Inc.*
Divine, Robert S. — *O'Shea, Divine & Company, Inc.*
Dixon, Aris — *CPS Inc.*
Do, Sonnie — *Whitney & Associates, Inc.*
Drexler, Robert — *Robert Drexler Associates, Inc.*
Drury, James J. — *Spencer Stuart*
Dugan, John H. — *J.H. Dugan and Associates, Inc.*
Duggan, James P. — *Slayton International, Inc.*
Dunman, Betsy L. — *Crawford & Crofford*
Dussick, Vince — *Dussick Management Associates*
Dwyer, Julie — *CPS Inc.*
Dykstra, Nicolette — *CPS Inc.*
Eason, James — *JRL Executive Recruiters*
Eason, Larry E. — *JRL Executive Recruiters*
Eberly, Carrie — *Accounting Resources, Inc.*
Edwards, Verba L. — *Wing Tips & Pumps, Inc.*
Eggena, Roger — *Phillips Resource Group*
Ehrhart, Jennifer — *ADOW's Executeam*
Erickson, Elaine — *Kenzer Corp.*
Ervin, Darlene — *CPS Inc.*
Fancher, Robert L. — *Bason Associates Inc.*
Faure, Michel — *The Caldwell Partners Amrop International*
Fill, Clifford G. — *D.S.A. - Dixie Search Associates*
Fill, Ellyn H. — *D.S.A. - Dixie Search Associates*

Fincher, Richard P. — *Phase II Management*
Fisher, Neal — *Fisher Personnel Management Services*
Flanagan, Robert M. — *Robert M. Flanagan & Associates, Ltd.*
Fogarty, Michael — *CPS Inc.*
Foy, James — *Foy, Schneid & Daniel, Inc.*
Frazier, John — *Cochran, Cochran & Yale, Inc.*
Friedman, Helen E. — *McCormack & Farrow*
Galante, Suzanne M. — *Vlcek & Company, Inc.*
Gallagher, Marilyn — *Hogan Acquisitions*
Garfinkle, Steven M. — *Battalia Winston International*
Gates, Douglas H. — *Skott/Edwards Consultants, Inc.*
Gauthier, Robert C. — *Columbia Consulting Group*
Gibson, Bruce — *Gibson & Company Inc.*
Gilmore, Lori — *CPS Inc.*
Glancey, Thomas F. — *Gordon Wahls Company*
Goldenberg, Susan — *Grant Cooper and Associates*
Goodman, Dawn M. — *Bason Associates Inc.*
Gorfinkle, Gayle — *Executive Search International*
Grady, James — *Search West, Inc.*
Graham, Dale — *CPS Inc.*
Granger, Lisa D. — *D.S.A. - Dixie Search Associates*
Grantham, John — *Grantham & Co., Inc.*
Grassl, Peter O. — *Bowman & Marshall, Inc.*
Green, Jane — *Phillips Resource Group*
Grenier, Glorianne — *CPS Inc.*
Grzybowski, Jill — *CPS Inc.*
Gurtin, Kay L. — *Executive Options, Ltd.*
Hailey, H.M. — *Damon & Associates, Inc.*
Hardison, Richard L. — *Hardison & Company*
Harkins, Robert E. — *Robert Harkins Associates, Inc.*
Harrison, Priscilla — *Phillips Resource Group*
Hart, Robert T. — *D.E. Foster Partners Inc.*
Harvey, Mike — *Advanced Executive Resources*
Haystead, Steve — *Advanced Executive Resources*
Hazerjian, Cynthia — *CPS Inc.*
Heafey, Bill — *CPS Inc.*
Hecker, Henry C. — *Hogan Acquisitions*
Hellebusch, Jerry — *Morgan Hunter Corp.*
Heneghan, Donald A. — *Allerton Heneghan & O'Neill*
Herman, Pat — *Whitney & Associates, Inc.*
Hicks, Albert M. — *Phillips Resource Group*
Hoevel, Michael J. — *Poirier, Hoevel & Co.*
Hogan, Larry H. — *Hogan Acquisitions*
Holden, Richard B. — *Ames Personnel Consultants, Inc.*
Hughes, James J. — *R.P. Barone Associates*
Hunter, Gabe — *Phillips Resource Group*
Iacovelli, Heather — *CPS Inc.*
Inzinna, Dennis — *AlternaStaff*
Irish, Alan — *CPS Inc.*
Jablo, Steven — *Dieckmann & Associates, Ltd.*
Jacobson, Donald — *Hunt Ltd.*
James, Bruce — *Roberson and Company*
James, Richard — *Criterion Executive Search, Inc.*
Jansen, Douglas L. — *Search Northwest Associates*
Jensen, Stephanie — *Don Richard Associates of Tidewater, Inc.*
Joffe, Barry — *Bason Associates Inc.*
Johnson, Douglas — *Quality Search*
Johnson, John F. — *Lamalie Amrop International*
Johnson, Robert J. — *Quality Search*
Jones, Gary — *BGB Associates*
Kader, Richard — *Richard Kader & Associates*
Kanrich, Susan Azaria — *AlternaStaff*
Karalis, William — *CPS Inc.*
Kehoe, Mike — *CPS Inc.*
Kenzer, Robert D. — *Kenzer Corp.*
Kern, Jerry L. — *ADOW's Executeam*
Kern, Kathleen G. — *ADOW's Executeam*
Kilcoyne, Pat — *CPS Inc.*
Kinney, Carol — *Dussick Management Associates*
Kinser, Richard E. — *Richard Kinser & Associates*
Kishbaugh, Herbert S. — *Kishbaugh Associates International*
Kkorzyniewski, Nicole — *CPS Inc.*
Klopfenstein, Edward L. — *Crowder & Company*
Klumpjan, Sonja — *CPS Inc.*
Koehler, Frank R. — *The Koehler Group*
Laird, Cheryl — *CPS Inc.*
Lamson-Gran, Jill — *Accounting Resources, Inc.*
Langer, Joel A. — *Langer Associates, Inc.*
Leahy, Jan — *CPS Inc.*
Leslie, William H. — *Boyden/Zay & Company*
Lofthouse, Cindy — *CPS Inc.*
Logan, Valarie A. — *D.S.A. - Dixie Search Associates*
Lotufo, Donald A. — *D.A.L. Associates, Inc.*
MacDougall, Andrew J. — *Spencer Stuart*
Maer, Harry — *Kenzer Corp.*
Magee, Charles R. — *Dieck, Mueller & Associates, Inc.*
Magee, Harrison R. — *Bowden & Company, Inc.*
Mangum, William T. — *Thomas Mangum Company*

Manns, Alex — *Crawford & Crofford*
Marino, Chester — *Cochran, Cochran & Yale, Inc.*
Marshall, Gerald — *Blair/Tech Recruiters*
Martens, Maxine — *Rene Plessner Associates, Inc.*
Mayes, Kay H. — *John Shell Associates, Inc.*
McAndrews, Kathy — *CPS Inc.*
McCorkle, Sam B. — *Morton, McCorkle & Associates, Inc.*
McDonnell, Julie — *Technical Personnel of Minnesota*
McGrath, Robert E. — *Robert E. McGrath & Associates*
McGuire, Bud — *Search West, Inc.*
McGuire, Corey — *Peter W. Ambler Company*
McIntyre, Joel — *Phillips Resource Group*
McNear, Jeffrey E. — *Barrett Partners*
Meagher, Patricia G. — *Spencer Stuart*
Meltzer, Andrea Y. — *Executive Options, Ltd.*
Mertensotto, Chuck H. — *Whitney & Associates, Inc.*
Metz, Alex — *Hunt Ltd.*
Michaels, Joseph — *CPS Inc.*
Mierzwinski, John — *Industrial Recruiters Associates, Inc.*
Miller, George N. — *Hite Executive Search*
Miller, Michael R. — *Lynch Miller Moore Partners, Inc.*
Mitton, Bill — *Executive Resource, Inc.*
Mohr, Brian — *CPS Inc.*
Molitor, John L. — *Barrett Partners*
Moore, Thomas — *Aureus Group*
Moran, Gayle — *Dussick Management Associates*
Morris, Kristine A. — *Morris & Berger*
Morton, Robert C. — *Morton, McCorkle & Associates, Inc.*
Mueller, Michael S. — *Dieck, Mueller & Associates, Inc.*
Mydlach, Renee — *CPS Inc.*
Neelin, Sharon — *The Caldwell Partners Amrop International*
Neidhart, Craig C. — *TNS Partners, Inc.*
Nelson, Barbara — *Herman Smith Executive Initiatives Inc.*
Nordland, Martin N. — *Horton International*
Normann, Amy — *Robert M. Flanagan & Associates, Ltd.*
O'Connell, Mary — *CPS Inc.*
Oberg, Roy — *The Danbrook Group, Inc.*
Ottenritter, Chris — *CPS Inc.*
Palmer, Melissa — *Don Richard Associates of Tampa, Inc.*
Parker, Murray B. — *The Borton Wallace Company*
Parr, James A. — *KPMG Management Consulting*
Pedley, Jill — *CPS Inc.*
Perkins, Daphne — *CPS Inc.*
Peters, James N. — *TNS Partners, Inc.*
Peterson, John — *CPS Inc.*
Pickering, Dale — *Agri-Tech Personnel, Inc.*
Pitts, Charles — *Contemporary Management Services, Inc.*
Plessner, Rene — *Rene Plessner Associates, Inc.*
Poirier, Roland — *Poirier, Hoevel & Co.*
Pomerance, Mark — *CPS Inc.*
Porada, Stephen D. — *CAP Inc.*
Probert, William W. — *Ward Howell International, Inc.*
Rachels, John W. — *Southwestern Professional Services*
Rapoport, William — *Blair/Tech Recruiters*
Rathbone, Kenneth J. — *Blair/Tech Recruiters*
Raymond, Jean — *The Caldwell Partners Amrop International*
Reddicks, Nate — *Search West, Inc.*
Rendl, Ric — *CPS Inc.*
Reyman, Susan — *S. Reyman & Associates Ltd.*
Riederer, Larry — *CPS Inc.*
Rizzo, L. Donald — *R.P. Barone Associates*
Roberts, Derek J. — *Ward Howell International, Inc.*
Roberts, William — *Cochran, Cochran & Yale, Inc.*
Robertson, William R. — *Ward Howell International, Inc.*
Robison, John H. — *Robison & Associates*
Rodgers, Kathi — *St. Lawrence International, Inc.*
Russell, Robin E. — *Kenzer Corp.*
Sahlas, Chrissy — *CPS Inc.*
Saletra, Andrew — *CPS Inc.*
Sanders, Natalie — *CPS Inc.*
Sayers, Bruce D. — *Brackin & Sayers Associates*
Scalamera, Tom — *CPS Inc.*
Scharett, Carol — *St. Lawrence International, Inc.*
Schiavone, Mary Rose — *Canny, Bowen Inc.*
Schlpma, Christine — *Advanced Executive Resources*
Schroeder, John W. — *Spencer Stuart*
Schueneman, David — *CPS Inc.*
Segal, Eric B. — *Kenzer Corp.*
Selko, Philip W. — *Hogan Acquisitions*
Serwat, Leonard A. — *Spencer Stuart*
Sevilla, Claudio A. — *Crawford & Crofford*
Shapiro, Elaine — *CPS Inc.*
Shea, John — *ALTCO Temporary Services*
Shea, John — *The ALTCO Group*
Shell, John C. — *John Shell Associates, Inc.*
Shoemaker, Larry C. — *Shoemaker & Associates*
Siegel, Pamela — *Executive Options, Ltd.*
Signer, Julie — *CPS Inc.*

Silverman, Paul M. — *The Marshall Group*
Simmons, Gerald J. — *Handy HRM Corp.*
Snyder, Thomas J. — *Spencer Stuart*
Sobczak, Ronald — *Search Enterprises, Inc.*
Stern, Stephen — *CPS Inc.*
Sterner, Doug — *CPS Inc.*
Stiles, Jack D. — *Sanford Rose Associates*
Stiles, Timothy — *Sanford Rose Associates*
Stone, Susan L. — *Stone Enterprises Ltd.*
Stoneham, Herbert E.C. — *Stoneham Associates Corp.*
Stricker, Sidney G. — *Stricker & Zagor*
Sumurdy, Melinda — *Kenzer Corp.*
Sur, William K. — *Canny, Bowen Inc.*
ten Cate, Herman H. — *Stoneham Associates Corp.*
Theobald, David B. — *Theobald & Associates*
Thielman, Joseph — *Barrett Partners*
Thomas, Cheryl M. — *CPS Inc.*
Thomas, Kim — *CPS Inc.*
Thompson, James R. — *Gordon Wahls Company*
Tovrog, Dan — *CPS Inc.*
Truemper, Dean — *CPS Inc.*
Truitt, Thomas B. — *Southwestern Professional Services*
Tullberg, Tina — *CPS Inc.*
Turner, Edward K. — *Don Richard Associates of Charlotte*
Tweed, Janet — *Gilbert Tweed/INESA*
Vann, Dianne — *The Button Group*
Visnich, L. Christine — *Bason Associates Inc.*
Vlcek, Thomas J. — *Vlcek & Company, Inc.*
Vogel, Michael S. — *Vogel Associates*
Waldoch, D. Mark — *Barnes Development Group, LLC*
Wertel, Ronald E. — *Gordon Wahls Company*
Whitney, David L. — *Whitney & Associates, Inc.*
Wilkinson, William R. — *Wilkinson & Ives*
Williams, Angie — *Whitney & Associates, Inc.*
Williams, Gary L. — *Barnes Development Group, LLC*
Williams, Lis — *Executive Options, Ltd.*
Winograd, Glenn — *Criterion Executive Search, Inc.*
Winston, Susan — *CPS Inc.*
Zilliacus, Patrick W. — *Larsen, Zilliacus & Associates, Inc.*

## 24. Pharmaceutical/Medical

Abbatiello, Christine Murphy — *Winter, Wyman & Company*
Abby, Daniel — *Bill Hahn Group, Inc.*
Adams, Jeffrey C. — *Telford, Adams & Alexander/Jeffrey C. Adams & Co., Inc.*
Ainsworth, Lawrence — *Search West, Inc.*
Albers, Joan — *Carver Search Consultants*
Alekel, Karren — *ALW Research International*
Allen, Cynthia — *Roberson and Company*
Allerton, Donald T. — *Allerton Heneghan & O'Neill*
Altreuter, Ken — *ALTCO Temporary Services*
Altreuter, Kenneth — *The ALTCO Group*
Altreuter, Rose — *ALTCO Temporary Services*
Altreuter, Rose — *The ALTCO Group*
Ambert, Amadol — *Bryant Research*
Anderson, Richard — *Grant Cooper and Associates*
Anderson, Roger J. — *BioQuest, Inc.*
Anderson, Thomas — *Paul J. Biestek Associates, Inc.*
Andrews, J. Douglas — *Clarey & Andrews, Inc.*
Andrick, Patty — *CPS Inc.*
Apostle, George — *Search Dynamics, Inc.*
Argentin, Jo — *Executive Placement Consultants, Inc.*
Arms, Douglas — *TOPAZ International, Inc.*
Arnold, Jerry — *Houtz-Strawn Associates, Inc.*
Aronin, Michael — *Fisher-Todd Associates*
Ascher, Susan P. — *The Ascher Group*
Aston, Kathy — *Marra Peters & Partners*
Atkinson, S. Graham — *Raymond Karsan Associates*
Aydelotte, G. Thomas — *Ingram & Aydelotte Inc.*
Bagg, Keith — *Keith Bagg & Associates Inc.*
Bailey, David O. — *Paul Ray Berndtson*
Bailey, William A. — *TNS Partners, Inc.*
Baird, Blaine T. — *Physicians Search, Inc.*
Baitler, Simon C. — *The Stevenson Group of Delaware Inc.*
Baker, Gary M. — *Cochran, Cochran & Yale, Inc.*
Balch, Randy — *CPS Inc.*
Baldwin, Keith R. — *The Baldwin Group*
Baran, Helena — *Michael J. Cavanagh and Associates*
Barnes, Roanne L. — *Barnes Development Group, LLC*
Baron, Jon C. — *MSI International*
Barone, Marialice — *Barone-O'Hara Associates*
Barthold, James A. — *McNichol Associates*
Bason, Maurice L. — *Bason Associates Inc.*
Bassman, Robert — *Kaye-Bassman International Corp.*
Bassman, Sandy — *Kaye-Bassman International Corp.*
Battalia, O. William — *Battalia Winston International*
Bearman, Linda — *Grant Cooper and Associates*
Beaver, Robert W. — *Executive Manning Corporation*

Belford, Paul — *JDG Associates, Ltd.*
Bellano, Robert W. — *Stanton Chase International*
Bennett, Delora — *Genesis Personnel Service, Inc.*
Benson, Kate — *Rene Plessner Associates, Inc.*
Berger, Jay V. — *Morris & Berger*
Berke, Carl E. — *The Cassie Group*
Berry, Harold B. — *The Hindman Company*
Besen, Douglas — *Besen Associates Inc.*
Biestek, Paul J. — *Paul J. Biestek Associates, Inc.*
Billington, Brian — *Billington & Associates*
Billington, William H. — *Spriggs & Company, Inc.*
Billotti, Lisa — *Bryant Research*
Blair, Kelly A. — *The Caldwell Partners Amrop International*
Blakslee, Jan H. — *J: Blakslee International, Ltd.*
Blanton, Thomas — *Blanton and Company*
Bloomer, James E. — *L.W. Foote Company*
Boccuzi, Joseph H. — *Spencer Stuart*
Borman, Theodore H. — *Lamalie Amrop International*
Boyer, Heath C. — *Spencer Stuart*
Boyle, Russell E. — *Egon Zehnder International Inc.*
Brackenbury, Robert — *Bowman & Marshall, Inc.*
Brackin, James B. — *Brackin & Sayers Associates*
Brady, Robert — *CPS Inc.*
Brandeis, Richard — *CPS Inc.*
Bratches, Howard — *Thorndike Deland Associates*
Brazil, Kathy — *Bryant Research*
Brieger, Steve — *Thorne, Brieger Associates Inc.*
Brocaglia, Joyce — *Alta Associates, Inc.*
Brooks, Natalie — *Raymond Karsan Associates*
Brophy, Melissa — *Maximum Management Corp.*
Brown, Larry C. — *Horton International*
Brown, S. Ross — *Egon Zehnder International Inc.*
Brudno, Robert J. — *Savoy Partners, Ltd.*
Brunelle, Francis W.H. — *The Caldwell Partners Amrop International*
Bruno, Deborah F. — *The Hindman Company*
Bryant, Richard D. — *Bryant Associates, Inc.*
Bryant, Thomas — *Bryant Research*
Bryza, Robert M. — *Robert Lowell International*
Buckles, Donna — *Cochran, Cochran & Yale, Inc.*
Budill, Edward — *Professional Search Consultants*
Bueschel, David A. — *Shepherd Bueschel & Provus, Inc.*
Burchill, Greg — *BGB Associates*
Burfield, Elaine — *Skott/Edwards Consultants, Inc.*
Burke, John — *The Experts*
Burns, Alan — *The Enns Partners Inc.*
Button, David R. — *The Button Group*
Cahill, Peter M. — *Peter M. Cahill Associates, Inc.*
Call, David — *Cochran, Cochran & Yale, Inc.*
Callahan, Wanda — *Cochran, Cochran & Yale, Inc.*
Callihan, Diana L. — *Search Northwest Associates*
Campbell, Robert Scott — *Wellington Management Group*
Campbell, W. Ross — *Egon Zehnder International Inc.*
Carideo, Joseph — *Thorndike Deland Associates*
Carlson, Judith — *Bowman & Marshall, Inc.*
Carrott, Gregory T. — *Egon Zehnder International Inc.*
Carter, Jon F. — *Egon Zehnder International Inc.*
Cassie, Ronald L. — *The Cassie Group*
Caudill, Nancy — *Webb, Johnson Associates, Inc.*
Causey, Andrea C. — *MSI International*
Cavanagh, Michael J. — *Michael J. Cavanagh and Associates*
Cavolina, Michael — *Carver Search Consultants*
Celenza, Catherine — *CPS Inc.*
Chan, Margaret — *Webb, Johnson Associates, Inc.*
Chargar, Frances — *Hunt Ltd.*
Charles, Ronald D. — *The Caldwell Partners Amrop International*
Christiansen, Amy — *CPS Inc.*
Christiansen, Doug — *CPS Inc.*
Chua, Jackie — *Keith Bagg & Associates Inc.*
Cizek, John T. — *Cizek Associates, Inc.*
Clarey, Jack R. — *Clarey & Andrews, Inc.*
Clark, Elliot H. — *Raymond Karsan Associates*
Clark, James — *CPS Inc.*
Clauhsen, Elizabeth A. — *Savoy Partners, Ltd.*
Cohen, Pamela — *TOPAZ International, Inc.*
Colman, Michael — *Executive Placement Consultants, Inc.*
Colucci, Bart A. — *Colucci, Blendow and Johnson, Inc.*
Connaghan, Linda — *Bowman & Marshall, Inc.*
Cottingham, R.L. — *Marvin L. Silcott & Associates, Inc.*
Coulman, Karen — *CPS Inc.*
Cowan, Roberta — *Drew Associates International*
Cragg, Barbara R. — *Southwestern Professional Services*
Cramer, Barbara Lee — *Physicians Search, Inc.*
Crean, Jeremiah N. — *Bryant Research*
Critchley, Walter — *Cochran, Cochran & Yale, Inc.*
Crowell, Elizabeth — *H.M. Long International, Ltd.*
Crumpley, Jim — *Jim Crumpley & Associates*
Cruz, Catherine — *TOPAZ International, Inc.*
Cunningham, Sheila — *Adams & Associates International*

Czepiel, Susan — *CPS Inc.*
D'Alessio, Gary A. — *Chicago Legal Search, Ltd.*
Dabich, Thomas M. — *Robert Harkins Associates, Inc.*
Daniel, Beverly — *Foy, Schneid & Daniel, Inc.*
de Palacios, Jeannette C. — *J. Palacios & Associates, Inc.*
Deal, Leslie — *Bryant Research*
Debrueys, Lee G. — *MSI International*
DeFrancesco, Mary Ellen — *The Onstott Group, Inc.*
DeHart, Donna — *Tower Consultants, Ltd.*
Del Pino, William — *National Search, Inc.*
Del Prete, Karen — *Gilbert Tweed/INESA*
Del'Ange, Gabrielle N. — *MSI International*
Delvani-Hart, Angela — *F-O-R-T-U-N-E Personnel Consultants of Nashua, Inc.*
deMartino, Cathy — *Lucas Associates*
Demchak, James P. — *Sandhurst Associates*
Desgrosellier, Gary P. — *Personnel Unlimited/Executive Search*
Desmond, Dennis — *Beall & Company, Inc.*
Detore, Robert R. — *Drew Associates International*
DiMarchi, Paul — *DiMarchi Partners, Inc.*
Dingman, Bruce — *Robert W. Dingman Company, Inc.*
Dingman, Robert W. — *Robert W. Dingman Company, Inc.*
Divine, Robert S. — *O'Shea, Divine & Company, Inc.*
Dixon, Aris — *CPS Inc.*
Do, Sonnie — *Whitney & Associates, Inc.*
Domann, William A. — *The Domann Organization*
Dotson, M. Ileen — *Dotson & Associates*
Drexler, Robert — *Robert Drexler Associates, Inc.*
DuBois, Joseph W. — *Horizon Medical Search of New Hampshire*
Dulet, Donna — *Bryant Research*
Dussick, Vince — *Dussick Management Associates*
Dwyer, Julie — *CPS Inc.*
Dykstra, Nicolette — *CPS Inc.*
Eason, James — *JRL Executive Recruiters*
Eason, Larry E. — *JRL Executive Recruiters*
Ebeling, John A. — *Gilbert Tweed/INESA*
Edwards, Douglas W. — *Egon Zehnder International Inc.*
Edwards, Verba L. — *Wing Tips & Pumps, Inc.*
Ehrgott, Elizabeth — *The Ascher Group*
Eibeler, C. — *Amherst Personnel Group Inc.*
Ellis, Ted K. — *The Hindman Company*
Emmott, Carol B. — *Spencer Stuart*
Enfield, Jerry J. — *Executive Manning Corporation*
England, Mark — *Austin-McGregor International*
Enns, George — *The Enns Partners Inc.*
Erstling, Gregory — *Normyle/Erstling Health Search Group*
Ervin, Darlene — *CPS Inc.*
Fancher, Robert L. — *Bason Associates Inc.*
Feder, Gwen — *Egon Zehnder International Inc.*
Ferguson, Robert — *Bill Hahn Group, Inc.*
Fifield, George C. — *Egon Zehnder International Inc.*
Fincher, Richard P. — *Phase II Management*
Fischer, John C. — *Horton International*
Flora, Dodi — *Crawford & Crofford*
Fogarty, Michael — *CPS Inc.*
Foreman, David C. — *Koontz, Jeffries & Associates, Inc.*
Fotino, Anne — *Normyle/Erstling Health Search Group*
Fowler, Jim — *First Search America, Inc.*
Frazier, John — *Cochran, Cochran & Yale, Inc.*
Freier, Bruce — *Executive Referral Services, Inc.*
French, William G. — *Preng & Associates, Inc.*
Friedman, Donna L. — *Tower Consultants, Ltd.*
Friedman, Helen E. — *McCormack & Farrow*
Gaines, Ronni L. — *TOPAZ International, Inc.*
Galante, Suzanne M. — *Vlcek & Company, Inc.*
Gallagher, Terence M. — *Battalia Winston International*
Gallin, Larry — *Gallin Associates*
Garfinkle, Steven M. — *Battalia Winston International*
Gauthier, Robert C. — *Columbia Consulting Group*
George, Delores F. — *Delores F. George Human Resource Management & Consulting Industry*
Gerson, Russ D. — *Webb, Johnson Associates, Inc.*
Gilbert, Jerry — *Gilbert & Van Campen International*
Giles, Joe L. — *Joe L. Giles and Associates, Inc.*
Gill, Patricia — *Columbia Consulting Group*
Gilmartin, William — *Hockett Associates, Inc.*
Gilmore, Lori — *CPS Inc.*
Gladstone, Arthur — *Executive Referral Services, Inc.*
Goar, Duane R. — *Sandhurst Associates*
Goebel, George A. — *John Kurosky & Associates*
Goldman, Michael L. — *Strategic Associates, Inc.*
Goldson, Bob — *The McCormick Group, Inc.*
Gonye, Peter K. — *Egon Zehnder International Inc.*
Goodman, Dawn M. — *Bason Associates Inc.*
Goodman, Victor — *Anderson Sterling Associates*
Gordon, Gerald L. — *E.G. Jones Associates, Ltd.*
Gorfinkle, Gayle — *Executive Search International*
Gourlay, Debra — *Rene Plessner Associates, Inc.*

Marks, Russell E. — *Webb, Johnson Associates, Inc.*
Marra, John — *Marra Peters & Partners*
Marra, John — *Marra Peters & Partners*
Marshall, Gerald — *Blair/Tech Recruiters*
Martin, Ellen — *Hunt Ltd.*
Martin, Jon — *Egon Zehnder International Inc.*
Marumoto, William H. — *The Interface Group, Ltd./Boyden*
Mashakas, Elizabeth — *TOPAZ International, Inc.*
Mason, William E. — *John Kurosky & Associates*
Matheny, Robert P. — *MSI International*
Matti, Suzy — *Southwestern Professional Services*
McAlpine, Bruce — *Keith Bagg & Associates Inc.*
McAndrews, Kathy — *CPS Inc.*
McBride, Jonathan E. — *McBride Associates, Inc.*
McCabe, Christopher — *Raymond Karsan Associates*
McConnell, Greg — *Winter, Wyman & Company*
McCreary, Charles — *Austin-McGregor International*
McDonald, Scott A. — *McDonald Associates International*
McDonald, Stanleigh B. — *McDonald Associates International*
McDonnell, Julie — *Technical Personnel of Minnesota*
McGann, Paul L. — *The Cassie Group*
McGuire, Corey — *Peter W. Ambler Company*
McLean, B. Keith — *Price Waterhouse*
McMillin, Bob — *Price Waterhouse*
McNamara, Timothy C. — *Columbia Consulting Group*
McNichol, John — *McNichol Associates*
Meagher, Patricia G. — *Spencer Stuart*
Mefford, Bob — *Executive Manning Corporation*
Meier, J. Dale — *Grant Cooper and Associates*
Meiland, A. Daniel — *Egon Zehnder International Inc.*
Menk, Carl W. — *Canny, Bowen Inc.*
Mertensotto, Chuck H. — *Whitney & Associates, Inc.*
Messett, William J. — *Messett Associates, Inc.*
Michaels, Joseph — *CPS Inc.*
Michaels, Stewart — *TOPAZ International, Inc.*
Middleton, Alfred E. — *The Neil Michael Group, Inc.*
Mikula, Linda — *Schweichler Associates, Inc.*
Miller, Elaine — *Search West, Inc.*
Miller, Julie — *Southwestern Professional Services*
Miller, Michael R. — *Lynch Miller Moore Partners, Inc.*
Miller, Roy — *The Enns Partners Inc.*
Milton, Suzanne — *Marra Peters & Partners*
Mirtz, P. John — *Mirtz Morice, Inc.*
Mitton, Bill — *Executive Resource, Inc.*
Mohr, Brian — *CPS Inc.*
Moore, Mark — *Wheeler, Moore & Elam Co.*
Moran, Gayle — *Dussick Management Associates*
Moran, Robert — *A.T. Kearney, Inc.*
Morgan, Gary — *National Search, Inc.*
Morice, James L. — *Mirtz Morice, Inc.*
Morris, Kristine A. — *Morris & Berger*
Morris, Paul T. — *The Morris Group*
Moses, Jerry — *J.M. Eagle Partners Ltd.*
Mueller-Maerki, Fortunat F. — *Egon Zehnder International Inc.*
Muendel, H. Edward — *Stanton Chase International*
Mursuli, Meredith — *Lasher Associates*
Mustin, Joyce M. — *J: Blakslee International, Ltd.*
Mydlach, Renee — *CPS Inc.*
Neff, Thomas J. — *Spencer Stuart*
Neill, Wellden K. — *Sampson Neill & Wilkins Inc.*
Newcorn, Andrew R. — *The Neil Michael Group, Inc.*
Noll, Robert J. — *The Hindman Company*
Nordland, Martin N. — *Horton International*
Norman, Randy — *Austin-McGregor International*
Norsell, Paul E. — *Paul Norsell & Associates, Inc.*
Nutter, Roger — *Raymond Karsan Associates*
O'Brien, John G. — *CanMed Consultants Inc.*
O'Connell, Mary — *CPS Inc.*
O'Donnell, James H. — *MSI International*
O'Hara, Daniel M. — *Lynch Miller Moore Partners, Inc.*
O'Hara, James J. — *Barone-O'Hara Associates*
O'Reilly, Jack — *Catalyx Group*
Ogilvie, Kit — *Howard Fischer Associates, Inc.*
Olsen, Carl — *A.T. Kearney, Inc.*
Oppenheim, Norman J. — *F-O-R-T-U-N-E Personnel Consultants of Nashua, Inc.*
Ottenritter, Chris — *CPS Inc.*
Pace, Susan A. — *Horton International*
Pacini, Lauren R. — *Hite Executive Search*
Padilla, Jose Sanchez — *Egon Zehnder International Inc.*
Page, Linda M. — *Wargo and Co., Inc.*
Palmer, Carlton A. — *Beall & Company, Inc.*
Palmer, James H. — *The Hindman Company*
Pappas, Jim — *Search Dynamics, Inc.*
Park, Dabney G. — *Mark Stanley & Company*
Parry, William H. — *Horton International*
Pastrana, Dario — *Egon Zehnder International Inc.*
Payette, Pierre — *Egon Zehnder International Inc.*

Peck, David W. — *The Peck Consultancy*
Pedley, Jill — *CPS Inc.*
Peeney, James D. — *Peeney Associates*
Pelisson, Charles — *Marra Peters & Partners*
Percival, Chris — *Chicago Legal Search, Ltd.*
Perkins, Daphne — *CPS Inc.*
Persky, Barry — *Barry Persky & Company, Inc.*
Peterson, John — *CPS Inc.*
Phillips, Scott K. — *Phillips & Ford, Inc.*
Pickering, Dale — *Agri-Tech Personnel, Inc.*
Pickford, Stephen T. — *The Corporate Staff, Inc.*
Pinkman, Karen N. — *Skott/Edwards Consultants, Inc.*
Pinson, Stephanie L. — *Gilbert Tweed/INESA*
Pitcher, Brian D. — *Skott/Edwards Consultants, Inc.*
Pitts, Charles — *Contemporary Management Services, Inc.*
Plimpton, Ralph L. — *R L Plimpton Associates*
Plummer, Winkie Donovan — *McManners Associates, Inc.*
Pomerance, Mark — *CPS Inc.*
Pomeroy, T. Lee — *Egon Zehnder International Inc.*
Porada, Stephen D. — *CAP Inc.*
Porter, Albert — *The Experts*
Porter, Donald — *Amherst Personnel Group Inc.*
Poster, Lawrence D. — *Catalyx Group*
Prencipe, V. Michael — *Raymond Karsan Associates*
Probert, William W. — *Ward Howell International, Inc.*
Provus, Barbara L. — *Shepherd Bueschel & Provus, Inc.*
Rabe, William — *Sales Executives Inc.*
Rabinowitz, Peter A. — *P.A.R. Associates Inc.*
Raheja, Marc C. — *CanMed Consultants Inc.*
Ramsey, John H. — *Mark Stanley & Company*
Randell, James E. — *Randell-Heiken, Inc.*
Range, Mary Jane — *Ingram & Aydelotte Inc.*
Rapoport, William — *Blair/Tech Recruiters*
Rathborne, Kenneth J. — *Blair/Tech Recruiters*
Rauch, Carl W. — *Physicians Search, Inc.*
Rauch, Cliff — *Physicians Search, Inc.*
Raymond, Anne — *Anderson Sterling Associates*
Raymond, Jean — *The Caldwell Partners Amrop International*
Reddick, David C. — *Horton International*
Redler, Rhonda — *National Search, Inc.*
Reiser, Ellen — *Thorndike Deland Associates*
Reiss, Matt — *National Search, Inc.*
Rendl, Ric — *CPS Inc.*
Renner, Sandra L. — *Spectra International Inc.*
Reyman, Susan — *S. Reyman & Associates Ltd.*
Riederer, Larry — *CPS Inc.*
Riley, James — *Hunt Ltd.*
Rimmel, James E. — *The Hindman Company*
Rizzo, L. Donald — *R.P. Barone Associates*
Roberts, Carl R. — *Southwestern Professional Services*
Roberts, Nick P. — *Spectrum Search Associates, Inc.*
Roberts, Scott B. — *Wargo and Co., Inc.*
Roberts, William — *Cochran, Cochran & Yale, Inc.*
Robertson, William R. — *Ward Howell International, Inc.*
Robinson, Bruce — *Bruce Robinson Associates*
Robinson, Eric B. — *Bruce Robinson Associates*
Romanchek, Walter R. — *Wellington Management Group*
Rosen, Salene — *Bryant Research*
Rosenfeld, Martin J. — *Sanford Rose Associates*
Rosenthal, Charles — *National Search, Inc.*
Ross, Mark S. — *Herman Smith Executive Initiatives Inc.*
Rossi, Silvio — *Keith Bagg & Associates Inc.*
Rozner, Burton L. — *Oliver & Rozner Associates, Inc.*
Rubinstein, Alan J. — *Chicago Legal Search, Ltd.*
Runquist, U.W. — *Webb, Johnson Associates, Inc.*
Russo, Karen — *K. Russo Associates*
Russo, Karen — *Maximum Management Corp.*
Sabat, Lori S. — *Alta Associates, Inc.*
Sacerdote, John — *Raymond Karsan Associates*
Sahlas, Chrissy — *CPS Inc.*
Saletra, Andrew — *CPS Inc.*
Salvagno, Michael J. — *The Cambridge Group Ltd*
Samet, Saul — *Fisher-Todd Associates*
Sampson, Martin C. — *Sampson Neill & Wilkins Inc.*
Sanders, Natalie — *CPS Inc.*
Sanders, Spencer H. — *Battalia Winston International*
Sandor, Richard J. — *Flynn, Hannock, Incorporated*
Sarn, Allan G. — *Allan Sarn Associates Inc.*
Savage, Edward J. — *Stanton Chase International*
Savard, Robert F. — *The Stevenson Group of Delaware Inc.*
Sawhill, Louise B. — *Paul Ray Berndtson*
Sayers, Bruce D. — *Brackin & Sayers Associates*
Scalamera, Tom — *CPS Inc.*
Schaefer, Frederic M. — *A.T. Kearney, Inc.*
Schaefer, Robert — *Search Enterprises, Inc.*
Schappell, Marc P. — *Egon Zehnder International Inc.*
Scherck, Henry J. — *Ward Howell International, Inc.*
Schiavone, Mary Rose — *Canny, Bowen Inc.*

Schmidt, Frank B. — *F.B. Schmidt International*
Schroeder, Lee — *Blau Kaptain Schroeder*
Schroeder, Steven J. — *Blau Kaptain Schroeder*
Schueneman, David — *CPS Inc.*
Schwartz, Carole — *A.T. Kearney, Inc.*
Semyan, John K. — *TNS Partners, Inc.*
Sennello, Gendra — *National Search, Inc.*
Sevilla, Claudio A. — *Crawford & Crofford*
Shapiro, Elaine — *CPS Inc.*
Shea, John — *ALTCO Temporary Services*
Shea, John — *The ALTCO Group*
Shea, Kathleen M. — *The Penn Partners, Incorporated*
Sheedy, Edward J. — *Dieckmann & Associates, Ltd.*
Shelton, Sandra — *National Search, Inc.*
Shemin, Grace — *Maximum Management Corp.*
Shepherd, Daniel M. — *Shepherd Bueschel & Provus, Inc.*
Sherwin, Thomas — *Barone-O'Hara Associates*
Shield, Nancy — *Maximum Management Corp.*
Shipherd, John T. — *The Cassie Group*
Shirilla, Robert M. — *F.B. Schmidt International*
Shoemaker, Larry C. — *Shoemaker & Associates*
Shultz, Deborah M. — *Blau Kaptain Schroeder*
Sibbald, John R. — *John Sibbald Associates, Inc.*
Sibul, Shelly Remen — *Chicago Legal Search, Ltd.*
Signer, Julie — *CPS Inc.*
Silcott, Marvin L. — *Marvin L. Silcott & Associates, Inc.*
Sill, Igor M. — *Geneva Group International*
Sill, Igor M. — *Geneva Group International*
Skunda, Donna M. — *Allerton Heneghan & O'Neill*
Slater, Ronald E. — *A.T. Kearney, Inc.*
Smead, Michelle M. — *A.T. Kearney, Inc.*
Smirnov, Tatiana — *Allan Sarn Associates Inc.*
Smith, Grant — *Price Waterhouse*
Smith, John F. — *The Penn Partners, Incorporated*
Snelgrove, Geiger — *National Search, Inc.*
Snodgrass, Stephen — *DeFrain, Mayer, Lee & Burgess LLC*
Snyder, James F. — *Snyder & Company*
Sobczak, Ronald — *Search Enterprises, Inc.*
Soggs, Cheryl Pavick — *A.T. Kearney, Inc.*
Solomon Ph.D., Neil M. — *The Neil Michael Group, Inc.*
Spadavecchia, Jennifer — *Alta Associates, Inc.*
Speck, Michael J. — *Lovas Stanley/Paul Ray Berndtson Inc.*
Spriggs, Robert D. — *Spriggs & Company, Inc.*
Stark, Jeff — *Thorne, Brieger Associates Inc.*
Statson, Dale E. — *Sales Executives Inc.*
Stein, Terry W. — *Stewart, Stein and Scott, Ltd.*
Steinman, Stephen — *The Stevenson Group of New Jersey*
Stenholm, Gilbert R. — *Spencer Stuart*
Stephanian, Armand A. — *Paul Ray Berndtson*
Stephenson, Don L. — *Ells Personnel System Inc.*
Stern, Stephen — *CPS Inc.*
Sterner, Doug — *CPS Inc.*
Stewart, Jan J. — *Egon Zehnder International Inc.*
Stewart, Jeffrey O. — *Stewart, Stein and Scott, Ltd.*
Stiles, Judy — *MedQuest Associates*
Stinson, R.J. — *Sampson Neill & Wilkins Inc.*
Stone, Susan L. — *Stone Enterprises Ltd.*
Stouffer, Kenneth — *Keith Bagg & Associates Inc.*
Stratmeyer, Karin Bergwall — *Princeton Entrepreneurial Resources*
Strawn, William — *Houtz-Strawn Associates, Inc.*
Stringer, Dan P. — *D.E. Foster Partners Inc.*
Strom, Mark N. — *Search Advisors International Corp.*
Sullivan, James — *Search Enterprises, Inc.*
Sur, William K. — *Canny, Bowen Inc.*
Swanson, Dick — *Raymond Karsan Associates*
Swatts, Stone — *F-O-R-T-U-N-E Personnel Consultants of Huntsville, Inc.*
Sweeney, James W. — *Sweeney Harbert & Mummert, Inc.*
Swidler, J. Robert — *Egon Zehnder International Inc.*
Taylor, Kenneth W. — *Egon Zehnder International Inc.*
Teas, John — *Southwestern Professional Services*
Teinert, Jay — *Damon & Associates, Inc.*
Telford, John H. — *Telford, Adams & Alexander/Telford & Co., Inc.*
Templin, Robert E. — *Gilbert Tweed/INESA*
Theobald, David B. — *Theobald & Associates*
Tholke, William E. — *Canny, Bowen Inc.*
Thomas, Cheryl M. — *CPS Inc.*
Thomas, John T. — *Ward Howell International, Inc.*
Thomas, Kim — *CPS Inc.*
Thomas, Terry — *Montague Enterprises*
Thompson, Kenneth L. — *McCormack & Farrow*
Tovrog, Dan — *CPS Inc.*
Tracy, Ronald O. — *Egon Zehnder International Inc.*
Trosin, Walter R. — *Johnson Smith & Knisely Accord*
Truemper, Dean — *CPS Inc.*
Truex, John F. — *Morton, McCorkle & Associates, Inc.*
Tullberg, Tina — *CPS Inc.*
Tunney, William — *Grant Cooper and Associates*

Tursi, Deborah J. — *The Corporate Connection, Ltd.*
Tutwiler, Stephen — *Don Richard Associates of Tampa, Inc.*
Tweed, Janet — *Gilbert Tweed/INESA*
Twiste, Craig — *Raymond Karsan Associates*
Ulbert, Nancy — *Aureus Group*
Vachon, David A. — *McNichol Associates*
Vainblat, Galina — *Foy, Schneid & Daniel, Inc.*
Valenta, Joseph — *Princeton Entrepreneurial Resources*
Van Campen, Jerry — *Gilbert & Van Campen International*
Van Clieaf, Mark — *MVC Associates International*
Vande-Water, Katie — *J. Robert Scott*
Vann, Dianne — *The Button Group*
Velten, Mark — *Hunt Advisory Services*
Velten, Mark — *Hunt Ltd.*
Venable, William W. — *Thorndike Deland Associates*
Vergara, Gail H. — *Spencer Stuart*
Virgili, Franca — *Johnson Smith & Knisely Accord*
Visnich, L. Christine — *Bason Associates Inc.*
Vlcek, Thomas J. — *Vlcek & Company, Inc.*
Vogel, Michael S. — *Vogel Associates*
Volk, Richard — *MSI International*
Wakefield, Scott — *National Search, Inc.*
Waldoch, D. Mark — *Barnes Development Group, LLC*
Wall, David — *Southwestern Professional Services*
Warren, Sylvia W. — *Thorndike Deland Associates*
Wasson, Thomas W. — *Spencer Stuart*
Waters, Peter D. — *John Kurosky & Associates*
Webb, George H. — *Webb, Johnson Associates, Inc.*
Weber, Jurgen — *BioQuest, Inc.*
Weiner, Arlene — *Sanford Rose Associates*
Weiner, Arthur — *Sanford Rose Associates*
Weisler, Nancy — *National Search, Inc.*
Weissman-Rosenthal, Abbe — *ALW Research International*
Weisz, Laura — *Anderson Sterling Associates*
Weller, Paul S. — *Mark Stanley & Company*
Werner, Bonnie — *H.M. Long International, Ltd.*
White, Patricia D. — *MSI International*
Whitney, David L. — *Whitney & Associates, Inc.*
Wilkins, Walter K. — *Sampson Neill & Wilkins Inc.*
Wilkinson, Barbara — *Beall & Company, Inc.*
Williams, Angie — *Whitney & Associates, Inc.*
Williams, Gary L. — *Barnes Development Group, LLC*
Williams, Laurelle N. — *MSI International*
Williams, Roger K. — *Williams, Roth & Krueger Inc.*
Williams, Walter E. — *Canny, Bowen Inc.*
Willis, William H. — *William Willis Worldwide Inc.*
Winitz, Joel — *GSW Consulting Group, Inc.*
Winitz, Marla — *GSW Consulting Group, Inc.*
Winnewisser, William E. — *Accounting & Computer Personnel*
Winston, Dale — *Battalia Winston International*
Winston, Susan — *CPS Inc.*
Winter, Peter — *Catalyx Group*
Wisch, Steven C. — *MB Inc. Interim Executive Division*
Wise, J. Herbert — *Sandhurst Associates*
Wolf, Stephen M. — *Byron Leonard International, Inc.*
Wood, John S. — *Egon Zehnder International Inc.*
Wright, Leslie — *The Stevenson Group of New Jersey*
Wyatt, James — *Wyatt & Jaffe*
Yard, Allan S. — *Bryant Research*
Yilmaz, Muriel — *Dinte Resources, Incorporated*
Young, Alexander — *Messett Associates, Inc.*
Zander, Barry W. — *MSI International*
Zaslav, Debra M. — *Telford, Adams & Alexander/Telford & Co., Inc.*
Zetter, Roger — *Hunt Ltd.*
Zila, Laurie M. — *Princeton Entrepreneurial Resources*
Zilliacus, Patrick W. — *Larsen, Zilliacus & Associates, Inc.*
Zingaro, Ron — *Zingaro and Company*
Zivic, Janis M. — *Spencer Stuart*
Zoppo, Dorathea — *Bill Hahn Group, Inc.*
Zucker, Nancy — *Maximum Management Corp.*

## 25. Public Administration

Adams, Jeffrey C. — *Telford, Adams & Alexander/Jeffrey C. Adams & Co., Inc.*
Antil, Pamela W. — *Norman Roberts & Associates, Inc.*
Bailey, William A. — *TNS Partners, Inc.*
Baker-Greene, Edward — *Isaacson, Miller*
Bason, Maurice L. — *Bason Associates Inc.*
Belford, Paul — *JDG Associates, Ltd.*
Bennett, Richard T. — *Isaacson, Miller*
Berger, Emanuel — *Isaacson, Miller*
Berger, Jay V. — *Morris & Berger*
Bittman, Beth M. — *Norman Roberts & Associates, Inc.*
Blair, Kelly A. — *The Caldwell Partners Amrop International*
Brown, Jeffrey W. — *Comprehensive Search*
Brunelle, Francis W.H. — *The Caldwell Partners Amrop International*

Caldwell, C. Douglas — *The Caldwell Partners Amrop International*
Charles, Ronald D. — *The Caldwell Partners Amrop International*
Chauvin, Ralph A. — *The Caldwell Partners Amrop International*
Christenson, H. Alan — *Christenson & Hutchison*
Collard, Joseph A. — *Spencer Stuart*
Cronin, Richard J. — *Hodge-Cronin & Associates, Inc.*
Divine, Robert S. — *O'Shea, Divine & Company, Inc.*
Edell, David E. — *The Development Resource Group Incorporated*
Fancher, Robert L. — *Bason Associates Inc.*
Fawcett, Anne M. — *The Caldwell Partners Amrop International*
Frank, Valerie S. — *Norman Roberts & Associates, Inc.*
George, Delores F. — *Delores F. George Human Resource Management & Consulting Industry*
Gilbert, Jerry — *Gilbert & Van Campen International*
Goodman, Dawn M. — *Bason Associates Inc.*
Halyburton, Robert R. — *The Halyburton Co., Inc.*
Hamilton, Timothy — *The Caldwell Partners Amrop International*
Hauser, Martha — *Spencer Stuart*
Hay, William E. — *William E. Hay & Company*
Hildebrand, Thomas B. — *Professional Resources Group, Inc.*
Hite, William A. — *Hite Executive Search*
Hutchison, William K. — *Christenson & Hutchison*
Joffe, Barry — *Bason Associates Inc.*
Johnson, Maxene — *Norman Roberts & Associates, Inc.*
Kelly, Donna J. — *Accountants Executive Search*
Kershaw, Lisa — *Tanton Mitchell/Paul Ray Berndtson*
King, Thomas — *Morgan Hunter Corp.*
Krejci, Stanley L. — *The Interface Group, Ltd./Boyden*
Kuper, Keith D. — *Christenson & Hutchison*
Leslie, William H. — *Boyden/Zay & Company*
Love, David M. — *Paul Ray Berndtson*
Low, Linda — *The Development Resource Group Incorporated*
Manns, Alex — *Crawford & Crofford*
Massey, H. Heath — *Robison & Associates*
McCormack, Joseph A. — *McCormack & Associates*
McIntyre, Alex D. — *Norman Roberts & Associates, Inc.*
McLean, B. Keith — *Price Waterhouse*
Miller, Arnie — *Isaacson, Miller*
Morris, Kristine A. — *Morris & Berger*
Myers, Kay — *Signature Staffing*
Neher, Robert L. — *Intech Summit Group, Inc.*
Nelson, Barbara — *Herman Smith Executive Initiatives Inc.*
Patton, Mitchell — *Patton/Perry Associates, Inc.*
Peternell, Melanie — *Signature Staffing*
Pinson, Stephanie L. — *Gilbert Tweed/INESA*
Ray, Paul R. — *Paul Ray Berndtson*
Raymond, Jean — *The Caldwell Partners Amrop International*
Regeuye, Peter J. — *Accountants Executive Search*
Roberts, Norman C. — *Norman Roberts & Associates, Inc.*
Robins, Jeri N. — *Nagler, Robins & Poe, Inc.*
Robison, John H. — *Robison & Associates*
Ross, Mark S. — *Herman Smith Executive Initiatives Inc.*
Rozan, Naomi — *Comprehensive Search*
Shervey, Brent C. — *O'Callaghan Honey/Paul Ray Berndtson, Inc.*
Smith, Herman M. — *Herman Smith Executive Initiatives Inc.*
Strom, Mark N. — *Search Advisors International Corp.*
Taylor, Charles E. — *Lamalie Amrop International*
Telford, John H. — *Telford, Adams & Alexander/Telford & Co., Inc.*
Truex, John F. — *Morton, McCorkle & Associates, Inc.*
Vennat, Manon — *Spencer Stuart*
Visnich, L. Christine — *Bason Associates Inc.*
Yilmaz, Muriel — *Dinte Resources, Incorporated*
Zaslav, Debra M. — *Telford, Adams & Alexander/Telford & Co., Inc.*
Zivic, Janis M. — *Spencer Stuart*
Zonis, Hildy R. — *Accountants Executive Search*

## 26. Publishing/Media

Abbatiello, Christine Murphy — *Winter, Wyman & Company*
Abbott, Peter — *The Abbott Group, Inc.*
Acquaviva, Jay — *Winter, Wyman & Company*
Alekel, Karren — *ALW Research International*
Aronin, Michael — *Fisher-Todd Associates*
Ascher, Susan P. — *The Ascher Group*
Aydelotte, G. Thomas — *Ingram & Aydelotte Inc.*
Baillou, Astrid — *Richard Kinser & Associates*
Barnum, Toni M. — *Stone Murphy & Olson*
Barr, Ronald — *Search West, Inc.*
Barton, Gary R. — *Barton Raben, Inc.*
Bellano, Robert W. — *Stanton Chase International*
Berenblum, Marvin B. — *Heidrick & Struggles, Inc.*
Berk-Levine, Margo — *MB Inc. Interim Executive Division*
Bishop, Susan — *Bishop Partners*
Borland, James — *Goodrich & Sherwood Associates, Inc.*
Brackenbury, Robert — *Bowman & Marshall, Inc.*
Brackin, James B. — *Brackin & Sayers Associates*
Bratches, Howard — *Thorndike Deland Associates*
Brocaglia, Joyce — *Alta Associates, Inc.*

Brophy, Melissa — *Maximum Management Corp.*
Brovender, Claire — *Winter, Wyman & Company*
Brown, Buzz — *Brown, Bernardy, Van Remmen, Inc.*
Brudno, Robert J. — *Savoy Partners, Ltd.*
Buck, Charles — *Charles Buck & Associates*
Burchill, Greg — *BGB Associates*
Burmaster, Holly — *Winter, Wyman & Company*
Burns, Alan — *The Enns Partners Inc.*
Cahill, James P. — *Thorndike Deland Associates*
Callahan, Wanda — *Cochran, Cochran & Yale, Inc.*
Campbell, Patricia A. — *The Onstott Group, Inc.*
Carideo, Joseph — *Thorndike Deland Associates*
Carlson, Judith — *Bowman & Marshall, Inc.*
Caruso, Kathy — *Accounting Resources, Inc.*
Chargar, Frances — *Hunt Ltd.*
Citrin, James M. — *Spencer Stuart*
Cizek, John T. — *Cizek Associates, Inc.*
Claushen, Elizabeth A. — *Savoy Partners, Ltd.*
Cohen, Luis Lezama — *Paul Ray Berndtson*
Colling, Douglas — *KPMG Management Consulting*
Combs, Stephen L. — *Juntunen-Combs-Poirier*
Connaghan, Linda — *Bowman & Marshall, Inc.*
Cooke, Katherine H. — *Horton International*
Cornehlsen, James H. — *Lamalie Amrop International*
Corrigan, Gerald F. — *The Corrigan Group*
Cragg, Barbara R. — *Southwestern Professional Services*
Crane, Howard C. — *Chartwell Partners International, Inc.*
Cronin, Richard J. — *Hodge-Cronin & Associates, Inc.*
Cunningham, Robert Y. — *Goodrich & Sherwood Associates, Inc.*
Dalton, Bret — *Robert W. Dingman Company, Inc.*
Danforth, W. Michael — *Hyde Danforth Wold & Co.*
Danoff, Audrey — *Don Richard Associates of Tidewater, Inc.*
Davis, Bert — *Bert Davis Executive Search, Inc.*
Davis, Orlin R. — *Heidrick & Struggles, Inc.*
de Bardin, Francesca — *F.L. Taylor & Company, Inc.*
Diaz-Joslyn, Mabel — *Walker Communications*
DiMarchi, Paul — *DiMarchi Partners, Inc.*
Dingman, Bruce — *Robert W. Dingman Company, Inc.*
Dingman, Robert W. — *Robert W. Dingman Company, Inc.*
Dinte, Paul — *Dinte Resources, Incorporated*
Divine, Robert S. — *O'Shea, Divine & Company, Inc.*
Do, Sonnie — *Whitney & Associates, Inc.*
Doele, Donald C. — *Goodrich & Sherwood Associates, Inc.*
Dotson, M. Ileen — *Dotson & Associates*
Dougherty, Bridget L. — *Wellington Management Group*
Drury, James J. — *Spencer Stuart*
Eberly, Carrie — *Accounting Resources, Inc.*
Ehrgott, Elizabeth — *The Ascher Group*
England, Mark — *Austin-McGregor International*
Enns, George — *The Enns Partners Inc.*
Feldman, Abe — *A.E. Feldman Associates*
Ferneborg, Jay W. — *Ferneborg & Associates, Inc.*
Ferneborg, John R. — *Ferneborg & Associates, Inc.*
Ferrari, S. Jay — *Ferrari Search Group*
Fixler, Eugene — *Ariel Recruitment Associates*
Flanagan, Robert M. — *Robert M. Flanagan & Associates, Ltd.*
Flannery, Peter — *Jonas, Walters & Assoc., Inc.*
Flowers, John E. — *Balfour Associates*
Frazier, John — *Cochran, Cochran & Yale, Inc.*
Gaines, Jay — *Jay Gaines & Company, Inc.*
Galante, Suzanne M. — *Vlcek & Company, Inc.*
Gallagher, Marilyn — *Hogan Acquisitions*
Gardiner, E. Nicholas P. — *Gardiner International*
Garfinkle, Steven M. — *Battalia Winston International*
Gauthier, Robert C. — *Columbia Consulting Group*
George, Delores F. — *Delores F. George Human Resource Management & Consulting Industry*
Gill, Patricia — *Columbia Consulting Group*
Glacy, Kurt — *Winter, Wyman & Company*
Glancey, Thomas F. — *Gordon Wahls Company*
Grantham, John — *Grantham & Co., Inc.*
Grassl, Peter O. — *Bowman & Marshall, Inc.*
Gray, Annie — *Annie Gray Associates, Inc./The Executive Search Firm*
Hall, Robert — *Don Richard Associates of Tidewater, Inc.*
Hallock, Peter B. — *Goodrich & Sherwood Associates, Inc.*
Hanson, Grant M. — *Goodrich & Sherwood Associates, Inc.*
Havas, Judy — *Heidrick & Struggles, Inc.*
Havener, Donald Clarke — *The Abbott Group, Inc.*
Hecker, Henry C. — *Hogan Acquisitions*
Heiken, Barbara E. — *Randell-Heiken, Inc.*
Hellebusch, Jerry — *Morgan Hunter Corp.*
Herman, Pat — *Whitney & Associates, Inc.*
Hite, William A. — *Hite Executive Search*
Hoevel, Michael J. — *Poirier, Hoevel & Co.*
Hogan, Larry H. — *Hogan Acquisitions*
Hopkins, Chester A. — *Handy HRM Corp.*
Hoppert, Phil — *Wargo and Co., Inc.*

Thielman, Joseph — *Barrett Partners*
Thompson, Brett — *Southwestern Professional Services*
Thompson, Carlton W. — *Spencer Stuart*
Thompson, James R. — *Gordon Wahls Company*
Thompson, Kenneth L. — *McCormack & Farrow*
Timoney, Laura — *Bishop Partners*
Trueblood, Brian G. — *TNS Partners, Inc.*
Tucker, Thomas A. — *The Thomas Tucker Company*
Turner, Edward K. — *Don Richard Associates of Charlotte*
Ulbert, Nancy — *Aureus Group*
Van Clieaf, Mark — *MVC Associates International*
Van Remmen, Roger — *Brown, Bernardy, Van Remmen, Inc.*
Velten, Mark — *Hunt Advisory Services*
Velten, Mark — *Hunt Ltd.*
Venable, William W. — *Thorndike Deland Associates*
Virgili, Franca — *Johnson Smith & Knisely Accord*
Vlcek, Thomas J. -- *Vlcek & Company, Inc.*
Vojta, Marilyn B. — *James Mead & Company*
von Stein, Scott — *Wilkinson & Ives*
Walker, Martin S. — *Walker Communications*
Wall, David — *Southwestern Professional Services*
Walters, William F. — *Jonas, Walters & Assoc., Inc.*
Ware, John C. — *Spencer Stuart*
Warren, Sylvia W. — *Thorndike Deland Associates*
Warter, Mark — *Isaacson, Miller*
Wein, Michael S. — *Media Management Resources, Inc.*
Wein, William — *InterimManagement Solutions, Inc.*
Wein, William — *Media Management Resources, Inc.*
Weissman-Rosenthal, Abbe — *ALW Research International*
Welch, Dale — *Winter, Wyman & Company*
Wertel, Ronald E. — *Gordon Wahls Company*
Wexler, Rona — *Ariel Recruitment Associates*
Whitney, David L. — *Whitney & Associates, Inc.*
Wier, Daniel — *Horton International*
Wilder, Richard B. — *Columbia Consulting Group*
Williams, Angie — *Whitney & Associates, Inc.*
Willis, William H. — *William Willis Worldwide Inc.*
Winitz, Joel — *GSW Consulting Group, Inc.*
Winitz, Marla — *GSW Consulting Group, Inc.*
Winter, Peter — *Catalyx Group*
Wright, Charles D. — *Goodrich & Sherwood Associates, Inc.*
Zee, Wanda — *Tesar-Reynes, Inc.*
Zetter, Roger — *Hunt Ltd.*
Zinn, Donald — *Bishop Partners*
Zivic, Janis M. — *Spencer Stuart*
Zonis, Hildy R. — *Accountants Executive Search*
Zucker, Nancy — *Maximum Management Corp.*

## 27. Real Estate

Abbatiello, Christine Murphy — *Winter, Wyman & Company*
Adams, Jeffrey C. — *Telford, Adams & Alexander/Jeffrey C. Adams & Co., Inc.*
Adams, Michael — *CG & Associates*
Alexander, John T. — *Telford, Adams & Alexander/Human Resource Services*
Allen, Scott — *Chrisman & Company, Incorporated*
Antil, Pamela W. — *Norman Roberts & Associates, Inc.*
Bader, Sam — *Bader Research Corporation*
Baran, Helena — *Michael J. Cavanagh and Associates*
Barton, Gary R. — *Barton Raben, Inc.*
Beck, Barbara S. — *Rhodes Associates*
Beckvold, John B. — *Atlantic Search Group, Inc.*
Berger, Jay V. — *Morris & Berger*
Berne, Marlene — *The Whitney Group*
Bittman, Beth M. — *Norman Roberts & Associates, Inc.*
Bladon, Andrew — *Don Richard Associates of Tampa, Inc.*
Bogard, Nicholas C. — *The Onstott Group, Inc.*
Bourrie, Sharon D. — *Chartwell Partners International, Inc.*
Brown, D. Perry — *Don Richard Associates of Washington, D.C., Inc.*
Brown, Ronald — *Richard, Wayne and Roberts*
Bruce, Michael C. — *Spencer Stuart*
Buchalter, Allyson — *The Whitney Group*
Burns, Terence N. — *D.E. Foster Partners Inc.*
Button, David R. — *The Button Group*
Caldwell, C. Douglas — *The Caldwell Partners Amrop International*
Cannavo, Louise — *The Whitney Group*
Casey, Jean — *Peter W. Ambler Company*
Cavanagh, Michael J. — *Michael J. Cavanagh and Associates*
Christenson, H. Alan — *Christenson & Hutchison*
Clark, Evan — *The Whitney Group*
Cole, Kevin — *Don Richard Associates of Washington, D.C., Inc.*
Collard, Joseph A. — *Spencer Stuart*
Corso, Glen S. — *Chartwell Partners International, Inc.*
Cramer, Paul J. — *C/R Associates*
Crath, Paul F. — *Price Waterhouse*
Crawford, Cassondra — *Don Richard Associates of Washington, D.C., Inc.*

Crystal, Jonathan A. — *Spencer Stuart*
Davis, Robert — *CG & Associates*
Delmonico, Laura — *A.J. Burton Group, Inc.*
Demchak, James P. — *Sandhurst Associates*
Desmond, Dennis — *Beall & Company, Inc.*
deWilde, David M. — *Chartwell Partners International, Inc.*
DiMarchi, Paul — *DiMarchi Partners, Inc.*
Divine, Robert S. — *O'Shea, Divine & Company, Inc.*
Do, Sonnie — *Whitney & Associates, Inc.*
Doan, Lisa — *Rhodes Associates*
Dorsey, Jim — *Ryan, Miller & Associates Inc.*
Dowell, Mary K. — *Professional Search Associates*
Dremely, Mark — *Richard, Wayne and Roberts*
Dunn, Mary Helen — *Paul Ray Berndtson*
Farish, John G. — *Paul Ray Berndtson*
Fawcett, Anne M. — *The Caldwell Partners Amrop International*
Feldman, Kimberley — *Atlantic Search Group, Inc.*
Ferneborg, Jay W. — *Ferneborg & Associates, Inc.*
Ferneborg, John R. — *Ferneborg & Associates, Inc.*
Flora, Dodi — *Crawford & Crofford*
Frank, Valerie S. — *Norman Roberts & Associates, Inc.*
Fribush, Richard — *A.J. Burton Group, Inc.*
Fulton, Christine N. — *Highland Search Group, L.L.C.*
George, Delores F. — *Delores F. George Human Resource Management & Consulting Industry*
Gerevas, Ronald E. — *Spencer Stuart*
Gerevas, Ronald E. — *Spencer Stuart*
Gilbert, Jerry — *Gilbert & Van Campen International*
Goar, Duane R. — *Sandhurst Associates*
Goldstein, Gary — *The Whitney Group*
Gordon, Gerald L. — *E.G. Jones Associates, Ltd.*
Gordon, Teri — *Don Richard Associates of Washington, D.C., Inc.*
Graves, Rosemarie — *Don Richard Associates of Washington, D.C., Inc.*
Gray, David — *CG & Associates*
Greene, Luke — *Broward-Dobbs, Inc.*
Groom, Charles C. — *CG & Associates*
Gurtin, Kay L. — *Executive Options, Ltd.*
Gwin, Ric — *Southwestern Professional Services*
Hall, Peter V. — *Chartwell Partners International, Inc.*
Hardison, Richard L. — *Hardison & Company*
Hargis, N. Leann — *Montgomery Resources, Inc.*
Harris, Ethel S. — *Don Richard Associates of Charlotte*
Harris, Julia — *The Whitney Group*
Harvey, Mike — *Advanced Executive Resources*
Haughton, Michael — *DeFrain, Mayer, Lee & Burgess LLC*
Hauswirth, Jeffrey M. — *Spencer Stuart*
Haystead, Steve — *Advanced Executive Resources*
Hellebusch, Jerry — *Morgan Hunter Corp.*
Hemingway, Stuart C. — *Robison & Associates*
Hensley, Gayla — *Atlantic Search Group, Inc.*
Herman, Pat — *Whitney & Associates, Inc.*
Hetherman, Margaret F. — *Highland Search Group, L.L.C.*
Holden, Richard — *Hornberger Management Company*
Hornberger, Frederick C. — *Hornberger Management Company*
Howell, Robert B. — *Atlantic Search Group, Inc.*
Howell, Robert B. — *Atlantic Search Group, Inc.*
Hudson, Reginald M. — *Search Bureau International*
Hunter, Sue J. — *Robison & Associates*
Hutchison, William K. — *Christenson & Hutchison*
Illsley, Hugh G. — *Ward Howell International, Inc.*
Jernigan, Susan N. — *Sockwell & Associates*
Jones, Daniel F. — *Atlantic Search Group, Inc.*
Juratovac, Michael — *Montgomery Resources, Inc.*
Kalus, Lisa — *Lisa Kalus & Associates, Inc.*
Kassouf, Connie — *The Whitney Group*
Kelly, Donna J. — *Accountants Executive Search*
Kelly, Peter W. — *R. Rollo Associates*
King, Bill — *The McCormick Group, Inc.*
King, Thomas — *Morgan Hunter Corp.*
Kinser, Richard E. — *Richard Kinser & Associates*
Knight, Russell — *Hornberger Management Company*
Krauser, H. James — *Spencer Stuart*
Kucewicz, William — *Search West, Inc.*
Kuo, Linda — *Montgomery Resources, Inc.*
Kuper, Keith D. — *Christenson & Hutchison*
Larsen, Richard F. — *Larsen, Zilliacus & Associates, Inc.*
Lasher, Charles M. — *Lasher Associates*
Lazaro, Alicia C. — *The Whitney Group*
Lee, Roger — *Montgomery Resources, Inc.*
Leff, Lisa A. — *Berger and Leff*
Letcher, Harvey D. — *Sandhurst Associates*
Lewis, Jon A. — *Sandhurst Associates*
Lewis, Marc D. — *Handy HRM Corp.*
Linde, Rick — *Battalia Winston International*
Line, Joseph T. — *Sharrow & Associates*
Litt-Peck, Michelle — *The Whitney Group*

Littman, Stephen — *Rhodes Associates*
Long, William G. — *McDonald, Long & Associates, Inc.*
Lyons, Jane A. — *Rhodes Associates*
Lyons, Michele R. — *R. Rollo Associates*
MacDougall, Andrew J. — *Spencer Stuart*
Manzo, Renee — *Atlantic Search Group, Inc.*
Mathias, William J. — *Preng & Associates, Inc.*
Mauer, Kristin — *Montgomery Resources, Inc.*
Mayes, Kay H. — *John Shell Associates, Inc.*
McAteer, Thomas — *Montgomery Resources, Inc.*
McConnell, Greg — *Winter, Wyman & Company*
McCormick, Brian — *The McCormick Group, Inc.*
McCormick, William J. — *The McCormick Group, Inc.*
McFadden, Ashton S. — *Johnson Smith & Knisely Accord*
McGuire, Corey — *Peter W. Ambler Company*
McKinnis, Paul D. — *Paul Ray Berndtson*
McNear, Jeffrey E. — *Barrett Partners*
Meltzer, Andrea Y. — *Executive Options, Ltd.*
Mertensotto, Chuck H. — *Whitney & Associates, Inc.*
Messett, William J. — *Messett Associates, Inc.*
Meyers, Steven — *Montgomery Resources, Inc.*
Millonzi, Joel C. — *Johnson Smith & Knisely Accord*
Molitor, John L. — *Barrett Partners*
Moran, Gail — *Comprehensive Search*
Morris, Kristine A. — *Morris & Berger*
Mursuli, Meredith — *Lasher Associates*
Nass, Martin D. — *Lamalie Amrop International*
Neidhart, Craig C. — *TNS Partners, Inc.*
Nelson, Garry A. — *Rhodes Associates*
Nevins, Patricia — *Rhodes Associates*
Nunziata, Peter — *Atlantic Search Group, Inc.*
O'Callaghan, Terry K. — *O'Callaghan Honey/Paul Ray Berndtson, Inc.*
O'Hara, Daniel M. — *Lynch Miller Moore Partners, Inc.*
Ogden, Dayton — *Spencer Stuart*
Olsen, Robert F. — *Robert Connelly and Associates Incorporated*
Ott, George W. — *Ott & Hansen, Inc.*
Palmer, Carlton A. — *Beall & Company, Inc.*
Palmer, Melissa — *Don Richard Associates of Tampa, Inc.*
Papciak, Dennis J. — *Temporary Accounting Personnel*
Park, Dabney G. — *Mark Stanley & Company*
Pepe, Leonida — *Butterfass, Pepe & MacCallan Inc.*
Phillips, Donald L. — *O'Shea, Divine & Company, Inc.*
Phillips, James L. — *Highland Search Group, L.L.C.*
Potter, Steven B. — *Highland Search Group, L.L.C.*
Powell, Leslie — *Rhodes Associates*
Prior, Donald — *The Caldwell Partners Amrop International*
Pugrant, Mark A. — *Grant/Morgan Associates, Inc.*
Rabinowitz, Peter A. — *P.A.R. Associates Inc.*
Ramsey, John H. — *Mark Stanley & Company*
Rauch, Carl W. — *Physicians Search, Inc.*
Rauch, Cliff — *Physicians Search, Inc.*
Reeves, William B. — *Spencer Stuart*
Regeuye, Peter J. — *Accountants Executive Search*
Rich, Lyttleton — *Sockwell & Associates*
Roberts, Carl R. — *Southwestern Professional Services*
Roberts, Nick P. — *Spectrum Search Associates, Inc.*
Roberts, Norman C. — *Norman Roberts & Associates, Inc.*
Robins, Jeri N. — *Nagler, Robins & Poe, Inc.*
Robison, John H. — *Robison & Associates*
Rollo, Robert S. — *R. Rollo Associates*
Ropes, John — *Ropes Associates, Inc.*
Ross, Mark S. — *Herman Smith Executive Initiatives Inc.*
Rozan, Naomi — *Comprehensive Search*
Rustin, Beth — *The Whitney Group*
Ryan, Lee — *Ryan, Miller & Associates Inc.*
Sarn, Allan G. — *Allan Sarn Associates Inc.*
Sathe, Mark A. — *Sathe & Associates, Inc.*
Saxner, David — *DSA, Inc.*
Schlpma, Christine — *Advanced Executive Resources*
Schroeder, John W. — *Spencer Stuart*
Shaw, Ken — *Hornberger Management Company*
Shell, John C. — *John Shell Associates, Inc.*
Shen, Eugene Y. — *The Whitney Group*
Siegel, Pamela — *Executive Options, Ltd.*
Simon, Penny B. — *Paul Ray Berndtson*
Skirbe, Douglas — *Rhodes Associates*
Smirnov, Tatiana — *Allan Sarn Associates Inc.*
Smith, Ethan L. — *Highland Search Group, L.L.C.*
Smith, Herman M. — *Herman Smith Executive Initiatives Inc.*
Snodgrass, Stephen — *DeFrain, Mayer, Lee & Burgess LLC*
Sockwell, J. Edgar — *Sockwell & Associates*
Stevens, Tracey — *Don Richard Associates of Washington, D.C., Inc.*
Stoll, Steven G. — *Sharrow & Associates*
Strassman, Mark — *Don Richard Associates of Washington, D.C., Inc.*
Taylor, Ernest A. — *Ward Howell International, Inc.*
Telford, John H. — *Telford, Adams & Alexander/Telford & Co., Inc.*
Thielman, Joseph — *Barrett Partners*

Tierney, Eileen — *The Whitney Group*
Tracey, Jack — *Management Assistance Group, Inc.*
Tryon, Katey — *DeFrain, Mayer, Lee & Burgess LLC*
Turner, Edward K. — *Don Richard Associates of Charlotte*
Tweed, Janet — *Gilbert Tweed/INESA*
Van Clieaf, Mark — *MVC Associates International*
Vann, Dianne — *The Button Group*
Vognsen, Rikke — *DSA, Inc.*
Vossler, James — *A.J. Burton Group, Inc.*
Walker, Craig H. — *A.J. Burton Group, Inc.*
Waxman, Bruce — *Ryan, Miller & Associates Inc.*
Weed, William H. — *Paul Ray Berndtson*
Weller, Paul S. — *Mark Stanley & Company*
Whiting, Anthony — *Johnson Smith & Knisely Accord*
Whitney, David L. — *Whitney & Associates, Inc.*
Wier, Daniel — *Horton International*
Wilder, Barry — *Rhodes Associates*
Wilkinson, Barbara — *Beall & Company, Inc.*
Williams, Angie — *Whitney & Associates, Inc.*
Williams, Dave — *The McCormick Group, Inc.*
Williams, Lis — *Executive Options, Ltd.*
Williams, Nicole — *Richard, Wayne and Roberts*
Williams, Walter E. — *Canny, Bowen Inc.*
Willis, William H. — *William Willis Worldwide Inc.*
Winter, Robert — *The Whitney Group*
Wise, J. Herbert — *Sandhurst Associates*
Yilmaz, Muriel — *Dinte Resources, Incorporated*
Young, Alexander — *Messett Associates, Inc.*
Zarkin, Norman — *Rhodes Associates*
Zarkin, Norman — *The Zarkin Group, Inc.*
Zaslav, Debra M. — *Telford, Adams & Alexander/Telford & Co., Inc.*
Zonis, Hildy R. — *Accountants Executive Search*

## 28. Transportation

Abbott, Peter — *The Abbott Group, Inc.*
Adams, Jeffrey C. — *Telford, Adams & Alexander/Jeffrey C. Adams & Co., Inc.*
Argentin, Jo — *Executive Placement Consultants, Inc.*
Aronin, Michael — *Fisher-Todd Associates*
Austin, Jessica L. — *D.S.A. - Dixie Search Associates*
Baker-Greene, Edward — *Isaacson, Miller*
Baran, Helena — *Michael J. Cavanagh and Associates*
Barnes, Richard E. — *Barnes Development Group, LLC*
Barnes, Roanne L. — *Barnes Development Group, LLC*
Baron, Len — *Industrial Recruiters Associates, Inc.*
Barthold, James A. — *McNichol Associates*
Barton, Gary R. — *Barton Raben, Inc.*
Bassman, Robert — *Kaye-Bassman International Corp.*
Bassman, Sandy — *Kaye-Bassman International Corp.*
Bauman, Martin H. — *Martin H. Bauman Associates, Inc.*
Berger, Emanuel — *Isaacson, Miller*
Bermea, Jose — *Gaffney Management Consultants*
Berry, Harold B. — *The Hindman Company*
Billington, Brian — *Billington & Associates*
Bitar, Edward — *The Interface Group, Ltd./Boyden*
Bittman, Beth M. — *Norman Roberts & Associates, Inc.*
Bliley, Jerry — *Spencer Stuart*
Bourrie, Sharon D. — *Chartwell Partners International, Inc.*
Bowen, Tad — *Executive Search International*
Brackin, James B. — *Brackin & Sayers Associates*
Brady, Colin S. — *Ward Howell International, Inc.*
Briggs, Adam — *Horton International*
Brown, Buzz — *Brown, Bernardy, Van Remmen, Inc.*
Bruno, Deborah F. — *The Hindman Company*
Bryza, Robert M. — *Robert Lowell International*
Burchill, Greg — *BGB Associates*
Burns, Alan — *The Enns Partners Inc.*
Caruso, Kathy — *Accounting Resources, Inc.*
Case, David — *Case Executive Search*
Casey, Jean — *Peter W. Ambler Company*
Cavanagh, Michael J. — *Michael J. Cavanagh and Associates*
Chargar, Frances — *Hunt Ltd.*
Chauvin, Ralph A. — *The Caldwell Partners Amrop International*
Collard, Joseph A. — *Spencer Stuart*
Colman, Michael — *Executive Placement Consultants, Inc.*
Crath, Paul F. — *Price Waterhouse*
Crowder, Edward W. — *Crowder & Company*
Czamanske, Paul W. — *Compass Group Ltd.*
Damon, Robert A. — *Spencer Stuart*
Danforth, W. Michael — *Hyde Danforth Wold & Co.*
Davidson, Arthur J. — *Lamalie Amrop International*
Davis, G. Gordon — *Davis & Company*
DeGioia, Joseph — *JDG Associates, Ltd.*
Delaney, Patrick J. — *Sensible Solutions, Inc.*
deMartino, Cathy — *Lucas Associates*
Demchak, James P. — *Sandhurst Associates*
deWilde, David M. — *Chartwell Partners International, Inc.*
Dickey, Chet W. — *Bowden & Company, Inc.*

Do, Sonnie — *Whitney & Associates, Inc.*
Dreifus, Donald — *Search West, Inc.*
Drexler, Robert — *Robert Drexler Associates, Inc.*
Drury, James J. — *Spencer Stuart*
Dudley, Robert — *Sanford Rose Associates*
Eason, James — *JRL Executive Recruiters*
Eason, Larry E. — *JRL Executive Recruiters*
Eberly, Carrie — *Accounting Resources, Inc.*
Ellis, Ted K. — *The Hindman Company*
Enns, George — *The Enns Partners Inc.*
Faure, Nicole — *The Caldwell Partners Amrop International*
Ferneborg, Jay W. — *Ferneborg & Associates, Inc.*
Ferneborg, John R. — *Ferneborg & Associates, Inc.*
Fill, Clifford G. — *D.S.A. - Dixie Search Associates*
Fill, Ellyn H. — *D.S.A. - Dixie Search Associates*
Fisher, Neal — *Fisher Personnel Management Services*
Flora, Dodi — *Crawford & Crofford*
Forest, Adam — *McCormack & Associates*
Frank, Valerie S. — *Norman Roberts & Associates, Inc.*
French, William G. — *Preng & Associates, Inc.*
Fribush, Richard — *A.J. Burton Group, Inc.*
Friedman, Helen E. — *McCormack & Farrow*
Gabriel, David L. — *The Arcus Group*
Gaffney, Keith — *Gaffney Management Consultants*
Gaffney, William — *Gaffney Management Consultants*
Gallagher, Marilyn — *Hogan Acquisitions*
Garcia, Samuel K. — *Southwestern Professional Services*
Gardiner, E. Nicholas P. — *Gardiner International*
George, Delores F. — *Delores F. George Human Resource Management & Consulting Industry*
Gilchrist, Robert J. — *Horton International*
Giles, Joe L. — *Joe L. Giles and Associates, Inc.*
Gill, Patricia — *Columbia Consulting Group*
Girsinger, Linda — *Industrial Recruiters Associates, Inc.*
Goar, Duane R. — *Sandhurst Associates*
Goldsmith, Fred J. — *Fred J. Goldsmith Associates*
Gordon, Gerald L. — *E.G. Jones Associates, Ltd.*
Gorfinkle, Gayle — *Executive Search International*
Granger, Lisa D. — *D.S.A. - Dixie Search Associates*
Grantham, John — *Grantham & Co., Inc.*
Hansen, David G. — *Ott & Hansen, Inc.*
Harbert, David O. — *Sweeney Harbert & Mummert, Inc.*
Havener, Donald Clarke — *The Abbott Group, Inc.*
Hay, William E. — *William E. Hay & Company*
Hecker, Henry C. — *Hogan Acquisitions*
Heller, Steven A. — *Martin H. Bauman Associates, Inc.*
Hellinger, Audrey — *Martin H. Bauman Associates, Inc.*
Helminiak, Audrey — *Gaffney Management Consultants*
Hemingway, Stuart C. — *Robison & Associates*
Heneghan, Donald A. — *Allerton Heneghan & O'Neill*
Herman, Pat — *Whitney & Associates, Inc.*
Hermanson, Shelley — *Ells Personnel System Inc.*
Hillen, Skip — *The McCormick Group, Inc.*
Hindman, Neil C. — *The Hindman Company*
Hite, William A. — *Hite Executive Search*
Hogan, Larry H. — *Hogan Acquisitions*
Hoppert, Phil — *Wargo and Co., Inc.*
Ingram, D. John — *Ingram & Aydelotte Inc.*
Jackson, Clarke H. — *The Caldwell Partners Amrop International*
Jacobson, Donald — *Hunt Advisory Services*
Jacobson, Donald — *Hunt Ltd.*
James, Bruce — *Roberson and Company*
Johnson, David — *Gaffney Management Consultants*
Johnson, Kathleen A. — *Barton Raben, Inc.*
Johnson, Rocky — *A.T. Kearney, Inc.*
Jones, Barbara J. — *Kaye-Bassman International Corp.*
Jones, Gary — *BGB Associates*
Kaye, Jeffrey — *Kaye-Bassman International Corp.*
Keeton, Susan G. — *The Corporate Connection, Ltd.*
Kelly, Peter W. — *R. Rollo Associates*
Kelly, Sheri — *Strategic Associates, Inc.*
Kershaw, Lisa — *Tanton Mitchell/Paul Ray Berndtson*
Kinser, Richard E. — *Richard Kinser & Associates*
Klopfenstein, Edward L. — *Crowder & Company*
Kopsick, Joseph M. — *Spencer Stuart*
Lamson-Gran, Jill — *Accounting Resources, Inc.*
Leland, Paul — *McInturff & Associates, Inc.*
Letcher, Harvey D. — *Sandhurst Associates*
Lewis, Jon A. — *Sandhurst Associates*
Line, Joseph T. — *Sharrow & Associates*
Lipe, Jerold L. — *Compass Group Ltd.*
Little, Suzaane — *Don Richard Associates of Tampa, Inc.*
Logan, Valarie A. — *D.S.A. - Dixie Search Associates*
Lyons, Michele R. — *R. Rollo Associates*
MacDougall, Andrew J. — *Spencer Stuart*
Magee, Harrison R. — *Bowden & Company, Inc.*
Malcolm, Rod — *The Enns Partners Inc.*
Manns, Alex — *Crawford & Crofford*

Mark, John L. — *J.L. Mark Associates, Inc.*
Martin, Ellen — *Hunt Ltd.*
Massey, H. Heath — *Robison & Associates*
McDermott, Richard A. — *Paul Ray Berndtson*
McGuire, Corey — *Peter W. Ambler Company*
McInturff, Robert — *McInturff & Associates, Inc.*
McKnight, Amy E. — *Chartwell Partners International, Inc.*
McNamara, Timothy C. — *Columbia Consulting Group*
McNear, Jeffrey E. — *Barrett Partners*
McNichol, John — *McNichol Associates*
Mertensotto, Chuck H. — *Whitney & Associates, Inc.*
Metz, Alex — *Hunt Ltd.*
Miller, Arnie — *Isaacson, Miller*
Miller, Roy — *The Enns Partners Inc.*
Mogul, Gene — *Mogul Consultants, Inc.*
Molitor, John L. — *Barrett Partners*
Myers, Kay — *Signature Staffing*
Neff, Thomas J. — *Spencer Stuart*
Neidhart, Craig C. — *TNS Partners, Inc.*
Nelson, Barbara — *Herman Smith Executive Initiatives Inc.*
Neuberth, Jeffrey G. — *Canny, Bowen Inc.*
Nielsen, Sue — *Ells Personnel System Inc.*
Noll, Robert J. — *The Hindman Company*
Nordland, Martin N. — *Horton International*
O'Hara, Daniel M. — *Lynch Miller Moore Partners, Inc.*
Ogden, Dayton — *Spencer Stuart*
Oller, Jose E. — *Ward Howell International, Inc.*
Owens, Ken — *F-O-R-T-U-N-E Personnel Consultants of Huntsville, Inc.*
Page, G. Schuyler — *A.T. Kearney, Inc.*
Page, Linda M. — *Wargo and Co., Inc.*
Palmer, James H. — *The Hindman Company*
Palmlund, David W. — *Lamalie Amrop International*
Pappas, Jim — *Search Dynamics, Inc.*
Patton, Mitchell — *Patton/Perry Associates, Inc.*
Paul, Lisa D. — *Merit Resource Group, Inc.*
Persky, Barry — *Barry Persky & Company, Inc.*
Peternell, Melanie — *Signature Staffing*
Peters, James N. — *TNS Partners, Inc.*
Phelps, Gene L. — *McCormack & Farrow*
Phillips, Donald L. — *O'Shea, Divine & Company, Inc.*
Pickering, Dale — *Agri-Tech Personnel, Inc.*
Pinson, Stephanie L. — *Gilbert Tweed/INESA*
Plummer, Winkie Donovan — *McManners Associates, Inc.*
Porter, Ken — *Tourism Development International*
Proct, Nina — *Martin H. Bauman Associates, Inc.*
Raab, Julie — *Dunhill Professional Search of Irvine, Inc.*
Regehly, Herbert L. — *The IMC Group of Companies Ltd.*
Reyman, Susan — *S. Reyman & Associates Ltd.*
Rieger, Louis J. — *Spencer Stuart*
Riley, James — *Hunt Ltd.*
Rimmel, James E. — *The Hindman Company*
Roberts, Norman C. — *Norman Roberts & Associates, Inc.*
Roberts, Scott B. — *Wargo and Co., Inc.*
Robison, John H. — *Robison & Associates*
Rogers, Leah — *Dinte Resources, Incorporated*
Rollo, Robert S. — *R. Rollo Associates*
Ross, Mark S. — *Herman Smith Executive Initiatives Inc.*
Rozner, Burton L. — *Oliver & Rozner Associates, Inc.*
Sayers, Bruce D. — *Brackin & Sayers Associates*
Schaefer, Frederic M. — *A.T. Kearney, Inc.*
Schroeder, John W. — *Spencer Stuart*
Schwartz, Carole — *A.T. Kearney, Inc.*
Selko, Philip W. — *Hogan Acquisitions*
Serwat, Leonard A. — *Spencer Stuart*
Sibbald, John R. — *John Sibbald Associates, Inc.*
Silvas, Stephen D. — *Roberson and Company*
Simmons, Gerald J. — *Handy HRM Corp.*
Skunda, Donna M. — *Allerton Heneghan & O'Neill*
Slater, Ronald E. — *A.T. Kearney, Inc.*
Slaughter, Katherine T. — *Compass Group Ltd.*
Slayton, Richard C. — *Slayton International, Inc.*
Slayton, Richard S. — *Slayton International, Inc.*
Slosar, John M. — *Canny, Bowen Inc.*
Smead, Michelle M. — *A.T. Kearney, Inc.*
Smith, Herman M. — *Herman Smith Executive Initiatives Inc.*
Snodgrass, Stephen — *DeFrain, Mayer, Lee & Burgess LLC*
Spadavecchia, Jennifer — *Alta Associates, Inc.*
Spriggs, Robert D. — *Spriggs & Company, Inc.*
Steck, Frank T. — *A.T. Kearney, Inc.*
Stein, Terry W. — *Stewart, Stein and Scott, Ltd.*
Stewart, Jeffrey O. — *Stewart, Stein and Scott, Ltd.*
Stewart, Ross M. — *Human Resources Network Partners Inc.*
Stone, Susan L. — *Stone Enterprises Ltd.*
Stoneham, Herbert E.C. — *Stoneham Associates Corp.*
Sturtz, James W. — *Compass Group Ltd.*
Telford, John H. — *Telford, Adams & Alexander/Telford & Co., Inc.*
ten Cate, Herman H. — *Stoneham Associates Corp.*

## 29. Utilities/Nuclear

## 30. Venture Capital

England, Mark — *Austin-McGregor International*
Enns, George — *The Enns Partners Inc.*
Erickson, Elaine — *Kenzer Corp.*
Fancher, Robert L. — *Bason Associates Inc.*
Farrow, Jerry M. — *McCormack & Farrow*
Feldman, Abe — *A.E. Feldman Associates*
Ferneborg, Jay W. — *Ferneborg & Associates, Inc.*
Ferneborg, John R. — *Ferneborg & Associates, Inc.*
Ferrari, S. Jay — *Ferrari Search Group*
Fischer, John C. — *Horton International*
Fisher, Neal — *Fisher Personnel Management Services*
Foote, Leland W. — *L.W. Foote Company*
Foreman, Rebecca — *Aubin International*
Freier, Bruce — *Executive Referral Services, Inc.*
Fribush, Richard — *A.J. Burton Group, Inc.*
Fulton, Christine N. — *Highland Search Group, L.L.C.*
Furlong, James W. — *Furlong Search, Inc.*
Furlong, James W. — *Furlong Search, Inc.*
Furlong, James W. — *Furlong Search, Inc.*
Gabriel, David L. — *The Arcus Group*
Gaffney, Keith — *Gaffney Management Consultants*
Gaffney, William — *Gaffney Management Consultants*
Gallagher, Marilyn — *Hogan Acquisitions*
Garfinkle, Steven M. — *Battalia Winston International*
Gibbs, John S. — *Spencer Stuart*
Gilbert, Jerry — *Gilbert & Van Campen International*
Gilbert, Patricia G. — *Lynch Miller Moore Partners, Inc.*
Gill, Patricia — *Columbia Consulting Group*
Gill, Susan — *Plummer & Associates, Inc.*
Gilmartin, William — *Hockett Associates, Inc.*
Gilreath, James M. — *Gilreath Weatherby, Inc.*
Glass, Lori — *The Executive Source*
Gobert, Larry — *Professional Search Consultants*
Goldenberg, Susan — *Grant Cooper and Associates*
Goldstein, Gary — *The Whitney Group*
Goodman, Dawn M. — *Bason Associates Inc.*
Gorfinkle, Gayle — *Executive Search International*
Gow, Roderick C. — *Lamalie Amrop International*
Grantham, Philip H. — *Columbia Consulting Group*
Gray, Mark — *Executive Referral Services, Inc.*
Hall, Peter V. — *Chartwell Partners International, Inc.*
Hallock, Peter B. — *Goodrich & Sherwood Associates, Inc.*
Halvorsen, Kara — *Chrisman & Company, Incorporated*
Hansen, David G. — *Ott & Hansen, Inc.*
Hanson, Grant M. — *Goodrich & Sherwood Associates, Inc.*
Hardison, Richard L. — *Hardison & Company*
Hardy, Thomas G. — *Spencer Stuart*
Hargis, N. Leann — *Montgomery Resources, Inc.*
Harris, Julia — *The Whitney Group*
Havener, Donald Clarke — *The Abbott Group, Inc.*
Hecker, Henry C. — *Hogan Acquisitions*
Heller, Steven A. — *Martin H. Bauman Associates, Inc.*
Hellinger, Audrey — *Martin H. Bauman Associates, Inc.*
Helminiak, Audrey — *Gaffney Management Consultants*
Herman, Pat — *Whitney & Associates, Inc.*
Hetherman, Margaret F. — *Highland Search Group, L.L.C.*
Higdon, Henry G. — *Higdon Prince Inc.*
Hockett, William — *Hockett Associates, Inc.*
Hogan, Larry H. — *Hogan Acquisitions*
Holt, Carol — *Bartholdi & Company, Inc.*
Holzberger, Georges L. — *Highland Search Group, L.L.C.*
Hopkinson, Dana — *Winter, Wyman & Company*
Horton, Robert H. — *Horton International*
Houchins, William N. — *Christian & Timbers*
Hoyda, Louis A. — *Thorndike Deland Associates*
Hughes, Cathy N. — *The Ogdon Partnership*
Hypes, Richard G. — *Lynch Miller Moore Partners, Inc.*
Ingram, D. John — *Ingram & Aydelotte Inc.*
Ives, Richard K. — *Wilkinson & Ives*
Joffe, Barry — *Bason Associates Inc.*
Johnson, David — *Gaffney Management Consultants*
Johnson, Kathleen A. — *Barton Raben, Inc.*
Johnson, Ronald S. — *Ronald S. Johnson Associates, Inc.*
Jones, Edward G. — *E.G. Jones Associates, Ltd.*
Juratovac, Michael — *Montgomery Resources, Inc.*
Juska, Frank — *Rusher, Loscavio & LoPresto*
Kaptain, John — *Blau Kaptain Schroeder*
Kassouf, Connie — *The Whitney Group*
Kelly, Peter W. — *R. Rollo Associates*
Kenzer, Robert D. — *Kenzer Corp.*
Kieffer, Michael C. — *Witt/Kieffer, Ford, Hadelman & Lloyd*
Knight, Liz — *Plummer & Associates, Inc.*
Knisely, Gary — *Johnson Smith & Knisely Accord*
Kohn, Adam P. — *Christian & Timbers*
Kopsick, Joseph M. — *Spencer Stuart*
Kossuth, David — *Kossuth & Associates, Inc.*
Kossuth, Jane — *Kossuth & Associates, Inc.*
Krauser, H. James — *Spencer Stuart*

Krejci, Stanley L. — *The Interface Group, Ltd./Boyden*
Kuo, Linda — *Montgomery Resources, Inc.*
Land, Shaun — *Dunhill Professional Search of Irvine, Inc.*
Larsen, Richard F. — *Larsen, Zilliacus & Associates, Inc.*
Lasher, Charles M. — *Lasher Associates*
Lazaro, Alicia C. — *The Whitney Group*
Lee, Roger — *Montgomery Resources, Inc.*
Leetma, Imbi — *Stanton Chase International*
Leslie, William H. — *Boyden/Zay & Company*
Lewis, Jon A. — *Sandhurst Associates*
Lewis, Marc D. — *Handy HRM Corp.*
Litt-Peck, Michelle — *The Whitney Group*
Littman, Stephen — *Rhodes Associates*
Long, William G. — *McDonald, Long & Associates, Inc.*
LoPresto, Robert L. — *Rusher, Loscavio & LoPresto*
Lucht, John — *The John Lucht Consultancy Inc.*
Lynch, Michael C. — *Lynch Miller Moore Partners, Inc.*
Lyons, Jane A. — *Rhodes Associates*
Lyons, Michele R. — *R. Rollo Associates*
Macdonald, G. William — *The Macdonald Group, Inc.*
Mackenna, Kathy — *Plummer & Associates, Inc.*
Mader, Stephen P. — *Christian & Timbers*
Maer, Harry — *Kenzer Corp.*
Magee, Harrison R. — *Bowden & Company, Inc.*
Malcolm, Rod — *The Enns Partners Inc.*
Mancino, Gene — *Blau Kaptain Schroeder*
Marks, Ira — *Strategic Alternatives*
Marks, Sarah J. — *The Executive Source*
Marumoto, William H. — *The Interface Group, Ltd./Boyden*
Mather, David R. — *Christian & Timbers*
Mauer, Kristin — *Montgomery Resources, Inc.*
Mazza, David B. — *Mazza & Riley, Inc.*
McAteer, Thomas — *Montgomery Resources, Inc.*
McBride, Jonathan E. — *McBride Associates, Inc.*
McCann, Cornelia B. — *Spencer Stuart*
McCreary, Charles — *Austin-McGregor International*
McFadden, Ashton S. — *Johnson Smith & Knisely Accord*
McManus, Paul — *Aubin International*
McSherry, James F. — *Battalia Winston International*
Mertensotto, Chuck H. — *Whitney & Associates, Inc.*
Meyers, Steven — *Montgomery Resources, Inc.*
Miller, Michael R. — *Lynch Miller Moore Partners, Inc.*
Miller, Roy — *The Enns Partners Inc.*
Millonzi, Joel C. — *Johnson Smith & Knisely Accord*
Molnar, Robert A. — *Johnson Smith & Knisely Accord*
Montgomery, James M. — *Houze, Shourds & Montgomery, Inc.*
Moore, Mark — *Wheeler, Moore & Elam Co.*
Morton, Robert C. — *Morton, McCorkle & Associates, Inc.*
Muendel, H. Edward — *Stanton Chase International*
Murphy, Cornelius J. — *Goodrich & Sherwood Associates, Inc.*
Mursuli, Meredith — *Lasher Associates*
Mustin, Joyce M. — *J: Blakslee International, Ltd.*
Nagler, Leon G. — *Nagler, Robins & Poe, Inc.*
Neff, Thomas J. — *Spencer Stuart*
Nelson, Garry A. — *Rhodes Associates*
Nephew, Robert — *Christian & Timbers*
Nevins, Patricia — *Rhodes Associates*
Norman, Randy — *Austin-McGregor International*
O'Hara, Daniel M. — *Lynch Miller Moore Partners, Inc.*
O'Reilly, Jack — *Catalyx Group*
Ocon, Olga — *Busch International*
Ogdon, Thomas H. — *The Ogdon Partnership*
Onstott, Joseph E. — *The Onstott Group, Inc.*
Palma, Frank R. — *Goodrich & Sherwood Associates, Inc.*
Palmer, Carlton A. — *Beall & Company, Inc.*
Patton, Mitchell — *Patton/Perry Associates, Inc.*
Paul, Lisa D. — *Merit Resource Group, Inc.*
Pepe, Leonida — *Butterfass, Pepe & MacCallan Inc.*
Percival, Chris — *Chicago Legal Search, Ltd.*
Peters, James N. — *TNS Partners, Inc.*
Pettway, Samuel H. — *Spencer Stuart*
Pfannkuche, Anthony V. — *Spencer Stuart*
Phelps, Gene L. — *McCormack & Farrow*
Phillips, James L. — *Highland Search Group, L.L.C.*
Phillips, Richard K. — *Handy HRM Corp.*
Phillips, Scott K. — *Phillips & Ford, Inc.*
Pierson, Edward J. — *Johnson Smith & Knisely Accord*
Pinkman, Karen N. — *Skott/Edwards Consultants, Inc.*
Plazza, Richard C. — *The Executive Source*
Plummer, John — *Plummer & Associates, Inc.*
Poster, Lawrence D. — *Catalyx Group*
Potter, Steven B. — *Highland Search Group, L.L.C.*
Powell, Leslie — *Rhodes Associates*
Preschlack, Jack E. — *Spencer Stuart*
Price, Andrew G. — *The Thomas Tucker Company*
Prince, Marilyn L. — *Higdon Prince Inc.*
Proct, Nina — *Martin H. Bauman Associates, Inc.*
Provus, Barbara L. — *Shepherd Bueschel & Provus, Inc.*

# Function Specialization Index by Recruiter

# Function Specialization Index by Recruiter

This index is arranged into 10 selected business functions, including the generalist category, and provides a breakdown of the primary and secondary lines of function specializations of each executive recruiter. Many recruiters have multiple listings in this index depending on the various specializations in which they are engaged. *Recruiters listed in the generalist category serve all function specializations.*

1. Generalist
2. Administration
3. Engineering
4. Finance/Accounting
5. General Management

6. Human Resources
7. Marketing
8. Research/Development
9. Sales
10. Women/Minorities

## 1. Generalist

Abbatiello, Christine Murphy — *Winter, Wyman & Company*
Abbott, Dale — *Mixtec Group*
Abbott, Peter — *The Abbott Group, Inc.*
Abe, Sherman — *Korn/Ferry International*
Abell, Vincent W. — *MSI International*
Abruzzo, James — *A.T. Kearney, Inc.*
Adams, Amy — *Richard, Wayne and Roberts*
Adams, Gary — *Management Recruiters International, Inc.*
Adams, Jeffrey C. — *Telford, Adams & Alexander/Jeffrey C. Adams & Co., Inc.*
Adams, Michael — *CG & Associates*
Adelson, Duane — *Stanton Chase International*
Afforde, Sharon Gould — *Jacobson Associates*
Agins, Ted — *National Restaurant Search, Inc.*
Aki, Alvin W. — *MSI International*
Akin, Gary K. — *Management Recruiters International, Inc.*
Akin, J.R. — *J.R. Akin & Company Inc.*
Albanese, Matt J. — *Management Recruiters International, Inc.*
Albores, Sergio — *Management Recruiters International, Inc.*
Albrecht, Franke M. — *Management Recruiters International, Inc.*
Albright, Cindy — *Summerfield Associates, Inc.*
Alden, Brian R. — *MSI International*
Alderman, Douglas — *Management Recruiters International, Inc.*
Alekel, Karren — *ALW Research International*
Alexander, Craig R. — *Management Recruiters International, Inc.*
Alexander, John T. — *Telford, Adams & Alexander/Human Resource Services*
Alexander, Raymond — *Howard Fischer Associates, Inc.*
Alfano, Anthony J. — *Russell Reynolds Associates, Inc.*
Allard, Susan — *Allard Associates*
Allen, Cynthia — *Roberson and Company*
Allen, Donald — *D.S. Allen Associates, Inc.*
Allen, Douglas — *Sullivan & Associates*
Allen, John L. — *Heidrick & Struggles, Inc.*
Allen, Scott — *Chrisman & Company, Incorporated*
Allerton, Donald T. — *Allerton Heneghan & O'Neill*
Alley, Glenwood — *Management Recruiters International, Inc.*
Allgire, Mary L. — *Kenzer Corp.*
Allred, J. Michael — *Spencer Stuart*
Alpeyrie, Jean-Louis — *Heidrick & Struggles, Inc.*
Alphonse-Charles, Maureen — *Pendleton James and Associates, Inc.*
Altieri, Robert J. — *Longshore & Simmons, Inc.*
Alvey, Frank C. — *Robert Sage Recruiting*
Ambler, Peter W. — *Peter W. Ambler Company*
Ameen, Edward N. — *Management Recruiters International, Inc.*
Ames, George C. — *Ames O'Neill Associates*
Amsterdam, Gail E. — *D.E. Foster Partners Inc.*
Ancona, Donald J. — *Management Recruiters International, Inc.*
Anderson, David C. — *Heidrick & Struggles, Inc.*
Anderson, Dennis — *Andcor Human Resources*
Anderson, Glenn G. — *Lamalie Amrop International*
Anderson, Janet — *Professional Alternatives, Inc.*
Anderson, Jim L. — *Management Recruiters International, Inc.*
Anderson, Richard — *Grant Cooper and Associates*
Anderson, Thomas — *Paul J. Biestek Associates, Inc.*
Andre, Jacques P. — *Paul Ray Berndtson*
Andre, Richard — *The Andre Group, Inc.*
Andrews, J. Douglas — *Clarey & Andrews, Inc.*
Andrews, Laura L. — *Stricker & Zagor*
Andujo, Michele M. — *Chrisman & Company, Incorporated*
Angel, Steven R. — *Management Recruiters International, Inc.*
Angell, Tryg R. — *Tryg R. Angell Ltd.*
Anglade, Jennifer — *Korn/Ferry International*
Angott, Mark R. — *Management Recruiters International, Inc.*
Ankeney, Dan R. — *Management Recruiters International, Inc.*
Annesi, Jerry — *Management Recruiters International, Inc.*
Anterasian, Kathy — *Egon Zehnder International Inc.*
Antil, Pamela W. — *Norman Roberts & Associates, Inc.*
Appleton, Diane — *Management Recruiters International, Inc.*
Archer, John W. — *Russell Reynolds Associates, Inc.*
Archer, Sandra F. — *Ryan, Miller & Associates Inc.*
Ardi, Dana B. — *Paul Ray Berndtson*
Argenio, Michelangelo — *Spencer Stuart*
Arms, Douglas — *TOPAZ International, Inc.*
Arms, Douglas — *TOPAZ Legal Solutions*
Arnold, David — *Christian & Timbers*
Arnold, David J. — *Heidrick & Struggles, Inc.*
Arnold, Janet N. — *Management Recruiters International, Inc.*
Arnold, Sheridan J. — *William B. Arnold Associates*
Arnold, William B. — *William B. Arnold Associates*
Aronin, Michael — *Fisher-Todd Associates*
Arons, Richard — *Korn/Ferry International*
Arozarena, Elaine — *Russell Reynolds Associates, Inc.*
Arrington, Renee — *Paul Ray Berndtson*
Arseneault, Daniel S. — *MSI International*
Artimovich, Lee J. — *Korn/Ferry International*
Ascher, Susan P. — *The Ascher Group*

Ashton, Edward J. — *E.J. Ashton & Associates, Ltd.*
Aslaksen, James G. — *Lamalie Amrop International*
Asquith, Peter S. — *Ames Personnel Consultants, Inc.*
Aston, Kathy — *Marra Peters & Partners*
Atkeson, George G. — *Ward Howell International, Inc.*
Atkins, Laurie — *Battalia Winston International*
Atkinson, S. Graham — *Raymond Karsan Associates*
Attell, Harold — *A.E. Feldman Associates*
Aubin, Richard E. — *Aubin International*
Austin, Jessica L. — *D.S.A. - Dixie Search Associates*
Aydelotte, G. Thomas — *Ingram & Aydelotte Inc.*
Azzani, Eunice — *Korn/Ferry International*
Bacher, Philip J. — *Handy HRM Corp.*
Bacigalupo, Terry — *Management Recruiters International, Inc.*
Bacon, Michael — *Management Recruiters International, Inc.*
Badger, Fred H. — *The Badger Group*
Bagley, James W. — *Russell Reynolds Associates, Inc.*
Bailey, David O. — *Paul Ray Berndtson*
Bailey, Joseph N. — *Russell Reynolds Associates, Inc.*
Bailey, Linda S. — *Kenzer Corp.*
Bailey, Lisa — *Nordeman Grimm, Inc.*
Bailey, William A. — *TNS Partners, Inc.*
Baillou, Astrid — *Richard Kinser & Associates*
Baird, Blaine T. — *Physicians Search, Inc.*
Baitler, Simon C. — *The Stevenson Group of Delaware Inc.*
Baker, Charles E. — *Kenzer Corp.*
Baker, Gerry — *Baker, Harris & Partners Limited*
Baker, Jerry H. — *Schuyler, Frye & Baker, Inc.*
Baker, Jim — *Southwestern Professional Services*
Baker, Judith — *Search Consultants International, Inc.*
Baker, Kerry — *Management Recruiters International, Inc.*
Baker, Walter U. — *Lamalie Amrop International*
Baker-Greene, Edward — *Isaacson, Miller*
Bakker, Robert E. — *Management Recruiters International, Inc.*
Baldi, Virgil — *Korn/Ferry International*
Baldwin, Keith R. — *The Baldwin Group*
Balkin, Linda E. — *Witt/Kieffer, Ford, Hadelman & Lloyd*
Ballantine, Caroline B. — *Heidrick & Struggles, Inc.*
Ballein, Kathleen M. — *Witt/Kieffer, Ford, Hadelman & Lloyd*
Ballenger, Michael — *Heidrick & Struggles, Inc.*
Banks, Renate — *Management Recruiters International, Inc.*
Baran, Helena — *Michael J. Cavanagh and Associates*
Baranski, David J. — *Management Recruiters International, Inc.*
Baranski, Glenda A. — *Management Recruiters International, Inc.*
Barao, Thomas — *Korn/Ferry International*
Barber, Toni L. — *MSI International*
Barbosa, Franklin J. — *Boyden*
Barger, H. Carter — *Barger & Sargeant, Inc.*
Bargholz, Harry — *Management Recruiters International, Inc.*
Barick, Bradford L. — *Management Recruiters International, Inc.*
Barick, Linda R. — *Management Recruiters International, Inc.*
Barker, Mary J. — *Management Recruiters International, Inc.*
Barker, Mary J. — *Management Recruiters International, Inc.*
Barlow, Ken H. — *The Cherbonnier Group, Inc.*
Barnes, Richard E. — *Barnes Development Group, LLC*
Barnes, Roanne L. — *Barnes Development Group, LLC*
Barnett, Barney O. — *Management Recruiters International, Inc.*
Barnett, Kim M. — *Management Recruiters International, Inc.*
Barnett-Flint, Juliet — *Heidrick & Struggles, Inc.*
Barnette, Dennis A. — *Heidrick & Struggles, Inc.*
Barnum, Toni M. — *Stone Murphy & Olson*
Baron, Harvey J. — *Management Recruiters International, Inc.*
Baron, Jon C. — *MSI International*
Baron, Len — *Industrial Recruiters Associates, Inc.*
Barone, Marialice — *Barone-O'Hara Associates*
Barowsky, Diane M. — *Lamalie Amrop International*
Barrett, Betsy — *Russell Reynolds Associates, Inc.*
Barrett, Dan E. — *Management Recruiters International, Inc.*
Barrett, J. David — *Heidrick & Struggles, Inc.*
Barth, Cynthia P. — *Longshore & Simmons, Inc.*
Barthold, James A. — *McNichol Associates*
Bartholdi, Ted — *Bartholdi & Company, Inc.*
Bartholdi, Theodore G. — *Bartholdi & Company, Inc.*
Barton, Gary R. — *Barton Raben, Inc.*
Bascom, Roger C. — *Management Recruiters International, Inc.*
Bascom, Shirley R. — *Management Recruiters International, Inc.*
Bason, Maurice L. — *Bason Associates Inc.*
Bass, Nate — *Jacobson Associates*
Bassler, John P. — *Korn/Ferry International*
Bassman, Bob W. — *Management Recruiters International, Inc.*
Bassman, Robert — *Kaye-Bassman International Corp.*
Bassman, Sandy — *Kaye-Bassman International Corp.*
Bassman, Sandy M. — *Management Recruiters International, Inc.*
Bastoky, Bruce M. — *January Management Group, Inc.*
Bates, Nina — *Allard Associates*
Battalia, O. William — *Battalia Winston International*
Bauer, Bob — *Management Recruiters International, Inc.*
Baugh, Amy — *Richard, Wayne and Roberts*

Bauman, Martin H. — *Martin H. Bauman Associates, Inc.*
Bawulski, Fred B. — *Management Recruiters International, Inc.*
Baxter, Robert — *Korn/Ferry International*
Beal, Richard D. — *A.T. Kearney, Inc.*
Beall, Charles P. — *Beall & Company, Inc.*
Beals, Calvin H. — *Management Recruiters International, Inc.*
Bean, Bob — *Management Recruiters International, Inc.*
Bearman, Linda — *Grant Cooper and Associates*
Beatty, Jane — *Paul Ray Berndtson*
Beaudin, Elizabeth C. — *Callan Associates, Ltd.*
Beaudine, Frank R. — *Eastman & Beaudine*
Beaudine, Frank R. — *Eastman & Beaudine*
Beaudine, Robert E. — *Eastman & Beaudine*
Beaupre, Joseph — *Price Waterhouse*
Beaver, Bentley H. — *The Onstott Group, Inc.*
Beaver, Robert W. — *Executive Manning Corporation*
Beck, Barbara S. — *Rhodes Associates*
Bedford, Jennifer — *Korn/Ferry International*
Beer, John — *People Management Northeast Incorporated*
Beerman, Joan — *Kenzer Corp.*
Beeson, William B. — *Lawrence-Leiter and Company*
Behringer, Neail — *Neail Behringer Consultants*
Beir, Ellen Haupt — *Korn/Ferry International*
Belden, Charles P. — *Raymond Karsan Associates*
Belfrey, Edward — *Dunhill Professional Search of Irvine, Inc.*
Bell, Cathy — *Management Recruiters International, Inc.*
Bell, Danny — *Management Recruiters International, Inc.*
Bell, Jeffrey G. — *Norman Broadbent International, Inc.*
Bell, Lindy — *F-O-R-T-U-N-E Personnel Consultants of Huntsville, Inc.*
Bell, Lisa — *Winter, Wyman & Company*
Bell, Michael — *Spencer Stuart*
Bellano, Robert W. — *Stanton Chase International*
Belle Isle, Charles — *Belle Isle, Djandji Inc.*
Bellview, Louis P. — *Management Recruiters International, Inc.*
Bellview, Sibyl M. — *Management Recruiters International, Inc.*
Benabou, Donna — *Kenzer Corp.*
Bennett, Jo — *Battalia Winston International*
Bennett, Joan — *Adams & Associates International*
Bennett, Ness — *Technical Connections Inc.*
Benson, Kate — *Rene Plessner Associates, Inc.*
Bentley, David W. — *Nordeman Grimm, Inc.*
Berarducci, Arthur — *Heidrick & Struggles, Inc.*
Berenblum, Marvin B. — *Heidrick & Struggles, Inc.*
Berger, Emanuel — *Isaacson, Miller*
Berger, Jay V. — *Morris & Berger*
Berger, Judith E. — *MDR Associates, Inc.*
Berk-Levine, Margo — *MB Inc. Interim Executive Division*
Berkowitz, Carol — *Career Management International*
Berlet, William — *KPMG Executive Search*
Berman, Kenneth D. — *MSI International*
Bermea, Jose — *Gaffney Management Consultants*
Berne, Marlene — *The Whitney Group*
Bernstein, Charles Page — *Paul Ray Berndtson*
Berrong, Barbie H. — *Management Recruiters International, Inc.*
Berrong, Ray — *Management Recruiters International, Inc.*
Berry, Chuck — *Management Recruiters International, Inc.*
Berry, Harold B. — *The Hindman Company*
Berry, John R. — *Heidrick & Struggles, Inc.*
Bertok, Ken — *The Wentworth Company, Inc.*
Bertsch, Phil L. — *Management Recruiters International, Inc.*
Bertsch, Phil L. — *Management Recruiters International, Inc.*
Besen, Douglas — *Besen Associates Inc.*
Bethmann, James M. — *Russell Reynolds Associates, Inc.*
Bhimpure, Anita — *Career Management International*
Bicknese, Elizabeth — *Heidrick & Struggles, Inc.*
Biddix, Maryanne — *Tyler & Company*
Biegel, Sandy — *Evie Kreisler & Associates, Inc.*
Biestek, Paul J. — *Paul J. Biestek Associates, Inc.*
Biggins, J. Veronica — *Heidrick & Struggles, Inc.*
Biggins, Joseph — *Winter, Wyman & Company*
Billingsly, Dorothy M. — *DHR International, Inc.*
Billington, William H. — *Spriggs & Company, Inc.*
Bilz, Deirdre — *Johnson Smith & Knisely Accord*
Bird, Len L. — *Management Recruiters International, Inc.*
Bishop, B. Susan — *DHR International, Inc.*
Bishop, James F. — *Burke, O'Brien & Bishop Associates, Inc.*
Bishop, Sandy — *Management Recruiters International, Inc.*
Bishop, Susan — *Bishop Partners*
Biskin, Donald — *Heidrick & Struggles, Inc.*
Bitar, Edward — *The Interface Group, Ltd./Boyden*
Bittman, Beth M. — *Norman Roberts & Associates, Inc.*
Bizick, Ron — *Management Recruiters International, Inc.*
Black, Douglas E. — *MSI International*
Black, Frank S. — *Management Recruiters International, Inc.*
Black, James L. — *DHR International, Inc.*
Black, Nancy C. — *Assisting Professionals, Inc.*
Blackmon, Sharon — *The Abbott Group, Inc.*

Blackshaw, Brian M. — *Blackshaw, Olmstead & Lynch*
Bladon, Andrew — *Don Richard Associates of Tampa, Inc.*
Blair, Kelly A. — *The Caldwell Partners Amrop International*
Blake, Eileen — *Howard Fischer Associates, Inc.*
Blakslee, Jan H. — *J: Blakslee International, Ltd.*
Blanton, Thomas — *Blanton and Company*
Blecksmith, Edward — *Korn/Ferry International*
Blessing, Marc L. — *Management Recruiters International, Inc.*
Bliley, Jerry — *Spencer Stuart*
Block, Randy — *Block & Associates*
Bloom, Howard C. — *The Howard C. Bloom Co.*
Bloom, Joyce — *The Howard C. Bloom Co.*
Bloomer, James E. — *L.W. Foote Company*
Blue, C. David — *Management Recruiters International, Inc.*
Blumenthal, Deborah — *Paul Ray Berndtson*
Blumenthal, Paula — *J.P. Canon Associates*
Boag, John — *Norm Sanders Associates*
Boal, Robert A. — *Management Recruiters International, Inc.*
Boccuzi, Joseph H. — *Spencer Stuart*
Bodnar, Beverly — *Management Recruiters International, Inc.*
Bodnar, Robert J. — *Management Recruiters International, Inc.*
Boehmer, Jack — *KPMG Executive Search*
Boerkoel, Timothy B. — *Russell Reynolds Associates, Inc.*
Bogard, Nicholas C. — *The Onstott Group, Inc.*
Bohle, John B. — *Paul Ray Berndtson*
Bohn, Steve J. — *MSI International*
Bolger, Thomas — *Korn/Ferry International*
Bolls, Rich — *Management Recruiters International, Inc.*
Bommarito, Bob C. — *Management Recruiters International, Inc.*
Bond, James L. — *People Management Northeast Incorporated*
Bonifield, Len — *Bonifield Associates*
Bonnell, William R. — *Bonnell Associates Ltd.*
Bonner, Barbara — *Mixtec Group*
Bonner, Rodney D. — *Management Recruiters International, Inc.*
Boone, James E. — *Korn/Ferry International*
Booth, Otis — *A.T. Kearney, Inc.*
Bopray, Pat — *Personnel Unlimited/Executive Search*
Borel, David P. — *Management Recruiters International, Inc.*
Borenstine, Alvin — *Synergistics Associates Ltd.*
Borland, James — *Goodrich & Sherwood Associates, Inc.*
Borman, Theodore H. — *Lamalie Amrop International*
Bormann, Cindy Ann — *MSI International*
Bos, Marijo — *Russell Reynolds Associates, Inc.*
Bostic, James E. — *Phillips Resource Group*
Bostick, Tim — *Paul Ray Berndtson*
Bothereau, Elizabeth A. — *Kenzer Corp.*
Boucher, Greg — *Southwestern Professional Services*
Bouer, Judy — *Baker Scott & Company*
Bourbeau, Paul J. — *Boyden*
Bourbonnais, Jean-Pierre — *Ward Howell International, Inc.*
Bourque, Jack J. — *Management Recruiters International, Inc.*
Bourrie, Sharon D. — *Chartwell Partners International, Inc.*
Bovich, Maryann C. — *Higdon Prince Inc.*
Bowen, Tad — *Executive Search International*
Bowen, William J. — *Heidrick & Struggles, Inc.*
Boxberger, Michael D. — *Korn/Ferry International*
Boyer, Dennis M. — *Heidrick & Struggles, Inc.*
Boyer, Heath C. — *Spencer Stuart*
Boyle, Russell E. — *Egon Zehnder International Inc.*
Braak, Diana — *Kincannon & Reed*
Brackin, James B. — *Brackin & Sayers Associates*
Bradshaw, John W. — *A.T. Kearney, Inc.*
Bradshaw, Monte — *Christian & Timbers*
Brady, Colin S. — *Ward Howell International, Inc.*
Brand, John E. — *Management Recruiters International, Inc.*
Brand, Karen M. — *Management Recruiters International, Inc.*
Brandjes, Michael J. — *Brandjes Associates*
Brandon, Irwin — *Hadley Lockwood, Inc.*
Brassard, Phillipe — *KPMG Executive Search*
Bratches, Howard — *Thorndike Deland Associates*
Braun, Jerold — *Jerold Braun & Associates*
Breault, Larry J. — *Management Recruiters International, Inc.*
Brennan, Patrick J. — *Handy HRM Corp.*
Brennan, Vincent F. — *Korn/Ferry International*
Brennecke, Richard C. — *Management Recruiters International, Inc.*
Brenner, Mary — *Prestige Inc.*
Brenner, Michael — *Lamalie Amrop International*
Brent, Art — *Goodrich & Sherwood Associates, Inc.*
Brenzel, John A. — *TASA International*
Brieger, Steve — *Thorne, Brieger Associates Inc.*
Briggs, Adam — *Horton International*
Bright, Timothy — *MSI International*
Brindise, Michael J. — *Dynamic Search Systems, Inc.*
Briody, Steve — *Management Recruiters International, Inc.*
Broadhurst, Austin — *Russell Reynolds Associates, Inc.*
Brock, John — *Korn/Ferry International*
Brock, Rufus C. — *Management Recruiters International, Inc.*
Brooks, Bernard E. — *Mruk & Partners/EMA Partners Int'l*

Citarella, Richard A. — *A.T. Kearney, Inc.*
Citera, Tom — *Howe-Lewis International*
Citrin, James M. — *Spencer Stuart*
Cizek, John T. — *Cizek Associates, Inc.*
Cizek, Marti J. — *Cizek Associates, Inc.*
Clarey, Jack R. — *Clarey & Andrews, Inc.*
Clarey, William A. — *Preng & Associates, Inc.*
Clark, Bruce M. — *IMCOR, Inc.*
Clark, Donald B. — *Paul Ray Berndtson*
Clark, Elliot H. — *Raymond Karsan Associates*
Clark, Evan — *The Whitney Group*
Clark, James D. — *Management Recruiters International, Inc.*
Clark, John Edward — *Management Recruiters International, Inc.*
Clark, Linda — *Kenzer Corp.*
Clark, Ronda — *Management Recruiters International, Inc.*
Clark, W. Christopher — *Heidrick & Struggles, Inc.*
Claude, Abe — *Paul Ray Berndtson*
Clauhsen, Elizabeth A. — *Savoy Partners, Ltd.*
Clayborne, Paul — *Prestige Inc.*
Cleary, Thomas R. — *ARJay & Associates*
Cleeve, Coleen — *Howe-Lewis International*
Clegg, Cynthia — *Horton International*
Clemens, William B. — *Norman Broadbent International, Inc.*
Clemens, William B. — *Norman Broadbent International, Inc.*
Clement, Norman — *Korn/Ferry International*
Clingan, Bob H. — *Management Recruiters International, Inc.*
Close, E. Wade — *Boyden*
Cobb, Lynn A. — *Management Recruiters International, Inc.*
Cobb, Mark A. — *Management Recruiters International, Inc.*
Cochran, Corinne — *Early Cochran & Olson, Inc.*
Coelyn, Ronald H. — *Spencer Stuart*
Coff, Scott — *Johnson Smith & Knisely Accord*
Coffey, Patty — *Winter, Wyman & Company*
Coffman, Brian — *Kossuth & Associates, Inc.*
Cohen, Kasumi — *Korn/Ferry International*
Cohen, Luis Lezama — *Paul Ray Berndtson*
Cohen, Michael R. — *Intech Summit Group, Inc.*
Cohen, Pamela — *TOPAZ International, Inc.*
Cohen, Pamela — *TOPAZ Legal Solutions*
Cohen, Richard — *Management Recruiters International, Inc.*
Cohen, Robert C. — *Intech Summit Group, Inc.*
Colavito, Joseph W. — *Lamalie Amrop International*
Colborne, Janis M. — *AJM Professional Services*
Cole, Les C. — *Management Recruiters International, Inc.*
Cole, Ronald J. — *Cole, Warren & Long, Inc.*
Colella, Thomas V. — *Korn/Ferry International*
Coleman, J. Gregory — *Korn/Ferry International*
Coleman, J. Kevin — *J. Kevin Coleman & Associates, Inc.*
Coleman, John A. — *Canny, Bowen Inc.*
Coleman, Michael M. — *Coleman Legal Search Consultants*
Coleman, Neil F. — *Management Recruiters International, Inc.*
Coleman, Scott A. — *Kenzer Corp.*
Collard, Joseph A. — *Spencer Stuart*
Colling, Douglas — *KPMG Executive Search*
Colling, Douglas — *KPMG Management Consulting*
Collins, Tom — *J.B. Homer Associates, Inc.*
Collis, Martin — *E.L. Shore & Associates Ltd.*
Colosimo, Chris — *Richard, Wayne and Roberts*
Coltrane, Michael — *Richard, Wayne and Roberts*
Colucci, Bart A. — *Colucci, Blendow and Johnson, Inc.*
Combs, Stephen L. — *Juntunen-Combs-Poirier*
Cona, Joseph A. — *Cona Personnel Search*
Conard, Rodney J. — *Conard Associates, Inc.*
Condit, Madeleine — *Korn/Ferry International*
Cone, Dan P. — *Management Recruiters International, Inc.*
Connelly, Heather — *The Caldwell Partners Amrop International*
Connelly, Kevin M. — *Spencer Stuart*
Connelly, Laura J. — *Management Recruiters International, Inc.*
Connelly, Scott — *Technical Connections Inc.*
Connelly, Thomas A. — *Korn/Ferry International*
Conner, John — *Flex Execs Management Solutions*
Connet, Mel — *Heidrick & Struggles, Inc.*
Connolly, Michael R. — *Management Recruiters International, Inc.*
Connors, Claire — *Korn/Ferry International*
Conover, Jo — *TASA International*
Conway, William P. — *Phillips Resource Group*
Cook, Dan — *Management Recruiters International, Inc.*
Cook, Dennis — *Korn/Ferry International*
Cook, Nancy L. — *The Diversified Search Companies*
Cook, Patricia — *Heidrick & Struggles, Inc.*
Cooke, Jeffrey R. — *Jonas, Walters & Assoc., Inc.*
Cooke, Katherine H. — *Horton International*
Cooksey, Ben — *Management Recruiters International, Inc.*
Cooper, Bill — *Management Recruiters International, Inc.*
Cooper, Larry W. — *Management Recruiters International, Inc.*
Cooper, William — *Search West, Inc.*
Copeland, Linda K. — *Management Recruiters International, Inc.*
Cordaro, Concetta — *Flynn, Hannock, Incorporated*

Corey, Michael J. — *Ward Howell International, Inc.*
Corey, Michael J. — *Witt/Kieffer, Ford, Hadelman & Lloyd*
Corey, Patrick M. — *Ward Howell International, Inc.*
Cornehlsen, James H. — *Lamalie Amrop International*
Cornfoot, Jim L. — *Management Recruiters International, Inc.*
Corrigan, Gerald F. — *The Corrigan Group*
Corso, Glen S. — *Chartwell Partners International, Inc.*
Corwin, J. Blade — *Seitchik Corwin and Seitchik, Inc.*
Costa, Cynthia A. — *MSI International*
Costa, Frances — *Gilbert Tweed/INESA*
Coston, Bruce G. — *MSI International*
Cotter, L.L. — *IMCOR, Inc.*
Cotterell, Dirk A. — *Management Recruiters International, Inc.*
Cottick, Ron — *Management Recruiters International, Inc.*
Cottingham, R.L. — *Marvin L. Silcott & Associates, Inc.*
Cowan, Roberta — *Drew Associates International*
Cowling, Wes — *Management Recruiters International, Inc.*
Cox, Mark M. — *Witt/Kieffer, Ford, Hadelman & Lloyd*
Cox, William — *E.J. Ashton & Associates, Ltd.*
Cozzillio, Larry — *The Andre Group, Inc.*
Crabtree, Bonnie — *Korn/Ferry International*
Cragg, Barbara R. — *Southwestern Professional Services*
Cramer, Katherine M. — *Pendleton James and Associates, Inc.*
Crane, Howard C. — *Chartwell Partners International, Inc.*
Crath, Paul F. — *Price Waterhouse*
Crawford, Dick B. — *Management Recruiters International, Inc.*
Crigler, Jim — *Management Recruiters International, Inc.*
Cripe, Joyce — *Mixtec Group*
Crist, Peter — *Crist Partners, Ltd.*
Cronin, Richard J. — *Hodge-Cronin & Associates, Inc.*
Crowder, Edward W. — *Crowder & Company*
Crowell, Elizabeth — *H.M. Long International, Ltd.*
Crownover, Kathryn L. — *MSI International*
Crumbaker, Robert H. — *Lamalie Amrop International*
Crump, William G. — *Paul Ray Berndtson*
Cruz, Catherine — *TOPAZ International, Inc.*
Cruz, Catherine — *TOPAZ Legal Solutions*
Crystal, Jonathan A. — *Spencer Stuart*
Csorba, Les — *A.T. Kearney, Inc.*
Cuellar, Paulina Robles — *Paul Ray Berndtson*
Cuellar, Scott R. — *Russell Reynolds Associates, Inc.*
Culp, Thomas C. — *The Diversified Search Companies*
Cummings, Harry J. — *Sanford Rose Associates*
Cundick, Jeff L. — *Management Recruiters International, Inc.*
Cunneff, Harry J. — *Management Recruiters International, Inc.*
Cunningham, Claudia — *Korn/Ferry International*
Cunningham, Lawrence — *Howard Fischer Associates, Inc.*
Cunningham, Robert Y. — *Goodrich & Sherwood Associates, Inc.*
Cunningham, Sheila — *Adams & Associates International*
Curlett, Lisa — *Korn/Ferry International*
Currence, Anna — *Kenzer Corp.*
Currie, Lawrence S. — *MSI International*
Cushman, Judith — *Marshall Consultants/West*
Czajkowski, John — *Management Recruiters International, Inc.*
Czamanske, Paul W. — *Executive Interim Management, Inc.*
Czamanske, Peter M. — *Executive Interim Management, Inc.*
D'Angelo, Ron E. — *Management Recruiters International, Inc.*
D'Elia, Arthur P. — *Korn/Ferry International*
D'Eramo, Tony P. — *Management Recruiters International, Inc.*
Dabich, Thomas M. — *Robert Harkins Associates, Inc.*
Dach, Bradley M. — *Management Recruiters International, Inc.*
Dalton, Bret — *Robert W. Dingman Company, Inc.*
Dalton, David R. — *MSI International*
Damon, Robert A. — *Spencer Stuart*
Dandurand, Jeff J. — *DHR International, Inc.*
Danforth, W. Michael — *Hyde Danforth Wold & Co.*
Daniel, Beverly — *Foy, Schneid & Daniel, Inc.*
Daniel, David S. — *Spencer Stuart*
Daniels, Alfred — *Alfred Daniels & Associates*
Darcy, Pat — *Paul Ray Berndtson*
Darter, Steven M. — *People Management Northeast Incorporated*
Daughety, Mac M. — *Management Recruiters International, Inc.*
Dautenhahn, Thomas — *Sanford Rose Associates*
David, Dodie — *Sullivan & Associates*
David, Jennifer — *Gilbert Tweed/INESA*
David, Paul — *Ward Howell International, Inc.*
Davidson, Arthur J. — *Lamalie Amrop International*
Davis, Bernel — *MSI International*
Davis, Evelyn C. — *EFL Associates*
Davis, G. Gordon — *Davis & Company*
Davis, Joan — *MSI International*
Davis, Joel C. — *MSI International*
Davis, John — *John J. Davis & Associates, Inc.*
Davis, John J. — *John J. Davis & Associates, Inc.*
Davis, Ken R. — *Management Recruiters International, Inc.*
Davis, Orlin R. — *Heidrick & Struggles, Inc.*
Davis, Robert — *CG & Associates*
Davison, Kristin — *Korn/Ferry International*

Davison, Patricia E. — *Lamalie Amrop International*
Davitt, John — *Korn/Ferry International*
de Bardin, Francesca — *F.L. Taylor & Company, Inc.*
de Cholnoky, Andrea — *Spencer Stuart*
De Kesel, Herman — *TASA International*
De Moch, Betty — *Search West, Inc.*
de Palacios, Jeannette C. — *J. Palacios & Associates, Inc.*
de Regt, John — *Heidrick & Struggles, Inc.*
de Tuede, Catherine — *Thomas A. Byrnes Associates*
Deal, Chuck H. — *Management Recruiters International, Inc.*
Debrueys, Lee G. — *MSI International*
DeCorrevont, James — *DeCorrevont & Associates*
DeCorrevont, James — *DeCorrevont & Associates*
DeCosta, Michael — *Korn/Ferry International*
Deering, Joseph — *U.S. Envirosearch*
DeFrancesco, Mary Ellen — *The Onstott Group, Inc.*
DeGioia, Joseph — *JDG Associates, Ltd.*
Dejong, Jack C. — *Management Recruiters International, Inc.*
Del Pino, William — *National Search, Inc.*
Del Prete, Karen — *Gilbert Tweed/INESA*
Del'Ange, Gabrielle N. — *MSI International*
Delaney, Patrick J. — *Sensible Solutions, Inc.*
Delin, Norm — *Management Recruiters International, Inc.*
Delman, Charles — *Korn/Ferry International*
DelNegro, Anthony T. — *DHR International, Inc.*
DelNegro, Anthony T. — *DHR International, Inc.*
DeLong, Art — *Richard Kader & Associates*
Demchak, James P. — *Sandhurst Associates*
Dennen, Bob E. — *Management Recruiters International, Inc.*
Dennen, Lorraine T. — *Management Recruiters International, Inc.*
Denney, Edward B. — *Denney & Company Incorporated*
Denney, Thomas L. — *Denney & Company Incorporated*
Densmore, Geraldine — *Michael Stern Associates Inc.*
Denson, Marsha — *Evie Kreisler & Associates, Inc.*
DeSanto, Constance E. — *Paul Ray Berndtson*
Desgrosellier, Gary P. — *Personnel Unlimited/Executive Search*
Desir, Etheline — *Tyler & Company*
Desmond, Dennis — *Beall & Company, Inc.*
Detore, Robert R. — *Drew Associates International*
Diamond, Peter — *Korn/Ferry International*
Diaz, Del J. — *Management Recruiters International, Inc.*
Diaz-Joslyn, Mabel — *Walker Communications*
Dickey, Arlene — *Kenzer Corp.*
Dickey, Chet W. — *Bowden & Company, Inc.*
Dickinson, Peter K. — *Shepherd Bueschel & Provus, Inc.*
Dickstein, Joel — *Management Recruiters International, Inc.*
Diduca, Tom A. — *Management Recruiters International, Inc.*
Dieck, Daniel W. — *Dieck, Mueller & Associates, Inc.*
Dieckmann, Ralph E. — *Dieckmann & Associates, Ltd.*
Dietz, David S. — *MSI International*
DiMarchi, Paul — *DiMarchi Partners, Inc.*
Dingman, Bruce — *Robert W. Dingman Company, Inc.*
Dingman, Robert W. — *Robert W. Dingman Company, Inc.*
Dinse, Beth — *Management Recruiters International, Inc.*
Dinte, Paul — *Dinte Resources, Incorporated*
Dipaolo, Jeff — *Management Recruiters International, Inc.*
Divine, Robert S. — *O'Shea, Divine & Company, Inc.*
Dixon, C.R. — *A la carte International*
Djandji, Guy N. — *Belle Isle, Djandji Inc.*
Doan, Lisa — *Rhodes Associates*
Doele, Donald C. — *Goodrich & Sherwood Associates, Inc.*
Dolezal, Dave — *Evie Kreisler & Associates, Inc.*
Doliva, Lauren M. — *Heidrick & Struggles, Inc.*
Domenico, Alfred J. — *Domenico/Bowman Associates*
Dominguez, Carl — *Heidrick & Struggles, Inc.*
Donnelly, George J. — *Ward Howell International, Inc.*
Donovan, Jerry E. — *Management Recruiters International, Inc.*
Doody, Michael F. — *Witt/Kieffer, Ford, Hadelman & Lloyd*
Dooley, James L. — *Management Recruiters International, Inc.*
Doran, Mary Ann — *Kenzer Corp.*
Dorsey, Jim — *Ryan, Miller & Associates Inc.*
Dougherty, Bridget L. — *Wellington Management Group*
Dougherty, Janice — *The McCormick Group, Inc.*
Dougherty, Lawrence J. — *Management Recruiters International, Inc.*
Douglas, Anne — *Prestige Inc.*
Doukas, Jon A. — *Professional Bank Services, Inc. D/B/A Executive Search, Inc.*
Dow, Lori — *Davidson, Laird & Associates*
Downs, James L. — *Sanford Rose Associates*
Dowrick, Jeanne A. — *Longshore & Simmons, Inc.*
Doyle, Bobby — *Richard, Wayne and Roberts*
Doyle, John P. — *Paul Ray Berndtson*
Dreifuss, Donald — *Search West, Inc.*
Dremely, Mark — *Richard, Wayne and Roberts*
Drennan, Ronald — *Ward Howell International, Inc.*
Driscoll, Donald L. — *Management Recruiters International, Inc.*
Drown, Clifford F. — *Management Recruiters International, Inc.*
Drummond-Hay, Peter — *Russell Reynolds Associates, Inc.*

Drury, James J. — *Spencer Stuart*
Duckworth, Donald R. — *Paul Ray Berndtson*
Ducruet, Linda K. — *Heidrick & Struggles, Inc.*
Dudley, Craig J. — *Paul Ray Berndtson*
Dudley, Robert — *Sanford Rose Associates*
Duggan, James P. — *Slayton International, Inc.*
Duke, Larry G. — *Management Recruiters International, Inc.*
Dukes, Ronald — *Heidrick & Struggles, Inc.*
Duley, Richard I. — *ARJay & Associates*
Dumesnil, Curtis — *Richard, Wayne and Roberts*
Dunbar, Geoffrey T. — *Heidrick & Struggles, Inc.*
Dunford, Michael S. — *Korn/Ferry International*
Dunlevie, Craig — *Korn/Ferry International*
Dunman, Betsy L. — *Crawford & Crofford*
Dunn, Ed L. — *Management Recruiters International, Inc.*
Dunn, Kathleen — *A.T. Kearney, Inc.*
Dunn, Mary Helen — *Paul Ray Berndtson*
Durakis, Charles A. — *C.A. Durakis Associates, Inc.*
Durakis, Charles A. — *C.A. Durakis Associates, Inc.*
Durakis, Charles A. — *C.A. Durakis Associates, Inc.*
Durand, Francois — *Ward Howell International, Inc.*
Dussick, Vince — *Dussick Management Associates*
Dykeman, James J. — *Management Recruiters International, Inc.*
Eagan, Karen L. — *Management Recruiters International, Inc.*
Eagan, Ridge — *Management Recruiters International, Inc.*
Earhart, William D. — *Sanford Rose Associates*
Earle, Paul W. — *Spencer Stuart*
Early, Alice C. — *Russell Reynolds Associates, Inc.*
Early, Bert H. — *Early Cochran & Olson, Inc.*
Eastham, Marvene M. — *Witt/Kieffer, Ford, Hadelman & Lloyd*
Eatman, Fred — *Management Recruiters International, Inc.*
Eatmon, Michael — *U.S. Envirosearch*
Ebeling, John A. — *Gilbert Tweed/INESA*
Eckhart, Ken — *Spencer Stuart*
Eden, Brooks D. — *Eden & Associates, Inc.*
Eden, Dianne — *Steeple Associates*
Eden, Don F. — *Management Recruiters International, Inc.*
Eden, Earl M. — *Eden & Associates, Inc.*
Edwards, Dorothy — *MSI International*
Edwards, Douglas W. — *Egon Zehnder International Inc.*
Edwards, Robert — *J.P. Canon Associates*
Edwards, Verba L. — *Wing Tips & Pumps, Inc.*
Ehrenzeller, Tony A. — *Management Recruiters International, Inc.*
Ehrgott, Elizabeth — *The Ascher Group*
Ehrhart, Jennifer — *ADOW's Executeam*
Eibeler, C. — *Amherst Personnel Group Inc.*
Eilertson, Douglas R. — *Sanford Rose Associates*
Eisert, Robert M. — *Sanford Rose Associates*
El-Darwish, Jill — *Winter, Wyman & Company*
Elam, Bill J. — *Management Recruiters International, Inc.*
Eldredge, L. Lincoln — *Lamalie Amrop International*
Elliott, A. Larry — *Heidrick & Struggles, Inc.*
Elliott, David H. — *Heidrick & Struggles, Inc.*
Elliott, Mark P. — *Lamalie Amrop International*
Ellis, Ronald A. — *Management Recruiters International, Inc.*
Ellis, Ted K. — *The Hindman Company*
Ellis, William — *Interspace Interactive Inc.*
Ellison, Richard — *Sanford Rose Associates*
Elston, William S. — *DHR International, Inc.*
Elwell, Richard F. — *Elwell & Associates Inc.*
Elwell, Stephen R. — *Elwell & Associates Inc.*
Emmott, Carol B. — *Spencer Stuart*
Empey, David G. — *Management Recruiters International, Inc.*
Endres, Robert — *Sanford Rose Associates*
Enfield, Jerry J. — *Executive Manning Corporation*
Engelgau, Elvita V. — *Management Recruiters International, Inc.*
Engelgau, Larry P. — *Management Recruiters International, Inc.*
England, Mark — *Austin-McGregor International*
Engman, Steven T. — *Lamalie Amrop International*
Enns, George — *The Enns Partners Inc.*
Ensminger, Barbara — *Management Recruiters International, Inc.*
Ensminger, Chub — *Management Recruiters International, Inc.*
Epstein, Kathy — *Canny, Bowen Inc.*
Erbes, Roysi — *Korn/Ferry International*
Erder, Debra — *Canny, Bowen Inc.*
Erickson, Elaine — *Kenzer Corp.*
Erickson, Mary R. — *Mary R. Erickson & Associates, Inc.*
Erlanger, Richard A. — *Erlanger Associates Inc.*
Erlien, Nancy B. — *Jacobson Associates*
Eskra, Michael D. — *Sanford Rose Associates*
Esty, Greg C. — *Management Recruiters International, Inc.*
Eustis, Lucy R. — *MSI International*
Evan-Cook, James W. — *Jacobson Associates*
Evans, Jeffrey — *Sullivan & Associates*
Evans, Robert M. — *TASA International*
Ezersky, Jane E. — *Highland Search Group, L.L.C.*
Fabbro, Vivian — *A.T. Kearney, Inc.*
Faber, Jill — *A.T. Kearney, Inc.*

Fagan, Mark — *Management Recruiters International, Inc.*
Fahlin, Kelly — *Winter, Wyman & Company*
Fair, Donna — *ProResource, Inc.*
Falk, John — *D.S. Allen Associates, Inc.*
Fancher, Robert L. — *Bason Associates Inc.*
Farber, Susan — *Heidrick & Struggles, Inc.*
Farish, John G. — *Paul Ray Berndtson*
Farkas, Denny P. — *Management Recruiters International, Inc.*
Farley, Antoinette L. — *Witt/Kieffer, Ford, Hadelman & Lloyd*
Farley, Leon A. — *Leon A. Farley Associates*
Farrar, Carolyn — *Sanford Rose Associates*
Farrar, Gary — *Sanford Rose Associates*
Farrow, Jerry M. — *McCormack & Farrow*
Faure, Nicole — *The Caldwell Partners Amrop International*
Fawcett, Anne M. — *The Caldwell Partners Amrop International*
Fazekas, John A. — *Korn/Ferry International*
Feder, Gwen — *Egon Zehnder International Inc.*
Fee, J. Curtis — *Spencer Stuart*
Felderman, Kenneth I. — *Lamalie Amrop International*
Feldman, Abe — *A.E. Feldman Associates*
Felton, Meg — *Korn/Ferry International*
Fennel, P.J. — *Heidrick & Struggles, Inc.*
Ferguson, Robert — *Bill Hahn Group, Inc.*
Ferneborg, Jay W. — *Ferneborg & Associates, Inc.*
Ferneborg, John R. — *Ferneborg & Associates, Inc.*
Ferry, Richard M. — *Korn/Ferry International*
Feyder, Michael — *A.T. Kearney, Inc.*
Fifield, George C. — *Egon Zehnder International Inc.*
Filko, Gary — *Management Recruiters International, Inc.*
Fill, Clifford G. — *D.S.A. - Dixie Search Associates*
Fill, Ellyn H. — *D.S.A. - Dixie Search Associates*
Fincher, Richard P. — *Phase II Management*
Fingers, David — *Bradford & Galt, Inc.*
Finn, Jacquelyn — *Jacquelyn Finn & Susan Schneider Associates, Inc.*
Fischer, Adam — *Howard Fischer Associates, Inc.*
Fischer, Howard M. — *Howard Fischer Associates, Inc.*
Fischer, Janet L. — *Boyden*
Fischer, John C. — *Horton International*
Fisher, Earl L. — *Management Recruiters International, Inc.*
Fisher, Neal — *Fisher Personnel Management Services*
Fitch, Lori — *R. Parker and Associates, Inc.*
Fixler, Eugene — *Ariel Recruitment Associates*
Flanagan, Dale M. — *Lamalie Amrop International*
Flanagan, Robert M. — *Robert M. Flanagan & Associates, Ltd.*
Flannery, Peter — *Jonas, Walters & Assoc., Inc.*
Flash, James — *Richard Kader & Associates*
Flask, A. Paul — *Korn/Ferry International*
Fleck, George — *Canny, Bowen Inc.*
Fleming, Joseph M. — *IMCOR, Inc.*
Fleming, Marco — *MSI International*
Fleming, Richard L. — *TASA International*
Flickinger, Susan V. — *Korn/Ferry International*
Flink, Debra — *Heidrick & Struggles, Inc.*
Flink, Debra K. — *Russell Reynolds Associates, Inc.*
Flinn, Richard A. — *Denney & Company Incorporated*
Flores, Agustin — *Ward Howell International, Inc.*
Flynn, Brian — *Korn/Ferry International*
Fogarty, Deirdre — *Paul Ray Berndtson*
Fogelgren, Stephen W. — *Management Recruiters International, Inc.*
Foley, Eileen — *Winter, Wyman & Company*
Foley, John J. — *Executive Outsourcing International*
Folkerth, Gene — *Gene Folkerth & Associates, Inc.*
Follrath, Noel — *Paul Ray Berndtson*
Fonfa, Ann — *S.R. Wolman Associates, Inc.*
Foote, Leland W. — *L.W. Foote Company*
Foote, Ray P. — *Heidrick & Struggles, Inc.*
Forbes, Kay Koob — *Sanford Rose Associates*
Forbes, Kenneth P. — *Sanford Rose Associates*
Ford, J. Daniel — *Witt/Kieffer, Ford, Hadelman & Lloyd*
Foreman, David C. — *Koontz, Jeffries & Associates, Inc.*
Foreman, Kathryn A. — *Paul Ray Berndtson*
Foreman, Rebecca — *Aubin International*
Forgosh, Jack H. — *Raymond Karsan Associates*
Forman, Donald R. — *Stanton Chase International*
Fosnot, Bob — *Management Recruiters International, Inc.*
Fosnot, Mike — *Management Recruiters International, Inc.*
Foster, Drew B. — *Management Recruiters International, Inc.*
Foster, Duke — *Korn/Ferry International*
Foster, Michael — *Sanford Rose Associates*
Foster, Robert — *Korn/Ferry International*
Foster, Torrey N. — *Lynch Miller Moore Partners, Inc.*
Fountain, Ray — *Management Recruiters International, Inc.*
Fowler, Jim — *First Search America, Inc.*
Fowler, Susan B. — *Russell Reynolds Associates, Inc.*
Fowler, Thomas A. — *The Hindman Company*
Fox, Amanda C. — *Paul Ray Berndtson*
Fox, Lucie — *Allard Associates*
Foy, James — *Foy, Schneid & Daniel, Inc.*

Foy, Richard — *Boyden*
Francis, David P. — *Heidrick & Struggles, Inc.*
Francis, Dwaine — *Francis & Associates*
Francis, Kay — *Francis & Associates*
Frank, Valerie S. — *Norman Roberts & Associates, Inc.*
Franklin, Cecilia — *Management Recruiters International, Inc.*
Franklin, Cleve — *Management Recruiters International, Inc.*
Franklin, John W. — *Russell Reynolds Associates, Inc.*
Franquemont, William R. — *EFL Associates*
Franzino, Michael — *TASA International*
Frazier, John — *Cochran, Cochran & Yale, Inc.*
Frazier, Steven M. — *Sanford Rose Associates*
Freda, Louis A. — *DHR International, Inc.*
Fredericks, Ward A. — *Mixtec Group*
Freedman, Howard — *Korn/Ferry International*
Freemon, Ted — *Management Recruiters International, Inc.*
French, William G. — *Preng & Associates, Inc.*
Frerichs, April — *Ryan, Miller & Associates Inc.*
Freud, John W. — *Paul Ray Berndtson*
Friar, Timothy K. — *Korn/Ferry International*
Friedman, Helen E. — *McCormack & Farrow*
Friedman, Janet — *Litchfield & Willis Inc.*
Friedman, Marcie W. — *Coleman Legal Search Consultants*
Friel, Thomas J. — *Heidrick & Struggles, Inc.*
Frieze, Stanley B. — *Stanley B. Frieze Company*
Frock, Suzanne D. — *Brandjes Associates*
Fruchtman, Gary K. — *Management Recruiters International, Inc.*
Fry, Edmund L. — *Witt/Kieffer, Ford, Hadelman & Lloyd*
Fry, John M. — *The Fry Group, Inc.*
Frye, Garland V. — *Schuyler, Frye & Baker, Inc.*
Fueglein, Hugo — *Korn/Ferry International*
Fuhrman, Katherine — *Richard, Wayne and Roberts*
Fuller, Craig L. — *Korn/Ferry International*
Fuller, Ev — *Management Recruiters International, Inc.*
Fuller, Robert L. — *Litchfield & Willis Inc.*
Fulton, Christine N. — *Highland Search Group, L.L.C.*
Funk, Robert William — *Korn/Ferry International*
Furlong, James W. — *Furlong Search, Inc.*
Furlong, James W. — *Furlong Search, Inc.*
Furlong, James W. — *Furlong Search, Inc.*
Futornick, Bill — *Paul Ray Berndtson*
Gabel, Gregory N. — *Canny, Bowen Inc.*
Gabler, Howard A. — *G.Z. Stephens Inc.*
Gabriel, David L. — *The Arcus Group*
Gadison, William — *Richard, Wayne and Roberts*
Gaffney, Keith — *Gaffney Management Consultants*
Gaffney, William — *Gaffney Management Consultants*
Gagan, Joan — *Gilbert Tweed/INESA*
Gaillard, Bill — *Management Recruiters International, Inc.*
Gaimster, Ann — *The Diversified Search Companies*
Gaines, Ronni L. — *TOPAZ International, Inc.*
Gaines, Ronni L. — *TOPAZ Legal Solutions*
Galante, Suzanne M. — *Vlcek & Company, Inc.*
Galinski, Paul — *E.J. Ashton & Associates, Ltd.*
Gallagher, David W. — *Lamalie Amrop International*
Gallagher, Jim — *Management Recruiters International, Inc.*
Gallagher, Marilyn — *Hogan Acquisitions*
Gallagher, Sallie — *Management Recruiters International, Inc.*
Gallagher, Terence M. — *Battalia Winston International*
Gandee, Bob — *Management Recruiters International, Inc.*
Gandee, Bob — *Management Recruiters International, Inc.*
Gandee, John R. — *Management Recruiters International, Inc.*
Gantar, Robert — *Howard Fischer Associates, Inc.*
Garcia, Joseph — *Management Recruiters International, Inc.*
Gardiner, E. Nicholas P. — *Gardiner International*
Gardner, J.W. — *Management Recruiters International, Inc.*
Gardner, John T. — *Heidrick & Struggles, Inc.*
Gardy, Susan H. — *Paul Ray Berndtson*
Garfinkle, Steven M. — *Battalia Winston International*
Gargalli, Claire W. — *The Diversified Search Companies*
Gariano, Robert J. — *Russell Reynolds Associates, Inc.*
Garman, Herb C. — *Management Recruiters International, Inc.*
Garrett, Donald L. — *Garrett Associates Inc.*
Garrett, Linda M. — *Garrett Associates Inc.*
Garrity, Irene — *Management Recruiters International, Inc.*
Gaskins, Kim — *Kenzer Corp.*
Gates, Douglas H. — *Skott/Edwards Consultants, Inc.*
Gates, Will — *Korn/Ferry International*
Gauss, James W. — *Witt/Kieffer, Ford, Hadelman & Lloyd*
Gauthier, Robert C. — *Columbia Consulting Group*
Gaxiola, Alejandro — *Smith Search, S.C.*
Gelfman, David — *Career Management International*
Genser, Elaina S. — *Witt/Kieffer, Ford, Hadelman & Lloyd*
George, Delores F. — *Delores F. George Human Resource
Management & Consulting Industry*
Gerber, Mark J. — *Wellington Management Group*
Gerevas, Ronald E. — *Spencer Stuart*
Gerevas, Ronald E. — *Spencer Stuart*

Hamdan, Mark — *Careernet of Florida, Inc.*
Hamer, Thurston — *Korn/Ferry International*
Hamilton, John R. — *A.T. Kearney, Inc.*
Hamilton, Timothy — *The Caldwell Partners Amrop International*
Hamm, Gary P. — *Witt/Kieffer, Ford, Hadelman & Lloyd*
Hancock, Deborah L. — *Morgan Hunter Corp.*
Hancock, Mimi — *Russell Reynolds Associates, Inc.*
Hand, Jean — *Management Recruiters International, Inc.*
Hanford, Michael — *Richard Kader & Associates*
Hanley, Maureen E. — *Gilbert Tweed/INESA*
Hanna, Dwight — *Cadillac Associates*
Hannock, Elwin W. — *Flynn, Hannock, Incorporated*
Hanrahan, Kevin R. — *Russell Reynolds Associates, Inc.*
Hansen, Bente K. — *DHR International, Inc.*
Hansen, Charles A. — *Management Recruiters International, Inc.*
Hansen, David G. — *Ott & Hansen, Inc.*
Hansen, Erik Lars — *Korn/Ferry International*
Hansen, Jan — *Management Recruiters International, Inc.*
Hansen, Martin L. — *Management Recruiters International, Inc.*
Hansen, Ty E. — *Blake, Hansen & Nye, Limited*
Hanson, Carrie — *U.S. Envirosearch*
Hanson, Grant M. — *Goodrich & Sherwood Associates, Inc.*
Hanson, Jeremy — *Korn/Ferry International*
Hanson, Lee — *Heidrick & Struggles, Inc.*
Hanson, Paul L. — *Ward Howell International, Inc.*
Hanson, Russell V. — *Management Recruiters International, Inc.*
Harap, David — *Korn/Ferry International*
Harbaugh, Paul J. — *International Management Advisors, Inc.*
Harbert, David O. — *Sweeney Harbert & Mummert, Inc.*
Hardbrod, Herbert — *Management Recruiters International, Inc.*
Hardison, Richard L. — *Hardison & Company*
Hardwick, Michael — *Management Recruiters International, Inc.*
Hardy, Thomas G. — *Spencer Stuart*
Harfenist, Harry — *Parker Page Group*
Harlow, John — *Korn/Ferry International*
Harmon, Tony — *Mixtec Group*
Haro, Adolfo Medina — *Egon Zehnder International Inc.*
Harrell, L. Parker — *Korn/Ferry International*
Harrington, Chip — *Management Recruiters International, Inc.*
Harrington, Joan — *Management Recruiters International, Inc.*
Harrington, Robert J. — *Sanford Rose Associates*
Harris, Bruce — *ProResource, Inc.*
Harris, Ethel S. — *Don Richard Associates of Charlotte*
Harris, Jack — *Baker, Harris & Partners Limited*
Harris, Jack L. — *Management Recruiters International, Inc.*
Harris, Julia — *The Whitney Group*
Harris, Melissa — *Paul Ray Berndtson*
Harris, Vicki M. — *Management Recruiters International, Inc.*
Harshman, Donald — *The Stevenson Group of New Jersey*
Hart, Andrew D. — *Russell Reynolds Associates, Inc.*
Hart, David — *Hadley Lockwood, Inc.*
Hart, Robert T. — *D.E. Foster Partners Inc.*
Hart, Susan S. — *Spencer Stuart*
Harty, Shirley Cox — *Paul Ray Berndtson*
Harvey, Jill — *MSI International*
Harvey, John K. — *Management Recruiters International, Inc.*
Harvey, Mike — *Advanced Executive Resources*
Harvey, Richard — *Price Waterhouse*
Hasler, Betty — *Heidrick & Struggles, Inc.*
Haughton, Michael — *DeFrain, Mayer, Lee & Burgess LLC*
Hauser, David E. — *Lamalie Amrop International*
Hauser, Jack — *Andcor Human Resources*
Hauser, Martha — *Spencer Stuart*
Hauswirth, Jeffrey M. — *Spencer Stuart*
Havas, Judy — *Heidrick & Struggles, Inc.*
Havener, Donald Clarke — *The Abbott Group, Inc.*
Hawfield, Sam G. — *Management Recruiters International, Inc.*
Hawkins, John T.W. — *Russell Reynolds Associates, Inc.*
Hawkins, Kirk V. — *Management Recruiters International, Inc.*
Hawksworth, A. Dwight — *A.D. & Associates Executive Search, Inc.*
Hay, Ian — *Korn/Ferry International*
Hay, William E. — *William E. Hay & Company*
Hayden, Dale — *Sanford Rose Associates*
Hayden, John — *Johnson Smith & Knisely Accord*
Hayden, Lynn — *Erlanger Associates Inc.*
Hayes, Stephen A. — *DHR International, Inc.*
Haystead, Steve — *Advanced Executive Resources*
Hazelton, Lisa M. — *Health Care Dimensions*
Heagy, Linda H. — *Paul Ray Berndtson*
Healey, Joseph T. — *Highland Search Group, L.L.C.*
Healy, Vanda K. — *Management Recruiters International, Inc.*
Healy, William C. — *Management Recruiters International, Inc.*
Heath, Jeffrey A. — *Management Recruiters International, Inc.*
Heavey, John — *Prestige Inc.*
Hebard, Roy — *Korn/Ferry International*
Hebel, Robert W. — *R.W. Hebel Associates*
Hebert, Guy J. — *Spencer Stuart*
Hecker, Henry C. — *Hogan Acquisitions*

Heckscher, Cindy P. — *The Diversified Search Companies*
Heideman, Mary Marren — *DeFrain, Mayer, Lee & Burgess LLC*
Heidrick, Gardner W. — *The Heidrick Partners, Inc.*
Heidrick, Robert L. — *The Heidrick Partners, Inc.*
Heiken, Barbara E. — *Randell-Heiken, Inc.*
Heintz, William — *Mixtec Group*
Heisser, Robert — *Management Recruiters International, Inc.*
Heldenbrand, Paul — *The McCormick Group, Inc.*
Helgeson, Burton H. — *Norm Sanders Associates*
Heller, Steven A. — *Martin H. Bauman Associates, Inc.*
Hellinger, Audrey — *Martin H. Bauman Associates, Inc.*
Helmholz, Steven W. — *Korn/Ferry International*
Helminiak, Audrey — *Gaffney Management Consultants*
Helt, Wally A. — *Management Recruiters International, Inc.*
Hemer, Craig — *Tanton Mitchell/Paul Ray Berndtson*
Hemingway, Stuart C. — *Robison & Associates*
Henard, John B. — *Lamalie Amrop International*
Henderson, Cathy — *Management Recruiters International, Inc.*
Henderson, Dale — *Management Recruiters International, Inc.*
Henderson, John — *Key Employment Services*
Henderson, Marc — *Prestige Inc.*
Henderson, William D. — *Russell Reynolds Associates, Inc.*
Hendon, Jill — *Korn/Ferry International*
Hendrickson, David L. — *Heidrick & Struggles, Inc.*
Hendrickson, Gary E. — *Management Recruiters International, Inc.*
Hendriks, Warren K. — *DHR International, Inc.*
Hendrixson, Ron — *Korn/Ferry International*
Heneghan, Donald A. — *Allerton Heneghan & O'Neill*
Henkel, John J. — *Management Recruiters International, Inc.*
Henkel, John J. — *Management Recruiters International, Inc.*
Henn, George W. — *G.W. Henn & Company*
Hennessy, Robert D. — *Korn/Ferry International*
Henry, Patrick — *F-O-R-T-U-N-E Personnel Consultants of Huntsville, Inc.*
Hensley, Bert — *Korn/Ferry International*
Hergenrather, Edmund R. — *Hergenrather & Company*
Hergenrather, Richard A. — *Hergenrather & Company*
Herget, James P. — *Lamalie Amrop International*
Herman, Eugene J. — *Earley Kielty and Associates, Inc.*
Hernandez, Luis A. — *CoEnergy, Inc.*
Herrmann, Jerry C. — *Management Recruiters International, Inc.*
Hertan, Richard L. — *Executive Manning Corporation*
Hertan, Wiliam A. — *Executive Manning Corporation*
Hertlein, James N.J. — *Boyden/Zay & Company*
Hess, David B. — *Sanford Rose Associates*
Hess, James C. — *The Diversified Search Companies*
Hess, Patricia — *Sanford Rose Associates*
Hessel, Gregory — *Korn/Ferry International*
Hetherman, Margaret F. — *Highland Search Group, L.L.C.*
Hettinger, Susan — *Kenzer Corp.*
Hetzel, William G. — *The Hetzel Group, Inc.*
Heuerman, James N. — *Korn/Ferry International*
Hewitt, Rives D. — *The Dalley Hewitt Company*
Hickman, Andrew — *Korn/Ferry International*
Hicks, Albert M. — *Phillips Resource Group*
Hicks, James L. — *MSI International*
Hicks, Mike — *Damon & Associates, Inc.*
Hicks, Nancy — *Paul Ray Berndtson*
Hicks, Timothy C. — *Korn/Ferry International*
Hidalgo, Rhonda — *Richard, Wayne and Roberts*
Hiebert, Wilf — *KPMG Executive Search*
Higdon, Henry G. — *Higdon Prince Inc.*
Higgins, David — *DHR International, Inc.*
Higgins, Donna — *Howard Fischer Associates, Inc.*
Higgins, John B. — *Higgins Associates, Inc.*
Hildebrand, Thomas B. — *Professional Resources Group, Inc.*
Hill, Emery — *MSI International*
Hill, Mike — *Tyler & Company*
Hill, Randall W. — *Heidrick & Struggles, Inc.*
Hillen, Skip — *The McCormick Group, Inc.*
Hiller, Steve — *The McCormick Group, Inc.*
Hilliker, Alan D. — *Egon Zehnder International Inc.*
Hillyer, Robert L. — *Executive Manning Corporation*
Hilton, Diane — *Richard, Wayne and Roberts*
Hilyard, Paul J. — *MSI International*
Hindman, Neil C. — *The Hindman Company*
Hingers, Marilyn H. — *Management Recruiters International, Inc.*
Hinkle, Dee — *Bradford & Galt, Inc.*
Hirsch, Julia C. — *Boyden*
Hirschbein, Don L. — *Management Recruiters International, Inc.*
Hirschey, K. David — *Andcor Human Resources*
Hite, William A. — *Hite Executive Search*
Hoagland, John H. — *Pendleton James and Associates, Inc.*
Hobart, John N. — *Paul Ray Berndtson*
Hobson, Mary L. — *EFL Associates*
Hockett, William — *Hockett Associates, Inc.*
Hodge, Jeff — *Heidrick & Struggles, Inc.*
Hodgson, Judy H. — *Management Recruiters International, Inc.*

Hodgson, Robert D. — *Management Recruiters International, Inc.*
Hoevel, Michael J. — *Poirier, Hoevel & Co.*
Hoffman, Brian — *Winter, Wyman & Company*
Hoffman, Mark — *Management Recruiters International, Inc.*
Hoffman, David H. — *DHR International, Inc.*
Hoffmann, David H. — *DHR International, Inc.*
Hogan, Edward — *Sanford Rose Associates*
Hogan, Larry H. — *Hogan Acquisitions*
Hohlstein, Jeff G. — *Management Recruiters International, Inc.*
Hohlstein, Jodi — *Management Recruiters International, Inc.*
Holden, Bradley J. — *Korn/Ferry International*
Holden, Richard — *Hornberger Management Company*
Holden, Richard B. — *Ames Personnel Consultants, Inc.*
Holland, Dave G. — *Management Recruiters International, Inc.*
Holland, Kathleen — *TOPAZ International, Inc.*
Holland, Kathleen — *TOPAZ Legal Solutions*
Holland, Richard G. — *Management Recruiters International, Inc.*
Hollinger, Bill A. — *Management Recruiters International, Inc.*
Hollinger, Lois — *Management Recruiters International, Inc.*
Hollingsworth, Leslie — *Brad Marks International*
Hollins, Howard D. — *MSI International*
Holloway, Linda — *Management Recruiters International, Inc.*
Holloway, Roger M. — *Management Recruiters International, Inc.*
Holmes, Lawrence J. — *Columbia Consulting Group*
Holmes, Len — *Management Recruiters International, Inc.*
Holodnak, William A. — *J. Robert Scott*
Holt, Carol — *Bartholdi & Company, Inc.*
Holt, Doug C. — *Management Recruiters International, Inc.*
Holupka, Gary F. — *Management Recruiters International, Inc.*
Holupka, Patricia Lampl — *Management Recruiters International, Inc.*
Holzberger, Georges L. — *Highland Search Group, L.L.C.*
Homer, Judy B. — *J.B. Homer Associates, Inc.*
Honer, Paul — *Johnson Smith & Knisely Accord*
Honey, W. Michael M. — *O'Callaghan Honey/Paul Ray Berndtson, Inc.*
Hooker, Lisa — *Paul Ray Berndtson*
Hopkins, Chester A. — *Handy HRM Corp.*
Hoppert, Phil — *Wargo and Co., Inc.*
Horgan, Thomas F. — *Nadzam, Lusk, Horgan & Associates, Inc.*
Hornberger, Frederick C. — *Hornberger Management Company*
Horton, Robert H. — *Horton International*
Horwitz, Sandy — *Kenzer Corp.*
Hoskins, Charles R. — *Heidrick & Struggles, Inc.*
Houchins, Gene E. — *Management Recruiters International, Inc.*
Houchins, William N. — *Christian & Timbers*
Hovey, Dick — *Management Recruiters International, Inc.*
Howard, Brian E. — *Management Recruiters International, Inc.*
Howard, Jill — *Health Care Dimensions*
Howard, Kathy S. — *Management Recruiters International, Inc.*
Howard, Leon — *Richard, Wayne and Roberts*
Howard, Richard H. — *Management Recruiters International, Inc.*
Howard, Susy — *The McCormick Group, Inc.*
Howe, Vance A. — *Ward Howell International, Inc.*
Howe, William S. — *Kenny, Kindler, Hunt & Howe*
Hoyda, Louis A. — *Thorndike Deland Associates*
Hucko, Donald S. — *Jonas, Walters & Assoc., Inc.*
Hudson, Kevin — *Raymond Karsan Associates*
Hudson, Reginald M. — *Search Bureau International*
Hudson, William — *Robert Sage Recruiting*
Hughes, Cathy N. — *The Ogdon Partnership*
Hughes, James J. — *R.P. Barone Associates*
Hughes, Kendall G. — *Hughes & Associates*
Hughes, Pat — *Kenzer Corp.*
Hulce, Colleen — *Korn/Ferry International*
Hume, David — *Bradford & Galt, Inc.*
Humphreys, Sidney — *Korn/Ferry International*
Hunt, James E. — *Kenny, Kindler, Hunt & Howe*
Hunt, Thomas — *MSI International*
Hunter, Durant A. — *Pendleton James and Associates, Inc.*
Hunter, Gabe — *Phillips Resource Group*
Hunter, Patricia — *Kenzer Corp.*
Hunter, Sharon W. — *Management Recruiters International, Inc.*
Hunter, Sue J. — *Robison & Associates*
Huntoon, Cliff — *Richard, Wayne and Roberts*
Huntting, Lisa — *Professional Alternatives, Inc.*
Hurd, J. Nicholas — *Russell Reynolds Associates, Inc.*
Hurley, Helen — *Management Recruiters International, Inc.*
Hursey, Bruce — *Management Recruiters International, Inc.*
Hurst, Joan E. — *Korn/Ferry International*
Hurt, Thomas E. — *Management Recruiters International, Inc.*
Hurt, Thomas E. — *Management Recruiters International, Inc.*
Hutchinson, Loretta M. — *Hutchinson Resources International*
Hutchinson, Richard H. — *Rurak & Associates, Inc.*
Hutchison, William K. — *Christenson & Hutchison*
Huttner, Leah — *Korn/Ferry International*
Hwang, Yvette — *MSI International*
Hyde, Mark D. — *MSI International*
Hyde, Tom G. — *Management Recruiters International, Inc.*

Hyde, W. Jerry — *Hyde Danforth Wold & Co.*
Hykes, Don A. — *A.T. Kearney, Inc.*
Hypes, Richard G. — *Lynch Miller Moore Partners, Inc.*
Ide, Ian — *Winter, Wyman & Company*
Ikle, A. Donald — *Ward Howell International, Inc.*
Illsley, Hugh G. — *Ward Howell International, Inc.*
Imely, Larry — *Christian & Timbers*
Incitti, Lance M. — *Management Recruiters International, Inc.*
Indiveri, Peter — *Kenzer Corp.*
Infantino, James — *Management Recruiters International, Inc.*
Infinger, Ronald E. — *Robison & Associates*
Ingalls, Joseph M. — *John Kurosky & Associates*
Inglis, William — *Korn/Ferry International*
Ingram, D. John — *Ingram & Aydelotte Inc.*
Inguagiato, Gregory — *MSI International*
Isenberg, Peter — *Management Recruiters International, Inc.*
Israel, Stephen — *Korn/Ferry International*
Issacs, Judith A. — *Grant Cooper and Associates*
Ives, Richard K. — *Wilkinson & Ives*
Ivey, Deborah M. — *MSI International*
Jablo, Steven — *Dieckmann & Associates, Ltd.*
Jackowitz, Todd — *J. Robert Scott*
Jackson, Barry — *Morgan Hunter Corp.*
Jackson, Carol — *The Wentworth Company, Inc.*
Jackson, Clarke H. — *The Caldwell Partners Amrop International*
Jackson, Clay — *Paul Ray Berndtson*
Jackson, James Greg — *Korn/Ferry International*
Jacob, Don C. — *Management Recruiters International, Inc.*
Jacobs, James W. — *Callan Associates, Ltd.*
Jacobs, Klaus — *TASA International*
Jacobs, Martin J. — *The Rubicon Group*
Jacobs, Mike — *Thorne, Brieger Associates Inc.*
Jacobson, Al — *KPMG Executive Search*
Jacobson, David N. — *Jacobson Associates*
Jacobson, Donald — *Hunt Ltd.*
Jacobson, Eric K. — *Management Recruiters International, Inc.*
Jacobson, Gregory — *Jacobson Associates*
Jacobson, Jewel — *Jacobson Associates*
Jacobson, Robert E. — *Management Recruiters International, Inc.*
Jadick, Theodore N. — *Heidrick & Struggles, Inc.*
Jaedike, Eldron — *Prestige Inc.*
Jaffe, Mark — *Wyatt & Jaffe*
Jambor, Hilary L. — *Korn/Ferry International*
James, Allison A. — *MSI International*
James, Bruce — *Roberson and Company*
James, E. Pendleton — *Pendleton James and Associates, Inc.*
James, Jane — *Canny, Bowen Inc.*
James, Michele — *Korn/Ferry International*
James, Richard — *Criterion Executive Search, Inc.*
Janecek, Robert — *Management Recruiters International, Inc.*
Janis, Laurence — *Integrated Search Solutions Group, LLC*
Jayne, Edward R. — *Heidrick & Struggles, Inc.*
Jeanes, Marshall M. — *IMCOR, Inc.*
Jelley, Sarah L. — *Pendleton James and Associates, Inc.*
Jenkins, Jeffrey N. — *Sanford Rose Associates*
Jensen, Christine K. — *John Kurosky & Associates*
Jensen, Debra — *Flex Execs Management Solutions*
Jernigan, Alice — *Ariel Recruitment Associates*
Jernigan, Susan N. — *Sockwell & Associates*
Jilka, Daniel L. — *Management Recruiters International, Inc.*
Jimenez, Gil C. — *Management Recruiters International, Inc.*
Joffe, Barry — *Bason Associates Inc.*
Johasky, Tom K. — *Management Recruiters International, Inc.*
Johnson, David — *Gaffney Management Consultants*
Johnson, Dennis R. — *Management Recruiters International, Inc.*
Johnson, Harold E. — *Norman Broadbent International, Inc.*
Johnson, John F. — *Lamalie Amrop International*
Johnson, John W. — *Webb, Johnson Associates, Inc.*
Johnson, Kathleen A. — *Barton Raben, Inc.*
Johnson, Maxene — *Norman Roberts & Associates, Inc.*
Johnson, Pete — *Morgan Hunter Corp.*
Johnson, Priscilla — *The Johnson Group, Inc.*
Johnson, Rocky — *A.T. Kearney, Inc.*
Johnson, Ron L. — *Management Recruiters International, Inc.*
Johnson, Ronald S. — *Ronald S. Johnson Associates, Inc.*
Johnson, S. Hope — *The Interface Group, Ltd./Boyden*
Johnson, Shirley E. — *The Heidrick Partners, Inc.*
Johnson, Walt W. — *Management Recruiters International, Inc.*
Johnston, Cindy — *Management Recruiters International, Inc.*
Johnston, James R. — *The Stevenson Group of Delaware Inc.*
Johnston, Philip D. — *Egon Zehnder International Inc.*
Jones, Barbara J. — *Kaye-Bassman International Corp.*
Jones, Dale E. — *Lamalie Amrop International*
Jones, Don — *Kenzer Corp.*
Jones, Donald K. — *Russell Reynolds Associates, Inc.*
Jones, Edgar — *A.T. Kearney, Inc.*
Jones, Edward G. — *E.G. Jones Associates, Ltd.*
Jones, Francis E. — *Earley Kielty and Associates, Inc.*

Jones, Gary — *BGB Associates*
Jones, Herschel — *Korn/Ferry International*
Jones, Jeffrey — *AJM Professional Services*
Jones, Jonathan C. — *The Ogdon Partnership*
Jones, Judy M. — *Management Recruiters International, Inc.*
Jones, Mike R. — *Management Recruiters International, Inc.*
Jones, Ronald T. — *ARJay & Associates*
Jordan, Stephen T. — *Paul Ray Berndtson*
Jose, Bill O. — *Management Recruiters International, Inc.*
Jose, Bill O. — *Management Recruiters International, Inc.*
Joubert, Pierre E. — *Boyden*
Joyce, Sheila M. — *Verkamp-Joyce Associates, Inc.*
Joys, David S. — *Heidrick & Struggles, Inc.*
Juarez, Maria Elena — *Amrop International*
Judd, Susan — *Korn/Ferry International*
Juelis, John J. — *Peeney Associates*
Juhan, Louise B. — *Korn/Ferry International*
Kacyn, Louis J. — *Egon Zehnder International Inc.*
Kader, Richard — *Richard Kader & Associates*
Kadin, Tom — *Kenzer Corp.*
Kahn, P. Frederick — *Heidrick & Struggles, Inc.*
Kaiser, Irene — *Dunhill Search International*
Kaiser, James G. — *Dunhill Search International*
Kalb, Lenny — *Career Management International*
Kalinowski, David — *Jacobson Associates*
Kampmann, Sara — *Johnson Smith & Knisely Accord*
Kaplan, Alexandra — *J.M. Eagle Partners Ltd.*
Kaplan, Gary — *Gary Kaplan & Associates*
Kaplan, Marc — *Gary Kaplan & Associates*
Kaplowitz, Marji — *Richard, Wayne and Roberts*
Kapur, Sharmila — *Korn/Ferry International*
Karsan, N.S. — *Raymond Karsan Associates*
Kashinsky, Richard J. — *Management Recruiters International, Inc.*
Kassouf, Connie — *The Whitney Group*
Katz, Art E. — *Management Recruiters International, Inc.*
Katz, Robert L. — *MSI International*
Katz, Rosalind N. — *ExecuScope Division of Russell Staffing Resources, Inc.*
Kaufman, Stuart — *Management Recruiters International, Inc.*
Kaufmann, Robert C. — *Spencer Stuart*
Kaun, Loren A. — *Management Recruiters International, Inc.*
Kayajian, Bob A. — *Management Recruiters International, Inc.*
Kaye, Jeff — *Management Recruiters International, Inc.*
Kaye, Jeffrey — *Kaye-Bassman International Corp.*
Kaye, Jerry — *Ward Howell International, Inc.*
Kean, Marjorie — *Korn/Ferry International*
Keating, Anne F. — *Korn/Ferry International*
Keating, Pierson — *Nordeman Grimm, Inc.*
Keefe, Donald J. — *TASA International*
Keegen, Joanne — *Evie Kreisler & Associates, Inc.*
Keen, Robert — *Management Recruiters International, Inc.*
Keesom, W. Peter — *Boyden/Zay & Company*
Keeton, Susan G. — *The Corporate Connection, Ltd.*
Keitel, Robert S. — *A.T. Kearney, Inc.*
Keller, Barbara — *Barton Raben, Inc.*
Keller, Lorraine L. — *Management Recruiters International, Inc.*
Keller, Peggy — *The McCormick Group, Inc.*
Kellerhals, Gloria — *Management Recruiters International, Inc.*
Kelley, Randall D. — *Spencer Stuart*
Kelly, Claudia L. — *Spencer Stuart*
Kelly, Elizabeth Ann — *Wellington Management Group*
Kelly, Kevin B. — *Russell Reynolds Associates, Inc.*
Kelly, Michael T. — *Russell Reynolds Associates, Inc.*
Kelly, Michael T. — *Russell Reynolds Associates, Inc.*
Kelly, Peter W. — *R. Rollo Associates*
Kelly, Roy P. — *Management Recruiters International, Inc.*
Kelsey, Micki — *Davidson, Laird & Associates*
Kelso, Patricia C. — *Barton Raben, Inc.*
Kemp, M. Scott — *M. Scott Kemp & Associates*
Kendall, Steven W. — *Management Recruiters International, Inc.*
Kendrick, M. Steven — *Lamalie Amrop International*
Kennedy, Michael — *The Danbrook Group, Inc.*
Kenny, Roger M. — *Kenny, Kindler, Hunt & Howe*
Kent, Melvin — *Melvin Kent & Associates, Inc.*
Kent, Vickey — *Professional Alternatives, Inc.*
Kenzer, Robert D. — *Kenzer Corp.*
Keogh, James — *Sanford Rose Associates*
Kepler, Charles W. — *Russell Reynolds Associates, Inc.*
Kerester, Jonathon — *Cadillac Associates*
Kern, Ann P. — *Korn/Ferry International*
Kern, Jerry L. — *ADOW's Executeam*
Kern, Kathleen G. — *ADOW's Executeam*
Kershaw, Lisa — *Tanton Mitchell/Paul Ray Berndtson*
Keshishian, Gregory — *Handy HRM Corp.*
Kettwig, David A. — *A.T. Kearney, Inc.*
Kieffer, Michael C. — *Witt/Kieffer, Ford, Hadelman & Lloyd*
Kielty, John L. — *Earley Kielty and Associates, Inc.*
Kiley, Phyllis — *National Search, Inc.*

Kiliper, Catherine G. — *Korn/Ferry International*
Kincannon, Kelly — *Kincannon & Reed*
Kindler, Peter A. — *Kenny, Kindler, Hunt & Howe*
King, Byron L. — *Management Recruiters International, Inc.*
King, Gary A. — *Management Recruiters International, Inc.*
King, James B. — *The Westminster Group, Inc.*
King, Stephen C. — *Boyden/Zay & Company*
Kingdom, Scott — *Korn/Ferry International*
Kingore, William C. — *DHR International, Inc.*
Kingsley, Kate — *Korn/Ferry International*
Kinley, David — *The Caldwell Partners Amrop International*
Kinney, Carol — *Dussick Management Associates*
Kinser, Richard E. — *Richard Kinser & Associates*
Kirby, James E. — *Management Recruiters International, Inc.*
Kirchgessner, Ken F. — *Management Recruiters International, Inc.*
Kirchner, Michael — *American Medical Consultants*
Kirkpatrick, Robert L. — *Reese Associates*
Kirschner, John — *Management Recruiters International, Inc.*
Kishbaugh, Herbert S. — *Kishbaugh Associates International*
Kissel, Jim R. — *Management Recruiters International, Inc.*
Kister, Edward A. — *Pendleton James and Associates, Inc.*
Kixmiller, David B. — *Heidrick & Struggles, Inc.*
Kizer, Jay R. — *Paul Ray Berndtson*
Klages, Constance W. — *International Management Advisors, Inc.*
Klauck, James J. — *Horton International*
Klavens, Cecile J. — *The Pickwick Group, Inc.*
Klavins, Larissa R. — *Dieckmann & Associates, Ltd.*
Klein, Gregory A. — *A.T. Kearney, Inc.*
Kleinstein, Jonah A. — *The Kleinstein Group*
Kline, James O. — *Management Recruiters International, Inc.*
Klock, Lawrence S. — *Russell Reynolds Associates, Inc.*
Klopfenstein, Edward L. — *Crowder & Company*
Klopmeyerr, Vanessa — *Kenzer Corp.*
Klos, Larry — *Management Recruiters International, Inc.*
Kluber, Bruce — *Richard, Wayne and Roberts*
Knapp, Ronald A. — *Knapp Consultants*
Knecht, Luke D. — *Russell Reynolds Associates, Inc.*
Knight, Gwen — *Richard, Wayne and Roberts*
Knight, Kim L. — *Telford, Adams & Alexander/The Knight Company*
Knight, Lisa — *Ward Howell International, Inc.*
Knight, Liz — *Plummer & Associates, Inc.*
Knight, Russell — *Hornberger Management Company*
Knisely, Gary — *Johnson Smith & Knisely Accord*
Knotts, Jerry — *Mixtec Group*
Knox, Andrew — *Korn/Ferry International*
Knutson, Rebecca J. — *Management Recruiters International, Inc.*
Koblentz, Joel M. — *Egon Zehnder International Inc.*
Kochmer, Sheila — *Management Recruiters International, Inc.*
Kochmer, Victor — *Management Recruiters International, Inc.*
Koenig, Joel S. — *Russell Reynolds Associates, Inc.*
Kohn, Adam P. — *Christian & Timbers*
Kohn, Carole — *Kenzer Corp.*
Kohn, Thomas C. — *Reflex Services, Inc.*
Kolburne, Barbara — *D.E. Foster Partners Inc.*
Kolder, Thomas R. — *Russell Reynolds Associates, Inc.*
Koletic, Rudy E. — *Management Recruiters International, Inc.*
Kolke, Rick — *Richard, Wayne and Roberts*
Kondra, Vernon J. — *The Douglas Reiter Company, Inc.*
Konker, David N. — *Russell Reynolds Associates, Inc.*
Koontz, Donald N. — *Koontz, Jeffries & Associates, Inc.*
Kopsick, Joseph M. — *Spencer Stuart*
Korkuch, Sandy — *Barone-O'Hara Associates*
Kornfeld, Warren — *Management Recruiters International, Inc.*
Kossuth, David — *Kossuth & Associates, Inc.*
Kossuth, Jane — *Kossuth & Associates, Inc.*
Kotick, Madeline — *The Stevenson Group of New Jersey*
Kotler, Herman — *Management Recruiters International, Inc.*
Kotler, Jerry R. — *Management Recruiters International, Inc.*
Kozlowski, Elaine K. — *Management Recruiters International, Inc.*
Kramer, Desni — *Management Recruiters International, Inc.*
Kratz, Steve — *Tyler & Company*
Kraus, Kathy — *Evie Kreisler & Associates, Inc.*
Krauser, H. James — *Spencer Stuart*
Kreisman, Charlotte — *Kenzer Corp.*
Krejci, Stanley L. — *The Interface Group, Ltd./Boyden*
Krell, Richard B. — *Russell Reynolds Associates, Inc.*
Krick, Terry L. — *Financial Resource Associates, Inc.*
Krieger, Dennis F. — *Seiden Krieger Associates, Inc.*
Kring, Kenneth L. — *Spencer Stuart*
Krinsky, Ira W. — *Korn/Ferry International*
Krochenski, Caren S. — *Management Recruiters International, Inc.*
Krochenski, Lynette — *Management Recruiters International, Inc.*
Krohn, Eileen — *The Stevenson Group of New Jersey*
Kruse, Kevin — *Korn/Ferry International*
Kucewicz, William — *Search West, Inc.*
Kuehnling, William A. — *Sanford Rose Associates*
Kuhl, Debra — *Paul Ray Berndtson*
Kuhl, Teresa — *Don Richard Associates of Tampa, Inc.*

Kuhnle, John H. — *Korn/Ferry International*
Kuhns, David — *Paul Ray Berndtson*
Kuntz, Bill — *Management Recruiters International, Inc.*
Kunzer, William J. — *Kunzer Associates, Ltd.*
Kuper, Keith D. — *Christenson & Hutchison*
Kurosky, John — *John Kurosky & Associates*
Kurtz, Michael E. — *MDR Associates, Inc.*
Kurz, Dick A. — *Management Recruiters International, Inc.*
Kush, Max — *Management Recruiters International, Inc.*
Kusin, Melanie B. — *Heidrick & Struggles, Inc.*
Kuypers, Arnold — *Lamalie Amrop International*
La Grow, Ronald E. — *DHR International, Inc.*
Laba, Marvin — *Marvin Laba & Associates*
Laba, Stuart M. — *Marvin Laba & Associates*
Labadie, Ernie B. — *Management Recruiters International, Inc.*
Lachance, Roger — *Laurendeau, Labrecque/Paul Ray Berndtson, Inc.*
Lachenauer, Bruce J. — *Heidrick & Struggles, Inc.*
LaFaye, Susan — *MSI International*
Laird, Meri — *Davidson, Laird & Associates*
Lajous, Luz — *Russell Reynolds Associates, Inc.*
Lake, Phillip R. — *U.S. Envirosearch*
Lalonde, Joel — *Management Recruiters International, Inc.*
Lamb, Angus K. — *Raymond Karsan Associates*
Lamb, Lynn M. — *F-O-R-T-U-N-E Personnel Consultants of Huntsville, Inc.*
Lamb, Peter S. — *Executive Resource, Inc.*
Lambert, Robert J. — *Heidrick & Struggles, Inc.*
Lampl, Joni — *Management Recruiters International, Inc.*
Lampl, Lisa — *Management Recruiters International, Inc.*
Lampl, Mark — *Korn/Ferry International*
Lampl, Richard — *Management Recruiters International, Inc.*
Lampl, Tom W. — *Management Recruiters International, Inc.*
Land, Shaun — *Dunhill Professional Search of Irvine, Inc.*
Landan, Joy — *Jacobson Associates*
Landon, Susan J. — *Lamalie Amrop International*
Landry, Leo G. — *MSI International*
Lane, Doug — *Management Recruiters International, Inc.*
Langer, Joel A. — *Langer Associates, Inc.*
Lankford, Charles — *MSI International*
Lannamann, Richard S. — *Russell Reynolds Associates, Inc.*
Lapat, Aaron D. — *J. Robert Scott*
Lapham, Lawrence L. — *Lawrence L. Lapham Inc.*
Lareau, Belle — *Management Recruiters International, Inc.*
Lareau, Jerry A. — *Management Recruiters International, Inc.*
Larsen, Bruce — *Prestige Inc.*
Larsen, Jack B. — *Jack B. Larsen & Associates*
Larsen, Richard F. — *Larsen, Zilliacus & Associates, Inc.*
Larson, Paul W. — *Paul Ray Berndtson*
Lasher, Charles M. — *Lasher Associates*
Lasse, Daniel C. — *Management Recruiters International, Inc.*
Latino, Irene K. — *Ward Howell International, Inc.*
LaTraverse, Jean J. — *Belle Isle, Djandji Inc.*
Latterell, Jeffrey D. — *Smith & Latterell (HRS, Inc.)*
Laubitz, Chris — *The Caldwell Partners Amrop International*
Lauderback, David R. — *A.T. Kearney, Inc.*
Laurendeau, Jean L. — *Laurendeau, Labrecque/Paul Ray Berndtson, Inc.*
Lautz, Lindsay A. — *Wilkinson & Ives*
Lavender, Jane — *Paul Ray Berndtson*
Lawler, Tim M. — *Management Recruiters International, Inc.*
Lawson, Bettye N. — *MSI International*
Lawson, Debra — *Management Recruiters International, Inc.*
Lawson, Ron S. — *Management Recruiters International, Inc.*
Layton, Bradford — *Bradford & Galt, Inc.*
Layton, Patrick R. — *MSI International*
Lazaro, Alicia C. — *The Whitney Group*
Lechner, David B. — *Management Recruiters International, Inc.*
LeComte, Andre — *Egon Zehnder International Inc.*
Lee, Barbara A. — *Management Recruiters International, Inc.*
Lee, Donna M. — *Kincannon & Reed*
Lee, Robert E. — *Management Recruiters International, Inc.*
Lee, Rodger A. — *Sanford Rose Associates*
Leetma, Imbi — *Stanton Chase International*
Lefebvre, Jean-Pierre — *Ward Howell International, Inc.*
Lehnst, Joh L. — *Management Recruiters International, Inc.*
LeMay, Steven E. — *Saber Consultants*
Lemke, Peter K. — *EFL Associates*
Lemon, Kay — *Management Recruiters International, Inc.*
Lence, Julie Anne — *MSI International*
Lenga, Bobbie — *Kenzer Corp.*
Lenkaitis, Lewis F. — *A.T. Kearney, Inc.*
Lennon, Roslyn J. — *Heidrick & Struggles, Inc.*
Lennox, Charles — *Price Waterhouse*
Leon, Jeffrey J. — *Russell Reynolds Associates, Inc.*
Lerner, Joel S. — *Sanford Rose Associates*
Leske, Lucy Apthorp — *Educational Management Network*
LesKovec, Charles S. — *MDR Associates, Inc.*
Leslie, William H. — *Boyden/Zay & Company*

Leszynski, Edward — *ProResource, Inc.*
Letcher, Harvey D. — *Sandhurst Associates*
Letson, Susan — *KPMG Executive Search*
Levine, Lois — *National Search, Inc.*
Levinson, Lauren — *The Danbrook Group, Inc.*
Levitt, Bob — *Management Recruiters International, Inc.*
Levitt, Muriel A. — *D.S. Allen Associates, Inc.*
Levy, Carlotta — *Evie Kreisler & Associates, Inc.*
Lew, Charles R. — *Coleman Lew & Associates, Inc.*
Lewis, Charles G. — *Longshore & Simmons, Inc.*
Lewis, Gretchen S. — *Heidrick & Struggles, Inc.*
Lewis, John — *Management Recruiters International, Inc.*
Lewis, Jon A. — *Sandhurst Associates*
Lewis, Marc D. — *Handy HRM Corp.*
Lewis, Mark — *Management Recruiters International, Inc.*
Lewis, Richard A. — *Cole, Warren & Long, Inc.*
Lieb, Donald F. — *Russell Reynolds Associates, Inc.*
Lieberman, Beverly — *Halbrecht Lieberman Associates, Inc.*
Liebowitz, Michael E. — *Highland Search Group, L.L.C.*
Lightner, Shayne — *Korn/Ferry International*
Liles, J.D. — *Management Recruiters International, Inc.*
Lincoln, Thomas C. — *Oppedisano & Company, Inc.*
Lindberg, Eric J. — *MSI International*
Linde, Rick — *Battalia Winston International*
Lindholst, Kai — *Egon Zehnder International Inc.*
Lindsay, M. Evan — *Heidrick & Struggles, Inc.*
Lindsay, Mary — *Norm Sanders Associates*
Lineback, Pam — *Management Recruiters International, Inc.*
Lineback, Robert — *Management Recruiters International, Inc.*
Lineback, Robert — *Management Recruiters International, Inc.*
Linton, Leonard M. — *Byron Leonard International, Inc.*
Lippman, Lloyd A. — *Career Management International*
Lissy, Elaine — *Paul Ray Berndtson*
Litchfield, Barbara H. — *Litchfield & Willis Inc.*
Litt-Peck, Michelle — *The Whitney Group*
Little, Suzaane — *Don Richard Associates of Tampa, Inc.*
Littman, Stephen — *Rhodes Associates*
Livesay, Christopher C. — *MSI International*
Livingston, Peter R. — *Livingston, Robert and Company Inc.*
Livolsi, Sebastian F. — *Management Recruiters International, Inc.*
Llaguno, Juan F. — *Korn/Ferry International*
Lloyd, John S. — *Witt/Kieffer, Ford, Hadelman & Lloyd*
Loeb, Stephen H. — *Grant Cooper and Associates*
Loewenstein, Victor H. — *Egon Zehnder International Inc.*
Logan, Valarie A. — *D.S.A. - Dixie Search Associates*
Logue, Kenneth F. — *Logue & Rice Inc.*
Lombardi, Nancy W. — *WTW Associates*
London, Gregory J. — *MSI International*
Lonergan, Mark W. — *Heidrick & Struggles, Inc.*
Long, Helga — *H.M. Long International, Ltd.*
Long, John P. — *John J. Davis & Associates, Inc.*
Long, Melanie — *National Search, Inc.*
Long, Thomas — *Egon Zehnder International Inc.*
Long, William G. — *McDonald, Long & Associates, Inc.*
Longmore, Marilyn — *Richard Kader & Associates*
Longoria, Janine — *Russell Reynolds Associates, Inc.*
Longshore, George F. — *Longshore & Simmons, Inc.*
Lonneke, John W. — *MSI International*
Lopez, Manney C. — *Management Recruiters International, Inc.*
Lopis, Roberta — *Richard, Wayne and Roberts*
Lord, Anthony W.G. — *Ward Howell International, Inc.*
Lorenz, Paula — *Kenzer Corp.*
Loscavio, J. Michael — *Rusher, Loscavio & LoPresto*
Lotufo, Donald A. — *D.A.L. Associates, Inc.*
Lotz, R. James — *International Management Advisors, Inc.*
Louden, Leo — *Winter, Wyman & Company*
Lovas, W. Carl — *Lovas Stanley/Paul Ray Berndtson Inc.*
Love, David M. — *Paul Ray Berndtson*
Love, Nolanda — *Evie Kreisler & Associates, Inc.*
Lovely, Edward — *The Stevenson Group of New Jersey*
Lowry, W. Randall — *Paul Ray Berndtson*
Lubawski, James — *Ward Howell International, Inc.*
Lucarelli, Joan — *The Onstott Group, Inc.*
Lucas, Charles C. — *The McAulay Firm*
Lucas, J. Curtis — *Korn/Ferry International*
Lucas, Ronnie L. — *MSI International*
Lucas, Thomas A. — *Management Recruiters International, Inc.*
Luce, Paul M. — *Management Recruiters International, Inc.*
Lucht, John — *The John Lucht Consultancy Inc.*
Luke, A. Wayne — *Heidrick & Struggles, Inc.*
Lumsby, George N. — *Boyden*
Lumsby, George N. — *International Management Advisors, Inc.*
Lunn, Jerry D. — *DHR International, Inc.*
Lusk, Theodore E. — *Nadzam, Lusk, Horgan & Associates, Inc.*
Lussier, Grant P. — *Heidrick & Struggles, Inc.*
Lynch, Anita F. — *Management Recruiters International, Inc.*
Lynch, Charles J. — *F-O-R-T-U-N-E Personnel Consultants of Nashua, Inc.*

Lynch, John — *Blackshaw, Olmstead & Lynch*
Lynch, John F. — *Management Recruiters International, Inc.*
Lynch, Michael C. — *Lynch Miller Moore Partners, Inc.*
Lynch, Sean E. — *Raymond Karsan Associates*
Lyons, Denis B.K. — *Spencer Stuart*
Lyons, Jane A. — *Rhodes Associates*
Lyons, Margaret — *Paul Ray Berndtson*
Lyons, Mary Fran — *Witt/Kieffer, Ford, Hadelman & Lloyd*
Lyons, Michele R. — *R. Rollo Associates*
Lyttle, Jordene — *The Caldwell Partners Amrop International*
MacArthur, Lauren — *Winter, Wyman & Company*
MacCallan, Deirdre — *Butterfass, Pepe & MacCallan Inc.*
MacCarthy, Ann — *Columbia Consulting Group*
Macdonald, G. William — *The Macdonald Group, Inc.*
Macdonald, Robert W. — *Russell Reynolds Associates, Inc.*
MacDougall, Andrew J. — *Spencer Stuart*
MacEachern, David — *Spencer Stuart*
MacGregor, Malcolm — *Boyden*
Machi, Mike T. — *Management Recruiters International, Inc.*
MacIntyre, Lisa W. — *Russell Reynolds Associates, Inc.*
MacKay, Malcolm — *Russell Reynolds Associates, Inc.*
Mackenna, Kathy — *Plummer & Associates, Inc.*
Mackenzie, Robert A. — *Management Recruiters International, Inc.*
Mackinlay, Marcelo D. — *Heidrick & Struggles, Inc.*
MacLane, Bruce W. — *Korn/Ferry International*
MacLean, B.A. — *The Diversified Search Companies*
MacLeod, Jill C. — *Lovas Stanley/Paul Ray Berndtson Inc.*
Mader, Stephen P. — *Christian & Timbers*
Maer, Harry — *Kenzer Corp.*
Magee, Charles — *Management Recruiters International, Inc.*
Magee, Charles R. — *Dieck, Mueller & Associates, Inc.*
Magee, Gerri — *Management Recruiters International, Inc.*
Magee, Harrison R. — *Bowden & Company, Inc.*
Magnusen, Hank F. — *Management Recruiters International, Inc.*
Mahaney, Joann — *Heidrick & Struggles, Inc.*
Maibach, Lisa W. — *Russell Reynolds Associates, Inc.*
Mainwaring, Andrew Brian — *Executive Search Consultants Corporation*
Maitland, Thomas M. — *DHR International, Inc.*
Mak, I. Paul — *Thomas A. Byrnes Associates*
Makrianes, James K. — *Webb, Johnson Associates, Inc.*
Malcolm, Doug C. — *Management Recruiters International, Inc.*
Malcolm, Rod — *The Enns Partners Inc.*
Malcom, John W. — *Johnson Smith & Knisely Accord*
Malfetti, Jim L. — *Management Recruiters International, Inc.*
Malfetti, Ro — *Management Recruiters International, Inc.*
Mallin, Ellen — *Howard Fischer Associates, Inc.*
Mallipudi, Anand — *Raymond Karsan Associates*
Malone, George V. — *Boyden*
Malone, Tom S. — *Management Recruiters International, Inc.*
Manassero, Henri J.P. — *International Management Advisors, Inc.*
Mangum, Jackie — *Thomas Mangum Company*
Mangum, William T. — *Thomas Mangum Company*
Mann, Douglas G. — *Ward Howell International, Inc.*
Manning, Jerry A. — *Management Recruiters International, Inc.*
Manning, Robert A. — *Management Recruiters International, Inc.*
Manns, Alex — *Crawford & Crofford*
Mansfield, Chris — *Paul Ray Berndtson*
Mansford, Keith — *Howard Fischer Associates, Inc.*
Manthey, Merv — *KPMG Executive Search*
Maphet, Harriet — *The Stevenson Group of New Jersey*
Marchette, Steve — *Juntunen-Combs-Poirier*
Marcus, Jane B. — *Russell Reynolds Associates, Inc.*
Marino, Jory J. — *Sullivan & Company*
Marion, Bradford B. — *Lamalie Amrop International*
Mark, John L. — *J.L. Mark Associates, Inc.*
Marks, Brad — *Brad Marks International*
Marks, Ira — *Strategic Alternatives*
Marks, Russell E. — *Webb, Johnson Associates, Inc.*
Marlow, William — *Straube Associates*
Marra, John — *Marra Peters & Partners*
Marra, John — *Marra Peters & Partners*
Marriott, Gloria A. — *Management Recruiters International, Inc.*
Marriott, Roger — *Management Recruiters International, Inc.*
Marshall, Neill P. — *Witt/Kieffer, Ford, Hadelman & Lloyd*
Marsteller, Franklin D. — *Spencer Stuart*
Martens, Maxine — *Rene Plessner Associates, Inc.*
Martin, Al — *KPMG Executive Search*
Martin, Charles E. — *Management Recruiters International, Inc.*
Martin, David — *The Guild Corporation*
Martin, Ellen — *Hunt Ltd.*
Martin, Geary D. — *Boyden/Zay & Company*
Martin, John G. — *Lamalie Amrop International*
Martin, Jon — *Egon Zehnder International Inc.*
Martin, Ken — *Spencer Stuart*
Martin, Lynne Koll — *Boyden*
Martin, Mary Lou — *Neail Behringer Consultants*
Martin, Nancy A. — *Educational Management Network*

Martin, Pat A. — *Management Recruiters International, Inc.*
Martin, Rande L. — *Management Recruiters International, Inc.*
Marumoto, William H. — *The Interface Group, Ltd./Boyden*
Marx, Dennis R. — *DHR International, Inc.*
Maschal, Charles E. — *Maschal/Connors, Inc.*
Mashack, Ted M. — *Management Recruiters International, Inc.*
Mashakas, Elizabeth — *TOPAZ International, Inc.*
Mashakas, Elizabeth — *TOPAZ Legal Solutions*
Maslan, Neal L. — *Ward Howell International, Inc.*
Mason, Eileen — *Management Recruiters International, Inc.*
Mason, Marlene — *Richard Kader & Associates*
Mason, William E. — *John Kurosky & Associates*
Masse, Laurence R. — *Ward Howell International, Inc.*
Massey, H. Heath — *Robison & Associates*
Massey, R. Bruce — *Bruce Massey & Partners Inc.*
Massung, Larry J. — *Management Recruiters International, Inc.*
Mastandrea, Pat — *Johnson Smith & Knisely Accord*
Matheny, Robert P. — *MSI International*
Mather, David R. — *Christian & Timbers*
Mathias, Kathy — *Stone Murphy & Olson*
Mathias, William J. — *Preng & Associates, Inc.*
Matthews, James M. — *Stanton Chase International*
Matthews, John C. — *Management Recruiters International, Inc.*
Matthews, Mary E. — *Nordeman Grimm, Inc.*
Matthews, William A. — *Heidrick & Struggles, Inc.*
Mattox, Robert D. — *Spencer Stuart*
Maurizio, Michael — *Management Recruiters International, Inc.*
Maxwell, Carol — *Paul Ray Berndtson*
May, Peter — *Mixtec Group*
Mayland, Tina — *Russell Reynolds Associates, Inc.*
Mazor, Elly — *Howard Fischer Associates, Inc.*
Mazza, David B. — *Mazza & Riley, Inc.*
Mazza, Leslie P. — *The Diversified Search Companies*
Mazzitelli, Teresa A. — *The Mazzitelli Group, Ltd.*
McAulay, A.L. — *The McAulay Firm*
McBride, Jonathan E. — *McBride Associates, Inc.*
McBryde, Marnie — *Spencer Stuart*
McBurney, Kevin — *The Caldwell Partners Amrop International*
McCabe, Christopher — *Raymond Karsan Associates*
McCallister, Jane T. — *Heidrick & Struggles, Inc.*
McCallister, Richard A. — *Boyden*
McCann, Cornelia B. — *Spencer Stuart*
McCarthy, David R. — *Spencer Stuart*
McCartney, Paul — *Korn/Ferry International*
McCarty, J. Rucker — *Heidrick & Struggles, Inc.*
McClain, Michael D. — *DHR International, Inc.*
McClearen, Bruce — *Tyler & Company*
McClement, John — *Korn/Ferry International*
McCloskey, Frank — *Korn/Ferry International*
McClure, James K. — *Korn/Ferry International*
McConnell, Greg — *Winter, Wyman & Company*
McConnell, Rod — *The McCormick Group, Inc.*
McCool, Anne G. — *Sullivan & Company*
McCorkle, Sam B. — *Morton, McCorkle & Associates, Inc.*
McCormack, Joseph A. — *McCormack & Associates*
McCormick, William J. — *The McCormick Group, Inc.*
McCoy, Horacio — *Korn/Ferry International*
McCoy, Millington F. — *Gould, McCoy & Chadick Incorporated*
McCreary, Charles — *Austin-McGregor International*
McCullough, Joe — *Management Recruiters International, Inc.*
McCurdy, Mark — *Summerfield Associates, Inc.*
McDermott, Richard A. — *Paul Ray Berndtson*
McDonald, Scott A. — *McDonald Associates International*
McDonald, Stanleigh B. — *McDonald Associates International*
McDonnell, Julie — *Technical Personnel of Minnesota*
McElhaney, Ron — *Management Recruiters International, Inc.*
McElhaney, Ronald W. — *Management Recruiters International, Inc.*
McElroy, John — *Management Recruiters International, Inc.*
McEwan, Paul — *Richard, Wayne and Roberts*
McEwen, Al — *Management Recruiters International, Inc.*
McFadden, Ashton S. — *Johnson Smith & Knisely Accord*
McFeely, Clarence E. — *McFeely Wackerle Shulman*
McGahey, Patricia M. — *Witt/Kieffer, Ford, Hadelman & Lloyd*
McGill, Robert — *The Caldwell Partners Amrop International*
McGonigle, Kevin M. — *Egon Zehnder International Inc.*
McGovern, Terence — *Korn/Ferry International*
McGue, Marsha S. — *Kenzer Corp.*
McGuigan, Walter J. — *Norm Sanders Associates*
McGuire, Corey — *Peter W. Ambler Company*
McGuire, D. — *The Gabriel Group*
McGuire, John J. — *Robert Sage Recruiting*
McHugh, Margaret — *Korn/Ferry International*
McIntyre, Alex D. — *Norman Roberts & Associates, Inc.*
McIntyre, Joel — *Phillips Resource Group*
McKay, W. John — *O'Callaghan Honey/Paul Ray Berndtson, Inc.*
McKie, Miles L. — *Russell Reynolds Associates, Inc.*
McKinnis, Paul D. — *Paul Ray Berndtson*

McKnight, Amy E. — *Chartwell Partners International, Inc.*
McKnight, Lourdes D. — *Sanford Rose Associates*
McLane, Brad — *Egon Zehnder International Inc.*
McLane, Thomas L. — *Russell Reynolds Associates, Inc.*
McLaughlin, John — *TASA International*
McLean, B. Keith — *Price Waterhouse*
McLean, Chris — *Chaloner Associates*
McLean, E. Peter — *Spencer Stuart*
McLeish, Robert H. — *Executive Search International*
McMahon, Mark J. — *A.T. Kearney, Inc.*
McManamon, Tim — *Rogers-McManamon Executive Search*
McManners, Donald E. — *McManners Associates, Inc.*
McManus, Paul — *Aubin International*
McMillin, Bob — *Price Waterhouse*
McNamara, Gerard P. — *Heidrick & Struggles, Inc.*
McNamara, Timothy C. — *Columbia Consulting Group*
McNamee, Erin — *Technical Connections Inc.*
McNerney, Kevin A. — *Heidrick & Struggles, Inc.*
McNichol, John — *McNichol Associates*
McNichols, Walter B. — *Gary Kaplan & Associates*
McNulty, Neil P. — *Management Recruiters International, Inc.*
McPherson, Stephen M. — *Ward Howell International, Inc.*
McPoyle, Thomas C. — *Sanford Rose Associates*
McQuoid, David — *A.T. Kearney, Inc.*
McRoberts, Dana L. — *Management Recruiters International, Inc.*
McSherry, James F. — *Battalia Winston International*
McSherry, Terrence J. — *Paul Ray Berndtson*
Meadley, Ronald J. — *Management Recruiters International, Inc.*
Meagher, Patricia G. — *Spencer Stuart*
Means, Wallace — *Management Recruiters International, Inc.*
Meany, Brian — *Herbert Mines Associates, Inc.*
Medinger, Ronald B. — *IMCOR, Inc.*
Medoff, Lynn — *C.A. Durakis Associates, Inc.*
Medtlie, Peder M. — *Management Recruiters International, Inc.*
Mefford, Bob — *Executive Manning Corporation*
Mehrbrodt, Al W. — *Management Recruiters International, Inc.*
Meier, J. Dale — *Grant Cooper and Associates*
Meiland, A. Daniel — *Egon Zehnder International Inc.*
Meister, Connie — *Management Recruiters International, Inc.*
Meister, Verle — *Management Recruiters International, Inc.*
Meitz, Bob L. — *Management Recruiters International, Inc.*
Meltzer, Andrea Y. — *Executive Options, Ltd.*
Mendoza, Guadalupe — *Ward Howell International, Inc.*
Menendez, Todd — *Don Richard Associates of Tampa, Inc.*
Menk, Carl W. — *Canny, Bowen Inc.*
Merrigan, Eileen M. — *Lamalie Amrop International*
Merriman, Mark — *Management Recruiters International, Inc.*
Meschke, Jason M. — *EFL Associates*
Messett, William J. — *Messett Associates, Inc.*
Messina, Kenneth — *Chestnut Hill Partners*
Mestepey, John — *A.T. Kearney, Inc.*
Mestre, Mercedes — *Korn/Ferry International*
Metz, Alex — *Hunt Ltd.*
Metz, Dan K. — *Russell Reynolds Associates, Inc.*
Meyer, Fred R. — *Management Recruiters International, Inc.*
Meyer, Michael F. — *Witt/Kieffer, Ford, Hadelman & Lloyd*
Meyer, Stacey — *Gary Kaplan & Associates*
Meyers, Maurice R. — *Management Recruiters International, Inc.*
Meyers, Mel — *DHR International, Inc.*
Meza, Anna — *Richard, Wayne and Roberts*
Michaels, Stewart — *TOPAZ International, Inc.*
Michaels, Stewart — *TOPAZ Legal Solutions*
Middleton, Alfred E. — *The Neil Michael Group, Inc.*
Mierzwinski, John — *Industrial Recruiters Associates, Inc.*
Miesemer, Arthur C. — *MSI International*
Miles, Kenneth T. — *MSI International*
Miles, Marybeth — *Winter, Wyman & Company*
Milius, Kent L. — *Management Recruiters International, Inc.*
Milkint, Margaret Resce — *Jacobson Associates*
Miller, Andrew S. — *Management Recruiters International, Inc.*
Miller, Benjamin J. — *MSI International*
Miller, Bert E. — *Management Recruiters International, Inc.*
Miller, George N. — *Hite Executive Search*
Miller, Joanna — *Korn/Ferry International*
Miller, Julie — *Southwestern Professional Services*
Miller, Michael R. — *Lynch Miller Moore Partners, Inc.*
Miller, Paul McG. — *Lamalie Amrop International*
Miller, Roy — *The Enns Partners Inc.*
Miller, Russel E. — *ARJay & Associates*
Millonzi, Joel C. — *Johnson Smith & Knisely Accord*
Milne, Robert P. — *Boyden/Zay & Company*
Milo, Bill — *Management Recruiters International, Inc.*
Milstein, Bonnie — *Marvin Laba & Associates*
Milton, Suzanne — *Marra Peters & Partners*
Mines, Herbert T. — *Herbert Mines Associates, Inc.*
Mirtz, P. John — *Mirtz Morice, Inc.*
Mitchell, F. Wayne — *Korn/Ferry International*
Mitchell, John R. — *Management Recruiters International, Inc.*

Mitchell, John T. — *Paul Ray Berndtson*
Mitchell, Katie — *Paul Ray Berndtson*
Mitchell, Kim — *Richard, Wayne and Roberts*
Mitchell, Kyle R. — *Tanton Mitchell/Paul Ray Berndtson*
Mitchell, Norman F. — *A.T. Kearney, Inc.*
Mitchell, Thomas M. — *Heidrick & Struggles, Inc.*
Mitros, George N. — *Mixtec Group*
Mockler, Nadine — *Part Time Resources, Inc.*
Moeller, Ed J. — *Management Recruiters International, Inc.*
Moerbe, Ed H. — *Stanton Chase International*
Moga, Michael — *Korn/Ferry International*
Mogul, Gene — *Mogul Consultants, Inc.*
Mohan, Jack — *Management Recruiters International, Inc.*
Mohan, Jack — *Management Recruiters International, Inc.*
Moliski, Robert — *Korn/Ferry International*
Molnar, Robert A. — *Johnson Smith & Knisely Accord*
Momtaz, Heba — *Evie Kreisler & Associates, Inc.*
Monaghan, Jill — *Paul Ray Berndtson*
Monahan, B. Roderick — *Lamalie Amrop International*
Mondragon, Philip — *Boyden*
Monogenis, Emanuel N. — *Heidrick & Struggles, Inc.*
Monroe, Kenneth D. — *Sanford Rose Associates*
Montgomery, Catherine C. — *Boyden*
Montgomery, James M. — *Houze, Shourds & Montgomery, Inc.*
Montigny, Paul F. — *Management Recruiters International, Inc.*
Mooney, Kelly — *Paul Ray Berndtson*
Mooney, Matt — *Paul Ray Berndtson*
Mooney, Penny P. — *Ward Howell International, Inc.*
Moore, Anne — *KPMG Executive Search*
Moore, David S. — *Lynch Miller Moore Partners, Inc.*
Moore, Denise — *Jonas, Walters & Assoc., Inc.*
Moore, Janice E. — *MSI International*
Moore, Lemuel R. — *MSI International*
Moore, Lynn W. — *Management Recruiters International, Inc.*
Moore, Mark — *Wheeler, Moore & Elam Co.*
Moore, Michael — *Agra Placements International Ltd.*
Moore, Mike — *Management Recruiters International, Inc.*
Moore, Richard C.E. — *Russell Reynolds Associates, Inc.*
Moors, Donald — *Coopers & Lybrand Consulting*
Moran, Gail — *Comprehensive Search*
Moran, Gayle — *Dussick Management Associates*
Moran, Robert — *A.T. Kearney, Inc.*
Moran, Thomas F. — *Ward Howell International, Inc.*
Morgan, Christopher — *Paul Ray Berndtson*
Morgan, Gary — *National Search, Inc.*
Morgan, Richard J. — *Morgan Samuels Co., Inc.*
Morgan, Richard S. — *Lovas Stanley/Paul Ray Berndtson Inc.*
Morgan, Vincent S. — *Johnson Smith & Knisely Accord*
Morice, James L. — *Mirtz Morice, Inc.*
Morin, Michelle — *Spencer Stuart*
Morrill, Nancy — *Winter, Wyman & Company*
Morris, David A. — *Heidrick & Struggles, Inc.*
Morris, David W. — *WTW Associates*
Morris, Kristine A. — *Morris & Berger*
Morrison, Janis L. — *Garrett Associates Inc.*
Morse, Aaron H. — *Management Recruiters International, Inc.*
Morse, Jeannine — *Management Recruiters International, Inc.*
Morse, Stephen W. — *Management Recruiters International, Inc.*
Morse, Steve — *Management Recruiters International, Inc.*
Morton, Robert C. — *Morton, McCorkle & Associates, Inc.*
Moschel, Evie — *S. Reyman & Associates Ltd.*
Moses, Brenda — *Paul Ray Berndtson*
Moses, Jerry — *J.M. Eagle Partners Ltd.*
Moss, Ethan — *Richard, Wayne and Roberts*
Mowatt, Virginia C. — *DHR International, Inc.*
Moxley, John H. — *Korn/Ferry International*
Moynihan, Kerry — *Korn/Ferry International*
Moyse, Richard G. — *Thorndike Deland Associates*
Mruk, Edwin S. — *Mruk & Partners/EMA Partners Int'l*
Mueller, Michael S. — *Dieck, Mueller & Associates, Inc.*
Mueller-Maerki, Fortunat F. — *Egon Zehnder International Inc.*
Muendel, H. Edward — *Stanton Chase International*
Mulcahey, Bob T. — *Management Recruiters International, Inc.*
Mullane, Patrick — *Kenzer Corp.*
Mullen, Edward — *Korn/Ferry International*
Muller, Sonja — *TASA International*
Mulligan, Robert P. — *William Willis Worldwide Inc.*
Mullings, Joe S. — *Management Recruiters International, Inc.*
Mummert, Dennis D. — *Sweeney Harbert & Mummert, Inc.*
Munguia, Rebecca — *Richard, Wayne and Roberts*
Murin, Rose Mary — *U.S. Envirosearch*
Murlas, Kim — *DHR International, Inc.*
Murphy, James F. — *Management Recruiters International, Inc.*
Murphy, Carrie — *Paul Ray Berndtson*
Murphy, Cornelius J. — *Goodrich & Sherwood Associates, Inc.*
Murphy, Gary J. — *Stone Murphy & Olson*
Murphy, Karen S. — *Flex Execs Management Solutions*
Murphy, Patrick — *Richard, Wayne and Roberts*

Murphy, Patrick J. — *P.J. Murphy & Associates, Inc.*
Murray, Cathy M. — *EFL Associates*
Murray, Virginia — *Baker, Harris & Partners Limited*
Mursuli, Meredith — *Lasher Associates*
Mustin, Joyce M. — *J: Blakslee International, Ltd.*
Myatt, James S. — *Sanford Rose Associates*
Myers, Kay — *Signature Staffing*
Myrick, Marilou — *ProResource, Inc.*
Myrick, Marilou — *ProResource, Inc.*
Nadherny, Christopher C. — *Spencer Stuart*
Nadherny, Ferdinand — *Russell Reynolds Associates, Inc.*
Nadzam, Richard — *Nadzam, Lusk, Horgan & Associates, Inc.*
Naff, Budd B. — *Management Recruiters International, Inc.*
Nagle, Charles L. — *Tyler & Company*
Nagler, Leon G. — *Nagler, Robins & Poe, Inc.*
Nahas, Caroline W. — *Korn/Ferry International*
Nahas, Robert — *Herbert Mines Associates, Inc.*
Nakatsuka, Walt — *Evie Kreisler & Associates, Inc.*
Napier, Ginger L. — *Preng & Associates, Inc.*
Nass, Martin D. — *Lamalie Amrop International*
Nathan, Catherine R. — *Ward Howell International, Inc.*
Nathanson, Barry F. — *Barry Nathanson Associates*
Naughtin, Terri — *Andcor Human Resources*
Nazzaro, Samuel G. — *Boyden*
Nederpelt, Jack H.B. — *Russell Reynolds Associates, Inc.*
Neelin, Sharon — *The Caldwell Partners Amrop International*
Neely, Alan S. — *Korn/Ferry International*
Neff, Thomas J. — *Spencer Stuart*
Nehiley, Jack J. — *Management Recruiters International, Inc.*
Neidhart, Craig C. — *TNS Partners, Inc.*
Neil, Colleen Ellen — *Korn/Ferry International*
Nein, Lawrence F. — *Lamalie Amrop International*
Nekervis, Nancy — *Evie Kreisler & Associates, Inc.*
Nelson, Garry A. — *Rhodes Associates*
Nelson, Rick J. — *Management Recruiters International, Inc.*
Nelson, Steve — *The McCormick Group, Inc.*
Nephew, Robert — *Christian & Timbers*
Nesbit, Robert G. — *Korn/Ferry International*
Neuberth, Jeffrey G. — *Canny, Bowen Inc.*
Neuffer, Bob P. — *Management Recruiters International, Inc.*
Neumann, Joan — *Gossage Regan Associates, Inc.*
Neumann, Pete — *Management Recruiters International, Inc.*
Neumann, Vicki A. — *Management Recruiters International, Inc.*
Neuwiler, Mark D. — *Saber Consultants*
Nevins, Patricia — *Rhodes Associates*
Newcomb, Andrew R. — *The Neil Michael Group, Inc.*
Newman, Arthur I. — *Lamalie Amrop International*
Newman, Jose L. — *Ward Howell International, Inc.*
Newman, Lynn — *Kishbaugh Associates International*
Newman, Mark — *Cole, Warren & Long, Inc.*
Newman, Maryann — *The Gabriel Group*
Newton, Stephen D. — *Russell Reynolds Associates, Inc.*
Nicastro, Kelley P. — *A la carte International*
Nichols, Nancy S. — *Heidrick & Struggles, Inc.*
Nicol, Peg — *Evie Kreisler & Associates, Inc.*
Nielsen, Bruce — *The Nielsen Healthcare Group*
Nielsen, Eric C. — *Russell Reynolds Associates, Inc.*
Nielsen, Sue — *Ells Personnel System Inc.*
Nixon, Sarah — *The Caldwell Partners Amrop International*
Noble, Jeffrey M. — *Management Recruiters International, Inc.*
Nocero, John — *ProResource, Inc.*
Noguchi, Yoshi — *Paul Ray Berndtson*
Nold, Robert — *Roberson and Company*
Noll, Robert J. — *The Hindman Company*
Noorani, Frank — *Management Recruiters International, Inc.*
Nordeman, Jacques C. — *Nordeman Grimm, Inc.*
Nordland, Martin N. — *Horton International*
Norman, Randy — *Austin-McGregor International*
Normann, Amy — *Robert M. Flanagan & Associates, Ltd.*
Norris, Ken — *A.T. Kearney, Inc.*
Norris, Ken — *Boyden*
Norsell, Paul E. — *Paul Norsell & Associates, Inc.*
Norton, Douglas — *Korn/Ferry International*
Norton, George F. — *Heidrick & Struggles, Inc.*
Norton, James B. — *GKR Americas, Inc.*
Nosal, David — *Korn/Ferry International*
Nosal, David A. — *Heidrick & Struggles, Inc.*
Nosky, Richard E. — *Ward Howell International, Inc.*
Novak, William J. — *Ward Howell International, Inc.*
Noyes, Kathleen M. — *Russell Reynolds Associates, Inc.*
Nunziata, Fred — *Eden & Associates, Inc.*
Nutter, Roger — *Raymond Karsan Associates*
Nye, David S. — *Blake, Hansen & Nye, Limited*
Nyhan, Alan — *Management Recruiters International, Inc.*
O'Brien, Anne Lim — *Heidrick & Struggles, Inc.*
O'Brien, Debbie A. — *Management Recruiters International, Inc.*
O'Brien, Lori — *Paul Ray Berndtson*
O'Brien, Marlon W.A. — *Management Recruiters International, Inc.*

O'Callaghan, Terry K. — *O'Callaghan Honey/Paul Ray Berndtson, Inc.*
O'Donnell, James H. — *MSI International*
O'Donnell, Timothy — *Ward Howell International, Inc.*
O'Donnell, Timothy W. — *Boyden*
O'Gorman, David J. — *DHR International, Inc.*
O'Halloran, Robert — *MSI International*
O'Hara, Daniel M. — *Lynch Miller Moore Partners, Inc.*
O'Hara, James J. — *Barone-O'Hara Associates*
O'Maley, Kimberlee — *Spencer Stuart*
O'Malley, Robert — *Raymond Karsan Associates*
O'Neill, David — *Korn/Ferry International*
O'Neill, James P. — *Allerton Heneghan & O'Neill*
O'Neill, Karen — *Ashton Computer Professionals Inc.*
O'Reilly, Bill — *Management Recruiters International, Inc.*
O'Reilly, Jack — *Catalyx Group*
O'Shea, Laurie A. — *The Heidrick Partners, Inc.*
O'Shea, Timothy J. — *Heidrick & Struggles, Inc.*
O'Such, Tracy — *Bishop Partners*
O'Toole, Dennis P. — *Dennis P. O'Toole & Associates Inc.*
Oakley, Mitch — *Management Recruiters International, Inc.*
Oberg, Roy — *The Danbrook Group, Inc.*
Oberting, Dave W. — *Management Recruiters International, Inc.*
Oberting, David J. — *Management Recruiters International, Inc.*
Ocon, Olga — *Busch International*
Odom, Philip — *Richard, Wayne and Roberts*
Ogden, Dayton — *Spencer Stuart*
Ogden, Thomas H. — *The Ogdon Partnership*
Ogilvie, Kit — *Howard Fischer Associates, Inc.*
Olesky, Beth Green — *Russell Reynolds Associates, Inc.*
Olin, Robyn — *Richard, Wayne and Roberts*
Olivares, Rebecca — *Paul Ray Berndtson*
Oliver, Phoebe — *Seiden Krieger Associates, Inc.*
Oliverio, Anthony P. — *Management Recruiters International, Inc.*
Oller, Jose E. — *Ward Howell International, Inc.*
Ollinger, Charles D. — *Heidrick & Struggles, Inc.*
Olmstead, George T. — *Blackshaw, Olmstead & Lynch*
Olsen, Carl — *A.T. Kearney, Inc.*
Olsen, Theodore J. — *Senior Careers Executive Search*
Olson, A. Andrew — *Paul Ray Berndtson*
Olson, B. Tucker — *Early Cochran & Olson, Inc.*
Olson, Nels — *Korn/Ferry International*
Ongirski, Richard P. — *Raymond Karsan Associates*
Onstott, Joseph E. — *The Onstott Group, Inc.*
Oppedisano, Edward — *Oppedisano & Company, Inc.*
Oppenheim, Norman J. — *F-O-R-T-U-N-E Personnel Consultants of Nashua, Inc.*
Oppenheimer, Janet — *Paul Ray Berndtson*
Orkin, Ralph — *Sanford Rose Associates*
Orkin, Sheilah — *Sanford Rose Associates*
Orner, Ted A. — *Russell Reynolds Associates, Inc.*
Orr, Don — *Orr Executive Search*
Orr, Steve — *Management Recruiters International, Inc.*
Oster, Joan — *Management Recruiters International, Inc.*
Oster, Rush R. — *Management Recruiters International, Inc.*
Oswald, Mark G. — *Canny, Bowen Inc.*
Ott, George W. — *Ott & Hansen, Inc.*
Otto, Karen E. — *Witt/Kieffer, Ford, Hadelman & Lloyd*
Owen, Jamie L. — *Management Recruiters International, Inc.*
Owens, LaMonte — *LaMonte Owens & Company*
Owens, Reggie R. — *The Gabriel Group*
Pace, Susan A. — *Horton International*
Pacheco, Ricardo — *Amrop International*
Pacini, Lauren R. — *Hite Executive Search*
Padilla, Jose Sanchez — *Egon Zehnder International Inc.*
Pagan, Vernon R. — *Management Recruiters International, Inc.*
Page, G. Schuyler — *A.T. Kearney, Inc.*
Page, Linda — *Jonas, Walters & Assoc., Inc.*
Page, Linda M. — *Wargo and Co., Inc.*
Palazio, Carla — *A.T. Kearney, Inc.*
Palma, Frank R. — *Goodrich & Sherwood Associates, Inc.*
Palmer, Carlton A. — *Beall & Company, Inc.*
Palmer, James H. — *The Hindman Company*
Palmer, Melissa — *Don Richard Associates of Tampa, Inc.*
Palmieri, Cathryn C. — *Korn/Ferry International*
Palmlund, David W. — *Lamalie Amrop International*
Paolotti, Susan — *Kenzer Corp.*
Papayanopulos, Manuel — *Korn/Ferry International*
Pappalardo, Charles — *Christian & Timbers*
Pappas, Timothy C. — *Jonas, Walters & Assoc., Inc.*
Pardo, Maria Elena — *Smith Search, S.C.*
Parfitt, William C. — *Parfitt Recruiting and Consulting*
Paris, Stephen — *Richard, Wayne and Roberts*
Park, Cleve A. — *Management Recruiters International, Inc.*
Park, Dabney G. — *Mark Stanley & Company*
Parker, P. Grant — *Raymond Karsan Associates*
Parker, Roberta — *R. Parker and Associates, Inc.*
Parker, Stephen B. — *Russell Reynolds Associates, Inc.*

Parr, James A. — *KPMG Executive Search*
Parr, James A. — *KPMG Management Consulting*
Parris, Ed — *Management Recruiters International, Inc.*
Parry, Heather — *Richard, Wayne and Roberts*
Parry, William H. — *Horton International*
Pasahow, David — *Heidrick & Struggles, Inc.*
Pastrana, Dario — *Egon Zehnder International Inc.*
Patence, David W. — *Handy HRM Corp.*
Patlovich, Michael J. — *Witt/Kieffer, Ford, Hadelman & Lloyd*
Patrick, Donald R. — *Sanford Rose Associates*
Patterson, Brenda — *Management Recruiters International, Inc.*
Patton, Mitchell — *Patton/Perry Associates, Inc.*
Paul, Linda — *Gilbert Tweed/INESA*
Paul, Lisa D. — *Merit Resource Group, Inc.*
Pawlik, Cynthia — *Paul Ray Berndtson*
Paxton, James W. — *Stanton Chase International*
Payette, Pierre — *Egon Zehnder International Inc.*
Payne, Mary A. — *Management Recruiters International, Inc.*
Payne, Tom H. — *Management Recruiters International, Inc.*
Paynter, Sandra L. — *Ward Howell International, Inc.*
Pearcy, Marsha G. — *Russell Reynolds Associates, Inc.*
Pearson, Robert L. — *Lamalie Amrop International*
Peasback, David R. — *Canny, Bowen Inc.*
Pease, Samuel C. — *Heidrick & Struggles, Inc.*
Peck, Linda — *The Peck Consultancy*
Pecot, Jack L. — *Management Recruiters International, Inc.*
Pederson, Terre — *Richard, Wayne and Roberts*
Peeney, James D. — *Peeney Associates*
Pelisson, Charles — *Marra Peters & Partners*
Pelton, Margaret — *Price Waterhouse*
Penfield, G. Jeff — *Management Recruiters International, Inc.*
Penfield, Marian — *Management Recruiters International, Inc.*
Peniche, Pedro — *Amrop International*
Pepe, Leonida — *Butterfass, Pepe & MacCallan Inc.*
Percifield, J. Michael — *Management Recruiters International, Inc.*
Peretz, Jamie — *Nordeman Grimm, Inc.*
Perez, Christina — *Orr Executive Search*
Perkey, Richard — *Korn/Ferry International*
Perkins, Bob — *Richard, Wayne and Roberts*
Perlman, Tali — *Coleman Legal Search Consultants*
Perry, Darrell L. — *Management Recruiters International, Inc.*
Perry, Richard — *McManners Associates, Inc.*
Perry, Robert H. — *R.H. Perry & Associates, Inc.*
Perry, Wayne B. — *Bruce Massey & Partners Inc.*
Perryman, Ben — *Paul Ray Berndtson*
Persico, Victor J. — *Management Recruiters International, Inc.*
Persky, Barry — *Barry Persky & Company, Inc.*
Pessin, Mark — *Evie Kreisler & Associates, Inc.*
Peternell, Melanie — *Signature Staffing*
Peters, James N. — *TNS Partners, Inc.*
Peterson, Bruce — *Korn/Ferry International*
Peterson, Dave A. — *Management Recruiters International, Inc.*
Peterson, Diana K. — *Management Recruiters International, Inc.*
Peterson, John A. — *Management Recruiters International, Inc.*
Peterson, Priscilla J. — *Management Recruiters International, Inc.*
Petrides, Andrew S. — *ARJay & Associates*
Pettersson, Tara L. — *Lamalie Amrop International*
Pettibone, Linda — *Herbert Mines Associates, Inc.*
Petty, J. Scott — *The Arcus Group*
Peyton, Leslie — *Korn/Ferry International*
Pfannkuche, Anthony V. — *Spencer Stuart*
Pfau, Madelaine — *Heidrick & Struggles, Inc.*
Pfeiffer, Irene — *Price Waterhouse*
Pfeiffer, Leonard — *Korn/Ferry International*
Pfister, Shelli — *Jack B. Larsen & Associates*
Phelps, Gene L. — *McCormack & Farrow*
Philips, Ann — *Management Recruiters International, Inc.*
Phillips, Anna W. — *Witt/Kieffer, Ford, Hadelman & Lloyd*
Phillips, Donald L. — *O'Shea, Divine & Company, Inc.*
Phillips, James L. — *Highland Search Group, L.L.C.*
Phillips, Whitney — *Korn/Ferry International*
Pickering, Dorothy C. — *Livingston, Robert and Company Inc.*
Pickford, Stephen T. — *The Corporate Staff, Inc.*
Pieh, Jerry — *Isaacson, Miller*
Pierce, Nicholas J. — *Paul Ray Berndtson*
Pierce, Richard — *Russell Reynolds Associates, Inc.*
Pierpont, Elizabeth H. — *Russell Reynolds Associates, Inc.*
Piers, Robert L. — *TASA International*
Pierson, Edward J. — *Johnson Smith & Knisely Accord*
Pike, Dick F. — *Management Recruiters International, Inc.*
Pimentel, Alberto — *Korn/Ferry International*
Pinson, Liz A. — *Management Recruiters International, Inc.*
Pinson, Stephanie L. — *Gilbert Tweed/INESA*
Pirhalla, Denise — *Kenzer Corp.*
Pistole, Ingrid — *Richard, Wayne and Roberts*
Pitcher, Brian D. — *Skott/Edwards Consultants, Inc.*
Pitchford, Jim J. — *Management Recruiters International, Inc.*
Pittard, Patrick S. — *Heidrick & Struggles, Inc.*

Pitto, Lili — *Ryan, Miller & Associates Inc.*
Pitts, Charles — *Contemporary Management Services, Inc.*
Pizzariello, Ann Marie — *Conex Incorporated*
Plagge, Cheryl L. — *Management Recruiters International, Inc.*
Platte, John D. — *Russell Reynolds Associates, Inc.*
Plecash, Bob — *Management Recruiters International, Inc.*
Plessner, Rene — *Rene Plessner Associates, Inc.*
Plotner, George A. — *Management Recruiters International, Inc.*
Plummer, John — *Plummer & Associates, Inc.*
Plummer, Winkie Donovan — *McManners Associates, Inc.*
Pocs, Martin M. — *DHR International, Inc.*
Poirier, Frank — *Juntunen-Combs-Poirier*
Poirier, Roland — *Poirier, Hoevel & Co.*
Polachi, Charles A. — *Fenwick Partners*
Polachi, Peter V. — *Fenwick Partners*
Poloni, James A. — *Management Recruiters International, Inc.*
Polvere, Gary T. — *Management Recruiters International, Inc.*
Pomeroy, T. Lee — *Egon Zehnder International Inc.*
Poore, Larry D. — *Ward Howell International, Inc.*
Pope, John S. — *DHR International, Inc.*
Poracky, John W. — *M. Wood Company*
Porter, Albert — *The Experts*
Porter, Donald — *Amherst Personnel Group Inc.*
Posner, Gary J. — *Educational Management Network*
Poster, Lawrence D. — *Catalyx Group*
Postles, Doris W. — *Longshore & Simmons, Inc.*
Potenza, Gregory — *Mixtec Group*
Potter, Douglas C. — *Stanton Chase International*
Potter, Steven B. — *Highland Search Group, L.L.C.*
Powell, Leslie — *Rhodes Associates*
Powell, Lloyd — *KPMG Executive Search*
Powell, Marie — *Kenzer Corp.*
Powers-Johnson, Allyson — *Johnson Smith & Knisely Accord*
Pratt, Michael W. — *Management Recruiters International, Inc.*
Prencipe, V. Michael — *Raymond Karsan Associates*
Preng, David E. — *Preng & Associates, Inc.*
Prentiss, Michael C. — *Management Recruiters International, Inc.*
Preschlack, Jack E. — *Spencer Stuart*
Press, Fred — *Adept Tech Recruiting*
Price, Andrew G. — *The Thomas Tucker Company*
Price, P. Anthony — *Russell Reynolds Associates, Inc.*
Priem, Windle B. — *Korn/Ferry International*
Priftis, Anthony — *Evie Kreisler & Associates, Inc.*
Prince, Marilyn L. — *Higdon Prince Inc.*
Prior, Donald — *The Caldwell Partners Amrop International*
Probert, William W. — *Ward Howell International, Inc.*
Proct, Nina — *Martin H. Bauman Associates, Inc.*
Proctor, Robert A. — *Heidrick & Struggles, Inc.*
Provost, Ed — *Management Recruiters International, Inc.*
Provost, Vicky L. — *Management Recruiters International, Inc.*
Provus, Barbara L. — *Shepherd Bueschel & Provus, Inc.*
Pryde, Marcia P. — *A.T. Kearney, Inc.*
Pryor, Keith — *The Diversified Search Companies*
Puente, Fred J. — *Management Recruiters International, Inc.*
Pugh, Judith Geist — *InterimManagement Solutions, Inc.*
Putrim, Tom — *Paul Ray Berndtson*
Quatrone, Olivia S. — *Heidrick & Struggles, Inc.*
Quick, Roger A. — *Norman Broadbent International, Inc.*
Quinn, Frank A. — *Management Recruiters International, Inc.*
Quinn, John — *Paul Ray Berndtson*
Quinn, Nola — *Technical Connections Inc.*
Quitel, Scott M. — *Management Recruiters International, Inc.*
Raab, Julie — *Dunhill Professional Search of Irvine, Inc.*
Raben, Steven — *Paul Ray Berndtson*
Rabinowitz, Peter A. — *P.A.R. Associates Inc.*
Rackley, Eugene M. — *Heidrick & Struggles, Inc.*
Radawicz, Angela — *Mixtec Group*
Radden, David B. — *Paul Ray Berndtson*
Radford-Oster, Deborah — *Morgan Hunter Corp.*
Raffin, Robert P. — *Management Recruiters International, Inc.*
Raiber, Laurie Altman — *The IMC Group of Companies Ltd.*
Ralston, Doug O. — *Management Recruiters International, Inc.*
Ramler, Carolyn S. — *The Corporate Connection, Ltd.*
Ramsey, John H. — *Mark Stanley & Company*
Ranberger, Mike J. — *Management Recruiters International, Inc.*
Randell, James E. — *Randell-Heiken, Inc.*
Ratigan, Charles C. — *Heidrick & Struggles, Inc.*
Rattner, Kenneth L. — *Heidrick & Struggles, Inc.*
Rauch, Ben — *Korn/Ferry International*
Ravenel, Lavinia — *MSI International*
Ray, Breck — *Paul Ray Berndtson*
Ray, Marianne C. — *Callan Associates, Ltd.*
Ray, Paul R. — *Paul Ray Berndtson*
Ray, Paul R. — *Paul Ray Berndtson*
Raymond, Allan H. — *Korn/Ferry International*
Raymond, Barry — *Raymond Karsan Associates*
Raymond, Jean — *The Caldwell Partners Amrop International*
Reagan, Paul W. — *Management Recruiters International, Inc.*

Recsetar, Steven — *DHR International, Inc.*
Reddick, David C. — *Horton International*
Redding, Denise — *The Douglas Reiter Company, Inc.*
Redler, Rhonda — *National Search, Inc.*
Redmond, Andrea — *Russell Reynolds Associates, Inc.*
Redwood, Guy W. — *Bruce Massey & Partners Inc.*
Reece, Christopher S. — *Reece & Mruk Partners*
Reed, David Q. — *Management Recruiters International, Inc.*
Reed, Ruthann — *Spectra International Inc.*
Reed, William D. — *Russell Reynolds Associates, Inc.*
Reeder, Michael S. — *Lamalie Amrop International*
Reese, Charles D. — *Reese Associates*
Reeves, Ron C. — *Management Recruiters International, Inc.*
Reeves, William B. — *Spencer Stuart*
Referente, Gwen — *Richard, Wayne and Roberts*
Regan, Muriel — *Gossage Regan Associates, Inc.*
Reid, Gary — *KPMG Executive Search*
Reilly, John — *The McCormick Group, Inc.*
Reilly, Robert E. — *DHR International, Inc.*
Reimenschneider, Donald — *Evie Kreisler & Associates, Inc.*
Reimer, Marvin — *Management Recruiters International, Inc.*
Reiser, Ellen — *Thorndike Deland Associates*
Reiss, Matt — *National Search, Inc.*
Reiter, Douglas — *The Douglas Reiter Company, Inc.*
Reiter, Harold D. — *Herbert Mines Associates, Inc.*
Reitkopp, Ellen — *Management Recruiters International, Inc.*
Reitkopp, Howard H. — *Management Recruiters International, Inc.*
Remick, Tierney Boyd — *Russell Reynolds Associates, Inc.*
Renick, Paula — *Kenzer Corp.*
Ressler, Dan R. — *Management Recruiters International, Inc.*
Reyes, Randolph G. — *Management Recruiters International, Inc.*
Reyman, Susan — *S. Reyman & Associates Ltd.*
Reynolds, Bud O. — *Management Recruiters International, Inc.*
Reynolds, Catherine — *Winter, Wyman & Company*
Reynolds, Gregory P. — *Roberts Ryan and Bentley*
Reynolds, Juli Ann — *Korn/Ferry International*
Reynolds, Susan F. — *Heidrick & Struggles, Inc.*
Rheude, Jim — *Management Recruiters International, Inc.*
Rice, Jim K. — *Management Recruiters International, Inc.*
Rice, John — *Paul Ray Berndtson*
Rice, Raymond D. — *Logue & Rice Inc.*
Rich, Kenneth M. — *Paul Ray Berndtson*
Rich, Lyttleton — *Sockwell & Associates*
Richard, Albert L. — *Human Resources Inc.*
Richards, Wes — *Heidrick & Struggles, Inc.*
Richardson, David M. — *DHR International, Inc.*
Richardson, J. Rick — *Spencer Stuart*
Richardson, Paul C. — *Korn/Ferry International*
Richardson, Tony R. — *Management Recruiters International, Inc.*
Rieger, Louis J. — *Spencer Stuart*
Riggs, David T. — *Management Recruiters International, Inc.*
Riggs, Lena — *Management Recruiters International, Inc.*
Rijke, R. Fred — *TASA International*
Riley, Elizabeth G. — *Mazza & Riley, Inc.*
Riley, James — *Hunt Ltd.*
Riley, Jeffrey K. — *EFL Associates*
Rimmel, James E. — *The Hindman Company*
Rimmele, Michael — *The Bankers Group*
Ring, Paul R. — *Sanford Rose Associates*
Rio, Monica — *Management Recruiters International, Inc.*
Rippey, George E. — *Heidrick & Struggles, Inc.*
Rittenberg, Richard S. — *D.E. Foster Partners Inc.*
Rivard, Dick — *Management Recruiters International, Inc.*
Rivas, Alberto F. — *Boyden*
Rivera, Elba R. — *Raymond Karsan Associates*
Rivers, Geri — *Chrisman & Company, Incorporated*
Rizk, Nyla — *Spencer Stuart*
Rizzo, L. Donald — *R.P. Barone Associates*
Roach, Ronald R. — *Sanford Rose Associates*
Robert, Diana — *Korn/Ferry International*
Roberts, Carl R. — *Southwestern Professional Services*
Roberts, Derek J. — *Ward Howell International, Inc.*
Roberts, Gary — *A.T. Kearney, Inc.*
Roberts, Jane — *Paul Ray Berndtson*
Roberts, Kenneth — *The Rubicon Group*
Roberts, Mitch — *A.E. Feldman Associates*
Roberts, Nick P. — *Spectrum Search Associates, Inc.*
Roberts, Norman C. — *Norman Roberts & Associates, Inc.*
Roberts, Raymond R. — *MSI International*
Roberts, Richard F. — *Management Recruiters International, Inc.*
Roberts, Scott B. — *Wargo and Co., Inc.*
Robertson, Bruce J. — *Norman Broadbent International, Inc.*
Robertson, John H.C. — *Sanford Rose Associates*
Robertson, William R. — *Ward Howell International, Inc.*
Robertson, William W. — *Marvin L. Silcott & Associates, Inc.*
Robins, Jeri N. — *Nagler, Robins & Poe, Inc.*
Robinson, Adrienne — *R L Plimpton Associates*
Robinson, Bruce — *Bruce Robinson Associates*

Robinson, Eric B. — *Bruce Robinson Associates*
Robison, John H. — *Robison & Associates*
Robson, Ridgely — *Accounting Personnel Consultants*
Roche, Gerard R. — *Heidrick & Struggles, Inc.*
Rodebaugh, Karen — *Management Recruiters International, Inc.*
Rodebaugh, Thomas L. — *Management Recruiters International, Inc.*
Rodetsky, Laurie — *Bradford & Galt, Inc.*
Rodgers, Kathi — *St. Lawrence International, Inc.*
Rodgers, Sarah J. — *Management Recruiters International, Inc.*
Rodney, Brett — *MSI International*
Rodriguez, Carlos R. — *Management Recruiters International, Inc.*
Rodriguez, Josie — *R. Parker and Associates, Inc.*
Rodriguez, Steven — *Spencer Stuart*
Roethlein, John — *Management Recruiters International, Inc.*
Roethlein, Lorian E. — *Management Recruiters International, Inc.*
Rogan, John P. — *Russell Reynolds Associates, Inc.*
Rogers, Gay — *Rogers-McManamon Executive Search*
Rogers, Leah — *Dinte Resources, Incorporated*
Rohan, James E. — *J.P. Canon Associates*
Rohan, Kevin A. — *J.P. Canon Associates*
Rojas-Magnon, Carlos — *Amrop International*
Roll, Bill — *Management Recruiters International, Inc.*
Rollo, Robert S. — *R. Rollo Associates*
Romaine, Stanley J. — *Mixtec Group*
Romanchek, Walter R. — *Wellington Management Group*
Romanello, Daniel P. — *Spencer Stuart*
Romaniw, Michael J. — *A la carte International*
Romaniw, Michael J. — *A la carte International*
Romaniw, Michael J. — *A la carte International*
Romano, Darren G. — *Korn/Ferry International*
Romanowicz, Jill — *Howard Fischer Associates, Inc.*
Ropes, John — *Ropes Associates, Inc.*
Rose, Sanford M. — *Sanford Rose Associates*
Rosemarin, Gloria J. — *Barrington Hart, Inc.*
Rosenberg, Esther — *Howe-Lewis International*
Rosenfeld, Martin J. — *Sanford Rose Associates*
Rosenthal, Andrea — *Korn/Ferry International*
Rosenthal, Charles — *National Search, Inc.*
Rosenwald, Tom H. — *Heidrick & Struggles, Inc.*
Rosica, John — *Management Recruiters International, Inc.*
Ross, Garland E. — *Management Recruiters International, Inc.*
Ross, Lawrence — *Lovas Stanley/Paul Ray Berndtson Inc.*
Ross, Marc A. — *Flowers & Associates*
Ross, Mark S. — *Herman Smith Executive Initiatives Inc.*
Ross, Martin B. — *Ward Howell International, Inc.*
Ross, Sheila L. — *Ward Howell International, Inc.*
Ross, William J. — *Flowers & Associates*
Rossi, George A. — *Heidrick & Struggles, Inc.*
Rossman, Paul R. — *Management Recruiters International, Inc.*
Rotella, Marshall W. — *The Corporate Connection, Ltd.*
Roth, Robert J. — *Williams, Roth & Krueger Inc.*
Rothenberg, Paul — *The McCormick Group, Inc.*
Rothfeld, Robert — *A.E. Feldman Associates*
Rothman, Jeffrey — *ProResource, Inc.*
Rothschild, John S. — *Heidrick & Struggles, Inc.*
Rothwell, Amy — *Howard Fischer Associates, Inc.*
Rottblatt, Michael — *Korn/Ferry International*
Rowe, Thomas A. — *Korn/Ferry International*
Rowe, William D. — *D.E. Foster Partners Inc.*
Rowell, Roger — *Halbrecht Lieberman Associates, Inc.*
Rowells, Michael — *MSI International*
Rowenhorst, Brenda — *The Bren Group*
Roy, Gary P. — *Management Recruiters International, Inc.*
Rozan, Naomi — *Comprehensive Search*
Rozner, Burton L. — *Oliver & Rozner Associates, Inc.*
Rubin, Marcey S. — *Kenzer Corp.*
Rubinstein, Walter — *Technical Connections Inc.*
Rudin, Harold — *Management Recruiters International, Inc.*
Rudin, Myra — *Management Recruiters International, Inc.*
Rudolph, Arlyn B. — *Management Recruiters International, Inc.*
Rudolph, Kenneth — *Kossuth & Associates, Inc.*
Rudzinsky, Howard — *Louis Rudzinsky Associates*
Rudzinsky, Jeffrey — *Louis Rudzinsky Associates*
Ruello, Brenda L. — *Heidrick & Struggles, Inc.*
Rumson, Barbara — *Management Recruiters International, Inc.*
Rumson, Paul M. — *Management Recruiters International, Inc.*
Runquist, U.W. — *Webb, Johnson Associates, Inc.*
Rupert, Jim — *Management Recruiters International, Inc.*
Rurak, Zbigniew T. — *Rurak & Associates, Inc.*
Ruschak, Randy R. — *Management Recruiters International, Inc.*
Rusher, William H. — *Rusher, Loscavio & LoPresto*
Russell, Carol — *ExecuScope Division of Russell Staffing Resources, Inc.*
Russell, Richard A. — *Executive Search Consultants Corporation*
Russell, Robin E. — *Kenzer Corp.*
Russell, Sam — *The Guild Corporation*
Russell, Susan Anne — *Executive Search Consultants Corporation*
Rust, John R. — *DHR International, Inc.*

Rustad, Binth — *Educational Management Network*
Rustin, Beth — *The Whitney Group*
Ryan, Joseph W. — *Skott/Edwards Consultants, Inc.*
Ryan, Mary L. — *Summerfield Associates, Inc.*
Sabados, Terri — *Management Recruiters International, Inc.*
Sacerdote, John — *Raymond Karsan Associates*
Sackmary, Marcia — *Sanford Rose Associates*
Sackmary, Steven — *Sanford Rose Associates*
Sahagian, John — *Human Resources Inc.*
Salikof, Allen B. — *Management Recruiters International, Inc.*
Salikof, Kaye R. — *Management Recruiters International, Inc.*
Salinger, Helen — *Gilbert Tweed/INESA*
Samet, Saul — *Fisher-Todd Associates*
Sammons, James A. — *Prestige Inc.*
Samuels, Lewis J. — *Morgan Samuels Co., Inc.*
Sanders, Dave A. — *Management Recruiters International, Inc.*
Sanders, Norman D. — *Norm Sanders Associates*
Sanders, Spencer H. — *Battalia Winston International*
Sanderson, Jeffrey M. — *Sullivan & Company*
Sandor, Richard J. — *Flynn, Hannock, Incorporated*
Sarafa, Sam N. — *Management Recruiters International, Inc.*
Sathe, Mark A. — *Sathe & Associates, Inc.*
Sauer, Robert C. — *Heidrick & Struggles, Inc.*
Savage, Edward J. — *Stanton Chase International*
Savard, Robert F. — *The Stevenson Group of Delaware Inc.*
Savereid, Lisa — *Isaacson, Miller*
Sawhill, Louise B. — *Paul Ray Berndtson*
Sawhook, Danny — *Richard, Wayne and Roberts*
Sawyer, Deborah A. — *Heidrick & Struggles, Inc.*
Sawyer, Patricia L. — *Smith & Sawyer Inc.*
Saxner, David — *DSA, Inc.*
Saydah, Robert F. — *Heidrick & Struggles, Inc.*
Sayers, Bruce D. — *Brackin & Sayers Associates*
Saylor, Bill E. — *Management Recruiters International, Inc.*
Scarbrough, Debbi — *Evie Kreisler & Associates, Inc.*
Schaad, Carl A. — *Heidrick & Struggles, Inc.*
Schaefer, Frederic M. — *A.T. Kearney, Inc.*
Schaller, F. William — *Sanford Rose Associates*
Schaller, Karen — *Sanford Rose Associates*
Schappell, Marc P. — *Egon Zehnder International Inc.*
Scharett, Carol — *St. Lawrence International, Inc.*
Scharringhausen, Michael — *Saber Consultants*
Schedra, Sharon — *Earley Kielty and Associates, Inc.*
Schegg, Paul — *Goodrich & Sherwood Associates, Inc.*
Scheidt, Sandi — *Paul Ray Berndtson*
Scheidt, Sandra L. — *The Heidrick Partners, Inc.*
Scherck, Henry J. — *Ward Howell International, Inc.*
Schiavone, Mary Rose — *Canny, Bowen Inc.*
Schiffer, Stewart — *Career Management International*
Schlanger, Ruth — *Richard, Wayne and Roberts*
Schlecht, Nancy — *Morgan Samuels Co., Inc.*
Schlosser, John R. — *Heidrick & Struggles, Inc.*
Schlpma, Christine — *Advanced Executive Resources*
Schmidt, Jeri E. — *Blake, Hansen & Nye, Limited*
Schmidt, Michelle C. — *Sanford Rose Associates*
Schmidt, Paul — *Paul Ray Berndtson*
Schmidt, Peter R. — *Boyden*
Schmidt, Peter R. — *Boyden*
Schmidt, Robert C. — *Management Recruiters International, Inc.*
Schmidt, Timothy G. — *Sanford Rose Associates*
Schmidt, William C. — *Christian & Timbers*
Schneider, Susan — *Jacquelyn Finn & Susan Schneider Associates, Inc.*
Schneider, Thomas P. — *WTW Associates*
Schneider, Tom J. — *Management Recruiters International, Inc.*
Schneiderman, Gerald — *Management Resource Associates, Inc.*
Schneidermeyer, Phil — *Korn/Ferry International*
Schneirov, Miriam A. — *Coleman Legal Search Consultants*
Schoen, Stephen G. — *MDR Associates, Inc.*
Schoenwetter, Carrie — *Management Recruiters International, Inc.*
Schoettle, Michael B. — *Heidrick & Struggles, Inc.*
Schoff, Frank J. — *Management Recruiters International, Inc.*
Schonberg, Alan R. — *Management Recruiters International, Inc.*
Schor, Neil D. — *Kenzer Corp.*
Schostak, Glen — *Korn/Ferry International*
Schramm, Walter M. — *Executive Outsourcing International*
Schreiber, Stuart M. — *Heidrick & Struggles, Inc.*
Schroeder, James L. — *Korn/Ferry International*
Schroeder, John W. — *Spencer Stuart*
Schroeder, Victoria — *Paul Ray Berndtson*
Schulte, Bernard — *Korn/Ferry International*
Schultz, Roger C. — *Management Recruiters International, Inc.*
Schuyler, Lambert — *Schuyler, Frye & Baker, Inc.*
Schwam, Carol — *A.E. Feldman Associates*
Schwartz, Carole — *A.T. Kearney, Inc.*
Schwartz, Harry — *Jacobson Associates*
Schwartz, Jay S. — *Management Recruiters International, Inc.*
Schwartz, Stephen D. — *Management Recruiters International, Inc.*

Schwartz, Susan — *Korn/Ferry International*
Schwartz, Vincent P. — *Slayton International, Inc.*
Scognamillo, Sandra V. — *Witt/Kieffer, Ford, Hadelman & Lloyd*
Scott, Alison — *Korn/Ferry International*
Scott, Evan — *Howard Fischer Associates, Inc.*
Scott, George W. — *Raymond Karsan Associates*
Scott, Jack — *Korn/Ferry International*
Scott, Ron — *Richard Kader & Associates*
Scroggins, Stephen R. — *Russell Reynolds Associates, Inc.*
Scullin, Richard — *Eden & Associates, Inc.*
Seals, Sonny — *A.T. Kearney, Inc.*
Sears, Kirk — *Management Recruiters International, Inc.*
Sears, Rick — *Management Recruiters International, Inc.*
Seco, William — *Seco & Zetto Associates, Inc.*
Seebeck, Robert F. — *Russell Reynolds Associates, Inc.*
Seefeld, David — *Management Recruiters International, Inc.*
Segal, Eric B. — *Kenzer Corp.*
Seibert, Nancy — *Tyler & Company*
Seiden, Steven A. — *Seiden Krieger Associates, Inc.*
Seitchik, Jack — *Seitchik Corwin and Seitchik, Inc.*
Seitchik, William — *Seitchik Corwin and Seitchik, Inc.*
Seitz, Charles J. — *Neail Behringer Consultants*
Sekera, Roger I. — *A.T. Kearney, Inc.*
Selbst, Denise — *Richard, Wayne and Roberts*
Selko, Philip W. — *Hogan Acquisitions*
Seltzer, Deborah Coogan — *Paul Ray Berndtson*
Semmes, John R. — *Management Recruiters International, Inc.*
Semyan, John K. — *TNS Partners, Inc.*
Sennello, Gendra — *National Search, Inc.*
Serota, Joel — *Kenzer Corp.*
Serwat, Leonard A. — *Spencer Stuart*
Sessa, Beth — *Richard, Wayne and Roberts*
Sessa, Vincent J. — *Integrated Search Solutions Group, LLC*
Settles, Barbara Z. — *Lamalie Amrop International*
Sevilla, Claudio A. — *Crawford & Crofford*
Sewell, Danny J. — *Management Recruiters International, Inc.*
Seweloh, Theodore W. — *The Heidrick Partners, Inc.*
Shabot, David — *Korn/Ferry International*
Shake, Samuel D. — *DHR International, Inc.*
Sharp, Paul S. — *Management Recruiters International, Inc.*
Shattuck, Merrill B. — *M.B. Shattuck and Associates, Inc.*
Shaw, Eric D. — *Management Recruiters International, Inc.*
Shaw, Ken — *Hornberger Management Company*
Shea, Kathleen M. — *The Penn Partners, Incorporated*
Shearer, Gary F. — *Management Recruiters International, Inc.*
Sheedy, Edward J. — *Dieckmann & Associates, Ltd.*
Sheehan, Arthur — *Management Recruiters International, Inc.*
Sheehan, Patricia — *Management Recruiters International, Inc.*
Shelton, Sandra — *National Search, Inc.*
Shen, Eugene Y. — *The Whitney Group*
Shenfield, Peter — *Baker, Harris & Partners Limited*
Shepard, Michael J. — *MSI International*
Shepherd, Daniel M. — *Shepherd Bueschel & Provus, Inc.*
Shepherd, Gail L. — *Shepherd Bueschel & Provus, Inc.*
Sheridan, Kenneth T. — *Management Recruiters International, Inc.*
Sheridan, Theresa — *Management Recruiters International, Inc.*
Sherman, Daniel A. — *Goodwin & Company*
Sherrill, Lee S. — *Management Recruiters International, Inc.*
Sherry, Joan — *Korn/Ferry International*
Shervey, Brent C. — *O'Callaghan Honey/Paul Ray Berndtson, Inc.*
Sherwin, Thomas — *Barone-O'Hara Associates*
Sherwood, Andrew — *Goodrich & Sherwood Associates, Inc.*
Shimp, David J. — *Lamalie Amrop International*
Shockey, William — *Korn/Ferry International*
Shoemaker, Fred W. — *MSI International*
Shoemaker, Larry C. — *Shoemaker & Associates*
Shore, Earl L. — *E.L. Shore & Associates Ltd.*
Shourds, Mary E. — *Houze, Shourds & Montgomery, Inc.*
Shulman, Melvin — *McFeely Wackerle Shulman*
Shultz, Susan F. — *SSA Executive Search International*
Sibbald, John R. — *John Sibbald Associates, Inc.*
Siegel, Fred — *Conex Incorporated*
Siegel, Pamela — *Executive Options, Ltd.*
Sierra, Rafael A. — *Lamalie Amrop International*
Sigurdson, Eric J. — *Russell Reynolds Associates, Inc.*
Silkiner, David S. — *Paul Ray Berndtson*
Silvas, Stephen D. — *Roberson and Company*
Silver, Lee A. — *L.A. Silver Associates, Inc.*
Silverman, Paul M. — *The Marshall Group*
Silverstein, Michael L. — *Management Recruiters International, Inc.*
Simmonds, David — *Coopers & Lybrand Consulting*
Simmons, Gerald J. — *Handy HRM Corp.*
Simmons, Jeffrey — *Kenzer Corp.*
Simmons, Tom — *Spencer Stuart*
Simmons, Vicki — *Richard, Wayne and Roberts*
Simon, John — *John J. Davis & Associates, Inc.*
Simon, Penny B. — *Paul Ray Berndtson*
Simon, William — *Korn/Ferry International*

Simpson, Kent T. — *Management Recruiters International, Inc.*
Sims, John — *Management Recruiters International, Inc.*
Sinclair, Amy — *Fisher Personnel Management Services*
Sinclair, Tom — *Coopers & Lybrand Consulting*
Singleton, Robin — *Tyler & Company*
Sitarski, Stan — *Howard Fischer Associates, Inc.*
Skirbe, Douglas — *Rhodes Associates*
Sklover, Bruce — *Professional Assignments of New York, Inc.*
Skunda, Donna M. — *Allerton Heneghan & O'Neill*
Slater, Ronald E. — *A.T. Kearney, Inc.*
Slayton, Richard S. — *Slayton International, Inc.*
Smead, Michelle M. — *A.T. Kearney, Inc.*
Smith, Adam M. — *The Abbott Group, Inc.*
Smith, Ana Luz — *Smith Search, S.C.*
Smith, Barry S. — *Management Recruiters International, Inc.*
Smith, Carroll V. — *Management Recruiters International, Inc.*
Smith, Cheryl — *Barton Raben, Inc.*
Smith, Cheryl — *KPMG Executive Search*
Smith, Cheryl — *ProResource, Inc.*
Smith, Clawson — *Ward Howell International, Inc.*
Smith, David P. — *Smith & Latterell (HRS, Inc.)*
Smith, Douglas M. — *Ward Howell International, Inc.*
Smith, Eric E. — *Management Recruiters International, Inc.*
Smith, Ethan L. — *Highland Search Group, L.L.C.*
Smith, Gin-Nie — *Management Recruiters International, Inc.*
Smith, Grant — *Price Waterhouse*
Smith, Herbert C. — *H C Smith Ltd.*
Smith, Herman D. — *Management Recruiters International, Inc.*
Smith, Herman M. — *Herman Smith Executive Initiatives Inc.*
Smith, John E. — *Smith Search, S.C.*
Smith, John F. — *The Penn Partners, Incorporated*
Smith, Margaret A. — *MSI International*
Smith, Mark L. — *Korn/Ferry International*
Smith, Matthew — *Korn/Ferry International*
Smith, Melanie F. — *The Heidrick Partners, Inc.*
Smith, Mike W. — *Management Recruiters International, Inc.*
Smith, Monica L. — *Analysts Resources, Inc.*
Smith, Perry V. — *Management Recruiters International, Inc.*
Smith, R. Michael — *Smith James Group, Inc.*
Smith, Rebecca Ruben — *H C Smith Ltd.*
Smith, Robert L. — *Smith & Sawyer Inc.*
Smith, Scott B. — *Ward Howell International, Inc.*
Smith, Shellie L. — *The Heidrick Partners, Inc.*
Smith, Steve L. — *Management Recruiters International, Inc.*
Snedden, Al — *Management Recruiters International, Inc.*
Snelgrove, Geiger — *National Search, Inc.*
Snellbaker, Mary W. — *Management Recruiters International, Inc.*
Snider, George R. — *Sanford Rose Associates*
Snodgrass, Stephen — *DeFrain, Mayer, Lee & Burgess LLC*
Snook, Maria P. — *Management Recruiters International, Inc.*
Snook, Marvin G. — *Management Recruiters International, Inc.*
Snyder, C. Edward — *Horton International*
Snyder, James F. — *Snyder & Company*
Snyder, Thomas J. — *Spencer Stuart*
Sockwell, J. Edgar — *Sockwell & Associates*
Soggs, Cheryl Pavick — *A.T. Kearney, Inc.*
Sola, George L. — *A.T. Kearney, Inc.*
Solomon Ph.D., Neil M. — *The Neil Michael Group, Inc.*
Solomon, Christina — *Richard, Wayne and Roberts*
Solters, Jeanne — *The Guild Corporation*
Somers, Donald A. — *Management Recruiters International, Inc.*
Somers, Scott D. — *Paul Ray Berndtson*
Songy, Al — *U.S. Envirosearch*
Soth, Mark H. — *Management Recruiters International, Inc.*
Southerland, Keith C. — *Witt/Kieffer, Ford, Hadelman & Lloyd*
Soutouras, James — *Smith James Group, Inc.*
Sowerbutt, Richard S. — *Hite Executive Search*
Spangenberg, J. Brand — *The Brand Company, Inc.*
Spangenberg, Sigrid — *The Brand Company, Inc.*
Spangler, Lloyd — *Cole, Warren & Long, Inc.*
Spann, Richard E. — *Goodrich & Sherwood Associates, Inc.*
Speck, Michael J. — *Lovas Stanley/Paul Ray Berndtson Inc.*
Spellacy, James P. — *Management Recruiters International, Inc.*
Spellman, Frances — *Kenzer Corp.*
Spence, Gene L. — *Heidrick & Struggles, Inc.*
Spence, Joseph T. — *Russell Reynolds Associates, Inc.*
Spencer, Frank — *Kenzer Corp.*
Sperry, Elizabeth B. — *Korn/Ferry International*
Spiegel, Deborah — *Kenzer Corp.*
Spiegel, Gay — *L.A. Silver Associates, Inc.*
Spitz, Grant — *The Caldwell Partners Amrop International*
Spitz, Richard — *Korn/Ferry International*
Splaine, Charles — *Splaine & Associates, Inc.*
Sponseller, Vern — *Richard Kader & Associates*
Sprague, David — *Michael Stern Associates Inc.*
Sprau, Collin L. — *Paul Ray Berndtson*
Spriggs, Robert D. — *Spriggs & Company, Inc.*
Springer, Mark H. — *M.H. Springer & Associates Incorporated*

Sprowls, Linda — *Allard Associates*
Srolis, Robert B. — *Raymond Karsan Associates*
St. Denis, Robert A. — *Sanford Rose Associates*
St. John, J. Burke — *Heidrick & Struggles, Inc.*
Stack, James K. — *Boyden*
Stackhouse, P. John — *Heidrick & Struggles, Inc.*
Stafford, Charles B. — *Management Recruiters International, Inc.*
Stahl, Cynthia — *Plummer & Associates, Inc.*
Standard, Gail — *Comprehensive Search*
Stanislaw, Robert J. — *DHR International, Inc.*
Stanley, Paul R.A. — *Lovas Stanley/Paul Ray Berndtson Inc.*
Stanley, Wade — *Management Recruiters International, Inc.*
Stark, Gary L. — *Management Recruiters International, Inc.*
Stark, Jeff — *Thorne, Brieger Associates Inc.*
Starner, William S. — *Fenwick Partners*
Starr, Anna — *Richard, Wayne and Roberts*
Steck, Frank T. — *A.T. Kearney, Inc.*
Steele, Kevin — *Winter, Wyman & Company*
Steenerson, Thomas L. — *MSI International*
Stein, Neil A. — *R.H. Perry & Associates, Inc.*
Stein, Terry W. — *Stewart, Stein and Scott, Ltd.*
Steinem, Andy — *Dahl-Morrow International*
Steinem, Barbara — *Dahl-Morrow International*
Steinman, Stephen — *The Stevenson Group of New Jersey*
Stemphoski, Ronald L. — *The Diversified Search Companies*
Stenberg, Edward — *Winter, Wyman & Company*
Stenholm, Gilbert R. — *Spencer Stuart*
Stephanian, Armand A. — *Paul Ray Berndtson*
Stephens, Roberto Salinas — *Smith Search, S.C.*
Stephenson, Craig — *Korn/Ferry International*
Stephenson, Don L. — *Ells Personnel System Inc.*
Stephenson, Mike — *Evie Kreisler & Associates, Inc.*
Sterling, Cheryl E. — *Management Recruiters International, Inc.*
Sterling, Jay — *Earley Kielty and Associates, Inc.*
Sterling, Ronald — *Management Recruiters International, Inc.*
Sterling, Sally M. — *Heidrick & Struggles, Inc.*
Stern, Leslie W. — *Sullivan & Company*
Stern, Michael I. — *Michael Stern Associates Inc.*
Stern, Ronni — *Kenzer Corp.*
Stevens, David — *Johnson Smith & Knisely Accord*
Stevens, Glenn — *Korn/Ferry International*
Stevens, Robin — *Paul Ray Berndtson*
Stevenson, Jani — *Howard Fischer Associates, Inc.*
Stevenson, Julianne M. — *Russell Reynolds Associates, Inc.*
Stevenson, Terry — *Bartholdi & Company, Inc.*
Stewart, Jan J. — *Egon Zehnder International Inc.*
Stewart, Jeffrey O. — *Stewart, Stein and Scott, Ltd.*
Stewart, Ross M. — *Human Resources Network Partners Inc.*
Stewart, Steve — *Management Recruiters International, Inc.*
Stewart, Wilf — *KPMG Executive Search*
Stiles, Jack D. — *Sanford Rose Associates*
Stiles, Timothy — *Sanford Rose Associates*
Stirn, Bradley A. — *Spencer Stuart*
Stivk, Barbara A. — *Thornton Resources*
Stoessel, Robert J. — *Management Recruiters International, Inc.*
Stokes, John — *Nordeman Grimm, Inc.*
Stoltz, Dick — *Management Recruiters International, Inc.*
Stone, Kayla — *Korn/Ferry International*
Stone, Robert Ryder — *Lamalie Amrop International*
Stone, Susan L. — *Stone Enterprises Ltd.*
Stoneham, Herbert E.C. — *Stoneham Associates Corp.*
Storbeck, Shelly — *A.T. Kearney, Inc.*
Storment, John H. — *Management Recruiters International, Inc.*
Stoy, Roger M. — *Heidrick & Struggles, Inc.*
Strain, Stephen R. — *Spencer Stuart*
Stratman, Sandy L. — *Management Recruiters International, Inc.*
Stratmeyer, Karin Bergwall — *Princeton Entrepreneurial Resources*
Straube, Stanley H. — *Straube Associates*
Strayhorn, Larry — *Management Recruiters International, Inc.*
Strayhorn, Patricia — *Management Recruiters International, Inc.*
Stricker, Sidney G. — *Stricker & Zagor*
Stringer, Dann P. — *D.E. Foster Partners Inc.*
Strobo, Ray S. — *Management Recruiters International, Inc.*
Strobridge, Richard P. — *F.L. Taylor & Company, Inc.*
Strom, Mark N. — *Search Advisors International Corp.*
Stroup, Jonathan C. — *Egon Zehnder International Inc.*
Stuart, Karen M. — *Reflex Services, Inc.*
Stubberfield, Lee — *Management Recruiters International, Inc.*
Stubbs, Judy N. — *Lamalie Amrop International*
Sturges, J.S. — *Contract Professionals*
Stutt, Brian — *Richard, Wayne and Roberts*
Suit-Terry, J.A. — *Management Recruiters International, Inc.*
Sullivan, Brian M. — *Sullivan & Company*
Sullivan, Catherine — *Korn/Ferry International*
Sullivan, Dennis — *Sullivan & Associates*
Sullivan, Joseph J. — *Joe Sullivan & Associates, Inc.*
Sullivan, Robert — *Korn/Ferry International*
Summerlin, Gerald — *Management Recruiters International, Inc.*

Summers, Burke — *The McCormick Group, Inc.*
Sumurdy, Melinda — *Kenzer Corp.*
Sur, William K. — *Canny, Bowen Inc.*
Sussman, Lynda — *Gilbert Tweed/INESA*
Sutter, Terry A. — *Russell Reynolds Associates, Inc.*
Sutton, Robert J. — *The Caldwell Partners Amrop International*
Swan, Richard A. — *Witt/Kieffer, Ford, Hadelman & Lloyd*
Swanson, Dick — *Raymond Karsan Associates*
Swanson, Jarl — *The Gabriel Group*
Swanson, Kris — *Flex Execs Management Solutions*
Swaringen, Mac — *Management Recruiters International, Inc.*
Sweeney, James W. — *Sweeney Harbert & Mummert, Inc.*
Sweeney, Sean K. — *Bonifield Associates*
Sweet, Charles W. — *A.T. Kearney, Inc.*
Swidler, J. Robert — *Egon Zehnder International Inc.*
Swystun, Karen — *Price Waterhouse*
Sykes, Hugh L. — *Management Recruiters International, Inc.*
Szafran, Jack — *U.S. Envirosearch*
Takacs, Gloria — *Gilbert & Van Campen International*
Talbot, Matt T. — *Management Recruiters International, Inc.*
Talbot, Norman — *Management Recruiters International, Inc.*
Tallent, Diane — *Evie Kreisler & Associates, Inc.*
Tames, Rodolfo — *Amrop International*
Tanabe, Sharon — *Korn/Ferry International*
Tanenbaum, Ray — *Kenzer Corp.*
Tanton, John E. — *Tanton Mitchell/Paul Ray Berndtson*
Tappan, Michael A. — *Ward Howell International, Inc.*
Tardugno, Carl — *Management Recruiters International, Inc.*
Tate, Robert H. — *Paul Ray Berndtson*
Taylor, Charles E. — *Lamalie Amrop International*
Taylor, Conrad G. — *MSI International*
Taylor, Ernest A. — *Ward Howell International, Inc.*
Taylor, Kenneth W. — *Egon Zehnder International Inc.*
Taylor, Richard — *Korn/Ferry International*
Taylor, Walt W. — *Management Recruiters International, Inc.*
Taylor-Gordon, Elaine — *Kenzer Corp.*
Teas, John — *Southwestern Professional Services*
Teinert, Jay — *Damon & Associates, Inc.*
Telford, John H. — *Telford, Adams & Alexander/Telford & Co., Inc.*
Tello, Fernando — *Korn/Ferry International*
Temple, John D. — *The Hindman Company*
ten Cate, Herman H. — *Stoneham Associates Corp.*
Terry, Douglas — *Jacobson Associates*
Tessin, Cy — *Management Recruiters International, Inc.*
Teter, Sandra — *The Danbrook Group, Inc.*
Theobald, David B. — *Theobald & Associates*
Thiras, Ted — *Mixtec Group*
Tholke, William E. — *Canny, Bowen Inc.*
Thomas, Bill — *Management Recruiters International, Inc.*
Thomas, Christine S. — *Lovas Stanley/Paul Ray Berndtson Inc.*
Thomas, Donald — *Mixtec Group*
Thomas, Ian — *International Staffing Consultants, Inc.*
Thomas, Jeffrey — *Fairfaxx Corporation*
Thomas, John T. — *Ward Howell International, Inc.*
Thomas, Kurt J. — *P.J. Murphy & Associates, Inc.*
Thomas, Terry — *Montague Enterprises*
Thomas, William — *Mixtec Group*
Thompson, Carlton W. — *Spencer Stuart*
Thompson, Dave — *Battalia Winston International*
Thompson, James R. — *Gordon Wahls Company*
Thompson, Jim E. — *Management Recruiters International, Inc.*
Thompson, John T. — *Heidrick & Struggles, Inc.*
Thompson, Kenneth L. — *McCormack & Farrow*
Thompson, Timothy W. — *Korn/Ferry International*
Thomson, Alexander G. — *Russell Reynolds Associates, Inc.*
Thornton, John C. — *Thornton Resources*
Thorpe, David L. — *IMCOR, Inc.*
Thrower, Tom S. — *Management Recruiters International, Inc.*
Tierney, Eileen — *The Whitney Group*
Tillman, J. Robert — *Russell Reynolds Associates, Inc.*
Timms, Alan R. — *DHR International, Inc.*
Timoney, Laura — *Bishop Partners*
Tingle, Trina A. — *MSI International*
Tinucci, Crystal M. — *Witt/Kieffer, Ford, Hadelman & Lloyd*
Tipping, William M. — *Ward Howell International, Inc.*
Titterington, Catherine F. — *MSI International*
Titus, Dave — *Management Recruiters International, Inc.*
Tobin, Jim — *Barton Raben, Inc.*
Tobin, William — *Korn/Ferry International*
Tokarcik, Patricia — *ProResource, Inc.*
Tolle, David W. — *Management Recruiters International, Inc.*
Toms, Evangeline — *Nordeman Grimm, Inc.*
Toole, Mary — *Management Recruiters International, Inc.*
Toole, Tom J. — *Management Recruiters International, Inc.*
Toson, James — *Prestige Inc.*
Tracey, Garvis — *Key Employment Services*
Tracey, Jack — *Management Assistance Group, Inc.*
Tracy, Ronald O. — *Egon Zehnder International Inc.*

Trapp, Ed — *Management Recruiters International, Inc.*
Trautman, William E. — *A.T. Kearney, Inc.*
Trautman, William E. — *Boyden*
Travis, Ed — *Management Recruiters International, Inc.*
Tribbett, Charles A. — *Russell Reynolds Associates, Inc.*
Tripp, William J. — *Management Recruiters International, Inc.*
Trosin, Walter R. — *Johnson Smith & Knisely Accord*
Trott, Kathryn — *Allard Associates*
Trott, Kathryn — *Allard Associates*
Trueblood, Brian G. — *TNS Partners, Inc.*
Truex, John F. — *Morton, McCorkle & Associates, Inc.*
Tryon, Katey — *DeFrain, Mayer, Lee & Burgess LLC*
Tucci, Joseph — *Fairfaxx Corporation*
Tucker, Thomas A. — *The Thomas Tucker Company*
Tufenkjian, Richard — *C.A. Durakis Associates, Inc.*
Tunney, William — *Grant Cooper and Associates*
Turnblacer, John — *The Gabriel Group*
Turner, Allan W. — *Management Recruiters International, Inc.*
Turner, Brad — *Management Recruiters International, Inc.*
Turner, Elaine — *Witt/Kieffer, Ford, Hadelman & Lloyd*
Tutwiler, Stephen — *Don Richard Associates of Tampa, Inc.*
Tweed, Janet — *Gilbert Tweed/INESA*
Twiste, Craig — *Raymond Karsan Associates*
Tydings, Mary C. — *Russell Reynolds Associates, Inc.*
Tyler, J. Larry — *Tyler & Company*
Tyler, Jackie — *Kenzer Corp.*
Tyson, Richard L. — *Bonifield Associates*
Uhl, Jack N. — *Management Recruiters International, Inc.*
Unger, Mike A. — *Management Recruiters International, Inc.*
Unger, Paul T. — *A.T. Kearney, Inc.*
Unger, Stephen A. — *Spencer Stuart*
Uniacke, Keith J. — *Management Recruiters International, Inc.*
Unterberg, Edward L. — *Russell Reynolds Associates, Inc.*
Utroska, Donald R. — *Lamalie Amrop International*
Vachon, David A. — *McNichol Associates*
Vainblat, Galina — *Foy, Schneid & Daniel, Inc.*
Vairo, Leonard A. — *Christian & Timbers*
Valdes, Ma. Elena — *Korn/Ferry International*
Valenta, Joseph — *Princeton Entrepreneurial Resources*
Valente, Joe J. — *Management Recruiters International, Inc.*
Valente, Sam — *Management Recruiters International, Inc.*
Valle, Javier — *A.T. Kearney, Inc.*
Van Alstine, Catherine — *Tanton Mitchell/Paul Ray Berndtson*
Van Alstyne, Susan — *Richard, Wayne and Roberts*
Van Campen, Jerry — *Gilbert & Van Campen International*
Van Campen, Stephen B. — *Gilbert & Van Campen International*
Van Clieaf, Mark — *MVC Associates International*
van de Wetering, Shirley — *The Caldwell Partners Amrop International*
Van Horn, Carol — *R. Parker and Associates, Inc.*
Van Nus, Robert — *Coopers & Lybrand Consulting*
Van Someren, Chris — *Korn/Ferry International*
van Someren, Christian — *Johnson Smith & Knisely Accord*
Van Steenkiste, Julie — *Davidson, Laird & Associates*
Van Wick, Mike — *Management Recruiters International, Inc.*
Vande-Water, Katie — *J. Robert Scott*
Vann, Dianne — *The Button Group*
Varian, Veronica — *Management Recruiters International, Inc.*
Vaughan, David B. — *Dunhill Professional Search of Irvine, Inc.*
Vautour, Eric L. — *Russell Reynolds Associates, Inc.*
Velline, Ena A. — *Paul Ray Berndtson*
Velten, Mark — *Hunt Ltd.*
Venable, William W. — *Thorndike Deland Associates*
Vennat, Manon — *Spencer Stuart*
Vergara, Gail H. — *Spencer Stuart*
Vergari, Jane — *Herbert Mines Associates, Inc.*
Verkamp, James Franklin — *Verkamp-Joyce Associates, Inc.*
Vermillion, Mike W. — *Management Recruiters International, Inc.*
Vernon, Jack H. — *Russell Reynolds Associates, Inc.*
Verrill-Schlager, Martha — *Korn/Ferry International*
Vet, Jan — *Korn/Ferry International*
Vierkant, Nona E. — *Management Recruiters International, Inc.*
Vierkant, Robert — *Management Recruiters International, Inc.*
Viglino, Victor P. — *DHR International, Inc.*
Villareal, Morey — *Villareal & Associates, Inc.*
Vincelette, Kathy A. — *Raymond Karsan Associates*
Vinnedge, Sandra — *U.S. Envirosearch*
Virgili, Franca — *Johnson Smith & Knisely Accord*
Visnich, L. Christine — *Bason Associates Inc.*
Visokey, Dale M. — *Russell Reynolds Associates, Inc.*
Vlasek, Ray D. — *Management Recruiters International, Inc.*
Vlcek, Thomas J. — *Vlcek & Company, Inc.*
Vogel, Emil — *Tarnow International*
Vognsen, Rikke — *DSA, Inc.*
Volk, Richard — *MSI International*
Volz, Scott — *Management Recruiters International, Inc.*
Von Der Ahe, Christopher — *Korn/Ferry International*
von der Linden, James A. — *Pendleton James and Associates, Inc.*

von Seldeneck, Judith M. — *The Diversified Search Companies*
von Stein, Scott — *Wilkinson & Ives*
Wackerle, Frederick W. — *McFeely Wackerle Shulman*
Wagman, Marc E. — *Management Recruiters International, Inc.*
Wagner, Robert — *Korn/Ferry International*
Waindle, Maureen — *Paul Ray Berndtson*
Wait, Kristin — *Korn/Ferry International*
Waitkus, Karen — *Richard, Wayne and Roberts*
Wakefield, Scott — *National Search, Inc.*
Wakeham, Robin — *Korn/Ferry International*
Walburger, Gary — *Korn/Ferry International*
Waldman, Noah H. — *Lamalie Amrop International*
Waldoch, D. Mark — *Barnes Development Group, LLC*
Waldrop, Gary R. — *MSI International*
Walker, Don — *Richard, Wayne and Roberts*
Walker, Judy — *Richard, Wayne and Roberts*
Walker, Martin S. — *Walker Communications*
Walker, Richard — *Bradford & Galt, Inc.*
Walker, Ronald H. — *Korn/Ferry International*
Wall, David — *Southwestern Professional Services*
Wallace, Alec — *Tanton Mitchell/Paul Ray Berndtson*
Wallace, Charles E. — *Heidrick & Struggles, Inc.*
Wallace, Dennis M. — *Sanford Rose Associates*
Wallace, Mark J. — *Management Recruiters International, Inc.*
Wallis, Barry — *Bradford & Galt, Inc.*
Walter, Mary Ann — *Spencer Stuart*
Walters, William F. — *Jonas, Walters & Assoc., Inc.*
Walther, Linda S. — *MSI International*
Walton, Bruce H. — *Heidrick & Struggles, Inc.*
Walton, James H. — *Management Recruiters International, Inc.*
Walton, Terry P. — *Heidrick & Struggles, Inc.*
Wanless, Theresa — *The Caldwell Partners Amrop International*
Ward, Ted — *Korn/Ferry International*
Ward, William F. — *Heidrick & Struggles, Inc.*
Wardell, Charles W.B. — *Lamalie Amrop International*
Ware, John C. — *Spencer Stuart*
Wargo, G. Rick — *A.T. Kearney, Inc.*
Waring, David C. — *Russell Reynolds Associates, Inc.*
Warren, Lester A. — *Management Recruiters International, Inc.*
Warren, Linda — *Prestige Inc.*
Warren, Richard B. — *Cole, Warren & Long, Inc.*
Warren, Sylvia W. — *Thorndike Deland Associates*
Wasp, Warren T. — *WTW Associates*
Wasson, Thomas W. — *Spencer Stuart*
Watkins, Jeffrey P. — *Paul Ray Berndtson*
Watkins, Thomas M. — *Lamalie Amrop International*
Watson, Stephen — *Paul Ray Berndtson*
Watson, Wally — *Management Recruiters International, Inc.*
Watt, Jennifer — *The McCormick Group, Inc.*
Watters, John T. — *DHR International, Inc.*
Wattier, David — *Key Employment Services*
Waxman, Bruce — *Ryan, Miller & Associates Inc.*
Wayne, Victoria P. — *Korn/Ferry International*
Webb, Don W. — *Management Recruiters International, Inc.*
Webb, George H. — *Webb, Johnson Associates, Inc.*
Webb, Pat A. — *Management Recruiters International, Inc.*
Webb, Shawn K. — *MSI International*
Webb, Verna F. — *Management Recruiters International, Inc.*
Weber, Fred — *J.B. Homer Associates, Inc.*
Weber, Fritz — *Management Recruiters International, Inc.*
Weber, James K. — *Management Recruiters International, Inc.*
Weber, Machelle — *Paul Ray Berndtson*
Weed, William H. — *Paul Ray Berndtson*
Weidener, Andrew E. — *Paul Ray Berndtson*
Weiler, Tom — *Executive Placement Consultants, Inc.*
Wein, Michael S. — *InterimManagement Solutions, Inc.*
Wein, William — *InterimManagement Solutions, Inc.*
Weiner, Arlene — *Sanford Rose Associates*
Weiner, Arthur — *Sanford Rose Associates*
Weir, Norma — *Paul Ray Berndtson*
Weisler, Nancy — *National Search, Inc.*
Weiss, Karen — *D.E. Foster Partners Inc.*
Weissman-Rosenthal, Abbe — *ALW Research International*
Welch, Robert H. — *Heidrick & Struggles, Inc.*
Welch, Sarah — *Korn/Ferry International*
Weller, Paul S. — *Mark Stanley & Company*
Wellman, Michael — *Korn/Ferry International*
Wendorff, Tom — *Kenzer Corp.*
Wentworth, John — *The Wentworth Company, Inc.*
Wentz, Terry M. — *Management Recruiters International, Inc.*
Werner, Bonnie — *H.M. Long International, Ltd.*
Wert, Marty — *Parfitt Recruiting and Consulting*
Wertel, Ronald E. — *Gordon Wahls Company*
Wertheim, M. Chris — *Witt/Kieffer, Ford, Hadelman & Lloyd*
Wesley, Terry R. — *Management Recruiters International, Inc.*
Wessel, Michael J. — *Spectra International Inc.*
West, Nancy — *Health Care Dimensions*
Westberry, David M. — *Lamalie Amrop International*

Westerfield, Putney — *Boyden*
Wexler, Rona — *Ariel Recruitment Associates*
Whalen, Kathleen — *The Nielsen Healthcare Group*
Whaley, Robert B. — *TASA International*
Wheel, Eric — *Management Recruiters International, Inc.*
Wheeler, Mary T. — *Lamalie Amrop International*
Whitaker, Charles — *Evie Kreisler & Associates, Inc.*
Whitcomb, Nancy C. — *Educational Management Network*
White, Jonathan — *Spencer Stuart*
White, Jonathan O. — *The Badger Group*
White, Patricia D. — *MSI International*
White, Richard B. — *Spencer Stuart*
White, William C. — *Venture Resources Inc.*
Whiting, Anthony — *Johnson Smith & Knisely Accord*
Whitley, Sue Ann — *Roberts Ryan and Bentley*
Whitley, Tom H. — *Management Recruiters International, Inc.*
Whittall, Barbara — *Heidrick & Struggles, Inc.*
Wicklund, Grant — *Heidrick & Struggles, Inc.*
Wieder, Thomas A. — *Management Recruiters International, Inc.*
Wieland, Patrick — *Bradford & Galt, Inc.*
Wier, Daniel — *Horton International*
Wierichs, Jeffrey C. — *TASA International*
Wilbanks, George R. — *Russell Reynolds Associates, Inc.*
Wilcox, Jan — *Kenzer Corp.*
Wilder, Barry — *Rhodes Associates*
Wilder, Richard B. — *Columbia Consulting Group*
Wile, Harold — *Kenzer Corp.*
Wilkie, Glenn — *Korn/Ferry International*
Wilkinson, Barbara — *Beall & Company, Inc.*
Wilkinson, William R. — *Wilkinson & Ives*
Willcox, David R. — *Senior Careers Executive Search*
Williams, Alexander H. — *Witt/Kieffer, Ford, Hadelman & Lloyd*
Williams, Barbara — *Kenzer Corp.*
Williams, Brad — *Winter, Wyman & Company*
Williams, Ellen — *Korn/Ferry International*
Williams, Gary L. — *Barnes Development Group, LLC*
Williams, Harry D. — *Jacobson Associates*
Williams, Kenneth C. — *Management Recruiters International, Inc.*
Williams, Larry — *Management Recruiters International, Inc.*
Williams, Laura — *Paul Ray Berndtson*
Williams, Laurelle N. — *MSI International*
Williams, Lis — *Executive Options, Ltd.*
Williams, Lynn — *Korn/Ferry International*
Williams, Nicole — *Richard, Wayne and Roberts*
Williams, Richard — *Blackshaw, Olmstead & Lynch*
Williams, Roger K. — *Williams, Roth & Krueger Inc.*
Williams, Scott D. — *Heidrick & Struggles, Inc.*
Williams, Walter E. — *Canny, Bowen Inc.*
Williamson, Frank — *Management Recruiters International, Inc.*
Willis, William H. — *William Willis Worldwide Inc.*
Willner, Nannette — *S.R. Wolman Associates, Inc.*
Wilson, Derrick — *Thornton Resources*
Wilson, Helen S. — *The Diversified Search Companies*
Wilson, John C. — *Russell Reynolds Associates, Inc.*
Wilson, Patricia L. — *Leon A. Farley Associates*
Wilson, Robert J. — *Coleman Lew & Associates, Inc.*
Wilson, Thomas H. — *Lamalie Amrop International*
Wimer, Thomas W. — *DHR International, Inc.*
Windle, Mary — *Evie Kreisler & Associates, Inc.*
Winfrey, James — *Korn/Ferry International*
Winitz, Joel — *GSW Consulting Group, Inc.*
Winitz, Marla — *GSW Consulting Group, Inc.*
Winograd, Glenn — *Criterion Executive Search, Inc.*
Winslow, Lawrence J. — *DHR International, Inc.*
Winston, Dale — *Battalia Winston International*
Winter, Peter — *Catalyx Group*
Winter, Robert — *The Whitney Group*
Wirtshafter, Linda — *Grant Cooper and Associates*
Wise, Anne — *U.S. Envirosearch*
Wise, J. Herbert — *Sandhurst Associates*
Wise, Ronald L. — *Management Recruiters International, Inc.*
Wiseman, Bonnie — *Witt/Kieffer, Ford, Hadelman & Lloyd*
Witte, David L. — *Ward Howell International, Inc.*
Wittenberg, Laura L. — *Boyden*
Wold, Ted W. — *Hyde Danforth Wold & Co.*
Wolf, Stephen M. — *Byron Leonard International, Inc.*
Wolfe, David — *Kenzer Corp.*
Wolfram, David A. — *EFL Associates*
Wollman, Harry — *Howard Fischer Associates, Inc.*
Wolman, Stephen R. — *S.R. Wolman Associates, Inc.*
Wolters, Tony A. — *Management Recruiters International, Inc.*
Womack, Joseph — *The Bankers Group*
Wood, Allison — *Korn/Ferry International*
Wood, John S. — *Egon Zehnder International Inc.*
Wood, Martin F. — *Lamalie Amrop International*
Wood, Milton M. — *M. Wood Company*
Wood, Steven N. — *DHR International, Inc.*
Woodruff, Mark S. — *Management Recruiters International, Inc.*

Woodrum, Robert L. — Korn/Ferry International
Wooller, Edmund A.M. — Windsor International
Woollett, James — Rusher, Loscavio & LoPresto
Worth, Janet M. — Witt/Kieffer, Ford, Hadelman & Lloyd
Wozniak, Bernard D. — Sanford Rose Associates
Wozniak, Jane K. — Sanford Rose Associates
Wright, Anne B. — Management Recruiters International, Inc.
Wright, Charles D. — Goodrich & Sherwood Associates, Inc.
Wright, Doug — Management Recruiters International, Inc.
Wright, Leslie — The Stevenson Group of New Jersey
Wright, Linus — Paul Ray Berndtson
Wrynn, Robert F. — MSI International
Wyatt, James — Wyatt & Jaffe
Wyatt, Janice — Korn/Ferry International
Wynkoop, Mary — Tyler & Company
Wyser-Pratte, Anne — Heidrick & Struggles, Inc.
Yamada, Steven — Korn/Ferry International
Yamvaketis, Stephen — John Kurosky & Associates
Yang, George — Technical Connections Inc.
Yilmaz, Muriel — Dinte Resources, Incorporated
Yoon, Kyung — Heidrick & Struggles, Inc.
Young, Alexander — Messett Associates, Inc.
Young, Arthur L. — Management Recruiters International, Inc.
Young, Charles E. — Flowers & Associates
Young, Laurie — Part Time Resources, Inc.
Young, Mark — D.E. Foster Partners Inc.
Young, Mimi — Educational Management Network
Young, Nick — Spencer Stuart
Young, Susan M. — Management Recruiters International, Inc.
Young, Van G. — Heidrick & Struggles, Inc.
Young, Wayne T. — Management Recruiters International, Inc.
Youngs, Donald L. — Youngs & Company
Yowe, Mark — Heidrick & Struggles, Inc.
Yturbe, Rafael — Russell Reynolds Associates, Inc.
Zaffrann, Craig S. — P.J. Murphy & Associates, Inc.
Zahradka, James F. — P.J. Murphy & Associates, Inc.
Zaleta, Andrew R. — A.T. Kearney, Inc.
Zander, Barry W. — MSI International
Zanotti, Les V. — Management Recruiters International, Inc.
Zaring, David J. — Management Recruiters International, Inc.
Zarkin, Norman — Rhodes Associates
Zaslav, Debra M. — Telford, Adams & Alexander/Telford & Co., Inc.
Zavala, Lorenzo — Russell Reynolds Associates, Inc.
Zawicki, David — Management Recruiters International, Inc.
Zay, Thomas C. — Boyden/Zay & Company
Zay, Thomas C. — Boyden/Zay & Company
Zellner, Paul A. — Paul Ray Berndtson
Zenzer, Anne — Witt/Kieffer, Ford, Hadelman & Lloyd
Zerkle, John P. — Management Recruiters International, Inc.
Zerkle, John P. — Management Recruiters International, Inc.
Zetter, Roger — Hunt Ltd.
Zetto, Kathryn — Seco & Zetto Associates, Inc.
Zila, Laurie M. — Princeton Entrepreneurial Resources
Zilliacus, Patrick W. — Larsen, Zilliacus & Associates, Inc.
Ziluck, Scott W. — Management Recruiters International, Inc.
Zimmerman, Joan C. — G.Z. Stephens Inc.
Zinn, Donald — Bishop Partners
Zivic, Janis M. — Spencer Stuart
Zona, Henry F. — Zona & Associates, Inc.
Zoppo, Dorathea — Bill Hahn Group, Inc.
Zucchiatti, Elizabeth — The Caldwell Partners Amrop International
Zwiff, Jeffrey G. — Johnson Smith & Knisely Accord

## 2. Administration

Abell, Vincent W. — MSI International
Abruzzo, James — A.T. Kearney, Inc.
Adams, Michael — CG & Associates
Adkisson, Billy D. — James Russell, Inc.
Akin, J.R. — J.R. Akin & Company Inc.
Albers, Joan — Carver Search Consultants
Alden, Brian R. — MSI International
Alexander, John T. — Telford, Adams & Alexander/Human
    Resource Services
Allard, Susan — Allard Associates
Allen, David A. — Intech Summit Group, Inc.
Allgire, Mary L. — Kenzer Corp.
Altreuter, Rose — The ALTCO Group
Ambler, Peter W. — Peter W. Ambler Company
Anderson, Richard — Grant Cooper and Associates
Andrews, J. Douglas — Clarey & Andrews, Inc.
Andrews, Laura L. — Stricker & Zagor
Antil, Pamela W. — Norman Roberts & Associates, Inc.
Apostle, George — Search Dynamics, Inc.
Aquavella, Charles P. — CPA & Associates
Aronin, Michael — Fisher-Todd Associates
Arseneault, Daniel S. — MSI International
Ascher, Susan P. — The Ascher Group
Ashton, Edward J. — E.J. Ashton & Associates, Ltd.

Aston, Kathy — Marra Peters & Partners
Attell, Harold — A.E. Feldman Associates
Bachmeier, Kevin — Agra Placements International Ltd.
Bagg, Mary — Keith Bagg & Associates Inc.
Bailey, William A. — TNS Partners, Inc.
Baker, Gary M. — Cochran, Cochran & Yale, Inc.
Baker-Greene, Edward — Isaacson, Miller
Baran, Helena — Michael J. Cavanagh and Associates
Barber, Toni L. — MSI International
Barlow, Ken H. — The Cherbonnier Group, Inc.
Barnes, Richard E. — Barnes Development Group, LLC
Barnes, Roanne L. — Barnes Development Group, LLC
Baron, Jon C. — MSI International
Barowsky, Diane M. — Lamalie Amrop International
Barr, Ronald — Search West, Inc.
Barthold, James A. — McNichol Associates
Barton, Gary R. — Barton Raben, Inc.
Bason, Maurice L. — Bason Associates Inc.
Bass, Nate — Jacobson Associates
Bates, Nina — Allard Associates
Bauman, Martin H. — Martin H. Bauman Associates, Inc.
Bearman, Linda — Grant Cooper and Associates
Beaudin, Elizabeth C. — Callan Associates, Ltd.
Behringer, Neail — Neail Behringer Consultants
Belford, Paul — JDG Associates, Ltd.
Bellshaw, David — Isaacson, Miller
Bennett, Delora — Genesis Personnel Service, Inc.
Bennett, Richard T. — Isaacson, Miller
Benson, Kate — Rene Plessner Associates, Inc.
Bergen, Anthony M. — CFO Associates, Inc.
Berger, Emanuel — Isaacson, Miller
Berman, Kenneth D. — MSI International
Bertoux, Michael P. — Wilcox, Bertoux & Miller
Besen, Douglas — Besen Associates Inc.
Billington, Brian — Billington & Associates
Bittman, Beth M. — Norman Roberts & Associates, Inc.
Black, Douglas E. — MSI International
Bladon, Andrew — Don Richard Associates of Tampa, Inc.
Bluhm, Claudia — Schweichler Associates, Inc.
Bogard, Nicholas C. — The Onstott Group, Inc.
Bohn, Steve J. — MSI International
Bonifield, Len — Bonifield Associates
Book, Cheryl — Aureus Group
Borland, James — Goodrich & Sherwood Associates, Inc.
Bormann, Cindy Ann — MSI International
Bostic, James E. — Phillips Resource Group
Bovee, Camille — Search West, Inc.
Brackin, James B. — Brackin & Sayers Associates
Brandjes, Michael J. — Brandjes Associates
Brieger, Steve — Thorne, Brieger Associates Inc.
Bright, Timothy — MSI International
Brinson, Robert — MSI International
Brodie, Ricki R. — MSI International
Brown, Charlene N. — Accent on Achievement, Inc.
Brown, Larry C. — Horton International
Brown, Lawrence Anthony — MSI International
Brown, Michael R. — MSI International
Brudno, Robert J. — Savoy Partners, Ltd.
Bryza, Robert M. — Robert Lowell International
Buck, Charles — Charles Buck & Associates
Bullock, Conni — Earley Kielty and Associates, Inc.
Burchill, Barb — BGB Associates
Burden, Gene — The Cherbonnier Group, Inc.
Burke, John — The Experts
Burnett, Rebecca J. — MSI International
Burns, Alan — The Enns Partners Inc.
Burns, Terence N. — D.E. Foster Partners Inc.
Bush, Martha A. — MSI International
Busterna, Charles — The KPA Group
Caldwell, William R. — Pearson, Caldwell & Farnsworth, Inc.
Callan, Robert M. — Callan Associates, Ltd.
Callihan, Diana L. — Search Northwest Associates
Campbell, Robert Scott — Wellington Management Group
Cappe, Richard R. — Roberts Ryan and Bentley
Cargo, Catherine — MSI International
Carpenter, Harold G. — MSI International
Carter, Christine C. — Health Care Dimensions
Casal, Daniel G. — Bonifield Associates
Casey, Jean — Peter W. Ambler Company
Cass, Kathryn H. — Don Richard Associates of Tidewater, Inc.
Cassie, Ronald L. — The Cassie Group
Cattanach, Bruce B. — Horton International
Causey, Andrea C. — MSI International
Cavanagh, Michael J. — Michael J. Cavanagh and Associates
Cesafsky, Barry R. — Lamalie Amrop International
Chandler, Robert C. — Ward Howell International, Inc.
Chappell, Peter — The Bankers Group
Chatterjie, Alok — MSI International

Chavous, C. Crawford — *Phillips Resource Group*
Cherbonnier, L. Michael — *The Cherbonnier Group, Inc.*
Chorman, Marilyn A. — *Hite Executive Search*
Chua, Jackie — *Keith Bagg & Associates Inc.*
Cizek, John T. — *Cizek Associates, Inc.*
Cizek, Marti J. — *Cizek Associates, Inc.*
Clarey, Jack R. — *Clarey & Andrews, Inc.*
Clauhsen, Elizabeth A. — *Savoy Partners, Ltd.*
Clemens, William B. — *Norman Broadbent International, Inc.*
Clemens, William B. — *Norman Broadbent International, Inc.*
Clovis, James R. — *Handy HRM Corp.*
Coffman, Brian — *Kossuth & Associates, Inc.*
Cohen, Michael R. — *Intech Summit Group, Inc.*
Cohen, Robert C. — *Intech Summit Group, Inc.*
Colasanto, Frank M. — *W.R. Rosato & Associates, Inc.*
Cole, Elizabeth — *MSI International*
Colling, Douglas — *KPMG Management Consulting*
Collins, Mollie P. — *Belvedere Partners*
Colucci, Bart A. — *Colucci, Blendow and Johnson, Inc.*
Cona, Joseph A. — *Cona Personnel Search*
Connelly, Kevin M. — *Spencer Stuart*
Conway, William P. — *Phillips Resource Group*
Cooke, Jeffrey R. — *Jonas, Walters & Assoc., Inc.*
Corrigan, Gerald F. — *The Corrigan Group*
Corso, Glen S. — *Chartwell Partners International, Inc.*
Costa, Cynthia A. — *MSI International*
Costick, Kathryn J. — *John Sibbald Associates, Inc.*
Coston, Bruce G. — *MSI International*
Cottingham, R.L. — *Marvin L. Silcott & Associates, Inc.*
Cox, James O. — *MSI International*
Cox, William — *E.J. Ashton & Associates, Ltd.*
Cramer, Paul J. — *C/R Associates*
Crath, Paul F. — *Price Waterhouse*
Creger, Elizabeth — *Search West, Inc.*
Crowell, Elizabeth — *H.M. Long International, Ltd.*
Crownover, Kathryn L. — *MSI International*
Crystal, Jonathan A. — *Spencer Stuart*
Cunningham, Robert Y. — *Goodrich & Sherwood Associates, Inc.*
Currie, Lawrence S. — *MSI International*
Dalton, David R. — *MSI International*
Daniels, Alfred — *Alfred Daniels & Associates*
Dannenberg, Richard A. — *Roberts Ryan and Bentley*
Davis, Bernel — *MSI International*
Davis, G. Gordon — *Davis & Company*
Davis, Robert — *CG & Associates*
Dawson, Joe — *S.C. International, Ltd.*
de Cholnoky, Andrea — *Spencer Stuart*
Debrueys, Lee G. — *MSI International*
DeCorrevont, James — *DeCorrevont & Associates*
DeCorrevont, James — *DeCorrevont & Associates*
Deering, Joseph — *U.S. Envirosearch*
DeGioia, Joseph — *JDG Associates, Ltd.*
DeHart, Donna — *Tower Consultants, Ltd.*
Del Pino, William — *National Search, Inc.*
Del'Ange, Gabrielle N. — *MSI International*
Delaney, Patrick J. — *Sensible Solutions, Inc.*
Della Monica, Vincent — *Search West, Inc.*
Desmond, Dennis — *Beall & Company, Inc.*
deVry, Kimberly A. — *Tower Consultants, Ltd.*
Dietz, David S. — *MSI International*
Dingman, Bruce — *Robert W. Dingman Company, Inc.*
Dingman, Robert W. — *Robert W. Dingman Company, Inc.*
Dinwiddie, Jill — *Belvedere Partners*
Diskin, Rochelle — *Search West, Inc.*
Divine, Robert S. — *O'Shea, Divine & Company, Inc.*
Doele, Donald C. — *Goodrich & Sherwood Associates, Inc.*
Doman, Matthew — *S.C. International, Ltd.*
Doody, Michael F. — *Witt/Kieffer, Ford, Hadelman & Lloyd*
Doukas, Jon A. — *Professional Bank Services, Inc. D/B/A Executive Search, Inc.*
Dow, Lori — *Davidson, Laird & Associates*
Dreifus, Donald — *Search West, Inc.*
Drury, James J. — *Spencer Stuart*
Dunman, Betsy L. — *Crawford & Crofford*
Earle, Paul W. — *Spencer Stuart*
Eastham, Marvene M. — *Witt/Kieffer, Ford, Hadelman & Lloyd*
Eatmon, Michael — *U.S. Envirosearch*
Eden, Brooks D. — *Eden & Associates, Inc.*
Eden, Dianne — *Steeple Associates*
Eden, Earl M. — *Eden & Associates, Inc.*
Edwards, Dorothy — *MSI International*
Edwards, Verba L. — *Wing Tips & Pumps, Inc.*
Eggena, Roger — *Phillips Resource Group*
Ehrgott, Elizabeth — *The Ascher Group*
Ehrhart, Jennifer — *ADOW's Executeam*
Einsele, Neil — *Agra Placements International Ltd.*
Emmott, Carol B. — *Spencer Stuart*
Enns, George — *The Enns Partners Inc.*

Erickson, Elaine — *Kenzer Corp.*
Erwin, Lee — *Agra Placements International Ltd.*
Eustis, Lucy R. — *MSI International*
Faber, Jill — *A.T. Kearney, Inc.*
Fancher, Robert L. — *Bason Associates Inc.*
Farley, Antoinette L. — *Witt/Kieffer, Ford, Hadelman & Lloyd*
Farnsworth, John A. — *Pearson, Caldwell & Farnsworth, Inc.*
Farrow, Jerry M. — *McCormack & Farrow*
Federman, Jack R. — *W.R. Rosato & Associates, Inc.*
Feldman, Abe — *A.E. Feldman Associates*
Ferneborg, Jay W. — *Ferneborg & Associates, Inc.*
Ferneborg, John R. — *Ferneborg & Associates, Inc.*
Ferrara, David M. — *Intech Summit Group, Inc.*
Fixler, Eugene — *Ariel Recruitment Associates*
Flanagan, Robert M. — *Robert M. Flanagan & Associates, Ltd.*
Flannery, Peter — *Jonas, Walters & Assoc., Inc.*
Fleming, Marco — *MSI International*
Fletcher, Karen — *Don Richard Associates of Tidewater, Inc.*
Flora, Dodi — *Crawford & Crofford*
Flynn, Jack — *Executive Search Consultants Corporation*
Follmer, Gary — *Agra Placements International Ltd.*
Fonfa, Ann — *S.R. Wolman Associates, Inc.*
Ford, J. Daniel — *Witt/Kieffer, Ford, Hadelman & Lloyd*
Foreman, David C. — *Koontz, Jeffries & Associates, Inc.*
Forman, Donald R. — *Stanton Chase International*
Fowler, Jim — *First Search America, Inc.*
Fox, Lucie — *Allard Associates*
Frank, Valerie S. — *Norman Roberts & Associates, Inc.*
Fredericks, Ward A. — *Mixtec Group*
French, William G. — *Preng & Associates, Inc.*
Frock, Suzanne D. — *Brandjes Associates*
Gaffney, Denise O'Grady — *Isaacson, Miller*
Galante, Suzanne M. — *Vlcek & Company, Inc.*
Galinski, Paul — *E.J. Ashton & Associates, Ltd.*
Gallagher, Marilyn — *Hogan Acquisitions*
Gallagher, Terence M. — *Battalia Winston International*
Galvani, Frank J. — *MSI International*
Gardner, Catherine — *Aureus Group*
Garrett, Donald L. — *Garrett Associates Inc.*
Garrett, Linda M. — *Garrett Associates Inc.*
Geiger, Jan — *Wilcox, Bertoux & Miller*
George, Delores F. — *Delores F. George Human Resource Management & Consulting Industry*
Gerber, Mark J. — *Wellington Management Group*
Gerevas, Ronald E. — *Spencer Stuart*
Gerevas, Ronald E. — *Spencer Stuart*
Gettys, James R. — *International Staffing Consultants, Inc.*
Giacalone, Louis — *Allard Associates*
Gibbs, John S. — *Spencer Stuart*
Gilbert, Robert — *U.S. Envirosearch*
Gill, Susan — *Plummer & Associates, Inc.*
Gladstone, Martin J. — *MSI International*
Glancey, Thomas F. — *Gordon Wahls Company*
Gold, Stacey — *Earley Kielty and Associates, Inc.*
Goldenberg, Sheryl — *Neail Behringer Consultants*
Goldenberg, Susan — *Grant Cooper and Associates*
Gooch, Randy — *Richard, Wayne and Roberts*
Goodman, Dawn M. — *Bason Associates Inc.*
Goodman, Julie — *Search West, Inc.*
Goodridge, Benjamin — *S.C. International, Ltd.*
Gordon, Gerald L. — *E.G. Jones Associates, Ltd.*
Gordon, Teri — *Don Richard Associates of Washington, D.C., Inc.*
Gostyla, Rick — *Spencer Stuart*
Gourlay, Debra — *Rene Plessner Associates, Inc.*
Grady, James — *Search West, Inc.*
Graver, Merialee — *Accounting Personnel Consultants*
Gray, Annie — *Annie Gray Associates, Inc./The Executive Search Firm*
Gray, David — *CG & Associates*
Gray, Mark — *Executive Referral Services, Inc.*
Greebe, Neil — *Flowers & Associates*
Green, Jane — *Phillips Resource Group*
Groom, Charles C. — *CG & Associates*
Groover, David — *MSI International*
Gulley, Marylyn — *MSI International*
Haas, Margaret P. — *Haas International, Inc.*
Hadelman, Jordan M. — *Witt/Kieffer, Ford, Hadelman & Lloyd*
Hallock, Peter B. — *Goodrich & Sherwood Associates, Inc.*
Hancock, Deborah L. — *Morgan Hunter Corp.*
Hanson, Carrie — *U.S. Envirosearch*
Hanson, Grant M. — *Goodrich & Sherwood Associates, Inc.*
Harbert, David O. — *Sweeney Harbert & Mummert, Inc.*
Harris, Ethel S. — *Don Richard Associates of Charlotte*
Harrison, Priscilla — *Phillips Resource Group*
Hart, Robert T. — *D.E. Foster Partners Inc.*
Harvey, Jill — *MSI International*
Harvey, Richard — *Price Waterhouse*
Hay, William E. — *William E. Hay & Company*

McRae, O. Jon — *Jon McRae & Associates, Inc.*
Meagher, Patricia G. — *Spencer Stuart*
Meier, J. Dale — *Grant Cooper and Associates*
Messett, William J. — *Messett Associates, Inc.*
Mestepey, John — *A.T. Kearney, Inc.*
Meyer, Stacey — *Gary Kaplan & Associates*
Meyer, William — *Agra Placements International Ltd.*
Miesemer, Arthur C. — *MSI International*
Miles, Kenneth T. — *MSI International*
Miller, Arnie — *Isaacson, Miller*
Miller, Benjamin J. — *MSI International*
Miller, Diane D. — *Wilcox, Bertoux & Miller*
Miller, George N. — *Hite Executive Search*
Miller, Laura — *Accounting Personnel Consultants*
Miller, Roy — *The Enns Partners Inc.*
Millonzi, Joel C. — *Johnson Smith & Knisely Accord*
Milton, Suzanne — *Marra Peters & Partners*
Mockler, Nadine — *Part Time Resources, Inc.*
Moerbe, Ed H. — *Stanton Chase International*
Moore, Denise — *Jonas, Walters & Assoc., Inc.*
Moore, Lemuel R. — *MSI International*
Moore, Mark — *Wheeler, Moore & Elam Co.*
Moore, Michael — *Agra Placements International Ltd.*
Moran, Gail — *Comprehensive Search*
Moran, Robert — *A.T. Kearney, Inc.*
Morgan, Gary — *National Search, Inc.*
Morrison, Janis L. — *Garrett Associates Inc.*
Moseley, Monroe — *Isaacson, Miller*
Muendel, H. Edward –- *Stanton Chase International*
Mulligan, Robert P. — *William Willis Worldwide Inc.*
Murin, Rose Mary — *U.S. Envirosearch*
Murphy, Cornelius J. — *Goodrich & Sherwood Associates, Inc.*
Murphy, Patrick J. — *P.J. Murphy & Associates, Inc.*
Murphy, Timothy D. — *MSI International*
Nagler, Leon G. — *Nagler, Robins & Poe, Inc.*
Nathanson, Barry F. — *Barry Nathanson Associates*
Neckanoff, Sharon — *Search West, Inc.*
Neher, Robert L. — *Intech Summit Group, Inc.*
Neri, Gene — *S.C. International, Ltd.*
Neuberth, Jeffrey G. — *Canny, Bowen Inc.*
Newbold, Michael — *Agra Placements International Ltd.*
Nielsen, Sue — *Ells Personnel System Inc.*
Nold, Robert — *Roberson and Company*
Nordland, Martin N. — *Horton International*
Normann, Amy — *Robert M. Flanagan & Associates, Ltd.*
Norsell, Paul E. — *Paul Norsell & Associates, Inc.*
Nye, David S. — *Blake, Hansen & Nye, Limited*
O'Donnell, James H. — *MSI International*
O'Hara, Daniel M. — *Lynch Miller Moore Partners, Inc.*
O'Toole, Dennis P. — *Dennis P. O'Toole & Associates Inc.*
Oddo, Judith — *Accounting Personnel Consultants*
Ogdon, Thomas H. — *The Ogdon Partnership*
Ohman, Gregory L. — *Pearson, Caldwell & Farnsworth, Inc.*
Oliver, Phoebe — *Seiden Krieger Associates, Inc.*
Oller, Jose E. — *Ward Howell International, Inc.*
Ott, George W. — *Ott & Hansen, Inc.*
Pacini, Lauren R. — *Hite Executive Search*
Page, Linda –- *Jonas, Walters & Assoc., Inc.*
Palma, Frank R. — *Goodrich & Sherwood Associates, Inc.*
Palmer, Carlton A. — *Beall & Company, Inc.*
Palmer, Melissa — *Don Richard Associates of Tampa, Inc.*
Papciak, Dennis J. — *Accounting Personnel Associates, Inc.*
Papciak, Dennis J. — *Temporary Accounting Personnel*
Pappas, Jim — *Search Dynamics, Inc.*
Pappas, Timothy C. — *Jonas, Walters & Assoc., Inc.*
Parr, James A. — *KPMG Management Consulting*
Patence, David W. — *Handy HRM Corp.*
Patton, Mitchell — *Patton/Perry Associates, Inc.*
Pearson, John R. — *Pearson, Caldwell & Farnsworth, Inc.*
Peeney, James D. — *Peeney Associates*
Pelisson, Charles — *Marra Peters & Partners*
Perry, Wayne B. — *Bruce Massey & Partners Inc.*
Persky, Barry — *Barry Persky & Company, Inc.*
Peters, James N. — *TNS Partners, Inc.*
Pettway, Samuel H. — *Spencer Stuart*
Pfeiffer, Irene — *Price Waterhouse*
Phillips, Donald L. — *O'Shea, Divine & Company, Inc.*
Pickering, Dale — *Agri-Tech Personnel, Inc.*
Pickford, Stephen T. — *The Corporate Staff, Inc.*
Pierson, Edward J. — *Johnson Smith & Knisely Accord*
Pinkman, Karen N. — *Skott/Edwards Consultants, Inc.*
Pitcher, Brian D. — *Skott/Edwards Consultants, Inc.*
Plessner, Rene — *Rene Plessner Associates, Inc.*
Poirier, Roland — *Poirier, Hoevel & Co.*
Porter, Albert — *The Experts*
Posner, Gary J. — *Educational Management Network*
Potenza, Gregory — *Mixtec Group*
Potter, Douglas C. — *Stanton Chase International*

Prados, Daniel — *Accounting Personnel Consultants*
Prince, Marilyn L. — *Higdon Prince Inc.*
Proct, Nina — *Martin H. Bauman Associates, Inc.*
Pugh, Judith Geist — *InterimManagement Solutions, Inc.*
Pugrant, Mark A. — *Grant/Morgan Associates, Inc.*
Quick, Roger A. — *Norman Broadbent International, Inc.*
Rabinowitz, Peter A. — *P.A.R. Associates Inc.*
Radawicz, Angela — *Mixtec Group*
Radford-Oster, Deborah — *Morgan Hunter Corp.*
Rauch, Carl W. — *Physicians Search, Inc.*
Rauch, Cliff — *Physicians Search, Inc.*
Ray, Marianne C. — *Callan Associates, Ltd.*
Redding, Denise — *The Douglas Reiter Company, Inc.*
Redler, Rhonda — *National Search, Inc.*
Redwood, Guy W. — *Bruce Massey & Partners Inc.*
Reece, Christopher S. — *Reece & Mruk Partners*
Regan, Thomas J. — *Tower Consultants, Ltd.*
Reiss, Matt — *National Search, Inc.*
Reiter, Douglas — *The Douglas Reiter Company, Inc.*
Renick, Cynthia L. — *Morgan Hunter Corp.*
Reticker, Peter — *MSI International*
Reyman, Susan — *S. Reyman & Associates Ltd.*
Reynolds, Gregory P. — *Roberts Ryan and Bentley*
Rice, Douglas — *Agra Placements International Ltd.*
Rice, Raymond D. — *Logue & Rice Inc.*
Rich, Lyttleton — *Sockwell & Associates*
Rieger, Louis J. — *Spencer Stuart*
Rimmele, Michael — *The Bankers Group*
Rinker, Jim — *Southwestern Professional Services*
Roberts, Kenneth — *The Rubicon Group*
Roberts, Mitch — *A.E. Feldman Associates*
Roberts, Nick P. — *Spectrum Search Associates, Inc.*
Roberts, Norman C. — *Norman Roberts & Associates, Inc.*
Roberts, Raymond R. — *MSI International*
Robinson, Bruce — *Bruce Robinson Associates*
Robison, John H. — *Robison & Associates*
Rodgers, John — *Agra Placements International Ltd.*
Rodgers, Kathi — *St. Lawrence International, Inc.*
Rodney, Brett — *MSI International*
Rollins, Scott — *S.C. International, Ltd.*
Romaine, Stanley J. — *Mixtec Group*
Romanchek, Walter R. — *Wellington Management Group*
Rosato, William R. — *W.R. Rosato & Associates, Inc.*
Rosenthal, Charles — *National Search, Inc.*
Ross, William J. — *Flowers & Associates*
Rossi, Silvio — *Keith Bagg & Associates*
Roth, Robert J. — *Williams, Roth & Krueger Inc.*
Rothfeld, Robert — *A.E. Feldman Associates*
Rowells, Michael — *MSI International*
Rudolph, Kenneth — *Kossuth & Associates, Inc.*
Rusher, William H. — *Rusher, Loscavio & LoPresto*
Russell, Richard A. — *Executive Search Consultants Corporation*
Russell, Robin E. — *Kenzer Corp.*
Russell, Susan Anne — *Executive Search Consultants Corporation*
Rustad, Binth — *Educational Management Network*
Ryan, Lee — *Ryan, Miller & Associates Inc.*
Sacerdote, John — *Raymond Karsan Associates*
Salvagno, Michael J. — *The Cambridge Group Ltd*
Sapperstein, Jerry S. — *CFO Associates, Inc.*
Sathe, Mark A. — *Sathe & Associates, Inc.*
Sayers, Bruce D. — *Brackin & Sayers Associates*
Schachter, Laura J. — *Professional Placement Associates, Inc.*
Scharett, Carol — *St. Lawrence International, Inc.*
Schedra, Sharon — *Earley Kielty and Associates, Inc.*
Schiavone, Mary Rose — *Canny, Bowen Inc.*
Schneider, Margo — *Search West, Inc.*
Schneider, Perry — *Agra Placements International Ltd.*
Schwam, Carol — *A.E. Feldman Associates*
Schwartz, Carole — *A.T. Kearney, Inc.*
Segal, Eric B. — *Kenzer Corp.*
Seiden, Steven A. — *Seiden Krieger Associates, Inc.*
Seitz, Charles J. — *Neail Behringer Consultants*
Sekera, Roger I. — *A.T. Kearney, Inc.*
Selko, Philip W. — *Hogan Acquisitions*
Sennello, Gendra — *National Search, Inc.*
Serwat, Leonard A. — *Spencer Stuart*
Sevilla, Claudio A. — *Crawford & Crofford*
Shattuck, Merrill B. — *M.B. Shattuck and Associates, Inc.*
Shelton, Sandra — *National Search, Inc.*
Shenfield, Peter — *Baker, Harris & Partners Limited*
Shepard, Michael J. — *MSI International*
Shervey, Brent C. — *O'Callaghan Honey/Paul Ray Berndtson, Inc.*
Sherwood, Andrew — *Goodrich & Sherwood Associates, Inc.*
Shipherd, John T. — *The Cassie Group*
Shoemaker, Larry C. — *Shoemaker & Associates*
Shulman, Melvin — *McFeely Wackerle Shulman*
Silver, Lee A. — *L.A. Silver Associates, Inc.*
Simmons, Sandra K. — *MSI International*

## 3. Engineering

Arseneault, Daniel S. — *MSI International*
Ashton, Barbara L. — *Ashton Computer Professionals Inc.*
Asquith, Peter S. — *Ames Personnel Consultants, Inc.*
Aston, Kathy — *Marra Peters & Partners*
Attell, Harold — *A.E. Feldman Associates*
Austin, Jessica L. — *D.S.A. - Dixie Search Associates*
Bachmeier, Kevin — *Agra Placements International Ltd.*
Badger, Fred H. — *The Badger Group*
Baer, Kenneth — *Source  Services Corporation*
Bagg, Keith — *Keith Bagg & Associates Inc.*
Baglio, Robert — *Source  Services Corporation*
Baier, Rebecca — *Source  Services Corporation*
Bailey, William A. — *TNS Partners, Inc.*
Baird, David W. — *D.W. Baird & Associates*
Baird, John — *Professional Search Consultants*
Baker, Gerry — *Baker, Harris & Partners Limited*
Baker, Judith — *Search Consultants International, Inc.*
Baker, S. Joseph — *Search Consultants International, Inc.*
Bakken, Mark — *Source  Services Corporation*
Balch, Randy — *CPS Inc.*
Balchumas, Charles — *Source  Services Corporation*
Balter, Sidney — *Source  Services Corporation*
Baltin, Carrie — *Search West, Inc.*
Banko, Scott — *Source  Services Corporation*
Baran, Helena — *Michael J. Cavanagh and Associates*
Baranowski, Peter — *Source  Services Corporation*
Barber, Toni L. — *MSI International*
Barbosa, Franklin J. — *Boyden*
Barlow, Ken H. — *The Cherbonnier Group, Inc.*
Barnaby, Richard — *Source  Services Corporation*
Barnes, Richard E. — *Barnes Development Group, LLC*
Barnes, Roanne L. — *Barnes Development Group, LLC*
Barnum, Toni M. — *Stone Murphy & Olson*
Baron, Jon C. — *MSI International*
Baron, Len — *Industrial Recruiters Associates, Inc.*
Barone, Marialice — *Barone-O'Hara Associates*
Barr, Ronald — *Search West, Inc.*
Bartels, Fredrick — *Source  Services Corporation*
Bartfield, Philip — *Source  Services Corporation*
Barthold, James A. — *McNichol Associates*
Bartholdi, Ted — *Bartholdi & Company, Inc.*
Bartholdi, Theodore G. — *Bartholdi & Company, Inc.*
Barton, James — *Source  Services Corporation*
Bason, Maurice L. — *Bason Associates Inc.*
Batte, Carol — *Source  Services Corporation*
Bauman, Martin H. — *Martin H. Bauman Associates, Inc.*
Beal, Richard D. — *A.T. Kearney, Inc.*
Bearman, Linda — *Grant Cooper and Associates*
Beaudin, Elizabeth C. — *Callan Associates, Ltd.*
Beaver, Bentley H. — *The Onstott Group, Inc.*
Beaver, Robert — *Source  Services Corporation*
Belden, Jeannette — *Source  Services Corporation*
Benjamin, Maurita — *Source  Services Corporation*
Bennett, Delora — *Genesis Personnel Service, Inc.*
Bennett, Jo — *Battalia Winston International*
Bennett, Joan — *Adams & Associates International*
Benson, Edward — *Source  Services Corporation*
Berger, Jeffrey — *Source  Services Corporation*
Berman, Kenneth D. — *MSI International*
Bermea, Jose — *Gaffney Management Consultants*
Bernard, Bryan — *Source  Services Corporation*
Bernas, Sharon — *Source  Services Corporation*
Besen, Douglas — *Besen Associates Inc.*
Betts, Suzette — *Source  Services Corporation*
Bickett, Nicole — *Source  Services Corporation*
Bidelman, Richard — *Source  Services Corporation*
Biestek, Paul J. — *Paul J. Biestek Associates, Inc.*
Biolsi, Joseph — *Source  Services Corporation*
Birns, Douglas — *Source  Services Corporation*
Bitar, Edward — *The Interface Group, Ltd./Boyden*
Bittman, Beth M. — *Norman Roberts & Associates, Inc.*
Black, Douglas E. — *MSI International*
Blackmon, Sharon — *The Abbott Group, Inc.*
Blakslee, Jan H. — *J: Blakslee International, Ltd.*
Bland, Walter — *Source  Services Corporation*
Blanton, Thomas — *Blanton and Company*
Blassaras, Peggy — *Source  Services Corporation*
Blecker, Jay — *TSS Consulting, Ltd.*
Blickle, Michael — *Source  Services Corporation*
Blim, Barbara — *JDG Associates, Ltd.*
Bloch, Suzanne — *Source  Services Corporation*
Blocher, John — *Source  Services Corporation*
Bloom, Howard C. — *Hernand & Partners*
Bloom, Joyce — *Hernand & Partners*
Bloomer, James E. — *L.W. Foote Company*
Bluhm, Claudia — *Schweichler Associates, Inc.*
Blunt, Peter — *Hernand & Partners*
Boczany, William J. — *The Guild Corporation*

Boesel, James — *Logix Partners*
Boesel, Jim — *Logix, Inc.*
Bohn, Steve J. — *MSI International*
Booth, Ronald — *Source  Services Corporation*
Bormann, Cindy Ann — *MSI International*
Bostic, James E. — *Phillips Resource Group*
Bosward, Allan — *Source  Services Corporation*
Bourbeau, Paul J. — *Boyden*
Bradshaw, John W. — *A.T. Kearney, Inc.*
Brady, Robert — *CPS Inc.*
Bragg, Garry — *The McCormick Group, Inc.*
Brandeis, Richard — *CPS Inc.*
Brassard, Gary — *Source  Services Corporation*
Bremer, Brian — *Source  Services Corporation*
Brentari, Michael — *Search Consultants International, Inc.*
Brewster, Edward — *Source  Services Corporation*
Brieger, Steve — *Thorne, Brieger Associates Inc.*
Briggs, Adam — *Horton International*
Bright, Timothy — *MSI International*
Brinson, Robert — *MSI International*
Brockman, Dan B. — *Dan B. Brockman Recruiters*
Brodie, Ricki R. — *MSI International*
Bronger, Patricia — *Source  Services Corporation*
Brooks, Charles — *Corporate Recruiters Ltd.*
Brooks, Kimberllay — *Corporate Recruiters Ltd.*
Brovender, Claire — *Winter, Wyman & Company*
Brown, Clifford — *Source  Services Corporation*
Brown, Daniel — *Source  Services Corporation*
Brown, Lawrence Anthony — *MSI International*
Brown, Michael R. — *MSI International*
Brown, Sandra E. — *MSI International*
Brown, Steven — *Source  Services Corporation*
Browne, Michael — *Source  Services Corporation*
Brudno, Robert J. — *Savoy Partners, Ltd.*
Brunner, Terry — *Source  Services Corporation*
Brunson, Therese — *Kors Montgomery International*
Bryant, Richard D. — *Bryant Associates, Inc.*
Bryza, Robert M. — *Robert Lowell International*
Buckles, Donna — *Cochran, Cochran & Yale, Inc.*
Budill, Edward — *Professional Search Consultants*
Burch, Donald — *Source  Services Corporation*
Burchill, Greg — *BGB Associates*
Burden, Gene — *The Cherbonnier Group, Inc.*
Burke, George M. — *The Burke Group*
Burke, John — *The Experts*
Burnett, Rebecca J. — *MSI International*
Burris, James C. — *Boyden*
Busch, Jack — *Busch International*
Bush, Martha A. — *MSI International*
Button, David R. — *The Button Group*
Buttrey, Daniel — *Source  Services Corporation*
Buzolits, Patrick — *Source  Services Corporation*
Cafero, Les — *Source  Services Corporation*
Cahill, Peter M. — *Peter M. Cahill Associates, Inc.*
Call, David — *Cochran, Cochran & Yale, Inc.*
Callan, Robert M. — *Callan Associates, Ltd.*
Callihan, Diana L. — *Search Northwest Associates*
Campbell, E. — *Source  Services Corporation*
Campbell, Jeff — *Source  Services Corporation*
Cargo, Catherine — *MSI International*
Carlson, Eric — *Source  Services Corporation*
Carnal, Rick — *Source  Services Corporation*
Carpenter, Harold G. — *MSI International*
Carter, Linda — *Source  Services Corporation*
Carvalho-Esteves, Maria — *Source  Services Corporation*
Case, David — *Case Executive Search*
Cassie, Ronald L. — *The Cassie Group*
Cast, Donald — *Dunhill Search International*
Castle, Lisa — *Source  Services Corporation*
Causey, Andrea C. — *MSI International*
Cavanagh, Michael J. — *Michael J. Cavanagh and Associates*
Cavolina, Michael — *Carver Search Consultants*
Celenza, Catherine — *CPS Inc.*
Cersosimo, Rocco — *Source  Services Corporation*
Chase, James — *Source  Services Corporation*
Chatterjie, Alok — *MSI International*
Chavous, C. Crawford — *Phillips Resource Group*
Cheah, Victor — *Source  Services Corporation*
Cherbonnier, L. Michael — *TCG International, Inc.*
Cherbonnier, L. Michael — *The Cherbonnier Group, Inc.*
Christian, Jeffrey E. — *Christian & Timbers*
Christiansen, Amy — *CPS Inc.*
Christiansen, Doug — *CPS Inc.*
Christman, Joel — *Source  Services Corporation*
Chronopoulos, Dennis — *Source  Services Corporation*
Cizek, John T. — *Cizek Associates, Inc.*
Cizek, Marti J. — *Cizek Associates, Inc.*
Clarey, William A. — *Preng & Associates, Inc.*

Clark, James — *CPS Inc.*
Clauhsen, Elizabeth A. — *Savoy Partners, Ltd.*
Clawson, Bob — *Source Services Corporation*
Clawson, Robert — *Source Services Corporation*
Cleary, Thomas R. — *ARJay & Associates*
Clegg, Cynthia — *Horton International*
Cline, Mark — *NYCOR Search, Inc.*
Close, E. Wade — *Boyden*
Cocconi, Alan — *Source Services Corporation*
Cochran, Hale — *Fenwick Partners*
Cochrun, James — *Source Services Corporation*
Coffman, Brian — *Kossuth & Associates, Inc.*
Cohen, Michael R. — *Intech Summit Group, Inc.*
Cohen, Robert C. — *Intech Summit Group, Inc.*
Cole, Elizabeth — *MSI International*
Cole, Rosalie — *Source Services Corporation*
Coleman, J. Kevin — *J. Kevin Coleman & Associates, Inc.*
Collard, Joseph A. — *Spencer Stuart*
Colling, Douglas — *KPMG Management Consulting*
Collins, Scott — *Source Services Corporation*
Collis, Gerald — *TSS Consulting, Ltd.*
Colosimo, Chris — *Richard, Wayne and Roberts*
Colucci, Bart A. — *Colucci, Blendow and Johnson, Inc.*
Comai, Christine — *Source Services Corporation*
Combs, Stephen L. — *Juntunen-Combs-Poirier*
Combs, Thomas — *Source Services Corporation*
Cona, Joseph A. — *Cona Personnel Search*
Coneys, Bridget — *Source Services Corporation*
Conway, William P. — *Phillips Resource Group*
Cook, Charlene — *Source Services Corporation*
Cooke, Jeffrey R. — *Jonas, Walters & Assoc., Inc.*
Costa, Cynthia A. — *MSI International*
Costello, Andrea L. — *Gallin Associates*
Costello, Jack — *Gallin Associates*
Coston, Bruce G. — *MSI International*
Cotugno, James — *Source Services Corporation*
Coughlin, Stephen — *Source Services Corporation*
Coulman, Karen — *CPS Inc.*
Cox, James O. — *MSI International*
Cragg, Barbara R. — *Southwestern Professional Services*
Cram, Noel — *R.P. Barone Associates*
Crath, Paul F. — *Price Waterhouse*
Crowder, Edward W. — *Crowder & Company*
Crowell, Elizabeth — *H.M. Long International, Ltd.*
Crownover, Kathryn L. — *MSI International*
Crumpley, Jim — *Jim Crumpley & Associates*
Crumpton, Marc — *Logix Partners*
Crumpton, Marc — *Logix, Inc.*
Cruse, O.D. — *Spencer Stuart*
Cuddy, Patricia — *Source Services Corporation*
Cunningham, Sheila — *Adams & Associates International*
Cuomo, Frank — *Frank Cuomo and Associates, Inc.*
Curren, Camella — *Source Services Corporation*
Currie, Lawrence S. — *MSI International*
Cutka, Matthew — *Source Services Corporation*
Czamanske, Paul W. — *Compass Group Ltd.*
Czepiel, Susan — *CPS Inc.*
Dalton, David R. — *MSI International*
Danforth, Monica — *Search Consultants International, Inc.*
Daniel, Beverly — *Foy, Schneid & Daniel, Inc.*
Dankberg, Iris — *Source Services Corporation*
Darnell, Nadine — *Brennan Associates*
Davis, Bernel — *MSI International*
Davis, C. Scott — *Source Services Corporation*
Davis, Elease — *Source Services Corporation*
Davis, G. Gordon — *Davis & Company*
Davis, Joel C. — *MSI International*
Davis, Robert — *CG & Associates*
Dawson, William — *Source Services Corporation*
de Palacios, Jeannette C. — *J. Palacios & Associates, Inc.*
Debrueys, Lee G. — *MSI International*
Debus, Wayne — *Source Services Corporation*
Deck, Jack — *Source Services Corporation*
Deering, Joseph — *U.S. Envirosearch*
DeGioia, Joseph — *JDG Associates, Ltd.*
Del'Ange, Gabrielle N. — *MSI International*
Delaney, Patrick — *Search West, Inc.*
Delaney, Patrick J. — *Sensible Solutions, Inc.*
Delvani-Hart, Angela — *F-O-R-T-U-N-E Personnel Consultants of Nashua, Inc.*
DeMarco, Robert — *Source Services Corporation*
deMartino, Cathy — *Lucas Associates*
Desgrosellier, Gary P. — *Personnel Unlimited/Executive Search*
Desmond, Dennis — *Beall & Company, Inc.*
Desmond, Mary — *Source Services Corporation*
Dever, Mary — *Source Services Corporation*
Devito, Alice — *Source Services Corporation*
Di Filippo, Thomas — *Source Services Corporation*

Diers, Gary — *Source Services Corporation*
Dietz, David S. — *MSI International*
Dittmar, Richard — *Source Services Corporation*
Divine, Robert S. — *O'Shea, Divine & Company, Inc.*
Dixon, Aris — *CPS Inc.*
Dobrow, Samuel — *Source Services Corporation*
Donahue, Debora — *Source Services Corporation*
Donnelly, Patti — *Source Services Corporation*
Dorfner, Martin — *Source Services Corporation*
Dornblut, Cindy — *Ashton Computer Professionals Inc.*
Dougherty, Bridget L. — *Wellington Management Group*
Dow, Lori — *Davidson, Laird & Associates*
Dowlatzadch, Homayoun — *Source Services Corporation*
Downs, William — *Source Services Corporation*
Doyle, Bobby — *Richard, Wayne and Roberts*
Doyle, Marie — *Spectra International Inc.*
Dreslinski, Robert S. — *Sharrow & Associates*
Drexler, Robert — *Robert Drexler Associates, Inc.*
Duelks, John — *Source Services Corporation*
Dugan, John H. — *J.H. Dugan and Associates, Inc.*
Duggan, James P. — *Slayton International, Inc.*
Duley, Richard I. — *ARJay & Associates*
Duncan, Dana — *Source Services Corporation*
Dunlow, Aimee — *Source Services Corporation*
Dunman, Betsy L. — *Crawford & Crofford*
Dupont, Rick — *Source Services Corporation*
Dwyer, Julie — *CPS Inc.*
Dykstra, Nicolette — *CPS Inc.*
Eason, James — *JRL Executive Recruiters*
Eason, Larry E. — *JRL Executive Recruiters*
Eatmon, Michael — *U.S. Envirosearch*
Eden, Brooks D. — *Eden & Associates, Inc.*
Edmond, Bruce — *Corporate Recruiters Ltd.*
Edwards, Dorothy — *MSI International*
Edwards, Robert — *J.P. Canon Associates*
Edwards, Verba L. — *Wing Tips & Pumps, Inc.*
Eggena, Roger — *Phillips Resource Group*
Eggert, Scott — *Source Services Corporation*
Ehrhart, Jennifer — *ADOW's Executeam*
Einsele, Neil — *Agra Placements International Ltd.*
Eiseman, Joe — *Source Services Corporation*
Eiseman, Joe — *Source Services Corporation*
Eiseman, Joe — *Source Services Corporation*
Ellis, Patricia — *Source Services Corporation*
Ellis, William — *Interspace Interactive Inc.*
Emerson, Randall — *Source Services Corporation*
England, Mark — *Austin-McGregor International*
Engle, Bryan — *Source Services Corporation*
Ervin, Darlene — *CPS Inc.*
Ervin, Russell — *Source Services Corporation*
Erwin, Lee — *Agra Placements International Ltd.*
Eton, Steven — *Search West, Inc.*
Eustis, Lucy R. — *MSI International*
Evans, Timothy — *Source Services Corporation*
Fagerstrom, Jon — *Source Services Corporation*
Fair, Donna — *ProResource, Inc.*
Fales, Scott — *Source Services Corporation*
Falk, John — *D.S. Allen Associates, Inc.*
Fancher, Robert L. — *Bason Associates Inc.*
Fanning, Paul — *Source Services Corporation*
Farler, Wiley — *Source Services Corporation*
Farley, Leon A. — *Leon A. Farley Associates*
Farrow, Jerry M. — *McCormack & Farrow*
Farthing, Andrew R. — *Parfitt Recruiting and Consulting*
Fechheimer, Peter — *Source Services Corporation*
Ferguson, Kenneth — *Source Services Corporation*
Ferguson, Lauren — *Search West, Inc.*
Field, Andrew — *Source Services Corporation*
Fill, Clifford G. — *D.S.A. - Dixie Search Associates*
Fill, Ellyn H. — *D.S.A. - Dixie Search Associates*
Fincher, Richard P. — *Phase II Management*
Finkel, Leslie — *Source Services Corporation*
Finnerty, James — *Source Services Corporation*
Fiore, Richard — *Search Consultants International, Inc.*
Fischer, Janet L. — *Boyden*
Fishback, Joren — *Derek Associates, Inc.*
Fisher, Neal — *Fisher Personnel Management Services*
Fitzgerald, Brian — *Source Services Corporation*
Flannery, Peter — *Jonas, Walters & Assoc., Inc.*
Fleming, Marco — *MSI International*
Flora, Dodi — *Crawford & Crofford*
Florio, Robert — *Southwestern Professional Services*
Flowers, Hayden — *Southwestern Professional Services*
Flowers, John E. — *Balfour Associates*
Fogarty, Michael — *CPS Inc.*
Folkerth, Gene — *Gene Folkerth & Associates, Inc.*
Follmer, Gary — *Agra Placements International Ltd.*
Foreman, David C. — *Koontz, Jeffries & Associates, Inc.*

Forest, Adam — *McCormack & Associates*
Forestier, Lois — *Source Services Corporation*
Forman, Donald R. — *Stanton Chase International*
Foster, Bradley — *Source Services Corporation*
Foster, John — *Source Services Corporation*
Fotia, Frank — *JDG Associates, Ltd.*
Fowler, Jim — *First Search America, Inc.*
Foy, Richard — *Boyden*
Francis, Brad — *Source Services Corporation*
Frank, Valerie S. — *Norman Roberts & Associates, Inc.*
Frantino, Michael — *Source Services Corporation*
Frazier, John — *Cochran, Cochran & Yale, Inc.*
Frederick, Dianne — *Source Services Corporation*
Freeh, Thomas — *Source Services Corporation*
French, William G. — *Preng & Associates, Inc.*
Friedman, Deborah — *Source Services Corporation*
Friedman, Helen E. — *McCormack & Farrow*
Fuhrman, Dennis — *Source Services Corporation*
Fujino, Rickey — *Source Services Corporation*
Fulger, Herbert — *Source Services Corporation*
Furlong, James W. — *Furlong Search, Inc.*
Furlong, James W. — *Furlong Search, Inc.*
Furlong, James W. — *Furlong Search, Inc.*
Fyhrie, David — *Source Services Corporation*
Gabriel, David L. — *The Arcus Group*
Gaffney, Keith — *Gaffney Management Consultants*
Gaffney, Megan — *Source Services Corporation*
Gaffney, William — *Gaffney Management Consultants*
Galante, Suzanne M. — *Vlcek & Company, Inc.*
Gale, Rhoda E. — *E.G. Jones Associates, Ltd.*
Gallagher, Marilyn — *Hogan Acquisitions*
Gallin, Larry — *Gallin Associates*
Galvani, Frank J. — *MSI International*
Gamble, Ira — *Source Services Corporation*
Garcia, Samuel K. — *Southwestern Professional Services*
Gardner, Michael — *Source Services Corporation*
Gares, Conrad — *TSS Consulting, Ltd.*
Garfinkle, Steven M. — *Battalia Winston International*
Garrett, Donald L. — *Garrett Associates Inc.*
Garrett, Linda M. — *Garrett Associates Inc.*
Garrett, Mark — *Source Services Corporation*
Gennawey, Robert — *Source Services Corporation*
Gerbosi, Karen — *Hernand & Partners*
Gettys, James R. — *International Staffing Consultants, Inc.*
Giesy, John — *Source Services Corporation*
Gilbert, Robert — *U.S. Envirosearch*
Gilchrist, Robert J. — *Horton International*
Giles, Joe L. — *Joe L. Giles and Associates, Inc.*
Gilinsky, David — *Source Services Corporation*
Gillespie, Thomas — *Professional Search Consultants*
Gilmartin, William — *Hockett Associates, Inc.*
Gilmore, Lori — *CPS Inc.*
Gilreath, James M. — *Gilreath Weatherby, Inc.*
Glacy, Kurt — *Winter, Wyman & Company*
Gladstone, Martin J. — *MSI International*
Glancey, Thomas F. — *Gordon Wahls Company*
Glass, Sharon — *Logix Partners*
Glass, Sharon — *Logix, Inc.*
Glickman, Leenie — *Source Services Corporation*
Gloss, Frederick C. — *F. Gloss International*
Gluzman, Arthur — *Source Services Corporation*
Gnatowski, Bruce — *Source Services Corporation*
Gold, Stanley — *Search West, Inc.*
Goldenberg, Susan — *Grant Cooper and Associates*
Goldsmith, Fred J. — *Fred J. Goldsmith Associates*
Gomez, Paul — *ARJay & Associates*
Goodman, Dawn M. — *Bason Associates Inc.*
Goodman, Victor — *Anderson Sterling Associates*
Goodwin, Gary — *Source Services Corporation*
Gordon, Trina D. — *Boyden*
Gorman, Patrick — *Source Services Corporation*
Gostyla, Rick — *Spencer Stuart*
Gould, Adam — *Logix Partners*
Gould, Adam — *Logix, Inc.*
Gould, Dana — *Logix Partners*
Gould, Dana — *Logix, Inc.*
Gourley, Timothy — *Source Services Corporation*
Grado, Eduardo — *Source Services Corporation*
Graff, Jack — *Source Services Corporation*
Graham, Dale — *CPS Inc.*
Graham, Shannon — *Source Services Corporation*
Grandinetti, Suzanne — *Source Services Corporation*
Granger, Lisa D. — *D.S.A. - Dixie Search Associates*
Grantham, Philip H. — *Columbia Consulting Group*
Gray, David — *CG & Associates*
Gray, Heather — *Source Services Corporation*
Gray, Russell — *Source Services Corporation*
Graziano, Lisa — *Source Services Corporation*

Grebenstein, Charles R. — *Skott/Edwards Consultants, Inc.*
Green, Jane — *Phillips Resource Group*
Green, Jean — *Broward-Dobbs, Inc.*
Green, Marc — *TSS Consulting, Ltd.*
Greene, Frederick J. — *Boyden*
Greene, Luke — *Broward-Dobbs, Inc.*
Grenier, Glorianne — *CPS Inc.*
Gresia, Paul — *Source Services Corporation*
Groner, David — *Source Services Corporation*
Groom, Charles C. — *CG & Associates*
Groover, David — *MSI International*
Grossman, James — *Source Services Corporation*
Grossman, Martin — *Source Services Corporation*
Grumulaitis, Leo — *Source Services Corporation*
Grzybowski, Jill — *CPS Inc.*
Guc, Stephen — *Source Services Corporation*
Gude, John S. — *Boyden*
Gulley, Marylyn — *MSI International*
Guthrie, Stuart — *Source Services Corporation*
Hacker-Taylor, Dianna — *Source Services Corporation*
Haider, Martin — *Source Services Corporation*
Hales, Daphne — *Source Services Corporation*
Hall, Robert — *Don Richard Associates of Tidewater, Inc.*
Haller, Mark — *Source Services Corporation*
Hamdan, Mark — *Careernet of Florida, Inc.*
Hamm, Gary — *Source Services Corporation*
Hammes, Betsy — *Search Enterprises, Inc.*
Hanley, Steven — *Source Services Corporation*
Hanna, Remon — *Source Services Corporation*
Hansen, David G. — *Ott & Hansen, Inc.*
Hansen, Ty E. — *Blake, Hansen & Nye, Limited*
Hanson, Carrie — *U.S. Envirosearch*
Harbaugh, Paul J. — *International Management Advisors, Inc.*
Hardison, Richard L. — *Hardison & Company*
Harkins, Robert E. — *Robert Harkins Associates, Inc.*
Harp, Kimberly — *Source Services Corporation*
Harris, Bruce — *ProResource, Inc.*
Harrison, Patricia — *Source Services Corporation*
Harrison, Priscilla — *Phillips Resource Group*
Hart, Crystal — *Source Services Corporation*
Hart, James — *Source Services Corporation*
Harvey, Jill — *MSI International*
Harvey, Mike — *Advanced Executive Resources*
Harvey, Richard — *Price Waterhouse*
Harwood, Brian — *Source Services Corporation*
Haselby, James — *Source Services Corporation*
Hasten, Lawrence — *Source Services Corporation*
Haughton, Michael — *DeFrain, Mayer, Lee & Burgess LLC*
Hauswirth, Jeffrey M. — *Spencer Stuart*
Hauver, Scott — *Logix Partners*
Havener, Donald Clarke — *The Abbott Group, Inc.*
Hawksworth, A. Dwight — *A.D. & Associates Executive Search, Inc.*
Hayes, Lee — *Source Services Corporation*
Hayes, Stacy — *The McCormick Group, Inc.*
Haystead, Steve — *Advanced Executive Resources*
Hazerjian, Cynthia — *CPS Inc.*
Heafey, Bill — *CPS Inc.*
Hebel, Robert W. — *R.W. Hebel Associates*
Hecker, Henry C. — *Hogan Acquisitions*
Heinrich, Scott — *Source Services Corporation*
Heiser, Charles S. — *The Cassie Group*
Hellinger, Audrey — *Martin H. Bauman Associates, Inc.*
Helminiak, Audrey — *Gaffney Management Consultants*
Henneberry, Ward — *Source Services Corporation*
Hennig, Sandra M. — *MSI International*
Henry, Patrick — *F-O-R-T-U-N-E Personnel Consultants of Huntsville, Inc.*
Henshaw, Robert — *F-O-R-T-U-N-E Personnel Consultants of Huntsville, Inc.*
Hernand, Warren L. — *Hernand & Partners*
Hernandez, Luis A. — *CoEnergy, Inc.*
Hernandez, Ruben — *Source Services Corporation*
Heroux, David — *Source Services Corporation*
Hertlein, James N.J. — *Boyden/Zay & Company*
Herzog, Sarah — *Source Services Corporation*
Hicks, Albert M. — *Phillips Resource Group*
Hicks, James L. — *MSI International*
Hight, Susan — *Source Services Corporation*
Hilbert, Laurence — *Source Services Corporation*
Hilgenberg, Thomas — *Source Services Corporation*
Hill, Emery — *MSI International*
Hillen, Skip — *The McCormick Group, Inc.*
Hillyer, Carolyn — *Source Services Corporation*
Hilton, Diane — *Richard, Wayne and Roberts*
Hilyard, Paul J. — *MSI International*
Hinojosa, Oscar — *Source Services Corporation*
Hirsch, Julia C. — *Boyden*
Hockett, William — *Hockett Associates, Inc.*

Hodges, Robert J. — *Sampson Neill & Wilkins Inc.*
Hoffman, Stephen — *Source Services Corporation*
Hofner, Andrew — *Source Services Corporation*
Hogan, Larry H. — *Hogan Acquisitions*
Holden, Richard B. — *Ames Personnel Consultants, Inc.*
Hollins, Howard D. — *MSI International*
Holmes, Lawrence J. — *Columbia Consulting Group*
Holt, Carol — *Bartholdi & Company, Inc.*
Holtz, Gene — *Agra Placements International Ltd.*
Hopgood, Earl — *JDG Associates, Ltd.*
Hoppert, Phil — *Wargo and Co., Inc.*
Hostetter, Kristi — *Source Services Corporation*
Houchins, William N. — *Christian & Timbers*
Houterloot, Tim — *Source Services Corporation*
Houver, Scott — *Logix, Inc.*
Hubert, David L. — *ARJay & Associates*
Hucko, Donald S. — *Jonas, Walters & Assoc., Inc.*
Hudson, Reginald M. — *Search Bureau International*
Hughes, Barbara — *Source Services Corporation*
Hughes, James J. — *R.P. Barone Associates*
Hughes, Randall — *Source Services Corporation*
Hull, Chuck — *Winter, Wyman & Company*
Hult, Dana — *Source Services Corporation*
Humphrey, Titus — *Source Services Corporation*
Hunt, Thomas — *MSI International*
Hunter, Gabe — *Phillips Resource Group*
Hunter, Sue J. — *Robison & Associates*
Huntoon, Cliff — *Richard, Wayne and Roberts*
Hurley, Janeen — *Winter, Wyman & Company*
Hurtado, Jaime — *Source Services Corporation*
Hutton, Thomas J. — *The Thomas Tucker Company*
Hwang, Yvette — *MSI International*
Hyde, Mark D. — *MSI International*
Hyde, W. Jerry — *Hyde Danforth Wold & Co.*
Hykes, Don A. — *A.T. Kearney, Inc.*
Hylas, Lisa — *Source Services Corporation*
Iacovelli, Heather — *CPS Inc.*
Iammatteo, Enzo — *Keith Bagg & Associates Inc.*
Imhof, Kirk — *Source Services Corporation*
Infinger, Ronald E. — *Robison & Associates*
Inger, Barry — *Source Services Corporation*
Inguagiato, Gregory — *MSI International*
Inskeep, Thomas — *Source Services Corporation*
Intravaia, Salvatore — *Source Services Corporation*
Inzinna, Dennis — *AlternaStaff*
Irish, Alan — *CPS Inc.*
Irvine, Robert — *Keith Bagg & Associates Inc.*
Irwin, Mark — *Source Services Corporation*
Issacs, Judith A. — *Grant Cooper and Associates*
Ives, Richard K. — *Wilkinson & Ives*
Ivey, Deborah M. — *MSI International*
Jablo, Steven — *Dieckmann & Associates, Ltd.*
Jackson, W.T. — *Sampson Neill & Wilkins Inc.*
Jacobs, Martin J. — *The Rubicon Group*
Jacobs, Mike — *Thorne, Brieger Associates Inc.*
Jacobson, Hayley — *Source Services Corporation*
Jadulang, Vincent — *Source Services Corporation*
Jaffe, Mark — *Wyatt & Jaffe*
James, Allison A. — *MSI International*
James, Bruce — *Roberson and Company*
James, Richard — *Criterion Executive Search, Inc.*
Jansen, Douglas L. — *Search Northwest Associates*
Januleski, Geoff — *Source Services Corporation*
Jeltema, John — *Source Services Corporation*
Jensen, Robert — *Source Services Corporation*
Jensen, Stephanie — *Don Richard Associates of Tidewater, Inc.*
Joffe, Barry — *Bason Associates Inc.*
Johnson, David — *Gaffney Management Consultants*
Johnson, Douglas — *Quality Search*
Johnson, Greg — *Source Services Corporation*
Johnson, John W. — *Webb, Johnson Associates, Inc.*
Johnson, Michael E. — *Sharrow & Associates*
Johnson, Peter — *Winter, Wyman & Company*
Johnson, Robert J. — *Quality Search*
Johnstone, Grant — *Source Services Corporation*
Jones, Gary — *BGB Associates*
Jones, Rodney — *Source Services Corporation*
Jones, Ronald T. — *ARJay & Associates*
Joubert, Pierre E. — *Boyden*
Joyce, William J. — *The Guild Corporation*
Juelis, John J. — *Peeney Associates*
Juska, Frank — *Rusher, Loscavio & LoPresto*
Kader, Richard — *Richard Kader & Associates*
Kaiser, Donald J. — *Dunhill Search International*
Kalus, Lisa — *Lisa Kalus & Associates, Inc.*
Kanrich, Susan Azaria — *AlternaStaff*
Kaplan, Traci — *Source Services Corporation*
Karalis, William — *CPS Inc.*

Kasmouski, Steve — *Winter, Wyman & Company*
Kasprzyk, Michael — *Source Services Corporation*
Katz, Robert L. — *MSI International*
Keesom, W. Peter — *Boyden/Zay & Company*
Kehoe, Mike — *CPS Inc.*
Kelly, Robert — *Source Services Corporation*
Kelly, Susan D. — *S.D. Kelly & Associates, Inc.*
Kelsey, Micki — *Davidson, Laird & Associates*
Kennedy, Craig — *Source Services Corporation*
Kennedy, Paul — *Source Services Corporation*
Kennedy, Walter — *Source Services Corporation*
Kennedy, Walter — *Source Services Corporation*
Kenney, Jeanne — *Source Services Corporation*
Kern, Jerry L. — *ADOW's Executeam*
Kern, Kathleen G. — *ADOW's Executeam*
Kerr, John — *Search West, Inc.*
Kilcoyne, Pat — *CPS Inc.*
King, Bill — *The McCormick Group, Inc.*
King, Joyce L. — *MSI International*
King, Shannon — *Source Services Corporation*
Kinser, Richard E. — *Richard Kinser & Associates*
Kirkpatrick, Robert L. — *Reese Associates*
Kirschner, Alan — *Source Services Corporation*
Kkorzyniewski, Nicole — *CPS Inc.*
Klages, Constance W. — *International Management Advisors, Inc.*
Klauck, James J. — *Horton International*
Klein, Gary I. — *Johnson Smith & Knisely Accord*
Klein, Gregory A. — *A.T. Kearney, Inc.*
Kleinstein, Scott — *Source Services Corporation*
Klopfenstein, Edward L. — *Crowder & Company*
Klumpjan, Sonja — *CPS Inc.*
Klusman, Edwin — *Source Services Corporation*
Knoll, Robert — *Source Services Corporation*
Knotts, Jerry — *Mixtec Group*
Kochert, Don — *Summerfield Associates, Inc.*
Koczak, John — *Source Services Corporation*
Kohn, Adam P. — *Christian & Timbers*
Kohonoski, Michael M. — *The Guild Corporation*
Kondra, Vernon J. — *The Douglas Reiter Company, Inc.*
Koontz, Donald N. — *Koontz, Jeffries & Associates, Inc.*
Kopsick, Joseph M. — *Spencer Stuart*
Korkuch, Sandy — *Barone-O'Hara Associates*
Kors, R. Paul — *Kors Montgomery International*
Kossuth, David — *Kossuth & Associates, Inc.*
Kossuth, Jane — *Kossuth & Associates, Inc.*
Kouble, Tim — *Logix Partners*
Kouble, Tim — *Logix, Inc.*
La Chance, Ronald — *Source Services Corporation*
LaCharite, Danielle — *The Guild Corporation*
LaFaye, Susan — *MSI International*
Laird, Cheryl — *CPS Inc.*
Laird, Meri — *Davidson, Laird & Associates*
Lake, Phillip R. — *U.S. Envirosearch*
Lamb, Lynn M. — *F-O-R-T-U-N-E Personnel Consultants of Huntsville, Inc.*
Lambert, William — *Source Services Corporation*
Lamia, Michael — *Source Services Corporation*
Lanctot, William D. — *Corporate Resources Professional Placement*
Land, Shaun — *Dunhill Professional Search of Irvine, Inc.*
Landry, Leo G. — *MSI International*
Langan, Marion — *Logix Partners*
Langford, Robert W. — *F-O-R-T-U-N-E Personnel Consultants of Huntsville, Inc.*
Lankford, Charles — *MSI International*
Lapointe, Fabien — *Source Services Corporation*
Larsen, Jack B. — *Jack B. Larsen & Associates*
Lasher, Charles M. — *Lasher Associates*
Laskin, Sandy — *Source Services Corporation*
Latterell, Jeffrey D. — *Smith & Latterell (HRS, Inc.)*
Lautz, Lindsay A. — *Wilkinson & Ives*
Laverty, William — *Source Services Corporation*
Lawrence, David — *Agra Placements International Ltd.*
Lawson, Bettye N. — *MSI International*
Layton, Patrick R. — *MSI International*
Lazar, Miriam — *Source Services Corporation*
Leahy, Jan — *CPS Inc.*
Leblanc, Danny — *Source Services Corporation*
Lebo, Terry — *Agra Placements International Ltd.*
Lee, Everett — *Source Services Corporation*
Leigh, Rebecca — *Source Services Corporation*
Leighton, Mark — *Source Services Corporation*
Leininger, Dennis — *Key Employment Services*
LemMou, Paul — *International Staffing Consultants, Inc.*
Lence, Julie Anne — *MSI International*
Lenkaitis, Lewis F. — *A.T. Kearney, Inc.*
Leslie, William H. — *Boyden/Zay & Company*
Leszynski, Edward — *ProResource, Inc.*
Lettrii, Mary — *BioQuest, Inc.*

Levenson, Laurel — *Source Services Corporation*
Levine, Irwin — *Source Services Corporation*
Levitt, Muriel A. — *D.S. Allen Associates, Inc.*
Lewicki, Christopher — *MSI International*
Lewis, Daniel — *Source Services Corporation*
Lewis, Susan — *Logix Partners*
Lewis, Susan — *Logix, Inc.*
Liebross, Eric — *Source Services Corporation*
Lin, Felix — *Source Services Corporation*
Lindberg, Eric J. — *MSI International*
Linton, Leonard M. — *Byron Leonard International, Inc.*
Lipe, Jerold L. — *Compass Group Ltd.*
Lipuma, Thomas — *Source Services Corporation*
Little, Gary — *Agra Placements International Ltd.*
Livesay, Christopher C. — *MSI International*
Loeb, Stephen H. — *Grant Cooper and Associates*
Lofthouse, Cindy — *CPS Inc.*
Logan, Valarie A. — *D.S.A. - Dixie Search Associates*
London, Gregory J. — *MSI International*
Long, Helga — *H.M. Long International, Ltd.*
Long, John — *Source Services Corporation*
Long, Mark — *Source Services Corporation*
Long, William G. — *McDonald, Long & Associates, Inc.*
LoPresto, Robert L. — *Rusher, Loscavio & LoPresto*
Loria, Frank — *Accounting Personnel Consultants*
Lotufo, Donald A. — *D.A.L. Associates, Inc.*
Lotz, R. James — *International Management Advisors, Inc.*
Lovell, Robert W. — *John Kurosky & Associates*
Lucarelli, Joan — *The Onstott Group, Inc.*
Lucas, Ronnie L. — *MSI International*
Luce, Daniel — *Source Services Corporation*
Lucht, John — *The John Lucht Consultancy Inc.*
Lucien, David — *Accounting Personnel Consultants*
Ludder, Mark — *Source Services Corporation*
Ludlow, Michael — *Source Services Corporation*
Lumsby, George N. — *International Management Advisors, Inc.*
Lundy, Martin — *Source Services Corporation*
Lynn, Donald — *Frank Cuomo and Associates, Inc.*
Lyons, Michael — *Source Services Corporation*
MacEachern, David — *Spencer Stuart*
MacGregor, Malcolm — *Boyden*
MacJadyen, David J. — *Sharrow & Associates*
MacMillan, James — *Source Services Corporation*
MacPherson, Holly — *Source Services Corporation*
Macrides, Michael — *Source Services Corporation*
Mader, Stephen P. — *Christian & Timbers*
Maggio, Mary — *Source Services Corporation*
Maher, William J. — *Johnson Smith & Knisely Accord*
Mahmoud, Sophia — *Source Services Corporation*
Maiers, Robert — *Key Employment Services*
Mairn, Todd — *Source Services Corporation*
Malone, George V. — *Boyden*
Manassero, Henri J.P. — *International Management Advisors, Inc.*
Manns, Alex — *Crawford & Crofford*
Marchette, Steve — *Juntunen-Combs-Poirier*
Marino, Chester — *Cochran, Cochran & Yale, Inc.*
Marion, Michael — *S.D. Kelly & Associates, Inc.*
Marks, Ira — *Strategic Alternatives*
Marks, Russell E. — *Webb, Johnson Associates, Inc.*
Marlow, William — *Straube Associates*
Marra, John — *Marra Peters & Partners*
Marra, John — *Marra Peters & Partners*
Marshall, Gerald — *Blair/Tech Recruiters*
Martin, David — *The Guild Corporation*
Martin, Geary D. — *Boyden/Zay & Company*
Martin, James — *Spectra International Inc.*
Martin, Lynne Koll — *Boyden*
Martin, Paula — *MSI International*
Martines, James — *Sharrow & Associates*
Marwil, Jennifer — *Source Services Corporation*
Maschal, Charles E. — *Maschal/Connors, Inc.*
Mason, William E. — *John Kurosky & Associates*
Massey, H. Heath — *Robison & Associates*
Massey, R. Bruce — *Bruce Massey & Partners Inc.*
Matheny, Robert P. — *MSI International*
Mather, David R. — *Christian & Timbers*
Mathias, Douglas — *Source Services Corporation*
Mathias, William J. — *Preng & Associates, Inc.*
Mathis, Carrie — *Source Services Corporation*
Mattingly, Kathleen — *Source Services Corporation*
Max, Bruno — *RBR Associates, Inc.*
Maxwell, John — *Source Services Corporation*
May, Peter — *Mixtec Group*
Mayer, Thomas — *Source Services Corporation*
McAndrews, Kathy — *CPS Inc.*
McCallister, Richard A. — *Boyden*
McCarthy, Laura — *Source Services Corporation*
McComas, Kelly E. — *The Guild Corporation*

McCorkle, Sam B. — *Morton, McCorkle & Associates, Inc.*
McCormack, William Reed — *MSI International*
McCormick, Brian — *The McCormick Group, Inc.*
McCormick, Joseph — *Source Services Corporation*
McCormick, William J. — *The McCormick Group, Inc.*
McCreary, Charles — *Austin-McGregor International*
McDonald, Gary E. — *Agra Placements International Ltd.*
McDonald, John R. — *TSS Consulting, Ltd.*
McDonald, Scott A. — *McDonald Associates International*
McDonald, Stanleigh B. — *McDonald Associates International*
McDonnell, Julie — *Technical Personnel of Minnesota*
McGann, Paul L. — *The Cassie Group*
McGinnis, Rita — *Source Services Corporation*
McGoldrick, Terrence — *Source Services Corporation*
McGrath, Robert E. — *Robert E. McGrath & Associates*
McGuire, Bud — *Search West, Inc.*
McGuire, Corey — *Peter W. Ambler Company*
McHugh, Keith — *Source Services Corporation*
McIntosh, Arthur — *Source Services Corporation*
McIntosh, Tad — *Source Services Corporation*
McIntyre, Alex D. — *Norman Roberts & Associates, Inc.*
McIntyre, Joel — *Phillips Resource Group*
McKinney, Julia — *Source Services Corporation*
McMahan, Stephen — *Source Services Corporation*
McMahan, Stephen — *Source Services Corporation*
McManamon, Tim — *Rogers-McManamon Executive Search*
McMillin, Bob — *Price Waterhouse*
McNamara, Timothy C. — *Columbia Consulting Group*
McNear, Jeffrey E. — *Barrett Partners*
McNichol, John — *McNichol Associates*
McThrall, David — *TSS Consulting, Ltd.*
Meara, Helen — *Source Services Corporation*
Meehan, John — *Source Services Corporation*
Meier, J. Dale — *Grant Cooper and Associates*
Mendelson, Jeffrey — *Source Services Corporation*
Mendoza-Green, Robin — *Source Services Corporation*
Messina, Marco — *Source Services Corporation*
Meyer, William — *Agra Placements International Ltd.*
Michaels, Joseph — *CPS Inc.*
Mierzwinski, John — *Industrial Recruiters Associates, Inc.*
Miesemer, Arthur C. — *MSI International*
Miles, Kenneth T. — *MSI International*
Miller, Benjamin J. — *MSI International*
Miller, Elaine — *Search West, Inc.*
Miller, Larry — *Source Services Corporation*
Miller, Russel E. — *ARJay & Associates*
Miller, Timothy — *Source Services Corporation*
Milligan, Dale — *Source Services Corporation*
Mills, John — *Source Services Corporation*
Milner, Carol — *Source Services Corporation*
Milton, Suzanne — *Marra Peters & Partners*
Miras, Cliff — *Source Services Corporation*
Miras, Cliff — *Source Services Corporation*
Mitchell, Norman F. — *A.T. Kearney, Inc.*
Mittwol, Myles — *Source Services Corporation*
Moerbe, Ed H. — *Stanton Chase International*
Mogul, Gene — *Mogul Consultants, Inc.*
Mohr, Brian — *CPS Inc.*
Molitor, John L. — *Barrett Partners*
Mollichelli, David — *Source Services Corporation*
Mondragon, Philip — *Boyden*
Montgomery, Catherine C. — *Boyden*
Moore, Craig — *Source Services Corporation*
Moore, Denise — *Jonas, Walters & Assoc., Inc.*
Moore, Dianna — *Source Services Corporation*
Moore, Lemuel R. — *MSI International*
Moore, Mark — *Wheeler, Moore & Elam Co.*
Moore, Michael — *Agra Placements International Ltd.*
Moore, Suzanne — *Source Services Corporation*
Moore, Thomas — *Aureus Group*
Moran, Douglas — *Source Services Corporation*
Moran, Robert — *A.T. Kearney, Inc.*
Morato, Rene — *Source Services Corporation*
Moretti, Denise — *Source Services Corporation*
Morgan, Vincent S. — *Johnson Smith & Knisely Accord*
Moriarty, Mike — *Source Services Corporation*
Morris, Scott — *Source Services Corporation*
Morrison, Janis L. — *Garrett Associates Inc.*
Morrow, Melanie — *Source Services Corporation*
Morton, Robert C. — *Morton, McCorkle & Associates, Inc.*
Mott, Greg — *Source Services Corporation*
Msidment, Roger — *Source Services Corporation*
Mueller, Colleen — *Source Services Corporation*
Muendel, H. Edward — *Stanton Chase International*
Mulligan, Robert P. — *William Willis Worldwide Inc.*
Murin, Rose Mary — *U.S. Envirosearch*
Murphy, Corinne — *Source Services Corporation*
Murphy, Gary J. — *Stone Murphy & Olson*

Murphy, James — *Source Services Corporation*
Murphy, Timothy D. — *MSI International*
Murry, John — *Source Services Corporation*
Mursuli, Meredith — *Lasher Associates*
Mustin, Joyce M. — *J: Blakslee International, Ltd.*
Mydlach, Renee — *CPS Inc.*
Myrick, Marilou — *ProResource, Inc.*
Myrick, Marilou — *ProResource, Inc.*
Nabers, Karen — *Source Services Corporation*
Nagler, Leon G. — *Nagler, Robins & Poe, Inc.*
Nagy, Les — *Source Services Corporation*
Napier, Ginger L. — *Preng & Associates, Inc.*
Nazzaro, Samuel G. — *Boyden*
Necessary, Rick — *Source Services Corporation*
Needham, Karen — *Source Services Corporation*
Neff, Herbert — *Source Services Corporation*
Neill, Wellden K. — *Sampson Neill & Wilkins Inc.*
Nelson, Barbara — *Herman Smith Executive Initiatives Inc.*
Nelson, Hitch — *Source Services Corporation*
Nelson, Mary — *Source Services Corporation*
Nelson-Folkersen, Jeffrey — *Source Services Corporation*
Nephew, Robert — *Christian & Timbers*
Neuberth, Jeffrey G. — *Canny, Bowen Inc.*
Neuwald, Debrah — *Source Services Corporation*
Newbold, Michael — *Agra Placements International Ltd.*
Newlon, Jay — *Logix, Inc.*
Newton, Jay — *Logix Partners*
Nocero, John — *ProResource, Inc.*
Nolan, Jean M. — *S.D. Kelly & Associates, Inc.*
Nolan, Robert — *Source Services Corporation*
Nold, Robert — *Roberson and Company*
Nolen, Shannon — *Source Services Corporation*
Nordland, Martin N. — *Horton International*
Norman, Randy — *Austin-McGregor International*
Norsell, Paul E. — *Paul Norsell & Associates, Inc.*
Nymark, John — *NYCOR Search, Inc.*
Nymark, Paul — *NYCOR Search, Inc.*
O'Brien, Susan — *Source Services Corporation*
O'Connell, Mary — *CPS Inc.*
O'Donnell, James H. — *MSI International*
O'Donnell, Timothy W. — *Boyden*
O'Hara, James J. — *Barone-O'Hara Associates*
O'Toole, Dennis P. — *Dennis P. O'Toole & Associates Inc.*
Oakes, Meg B. — *D.P. Parker and Associates*
Oaks, Robert — *Search West, Inc.*
Oberg, Roy — *The Danbrook Group, Inc.*
Occhiboi, Emil — *Source Services Corporation*
Ocon, Olga — *Busch International*
Oddo, Judith — *Accounting Personnel Consultants*
Olsen, Carl — *A.T. Kearney, Inc.*
Olsen, David — *Search Enterprises South, Inc.*
Olsen, Robert — *Source Services Corporation*
Olsen, Robert F. — *Robert Connelly and Associates Incorporated*
Orr, Stacie — *Source Services Corporation*
Ottenritter, Chris — *CPS Inc.*
Ouellette, Christopher — *Source Services Corporation*
Owen, Christopher — *Source Services Corporation*
Owen, John — *Key Employment Services*
Owens, Ken — *F-O-R-T-U-N-E Personnel Consultants of Huntsville, Inc.*
Pachowitz, John — *Source Services Corporation*
Pacini, Lauren R. — *Hite Executive Search*
Page, Linda — *Jonas, Walters & Assoc., Inc.*
Page, Linda M. — *Wargo and Co., Inc.*
Paliwoda, William — *Source Services Corporation*
Palmer, Carlton A. — *Beall & Company, Inc.*
Pappas, Jim — *Search Dynamics, Inc.*
Pappas, Timothy C. — *Jonas, Walters & Assoc., Inc.*
Paradise, Malcolm — *Source Services Corporation*
Parent, Martine L. — *O'Callaghan Honey/Paul Ray Berndtson, Inc.*
Parente, James — *Source Services Corporation*
Parker, David P. — *D.P. Parker and Associates*
Parker, Murray B. — *The Borton Wallace Company*
Parkin, Myrna — *S.D. Kelly & Associates, Inc.*
Parr, James A. — *KPMG Management Consulting*
Parroco, Jason — *Source Services Corporation*
Patel, Shailesh — *Source Services Corporation*
Paternie, Patrick — *Source Services Corporation*
Paul, Kathleen — *Source Services Corporation*
Peal, Matthew — *Source Services Corporation*
Peasback, David R. — *Canny, Bowen Inc.*
Peckenpaugh, Ann D. — *Schweichler Associates, Inc.*
Pedley, Jill — *CPS Inc.*
Peeney, James D. — *Peeney Associates*
Pelisson, Charles — *Marra Peters & Partners*
Pelkey, Chris — *The McCormick Group, Inc.*
Perkins, Bob — *Richard, Wayne and Roberts*
Perkins, Daphne — *CPS Inc.*

Perry, Carolyn — *Source Services Corporation*
Perry, Wayne B. — *Bruce Massey & Partners Inc.*
Persky, Barry — *Barry Persky & Company, Inc.*
Peters, James N. — *TNS Partners, Inc.*
Peters, Kevin — *Source Services Corporation*
Petersen, Richard — *Source Services Corporation*
Peterson, John — *CPS Inc.*
Petrides, Andrew S. — *ARJay & Associates*
Petty, J. Scott — *The Arcus Group*
Pfeiffer, Irene — *Price Waterhouse*
Pfister, Shelli — *Jack B. Larsen & Associates*
Phillips, Bill — *Dunhill Search International*
Phillips, Donald L. — *O'Shea, Divine & Company, Inc.*
Pickering, Dale — *Agri-Tech Personnel, Inc.*
Pierce, Matthew — *Source Services Corporation*
Pillow, Charles — *Source Services Corporation*
Pineda, Rosanna — *Source Services Corporation*
Pirro, Sheri — *Source Services Corporation*
Pitcher, Brian D. — *Skott/Edwards Consultants, Inc.*
Pitts, Charles — *Contemporary Management Services, Inc.*
Plant, Jerry — *Source Services Corporation*
Poe, James B. — *Nagler, Robins & Poe, Inc.*
Poirier, Frank — *Juntunen-Combs-Poirier*
Polacek, Frank — *Search Enterprises South, Inc.*
Pomerance, Mark — *CPS Inc.*
Pompeo, Paul — *Search West, Inc.*
Porada, Stephen D. — *CAP Inc.*
Porter, Albert — *The Experts*
Porter, Nanci — *Eastridge InfoTech*
Pototo, Brian — *Source Services Corporation*
Potter, Douglas C. — *Stanton Chase International*
Powell, Danny — *Source Services Corporation*
Powell, Gregory — *Source Services Corporation*
Power, Michael — *Source Services Corporation*
Pregeant, David — *Source Services Corporation*
Preng, David E. — *Preng & Associates, Inc.*
Preusse, Eric — *Source Services Corporation*
Price, Andrew G. — *The Thomas Tucker Company*
Price, Carl — *Source Services Corporation*
Proct, Nina — *Martin H. Bauman Associates, Inc.*
Prosser, Shane — *Search Consultants International, Inc.*
Pugliese, Vincent — *Search West, Inc.*
Quinlan, Lynne — *Winter, Wyman & Company*
Raab, Julie — *Dunhill Professional Search of Irvine, Inc.*
Radawicz, Angela — *Mixtec Group*
Rapoport, William — *Blair/Tech Recruiters*
Rasmussen, Timothy — *Source Services Corporation*
Ratajczak, Paul — *Source Services Corporation*
Rathborne, Kenneth J. — *Blair/Tech Recruiters*
Ray, Marianne C. — *Callan Associates, Ltd.*
Raymond, Anne — *Anderson Sterling Associates*
Reardon, Joseph — *Source Services Corporation*
Reddicks, Nate — *Search West, Inc.*
Redding, Denise — *The Douglas Reiter Company, Inc.*
Redwood, Guy W. — *Bruce Massey & Partners Inc.*
Reed, Ruthann — *Spectra International Inc.*
Reed, Susan — *Source Services Corporation*
Regehly, Herbert L. — *The IMC Group of Companies Ltd.*
Reid, Katherine — *Source Services Corporation*
Reid, Scott — *Source Services Corporation*
Reiter, Douglas — *The Douglas Reiter Company, Inc.*
Rendl, Ric — *CPS Inc.*
Renfroe, Ann-Marie — *Source Services Corporation*
Renick, Cynthia L. — *Morgan Hunter Corp.*
Rennell, Thomas — *Source Services Corporation*
Renteria, Elizabeth — *Source Services Corporation*
Renwick, David — *John Kurosky & Associates*
Resnic, Alan — *Source Services Corporation*
Reticker, Peter — *MSI International*
Reyman, Susan — *S. Reyman & Associates Ltd.*
Reynolds, Gregory P. — *Roberts Ryan and Bentley*
Reynolds, Laura — *Source Services Corporation*
Rhoades, Michael — *Source Services Corporation*
Rice, Douglas — *Agra Placements International Ltd.*
Richard, Ryan — *Logix Partners*
Richard, Ryan — *Logix, Inc.*
Riederer, Larry — *CPS Inc.*
Rinaldi, Michael D. — *D.P. Parker and Associates*
Rios, Vince — *Source Services Corporation*
Rios, Vincent — *Source Services Corporation*
Rivas, Alberto F. — *Boyden*
Rivers, Geri — *Chrisman & Company, Incorporated*
Rizzo, L. Donald — *R.P. Barone Associates*
Robb, Tammy — *Source Services Corporation*
Roberts, Clifford — *Search Enterprises, Inc.*
Roberts, Norman C. — *Norman Roberts & Associates, Inc.*
Roberts, Raymond R. — *MSI International*
Roberts, Scott B. — *Wargo and Co., Inc.*

Robertson, Sherry — *Source Services Corporation*
Robinette, Paul — *Hernand & Partners*
Robins, Jeri N. — *Nagler, Robins & Poe, Inc.*
Robinson, Bruce — *Bruce Robinson Associates*
Robinson, Tonya — *Source Services Corporation*
Robison, John H. — *Robison & Associates*
Rockwell, Bruce — *Source Services Corporation*
Rodgers, John — *Agra Placements International Ltd.*
Rodgers, Kathi — *St. Lawrence International, Inc.*
Rodney, Brett — *MSI International*
Rodriguez, Manuel — *Source Services Corporation*
Romanello, Daniel P. — *Spencer Stuart*
Ropella, Patrick B. — *Ropella & Associates*
Rosen, Mitchell — *Source Services Corporation*
Rosenstein, Michele — *Source Services Corporation*
Ross, Marc A. — *Flowers & Associates*
Ross, Mark S. — *Herman Smith Executive Initiatives Inc.*
Ross, William J. — *Flowers & Associates*
Rossi, Silvio — *Keith Bagg & Associates Inc.*
Roth, Robert J. — *Williams, Roth & Krueger Inc.*
Rothenbush, Clayton — *Source Services Corporation*
Rothman, Jeffrey — *ProResource, Inc.*
Roussel, Vicki — *Logix Partners*
Roussel, Vicki J. — *Logix, Inc.*
Rowells, Michael — *MSI International*
Rowland, James — *Source Services Corporation*
Rozentsvayg, Michael — *Logix Partners*
Rozentsvayg, Michael — *Logix, Inc.*
Rudolph, Kenneth — *Kossuth & Associates, Inc.*
Rudzinsky, Howard — *Louis Rudzinsky Associates*
Rudzinsky, Jeffrey — *Louis Rudzinsky Associates*
Runge, Gary — *Search Enterprises South, Inc.*
Rurak, Zbigniew T. — *Rurak & Associates, Inc.*
Rusher, William H. — *Rusher, Loscavio & LoPresto*
Russell, Sam — *The Guild Corporation*
Ryan, David — *Source Services Corporation*
Ryan, Kathleen — *Source Services Corporation*
Ryan, Mark — *Source Services Corporation*
Sacerdote, John — *Raymond Karsan Associates*
Sadaj, Michael — *Source Services Corporation*
Sahlas, Chrissy — *CPS Inc.*
Salet, Michael — *Source Services Corporation*
Saletra, Andrew — *CPS Inc.*
Sampson, Martin C. — *Sampson Neill & Wilkins Inc.*
Samsel, Randy — *Source Services Corporation*
Samuelson, Robert — *Source Services Corporation*
Sanchez, William — *Source Services Corporation*
Sandbloom, Kenneth — *Search Enterprises South, Inc.*
Sanders, Natalie — *CPS Inc.*
Sanders, Spencer H. — *Battalia Winston International*
Sangster, Jeffrey — *F-O-R-T-U-N-E Personnel Consultants of Manatee County*
Santiago, Benefrido — *Source Services Corporation*
Sapers, Mark — *Source Services Corporation*
Saposhnik, Doron — *Source Services Corporation*
Sardella, Sharon — *Source Services Corporation*
Sathe, Mark A. — *Sathe & Associates, Inc.*
Savela, Edward — *Source Services Corporation*
Saxner, David — *DSA, Inc.*
Scalamera, Tom — *CPS Inc.*
Schaefer, Robert — *Search Enterprises, Inc.*
Scharett, Carol — *St. Lawrence International, Inc.*
Schiavone, Mary Rose — *Canny, Bowen Inc.*
Schlpma, Christine — *Advanced Executive Resources*
Schmidt, Jeri E. — *Blake, Hansen & Nye, Limited*
Schmidt, Peter R. — *Boyden*
Schmidt, William C. — *Christian & Timbers*
Schneider, Perry — *Agra Placements International Ltd.*
Schneiderman, Gerald — *Management Resource Associates, Inc.*
Schrenzel, Benjamin — *Parfitt Recruiting and Consulting*
Schroeder, James — *Source Services Corporation*
Schroeder, Steven J. — *Blau Kaptain Schroeder*
Schueneman, David — *CPS Inc.*
Schultz, Randy — *Source Services Corporation*
Schwalbach, Robert — *Source Services Corporation*
Schwam, Carol — *A.E. Feldman Associates*
Schweichler, Lee J. — *Schweichler Associates, Inc.*
Schwinden, William — *Source Services Corporation*
Scimone, James — *Source Services Corporation*
Scimone, Jim — *Source Services Corporation*
Scoff, Barry — *Source Services Corporation*
Scrivines, Hank — *Search Northwest Associates*
Seamon, Kenneth — *Source Services Corporation*
Selker, Gregory L. — *Christian & Timbers*
Selko, Philip W. — *Hogan Acquisitions*
Sell, David — *Source Services Corporation*
Selvaggi, Esther — *Source Services Corporation*
Semple, David — *Source Services Corporation*

Serba, Kerri — *Source Services Corporation*
Sevilla, Claudio A. — *Crawford & Crofford*
Shackleford, David — *Source Services Corporation*
Shamir, Ben — *S.D. Kelly & Associates, Inc.*
Shanks, Jennifer — *Source Services Corporation*
Shapanka, Samuel — *Source Services Corporation*
Shapiro, Elaine — *CPS Inc.*
Shattuck, Merrill B. — *M.B. Shattuck and Associates, Inc.*
Shawhan, Heather — *Source Services Corporation*
Shea, John — *ALTCO Temporary Services*
Shea, John — *The ALTCO Group*
Shelton, Jonathan — *Source Services Corporation*
Shenfield, Peter — *Baker, Harris & Partners Limited*
Shepard, Michael J. — *MSI International*
Sherwin, Thomas — *Barone-O'Hara Associates*
Shipherd, John T. — *The Cassie Group*
Shoemaker, Fred W. — *MSI International*
Shoemaker, Larry C. — *Shoemaker & Associates*
Sibbald, John R. — *John Sibbald Associates, Inc.*
Siegel, RitaSue — *RitaSue Siegel Resources Inc.*
Signer, Julie — *CPS Inc.*
Siker, Paul W. — *The Guild Corporation*
Silcott, Marvin L. — *Marvin L. Silcott & Associates, Inc.*
Sill, Igor M. — *Geneva Group International*
Sill, Igor M. — *Geneva Group International*
Silvas, Stephen D. — *Roberson and Company*
Silver, Kit — *Source Services Corporation*
Silver, Lee A. — *L.A. Silver Associates, Inc.*
Simankov, Dmitry — *Logix, Inc.*
Simmons, Deborah — *Source Services Corporation*
Simmons, Sandra K. — *MSI International*
Sinclair, Amy — *Fisher Personnel Management Services*
Sirena, Evelyn — *Source Services Corporation*
Sjogren, Dennis — *Agra Placements International Ltd.*
Skunda, Donna M. — *Allerton Heneghan & O'Neill*
Slater, Ronald E. — *A.T. Kearney, Inc.*
Slaughter, Katherine T. — *Compass Group Ltd.*
Slayton, Richard C. — *Slayton International, Inc.*
Sloan, Scott — *Source Services Corporation*
Slosar, John M. — *Canny, Bowen Inc.*
Smith, Adam M. — *The Abbott Group, Inc.*
Smith, Cheryl — *ProResource, Inc.*
Smith, David P. — *Smith & Latterell (HRS, Inc.)*
Smith, Grant — *Price Waterhouse*
Smith, Ian — *International Staffing Consultants, Inc.*
Smith, Kevin — *F-O-R-T-U-N-E Personnel Consultants of Manatee County*
Smith, Lawrence — *Source Services Corporation*
Smith, Margaret A. — *MSI International*
Smith, Timothy — *Source Services Corporation*
Smock, Cynthia — *Source Services Corporation*
Smoller, Howard — *Source Services Corporation*
Snodgrass, Stephen — *DeFrain, Mayer, Lee & Burgess LLC*
Snowden, Charles — *Source Services Corporation*
Snowhite, Rebecca — *Source Services Corporation*
Snyder, James F. — *Snyder & Company*
Sobczak, Ronald — *Search Enterprises, Inc.*
Sochacki, Michael — *Source Services Corporation*
Soggs, Cheryl Pavick — *A.T. Kearney, Inc.*
Sola, George L. — *A.T. Kearney, Inc.*
Solters, Jeanne — *The Guild Corporation*
Song, Louis — *Source Services Corporation*
Songy, Al — *U.S. Envirosearch*
Sorgen, Jay — *Source Services Corporation*
Sostilio, Louis — *Source Services Corporation*
Sowerbutt, Richard S. — *Hite Executive Search*
Spanninger, Mark J. — *The Guild Corporation*
Spector, Michael — *Source Services Corporation*
Spencer, John — *Source Services Corporation*
Spencer, John — *Source Services Corporation*
Spiegel, Gay — *L.A. Silver Associates, Inc.*
Spoutz, Paul — *Source Services Corporation*
Spriggs, Robert D. — *Spriggs & Company, Inc.*
St. Martin, Peter — *Source Services Corporation*
Staats, Dave — *Southwestern Professional Services*
Stack, James K. — *Boyden*
Stack, Richard — *Source Services Corporation*
Staehely, Janna — *Southwestern Professional Services*
Stark, Jeff — *Thorne, Brieger Associates Inc.*
Starr, Anna — *Richard, Wayne and Roberts*
Steenerson, Thomas L. — *MSI International*
Stephens, Andrew — *Source Services Corporation*
Stephens, John — *Source Services Corporation*
Stephenson, Don L. — *Ells Personnel System Inc.*
Stern, Stephen — *CPS Inc.*
Sterner, Doug — *CPS Inc.*
Stevenson, Terry — *Bartholdi & Company, Inc.*
Stewart, Ross M. — *Human Resources Network Partners Inc.*

Yeaton, Robert — *Source Services Corporation*
Youlano, John — *Personnel Unlimited/Executive Search*
Young, Charles E. — *Flowers & Associates*
Young, Heather — *The Guild Corporation*
Youngberg, David — *Source Services Corporation*
Zander, Barry W. — *MSI International*
Zarnoski, Hank — *Dunhill Search International*
Zatman, Allen — *Search Enterprises South, Inc.*
Zatzick, Michael — *Search West, Inc.*
Zavrel, Mark — *Source Services Corporation*
Zay, Thomas C. — *Boyden/Zay & Company*
Zegel, Gary — *Source Services Corporation*
Zell, David M. — *Logix Partners*
Zera, Ronald J. — *Spencer Stuart*
Zilliacus, Patrick W. — *Larsen, Zilliacus & Associates, Inc.*
Zimbal, Mark — *Source Services Corporation*
Zimont, Scott — *Source Services Corporation*
Zingaro, Ron — *Zingaro and Company*
Zivic, Janis M. — *Spencer Stuart*

## 4. Finance/Accounting

Abbott, Peter — *The Abbott Group, Inc.*
Abell, Vincent W. — *MSI International*
Abernathy, Donald E. — *Don Richard Associates of Charlotte*
Abramson, Roye — *Source Services Corporation*
Ackerman, Larry R. — *Spectrum Search Associates, Inc.*
Adams, Amy — *Richard, Wayne and Roberts*
Adams, Len — *The KPA Group*
Adams, Michael — *CG & Associates*
Adams, Ralda F. — *Hospitality International*
Akin, J.R. — *J.R. Akin & Company Inc.*
Albert, Richard — *Source Services Corporation*
Alden, Brian R. — *MSI International*
Alexander, John T. — *Telford, Adams & Alexander/Human Resource Services*
Alford, Holly — *Source Services Corporation*
Allen, David A. — *Intech Summit Group, Inc.*
Allgire, Mary L. — *Kenzer Corp.*
Alringer, Marc — *Source Services Corporation*
Altreuter, Rose — *ALTCO Temporary Services*
Altreuter, Rose — *The ALTCO Group*
Ambler, Peter W. — *Peter W. Ambler Company*
Amico, Robert — *Source Services Corporation*
Amsterdam, Gail E. — *D.E. Foster Partners Inc.*
Anderson, Janet — *Professional Alternatives, Inc.*
Anderson, Mary — *Source Services Corporation*
Anderson, Matthew — *Source Services Corporation*
Anderson, Richard — *Grant Cooper and Associates*
Anderson, Roger J. — *BioQuest, Inc.*
Anderson, Shawn — *Temporary Accounting Personnel, Inc.*
Andrews, J. Douglas — *Clarey & Andrews, Inc.*
Andrews, Laura L. — *Stricker & Zagor*
Andujo, Michele M. — *Chrisman & Company, Incorporated*
Angell, Tryg R. — *Tryg R. Angell Ltd.*
Antil, Pamela W. — *Norman Roberts & Associates, Inc.*
Anwar, Tarin — *Jay Gaines & Company, Inc.*
Aquavella, Charles P. — *CPA & Associates*
Archer, Sandra F. — *Ryan, Miller & Associates Inc.*
Argenio, Michelangelo — *Spencer Stuart*
Argentin, Jo — *Executive Placement Consultants, Inc.*
Arnold, Jerry — *Houtz-Strawn Associates, Inc.*
Aronow, Lawrence E. — *Aronow Associates, Inc.*
Arseneault, Daniel S. — *MSI International*
Ascher, Susan P. — *The Ascher Group*
Ashton, Edward J. — *E.J. Ashton & Associates, Ltd.*
Asquith, Peter S. — *Ames Personnel Consultants, Inc.*
Aston, Kathy — *Marra Peters & Partners*
Attell, Harold — *A.E. Feldman Associates*
Austin, Jessica L. — *D.S.A. - Dixie Search Associates*
Aydelotte, G. Thomas — *Ingram & Aydelotte Inc.*
Bachmeier, Kevin — *Agra Placements International Ltd.*
Bacorn, Debra — *Accountants on Call*
Badger, Fred H. — *The Badger Group*
Baer, Kenneth — *Source Services Corporation*
Bagg, Mary — *Keith Bagg & Associates Inc.*
Baglio, Robert — *Source Services Corporation*
Bagwell, Bruce — *Intersource, Ltd.*
Baier, Rebecca — *Source Services Corporation*
Bailey, William A. — *TNS Partners, Inc.*
Baker, Gary M. — *Cochran, Cochran & Yale, Inc.*
Baker, Gary M. — *Temporary Accounting Personnel, Inc.*
Baker-Greene, Edward — *Isaacson, Miller*
Bakken, Mark — *Source Services Corporation*
Balchumas, Charles — *Source Services Corporation*
Baldock, Robert G. — *Lovas Stanley/Paul Ray Berndtson Inc.*
Balter, Sidney — *Source Services Corporation*
Banko, Scott — *Source Services Corporation*
Baran, Helena — *Michael J. Cavanagh and Associates*

Baranowski, Peter — *Source Services Corporation*
Barber, Toni L. — *MSI International*
Barbosa, Franklin J. — *Boyden*
Barger, H. Carter — *Barger & Sargeant, Inc.*
Barlow, Ken H. — *The Cherbonnier Group, Inc.*
Barnaby, Richard — *Source Services Corporation*
Barnes, Richard E. — *Barnes Development Group, LLC*
Barnes, Roanne L. — *Barnes Development Group, LLC*
Barnum, Toni M. — *Stone Murphy & Olson*
Baron, Jon C. — *MSI International*
Baron, Len — *Industrial Recruiters Associates, Inc.*
Barowsky, Diane M. — *Lamalie Amrop International*
Barr, Ronald — *Search West, Inc.*
Barrett, J. David — *Heidrick & Struggles, Inc.*
Barrucci, Jim — *Winter, Wyman & Company*
Bartels, Fredrick — *Source Services Corporation*
Bartfield, Philip — *Source Services Corporation*
Barthold, James A. — *McNichol Associates*
Bartholdi, Ted — *Bartholdi & Company, Inc.*
Bartholdi, Theodore G. — *Bartholdi & Company, Inc.*
Barton, Gary R. — *Barton Raben, Inc.*
Barton, James — *Source Services Corporation*
Bason, Maurice L. — *Bason Associates Inc.*
Bass, Nate — *Jacobson Associates*
Bates, Scott W. — *Kittleman & Associates*
Battalia, O. William — *Battalia Winston International*
Batte, Carol — *Source Services Corporation*
Battistoni, Bea — *Accountants on Call*
Battistoni, Bea — *Accountants on Call*
Bauman, Martin H. — *Martin H. Bauman Associates, Inc.*
Bearman, Linda — *Grant Cooper and Associates*
Beaudin, Elizabeth C. — *Callan Associates, Ltd.*
Beaulieu, Genie A. — *Romac & Associates*
Beaver, Bentley H. — *The Onstott Group, Inc.*
Beaver, Robert — *Source Services Corporation*
Beck, Jerry — *Financial Search Corporation*
Beckvold, John B. — *Atlantic Search Group, Inc.*
Belden, Jeannette — *Source Services Corporation*
Bell, Jeffrey G. — *Norman Broadbent International, Inc.*
Bellano, Robert W. — *Stanton Chase International*
Benjamin, Maurita — *Source Services Corporation*
Bennett, Delora — *Genesis Personnel Service, Inc.*
Bennett, Jo — *Battalia Winston International*
Benson, Edward — *Source Services Corporation*
Benson, Kate — *Rene Plessner Associates, Inc.*
Bergen, Anthony M. — *CFO Associates, Inc.*
Berger, Emanuel — *Isaacson, Miller*
Berger, Jeffrey — *Source Services Corporation*
Berlin, Marc — *Accountants on Call*
Berman, Kenneth D. — *MSI International*
Bernard, Bryan — *Source Services Corporation*
Bernas, Sharon — *Source Services Corporation*
Bettick, Michael J. — *A.J. Burton Group, Inc.*
Betts, Suzette — *Source Services Corporation*
Bickett, Nicole — *Source Services Corporation*
Bidelman, Richard — *Source Services Corporation*
Billington, Brian — *Billington & Associates*
Biolsi, Joseph — *Source Services Corporation*
Birns, Douglas — *Source Services Corporation*
Bitar, Edward — *The Interface Group, Ltd./Boyden*
Black, Douglas E. — *MSI International*
Bladon, Andrew — *Don Richard Associates of Tampa, Inc.*
Blair, Susan — *Simpson Associates*
Blakslee, Jan H. — *J: Blakslee International, Ltd.*
Bland, Walter — *Source Services Corporation*
Blassaras, Peggy — *Source Services Corporation*
Blickle, Michael — *Source Services Corporation*
Bliley, Jerry — *Spencer Stuart*
Bloch, Suzanne — *Source Services Corporation*
Blocher, John — *Source Services Corporation*
Bluhm, Claudia — *Schweichler Associates, Inc.*
Boccella, Ralph — *Susan C. Goldberg Associates*
Boczany, William J. — *The Guild Corporation*
Bodner, Marilyn — *Bodner, Inc.*
Bogard, Nicholas C. — *The Onstott Group, Inc.*
Bohn, Steve J. — *MSI International*
Bond, Robert J. — *Romac & Associates*
Bonifield, Len — *Bonifield Associates*
Bonnell, William R. — *Bonnell Associates Ltd.*
Booth, Ronald — *Source Services Corporation*
Borland, James — *Goodrich & Sherwood Associates, Inc.*
Bormann, Cindy Ann — *MSI International*
Bosward, Allan — *Source Services Corporation*
Bourbeau, Paul J. — *Boyden*
Bourrie, Sharon D. — *Chartwell Partners International, Inc.*
Bovich, Maryann C. — *Higdon Prince Inc.*
Boyd, Michael — *Accountants on Call*
Boyd, Sara — *Accountants on Call*

Boyd, Sara — *Accountants on Call*
Boyer, Heath C. — *Spencer Stuart*
Brackenbury, Robert — *Bowman & Marshall, Inc.*
Brackin, James B. — *Brackin & Sayers Associates*
Brandjes, Michael J. — *Brandjes Associates*
Brassard, Gary — *Source Services Corporation*
Bratches, Howard — *Thorndike Deland Associates*
Bremer, Brian — *Source Services Corporation*
Brewster, Edward — *Source Services Corporation*
Brieger, Steve — *Thorne, Brieger Associates Inc.*
Briggs, Adam — *Horton International*
Bright, Timothy — *MSI International*
Brinson, Robert — *MSI International*
Brocaglia, Joyce — *Alta Associates, Inc.*
Brodie, Ricki R. — *MSI International*
Bronger, Patricia — *Source Services Corporation*
Brown, Charlene N. — *Accent on Achievement, Inc.*
Brown, Clifford — *Source Services Corporation*
Brown, D. Perry — *Don Richard Associates of Washington, D.C., Inc.*
Brown, Daniel — *Source Services Corporation*
Brown, Franklin Key — *Handy HRM Corp.*
Brown, Larry C. — *Horton International*
Brown, Lawrence Anthony — *MSI International*
Brown, Michael R. — *MSI International*
Brown, Steven — *Source Services Corporation*
Browne, Michael — *Source Services Corporation*
Brudno, Robert J. — *Savoy Partners, Ltd.*
Brunner, Terry — *Source Services Corporation*
Bryant, Henry — *D. Brown and Associates, Inc.*
Bryant, Richard D. — *Bryant Associates, Inc.*
Bryza, Robert M. — *Robert Lowell International*
Brzowski, John — *Financial Search Corporation*
Buchsbaum, Deborah — *Accountants on Call*
Bueschel, David A. — *Shepherd Bueschel & Provus, Inc.*
Bullock, Conni — *Earley Kielty and Associates, Inc.*
Bump, Gerald J. — *D.E. Foster Partners Inc.*
Burch, Donald — *Source Services Corporation*
Burchard, Stephen R. — *Burchard & Associates, Inc.*
Burchill, Barb — *BGB Associates*
Burchill, Greg — *BGB Associates*
Burden, Gene — *The Cherbonnier Group, Inc.*
Burfield, Elaine — *Skott/Edwards Consultants, Inc.*
Burke, John — *The Experts*
Burnett, Rebecca J. — *MSI International*
Burns, Alan — *The Enns Partners Inc.*
Burns, Terence N. — *D.E. Foster Partners Inc.*
Burris, James C. — *Boyden*
Busch, Jack — *Busch International*
Bush, Martha A. — *MSI International*
Busterna, Charles — *The KPA Group*
Butcher, Pascale — *F-O-R-T-U-N-E Personnel Consultants of Manatee County*
Butler, Kirby B. — *The Butlers Company Insurance Recruiters*
Butterfass, Stanley — *Butterfass, Pepe & MacCallan Inc.*
Buttrey, Daniel — *Source Services Corporation*
Buzolits, Patrick — *Source Services Corporation*
Bye, Randy — *Romac & Associates*
Byrnes, Thomas A. — *Thomas A. Byrnes Associates*
Cafero, Les — *Source Services Corporation*
Caldwell, William R. — *Pearson, Caldwell & Farnsworth, Inc.*
Calivas, Kay — *A.J. Burton Group, Inc.*
Callan, Robert M. — *Callan Associates, Ltd.*
Campbell, E. — *Source Services Corporation*
Campbell, Gary — *Romac & Associates*
Campbell, Jeff — *Source Services Corporation*
Campbell, Robert Scott — *Wellington Management Group*
Cannavino, John J. — *Financial Resource Associates, Inc.*
Cannon, Alexis — *Richard, Wayne and Roberts*
Cannon, Alicia — *Accountants on Call*
Cannon, Alicia — *Accountants on Call*
Capizzi, Salvatore — *Winter, Wyman & Company*
Cargo, Catherine — *MSI International*
Carideo, Joseph — *Thorndike Deland Associates*
Carlson, Eric — *Source Services Corporation*
Carlson, Judith — *Bowman & Marshall, Inc.*
Carnal, Rick — *Source Services Corporation*
Carpenter, Harold G. — *MSI International*
Carter, Christine C. — *Health Care Dimensions*
Carter, Linda — *Source Services Corporation*
Caruso, Kathy — *Accounting Resources, Inc.*
Carvalho-Esteves, Maria — *Source Services Corporation*
Casal, Daniel G. — *Bonifield Associates*
Casey, Darren — *Parfitt Recruiting and Consulting*
Cashen, Anthony B. — *Lamalie Amrop International*
Cass, Kathryn H. — *Don Richard Associates of Tidewater, Inc.*
Cassie, Ronald L. — *The Cassie Group*
Castine, Michael P. — *Spencer Stuart*
Castle, Lisa — *Source Services Corporation*

Cattanach, Bruce B. — *Horton International*
Causey, Andrea C. — *MSI International*
Cavanagh, Michael J. — *Michael J. Cavanagh and Associates*
Cersosimo, Rocco — *Source Services Corporation*
Chappell, Peter — *The Bankers Group*
Chase, James — *Source Services Corporation*
Chatterjie, Alok — *MSI International*
Chattin, Norma Anne — *Accountants on Call*
Cheah, Victor — *Source Services Corporation*
Cherbonnier, L. Michael — *TCG International, Inc.*
Cherbonnier, L. Michael — *The Cherbonnier Group, Inc.*
Chesla, Garry — *Executive Referral Services, Inc.*
Cho, Ui — *Richard, Wayne and Roberts*
Christenson, H. Alan — *Christenson & Hutchison*
Christman, Joel — *Source Services Corporation*
Chronopoulos, Dennis — *Source Services Corporation*
Cinquemano, Teri — *Accounting Personnel Consultants*
Citarella, Richard A. — *A.T. Kearney, Inc.*
Cizek, John T. — *Cizek Associates, Inc.*
Cizek, Marti J. — *Cizek Associates, Inc.*
Clarey, Jack R. — *Clarey & Andrews, Inc.*
Clarey, William A. — *Preng & Associates, Inc.*
Clauhsen, Elizabeth A. — *Savoy Partners, Ltd.*
Clawson, Bob — *Source Services Corporation*
Clawson, Robert — *Source Services Corporation*
Clegg, Cynthia — *Horton International*
Clemens, William B. — *Norman Broadbent International, Inc.*
Clemens, William B. — *Norman Broadbent International, Inc.*
Close, E. Wade — *Boyden*
Cocchiaro, Richard — *Romac & Associates*
Cocconi, Alan — *Source Services Corporation*
Cochran, Hale — *Fenwick Partners*
Cochrun, James — *Source Services Corporation*
Coffman, Brian — *Kossuth & Associates, Inc.*
Cohen, Michael R. — *Intech Summit Group, Inc.*
Cohen, Robert C. — *Intech Summit Group, Inc.*
Colborne, Janis M. — *AJM Professional Services*
Cole, Elizabeth — *MSI International*
Cole, Kevin — *Don Richard Associates of Washington, D.C., Inc.*
Cole, Rosalie — *Source Services Corporation*
Coleman, J. Kevin — *J. Kevin Coleman & Associates, Inc.*
Coleman, John A. — *Canny, Bowen Inc.*
Collard, Joseph A. — *Spencer Stuart*
Collier, David — *Parfitt Recruiting and Consulting/PRO TEM*
Colling, Douglas — *KPMG Management Consulting*
Collins, Robert — *Financial Search Corporation*
Collins, Scott — *Source Services Corporation*
Collins, Stephen — *The Johnson Group, Inc.*
Colman, Michael — *Executive Placement Consultants, Inc.*
Colucci, Bart A. — *Colucci, Blendow and Johnson, Inc.*
Comai, Christine — *Source Services Corporation*
Combs, Thomas — *Source Services Corporation*
Commersoli, Al — *Executive Referral Services, Inc.*
Cona, Joseph A. — *Cona Personnel Search*
Conard, Rodney J. — *Conard Associates, Inc.*
Coneys, Bridget — *Source Services Corporation*
Connaghan, Linda — *Bowman & Marshall, Inc.*
Connelly, Kevin M. — *Spencer Stuart*
Conner, John — *Flex Execs Management Solutions*
Cook, Charlene — *Source Services Corporation*
Cooke, Jeffrey R. — *Jonas, Walters & Assoc., Inc.*
Cooke, Katherine H. — *Horton International*
Coon, David — *Don Richard Associates of Richmond, Inc.*
Cooper, David C. — *David C. Cooper and Associates, Inc.*
Cordaro, Concetta — *Flynn, Hannock, Incorporated*
Cornehlsen, James H. — *Lamalie Amrop International*
Corrigan, Gerald F. — *The Corrigan Group*
Corso, Glen S. — *Chartwell Partners International, Inc.*
Costa, Cynthia A. — *MSI International*
Coston, Bruce G. — *MSI International*
Cotugno, James — *Source Services Corporation*
Coughlin, Stephen — *Source Services Corporation*
Courtney, Brendan A.J. — *A.J. Burton Group, Inc.*
Cox, James O. — *MSI International*
Cox, William — *E.J. Ashton & Associates, Ltd.*
Coyle, Hugh F. — *A.J. Burton Group, Inc.*
Cramer, Paul J. — *C/R Associates*
Crane, Howard C. — *Chartwell Partners International, Inc.*
Crath, Paul F. — *Price Waterhouse*
Crawford, Cassondra — *Don Richard Associates of Washington, D.C., Inc.*
Creger, Elizabeth — *Search West, Inc.*
Crist, Peter — *Crist Partners, Ltd.*
Critchley, Walter — *Temporary Accounting Personnel, Inc.*
Crowder, Edward W. — *Crowder & Company*
Crownover, Kathryn L. — *MSI International*
Crumbaker, Robert H. — *Lamalie Amrop International*
Cruse, O.D. — *Spencer Stuart*

Hart, James — *Source Services Corporation*
Hart, Robert T. — *D.E. Foster Partners Inc.*
Harvey, Jill — *MSI International*
Harvey, Mike — *Advanced Executive Resources*
Harvey, Richard — *Price Waterhouse*
Harwood, Brian — *Source Services Corporation*
Haselby, James — *Source Services Corporation*
Hasten, Lawrence — *Source Services Corporation*
Haughton, Michael — *DeFrain, Mayer, Lee & Burgess LLC*
Hauser, Martha — *Spencer Stuart*
Havener, Donald Clarke — *The Abbott Group, Inc.*
Hawkins, W. Davis — *Spencer Stuart*
Hawksworth, A. Dwight — *A.D. & Associates Executive Search, Inc.*
Hay, William E. — *William E. Hay & Company*
Hayes, Lee — *Source Services Corporation*
Haystead, Steve — *Advanced Executive Resources*
Hazelton, Lisa M. — *Health Care Dimensions*
Healey, Joseph T. — *Highland Search Group, L.L.C.*
Hebel, Robert W. — *R.W. Hebel Associates*
Hecker, Henry C. — *Hogan Acquisitions*
Heinrich, Scott — *Source Services Corporation*
Heiser, Charles S. — *The Cassie Group*
Hellebusch, Jerry — *Morgan Hunter Corp.*
Hellinger, Audrey — *Martin H. Bauman Associates, Inc.*
Henderson, John — *Key Employment Services*
Heneghan, Donald A. — *Allerton Heneghan & O'Neill*
Henneberry, Ward — *Source Services Corporation*
Hennig, Sandra M. — *MSI International*
Hensley, Gayla — *Atlantic Search Group, Inc.*
Herget, James P. — *Lamalie Amrop International*
Herman, Beth — *Accountants on Call*
Herman, Eugene J. — *Earley Kielty and Associates, Inc.*
Herman, Pat — *Whitney & Associates, Inc.*
Hernandez, Ruben — *Source Services Corporation*
Heroux, David — *Source Services Corporation*
Herrod, Vicki — *Accountants on Call*
Herzog, Sarah — *Source Services Corporation*
Hetherman, Margaret F. — *Highland Search Group, L.L.C.*
Hewitt, Rives D. — *The Dalley Hewitt Company*
Hicks, James L. — *MSI International*
Higdon, Henry G. — *Higdon Prince Inc.*
Higgins, John B. — *Higgins Associates, Inc.*
Hight, Susan — *Source Services Corporation*
Hilbert, Laurence — *Source Services Corporation*
Hildebrand, Thomas B. — *Professional Resources Group, Inc.*
Hilgenberg, Thomas — *Source Services Corporation*
Hill, Emery — *MSI International*
Hillyer, Carolyn — *Source Services Corporation*
Hilyard, Paul J. — *MSI International*
Hinojosa, Oscar — *Source Services Corporation*
Hirsch, Julia C. — *Boyden*
Hites, Susan — *Accountants on Call*
Hockett, William — *Hockett Associates, Inc.*
Hodge, Jeff — *Heidrick & Struggles, Inc.*
Hoevel, Michael J. — *Poirier, Hoevel & Co.*
Hoffman, Sharon L. — *Accountants on Call*
Hoffman, Stephen — *Source Services Corporation*
Hoffmeir, Patricia A. — *Gilbert Tweed/INESA*
Hofner, Andrew — *Source Services Corporation*
Hogan, Larry H. — *Hogan Acquisitions*
Holden, Richard B. — *Ames Personnel Consultants, Inc.*
Hollins, Howard D. — *MSI International*
Holodnak, William A. — *J. Robert Scott*
Holt, Carol — *Bartholdi & Company, Inc.*
Holtz, Gene — *Agra Placements International Ltd.*
Holzberger, Georges L. — *Highland Search Group, L.L.C.*
Homrich, Patricia J. — *David C. Cooper and Associates, Inc.*
Hopkinson, Dana — *Winter, Wyman & Company*
Hoppert, Phil — *Wargo and Co., Inc.*
Hostetter, Kristi — *Source Services Corporation*
Houterloot, Tim — *Source Services Corporation*
Howard, Jill — *Health Care Dimensions*
Howard, Leon — *Richard, Wayne and Roberts*
Howard, Marybeth — *Accounting & Bookkeeping Personnel, Inc.*
Howe, Theodore — *Romac & Associates*
Howell, Robert B. — *Atlantic Search Group, Inc.*
Howell, Robert B. — *Atlantic Search Group, Inc.*
Hoyda, Louis A. — *Thorndike Deland Associates*
Hubert, David L. — *ARJay & Associates*
Hucko, Donald S. — *Jonas, Walters & Assoc., Inc.*
Hudson, Reginald M. — *Search Bureau International*
Hughes, Barbara — *Source Services Corporation*
Hughes, Cathy N. — *The Ogdon Partnership*
Hughes, Kevin R. — *Handy HRM Corp.*
Hughes, Randall — *Source Services Corporation*
Hult, Dana — *Source Services Corporation*
Humphrey, Titus — *Source Services Corporation*
Hunt, Thomas — *MSI International*

Hunter, Steven — *Diamond Tax Recruiting*
Huntting, Lisa — *Professional Alternatives, Inc.*
Hurtado, Jaime — *Source Services Corporation*
Huss, Juli — *Accountants on Call*
Hutchison, Richard H. — *Rurak & Associates, Inc.*
Hutchison, William K. — *Christenson & Hutchison*
Hwang, Yvette — *MSI International*
Hyde, Mark D. — *MSI International*
Hyde, W. Jerry — *Hyde Danforth Wold & Co.*
Hykes, Don A. — *A.T. Kearney, Inc.*
Hylas, Lisa — *Source Services Corporation*
Hypes, Richard G. — *Lynch Miller Moore Partners, Inc.*
Iammatteo, Enzo — *Keith Bagg & Associates Inc.*
Imely, Larry — *Christian & Timbers*
Imhof, Kirk — *Source Services Corporation*
Infinger, Ronald E. — *Robison & Associates*
Inger, Barry — *Source Services Corporation*
Ingram, D. John — *Ingram & Aydelotte Inc.*
Inguagiato, Gregory — *MSI International*
Inskeep, Thomas — *Source Services Corporation*
Intravaia, Salvatore — *Source Services Corporation*
Inzitari, Gloria — *Accountants on Call*
Irvine, Robert — *Keith Bagg & Associates Inc.*
Irwin, Mark — *Source Services Corporation*
Isaacson, John — *Isaacson, Miller*
Issacs, Judith A. — *Grant Cooper and Associates*
Ives, Richard K. — *Wilkinson & Ives*
Ivey, Deborah M. — *MSI International*
Jacobs, Judith — *The Rubicon Group*
Jacobs, Martin J. — *The Rubicon Group*
Jacobs, Mike — *Thorne, Brieger Associates Inc.*
Jacobson, Hayley — *Source Services Corporation*
Jadulang, Vincent — *Source Services Corporation*
James, Allison A. — *MSI International*
James, Richard — *Criterion Executive Search, Inc.*
Januleski, Geoff — *Source Services Corporation*
Jeltema, John — *Source Services Corporation*
Jensen, Debra — *Flex Execs Management Solutions*
Jensen, Robert — *Source Services Corporation*
Jernigan, Alice — *Ariel Recruitment Associates*
Jernigan, Susan N. — *Sockwell & Associates*
Joffe, Barry — *Bason Associates Inc.*
Johnson, Brian — *A.J. Burton Group, Inc.*
Johnson, David — *Gaffney Management Consultants*
Johnson, Greg — *Source Services Corporation*
Johnson, John F. — *Lamalie Amrop International*
Johnson, John W. — *Webb, Johnson Associates, Inc.*
Johnson, Kathleen A. — *Barton Raben, Inc.*
Johnson, Keith — *Romac & Associates*
Johnson, Priscilla — *The Johnson Group, Inc.*
Johnstone, Grant — *Source Services Corporation*
Jones, Daniel F. — *Atlantic Search Group, Inc.*
Jones, Francis E. — *Earley Kielty and Associates, Inc.*
Jones, Gary — *BGB Associates*
Jones, Jeffrey — *AJM Professional Services*
Jones, Jonathan C. — *The Ogdon Partnership*
Jones, Rodney — *Source Services Corporation*
Jones, Ronald T. — *ARJay & Associates*
Joubert, Pierre E. — *Boyden*
Joyce, William J. — *The Guild Corporation*
Judge, Alfred L. — *The Cambridge Group Ltd*
Juelis, John J. — *Peeney Associates*
Juratovac, Michael — *Montgomery Resources, Inc.*
Justiss, Ted W. — *David C. Cooper and Associates, Inc.*
Kader, Richard — *Richard Kader & Associates*
Kaiser, Donald J. — *Dunhill Search International*
Kalinowski, David — *Jacobson Associates*
Kanal, David S. — *Johnson Smith & Knisely Accord*
Kane, Frank — *A.J. Burton Group, Inc.*
Kantor, Richard — *Search West, Inc.*
Kaplan, Gary — *Gary Kaplan & Associates*
Kaplan, Marc — *Gary Kaplan & Associates*
Kaplan, Traci — *Source Services Corporation*
Karr, Cynthia L. — *Howard Karr & Associates, Inc.*
Karr, Howard L. — *Howard Karr & Associates, Inc.*
Kasprzyk, Michael — *Source Services Corporation*
Katz, Robert L. — *MSI International*
Keesom, W. Peter — *Boyden/Zay & Company*
Keith, Stephanie — *Southwestern Professional Services*
Keller, Barbara — *Barton Raben, Inc.*
Kelly, Claudia L. — *Spencer Stuart*
Kelly, Donna J. — *Accountants Executive Search*
Kelly, Elizabeth Ann — *Wellington Management Group*
Kelly, Robert — *Source Services Corporation*
Kelso, Patricia C. — *Barton Raben, Inc.*
Kennedy, Craig — *Source Services Corporation*
Kennedy, Michael — *The Danbrook Group, Inc.*
Kennedy, Paul — *Source Services Corporation*

MacCallan, Deirdre — *Butterfass, Pepe & MacCallan Inc.*
MacCarthy, Ann — *Columbia Consulting Group*
MacGregor, Malcolm — *Boyden*
Mackenna, Kathy — *Plummer & Associates, Inc.*
MacMillan, James — *Source Services Corporation*
MacPherson, Holly — *Source Services Corporation*
Macrides, Michael — *Source Services Corporation*
Madaras, Debra — *Financial Resource Associates, Inc.*
Mader, Stephen P. — *Christian & Timbers*
Maer, Harry — *Kenzer Corp.*
Maggio, Mary — *Source Services Corporation*
Maher, William J. — *Johnson Smith & Knisely Accord*
Mahmoud, Sophia — *Source Services Corporation*
Mainwaring, Andrew Brian — *Executive Search Consultants Corporation*
Mairn, Todd — *Source Services Corporation*
Mak, I. Paul — *Thomas A. Byrnes Associates*
Malcolm, Rod — *The Enns Partners Inc.*
Malone, George V. — *Boyden*
Manassero, Henri J.P. — *International Management Advisors, Inc.*
Mancos, Barbara — *Accountants on Call*
Manns, Alex — *Crawford & Crofford*
Manzo, Renee — *Atlantic Search Group, Inc.*
Maphet, Harriet — *The Stevenson Group of New Jersey*
Marion, Bradford B. — *Lamalie Amrop International*
Marks, Russell E. — *Webb, Johnson Associates, Inc.*
Marlow, William — *Straube Associates*
Marra, John — *Marra Peters & Partners*
Marra, John — *Marra Peters & Partners*
Marshall, John — *Accountants on Call*
Martens, Maxine — *Rene Plessner Associates, Inc.*
Martin, David — *The Guild Corporation*
Martin, Geary D. — *Boyden/Zay & Company*
Martin, Kenneth — *Winter, Wyman & Company*
Martin, Lynne Koll — *Boyden*
Martin, Nancy A. — *Educational Management Network*
Martin, Paula — *MSI International*
Marumoto, William H. — *The Interface Group, Ltd./Boyden*
Marwil, Jennifer — *Source Services Corporation*
Maschal, Charles E. — *Maschal/Connors, Inc.*
Mason, William E. — *John Kurosky & Associates*
Massey, H. Heath — *Robison & Associates*
Massey, R. Bruce — *Bruce Massey & Partners Inc.*
Matheny, Robert P. — *MSI International*
Mather, David R. — *Christian & Timbers*
Mathias, Douglas — *Source Services Corporation*
Mathias, William J. — *Preng & Associates, Inc.*
Mathis, Carrie — *Source Services Corporation*
Matthews, Nadie — *Accountants on Call*
Mattingly, Kathleen — *Source Services Corporation*
Matueny, Robert — *Ryan, Miller & Associates Inc.*
Mauer, Kristin — *Montgomery Resources, Inc.*
Maxwell, John — *Source Services Corporation*
May, Peter — *Mixtec Group*
Mayer, Thomas — *Source Services Corporation*
Mayes, Kay H. — *John Shell Associates, Inc.*
Maynard, Raun — *Accountants on Call*
Mazza, David B. — *Mazza & Riley, Inc.*
Mazzocchi, Jonathan — *Winter, Wyman & Company*
McAlpine, Bruce — *Keith Bagg & Associates Inc.*
McAteer, Thomas — *Montgomery Resources, Inc.*
McBride, Jonathan E. — *McBride Associates, Inc.*
McBryde, Marnie — *Spencer Stuart*
McCallister, Richard A. — *Boyden*
McCarthy, Laura — *Source Services Corporation*
McComas, Kelly E. — *The Guild Corporation*
McCormack, William Reed — *MSI International*
McCormick, Brian — *The McCormick Group, Inc.*
McCormick, Cyndi — *Winter, Wyman & Company*
McCormick, Joseph — *Source Services Corporation*
McCormick, William J. — *The McCormick Group, Inc.*
McCreary, Charles — *Austin-McGregor International*
McCutcheon, C. Scott — *John Kurosky & Associates*
McDaniel, Debra A. — *Simpson Associates*
McDonald, Gary E. — *Agra Placements International Ltd.*
McDonald, Scott A. — *McDonald Associates International*
McDonald, Stanleigh B. — *McDonald Associates International*
McDonnell, Julie — *Technical Personnel of Minnesota*
McFadden, Ashton S. — *Johnson Smith & Knisely Accord*
McGinnis, Rita — *Source Services Corporation*
McGoldrick, Terrence — *Source Services Corporation*
McHugh, Keith — *Source Services Corporation*
McIntosh, Arthur — *Source Services Corporation*
McIntosh, Tad — *Source Services Corporation*
McIntyre, Alex D. — *Norman Roberts & Associates, Inc.*
McKinney, Julia — *Source Services Corporation*
McKnight, Amy E. — *Chartwell Partners International, Inc.*
McLaughlin, John — *Romac & Associates*

McLean, E. Peter — *Spencer Stuart*
McMahan, Stephen — *Source Services Corporation*
McMahan, Stephen — *Source Services Corporation*
McMillin, Bob — *Price Waterhouse*
McNamara, Timothy C. — *Columbia Consulting Group*
McNear, Jeffrey E. — *Barrett Partners*
McNichol, John — *McNichol Associates*
McNichols, Walter B. — *Gary Kaplan & Associates*
McQuoid, David — *A.T. Kearney, Inc.*
McRae, O. Jon — *Jon McRae & Associates, Inc.*
Meagher, Patricia G. — *Spencer Stuart*
Meany, Brian — *Herbert Mines Associates, Inc.*
Meara, Helen — *Source Services Corporation*
Meehan, John — *Source Services Corporation*
Meehan, Robert — *A.J. Burton Group, Inc.*
Meier, J. Dale — *Grant Cooper and Associates*
Meltzer, Andrea Y. — *Executive Options, Ltd.*
Mendelson, Jeffrey — *Source Services Corporation*
Mendoza-Green, Robin — *Source Services Corporation*
Menendez, Todd — *Don Richard Associates of Tampa, Inc.*
Merrifield, Gary — *Accountants on Call*
Merrigan, Eileen M. — *Lamalie Amrop International*
Mertensotto, Chuck H. — *Whitney & Associates, Inc.*
Messett, William J. — *Messett Associates, Inc.*
Messina, Marco — *Source Services Corporation*
Mestepey, John — *A.T. Kearney, Inc.*
Meyer, Marjorie — *Accountants on Call*
Meyer, Stacey — *Gary Kaplan & Associates*
Meyer, William — *Agra Placements International Ltd.*
Meyers, Steven — *Montgomery Resources, Inc.*
Meza, Anna — *Richard, Wayne and Roberts*
Mierzwinski, John — *Industrial Recruiters Associates, Inc.*
Miesemer, Arthur C. — *MSI International*
Miles, Kenneth T. — *MSI International*
Miller, Arnie — *Isaacson, Miller*
Miller, Benjamin J. — *MSI International*
Miller, David — *Temporary Accounting Personnel, Inc.*
Miller, Harold B. — *MSI International*
Miller, Larry — *Source Services Corporation*
Miller, Laura — *Accounting Personnel Consultants*
Miller, Michael R. — *Lynch Miller Moore Partners, Inc.*
Miller, Roy — *The Enns Partners Inc.*
Miller, Russel E. — *ARJay & Associates*
Miller, Timothy — *Source Services Corporation*
Milligan, Dale — *Source Services Corporation*
Millonzi, Joel C. — *Johnson Smith & Knisely Accord*
Mills, John — *Source Services Corporation*
Milner, Carol — *Source Services Corporation*
Milstein, Bonnie — *Marvin Laba & Associates*
Milton, Suzanne — *Marra Peters & Partners*
Mines, Herbert T. — *Herbert Mines Associates, Inc.*
Miras, Cliff — *Source Services Corporation*
Miras, Cliff — *Source Services Corporation*
Mitchell, John — *Romac & Associates*
Mitton, Bill — *Executive Resource, Inc.*
Mittwol, Myles — *Source Services Corporation*
Mochwart, Donald — *Drummond Associates, Inc.*
Mockler, Nadine — *Part Time Resources, Inc.*
Molitor, John L. — *Barrett Partners*
Mollichelli, David — *Source Services Corporation*
Mondragon, Philip — *Boyden*
Montgomery, Catherine C. — *Boyden*
Montgomery, James M. — *Houze, Shourds & Montgomery, Inc.*
Moore, Craig — *Source Services Corporation*
Moore, David S. — *Lynch Miller Moore Partners, Inc.*
Moore, Denise — *Jonas, Walters & Assoc., Inc.*
Moore, Dianna — *Source Services Corporation*
Moore, Janice E. — *MSI International*
Moore, Lemuel R. — *MSI International*
Moore, Mark — *Wheeler, Moore & Elam Co.*
Moore, Michael — *Agra Placements International Ltd.*
Moore, Suzanne — *Source Services Corporation*
Moran, Douglas — *Source Services Corporation*
Morato, Rene — *Source Services Corporation*
Moretti, Denise — *Source Services Corporation*
Morgan, David G. — *Morgan Stampfl, Inc.*
Morgan, Donald T. — *MSI International*
Morgan, Gary — *National Search, Inc.*
Moriarty, Mike — *Source Services Corporation*
Morris, Scott — *Source Services Corporation*
Morrison, Janis L. — *Garrett Associates Inc.*
Morrow, Melanie — *Source Services Corporation*
Morrow, Miles — *Key Employment Services*
Morton, Robert C. — *Morton, McCorkle & Associates, Inc.*
Moseley, Monroe — *Isaacson, Miller*
Mott, Greg — *Source Services Corporation*
Msidment, Roger — *Source Services Corporation*
Mueller, Colleen — *Source Services Corporation*

Muendel, H. Edward — *Stanton Chase International*
Muller, Charles A. — *AJM Professional Services*
Mummert, Dennis D. — *Sweeney Harbert & Mummert, Inc.*
Munguia, Rebecca — *Richard, Wayne and Roberts*
Murin, Rose Mary — *U.S. Envirosearch*
Murphy, Corinne — *Source Services Corporation*
Murphy, Cornelius J. — *Goodrich & Sherwood Associates, Inc.*
Murphy, Gary J. — *Stone Murphy & Olson*
Murphy, James — *Source Services Corporation*
Murphy, Karen S. — *Flex Execs Management Solutions*
Murphy, Patrick J. — *P.J. Murphy & Associates, Inc.*
Murphy, Timothy D. — *MSI International*
Murray, Virginia — *Baker, Harris & Partners Limited*
Murry, John — *Source Services Corporation*
Mursuli, Meredith — *Lasher Associates*
Mustin, Joyce M. — *J: Blakslee International, Ltd.*
Myers, Kay — *Signature Staffing*
Myrick, Marilou — *ProResource, Inc.*
Myrick, Marilou — *ProResource, Inc.*
Nabers, Karen — *Source Services Corporation*
Nadherny, Christopher C. — *Spencer Stuart*
Nagler, Leon G. — *Nagler, Robins & Poe, Inc.*
Nagy, Les — *Source Services Corporation*
Nahas, Robert — *Herbert Mines Associates, Inc.*
Napier, Ginger L. — *Preng & Associates, Inc.*
Nass, Martin D. — *Lamalie Amrop International*
Nathanson, Barry F. — *Barry Nathanson Associates*
Nazzaro, Samuel G. — *Boyden*
Neblett, Jon — *Don Richard Associates of Richmond, Inc.*
Necessary, Rick — *Source Services Corporation*
Neckanoff, Sharon — *Search West, Inc.*
Needham, Karen — *Source Services Corporation*
Neff, Herbert — *Source Services Corporation*
Nein, Lawrence F. — *Lamalie Amrop International*
Nelson, Barbara — *Herman Smith Executive Initiatives Inc.*
Nelson, Hitch — *Source Services Corporation*
Nelson, Mary — *Source Services Corporation*
Nelson-Folkersen, Jeffrey — *Source Services Corporation*
Nephew, Robert — *Christian & Timbers*
Neuberth, Jeffrey G. — *Canny, Bowen Inc.*
Neuwald, Debrah — *Source Services Corporation*
Newbold, Michael — *Agra Placements International Ltd.*
Newman, Lynn — *Kishbaugh Associates International*
Nielsen, Sue — *Ells Personnel System Inc.*
Nitti, Jacqueline — *ALTCO Temporary Services*
Nocero, John — *ProResource, Inc.*
Nolan, Michael W. — *Accounting & Bookkeeping Personnel, Inc.*
Nolan, Robert — *Source Services Corporation*
Nolen, Shannon — *Source Services Corporation*
Nordland, Martin N. — *Horton International*
Norman, Randy — *Austin-McGregor International*
Normann, Amy — *Robert M. Flanagan & Associates, Ltd.*
Norsell, Paul E. — *Paul Norsell & Associates, Inc.*
Nunziata, Fred — *Eden & Associates, Inc.*
Nunziata, Peter — *Atlantic Search Group, Inc.*
Nye, David S. — *Blake, Hansen & Nye, Limited*
O'Brien, John G. — *CanMed Consultants Inc.*
O'Brien, Susan — *Source Services Corporation*
O'Connell, Bridget — *Accountants on Call*
O'Connell, Michael — *Ryan, Miller & Associates Inc.*
O'Connell, William — *Winter, Wyman & Company*
O'Donnell, James H. — *MSI International*
O'Donnell, Timothy W. — *Boyden*
O'Halloran, Robert — *MSI International*
O'Hara, Daniel M. — *Lynch Miller Moore Partners, Inc.*
O'Maley, Kimberlee — *Spencer Stuart*
O'Meally, Diane — *Accountants on Call*
O'Neill, James P. — *Allerton Heneghan & O'Neill*
O'Neill, Stephen A. — *Harris Heery & Associates*
O'Toole, Dennis P. — *Dennis P. O'Toole & Associates Inc.*
Occhiboi, Emil — *Source Services Corporation*
Ocon, Olga — *Busch International*
Oddo, Judith — *Accounting Personnel Consultants*
Ogden, Thomas H. — *The Ogdon Partnership*
Ohman, Gregory L. — *Pearson, Caldwell & Farnsworth, Inc.*
Olin, Robyn — *Richard, Wayne and Roberts*
Oliver, Phoebe — *Seiden Krieger Associates, Inc.*
Olmstead, George T. — *Blackshaw, Olmstead & Lynch*
Olsen, Robert — *Source Services Corporation*
Onstott, Joseph E. — *The Onstott Group, Inc.*
Oppedisano, Edward — *Oppedisano & Company, Inc.*
Orr, Stacie — *Source Services Corporation*
Ott, George W. — *Ott & Hansen, Inc.*
Ouellette, Christopher — *Source Services Corporation*
Owen, Christopher — *Source Services Corporation*
Pace, Susan A. — *Horton International*
Pachowitz, John — *Source Services Corporation*
Page, G. Schuyler — *A.T. Kearney, Inc.*

Page, Linda — *Jonas, Walters & Assoc., Inc.*
Page, Linda M. — *Wargo and Co., Inc.*
Palazio, Carla — *A.T. Kearney, Inc.*
Paliwoda, William — *Source Services Corporation*
Palma, Frank R. — *Goodrich & Sherwood Associates, Inc.*
Palmer, Carlton A. — *Beall & Company, Inc.*
Palmer, Melissa — *Don Richard Associates of Tampa, Inc.*
Palmlund, David W. — *Lamalie Amrop International*
Papciak, Dennis J. — *Accounting Personnel Associates, Inc.*
Papciak, Dennis J. — *Temporary Accounting Personnel*
Pappas, Timothy C. — *Jonas, Walters & Assoc., Inc.*
Paradise, Malcolm — *Source Services Corporation*
Parbs, Michael — *Accountants on Call*
Parbs, Michael — *Accountants on Call*
Parente, James — *Source Services Corporation*
Parfitt, William C. — *Parfitt Recruiting and Consulting/PRO TEM*
Park, Dabney G. — *Mark Stanley & Company*
Parr, James A. — *KPMG Management Consulting*
Parroco, Jason — *Source Services Corporation*
Patel, Shailesh — *Source Services Corporation*
Patence, David W. — *Handy HRM Corp.*
Paternie, Patrick — *Source Services Corporation*
Patton, Mitchell — *Patton/Perry Associates, Inc.*
Paul, Kathleen — *Source Services Corporation*
Payne, Robert — *Winter, Wyman & Company*
Peal, Matthew — *Source Services Corporation*
Pearson, John R. — *Pearson, Caldwell & Farnsworth, Inc.*
Pearson, Robert L. — *Lamalie Amrop International*
Peasback, David R. — *Canny, Bowen Inc.*
Pease, Edward — *Don Richard Associates of Georgia, Inc.*
Peckenpaugh, Ann D. — *Schweichler Associates, Inc.*
Peeney, James D. — *Peeney Associates*
Pelisson, Charles — *Marra Peters & Partners*
Pelletier, Jacques F. — *Roth Young Personnel Service of Boston, Inc.*
Pepe, Leonida — *Butterfass, Pepe & MacCallan Inc.*
Perron, Daniel — *Accountants on Call*
Perry, Carolyn — *Source Services Corporation*
Perry, Wayne B. — *Bruce Massey & Partners Inc.*
Persky, Barry — *Barry Persky & Company, Inc.*
Peternell, Melanie — *Signature Staffing*
Peters, James N. — *TNS Partners, Inc.*
Peters, Kevin — *Source Services Corporation*
Peters, Todd — *Morgan Hunter Corp.*
Petersen, Richard — *Source Services Corporation*
Pettibone, Linda — *Herbert Mines Associates, Inc.*
Pettway, Samuel H. — *Spencer Stuart*
Petty, J. Scott — *The Arcus Group*
Pfannkuche, Anthony V. — *Spencer Stuart*
Pfeiffer, Irene — *Price Waterhouse*
Pfister, Shelli — *Jack B. Larsen & Associates*
Phillips, Donald — *Accountants on Call*
Phillips, Donald L. — *O'Shea, Divine & Company, Inc.*
Phillips, James L. — *Highland Search Group, L.L.C.*
Phillips, Richard K. — *Handy HRM Corp.*
Phillips, Scott K. — *Phillips & Ford, Inc.*
Pickering, Dale — *Agri-Tech Personnel, Inc.*
Pickford, Stephen T. — *The Corporate Staff, Inc.*
Pierce, Matthew — *Source Services Corporation*
Pierson, Edward J. — *Johnson Smith & Knisely Accord*
Pillow, Charles — *Source Services Corporation*
Pineda, Rosanna — *Source Services Corporation*
Pinkman, Karen N. — *Skott/Edwards Consultants, Inc.*
Pirro, Sheri — *Source Services Corporation*
Pitcher, Brian D. — *Skott/Edwards Consultants, Inc.*
Pitto, Lili — *Ryan, Miller & Associates Inc.*
Plant, Jerry — *Source Services Corporation*
Plessner, Rene — *Rene Plessner Associates, Inc.*
Plimpton, Ralph L. — *R L Plimpton Associates*
Plummer, John — *Plummer & Associates, Inc.*
Poe, James B. — *Nagler, Robins & Poe, Inc.*
Poirier, Roland — *Poirier, Hoevel & Co.*
Poracky, John W. — *M. Wood Company*
Porter, Albert — *The Experts*
Posner, Gary J. — *Educational Management Network*
Potenza, Gregory — *Mixtec Group*
Pototo, Brian — *Source Services Corporation*
Potter, Steven B. — *Highland Search Group, L.L.C.*
Powell, Danny — *Source Services Corporation*
Powell, Gregory — *Source Services Corporation*
Power, Michael — *Source Services Corporation*
Prados, Daniel — *Accounting Personnel Consultants*
Pregeant, David — *Source Services Corporation*
Preng, David E. — *Preng & Associates, Inc.*
Press, Fred — *Adept Tech Recruiting*
Preusse, Eric — *Source Services Corporation*
Price, Carl — *Source Services Corporation*
Prince, Marilyn L. — *Higdon Prince Inc.*

Proct, Nina — *Martin H. Bauman Associates, Inc.*
Pryde, Marcia P. — *A.T. Kearney, Inc.*
Pugh, Judith Geist — *InterimManagement Solutions, Inc.*
Pugrant, Mark A. — *Grant/Morgan Associates, Inc.*
Rabinowitz, Peter A. — *P.A.R. Associates Inc.*
Radawicz, Angela — *Mixtec Group*
Radice, Joseph — *Hospitality International*
Raheja, Marc C. — *CanMed Consultants Inc.*
Ramsey, John H. — *Mark Stanley & Company*
Rasmussen, Timothy — *Source Services Corporation*
Ratajczak, Paul — *Source Services Corporation*
Ravenel, Lavinia — *MSI International*
Ray, Marianne C. — *Callan Associates, Ltd.*
Raymond, Anne — *Anderson Sterling Associates*
Reardon, Joseph — *Source Services Corporation*
Reddick, David C. — *Horton International*
Redding, Denise — *The Douglas Reiter Company, Inc.*
Redler, Rhonda — *National Search, Inc.*
Redwood, Guy W. — *Bruce Massey & Partners Inc.*
Reece, Christopher S. — *Reece & Mruk Partners*
Reed, Susan — *Source Services Corporation*
Reeves, William B. — *Spencer Stuart*
Regehly, Herbert L. — *The IMC Group of Companies Ltd.*
Regeuye, Peter J. — *Accountants Executive Search*
Reid, Katherine — *Source Services Corporation*
Reid, Scott — *Source Services Corporation*
Reinhart, Jeaneen — *Accountants on Call*
Reiser, Ellen — *Thorndike Deland Associates*
Reiss, Matt — *National Search, Inc.*
Reiter, Douglas — *The Douglas Reiter Company, Inc.*
Reiter, Harold D. — *Herbert Mines Associates, Inc.*
Renfroe, Ann-Marie — *Source Services Corporation*
Rennell, Thomas — *Source Services Corporation*
Renner, Sandra L. — *Spectra International Inc.*
Renteria, Elizabeth — *Source Services Corporation*
Resnic, Alan — *Source Services Corporation*
Reticker, Peter — *MSI International*
Reyman, Susan — *S. Reyman & Associates Ltd.*
Reynolds, Laura — *Source Services Corporation*
Rhoades, Michael — *Source Services Corporation*
Rice, Douglas — *Agra Placements International Ltd.*
Rice, Marie — *Jay Gaines & Company, Inc.*
Rice, Raymond D. — *Logue & Rice Inc.*
Rich, Lyttleton — *Sockwell & Associates*
Rieger, Louis J. — *Spencer Stuart*
Riley, Elizabeth G. — *Mazza & Riley, Inc.*
Rimmele, Michael — *The Bankers Group*
Rinker, Jim — *Southwestern Professional Services*
Rios, Vince — *Source Services Corporation*
Rios, Vincent — *Source Services Corporation*
Rivas, Alberto F. — *Boyden*
Robb, Tammy — *Source Services Corporation*
Roberts, Carl R. — *Southwestern Professional Services*
Roberts, Kenneth — *The Rubicon Group*
Roberts, Mitch — *A.E. Feldman Associates*
Roberts, Nick P. — *Spectrum Search Associates, Inc.*
Roberts, Norman C. — *Norman Roberts & Associates, Inc.*
Roberts, Raymond R. — *MSI International*
Roberts, Scott B. — *Wargo and Co., Inc.*
Robertson, Sherry — *Source Services Corporation*
Robertson, William R. — *Ward Howell International, Inc.*
Robins, Jeri N. — *Nagler, Robins & Poe, Inc.*
Robinson, Bruce — *Bruce Robinson Associates*
Robinson, Tonya — *Source Services Corporation*
Robison, John H. — *Robison & Associates*
Rockwell, Bruce — *Source Services Corporation*
Rodgers, John — *Agra Placements International Ltd.*
Rodney, Brett — *MSI International*
Rodriguez, Manuel — *Source Services Corporation*
Romaine, Stanley J. — *Mixtec Group*
Romanchek, Walter R. — *Wellington Management Group*
Romanello, Daniel P. — *Spencer Stuart*
Rorech, Maureen — *Romac & Associates*
Rosemarin, Gloria J. — *Barrington Hart, Inc.*
Rosen, Mark — *Winter, Wyman & Company*
Rosen, Mitchell — *Source Services Corporation*
Rosenstein, Michele — *Source Services Corporation*
Rosenthal, Charles — *National Search, Inc.*
Ross, John — *Morgan Stampfl, Inc.*
Ross, Lawrence — *Lovas Stanley/Paul Ray Berndtson Inc.*
Ross, Mark S. — *Herman Smith Executive Initiatives Inc.*
Ross, William J. — *Flowers & Associates*
Rossi, Silvio — *Keith Bagg & Associates Inc.*
Rossi, Thomas — *Southwestern Professional Services*
Roth, Robert J. — *Williams, Roth & Krueger Inc.*
Rothenbush, Clayton — *Source Services Corporation*
Rothfeld, Robert — *A.E. Feldman Associates*
Rothman, Jeffrey — *ProResource, Inc.*

Rowe, Thomas A. — *Korn/Ferry International*
Rowe, William D. — *D.E. Foster Partners Inc.*
Rowells, Michael — *MSI International*
Rowland, James — *Source Services Corporation*
Rudolph, Kenneth — *Kossuth & Associates, Inc.*
Rumson, Paul — *Roth Young Personnel Service of Boston, Inc.*
Rurak, Zbigniew T. — *Rurak & Associates, Inc.*
Russell, Robin E. — *Kenzer Corp.*
Russell, Sam — *The Guild Corporation*
Rustad, Binth — *Educational Management Network*
Ryan, David — *Source Services Corporation*
Ryan, Kathleen — *Source Services Corporation*
Ryan, Lee — *Ryan, Miller & Associates Inc.*
Ryan, Mark — *Source Services Corporation*
Ryckaert, Terri — *Financial Search Corporation*
Sabat, Lori S. — *Alta Associates, Inc.*
Sacerdote, John — *Raymond Karsan Associates*
Sadaj, Michael — *Source Services Corporation*
Sahe, Mark — *Accountants on Call*
Salet, Michael — *Source Services Corporation*
Salvagno, Michael J. — *The Cambridge Group Ltd*
Samsel, Randy — *Source Services Corporation*
Samuelson, Robert — *Source Services Corporation*
Sanchez, William — *Source Services Corporation*
Sanders, Spencer H. — *Battalia Winston International*
Saner, Harold — *Romac & Associates*
Santiago, Benefrido — *Source Services Corporation*
Sapers, Mark — *Source Services Corporation*
Saposhnik, Doron — *Source Services Corporation*
Sapperstein, Jerry S. — *CFO Associates, Inc.*
Sardella, Sharon — *Source Services Corporation*
Sathe, Mark A. — *Sathe & Associates, Inc.*
Sauer, Harry J. — *Romac & Associates*
Savage, Edward J. — *Stanton Chase International*
Savage, Julie — *Winter, Wyman & Company*
Savela, Edward — *Source Services Corporation*
Sawyer, Patricia L. — *Smith & Sawyer Inc.*
Saxner, David — *DSA, Inc.*
Sayers, Bruce D. — *Brackin & Sayers Associates*
Schaefer, Brett — *Accountants on Call*
Schedra, Sharon — *Earley Kielty and Associates, Inc.*
Schiavone, Mary Rose — *Canny, Bowen Inc.*
Schiffer, Stewart — *Career Management International*
Schlpma, Christine — *Advanced Executive Resources*
Schmidt, Jeri E. — *Blake, Hansen & Nye, Limited*
Schmidt, Peter R. — *Boyden*
Schneider, Perry — *Agra Placements International Ltd.*
Schneider, Victor — *Accountants on Call*
Schneiderman, Gerald — *Management Resource Associates, Inc.*
Schoppergrell, Holly — *Don Richard Associates of Charlotte*
Schroeder, James — *Source Services Corporation*
Schroeder, John W. — *Spencer Stuart*
Schuckman, Louis — *Accountants on Call*
Schultz, Randy — *Source Services Corporation*
Schwalbach, Robert — *Source Services Corporation*
Schwam, Carol — *A.E. Feldman Associates*
Schwartz, Carole — *A.T. Kearney, Inc.*
Schwarzkopf, A. Renee — *David C. Cooper and Associates, Inc.*
Schweichler, Lee J. — *Schweichler Associates, Inc.*
Schwinden, William — *Source Services Corporation*
Scimone, James — *Source Services Corporation*
Scimone, Jim — *Source Services Corporation*
Scoff, Barry — *Source Services Corporation*
Scothon, Alan — *Romac & Associates*
Seamon, Kenneth — *Source Services Corporation*
Segal, Eric B. — *Kenzer Corp.*
Seiden, Steven A. — *Seiden Krieger Associates, Inc.*
Seitz, Charles J. — *Neail Behringer Consultants*
Sekera, Roger I. — *A.T. Kearney, Inc.*
Selbach, Barbara — *Spencer Stuart*
Selko, Philip W. — *Hogan Acquisitions*
Sell, David — *Source Services Corporation*
Selvaggi, Esther — *Source Services Corporation*
Semple, David — *Source Services Corporation*
Semyan, John K. — *TNS Partners, Inc.*
Sennello, Gendra — *National Search, Inc.*
Serba, Kerri — *Source Services Corporation*
Serwat, Leonard A. — *Spencer Stuart*
Sevilla, Claudio A. — *Crawford & Crofford*
Shackleford, David — *Source Services Corporation*
Shanks, Jennifer — *Source Services Corporation*
Shapanka, Samuel — *Source Services Corporation*
Shawhan, Heather — *Source Services Corporation*
Shea, Christopher J. — *Ingram & Aydelotte Inc.*
Sheedy, Edward J. — *Dieckmann & Associates, Ltd.*
Sheets, Russel — *Accountants on Call*
Shell, John C. — *John Shell Associates, Inc.*
Shelton, Jonathan — *Source Services Corporation*

Truitt, Thomas B. — *Southwestern Professional Services*
Truvillion, Mary — *Accountants on Call*
Tryon, Katey — *DeFrain, Mayer, Lee & Burgess LLC*
Tscelli, Maureen — *Source Services Corporation*
Tschan, Stephen — *Source Services Corporation*
Tucci, Joseph — *Fairfaxx Corporation*
Tucker, Thomas A. — *The Thomas Tucker Company*
Tunney, William — *Grant Cooper and Associates*
Turner, Edward K. — *Don Richard Associates of Charlotte*
Turner, Marilyn — *Temporary Accounting Personnel Inc.*
Turner, Michael — *Rocky Mountain Recruiters, Inc.*
Turner, Raymond — *Source Services Corporation*
Tutwiler, Stephen — *Don Richard Associates of Tampa, Inc.*
Tweed, Janet — *Gilbert Tweed/INESA*
Twomey, James — *Source Services Corporation*
Tyler, Janet — *Accountants on Call*
Tyson, Richard L. — *Bonifield Associates*
Ulbert, Nancy — *Aureus Group*
Unger, Stephen A. — *Spencer Stuart*
Uzzel, Linda — *Source Services Corporation*
Vacca, Domenic — *Romac & Associates*
Vachon, David A. — *McNichol Associates*
Vainblat, Galina — *Foy, Schneid & Daniel, Inc.*
Valenta, Joseph — *Princeton Entrepreneurial Resources*
Van Alstine, Catherine — *Tanton Mitchell/Paul Ray Berndtson*
Van Alstyne, Susan — *Richard, Wayne and Roberts*
Van Campen, Jerry — *Gilbert & Van Campen International*
Van Norman, Ben — *Source Services Corporation*
Van Steenkiste, Julie — *Davidson, Laird & Associates*
Vandenbulcke, Cynthia — *Source Services Corporation*
Varney, Monique — *Source Services Corporation*
Varrichio, Michael — *Source Services Corporation*
Velez, Hector — *Source Services Corporation*
Venable, William W. — *Thorndike Deland Associates*
Vennat, Manon — *Spencer Stuart*
Vergara, Gail H. — *Spencer Stuart*
Vergari, Jane — *Herbert Mines Associates, Inc.*
Vilella, Paul — *Source Services Corporation*
Villella, Paul — *Source Services Corporation*
Vinett-Hessel, Deirde — *Source Services Corporation*
Vinnedge, Sandra — *U.S. Envirosearch*
Violette, Bradley — *Accountants on Call*
Visnich, L. Christine — *Bason Associates Inc.*
Visotsky, Thomas — *Don Richard Associates of Richmond, Inc.*
Viviano, Cathleen — *Source Services Corporation*
Vlcek, Thomas J. — *Vlcek & Company, Inc.*
Vognsen, Rikke — *DSA, Inc.*
Voigt, John A. — *Romac & Associates*
Volk, Richard — *MSI International*
Vossler, James — *A.J. Burton Group, Inc.*
Wade, Christy — *Source Services Corporation*
Waggoner, Lisa — *Intersource, Ltd.*
Waitkus, Karen — *Richard, Wayne and Roberts*
Wakefield, Scott — *National Search, Inc.*
Waldman, Noah H. — *Lamalie Amrop International*
Waldoch, D. Mark — *Barnes Development Group, LLC*
Waldon, Jeffrey — *Accountants on Call*
Waldon, Maita — *Accountants on Call*
Waldrop, Gary R. — *MSI International*
Walker, Ann — *Source Services Corporation*
Walker, Craig H. — *A.J. Burton Group, Inc.*
Walker, Don — *Richard, Wayne and Roberts*
Walker, Ewing J. — *Ward Howell International, Inc.*
Walker, Martin S. — *Walker Communications*
Walker, Rose — *Source Services Corporation*
Wallace, Alec — *Tanton Mitchell/Paul Ray Berndtson*
Wallace, Toby — *Source Services Corporation*
Walters, William F. — *Jonas, Walters & Assoc., Inc.*
Walther, Linda S. — *MSI International*
Ward, Les — *Source Services Corporation*
Ward, Madeleine — *LTM Associates*
Ward, Robert — *Source Services Corporation*
Warnock, Phyl — *Source Services Corporation*
Warren, Sylvia W. — *Thorndike Deland Associates*
Warter, Mark — *Isaacson, Miller*
Watkins, Thomas M. — *Lamalie Amrop International*
Watson, James — *MSI International*
Waxman, Bruce — *Ryan, Miller & Associates Inc.*
Waxman, Kathleen — *Accountants on Call*
Waymire, Pamela — *Source Services Corporation*
Wayne, Cary S. — *ProSearch Inc.*
Webb, George H. — *Webb, Johnson Associates, Inc.*
Webb, Shawn K. — *MSI International*
Webber, Edward — *Source Services Corporation*
Weber, Jurgen — *BioQuest, Inc.*
Weeks, Glenn — *Source Services Corporation*
Wein, Michael S. — *InterimManagement Solutions, Inc.*
Weinberg, Melvin — *Romac & Associates*

Weis, Theodore — *Source Services Corporation*
Weisler, Nancy — *National Search, Inc.*
Weiss, Elizabeth — *Source Services Corporation*
Weisz, Laura — *Anderson Sterling Associates*
Welch, David — *Isaacson, Miller*
Weller, Paul S. — *Mark Stanley & Company*
Wenz, Alexander — *Source Services Corporation*
Wertel, Ronald E. — *Gordon Wahls Company*
Wessling, Jerry — *Source Services Corporation*
West, Nancy — *Health Care Dimensions*
West, Vikki Lynn — *Accounting & Bookkeeping Personnel, Inc.*
Westerfield, Putney — *Boyden*
Wexler, Rona — *Ariel Recruitment Associates*
Wheatley, William — *Drummond Associates, Inc.*
Wheeler, Gerard H. — *A.J. Burton Group, Inc.*
Wheeler, Mary T. — *Lamalie Amrop International*
Whitcomb, Nancy C. — *Educational Management Network*
White, Jeffrey E. — *Simpson Associates*
White, Jonathan O. — *The Badger Group*
White, Kimberly — *Executive Referral Services, Inc.*
White, Patricia D. — *MSI International*
White, William C. — *Venture Resources Inc.*
Whitfield, Jack — *Source Services Corporation*
Whiting, Anthony — *Johnson Smith & Knisely Accord*
Whitney, David L. — *Whitney & Associates, Inc.*
Whitton, Paula L. — *Pearson, Caldwell & Farnsworth, Inc.*
Wichlei, Alan — *Isaacson, Miller*
Wier, Daniel — *Horton International*
Wilcox, Fred T. — *Wilcox, Bertoux & Miller*
Wilcox, Karen — *Isaacson, Miller*
Wilder, Richard B. — *Columbia Consulting Group*
Wilensky, Joel H. — *Joel H. Wilensky Associates, Inc.*
Wilkinson, Barbara — *Beall & Company, Inc.*
Wilkinson, William R. — *Wilkinson & Ives*
Willbrandt, Curt — *Source Services Corporation*
Williams, Alexander H. — *Witt/Kieffer, Ford, Hadelman & Lloyd*
Williams, Angie — *Whitney & Associates, Inc.*
Williams, Gary L. — *Barnes Development Group, LLC*
Williams, Harry D. — *Jacobson Associates*
Williams, John — *Source Services Corporation*
Williams, Laurelle N. — *MSI International*
Williams, Lis — *Executive Options, Ltd.*
Williams, Michelle Cruz — *Isaacson, Miller*
Williams, Roger K. — *Williams, Roth & Krueger Inc.*
Williams, Walter E. — *Canny, Bowen Inc.*
Willis, William H. — *William Willis Worldwide Inc.*
Wilson, Joyce — *Source Services Corporation*
Wilson, Patricia L. — *Leon A. Farley Associates*
Wilson, Thomas H. — *Lamalie Amrop International*
Wingate, Mary — *Source Services Corporation*
Winitz, Joel — *GSW Consulting Group, Inc.*
Winitz, Marla — *GSW Consulting Group, Inc.*
Winkowski, Stephen — *Source Services Corporation*
Winnewisser, William E. — *Accounting & Computer Personnel*
Winnicki, Kimberly — *Source Services Corporation*
Winograd, Glenn — *Criterion Executive Search, Inc.*
Winston, Dale — *Battalia Winston International*
Wisch, Steven C. — *MB Inc. Interim Executive Division*
Wise, Anne — *U.S. Envirosearch*
Wise, J. Herbert — *Sandhurst Associates*
Wittenberg, Laura L. — *Boyden*
Witzgall, William — *Source Services Corporation*
Wolf, Donald — *Source Services Corporation*
Wolf, Stephen M. — *Byron Leonard International, Inc.*
Wolfe, Peter — *Source Services Corporation*
Womack, Joseph — *The Bankers Group*
Wood, Gary — *Source Services Corporation*
Wood, Martin F. — *Lamalie Amrop International*
Woods, Craig — *Source Services Corporation*
Wooller, Edmund A.M. — *Windsor International*
Woomer, Jerome — *Source Services Corporation*
Workman, David — *Source Services Corporation*
Wright, Carl A.J. — *A.J. Burton Group, Inc.*
Wright, Charles D. — *Goodrich & Sherwood Associates, Inc.*
Wright, Leslie — *The Stevenson Group of New Jersey*
Wrynn, Robert F. — *MSI International*
Wujciak, Sandra — *Accountants on Call*
Wycoff-Viola, Amy — *Source Services Corporation*
Yeaton, Robert — *Source Services Corporation*
Young, Alexander — *Messett Associates, Inc.*
Young, Heather — *The Guild Corporation*
Young, Laurie — *Part Time Resources, Inc.*
Young, Mimi — *Educational Management Network*
Youngberg, David — *Source Services Corporation*
Youngs, Donald L. — *Youngs & Company*
Zaffrann, Craig S. — *P.J. Murphy & Associates, Inc.*
Zahradka, James F. — *P.J. Murphy & Associates, Inc.*
Zander, Barry W. — *MSI International*

Zavat, Marc — *Ryan, Miller & Associates Inc.*
Zavrel, Mark — *Source Services Corporation*
Zay, Thomas C. — *Boyden/Zay & Company*
Zegel, Gary — *Source Services Corporation*
Zera, Ronald J. — *Spencer Stuart*
Zila, Laurie M. — *Princeton Entrepreneurial Resources*
Zimbal, Mark — *Source Services Corporation*
Zimont, Scott — *Source Services Corporation*
Zingaro, Ron — *Zingaro and Company*
Zivic, Janis M. — *Spencer Stuart*
Zona, Henry F. — *Zona & Associates, Inc.*
Zonis, Hildy R. — *Accountants Executive Search*
Zwiff, Jeffrey G. — *Johnson Smith & Knisely Accord*

## 5. General Management

Abbott, Dale — *Mixtec Group*
Abbott, Peter — *The Abbott Group, Inc.*
Abell, Vincent W. — *MSI International*
Adams, Michael — *CG & Associates*
Adams, Ralda F. — *Hospitality International*
Adkisson, Billy D. — *James Russell, Inc.*
Agins, Ted — *National Restaurant Search, Inc.*
Akin, J.R. — *J.R. Akin & Company Inc.*
Albers, Joan — *Carver Search Consultants*
Alden, Brian R. — *MSI International*
Alekel, Karren — *ALW Research International*
Alexander, John T. — *Telford, Adams & Alexander/Human Resource Services*
Allard, Susan — *Allard Associates*
Allen, David A. — *Intech Summit Group, Inc.*
Allen, Donald — *D.S. Allen Associates, Inc.*
Allerton, Donald T. — *Allerton Heneghan & O'Neill*
Allgire, Mary L. — *Kenzer Corp.*
Allred, J. Michael — *Spencer Stuart*
Amato, Joseph — *Amato & Associates, Inc.*
Ambler, Peter W. — *Peter W. Ambler Company*
Amsterdam, Gail E. — *D.E. Foster Partners Inc.*
Anderson, Glenn G. — *Lamalie Amrop International*
Anderson, Richard — *Grant Cooper and Associates*
Anderson, Roger J. — *BioQuest, Inc.*
Anderson, Thomas — *Paul J. Biestek Associates, Inc.*
Andrews, J. Douglas — *Clarey & Andrews, Inc.*
Andrews, Laura L. — *Stricker & Zagor*
Andujo, Michele M. — *Chrisman & Company, Incorporated*
Antil, Pamela W. — *Norman Roberts & Associates, Inc.*
Anwar, Tarin — *Jay Gaines & Company, Inc.*
Apostle, George — *Search Dynamics, Inc.*
Aquavella, Charles P. — *CPA & Associates*
Argenio, Michelangelo — *Spencer Stuart*
Ariail, C. Bowling — *Ariail & Associates*
Ariail, Randolph C. — *Ariail & Associates*
Arnold, David — *Christian & Timbers*
Arnold, Jerry — *Houtz-Strawn Associates, Inc.*
Aronin, Michael — *Fisher-Todd Associates*
Aronow, Lawrence E. — *Aronow Associates, Inc.*
Arseneault, Daniel S. — *MSI International*
Ascher, Susan P. — *The Ascher Group*
Ashton, Barbara L. — *Ashton Computer Professionals Inc.*
Ashton, Edward J. — *E.J. Ashton & Associates, Ltd.*
Asquith, Peter S. — *Ames Personnel Consultants, Inc.*
Aston, Kathy — *Marra Peters & Partners*
Atkins, Laurie — *Battalia Winston International*
Attell, Harold — *A.E. Feldman Associates*
Austin, Jessica L. — *D.S.A. - Dixie Search Associates*
Aydelotte, G. Thomas — *Ingram & Aydelotte Inc.*
Bacher, Philip J. — *Handy HRM Corp.*
Bachmeier, Kevin — *Agra Placements International Ltd.*
Badger, Fred H. — *The Badger Group*
Bagg, Keith — *Keith Bagg & Associates Inc.*
Bailey, William A. — *TNS Partners, Inc.*
Baillou, Astrid — *Richard Kinser & Associates*
Baird, David W. — *D.W. Baird & Associates*
Baker, Gerry — *Baker, Harris & Partners Limited*
Baker, Judith — *Search Consultants International, Inc.*
Baker, S. Joseph — *Search Consultants International, Inc.*
Baker, Walter U. — *Lamalie Amrop International*
Baker-Greene, Edward — *Isaacson, Miller*
Baldock, Robert G. — *Lovas Stanley/Paul Ray Berndtson Inc.*
Balkin, Linda E. — *Witt/Kieffer, Ford, Hadelman & Lloyd*
Ballein, Kathleen M. — *Witt/Kieffer, Ford, Hadelman & Lloyd*
Barack, Brianne — *The Barack Group, Inc.*
Baran, Helena — *Michael J. Cavanagh and Associates*
Barber, Toni L. — *MSI International*
Barbosa, Franklin J. — *Boyden*
Barger, H. Carter — *Barger & Sargeant, Inc.*
Barlow, Ken H. — *The Cherbonnier Group, Inc.*
Barnes, Richard E. — *Barnes Development Group, LLC*
Barnes, Roanne L. — *Barnes Development Group, LLC*
Barnum, Toni M. — *Stone Murphy & Olson*

Baron, Jon C. — *MSI International*
Baron, Len — *Industrial Recruiters Associates, Inc.*
Barone, Marialice — *Barone-O'Hara Associates*
Barr, Ronald — *Search West, Inc.*
Barthold, James A. — *McNichol Associates*
Bartholdi, Ted — *Bartholdi & Company, Inc.*
Bartholdi, Theodore G. — *Bartholdi & Company, Inc.*
Barton, Gary R. — *Barton Raben, Inc.*
Bason, Maurice L. — *Bason Associates Inc.*
Bass, Nate — *Jacobson Associates*
Bates, Nina — *Allard Associates*
Bates, Scott W. — *Kittleman & Associates*
Battalia, O. William — *Battalia Winston International*
Bauman, Martin H. — *Martin H. Bauman Associates, Inc.*
Bean, Bill — *Professional Search Consultants*
Bearman, Linda — *Grant Cooper and Associates*
Beaudin, Elizabeth C. — *Callan Associates, Ltd.*
Beaver, Bentley H. — *The Onstott Group, Inc.*
Beck, Charlotte — *Witt/Kieffer, Ford, Hadelman & Lloyd*
Behringer, Neail — *Neail Behringer Consultants*
Belford, Paul — *JDG Associates, Ltd.*
Belfrey, Edward — *Dunhill Professional Search of Irvine, Inc.*
Bell, Jeffrey G. — *Norman Broadbent International, Inc.*
Bellano, Robert W. — *Stanton Chase International*
Bellshaw, David — *Isaacson, Miller*
Bennett, Jo — *Battalia Winston International*
Bennett, Joan — *Adams & Associates International*
Bennett, Richard T. — *Isaacson, Miller*
Benson, Kate — *Rene Plessner Associates, Inc.*
Bergen, Anthony M. — *CFO Associates, Inc.*
Berger, Emanuel — *Isaacson, Miller*
Berk-Levine, Margo — *MB Inc. Interim Executive Division*
Berman, Kenneth D. — *MSI International*
Bermea, Jose — *Gaffney Management Consultants*
Berry, John R. — *Hedrick & Struggles, Inc.*
Bertoux, Michael P. — *Wilcox, Bertoux & Miller*
Besen, Douglas — *Besen Associates Inc.*
Biestek, Paul J. — *Paul J. Biestek Associates, Inc.*
Billington, Brian — *Billington & Associates*
Billington, William H. — *Spriggs & Company, Inc.*
Bishop, Susan — *Bishop Partners*
Bitar, Edward — *The Interface Group, Ltd./Boyden*
Bittman, Beth M. — *Norman Roberts & Associates, Inc.*
Black, Douglas E. — *MSI International*
Blackmon, Sharon — *The Abbott Group, Inc.*
Blakslee, Jan H. — *J: Blakslee International, Ltd.*
Blanton, Thomas — *Blanton and Company*
Blecker, Jay — *TSS Consulting, Ltd.*
Bliley, Jerry — *Spencer Stuart*
Bloomer, James E. — *L.W. Foote Company*
Bluhm, Claudia — *Schweichler Associates, Inc.*
Boczany, William J. — *The Guild Corporation*
Bogard, Nicholas C. — *The Onstott Group, Inc.*
Bohn, Steve J. — *MSI International*
Bole, J. Jeffrey — *William J. Christopher Associates, Inc.*
Bond, Allan — *Walden Associates*
Bonifield, Len — *Bonifield Associates*
Bonnell, William R. — *Bonnell Associates Ltd.*
Book, Cheryl — *Aureus Group*
Booth, Otis — *A.T. Kearney, Inc.*
Borland, James — *Goodrich & Sherwood Associates, Inc.*
Borman, Theodore H. — *Lamalie Amrop International*
Bormann, Cindy Ann — *MSI International*
Bostic, James E. — *Phillips Resource Group*
Bourbeau, Paul J. — *Boyden*
Bourrie, Sharon D. — *Chartwell Partners International, Inc.*
Bovich, Maryann C. — *Higdon Prince Inc.*
Bowen, Tad — *Executive Search International*
Boyer, Heath C. — *Spencer Stuart*
Brackin, James B. — *Brackin & Sayers Associates*
Brady, Colin S. — *Ward Howell International, Inc.*
Brandjes, Michael J. — *Brandjes Associates*
Bratches, Howard — *Thorndike Deland Associates*
Brennan, Jerry — *Brennan Associates*
Brennan, Patrick J. — *Handy HRM Corp.*
Brennen, Richard J. — *Spencer Stuart*
Brenner, Michael — *Lamalie Amrop International*
Brentari, Michael — *Search Consultants International, Inc.*
Brieger, Steve — *Thorne, Brieger Associates Inc.*
Briggs, Adam — *Horton International*
Bright, Timothy — *MSI International*
Brinson, Robert — *MSI International*
Brodie, Ricki R. — *MSI International*
Brown, Franklin Key — *Handy HRM Corp.*
Brown, Larry C. — *Horton International*
Brown, Lawrence Anthony — *MSI International*
Brown, Michael R. — *MSI International*
Brudno, Robert J. — *Savoy Partners, Ltd.*
Brunson, Therese — *Kors Montgomery International*

Bryant, Richard D. — *Bryant Associates, Inc.*
Bryza, Robert M. — *Robert Lowell International*
Buck, Charles — *Charles Buck & Associates*
Budill, Edward — *Professional Search Consultants*
Bueschel, David A. — *Shepherd Bueschel & Provus, Inc.*
Bullock, Conni — *Earley Kielty and Associates, Inc.*
Bump, Gerald J. — *D.E. Foster Partners Inc.*
Burchill, Greg — *BGB Associates*
Burden, Gene — *The Cherbonnier Group, Inc.*
Burfield, Elaine — *Skott/Edwards Consultants, Inc.*
Burke, George M. — *The Burke Group*
Burke, John — *The Experts*
Burnett, Rebecca J. — *MSI International*
Burns, Alan — *The Enns Partners Inc.*
Burns, Terence N. — *D.E. Foster Partners Inc.*
Burris, James C. — *Boyden*
Busch, Jack — *Busch International*
Bush, Martha A. — *MSI International*
Butler, Kirby B. — *The Butlers Company Insurance Recruiters*
Button, David R. — *The Button Group*
Byrnes, Thomas A. — *Thomas A. Byrnes Associates*
Cahill, Peter M. — *Peter M. Cahill Associates, Inc.*
Caldwell, William R. — *Pearson, Caldwell & Farnsworth, Inc.*
Call, David — *Cochran, Cochran & Yale, Inc.*
Callan, Robert M. — *Callan Associates, Ltd.*
Callen, John H. — *Ward Howell International, Inc.*
Callihan, Diana L. — *Search Northwest Associates*
Campbell, Patricia A. — *The Onstott Group, Inc.*
Campbell, Robert Scott — *Wellington Management Group*
Cappe, Richard R. — *Roberts Ryan and Bentley*
Carabelli, Paula — *Witt/Kieffer, Ford, Hadelman & Lloyd*
Carey, Dennis C. — *Spencer Stuart*
Cargo, Catherine — *MSI International*
Carideo, Joseph — *Thorndike Deland Associates*
Carpenter, Harold G. — *MSI International*
Carter, Christine C. — *Health Care Dimensions*
Casal, Daniel G. — *Bonifield Associates*
Casey, Darren — *Parfitt Recruiting and Consulting*
Casey, Jean — *Peter W. Ambler Company*
Cashen, Anthony B. — *Lamalie Amrop International*
Cass, Kathryn H. — *Don Richard Associates of Tidewater, Inc.*
Cassie, Ronald L. — *The Cassie Group*
Cattanach, Bruce B. — *Horton International*
Causey, Andrea C. — *MSI International*
Cavanagh, Michael J. — *Michael J. Cavanagh and Associates*
Cavolina, Michael — *Carver Search Consultants*
Chandler, Robert C. — *Ward Howell International, Inc.*
Chappell, Peter — *The Bankers Group*
Chatterjie, Alok — *MSI International*
Chavous, C. Crawford — *Phillips Resource Group*
Cherbonnier, L. Michael — *TCG International, Inc.*
Cherbonnier, L. Michael — *The Cherbonnier Group, Inc.*
Chesla, Garry — *Executive Referral Services, Inc.*
Chorman, Marilyn A. — *Hite Executive Search*
Christenson, H. Alan — *Christenson & Hutchison*
Christian, Jeffrey E. — *Christian & Timbers*
Christoff, Matthew J. — *Spencer Stuart*
Citera, Tom — *Howe-Lewis International*
Cizek, John T. — *Cizek Associates, Inc.*
Cizek, Marti J. — *Cizek Associates, Inc.*
Clarey, Jack R. — *Clarey & Andrews, Inc.*
Clarey, William A. — *Preng & Associates, Inc.*
Clark, Steven — *D.A. Kreuter Associates, Inc.*
Clauhsen, Elizabeth A. — *Savoy Partners, Ltd.*
Cleary, Thomas R. — *ARJay & Associates*
Cleeve, Coleen — *Howe-Lewis International*
Clegg, Cynthia — *Horton International*
Clemens, William B. — *Norman Broadbent International, Inc.*
Clemens, William B. — *Norman Broadbent International, Inc.*
Close, E. Wade — *Boyden*
Clovis, James R. — *Handy HRM Corp.*
Cochran, Hale — *Fenwick Partners*
Coffman, Brian — *Kossuth & Associates, Inc.*
Cohen, Michael R. — *Intech Summit Group, Inc.*
Cohen, Robert C. — *Intech Summit Group, Inc.*
Cole, Elizabeth — *MSI International*
Coleman, Gregory — *Strategic Associates, Inc.*
Coleman, J. Kevin — *J. Kevin Coleman & Associates, Inc.*
Coleman, John A. — *Canny, Bowen Inc.*
Collard, Joseph A. — *Spencer Stuart*
Collier, David — *Parfitt Recruiting and Consulting/PRO TEM*
Colling, Douglas — *KPMG Management Consulting*
Collis, Gerald — *TSS Consulting, Ltd.*
Colucci, Bart A. — *Colucci, Blendow and Johnson, Inc.*
Combs, Stephen L. — *Juntunen-Combs-Poirier*
Cona, Joseph A. — *Cona Personnel Search*
Conard, Rodney J. — *Conard Associates, Inc.*
Connelly, Kevin M. — *Spencer Stuart*
Conner, John — *Flex Execs Management Solutions*

Connolly, Cathryn — *Strategic Associates, Inc.*
Conway, William P. — *Phillips Resource Group*
Cooke, Jeffrey R. — *Jonas, Walters & Assoc., Inc.*
Cooke, Katherine H. — *Horton International*
Cordaro, Concetta — *Flynn, Hannock, Incorporated*
Corey, Michael J. — *Witt/Kieffer, Ford, Hadelman & Lloyd*
Cornehlsen, James H. — *Lamalie Amrop International*
Corrigan, Gerald F. — *The Corrigan Group*
Corso, Glen S. — *Chartwell Partners International, Inc.*
Costa, Cynthia A. — *MSI International*
Costick, Kathryn J. — *John Sibbald Associates, Inc.*
Coston, Bruce G. — *MSI International*
Cox, James O. — *MSI International*
Cox, Mark M. — *Witt/Kieffer, Ford, Hadelman & Lloyd*
Cox, William — *E.J. Ashton & Associates, Ltd.*
Crane, Howard C. — *Chartwell Partners International, Inc.*
Crath, Paul F. — *Price Waterhouse*
Cripe, Joyce — *Mixtec Group*
Crist, Peter — *Crist Partners, Ltd.*
Critchley, Walter — *Cochran, Cochran & Yale, Inc.*
Crowder, Edward W. — *Crowder & Company*
Crowell, Elizabeth — *H.M. Long International, Ltd.*
Crownover, Kathryn L. — *MSI International*
Crumbaker, Robert H. — *Lamalie Amrop International*
Crumpton, Marc — *Walden Associates*
Cruse, O.D. — *Spencer Stuart*
Crystal, Jonathan A. — *Spencer Stuart*
Cunningham, Robert Y. — *Goodrich & Sherwood Associates, Inc.*
Cunningham, Sheila — *Adams & Associates International*
Cuomo, Frank — *Frank Cuomo and Associates, Inc.*
Currie, Lawrence S. — *MSI International*
Cyphers, Ralph R. — *Strategic Associates, Inc.*
Czamanske, Paul W. — *Compass Group Ltd.*
Daily, John C. — *Handy HRM Corp.*
Dalton, Bret — *Robert W. Dingman Company, Inc.*
Dalton, David R. — *MSI International*
Damon, Richard E. — *Damon & Associates, Inc.*
Damon, Robert A. — *Spencer Stuart*
Danforth, Monica — *Search Consultants International, Inc.*
Daniel, Beverly — *Foy, Schneid & Daniel, Inc.*
Daniels, Alfred — *Alfred Daniels & Associates*
Daniels, David — *Search West, Inc.*
Davidson, Arthur J. — *Lamalie Amrop International*
Davis, Bernel — *MSI International*
Davis, Bert — *Bert Davis Executive Search, Inc.*
Davis, G. Gordon — *Davis & Company*
Davis, Robert — *CG & Associates*
Davison, Patricia E. — *Lamalie Amrop International*
de Cholnoky, Andrea — *Spencer Stuart*
de Palacios, Jeannette C. — *J. Palacios & Associates, Inc.*
de Tuede, Catherine — *Thomas A. Byrnes Associates*
Debrueys, Lee G. — *MSI International*
Deering, Joseph — *U.S. Envirosearch*
DeFrancesco, Mary Ellen — *The Onstott Group, Inc.*
DeFuniak, William S. — *DeFuniak & Edwards*
DeHart, Donna — *Tower Consultants, Ltd.*
Del Pino, William — *National Search, Inc.*
Del'Ange, Gabrielle N. — *MSI International*
Delaney, Patrick J. — *Sensible Solutions, Inc.*
DeLong, Art — *Richard Kader & Associates*
deMartino, Cathy — *Lucas Associates*
Densmore, Geraldine — *Michael Stern Associates Inc.*
Desmond, Dennis — *Beall & Company, Inc.*
deWilde, David M. — *Chartwell Partners International, Inc.*
Diaz-Joslyn, Mabel — *Walker Communications*
Dickerson, Scot — *Key Employment Services*
Dieckmann, Ralph E. — *Dieckmann & Associates, Ltd.*
Dietz, David S. — *MSI International*
DiMarchi, Paul — *DiMarchi Partners, Inc.*
Dingman, Bruce — *Robert W. Dingman Company, Inc.*
Dingman, Robert W. — *Robert W. Dingman Company, Inc.*
DiSalvo, Fred — *The Cambridge Group Ltd*
Divine, Robert S. — *O'Shea, Divine & Company, Inc.*
Dixon, C.R. — *A la carte International*
Doele, Donald C. — *Goodrich & Sherwood Associates, Inc.*
Domann, William A. — *The Domann Organization*
Donnelly, George J. — *Ward Howell International, Inc.*
Doody, Michael F. — *Witt/Kieffer, Ford, Hadelman & Lloyd*
Dotson, M. Ileen — *Dotson & Associates*
Dougherty, Bridget L. — *Wellington Management Group*
Dougherty, Janice — *The McCormick Group, Inc.*
Doukas, Jon A. — *Professional Bank Services, Inc. D/B/A Executive Search, Inc.*
Dow, Lori — *Davidson, Laird & Associates*
Dowell, Mary K. — *Professional Search Associates*
Dreifus, Donald — *Search West, Inc.*
Drexler, Robert — *Robert Drexler Associates, Inc.*
Dromeshauser, Peter — *Dromeshauser Associates*
Drury, James J. — *Spencer Stuart*

Groom, Charles C. — *CG & Associates*
Groover, David — *MSI International*
Gross, Howard — *Herbert Mines Associates, Inc.*
Guberman, Robert P. — *A.T. Kearney, Inc.*
Gude, John S. — *Boyden*
Gulley, Marylyn — *MSI International*
Gurtin, Kay L. — *Executive Options, Ltd.*
Haas, Margaret P. — *Haas International, Inc.*
Haberman, Joseph C. — *A.T. Kearney, Inc.*
Hadelman, Jordan M. — *Witt/Kieffer, Ford, Hadelman & Lloyd*
Hahn, William R. — *Bill Hahn Group, Inc.*
Hailey, H.M. — *Damon & Associates, Inc.*
Hall, Peter V. — *Chartwell Partners International, Inc.*
Hallock, Peter B. — *Goodrich & Sherwood Associates, Inc.*
Halvorsen, Jeanne M. — *Kittleman & Associates*
Halvorsen, Kara — *Chrisman & Company, Incorporated*
Halyburton, Robert R. — *The Halyburton Co., Inc.*
Hamdan, Mark — *Careernet of Florida, Inc.*
Hamm, Gary P. — *Witt/Kieffer, Ford, Hadelman & Lloyd*
Hanford, Michael — *Richard Kader & Associates*
Hanley, Maureen E. — *Gilbert Tweed/INESA*
Hannock, Elwin W. — *Flynn, Hannock, Incorporated*
Hansen, David G. — *Ott & Hansen, Inc.*
Hansen, Ty E. — *Blake, Hansen & Nye, Limited*
Hanson, Carrie — *U.S. Envirosearch*
Hanson, Grant M. — *Goodrich & Sherwood Associates, Inc.*
Harbaugh, Paul J. — *International Management Advisors, Inc.*
Harbert, David O. — *Sweeney Harbert & Mummert, Inc.*
Hardison, Richard L. — *Hardison & Company*
Harelick, Arthur S. — *Ashway, Ltd.*
Harkins, Robert E. — *Robert Harkins Associates, Inc.*
Harris, Bruce — *ProResource, Inc.*
Harris, Ethel S. — *Don Richard Associates of Charlotte*
Harrison, Joel — *D.A. Kreuter Associates, Inc.*
Harrison, Priscilla — *Phillips Resource Group*
Harshman, Donald — *The Stevenson Group of New Jersey*
Hart, Robert T. — *D.E. Foster Partners Inc.*
Harvey, Jill — *MSI International*
Harvey, Mike — *Advanced Executive Resources*
Harvey, Richard — *Price Waterhouse*
Hauck, Fred P. — *The Cassie Group*
Haughton, Michael — *DeFrain, Mayer, Lee & Burgess LLC*
Hauser, Martha — *Spencer Stuart*
Hauswirth, Jeffrey M. — *Spencer Stuart*
Havener, Donald Clarke — *The Abbott Group, Inc.*
Hawksworth, A. Dwight — *A.D. & Associates Executive Search, Inc.*
Hay, William E. — *William E. Hay & Company*
Haystead, Steve — *Advanced Executive Resources*
Hazelton, Lisa M. — *Health Care Dimensions*
Healey, Joseph T. — *Highland Search Group, L.L.C.*
Hebel, Robert W. — *R.W. Hebel Associates*
Hecker, Henry C. — *Hogan Acquisitions*
Heiken, Barbara E. — *Randell-Heiken, Inc.*
Heintz, William — *Mixtec Group*
Heiser, Charles S. — *The Cassie Group*
Hellinger, Audrey — *Martin H. Bauman Associates, Inc.*
Helminiak, Audrey — *Gaffney Management Consultants*
Hemingway, Stuart C. — *Robison & Associates*
Henard, John B. — *Lamalie Amrop International*
Heneghan, Donald A. — *Allerton Heneghan & O'Neill*
Hennig, Sandra M. — *MSI International*
Henshaw, Robert — *F-O-R-T-U-N-E Personnel Consultants of Huntsville, Inc.*
Herget, James P. — *Lamalie Amrop International*
Herman, Eugene J. — *Earley Kielty and Associates, Inc.*
Hermsmeyer, Rex — *Hitchens & Foster, Inc.*
Hertlein, James N.J. — *Boyden/Zay & Company*
Herz, Stanley — *Stanley Herz and Company, Inc.*
Hetherman, Margaret F. — *Highland Search Group, L.L.C.*
Hewitt, Rives D. — *The Dalley Hewitt Company*
Hicks, Albert M. — *Phillips Resource Group*
Hicks, James L. — *MSI International*
Higdon, Henry G. — *Higdon Prince Inc.*
Higgins, John B. — *Higgins Associates, Inc.*
Hildebrand, Thomas B. — *Professional Resources Group, Inc.*
Hill, Emery — *MSI International*
Hillen, Skip — *The McCormick Group, Inc.*
Hilyard, Paul J. — *MSI International*
Hirsch, Julia C. — *Boyden*
Hockett, William — *Hockett Associates, Inc.*
Hodges, Robert J. — *Sampson Neill & Wilkins Inc.*
Hoevel, Michael J. — *Poirier, Hoevel & Co.*
Hoffmeir, Patricia A. — *Gilbert Tweed/INESA*
Hogan, Larry H. — *Hogan Acquisitions*
Holden, Richard B. — *Ames Personnel Consultants, Inc.*
Hollins, Howard D. — *MSI International*
Holmes, Lawrence J. — *Columbia Consulting Group*
Holodnak, William A. — *J. Robert Scott*
Holt, Carol — *Bartholdi & Company, Inc.*

Holtz, Gene — *Agra Placements International Ltd.*
Holzberger, Georges L. — *Highland Search Group, L.L.C.*
Hopgood, Earl — *JDG Associates, Ltd.*
Hopkins, Chester A. — *Handy HRM Corp.*
Hoppert, Phil — *Wargo and Co., Inc.*
Horton, Robert H. — *Horton International*
Houchins, William N. — *Christian & Timbers*
Houtz, Kenneth — *Houtz-Strawn Associates, Inc.*
Howard, Jill — *Health Care Dimensions*
Hoyda, Louis A. — *Thorndike Deland Associates*
Hucko, Donald S. — *Jonas, Walters & Assoc., Inc.*
Hudson, Reginald M. — *Search Bureau International*
Hughes, Cathy N. — *The Ogdon Partnership*
Hughes, Donald J. — *Hughes & Company*
Hughes, James J. — *R.P. Barone Associates*
Hunt, Thomas — *MSI International*
Hunter, Gabe — *Phillips Resource Group*
Hunter, John B. — *John Sibbald Associates, Inc.*
Hunter, Sue J. — *Robison & Associates*
Hutchison, Richard H. — *Rurak & Associates, Inc.*
Hutchison, William K. — *Christenson & Hutchison*
Hutton, Thomas J. — *The Thomas Tucker Company*
Hwang, Yvette — *MSI International*
Hyde, Mark D. — *MSI International*
Hyde, W. Jerry — *Hyde Danforth Wold & Co.*
Hykes, Don A. — *A.T. Kearney, Inc.*
Hypes, Richard G. — *Lynch Miller Moore Partners, Inc.*
Iammatteo, Enzo — *Keith Bagg & Associates Inc.*
Ikle, A. Donald — *Ward Howell International, Inc.*
Imely, Larry — *Christian & Timbers*
Infinger, Ronald E. — *Robison & Associates*
Ingram, D. John — *Ingram & Aydelotte Inc.*
Inguagiato, Gregory — *MSI International*
Inzinna, Dennis — *AlternaStaff*
Irvine, Robert — *Keith Bagg & Associates Inc.*
Isaacson, John — *Isaacson, Miller*
Issacs, Judith A. — *Grant Cooper and Associates*
Ives, Richard K. — *Wilkinson & Ives*
Ivey, Deborah M. — *MSI International*
Jablo, Steven — *Dieckmann & Associates, Ltd.*
Jackson, W.T. — *Sampson Neill & Wilkins Inc.*
Jacobs, Judith — *The Rubicon Group*
Jacobs, Martin J. — *The Rubicon Group*
Jacobs, Mike — *Thorne, Brieger Associates Inc.*
Jacobson, Donald — *Hunt Advisory Services*
Jaffe, Mark — *Wyatt & Jaffe*
James, Allison A. — *MSI International*
James, Bruce — *Roberson and Company*
Jeffers, Carol S. — *John Sibbald Associates, Inc.*
Jensen, Debra — *Flex Execs Management Solutions*
Jernigan, Alice — *Ariel Recruitment Associates*
Jernigan, Susan N. — *Sockwell & Associates*
Jessamy, Howard T. — *Witt/Kieffer, Ford, Hadelman & Lloyd*
Joffe, Barry — *Bason Associates Inc.*
Johnson, David — *Gaffney Management Consultants*
Johnson, Douglas — *Quality Search*
Johnson, Harold E. — *Norman Broadbent International, Inc.*
Johnson, Janet — *Normyle/Erstling Health Search Group*
Johnson, John F. — *Lamalie Amrop International*
Johnson, John W. — *Webb, Johnson Associates, Inc.*
Johnson, Kathleen A. — *Barton Raben, Inc.*
Johnson, Maxene — *Norman Roberts & Associates, Inc.*
Johnson, Priscilla — *The Johnson Group, Inc.*
Johnson, Robert J. — *Quality Search*
Johnson, Rocky — *A.T. Kearney, Inc.*
Johnson, S. Hope — *The Interface Group, Ltd./Boyden*
Johnson, Stephanie — *Carver Search Consultants*
Jones, Francis E. — *Earley Kielty and Associates, Inc.*
Jones, Gary — *BGB Associates*
Jones, Jonathan C. — *The Ogdon Partnership*
Jones, Ronald T. — *ARJay & Associates*
Joubert, Pierre E. — *Boyden*
Joyce, William J. — *The Guild Corporation*
Juelis, John J. — *Peeney Associates*
Juska, Frank — *Rusher, Loscavio & LoPresto*
Kaiser, Donald J. — *Dunhill Search International*
Kalinowski, David — *Jacobson Associates*
Kanal, David S. — *Johnson Smith & Knisely Accord*
Kanrich, Susan Azaria — *AlternaStaff*
Kaplan, Gary — *Gary Kaplan & Associates*
Kaplan, Marc — *Gary Kaplan & Associates*
Kaptain, John — *Blau Kaptain Schroeder*
Katz, Robert L. — *MSI International*
Keesom, W. Peter — *Boyden/Zay & Company*
Keitel, Robert S. — *A.T. Kearney, Inc.*
Keller, Barbara — *Barton Raben, Inc.*
Kelly, Elizabeth Ann — *Wellington Management Group*
Kelly, Sheri — *Strategic Associates, Inc.*
Kelly, Susan D. — *S.D. Kelly & Associates, Inc.*

Kennedy, Michael — *The Danbrook Group, Inc.*
Kenzer, Robert D. — *Kenzer Corp.*
Kern, Jerry L. — *ADOW's Executeam*
Kern, Kathleen G. — *ADOW's Executeam*
Kershaw, Lisa — *Tanton Mitchell/Paul Ray Berndtson*
Kettwig, David A. — *A.T. Kearney, Inc.*
Kieffer, Michael C. — *Witt/Kieffer, Ford, Hadelman & Lloyd*
Kielty, John L. — *Earley Kielty and Associates, Inc.*
Kilcullen, Brian A. — *D.A. Kreuter Associates, Inc.*
Kile, Robert W. — *Rusher, Loscavio & LoPresto*
Kiley, Phyllis — *National Search, Inc.*
King, Bill — *The McCormick Group, Inc.*
King, Joyce L. — *MSI International*
King, Richard M. — *Kittleman & Associates*
King, Stephen C. — *Boyden/Zay & Company*
King, Steven — *Ashway, Ltd.*
Kinser, Richard E. — *Richard Kinser & Associates*
Kirkpatrick, Robert L. — *Reese Associates*
Kirschman, David R. — *Physician Executive Management Center*
Kishbaugh, Herbert S. — *Kishbaugh Associates International*
Klages, Constance W. — *International Management Advisors, Inc.*
Klauck, James J. — *Horton International*
Klavens, Cecile J. — *The Pickwick Group, Inc.*
Klavins, Larissa R. — *Dieckmann & Associates, Ltd.*
Klein, Gary I. — *Johnson Smith & Knisely Accord*
Klein, Gregory A. — *A.T. Kearney, Inc.*
Klopfenstein, Edward L. — *Crowder & Company*
Knight, Kim L. — *Telford, Adams & Alexander/The Knight Company*
Knisely, Gary — *Johnson Smith & Knisely Accord*
Knotts, Jerry — *Mixtec Group*
Kochert, Don — *Summerfield Associates, Inc.*
Koehler, Cathy — *Ells Personnel System Inc.*
Kohn, Adam P. — *Christian & Timbers*
Kohonoski, Michael M. — *The Guild Corporation*
Kondra, Vernon J. — *The Douglas Reiter Company, Inc.*
Koontz, Donald N. — *Koontz, Jeffries & Associates, Inc.*
Kopsick, Joseph M. — *Spencer Stuart*
Korkuch, Sandy — *Barone-O'Hara Associates*
Kors, R. Paul — *Kors Montgomery International*
Kossuth, David — *Kossuth & Associates, Inc.*
Kossuth, Jane — *Kossuth & Associates, Inc.*
Kotick, Madeline — *The Stevenson Group of New Jersey*
Krauser, H. James — *Spencer Stuart*
Krejci, Stanley L. — *The Interface Group, Ltd./Boyden*
Kreps, Charles D. — *Normyle/Erstling Health Search Group*
Kreuter, Daniel A. — *D.A. Kreuter Associates, Inc.*
Kreutz, Gary L. — *Kreutz Consulting Group, Inc.*
Krieger, Dennis F. — *Seiden Krieger Associates, Inc.*
Kring, Kenneth L. — *Spencer Stuart*
Krohn, Eileen — *The Stevenson Group of New Jersey*
Kropp, Randy — *Ells Personnel System Inc.*
Kuper, Keith D. — *Christenson & Hutchison*
Kuypers, Arnold — *Lamalie Amrop International*
Laba, Marvin — *Marvin Laba & Associates*
Laba, Stuart M. — *Marvin Laba & Associates*
LaCharite, Danielle — *The Guild Corporation*
LaFaye, Susan — *MSI International*
Laird, Meri — *Davidson, Laird & Associates*
Lake, Phillip R. — *U.S. Envirosearch*
Lamb, Lynn M. — *F-O-R-T-U-N-E Personnel Consultants of Huntsville, Inc.*
Land, Shaun — *Dunhill Professional Search of Irvine, Inc.*
Landon, Susan J. — *Lamalie Amrop International*
Langer, Joel A. — *Langer Associates, Inc.*
Langford, Robert W. — *F-O-R-T-U-N-E Personnel Consultants of Huntsville, Inc.*
Lankford, Charles — *MSI International*
Larsen, Jack B. — *Jack B. Larsen & Associates*
Larsen, Richard F. — *Larsen, Zilliacus & Associates, Inc.*
Lasher, Charles M. — *Lasher Associates*
Lauderback, David R. — *A.T. Kearney, Inc.*
Lautz, Lindsay A. — *Wilkinson & Ives*
Lawner, Harvey — *Walden Associates*
Lawrance, Susanne — *Sharrow & Associates*
Lawrence, David — *Agra Placements International Ltd.*
Lawson, Bettye N. — *MSI International*
Layton, Patrick R. — *MSI International*
Lebo, Terry — *Agra Placements International Ltd.*
Leetma, Imbi — *Stanton Chase International*
Leininger, Dennis — *Key Employment Services*
Leland, Paul — *McInturff & Associates, Inc.*
Lence, Julie Anne — *MSI International*
Lenkaitis, Lewis F. — *A.T. Kearney, Inc.*
Leonard, Linda — *Harris Heery & Associates*
Leslie, William H. — *Boyden/Zay & Company*
Leszynski, Edward — *ProResource, Inc.*
Lettrii, Mary — *BioQuest, Inc.*
Levine, Alan M. — *MB Inc. Interim Executive Division*
Levine, Lois — *National Search, Inc.*

Levinson, Lauren — *The Danbrook Group, Inc.*
Levitt, Muriel A. — *D.S. Allen Associates, Inc.*
Lewicki, Christopher — *MSI International*
Lewis, Jon A. — *Sandhurst Associates*
Lewis, Marc D. — *Handy HRM Corp.*
Liebowitz, Michael E. — *Highland Search Group, L.L.C.*
Lindberg, Eric J. — *MSI International*
Linde, Rick — *Battalia Winston International*
Lindenmuth, Mary — *Search West, Inc.*
Linton, Leonard M. — *Byron Leonard International, Inc.*
Lipe, Jerold L. — *Compass Group Ltd.*
Lippman, Lloyd A. — *Career Management International*
Little, Gary — *Agra Placements International Ltd.*
Livesay, Christopher C. — *MSI International*
Lloyd, John S. — *Witt/Kieffer, Ford, Hadelman & Lloyd*
Loeb, Stephen H. — *Grant Cooper and Associates*
Logan, Valarie A. — *D.S.A. - Dixie Search Associates*
Logue, Kenneth F. — *Logue & Rice Inc.*
London, Gregory J. — *MSI International*
Long, Helga — *H.M. Long International, Ltd.*
Long, John P. — *John J. Davis & Associates, Inc.*
Long, Melanie — *National Search, Inc.*
Long, William G. — *McDonald, Long & Associates, Inc.*
LoPresto, Robert L. — *Rusher, Loscavio & LoPresto*
Loria, Frank — *Accounting Personnel Consultants*
Loscavio, J. Michael — *Rusher, Loscavio & LoPresto*
Lotufo, Donald A. — *D.A.L. Associates, Inc.*
Lotz, R. James — *International Management Advisors, Inc.*
Lovas, W. Carl — *Lovas Stanley/Paul Ray Berndtson Inc.*
Lovely, Edward — *The Stevenson Group of New Jersey*
Low, Linda — *The Development Resource Group Incorporated*
Lucarelli, Joan — *The Onstott Group, Inc.*
Lucas, Ronnie L. — *MSI International*
Lucht, John — *The John Lucht Consultancy Inc.*
Lumsby, George N. — *International Management Advisors, Inc.*
Lynch, Michael C. — *Lynch Miller Moore Partners, Inc.*
Lynn, Donald — *Frank Cuomo and Associates, Inc.*
Lyons, Denis B.K. — *Spencer Stuart*
MacCarthy, Ann — *Columbia Consulting Group*
Macdonald, G. William — *The Macdonald Group, Inc.*
MacEachern, David — *Spencer Stuart*
MacGregor, Malcolm — *Boyden*
MacJadyen, David J. — *Sharrow & Associates*
Mackenna, Kathy — *Plummer & Associates, Inc.*
Mackey-Ross, Christine — *Witt/Kieffer, Ford, Hadelman & Lloyd*
Mader, Stephen P. — *Christian & Timbers*
Maer, Harry — *Kenzer Corp.*
Maher, William J. — *Johnson Smith & Knisely Accord*
Mak, I. Paul — *Thomas A. Byrnes Associates*
Malcolm, Rod — *The Enns Partners Inc.*
Malcom, John W. — *Johnson Smith & Knisely Accord*
Malone, George V. — *Boyden*
Manassero, Henri J.P. — *International Management Advisors, Inc.*
Mancino, Gene — *Blau Kaptain Schroeder*
Manns, Alex — *Crawford & Crofford*
Maphet, Harriet — *The Stevenson Group of New Jersey*
Marchette, Steve — *Juntunen-Combs-Poirier*
Marion, Bradford B. — *Lamalie Amrop International*
Marion, Michael — *S.D. Kelly & Associates, Inc.*
Marks, Ira — *Strategic Alternatives*
Marks, Russell E. — *Webb, Johnson Associates, Inc.*
Marlow, William — *Straube Associates*
Marra, John — *Marra Peters & Partners*
Marra, John — *Marra Peters & Partners*
Marshall, Neill P. — *Witt/Kieffer, Ford, Hadelman & Lloyd*
Martens, Maxine — *Rene Plessner Associates, Inc.*
Martin, David — *The Guild Corporation*
Martin, Geary D. — *Boyden/Zay & Company*
Martin, Lynne Koll — *Boyden*
Martin, Mary Lou — *Neail Behringer Consultants*
Martin, Paula — *MSI International*
Marumoto, William H. — *The Interface Group, Ltd./Boyden*
Maschal, Charles E. — *Maschal/Connors, Inc.*
Maslan, Neal L. — *Ward Howell International, Inc.*
Mason, William E. — *John Kurosky & Associates*
Massey, H. Heath — *Robison & Associates*
Massey, R. Bruce — *Bruce Massey & Partners Inc.*
Matheny, Robert P. — *MSI International*
Mather, David R. — *Christian & Timbers*
Mathias, William J. — *Preng & Associates, Inc.*
Max, Bruno — *RBR Associates, Inc.*
May, Peter — *Mixtec Group*
Mazza, David B. — *Mazza & Riley, Inc.*
McBride, Jonathan E. — *McBride Associates, Inc.*
McBryde, Marnie — *Spencer Stuart*
McCallister, Richard A. — *Boyden*
McCarthy, David R. — *Spencer Stuart*
McComas, Kelly E. — *The Guild Corporation*
McCorkle, Sam B. — *Morton, McCorkle & Associates, Inc.*

McCormack, Joseph A. — *McCormack & Associates*
McCormack, William Reed — *MSI International*
McCormick, Brian — *The McCormick Group, Inc.*
McCormick, William J. — *The McCormick Group, Inc.*
McCreary, Charles — *Austin-McGregor International*
McDonald, Gary E. — *Agra Placements International Ltd.*
McDonald, John R. — *TSS Consulting, Ltd.*
McDonald, Scott A. — *McDonald Associates International*
McDonald, Stanleigh B. — *McDonald Associates International*
McDonnell, Julie — *Technical Personnel of Minnesota*
McFadden, Ashton S. — *Johnson Smith & Knisely Accord*
McGahey, Patricia M. — *Witt/Kieffer, Ford, Hadelman & Lloyd*
McGrath, Thomas F. — *Spriggs & Company, Inc.*
McGuire, Bud — *Search West, Inc.*
McGuire, Corey — *Peter W. Ambler Company*
McInturff, Robert — *McInturff & Associates, Inc.*
McIntyre, Alex D. — *Norman Roberts & Associates, Inc.*
McIntyre, Joel — *Phillips Resource Group*
McLean, E. Peter — *Spencer Stuart*
McMillin, Bob — *Price Waterhouse*
McNichol, John — *McNichol Associates*
McNichols, Walter B. — *Gary Kaplan & Associates*
McRae, O. Jon — *Jon McRae & Associates, Inc.*
McSherry, James F. — *Battalia Winston International*
McThrall, David — *TSS Consulting, Ltd.*
Mead, James D. — *James Mead & Company*
Meagher, Patricia G. — *Spencer Stuart*
Meany, Brian — *Herbert Mines Associates, Inc.*
Meier, J. Dale — *Grant Cooper and Associates*
Meltzer, Andrea Y. — *Executive Options, Ltd.*
Menk, Carl W. — *Canny, Bowen Inc.*
Merkuris, Jennifer — *Aureus Group*
Messett, William J. — *Messett Associates, Inc.*
Mestepey, John — *A.T. Kearney, Inc.*
Metz, Alex — *Hunt Ltd.*
Meyer, Michael F. — *Witt/Kieffer, Ford, Hadelman & Lloyd*
Meyer, Stacey — *Gary Kaplan & Associates*
Meyer, William — *Agra Placements International Ltd.*
Mierzwinski, John — *Industrial Recruiters Associates, Inc.*
Miesemer, Arthur C. — *MSI International*
Mikula, Linda — *Schweichler Associates, Inc.*
Miles, Kenneth T. — *MSI International*
Miller, Arnie — *Isaacson, Miller*
Miller, Benjamin J. — *MSI International*
Miller, Diane D. — *Wilcox, Bertoux & Miller*
Miller, Michael R. — *Lynch Miller Moore Partners, Inc.*
Miller, Paul McG. — *Lamalie Amrop International*
Miller, Roy — *The Enns Partners Inc.*
Miller, Russel E. — *ARJay & Associates*
Millonzi, Joel C. — *Johnson Smith & Knisely Accord*
Milstein, Bonnie — *Marvin Laba & Associates*
Milton, Suzanne — *Marra Peters & Partners*
Mines, Herbert T. — *Herbert Mines Associates, Inc.*
Mitchell, Kyle R. — *Tanton Mitchell/Paul Ray Berndtson*
Mockler, Nadine — *Part Time Resources, Inc.*
Mogul, Gene — *Mogul Consultants, Inc.*
Mondragon, Philip — *Boyden*
Montgomery, Catherine C. — *Boyden*
Montgomery, James M. — *Houze, Shourds & Montgomery, Inc.*
Moore, David S. — *Lynch Miller Moore Partners, Inc.*
Moore, Denise — *Jonas, Walters & Assoc., Inc.*
Moore, Lemuel R. — *MSI International*
Moore, Mark — *Wheeler, Moore & Elam Co.*
Moore, Michael — *Agra Placements International Ltd.*
Moran, Gail — *Comprehensive Search*
Morgan, Gary — *National Search, Inc.*
Morgan, Richard S. — *Lovas Stanley/Paul Ray Berndtson Inc.*
Morgan, Vincent S. — *Johnson Smith & Knisely Accord*
Morrison, Janis L. — *Garrett Associates Inc.*
Morton, Robert C. — *Morton, McCorkle & Associates, Inc.*
Moseley, Monroe — *Isaacson, Miller*
Muendel, H. Edward — *Stanton Chase International*
Mulligan, Robert P. — *William Willis Worldwide Inc.*
Mummert, Dennis D. — *Sweeney Harbert & Mummert, Inc.*
Murin, Rose Mary — *U.S. Envirosearch*
Murphy, Cornelius J. — *Goodrich & Sherwood Associates, Inc.*
Murphy, Gary J. — *Stone Murphy & Olson*
Murphy, Karen S. — *Flex Execs Management Solutions*
Murphy, Patrick J. — *P.J. Murphy & Associates, Inc.*
Murphy, Timothy D. — *MSI International*
Mursuli, Meredith — *Lasher Associates*
Mustin, Joyce M. — *J: Blakslee International, Ltd.*
Myrick, Marilou — *ProResource, Inc.*
Myrick, Marilou — *ProResource, Inc.*
Nadherny, Christopher C. — *Spencer Stuart*
Nagler, Leon G. — *Nagler, Robins & Poe, Inc.*
Nahas, Robert — *Herbert Mines Associates, Inc.*
Napier, Ginger L. — *Preng & Associates, Inc.*
Nass, Martin D. — *Lamalie Amrop International*

Nathanson, Barry F. — *Barry Nathanson Associates*
Nazzaro, Samuel G. — *Boyden*
Neff, Thomas J. — *Spencer Stuart*
Neher, Robert L. — *Intech Summit Group, Inc.*
Neill, Wellden K. — *Sampson Neill & Wilkins Inc.*
Nein, Lawrence F. — *Lamalie Amrop International*
Nelson, Barbara — *Herman Smith Executive Initiatives Inc.*
Nephew, Robert — *Christian & Timbers*
Neuberth, Jeffrey G. — *Canny, Bowen Inc.*
Newbold, Michael — *Agra Placements International Ltd.*
Newman, Arthur I. — *Lamalie Amrop International*
Newman, Lynn — *Kishbaugh Associates International*
Nicastro, Kelley P. — *A la carte International*
Nocero, John — *ProResource, Inc.*
Nordland, Martin N. — *Horton International*
Norman, Randy — *Austin-McGregor International*
Norsell, Paul E. — *Paul Norsell & Associates, Inc.*
Nye, David S. — *Blake, Hansen & Nye, Limited*
O'Brien, Anne Lim — *Heidrick & Struggles, Inc.*
O'Brien, John G. — *CanMed Consultants Inc.*
O'Donnell, James H. — *MSI International*
O'Donnell, Timothy W. — *Boyden*
O'Hara, Daniel M. — *Lynch Miller Moore Partners, Inc.*
O'Hara, James J. — *Barone-O'Hara Associates*
O'Maley, Kimberlee — *Spencer Stuart*
O'Neill, James P. — *Allerton Heneghan & O'Neill*
O'Neill, Stephen A. — *Harris Heery & Associates*
O'Reilly, Jack — *Catalyx Group*
O'Such, Tracy — *Bishop Partners*
O'Toole, Dennis P. — *Dennis P. O'Toole & Associates Inc.*
Oakes, Meg B. — *D.P. Parker and Associates*
Oberg, Roy — *The Danbrook Group, Inc.*
Ocon, Olga — *Busch International*
Ogden, Dayton — *Spencer Stuart*
Ogdon, Thomas H. — *The Ogdon Partnership*
Ohman, Gregory L. — *Pearson, Caldwell & Farnsworth, Inc.*
Oliver, Phoebe — *Seiden Krieger Associates, Inc.*
Oller, Jose E. — *Ward Howell International, Inc.*
Olmstead, George T. — *Blackshaw, Olmstead & Lynch*
Olsen, Carl — *A.T. Kearney, Inc.*
Olsen, David G. — *Handy HRM Corp.*
Onstott, Joseph E. — *The Onstott Group, Inc.*
Oppenheim, Jeffrey — *Roth Young Personnel Service of Boston, Inc.*
Osborn, Jim — *Southwestern Professional Services*
Oswald, Mark G. — *Canny, Bowen Inc.*
Ott, George W. — *Ott & Hansen, Inc.*
Otto, Karen E. — *Witt/Kieffer, Ford, Hadelman & Lloyd*
Owens, Ken — *F-O-R-T-U-N-E Personnel Consultants of Huntsville, Inc.*
Pacini, Lauren R. — *Hite Executive Search*
Page, Linda — *Jonas, Walters & Assoc., Inc.*
Page, Linda M. — *Wargo and Co., Inc.*
Palazio, Carla — *A.T. Kearney, Inc.*
Palma, Frank R. — *Goodrich & Sherwood Associates, Inc.*
Palmer, Carlton A. — *Beall & Company, Inc.*
Palmlund, David W. — *Lamalie Amrop International*
Pappas, Jim — *Search Dynamics, Inc.*
Pappas, Timothy C. — *Jonas, Walters & Assoc., Inc.*
Parfitt, William C. — *Parfitt Recruiting and Consulting/PRO TEM*
Park, Dabney G. — *Mark Stanley & Company*
Parker, David P. — *D.P. Parker and Associates*
Parker, Roberta — *R. Parker and Associates, Inc.*
Parkin, Myrna — *S.D. Kelly & Associates, Inc.*
Parr, James A. — *KPMG Management Consulting*
Parry, William H. — *Horton International*
Patence, David W. — *Handy HRM Corp.*
Patlovich, Michael J. — *Witt/Kieffer, Ford, Hadelman & Lloyd*
Patton, Mitchell — *Patton/Perry Associates, Inc.*
Pearson, John R. — *Pearson, Caldwell & Farnsworth, Inc.*
Pearson, Robert L. — *Lamalie Amrop International*
Peasback, David R. — *Canny, Bowen Inc.*
Peckenpaugh, Ann D. — *Schweichler Associates, Inc.*
Peeney, James D. — *Peeney Associates*
Pelisson, Charles — *Marra Peters & Partners*
Pelletier, Jacques F. — *Roth Young Personnel Service of Boston, Inc.*
Perez, Christina — *Orr Executive Search*
Perry, Wayne B. — *Bruce Massey & Partners Inc.*
Persky, Barry — *Barry Persky & Company, Inc.*
Peternich, Tracy — *Simpson Associates*
Peters, James N. — *TNS Partners, Inc.*
Petrides, Andrew S. — *ARJay & Associates*
Pettersson, Tara L. — *Lamalie Amrop International*
Pettibone, Linda — *Herbert Mines Associates, Inc.*
Pettway, Samuel H. — *Spencer Stuart*
Pfannkuche, Anthony V. — *Spencer Stuart*
Pfeiffer, Irene — *Price Waterhouse*
Pfister, Shelli — *Jack B. Larsen & Associates*
Phelps, Gene L. — *McCormack & Farrow*
Phillips, Anna W. — *Witt/Kieffer, Ford, Hadelman & Lloyd*

Phillips, Donald L. — *O'Shea, Divine & Company, Inc.*
Phillips, James L. — *Highland Search Group, L.L.C.*
Phillips, Richard K. — *Handy HRM Corp.*
Phillips, Scott K. — *Phillips & Ford, Inc.*
Pickens, Barbara — *Johnson Smith & Knisely Accord*
Pickering, Dale — *Agri-Tech Personnel, Inc.*
Pickford, Stephen T. — *The Corporate Staff, Inc.*
Pierson, Edward J. — *Johnson Smith & Knisely Accord*
Pinkman, Karen N. — *Skott/Edwards Consultants, Inc.*
Pitcher, Brian D. — *Skott/Edwards Consultants, Inc.*
Plessner, Rene — *Rene Plessner Associates, Inc.*
Plimpton, Ralph L. — *R L Plimpton Associates*
Plummer, John — *Plummer & Associates, Inc.*
Poe, James B. — *Nagler, Robins & Poe, Inc.*
Poirier, Frank — *Juntunen-Combs-Poirier*
Poirier, Roland — *Poirier, Hoevel & Co.*
Poracky, John W. — *M. Wood Company*
Porada, Stephen D. — *CAP Inc.*
Porter, Albert — *The Experts*
Porter, Ken — *Tourism Development International*
Poster, Lawrence D. — *Catalyx Group*
Potenza, Gregory — *Mixtec Group*
Potter, Steven B. — *Highland Search Group, L.L.C.*
Preng, David E. — *Preng & Associates, Inc.*
Preschlack, Jack E. — *Spencer Stuart*
Prince, Marilyn L. — *Higdon Prince Inc.*
Proct, Nina — *Martin H. Bauman Associates, Inc.*
Prosser, Shane — *Search Consultants International, Inc.*
Pryde, Marcia P. — *A.T. Kearney, Inc.*
Pugliese, Vincent — *Search West, Inc.*
Quick, Roger A. — *Norman Broadbent International, Inc.*
Raab, Julie — *Dunhill Professional Search of Irvine, Inc.*
Rabe, William — *Sales Executives Inc.*
Rabinowitz, Peter A. — *P.A.R. Associates Inc.*
Radawicz, Angela — *Mixtec Group*
Radice, Joseph — *Hospitality International*
Raheja, Marc C. — *CanMed Consultants Inc.*
Raiber, Laurie Altman — *The IMC Group of Companies Ltd.*
Ramsey, John H. — *Mark Stanley & Company*
Randell, James E. — *Randell-Heiken, Inc.*
Range, Mary Jane — *Ingram & Aydelotte Inc.*
Ray, Marianne C. — *Callan Associates, Ltd.*
Raymond, Anne — *Anderson Sterling Associates*
Reddick, David C. — *Horton International*
Redding, Denise — *The Douglas Reiter Company, Inc.*
Redler, Rhonda — *National Search, Inc.*
Redwood, Guy W. — *Bruce Massey & Partners Inc.*
Reece, Christopher S. — *Reece & Mruk Partners*
Reeder, Michael S. — *Lamalie Amrop International*
Reeves, William B. — *Spencer Stuart*
Regehly, Herbert L. — *The IMC Group of Companies Ltd.*
Reiser, Ellen — *Thorndike Deland Associates*
Reiss, Matt — *National Search, Inc.*
Reiter, Douglas — *The Douglas Reiter Company, Inc.*
Reiter, Harold D. — *Herbert Mines Associates, Inc.*
Renick, Cynthia L. — *Morgan Hunter Corp.*
Reticker, Peter — *MSI International*
Reyman, Susan — *S. Reyman & Associates Ltd.*
Reynolds, Gregory P. — *Roberts Ryan and Bentley*
Rice, Douglas — *Agra Placements International Ltd.*
Rice, Marie — *Jay Gaines & Company, Inc.*
Rice, Raymond D. — *Logue & Rice Inc.*
Rich, Lyttleton — *Sockwell & Associates*
Richards, Sharon — *The Barack Group, Inc.*
Richardson, J. Rick — *Spencer Stuart*
Rieger, Louis J. — *Spencer Stuart*
Riley, Elizabeth G. — *Mazza & Riley, Inc.*
Rimmele, Michael — *The Bankers Group*
Rinaldi, Michael D. — *D.P. Parker and Associates*
Rinker, Jim — *Southwestern Professional Services*
Rivas, Alberto F. — *Boyden*
Rivers, Geri — *Chrisman & Company, Incorporated*
Rizzo, L. Donald — *R.P. Barone Associates*
Roberts, Mitch — *A.E. Feldman Associates*
Roberts, Nick P. — *Spectrum Search Associates, Inc.*
Roberts, Norman C. — *Norman Roberts & Associates, Inc.*
Roberts, Raymond R. — *MSI International*
Roberts, Scott B. — *Wargo and Co., Inc.*
Robertson, William R. — *Ward Howell International, Inc.*
Robins, Jeri N. — *Nagler, Robins & Poe, Inc.*
Robinson, Bruce — *Bruce Robinson Associates*
Robison, John H. — *Robison & Associates*
Rodgers, John — *Agra Placements International Ltd.*
Rodgers, Kathi — *St. Lawrence International, Inc.*
Rodney, Brett — *MSI International*
Rodriguez, Josie — *R. Parker and Associates, Inc.*
Romaine, Stanley J. — *Mixtec Group*
Romanchek, Walter R. — *Wellington Management Group*
Romanello, Daniel P. — *Spencer Stuart*

Romaniw, Michael J. — *A la carte International*
Romaniw, Michael J. — *A la carte International*
Romaniw, Michael J. — *A la carte International*
Ropella, Patrick B. — *Ropella & Associates*
Rosemarin, Gloria J. — *Barrington Hart, Inc.*
Rosenberg, Esther — *Howe-Lewis International*
Rosenthal, Charles — *National Search, Inc.*
Ross, Lawrence — *Lovas Stanley/Paul Ray Berndtson Inc.*
Ross, Marc A. — *Flowers & Associates*
Ross, Mark S. — *Herman Smith Executive Initiatives Inc.*
Ross, Martin B. — *Ward Howell International, Inc.*
Ross, William J. — *Flowers & Associates*
Rossi, Silvio — *Keith Bagg & Associates Inc.*
Roth, Robert J. — *Williams, Roth & Krueger Inc.*
Roth, William — *Harris Heery & Associates*
Rothfeld, Robert — *A.E. Feldman Associates*
Rothman, Jeffrey — *ProResource, Inc.*
Rowe, William D. — *D.E. Foster Partners Inc.*
Rowells, Michael — *MSI International*
Rudolph, Kenneth — *Kossuth & Associates, Inc.*
Rudzinsky, Howard — *Louis Rudzinsky Associates*
Rumson, Paul — *Roth Young Personnel Service of Boston, Inc.*
Rurak, Zbigniew T. — *Rurak & Associates, Inc.*
Russell, Richard A. — *Executive Search Consultants Corporation*
Russell, Robin E. — *Kenzer Corp.*
Russell, Sam — *The Guild Corporation*
Russell, Susan Anne — *Executive Search Consultants Corporation*
Sacerdote, John — *Raymond Karsan Associates*
Safnuk, Donald — *Corporate Recruiters Ltd.*
Sampson, Martin C. — *Sampson Neill & Wilkins Inc.*
Sanders, Spencer H. — *Battalia Winston International*
Sangster, Jeffrey — *F-O-R-T-U-N-E Personnel Consultants of Manatee County*
Sapperstein, Jerry S. — *CFO Associates, Inc.*
Sathe, Mark A. — *Sathe & Associates, Inc.*
Savage, Edward J. — *Stanton Chase International*
Sawyer, Patricia L. — *Smith & Sawyer Inc.*
Sayers, Bruce D. — *Brackin & Sayers Associates*
Schaefer, Frederic M. — *A.T. Kearney, Inc.*
Schaefer, Robert — *Search Enterprises, Inc.*
Scharett, Carol — *St. Lawrence International, Inc.*
Schedra, Sharon — *Earley Kielty and Associates, Inc.*
Schlpma, Christine — *Advanced Executive Resources*
Schmidt, Jeri E. — *Blake, Hansen & Nye, Limited*
Schmidt, Peter R. — *Boyden*
Schmidt, William C. — *Christian & Timbers*
Schneider, Perry — *Agra Placements International Ltd.*
Schneiderman, Gerald — *Management Resource Associates, Inc.*
Schroeder, John W. — *Spencer Stuart*
Schroeder, Lee — *Blau Kaptain Schroeder*
Schroeder, Steven J. — *Blau Kaptain Schroeder*
Schuette, Dorothy — *Harris Heery & Associates*
Schwam, Carol — *A.E. Feldman Associates*
Schweichler, Lee J. — *Schweichler Associates, Inc.*
Scognamillo, Sandra V. — *Witt/Kieffer, Ford, Hadelman & Lloyd*
Scrivines, Hank — *Search Northwest Associates*
Seals, Sonny — *A.T. Kearney, Inc.*
Segal, Eric B. — *Kenzer Corp.*
Seiden, Steven A. — *Seiden Krieger Associates, Inc.*
Seitz, Charles J. — *Neail Behringer Consultants*
Sekera, Roger I. — *A.T. Kearney, Inc.*
Selker, Gregory L. — *Christian & Timbers*
Selko, Philip W. — *Hogan Acquisitions*
Semyan, John K. — *TNS Partners, Inc.*
Sennello, Gendra — *National Search, Inc.*
Serwat, Leonard A. — *Spencer Stuart*
Settles, Barbara Z. — *Lamalie Amrop International*
Sevilla, Claudio A. — *Crawford & Crofford*
Shamir, Ben — *S.D. Kelly & Associates, Inc.*
Sheedy, Edward J. — *Dieckmann & Associates, Ltd.*
Shelton, Sandra — *National Search, Inc.*
Shenfield, Peter — *Baker, Harris & Partners Limited*
Shepard, Michael J. — *MSI International*
Shepherd, Daniel M. — *Shepherd Bueschel & Provus, Inc.*
Shervey, Brent C. — *O'Callaghan Honey/Paul Ray Berndtson, Inc.*
Sherwin, Thomas — *Barone-O'Hara Associates*
Sherwood, Andrew — *Goodrich & Sherwood Associates, Inc.*
Shimp, David J. — *Lamalie Amrop International*
Shipherd, John T. — *The Cassie Group*
Shoemaker, Larry C. — *Shoemaker & Associates*
Shultz, Deborah M. — *Blau Kaptain Schroeder*
Sibbald, John R. — *John Sibbald Associates, Inc.*
Siegel, Pamela — *Executive Options, Ltd.*
Sierra, Rafael A. — *Lamalie Amrop International*
Siker, Paul W. — *The Guild Corporation*
Sill, Igor M. — *Geneva Group International*
Sill, Igor M. — *Geneva Group International*
Silvas, Stephen D. — *Roberson and Company*
Silver, Lee A. — *L.A. Silver Associates, Inc.*

Simmons, Gerald J. — *Handy HRM Corp.*
Simmons, Sandra K. — *MSI International*
Sinclair, Amy — *Fisher Personnel Management Services*
Sine, Mark — *Hospitality International*
Singer, Glenn — *Witt/Kieffer, Ford, Hadelman & Lloyd*
Sjogren, Dennis — *Agra Placements International Ltd.*
Skunda, Donna M. — *Allerton Heneghan & O'Neill*
Slaughter, Katherine T. — *Compass Group Ltd.*
Slayton, Richard C. — *Slayton International, Inc.*
Smead, Michelle M. — *A.T. Kearney, Inc.*
Smith, Adam M. — *The Abbott Group, Inc.*
Smith, Cheryl — *ProResource, Inc.*
Smith, David P. — *Smith & Latterell (HRS, Inc.)*
Smith, Douglas M. — *Ward Howell International, Inc.*
Smith, Ethan L. — *Highland Search Group, L.L.C.*
Smith, Grant — *Price Waterhouse*
Smith, Herman M. — *Herman Smith Executive Initiatives Inc.*
Smith, Margaret A. — *MSI International*
Smith, Marvin E. — *Parfitt Recruiting and Consulting*
Smith, Robert L. — *Smith & Sawyer Inc.*
Smith, Toni S. — *Spencer Stuart*
Snelgrove, Geiger — *National Search, Inc.*
Snodgrass, Stephen — *DeFrain, Mayer, Lee & Burgess LLC*
Snyder, James F. — *Snyder & Company*
Snyder, Thomas J. — *Spencer Stuart*
Sockwell, J. Edgar — *Sockwell & Associates*
Soggs, Cheryl Pavick — *A.T. Kearney, Inc.*
Sola, George L. — *A.T. Kearney, Inc.*
Solters, Jeanne — *The Guild Corporation*
Songy, Al — *U.S. Envirosearch*
Southerland, Keith C. — *Witt/Kieffer, Ford, Hadelman & Lloyd*
Sowerbutt, Richard S. — *Hite Executive Search*
Spann, Richard E. — *Goodrich & Sherwood Associates, Inc.*
Spanninger, Mark J. — *The Guild Corporation*
Speck, Michael J. — *Lovas Stanley/Paul Ray Berndtson Inc.*
Spicer, Merrilyn — *Search West, Inc.*
Spiegel, Gay — *L.A. Silver Associates, Inc.*
Sprague, David — *Michael Stern Associates Inc.*
Spriggs, Robert D. — *Spriggs & Company, Inc.*
Sprowls, Linda — *Allard Associates*
Stack, James K. — *Boyden*
Stafford, Susan — *Hospitality International*
Stahl, Cynthia — *Plummer & Associates, Inc.*
Stanley, Paul R.A. — *Lovas Stanley/Paul Ray Berndtson Inc.*
Stark, Jeff — *Thorne, Brieger Associates Inc.*
Statson, Dale E. — *Sales Executives Inc.*
Steck, Frank T. — *A.T. Kearney, Inc.*
Steenerson, Thomas L. — *MSI International*
Stein, Terry W. — *Stewart, Stein and Scott, Ltd.*
Steinman, Stephen — *The Stevenson Group of New Jersey*
Stenholm, Gilbert R. — *Spencer Stuart*
Sterling, Jay — *Earley Kielty and Associates, Inc.*
Stern, Michael I. — *Michael Stern Associates Inc.*
Stevenson, Terry — *Bartholdi & Company, Inc.*
Stewart, Jeffrey O. — *Stewart, Stein and Scott, Ltd.*
Stewart, Ross M. — *Human Resources Network Partners Inc.*
Stiles, Judy — *MedQuest Associates*
Stinson, R.J. — *Sampson Neill & Wilkins Inc.*
Stivk, Barbara A. — *Thornton Resources*
Stone, Robert Ryder — *Lamalie Amrop International*
Stouffer, Dale — *Agra Placements International Ltd.*
Stratmeyer, Karin Bergwall — *Princeton Entrepreneurial Resources*
Straube, Stanley H. — *Straube Associates*
Strawn, William — *Houtz-Strawn Associates, Inc.*
Stricker, Sidney G. — *Stricker & Zagor*
Stringer, Dann P. — *D.E. Foster Partners Inc.*
Strom, Mark N. — *Search Advisors International Corp.*
Strong, Duane K. — *Executive Resource, Inc.*
Strong, Robert W. — *The Barack Group, Inc.*
Stubbs, Judy N. — *Lamalie Amrop International*
Sturtz, James W. — *Compass Group Ltd.*
Stutt, Brian — *Richard, Wayne and Roberts*
Sullivan, James — *Search Enterprises, Inc.*
Sullivan, Kay — *Rusher, Loscavio & LoPresto*
Summerfield-Beall, Dotty — *Summerfield Associates, Inc.*
Summers, Burke — *The McCormick Group, Inc.*
Sumurdy, Melinda — *Kenzer Corp.*
Sur, William K. — *Canny, Bowen Inc.*
Sussman, Lynda — *Gilbert Tweed/INESA*
Swan, Richard A. — *Witt/Kieffer, Ford, Hadelman & Lloyd*
Swanson, Dick — *Raymond Karsan Associates*
Swanson, Kris — *Flex Execs Management Solutions*
Swatts, Stone — *F-O-R-T-U-N-E Personnel Consultants of Huntsville, Inc.*
Sweeney, James W. — *Sweeney Harbert & Mummert, Inc.*
Sweeney, Sean K. — *Bonifield Associates*
Swick, Jan — *TSS Consulting, Ltd.*
Szafran, Jack — *U.S. Envirosearch*
Tabisz, Susanne — *Executive Referral Services, Inc.*

Taft, Steven D. — *The Guild Corporation*
Takacs, David L. — *Gilbert & Van Campen International*
Taylor, Charles E. — *Lamalie Amrop International*
Taylor, Conrad G. — *MSI International*
Taylor, Ernest A. — *Ward Howell International, Inc.*
Teinert, Jay — *Damon & Associates, Inc.*
Templin, Robert E. — *Gilbert Tweed/INESA*
Teter, Sandra — *The Danbrook Group, Inc.*
Theobald, David B. — *Theobald & Associates*
Thies, Gary — *S.D. Kelly & Associates, Inc.*
Thiras, Ted — *Mixtec Group*
Tholke, William E. — *Canny, Bowen Inc.*
Thomas, Christine S. — *Lovas Stanley/Paul Ray Berndtson Inc.*
Thomas, Donald — *Mixtec Group*
Thomas, Jeffrey — *Fairfaxx Corporation*
Thomas, John T. — *Ward Howell International, Inc.*
Thomas, Kurt J. — *P.J. Murphy & Associates, Inc.*
Thomas, Terry — *Montague Enterprises*
Thomas, William — *Mixtec Group*
Thompson, Carlton W. — *Spencer Stuart*
Thompson, Dave — *Battalia Winston International*
Thompson, James R. — *Gordon Wahls Company*
Thompson, John R. — *MSI International*
Thompson, Kenneth L. — *McCormack & Farrow*
Thornton, John C. — *Thornton Resources*
Timoney, Laura — *Bishop Partners*
Tinucci, Crystal M. — *Witt/Kieffer, Ford, Hadelman & Lloyd*
Tipp, George — *Intech Summit Group, Inc.*
Titterington, Catherine F. — *MSI International*
Tokarcik, Patricia — *ProResource, Inc.*
Tokash, Ronald E. — *MSI International*
Tracey, Jack — *Management Assistance Group, Inc.*
Trosin, Walter R. — *Johnson Smith & Knisely Accord*
Trott, Kathryn — *Allard Associates*
Trott, Kathryn — *Allard Associates*
Truax, Kevin — *Key Employment Services*
Trueblood, Brian G. — *TNS Partners, Inc.*
Truex, John F. — *Morton, McCorkle & Associates, Inc.*
Truitt, Thomas B. — *Southwestern Professional Services*
Tryon, Katey — *DeFrain, Mayer, Lee & Burgess LLC*
Tucci, Joseph — *Fairfaxx Corporation*
Tucker, Thomas A. — *The Thomas Tucker Company*
Tunney, William — *Grant Cooper and Associates*
Turner, Edward K. — *Don Richard Associates of Charlotte*
Tutwiler, Stephen — *Don Richard Associates of Tampa, Inc.*
Tweed, Janet — *Gilbert Tweed/INESA*
Tyson, Richard L. — *Bonifield Associates*
Ulbert, Nancy — *Aureus Group*
Unger, Stephen A. — *Spencer Stuart*
Utroska, Donald R. — *Lamalie Amrop International*
Vachon, David A. — *McNichol Associates*
Vainblat, Galina — *Foy, Schneid & Daniel, Inc.*
Valenta, Joseph — *Princeton Entrepreneurial Resources*
Van Campen, Jerry — *Gilbert & Van Campen International*
Van Clieaf, Mark — *MVC Associates International*
Van Horn, Carol — *R. Parker and Associates, Inc.*
van Someren, Christian — *Johnson Smith & Knisely Accord*
Vann, Dianne — *The Button Group*
Velten, Mark — *Hunt Advisory Services*
Venable, William W. — *Thorndike Deland Associates*
Vennat, Manon — *Spencer Stuart*
Vergara, Gail H. — *Spencer Stuart*
Vergari, Jane — *Herbert Mines Associates, Inc.*
Vinnedge, Sandra — *U.S. Envirosearch*
Virgili, Franca — *Johnson Smith & Knisely Accord*
Visnich, L. Christine — *Bason Associates Inc.*
Vlcek, Thomas J. — *Vlcek & Company, Inc.*
Vojta, Marilyn B. — *James Mead & Company*
Volk, Richard — *MSI International*
Wakefield, Scott — *National Search, Inc.*
Waldman, Noah H. — *Lamalie Amrop International*
Waldoch, D. Mark — *Barnes Development Group, LLC*
Waldrop, Gary R. — *MSI International*
Walker, Ewing J. — *Ward Howell International, Inc.*
Walker, Martin S. — *Walker Communications*
Wallace, Alec — *Tanton Mitchell/Paul Ray Berndtson*
Walters, William F. — *Jonas, Walters & Assoc., Inc.*
Walther, Linda S. — *MSI International*
Ward, Madeleine — *LTM Associates*
Wardell, Charles W.B. — *Lamalie Amrop International*
Ware, John C. — *Spencer Stuart*
Wargo, G. Rick — *A.T. Kearney, Inc.*
Warren, Sylvia W. — *Thorndike Deland Associates*
Warter, Mark — *Isaacson, Miller*
Wassill, Larry — *Corporate Recruiters Ltd.*
Waters, Peter D. — *John Kurosky & Associates*
Watkins, Thomas M. — *Lamalie Amrop International*
Watson, James — *MSI International*
Wayne, Cary S. — *ProSearch Inc.*

Webb, George H. — *Webb, Johnson Associates, Inc.*
Webb, Shawn K. — *MSI International*
Weber, Jurgen — *BioQuest, Inc.*
Wein, Michael S. — *InterimManagement Solutions, Inc.*
Wein, Michael S. — *Media Management Resources, Inc.*
Wein, William — *InterimManagement Solutions, Inc.*
Wein, William — *Media Management Resources, Inc.*
Weisler, Nancy — *National Search, Inc.*
Weiss, Jeffrey — *Search West, Inc.*
Weissman-Rosenthal, Abbe — *ALW Research International*
Weisz, Laura — *Anderson Sterling Associates*
Welch, David — *Isaacson, Miller*
Weller, Paul S. — *Mark Stanley & Company*
Werner, Bonnie — *H.M. Long International, Ltd.*
Wertel, Ronald E. — *Gordon Wahls Company*
West, Nancy — *Health Care Dimensions*
Westerfield, Putney — *Boyden*
Weston, Corinne F. — *D.A. Kreuter Associates, Inc.*
Wexler, Rona — *Ariel Recruitment Associates*
White, Jonathan O. — *The Badger Group*
White, Kimberly — *Executive Referral Services, Inc.*
White, Patricia D. — *MSI International*
White, Richard B. — *Spencer Stuart*
White, William C. — *Venture Resources Inc.*
Whiting, Anthony — *Johnson Smith & Knisely Accord*
Whitton, Paula L. — *Pearson, Caldwell & Farnsworth, Inc.*
Wichansky, Mark — *TSS Consulting, Ltd.*
Wichlei, Alan — *Isaacson, Miller*
Wier, Daniel — *Horton International*
Wilcox, Fred T. — *Wilcox, Bertoux & Miller*
Wilcox, Karen — *Isaacson, Miller*
Wilder, Richard B. — *Columbia Consulting Group*
Wilkins, Walter K. — *Sampson Neill & Wilkins Inc.*
Wilkinson, Barbara — *Beall & Company, Inc.*
Wilkinson, William R. — *Wilkinson & Ives*
Williams, Alexander H. — *Witt/Kieffer, Ford, Hadelman & Lloyd*
Williams, Gary L. — *Barnes Development Group, LLC*
Williams, Harry D. — *Jacobson Associates*
Williams, Laurelle N. — *MSI International*
Williams, Lis — *Executive Options, Ltd.*
Williams, Michelle Cruz — *Isaacson, Miller*
Williams, Roger K. — *Williams, Roth & Krueger Inc.*
Williams, Walter E. — *Canny, Bowen Inc.*
Willis, William H. — *William Willis Worldwide Inc.*
Willner, Nannette — *S.R. Wolman Associates, Inc.*
Wilson, Derrick — *Thornton Resources*
Wilson, Patricia L. — *Leon A. Farley Associates*
Winitz, Joel — *GSW Consulting Group, Inc.*
Winitz, Marla — *GSW Consulting Group, Inc.*
Winnewisser, William E. — *Accounting & Computer Personnel*
Winograd, Glenn — *Criterion Executive Search, Inc.*
Winston, Dale — *Battalia Winston International*
Winter, Peter — *Catalyx Group*
Wisch, Steven C. — *MB Inc. Interim Executive Division*
Wise, Anne — *U.S. Envirosearch*
Wiseman, Bonnie — *Witt/Kieffer, Ford, Hadelman & Lloyd*
Witte, David L. — *Ward Howell International, Inc.*
Wittenberg, Laura L. — *Boyden*
Wolf, Craig — *Aureus Group*
Wolf, Stephen M. — *Byron Leonard International, Inc.*
Wolman, Stephen R. — *S.R. Wolman Associates, Inc.*
Womack, Joseph — *The Bankers Group*
Wood, Martin F. — *Lamalie Amrop International*
Wood, Milton N. — *M. Wood Company*
Woody, Jacqueline K. — *Aureus Group*
Wooller, Edmund A.M. — *Windsor International*
Woollett, James — *Rusher, Loscavio & LoPresto*
Worth, Janet M. — *Witt/Kieffer, Ford, Hadelman & Lloyd*
Wright, Charles D. — *Goodrich & Sherwood Associates, Inc.*
Wright, Leslie — *The Stevenson Group of New Jersey*
Wrynn, Robert F. — *MSI International*
Wyatt, James — *Wyatt & Jaffe*
Young, Alexander — *Messett Associates, Inc.*
Young, Charles E. — *Flowers & Associates*
Young, Heather — *The Guild Corporation*
Young, Laurie — *Part Time Resources, Inc.*
Youngs, Donald L. — *Youngs & Company*
Zaffrann, Craig S. — *P.J. Murphy & Associates, Inc.*
Zahradka, James F. — *P.J. Murphy & Associates, Inc.*
Zak, Adam — *Adams & Associates International*
Zander, Barry W. — *MSI International*
Zarkin, Norman — *The Zarkin Group, Inc.*
Zarnoski, Hank — *Dunhill Search International*
Zay, Thomas C. — *Boyden/Zay & Company*
Zay, Thomas C. — *Boyden/Zay & Company*
Zenzer, Anne — *Witt/Kieffer, Ford, Hadelman & Lloyd*
Zera, Ronald J. — *Spencer Stuart*
Zila, Laurie M. — *Princeton Entrepreneurial Resources*
Zilliacus, Patrick W. — *Larsen, Zilliacus & Associates, Inc.*

Zingaro, Ron — *Zingaro and Company*
Zinn, Donald — *Bishop Partners*
Zivic, Janis M. — *Spencer Stuart*
Zona, Henry F. — *Zona & Associates, Inc.*
Zwiff, Jeffrey G. — *Johnson Smith & Knisely Accord*

## 6. Human Resources

Abbott, Peter — *The Abbott Group, Inc.*
Abruzzo, James — *A.T. Kearney, Inc.*
Adams, Len — *The KPA Group*
Adams, Ralda F. — *Hospitality International*
Akin, J.R. — *J.R. Akin & Company Inc.*
Alekel, Karren — *ALW Research International*
Alexander, John T. — *Telford, Adams & Alexander/Human Resource Services*
Allen, David A. — *Intech Summit Group, Inc.*
Allen, Rita B. — *R.D. Gatti & Associates, Incorporated*
Allerton, Donald T. — *Allerton Heneghan & O'Neill*
Allgire, Mary L. — *Kenzer Corp.*
Altreuter, Ken — *ALTCO Temporary Services*
Altreuter, Kenneth — *The ALTCO Group*
Altreuter, Rose — *ALTCO Temporary Services*
Altreuter, Rose — *The ALTCO Group*
Ambler, Peter W. — *Peter W. Ambler Company*
Ames, George C. — *Ames O'Neill Associates*
Amsterdam, Gail E. — *D.E. Foster Partners Inc.*
Anderson, Janet — *Professional Alternatives, Inc.*
Anderson, Richard — *Grant Cooper and Associates*
Anderson, Shawn — *Temporary Accounting Personnel, Inc.*
Anderson, Thomas — *Paul J. Biestek Associates, Inc.*
Andre, Richard — *The Andre Group, Inc.*
Andrews, J. Douglas — *Clarey & Andrews, Inc.*
Andrews, Laura L. — *Stricker & Zagor*
Andujo, Michele M. — *Chrisman & Company, Incorporated*
Angell, Tryg R. — *Tryg R. Angell Ltd.*
Aquavella, Charles P. — *CPA & Associates*
Argentin, Jo — *Executive Placement Consultants, Inc.*
Ascher, Susan P. — *The Ascher Group*
Asquith, Peter S. — *Ames Personnel Consultants, Inc.*
Aston, Kathy — *Marra Peters & Partners*
Atkins, Laurie — *Battalia Winston International*
Attell, Harold — *A.E. Feldman Associates*
Austin, Jessica L. — *D.S.A. - Dixie Search Associates*
Aydelotte, G. Thomas — *Ingram & Aydelotte Inc.*
Bacher, Philip J. — *Handy HRM Corp.*
Bachmeier, Kevin — *Agra Placements International Ltd.*
Bagg, Mary — *Keith Bagg & Associates Inc.*
Bagwell, Bruce — *Intersource, Ltd.*
Bailey, William A. — *TNS Partners, Inc.*
Baker, Gary M. — *Temporary Accounting Personnel, Inc.*
Baker-Greene, Edward — *Isaacson, Miller*
Banker, Judith G. — *R.D. Gatti & Associates, Incorporated*
Baran, Helena — *Michael J. Cavanagh and Associates*
Barbosa, Franklin J. — *Boyden*
Barnes, Richard E. — *Barnes Development Group, LLC*
Barnes, Roanne L. — *Barnes Development Group, LLC*
Barnum, Toni M. — *Stone Murphy & Olson*
Barthold, James A. — *McNichol Associates*
Barton, Gary R. — *Barton Raben, Inc.*
Bason, Maurice L. — *Bason Associates Inc.*
Battalia, O. William — *Battalia Winston International*
Bauman, Martin H. — *Martin H. Bauman Associates, Inc.*
Bearman, Linda — *Grant Cooper and Associates*
Beaudin, Elizabeth C. — *Callan Associates, Ltd.*
Beaver, Bentley H. — *The Onstott Group, Inc.*
Belford, Paul — *JDG Associates, Ltd.*
Bell, Michael — *Spencer Stuart*
Bellano, Robert W. — *Stanton Chase International*
Bennett, Jo — *Battalia Winston International*
Benson, Kate — *Rene Plessner Associates, Inc.*
Berger, Emanuel — *Isaacson, Miller*
Berk-Levine, Margo — *MB Inc. Interim Executive Division*
Besen, Douglas — *Besen Associates Inc.*
Biestek, Paul J. — *Paul J. Biestek Associates, Inc.*
Billington, Brian — *Billington & Associates*
Billington, William H. — *Spriggs & Company, Inc.*
Bishop, Barbara — *The Executive Source*
Bittman, Beth M. — *Norman Roberts & Associates, Inc.*
Blackmon, Sharon — *The Abbott Group, Inc.*
Blair, Susan — *Simpson Associates*
Blakslee, Jan H. — *J: Blakslee International, Ltd.*
Blanton, Thomas — *Blanton and Company*
Bliley, Jerry — *Spencer Stuart*
Bloomfield, Mary — *R.D. Gatti & Associates, Incorporated*
Bluhm, Claudia — *Schweichler Associates, Inc.*
Bogard, Nicholas C. — *The Onstott Group, Inc.*
Bonifield, Len — *Bonifield Associates*
Bonnell, William R. — *Bonnell Associates Ltd.*
Borland, James — *Goodrich & Sherwood Associates, Inc.*

Bostic, James E. — *Phillips Resource Group*
Bourbeau, Paul J. — *Boyden*
Bourrie, Sharon D. — *Chartwell Partners International, Inc.*
Boyer, Heath C. — *Spencer Stuart*
Brackin, James B. — *Brackin & Sayers Associates*
Brandjes, Michael J. — *Brandjes Associates*
Bratches, Howard — *Thorndike Deland Associates*
Brieger, Steve — *Thorne, Brieger Associates Inc.*
Briggs, Adam — *Horton International*
Brooks, Natalie — *Raymond Karsan Associates*
Brophy, Melissa — *Maximum Management Corp.*
Brown, Charlene N. — *Accent on Achievement, Inc.*
Brown, Larry C. — *Horton International*
Brudno, Robert J. — *Savoy Partners, Ltd.*
Bryant, Richard D. — *Bryant Associates, Inc.*
Bryza, Robert M. — *Robert Lowell International*
Buck, Charles — *Charles Buck & Associates*
Bullock, Conni — *Earley Kielty and Associates, Inc.*
Bump, Gerald J. — *D.E. Foster Partners Inc.*
Burchard, Stephen R. — *Burchard & Associates, Inc.*
Burchill, Barb — *BGB Associates*
Burchill, Greg — *BGB Associates*
Burfield, Elaine — *Skott/Edwards Consultants, Inc.*
Burke, J. Michael — *Merit Resource Group, Inc.*
Burke, John — *The Experts*
Burns, Alan — *The Enns Partners Inc.*
Burns, Terence N. — *D.E. Foster Partners Inc.*
Burris, James C. — *Boyden*
Busterna, Charles — *The KPA Group*
Butler, Kirby B. — *The Butlers Company Insurance Recruiters*
Butterfass, Stanley — *Butterfass, Pepe & MacCallan Inc.*
Byrnes, Thomas A. — *Thomas A. Byrnes Associates*
Cahill, Peter M. — *Peter M. Cahill Associates, Inc.*
Caldwell, William R. — *Pearson, Caldwell & Farnsworth, Inc.*
Callan, Robert M. — *Callan Associates, Ltd.*
Campbell, Patricia A. — *The Onstott Group, Inc.*
Campbell, Robert Scott — *Wellington Management Group*
Carideo, Joseph — *Thorndike Deland Associates*
Carrigan, Maureen — *R.D. Gatti & Associates, Incorporated*
Carter, Christine C. — *Health Care Dimensions*
Casey, Jean — *Peter W. Ambler Company*
Cass, Kathryn H. — *Don Richard Associates of Tidewater, Inc.*
Cassie, Ronald L. — *The Cassie Group*
Cattanach, Bruce B. — *Horton International*
Cavanagh, Michael J. — *Michael J. Cavanagh and Associates*
Chappell, Peter — *The Bankers Group*
Chavous, C. Crawford — *Phillips Resource Group*
Cherbonnier, L. Michael — *The Cherbonnier Group, Inc.*
Chesla, Garry — *Executive Referral Services, Inc.*
Chorman, Marilyn A. — *Hite Executive Search*
Cizek, John T. — *Cizek Associates, Inc.*
Cizek, Marti J. — *Cizek Associates, Inc.*
Clarey, Jack R. — *Clarey & Andrews, Inc.*
Clarey, William A. — *Preng & Associates, Inc.*
Clauhsen, Elizabeth A. — *Savoy Partners, Ltd.*
Cleeve, Coleen — *Howe-Lewis International*
Clegg, Cynthia — *Horton International*
Close, E. Wade — *Boyden*
Clovis, James R. — *Handy HRM Corp.*
Coffman, Brian — *Kossuth & Associates, Inc.*
Coleman, Gregory — *Strategic Associates, Inc.*
Coleman, J. Kevin — *J. Kevin Coleman & Associates, Inc.*
Collard, Joseph A. — *Spencer Stuart*
Collier, David — *Parfitt Recruiting and Consulting/PRO TEM*
Colling, Douglas — *KPMG Management Consulting*
Colman, Michael — *Executive Placement Consultants, Inc.*
Colucci, Bart A. — *Colucci, Blendow and Johnson, Inc.*
Commersoli, Al — *Executive Referral Services, Inc.*
Conner, John — *Flex Execs Management Solutions*
Conway, William P. — *Phillips Resource Group*
Cooke, Jeffrey R. — *Jonas, Walters & Assoc., Inc.*
Cooke, Katherine H. — *Horton International*
Cordaro, Concetta — *Flynn, Hannock, Incorporated*
Corrigan, Gerald F. — *The Corrigan Group*
Costick, Kathryn J. — *John Sibbald Associates, Inc.*
Cozzillio, Larry — *The Andre Group, Inc.*
Cragg, Barbara R. — *Southwestern Professional Services*
Cramer, Paul J. — *C/R Associates*
Crane, Howard C. — *Chartwell Partners International, Inc.*
Crath, Paul F. — *Price Waterhouse*
Critchley, Walter — *Cochran, Cochran & Yale, Inc.*
Critchley, Walter — *Temporary Accounting Personnel, Inc.*
Crowder, Edward W. — *Crowder & Company*
Crowell, Elizabeth — *H.M. Long International, Ltd.*
Cunningham, Robert Y. — *Goodrich & Sherwood Associates, Inc.*
Czamanske, Paul W. — *Compass Group Ltd.*
D'Ambrosio, Nicholas — *Alexander Ross Inc.*
Daniel, Beverly — *Foy, Schneid & Daniel, Inc.*
Dankowski, Thomas A. — *Dankowski and Associates, Inc.*

Davis, G. Gordon — *Davis & Company*
Dawson, Joe — *S.C. International, Ltd.*
de Bardin, Francesca — *F.L. Taylor & Company, Inc.*
de Palacios, Jeannette C. — *J. Palacios & Associates, Inc.*
de Tuede, Catherine — *Thomas A. Byrnes Associates*
DeCorrevont, James — *DeCorrevont & Associates*
DeCorrevont, James — *DeCorrevont & Associates*
DeFrancesco, Mary Ellen — *The Onstott Group, Inc.*
DeHart, Donna — *Tower Consultants, Ltd.*
Del Pino, William — *National Search, Inc.*
Delaney, Patrick J. — *Sensible Solutions, Inc.*
DeLong, Art — *Richard Kader & Associates*
Demchak, James P. — *Sandhurst Associates*
Densmore, Geraldine — *Michael Stern Associates Inc.*
Desgrosellier, Gary P. — *Personnel Unlimited/Executive Search*
Desmond, Dennis — *Beall & Company, Inc.*
deVry, Kimberly A. — *Tower Consultants, Ltd.*
deWilde, David M. — *Chartwell Partners International, Inc.*
Dieckmann, Ralph E. — *Dieckmann & Associates, Ltd.*
Dingman, Bruce — *Robert W. Dingman Company, Inc.*
Dingman, Robert W. — *Robert W. Dingman Company, Inc.*
DiSalvo, Fred — *The Cambridge Group Ltd*
Divine, Robert S. — *O'Shea, Divine & Company, Inc.*
Dixon, C.R. — *A la carte International*
Doele, Donald C. — *Goodrich & Sherwood Associates, Inc.*
Doman, Matthew — *S.C. International, Ltd.*
Doody, Michael F. — *Witt/Kieffer, Ford, Hadelman & Lloyd*
Dougherty, Bridget L. — *Wellington Management Group*
Doukas, Jon A. — *Professional Bank Services, Inc. D/B/A Executive Search, Inc.*
Dow, Lori — *Davidson, Laird & Associates*
Dowell, Mary K. — *Professional Search Associates*
Doyle, John P. — *Paul Ray Berndtson*
Drury, James J. — *Spencer Stuart*
Duley, Richard I. — *ARJay & Associates*
Earle, Paul W. — *Spencer Stuart*
Eason, James — *JRL Executive Recruiters*
Eason, Larry E. — *JRL Executive Recruiters*
Eastham, Marvene M. — *Witt/Kieffer, Ford, Hadelman & Lloyd*
Ebeling, John A. — *Gilbert Tweed/INESA*
Eden, Brooks D. — *Eden & Associates, Inc.*
Eden, Dianne — *Steeple Associates*
Edwards, Verba L. — *Wing Tips & Pumps, Inc.*
Eggena, Roger — *Phillips Resource Group*
Ehrgott, Elizabeth — *The Ascher Group*
Ehrhart, Jennifer — *ADOW's Executeam*
Einsele, Neil — *Agra Placements International Ltd.*
Eldredge, L. Lincoln — *Lamalie Amrop International*
Elliott, Mark P. — *Lamalie Amrop International*
Ellis, David — *Don Richard Associates of Georgia, Inc.*
Ellis, William — *Interspace Interactive Inc.*
Emmott, Carol B. — *Spencer Stuart*
England, Mark — *Austin-McGregor International*
Enns, George — *The Enns Partners Inc.*
Erickson, Elaine — *Kenzer Corp.*
Erwin, Lee — *Agra Placements International Ltd.*
Faber, Jill — *A.T. Kearney, Inc.*
Fair, Donna — *ProResource, Inc.*
Fancher, Robert L. — *Bason Associates Inc.*
Farley, Antoinette L. — *Witt/Kieffer, Ford, Hadelman & Lloyd*
Farley, Leon A. — *Leon A. Farley Associates*
Farnsworth, John A. — *Pearson, Caldwell & Farnsworth, Inc.*
Farrow, Jerry M. — *McCormack & Farrow*
Feldman, Abe — *A.E. Feldman Associates*
Ferneborg, Jay W. — *Ferneborg & Associates, Inc.*
Ferneborg, John R. — *Ferneborg & Associates, Inc.*
Ferrari, S. Jay — *Ferrari Search Group*
Fill, Clifford G. — *D.S.A. - Dixie Search Associates*
Fill, Ellyn H. — *D.S.A. - Dixie Search Associates*
Fischer, Janet L. — *Boyden*
Fischer, John C. — *Horton International*
Fisher, Neal — *Fisher Personnel Management Services*
Fixler, Eugene — *Ariel Recruitment Associates*
Flanagan, Robert M. — *Robert M. Flanagan & Associates, Ltd.*
Flanders, Karen — *Advanced Information Management*
Flannery, Peter — *Jonas, Walters & Assoc., Inc.*
Fleming, Richard — *R.D. Gatti & Associates, Incorporated*
Flora, Dodi — *Crawford & Crofford*
Flowers, John E. — *Balfour Associates*
Folkerth, Gene — *Gene Folkerth & Associates, Inc.*
Follmer, Gary — *Agra Placements International Ltd.*
Fonfa, Ann — *S.R. Wolman Associates, Inc.*
Ford, J. Daniel — *Witt/Kieffer, Ford, Hadelman & Lloyd*
Ford, Sandra D. — *Phillips & Ford, Inc.*
Foreman, David C. — *Koontz, Jeffries & Associates, Inc.*
Forest, Adam — *McCormack & Associates*
Fox, Amanda — *Paul Ray Berndtson*
Foy, James — *Foy, Schneid & Daniel, Inc.*
Foy, Richard — *Boyden*

Francis, Joseph — *Hospitality International*
Frank, Valerie S. — *Norman Roberts & Associates, Inc.*
Frazier, John — *Cochran, Cochran & Yale, Inc.*
French, William G. — *Preng & Associates, Inc.*
Friedman, Donna L. — *Tower Consultants, Ltd.*
Friedman, Helen E. — *McCormack & Farrow*
Frock, Suzanne D. — *Brandjes Associates*
Fulton, Christine N. — *Highland Search Group, L.L.C.*
Gabel, Gregory N. — *Canny, Bowen Inc.*
Gabriel, David L. — *The Arcus Group*
Gaffney, Denise O'Grady — *Isaacson, Miller*
Gaines, Jay — *Jay Gaines & Company, Inc.*
Galante, Suzanne M. — *Vlcek & Company, Inc.*
Gallagher, Terence M. — *Battalia Winston International*
Garfinkle, Steven M. — *Battalia Winston International*
Garrett, Donald L. — *Garrett Associates Inc.*
Garrett, Linda M. — *Garrett Associates Inc.*
Gatti, Robert D. — *R.D. Gatti & Associates, Incorporated*
Gauny, Brian — *Merit Resource Group, Inc.*
Gauthier, Robert C. — *Columbia Consulting Group*
Gelfman, David — *Career Management International*
George, Delores F. — *Delores F. George Human Resource Management & Consulting Industry*
Gerevas, Ronald E. — *Spencer Stuart*
Gerevas, Ronald E. — *Spencer Stuart*
Gettys, James R. — *International Staffing Consultants, Inc.*
Gibbs, John S. — *Spencer Stuart*
Gilbert, Elaine — *Herbert Mines Associates, Inc.*
Gilbert, Jerry — *Gilbert & Van Campen International*
Gilbert, Patricia G. — *Lynch Miller Moore Partners, Inc.*
Giles, Joe L. — *Joe L. Giles and Associates, Inc.*
Gill, Patricia — *Columbia Consulting Group*
Gillespie, Thomas — *Professional Search Consultants*
Gilreath, James M. — *Gilreath Weatherby, Inc.*
Gladstone, Arthur — *Executive Referral Services, Inc.*
Glass, Lori — *The Executive Source*
Glatman, Marcia — *HRD Consultants, Inc.*
Glennie, Francisco — *Ward Howell International, Inc.*
Glueck, Sharon — *Career Temps, Inc.*
Goar, Duane R. — *Sandhurst Associates*
Gold, Stacey — *Earley Kielty and Associates, Inc.*
Goldberg, Bret — *Roth Young Personnel Service of Boston, Inc.*
Goldenberg, Susan — *Grant Cooper and Associates*
Goldsmith, Fred J. — *Fred J. Goldsmith Associates*
Gomez, Paul — *ARJay & Associates*
Goodman, Dawn M. — *Bason Associates Inc.*
Goodman, Victor — *Anderson Sterling Associates*
Goodridge, Benjamin — *S.C. International, Ltd.*
Gordon, Teri — *Don Richard Associates of Washington, D.C., Inc.*
Gordon, Trina D. — *Boyden*
Gostyla, Rick — *Spencer Stuart*
Gourlay, Debra — *Rene Plessner Associates, Inc.*
Granger, Lisa D. — *D.S.A. - Dixie Search Associates*
Grantham, John — *Grantham & Co., Inc.*
Grantham, Philip H. — *Columbia Consulting Group*
Gray, Annie — *Annie Gray Associates, Inc./The Executive Search Firm*
Gray, Mark — *Executive Referral Services, Inc.*
Greco, Patricia — *Howe-Lewis International*
Green, Jane — *Phillips Resource Group*
Green, Jean — *Broward-Dobbs, Inc.*
Greene, Frederick J. — *Boyden*
Gross, Howard — *Herbert Mines Associates, Inc.*
Gude, John S. — *Boyden*
Gurtin, Kay L. — *Executive Options, Ltd.*
Haas, Margaret P. — *Haas International, Inc.*
Haberman, Joseph C. — *A.T. Kearney, Inc.*
Hadelman, Jordan M. — *Witt/Kieffer, Ford, Hadelman & Lloyd*
Halladay, Patti — *Intersource, Ltd.*
Hallock, Peter B. — *Goodrich & Sherwood Associates, Inc.*
Halvorsen, Kara — *Chrisman & Company, Incorporated*
Hamdan, Mark — *Careernet of Florida, Inc.*
Hanford, Michael — *Richard Kader & Associates*
Hanley, Maureen E. — *Gilbert Tweed/INESA*
Hanna, Rodney — *Merit Resource Group, Inc.*
Hannock, Elwin W. — *Flynn, Hannock, Incorporated*
Hansen, David G. — *Ott & Hansen, Inc.*
Hansen, Ty E. — *Blake, Hansen & Nye, Limited*
Hanson, Grant M. — *Goodrich & Sherwood Associates, Inc.*
Harbaugh, Paul J. — *International Management Advisors, Inc.*
Harbert, David O. — *Sweeney Harbert & Mummert, Inc.*
Hardison, Richard L. — *Hardison & Company*
Harkins, Robert E. — *Robert Harkins Associates, Inc.*
Harris, Bruce — *ProResource, Inc.*
Harris, Ethel S. — *Don Richard Associates of Charlotte*
Harris, Jack — *Baker, Harris & Partners Limited*
Harrison, Priscilla — *Phillips Resource Group*
Harshman, Donald — *The Stevenson Group of New Jersey*
Hart, Robert T. — *D.E. Foster Partners Inc.*

Hartzman, Deborah — *Advanced Information Management*
Harvey, Mike — *Advanced Executive Resources*
Harvey, Richard — *Price Waterhouse*
Haughton, Michael — *DeFrain, Mayer, Lee & Burgess LLC*
Hauser, Martha — *Spencer Stuart*
Hauswirth, Jeffrey M. — *Spencer Stuart*
Havener, Donald Clarke — *The Abbott Group, Inc.*
Hawksworth, A. Dwight — *A.D. & Associates Executive Search, Inc.*
Hay, William E. — *William E. Hay & Company*
Haystead, Steve — *Advanced Executive Resources*
Healey, Joseph T. — *Highland Search Group, L.L.C.*
Hebel, Robert W. — *R.W. Hebel Associates*
Heideman, Mary Marren — *DeFrain, Mayer, Lee & Burgess LLC*
Heiken, Barbara E. — *Randell-Heiken, Inc.*
Heiser, Charles S. — *The Cassie Group*
Hellinger, Audrey — *Martin H. Bauman Associates, Inc.*
Helminiak, Audrey — *Gaffney Management Consultants*
Hemingway, Stuart C. — *Robison & Associates*
Heneghan, Donald A. — *Allerton Heneghan & O'Neill*
Henshaw, Robert — *F-O-R-T-U-N-E Personnel Consultants of Huntsville, Inc.*
Herget, James P. — *Lamalie Amrop International*
Herman, Eugene J. — *Earley Kielty and Associates, Inc.*
Hertlein, James N.J. — *Boyden/Zay & Company*
Hetherman, Margaret F. — *Highland Search Group, L.L.C.*
Hewitt, Rives D. — *The Dalley Hewitt Company*
Hicks, Albert M. — *Phillips Resource Group*
Higdon, Henry G. — *Higdon Prince Inc.*
Hildebrand, Thomas B. — *Professional Resources Group, Inc.*
Hillen, Skip — *The McCormick Group, Inc.*
Hirsch, Julia C. — *Boyden*
Hoevel, Michael J. — *Poirier, Hoevel & Co.*
Holden, Richard B. — *Ames Personnel Consultants, Inc.*
Holodnak, William A. — *J. Robert Scott*
Holtz, Gene — *Agra Placements International Ltd.*
Holzberger, Georges L. — *Highland Search Group, L.L.C.*
Hoppert, Phil — *Wargo and Co., Inc.*
Hoyda, Louis A. — *Thorndike Deland Associates*
Hucko, Donald S. — *Jonas, Walters & Assoc., Inc.*
Hudson, Reginald M. — *Search Bureau International*
Hughes, Cathy N. — *The Ogdon Partnership*
Hughes, Donald J. — *Hughes & Company*
Hughes, Kevin R. — *Handy HRM Corp.*
Hunter, Gabe — *Phillips Resource Group*
Hunter, John B. — *John Sibbald Associates, Inc.*
Hunter, Sue J. — *Robison & Associates*
Huntting, Lisa — *Professional Alternatives, Inc.*
Hutchison, Richard H. — *Rurak & Associates, Inc.*
Hyde, W. Jerry — *Hyde Danforth Wold & Co.*
Hykes, Don A. — *A.T. Kearney, Inc.*
Ingram, D. John — *Ingram & Aydelotte Inc.*
Inzinna, Dennis — *AlternaStaff*
Isaacson, John — *Isaacson, Miller*
Issacs, Judith A. — *Grant Cooper and Associates*
Ives, Richard K. — *Wilkinson & Ives*
Jacobs, Judith — *The Rubicon Group*
Jacobs, Mike — *Thorne, Brieger Associates Inc.*
Jaffe, Mark — *Wyatt & Jaffe*
James, Bruce — *Roberson and Company*
Janis, Laurence — *Integrated Search Solutions Group, LLC*
Jensen, Debra — *Flex Execs Management Solutions*
Jernigan, Alice — *Ariel Recruitment Associates*
Jernigan, Susan N. — *Sockwell & Associates*
Joffe, Barry — *Bason Associates Inc.*
Johnson, David — *Gaffney Management Consultants*
Johnson, Douglas — *Quality Search*
Johnson, Harold E. — *Norman Broadbent International, Inc.*
Johnson, John F. — *Lamalie Amrop International*
Johnson, John W. — *Webb, Johnson Associates, Inc.*
Johnson, Julie — *International Staffing Consultants, Inc.*
Johnson, Kathleen A. — *Barton Raben, Inc.*
Johnson, Priscilla — *The Johnson Group, Inc.*
Johnson, Robert J. — *Quality Search*
Johnson, S. Hope — *The Interface Group, Ltd./Boyden*
Jones, B.J. — *Intersource, Ltd.*
Jones, Francis E. — *Earley Kielty and Associates, Inc.*
Jones, Gary — *BGB Associates*
Jones, Jonathan C. — *The Ogdon Partnership*
Jones, Ronald T. — *ARJay & Associates*
Joubert, Pierre E. — *Boyden*
Juelis, John J. — *Peeney Associates*
Kaiser, Donald J. — *Dunhill Search International*
Kaiser, Irene — *Dunhill Search International*
Kaiser, James G. — *Dunhill Search International*
Kalb, Lenny — *Career Management International*
Kanal, David S. — *Johnson Smith & Knisely Accord*
Kanrich, Susan Azaria — *AlternaStaff*
Kaplan, Gary — *Gary Kaplan & Associates*

Kaplan, Marc — *Gary Kaplan & Associates*
Keesom, W. Peter — *Boyden/Zay & Company*
Kelly, Elizabeth Ann — *Wellington Management Group*
Kelso, Patricia C. — *Barton Raben, Inc.*
Kent, Vickey — *Professional Alternatives, Inc.*
Kenzer, Robert D. — *Kenzer Corp.*
Kern, Jerry L. — *ADOW's Executeam*
Kern, Kathleen G. — *ADOW's Executeam*
Kershaw, Lisa — *Tanton Mitchell/Paul Ray Berndtson*
Kettwig, David A. — *A.T. Kearney, Inc.*
Kiedel, Michelle — *Winter, Wyman & Company*
Kieffer, Michael C. — *Witt/Kieffer, Ford, Hadelman & Lloyd*
Kielty, John L. — *Earley Kielty and Associates, Inc.*
Kiley, Phyllis — *National Search, Inc.*
King, Bill — *The McCormick Group, Inc.*
Kinley, Kathy — *Intech Summit Group, Inc.*
Kinser, Richard E. — *Richard Kinser & Associates*
Kirkpatrick, Robert L. — *Reese Associates*
Kishbaugh, Herbert S. — *Kishbaugh Associates International*
Klages, Constance W. — *International Management Advisors, Inc.*
Klauck, James J. — *Horton International*
Klavens, Cecile J. — *The Pickwick Group, Inc.*
Klein, Gary I. — *Johnson Smith & Knisely Accord*
Klein, Gregory A. — *A.T. Kearney, Inc.*
Klopfenstein, Edward L. — *Crowder & Company*
Knight, Kim L. — *Telford, Adams & Alexander/The Knight Company*
Knisely, Gary — *Johnson Smith & Knisely Accord*
Kochert, Don — *Summerfield Associates, Inc.*
Koehler, Cathy — *Ells Personnel System Inc.*
Koehler, Frank R. — *The Koehler Group*
Kondra, Vernon J. — *The Douglas Reiter Company, Inc.*
Koontz, Donald N. — *Koontz, Jeffries & Associates, Inc.*
Kopsick, Joseph M. — *Spencer Stuart*
Kossuth, David — *Kossuth & Associates, Inc.*
Kossuth, Jane — *Kossuth & Associates, Inc.*
Kotick, Madeline — *The Stevenson Group of New Jersey*
Krejci, Stanley L. — *The Interface Group, Ltd./Boyden*
Krieger, Dennis F. — *Seiden Krieger Associates, Inc.*
Kring, Kenneth L. — *Spencer Stuart*
Krohn, Eileen — *The Stevenson Group of New Jersey*
Kropp, Randy — *Ells Personnel System Inc.*
Kuhl, Teresa — *Don Richard Associates of Tampa, Inc.*
Kuypers, Arnold — *Lamalie Amrop International*
Laba, Marvin — *Marvin Laba & Associates*
Laba, Stuart M. — *Marvin Laba & Associates*
Lang, Vicki J. — *Morgan Hunter Corp.*
Langer, Joel A. — *Langer Associates, Inc.*
Larkin, Kathleen — *Winter, Wyman & Company*
Larsen, Jack B. — *Jack B. Larsen & Associates*
Larsen, Richard F. — *Larsen, Zilliacus & Associates, Inc.*
Lasher, Charles M. — *Lasher Associates*
Lauerman, Fred J. — *Development Search Specialists*
Lautz, Lindsay A. — *Wilkinson & Ives*
Lawrence, David — *Agra Placements International Ltd.*
Lebo, Terry — *Agra Placements International Ltd.*
Lee, Janice — *Summerfield Associates, Inc.*
Leetma, Imbi — *Stanton Chase International*
Leininger, Dennis — *Key Employment Services*
Lenkaitis, Lewis F. — *A.T. Kearney, Inc.*
Leske, Lucy A. — *Educational Management Network*
Leske, Lucy Apthorp — *Educational Management Network*
Leslie, William H. — *Boyden/Zay & Company*
Leszynski, Edward — *ProResource, Inc.*
Letcher, Harvey D. — *Sandhurst Associates*
Levine, Lois — *National Search, Inc.*
Lewis, Jon A. — *Sandhurst Associates*
Lichtenstein, Ben — *Alexander Ross Inc.*
Linde, Rick — *Battalia Winston International*
Lindegren, Joan — *Winter, Wyman & Company*
Linton, Leonard M. — *Byron Leonard International, Inc.*
Lipe, Jerold L. — *Compass Group Ltd.*
Lippman, Lloyd A. — *Career Management International*
Little, Gary — *Agra Placements International Ltd.*
Lloyd, John S. — *Witt/Kieffer, Ford, Hadelman & Lloyd*
Loeb, Stephen H. — *Grant Cooper and Associates*
Logan, Valarie A. — *D.S.A. - Dixie Search Associates*
Logue, Kenneth F. — *Logue & Rice Inc.*
Long, Helga — *H.M. Long International, Ltd.*
Long, Melanie — *National Search, Inc.*
Long, William G. — *McDonald, Long & Associates, Inc.*
Loria, Frank — *Accounting Personnel Consultants*
Lotufo, Donald A. — *D.A.L. Associates, Inc.*
Lotz, R. James — *International Management Advisors, Inc.*
Lovely, Edward — *The Stevenson Group of New Jersey*
Loving, Vikki — *Intersource, Ltd.*
Lucarelli, Joan — *The Onstott Group, Inc.*
Lucht, John — *The John Lucht Consultancy Inc.*
Lumsby, George N. — *International Management Advisors, Inc.*
MacCarthy, Ann — *Columbia Consulting Group*

Macdonald, G. William — *The Macdonald Group, Inc.*
MacEachern, David — *Spencer Stuart*
MacGregor, Malcolm — *Boyden*
Mackenna, Kathy — *Plummer & Associates, Inc.*
Mader, Stephen P. — *Christian & Timbers*
Maer, Harry — *Kenzer Corp.*
Maher, William J. — *Johnson Smith & Knisely Accord*
Mahr, Toni — *K. Russo Associates*
Mainwaring, Andrew Brian — *Executive Search Consultants Corporation*
Mak, I. Paul — *Thomas A. Byrnes Associates*
Malcolm, Rod — *The Enns Partners Inc.*
Malcom, John W. — *Johnson Smith & Knisely Accord*
Malone, George V. — *Boyden*
Manassero, Henri J.P. — *International Management Advisors, Inc.*
Manns, Alex — *Crawford & Crofford*
Manzo, Romero — *The Prairie Group*
Maphet, Harriet — *The Stevenson Group of New Jersey*
Marion, Bradford B. — *Lamalie Amrop International*
Marks, Paula — *Alexander Ross Inc.*
Marks, Russell E. — *Webb, Johnson Associates, Inc.*
Marks, Sarah J. — *The Executive Source*
Marlow, William — *Straube Associates*
Marra, John — *Marra Peters & Partners*
Marra, John — *Marra Peters & Partners*
Martens, Maxine — *Rene Plessner Associates, Inc.*
Martin, Bette — *R.D. Gatti & Associates, Incorporated*
Martin, Lynne Koll — *Boyden*
Martin, Mary Lou — *Neail Behringer Consultants*
Martin, Nancy A. — *Educational Management Network*
Marumoto, William H. — *The Interface Group, Ltd./Boyden*
Maschal, Charles E. — *Maschal/Connors, Inc.*
Massey, H. Heath — *Robison & Associates*
Massey, R. Bruce — *Bruce Massey & Partners Inc.*
Mather, David R. — *Christian & Timbers*
Mathias, William J. — *Preng & Associates, Inc.*
McBride, Jonathan E. — *McBride Associates, Inc.*
McCallister, Richard A. — *Boyden*
McCorkle, Sam B. — *Morton, McCorkle & Associates, Inc.*
McCormick, Brian — *The McCormick Group, Inc.*
McCreary, Charles — *Austin-McGregor International*
McDaniel, Debra A. — *Simpson Associates*
McDonald, Gary E. — *Agra Placements International Ltd.*
McDonald, Stanleigh B. — *McDonald Associates International*
McDonnell, Julie — *Technical Personnel of Minnesota*
McFadden, Ashton S. — *Johnson Smith & Knisely Accord*
McGrath, Thomas F. — *Spriggs & Company, Inc.*
McGuire, Corey — *Peter W. Ambler Company*
McIntyre, Alex D. — *Norman Roberts & Associates, Inc.*
McIntyre, Joel — *Phillips Resource Group*
McKell, Linda — *Advanced Information Management*
McMillin, Bob — *Price Waterhouse*
McNichol, John — *McNichol Associates*
McNichols, Walter B. — *Gary Kaplan & Associates*
McQuoid, David — *A.T. Kearney, Inc.*
McSherry, James F. — *Battalia Winston International*
Meagher, Patricia G. — *Spencer Stuart*
Meany, Brian — *Herbert Mines Associates, Inc.*
Meier, J. Dale — *Grant Cooper and Associates*
Meltzer, Andrea Y. — *Executive Options, Ltd.*
Menendez, Todd — *Don Richard Associates of Tampa, Inc.*
Menk, Carl W. — *Canny, Bowen Inc.*
Messett, William J. — *Messett Associates, Inc.*
Mestepey, John — *A.T. Kearney, Inc.*
Meyer, Michael F. — *Witt/Kieffer, Ford, Hadelman & Lloyd*
Meyer, Stacey — *Gary Kaplan & Associates*
Meyer, William — *Agra Placements International Ltd.*
Miller, Arnie — *Isaacson, Miller*
Miller, David — *Temporary Accounting Personnel, Inc.*
Miller, George N. — *Hite Executive Search*
Miller, Roy — *The Enns Partners Inc.*
Miller, Russel E. — *ARJay & Associates*
Millonzi, Joel C. — *Johnson Smith & Knisely Accord*
Milstein, Bonnie — *Marvin Laba & Associates*
Milton, Suzanne — *Marra Peters & Partners*
Mines, Herbert T. — *Herbert Mines Associates, Inc.*
Mitton, Bill — *Executive Resource, Inc.*
Mockler, Nadine — *Part Time Resources, Inc.*
Mondragon, Philip — *Boyden*
Montgomery, Catherine C. — *Boyden*
Montgomery, James M. — *Houze, Shourds & Montgomery, Inc.*
Moore, Denise — *Jonas, Walters & Assoc., Inc.*
Moore, Mark — *Wheeler, Moore & Elam Co.*
Moore, Michael — *Agra Placements International Ltd.*
Moran, Robert — *A.T. Kearney, Inc.*
Morgan, Beverly — *Winter, Wyman & Company*
Morgan, Gary — *National Search, Inc.*
Morgan, Richard S. — *Lovas Stanley/Paul Ray Berndtson Inc.*
Morris, Paul T. — *The Morris Group*

Schmidt, Jeri E. — *Blake, Hansen & Nye, Limited*
Schmidt, Peter R. — *Boyden*
Schneider, Perry — *Agra Placements International Ltd.*
Schneiderman, Gerald — *Management Resource Associates, Inc.*
Schroeder, John W. — *Spencer Stuart*
Schwam, Carol — *A.E. Feldman Associates*
Schwartz, Carole — *A.T. Kearney, Inc.*
Schweichler, Lee J. — *Schweichler Associates, Inc.*
Scott, Mark S. — *The Prairie Group*
Segal, Eric B. — *Kenzer Corp.*
Seiden, Steven A. — *Seiden Krieger Associates, Inc.*
Sekera, Roger I. — *A.T. Kearney, Inc.*
Semyan, John K. — *TNS Partners, Inc.*
Sennello, Gendra — *National Search, Inc.*
Serwat, Leonard A. — *Spencer Stuart*
Sessa, Vincent J. — *Integrated Search Solutions Group, LLC*
Settles, Barbara Z. — *Lamalie Amrop International*
Shattuck, Merrill B. — *M.B. Shattuck and Associates, Inc.*
Shea, John — *The ALTCO Group*
Sheedy, Edward J. — *Dieckmann & Associates, Ltd.*
Shelton, Sandra — *National Search, Inc.*
Shemin, Grace — *Maximum Management Corp.*
Shenfield, Peter — *Baker, Harris & Partners Limited*
Shervey, Brent C. — *O'Callaghan Honey/Paul Ray Berndtson, Inc.*
Sherwood, Andrew — *Goodrich & Sherwood Associates, Inc.*
Shield, Nancy — *Maximum Management Corp.*
Shipherd, John T. — *The Cassie Group*
Shoemaker, Larry C. — *Shoemaker & Associates*
Sibbald, John R. — *John Sibbald Associates, Inc.*
Siegel, Pamela — *Executive Options, Ltd.*
Silcott, Marvin L. — *Marvin L. Silcott & Associates, Inc.*
Silvas, Stephen D. — *Roberson and Company*
Silver, Lee A. — *L.A. Silver Associates, Inc.*
Simmons, Vicki — *Richard, Wayne and Roberts*
Sinclair, Amy — *Fisher Personnel Management Services*
Sine, Mark — *Hospitality International*
Sjogren, Dennis — *Agra Placements International Ltd.*
Sklover, Bruce — *Professional Assignments of New York, Inc.*
Slaughter, Katherine T. — *Compass Group Ltd.*
Slayton, Richard C. — *Slayton International, Inc.*
Slosar, John M. — *Canny, Bowen Inc.*
Smead, Michelle M. — *A.T. Kearney, Inc.*
Smirnov, Tatiana — *Allan Sarn Associates Inc.*
Smith, Adam M. — *The Abbott Group, Inc.*
Smith, Cheryl — *Barton Raben, Inc.*
Smith, Cheryl — *ProResource, Inc.*
Smith, David P. — *Smith & Latterell (HRS, Inc.)*
Smith, Ethan L. — *Highland Search Group, L.L.C.*
Smith, Grant — *Price Waterhouse*
Smith, Herman M. — *Herman Smith Executive Initiatives Inc.*
Smith, Marvin E. — *Parfitt Recruiting and Consulting*
Smith, Richard — *S.C. International, Ltd.*
Smith, Robert L. — *Smith & Sawyer Inc.*
Smyth, Brendan — *Simpson Associates*
Snelgrove, Geiger — *National Search, Inc.*
Snodgrass, Stephen — *DeFrain, Mayer, Lee & Burgess LLC*
Snyder, James F. — *Snyder & Company*
Sockwell, J. Edgar — *Sockwell & Associates*
Soggs, Cheryl Pavick — *A.T. Kearney, Inc.*
Sorg, Leslie — *The McCormick Group, Inc.*
Spann, Richard E. — *Goodrich & Sherwood Associates, Inc.*
Spiegel, Gay — *L.A. Silver Associates, Inc.*
Sprague, David — *Michael Stern Associates Inc.*
Spriggs, Robert D. — *Spriggs & Company, Inc.*
Stack, James K. — *Boyden*
Stafford, Susan — *Hospitality International*
Stanley, Paul R.A. — *Lovas Stanley/Paul Ray Berndtson Inc.*
Stark, Jeff — *Thorne, Brieger Associates Inc.*
Stein, Terry W. — *Stewart, Stein and Scott, Ltd.*
Steinman, Stephen — *The Stevenson Group of New Jersey*
Stenholm, Gilbert R. — *Spencer Stuart*
Sterling, Jay — *Earley Kielty and Associates, Inc.*
Stern, Michael I. — *Michael Stern Associates Inc.*
Stewart, Jeffrey O. — *Stewart, Stein and Scott, Ltd.*
Stewart, Ross M. — *Human Resources Network Partners Inc.*
Stivk, Barbara A. — *Thornton Resources*
Stouffer, Dale — *Agra Placements International Ltd.*
Stratmeyer, Karin Bergwall — *Princeton Entrepreneurial Resources*
Straube, Stanley H. — *Straube Associates*
Stricker, Sidney G. — *Stricker & Zagor*
Strobridge, Richard P. — *F.L. Taylor & Company, Inc.*
Strom, Mark N. — *Search Advisors International Corp.*
Stubbs, Judy N. — *Lamalie Amrop International*
Sturtz, James W. — *Compass Group Ltd.*
Sullivan, Kay — *Rusher, Loscavio & LoPresto*
Summerfield-Beall, Dotty — *Summerfield Associates, Inc.*
Sumurdy, Melinda — *Kenzer Corp.*
Sur, William K. — *Canny, Bowen Inc.*
Sussman, Lynda — *Gilbert Tweed/INESA*

Swan, Richard A. — *Witt/Kieffer, Ford, Hadelman & Lloyd*
Swanson, Dick — *Raymond Karsan Associates*
Swanson, Kris — *Flex Execs Management Solutions*
Sweeney, James W. — *Sweeney Harbert & Mummert, Inc.*
Takacs, Gloria — *Gilbert & Van Campen International*
Teinert, Jay — *Damon & Associates, Inc.*
Templin, Robert E. — *Gilbert Tweed/INESA*
Theobald, David B. — *Theobald & Associates*
Tholke, William E. — *Canny, Bowen Inc.*
Thomas, Christine S. — *Lovas Stanley/Paul Ray Berndtson Inc.*
Thomas, Jeffrey — *Fairfaxx Corporation*
Thomas, Kurt J. — *P.J. Murphy & Associates, Inc.*
Thompson, Brett — *Southwestern Professional Services*
Thompson, Dave — *Battalia Winston International*
Thompson, Kenneth L. — *McCormack & Farrow*
Thornton, John C. — *Thornton Resources*
Tobin, Jim — *Barton Raben, Inc.*
Tokarcik, Patricia — *ProResource, Inc.*
Tracey, Jack — *Management Assistance Group, Inc.*
Trosin, Walter R. — *Johnson Smith & Knisely Accord*
Troup, Roger — *The McCormick Group, Inc.*
Trueblood, Brian G. — *TNS Partners, Inc.*
Truex, John F. — *Morton, McCorkle & Associates, Inc.*
Tryon, Katey — *DeFrain, Mayer, Lee & Burgess LLC*
Tucci, Joseph — *Fairfaxx Corporation*
Tucker, Thomas A. — *The Thomas Tucker Company*
Tunney, William — *Grant Cooper and Associates*
Turner, Edward K. — *Don Richard Associates of Charlotte*
Tweed, Janet — *Gilbert Tweed/INESA*
Ulbert, Nancy — *Aureus Group*
Unger, Paul T. — *A.T. Kearney, Inc.*
Unger, Stephen A. — *Spencer Stuart*
Vachon, David A. — *McNichol Associates*
Vainblat, Galina — *Foy, Schneid & Daniel, Inc.*
Valenta, Joseph — *Princeton Entrepreneurial Resources*
Van Campen, Jerry — *Gilbert & Van Campen International*
Van Clieaf, Mark — *MVC Associates International*
van Someren, Christian — *Johnson Smith & Knisely Accord*
Vaughan, David B. — *Dunhill Professional Search of Irvine, Inc.*
Venable, William W. — *Thorndike Deland Associates*
Vennat, Manon — *Spencer Stuart*
Vergara, Gail H. — *Spencer Stuart*
Vergari, Jane — *Herbert Mines Associates, Inc.*
Virgili, Franca — *Johnson Smith & Knisely Accord*
Visnich, L. Christine — *Bason Associates Inc.*
Vlcek, Thomas J. — *Vlcek & Company, Inc.*
Vogel, Michael S. — *Vogel Associates*
Waggoner, Lisa — *Intersource, Ltd.*
Wakefield, Scott — *National Search, Inc.*
Waldoch, D. Mark — *Barnes Development Group, LLC*
Walker, Ewing J. — *Ward Howell International, Inc.*
Wall, David — *Southwestern Professional Services*
Wallace, Alec — *Tanton Mitchell/Paul Ray Berndtson*
Walters, William F. — *Jonas, Walters & Assoc., Inc.*
Wargo, G. Rick — *A.T. Kearney, Inc.*
Warren, Sylvia W. — *Thorndike Deland Associates*
Warter, Mark — *Isaacson, Miller*
Watkins, Thomas M. — *Lamalie Amrop International*
Watson, Peggy — *Advanced Information Management*
Wayne, Cary S. — *ProSearch Inc.*
Webb, George H. — *Webb, Johnson Associates, Inc.*
Weisler, Nancy — *National Search, Inc.*
Weissman-Rosenthal, Abbe — *ALW Research International*
Weisz, Laura — *Anderson Sterling Associates*
Welch, David — *Isaacson, Miller*
Weller, Paul S. — *Mark Stanley & Company*
Werner, Bonnie — *H.M. Long International, Ltd.*
Westerfield, Putney — *Boyden*
Wexler, Rona — *Ariel Recruitment Associates*
Whitcomb, Nancy C. — *Educational Management Network*
White, Jeffrey E. — *Simpson Associates*
White, Kimberly — *Executive Referral Services, Inc.*
White, William C. — *Venture Resources Inc.*
Whiting, Anthony — *Johnson Smith & Knisely Accord*
Whitley, Sue Ann — *Roberts Ryan and Bentley*
Whitton, Paula L. — *Pearson, Caldwell & Farnsworth, Inc.*
Wichlei, Alan — *Isaacson, Miller*
Wier, Daniel — *Horton International*
Wilcox, Karen — *Isaacson, Miller*
Wilder, Richard B. — *Columbia Consulting Group*
Wilkinson, Barbara — *Beall & Company, Inc.*
Wilkinson, William R. — *Wilkinson & Ives*
Williams, Alexander H. — *Witt/Kieffer, Ford, Hadelman & Lloyd*
Williams, Gary L. — *Barnes Development Group, LLC*
Williams, Lis — *Executive Options, Ltd.*
Williams, Michelle Cruz — *Isaacson, Miller*
Williams, Roger K. — *Williams, Roth & Krueger Inc.*
Williams, Walter E. — *Canny, Bowen Inc.*
Willis, William H. — *William Willis Worldwide Inc.*

## 7. Marketing

Bueschel, David A. — *Shepherd Bueschel & Provus, Inc.*
Bullock, Conni — *Earley Kielty and Associates, Inc.*
Bump, Gerald J. — *D.E. Foster Partners Inc.*
Burchill, Greg — *BGB Associates*
Burden, Gene — *The Cherbonnier Group, Inc.*
Burke, John — *The Experts*
Burnett, Rebecca J. — *MSI International*
Burns, Alan — *The Enns Partners Inc.*
Burns, Terence N. — *D.E. Foster Partners Inc.*
Burris, James C. — *Boyden*
Busch, Jack — *Busch International*
Bush, Martha A. — *MSI International*
Busterna, Charles — *The KPA Group*
Butler, Kirby B. — *The Butlers Company Insurance Recruiters*
Butterfass, Stanley — *Butterfass, Pepe & MacCallan Inc.*
Button, David R. — *The Button Group*
Byrnes, Thomas A. — *Thomas A. Byrnes Associates*
Cahill, Peter M. — *Peter M. Cahill Associates, Inc.*
Caldwell, William R. — *Pearson, Caldwell & Farnsworth, Inc.*
Callahan, Wanda — *Cochran, Cochran & Yale, Inc.*
Callan, Robert M. — *Callan Associates, Ltd.*
Campbell, Patricia A. — *The Onstott Group, Inc.*
Campbell, Robert Scott — *Wellington Management Group*
Cargo, Catherine — *MSI International*
Carideo, Joseph — *Thorndike Deland Associates*
Carpenter, Harold G. — *MSI International*
Carter, Christine C. — *Health Care Dimensions*
Casal, Daniel G. — *Bonifield Associates*
Casey, Jean — *Peter W. Ambler Company*
Cashen, Anthony B. — *Lamalie Amrop International*
Cassie, Ronald L. — *The Cassie Group*
Causey, Andrea C. — *MSI International*
Cavanagh, Michael J. — *Michael J. Cavanagh and Associates*
Cavolina, Michael — *Carver Search Consultants*
Cavriani, Randolph — *Search West, Inc.*
Center, Linda — *The Search Center Inc.*
Chappell, Peter — *The Bankers Group*
Chatterjie, Alok — *MSI International*
Chavous, C. Crawford — *Phillips Resource Group*
Cherbonnier, L. Michael — *TCG International, Inc.*
Cherbonnier, L. Michael — *The Cherbonnier Group, Inc.*
Christenson, H. Alan — *Christenson & Hutchison*
Christian, Jeffrey E. — *Christian & Timbers*
Christoff, Matthew J. — *Spencer Stuart*
Chua, Jackie — *Keith Bagg & Associates Inc.*
Citarella, Richard A. — *A.T. Kearney, Inc.*
Citera, Tom — *Howe-Lewis International*
Citrin, Lea — *K.L. Whitney Company*
Cizek, John T. — *Cizek Associates, Inc.*
Cizek, Marti J. — *Cizek Associates, Inc.*
Clark, Steven — *D.A. Kreuter Associates, Inc.*
Clauhsen, Elizabeth A. — *Savoy Partners, Ltd.*
Cleary, Thomas R. — *ARJay & Associates*
Cleeve, Coleen — *Howe-Lewis International*
Clegg, Cynthia — *Horton International*
Close, E. Wade — *Boyden*
Cochran, Hale — *Fenwick Partners*
Coffman, Brian — *Kossuth & Associates, Inc.*
Cohen, Michael R. — *Intech Summit Group, Inc.*
Cohen, Robert C. — *Intech Summit Group, Inc.*
Colasanto, Frank M. — *W.R. Rosato & Associates, Inc.*
Cole, Elizabeth — *MSI International*
Coleman, J. Kevin — *J. Kevin Coleman & Associates, Inc.*
Collard, Joseph A. — *Spencer Stuart*
Collier, David — *Parfitt Recruiting and Consulting/PRO TEM*
Colling, Douglas — *KPMG Management Consulting*
Collis, Gerald — *TSS Consulting, Ltd.*
Colucci, Bart A. — *Colucci, Blendow and Johnson, Inc.*
Combs, Stephen L. — *Juntunen-Combs-Poirier*
Conard, Rodney J. — *Conard Associates, Inc.*
Conner, John — *Flex Execs Management Solutions*
Connor, Michele — *Abraham & London, Ltd.*
Conway, William P. — *Phillips Resource Group*
Cooke, Jeffrey R. — *Jonas, Walters & Assoc., Inc.*
Cooke, Katherine H. — *Horton International*
Cordaro, Concetta — *Flynn, Hannock, Incorporated*
Cornehlsen, James H. — *Lamalie Amrop International*
Corrigan, Gerald F. — *The Corrigan Group*
Corso, Glen S. — *Chartwell Partners International, Inc.*
Costa, Cynthia A. — *MSI International*
Coston, Bruce G. — *MSI International*
Cox, James O. — *MSI International*
Cox, William — *E.J. Ashton & Associates, Ltd.*
Crane, Howard C. — *Chartwell Partners International, Inc.*
Crath, Paul F. — *Price Waterhouse*
Creger, Elizabeth — *Search West, Inc.*
Critchley, Walter — *Cochran, Cochran & Yale, Inc.*
Crowder, Edward W. — *Crowder & Company*

Crowell, Elizabeth — *H.M. Long International, Ltd.*
Crownover, Kathryn L. — *MSI International*
Crumbaker, Robert H. — *Lamalie Amrop International*
Cruse, O.D. — *Spencer Stuart*
Crystal, Jonathan A. — *Spencer Stuart*
Cunningham, Robert Y. — *Goodrich & Sherwood Associates, Inc.*
Cunningham, Sheila — *Adams & Associates International*
Cuomo, Frank — *Frank Cuomo and Associates, Inc.*
Currie, Lawrence S. — *MSI International*
Czamanske, Paul W. — *Compass Group Ltd.*
Dalton, Bret — *Robert W. Dingman Company, Inc.*
Dalton, David R. — *MSI International*
Damon, Richard E. — *Damon & Associates, Inc.*
Damon, Robert A. — *Spencer Stuart*
Danforth, Monica — *Search Consultants International, Inc.*
Daniel, Beverly — *Foy, Schneid & Daniel, Inc.*
Daniels, Alfred — *Alfred Daniels & Associates*
Daniels, David — *Search West, Inc.*
Daniels, Leonard — *Placement Associates Inc.*
Dannenberg, Richard A. — *Roberts Ryan and Bentley*
Danoff, Audrey — *Don Richard Associates of Tidewater, Inc.*
Davis, Bernel — *MSI International*
Davis, Bert — *Bert Davis Executive Search, Inc.*
Davis, G. Gordon — *Davis & Company*
Davison, Patricia E. — *Lamalie Amrop International*
de Bardin, Francesca — *F.L. Taylor & Company, Inc.*
de Palacios, Jeannette C. — *J. Palacios & Associates, Inc.*
de Tuede, Catherine — *Thomas A. Byrnes Associates*
Debrueys, Lee G. — *MSI International*
DeCorrevont, James — *DeCorrevont & Associates*
DeCorrevont, James — *DeCorrevont & Associates*
Deering, Joseph — *U.S. Envirosearch*
DeFrancesco, Mary Ellen — *The Onstott Group, Inc.*
DeHart, Donna — *Tower Consultants, Ltd.*
Del Pino, William — *National Search, Inc.*
Del'Ange, Gabrielle N. — *MSI International*
Delaney, Patrick J. — *Sensible Solutions, Inc.*
Della Monica, Vincent — *Search West, Inc.*
DeLong, Art — *Richard Kader & Associates*
deMartino, Cathy — *Lucas Associates*
Demchak, James P. — *Sandhurst Associates*
Densmore, Geraldine — *Michael Stern Associates Inc.*
Desgrosellier, Gary P. — *Personnel Unlimited/Executive Search*
Desmond, Dennis — *Beall & Company, Inc.*
deWilde, David M. — *Chartwell Partners International, Inc.*
Diaz-Joslyn, Mabel — *Walker Communications*
Dietz, David S. — *MSI International*
DiMarchi, Paul — *DiMarchi Partners, Inc.*
Dingman, Bruce — *Robert W. Dingman Company, Inc.*
Dingman, Robert W. — *Robert W. Dingman Company, Inc.*
DiSalvo, Fred — *The Cambridge Group Ltd*
Diskin, Rochelle — *Search West, Inc.*
Divine, Robert S. — *O'Shea, Divine & Company, Inc.*
Dixon, C.R. — *A la carte International*
Doele, Donald C. — *Goodrich & Sherwood Associates, Inc.*
Donahie, Stephen — *Search West, Inc.*
Doody, Michael F. — *Witt/Kieffer, Ford, Hadelman & Lloyd*
Dornblut, Cindy — *Ashton Computer Professionals Inc.*
Dotson, M. Ileen — *Dotson & Associates*
Dougherty, Bridget L. — *Wellington Management Group*
Dougherty, Janice — *The McCormick Group, Inc.*
Dowell, Mary K. — *Professional Search Associates*
Dreifus, Donald — *Search West, Inc.*
Dromeshauser, Peter — *Dromeshauser Associates*
Drury, James J. — *Spencer Stuart*
Dugan, John H. — *J.H. Dugan and Associates, Inc.*
Duley, Richard I. — *ARJay & Associates*
Dunman, Betsy L. — *Crawford & Crofford*
Dussick, Vince — *Dussick Management Associates*
Earle, Paul W. — *Spencer Stuart*
Eastham, Marvene M. — *Witt/Kieffer, Ford, Hadelman & Lloyd*
Eatmon, Michael — *U.S. Envirosearch*
Ebeling, John A. — *Gilbert Tweed/INESA*
Eden, Brooks D. — *Eden & Associates, Inc.*
Eden, Dianne — *Steeple Associates*
Edmond, Bruce — *Corporate Recruiters Ltd.*
Edwards, Dorothy — *MSI International*
Edwards, Verba L. — *Wing Tips & Pumps, Inc.*
Eggena, Roger — *Phillips Resource Group*
Ehrgott, Elizabeth — *The Ascher Group*
Ehrhart, Jennifer — *ADOW's Executeam*
Eibeler, C. — *Amherst Personnel Group Inc.*
Einsele, Neil — *Agra Placements International Ltd.*
Eldredge, L. Lincoln — *Lamalie Amrop International*
Elliott, Mark P. — *Lamalie Amrop International*
Ellis, William — *Interspace Interactive Inc.*
Emmott, Carol B. — *Spencer Stuart*
England, Mark — *Austin-McGregor International*

Haystead, Steve — *Advanced Executive Resources*
Hazelton, Lisa M. — *Health Care Dimensions*
Hebel, Robert W. — *R.W. Hebel Associates*
Hecker, Henry C. — *Hogan Acquisitions*
Heery, William — *Harris Heery & Associates*
Heiken, Barbara E. — *Randell-Heiken, Inc.*
Heintz, William — *Mixtec Group*
Heiser, Charles S. — *The Cassie Group*
Hellinger, Audrey — *Martin H. Bauman Associates, Inc.*
Helminiak, Audrey — *Gaffney Management Consultants*
Hemingway, Stuart C. — *Robison & Associates*
Henard, John B. — *Lamalie Amrop International*
Heneghan, Donald A. — *Allerton Heneghan & O'Neill*
Hennig, Sandra M. — *MSI International*
Herget, James P. — *Lamalie Amrop International*
Herman, Eugene J. — *Earley Kielty and Associates, Inc.*
Hernandez, Luis A. — *CoEnergy, Inc.*
Hewitt, Rives D. — *The Dalley Hewitt Company*
Hicks, Albert M. — *Phillips Resource Group*
Hicks, James L. — *MSI International*
Higdon, Henry G. — *Higdon Prince Inc.*
Higgins, John B. — *Higgins Associates, Inc.*
Hildebrand, Thomas B. — *Professional Resources Group, Inc.*
Hill, Emery — *MSI International*
Hillen, Skip — *The McCormick Group, Inc.*
Hilyard, Paul J. — *MSI International*
Hirsch, Julia C. — *Boyden*
Hnatuik, Ivan — *Corporate Recruiters Ltd.*
Hockett, William — *Hockett Associates, Inc.*
Hodges, Robert J. — *Sampson Neill & Wilkins Inc.*
Hoevel, Michael J. — *Poirier, Hoevel & Co.*
Hoffmeir, Patricia A. — *Gilbert Tweed/INESA*
Hogan, Larry H. — *Hogan Acquisitions*
Holden, Richard B. — *Ames Personnel Consultants, Inc.*
Holland, John H. — *Sloan & Associates*
Hollins, Howard D. — *MSI International*
Holmes, Lawrence J. — *Columbia Consulting Group*
Holt, Carol — *Bartholdi & Company, Inc.*
Holtz, Gene — *Agra Placements International Ltd.*
Hopgood, Earl — *JDG Associates, Ltd.*
Hoppert, Phil — *Wargo and Co., Inc.*
Horner, Gregory — *Corporate Recruiters Ltd.*
Houchins, William N. — *Christian & Timbers*
Houtz, Kenneth — *Houtz-Strawn Associates, Inc.*
Howard, Jill — *Health Care Dimensions*
Hoyda, Louis A. — *Thorndike Deland Associates*
Hucko, Donald S. — *Jonas, Walters & Assoc., Inc.*
Hudson, Reginald M. — *Search Bureau International*
Hughes, Cathy N. — *The Ogdon Partnership*
Hughes, Donald J. — *Hughes & Company*
Hughes, James J. — *R.P. Barone Associates*
Humphrey, Joan — *Abraham & London, Ltd.*
Hunt, Thomas — *MSI International*
Hunter, Gabe — *Phillips Resource Group*
Hunter, Sue J. — *Robison & Associates*
Huntting, Lisa — *Professional Alternatives, Inc.*
Hutchison, Richard H. — *Rurak & Associates, Inc.*
Hutchison, William K. — *Christenson & Hutchison*
Hwang, Yvette — *MSI International*
Hyde, Mark D. — *MSI International*
Hyde, W. Jerry — *Hyde Danforth Wold & Co.*
Hykes, Don A. — *A.T. Kearney, Inc.*
Hypes, Richard G. — *Lynch Miller Moore Partners, Inc.*
Iammatteo, Enzo — *Keith Bagg & Associates Inc.*
Iannacone, Kelly — *Abraham & London, Ltd.*
Imely, Larry — *Christian & Timbers*
Ingram, D. John — *Ingram & Aydelotte Inc.*
Inguagiato, Gregory — *MSI International*
Irvine, Robert — *Keith Bagg & Associates Inc.*
Issacs, Judith A. — *Grant Cooper and Associates*
Ives, Richard K. — *Wilkinson & Ives*
Ivey, Deborah M. — *MSI International*
Jablo, Steven — *Dieckmann & Associates, Ltd.*
Jackson, Bruce — *Noble & Associates Inc.*
Jackson, W.T. — *Sampson Neill & Wilkins Inc.*
Jacobs, Judith — *The Rubicon Group*
Jacobs, Martin J. — *The Rubicon Group*
Jacobs, Mike — *Thorne, Brieger Associates Inc.*
Jaffe, Mark — *Wyatt & Jaffe*
James, Allison A. — *MSI International*
James, Bruce — *Roberson and Company*
Janis, Laurence — *Integrated Search Solutions Group, LLC*
Jensen, Debra — *Flex Execs Management Solutions*
Jernigan, Alice — *Ariel Recruitment Associates*
Jernigan, Susan N. — *Sockwell & Associates*
Joffe, Barry — *Bason Associates Inc.*
Johnson, David — *Gaffney Management Consultants*
Johnson, Douglas — *Quality Search*
Johnson, Janet — *Normyle/Erstling Health Search Group*

Johnson, John W. — *Webb, Johnson Associates, Inc.*
Johnson, Julie — *International Staffing Consultants, Inc.*
Johnson, Kathleen A. — *Barton Raben, Inc.*
Johnson, Priscilla — *The Johnson Group, Inc.*
Johnson, Robert J. — *Quality Search*
Johnson, S. Hope — *The Interface Group, Ltd./Boyden*
Johnson, Stephanie — *Carver Search Consultants*
Jones, Francis E. — *Earley Kielty and Associates, Inc.*
Jones, Gary — *BGB Associates*
Jones, Jonathan C. — *The Ogdon Partnership*
Jones, Ronald T. — *ARJay & Associates*
Joubert, Pierre E. — *Boyden*
Judy, William — *Search West, Inc.*
Juelis, John J. — *Peeney Associates*
Kader, Richard — *Richard Kader & Associates*
Kaiser, Donald J. — *Dunhill Search International*
Kaiser, James G. — *Dunhill Search International*
Kalinowski, David — *Jacobson Associates*
Kanal, David S. — *Johnson Smith & Knisely Accord*
Kanovsky, Gerald — *Career Consulting Group, Inc.*
Kanovsky, Marlene — *Career Consulting Group, Inc.*
Kaplan, Gary — *Gary Kaplan & Associates*
Kaplan, Marc — *Gary Kaplan & Associates*
Kaptain, John — *Blau Kaptain Schroeder*
Kashiwagi, Keiko — *The Repovich-Reynolds Group*
Katz, Robert L. — *MSI International*
Keesom, W. Peter — *Boyden/Zay & Company*
Keller, Barbara — *Barton Raben, Inc.*
Kelly, Claudia L. — *Spencer Stuart*
Kelly, Elizabeth Ann — *Wellington Management Group*
Kelly, Susan D. — *S.D. Kelly & Associates, Inc.*
Kelso, Patricia C. — *Barton Raben, Inc.*
Kennedy, Michael — *The Danbrook Group, Inc.*
Kent, Vickey — *Professional Alternatives, Inc.*
Kenzer, Robert D. — *Kenzer Corp.*
Kern, Jerry L. — *ADOW's Executeam*
Kern, Kathleen G. — *ADOW's Executeam*
Kershaw, Lisa — *Tanton Mitchell/Paul Ray Berndtson*
Kettwig, David A. — *A.T. Kearney, Inc.*
Kick, James W. — *The Prairie Group*
Kieffer, Michael C. — *Witt/Kieffer, Ford, Hadelman & Lloyd*
Kielty, John L. — *Earley Kielty and Associates, Inc.*
Kilcullen, Brian A. — *D.A. Kreuter Associates, Inc.*
Kiley, Phyllis — *National Search, Inc.*
King, Bill — *The McCormick Group, Inc.*
King, Joyce L. — *MSI International*
King, Richard M. — *Kittleman & Associates*
Kinney, Carol — *Dussick Management Associates*
Kinser, Richard E. — *Richard Kinser & Associates*
Kirkpatrick, Robert L. — *Reese Associates*
Kishbaugh, Herbert S. — *Kishbaugh Associates International*
Klages, Constance W. — *International Management Advisors, Inc.*
Klauck, James J. — *Horton International*
Klavens, Cecile J. — *The Pickwick Group, Inc.*
Klavins, Larissa R. — *Dieckmann & Associates, Ltd.*
Klein, Gary I. — *Johnson Smith & Knisely Accord*
Klein, Gregory A. — *A.T. Kearney, Inc.*
Klopfenstein, Edward L. — *Crowder & Company*
Knisely, Gary — *Johnson Smith & Knisely Accord*
Kobayashi, Raelen — *The Repovich-Reynolds Group*
Kohn, Adam P. — *Christian & Timbers*
Kondra, Vernon J. — *The Douglas Reiter Company, Inc.*
Konkolski, Laurie — *The Paladin Companies, Inc.*
Koontz, Donald N. — *Koontz, Jeffries & Associates, Inc.*
Kopsick, Joseph M. — *Spencer Stuart*
Korkuch, Sandy — *Barone-O'Hara Associates*
Kors, R. Paul — *Kors Montgomery International*
Kossuth, David — *Kossuth & Associates, Inc.*
Kossuth, Jane — *Kossuth & Associates, Inc.*
Kotick, Madeline — *The Stevenson Group of New Jersey*
Krauser, H. James — *Spencer Stuart*
Krejci, Stanley L. — *The Interface Group, Ltd./Boyden*
Kreps, Charles D. — *Normyle/Erstling Health Search Group*
Kreuter, Daniel A. — *D.A. Kreuter Associates, Inc.*
Kreutz, Gary L. — *Kreutz Consulting Group, Inc.*
Krieger, Dennis F. — *Seiden Krieger Associates, Inc.*
Kring, Kenneth L. — *Spencer Stuart*
Krohn, Eileen — *The Stevenson Group of New Jersey*
Kuper, Keith D. — *Christenson & Hutchison*
Kuypers, Arnold — *Lamalie Amrop International*
Laba, Marvin — *Marvin Laba & Associates*
Laba, Stuart M. — *Marvin Laba & Associates*
LaFaye, Susan — *MSI International*
Lake, Phillip R. — *U.S. Envirosearch*
Land, Shaun — *Dunhill Professional Search of Irvine, Inc.*
Langer, Joel A. — *Langer Associates, Inc.*
Lankford, Charles — *MSI International*
Larsen, William G. — *The Paladin Companies, Inc.*
Lasher, Charles M. — *Lasher Associates*

Laub, Stuart R. — *Abraham & London, Ltd.*
Lauderback, David R. — *A.T. Kearney, Inc.*
Lautz, Lindsay A. — *Wilkinson & Ives*
Lawrence, David — *Agra Placements International Ltd.*
Lawson, Bettye N. — *MSI International*
Layton, Patrick R. — *MSI International*
Lebo, Terry — *Agra Placements International Ltd.*
Leetma, Imbi — *Stanton Chase International*
Leininger, Dennis — *Key Employment Services*
Lence, Julie Anne — *MSI International*
Lenkaitis, Lewis F. — *A.T. Kearney, Inc.*
Leonard, Linda — *Harris Heery & Associates*
Leslie, William H. — *Boyden/Zay & Company*
Leszynski, Edward — *ProResource, Inc.*
Letcher, Harvey D. — *Sandhurst Associates*
Lettrii, Mary — *BioQuest, Inc.*
Levine, Alan M. — *MB Inc. Interim Executive Division*
Levine, Lois — *National Search, Inc.*
Levinson, Lauren — *The Danbrook Group, Inc.*
Levitt, Muriel A. — *D.S. Allen Associates, Inc.*
Lewicki, Christopher — *MSI International*
Lewis, Jon A. — *Sandhurst Associates*
Lindberg, Eric J. — *MSI International*
Linde, Rick — *Battalia Winston International*
Linton, Leonard M. — *Byron Leonard International, Inc.*
Lippman, Lloyd A. — *Career Management International*
Little, Gary — *Agra Placements International Ltd.*
Livesay, Christopher C. — *MSI International*
Loeb, Stephen H. — *Grant Cooper and Associates*
Logan, Valarie A. — *D.S.A. - Dixie Search Associates*
London, Gregory J. — *MSI International*
Long, Benjamin H. — *Travaille Executive Search*
Long, Helga — *H.M. Long International, Ltd.*
Long, Melanie — *National Search, Inc.*
Long, William G. — *McDonald, Long & Associates, Inc.*
Longmore, Marilyn — *Richard Kader & Associates*
LoPresto, Robert L. — *Rusher, Loscavio & LoPresto*
Lotufo, Donald A. — *D.A.L. Associates, Inc.*
Lotz, R. James — *International Management Advisors, Inc.*
Lovely, Edward — *The Stevenson Group of New Jersey*
Lucarelli, Joan — *The Onstott Group, Inc.*
Lucas, Ronnie L. — *MSI International*
Lucht, John — *The John Lucht Consultancy Inc.*
Lumsby, George N. — *International Management Advisors, Inc.*
Lynch, Michael C. — *Lynch Miller Moore Partners, Inc.*
Lynn, Donald — *Frank Cuomo and Associates, Inc.*
Lyons, Denis B.K. — *Spencer Stuart*
MacCarthy, Ann — *Columbia Consulting Group*
MacGregor, Malcolm — *Boyden*
MacJadyen, David J. — *Sharrow & Associates*
Mackenna, Kathy — *Plummer & Associates, Inc.*
Mader, Stephen P. — *Christian & Timbers*
Maer, Harry — *Kenzer Corp.*
Magnani, Susan — *The Search Center Inc.*
Maher, William J. — *Johnson Smith & Knisely Accord*
Mak, I. Paul — *Thomas A. Byrnes Associates*
Malcolm, Rod — *The Enns Partners Inc.*
Malcom, John W. — *Johnson Smith & Knisely Accord*
Malone, George V. — *Boyden*
Manassero, Henri J.P. — *International Management Advisors, Inc.*
Mancino, Gene — *Blau Kaptain Schroeder*
Manns, Alex — *Crawford & Crofford*
Maphet, Harriet — *The Stevenson Group of New Jersey*
Marchette, Steve — *Juntunen-Combs-Poirier*
Marion, Bradford B. — *Lamalie Amrop International*
Marion, Michael — *S.D. Kelly & Associates, Inc.*
Marks, Ira — *Strategic Alternatives*
Marks, Russell E. — *Webb, Johnson Associates, Inc.*
Marlow, William — *Straube Associates*
Marra, John — *Marra Peters & Partners*
Marra, John — *Marra Peters & Partners*
Marshall, Larry — *Marshall Consultants, Inc.*
Martens, Maxine — *Rene Plessner Associates, Inc.*
Martin, Geary D. — *Boyden/Zay & Company*
Martin, Lynne Koll — *Boyden*
Martin, Paula — *MSI International*
Marumoto, William H. — *The Interface Group, Ltd./Boyden*
Maschal, Charles E. — *Maschal/Connors, Inc.*
Massey, R. Bruce — *Bruce Massey & Partners Inc.*
Matheny, Robert P. — *MSI International*
Mather, David R. — *Christian & Timbers*
Matti, Suzy — *Southwestern Professional Services*
Max, Bruno — *RBR Associates, Inc.*
May, Peter — *Mixtec Group*
Mazza, David B. — *Mazza & Riley, Inc.*
McAleavy, Steve — *Search Consultants International, Inc.*
McBride, Jonathan E. — *McBride Associates, Inc.*
McBryde, Marnie — *Spencer Stuart*
McCallister, Richard A. — *Boyden*

McCandless, Hugh — *Marshall Consultants, Inc.*
McCorkle, Sam B. — *Morton, McCorkle & Associates, Inc.*
McCormack, William Reed — *MSI International*
McCormick, Brian — *The McCormick Group, Inc.*
McCormick, William J. — *The McCormick Group, Inc.*
McCreary, Charles — *Austin-McGregor International*
McDaniel, Debra A. — *Simpson Associates*
McDonald, Gary E. — *Agra Placements International Ltd.*
McDonald, John R. — *TSS Consulting, Ltd.*
McDonald, Scott A. — *McDonald Associates International*
McDonald, Stanleigh B. — *McDonald Associates International*
McDonnell, Julie — *Technical Personnel of Minnesota*
McFadden, Ashton S. — *Johnson Smith & Knisely Accord*
McGann, Paul L. — *The Cassie Group*
McGrath, Robert E. — *Robert E. McGrath & Associates*
McGrath, Thomas F. — *Spriggs & Company, Inc.*
McGuire, Corey — *Peter W. Ambler Company*
McIntyre, Joel — *Phillips Resource Group*
McKnight, Amy E. — *Chartwell Partners International, Inc.*
McManamon, Tim — *Rogers-McManamon Executive Search*
McMillin, Bob — *Price Waterhouse*
McNamara, Timothy C. — *Columbia Consulting Group*
McNichol, John — *McNichol Associates*
McNichols, Walter B. — *Gary Kaplan & Associates*
McThrall, David — *TSS Consulting, Ltd.*
Mead, James D. — *James Mead & Company*
Meagher, Patricia G. — *Spencer Stuart*
Meany, Brian — *Herbert Mines Associates, Inc.*
Meier, J. Dale — *Grant Cooper and Associates*
Meltzer, Andrea Y. — *Executive Options, Ltd.*
Menk, Carl W. — *Canny, Bowen Inc.*
Merrigan, Eileen M. — *Lamalie Amrop International*
Messett, William J. — *Messett Associates, Inc.*
Mestepey, John — *A.T. Kearney, Inc.*
Meyer, Stacey — *Gary Kaplan & Associates*
Meyer, William — *Agra Placements International Ltd.*
Mierzwinski, John — *Industrial Recruiters Associates, Inc.*
Miesemer, Arthur C. — *MSI International*
Mikula, Linda — *Schweichler Associates, Inc.*
Miles, Kenneth T. — *MSI International*
Mill, Christopher A. — *The Paladin Companies, Inc.*
Miller, Benjamin J. — *MSI International*
Miller, Brett — *The McCormick Group, Inc.*
Miller, Michael R. — *Lynch Miller Moore Partners, Inc.*
Miller, Paul McG. — *Lamalie Amrop International*
Miller, Roy — *The Enns Partners Inc.*
Miller, Russel E. — *ARJay & Associates*
Millonzi, Joel C. — *Johnson Smith & Knisely Accord*
Milstein, Bonnie — *Marvin Laba & Associates*
Milton, Suzanne — *Marra Peters & Partners*
Mines, Herbert T. — *Herbert Mines Associates, Inc.*
Mitros, George N. — *Mixtec Group*
Mockler, Nadine — *Part Time Resources, Inc.*
Moerbe, Ed H. — *Stanton Chase International*
Mogul, Gene — *Mogul Consultants, Inc.*
Mondragon, Philip — *Boyden*
Montgomery, Catherine C. — *Boyden*
Montgomery, James M. — *Houze, Shourds & Montgomery, Inc.*
Moore, David S. — *Lynch Miller Moore Partners, Inc.*
Moore, Denise — *Jonas, Walters & Assoc., Inc.*
Moore, Lemuel R. — *MSI International*
Moore, Mark — *Wheeler, Moore & Elam Co.*
Moore, Michael — *Agra Placements International Ltd.*
Moran, Carla — *Key Employment Services*
Moran, Gail — *Comprehensive Search*
Moran, Gayle — *Dussick Management Associates*
Morgan, Gary — *National Search, Inc.*
Morgan, Richard — *Lovas Stanley/Paul Ray Berndtson Inc.*
Morgan, Vincent S. — *Johnson Smith & Knisely Accord*
Morris, Paul T. — *The Morris Group*
Morrison, Janis L. — *Garrett Associates Inc.*
Morton, Robert C. — *Morton, McCorkle & Associates, Inc.*
Morton, Sheila Ann — *Sloan & Associates*
Moyer, David S. — *Moyer, Sherwood Associates, Inc.*
Muendel, H. Edward — *Stanton Chase International*
Mulligan, Robert P. — *William Willis Worldwide Inc.*
Mummert, Dennis D. — *Sweeney Harbert & Mummert, Inc.*
Murin, Rose Mary — *U.S. Envirosearch*
Murphy, Cornelius J. — *Goodrich & Sherwood Associates, Inc.*
Murphy, Gary J. — *Stone Murphy & Olson*
Murphy, Karen S. — *Flex Execs Management Solutions*
Murphy, Patrick J. — *P.J. Murphy & Associates, Inc.*
Murphy, Timothy D. — *MSI International*
Mursuli, Meredith — *Lasher Associates*
Mustin, Joyce M. — *J: Blakslee International, Ltd.*
Myers, Kay — *Signature Staffing*
Myrick, Marilou — *ProResource, Inc.*
Myrick, Marilou — *ProResource, Inc.*
Nadherny, Christopher C. — *Spencer Stuart*

Nagler, Leon G. — *Nagler, Robins & Poe, Inc.*
Nahas, Robert — *Herbert Mines Associates, Inc.*
Nathanson, Barry F. — *Barry Nathanson Associates*
Nazzaro, Samuel G. — *Boyden*
Neill, Wellden K. — *Sampson Neill & Wilkins Inc.*
Nein, Lawrence F. — *Lamalie Amrop International*
Nelson, Barbara — *Herman Smith Executive Initiatives Inc.*
Nephew, Robert — *Christian & Timbers*
Neuberth, Jeffrey G. — *Canny, Bowen Inc.*
Newbold, Michael — *Agra Placements International Ltd.*
Newman, Lynn — *Kishbaugh Associates International*
Nicastro, Kelley P. — *A la carte International*
Nitti, Jacqueline — *ALTCO Temporary Services*
Noble, Donald H. — *Noble & Associates Inc.*
Nocero, John — *ProResource, Inc.*
Nolan, Jean M. — *S.D. Kelly & Associates, Inc.*
Nold, Robert — *Roberson and Company*
Nordland, Martin N. — *Horton International*
Norman, Randy — *Austin-McGregor International*
Normann, Amy — *Robert M. Flanagan & Associates, Ltd.*
Norsell, Paul E. — *Paul Norsell & Associates, Inc.*
Nunziata, Fred — *Eden & Associates, Inc.*
O'Brien, John G. — *CanMed Consultants Inc.*
O'Donnell, James H. — *MSI International*
O'Donnell, Timothy W. — *Boyden*
O'Hara, Daniel M. — *Lynch Miller Moore Partners, Inc.*
O'Hara, James J. — *Barone-O'Hara Associates*
O'Maley, Kimberlee — *Spencer Stuart*
O'Neill, James P. — *Allerton Heneghan & O'Neill*
O'Neill, Stephen A. — *Harris Heery & Associates*
O'Such, Tracy — *Bishop Partners*
O'Toole, Dennis P. — *Dennis P. O'Toole & Associates Inc.*
Oakes, Meg B. — *D.P. Parker and Associates*
Ocon, Olga — *Busch International*
Ogdon, Thomas H. — *The Ogdon Partnership*
Ohman, Gregory L. — *Pearson, Caldwell & Farnsworth, Inc.*
Oliver, Phoebe — *Seiden Krieger Associates, Inc.*
Oller, Jose E. — *Ward Howell International, Inc.*
Olmstead, George T. — *Blackshaw, Olmstead & Lynch*
Olsen, Carl — *A.T. Kearney, Inc.*
Onstott, Joseph E. — *The Onstott Group, Inc.*
Oppenheim, Jeffrey — *Roth Young Personnel Service of Boston, Inc.*
Oswald, Mark G. — *Canny, Bowen Inc.*
Owens, Ken — *F-O-R-T-U-N-E Personnel Consultants of Huntsville, Inc.*
Pace, Susan A. — *Horton International*
Pacini, Lauren R. — *Hite Executive Search*
Page, Linda — *Jonas, Walters & Assoc., Inc.*
Page, Linda M. — *Wargo and Co., Inc.*
Palma, Frank R. — *Goodrich & Sherwood Associates, Inc.*
Palmer, Carlton A. — *Beall & Company, Inc.*
Palmlund, David W. — *Lamalie Amrop International*
Pamplin, LaShana — *The Repovich-Reynolds Group*
Pappas, Jim — *Search Dynamics, Inc.*
Pappas, Timothy C. — *Jonas, Walters & Assoc., Inc.*
Parfitt, William C. — *Parfitt Recruiting and Consulting/PRO TEM*
Parker, David P. — *D.P. Parker and Associates*
Parker, Roberta — *R. Parker and Associates, Inc.*
Parkin, Myrna — *S.D. Kelly & Associates, Inc.*
Parr, James A. — *KPMG Management Consulting*
Parry, William H. — *Horton International*
Patence, David W. — *Handy HRM Corp.*
Patton, Mitchell — *Patton/Perry Associates, Inc.*
Pearson, John R. — *Pearson, Caldwell & Farnsworth, Inc.*
Pearson, Robert L. — *Lamalie Amrop International*
Peckenpaugh, Ann D. — *Schweichler Associates, Inc.*
Peeney, James D. — *Peeney Associates*
Pelisson, Charles — *Marra Peters & Partners*
Pelkey, Chris — *The McCormick Group, Inc.*
Pelletier, Jacques F. — *Roth Young Personnel Service of Boston, Inc.*
Pepe, Leonida — *Butterfass, Pepe & MacCallan Inc.*
Perez, Christina — *Orr Executive Search*
Perry, Wayne B. — *Bruce Massey & Partners Inc.*
Persky, Barry — *Barry Persky & Company, Inc.*
Peternell, Melanie — *Signature Staffing*
Peternich, Tracy — *Simpson Associates*
Peters, James N. — *TNS Partners, Inc.*
Pettersson, Tara L. — *Lamalie Amrop International*
Pettibone, Linda — *Herbert Mines Associates, Inc.*
Pettway, Samuel H. — *Spencer Stuart*
Petty, J. Scott — *The Arcus Group*
Pfeiffer, Irene — *Price Waterhouse*
Phelps, Gene L. — *McCormack & Farrow*
Phillips, Donald L. — *O'Shea, Divine & Company, Inc.*
Phillips, Scott K. — *Phillips & Ford, Inc.*
Pickens, Barbara — *Johnson Smith & Knisely Accord*
Pickering, Dale — *Agri-Tech Personnel, Inc.*
Pickford, Stephen T. — *The Corporate Staff, Inc.*
Pierson, Edward J. — *Johnson Smith & Knisely Accord*

Pinkman, Karen N. — *Skott/Edwards Consultants, Inc.*
Pitcher, Brian D. — *Skott/Edwards Consultants, Inc.*
Plessner, Rene — *Rene Plessner Associates, Inc.*
Plummer, John — *Plummer & Associates, Inc.*
Podway, Hope — *Search West, Inc.*
Poe, James B. — *Nagler, Robins & Poe, Inc.*
Poirier, Frank — *Juntunen-Combs-Poirier*
Poirier, Roland — *Poirier, Hoevel & Co.*
Pompeo, Paul — *Search West, Inc.*
Porada, Stephen D. — *CAP Inc.*
Porter, Albert — *The Experts*
Porter, Donald — *Amherst Personnel Group Inc.*
Potenza, Gregory — *Mixtec Group*
Potter, Douglas C. — *Stanton Chase International*
Price, Andrew G. — *The Thomas Tucker Company*
Prince, Marilyn L. — *Higdon Prince Inc.*
Proct, Nina — *Martin H. Bauman Associates, Inc.*
Prosser, Shane — *Search Consultants International, Inc.*
Provus, Barbara L. — *Shepherd Bueschel & Provus, Inc.*
Pryde, Marcia P. — *A.T. Kearney, Inc.*
Pugh, Judith Geist — *InterimManagement Solutions, Inc.*
Raab, Julie — *Dunhill Professional Search of Irvine, Inc.*
Rabe, William — *Sales Executives Inc.*
Rabinowitz, Peter A. — *P.A.R. Associates Inc.*
Radawicz, Angela — *Mixtec Group*
Radice, Joseph — *Hospitality International*
Raheja, Marc C. — *CanMed Consultants Inc.*
Raiber, Laurie Altman — *The IMC Group of Companies Ltd.*
Randell, James E. — *Randell-Heiken, Inc.*
Ray, Marianne C. — *Callan Associates, Ltd.*
Raymond, Anne — *Anderson Sterling Associates*
Reddick, David C. — *Horton International*
Redding, Denise — *The Douglas Reiter Company, Inc.*
Redler, Rhonda — *National Search, Inc.*
Redwood, Guy W. — *Bruce Massey & Partners Inc.*
Reece, Christopher S. — *Reece & Mruk Partners*
Reed, Ruthann — *Spectra International Inc.*
Reeder, Michael S. — *Lamalie Amrop International*
Reeves, William B. — *Spencer Stuart*
Regehly, Herbert L. — *The IMC Group of Companies Ltd.*
Reiser, Ellen — *Thorndike Deland Associates*
Reiss, Matt — *National Search, Inc.*
Reiter, Douglas — *The Douglas Reiter Company, Inc.*
Reiter, Harold D. — *Herbert Mines Associates, Inc.*
Renick, Cynthia L. — *Morgan Hunter Corp.*
Renwick, David — *John Kurosky & Associates*
Reticker, Peter — *MSI International*
Reyman, Susan — *S. Reyman & Associates Ltd.*
Reynes, Tony — *Tesar-Reynes, Inc.*
Reynolds, Gregory P. — *Roberts Ryan and Bentley*
Reynolds, Smooch S. — *The Repovich-Reynolds Group*
Rice, Douglas — *Agra Placements International Ltd.*
Rice, Marie — *Jay Gaines & Company, Inc.*
Rich, Lyttleton — *Sockwell & Associates*
Richards, Robert A. — *Sloan & Associates*
Richards, Sharon — *The Barack Group, Inc.*
Richardson, J. Rick — *Spencer Stuart*
Rieger, Louis J. — *Spencer Stuart*
Riley, Elizabeth G. — *Mazza & Riley, Inc.*
Rimmele, Michael — *The Bankers Group*
Rinaldi, Michael D. — *D.P. Parker and Associates*
Rinker, Jim — *Southwestern Professional Services*
Rivas, Alberto F. — *Boyden*
Rizzo, L. Donald — *R.P. Barone Associates*
Roberts, Mitch — *A.E. Feldman Associates*
Roberts, Norman C. — *Norman Roberts & Associates, Inc.*
Roberts, Raymond R. — *MSI International*
Roberts, Scott B. — *Wargo and Co., Inc.*
Roberts, William — *Cochran, Cochran & Yale, Inc.*
Robertson, Bruce J. — *Norman Broadbent International, Inc.*
Robins, Jeri N. — *Nagler, Robins & Poe, Inc.*
Robinson, Bruce — *Bruce Robinson Associates*
Robison, John H. — *Robison & Associates*
Rodgers, John — *Agra Placements International Ltd.*
Rodgers, Kathi — *St. Lawrence International, Inc.*
Rodney, Brett — *MSI International*
Rodriguez, Josie — *R. Parker and Associates, Inc.*
Romaine, Stanley J. — *Mixtec Group*
Romanchek, Walter R. — *Wellington Management Group*
Romanello, Daniel P. — *Spencer Stuart*
Romaniw, Michael J. — *A la carte International*
Romaniw, Michael J. — *A la carte International*
Romaniw, Michael J. — *A la carte International*
Ropella, Patrick B. — *Ropella & Associates*
Rosato, William R. — *W.R. Rosato & Associates, Inc.*
Rosemarin, Gloria J. — *Barrington Hart, Inc.*
Rosen, Elayne — *Noble & Associates Inc.*
Rosenberg, Esther — *Howe-Lewis International*
Rosenthal, Charles — *National Search, Inc.*

Ross, Lawrence — *Lovas Stanley/Paul Ray Berndtson Inc.*
Ross, Mark S. — *Herman Smith Executive Initiatives Inc.*
Rossi, Silvio — *Keith Bagg & Associates Inc.*
Roth, Robert J. — *Williams, Roth & Krueger Inc.*
Roth, William — *Harris Heery & Associates*
Rothfeld, Robert — *A.E. Feldman Associates*
Rothman, Jeffrey — *ProResource, Inc.*
Rowells, Michael — *MSI International*
Rudolph, Kenneth — *Kossuth & Associates, Inc.*
Rudzinsky, Howard — *Louis Rudzinsky Associates*
Rumson, Paul — *Roth Young Personnel Service of Boston, Inc.*
Rurak, Zbigniew T. — *Rurak & Associates, Inc.*
Rusher, William H. — *Rusher, Loscavio & LoPresto*
Russell, Robin E. — *Kenzer Corp.*
Sacerdote, John — *Raymond Karsan Associates*
Samet, Saul — *Fisher-Todd Associates*
Sampson, Martin C. — *Sampson Neill & Wilkins Inc.*
Sanders, Spencer H. — *Battalia Winston International*
Sapperstein, Jerry S. — *CFO Associates, Inc.*
Sathe, Mark A. — *Sathe & Associates, Inc.*
Savage, Edward J. — *Stanton Chase International*
Sawyer, Patricia L. — *Smith & Sawyer Inc.*
Sayers, Bruce D. — *Brackin & Sayers Associates*
Schaefer, Frederic M. — *A.T. Kearney, Inc.*
Scharett, Carol — *St. Lawrence International, Inc.*
Schedra, Sharon — *Earley Kielty and Associates, Inc.*
Schiavone, Mary Rose — *Canny, Bowen Inc.*
Schiffer, Stewart — *Career Management International*
Schlpma, Christine — *Advanced Executive Resources*
Schmidt, Frank B. — *F.B. Schmidt International*
Schmidt, Jeri E. — *Blake, Hansen & Nye, Limited*
Schmidt, Peter R. — *Boyden*
Schmidt, William C. — *Christian & Timbers*
Schneider, Margo — *Search West, Inc.*
Schneider, Perry — *Agra Placements International Ltd.*
Schneiderman, Gerald — *Management Resource Associates, Inc.*
Schnierow, Beryl — *Tesar-Reynes, Inc.*
Schroeder, John W. — *Spencer Stuart*
Schroeder, Lee — *Blau Kaptain Schroeder*
Schroeder, Steven J. — *Blau Kaptain Schroeder*
Schuette, Dorothy — *Harris Heery & Associates*
Schwam, Carol — *A.E. Feldman Associates*
Schwartz, Carole — *A.T. Kearney, Inc.*
Schweichler, Lee J. — *Schweichler Associates, Inc.*
Seals, Sonny — *A.T. Kearney, Inc.*
Seco, William — *Seco & Zetto Associates, Inc.*
Segal, Eric B. — *Kenzer Corp.*
Seiden, Steven A. — *Seiden Krieger Associates, Inc.*
Seitz, Charles J. — *Neail Behringer Consultants*
Sekera, Roger I. — *A.T. Kearney, Inc.*
Selbach, Barbara — *Spencer Stuart*
Selker, Gregory L. — *Christian & Timbers*
Selko, Philip W. — *Hogan Acquisitions*
Semyan, John K. — *TNS Partners, Inc.*
Sennello, Gendra — *National Search, Inc.*
Serwat, Leonard A. — *Spencer Stuart*
Sessa, Vincent J. — *Integrated Search Solutions Group, LLC*
Settles, Barbara Z. — *Lamalie Amrop International*
Sevilla, Claudio A. — *Crawford & Crofford*
Shamir, Ben — *S.D. Kelly & Associates, Inc.*
Shattuck, Merrill B. — *M.B. Shattuck and Associates, Inc.*
Sheedy, Edward J. — *Dieckmann & Associates, Ltd.*
Shelton, Sandra — *National Search, Inc.*
Shenfield, Peter — *Baker, Harris & Partners Limited*
Shepard, Michael J. — *MSI International*
Shepherd, Daniel M. — *Shepherd Bueschel & Provus, Inc.*
Sher, Lawrence — *M.A. Churchill & Associates, Inc.*
Shervey, Brent C. — *O'Callaghan Honey/Paul Ray Berndtson, Inc.*
Sherwin, Thomas — *Barone-O'Hara Associates*
Sherwood, Andrew — *Goodrich & Sherwood Associates, Inc.*
Shimp, David J. — *Lamalie Amrop International*
Shipherd, John T. — *The Cassie Group*
Shirilla, Robert M. — *F.B. Schmidt International*
Shoemaker, Larry C. — *Shoemaker & Associates*
Shulman, Barry — *Shulman Associates*
Shultz, Deborah M. — *Blau Kaptain Schroeder*
Sibbald, John R. — *John Sibbald Associates, Inc.*
Siegel, Pamela — *Executive Options, Ltd.*
Siegel, RitaSue — *RitaSue Siegel Resources Inc.*
Sierra, Rafael A. — *Lamalie Amrop International*
Sill, Igor M. — *Geneva Group International*
Sill, Igor M. — *Geneva Group International*
Silver, Lee A. — *L.A. Silver Associates, Inc.*
Simmons, Anneta — *F-O-R-T-U-N-E Personnel Consultants of Huntsville, Inc.*
Simmons, Gerald J. — *Handy HRM Corp.*
Simmons, Sandra K. — *MSI International*
Sinclair, Amy — *Fisher Personnel Management Services*
Sine, Mark — *Hospitality International*

Sjogren, Dennis — *Agra Placements International Ltd.*
Sklover, Bruce — *Professional Assignments of New York, Inc.*
Skunda, Donna M. — *Allerton Heneghan & O'Neill*
Slater, Ronald E. — *A.T. Kearney, Inc.*
Slaughter, Katherine T. — *Compass Group Ltd.*
Slayton, Richard C. — *Slayton International, Inc.*
Sloan, Michael D. — *Sloan & Associates*
Slocum, Ann Marie — *K.L. Whitney Company*
Smead, Michelle M. — *A.T. Kearney, Inc.*
Smith, Adam M. — *The Abbott Group, Inc.*
Smith, Cheryl — *Barton Raben, Inc.*
Smith, Cheryl — *ProResource, Inc.*
Smith, David P. — *Smith & Latterell (HRS, Inc.)*
Smith, Grant — *Price Waterhouse*
Smith, Margaret A. — *MSI International*
Smith, Monica S. — *Analysts Resources, Inc.*
Smith, Robert L. — *Smith & Sawyer Inc.*
Smyth, Brendan — *Simpson Associates*
Snelgrove, Geiger — *National Search, Inc.*
Snodgrass, Stephen — *DeFrain, Mayer, Lee & Burgess LLC*
Snyder, James F. — *Snyder & Company*
Snyder, Thomas J. — *Spencer Stuart*
Sockwell, J. Edgar — *Sockwell & Associates*
Soggs, Cheryl Pavick — *A.T. Kearney, Inc.*
Sola, George L. — *A.T. Kearney, Inc.*
Songy, Al — *U.S. Envirosearch*
Sowerbutt, Richard S. — *Hite Executive Search*
Spann, Richard E. — *Goodrich & Sherwood Associates, Inc.*
Speck, Michael J. — *Lovas Stanley/Paul Ray Berndtson Inc.*
Spicher, John — *M.A. Churchill & Associates, Inc.*
Spiegel, Gay — *L.A. Silver Associates, Inc.*
Sprague, David — *Michael Stern Associates Inc.*
Sprau, Collin L. — *Paul Ray Berndtson*
Spriggs, Robert D. — *Spriggs & Company, Inc.*
Sprowls, Linda — *Allard Associates*
Stack, James K. — *Boyden*
Stafford, Susan — *Hospitality International*
Stark, Jeff — *Thorne, Brieger Associates Inc.*
Statson, Dale E. — *Sales Executives Inc.*
Steck, Frank T. — *A.T. Kearney, Inc.*
Steenerson, Thomas L. — *MSI International*
Stein, Terry W. — *Stewart, Stein and Scott, Ltd.*
Steinman, Stephen — *The Stevenson Group of New Jersey*
Stenholm, Gilbert R. — *Spencer Stuart*
Sterling, Jay — *Earley Kielty and Associates, Inc.*
Stern, Michael I. — *Michael Stern Associates Inc.*
Stevenson, Terry — *Bartholdi & Company, Inc.*
Stewart, Jeffrey O. — *Stewart, Stein and Scott, Ltd.*
Stewart, Ross M. — *Human Resources Network Partners Inc.*
Stiles, Judy — *MedQuest Associates*
Stinson, R.J. — *Sampson Neill & Wilkins Inc.*
Stivk, Barbara A. — *Thornton Resources*
Stoll, Steven G. — *Sharrow & Associates*
Stone, Robert Ryder — *Lamalie Amrop International*
Stone, Susan L. — *Stone Enterprises Ltd.*
Stouffer, Dale — *Agra Placements International Ltd.*
Stratmeyer, Karin Bergwall — *Princeton Entrepreneurial Resources*
Straube, Stanley H. — *Straube Associates*
Strawn, William — *Houtz-Strawn Associates, Inc.*
Stricker, Sidney G. — *Stricker & Zagor*
Stringer, Dann P. — *D.E. Foster Partners Inc.*
Strobridge, Richard P. — *F.L. Taylor & Company, Inc.*
Strom, Mark N. — *Search Advisors International Corp.*
Strong, Robert W. — *The Barack Group, Inc.*
Stubbs, Judy N. — *Lamalie Amrop International*
Sturtz, James W. — *Compass Group Ltd.*
Stutt, Brian — *Richard, Wayne and Roberts*
Sullivan, Kay — *Rusher, Loscavio & LoPresto*
Summers, Burke — *The McCormick Group, Inc.*
Sumurdy, Melinda — *Kenzer Corp.*
Sur, William K. — *Canny, Bowen Inc.*
Swan, Richard A. — *Witt/Kieffer, Ford, Hadelman & Lloyd*
Swanson, Dick — *Raymond Karsan Associates*
Swanson, Kris — *Flex Execs Management Solutions*
Swatts, Stone — *F-O-R-T-U-N-E Personnel Consultants of Huntsville, Inc.*
Sweeney, James W. — *Sweeney Harbert & Mummert, Inc.*
Sweeney, Sean K. — *Bonifield Associates*
Swick, Jan — *TSS Consulting, Ltd.*
Szafran, Jack — *U.S. Envirosearch*
Takacs, Gloria — *Gilbert & Van Campen International*
Taylor, Conrad G. — *MSI International*
Taylor, Ernest A. — *Ward Howell International, Inc.*
Teas, John — *Southwestern Professional Services*
Teinert, Jay — *Damon & Associates, Inc.*
Templin, Robert E. — *Gilbert Tweed/INESA*
Tesar, Bob — *Tesar-Reynes, Inc.*
Theobald, David B. — *Theobald & Associates*
Thies, Gary — *S.D. Kelly & Associates, Inc.*

Thiras, Ted — *Mixtec Group*
Tholke, William E. — *Canny, Bowen Inc.*
Thomas, Christine S. — *Lovas Stanley/Paul Ray Berndtson Inc.*
Thomas, Jeffrey — *Fairfaxx Corporation*
Thomas, John T. — *Ward Howell International, Inc.*
Thomas, Kurt J. — *P.J. Murphy & Associates, Inc.*
Thomas, Terry — *Montague Enterprises*
Thompson, Brett — *Southwestern Professional Services*
Thompson, Dave — *Battalia Winston International*
Thompson, James R. — *Gordon Wahls Company*
Thompson, John R. — *MSI International*
Thompson, Kenneth L. — *McCormack & Farrow*
Thornton, John C. — *Thornton Resources*
Timoney, Laura — *Bishop Partners*
Tipp, George — *Intech Summit Group, Inc.*
Titterington, Catherine F. — *MSI International*
Tokarcik, Patricia — *ProResource, Inc.*
Tokash, Ronald E. — *MSI International*
Tonjuk, Tina — *The Paladin Companies, Inc.*
Tracey, Jack — *Management Assistance Group, Inc.*
Trosin, Walter R. — *Johnson Smith & Knisely Accord*
Trott, Kathryn — *Allard Associates*
Trott, Kathryn — *Allard Associates*
Trueblood, Brian G. — *TNS Partners, Inc.*
Truex, John F. — *Morton, McCorkle & Associates, Inc.*
Tryon, Katey — *DeFrain, Mayer, Lee & Burgess LLC*
Tucci, Joseph — *Fairfaxx Corporation*
Tucker, Thomas A. — *The Thomas Tucker Company*
Tunney, William — *Grant Cooper and Associates*
Tweed, Janet — *Gilbert Tweed/INESA*
Tyson, Richard L. — *Bonifield Associates*
Unger, Paul T. — *A.T. Kearney, Inc.*
Unger, Stephen A. — *Spencer Stuart*
Utroska, Donald R. — *Lamalie Amrop International*
Vachon, David A. — *McNichol Associates*
Vainblat, Galina — *Foy, Schneid & Daniel, Inc.*
Valenta, Joseph — *Princeton Entrepreneurial Resources*
Van Alstine, Catherine — *Tanton Mitchell/Paul Ray Berndtson*
Van Campen, Jerry — *Gilbert & Van Campen International*
Van Clieaf, Mark — *MVC Associates International*
Van Horn, Carol — *R. Parker and Associates, Inc.*
Van Remmen, Roger — *Brown, Bernardy, Van Remmen, Inc.*
van Someren, Christian — *Johnson Smith & Knisely Accord*
Vann, Dianne — *The Button Group*
Vaughan, David B. — *Dunhill Professional Search of Irvine, Inc.*
Venable, William W. — *Thorndike Deland Associates*
Vennat, Manon — *Spencer Stuart*
Vergara, Gail H. — *Spencer Stuart*
Vergari, Jane — *Herbert Mines Associates, Inc.*
Vinnedge, Sandra — *U.S. Envirosearch*
Virgili, Franca — *Johnson Smith & Knisely Accord*
Visnich, L. Christine — *Bason Associates Inc.*
Vlcek, Thomas J. — *Vlcek & Company, Inc.*
Vogus, Jerry — *Cumberland Group Inc.*
Vojta, Marilyn B. — *James Mead & Company*
Volk, Richard — *MSI International*
Wakefield, Scott — *National Search, Inc.*
Waldman, Noah H. — *Lamalie Amrop International*
Waldoch, D. Mark — *Barnes Development Group, LLC*
Waldrop, Gary R. — *MSI International*
Walker, Ewing J. — *Ward Howell International, Inc.*
Walker, Martin S. — *Walker Communications*
Wall, David — *Southwestern Professional Services*
Walsh, Patty — *Abraham & London, Ltd.*
Walters, William F. — *Jonas, Walters & Assoc., Inc.*
Walther, Linda S. — *MSI International*
Wardell, Charles W.B. — *Lamalie Amrop International*
Ware, John C. — *Spencer Stuart*
Wargo, G. Rick — *A.T. Kearney, Inc.*
Warren, Sylvia W. — *Thorndike Deland Associates*
Wasserman, Harvey — *Churchill and Affiliates, Inc.*
Waters, Peter D. — *John Kurosky & Associates*
Watkins, Thomas M. — *Lamalie Amrop International*
Watson, James — *MSI International*
Wayne, Cary S. — *ProSearch Inc.*
Webb, George H. — *Webb, Johnson Associates, Inc.*
Webb, Shawn K. — *MSI International*
Weber, Jurgen — *BioQuest, Inc.*
Wein, Michael S. — *InterimManagement Solutions, Inc.*
Wein, Michael S. — *Media Management Resources, Inc.*
Wein, William — *InterimManagement Solutions, Inc.*
Wein, William — *Media Management Resources, Inc.*
Weintraub, Lynn — *The Paladin Companies, Inc.*
Weisler, Nancy — *National Search, Inc.*
Weissman-Rosenthal, Abbe — *ALW Research International*
Weisz, Laura — *Anderson Sterling Associates*
Werner, Bonnie — *H.M. Long International, Ltd.*
Wertel, Ronald E. — *Gordon Wahls Company*
West, Nancy — *Health Care Dimensions*

Westerfield, Putney — *Boyden*
Weston, Corinne F. — *D.A. Kreuter Associates, Inc.*
Wexler, Rona — *Ariel Recruitment Associates*
White, Jeffrey E. — *Simpson Associates*
White, Jonathan O. — *The Badger Group*
White, Patricia D. — *MSI International*
White, Richard B. — *Spencer Stuart*
White, William C. — *Venture Resources Inc.*
Whiting, Anthony — *Johnson Smith & Knisely Accord*
Whitley, Sue Ann — *Roberts Ryan and Bentley*
Whitney, Kenneth L. — *K.L. Whitney Company*
Whitton, Paula L. — *Pearson, Caldwell & Farnsworth, Inc.*
Wichansky, Mark — *TSS Consulting, Ltd.*
Wier, Daniel — *Horton International*
Wilder, Richard B. — *Columbia Consulting Group*
Wilkins, Walter K. — *Sampson Neill & Wilkins Inc.*
Wilkinson, Barbara — *Beall & Company, Inc.*
Wilkinson, William R. — *Wilkinson & Ives*
Williams, Alexander H. — *Witt/Kieffer, Ford, Hadelman & Lloyd*
Williams, Dave — *The McCormick Group, Inc.*
Williams, Gary L. — *Barnes Development Group, LLC*
Williams, Harry D. — *Jacobson Associates*
Williams, Laurelle N. — *MSI International*
Williams, Lis — *Executive Options, Ltd.*
Williams, Roger K. — *Williams, Roth & Krueger Inc.*
Williams, Walter E. — *Canny, Bowen Inc.*
Willis, William H. — *William Willis Worldwide Inc.*
Willner, Nannette — *S.R. Wolman Associates, Inc.*
Wilson, Derrick — *Thornton Resources*
Wilson, Patricia L. — *Leon A. Farley Associates*
Winitz, Joel — *GSW Consulting Group, Inc.*
Winitz, Marla — *GSW Consulting Group, Inc.*
Winston, Dale — *Battalia Winston International*
Wisch, Steven C. — *MB Inc. Interim Executive Division*
Wise, Anne — *U.S. Envirosearch*
Wise, J. Herbert — *Sandhurst Associates*
Wittenberg, Laura L. — *Boyden*
Wolf, Stephen M. — *Byron Leonard International, Inc.*
Wolman, Stephen R. — *S.R. Wolman Associates, Inc.*
Womack, Joseph — *The Bankers Group*
Wood, Martin F. — *Lamalie Amrop International*
Wood, Milton M. — *M. Wood Company*
Wooller, Edmund A.M. — *Windsor International*
Woollett, James — *Rusher, Loscavio & LoPresto*
Wren, Jay — *Jay Wren & Associates*
Wren, Shelly J. — *Sloan & Associates*
Wright, Charles D. — *Goodrich & Sherwood Associates, Inc.*
Wright, Leslie — *The Stevenson Group of New Jersey*
Wrynn, Robert F. — *MSI International*
Wyatt, James — *Wyatt & Jaffe*
Wylie, Pamela — *M.A. Churchill & Associates, Inc.*
Young, Alexander — *Messett Associates, Inc.*
Young, Laurie — *Part Time Resources, Inc.*
Young, Lesley — *Search West, Inc.*
Zaffrann, Craig S. — *P.J. Murphy & Associates, Inc.*
Zahradka, James F. — *P.J. Murphy & Associates, Inc.*
Zander, Barry W. — *MSI International*
Zarkin, Norman — *The Zarkin Group, Inc.*
Zay, Thomas C. — *Boyden/Zay & Company*
Zay, Thomas C. — *Boyden/Zay & Company*
Zee, Wanda — *Tesar-Reynes, Inc.*
Zera, Ronald J. — *Spencer Stuart*
Zetto, Kathryn — *Seco & Zetto Associates, Inc.*
Zila, Laurie M. — *Princeton Entrepreneurial Resources*
Zilliacus, Patrick W. — *Larsen, Zilliacus & Associates, Inc.*
Zingaro, Ron — *Zingaro and Company*
Zinn, Donald — *Bishop Partners*
Zona, Henry F. — *Zona & Associates, Inc.*
Zwiff, Jeffrey G. — *Johnson Smith & Knisely Accord*

## 8. Research/Development

Abbott, Dale — *Mixtec Group*
Abbott, Peter — *The Abbott Group, Inc.*
Alekel, Karren — *ALW Research International*
Allen, David A. — *Intech Summit Group, Inc.*
Allerton, Donald T. — *Allerton Heneghan & O'Neill*
Allgire, Mary L. — *Kenzer Corp.*
Altreuter, Ken — *ALTCO Temporary Services*
Altreuter, Kenneth — *The ALTCO Group*
Ambert, Amadol — *Bryant Research*
Ambler, Peter W. — *Peter W. Ambler Company*
Ames, George C. — *Ames O'Neill Associates*
Anderson, Dean C. — *Corporate Resources Professional Placement*
Anderson, Roger J. — *BioQuest, Inc.*
Anderson, Thomas — *Paul J. Biestek Associates, Inc.*
Andrews, Laura L. — *Stricker & Zagor*
Andrick, Patty — *CPS Inc.*
Angell, Tryg R. — *Tryg R. Angell Ltd.*
Apostle, George — *Search Dynamics, Inc.*

Ariail, C. Bowling — *Ariail & Associates*
Ariail, Randolph C. — *Ariail & Associates*
Arnold, David — *Christian & Timbers*
Arnold, Jerry — *Houtz-Strawn Associates, Inc.*
Aronin, Michael — *Fisher-Todd Associates*
Ashton, Barbara L. — *Ashton Computer Professionals Inc.*
Asquith, Peter S. — *Ames Personnel Consultants, Inc.*
Aston, Kathy — *Marra Peters & Partners*
Attell, Harold — *A.E. Feldman Associates*
Austin, Jessica L. — *D.S.A. - Dixie Search Associates*
Bachmeier, Kevin — *Agra Placements International Ltd.*
Badger, Fred H. — *The Badger Group*
Bagg, Keith — *Keith Bagg & Associates Inc.*
Baird, David W. — *D.W. Baird & Associates*
Baker, Gerry — *Baker, Harris & Partners Limited*
Balch, Randy — *CPS Inc.*
Baltin, Carrie — *Search West, Inc.*
Barbosa, Franklin J. — *Boyden*
Barlow, Ken H. — *The Cherbonnier Group, Inc.*
Barnes, Richard E. — *Barnes Development Group, LLC*
Barnes, Roanne L. — *Barnes Development Group, LLC*
Baron, Len — *Industrial Recruiters Associates, Inc.*
Barone, Marialice — *Barone-O'Hara Associates*
Barr, Ronald — *Search West, Inc.*
Bartholi, James A. — *McNichol Associates*
Bartholdi, Ted — *Bartholdi & Company, Inc.*
Bartholdi, Theodore G. — *Bartholdi & Company, Inc.*
Bason, Maurice L. — *Bason Associates Inc.*
Bass, Nate — *Jacobson Associates*
Bates, Nina — *Allard Associates*
Bauman, Martin H. — *Martin H. Bauman Associates, Inc.*
Beal, Richard D. — *A.T. Kearney, Inc.*
Beaudin, Elizabeth C. — *Callan Associates, Ltd.*
Beaver, Bentley H. — *The Onstott Group, Inc.*
Benson, Kate — *Rene Plessner Associates, Inc.*
Berke, Carl E. — *The Cassie Group*
Bermea, Jose — *Gaffney Management Consultants*
Besen, Douglas — *Besen Associates Inc.*
Biestek, Paul J. — *Paul J. Biestek Associates, Inc.*
Billotti, Lisa — *Bryant Research*
Bladon, Andrew — *Don Richard Associates of Tampa, Inc.*
Blakslee, Jan H. — *J: Blakslee International, Ltd.*
Blanton, Thomas — *Blanton and Company*
Blim, Barbara — *JDG Associates, Ltd.*
Bloomer, James E. — *L.W. Foote Company*
Bluhm, Claudia — *Schweichler Associates, Inc.*
Boczany, William J. — *The Guild Corporation*
Bonifield, Len — *Bonifield Associates*
Bonner, Barbara — *Mixtec Group*
Borden, Stuart — *M.A. Churchill & Associates, Inc.*
Borman, Theodore H. — *Lamalie Amrop International*
Bostic, James E. — *Phillips Resource Group*
Bourbeau, Paul J. — *Boyden*
Bradshaw, John W. — *A.T. Kearney, Inc.*
Brady, Robert — *CPS Inc.*
Brandeis, Richard — *CPS Inc.*
Brandjes, Michael J. — *Brandjes Associates*
Brazil, Kathy — *Bryant Research*
Brennan, Timothy — *Brennan Associates*
Brennen, Richard J. — *Spencer Stuart*
Brentari, Michael — *Search Consultants International, Inc.*
Brieger, Steve — *Thorne, Brieger Associates Inc.*
Briggs, Adam — *Horton International*
Brooks, Kimberllay — *Corporate Recruiters Ltd.*
Brown, Franklin Key — *Handy HRM Corp.*
Bryant, Richard D. — *Bryant Associates, Inc.*
Bryant, Thomas — *Bryant Research*
Bryza, Robert M. — *Robert Lowell International*
Bullock, Conni — *Earley Kielty and Associates, Inc.*
Burden, Gene — *The Cherbonnier Group, Inc.*
Burfield, Elaine — *Skott/Edwards Consultants, Inc.*
Burke, George M. — *The Burke Group*
Burke, John — *The Experts*
Burris, James C. — *Boyden*
Busch, Jack — *Busch International*
Butler, Kirby B. — *The Butlers Company Insurance Recruiters*
Button, David R. — *The Button Group*
Byrnes, Thomas A. — *Thomas A. Byrnes Associates*
Cahill, Peter M. — *Peter M. Cahill Associates, Inc.*
Callan, Robert M. — *Callan Associates, Ltd.*
Callihan, Diana L. — *Search Northwest Associates*
Campbell, Robert Scott — *Wellington Management Group*
Carter, Christine C. — *Health Care Dimensions*
Casal, Daniel G. — *Bonifield Associates*
Cavolina, Michael — *Carver Search Consultants*
Celenza, Catherine — *CPS Inc.*
Chavous, C. Crawford — *Phillips Resource Group*
Cherbonnier, L. Michael — *TCG International, Inc.*
Cherbonnier, L. Michael — *The Cherbonnier Group, Inc.*

Christian, Jeffrey E. — *Christian & Timbers*
Christiansen, Amy — *CPS Inc.*
Christiansen, Doug — *CPS Inc.*
Cizek, John T. — *Cizek Associates, Inc.*
Cizek, Marti J. — *Cizek Associates, Inc.*
Clarey, William A. — *Preng & Associates, Inc.*
Clark, James — *CPS Inc.*
Cleary, Thomas R. — *ARJay & Associates*
Cline, Mark — *NYCOR Search, Inc.*
Close, E. Wade — *Boyden*
Cochran, Hale — *Fenwick Partners*
Coffman, Brian — *Kossuth & Associates, Inc.*
Cohen, Michael R. — *Intech Summit Group, Inc.*
Cohen, Robert C. — *Intech Summit Group, Inc.*
Colasanto, Frank M. — *W.R. Rosato & Associates, Inc.*
Colling, Douglas — *KPMG Management Consulting*
Colucci, Bart A. — *Colucci, Blendow and Johnson, Inc.*
Combs, Stephen L. — *Juntunen-Combs-Poirier*
Conway, William P. — *Phillips Resource Group*
Cooke, Jeffrey R. — *Jonas, Walters & Assoc., Inc.*
Coulman, Karen — *CPS Inc.*
Cram, Noel — *R.P. Barone Associates*
Crath, Paul F. — *Price Waterhouse*
Crean, Jeremiah N. — *Bryant Research*
Cripe, Joyce — *Mixtec Group*
Critchley, Walter — *Cochran, Cochran & Yale, Inc.*
Crowell, Elizabeth — *H.M. Long International, Ltd.*
Crumpley, Jim — *Jim Crumpley & Associates*
Cruse, O.D. — *Spencer Stuart*
Czamanske, Paul W. — *Compass Group Ltd.*
Czepiel, Susan — *CPS Inc.*
Daily, John C. — *Handy HRM Corp.*
Daniels, Alfred — *Alfred Daniels & Associates*
Daniels, David — *Search West, Inc.*
Davis, Bert — *Bert Davis Executive Search, Inc.*
Davis, G. Gordon — *Davis & Company*
de Cholnoky, Andrea — *Spencer Stuart*
Deal, Leslie — *Bryant Research*
DeFrancesco, Mary Ellen — *The Onstott Group, Inc.*
DeGioia, Joseph — *JDG Associates, Ltd.*
Del Pino, William — *National Search, Inc.*
Delaney, Patrick — *Search West, Inc.*
DeLong, Art — *Richard Kader & Associates*
Desmond, Dennis — *Beall & Company, Inc.*
Diaz-Joslyn, Mabel — *Walker Communications*
DiMarchi, Paul — *DiMarchi Partners, Inc.*
Divine, Robert S. — *O'Shea, Divine & Company, Inc.*
Dixon, Aris — *CPS Inc.*
Dixon, C.R. — *A la carte International*
Domann, William A. — *The Domann Organization*
Dornblut, Cindy — *Ashton Computer Professionals Inc.*
Drexler, Robert — *Robert Drexler Associates, Inc.*
Dugan, John H. — *J.H. Dugan and Associates, Inc.*
Dulet, Donna — *Bryant Research*
Duley, Richard I. — *ARJay & Associates*
Dunman, Betsy L. — *Crawford & Crofford*
Dussick, Vince — *Dussick Management Associates*
Dwyer, Julie — *CPS Inc.*
Dykstra, Nicolette — *CPS Inc.*
Earle, Paul W. — *Spencer Stuart*
Eason, James — *JRL Executive Recruiters*
Eason, Larry E. — *JRL Executive Recruiters*
Ebeling, John A. — *Gilbert Tweed/INESA*
Edmond, Bruce — *Corporate Recruiters Ltd.*
Edwards, Verba L. — *Wing Tips & Pumps, Inc.*
Eggena, Roger — *Phillips Resource Group*
Einsele, Neil — *Agra Placements International Ltd.*
Eldredge, L. Lincoln — *Lamalie Amrop International*
England, Mark — *Austin-McGregor International*
Erickson, Elaine — *Kenzer Corp.*
Ervin, Darlene — *CPS Inc.*
Erwin, Lee — *Agra Placements International Ltd.*
Fair, Donna — *ProResource, Inc.*
Fancher, Robert L. — *Bason Associates Inc.*
Federman, Jack R. — *W.R. Rosato & Associates, Inc.*
Felderman, Kenneth I. — *Lamalie Amrop International*
Ferguson, Lauren — *Search West, Inc.*
Ferrara, David M. — *Intech Summit Group, Inc.*
Fill, Clifford G. — *D.S.A. - Dixie Search Associates*
Fill, Ellyn H. — *D.S.A. - Dixie Search Associates*
Fincher, Richard P. — *Phase II Management*
Fiore, Richard — *Search Consultants International, Inc.*
Fischer, Janet L. — *Boyden*
Fisher, Neal — *Fisher Personnel Management Services*
Flanders, Karen — *Advanced Information Management*
Flannery, Peter — *Jonas, Walters & Assoc., Inc.*
Fogarty, Michael — *CPS Inc.*
Folkerth, Gene — *Gene Folkerth & Associates, Inc.*
Follmer, Gary — *Agra Placements International Ltd.*

Fonfa, Ann — *S.R. Wolman Associates, Inc.*
Foreman, David C. — *Koontz, Jeffries & Associates, Inc.*
Fotia, Frank — *JDG Associates, Ltd.*
Fovhez, Michael J.P. — *Sloan & Associates*
Fowler, Jim — *First Search America, Inc.*
Fox, Lucie — *Allard Associates*
Foy, Richard — *Boyden*
Frazier, John — *Cochran, Cochran & Yale, Inc.*
French, William G. — *Preng & Associates, Inc.*
Friedman, Helen E. — *McCormack & Farrow*
Frock, Suzanne D. — *Brandjes Associates*
Fulton, Christine N. — *Highland Search Group, L.L.C.*
Furlong, James W. — *Furlong Search, Inc.*
Furlong, James W. — *Furlong Search, Inc.*
Furlong, James W. — *Furlong Search, Inc.*
Gaffney, Keith — *Gaffney Management Consultants*
Gaffney, William — *Gaffney Management Consultants*
Galante, Suzanne M. — *Vlcek & Company, Inc.*
Gale, Rhoda E. — *E.G. Jones Associates, Ltd.*
Gallin, Larry — *Gallin Associates*
Garfinkle, Steven M. — *Battalia Winston International*
Garrett, Donald L. — *Garrett Associates Inc.*
Garrett, Linda M. — *Garrett Associates Inc.*
Gauthier, Robert C. — *Columbia Consulting Group*
George, Delores F. — *Delores F. George Human Resource Management & Consulting Industry*
Gilchrist, Robert J. — *Horton International*
Giles, Joe L. — *Joe L. Giles and Associates, Inc.*
Gill, Patricia — *Columbia Consulting Group*
Gilmartin, William — *Hockett Associates, Inc.*
Gilmore, Lori — *CPS Inc.*
Gladstone, Arthur — *Executive Referral Services, Inc.*
Gloss, Frederick C. — *F. Gloss International*
Gold, Stacey — *Earley Kielty and Associates, Inc.*
Gold, Stanley — *Search West, Inc.*
Goldenberg, Susan — *Grant Cooper and Associates*
Gomez, Paul — *ARJay & Associates*
Goodman, Dawn M. — *Bason Associates Inc.*
Goodman, Victor — *Anderson Sterling Associates*
Gordon, Trina D. — *Boyden*
Gostyla, Rick — *Spencer Stuart*
Gould, Dana — *Logix, Inc.*
Gourlay, Debra — *Rene Plessner Associates, Inc.*
Graham, Dale — *CPS Inc.*
Granger, Lisa D. — *D.S.A. - Dixie Search Associates*
Grantham, John — *Grantham & Co., Inc.*
Grantham, Philip H. — *Columbia Consulting Group*
Gray, Mark — *Executive Referral Services, Inc.*
Grebenstein, Charles R. — *Skott/Edwards Consultants, Inc.*
Green, Jane — *Phillips Resource Group*
Greene, Frederick J. — *Boyden*
Grenier, Glorianne — *CPS Inc.*
Grzybowski, Jill — *CPS Inc.*
Gude, John S. — *Boyden*
Hall, Robert — *Don Richard Associates of Tidewater, Inc.*
Hanford, Michael — *Richard Kader & Associates*
Harbaugh, Paul J. — *International Management Advisors, Inc.*
Harbert, David O. — *Sweeney Harbert & Mummert, Inc.*
Hardison, Richard L. — *Hardison & Company*
Harris, Bruce — *ProResource, Inc.*
Harrison, Priscilla — *Phillips Resource Group*
Hart, Robert T. — *D.E. Foster Partners Inc.*
Harvey, Mike — *Advanced Executive Resources*
Hauck, Fred P. — *The Cassie Group*
Hauswirth, Jeffrey M. — *Spencer Stuart*
Havener, Donald Clarke — *The Abbott Group, Inc.*
Hawksworth, A. Dwight — *A.D. & Associates Executive Search, Inc.*
Haystead, Steve — *Advanced Executive Resources*
Hazerjian, Cynthia — *CPS Inc.*
Heafey, Bill — *CPS Inc.*
Hebel, Robert W. — *R.W. Hebel Associates*
Heintz, William — *Mixtec Group*
Hellinger, Audrey — *Martin H. Bauman Associates, Inc.*
Helminiak, Audrey — *Gaffney Management Consultants*
Heneghan, Donald A. — *Allerton Heneghan & O'Neill*
Herget, James P. — *Lamalie Amrop International*
Herman, Eugene J. — *Earley Kielty and Associates, Inc.*
Hetherman, Margaret F. — *Highland Search Group, L.L.C.*
Hicks, Albert M. — *Phillips Resource Group*
Hirsch, Julia C. — *Boyden*
Hockett, William — *Hockett Associates, Inc.*
Hodges, Robert J. — *Sampson Neill & Wilkins Inc.*
Hoffmeir, Patricia A. — *Gilbert Tweed/INESA*
Holden, Richard B. — *Ames Personnel Consultants, Inc.*
Holland, John H. — *Sloan & Associates*
Holmes, Lawrence J. — *Columbia Consulting Group*
Holt, Carol — *Bartholdi & Company, Inc.*
Holtz, Gene — *Agra Placements International Ltd.*
Hopgood, Earl — *JDG Associates, Ltd.*

Hoppert, Phil — *Wargo and Co., Inc.*
Houtz, Kenneth — *Houtz-Strawn Associates, Inc.*
Hucko, Donald S. — *Jonas, Walters & Assoc., Inc.*
Hudson, Reginald M. — *Search Bureau International*
Hunter, Gabe — *Phillips Resource Group*
Hutchison, Richard H. — *Rurak & Associates, Inc.*
Hutton, Thomas J. — *The Thomas Tucker Company*
Hykes, Don A. — *A.T. Kearney, Inc.*
Iacovelli, Heather — *CPS Inc.*
Iammatteo, Enzo — *Keith Bagg & Associates Inc.*
Imely, Larry — *Christian & Timbers*
Inzinna, Dennis — *AlternaStaff*
Irish, Alan — *CPS Inc.*
Irvine, Robert — *Keith Bagg & Associates Inc.*
Ives, Richard K. — *Wilkinson & Ives*
Jable, Maria C. — *Bryant Research*
Jablo, Steven — *Dieckmann & Associates, Ltd.*
Jackson, W.T. — *Sampson Neill & Wilkins Inc.*
Jacobs, Martin J. — *The Rubicon Group*
Jacobs, Mike — *Thorne, Brieger Associates Inc.*
Jaffe, Mark — *Wyatt & Jaffe*
James, Richard — *Criterion Executive Search, Inc.*
Jansen, Douglas L. — *Search Northwest Associates*
Joffe, Barry — *Bason Associates Inc.*
Johnson, David — *Gaffney Management Consultants*
Johnson, Douglas — *Quality Search*
Johnson, John W. — *Webb, Johnson Associates, Inc.*
Johnson, Michael E. — *Sharrow & Associates*
Johnson, Robert J. — *Quality Search*
Johnson, S. Hope — *The Interface Group, Ltd./Boyden*
Jones, Francis E. — *Earley Kielty and Associates, Inc.*
Jones, Ronald T. — *ARJay & Associates*
Joubert, Pierre E. — *Boyden*
Joyce, William J. — *The Guild Corporation*
Juelis, John J. — *Peeney Associates*
Kalinowski, David — *Jacobson Associates*
Kanrich, Susan Azaria — *AlternaStaff*
Kaplan, Gary — *Gary Kaplan & Associates*
Kaplan, Marc — *Gary Kaplan & Associates*
Kaptain, John — *Blau Kaptain Schroeder*
Karalis, William — *CPS Inc.*
Keesom, W. Peter — *Boyden/Zay & Company*
Kehoe, Mike — *CPS Inc.*
Kelly, Elizabeth Ann — *Wellington Management Group*
Kenzer, Robert D. — *Kenzer Corp.*
Kern, Jerry L. — *ADOW's Executeam*
Kerr, John — *Search West, Inc.*
Kielty, John L. — *Earley Kielty and Associates, Inc.*
Kilcoyne, Pat — *CPS Inc.*
Kiley, Phyllis — *National Search, Inc.*
Kinney, Carol — *Dussick Management Associates*
Kinser, Richard E. — *Richard Kinser & Associates*
Kirkpatrick, Robert L. — *Reese Associates*
Kishbaugh, Herbert S. — *Kishbaugh Associates International*
Kkorzyniewski, Nicole — *CPS Inc.*
Klages, Constance W. — *International Management Advisors, Inc.*
Klauck, James J. — *Horton International*
Klein, Gregory A. — *A.T. Kearney, Inc.*
Klumpjan, Sonja — *CPS Inc.*
Knisely, Gary — *Johnson Smith & Knisely Accord*
Knotts, Jerry — *Mixtec Group*
Kohn, Adam P. — *Christian & Timbers*
Kohonoski, Michael M. — *The Guild Corporation*
Koontz, Donald N. — *Koontz, Jeffries & Associates, Inc.*
Kopsick, Joseph M. — *Spencer Stuart*
Korkuch, Sandy — *Barone-O'Hara Associates*
Kossuth, David — *Kossuth & Associates, Inc.*
Kossuth, Jane — *Kossuth & Associates, Inc.*
Kreutz, Gary L. — *Kreutz Consulting Group, Inc.*
Kuhl, Teresa — *Don Richard Associates of Tampa, Inc.*
LaCharite, Danielle — *The Guild Corporation*
Laird, Cheryl — *CPS Inc.*
Laird, Meri — *Davidson, Laird & Associates*
Lanctot, William D. — *Corporate Resources Professional Placement*
Land, Shaun — *Dunhill Professional Search of Irvine, Inc.*
Langan, Marion — *Logix, Inc.*
Langer, Joel A. — *Langer Associates, Inc.*
Lasher, Charles M. — *Lasher Associates*
Lawrence, David — *Agra Placements International Ltd.*
Leahy, Jan — *CPS Inc.*
Lebo, Terry — *Agra Placements International Ltd.*
Leininger, Dennis — *Key Employment Services*
Lejeune, Jeanette — *F-O-R-T-U-N-E Personnel Consultants of Huntsville, Inc.*
Lenkaitis, Lewis F. — *A.T. Kearney, Inc.*
Leszynski, Edward — *ProResource, Inc.*
Lettrii, Mary — *BioQuest, Inc.*
Levine, Lois — *National Search, Inc.*

Linton, Leonard M. — *Byron Leonard International, Inc.*
Little, Gary — *Agra Placements International Ltd.*
Lofthouse, Cindy — *CPS Inc.*
Logan, Valarie A. — *D.S.A. - Dixie Search Associates*
Long, Helga — *H.M. Long International, Ltd.*
Long, Melanie — *National Search, Inc.*
LoPresto, Robert L. — *Rusher, Loscavio & LoPresto*
Loria, Frank — *Accounting Personnel Consultants*
Loscavio, J. Michael — *Rusher, Loscavio & LoPresto*
Lotufo, Donald A. — *D.A.L. Associates, Inc.*
Lotz, R. James — *International Management Advisors, Inc.*
Lovell, Robert W. — *John Kurosky & Associates*
Lucarelli, Joan — *The Onstott Group, Inc.*
Lucht, John — *The John Lucht Consultancy Inc.*
Lumsby, George N. — *International Management Advisors, Inc.*
Macdonald, G. William — *The Macdonald Group, Inc.*
MacGregor, Malcolm — *Boyden*
Mader, Stephen P. — *Christian & Timbers*
Maer, Harry — *Kenzer Corp.*
Maher, William J. — *Johnson Smith & Knisely Accord*
Malone, George V. — *Boyden*
Manassero, Henri J.P. — *International Management Advisors, Inc.*
Mancino, Gene — *Blau Kaptain Schroeder*
Mann, Carol — *Bryant Research*
Marchette, Steve — *Juntunen-Combs-Poirier*
Marino, Chester — *Cochran, Cochran & Yale, Inc.*
Marks, Ira — *Strategic Alternatives*
Marks, Russell E. — *Webb, Johnson Associates, Inc.*
Marra, John — *Marra Peters & Partners*
Marra, John — *Marra Peters & Partners*
Marshall, Gerald — *Blair/Tech Recruiters*
Martin, David — *The Guild Corporation*
Martin, Geary D. — *Boyden/Zay & Company*
Martin, Lynne Koll — *Boyden*
Maschal, Charles E. — *Maschal/Connors, Inc.*
Mason, William E. — *John Kurosky & Associates*
Massey, R. Bruce — *Bruce Massey & Partners Inc.*
Mather, David R. — *Christian & Timbers*
Mathias, William J. — *Preng & Associates, Inc.*
May, Peter — *Mixtec Group*
McAndrews, Kathy — *CPS Inc.*
McBride, Jonathan E. — *McBride Associates, Inc.*
McCallister, Richard A. — *Boyden*
McComas, Kelly E. — *The Guild Corporation*
McCormick, William J. — *The McCormick Group, Inc.*
McCreary, Charles — *Austin-McGregor International*
McDonald, Gary E. — *Agra Placements International Ltd.*
McDonnell, Julie — *Technical Personnel of Minnesota*
McFadden, Ashton S. — *Johnson Smith & Knisely Accord*
McGann, Paul L. — *The Cassie Group*
McGuire, Bud — *Search West, Inc.*
McIntyre, Joel — *Phillips Resource Group*
McManamon, Tim — *Rogers-McManamon Executive Search*
McNamara, Timothy C. — *Columbia Consulting Group*
McNichol, John — *McNichol Associates*
McNichols, Walter B. — *Gary Kaplan & Associates*
Meyer, Stacey — *Gary Kaplan & Associates*
Meyer, William — *Agra Placements International Ltd.*
Michaels, Joseph — *CPS Inc.*
Mierzwinski, John — *Industrial Recruiters Associates, Inc.*
Mikula, Linda — *Schweichler Associates, Inc.*
Miller, Elaine — *Search West, Inc.*
Miller, Russel E. — *ARJay & Associates*
Millonzi, Joel C. — *Johnson Smith & Knisely Accord*
Milton, Suzanne — *Marra Peters & Partners*
Mitchell, Norman F. — *A.T. Kearney, Inc.*
Mitros, George N. — *Mixtec Group*
Mockler, Nadine — *Part Time Resources, Inc.*
Mogul, Gene — *Mogul Consultants, Inc.*
Mohr, Brian — *CPS Inc.*
Mondragon, Philip — *Boyden*
Montgomery, Catherine C. — *Boyden*
Moore, Denise — *Jonas, Walters & Assoc., Inc.*
Moore, Mark — *Wheeler, Moore & Elam Co.*
Moore, Michael — *Agra Placements International Ltd.*
Moran, Gayle — *Dussick Management Associates*
Moran, Robert — *A.T. Kearney, Inc.*
Morgan, Gary — *National Search, Inc.*
Morgan, Richard S. — *Lovas Stanley/Paul Ray Berndtson Inc.*
Morgan, Vincent S. — *Johnson Smith & Knisely Accord*
Morris, Paul T. — *The Morris Group*
Morrison, Janis L. — *Garrett Associates Inc.*
Morton, Robert C. — *Morton, McCorkle & Associates, Inc.*
Morton, Sheila Ann — *Sloan & Associates*
Muendel, H. Edward — *Stanton Chase International*
Mulligan, Robert P. — *William Willis Worldwide Inc.*
Mummert, Dennis D. — *Sweeney Harbert & Mummert, Inc.*
Mursuli, Meredith — *Lasher Associates*
Mustin, Joyce M. — *J: Blakslee International, Ltd.*

Mydlach, Renee — *CPS Inc.*
Myrick, Marilou — *ProResource, Inc.*
Myrick, Marilou — *ProResource, Inc.*
Nagler, Leon G. — *Nagler, Robins & Poe, Inc.*
Nathanson, Barry F. — *Barry Nathanson Associates*
Nazzaro, Samuel G. — *Boyden*
Neill, Wellden K. — *Sampson Neill & Wilkins Inc.*
Newbold, Michael — *Agra Placements International Ltd.*
Newman, Lynn — *Kishbaugh Associates International*
Nicastro, Kelley P. — *A la carte International*
Nocero, John — *ProResource, Inc.*
Nordland, Martin N. — *Horton International*
Norman, Randy — *Austin-McGregor International*
Norsell, Paul E. — *Paul Norsell & Associates, Inc.*
Nymark, John — *NYCOR Search, Inc.*
Nymark, Paul — *NYCOR Search, Inc.*
O'Brien, John G. — *CanMed Consultants Inc.*
O'Brien, Maggie — *Advanced Information Management*
O'Connell, Mary — *CPS Inc.*
O'Donnell, Timothy W. — *Boyden*
O'Hara, Daniel M. — *Lynch Miller Moore Partners, Inc.*
O'Hara, James J. — *Barone-O'Hara Associates*
O'Reilly, Jack — *Catalyx Group*
Oakes, Meg B. — *D.P. Parker and Associates*
Oaks, Robert — *Search West, Inc.*
Ocon, Olga — *Busch International*
Ogden, Thomas H. — *The Ogdon Partnership*
Olsen, Carl — *A.T. Kearney, Inc.*
Oppenheim, Jeffrey — *Roth Young Personnel Service of Boston, Inc.*
Ottenritter, Chris — *CPS Inc.*
Page, Linda — *Jonas, Walters & Assoc., Inc.*
Page, Linda M. — *Wargo and Co., Inc.*
Palmer, Carlton A. — *Beall & Company, Inc.*
Palmlund, David W. — *Lamalie Amrop International*
Pappas, Jim — *Search Dynamics, Inc.*
Pappas, Timothy C. — *Jonas, Walters & Assoc., Inc.*
Parker, David P. — *D.P. Parker and Associates*
Parker, Murray B. — *The Borton Wallace Company*
Parr, James A. — *KPMG Management Consulting*
Parry, William H. — *Horton International*
Peckenpaugh, Ann D. — *Schweichler Associates, Inc.*
Pedley, Jill — *CPS Inc.*
Peeney, James D. — *Peeney Associates*
Pelisson, Charles — *Marra Peters & Partners*
Perez, Christina — *Orr Executive Search*
Perkins, Daphne — *CPS Inc.*
Perry, Wayne B. — *Bruce Massey & Partners Inc.*
Persky, Barry — *Barry Persky & Company, Inc.*
Peterson, John — *CPS Inc.*
Phillips, Richard K. — *Handy HRM Corp.*
Pickering, Dale — *Agri-Tech Personnel, Inc.*
Pitcher, Brian D. — *Skott/Edwards Consultants, Inc.*
Plessner, Rene — *Rene Plessner Associates, Inc.*
Plimpton, Ralph L. — *R L Plimpton Associates*
Poirier, Frank — *Juntunen-Combs-Poirier*
Pomerance, Mark — *CPS Inc.*
Porter, Albert — *The Experts*
Poster, Lawrence D. — *Catalyx Group*
Preng, David E. — *Preng & Associates, Inc.*
Price, Andrew G. — *The Thomas Tucker Company*
Proct, Nina — *Martin H. Bauman Associates, Inc.*
Prosser, Shane — *Search Consultants International, Inc.*
Raab, Julie — *Dunhill Professional Search of Irvine, Inc.*
Radawicz, Angela — *Mixtec Group*
Raheja, Marc C. — *CanMed Consultants Inc.*
Raiber, Laurie Altman — *The IMC Group of Companies Ltd.*
Rapoport, William — *Blair/Tech Recruiters*
Rathborne, Kenneth J. — *Blair/Tech Recruiters*
Ray, Marianne C. — *Callan Associates, Ltd.*
Raymond, Anne — *Anderson Sterling Associates*
Reddicks, Nate — *Search West, Inc.*
Redler, Rhonda — *National Search, Inc.*
Redwood, Guy W. — *Bruce Massey & Partners Inc.*
Reece, Christopher S. — *Reece & Mruk Partners*
Reed, Ruthann — *Spectra International Inc.*
Regehly, Herbert L. — *The IMC Group of Companies Ltd.*
Reiss, Matt — *National Search, Inc.*
Rendl, Ric — *CPS Inc.*
Rice, Douglas — *Agra Placements International Ltd.*
Richards, Robert A. — *Sloan & Associates*
Riederer, Larry — *CPS Inc.*
Rinaldi, Michael D. — *D.P. Parker and Associates*
Rivas, Alberto F. — *Boyden*
Rizzo, L. Donald — *R.P. Barone Associates*
Roberts, Kenneth — *The Rubicon Group*
Roberts, Mitch — *A.E. Feldman Associates*
Roberts, Scott B. — *Wargo and Co., Inc.*
Robinson, Bruce — *Bruce Robinson Associates*

Robison, John H. — *Robison & Associates*
Rodgers, John — *Agra Placements International Ltd.*
Rodgers, Kathi — *St. Lawrence International, Inc.*
Romanchek, Walter R. — *Wellington Management Group*
Romanello, Daniel P. — *Spencer Stuart*
Romaniw, Michael J. — *A la carte International*
Romaniw, Michael J. — *A la carte International*
Romaniw, Michael J. — *A la carte International*
Ropella, Patrick B. — *Ropella & Associates*
Rosato, William R. — *W.R. Rosato & Associates, Inc.*
Rosen, Salene — *Bryant Research*
Rosenthal, Charles — *National Search, Inc.*
Ross, Martin B. — *Ward Howell International, Inc.*
Rossi, Silvio — *Keith Bagg & Associates Inc.*
Roth, Robert J. — *Williams, Roth & Krueger Inc.*
Rothman, Jeffrey — *ProResource, Inc.*
Rudolph, Kenneth — *Kossuth & Associates, Inc.*
Rudzinsky, Howard — *Louis Rudzinsky Associates*
Rudzinsky, Jeffrey — *Louis Rudzinsky Associates*
Rurak, Zbigniew T. — *Rurak & Associates, Inc.*
Russell, Robin E. — *Kenzer Corp.*
Russell, Sam — *The Guild Corporation*
Sacerdote, John — *Raymond Karsan Associates*
Sahlas, Chrissy — *CPS Inc.*
Saletra, Andrew — *CPS Inc.*
Sampson, Martin C. — *Sampson Neill & Wilkins Inc.*
Sanders, Natalie — *CPS Inc.*
Sanders, Spencer H. — *Battalia Winston International*
Sangster, Jeffrey — *F-O-R-T-U-N-E Personnel Consultants of Manatee County*
Scalamera, Tom — *CPS Inc.*
Schaefer, Robert — *Search Enterprises, Inc.*
Scharett, Carol — *St. Lawrence International, Inc.*
Schedra, Sharon — *Earley Kielty and Associates, Inc.*
Schiavone, Mary Rose — *Canny, Bowen Inc.*
Schlpma, Christine — *Advanced Executive Resources*
Schmidt, Jeri E. — *Blake, Hansen & Nye, Limited*
Schmidt, Peter R. — *Boyden*
Schneider, Perry — *Agra Placements International Ltd.*
Schneiderman, Gerald — *Management Resource Associates, Inc.*
Schroeder, Lee — *Blau Kaptain Schroeder*
Schroeder, Steven J. — *Blau Kaptain Schroeder*
Schueneman, David — *CPS Inc.*
Schwam, Carol — *A.E. Feldman Associates*
Schweichler, Lee J. — *Schweichler Associates, Inc.*
Scrivines, Hank — *Search Northwest Associates*
Segal, Eric B. — *Kenzer Corp.*
Selker, Gregory L. — *Christian & Timbers*
Sennello, Gendra — *National Search, Inc.*
Sevilla, Claudio A. — *Crawford & Crofford*
Shapiro, Elaine — *CPS Inc.*
Shattuck, Merrill B. — *M.B. Shattuck and Associates, Inc.*
Shea, John — *ALTCO Temporary Services*
Shea, John — *The ALTCO Group*
Shelton, Sandra — *National Search, Inc.*
Sher, Lawrence — *M.A. Churchill & Associates, Inc.*
Sherwin, Thomas — *Barone-O'Hara Associates*
Shoemaker, Larry C. — *Shoemaker & Associates*
Shultz, Deborah M. — *Blau Kaptain Schroeder*
Sibbald, John R. — *John Sibbald Associates, Inc.*
Signer, Julie — *CPS Inc.*
Siker, Paul W. — *The Guild Corporation*
Silcott, Marvin L. — *Marvin L. Silcott & Associates, Inc.*
Sill, Igor M. — *Geneva Group International*
Sill, Igor M. — *Geneva Group International*
Silver, Lee A. — *L.A. Silver Associates, Inc.*
Sjogren, Dennis — *Agra Placements International Ltd.*
Skunda, Donna M. — *Allerton Heneghan & O'Neill*
Slater, Ronald E. — *A.T. Kearney, Inc.*
Slaughter, Katherine T. — *Compass Group Ltd.*
Slayton, Richard C. — *Slayton International, Inc.*
Sloan, Michael D. — *Sloan & Associates*
Smith, Adam M. — *The Abbott Group, Inc.*
Smith, Cheryl — *ProResource, Inc.*
Smith, David P. — *Smith & Latterell (HRS, Inc.)*
Smith, Herman M. — *Herman Smith Executive Initiatives Inc.*
Snelgrove, Geiger — *National Search, Inc.*
Snyder, James F. — *Snyder & Company*
Soggs, Cheryl Pavick — *A.T. Kearney, Inc.*
Sola, George L. — *A.T. Kearney, Inc.*
Solters, Jeanne — *The Guild Corporation*
Sowerbutt, Richard S. — *Hite Executive Search*
Spanninger, Mark J. — *The Guild Corporation*
Spicher, John — *M.A. Churchill & Associates, Inc.*
Spiegel, Gay — *L.A. Silver Associates, Inc.*
Spriggs, Robert D. — *Spriggs & Company, Inc.*
Sprowls, Linda — *Allard Associates*
Staats, Dave — *Southwestern Professional Services*
Stack, James K. — *Boyden*

Stanley, Paul R.A. — *Lovas Stanley/Paul Ray Berndtson Inc.*
Stark, Jeff — *Thorne, Brieger Associates Inc.*
Stein, Terry W. — *Stewart, Stein and Scott, Ltd.*
Stenholm, Gilbert R. — *Spencer Stuart*
Stephenson, Don L. — *Ells Personnel System Inc.*
Sterling, Jay — *Earley Kielty and Associates, Inc.*
Stern, Stephen — *CPS Inc.*
Sterner, Doug — *CPS Inc.*
Stevenson, Terry — *Bartholdi & Company, Inc.*
Stewart, Jeffrey O. — *Stewart, Stein and Scott, Ltd.*
Stewart, Ross M. — *Human Resources Network Partners Inc.*
Stiles, Judy — *MedQuest Associates*
Stinson, R.J. — *Sampson Neill & Wilkins Inc.*
Stone, Susan L. — *Stone Enterprises Ltd.*
Stouffer, Dale — *Agra Placements International Ltd.*
Strawn, William — *Houtz-Strawn Associates, Inc.*
Stricker, Sidney G. — *Stricker & Zagor*
Strom, Mark N. — *Search Advisors International Corp.*
Strong, Duane K. — *Executive Resource, Inc.*
Stubbs, Judy N. — *Lamalie Amrop International*
Sturtz, James W. — *Compass Group Ltd.*
Sullivan, James — *Search Enterprises, Inc.*
Sullivan, Kay — *Rusher, Loscavio & LoPresto*
Sumurdy, Melinda — *Kenzer Corp.*
Sur, William K. — *Canny, Bowen Inc.*
Swanson, Dick — *Raymond Karsan Associates*
Swatts, Stone — *F-O-R-T-U-N-E Personnel Consultants of Huntsville, Inc.*
Sweeney, James W. — *Sweeney Harbert & Mummert, Inc.*
Sweeney, Sean K. — *Bonifield Associates*
Taft, Steven D. — *The Guild Corporation*
Teinert, Jay — *Damon & Associates, Inc.*
Templin, Robert E. — *Gilbert Tweed/INESA*
Tholke, William E. — *Canny, Bowen Inc.*
Thomas, Cheryl M. — *CPS Inc.*
Thomas, Donald — *Mixtec Group*
Thomas, Kim — *CPS Inc.*
Thompson, Kenneth L. — *McCormack & Farrow*
To, Raymond — *Corporate Recruiters Ltd.*
Tokarcik, Patricia — *ProResource, Inc.*
Tovrog, Dan — *CPS Inc.*
Tracey, Jack — *Management Assistance Group, Inc.*
Trosin, Walter R. — *Johnson Smith & Knisely Accord*
Trott, Kathryn — *Allard Associates*
Truemper, Dean — *CPS Inc.*
Tucker, Thomas A. — *The Thomas Tucker Company*
Tullberg, Tina — *CPS Inc.*
Tweed, Janet — *Gilbert Tweed/INESA*
Tyson, Richard L. — *Bonifield Associates*
Unger, Paul T. — *A.T. Kearney, Inc.*
Unger, Stephen A. — *Spencer Stuart*
Vachon, David A. — *McNichol Associates*
Van Steenkiste, Julie — *Davidson, Laird & Associates*
Vann, Dianne — *The Button Group*
Vergara, Gail H. — *Spencer Stuart*
Virgili, Franca — *Johnson Smith & Knisely Accord*
Visnich, L. Christine — *Bason Associates Inc.*
Vlcek, Thomas J. — *Vlcek & Company, Inc.*
Wakefield, Scott — *National Search, Inc.*
Waldoch, D. Mark — *Barnes Development Group, LLC*
Walker, Martin S. — *Walker Communications*
Walters, William F. — *Jonas, Walters & Assoc., Inc.*
Ware, John C. — *Spencer Stuart*
Wargo, G. Rick — *A.T. Kearney, Inc.*
Waters, Peter D. — *John Kurosky & Associates*
Wayne, Cary S. — *ProSearch Inc.*
Webb, George H. — *Webb, Johnson Associates, Inc.*
Weber, Jurgen — *BioQuest, Inc.*
Wein, Michael S. — *InterimManagement Solutions, Inc.*
Wein, Michael S. — *Media Management Resources, Inc.*
Wein, William — *Media Management Resources, Inc.*
Weisler, Nancy — *National Search, Inc.*
Weiss, Jeffrey — *Search West, Inc.*
Weissman-Rosenthal, Abbe — *ALW Research International*
Weisz, Laura — *Anderson Sterling Associates*
Werner, Bonnie — *H.M. Long International, Ltd.*
Westerfield, Putney — *Boyden*
White, Jonathan O. — *The Badger Group*
White, William C. — *Venture Resources Inc.*
Whiting, Anthony — *Johnson Smith & Knisely Accord*
Wilkins, Walter K. — *Sampson Neill & Wilkins Inc.*
Wilkinson, Barbara — *Beall & Company, Inc.*
Wilkinson, William R. — *Wilkinson & Ives*
Williams, Gary L. — *Barnes Development Group, LLC*
Williams, Harry D. — *Jacobson Associates*
Williams, Roger K. — *Williams, Roth & Krueger Inc.*
Willis, William H. — *William Willis Worldwide Inc.*
Willner, Nannette — *S.R. Wolman Associates, Inc.*
Winitz, Joel — *GSW Consulting Group, Inc.*

Cannavo, Louise — *The Whitney Group*
Cargo, Catherine — *MSI International*
Carideo, Joseph — *Thorndike Deland Associates*
Carpenter, Harold G. — *MSI International*
Carter, Christine C. — *Health Care Dimensions*
Casal, Daniel G. — *Bonifield Associates*
Casey, Jean — *Peter W. Ambler Company*
Cassie, Ronald L. — *The Cassie Group*
Cattanach, Bruce B. — *Horton International*
Causey, Andrea C. — *MSI International*
Cavolina, Michael — *Carver Search Consultants*
Cavriani, Randolph — *Search West, Inc.*
Celenza, Catherine — *CPS Inc.*
Chappell, Peter — *The Bankers Group*
Chatterjie, Alok — *MSI International*
Chavous, C. Crawford — *Phillips Resource Group*
Cherbonnier, L. Michael — *TCG International, Inc.*
Cherbonnier, L. Michael — *The Cherbonnier Group, Inc.*
Christenson, H. Alan — *Christenson & Hutchison*
Christian, Jeffrey E. — *Christian & Timbers*
Christiansen, Amy — *CPS Inc.*
Christiansen, Doug — *CPS Inc.*
Citarella, Richard A. — *A.T. Kearney, Inc.*
Citrin, Lea — *K.L. Whitney Company*
Cizek, John T. — *Cizek Associates, Inc.*
Cizek, Marti J. — *Cizek Associates, Inc.*
Clanton, Diane — *Clanton & Co.*
Clark, Evan — *The Whitney Group*
Clark, James — *CPS Inc.*
Clark, Steven — *D.A. Kreuter Associates, Inc.*
Clauhsen, Elizabeth A. — *Savoy Partners, Ltd.*
Cleary, Thomas R. — *ARJay & Associates*
Close, E. Wade — *Boyden*
Cochran, Hale — *Fenwick Partners*
Coffman, Brian — *Kossuth & Associates, Inc.*
Cohen, Michael R. — *Intech Summit Group, Inc.*
Cohen, Robert C. — *Intech Summit Group, Inc.*
Colasanto, Frank M. — *W.R. Rosato & Associates, Inc.*
Cole, Elizabeth — *MSI International*
Collard, Joseph A. — *Spencer Stuart*
Collier, David — *Parfitt Recruiting and Consulting/PRO TEM*
Colling, Douglas — *KPMG Management Consulting*
Colucci, Bart A. — *Colucci, Blendow and Johnson, Inc.*
Combs, Stephen L. — *Juntunen-Combs-Poirier*
Conner, John — *Flex Execs Management Solutions*
Connor, Michele — *Abraham & London, Ltd.*
Conway, William P. — *Phillips Resource Group*
Cooke, Jeffrey R. — *Jonas, Walters & Assoc., Inc.*
Cooke, Katherine H. — *Horton International*
Cornehlsen, James H. — *Lamalie Amrop International*
Corrigan, Gerald F. — *The Corrigan Group*
Costa, Cynthia A. — *MSI International*
Coston, Bruce G. — *MSI International*
Coulman, Karen — *CPS Inc.*
Cox, James O. — *MSI International*
Cox, William — *E.J. Ashton & Associates, Ltd.*
Cragg, Barbara R. — *Southwestern Professional Services*
Crane, Howard C. — *Chartwell Partners International, Inc.*
Crath, Paul F. — *Price Waterhouse*
Creger, Elizabeth — *Search West, Inc.*
Critchley, Walter — *Cochran, Cochran & Yale, Inc.*
Crowder, Edward W. — *Crowder & Company*
Crownover, Kathryn L. — *MSI International*
Cruse, O.D. — *Spencer Stuart*
Crystal, Jonathan A. — *Spencer Stuart*
Cunningham, Robert Y. — *Goodrich & Sherwood Associates, Inc.*
Cuomo, Frank — *Frank Cuomo and Associates, Inc.*
Currie, Lawrence S. — *MSI International*
Czamanske, Paul W. — *Compass Group Ltd.*
Czepiel, Susan — *CPS Inc.*
Dalton, Bret — *Robert W. Dingman Company, Inc.*
Dalton, David R. — *MSI International*
Damon, Richard E. — *Damon & Associates, Inc.*
Damon, Robert A. — *Spencer Stuart*
Daniels, Alfred — *Alfred Daniels & Associates*
Daniels, David — *Search West, Inc.*
Danoff, Audrey — *Don Richard Associates of Tidewater, Inc.*
Darnell, Nadine — *Brennan Associates*
Davis, Bernel — *MSI International*
Davis, Bert — *Bert Davis Executive Search, Inc.*
Davis, G. Gordon — *Davis & Company*
Davison, Patricia E. — *Lamalie Amrop International*
de Bardin, Francesca — *F.L. Taylor & Company, Inc.*
de Cholnoky, Andrea — *Spencer Stuart*
de Palacios, Jeannette C. — *J. Palacios & Associates, Inc.*
de Tuede, Catherine — *Thomas A. Byrnes Associates*
Debrueys, Lee G. — *MSI International*
DeCorrevont, James — *DeCorrevont & Associates*
DeCorrevont, James — *DeCorrevont & Associates*

Deering, Joseph — *U.S. Envirosearch*
DeFrancesco, Mary Ellen — *The Onstott Group, Inc.*
DeHart, Donna — *Tower Consultants, Ltd.*
Del Pino, William — *National Search, Inc.*
Del'Ange, Gabrielle N. — *MSI International*
Delaney, Patrick J. — *Sensible Solutions, Inc.*
DeLong, Art — *Richard Kader & Associates*
deMartino, Cathy — *Lucas Associates*
Demchak, James P. — *Sandhurst Associates*
Densmore, Geraldine — *Michael Stern Associates Inc.*
Desgrosellier, Gary P. — *Personnel Unlimited/Executive Search*
Desmond, Dennis — *Beall & Company, Inc.*
Diaz-Joslyn, Mabel — *Walker Communications*
Dietz, David S. — *MSI International*
DiMarchi, Paul — *DiMarchi Partners, Inc.*
Dingman, Bruce — *Robert W. Dingman Company, Inc.*
Dingman, Robert W. — *Robert W. Dingman Company, Inc.*
DiSalvo, Fred — *The Cambridge Group Ltd*
Divine, Robert S. — *O'Shea, Divine & Company, Inc.*
Dixon, Aris — *CPS Inc.*
Doele, Donald C. — *Goodrich & Sherwood Associates, Inc.*
Donahie, Stephen — *Search West, Inc.*
Dornblut, Cindy — *Ashton Computer Professionals Inc.*
Dotson, M. Ileen — *Dotson & Associates*
Dougherty, Bridget L. — *Wellington Management Group*
Dougherty, Janice — *The McCormick Group, Inc.*
Dow, Lori — *Davidson, Laird & Associates*
Dowell, Mary K. — *Professional Search Associates*
Dromeshauser, Peter — *Dromeshauser Associates*
Drury, James J. — *Spencer Stuart*
Dugan, John H. — *J.H. Dugan and Associates, Inc.*
Duggan, James P. — *Slayton International, Inc.*
Duley, Richard I. — *ARJay & Associates*
Dunlop, Eric — *Southwestern Professional Services*
Dunman, Betsy L. — *Crawford & Crofford*
Dussick, Vince — *Dussick Management Associates*
Dwyer, Julie — *CPS Inc.*
Dykstra, Nicolette — *CPS Inc.*
Earle, Paul W. — *Spencer Stuart*
Eatmon, Michael — *U.S. Envirosearch*
Ebeling, John A. — *Gilbert Tweed/INESA*
Eden, Dianne — *Steeple Associates*
Edmond, Bruce — *Corporate Recruiters Ltd.*
Edwards, Dorothy — *MSI International*
Edwards, Verba L. — *Wing Tips & Pumps, Inc.*
Eggena, Roger — *Phillips Resource Group*
Eibeler, C. — *Amherst Personnel Group Inc.*
Einsele, Neil — *Agra Placements International Ltd.*
Eldredge, L. Lincoln — *Lamalie Amrop International*
Elliott, Mark P. — *Lamalie Amrop International*
Ellis, William — *Interspace Interactive Inc.*
Emmott, Carol B. — *Spencer Stuart*
England, Mark — *Austin-McGregor International*
Engman, Steven T. — *Lamalie Amrop International*
Enns, George — *The Enns Partners Inc.*
Erickson, Elaine — *Kenzer Corp.*
Erstling, Gregory — *Normyle/Erstling Health Search Group*
Ervin, Darlene — *CPS Inc.*
Ervin, James — *Search West, Inc.*
Erwin, Lee — *Agra Placements International Ltd.*
Eton, Steven — *Search West, Inc.*
Eustis, Lucy R. — *MSI International*
Ezersky, Jane E. — *Highland Search Group, L.L.C.*
Faber, Jill — *A.T. Kearney, Inc.*
Falk, John — *D.S. Allen Associates, Inc.*
Fancher, Robert L. — *Bason Associates Inc.*
Farley, Leon A. — *Leon A. Farley Associates*
Farnsworth, John A. — *Pearson, Caldwell & Farnsworth, Inc.*
Farrow, Jerry M. — *McCormack & Farrow*
Federman, Jack R. — *W.R. Rosato & Associates, Inc.*
Feldman, Abe — *A.E. Feldman Associates*
Ferneborg, Jay W. — *Ferneborg & Associates, Inc.*
Ferneborg, John R. — *Ferneborg & Associates, Inc.*
Ferrari, S. Jay — *Ferrari Search Group*
Feyder, Michael — *A.T. Kearney, Inc.*
Fill, Clifford G. — *D.S.A. - Dixie Search Associates*
Fill, Ellyn H. — *D.S.A. - Dixie Search Associates*
Fincher, Richard P. — *Phase II Management*
Fischer, Janet L. — *Boyden*
Fishback, Joren — *Derek Associates, Inc.*
Fisher, Neal — *Fisher Personnel Management Services*
Fitch, Lori — *R. Parker and Associates, Inc.*
Fixler, Eugene — *Ariel Recruitment Associates*
Flanagan, John — *Lamalie Amrop International*
Flanagan, Robert M. — *Robert M. Flanagan & Associates, Ltd.*
Flannery, Peter — *Jonas, Walters & Assoc., Inc.*
Fleming, Marco — *MSI International*
Flora, Dodi — *Crawford & Crofford*
Flowers, John E. — *Balfour Associates*

Fogarty, Michael — *CPS Inc.*
Follmer, Gary — *Agra Placements International Ltd.*
Fonfa, Ann — *S.R. Wolman Associates, Inc.*
Foreman, David C. — *Koontz, Jeffries & Associates, Inc.*
Forest, Adam — *McCormack & Associates*
Forman, Donald R. — *Stanton Chase International*
Foster, Torrey N. — *Lynch Miller Moore Partners, Inc.*
Fotino, Anne — *Normyle/Erstling Health Search Group*
Fovhez, Michael J.P. — *Sloan & Associates*
Fowler, Jim — *First Search America, Inc.*
Fox, Lucie — *Allard Associates*
Foy, Richard — *Boyden*
Francis, Joseph — *Hospitality International*
Frazier, John — *Cochran, Cochran & Yale, Inc.*
Fredericks, Ward A. — *Mixtec Group*
French, Ted — *Spectra International Inc.*
French, William G. — *Preng & Associates, Inc.*
Friedman, Helen E. — *McCormack & Farrow*
Fulton, Christine N. — *Highland Search Group, L.L.C.*
Furlong, James W. — *Furlong Search, Inc.*
Furlong, James W. — *Furlong Search, Inc.*
Furlong, James W. — *Furlong Search, Inc.*
Gabel, Gregory N. — *Canny, Bowen Inc.*
Gaines, Jay — *Jay Gaines & Company, Inc.*
Galante, Suzanne M. — *Vlcek & Company, Inc.*
Gale, Rhoda E. — *E.G. Jones Associates, Ltd.*
Galinski, Paul — *E.J. Ashton & Associates, Ltd.*
Gallagher, David W. — *Lamalie Amrop International*
Gallagher, Terence M. — *Battalia Winston International*
Gallin, Larry — *Gallin Associates*
Galvani, Frank J. — *MSI International*
Garcia, Samuel K. — *Southwestern Professional Services*
Garfinkle, Steven M. — *Battalia Winston International*
Garrett, Donald L. — *Garrett Associates Inc.*
Garrett, Linda M. — *Garrett Associates Inc.*
Gelfman, David — *Career Management International*
George, Delores F. — *Delores F. George Human Resource Management & Consulting Industry*
Gerevas, Ronald E. — *Spencer Stuart*
Gerevas, Ronald E. — *Spencer Stuart*
Germain, Valerie — *Jay Gaines & Company, Inc.*
Giacalone, Louis — *Allard Associates*
Gibbs, John S. — *Spencer Stuart*
Gilbert, Elaine — *Herbert Mines Associates, Inc.*
Gilbert, Jerry — *Gilbert & Van Campen International*
Gilbert, Robert — *U.S. Envirosearch*
Gill, Patricia — *Columbia Consulting Group*
Gillespie, Thomas — *Professional Search Consultants*
Gilmartin, William — *Hockett Associates, Inc.*
Gilmore, Lori — *CPS Inc.*
Gladstone, Arthur — *Executive Referral Services, Inc.*
Gladstone, Martin J. — *MSI International*
Glancey, Thomas F. — *Gordon Wahls Company*
Gloss, Frederick C. — *F. Gloss International*
Goar, Duane R. — *Sandhurst Associates*
Goedtke, Steven — *Southwestern Professional Services*
Gold, Stacey — *Earley Kielty and Associates, Inc.*
Goldberg, Bret — *Roth Young Personnel Service of Boston, Inc.*
Goldenberg, Sheryl — *Neail Behringer Consultants*
Goldenberg, Susan — *Grant Cooper and Associates*
Goldsmith, Fred J. — *Fred J. Goldsmith Associates*
Goldstein, Gary — *The Whitney Group*
Goldstein, Steve — *R. Parker and Associates, Inc.*
Gomez, Paul — *ARJay & Associates*
Goodman, Dawn M. — *Bason Associates Inc.*
Goodman, Victor — *Anderson Sterling Associates*
Gordon, Gerald L. — *E.G. Jones Associates, Ltd.*
Gordon, Trina D. — *Boyden*
Gostyla, Rick — *Spencer Stuart*
Gourlay, Debra — *Rene Plessner Associates, Inc.*
Gow, Roderick C. — *Lamalie Amrop International*
Grady, James — *Search West, Inc.*
Graham, Dale — *CPS Inc.*
Granger, Lisa D. — *D.S.A. - Dixie Search Associates*
Grantham, John — *Grantham & Co., Inc.*
Gray, Mark — *Executive Referral Services, Inc.*
Greebe, Neil — *Flowers & Associates*
Green, Jane — *Phillips Resource Group*
Greene, Frederick J. — *Boyden*
Grenier, Glorianne — *CPS Inc.*
Grey, Cort — *The McCormick Group, Inc.*
Groover, David — *MSI International*
Gross, Howard — *Herbert Mines Associates, Inc.*
Grzybowski, Jill — *CPS Inc.*
Gude, John S. — *Boyden*
Gulley, Marylyn — *MSI International*
Haas, Margaret P. — *Haas International, Inc.*
Hailey, H.M. — *Damon & Associates, Inc.*
Hall, Peter V. — *Chartwell Partners International, Inc.*

Hallock, Peter B. — *Goodrich & Sherwood Associates, Inc.*
Halyburton, Robert R. — *The Halyburton Co., Inc.*
Hamdan, Mark — *Careernet of Florida, Inc.*
Hanford, Michael — *Richard Kader & Associates*
Hanley, Maureen E. — *Gilbert Tweed/INESA*
Hansen, Ty E. — *Blake, Hansen & Nye, Limited*
Hanson, Carrie — *U.S. Envirosearch*
Hanson, Grant M. — *Goodrich & Sherwood Associates, Inc.*
Harbert, David O. — *Sweeney Harbert & Mummert, Inc.*
Hardison, Richard L. — *Hardison & Company*
Harmon, Tony — *Mixtec Group*
Harris, Julia — *The Whitney Group*
Harrison, Joel — *D.A. Kreuter Associates, Inc.*
Harrison, Priscilla — *Phillips Resource Group*
Harshman, Donald — *The Stevenson Group of New Jersey*
Hart, Robert T. — *D.E. Foster Partners Inc.*
Harvey, Jill — *MSI International*
Harvey, Joy — *Key Employment Services*
Harvey, Mike — *Advanced Executive Resources*
Harvey, Richard — *Price Waterhouse*
Haughton, Michael — *DeFrain, Mayer, Lee & Burgess LLC*
Hauser, Martha — *Spencer Stuart*
Hauswirth, Jeffrey M. — *Spencer Stuart*
Havener, Donald Clarke — *The Abbott Group, Inc.*
Hawksworth, A. Dwight — *A.D. & Associates Executive Search, Inc.*
Hayes, Stacy — *The McCormick Group, Inc.*
Haystead, Steve — *Advanced Executive Resources*
Hazelton, Lisa M. — *Health Care Dimensions*
Hazerjian, Cynthia — *CPS Inc.*
Heafey, Bill — *CPS Inc.*
Healey, Joseph T. — *Highland Search Group, L.L.C.*
Hebel, Robert W. — *R.W. Hebel Associates*
Heiken, Barbara E. — *Randell-Heiken, Inc.*
Heintz, William — *Mixtec Group*
Heiser, Charles S. — *The Cassie Group*
Hellinger, Audrey — *Martin H. Bauman Associates, Inc.*
Helminiak, Audrey — *Gaffney Management Consultants*
Henard, John B. — *Lamalie Amrop International*
Hennig, Sandra M. — *MSI International*
Herget, James P. — *Lamalie Amrop International*
Herman, Eugene J. — *Earley Kielty and Associates, Inc.*
Hetherman, Margaret F. — *Highland Search Group, L.L.C.*
Hicks, Albert M. — *Phillips Resource Group*
Hicks, James L. — *MSI International*
Hill, Emery — *MSI International*
Hillen, Skip — *The McCormick Group, Inc.*
Hilyard, Paul J. — *MSI International*
Hirsch, Julia C. — *Boyden*
Hnatuik, Ivan — *Corporate Recruiters Ltd.*
Hockett, William — *Hockett Associates, Inc.*
Hodges, Robert J. — *Sampson Neill & Wilkins Inc.*
Hoevel, Michael J. — *Poirier, Hoevel & Co.*
Holden, Richard B. — *Ames Personnel Consultants, Inc.*
Holland, John H. — *Sloan & Associates*
Hollins, Howard D. — *MSI International*
Holmes, Lawrence J. — *Columbia Consulting Group*
Holt, Carol — *Bartholdi & Company, Inc.*
Holtz, Gene — *Agra Placements International Ltd.*
Holzberger, Georges L. — *Highland Search Group, L.L.C.*
Hoppert, Phil — *Wargo and Co., Inc.*
Horner, Gregory — *Corporate Recruiters Ltd.*
Houchins, William N. — *Christian & Timbers*
Howard, Jill — *Health Care Dimensions*
Hoyda, Louis A. — *Thorndike Deland Associates*
Hucko, Donald S. — *Jonas, Walters & Assoc., Inc.*
Hudson, Reginald M. — *Search Bureau International*
Hughes, Cathy N. — *The Ogdon Partnership*
Hughes, David — *Southwestern Professional Services*
Hughes, Donald J. — *Hughes & Company*
Humphrey, Joan — *Abraham & London, Ltd.*
Hunt, Thomas — *MSI International*
Hunter, Gabe — *Phillips Resource Group*
Hunter, Sue J. — *Robison & Associates*
Hutchins, Richard H. — *Rurak & Associates, Inc.*
Hutchison, William K. — *Christenson & Hutchison*
Hwang, Yvette — *MSI International*
Hyde, Mark D. — *MSI International*
Hyde, W. Jerry — *Hyde Danforth Wold & Co.*
Hykes, Don A. — *A.T. Kearney, Inc.*
Iacovelli, Heather — *CPS Inc.*
Iammatteo, Enzo — *Keith Bagg & Associates Inc.*
Iannacone, Kelly — *Abraham & London, Ltd.*
Imely, Larry — *Christian & Timbers*
Inguagiato, Gregory — *MSI International*
Irish, Alan — *CPS Inc.*
Irvine, Robert — *Keith Bagg & Associates Inc.*
Issacs, Judith A. — *Grant Cooper and Associates*
Ives, Richard K. — *Wilkinson & Ives*
Ivey, Deborah M. — *MSI International*

Jackson, W.T. — *Sampson Neill & Wilkins Inc.*
Jacobs, Judith — *The Rubicon Group*
Jacobs, Mike — *Thorne, Brieger Associates Inc.*
James, Allison A. — *MSI International*
James, Bruce — *Roberson and Company*
Janis, Laurence — *Integrated Search Solutions Group, LLC*
Jensen, Debra — *Flex Execs Management Solutions*
Jernigan, Alice — *Ariel Recruitment Associates*
Jernigan, Susan N. — *Sockwell & Associates*
Joffe, Barry — *Bason Associates Inc.*
Johnson, David — *Gaffney Management Consultants*
Johnson, Douglas — *Quality Search*
Johnson, Janet — *Normyle/Erstling Health Search Group*
Johnson, John W. — *Webb, Johnson Associates, Inc.*
Johnson, Julie — *International Staffing Consultants, Inc.*
Johnson, Kathleen A. — *Barton Raben, Inc.*
Johnson, Priscilla — *The Johnson Group, Inc.*
Johnson, Robert J. — *Quality Search*
Johnson, Stephanie — *Carver Search Consultants*
Jones, Francis E. — *Earley Kielty and Associates, Inc.*
Jones, Gary — *BGB Associates*
Jones, Jonathan C. — *The Ogdon Partnership*
Jones, Ronald T. — *ARJay & Associates*
Joubert, Pierre E. — *Boyden*
Judy, William — *Search West, Inc.*
Juelis, John J. — *Peeney Associates*
Kader, Richard — *Richard Kader & Associates*
Kaiser, Donald J. — *Dunhill Search International*
Kalinowski, David — *Jacobson Associates*
Kanal, David S. — *Johnson Smith & Knisely Accord*
Kanovsky, Gerald — *Career Consulting Group, Inc.*
Kanovsky, Marlene — *Career Consulting Group, Inc.*
Kaplan, Gary — *Gary Kaplan & Associates*
Kaplan, Marc — *Gary Kaplan & Associates*
Karalis, William — *CPS Inc.*
Kassouf, Connie — *The Whitney Group*
Katz, Robert L. — *MSI International*
Keesom, W. Peter — *Boyden/Zay & Company*
Kehoe, Mike — *CPS Inc.*
Keller, Barbara — *Barton Raben, Inc.*
Kelly, Elizabeth Ann — *Wellington Management Group*
Kelly, Susan D. — *S.D. Kelly & Associates, Inc.*
Kennedy, Michael — *The Danbrook Group, Inc.*
Kenzer, Robert D. — *Kenzer Corp.*
Kershaw, Lisa — *Tanton Mitchell/Paul Ray Berndtson*
Kettwig, David A. — *A.T. Kearney, Inc.*
Kick, James W. — *The Prairie Group*
Kielty, John L. — *Earley Kielty and Associates, Inc.*
Kilcoyne, Pat — *CPS Inc.*
Kilcullen, Brian A. — *D.A. Kreuter Associates, Inc.*
Kiley, Phyllis — *National Search, Inc.*
King, Bill — *The McCormick Group, Inc.*
King, Joyce L. — *MSI International*
Kinney, Carol — *Dussick Management Associates*
Kirkpatrick, Robert L. — *Reese Associates*
Kishbaugh, Herbert S. — *Kishbaugh Associates International*
Kkorzyniewski, Nicole — *CPS Inc.*
Klauck, James J. — *Horton International*
Klein, Gary I. — *Johnson Smith & Knisely Accord*
Klein, Gregory A. — *A.T. Kearney, Inc.*
Klopfenstein, Edward L. — *Crowder & Company*
Klumpjan, Sonja — *CPS Inc.*
Knisely, Gary — *Johnson Smith & Knisely Accord*
Kohn, Adam P. — *Christian & Timbers*
Kolke, Rick — *Richard, Wayne and Roberts*
Koontz, Donald N. — *Koontz, Jeffries & Associates, Inc.*
Kopsick, Joseph M. — *Spencer Stuart*
Korkuch, Sandy — *Barone-O'Hara Associates*
Kors, R. Paul — *Kors Montgomery International*
Kossuth, David — *Kossuth & Associates, Inc.*
Kossuth, Jane — *Kossuth & Associates, Inc.*
Kotick, Madeline — *The Stevenson Group of New Jersey*
Kreps, Charles D. — *Normyle/Erstling Health Search Group*
Kreuter, Daniel A. — *D.A. Kreuter Associates, Inc.*
Kring, Kenneth L. — *Spencer Stuart*
Krohn, Eileen — *The Stevenson Group of New Jersey*
Krostangel, Thomas — *Personnel Unlimited/Executive Search*
Kuper, Keith D. — *Christenson & Hutchison*
Laba, Marvin — *Marvin Laba & Associates*
Laba, Stuart M. — *Marvin Laba & Associates*
LaFaye, Susan — *MSI International*
Laird, Cheryl — *CPS Inc.*
Laird, Meri — *Davidson, Laird & Associates*
Lake, Phillip R. — *U.S. Envirosearch*
Land, Shaun — *Dunhill Professional Search of Irvine, Inc.*
Langford, Robert W. — *F-O-R-T-U-N-E Personnel Consultants of Huntsville, Inc.*
Lankford, Charles — *MSI International*
Larsen, Jack B. — *Jack B. Larsen & Associates*

Larsen, Richard F. — *Larsen, Zilliacus & Associates, Inc.*
Lasher, Charles M. — *Lasher Associates*
Laub, Stuart R. — *Abraham & London, Ltd.*
Lauderback, David R. — *A.T. Kearney, Inc.*
Lautz, Lindsay A. — *Wilkinson & Ives*
Lawrance, Susanne — *Sharrow & Associates*
Lawrence, David — *Agra Placements International Ltd.*
Lawson, Bettye N. — *MSI International*
Layton, Patrick R. — *MSI International*
Lazaro, Alicia C. — *The Whitney Group*
Leahy, Jan — *CPS Inc.*
Lebo, Terry — *Agra Placements International Ltd.*
Leetma, Imbi — *Stanton Chase International*
Leininger, Dennis — *Key Employment Services*
Lence, Julie Anne — *MSI International*
Lenkaitis, Lewis F. — *A.T. Kearney, Inc.*
Letcher, Harvey D. — *Sandhurst Associates*
Lettrii, Mary — *BioQuest, Inc.*
Levine, Alan M. — *MB Inc. Interim Executive Division*
Levine, Lois — *National Search, Inc.*
Levinson, Lauren — *The Danbrook Group, Inc.*
Levitt, Muriel A. — *D.S. Allen Associates, Inc.*
Lewicki, Christopher — *MSI International*
Lewis, Jon A. — *Sandhurst Associates*
Lewis, Sandee — *Southwestern Professional Services*
Lewis, Sean — *Southwestern Professional Services*
Liebowitz, Michael E. — *Highland Search Group, L.L.C.*
Lindberg, Eric J. — *MSI International*
Linde, Rick — *Battalia Winston International*
Linton, Leonard M. — *Byron Leonard International, Inc.*
Lipe, Jerold L. — *Compass Group Ltd.*
Litt-Peck, Michelle — *The Whitney Group*
Little, Elizabeth A. — *Financial Resource Associates, Inc.*
Little, Gary — *Agra Placements International Ltd.*
Livesay, Christopher C. — *MSI International*
Loeb, Stephen H. — *Grant Cooper and Associates*
Lofthouse, Cindy — *CPS Inc.*
Logan, Valarie A. — *D.S.A. - Dixie Search Associates*
London, Gregory J. — *MSI International*
Long, Melanie — *National Search, Inc.*
Long, William G. — *McDonald, Long & Associates, Inc.*
Longmore, Marilyn — *Richard Kader & Associates*
LoPresto, Robert L. — *Rusher, Loscavio & LoPresto*
Lotufo, Donald A. — *D.A.L. Associates, Inc.*
Lovely, Edward — *The Stevenson Group of New Jersey*
Lucarelli, Joan — *The Onstott Group, Inc.*
Lucas, Ronnie L. — *MSI International*
Lucht, John — *The John Lucht Consultancy Inc.*
Lynn, Donald — *Frank Cuomo and Associates, Inc.*
MacCarthy, Ann — *Columbia Consulting Group*
MacGregor, Malcolm — *Boyden*
MacJadyen, David J. — *Sharrow & Associates*
Mackin, Michael — *D. Brown and Associates, Inc.*
Mader, Stephen P. — *Christian & Timbers*
Maer, Harry — *Kenzer Corp.*
Maher, William J. — *Johnson Smith & Knisely Accord*
Mak, I. Paul — *Thomas A. Byrnes Associates*
Malcolm, Rod — *The Enns Partners Inc.*
Malcom, John W. — *Johnson Smith & Knisely Accord*
Malone, George V. — *Boyden*
Manes, Kathy — *Dunhill Professional Search of Irvine, Inc.*
Manns, Alex — *Crawford & Crofford*
Maphet, Harriet — *The Stevenson Group of New Jersey*
Marchette, Steve — *Juntunen-Combs-Poirier*
Marion, Bradford B. — *Lamalie Amrop International*
Marion, Michael — *S.D. Kelly & Associates, Inc.*
Marks, Ira — *Strategic Alternatives*
Marks, Russell E. — *Webb, Johnson Associates, Inc.*
Marra, John — *Marra Peters & Partners*
Marra, John — *Marra Peters & Partners*
Martens, Maxine — *Rene Plessner Associates, Inc.*
Martin, Geary D. — *Boyden/Zay & Company*
Martin, Lynne Koll — *Boyden*
Martin, Paula — *MSI International*
Marye, George — *Damon & Associates, Inc.*
Maschal, Charles E. — *Maschal/Connors, Inc.*
Massey, H. Heath — *Robison & Associates*
Matheny, Robert P. — *MSI International*
Mather, David R. — *Christian & Timbers*
Matti, Suzy — *Southwestern Professional Services*
Max, Bruno — *RBR Associates, Inc.*
May, Peter — *Mixtec Group*
Mazza, David B. — *Mazza & Riley, Inc.*
McAndrews, Kathy — *CPS Inc.*
McBride, Jonathan E. — *McBride Associates, Inc.*
McBryde, Marnie — *Spencer Stuart*
McCallister, Richard A. — *Boyden*
McCorkle, Sam B. — *Morton, McCorkle & Associates, Inc.*
McCormack, William Reed — *MSI International*

McCormick, Brian — *The McCormick Group, Inc.*
McCormick, William J. — *The McCormick Group, Inc.*
McCreary, Charles — *Austin-McGregor International*
McDaniel, Debra A. — *Simpson Associates*
McDonald, Gary E. — *Agra Placements International Ltd.*
McDonald, Scott A. — *McDonald Associates International*
McDonald, Stanleigh B. — *McDonald Associates International*
McDonnell, Julie — *Technical Personnel of Minnesota*
McEwan, Paul — *Richard, Wayne and Roberts*
McFadden, Ashton S. — *Johnson Smith & Knisely Accord*
McGann, Paul L. — *The Cassie Group*
McGrath, Thomas F. — *Spriggs & Company, Inc.*
McGuire, Corey — *Peter W. Ambler Company*
McIntyre, Joel — *Phillips Resource Group*
McKnight, Amy E. — *Chartwell Partners International, Inc.*
McMillin, Bob — *Price Waterhouse*
McNichol, John — *McNichol Associates*
McNichols, Walter B. — *Gary Kaplan & Associates*
McSherry, James F. — *Battalia Winston International*
Mead, James D. — *James Mead & Company*
Meagher, Patricia G. — *Spencer Stuart*
Meany, Brian — *Herbert Mines Associates, Inc.*
Meier, J. Dale — *Grant Cooper and Associates*
Merrigan, Eileen M. — *Lamalie Amrop International*
Mestepey, John — *A.T. Kearney, Inc.*
Meyer, Stacey — *Gary Kaplan & Associates*
Meyer, William — *Agra Placements International Ltd.*
Michaels, Joseph — *CPS Inc.*
Mierzwinski, John — *Industrial Recruiters Associates, Inc.*
Miesemer, Arthur C. — *MSI International*
Mikula, Linda — *Schweichler Associates, Inc.*
Miles, Kenneth T. — *MSI International*
Miller, Benjamin J. — *MSI International*
Miller, Brett — *The McCormick Group, Inc.*
Miller, Julie — *Southwestern Professional Services*
Miller, Kenneth A. — *Computer Network Resources, Inc.*
Miller, Paul McG. — *Lamalie Amrop International*
Miller, Roy — *The Enns Partners Inc.*
Miller, Russel E. — *ARJay & Associates*
Millonzi, Joel C. — *Johnson Smith & Knisely Accord*
Milstein, Bonnie — *Marvin Laba & Associates*
Milton, Suzanne — *Marra Peters & Partners*
Mines, Herbert T. — *Herbert Mines Associates, Inc.*
Mitros, George N. — *Mixtec Group*
Mockler, Nadine — *Part Time Resources, Inc.*
Moerbe, Ed H. — *Stanton Chase International*
Mogul, Gene — *Mogul Consultants, Inc.*
Mohr, Brian — *CPS Inc.*
Mondragon, Philip — *Boyden*
Montgomery, Catherine C. — *Boyden*
Moore, Denise — *Jonas, Walters & Assoc., Inc.*
Moore, Lemuel R. — *MSI International*
Moore, Mark — *Wheeler, Moore & Elam Co.*
Moore, Michael — *Agra Placements International Ltd.*
Moran, Carla — *Key Employment Services*
Moran, Gail — *Comprehensive Search*
Moran, Gayle — *Dussick Management Associates*
Morgan, Gary — *National Search, Inc.*
Morgan, Richard S. — *Lovas Stanley/Paul Ray Berndtson Inc.*
Morgan, Vincent S. — *Johnson Smith & Knisely Accord*
Morris, Paul T. — *The Morris Group*
Morrison, Janis L. — *Garrett Associates Inc.*
Morton, Robert C. — *Morton, McCorkle & Associates, Inc.*
Morton, Sheila Ann — *Sloan & Associates*
Mouchet, Marcus — *Commonwealth Consultants*
Moyse, Richard G. — *Thorndike Deland Associates*
Muendel, H. Edward — *Stanton Chase International*
Mummert, Dennis D. — *Sweeney Harbert & Mummert, Inc.*
Murin, Rose Mary — *U.S. Envirosearch*
Murphy, Cornelius J. — *Goodrich & Sherwood Associates, Inc.*
Murphy, Karen S. — *Flex Execs Management Solutions*
Murphy, Patrick J. — *P.J. Murphy & Associates, Inc.*
Murphy, Timothy D. — *MSI International*
Mursuli, Meredith — *Lasher Associates*
Mydlach, Renee — *CPS Inc.*
Nadherny, Christopher C. — *Spencer Stuart*
Nagler, Leon G. — *Nagler, Robins & Poe, Inc.*
Nahas, Robert — *Herbert Mines Associates, Inc.*
Nathanson, Barry F. — *Barry Nathanson Associates*
Nazzaro, Samuel G. — *Boyden*
Neill, Wellden K. — *Sampson Neill & Wilkins Inc.*
Nelson, Barry — *Herman Smith Executive Initiatives Inc.*
Nephew, Robert — *Christian & Timbers*
Neuberth, Jeffrey G. — *Canny, Bowen Inc.*
Newbold, Michael — *Agra Placements International Ltd.*
Newman, Lynn — *Kishbaugh Associates International*
Nicastro, Kelley P. — *A la carte International*
Nolan, Jean M. — *S.D. Kelly & Associates, Inc.*
Nold, Robert — *Roberson and Company*

Norman, Randy — *Austin-McGregor International*
Normann, Amy — *Robert M. Flanagan & Associates, Ltd.*
Norsell, Paul E. — *Paul Norsell & Associates, Inc.*
O'Brien, John G. — *CanMed Consultants Inc.*
O'Connell, Mary — *CPS Inc.*
O'Donnell, James H. — *MSI International*
O'Donnell, Timothy W. — *Boyden*
O'Hara, Daniel M. — *Lynch Miller Moore Partners, Inc.*
O'Hara, James J. — *Barone-O'Hara Associates*
O'Maley, Kimberlee — *Spencer Stuart*
O'Such, Tracy — *Bishop Partners*
O'Toole, Dennis P. — *Dennis P. O'Toole & Associates Inc.*
Oberg, Roy — *The Danbrook Group, Inc.*
Ocon, Olga — *Busch International*
Ogden, Thomas H. — *The Ogdon Partnership*
Ohman, Gregory L. — *Pearson, Caldwell & Farnsworth, Inc.*
Olsen, Carl — *A.T. Kearney, Inc.*
Onstott, Joseph E. — *The Onstott Group, Inc.*
Oppenheim, Jeffrey — *Roth Young Personnel Service of Boston, Inc.*
Oswald, Mark G. — *Canny, Bowen Inc.*
Ottenritter, Chris — *CPS Inc.*
Owens, Ken — *F-O-R-T-U-N-E Personnel Consultants of Huntsville, Inc.*
Pace, Susan A. — *Horton International*
Pacini, Lauren R. — *Hite Executive Search*
Page, Linda — *Jonas, Walters & Assoc., Inc.*
Page, Linda M. — *Wargo and Co., Inc.*
Palma, Frank R. — *Goodrich & Sherwood Associates, Inc.*
Palmer, Carlton A. — *Beall & Company, Inc.*
Palmlund, David W. — *Lamalie Amrop International*
Panetta, Timothy — *Commonwealth Consultants*
Pappas, Jim — *Search Dynamics, Inc.*
Pappas, Timothy C. — *Jonas, Walters & Assoc., Inc.*
Parfitt, William C. — *Parfitt Recruiting and Consulting/PRO TEM*
Park, Dabney G. — *Mark Stanley & Company*
Parker, Roberta — *R. Parker and Associates, Inc.*
Parkin, Myrna — *S.D. Kelly & Associates, Inc.*
Parr, James A. — *KPMG Management Consulting*
Parry, William H. — *Horton International*
Patence, David W. — *Handy HRM Corp.*
Patton, Mitchell — *Patton/Perry Associates, Inc.*
Pearson, John R. — *Pearson, Caldwell & Farnsworth, Inc.*
Pearson, Robert L. — *Lamalie Amrop International*
Peckenpaugh, Ann D. — *Schweichler Associates, Inc.*
Pedley, Jill — *CPS Inc.*
Peeney, James D. — *Peeney Associates*
Pelisson, Charles — *Marra Peters & Partners*
Pelkey, Chris — *The McCormick Group, Inc.*
Pelletier, Jacques F. — *Roth Young Personnel Service of Boston, Inc.*
Perez, Christina — *Orr Executive Search*
Perkins, Daphne — *CPS Inc.*
Persky, Barry — *Barry Persky & Company, Inc.*
Peters, James N. — *TNS Partners, Inc.*
Peterson, John — *CPS Inc.*
Pettersson, Tara L. — *Lamalie Amrop International*
Pettibone, Linda — *Herbert Mines Associates, Inc.*
Pettway, Samuel H. — *Spencer Stuart*
Pfeiffer, Irene — *Price Waterhouse*
Pfister, Shelli — *Jack B. Larsen & Associates*
Phelps, Gene L. — *McCormack & Farrow*
Phillips, Donald L. — *O'Shea, Divine & Company, Inc.*
Phillips, James L. — *Highland Search Group, L.L.C.*
Pickens, Barbara — *Johnson Smith & Knisely Accord*
Pickering, Dale — *Agri-Tech Personnel, Inc.*
Pickford, Stephen T. — *The Corporate Staff, Inc.*
Pierson, Edward J. — *Johnson Smith & Knisely Accord*
Pinkman, Karen N. — *Skott/Edwards Consultants, Inc.*
Pitcher, Brian D. — *Skott/Edwards Consultants, Inc.*
Plessner, Rene — *Rene Plessner Associates, Inc.*
Podway, Hope — *Search West, Inc.*
Poirier, Frank — *Juntunen-Combs-Poirier*
Poirier, Roland — *Poirier, Hoevel & Co.*
Pomerance, Mark — *CPS Inc.*
Pompeo, Paul — *Search West, Inc.*
Poracky, John W. — *M. Wood Company*
Porter, Albert — *The Experts*
Porter, Donald — *Amherst Personnel Group Inc.*
Porter, Nanci — *Eastridge InfoTech*
Potter, Douglas C. — *Stanton Chase International*
Potter, Steven B. — *Highland Search Group, L.L.C.*
Prince, Marilyn L. — *Higdon Prince Inc.*
Proct, Nina — *Martin H. Bauman Associates, Inc.*
Provus, Barbara L. — *Shepherd Bueschel & Provus, Inc.*
Pryde, Marcia D. — *A.T. Kearney, Inc.*
Pugliese, Vincent — *Search West, Inc.*
Raab, Julie — *Dunhill Professional Search of Irvine, Inc.*
Rabe, William — *Sales Executives Inc.*
Rachels, John W. — *Southwestern Professional Services*
Radawicz, Angela — *Mixtec Group*

Radice, Joseph — *Hospitality International*
Raheja, Marc C. — *CanMed Consultants Inc.*
Raiber, Laurie Altman — *The IMC Group of Companies Ltd.*
Ramsey, John H. — *Mark Stanley & Company*
Randell, James E. — *Randell-Heiken, Inc.*
Ray, Marianne C. — *Callan Associates, Ltd.*
Raymond, Anne — *Anderson Sterling Associates*
Reddick, David C. — *Horton International*
Reddicks, Nate — *Search West, Inc.*
Redler, Rhonda — *National Search, Inc.*
Reece, Christopher S. — *Reece & Mruk Partners*
Reeder, Michael S. — *Lamalie Amrop International*
Regehly, Herbert L. — *The IMC Group of Companies Ltd.*
Reiser, Ellen — *Thorndike Deland Associates*
Reiss, Matt — *National Search, Inc.*
Reiter, Harold D. — *Herbert Mines Associates, Inc.*
Rendl, Ric — *CPS Inc.*
Renick, Cynthia L. — *Morgan Hunter Corp.*
Renwick, David — *John Kurosky & Associates*
Reticker, Peter — *MSI International*
Reyman, Susan — *S. Reyman & Associates Ltd.*
Rice, Douglas — *Agra Placements International Ltd.*
Rice, Marie — *Jay Gaines & Company, Inc.*
Rich, Lyttleton — *Sockwell & Associates*
Richards, Robert A. — *Sloan & Associates*
Riederer, Larry — *CPS Inc.*
Riley, Elizabeth G. — *Mazza & Riley, Inc.*
Rimmele, Michael — *The Bankers Group*
Rinker, Jim — *Southwestern Professional Services*
Rivas, Alberto F. — *Boyden*
Rizzo, L. Donald — *R.P. Barone Associates*
Roberts, Carl R. — *Southwestern Professional Services*
Roberts, Mitch — *A.E. Feldman Associates*
Roberts, Raymond R. — *MSI International*
Roberts, Scott B. — *Wargo and Co., Inc.*
Roberts, William — *Cochran, Cochran & Yale, Inc.*
Robins, Jeri N. — *Nagler, Robins & Poe, Inc.*
Robinson, Bruce — *Bruce Robinson Associates*
Robison, John H. — *Robison & Associates*
Rodgers, John — *Agra Placements International Ltd.*
Rodgers, Kathi — *St. Lawrence International, Inc.*
Rodney, Brett — *MSI International*
Rodriguez, Josie — *R. Parker and Associates, Inc.*
Romaine, Stanley J. — *Mixtec Group*
Romanchek, Walter R. — *Wellington Management Group*
Romanello, Daniel P. — *Spencer Stuart*
Romaniw, Michael J. — *A la carte International*
Romaniw, Michael J. — *A la carte International*
Romaniw, Michael J. — *A la carte International*
Ropella, Patrick B. — *Ropella & Associates*
Rosato, William R. — *W.R. Rosato & Associates, Inc.*
Rosemarin, Gloria J. — *Barrington Hart, Inc.*
Rosenthal, Charles — *National Search, Inc.*
Ross, Lawrence — *Lovas Stanley/Paul Ray Berndtson Inc.*
Ross, Marc A. — *Flowers & Associates*
Ross, William J. — *Flowers & Associates*
Rossi, Silvio — *Keith Bagg & Associates Inc.*
Rossi, Thomas — *Southwestern Professional Services*
Roth, Robert J. — *Williams, Roth & Krueger Inc.*
Rothfeld, Robert — *A.E. Feldman Associates*
Rowells, Michael — *MSI International*
Rudolph, Kenneth — *Kossuth & Associates, Inc.*
Rudzinsky, Howard — *Louis Rudzinsky Associates*
Rumson, Paul — *Roth Young Personnel Service of Boston, Inc.*
Rurak, Zbigniew T. — *Rurak & Associates, Inc.*
Rusher, William H. — *Rusher, Loscavio & LoPresto*
Russell, Robin E. — *Kenzer Corp.*
Rustin, Beth — *The Whitney Group*
Sacerdote, John — *Raymond Karsan Associates*
Sahlas, Chrissy — *CPS Inc.*
Saletra, Andrew — *CPS Inc.*
Sampson, Martin C. — *Sampson Neill & Wilkins Inc.*
Sanders, Natalie — *CPS Inc.*
Sanders, Spencer H. — *Battalia Winston International*
Sapperstein, Jerry S. — *CFO Associates, Inc.*
Sathe, Mark A. — *Sathe & Associates, Inc.*
Savage, Edward J. — *Stanton Chase International*
Sawyer, Patricia L. — *Smith & Sawyer Inc.*
Sayers, Bruce D. — *Brackin & Sayers Associates*
Scalamera, Tom — *CPS Inc.*
Schaefer, Frederic M. — *A.T. Kearney, Inc.*
Scharett, Carol — *St. Lawrence International, Inc.*
Schedra, Sharon — *Earley Kielty and Associates, Inc.*
Schiavone, Mary Rose — *Canny, Bowen Inc.*
Schlpma, Christine — *Advanced Executive Resources*
Schmidt, Jeri E. — *Blake, Hansen & Nye, Limited*
Schmidt, Peter R. — *Boyden*
Schmidt, William C. — *Christian & Timbers*
Schneider, Perry — *Agra Placements International Ltd.*

Schneiderman, Gerald — *Management Resource Associates, Inc.*
Schroeder, Steven J. — *Blau Kaptain Schroeder*
Schueneman, David — *CPS Inc.*
Schwam, Carol — *A.E. Feldman Associates*
Schwartz, Carole — *A.T. Kearney, Inc.*
Schweichler, Lee J. — *Schweichler Associates, Inc.*
Seals, Sonny — *A.T. Kearney, Inc.*
Seco, William — *Seco & Zetto Associates, Inc.*
Segal, Eric B. — *Kenzer Corp.*
Seitz, Charles J. — *Neail Behringer Consultants*
Sekera, Roger I. — *A.T. Kearney, Inc.*
Selker, Gregory L. — *Christian & Timbers*
Semyan, John K. — *TNS Partners, Inc.*
Sennello, Gendra — *National Search, Inc.*
Serwat, Leonard A. — *Spencer Stuart*
Sessa, Vincent J. — *Integrated Search Solutions Group, LLC*
Settles, Barbara Z. — *Lamalie Amrop International*
Sevilla, Claudio A. — *Crawford & Crofford*
Shamir, Ben — *S.D. Kelly & Associates, Inc.*
Shapiro, Elaine — *CPS Inc.*
Shelton, Sandra — *National Search, Inc.*
Shen, Eugene Y. — *The Whitney Group*
Shepard, Michael J. — *MSI International*
Shepherd, Daniel M. — *Shepherd Bueschel & Provus, Inc.*
Sher, Lawrence — *M.A. Churchill & Associates, Inc.*
Sherwin, Thomas — *Barone-O'Hara Associates*
Sherwood, Andrew — *Goodrich & Sherwood Associates, Inc.*
Shimp, David J. — *Lamalie Amrop International*
Shipherd, John T. — *The Cassie Group*
Shoemaker, Larry C. — *Shoemaker & Associates*
Sibbald, John R. — *John Sibbald Associates, Inc.*
Siegel, RitaSue — *RitaSue Siegel Resources Inc.*
Sierra, Rafael A. — *Lamalie Amrop International*
Signer, Julie — *CPS Inc.*
Sill, Igor M. — *Geneva Group International*
Sill, Igor M. — *Geneva Group International*
Silvas, Stephen D. — *Roberson and Company*
Silver, Lee A. — *L.A. Silver Associates, Inc.*
Simmons, Anneta — *F-O-R-T-U-N-E Personnel Consultants of Huntsville, Inc.*
Simmons, Gerald J. — *Handy HRM Corp.*
Simmons, Sandra K. — *MSI International*
Sinclair, Amy — *Fisher Personnel Management Services*
Sine, Mark — *Hospitality International*
Sjogren, Dennis — *Agra Placements International Ltd.*
Slater, Ronald E. — *A.T. Kearney, Inc.*
Slaughter, Katherine T. — *Compass Group Ltd.*
Sloan, Michael D. — *Sloan & Associates*
Slocum, Ann Marie — *K.L. Whitney Company*
Smead, Michelle M. — *A.T. Kearney, Inc.*
Smith, Adam M. — *The Abbott Group, Inc.*
Smith, Cheryl — *Barton Raben, Inc.*
Smith, David P. — *Smith & Latterell (HRS, Inc.)*
Smith, Ethan L. — *Highland Search Group, L.L.C.*
Smith, Grant — *Price Waterhouse*
Smith, Margaret A. — *MSI International*
Smith, Monica L. — *Analysts Resources, Inc.*
Smith, Robert L. — *Smith & Sawyer Inc.*
Smyth, Brendan — *Simpson Associates*
Snelgrove, Geiger — *National Search, Inc.*
Snodgrass, Stephen — *DeFrain, Mayer, Lee & Burgess LLC*
Snyder, James F. — *Snyder & Company*
Snyder, Thomas J. — *Spencer Stuart*
Sockwell, J. Edgar — *Sockwell & Associates*
Soggs, Cheryl Pavick — *A.T. Kearney, Inc.*
Sola, George L. — *A.T. Kearney, Inc.*
Songy, Al — *U.S. Envirosearch*
Sowerbutt, Richard S. — *Hite Executive Search*
Spann, Richard E. — *Goodrich & Sherwood Associates, Inc.*
Speck, Michael J. — *Lovas Stanley/Paul Ray Berndtson Inc.*
Spicher, John — *M.A. Churchill & Associates, Inc.*
Spiegel, Gay — *L.A. Silver Associates, Inc.*
Sponseller, Vern — *Richard Kader & Associates*
Sprague, David — *Michael Stern Associates Inc.*
Sprau, Collin L. — *Paul Ray Berndtson*
Spriggs, Robert D. — *Spriggs & Company, Inc.*
Sprowls, Linda — *Allard Associates*
Stack, James K. — *Boyden*
Stafford, Susan — *Hospitality International*
Stark, Jeff — *Thorne, Brieger Associates Inc.*
Statson, Dale E. — *Sales Executives Inc.*
Steck, Frank T. — *A.T. Kearney, Inc.*
Steenerson, Thomas L. — *MSI International*
Stein, Terry W. — *Stewart, Stein and Scott, Ltd.*
Steinman, Stephen — *The Stevenson Group of New Jersey*
Stenholm, Gilbert R. — *Spencer Stuart*
Sterling, Jay — *Earley Kielty and Associates, Inc.*
Stern, Michael I. — *Michael Stern Associates Inc.*
Stern, Stephen — *CPS Inc.*

Sterner, Doug — *CPS Inc.*
Stevenson, Terry — *Bartholdi & Company, Inc.*
Stewart, Jeffrey O. — *Stewart, Stein and Scott, Ltd.*
Stewart, Ross M. — *Human Resources Network Partners Inc.*
Stiles, Judy — *MedQuest Associates*
Stinson, R.J. — *Sampson Neill & Wilkins Inc.*
Stoll, Steven G. — *Sharrow & Associates*
Stone, Robert Ryder — *Lamalie Amrop International*
Stone, Susan L. — *Stone Enterprises Ltd.*
Stouffer, Dale — *Agra Placements International Ltd.*
Stricker, Sidney G. — *Stricker & Zagor*
Strobridge, Richard P. — *F.L. Taylor & Company, Inc.*
Strom, Mark N. — *Search Advisors International Corp.*
Stubbs, Judy N. — *Lamalie Amrop International*
Sturtz, James W. — *Compass Group Ltd.*
Sullivan, Kay — *Rusher, Loscavio & LoPresto*
Summers, Burke — *The McCormick Group, Inc.*
Sumurdy, Melinda — *Kenzer Corp.*
Sur, William K. — *Canny, Bowen Inc.*
Swanson, Dick — *Raymond Karsan Associates*
Swanson, Kris — *Flex Execs Management Solutions*
Swatts, Stone — *F-O-R-T-U-N-E Personnel Consultants of Huntsville, Inc.*
Sweeney, James W. — *Sweeney Harbert & Mummert, Inc.*
Sweeney, Sean K. — *Bonifield Associates*
Szafran, Jack — *U.S. Envirosearch*
Takacs, Gloria — *Gilbert & Van Campen International*
Taylor, Conrad G. — *MSI International*
Taylor, Ernest A. — *Ward Howell International, Inc.*
Teas, John — *Southwestern Professional Services*
Teinert, Jay — *Damon & Associates, Inc.*
Teter, Sandra — *The Danbrook Group, Inc.*
Theobald, David B. — *Theobald & Associates*
Thies, Gary — *S.D. Kelly & Associates, Inc.*
Thiras, Ted — *Mixtec Group*
Tholke, William E. — *Canny, Bowen Inc.*
Thomas, Cheryl M. — *CPS Inc.*
Thomas, Christine S. — *Lovas Stanley/Paul Ray Berndtson Inc.*
Thomas, Jeffrey — *Fairfaxx Corporation*
Thomas, John T. — *Ward Howell International, Inc.*
Thomas, Kim — *CPS Inc.*
Thomas, Kurt J. — *P.J. Murphy & Associates, Inc.*
Thompson, Brett — *Southwestern Professional Services*
Thompson, Dave — *Battalia Winston International*
Thompson, James R. — *Gordon Wahls Company*
Thompson, John R. — *MSI International*
Tierney, Eileen — *The Whitney Group*
Timoney, Laura — *Bishop Partners*
Tipp, George — *Intech Summit Group, Inc.*
Titterington, Catherine F. — *MSI International*
Tokash, Ronald E. — *MSI International*
Tovrog, Dan — *CPS Inc.*
Tracey, Jack — *Management Assistance Group, Inc.*
Trosin, Walter R. — *Johnson Smith & Knisely Accord*
Trott, Kathryn — *Allard Associates*
Trott, Kathryn — *Allard Associates*
Trueblood, Brian G. — *TNS Partners, Inc.*
Truemper, Dean — *CPS Inc.*
Truex, John F. — *Morton, McCorkle & Associates, Inc.*
Tryon, Katey — *DeFrain, Mayer, Lee & Burgess LLC*
Tucci, Joseph — *Fairfaxx Corporation*
Tullberg, Tina — *CPS Inc.*
Tunney, William — *Grant Cooper and Associates*
Tursi, Deborah J. — *The Corporate Connection, Ltd.*
Tweed, Janet — *Gilbert Tweed/INESA*
Tyson, Richard L. — *Bonifield Associates*
Unger, Paul T. — *A.T. Kearney, Inc.*
Unger, Stephen A. — *Spencer Stuart*
Vachon, David A. — *McNichol Associates*
Van Alstine, Catherine — *Tanton Mitchell/Paul Ray Berndtson*
Van Campen, Jerry — *Gilbert & Van Campen International*
Van Horn, Carol — *R. Parker and Associates, Inc.*
van Someren, Christian — *Johnson Smith & Knisely Accord*
Vann, Dianne — *The Button Group*
Vaughan, David B. — *Dunhill Professional Search of Irvine, Inc.*
Venable, William W. — *Thorndike Deland Associates*
Vergari, Jane — *Herbert Mines Associates, Inc.*
Vinnedge, Sandra — *U.S. Envirosearch*
Virgili, Franca — *Johnson Smith & Knisely Accord*
Visnich, L. Christine — *Bason Associates Inc.*
Vlcek, Thomas J. — *Vlcek & Company, Inc.*
Vogus, Jerry — *Cumberland Group Inc.*
Vojta, Marilyn B. — *James Mead & Company*
Volk, Richard — *MSI International*
Wakefield, Scott — *National Search, Inc.*
Waldman, Noah H. — *Lamalie Amrop International*
Waldoch, D. Mark — *Barnes Development Group, LLC*
Waldrop, Gary R. — *MSI International*
Walker, Martin S. — *Walker Communications*

Wall, David — *Southwestern Professional Services*
Walsh, Patty — *Abraham & London, Ltd.*
Walters, William F. — *Jonas, Walters & Assoc., Inc.*
Walther, Linda S. — *MSI International*
Ward, Madeleine — *LTM Associates*
Wardell, Charles W.B. — *Lamalie Amrop International*
Wargo, G. Rick — *A.T. Kearney, Inc.*
Warren, Sylvia W. — *Thorndike Deland Associates*
Wasserman, Harvey — *Churchill and Affiliates, Inc.*
Wassill, Larry — *Corporate Recruiters Ltd.*
Waters, Peter D. — *John Kurosky & Associates*
Watson, James — *MSI International*
Wayne, Cary S. — *ProSearch Inc.*
Webb, George H. — *Webb, Johnson Associates, Inc.*
Webb, Shawn K. — *MSI International*
Weber, Jurgen — *BioQuest, Inc.*
Wein, Michael S. — *InterimManagement Solutions, Inc.*
Wein, Michael S. — *Media Management Resources, Inc.*
Wein, William — *InterimManagement Solutions, Inc.*
Wein, William — *Media Management Resources, Inc.*
Weisler, Nancy — *National Search, Inc.*
Weissman-Rosenthal, Abbe — *ALW Research International*
Weisz, Laura — *Anderson Sterling Associates*
Weller, Paul S. — *Mark Stanley & Company*
Wertel, Ronald E. — *Gordon Wahls Company*
West, Nancy — *Health Care Dimensions*
Westerfield, Putney — *Boyden*
Weston, Corinne F. — *D.A. Kreuter Associates, Inc.*
Wexler, Rona — *Ariel Recruitment Associates*
White, Jeffrey E. — *Simpson Associates*
White, Jonathan O. — *The Badger Group*
White, Kimberly — *Executive Referral Services, Inc.*
White, Patricia D. — *MSI International*
White, Richard B. — *Spencer Stuart*
White, William C. — *Venture Resources Inc.*
Whiting, Anthony — *Johnson Smith & Knisely Accord*
Whitley, Sue Ann — *Roberts Ryan and Bentley*
Whitney, Kenneth L. — *K.L. Whitney Company*
Whitton, Paula L. — *Pearson, Caldwell & Farnsworth, Inc.*
Wier, Daniel — *Horton International*
Wilkins, Walter K. — *Sampson Neill & Wilkins Inc.*
Wilkinson, Barbara — *Beall & Company, Inc.*
Wilkinson, William R. — *Wilkinson & Ives*
Williams, Dave — *The McCormick Group, Inc.*
Williams, Gary L. — *Barnes Development Group, LLC*
Williams, Harry D. — *Jacobson Associates*
Williams, Laurelle N. — *MSI International*
Williams, Roger K. — *Williams, Roth & Krueger Inc.*
Williams, Walter E. — *Canny, Bowen Inc.*
Willis, William H. — *William Willis Worldwide Inc.*
Willner, Nannette — *S.R. Wolman Associates, Inc.*
Wilson, Patricia L. — *Leon A. Farley Associates*
Winitz, Joel — *GSW Consulting Group, Inc.*
Winitz, Marla — *GSW Consulting Group, Inc.*
Winston, Dale — *Battalia Winston International*
Winston, Susan — *CPS Inc.*
Winter, Robert — *The Whitney Group*
Wisch, Steven C. — *MB Inc. Interim Executive Division*
Wise, Anne — *U.S. Envirosearch*
Wise, J. Herbert — *Sandhurst Associates*
Wittenberg, Laura L. — *Boyden*
Wolf, Stephen M. — *Byron Leonard International, Inc.*
Wolman, Stephen R. — *S.R. Wolman Associates, Inc.*
Womack, Joseph — *The Bankers Group*
Wood, Martin F. — *Lamalie Amrop International*
Wood, Milton M. — *M. Wood Company*
Wooller, Edmund A.M. — *Windsor International*
Woollett, James — *Rusher, Loscavio & LoPresto*
Wren, Jay — *Jay Wren & Associates*
Wren, Shelly J. — *Sloan & Associates*
Wright, Charles D. — *Goodrich & Sherwood Associates, Inc.*
Wright, Leslie — *The Stevenson Group of New Jersey*
Wrynn, Robert F. — *MSI International*
Wyatt, James — *Wyatt & Jaffe*
Wylie, Pamela — *M.A. Churchill & Associates, Inc.*
Young, Laurie — *Part Time Resources, Inc.*
Young, Lesley — *Search West, Inc.*
Zaffrann, Craig S. — *P.J. Murphy & Associates, Inc.*
Zahradka, James F. — *P.J. Murphy & Associates, Inc.*
Zander, Barry W. — *MSI International*
Zarkin, Norman — *The Zarkin Group, Inc.*
Zatzick, Michael — *Search West, Inc.*
Zay, Thomas C. — *Boyden/Zay & Company*
Zera, Ronald J. — *Spencer Stuart*
Zetto, Kathryn — *Seco & Zetto Associates, Inc.*
Zingaro, Ron — *Zingaro and Company*
Zinn, Donald — *Bishop Partners*
Zona, Henry F. — *Zona & Associates, Inc.*
Zwiff, Jeffrey G. — *Johnson Smith & Knisely Accord*

## 10. Women/Minorities

Abbott, Peter — *The Abbott Group, Inc.*
Adams, Ralda F. — *Hospitality International*
Akin, J.R. — *J.R. Akin & Company Inc.*
Alekel, Karren — *ALW Research International*
Allard, Susan — *Allard Associates*
Allerton, Donald T. — *Allerton Heneghan & O'Neill*
Altreuter, Ken — *ALTCO Temporary Services*
Altreuter, Rose — *ALTCO Temporary Services*
Altreuter, Rose — *The ALTCO Group*
Andrick, Patty — *CPS Inc.*
Antil, Pamela W. — *Norman Roberts & Associates, Inc.*
Argentin, Jo — *Executive Placement Consultants, Inc.*
Arms, Douglas — *TOPAZ International, Inc.*
Arms, Douglas — *TOPAZ Legal Solutions*
Arnold, David — *Christian & Timbers*
Aronin, Michael — *Fisher-Todd Associates*
Ascher, Susan P. — *The Ascher Group*
Ast, Steven T. — *Ast/Bryant*
Attell, Harold — *A.E. Feldman Associates*
Baker, Gary M. — *Cochran, Cochran & Yale, Inc.*
Baker-Greene, Edward — *Isaacson, Miller*
Balch, Randy — *CPS Inc.*
Barbosa, Franklin J. — *Boyden*
Barnum, Toni M. — *Stone Murphy & Olson*
Baron, Len — *Industrial Recruiters Associates, Inc.*
Barthold, James A. — *McNichol Associates*
Bates, Scott W. — *Kittleman & Associates*
Bauman, Martin H. — *Martin H. Bauman Associates, Inc.*
Beaudin, Elizabeth C. — *Callan Associates, Ltd.*
Bellshaw, David — *Isaacson, Miller*
Bennett, Delora — *Genesis Personnel Service, Inc.*
Bennett, Jo — *Battalia Winston International*
Bennett, Richard T. — *Isaacson, Miller*
Berger, Emanuel — *Isaacson, Miller*
Berke, Carl E. — *The Cassie Group*
Bermea, Jose — *Gaffney Management Consultants*
Besen, Douglas — *Besen Associates Inc.*
Bishop, Susan — *Bishop Partners*
Bitar, Edward — *The Interface Group, Ltd./Boyden*
Bittman, Beth M. — *Norman Roberts & Associates, Inc.*
Blackmon, Sharon — *The Abbott Group, Inc.*
Blakslee, Jan H. — *J: Blakslee International, Ltd.*
Bostic, James E. — *Phillips Resource Group*
Bourbeau, Paul J. — *Boyden*
Bourrie, Sharon D. — *Chartwell Partners International, Inc.*
Bovich, Maryann C. — *Higdon Prince Inc.*
Brady, Robert — *CPS Inc.*
Brandeis, Richard — *CPS Inc.*
Brown, Charlene N. — *Accent on Achievement, Inc.*
Brudno, Robert J. — *Savoy Partners, Ltd.*
Bryant, Christopher P. — *Ast/Bryant*
Bryant, Richard D. — *Bryant Associates, Inc.*
Bryza, Robert M. — *Robert Lowell International*
Bullock, Conni — *Earley Kielty and Associates, Inc.*
Burchill, Greg — *BGB Associates*
Burfield, Elaine — *Skott/Edwards Consultants, Inc.*
Burns, Terence N. — *D.E. Foster Partners Inc.*
Burris, James C. — *Boyden*
Butterfass, Stanley — *Butterfass, Pepe & MacCallan Inc.*
Byrnes, Thomas A. — *Thomas A. Byrnes Associates*
Call, David — *Cochran, Cochran & Yale, Inc.*
Callahan, Wanda — *Cochran, Cochran & Yale, Inc.*
Callan, Robert M. — *Callan Associates, Ltd.*
Campbell, Patricia A. — *The Onstott Group, Inc.*
Case, David — *Case Executive Search*
Cassie, Ronald L. — *The Cassie Group*
Celenza, Catherine — *CPS Inc.*
Chappell, Peter — *The Bankers Group*
Chavous, C. Crawford — *Phillips Resource Group*
Chesla, Garry — *Executive Referral Services, Inc.*
Chorman, Marilyn A. — *Hite Executive Search*
Christian, Jeffrey E. — *Christian & Timbers*
Christiansen, Amy — *CPS Inc.*
Christiansen, Doug — *CPS Inc.*
Citera, Tom — *Howe-Lewis International*
Cizek, Marti J. — *Cizek Associates, Inc.*
Clark, James — *CPS Inc.*
Clauhsen, Elizabeth A. — *Savoy Partners, Ltd.*
Cleeve, Coleen — *Howe-Lewis International*
Close, E. Wade — *Boyden*
Coffman, Brian — *Kossuth & Associates, Inc.*
Cohen, Pamela — *TOPAZ International, Inc.*
Cohen, Pamela — *TOPAZ Legal Solutions*
Collins, Mollie P. — *Belvedere Partners*
Collins, Stephen — *The Johnson Group, Inc.*
Colman, Michael — *Executive Placement Consultants, Inc.*
Commersoli, Al — *Executive Referral Services, Inc.*

Connolly, Cathryn — *Strategic Associates, Inc.*
Conway, William P. — *Phillips Resource Group*
Cordaro, Concetta — *Flynn, Hannock, Incorporated*
Corso, Glen S. — *Chartwell Partners International, Inc.*
Costello, Andrea L. — *Gallin Associates*
Costick, Kathryn J. — *John Sibbald Associates, Inc.*
Coulman, Karen — *CPS Inc.*
Cragg, Barbara R. — *Southwestern Professional Services*
Critchley, Walter — *Cochran, Cochran & Yale, Inc.*
Crowder, Edward W. — *Crowder & Company*
Cruse, O.D. — *Spencer Stuart*
Cruz, Catherine — *TOPAZ International, Inc.*
Cruz, Catherine — *TOPAZ Legal Solutions*
Crystal, Jonathan A. — *Spencer Stuart*
Curtis, Ellissa — *Cochran, Cochran & Yale, Inc.*
Czamanske, Paul W. — *Compass Group Ltd.*
Czepiel, Susan — *CPS Inc.*
D'Alessio, Gary A. — *Chicago Legal Search, Ltd.*
Daum, Julie — *Spencer Stuart*
Davis, Bert — *Bert Davis Executive Search, Inc.*
de Tuede, Catherine — *Thomas A. Byrnes Associates*
DeCorrevont, James — *DeCorrevont & Associates*
DeCorrevont, James — *DeCorrevont & Associates*
Deering, Joseph — *U.S. Envirosearch*
DeHart, Donna — *Tower Consultants, Ltd.*
Del Pino, William — *National Search, Inc.*
DeLong, Art — *Richard Kader & Associates*
deVry, Kimberly A. — *Tower Consultants, Ltd.*
deWilde, David M. — *Chartwell Partners International, Inc.*
Diaz-Joslyn, Mabel — *Walker Communications*
Dieckmann, Ralph E. — *Dieckmann & Associates, Ltd.*
Dixon, Aris — *CPS Inc.*
Dotson, M. Ileen — *Dotson & Associates*
Dougherty, Bridget L. — *Wellington Management Group*
Dow, Lori — *Davidson, Laird & Associates*
Dugan, John H. — *J.H. Dugan and Associates, Inc.*
Dussick, Vince — *Dussick Management Associates*
Dwyer, Julie — *CPS Inc.*
Dykstra, Nicolette — *CPS Inc.*
Earle, Paul W. — *Spencer Stuart*
Eatmon, Michael — *U.S. Envirosearch*
Ebeling, John A. — *Gilbert Tweed/INESA*
Edwards, Verba L. — *Wing Tips & Pumps, Inc.*
Ehrgott, Elizabeth — *The Ascher Group*
Ehrhart, Jennifer — *ADOW's Executeam*
Eibeler, C. — *Amherst Personnel Group Inc.*
Ellis, William — *Interspace Interactive Inc.*
England, Mark — *Austin-McGregor International*
Ervin, Darlene — *CPS Inc.*
Ezersky, Jane E. — *Highland Search Group, L.L.C.*
Fairlie, Suzanne F. — *ProSearch, Inc.*
Feldman, Abe — *A.E. Feldman Associates*
Ferrari, S. Jay — *Ferrari Search Group*
Fischer, Janet L. — *Boyden*
Flanders, Karen — *Advanced Information Management*
Fogarty, Michael — *CPS Inc.*
Fonfa, Ann — *S.R. Wolman Associates, Inc.*
Ford, Sandra D. — *Phillips & Ford, Inc.*
Foreman, David C. — *Koontz, Jeffries & Associates, Inc.*
Forest, Adam — *McCormack & Associates*
Foy, Richard — *Boyden*
Francis, Joseph — *Hospitality International*
Frank, Valerie S. — *Norman Roberts & Associates, Inc.*
Frazier, John — *Cochran, Cochran & Yale, Inc.*
Freier, Bruce — *Executive Referral Services, Inc.*
Friedman, Donna L. — *Tower Consultants, Ltd.*
Friedman, Helen E. — *McCormack & Farrow*
Fulton, Christine N. — *Highland Search Group, L.L.C.*
Gabel, Gregory N. — *Canny, Bowen Inc.*
Gabriel, David L. — *The Arcus Group*
Gaffney, Denise O'Grady — *Isaacson, Miller*
Gaffney, Keith — *Gaffney Management Consultants*
Gaffney, William — *Gaffney Management Consultants*
Gaines, Ronni L. — *TOPAZ International, Inc.*
Gaines, Ronni L. — *TOPAZ Legal Solutions*
Galante, Suzanne M. — *Vlcek & Company, Inc.*
Gallagher, Terence M. — *Battalia Winston International*
Garfinkle, Steven M. — *Battalia Winston International*
Garrett, Donald L. — *Garrett Associates Inc.*
Garrett, Linda M. — *Garrett Associates Inc.*
George, Delores F. — *Delores F. George Human Resource Management & Consulting Industry*
Giacalone, Louis — *Allard Associates*
Gilbert, Jerry — *Gilbert & Van Campen International*
Gilbert, Robert — *U.S. Envirosearch*
Giles, Joe L. — *Joe L. Giles and Associates, Inc.*
Gill, Patricia — *Columbia Consulting Group*
Gilmore, Lori — *CPS Inc.*
Girsinger, Linda — *Industrial Recruiters Associates, Inc.*

Gold, Stacey — *Earley Kielty and Associates, Inc.*
Goldman, Michael L. — *Strategic Associates, Inc.*
Goodman, Victor — *Anderson Sterling Associates*
Gordon, Trina D. — *Boyden*
Graham, Dale — *CPS Inc.*
Gray, Mark — *Executive Referral Services, Inc.*
Greco, Patricia — *Howe-Lewis International*
Greene, Frederick J. — *Boyden*
Grenier, Glorianne — *CPS Inc.*
Grzybowski, Jill — *CPS Inc.*
Gude, John S. — *Boyden*
Gurtin, Kay L. — *Executive Options, Ltd.*
Hall, Peter V. — *Chartwell Partners International, Inc.*
Halvorsen, Jeanne M. — *Kittleman & Associates*
Hanford, Michael — *Richard Kader & Associates*
Hanson, Carrie — *U.S. Envirosearch*
Harbaugh, Paul J. — *International Management Advisors, Inc.*
Hard, Sally Ann — *Ast/Bryant*
Hardison, Richard L. — *Hardison & Company*
Hart, Robert T. — *D.E. Foster Partners Inc.*
Hartzman, Deborah — *Advanced Information Management*
Harvey, Mike — *Advanced Executive Resources*
Hatcher, Joe B. — *Ast/Bryant*
Hauck, Fred P. — *The Cassie Group*
Hauser, Martha — *Spencer Stuart*
Havener, Donald Clarke — *The Abbott Group, Inc.*
Hawksworth, A. Dwight — *A.D. & Associates Executive Search, Inc.*
Hay, William E. — *William E. Hay & Company*
Haystead, Steve — *Advanced Executive Resources*
Hazerjian, Cynthia — *CPS Inc.*
Heafey, Bill — *CPS Inc.*
Heiken, Barbara E. — *Randell-Heiken, Inc.*
Heiser, Charles S. — *The Cassie Group*
Hellinger, Audrey — *Martin H. Bauman Associates, Inc.*
Helminiak, Audrey — *Gaffney Management Consultants*
Hemingway, Stuart C. — *Robison & Associates*
Heneghan, Donald A. — *Allerton Heneghan & O'Neill*
Herman, Eugene J. — *Earley Kielty and Associates, Inc.*
Hermanson, Shelley — *Ells Personnel System Inc.*
Hicks, Albert M. — *Phillips Resource Group*
Higdon, Henry G. — *Higdon Prince Inc.*
Hirsch, Julia C. — *Boyden*
Hoevel, Michael J. — *Poirier, Hoevel & Co.*
Holland, Kathleen — *TOPAZ International, Inc.*
Holland, Kathleen — *TOPAZ Legal Solutions*
Hudson, Reginald M. — *Search Bureau International*
Hughes, Cathy N. — *The Ogdon Partnership*
Hunter, Gabe — *Phillips Resource Group*
Iacovelli, Heather — *CPS Inc.*
Irish, Alan — *CPS Inc.*
Isaacson, John — *Isaacson, Miller*
James, Richard — *Criterion Executive Search, Inc.*
Jeffers, Carol S. — *John Sibbald Associates, Inc.*
Johnson, David — *Gaffney Management Consultants*
Johnson, Douglas — *Quality Search*
Johnson, Maxene — *Norman Roberts & Associates, Inc.*
Johnson, Priscilla — *The Johnson Group, Inc.*
Johnson, Robert J. — *Quality Search*
Johnson, S. Hope — *The Interface Group, Ltd./Boyden*
Jones, Francis E. — *Earley Kielty and Associates, Inc.*
Jones, Gary — *BGB Associates*
Joubert, Pierre E. — *Boyden*
Juelis, John J. — *Peeney Associates*
Kader, Richard — *Richard Kader & Associates*
Karalis, William — *CPS Inc.*
Kehoe, Mike — *CPS Inc.*
Kelly, Claudia L. — *Spencer Stuart*
Kelly, Sheri — *Strategic Associates, Inc.*
Kelsey, Micki — *Davidson, Laird & Associates*
Kern, Jerry L. — *ADOW's Executeam*
Kern, Kathleen G. — *ADOW's Executeam*
Kielty, John L. — *Earley Kielty and Associates, Inc.*
Kilcoyne, Pat — *CPS Inc.*
Kiley, Phyllis — *National Search, Inc.*
King, Richard M. — *Kittleman & Associates*
Kinley, Kathy — *Intech Summit Group, Inc.*
Kinney, Carol — *Dussick Management Associates*
Kkorzyniewski, Nicole — *CPS Inc.*
Klages, Constance W. — *International Management Advisors, Inc.*
Klavens, Cecile J. — *The Pickwick Group, Inc.*
Klein, Gary I. — *Johnson Smith & Knisely Accord*
Klopfenstein, Edward L. — *Crowder & Company*
Klumpjan, Sonja — *CPS Inc.*
Knisely, Gary — *Johnson Smith & Knisely Accord*
Kohn, Adam P. — *Christian & Timbers*
Koontz, Donald N. — *Koontz, Jeffries & Associates, Inc.*
Kossuth, David — *Kossuth & Associates, Inc.*
Kossuth, Jane — *Kossuth & Associates, Inc.*
Krejci, Stanley L. — *The Interface Group, Ltd./Boyden*

Kreutz, Gary L. — *Kreutz Consulting Group, Inc.*
Kring, Kenneth L. — *Spencer Stuart*
Laird, Cheryl — *CPS Inc.*
Laird, Meri — *Davidson, Laird & Associates*
Lake, Phillip R. — *U.S. Envirosearch*
Lautz, Lindsay A. — *Wilkinson & Ives*
Leahy, Jan — *CPS Inc.*
Leininger, Dennis — *Key Employment Services*
Levine, Lois — *National Search, Inc.*
Lipe, Jerold L. — *Compass Group Ltd.*
Lofthouse, Cindy — *CPS Inc.*
Logue, Kenneth F. — *Logue & Rice Inc.*
Long, Melanie — *National Search, Inc.*
Long, William G. — *McDonald, Long & Associates, Inc.*
Longmore, Marilyn — *Richard Kader & Associates*
Loomis, Ruth L. — *Ast/Bryant*
Lotz, R. James — *International Management Advisors, Inc.*
Loving, Vikki — *Intersource, Ltd.*
Lucarelli, Joan — *The Onstott Group, Inc.*
Lucht, John — *The John Lucht Consultancy Inc.*
Lumsby, George N. — *International Management Advisors, Inc.*
MacCallan, Deirdre — *Butterfass, Pepe & MacCallan Inc.*
MacGregor, Malcolm — *Boyden*
Mainwaring, Andrew Brian — *Executive Search Consultants Corporation*
Mak, I. Paul — *Thomas A. Byrnes Associates*
Malcom, John W. — *Johnson Smith & Knisely Accord*
Malone, George V. — *Boyden*
Manassero, Henri J.P. — *International Management Advisors, Inc.*
Marino, Chester — *Cochran, Cochran & Yale, Inc.*
Marks, Ira — *Strategic Alternatives*
Marlow, William — *Straube Associates*
Martin, Lynne Koll — *Boyden*
Marumoto, William H. — *The Interface Group, Ltd./Boyden*
Mashakas, Elizabeth — *TOPAZ International, Inc.*
Mashakas, Elizabeth — *TOPAZ Legal Solutions*
Mather, David R. — *Christian & Timbers*
McAndrews, Kathy — *CPS Inc.*
McCallister, Richard A. — *Boyden*
McCarthy, David R. — *Spencer Stuart*
McCormack, Joseph A. — *McCormack & Associates*
McCreary, Charles — *Austin-McGregor International*
McDonald, Scott A. — *McDonald Associates International*
McDonald, Stanleigh B. — *McDonald Associates International*
McGann, Paul L. — *The Cassie Group*
McIntyre, Alex D. — *Norman Roberts & Associates, Inc.*
McIntyre, Joel — *Phillips Resource Group*
McKell, Linda — *Advanced Information Management*
McKnight, Amy E. — *Chartwell Partners International, Inc.*
McNamara, Timothy C. — *Columbia Consulting Group*
McNichol, John — *McNichol Associates*
McSherry, James F. — *Battalia Winston International*
Meagher, Patricia G. — *Spencer Stuart*
Meltzer, Andrea Y. — *Executive Options, Ltd.*
Messett, William J. — *Messett Associates, Inc.*
Michaels, Joseph — *CPS Inc.*
Michaels, Stewart — *TOPAZ International, Inc.*
Michaels, Stewart — *TOPAZ Legal Solutions*
Mierzwinski, John — *Industrial Recruiters Associates, Inc.*
Miller, Arnie — *Isaacson, Miller*
Miller, George N. — *Hite Executive Search*
Mohr, Brian — *CPS Inc.*
Mondragon, Philip — *Boyden*
Montgomery, Catherine C. — *Boyden*
Montgomery, James M. — *Houze, Shourds & Montgomery, Inc.*
Moore, Michael — *Agra Placements International Ltd.*
Moran, Gayle — *Dussick Management Associates*
Morgan, Gary — *National Search, Inc.*
Morris, Paul T. — *The Morris Group*
Morrison, Janis L. — *Garrett Associates Inc.*
Moseley, Monroe — *Isaacson, Miller*
Murin, Rose Mary — *U.S. Envirosearch*
Murphy, Gary J. — *Stone Murphy & Olson*
Murray, Virginia — *Baker, Harris & Partners Limited*
Mustin, Joyce M. — *J: Blakslee International, Ltd.*
Mydlach, Renee — *CPS Inc.*
Napier, Ginger L. — *Preng & Associates, Inc.*
Nazzaro, Samuel G. — *Boyden*
Nelson, Barbara — *Herman Smith Executive Initiatives Inc.*
Neuberth, Jeffrey G. — *Canny, Bowen Inc.*
Nicastro, Kelley P. — *A la carte International*
Nielsen, Sue — *Ells Personnel System Inc.*
Nitti, Jacqueline — *ALTCO Temporary Services*
Norman, Randy — *Austin-McGregor International*
O'Brien, Maggie — *Advanced Information Management*
O'Connell, Mary — *CPS Inc.*
O'Donnell, Timothy W. — *Boyden*
O'Neill, James P. — *Allerton Heneghan & O'Neill*
O'Such, Tracy — *Bishop Partners*

Oswald, Mark G. — *Canny, Bowen Inc.*
Ott, George W. — *Ott & Hansen, Inc.*
Ottenritter, Chris — *CPS Inc.*
Owens, LaMonte — *LaMonte Owens & Company*
Papciak, Dennis J. — *Accounting Personnel Associates, Inc.*
Peasback, David R. — *Canny, Bowen Inc.*
Peckenpaugh, Ann D. — *Schweichler Associates, Inc.*
Pedley, Jill — *CPS Inc.*
Peeney, James D. — *Peeney Associates*
Pelton, Margaret — *Price Waterhouse*
Pepe, Leonida — *Butterfass, Pepe & MacCallan Inc.*
Percival, Chris — *Chicago Legal Search, Ltd.*
Perez, Christina — *Orr Executive Search*
Perkins, Daphne — *CPS Inc.*
Peternich, Tracy — *Simpson Associates*
Peterson, John — *CPS Inc.*
Pettway, Samuel H. — *Spencer Stuart*
Phelps, Gene L. — *McCormack & Farrow*
Phillips, Donald L. — *O'Shea, Divine & Company, Inc.*
Pierson, Edward J. — *Johnson Smith & Knisely Accord*
Pinkman, Karen N. — *Skott/Edwards Consultants, Inc.*
Pitcher, Brian D. — *Skott/Edwards Consultants, Inc.*
Poirier, Roland — *Poirier, Hoevel & Co.*
Pomerance, Mark — *CPS Inc.*
Poore, Larry D. — *Ward Howell International, Inc.*
Porter, Donald — *Amherst Personnel Group Inc.*
Prince, Marilyn L. — *Higdon Prince Inc.*
Proct, Nina — *Martin H. Bauman Associates, Inc.*
Provus, Barbara L. — *Shepherd Bueschel & Provus, Inc.*
Raab, Julie — *Dunhill Professional Search of Irvine, Inc.*
Rabinowitz, Peter A. — *P.A.R. Associates Inc.*
Radice, Joseph — *Hospitality International*
Randell, James E. — *Randell-Heiken, Inc.*
Ray, Marianne C. — *Callan Associates, Ltd.*
Raymond, Anne — *Anderson Sterling Associates*
Redler, Rhonda — *National Search, Inc.*
Reece, Christopher S. — *Reece & Mruk Partners*
Regan, Thomas J. — *Tower Consultants, Ltd.*
Reiss, Matt — *National Search, Inc.*
Rendl, Ric — *CPS Inc.*
Renick, Cynthia L. — *Morgan Hunter Corp.*
Reynolds, Gregory P. — *Roberts Ryan and Bentley*
Rice, Raymond D. — *Logue & Rice Inc.*
Riederer, Larry — *CPS Inc.*
Rieger, Louis J. — *Spencer Stuart*
Rimmele, Michael — *The Bankers Group*
Rivas, Alberto F. — *Boyden*
Rivers, Geri — *Chrisman & Company, Incorporated*
Roberts, Mitch — *A.E. Feldman Associates*
Roberts, Norman C. — *Norman Roberts & Associates, Inc.*
Roberts, William — *Cochran, Cochran & Yale, Inc.*
Robins, Jeri N. — *Nagler, Robins & Poe, Inc.*
Robinson, Bruce — *Bruce Robinson Associates*
Robinson, Eric B. — *Bruce Robinson Associates*
Rosenberg, Esther — *Howe-Lewis International*
Rosenthal, Charles — *National Search, Inc.*
Rothfeld, Robert — *A.E. Feldman Associates*
Rubinstein, Alan J. — *Chicago Legal Search, Ltd.*
Rudolph, Kenneth — *Kossuth & Associates, Inc.*
Sacerdote, John — *Raymond Karsan Associates*
Sahlas, Chrissy — *CPS Inc.*
Saletra, Andrew — *CPS Inc.*
Sanders, Natalie — *CPS Inc.*
Sawyer, Patricia L. — *Smith & Sawyer Inc.*
Scalamera, Tom — *CPS Inc.*
Schedra, Sharon — *Earley Kielty and Associates, Inc.*
Schiavone, Mary Rose — *Canny, Bowen Inc.*
Schlpma, Christine — *Advanced Executive Resources*
Schmidt, Peter R. — *Boyden*
Schroeder, John W. — *Spencer Stuart*
Schueneman, David — *CPS Inc.*
Schwam, Carol — *A.E. Feldman Associates*
Scullin, Richard — *Eden & Associates, Inc.*
Seco, William — *Seco & Zetto Associates, Inc.*
Selker, Gregory L. — *Christian & Timbers*
Sennello, Gendra — *National Search, Inc.*
Serwat, Leonard A. — *Spencer Stuart*
Shapiro, Elaine — *CPS Inc.*
Sharf, Bernard — *Search Associates, Inc.*
Shea, John — *ALTCO Temporary Services*
Shelton, Sandra — *National Search, Inc.*
Shipherd, John T. — *The Cassie Group*
Shoemaker, Larry C. — *Shoemaker & Associates*
Shultz, Susan F. — *SSA Executive Search International*
Sibbald, John R. — *John Sibbald Associates, Inc.*
Sibul, Shelly Remen — *Chicago Legal Search, Ltd.*

Siegel, Pamela — *Executive Options, Ltd.*
Signer, Julie — *CPS Inc.*
Silcott, Marvin L. — *Marvin L. Silcott & Associates, Inc.*
Sinclair, Amy — *Fisher Personnel Management Services*
Sine, Mark — *Hospitality International*
Skunda, Donna M. — *Allerton Heneghan & O'Neill*
Slaughter, Katherine T. — *Compass Group Ltd.*
Smith, Adam M. — *The Abbott Group, Inc.*
Smith, David P. — *Smith & Latterell (HRS, Inc.)*
Snelgrove, Geiger — *National Search, Inc.*
Songy, Al — *U.S. Envirosearch*
Stack, James K. — *Boyden*
Stafford, Susan — *Hospitality International*
Stein, Terry W. — *Stewart, Stein and Scott, Ltd.*
Sterling, Jay — *Earley Kielty and Associates, Inc.*
Stern, Stephen — *CPS Inc.*
Sterner, Doug — *CPS Inc.*
Stewart, Ross M. — *Human Resources Network Partners Inc.*
Straube, Stanley H. — *Straube Associates*
Stringer, Dann P. — *D.E. Foster Partners Inc.*
Strom, Mark N. — *Search Advisors International Corp.*
Sturtz, James W. — *Compass Group Ltd.*
Sullivan, Kay — *Rusher, Loscavio & LoPresto*
Summerfield-Beall, Dotty — *Summerfield Associates, Inc.*
Sur, William K. — *Canny, Bowen Inc.*
Sussman, Lynda — *Gilbert Tweed/INESA*
Swanson, Dick — *Raymond Karsan Associates*
Szafran, Jack — *U.S. Envirosearch*
Takacs, Gloria — *Gilbert & Van Campen International*
Tholke, William E. — *Canny, Bowen Inc.*
Thomas, Cheryl M. — *CPS Inc.*
Thomas, Kim — *CPS Inc.*
Timoney, Laura — *Bishop Partners*
Tipping, William M. — *Ward Howell International, Inc.*
Torbert, Laura — *Temporary Accounting Personnel Inc.*
Tovrog, Dan — *CPS Inc.*
Trosin, Walter R. — *Johnson Smith & Knisely Accord*
Trott, Kathryn — *Allard Associates*
Trott, Kathryn — *Allard Associates*
Truemper, Dean — *CPS Inc.*
Truex, John F. — *Morton, McCorkle & Associates, Inc.*
Tullberg, Tina — *CPS Inc.*
Turner, Marilyn — *Temporary Accounting Personnel Inc.*
Vachon, David A. — *McNichol Associates*
Van Campen, Jerry — *Gilbert & Van Campen International*
Vennat, Manon — *Spencer Stuart*
Vergara, Gail H. — *Spencer Stuart*
Vinnedge, Sandra — *U.S. Envirosearch*
Vlcek, Thomas J. — *Vlcek & Company, Inc.*
Waggoner, Lisa — *Intersource, Ltd.*
Wakefield, Scott — *National Search, Inc.*
Walker, Ewing J. — *Ward Howell International, Inc.*
Walker, Martin S. — *Walker Communications*
Warter, Mark — *Isaacson, Miller*
Watson, Peggy — *Advanced Information Management*
Wein, Michael S. — *Media Management Resources, Inc.*
Wein, William — *Media Management Resources, Inc.*
Weisler, Nancy — *National Search, Inc.*
Weissman-Rosenthal, Abbe — *ALW Research International*
Weisz, Laura — *Anderson Sterling Associates*
Welch, David — *Isaacson, Miller*
Westerfield, Putney — *Boyden*
White, Kimberly — *Executive Referral Services, Inc.*
Whitley, Sue Ann — *Roberts Ryan and Bentley*
Wichlei, Alan — *Isaacson, Miller*
Wier, Daniel — *Horton International*
Wilcox, Karen — *Isaacson, Miller*
Williams, Lis — *Executive Options, Ltd.*
Williams, Michelle Cruz — *Isaacson, Miller*
Willner, Nannette — *S.R. Wolman Associates, Inc.*
Wilson, Patricia L. — *Leon A. Farley Associates*
Winograd, Glenn — *Criterion Executive Search, Inc.*
Winston, Dale — *Battalia Winston International*
Winston, Susan — *CPS Inc.*
Wise, Anne — *U.S. Envirosearch*
Wittenberg, Laura L. — *Boyden*
Wolman, Stephen R. — *S.R. Wolman Associates, Inc.*
Womack, Joseph — *The Bankers Group*
Woodward, Lee — *Search Associates, Inc.*
Young, Alexander — *Messett Associates, Inc.*
Zera, Ronald J. — *Spencer Stuart*
Zetto, Kathryn — *Seco & Zetto Associates, Inc.*
Zilliacus, Patrick W. — *Larsen, Zilliacus & Associates, Inc.*
Zinn, Donald — *Bishop Partners*
Zivic, Janis M. — *Spencer Stuart*

# Geographic Index

## Alabama
### Birmingham
Blanton, Thomas — *Blanton and Company*
Martin, Charles E. — *Management Recruiters International, Inc.*
Martin, Pat A. — *Management Recruiters International, Inc.*
### Huntsville
Banks, Renate — *Management Recruiters International, Inc.*
Bell, Lindy — *F-O-R-T-U-N-E Personnel Consultants of Huntsville, Inc.*
Henry, Patrick — *F-O-R-T-U-N-E Personnel Consultants of Huntsville, Inc.*
Henshaw, Robert — *F-O-R-T-U-N-E Personnel Consultants of Huntsville, Inc.*
Lamb, Lynn M. — *F-O-R-T-U-N-E Personnel Consultants of Huntsville, Inc.*
Langford, Robert W. — *F-O-R-T-U-N-E Personnel Consultants of Huntsville, Inc.*
Lejeune, Jeanette — *F-O-R-T-U-N-E Personnel Consultants of Huntsville, Inc.*
Owens, Ken — *F-O-R-T-U-N-E Personnel Consultants of Huntsville, Inc.*
Simmons, Anneta — *F-O-R-T-U-N-E Personnel Consultants of Huntsville, Inc.*
Swatts, Stone — *F-O-R-T-U-N-E Personnel Consultants of Huntsville, Inc.*
### Mobile
Brock, Rufus C. — *Management Recruiters International, Inc.*

## Alaska
### Kenai
Morse, Aaron H. — *Management Recruiters International, Inc.*
Morse, Jeannine — *Management Recruiters International, Inc.*

## Arizona
### Nogales
Garcia, Joseph — *Management Recruiters International, Inc.*
### Phoenix
Balchumas, Charles — *Source Services Corporation*
Blecker, Jay — *TSS Consulting, Ltd.*
Booth, Ronald — *Source Services Corporation*
Bruno, David A. — *DHR International, Inc.*
Cizek, Marti J. — *Cizek Associates, Inc.*
Collins, Scott — *Source Services Corporation*
Collis, Gerald — *TSS Consulting, Ltd.*
Debus, Wayne — *Source Services Corporation*
Faber, Jill — *A.T. Kearney, Inc.*
Gabbay, Steve — *Accounting & Bookkeeping Personnel, Inc.*
Gares, Conrad — *TSS Consulting, Ltd.*
Goldman, Elaine — *Phyllis Hawkins & Associates, Inc.*
Graff, Jack — *Source Services Corporation*
Green, Marc — *TSS Consulting, Ltd.*
Hawkins, Phyllis — *Phyllis Hawkins & Associates, Inc.*
Howard, Marybeth — *Accounting & Bookkeeping Personnel, Inc.*
Howe, Vance A. — *Ward Howell International, Inc.*
Jones, B.J. — *Intersource, Ltd.*
Kuzmick, John — *Accountants on Call*
McDonald, John R. — *TSS Consulting, Ltd.*
McThrall, David — *TSS Consulting, Ltd.*
Meyer, Marjorie — *Accountants on Call*
Meyer, Michael F. — *Witt/Kieffer, Ford, Hadelman & Lloyd*
Nolan, Michael W. — *Accounting & Bookkeeping Personnel, Inc.*
Nosky, Richard E. — *Ward Howell International, Inc.*
Orr, Don — *Orr Executive Search*
Perez, Christina — *Orr Executive Search*
Petersen, Richard — *Source Services Corporation*
Robertson, Sherry — *Source Services Corporation*
Shultz, Susan F. — *SSA Executive Search International*
Spector, Michael — *Source Services Corporation*
Swick, Jan — *TSS Consulting, Ltd.*
Weeks, Glenn — *Source Services Corporation*
Weis, Theodore — *Source Services Corporation*
Wertheim, M. Chris — *Witt/Kieffer, Ford, Hadelman & Lloyd*
West, Vikki Lynn — *Accounting & Bookkeeping Personnel, Inc.*
Wichansky, Mark — *TSS Consulting, Ltd.*
Wimer, Thomas W. — *DHR International, Inc.*
### Scottsdale
Allen, Cynthia — *Roberson and Company*
Bartholdi, Theodore G. — *Bartholdi & Company, Inc.*
Doyle, Marie — *Spectra International Inc.*
Franquemont, William R. — *EFL Associates*
French, Ted — *Spectra International Inc.*
Govig, Dick A. — *Management Recruiters International, Inc.*
Govig, Todd — *Management Recruiters International, Inc.*
Jacobs, Judith — *The Rubicon Group*
Jacobs, Martin J. — *The Rubicon Group*
James, Bruce — *Roberson and Company*
Lence, Julie Anne — *Spectra International Inc.*
Margolis, Michael — *Spectra International Inc.*
Martin, James — *Spectra International Inc.*
Nold, Robert — *Roberson and Company*
Reed, Ruthann — *Spectra International Inc.*

Renner, Sandra L. — *Spectra International Inc.*
Roberts, Kenneth — *The Rubicon Group*
Rowenhorst, Brenda — *The Bren Group*
Silvas, Stephen D. — *Roberson and Company*
Wessel, Michael J. — *Spectra International Inc.*
Wilder, Richard B. — *Columbia Consulting Group*
### Tempe
Coltrane, Michael — *Richard, Wayne and Roberts*
Murphy, Patrick — *Richard, Wayne and Roberts*
### Tucson
Dejong, Jack C. — *Management Recruiters International, Inc.*
Etter, Duane A. — *Accounting & Bookkeeping Personnel, Inc.*
Garman, Herb C. — *Management Recruiters International, Inc.*
Roethlein, John — *Management Recruiters International, Inc.*
Roethlein, Lorian E. — *Management Recruiters International, Inc.*

## Arkansas
### Conway
Hatcher, Joe B. — *Ast/Bryant*
### Fayetteville
Bulla, Steven W. — *Management Recruiters International, Inc.*
### Little Rock
Hall, Earl R. — *Management Recruiters International, Inc.*
Hall, Noel K. — *Management Recruiters International, Inc.*
### Paragould
Woodruff, Mark S. — *Management Recruiters International, Inc.*
### Rogers
McEwen, Al — *Management Recruiters International, Inc.*

## California
### Agoura Hills
Schmidt, Frank B. — *F.B. Schmidt International*
Shirilla, Robert M. — *F.B. Schmidt International*
### Anderson
Connolly, Michael R. — *Management Recruiters International, Inc.*
### Aptos
Henderson, Cathy — *Management Recruiters International, Inc.*
Henderson, Dale — *Management Recruiters International, Inc.*
### Arcadia
Knight, Kim L. — *Telford, Adams & Alexander/The Knight Company*
### Auburn
Norsell, Paul E. — *Paul Norsell & Associates, Inc.*
### Berkeley
Howard, Richard H. — *Management Recruiters International, Inc.*
### Beverly Hills
Baitler, Simon C. — *The Stevenson Group of Delaware Inc.*
Morgan, Richard J. — *Morgan Samuels Co., Inc.*
Samuels, Lewis J. — *Morgan Samuels Co., Inc.*
Schlecht, Nancy — *Morgan Samuels Co., Inc.*
### Burbank
DeMario, William — *Accountants on Call*
O'Meally, Diane — *Accountants on Call*
Shaw, Eric D. — *Management Recruiters International, Inc.*
### Burlingame
Hirschbein, Don L. — *Management Recruiters International, Inc.*
### Carmel
Dugan, John H. — *J.H. Dugan and Associates, Inc.*
### Citrus Heights
Schaller, F. William — *Sanford Rose Associates*
Schaller, Karen — *Sanford Rose Associates*
### City of Industry
Tice, Diane — *Accountants on Call*
### Clovis
Albers, Joan — *Carver Search Consultants*
Cavolina, Michael — *Carver Search Consultants*
Hendrickson, Gary E. — *Management Recruiters International, Inc.*
Johnson, Stephanie — *Carver Search Consultants*
Lemon, Kay — *Management Recruiters International, Inc.*
### Corte Madera
Bluhm, Claudia — *Schweichler Associates, Inc.*
Blunt, Peter — *Hernand & Partners*
Gerbosi, Karen — *Hernand & Partners*
Hernand, Warren L. — *Hernand & Partners*
Mikula, Linda — *Schweichler Associates, Inc.*
Peckenpaugh, Ann D. — *Schweichler Associates, Inc.*
Schweichler, Lee J. — *Schweichler Associates, Inc.*
### Costa Mesa
Farrow, Jerry M. — *McCormack & Farrow*
Friedman, Helen E. — *McCormack & Farrow*
Johnson, Walt W. — *Management Recruiters International, Inc.*
Nelson, Rick J. — *Management Recruiters International, Inc.*
Phelps, Gene L. — *McCormack & Farrow*
Telford, John H. — *Telford, Adams & Alexander/Telford & Co., Inc.*
Thompson, Kenneth L. — *McCormack & Farrow*
Zaslav, Debra M. — *Telford, Adams & Alexander/Telford & Co., Inc.*

Groban, Jack — *A.T. Kearney, Inc.*
Hanna, Remon — *Source Services Corporation*
Hansen, Erik Lars — *Korn/Ferry International*
Harris, Melissa — *Paul Ray Berndtson*
Hartzman, Deborah — *Advanced Information Management*
Havas, Judy — *Heidrick & Struggles, Inc.*
Hendrixson, Ron — *Korn/Ferry International*
Hensley, Bert — *Korn/Ferry International*
Hicks, Nancy — *Paul Ray Berndtson*
Hill, Randall W. — *Heidrick & Struggles, Inc.*
Hoevel, Michael J. — *Poirier, Hoevel & Co.*
Hollingsworth, Leslie — *Brad Marks International*
Hulce, Colleen — *Korn/Ferry International*
Hunter, Patricia — *Kenzer Corp.*
Hurtado, Jaime — *Source Services Corporation*
Inglis, William — *Korn/Ferry International*
Johnson, Maxene — *Norman Roberts & Associates, Inc.*
Johnson, Ronald S. — *Ronald S. Johnson Associates, Inc.*
Judd, Susan — *Korn/Ferry International*
Katz, Cyndi — *Search West, Inc.*
Kelly, Peter W. — *R. Rollo Associates*
Kerester, Jonathon — *Cadillac Associates*
Klopmeyerr, Vanessa — *Kenzer Corp.*
Knox, Andrew — *Korn/Ferry International*
Koenig, Joel S. — *Russell Reynolds Associates, Inc.*
Krell, Richard B. — *Russell Reynolds Associates, Inc.*
Krinsky, Ira W. — *Korn/Ferry International*
Kucewicz, William — *Search West, Inc.*
Laba, Marvin — *Marvin Laba & Associates*
Lambert, Robert J. — *Heidrick & Struggles, Inc.*
Lane, Sheri — *Ryan, Miller & Associates Inc.*
Larsen, Richard F. — *Larsen, Zilliacus & Associates, Inc.*
Larson, Paul W. — *Paul Ray Berndtson*
Leetma, Imbi — *Stanton Chase International*
Levy, Carlotta — *Evie Kreisler & Associates, Inc.*
Lightner, Shayne — *Korn/Ferry International*
Lin, Felix — *Source Services Corporation*
Lissy, Elaine — *Paul Ray Berndtson*
Love, Nolanda — *Evie Kreisler & Associates, Inc.*
Lyons, Michele R. — *R. Rollo Associates*
MacKinnon, Helen — *Technical Connections Inc.*
Marks, Brad — *Brad Marks International*
Matueny, Robert — *Ryan, Miller & Associates Inc.*
McClain, Michael D. — *DHR International, Inc.*
McCormack, Joseph A. — *McCormack & Associates*
McHugh, Keith — *Source Services Corporation*
McIntyre, Alex D. — *Norman Roberts & Associates, Inc.*
McNamee, Erin — *Technical Connections Inc.*
Milstein, Bonnie — *Marvin Laba & Associates*
Mitchell, Thomas M. — *Heidrick & Struggles, Inc.*
Momtaz, Heba — *Evie Kreisler & Associates, Inc.*
Moxley, John H. — *Korn/Ferry International*
Mullen, Edward — *Korn/Ferry International*
Nahas, Caroline W. — *Korn/Ferry International*
Nekervis, Nancy — *Evie Kreisler & Associates, Inc.*
Nolen, Shannon — *Source Services Corporation*
O'Brien, Maggie — *Advanced Information Management*
O'Connell, Michael — *Ryan, Miller & Associates Inc.*
O'Shea, Timothy J. — *Heidrick & Struggles, Inc.*
Olivares, Rebecca — *Paul Ray Berndtson*
Peters, Kevin — *Source Services Corporation*
Pfannkuche, Anthony V. — *Spencer Stuart*
Phillips, Whitney — *Korn/Ferry International*
Pimentel, Alberto — *Korn/Ferry International*
Podway, Hope — *Search West, Inc.*
Poirier, Roland — *Poirier, Hoevel & Co.*
Pugliese, Vincent — *Search West, Inc.*
Quinn, Nola — *Technical Connections Inc.*
Radden, David B. — *Paul Ray Berndtson*
Reynolds, Susan F. — *Heidrick & Struggles, Inc.*
Rivers, Geri — *Chrisman & Company, Incorporated*
Roberts, Nick P. — *Spectrum Search Associates, Inc.*
Roberts, Norman C. — *Norman Roberts & Associates, Inc.*
Roberts, Richard F. — *Management Recruiters International, Inc.*
Rodriguez, Steven — *Spencer Stuart*
Rollo, Robert S. — *R. Rollo Associates*
Rosenthal, Andrea — *Korn/Ferry International*
Rubinstein, Walter — *Technical Connections Inc.*
Russell, Robin E. — *Kenzer Corp.*
Ryan, Lee — *Ryan, Miller & Associates Inc.*
Santiago, Benefrido — *Source Services Corporation*
Saposhnik, Doron — *Source Services Corporation*
Savage, Edward J. — *Stanton Chase International*
Schlosser, John R. — *Heidrick & Struggles, Inc.*
Schoettle, Michael B. — *Heidrick & Struggles, Inc.*
Shanks, Jennifer — *Source Services Corporation*
Shawhan, Heather — *Source Services Corporation*
Simmons, Jeffrey — *Kenzer Corp.*
Simon, William — *Korn/Ferry International*
Somers, Scott D. — *Paul Ray Berndtson*
Spencer, John — *Source Services Corporation*

Spencer, John — *Source Services Corporation*
Spitz, Richard — *Korn/Ferry International*
Stephanian, Armand A. — *Paul Ray Berndtson*
Sullivan, Catherine — *Korn/Ferry International*
Tallent, Diane — *Evie Kreisler & Associates, Inc.*
Tanabe, Sharon — *Korn/Ferry International*
Thompson, Leslie — *Source Services Corporation*
Thrower, Troy — *Source Services Corporation*
Unger, Stephen A. — *Spencer Stuart*
Van Remmen, Roger — *Brown, Bernardy, Van Remmen, Inc.*
Vandenbulcke, Cynthia — *Source Services Corporation*
Velline, Ena A. — *Paul Ray Berndtson*
Vet, Jan — *Korn/Ferry International*
Virgili, Franca — *Johnson Smith & Knisely Accord*
Von Der Ahe, Christopher — *Korn/Ferry International*
Wagner, Robert — *Korn/Ferry International*
Walburger, Gary — *Korn/Ferry International*
Waxman, Bruce — *Ryan, Miller & Associates Inc.*
Weiss, Jeffrey — *Search West, Inc.*
Wier, Daniel — *Horton International*
Windle, Mary — *Evie Kreisler & Associates, Inc.*
Yang, George — *Technical Connections Inc.*
Zatzick, Michael — *Search West, Inc.*
Zilliacus, Patrick W. — *Larsen, Zilliacus & Associates, Inc.*

**Los Gatos**
Goodere, Greg — *Splaine & Associates, Inc.*
Splaine, Charles — *Splaine & Associates, Inc.*

**Manhattan Beach**
Fisher, Neal — *Fisher Personnel Management Services*
Sinclair, Amy — *Fisher Personnel Management Services*

**Menlo Park**
Barnett-Flint, Juliet — *Heidrick & Struggles, Inc.*
Campbell, Thomas J. — *Heidrick & Struggles, Inc.*
Connet, Mel — *Heidrick & Struggles, Inc.*
Friel, Thomas J. — *Heidrick & Struggles, Inc.*
Gostyla, Rick — *Spencer Stuart*
Harlow, John — *Korn/Ferry International*
Kelly, Michael T. — *Russell Reynolds Associates, Inc.*
Kixmiller, David B. — *Heidrick & Struggles, Inc.*
Lewis, Gretchen S. — *Heidrick & Struggles, Inc.*
Lonergan, Mark W. — *Heidrick & Struggles, Inc.*
Lundburg, Kirk — *Accountemps (division of Robert Half International)*
Mahaney, Joann — *Heidrick & Struggles, Inc.*
O'Reilly, Jack — *Catalyx Group*
Richards, Wes — *Heidrick & Struggles, Inc.*
Rizk, Nyla — *Spencer Stuart*
Scott, Alison — *Korn/Ferry International*
Stirn, Bradley A. — *Spencer Stuart*
Strain, Stephen R. — *Spencer Stuart*
Thompson, John T. — *Heidrick & Struggles, Inc.*
Ware, John C. — *Spencer Stuart*
Yoon, Kyung — *Heidrick & Struggles, Inc.*

**Mill Valley**
Blakslee, Jan H. — *J: Blakslee International, Ltd.*
Block, Randy — *Block & Associates*
Mustin, Joyce M. — *J: Blakslee International, Ltd.*
Wheel, Eric — *Management Recruiters International, Inc.*

**Milpitas**
Mallipudi, Anand — *Raymond Karsan Associates*

**Mission Viejo**
Miller, Kenneth A. — *Computer Network Resources, Inc.*

**Monterey**
Kashinsky, Richard J. — *Management Recruiters International, Inc.*

**Morro Bay**
Glaza, Ron — *Management Recruiters International, Inc.*

**Mountain View**
McKell, Linda — *Advanced Information Management*
Watson, Peggy — *Advanced Information Management*

**Newport Beach**
Cronin, Dolores — *Corporate Careers, Inc.*
Davis, G. Gordon — *Davis & Company*
Divine, Robert S. — *O'Shea, Divine & Company, Inc.*
Galante, Suzanne M. — *Vlcek & Company, Inc.*
Gettys, James R. — *International Staffing Consultants, Inc.*
Goldfarb-Lee, Terry — *O'Shea, Divine & Company, Inc.*
Gordon, Elliot — *Korn/Ferry International*
Harap, David — *Korn/Ferry International*
Johnson, Julie — *International Staffing Consultants, Inc.*
LemMou, Paul — *International Staffing Consultants, Inc.*
Phillips, Donald L. — *O'Shea, Divine & Company, Inc.*
Reno, Geri — *Corporate Careers, Inc.*
Smith, Ian — *International Staffing Consultants, Inc.*
Thomas, Ian — *International Staffing Consultants, Inc.*
Tyler, Janet — *Accountants on Call*
Vlcek, Thomas J. — *Vlcek & Company, Inc.*

**Northridge**
Furlong, James W. — *Furlong Search, Inc.*

Ives, Richard K. — *Wilkinson & Ives*
Jozwik, Peter — *The Search Firm, Inc.*
Juratovac, Michael — *Montgomery Resources, Inc.*
Juska, Frank — *Rusher, Loscavio & LoPresto*
Kampmann, Sara — *Johnson Smith & Knisely Accord*
Katz, Rosalind N. — *ExecuScope Division of Russell Staffing Resources, Inc.*
Kenney, Jeanne — *Source Services Corporation*
Kile, Robert W. — *Rusher, Loscavio & LoPresto*
Kingsley, Kate — *Korn/Ferry International*
Kuo, Linda — *Montgomery Resources, Inc.*
Larsen, William G. — *The Paladin Companies, Inc.*
Lautz, Lindsay A. — *Wilkinson & Ives*
Lee, Roger — *Montgomery Resources, Inc.*
Leff, Lisa A. — *Berger and Leff*
Lettrii, Mary — *BioQuest, Inc.*
Loscavio, J. Michael — *Rusher, Loscavio & LoPresto*
MacPherson, Holly — *Source Services Corporation*
Mahmoud, Sophia — *Source Services Corporation*
Maibach, Lisa W. — *Russell Reynolds Associates, Inc.*
Marchette, Steve — *Juntunen-Combs-Poirier*
Martin, Lynne Koll — *Boyden*
Mauer, Kristin — *Montgomery Resources, Inc.*
McAteer, Thomas — *Montgomery Resources, Inc.*
McKnight, Amy E. — *Chartwell Partners International, Inc.*
McLaughlin, John — *Romac & Associates*
Metz, Dan K. — *Russell Reynolds Associates, Inc.*
Meyers, Steven — *Montgomery Resources, Inc.*
Mill, Christopher A. — *The Paladin Companies, Inc.*
Nosal, David — *Korn/Ferry International*
Nosal, David A. — *Heidrick & Struggles, Inc.*
O'Maley, Kimberlee — *Spencer Stuart*
O'Neill, David — *Korn/Ferry International*
Pearson, John R. — *Pearson, Caldwell & Farnsworth, Inc.*
Poirier, Frank — *Juntunen-Combs-Poirier*
Pompeo, Paul — *Search West, Inc.*
Price, Andrew G. — *The Thomas Tucker Company*
Price, P. Anthony — *Russell Reynolds Associates, Inc.*
Rusher, William H. — *Rusher, Loscavio & LoPresto*
Russell, Carol — *ExecuScope Division of Russell Staffing Resources, Inc.*
Sanchez, William — *Source Services Corporation*
Saydah, Robert F. — *Heidrick & Struggles, Inc.*
Schneider, James — *The Search Firm, Inc.*
Schulte, Bernard — *Korn/Ferry International*
Scott, Jack — *Korn/Ferry International*
Seitchik, Jack — *Seitchik Corwin and Seitchik, Inc.*
Shattuck, Merrill B. — *M.B. Shattuck and Associates, Inc.*
Shulman, Barry — *Shulman Associates*
Shulman, Melvin — *McFeely Wackerle Shulman*
Sill, Igor M. — *Geneva Group International*
Stack, James K. — *Boyden*
Theobald, David B. — *Theobald & Associates*
Thompson, Dave — *Battalia Winston International*
Timms, Alan R. — *DHR International, Inc.*
Trott, Kathryn — *Allard Associates*
Tucker, Thomas A. — *The Thomas Tucker Company*
Van Norman, Ben — *Source Services Corporation*
von Stein, Scott — *Wilkinson & Ives*
Walter, Mary Ann — *Spencer Stuart*
Wayne, Victoria P. — *Korn/Ferry International*
Weber, Jurgen — *BioQuest, Inc.*
Webster, Robert C. — *The Lawsmiths of Northern California, Inc.*
Weintraub, Lynn — *The Paladin Companies, Inc.*
Westerfield, Putney — *Boyden*
White, Jonathan — *Spencer Stuart*
Wilkinson, William R. — *Wilkinson & Ives*
Wilson, John C. — *Russell Reynolds Associates, Inc.*
Wilson, Patricia L. — *Leon A. Farley Associates*
Yamada, Steven — *Korn/Ferry International*
Yowe, Mark — *Heidrick & Struggles, Inc.*
Zivic, Janis M. — *Spencer Stuart*

**San Jose**
Boyd, Michael — *Accountants on Call*
Rosica, John — *Management Recruiters International, Inc.*
Schuckman, Louis — *Accountants on Call*

**San Juan Capistrano**
McManamon, Tim — *Rogers-McManamon Executive Search*
Rogers, Gay — *Rogers-McManamon Executive Search*

**San Luis Obispo**
Bunker, Ralph L. — *Management Recruiters International, Inc.*

**San Mateo**
Ferneborg, Jay W. — *Ferneborg & Associates, Inc.*
Ferneborg, John R. — *Ferneborg & Associates, Inc.*
Karr, Cynthia L. — *Howard Karr & Associates, Inc.*
Karr, Howard L. — *Howard Karr & Associates, Inc.*
Pickford, Stephen T. — *The Corporate Staff, Inc.*

**San Pedro**
Bertok, Ken — *The Wentworth Company, Inc.*
Chambers, Robert — *The Wentworth Company, Inc.*

Jackson, Carol — *The Wentworth Company, Inc.*
Wentworth, John — *The Wentworth Company, Inc.*

**Santa Ana**
Endres, Robert — *Sanford Rose Associates*

**Santa Barbara**
Mehrbrodt, Al W. — *Management Recruiters International, Inc.*
Myatt, James S. — *Sanford Rose Associates*

**Santa Clara**
Horgan, Thomas F. — *Nadzam, Lusk, Horgan & Associates, Inc.*
Lusk, Theodore E. — *Nadzam, Lusk, Horgan & Associates, Inc.*
Nadzam, Richard — *Nadzam, Lusk, Horgan & Associates, Inc.*

**Santa Clarita**
Parry, William H. — *Horton International*

**Santa Monica**
Bryant, Christopher P. — *Ast/Bryant*
Corrigan, Gerald F. — *The Corrigan Group*
Loomis, Ruth L. — *Ast/Bryant*

**Sherman Oaks**
Biolsi, Joseph — *Source Services Corporation*
Cook, Charlene — *Source Services Corporation*
Fanning, Paul — *Source Services Corporation*
Goldsmith, Fred J. — *Fred J. Goldsmith Associates*
Hasten, Lawrence — *Source Services Corporation*
Heroux, David — *Source Services Corporation*
Ratajczak, Paul — *Source Services Corporation*
Renteria, Elizabeth — *Source Services Corporation*
Trimble, Patricia — *Source Services Corporation*

**Solvang**
Hergenrather, Edmund R. — *Hergenrather & Company*

**Sunnyvale**
Beaver, Robert — *Source Services Corporation*
Bosward, Allan — *Source Services Corporation*
Fechheimer, Peter — *Source Services Corporation*
Fujino, Rickey — *Source Services Corporation*
Gamble, Ira — *Source Services Corporation*
Gray, Russell — *Source Services Corporation*
Hoffman, Stephen — *Source Services Corporation*
Hughes, Barbara — *Source Services Corporation*
Humphrey, Titus — *Source Services Corporation*
McKnight, Lourdes D. — *Sanford Rose Associates*
Nelson, Hitch — *Source Services Corporation*
Pregeant, David — *Source Services Corporation*
Rosen, Mitchell — *Source Services Corporation*
Schwalbach, Robert — *Source Services Corporation*
Silver, Kit — *Source Services Corporation*

**Tarzana**
Goodman, Victor — *Anderson Sterling Associates*
Raymond, Anne — *Anderson Sterling Associates*
Weisz, Laura — *Anderson Sterling Associates*

**Tiburon**
Thomas, Terry — *Montague Enterprises*

**Torrance**
Berlin, Marc — *Accountants on Call*
Hagerthy, Michael J. — *IMCOR, Inc.*

**Valley Center**
Heiser, Charles S. — *The Cassie Group*

**Van Nuys**
Sharf, Bernard — *Search Associates, Inc.*
Woodward, Lee — *Search Associates, Inc.*

**Walnut Creek**
Waxman, Kathleen — *Accountants on Call*

**Westlake Village**
Abbott, Dale — *Mixtec Group*
Baltin, Carrie — *Search West, Inc.*
Bonner, Barbara — *Mixtec Group*
Bovee, Camille — *Search West, Inc.*
Cripe, Joyce — *Mixtec Group*
Dalton, Bret — *Robert W. Dingman Company, Inc.*
Delaney, Patrick — *Search West, Inc.*
Della Monica, Vincent — *Search West, Inc.*
Dingman, Bruce — *Robert W. Dingman Company, Inc.*
Dingman, Robert W. — *Robert W. Dingman Company, Inc.*
Diskin, Rochelle — *Search West, Inc.*
Donahie, Stephen — *Search West, Inc.*
Fredericks, Ward A. — *Mixtec Group*
Harmon, Tony — *Mixtec Group*
Kantor, Richard — *Search West, Inc.*
Knotts, Jerry — *Mixtec Group*
Kracker, Robert — *Search West, Inc.*
Linton, Leonard M. — *Byron Leonard International, Inc.*
May, Peter — *Mixtec Group*
Miller, Elaine — *Search West, Inc.*
Mitros, George N. — *Mixtec Group*
Neckanoff, Sharon — *Search West, Inc.*
Potenza, Gregory — *Mixtec Group*
Radawicz, Angela — *Mixtec Group*
Robinette, Paul — *Hernand & Partners*
Romaine, Stanley J. — *Mixtec Group*

Schneider, Margo — *Search West, Inc.*
Thiras, Ted — *Mixtec Group*
Thomas, William — *Mixtec Group*
White, William C. — *Venture Resources Inc.*
Wolf, Stephen M. — *Byron Leonard International, Inc.*
Young, Lesley — *Search West, Inc.*

**Woodland Hills**
Loper, Doris — *Mortgage & Financial Personnel Services*
Maynard, Raun — *Accountants on Call*
Sherman, Robert R. — *Mortgage & Financial Personnel Services*
Springer, Mark H. — *M.H. Springer & Associates Incorporated*

## Canada
### Calgary, Alberta
Hamilton, Timothy — *The Caldwell Partners Amrop International*
Honey, W. Michael M. — *O'Callaghan Honey/Paul Ray Berndtson, Inc.*
Manthey, Merv — *KPMG Executive Search*
McKay, W. John — *O'Callaghan Honey/Paul Ray Berndtson, Inc.*
O'Callaghan, Terry K. — *O'Callaghan Honey/Paul Ray Berndtson, Inc.*
Parent, Martine L. — *O'Callaghan Honey/Paul Ray Berndtson, Inc.*
Pfeiffer, Irene — *Price Waterhouse*
Shervey, Brent C. — *O'Callaghan Honey/Paul Ray Berndtson, Inc.*
Sutton, Robert J. — *The Caldwell Partners Amrop International*
van de Wetering, Shirley — *The Caldwell Partners Amrop International*

### Edmonton, Alberta
Harvey, Richard — *Price Waterhouse*
Jacobson, Al — *KPMG Executive Search*
Simmonds, David — *Coopers & Lybrand Consulting*

### Halifax, Nova Scotia
Hall, George — *Coopers & Lybrand Consulting*
Letson, Susan — *KPMG Executive Search*

### Mississauga, Ontario
O'Brien, John G. — *CanMed Consultants Inc.*
Raheja, Marc C. — *CanMed Consultants Inc.*

### Montreal, Quebec
Beaupre, Joseph — *Price Waterhouse*
Belle Isle, Charles — *Belle Isle, Djandji Inc.*
Bourbeau, Paul J. — *Boyden*
Bourbonnais, Jean-Pierre — *Ward Howell International, Inc.*
Brassard, Phillipe — *KPMG Executive Search*
Champoux, Yves — *Ward Howell International, Inc.*
Djandji, Guy N. — *Belle Isle, Djandji Inc.*
Drennan, Ronald — *Ward Howell International, Inc.*
Durand, Francois — *Ward Howell International, Inc.*
Faure, Nicole — *The Caldwell Partners Amrop International*
Gosselin, Jocelyne — *The Caldwell Partners Amrop International*
Hebert, Guy J. — *Spencer Stuart*
Johnston, Philip D. — *Egon Zehnder International Inc.*
Joubert, Pierre E. — *Boyden*
Krecklo, Brian Douglas — *Krecklo & Associates Inc.*
Labrecque, Bernard F. — *Laurendeau, Labrecque/Paul Ray Berndtson, Inc.*
Lachance, Roger — *Laurendeau, Labrecque/Paul Ray Berndtson, Inc.*
LaTraverse, Jean J. — *Belle Isle, Djandji Inc.*
Laurendeau, Jean L. — *Laurendeau, Labrecque/Paul Ray Berndtson, Inc.*
LeComte, Andre — *Egon Zehnder International Inc.*
Lefebvre, Jean-Pierre — *Ward Howell International, Inc.*
Payette, Pierre — *Egon Zehnder International Inc.*
Raymond, Jean — *The Caldwell Partners Amrop International*
Swidler, J. Robert — *Egon Zehnder International Inc.*
Vennat, Manon — *Spencer Stuart*

### Nepean, Ontario
Winter, Peter — *Catalyx Group*

### North York, Ontario
Nagy, Les — *Source Services Corporation*

### Ottawa, Ontario
Morgan, Richard S. — *Lovas Stanley/Paul Ray Berndtson Inc.*
Reid, Gary — *KPMG Executive Search*

### Saint John, New Brunswick
Moors, Donald — *Coopers & Lybrand Consulting*

### Saskatoon, Saskatchewan
Hiebert, Wilf — *KPMG Executive Search*

### St. John's, Newfoundland
Powell, Lloyd — *KPMG Executive Search*

### Toronto, Ontario
Bagg, Keith — *Keith Bagg & Associates Inc.*
Bagg, Mary — *Keith Bagg & Associates Inc.*
Baker, Gerry — *Baker, Harris & Partners Limited*
Baldock, Robert G. — *Lovas Stanley/Paul Ray Berndtson Inc.*
Baran, Helena — *Michael J. Cavanagh and Associates*
Bell, Michael — *Spencer Stuart*
Berlet, William — *KPMG Executive Search*
Blair, Kelly A. — *The Caldwell Partners Amrop International*
Bliley, Jerry — *Spencer Stuart*

Brunelle, Francis W.H. — *The Caldwell Partners Amrop International*
Burns, Alan — *The Enns Partners Inc.*
Caldwell, C. Douglas — *The Caldwell Partners Amrop International*
Campbell, Margaret — *Coopers & Lybrand Consulting*
Campbell, W. Ross — *Egon Zehnder International Inc.*
Caplan, Deborah — *Price Waterhouse*
Carver, Graham — *Cambridge Management Planning*
Cavanagh, Michael J. — *Michael J. Cavanagh and Associates*
Charles, Ronald D. — *The Caldwell Partners Amrop International*
Chauvin, Ralph A. — *The Caldwell Partners Amrop International*
Chua, Jackie — *Keith Bagg & Associates Inc.*
Colling, Douglas — *KPMG Executive Search*
Colling, Douglas — *KPMG Management Consulting*
Collis, Martin — *E.L. Shore & Associates Ltd.*
Connelly, Heather — *The Caldwell Partners Amrop International*
Cook, Dennis — *Korn/Ferry International*
Crath, Paul F. — *Price Waterhouse*
Densmore, Geraldine — *Michael Stern Associates Inc.*
Enns, George — *The Enns Partners Inc.*
Fawcett, Anne M. — *The Caldwell Partners Amrop International*
Fennel, P.J. — *Heidrick & Struggles, Inc.*
Gillies, Margaret — *KPMG Executive Search*
Graham, Craig — *Ward Howell International, Inc.*
Graham, Robert — *Cambridge Management Planning*
Hamar, Rolie C. — *Accountants on Call*
Harris, Jack — *Baker, Harris & Partners Limited*
Hauswirth, Jeffrey M. — *Spencer Stuart*
Hay, Ian — *Korn/Ferry International*
Humphreys, Sidney — *Korn/Ferry International*
Hussey, Wayne — *Krecklo & Associates Inc.*
Iammatteo, Enzo — *Keith Bagg & Associates Inc.*
Illsley, Hugh G. — *Ward Howell International, Inc.*
Irvine, Robert — *Keith Bagg & Associates Inc.*
Kinley, David — *The Caldwell Partners Amrop International*
Knight, Lisa — *Ward Howell International, Inc.*
Laubitz, Chris — *The Caldwell Partners Amrop International*
Lennox, Charles — *Price Waterhouse*
Long, Thomas — *Egon Zehnder International Inc.*
Lovas, W. Carl — *Lovas Stanley/Paul Ray Berndtson Inc.*
Lyttle, Jordene — *The Caldwell Partners Amrop International*
MacDougall, Andrew J. — *Spencer Stuart*
MacEachern, David — *Spencer Stuart*
Mackinlay, Marcelo D. — *Heidrick & Struggles, Inc.*
MacLeod, Jill C. — *Lovas Stanley/Paul Ray Berndtson Inc.*
Malcolm, Rod — *The Enns Partners Inc.*
Martin, Jon — *Egon Zehnder International Inc.*
Massey, R. Bruce — *Bruce Massey & Partners Inc.*
McAlpine, Bruce — *Keith Bagg & Associates Inc.*
McGill, Robert — *The Caldwell Partners Amrop International*
McLean, B. Keith — *Price Waterhouse*
Miller, Roy — *The Enns Partners Inc.*
Moga, Michael — *Korn/Ferry International*
Moore, Richard C.E. — *Russell Reynolds Associates, Inc.*
Morin, Michelle — *Spencer Stuart*
Murray, Virginia — *Baker, Harris & Partners Limited*
Nederpelt, Jack H.B. — *Russell Reynolds Associates, Inc.*
Neelin, Sharon — *The Caldwell Partners Amrop International*
Neil, Colleen Ellen — *Korn/Ferry International*
Nelson, Barbara — *Herman Smith Executive Initiatives Inc.*
Nixon, Sarah — *The Caldwell Partners Amrop International*
Parr, James A. — *KPMG Executive Search*
Parr, James A. — *KPMG Management Consulting*
Pasahow, David — *Heidrick & Struggles, Inc.*
Paynter, Sandra L. — *Ward Howell International, Inc.*
Pelton, Margaret — *Price Waterhouse*
Perry, Wayne B. — *Bruce Massey & Partners Inc.*
Probert, William W. — *Ward Howell International, Inc.*
Redwood, Guy W. — *Bruce Massey & Partners Inc.*
Roberts, Derek J. — *Ward Howell International, Inc.*
Ross, Lawrence — *Lovas Stanley/Paul Ray Berndtson Inc.*
Ross, Mark S. — *Herman Smith Executive Initiatives Inc.*
Ross, Sheila L. — *Ward Howell International, Inc.*
Rossi, Silvio — *Keith Bagg & Associates Inc.*
Shenfield, Peter — *Baker, Harris & Partners Limited*
Shore, Earl L. — *E.L. Shore & Associates Ltd.*
Sinclair, Tom — *Coopers & Lybrand Consulting*
Smith, Cheryl — *KPMG Executive Search*
Smith, Herman M. — *Herman Smith Executive Initiatives Inc.*
Speck, Michael J. — *Lovas Stanley/Paul Ray Berndtson Inc.*
Sprague, David — *Michael Stern Associates Inc.*
Stackhouse, P. John — *Heidrick & Struggles, Inc.*
Stanley, Paul R.A. — *Lovas Stanley/Paul Ray Berndtson Inc.*
Stern, Michael I. — *Michael Stern Associates Inc.*
Stewart, Jan J. — *Egon Zehnder International Inc.*
Stewart, Wilf — *KPMG Executive Search*
Stoneham, Herbert E.C. — *Stoneham Associates Corp.*
Stouffer, Kenneth — *Keith Bagg & Associates Inc.*
ten Cate, Herman H. — *Stoneham Associates Corp.*
Thomas, Christine S. — *Lovas Stanley/Paul Ray Berndtson Inc.*

Van Clieaf, Mark — *MVC Associates International*
Wanless, Theresa — *The Caldwell Partners Amrop International*
Whittall, Barbara — *Heidrick & Struggles, Inc.*
Wilkie, Glenn — *Korn/Ferry International*
Zucchiatti, Elizabeth — *The Caldwell Partners Amrop International*

### Vancouver, British Columbia
Ashton, Barbara L. — *Ashton Computer Professionals Inc.*
Brooks, Charles — *Corporate Recruiters Ltd.*
Brooks, Kimberllay — *Corporate Recruiters Ltd.*
Christie, Ian — *The Caldwell Partners Amrop International*
Dornblut, Cindy — *Ashton Computer Professionals Inc.*
Edmond, Bruce — *Corporate Recruiters Ltd.*
Gibbons, Betsy — *The Caldwell Partners Amrop International*
Hemer, Craig — *Tanton Mitchell/Paul Ray Berndtson*
Hnatuik, Ivan — *Corporate Recruiters Ltd.*
Horner, Gregory — *Corporate Recruiters Ltd.*
Jackson, Clarke H. — *The Caldwell Partners Amrop International*
Kershaw, Lisa — *Tanton Mitchell/Paul Ray Berndtson*
Leigh, Daniel S. — *Accountants on Call*
McBurney, Kevin — *The Caldwell Partners Amrop International*
McMillin, Bob — *Price Waterhouse*
Mitchell, Kyle R. — *Tanton Mitchell/Paul Ray Berndtson*
Moore, Anne — *KPMG Executive Search*
O'Neill, Karen — *Ashton Computer Professionals Inc.*
Prior, Donald — *The Caldwell Partners Amrop International*
Safnuk, Donald — *Corporate Recruiters Ltd.*
Smith, Grant — *Price Waterhouse*
Spitz, Grant — *The Caldwell Partners Amrop International*
Tanton, John E. — *Tanton Mitchell/Paul Ray Berndtson*
To, Raymond — *Corporate Recruiters Ltd.*
Van Alstine, Catherine — *Tanton Mitchell/Paul Ray Berndtson*
Van Nus, Robert — *Coopers & Lybrand Consulting*
Wallace, Alec — *Tanton Mitchell/Paul Ray Berndtson*
Wassill, Larry — *Corporate Recruiters Ltd.*

### Waterloo, Ontario
Boehmer, Jack — *KPMG Executive Search*

### Winnipeg, Manitoba
Martin, Al — *KPMG Executive Search*
Swystun, Karen — *Price Waterhouse*

## Colorado
### Boulder
Arnold, Janet N. — *Management Recruiters International, Inc.*
Hunter, Sharon W. — *Management Recruiters International, Inc.*
Parker, Murray B. — *The Borton Wallace Company*

### Colorado Springs
Carter, Christine C. — *Health Care Dimensions*
Hazelton, Lisa M. — *Health Care Dimensions*
Howard, Jill — *Health Care Dimensions*
Merriman, Mark — *Management Recruiters International, Inc.*
Reynolds, Bud O. — *Management Recruiters International, Inc.*
West, Nancy — *Health Care Dimensions*

### Denver
Arnold, Sheridan J. — *William B. Arnold Associates*
Arnold, William B. — *William B. Arnold Associates*
DiMarchi, Paul — *DiMarchi Partners, Inc.*
Kirschner, John — *Management Recruiters International, Inc.*
Maitland, Thomas M. — *DHR International, Inc.*
Mark, John L. — *J.L. Mark Associates, Inc.*
Pocs, Martin M. — *DHR International, Inc.*
Pryde, Marcia P. — *A.T. Kearney, Inc.*
Roberts, Gary — *A.T. Kearney, Inc.*
Sahe, Mark — *Accountants on Call*
Schaefer, Frederic M. — *A.T. Kearney, Inc.*
Torbert, Laura — *Temporary Accounting Personnel Inc.*
Turner, Marilyn — *Temporary Accounting Personnel Inc.*
Turner, Michael — *Rocky Mountain Recruiters, Inc.*
Winslow, Lawrence J. — *DHR International, Inc.*

### Englewood
Christian, Kevin — *Management Recruiters International, Inc.*
Davis, C. Scott — *Source Services Corporation*
Ellis, Patricia — *Source Services Corporation*
Field, Andrew — *Source Services Corporation*
Francis, Brad — *Source Services Corporation*
Graham, Shannon — *Source Services Corporation*
Haider, Martin — *Source Services Corporation*
Harp, Kimberly — *Source Services Corporation*
Heisser, Robert — *Management Recruiters International, Inc.*
Hobson, Mary L. — *EFL Associates*
Milius, Kent L. — *Management Recruiters International, Inc.*
Pugh, Judith Geist — *InterimManagement Solutions, Inc.*
Reynolds, Laura — *Source Services Corporation*
Riley, Jeffrey K. — *EFL Associates*
Sell, David — *Source Services Corporation*
Spoutz, Paul — *Source Services Corporation*
Stiles, Judy — *MedQuest Associates*
Trimble, Rhonda — *Source Services Corporation*
Wein, Michael S. — *InterimManagement Solutions, Inc.*
Wein, Michael S. — *Media Management Resources, Inc.*
Wein, William — *InterimManagement Solutions, Inc.*

Wein, William — *Media Management Resources, Inc.*
Woomer, Jerome — *Source Services Corporation*

### Evergreen
Neumann, Pete — *Management Recruiters International, Inc.*
Neumann, Vicki A. — *Management Recruiters International, Inc.*

### Franktown
Empey, David G. — *Management Recruiters International, Inc.*

### Greenwood Village
Greco, Maria — *R L Plimpton Associates*
Plimpton, Ralph L. — *R L Plimpton Associates*
Robinson, Adrienne — *R L Plimpton Associates*

### Lakewood
Bonner, Rodney D. — *Management Recruiters International, Inc.*
Deering, Joseph — *U.S. Envirosearch*
Eatmon, Michael — *U.S. Envirosearch*
Gilbert, Robert — *U.S. Envirosearch*
Hanson, Carrie — *U.S. Envirosearch*
Lake, Phillip R. — *U.S. Envirosearch*
Murin, Rose Mary — *U.S. Envirosearch*
Songy, Al — *U.S. Envirosearch*
Szafran, Jack — *U.S. Envirosearch*
Vinnedge, Sandra — *U.S. Envirosearch*
Wise, Anne — *U.S. Envirosearch*

### Leadville
Stevenson, Terry — *Bartholdi & Company, Inc.*

### Westminster
Kellerhals, Gloria — *Management Recruiters International, Inc.*

## Connecticut
### Avon
Beer, John — *People Management Northeast Incorporated*
Bond, James L. — *People Management Northeast Incorporated*
Briggs, Adam — *Horton International*
Brown, Larry C. — *Horton International*
Clegg, Cynthia — *Horton International*
Cooke, Katherine H. — *Horton International*
Darter, Steven M. — *People Management Northeast Incorporated*
Fischer, John C. — *Horton International*
Gilchrist, Robert J. — *Horton International*
Horton, Robert H. — *Horton International*
Klauck, James J. — *Horton International*
Pace, Susan A. — *Horton International*
Snyder, James F. — *Snyder & Company*

### Colchester
Gionta, Michael E. — *Management Recruiters International, Inc.*

### Cos Cob
Mockler, Nadine — *Part Time Resources, Inc.*
Young, Laurie — *Part Time Resources, Inc.*

### Cromwell
Cole, Les C. — *Management Recruiters International, Inc.*

### Danbury
Connor, Michele — *Abraham & London, Ltd.*
Humphrey, Joan — *Abraham & London, Ltd.*
Iannacone, Kelly — *Abraham & London, Ltd.*
Laub, Stuart R. — *Abraham & London, Ltd.*

### Fairfield
Oster, Joan — *Management Recruiters International, Inc.*
Oster, Rush R. — *Management Recruiters International, Inc.*

### Greenwich
Arnold, David J. — *Heidrick & Struggles, Inc.*
Berenblum, Marvin B. — *Heidrick & Struggles, Inc.*
Brown, John T. — *Management Recruiters International, Inc.*
de Regt, John — *Heidrick & Struggles, Inc.*
Ducruet, Linda K. — *Heidrick & Struggles, Inc.*
Erlanger, Richard A. — *Erlanger Associates Inc.*
Foote, Ray P. — *Heidrick & Struggles, Inc.*
Hendrickson, David L. — *Heidrick & Struggles, Inc.*
Livingston, Peter R. — *Livingston, Robert and Company Inc.*
Lynch, John — *Blackshaw, Olmstead & Lynch*
Mahr, Toni — *K. Russo Associates*
Mulligan, Robert P. — *William Willis Worldwide Inc.*
Pickering, Dorothy C. — *Livingston, Robert and Company Inc.*
Rippey, George E. — *Heidrick & Struggles, Inc.*
Russo, Karen — *K. Russo Associates*
Willis, William H. — *William Willis Worldwide Inc.*

### Hamden
Bartone, Robert J. — *MRG Search & Placement Inc.*
Clark, Gary — *MRG Search & Placement Inc.*
Culotta, Jonathan — *MRG Search & Placement Inc.*

### Hartford
Brown, Clifford — *Source Services Corporation*
Harwood, Brian — *Source Services Corporation*
Inzitari, Gloria — *Accountants on Call*
McCormick, Joseph — *Source Services Corporation*
Needham, Karen — *Source Services Corporation*
Simon, Bernard — *Accountants on Call*
Tenero, Kymberly — *Source Services Corporation*

Kuhnle, John H. — *Korn/Ferry International*
Landau, David — *Klein, Landau, Romm & North*
Lerner, Alyssa — *Klein, Landau, Romm & North*
Long, Benjamin H. — *Travaille Executive Search*
Low, Linda — *The Development Resource Group Incorporated*
Marumoto, William H. — *The Interface Group, Ltd./Boyden*
McBride, Jonathan E. — *McBride Associates, Inc.*
Moynihan, Kerry — *Korn/Ferry International*
North, Liz — *Klein, Landau, Romm & North*
Norton, Douglas — *Korn/Ferry International*
Nye, David S. — *Blake, Hansen & Nye, Limited*
Olson, Nels — *Korn/Ferry International*
Pearcy, Marsha G. — *Russell Reynolds Associates, Inc.*
Perry, Robert H. — *R.H. Perry & Associates, Inc.*
Pfeiffer, Leonard — *Korn/Ferry International*
Romm, Barry — *Klein, Landau, Romm & North*
Rurak, Zbigniew T. — *Rurak & Associates, Inc.*
Schneider, Susan — *Jacquelyn Finn & Susan Schneider Associates, Inc.*
Sellery, Robert A. — *Robert Sellery Associates, Ltd.*
Sherman, Daniel A. — *Goodwin & Company*
Stein, Neil A. — *R.H. Perry & Associates, Inc.*
Sterling, Sally M. — *Heidrick & Struggles, Inc.*
Stevens, Tracey — *Don Richard Associates of Washington, D.C., Inc.*
Stoy, Roger M. — *Heidrick & Struggles, Inc.*
Strassman, Mark — *Don Richard Associates of Washington, D.C., Inc.*
Stringer, Dann P. — *D.E. Foster Partners Inc.*
Szubielski, Ellen — *Klein, Landau, Romm & North*
Tobin, William — *Korn/Ferry International*
Tydings, Mary C. — *Russell Reynolds Associates, Inc.*
Vautour, Eric L. — *Russell Reynolds Associates, Inc.*
Verrill-Schlager, Martha — *Korn/Ferry International*
Vilella, Paul — *Source  Services Corporation*
Walker, Ronald H. — *Korn/Ferry International*
Weller, Paul S. — *Mark Stanley & Company*

## Florida

### Altamonte Springs
Cannavino, John J. — *Financial Resource Associates, Inc.*
Krick, Terry L. — *Financial Resource Associates, Inc.*
Little, Elizabeth A. — *Financial Resource Associates, Inc.*
Madaras, Debra — *Financial Resource Associates, Inc.*

### Bartow
Titus, Dave — *Management Recruiters International, Inc.*

### Boca Raton
Labadie, Ernie B. — *Management Recruiters International, Inc.*
Marra, John — *Marra Peters & Partners*
Schneiderman, Gerald — *Management Resource Associates, Inc.*

### Bonita Springs
Shearer, Gary F. — *Management Recruiters International, Inc.*

### Bradenton
Moore, Lynn W. — *Management Recruiters International, Inc.*

### Clearwater
Butler, Kirby B. — *The Butlers Company Insurance Recruiters*
Costello, Andrea L. — *Gallin Associates*
Costello, Jack — *Gallin Associates*
Gallin, Larry — *Gallin Associates*
Gleason-Lianopolis, Helen W. — *Management Recruiters International, Inc.*
Monroe, Kenneth D. — *Sanford Rose Associates*

### Coral Gables
Hamdan, Mark — *Careernet of Florida, Inc.*
Park, Dabney G. — *Mark Stanley & Company*
Perron, Daniel — *Accountants on Call*
Ramsey, John H. — *Mark Stanley & Company*
Small, Ellyn — *Accountants on Call*
Weber, James K. — *Management Recruiters International, Inc.*

### Coral Springs
Del Pino, William — *National Search, Inc.*
Kiley, Phyllis — *National Search, Inc.*
Levine, Lois — *National Search, Inc.*
Long, Melanie — *National Search, Inc.*
Morgan, Gary — *National Search, Inc.*
Olsen, David — *Search Enterprises South, Inc.*
Polacek, Frank — *Search Enterprises South, Inc.*
Redler, Rhonda — *National Search, Inc.*
Reiss, Matt — *National Search, Inc.*
Rosenthal, Charles — *National Search, Inc.*
Runge, Gary — *Search Enterprises South, Inc.*
Sandbloom, Kenneth — *Search Enterprises South, Inc.*
Sennello, Gendra — *National Search, Inc.*
Shelton, Sandra — *National Search, Inc.*
Snelgrove, Geiger — *National Search, Inc.*
Wakefield, Scott — *National Search, Inc.*
Weisler, Nancy — *National Search, Inc.*
Zatman, Allen — *Search Enterprises South, Inc.*

### Englewood
Hansen, Ty E. — *Blake, Hansen & Nye, Limited*

### Fernandina Beach
Richard, Albert L. — *Human Resources Inc.*

### Fort Lauderdale
Beaver, Robert W. — *Executive Manning Corporation*
Dickstein, Joel — *Management Recruiters International, Inc.*
Enfield, Jerry J. — *Executive Manning Corporation*
Hertan, Richard L. — *Executive Manning Corporation*
Hertan, Wiliam A. — *Executive Manning Corporation*
Hillyer, Robert L. — *Executive Manning Corporation*
Johasky, Tom K. — *Management Recruiters International, Inc.*
Kirchner, Michael — *American Medical Consultants*
Lasher, Charles M. — *Lasher Associates*
Mefford, Bob — *Executive Manning Corporation*
Mursini, Meredith — *Lasher Associates*
Porter, Ken — *Tourism Development International*
Ropes, John — *Ropes Associates, Inc.*
Sutter, Howard — *Romac & Associates*
Viglino, Victor P. — *DHR International, Inc.*

### Fort Myers
Akin, J.R. — *J.R. Akin & Company Inc.*
Beals, Calvin H. — *Management Recruiters International, Inc.*

### Ft. Lauderdale
Baer, Kenneth — *Source  Services Corporation*
Bloch, Suzanne — *Source  Services Corporation*
Scimone, Jim — *Source  Services Corporation*

### Indialantic
Cinco, Larry — *Management Recruiters International, Inc.*
Cinco, Susan M. — *Management Recruiters International, Inc.*

### Jacksonville
Bragg, Garry — *The McCormick Group, Inc.*
Gwin, Ric — *Southwestern Professional Services*
Hansen, Charles A. — *Management Recruiters International, Inc.*
Hoskins, Charles R. — *Heidrick & Struggles, Inc.*
Keith, Stephanie — *Southwestern Professional Services*
Lee, Barbara A. — *Management Recruiters International, Inc.*
Lee, Robert E. — *Management Recruiters International, Inc.*
Matti, Suzy — *Southwestern Professional Services*
Norton, George F. — *Heidrick & Struggles, Inc.*
Walton, Terry P. — *Heidrick & Struggles, Inc.*

### Jupiter
Ellis, Ronald A. — *Management Recruiters International, Inc.*

### Largo
DeCorrevont, James — *DeCorrevont & Associates*

### Longwood
Aki, Alvin W. — *MSI International*
Bohn, Steve J. — *MSI International*
Brown, Sandra E. — *MSI International*
Clark, John Edward — *Management Recruiters International, Inc.*
Davis, Joel C. — *MSI International*
Fleming, Marco — *MSI International*
Landry, Leo G. — *MSI International*
Shoemaker, Fred W. — *MSI International*
Walther, Linda S. — *MSI International*

### Maitland
Brown, Arlene — *Management Recruiters International, Inc.*
Brown, Tom — *Management Recruiters International, Inc.*

### Miami
Berger, Judith E. — *MDR Associates, Inc.*
Connelly, Thomas A. — *Korn/Ferry International*
Diaz, Del J. — *Management Recruiters International, Inc.*
Dunn, Kathleen — *A.T. Kearney, Inc.*
Gerstl, Ronald — *Maxecon Executive Search Consultants*
Harfenist, Harry — *Parker Page Group*
Jones, Edgar — *A.T. Kearney, Inc.*
Kean, Marjorie — *Korn/Ferry International*
LesKovec, Charles S. — *MDR Associates, Inc.*
Messett, William J. — *Messett Associates, Inc.*
Mestepey, John — *A.T. Kearney, Inc.*
Moran, Robert — *A.T. Kearney, Inc.*
Norris, Ken — *A.T. Kearney, Inc.*
Osinski, Martin H. — *American Medical Consultants*
Palazio, Carla — *A.T. Kearney, Inc.*
Schoen, Stephen G. — *MDR Associates, Inc.*
Young, Alexander — *Messett Associates, Inc.*
Young, Mark — *D.E. Foster Partners Inc.*

### Miami Lakes
Ankus, Joseph E. — *H. Hertner Associates, Inc.*
Dunman, Betsy L. — *Crawford & Crofford*
Flora, Dodi — *Crawford & Crofford*
Glueck, Sharon — *Career Temps, Inc.*
Grossman, Martin — *Source  Services Corporation*
Hernandez, Ruben — *Source  Services Corporation*
Hertner, Herbert H. — *H. Hertner Associates, Inc.*
Hertner, Pamela R. — *H. Hertner Associates, Inc.*
Hylas, Lisa — *Source  Services Corporation*
La Chance, Ronald — *Source  Services Corporation*
Lamia, Michael — *Source  Services Corporation*
Manns, Alex — *Crawford & Crofford*
Morato, Rene — *Source  Services Corporation*
Mullings, Joe S. — *Management Recruiters International, Inc.*
Neff, Herbert — *Source  Services Corporation*

Goodwin, Joe D. — *Lamalie Amrop International*
Gordon, Jacqueline — *Evie Kreisler & Associates, Inc.*
Gray, Lisa — *Evie Kreisler & Associates, Inc.*
Green, Jean — *Broward-Dobbs, Inc.*
Greene, Luke — *Broward-Dobbs, Inc.*
Groover, David — *MSI International*
Hailes, Brian — *Russell Reynolds Associates, Inc.*
Hales, Daphne — *Source Services Corporation*
Hall, Thomas H. — *Korn/Ferry International*
Harty, Shirley Cox — *Paul Ray Berndtson*
Harvey, Jill — *MSI International*
Hauser, David E. — *Lamalie Amrop International*
Hauser, Martha — *Spencer Stuart*
Hawksworth, A. Dwight — *A.D. & Associates Executive Search, Inc.*
Hendon, Jill — *Korn/Ferry International*
Hennig, Sandra M. — *MSI International*
Herman, Beth — *Accountants on Call*
Hewitt, Rives D. — *The Dalley Hewitt Company*
Hicks, James L. — *MSI International*
Holland, Richard G. — *Management Recruiters International, Inc.*
Homrich, Patricia J. — *David C. Cooper and Associates, Inc.*
Houchins, Gene E. — *Management Recruiters International, Inc.*
Hurst, Joan E. — *Korn/Ferry International*
Hyde, Mark D. — *MSI International*
Jacobson, Gregory — *Jacobson Associates*
Jones, Dale E. — *Lamalie Amrop International*
Juhan, Louise B. — *Korn/Ferry International*
Justiss, Ted W. — *David C. Cooper and Associates, Inc.*
Katz, Robert L. — *MSI International*
Keesom, W. Peter — *Boyden/Zay & Company*
Kelly, Kevin B. — *Russell Reynolds Associates, Inc.*
King, Joyce L. — *MSI International*
Klein, Jill S. — *David C. Cooper and Associates, Inc.*
Kloess, Janice Sciulli — *David C. Cooper and Associates, Inc.*
Koblentz, Joel M. — *Egon Zehnder International Inc.*
Kratz, Steve — *Tyler & Company*
Krull, Joan R. — *Lawstaf Legal Search, Inc.*
Kuhl, Debra — *Paul Ray Berndtson*
Leslie, William H. — *Boyden/Zay & Company*
Lindberg, Eric J. — *MSI International*
Lindsay, M. Evan — *Heidrick & Struggles, Inc.*
London, Gregory J. — *MSI International*
Luke, A. Wayne — *Heidrick & Struggles, Inc.*
MacLane, Bruce W. — *Korn/Ferry International*
Malcolm, Doug C. — *Management Recruiters International, Inc.*
Martin, Geary D. — *Boyden/Zay & Company*
Matthews, William A. — *Heidrick & Struggles, Inc.*
Mattox, Robert D. — *Spencer Stuart*
Mayland, Tina — *Russell Reynolds Associates, Inc.*
McCarty, J. Rucker — *Heidrick & Struggles, Inc.*
McClearen, Bruce — *Tyler & Company*
McConnell, Greg — *Winter, Wyman & Company*
McCormack, William Reed — *MSI International*
McGonigle, Kevin M. — *Egon Zehnder International Inc.*
McGue, Marsha S. — *Kenzer Corp.*
McKinnis, Paul D. — *Paul Ray Berndtson*
McRae, O. Jon — *Jon McRae & Associates, Inc.*
Miles, Kenneth T. — *MSI International*
Miller, Harold B. — *MSI International*
Milligan, Dale — *Source Services Corporation*
Milne, Robert P. — *Boyden/Zay & Company*
Mitchell, John T. — *Paul Ray Berndtson*
Mitchell, Norman F. — *A.T. Kearney, Inc.*
Monaghan, Jill — *Paul Ray Berndtson*
Mooney, Matt — *Paul Ray Berndtson*
Moore, Janice E. — *MSI International*
Moore, Lemuel R. — *MSI International*
Morgan, Donald T. — *MSI International*
Morrison, Janis L. — *Garrett Associates Inc.*
Mouchet, Marcus — *Commonwealth Consultants*
Murphy, James — *Source Services Corporation*
Murphy, Timothy D. — *MSI International*
Nagle, Charles L. — *Tyler & Company*
Neely, Alan S. — *Korn/Ferry International*
Norton, James B. — *GKR Americas, Inc.*
O'Donnell, James H. — *MSI International*
O'Halloran, Robert — *MSI International*
Olmstead, George T. — *Blackshaw, Olmstead & Lynch*
Panetta, Timothy — *Commonwealth Consultants*
Parker, Stephen B. — *Russell Reynolds Associates, Inc.*
Pease, Edward — *Don Richard Associates of Georgia, Inc.*
Perkey, Richard — *Korn/Ferry International*
Pettway, Samuel H. — *Spencer Stuart*
Pierce, Nicholas J. — *Paul Ray Berndtson*
Pirhalla, Denise — *Kenzer Corp.*
Pittard, Patrick S. — *Heidrick & Struggles, Inc.*
Powell, Marie — *Kenzer Corp.*
Rackley, Eugene M. — *Heidrick & Struggles, Inc.*
Ravenel, Lavinia — *MSI International*
Reeder, Michael S. — *Lamalie Amrop International*
Reeves, William B. — *Spencer Stuart*
Reimenschneider, Donald — *Evie Kreisler & Associates, Inc.*

Reticker, Peter — *MSI International*
Robert, Diana — *Korn/Ferry International*
Roberts, Jane — *Paul Ray Berndtson*
Robertson, William R. — *Ward Howell International, Inc.*
Salet, Michael — *Source Services Corporation*
Savela, Edward — *Source Services Corporation*
Sawhill, Louise B. — *Paul Ray Berndtson*
Sawyer, Deborah A. — *Heidrick & Struggles, Inc.*
Scarbrough, Debbi — *Evie Kreisler & Associates, Inc.*
Scheidt, Sandi — *Paul Ray Berndtson*
Schor, Neil D. — *Kenzer Corp.*
Schuyler, Lambert — *Schuyler, Frye & Baker, Inc.*
Schwartz, Harry — *Jacobson Associates*
Schwarzkopf, A. Renee — *David C. Cooper and Associates, Inc.*
Seals, Sonny — *A.T. Kearney, Inc.*
Seibert, Nancy — *Tyler & Company*
Seltzer, Deborah Coogan — *Paul Ray Berndtson*
Semple, David — *Source Services Corporation*
Serio, Judith A. — *Lawstaf Legal Search, Inc.*
Shepard, Michael J. — *MSI International*
Shoemaker, Larry C. — *Shoemaker & Associates*
Sierra, Rafael A. — *Lamalie Amrop International*
Silkiner, David S. — *Paul Ray Berndtson*
Simmons, Sandra K. — *MSI International*
Singleton, Robin — *Tyler & Company*
Soggs, Cheryl Pavick — *A.T. Kearney, Inc.*
Spence, Joseph T. — *Russell Reynolds Associates, Inc.*
St. Martin, Peter — *Source Services Corporation*
Steenerson, Thomas L. — *MSI International*
Stevens, Robin — *Paul Ray Berndtson*
Stroup, Jonathan C. — *Egon Zehnder International Inc.*
Taylor, Conrad G. — *MSI International*
Taylor, Ernest A. — *Ward Howell International, Inc.*
Thompson, John R. — *MSI International*
Tingle, Trina A. — *MSI International*
Tipping, William M. — *Ward Howell International, Inc.*
Tyler, J. Larry — *Tyler & Company*
Volk, Richard — *MSI International*
Waindle, Maureen — *Paul Ray Berndtson*
Waldman, Noah H. — *Lamalie Amrop International*
Waldrop, Gary R. — *MSI International*
Watkins, Jeffrey P. — *Paul Ray Berndtson*
Watson, James — *MSI International*
Webb, Shawn K. — *MSI International*
Weidener, Andrew E. — *Paul Ray Berndtson*
White, Patricia D. — *MSI International*
Wile, Harold — *Kenzer Corp.*
Williams, Richard — *Blackshaw, Olmstead & Lynch*
Wooller, Edmund A.M. — *Windsor International*
Wrynn, Robert F. — *MSI International*
Wynkoop, Mary — *Tyler & Company*
Zay, Thomas C. — *Boyden/Zay & Company*

**Columbus**
Silverstein, Michael L. — *Management Recruiters International, Inc.*
**Cumming**
Barrett, Dan E. — *Management Recruiters International, Inc.*
**Dalton**
Webb, Don W. — *Management Recruiters International, Inc.*
Webb, Verna F. — *Management Recruiters International, Inc.*
**Duluth**
Eason, James — *JRL Executive Recruiters*
Riggs, David T. — *Management Recruiters International, Inc.*
Riggs, Lena — *Management Recruiters International, Inc.*
**LaGrange**
Brown, Jeffrey W. — *Comprehensive Search*
Moran, Gail — *Comprehensive Search*
Rozan, Naomi — *Comprehensive Search*
Standard, Gail — *Comprehensive Search*
**Lithia Springs**
Kendall, Steven W. — *Management Recruiters International, Inc.*
**Marietta**
Austin, Jessica L. — *D.S.A. - Dixie Search Associates*
Dougherty, Lawrence J. — *Management Recruiters International, Inc.*
Fill, Clifford G. — *D.S.A. - Dixie Search Associates*
Fill, Ellyn H. — *D.S.A. - Dixie Search Associates*
Granger, Lisa D. — *D.S.A. - Dixie Search Associates*
Kirby, James E. — *Management Recruiters International, Inc.*
Logan, Valarie A. — *D.S.A. - Dixie Search Associates*
**Norcross**
Patrick, Donald R. — *Sanford Rose Associates*
Rivard, Dick — *Management Recruiters International, Inc.*
**Peachtree City**
Wise, Ronald L. — *Management Recruiters International, Inc.*
**Perry**
Wentz, Terry M. — *Management Recruiters International, Inc.*
**Roswell**
Bagwell, Bruce — *Intersource, Ltd.*
Beall, Charles P. — *Beall & Company, Inc.*
Burnette, Dennis W. — *Sanford Rose Associates*

Jacobson, Jewel — *Jacobson Associates*
Jambor, Hilary L. — *Korn/Ferry International*
Jeffers, Carol S. — *John Sibbald Associates, Inc.*
Johnson, Shirley E. — *The Heidrick Partners, Inc.*
Jones, Suzanne English — *Vera L. Rast Partners, Inc.*
Kacyn, Louis J. — *Egon Zehnder International Inc.*
Kahn, P. Frederick — *Heidrick & Struggles, Inc.*
Keegen, Joanne — *Evie Kreisler & Associates, Inc.*
Kepler, Charles W. — *Russell Reynolds Associates, Inc.*
Kettwig, David A. — *A.T. Kearney, Inc.*
King, Richard M. — *Kittleman & Associates*
Kingdom, Scott — *Korn/Ferry International*
Kingore, William C. — *DHR International, Inc.*
Klavins, Larissa R. — *Dieckmann & Associates, Ltd.*
Klein, Gregory A. — *A.T. Kearney, Inc.*
Kleinstein, Scott — *Source Services Corporation*
Klock, Lawrence S. — *Russell Reynolds Associates, Inc.*
Knecht, Luke D. — *Russell Reynolds Associates, Inc.*
Kolder, Thomas R. — *Russell Reynolds Associates, Inc.*
Konkolski, Laurie — *The Paladin Companies, Inc.*
Kopsick, Joseph M. — *Spencer Stuart*
Kraus, Kathy — *Evie Kreisler & Associates, Inc.*
Lachenauer, Bruce J. — *Heidrick & Struggles, Inc.*
Landan, Joy — *Jacobson Associates*
Lenga, Bobbie — *Kenzer Corp.*
Lennon, Roslyn J. — *Heidrick & Struggles, Inc.*
Lindholst, Kai — *Egon Zehnder International Inc.*
Longoria, Janine — *Russell Reynolds Associates, Inc.*
Lorenz, Paula — *Kenzer Corp.*
Lubawski, James — *Ward Howell International, Inc.*
Lucas, J. Curtis — *Korn/Ferry International*
Lynch, Michael C. — *Lynch Miller Moore Partners, Inc.*
Lyons, Margaret — *Paul Ray Berndtson*
Mainwaring, Andrew Brian — *Executive Search Consultants Corporation*
Mansfield, Chris — *Paul Ray Berndtson*
Marcus, Jane B. — *Russell Reynolds Associates, Inc.*
Marion, Bradford B. — *Lamalie Amrop International*
Marx, Dennis R. — *DHR International, Inc.*
Maxwell, Carol — *Paul Ray Berndtson*
McCallister, Richard A. — *Boyden*
McCloskey, Frank — *Korn/Ferry International*
McDermott, Richard A. — *Paul Ray Berndtson*
McFeely, Clarence E. — *McFeely Wackerle Shulman*
McKie, Miles L. — *Russell Reynolds Associates, Inc.*
McLane, Brad — *Egon Zehnder International Inc.*
McNear, Jeffrey E. — *Barrett Partners*
McSherry, James F. — *Battalia Winston International*
McSherry, Terrence J. — *Paul Ray Berndtson*
Meagher, Patricia G. — *Spencer Stuart*
Milkint, Margaret Resce — *Jacobson Associates*
Miller, Michael R. — *Lynch Miller Moore Partners, Inc.*
Miller, Paul McG. — *Lamalie Amrop International*
Moliski, Robert — *Korn/Ferry International*
Molitor, John L. — *Barrett Partners*
Moore, David S. — *Lynch Miller Moore Partners, Inc.*
Morgan, Christopher — *Paul Ray Berndtson*
Moschel, Evie — *S. Reyman & Associates Ltd.*
Mowatt, Virginia C. — *DHR International, Inc.*
Mullane, Patrick — *Kenzer Corp.*
Murlas, Kim — *DHR International, Inc.*
Murphy, Carrie — *Paul Ray Berndtson*
Nadherny, Christopher C. — *Spencer Stuart*
Nadherny, Ferdinand — *Russell Reynolds Associates, Inc.*
Nakatsuka, Walt — *Evie Kreisler & Associates, Inc.*
Nein, Lawrence F. — *Lamalie Amrop International*
O'Donnell, Timothy W. — *Boyden*
O'Gorman, David J. — *DHR International, Inc.*
O'Hara, Daniel M. — *Lynch Miller Moore Partners, Inc.*
O'Neill, James P. — *Allerton Heneghan & O'Neill*
O'Shea, Laurie A. — *The Heidrick Partners, Inc.*
Olsen, Robert — *Source Services Corporation*
Olson, A. Andrew — *Paul Ray Berndtson*
Olson, B. Tucker — *Early Cochran & Olson, Inc.*
Olson, Cherene — *The Paladin Companies, Inc.*
Oppenheimer, Janet — *Paul Ray Berndtson*
Pappas, Jim — *Search Dynamics, Inc.*
Pawlik, Cynthia — *Paul Ray Berndtson*
Pearson, Robert L. — *Lamalie Amrop International*
Percival, Chris — *Chicago Legal Search, Ltd.*
Pierce, Richard — *Russell Reynolds Associates, Inc.*
Poore, Larry D. — *Ward Howell International, Inc.*
Pope, John S. — *DHR International, Inc.*
Poracky, John W. — *M. Wood Company*
Preschlack, Jack E. — *Spencer Stuart*
Provus, Barbara L. — *Shepherd Bueschel & Provus, Inc.*
Quick, Roger A. — *Norman Broadbent International, Inc.*
Quinn, John — *Paul Ray Berndtson*
Rast, Vera L. — *Vera L. Rast Partners, Inc.*
Ratigan, Charles C. — *Heidrick & Struggles, Inc.*
Rattner, Kenneth L. — *Heidrick & Struggles, Inc.*
Recsetar, Steven — *DHR International, Inc.*

Redmond, Andrea — *Russell Reynolds Associates, Inc.*
Reilly, Robert E. — *DHR International, Inc.*
Remick, Tierney Boyd — *Russell Reynolds Associates, Inc.*
Reyman, Susan — *S. Reyman & Associates Ltd.*
Reynes, Tony — *Tesar-Reynes, Inc.*
Rimmele, Michael — *The Bankers Group*
Rosemarin, Gloria J. — *Barrington Hart, Inc.*
Roth, Robert J. — *Williams, Roth & Krueger Inc.*
Rothschild, John S. — *Heidrick & Struggles, Inc.*
Rubin, Marcey S. — *Kenzer Corp.*
Rubinstein, Alan J. — *Chicago Legal Search, Ltd.*
Russell, Richard A. — *Executive Search Consultants Corporation*
Russell, Susan Anne — *Executive Search Consultants Corporation*
Rust, John R. — *DHR International, Inc.*
Ryan, David — *Source Services Corporation*
Saxner, David — *DSA, Inc.*
Scheidt, Sandra L. — *The Heidrick Partners, Inc.*
Schmidt, Paul — *Paul Ray Berndtson*
Schnierow, Beryl — *Tesar-Reynes, Inc.*
Schroeder, James L. — *Korn/Ferry International*
Schroeder, Victoria — *Paul Ray Berndtson*
Schwartz, Vincent P. — *Slayton International, Inc.*
Seebeck, Robert F. — *Russell Reynolds Associates, Inc.*
Serwat, Leonard A. — *Spencer Stuart*
Seweloh, Theodore W. — *The Heidrick Partners, Inc.*
Sheedy, Edward J. — *Dieckmann & Associates, Ltd.*
Shepherd, Daniel M. — *Shepherd Bueschel & Provus, Inc.*
Shepherd, Gail L. — *Shepherd Bueschel & Provus, Inc.*
Shimp, David J. — *Lamalie Amrop International*
Sibbald, John R. — *John Sibbald Associates, Inc.*
Sibul, Shelly Remen — *Chicago Legal Search, Ltd.*
Sigurdson, Eric J. — *Russell Reynolds Associates, Inc.*
Skunda, Donna M. — *Allerton Heneghan & O'Neill*
Slater, Ronald E. — *A.T. Kearney, Inc.*
Slayton, Richard C. — *Slayton International, Inc.*
Slayton, Richard S. — *Slayton International, Inc.*
Sloan, Scott — *Source Services Corporation*
Smead, Michelle M. — *A.T. Kearney, Inc.*
Smith, Matthew — *Korn/Ferry International*
Smith, Melanie F. — *The Heidrick Partners, Inc.*
Smith, Shellie L. — *The Heidrick Partners, Inc.*
Smith, Toni S. — *Spencer Stuart*
Snyder, Thomas J. — *Spencer Stuart*
Sola, George L. — *A.T. Kearney, Inc.*
Spellman, Frances — *Kenzer Corp.*
Sperry, Elizabeth B. — *Korn/Ferry International*
Sprau, Collin L. — *Paul Ray Berndtson*
Steck, Frank T. — *A.T. Kearney, Inc.*
Stenholm, Gilbert R. — *Spencer Stuart*
Stern, Ronni — *Kenzer Corp.*
Stone, Susan L. — *Stone Enterprises Ltd.*
Sweet, Charles W. — *A.T. Kearney, Inc.*
Sweet, Randall — *Source Services Corporation*
Tabisz, Susanne — *Executive Referral Services, Inc.*
Tate, Robert H. — *Paul Ray Berndtson*
Taylor, Kenneth W. — *Egon Zehnder International Inc.*
Terry, Douglas — *Jacobson Associates*
Tesar, Bob — *Tesar-Reynes, Inc.*
Thielman, Joseph — *Barrett Partners*
Thomas, John T. — *Ward Howell International, Inc.*
Tillman, J. Robert — *Russell Reynolds Associates, Inc.*
Tonjuk, Tina — *The Paladin Companies, Inc.*
Tracy, Ronald O. — *Egon Zehnder International Inc.*
Trefzer, Kristie — *Source Services Corporation*
Trent, Alex — *Vera L. Rast Partners, Inc.*
Tribbett, Charles A. — *Russell Reynolds Associates, Inc.*
Tyler, Jackie — *Kenzer Corp.*
Unterberg, Edward L. — *Russell Reynolds Associates, Inc.*
Utroska, Donald R. — *Lamalie Amrop International*
Vergara, Gail H. — *Spencer Stuart*
Visokey, Dale M. — *Russell Reynolds Associates, Inc.*
Vognsen, Rikke — *DSA, Inc.*
Wackerle, Frederick W. — *McFeely Wackerle Shulman*
Wargo, G. Rick — *A.T. Kearney, Inc.*
Waring, David C. — *Russell Reynolds Associates, Inc.*
Weber, Machelle — *Paul Ray Berndtson*
Weir, Norma — *Paul Ray Berndtson*
White, Kimberly — *Executive Referral Services, Inc.*
Williams, Barbara — *Kenzer Corp.*
Williams, Roger K. — *Williams, Roth & Krueger Inc.*
Wittenberg, Laura L. — *Boyden*
Womack, Joseph — *The Bankers Group*
Wood, Milton M. — *M. Wood Company*
Wycoff-Viola, Amy — *Source Services Corporation*
Zaleta, Andrew R. — *A.T. Kearney, Inc.*
Zee, Wanda — *Tesar-Reynes, Inc.*
Zellner, Paul A. — *Paul Ray Berndtson*

**Deerfield**
Higgins, John B. — *Higgins Associates, Inc.*
**DeKalb**
Clark, James — *CPS Inc.*

Riederer, Larry — *CPS Inc.*
Sahlas, Chrissy — *CPS Inc.*
Saletra, Andrew — *CPS Inc.*
Sanders, Natalie — *CPS Inc.*
Scalamera, Tom — *CPS Inc.*
Schueneman, David — *CPS Inc.*
Scott, Mark S. — *The Prairie Group*
Signer, Julie — *CPS Inc.*
Stern, Stephen — *CPS Inc.*
Sterner, Doug — *CPS Inc.*
Thomas, Cheryl M. — *CPS Inc.*
Thomas, Kim — *CPS Inc.*
Tovrog, Dan — *CPS Inc.*
Truemper, Dean — *CPS Inc.*
Tullberg, Tina — *CPS Inc.*
Winston, Susan — *CPS Inc.*

### Westmont
Hammes, Betsy — *Search Enterprises, Inc.*
Roberts, Clifford — *Search Enterprises, Inc.*
Schaefer, Robert — *Search Enterprises, Inc.*
Sobczak, Ronald — *Search Enterprises, Inc.*
Sullivan, James — *Search Enterprises, Inc.*
Trivedi, Jay — *Search Enterprises, Inc.*
Tully, Thomas — *Search Enterprises, Inc.*

## Indiana
### Angola
Joyce, James — *Sharrow & Associates*
### Carmel
Ceryak, George V. — *Management Recruiters International, Inc.*
Rheude, Jim — *Management Recruiters International, Inc.*
Robertson, John H.C. — *Sanford Rose Associates*
### Columbus
Evans, Robert M. — *TASA International*
Percifield, J. Michael — *Management Recruiters International, Inc.*
Piers, Robert L. — *TASA International*
### Danville
Gonzalez-Miller, Laura — *Management Recruiters International, Inc.*
Miller, Bert E. — *Management Recruiters International, Inc.*
### Elkhart
Alvey, Frank C. — *Robert Sage Recruiting*
Hudson, William — *Robert Sage Recruiting*
McGuire, John J. — *Robert Sage Recruiting*
### Evansville
Caldemeyer, Marjorie L. — *Management Recruiters International, Inc.*
### Fort Wayne
Rudin, Harold — *Management Recruiters International, Inc.*
Rudin, Myra — *Management Recruiters International, Inc.*
### Indianapolis
Bickett, Nicole — *Source Services Corporation*
Blassaras, Peggy — *Source Services Corporation*
Brassard, Gary — *Source Services Corporation*
Emerson, Randall — *Source Services Corporation*
Herrod, Vicki — *Accountants on Call*
Houterloot, Tim — *Source Services Corporation*
Kuntz, Bill — *Management Recruiters International, Inc.*
Long, Mark — *Source Services Corporation*
Necessary, Rick — *Source Services Corporation*
Patterson, Brenda — *Management Recruiters International, Inc.*
Walker, Ann — *Source Services Corporation*
### Long Beach
DeFuniak, William S. — *DeFuniak & Edwards*
### Newburgh
Berrong, Barbie H. — *Management Recruiters International, Inc.*
Berrong, Ray — *Management Recruiters International, Inc.*
Forbes, Kay Koob — *Sanford Rose Associates*
Forbes, Kenneth P. — *Sanford Rose Associates*
### Noblesville
Isenberg, Peter — *Management Recruiters International, Inc.*
### Peru
Holtz, Gene — *Agra Placements International Ltd.*
Lawrence, David — *Agra Placements International Ltd.*
Rice, Douglas — *Agra Placements International Ltd.*
Rodgers, John — *Agra Placements International Ltd.*
Stouffer, Dale — *Agra Placements International Ltd.*
### Richmond
Martin, Rande L. — *Management Recruiters International, Inc.*

## Iowa
### Bettendorf
Herrmann, Jerry C. — *Management Recruiters International, Inc.*
### Cedar Rapids
Weber, Fritz — *Management Recruiters International, Inc.*
### Centerville
Hovey, Dick — *Management Recruiters International, Inc.*
### Clive
Vermillion, Mike W. — *Management Recruiters International, Inc.*

### Dubuque
Pratt, Michael W. — *Management Recruiters International, Inc.*
### Fairfield
Soth, Mark H. — *Management Recruiters International, Inc.*
### Mason City
Plagge, Cheryl L. — *Management Recruiters International, Inc.*
### Sioux City
Hurley, Helen — *Management Recruiters International, Inc.*
Rupert, Jim — *Management Recruiters International, Inc.*
### Spencer
Dach, Bradley M. — *Management Recruiters International, Inc.*
### West Des Moines
Dickerson, Scot — *Key Employment Services*
Erwin, Lee — *Agra Placements International Ltd.*
Follmer, Gary — *Agra Placements International Ltd.*
Francis, Dwaine — *Francis & Associates*
Francis, Kay — *Francis & Associates*
Harvey, Joy — *Key Employment Services*
Henderson, John — *Key Employment Services*
Hildebrand, Thomas B. — *Professional Resources Group, Inc.*
Lebo, Terry — *Agra Placements International Ltd.*
Leininger, Dennis — *Key Employment Services*
Maiers, Robert — *Key Employment Services*
Moore, Michael — *Agra Placements International Ltd.*
Moran, Carla — *Key Employment Services*
Morrow, Miles — *Key Employment Services*
Owen, John — *Key Employment Services*
Tracey, Garvis — *Key Employment Services*
Truax, Kevin — *Key Employment Services*
Wattier, David — *Key Employment Services*
### Williamsburg
Lehnst, Joh L. — *Management Recruiters International, Inc.*

## Kansas
### Lenexa
Turner, Brad — *Management Recruiters International, Inc.*
### Overland Park
Berger, Jeffrey — *Source Services Corporation*
Blocher, John — *Source Services Corporation*
Brackenbury, Robert — *Bowman & Marshall, Inc.*
Buda, Danny — *Management Recruiters International, Inc.*
Carlson, Judith — *Bowman & Marshall, Inc.*
Connaghan, Linda — *Bowman & Marshall, Inc.*
Davis, Evelyn C. — *EFL Associates*
Fingers, David — *Bradford & Galt, Inc.*
Grassl, Peter O. — *Bowman & Marshall, Inc.*
Griffen, Leslie G. — *EFL Associates*
Grossman, James — *Source Services Corporation*
Hancock, Deborah L. — *Morgan Hunter Corp.*
Haselby, James — *Source Services Corporation*
Haughton, Michael — *DeFrain, Mayer, Lee & Burgess LLC*
Heideman, Mary Marren — *DeFrain, Mayer, Lee & Burgess LLC*
Hellebusch, Jerry — *Morgan Hunter Corp.*
Hillyer, Carolyn — *Source Services Corporation*
Howard, Brian E. — *Management Recruiters International, Inc.*
Howard, Kathy S. — *Management Recruiters International, Inc.*
Jackson, Barry — *Morgan Hunter Corp.*
Johnson, Pete — *Morgan Hunter Corp.*
King, Thomas — *Morgan Hunter Corp.*
Kvasnicka, Jay Allen — *Morgan Hunter Corp.*
Lang, Vicki L. — *Morgan Hunter Corp.*
Lemke, Peter K. — *EFL Associates*
Meschke, Jason M. — *EFL Associates*
Msidment, Roger — *Source Services Corporation*
Murray, Cathy M. — *EFL Associates*
Myers, Kay — *Signature Staffing*
Peternell, Melanie — *Signature Staffing*
Peters, Todd — *Morgan Hunter Corp.*
Radford-Oster, Deborah — *Morgan Hunter Corp.*
Renick, Cynthia L. — *Morgan Hunter Corp.*
Robb, Tammy — *Source Services Corporation*
Rowland, James — *Source Services Corporation*
Ryan, Kathleen — *Source Services Corporation*
Snodgrass, Stephen — *DeFrain, Mayer, Lee & Burgess LLC*
Tilley, Kyle — *Source Services Corporation*
Tryon, Katey — *DeFrain, Mayer, Lee & Burgess LLC*
Viviano, Cathleen — *Source Services Corporation*
Wagman, Marc E. — *Management Recruiters International, Inc.*
Wolfram, David A. — *EFL Associates*
### Shawnee-Mission
Beeson, William B. — *Lawrence-Leiter and Company*
### Topeka
Hawkins, Kirk V. — *Management Recruiters International, Inc.*
### Wichita
Reimer, Marvin — *Management Recruiters International, Inc.*

## Kentucky

## Crestview Hills
Kern, Jerry L. — *ADOW's Executeam*
## Danville
Smith, Mike W. — *Management Recruiters International, Inc.*
## Florence
Stoll, Steven G. — *Sharrow & Associates*
## Lexington
Simpson, Kent T. — *Management Recruiters International, Inc.*
## Louisville
Angel, Steven R. — *Management Recruiters International, Inc.*
Berry, Harold B. — *The Hindman Company*
Brenzel, John A. — *TASA International*
Bruno, Deborah F. — *The Hindman Company*
Doukas, Jon A. — *Professional Bank Services, Inc. D/B/A Executive Search, Inc.*
Grasch, Jerry E. — *The Hindman Company*
Hindman, Neil C. — *The Hindman Company*
Keefe, Donald J. — *TASA International*
Lerner, Joel S. — *Sanford Rose Associates*
Mattingly, Kathleen — *Source Services Corporation*
Moore, Dianna — *Source Services Corporation*
Moriarty, Mike — *Source Services Corporation*
Noll, Robert J. — *Source Services Corporation*
Palmer, James H. — *The Hindman Company*
Parroco, Jason — *Source Services Corporation*
Robinson, Tonya — *Source Services Corporation*
Temple, John D. — *The Hindman Company*
Williams, John — *Source Services Corporation*
Workman, David — *Source Services Corporation*
## Richmond
Lawson, Ron S. — *Management Recruiters International, Inc.*
## Russell
Pinson, Liz A. — *Management Recruiters International, Inc.*
## Shelbyville
Barnett, Barney O. — *Management Recruiters International, Inc.*
## Lousiana
### Baton Rouge
Franklin, Cecilia — *Management Recruiters International, Inc.*
Franklin, Cleve — *Management Recruiters International, Inc.*
### Mandeville
Schmidt, Michelle C. — *Sanford Rose Associates*
Schmidt, Timothy G. — *Sanford Rose Associates*
### Metairie
Ameen, Edward N. — *Management Recruiters International, Inc.*
Luce, Paul M. — *Management Recruiters International, Inc.*
### Monroe
Causey, Andrea C. — *MSI International*
Hollins, Howard D. — *MSI International*
Hursey, Bruce — *Management Recruiters International, Inc.*
Lawson, Bettye N. — *MSI International*
Matheny, Robert P. — *MSI International*
Williams, Laurelle N. — *MSI International*
### New Orleans
Baron, Jon C. — *MSI International*
Carpenter, Harold G. — *MSI International*
Cinquemano, Teri — *Accounting Personnel Consultants*
Coston, Bruce G. — *MSI International*
Davis, Bernel — *MSI International*
Debrueys, Lee G. — *MSI International*
Dietz, David S. — *MSI International*
Eustis, Lucy R. — *MSI International*
Graver, Merialee — *Accounting Personnel Consultants*
Gulley, Marylyn — *MSI International*
Hunt, Thomas — *MSI International*
Ivey, Deborah M. — *MSI International*
Jackson, Pam — *Accounting Personnel Consultants*
James, Allison A. — *MSI International*
Kerth, Norman — *Accounting Personnel Consultants*
LaFaye, Susan — *MSI International*
Lence, Julie Anne — *MSI International*
Loria, Frank — *Accounting Personnel Consultants*
Lucien, David — *Accounting Personnel Consultants*
Miller, Laura — *Accounting Personnel Consultants*
Oddo, Judith — *Accounting Personnel Consultants*
Prados, Daniel — *Accounting Personnel Consultants*
Roberts, Raymond R. — *MSI International*
Robson, Ridgely — *Accounting Personnel Consultants*
Rowells, Michael — *MSI International*
Smith, Margaret A. — *MSI International*

Theard, Susan — *Romac & Associates*
Titterington, Catherine F. — *MSI International*
## Shreveport
Magee, Charles — *Management Recruiters International, Inc.*
Magee, Gerri — *Management Recruiters International, Inc.*
## Slidell
Pecot, Jack L. — *Management Recruiters International, Inc.*
## Maine
### Brunswick
Asquith, Peter S. — *Ames Personnel Consultants, Inc.*
Holden, Richard B. — *Ames Personnel Consultants, Inc.*
### Portland
Beaulieu, Genie A. — *Romac & Associates*
LaPierre, Louis — *Romac & Associates*
Struzziero, Ralph E. — *Romac & Associates*
## Maryland
### Annapolis
Abbott, Peter — *The Abbott Group, Inc.*
Blackmon, Sharon — *The Abbott Group, Inc.*
Czajkowski, John — *Management Recruiters International, Inc.*
Havener, Donald Clarke — *The Abbott Group, Inc.*
Smith, Adam M. — *The Abbott Group, Inc.*
### Baltimore
Balter, Sidney — *Source Services Corporation*
Bettick, Michael J. — *A.J. Burton Group, Inc.*
Brandjes, Michael J. — *Brandjes Associates*
Burton, Linda — *Management Recruiters International, Inc.*
Calivas, Kay — *A.J. Burton Group, Inc.*
Campbell, E. — *Source Services Corporation*
Courtney, Brendan A.J. — *A.J. Burton Group, Inc.*
Coyle, Hugh F. — *A.J. Burton Group, Inc.*
D'Angelo, Ron E. — *Management Recruiters International, Inc.*
Davis, Ken R. — *Management Recruiters International, Inc.*
Delmonico, Laura — *A.J. Burton Group, Inc.*
Edwards, Randolph J. — *DeFuniak & Edwards*
Engle, Bryan — *Source Services Corporation*
Fribush, Richard — *A.J. Burton Group, Inc.*
Frock, Suzanne D. — *Brandjes Associates*
Gauthier, Robert C. — *Columbia Consulting Group*
Grantham, Philip H. — *Columbia Consulting Group*
Holmes, Lawrence J. — *Columbia Consulting Group*
Johnson, Brian — *A.J. Burton Group, Inc.*
Klein, Brandon — *A.J. Burton Group, Inc.*
Lazar, Miriam — *Source Services Corporation*
Matthews, James M. — *Stanton Chase International*
McNamara, Timothy C. — *Columbia Consulting Group*
Meehan, Robert — *A.J. Burton Group, Inc.*
Muendel, H. Edward — *Stanton Chase International*
Paxton, James W. — *Stanton Chase International*
Rosenstein, Michele — *Source Services Corporation*
Scranton, Lisa — *A.J. Burton Group, Inc.*
Sindler, Jay — *A.J. Burton Group, Inc.*
Walker, Craig H. — *A.J. Burton Group, Inc.*
Wheeler, Gerard H. — *A.J. Burton Group, Inc.*
Winnicki, Kimberly — *Source Services Corporation*
Wright, Carl A.J. — *A.J. Burton Group, Inc.*
### Bethesda
Jessamy, Howard T. — *Witt/Kieffer, Ford, Hadelman & Lloyd*
McGahey, Patricia M. — *Witt/Kieffer, Ford, Hadelman & Lloyd*
Phillips, Anna W. — *Witt/Kieffer, Ford, Hadelman & Lloyd*
Pugrant, Mark A. — *Grant/Morgan Associates, Inc.*
Reynolds, Gregory P. — *Roberts Ryan and Bentley*
### Chevy Chase
Kane, Frank — *A.J. Burton Group, Inc.*
Prentiss, Michael C. — *Management Recruiters International, Inc.*
Tootsey, Mark A. — *A.J. Burton Group, Inc.*
Vossler, James — *A.J. Burton Group, Inc.*
### Columbia
Durakis, Charles A. — *C.A. Durakis Associates, Inc.*
Gostin, Howard I. — *Sanford Rose Associates*
Houchins, William N. — *Christian & Timbers*
Reyes, Randolph G. — *Management Recruiters International, Inc.*
### Ellicott City
Bell, Cathy — *Management Recruiters International, Inc.*
Bell, Danny — *Management Recruiters International, Inc.*
### Frederick
Webb, Pat A. — *Management Recruiters International, Inc.*
### Hanover
Stubberfield, Lee — *Management Recruiters International, Inc.*
### Landover
Graves, Rosemarie — *Don Richard Associates of Washington, D.C., Inc.*
### Lutherville
Baird, David W. — *D.W. Baird & Associates*
Buck, Walter J. — *E.G. Jones Associates, Ltd.*

Gale, Rhoda E. — *E.G. Jones Associates, Ltd.*
Gordon, Gerald L. — *E.G. Jones Associates, Ltd.*
Jones, Edward G. — *E.G. Jones Associates, Ltd.*
**Mitchellville**
MacJadyen, David J. — *Sharrow & Associates*
**Rockville**
Belford, Paul — *JDG Associates, Ltd.*
Blim, Barbara — *JDG Associates, Ltd.*
Brown, D. Perry — *Don Richard Associates of Washington, D.C., Inc.*
DeGioia, Joseph — *JDG Associates, Ltd.*
Fotia, Frank — *JDG Associates, Ltd.*
Hopgood, Earl — *JDG Associates, Ltd.*
**Salisbury**
Puente, Fred J. — *Management Recruiters International, Inc.*
**Silver Spring**
Black, Frank S. — *Management Recruiters International, Inc.*
Hingers, Marilyn H. — *Management Recruiters International, Inc.*
Max, Bruno — *RBR Associates, Inc.*
**Timonium**
McPoyle, Thomas C. — *Sanford Rose Associates*
**Towson**
Cappe, Richard R. — *Roberts Ryan and Bentley*
Dannenberg, Richard A. — *Roberts Ryan and Bentley*
## Massachusetts
**Andover**
Kishbaugh, Herbert S. — *Kishbaugh Associates International*
Newman, Lynn — *Kishbaugh Associates International*
**Boston**
Allen, John L. — *Heidrick & Struggles, Inc.*
Alphonse-Charles, Maureen — *Pendleton James and Associates, Inc.*
Baker-Greene, Edward — *Isaacson, Miller*
Barao, Thomas — *Korn/Ferry International*
Beckvold, John B. — *Atlantic Search Group, Inc.*
Bellshaw, David — *Isaacson, Miller*
Bennett, Richard T. — *Isaacson, Miller*
Berarducci, Arthur — *Heidrick & Struggles, Inc.*
Berger, Emanuel — *Isaacson, Miller*
Bilz, Deirdre — *Johnson Smith & Knisely Accord*
Birns, Douglas — *Source Services Corporation*
Bond, Robert J. — *Romac & Associates*
Burke, Sally — *Chaloner Associates*
Celenza, Catherine — *CPS Inc.*
Chaloner, Edward — *Chaloner Associates*
Cramer, Katherine M. — *Pendleton James and Associates, Inc.*
Cuddy, Brian C. — *Romac & Associates*
Czepiel, Susan — *CPS Inc.*
DeCosta, Michael — *Korn/Ferry International*
Epstein, Kathy — *Canny, Bowen Inc.*
Fazekas, John A. — *Korn/Ferry International*
Feldman, Kimberley — *Atlantic Search Group, Inc.*
Fioretti, Kim — *Accountants on Call*
Flynn, Brian — *Korn/Ferry International*
Gaffney, Denise O'Grady — *Isaacson, Miller*
Gleckman, Mark — *Winter, Wyman & Company*
Gourley, Timothy — *Source Services Corporation*
Greenfield, Art — *Management Recruiters International, Inc.*
Hallagan, Robert E. — *Heidrick & Struggles, Inc.*
Hazerjian, Cynthia — *CPS Inc.*
Hensley, Gayla — *Atlantic Search Group, Inc.*
Hoagland, John H. — *Pendleton James and Associates, Inc.*
Holodnak, William A. — *J. Robert Scott*
Hopkinson, Dana — *Winter, Wyman & Company*
Howell, Robert B. — *Atlantic Search Group, Inc.*
Howell, Robert B. — *Atlantic Search Group, Inc.*
Hunter, Durant A. — *Pendleton James and Associates, Inc.*
Hurd, J. Nicholas — *Russell Reynolds Associates, Inc.*
Isaacson, John — *Isaacson, Miller*
Jackowitz, Todd — *J. Robert Scott*
Jones, Daniel F. — *Atlantic Search Group, Inc.*
Lapat, Aaron D. — *J. Robert Scott*
Manzo, Renee — *Atlantic Search Group, Inc.*
Martin, Kenneth — *Winter, Wyman & Company*
McClure, James K. — *Korn/Ferry International*
McLean, Chris — *Chaloner Associates*
McMahan, Stephen — *Source Services Corporation*
Miller, Arnie — *Isaacson, Miller*
Mohan, Jack — *Management Recruiters International, Inc.*
Moseley, Monroe — *Isaacson, Miller*
Nehiley, Jack J. — *Management Recruiters International, Inc.*
Nunziata, Peter — *Atlantic Search Group, Inc.*
O'Connell, Mary — *CPS Inc.*
O'Connell, William — *Winter, Wyman & Company*
Ollinger, Charles D. — *Heidrick & Struggles, Inc.*
Orr, Stacie — *Source Services Corporation*
Oswald, Mark G. — *Canny, Bowen Inc.*
Ouellette, Christopher — *Source Services Corporation*
Pease, Samuel C. — *Heidrick & Struggles, Inc.*
Pieh, Jerry — *Isaacson, Miller*

Rabinowitz, Peter A. — *P.A.R. Associates Inc.*
Reardon, Joseph — *Source Services Corporation*
Reed, William D. — *Russell Reynolds Associates, Inc.*
Resnic, Alan — *Source Services Corporation*
Reynolds, Catherine — *Winter, Wyman & Company*
Reynolds, Juli Ann — *Korn/Ferry International*
Rosen, Mark — *Winter, Wyman & Company*
Rossi, George A. — *Heidrick & Struggles, Inc.*
Savage, Julie — *Winter, Wyman & Company*
Savereid, Lisa — *Isaacson, Miller*
Schaad, Carl A. — *Heidrick & Struggles, Inc.*
Serba, Kerri — *Source Services Corporation*
Shabot, David — *Korn/Ferry International*
Shapiro, Elaine — *CPS Inc.*
Smith, Mark L. — *Korn/Ferry International*
Smith, Timothy — *Source Services Corporation*
Sostilio, Louis — *Source Services Corporation*
Stevenson, Julianne M. — *Russell Reynolds Associates, Inc.*
Sullivan, Robert — *Korn/Ferry International*
Thomson, Alexander G. — *Russell Reynolds Associates, Inc.*
Tscelli, Maureen — *Source Services Corporation*
Vande-Water, Katie — *J. Robert Scott*
Vernon, Jack H. — *Russell Reynolds Associates, Inc.*
von der Linden, James A. — *Pendleton James and Associates, Inc.*
Wakeham, Robin — *Korn/Ferry International*
Walton, Bruce H. — *Heidrick & Struggles, Inc.*
Warter, Mark — *Isaacson, Miller*
Webber, Edward — *Source Services Corporation*
Welch, David — *Isaacson, Miller*
Welch, Sarah — *Korn/Ferry International*
Wichlei, Alan — *Isaacson, Miller*
Wilcox, Karen — *Isaacson, Miller*
Williams, Michelle Cruz — *Isaacson, Miller*
Williams, Walter E. — *Canny, Bowen Inc.*
Wyatt, Janice — *Korn/Ferry International*
Zegel, Gary — *Source Services Corporation*
**Braintree**
Morse, Steve — *Management Recruiters International, Inc.*
**Burlington**
Browne, Michael — *Source Services Corporation*
Cheah, Victor — *Source Services Corporation*
Chronopoulos, Dennis — *Source Services Corporation*
Di Filippo, Thomas — *Source Services Corporation*
Finnerty, James — *Source Services Corporation*
Glickman, Leenie — *Source Services Corporation*
Inger, Barry — *Source Services Corporation*
Lundy, Martin — *Source Services Corporation*
Macrides, Michael — *Source Services Corporation*
Mader, Stephen P. — *Christian & Timbers*
Moore, Craig — *Source Services Corporation*
Murry, John — *Source Services Corporation*
Nephew, Robert — *Christian & Timbers*
Patlovich, Michael J. — *Witt/Kieffer, Ford, Hadelman & Lloyd*
Twomey, James — *Source Services Corporation*
Vairo, Leonard A. — *Christian & Timbers*
Winkowski, Stephen — *Source Services Corporation*
**Cambridge**
Denney, Edward B. — *Denney & Company Incorporated*
Tufenkjian, Richard — *C.A. Durakis Associates, Inc.*
**Dedham**
Kelly, Susan D. — *S.D. Kelly & Associates, Inc.*
Marion, Michael — *S.D. Kelly & Associates, Inc.*
Nolan, Jean M. — *S.D. Kelly & Associates, Inc.*
Parkin, Myrna — *S.D. Kelly & Associates, Inc.*
Shamir, Ben — *S.D. Kelly & Associates, Inc.*
Thies, Gary — *S.D. Kelly & Associates, Inc.*
**Framingham**
Sherwin, Thomas — *Barone-O'Hara Associates*
Silver, Lee A. — *L.A. Silver Associates, Inc.*
Spiegel, Gay — *L.A. Silver Associates, Inc.*
**Lexington**
Cochran, Hale — *Fenwick Partners*
Germaine, Debra — *Fenwick Partners*
Polachi, Charles A. — *Fenwick Partners*
Polachi, Peter V. — *Fenwick Partners*
Rudzinsky, Howard — *Louis Rudzinsky Associates*
Rudzinsky, Jeffrey — *Louis Rudzinsky Associates*
Starner, William S. — *Fenwick Partners*
**Manchester-by-the-Sea**
Gilreath, James M. — *Gilreath Weatherby, Inc.*
**Medfield**
Allen, Rita B. — *R.D. Gatti & Associates, Incorporated*
Banker, Judith G. — *R.D. Gatti & Associates, Incorporated*
Bloomfield, Mary — *R.D. Gatti & Associates, Incorporated*
Carrigan, Maureen — *R.D. Gatti & Associates, Incorporated*
Fleming, Richard — *R.D. Gatti & Associates, Incorporated*
Gatti, Robert D. — *R.D. Gatti & Associates, Incorporated*
Martin, Bette — *R.D. Gatti & Associates, Incorporated*
Nathan, Gerri — *R.D. Gatti & Associates, Incorporated*

Czamanske, Paul W. — *Executive Interim Management, Inc.*
Czamanske, Peter M. — *Executive Interim Management, Inc.*
David, Dodie — *Sullivan & Associates*
Evans, Jeffrey — *Sullivan & Associates*
Slaughter, Katherine T. — *Compass Group Ltd.*
Sturtz, James W. — *Compass Group Ltd.*
Sullivan, Dennis — *Sullivan & Associates*

**Blissfield**
Snellbaker, Mary W. — *Management Recruiters International, Inc.*

**Bloomfield Hills**
Black, Nancy C. — *Assisting Professionals, Inc.*
Carlson, Sharon A. — *Assisting Professionals, Inc.*
Crowder, Edward W. — *Crowder & Company*
Kemp, M. Scott — *M. Scott Kemp & Associates*
Klopfenstein, Edward L. — *Crowder & Company*

**Center Line**
Dreslinski, Robert S. — *Sharrow & Associates*
Johnson, Michael E. — *Sharrow & Associates*
Keefer, Russell R. — *Sharrow & Associates*
Lawrance, Susanne — *Sharrow & Associates*
Line, Joseph T. — *Sharrow & Associates*
Martines, James — *Sharrow & Associates*

**Dearborn**
Kozlowski, Elaine K. — *Management Recruiters International, Inc.*
Tripp, William J. — *Management Recruiters International, Inc.*

**Detroit**
Giles, Joe L. — *Joe L. Giles and Associates, Inc.*
Lawson, Debra — *Management Recruiters International, Inc.*

**Farmington Hills**
Neman, Nancy — *Phyllis Hawkins & Associates, Inc.*

**Flint**
Reed, David Q. — *Management Recruiters International, Inc.*

**Grand Rapids**
Anderson, Matthew — *Source  Services Corporation*
Combs, Thomas — *Source  Services Corporation*
Fales, Scott — *Source  Services Corporation*
Harvey, Mike — *Advanced Executive Resources*
Haystead, Steve — *Advanced Executive Resources*
Mairn, Todd — *Source  Services Corporation*
Meadley, Ronald J. — *Management Recruiters International, Inc.*
Peal, Matthew — *Source  Services Corporation*
Schlpma, Christine — *Advanced Executive Resources*
Sochacki, Michael — *Source  Services Corporation*
Trewhella, Michael — *Source  Services Corporation*
Willbrandt, Curt — *Source  Services Corporation*

**Grosse Pointe**
Whitley, Sue Ann — *Roberts Ryan and Bentley*

**Grosse Pointe Park**
Case, David — *Case Executive Search*

**Holland**
Bakker, Robert E. — *Management Recruiters International, Inc.*

**Holt**
Peterson, John A. — *Management Recruiters International, Inc.*
Peterson, Priscilla J. — *Management Recruiters International, Inc.*

**Houghton**
Harris, Jack L. — *Management Recruiters International, Inc.*
Harris, Vicki M. — *Management Recruiters International, Inc.*

**Kalamazoo**
Tessin, Cy — *Management Recruiters International, Inc.*

**Livonia**
Eden, Don F. — *Management Recruiters International, Inc.*

**Marine City**
Bommarito, Bob C. — *Management Recruiters International, Inc.*

**Muskegon**
Mitchell, John R. — *Management Recruiters International, Inc.*

**Oak Park**
Rosenfeld, Martin J. — *Sanford Rose Associates*

**Rochester Hills**
Angott, Mark R. — *Management Recruiters International, Inc.*

**Southfield**
Brunner, Terry — *Source  Services Corporation*
Buzolits, Patrick — *Source  Services Corporation*
Comai, Christine — *Source  Services Corporation*
Dow, Lori — *Davidson, Laird & Associates*
Foster, Bradley — *Source  Services Corporation*
Gluzman, Arthur — *Source  Services Corporation*
Guc, Stephen — *Source  Services Corporation*
Kelsey, Micki — *Davidson, Laird & Associates*
Klusman, Edwin — *Source  Services Corporation*
Laird, Meri — *Davidson, Laird & Associates*
Lewis, Daniel — *Source  Services Corporation*
Swanner, William — *Source  Services Corporation*
Van Steenkiste, Julie — *Davidson, Laird & Associates*

**Traverse City**
Barker, Mary J. — *Management Recruiters International, Inc.*

**Troy**
Brown, Charlene N. — *Accent on Achievement, Inc.*
Colborne, Janis M. — *AJM Professional Services*
Cole, Sharon A. — *AJM Professional Services*
Edwards, Verba L. — *Wing Tips & Pumps, Inc.*
Jones, Jeffrey — *AJM Professional Services*
Moeller, Ed J. — *Management Recruiters International, Inc.*
Muller, Charles A. — *AJM Professional Services*
Rabe, William — *Sales Executives Inc.*
Roehrig, Kurt W. — *AJM Professional Services*
Statson, Dale E. — *Sales Executives Inc.*

## Minnesota
**Bloomington**
Kennedy, Walter — *Source  Services Corporation*

**Chanhassen**
Ancona, Donald J. — *Management Recruiters International, Inc.*

**Minneapolis**
Anderson, Janet — *Professional Alternatives, Inc.*
Artimovich, Lee J. — *Korn/Ferry International*
Bachmeier, Kevin — *Agra Placements International Ltd.*
Baker, Charles E. — *Kenzer Corp.*
Barnum, Toni M. — *Stone Murphy & Olson*
Bothereau, Elizabeth A. — *Kenzer Corp.*
Chandler, Cynthia — *Kenzer Corp.*
Cline, Mark — *NYCOR Search, Inc.*
Coleman, Scott A. — *Kenzer Corp.*
Do, Sonnie — *Whitney & Associates, Inc.*
Erickson, Mary R. — *Mary R. Erickson & Associates, Inc.*
Getzkin, Helen — *Korn/Ferry International*
Hanson, Jeremy — *Korn/Ferry International*
Herman, Pat — *Whitney & Associates, Inc.*
Hettinger, Susan — *Kenzer Corp.*
Huntting, Lisa — *Professional Alternatives, Inc.*
Hykes, Don A. — *A.T. Kearney, Inc.*
Johnson, Keith — *Romac & Associates*
Kelly, Michael T. — *Russell Reynolds Associates, Inc.*
Kennedy, Walter — *Source  Services Corporation*
Kent, Vickey — *Professional Alternatives, Inc.*
Kruchoski, Jan — *Accountants on Call*
Macdonald, Robert W. — *Russell Reynolds Associates, Inc.*
Mathias, Kathy — *Stone Murphy & Olson*
McDonnell, Julie — *Technical Personnel of Minnesota*
McQuoid, David — *A.T. Kearney, Inc.*
Mertensotto, Chuck H. — *Whitney & Associates, Inc.*
Murphy, Gary J. — *Stone Murphy & Olson*
Nymark, John — *NYCOR Search, Inc.*
Nymark, Paul — *NYCOR Search, Inc.*
Olsen, Robert F. — *Robert Connelly and Associates Incorporated*
Raymond, Allan H. — *Korn/Ferry International*
Sathe, Mark A. — *Sathe & Associates, Inc.*
Schoenwetter, Carrie — *Management Recruiters International, Inc.*
Sjogren, Dennis — *Agra Placements International Ltd.*
Stein, Terry W. — *Stewart, Stein and Scott, Ltd.*
Stewart, Jeffrey O. — *Stewart, Stein and Scott, Ltd.*
Whitney, David L. — *Whitney & Associates, Inc.*
Williams, Angie — *Whitney & Associates, Inc.*
Wujciak, Sandra — *Accountants on Call*

**Minnetonka**
Delin, Norm — *Management Recruiters International, Inc.*
Hermanson, Shelley — *Ells Personnel System Inc.*
Jaffe, Mark — *Wyatt & Jaffe*
Koehler, Cathy — *Ells Personnel System Inc.*
Kropp, Randy — *Ells Personnel System Inc.*
Nielsen, Sue — *Ells Personnel System Inc.*
Stephenson, Don L. — *Ells Personnel System Inc.*
Welsh, Jason — *Ells Personnel System Inc.*
Wyatt, James — *Wyatt & Jaffe*

**Plymouth**
Anderson, Dean C. — *Corporate Resources Professional Placement*
Lanctot, William D. — *Corporate Resources Professional Placement*

**Rochester**
Vierkant, Nona E. — *Management Recruiters International, Inc.*
Vierkant, Robert — *Management Recruiters International, Inc.*

**St. Paul**
Lauerman, Fred J. — *Development Search Specialists*

**Wayzata**
Anderson, Dennis — *Andcor Human Resources*
Hauser, Jack — *Andcor Human Resources*
Hirschey, K. David — *Andcor Human Resources*
Mazzitelli, Teresa A. — *The Mazzitelli Group, Ltd.*
Naughtin, Terri — *Andcor Human Resources*

**Winona**
Crigler, Jim — *Management Recruiters International, Inc.*

## Mississippi
**Jackson**
Gardner, J.W. — *Management Recruiters International, Inc.*
Van Wick, Mike — *Management Recruiters International, Inc.*

**East Brunswick**
Berkowitz, Carol — *Career Management International*
Bhimpure, Anita — *Career Management International*
Gelfman, David — *Career Management International*
Kalb, Lenny — *Career Management International*
Lippman, Lloyd A. — *Career Management International*
Marshall, Gerald — *Blair/Tech Recruiters*
Rapoport, William — *Blair/Tech Recruiters*
Rathborne, Kenneth J. — *Blair/Tech Recruiters*
Ravit, Alan — *Career Management International*
Schiffer, Stewart — *Career Management International*

**Edison**
Abramson, Roye — *Source  Services Corporation*
Altreuter, Ken — *ALTCO Temporary Services*
Altreuter, Kenneth — *The ALTCO Group*
Altreuter, Rose — *ALTCO Temporary Services*
Altreuter, Rose — *The ALTCO Group*
Cannon, Alicia — *Accountants on Call*
Carvalho-Esteves, Maria — *Source  Services Corporation*
Castle, Lisa — *Source  Services Corporation*
Cuddy, Patricia — *Source  Services Corporation*
Frantino, Michael — *Source  Services Corporation*
Jones, Rodney — *Source  Services Corporation*
Miras, Cliff — *Source  Services Corporation*
Nitti, Jacqueline — *ALTCO Temporary Services*
Reed, Susan — *Source  Services Corporation*
Scoff, Barry — *Source  Services Corporation*
Shea, John — *ALTCO Temporary Services*
Shea, John — *The ALTCO Group*

**Emerson**
Ambert, Amadol — *Bryant Research*
Billotti, Lisa — *Bryant Research*
Brazil, Kathy — *Bryant Research*
Bryant, Thomas — *Bryant Research*
Crean, Jeremiah N. — *Bryant Research*
Deal, Leslie — *Bryant Research*
Dulet, Donna — *Bryant Research*
Jable, Maria C. — *Bryant Research*
Mann, Carol — *Bryant Research*
Rosen, Salene — *Bryant Research*
Yard, Allan S. — *Bryant Research*

**Englewood Cliffs**
Harshman, Donald — *The Stevenson Group of New Jersey*
Kotick, Madeline — *The Stevenson Group of New Jersey*
Krohn, Eileen — *The Stevenson Group of New Jersey*
Lovely, Edward — *The Stevenson Group of New Jersey*
Maphet, Harriet — *The Stevenson Group of New Jersey*
Steinman, Stephen — *The Stevenson Group of New Jersey*
Wright, Leslie — *The Stevenson Group of New Jersey*

**Fanwood**
Juelis, John J. — *Peeney Associates*
Peeney, James D. — *Peeney Associates*

**Flemington**
Brocaglia, Joyce — *Alta Associates, Inc.*
Cahoon, D.B. — *Sanford Rose Associates*
Sabat, Lori S. — *Alta Associates, Inc.*
Spadavecchia, Jennifer — *Alta Associates, Inc.*

**Florham Park**
Laba, Stuart M. — *Marvin Laba & Associates*

**Hackensack**
Drexler, Robert — *Robert Drexler Associates, Inc.*

**Haddonfield**
Kelly, Roy P. — *Management Recruiters International, Inc.*

**Harrington Park**
Seco, William — *Seco & Zetto Associates, Inc.*
Zetto, Kathryn — *Seco & Zetto Associates, Inc.*

**Hazlet**
Boag, John — *Norm Sanders Associates*
Helgeson, Burton H. — *Norm Sanders Associates*
Lindsay, Mary — *Norm Sanders Associates*
McGuigan, Walter J. — *Norm Sanders Associates*
Sanders, Norman D. — *Norm Sanders Associates*

**Hope**
Magnusen, Hank F. — *Management Recruiters International, Inc.*

**Iselin**
Gallagher, Terence M. — *Battalia Winston International*
Kleinstein, Jonah A. — *The Kleinstein Group*

**Livingston**
Silverstein, Rita — *Accountants on Call*

**Mahwah**
Butterfass, Stanley — *Butterfass, Pepe & MacCallan Inc.*
MacCallan, Deirdre — *Butterfass, Pepe & MacCallan Inc.*
Pepe, Leonida — *Butterfass, Pepe & MacCallan Inc.*

**Marlton**
Bonifield, Len — *Bonifield Associates*
Casal, Daniel G. — *Bonifield Associates*
Sweeney, Sean K. — *Bonifield Associates*
Tyson, Richard L. — *Bonifield Associates*

**Medford**
Talbot, Matt T. — *Management Recruiters International, Inc.*
Talbot, Norman — *Management Recruiters International, Inc.*

**Metuchen**
Noorani, Frank — *Management Recruiters International, Inc.*

**Millburn**
Aston, Kathy — *Marra Peters & Partners*
Marra, John — *Marra Peters & Partners*
Milton, Suzanne — *Marra Peters & Partners*
Pelisson, Charles — *Marra Peters & Partners*

**Montclair**
Cowan, Roberta — *Drew Associates International*
Detore, Robert R. — *Drew Associates International*
Grady, Richard F. — *Drew Associates International*

**Morristown**
Barbosa, Franklin J. — *Boyden*
Burfield, Elaine — *Skott/Edwards Consultants, Inc.*
Burkland, Skott B. — *Skott/Edwards Consultants, Inc.*
Burris, James C. — *Boyden*
Eden, Dianne — *Steeple Associates*
Grebenstein, Charles R. — *Skott/Edwards Consultants, Inc.*
Malone, George V. — *Boyden*
Montgomery, Catherine C. — *Boyden*
Pitcher, Brian D. — *Skott/Edwards Consultants, Inc.*
Ryan, Joseph W. — *Skott/Edwards Consultants, Inc.*
Schmidt, Peter R. — *Boyden*
Young, Susan M. — *Management Recruiters International, Inc.*
Young, Wayne T. — *Management Recruiters International, Inc.*

**Mount Laurel**
Ruschak, Randy R. — *Management Recruiters International, Inc.*

**Mountain Lakes**
Besen, Douglas — *Besen Associates Inc.*

**Mountainside**
Malfetti, Jim L. — *Management Recruiters International, Inc.*
Malfetti, Ro — *Management Recruiters International, Inc.*

**New Providence**
Miller, Andrew S. — *Management Recruiters International, Inc.*

**North Caldwell**
Citrin, Lea — *K.L. Whitney Company*
Slocum, Ann Marie — *K.L. Whitney Company*
Whitney, Kenneth L. — *K.L. Whitney Company*

**Paramus**
Eiseman, Joe — *Source  Services Corporation*
Lebovits, Neil — *Accountants on Call*

**Parlin**
Hardbrod, Herbert — *Management Recruiters International, Inc.*

**Parsippany**
Barton, James — *Source  Services Corporation*
Bergen, Anthony M. — *CFO Associates, Inc.*
Bouer, Judy — *Baker Scott & Company*
Cotugno, James — *Source  Services Corporation*
Eiseman, Joe — *Source  Services Corporation*
Graziano, Lisa — *Source  Services Corporation*
Hanson, Grant M. — *Goodrich & Sherwood Associates, Inc.*
Liebross, Eric — *Source  Services Corporation*
Lipuma, Thomas — *Source  Services Corporation*
Mendoza-Green, Robin — *Source  Services Corporation*
Mittwol, Myles — *Source  Services Corporation*
Palma, Frank R. — *Goodrich & Sherwood Associates, Inc.*
Perry, Carolyn — *Source  Services Corporation*
Plant, Jerry — *Source  Services Corporation*
Renfroe, Ann-Marie — *Source  Services Corporation*
Sapperstein, Jerry S. — *CFO Associates, Inc.*
Tankson, Dawn — *Source  Services Corporation*

**Pompton Lakes**
Zawicki, David — *Management Recruiters International, Inc.*

**Princeton**
Arons, Richard — *Korn/Ferry International*
Barone, Marialice — *Barone-O'Hara Associates*
Bartfield, Philip — *Source  Services Corporation*
Bishop, James F. — *Burke, O'Brien & Bishop Associates, Inc.*
Bremer, Brian — *Source  Services Corporation*
Brooks, Natalie — *Raymond Karsan Associates*
Callaway, Lisa — *Korn/Ferry International*
Cannon, Alicia — *Accountants on Call*
Carrara, Gilbert J. — *Korn/Ferry International*
Doele, Donald C. — *Goodrich & Sherwood Associates, Inc.*
Gill, Patricia — *Columbia Consulting Group*
Kaptain, John — *Blau Kaptain Schroeder*
Korkuch, Sandy — *Barone-O'Hara Associates*
Mancino, Gene — *Blau Kaptain Schroeder*
Meara, Helen — *Source  Services Corporation*
Miras, Cliff — *Source  Services Corporation*
O'Hara, James J. — *Barone-O'Hara Associates*
Schostak, Glen — *Korn/Ferry International*
Stratmeyer, Karin Bergwall — *Princeton Entrepreneurial Resources*

Valenta, Joseph — *Princeton Entrepreneurial Resources*
Zila, Laurie M. — *Princeton Entrepreneurial Resources*
**Red Bank**
Unger, Mike A. — *Management Recruiters International, Inc.*
**Rochelle Park**
Erstling, Gregory — *Normyle/Erstling Health Search Group*
Fotino, Anne — *Normyle/Erstling Health Search Group*
Johnson, Janet — *Normyle/Erstling Health Search Group*
Kreps, Charles D. — *Normyle/Erstling Health Search Group*
**Rutherford**
Macdonald, G. William — *The Macdonald Group, Inc.*
**Saddle Brook**
Buchsbaum, Deborah — *Accountants on Call*
Krutzsch, Linda — *Accountants on Call*
Libes, Dory — *Accountants on Call*
Libes, Stewart C. — *Accountants on Call*
**Secaucus**
Robinson, Bruce — *Bruce Robinson Associates*
Robinson, Eric B. — *Bruce Robinson Associates*
Silverberg, Alisa — *Accountants on Call*
**Short Hills**
Davis, John J. — *John J. Davis & Associates, Inc.*
**Shrewsbury**
Alderman, Douglas — *Management Recruiters International, Inc.*
Sabados, Terri — *Management Recruiters International, Inc.*
**Sparta**
Incitti, Lance M. — *Management Recruiters International, Inc.*
**Springfield**
Allen, Donald — *D.S. Allen Associates, Inc.*
Gikas, Bill — *Tarnow International*
Vogel, Emil — *Tarnow International*
**Stanhope**
Young, Arthur L. — *Management Recruiters International, Inc.*
**Summit**
Foreman, David C. — *Koontz, Jeffries & Associates, Inc.*
Koontz, Donald N. — *Koontz, Jeffries & Associates, Inc.*
**Tennent**
Porada, Stephen D. — *CAP Inc.*
**Upper Montclair**
Hodges, Robert J. — *Sampson Neill & Wilkins Inc.*
Jackson, W.T. — *Sampson Neill & Wilkins Inc.*
Neill, Wellden K. — *Sampson Neill & Wilkins Inc.*
Richardson, David M. — *DHR International, Inc.*
Sampson, Martin C. — *Sampson Neill & Wilkins Inc.*
Stinson, R.J. — *Sampson Neill & Wilkins Inc.*
Wilkins, Walter K. — *Sampson Neill & Wilkins Inc.*
**Verona**
Ascher, Susan P. — *The Ascher Group*
Ehrgott, Elizabeth — *The Ascher Group*
**Wall**
Abby, Daniel — *Bill Hahn Group, Inc.*
Ferguson, Robert — *Bill Hahn Group, Inc.*
Hahn, William R. — *Bill Hahn Group, Inc.*
Zoppo, Dorathea — *Bill Hahn Group, Inc.*
**West Orange**
Arms, Douglas — *TOPAZ International, Inc.*
Arms, Douglas — *TOPAZ Legal Solutions*
Cohen, Pamela — *TOPAZ International, Inc.*
Cohen, Pamela — *TOPAZ Legal Solutions*
Cruz, Catherine — *TOPAZ International, Inc.*
Cruz, Catherine — *TOPAZ Legal Solutions*
Ebeling, John A. — *Gilbert Tweed/INESA*
Gaines, Ronni L. — *TOPAZ International, Inc.*
Gaines, Ronni L. — *TOPAZ Legal Solutions*
Greenwald, Jane K. — *Gilbert Tweed/INESA*
Hanley, Maureen E. — *Gilbert Tweed/INESA*
Holland, Kathleen — *TOPAZ International, Inc.*
Holland, Kathleen — *TOPAZ Legal Solutions*
Mashakas, Elizabeth — *TOPAZ International, Inc.*
Mashakas, Elizabeth — *TOPAZ Legal Solutions*
Michaels, Stewart — *TOPAZ International, Inc.*
Michaels, Stewart — *TOPAZ Legal Solutions*
Paul, Linda — *Gilbert Tweed/INESA*
Pinson, Stephanie L. — *Gilbert Tweed/INESA*
**West Trenton**
Bodnar, Beverly — *Management Recruiters International, Inc.*
Bodnar, Robert J. — *Management Recruiters International, Inc.*
**Woodbridge**
Cram, Noel — *R.P. Barone Associates*
Hughes, James J. — *R.P. Barone Associates*
Rizzo, L. Donald — *R.P. Barone Associates*

**New Mexico**
**Albuquerque**
Schneider, Tom J. — *Management Recruiters International, Inc.*
Schroeder, Steven J. — *Blau Kaptain Schroeder*

**New York**
**Albany**
Kayajian, Bob A. — *Management Recruiters International, Inc.*
Mulcahey, Bob T. — *Management Recruiters International, Inc.*
**Auburn**
Dunn, Ed L. — *Management Recruiters International, Inc.*
**Bath**
Lewis, Mark — *Management Recruiters International, Inc.*
**Binghamton**
Clingan, Bob H. — *Management Recruiters International, Inc.*
Wallace, Mark J. — *Management Recruiters International, Inc.*
**Brooklyn**
Hutchinson, Loretta M. — *Hutchinson Resources International*
**Buffalo**
Cramer, Paul J. — *C/R Associates*
**Cortland**
Adams, Ralda F. — *Hospitality International*
Sine, Mark — *Hospitality International*
Stafford, Susan — *Hospitality International*
**Farmington**
Plecash, Bob — *Management Recruiters International, Inc.*
**Fayetteville**
Atkinson, S. Graham — *Raymond Karsan Associates*
**Great Neck**
Attell, Harold — *A.E. Feldman Associates*
Feldman, Abe — *A.E. Feldman Associates*
Frieze, Stanley B. — *Stanley B. Frieze Company*
Kaufman, Stuart — *Management Recruiters International, Inc.*
Kotler, Herman — *Management Recruiters International, Inc.*
Nathanson, Barry F. — *Barry Nathanson Associates*
Roberts, Mitch — *A.E. Feldman Associates*
Rothfeld, Robert — *A.E. Feldman Associates*
Schwam, Carol — *A.E. Feldman Associates*
**Greenwood Lake**
Chermak, Carolyn A. — *Management Recruiters International, Inc.*
**Harrison**
Zarkin, Norman — *The Zarkin Group, Inc.*
**Hauppauge**
Ames, George C. — *Ames O'Neill Associates*
**Hawthorne**
Foy, Richard — *Boyden*
**Hicksville**
Eibeler, C. — *Amherst Personnel Group Inc.*
Porter, Donald — *Amherst Personnel Group Inc.*
**Huntington Station**
Levitt, Bob — *Management Recruiters International, Inc.*
**Jericho**
Mogul, Gene — *Mogul Consultants, Inc.*
Targovnik, Andrew — *Accountants on Call*
**Larchmont**
O'Toole, Dennis P. — *Dennis P. O'Toole & Associates Inc.*
**Madrid**
Infantino, James — *Management Recruiters International, Inc.*
**New York**
Abruzzo, James — *A.T. Kearney, Inc.*
Adams, Len — *The KPA Group*
Alfano, Anthony J. — *Russell Reynolds Associates, Inc.*
Alpeyrie, Jean-Louis — *Heidrick & Struggles, Inc.*
Amsterdam, Gail E. — *D.E. Foster Partners Inc.*
Andre, Jacques P. — *Paul Ray Berndtson*
Andrews, Laura L. — *Stricker & Zagor*
Anglade, Jennifer — *Korn/Ferry International*
Anwar, Tarin — *Jay Gaines & Company, Inc.*
Archer, John W. — *Russell Reynolds Associates, Inc.*
Argenio, Michelangelo — *Spencer Stuart*
Aronin, Michael — *Fisher-Todd Associates*
Aronow, Lawrence E. — *Aronow Associates, Inc.*
Arozarena, Elaine — *Russell Reynolds Associates, Inc.*
Atkins, Laurie — *Battalia Winston International*
Aydelotte, G. Thomas — *Ingram & Aydelotte Inc.*
Bacher, Philip J. — *Handy HRM Corp.*
Bader, Sam — *Bader Research Corporation*
Bagley, James W. — *Russell Reynolds Associates, Inc.*
Bailey, David O. — *Paul Ray Berndtson*
Bailey, Joseph W. — *Russell Reynolds Associates, Inc.*
Bailey, Lisa — *Nordeman Grimm, Inc.*
Baillou, Astrid — *Richard Kinser & Associates*
Barack, Brianne — *The Barack Group, Inc.*
Barrett, J. David — *Heidrick & Struggles, Inc.*
Battalia, O. William — *Battalia Winston International*
Bauman, Martin H. — *Martin H. Bauman Associates, Inc.*
Beck, Barbara S. — *Rhodes Associates*
Beerman, Joan — *Kenzer Corp.*
Behringer, Neail — *Neail Behringer Consultants*
Beir, Ellen Haupt — *Korn/Ferry International*
Bell, Jeffrey G. — *Norman Broadbent International, Inc.*

Bell, Peter P. — *Cantor Concern Staffing Options, Inc.*
Benabou, Donna — *Kenzer Corp.*
Bennett, Jo — *Battalia Winston International*
Benson, Kate — *Rene Plessner Associates, Inc.*
Bentley, David W. — *Nordeman Grimm, Inc.*
Berger, Joel — *Meridian Legal Search*
Berk-Levine, Margo — *MB Inc. Interim Executive Division*
Berne, Marlene — *The Whitney Group*
Bishop, Barbara — *The Executive Source*
Bishop, Susan — *Bishop Partners*
Blair, Susan — *Simpson Associates*
Blumenthal, Deborah — *Paul Ray Berndtson*
Blumenthal, Paula — *J.P. Canon Associates*
Boccuzi, Joseph H. — *Spencer Stuart*
Bodner, Marilyn — *Bodner, Inc.*
Boerkoel, Timothy B. — *Russell Reynolds Associates, Inc.*
Borland, James — *Goodrich & Sherwood Associates, Inc.*
Borman, Theodore H. — *Lamalie Amrop International*
Bovich, Maryann C. — *Higdon Prince Inc.*
Boyle, Russell E. — *Egon Zehnder International Inc.*
Brandon, Irwin — *Hadley Lockwood, Inc.*
Bratches, Howard — *Thorndike Deland Associates*
Brennan, Patrick J. — *Handy HRM Corp.*
Brennan, Vincent F. — *Korn/Ferry International*
Brenner, Michael — *Lamalie Amrop International*
Brieger, Steve — *Thorne, Brieger Associates Inc.*
Brink, James — *Noble & Associates Inc.*
Broadhurst, Austin — *Russell Reynolds Associates, Inc.*
Brooks, Bernard E. — *Mruk & Partners/EMA Partners Int'l*
Brophy, Melissa — *Maximum Management Corp.*
Brown, David — *Korn/Ferry International*
Brown, Debra J. — *Norman Broadbent International, Inc.*
Brown, Franklin Key — *Handy HRM Corp.*
Brown, Hobson — *Russell Reynolds Associates, Inc.*
Buchalter, Allyson — *The Whitney Group*
Buck, Charles — *Charles Buck & Associates*
Bullard, Roger C. — *Russell Reynolds Associates, Inc.*
Bullock, Conni — *Earley Kielty and Associates, Inc.*
Burnett, Brendan G. — *Sullivan & Company*
Busterna, Charles — *The KPA Group*
Butler, Kevin M. — *Russell Reynolds Associates, Inc.*
Cahill, James P. — *Thorndike Deland Associates*
Callen, John H. — *Ward Howell International, Inc.*
Cannavo, Louise — *The Whitney Group*
Cantor, Bill — *Cantor Concern Staffing Options, Inc.*
Carideo, Joseph — *Thorndike Deland Associates*
Carpenter, James J. — *Russell Reynolds Associates, Inc.*
Cashen, Anthony B. — *Lamalie Amrop International*
Castine, Michael P. — *Spencer Stuart*
Caudill, Nancy — *Webb, Johnson Associates, Inc.*
Celentano, James — *Korn/Ferry International*
Chadick, Susan L. — *Gould, McCoy & Chadick Incorporated*
Chamberlin, Brooks T. — *Korn/Ferry International*
Chan, Margaret — *Webb, Johnson Associates, Inc.*
Chargar, Frances — *Hunt Ltd.*
Chase, Kevin — *Paul Ray Berndtson*
Cicchino, William M. — *Lamalie Amrop International*
Citera, Tom — *Howe-Lewis International*
Clark, Evan — *The Whitney Group*
Claude, Abe — *Paul Ray Berndtson*
Cleeve, Coleen — *Howe-Lewis International*
Clemens, William B. — *Norman Broadbent International, Inc.*
Clovis, James R. — *Handy HRM Corp.*
Coff, Scott — *Johnson Smith & Knisely Accord*
Cohen, Richard — *Management Recruiters International, Inc.*
Colasanto, Frank M. — *W.R. Rosato & Associates, Inc.*
Coleman, J. Gregory — *Korn/Ferry International*
Coleman, John A. — *Canny, Bowen Inc.*
Collins, Stephen — *The Johnson Group, Inc.*
Collins, Tom — *J.B. Homer Associates, Inc.*
Cook, Patricia — *Heidrick & Struggles, Inc.*
Cornehlsen, James H. — *Lamalie Amrop International*
Costa, Frances — *Gilbert Tweed/INESA*
Crowell, Elizabeth — *H.M. Long International, Ltd.*
Crump, William G. — *Paul Ray Berndtson*
Cunningham, Robert Y. — *Goodrich & Sherwood Associates, Inc.*
Curlett, Lisa — *Korn/Ferry International*
Currence, Anna — *Kenzer Corp.*
D'Ambrosio, Nicholas — *Alexander Ross Inc.*
D'Elia, Arthur P. — *Korn/Ferry International*
Daily, John C. — *Handy HRM Corp.*
Damon, Robert A. — *Spencer Stuart*
Daniel, Beverly — *Foy, Schneid & Daniel, Inc.*
Daniel, David S. — *Spencer Stuart*
Daniels, Leonard — *Placement Associates Inc.*
Darcy, Pat — *Paul Ray Berndtson*
Daum, Julie — *Spencer Stuart*
David, Jennifer — *Gilbert Tweed/INESA*
Davis, Bert — *Bert Davis Executive Search, Inc.*
Davis, John — *John J. Davis & Associates, Inc.*
Davis, Orlin R. — *Heidrick & Struggles, Inc.*
de Bardin, Francesca — *F.L. Taylor & Company, Inc.*

de Cholnoky, Andrea — *Spencer Stuart*
Del Prete, Karen — *Gilbert Tweed/INESA*
Delman, Charles — *Korn/Ferry International*
DelNegro, Anthony T. — *DHR International, Inc.*
Diaz-Joslyn, Mabel — *Walker Communications*
DiPiazza, Joseph — *Boyden*
Doan, Lisa — *Rhodes Associates*
Dotson, M. Ileen — *Dotson & Associates*
Drummond-Hay, Peter — *Russell Reynolds Associates, Inc.*
Dunn, Mary Helen — *Paul Ray Berndtson*
Early, Alice C. — *Russell Reynolds Associates, Inc.*
Edell, David E. — *The Development Resource Group Incorporated*
Edwards, Robert — *J.P. Canon Associates*
Ellis, William — *Interspace Interactive Inc.*
Erder, Debra — *Canny, Bowen Inc.*
Erickson, Elaine — *Kenzer Corp.*
Ezersky, Jane E. — *Highland Search Group, L.L.C.*
Farrell, Barbara — *The Barack Group, Inc.*
Feder, Gwen — *Egon Zehnder International Inc.*
Federman, Jack R. — *W.R. Rosato & Associates, Inc.*
Felton, Meg — *Korn/Ferry International*
Fienberg, Chester — *Drummond Associates, Inc.*
Fitch, Lori — *R. Parker and Associates, Inc.*
Fixler, Eugene — *Ariel Recruitment Associates*
Flanagan, Dale M. — *Lamalie Amrop International*
Flink, Debra — *Heidrick & Struggles, Inc.*
Flink, Debra K. — *Russell Reynolds Associates, Inc.*
Fogarty, Deirdre — *Paul Ray Berndtson*
Fonfa, Ann — *S.R. Wolman Associates, Inc.*
Forestier, Lois — *Source Services Corporation*
Foster, Dwight E. — *D.E. Foster Partners Inc.*
Foster, Robert — *Korn/Ferry International*
Fowler, Susan B. — *Russell Reynolds Associates, Inc.*
Foy, James — *Foy, Schneid & Daniel, Inc.*
Francis, David P. — *Heidrick & Struggles, Inc.*
Francis, Joseph — *Hospitality International*
Franzino, Michael — *TASA International*
Freedman, Howard — *Korn/Ferry International*
Friedman, Lesley M. — *Special Counsel International*
Frumess, Gregory — *D.E. Foster Partners Inc.*
Fry, John M. — *The Fry Group, Inc.*
Fulton, Christine N. — *Highland Search Group, L.L.C.*
Gabel, Gregory N. — *Canny, Bowen Inc.*
Gabler, Howard A. — *G.Z. Stephens Inc.*
Gagan, Joan — *Gilbert Tweed/INESA*
Gaines, Jay — *Jay Gaines & Company, Inc.*
Gardiner, E. Nicholas P. — *Gardiner International*
Gardner, Michael — *Source Services Corporation*
Gardy, Susan H. — *Paul Ray Berndtson*
Gates, Douglas H. — *Skott/Edwards Consultants, Inc.*
Germain, Valerie — *Jay Gaines & Company, Inc.*
Gerson, Russ D. — *Webb, Johnson Associates, Inc.*
Giacalone, Louis — *Allard Associates*
Gibbs, John S. — *Spencer Stuart*
Gilbert, Elaine — *Herbert Mines Associates, Inc.*
Gilbert, Jerry — *Gilbert & Van Campen International*
Glass, Lori — *The Executive Source*
Gold, Stacey — *Earley Kielty and Associates, Inc.*
Goldenberg, Sheryl — *Neail Behringer Consultants*
Goldstein, Gary — *The Whitney Group*
Goldstein, Steve — *R. Parker and Associates, Inc.*
Gonye, Peter K. — *Egon Zehnder International Inc.*
Gonzalez, Naomi — *McManners Associates, Inc.*
Goodwin, Gary — *Source Services Corporation*
Gossage, Wayne — *Gossage Regan Associates, Inc.*
Gottenberg, Norbert A. — *Norman Broadbent International, Inc.*
Gould, William E. — *Gould, McCoy & Chadick Incorporated*
Gourlay, Debra — *Rene Plessner Associates, Inc.*
Gow, Roderick C. — *Lamalie Amrop International*
Graf, Debra — *Kenzer Corp.*
Grand, Gordon — *Russell Reynolds Associates, Inc.*
Greco, Patricia — *Howe-Lewis International*
Greenberg, Ruth — *Kenzer Corp.*
Greene, Wallace — *Korn/Ferry International*
Grey, Fred — *J.B. Homer Associates, Inc.*
Grieco, Joseph — *Goodrich & Sherwood Associates, Inc.*
Griffin, Gilroye A. — *Paul Ray Berndtson*
Grimm, Peter G. — *Nordeman Grimm, Inc.*
Gross, Howard — *Herbert Mines Associates, Inc.*
Gross, Kathy — *Evie Kreisler & Associates, Inc.*
Gustafson, Eric P. — *Korn/Ferry International*
Haas, Margaret P. — *Haas International, Inc.*
Harbaugh, Paul J. — *International Management Advisors, Inc.*
Hardy, Thomas G. — *Spencer Stuart*
Harelick, Arthur S. — *Ashway, Ltd.*
Harris, Julia — *The Whitney Group*
Hart, Andrew D. — *Russell Reynolds Associates, Inc.*
Hart, David — *Hadley Lockwood, Inc.*
Hawkins, W. Davis — *Spencer Stuart*
Hayden, John — *Johnson Smith & Knisely Accord*
Healey, Joseph T. — *Highland Search Group, L.L.C.*
Heath, Jeffrey A. — *Management Recruiters International, Inc.*

Winter, Robert — *The Whitney Group*
Wisch, Steven C. — *MB Inc. Interim Executive Division*
Witte, David L. — *Ward Howell International, Inc.*
Wolfe, David — *Kenzer Corp.*
Wolman, Stephen R. — *S.R. Wolman Associates, Inc.*
Wood, John S. — *Egon Zehnder International Inc.*
Woodrum, Robert L. — *Korn/Ferry International*
Wyser-Pratte, Anne — *Heidrick & Struggles, Inc.*
Young, Van G. — *Heidrick & Struggles, Inc.*
Zarkin, Norman — *Rhodes Associates*
Zetter, Roger — *Hunt Ltd.*
Zimmerman, Joan C. — *G.Z. Stephens Inc.*
Zinn, Donald — *Bishop Partners*
Zona, Henry F. — *Zona & Associates, Inc.*
Zonis, Hildy R. — *Accountants Executive Search*
Zucker, Nancy — *Maximum Management Corp.*
Zwiff, Jeffrey G. — *Johnson Smith & Knisely Accord*

**North Salem**
Flanagan, Robert M. — *Robert M. Flanagan & Associates, Ltd.*
Normann, Amy — *Robert M. Flanagan & Associates, Ltd.*

**Northport**
Livolsi, Sebastian F. — *Management Recruiters International, Inc.*

**Pearl River**
Malone, Tom S. — *Management Recruiters International, Inc.*
Varian, Veronica — *Management Recruiters International, Inc.*

**Port Washington**
Janis, Laurence — *Integrated Search Solutions Group, LLC*
Sessa, Vincent J. — *Integrated Search Solutions Group, LLC*

**Rochester**
Anderson, Shawn — *Temporary Accounting Personnel, Inc.*
Annesi, Jerry — *Management Recruiters International, Inc.*
Baker, Gary M. — *Cochran, Cochran & Yale, Inc.*
Baker, Gary M. — *Temporary Accounting Personnel, Inc.*
Brent, Art — *Goodrich & Sherwood Associates, Inc.*
Buckles, Donna — *Cochran, Cochran & Yale, Inc.*
Call, David — *Cochran, Cochran & Yale, Inc.*
Callahan, Wanda — *Cochran, Cochran & Yale, Inc.*
Critchley, Walter — *Cochran, Cochran & Yale, Inc.*
Critchley, Walter — *Temporary Accounting Personnel, Inc.*
Curtis, Ellissa — *Cochran, Cochran & Yale, Inc.*
Frazier, John — *Cochran, Cochran & Yale, Inc.*
Marino, Chester — *Cochran, Cochran & Yale, Inc.*
Miller, David — *Temporary Accounting Personnel, Inc.*
Murphy, Cornelius J. — *Goodrich & Sherwood Associates, Inc.*
Roberts, William — *Cochran, Cochran & Yale, Inc.*

**Rockville Centre**
Wieder, Thomas A. — *Management Recruiters International, Inc.*

**Rome**
Tardugno, Carl — *Management Recruiters International, Inc.*

**Rye Brook**
Schachter, Laura J. — *Professional Placement Associates, Inc.*

**Scarsdale**
Cuomo, Frank — *Frank Cuomo and Associates, Inc.*
Long, William G. — *McDonald, Long & Associates, Inc.*
Lynn, Donald — *Frank Cuomo and Associates, Inc.*
Press, Fred — *Adept Tech Recruiting*

**Somers**
Gorman, T. Patrick — *Techsearch Services, Inc.*
Herz, Stanley — *Stanley Herz and Company, Inc.*
Taft, David G. — *Techsearch Services, Inc.*

**Southampton**
Jose, Bill O. — *Management Recruiters International, Inc.*
Lareau, Belle — *Management Recruiters International, Inc.*
Lareau, Jerry A. — *Management Recruiters International, Inc.*

**Southold**
Sullivan, Joseph J. — *Joe Sullivan & Associates, Inc.*

**Stone Ridge**
Mackenzie, Robert A. — *Management Recruiters International, Inc.*

**Syracuse**
Rodgers, Kathi — *St. Lawrence International, Inc.*
Scharett, Carol — *St. Lawrence International, Inc.*
Winnewisser, William E. — *Accounting & Computer Personnel*

**Tarrytown**
Neuffer, Bob P. — *Management Recruiters International, Inc.*

**White Plains**
Bland, Walter — *Source Services Corporation*
Burch, Donald — *Source Services Corporation*
Devito, Alice — *Source Services Corporation*
Eiseman, Joe — *Source Services Corporation*
Langer, Joel A. — *Langer Associates, Inc.*
Laskin, Sandy — *Source Services Corporation*
Maggio, Mary — *Source Services Corporation*
Occhiboi, Emil — *Source Services Corporation*
Paliwoda, William — *Source Services Corporation*
Parente, James — *Source Services Corporation*
Patel, Shailesh — *Source Services Corporation*
Sirena, Evelyn — *Source Services Corporation*

**Whitesboro**
Maurizio, Michael — *Management Recruiters International, Inc.*

**Woodbury**
Jose, Bill O. — *Management Recruiters International, Inc.*
Kornfeld, Warren — *Management Recruiters International, Inc.*

**North Carolina**

**Asheville**
Rumson, Barbara — *Management Recruiters International, Inc.*
Rumson, Paul M. — *Management Recruiters International, Inc.*

**Boiling Springs**
Holland, Dave G. — *Management Recruiters International, Inc.*
Sherrill, Lee S. — *Management Recruiters International, Inc.*

**Boone**
Driscoll, Donald L. — *Management Recruiters International, Inc.*

**Bunn**
Cone, Dan P. — *Management Recruiters International, Inc.*

**Burlington**
Pike, Dick F. — *Management Recruiters International, Inc.*

**Cary**
Cleary, Thomas R. — *ARJay & Associates*
Duley, Richard I. — *ARJay & Associates*
Gomez, Paul — *ARJay & Associates*
Miller, Russel E. — *ARJay & Associates*
Petrides, Andrew S. — *ARJay & Associates*

**Cedar Mountain**
Schoff, Frank J. — *Management Recruiters International, Inc.*

**Chapel Hill**
Grantham, John — *Grantham & Co., Inc.*

**Charlotte**
Abernathy, Donald E. — *Don Richard Associates of Charlotte*
Buttrey, Daniel — *Source Services Corporation*
Carrick, Kenneth D. — *Coleman Lew & Associates, Inc.*
Coughlin, Stephen — *Source Services Corporation*
Dewing, Jesse J. — *Don Richard Associates of Charlotte*
Downs, James L. — *Sanford Rose Associates*
Duke, Larry G. — *Management Recruiters International, Inc.*
Foster, Brian Scott — *Don Richard Associates of Charlotte*
Fuller, Ev — *Management Recruiters International, Inc.*
Gregory, Mark — *Accountants on Call*
Haigler, Lisa S. — *Don Richard Associates of Charlotte*
Halyburton, Robert R. — *The Halyburton Co., Inc.*
Harris, Ethel S. — *Don Richard Associates of Charlotte*
Hemingway, Stuart C. — *Robison & Associates*
Hill, Emery — *MSI International*
Hunter, Sue J. — *Robison & Associates*
Infinger, Ronald E. — *Robison & Associates*
Jernigan, Susan N. — *Sockwell & Associates*
Kelly, Robert — *Source Services Corporation*
Lew, Charles E. — *Coleman Lew & Associates, Inc.*
Lewis, John — *Management Recruiters International, Inc.*
Lucas, Charles C. — *The McAulay Firm*
MacMillan, James — *Source Services Corporation*
Massey, H. Heath — *Robison & Associates*
McAulay, A.L. — *The McAulay Firm*
McKinney, Julia — *Source Services Corporation*
Means, Wallace — *Management Recruiters International, Inc.*
Murphy, Corinne — *Source Services Corporation*
Oberting, Dave W. — *Management Recruiters International, Inc.*
Patton, Mitchell — *Patton/Perry Associates, Inc.*
Quinn, Frank A. — *Management Recruiters International, Inc.*
Rich, Lyttleton — *Sockwell & Associates*
Robison, John H. — *Robison & Associates*
Schoppergrell, Holly — *Don Richard Associates of Charlotte*
Sockwell, J. Edgar — *Sockwell & Associates*
Turner, Edward K. — *Don Richard Associates of Charlotte*
Wilson, Robert J. — *Coleman Lew & Associates, Inc.*

**Cornelius**
Hawfield, Sam G. — *Management Recruiters International, Inc.*

**Durham**
Philips, Ann — *Management Recruiters International, Inc.*

**Emerald Isle**
Liles, J.D. — *Management Recruiters International, Inc.*

**Enfield**
Snook, Maria P. — *Management Recruiters International, Inc.*
Snook, Marvin G. — *Management Recruiters International, Inc.*

**Fayetteville**
Semmes, John R. — *Management Recruiters International, Inc.*

**Gastonia**
Deal, Chuck H. — *Management Recruiters International, Inc.*
Halek, Frederick D. — *Sanford Rose Associates*

**Greensboro**
Ariail, C. Bowling — *Ariail & Associates*
Ariail, Randolph C. — *Ariail & Associates*
Harrington, Robert J. — *Sanford Rose Associates*
Oakley, Mitch — *Management Recruiters International, Inc.*

**Hickory**
Gaillard, Bill — *Management Recruiters International, Inc.*
King, Byron L. — *Management Recruiters International, Inc.*
Volz, Scott — *Management Recruiters International, Inc.*

**High Point**
Smith, Gin-Nie — *Management Recruiters International, Inc.*
Smith, Steve L. — *Management Recruiters International, Inc.*

**Kannapolis**
Swaringen, Mac — *Management Recruiters International, Inc.*
Whitley, Tom H. — *Management Recruiters International, Inc.*

**Kinston**
Daugherty, Mac M. — *Management Recruiters International, Inc.*
Thomas, Bill — *Management Recruiters International, Inc.*
Turner, Allan W. — *Management Recruiters International, Inc.*

**Louisburg**
Perry, Darrell L. — *Management Recruiters International, Inc.*

**Madison**
Summerlin, Gerald — *Management Recruiters International, Inc.*

**Matthews**
Camp, David K. — *Management Recruiters International, Inc.*

**Mooresville**
Sykes, Hugh L. — *Management Recruiters International, Inc.*

**Mount Airy**
Hackett, Don F. — *Management Recruiters International, Inc.*

**New Bern**
Eatman, Fred — *Management Recruiters International, Inc.*

**Pinehurst**
Wright, Anne B. — *Management Recruiters International, Inc.*
Wright, Doug — *Management Recruiters International, Inc.*

**Raleigh**
Bye, Randy — *Romac & Associates*
Stanley, Wade — *Management Recruiters International, Inc.*
Twiste, Craig — *Raymond Karsan Associates*

**Rocky Mount**
Manning, Robert A. — *Management Recruiters International, Inc.*
Sewell, Danny J. — *Management Recruiters International, Inc.*

**Statesville**
Coleman, Neil F. — *Management Recruiters International, Inc.*

**Wilmington**
Bargholz, Harry — *Management Recruiters International, Inc.*

**Winston-Salem**
Jones, Judy M. — *Management Recruiters International, Inc.*
Jones, Mike R. — *Management Recruiters International, Inc.*
LaValle, Michael — *Romac & Associates*

## Ohio

**Akron**
Eilertson, Douglas R. — *Sanford Rose Associates*
Gerst, Tom J. — *Management Recruiters International, Inc.*
Leszynski, Edward — *ProResource, Inc.*
Rose, Sanford M. — *Sanford Rose Associates*
Snider, George R. — *Sanford Rose Associates*

**Beachwood**
Falk, John — *D.S. Allen Associates, Inc.*

**Berea**
DeLong, Art — *Richard Kader & Associates*
Flash, James — *Richard Kader & Associates*
Hanford, Michael — *Richard Kader & Associates*
Kader, Richard — *Richard Kader & Associates*
Longmore, Marilyn — *Richard Kader & Associates*
Mason, Marlene — *Richard Kader & Associates*
Scott, Ron — *Richard Kader & Associates*
Sponseller, Vern — *Richard Kader & Associates*

**Blue Ash**
Ehrhart, Jennifer — *ADOW's Executeam*

**Boardman**
Somers, Donald A. — *Management Recruiters International, Inc.*

**Brunswick**
Boal, Robert A. — *Management Recruiters International, Inc.*

**Canfield**
Ellison, Richard — *Sanford Rose Associates*
Rimmel, James E. — *The Hindman Company*

**Canton**
Kuehnling, William A. — *Sanford Rose Associates*

**Chagrin Falls**
Gallagher, Marilyn — *Hogan Acquisitions*
Hecker, Henry C. — *Hogan Acquisitions*
Hogan, Larry H. — *Hogan Acquisitions*
Selko, Philip W. — *Hogan Acquisitions*

**Cincinnati**
Bason, Maurice L. — *Bason Associates Inc.*
Bennett, Delora — *Genesis Personnel Service, Inc.*
Canan, Bruce — *The Nielsen Healthcare Group*
Christman, Joel — *Source Services Corporation*
D'Eramo, Tony P. — *Management Recruiters International, Inc.*

Davis, Elease — *Source Services Corporation*
Fancher, Robert L. — *Bason Associates Inc.*
Florio, Robert — *Source Services Corporation*
Frederick, Dianne — *Source Services Corporation*
Goodman, Dawn M. — *Bason Associates Inc.*
Hacker-Taylor, Dianna — *Source Services Corporation*
Haller, Mark — *Source Services Corporation*
Joffe, Barry — *Bason Associates Inc.*
Johnson, Greg — *Source Services Corporation*
Kern, Kathleen G. — *ADOW's Executeam*
Koczak, John — *Source Services Corporation*
Lambert, William — *Source Services Corporation*
Laverty, William — *Source Services Corporation*
McCullough, Joe — *Management Recruiters International, Inc.*
Merrifield, Gary — *Accountants on Call*
Nutter, Roger — *Raymond Karsan Associates*
O'Reilly, Bill — *Management Recruiters International, Inc.*
Snowhite, Rebecca — *Source Services Corporation*
Sweeney, Anne — *Source Services Corporation*
Visnich, L. Christine — *Bason Associates Inc.*
Witzgall, William — *Source Services Corporation*

**Cleveland**
Anderson, Glenn G. — *Lamalie Amrop International*
Arnold, David — *Christian & Timbers*
Blessing, Marc L. — *Management Recruiters International, Inc.*
Bradshaw, Monte — *Christian & Timbers*
Chorman, Marilyn A. — *Hite Executive Search*
Christian, Jeffrey E. — *Christian & Timbers*
Crumbaker, Robert H. — *Lamalie Amrop International*
Dickey, Chet W. — *Bowden & Company, Inc.*
Dipaolo, Jeff — *Management Recruiters International, Inc.*
Elliott, Mark P. — *Lamalie Amrop International*
Fair, Donna — *ProResource, Inc.*
Felderman, Kenneth I. — *Lamalie Amrop International*
Ferrari, S. Jay — *Ferrari Search Group*
Fogelgren, Stephen W. — *Management Recruiters International, Inc.*
Gandee, Bob — *Management Recruiters International, Inc.*
Gandee, Bob — *Management Recruiters International, Inc.*
Gregor, Joie A. — *Heidrick & Struggles, Inc.*
Hamilton, John R. — *A.T. Kearney, Inc.*
Harris, Bruce — *ProResource, Inc.*
Herget, James P. — *Lamalie Amrop International*
Hite, William A. — *Hite Executive Search*
Imely, Larry — *Christian & Timbers*
Jacobson, Robert E. — *Management Recruiters International, Inc.*
Johnson, John F. — *Lamalie Amrop International*
Kohn, Adam P. — *Christian & Timbers*
Lauderback, David R. — *A.T. Kearney, Inc.*
Lenkaitis, Lewis F. — *A.T. Kearney, Inc.*
Magee, Harrison R. — *Bowden & Company, Inc.*
McNamara, Gerard P. — *Heidrick & Struggles, Inc.*
Miller, George N. — *Hite Executive Search*
Montigny, Paul F. — *Management Recruiters International, Inc.*
Myrick, Marilou — *ProResource, Inc.*
Nocero, John — *ProResource, Inc.*
Pacini, Lauren R. — *Hite Executive Search*
Pappalardo, Charles — *Christian & Timbers*
Park, Cleve A. — *Management Recruiters International, Inc.*
Sauer, Robert C. — *Heidrick & Struggles, Inc.*
Schmidt, William C. — *Christian & Timbers*
Schonberg, Alan R. — *Management Recruiters International, Inc.*
Selker, Gregory L. — *Christian & Timbers*
Smith, Cheryl — *ProResource, Inc.*
Sowerbutt, Richard S. — *Hite Executive Search*
Taylor, Charles E. — *Lamalie Amrop International*
Tokarcik, Patricia — *ProResource, Inc.*
Wallace, Richard — *Heidrick & Struggles, Inc.*
Wesley, Terry R. — *Management Recruiters International, Inc.*
Wood, Martin F. — *Lamalie Amrop International*

**Columbus**
Earhart, William D. – - *Sanford Rose Associates*
Eggert, Scott — *Source Services Corporation*
Giesy, John — *Source Services Corporation*
Henn, George W. — *G.W. Henn & Company*
Hostetter, Kristi — *Source Services Corporation*
Marshall, John — *Accountants on Call*
Meyers, Mel — *DHR International, Inc.*
Mills, John — *Source Services Corporation*
Morris, Scott — *Source Services Corporation*
Myrick, Marilou — *ProResource, Inc.*
O'Brien, Susan — *Source Services Corporation*
Oberting, David J. — *Management Recruiters International, Inc.*
Pirro, Sheri — *Source Services Corporation*
Rothenbush, Clayton — *Source Services Corporation*
Sheets, Russel — *Accountants on Call*
Shelton, Jonathan — *Source Services Corporation*
Stoltz, Dick — *Management Recruiters International, Inc.*

**Dayton**
Blickle, Michael — *Source Services Corporation*
Folkerth, Gene — *Gene Folkerth & Associates, Inc.*
Johnson, Douglas — *Quality Search*

Johnson, Robert J. — *Quality Search*
Kotler, Jerry R. — *Management Recruiters International, Inc.*
Marwil, Jennifer — *Source Services Corporation*
McGoldrick, Terrence — *Source Services Corporation*
Noble, Jeffrey M. — *Management Recruiters International, Inc.*
Rhoades, Michael — *Source Services Corporation*
Ring, Paul R. — *Sanford Rose Associates*
Rockwell, Bruce — *Source Services Corporation*
Schroeder, James — *Source Services Corporation*
Scothon, Alan — *Romac & Associates*
Smith, Lawrence — *Source Services Corporation*
Tobin, Christopher — *Source Services Corporation*
Uzzel, Linda — *Source Services Corporation*
Waymire, Pamela — *Source Services Corporation*
Wessling, Jerry — *Source Services Corporation*

### Dublin
Bastoky, Bruce M. — *January Management Group, Inc.*
Kent, Melvin — *Melvin Kent & Associates, Inc.*

### Euclid
Orkin, Ralph — *Sanford Rose Associates*
Orkin, Sheilah — *Sanford Rose Associates*

### Hudson
Cummings, Harry J. — *Sanford Rose Associates*

### Independence
Banko, Scott — *Source Services Corporation*
Barnaby, Richard — *Source Services Corporation*
Bernas, Sharon — *Source Services Corporation*
Carnal, Rick — *Source Services Corporation*
Fulger, Herbert — *Source Services Corporation*
Gilinsky, David — *Source Services Corporation*
Mayer, Thomas — *Source Services Corporation*
Miller, Timothy — *Source Services Corporation*
Morrow, Melanie — *Source Services Corporation*
Rio, Monica — *Management Recruiters International, Inc.*
Samsel, Randy — *Source Services Corporation*
Seamon, Kenneth — *Source Services Corporation*
Tschan, Stephen — *Source Services Corporation*
Wood, Gary — *Source Services Corporation*

### Lima
Dautenhahn, Thomas — *Sanford Rose Associates*

### Maumee
Greebe, Neil — *Flowers & Associates*
Ross, Marc A. — *Flowers & Associates*
Ross, William J. — *Flowers & Associates*
Young, Charles E. — *Flowers & Associates*

### Mentor
Sterling, Cheryl E. — *Management Recruiters International, Inc.*
Sterling, Ronald — *Management Recruiters International, Inc.*

### Middletown
Plotner, George A. — *Management Recruiters International, Inc.*

### No. Ridgeville
Dankowski, Thomas A. — *Dankowski and Associates, Inc.*

### North Canton
Bascom, Roger C. — *Management Recruiters International, Inc.*
Bascom, Shirley R. — *Management Recruiters International, Inc.*

### North Ridgeville
Spellacy, James P. — *Management Recruiters International, Inc.*

### Shaker Heights
Johnston, Cindy — *Management Recruiters International, Inc.*
Smith, Herbert C. — *H C Smith Ltd.*
Smith, Rebecca Ruben — *H C Smith Ltd.*

### Sidney
Uniacke, Keith J. — *Management Recruiters International, Inc.*

### Solon
Barnett, Kim M. — *Management Recruiters International, Inc.*

### Toledo
Fruchtman, Gary K. — *Management Recruiters International, Inc.*

### Willoughby Hills
Wayne, Cary S. — *ProSearch Inc.*

### Wilmington
Walton, James H. — *Management Recruiters International, Inc.*

## Oklahoma
### Oklahoma City
Roy, Gary P. — *Management Recruiters International, Inc.*
Suit-Terry, J.A. — *Management Recruiters International, Inc.*

### Tulsa
Villareal, Morey — *Villareal & Associates, Inc.*
Wolters, Tony A. — *Management Recruiters International, Inc.*
Wozniak, Bernard D. — *Sanford Rose Associates*
Wozniak, Jane K. — *Sanford Rose Associates*

## Oregon
### Bend
Lopez, Manney C. — *Management Recruiters International, Inc.*

### Clackamas
Callihan, Diana L. — *Search Northwest Associates*
Jansen, Douglas L. — *Search Northwest Associates*
Scrivines, Hank — *Search Northwest Associates*

### Hillsboro
Furlong, James W. — *Furlong Search, Inc.*

### Portland
Belden, Jeannette — *Source Services Corporation*
Bryant, Henry — *D. Brown and Associates, Inc.*
Conners, Theresa — *D. Brown and Associates, Inc.*
Decker, Richard — *D. Brown and Associates, Inc.*
Diers, Gary — *Source Services Corporation*
Engelgau, Elvita P. — *Management Recruiters International, Inc.*
Engelgau, Larry P. — *Management Recruiters International, Inc.*
Ervin, Russell — *Source Services Corporation*
Gelinas, Lynn — *D. Brown and Associates, Inc.*
Irwin, Mark — *Source Services Corporation*
Kennedy, Craig — *Source Services Corporation*
Kondra, Vernon J. — *The Douglas Reiter Company, Inc.*
Leben, Sally — *D. Brown and Associates, Inc.*
Mackin, Michael — *D. Brown and Associates, Inc.*
Mathias, Douglas — *Source Services Corporation*
Moran, Douglas — *Source Services Corporation*
Redding, Denise — *The Douglas Reiter Company, Inc.*
Reiter, Douglas — *The Douglas Reiter Company, Inc.*
Romo, Dorothy — *D. Brown and Associates, Inc.*
Simmons, Deborah — *Source Services Corporation*
Stiles, Jack D. — *Sanford Rose Associates*
Stiles, Timothy — *Sanford Rose Associates*

## Pennsylvania
### Allentown
Filko, Gary — *Management Recruiters International, Inc.*

### Bethlehem
Meyer, Fred R. — *Management Recruiters International, Inc.*

### Bryn Mawr
Morris, Paul T. — *The Morris Group*

### Buckingham
Eisert, Robert M. — *Sanford Rose Associates*

### Carlisle
Sears, Rick — *Management Recruiters International, Inc.*

### Chinchilla
Kochmer, Sheila — *Management Recruiters International, Inc.*
Kochmer, Victor — *Management Recruiters International, Inc.*

### Conshohocken
Altieri, Robert J. — *Longshore & Simmons, Inc.*
Barth, Cynthia P. — *Longshore & Simmons, Inc.*
Clark, Steven — *D.A. Kreuter Associates, Inc.*
Dowrick, Jeanne A. — *Longshore & Simmons, Inc.*
Harrison, Joel — *D.A. Kreuter Associates, Inc.*
Kilcullen, Brian A. — *D.A. Kreuter Associates, Inc.*
Kreuter, Daniel A. — *D.A. Kreuter Associates, Inc.*
Lewis, Charles G. — *Longshore & Simmons, Inc.*
Longshore, George F. — *Longshore & Simmons, Inc.*
Postles, Doris W. — *Longshore & Simmons, Inc.*
Weston, Corinne F. — *D.A. Kreuter Associates, Inc.*

### Doylestown
Berke, Carl E. — *The Cassie Group*

### Easton
Cassie, Ronald L. — *The Cassie Group*
Kush, Max — *Management Recruiters International, Inc.*

### Ephrata
Dabich, Thomas M. — *Robert Harkins Associates, Inc.*
Harkins, Robert E. — *Robert Harkins Associates, Inc.*

### Erie
Larsen, Jack B. — *Jack B. Larsen & Associates*
Pfister, Shelli — *Jack B. Larsen & Associates*
Roach, Ronald R. — *Sanford Rose Associates*

### Exton
Lynch, Anita F. — *Management Recruiters International, Inc.*
Lynch, John F. — *Management Recruiters International, Inc.*

### Feasterville
Wasserman, Harvey — *Churchill and Affiliates, Inc.*

### Harrisburg
Milo, Bill — *Management Recruiters International, Inc.*

### Huntingdon Valley
Vogel, Michael S. — *Vogel Associates*

### King of Prussia
Cozzillio, Larry — *The Andre Group, Inc.*
Donnelly, Patti — *Source Services Corporation*
Finkel, Leslie — *Source Services Corporation*
Hight, Susan — *Source Services Corporation*
Inskeep, Thomas — *Source Services Corporation*
Januleski, Geoff — *Source Services Corporation*
Libes, Mark S. — *Accountants on Call*
Moretti, Denise — *Source Services Corporation*
Nolan, Robert — *Source Services Corporation*

Reid, Katherine — *Source  Services Corporation*
Selvaggi, Esther — *Source  Services Corporation*
Shackleford, David — *Source  Services Corporation*
Storm, Deborah — *Source  Services Corporation*

**Lancaster**
Rodebaugh, Karen — *Management Recruiters International, Inc.*
Rodebaugh, Thomas L. — *Management Recruiters International, Inc.*

**Lansdowne**
Flowers, John E. — *Balfour Associates*

**McMurray**
Fosnot, Bob — *Management Recruiters International, Inc.*
Fosnot, Mike — *Management Recruiters International, Inc.*

**Media**
Glancey, Thomas F. — *Gordon Wahls Company*
Thompson, James R. — *Gordon Wahls Company*
Wertel, Ronald E. — *Gordon Wahls Company*

**Monroeville**
Belden, Charles P. — *Raymond Karsan Associates*

**Montoursville**
Helt, Wally A. — *Management Recruiters International, Inc.*

**Murrysville**
Williamson, Frank — *Management Recruiters International, Inc.*

**Newtown Square**
Bishop, Sandy — *Management Recruiters International, Inc.*

**Paoli**
Eden, Brooks D. — *Eden & Associates, Inc.*
Eden, Earl M. — *Eden & Associates, Inc.*
Nunziata, Fred — *Eden & Associates, Inc.*
Scullin, Richard — *Eden & Associates, Inc.*

**Philadelphia**
Alexander, Raymond — *Howard Fischer Associates, Inc.*
Barthold, James A. — *McNichol Associates*
Bassler, John P. — *Korn/Ferry International*
Blake, Eileen — *Howard Fischer Associates, Inc.*
Boyer, Heath C. — *Spencer Stuart*
Campbell, Robert Scott — *Wellington Management Group*
Carey, Dennis C. — *Spencer Stuart*
Cole, Ronald J. — *Cole, Warren & Long, Inc.*
Coleman, Michael M. — *Coleman Legal Search Consultants*
Cook, Nancy L. — *The Diversified Search Companies*
Culp, Thomas C. — *The Diversified Search Companies*
Cunningham, Lawrence — *Howard Fischer Associates, Inc.*
Dougherty, Bridget L. — *Wellington Management Group*
Fischer, Adam — *Howard Fischer Associates, Inc.*
Fischer, Howard M. — *Howard Fischer Associates, Inc.*
Friedman, Marcie W. — *Coleman Legal Search Consultants*
Gaimster, Ann — *The Diversified Search Companies*
Gantar, Donna — *Howard Fischer Associates, Inc.*
Gargalli, Claire W. — *The Diversified Search Companies*
Gerber, Mark J. — *Wellington Management Group*
Gibb, Jeffrey B. — *Coleman Legal Search Consultants*
Goldsmith, Phillip R. — *The Diversified Search Companies*
Heckscher, Cindy P. — *The Diversified Search Companies*
Hennessy, Robert D. — *Korn/Ferry International*
Hess, James C. — *The Diversified Search Companies*
Higgins, Donna — *Howard Fischer Associates, Inc.*
Huttner, Leah — *Korn/Ferry International*
Kelly, Elizabeth Ann — *Wellington Management Group*
Koehler, Frank R. — *The Koehler Group*
Kring, Kenneth L. — *Spencer Stuart*
Lewis, Richard A. — *Cole, Warren & Long, Inc.*
Libes, Mark S. — *Accountants on Call*
Lucas, Thomas A. — *Management Recruiters International, Inc.*
MacLean, B.A. — *The Diversified Search Companies*
Mallin, Ellen — *Howard Fischer Associates, Inc.*
Mansford, Keith — *Howard Fischer Associates, Inc.*
Marsteller, Franklin D. — *Spencer Stuart*
Martin, Ken — *Spencer Stuart*
Mazor, Elly — *Howard Fischer Associates, Inc.*
Mazza, Leslie P. — *The Diversified Search Companies*
McCann, Cornelia B. — *Spencer Stuart*
McCarthy, David R. — *Spencer Stuart*
McGuire, D. — *The Gabriel Group*
McNichol, John — *McNichol Associates*
Newman, Mark — *Cole, Warren & Long, Inc.*
Newman, Maryann — *The Gabriel Group*
Ogilvie, Kit — *Howard Fischer Associates, Inc.*
Owens, LaMonte — *LaMonte Owens & Company*
Owens, Reggie R. — *The Gabriel Group*
Perlman, Tali — *Coleman Legal Search Consultants*
Pryor, Keith — *The Diversified Search Companies*
Quitel, Scott M. — *Management Recruiters International, Inc.*
Romanchek, Walter R. — *Wellington Management Group*
Romanowicz, Jill — *Howard Fischer Associates, Inc.*
Rothwell, Amy — *Howard Fischer Associates, Inc.*
Salikof, Allen B. — *Management Recruiters International, Inc.*
Salikof, Kaye R. — *Management Recruiters International, Inc.*
Sauer, Harry J. — *Romac & Associates*

Schneirov, Miriam A. — *Coleman Legal Search Consultants*
Scott, Evan — *Howard Fischer Associates, Inc.*
Shea, Kathleen M. — *The Penn Partners, Incorporated*
Sitarski, Stan — *Howard Fischer Associates, Inc.*
Smith, John F. — *The Penn Partners, Incorporated*
Spangler, Lloyd — *Cole, Warren & Long, Inc.*
Stemphoski, Ronald L. — *The Diversified Search Companies*
Stevenson, Jani — *Howard Fischer Associates, Inc.*
Swanson, Jarl — *The Gabriel Group*
Turnblacer, John — *The Gabriel Group*
Vachon, David A. — *McNichol Associates*
von Seldeneck, Judith M. — *The Diversified Search Companies*
Warren, Richard B. — *Cole, Warren & Long, Inc.*
Wilson, Helen S. — *The Diversified Search Companies*
Wollman, Harry — *Howard Fischer Associates, Inc.*

**Pittsburgh**
Adams, Michael — *CG & Associates*
Bizick, Ron — *Management Recruiters International, Inc.*
Brackin, James B. — *Brackin & Sayers Associates*
Cersosimo, Rocco — *Source  Services Corporation*
Close, E. Wade — *Boyden*
Connelly, Laura J. — *Management Recruiters International, Inc.*
Davis, Robert — *CG & Associates*
Denney, Thomas L. — *Denney & Company Incorporated*
Dorfner, Martin — *Source  Services Corporation*
Farler, Wiley — *Source  Services Corporation*
Flinn, Richard A. — *Denney & Company Incorporated*
Gallagher, Jim — *Management Recruiters International, Inc.*
Gallagher, Sallie — *Management Recruiters International, Inc.*
Gray, David — *CG & Associates*
Groom, Charles C. — *CG & Associates*
Hallam, Andy J. — *Management Recruiters International, Inc.*
Holupka, Gary F. — *Management Recruiters International, Inc.*
Holupka, Patricia Lampl — *Management Recruiters International, Inc.*
Kohn, Thomas C. — *Reflex Services, Inc.*
Latterell, Jeffrey D. — *Smith & Latterell (HRS, Inc.)*
MacGregor, Malcolm — *Boyden*
Nazzaro, Samuel G. — *Boyden*
Norris, Ken — *Boyden*
Papciak, Dennis J. — *Accounting Personnel Associates, Inc.*
Papciak, Dennis J. — *Temporary Accounting Personnel*
Reid, Scott — *Source  Services Corporation*
Rossman, Paul R. — *Management Recruiters International, Inc.*
Rothman, Jeffrey — *ProResource, Inc.*
Sayers, Bruce D. — *Brackin & Sayers Associates*
Smith, David P. — *Smith & Latterell (HRS, Inc.)*
Smock, Cynthia — *Source  Services Corporation*
Stivk, Barbara A. — *Thornton Resources*
Stuart, Karen M. — *Reflex Services, Inc.*
Thornton, John C. — *Thornton Resources*
Trice, Renee — *Source  Services Corporation*
Wilson, Derrick — *Thornton Resources*

**Plymouth Meeting**
Fairlie, Suzanne F. — *ProSearch, Inc.*

**Sewickley**
Lampl, Joni — *Management Recruiters International, Inc.*
Lampl, Richard — *Management Recruiters International, Inc.*

**Southampton**
Borden, Stuart — *M.A. Churchill & Associates, Inc.*
Frazier, Steven M. — *Sanford Rose Associates*
Sher, Lawrence — *M.A. Churchill & Associates, Inc.*
Spicher, John — *M.A. Churchill & Associates, Inc.*
Wylie, Pamela — *M.A. Churchill & Associates, Inc.*

**Southeastern**
Zerkle, John P. — *Management Recruiters International, Inc.*

**Strafford**
DiGiovanni, Charles — *Penn Search*

**Trevose**
Bass, Nate — *Jacobson Associates*
Kalinowski, David — *Jacobson Associates*
Williams, Harry D. — *Jacobson Associates*

**Upper St. Clair**
Uhl, Jack N. — *Management Recruiters International, Inc.*

**Valley Forge**
Hamm, Mary Kay — *Romac & Associates*

**Villanova**
DeHart, Donna — *Tower Consultants, Ltd.*
deVry, Kimberly A. — *Tower Consultants, Ltd.*
Friedman, Donna L. — *Tower Consultants, Ltd.*

**Warminster**
Mashack, Ted M. — *Management Recruiters International, Inc.*

**Wayne**
Brown, Kevin P. — *Raymond Karsan Associates*
Cerasoli, Philip A. — *Experience-On-Tap Inc.*
Chojnacki, Bindi — *Raymond Karsan Associates*
Clark, Elliot H. — *Raymond Karsan Associates*
Ford, Sandra D. — *Phillips & Ford, Inc.*
Forgosh, Jack H. — *Raymond Karsan Associates*

**Bellaire**
Drown, Clifford F. — *Management Recruiters International, Inc.*
**Canyon Lake**
Penfield, G. Jeff — *Management Recruiters International, Inc.*
Penfield, Marian — *Management Recruiters International, Inc.*
**Dallas**
Adelson, Duane — *Stanton Chase International*
Alford, Holly — *Source  Services Corporation*
Ambler, Peter W. — *Peter W. Ambler Company*
Anderson, David C. — *Heidrick & Struggles, Inc.*
Baier, Rebecca — *Source Services Corporation*
Bailey, William A. — *TNS Partners, Inc.*
Bakken, Mark — *Source Services Corporation*
Bassman, Bob W. — *Management Recruiters International, Inc.*
Bassman, Robert — *Kaye-Bassman International Corp.*
Bassman, Sandy — *Kaye-Bassman International Corp.*
Bassman, Sandy M. — *Management Recruiters International, Inc.*
Beal, Richard D. — *A.T. Kearney, Inc.*
Beaudine, Frank R. — *Eastman & Beaudine*
Beaudine, Robert E. — *Eastman & Beaudine*
Bethmann, James M. — *Russell Reynolds Associates, Inc.*
Bloom, Howard C. — *Hernand & Partners*
Bloom, Howard C. — *The Howard C. Bloom Co.*
Bloom, Joyce — *Hernand & Partners*
Bloom, Joyce — *The Howard C. Bloom Co.*
Bolger, Thomas — *Korn/Ferry International*
Brennan, Jerry — *Brennan Associates*
Brennan, Timothy — *Brennan Associates*
Brown, Steven — *Source  Services Corporation*
Bryza, Robert M. — *Robert Lowell International*
Buntrock, George E. — *Management Recruiters International, Inc.*
Burkholder, John A. — *Management Recruiters International, Inc.*
Bush, R. Stuart — *Russell Reynolds Associates, Inc.*
Carter, Linda — *Source  Services Corporation*
Casey, Jean — *Peter W. Ambler Company*
Clark, Linda — *Kenzer Corp.*
Cotter, L.L. — *IMCOR, Inc.*
Cottingham, R.L. — *Marvin L. Silcott & Associates, Inc.*
Cruse, O.D. — *Spencer Stuart*
Damon, Richard E. — *Damon & Associates, Inc.*
Dandurand, Jeff J. — *DHR International, Inc.*
Danforth, W. Michael — *Hyde Danforth Wold & Co.*
Darnell, Nadine — *Brennan Associates*
Davison, Patricia E. — *Lamalie Amrop International*
Demchak, James P. — *Sandhurst Associates*
Diamond, Peter — *Korn/Ferry International*
Doran, Mary Ann — *Kenzer Corp.*
Duncan, Dana — *Source  Services Corporation*
Dunlow, Aimee — *Source  Services Corporation*
Dupont, Rick — *Source  Services Corporation*
Eldredge, L. Lincoln — *Lamalie Amrop International*
England, Mark — *Austin-McGregor International*
Engman, Steven T. — *Lamalie Amrop International*
Ferris, Sheri Rae — *Accountants on Call*
Fitzgerald, Brian — *Source  Services Corporation*
Forman, Donald R. — *Stanton Chase International*
Funk, Robert William — *Korn/Ferry International*
Gabriel, David L. — *The Arcus Group*
Goar, Duane R. — *Sandhurst Associates*
Goodspeed, Peter W. — *Witt/Kieffer, Ford, Hadelman & Lloyd*
Grado, Eduardo — *Source  Services Corporation*
Grumulaitis, Leo — *Source  Services Corporation*
Hagler, Holly — *Heidrick & Struggles, Inc.*
Hailey, H.M. — *Damon & Associates, Inc.*
Halstead, Frederick A. — *Ward Howell International, Inc.*
Hamm, Gary — *Source  Services Corporation*
Harrison, Patricia — *Source  Services Corporation*
Hessel, Gregory — *Korn/Ferry International*
Hickman, Andrew — *Korn/Ferry International*
Hicks, Mike — *Damon & Associates, Inc.*
Hill, Mike — *Tyler & Company*
Hinojosa, Oscar — *Source  Services Corporation*
Hyde, W. Jerry — *Hyde Danforth Wold & Co.*
Jenkins, Jeffrey N. — *Sanford Rose Associates*
Johnson, Rocky — *A.T. Kearney, Inc.*
Jones, Barbara J. — *Kaye-Bassman International Corp.*
Jones, Don — *Kenzer Corp.*
Jordan, Stephen T. — *Paul Ray Berndtson*
Kaye, Jeff — *Management Recruiters International, Inc.*
Kaye, Jeffrey — *Kaye-Bassman International Corp.*
Kelley, Randall D. — *Spencer Stuart*
Kendrick, M. Steven — *Lamalie Amrop International*
Kennedy, Michael — *The Danbrook Group, Inc.*
Kohn, Carole — *Kenzer Corp.*
Konker, David N. — *Russell Reynolds Associates, Inc.*
Kuypers, Arnold — *Lamalie Amrop International*
Lavender, Jane — *Paul Ray Berndtson*
Leblanc, Danny — *Source  Services Corporation*
Lee, Everett — *Source  Services Corporation*
Letcher, Harvey D. — *Sandhurst Associates*

Levinson, Lauren — *The Danbrook Group, Inc.*
Lewis, Jon A. — *Sandhurst Associates*
Lieb, Donald F. — *Russell Reynolds Associates, Inc.*
Lineback, Pam — *Management Recruiters International, Inc.*
Lineback, Robert — *Management Recruiters International, Inc.*
Lineback, Robert — *Management Recruiters International, Inc.*
Love, David M. — *Paul Ray Berndtson*
Marshall, Neill P. — *Witt/Kieffer, Ford, Hadelman & Lloyd*
Martin, John G. — *Lamalie Amrop International*
Marye, George — *Damon & Associates, Inc.*
Mathis, Carrie — *Source  Services Corporation*
McCartney, Paul — *Korn/Ferry International*
McCreary, Charles — *Austin-McGregor International*
McGinnis, Rita — *Source  Services Corporation*
McGuire, Corey — *Peter W. Ambler Company*
McIntosh, Arthur — *Source  Services Corporation*
McIntosh, Tad — *Source  Services Corporation*
Mitchell, F. Wayne — *Korn/Ferry International*
Mitchell, John — *Romac & Associates*
Mitchell, Katie — *Paul Ray Berndtson*
Moerbe, Ed H. — *Stanton Chase International*
Monahan, B. Roderick — *Lamalie Amrop International*
Moore, Mark — *Wheeler, Moore & Elam Co.*
Mott, Greg — *Source  Services Corporation*
Mueller, Colleen — *Source  Services Corporation*
Neidhart, Craig C. — *TNS Partners, Inc.*
Norman, Randy — *Austin-McGregor International*
Novak, William J. — *Ward Howell International, Inc.*
Oberg, Roy — *The Danbrook Group, Inc.*
Oller, Jose E. — *Ward Howell International, Inc.*
Page, G. Schuyler — *A.T. Kearney, Inc.*
Palmlund, David W. — *Lamalie Amrop International*
Pessin, Mark — *Evie Kreisler & Associates, Inc.*
Peters, James N. — *TNS Partners, Inc.*
Pfau, Madelaine — *Heidrick & Struggles, Inc.*
Pillow, Charles — *Source  Services Corporation*
Potter, Douglas C. — *Stanton Chase International*
Priftis, Anthony — *Evie Kreisler & Associates, Inc.*
Robertson, William W. — *Marvin L. Silcott & Associates, Inc.*
Rowe, William D. — *D.E. Foster Partners Inc.*
Schaefer, Brett — *Accountants on Call*
Schroeder, John W. — *Spencer Stuart*
Semyan, John K. — *TNS Partners, Inc.*
Settles, Barbara Z. — *Lamalie Amrop International*
Silcott, Marvin L. — *Marvin L. Silcott & Associates, Inc.*
Smith, Perry V. — *Management Recruiters International, Inc.*
Southerland, Keith C. — *Witt/Kieffer, Ford, Hadelman & Lloyd*
Stephenson, Mike — *Evie Kreisler & Associates, Inc.*
Stewart, Ross M. — *Human Resources Network Partners Inc.*
Stone, Kayla — *Korn/Ferry International*
Strander, Dervin — *Source  Services Corporation*
Stubbs, Judy N. — *Lamalie Amrop International*
Sumurdy, Melinda — *Kenzer Corp.*
Susoreny, Samali — *Source  Services Corporation*
Sutter, Terry A. — *Russell Reynolds Associates, Inc.*
Teinert, Jay — *Damon & Associates, Inc.*
Teter, Sandra — *The Danbrook Group, Inc.*
Thompson, Jim E. — *Management Recruiters International, Inc.*
Trueblood, Brian G. — *TNS Partners, Inc.*
Varrichio, Michael — *Source  Services Corporation*
Vlasek, Ray D. — *Management Recruiters International, Inc.*
Wallace, Toby — *Source  Services Corporation*
Ward, Les — *Source  Services Corporation*
Ward, William F. — *Heidrick & Struggles, Inc.*
Watkins, Thomas M. — *Lamalie Amrop International*
Watson, Stephen — *Paul Ray Berndtson*
Weiss, Elizabeth — *Source  Services Corporation*
Westberry, David M. — *Lamalie Amrop International*
Whitaker, Charles — *Evie Kreisler & Associates, Inc.*
Wicklund, Grant — *Heidrick & Struggles, Inc.*
Williams, Scott D. — *Heidrick & Struggles, Inc.*
Wingate, Mary — *Source  Services Corporation*
Wise, J. Herbert — *Sandhurst Associates*
Wold, Ted W. — *Hyde Danforth Wold & Co.*
Wood, Allison — *Korn/Ferry International*
Worth, Janet M. — *Witt/Kieffer, Ford, Hadelman & Lloyd*
Wright, Linus — *Paul Ray Berndtson*
Zera, Ronald J. — *Spencer Stuart*

**Fort Worth**
Arrington, Renee — *Paul Ray Berndtson*
Bostick, Tim — *Paul Ray Berndtson*
Hobart, John N. — *Paul Ray Berndtson*
Hughes, Kendall G. — *Hughes & Associates*
Kizer, Jay R. — *Paul Ray Berndtson*
Mooney, Kelly — *Paul Ray Berndtson*
Perryman, Ben — *Paul Ray Berndtson*
Ray, Breck — *Paul Ray Berndtson*
Ray, Paul R. — *Paul Ray Berndtson*
Ray, Paul R. — *Paul Ray Berndtson*
Rice, John — *Paul Ray Berndtson*

## Friendswood
Bellview, Louis P. — *Management Recruiters International, Inc.*
Bellview, Sibyl M. — *Management Recruiters International, Inc.*

## Houston
Adams, Amy — *Richard, Wayne and Roberts*
Akin, Gary K. — *Management Recruiters International, Inc.*
Albrecht, Franke M. — *Management Recruiters International, Inc.*
Baird, John — *Professional Search Consultants*
Baker, Judith — *Search Consultants International, Inc.*
Baker, S. Joseph — *Search Consultants International, Inc.*
Barton, Gary R. — *Barton Raben, Inc.*
Batte, Carol — *Source Services Corporation*
Battistoni, Bea — *Accountants on Call*
Baugh, Amy — *Richard, Wayne and Roberts*
Bean, Bill — *Professional Search Consultants*
Bernard, Bryan — *Source Services Corporation*
Betts, Suzette — *Source Services Corporation*
Bird, Len L. — *Management Recruiters International, Inc.*
Block, Laurie — *Richard, Wayne and Roberts*
Bolls, Rich — *Management Recruiters International, Inc.*
Bradshaw, John W. — *A.T. Kearney, Inc.*
Brentari, Michael — *Search Consultants International, Inc.*
Brock, John — *Korn/Ferry International*
Brown, Floyd — *Richard, Wayne and Roberts*
Brown, Ronald — *Richard, Wayne and Roberts*
Browndyke, Chip — *Paul Ray Berndtson*
Brunson, Therese — *Kors Montgomery International*
Budill, Edward — *Professional Search Consultants*
Cannon, Alexis — *Richard, Wayne and Roberts*
Center, Linda — *The Search Center Inc.*
Cherbonnier, L. Michael — *TCG International, Inc.*
Cherbonnier, L. Michael — *The Cherbonnier Group, Inc.*
Cho, Ui — *Richard, Wayne and Roberts*
Christiana, Jack — *Richard, Wayne and Roberts*
Clarey, William A. — *Preng & Associates, Inc.*
Collard, Joseph A. — *Spencer Stuart*
Colosimo, Chris — *Richard, Wayne and Roberts*
Cooksey, Ben — *Management Recruiters International, Inc.*
Copeland, Linda K. — *Management Recruiters International, Inc.*
Crownover, Kathryn L. — *MSI International*
Crystal, Jonathan A. — *Spencer Stuart*
Csorba, Les — *A.T. Kearney, Inc.*
Dalton, David R. — *MSI International*
Danforth, Monica — *Search Consultants International, Inc.*
Donnelly, George J. — *Ward Howell International, Inc.*
Doyle, Bobby — *Richard, Wayne and Roberts*
Dremely, Mark — *Richard, Wayne and Roberts*
Dumesnil, Curtis — *Richard, Wayne and Roberts*
Eastham, Marvene M. — *Witt/Kieffer, Ford, Hadelman & Lloyd*
Edwards, Dorothy — *MSI International*
Fiore, Richard — *Search Consultants International, Inc.*
French, William G. — *Preng & Associates, Inc.*
Freud, John W. — *Paul Ray Berndtson*
Friedman, Janet — *Litchfield & Willis Inc.*
Fry, Edmund L. — *Witt/Kieffer, Ford, Hadelman & Lloyd*
Fuhrman, Katherine — *Richard, Wayne and Roberts*
Fuller, Robert L. — *Litchfield & Willis Inc.*
Gadison, William — *Richard, Wayne and Roberts*
Gillespie, Thomas — *Professional Search Consultants*
Gobert, Larry — *Professional Search Consultants*
Golding, Robert L. — *Lamalie Amrop International*
Gooch, Randy — *Richard, Wayne and Roberts*
Gray, Heather — *Source Services Corporation*
Griffin, John A. — *Heidrick & Struggles, Inc.*
Hadfield, Sheri — *Paul Ray Berndtson*
Hernandez, Luis A. — *CoEnergy, Inc.*
Hertlein, James N.J. — *Boyden/Zay & Company*
Hidalgo, Rhonda — *Richard, Wayne and Roberts*
Hilton, Diane — *Richard, Wayne and Roberts*
Howard, Leon — *Richard, Wayne and Roberts*
Huntoon, Cliff — *Richard, Wayne and Roberts*
Jackson, Clay — *Paul Ray Berndtson*
Johnson, Kathleen A. — *Barton Raben, Inc.*
Johnstone, Grant — *Source Services Corporation*
Kaplowitz, Marji — *Richard, Wayne and Roberts*
Keller, Barbara — *Barton Raben, Inc.*
Kelso, Patricia C. — *Barton Raben, Inc.*
King, Stephen C. — *Boyden/Zay & Company*
Kluber, Bruce — *Richard, Wayne and Roberts*
Knight, Gwen — *Richard, Wayne and Roberts*
Kolke, Rick — *Richard, Wayne and Roberts*
Kors, R. Paul — *Kors Montgomery International*
LeMay, Steven E. — *Saber Consultants*
Litchfield, Barbara H. — *Litchfield & Willis Inc.*
Lopis, Roberta — *Richard, Wayne and Roberts*
Lowry, W. Randall — *Paul Ray Berndtson*
Luce, Daniel — *Source Services Corporation*
Magnani, Susan — *The Search Center Inc.*
Mathias, William J. — *Preng & Associates, Inc.*
McAleavy, Steve — *Search Consultants International, Inc.*
McEwan, Paul — *Richard, Wayne and Roberts*

Meza, Anna — *Richard, Wayne and Roberts*
Mitchell, Kim — *Richard, Wayne and Roberts*
Morris, David A. — *Heidrick & Struggles, Inc.*
Moses, Brenda — *Paul Ray Berndtson*
Moss, Ethan — *Richard, Wayne and Roberts*
Munguia, Rebecca — *Richard, Wayne and Roberts*
Napier, Ginger L. — *Preng & Associates, Inc.*
Neuwiler, Mark D. — *Saber Consultants*
Newman, Arthur I. — *Lamalie Amrop International*
Newton, Stephen D. — *Russell Reynolds Associates, Inc.*
Nielsen, Eric C. — *Russell Reynolds Associates, Inc.*
O'Brien, Lori — *Paul Ray Berndtson*
Odom, Philip — *Richard, Wayne and Roberts*
Olin, Robyn — *Richard, Wayne and Roberts*
Orner, Ted A. — *Russell Reynolds Associates, Inc.*
Paris, Stephen — *Richard, Wayne and Roberts*
Parry, Heather — *Richard, Wayne and Roberts*
Pederson, Terre — *Richard, Wayne and Roberts*
Perkins, Bob — *Richard, Wayne and Roberts*
Peterson, Bruce — *Korn/Ferry International*
Pettersson, Tara L. — *Lamalie Amrop International*
Petty, J. Scott — *The Arcus Group*
Pistole, Ingrid — *Richard, Wayne and Roberts*
Powell, Danny — *Source Services Corporation*
Preng, David E. — *Preng & Associates, Inc.*
Prosser, Shane — *Search Consultants International, Inc.*
Raben, Steven — *Paul Ray Berndtson*
Referente, Gwen — *Richard, Wayne and Roberts*
Rieger, Louis J. — *Spencer Stuart*
Samuelson, Robert — *Source Services Corporation*
Sawhook, Danny — *Richard, Wayne and Roberts*
Scharringhausen, Michael — *Saber Consultants*
Schlanger, Ruth — *Richard, Wayne and Roberts*
Selbst, Denise — *Richard, Wayne and Roberts*
Sessa, Beth — *Richard, Wayne and Roberts*
Simmons, Tom — *Spencer Stuart*
Simmons, Vicki — *Richard, Wayne and Roberts*
Smith, Cheryl — *Barton Raben, Inc.*
Smith, Eric E. — *Management Recruiters International, Inc.*
Solomon, Christina — *Richard, Wayne and Roberts*
Starr, Anna — *Richard, Wayne and Roberts*
Stutt, Brian — *Richard, Wayne and Roberts*
Tanner, Frank — *Source Services Corporation*
Tobin, Jim — *Barton Raben, Inc.*
Van Alstyne, Susan — *Richard, Wayne and Roberts*
Wade, Christy — *Source Services Corporation*
Waitkus, Karen — *Richard, Wayne and Roberts*
Walker, Don — *Richard, Wayne and Roberts*
Walker, Ewing J. — *Ward Howell International, Inc.*
Walker, Judy — *Richard, Wayne and Roberts*
Williams, Laura — *Paul Ray Berndtson*
Williams, Nicole — *Richard, Wayne and Roberts*
Wilson, Thomas H. — *Lamalie Amrop International*
Winfrey, James — *Korn/Ferry International*
Zay, Thomas C. — *Boyden/Zay & Company*
Zimont, Scott — *Source Services Corporation*

## Irving
Bormann, Cindy Ann — *MSI International*
Bright, Timothy — *MSI International*
Davis, Joan — *MSI International*
Fowler, Thomas A. — *The Hindman Company*
Freemon, Ted — *Management Recruiters International, Inc.*
Hilyard, Paul J. — *MSI International*
Jacobson, Eric K. — *Management Recruiters International, Inc.*
Lankford, Charles — *MSI International*
Layton, Patrick R. — *MSI International*
Lonneke, John W. — *MSI International*
Lucas, Ronnie L. — *MSI International*
Miller, Benjamin J. — *MSI International*
Roll, Bill — *Management Recruiters International, Inc.*

## Lewisviile
Kramer, Desni — *Management Recruiters International, Inc.*

## Lubbock
Warren, Lester A. — *Management Recruiters International, Inc.*

## New Braunfels
Rice, Jim K. — *Management Recruiters International, Inc.*

## Plano
Appleton, Diane — *Management Recruiters International, Inc.*
Button, David R. — *The Button Group*
Hardison, Richard L. — *Hardison & Company*
Jacob, Don C. — *Management Recruiters International, Inc.*
McRoberts, Dana L. — *Management Recruiters International, Inc.*
Vann, Dianne — *The Button Group*

## Richardson
Flowers, Hayden — *Southwestern Professional Services*

## Round Rock
Hohlstein, Jeff G. — *Management Recruiters International, Inc.*
Hohlstein, Jodi — *Management Recruiters International, Inc.*

**San Antonio**
Carrigan, Denise — *Management Recruiters International, Inc.*
Cornfoot, Jim L. — *Management Recruiters International, Inc.*
Goicoechea, Lydia — *Management Recruiters International, Inc.*
Goicoechea, Sam — *Management Recruiters International, Inc.*
Jimenez, Gil C. — *Management Recruiters International, Inc.*
Sheridan, Kenneth T. — *Management Recruiters International, Inc.*
Sheridan, Theresa — *Management Recruiters International, Inc.*
**San Marcos**
Berry, Chuck — *Management Recruiters International, Inc.*
**Seven Points**
Youngs, Donald L. — *Youngs & Company*
**Stafford**
Gandee, John R. — *Management Recruiters International, Inc.*
**The Colony**
Aquavella, Charles P. — *CPA & Associates*
**Woodlands**
Krochenski, Caren S. — *Management Recruiters International, Inc.*
Krochenski, Lynette — *Management Recruiters International, Inc.*

**Utah**
**Ogden**
Manning, Jerry A. — *Management Recruiters International, Inc.*
**Park City**
Esty, Greg C. — *Management Recruiters International, Inc.*
Lee, Rodger A. — *Sanford Rose Associates*
**Provo**
Massung, Larry J. — *Management Recruiters International, Inc.*
**Salt Lake City**
Cotterell, Dirk A. — *Management Recruiters International, Inc.*
Dever, Mary — *Source Services Corporation*
Donahue, Debora — *Source Services Corporation*
Imhof, Kirk — *Source Services Corporation*
Sadaj, Michael — *Source Services Corporation*
Tanner, Gary — *Source Services Corporation*
Warnock, Phyl — *Source Services Corporation*

**Vermont**
**Burlington**
Nyhan, Alan — *Management Recruiters International, Inc.*

**Virginia**
**Alexandria**
Guberman, Robert P. — *A.T. Kearney, Inc.*
Haberman, Joseph C. — *A.T. Kearney, Inc.*
Hughes, Donald J. — *Hughes & Company*
Prencipe, V. Michael — *Raymond Karsan Associates*
Sekera, Roger I. — *A.T. Kearney, Inc.*
Storbeck, Shelly — *A.T. Kearney, Inc.*
Unger, Paul T. — *A.T. Kearney, Inc.*
**Arlington**
Carr, W. Lyles — *The McCormick Group, Inc.*
Donovan, Jerry E. — *Management Recruiters International, Inc.*
Grey, Cort — *The McCormick Group, Inc.*
Hayes, Stacy — *The McCormick Group, Inc.*
Heldenbrand, Paul — *The McCormick Group, Inc.*
Howard, Susy — *The McCormick Group, Inc.*
King, Bill — *The McCormick Group, Inc.*
McConnell, Rod — *The McCormick Group, Inc.*
McCormick, Brian — *The McCormick Group, Inc.*
Miller, Brett — *The McCormick Group, Inc.*
Nelson, Steve — *The McCormick Group, Inc.*
Pelkey, Chris — *The McCormick Group, Inc.*
Reilly, John — *The McCormick Group, Inc.*
Rothenberg, Paul — *The McCormick Group, Inc.*
Sorg, Leslie — *The McCormick Group, Inc.*
Summers, Burke — *The McCormick Group, Inc.*
Troup, Roger — *The McCormick Group, Inc.*
Voigt, John A. — *Romac & Associates*
Watt, Jennifer — *The McCormick Group, Inc.*
Williams, Dave — *The McCormick Group, Inc.*
**Bristol**
Ellis, Ted K. — *The Hindman Company*
**Fairfax**
Ehrenzeller, Tony A. — *Management Recruiters International, Inc.*
**Fredericksburg**
McCormick, William J. — *The McCormick Group, Inc.*
**Herndon**
Fossett, Gary J. — *John Michael Associates*
Kurtz, Michael E. — *MDR Associates, Inc.*
Persinger, Andrea J. — *John Michael Associates*
**Leesburg**
Gilmore, Jerry W. — *Management Recruiters International, Inc.*
Gilmore, Pam — *Management Recruiters International, Inc.*
**Lynchburg**
Blue, C. David — *Management Recruiters International, Inc.*
**Manassas**
Ranberger, Mike J. — *Management Recruiters International, Inc.*

**Martinsville**
Gurley, Herschel — *Management Recruiters International, Inc.*
Matthews, John C. — *Management Recruiters International, Inc.*
**McLean**
Boczany, William J. — *The Guild Corporation*
Cole, Kevin — *Don Richard Associates of Washington, D.C., Inc.*
Dinte, Paul — *Dinte Resources, Incorporated*
Gordon, Teri — *Don Richard Associates of Washington, D.C., Inc.*
Joyce, William J. — *The Guild Corporation*
Kohonoski, Michael M. — *The Guild Corporation*
LaCharite, Danielle — *The Guild Corporation*
Martin, David — *The Guild Corporation*
McComas, Kelly E. — *The Guild Corporation*
Reitkopp, Ellen — *Management Recruiters International, Inc.*
Reitkopp, Howard H. — *Management Recruiters International, Inc.*
Rogers, Leah — *Dinte Resources, Incorporated*
Russell, Sam — *The Guild Corporation*
Shontell, William — *Don Richard Associates of Washington, D.C., Inc.*
Siker, Paul W. — *The Guild Corporation*
Solters, Jeanne — *The Guild Corporation*
Spanninger, Mark J. — *The Guild Corporation*
Taft, Steven D. — *The Guild Corporation*
Yilmaz, Muriel — *Dinte Resources, Incorporated*
Young, Heather — *The Guild Corporation*
**Reston**
Holt, Carol — *Bartholdi & Company, Inc.*
Steinem, Andy — *Dahl-Morrow International*
Steinem, Barbara — *Dahl-Morrow International*
**Richmond**
Beck, Michael — *Don Richard Associates of Richmond, Inc.*
Chattin, Norma Anne — *Accountants on Call*
Coon, David — *Don Richard Associates of Richmond, Inc.*
Gregory, Stephen — *Don Richard Associates of Richmond, Inc.*
Hall, Marty B. — *Catlin-Wells & White*
Keeton, Susan G. — *The Corporate Connection, Ltd.*
Neblett, Jon — *Don Richard Associates of Richmond, Inc.*
Ramler, Carolyn S. — *The Corporate Connection, Ltd.*
Rotella, Marshall W. — *The Corporate Connection, Ltd.*
Schwartz, Jay S. — *Management Recruiters International, Inc.*
Tursi, Deborah J. — *The Corporate Connection, Ltd.*
Visotsky, Thomas — *Don Richard Associates of Richmond, Inc.*
**Roanoke**
Sharp, Paul S. — *Management Recruiters International, Inc.*
**Suffolk**
McNulty, Neil P. — *Management Recruiters International, Inc.*
**Vienna**
Abell, Vincent W. — *MSI International*
Alden, Brian R. — *MSI International*
Baglio, Robert — *Source Services Corporation*
Benjamin, Maurita — *Source Services Corporation*
Braak, Diana — *Kincannon & Reed*
Bush, Martha A. — *MSI International*
Cargo, Catherine — *MSI International*
Chatterjie, Alok — *MSI International*
Christy, Michael T. — *Heidrick & Struggles, Inc.*
Cole, Elizabeth — *MSI International*
Coneys, Bridget — *Source Services Corporation*
Dawson, William — *Source Services Corporation*
Elliott, A. Larry — *Heidrick & Struggles, Inc.*
Foster, John — *Source Services Corporation*
Gaffney, Megan — *Source Services Corporation*
Gloss, Frederick C. — *F. Gloss International*
Gnatowski, Bruce — *Source Services Corporation*
Gresia, Paul — *Source Services Corporation*
Hanley, Steven — *Source Services Corporation*
Jayne, Edward R. — *Heidrick & Struggles, Inc.*
Kaplan, Traci — *Source Services Corporation*
Kasprzyk, Michael — *Source Services Corporation*
Kincannon, Kelly — *Kincannon & Reed*
Lee, Donna M. — *Kincannon & Reed*
Lewicki, Christopher — *MSI International*
Logue, Kenneth F. — *Logue & Rice Inc.*
Ludder, Mark — *Source Services Corporation*
Martin, Paula — *MSI International*
McCarthy, Laura — *Source Services Corporation*
McNerney, Kevin A. — *Heidrick & Struggles, Inc.*
Meehan, John — *Source Services Corporation*
Miesemer, Arthur C. — *MSI International*
Moore, Suzanne — *Source Services Corporation*
Nelson, Mary — *Source Services Corporation*
Owen, Christopher — *Source Services Corporation*
Parbs, Michael — *Accountants on Call*
Powell, Gregory — *Source Services Corporation*
Rice, Raymond D. — *Logue & Rice Inc.*
Snowden, Charles — *Source Services Corporation*
Stephens, Andrew — *Source Services Corporation*
Tokash, Ronald E. — *MSI International*
Velez, Hector — *Source Services Corporation*

Douglas, Anne — *Prestige Inc.*
Heavey, John — *Prestige Inc.*
Henderson, Marc — *Prestige Inc.*
Jaedike, Eldron — *Prestige Inc.*
Larsen, Bruce — *Prestige Inc.*
Sammons, James A. — *Prestige Inc.*
Toson, James — *Prestige Inc.*
Warren, Linda — *Prestige Inc.*

**Seymour**
Dieck, Daniel W. — *Dieck, Mueller & Associates, Inc.*
Magee, Charles R. — *Dieck, Mueller & Associates, Inc.*
Mueller, Michael S. — *Dieck, Mueller & Associates, Inc.*

**Wausau**
Knutson, Rebecca J. — *Management Recruiters International, Inc.*

**Wauwatosa**
Mancos, Barbara — *Accountants on Call*

## Wyoming

**Cheyenne**
Meister, Connie — *Management Recruiters International, Inc.*
Meister, Verle — *Management Recruiters International, Inc.*

## Mexico

**Cuernavaca, Moreios**
Albores, Sergio — *Management Recruiters International, Inc.*

**Garza Garcia, N.L.**
Carrillo, Jose — *Amrop International*
Pacheco, Ricardo — *Amrop International*

**Guadalajara, Jal.**
Gaxiola, Alejandro — *Smith Search, S.C.*

**Mexico City D.F.**
Valle, Javier — *A.T. Kearney, Inc.*

**Mexico City, D.F.**
Cohen, Luis Lezama — *Paul Ray Berndtson*
Cuellar, Paulina Robles — *Paul Ray Berndtson*

Dudley, Craig J. — *Paul Ray Berndtson*
Flores, Agustin — *Ward Howell International, Inc.*
Gitlin, Bernardo — *Boyden*
Glennie, Francisco — *Ward Howell International, Inc.*
Graue, Monica — *Korn/Ferry International*
Hamer, Thurston — *Korn/Ferry International*
Haro, Adolfo Medina — *Egon Zehnder International Inc.*
Juarez, Maria Elena — *Amrop International*
Lajous, Luz — *Russell Reynolds Associates, Inc.*
Lussier, Grant P. — *Heidrick & Struggles, Inc.*
McCoy, Horacio — *Korn/Ferry International*
Mendoza, Guadalupe — *Ward Howell International, Inc.*
Mondragon, Philip — *Boyden*
Newman, Jose L. — *Ward Howell International, Inc.*
Padilla, Jose Sanchez — *Egon Zehnder International Inc.*
Papayanopulos, Manuel — *Korn/Ferry International*
Pardo, Maria Elena — *Smith Search, S.C.*
Pastrana, Dario — *Egon Zehnder International Inc.*
Peniche, Pedro — *Amrop International*
Rivas, Alberto F. — *Boyden*
Rojas-Magnon, Carlos — *Amrop International*
Romaniw, Michael J. — *A la carte International*
Smith, John E. — *Smith Search, S.C.*
Stephens, Roberto Salinas — *Smith Search, S.C.*
Tames, Rodolfo — *Amrop International*
Tello, Fernando — *Korn/Ferry International*
Valdes, Ma. Elena — *Korn/Ferry International*
Yturbe, Rafael — *Russell Reynolds Associates, Inc.*
Zavala, Lorenzo — *Russell Reynolds Associates, Inc.*

**Monterrey, N.L.**
Gonzalez, Romulo H. — *Korn/Ferry International*
Gonzalez de Coindreau, Alicia M. — *Korn/Ferry International*
Gonzalez de la Rocha, Sergio — *Korn/Ferry International*
Llaguno, Juan F. — *Korn/Ferry International*

**Villa Corregidora, Qro.**
Smith, Ana Luz — *Smith Search, S.C.*

# Appendix: Job-Search Resources

If you would like more information about executive recruiters, or if you would like to order other career strategy guides and subscribe to our online *Job-Seekers Network*, please refer to the following Hunt-Scanlon publications. To learn more about these products and ordering information, please call (800) 477-1199 toll free today!

- Executive Recruiters of North America
- Executive Search Review
- Headhunter News (at www.recruiterlink.com)
- The Job-Seekers Network (at www.recruiterlink.com)
- The Kingmaker
- The Select Guide to Human Resource Executives
- Silicon Valley Recruiters
- Wall $treet Recruiters
- Workplace America (at www.recruiterlink.com)